PETERSON'S PRIVATE SECONDARY SCHOOLS 2013–14

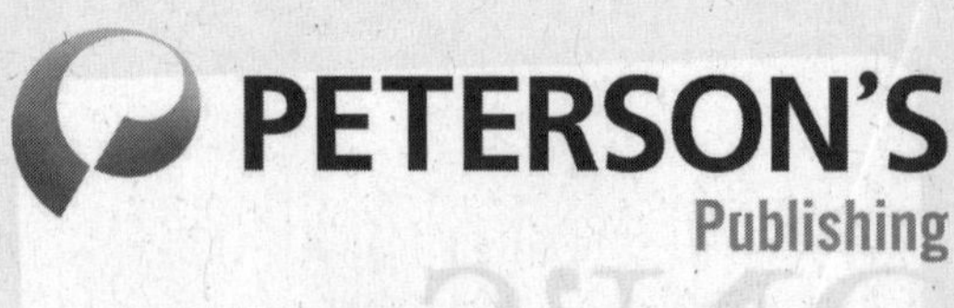

About Peterson's Publishing

Peterson's Publishing provides the accurate, dependable, high-quality education content and guidance you need to succeed. No matter where you are on your academic or professional path, you can rely on Peterson's print and digital publications for the most up-to-date education exploration data, expert test-prep tools, and top-notch career success resources—everything you need to achieve your goals.

Visit us online at **www.petersonspublishing.com** and let Peterson's help you achieve your goals.

For more information, contact Peterson's Publishing, 800-338-3282 Ext. 54229; or find us on the World Wide Web at www.petersonspublishing.com.

Previous editions published as *Peterson's Guide to Independent Secondary Schools* © 1980, 1981, 1982, 1983, 1984, 1985, 1986, 1987, 1988, 1989, 1990, 1991, 1992 and as *Peterson's Private Secondary Schools* © 1993, 1994, 1995, 1996, 1997, 1998, 1999, 2000, 2001, 2002, 2003, 2004, 2005, 2006, 2007, 2008, 2009, 2010, 2011, 2012

Cover photo courtesy of Lauralton Hall.

Bernadette Webster, Managing Editor; Jill C. Schwartz, Editor; Christine Lucas, Research Project Manager; James Ranish, Research Associate; Phyllis Johnson, Software Engineer; Ray Golaszewski, Publishing Operations Manager; Linda M. Williams, Composition Manager; Nadeen Kabia, Fulfillment Coordinator

ISSN 1544-2330
ISBN-13: 978-0-7689-3627-8
ISBN-10: 0-7689-3627-6

Printed in the United States of America

10 9 8 7 6 5 4 3 2 1 15 14 13

Thirty-fourth Edition

By producing this book on recycled paper (40% post-consumer waste) 98 trees were saved.

Certified Chain of Custody

60% Certified Fiber Sourcing and
40% Post-Consumer Recycled

www.sfiprogram.org

*This label applies to the text stock.

Sustainability—Its Importance to Peterson's Publishing

What does sustainability mean to Peterson's? As a leading publisher, we are aware that our business has a direct impact on vital resources—most especially the trees that are used to make our books. Peterson's Publishing is proud that its products are certified by the Sustainable Forestry Initiative (SFI) chain-of-custody standard and that all of its books are printed on paper that is 40% post-consumer waste using vegetable-based ink.

Being a part of the Sustainable Forestry Initiative (SFI) means that all of our vendors—from paper suppliers to printers—have undergone rigorous audits to demonstrate that they are maintaining a sustainable environment.

Peterson's Publishing continuously strives to find new ways to incorporate sustainability throughout all aspects of its business.

Contents

INDEX

A Note from the Editors of Peterson's Publishing

Peterson's Private Secondary Schools 2013–14 is the authoritative source of information for parents and students who are exploring the alternative of privately provided education. In this edition, you will find information for more than 1,100 schools worldwide. The data published in this guide are obtained directly from the schools themselves to help you make a fully informed decision.

If you've decided to look into private schooling for your son or daughter but aren't sure how to begin, relax. You won't have to go it alone. **What You Should Know About Private Education** can help you plan your search and demystify the admission process. In the articles that follow, you'll find valuable advice from admission experts about applying to private secondary schools and choosing the school that's right for your child.

Schools will be pleased to know that Peterson's helped you in your private secondary school selection.

In "Why Choose an Independent School?" Patrick F. Bassett, President of the National Association of Independent Schools (NAIS), describes the reasons why an increasing number of families are considering private schooling.

If you want a private education for your child but are hesitant about sending him or her away to a boarding school, read "Another Option: Independent Day Schools" where Lila Lohr, former Head of School at Princeton Day School in Princeton, New Jersey, discusses the benefits of day schools.

From Howard and Matthew Greenes' "The Contemporary Boarding School: Change and Adaptability" to The Association of Boarding Schools' (TABS) "Study Confirms Benefits of Boarding School"—if you are having doubts about boarding schools, you'll want to check out these articles!

Mark Meyer-Braun, Former Head of School at the Outdoor Academy, offers "Semester Schools: Great Opportunities," which explores various options for students to spend an exciting semester in a new "school-away-from-school."

If you are considering a special needs or therapeutic school for your child, you will want to read "Why a Therapeutic or Special Needs School?" by Diederik van Renesse, an educational consultant who specializes in this area.

To help you compare private schools and make the best choice for your child, check out "Finding the Perfect Match" by Helene Reynolds, a former educational planning and placement counselor.

"Plan a Successful School Search" gives you an overview of the admission process.

If the admission application forms have you baffled and confused, read "Understanding the Admission Application Form," by Gregg W. M. Maloberti, Dean of Admission at The Lawrenceville School.

For the lowdown on standardized testing, Heather Hoerle, Executive Director of the Secondary School Admission Test Board (SSATB), describes the two tests most often required by private schools and the role that tests play in admission decisions in "About Standardized Tests."

In "Paying for a Private Education," Mark Mitchell, Vice President, School Information Services at NAIS, shares some thoughts on financing options.

Finally, "How to Use This Guide" gives you all the information you need on how to make *Peterson's Private Secondary Schools 2013–14* work for you!

Next up, the **Quick-Reference Chart,** "Private Secondary Schools At-a-Glance," lists schools by state, U.S. territory, or country and provides essential information about a school's students, range of grade levels, enrollment figures, faculty, and special offerings.

The **School Profiles** follow, and it's here you can learn more about particular schools. *Peterson's Private Secondary Schools 2013–14* contains three **School Profiles** sections—one for traditional college-preparatory and general academic schools, one for special needs schools that serve students with a variety of special learning and social needs, and one for junior boarding schools that serve students in middle school grades. Many schools have chosen to submit a display ad, which appears near their profile and offers specific information the school wants you to know.

Close-Ups follow each **School Profiles** section and feature expanded two-page school descriptions written exclusively for this guide. There is a reference at the end of a profile directing you to that school's **Close-Up.**

Summer programs are more important than ever for teens. Aside from looking good on a college application, they can be extremely transformative—helping students develop leadership skills, gain greater self-knowledge, and cultivate friendships with peers from across the country or around the world. Finding meaningful summer programs for teens can often be challenging. *Peterson's Private Secondary Schools* guide offers a Summer Programs section that includes two-page descriptions, complete with photos, of exciting opportunities taking place at private schools in the United States and abroad during the summer months. You'll find great information about program offerings, facilities, staff, costs, and much more.

The **Specialized Directories** are generated from responses to Peterson's annual school survey. These directories group schools by the categories considered most important when choosing a private school, including type, entrance requirements, curricula, financial aid data, and special programs.

Finally, in the **Index** you'll find the "Alphabetical Listing of Schools" for the page references of schools that have already piqued your interest.

Peterson's publishes a full line of resources to help guide you and your family through the private secondary school admission process. Peterson's publications can be found at your local bookstore and library and your school guidance office, and you can access us online at www.petersonspublishing.com. Peterson's books are also available as eBooks.

Join Peterson's Private Schools conversation at www.facebook.com/petersonspublishing. The resources of Peterson's Publishing are available to help you with your private school search.

We welcome any comments or suggestions you may have about this publication. Please send us an e-mail at custsvc@petersons.com. Your feedback will help us make your educational dreams possible.

Schools will be pleased to know that Peterson's Publishing helped you in your private secondary school selection. Admission staff members are more than happy to answer questions, address specific problems, and help in any way they can. The editors at Peterson's Publishing wish you great success in your search!

What You Should Know About Private Education

Why Choose an Independent School?

Patrick F. Bassett
President of the National Association of Independent Schools (NAIS)

Why do families choose independent private schools for their children? Many cite the intimate school size and setting, individualized attention, and high academic standards.

Recent research highlights the success of independent school graduates, who outperform graduates from all other types of schools in a whole host of categories, reflecting exceptional preparation for academic and civic life.

Although nearly all independent school graduates go on to attend college, *The Freshman Survey Trends Report*, a study conducted by the Higher Education Research Institute, found that 85 percent of students who attended independent schools that belong to the National Association of Independent Schools (NAIS) went on to attend "very high" or "highly selective" colleges and universities. This "persistence factor" is largely attributable to attending a school with high expectations for all students and a culture that reinforces achievement. The ethos of independent schools contributes to this equation, since everybody is expected to work hard and succeed academically.

NAIS school graduates were also more engaged with their communities than students from other types of schools. Forty-one percent of NAIS graduates said they expected to participate in volunteer or community activities in college, compared to just 24 percent of the whole group. NAIS graduates were also far more inclined to consider "keeping up-to-date with political affairs" essential (46 percent NAIS, 31 percent all).

Another study, the *National Educational Longitudinal Study* (conducted by the U.S. Department of Education) tracked students from public schools, parochial schools, NAIS independent schools, and other private schools from the time they were eighth graders in 1988 until the year 2000. Nearly all of the NAIS students in the NELS study had pursued postsecondary education by their mid-20s. More than three quarters had graduated from a college or university, including 8 percent who completed master's degrees, and 1.5 percent who achieved a Ph.D. or professional degree (e.g., M.D. or LL.B.) by their mid-20s.

Perhaps the most significant factor that distinguished NAIS graduates from graduates of other types of schools was the strength of their commitment to community service and active civic participation. While slightly more than 1 out of 5 survey participants reported volunteering for civic events, nearly one third of NAIS school graduates said that they regularly participated in voluntary activities in their communities. NAIS students were also nearly twice as likely to volunteer to work for political campaigns and political causes. And NAIS students were committed to exercising their civic duty as voters. Whereas slightly more than half of all NELS participants voted in the presidential election before the study, more than 75 percent of NAIS school graduates registered their voices.

With independent schools, you have the opportunity to choose a school with a philosophy, values, and approach to teaching that is the right fit for your child.

Another factor that contributes to the success of students in independent schools is the partnership with families. This coalescing of parental and school voices helps children prosper because the key adults in their lives reinforce a common set of values and speak with a common voice. Indeed, the great achievement of American education is that it offers families many choices of schooling so that they can find a school with a voice and vision to match their own.

Each independent school has a unique mission, culture, and personality. There are day schools, boarding schools, and combination day-boarding schools. Some independent schools have a few dozen students; others have several thousand. Some are coed; others are single-sex. Some independent schools have a religious affiliation; some are nonsectarian. Most serve students of average to exceptional academic ability, but some serve exclusively those with learning differences, and others serve highly gifted students. The vast majority of independent schools are college-prep.

With independent schools, you have the opportunity to choose a school with a philosophy, values, and approach to teaching that is the right fit for your child.

Make the choice of a lifetime. Choose an independent school.

Another Option: Independent Day Schools

Lila Lohr

For those of us who are fortunate enough to be able to send our children to an independent day school, it seems to offer the best of both worlds. Our children are able to reap the enormous benefits of an independent school education and we, as parents, are able to continue to play a vital, daily role in the education of our children. Parents enjoy being seen as partners with day schools in educating their children.

As more and more independent day schools have sprung up in communities across the country, more and more parents are choosing to send their children to them, even when it might involve a lengthy daily commute. Contrary to some old stereotypes, parents of independent school students are not all cut from the same mold, living in the same neighborhood with identical dreams and aspirations for their children. Independent school parents represent a wide range of interests, attitudes, and parenting styles.

They also have several things in common. Most parents send their children to independent day schools because they think their children will get a better education in a safe, value-laden environment. Many parents are willing to pay substantial annual tuition because they believe their children will be held to certain standards, challenged academically, and thoroughly prepared for college.

This willingness to make what are, for many, substantial financial sacrifices reflects the recognition that much of one's character is formed in school. Concerned parents want their children to go to schools where values are discussed and reinforced. They seek schools that have clear expectations and limits. The nonpublic status allows independent schools to establish specific standards of behavior and performance and to suspend or expel students who don't conform to those expectations.

Understanding the power of adolescent peer pressure, parents are eager to have their children go to school with other teens who are academically ambitious and required to behave. They seek an environment where it is "cool" to be smart, to work hard, and to be involved in the school community. In independent day schools, students spend their evenings doing homework, expect to be called on in class, and participate in sports or clubs.

Successful independent schools, whether elementary or high school, large or small, single-sex or coed, recognize the importance of a school-parent partnership in educating each child. Experienced faculty members and administrators readily acknowledge that, while they are experts on education, parents are the experts on their own children. Gone are the days when parents simply dropped their children off in the morning, picked them up at the end of the day, and assumed the school would do the educating. Clearly, children benefit enormously when their parents and teachers work together, sharing their observations and concerns openly and frequently.

Most independent schools welcome and encourage parental involvement and support.

Independent schools encourage this two-way give-and-take and are committed to taking it well beyond the public school model. Annual back-to-school nights are attended by more than 90 percent of parents. Teacher-parent and student-teacherparent conferences, extensive written comments as part of the report cards, and adviser systems that encourage close faculty-student relationships are all structures that facilitate this parent-school partnership. Although more and more independent school parents work full-time, they make time for these critical opportunities to sit down and discuss their children's progress.

Most independent schools welcome and encourage parental involvement and support. Although the individual structures vary from school to school, most include opportunities beyond making cookies and chaperoning dances. Many parents enjoy being involved in community service projects, working on school fund raisers, participating in admission activities, sharing their expertise in appropriate academic classes, and even offering student internships. Most schools have made a concerted effort to structure specific opportunities for working parents to participate in the life of the school.

Independent day schools recognize the benefits of parent volunteers and of extending themselves so that parents feel that they are an important part of the school family. Buddy systems that pair new parents with families who have been at the school for several years help ease the transition for families who are new to the independent school sector.

Independent schools have also responded to increased parental interest in programs focusing on parenting skills. Recognizing the inherent difficulties of raising children, independent day schools have provided forums for discussing and learning about drugs, depression, stress management, peer pressure, and the like. Book groups, panel discussions, and workshops provide important opportunities for parents to share their concerns and to get to know the parents of their children's classmates. Schools recognize that this parent-to-parent communication and networking strengthens the entire school community.

Many current day school parents would contend that when you choose an independent day school for your child you are really choosing a school for the entire family. The students become so involved in their academic and extracurricular activities and the parents spend so much time at school supporting those activities that it does become the entire family's school.

Lila Lohr is a former Head of School at Princeton Day School in Princeton, New Jersey, and the Friends School of Baltimore in Baltimore, Maryland. She has been a teacher and an administrator in independent day schools for more than thirty years and is the mother of 3 independent day school graduates.

The Contemporary Boarding School: Change and Adaptability

Howard Greene
Matthew Greene

One of the most telling characteristics of the independent schools since their inception has been their ability to adapt to the significant social, political, and economic movements that have defined the evolutionary unfolding of an extraordinary nation. Those boarding schools that have survived and flourished over time have done so by adapting their curricula, the composition of their student bodies, and their facilities and resources to continue their role in training future leaders, regardless of their social, religious, and economic backgrounds.

How does this continuous state of adaptation and development translate to contemporary boarding school programs and populations? What do these schools stand for? How do they accomplish their primary goals? Here are the key features you should take note of as you consider this unique form of education.

Diversity

The American boarding school is viewed worldwide as an outstanding venue for students to obtain a first-rate education while they interact with a broad mix of other people. The resources and facilities are unmatched in any other country. Currently, more than 11,000 of the enrolled students in NAIS boarding schools are foreign nationals. Some of the larger, internationally recognized American schools enroll a large number of geographically diverse students.

The modern boarding school is, in fact, far more diverse than the local public schools that the majority of American students attend. Significant socioeconomic and continuing racial and ethnic segregation has resulted in homogeneous student bodies in many public school districts across the country. By contrast, boarding schools have a commitment to enroll outstanding students of all economic and social circumstances.

A Sense of Community

School leaders, when asked what defines their particular school, often refer to the power of community that envelops students, teachers, deans and administrators, coaches, and staff members. How valuable this is to all parties, especially to young men and women caught up in today's frenzied, competitive, and disjointed culture where it is easy to feel overwhelmed and uncertain. The desire to be in an environment where peers and adults are engaged with one another in a caring and supportive culture is a driving force for many who feel disconnected from, or simply not fully engaged with, the people and programs in their current school.

A Beacon of Educational Standards

Boarding schools have always set their own standards of educational attainment and pedagogy. Since they are not regulated by state educational bodies or influenced by the agendas of individual or party politics, the school professionals can design an academic and nonacademic curriculum that reflects the standards and goals they have set for their students.

Building Character

While all boarding schools have as their historic mission preparing students for university entrance and a successful academic experience, most have loftier goals in mind. Character is as important as acquired information and credits. Schools emphasize the development of critical thinking and analytical skills, an open mind to new and different ideas and opinions, excellent writing and oral skills, and an ability to think in mathematical and scientific terms. Most boarding schools look beyond these critical intellectual skills to the emotional, social, moral, and intellectual components of the education of the students in their charge. The residential community becomes a vital and active force in developing and honing these crucial skills. Every day, an individual might be called upon to make a decision in the classroom, on the playing field, or in the dormitory or dining hall that can have either a negative or positive impact on another student or the larger community.

The ultimate goal of the boarding school is not to create privileged adolescents who think and act alike but rather to consider the whole child at a critical stage in his or her moral and social development. There is a powerful force of stated ideals in the community at large that can be drawn on to help guide a young woman or man who has to decide how to behave in social situations, the classroom, the playing field, the dormitory, or even at home.

Boarding Schools as a Partnership

The Board of Trustees' Role

The members of the Board of Trustees are committed volunteers who have been elected to work as a cohesive group in overseeing the well-being of the school. The board is a legal entity charged with the responsibility of making certain the school is in sound fiscal and administrative condition and is fulfilling its stated mission. The board oversees the work of the head of school in the broadest sense and determines if he or she is responsibly managing the school. Typically, board members are recent and older graduates, parents of past and current students, or professional experts, all of whom work together to ensure that the school functions soundly on both an educational and financial basis. Boards generally choose their own members on the basis of a commitment to that institution's mission and purposes.

An independent school that is functioning well is, in large measure, the result of a healthy working relationship between the board and the senior management of the school. Together they review the annual operating budget, consider current and long-term strategic planning, and oversee fund-raising—in particular, capital campaigns to enlarge the school's endowment and physical facilities.

A number of schools include students in board meetings and specific committees. Typically, this includes the president of the student council who attends the general board meetings and student leaders who are active members of the student life committee. Their voices play a helpful role in determining school policies, rules, activities, and programs. In addition to the value added to the school community, these students gain a significant learning experience from such a deliberative process.

The School Head's Role

The head of school, reporting to the Board of Trustees, is the chief executive officer and is responsible for the operation of the school. It is his or her responsibility to execute the broad range of academic and noncurricular programs with the assistance of the faculty and other senior administrators, to hire and fire, to lead the faculty, to maintain a sound fiscal operation, to raise money from outside sources, and to serve as the educational visionary for the institution. A successfully run boarding school is a reflection of the mutual respect and effective working relationship between the head and the trustees.

In reviewing the merits of any boarding school for your child, be certain to learn about the relationship between the school head and the board, as well as the composition of the board. The days of a head staying at a school for twenty or thirty years are long gone, though some sitting heads have been in their position for close to that length of time. The norm these days is closer to the decade mark for a successful head running a well-managed school. A long-established or new head is not necessarily a sign either of school strength or weakness. Look beyond a head's tenure to seek out his or her experience level, accomplishments, energy, philosophy, and personal impact on a school.

The Faculty's Role

The opportunity to teach, counsel, and coach students in an intimate setting is what attracts most teachers to boarding schools. It is common practice for a faculty member in her role as dormitory parent, adviser, classroom teacher, coach, or administrator to seek out students whom she identifies as needing her help through the daily interaction that is part and parcel of the boarding life.

Boarding school teachers play an active and respected role in the affairs of their school. They serve on committees that set academic programs, grading standards, requirements for graduation, and standards of behavior. Faculty members work through academic departments to be certain that students are gaining a comprehensive and coherent education.

It is not happenstance that the great majority of boarding school teachers are graduates of strong liberal arts colleges and, most frequently, have graduate degrees in their particular discipline. A great many also played a sport at the intercollegiate level or were actively engaged in campus governance or the arts. The boarding school offers the teacher who loves her academic subject and has other talents the opportunity to share her enthusiasm with her students. The independent status of the school encourages the dedicated teacher to create and deliver a stimulating, effective curriculum that is usually free of topics, content, or lesson plans mandated by outside sources and without an end goal of preparation for standardized testing.

The Students' Role

Despite its traditions and culture, a school can, and often in large part does, reinvent itself every four years as new classes of students enter the school, gradually assume leadership responsibilities, and graduate, making room for new students to take their places. What an individual school "is" represents a shifting target because of the constant influx and egress of students. For prospective students, who those students are when they arrive constitutes one of the most significant influences on the boarding school experience and whether or not it is a good one.

Students in boarding schools today sit in on board meetings, judge fellow students on disciplinary committees, edit papers and yearbooks, serve as proctors or resident advisers in dormitories, and captain sports teams. They also conduct independent study projects, work with faculty as teaching assistants, guide tours on campus, talk with accreditation committees, and babysit faculty members' children. Students are active in community service projects on campus, in town, and around the world. They start new clubs, raise money for capital campaigns, and publish scientific research. They protest, vote, and serve as peer mediators and advisers. They sit around seminar tables discussing advanced literature and historical topics. They speak their minds, challenging faculty and administrators to improve courses, revise standards, and maintain their composure. Students at boarding schools are clearly not passive recipients; rather they are active participants in all aspects of school and community life.

The Parents' Role

One of the major changes in the boarding school partnership in recent years is the more active role that parents play. In past generations when the schools were more homogeneous in their student composition, parents were basically expected to leave the care and education of their children to the school's head and faculty. They were reassured that the moral, spiritual, and intellectual training of their offspring would be seen to. This is a far cry from the relationship contemporary parents, school administrators, and teachers understand as a partnership. Parents expect regular communications from their child's teachers and house advisers regarding student progress or any personal or academic difficulties. Heads of school and deans acknowledge that there is a regular flow of telephone calls and e-mails from the concerned parent. There is greater communication with parents regarding campus events and specific information about their child's engagement and performance.

Parenting a boarding school student involves a balancing act between being overly involved and too distant. Parents should neither assume that boarding schools will take over all parental and educational responsibilities for their children nor seek to insinuate themselves into every aspect of a student's school life. Parents should be watchful, involved, supportive, and attuned to the messages both the school and student are sending regarding the most appropriate and desirable level of engagement.

Schools also acknowledge that past and current parents are a major source of the financial support that enables them to carry on their stated purposes at the highest level of quality. Parents play a significant role in supporting fund-raising efforts and sponsoring events for current and prospective students and their parents. Most boarding schools have established parent committees that help to keep an open line of communication with the school's administrative leaders regarding parental concerns and recommendations for effective support of the students.

The Student Experience

Rather than interpreting discipline strictly as a punitive concept, schools use discipline as a teaching and learning tool. The community of faculty, deans, and students works together to establish agreeable rules of behavior. Each student must abide by this community ethos and, in the process of doing so, learns much about the interests and needs of others, the responsibility of an individual toward the common good, and the self-discipline and restraint that make this possible. The rewards are ample: a sense of responsibility and empowerment and the freedom to carry on one's daily life of activities and studies and time for friends. Those who break the rules find there is a response from the community and that appropriate action is taken.

Students play a major role in the smooth running of their school. Any school head will quickly confirm that his or her students are never shy or reluctant to make their voices heard on issues that affect their lives. Boarding students take it as fact that articulating their opinions to their teachers and administrators is a fundamental right.

---

*Howard R. Greene, M.A., M.Ed., and Matthew W. Greene, Ph.D., have been providing personalized admissions counseling to guide students to the right secondary school, college, or graduate school for more than 35 years. They are the hosts of two PBS specials on college admission and have written numerous books, including the **Greenes' Guides to Educational Planning Series.***

Originally published in a slightly different form in The Greenes' Guide to Boarding Schools (Princeton: Peterson's, 2006), 9-19. Reprinted by permission of the authors.

Study Confirms Benefits of Boarding School

Many people have long sung the praises of the boarding school experience. The high-level academics, the friendships, and the life lessons learned are without rival at private day or public schools, they say.

Now, a study released by The Association of Boarding Schools (TABS), a nonprofit organization of independent, college-preparatory schools, validates these claims. Not only do boarding school students spend more time studying (and less time watching TV), they are also better prepared for college and progress more quickly in their careers than their counterparts who attended private day or public schools.

The survey, which was conducted by the Baltimore-based research firm the Art & Science Group, involved interviews with 1,000 students and alumni from boarding schools, 1,100 from public schools, and 600 from private day schools (including independent day and parochial schools).

The results not only affirm the benefits enjoyed by boarding school graduates but those bestowed upon current boarding school students as well. "The study helps us better understand how the opportunities for interaction and learning beyond the classroom found at boarding schools impact a student's life at school and into adulthood," explained Steve Ruzicka, former TABS executive director. Ruzicka said the survey also provides boarding school alumni with empirical data to help when considering their children's educational options.

Rigorous Academics Prevail

Why do students apply to boarding schools? The TABS study found that the primary motivation for both applicants and their parents is the promise of a better education. And, happily, the vast majority of current and past students surveyed reported that their schools deliver on this promise. Current students indicated significantly higher levels of satisfaction with their academic experience at boarding schools than their peers at public and private day schools by more than ten percentage points (54 percent of boarding students versus 42 percent of private day students and 40 percent of public school students). Boarders reported in greater relative percentages that they find their schools academically challenging, that their peers are more motivated, and the quality of teaching is very high.

But the boarding environment is valued just as much for the opportunities for interaction and learning beyond the classroom. Interactions in the dining room, the dormitory, and on the playing field both complement and supplement academics, exposing students to a broad geographic and socioeconomic spectrum, challenging their boundaries, and broadening their vision of the world.

The Boarding School Boost

The 24/7 life at boarding schools also gives students a significant leg up when they attend college, the survey documents.

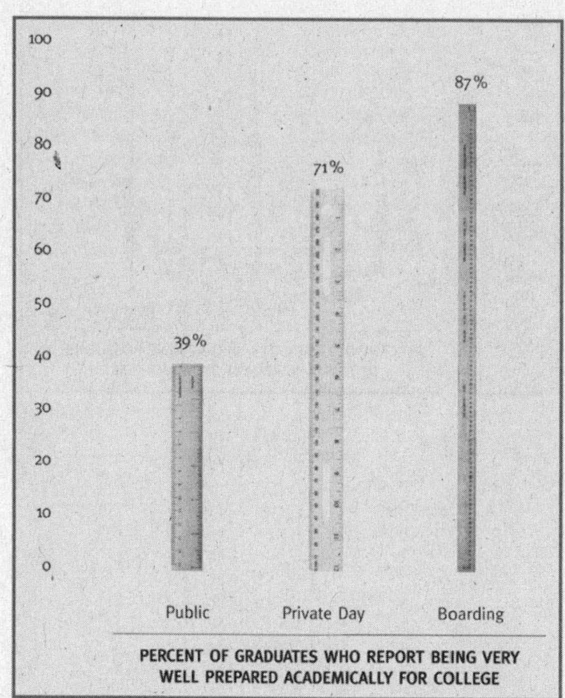

PERCENT OF GRADUATES WHO REPORT BEING VERY WELL PREPARED ACADEMICALLY FOR COLLEGE

Some 87 percent of boarding school graduates said they were very well prepared academically for college, with only 71 percent of private day and just 39 percent of public school alumni saying the same. And 78 percent of boarders reported that their schools also helped better prepare them to face the nonacademic aspects of college life, such as independence, social life, and time management. Only 36 percent of private day graduates and 23 percent of public school graduates said the same.

The TABS survey also documented that a larger percentage of boarding school graduates go on to earn advanced degrees once they finish college: 50 percent, versus 36 percent of private day and 21 percent of public school alumni.

Beyond college, boarding school graduates also reap greater benefits from their on-campus experiences, advancing faster and further in their careers comparatively. The study scrutinized former boarders versus private day and public school graduates in terms of achieving positions in top management and found that by midcareer, 44 percent of boarding school graduates had reached positions in top management versus 33 percent of private day school graduates and 27 percent of public school graduates.

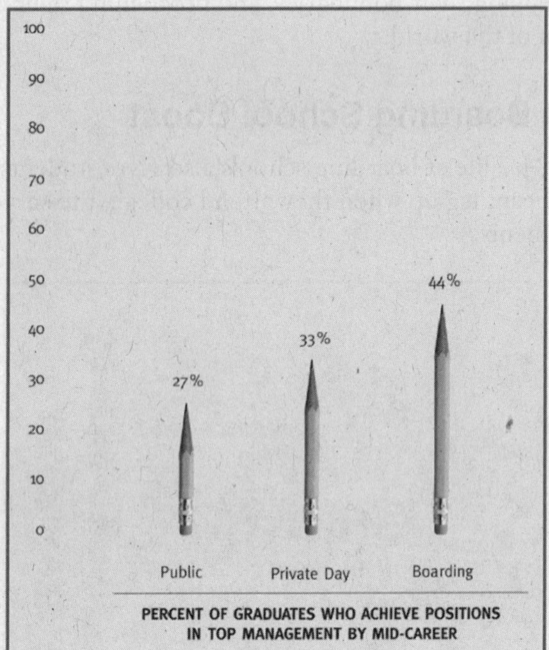

PERCENT OF GRADUATES WHO ACHIEVE POSITIONS IN TOP MANAGEMENT BY MID-CAREER

By late in their careers, more than half of the surveyed boarding school sample, 52 percent, held positions in top management as opposed to 39 percent of private day and 27 percent of public school graduates.

But perhaps the most compelling statistic that the study produced is the extremely high percentage—some 90 percent—of boarding school alumni who say they would, if given the opportunity, repeat their boarding school experience. This alone is a strong argument that validates the enduring value of the boarding school model. It is hoped that the study will help dispel many of the myths and stereotypes that have dogged the image of boarding schools over the last century and spread the good news that boarding schools today are diverse, exciting places for bright, well-adjusted students who are looking for success in their academic lives—and beyond.

For more information on TABS visit the Web site at www.schools.com.

Used by permission of The Association of Boarding Schools.

Semester Schools: Great Opportunities

Mark Meyer-Braun
Former Head of School, The Outdoor Academy

Over the last twenty years, there has been tremendous growth in the range of educational opportunities available to young Americans. The advent of semester schools has played no small part in this trend. Similar in many ways to semester-abroad programs, semester schools provide secondary school students the opportunity to leave their home school for half an academic year to have a very different kind of experience—the experience of living and learning within a small community, among diverse students, and in a new and different place. The curricula of such schools tend to be thematic, interdisciplinary, rigorous, and experiential.

At semester schools, students have a full-immersion experience in a tightly knit learning community.

What Are the Benefits?

As a starting point for their programs, semester schools have embraced many of the qualities typical of independent schools. In fact, a number of semester schools were developed as extension programs by existing independent schools, providing unusual opportunities to their own students and those from other schools. Other semester schools have grown from independent educational organizations or foundations that bring their own educational interests and expertise to their semester programs. In both cases, semester schools provide the kind of challenging environment for which independent schools are known.

Across the board, semester school programs provide students with exceptional opportunities for contact with their teachers. Individual instruction and intimate classes are common, as is contact with teachers outside the classroom. At semester schools, students have a full-immersion experience in a tightly knit learning community. In such a setting, teachers are able to challenge each student in his or her own area of need, mentoring students to both academic and personal fulfillment.

Semester schools have developed around specialized curricular interests, often involving unique offerings or nontraditional subjects. In almost every case, these specialized curricula are related to the school's location. Indeed, place-based learning is a common thread in semester school education. Whether in New York City or the Appalachian Mountains, semester schools enable students to cultivate a sense of place and develop greater sensitivity to their surroundings. This is often accomplished through a combination of experiential education and traditional instruction. Students develop academic knowledge and practical skills in tandem through active participation in intellectual discourse, creative projects, hands-on exercises, and service learning opportunities. Throughout, emphasis is placed on the importance of combining intellectual exploration with thoughtful self-reflection, often facilitated by journaling exercises or group processing activities.

At semester schools, students inevitably learn their most important lessons through their membership in the school community. Living closely with peers and teachers and working together for the benefit of the group enables students to develop extraordinary communication skills and high levels of interpersonal accountability. Through this experience, students gain invaluable leadership and cooperation skills.

Ultimately, semester schools seek to impart translatable skills to their students. The common goal is for students to return to their schools and families with greater motivation, empathy, self-knowledge, and self-determination. These skills help to prepare students for the college experience and beyond. In addition, semester school participants report that their experiences helped to distinguish them in the college application process. Semester school programs are certainly not for everybody, but they serve an important role for students who are seeking something beyond the ordinary—students who wish to know themselves and the world in a profound way. All of the following semester school programs manifest these same values in their own distinctive way.

CITYterm

CITYterm, founded in 1996, is an interdisciplinary, experience-based program that takes 30 juniors and seniors from across the country and engages them in a semester-long study of New York City. CITYterm students typically spend three days a week in the classroom, reading, writing, and thinking about New York City, and three days a week in the city working on projects, studying diverse neighborhoods, or meeting with politicians, urban historians, authors, artists, actors, and various city experts. Much of the excitement of CITYterm comes from experiencing firsthand in the city what has been studied in the classroom. Many of the projects are done in collaborative teams where the groups engage not only in formal academic research at the city's libraries but also use the resources of New York City's residents and institutions to gather the information necessary for presentations. Students come to see themselves as the active creators of their own learning both in the classroom and in the world. Learn more about CITYterm by visiting www.cityterm.org.

Conserve School

Conserve School is a semester school for high school juniors that is focused on the theme of environmental stewardship. Attending Conserve School gives high school students a one-semester opportunity to step out of their regular school and into a unique educational setting, while still continuing their required academic studies. Conserve School's challenging, college-prep curriculum immerses high school juniors in environmental history, nature literature, and the science of conservation. Because Conserve School is located on a 1,200-acre wilderness campus, a significant portion of the curriculum is delivered via outdoors, hands-on, active learning. Conserve School is located just west of Land O' Lakes, Wisconsin, near the border of Michigan's Upper Peninsula. Learn more about the Conserve School at www.conserveschool.org/.

The Island School

The Island School, founded in 1999 by The Lawrenceville School, is an independent academic program in the Bahamas for high school sophomores or juniors. The fourteen-week academic course of study includes honors classes in science, field research (a laboratory science), history, math, art, English literature, and physical/outdoor education and a weekly community service component. All courses are place-based and explicitly linked, taking advantage of the school's surroundings to both deepen understandings of complex academic and social issues and to make those understandings lasting by connecting course content with experience. Students apply their investigative, interpretive, and problem-solving skills during four- and eight-day kayaking expeditions, SCUBA diving opportunities, teaching environmental issues to local students, and in daily life at the school. In addition to traditional

classroom assessments, students conduct research on mangrove communities, coastal management, artificial reefs, permaculture, and marine protected areas. These projects support national research and are conducted under the auspices of the Bahamian government. At the conclusion of the semester, students present their work to a panel of visiting scientists and educators, including local and national government officials from the Bahamas. The opportunity to interact with the local community through research, outreach, and the rigorous physical and academic schedule creates a transformative experience for students. The admissions process is competitive, and selected students demonstrate solid academic performance, leadership potential, and a high degree of self-motivation. Contact The Island School for more information at www.islandschool.org.

Chewonki Semester School

The Chewonki Semester School (formerly Maine Coast Semester) offers a small group of eleventh-grade students the chance to live and work on a 400-acre saltwater peninsula with the goal of exploring the natural world through courses in natural science, environmental issues, literature and writing, art, history, mathematics, and foreign language. Since 1988, this semester school has welcomed students from more than 230 public and private schools across the country and in Canada. The Chewonki community is small—39 students and 20 faculty members—and the application process is competitive. In addition to their studies, students work for several hours each afternoon on an organic farm, in a wood lot, or on maintenance and construction projects. Students who attend are highly motivated, capable, and willing to take the risk of leaving friends and family for a portion of their high school career. They enjoy hard work, both intellectual and physical, and they demonstrate a tangible desire to contribute to the world. Chewonki students return to their schools with self-confidence, an appreciation for the struggles and rewards of community living, and an increased sense of ownership of their education. For information on the Chewonki Semester School, go to www.chewonki.org.

The Mountain School

The Mountain School of Milton Academy, founded in 1984, hosts 45 high school juniors from private and public schools throughout the United States who have chosen to spend four months on a working organic farm in Vermont. Courses provide a demanding and integrated learning experience, taking full advantage of the school's small size and mountain campus. Students and adults develop a social contract of mutual trust that expects individual and communal responsibility, models the values of simplicity and sustainability, and challenges teenagers to engage in meaningful work. Students live with teachers in small houses and help make important decisions concerning how to live together and manage the farm. Courses offered include English, environmental science, U.S. history, and all levels of math, physics, chemistry, Spanish, French, Latin, studio art, and humanities. To learn more, please visit the Web site at www. mountainschool.org.

The Outdoor Academy of the Southern Appalachians

The Outdoor Academy offers tenth-grade and select eleventh-grade students from across the country a semester away in the mountains of North Carolina. Arising from more than eighty years of experiential education at Eagle's Nest Foundation, this school-away-from-school provides a college-preparatory curriculum along with special offerings in environmental education, outdoor leadership, the arts, and community service. Each semester, up to 35 students embrace the Southern Appalachians as a unique ecological, historical, and cultural American region. In this setting, students and teachers live as a close-knit community, and lessons of cooperation and responsibility abound. Students develop a healthy work ethic as course work and projects are pursued both in and out of the classroom. Courses in English, mathematics, science, history, foreign language, visual and performing arts, and music emphasize hands-on and cooperative learning. Classes often meet outside on the 180-acre wooded campus or in nearby national wilderness areas, where the natural world enhances intellectual pursuits. On weekends and extended trips, the outdoor leadership program teaches hiking, backpacking, caving, canoeing, and rock-climbing skills. The Outdoor Academy is open to students from both public and private secondary schools and is accredited by the Southern Association of Colleges and Schools. Learn more about The Outdoor Academy at www.enf.org/outdoor_academy/academic_program.

The Oxbow School

The Oxbow School in Napa, California, is a one-semester visual arts program for high school juniors and seniors from public and private schools nationwide. Oxbow offers students a unique educational experience focused on in-depth study in sculpture, printmaking, drawing and painting, and photography and digital media, including animation. The interdisciplinary, project-based curriculum emphasizes experiential learning, critical thinking, and the development of research skills as a means of focused artistic inquiry. Each semester, 2 Visiting Artists are invited to work collaboratively with students and teachers. By engaging students in the creative process, Oxbow fosters a deep appreciation for creativity in all areas of life beyond the classroom. Since its founding in 1998, students who have spent a semester at The Oxbow School have matriculated to leading universities, colleges, and independent colleges of art and design around the country. Learn more at www.oxbowschool.org.

The Rocky Mountain Semester

The Rocky Mountain Semester (RMS) at the High Mountain Institute is an opportunity for high school juniors to examine the human relationship to the natural world through a combination of rigorous academics and extended wilderness expeditions. During the 110-day program, up to 38 students spend five weeks backpacking, skiing, and studying throughout the wilderness of Colorado and Utah. The remainder of the semester is spent on campus near Leadville, Colorado, where students pursue a rigorous course of study and learn how to live successfully in a small community environment. While at the RMS, most students take five or six classes—the only required elective is Practices and Principles: Ethics of the Natural World. It is in this class that students are taught the theoretical foundations for all that is done in the field, examine the human relationship to the natural world, and learn the skills necessary to travel safely and comfortably in remote settings. Students may also take literature of the natural world, natural science, U.S. history or AP U.S. history, Spanish or French, and mathematics.

Interested students can learn more about The Rocky Mountain Semester at www.hminet.org/RockyMountainSemester.

The Woolman Semester

The Woolman Semester is a community-based, sixteen-week, interdisciplinary program for high school juniors and seniors and first-year postgraduates. The mission of the school is to weave together peace, sustainability, and social action into an intensely rigorous academic experience. The school is located at the Sierra Friends Center in Nevada City, California, on a 230-acre campus complete with forests, fields, gardens, and livestock to use as a living laboratory, as well as for the wood chopping and lettuce harvesting of daily life. Classes generally meet in the morning, while labs, study groups, and farm work take place in the afternoon. Students and faculty members also participate in a two-week service project and a one-week wilderness trip. Get all the information on The Woolman Semester program at www.woolman.org.

The author wishes to acknowledge and thank all the semester school programs for contributing their school profiles and collaborating in order to spread the word about semester school education.

Why a Therapeutic or Special Needs School?

Diederik van Renesse

Families contact me when a son or daughter is experiencing increased difficulties in school or has shown a real change in attitude at home. Upon further discussion, parents often share the fact that they have spoken with their child's teachers and have held meetings to establish support systems in the school and at home. Evaluations, medications, therapists, and motivational counseling are but a few of the multiple approaches that parents and educators take—yet in some cases, the downward spiral continues. Anxiety builds in the student and family members; school avoidance and increased family turmoil reach a point where the situation is intolerable, and alternatives must be explored—be it a special needs school, a therapeutic school, or a combination of both.

Some families seek the help of an independent education consultant to identify the most appropriate setting.

But should that school be a day or residential school, and how do parents decide which will best meet their child's needs? Resources such as *Peterson's Private Secondary Schools*, the Internet, guidance/school counselors, and therapists are valuable; however, the subtle nuances involved in determining the environment that will best serve the child are difficult to ascertain. Some families seek the help of an independent education consultant to identify the most appropriate setting. Many independent education consultants specialize in working with children who have special needs such as learning differences, anxiety disorders, emotional issues, ADHD, opposition, defiance, school phobia, drug or alcohol abuse, Asperger Syndrome, autism, and more. Consultants have frequent contact with the schools, and they work closely with parents during the enrollment process.

Given the broad spectrum of needs presented by individual students, many parents question whether there is indeed a day school that can meet the needs of their child. The answer often depends on location, space availability, willingness to relocate, and appropriateness of the options. While there are many day school options throughout the United States, there are even more residential or boarding options. Clearly the decision to have your child attend a residential school is not made easily. As a family you may feel as though you do not have a choice—but you should undertake a thorough assessment of all the day options and how they might meet the majority of your child's needs.

When the primary concerns are learning differences, many local options (though often small and issue-specific) are available to families. Local counselors are often valuable resources as are local chapters of national LD organizations. If you come up with a variety of options, carefully compare them by visiting the schools and meeting with the specialists at each school—those individuals who will work directly with your child.

With the day options, it is important to keep the following factors in mind: program and staff credentials, transportation time to and from the school, availability of additional resources (support services) in or outside the school setting, sports and extracurricular offerings, facilities and accessibility, and your child's potential peer group. You will also need to assess many of these factors when considering residential schools, although most residential schools are more self-contained than day schools. Also significant is whether the school has been approved by and accepts funding from its state and/or school district.

For families who cannot avail themselves of local day options or whose child is best served in a residential setting, an even greater spectrum of options is available. These range from traditional boarding schools with built-in academic support services to therapeutic boarding schools, wilderness or outdoor therapeutic programs, emotional growth or behavior modification schools, transitional or independent living programs, and even residential treatment centers, hospitals, or other health facilities.

Given the breadth of the residential schools or programs, most families are best served by a team that includes not only the parents (and at times the student), but also the professionals who have taught, counseled, and worked closely with the child. Together, the team can identify the specific needs, deficits, or behavioral issues that must be addressed, and they can work together to match those with the appropriate schools. As with day schools, you should arrange to visit the facilities so that you are well-informed about each option and will be comfortable with your final decision. These visits are not only opportunities for you to meet the staff and students, but also for you and your child to begin a relationship that will continue when your child is enrolled.

There is no question that seeking alternative options, whether they are special needs or therapeutic, is a daunting task. However, with the help of expert resources and reliable professionals, the right school can make a significant and lasting impact on your child's health and well-being.

Diederik van Renesse is a Senior Partner at Steinbrecher & Partners Educational Consulting Services in Westport, Connecticut. A former teacher, admission director, and private school counselor, he now specializes in helping families throughout the United States and abroad with youngsters who require special needs or alternative schools or who need interventions and therapeutic settings.

Finding the Perfect Match

Helene Reynolds

One of the real benefits of independent education is that it allows you to deliberately seek out and choose a school community for your child. If you are like most parents, you want your child's school years to reflect an appropriate balance of academic challenge, social development, and exploration into athletics and the arts. You hope that through exposure to new ideas and sound mentoring your child will develop an awareness of individual social responsibility, as well as the study skills and work ethic to make a contribution to his or her world. It is every parent's fondest wish to have the school experience spark those areas of competence that can be pursued toward excellence and distinction.

An increasing number of parents realize that this ideal education is found outside their public school system, that shrinking budgets, divisive school boards, and overcrowded classrooms have resulted in schools where other agendas vie with education for attention and money. In this environment there is less time and energy for teachers to focus on individual needs.

The decision to choose a private school can be made for as many different reasons as there are families making the choice. Perhaps your child would benefit from smaller classes or accelerated instruction. Perhaps your child has needs or abilities that can be more appropriately addressed in a specialized environment. Perhaps you are concerned about the academic quality of your local public school and the impact it may have on your child's academic future. Or perhaps you feel that a private school education is a gift you can give your child to guide him or her toward a more successful future.

Every child is an individual, and this makes school choice a process unique to each family. The fact that your father attended a top-flight Eastern boarding school to prepare for the Ivy League does not necessarily make this educational course suitable for all of his grandchildren. In addition to determining the school's overall quality, you must explore the appropriateness of philosophy, curriculum, level of academic difficulty, and style before making your selection. The right school is the school where your child will thrive, and a famous name and a hallowed reputation are not necessarily the

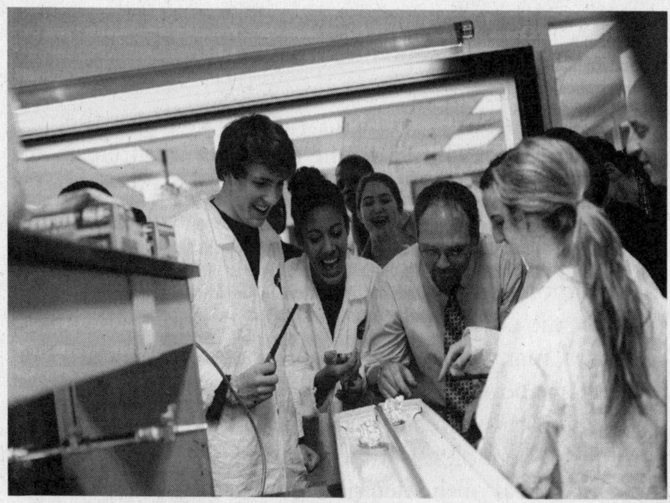

factors that define the right environment. The challenge is in discovering what the factors are that make the match between your child and his or her school the right one.

No matter how good its quality and reputation, a single school is unlikely to be able to meet the needs of all children. The question remains: How do families begin their search with confidence so they will find what they are looking for? How do they make the right connection?

As a parent, there are a number of steps you can follow to establish a reasoned and objective course of information gathering that will lead to a subjective discussion of this information and the way it applies to the student in question. This can only occur if the first step is done thoroughly and in an orderly manner. Ultimately, targeting a small group of schools, any of which could be an excellent choice, is only possible after information gathering and discussion have taken place. With work and a little luck, the result of this process is a school with an academically sound and challenging program based on an educational philosophy that is an extension of the family's views and which will provide an emotionally and socially supportive milieu for the child.

Step 1: Identify Student Needs

Often the decision to change schools seems to come out of the blue, but, in retrospect, it can be seen as a decision the family has been leading up to for some time. I would urge parents to decide on their own goals for the search first and to make sure, if possible, that they can work in concert toward meeting these goals before introducing the idea to their child. These goals are as different as the parents who hold them. For one parent, finding a school with a state-of-the-art computer program is a high priority. For another, finding a school with a full dance and music program is important. Others will be most concerned about finding a school that has the best record of college acceptances and highest SAT or ACT scores.

Once you have decided your own goals for the search, bring the child into the discussion. I often say to parents that the decision to explore is *not* the decision to change schools but only the decision to gather information and consider options. It is important to be aware that everyone has an individual style of decision making and that the decision to make a change is loaded with concerns, many of which will not be discovered until the process has begun.

If you have already made the decision to change your child's school, it is important to let your child know that this aspect of the decision is open to discussion but not to negotiation. It is equally important that you let your child know that he or she will have responsibility in choosing the specific school. Without that knowledge, your son or daughter may feel that he or she has no control over the course of his or her own life.

If you have already made the decision to change your child's school, it is important to let your child know that this aspect of the decision is open to discussion but not to negotiation.

Some students are responsible enough to take the lead in the exploration; some are too young to do so. But in all cases, children need reassurance about their future and clarity about the reasons for considering other school settings. Sometimes the situation is fraught with disparate opinions that can turn school choice into a family battleground, one in which the child is the ultimate casualty. It is always important to keep in mind that the welfare of the child is the primary goal.

The knowledge that each individual has his or her own agenda and way of making decisions should be warning enough to pursue some preliminary discussion so that you, as parents, can avoid the pitfall of conflicting goals and maintain a united front and a reasonably directed course of action. The family discussion should be energetic, and differences of opinion should be encouraged as healthy and necessary and expressed in a climate of trust and respect.

There are many reasons why you may, at this point, decide to involve a professional educational consultant. Often this choice is made to provide a neutral ground where you and your child can both speak and be heard. Another reason is to make sure that you have established a sound course of exploration that takes both your own and your child's needs into consideration. Consultants who are up-to-date on school information, who have visited each campus, and who are familiar with the situations of their clients can add immeasurably to the process. They can provide a reality check, reinforcement of personal impressions, and experience-based information support for people who are doing a search of this type for the first time. All the research in the world cannot replace the experience and industry knowledge of a seasoned professional. In addition, if the specific circumstances of the placement are delicate, the educational consultant is in a position to advocate for your child during the placement process. There are also situations in which a family in crisis doesn't have the time or the ability to approach school choice in a deliberate and objective manner.

These are some of the many reasons to engage the services of a consultant, but it is the family guidance aspect that most families overlook at the start of the process and value most highly after they have completed it. A good consultant provides neutral ground and information backup that are invaluable.

Step 2: Evaluate Your Child's Academic Profile

If your child's academic profile raises questions about his or her ability, learning style, or emotional profile, get a professional evaluation to make sure that your expectations for your child are congruent with the child's actual abilities and needs.

Start gathering information about your child from the current school. Ask guidance counselors and teachers for their observations, and request a formal meeting to review the standardized testing that virtually every school administers. Question their views of your child's behavior, attentiveness, and areas of strength and weakness. Make sure you fully understand the reasons behind their recommendations. Do not feel shy about calling back to ask questions at a later date, after you have had time to think and consider this important information. Your child's future may depend on the decisions you are making; don't hesitate to keep asking until you have the information you need.

If a picture of concern emerges, ask the guidance counselor, other parents, or your pediatrician for suggestions regarding learning specialists or psychologists in the community who work with children and can provide an evaluation of their academic ability, academic achievement, and learning style. The evaluation should be reviewed in-depth with the specialist, who should be asked about specific recommendations for changes in the youngster's schooling.

Remember, as the parent, it is ultimately your responsibility to weigh the ideas of others and to decide if the difficulty lies with your child or the environment, either of which could indicate a need for a change of school.

Step 3: Review the Goals of Placement

Discuss your differences of opinion about making a change. Identify a list of schools that creates a ballpark of educational possibilities. (An educational consultant can also be helpful at this stage.)

It is important that both you and your child take the time to consider what characteristics, large and small, you would like in the new school and which you would like to avoid. As you each make lists of priorities and discuss them, the process of school choice enters the subjective arena. The impersonal descriptions of school environments transform into very personal visualizations of the ways you and your child view the child in a new setting.

A chance to play ice hockey, a series of courses in Mandarin Chinese, the opportunity to take private flute lessons, or a desire to meet others from all over the world may sound like a bizarre mix of criteria, but the desire to explore and find all of these options in a single environment expresses the expansiveness of the student's mind and the areas he or she wants to perfect, try out, or explore. Don't expect perfectly logical thinking from your child as he or she considers options; don't take everything he or she says literally or too seriously. Open and respectful discussion will allow a child to embrace a new possibility one day and reject it the next—this is part of the process of decision making and affirmation and part of the fun of exploration.

Step 4: Set an Itinerary

Set an itinerary for visits and interviews so that you and your child can compare campuses and test your preconceived ideas of the schools you have researched against the reality of the campus community; forward standardized testing scores and transcripts to the schools prior to visits so that the admission office has pertinent information in advance of your meeting.

In order to allow your child the freedom to form opinions about the schools you visit, you may want to keep these pointers in mind:

- Parents should allow their child to be front and center during the visits and interviews—allow your child to answer questions, even if they leave out details you think are important.
- Parents should stay in the background and have confidence that the admission officers know how to engage kids in conversation.
- This may be the first time your child has been treated by a school as an individual and responsible person—enjoy watching him or her adjust to this as an observer, not as a protector or participant.
- Don't let your own anxiety ruin your child's experience.
- Discuss dress in advance so it doesn't become the issue and focus of the trip.

Keep your ideas and impressions to yourself and allow your child first shot at verbalizing opinions. Remember that immediate reactions are not final decisions; often the first response is only an attempt to process the experience.

Step 5: Use the Application Process for Personal Guidance

Make sure your child uses the application process not only to satisfy the school's need for information but also to continue the personal guidance process of working through and truly understanding his or her goals and expectations.

Application questions demand your child's personal insight and exploration. Addressing questions about significant experiences, people who have influenced his or her life, or selecting four words that best describe him or her are ways of coming to grips with who your child is and what he or she wants to accomplish both at the new school and in life. Although parents want their children to complete seamless and perfect applications, it is important to remember that the application must be the work of the child and that the parent has an excellent opportunity to discuss the questions and answers to help guide the student in a positive and objective self-review.

It is more important that the application essays accurately reflect the personality and values of the student than that they be technically flawless. Since the school is basing part of its acceptance decision on the contents of the application, the school needs to meet the real student in the application. The child's own determination of what it is important for the school to know about them is crucial to this process. That being said, parents can play an important role in helping the child understand the difference between unnecessarily brutal honesty and putting his or her best foot forward.

Step 6: Trust Your Observations

Although the process of school exploration depends on objectivity, it is rare that a family will embrace a school solely because of its computer labs, endowment, library, SAT or ACT scores, or football team. These objective criteria frame the search, but it tends to be the intangibles that determine the decision. It is the subjective—instinctive responses to events on campus, people met, quality of interview, unfathomable vibes—that makes the match.

It is important to review what aspects of the school environment made you feel at home. These questions apply equally to parent and child. Did you like the people you met on campus? Was the tour informational but informal, with students stopping to greet you or the tour guide? Was the tone of the campus (austere or homey, modern or traditional) consistent with the kind of educational atmosphere you are looking for? Are the sports facilities beyond your wildest expectation? Does the college-sending record give you confidence that your child will find an intellectually comfortable peer group? How long do the teachers tend to stay with the school, and do they send their own children there? If it is a boarding school, do teachers live on campus? How homey is the dorm setup?

The most fundamental questions are: Do people in the school community like where they are, trust each other, have respect for each other, and feel comfortable there? Is it a family you would care to join? These subjective responses will help you recognize which schools will make your child feel he or she is part of the community, where he or she will fit in and be respected for who he or she is and wants to become.

Helene Reynolds is a former educational consultant from Princeton, New Jersey.

Plan a Successful School Search

Application deadlines, entrance exams, interviews, and acceptance or rejection letters—these are some of the challenges you can expect to encounter when applying to private schools. The school search may seem daunting, but it doesn't have to be. Here are some tips to help get you on your way.

The first step is to gather information, preferably in the spring before you plan on applying. *Peterson's Private Secondary Schools*, with vital statistics on more than 1,100 leading private schools in the United States and abroad, can help you evaluate schools, clarify your choices, and hone your search.

If you're considering boarding schools, you may also want to obtain a free copy of the *Boarding Schools Directory* from The Association of Boarding Schools (TABS) by calling 828-258-5354 or visiting TABS's Web site (www.boardingschools.com).

Visiting Schools

The next step is to start a list of schools that pique your or your child's interest. You'll want to call, fax, e-mail, or write to admission offices for catalogs and applications. At this stage, don't let cost rule out choices. You'll learn more about the school later—the financing resources it makes available to students and its policies of awarding aid.

With school brochures and catalogs in hand, start planning fall visits and interviews. Review your school calendar, noting Saturdays, holidays, and vacations. Try to plan interviews for these days off. Each interview could last about 3 hours, as campus tours and other activities are often included.

Once you have determined which schools you want to see, where they are, and in what order you want to see them, call each school to set the interview date and time.

Keep in mind that there is no "magic number" of schools to see. Some students interview at and apply to only one school, feeling that if they are not accepted, they will stay at their current school. Some students interview at many, thinking that considering a large number and a variety of schools will help them focus on real needs and desires.

After you've made an appointment to visit the school, reread the school's catalog and, if possible, its description in this guide, and check out its Web site so that facts about the school will be fresh in your mind when you visit.

The Application Process

Once the fact-finding is completed, your child will need to work on applications. Most schools have January or February deadlines, so it pays to begin filling out forms in November.

Applications may ask for all or some of the following: school records, references from teachers, a student statement, a writing sample or essay, an application fee, and medical history form.

If you are working with a hard-copy form, make photocopies of all application pages before your child begins to complete them. That way, he or she will have at least one copy for use as a rough draft. Also make copies of each completed application for your records.

References are usually written on specific school forms and are considered confidential. To ensure confidentiality, people providing references mail their comments directly to the school. A school may require four or five references—three academic references, usually from an English teacher, a math teacher, and one other teacher, and one or two references from other evaluators who know your child's strengths in areas other than academics. Ask these people in advance if they will write on your child's behalf. Give reference-writers appropriate forms with any special instructions and stamped envelopes addressed to the school; be sure to provide as much lead time before the deadline as possible.

The student application is completed on a special form and consists of factual family information, as well as some long or short essay questions. As tempting as it may be to help, let your child do the writing. The schools need to see the student's style, mechanical skills, and the way he or she looks at life and education. Some schools require a corrected writing sample from an English assignment. In this case, have your child ask his or her English teacher to help choose his or her best work.

For additional information on applications, including the common application forms, check out "Understanding the Admission Application Form" on page 25.

Most schools have January or February deadlines, so it pays to begin filling out forms in November.

Once the applications are mailed or submitted online, the hard part is done. Ask admission officers when you can expect to hear their decisions. Most schools will let you know in early March. While you wait, you may want to remind your son or daughter that being turned down by a school is not a statement about his or her worth. Schools have many different objectives in putting a class together. And that's a lesson that will come in handy when you face the college application process.

Understanding the Admission Application Form

Gregg W. M. Maloberti
Dean of Admission
The Lawrenceville School
Lawrenceville, New Jersey

Students applying to independent schools are presented with a myriad of options when it comes time to choose the method of completing the application process. Where once each school issued and required its own paper application, many schools now accept common applications such as the Secondary Schools Application from SSAT (Secondary School Admission Test), the Admission Application Form from TABS (The Association of Boarding Schools), or various other online application forms sponsored by individual schools and placement programs. With so many options, many applicants and parents are perplexed as to which method to employ, and others worry that the choice of one method over another may have a negative effect on their chances of admission. Understanding more about why these changes came about and how they save applicants and schools time and money may help applicants and their parents make an informed choice about which method to use.

The recent developments and innovations in independent school applications mirror the changes that have occurred at the college level. The College Board's Common Application is accepted at over 300 colleges and is available online. The Internet has accelerated the interest in online applications. At the same time, students are much more accustomed to writing on a computer than they once were with pen and paper. Concerns about the financial and environmental costs of a paper-based application that travels from the printer to the school, to the candidate, to the candidate's school, and back to the admission office by mail or courier contribute to the idea that the time of an online commonly accepted application has come.

The Standard Application Online (SAO) is available on the SSAT Web site at www.ssat.org/ssat/apply-appservice.html. The Boarding Schools Admission Application Form is available in the TABS Boarding Schools Directory and in electronic form from the TABS Web site: http://www.boardingschools.com/how-to-apply/application.aspx.

There are a few schools that accept only the recommendation forms from the Admission Application Form. It's best to check with each school to find out which forms are preferred. The list of schools accepting the Secondary Schools Application from SSAT is available at this SSAT Web site: http://www.ssat.org/ssat/apply-appservice.html.

Common Applications Make Sense

Anxious parents' lingering doubts about the use of one of the common application forms are hard to ignore: Will the substitution of the common application for the individual school's application cause the admission committee to be offended and compromise my child's chances for admission? Parents should rest assured that schools agreeing to accept the common application forms believe that a fair and effective admission decision can be made on the basis of the common form and that its use in no way erodes the quality of their selection process.

How Does the Common Application Differ?

All applications begin with a biographical sketch of the candidate: name, address, birth date, mailing address, parents' names, and schools attended. Information regarding sibling or legacy relationships, interest in financial aid, citizenship, language spoken, and even racial and ethnic diversity is collected as well. Except for the order in which these questions appear, there is little variation in these question types from one school's application to another. The common application forms certainly relieve candidates of the burden of providing the very same biographical information over and over again.

The second section of an application generally reveals a candidate's accomplishments and ambitions. Often, the applicants are asked to catalog their interests and activities in list or narrative form. Schools want to know what the candidate has done, for how long, with whom, and to what distinction, if any. In a few cases, some schools ask for a series of short answers to a combination of questions or look for the applicant to complete a sentence. There are generally no "right" answers to these questions—but honest answers can help the school begin to characterize the applicant's curiosity, maturity, ambition, and self-esteem. Here again, great similarity exists in the manner and style with which this information is gathered. While the common application forms ask these question types in a more direct manner, they are no less effective than the individual school's application, and their use affords a candidate a genuine measure of efficiency without compromising individuality.

Schools that advocate the use of their own applications over that of the common application forms often bitterly defend the third and final portion of their applications since it generally includes essay questions. With few exceptions, these questions, while occasionally posed in a unique or original manner, seek to probe much the same territory covered by the three choices listed in the essay section of the common application forms:

1. Describe a person you admire or who has influenced you a great deal.
2. What makes you the interesting person that you are?
3. Explain the impact of an event or activity that has created a change in your life or in your way of thinking.

Many schools that use the common applications require a supplement that affords an opportunity for candidates to provide information that is not requested by the common applications.

While the candidate's ability to write well is certainly under review in the essay question, the exercise investigates a candidate's values and explores the individual experiences that have shaped his or her character. These questions give candidates a chance to reveal such qualities as independence, self-reliance, creativity, originality, humility, generosity, curiosity, and genius. Viewed in this light, answering these questions becomes a tall order. The best advice may be to just answer them. In addition, candidates should recognize that although the content of their essays is always of interest, grammar, spelling, punctuation, organization, and the inclusion of evidence or examples are of equal importance.

Candidates who come from disadvantaged backgrounds often find this section of the application the most challenging and occasionally exclusionary. Some schools assume that all applicants have access to opportunities such as summer camps, music instruction, and periodicals and newspapers. Whatever the case, the common application forms attempt to be more inclusive of a broader set of experiences. In fact, many outreach agencies who seek to identify and place disadvantaged students in independent schools have either used one of the existing common application forms or have developed their own applications in lieu of individual school application forms.

If a student fears that using one of the common applications will somehow fail to convey a unique aspect of his or her individuality or that the essay question answers will not speak to the unique qualities of why a particular school might be a good match, he or she may want to think about including an extra essay. Just because a candidate uses a common application does not mean that he or she must use a common approach to completing it. Imagine how welcome a splash of creativity might be to an individual reader or committee of admission officers who may read hundreds or even thousands of applications each admission season. An application that parrots the list of school courses, sports, and activities offers little insight into the candidate. A well-written application will be as unique as the individual who wrote it.

Applicants and their parents are not the only winners when a common application form is used. The teachers who dutifully complete countless recommendation forms enjoy the convenience of having to complete only one form for each of their students applying to independent schools. Practically speaking, if there is ever a time that a student wants to be in good favor with his or her teacher, it is the moment at which a reference is being given. Using a common application makes the process of applying to multiple schools a much more manageable endeavor. When there is only one form to complete, most teachers will provide longer and more informative answers that are far more helpful to admission officers. Common applications are a great remedy for the fatigue and frustration endured by teachers who have been overwhelmed by a barrage of recommendation forms. Currently, there are even more schools accepting common recommendation forms than there are schools accepting the entire Secondary School Application or the Admission Application Form. Before discounting the benefits of a common application, be sure to consider at least the use of the recommendation forms.

Using a common application makes the process of applying to multiple schools a much more manageable endeavor.

Counselors and Consultants Speak Out

Lee Carey, Director of Admissions and Secondary School Counseling at Shore Country Day School in Beverly, Massachusetts, has been advising eighth-graders for many years and finds the workload associated with the application process unreasonable for most of her students. "It is inconceivable to expect a 14-year-old student to write upwards of eight individual essays, all of top quality. From taking time for school visits, making up missed schoolwork, organizing forms, completing paperwork, and polishing writing, the act of applying to secondary schools becomes a whole second job for eighth- and ninth-grade students." Considering that the average application includes up to ten documents, some of which must pass between the applicant, the sending school, and back to the applicant or the receiving school, an eighth grader and his or her parents are now looking at completing more than eighty documents! On top of the testing process and applying for financial aid, this amounts to an enormous administrative challenge.

Karl Koenigsbauer, Director of Secondary School Placement, Eaglebrook School in Deerfield, Massachusetts, agrees that the common application forms make the process more efficient, but he worries about how they might erode the process as well. "My goal is to help students find the school that will be the best match for their abilities and interests. The essay questions from some schools really help the candidate to understand more about what qualities of mind and spirit a school values. When a candidate comes to me and says a particular question is too difficult, too simplistic, or just plain confusing, it gives me an opportunity to help him or her see how that question represents the identity of that particular school and why it may or may not be a good match. I worry that the common application forms will homogenize the application process to the point where I lose this opportunity to fine-tune the placement process."

Faith Howland, an independent educational consultant in Boston, Massachusetts, and a member of the Independent Educational Consultants Association (IECA), works with families to find the right school and is also often contacted for help when a student's first round of applications has not been successful. "The application process can be near overwhelming for 13- and 14-year-olds. To write as many as eight different applications, each with different essays, just when you are expected to get great grades and continue your sports commitments and other extracurricular activities—not to mention working to prepare for entrance tests. This is high stress! Use of a common application form would be supportive to students and would be extremely helpful in streamlining the teacher recommendations. For those kids who need to submit a second round of applications, the common application forms could be invaluable. These youngsters are coping with disappointment while needing to research new possibilities. If schools were willing to share the common application forms, it's conceivable that many more students who might simply give up if not successful on their first applications could be placed."

Many Schools, One Application

Increased acceptance of the Secondary Schools Application and the Admission Application Form could lead to a marked increase in applications. Common applications are especially helpful to the candidate who fails to earn any acceptance letters at the end of the application process. Traditionally, if a candidate wants to apply to a new list of schools, he or she must start from scratch and complete a new set of forms. Common applications certainly speed up this process, and in the case of the Secondary School Application from SSAT, sending an application to an additional school is as easy as sending the test scores. Candidates simply sign in to their accounts and select another school.

More than half of the candidates who apply to independent schools come from public schools and may not enjoy the benefit of placement counselors at their schools nor do they seek the advice of independent counselors. Regardless, most candidates are well served in using one of the common application forms when applying to multiple schools. One strategy may be to complete a few individual applications and then submit one of the common application forms to a few other schools—identifying some additional options and increasing the likelihood of having meaningful choices after the decision letters are mailed. Many candidates find it much easier to figure out which school they want once they know which school wants them.

Few schools realize how difficult the application process can be for families who are applying to more than one school. Common application forms make the process of applying to multiple schools a much more manageable endeavor. The use of a common application form affords families much more time and energy to devote to other aspects of the application and interview process. By reducing the duplicated paperwork of recommendations and the need to complete so many essays, applicants and their parents are granted a greater opportunity to discuss the real issues surrounding school selection, such as the compatibility of curriculum, style of teaching, and program offerings. Rather than creating folders for each school and chasing down multiple letters of recommendation, applicants and their parents can focus on just a few essays and remove the stress associated with sorting and tracking multiple documents.

Candidates and their families can be assured of the professionalism of admission officers and feel free to use one of the common applications. The Secondary School Application and the Admission Application Form represent the efforts of the very best admission officers who have put the interests of the applicant at the fore—shifting the focus away from the school and back to the candidate. Candidates can be confident that the common application form will more than adequately allow them to make a strong case for their own admission at any school accepting the form.

About Standardized Tests

Heather Hoerle
Executive Director
Secondary School Admission Test Board (SSATB)

Mention the word "testing" to even the most capable student, and he or she is likely to freeze in fear. It's no wonder, then, that standardized testing in the independent school admission process causes nail-biting among students and parents alike.

You may be wondering why private schools test prospective students in the first place. In most cases, standardized testing is used to evaluate a student's ability to perform outside of the classroom. Often, testing helps schools to understand whether they have an appropriate program for applicants. In some cases, private schools find they are best equipped to serve students with test results that fit within a specific range or percentile. Note that standardized testing is also used to place accepted students into appropriate classes in their new school.

Often, testing helps schools to understand whether they have an appropriate program for applicants.

Years ago, I took the Secondary School Admission Test (SSAT) as part of the admission process to a boarding school. After my scores came back, my grim-faced mother called the boarding school's admission director to discuss the results. Much to her relief and surprise, I was accepted by the school in spite of mediocre quantitative testing. Indeed, the strength of my application assured school officials that I was ready for their academic challenge, despite the "average" test results. The SSAT, while an important part of my application, did not tell admission officials about my motivation, nor did it yield any information about my academic and creative achievements.

While it is true that some schools assign a great deal of importance to standardized testing, it is just as true that many schools regard testing as only one part of the application process. Many private schools place equal value on the applicant's campus interview, the student's record of achievement, teacher recommendations, and student/parent written statements. In short, test scores cannot tell an individual's full story, and admission officials recognize this limitation, even as they require standardized testing.

The tests that are most frequently used by private secondary schools are the Secondary School Admission Test Board's SSAT and the Educational Records Bureau's Independent School Entrance Exam (ISEE).

Taking the SSAT

The SSAT, which is used to evaluate applicants for admission to grades 5–11, is a multiple-choice test that measures students' abilities in math and verbal areas and enables counselors to compare students' scores with those of private school applicants and the national school population. The SSAT takes more than 2 hours to complete. Two levels are administered. The lower level exam is taken by students in grades 5–7. The upper level is administered to students in grades 8–11. Students' scores are compared only to students in the same grade. The exam contains multiple-choice questions and a writing sample.

The SSAT is given nationally at more than 600 test sites in all fifty states on selected Saturdays during the school year (in October, November, December, January, February, March, April, and June). It is also given internationally in November, December, January, March, and April.

Applicants can arrange to have SSAT scores sent to several different schools. Registration forms and details about specific test sites, dates, and fees are available at www.ssat.org or by calling 609-683-4440. You can download a free copy of the *SSAT Student Guide* from the Web site. The Secondary School Admission Test Board also sells *Preparing and Applying for Independent School Admission and the SSAT,* a sample test booklet that contains an actual test form for student practice, for a small fee.

Taking the ISEE

The ISEE is used to assess the math and verbal abilities and achievement of students entering grades 5 through 12. The test is administered at three levels: a lower level for students applying to grades 5 and 6; a middle level for those students applying to grades 7 and 8; and an upper level for students applying to grades 9 through 12. Students' scores are compared only to students in the same grade.

The test, which takes about 3 hours to complete, has two components—a multiple-choice segment and a 30-minute essay. The essay, although not scored, gives schools a chance to see a student's writing on an informal topic. The turnaround time for score reporting is seven to ten business days.

The ISEE is administered at sites across the United States and abroad on dates chosen by the schools. Families can obtain test dates and locations by requesting a free student guide from the Educational Records Bureau online at http://erblearn.org. The Educational Records Bureau also publishes *What to Expect on the ISEE*, a sample test booklet that contains half-length practice tests.

How Important Are the Tests?

Parents may want to assure their child that his or her fate does not rely solely on test performance. According to admission counselors, test results are only one part of the admission process. Test scores may not directly relate to the grades a student is capable of achieving in school, and tests cannot measure motivation. Because admission representatives know that a student can contribute to the life of the school community in many different ways, they are careful to keep all of an applicant's talents, abilities, and achievements in mind when evaluating his or her potential for success.

Attention Students: Worried About Taking the SSAT or ISEE?

Here are a few tips to help ban the testing blues.

- Get plenty of rest the day before the test. You will need all of your concentration on the test date, and fatigue can wreak havoc on your ability to focus.
- Eat a meal before you take the test. Your brain needs the energy that food provides!
- Carefully read the materials provided by the sponsoring test group several days before testing is scheduled. Often a "practice test" is included in your registration materials and can be helpful in preparing you for the upcoming test.
- Be well prepared. Advance registration materials offer plenty of guidance on what you will need to bring to the test, such as your registration ticket and No. 2 pencils.
- Allow plenty of time to get to your test site. Be sure that you have directions to the test center, and arrive ahead of the test administration time in order to register on-site, find a bathroom, and get acclimated to the setting.
- As you are taking the test, do not get hung up on hard questions. Skip them and move on. If you have time at the end of each test section, return to unanswered questions and try again.
- Don't forget personal "comfort" items. If you have a cold, be sure to bring tissues and cough drops along. Have extra money on hand, since you may want something to drink during the break. Wear layers, just in case you get too hot or too cold while taking the test.
- Finally, relax! While it is important to do your best work on standardized tests, your future does not depend solely on your test results.

Paying for a Private Education

Mark J. Mitchell
Vice President, School Information Services
National Association of Independent Schools (NAIS)

Imagine asking a car dealer to sell you a $15,000 sedan for $5000 because that is all you can afford. When you buy a car, you know that you will be paying more than it cost to design, build, ship, and sell the car. The sales staff will not offer you a price based on your income. At best, you may receive discounts, rebates, or other incentives that allow you to pay the lowest price the dealer is willing to accept. As a buyer, you even accept the notion that the car's value will depreciate as soon as you drive it off the lot. No matter how you look at it, you pay more than the car cost to make and ultimately more than it's worth.

Tuition at many private schools can easily approach the cost of a new car; however, paying for a private school education is not the same as buying a car. One difference is the availability of financial aid at thousands of schools in the United States and abroad to help offset the tuition. Imagine asking a school to accept $5000 for a $15,000 tuition because that is all you can afford to pay. That is exactly what private schools that provide need-based financial aid programs accomplish. Learning about the financing options and procedures available at private schools can make this imagined scenario a reality for many families.

Need-Based Financial Aid

Many private schools offer assistance to families who demonstrate financial need. In fact, for a recent academic year, schools that belonged to the National Association of Independent Schools (NAIS) provided more than $1 trillion in need-based financial aid to nearly 18 percent of their students. For 2010–11, the average grant for boarding school students was $20,630 and the average grant for day school students was $10,054. These need-based grants do not need to be repaid and are used to offset the school's tuition. Schools make this substantial commitment as one way of ensuring a socio-economically diverse student body and to help ensure that every student qualified for admission has the best chance to enroll, regardless of his or her financial circumstances.

How Financial Need Is Determined

Many schools use a process of determining financial need that requires the completion of applications and the submission of tax forms and other documentation to help them decide how much help each family needs. Currently, more than 2,400 schools nationwide ask families to complete The School and Student Service (SSS) Parents' Financial Statement (PFS) online at www.nais.org to determine eligibility for aid. The PFS gathers information about family size, income and expenses, parents' assets and indebtedness, and the child's assets. From this and other information, schools are provided with an estimate of the amount of discretionary income (after several allowances are made for basic necessities) available for education costs. Schools review each case individually and use this estimate, along with such supporting documentation as most recent income tax forms, to make a final decision on your need for a financial aid grant. For more information, please visit www.nais.org/go/parents.

The amount of a need-based financial aid award varies from person to person and school to school. Just as individuals have different financial resources and obligations that dictate their need for assistance, schools have different resources and policies that dictate their ability to meet your financial need. Tuition costs, endowment incomes, and the school's philosophy about financial aid are a few of the things that can affect how much aid a school can offer. If your decision to send your child to a private school depends heavily on getting financial help, you would benefit from applying for aid at more than one school.

Merit-Based Awards

While the majority of aid offered is based on a family's financial situation, not everyone who receives financial assistance must demonstrate financial need. Private schools offer millions of dollars in merit-based scholarships to thousands of students. In the 2009–10 academic year, 275 NAIS-member schools awarded an average annual merit award worth $4597 to students, totaling more than $35.7 million. Even with this level of commitment, such awards are rare (just 5.4 percent of all enrolled students receive this type of aid) and, therefore, highly competitive. They may serve to reward demonstrated talents or achievements in areas ranging from academics to athletics to the arts.

Some additional resources may be available from organizations and agencies in your community. Civic and religious groups, foundations, and even your employer may sponsor scholarships for students at private schools. Unfortunately, these options tend to be few and far between, limited in number and size of award. Be sure to ask a financial aid officer at the school(s) in which you are interested if he or she is aware of such organizations and opportunities.

The financial aid officer at the school is the best source of information about your options.

Whether it is offered by the school or a local organization, be sure to understand the requirements or conditions on which a merit-based scholarship is based. Ask if the award is renewable and, if so, under what conditions. Often, certain criteria must be met (such as minimum GPA, community service, or participation in activities) to ensure renewal of the award in subsequent years. (Some merit awards are available for just one year.)

Tuition Financing Options

Whether or not you qualify for grants or scholarships, another way to get financial help involves finding ways to make tuition payments easier on your family's monthly budget. One common option is the tuition payment plan. These plans allow you to spread tuition payments (less any forms of financial aid you receive) over a period of eight to ten months. In most cases, payments start before the school year begins, but this method can be more feasible than coming up with one or two lump sum payments before the beginning of the school year. Payment plans may be administered by the schools themselves or by a private company approved by the school. They do not normally require credit checks or charge interest; however, they typically charge an application or service fee, which may include tuition insurance. Additional information about tuition payment plans is available on the NAIS Web site at http://sss.nais.org/Parents/Support/Pages/FAQs-for-Families.aspx.

Since a high-quality education is one of the best investments they can make in their child's future, many parents finance the cost just as they would any other important expense. A number of schools, banks, and other agencies offer tuition loan programs specifically for elementary and secondary school expenses. While such loans are subject to credit checks and must be repaid with interest, they tend to offer rates and terms that are more favorable than those of other consumer loans. It pays to compare the details of more than one type of loan program to find the best one for your needs. Although they should always be regarded as an option of last resort, tuition loan programs can be helpful. Of course, every family must consider both the short- and long-term costs of borrowing and make its decision part of a larger plan for education financing.

A Final Word

Although the primary responsibility to pay for school costs rests with the family, there are options available if you need help. As you can see, financing a private school education can result in a partnership between the family, the school, and sometimes outside agencies or companies, with each making an effort to provide ways to meet the costs. The financial aid officer at the school is the best source of information about your options and is willing to help you in every way he or she can. Always go to the financial aid officer at a school in which you are interested whenever you have any questions or concerns about programs or the application process. Understanding your responsibilities, meeting deadlines, and learning about the full range of options is your best strategy for obtaining assistance. Although there are no guarantees, with proper planning and by asking the right questions, your family just might get the high-quality private education for less.

How to Use This Guide

Quick-Reference Chart

"Private Secondary Schools At-a-Glance" presents data listed in alphabetical order by state and U.S. territories; schools in Canada and other countries follow state listings. If your search is limited to a specific state, turn to the appropriate section and scan the chart for quick information about each school in that state: Are students boarding, day, or both? Is it coeducational? What grade levels are offered? How many students are enrolled? What is the student/faculty ratio? How many sports are offered? Does the school offer Advanced Placement test preparation?

School Profiles and Displays

The **School Profiles** and **Displays** contain basic information about the schools and are listed alphabetically in each section. An outline of a **School Profile** follows. The items of information found under each section heading are defined and displayed. Any item discussed below that is omitted from a **School Profile** either does not apply to that particular school or is one for which no information was supplied.

Heading Name and address of school, along with the name of the Head of School.

General Information Type (boys', girls', coeducational, boarding/day, distance learning) and academic emphasis, religious affiliation, grades, founding date, campus setting, nearest major city, housing, campus size, total number of buildings, accreditation and memberships, languages of instruction, endowment, enrollment, upper school average class size, upper school faculty-student ratio, number of required school days per year (Upper School), number of days per week Upper School students typically attend, and length of the average school day.

Upper School Student Profile Breakdown by grade, gender, boarding/day, geography, and religion.

Faculty Total number; breakdown by gender, number with advanced degrees, and number who reside on campus.

Subjects Offered Academic and general subjects.

Graduation Requirements Subjects and other requirements, including community service.

Special Academic Programs Honors and Advanced Placement courses, accelerated programs, study at local college for college credit, study abroad, independent study, ESL programs, programs for gifted/remedial students and students with learning disabilities.

College Admission Counseling Number of recent graduates, representative list of colleges attended. May include mean or median SAT/ACT scores and percentage of students scoring over 600 on each section of the SAT, over 1800 on the combined SAT, or over 26 on the composite ACT.

Student Life Dress code, student council, discipline, and religious service attendance requirements.

Summer Programs Programs offered and focus; location; open to boys, girls, or both and availability to students from other schools; usual enrollment; program dates and application deadlines.

Tuition and Aid Costs, available financial aid.

Admissions New-student figures, admissions requirements, application deadlines, fees.

Athletics Sports, levels, and gender; number of PE instructors, coaches, and athletic trainers.

Computers List of classes that use computers, campus technology, and availability of student e-mail accounts, online student grades, and a published electronic and media policy.

Contact Person to whom inquiries should be addressed.

Displays, provided by school administrators, present information designed to complement the data already appearing in the **School Profile.**

Close-Ups

Close-Ups, written expressly for Peterson's Publishing by school administrators, provide in-depth information about the schools that have chosen to submit them. These descriptions are all in the same format to provide maximum comparability. **Close-Ups** follow each **School Profile** section; there is a page reference at the end of a **School Profile** directing you to that school's **Close-Up** as well as its **Summer Program Close-Up,** if one was provided. Schools are listed alphabetically in each section.

Special Needs Schools

One of the great strengths of private schools is their variety. This section is dedicated to the belief that there is an appropriate school setting for every child, one in which he or she will thrive academically, socially, and emotionally. The task for parents, counselors, and educators is to know the child's needs and the schools' resources well enough to make the right match.

Schools in this section serve those students who may have special challenges, including learning differences, dyslexia, language delay, attention deficit disorders, social maladjustment to family and surroundings, or emotional disturbances; these students may need individual attention or are underachieving for some other reason. Parents of children who lag significantly behind their grade level in basic academic skills or who have little or no motivation for schoolwork will also want to consult this section. (For easy reference, schools that offer extra help for students are identified in two directories: "Schools Reporting Programs for Students with Special Needs" and "Schools Reporting That They Accommodate Underachievers.") The schools included here chose to be in this section because they consider special needs education to be their primary focus. It is the mission of these schools, whose curricula and methodologies vary widely, to uncover a student's strengths and, with appropriate academic, social, and psychological counseling, enable him or her to succeed.

Junior Boarding Schools

As parents know, the early adolescent years are ones of tremendous physical and emotional change. Junior boarding schools specialize in this crucial period by taking advantage of children's natural curiosity, zest for learning, and growing self-awareness. While junior boarding schools enroll students with a wide range of academic abilities and levels of emotional self-assurance, their goal is to meet each youngster's individual needs within a supportive community. They accomplish this through low student-teacher ratios and enrollment numbers deliberately kept low.

The boarding schools featured in this section serve students in the middle school grades (6–9); some offer primary programs as well. For more information about junior boarding schools, visit the Junior Boarding Schools Association Web site at www.jbsa.org.

Summer Programs

The Summer Programs section offers Close-Ups of exciting summer programs that are taking place at private schools throughout the United States and abroad. These two-page in-depth descriptions provide details on the summer program's background and philosophy, program offerings, location, staff, facilities, daily schedule, extra opportunities and activities, medical care, transportation, costs, financial aid, application timetable, and contact information. The photos included in the Summer Program Close-Ups offer a glimpse of the facilities, surroundings, and faces of program participants. Those schools whose summer program descriptions are included in this section have paid a fee to Peterson's Publishing to provide this information to you.

Specialized Directories

These directories are compiled from the information gathered in *Peterson's Annual Survey of Private Secondary Schools*. The schools that did not return a survey or provided incomplete data are not fully represented in these directories. For ease of reference, the directories are grouped by category: type, curricula, financial data, special programs, and special needs.

Index

The "Alphabetical Listing of Schools" shows page numbers for School Profiles in regular type, page numbers for Displays in *italics*, and page numbers for Close-Ups in **boldface** type.

Data Collection Procedures

The data contained in *Peterson's Private Secondary Schools 2013–14* **School Profiles, Quick-Reference Chart, Specialized Directories,** and **Index** were collected through *Peterson's Annual Survey of Private Secondary Schools* during fall 2012. Also included were schools that submitted information for the 2011–12 data collection effort but did not submit updates in the fall of 2012. Questionnaires were posted online. With minor exceptions, data for those schools that responded to the questionnaire were submitted by officials at the schools themselves. All usable information received in time for publication has been included. The omission of a particular item from a **School Profile** means that it is either not applicable to that school or not available or usable. Because of Peterson's extensive system of checking data, we believe that the information presented in this guide is accurate. However, errors and omissions are possible in a data collection and processing endeavor of this scope. Therefore, students and parents should check with a specific school at the time of application to verify all pertinent information.

Criteria for Inclusion in This Book

Most schools in this book have curricula that are primarily college preparatory. If a school is accredited or is a candidate for accreditation by a regional accrediting group, including the European Council of International Schools, and/or is approved by a state Department of Education, and/or is a member of the National Association of Independent Schools or the European Council of International Schools, then such accreditation, approval, or membership is stated. Schools appearing in the **Special Needs Schools** section may not have such accreditation or approval.

Quick-Reference Chart

Private Secondary Schools At-a-Glance

	STUDENTS ACCEPTED				GRADES			STUDENT/FACULTY			SCHOOL OFFERINGS	
	BOARDING		DAY									
	Boys	Girls	Boys	Girls	Lower	Middle	Upper	Total	Upper	Student/Faculty Ratio	Advanced Placement Preparation	Sports
UNITED STATES												
Alabama												
Bayside Academy, Daphne	X	X	X	X	PK–6	7–8	9–12	727	251	9:1	X	29
Briarwood Christian High School, Birmingham	X	X	X	X	K–6	7–8	9–12	1,967	589	23:1	X	18
Edgewood Academy, Elmore	X	X	X	X	K–5	6–8	9–12	275	99	14:1	X	12
Madison Academy, Madison	X	X	X	X	PS–6	–	7–12	900	450	15:1		9
Marion Academy, Marion	X	X	X	X	K–3	4–6	7–12	96	50	8:1		8
Mars Hill Bible School, Florence	X	X	X	X	K4–4	5–8	9–12	540	198	14:1	X	11
McGill-Toolen Catholic High School, Mobile	X	X	X	X	–	–	9–12	1,135	1,135	14:1	X	14
Pickens Academy, Carrollton	X	X	X	X	K4–6	–	7–12	265	151	20:1		12
Randolph School, Huntsville	X	X	X	X	K–4	5–8	9–12	1,001	366	10:1	X	17
St. Paul's Episcopal School, Mobile	X	X	X	X	PK–4	5–8	9–12	1,222	381	12:1	X	18
Alaska												
Grace Christian School, Anchorage	X	X	X	X	K–6	7–8	9–12	617	213	15:1	X	8
Arizona												
Blueprint Education, Glendale	X	X	X	X	–	–					X	
Brophy College Preparatory, Phoenix	X	X	X	X	–	6–7	9–12	1,348	1,291	15:1	X	44
Copper Canyon Academy, Rimrock	X	X	X	X	–	–	9–12	90	90	10:1		20
Phoenix Christian Unified Schools, Phoenix	X	X	X	X	PS–5	6–8	9–12	380	213	20:1	X	17
Phoenix Country Day School, Paradise Valley	X	X	X	X	PK–4	5–8	9–12	724	251	8:1	X	24
St. Gregory College Preparatory School, Tucson	X	X	X	X	–	6–8	9–12	299	189	9:1	X	23
Saint Mary's High School, Phoenix	X	X	X	X	–	–	9–12	504	504	15:1	X	18
Salpointe Catholic High School, Tucson	X	X	X	X	–	–	9–12	1,094	1,094	15:1	X	39
Scottsdale Christian Academy, Phoenix	X	X	X	X	PK–5	6–8	9–12	821	284	13:1	X	15
Southwestern Academy, Rimrock	X	X	X	X	–	–	9–PG	27	27	4:1	X	53
Tri-City Christian Academy, Chandler	X	X	X	X	K4–6	7–8	9–12	304	92	16:1		4
Valley Lutheran High School, Phoenix	X	X	X	X	–	–	9–12	184	184	10:1	X	16
Arkansas												
Episcopal Collegiate School, Little Rock	X	X	X	X	PK–5	6–8	9–12	763	228	10:1	X	16
California												
Academy of Our Lady of Peace, San Diego	X	X	X	X	–	–	9–12	750	750	14:1	X	11
Alverno High School, Sierra Madre	X	X	X	X	–	–	9–12	174	174	12:1	X	10
Anacapa School, Santa Barbara	X	X	X	X	7–8	–	9–12	49	37	9:1	X	23
Archbishop Mitty High School, San Jose	X	X	X	X	–	–	9–12	1,712	1,712	17:1	X	27
Army and Navy Academy, Carlsbad	X	X	X	X	7–9	–	10–12	307	233	15:1	X	28
Arroyo Pacific Academy, Arcadia	X	X	X	X	–	–				8:1	X	18
The Athenian School, Danville	X	X	X	X	–	6–8	9–12	471	306	10:1	X	15
Bakersfield Christian High School, Bakersfield	X	X	X	X	–	–	9–12	436	436	17:1	X	15
The Bay School of San Francisco, San Francisco	X	X	X	X	–	–	9–12	305	305	8:1		
Bellarmine College Preparatory, San Jose	X	X	X	X	–	–	9–12	1,600	1,600	13:1	X	23
Bishop Conaty-Our Lady of Loretto High School, Los Angeles	X	X	X	X	–	–	9–12	326	326	12:1	X	5
Bishop Montgomery High School, Torrance	X	X	X	X	–	–	9–12	975	975	22:1	X	17
Bishop O'Dowd High School, Oakland	X	X	X	X	–	–	9–12	1,144	1,144	15:1	X	34
The Bishop's School, La Jolla	X	X	X	X	–	6–8	9–12	800	558	14:1	X	18
Bridges Academy, Studio City	X	X	X	X	–	5–8	9–12	134	76	8:1		3
Calvin Christian High School, Escondido	X	X	X	X	PK–5	6–8	9–12	491	162	17:1	X	11
Campbell Hall (Episcopal), North Hollywood	X	X	X	X	K–6	7–8	9–12	1,085	533	8:1	X	20
Capistrano Valley Christian Schools, San Juan Capistrano	X	X	X	X	JK–6	7–8	9–12	456	192	13:1	X	14
Carondelet High School, Concord	X	X	X	X	–	–	9–12	800	800	15:1	X	22
Castilleja School, Palo Alto	X	X	X	X	–	6–8	9–12	451	258	6:1	X	14
Central Catholic High School, Modesto	X	X	X	X	–	–	9–12	389	389	14:1	X	15
Chadwick School, Palos Verdes Peninsula	X	X	X	X	K–6	7–8	9–12	830	357	6:1	X	20
Chaminade College Preparatory, West Hills	X	X	X	X	–	6–8	9–12	2,028	1,330	16:1	X	25
Children's Creative and Performing Arts Academy of San Diego, San Diego	X	X	X	X	K–5	6–8	9–12	265	115	15:1	X	30
Chinese Christian Schools, Alameda	X	X	X	X	K–5	6–8	9–12	640	220	8:1	X	18
Contra Costa Christian High School, Walnut Creek	X	X	X	X	K–5	6–8	9–12	230	95	10:1	X	5
Crespi Carmelite High School, Encino	X	X	X	X	–	–	9–12	565	565	14:1	X	17
Crossroads School for Arts & Sciences, Santa Monica	X	X	X	X	K–5	6–8	9–12	1,154	506	11:1		21
Crystal Springs Uplands School, Hillsborough	X	X	X	X	–	6–8	9–12	350	250	9:1		24

Private Secondary Schools At-a-Glance

	STUDENTS ACCEPTED				GRADES			STUDENT/FACULTY			SCHOOL OFFERINGS	
	BOARDING		DAY									
	Boys	Girls	Boys	Girls	Lower	Middle	Upper	Total	Upper	Student/Faculty Ratio	Advanced Placement Preparation	Sports
Damien High School, La Verne	X	X	X	X	–	–	9–12	922	922	20:1	X	27
De La Salle High School, Concord	X	X	X	X	–	–	9–12	1,021	1,021	28:1	X	19
Eldorado Emerson Private School, Orange	X	X	X	X	K–6	–	7–12	150	80	18:1	X	7
Faith Christian High School, Yuba City	X	X	X	X	–	–	9–12	100	100	12:1	X	7
Flintridge Preparatory School, La Canada Flintridge	X	X	X	X	–	7–8	9–12	500	400	13:1	X	17
Fresno Christian Schools, Fresno	X	X	X	X	K–6	7–8	9–12	512	186	12:1	X	17
The Frostig School, Pasadena	X	X	X	X	1–5	6–8	9–12	95	48	6:1		4
Grace Brethren School, Simi Valley	X	X	X	X	K–6	7–8	9–12	840	290	11:1	X	17
The Grauer School, Encinitas	X	X	X	X	–	6–8	9–12	160	88	6:1	X	54
The Harker School, San Jose	X	X	X	X	K–5	6–8	9–12	1,819	727	10:1	X	21
Harvard-Westlake School, Studio City	X	X	X	X	–	7–8	9–12	1,605	1,178	8:1	X	21
Head-Royce School, Oakland	X	X	X	X	K–5	6–8	9–12	876	356	9:1	X	20
Hebrew Academy, Huntington Beach	X	X	X	X	N–5	6–8	9–12	259	21	4:1	X	14
Heritage Christian School, North Hills	X	X	X	X	–	7–8	9–12	911	697	22:1	X	11
Highland Hall Waldorf School, Northridge	X	X	X	X	N–6	7–8	9–12	225	80	6:1		6
Idyllwild Arts Academy, Idyllwild	X	X	X	X	–	–	9–PG	295	295	12:1	X	38
Immaculate Heart High School and Middle School, Los Angeles	X	X	X	X	–	6–8	9–12	550	550	16:1		
International High School, San Francisco	X	X	X	X	PK–5	6–8	9–12	1,021	313	10:1		24
Junipero Serra High School, San Mateo	X	X	X	X	–	–	9–12	900	900	27:1	X	28
Kings Christian School, Lemoore	X	X	X	X	PK–6	7–8	9–12	294	80	11:1	X	17
La Cheim School, Antioch	X	X	X	X	1–5	6–8	9–12	15	6			2
La Jolla Country Day School, La Jolla	X	X	X	X	N–4	5–8	9–12	1,170	492	16:1	X	29
La Salle High School, Pasadena	X	X	X	X	–	–	9–12	710	710	11:1	X	20
Laurel Springs School, Ojai	X	X	X	X	K–5	6–8	9–12	1,529	876	1:1	X	
Linfield Christian School, Temecula	X	X	X	X	JK–5	6–8	9–12	758	319	15:1	X	12
Lodi Academy, Lodi	X	X	X	X	–	–	9–12	95	95	13:1	X	6
Los Angeles Lutheran High School, Sylmar	X	X	X	X	K–6	7–8	9–12	397	146	10:1	X	20
Louisville High School, Woodland Hills	X	X	X	X	–	–	9–12	428	428	25:1	X	15
Lutheran High School of San Diego, Chula Vista	X	X	X	X	–	–	9–12	88	88	12:1	X	6
Lycee International de Los Angeles, Burbank	X	X	X	X	PK–5	6–8	9–12	934	103	4:1		8
Maranatha High School, Pasadena	X	X	X	X	–	–	9–12	655	655	13:1	X	22
Marymount High School, Los Angeles	X	X	X	X	–	–	9–12	372	372	7:1	X	20
Mercy High School College Preparatory, San Francisco	X	X	X	X	–	–	9–12	394	394	14:1	X	11
Mesa Grande Seventh-Day Academy, Calimesa	X	X	X	X	K–6	7–8	9–12	265	119	10:1		9
Midland School, Los Olivos	X	X	X	X	–	–	9–12	80	80	5:1	X	19
Modesto Christian School, Modesto	X	X	X	X	K–5	6–8	9–12	580	280	11:1	X	13
Moreau Catholic High School, Hayward	X	X	X	X	–	–	9–12	896	896	18:1	X	22
Notre Dame Academy, Los Angeles	X	X	X	X	–	–	9–12			13:1	X	10
Notre Dame High School, San Jose	X	X	X	X	–	–	9–12	626	626	11:1	X	12
Oak Grove School, Ojai	X	X	X	X	PK–6	7–8	9–12	209	53	7:1	X	15
Ojai Valley School, Ojai	X	X	X	X	PK–5	6–8	9–12	288	109	6:1	X	31
Orinda Academy, Orinda	X	X	X	X	–	6–8	9–12	90	77	9:1	X	4
Pacific Academy, Encinitas	X	X	X	X	–	7–8	9–12	21	20	5:1	X	
Palma School, Salinas	X	X	X	X	–	7–8	9–12	534	402	15:1	X	13
Palo Alto Preparatory School, Mountain View	X	X	X	X	–	–	8–12	65	65	6:1	X	
Paradise Adventist Academy, Paradise	X	X	X	X	K–4	5–8	9–12	196	81	8:1		5
Patten Academy of Christian Education, Oakland	X	X	X	X	K–5	6–8	9–12	117	44	6:1		2
Providence High School, Burbank	X	X	X	X	–	–	9–12	417	417	9:1	X	17
Ramona Convent Secondary School, Alhambra	X	X	X	X	–	7–8	9–12	272	258	9:1	X	8
Redwood Christian Schools, Castro Valley	X	X	X	X	K–5	6–8	9–12	648	260	10:1	X	8
Rolling Hills Preparatory School, San Pedro	X	X	X	X	–	6–8	9–12	225	130	9:1	X	21
Sacramento Adventist Academy, Carmichael	X	X	X	X	K–6	7–8	9–12	222	107	12:1	X	6
Sacramento Country Day School, Sacramento	X	X	X	X	PK–5	6–8	9–12	469	135	9:1	X	15
Saddleback Valley Christian School, San Juan Capistrano	X	X	X	X	JK–6	7–8	9–12	911	376	15:1	X	14
Sage Hill School, Newport Coast	X	X	X	X	–	–	9–12	466	466	10:1	X	13
Saint Anthony High School, Long Beach	X	X	X	X	–	–	9–12	480	480	19:1	X	22
St. Augustine High School, San Diego	X	X	X	X	–	–	9–12	700	700	28:1	X	43
St. Bernard's Catholic School, Eureka	X	X	X	X	K–8	–	9–12	300	150	12:1	X	11
St. Catherine's Academy, Anaheim	X	X	X	X	K–6	7–8		157	81	14:1		24
Saint Elizabeth High School, Oakland	X	X	X	X	–	–	9–12	142	142	15:1	X	7
Saint Francis High School, La Canada Flintridge	X	X	X	X	–	–	9–12	671	671	15:1	X	10
Saint Lawrence Academy, Santa Clara	X	X	X	X	–	–	9–12	250	250	15:1		9
Saint Lucy's Priory High School, Glendora	X	X	X	X	–	–	9–12	647	647	17:1	X	18
St. Michael's Preparatory School of the Norbertine Fathers, Silverado	X	X	X	X	–	–	9–12	66	66	3:1	X	11
Saint Patrick - Saint Vincent High School, Vallejo	X	X	X	X	–	–	9–12	502	502	30:1	X	15
Salesian High School, Richmond	X	X	X	X	–	–	9–12	473	473	18:1	X	15
San Domenico School, San Anselmo	X	X	X	X	PK–5	6–8	9–12	598	163	5:1	X	12

Private Secondary Schools At-a-Glance

	STUDENTS ACCEPTED				GRADES			STUDENT/FACULTY			SCHOOL OFFERINGS	
	BOARDING		DAY									
	Boys	Girls	Boys	Girls	Lower	Middle	Upper	Total	Upper	Student/Faculty Ratio	Advanced Placement Preparation	Sports
Santa Catalina School, Monterey	X	X	X	X	–	–	9–12	258	258	8:1	X	31
Sonoma Academy, Santa Rosa	X	X	X	X	–	–	9–12	246	492	12:1	X	26
Southwestern Academy, San Marino	X	X	X	X	–	–			120	6:1	X	34
Stevenson School, Pebble Beach	X	X	X	X	K–5	6–8	9–12	747	520	10:1	X	34
Summerfield Waldorf School, Santa Rosa	X	X	X	X	K–6	7–8	9–12	385	99	7:1		5
The Thacher School, Ojai	X	X	X	X	–	–	9–12	246	246	6:1	X	40
THINK Global School, San Francisco	X	X	X	X	–	–	9–12	36	36	3:1		
Tri-City Christian Schools, Vista	X	X	X	X	PK–6	7–8	9–12	571	220	12:1	X	22
Valley Christian High School, San Jose	X	X	X	X	K–5	6–8	9–12	2,400	1,375	17:1	X	20
The Webb Schools, Claremont	X	X	X	X	–	–	9–12	410	410	8:1	X	39
Westridge School, Pasadena	X	X	X	X	4–6	7–8	9–12	480	256	6:1	X	19
Windward School, Los Angeles	X	X	X	X	–	7–8	9–12	541	369	7:1	X	5
York School, Monterey	X	X	X	X	–	–	8–12	225	225	8:1	X	20
Colorado												
Alexander Dawson School, Lafayette	X	X	X	X	K–4	5–8	9–12	453	183	7:1	X	43
The Colorado Springs School, Colorado Springs	X	X	X	X	PK–5	6–8	9–12	302	104	6:1	X	22
Denver Academy, Denver	X	X	X	X	1–6	7–8	9–12	354	200	8:1		28
Denver Christian High School, Denver	X	X	X	X	–	–	9–12	150	150	19:1		11
Fountain Valley School of Colorado, Colorado Springs	X	X	X	X	–	–	9–12	23,624	236	5:1	X	43
Front Range Christian High School, Littleton	X	X	X	X	PK–6	7–8	9–12	391	169	7:1	X	18
Humanex Academy, Englewood	X	X	X	X	–	6–8	9–12		2	8:1		16
Kent Denver School, Englewood	X	X	X	X	–	6–8	9–12	672	449	7:1	X	28
Regis Jesuit High School, Girls Division, Aurora	X	X	X	X	–	–		1,700	1,700	8:1	X	27
Telluride Mountain School, Telluride	X	X	X	X	PK–4	5–8	9–12	100	18	10:1		30
Temple Grandin School, Boulder	X	X	X	X	–	6–8	8–12	20	13	4:1		
Connecticut												
Chase Collegiate School, Waterbury	X	X	X	X	PK–5	6–8	9–12	440	194	6:1	X	31
Choate Rosemary Hall, Wallingford	X	X	X	X	–	–	9–12	864	864	6:1	X	41
Convent of the Sacred Heart, Greenwich	X	X	X	X	PS–4	5–8	9–12	776	300	7:1	X	23
Eagle Hill School, Greenwich	X	X	X	X	1–6	–	7–9	230	115	4:1		33
The Ethel Walker School, Simsbury	X	X	X	X	–	6–8	9–12	260	221	6:1	X	43
Fairfield College Preparatory School, Fairfield	X	X	X	X	–	–	9–12	896	896	18:1	X	32
The Glenholme School, Devereux Connecticut, Washington	X	X	X	X	5–6	7–8	9–PG	89	75	10:1		44
Holy Cross High School, Waterbury	X	X	X	X	–	–	9–12	630	630	15:1	X	24
Hopkins School, New Haven	X	X	X	X	–	7–8	9–12	709	554	6:1	X	38
Kent School, Kent	X	X	X	X	–	–	9–PG	565	565	7:1	X	43
King Low Heywood Thomas, Stamford	X	X	X	X	PK–5	6–8	9–12	684	324	8:1	X	21
Kingswood-Oxford School, West Hartford	X	X	X	X	–	6–8	9–12	499	345	8:1	X	20
Lauralton Hall, Milford	X	X	X	X	–	–	9–12	465	465	12:1		18
The Marvelwood School, Kent	X	X	X	X	–	–	9–12	165	165	4:1	X	34
Miss Porter's School, Farmington	X	X	X	X	–	–	9–12	306	306	7:1	X	40
Northwest Catholic High School, West Hartford	X	X	X	X	–	–	9–12	603	603	12:1	X	32
The Norwich Free Academy, Norwich	X	X	X	X	–	–	9–12	2,265		22:1	X	36
The Oxford Academy, Westbrook	X	X	X	X	–	–	9–PG	38	38	1:1	X	20
The Rectory School, Pomfret	X	X	X	X	1–4	5–9		251	178	4:1		38
Rumsey Hall School, Washington Depot	X	X	X	X	K–5	6–9		333	221	8:1		48
St. Bernard High School, Uncasville	X	X	X	X	–	6–8	9–12	369	261	12:1		24
St. Joseph High School, Trumbull	X	X	X	X	–	–	9–12	830	830	14:1	X	17
The Taft School, Watertown	X	X	X	X	–	–	9–PG	586	586	5:1	X	46
Watkinson School, Hartford	X	X	X	X	–	6–8	9–PG	240	165	6:1	X	30
Wellspring Foundation, Bethlehem	X	X	X	X	1–6	–	7–12	51				
Westminster School, Simsbury	X	X	X	X	–	–	9–PG	390	390	6:1	X	34
Westover School, Middlebury	X	X	X	X	–	–	9–12	209	209	12:1	X	48
The Williams School, New London	X	X	X	X	–	7–8	9–12	238	187	9:1	X	18
The Woodhall School, Bethlehem	X	X	X	X	–	–	9–PG	39	39	4:1	X	35
Delaware												
Salesianum School, Wilmington	X	X	X	X	–	–	9–12	970	970	12:1	X	22
Tower Hill School, Wilmington	X	X	X	X	PS–4	5–8	9–12	748	244	6:1	X	21
Wilmington Christian School, Hockessin	X	X	X	X	PK–5	6–8	9–12	517	231	15:1	X	12
District of Columbia												
Edmund Burke School, Washington	X	X	X	X	–	6–8	9–12	297	212	6:1	X	17
Georgetown Day School, Washington	X	X	X	X	PK–5	6–8	9–12	1,075	500	7:1	X	9
Georgetown Visitation Preparatory School, Washington	X	X	X	X	–	–	9–12	490	490	10:1	X	19
Gonzaga College High School, Washington	X	X	X	X	–	–	9–12	958	958	15:1	X	33
The Lab School of Washington, Washington	X	X	X	X	1–6	7–8	9–12	344	119	8:1		10
St. Albans School, Washington	X	X	X	X	4–8	–	9–12	586	322	7:1	X	34
Washington International School, Washington	X	X	X	X	PK–5	6–8	9–12	901	263	7.5:1		10

Private Secondary Schools At-a-Glance

	STUDENTS ACCEPTED				GRADES			STUDENT/FACULTY			SCHOOL OFFERINGS	
	BOARDING		DAY									
	Boys	Girls	Boys	Girls	Lower	Middle	Upper	Total	Upper	Student/Faculty Ratio	Advanced Placement Preparation	Sports
Florida												
American Academy, Plantation	X	X	X	X	1–6	7–8	9–12	297	150	12:1		21
American Heritage School, Delray Beach	X	X	X	X	PK–5	–	6–12	1,035	800	10:1	X	21
American Heritage School, Plantation	X	X	X	X	PK–6	–	7–12	2,345	1,608	15:1	X	19
The American School in El Salvador, Miami	X	X	X	X	PK–5	6–8	9–12	1,605	451	18:1	X	7
Belen Jesuit Preparatory School, Miami	X	X	X	X	–	6–8	9–12	1,497	906	13:1	X	19
Berkeley Preparatory School, Tampa	X	X	X	X	PK–5	6–8	9–12	1,290	565	9:1	X	28
Bishop John J. Snyder High School, Jacksonville	X	X	X	X	–	–	9–12	481	481	15:1	X	16
Bishop Kenny High School, Jacksonville	X	X	X	X	–	–	9–12	1,210	1,210	17:1	X	18
The Bolles School, Jacksonville	X	X	X	X	PK–5	6–8	9–12	1,648	781	10:1	X	18
Bradenton Christian School, Bradenton	X	X	X	X	PK–5	6–8	9–12	542	161	14:1	X	16
Canterbury School, Fort Myers	X	X	X	X	PK–6	7–8	9–12	580	199	10:1	X	13
The Canterbury School of Florida, St. Petersburg	X	X	X	X	PK–4	5–8	9–12	433	165	7:1	X	35
Cardinal Mooney Catholic High School, Sarasota	X	X	X	X	–	–	9–12	467	467	13:1	X	18
Cardinal Newman High School, West Palm Beach	X	X	X	X	–	–	9–12	517	517	25:1	X	18
Christopher Columbus High School, Miami	X	X	X	X	–	–	9–12	1,357	1,357	17:1	X	18
The Community School of Naples, Naples	X	X	X	X	PK–5	6–8	9–12	706	286	8:1	X	18
Donna Klein Jewish Academy, Boca Raton	X	X	X	X	PK–4	5–8	9–12	670	139	6:1	X	15
Episcopal High School of Jacksonville, Jacksonville	X	X	X	X	–	6–8	9–12	857	566	10:1	X	22
Father Lopez High School, Daytona Beach	X	X	X	X	–	–	9–12	407	407	13:1	X	20
The First Academy, Orlando	X	X	X	X	K4–6	7–8	9–12	989	398	17:1	X	22
Forest Lake Academy, Apopka	X	X	X	X	–	–	9–12	389	389	12:1		13
Foundation Academy, Winter Garden	X	X	X	X	K–5	6–8	9–12	496	128	14:1	X	12
Glades Day School, Belle Glade	X	X	X	X	PK–6	7–8	9–12	339	136	15:1	X	11
Jesuit High School of Tampa, Tampa	X	X	X	X	–	–	9–12	752	752	13:1	X	18
Keswick Christian School, St. Petersburg	X	X	X	X	–5	6–8	9–12	430	115	15:1	X	20
Palmer Trinity School, Palmetto Bay	X	X	X	X	–	6–8	9–12	660	381	50:1	X	27
Pensacola Catholic High School, Pensacola	X	X	X	X	–	–	9–12	595	595	18:1	X	9
Pine Crest School, Fort Lauderdale	X	X	X	X	PK–5	6–8	9–12	1,755	806	14:1	X	21
Ransom Everglades School, Miami	X	X	X	X	–	6–8	9–12	1,075	613	10:1	X	22
Saddlebrook Preparatory School, Wesley Chapel	X	X	X	X	3–5	6–8	9–12	85	68	8:1		1
St. Brendan High School, Miami	X	X	X	X	–	–	9–12	1,118	1,118	15:1	X	11
Saint Stephen's Episcopal School, Bradenton	X	X	X	X	PK–6	7–8	9–12	654	261	11:1	X	33
St. Thomas Aquinas High School, Fort Lauderdale	X	X	X	X	–	–	9–12	2,239	2,239	18:1	X	30
Trinity Preparatory School, Winter Park	X	X	X	X	–	6–8	9–12	860	512	9:1	X	21
University School of Nova Southeastern University, Fort Lauderdale	X	X	X	X	PK–5	6–8	9–12	1,885	714	11:1	X	19
Georgia												
Augusta Christian School (I), Martinez	X	X	X	X	K–5	6–8	9–12	572	249	10:1	X	13
Augusta Preparatory Day School, Martinez	X	X	X	X	PS–4	5–8	9–12	528	201	9:1		10
Blessed Trinity High School, Roswell	X	X	X	X	–	–	9–12	965	965	14:1	X	17
Brookstone School, Columbus	X	X	X	X	PK–5	6–8	9–12	799	307	10:1	X	12
Bulloch Academy, Statesboro	X	X	X	X	PK–5	6–8	9–12	498	161	17:1	X	17
Darlington School, Rome	X	X	X	X	PK–4	5–8	9–PG	848	477	13:1	X	42
Eaton Academy, Roswell	X	X	X	X	K–5	6–8	9–12	80	40	5:1		34
First Presbyterian Day School, Macon	X	X	X	X	PK–5	6–8	9–12	949	326	12:1	X	17
Flint River Academy, Woodbury	X	X	X	X	–5	6–8	9–12	312	91	14:1	X	15
Frederica Academy, St. Simons Island	X	X	X	X	PK–5	6–8	9–12	412	146	9:1	X	19
The Galloway School, Atlanta	X	X	X	X	P3–4	5–8	9–12	747	250	9:1	X	13
George Walton Academy, Monroe	X	X	X	X	K4–5	6–8	9–12	878	316	12:1	X	19
The Heritage School, Newnan	X	X	X	X	PK–4	5–8	9–12	428	166	8:1	X	29
The Howard School, Atlanta	X	X	X	X	PK–5	6–8	9–12	244	73	8:1		6
John Hancock Academy, Sparta	X	X	X	X	K–5	6–8	9–12	122	44	8:1		12
Landmark Christian School, Fairburn	X	X	X	X	K4–5	6–8	9–12	842	246	8:1	X	15
The Lovett School, Atlanta	X	X	X	X	K–5	6–8	9–12	1,610	600	8:1	X	45
Marist School, Atlanta	X	X	X	X	–	–	7–12	1,081	1,081	11:1	X	18
Mill Springs Academy, Alpharetta	X	X	X	X	1–5	6–8	9–12	321	145	4:1		23
Mt. De Sales Academy, Macon	X	X	X	X	–	6–8	9–12	662	421	9:1		16
Mount Vernon Presbyterian School, Atlanta	X	X	X	X	–							
Piedmont Academy, Monticello	X	X	X	X	1–5	6–8	9–12	270	105	13:1		9
Pinecrest Academy, Cumming	X	X	X	X	PK–5	6–8	9–12	752	237	10:1	X	12
Riverside Military Academy, Gainesville	X	X	X	X	–	7–8	9–12	423	338	14:1	X	57
St. Pius X Catholic High School, Atlanta	X	X	X	X	–	–	9–12	1,100	1,100	12:1	X	23
Stratford Academy, Macon	X	X	X	X	1–5	6–8	9–12	962	318	13:1	X	21
Whitefield Academy, Mableton	X	X	X	X	PK–4	5–8	9–12	649	218	18:1	X	20
Hawaii												
ASSETS School, Honolulu	X	X	X	X	K–8	–	9–12	339	117	8:1		30
Hawaii Baptist Academy, Honolulu	X	X	X	X	K–6	7–8	9–12	1,138	474	17:1	X	22

Private Secondary Schools At-a-Glance	STUDENTS ACCEPTED				GRADES			STUDENT/FACULTY			SCHOOL OFFERINGS	
	BOARDING		DAY									
	Boys	Girls	Boys	Girls	Lower	Middle	Upper	Total	Upper	Student/Faculty Ratio	Advanced Placement Preparation	Sports
Ho'Ala School, Wahiawa	X	X	X	X	K–5	6–8	9–12	65	15		X	4
Lutheran High School of Hawaii, Honolulu	X	X	X	X	–	–	9–12	68	68	7:1	X	23
Maui Preparatory Academy, Lahaina	X	X	X	X	PK–5	6–8	9–12	200	55	5:1	X	13
Mid-Pacific Institute, Honolulu	X	X	X	X	K–5	6–8	9–12	1,550	840	20:1	X	31
Punahou School, Honolulu	X	X	X	X	K–5	6–8	9–12	3,743	1,713	11:1	X	21
St. Anthony's Junior-Senior High School, Wailuku	X	X	X	X	–	7–8	9–12	155	106	10:1	X	28
Seabury Hall, Makawao	X	X	X	X	–	6–8	9–12	443	311	11:1	X	15
Idaho												
Bishop Kelly High School, Boise	X	X	X	X	–	–	9–12	680	680	18:1	X	21
Cole Valley Christian High School, Meridian	X	X	X	X	PK–6	7–8	9–12	801	245	10:1	X	10
Turning Winds Academic Institute, Bonners Ferry	X	X	X	X	–	–			42	7:1		27
Illinois												
Alleman High School, Rock Island	X	X	X	X	–	–	9–12	467	467			
Benet Academy, Lisle	X	X	X	X	–	–	9–12	1,339	1,339	18:1	X	24
The Chicago Academy for the Arts, Chicago	X	X	X	X	–	–	9–12	146	146	15:1	X	
Chicago Waldorf School, Chicago	X	X	X	X	1–5	6–8	9–12	279	71			6
Elgin Academy, Elgin	X	X	X	X	PS–4	5–8	9–12	432	144	5:1	X	13
The Governor French Academy, Belleville	X	X	X	X	K–8	–	9–12	164	44	6:1	X	6
Immaculate Conception School, Elmhurst	X	X	X	X	–	–	9–12	340	340	8:1	X	22
Josephinum Academy, Chicago	X	X	X	X	–	–	9–12	187	187	9:1	X	7
The Latin School of Chicago, Chicago	X	X	X	X	JK–4	5–8	9–12	1,110	430	8:1	X	25
Luther North College Prep, Chicago	X	X	X	X	–	–	9–12	180	180	16:1	X	10
Marian Central Catholic High School, Woodstock	X	X	X	X	–	–	9–12	691	691	18:1	X	16
Marmion Academy, Aurora	X	X	X	X	–	–	9–12	523	523	11:1	X	22
Mother McAuley High School, Chicago	X	X	X	X	–	–	9–12	1,215	1,215	17:1	X	20
Nazareth Academy, LaGrange Park	X	X	X	X	–	–	9–12	802	802	18:1	X	16
North Shore Country Day School, Winnetka	X	X	X	X	PK–5	6–8	9–12	510	210	8:1	X	15
Notre Dame College Prep, Niles	X	X	X	X	–	–	9–12	793	793	17:1	X	27
Roycemore School, Evanston	X	X	X	X	PK–4	5–8	9–12	292	96	5:1	X	7
Sacred Heart/Griffin High School, Springfield	X	X	X	X	–	–	9–12	781	781	24:1	X	15
Saint Anthony High School, Effingham	X	X	X	X	–	–	9–12	190	190	10:1	X	13
Saint Joseph High School, Westchester	X	X	X	X	–	–	9–12	524	524	16:1	X	19
Saint Patrick High School, Chicago	X	X	X	X	–	–	9–12	710	710	17:1	X	16
Saint Viator High School, Arlington Heights	X	X	X	X	–	–	9–12	990	990	18:1		18
Timothy Christian High School, Elmhurst	X	X	X	X	K–6	7–8	9–12	1,052	381	13:1	X	12
University of Chicago Laboratory Schools, Chicago	X	X	X	X	N–5	6–8	9–12	1,825	516	10:1	X	15
Wheaton Academy, West Chicago	X	X	X	X	–	–	9–12	640	640	15:1	X	33
The Willows Academy, Des Plaines	X	X	X	X	–	6–8	9–12	230	150	10:1	X	8
Indiana												
Bishop Luers High School, Fort Wayne	X	X	X	X	–	–	9–12	596	596	17:1	X	21
Cathedral High School, Indianapolis	X	X	X	X	–	–	9–12	1,255	1,255	13:1	X	31
Concordia Lutheran High School, Fort Wayne	X	X	X	X	–	–	9–12	691	691	17:1	X	22
Lutheran High School of Indianapolis, Indianapolis	X	X	X	X	–	–	9–12	216	216	15:1	X	17
Marian High School, Mishawaka	X	X	X	X	–	–	9–12	719	719	24:1	X	30
Oldenburg Academy, Oldenburg	X	X	X	X	–	–	9–12	202	202	12:1	X	14
Iowa												
Alpha Omega Academy, Rock Rapids	X	X	X	X	K–5	6–8	9–12	2,350	1,600	52:1		
Dowling Catholic High School, West Des Moines	X	X	X	X	–	–	9–12	1,400	1,400	18:1	X	21
Maharishi School of the Age of Enlightenment, Fairfield	X	X	X	X	PS–6	7–8	9–12	213	91	12:1		33
Saint Albert Junior-Senior High School, Council Bluffs	X	X	X	X	PK–6	7–8	9–12	752	215	11:1	X	16
Kansas												
Hyman Brand Hebrew Academy of Greater Kansas City, Overland Park	X	X	X	X	K–5	6–8	9–12	228	49	5:1	X	4
Immaculata High School, Leavenworth	X	X	X	X	–	–	9–12	122	122	9:1		14
Independent School, Wichita	X	X	X	X	PK–5	6–8	9–12	511	210	8:1	X	16
Maur Hill-Mount Academy, Atchison	X	X	X	X	–	–	9–12	195	195	9:1	X	35
Saint Thomas Aquinas High School, Overland Park	X	X	X	X	–	–	9–12	937	937	15:1	X	20
St. Xavier Catholic School, Junction City	X	X	X	X	–	–						5
Kentucky												
Beth Haven Christian School, Louisville	X	X	X	X	K4–5	6–8	9–12	211	60	9:1		7
Calvary Christian School, Covington	X	X	X	X	K4–6	7–8	9–12	359	108	8:1	X	22
Community Christian Academy, Independence	X	X	X	X	PS–6	7–8	9–12	268	61	15:1		6
Kentucky Country Day School, Louisville	X	X	X	X	JK–4	5–8	9–12	942	287	7:1	X	20
Landmark Christian Academy, Louisville	X	X	X	X	K4–6	7–8	9–12	130	28	11:1		4
Lexington Catholic High School, Lexington	X	X	X	X	–	–	9–12	802	802	14:1	X	22
Louisville Collegiate School, Louisville	X	X	X	X	JK–5	6–8	9–12	720		8:1	X	15
Oneida Baptist Institute, Oneida	X	X	X	X	–	6–8	9–12	275	210	11:1	X	10

Private Secondary Schools At-a-Glance

	STUDENTS ACCEPTED				GRADES			STUDENT/FACULTY			SCHOOL OFFERINGS	
	BOARDING		DAY									
	Boys	Girls	Boys	Girls	Lower	Middle	Upper	Total	Upper	Student/Faculty Ratio	Advanced Placement Preparation	Sports
St. Francis High School, Louisville	X	X	X	X	–	–	9–12	136	136	7:1	X	26
Trinity High School, Louisville	X	X	X	X	–	–	9–12	1,320	1,320	12:1	X	48
Whitefield Academy, Louisville	X	X	X	X	PS–5	6–8	9–12	731	199	20:1	X	17
Louisiana												
Academy of the Sacred Heart, New Orleans	X	X	X	X	1–4	5–8	9–12	620	202	16:1	X	22
Holy Cross School, New Orleans	X	X	X	X	–	5–7	8–12	980	680	13:1	X	27
Holy Savior Menard Catholic High School, Alexandria	X	X	X	X	–	7–8	9–12	480	298	12:1	X	15
St. Joseph's Academy, Baton Rouge	X	X	X	X	–	–	9–12	1,022	1,022	15:1	X	25
St. Martin's Episcopal School, Metairie	X	X	X	X	PK–5	6–8	9–12	526	235	8:1	X	17
Westminster Christian Academy, Opelousas	X	X	X	X	PK–6	7–8	9–12	1,123	245	13:1	X	13
Maine												
Cheverus High School, Portland	X	X	X	X	–	–	9–12	504	504	12:1	X	26
Fryeburg Academy, Fryeburg	X	X	X	X	–	–	9–PG	681	681	10:1	X	63
George Stevens Academy, Blue Hill	X	X	X	X	–	–	9–12	313	313	10:1	X	53
Gould Academy, Bethel	X	X	X	X	–	–	9–PG	232	232	6:1	X	12
Kents Hill School, Kents Hill	X	X	X	X	–	–	9–PG	250	250	6:1	X	37
Lee Academy, Lee	X	X	X	X	–	–	9–PG	268	268	12:1	X	51
Lincoln Academy, Newcastle	X	X	X	X	–	–	9–12	500	500	13:1	X	17
Maine Central Institute, Pittsfield	X	X	X	X	–	–	9–PG	455	455	14:1	X	26
North Yarmouth Academy, Yarmouth	X	X	X	X	–	5–8	9–12	280	190	8:1	X	19
Saint Dominic Academy, Auburn	X	X	X	X	PK–6	7–8	9–12	571	203	12:1	X	15
Waynflete School, Portland	X	X	X	X	PK–5	6–8	9–12	567	259	12:1		23
Maryland												
Academy of the Holy Cross, Kensington	X	X	X	X	–	–	9–12	528	528	14:1	X	20
Archbishop Curley High School, Baltimore	X	X	X	X	–	–	9–12	526	526	14:1	X	19
The Baltimore Actors' Theatre Conservatory, Baltimore	X	X	X	X	3–5	7–8	9–12	24	10	3:1	X	
Baltimore Lutheran School, Towson	X	X	X	X	–	6–8	9–12	240	178	12:1	X	18
Barrie School, Silver Spring	X	X	X	X	N–5	6–8	9–12	293	54	8:1	X	11
The Bryn Mawr School for Girls, Baltimore	X	X	X	X	K–5	6–8	9–12	700	290	6:1	X	41
Calvert Hall College High School, Baltimore	X	X	X	X	–	–	9–12	1,188	1,188	12:1	X	35
The Catholic High School of Baltimore, Baltimore	X	X	X	X	–	–	9–12	299	299	12:1	X	17
DeMatha Catholic High School, Hyattsville	X	X	X	X	–	–	9–12	884	884	13:1	X	24
Elizabeth Seton High School, Bladensburg	X	X	X	X	–	–	9–12	575	575	13:1	X	38
Garrison Forest School, Owings Mills	X	X	X	X	N–5	6–8	9–12	652	299	9:1	X	28
Georgetown Preparatory School, North Bethesda	X	X	X	X	–	–	9–12	490	490	8:1	X	51
Gilman School, Baltimore	X	X	X	X	K–5	6–8	9–12	1,034	465	8:1	X	26
Glenelg Country School, Ellicott City	X	X	X	X	PK–5	6–8	9–12	768	281	6:1	X	27
The Gunston School, Centreville	X	X	X	X	–	–	9–12	148	148	6:1	X	16
Institute of Notre Dame, Baltimore	X	X	X	X	–	–	9–12	384	384	11:1	X	32
Landon School, Bethesda	X	X	X	X	3–5	6–8	9–12	680	336	6:1	X	25
Loyola-Blakefield, Baltimore	X	X	X	X	–	6–8	9–12	988	749	10:1	X	24
McDonogh School, Owings Mills	X	X	X	X	K–4	5–8	9–12	1,289	588	9:1	X	28
The Nora School, Silver Spring	X	X	X	X	–	–	9–12	60	60	5:1		27
The Park School of Baltimore, Baltimore	X	X	X	X	PK–5	6–8	9–12	850	305	7:1	X	17
Roland Park Country School, Baltimore	X	X	X	X	K–5	6–8	9–12	650	287	7:1	X	25
St. Andrew's Episcopal School, Potomac	X	X	X	X	PS–3	4–8	9–12	506	248	6:1	X	16
Saint Mary's High School, Annapolis	X	X	X	X	–	–	9–12	485	485	15:1	X	20
St. Timothy's School, Stevenson	X	X	X	X	–	–	9–12	157	157	6:1		22
Sandy Spring Friends School, Sandy Spring	X	X	X	X	PK–5	6–8	9–12	572	263	8:1	X	41
Severn School, Severna Park	X	X	X	X	–	6–8	9–12	582	397	8:1	X	27
Worcester Preparatory School, Berlin	X	X	X	X	PK–5	6–8	9–12	532	200	9:1	X	13
Massachusetts												
Beaver Country Day School, Chestnut Hill	X	X	X	X	–	6–8	9–12	451	326	8:1		23
Berkshire School, Sheffield	X	X	X	X	–	–	9–PG		386	5:1	X	36
Bishop Stang High School, North Dartmouth	X	X	X	X	–	–	9–12	667	667	13:1	X	33
Boston Trinity Academy, Boston	X	X	X	X	–	6–8	9–12	213	163	8:1	X	9
Boston University Academy, Boston	X	X	X	X	–	–	9–12	167	167	8:1		13
Brimmer and May School, Chestnut Hill	X	X	X	X	PK–5	6–8	9–12	398	134	6:1	X	18
The British School of Boston, Boston	X	X	X	X	PK–3	4–8	9–12	383	59	3:1		20
Brooks School, North Andover	X	X	X	X	–	–	9–12	370	37	5:1	X	19
Buxton School, Williamstown	X	X	X	X	–	–	9–12	90	90	4:1		24
Cape Cod Academy, Osterville	X	X	X	X	PK–5	6–8	9–12	317	155	4:1	X	18
Central Catholic High School, Lawrence	X	X	X	X	–	–	9–12	1,340	1,340	24:1	X	32
Concord Academy, Concord	X	X	X	X	–	–	9–12	370	370	6:1		35
Cushing Academy, Ashburnham	X	X	X	X	–	–	9–PG	445	445	8:1	X	40
Dana Hall School, Wellesley	X	X	X	X	–	6–8	9–12	475	356	9:1	X	41
Deerfield Academy, Deerfield	X	X	X	X	–	–	9–PG	630	630	6:1	X	46

Private Secondary Schools At-a-Glance

	STUDENTS ACCEPTED				GRADES			STUDENT/FACULTY			SCHOOL OFFERINGS	
	BOARDING		DAY									
	Boys	Girls	Boys	Girls	Lower	Middle	Upper	Total	Upper	Student/Faculty Ratio	Advanced Placement Preparation	Sports
Dexter School, Brookline	X	X	X	X	–6	7–8	9–12	415	145	7:1	X	16
Eaglebrook School, Deerfield	X	X	X	X	–	6–9		253	223	4:1		64
Eagle Hill School, Hardwick	X	X	X	X	–	8–	9–12	205	193	4:1		39
Falmouth Academy, Falmouth	X	X	X	X	–	7–8	9–12	186	111	4:1	X	3
Fay School, Southborough	X	X	X	X	PK–6	–	7–9	450		8:1		39
The Fessenden School, West Newton	X	X	X	X	K–4	5–6	7–9	475	197	7:1		24
Gann Academy (The New Jewish High School of Greater Boston), Waltham	X	X	X	X	–	–	9–12	311	311	5:1	X	14
Holyoke Catholic High School, Chicopee	X	X	X	X	–	–	9–12	298	298	10:1	X	19
The Judge Rotenberg Educational Center, Canton	X	X	X	X	–	–			130			3
Matignon High School, Cambridge	X	X	X	X	–	–	9–12	464	464	18:1	X	26
Middlesex School, Concord	X	X	X	X	–	–	9–12	375	375	6:1	X	22
Milton Academy, Milton	X	X	X	X	K–5	6–8	9–12	980	675	5:1	X	28
Noble and Greenough School, Dedham	X	X	X	X	–	7–8	9–12	594	475	7:1	X	8
Phillips Academy (Andover), Andover	X	X	X	X	–	–	9–PG	1,143	1,143	5:1	X	48
The Pingree School, South Hamilton	X	X	X	X	–	–	9–12	334	334	7:1	X	32
Pioneer Valley Christian School, Springfield	X	X	X	X	PS–5	6–8	9–12	265	77	4.5:1	X	10
The Rivers School, Weston	X	X	X	X	–	6–8	9–12	479	359	6:1	X	18
The Roxbury Latin School, West Roxbury	X	X	X	X	–	–	7–12	297	297	7:1	X	10
St. John's Preparatory School, Danvers	X	X	X	X	–	–	9–12	1,200	1,200	12:1	X	47
Southfield School, Brookline	X	X	X	X	PK–6	7–8	9–12	319	82	7:1	X	18
The Sudbury Valley School, Framingham	X	X	X	X	–	–		160		16:1		
Valley View School, North Brookfield	X	X	X	X	–	5–8	9–12	56	26	6:1		48
Waldorf High School of Massachusetts Bay, Belmont	X	X	X	X	–	–	9–12	57	57	7:1		4
Walnut Hill School for the Arts, Natick	X	X	X	X	–	–	9–12	298	298	6:1	X	11
The Williston Northampton School, Easthampton	X	X	X	X	–	7–8	9–PG	534	454	6:1	X	39
The Woodward School, Quincy	X	X	X	X	–	6–8	9–12	125	81	8:1	X	3
Michigan												
Brother Rice High School, Bloomfield Hills	X	X	X	X	–	–	9–12	675	675	13:1	X	26
Gabriel Richard Catholic High School, Riverview	X	X	X	X	–	–	9–12	309	309	17:1	X	17
Greenhills School, Ann Arbor	X	X	X	X	–	6–8	9–12	556	321	8:1	X	15
Interlochen Arts Academy, Interlochen	X	X	X	X	–	–	9–PG	471	471	6:1	X	
Jean and Samuel Frankel Jewish Academy of Metropolitan Detroit, West Bloomfield	X	X	X	X	–	–	9–12	230	230		X	
Kalamazoo Christian High School, Kalamazoo	X	X	X	X	K–5	5–8	9–12	810	250	12:1	X	17
Lutheran High School Northwest, Rochester Hills	X	X	X	X	–	–	9–12	300	300	15:1	X	20
Powers Catholic High School, Flint	X	X	X	X	–	–	9–12	511	511	18:1	X	29
St. Mary's Preparatory School, Orchard Lake	X	X	X	X	–	–	9–12	480	480	10:1	X	44
Southfield Christian High School, Southfield	X	X	X	X	PK–5	6–8	9–12	567	198	20:1	X	12
University Liggett School, Grosse Pointe Woods	X	X	X	X	PK–5	6–8	9–12	616	282	8:1		16
University of Detroit Jesuit High School and Academy, Detroit	X	X	X	X	–	7–8	9–12	873	751	14:1	X	18
The Valley School, Swartz Creek	X	X	X	X	PK–4	5–8	9–12	62	17	8:1		9
West Catholic High School, Grand Rapids	X	X	X	X	–	–	9–12	437	437	30:1	X	22
Minnesota												
The Blake School, Hopkins	X	X	X	X	PK–5	6–8	9–12	1,372	529	8:1	X	15
Breck School, Minneapolis	X	X	X	X	PK–4	5–8	9–12	1,127	402	11:1	X	19
Cotter Schools, Winona	X	X	X	X	–	7–8	9–12	380	298	11:1		29
St. Croix Schools, West St. Paul	X	X	X	X	–	6–8	9–12	500	440	15:1	X	38
Saint John's Preparatory School, Collegeville	X	X	X	X	6–6	7–8	9–PG	315	233	10:1	X	50
St. Paul Academy and Summit School, St. Paul	X	X	X	X	K–5	6–8	9–12	884	373	7:1		25
Saint Thomas Academy, Mendota Heights	X	X	X	X	–	7–8	9–12	671	546	10:1	X	30
Shattuck-St. Mary's School, Faribault	X	X	X	X	–	6–8	9–PG	438	398	9:1	X	29
Mississippi												
Canton Academy, Canton	X	X	X	X	–6	–	7–12	333	166	17:1		21
Chamberlain-Hunt Academy, Port Gibson	X	X	X	X	–	7–9	10–12	90	54	5:1		44
Jackson Preparatory School, Jackson	X	X	X	X	–	6–9	10–12	800	375	13:1	X	15
St. Stanislaus College, Bay St. Louis	X	X	X	X	–	7–8	9–PG	352	250	12:1	X	34
SBEC (Southern Baptist Educational Center), Southaven	X	X	X	X	PK–6	–	7–12	1,077	474	13:1	X	14
Vicksburg Catholic School, Vicksburg	X	X	X	X	PK–6	–	7–12	569	253	10:1	X	13
Missouri												
Chaminade College Preparatory School, St. Louis	X	X	X	X	–	6–8	9–12	775	499	10:1	X	21
John Burroughs School, St. Louis	X	X	X	X	–	7–8	9–12	600	405	7:1	X	27
Lutheran High School North, St. Louis	X	X	X	X	–	–	9–12	311	311	10:1	X	13
Missouri Military Academy, Mexico	X	X	X	X	–	6–8	9–PG	232	186	11:1	X	42
MU High School, Columbia	X	X	X	X	–	–					X	
Nerinx Hall, Webster Groves	X	X	X	X	–	–	9–12	628	628	12:1	X	13
New Covenant Academy, Springfield	X	X	X	X	JK–6	7–8	9–12	371	92	10:1		6

Private Secondary Schools At-a-Glance

	STUDENTS ACCEPTED				GRADES			STUDENT/FACULTY			SCHOOL OFFERINGS	
	BOARDING		DAY									
	Boys	Girls	Boys	Girls	Lower	Middle	Upper	Total	Upper	Student/Faculty Ratio	Advanced Placement Preparation	Sports
Saint Teresa's Academy, Kansas City	X	X	X	X	–	–	9–12	580	580	12:1	X	25
Thomas Jefferson School, St. Louis	X	X	X	X	–	7–8	9–PG	91	68	6:1	X	9
Valle Catholic High School, Ste. Genevieve	X	X	X	X	–	–	9–12	134	134	9:1	X	14
Vianney High School, St. Louis	X	X	X	X	–	–	9–12	640	640	13:1	X	22
Villa Duchesne and Oak Hill School, St. Louis	X	X	X	X	JK–6	7–8	9–12	640	297	9:1	X	13
Montana												
Butte Central Catholic High School, Butte	X	X	X	X	–	–	9–12	134	134	12:1	X	11
Manhattan Christian High School, Manhattan	X	X	X	X	PK–5	6–8	9–12	290	87	8:1	X	8
Nebraska												
Mount Michael Benedictine School, Elkhorn	X	X	X	X	–	–	9–12	221	221	10:1	X	22
Nebraska Christian Schools, Central City	X	X	X	X	K–6	7–8	9–12	196	124	10:1		6
Scotus Central Catholic High School, Columbus	X	X	X	X	–	7–8	9–12	396	258	14:1	X	13
Nevada												
Faith Lutheran High School, Las Vegas	X	X	X	X	–	6–8	9–12	1,390	749	17:1	X	22
The Meadows School, Las Vegas	X	X	X	X	PK–5	6–8	9–12	891	261	11:1	X	15
Sage Ridge School, Reno	X	X	X	X	–	5–8	9–12	215	85	6:1	X	15
New Hampshire												
Bishop Brady High School, Concord	X	X	X	X	–	–	9–12	365	365	16:1	X	30
Bishop Guertin High School, Nashua	X	X	X	X	–	–	9–12	900	900		X	35
Cardigan Mountain School, Canaan	X	X	X	X	–	6–9		215	192	4:1		41
The Derryfield School, Manchester	X	X	X	X	–	6–8	9–12	363	248	8:1	X	26
Dublin Christian Academy, Dublin	X	X	X	X	K–6	7–8	9–12	88	52	8:1	X	10
Dublin School, Dublin	X	X	X	X	–	–	9–12	140	140	4:1	X	70
Hampshire Country School, Rindge	X	X	X	X	3–6	–	7–12	21	17	2:1		24
Kimball Union Academy, Meriden	X	X	X	X	–	–	9–PG	314	314	6:1	X	38
Portsmouth Christian Academy, Dover	X	X	X	X	PK–5	6–8	9–12	617	181	13:1	X	16
Proctor Academy, Andover	X	X	X	X	–	–	9–12	360	360	5:1	X	57
St. Thomas Aquinas High School, Dover	X	X	X	X	–	–	9–12	630	630	14:1	X	18
Tilton School, Tilton	X	X	X	X	–	–	9–PG	241	241	6:1	X	28
Trinity High School, Manchester	X	X	X	X	–	–	9–12	447	447	12:1	X	22
New Jersey												
Bishop Eustace Preparatory School, Pennsauken	X	X	X	X	–	–	9–12	700	700	13:1	X	20
Blair Academy, Blairstown	X	X	X	X	–	–	9–PG	450	450	6:1	X	43
Christian Brothers Academy, Lincroft	X	X	X	X	–	–	9–12	997	997	15:1	X	15
Delbarton School, Morristown	X	X	X	X	–	7–8	9–12	554	487	10:1	X	28
Hawthorne Christian Academy, Hawthorne	X	X	X	X	PS–5	6–8	9–12	496	150	7:1	X	10
The Hudson School, Hoboken	X	X	X	X	–	5–8	9–12	185	85	4:1	X	15
Immaculata High School, Somerville	X	X	X	X	–	–	9–12	690	690	13:1	X	12
The Lawrenceville School, Lawrenceville	X	X	X	X	–	–	9–PG	819	819	8:1		51
Marylawn of the Oranges, South Orange	X	X	X	X	–	6–8	9–12	145	123	15:1	X	14
Monsignor Donovan High School, Toms River	X	X	X	X	–	–	9–12	726	726	15:1	X	23
Montclair Kimberley Academy, Montclair	X	X	X	X	PK–3	4–8	9–12	1,031	249	6:1	X	21
Moorestown Friends School, Moorestown	X	X	X	X	PS–4	5–8	9–12	715	294	9:1	X	17
Morristown-Beard School, Morristown	X	X	X	X	–	6–8	9–12	557	401	7:1	X	21
Mt. Saint Dominic Academy, Caldwell	X	X	X	X	–	–	9–12	315	315	12:1	X	20
Newark Academy, Livingston	X	X	X	X	–	6–8	9–12	580	40	12:1	X	32
Notre Dame High School, Lawrenceville	X	X	X	X	–	–	9–12	1,299	1,299	13:1	X	30
Our Lady of Mercy Academy, Newfield	X	X	X	X	–	–	9–12	150	150	11:1		17
Peddie School, Hightstown	X	X	X	X	–	–	9–PG	550	550	6:1	X	27
The Pennington School, Pennington	X	X	X	X	–	6–8	9–12	485	388	8:1	X	25
The Pingry School, Martinsville	X	X	X	X	K–5	6–8	9–12	1,077	550	8:1	X	25
Pope John XXIII Regional High School, Sparta	X	X	X	X	–	–	8–12	972	972	13:1	X	19
Ranney School, Tinton Falls	X	X	X	X	N–5	6–8	9–12	821	271	9:1	X	24
Saint Augustine Preparatory School, Richland	X	X	X	X	–	–	9–12	682	682	12:1	X	23
Saint Joseph High School, Metuchen	X	X	X	X	–	–	9–12	760	760	16:1	X	24
Villa Victoria Academy, Ewing	X	X	X	X	PK–6	7–8	9–12	202	67	6:1	X	10
Villa Walsh Academy, Morristown	X	X	X	X	–	7–8	9–12	260	230	8:1	X	11
New Mexico												
Menaul School, Albuquerque	X	X	X	X	–	6–8	9–12	185	122	9:1	X	13
Sandia Preparatory School, Albuquerque	X	X	X	X	–	6–8	9–12	625	360	10:1		32
Santa Fe Preparatory School, Santa Fe	X	X	X	X	–	7–8	9–12	303	204	16:1	X	16
New York												
Allendale Columbia School, Rochester	X	X	X	X	N–5	6–8	9–12	363	135		X	11
All Hallows High School, Bronx	X	X	X	X	–	–	9–12	654	654	15:1		14
Bay Ridge Preparatory School, Brooklyn	X	X	X	X	K–5	6–8	9–12			7:1	X	13

Private Secondary Schools At-a-Glance

	STUDENTS ACCEPTED				GRADES			STUDENT/FACULTY			SCHOOL OFFERINGS	
	BOARDING		DAY									
	Boys	Girls	Boys	Girls	Lower	Middle	Upper	Total	Upper	Student/Faculty Ratio	Advanced Placement Preparation	Sports
The Beekman School, New York	X	X	X	X	–	–	9–PG	80	80	8:1	X	
The Birch Wathen Lenox School, New York	X	X	X	X	K–5	6–8	9–12	570	170	15:1	X	26
The Brearley School, New York	X	X	X	X	K–4	5–8	9–12	688	213	6:1	X	26
Buffalo Academy of the Sacred Heart, Buffalo	X	X	X	X	–	–	9–12	407	407	10:1	X	25
Cascadilla School, Ithaca	X	X	X	X	–	–	9–PG	50	50	6:1	X	51
Catholic Central High School, Troy	X	X	X	X	–	7–8	9–12	520	415	12:1	X	17
Christian Brothers Academy, Syracuse	X	X	X	X	–	–	7–12	750	750		X	18
Christian Central Academy, Williamsville	X	X	X	X	K–5	6–8	9–12	370	104	10:1	X	11
Convent of the Sacred Heart, New York	X	X	X	X	PK–4	5–8	9–12	698	208	10:1	X	23
Darrow School, New Lebanon	X	X	X	X	–	–				4:1	X	26
Doane Stuart School, Rensselaer	X	X	X	X	N–4	5–8	9–12	302	154	7:1	X	23
Dominican Academy, New York	X	X	X	X	–	–	9–12	209	209	8:1	X	9
Emma Willard School, Troy	X	X	X	X	–	–	9–PG	329	329	5.5:1	X	37
Fontbonne Hall Academy, Brooklyn	X	X	X	X	–	–	9–12	486	486	13:1	X	17
Fordham Preparatory School, Bronx	X	X	X	X	–	–	9–12	955	955	11:1	X	23
French-American School of New York, Mamaroneck	X	X	X	X	N–5	6–8	9–12	848	186	7:1	X	8
Friends Academy, Locust Valley	X	X	X	X	N–5	6–8	9–12	775	371	8:1	X	18
The Harley School, Rochester	X	X	X	X	N–4	5–8	9–12	513	163	7:1	X	15
The Harvey School, Katonah	X	X	X	X	–	6–8	9–12	334	248	6:1	X	23
Hebrew Academy of the Five Towns & Rockaway, Cedarhurst	X	X	X	X	–	–	9–12	388	388		X	7
The Hewitt School, New York	X	X	X	X	K–3	4–7	8–12	520	115	7:1	X	11
Holy Angels Academy, Buffalo	X	X	X	X	–	6–8	9–12	242	224	10:1	X	24
Holy Trinity Diocesan High School, Hicksville	X	X	X	X	–	–	9–12	1,351	1,351	17:1	X	24
Houghton Academy, Houghton	X	X	X	X	–	6–8	9–PG	134	112	8:1	X	15
Iona Preparatory School, New Rochelle	X	X	X	X	–	–	9–12	785	785	13:1	X	36
The Kew-Forest School, Forest Hills	X	X	X	X	N–6	7–8	9–12	243	98	8:1	X	17
La Scuola D'Italia Guglielmo Marconi, New York	X	X	X	X	PK–5	6–8	9–12	261	44		X	4
Long Island Lutheran Middle and High School, Brookville	X	X	X	X	–	6–8	9–12	595	402	9:1	X	23
Loyola School, New York	X	X	X	X	–	–	9–12	202	202	9:1	X	16
Maplebrook School, Amenia	X	X	X	X	–	–		70	60	8:1		41
Martin Luther High School, Maspeth	X	X	X	X	–	6–8	9–12	212	170	12:1	X	18
The Mary Louis Academy, Jamaica Estates	X	X	X	X	–	–	9–12	909	909	13:1	X	27
Mount Mercy Academy, Buffalo	X	X	X	X	–	–	9–12	244	244	20:1	X	12
Northwood School, Lake Placid	X	X	X	X	–	–	9–12	182	182	6:1	X	49
Oakwood Friends School, Poughkeepsie	X	X	X	X	–	6–8	9–12	125	105	4:1	X	32
The Park School of Buffalo, Snyder	X	X	X	X	PK–4	5–8	9–12	250	110	8:1	X	31
Professional Children's School, New York	X	X	X	X	–	6–8	9–12	193	161	8:1		
Regis High School, New York	X	X	X	X	–	–	9–12	530	530	15:1	X	8
Riverdale Country School, Bronx	X	X	X	X	PK–5	6–8	9–12	1,125	500	8:1		22
Ross School, East Hampton	X	X	X	X	N–5	6–8	9–12	618	344	7:1	X	21
Rye Country Day School, Rye	X	X	X	X	PK–4	5–8	9–12	886	393	7:1	X	32
Smith School, New York	X	X	X	X	–	7–8	9–12	57	42	4:1		7
Soundview Preparatory School, Yorktown Heights	X	X	X	X	–	6–8	9–12	70	58	4:1	X	8
The Spence School, New York	X	X	X	X	K–4	5–8	9–12	720	237	7:1	X	13
The Storm King School, Cornwall-on-Hudson	X	X	X	X	–	8–8	9–12	127	120	6:1	X	64
Trinity-Pawling School, Pawling	X	X	X	X	–	7–8	9–PG	293	265	8:1	X	40
The Waldorf School of Garden City, Garden City	X	X	X	X	N–5	6–8	9–12	350	105	5:1	X	14
The Waldorf School of Saratoga Springs, Saratoga Springs	X	X	X	X	PK–8	–	9–12	252	47	3:1		11
The Windsor School, Flushing	X	X	X	X	–	6–8	9–13	152	148	14:1	X	11
Winston Preparatory School, New York	X	X	X	X	–	6–8	9–12	191	148	3:1		13
Xaverian High School, Brooklyn	X	X	X	X	–	6–8	9–12	1,088	919	26:1	X	35
York Preparatory School, New York	X	X	X	X	–	6–8	9–12	358	262	6:1	X	26
North Carolina												
Arthur Morgan School, Burnsville	X	X	X	X	–	7–9		27	24	2:1		26
Bishop McGuinness Catholic High School, Kernersville	X	X	X	X	–	–	9–12	549	549	15:1	X	16
Cannon School, Concord	X	X	X	X	PK–4	5–8	9–12	905		9:1	X	21
Cape Fear Academy, Wilmington	X	X	X	X	PK–5	6–8	9–12	601	239	8:1	X	13
Cardinal Gibbons High School, Raleigh	X	X	X	X	–	–	9–12	1,192	1,192	14:1	X	28
Carolina Day School, Asheville	X	X	X	X	PK–5	6–8	9–12	610	170	6:1	X	13
Charlotte Country Day School, Charlotte	X	X	X	X	PK–4	5–8	9–12	1,622	488	12:1		21
Charlotte Latin School, Charlotte	X	X	X	X	K–5	6–8	9–12	1,402	495	8:1	X	20
Durham Academy, Durham	X	X	X	X	PK–4	5–8	9–12	1,165	406	12:1	X	25
Fayetteville Academy, Fayetteville	X	X	X	X	PK–5	6–8	9–12	378	137	14:1	X	12
Forsyth Country Day School, Lewisville	X	X	X	X	PK–4	5–8	9–12	776	319	12:1	X	17
Gaston Day School, Gastonia	X	X	X	X	PS–4	5–8	9–12	495	145	7:1	X	16
Harrells Christian Academy, Harrells	X	X	X	X	K–5	6–8	9–12	404	146	9:1	X	9
Noble Academy, Greensboro	X	X	X	X	K–6	7–9	10–12	163	39	9:1		8

Private Secondary Schools At-a-Glance

	STUDENTS ACCEPTED				GRADES			STUDENT/FACULTY			SCHOOL OFFERINGS	
	BOARDING		DAY									
	Boys	Girls	Boys	Girls	Lower	Middle	Upper	Total	Upper	Student/Faculty Ratio	Advanced Placement Preparation	Sports
The O'Neal School, Southern Pines	X	X	X	X	PK–5	6–8	9–12	435	168	12:1	X	10
Ravenscroft School, Raleigh	X	X	X	X	PK–5	6–8	9–12	1,210	459	8:1	X	22
Saint Mary's School, Raleigh	X	X	X	X	–	–	9–12	237	237	8:1	X	15
Salem Academy, Winston-Salem	X	X	X	X	–	–	9–12	160	160	7:1	X	22
Westchester Country Day School, High Point	X	X	X	X	PK–5	6–8	9–12	384	142	6:1	X	15
Northern Mariana Islands												
Mount Carmel School, Saipan	X	X	X	X	1–5	6–8	9–12	378	146	20:1	X	11
Ohio												
Bishop Fenwick High School, Franklin	X	X	X	X	–	–	9–12	553	553	14:1	X	24
Cincinnati Country Day School, Cincinnati	X	X	X	X	PK–5	6–8	9–12	830	270	9:1	X	14
Columbus School for Girls, Columbus	X	X	X	X	PK–5	6–8	9–12	573	211	9:1	X	44
Elyria Catholic High School, Elyria	X	X	X	X	–	–	9–12	486	486	14:1	X	16
Gilmour Academy, Gates Mills	X	X	X	X	PK–6	7–8	9–12	689	433	9:1	X	37
Hawken School, Gates Mills	X	X	X	X	PS–5	6–8	9–12	972	424	9:1	X	17
Lawrence School, Sagamore Hills	X	X	X	X	K–6	7–8	9–12	280	136	11:1		11
Lehman High School, Sidney	X	X	X	X	–	–	9–12	205	205	15:1	X	15
Padua Franciscan High School, Parma	X	X	X	X	–	–	9–12	805	805	19:1	X	42
St. Francis de Sales High School, Toledo	X	X	X	X	–	–	9–12	612	612	14:1	X	17
Saint Joseph Academy High School, Cleveland	X	X	X	X	–	–			665	12:1	X	17
Saint Ursula Academy, Toledo	X	X	X	X	–	7–8	9–12	549	522	16:1	X	31
The Seven Hills School, Cincinnati	X	X	X	X	PK–5	6–8	9–12	1,011	305	9:1	X	13
Stephen T. Badin High School, Hamilton	X	X	X	X	–	–	9–12	509	509	19:1	X	18
The Summit Country Day School, Cincinnati	X	X	X	X	PK–4	5–8	9–12	1,071	382	9:1	X	19
Trinity High School, Garfield Heights	X	X	X	X	–	–	9–12	352	352	10:1	X	15
Villa Angela-St. Joseph High School, Cleveland	X	X	X	X	–	–	9–12	310	310	15:1	X	21
Oklahoma												
Bishop McGuinness Catholic High School, Oklahoma City	X	X	X	X	9–10	–	11–12	681	338	12:1	X	19
Holland Hall, Tulsa	X	X	X	X	PK–3	4–8	9–12	995	333	9:1	X	20
Rejoice Christian Schools, Owasso	X	X	X	X	P3–5	6–8	9–12	713	84	12:1		19
Oregon												
Blanchet School, Salem	X	X	X	X	–	6–8	9–12	363	249	15:1	X	15
Canyonville Christian Academy, Canyonville	X	X	X	X	–	–			124	9:1	X	11
Cascades Academy of Central Oregon, Bend	X	X	X	X	K–5	6–8	9–12	143	23	6:1		
The Catlin Gabel School, Portland	X	X	X	X	PS–5	6–8	9–12	753	309	8:1		49
Christa McAuliffe Academy School of Arts and Sciences, Lake Oswego	X	X	X	X	K–5	6–8	9–12	108	91	25:1	X	
De La Salle North Catholic High School, Portland	X	X	X	X	–	–	9–12	322	322	17:1	X	
Northwest Academy, Portland	X	X	X	X	–	6–8	9–12	163	68	4:1		9
Oregon Episcopal School, Portland	X	X	X	X	PK–5	6–8	9–12	851	311	7:1	X	22
Pacific Crest Community School, Portland	X	X	X	X	–	6–8	9–12	85	60	9:1		12
St. Mary's School, Medford	X	X	X	X	–	6–8	9–12	468	332	11:1	X	25
Salem Academy, Salem	X	X	X	X	K–5	6–8	9–12	594	228	9:1	X	12
Wellsprings Friends School, Eugene	X	X	X	X	–	–	9–12	60	60	8:1		9
Windells Academy, Brightwood	X	X	X	X	–	–	9–12	25	25	7:1		3
Pennsylvania												
Academy of Notre Dame de Namur, Villanova	X	X	X	X	–	6–8	9–12	519	392	8:1		18
Academy of the New Church Boys' School, Bryn Athyn	X	X	X	X	–	–	9–12	118	118	8:1	X	6
Academy of the New Church Girls' School, Bryn Athyn	X	X	X	X	–	–	9–12	86	86	8:1	X	9
The Agnes Irwin School, Rosemont	X	X	X	X	PK–4	5–8	9–12	701	292	6:1	X	27
Camphill Special School, Glenmoore	X	X	X	X	K–5	6–8	9–13	115	57	5:1		
Cardinal O'Hara High School, Springfield	X	X	X	X	–	–			1,289	21:1	X	21
Cathedral Preparatory School, Erie	X	X	X	X	–	–	9–12	581	581	13:1	X	23
Christopher Dock Mennonite High School, Lansdale	X	X	X	X	–	–	9–12	343	343	11:1	X	12
The Church Farm School, Exton	X	X	X	X	–	7–8	9–12	193	162	6:1	X	16
The Concept School, Westtown	X	X	X	X	–	5–8	9–12	19	13	4:1		11
Country Day School of the Sacred Heart, Bryn Mawr	X	X	X	X	PK–4	5–8	9–12	307	165	8:1	X	11
Devon Preparatory School, Devon	X	X	X	X	–	6–8	9–12	260	196	10:1	X	10
DuBois Central Catholic High School/Middle School, DuBois	X	X	X	X	–	6–8	9–12	241	161	14:1		
Friends' Central School, Wynnewood	X	X	X	X	N–4	5–8	9–12	832	392	8:1		25
Germantown Friends School, Philadelphia	X	X	X	X	K–5	6–8	9–12	861	353	9:1		16
Grier School, Tyrone	X	X	X	X	–	7–8	9–PG	290	252	7:1	X	40
The Harrisburg Academy, Wormleysburg	X	X	X	X	PS–4	5–8	9–12	400	90	8:1	X	8
The Hill School, Pottstown	X	X	X	X	–	–	9–PG	494	494	7:1	X	25
The Hill Top Preparatory School, Rosemont	X	X	X	X	–	5–9	10–12	78	42	6:1		26
Holy Ghost Preparatory School, Bensalem	X	X	X	X	–	–	9–12	480	480	11:1	X	19

Private Secondary Schools At-a-Glance	STUDENTS ACCEPTED				GRADES			STUDENT/FACULTY			SCHOOL OFFERINGS	
	BOARDING		DAY									
	Boys	Girls	Boys	Girls	Lower	Middle	Upper	Total	Upper	Student/Faculty Ratio	Advanced Placement Preparation	Sports
Jack M. Barrack Hebrew Academy, Bryn Mawr	X	X	X	X	–	6–8	9–12	274	205	15:1	X	14
Lancaster Country Day School, Lancaster	X	X	X	X	PS–5	6–8	9–12	599	204	8:1	X	20
Lancaster Mennonite High School, Lancaster	X	X	X	X	PK–5	6–8	9–12	638	638	15:1	X	11
Lansdale Catholic High School, Lansdale	X	X	X	X	–	–	9–12	763	763		X	25
Lehigh Valley Christian High School, Catasauqua	X	X	X	X	–	–	9–12	125	125	7:1	X	8
Malvern Preparatory School, Malvern	X	X	X	X	–	6–8	9–12	595	434	9:1	X	17
MMI Preparatory School, Freeland	X	X	X	X	–	6–8	9–12	257	161	11:1	X	11
Moravian Academy, Bethlehem	X	X	X	X	PK–5	6–8	9–12	775	300	7:1	X	14
Mount Saint Joseph Academy, Flourtown	X	X	X	X	–	–	9–12	550	550	10:1	X	14
Notre Dame Junior/Senior High School, East Stroudsburg	X	X	X	X	–	–	7–12	233	233	15:1	X	14
The Oakland School, Pittsburgh	X	X	X	X	–	–	8–12	40	40	6:1		32
The Pathway School, Norristown	X	X	X	X	–	–		125	64	6:1		5
Philadelphia-Montgomery Christian Academy, Erdenheim	X	X	X	X	PK–5	6–8	9–12	304	124	10:1	X	8
St. Joseph's Preparatory School, Philadelphia	X	X	X	X	–	–	9–12	993	993	16:1	X	32
Shady Side Academy, Pittsburgh	X	X	X	X	PK–5	6–8	9–12	931	489	8:1	X	25
The Shipley School, Bryn Mawr	X	X	X	X	PK–5	6–8	9–12	834	342	7:1	X	25
Valley Forge Military Academy & College, Wayne	X	X	X	X	–	7–8	9–PG	248	227	11:1	X	36
Villa Joseph Marie High School, Holland	X	X	X	X	–	–	9–12	367	367	10:1	X	14
Villa Maria Academy, Erie	X	X	X	X	–	–	9–12	323	323	10:1	X	13
Westtown School, West Chester	X	X	X	X	PK–5	6–8	9–12	642	374	8:1	X	36
Woodlynde School, Strafford	X	X	X	X	K–5	6–8	9–12	262	100	5:1		8
Wyoming Seminary, Kingston	X	X	X	X	PS–8	–	9–PG	756	419	8:1	X	24
York Catholic High School, York	X	X	X	X	–	7–8	9–12	636	440	16:1	X	19
Puerto Rico												
Baldwin School of Puerto Rico, Bayamón	X	X	X	X	PK–5	6–8	9–12	809	191	8:1	X	12
Colegio San Jose, San Juan	X	X	X	X	–	7–8	9–12	502	345		X	13
Commonwealth Parkville School, San Juan	X	X	X	X	PS–6	7–8	9–12	672	174	7:1	X	28
Guamani Private School, Guayama	X	X	X	X	1–6	7–8	9–12	606	164	13:1	X	6
Wesleyan Academy, Guaynabo	X	X	X	X	PK–6	7–8	9–12	927	197	23:1	X	8
Rhode Island												
Lincoln School, Providence	X	X	X	X	N–5	6–8	9–12	337	157	4:1	X	9
Mount Saint Charles Academy, Woonsocket	X	X	X	X	–	–	7–12	774	774	18:1	X	27
Portsmouth Abbey School, Portsmouth	X	X	X	X	–	–	9–12	357	357	7:1	X	24
The Prout School, Wakefield	X	X	X	X	–	–	9–12	640	640	18:1	X	27
Providence Country Day School, East Providence	X	X	X	X	–	6–8	9–12	201	165	7:1	X	19
St. Andrew's School, Barrington	X	X	X	X	3–5	6–8	9–PG	215	181	5:1	X	32
St. George's School, Middletown	X	X	X	X	–	–	9–12	365	365	6:1	X	21
The Wheeler School, Providence	X	X	X	X	N–5	6–8	9–12	839	343	8:1	X	15
South Carolina												
Christ Church Episcopal School, Greenville	X	X	X	X	K–4	5–8	9–12	1,095	388	9:1		16
Porter-Gaud School, Charleston	X	X	X	X	1–5	6–8	9–12	889	342	12:1	X	26
St. Joseph's Catholic School, Greenville	X	X	X	X	–	6–8	9–12	644	395	13:1	X	17
Spartanburg Day School, Spartanburg	X	X	X	X	PK–4	5–8	9–12	449	145	9:1	X	17
Wilson Hall, Sumter	X	X	X	X	PS–5	6–8	9–12	825	248	13:1	X	34
South Dakota												
Freeman Academy, Freeman	X	X	X	X	1–4	5–8	9–12	79	46	5:1		7
Sunshine Bible Academy, Miller	X	X	X	X	K–5	6–8	9–12	86	65	9:1		12
Tennessee												
Bachman Academy, McDonald	X	X	X	X	–	6–8	9–PG	35	26	3:1		40
Battle Ground Academy, Franklin	X	X	X	X	K–4	5–8	9–12	846	323	11:1	X	30
Briarcrest Christian High School, Eads	X	X	X	X	PK–5	6–8	9–12	1,649	553	14:1	X	20
Chattanooga Christian School, Chattanooga	X	X	X	X	K–5	6–8	9–12	1,156	443	17:1	X	18
Christian Academy of Knoxville, Knoxville	X	X	X	X	PK–5	6–8	9–12	1,158	430	17:1		15
Clarksville Academy, Clarksville	X	X	X	X	PK–5	6–8	9–12	566	190	7:1	X	12
Columbia Academy, Columbia	X	X	X	X	K–6	–	7–12	623	261	10:1	X	15
Currey Ingram Academy, Brentwood	X	X	X	X	K–4	5–8	9–12	299	64	4:1		8
Davidson Academy, Nashville	X	X	X	X	PK–6	7–8	9–12				X	16
Donelson Christian Academy, Nashville	X	X	X	X	K4–5	6–8	9–12	735	237	16:1	X	18
Ezell-Harding Christian School, Antioch	X	X	X	X	PK–4	5–8	9–12	648	207	12:1	X	15
Father Ryan High School, Nashville	X	X	X	X	–	–	9–12	948	948	12:1	X	30
Girls Preparatory School, Chattanooga	X	X	X	X	–	6–8	9–12	590	345	8:1	X	45
Grace Baptist Academy, Chattanooga	X	X	X	X	K4–5	6–8	9–12	572	161	12:1	X	16
The King's Academy, Seymour	X	X	X	X	K4–5	6–8	9–12	471	169	14:1	X	25
Memphis Catholic High School and Middle School, Memphis	X	X	X	X	–	7–8	9–12	190	154	15:1		
Middle Tennessee Christian School, Murfreesboro	X	X	X	X	PK–6	7–8	9–12	665	200	18:1	X	13

Private Secondary Schools At-a-Glance

	STUDENTS ACCEPTED				GRADES			STUDENT/FACULTY			SCHOOL OFFERINGS	
	BOARDING		DAY									
	Boys	Girls	Boys	Girls	Lower	Middle	Upper	Total	Upper	Student/Faculty Ratio	Advanced Placement Preparation	Sports
Montgomery Bell Academy, Nashville	X	X	X	X	–	7–8	9–12	715	486	8:1	X	38
Notre Dame High School, Chattanooga	X	X	X	X	–	–	9–12	407	407	10:1	X	42
St. Andrew's–Sewanee School, Sewanee	X	X	X	X	–	6–8	9–12	248	186	4:1	X	57
St. Benedict at Auburndale, Cordova	X	X	X	X	–	–	9–12	982	982	16:1	X	24
St. George's Independent School, Collierville	X	X	X	X	PK–5	6–8	9–12	1,195	389	7:1	X	16
St. Mary's Episcopal School, Memphis	X	X	X	X	PK–4	5–8	9–12	846	243	13:1	X	12
Trinity Christian Academy, Jackson	X	X	X	X	PS–5	6–8	9–12	751	241	10:1		13
University School of Jackson, Jackson	X	X	X	X	PK–5	6–8	9–12	1,196	348	13:1	X	16
Webb School of Knoxville, Knoxville	X	X	X	X	K–5	6–8	9–12	1,023	455	10:1	X	19
Texas												
The Awty International School, Houston	X	X	X	X	PK–5	6–8	9–12	1,489	415	18:1		18
The Brook Hill School, Bullard	X	X	X	X	PK–5	6–8	9–12	519	191	9:1	X	20
The Canterbury Episcopal School, DeSoto	X	X	X	X	K–6	7–8	9–12	251	80	11:1	X	11
Central Catholic High School, San Antonio	X	X	X	X	–	–	9–12	558	558	20:1	X	20
Cistercian Preparatory School, Irving	X	X	X	X	–	5–8	9–12	348	175	7:1	X	14
Dallas Christian School, Mesquite	X	X	X	X	PK–5	6–8	9–12	585	222	12:1		12
Duchesne Academy of the Sacred Heart, Houston	X	X	X	X	PK–4	5–8	9–12	681	229	7:1	X	14
Episcopal High School, Bellaire	X	X	X	X	–	–	9–12	673	673	9:1	X	23
Fairhill School, Dallas	X	X	X	X	1–5	6–8	9–12	220	90	12:1		7
First Baptist Academy, Dallas	X	X	X	X	PK–5	6–8	9–12	239	87	8:1	X	14
Fort Worth Christian School, North Richland Hills	X	X	X	X	PK–5	6–8	9–12	870	364	14:1	X	16
Fort Worth Country Day School, Fort Worth	X	X	X	X	K–4	5–8	9–12	1,110	403	10:1	X	26
Gateway School, Arlington	X	X	X	X	–	–				8:1		6
Greenhill School, Addison	X	X	X	X	PK–4	5–8	9–12	1,279	468	7:1	X	29
The Hockaday School, Dallas	X	X	X	X	PK–4	5–8	9–12	1,086	478	15:1	X	42
Houston Learning Academy-North Houston, Houston	X	X	X	X	–	–	9–12	30	30	5:1		
Huntington-Surrey School, Austin	X	X	X	X	–	–8	9–12	42	40	4:1		
Hyde Park Baptist School, Austin	X	X	X	X	PK–5	6–8	9–12	568	259	12:1	X	14
Lakehill Preparatory School, Dallas	X	X	X	X	K–4	5–8	9–12	400	110	10:1	X	15
Loretto Academy, El Paso	X	X	X	X	PK–5	6–8	9–12	636	365	20:1	X	13
Marine Military Academy, Harlingen	X	X	X	X	–	–	8–12	250	250	13:1	X	40
Memorial Hall School, Houston	X	X	X	X	–	6–8	9–12	75	70	14:1		11
North Central Texas Academy, Granbury	X	X	X	X	K–5	6–8	9–12	170	65	7:1		17
The Oakridge School, Arlington	X	X	X	X	PS–4	5–8	9–12	858	314	11:1	X	23
Parish Episcopal School, Dallas	X	X	X	X	PK–4	5–8	9–12	1,100				22
Presbyterian Pan American School, Kingsville	X	X	X	X	–	–	9–12	163	163	10:1		19
Prestonwood Christian Academy, Plano	X	X	X	X	PK–4	5–8	9–12	1,472	491	11:1	X	13
River Oaks Baptist School, Houston	X	X	X	X	K–4	5–8		732	160			
St. Agnes Academy, Houston	X	X	X	X	–	–	9–12	890	890	15:1	X	19
St. Anthony Catholic High School, San Antonio	X	X	X	X	–	–	9–12	391	391	12:1	X	14
St. Mark's School of Texas, Dallas	X	X	X	X	1–4	5–8	9–12	851	367	8:1	X	41
Saint Mary's Hall, San Antonio	X	X	X	X	PK–5	6–8	9–PG	991	390	6:1	X	21
St. Pius X High School, Houston	X	X	X	X	–	–	9–12	649	649	12:1	X	17
St. Stephen's Episcopal School, Austin	X	X	X	X	–	6–8	9–12	669	464	8:1	X	39
St. Thomas High School, Houston	X	X	X	X	–	–	9–12	752	752	14:1	X	18
San Marcos Baptist Academy, San Marcos	X	X	X	X	–	7–8	9–12	287	240	7:1	X	24
Shelton School and Evaluation Center, Dallas	X	X	X	X	PS–4	5–8	9–12	868	262	8:1		11
Southwest Christian School, Inc., Fort Worth	X	X	X	X	PK–6	7–8	9–12	861	297	11:1	X	21
Spring Creek Academy, Plano	X	X	X	X	K–5	6–8	9–12			6:1	X	
The Tenney School, Houston	X	X	X	X	–	6–8	9–12	55	42	2:1	X	
TMI - The Episcopal School of Texas, San Antonio	X	X	X	X	–	6–8	9–12	435	300	10:1	X	21
Tyler Street Christian Academy, Dallas	X	X	X	X	P3–6	7–8	9–12	198	47	13:1	X	16
The Ursuline Academy of Dallas, Dallas	X	X	X	X	–	–	9–12	800	800	10:1	X	14
Westbury Christian School, Houston	X	X	X	X	PK–6	7–8	9–12	579	267	10:1	X	13
The Winston School San Antonio, San Antonio	X	X	X	X	K–6	7–8	9–12	197	92	8:1		14
Utah												
Concordia Preparatory School, Riverton	X	X	X	X	–	–	9–12	58	58	3:1	X	14
Intermountain Christian School, Salt Lake City	X	X	X	X	PK–5	6–8	9–12	277	60	8:1	X	5
Realms of Inquiry, Murray	X	X	X	X	–	6–8	9–12	22	12	7:1		62
Rowland Hall, Salt Lake City	X	X	X	X	PK–5	6–8	9–12	980	310	8:1	X	30
Wasatch Academy, Mt. Pleasant	X	X	X	X	–	7–8	9–PG	304	290	10:1	X	69
The Waterford School, Sandy	X	X	X	X	PK–5	6–8	9–12	875	251	5:1	X	23
Vermont												
Burr and Burton Academy, Manchester	X	X	X	X	–	–	9–12	680	680	12:1	X	25
The Greenwood School, Putney	X	X	X	X	–	6–8	9–12	45	26	2:1		68
Lyndon Institute, Lyndon Center	X	X	X	X	–	–	9–12		626	10:1	X	35
Stratton Mountain School, Stratton Mountain	X	X	X	X	–	7–8	9–PG	124	101	6:1		16

Private Secondary Schools At-a-Glance

	STUDENTS ACCEPTED: BOARDING		STUDENTS ACCEPTED: DAY		GRADES			STUDENT/FACULTY			SCHOOL OFFERINGS	
	Boys	Girls	Boys	Girls	Lower	Middle	Upper	Total	Upper	Student/Faculty Ratio	Advanced Placement Preparation	Sports
Virgin Islands												
St. Croix Country Day School, Kingshill	X	X	X	X	N–6	7–8	9–12	413	144	12:1	X	12
Virginia												
Bishop Denis J. O'Connell High School, Arlington	X	X	X	X	–	–		1,221	1,221	12:1	X	24
Bishop Ireton High School, Alexandria	X	X	X	X	–	–	9–12	825	825	14:1	X	24
Cape Henry Collegiate School, Virginia Beach	X	X	X	X	PK–5	6–8	9–12	835	397	10:1	X	45
Carlisle School, Axton	X	X	X	X	PK–5	6–8	9–12	549	174	7:1	X	17
Christchurch School, Christchurch	X	X	X	X	1–4	5–8	9–12	221	221	6:1	X	37
The Collegiate School, Richmond	X	X	X	X	K–4	5–8	9–12	1,602	521	15:1	X	24
Eastern Mennonite High School, Harrisonburg	X	X	X	X	K–5	6–8	9–12	385	218	10:1	X	11
Episcopal High School, Alexandria	X	X	X	X	–	–	9–12	435	435	6:1	X	44
Fishburne Military School, Waynesboro	X	X	X	X	–	7–8	9–12	170	155	9:1	X	12
Flint Hill School, Oakton	X	X	X	X	JK–4	5–8	9–12	1,099	513	7:1	X	35
Foxcroft School, Middleburg	X	X	X	X	–	–	9–12	160	160	7:1	X	34
Hargrave Military Academy, Chatham	X	X	X	X	–	7–9	10–PG	310	260	12:1	X	49
Little Keswick School, Keswick	X	X	X	X	–	–		34		3:1		13
Miller School of Albemarle, Charlottesville	X	X	X	X	–	8–8	9–12	173	153	6:1	X	43
Norfolk Academy, Norfolk	X	X	X	X	1–6	7–9	10–12	1,248	379	10:1	X	22
Oakland School, Keswick	X	X	X	X	–	–				5:1		44
Randolph-Macon Academy, Front Royal	X	X	X	X	–	6–8	9–PG	367	294	9:1	X	27
St. Anne's–Belfield School, Charlottesville	X	X	X	X	PK–4	5–8	9–12	869	347	8:1	X	22
St. Stephen's & St. Agnes School, Alexandria	X	X	X	X	JK–5	6–8	9–12	1,143	453	9:1	X	28
Stuart Hall, Staunton	X	X	X	X	PK–5	6–8	9–12	300	125	12:1	X	13
Tandem Friends School, Charlottesville	X	X	X	X	–	5–8	9–12	207	109	6:1	X	11
Tidewater Academy, Wakefield	X	X	X	X	PK–5	6–7	8–12	153	62	15:1	X	7
Wakefield School, The Plains	X	X	X	X	PS–5	6–8	9–12	397	152	16:1	X	16
Walsingham Academy, Williamsburg	X	X	X	X	PK–7	–	8–12	533	220	7:1	X	12
Washington												
Annie Wright School, Tacoma	X	X	X	X	PS–5	6–8	9–12	443	162	5:1		7
Chrysalis School, Woodinville	X	X	X	X	K–6	7–8	9–12	165	108	4:1		
Crosspoint Academy, Bremerton	X	X	X	X	K–6	7–8	9–12	253	96	8:1		8
Explorations Academy, Bellingham	X	X	X	X	–	–		33	33	7:1	X	
The Northwest School, Seattle	X	X	X	X	–	6–8	9–12	478	339	9:1		14
The Overlake School, Redmond	X	X	X	X	–	5–8	9–12	521	297	9:1	X	38
Seattle Academy of Arts and Sciences, Seattle	X	X	X	X	–	6–8	9–12	686	441	9:1		23
Shoreline Christian, Shoreline	X	X	X	X	PS–6	7–8	9–12	212	76	7:1		6
University Prep, Seattle	X	X	X	X	–	6–8	9–12	511	302	9:1		33
West Sound Academy, Poulsbo	X	X	X	X	–	6–8	9–12	92	66	7:1		10
West Virginia												
The Linsly School, Wheeling	X	X	X	X	5–8	–	9–12	450	296	9:1	X	47
Wisconsin												
Catholic Central High School, Burlington	X	X	X	X	–	–	9–12	168	168	9:1	X	23
Fox Valley Lutheran High School, Appleton	X	X	X	X	–	–	9–12	542	542	14:1	X	14
Saint Joan Antida High School, Milwaukee	X	X	X	X	–	–	9–12	250	250	14:1	X	7
St. Lawrence Seminary High School, Mount Calvary	X	X	X	X	–	–	9–12	191	191	9:1		26
University School of Milwaukee, Milwaukee	X	X	X	X	PK–4	5–8	9–12	1,082	364	9:1	X	16
Wyoming												
The Journeys School of Teton Science School, Jackson	X	X	X	X	K–5	6–8	9–12	152	42	7:1		30
CANADA												
The Academy for Gifted Children (PACE), Richmond Hill, ON	X	X	X	X	1–3	4–7	8–12	298	113	15:1	X	46
Académie Ste Cécile International School, Windsor, ON	X	X	X	X	JK–8	–	9–12	236	113	15:1	X	25
Arrowsmith School, Toronto, ON	X	X	X	X	1–5	6–9	10–12	75	20	10:1		
Balmoral Hall School, Winnipeg, MB	X	X	X	X	N–5	6–8	9–12	451	152	7:1	X	67
Bayview Glen School, Toronto, ON	X	X	X	X	–5	6–8	9–12			22:1	X	
Bearspaw Christian School, Calgary, AB	X	X	X	X	K–6	7–9	10–12	559	116	10:1		15
Bishop's College School, Sherbrooke, QC	X	X	X	X	–	7–9	10–12	216	138	7:1	X	47
Brentwood College School, Mill Bay, BC	X	X	X	X	–	–	9–12	435	435	9:1	X	43
Central Alberta Christian High School, Lacombe, AB	X	X	X	X	–	–	10–12	108	108	13:1		22
The Country Day School, King City, ON	X	X	X	X	JK–6	7–8	9–12	720	300	9:1	X	30
Crawford Adventist Academy, Willowdale, ON	X	X	X	X	JK–6	7–8	9–12	354	151	16:1	X	13
Foothills Academy, Calgary, AB	X	X	X	X	1–6	7–8	9–12	200	114	12:1		46
Great Lakes Christian High School, Beamsville, ON	X	X	X	X	–	–	9–12	94	94	10:1		19
Heritage Christian Academy, Calgary, AB	X	X	X	X	K–6	7–9	10–12	568	121	9:1		16

Private Secondary Schools At-a-Glance

	STUDENTS ACCEPTED				GRADES			STUDENT/FACULTY			SCHOOL OFFERINGS	
	BOARDING		DAY									
	Boys	Girls	Boys	Girls	Lower	Middle	Upper	Total	Upper	Student/Faculty Ratio	Advanced Placement Preparation	Sports
Heritage Christian School, Jordan, ON	X	X	X	X	K–8	–	9–12	610	180	15:1		5
Holy Trinity School, Richmond Hill, ON	X	X	X	X	JK–6	7–8	9–12	750	400		X	
Kingsway College, Oshawa, ON	X	X	X	X	–	–	9–12	189	189	13:1		17
Lakefield College School, Lakefield, ON	X	X	X	X	–	8–8	9–12	365	351	7:1	X	39
The Laureate Academy, Winnipeg, MB	X	X	X	X	1–5	6–8	9–12	80	35	6:1		36
Linden Christian School, Winnipeg, MB	X	X	X	X	K–4	5–8	9–12	876	271	13:1		21
Luther College High School, Regina, SK	X	X	X	X	–	–	9–12	416	416	16:1		21
Meadowridge School, Maple Ridge, BC	X	X	X	X	JK–5	–	6–12	540	290	12:1		12
Mennonite Collegiate Institute, Gretna, MB	X	X	X	X	–	7–8	9–12	130	120	13:1	X	14
Miss Edgar's and Miss Cramp's School, Montreal, QC	X	X	X	X	K–5	6–8	9–11	335	115	9:1	X	26
MPS Etobicoke, Toronto, ON	X	X	X	X	JK–6	7–8	9–12	255	118	18:1		27
Niagara Christian Community of Schools, Fort Erie, ON	X	X	X	X	–	6–8	9–12	166	146	16:1		21
North Toronto Christian School, Toronto, ON	X	X	X	X	JK–6	7–8	9–12	488	216	15:1		27
Parkview Adventist Academy, Lacombe, AB	X	X	X	X	–	–		107	107	10:1		8
Peoples Christian Academy, Markham, ON	X	X	X	X	JK–5	6–8	9–12	339	110	10:1		10
Pickering College, Newmarket, ON	X	X	X	X	JK–8	–	9–12	373	217	9:1		49
Pinehurst School, St. Catharines, ON	X	X	X	X	7–8	9–10	11–12	22	13	10:1		71
Queen Margaret's School, Duncan, BC	X	X	X	X	PS–7	–	8–12	316	146	8:1	X	68
Quinte Christian High School, Belleville, ON	X	X	X	X	–	–	9–12	161	161	15:1		8
Ridley College, St. Catharines, ON	X	X	X	X	JK–8	–	9–PG	630	446	7:1	X	78
Rockway Mennonite Collegiate, Kitchener, ON	X	X	X	X	–	7–8	9–12	285	243	10:1		30
Rothesay Netherwood School, Rothesay, NB	X	X	X	X	–	6–8	9–12	265	204	8:1		48
Royal Canadian College, Vancouver, BC	X	X	X	X	–	9–10	11–12	88	80	15:1		5
Rundle College, Calgary, AB	X	X	X	X	PK–6	7–9	10–12	811	246	14:1		23
Sacred Heart School of Halifax, Halifax, NS	X	X	X	X	K–6	–	7–12	461	258	15:1	X	17
St. Andrew's College, Aurora, ON	X	X	X	X	–	5–8	9–12	614	446	9:1	X	62
St. George's School, Vancouver, BC	X	X	X	X	1–7	–	8–12	1,157	761	10:1	X	33
St. George's School of Montreal, Montreal, QC	X	X	X	X	K–6	–	7–11	426	236	15:1	X	45
St. John's-Ravenscourt School, Winnipeg, MB	X	X	X	X	K–5	6–8	9–12	822	374	9:1	X	15
St. Jude's School, Kitchener, ON	X	X	X	X	1–6	7–9	10–12	30	10	6:1		13
St. Michael's College School, Toronto, ON	X	X	X	X	–	7–8	9–12	1,078	882	16:1	X	32
St. Patrick's Regional Secondary, Vancouver, BC	X	X	X	X	–	–		500	506		X	6
St. Paul's High School, Winnipeg, MB	X	X	X	X	–	–	9–12	596	596	14:1	X	21
Scholar's Hall Preparatory School, Kitchener, ON	X	X	X	X	JK–3	4–8	9–12	105	35	10:1		23
Shawnigan Lake School, Shawnigan Lake, BC	X	X	X	X	–	–	8–12	453	453	8:1	X	46
Shoore Centre for Learning, Toronto, ON	X	X	X	X	–	6–8	9–12	30	22	6:1		
Signet Christian School, North York, ON	X	X	X	X	JK–8	–	9–12	40	22	5:1		9
Solomon College, Edmonton, AB	X	X	X	X	–	–		25	25	10:1		
Strathcona-Tweedsmuir School, Okotoks, AB	X	X	X	X	1–6	7–9	10–12	667	243	9:1		25
Tapply Binet College, Ancaster, ON	X	X	X	X	–	–		17	11	3:1		1
Trinity College School, Port Hope, ON	X	X	X	X	–	5–8	9–12	545	450	8:1	X	41
Upper Canada College, Toronto, ON	X	X	X	X	–7	–	8–12	1,154	738	8:1		53
Venta Preparatory School, Ottawa, ON	X	X	X	X	1–7	–	8–10	82	23	6:1		14
West Island College, Calgary, AB	X	X	X	X	–	7–9	10–12	451	238	17:1	X	35
INTERNATIONAL												
Brazil												
Escola Americana de Campinas, Campinas-SP	X	X	X	X	PK–5	6–8	9–12	300	162	7:1	X	27
Colombia												
Colegio Bolivar, Cali	X	X	X	X	PK–5	6–8	9–12	1,228	378	9:1	X	13
Czech Republic												
The English College in Prague, Prague	X	X	X	X	8–9	10–11	12–13	360	150	11:1		
Ecuador												
Alliance Academy, Quito	X	X	X	X	PK–6	7–8	9–12	604	208	7:1	X	27
Germany												
Munich International School, Starnberg	X	X	X	X	PK–4	5–8	9–12	1,206	424	6:1		23
Greece												
Pinewood - The International School of Thessaloniki, Greece, Thessaloniki	X	X	X	X	PK–5	6–8	9–12	205	75	5:1		17
Italy												
Marymount International School, Rome	X	X	X	X	PK–5	6–8	9–12	624	212	15:1		7
St. Stephen's School, Rome, Rome	X	X	X	X	–	–	9–PG	259	259	7:1	X	7

Private Secondary Schools At-a-Glance

	STUDENTS ACCEPTED				GRADES			STUDENT/FACULTY			SCHOOL OFFERINGS	
	BOARDING		DAY									
	Boys	Girls	Boys	Girls	Lower	Middle	Upper	Total	Upper	Student/Faculty Ratio	Advanced Placement Preparation	Sports
Japan												
Columbia International School, Tokorozawa, Saitama	X	X	X	X	1–6	7–9	10–12	278	73	12:1	X	48
Saint Maur International School, Yokohama	X	X	X	X	PK–5	6–8	9–12	406	114	4:1	X	6
Seisen International School, Tokyo	X	X	X	X	K–6	7–8	9–12	613	171	7:1		12
Mexico												
The American School Foundation, Mexico City, D.F.	X	X	X	X	1–5	6–8	9–12	2,571	733	11:1	X	7
Netherlands												
International School of Amsterdam, Amstelveen	X	X	X	X	PS–5	6–8	9–12	1,008	246	5:1		17
Senegal												
Dakar Academy, Dakar	X	X	X	X	K–5	7–8	9–12	218	105	6:1	X	6
Switzerland												
TASIS, The American School in Switzerland, Montagnola-Lugano	X	X	X	X	1–5	6–8	9–PG	642	339	5:1	X	35
Zurich International School, Wdenswil	X	X	X	X	PS–5	6–8	9–13	1,493	460	7:1	X	29
Taiwan												
Taipei American School, Taipei	X	X	X	X	PK–5	6–8	9–12	2,235	884	9:1	X	12
Thailand												
International School Bangkok, Pakkret	X	X	X	X	PK–5	6–8	9–12	1,840	703	10:1	X	15
Turkey												
Istanbul International Community School, Istanbul	X	X	X	X	1–6	–	7–12	555	239	9:1		10
United Kingdom												
Brockwood Park School, Alresford	X	X	X	X	–	–		65	65	7:1		
The International School of London, London	X	X	X	X	K–5	6–10	11–12	340	60	8:1		7
Merchiston Castle School, Edinburgh	X	X	X	X	–	–			174	9:1		46
TASIS The American School in England, Thorpe, Surrey	X	X	X	X	N–4	5–8	9–13	750	390	8:1	X	44
Zambia												
American International School, Lusaka, Lusaka	X	X	X	X	6–8	9–10	11–12	257	72	7:1		21

Traditional Day and Boarding Schools

ACADEMY AT THE LAKES

2331 Collier Parkway
Land O'Lakes, Florida 34639

Head of School: Mr. Mark Heller

General Information Coeducational day college-preparatory and arts school. Grades PK–12. Founded: 1992. Setting: suburban. Nearest major city is Tampa. 9-acre campus. 9 buildings on campus. Approved or accredited by Southern Association of Colleges and Schools and Florida Department of Education. Member of National Association of Independent Schools and Secondary School Admission Test Board. Total enrollment: 404. Upper school average class size: 14. Upper school faculty-student ratio: 1:5. There are 176 required school days per year for Upper School students. Upper School students typically attend 5 days per week. The average school day consists of 7 hours and 15 minutes.

Upper School Student Profile Grade 9: 30 students (14 boys, 16 girls); Grade 10: 33 students (13 boys, 20 girls); Grade 11: 40 students (23 boys, 17 girls); Grade 12: 23 students (12 boys, 11 girls).

Faculty School total: 57. In upper school: 12 men, 16 women; 19 have advanced degrees.

Graduation Requirements Standard curriculum.

Special Academic Programs 9 Advanced Placement exams for which test preparation is offered; honors section; ESL (10 students enrolled).

College Admission Counseling 30 students graduated in 2011; all went to college, including Gettysburg College; Rollins College; The University of Tampa; University of South Florida; Wake Forest University.

Student Life Upper grades have specified standards of dress, student council, honor system. Discipline rests primarily with faculty.

Tuition and Aid Day student tuition: $16,990. Tuition installment plan (monthly payment plans). Merit scholarship grants, need-based scholarship grants available. In 2011–12, 24% of upper-school students received aid.

Admissions Traditional secondary-level entrance grade is 9. For fall 2011, 44 students applied for upper-level admission, 36 were accepted, 26 enrolled. SSAT required. Deadline for receipt of application materials: none. Application fee required: $50. Interview required.

Athletics Interscholastic: baseball (boys), basketball (b,g), cheering (g), cross-country running (b,g), football (b), golf (b,g), physical fitness (b,g), physical training (b,g), soccer (b,g), softball (g), strength & conditioning (b,g), swimming and diving (b,g), tennis (b,g), touch football (b), track and field (b,g), volleyball (g), weight training (b,g), winter soccer (b,g); coed interscholastic: physical fitness, physical training, soccer, strength & conditioning, weight training. 3 PE instructors, 11 coaches, 1 athletic trainer.

Computers Computer network features include on-campus library services, Internet access, wireless campus network, Internet filtering or blocking technology. Students grades are available online. The school has a published electronic and media policy.

Contact Mrs. Melissa Starkey, Associate Director of Admissions. 813-909-7919. Fax: 813-949-0563. E-mail: mstarkey@academyatthelakes.org. Web site: www.academyatthelakes.org/

THE ACADEMY FOR GIFTED CHILDREN (PACE)

12 Bond Crescent
Richmond Hill, Ontario L4E 3K2, Canada

Head of School: Barbara Rosenberg

General Information Coeducational day college-preparatory and differentiated curriculum for Intellectually gifted students school. Grades 1–12. Founded: 1993. Setting: suburban. Nearest major city is Toronto, Canada. 3-acre campus. 2 buildings on campus. Approved or accredited by Ontario Ministry of Education and Ontario Department of Education. Language of instruction: English. Total enrollment: 298. Upper school average class size: 17. Upper school faculty-student ratio: 1:15. There are 187 required school days per year for Upper School students. Upper School students typically attend 5 days per week. The average school day consists of 6 hours.

Upper School Student Profile Grade 8: 31 students (20 boys, 11 girls); Grade 9: 16 students (11 boys, 5 girls); Grade 10: 23 students (11 boys, 12 girls); Grade 11: 27 students (17 boys, 10 girls); Grade 12: 16 students (10 boys, 6 girls).

Faculty School total: 27. In upper school: 5 men, 7 women; 4 have advanced degrees.

Subjects Offered 20th century world history, Advanced Placement courses, algebra, analytic geometry, biology, calculus, calculus-AP, Canadian geography, Canadian history, Canadian law, career education, chemistry, chemistry-AP, civics, computer programming, computer science, computer science-AP, computer studies, dramatic arts, English, finite math, French, French as a second language, geometry, health education, language, law, literature, mathematics, modern Western civilization, music, philosophy, physical education, physics, science, sociology, visual arts, world civilizations, writing.

Graduation Requirements Advanced chemistry, advanced math, algebra, analytic geometry, biology, calculus, Canadian geography, Canadian history, Canadian literature, career education, chemistry, civics, English literature, French as a second language, healthful living, law, music, philosophy, pre-algebra, pre-calculus, science, scuba diving, senior humanities, social sciences, sociology, theater arts, visual arts, minimum of 40 hours of community service, OSSLT.

Special Academic Programs 5 Advanced Placement exams for which test preparation is offered; honors section; independent study; academic accommodation for the gifted.

College Admission Counseling 22 students graduated in 2012; all went to college, including Harvard University; McMaster University; Queen's University at Kingston; The University of Western Ontario; University of Toronto; University of Waterloo. Median SAT critical reading: 780, median SAT math: 800, median SAT writing: 780, median combined SAT: 2360. 100% scored over 600 on SAT critical reading, 100% scored over 600 on SAT math, 100% scored over 600 on SAT writing, 100% scored over 1800 on combined SAT.

Student Life Upper grades have specified standards of dress, student council, honor system. Discipline rests primarily with faculty.

Tuition and Aid Day student tuition: CAN$11,500. Guaranteed tuition plan. Tuition installment plan (monthly payment plans).

Admissions Traditional secondary-level entrance grade is 8. For fall 2012, 14 students applied for upper-level admission, 6 were accepted, 6 enrolled. Psychoeducational evaluation, Wechsler Individual Achievement Test, WISC III or other aptitude measures; standardized achievement test and WISC-R required. Deadline for receipt of application materials: none. No application fee required. On-campus interview required.

Athletics Interscholastic: badminton (boys, girls), ball hockey (b), baseball (b,g), basketball (b,g), flag football (b), floor hockey (b), golf (b,g), independent competitive sports (b,g), indoor soccer (b,g), sailboarding (b,g), soccer (b,g), softball (b,g), tennis (b,g), track and field (b,g), volleyball (b,g), winter soccer (b,g); intramural: badminton (b,g), basketball (b,g), soccer (b,g), softball (b,g); coed interscholastic: badminton, baseball, bowling, cross-country running, flag football, Frisbee, indoor soccer, sailboarding, tennis, ultimate Frisbee; coed intramural: alpine skiing, badminton, ball hockey, basketball, blading, climbing, cooperative games, cross-country running, curling, dance, diving, floor hockey, handball, ice skating, indoor soccer, jogging, jump rope, life saving, martial arts, outdoor activities, outdoor education, outdoor skills, physical fitness, rock climbing, ropes courses, scuba diving, skiing (cross-country), skiing (downhill), snowboarding, snowshoeing, ultimate Frisbee, volleyball, wall climbing, yoga. 2 PE instructors, 10 coaches.

Computers Computers are regularly used in career exploration, desktop publishing, digital applications, English, information technology, keyboarding, news writing, newspaper, programming, science, technology, theater, writing, yearbook classes. Computer network features include Internet access, wireless campus network, Internet filtering or blocking technology. Computer access in designated common areas is available to students. Students grades are available online. The school has a published electronic and media policy.

Contact Barbara Rosenberg, Director. 905-773-3997. Fax: 905-773-4722. Web site: www.pace.on.ca

ACADEMY OF HOLY ANGELS

6600 Nicollet Avenue South
Richfield, Minnesota 55423-2498

Head of School: Mr. Thomas C. Shipley

General Information Coeducational day college-preparatory, arts, business, religious studies, and technology school, affiliated with Roman Catholic Church. Grades 9–12. Founded: 1877. Setting: suburban. Nearest major city is Minneapolis. 26-acre campus. 2 buildings on campus. Approved or accredited by North Central Association of Colleges and Schools. Endowment: $1 million. Total enrollment: 845. Upper school average class size: 20. Upper school faculty-student ratio: 1:13.

Upper School Student Profile 80% of students are Roman Catholic.

Faculty School total: 63. In upper school: 30 men, 30 women; 29 have advanced degrees.

Subjects Offered Algebra, American history, American literature, anatomy, art, art history, astronomy, Bible studies, biology, broadcasting, business, business skills, calculus, ceramics, chemistry, computer math, computer programming, computer science, dance, drafting, drama, economics, electronics, English, English literature, environmental science, ethics, European history, expository writing, fine arts, French, geography, geometry, German, government/civics, grammar, health, history, home economics, industrial arts, journalism, mathematics, mechanical drawing, music, photography, physical education, physics, physiology, psychology, religion, Russian, science, social sciences, social studies, sociology, Spanish, speech, theater, theology, trigonometry, typing, world history, world literature, writing.

Graduation Requirements Arts and fine arts (art, music, dance, drama), business skills (includes word processing), English, mathematics, physical education (includes health), religion (includes Bible studies and theology), science, social sciences, social studies (includes history).

Special Academic Programs Advanced Placement exam preparation; honors section; independent study; study at local college for college credit; study abroad; academic accommodation for the gifted, the musically talented, and the artistically talented.

College Admission Counseling 183 students graduated in 2011; 174 went to college, including College of Saint Benedict; Iowa State University of Science and Technology; Saint John's University; University of Minnesota, Duluth; University of Minnesota, Twin Cities Campus; University of Wisconsin–Madison. Other: 2 went to work, 2 entered military service, 5 had other specific plans. Mean SAT critical reading: 577, mean SAT math: 606, mean composite ACT: 25.

Student Life Upper grades have uniform requirement, student council, honor system. Discipline rests equally with students and faculty. Attendance at religious services is required.

Tuition and Aid Day student tuition: $11,875. Tuition installment plan (monthly payment plans, individually arranged payment plans, quarterly payment plan). Need-based scholarship grants, minority student scholarships, single-parent family scholarships available. In 2011–12, 37% of upper-school students received aid. Total amount of financial aid awarded in 2011–12: $1,000,000.

Admissions Traditional secondary-level entrance grade is 9. For fall 2011, 325 students applied for upper-level admission, 320 were accepted, 206 enrolled. ACT-Explore required. Deadline for receipt of application materials: January 21. No application fee required. Interview recommended.

Athletics Interscholastic: baseball (boys), basketball (b,g), cross-country running (b,g), danceline (g), football (b), golf (b,g), ice hockey (b,g), soccer (b,g), softball (g), tennis (b,g), track and field (b,g), volleyball (g); intramural: lacrosse (g); coed interscholastic: bowling; coed intramural: football. 3 PE instructors, 27 coaches, 1 athletic trainer.

Computers Computers are regularly used in English, foreign language, mathematics, science, yearbook classes. Computer network features include on-campus library services, online commercial services, Internet access. The school has a published electronic and media policy.

Contact Ms. Meg Angevine, Assistant Director of Admissions. 612-798-0764. Fax: 612-798-2610. E-mail: mangevine@academyofholyangels.org. Web site: www.academyofholyangels.org

ACADEMY OF NOTRE DAME DE NAMUR

560 Sproul Road
Villanova, Pennsylvania 19085-1220

Head of School: Mrs. Veronica Collins Harrington

General Information Girls' day college-preparatory, arts, and religious studies school, affiliated with Roman Catholic Church. Grades 6–12. Founded: 1856. Setting: suburban. Nearest major city is Philadelphia. 38-acre campus. 9 buildings on campus. Approved or accredited by Middle States Association of Colleges and Schools, National Catholic Education Association, Pennsylvania Association of Independent Schools, and Pennsylvania Department of Education. Member of National Association of Independent Schools. Endowment: $5 million. Total enrollment: 519. Upper school average class size: 15. Upper school faculty-student ratio: 1:8. There are 170 required school days per year for Upper School students. Upper School students typically attend 5 days per week. The average school day consists of 6 hours and 45 minutes.

Upper School Student Profile Grade 9: 99 students (99 girls); Grade 10: 98 students (98 girls); Grade 11: 89 students (89 girls); Grade 12: 106 students (106 girls). 88% of students are Roman Catholic.

Faculty School total: 62. In upper school: 9 men, 45 women; 39 have advanced degrees.

Subjects Offered Advanced biology, American history-AP, Bible, biology, biology-AP, calculus, calculus-AP, ceramics, chemistry, chemistry-AP, choral music, Christian and Hebrew scripture, Christian ethics, comparative government and politics-AP, computer skills, contemporary history, dance, economics, English, English literature, English literature and composition-AP, environmental science, French, French language-AP, geometry, government and politics-AP, health, health education, Hebrew scripture, instrumental music, journalism, Latin, Latin-AP, literature, literature and composition-AP, mathematics, multimedia design, music, music performance, music theory, music theory-AP, music-AP, physical education, physics-AP, pre-algebra, pre-calculus, psychology, SAT/ACT preparation, Spanish, Spanish language-AP, Spanish-AP, studio art-AP, U.S. government and politics-AP, U.S. history-AP, United States government-AP, visual and performing arts, world cultures.

Graduation Requirements Art, English, foreign language, guidance, mathematics, music, physical education (includes health), religion (includes Bible studies and theology), science, social studies (includes history), 40 hours of social service.

Special Academic Programs Honors section; independent study; study at local college for college credit; study abroad; academic accommodation for the gifted, the musically talented, and the artistically talented.

College Admission Counseling 100 students graduated in 2012; all went to college, including Boston College; Georgetown University; Penn State University Park; Saint Joseph's University; University of Delaware; Villanova University. Median SAT critical reading: 600, median SAT math: 600, median SAT writing: 630, median combined SAT: 1820, median composite ACT: 26. 51% scored over 600 on SAT critical reading, 56% scored over 600 on SAT math, 64% scored over 600 on SAT writing, 55% scored over 1800 on combined SAT, 37% scored over 26 on composite ACT.

Student Life Upper grades have uniform requirement, student council, honor system. Discipline rests primarily with faculty. Attendance at religious services is required.

Summer Programs Enrichment, advancement, sports, computer instruction programs offered; session focuses on academic enrichment; held on campus; accepts boys and girls; open to students from other schools. 50 students usually enrolled. 2013 schedule: June 25 to July 16. Application deadline: June 1.

Tuition and Aid Day student tuition: $16,932–$19,646. Tuition installment plan (Insured Tuition Payment Plan, monthly payment plans, quarterly and semi-annual payment plans). Merit scholarship grants, need-based scholarship grants available. In 2012–13, 32% of upper-school students received aid; total upper-school merit-scholarship money awarded: $370,500. Total amount of financial aid awarded in 2012–13: $449,500.

Admissions Traditional secondary-level entrance grade is 9. For fall 2012, 351 students applied for upper-level admission, 268 were accepted, 170 enrolled. High School Placement Test required. Deadline for receipt of application materials: December 17. Application fee required: $40. Interview required.

Athletics Interscholastic: basketball, crew, cross-country running, dance, diving, field hockey, golf, lacrosse, rowing, soccer, softball, swimming and diving, tennis, track and field, volleyball, winter (indoor) track; intramural: dance, kickball, modern dance. 2 PE instructors, 31 coaches, 1 athletic trainer.

Computers Computers are regularly used in all classes. Computer network features include on-campus library services, online commercial services, Internet access, wireless campus network, Internet filtering or blocking technology, Smart Boards in classrooms. Student e-mail accounts are available to students. Students grades are available online. The school has a published electronic and media policy.

Contact Mrs. Diane Sander, Director of Admissions. 610-971-0498. Fax: 610-687-1912. E-mail: dsander@ndapa.org. Web site: www.ndapa.org

ACADEMY OF OUR LADY OF PEACE

4860 Oregon Street
San Diego, California 92116-1393

Head of School: Mr. John Galvan

General Information Girls' day college-preparatory, arts, religious studies, and technology school, affiliated with Roman Catholic Church. Grades 9–12. Founded: 1882. Setting: urban. 20-acre campus. 7 buildings on campus. Approved or accredited by Western Association of Schools and Colleges, Western Catholic Education Association, and California Department of Education. Endowment: $250,000. Total enrollment: 750. Upper school average class size: 28. Upper school faculty-student ratio: 1:14. There are 180 required school days per year for Upper School students. Upper School students typically attend 5 days per week. The average school day consists of 6 hours and 45 minutes.

Upper School Student Profile Grade 9: 193 students (193 girls); Grade 10: 181 students (181 girls); Grade 11: 190 students (190 girls); Grade 12: 186 students (186 girls). 91% of students are Roman Catholic.

Faculty School total: 53. In upper school: 11 men, 42 women; 35 have advanced degrees.

Subjects Offered Algebra, American literature, art, Bible studies, biology, biology-AP, British literature, calculus, calculus-AP, campus ministry, ceramics, chemistry, chemistry-AP, dance, drama, economics, English, English language and composition-AP, English literature and composition-AP, ethics, fitness, French, French language-AP, French-AP, genetics, geometry, government, graphic arts, health, marine science, music appreciation, music theory-AP, painting, physical education, physics, pre-calculus, psychology, Spanish, Spanish language-AP, Spanish literature-AP, speech, studio art-AP, study skills, U.S. government and politics-AP, U.S. history, U.S. history-AP, video film production, Western civilization, yearbook, yoga.

Graduation Requirements Arts and fine arts (art, music, dance, drama), English, foreign language, mathematics, physical education (includes health), religion (includes Bible studies and theology), science, social sciences, social studies (includes history), speech, 75 hours of community service, 9-11 reflection paper required for seniors.

Special Academic Programs 13 Advanced Placement exams for which test preparation is offered; honors section.

College Admission Counseling 161 students graduated in 2012; 160 went to college, including Saint Mary's College of California; San Diego State University; Sonoma State University; University of California, Davis; University of San Diego; University of San Francisco. Other: 1 had other specific plans. Median SAT critical reading: 540, median SAT math: 520, median SAT writing: 550, median combined SAT: 1610. 34% scored over 600 on SAT critical reading, 22% scored over 600 on SAT math, 37% scored over 600 on SAT writing, 50% scored over 1800 on combined SAT, 10% scored over 26 on composite ACT.

Student Life Upper grades have uniform requirement, student council, honor system. Discipline rests equally with students and faculty. Attendance at religious services is required.

Summer Programs Enrichment, advancement programs offered; session focuses on advancement and remediation/make-up; held on campus; accepts girls; open to students from other schools. 200 students usually enrolled. 2013 schedule: June 10 to July 19. Application deadline: May 1.

Tuition and Aid Day student tuition: $13,360. Tuition installment plan (FACTS Tuition Payment Plan). Need-based scholarship grants available. In 2012–13, 50% of upper-school students received aid. Total amount of financial aid awarded in 2012–13: $2,400,000.

Admissions Traditional secondary-level entrance grade is 9. For fall 2012, 248 students applied for upper-level admission, 223 were accepted, 210 enrolled. High School

Placement Test required. Deadline for receipt of application materials: none. Application fee required: $50. On-campus interview required.

Athletics Interscholastic: basketball, cheering, cross-country running, golf, gymnastics, soccer, softball, swimming and diving, tennis, track and field, volleyball. 4 PE instructors, 16 coaches.

Computers Computers are regularly used in computer applications, media production, music, music technology, photography, Web site design, word processing classes. Computer network features include on-campus library services, online commercial services, Internet access, wireless campus network, Internet filtering or blocking technology. Campus intranet, student e-mail accounts, and computer access in designated common areas are available to students. Students grades are available online. The school has a published electronic and media policy.

Contact Mrs. Melissa Acosta, Admissions Coordinator/ Registrar. 619-725-9149. Fax: 619-297-2473. E-mail: macosta@aolp.org. Web site: www.aolp.org

ACADEMY OF THE HOLY CROSS

4920 Strathmore Avenue
Kensington, Maryland 20895-1299

Head of School: Dr. Claire M. Helm

General Information Girls' day college-preparatory, arts, and religious studies school, affiliated with Roman Catholic Church. Grades 9–12. Founded: 1868. Setting: suburban. Nearest major city is Rockville. 28-acre campus. 2 buildings on campus. Approved or accredited by Association of Independent Schools of Greater Washington, International Baccalaureate Organization, Middle States Association of Colleges and Schools, National Catholic Education Association, and Maryland Department of Education. Upper school average class size: 20. Upper school faculty-student ratio: 1:14. There are 175 required school days per year for Upper School students. Upper School students typically attend 5 days per week. The average school day consists of 7 hours.

Upper School Student Profile Grade 9: 126 students (126 girls); Grade 10: 136 students (136 girls); Grade 11: 154 students (154 girls); Grade 12: 112 students (112 girls). 81% of students are Roman Catholic.

Faculty School total: 50. In upper school: 11 men, 39 women.

Subjects Offered Acting, Advanced Placement courses, African studies, algebra, American history, American literature, Arabic, art, art history-AP, Asian studies, biology, biology-AP, calculus, calculus-AP, ceramics, chemistry, chemistry-AP, Christian scripture, computer science, concert choir, creative writing, design, drama, drawing, earth science, economics, English, English language and composition-AP, English literature, English literature and composition-AP, environmental science, ethnic studies, expository writing, fine arts, forensics, French, genetics, geography, geometry, government/civics, grammar, health, Hebrew scripture, history, history of the Catholic Church, honors English, honors geometry, humanities, instrumental music, jazz dance, Latin, Latin American studies, madrigals, mathematics, moral theology, music, music appreciation, musical theater, musical theater dance, painting, peace studies, personal finance, photography, physical education, physical science, physics, physiology, precalculus, psychology, public speaking, religion, religious studies, science, sculpture, Shakespeare, social sciences, social studies, Spanish, sports medicine, statistics, studio art, studio art-AP, tap dance, technology, theater, theater design and production, theology, trigonometry, U.S. government, U.S. government and politics-AP, U.S. history, U.S. history-AP, Web site design, world history, world studies.

Graduation Requirements Art, electives, English, foreign language, mathematics, performing arts, physical education (includes health), science, senior project, social sciences, social studies (includes history), theology, Christian service commitment, senior project internship.

Special Academic Programs International Baccalaureate program; Advanced Placement exam preparation; honors section; independent study; academic accommodation for the gifted and the artistically talented.

College Admission Counseling 138 students graduated in 2012; all went to college, including Penn State University Park; The Catholic University of America; Towson University; University of Dayton; University of Maryland, College Park; University of South Carolina. Mean SAT critical reading: 557, mean SAT math: 543, mean SAT writing: 566, mean combined SAT: 1666, mean composite ACT: 24.

Student Life Upper grades have uniform requirement, student council, honor system. Discipline rests equally with students and faculty. Attendance at religious services is required.

Summer Programs Enrichment, advancement, sports, art/fine arts, computer instruction programs offered; session focuses on enrichment and athletic skill-building; held on campus; accepts girls; open to students from other schools. 200 students usually enrolled.

Tuition and Aid Day student tuition: $18,500. Tuition installment plan (individually arranged payment plans). Tuition reduction for siblings, merit scholarship grants, need-based scholarship grants, alumnae stipends available. In 2012–13, 72% of upper-school students received aid.

Admissions Traditional secondary-level entrance grade is 9. High School Placement Test required. Deadline for receipt of application materials: December 7. Application fee required: $60. On-campus interview required.

Athletics Interscholastic: archery, basketball, crew, cross-country running, diving, equestrian sports, field hockey, golf, ice hockey, lacrosse, soccer, softball, swimming and diving, tennis, track and field, volleyball; intramural: basketball, cheering, dance, dance team, kayaking, lacrosse, soccer. 2 PE instructors, 35 coaches, 1 athletic trainer.

Computers Computers are regularly used in art, foreign language, mathematics, science, social sciences classes. Computer network features include on-campus library services, online commercial services, Internet access, wireless campus network, Internet filtering or blocking technology. Student e-mail accounts and computer access in designated common areas are available to students. Students grades are available online. The school has a published electronic and media policy.

Contact Mrs. Gracie Smith, Director of Admissions. 301-929-6442. Fax: 301-929-6440. E-mail: admissions@ahctartans.org. Web site: www.ahctartans.org

ACADEMY OF THE NEW CHURCH BOYS' SCHOOL

2815 Benade Circle
Box 707
Bryn Athyn, Pennsylvania 19009

Head of School: Mr. Jeremy T. Irwin

General Information Boys' boarding and day college-preparatory, arts, and religious studies school, affiliated with Church of the New Jerusalem. Grades 9–12. Founded: 1887. Setting: suburban. Nearest major city is Philadelphia. Students are housed in single-sex dormitories. 200-acre campus. 8 buildings on campus. Approved or accredited by Middle States Association of Colleges and Schools and Pennsylvania Department of Education. Member of National Association of Independent Schools. Endowment: $200 million. Total enrollment: 118. Upper school average class size: 15. Upper school faculty-student ratio: 1:8. There are 175 required school days per year for Upper School students. Upper School students typically attend 5 days per week. The average school day consists of 7 hours and 15 minutes.

Upper School Student Profile Grade 9: 25 students (25 boys); Grade 10: 31 students (31 boys); Grade 11: 27 students (27 boys); Grade 12: 35 students (35 boys). 35% of students are boarding students. 75% are state residents. 18 states are represented in upper school student body. 4% are international students. International students from China and Republic of Korea; 2 other countries represented in student body. 85% of students are Church of the New Jerusalem.

Faculty School total: 40. In upper school: 20 men, 20 women; 35 have advanced degrees; 10 reside on campus.

Subjects Offered Advanced chemistry, Advanced Placement courses, African-American literature, algebra, American history, American history-AP, American literature, American literature-AP, anatomy, anatomy and physiology, ancient world history, art, art history, Bible studies, biology, British literature, calculus, calculus-AP, ceramics, chemistry, civics, computer programming, computer science, creative writing, dance, drama, ecology, English, English literature, English literature-AP, environmental science, European history, expository writing, fine arts, French, geometry, German, government/civics, grammar, health, history, honors U.S. history, industrial arts, journalism, Latin, mathematics, music, music theater, musical theater, philosophy, photography, physical education, physical science, physics, physiology, portfolio art, precalculus, printmaking, probability and statistics, religion, religious education, religious studies, science, sculpture, senior project, social sciences, social studies, sociology, Spanish, speech, statistics, studio art, theater, theater arts, theater design and production, theater production, theology, trigonometry, U.S. history-AP, vocal ensemble, vocal music, women in literature, world history, world literature.

Graduation Requirements Arts and fine arts (art, music, dance, drama), English, foreign language, mathematics, physical education (includes health), religion (includes Bible studies and theology), science, social sciences, social studies (includes history).

Special Academic Programs Advanced Placement exam preparation; honors section; independent study; study at local college for college credit; academic accommodation for the gifted, the musically talented, and the artistically talented; remedial reading and/or remedial writing; remedial math; programs in English, mathematics, general development for dyslexic students; ESL (6 students enrolled).

College Admission Counseling 35 students graduated in 2012; 33 went to college, including Arcadia University; Bryn Athyn College of the New Church; Gettysburg College; Penn State University Park; Virginia Polytechnic Institute and State University; West Chester University of Pennsylvania. Other: 2 entered military service. Median SAT critical reading: 540, median SAT math: 560, median SAT writing: 530, median combined SAT: 1630. 28% scored over 600 on SAT critical reading, 33% scored over 600 on SAT math, 31% scored over 600 on SAT writing, 31% scored over 1800 on combined SAT.

Student Life Upper grades have specified standards of dress, student council. Discipline rests primarily with faculty. Attendance at religious services is required.

Summer Programs Sports programs offered; held on campus; accepts boys and girls; open to students from other schools. 110 students usually enrolled. 2013 schedule: July 11 to August 1. Application deadline: June 1.

Tuition and Aid Day student tuition: $14,040; 7-day tuition and room/board: $20,480. Tuition installment plan (monthly payment plans, individually arranged payment plans, term payment plan). Need-based scholarship grants available. In 2012–13, 60% of upper-school students received aid. Total amount of financial aid awarded in 2012–13: $750,000.

Admissions Traditional secondary-level entrance grade is 9. For fall 2012, 50 students applied for upper-level admission, 39 were accepted, 34 enrolled. Iowa Subtests,

PSAT, SAT or SSAT required. Deadline for receipt of application materials: none. Application fee required: $50. Interview required.

Athletics Interscholastic: baseball, basketball, football, ice hockey, lacrosse, wrestling. 1 PE instructor, 6 coaches, 1 athletic trainer.

Computers Computers are regularly used in English, foreign language, history, mathematics, science classes. Computer network features include on-campus library services, online commercial services, Internet access, wireless campus network, Internet filtering or blocking technology. Campus intranet, student e-mail accounts, and computer access in designated common areas are available to students. Students grades are available online. The school has a published electronic and media policy.

Contact Denise DiFiglia, Director of Admissions. 267-502-4855. Web site: www.ancss.org

ACADEMY OF THE NEW CHURCH GIRLS' SCHOOL

2815 Benade Circle
Box 707
Bryn Athyn, Pennsylvania 19009

Head of School: Susan O. Odhner

General Information Girls' boarding and day college-preparatory, general academic, arts, and religious studies school, affiliated with Church of the New Jerusalem, Christian faith. Grades 9–12. Founded: 1884. Setting: suburban. Nearest major city is Philadelphia. Students are housed in single-sex dormitories. 200-acre campus. 8 buildings on campus. Approved or accredited by Middle States Association of Colleges and Schools and Pennsylvania Department of Education. Member of National Association of Independent Schools. Endowment: $200 million. Total enrollment: 86. Upper school average class size: 15. Upper school faculty-student ratio: 1:8. There are 175 required school days per year for Upper School students. Upper School students typically attend 5 days per week. The average school day consists of 7 hours and 15 minutes.

Upper School Student Profile Grade 9: 22 students (22 girls); Grade 10: 15 students (15 girls); Grade 11: 25 students (25 girls); Grade 12: 24 students (24 girls). 33% of students are boarding students. 75% are state residents. 13 states are represented in upper school student body. 13% are international students. International students from Canada, China, and Republic of Korea; 3 other countries represented in student body. 85% of students are Church of the New Jerusalem, Christian.

Faculty School total: 40. In upper school: 20 men, 20 women; 36 have advanced degrees; 10 reside on campus.

Subjects Offered Advanced chemistry, Advanced Placement courses, African-American literature, algebra, American history, American history-AP, American literature, anatomy, ancient history, ancient world history, art, art history, Bible studies, biology, British literature, calculus, calculus-AP, chemistry, civics, computer science, creative writing, drafting, drama, dramatic arts, drawing, ecology, ecology, environmental systems, economics, English, English literature, English literature-AP, English-AP, European history, expository writing, film studies, fine arts, French, geometry, government/civics, grammar, health, history, honors algebra, honors English, honors geometry, honors U.S. history, human anatomy, Latin, mathematics, medieval history, music, painting, philosophy, photography, physical education, physical science, physics, physiology, pre-calculus, printmaking, religion, science, sculpture, senior project, social sciences, social studies, Spanish, speech, stained glass, statistics-AP, theater, theology, trigonometry, women in literature, world history, world literature.

Graduation Requirements Arts and fine arts (art, music, dance, drama), English, foreign language, mathematics, physical education (includes health), religion (includes Bible studies and theology), science, social sciences, social studies (includes history).

Special Academic Programs Advanced Placement exam preparation; honors section; independent study; study at local college for college credit; academic accommodation for the gifted, the musically talented, and the artistically talented; remedial reading and/or remedial writing; remedial math; special instructional classes for students with Attention Deficit Disorder and learning-disabled children; ESL (8 students enrolled).

College Admission Counseling 35 students graduated in 2012; all went to college, including Arcadia University; Bryn Athyn College of the New Church; Gettysburg College; Penn State University Park; Virginia Polytechnic Institute and State University; West Chester University of Pennsylvania. Median SAT critical reading: 540, median SAT math: 560, median SAT writing: 530, median combined SAT: 1630. 28% scored over 600 on SAT critical reading, 33% scored over 600 on SAT math, 31% scored over 600 on SAT writing, 31% scored over 1800 on combined SAT.

Student Life Upper grades have uniform requirement, student council. Discipline rests primarily with faculty. Attendance at religious services is required.

Summer Programs Sports programs offered; held on campus; accepts boys and girls; open to students from other schools. 130 students usually enrolled. 2013 schedule: July 11 to August 1. Application deadline: June 1.

Tuition and Aid Day student tuition: $14,040; 7-day tuition and room/board: $20,480. Tuition installment plan (monthly payment plans, individually arranged payment plans, term payment plan). Need-based scholarship grants, need-based loans, middle-income loans available. In 2012–13, 60% of upper-school students received aid. Total amount of financial aid awarded in 2012–13: $750,000.

Admissions Traditional secondary-level entrance grade is 9. For fall 2012, 49 students applied for upper-level admission, 40 were accepted, 37 enrolled. Iowa Subtests, PSAT, SAT or SSAT required. Deadline for receipt of application materials: none. Application fee required: $50. Interview required.

Athletics Interscholastic: basketball, dance team, field hockey, ice hockey, lacrosse, soccer, softball, tennis, volleyball. 1 PE instructor, 6 coaches, 1 athletic trainer.

Computers Computers are regularly used in English, foreign language, history, Latin, mathematics, science classes. Computer network features include on-campus library services, online commercial services, Internet access, wireless campus network, Internet filtering or blocking technology. Campus intranet and student e-mail accounts are available to students.

Contact Denise DiFiglia, Director of Admissions. 267-502-4855. Fax: 267-502-2617. E-mail: denise.difiglia@ancss.org. Web site: www.ancss.org

ACADEMY OF THE SACRED HEART

1821 Academy Road
Grand Coteau, Louisiana 70541

Head of School: Sr. Lynne Lieux, RSCJ

General Information Girls' boarding and coeducational day college-preparatory, arts, religious studies, bilingual studies, technology, and liberal arts and sciences school, affiliated with Roman Catholic Church. Boarding girls grades 7–12, day boys grades PK–9, day girls grades PK–12. Founded: 1821. Setting: small town. Nearest major city is Lafayette. Students are housed in single-sex dormitories. 250-acre campus. 9 buildings on campus. Approved or accredited by Independent Schools Association of the Southwest, Ohio Catholic Schools Accreditation Association (OCSAA), and Louisiana Department of Education. Endowment: $8 million. Total enrollment: 481. Upper school average class size: 18. Upper school faculty-student ratio: 1:10. There are 180 required school days per year for Upper School students. Upper School students typically attend 5 days per week. The average school day consists of 6 hours.

Upper School Student Profile Grade 9: 49 students (9 boys, 40 girls); Grade 10: 29 students (29 girls); Grade 11: 28 students (28 girls); Grade 12: 30 students (30 girls). 19% of students are boarding students. 80% are state residents. 6 states are represented in upper school student body. 5% are international students. International students from Brazil, China, Mexico, Republic of Korea, and Taiwan. 90% of students are Roman Catholic.

Faculty School total: 50. In upper school: 6 men, 20 women; 14 have advanced degrees; 3 reside on campus.

Subjects Offered Advanced math, Advanced Placement courses, algebra, American literature, art appreciation, biology, biology-AP, British literature, British literature (honors), calculus, calculus-AP, chemistry, chorus, creative dance, creative writing, dance, drama, English, English literature-AP, environmental science, equestrian sports, equine science, ESL, ethical decision making, fine arts, French, French language-AP, French-AP, geometry, government-AP, government/civics, health, independent study, mathematics, moral reasoning, music theater, photography, physical education, physics, play production, pottery, pre-algebra, religion and culture, scripture, social justice, social sciences, Spanish, Spanish language-AP, Spanish-AP, studio art, theater, U.S. government, U.S. government and politics-AP, U.S. history, U.S. history-AP, women's studies, world history, world history-AP, yearbook.

Graduation Requirements Arts and fine arts (art, music, dance, drama), English, foreign language, mathematics, physical education (includes health), religion (includes Bible studies and theology), science, social sciences, social studies (includes history), May project. Community service is required.

Special Academic Programs International Baccalaureate program; Advanced Placement exam preparation; honors section; independent study; term-away projects; study at local college for college credit; domestic exchange program; study abroad; academic accommodation for the gifted, the musically talented, and the artistically talented; ESL (13 students enrolled).

College Admission Counseling 29 students graduated in 2011; all went to college, including Baylor University; Louisiana State University and Agricultural and Mechanical College; Loyola University New Orleans; Tulane University; University of Louisiana at Lafayette. Mean composite ACT: 25.

Student Life Upper grades have uniform requirement, student council, honor system. Discipline rests primarily with faculty. Attendance at religious services is required.

Tuition and Aid Day student tuition: $11,350–$12,600; 5-day tuition and room/board: $15,700; 7-day tuition and room/board: $17,000–$18,000. Tuition installment plan (monthly payment plans, individually arranged payment plans, 1 ayment, 2 payments, monthly payment plan for day students). Tuition reduction for siblings, merit scholarship grants, need-based scholarship grants available. In 2011–12, 16% of upper-school students received aid; total upper-school merit-scholarship money awarded: $7500.

Admissions Traditional secondary-level entrance grade is 9. For fall 2011, 34 students applied for upper-level admission, 30 were accepted, 28 enrolled. Metropolitan Achievement Short Form and Stanford Achievement Test required. Deadline for receipt of application materials: none. Application fee required: $100. Interview recommended.

Athletics Interscholastic: aquatics (girls), baseball (b), basketball (b,g), cheering (g), cross-country running (g), dance (g), dance team (g), dressage (b,g), equestrian sports (b,g), golf (b,g), horseback riding (b,g), soccer (b,g), softball (g), swimming and diving (b,g), tennis (b,g), track and field (b,g), volleyball (g). 3 PE instructors, 5 coaches.

Computers Computers are regularly used in all academic classes. Computer network features include on-campus library services, online commercial services, Internet access, wireless campus network, Internet filtering or blocking technology. Student e-mail accounts and computer access in designated common areas are available to students. Students grades are available online. The school has a published electronic and media policy.

Contact D'Lane Wimberley Thomas, Director of Admissions. 337-662-5275 Ext. 5009. Fax: 337-662-3011. E-mail: admissions@sshcoteau.org. Web site: www.sshcoteau.org

ACADEMY OF THE SACRED HEART

4521 St. Charles Avenue
New Orleans, Louisiana 70115-4831

Head of School: Dr. Timothy Matthew Burns

General Information Girls' day college-preparatory, arts, religious studies, bilingual studies, and technology school, affiliated with Roman Catholic Church. Grades PK–12. Founded: 1887. Setting: urban. 7-acre campus. 3 buildings on campus. Approved or accredited by Independent Schools Association of the Southwest, National Catholic Education Association, Network of Sacred Heart Schools, Southern Association of Colleges and Schools, and Louisiana Department of Education. Member of National Association of Independent Schools. Endowment: $7.7 million. Total enrollment: 620. Upper school average class size: 16. Upper school faculty-student ratio: 1:16. There are 178 required school days per year for Upper School students. Upper School students typically attend 5 days per week. The average school day consists of 6 hours and 30 minutes.

Upper School Student Profile Grade 9: 47 students (47 girls); Grade 10: 54 students (54 girls); Grade 11: 57 students (57 girls); Grade 12: 44 students (44 girls). 88% of students are Roman Catholic.

Faculty School total: 101. In upper school: 9 men, 19 women; 19 have advanced degrees.

Subjects Offered Advanced chemistry, algebra, American government, American history, American history-AP, American literature, American literature-AP, anatomy and physiology, art, astronomy, athletics, basketball, biology, biology-AP, calculus, calculus-AP, campus ministry, Catholic belief and practice, ceramics, cheerleading, chemistry, chemistry-AP, clayworking, college admission preparation, college awareness, college counseling, college planning, computer applications, computer education, computer processing, computer resources, computer science, computer skills, computer studies, creative writing, drawing, electives, English, English literature, English literature-AP, English-AP, foreign language, French, French-AP, geometry, government, government-AP, guidance, history of the Catholic Church, honors algebra, honors English, honors geometry, honors U.S. history, honors world history, painting, peer counseling, pre-calculus, religion, robotics, social justice, Spanish, Spanish-AP, U.S. government, U.S. government and politics-AP, U.S. history, U.S. history-AP, video communication, Web site design, world history, world history-AP, world religions.

Graduation Requirements Advanced Placement courses, algebra, American government, American literature, arts and fine arts (art, music, dance, drama), athletics, Basic programming, British literature, calculus, career/college preparation, computer applications, computer literacy, electives, English, foreign language, geometry, guidance, moral theology, peer counseling, physical education (includes health), physics, religion (includes Bible studies and theology), robotics, science, scripture, social justice, social studies (includes history), U.S. government, yearbook, senior speech, 50 hours of required community service.

Special Academic Programs Advanced Placement exam preparation; honors section; study at local college for college credit; domestic exchange program (with Network of Sacred Heart Schools).

College Admission Counseling 44 students graduated in 2012; all went to college, including College of Charleston; Louisiana State University and Agricultural and Mechanical College; Spring Hill College; Tulane University; University of Mississippi; Washington and Lee University.

Student Life Upper grades have uniform requirement, student council, honor system. Discipline rests equally with students and faculty. Attendance at religious services is required.

Summer Programs Enrichment, sports, art/fine arts programs offered; session focuses on arts, creative writing, robotics, strength and conditioning; held both on and off campus; held at Upper School campus, gym, area tracks; accepts girls; not open to students from other schools. 18 students usually enrolled. 2013 schedule: June to August.

Tuition and Aid Day student tuition: $14,300. Tuition installment plan (The Tuition Plan, individually arranged payment plans, bank loan). Merit scholarship grants, need-based scholarship grants available. In 2012–13, 27% of upper-school students received aid; total upper-school merit-scholarship money awarded: $20,650. Total amount of financial aid awarded in 2012–13: $264,600.

Admissions Traditional secondary-level entrance grade is 9. Achievement tests, admissions testing, ERB, OLSAT/Stanford or PSAT or SAT for applicants to grade 11 and 12 required. Deadline for receipt of application materials: none. Application fee required: $50. Interview required.

Athletics Interscholastic: aerobics, ballet, baseball, basketball, cheering, cross-country running, fitness, golf, indoor track & field, physical fitness, sailing, soccer, softball, strength & conditioning, swimming and diving, tennis, track and field, volleyball; intramural: aerobics, cooperative games, fitness, jogging, outdoor activities, outdoor recreation, physical fitness. 5 PE instructors, 14 coaches, 1 athletic trainer.

Computers Computers are regularly used in all classes. Computer network features include on-campus library services, online commercial services, Internet access, wireless campus network, Internet filtering or blocking technology. Campus intranet, student e-mail accounts, and computer access in designated common areas are available to students. Students grades are available online. The school has a published electronic and media policy.

Contact Ms. Christy Sevante, Admission Director. 504-269-1214. Fax: 504-896-7880. E-mail: csevante@ashrosary.org. Web site: www.ashrosary.org

ACADEMY OF THE SACRED HEART

1250 Kensington Road
Bloomfield Hills, Michigan 48304-3029

Head of School: Bridget Bearss, RSCJ

General Information Coeducational day college-preparatory, arts, religious studies, technology, experiential learning, and community service school, affiliated with Roman Catholic Church. Boys grades N–8, girls grades N–12. Founded: 1851. Setting: suburban. Nearest major city is Detroit. 44-acre campus. 1 building on campus. Approved or accredited by Michigan Department of Education. Endowment: $3.4 million. Total enrollment: 493. Upper school average class size: 12. Upper school faculty-student ratio: 1:7. There are 180 required school days per year for Upper School students. Upper School students typically attend 5 days per week. The average school day consists of 7 hours.

Upper School Student Profile Grade 9: 39 students (39 girls); Grade 10: 29 students (29 girls); Grade 11: 27 students (27 girls); Grade 12: 32 students (32 girls). 63% of students are Roman Catholic.

Faculty School total: 79. In upper school: 11 men, 13 women; 14 have advanced degrees.

Subjects Offered 20th century history, Advanced Placement courses, algebra, American literature, art, art history, biology, calculus, calculus-AP, chemistry, child development, clayworking, community service, computer applications, computer graphics, concert band, concert choir, crafts, creative writing, earth science, economics, English literature, English literature-AP, English-AP, environmental science, European history, European history-AP, forensics, French, genetics, geometry, global studies, government/civics, health, health and wellness, honors algebra, honors geometry, interior design, jewelry making, Latin, literature, mathematics, photography, physical education, physical science, physics, pre-calculus, psychology, publications, social studies, sociology, Spanish, theater, theology, U.S. history, U.S. history-AP, video, Web site design, world history, world literature.

Graduation Requirements Arts and fine arts (art, music, dance, drama), computer applications, foreign language, government, health and wellness, literature, mathematics, physical education (includes health), science, social studies (includes history), theology, U.S. government, U.S. history, world history, world literature, Project Term, First Year Experience (arts lab). Community service is required.

Special Academic Programs 3 Advanced Placement exams for which test preparation is offered; honors section; independent study; term-away projects; domestic exchange program (with Network of Sacred Heart Schools); academic accommodation for the gifted, the musically talented, and the artistically talented.

College Admission Counseling 34 students graduated in 2011; all went to college, including Dartmouth College; Fordham University; Michigan State University; University of Michigan; Washington University in St. Louis. Mean SAT critical reading: 545, mean SAT math: 527, mean SAT writing: 563, mean composite ACT: 25.

Student Life Upper grades have uniform requirement, student council, honor system. Discipline rests primarily with faculty. Attendance at religious services is required.

Tuition and Aid Day student tuition: $19,900. Tuition installment plan (Salie Mae Tuition Plan). Tuition reduction for siblings, merit scholarship grants, need-based scholarship grants available. In 2011–12, 51% of upper-school students received aid; total upper-school merit-scholarship money awarded: $8000. Total amount of financial aid awarded in 2011–12: $834,755.

Admissions Traditional secondary-level entrance grade is 9. For fall 2011, 35 students applied for upper-level admission, 29 were accepted, 17 enrolled. Scholastic Testing Service High School Placement Test or Stanford Achievement Test required. Deadline for receipt of application materials: none. Application fee required: $50. On-campus interview required.

Athletics Interscholastic: basketball, dance team, equestrian sports, field hockey, figure skating, golf, lacrosse, skiing (downhill), softball, tennis, volleyball. 1 PE instructor, 13 coaches.

Computers Computers are regularly used in all academic classes. Computer network features include on-campus library services, online commercial services, Internet access, wireless campus network, Internet filtering or blocking technology, tablet PC program with wireless network and print services, classroom multimedia services, computer in each classroom. Campus intranet, student e-mail accounts, and computer access in designated common areas are available to students. Students grades are available online. The school has a published electronic and media policy.

Contact Barbara Lopiccolo, Director of Admissions. 248-646-8900 Ext. 129. Fax: 248-646-4143. E-mail: blopiccolo@ashmi.org. Web site: www.ashmi.org

ACADÉMIE STE CÉCILE INTERNATIONAL SCHOOL

925 Cousineau Road
Windsor, Ontario N9G 1V8, Canada

Head of School: Mlle. Thérèse H. Gadoury

General Information Coeducational boarding and day college-preparatory, arts, and bilingual studies school, affiliated with Roman Catholic Church. Boarding grades 6–12, day grades JK–12. Founded: 1993. Setting: suburban. Nearest major city is Toronto, Canada. Students are housed in single-sex by floor dormitories. 30-acre campus. 2 buildings on campus. Approved or accredited by International Baccalaureate Organization, Ontario Ministry of Education, The Association of Boarding Schools, and Ontario Department of Education. Languages of instruction: English and French. Total enrollment: 236. Upper school average class size: 15. Upper school faculty-student ratio: 1:15. There are 180 required school days per year for Upper School students. Upper School students typically attend 5 days per week. The average school day consists of 6 hours and 15 minutes.

Upper School Student Profile Grade 9: 19 students (10 boys, 9 girls); Grade 10: 29 students (10 boys, 19 girls); Grade 11: 38 students (15 boys, 23 girls); Grade 12: 34 students (24 boys, 10 girls). 45% of students are boarding students. 2% are province residents. 2 provinces are represented in upper school student body. 45% are international students. International students from China, Hong Kong, Mexico, Taiwan, and United States; 2 other countries represented in student body. 70% of students are Roman Catholic.

Faculty School total: 50. In upper school: 13 men, 11 women; 10 have advanced degrees; 4 reside on campus.

Subjects Offered Accounting, advanced chemistry, advanced computer applications, advanced math, algebra, art, art education, art history, audio visual/media, ballet, basketball, biology, business technology, calculus, campus ministry, career education, careers, Catholic belief and practice, chemistry, choir, choral music, civics, classical music, computer information systems, computer programming, computer science, concert band, concert bell choir, concert choir, creative dance, creative drama, creative thinking, creative writing, critical thinking, critical writing, dance, dance performance, decision making skills, desktop publishing, desktop publishing, ESL, discrete mathematics, drama performance, drama workshop, dramatic arts, drawing, drawing and design, driver education, earth science, economics, English, English literature, environmental studies, ethics, expository writing, family living, French, French studies, geography, geometry, German, golf, handbells, health and wellness, health education, history, history of dance, history of music, history of religion, history of the Catholic Church, honors algebra, honors English, honors geometry, honors world history, instrumental music, International Baccalaureate courses, Internet, Internet research, intro to computers, Italian, jazz band, jazz dance, journalism, keyboarding, Latin, leadership, library skills, Life of Christ, literature, literature and composition-AP, mathematics, media studies, music, music appreciation, music composition, music history, music performance, music theory, organ, painting, philosophy, photography, physical education, physics, piano, poetry, prayer/spirituality, pre-algebra, pre-calculus, probability and statistics, public speaking, reading, reading/study skills, religion, research skills, SAT preparation, science, sculpture, Shakespeare, social studies, softball, Spanish, stage and body movement, stained glass, strings, student government, swimming, tennis, TOEFL preparation, track and field, values and decisions, visual arts, vocal ensemble, voice, volleyball, wind ensemble, wind instruments, world religions, writing, yearbook.

Graduation Requirements Ontario Ministry of Education requirements.

Special Academic Programs International Baccalaureate program; Advanced Placement exam preparation; honors section; accelerated programs; academic accommodation for the gifted, the musically talented, and the artistically talented; remedial reading and/or remedial writing; remedial math; ESL (40 students enrolled).

College Admission Counseling 35 students graduated in 2012; they went to McMaster University; The University of British Columbia; The University of Western Ontario; University of Toronto; University of Waterloo; University of Windsor. Other: 35 entered a postgraduate year. Mean SAT critical reading: 593, mean SAT math: 724, mean SAT writing: 615. 67% scored over 600 on SAT critical reading, 83% scored over 600 on SAT math, 67% scored over 600 on SAT writing.

Student Life Upper grades have uniform requirement, student council, honor system. Discipline rests primarily with faculty.

Summer Programs Remediation, enrichment, advancement, ESL, art/fine arts programs offered; session focuses on ESL; held on campus; accepts boys and girls; open to students from other schools. 25 students usually enrolled. 2013 schedule: July 2 to August 31. Application deadline: May 31.

Tuition and Aid Day student tuition: CAN$13,850; 7-day tuition and room/board: CAN$45,500. Tuition installment plan (Insured Tuition Payment Plan). Tuition reduction for siblings, merit scholarship grants available. In 2012–13, 5% of upper-school students received aid; total upper-school merit-scholarship money awarded: CAN$4500. Total amount of financial aid awarded in 2012–13: CAN$15,000.

Admissions Traditional secondary-level entrance grade is 9. For fall 2012, 25 students applied for upper-level admission, 21 were accepted, 18 enrolled. Deadline for receipt of application materials: none. Application fee required: CAN$300. Interview recommended.

Athletics Interscholastic: aquatics (boys, girls), badminton (b,g), basketball (b,g), equestrian sports (b,g), golf (b,g), horseback riding (b,g), ice hockey (g), independent competitive sports (b,g), modern dance (b,g), physical fitness (b,g), soccer (b,g), softball (b,g), swimming and diving (b,g), tennis (b,g), volleyball (b,g); intramural: aquatics (b,g), badminton (b,g), ballet (g), basketball (b,g), bowling (b,g), cross-country running (b,g), dance (b,g), dressage (b,g), equestrian sports (b,g), golf (b,g), horseback riding (b,g), paddle tennis (b,g), soccer (b,g), softball (b,g), swimming and diving (b,g), table tennis (b,g), tennis (b,g), volleyball (b,g); coed interscholastic: aquatics, badminton, basketball, dressage, equestrian sports, fitness, golf, horseback riding, indoor track & field, modern dance, physical fitness, soccer, softball, swimming and diving, tennis, volleyball; coed intramural: aquatics, badminton, basketball, bowling, cross-country running, dance, dressage, equestrian sports, floor hockey, golf, horseback riding, modern dance, soccer, softball, swimming and diving, tennis, volleyball. 2 PE instructors, 8 coaches.

Computers Computers are regularly used in accounting, business, desktop publishing, ESL, information technology, mathematics classes. Computer network features include Internet access, wireless campus network.

Contact Ms. Gwen A. Gatt, Admissions Clerk. 519-969-1291. Fax: 519-969-7953. E-mail: info@stececile.ca. Web site: www.stececile.ca

THE AGNES IRWIN SCHOOL

Ithan Avenue and Conestoga Road
Rosemont, Pennsylvania 19010

Head of School: Dr. Mary F. Seppala

General Information Girls' day college-preparatory school. Grades PK–12. Founded: 1869. Setting: suburban. Nearest major city is Philadelphia. 18-acre campus. 5 buildings on campus. Approved or accredited by Middle States Association of Colleges and Schools, National Independent Private Schools Association, Pennsylvania Association of Independent Schools, and Pennsylvania Department of Education. Member of National Association of Independent Schools, Secondary School Admission Test Board, and National Coalition of Girls' Schools. Endowment: $22.4 million. Total enrollment: 701. Upper school average class size: 15. Upper school faculty-student ratio: 1:6. There are 162 required school days per year for Upper School students. Upper School students typically attend 5 days per week. The average school day consists of 6 hours and 5 minutes.

Upper School Student Profile Grade 9: 73 students (73 girls); Grade 10: 84 students (84 girls); Grade 11: 69 students (69 girls); Grade 12: 66 students (66 girls).

Faculty School total: 110. In upper school: 15 men, 41 women; 43 have advanced degrees.

Subjects Offered 20th century world history, advanced studio art-AP, algebra, American history, American history-AP, American literature, American literature-AP, Asian studies, bioethics, biology, biology-AP, calculus, calculus-AP, chemistry, chemistry-AP, computer programming, dance, drama, economics, English, English language-AP, English literature, English literature and composition-AP, environmental science-AP, European history, European history-AP, finite math, French, French-AP, geometry, Greek, health, history, Latin, Latin-AP, media arts, media studies, Middle East, Middle Eastern history, music theory, photo shop, photography, physical education, physics, physics-AP, pre-calculus, public speaking, robotics, Spanish, Spanish-AP, statistics, studio art, theater arts, trigonometry.

Graduation Requirements Arts and fine arts (art, music, dance, drama), English, foreign language, history, mathematics, physical education (includes health), science, Senior assembly given by each girl before graduation. Community service is required.

Special Academic Programs 13 Advanced Placement exams for which test preparation is offered; honors section; independent study; term-away projects; study abroad; academic accommodation for the gifted.

College Admission Counseling 58 students graduated in 2012; all went to college, including Duke University; Franklin & Marshall College; Massachusetts Institute of Technology; University of Pennsylvania; University of Richmond. 81% scored over 600 on SAT critical reading, 72% scored over 600 on SAT math, 88% scored over 600 on SAT writing.

Student Life Upper grades have uniform requirement, student council, honor system. Discipline rests equally with students and faculty.

Summer Programs Remediation, enrichment, advancement, sports, art/fine arts, computer instruction programs offered; session focuses on arts, academics, and athletics; held on campus; accepts boys and girls; open to students from other schools. 1,000 students usually enrolled. 2013 schedule: June 15 to July 31. Application deadline: none.

Tuition and Aid Day student tuition: $29,300. Tuition installment plan (monthly payment plans). Need-based scholarship grants available. In 2012–13, 23% of upper-school students received aid. Total amount of financial aid awarded in 2012–13: $1,389,400.

Admissions Traditional secondary-level entrance grade is 9. For fall 2012, 93 students applied for upper-level admission, 48 were accepted, 33 enrolled. ISEE, SSAT or WISC-R or WISC-III required. Deadline for receipt of application materials: December 15. Application fee required: $50. Interview required.

Athletics Interscholastic: basketball, crew, cross-country running, diving, field hockey, golf, independent competitive sports, lacrosse, running, soccer, softball, squash, swimming and diving, tennis, track and field, volleyball; intramural: aerobics, aerobics/Nautilus, ballet, crew, dance, fitness, modern dance, Nautilus, physical fitness, physical training, strength & conditioning, weight training. 4 PE instructors, 27 coaches, 1 athletic trainer.

Computers Computers are regularly used in art, English, foreign language, history, mathematics, media arts, photography, science, yearbook classes. Computer network features include on-campus library services, online commercial services, Internet access, wireless campus network, online databases. Campus intranet, student e-mail accounts, and computer access in designated common areas are available to students. The school has a published electronic and media policy.

Contact Mrs. Sally B. Keidel, Assistant Head of School for Enrollment and External Relations. 610-525-8400. Fax: 610-525-8908. E-mail: skeidel@agnesirwin.org. Web site: www.agnesirwin.org

ALEXANDER DAWSON SCHOOL

10455 Dawson Drive
Lafayette, Colorado 80026

Head of School: Mr. George Moore

General Information Coeducational day college-preparatory, arts, technology, and engineering, global studies school. Grades K–12. Founded: 1970. Setting: rural. Nearest major city is Boulder. 113-acre campus. 11 buildings on campus. Approved or accredited by Association of Colorado Independent Schools and Colorado Department of Education. Member of National Association of Independent Schools and Secondary School Admission Test Board. Total enrollment: 453. Upper school average class size: 15. Upper school faculty-student ratio: 1:7. There are 172 required school days per year for Upper School students. Upper School students typically attend 5 days per week. The average school day consists of 9 hours and 30 minutes.

Upper School Student Profile Grade 9: 62 students (27 boys, 35 girls); Grade 10: 43 students (23 boys, 20 girls); Grade 11: 44 students (25 boys, 19 girls); Grade 12: 44 students (17 boys, 27 girls).

Faculty School total: 53. In upper school: 17 men, 10 women; 23 have advanced degrees.

Subjects Offered Algebra, American history, American literature, art, art history, biology, calculus, ceramics, chemistry, Chinese, computer math, computer multimedia, computer programming, computer science, creative writing, dance, drafting, drama, earth science, economics, English, English literature, European history, expository writing, fine arts, French, geography, geometry, government-AP, government/civics, grammar, health, history, industrial arts, journalism, Latin, mathematics, mechanical drawing, music, photography, physical education, physics, science, social sciences, social studies, Spanish, speech, theater, trigonometry, world history, world literature, writing.

Graduation Requirements Arts and fine arts (art, music, dance, drama), computer science, English, foreign language, history, mathematics, science, sports.

Special Academic Programs 15 Advanced Placement exams for which test preparation is offered; honors section; independent study; term-away projects; study at local college for college credit; study abroad; academic accommodation for the gifted, the musically talented, and the artistically talented; remedial reading and/or remedial writing; remedial math; special instructional classes for deaf students.

College Admission Counseling 38 students graduated in 2012; all went to college, including Middlebury College; Pomona College; University of Denver; Wellesley College. Mean SAT critical reading: 616, mean SAT math: 620, mean composite ACT: 27.

Student Life Upper grades have specified standards of dress, student council, honor system. Discipline rests equally with students and faculty.

Tuition and Aid Day student tuition: $20,550. Tuition installment plan (Insured Tuition Payment Plan, monthly payment plans, individually arranged payment plans). Need-based scholarship grants, need-based loans available. In 2012–13, 18% of upper-school students received aid. Total amount of financial aid awarded in 2012–13: $1,300,000.

Admissions Traditional secondary-level entrance grade is 9. For fall 2012, 45 students applied for upper-level admission, 31 were accepted, 24 enrolled. Deadline for receipt of application materials: none. Application fee required: $75. Interview required.

Athletics Interscholastic: baseball (boys), basketball (b,g), lacrosse (b), soccer (b,g), swimming and diving (b,g), synchronized swimming (g), tennis (b,g), track and field (b,g), volleyball (g); intramural: lacrosse (b); coed interscholastic: bicycling, canoeing/kayaking, cross-country running, equestrian sports, golf, kayaking, martial arts, paddling, skiing (downhill), Special Olympics; coed intramural: aerobics, aerobics/dance, backpacking, Circus, climbing, dance, equestrian sports, fitness, flag football, football, Frisbee, golf, hiking/backpacking, indoor soccer, martial arts, modern dance, outdoor activities, outdoor education, outdoor recreation, outdoor skills, physical fitness, rafting, rock climbing, ropes courses, running, strength & conditioning, weight lifting. 3 PE instructors, 22 coaches, 1 athletic trainer.

Computers Computers are regularly used in art, engineering, mathematics, science classes. Computer network features include on-campus library services, online commercial services, Internet access, wireless campus network, Internet filtering or blocking technology. Student e-mail accounts and computer access in designated common areas are available to students. Students grades are available online. The school has a published electronic and media policy.

Contact Ms. Denise LaRusch, Assistant to the Director of Admissions. 303-665-6679. Fax: 303-381-0415. E-mail: dlarusch@dawsonschool.org. Web site: www.dawsonschool.org

ALLEMAN HIGH SCHOOL

1103 40th Street
Rock Island, Illinois 61201-3114

Head of School: Mr. Colin Letendre

General Information college-preparatory school, affiliated with Roman Catholic Church. Approved or accredited by Illinois Department of Education. Total enrollment: 467. Upper school average class size: 18.

Upper School Student Profile 94.5% of students are Roman Catholic.

Student Life Attendance at religious services is required.

Admissions Application fee required: $25.

Contact 309-786-7793. Fax: 309-786-7834. Web site: www.allemanhighschool.org

ALLENDALE COLUMBIA SCHOOL

519 Allens Creek Road
Rochester, New York 14618

Head of School: Mick Gee

General Information Coeducational day college-preparatory school. Grades N–12. Founded: 1890. Setting: suburban. 33-acre campus. 5 buildings on campus. Approved or accredited by New York State Association of Independent Schools. Member of National Association of Independent Schools. Endowment: $15 million. Total enrollment: 363. There are 165 required school days per year for Upper School students. Upper School students typically attend 5 days per week. The average school day consists of 6 hours and 30 minutes.

Upper School Student Profile Grade 9: 36 students (16 boys, 20 girls); Grade 10: 43 students (22 boys, 21 girls); Grade 11: 28 students (14 boys, 14 girls); Grade 12: 28 students (15 boys, 13 girls).

Faculty School total: 58. In upper school: 11 men, 17 women; 23 have advanced degrees.

Subjects Offered Advanced Placement courses, advanced studio art-AP, algebra, American history, American history-AP, American literature, American literature-AP, art, art-AP, astronomy, bioethics, biology, biology-AP, calculus, calculus-AP, chemistry, chemistry-AP, composition-AP, computer science, digital art, discrete mathematics, earth science, economics, English, English language and composition-AP, English literature, environmental science, environmental science-AP, European history, European history-AP, expository writing, French, French-AP, genetics, geology, geometry, government/civics, grammar, health, history, history of China and Japan, jazz ensemble, Latin, Latin-AP, mathematics, mathematics-AP, music, photography, physical education, physics, physics-AP, pre-calculus, probability and statistics, science, social studies, Spanish, Spanish-AP, statistics-AP, U.S. history, U.S. history-AP, world history, writing.

Graduation Requirements Art, arts, computer science, English, foreign language, history, mathematics, physical education (includes health), science, participation in at least one team sport in both 9th and 10th grade.

Special Academic Programs 19 Advanced Placement exams for which test preparation is offered; independent study.

College Admission Counseling 34 students graduated in 2012; 33 went to college, including Boston College; Cornell University; Nazareth College of Rochester; New York University; Rochester Institute of Technology; University of Rochester. Other: 1 had other specific plans. Mean SAT critical reading: 623, mean SAT math: 645, mean SAT writing: 622. 51% scored over 600 on SAT critical reading, 62% scored over 600 on SAT math, 58% scored over 600 on SAT writing.

Student Life Upper grades have specified standards of dress, student council. Discipline rests primarily with faculty.

Summer Programs Enrichment, sports, art/fine arts programs offered; held on campus; accepts boys and girls; open to students from other schools. 550 students usually enrolled. 2013 schedule: June 10 to August 23. Application deadline: none.

Tuition and Aid Day student tuition: $5025–$20,250. Tuition installment plan (FACTS Tuition Payment Plan). Need-based scholarship grants available. In 2012–13, 50% of upper-school students received aid. Total amount of financial aid awarded in 2012–13: $840,990.

Admissions Traditional secondary-level entrance grade is 9. For fall 2012, 57 students applied for upper-level admission, 31 were accepted, 26 enrolled. ERB - verbal abilities, reading comprehension, quantitative abilities (level F, form 1), essay, math and English placement tests, school's own exam or writing sample required. Deadline for receipt of application materials: none. Application fee required: $50. Interview required.

Athletics Interscholastic: baseball (boys), basketball (b,g), cross-country running (b,g), soccer (b,g), softball (g), tennis (b,g), volleyball (g); coed interscholastic: bowling, golf, swimming and diving, track and field. 4 PE instructors.

Computers Computers are regularly used in all academic classes. Computer network features include on-campus library services, Internet access, wireless campus network, Internet filtering or blocking technology, county-wide library services. Student e-mail accounts and computer access in designated common areas are available to students. The school has a published electronic and media policy.

Contact Karyn Vella, Director of Admissions. 585-641-5344. Fax: 585-383-1191. E-mail: admissions@allendalecolumbia.org. Web site: www.allendalecolumbia.org

ALL HALLOWS HIGH SCHOOL

111 East 164th Street
Bronx, New York 10452-9402

Head of School: Mr. Paul P. Krebbs

General Information Boys' day college-preparatory, general academic, business, and religious studies school, affiliated with Roman Catholic Church. Grades 9–12. Founded: 1909. Setting: urban. 1 building on campus. Approved or accredited by Christian Brothers Association, Middle States Association of Colleges and Schools, and New York Department of Education. Total enrollment: 654. Upper school average class size: 27. Upper school faculty-student ratio: 1:15. There are 180 required school days per year for Upper School students. Upper School students typically attend 5 days per week. The average school day consists of 6 hours and 8 minutes.

Upper School Student Profile 85% of students are Roman Catholic.

Faculty School total: 42. In upper school: 37 men, 5 women; 33 have advanced degrees.

Subjects Offered Algebra, American history, art, Bible studies, biology, calculus, chemistry, computer science, economics, English, English literature, environmental science, geometry, government/civics, grammar, history, humanities, Latin, mathematics, media studies, physical education, physics, political science, religion, science, social studies, Spanish, speech, trigonometry.

Graduation Requirements Arts and fine arts (art, music, dance, drama), business skills (includes word processing), computer science, English, foreign language, mathematics, physical education (includes health), religion (includes Bible studies and theology), science, social sciences, social studies (includes history). Community service is required.

Special Academic Programs Remedial reading and/or remedial writing; remedial math.

College Admission Counseling 154 students graduated in 2012; all went to college.

Student Life Upper grades have specified standards of dress, student council, honor system. Discipline rests primarily with faculty. Attendance at religious services is required.

Tuition and Aid Merit scholarship grants available.

Admissions School's own exam required. Deadline for receipt of application materials: none. No application fee required. On-campus interview required.

Athletics Interscholastic: baseball, basketball, bowling, cross-country running, fencing, golf, indoor track & field, soccer, track and field, winter (indoor) track; intramural: field hockey, flag football, indoor soccer, lacrosse. 1 PE instructor, 4 coaches.

Computers Computers are regularly used in English, history, mathematics, media studies, science classes. Computer resources include on-campus library services, Internet access.

Contact Mr. Sean Sullivan, Principal. 718-293-4545. Fax: 718-293-8634. E-mail: alhallow@aol.com. Web site: www.allhallows.org

ALLIANCE ACADEMY

Casilla 17-11-06186
Quito, Ecuador

Head of School: Dr. David Wells

General Information Coeducational boarding and day and distance learning college-preparatory, arts, and religious studies school, affiliated with Christian faith. Boarding grades 7–12, day grades PK–12. Distance learning grades 10–12. Founded: 1929. Setting: urban. Students are housed in single-sex by floor dormitories and mission agency dormitories. 8-acre campus. 6 buildings on campus. Approved or accredited by Association of American Schools in South America, Association of Christian Schools International, and Southern Association of Colleges and Schools. Language of instruction: English. Total enrollment: 604. Upper school average class size: 15. Upper school faculty-student ratio: 1:7. There are 200 required school days per year for Upper School students. Upper School students typically attend 5 days per week. The average school day consists of 6 hours and 30 minutes.

Upper School Student Profile Grade 9: 51 students (27 boys, 24 girls); Grade 10: 60 students (26 boys, 34 girls); Grade 11: 44 students (14 boys, 30 girls); Grade 12: 53 students (27 boys, 26 girls). 1% of students are boarding students. 34% are international students. International students from Canada, China, Japan, Republic of Korea, Taiwan, and United States; 9 other countries represented in student body. 40% of students are Christian faith.

Faculty School total: 91. In upper school: 21 men, 24 women; 14 have advanced degrees; 3 reside on campus.

Subjects Offered Algebra, American history, American literature, art, auto mechanics, band, Bible, Bible as literature, Bible studies, biology, biology-AP, business, calculus, calculus-AP, chemistry, choir, Christian doctrine, Christian ethics, Christian studies, church history, computer applications, computer art, computer programming, computer science, concert band, creative writing, debate, desktop publishing, drama, earth science, economics, English, English as a foreign language, English language-AP, English literature, English literature-AP, ESL, family and consumer science, fine arts, French, French as a second language, geography, geometry, government/civics, grammar, health, health education, history, home economics, industrial arts, journalism, keyboarding, Life of Christ, marching band, mathematics, music, novels, photography, physical education, physics, pre-algebra, pre-calculus, public speaking, religion, religion and culture, science, senior seminar, small engine repair, social sciences, social studies, Spanish, Spanish literature, Spanish literature-AP, speech, speech and debate, theater, trigonometry, video communication, vocal ensemble, woodworking, world geography, world history, world religions, writing, yearbook.

Graduation Requirements 1 1/2 elective credits, algebra, arts and fine arts (art, music, dance, drama), comparative government and politics, computer applications, English, foreign language, health education, mathematics, physical education (includes health), religion (includes Bible studies and theology), science, social sciences, social studies (includes history), U.S. government and politics, U.S. history.

Special Academic Programs 12 Advanced Placement exams for which test preparation is offered; independent study; study at local college for college credit; academic accommodation for the gifted; remedial reading and/or remedial writing; remedial math; programs in English, mathematics, general development for dyslexic students; special instructional classes for students with developmental and/or learning disabilities; ESL (52 students enrolled).

College Admission Counseling 52 students graduated in 2012; 39 went to college, including Azusa Pacific University; Calvin College; John Brown University; Simpson University; Worcester Polytechnic Institute. Other: 4 went to work, 2 entered military service, 7 had other specific plans. Median SAT critical reading: 495, median SAT math: 517, median SAT writing: 496, median combined SAT: 1508, median composite ACT: 22. 36% scored over 600 on SAT critical reading, 29% scored over 600 on SAT math, 30% scored over 600 on SAT writing, 32% scored over 1800 on combined SAT, 26% scored over 26 on composite ACT.

Student Life Upper grades have specified standards of dress, student council, honor system. Discipline rests primarily with faculty. Attendance at religious services is required.

Summer Programs Remediation, ESL, sports programs offered; session focuses on ESL; held on campus; accepts boys and girls; not open to students from other schools. 27 students usually enrolled. 2013 schedule: June 25 to August 3. Application deadline: June 12.

Tuition and Aid Day student tuition: $9900. Tuition installment plan (monthly payment plans, individually arranged payment plans). Tuition reduction for siblings, need-based scholarship grants, paying campus jobs, tuition reduction for children of missionaries, two full scholarships for children of Ecuadorian military personnel available. In 2012–13, 30% of upper-school students received aid. Total amount of financial aid awarded in 2012–13: $800,000.

Admissions Traditional secondary-level entrance grade is 9. For fall 2012, 46 students applied for upper-level admission, 28 were accepted, 26 enrolled. English entrance exam, English proficiency, WRAT or writing sample required. Deadline for receipt of application materials: none. Application fee required: $100. On-campus interview required.

Athletics Interscholastic: basketball (boys, girls), soccer (b,g), volleyball (b,g); intramural: badminton (b,g), ball hockey (b), horseshoes (b), in-line hockey (b), modern dance (g), table tennis (b,g); coed intramural: backpacking, basketball, bocce, climbing, croquet, field hockey, flag football, floor hockey, football, hiking/backpacking, indoor soccer, kickball, martial arts, outdoor adventure, paddle tennis, running, soccer, softball, strength & conditioning, table tennis, volleyball, wall climbing. 2 PE instructors, 1 coach.

Computers Computers are regularly used in basic skills, business education, career exploration, college planning, computer applications, design, desktop publishing, desktop publishing, ESL, digital applications, graphic design, independent study, information technology, introduction to technology, keyboarding, lab/keyboard, language development, media arts, media production, media services, photography, photojournalism, programming, publications, technology, video film production, word processing, writing, yearbook classes. Computer network features include on-campus library services, online commercial services, Internet access, wireless campus network, Internet filtering or blocking technology. Campus intranet, student e-mail accounts, and computer access in designated common areas are available to students. Students grades are available online. The school has a published electronic and media policy.

Contact Mrs. Alexandra Chavez, Director of Admissions. 593-2-226-6985. Fax: 593-2-226-4350. E-mail: achavez@alliance.k12.ec. Web site: www.alliance.k12.ec

ALLISON ACADEMY

1881 Northeast 164th Street
North Miami Beach, Florida 33162

Head of School: Dr. Sarah F. Allison

General Information Coeducational day college-preparatory, general academic, arts, business, and English for Speakers of Other Languages school. Grades 6–12. Founded: 1983. Setting: urban. Nearest major city is Miami. 1-acre campus. 2 buildings

on campus. Approved or accredited by Association of Independent Schools of Florida, National Council for Private School Accreditation, Southern Association of Colleges and Schools, and Florida Department of Education. Total enrollment: 91. Upper school average class size: 15. Upper school faculty-student ratio: 1:10. There are 180 required school days per year for Upper School students. Upper School students typically attend 5 days per week. The average school day consists of 5 hours and 50 minutes.
Upper School Student Profile Grade 9: 17 students (13 boys, 4 girls); Grade 10: 17 students (12 boys, 5 girls); Grade 11: 15 students (12 boys, 3 girls); Grade 12: 21 students (13 boys, 8 girls).
Faculty School total: 11. In upper school: 5 men, 6 women; 5 have advanced degrees.
Subjects Offered Advanced Placement courses, algebra, American government, American history, art history, arts, biology, chemistry, chorus, computer science, consumer mathematics, creative drama, drama, drawing, ecology, environmental systems, economics, economics and history, English, English language and composition-AP, English literature, environmental science, ESL, fine arts, French, French language-AP, general math, geography, geometry, health education, history, humanities, life management skills, life skills, mathematics, painting, peer counseling, physical education, physical science, physics, pre-calculus, psychology, reading, reading/study skills, SAT/ACT preparation, science, social sciences, social studies, Spanish, sports, trigonometry, world cultures, writing, yearbook.
Graduation Requirements Algebra, American government, arts and fine arts (art, music, dance, drama), business skills (includes word processing), chemistry, computer applications, computer science, creative writing, current events, drama, earth and space science, economics, English, English literature, environmental education, foreign language, health education, life management skills, mathematics, physical education (includes health), psychology, SAT/ACT preparation, science, social sciences, social studies (includes history), Spanish, U.S. history, world history, 75 hours of community service.
Special Academic Programs 1 Advanced Placement exam for which test preparation is offered; honors section; accelerated programs; study at local college for college credit; academic accommodation for the gifted, the musically talented, and the artistically talented; remedial reading and/or remedial writing; remedial math; programs in English, mathematics, general development for dyslexic students; special instructional classes for students with learning disabilities, dyslexia, and Attention Deficit Disorder; ESL (3 students enrolled).
College Admission Counseling 22 students graduated in 2011; 17 went to college, including Barry University; Broward College; Florida International University; Miami Dade College. Other: 2 went to work, 1 entered military service, 2 had other specific plans. Median SAT critical reading: 500, median SAT math: 510, median composite ACT: 19. 16% scored over 600 on SAT critical reading, 15% scored over 600 on SAT math, 8% scored over 26 on composite ACT.
Student Life Upper grades have uniform requirement, student council. Discipline rests primarily with faculty.
Tuition and Aid Day student tuition: $14,000. Tuition installment plan (Insured Tuition Payment Plan, monthly payment plans, individually arranged payment plans). Tuition reduction for siblings, merit scholarship grants, need-based scholarship grants available. In 2011–12, 26% of upper-school students received aid; total upper-school merit-scholarship money awarded: $32,000. Total amount of financial aid awarded in 2011–12: $105,000.
Admissions Traditional secondary-level entrance grade is 9. Admissions testing, CAT, CTBS (or similar from their school), Woodcock-Johnson or Woodcock-Johnson Revised Achievement Test required. Deadline for receipt of application materials: none. Application fee required: $450. Interview required.
Athletics Interscholastic: basketball (boys), swimming and diving (b), tennis (b,g), walking (g), weight training (b); intramural: basketball (b,g), golf (b), martial arts (b,g), soccer (b,g), softball (b,g), swimming and diving (b,g), table tennis (b,g), tennis (b,g), walking (g); coed interscholastic: bowling, flag football, kickball, physical fitness, tennis; coed intramural: badminton, martial arts, physical fitness, soccer, softball, swimming and diving, table tennis, tennis, volleyball. 2 PE instructors, 2 coaches.
Computers Computers are regularly used in art, business applications, computer applications, current events, drawing and design, English, foreign language, geography, health, history, keyboarding, life skills, mathematics, psychology, reading, SAT preparation, science, Spanish, word processing classes. Computer resources include on-campus library services, online commercial services, Internet access, wireless campus network. Computer access in designated common areas is available to students. Students grades are available online. The school has a published electronic and media policy.
Contact Margaret Sheriff, Administrator. 305-940-3922. Fax: 305-940-1820. E-mail: thenewsheriff@gmail.com. Web site: www.allisonacademy.com

ALPHA OMEGA ACADEMY

804 North Second Avenue East
Rock Rapids, Iowa 51246

Head of School: Dr. Deborah K. Secord

General Information Coeducational day and distance learning college-preparatory, general academic, and distance learning school, affiliated with Christian faith. Grades K–12. Distance learning grades K–12. Founded: 1992. Setting: small town. Approved or accredited by CITA (Commission on International and Trans-Regional Accreditation) and North Central Association of Colleges and Schools. Total enrollment: 2,350. Upper school faculty-student ratio: 1:52. Upper School students typically attend 5 days per week.
Faculty School total: 36. In upper school: 14 men, 19 women; 6 have advanced degrees.
Subjects Offered Accounting, algebra, American government, American history, American literature, art, Bible, biology, British literature, calculus, career planning, chemistry, civics, consumer mathematics, earth science, English, English composition, English literature, French, general math, general science, geography, geometry, health, history, home economics, language arts, mathematics, music appreciation, music theory, physical fitness, science, Spanish, state history, world geography, world history.
Graduation Requirements 1 1/2 elective credits, algebra, biology, chemistry, language arts, mathematics, physical education (includes health), science, social studies (includes history), one credit of Bible.
Special Academic Programs Accelerated programs; independent study; remedial math.
College Admission Counseling 250 students graduated in 2012.
Student Life Upper grades have honor system. Discipline rests primarily with faculty.
Summer Programs Remediation programs offered; session focuses on credit recovery; accepts boys and girls; open to students from other schools.
Tuition and Aid Day student tuition: $600–$3000. Tuition installment plan (Six Month Payment Plan, Two Payment Plan). Tuition reduction for siblings available.
Admissions Math and English placement tests or placement test required. Deadline for receipt of application materials: none. Application fee required: $185. Interview required.
Athletics 2 PE instructors.
Computers Computers are regularly used in accounting, Bible studies, business skills, career technology, college planning, English, foreign language, French, geography, health, history, mathematics, music, science, social sciences, social studies, Spanish classes. Students grades are available online. The school has a published electronic and media policy.
Contact Mrs. Robin Inlow, Continuous Improvement Coordinator. 800-682-7396 Ext. 6253. Fax: 712-472-6830. E-mail: rinlow@aoacademy.com. Web site: www.aoacademy.com

ALVERNO HIGH SCHOOL

200 North Michillinda Avenue
Sierra Madre, California 91024

Head of School: Ms. Ann M. Gillick

General Information Girls' day college-preparatory, arts, religious studies, and technology school, affiliated with Roman Catholic Church. Grades 9–12. Founded: 1960. Setting: suburban. Nearest major city is Pasadena. 13-acre campus. 8 buildings on campus. Approved or accredited by California Association of Independent Schools, National Catholic Education Association, Western Association of Schools and Colleges, and California Department of Education. Upper school average class size: 18. Upper school faculty-student ratio: 1:12. There are 181 required school days per year for Upper School students. Upper School students typically attend 5 days per week. The average school day consists of 7 hours and 45 minutes.
Upper School Student Profile Grade 9: 53 students (53 girls); Grade 10: 39 students (39 girls); Grade 11: 37 students (37 girls); Grade 12: 45 students (45 girls). 65% of students are Roman Catholic.
Faculty School total: 17. In upper school: 4 men, 13 women; 11 have advanced degrees.
Subjects Offered ACT preparation, advanced biology, advanced chemistry, advanced studio art-AP, algebra, American literature, band, biology-AP, British literature (honors), calculus-AP, Catholic belief and practice, ceramics, choir, college counseling, conceptual physics, dance, dramatic arts, driver education, earth science, English language-AP, English literature-AP, European history-AP, finite math, fitness, freshman seminar, geometry, health, history of the Catholic Church, honors algebra, honors English, honors geometry, honors U.S. history, honors world history, human geography - AP, improvisation, language-AP, leadership and service, literature and composition-AP, literature-AP, Mandarin, modern European history-AP, multicultural studies, musical theater, photography, pre-calculus, religion, SAT preparation, science, senior project, Shakespeare, social studies, softball, Spanish-AP, sports conditioning, stagecraft, student government, studio art-AP, technology/design, theater arts, theater design and production, track and field, trigonometry, U.S. history-AP, United States government-AP, video film production, visual and performing arts, world literature, world religions, writing, yearbook, zoology.
Graduation Requirements Completion of 140 service hours.
Special Academic Programs 11 Advanced Placement exams for which test preparation is offered; honors section; independent study; academic accommodation for the gifted; remedial reading and/or remedial writing; remedial math; programs in English, mathematics, general development for dyslexic students.
College Admission Counseling 45 students graduated in 2012; 44 went to college, including California State Polytechnic University, Pomona; Marymount College, Palos Verdes, California; University of California, Davis; University of California, Riverside; University of La Verne. Other: 1 entered military service.

Student Life Upper grades have uniform requirement, student council, honor system. Discipline rests primarily with faculty. Attendance at religious services is required.
Summer Programs Remediation, enrichment, advancement, sports, art/fine arts, rigorous outdoor training, computer instruction programs offered; session focuses on to empower each young woman to be exactly the person she wants to be; held on campus; accepts girls; open to students from other schools. 100 students usually enrolled. 2013 schedule: June 18 to July 18. Application deadline: June 1.
Tuition and Aid Day student tuition: $13,500. Tuition installment plan (FACTS Tuition Payment Plan, monthly payment plans). Tuition reduction for siblings, merit scholarship grants, need-based scholarship grants available. In 2012–13, 40% of upper-school students received aid; total upper-school merit-scholarship money awarded: $172,198. Total amount of financial aid awarded in 2012–13: $253,313.
Admissions Traditional secondary-level entrance grade is 9. For fall 2012, 118 students applied for upper-level admission, 116 were accepted, 53 enrolled. High School Placement Test (closed version) from Scholastic Testing Service required. Deadline for receipt of application materials: January 18. Application fee required: $75. On-campus interview required.
Athletics Interscholastic: aquatics, basketball, cross-country running, soccer, softball, volleyball; intramural: aerobics/dance, dance, modern dance, self defense. 1 PE instructor, 4 coaches.
Computers Computers are regularly used in all academic classes. Computer network features include on-campus library services, Internet access, wireless campus network, Internet filtering or blocking technology. Students grades are available online. The school has a published electronic and media policy.
Contact Ms. Sara McCarthy, Director of Admissions and Public Relations. 626-355-3463 Ext. 235. Fax: 626-355-3153. E-mail: smccarthy@alverno-hs.org. Web site: myalverno.org/

AMERICAN ACADEMY

Plantation, Florida
See Special Needs Schools section.

THE AMERICAN BOYCHOIR SCHOOL

Princeton, New Jersey
See Junior Boarding Schools section.

AMERICAN HERITAGE SCHOOL

6200 Linton Boulevard
Delray Beach, Florida 33484

Head of School: Robert Stone

General Information Coeducational day college-preparatory, arts, technology, and pre-medical, pre-law, pre-engineering school. Grades PK–12. Founded: 1994. Setting: suburban. Nearest major city is Fort Lauderdale. 40-acre campus. 8 buildings on campus. Approved or accredited by Association of Independent Schools of Florida, Southern Association of Colleges and Schools, and Florida Department of Education. Member of National Association of Independent Schools. Total enrollment: 1,035. Upper school average class size: 17. Upper school faculty-student ratio: 1:10. There are 175 required school days per year for Upper School students. Upper School students typically attend 5 days per week. The average school day consists of 6 hours and 30 minutes.
Upper School Student Profile Grade 6: 68 students (38 boys, 30 girls); Grade 7: 80 students (45 boys, 35 girls); Grade 8: 79 students (57 boys, 22 girls); Grade 9: 148 students (79 boys, 69 girls); Grade 10: 148 students (75 boys, 73 girls); Grade 11: 129 students (66 boys, 63 girls); Grade 12: 148 students (82 boys, 66 girls).
Faculty School total: 104. In upper school: 24 men, 52 women; 55 have advanced degrees.
Subjects Offered Acting, algebra, American government, American history, American history-AP, American legal systems, American literature, American literature-AP, anatomy and physiology, architectural drawing, art, band, biology, biology-AP, calculus-AP, ceramics, chemistry, chemistry-AP, Chinese, chorus, community service, computer graphics, computer science, computer science-AP, constitutional law, costumes and make-up, creative writing, dance, digital photography, drama, drawing, economics, engineering, English, English language and composition-AP, English literature, English literature and composition-AP, environmental science, environmental science-AP, ESL, film and literature, fine arts, forensics, French, French-AP, geometry, graphic design, guitar, honors algebra, honors English, honors geometry, honors U.S. history, honors world history, journalism, law studies, Mandarin, mathematics, multimedia, multimedia design, music theory-AP, oceanography, orchestra, painting, photography, physical education, physics, physics-AP, portfolio art, pre-algebra, pre-calculus, probability and statistics, psychology, psychology-AP, public policy, research skills, SAT/ACT preparation, science, sculpture, set design, Spanish, Spanish-AP, speech and debate, sports medicine, stagecraft, statistics-AP, studio art, theater, U.S. government and politics-AP, vocal music, Web site design, weight training, world history, world history-AP, world literature, writing, writing, yearbook.
Graduation Requirements Arts and fine arts (art, music, dance, drama), English, foreign language, mathematics, physical education (includes health), science, social studies (includes history), acceptance to a 4-year college. Community service is required.
Special Academic Programs 16 Advanced Placement exams for which test preparation is offered; honors section; academic accommodation for the gifted, the musically talented, and the artistically talented; remedial reading and/or remedial writing; remedial math; programs in English, mathematics, general development for dyslexic students; special instructional classes for deaf students, blind students; ESL (95 students enrolled).
College Admission Counseling 147 students graduated in 2012; 145 went to college, including Florida Atlantic University; Florida Gulf Coast University; Florida State University; Palm Beach Atlantic University; University of Central Florida; University of Florida. Other: 1 entered military service, 1 had other specific plans. Median SAT critical reading: 530, median SAT math: 550, median SAT writing: 540, median combined SAT: 540. 23% scored over 600 on SAT critical reading, 33% scored over 600 on SAT math, 32% scored over 600 on SAT writing, 25% scored over 1800 on combined SAT.
Student Life Upper grades have uniform requirement, student council. Discipline rests primarily with faculty.
Summer Programs Remediation, enrichment, advancement, ESL programs offered; session focuses on academics; held on campus; accepts boys and girls; open to students from other schools. 50 students usually enrolled. 2013 schedule: June 4 to August 3. Application deadline: none.
Tuition and Aid Day student tuition: $20,000. Tuition installment plan (monthly payment plans, semester payment plan, yearly). Tuition reduction for siblings, merit scholarship grants, need-based scholarship grants, academic awards, fine arts awards available. In 2012–13, 17% of upper-school students received aid; total upper-school merit-scholarship money awarded: $334,955. Total amount of financial aid awarded in 2012–13: $1,602,000.
Admissions Traditional secondary-level entrance grade is 9. For fall 2012, 669 students applied for upper-level admission, 245 were accepted, 179 enrolled. Slossen Intelligence and Stanford Achievement Test required. Deadline for receipt of application materials: none. Application fee required: $100. On-campus interview required.
Athletics Interscholastic: baseball (boys), basketball (b,g), broomball (g), cross-country running (b,g), dance (b,g), diving (b,g), football (b), golf (b,g), lacrosse (b), soccer (b,g), softball (g), swimming and diving (b,g), tennis (b,g), track and field (b,g), volleyball (g), water polo (b), weight training (b,g), winter soccer (b,g), wrestling (b); coed interscholastic: cheering, physical fitness. 3 PE instructors, 2 athletic trainers.
Computers Computers are regularly used in all academic, college planning, computer applications, desktop publishing, digital applications, drawing and design, economics, English, ESL, foreign language, French, geography, graphic design, history, human geography - AP, journalism, keyboarding, library, literary magazine, mathematics, media arts, media production, multimedia, music, music technology, newspaper, photography, programming, psychology, reading, SAT preparation, science, social sciences, social studies, Spanish, speech, video film production, Web site design, writing, yearbook classes. Computer network features include on-campus library services, online commercial services, Internet access, wireless campus network, Internet filtering or blocking technology, Questia, Noodle Tools, Naviance, Lexis-Nexus, Quia, ProQuest/SIRS, Turnitin, Cengage Learning Gale, Learning Today, Nettrekker, EBSCOhost, Accelerated Reader. Student e-mail accounts and computer access in designated common areas are available to students. Students grades are available online. The school has a published electronic and media policy.
Contact Mr. Harold Bailey, DD, Director of Admissions. 561-495-7272 Ext. 236. Fax: 561-495-4192. E-mail: harold.bailey@ahschool.com. Web site: www.ahschool.com

See Display on next page and Close-Up on page 542.

AMERICAN HERITAGE SCHOOL

12200 West Broward Boulevard
Plantation, Florida 33325

Head of School: William R. Laurie

General Information Coeducational day college-preparatory, arts, technology, pre-medical, pre-law, pre-engineering, bio-medical, arts, and journalism, broadcasting school. Grades PK–12. Founded: 1969. Setting: suburban. Nearest major city is Fort Lauderdale. 40-acre campus. 5 buildings on campus. Approved or accredited by Association of Independent Schools of Florida, CITA (Commission on International and Trans-Regional Accreditation), Southern Association of Colleges and Schools, and Florida Department of Education. Total enrollment: 2,345. Upper school average class size: 19. Upper school faculty-student ratio: 1:15. There are 175 required school days per year for Upper School students. Upper School students typically attend 5 days per week. The average school day consists of 7 hours and 15 minutes.
Upper School Student Profile Grade 7: 149 students (75 boys, 74 girls); Grade 8: 176 students (98 boys, 78 girls); Grade 9: 342 students (184 boys, 158 girls); Grade 10: 320 students (183 boys, 137 girls); Grade 11: 326 students (162 boys, 164 girls); Grade 12: 295 students (138 boys, 157 girls).

Faculty School total: 171. In upper school: 42 men, 72 women; 61 have advanced degrees.

Subjects Offered Acting, algebra, American government, American history, American history-AP, American legal systems, American literature, American literature-AP, anatomy and physiology, architectural drawing, architecture, art, band, biology, biology-AP, business law, calculus-AP, ceramics, chemistry, chemistry-AP, Chinese, chorus, community service, computer graphics, computer science, computer science-AP, constitutional law, costumes and make-up, creative writing, dance, drama, drawing, economics, economics-AP, engineering, English, English language and composition-AP, English literature, English literature and composition-AP, environmental science, environmental science-AP, ESL, European history-AP, fine arts, forensics, French, French language-AP, French-AP, geometry, government-AP, graphic design, guitar, honors algebra, honors English, honors geometry, honors U.S. history, honors world history, human geography - AP, journalism, law studies, literary magazine, mathematics, music theory, music theory-AP, oceanography, orchestra, organic chemistry, painting, photography, physical education, physics, physics-AP, portfolio art, pre-algebra, pre-calculus, probability and statistics, psychology, psychology-AP, public speaking, research, research skills, SAT preparation, SAT/ACT preparation, science, sculpture, set design, sociology, Spanish, Spanish-AP, speech and debate, stage design, stagecraft, statistics-AP, studio art, technical theater, theater, U.S. government and politics-AP, video film production, visual arts, vocal music, Web site design, weight training, world history, world history-AP, world literature, writing, writing, yearbook.

Graduation Requirements Arts and fine arts (art, music, dance, drama), English, foreign language, mathematics, physical education (includes health), science, social studies (includes history), acceptance to a 4-year college. Community service is required.

Special Academic Programs Advanced Placement exam preparation; honors section; academic accommodation for the gifted, the musically talented, and the artistically talented; ESL (42 students enrolled).

College Admission Counseling 266 students graduated in 2012; all went to college, including Florida International University; Florida State University; Nova Southeastern University; University of Central Florida; University of Florida; University of Miami. Mean SAT critical reading: 559, mean SAT math: 580, mean SAT writing: 595, mean composite ACT: 27. 43% scored over 600 on SAT critical reading, 49% scored over 600 on SAT math, 49% scored over 600 on SAT writing, 48% scored over 26 on composite ACT.

Student Life Upper grades have uniform requirement, student council. Discipline rests primarily with faculty.

Summer Programs Remediation, enrichment, advancement, ESL, art/fine arts, computer instruction programs offered; session focuses on academics; held on campus; accepts boys and girls; open to students from other schools. 500 students usually enrolled. 2013 schedule: June 10 to August 9. Application deadline: none.

Tuition and Aid Day student tuition: $21,269–$22,954. Tuition installment plan (monthly payment plans, Semester payment plan, yearly). Tuition reduction for siblings, merit scholarship grants, need-based scholarship grants available. In 2012–13, 22% of upper-school students received aid; total upper-school merit-scholarship money awarded: $3,800,000. Total amount of financial aid awarded in 2012–13: $3,800,000.

Admissions Traditional secondary-level entrance grade is 9. Slossen Intelligence and Stanford Achievement Test required. Deadline for receipt of application materials: none. Application fee required: $100. On-campus interview required.

Athletics Interscholastic: baseball (boys), basketball (b,g), cross-country running (b,g), diving (b,g), football (b), golf (b,g), lacrosse (b,g), soccer (b,g), softball (g), swimming and diving (b,g), tennis (b,g), track and field (b,g), volleyball (b,g), weight training (b,g), winter soccer (b,g), wrestling (b); coed interscholastic: cheering, physical fitness, physical training. 4 PE instructors, 6 coaches.

Computers Computers are regularly used in all academic classes. Computer network features include on-campus library services, online commercial services, Internet access, wireless campus network, Internet filtering or blocking technology, Questia, iPads used by students and teachers on school Intranet. Campus intranet, student e-mail accounts, and computer access in designated common areas are available to students. Students grades are available online. The school has a published electronic and media policy.

Contact William R. Laurie, President. 954-472-0022 Ext. 3062. Fax: 954-472-3088. E-mail: admissions@ahschool.com. Web site: www.ahschool.com

See Display below and Close-Up on page 542.

AMERICAN INTERNATIONAL SCHOOL, LUSAKA

PO Box 320176
Lusaka, Zambia

Head of School: Mr. Thomas J. Pado

General Information Coeducational day college-preparatory school. Grades 6–12. Founded: 1986. Setting: suburban. 12-acre campus. 11 buildings on campus. Approved or accredited by Council of International Schools, International Baccalaureate Organization, and Middle States Association of Colleges and Schools. Member of European Council of International Schools. Language of instruction: English. Total enrollment: 257. Upper school average class size: 18. Upper school faculty-student ratio: 1:7. There are 180 required school days per year for Upper School students. Upper School students typically attend 5 days per week. The average school day consists of 5 hours and 50 minutes.

Upper School Student Profile Grade 9: 33 students (20 boys, 13 girls); Grade 10: 33 students (21 boys, 12 girls); Grade 11: 39 students (23 boys, 16 girls); Grade 12: 33 students (18 boys, 15 girls).

Faculty School total: 39. In upper school: 15 men, 21 women; 19 have advanced degrees.
Subjects Offered International Baccalaureate courses.
Graduation Requirements International Baccalaureate courses.
Special Academic Programs International Baccalaureate program; ESL (16 students enrolled).
College Admission Counseling 35 students graduated in 2012; 31 went to college. Other: 1 entered military service, 3 had other specific plans. Median SAT critical reading: 530, median SAT math: 520, median SAT writing: 540, median combined SAT: 1610, median composite ACT: 23. 26.7% scored over 600 on SAT critical reading, 26.7% scored over 600 on SAT math, 40% scored over 600 on SAT writing, 33.3% scored over 1800 on combined SAT, 27.8% scored over 26 on composite ACT.
Student Life Upper grades have student council, honor system. Discipline rests primarily with faculty.
Tuition and Aid Day student tuition: $17,100.
Admissions Traditional secondary-level entrance grade is 11. For fall 2012, 12 students applied for upper-level admission, 11 were accepted, 10 enrolled. English Composition Test for ESL students required. Deadline for receipt of application materials: none. No application fee required.
Athletics Intramural: badminton (boys, girls), basketball (b,g), climbing (b,g), cross-country running (b,g), dance (b,g), field hockey (b,g), fitness (b,g), floor hockey (b,g), Frisbee (b,g), handball (b,g), indoor soccer (b,g), rugby (b), soccer (b,g), swimming and diving (b,g), tennis (b,g), triathlon (b,g), ultimate Frisbee (b,g), volleyball (b,g), wall climbing (b,g), water polo (b,g), weight training (b,g); coed intramural: badminton, basketball, climbing, cross-country running, dance, field hockey, fitness, floor hockey, Frisbee, handball, indoor soccer, soccer, swimming and diving, tennis, triathlon, ultimate Frisbee, volleyball, wall climbing, water polo, weight training. 3 PE instructors, 14 coaches.
Computers Computers are regularly used in all classes. Computer network features include on-campus library services, Internet access, wireless campus network, Internet filtering or blocking technology. Campus intranet is available to students. Students grades are available online. The school has a published electronic and media policy.

THE AMERICAN SCHOOL FOUNDATION

Bondojito 215
Colonia Las Americas
Mexico City, D.F. 01120, Mèxico

Head of School: Mr. Paul Williams

General Information Coeducational day college-preparatory, Mexican Program Curriculum, and U.S. program curriculum school. Grades PK–12. Founded: 1888. Setting: urban. Nearest major city is Mexico City, Mexico. 17-acre campus. 4 buildings on campus. Approved or accredited by International Baccalaureate Organization, Ministry of Education, Mexico; Southern Association of Colleges and Schools, and Universidad Nacional Autonoma de Mexico. Affiliate member of National Association of Independent Schools; member of Secondary School Admission Test Board. Languages of instruction: English and Spanish. Endowment: 141.3 million Mexican pesos. Total enrollment: 2,571. Upper school average class size: 18. Upper school faculty-student ratio: 1:11. There are 181 required school days per year for Upper School students. Upper School students typically attend 5 days per week. The average school day consists of 6 hours and 45 minutes.
Upper School Student Profile Grade 9: 186 students (105 boys, 81 girls); Grade 10: 174 students (78 boys, 96 girls); Grade 11: 193 students (89 boys, 104 girls); Grade 12: 180 students (96 boys, 84 girls).
Faculty School total: 217. In upper school: 36 men, 28 women; 40 have advanced degrees.
Subjects Offered Advanced Placement courses, algebra, American history, American literature, anatomy, art, art history, biology, calculus, ceramics, chemistry, computer programming, computer science, drafting, drama, earth science, ecology, economics, English, English literature, European history, expository writing, film, fine arts, French, geography, geometry, government/civics, grammar, health, history, humanities, journalism, mathematics, Mexican history, music, philosophy, photography, physical education, physics, physiology, psychology, science, social sciences, social studies, Spanish, speech, statistics, trigonometry, world history, world literature, writing.
Graduation Requirements English, foreign language, health, humanities, mathematics, physical education (includes health), science, social studies (includes history), technology, IB Personal Project (10th grade).
Special Academic Programs International Baccalaureate program; 12 Advanced Placement exams for which test preparation is offered; independent study; remedial reading and/or remedial writing; programs in English, mathematics, general development for dyslexic students; special instructional classes for learning disabilities (LD), Attention Deficit Hyperactivity Disorder (ADHD), and speech and language disorders.
College Admission Counseling 182 students graduated in 2012; 149 went to college, including Instituto Tecnologico Autonomo de Mexico, Instituto Tecnologico y de Estudios Superiores de Monterrey, Campus Santa Fe; New York University, Northeastern University, School of the Art Institute of Chicago, Universidad Iberoamericana. Other: 22 had other specific plans. Median SAT critical reading: 570, median SAT math: 610, median SAT writing: 570, median combined SAT: 1750, median composite ACT: 27. 38.5% scored over 600 on SAT critical reading, 58.2% scored over 600 on SAT math, 41% scored over 600 on SAT writing, 40.2% scored over 1800 on combined SAT, 53.9% scored over 26 on composite ACT.
Student Life Upper grades have specified standards of dress, student council. Discipline rests primarily with faculty.
Tuition and Aid Day student tuition: 162,550 Mexican pesos. Tuition installment plan (monthly payment plans, Tuition Insurance). Need-based scholarship grants available. In 2012–13, 14% of upper-school students received aid. Total amount of financial aid awarded in 2012–13: 7,534,193 Mexican pesos.
Admissions Traditional secondary-level entrance grade is 10. For fall 2012, 220 students applied for upper-level admission, 102 were accepted, 92 enrolled. Essay and NWEA tests in math, reading, and language required. Deadline for receipt of application materials: none. Application fee required: 1000 Mexican pesos. On-campus interview required.
Athletics Interscholastic: basketball (boys, girls), dance team (g), football (b), soccer (b,g), swimming and diving (b,g), volleyball (g); coed interscholastic: running. 2 PE instructors, 20 coaches, 1 athletic trainer.
Computers Computers are regularly used in all classes. Computer network features include on-campus library services, online commercial services, Internet access, wireless campus network, Internet filtering or blocking technology. Campus intranet, student e-mail accounts, and computer access in designated common areas are available to students. Students grades are available online. The school has a published electronic and media policy.
Contact Patricia Hubp, Director of Admission. 52-555-227-4900. Fax: 52-55273-4357. E-mail: martindehubp@asf.edu.mx. Web site: www.asf.edu.mx

THE AMERICAN SCHOOL IN EL SALVADOR

VIPSAL 1352
Miami, Florida 33102-5364

Head of School: Mr. Ken Templeton

General Information Coeducational day college-preparatory school. Grades PK–12. Founded: 1946. Setting: urban. Nearest major city is San Salvador, El Salvador. 15-acre campus. 5 buildings on campus. Approved or accredited by Florida Department of Education. Member of National Association of Independent Schools. Total enrollment: 1,605. Upper school average class size: 21. Upper school faculty-student ratio: 1:18. There are 185 required school days per year for Upper School students. Upper School students typically attend 5 days per week. The average school day consists of 5 hours and 55 minutes.
Faculty School total: 170. In upper school: 22 men, 24 women; 15 have advanced degrees.
Subjects Offered Advanced Placement courses, advanced studio art-AP, algebra, American government, American history-AP, American literature-AP, ancient world history, art, art-AP, biology, biology-AP, calculus, calculus-AP, chemistry, chemistry-AP, college counseling, comparative government and politics-AP, Eastern world civilizations, English, English language and composition-AP, English language-AP, English literature, English literature and composition-AP, environmental science, French, French language-AP, geometry, health, honors algebra, honors English, honors U.S. history, honors world history, Italian, Latin American history, life science, life skills, philosophy, photography, physical education, physical science, physics, physics-AP, pre-algebra, pre-calculus, psychology, psychology-AP, SAT preparation, service learning/internship, Spanish, Spanish language-AP, Spanish literature-AP, study skills, U.S. history-AP.
Special Academic Programs Advanced Placement exam preparation.
College Admission Counseling 103 students graduated in 2012; 102 went to college, including Florida International University; Loyola University New Orleans; Savannah College of Art and Design; Texas Christian University; Trinity University.
Student Life Upper grades have uniform requirement, student council, honor system. Discipline rests primarily with faculty.
Summer Programs Remediation, enrichment programs offered; session focuses on remedial work; held on campus; accepts boys and girls; open to students from other schools. 100 students usually enrolled. 2013 schedule: June to July. Application deadline: May.
Tuition and Aid Day student tuition: $7937. Tuition installment plan (monthly payment plans).
Admissions Traditional secondary-level entrance grade is 9. Academic Profile Tests, admissions testing, any standardized test or Iowa Test, CTBS, or TAP required. Deadline for receipt of application materials: none. Application fee required: $50. On-campus interview required.
Athletics Interscholastic: basketball (boys, girls), cross-country running (b,g), handball (b,g), soccer (b,g), table tennis (b,g), volleyball (b,g), wall climbing (b,g); intramural: basketball (b,g), handball (b,g), soccer (b,g), table tennis (b,g), volleyball (b,g); coed interscholastic: cross-country running; coed intramural: basketball, soccer, table tennis, volleyball. 10 PE instructors, 30 coaches.
Computers Computer resources include on-campus library services, Internet access, wireless campus network, Internet filtering or blocking technology. Student e-mail accounts and computer access in designated common areas are available to students. Students grades are available online.

Contact Mrs. Yolanda Lopez, Director of Admissions. 503-252-8822 Ext. 0. Fax: 503-252-8822 Ext. 2. E-mail: lopez.yolanda@amschool.edu.sv. Web site: www.amschool.edu.sv

THE AMERICAN SCHOOL IN LONDON

One Waverley Place
London NW8 0NP, United Kingdom

Head of School: Coreen R. Hester

General Information Coeducational day college-preparatory school. Grades PK–12. Founded: 1951. Setting: urban. 3-acre campus. 1 building on campus. Approved or accredited by Middle States Association of Colleges and Schools. Affiliate member of National Association of Independent Schools; member of Secondary School Admission Test Board. Language of instruction: English. Endowment: £12 million. Total enrollment: 1,350. Upper school average class size: 15. Upper school faculty-student ratio: 1:10. There are 172 required school days per year for Upper School students. Upper School students typically attend 5 days per week. The average school day consists of 5 hours and 50 minutes.

Upper School Student Profile Grade 9: 127 students (68 boys, 59 girls); Grade 10: 123 students (66 boys, 57 girls); Grade 11: 115 students (67 boys, 48 girls); Grade 12: 103 students (56 boys, 47 girls).

Faculty School total: 112. In upper school: 17 men, 30 women; 36 have advanced degrees.

Subjects Offered Acting, African studies, algebra, American literature, anatomy and physiology, Arabic, architectural drawing, art, art history-AP, astronomy, biology, biology-AP, British literature, calculus, calculus-AP, chemistry, chemistry-AP, Chinese, Chinese studies, computer applications, computer science-AP, concert band, concert choir, dance, digital imaging, digital music, digital photography, drawing, ecology, economics, environmental science, European history, European history-AP, film, French, French language-AP, French literature-AP, genetics, geometry, German, health, human geography - AP, independent study, Japanese, jazz band, journalism, Latin, macro/microeconomics-AP, Middle East, modern European history-AP, music theory-AP, mythology, orchestra, painting, photography, physical education, physics-AP, play production, poetry, pre-calculus, psychology, psychology-AP, Russian, Russian literature, Russian studies, Shakespeare, Spanish, Spanish language-AP, Spanish literature-AP, statistics-AP, studio art-AP, trigonometry, U.S. history, U.S. history-AP, video and animation, video film production, world civilizations, world geography, writing, yearbook.

Graduation Requirements Arts and fine arts (art, music, dance, drama), English, foreign language, mathematics, physical education (includes health), science, social studies (includes history), technology.

Special Academic Programs Advanced Placement exam preparation; independent study; programs in general development for dyslexic students; ESL (41 students enrolled).

College Admission Counseling 111 students graduated in 2011; 109 went to college, including Brown University; Emory University, Oxford College; Georgetown University; New York University; Princeton University; University of Southern California. Other: 2 had other specific plans. Mean SAT critical reading: 659, mean SAT math: 669, mean SAT writing: 669.

Student Life Upper grades have student council, honor system. Discipline rests primarily with faculty.

Tuition and Aid Day student tuition: £22,550. Tuition installment plan (monthly payment plans, individually arranged payment plans). Need-based scholarship grants available. In 2011–12, 5% of upper-school students received aid. Total amount of financial aid awarded in 2011–12: £411,850.

Admissions ERB, ISEE, PSAT or SAT required. Deadline for receipt of application materials: none. Application fee required: £150.

Athletics Interscholastic: baseball (boys), basketball (b,g), cheering (g), crew (b,g), cross-country running (b,g), dance (g), field hockey (g), rugby (b), soccer (b,g), softball (g), swimming and diving (b,g), tennis (b,g), track and field (b,g), volleyball (b,g); coed interscholastic: golf; coed intramural: badminton, kickball, soccer, swimming and diving, tennis. 3 PE instructors, 52 coaches.

Computers Computers are regularly used in animation, English, foreign language, journalism, mathematics, media arts, media production, science, social studies, video film production, Web site design, yearbook classes. Computer network features include on-campus library services, Internet access, wireless campus network. Student e-mail accounts are available to students. Students grades are available online.

Contact Jodi Coats, Dean of Admissions. 44-20-7449-1221. Fax: 44-20-7449-1350. E-mail: admissions@asl.org. Web site: www.asl.org

ANACAPA SCHOOL

814 Santa Barbara Street
Santa Barbara, California 93101

Head of School: Mr. Gordon Sichi

General Information Coeducational day college-preparatory and arts school. Grades 7–12. Founded: 1981. Setting: urban. 2 buildings on campus. Approved or accredited by Western Association of Schools and Colleges and California Department of Education. Total enrollment: 49. Upper school average class size: 12. Upper school faculty-student ratio: 1:9. Upper School students typically attend 5 days per week. The average school day consists of 7 hours and 10 minutes.

Upper School Student Profile Grade 9: 13 students (6 boys, 7 girls); Grade 10: 4 students (2 boys, 2 girls); Grade 11: 8 students (6 boys, 2 girls); Grade 12: 12 students (4 boys, 8 girls).

Faculty School total: 12. In upper school: 5 men, 5 women; 4 have advanced degrees.

Special Academic Programs Advanced Placement exam preparation.

College Admission Counseling 11 students graduated in 2012; all went to college, including Santa Barbara City College; University of California, Los Angeles; Westmont College.

Student Life Upper grades have specified standards of dress, student council, honor system. Discipline rests primarily with faculty.

Tuition and Aid Tuition installment plan (individually arranged payment plans). Merit scholarship grants, need-based scholarship grants, paying campus jobs available. In 2012–13, 69% of upper-school students received aid.

Admissions Traditional secondary-level entrance grade is 9. For fall 2012, 6 students applied for upper-level admission, 6 were accepted, 5 enrolled. Deadline for receipt of application materials: none. Application fee required: $100. Interview required.

Athletics Coed Intramural: aquatics, backpacking, basketball, canoeing/kayaking, dance, fitness, flag football, hiking/backpacking, jogging, kayaking, outdoor activities, outdoor adventure, running, sailing, scuba diving, skiing (downhill), soccer, softball, squash, surfing, swimming and diving, table tennis, yoga.

Computers Computers are regularly used in all academic classes. Computer resources include Internet access, wireless campus network. Computer access in designated common areas is available to students. The school has a published electronic and media policy.

Contact Ms. Sheryn Sears, Executive Administrator. 805-965-0228. Fax: 805-899-2758. E-mail: anacapa@anacapaschool.org. Web site: www.anacapaschool.org

ANNIE WRIGHT SCHOOL

827 North Tacoma Avenue
Tacoma, Washington 98403

Head of School: Mr. Christian Sullivan

General Information Girls' boarding and coeducational day college-preparatory, arts, technology, and mathematics, science and music school, affiliated with Episcopal Church. Boarding girls grades 9–12, day boys grades PS–8, day girls grades PS–12. Founded: 1884. Setting: suburban. Nearest major city is Seattle. Students are housed in single-sex dormitories. 10-acre campus. 3 buildings on campus. Approved or accredited by International Baccalaureate Organization, National Association of Episcopal Schools, Northwest Accreditation Commission, Pacific Northwest Association of Independent Schools, The Association of Boarding Schools, and Washington Department of Education. Member of National Association of Independent Schools and Secondary School Admission Test Board. Endowment: $14.7 million. Total enrollment: 443. Upper school average class size: 12. Upper school faculty-student ratio: 1:5. There are 180 required school days per year for Upper School students. Upper School students typically attend 5 days per week. The average school day consists of 7 hours and 10 minutes.

Upper School Student Profile Grade 9: 34 students (34 girls); Grade 10: 44 students (44 girls); Grade 11: 44 students (44 girls); Grade 12: 40 students (40 girls). 55% of students are boarding students. 45% are state residents. 14 states are represented in upper school student body. 37% are international students. International students from China, Japan, Republic of Korea, Taiwan, and Thailand; 7 other countries represented in student body. 10% of students are members of Episcopal Church.

Faculty School total: 85. In upper school: 15 men, 20 women; 15 have advanced degrees; 6 reside on campus.

Subjects Offered Algebra, American history, American literature, anatomy, art, art history, biology, calculus, ceramics, chemistry, computer programming, computer science, creative writing, dance, drama, earth science, economics, English, English literature, ESL, fine arts, French, geometry, government/civics, health, history, Japanese, mathematics, music, music history, physical education, physics, religion, science, social studies, Spanish, theater, world history, world literature.

Graduation Requirements Arts and fine arts (art, music, dance, drama), English, history, mathematics, modern languages, physical education (includes health), religion (includes Bible studies and theology), science, social studies (includes history), swim safety test.

Special Academic Programs International Baccalaureate program; independent study; term-away projects; study abroad; ESL (46 students enrolled).

College Admission Counseling 31 students graduated in 2012; all went to college, including The George Washington University; University of San Francisco; University of Washington. Mean SAT critical reading: 599, mean SAT math: 667, mean SAT writing: 627.

Student Life Upper grades have uniform requirement, student council, honor system. Discipline rests equally with students and faculty.

Tuition and Aid Day student tuition: $23,870; 5-day tuition and room/board: $36,870; 7-day tuition and room/board: $46,950. Tuition installment plan (monthly payment plans, individually arranged payment plans). Merit scholarship grants, need-based scholarship grants available. In 2012–13, 8% of upper-school students received aid; total upper-school merit-scholarship money awarded: $324,578. Total amount of financial aid awarded in 2012–13: $915,093.

Admissions Traditional secondary-level entrance grade is 9. International English Language Test or TOEFL required. Deadline for receipt of application materials: February 8. Application fee required: $100. Interview required.

Athletics Interscholastic: basketball, cross-country running, golf, soccer, tennis, track and field, volleyball. 5 PE instructors, 10 coaches, 1 athletic trainer.

Computers Computers are regularly used in all academic classes. Computer network features include on-campus library services, Internet access. Student e-mail accounts are available to students. The school has a published electronic and media policy.

Contact Ms. Kanani Cockett, Admissions Associate. 253-284-8600. Fax: 253-572-3616. E-mail: kanani_cockett@aw.org. Web site: awschools.org/

ARCHBISHOP CURLEY HIGH SCHOOL

3701 Sinclair Lane
Baltimore, Maryland 21213

Head of School: Fr. Joseph Benicewicz

General Information Boys' day college-preparatory school, affiliated with Roman Catholic Church. Grades 9–12. Founded: 1961. Setting: urban. 33-acre campus. 3 buildings on campus. Approved or accredited by Middle States Association of Colleges and Schools and Maryland Department of Education. Endowment: $3.2 million. Total enrollment: 526. Upper school average class size: 22. Upper school faculty-student ratio: 1:14. Upper School students typically attend 5 days per week. The average school day consists of 6 hours and 30 minutes.

Upper School Student Profile Grade 9: 140 students (140 boys); Grade 10: 130 students (130 boys); Grade 11: 128 students (128 boys); Grade 12: 128 students (128 boys). 65% of students are Roman Catholic.

Faculty School total: 52. In upper school: 41 men, 11 women; 24 have advanced degrees.

Subjects Offered 20th century world history, 3-dimensional design, advanced chemistry, advanced computer applications, advanced math, algebra, American government, American history, American history-AP, American literature, analytic geometry, art, art appreciation, astronomy, band, Basic programming, biology, biology-AP, British literature, British literature (honors), business law, business mathematics, calculus, calculus-AP, campus ministry, Catholic belief and practice, chemistry, chemistry-AP, choral music, Christian and Hebrew scripture, Christian doctrine, Christian ethics, computer applications, computer studies, concert band, consumer law, consumer mathematics, earth science, English, English literature and composition-AP, environmental science, ethical decision making, European history, fine arts, French, freshman seminar, geography, geometry, government, government-AP, health, history of the Catholic Church, HTML design, instrumental music, jazz band, journalism, keyboarding, Latin, Life of Christ, music theory, photography, physical science, physics, physics-AP, pre-algebra, pre-calculus, probability and statistics, psychology, psychology-AP, reading/study skills, SAT/ACT preparation, Spanish, Spanish language-AP, U.S. government and politics-AP.

Graduation Requirements Algebra, American government, American history, art appreciation, biology, British literature, chemistry, church history, computer applications, English, foreign language, geometry, keyboarding, Life of Christ, physical fitness, physics, world history, world religions, 30 hours of community service with a written paper.

Special Academic Programs Advanced Placement exam preparation; honors section; independent study; study at local college for college credit; remedial reading and/or remedial writing; remedial math; programs in English, mathematics for dyslexic students.

College Admission Counseling 123 students graduated in 2012; they went to Loyola University Maryland; Mount St. Mary's University; Stevenson University; Towson University; University of Maryland, College Park; York College of Pennsylvania.

Student Life Upper grades have specified standards of dress, student council, honor system. Discipline rests primarily with faculty. Attendance at religious services is required.

Summer Programs Remediation, enrichment, advancement, sports, art/fine arts, computer instruction programs offered; held on campus; accepts boys and girls; open to students from other schools. 2013 schedule: June 15 to August 9. Application deadline: June 15.

Tuition and Aid Day student tuition: $11,500. Tuition installment plan (FACTS Tuition Payment Plan, monthly payment plans, individually arranged payment plans). Tuition reduction for siblings, merit scholarship grants, need-based scholarship grants, paying campus jobs available.

Admissions Traditional secondary-level entrance grade is 9. For fall 2012, 300 students applied for upper-level admission, 140 enrolled. High School Placement Test (closed version) from Scholastic Testing Service required. Deadline for receipt of application materials: December 31. Application fee required: $10. Interview required.

Athletics Interscholastic: baseball, basketball, cross-country running, football, golf, indoor track & field, lacrosse, soccer, tennis, track and field, volleyball, wrestling; intramural: basketball, flag football, Frisbee, handball, martial arts, touch football, weight lifting, weight training. 2 PE instructors, 32 coaches, 1 athletic trainer.

Computers Computers are regularly used in creative writing, English, graphic arts, journalism, library, photography, SAT preparation, science, technology classes. Computer network features include on-campus library services, Internet access, wireless campus network, Internet filtering or blocking technology. Student e-mail accounts are available to students. Students grades are available online. The school has a published electronic and media policy.

Contact Mr. John Tucker, Admissions Director. 410-485-5000 Ext. 289. Fax: 410-485-1090. E-mail: jtucker@archbishopcurley.org. Web site: www.archbishopcurley.org

ARCHBISHOP HOBAN HIGH SCHOOL

1 Holy Cross Boulevard
Akron, Ohio 44306

Head of School: Br. Kenneth Haders, CSC

General Information Coeducational day college-preparatory, arts, business, religious studies, technology, and family and consumer sciences school, affiliated with Roman Catholic Church. Grades 9–12. Founded: 1953. Setting: urban. 75-acre campus. 3 buildings on campus. Approved or accredited by National Catholic Education Association, North Central Association of Colleges and Schools, Ohio Catholic Schools Accreditation Association (OCSAA), and Ohio Department of Education. Endowment: $6 million. Total enrollment: 849. Upper school average class size: 23. Upper school faculty-student ratio: 1:13. There are 178 required school days per year for Upper School students. Upper School students typically attend 5 days per week. The average school day consists of 6 hours and 55 minutes.

Upper School Student Profile Grade 9: 220 students (109 boys, 111 girls); Grade 10: 215 students (110 boys, 105 girls); Grade 11: 197 students (95 boys, 102 girls); Grade 12: 216 students (96 boys, 120 girls). 82% of students are Roman Catholic.

Faculty School total: 56. In upper school: 26 men, 30 women; 48 have advanced degrees.

Subjects Offered Advanced Placement courses, advanced studio art-AP, algebra, American literature, anatomy and physiology, art, astronomy, biology, biology-AP, British literature, calculus-AP, Catholic belief and practice, ceramics, chemistry, chemistry-AP, child development, Chinese, choir, Christian and Hebrew scripture, church history, computer applications, computer graphics, conceptual physics, concert choir, desktop publishing, digital imaging, digital music, drawing, earth science, economics, electronic music, engineering, English, English literature and composition-AP, ensembles, environmental science, European history-AP, fine arts, food and nutrition, French, geometry, guitar, health education, history of the Catholic Church, honors algebra, honors English, honors geometry, honors world history, human anatomy, Italian, Latin, learning strategies, moral and social development, newspaper, orchestra, painting, philosophy, physical education, physics, physics-AP, pre-algebra, pre-calculus, printmaking, social justice, Spanish, statistics-AP, studio art, television, trigonometry, U.S. government, U.S. history, U.S. history-AP, values and decisions, Web site design, world cultures, world literature, yearbook.

Graduation Requirements Algebra, arts and fine arts (art, music, dance, drama), biology, economics, electives, English, health education, mathematics, physical education (includes health), religious studies, science, social studies (includes history), U.S. government, Christian service totaling 75 hours over four years.

Special Academic Programs 9 Advanced Placement exams for which test preparation is offered; honors section; academic accommodation for the gifted; remedial reading and/or remedial writing; remedial math.

College Admission Counseling 214 students graduated in 2011; 212 went to college, including Kent State University; Ohio University; The Ohio State University; The University of Akron; The University of Toledo; University of Dayton. Other: 1 went to work, 1 entered military service. Median SAT critical reading: 570, median SAT math: 570, median SAT writing: 560, median combined SAT: 1720, median composite ACT: 24. 44% scored over 600 on SAT critical reading, 46% scored over 600 on SAT math, 39% scored over 600 on SAT writing, 39% scored over 1800 on combined SAT, 40% scored over 26 on composite ACT.

Student Life Upper grades have specified standards of dress, student council, honor system. Discipline rests primarily with faculty. Attendance at religious services is required.

Tuition and Aid Day student tuition: $8880. Tuition installment plan (FACTS Tuition Payment Plan, individually arranged payment plans, Semester Payment Plan, Quarterly Payment Plan). Tuition reduction for siblings, merit scholarship grants, need-based scholarship grants, paying campus jobs available. In 2011–12, 40% of upper-school students received aid; total upper-school merit-scholarship money awarded: $250,000. Total amount of financial aid awarded in 2011–12: $2,200,000.

Admissions Traditional secondary-level entrance grade is 9. For fall 2011, 305 students applied for upper-level admission, 250 were accepted, 240 enrolled. High School Placement Test required. Deadline for receipt of application materials: none. No application fee required. Interview recommended.

Athletics Interscholastic: baseball (boys), basketball (b,g), bowling (b,g), cross-country running (b,g), dance team (g), football (b), golf (b,g), gymnastics (g), ice hockey (b), indoor track & field (b), lacrosse (b), soccer (b,g), softball (g), swimming and diving (b,g), tennis (b,g), track and field (b,g), volleyball (b,g), wrestling (b); intramural: flag football (g); coed interscholastic: cheering; coed intramural: basketball, strength & conditioning, ultimate Frisbee, weight training. 1 PE instructor, 1 athletic trainer.

Computers Computers are regularly used in desktop publishing, graphic design, newspaper, science, video film production, Web site design, yearbook classes. Computer network features include on-campus library services, Internet access, wireless campus network, Internet filtering or blocking technology. Campus intranet, student e-mail accounts, and computer access in designated common areas are available to students. Students grades are available online. The school has a published electronic and media policy.

Contact Mr. Christopher Fahey, Admissions Counselor. 330-773-6658 Ext. 215. Fax: 330-773-9100. E-mail: Faheyc@hoban.org. Web site: www.hoban.org

ARCHBISHOP MITTY HIGH SCHOOL

5000 Mitty Avenue
San Jose, California 95129

Head of School: Mr. Tim Brosnan

General Information Coeducational day college-preparatory, arts, religious studies, and technology school, affiliated with Roman Catholic Church. Grades 9–12. Founded: 1964. Setting: suburban. 24-acre campus. 11 buildings on campus. Approved or accredited by National Catholic Education Association, Western Association of Schools and Colleges, and California Department of Education. Endowment: $9.8 million. Total enrollment: 1,712. Upper school average class size: 27. Upper school faculty-student ratio: 1:17. There are 180 required school days per year for Upper School students. Upper School students typically attend 5 days per week. The average school day consists of 6 hours and 45 minutes.

Upper School Student Profile Grade 9: 448 students (233 boys, 215 girls); Grade 10: 464 students (216 boys, 248 girls); Grade 11: 410 students (191 boys, 219 girls); Grade 12: 390 students (178 boys, 212 girls). 75% of students are Roman Catholic.

Faculty School total: 110. In upper school: 55 men, 55 women; 70 have advanced degrees.

Subjects Offered 3-dimensional art, acting, American history-AP, American literature-AP, ancient world history, art, biology, biology-AP, British literature, calculus, calculus-AP, Catholic belief and practice, chemistry, chemistry-AP, choral music, chorus, church history, college placement, college writing, community service, computer graphics, computer multimedia, concert band, concert choir, drawing, economics and history, English, English language and composition-AP, English literature, English literature-AP, French, French language-AP, French literature-AP, French studies, French-AP, geometry, history-AP, honors algebra, honors English, honors geometry, honors U.S. history, honors world history, music, music appreciation, music theory-AP, philosophy, physics, physics-AP, political science, religion, social sciences, Spanish, Spanish language-AP, Spanish literature, Spanish literature-AP, student government, theater arts, U.S. government and politics, U.S. government and politics-AP, U.S. history, U.S. history-AP, U.S. literature, visual and performing arts, visual arts, world history.

Graduation Requirements Art, English, foreign language, mathematics, philosophy, physical education (includes health), religious studies, science, social sciences, 100 hours of Christian service.

Special Academic Programs 18 Advanced Placement exams for which test preparation is offered; honors section; study at local college for college credit; academic accommodation for the gifted, the musically talented, and the artistically talented.

College Admission Counseling 387 students graduated in 2012; all went to college, including California Polytechnic State University, San Luis Obispo; Santa Clara University; Stanford University; University of California, Berkeley; University of California, Davis; University of California, Los Angeles. Mean SAT critical reading: 602, mean SAT math: 603, mean SAT writing: 621, mean combined SAT: 1826, mean composite ACT: 26.

Student Life Upper grades have specified standards of dress, student council, honor system. Discipline rests primarily with faculty. Attendance at religious services is required.

Summer Programs Remediation, enrichment, advancement, sports, art/fine arts, computer instruction programs offered; session focuses on academics and athletics; held on campus; accepts boys and girls; open to students from other schools. 500 students usually enrolled. 2013 schedule: June 10 to July 20. Application deadline: May 31.

Tuition and Aid Day student tuition: $15,650. Tuition installment plan (SMART Tuition Payment Plan). Need-based scholarship grants, paying campus jobs available. In 2012–13, 20% of upper-school students received aid. Total amount of financial aid awarded in 2012–13: $3,000,000.

Admissions Traditional secondary-level entrance grade is 9. For fall 2012, 1,400 students applied for upper-level admission, 448 were accepted, 448 enrolled. High School Placement Test required. Deadline for receipt of application materials: December 14. Application fee required: $75.

Athletics Interscholastic: aquatics (boys, girls), badminton (b,g), baseball (b), basketball (b,g), cross-country running (b,g), dance team (g), diving (b,g), field hockey (g), football (b), golf (b,g), lacrosse (b), soccer (b,g), softball (g), swimming and diving (b,g), tennis (b,g), track and field (b,g), volleyball (b,g), water polo (b,g); weight training (b,g), winter soccer (b,g); intramural: roller hockey (b,g); coed interscholastic: physical fitness, strength & conditioning, wrestling; coed intramural: basketball, ice hockey, in-line hockey, table tennis. 4 PE instructors, 110 coaches, 2 athletic trainers.

Computers Computers are regularly used in all classes. Computer network features include on-campus library services, online commercial services, Internet access, wireless campus network, Internet filtering or blocking technology. Campus intranet, student e-mail accounts, and computer access in designated common areas are available to students. Students grades are available online. The school has a published electronic and media policy.

Contact Mrs. Lori Robowski, Assistant for Admissions. 408-342-4300. Fax: 408-342-4308. E-mail: admissions@mitty.com. Web site: www.mitty.com/

ARCHBISHOP RUMMEL HIGH SCHOOL

1901 Severn Avenue
Metairie, Louisiana 70001-2893

Head of School: Mr. Michael Scalco

General Information Boys' day college-preparatory, arts, religious studies, and technology school, affiliated with Roman Catholic Church. Grades 8–12. Founded: 1962. Setting: suburban. Nearest major city is New Orleans. 20-acre campus. 10 buildings on campus. Approved or accredited by Association for Experiential Education, National Catholic Education Association, Southern Association of Colleges and Schools, and Louisiana Department of Education. Total enrollment: 815. Upper school average class size: 27. Upper school faculty-student ratio: 1:14. There are 181 required school days per year for Upper School students. Upper School students typically attend 5 days per week. The average school day consists of 7 hours.

Upper School Student Profile Grade 8: 121 students (121 boys); Grade 9: 174 students (174 boys); Grade 10: 172 students (172 boys); Grade 11: 162 students (162 boys); Grade 12: 186 students (186 boys). 90% of students are Roman Catholic.

Faculty School total: 57. In upper school: 30 men, 27 women; 7 have advanced degrees.

Subjects Offered ACT preparation, advanced biology, advanced chemistry, advanced computer applications, advanced math, advanced studio art-AP, algebra, American government, American history, American history-AP, American literature, American literature-AP, anatomy, anatomy and physiology, ancient world history, art, art appreciation, art-AP, band, biology, British literature, British literature (honors), British literature-AP, calculus, calculus-AP, campus ministry, Catholic belief and practice, ceramics, chemistry, chemistry-AP, civics, computer applications, computer literacy, computer science, creative writing, economics, English, English language and composition-AP, English literature, English literature and composition-AP, environmental science, European history, European literature, fine arts, French, geography, geometry, government-AP, health education, history of the Catholic Church, honors algebra, honors English, honors geometry, honors U.S. history, honors world history, human anatomy, instrumental music, language arts, Latin, moral theology, physics, psychology, reading, sociology, Spanish, Spanish literature, speech, statistics-AP, street law, studio art, studio art-AP, U.S. government and politics-AP, U.S. history, U.S. history-AP, U.S. literature, United States government-AP, Web site design, Western civilization, world geography.

Graduation Requirements ACT preparation, advanced math, American history, art appreciation, biology, Catholic belief and practice, chemistry, civics, computer applications, computer literacy, computer science, English, environmental science, foreign language, geography, health education, history of the Catholic Church, physical education (includes health), physical science, physics, reading, U.S. history, Western civilization, world geography.

Special Academic Programs Advanced Placement exam preparation; honors section; programs in general development for dyslexic students.

College Admission Counseling 210 students graduated in 2011; 200 went to college, including Louisiana State University and Agricultural and Mechanical College; Loyola University New Orleans; Nicholls State University; University of Louisiana at Lafayette; University of New Orleans. Other: 2 entered military service.

Student Life Upper grades have uniform requirement, student council, honor system. Discipline rests primarily with faculty. Attendance at religious services is required.

Tuition and Aid Day student tuition: $7150. Tuition installment plan (monthly payment plans). Merit scholarship grants, need-based scholarship grants, paying campus jobs available. In 2011–12, 20% of upper-school students received aid.

Admissions High School Placement Test required. Deadline for receipt of application materials: January 8. Application fee required: $20. Interview required.

Athletics Interscholastic: baseball, basketball, bowling, cheering, cross-country running, field hockey, football, Frisbee, golf, hockey, in-line hockey, jogging, power lifting, rugby, soccer, strength & conditioning, swimming and diving, tennis, track and field, whiffle ball, wrestling; intramural: flag football. 10 PE instructors, 25 coaches, 2 athletic trainers.

Computers Computers are regularly used in computer applications, creative writing, English, multimedia, programming, reading, science classes. Computer resources include on-campus library services, Internet access, Internet filtering or blocking technology. Students grades are available online. The school has a published electronic and media policy.

Contact Joseph A. Serio, Director of Communications. 504-834-5592 Ext. 263. Fax: 504-833-2232. E-mail: jserio@rummelraiders.com. Web site: www.rummelraiders.com

ARENDELL PARROTT ACADEMY

PO Box 1297
Kinston, North Carolina 28503-1297

Head of School: Mr. Peter Cowen

General Information Coeducational day college-preparatory school. Grades PK–12. Founded: 1964. Setting: small town. 80-acre campus. 6 buildings on campus. Approved or accredited by Southern Association of Colleges and Schools and North Carolina Department of Education. Total enrollment: 788. Upper school average class size: 18. There are 178 required school days per year for Upper School students. Upper School students typically attend 5 days per week. The average school day consists of 6 hours and 20 minutes.

Faculty School total: 60. In upper school: 10 men, 21 women; 20 have advanced degrees.

Special Academic Programs Advanced Placement exam preparation; honors section; study at local college for college credit.

College Admission Counseling 54 students graduated in 2011; all went to college. Mean SAT critical reading: 611, mean SAT math: 600, mean SAT writing: 602, mean combined SAT: 1813.

Student Life Upper grades have specified standards of dress, student council, honor system. Discipline rests primarily with faculty.

Tuition and Aid Day student tuition: $9500. Tuition installment plan (monthly payment plans, individually arranged payment plans). Need-based scholarship grants available. In 2011–12, 17% of upper-school students received aid. Total amount of financial aid awarded in 2011–12: $260,000.

Admissions Traditional secondary-level entrance grade is 9. Deadline for receipt of application materials: none. Application fee required: $550. Interview required.

Athletics Interscholastic: baseball (boys), basketball (b,g), canoeing/kayaking (g), cross-country running (b,g), dance squad (g), field hockey (g), football (b), lacrosse (b), soccer (b,g), softball (g), swimming and diving (b,g), tennis (b,g), volleyball (g); coed interscholastic: dance, fitness, golf, physical fitness, physical training, strength & conditioning.

Computers Computer network features include on-campus library services, Internet access, wireless campus network, Internet filtering or blocking technology. Computer access in designated common areas is available to students. Students grades are available online. The school has a published electronic and media policy.

Contact Julie Rogers, Director of Admissions. 252-522-0410 Ext. 202. Fax: 919-522-0672. E-mail: jrogers@parrottacademy.org. Web site: www.parrottacademy.org

ARMBRAE ACADEMY

1400 Oxford Street
Halifax, Nova Scotia B3H 3Y8, Canada

Head of School: Gary D. O'Meara

General Information Coeducational day college-preparatory school. Grades K–12. Founded: 1887. Setting: urban. 2-acre campus. 3 buildings on campus. Approved or accredited by Canadian Association of Independent Schools, Canadian Educational Standards Institute, and Nova Scotia Department of Education. Language of instruction: English. Endowment: CAN$1 million. Total enrollment: 258. Upper school average class size: 22. Upper school faculty-student ratio: 1:9. There are 185 required school days per year for Upper School students. Upper School students typically attend 5 days per week. The average school day consists of 5 hours and 30 minutes.

Faculty School total: 35. In upper school: 5 men, 8 women; 5 have advanced degrees.

Subjects Offered Algebra, American history, art, biology, calculus, chemistry, computer science, earth science, economics, English, English literature, European history, French, geography, geology, geometry, government/civics, grammar, health, history, keyboarding, Mandarin, mathematics, music, physical education, physics, science, social studies, study skills, trigonometry, world literature, writing.

Graduation Requirements Computer science, English, foreign language, mathematics, physical education (includes health), science, social studies (includes history), 6 courses each in grades 11 and 12.

Special Academic Programs Advanced Placement exam preparation; accelerated programs; study at local college for college credit; academic accommodation for the artistically talented.

College Admission Counseling 20 students graduated in 2011; they went to Acadia University; Carleton University; Dalhousie University; McGill University; Queen's University at Kingston; St. Francis Xavier University.

Student Life Upper grades have uniform requirement, student council. Discipline rests equally with students and faculty.

Tuition and Aid Day student tuition: CAN$11,870. Tuition installment plan (monthly payment plans, term payment plan). Tuition reduction for siblings, bursaries, merit scholarship grants available. In 2011–12, 4% of upper-school students received aid; total upper-school merit-scholarship money awarded: CAN$2000. Total amount of financial aid awarded in 2011–12: CAN$60,000.

Admissions Traditional secondary-level entrance grade is 10. For fall 2011, 25 students applied for upper-level admission, 22 were accepted, 15 enrolled. CTBS (or similar from their school) required. Deadline for receipt of application materials: none. Application fee required: CAN$150. On-campus interview required.

Athletics Interscholastic: badminton (boys, girls), basketball (b,g), cross-country running (b,g), field hockey (g), ice hockey (b), soccer (b,g), swimming and diving (b,g), tennis (b,g), track and field (b,g), volleyball (b,g); intramural: badminton (b,g), cross-country running (b,g); coed interscholastic: curling, ice hockey; coed intramural: ice hockey. 2 PE instructors, 4 coaches.

Computers Computers are regularly used in all classes. Computer network features include on-campus library services, online commercial services, Internet access, wireless campus network. Campus intranet and student e-mail accounts are available to students. Students grades are available online. The school has a published electronic and media policy.

Contact Gary D. O'Meara, Headmaster. 902-423-7920. Fax: 902-423-9731. E-mail: head@armbrae.ns.ca. Web site: www.armbrae.ns.ca

ARMONA UNION ACADEMY

14435 Locust Street
PO Box 397
Armona, California 93202

Head of School: Mr. Erik Borges

General Information Coeducational day college-preparatory, general academic, and religious studies school, affiliated with Seventh-day Adventists. Grades K–12. Founded: 1904. Setting: small town. Nearest major city is Fresno. 20-acre campus. 5 buildings on campus. Approved or accredited by Western Association of Schools and Colleges and California Department of Education. Member of Secondary School Admission Test Board. Endowment: $98,000. Total enrollment: 138. Upper school average class size: 15. Upper school faculty-student ratio: 1:10. There are 180 required school days per year for Upper School students. Upper School students typically attend 5 days per week. The average school day consists of 7 hours and 45 minutes.

Upper School Student Profile 85% of students are Seventh-day Adventists.

Faculty School total: 13. In upper school: 5 men, 1 woman; 3 have advanced degrees.

Subjects Offered Algebra, American history, American literature, art, Bible studies, biology, chemistry, choir, community service, computer science, economics, English, English literature, geometry, government, mathematics, physical education, physical science, physics, religion, science, Spanish, world history, world literature, yearbook.

Graduation Requirements Arts and fine arts (art, music, dance, drama), business skills (includes word processing), computer science, English, foreign language, mathematics, physical education (includes health), religion (includes Bible studies and theology), science, social sciences, social studies (includes history). Community service is required.

Special Academic Programs Study at local college for college credit.

College Admission Counseling 11 students graduated in 2011; 9 went to college, including La Sierra University; Southern Adventist University; West Hills Community College. Other: 1 went to work, 1 entered military service.

Student Life Upper grades have specified standards of dress, student council. Discipline rests primarily with faculty. Attendance at religious services is required.

Tuition and Aid Day student tuition: $5140. Guaranteed tuition plan. Tuition installment plan (monthly payment plans, individually arranged payment plans). Tuition reduction for siblings, need-based scholarship grants available. In 2011–12, 60% of upper-school students received aid. Total amount of financial aid awarded in 2011–12: $50,000.

Admissions Traditional secondary-level entrance grade is 9. For fall 2011, 11 students applied for upper-level admission, 7 were accepted, 7 enrolled. Deadline for receipt of application materials: August 15. Application fee required: $75. Interview required.

Athletics Interscholastic: basketball (boys, girls), flag football (b,g), football (b,g), volleyball (b,g); intramural: basketball (b,g), flag football (b,g); coed interscholastic: baseball, outdoor education, soccer, softball, track and field; coed intramural: baseball, outdoor education, paddle tennis, soccer, softball, table tennis, track and field, volleyball.

Computers Computers are regularly used in English, history, mathematics, science, yearbook classes. Computer network features include on-campus library services, online commercial services, Internet access, wireless campus network, Internet filtering or blocking technology. Students grades are available online. The school has a published electronic and media policy.

Contact Mrs. Aniesha Kleinhammer, Registrar. 559-582-4468 Ext. 10. Fax: 559-582-6609. E-mail: auaregistrar@gmail.com. Web site: www.auaweb.com

ARMY AND NAVY ACADEMY

2605 Carlsbad Boulevard
PO Box 3000
Carlsbad, California 92018-3000

Head of School: Brig. Gen. Stephen M. Bliss, Retd.

General Information Boys' boarding and day college-preparatory, Junior ROTC, and military school. Grades 7–12. Founded: 1910. Setting: small town. Nearest major city is San Diego. Students are housed in single-sex dormitories. 16-acre campus. 34

buildings on campus. Approved or accredited by California Association of Independent Schools and Western Association of Schools and Colleges. Member of National Association of Independent Schools and Secondary School Admission Test Board. Endowment: $517,767. Total enrollment: 307. Upper school average class size: 15. Upper school faculty-student ratio: 1:15. There are 180 required school days per year for Upper School students. Upper School students typically attend 5 days per week. The average school day consists of 6 hours and 45 minutes.

Upper School Student Profile Grade 10: 75 students (75 boys); Grade 11: 74 students (74 boys); Grade 12: 84 students (84 boys). 90% of students are boarding students. 67% are state residents. 15 states are represented in upper school student body. 30% are international students. International students from China, Malaysia, Mexico, Russian Federation, Taiwan, and Viet Nam; 10 other countries represented in student body.

Faculty School total: 30. In upper school: 16 men, 14 women; 15 have advanced degrees.

Subjects Offered Advanced studio art-AP, algebra, art, biology, biology-AP, calculus-AP, chemistry, chemistry-AP, composition-AP, drama, economics, English, English literature-AP, English-AP, ESL, European history-AP, French, French-AP, geography, geometry, guitar, independent study, JROTC, marching band, media studies, music appreciation, music technology, photography, physical education, physics, physics-AP, pre-calculus, psychology-AP, Spanish, Spanish-AP, statistics-AP, studio art-AP, study skills, U.S. government, U.S. history, U.S. history-AP, video film production, weight training, world history, yearbook.

Graduation Requirements Arts and fine arts (art, music, dance, drama), electives, English, foreign language, lab science, leadership education training, mathematics, physical education (includes health), social studies (includes history).

Special Academic Programs 8 Advanced Placement exams for which test preparation is offered; honors section; independent study; special instructional classes for students with Attention Deficit Disorder and learning disabilities; ESL (30 students enrolled).

College Admission Counseling 61 students graduated in 2012; 56 went to college, including Montana State University; The University of Arizona; University of California, Irvine; University of California, Los Angeles; University of Colorado Boulder; University of San Diego. Other: 1 entered military service, 4 had other specific plans. Mean SAT critical reading: 453, mean SAT math: 491, mean SAT writing: 432. 8.8% scored over 600 on SAT critical reading, 21.5% scored over 600 on SAT math, 7.5% scored over 600 on SAT writing, 18.8% scored over 26 on composite ACT.

Student Life Upper grades have uniform requirement, student council, honor system. Discipline rests primarily with faculty.

Summer Programs Remediation, enrichment, ESL, sports, art/fine arts, rigorous outdoor training, computer instruction programs offered; session focuses on academic, JROTC leadership, and recreation; held on campus; accepts boys and girls; open to students from other schools. 300 students usually enrolled. 2013 schedule: June 30 to August 4. Application deadline: none.

Tuition and Aid Day student tuition: $19,500; 7-day tuition and room/board: $32,850. Tuition installment plan (individually arranged payment plans). Tuition reduction for siblings, need-based scholarship grants, military discount available. In 2012–13, 22% of upper-school students received aid. Total amount of financial aid awarded in 2012–13: $575,000.

Admissions Traditional secondary-level entrance grade is 10. For fall 2012, 124 students applied for upper-level admission, 69 were accepted, 64 enrolled. ISEE, Otis-Lennon School Ability Test, SSAT, Star-9 or TOEFL required. Deadline for receipt of application materials: none. Application fee required: $100. Interview required.

Athletics Interscholastic: aquatics, baseball, basketball, cross-country running, drill team, football, golf, in-line hockey, marksmanship, riflery, soccer, surfing, swimming and diving, tennis, track and field, water polo, weight lifting, wrestling; intramural: aquatics, combined training, fitness, hockey, independent competitive sports, JROTC drill, outdoor activities, outdoor recreation, physical fitness, physical training, strength & conditioning, surfing. 15 coaches, 1 athletic trainer.

Computers Computers are regularly used in media, music technology, video film production, yearbook classes. Computer network features include on-campus library services, Internet access, wireless campus network, Internet filtering or blocking technology. Computer access in designated common areas is available to students. Students grades are available online. The school has a published electronic and media policy.

Contact Candice Heidenrich, Director of Admissions. 888-762-2338. Fax: 760-434-5948. E-mail: admissions@armyandnavyacademy.org. Web site: www.armyandnavyacademy.org

ARROWSMITH SCHOOL

Toronto, Ontario, Canada

See Special Needs Schools section.

ARROYO PACIFIC ACADEMY

41 West Santa Clara Street
Arcadia, California 91007-0661

Head of School: Philip Clarke

General Information Coeducational day college-preparatory and arts school. Grades 9–12. Founded: 1998. Setting: suburban. 2 buildings on campus. Approved or accredited by Western Association of Schools and Colleges and California Department of Education. Upper school average class size: 12. Upper school faculty-student ratio: 1:8. There are 160 required school days per year for Upper School students. Upper School students typically attend 5 days per week. The average school day consists of 6 hours.

Faculty School total: 22. In upper school: 13 men, 9 women.

Subjects Offered Acting, advanced biology, advanced chemistry, advanced math, Advanced Placement courses, algebra, American government, American history, American history-AP, American literature, American literature-AP, American sign language, applied arts, applied music, art, ASB Leadership, athletics, basketball, biology-AP, British literature, broadcast journalism, broadcasting, business, business mathematics, calculus-AP, career and personal planning, career/college preparation, chemistry, chemistry-AP, China/Japan history, Chinese, Chinese history, Chinese literature, Chinese studies, choir, chorus, cinematography, classical music, college admission preparation, college counseling, college planning, college writing, computer art, computer education, computer graphics, computer music, computer skills, computer technologies, conceptual physics, creative arts, creative dance, creative drama, creative thinking, creative writing, culinary arts, dance, dance performance, digital art, digital music, drama, drama performance, dramatic arts, drawing, earth science, economics-AP, English, English language and composition-AP, English language-AP, English literature and composition-AP, English literature-AP, English-AP, environmental science, environmental science-AP, film, filmmaking, fine arts, fitness, food and nutrition, foreign language, forensics, geometry, government-AP, graphic design, health education, history, history of music, history-AP, instrumental music, instruments, intro to computers, introduction to digital multitrack recording techniques, introduction to technology, introduction to theater, jazz, jazz band, jazz ensemble, lab science, lab/keyboard, literature and composition-AP, macro/microeconomics-AP, Mandarin, mathematics-AP, media, media arts, media communications, media production, microeconomics-AP, modern Chinese history, music, music appreciation, music composition, music history, music performance, music technology, music theater, musical productions, musical theater, musical theater dance, nutrition, orchestra, outdoor education, participation in sports, personal finance, personal fitness, personal money management, photo shop, photography, photojournalism, physical education, physical fitness, physics, physics-AP, play production, play/screen writing, playwriting, playwriting and directing, poetry, pre-algebra, pre-calculus, psychology, SAT preparation, scene study, science, science and technology, sign language, Spanish, Spanish language-AP, Spanish-AP, stage and body movement, stage design, statistics, statistics-AP, student government, theater, theater arts, theater design and production, theater production, trigonometry, U.S. government, U.S. government and politics, U.S. government and politics-AP, U.S. history, U.S. history-AP, United States government-AP, video film production, visual and performing arts, visual arts, vocal ensemble, vocal music, voice, volleyball, world history, world history-AP.

Special Academic Programs 11 Advanced Placement exams for which test preparation is offered; independent study.

College Admission Counseling 50 students graduated in 2012; they went to Kent State University; University of California, Irvine; University of Southern California.

Student Life Upper grades have specified standards of dress, student council, honor system. Discipline rests primarily with faculty.

Summer Programs Remediation, enrichment, advancement, art/fine arts programs offered; held on campus; accepts boys and girls; open to students from other schools. 80 students usually enrolled. 2013 schedule: June 17 to July 23. Application deadline: June 7.

Tuition and Aid Day student tuition: $14,500. Tuition installment plan (FACTS Tuition Payment Plan).

Admissions Deadline for receipt of application materials: none. Application fee required: $150. Interview required.

Athletics Interscholastic: basketball (boys), flag football (b), rugby (b); intramural: cheering (g); coed interscholastic: soccer, tennis, track and field; coed intramural: aerobics, aerobics/dance, backpacking, dance, dance squad, dance team, fitness, hiking/backpacking, outdoor skills, outdoors, physical fitness.

Computers Computers are regularly used in all classes. Computer resources include Internet access, advanced photo/video design software. Campus intranet and computer access in designated common areas are available to students.

Contact Aling Zhang, Admissions Coordinator. 626-294-0661. E-mail: azhang@arroyopacific.org. Web site: www.arroyopacific.org/

ARTHUR MORGAN SCHOOL

Burnsville, North Carolina

See Junior Boarding Schools section.

ASSETS SCHOOL

Honolulu, Hawaii
See Special Needs Schools section.

THE ATHENIAN SCHOOL

2100 Mount Diablo Scenic Boulevard
Danville, California 94506

Head of School: Eric Feron Niles

General Information Coeducational boarding and day college-preparatory school. Boarding grades 9–12, day grades 6–12. Founded: 1965. Setting: suburban. Nearest major city is San Francisco. Students are housed in single-sex dormitories. 75-acre campus. 25 buildings on campus. Approved or accredited by California Association of Independent Schools, The Association of Boarding Schools, The College Board, Western Association of Schools and Colleges, and California Department of Education. Member of National Association of Independent Schools and Secondary School Admission Test Board. Endowment: $8 million. Total enrollment: 471. Upper school average class size: 15. Upper school faculty-student ratio: 1:10. Upper School students typically attend 5 days per week. The average school day consists of 5 hours and 35 minutes.

Upper School Student Profile Grade 9: 71 students (37 boys, 34 girls); Grade 10: 78 students (35 boys, 43 girls); Grade 11: 79 students (42 boys, 37 girls); Grade 12: 76 students (36 boys, 40 girls). 14% of students are boarding students. 90% are state residents. 1 state is represented in upper school student body. 13% are international students. International students from China, Japan, Republic of Korea, Russian Federation, Taiwan, and Viet Nam; 7 other countries represented in student body.

Faculty School total: 55. In upper school: 27 men, 24 women; 37 have advanced degrees; 20 reside on campus.

Subjects Offered African-American studies, algebra, American history, American literature, American literature-AP, anatomy, art, art history, Asian history, Asian literature, biology, calculus-AP, ceramics, chemistry, classical studies, college writing, community service, comparative cultures, comparative religion, computer programming, computer science, computer skills, contemporary history, creative writing, dance, dance performance, debate, drama, drama performance, drama workshop, drawing, earth science, ecology, economics, economics and history, English, English as a foreign language, English literature, English-AP, environmental studies, ESL, ethics, European history, European history-AP, expository writing, fencing, fine arts, French, French-AP, geography, geology, geometry, government/civics, graphic design, health, history, humanities, introduction to technology, jazz band, jewelry making, literary magazine, literature seminar, literature-AP, mathematics, modern European history-AP, music, music history, music performance, musical theater, painting, philosophy, photography, physical education, physics, science, science project, sculpture, sociology, Spanish, Spanish literature-AP, Spanish-AP, stained glass, statistics, statistics-AP, theater, theater design and production, trigonometry, U.S. history-AP, wilderness experience, world cultures, world history, world literature, writing, yearbook, yoga.

Graduation Requirements American history, arts and fine arts (art, music, dance, drama), English, foreign language, history, literature, mathematics, physical education (includes health), science, wilderness experience, world history. Community service is required.

Special Academic Programs Advanced Placement exam preparation; honors section; independent study; term-away projects; study at local college for college credit; domestic exchange program; study abroad; ESL (8 students enrolled).

College Admission Counseling 76 students graduated in 2012; 75 went to college, including Chapman University; Drexel University; New York University; University of California, Berkeley; University of California, Davis; University of California, Los Angeles. Other: 1 went to work. Median SAT critical reading: 610, median SAT math: 640, median SAT writing: 630, median combined SAT: 1890. 55% scored over 600 on SAT critical reading, 74% scored over 600 on SAT math, 66% scored over 600 on SAT writing, 62% scored over 1800 on combined SAT.

Student Life Upper grades have specified standards of dress, student council. Discipline rests equally with students and faculty.

Summer Programs Enrichment, advancement, ESL, sports, art/fine arts, computer instruction programs offered; session focuses on academic enrichment, sports, and ESL; held on campus; accepts boys and girls; open to students from other schools. 200 students usually enrolled. 2013 schedule: June 13 to August 3. Application deadline: none.

Tuition and Aid Day student tuition: $31,950; 5-day tuition and room/board: $50,800; 7-day tuition and room/board: $50,800. Tuition installment plan (Insured Tuition Payment Plan, monthly payment plans). Need-based scholarship grants available. In 2012–13, 22% of upper-school students received aid. Total amount of financial aid awarded in 2012–13: $2,002,000.

Admissions Traditional secondary-level entrance grade is 9. For fall 2012, 514 students applied for upper-level admission, 122 were accepted, 51 enrolled. International English Language Test, ISEE, SSAT or TOEFL required. Deadline for receipt of application materials: January 12. Application fee required: $75. Interview required.

Athletics Interscholastic: baseball (boys), basketball (b,g), cross-country running (b,g), golf (b), soccer (b,g), softball (g), swimming and diving (b,g), tennis (b,g); coed interscholastic: volleyball, wrestling; coed intramural: basketball, climbing, cross-country running, dance, fencing, weight training, yoga. 12 coaches.

Computers Computers are regularly used in English, foreign language, graphic design, history, humanities, information technology, library science, literary magazine, mathematics, publications, science, yearbook classes. Computer network features include on-campus library services, online commercial services, Internet access, wireless campus network, Internet filtering or blocking technology. Campus intranet, student e-mail accounts, and computer access in designated common areas are available to students. Students grades are available online. The school has a published electronic and media policy.

Contact Beverly Gomer, Associate Director of Admission. 925-362-7223. Fax: 925-362-7228. E-mail: bgomer@athenian.org. Web site: www.athenian.org

See Display on next page and Close-Up on page 544.

ATLANTA INTERNATIONAL SCHOOL

2890 North Fulton Drive
Atlanta, Georgia 30305

Head of School: Mr. Kevin Glass

General Information Coeducational day college-preparatory, bilingual studies, and International Baccalaureate school. Grades PK–12. Founded: 1984. Setting: urban. 10-acre campus. 4 buildings on campus. Approved or accredited by French Ministry of Education, Georgia Independent School Association, International Baccalaureate Organization, National Independent Private Schools Association, Southern Association of Colleges and Schools, Southern Association of Independent Schools, and Georgia Department of Education. Member of National Association of Independent Schools and European Council of International Schools. Endowment: $7.3 million. Total enrollment: 934. Upper school average class size: 16. Upper school faculty-student ratio: 1:8. Upper School students typically attend 5 days per week. The average school day consists of 6 hours and 30 minutes.

Upper School Student Profile Grade 9: 66 students (42 boys, 24 girls); Grade 10: 70 students (33 boys, 37 girls); Grade 11: 76 students (39 boys, 37 girls); Grade 12: 65 students (24 boys, 41 girls).

Faculty School total: 134.

Subjects Offered American history, art, biology, chemistry, Chinese, choir, chorus, computer science, contemporary issues, economics, English, English literature, ESL, fine arts, French, French as a second language, geography, German, health, integrated mathematics, International Baccalaureate courses, jazz band, lab/keyboard, Latin, math methods, mathematics, model United Nations, physical education, physics, SAT preparation, science, science and technology, social studies, Spanish, theater, theater arts, theory of knowledge, world history, yearbook.

Graduation Requirements Arts and fine arts (art, music, dance, drama), English, foreign language, mathematics, physical education (includes health), science, social studies (includes history), theory of knowledge, extended essay/research project. Community service is required.

Special Academic Programs International Baccalaureate program; independent study; term-away projects; study abroad; ESL (45 students enrolled).

College Admission Counseling 73 students graduated in 2011; 72 went to college, including Emory University; Georgetown University; Georgia Institute of Technology; McGill University; New York University; University of Georgia. Other: 1 had other specific plans. Mean SAT critical reading: 650, mean SAT math: 627.

Student Life Upper grades have specified standards of dress, student council. Discipline rests primarily with faculty.

Tuition and Aid Day student tuition: $18,092–$20,640. Tuition installment plan (Insured Tuition Payment Plan). Need-based scholarship grants available. In 2011–12, 14% of upper-school students received aid.

Admissions Traditional secondary-level entrance grade is 9. For fall 2011, 57 students applied for upper-level admission, 47 were accepted, 31 enrolled. Deadline for receipt of application materials: none. Application fee required: $100. Interview recommended.

Athletics Interscholastic: baseball (boys), basketball (b,g), cross-country running (b,g), soccer (b,g), swimming and diving (b,g), tennis (b,g), track and field (b,g), volleyball (g); intramural: strength & conditioning (b,g), track and field (b,g); coed intramural: basketball, fitness, jogging, volleyball. 9 PE instructors, 7 coaches, 3 athletic trainers.

Computers Computers are regularly used in all academic classes. Computer network features include Internet access, Internet filtering or blocking technology, server space for file storage, online classroom, multi-user learning software. Student e-mail accounts and computer access in designated common areas are available to students. Students grades are available online. The school has a published electronic and media policy.

Contact Ms. Charlotte Smith, Associate Director of Admission and Financial Aid. 404-841-3891. Fax: 404-841-3873. E-mail: csmith@aischool.org. Web site: www.aischool.org

ATLANTIS ACADEMY

Miami, Florida
See Special Needs Schools section.

AUGUSTA CHRISTIAN SCHOOL (I)

313 Baston Road
Martinez, Georgia 30907

Head of School: Dr. David M. Piccolo

General Information Coeducational day college-preparatory, arts, religious studies, and technology school. Grades K–12. Founded: 1958. Setting: suburban. Nearest major city is Augusta. 26-acre campus. 10 buildings on campus. Approved or accredited by Association of Christian Schools International, South Carolina Independent School Association, Southern Association of Colleges and Schools, and Georgia Department of Education. Total enrollment: 572. Upper school average class size: 18. Upper school faculty-student ratio: 1:10. There are 180 required school days per year for Upper School students. Upper School students typically attend 5 days per week. The average school day consists of 7 hours and 5 minutes.

Upper School Student Profile Grade 9: 56 students (30 boys, 26 girls); Grade 10: 64 students (34 boys, 30 girls); Grade 11: 69 students (37 boys, 32 girls); Grade 12: 60 students (33 boys, 27 girls).

Faculty School total: 55. In upper school: 13 men, 13 women; 3 have advanced degrees.

Subjects Offered Advanced chemistry, advanced computer applications, advanced math, Advanced Placement courses, algebra, American government, American history, American history-AP, American literature, anatomy and physiology, art, athletic training, athletics, band, baseball, basketball, Bible, Bible studies, biology, biology-AP, British literature, British literature-AP, calculus-AP, ceramics, cheerleading, chemistry, choir, choral music, chorus, Christian education, Christian studies, college counseling, comparative religion, computer education, computer skills, drama, drama performance, earth science, ecology, economics and history, electives, English, English composition, English literature, English literature-AP, English-AP, European history, French, general science, geography, geometry, government, grammar, health, health science, history, instrumental music, keyboarding, life skills, mathematics, mathematics-AP, music appreciation, musical productions, New Testament, physics, piano, pre-algebra, pre-calculus, public speaking, reading, remedial/makeup course work, SAT preparation, science, social studies, Spanish, speech, sports, state history, student government, swimming, U.S. government, U.S. history, U.S. history-AP, U.S. literature, volleyball, weight training, weightlifting, world history, wrestling, yearbook.

Graduation Requirements Bible, computers, electives, English, foreign language, mathematics, physical education (includes health), science, social studies (includes history), speech.

Special Academic Programs Advanced Placement exam preparation; honors section; study at local college for college credit; programs in English, mathematics for dyslexic students; ESL (14 students enrolled).

College Admission Counseling 67 students graduated in 2012; all went to college, including Augusta State University; Georgia Institute of Technology; Georgia Southern University; University of Georgia.

Student Life Upper grades have specified standards of dress, student council. Discipline rests primarily with faculty. Attendance at religious services is required.

Summer Programs Remediation programs offered; session focuses on academics; held on campus; accepts boys and girls; open to students from other schools.

Tuition and Aid Day student tuition: $1000–$12,300. Tuition installment plan (Insured Tuition Payment Plan, monthly payment plans, individually arranged payment plans). Tuition reduction for siblings, need-based scholarship grants available.

Admissions Traditional secondary-level entrance grade is 9. Stanford Achievement Test required. Deadline for receipt of application materials: none. Application fee required: $100. Interview required.

Athletics Interscholastic: baseball (boys), basketball (b,g), cheering (g), cross-country running (b,g), football (b), soccer (b,g), softball (g), swimming and diving (b,g), tennis (b,g), track and field (b,g), volleyball (g), wrestling (b); coed interscholastic: golf. 3 PE instructors.

Computers Computers are regularly used in computer applications, keyboarding, yearbook classes. Computer network features include on-campus library services, Internet access, wireless campus network, Internet filtering or blocking technology. Campus intranet is available to students. Students grades are available online. The school has a published electronic and media policy.

Contact Mrs. Lauren Banks, Director of Admissions. 706-863-2905 Ext. 111. Fax: 706-860-6618. E-mail: laurenbanks@augustachristian.org. Web site: www.augustachristian.org

AUGUSTA PREPARATORY DAY SCHOOL

285 Flowing Wells Road
Martinez, Georgia 30907

Head of School: Becky Gilmore

General Information Coeducational day college-preparatory school. Grades PS–12. Founded: 1960. Setting: suburban. Nearest major city is Augusta. 52-acre campus. 6 buildings on campus. Approved or accredited by Georgia Independent School Association, Southern Association of Colleges and Schools, and Southern Association of Independent Schools. Member of National Association of Independent Schools and Secondary School Admission Test Board. Endowment: $4 million. Total enrollment: 528. Upper school average class size: 11. Upper school faculty-student ratio: 1:9. There are 180 required school days per year for Upper School students. Upper School students typically attend 5 days per week. The average school day consists of 7 hours and 15 minutes.

Upper School Student Profile Grade 9: 43 students (21 boys, 22 girls); Grade 10: 66 students (33 boys, 33 girls); Grade 11: 51 students (25 boys, 26 girls); Grade 12: 48 students (24 boys, 24 girls).

Faculty School total: 65. In upper school: 15 men, 10 women; 18 have advanced degrees.

Subjects Offered 20th century world history, Advanced Placement courses, advanced studio art-AP, algebra, American history, American literature, art, biology, biology-AP, calculus, calculus-AP, chemistry, chemistry-AP, computer programming, debate, drama, ecology, economics, English, English literature, English literature-AP, European history-AP, French, French-AP, geometry, government, government/civics, grammar, Latin, Latin-AP, marine science, physics, pre-calculus, Russian, senior project, Spanish, Spanish-AP, statistics-AP, studio art-AP, theater design and production, U.S. history-AP, world history, zoology.

Graduation Requirements American government, American history, arts and fine arts (art, music, dance, drama), English, foreign language, mathematics, science, social studies (includes history).

Special Academic Programs Honors section; independent study; term-away projects; academic accommodation for the gifted.

College Admission Counseling 54 students graduated in 2012; all went to college, including Augusta State University; College of Charleston; Furman University; Georgia Institute of Technology; Mercer University; University of Georgia. Median SAT critical reading: 602, median SAT math: 602, median SAT writing: 603, median combined SAT: 1807, median composite ACT: 27. 50% scored over 600 on SAT critical reading, 50% scored over 600 on SAT math, 50% scored over 600 on SAT writing, 50% scored over 1800 on combined SAT, 50% scored over 26 on composite ACT.

Student Life Upper grades have specified standards of dress, student council, honor system. Discipline rests equally with students and faculty.

Summer Programs Enrichment, sports, art/fine arts programs offered; session focuses on enrichment/sports; held on campus; accepts boys and girls; open to students from other schools. 2013 schedule: June 6 to August 1.

Admissions Traditional secondary-level entrance grade is 9. For fall 2012, 25 students applied for upper-level admission, 24 were accepted, 20 enrolled. ERB CTP III required. Deadline for receipt of application materials: none. No application fee required.

Athletics Interscholastic: aquatics (boys, girls), baseball (b), basketball (b,g), cheering (g), cross-country running (b,g), fitness (b,g), football (b), golf (b), physical training (b,g), volleyball (g). 3 PE instructors, 1 athletic trainer.

Computers Computer network features include on-campus library services, online commercial services, Internet access, wireless campus network, Internet filtering or blocking technology. Campus intranet and computer access in designated common areas are available to students. Students grades are available online. The school has a published electronic and media policy.

Contact Rosie Herrmann, Director of Admission. 706-863-1906 Ext. 201. Fax: 706-863-6198. E-mail: admissions@augustaprep.org. Web site: www.augustaprep.org

AULDERN ACADEMY

990 Glovers Grove Church Road
Siler City, North Carolina 27344

Head of School: Ms. Jane Samuel

General Information Girls' boarding college-preparatory and arts school; primarily serves underachievers, students with learning disabilities, individuals with Attention Deficit Disorder, and individuals with emotional and behavioral problems. Grades 8–12. Founded: 2001. Setting: rural. Nearest major city is Chapel Hill. Students are housed in single-sex dormitories. 86-acre campus. 4 buildings on campus. Approved or accredited by National Independent Private Schools Association, Southern Association of Colleges and Schools, and North Carolina Department of Education. Total enrollment: 60. Upper school average class size: 10. Upper school faculty-student ratio: 1:10. There are 225 required school days per year for Upper School students. Upper School students typically attend 5 days per week. The average school day consists of 6 hours.

Upper School Student Profile Grade 9: 6 students (6 girls); Grade 10: 12 students (12 girls); Grade 11: 16 students (16 girls); Grade 12: 20 students (20 girls). 100% of students are boarding students. 10% are state residents. 18 states are represented in upper school student body.

Faculty School total: 7. In upper school: 4 men, 3 women; 1 has an advanced degree.

Subjects Offered Advanced math, Advanced Placement courses, algebra, American literature, art, arts and crafts, biology, biology-AP, British literature, ceramics, chemistry, choir, clayworking, college planning, dance, discrete mathematics, drawing, earth science, economics, English, English composition, English language and composition-AP, environmental science, environmental science-AP, equestrian sports, geometry, health, health education, honors algebra, honors English, honors geometry, honors U.S. history, honors world history, jewelry making, library assistant, life skills, nutrition, oil painting, painting, photography, physical education, physical fitness, pottery, pre-algebra, pre-calculus, printmaking, SAT preparation, science, sex education, sociology, Spanish, study skills, U.S. government, U.S. history, U.S. history-AP, world history.

Graduation Requirements Art, electives, English, foreign language, mathematics, physical education (includes health), science, social studies (includes history), 30 hours of community service.

Special Academic Programs Advanced Placement exam preparation; honors section; accelerated programs; independent study; academic accommodation for the gifted; remedial reading and/or remedial writing; remedial math; programs in English, mathematics for dyslexic students; special instructional classes for students with mild learning disabilities, mild Attention Deficit Disorder, mild behavioral and/or emotional problems (anxiety, depression).

College Admission Counseling 16 students graduated in 2011; 13 went to college, including Guilford College; High Point University; Meredith College; William Peace University. Other: 3 went to work. Mean SAT critical reading: 580, mean SAT math: 550.

Student Life Upper grades have specified standards of dress, student council, honor system. Discipline rests primarily with faculty.

Tuition and Aid 7-day tuition and room/board: $69,000. Guaranteed tuition plan. Tuition installment plan (monthly payment plans, individually arranged payment plans, Clark Educational Loans, Serenity Loans). Need-based scholarship grants available.

Admissions Traditional secondary-level entrance grade is 11. Battery of testing done through outside agency, comprehensive educational evaluation, psychoeducational evaluation, Stanford Achievement Test and WISC-III and Woodcock-Johnson required. Deadline for receipt of application materials: none. Application fee required: $1500. Interview recommended.

Athletics Intramural: basketball, bicycling, billiards, cheering, combined training, cooperative games, croquet, dance, fishing, fitness, fitness walking, flag football, horseback riding, indoor soccer, jogging, kickball, outdoor activities, outdoor adventure, outdoor education, outdoor recreation, physical fitness, roller skating, running, soccer, softball, strength & conditioning, table tennis, tennis, volleyball, walking, weight training, yoga.

Computers Computer resources include on-campus library services, Internet access, Internet filtering or blocking technology. Campus intranet, student e-mail accounts, and computer access in designated common areas are available to students.

Contact Ms. Amanda Woolard, Admission Coordinator. 919-837-2336 Ext. 200. Fax: 919-837-5284. E-mail: anamda.woolard@sequeltsi.com. Web site: www.auldern.com

THE AWTY INTERNATIONAL SCHOOL

7455 Awty School Lane
Houston, Texas 77055

Head of School: Dr. Stephen Codrington

General Information Coeducational day college-preparatory and bilingual studies school. Grades PK–12. Founded: 1956. Setting: urban. 25-acre campus. 16 buildings on campus. Approved or accredited by French Ministry of Education, Independent Schools Association of the Southwest, International Baccalaureate Organization, and Texas Department of Education. Member of National Association of Independent Schools, Secondary School Admission Test Board, and European Council of International Schools. Languages of instruction: English, French, and Spanish. Endowment: $3.9 million. Total enrollment: 1,489. Upper school average class size: 17. Upper school faculty-student ratio: 1:18. Upper School students typically attend 5 days per week.

Faculty School total: 186. In upper school: 24 men, 57 women; 63 have advanced degrees.

Subjects Offered Algebra, American history, Arabic, art, biology, calculus, chemistry, community service, computer programming, computer science, computer studies, drama, Dutch, English, ESL, fine arts, French, geography, geometry, German, grammar, history, Italian, Mandarin, mathematics, music, Norwegian, philosophy, physical education, physics, science, social sciences, social studies, Spanish, theater, theory of knowledge, trigonometry, world history, world literature, writing.

Graduation Requirements Arts and fine arts (art, music, dance, drama), computer science, English, foreign language, mathematics, physical education (includes health), science, social sciences, social studies (includes history), 4000-word extended essay. Community service is required.

Special Academic Programs International Baccalaureate program; ESL.

College Admission Counseling 92 students graduated in 2012; all went to college, including Georgetown University; McGill University; Princeton University; Rice University; University of Houston. Median SAT critical reading: 620, median SAT math: 640, median SAT writing: 640, median combined SAT: 1880, median composite ACT: 30. 69% scored over 600 on SAT critical reading, 81% scored over 600 on SAT math, 82% scored over 600 on SAT writing, 77% scored over 1800 on combined SAT, 83% scored over 26 on composite ACT.

Student Life Upper grades have uniform requirement, student council, honor system. Discipline rests primarily with faculty.

Tuition and Aid Day student tuition: $20,472. Tuition installment plan (monthly payment plans, individually arranged payment plans, semi-annual payment plan, Dewar Tuition Refund Plan). Need-based scholarship grants, need-based financial aid available. In 2012–13, 8% of upper-school students received aid. Total amount of financial aid awarded in 2012–13: $407,857.

Admissions Traditional secondary-level entrance grade is 9. For fall 2012, 222 students applied for upper-level admission, 131 were accepted, 89 enrolled. ISEE, OLSAT,

ERB and writing sample required. Deadline for receipt of application materials: January 31. Application fee required: $100. On-campus interview required.
Athletics Interscholastic: cheering (girls), dance squad (g), dance team (g); coed interscholastic: basketball, cross-country running, golf, running, soccer, tennis, track and field, volleyball, winter soccer; coed intramural: aerobics/dance, badminton, bicycling, fitness, table tennis, triathlon. 5 PE instructors, 7 coaches, 1 athletic trainer.
Computers Computers are regularly used in all academic classes. Computer network features include on-campus library services, online commercial services, Internet access, wireless campus network, Internet filtering or blocking technology. Computer access in designated common areas is available to students. Students grades are available online. The school has a published electronic and media policy.
Contact Mrs. Erika Benavente, Co-Director of Admissions. 713-328-5804. Fax: 713-686-4956. E-mail: ebenavente@awty.org. Web site: www.awty.org

BACHMAN ACADEMY

McDonald, Tennessee
See Special Needs Schools section.

BAKERSFIELD CHRISTIAN HIGH SCHOOL

12775 Stockdale Highway
Bakersfield, California 93314

Head of School: Mr. Stephen Dinger

General Information Coeducational day college-preparatory and religious studies school, affiliated with Christian faith. Grades 9–12. Founded: 1979. Setting: suburban. 47-acre campus. 9 buildings on campus. Approved or accredited by Association of Christian Schools International, Western Association of Schools and Colleges, and California Department of Education. Endowment: $500,000. Total enrollment: 436. Upper school average class size: 22. Upper school faculty-student ratio: 1:17. There are 180 required school days per year for Upper School students. Upper School students typically attend 5 days per week. The average school day consists of 7 hours.
Faculty School total: 44. In upper school: 21 men, 23 women; 7 have advanced degrees.
Subjects Offered Advanced Placement courses, advanced studio art-AP, agriculture, American literature, American literature-AP, Bible, biology, biology-AP, British literature, British literature-AP, calculus, calculus-AP, chemistry, chemistry-AP, choir, Christian ethics, comparative religion, computer animation, contemporary issues, digital photography, drama, economics, economics-AP, English, English literature, English literature-AP, English-AP, European history, European history-AP, foreign language, forensics, French, history-AP, human anatomy, introduction to literature, jazz band, performing arts, photography, physical science, physics, physics-AP, pre-calculus, Spanish, Spanish-AP, statistics, statistics-AP, studio art, studio art-AP, U.S. history, U.S. history-AP, video and animation, world history, world literature.
Graduation Requirements 40 hours community service.
Special Academic Programs Advanced Placement exam preparation; independent study.
Student Life Upper grades have specified standards of dress, student council, honor system. Discipline rests primarily with faculty. Attendance at religious services is required.
Tuition and Aid Day student tuition: $11,090. Tuition installment plan (FACTS Tuition Payment Plan, monthly payment plans, individually arranged payment plans). Tuition reduction for siblings, need-based financial aid available. In 2012–13, 33% of upper-school students received aid. Total amount of financial aid awarded in 2012–13: $170,000.
Admissions Traditional secondary-level entrance grade is 9. Deadline for receipt of application materials: none. Application fee required: $75. On-campus interview required.
Athletics Interscholastic: baseball (boys), basketball (b,g), cheering (g), football (b), golf (b,g), soccer (b,g), softball (g), tennis (b,g), volleyball (g), weight lifting (b), weight training (b,g), wrestling (b); coed interscholastic: cross-country running, swimming and diving, track and field. 10 coaches, 1 athletic trainer.
Computers Computer network features include on-campus library services, Internet access, Internet filtering or blocking technology. Computer access in designated common areas is available to students. Students grades are available online. The school has a published electronic and media policy.
Contact Mrs. Alice E. Abril, Director of Admissions. 661-410-7000. Fax: 661-410-7007. E-mail: aabril@bakersfieldchristian.com. Web site: www.bakersfieldchristian.com

BALDWIN SCHOOL OF PUERTO RICO

PO Box 1827
Bayam?Puerto Rico 00960-1827

Head of School: Mr. James Nelligan

General Information Coeducational day college-preparatory school. Grades PK–12. Founded: 1968. Setting: suburban. Nearest major city is San Juan. 23-acre campus. 6 buildings on campus. Approved or accredited by Middle States Association of Colleges and Schools and Puerto Rico Department of Education. Member of National Association of Independent Schools. Languages of instruction: English and Spanish. Total enrollment: 809. Upper school average class size: 20. Upper school faculty-student ratio: 1:8. There are 173 required school days per year for Upper School students. Upper School students typically attend 5 days per week. The average school day consists of 6 hours and 40 minutes.
Upper School Student Profile Grade 9: 51 students (28 boys, 23 girls); Grade 10: 50 students (27 boys, 23 girls); Grade 11: 49 students (24 boys, 25 girls); Grade 12: 41 students (13 boys, 28 girls).
Faculty School total: 90. In upper school: 7 men, 29 women; 20 have advanced degrees.
Subjects Offered Algebra, American history, American literature, art, biology, biology-AP, British literature, calculus, calculus-AP, chemistry, chemistry-AP, computer information systems, computer literacy, computer programming, computer science, computers, English, English literature, English literature-AP, environmental science, European history-AP, fine arts, French, French-AP, geography, geometry, grammar, history, mathematics, music, physical education, physics, pre-calculus, psychology, Puerto Rican history, science, social studies, Spanish, Spanish language-AP, Spanish literature-AP, study skills, visual arts, world literature, writing.
Graduation Requirements Algebra, American history, American literature, arts and fine arts (art, music, dance, drama), biology, British literature, chemistry, computer science, English, English literature, geometry, mathematics, physical education (includes health), Puerto Rican history, science, social studies (includes history), Spanish, Spanish literature, U.S. history, Western civilization, Spanish as a Second Language, Spanish.
Special Academic Programs Advanced Placement exam preparation.
College Admission Counseling 50 students graduated in 2012; all went to college, including Boston University; Harvard University; The George Washington University; Tufts University; United States Military Academy; University of Puerto Rico, Río Piedras. Median SAT critical reading: 587, median SAT math: 569, median SAT writing: 595.
Student Life Upper grades have uniform requirement, student council, honor system. Discipline rests equally with students and faculty.
Summer Programs Remediation, enrichment, ESL programs offered; session focuses on remediation; held on campus; accepts boys and girls; open to students from other schools. 170 students usually enrolled. 2013 schedule: June 1 to June 30. Application deadline: May 14.
Tuition and Aid Day student tuition: $11,030–$11,665. Guaranteed tuition plan. Tuition installment plan (annual payment plan, biannual payment plan, quartely payment plan). Tuition reduction for siblings, need-based scholarship grants, tuition reduction for children of staff, full scholarship program for eligible students, financial assistance for elegible students available. In 2012–13, 1% of upper-school students received aid. Total amount of financial aid awarded in 2012–13: $54,420.
Admissions Traditional secondary-level entrance grade is 9. For fall 2012, 25 students applied for upper-level admission, 22 were accepted, 19 enrolled. Brigance Test of Basic Skills and Stanford Achievement Test, Otis-Lennon required. Deadline for receipt of application materials: none. Application fee required: $150. On-campus interview recommended.
Athletics Interscholastic: baseball (boys), basketball (b,g), cheering (g), indoor soccer (b,g), soccer (b,g), swimming and diving (b,g), tennis (b,g), volleyball (b,g); intramural: flag football (b,g), touch football (b,g); coed interscholastic: golf, physical fitness. 6 PE instructors, 17 coaches, 1 athletic trainer.
Computers Computers are regularly used in English, history, mathematics, psychology, science, Spanish, technology classes. Computer network features include on-campus library services, Internet access, wireless campus network, Internet filtering or blocking technology. Computer access in designated common areas is available to students. Students grades are available online.
Contact Mrs. Ely Mej?, Director of Admissions. 787-720-2421 Ext. 239. Fax: 787-790-0619. E-mail: emejias@baldwin-school.org. Web site: www.baldwin-school.org

BALMORAL HALL SCHOOL

630 Westminster Avenue
Winnipeg, Manitoba R3C 3S1, Canada

Head of School: Mrs. Joanne Kamins

General Information Girls' boarding and day college-preparatory, arts, technology, and athletics/prep hockey school. Boarding grades 6–12, day grades N–12. Founded: 1901. Setting: urban. Students are housed in apartment-style residence. 12-acre campus. 2 buildings on campus. Approved or accredited by Canadian Association of Independent Schools, Canadian Educational Standards Institute, International Baccalaureate Organization, The Association of Boarding Schools, and Manitoba Department of Education. Affiliate member of National Association of Independent Schools; member of Secondary School Admission Test Board. Language of instruction: English. Endowment: CAN$1 million. Total enrollment: 451. Upper school average class size: 18. Upper school faculty-student ratio: 1:7. There are 183 required school days per year for Upper School students. Upper School students typically attend 5 days per week. The average school day consists of 5 hours.
Upper School Student Profile Grade 9: 25 students (25 girls); Grade 10: 37 students (37 girls); Grade 11: 44 students (44 girls); Grade 12: 46 students (46 girls). 13%

of students are boarding students. 85% are province residents. 3 provinces are represented in upper school student body. 10% are international students. International students from China, Hong Kong, Mexico, Republic of Korea, Sweden, and Taiwan; 2 other countries represented in student body.

Faculty School total: 47. In upper school: 9 men, 15 women; 7 have advanced degrees; 4 reside on campus.

Subjects Offered Acting, advanced math, Advanced Placement courses, advanced studio art-AP, advanced TOEFL/grammar, art, biology, biology-AP, calculus, calculus-AP, career and personal planning, career/college preparation, chemistry, chemistry-AP, choir, college planning, communications, community service, computer science, consumer mathematics, dance performance, debate, desktop publishing, digital art, digital photography, drama, driver education, English, English language and composition-AP, English literature, English literature and composition-AP, English literature-AP, English/composition-AP, ESL, ethics, French, French language-AP, French literature-AP, general science, geography, health, history, history-AP, jazz ensemble, mathematics, mathematics-AP, media arts, modern Western civilization, multimedia, music, musical theater, performing arts, personal development, physical education, physics, physics-AP, pre-calculus, psychology-AP, SAT/ACT preparation, science, social studies, Spanish, Spanish-AP, studio art-AP, technology, vocal ensemble, world affairs, world history.

Graduation Requirements Minimum of 10 hours per year of Service Learning participation in grades 9 through 12.

Special Academic Programs Advanced Placement exam preparation; honors section; accelerated programs; study at local college for college credit; academic accommodation for the gifted; ESL (19 students enrolled).

College Admission Counseling 35 students graduated in 2012; all went to college, including McGill University; Queen's University at Kingston; The University of Western Ontario; The University of Winnipeg; University of Manitoba; University of Toronto. Median SAT critical reading: 435, median SAT math: 590, median SAT writing: 445, median combined SAT: 1400, median composite ACT: 21. 7% scored over 600 on SAT critical reading, 43% scored over 600 on SAT math, 36% scored over 1800 on combined SAT, 23% scored over 26 on composite ACT.

Student Life Upper grades have uniform requirement, student council, honor system. Discipline rests primarily with faculty.

Tuition and Aid Day student tuition: CAN$14,700; 5-day tuition and room/board: CAN$30,400. Tuition installment plan (The Tuition Plan). Tuition reduction for siblings, bursaries, merit scholarship grants available. In 2012–13, 23% of upper-school students received aid; total upper-school merit-scholarship money awarded: CAN$14,000. Total amount of financial aid awarded in 2012–13: CAN$253,096.

Admissions Traditional secondary-level entrance grade is 9. School's own exam required. Deadline for receipt of application materials: none. Application fee required: CAN$150. Interview required.

Athletics Interscholastic: badminton, basketball, cross-country running, curling, Frisbee, golf, ice hockey, indoor track & field, outdoor skills, running, soccer, speedskating, track and field, ultimate Frisbee, volleyball; intramural: aerobics, aerobics/dance, aerobics/Nautilus, alpine skiing, backpacking, badminton, ballet, baseball, basketball, bicycling, bowling, broomball, cooperative games, Cosom hockey, cross-country running, curling, dance, dance team, fencing, field hockey, figure skating, fitness, fitness walking, flag football, floor hockey, Frisbee, golf, gymnastics, handball, hiking/backpacking, hockey, ice hockey, ice skating, in-line skating, indoor hockey, indoor track & field, jogging, jump rope, modern dance, netball, outdoor activities, outdoor education, outdoor skills, physical fitness, physical training, roller blading, rowing, rugby, running, skiing (cross-country), skiing (downhill), snowboarding, snowshoeing, soccer, softball, speedskating, strength & conditioning, swimming and diving, table tennis, tennis, track and field, ultimate Frisbee, volleyball, walking, wall climbing, weight training, yoga. 2 PE instructors, 4 coaches.

Computers Computers are regularly used in all classes. Computer network features include on-campus library services, Internet access, wireless campus network, Internet filtering or blocking technology. Campus intranet, student e-mail accounts, and computer access in designated common areas are available to students. Students grades are available online. The school has a published electronic and media policy.

Contact Ms. Bin Dong Jiang, Day Admissions Administrator. 204-784-1608. Fax: 204-774-5534. E-mail: bdjiang@balmoralhall.com. Web site: www.balmoralhall.com

THE BALTIMORE ACTORS' THEATRE CONSERVATORY

The Dumbarton House
300 Dumbarton Road
Baltimore, Maryland 21212-1532

Head of School: Walter E. Anderson

General Information Coeducational day and distance learning college-preparatory and arts school. Grades K–12. Distance learning grades 9–12. Founded: 1979. Setting: suburban. 35-acre campus. 3 buildings on campus. Approved or accredited by Association of Independent Maryland Schools, Middle States Association of Colleges and Schools, and Maryland Department of Education. Endowment: $200,000. Total enrollment: 24. Upper school average class size: 6. Upper school faculty-student ratio: 1:3. There are 175 required school days per year for Upper School students. Upper School students typically attend 5 days per week. The average school day consists of 7 hours and 30 minutes.

Upper School Student Profile Grade 9: 3 students (2 boys, 1 girl); Grade 11: 4 students (4 girls); Grade 12: 1 student (1 girl); Postgraduate: 2 students (1 boy, 1 girl).

Faculty School total: 12. In upper school: 2 men, 8 women; 9 have advanced degrees.

Subjects Offered Acting, algebra, American history-AP, ballet, biology-AP, British literature, chemistry, English language-AP, environmental science-AP, French, geometry, health science, music history, music theory-AP, novels, physics, pre-calculus, psychology, sociology, theater history, trigonometry, world history, world history-AP.

Graduation Requirements Algebra, American history, ballet, chemistry, English, French, geometry, modern dance, music history, music theory, physical science, psychology, sociology, theater history, world history, students are required to complete graduation requirements in the three performing arts areas of music, drama, and dance.

Special Academic Programs Advanced Placement exam preparation; honors section; accelerated programs; independent study; study at local college for college credit; academic accommodation for the gifted, the musically talented, and the artistically talented.

College Admission Counseling Colleges students went to include Nazareth College of Rochester. Median SAT critical reading: 600, median SAT math: 570, median composite ACT: 26.

Student Life Upper grades have uniform requirement, student council, honor system. Discipline rests primarily with faculty.

Summer Programs Remediation, art/fine arts programs offered; session focuses on music, drama, dance, and art; held off campus; held at theater in Oregon Ridge Park, Hunt Valley, Maryland; accepts boys and girls; open to students from other schools. 30 students usually enrolled. 2013 schedule: July 24 to August 8. Application deadline: none.

Tuition and Aid Day student tuition: $10,000. Tuition installment plan (SMART Tuition Payment Plan, FACTS Tuition Payment Plan, individually arranged payment plans). Need-based scholarship grants available. In 2012–13, 10% of upper-school students received aid. Total amount of financial aid awarded in 2012–13: $12,000.

Admissions Traditional secondary-level entrance grade is 9. For fall 2012, 50 students applied for upper-level admission, 15 were accepted, 7 enrolled. Any standardized test, English, French, and math proficiency and writing sample required. Deadline for receipt of application materials: April 3. Application fee required: $50. On-campus interview required.

Computers Computers are regularly used in college planning, creative writing, dance, desktop publishing, English, historical foundations for arts, history, independent study, introduction to technology, keyboarding, music, music technology, psychology, senior seminar, theater, theater arts, word processing, writing classes. Computer network features include Internet access, wireless campus network, Internet filtering or blocking technology. Student e-mail accounts are available to students. The school has a published electronic and media policy.

Contact Mr. Walter E. Anderson, Headmaster. 410-337-8519. Fax: 410-337-8582. E-mail: batpro@baltimoreactorstheatre.org. Web site: www.baltimoreactorstheatre.org

BALTIMORE LUTHERAN SCHOOL

1145 Concordia Drive
Towson, Maryland 21286-1796

Head of School: Mr. Alan Freeman

General Information Coeducational day and distance learning college-preparatory, arts, religious studies, and technology school, affiliated with Lutheran Church–Missouri Synod. Grades 6–12. Distance learning grades 9–12. Founded: 1965. Setting: suburban. Nearest major city is Baltimore. 25-acre campus. 5 buildings on campus. Approved or accredited by Association of Independent Maryland Schools, Middle States Association of Colleges and Schools, and Maryland Department of Education. Endowment: $1.3 million. Total enrollment: 240. Upper school average class size: 16. Upper school faculty-student ratio: 1:12. There are 174 required school days per year for Upper School students. Upper School students typically attend 5 days per week. The average school day consists of 6 hours and 45 minutes.

Upper School Student Profile 30% of students are Lutheran Church–Missouri Synod.

Faculty School total: 36. In upper school: 14 men, 15 women; 16 have advanced degrees.

Subjects Offered 20th century history, 3-dimensional art, acting, advanced biology, Advanced Placement courses, algebra, American government, American history, American literature, analytic geometry, anatomy, art, Bible studies, biology, biology-AP, brass choir, British literature, British literature (honors), calculus, chemistry, Chesapeake Bay studies, Christian doctrine, Christian scripture, church history, college counseling, college planning, computer education, computer graphics, computer programming, computers, concert band, concert choir, creative writing, digital photography, drama, drama performance, dramatic arts, drawing, drawing and design, earth science, ecology, economics, economics and history, English, English literature, English literature-AP, expository writing, French, geometry, German, government/civics, grammar, graphic arts, graphic design, health, honors English, independent study, intro to computers, jazz band, journalism, keyboarding, Latin, law, mathematics, music, painting, photography, physical education, physics, pre-algebra, psychology, religion, SAT/ACT preparation, science, social studies, Spanish, Spanish-AP, speech, studio art, theater, theology, trigonometry, Web site design, word processing, world history, world history-AP, world literature, writing, yearbook.

Graduation Requirements Arts and fine arts (art, music, dance, drama), English, foreign language, mathematics, physical education (includes health), religion (includes Bible studies and theology), science, social studies (includes history), technology.

Special Academic Programs 5 Advanced Placement exams for which test preparation is offered; honors section; independent study; study at local college for college credit; academic accommodation for the gifted; programs in English, mathematics for dyslexic students.

College Admission Counseling 79 students graduated in 2012; 78 went to college, including Brown University; Loyola University Maryland; The Johns Hopkins University; Towson University; University of Maryland, Baltimore County; University of Maryland, College Park. Other: 1 went to work. Mean SAT critical reading: 539, mean SAT math: 522, mean SAT writing: 545.

Student Life Upper grades have uniform requirement, student council, honor system. Discipline rests primarily with faculty. Attendance at religious services is required.

Summer Programs Remediation, sports programs offered; session focuses on general activities; held on campus; accepts boys and girls; open to students from other schools. 2013 schedule: June 12 to August 11.

Tuition and Aid Day student tuition: $10,950. Tuition installment plan (FACTS Tuition Payment Plan). Tuition reduction for siblings, merit scholarship grants, need-based scholarship grants, academic merit scholarships for students from Christian schools available. In 2012–13, 25% of upper-school students received aid; total upper-school merit-scholarship money awarded: $18,000. Total amount of financial aid awarded in 2012–13: $70,000.

Admissions Traditional secondary-level entrance grade is 9. For fall 2012, 85 students applied for upper-level admission, 70 were accepted, 40 enrolled. ISEE, school placement exam, TOEFL or SLEP and writing sample required. Deadline for receipt of application materials: none. Application fee required: $50. On-campus interview required.

Athletics Interscholastic: baseball (boys), basketball (b,g), cheering (g), cross-country running (b,g), field hockey (g), football (b), golf (b), indoor soccer (g), lacrosse (b,g), soccer (b,g), softball (g), tennis (b,g), track and field (b,g), volleyball (g), winter soccer (g), wrestling (b); coed intramural: skiing (downhill), snowboarding. 2 PE instructors, 5 coaches, 1 athletic trainer.

Computers Computers are regularly used in English, graphic design, history, independent study, journalism, library, mathematics, newspaper, photography, SAT preparation, social sciences, technology, writing, yearbook classes. Computer network features include on-campus library services, online commercial services, Internet access, wireless campus network, Internet filtering or blocking technology. Student e-mail accounts are available to students. Students grades are available online. The school has a published electronic and media policy.

Contact Mr. Jim Carter, Director of Admissions. 410-825-2323 Ext. 272. Fax: 410-825-2506. E-mail: jcarter@baltimorelutheran.org. Web site: www.baltimorelutheran.org

BARRIE SCHOOL

13500 Layhill Road
Silver Spring, Maryland 20906

Head of School: Mr. Charles Abelmann

General Information Coeducational day college-preparatory school. Grades N–12. Founded: 1932. Setting: suburban. Nearest major city is Washington, DC. 45-acre campus. 8 buildings on campus. Approved or accredited by Middle States Association of Colleges and Schools and Maryland Department of Education. Member of National Association of Independent Schools and Secondary School Admission Test Board. Endowment: $320,000. Total enrollment: 293. Upper school average class size: 15. Upper school faculty-student ratio: 1:8. There are 175 required school days per year for Upper School students. Upper School students typically attend 5 days per week. The average school day consists of 7 hours and 20 minutes.

Upper School Student Profile Grade 9: 14 students (12 boys, 2 girls); Grade 10: 11 students (8 boys, 3 girls); Grade 11: 11 students (5 boys, 6 girls); Grade 12: 18 students (7 boys, 11 girls).

Faculty School total: 34. In upper school: 10 men, 9 women; 13 have advanced degrees.

Subjects Offered Algebra, art, biology, calculus, calculus-AP, ceramics, chemistry, community service, drama, drawing, environmental science-AP, fitness, French, French-AP, geometry, health, health and wellness, history, humanities, illustration, instrumental music, music, painting, performing arts, physics, pre-calculus, sculpture, service learning/internship, Spanish, statistics-AP, studio art, world geography, world history, writing, yearbook.

Graduation Requirements Algebra, art, biology, chemistry, English, foreign language, health, history, humanities, mathematics, physics, pre-algebra, science, sports, U.S. history, 96 hours of community service.

Special Academic Programs 13 Advanced Placement exams for which test preparation is offered; independent study.

College Admission Counseling 22 students graduated in 2012; 21 went to college, including Babson College; Earlham College; St. Mary's College of Maryland; The College of Wooster; University of Maryland, Baltimore County; University of Maryland, College Park. Other: 1 had other specific plans. Mean SAT critical reading: 536, mean SAT math: 525, mean SAT writing: 541, mean combined SAT: 1602, mean composite ACT: 25. 21% scored over 600 on SAT critical reading, 26% scored over 600 on SAT math, 21% scored over 600 on SAT writing, 21% scored over 1800 on combined SAT, 17% scored over 26 on composite ACT.

Student Life Upper grades have student council. Discipline rests primarily with faculty.

Summer Programs Sports programs offered; session focuses on day camp; held on campus; accepts boys and girls; open to students from other schools. 700 students usually enrolled. 2013 schedule: June 17 to August 9. Application deadline: none.

Tuition and Aid Day student tuition: $26,100. Tuition installment plan (FACTS Tuition Payment Plan, monthly payment plans, The Tuition Refund Plan). Need-based scholarship grants, need-based financial aid grants available. In 2012–13, 47% of upper-school students received aid. Total amount of financial aid awarded in 2012–13: $539,950.

Admissions Traditional secondary-level entrance grade is 9. For fall 2012, 28 students applied for upper-level admission, 9 were accepted, 7 enrolled. ISEE, SSAT or TOEFL or SLEP required. Deadline for receipt of application materials: January 18. Application fee required: $50. Interview required.

Athletics Interscholastic: basketball (boys, girls), soccer (b); coed interscholastic: cross-country running, equestrian sports, horseback riding, outdoor activities, physical fitness, running, tennis, track and field, ultimate Frisbee. 4 coaches.

Computers Computers are regularly used in all classes. Computer network features include Internet access, wireless campus network, Internet filtering or blocking technology. Campus intranet, student e-mail accounts, and computer access in designated common areas are available to students. The school has a published electronic and media policy.

Contact Ms. Alyssa Jahn, Director of Admission. 301-576-2839. Fax: 301-576-2803. E-mail: ajahn@barrie.org. Web site: www.barrie.org

BATTLE GROUND ACADEMY

PO Box 1889
Franklin, Tennessee 37065-1889

Head of School: Dr. John W. Griffith

General Information Coeducational day college-preparatory, arts, and technology school. Grades K–12. Founded: 1889. Setting: suburban. Nearest major city is Nashville. 55-acre campus. 13 buildings on campus. Approved or accredited by Southern Association of Colleges and Schools, Southern Association of Independent Schools, and Tennessee Department of Education. Member of National Association of Independent Schools. Endowment: $8.3 million. Total enrollment: 846. Upper school average class size: 16. Upper school faculty-student ratio: 1:11. There are 180 required school days per year for Upper School students. Upper School students typically attend 5 days per week. The average school day consists of 7 hours and 15 minutes.

Upper School Student Profile Grade 6: 79 students (40 boys, 39 girls); Grade 7: 92 students (42 boys, 50 girls); Grade 8: 79 students (40 boys, 39 girls); Grade 9: 84 students (47 boys, 37 girls); Grade 10: 91 students (46 boys, 45 girls); Grade 11: 78 students (48 boys, 30 girls); Grade 12: 70 students (37 boys, 33 girls).

Faculty School total: 110. In upper school: 26 men, 20 women; 27 have advanced degrees.

Subjects Offered Accounting, algebra, American history, American literature, art, art history, biology, calculus, chemistry, chorus, computer applications, computer programming, computer science, drama, early childhood, economics, English, English literature, English literature and composition-AP, European history, fine arts, French, French-AP, geography, geometry, government/civics, grammar, health, history, Latin, mathematics, modern European history-AP, music, music history, physical education, physics, science, social studies, Spanish, speech, technical theater, theater, trigonometry, U.S. history, U.S. history-AP, world history, world history-AP, world literature, writing.

Graduation Requirements Arts and fine arts (art, music, dance, drama), computer science, English, foreign language, mathematics, physical education (includes health), science, social studies (includes history). Community service is required.

Special Academic Programs Advanced Placement exam preparation; honors section.

College Admission Counseling 90 students graduated in 2012; 88 went to college. Other: 1 entered military service, 1 had other specific plans. Mean SAT critical reading: 631, mean SAT math: 618, mean SAT writing: 604, mean combined SAT: 1853, mean composite ACT: 27.

Student Life Upper grades have uniform requirement, student council, honor system. Discipline rests primarily with faculty.

Summer Programs Remediation, enrichment, sports, art/fine arts, computer instruction programs offered; session focuses on remediation, enrichment, and sports; held both on and off campus; held at Local Farm; accepts boys and girls; open to students from other schools. 550 students usually enrolled. 2013 schedule: June 3 to July 27. Application deadline: none.

Tuition and Aid Day student tuition: $17,930. Tuition installment plan (The Tuition Plan, FACTS Tuition Payment Plan, individually arranged payment plans). Merit scholarship grants, need-based scholarship grants, paying campus jobs available. In 2012–13, 20% of upper-school students received aid. Total amount of financial aid awarded in 2012–13: $1,180,000.

Admissions Traditional secondary-level entrance grade is 9. ISEE required. Deadline for receipt of application materials: none. Application fee required: $50. Interview required.

Athletics Interscholastic: baseball (boys), basketball (b,g), cheering (g), cross-country running (b,g), dance team (g), fitness (b,g), football (b), golf (b,g), physical fitness (b,g), physical training (b,g), soccer (b,g), softball (g), strength & conditioning (b,g), swimming and diving (b,g), tennis (b,g), track and field (b,g), volleyball (g), weight training (b,g), wrestling (b); intramural: baseball (b,g), basketball (b,g), fitness (b,g), football (b), softball (g); coed interscholastic: bowling, fitness, marksmanship, riflery, trap and skeet; coed intramural: fitness, flag football, hiking/backpacking, mountain biking, outdoor activities, outdoor adventure, physical training, rock climbing, ropes courses, soccer. 1 PE instructor, 4 coaches, 1 athletic trainer.

Computers Computers are regularly used in art, college planning, desktop publishing, English, foreign language, geography, history, library, literary magazine, mathematics, newspaper, photography, SAT preparation, science, social studies, Spanish, study skills, technology, theater, writing classes. Computer network features include on-campus library services, online commercial services, Internet access, wireless campus network, Internet filtering or blocking technology. Campus intranet, student e-mail accounts, and computer access in designated common areas are available to students. Students grades are available online. The school has a published electronic and media policy.

Contact Robin Goertz, Director of Admissions. 615-567-9014. E-mail: robin.goertz@mybga.org. Web site: www.battlegroundacademy.org

BAYLOR SCHOOL

171 Baylor School Road
Chattanooga, Tennessee 37405

Head of School: Mr. Scott Wilson

General Information Coeducational boarding and day college-preparatory and arts school. Boarding grades 9–12, day grades 6–12. Founded: 1893. Setting: suburban. Nearest major city is Atlanta, GA. Students are housed in single-sex dormitories. 670-acre campus. 30 buildings on campus. Approved or accredited by Southern Association of Colleges and Schools, Southern Association of Independent Schools, The Association of Boarding Schools, and Tennessee Department of Education. Member of National Association of Independent Schools and Secondary School Admission Test Board. Endowment: $90 million. Total enrollment: 1,070. Upper school average class size: 14. Upper school faculty-student ratio: 1:8. There are 180 required school days per year for Upper School students. Upper School students typically attend 5 days per week. The average school day consists of 7 hours and 30 minutes.

Upper School Student Profile Grade 9: 165 students (84 boys, 81 girls); Grade 10: 200 students (103 boys, 97 girls); Grade 11: 199 students (101 boys, 98 girls); Grade 12: 192 students (102 boys, 90 girls). 38% of students are boarding students. 74% are state residents. 21 states are represented in upper school student body. 10% are international students. International students from Bermuda, China, Germany, Mexico, Republic of Korea, and Taiwan; 24 other countries represented in student body.

Faculty School total: 144. In upper school: 77 men, 67 women; 91 have advanced degrees; 45 reside on campus.

Subjects Offered Algebra, American history, American literature, anthropology, art, art history, art history-AP, art-AP, astronomy, biology, biology-AP, calculus-AP, ceramics, chemistry, chemistry-AP, computer math, computer science, computer science-AP, creative writing, dance, drama, driver education, economics, English, English language-AP, English literature, English literature-AP, environmental science, environmental science-AP, ethics, European history, European history-AP, film, fine arts, finite math, forensics, French, French-AP, genetics, geography, geometry, German, German-AP, government/civics, history, human geography - AP, Latin, Latin-AP, mathematics, music, photography, physical education, physics, physics-AP, religion, science, social studies, Spanish, Spanish-AP, speech, statistics, statistics-AP, theater, trigonometry, U.S. history-AP, video, world history, world literature.

Graduation Requirements Arts and fine arts (art, music, dance, drama), English, foreign language, mathematics, physical education (includes health), science, social studies (includes history), Leadership Baylor, summer reading, iPad School.

Special Academic Programs 22 Advanced Placement exams for which test preparation is offered; honors section; study abroad; academic accommodation for the gifted, the musically talented, and the artistically talented; special instructional classes for deaf students.

College Admission Counseling 162 students graduated in 2011; all went to college, including Georgia Institute of Technology; Sewanee: The University of the South; The University of Alabama; The University of Tennessee; University of Georgia; University of Illinois at Urbana–Champaign.

Student Life Upper grades have specified standards of dress, student council, honor system. Discipline rests primarily with faculty.

Tuition and Aid Day student tuition: $19,985; 7-day tuition and room/board: $40,705. Tuition installment plan (The Tuition Plan, Insured Tuition Payment Plan, Key Tuition Payment Plan, FACTS Tuition Payment Plan, monthly payment plans, individually arranged payment plans). Merit scholarship grants, need-based scholarship grants available. In 2011–12, 35% of upper-school students received aid; total upper-school merit-scholarship money awarded: $350,000. Total amount of financial aid awarded in 2011–12: $2,500,000.

Admissions Traditional secondary-level entrance grade is 9. For fall 2011, 89 students applied for upper-level admission, 47 were accepted, 38 enrolled. ISEE, SSAT or TOEFL required. Deadline for receipt of application materials: none. Application fee required: $75. Interview required.

Athletics Interscholastic: aquatics (boys, girls), baseball (b), basketball (b,g), bowling (b,g), cheering (g), crew (b,g), cross-country running (b,g), dance (g), dance team (g), diving (b,g), fencing (b,g), football (b), golf (b,g), lacrosse (b,g), modern dance (g), soccer (b,g), softball (g), swimming and diving (b,g), tennis (b,g), track and field (b,g), volleyball (g), wrestling (b); intramural: ballet (g), dance (g), weight lifting (b,g); coed interscholastic: aerobics/dance, rowing, running, strength & conditioning; coed intramural: backpacking, bicycling, canoeing/kayaking, climbing, fitness, fly fishing, Frisbee, hiking/backpacking, kayaking, mountain biking, mountaineering, ocean paddling, outdoor activities, outdoor adventure, outdoor education, physical fitness, rafting, rock climbing, scuba diving, ultimate Frisbee, wall climbing, wilderness survival. 4 PE instructors, 10 coaches, 2 athletic trainers.

Computers Computers are regularly used in art, English, history, mathematics, photography, publications, science, Spanish, technology, theater arts, writing, yearbook classes. Computer network features include on-campus library services, online commercial services, Internet access, wireless campus network, Internet filtering or blocking technology. Student e-mail accounts and computer access in designated common areas are available to students. Students grades are available online. The school has a published electronic and media policy.

Contact Ms. Cindy Clark, Boarding Admission Associate. 423-267-8505 Ext. 220. Fax: 423-757-2525. E-mail: cclark@baylorschool.org. Web site: www.baylorschool.org

BAY RIDGE PREPARATORY SCHOOL

7420 Fourth Avenue
Brooklyn, New York 11209

Head of School: Dr. Michael T. Dealy

General Information Coeducational day college-preparatory, general academic, and arts school. Grades K–12. Founded: 1998. Setting: urban. 1 building on campus. Approved or accredited by New York State Association of Independent Schools, New York State Board of Regents, and New York Department of Education. Member of National Association of Independent Schools. Upper school average class size: 17. Upper school faculty-student ratio: 1:7. Upper School students typically attend 5 days per week. The average school day consists of 6 hours and 15 minutes.

Faculty School total: 62. In upper school: 16 men, 15 women; 25 have advanced degrees.

Subjects Offered Algebra, American government, American history, American literature, ancient world history, art, art history, biology, calculus, chemistry, college admission preparation, college counseling, college writing, computer science, creative writing, earth science, economics, English, English literature, European history, European literature, geometry, health education, journalism, microbiology, modern history, music composition, physics, SAT preparation, Shakespeare, Spanish, statistics, U.S. government and politics.

Special Academic Programs Advanced Placement exam preparation; honors section; independent study; study at local college for college credit; academic accommodation for the gifted, the musically talented, and the artistically talented; remedial reading and/or remedial writing; remedial math; programs in English, mathematics, general development for dyslexic students.

Student Life Upper grades have specified standards of dress, honor system. Discipline rests primarily with faculty.

Tuition and Aid Tuition installment plan (FACTS Tuition Payment Plan, monthly payment plans). Tuition reduction for siblings, merit scholarship grants available.

Admissions Traditional secondary-level entrance grade is 9. For fall 2012, 75 students applied for upper-level admission, 20 were accepted, 15 enrolled. Deadline for receipt of application materials: none. Application fee required: $60. Interview required.

Athletics Interscholastic: baseball (boys), basketball (b,g), soccer (b,g); intramural: baseball (b), basketball (g), cheering (g), hockey (b), soccer (b,g), softball (g); coed interscholastic: squash; coed intramural: cross-country running, dance, dance squad, martial arts, squash, track and field, yoga. 3 PE instructors, 7 coaches.

Computers Computers are regularly used in college planning classes. Computer network features include Internet access, wireless campus network. Student e-mail accounts and computer access in designated common areas are available to students. Students grades are available online.

Contact Ms. Wendy Freeburn, Admissions Coordinator. 718-833-9090 Ext. 305. Fax: 718-833-6680. E-mail: admissions@bayridgeprep.org. Web site: www.bayridgeprep.org

THE BAY SCHOOL OF SAN FRANCISCO

35 Keyes Avenue, The Presidio of San Francisco
San Francisco, California 94129

Head of School: Mr. Timothy Johnson

General Information Coeducational day college-preparatory school. Grades 9–12. Founded: 2004. Setting: urban. 2 buildings on campus. Approved or accredited by California Association of Independent Schools, Western Association of Schools and Colleges, and California Department of Education. Member of National Association of Independent Schools and Secondary School Admission Test Board. Total enrollment: 305. Upper school average class size: 14. Upper school faculty-student ratio: 1:8. The average school day consists of 6 hours and 40 minutes.

Faculty School total: 38. In upper school: 17 men, 21 women; 27 have advanced degrees.

Graduation Requirements Senior Signature Project.

Student Life Upper grades have student council. Discipline rests equally with students and faculty.

Tuition and Aid Day student tuition: $37,600. Need-based scholarship grants available. In 2012–13, 30% of upper-school students received aid.

Admissions Traditional secondary-level entrance grade is 9. ISEE, PSAT or SAT for applicants to grade 11 and 12, SAT or SSAT required. Deadline for receipt of application materials: January 17. Application fee required: $90. Interview required.

Computers Computer network features include on-campus library services, Internet access, wireless campus network, Internet filtering or blocking technology. Student e-mail accounts are available to students.

Contact Ms. Brooke Wilson, Admission Associate. 415-684-8949. Fax: 415-561-5808. E-mail: admission@bayschoolsf.org. Web site: www.bayschoolsf.org/

BAYSIDE ACADEMY

303 Dryer Avenue
Daphne, Alabama 36526

Head of School: Mr. Peter B. Huestis

General Information Coeducational day college-preparatory, arts, and technology school. Grades PK–12. Founded: 1970. Setting: small town. Nearest major city is Mobile. 44-acre campus. 9 buildings on campus. Approved or accredited by Southern Association of Colleges and Schools, Southern Association of Independent Schools, and Alabama Department of Education. Total enrollment: 727. Upper school average class size: 18. Upper school faculty-student ratio: 1:9. There are 177 required school days per year for Upper School students. The average school day consists of 7 hours.

Faculty School total: 72. In upper school: 11 men, 15 women; 22 have advanced degrees.

Subjects Offered Advanced Placement courses, algebra, American history, American literature, art, art history, biology, biology-AP, calculus, chemistry, chemistry-AP, computer programming, computer science, creative writing, drama, economics, English, English literature, environmental science, European history, film, fine arts, French, genetics, geography, geometry, government/civics, grammar, histology, history, Latin, marine biology, mathematics, multimedia, music, photography, physical education, physics, science, social studies, Spanish, speech, theater, trigonometry, world history, world literature, writing.

Graduation Requirements Arts and fine arts (art, music, dance, drama), computer science, English, foreign language, mathematics, physical education (includes health), science, social studies (includes history).

Special Academic Programs 15 Advanced Placement exams for which test preparation is offered; honors section; independent study; study abroad; programs in English, mathematics, general development for dyslexic students.

College Admission Counseling 73 students graduated in 2012; 72 went to college, including Auburn University; College of Charleston; Rhodes College; The University of Alabama; Tulane University; Vanderbilt University. Other: 1 entered military service. 80% scored over 26 on composite ACT.

Student Life Upper grades have uniform requirement, student council, honor system. Discipline rests primarily with faculty.

Tuition and Aid Day student tuition: $10,300. Tuition installment plan (monthly payment plans, individually arranged payment plans). Need-based scholarship grants available. In 2012–13, 15% of upper-school students received aid.

Admissions Traditional secondary-level entrance grade is 9. For fall 2012, 23 students applied for upper-level admission, 18 were accepted, 14 enrolled. Otis-Lennon School Ability Test, Stanford Achievement Test and Stanford Achievement Test, Otis-Lennon School Ability Test required. Deadline for receipt of application materials: none. Application fee required: $100. Interview required.

Athletics Interscholastic: aerobics/dance (girls), aquatics (b,g), baseball (b), basketball (b,g), cheering (g), cross-country running (b,g), dance (g), dance squad (g), dance team (g), football (b), golf (b,g), indoor track (b,g), indoor track & field (b,g), soccer (b,g), softball (g), swimming and diving (b,g), tennis (b,g), track and field (b,g), volleyball (g); intramural: ballet (g), dance (g), dance team (g), football (b), soccer (b,g); coed intramural: ballet, basketball, bicycling, canoeing/kayaking, dance, equestrian sports, physical training, sailing, scuba diving, soccer, strength & conditioning, track and field, weight training, yoga. 6 PE instructors, 11 coaches, 1 athletic trainer.

Computers Computer network features include on-campus library services, online commercial services, Internet access, wireless campus network, Internet filtering or blocking technology. Campus intranet is available to students. Students grades are available online.

Contact Alan M. Foster, Director of Admissions. 251-338-6415. Fax: 251-338-6310. E-mail: afoster@baysideacademy.org. Web site: www.baysideacademy.org

BAYVIEW GLEN SCHOOL

275 Duncan Mill Road
Toronto, Ontario M3B 3H9, Canada

Head of School: Mrs. Eileen Daunt

General Information Coeducational day college-preparatory, general academic, arts, business, technology, and athletics school. Grades PK–12. Founded: 1962. Setting: urban. 40-acre campus. 1 building on campus. Approved or accredited by Canadian Association of Independent Schools, Conference of Independent Schools of Ontario, and Ontario Department of Education. Language of instruction: English. Upper school average class size: 22. Upper school faculty-student ratio: 1:22. Upper School students typically attend 5 days per week. The average school day consists of 7 hours.

Faculty School total: 100. In upper school: 18 men, 14 women.

Subjects Offered Advanced Placement courses, all academic.

Special Academic Programs Advanced Placement exam preparation.

Student Life Upper grades have uniform requirement, student council. Discipline rests primarily with faculty.

Tuition and Aid Day student tuition: CAN$21,200. Guaranteed tuition plan. Tuition installment plan (monthly payment plans, individually arranged payment plans). Bursaries, need-based scholarship grants available.

Admissions Admissions testing required. Application fee required. On-campus interview required.

Computers Computers are regularly used in all academic classes. Computer network features include on-campus library services, Internet access, wireless campus network, Internet filtering or blocking technology. Campus intranet, student e-mail accounts, and computer access in designated common areas are available to students. Students grades are available online. The school has a published electronic and media policy.

Contact Mrs. Judy Maxwell, Director of Admissions. 416-443-1030 Ext. 605. Fax: 416-443-1032. E-mail: jmaxwell@bayviewglen.ca. Web site:

BEARSPAW CHRISTIAN SCHOOL

15001 69 Street NW
Calgary, Alberta T3R 1C5, Canada

Head of School: Mr. Kelly Blake

General Information Coeducational day and distance learning college-preparatory, general academic, business, and religious studies school, affiliated with Christian faith. Grades K–12. Distance learning grades 1–12. Founded: 1991. Setting: rural. 40-acre campus. 3 buildings on campus. Approved or accredited by Association of Christian Schools International, Association of Independent Schools and Colleges of Alberta, and Alberta Department of Education. Language of instruction: English. Total enrollment: 559. Upper school average class size: 20. Upper school faculty-student ratio: 1:10. There are 177 required school days per year for Upper School students. The average school day consists of 6 hours and 45 minutes.

Upper School Student Profile Grade 10: 41 students (15 boys, 26 girls); Grade 11: 35 students (11 boys, 24 girls); Grade 12: 40 students (12 boys, 28 girls). 95% of students are Christian faith.

Faculty School total: 24. In upper school: 7 men, 17 women; 2 have advanced degrees.

Subjects Offered 20th century history, 20th century world history, acting, advanced chemistry, advanced math, algebra, applied music, art, athletic training, athletics, Bible studies, biology, business, business communications, business education, business law, calculus, Canadian history, Canadian law, career and personal planning, career education, chemistry, Christian education, Christianity, communication skills, computer applications, English composition, food and nutrition, foreign language, French as a second language, general math, health and wellness, keyboarding, media arts, physical education, physics, science, social studies, Spanish, world history.

Graduation Requirements Bible, English, mathematics, science, social studies (includes history).

Special Academic Programs Honors section; independent study; remedial math; special instructional classes for students with learning disabilities, Attention Deficit Disorder, emotional problems, and dyslexia.

College Admission Counseling 34 students graduated in 2012; they went to Trinity Western University; University of Alberta; University of Calgary; University of Victoria.

Student Life Upper grades have uniform requirement, student council, honor system. Discipline rests primarily with faculty. Attendance at religious services is required.

Summer Programs Sports programs offered; session focuses on basketball, volleyball, strength training; held on campus; accepts boys and girls; open to students from other schools. 60 students usually enrolled. 2013 schedule: July 15 to August 15. Application deadline: July 15.

Tuition and Aid Day student tuition: CAN$5765. Tuition installment plan (monthly payment plans, individually arranged payment plans). Tuition reduction for siblings, need-based scholarship grants available. In 2012–13, 16% of upper-school students received aid. Total amount of financial aid awarded in 2012–13: CAN$125,245.

Admissions Traditional secondary-level entrance grade is 10. For fall 2012, 11 students applied for upper-level admission, 7 were accepted, 7 enrolled. Achievement tests, admissions testing, CTB/McGraw-Hill/Macmillan Co-op Test, WAIS, WICS, Woodcock-Johnson and writing sample required. Deadline for receipt of application materials: September 30. Application fee required: CAN$400. Interview required.

Athletics Interscholastic: badminton (boys, girls), basketball (b,g), cross-country running (b,g), floor hockey (b,g), golf (b,g), indoor soccer (b,g), track and field (b,g), volleyball (b,g), wrestling (b); intramural: aerobics/dance (b,g), badminton (b,g), basketball (b,g), cross-country running (b,g), flag football (b,g), floor hockey (b,g), track and field (b,g), volleyball (b,g), wrestling (b,g); coed interscholastic: badminton, indoor soccer, soccer; coed intramural: aerobics/dance, badminton, ball hockey, basketball, flag football, floor hockey, handball, indoor soccer, strength & conditioning, volleyball. 2 PE instructors, 1 athletic trainer.

Computers Computers are regularly used in all academic classes. Computer network features include Internet access, wireless campus network, Internet filtering or blocking technology. Student e-mail accounts and computer access in designated common areas are available to students. Students grades are available online. The school has a published electronic and media policy.

Contact Mrs. Amie Lee, Registrar. 403-295-2566 Ext. 1102. Fax: 403-275-8170. E-mail: alee@bearspawschool.com. Web site: www.bearspawschool.com

BEAVER COUNTRY DAY SCHOOL

791 Hammond Street
Chestnut Hill, Massachusetts 02467

Head of School: Peter R. Hutton

General Information Coeducational day college-preparatory and arts school. Grades 6–12. Founded: 1920. Setting: suburban. Nearest major city is Boston. 17-acre campus. 3 buildings on campus. Approved or accredited by Association of Independent Schools in New England, New England Association of Schools and Colleges, The College Board, and Massachusetts Department of Education. Member of National Association of Independent Schools and Secondary School Admission Test Board. Endowment: $10 million. Total enrollment: 451. Upper school average class size: 15. Upper school faculty-student ratio: 1:8. Upper School students typically attend 5 days per week. The average school day consists of 7 hours and 40 minutes.

Upper School Student Profile Grade 9: 70 students (41 boys, 29 girls); Grade 10: 90 students (48 boys, 42 girls); Grade 11: 80 students (40 boys, 40 girls); Grade 12: 86 students (40 boys, 46 girls).

Faculty School total: 71. In upper school: 24 men, 34 women; 41 have advanced degrees.

Subjects Offered 20th century American writers, 20th century history, 20th century world history, 3-dimensional art, 3-dimensional design, acting, advanced biology, advanced chemistry, advanced math, algebra, American Civil War, American democracy, American foreign policy, American government, American history, American literature, American studies, anatomy and physiology, art, art history, arts, astronomy, athletics, bioethics, bioethics, DNA and culture, biology, biotechnology, business communications, business skills, calculus, career education internship, cell biology, ceramics, chamber groups, chemistry, child development, Chinese history, chorus, civil rights, Civil War, civil war history, classical music, college counseling, college placement, college writing, community service, comparative civilizations, comparative cultures, comparative government and politics, comparative politics, comparative religion, computer graphics, computer math, computer programming, computer skills, constitutional history of U.S., contemporary history, contemporary issues in science, costumes and make-up, creative writing, current history, dance, decision making skills, digital photography, diversity studies, DNA, drama, drawing and design, driver education, economics, English, English literature, equality and freedom, European civilization, European history, expository writing, fine arts, foreign language, foreign policy, French, French as a second language, French studies, functions, gender and religion, gender issues, general math, geography, geometry, geometry with art applications, government, government/civics, grammar, great books, health, history, Holocaust and other genocides, Holocaust studies, honors algebra, honors English, honors geometry, honors U.S. history, human biology, human sexuality, independent study, integrated mathematics, international affairs, jazz, jazz band, journalism, junior and senior seminars, Latin American history, Latin American studies, marketing, mathematics, Middle Eastern history, modern European history, music, musical theater, painting, peer counseling, philosophy, photography, physical education, physics, play production, poetry, pre-calculus, programming, psychology, science, Shakespeare, social justice, social studies, society, politics and law, Spanish, Spanish literature, squash, statistics, studio art, study skills, theater, trigonometry, typing, U.S. history, world history, writing.

Graduation Requirements Arts, English, foreign language, history, interdisciplinary studies, mathematics, science, 40 hours of community service.

Special Academic Programs Honors section; independent study.

College Admission Counseling 78 students graduated in 2012; all went to college, including Harvard University; Occidental College; Skidmore College; Smith College; Stanford University; University of Southern California.

Student Life Upper grades have student council, honor system. Discipline rests equally with students and faculty.

Tuition and Aid Day student tuition: $38,590. Tuition installment plan (Academic Management Services Plan, Key Tuition Payment Plan, monthly payment plans, individually arranged payment plans). Need-based scholarship grants available. In 2012–13, 26% of upper-school students received aid. Total amount of financial aid awarded in 2012–13: $3,335,098.

Admissions Traditional secondary-level entrance grade is 9. For fall 2012, 433 students applied for upper-level admission, 326 were accepted, 97 enrolled. ISEE or SSAT required. Deadline for receipt of application materials: January 15. Application fee required: $45. Interview required.

Athletics Interscholastic: baseball (boys), basketball (b,g), cross-country running (b,g), field hockey (g), ice hockey (g), lacrosse (b,g), soccer (b,g), softball (g), tennis (b,g), volleyball (g), wrestling (b); coed interscholastic: cross-country running, fencing, fitness, Frisbee, golf, squash, ultimate Frisbee; coed intramural: dance team, flag football, floor hockey, physical fitness, strength & conditioning, yoga. 2 PE instructors, 108 coaches, 1 athletic trainer.

Computers Computers are regularly used in art, English, foreign language, history, mathematics, science classes. Computer network features include on-campus library services, online commercial services, Internet access, wireless campus network, Internet filtering or blocking technology. Student e-mail accounts are available to students. Students grades are available online. The school has a published electronic and media policy.

Contact Nedda Bonassera, Admission Office Manager. 617-738-2725. Fax: 617-738-2767. E-mail: admission@bcdschool.org. Web site: www.bcdschool.org

THE BEEKMAN SCHOOL

220 East 50th Street
New York, New York 10022

Head of School: George Higgins

General Information Coeducational day college-preparatory, general academic, arts, and technology school. Grades 9–PG. Founded: 1925. Setting: urban. 1 building on campus. Approved or accredited by New York State Board of Regents and New York Department of Education. Total enrollment: 80. Upper school average class size: 8. Upper school faculty-student ratio: 1:8. There are 165 required school days per year for Upper School students. Upper School students typically attend 5 days per week. The average school day consists of 6 hours and 15 minutes.

Upper School Student Profile Grade 9: 15 students (8 boys, 7 girls); Grade 10: 19 students (11 boys, 8 girls); Grade 11: 21 students (12 boys, 9 girls); Grade 12: 25 students (13 boys, 12 girls); Postgraduate: 2 students (1 boy, 1 girl).

Faculty School total: 12. In upper school: 4 men, 8 women; 10 have advanced degrees.

Subjects Offered Advanced Placement courses, algebra, American history, anatomy and physiology, ancient world history, art, astronomy, bioethics, biology, business mathematics, calculus, calculus-AP, chemistry, computer animation, computer art, computer science, conceptual physics, creative writing, drama, drawing, Eastern religion and philosophy, ecology, economics, English, environmental science, ESL, European history, film, French, geometry, government, health, modern politics, modern world history, photography, physical education, physical science, physics, poetry, pre-calculus, psychology, SAT preparation, sculpture, Spanish, TOEFL preparation, trigonometry, U.S. history, video film production, Web site design, Western philosophy.

Graduation Requirements Art, computer technologies, electives, English, foreign language, health education, mathematics, physical education (includes health), science, social studies (includes history).

Special Academic Programs Advanced Placement exam preparation; honors section; accelerated programs; independent study; academic accommodation for the gifted, the musically talented, and the artistically talented; remedial reading and/or remedial writing; remedial math; programs in English, mathematics, general development for dyslexic students; ESL (4 students enrolled).

College Admission Counseling 28 students graduated in 2012; 27 went to college, including Arizona State University; Boston University; Fordham University; New York University; Sarah Lawrence College; University of Vermont. Other: 1 had other specific plans. Mean SAT critical reading: 556, mean SAT math: 519, mean SAT writing: 543. 33% scored over 600 on SAT critical reading, 27% scored over 600 on SAT math, 30% scored over 600 on SAT writing.

Student Life Upper grades have student council, honor system. Discipline rests primarily with faculty.

Summer Programs Remediation, enrichment, advancement, ESL programs offered; session focuses on academics; held on campus; accepts boys and girls; open to students from other schools. 35 students usually enrolled. 2013 schedule: July 1 to August 12. Application deadline: June 28.

Tuition and Aid Day student tuition: $34,500. Tuition installment plan (monthly payment plans, individually arranged payment plans).

Admissions Traditional secondary-level entrance grade is 9. For fall 2012, 39 students applied for upper-level admission, 38 were accepted, 33 enrolled. Deadline for

receipt of application materials: none. No application fee required. On-campus interview required.
Athletics 1 PE instructor.
Computers Computer resources include online commercial services, Internet access.
Contact George Higgins, Headmaster. 212-755-6666. Fax: 212-888-6085. E-mail: georgeh@beekmanschool.org. Web site: www.BeekmanSchool.org

See Display on this page and Close-Up on page 546.

BELEN JESUIT PREPARATORY SCHOOL

500 Southwest 127th Avenue
Miami, Florida 33184

Head of School: Fr. Pedro A. Suarez, SJ

General Information Boys' day college-preparatory and religious studies school, affiliated with Roman Catholic Church. Grades 6–12. Founded: 1854. Setting: urban. 32-acre campus. 3 buildings on campus. Approved or accredited by CITA (Commission on International and Trans-Regional Accreditation), Jesuit Secondary Education Association, National Catholic Education Association, Southern Association of Colleges and Schools, and Florida Department of Education. Endowment: $8 million. Total enrollment: 1,497. Upper school average class size: 25. Upper school faculty-student ratio: 1:13. There are 175 required school days per year for Upper School students. Upper School students typically attend 5 days per week. The average school day consists of 8 hours.
Upper School Student Profile Grade 9: 242 students (242 boys); Grade 10: 241 students (241 boys); Grade 11: 223 students (223 boys); Grade 12: 200 students (200 boys). 98% of students are Roman Catholic.
Faculty School total: 120. In upper school: 43 men, 34 women; 67 have advanced degrees.
Subjects Offered Advanced Placement courses, art, art history, biology, chemistry, composition, computers, English, English literature, French, history, mathematics, music, philosophy, physical education, physics, religion, science, social studies, Spanish.
Graduation Requirements Arts and fine arts (art, music, dance, drama), electives, English, foreign language, mathematics, philosophy, physical education (includes health), religion (includes Bible studies and theology), science, social sciences, social studies (includes history). Community service is required.
Special Academic Programs Advanced Placement exam preparation; honors section; study at local college for college credit.
College Admission Counseling 219 students graduated in 2012; all went to college, including Florida International University; Florida State University; Miami Dade College; Tallahassee Community College; University of Florida; University of Miami. Median SAT critical reading: 570, median SAT math: 595. Mean SAT writing: 562, mean composite ACT: 25. 27% scored over 600 on SAT critical reading, 26% scored over 600 on SAT math.
Student Life Upper grades have uniform requirement, student council. Discipline rests primarily with faculty.
Summer Programs Remediation, enrichment programs offered; session focuses on make-up courses; held on campus; accepts boys; not open to students from other schools. 200 students usually enrolled. 2013 schedule: June 19 to July 19.
Tuition and Aid Day student tuition: $12,800. Tuition installment plan (monthly payment plans). Need-based scholarship grants available. In 2012–13, 35% of upper-school students received aid. Total amount of financial aid awarded in 2012–13: $400,000.
Admissions Traditional secondary-level entrance grade is 9. For fall 2012, 108 students applied for upper-level admission, 71 were accepted, 54 enrolled. School's own exam required. Deadline for receipt of application materials: January 30. Application fee required: $60.
Athletics Interscholastic: baseball, basketball, bowling, crew, cross-country running, football, golf, lacrosse, soccer, swimming and diving, tennis, track and field, volleyball, water polo, wrestling; intramural: fencing, fishing, in-line hockey, weight training. 6 PE instructors, 22 coaches, 1 athletic trainer.
Computers Computers are regularly used in art, English, foreign language, history, mathematics, music, science classes. Computer network features include on-campus library services, online commercial services, Internet access, wireless campus network, Internet filtering or blocking technology. Campus intranet and student e-mail accounts are available to students. Students grades are available online. The school has a published electronic and media policy.
Contact Mrs. Chris Besil, Admissions Secretary. 786-621-4032. Fax: 786-621-4033. E-mail: admissions@belenjesuit.org. Web site: belenjesuit.org

BELLARMINE COLLEGE PREPARATORY

960 West Hedding Street
San Jose, California 95126

Head of School: Mr. Chris Meyercord

General Information Boys' day college-preparatory, arts, religious studies, and technology school, affiliated with Roman Catholic Church. Grades 9–12. Founded: 1851. Setting: suburban. 26-acre campus. 14 buildings on campus. Approved or accredited by National Catholic Education Association and Western Association of Schools and Colleges. Endowment: $57 million. Total enrollment: 1,600. Upper school average class size: 25. Upper school faculty-student ratio: 1:13. There are 170 required school days per year for Upper School students. Upper School students typically attend 5 days per week. The average school day consists of 6 hours and 25 minutes.

Upper School Student Profile Grade 9: 415 students (415 boys); Grade 10: 410 students (410 boys); Grade 11: 390 students (390 boys); Grade 12: 385 students (385 boys). 75% of students are Roman Catholic.

Faculty School total: 90. In upper school: 60 men, 30 women; 65 have advanced degrees.

Subjects Offered Algebra, American history, American literature, anatomy, art, arts, biology, calculus, ceramics, chemistry, community service, computer science, drama, English, English literature, ethics, European history, expository writing, fine arts, French, geography, geometry, government/civics, history, international relations, Latin, Mandarin, mathematics, music, physical education, physics, psychology, religion, science, social sciences, social studies, Spanish, speech, theater, theology, trigonometry, world history, world literature, writing.

Graduation Requirements Arts and fine arts (art, music, dance, drama), English, foreign language, mathematics, physical education (includes health), religion (includes Bible studies and theology), science, social sciences, social studies (includes history), 75 hours of Christian service.

Special Academic Programs Advanced Placement exam preparation; honors section; independent study; special instructional classes for students with learning disabilities and Attention Deficit Disorder.

College Admission Counseling 392 students graduated in 2012; 390 went to college, including California Polytechnic State University, San Luis Obispo; San Jose State University; Santa Clara University; University of California, Berkeley; University of California, Davis; University of Southern California. Other: 2 had other specific plans. Mean combined SAT: 1884, mean composite ACT: 27.

Student Life Upper grades have specified standards of dress, student council, honor system. Discipline rests primarily with faculty. Attendance at religious services is required.

Summer Programs Remediation, enrichment, advancement, sports, art/fine arts, computer instruction programs offered; session focuses on enrichment; held on campus; accepts boys and girls; open to students from other schools. 1,320 students usually enrolled. 2013 schedule: June 14 to July 21. Application deadline: June 14.

Tuition and Aid Day student tuition: $16,770. Tuition installment plan (FACTS Tuition Payment Plan, semester payment plan, 11 installment plan). Need-based scholarship grants available. In 2012–13, 24% of upper-school students received aid. Total amount of financial aid awarded in 2012–13: $3,700,000.

Admissions Traditional secondary-level entrance grade is 9. For fall 2012, 950 students applied for upper-level admission, 500 were accepted, 415 enrolled. High School Placement Test required. Deadline for receipt of application materials: December 15. Application fee required: $70.

Athletics Interscholastic: aquatics, baseball, basketball, cross-country running, diving, football, golf, ice hockey, lacrosse, soccer, swimming and diving, tennis, track and field, volleyball, water polo, wrestling; intramural: basketball, flag football, Frisbee, in-line hockey, indoor hockey, soccer, tai chi, touch football, yoga. 4 PE instructors, 15 coaches, 2 athletic trainers.

Computers Computers are regularly used in art, English, foreign language, mathematics, music, science classes. Computer network features include on-campus library services, online commercial services, Internet access, wireless campus network. Student e-mail accounts are available to students. Students grades are available online. The school has a published electronic and media policy.

Contact Terry Council, Admissions Assistant. 408-294-9224. Fax: 408-294-1894. E-mail: admissions@bcp.org. Web site: www.bcp.org

BENEDICTINE COLLEGE PREPARATORY

304 North Sheppard Street
Richmond, Virginia 23221

Head of School: Mr. Jesse Grapes

General Information Boys' day college-preparatory, arts, religious studies, Junior ROTC, and military school, affiliated with Roman Catholic Church. Grades 9–12. Founded: 1911. Setting: urban. 1-acre campus. 3 buildings on campus. Approved or accredited by National Catholic Education Association and Virginia Department of Education. Member of National Association of Independent Schools. Endowment: $1.5 million. Total enrollment: 277. Upper school average class size: 15. Upper school faculty-student ratio: 1:9. There are 180 required school days per year for Upper School students. Upper School students typically attend 5 days per week. The average school day consists of 7 hours and 30 minutes.

Upper School Student Profile Grade 9: 72 students (72 boys); Grade 10: 66 students (66 boys); Grade 11: 61 students (61 boys); Grade 12: 78 students (78 boys). 65% of students are Roman Catholic.

Faculty School total: 34. In upper school: 24 men, 10 women; 14 have advanced degrees.

Subjects Offered 3-dimensional art, advanced biology, advanced studio art-AP, algebra, American literature, anatomy and physiology, art, art-AP, band, biology, biology-AP, calculus, calculus-AP, Catholic belief and practice, chemistry, Christian doctrine, Christian scripture, communication arts, creative writing, discrete mathematics, economics, engineering, English, English literature, English literature and composition-AP, geography, geometry, graphic arts, human anatomy, journalism, JROTC, Latin, Latin-AP, moral theology, photography, photojournalism, physical education, physical science, physics, pre-calculus, psychology, religion, robotics, Spanish, statistics, U.S. and Virginia government, U.S. government, U.S. government and politics, U.S. government and politics-AP, U.S. history, U.S. history-AP, United States government-AP, world history, world literature, yearbook.

Graduation Requirements Arts and fine arts (art, music, dance, drama), electives, English, JROTC, lab science, language, mathematics, physical education (includes health), religion (includes Bible studies and theology), social studies (includes history), community service requirement.

Special Academic Programs Advanced Placement exam preparation; honors section; academic accommodation for the gifted and the artistically talented; remedial math.

College Admission Counseling 69 students graduated in 2011; 68 went to college, including The College of William and Mary; University of Notre Dame; University of Virginia; Virginia Polytechnic Institute and State University. Other: 1 went to work. Mean combined SAT: 1580, mean composite ACT: 22.

Student Life Upper grades have uniform requirement, student council, honor system. Discipline rests equally with students and faculty. Attendance at religious services is required.

Tuition and Aid Day student tuition: $14,700. Tuition installment plan (FACTS Tuition Payment Plan). Merit scholarship grants, need-based scholarship grants, full time employee tuition discount (1/2 price) for sons available. In 2011–12, 35% of upper-school students received aid; total upper-school merit-scholarship money awarded: $50,000. Total amount of financial aid awarded in 2011–12: $500,000.

Admissions Traditional secondary-level entrance grade is 9. For fall 2011, 138 students applied for upper-level admission, 115 were accepted, 89 enrolled. SSAT required. Deadline for receipt of application materials: none. Application fee required: $50. Interview required.

Athletics Interscholastic: baseball, basketball, boxing, cross-country running, football, golf, indoor track & field, JROTC drill, lacrosse, marksmanship, outdoor skills, riflery, soccer, swimming and diving, tennis, track and field, winter (indoor) track, wrestling; intramural: Frisbee, outdoor adventure, outdoor education, strength & conditioning, volleyball, weight lifting, weight training, wilderness survival, wildernessways. 27 coaches, 1 athletic trainer.

Computers Computers are regularly used in graphic arts, journalism, photojournalism, programming, yearbook classes. Computer resources include on-campus library services, Internet access, wireless campus network, Internet filtering or blocking technology. Student e-mail accounts are available to students. Students grades are available online. The school has a published electronic and media policy.

Contact Mrs. Sandy M. Carli, Associate Director of Admission. 804-342-1314. Fax: 804-342-1349. E-mail: scarli@benedictinecollegeprep.org. Web site: www.benedictinecollegeprep.org

BENEDICTINE HIGH SCHOOL

2900 Martin Luther King, Jr. Drive
Cleveland, Ohio 44104

Head of School: Mr. Joseph Gressock

General Information Boys' day college-preparatory and religious studies school, affiliated with Roman Catholic Church. Grades 9–12. Founded: 1927. Setting: urban. 13-acre campus. 3 buildings on campus. Approved or accredited by National Catholic Education Association, North Central Association of Colleges and Schools, Ohio Catholic Schools Accreditation Association (OCSAA), and Ohio Department of Education. Total enrollment: 352. Upper school average class size: 15. Upper school faculty-student ratio: 1:11. There are 180 required school days per year for Upper School students. Upper School students typically attend 5 days per week. The average school day consists of 6 hours and 30 minutes.

Upper School Student Profile Grade 9: 90 students (90 boys); Grade 10: 68 students (68 boys); Grade 11: 90 students (90 boys); Grade 12: 82 students (82 boys). 80% of students are Roman Catholic.

Faculty School total: 37. In upper school: 32 men, 5 women; 31 have advanced degrees.

Subjects Offered Advanced chemistry, advanced math, Advanced Placement courses, aesthetics, algebra, American literature, American literature-AP, analysis and differential calculus, analytic geometry, Ancient Greek, ancient history, ancient world history, art, athletic training, band, Basic programming, Bible studies, biology, biology-AP, British literature-AP, business education, business law, calculus, calculus-AP, Catholic belief and practice, Central and Eastern European history, ceramics, chemistry, choir, chorus, church history, Civil War, civil war history, classical Greek literature, classical language, computer education, computer graphics, computer information systems, computer literacy, computer programming, computer skills, computer-aided design, concert band, concert choir, current events, drawing, drawing and design, economics, electives, English, English literature and composition-AP, European history-AP, film studies, foreign language, French, geometry, German, government, government-AP, government/civics, government/civics-AP, graphic design, health, honors algebra, honors English, honors geometry, honors U.S. history, honors world history, human geography - AP, jazz band, journalism, keyboarding, lab science, Latin, Latin-AP, Life of Christ, marching band, marketing, moral theology, music, music appreciation, New Testament, painting, physical education, pre-calculus, probability and statistics, psychology, Russian, Shakespeare.

Graduation Requirements 1 1/2 elective credits, 20th century American writers, 20th century history, 20th century world history, algebra, American government, American history, American literature, ancient history, ancient world history, art, biology, British literature, chemistry, church history, computer applications, English, foreign language, geometry, physical education (includes health), physics, senior project, theology, U.S. history, world history, community service hours.

Special Academic Programs 8 Advanced Placement exams for which test preparation is offered; honors section; independent study; study at local college for college credit; study abroad; remedial reading and/or remedial writing; remedial math.

College Admission Counseling 79 students graduated in 2011; 75 went to college, including Bowling Green State University; Case Western Reserve University; Cleveland State University; Kent State University; The University of Akron; University of Dayton. Other: 2 went to work, 2 entered military service. Mean SAT critical reading: 554, mean SAT math: 526, mean SAT writing: 542, mean combined SAT: 1622, mean composite ACT: 22.

Student Life Upper grades have specified standards of dress, student council, honor system. Discipline rests primarily with faculty. Attendance at religious services is required.

Tuition and Aid Day student tuition: $9000. Tuition installment plan (monthly payment plans, individually arranged payment plans). Tuition reduction for siblings, merit scholarship grants, need-based scholarship grants, paying campus jobs available. In 2011–12, 73% of upper-school students received aid.

Admissions Traditional secondary-level entrance grade is 9. For fall 2011, 250 students applied for upper-level admission, 175 were accepted, 90 enrolled. High School Placement Test required. Deadline for receipt of application materials: none. Application fee required: $150. Interview recommended.

Athletics Interscholastic: baseball, basketball, bowling, cross-country running, football, golf, hockey, ice hockey, lacrosse, soccer, swimming and diving, track and field, wrestling; intramural: baseball, basketball, flag football, football, physical fitness, physical training, skiing (downhill), snowboarding, strength & conditioning, volleyball, weight lifting, weight training. 10 coaches, 2 athletic trainers.

Computers Computers are regularly used in computer applications, creative writing, current events, data processing, design, English, graphic design, history, independent study, information technology, library, mathematics, newspaper, technical drawing, yearbook classes. Computer network features include on-campus library services, online commercial services, Internet access, wireless campus network, Internet filtering or blocking technology. Student e-mail accounts are available to students. Students grades are available online. The school has a published electronic and media policy.

Contact Mr. Kieran Patton, Admissions and Advancement Director. 216-421-2080 Ext. 356. Fax: 216-421-1100. E-mail: patton@cbhs.net. Web site: www.cbhs.net

BENET ACADEMY

2200 Maple Avenue
Lisle, Illinois 60532

Head of School: Mr. Stephen A. Marth

General Information Coeducational day college-preparatory, arts, and religious studies school, affiliated with Roman Catholic Church. Grades 9–12. Founded: 1887. Setting: suburban. Nearest major city is Chicago. 54-acre campus. 8 buildings on campus. Approved or accredited by North Central Association of Colleges and Schools and Illinois Department of Education. Total enrollment: 1,339. Upper school average class size: 27. Upper school faculty-student ratio: 1:18. There are 176 required school days per year for Upper School students. Upper School students typically attend 5 days per week. The average school day consists of 6 hours and 30 minutes.

Upper School Student Profile Grade 9: 344 students (184 boys, 160 girls); Grade 10: 330 students (169 boys, 161 girls); Grade 11: 327 students (161 boys, 166 girls); Grade 12: 338 students (149 boys, 189 girls). 97% of students are Roman Catholic.

Faculty School total: 76. In upper school: 45 men, 31 women; 73 have advanced degrees.

Subjects Offered Algebra, American history, American literature, art history, biology, business, calculus, chemistry, computer programming, computer science, creative writing, drama, driver education, economics, English, European history, French, geography, geometry, German, government/civics, health, history, Latin, mathematics, music, physical education, physics, religion, science, Spanish, speech, statistics, trigonometry, U.S. history-AP, world history, world literature, writing.

Graduation Requirements Computer science, English, foreign language, mathematics, physical education (includes health), religion (includes Bible studies and theology), science, social studies (includes history).

Special Academic Programs 21 Advanced Placement exams for which test preparation is offered; honors section; study at local college for college credit; academic accommodation for the gifted.

College Admission Counseling 338 students graduated in 2012; 336 went to college, including Northwestern University; The University of Iowa; University of Illinois; University of Notre Dame. Other: 2 had other specific plans. Mean SAT critical reading: 632, mean SAT math: 647, mean SAT writing: 622, mean composite ACT: 28.

Student Life Upper grades have uniform requirement, student council. Discipline rests primarily with faculty. Attendance at religious services is required.

Summer Programs Computer instruction programs offered; session focuses on computer literacy skills for incoming freshmen; held on campus; accepts boys and girls; not open to students from other schools. 300 students usually enrolled.

Tuition and Aid Day student tuition: $9700. Tuition installment plan (monthly payment plans). Tuition reduction for siblings, need-based scholarship grants available. In 2012–13, 5% of upper-school students received aid.

Admissions Traditional secondary-level entrance grade is 9. For fall 2012, 550 students applied for upper-level admission, 430 were accepted, 345 enrolled. High School Placement Test required. Deadline for receipt of application materials: January 12. Application fee required: $35. On-campus interview required.

Athletics Interscholastic: baseball (boys), basketball (b,g), cheering (g), cross-country running (b,g), dance team (g), fishing (b), football (b), golf (b,g), lacrosse (b,g), pom squad (g), soccer (b,g), softball (g), strength & conditioning (b), swimming and diving (b,g), tennis (b,g), track and field (b,g), volleyball (b,g), yoga (g); intramural: weight training (b,g), yoga (g); coed interscholastic: ice hockey; coed intramural: bowling, flag football, Frisbee, table tennis. 4 PE instructors, 30 coaches, 1 athletic trainer.

Computers Computers are regularly used in English, history, mathematics, science, Spanish classes. Computer network features include on-campus library services, online commercial services, Internet access, Internet filtering or blocking technology. The school has a published electronic and media policy.

Contact Mr. James E. Brown, Assistant Principal. 630-969-6550. Fax: 630-719-2849. E-mail: jbrown@benet.org. Web site: www.benet.org/

BEN FRANKLIN ACADEMY

1585 Clifton Road
Atlanta, Georgia 30329

Head of School: Dr. Wood Smethurst

General Information Coeducational day college-preparatory school. Grades 9–12. Founded: 1987. Setting: urban. 3-acre campus. 2 buildings on campus. Approved or accredited by Georgia Independent School Association, Southern Association of Colleges and Schools, Southern Association of Independent Schools, and Georgia Department of Education. Total enrollment: 130. Upper school average class size: 1. Upper school faculty-student ratio: 1:2. There are 180 required school days per year for Upper School students. Upper School students typically attend 5 days per week. The average school day consists of 3 hours and 30 minutes.

Faculty School total: 29. In upper school: 12 men, 17 women; 15 have advanced degrees.

Subjects Offered 1 1/2 elective credits.

Graduation Requirements We have a work-study component in addition to the academic requirements.

Special Academic Programs Advanced Placement exam preparation; honors section; accelerated programs; academic accommodation for the gifted.

College Admission Counseling 40 students graduated in 2011; all went to college.

Student Life Upper grades have specified standards of dress. Discipline rests primarily with faculty.

Tuition and Aid Day student tuition: $23,250–$29,750. Tuition installment plan (individually arranged payment plans). Tuition reduction for siblings, need-based scholarship grants available. In 2011–12, 20% of upper-school students received aid.

Admissions Traditional secondary-level entrance grade is 10. Deadline for receipt of application materials: none. No application fee required. On-campus interview required.

Athletics Interscholastic: cross-country running (boys, girls), golf (b,g); coed interscholastic: basketball, cross-country running, Frisbee, golf, tennis, ultimate Frisbee.

Computers Computer resources include on-campus library services, Internet access, Internet filtering or blocking technology. Campus intranet and student e-mail accounts are available to students. The school has a published electronic and media policy.

Contact Dr. Martha B. Burdette, Dean of Studies. 404-633-7404. Fax: 404-321-0610. E-mail: bfa@benfranklinacademy.org. Web site: www.benfranklinacademy.org

BEREAN CHRISTIAN HIGH SCHOOL

245 El Divisadero Avenue
Walnut Creek, California 94598

Head of School: Mr. Nelson M. Noriega

General Information Coeducational day college-preparatory and religious studies school, affiliated with Baptist Church. Grades 9–12. Founded: 1969. Setting: suburban. Nearest major city is Oakland. 5-acre campus. 5 buildings on campus. Approved or accredited by Western Association of Schools and Colleges and California Department of Education. Total enrollment: 430. Upper school average class size: 430. Upper school faculty-student ratio: 1:14. There are 180 required school days per year for Upper School students. Upper School students typically attend 5 days per week. The average school day consists of 6 hours and 30 minutes.

Upper School Student Profile 50% of students are Baptist.
Faculty School total: 31. In upper school: 14 men, 17 women; 11 have advanced degrees.
Subjects Offered Algebra, anatomy, art, arts, Bible studies, biology, chemistry, choir, computer literacy, computer science, drama, economics, English, ethics, fine arts, geometry, government, health, mathematics, physical education, physics, physiology, pre-calculus, religion, science, social studies, Spanish, trigonometry, U.S. history, world history, world religions.
Special Academic Programs Advanced Placement exam preparation; independent study; study abroad.
College Admission Counseling 105 students graduated in 2011; 103 went to college. Other: 2 went to work.
Student Life Upper grades have specified standards of dress, student council, honor system. Discipline rests primarily with faculty.
Tuition and Aid Day student tuition: $7500. Tuition reduction for siblings, need-based scholarship grants available. In 2011–12, 5% of upper-school students received aid.
Admissions Traditional secondary-level entrance grade is 9. For fall 2011, 205 students applied for upper-level admission, 125 were accepted, 125 enrolled. Deadline for receipt of application materials: March. Application fee required: $345. On-campus interview required.
Athletics Interscholastic: baseball (boys), basketball (b,g), cheering (g), cross-country running (b,g), football (b), soccer (b,g), softball (g), swimming and diving (b,g), tennis (g), volleyball (b,g); coed interscholastic: golf. 2 PE instructors, 42 coaches.
Computers Computer network features include on-campus library services, Internet access, wireless campus network, Internet filtering or blocking technology. Student e-mail accounts are available to students. Students grades are available online.
Contact Nelson M. Noriega, Principal. 925-945-6464. E-mail: nnoriega@berean-eagles.org. Web site: www.berean-eagles.org

BERKELEY PREPARATORY SCHOOL

4811 Kelly Road
Tampa, Florida 33615

Head of School: Joseph W. Seivold

General Information Coeducational day college-preparatory, arts, religious studies, bilingual studies, and technology school, affiliated with Episcopal Church. Grades PK–12. Founded: 1960. Setting: suburban. 80-acre campus. 8 buildings on campus. Approved or accredited by Florida Council of Independent Schools, National Association of Episcopal Schools, Southern Association of Colleges and Schools, Southern Association of Independent Schools, The College Board, and Florida Department of Education. Member of National Association of Independent Schools and Secondary School Admission Test Board. Total enrollment: 1,290. Upper school average class size: 15. Upper school faculty-student ratio: 1:9. Upper School students typically attend 5 days per week. The average school day consists of 7 hours.
Faculty School total: 175. In upper school: 30 men, 38 women; 45 have advanced degrees.
Subjects Offered African history, algebra, American government, American history, American literature, art, art history, biology, biology-AP, calculus, calculus-AP, ceramics, chemistry, chemistry-AP, China/Japan history, community service, computer math, computer programming, computer science, creative writing, dance, drama, drama performance, drama workshop, early childhood, economics, English, English literature, English-AP, environmental science-AP, etymology, European history, expository writing, fine arts, French, French-AP, freshman seminar, geography, geometry, government/civics, grammar, guitar, health, history, history of China and Japan, honors algebra, honors English, honors geometry, instruments, Latin, Latin American history, Latin-AP, logic, Mandarin, math analysis, mathematics, media arts, microbiology, modern European history, modern European history-AP, music, performing arts, philosophy, physical education, physics, physics-AP, pre-calculus, psychology, religious studies, SAT preparation, science, social studies, Spanish, Spanish-AP, speech, stage design, statistics, statistics-AP, technical theater, television, theater, theater production, U.S. history, U.S. history-AP, video, video film production, Western civilization, world history, world literature, writing.
Graduation Requirements Arts and fine arts (art, music, dance, drama), computer science, English, foreign language, mathematics, physical education (includes health), religious studies, science, social studies (includes history). Community service is required.
Special Academic Programs Advanced Placement exam preparation; honors section; independent study; study abroad.
College Admission Counseling 150 students graduated in 2012; all went to college, including Boston College; Duke University; Harvard University; University of Florida; University of Michigan; Wake Forest University. Mean SAT critical reading: 616, mean SAT math: 633, mean SAT writing: 632, mean combined SAT: 1881, mean composite ACT: 28.
Student Life Upper grades have specified standards of dress, student council, honor system. Discipline rests equally with students and faculty.
Summer Programs Remediation, enrichment, advancement, sports, art/fine arts, computer instruction programs offered; session focuses on setting a fun pace for excellence; held on campus; accepts boys and girls; open to students from other schools. 3,000 students usually enrolled. 2013 schedule: June 4 to July 27. Application deadline: none.
Tuition and Aid Day student tuition: $20,110. Tuition installment plan (8-installment plan). Merit scholarship grants, need-based scholarship grants available. Total upper-school merit-scholarship money awarded for 2012–13: $8,600,000.
Admissions Traditional secondary-level entrance grade is 9. Otis-Lennon Mental Ability Test and SSAT required. Deadline for receipt of application materials: January 30. Application fee required: $75. On-campus interview required.
Athletics Interscholastic: baseball (boys), basketball (b,g), cheering (g), crew (b,g), cross-country running (b,g), dance squad (g), dance team (g), diving (b,g), football (b), golf (b,g), ice hockey (b), lacrosse (b), rowing (b,g), soccer (b,g), softball (g), swimming and diving (b,g), tennis (b,g), track and field (b,g), volleyball (b,g); coed interscholastic: weight lifting, wrestling; coed intramural: physical fitness, physical training, power lifting, project adventure, strength & conditioning, wall climbing, weight training. 14 PE instructors, 74 coaches, 2 athletic trainers.
Computers Computers are regularly used in art, English, foreign language, history, mathematics, music, science classes. Computer network features include on-campus library services, online commercial services, Internet access, wireless campus network, Internet filtering or blocking technology. Student e-mail accounts are available to students. Students grades are available online. The school has a published electronic and media policy.
Contact Janie McIlvaine, Director of Admissions. 813-885-1673. Fax: 813-886-6933. E-mail: mcilvjan@berkeleyprep.org. Web site: www.berkeleyprep.org

See Display on next page and Close-Up on page 548.

BERKSHIRE SCHOOL

245 North Undermountain Road
Sheffield, Massachusetts 01257

Head of School: Michael J. Maher

General Information Coeducational boarding and day college-preparatory, arts, and technology school. Grades 9–PG. Founded: 1907. Setting: rural. Nearest major city is Hartford, CT. Students are housed in single-sex dormitories. 400-acre campus. 37 buildings on campus. Approved or accredited by Association of Independent Schools in New England, New England Association of Schools and Colleges, and The Association of Boarding Schools. Member of National Association of Independent Schools and Secondary School Admission Test Board. Endowment: $91 million. Upper school average class size: 12. Upper school faculty-student ratio: 1:5. Upper School students typically attend 6 days per week. The average school day consists of 6 hours and 45 minutes.
Upper School Student Profile Grade 9: 63 students (35 boys, 28 girls); Grade 10: 109 students (66 boys, 43 girls); Grade 11: 102 students (56 boys, 46 girls); Grade 12: 96 students (54 boys, 42 girls); Postgraduate: 16 students (14 boys, 2 girls). 92% of students are boarding students. 8% are state residents. 27 states are represented in upper school student body. 18% are international students. International students from Canada, China, Mexico, Republic of Korea, Venezuela, and Viet Nam; 21 other countries represented in student body.
Faculty School total: 67. In upper school: 42 men, 25 women; 42 have advanced degrees; 49 reside on campus.
Subjects Offered 3-dimensional design, acting, Advanced Placement courses, algebra, American government, American history, American literature, anatomy, ancient history, animal behavior, art, art history, aviation, biology, calculus, ceramics, chemistry, Chinese, choral music, chorus, comparative government and politics, comparative religion, computer programming, constitutional law, creative writing, dance, digital art, drama, drawing and design, economics, English, English literature, environmental science, ESL, ethics, European history, expository writing, French, geology, geometry, health, history, instrumental music, Latin, mathematics, music, music technology, painting, philosophy, photography, physics, pre-calculus, psychology, science, Spanish, studio art, theater, trigonometry, world religions, writing.
Graduation Requirements Arts and fine arts (art, music, dance, drama), English, foreign language, history, mathematics, science. Community service is required.
Special Academic Programs 16 Advanced Placement exams for which test preparation is offered; honors section; independent study; study abroad; ESL (8 students enrolled).
College Admission Counseling 113 students graduated in 2012; all went to college, including Bates College; Colgate University; Connecticut College; Emory University; Hamilton College; Union College.
Student Life Upper grades have specified standards of dress, student council, honor system. Discipline rests equally with students and faculty.
Tuition and Aid Day student tuition: $39,900; 7-day tuition and room/board: $49,900. Tuition installment plan (Key Tuition Payment Plan, monthly payment plans). Need-based scholarship grants available. In 2012–13, 30% of upper-school students received aid. Total amount of financial aid awarded in 2012–13: $4,955,292.
Admissions Traditional secondary-level entrance grade is 9. For fall 2012, 1,012 students applied for upper-level admission, 374 were accepted, 149 enrolled. ACT, PSAT, SAT, SSAT or TOEFL required. Deadline for receipt of application materials: January 15. Application fee required: $75. Interview required.

Athletics Interscholastic: baseball (boys), basketball (b,g), crew (b,g), cross-country running (b,g), field hockey (g), football (b), ice hockey (b,g), lacrosse (b,g), soccer (b,g), softball (g), squash (b,g), tennis (b,g), track and field (b,g), volleyball (g); coed interscholastic: alpine skiing, golf, mountain biking; coed intramural: alpine skiing, canoeing/kayaking, climbing, dance, fly fishing, hiking/backpacking, kayaking, modern dance, mountaineering, outdoor adventure, outdoor education, outdoor skills, rappelling, rock climbing, ropes courses, skiing (cross-country), skiing (downhill), snowboarding, wilderness, wilderness survival. 2 athletic trainers.

Computers Computers are regularly used in art, English, foreign language, mathematics, music, science, technology classes. Computer network features include on-campus library services, online commercial services, Internet access, wireless campus network, Internet filtering or blocking technology, network printing, interactive Polyvision white boards (smart boards). Campus intranet and student e-mail accounts are available to students. Students grades are available online. The school has a published electronic and media policy.

Contact Ms. Karin Tucker, Assistant to Director of Admission. 413-229-1003. Fax: 413-229-1016. E-mail: admission@berkshireschool.org. Web site: www.berkshireschool.org

See Display on next page and Close-Up on page 550.

BETH HAVEN CHRISTIAN SCHOOL

5515 Johnsontown Road
Louisville, Kentucky 40272

Head of School: Ms. Melissa Pace

General Information Coeducational day college-preparatory and religious studies school, affiliated with Baptist Church. Grades K4–12. Founded: 1971. Setting: suburban. 2-acre campus. 1 building on campus. Approved or accredited by Association of Christian Schools International and Kentucky Department of Education. Total enrollment: 211. Upper school average class size: 18. Upper school faculty-student ratio: 1:9. There are 177 required school days per year for Upper School students. Upper School students typically attend 5 days per week. The average school day consists of 7 hours and 5 minutes.

Upper School Student Profile Grade 9: 9 students (5 boys, 4 girls); Grade 10: 12 students (8 boys, 4 girls); Grade 11: 18 students (10 boys, 8 girls); Grade 12: 21 students (13 boys, 8 girls). 65% of students are Baptist.

Faculty School total: 12. In upper school: 4 men, 3 women; 2 have advanced degrees.

Subjects Offered ACT preparation, Advanced Placement courses, algebra, American history, American literature, analytic geometry, art appreciation, Bible studies, biology, British literature (honors), business mathematics, calculus-AP, chemistry, computer applications, drama, dramatic arts, earth science, economics, English, English composition, English language and composition-AP, health, honors algebra, honors English, honors geometry, honors U.S. history, honors world history, independent study, journalism, keyboarding, lab science, psychology, psychology-AP, senior seminar, Spanish, speech, trigonometry, U.S. government and politics-AP, world geography, world history, yearbook.

Graduation Requirements ACT preparation, algebra, American government, American history, American literature, analytic geometry, arts appreciation, Bible, biology, British literature, chemistry, earth science, economics, English, language, physical education (includes health), world geography, world history.

Special Academic Programs Honors section; independent study; study at local college for college credit.

College Admission Counseling 26 students graduated in 2012; 24 went to college, including Abilene Christian University; Asbury University; Bellarmine University; Indiana University Bloomington; Jefferson Community and Technical College; University of Louisville. Other: 1 entered military service, 1 had other specific plans. Median composite ACT: 22. 5% scored over 26 on composite ACT.

Student Life Upper grades have uniform requirement, student council, honor system. Discipline rests primarily with faculty.

Summer Programs Remediation, sports programs offered; held on campus; accepts boys and girls; not open to students from other schools. 50 students usually enrolled. 2013 schedule: June 3 to August 16. Application deadline: June 3.

Tuition and Aid Day student tuition: $4575. Tuition installment plan (FACTS Tuition Payment Plan). Tuition reduction for siblings, need-based scholarship grants, two full-tuition memorial scholarships are awarded each year based on a combination of merit and need available. In 2012–13, 5% of upper-school students received aid. Total amount of financial aid awarded in 2012–13: $8000.

Admissions Traditional secondary-level entrance grade is 9. For fall 2012, 9 students applied for upper-level admission, 9 were accepted, 9 enrolled. Stanford Test of Academic Skills required. Deadline for receipt of application materials: none. Application fee required: $250. Interview required.

Athletics Interscholastic: baseball (boys), basketball (b,g), cheering (g), football (b), softball (g), volleyball (g); coed interscholastic: cross-country running. 1 PE instructor.

Computers Computers are regularly used in business applications, computer applications, English, journalism, yearbook classes. Computer network features include Internet access, Internet filtering or blocking technology. Computer access in designated common areas is available to students. Students grades are available online. The school has a published electronic and media policy.

Contact Ms. Lisa Vincent, Registrar. 502-937-3516. Fax: 502-937-3364. E-mail: lvincent@bethhaven.com. Web site: www.bethhaven.com/

THE BIRCH WATHEN LENOX SCHOOL

210 East 77th Street
New York, New York 10075

Head of School: Mr. Frank J. Carnabuci III

General Information Coeducational day college-preparatory school. Grades K–12. Founded: 1916. Setting: urban. 1 building on campus. Approved or accredited by New York Department of Education. Member of National Association of Independent Schools. Endowment: $7.2 million. Total enrollment: 570. Upper school average class size: 15. Upper school faculty-student ratio: 1:15. Upper School students typically attend 5 days per week. The average school day consists of 7 hours.

Upper School Student Profile Grade 9: 46 students (24 boys, 22 girls); Grade 10: 45 students (25 boys, 20 girls); Grade 11: 46 students (23 boys, 23 girls); Grade 12: 48 students (22 boys, 26 girls).

Faculty School total: 120. In upper school: 30 men, 85 women; 115 have advanced degrees.

Subjects Offered Algebra, American history, American history-AP, American literature, American literature-AP, art, art history, biology, calculus, ceramics, chemistry, community service, computer math, computer science, creative writing, dance, drama, driver education, economics, English, English literature, environmental science, European history, expository writing, fine arts, French, geography, geology, geometry, government/civics, grammar, industrial arts, Japanese, journalism, mathematics, music, philosophy, photography, physical education, physics, science, Shakespeare, social studies, Spanish, speech, swimming, theater, trigonometry, typing, world history, writing.

Graduation Requirements 20th century world history, arts and fine arts (art, music, dance, drama), computer science, English, foreign language, mathematics, physical education (includes health), science, social studies (includes history). Community service is required.

Special Academic Programs Advanced Placement exam preparation; honors section; independent study; study abroad; academic accommodation for the gifted, the musically talented, and the artistically talented.

College Admission Counseling 44 students graduated in 2012; all went to college, including Columbia University; Skidmore College; Trinity College; University of Pennsylvania; Vanderbilt University; Wesleyan University. Mean SAT critical reading: 650, mean SAT math: 650, mean SAT writing: 700.

Student Life Upper grades have uniform requirement, student council, honor system. Discipline rests equally with students and faculty.

Summer Programs Enrichment programs offered; session focuses on math and science; not open to students from other schools.

Tuition and Aid Day student tuition: $38,950. Tuition installment plan (Key Tuition Payment Plan, monthly payment plans, individually arranged payment plans). Merit scholarship grants, need-based scholarship grants available. In 2012–13, 17% of upper-school students received aid; total upper-school merit-scholarship money awarded: $100,000. Total amount of financial aid awarded in 2012–13: $1,200,000.

Admissions Traditional secondary-level entrance grade is 9. For fall 2012, 100 students applied for upper-level admission, 30 were accepted, 20 enrolled. ERB, ISEE, Math Placement Exam or writing sample required. Deadline for receipt of application materials: none. Application fee required: $50. On-campus interview required.

Athletics Interscholastic: baseball (boys), basketball (b,g), cross-country running (b,g), field hockey (g), hockey (b), ice hockey (b), lacrosse (b), soccer (b,g), softball (g), squash (b,g), swimming and diving (b,g), tennis (b,g), track and field (b,g), volleyball (g); intramural: aerobics (b,g), badminton (g), baseball (b), basketball (b,g), dance (b), ice hockey (b), indoor soccer (b), running (b,g), skiing (downhill) (b,g), soccer (b,g), softball (g), swimming and diving (b,g), tennis (b,g), track and field (b,g), volleyball (b,g); coed interscholastic: cross-country running, Frisbee, golf, ice hockey, indoor track & field, lacrosse, squash; coed intramural: bicycling, dance, golf, gymnastics, indoor track & field, skiing (cross-country), skiing (downhill). 5 PE instructors, 8 coaches.

Computers Computers are regularly used in all academic classes. Computer network features include on-campus library services, Internet access, wireless campus network, MOBY, Smartboard. Student e-mail accounts are available to students.

Contact Billie Williams, Admissions Coordinator. 212-861-0404. Fax: 212-879-3388. E-mail: bwilliams@bwl.org. Web site: www.bwl.org

See Close-Up on page 552.

BISHOP BLANCHET HIGH SCHOOL

8200 Wallingford Avenue North
Seattle, Washington 98103-4599

Head of School: Kristine Ann Brynildsen-Smith, EdD

General Information Coeducational day college-preparatory, arts, religious studies, and technology school, affiliated with Roman Catholic Church. Grades 9–12. Founded: 1954. Setting: urban. 9-acre campus. 1 building on campus. Approved or accredited by National Catholic Education Association, Northwest Accreditation Commission, and Washington Department of Education. Endowment: $5 million. Total enrollment: 989. Upper school average class size: 20. Upper school faculty-student ratio: 1:13. There are 180 required school days per year for Upper School students. Upper School students typically attend 5 days per week. The average school day consists of 7 hours and 30 minutes.

Upper School Student Profile Grade 9: 264 students (138 boys, 126 girls); Grade 10: 262 students (152 boys, 110 girls); Grade 11: 223 students (118 boys, 105 girls); Grade 12: 241 students (132 boys, 109 girls). 82% of students are Roman Catholic.

Faculty School total: 81. In upper school: 36 men, 45 women; 52 have advanced degrees.

Subjects Offered 20th century American writers, 20th century world history, 3-dimensional design, American foreign policy, American history-AP, American literature, anatomy and physiology, applied arts, art, arts and crafts, ASB Leadership, band, biology, business applications, calculus, calculus-AP, Catholic belief and practice, ceramics, chamber groups, chemistry, chemistry-AP, choral music, comparative religion, contemporary history, desktop publishing, discrete mathematics, drama, drama performance, economics, English composition, English literature, ethics, ethnic literature, ethnic studies, European history, family living, French, German, government, guitar, health, history of rock and roll, history of the Catholic Church, instrumental music, Japanese, jazz band, language arts, Life of Christ, literature, marching band, math analysis, musical productions, performing arts, personal finance, philosophy, photography, physical education, physics, psychology, religion, scripture, set design, Spanish, U.S. history, vocal ensemble.

Graduation Requirements Art, business education, English, foreign language, lab science, mathematics, physical education (includes health), religion (includes Bible studies and theology), social studies (includes history).

Special Academic Programs Advanced Placement exam preparation; honors section; study at local college for college credit; programs in general development for dyslexic students.

College Admission Counseling 224 students graduated in 2011; 215 went to college, including Gonzaga University; The University of Montana Western; University of Washington; Washington State University; Western Washington University. Other: 4 went to work, 5 had other specific plans.

Student Life Upper grades have specified standards of dress, student council. Discipline rests primarily with faculty. Attendance at religious services is required.

Tuition and Aid Day student tuition: $12,312. Tuition installment plan (monthly payment plans, individually arranged payment plans). Tuition reduction for siblings, merit scholarship grants, need-based scholarship grants, paying campus jobs available. In 2011–12, 40% of upper-school students received aid; total upper-school merit-scholarship money awarded: $120,000. Total amount of financial aid awarded in 2011–12: $1,600,000.

Admissions Traditional secondary-level entrance grade is 9. For fall 2011, 600 students applied for upper-level admission, 265 enrolled. ISEE required. Deadline for receipt of application materials: January 12. Application fee required: $25.

Athletics Interscholastic: baseball (boys), basketball (b,g), cheering (g), cross-country running (b,g), football (b), golf (b,g), lacrosse (b), soccer (b,g), softball (g), volleyball (g), wrestling (b); coed interscholastic: swimming and diving, tennis, track and field; coed intramural: alpine skiing, basketball, bowling, dance team, golf, hiking/backpacking, skiing (downhill), snowboarding, soccer, softball, strength & conditioning, table tennis, tennis, volleyball, weight lifting. 6 PE instructors, 1 athletic trainer.

Computers Computers are regularly used in accounting, business applications, business education, career exploration, college planning, computer applications, desktop publishing, foreign language, journalism, keyboarding, library skills, mathematics, newspaper, photography, science, video film production, word processing, yearbook classes. Computer network features include on-campus library services, online commercial services, Internet access, wireless campus network, Internet filtering or blocking technology, Internet Services with 2 ISP's totaling 60mbps bandwidth, Desktop monitoring software for library and labs, Web-based virtual classroom environment for all classes (Moodle. Student e-mail accounts and computer access in designated common areas are available to students. Students grades are available online. The school has a published electronic and media policy.

Contact Ann Alokolaro, Director of Admissions. 206-527-7741. Fax: 206-527-7712. E-mail: aalokola@bishopblanchet.org. Web site: www.bishopblanchet.org

BISHOP BRADY HIGH SCHOOL

25 Columbus Avenue
Concord, New Hampshire 03301

Head of School: Mr. Trevor Bonat

General Information Coeducational day college-preparatory school, affiliated with Roman Catholic Church. Grades 9–12. Founded: 1963. Setting: suburban. 8-acre campus. 1 building on campus. Approved or accredited by National Catholic Education Association, New England Association of Schools and Colleges, and New Hampshire Department of Education. Total enrollment: 365. Upper school average class size: 17. Upper school faculty-student ratio: 1:16. There are 180 required school days per year for Upper School students. Upper School students typically attend 5 days per week. The average school day consists of 6 hours and 30 minutes.

Upper School Student Profile Grade 9: 93 students (45 boys, 48 girls); Grade 10: 84 students (43 boys, 41 girls); Grade 11: 93 students (43 boys, 50 girls); Grade 12: 95 students (47 boys, 48 girls). 70% of students are Roman Catholic.

Faculty School total: 34. In upper school: 14 men, 20 women; 25 have advanced degrees.

Subjects Offered Advanced chemistry, advanced math, algebra, anatomy and physiology, art appreciation, arts, biology, biology-AP, calculus-AP, career/college preparation, chemistry, chemistry-AP, Christian scripture, civics, college awareness, college counseling, computer education, conceptual physics, drama, English, English literature-AP, English-AP, film studies, French-AP, freshman seminar, geometry, guidance, health education, history, history-AP, honors English, Latin, moral theology, music appreciation, musical theater, physical education, physics-AP, pre-calculus, probability and statistics, psychology, religious studies, research and reference, SAT preparation, social justice, Spanish-AP, theology, trigonometry, U.S. history-AP, world religions, writing.

Graduation Requirements Algebra, American literature, arts and fine arts (art, music, dance, drama), biology, chemistry, computer education, English, geometry, languages, physical education (includes health), science, social studies (includes history), theology, 90 hours of community service.

Special Academic Programs 8 Advanced Placement exams for which test preparation is offered; honors section; independent study; study at local college for college credit; academic accommodation for the gifted; ESL (25 students enrolled).

College Admission Counseling 97 students graduated in 2012; 93 went to college, including Boston College; Georgetown University; Saint Anselm College; University of New Hampshire; University of Notre Dame. Other: 4 entered military service. Mean SAT critical reading: 556, mean SAT math: 544, mean SAT writing: 552, mean composite ACT: 25. 30% scored over 600 on SAT critical reading, 30% scored over 600 on SAT math.

Student Life Upper grades have specified standards of dress, student council, honor system. Discipline rests primarily with faculty. Attendance at religious services is required.

Summer Programs Remediation, enrichment, advancement, sports programs offered; session focuses on football and conditioning, mathematics, study skills; held on campus; accepts boys and girls; open to students from other schools. 60 students usually enrolled. 2013 schedule: June 20 to August 15.

Tuition and Aid Day student tuition: $9800. Tuition installment plan (Insured Tuition Payment Plan, monthly payment plans, individually arranged payment plans). Tuition reduction for siblings, merit scholarship grants, need-based scholarship grants available. In 2012–13, 35% of upper-school students received aid.

Admissions Traditional secondary-level entrance grade is 9. For fall 2012, 135 students applied for upper-level admission, 130 were accepted, 81 enrolled. SSAT required. Deadline for receipt of application materials: June 15. Application fee required: $45. Interview required.

Athletics Interscholastic: alpine skiing (boys, girls), baseball (b), basketball (b,g), cheering (g), cross-country running (b,g), field hockey (g), football (b), golf (b,g), hockey (b), ice hockey (b), indoor track (b,g), lacrosse (b,g), skiing (downhill) (b,g), soccer (b,g), softball (g), swimming and diving (b,g), tennis (b,g), track and field (b,g); intramural: basketball (b,g); coed interscholastic: equestrian sports, juggling, outdoor activities, outdoor adventure; coed intramural: basketball, indoor track, outdoor activities, outdoor adventure, rock climbing, skiing (cross-country), skiing (downhill), snowboarding, strength & conditioning, table tennis, volleyball, weight lifting, weight training. 1 PE instructor.

Computers Computers are regularly used in business applications, college planning, journalism, literary magazine, newspaper classes. Computer network features include on-campus library services, online commercial services, Internet access, wireless campus network, Internet filtering or blocking technology. Student e-mail accounts and computer access in designated common areas are available to students. Students grades are available online. The school has a published electronic and media policy.

Contact Mrs. Lonna J. Abbott, Director of Admissions and Enrollment. 603-224-7419. Fax: 603-228-6664. E-mail: labbott@bishopbrady.edu. Web site: www.bishopbrady.edu

BISHOP CONATY-OUR LADY OF LORETTO HIGH SCHOOL

2900 West Pico Boulevard
Los Angeles, California 90006

Head of School: Mr. Richard A. Spicer

General Information Girls' day college-preparatory, general academic, arts, religious studies, and technology school, affiliated with Roman Catholic Church. Grades 9–12. Founded: 1923. Setting: urban. 3-acre campus. 2 buildings on campus. Approved or accredited by National Catholic Education Association, The College Board, Western Association of Schools and Colleges, Western Catholic Education Association, and California Department of Education. Endowment: $579,607. Total enrollment: 326. Upper school average class size: 21. Upper school faculty-student ratio: 1:12. There are 182 required school days per year for Upper School students. Upper School students typically attend 5 days per week. The average school day consists of 5 hours and 15 minutes.

Upper School Student Profile Grade 9: 62 students (62 girls); Grade 10: 108 students (108 girls); Grade 11: 77 students (77 girls); Grade 12: 79 students (79 girls). 91% of students are Roman Catholic.

Faculty School total: 22. In upper school: 7 men, 14 women; 16 have advanced degrees.

Subjects Offered Aerobics, algebra, American literature, anatomy and physiology, ASB Leadership, athletics, biology, British literature, Catholic belief and practice, ceramics, chemistry, Christian and Hebrew scripture, computer literacy, dance, dance performance, drama, drawing, drawing and design, economics, English, English language and composition-AP, European history-AP, French, geometry, government, government and politics-AP, health, honors algebra, honors English, honors geometry, integrated science, linear algebra, moral reasoning, painting, physical education, physics, pre-calculus, religion, senior project, social justice, Spanish, Spanish language-AP, statistics, trigonometry, U.S. government, U.S. history, U.S. history-AP, visual arts, Web site design, world history, world religions, yearbook.

Graduation Requirements Arts and fine arts (art, music, dance, drama), computer science, English, foreign language, mathematics, physical education (includes health), religion (includes Bible studies and theology), science, social studies (includes history), 100 hours of community service, senior project.

Special Academic Programs 6 Advanced Placement exams for which test preparation is offered; honors section; remedial reading and/or remedial writing; remedial math.

College Admission Counseling 68 students graduated in 2012; all went to college, including California State University, Northridge; Loyola Marymount University; Marymount College, Palos Verdes, California; Mount St. Mary's College; Santa Monica College; University of California, Riverside. Median SAT critical reading: 440, median SAT math: 390, median SAT writing: 440, median combined SAT: 1300, median composite ACT: 19. 6% scored over 600 on SAT critical reading, 2% scored over 600 on SAT math, 6% scored over 600 on SAT writing, 4% scored over 1800 on combined SAT, 11% scored over 26 on composite ACT.

Student Life Upper grades have uniform requirement, student council, honor system. Discipline rests primarily with faculty. Attendance at religious services is required.

Summer Programs Remediation, enrichment, advancement, art/fine arts, computer instruction programs offered; session focuses on make-up courses and strengthening incoming freshmen skills; held on campus; accepts boys and girls; open to students from other schools. 180 students usually enrolled. 2013 schedule: June 17 to July 26. Application deadline: June 10.

Tuition and Aid Day student tuition: $6325–$8350. Tuition installment plan (monthly payment plans, individually arranged payment plans). Tuition reduction for siblings, need-based scholarship grants, paying campus jobs available. In 2012–13, 91% of upper-school students received aid. Total amount of financial aid awarded in 2012–13: $593,619.

Admissions Traditional secondary-level entrance grade is 9. For fall 2012, 110 students applied for upper-level admission, 82 were accepted, 62 enrolled. High School Placement Test required. Deadline for receipt of application materials: August 15. Application fee required: $55. On-campus interview required.

Athletics Interscholastic: basketball, cross-country running, soccer, softball, volleyball. 3 coaches.

Computers Computers are regularly used in computer applications, Web site design, yearbook classes. Computer network features include on-campus library services, Internet access, wireless campus network, Internet filtering or blocking technology. Computer access in designated common areas is available to students. Students grades are available online. The school has a published electronic and media policy.

Contact Sr. Harriet Stellern, Director of Admissions. 323-737-0012 Ext. 103. Fax: 323-737-1749. E-mail: hstellern@bishopconatyloretto.org. Web site: www.bishopconatyloretto.org

BISHOP DENIS J. O'CONNELL HIGH SCHOOL

6600 Little Falls Road
Arlington, Virginia 22213

Head of School: Mrs. Katy Prebble

General Information Coeducational day college-preparatory, arts, business, religious studies, bilingual studies, and technology school, affiliated with Roman Catholic Church. Grades 9–12. Founded: 1957. Setting: suburban. Nearest major city is Washington, DC. 28-acre campus. 1 building on campus. Approved or accredited by National Catholic Education Association, Southern Association of Colleges and Schools, Southern Association of Independent Schools, Virginia Association of Independent Schools, and Virginia Department of Education. Member of Secondary School Admission Test Board. Total enrollment: 1,221. Upper school average class size: 19. Upper school faculty-student ratio: 1:12. There are 180 required school days per year for Upper School students. Upper School students typically attend 5 days per week. The average school day consists of 7 hours and 15 minutes.

Upper School Student Profile 83% of students are Roman Catholic.

Faculty School total: 110. In upper school: 73 have advanced degrees.

Subjects Offered Accounting, African American history, algebra, American history, American history-AP, American literature, analysis, art, art history, athletic training, Basic programming, Bible studies, biology, biology-AP, business, business technology, calculus, calculus-AP, chemistry, chemistry-AP, choir, choral music, chorus, church history, comparative government and politics-AP, comparative political systems-AP, computer graphics, computer multimedia, computer music, computer programming, computer science, computer science-AP, computer skills, creative writing, digital art, dramatic arts, driver education, earth science, East Asian history, ecology, economics, economics-AP, English, English language-AP, English literature, English literature-AP, environmental science-AP, European history, European history-AP, fine arts, forensics, French, French language-AP, French-AP, geography, geometry, German, German-AP, government and politics-AP, government-AP, government/civics, guitar, health, history, history of the Catholic Church, honors English, honors geometry, honors U.S. history, honors world history, introduction to theater, Italian, jazz band, journalism, Latin, Latin-AP, literature-AP, macro/microeconomics-AP, macroeconomics-AP, marketing, mathematics, media arts, microeconomics-AP, modern European history-AP, music, music theory-AP, music-AP, New Testament, newspaper, orchestra, painting, personal finance, personal fitness, photo shop, photography, photojournalism, physical education, physical fitness, physics, physics-AP, piano, play production, pre-calculus, probability, psychology, psychology-AP, public speaking, religion, remedial study skills, science, science research, social sciences, social studies, sociology, Spanish, Spanish language-AP, Spanish literature-AP, Spanish-AP, speech, speech and debate, sports conditioning, sports psychology, statistics, statistics-AP, student government, studio art-AP, theater arts, theater design and production, theology, trigonometry, U.S. and Virginia government-AP, U.S. and Virginia history, U.S. government, U.S. government and politics-AP, U.S. history, U.S. history-AP, United States government-AP, video film production, voice ensemble, Web site design, weight training, weightlifting, world history, world literature.

Graduation Requirements Arts and fine arts (art, music, dance, drama), computer science, English, foreign language, mathematics, physical education (includes health), religion (includes Bible studies and theology), science, social sciences, social studies (includes history), community service program incorporated into graduation requirements.

Special Academic Programs 26 Advanced Placement exams for which test preparation is offered; honors section; independent study; study at local college for college credit; academic accommodation for the gifted; remedial math; programs in general development for dyslexic students.

College Admission Counseling 281 students graduated in 2012; 279 went to college, including George Mason University; James Madison University; The College of William and Mary; University of Virginia; Virginia Commonwealth University; Virginia Polytechnic Institute and State University. Other: 1 entered military service, 1 had other specific plans. Median SAT critical reading: 563, median SAT math: 549, median SAT writing: 555, median combined SAT: 1667, median composite ACT: 29.

Student Life Upper grades have uniform requirement, student council, honor system. Discipline rests equally with students and faculty. Attendance at religious services is required.

Summer Programs Remediation, enrichment, advancement, sports, art/fine arts, computer instruction programs offered; held on campus; accepts boys and girls; open to students from other schools. 220 students usually enrolled. 2013 schedule: June 15 to August 15. Application deadline: none.

Tuition and Aid Day student tuition: $11,600–$15,350. Tuition installment plan (FACTS Tuition Payment Plan). Tuition reduction for siblings, merit scholarship grants, need-based scholarship grants, scholarship competition only for eighth graders currently enrolled in a Diocese of Arlington Catholic school available. In 2012–13, 30% of upper-school students received aid; total upper-school merit-scholarship money awarded: $30,000. Total amount of financial aid awarded in 2012–13: $1,500,000.

Admissions High School Placement Test required. Deadline for receipt of application materials: January 28. Application fee required: $50.

Athletics Interscholastic: baseball (boys), basketball (b,g), crew (b,g), cross-country running (b,g), dance team (g), diving (b,g), field hockey (g), football (b), ice hockey (b), lacrosse (b,g), soccer (b,g), softball (g), swimming and diving (b,g), tennis (b,g), track and field (b,g), volleyball (g), weight lifting (b,g), weight training (b,g), winter (indoor) track (b,g), wrestling (b); intramural: basketball (b,g), weight lifting (b,g); coed interscholastic: golf, ice hockey, sailing; coed intramural: crew, flag football, softball, ultimate Frisbee, volleyball. 7 PE instructors, 7 coaches, 1 athletic trainer.

Computers Computers are regularly used in accounting, all academic, art, business, computer applications, English, foreign language, health, history, mathematics, science, social sciences classes. Computer network features include on-campus library services, online commercial services, Internet access, wireless campus network, Internet filtering or blocking technology. Campus intranet, student e-mail accounts, and computer access in designated common areas are available to students. Students grades are available online. The school has a published electronic and media policy.

Contact Mr. Michael Cresson, Director of Admissions. 703-237-1433. Fax: 703-241-9066. E-mail: mcresson@bishopoconnell.org. Web site: www.bishopoconnell.org

BISHOP EUSTACE PREPARATORY SCHOOL

5552 Route 70
Pennsauken, New Jersey 08109-4798

Head of School: Br. James Beamesderfer, SAC

General Information Coeducational day college-preparatory, arts, religious studies, and technology school, affiliated with Roman Catholic Church. Grades 9–12. Founded: 1954. Setting: suburban. Nearest major city is Philadelphia, PA. 32-acre campus. 7 buildings on campus. Approved or accredited by Middle States Association of Colleges and Schools and New Jersey Department of Education. Endowment: $3.5 million. Total enrollment: 700. Upper school average class size: 20. Upper school faculty-student ratio: 1:13. There are 161 required school days per year for Upper School students. Upper School students typically attend 5 days per week. The average school day consists of 6 hours and 20 minutes.

Upper School Student Profile 88% of students are Roman Catholic.

Faculty School total: 57. In upper school: 26 men, 31 women; 44 have advanced degrees.

Subjects Offered Advanced chemistry, advanced computer applications, Advanced Placement courses, algebra, American history, American history-AP, American literature, anatomy, anatomy and physiology, applied music, art and culture, art history, band, Bible studies, biology, biology-AP, British literature, British literature (honors), calculus, calculus-AP, campus ministry, career education, career exploration, career/college preparation, chemistry, chemistry-AP, choir, Christian doctrine, Christian education, Christian ethics, Christian scripture, clinical chemistry, college counseling, college placement, college planning, comparative religion, computer education, computer science, creative writing, driver education, economics and history, electives, English, English literature, English literature and composition-AP, environmental science, environmental science-AP, ethics, European history-AP, film, film and literature, fine arts, French, French as a second language, gender issues, genetics, geometry, German, government and politics-AP, government/civics, grammar, health, history, honors algebra, honors English, honors geometry, honors U.S. history, honors world history, instrumental music, journalism, Latin, law, law studies, macroeconomics-AP, mathematics, mathematics-AP, music, music composition, music history, music theory, music theory-AP, physical education, physical science, physics, physics-AP, physiology, pre-calculus, psychology, psychology-AP, science, sex education, social studies, sociology, Spanish, Spanish-AP, statistics-AP, theology, trigonometry, U.S. government and politics-AP, U.S. history, U.S. history-AP, vocal music, women's studies, world affairs, world history, world religions.

Graduation Requirements Arts and fine arts (art, music, dance, drama), career exploration, computer science, English, foreign language, mathematics, physical education (includes health), religion (includes Bible studies and theology), science, social studies (includes history). Community service is required.

Special Academic Programs 16 Advanced Placement exams for which test preparation is offered; honors section; independent study; study at local college for college credit; academic accommodation for the gifted and the musically talented.

College Admission Counseling 181 students graduated in 2012; 180 went to college, including Drexel University; Loyola University Maryland; Rutgers, The State University of New Jersey, New Brunswick; Saint Joseph's University; The Catholic University of America; Villanova University. Other: 1 had other specific plans. 37% scored over 600 on SAT critical reading, 41% scored over 600 on SAT math, 38% scored over 600 on SAT writing.

Student Life Upper grades have uniform requirement, student council, honor system. Discipline rests primarily with faculty. Attendance at religious services is required.

Summer Programs Enrichment, advancement, sports programs offered; session focuses on student recruitment and enrichment for middle school students; advancement in math for current students; held on campus; accepts boys and girls; open to students from other schools. 150 students usually enrolled. 2013 schedule: June 17 to August 2. Application deadline: July 31.

Tuition and Aid Day student tuition: $15,400. Tuition installment plan (FACTS Tuition Payment Plan). Merit scholarship grants, need-based scholarship grants available. In 2012–13, 35% of upper-school students received aid; total upper-school merit-scholarship money awarded: $277,200. Total amount of financial aid awarded in 2012–13: $800,000.

Admissions Traditional secondary-level entrance grade is 9. High School Placement Test, math and English placement tests or placement test required. Deadline for receipt of application materials: none. Application fee required: $60.

Athletics Interscholastic: baseball (boys), basketball (b,g), bowling (b,g), cheering (g), crew (b,g), cross-country running (b,g), field hockey (g), football (b), ice hockey (b), indoor track & field (b,g), lacrosse (b,g), running (b,g), soccer (b,g), softball (g), swimming and diving (b,g), tennis (b,g), track and field (b,g); coed interscholastic: aquatics, diving, golf. 3 PE instructors, 61 coaches, 1 athletic trainer.

Computers Computers are regularly used in all academic classes. Computer network features include on-campus library services, online commercial services, Internet access, wireless campus network, Internet filtering or blocking technology. Campus intranet and computer access in designated common areas are available to students. Students grades are available online. The school has a published electronic and media policy.

Contact Mr. Nicholas Italiano, Director of Institutional Advancement. 856-662-2160 Ext. 252. Fax: 856-665-2184. E-mail: nitaliano@eustace.org. Web site: www.eustace.org

BISHOP FENWICK HIGH SCHOOL

4855 State Route 122
Franklin, Ohio 45005

Head of School: Mr. Trevor Block

General Information Coeducational day college-preparatory, arts, and religious studies school, affiliated with Roman Catholic Church. Grades 9–12. Founded: 1952. Setting: small town. Nearest major city is Cincinnati. 66-acre campus. 1 building on campus. Approved or accredited by National Catholic Education Association, North Central Association of Colleges and Schools, Ohio Catholic Schools Accreditation Association (OCSAA), and Ohio Department of Education. Upper school average class size: 24. Upper school faculty-student ratio: 1:14. There are 184 required school days per year for Upper School students. Upper School students typically attend 5 days per week. The average school day consists of 6 hours and 35 minutes.

Upper School Student Profile Grade 9: 145 students (80 boys, 65 girls); Grade 10: 130 students (73 boys, 57 girls); Grade 11: 160 students (98 boys, 62 girls); Grade 12: 118 students (61 boys, 57 girls). 88% of students are Roman Catholic.

Faculty School total: 40. In upper school: 18 men, 22 women; 23 have advanced degrees.

Subjects Offered Accounting, ACT preparation, algebra, American democracy, art, art-AP, athletic training, biology, botany, calculus-AP, career planning, cell biology, chemistry, choir, chorus, church history, college admission preparation, computer graphics, computer programming, concert band, creative writing, economics, engineering, English, English-AP, ensembles, film and literature, fine arts, French, functions, general business, geometry, government, government/civics-AP, health, honors algebra, honors English, honors geometry, integrated mathematics, jazz band, Latin, Latin-AP, leadership, marching band, mathematics, multimedia, music appreciation, mythology, physical education, physical science, physics, physiology, portfolio art, pre-algebra, psychology, publications, religion, science, social studies, Spanish, statistics, study skills, technology, theater, theater arts, trigonometry, U.S. history, U.S. history-AP, Web site design, world geography, world history, writing, yearbook, zoology.

Graduation Requirements Arts and fine arts (art, music, dance, drama), English, foreign language, mathematics, physical education (includes health), religion (includes Bible studies and theology), science, social studies (includes history), technology, community service, retreats, pass the Ohio Graduation Test.

Special Academic Programs Advanced Placement exam preparation; honors section; study at local college for college credit; academic accommodation for the gifted; special instructional classes for deaf students.

College Admission Counseling 124 students graduated in 2012; 122 went to college, including Miami University; Ohio University; The Ohio State University; University of Cincinnati; University of Dayton; Xavier University. Other: 1 went to work, 1 entered military service. Median SAT critical reading: 550, median SAT math: 560, median SAT writing: 530, median combined SAT: 1640. Mean composite ACT: 24. 37% scored over 600 on SAT critical reading, 39% scored over 600 on SAT math, 26% scored over 600 on SAT writing, 33% scored over 1800 on combined SAT, 38% scored over 26 on composite ACT.

Student Life Upper grades have uniform requirement, student council, honor system. Discipline rests primarily with faculty. Attendance at religious services is required.

Tuition and Aid Day student tuition: $8400. Tuition installment plan (FACTS Tuition Payment Plan). Tuition reduction for siblings, merit scholarship grants, need-based scholarship grants, paying campus jobs available. In 2012–13, 19% of upper-school students received aid.

Admissions Traditional secondary-level entrance grade is 9. High School Placement Test required. Deadline for receipt of application materials: December 1. No application fee required.

Athletics Interscholastic: baseball (boys), basketball (b,g), bowling (b,g), cheering (g), cross-country running (b,g), dance team (g), football (b), golf (b,g), lacrosse (b,g), soccer (b,g), softball (g), tennis (b,g), volleyball (b,g), weight training (b,g), wrestling (b); intramural: basketball (b), weight training (b,g); coed interscholastic: in-line hockey, roller hockey, swimming and diving, track and field; coed intramural: freestyle skiing, paint ball, skiing (downhill), snowboarding, strength & conditioning. 1 PE instructor, 62 coaches, 1 athletic trainer.

Computers Computers are regularly used in career exploration, career technology, college planning, engineering, graphic arts, graphic design, introduction to technology, multimedia, photography, publications, technology, video film production, Web site design, yearbook classes. Computer network features include on-campus library services, Internet access, wireless campus network, Internet filtering or blocking technology, laptop carts, iPad cart. Campus intranet and computer access in designated common areas are available to students. Students grades are available online. The school has a published electronic and media policy.

Contact Mrs. Betty Turvy, Director of Admissions. 513-428-0525. Fax: 513-727-1501. E-mail: bturvy@fenwickfalcons.org. Web site: www.fenwickfalcons.org

BISHOP GUERTIN HIGH SCHOOL

194 Lund Road
Nashua, New Hampshire 03060-4398

Head of School: Br. Mark Hilton, SC

General Information Coeducational day college-preparatory and religious studies school, affiliated with Roman Catholic Church. Grades 9–12. Founded: 1963. Setting: suburban. Nearest major city is Boston, MA. 1 building on campus. Approved or accredited by New England Association of Schools and Colleges and New Hampshire Department of Education. Total enrollment: 900. Upper school average class size: 20. Upper School students typically attend 5 days per week. The average school day consists of 6 hours and 30 minutes.

Upper School Student Profile 70% of students are Roman Catholic.

Subjects Offered 20th century history, acting, advanced chemistry, advanced computer applications, advanced math, algebra, American literature-AP, analysis and differential calculus, anatomy and physiology, art appreciation, art history, band, Bible studies, biology, biology-AP, British history, British literature, British literature (honors), business law, calculus, calculus-AP, campus ministry, career/college preparation, chemistry, chemistry-AP, chorus, Christian and Hebrew scripture, Christian doctrine, Christian education, Christian ethics, Christianity, church history, civics, college admission preparation, college counseling, college writing, community service, comparative government and politics, comparative government and politics-AP, comparative religion, computer applications, computer art, computer education, computer literacy, computer multimedia, computer processing, computer programming, computer programming-AP, computer science, computer technologies, computer-aided design, constitutional history of U.S., consumer economics, contemporary history, CPR, creative writing, death and loss, debate, desktop publishing, digital photography, discrete mathematics, dramatic arts, drawing, driver education, economics, emergency medicine, English, English composition, English literature, English literature and composition-AP, English-AP, environmental science, ethics, European history, fine arts, foreign language, French, geography, geometry, government/civics, grammar, health, health and wellness, health education, history, honors geometry, honors U.S. history, honors world history, human anatomy, human biology, human sexuality, instrumental music, journalism, Latin, Latin-AP, law, literary magazine, marching band, mechanics of writing, moral reasoning, moral theology, music, philosophy, physical education, physics, pre-calculus, psychology, religion, religious studies, science, senior seminar, Shakespeare, social studies, Spanish, statistics, studio art, studio art-AP, The 20th Century, theater, trigonometry, U.S. government and politics, U.S. government and politics-AP, U.S. history, U.S. history-AP, U.S. literature, world history, world literature.

Graduation Requirements Arts and fine arts (art, music, dance, drama), computer science, English, foreign language, mathematics, physical education (includes health), religion (includes Bible studies and theology), science, social studies (includes history).

Special Academic Programs 13 Advanced Placement exams for which test preparation is offered; honors section; study at local college for college credit; academic accommodation for the gifted.

College Admission Counseling 211 students graduated in 2012; 208 went to college. Other: 2 entered military service, 1 entered a postgraduate year. Median combined SAT: 1702, median composite ACT: 26.

Student Life Upper grades have uniform requirement, student council, honor system. Discipline rests primarily with faculty. Attendance at religious services is required.

Summer Programs Enrichment programs offered; held on campus; accepts boys and girls; not open to students from other schools. 40 students usually enrolled. 2013 schedule: July 1 to July 31. Application deadline: May 1.

Tuition and Aid Day student tuition: $12,150. Tuition installment plan (FACTS Tuition Payment Plan, individually arranged payment plans). Merit scholarship grants, need-based scholarship grants available. In 2012–13, 10% of upper-school students received aid.

Admissions Traditional secondary-level entrance grade is 9. High School Placement Test required. Deadline for receipt of application materials: January 6. Application fee required: $35.

Athletics Interscholastic: baseball (boys), basketball (b,g), cheering (b,g), cross-country running (b,g), field hockey (g), football (b), gymnastics (g), hockey (b,g), ice hockey (b,g), lacrosse (b), skiing (downhill) (b,g), soccer (b,g), softball (g), swimming and diving (b,g), tennis (b,g), track and field (b,g), volleyball (g), wrestling (b); intramural: crew (b,g); coed interscholastic: aquatics, cheering, golf, ice hockey, indoor track, nordic skiing, paint ball, skiing (downhill); coed intramural: aerobics/dance, basketball, bowling, crew, dance, fishing, freestyle skiing, golf, mountain biking, outdoor education, strength & conditioning, swimming and diving, table tennis, tennis, volleyball, weight lifting, weight training. 4 PE instructors, 55 coaches, 2 athletic trainers.

Computers Computers are regularly used in career education, career exploration, career technology, college planning, data processing, desktop publishing, independent study, information technology, introduction to technology, library, library science, library skills, literary magazine, multimedia, music, news writing, newspaper, programming, publications, publishing, research skills, stock market, technology, Web site design, word processing, yearbook classes. Computer network features include on-campus library services, online commercial services, Internet access, wireless campus network, Internet filtering or blocking technology. The school has a published electronic and media policy.

Contact Mrs. Alison Mueller '03, Director of Admissions. 603-889-4107 Ext. 4304. Fax: 603-889-0701. E-mail: admit@bghs.org. Web site: www.bghs.org

BISHOP IRETON HIGH SCHOOL

201 Cambridge Road
Alexandria, Virginia 22314-4899

Head of School: Mr. Timothy Hamer

General Information Coeducational day college-preparatory, arts, religious studies, and technology school, affiliated with Roman Catholic Church. Grades 9–12. Founded: 1964. Setting: suburban. 12-acre campus. 1 building on campus. Approved or accredited by National Catholic Education Association and Southern Association of Colleges and Schools. Total enrollment: 825. Upper school average class size: 24. Upper school faculty-student ratio: 1:14. There are 180 required school days per year for Upper School students. Upper School students typically attend 5 days per week. The average school day consists of 6 hours.

Upper School Student Profile Grade 9: 217 students (99 boys, 118 girls); Grade 10: 200 students (83 boys, 117 girls); Grade 11: 193 students (104 boys, 89 girls); Grade 12: 215 students (98 boys, 117 girls). 86% of students are Roman Catholic.

Faculty School total: 64. In upper school: 29 men, 35 women; 50 have advanced degrees.

Subjects Offered Advanced Placement courses, Catholic belief and practice, computer science, driver education, English, film, fine arts, foreign language, health, mathematics, physical education, religion, science, social studies.

Graduation Requirements Arts and fine arts (art, music, dance, drama), computer science, English, foreign language, mathematics, physical education (includes health), religion (includes Bible studies and theology), science, social studies (includes history), 60 hours of community service. Community service is required.

Special Academic Programs Advanced Placement exam preparation; honors section; academic accommodation for the musically talented; special instructional classes for students with Attention Deficit Disorder.

College Admission Counseling 203 students graduated in 2012; 201 went to college, including James Madison University; Longwood University; The College of William and Mary; University of Virginia; Virginia Commonwealth University; Virginia Polytechnic Institute and State University. Other: 2 had other specific plans. Mean SAT critical reading: 575, mean SAT math: 557, mean SAT writing: 579, mean combined SAT: 1711, mean composite ACT: 24.

Student Life Upper grades have uniform requirement, honor system. Discipline rests primarily with faculty. Attendance at religious services is required.

Summer Programs Remediation, enrichment, art/fine arts, computer instruction programs offered; session focuses on remediation; held on campus; accepts boys and girls; open to students from other schools. 50 students usually enrolled. 2013 schedule: June to July.

Tuition and Aid Day student tuition: $12,524–$16,868. Tuition installment plan (FACTS Tuition Payment Plan, monthly payment plans). Tuition reduction for siblings, merit scholarship grants, need-based scholarship grants available. In 2012–13, 15% of upper-school students received aid; total upper-school merit-scholarship money awarded: $139,500. Total amount of financial aid awarded in 2012–13: $580,000.

Admissions Traditional secondary-level entrance grade is 9. For fall 2012, 443 students applied for upper-level admission, 389 were accepted, 232 enrolled. High School Placement Test (closed version) from Scholastic Testing Service required. Deadline for receipt of application materials: January 28. Application fee required: $50.

Athletics Interscholastic: baseball (boys), basketball (b,g), field hockey (g), football (b), lacrosse (b,g), soccer (b,g), softball (g), swimming and diving (b,g), tennis (b,g), track and field (b,g), volleyball (g), water polo (b), winter (indoor) track (b,g), wrestling (b); intramural: weight training (b,g); coed interscholastic: cheering, crew, cross-country running, diving, golf, ice hockey, indoor track, water polo, weight training; coed intramural: skiing (downhill), table tennis. 4 PE instructors, 2 athletic trainers.

Computers Computers are regularly used in all academic classes. Computer network features include on-campus library services, online commercial services, Internet access, wireless campus network, Internet filtering or blocking technology. Student e-mail accounts and computer access in designated common areas are available to students. Students grades are available online. The school has a published electronic and media policy.

Contact Mr. Peter J. Hamer, Director of Admissions. 703-212-5190. Fax: 703-212-8173. E-mail: hamerp@bishopireton.org. Web site: www.bishopireton.org

BISHOP JOHN J. SNYDER HIGH SCHOOL

5001 Samaritan Way
Jacksonville, Florida 32210

Head of School: Deacon David Yazdiya

General Information Coeducational day college-preparatory school, affiliated with Roman Catholic Church. Grades 9–12. Founded: 2002. Setting: suburban. 50-acre campus. 14 buildings on campus. Approved or accredited by National Catholic Education Association, Southern Association of Colleges and Schools, and Florida Department of Education. Upper school average class size: 21. Upper school faculty-student ratio: 1:15. There are 180 required school days per year for Upper School students. Upper School students typically attend 5 days per week. The average school day consists of 6 hours and 47 minutes.

Upper School Student Profile Grade 9: 136 students (72 boys, 64 girls); Grade 10: 131 students (78 boys, 53 girls); Grade 11: 117 students (53 boys, 64 girls); Grade 12: 103 students (43 boys, 60 girls). 80% of students are Roman Catholic.

Faculty School total: 33. In upper school: 18 men, 15 women; 15 have advanced degrees.

Subjects Offered Advanced biology, advanced chemistry, Advanced Placement courses, algebra, American government, American history, American history-AP, American literature, American literature-AP, anatomy and physiology, applied skills, art, athletics, Basic programming, Bible, biology, biology-AP, British literature, British literature (honors), calculus-AP, campus ministry, chemistry-AP, Chinese, choir, choral music, Christian doctrine, church history, college admission preparation, college awareness, college counseling, college planning, composition-AP, computer skills, creative writing, debate, economics, economics-AP, English, English composition, English language and composition-AP, English literature and composition-AP, French, geography, geometry, government, government-AP, guidance, healthful living, history of the

Catholic Church, honors algebra, honors English, honors geometry, honors U.S. history, honors world history, Latin, marine science, physics, religious education, Spanish, speech and debate, statistics, studio art, the Web, U.S. history, U.S. history-AP, world history, world history-AP.

Graduation Requirements 20th century world history, world history.

Special Academic Programs 9 Advanced Placement exams for which test preparation is offered.

College Admission Counseling 103 students graduated in 2012; 101 went to college, including Florida State University; Georgia Southern University; University of Central Florida; University of Florida; University of North Florida; University of South Florida. Other: 1 went to work, 1 entered military service.

Student Life Upper grades have uniform requirement, student council, honor system. Discipline rests primarily with faculty. Attendance at religious services is required.

Summer Programs Remediation programs offered; held on campus; accepts boys and girls; not open to students from other schools. 15 students usually enrolled. 2013 schedule: June to July.

Tuition and Aid Day student tuition: $6780. Tuition installment plan (FACTS Tuition Payment Plan). Tuition reduction for siblings, need-based scholarship grants available. In 2012–13, 32% of upper-school students received aid. Total amount of financial aid awarded in 2012–13: $250,000.

Admissions Traditional secondary-level entrance grade is 9. For fall 2012, 485 students applied for upper-level admission, 485 were accepted, 482 enrolled. Explore required. Deadline for receipt of application materials: none. Application fee required: $375. Interview recommended.

Athletics Interscholastic: baseball (boys), basketball (b,g), cheering (b,g), cross-country running (b,g), diving (b,g), football (b), golf (b,g), lacrosse (b), soccer (b,g), softball (g), swimming and diving (b,g), tennis (b,g), track and field (b,g), volleyball (g), weight lifting (b), wrestling (b). 2 PE instructors, 23 coaches, 1 athletic trainer.

Computers Computers are regularly used in all academic classes. Computer resources include on-campus library services, Internet access, wireless campus network, Internet filtering or blocking technology. Students grades are available online.

Contact Mrs. Mary Anne Briggs, Assistant to the Principal. 904-771-1029. Fax: 904-908-8988. E-mail: maryannebriggs@bishopsnyder.org. Web site: www.bishopsnyder.org

BISHOP KELLY HIGH SCHOOL

7009 Franklin Road
Boise, Idaho 83709-0922

Head of School: Mr. Robert R. Wehde

General Information Coeducational day college-preparatory and religious studies school, affiliated with Roman Catholic Church. Grades 9–12. Founded: 1964. Setting: urban. 68-acre campus. 2 buildings on campus. Approved or accredited by National Catholic Education Association, Northwest Accreditation Commission, Western Catholic Education Association, and Idaho Department of Education. Endowment: $7.3 million. Total enrollment: 680. Upper school average class size: 21. Upper school faculty-student ratio: 1:18. There are 176 required school days per year for Upper School students. Upper School students typically attend 5 days per week. The average school day consists of 7 hours.

Upper School Student Profile Grade 9: 187 students (97 boys, 90 girls); Grade 10: 188 students (96 boys, 92 girls); Grade 11: 158 students (86 boys, 72 girls); Grade 12: 145 students (74 boys, 71 girls); Grade 13: 2 students (2 girls). 75% of students are Roman Catholic.

Faculty School total: 46. In upper school: 23 men, 23 women; 35 have advanced degrees.

Subjects Offered Advanced Placement courses, algebra, American government, American history-AP, art, art appreciation, art-AP, band, biology, biology-AP, calculus-AP, campus ministry, Catholic belief and practice, chemistry, chemistry-AP, choir, Christianity, comparative religion, computer applications, computer science-AP, conceptual physics, creative writing, drawing, earth science, economics, engineering, English, English-AP, fitness, French, geometry, health, history of the Catholic Church, horticulture, instrumental music, literature, moral reasoning, painting, physical education, physics, physics-AP, pottery, pre-algebra, pre-calculus, psychology, reading/study skills, religious education, religious studies, senior seminar, service learning/internship, social justice, Spanish, Spanish-AP, speech, speech and debate, sports medicine, statistics-AP, theater, theater arts, theology, U.S. history, video film production, weight training, world history, yearbook.

Graduation Requirements Computer science, English, foreign language, mathematics, physical education (includes health), religion (includes Bible studies and theology), science, social studies (includes history), 30 hours of community service.

Special Academic Programs Advanced Placement exam preparation; honors section; independent study; study at local college for college credit.

College Admission Counseling 150 students graduated in 2012; 148 went to college, including Boise State University; Gonzaga University; Santa Clara University; University of Idaho; University of Portland; University of Utah. Other: 2 went to work. Mean SAT critical reading: 579, mean SAT math: 601, mean SAT writing: 575, mean combined SAT: 1755.

Student Life Upper grades have specified standards of dress, student council, honor system. Discipline rests primarily with faculty. Attendance at religious services is required.

Tuition and Aid Day student tuition: $7080. Tuition installment plan (The Tuition Plan, monthly payment plans, individually arranged payment plans). Need-based scholarship grants available. In 2012–13, 79% of upper-school students received aid. Total amount of financial aid awarded in 2012–13: $997,049.

Admissions Traditional secondary-level entrance grade is 9. For fall 2012, 680 students applied for upper-level admission, 680 were accepted, 680 enrolled. Deadline for receipt of application materials: none. Application fee required: $205.

Athletics Interscholastic: baseball (boys), basketball (b,g), cheering (g), cross-country running (b,g), fitness (b,g), football (b), golf (b,g), ice hockey (b), lacrosse (b,g), physical fitness (b,g), skiing (downhill) (b,g), snowboarding (b,g), soccer (b,g), softball (g), swimming and diving (b,g), tennis (b,g), track and field (b,g), volleyball (g), weight lifting (b,g), weight training (b,g), wrestling (b). 2 PE instructors, 10 coaches, 1 athletic trainer.

Computers Computers are regularly used in economics, English, foreign language, history, journalism, mathematics, science classes. Computer network features include on-campus library services, Internet access, Internet filtering or blocking technology, Blackboard. Student e-mail accounts and computer access in designated common areas are available to students. Students grades are available online. The school has a published electronic and media policy.

Contact Mrs. Kelly Shockey, Director of Admissions. 208-375-6010. Fax: 208-375-3626. E-mail: kshockey@bk.org. Web site: www.bk.org

BISHOP KENNY HIGH SCHOOL

1055 Kingman Avenue
Jacksonville, Florida 32207

Head of School: Rev. Michael R. Houle

General Information Coeducational day college-preparatory school, affiliated with Roman Catholic Church. Grades 9–12. Founded: 1952. Setting: urban. 55-acre campus. 10 buildings on campus. Approved or accredited by Southern Association of Colleges and Schools. Total enrollment: 1,210. Upper school average class size: 22. Upper school faculty-student ratio: 1:17. There are 180 required school days per year for Upper School students. Upper School students typically attend 5 days per week. The average school day consists of 6 hours and 30 minutes.

Upper School Student Profile Grade 9: 308 students (147 boys, 161 girls); Grade 10: 323 students (162 boys, 161 girls); Grade 11: 283 students (127 boys, 156 girls); Grade 12: 293 students (143 boys, 150 girls). 85% of students are Roman Catholic.

Faculty School total: 71. In upper school: 23 men, 48 women; 49 have advanced degrees.

Subjects Offered Accounting, desktop publishing, technology, word processing.

Graduation Requirements Electives, English, foreign language, health, mathematics, performing arts, personal fitness, practical arts, religion (includes Bible studies and theology), science, social studies (includes history), service hour requirements.

Special Academic Programs Advanced Placement exam preparation; honors section.

College Admission Counseling 323 students graduated in 2012; all went to college, including Florida Atlantic University; Florida State University; University of Central Florida; University of Florida; University of North Florida; University of South Florida. Median SAT critical reading: 540, median SAT math: 520, median SAT writing: 520, median combined SAT: 1580, median composite ACT: 24. 20% scored over 600 on SAT critical reading, 19% scored over 600 on SAT math, 16% scored over 600 on SAT writing, 18% scored over 1800 on combined SAT, 27% scored over 26 on composite ACT.

Student Life Upper grades have uniform requirement, student council, honor system. Discipline rests primarily with faculty. Attendance at religious services is required.

Summer Programs Remediation, enrichment, sports programs offered; session focuses on enrichment/remediation; held on campus; accepts boys and girls; not open to students from other schools. 300 students usually enrolled. 2013 schedule: June 12 to July 11.

Tuition and Aid Day student tuition: $7020–$9900. Tuition installment plan (FACTS Tuition Payment Plan, individually arranged payment plans). Tuition reduction for siblings, need-based scholarship grants available. In 2012–13, 20% of upper-school students received aid.

Admissions Traditional secondary-level entrance grade is 9. ACT-Explore or Explore required. Deadline for receipt of application materials: none. Application fee required. On-campus interview required.

Athletics Interscholastic: baseball (boys), basketball (b,g), cheering (g), cross-country running (b,g), diving (b,g), drill team (g), football (b), golf (b,g), JROTC drill (b,g), riflery (b,g), soccer (b,g), softball (g), swimming and diving (b,g), tennis (b,g), track and field (b,g), volleyball (g), weight lifting (b), wrestling (b). 1 athletic trainer.

Computers Computers are regularly used in computer applications, journalism, keyboarding, newspaper, yearbook classes. Computer resources include on-campus library services, Internet access, Internet filtering or blocking technology, design software for Journalism and MultiMedia, CS4 Suite, 5 computer labs. The school has a published electronic and media policy.

Contact Mr. Caleb Kitchings, Director of Admissions. 904-398-7545. Fax: 904-398-5728. E-mail: admissions@bishopkenny.org. Web site: www.bishopkenny.org

BISHOP LUERS HIGH SCHOOL

333 East Paulding Road
Fort Wayne, Indiana 46816

Head of School: Mrs. Mary T. Keefer

General Information Coeducational day college-preparatory and religious studies school, affiliated with Roman Catholic Church; primarily serves individuals with Attention Deficit Disorder. Grades 9–12. Founded: 1958. Setting: urban. 5-acre campus. 1 building on campus. Approved or accredited by National Catholic Education Association, North Central Association of Colleges and Schools, and Indiana Department of Education. Total enrollment: 596. Upper school average class size: 25. Upper school faculty-student ratio: 1:17. There are 180 required school days per year for Upper School students. Upper School students typically attend 5 days per week. The average school day consists of 6 hours and 35 minutes.

Upper School Student Profile Grade 9: 181 students (93 boys, 88 girls); Grade 10: 148 students (91 boys, 57 girls); Grade 11: 125 students (60 boys, 65 girls); Grade 12: 142 students (77 boys, 65 girls). 89% of students are Roman Catholic.

Faculty School total: 31. In upper school: 10 men, 21 women; 18 have advanced degrees.

Subjects Offered 3-dimensional art, accounting, algebra, Bible, biology, biology-AP, business, business law, calculus-AP, chamber groups, chemistry, chemistry-AP, chorus, church history, computer applications, computer programming, concert band, creative writing, drawing, economics, English, French, geometry, government, health education, honors algebra, honors English, honors geometry, honors U.S. history, honors world history, Latin, music appreciation, music theory, painting, physical education, physics, physiology, pre-calculus, probability and statistics, psychology, sculpture, sociology, Spanish, speech communications, student government, student publications, study skills, theater arts, theater production, theology, trigonometry, U.S. history, world civilizations, world geography, world history.

Graduation Requirements Computers, English, mathematics, physical education (includes health), religion (includes Bible studies and theology), science, social studies (includes history).

Special Academic Programs Advanced Placement exam preparation; honors section; study at local college for college credit; academic accommodation for the gifted and the musically talented; remedial reading and/or remedial writing; remedial math.

College Admission Counseling 128 students graduated in 2012; 119 went to college, including Ball State University; Indiana University–Purdue University Fort Wayne; Indiana University Bloomington; Purdue University. Other: 5 went to work, 4 entered military service. Mean SAT critical reading: 483, mean SAT math: 486, mean SAT writing: 461, mean composite ACT: 22. 13.8% scored over 600 on SAT critical reading, 11.5% scored over 600 on SAT math, 6.9% scored over 600 on SAT writing.

Student Life Upper grades have specified standards of dress, student council. Discipline rests equally with students and faculty. Attendance at religious services is required.

Summer Programs Remediation, sports programs offered; session focuses on camps and enrichment; held on campus; accepts boys and girls; open to students from other schools. 250 students usually enrolled. 2013 schedule: June 15 to August 10. Application deadline: May 30.

Tuition and Aid Day student tuition: $4725. Tuition installment plan (FACTS Tuition Payment Plan). Tuition reduction for siblings, merit scholarship grants, need-based scholarship grants, paying campus jobs available. In 2012–13, 61% of upper-school students received aid.

Admissions Traditional secondary-level entrance grade is 9. Admissions testing required. Deadline for receipt of application materials: none. Application fee required: $120.

Athletics Interscholastic: baseball (boys), basketball (b,g), bowling (b,g), cheering (g), cross-country running (b,g), dance (g), dance team (g), diving (b,g), football (b), golf (b,g), lacrosse (b), riflery (b,g), running (b,g), soccer (b,g), softball (g), swimming and diving (b,g), tennis (b,g), track and field (b,g), volleyball (g), wrestling (g); intramural: lacrosse (b,g); coed intramural: lacrosse, riflery, weight training. 2 PE instructors, 25 coaches, 2 athletic trainers.

Computers Computers are regularly used in all academic, business, yearbook classes. Computer network features include on-campus library services, Internet access, Internet filtering or blocking technology. Students grades are available online. The school has a published electronic and media policy.

Contact Mrs. Jennifer Andorfer, Co-Director of Admissions and Public Relations. 260-456-1261 Ext. 3141. Fax: 260-456-1262. E-mail: jandorfer@bishopluers.org. Web site: www.bishopluers.org/

BISHOP MCGUINNESS CATHOLIC HIGH SCHOOL

1725 NC Highway 66 South
Kernersville, North Carolina 27284

Head of School: Mr. George L. Repass

General Information Coeducational day college-preparatory, arts, and religious studies school, affiliated with Roman Catholic Church. Grades 9–12. Founded: 1959. Setting: small town. Nearest major city is Winston-Salem. 42-acre campus. 2 buildings on campus. Approved or accredited by National Catholic Education Association, Southern Association of Colleges and Schools, The College Board, and North Carolina Department of Education. Member of National Association of Independent Schools. Endowment: $100,000. Total enrollment: 549. Upper school average class size: 18. Upper school faculty-student ratio: 1:15. There are 180 required school days per year for Upper School students. Upper School students typically attend 5 days per week. The average school day consists of 6 hours and 50 minutes.

Upper School Student Profile Grade 9: 142 students (87 boys, 55 girls); Grade 10: 152 students (81 boys, 71 girls); Grade 11: 111 students (69 boys, 42 girls); Grade 12: 144 students (76 boys, 68 girls). 75% of students are Roman Catholic.

Faculty School total: 36. In upper school: 20 men, 16 women; 31 have advanced degrees.

Subjects Offered Algebra, American history, anatomy, art history, arts, biology, biology-AP, calculus, calculus-AP, chemistry, chemistry-AP, community service, computer science, computer science-AP, creative writing, earth science, English, English language-AP, English literature and composition-AP, environmental science, European history-AP, fine arts, French, French language-AP, French-AP, geometry, health, Latin, Latin-AP, mathematics, music, music theory-AP, photography, physical education, physical science, physics, political science, religion, science, social studies, Spanish, Spanish-AP, statistics-AP, trigonometry, U.S. history-AP, world history.

Graduation Requirements 1 1/2 elective credits, arts and fine arts (art, music, dance, drama), English, foreign language, mathematics, physical education (includes health), religion (includes Bible studies and theology), science, social studies (includes history), all students must attend the retreat for their grade level; all seniors must complete the senior career project. Community service is required.

Special Academic Programs 16 Advanced Placement exams for which test preparation is offered; honors section; independent study; term-away projects; study at local college for college credit.

College Admission Counseling Colleges students went to include Appalachian State University; East Carolina University; North Carolina State University; The University of North Carolina at Chapel Hill; The University of North Carolina at Charlotte; The University of North Carolina Wilmington. Mean SAT critical reading: 553, mean SAT math: 539, mean SAT writing: 534, mean combined SAT: 1626, mean composite ACT: 24. 30% scored over 600 on SAT critical reading, 29% scored over 600 on SAT math, 20% scored over 600 on SAT writing, 27% scored over 1800 on combined SAT, 29% scored over 26 on composite ACT.

Student Life Upper grades have specified standards of dress, student council, honor system. Discipline rests primarily with faculty. Attendance at religious services is required.

Tuition and Aid Tuition installment plan (monthly payment plans, yearly, semester, and quarterly payment plans). Tuition reduction for siblings, need-based scholarship grants available. In 2012–13, 19% of upper-school students received aid. Total amount of financial aid awarded in 2012–13: $288,550.

Admissions Traditional secondary-level entrance grade is 9. For fall 2012, 182 students applied for upper-level admission, 172 were accepted, 154 enrolled. Achievement/Aptitude/Writing or High School Placement Test required. Deadline for receipt of application materials: none. Application fee required: $75. On-campus interview required.

Athletics Interscholastic: baseball (boys), basketball (b,g), cheering (g), fencing (b), football (b), lacrosse (b), soccer (b,g), softball (g), tennis (b,g), volleyball (g), wrestling (b); coed interscholastic: cross-country running, golf, swimming and diving, track and field, weight training. 3 PE instructors, 40 coaches, 1 athletic trainer.

Computers Computers are regularly used in accounting classes. Computer resources include on-campus library services, Internet access, Internet filtering or blocking technology. Student e-mail accounts and computer access in designated common areas are available to students. Students grades are available online. The school has a published electronic and media policy.

Contact Mr. Robert Belcher, Admissions Director. 336-564-1011. Fax: 336-564-1060. E-mail: rb@bmhs.us. Web site: www.bmhs.us

BISHOP MCGUINNESS CATHOLIC HIGH SCHOOL

801 Northwest 50th Street
Oklahoma City, Oklahoma 73118-6001

Head of School: Mr. David L. Morton

General Information Coeducational day college-preparatory, arts, business, religious studies, bilingual studies, and technology school, affiliated with Roman Catholic Church. Grades 9–12. Founded: 1950. Setting: urban. 20-acre campus. 4 buildings on campus. Approved or accredited by North Central Association of Colleges and Schools and Oklahoma Department of Education. Endowment: $957,041. Total enrollment: 681. Upper school average class size: 12. Upper school faculty-student ratio: 1:12. There are

177 required school days per year for Upper School students. Upper School students typically attend 5 days per week. The average school day consists of 6 hours and 10 minutes.

Upper School Student Profile Grade 11: 178 students (99 boys, 79 girls); Grade 12: 160 students (74 boys, 86 girls). 75% of students are Roman Catholic.

Faculty School total: 58. In upper school: 15 men, 13 women; 12 have advanced degrees.

Subjects Offered Algebra, American literature, American literature-AP, art, band, Bible studies, biology, biology-AP, business, business law, calculus-AP, Catholic belief and practice, ceramics, chemistry, chorus, church history, computer technologies, creative writing, culinary arts, current events, dance, debate, design, drama, drawing, economics, electives, English, English literature, English literature-AP, ethics, French, geometry, German, government, government-AP, health and wellness, history of the Catholic Church, honors algebra, honors English, honors geometry, introduction to theater, Latin, leadership, learning lab, macroeconomics-AP, newspaper, orchestra, painting, personal finance, photography, physical education, physical science, physics, physics-AP, physiology, practical arts, prayer/spirituality, pre-calculus, psychology, scripture, sociology, Spanish, speech, stagecraft, theater, U.S. history, U.S. history-AP, weight training, world history, world history-AP, world religions, writing workshop, yearbook.

Graduation Requirements Arts and fine arts (art, music, dance, drama), electives, English, foreign language, mathematics, physical education (includes health), practical arts, science, social studies (includes history), theology, 90 hours of Christian service.

Special Academic Programs 10 Advanced Placement exams for which test preparation is offered; honors section; academic accommodation for the gifted and the artistically talented; programs in English, mathematics for dyslexic students; special instructional classes for students with learning differences.

College Admission Counseling 178 students graduated in 2012; 169 went to college, including Oklahoma City University; Oklahoma State University; Texas Christian University; University of Arkansas; University of Notre Dame; University of Oklahoma. Other: 2 went to work, 1 entered military service, 3 entered a postgraduate year, 3 had other specific plans. Median SAT critical reading: 580, median SAT math: 540, median SAT writing: 590, median combined SAT: 1710, median composite ACT: 24. 44% scored over 600 on SAT critical reading, 33% scored over 600 on SAT math, 60% scored over 600 on SAT writing, 28.5% scored over 1800 on combined SAT, 33.8% scored over 26 on composite ACT.

Student Life Upper grades have uniform requirement, student council, honor system. Discipline rests primarily with faculty. Attendance at religious services is required.

Summer Programs Remediation, enrichment programs offered; session focuses on science enrichment, math enrichment and remediation; held on campus; accepts boys and girls; not open to students from other schools. 20 students usually enrolled.

Tuition and Aid Day student tuition: $8100. Tuition installment plan (FACTS Tuition Payment Plan). Need-based scholarship grants, paying campus jobs available. In 2012–13, 21% of upper-school students received aid. Total amount of financial aid awarded in 2012–13: $206,050.

Admissions Traditional secondary-level entrance grade is 11. For fall 2012, 14 students applied for upper-level admission, 14 were accepted, 14 enrolled. STS or writing sample required. Deadline for receipt of application materials: May 1. Application fee required: $375. On-campus interview required.

Athletics Interscholastic: baseball (boys), basketball (b,g), bowling (b,g), cheering (g), cross-country running (b,g), football (b), golf (b,g), indoor track & field (b,g), soccer (b,g), softball (g), swimming and diving (b,g), tennis (b,g), track and field (b,g), volleyball (g), weight training (b,g), winter (indoor) track (b,g), wrestling (b); coed interscholastic: dance team, physical fitness. 9 coaches, 1 athletic trainer.

Computers Computers are regularly used in all academic classes. Computer network features include on-campus library services, online commercial services, Internet access, wireless campus network, Internet filtering or blocking technology, laptop classroom computers, wireless printing, eBooks, and My Road. Student e-mail accounts and computer access in designated common areas are available to students. Students grades are available online. The school has a published electronic and media policy.

Contact Ms. Amy Hanson, 9th Grade Counselor. 405-842-6638 Ext. 225. Fax: 405-858-9550. E-mail: ahanson@bmchs.org. Web site: www.bmchs.org

BISHOP MONTGOMERY HIGH SCHOOL

5430 Torrance Boulevard
Torrance, California 90503

Head of School: Ms. Rosemary Distaso-Libbon

General Information Coeducational day college-preparatory, arts, religious studies, and technology school, affiliated with Roman Catholic Church. Grades 9–12. Founded: 1957. Setting: suburban. Nearest major city is Los Angeles. 27-acre campus. 9 buildings on campus. Approved or accredited by National Catholic Education Association, Western Association of Schools and Colleges, Western Catholic Education Association, and California Department of Education. Total enrollment: 975. Upper school average class size: 22. Upper school faculty-student ratio: 1:22. There are 180 required school days per year for Upper School students. Upper School students typically attend 5 days per week. The average school day consists of 6 hours and 10 minutes.

Upper School Student Profile Grade 9: 226 students (118 boys, 108 girls); Grade 10: 257 students (124 boys, 133 girls); Grade 11: 244 students (115 boys, 129 girls); Grade 12: 248 students (115 boys, 133 girls). 75% of students are Roman Catholic.

Faculty School total: 60. In upper school: 25 men, 33 women; 22 have advanced degrees.

Subjects Offered Advanced Placement courses, algebra, American history, American history-AP, American literature, anatomy, art, Bible studies, biology, calculus, chemistry, chorus, composition, computer science, drama, economics, English, English literature, English literature-AP, fine arts, French, geometry, government/civics, health, history, languages, literature, mathematics, physical education, physics, physics-AP, physiology, religion, science, social studies, Spanish, statistics, theater, weight training, world history, yearbook.

Graduation Requirements Arts and fine arts (art, music, dance, drama), business skills (includes word processing), computer science, English, mathematics, physical education (includes health), religion (includes Bible studies and theology), science, social studies (includes history).

Special Academic Programs Advanced Placement exam preparation; honors section.

College Admission Counseling 284 students graduated in 2012; all went to college, including California State University, Dominguez Hills; California State University, Long Beach; Loyola Marymount University; University of California, Irvine; University of California, Los Angeles; University of California, Riverside. Mean SAT critical reading: 527, mean SAT math: 527, mean SAT writing: 526.

Student Life Upper grades have uniform requirement, student council, honor system. Discipline rests primarily with faculty. Attendance at religious services is required.

Summer Programs Remediation, enrichment, advancement, sports, art/fine arts, computer instruction programs offered; session focuses on academic enrichment/remediation and athletic conditioning; held on campus; accepts boys and girls; not open to students from other schools. 900 students usually enrolled. 2013 schedule: June 20 to July 24. Application deadline: June 19.

Tuition and Aid Day student tuition: $7900. Tuition installment plan (monthly payment plans). Tuition reduction for siblings, financial need available. In 2012–13, 4% of upper-school students received aid. Total amount of financial aid awarded in 2012–13: $30,000.

Admissions Traditional secondary-level entrance grade is 9. High School Placement Test, Iowa Tests of Basic Skills and Stanford 9 required. Deadline for receipt of application materials: January 17. Application fee required: $100.

Athletics Interscholastic: baseball (boys), basketball (b,g), cheering (g), cross-country running (b,g), dance (g), dance team (g), football (b), golf (b,g), soccer (b,g), softball (g), strength & conditioning (b,g), tennis (b,g), volleyball (b,g); coed interscholastic: aerobics, surfing, swimming and diving, track and field. 3 PE instructors, 32 coaches, 2 athletic trainers.

Computers Computers are regularly used in library, newspaper, programming, publications, technology, Web site design classes. Computer network features include on-campus library services, Internet access, wireless campus network. Students grades are available online. The school has a published electronic and media policy.

Contact Mrs. Casey Dunn, Director of Admissions. 310-540-2021 Ext. 227. Fax: 310-543-5102. E-mail: cdunn@bmhs-la.org. Web site: www.bmhs-la.org

BISHOP MORA SALESIAN HIGH SCHOOL

960 South Soto Street
Los Angeles, California 90023

Head of School: Mr. Samuel Robles

General Information Boys' day college-preparatory, general academic, and religious studies school, affiliated with Roman Catholic Church. Grades 9–12. Founded: 1958. Setting: urban. 2 buildings on campus. Approved or accredited by Accrediting Commission for Schools, Western Association of Schools and Colleges, Western Catholic Education Association, and California Department of Education. Upper school average class size: 28. Upper school faculty-student ratio: 1:15. There are 188 required school days per year for Upper School students. The average school day consists of 6 hours and 50 minutes.

Upper School Student Profile Grade 9: 131 students (131 boys); Grade 10: 116 students (116 boys); Grade 11: 105 students (105 boys); Grade 12: 102 students (102 boys). 98% of students are Roman Catholic.

Faculty School total: 32. In upper school: 24 men, 8 women; 28 have advanced degrees.

Subjects Offered Advanced biology, advanced chemistry, advanced math, Advanced Placement courses, algebra, American history, American history-AP, American literature, anatomy and physiology, applied music, art, arts appreciation, athletic training, athletics, baseball, basketball, Bible studies, biology, biology-AP, British history, British literature, British literature (honors), business, calculus, calculus-AP, Catholic belief and practice, chemistry, chemistry-AP, Christianity, church history, cinematography, college admission preparation, college awareness, college counseling, college placement, college planning, computer applications, computer science, creative writing, drama, drawing, economics, economics-AP, English, English literature, English-AP, environmental science, ethics, European history, expository writing, fine arts, geometry, government/civics, grammar, health, health education, Hispanic literature, history, mathematics, music, physical education, physical science, physics, physics-AP, pre-algebra, pre-calculus, psychology, psychology-AP, religion, science, social studies, Spanish, Spanish-AP, speech and debate, theater, trigonometry, U.S. government and politics-AP, volleyball, weight training, world history, world literature, writing.

Graduation Requirements Arts and fine arts (art, music, dance, drama), computer science, English, foreign language, mathematics, physical education (includes health), religion (includes Bible studies and theology), religious studies, science, social studies (includes history), Christian service program.

Special Academic Programs Study at local college for college credit; academic accommodation for the musically talented and the artistically talented; remedial reading and/or remedial writing.

College Admission Counseling 87 students graduated in 2011; 86 went to college, including California State University, Los Angeles; Loyola Marymount University; University of California, Los Angeles; University of California, Riverside; Whittier College. Other: 1 entered military service.

Student Life Upper grades have uniform requirement, student council, honor system. Discipline rests equally with students and faculty. Attendance at religious services is required.

Tuition and Aid Day student tuition: $8900. Tuition installment plan (FACTS Tuition Payment Plan, monthly payment plans, individually arranged payment plans). Tuition reduction for siblings, merit scholarship grants, need-based scholarship grants available. In 2011–12, 75% of upper-school students received aid; total upper-school merit-scholarship money awarded: $2500. Total amount of financial aid awarded in 2011–12: $1,548,500.

Admissions Traditional secondary-level entrance grade is 9. ETS high school placement exam required. Deadline for receipt of application materials: April 1. Application fee required: $50. On-campus interview required.

Athletics Interscholastic: baseball, basketball, bicycling, cross-country running, football, golf, physical fitness, physical training, power lifting, running, soccer, track and field, volleyball, weight training, wrestling; intramural: aerobics/Nautilus, basketball, cheering, dance squad, dance team, soccer, yoga. 12 coaches, 1 athletic trainer.

Computers Computers are regularly used in design, desktop publishing, English, mathematics, word processing, writing, writing, yearbook classes. Computer network features include Internet access. Campus intranet and student e-mail accounts are available to students.

Contact Mr. Mark Johnson, Vice Principal/Director of Curriculum. 323-261-7124 Ext. 224. Fax: 213-261-7600. E-mail: johnson@mustangsla.org. Web site: www.mustangsla.org

BISHOP O'DOWD HIGH SCHOOL

9500 Stearns Avenue
Oakland, California 94605-4799

Head of School: Dr. Stephen Phelps

General Information Coeducational day college-preparatory, arts, religious studies, technology, and Environmental Science school, affiliated with Roman Catholic Church. Grades 9–12. Founded: 1951. Setting: urban. 8-acre campus. 12 buildings on campus. Approved or accredited by Western Association of Schools and Colleges, Western Catholic Education Association, and California Department of Education. Endowment: $1 million. Total enrollment: 1,144. Upper school average class size: 25. Upper school faculty-student ratio: 1:15. Upper School students typically attend 5 days per week. The average school day consists of 6 hours and 30 minutes.

Upper School Student Profile Grade 9: 295 students (142 boys, 153 girls); Grade 10: 322 students (159 boys, 163 girls); Grade 11: 252 students (123 boys, 129 girls); Grade 12: 273 students (129 boys, 144 girls). 55% of students are Roman Catholic.

Faculty School total: 79. In upper school: 41 men, 38 women; 55 have advanced degrees.

Subjects Offered Art, computer science, English, fine arts, foreign language, mathematics, physical education, religion, science, social studies.

Graduation Requirements Arts and fine arts (art, music, dance, drama), English, foreign language, mathematics, physical education (includes health), religion (includes Bible studies and theology), religious studies, science, social studies (includes history), 100 hour service learning project to be completed over all four years.

Special Academic Programs Advanced Placement exam preparation; honors section; academic accommodation for the gifted, the musically talented, and the artistically talented; remedial reading and/or remedial writing; remedial math; special instructional classes for students with ADD and dyslexia.

College Admission Counseling 296 students graduated in 2012; 294 went to college, including California Polytechnic State University, San Luis Obispo; San Francisco State University; University of California, Berkeley; University of California, Davis; University of California, Santa Cruz; University of Oregon. Other: 2 had other specific plans. Mean SAT critical reading: 566, mean SAT math: 565, mean SAT writing: 575.

Student Life Upper grades have specified standards of dress, student council. Discipline rests equally with students and faculty.

Summer Programs Remediation, computer instruction programs offered; session focuses on review; held on campus; accepts boys and girls; open to students from other schools. 120 students usually enrolled. 2013 schedule: June 13 to July 20. Application deadline: June 1.

Tuition and Aid Day student tuition: $14,440. Tuition installment plan (monthly payment plans, individually arranged payment plans). Tuition reduction for siblings, merit scholarship grants, need-based scholarship grants available. In 2012–13, 30% of upper-school students received aid; total upper-school merit-scholarship money awarded: $150,000. Total amount of financial aid awarded in 2012–13: $2,300,000.

Admissions Traditional secondary-level entrance grade is 9. For fall 2012, 700 students applied for upper-level admission, 460 were accepted, 295 enrolled. High School Placement Test and High School Placement Test (closed version) from Scholastic Testing Service required. Deadline for receipt of application materials: none. Application fee required: $90.

Athletics Interscholastic: aquatics (boys, girls), baseball (b), basketball (b,g), cheering (g), cross-country running (b,g), diving (b,g), football (b), golf (b,g), lacrosse (b,g), rugby (b,g), soccer (b,g), softball (g), strength & conditioning (b,g), swimming and diving (b,g), tennis (b,g), track and field (b,g), volleyball (g), water polo (b,g); intramural: basketball (b,g), dance squad (g), physical training (b,g), soccer (b,g), weight training (b,g); coed interscholastic: cross-country running, strength & conditioning; coed intramural: aerobics, aerobics/dance, alpine skiing, backpacking, bicycling, bowling, combined training, flag football, Frisbee, hiking/backpacking, mountain biking, skiing (downhill), snowboarding, weight training. 5 PE instructors, 36 coaches, 1 athletic trainer.

Computers Computers are regularly used in all academic, career exploration, library, library skills, mathematics, media arts, media production, newspaper, programming, research skills, science, video film production, yearbook classes. Computer network features include on-campus library services, online commercial services, Internet access, wireless campus network, Internet filtering or blocking technology, one to one laptop program—every student has a laptop on campus. Student e-mail accounts are available to students. Students grades are available online. The school has a published electronic and media policy.

Contact Mr. Tyler Kreitz, Director of Admissions. 510-577-9100. Fax: 510-638-3259. E-mail: tkreitz@bishopodowd.org. Web site: www.bishopodowd.org

BISHOP'S COLLEGE SCHOOL

80 Moulton Hill Road
PO Box 5001, Succ. Lennoxville
Sherbrooke, Quebec J1M 1Z8, Canada

Head of School: Mr. William Mitchell

General Information Coeducational boarding and day college-preparatory, arts, and bilingual studies school. Grades 7–12. Founded: 1836. Setting: small town. Nearest major city is Montreal, Canada. Students are housed in single-sex dormitories. 270-acre campus. 30 buildings on campus. Approved or accredited by Canadian Association of Independent Schools, Canadian Educational Standards Institute, Quebec Association of Independent Schools, The Association of Boarding Schools, and Quebec Department of Education. Affiliate member of National Association of Independent Schools. Languages of instruction: English and French. Endowment: CAN$15.6 million. Total enrollment: 216. Upper school average class size: 18. Upper school faculty-student ratio: 1:7. There are 180 required school days per year for Upper School students. Upper School students typically attend 6 days per week. The average school day consists of 8 hours.

Upper School Student Profile Grade 10: 32 students (18 boys, 14 girls); Grade 11: 64 students (37 boys, 27 girls); Grade 12: 42 students (27 boys, 15 girls). 75% of students are boarding students. 44% are province residents. 11 provinces are represented in upper school student body. 49% are international students. International students from Bahamas, China, France, Mexico, Saudi Arabia, and United States; 17 other countries represented in student body.

Faculty School total: 30. In upper school: 17 men, 13 women; 15 reside on campus.

Subjects Offered Algebra, art, biology, calculus, chemistry, computer science, creative writing, dance, drama, economics, English, environmental science, ESL, ethics, finite math, French, French as a second language, geography, geometry, history, mathematics, music, philosophy, physical education, physical science, physics, political science, religion, science, sociology, study skills, technology, theater, trigonometry, world history.

Graduation Requirements Follow Ministry of Quebec guidelines, follow Ministry of Ontario guidelines.

Special Academic Programs Advanced Placement exam preparation; term-away projects; study at local college for college credit; study abroad; academic accommodation for the gifted, the musically talented, and the artistically talented; remedial reading and/or remedial writing; remedial math; ESL (31 students enrolled).

College Admission Counseling 44 students graduated in 2012; 42 went to college, including Carleton University; Ryerson University; University of Guelph; University of Toronto. Other: 2 had other specific plans.

Student Life Upper grades have uniform requirement, student council, honor system. Discipline rests equally with students and faculty.

Summer Programs Remediation, advancement, ESL programs offered; session focuses on English or French as a Second Language and math; held on campus; accepts boys and girls; open to students from other schools. 150 students usually enrolled. 2013 schedule: July 1 to July 28. Application deadline: none.

Tuition and Aid Day student tuition: CAN$17,200; 7-day tuition and room/board: CAN$44,500. Tuition installment plan (monthly payment plans, individually arranged payment plans, single payment plan). Tuition reduction for siblings, bursaries, merit scholarship grants, need-based scholarship grants, need-based loans available.

Admissions Admissions testing or English for Non-native Speakers required. Deadline for receipt of application materials: none. Application fee required: CAN$100. Interview required.

Athletics Interscholastic: baseball (boys), football (b,g), gymnastics (g), hockey (b), ice hockey (b), softball (g); coed interscholastic: alpine skiing, aquatics, basketball, bicycling, climbing, cross-country running, equestrian sports, golf, horseback riding, independent competitive sports, nordic skiing, outdoor adventure, rugby, skiing (cross-country), skiing (downhill), soccer, swimming and diving, track and field; coed intramural: aerobics, alpine skiing, backpacking, badminton, basketball, climbing, Cosom hockey, curling, dance, figure skating, fitness, fitness walking, floor hockey, hiking/backpacking, hockey, horseback riding, ice hockey, ice skating, indoor hockey, jogging, mountain biking, outdoor activities, outdoor education, physical fitness, rock climbing, snowshoeing, squash, strength & conditioning, yoga. 1 PE instructor, 10 coaches, 1 athletic trainer.

Computers Computer network features include on-campus library services, Internet access, wireless campus network, Internet filtering or blocking technology, school-wide laptop initiative (included in tuition), fiber optic network. Student e-mail accounts are available to students. The school has a published electronic and media policy.

Contact Mrs. Ashli MacInnis, Director of Recruitment and Admissions. 819-566-0227 Ext. 296. Fax: 819-566-8123. E-mail: amacinnis@bishopscollegeschool.com. Web site: www.bishopscollegeschool.com

THE BISHOP'S SCHOOL

7607 La Jolla Boulevard
La Jolla, California 92037

Head of School: Aimeclaire Roche

General Information Coeducational day college-preparatory, arts, religious studies, and technology school, affiliated with Episcopal Church. Grades 6–12. Founded: 1909. Setting: suburban. Nearest major city is San Diego. 11-acre campus. 8 buildings on campus. Approved or accredited by California Association of Independent Schools, National Association of Episcopal Schools, Western Association of Schools and Colleges, and California Department of Education. Member of National Association of Independent Schools. Endowment: $27 million. Total enrollment: 800. Upper school average class size: 14. Upper school faculty-student ratio: 1:14. Upper School students typically attend 5 days per week. The average school day consists of 7 hours.

Upper School Student Profile Grade 9: 138 students (62 boys, 76 girls); Grade 10: 143 students (82 boys, 61 girls); Grade 11: 136 students (69 boys, 67 girls); Grade 12: 141 students (69 boys, 72 girls).

Faculty School total: 93. In upper school: 38 men, 45 women; 71 have advanced degrees.

Subjects Offered Acting, Advanced Placement courses, advanced studio art-AP, algebra, American history, American literature, art history, art history-AP, arts, ASB Leadership, biology, biology-AP, calculus, calculus-AP, ceramics, chemistry, chemistry-AP, Chinese, Chinese studies, chorus, community service, comparative government and politics-AP, comparative religion, computer programming, computer science, creative writing, dance, discrete mathematics, drama, drawing, earth science, ecology, economics, economics and history, economics-AP, English, English literature, environmental science, ethics, European history, European history-AP, forensics, French, French language-AP, French literature-AP, genetics, geography, geometry, government/civics, health, history, human anatomy, humanities, integrated mathematics, Internet, jazz band, journalism, Latin, Latin American studies, Latin-AP, literature and composition-AP, literature-AP, macro/microeconomics-AP, marine biology, mathematics, music, painting, philosophy, photography, physical education, physical science, physics, physics-AP, physiology, pre-algebra, pre-calculus, probability, programming, religious studies, Shakespeare, social studies, Spanish, Spanish language-AP, Spanish literature-AP, speech, speech and debate, stained glass, statistics, statistics-AP, studio art-AP, tap dance, theater, theater design and production, typing, U.S. government and politics-AP, U.S. history, U.S. history-AP, visual reality, world history, yearbook.

Graduation Requirements Arts and fine arts (art, music, dance, drama), computer science, English, foreign language, mathematics, physical education (includes health), religion (includes Bible studies and theology), science, social sciences, social studies (includes history), swimming test, computer proficiency. Community service is required.

Special Academic Programs Advanced Placement exam preparation; honors section; independent study; study abroad.

College Admission Counseling 133 students graduated in 2012; 129 went to college, including Boston College; Brown University; New York University; Stanford University; University of California, Berkeley; University of Southern California. Other: 4 had other specific plans. Median SAT critical reading: 670, median SAT math: 680, median SAT writing: 700, median combined SAT: 2080, median composite ACT: 31. 79% scored over 600 on SAT critical reading, 86% scored over 600 on SAT math, 83% scored over 600 on SAT writing, 83% scored over 1800 on combined SAT, 85% scored over 26 on composite ACT.

Student Life Upper grades have uniform requirement, student council, honor system. Discipline rests equally with students and faculty. Attendance at religious services is required.

Summer Programs Remediation, enrichment, advancement, sports, art/fine arts, computer instruction programs offered; held on campus; accepts boys and girls; open to students from other schools. 270 students usually enrolled. 2013 schedule: June 21 to July 21. Application deadline: June 21.

Tuition and Aid Day student tuition: $28,000. Tuition installment plan (FACTS Tuition Payment Plan, semester payment plans, Key Resources Achiever Loan). Need-based scholarship grants available. In 2012–13, 20% of upper-school students received aid. Total amount of financial aid awarded in 2012–13: $2,900,000.

Admissions Traditional secondary-level entrance grade is 9. For fall 2012, 390 students applied for upper-level admission, 226 were accepted, 175 enrolled. ISEE required. Deadline for receipt of application materials: February 1. Application fee required: $100. On-campus interview required.

Athletics Interscholastic: baseball (boys), basketball (b,g), cross-country running (b,g), equestrian sports (b,g), field hockey (g), football (b), golf (b,g), gymnastics (g), lacrosse (b,g), soccer (b,g), softball (g), swimming and diving (b,g), tennis (b,g), track and field (b,g), volleyball (b,g), water polo (b,g); intramural: weight training (b,g); coed interscholastic: sailing. 5 PE instructors, 38 coaches, 1 athletic trainer.

Computers Computers are regularly used in English, foreign language, history, journalism, library, music, science, yearbook classes. Computer network features include on-campus library services, online commercial services, Internet access.

Contact Kim Peckham, Director of Admissions and Financial Aid. 858-875-0809. Fax: 858-459-2990. E-mail: peckhamk@bishops.com. Web site: www.bishops.com

BISHOP STANG HIGH SCHOOL

500 Slocum Road
North Dartmouth, Massachusetts 02747-2999

Head of School: Mr. Peter V. Shaughnessy

General Information Coeducational day college-preparatory, arts, business, religious studies, technology, science, and arts school, affiliated with Roman Catholic Church. Grades 9–12. Founded: 1959. Setting: suburban. Nearest major city is New Bedford. 8-acre campus. 1 building on campus. Approved or accredited by New England Association of Schools and Colleges and Massachusetts Department of Education. Endowment: $2 million. Total enrollment: 667. Upper school average class size: 19. Upper school faculty-student ratio: 1:13. There are 180 required school days per year for Upper School students. Upper School students typically attend 5 days per week. The average school day consists of 6 hours and 30 minutes.

Upper School Student Profile Grade 9: 167 students (75 boys, 92 girls); Grade 10: 160 students (70 boys, 90 girls); Grade 11: 174 students (87 boys, 87 girls); Grade 12: 166 students (81 boys, 85 girls). 85% of students are Roman Catholic.

Faculty School total: 61. In upper school: 23 men, 38 women; 29 have advanced degrees.

Subjects Offered 3-dimensional design, advanced biology, algebra, American history, American literature, anatomy and physiology, art, biochemistry, bioethics, biology, biology-AP, calculus, calculus-AP, campus ministry, Catholic belief and practice, chemistry, chemistry-AP, chorus, church history, communications, community service, computer science, concert band, criminal justice, criminology, death and loss, driver education, ecology, English, English literature, English-AP, environmental science, fine arts, French, geometry, government/civics, health, history, history of the Catholic Church, instrumental music, introduction to theater, Latin, Life of Christ, marine biology, marketing, mathematics, mechanical drawing, media production, modern European history-AP, moral theology, music, oceanography, photography, physical education, physics, physics-AP, physiology, Portuguese, prayer/spirituality, psychology, psychology-AP, religion, religious studies, science, social sciences, social studies, sociology, Spanish, study skills, technical drawing, theater arts, trigonometry, Web authoring, world history, world literature, writing, yearbook.

Graduation Requirements Arts and fine arts (art, music, dance, drama), business skills (includes word processing), computer science, English, foreign language, mathematics, physical education (includes health), religion (includes Bible studies and theology), science, social sciences, social studies (includes history), service project. Community service is required.

Special Academic Programs 7 Advanced Placement exams for which test preparation is offered; honors section; remedial reading and/or remedial writing; remedial math; programs in English, mathematics, general development for dyslexic students.

College Admission Counseling 200 students graduated in 2012; 197 went to college, including Bridgewater State University; Northeastern University; Providence College; University of Massachusetts Amherst; University of Massachusetts Dartmouth; University of Rhode Island. Other: 2 went to work, 1 entered military service. Mean SAT critical reading: 546, mean SAT math: 537, mean SAT writing: 532, mean combined SAT: 1615.

Student Life Upper grades have uniform requirement, student council, honor system. Discipline rests primarily with faculty. Attendance at religious services is required.

Summer Programs Enrichment, sports, art/fine arts, computer instruction programs offered; session focuses on sport and activity camps; held on campus; accepts boys and girls; open to students from other schools. 200 students usually enrolled. 2013 schedule: July 1 to August 19. Application deadline: June.

Tuition and Aid Day student tuition: $8300. Tuition installment plan (FACTS Tuition Payment Plan, monthly payment plans). Merit scholarship grants, need-based scholarship grants available. In 2012–13, 27% of upper-school students received aid; total upper-school merit-scholarship money awarded: $12,500. Total amount of financial aid awarded in 2012–13: $500,000.

Admissions For fall 2012, 250 students applied for upper-level admission, 210 were accepted, 175 enrolled. Scholastic Testing Service High School Placement Test or SSAT required. Deadline for receipt of application materials: none. No application fee required. On-campus interview recommended.

Athletics Interscholastic: aquatics (boys, girls), baseball (b), basketball (b,g), cheering (g), cross-country running (b,g), diving (b,g), field hockey (g), fitness (b,g), football (b), ice hockey (b), lacrosse (b,g), soccer (b,g), softball (g), swimming and diving (b,g), tennis (b,g), track and field (b,g), volleyball (b,g), winter (indoor) track (b,g); coed interscholastic: golf, indoor track & field, physical fitness, sailing, strength & conditioning; coed intramural: climbing, crew, Frisbee, physical training, rowing, sailing, skiing (downhill), snowboarding, strength & conditioning, ultimate Frisbee, weight lifting, weight training. 1 PE instructor, 10 coaches, 1 athletic trainer.

Computers Computers are regularly used in all classes. Computer network features include on-campus library services, online commercial services, Internet access, wireless campus network, Internet filtering or blocking technology. Campus intranet, student e-mail accounts, and computer access in designated common areas are available to students. The school has a published electronic and media policy.

Contact Mrs. Christine Payette, Admissions Director. 508-996-5602 Ext. 424. Fax: 508-994-6756. E-mail: admits@bishopstang.com. Web site: www.bishopstang.com

THE BISHOP STRACHAN SCHOOL

298 Lonsdale Road
Toronto, Ontario M4V 1X2, Canada

Head of School: Ms. Deryn Lavell

General Information Girls' boarding and day and distance learning college-preparatory, arts, business, religious studies, and technology school, affiliated with Anglican Church of Canada. Boarding grades 7–12, day grades JK–12. Distance learning grades 9–12. Founded: 1867. Setting: urban. Students are housed in single-sex dormitories. 7-acre campus. 1 building on campus. Approved or accredited by Canadian Association of Independent Schools, Canadian Educational Standards Institute, The Association of Boarding Schools, and Ontario Department of Education. Affiliate member of National Association of Independent Schools; member of Secondary School Admission Test Board. Language of instruction: English. Endowment: CAN$12 million. Total enrollment: 891. Upper school average class size: 20. Upper school faculty-student ratio: 1:9. There are 184 required school days per year for Upper School students. Upper School students typically attend 5 days per week. The average school day consists of 6 hours and 10 minutes.

Upper School Student Profile Grade 6: 44 students (44 girls); Grade 7: 82 students (82 girls); Grade 8: 100 students (100 girls); Grade 9: 118 students (118 girls); Grade 10: 123 students (123 girls); Grade 11: 115 students (115 girls); Grade 12: 105 students (105 girls). 16% of students are boarding students. 90% are province residents. 6 provinces are represented in upper school student body. 10% are international students. International students from Bahamas, China, Ghana, Nepal, Republic of Korea, and United States; 14 other countries represented in student body. 30% of students are members of Anglican Church of Canada.

Faculty School total: 111. In upper school: 20 men, 61 women; 30 have advanced degrees; 5 reside on campus.

Subjects Offered Accounting, algebra, American history, aquatics, art, art history, biology, biology-AP, business, business skills, calculus, calculus-AP, Canadian geography, Canadian history, career and personal planning, career education, chemistry, chemistry-AP, computer programming, computer science, computer science-AP, creative writing, drama, earth science, ecology, economics, English, English language-AP, English literature, English literature-AP, environmental science, ESL, ethics, European history, expository writing, fine arts, French, French language-AP, geography, geometry, government/civics, graphic arts, health, history, Italian, Latin, macroeconomics-AP, Mandarin, mathematics, microeconomics-AP, music, philosophy, physical education, physics, religion, science, social sciences, social studies, Spanish, Spanish language-AP, statistics-AP, theater, trigonometry, U.S. history-AP, world history.

Graduation Requirements Arts, Canadian geography, Canadian history, career education, civics, English, French, mathematics, physical education (includes health), science, 40 hours of community service, completion of 30 credits from grade 9-12.

Special Academic Programs Advanced Placement exam preparation; honors section; accelerated programs; independent study; term-away projects; study abroad; academic accommodation for the gifted, the musically talented, and the artistically talented; ESL (12 students enrolled).

College Admission Counseling 122 students graduated in 2011; 121 went to college, including Cornell University; McGill University; Queen's University at Kingston; University of Southern California; University of Toronto; Yale University. Other: 1 had other specific plans. Mean SAT critical reading: 609, mean SAT math: 610, mean SAT writing: 599.

Student Life Upper grades have uniform requirement, student council, honor system. Discipline rests primarily with faculty.

Tuition and Aid Day student tuition: CAN$26,410; 7-day tuition and room/board: CAN$47,860. Tuition installment plan (monthly payment plans, 3-installment plan). Bursaries, merit scholarship grants, need-based scholarship grants available. In 2011–12, 5% of upper-school students received aid; total upper-school merit-scholarship money awarded: CAN$95,000. Total amount of financial aid awarded in 2011–12: CAN$500,000.

Admissions Traditional secondary-level entrance grade is 9. For fall 2011, 450 students applied for upper-level admission, 244 were accepted, 165 enrolled. Admissions testing, SSAT or TOEFL required. Deadline for receipt of application materials: none. Application fee required: CAN$180. Interview required.

Athletics Interscholastic: alpine skiing, aquatics, archery, artistic gym, badminton, basketball, cross-country running, curling, field hockey, golf, gymnastics, hockey, ice hockey, nordic skiing, rhythmic gymnastics, skiing (downhill), soccer, softball, swimming and diving, tennis, track and field, volleyball; intramural: aerobics, aerobics/dance, backpacking, ballet, canoeing/kayaking, climbing, cooperative games, crew, dance, fencing, fitness, hiking/backpacking, kayaking, life saving, modern dance, outdoor adventure, outdoor education, outdoor recreation, physical training, rappelling, rock climbing, ropes courses, rowing, running, self defense, synchronized swimming, wall climbing, weight training, wilderness survival, yoga. 11 PE instructors.

Computers Computers are regularly used in art, business studies, career education, career exploration, economics, English, foreign language, geography, history, mathematics, music, science classes. Computer network features include on-campus library services, Internet access, wireless campus network, Internet filtering or blocking technology, laptop program (grades 9-12). Campus intranet and student e-mail accounts are available to students. Students grades are available online. The school has a published electronic and media policy.

Contact Ms. Jenna Parrett, Administrative Assistant. 416-483-4325 Ext. 1220. Fax: 416-481-5632. E-mail: studentrecruiting@bss.on.ca. Web site: www.bss.on.ca

BLAIR ACADEMY

2 Park Street
Blairstown, New Jersey 07825

Head of School: T. Chandler Hardwick III

General Information Coeducational boarding and day college-preparatory, arts, and technology school, affiliated with Presbyterian Church. Boarding grades 9–PG, day grades 9–12. Founded: 1848. Setting: rural. Nearest major city is New York, NY. Students are housed in single-sex dormitories. 425-acre campus. 42 buildings on campus. Approved or accredited by Middle States Association of Colleges and Schools, The Association of Boarding Schools, and New Jersey Department of Education. Member of National Association of Independent Schools and Secondary School Admission Test Board. Endowment: $67 million. Total enrollment: 450. Upper school average class size: 11. Upper school faculty-student ratio: 1:6. Upper School students typically attend 6 days per week. The average school day consists of 6 hours and 45 minutes.

Upper School Student Profile Grade 9: 88 students (44 boys, 44 girls); Grade 10: 115 students (64 boys, 51 girls); Grade 11: 115 students (66 boys, 49 girls); Grade 12: 124 students (68 boys, 56 girls); Postgraduate: 7 students (5 boys, 2 girls). 80% of students are boarding students. 22 states are represented in upper school student body. 17% are international students. International students from China, Hong Kong, Republic of Korea, Spain, Thailand, and United Kingdom; 17 other countries represented in student body.

Faculty School total: 80. In upper school: 40 men, 27 women; 57 have advanced degrees; 78 reside on campus.

Subjects Offered 3-dimensional art, 3-dimensional design, advanced math, Advanced Placement courses, advanced studio art-AP, African history, algebra, American government, American history, American history-AP, American literature, anatomy, architectural drawing, architecture, art, art history-AP, art-AP, Asian studies, biochemistry, biology, biology-AP, biotechnology, calculus, calculus-AP, ceramics, chemistry, chemistry-AP, Chinese, comparative government and politics-AP, computer programming, computer science, computer science-AP, creative writing, dance, drafting, drama, drawing, drawing and design, driver education, economics, economics and history, economics-AP, English, English language-AP, English literature, English literature-AP, environmental science, environmental science-AP, ethics, European history, European history-AP, filmmaking, fine arts, French, French language-AP, geometry, government/civics, health, history, Japanese history, jazz band, Latin, marine biology, marine science, mathematics, mechanical drawing, music, music theory-AP, painting, philosophy, photography, physics, pre-calculus, psychology, religion, robotics, science, social studies, Spanish, Spanish language-AP, statistics-AP, theater, theology, world history, world history-AP, world literature, writing.

Graduation Requirements Arts and fine arts (art, music, dance, drama), biology, English, foreign language, mathematics, performing arts, religion (includes Bible studies and theology), science, social studies (includes history), U.S. history, athletic requirement.

Special Academic Programs 23 Advanced Placement exams for which test preparation is offered; honors section; independent study; study abroad.

College Admission Counseling 134 students graduated in 2012; 133 went to college, including Boston College; Cornell University; Lehigh University; New York

University; Syracuse University; University of Pennsylvania. Other: 1 entered a postgraduate year. Mean SAT critical reading: 610, mean SAT math: 620, mean SAT writing: 630.

Student Life Upper grades have specified standards of dress, student council, honor system. Discipline rests equally with students and faculty.

Tuition and Aid Day student tuition: $35,600; 7-day tuition and room/board: $49,500. Tuition installment plan (Key Tuition Payment Plan, monthly payment plans). Need-based scholarship grants, need-based loans available. In 2012–13, 32% of upper-school students received aid. Total amount of financial aid awarded in 2012–13: $5,100,000.

Admissions Traditional secondary-level entrance grade is 9. For fall 2012, 789 students applied for upper-level admission, 241 were accepted, 145 enrolled. SSAT or TOEFL required. Deadline for receipt of application materials: January 15. Application fee required: $50. On-campus interview required.

Athletics Interscholastic: alpine skiing (boys, girls), baseball (b), basketball (b,g), crew (b,g), cross-country running (b,g), field hockey (g), football (b), golf (b,g), indoor track (b,g), lacrosse (b,g), rowing (b,g), running (b,g), skiing (downhill) (b,g), soccer (b,g), softball (g), squash (b,g), swimming and diving (b,g), tennis (b,g), track and field (b,g), volleyball (g), winter (indoor) track (b,g), wrestling (b); intramural: basketball (b,g), crew (b,g), ice hockey (b,g), rowing (b,g), volleyball (g); coed intramural: alpine skiing, bicycling, canoeing/kayaking, dance, equestrian sports, fitness, flag football, golf, horseback riding, kayaking, life saving, modern dance, mountaineering, outdoor activities, outdoor adventure, outdoor education, outdoor skills, physical fitness, skiing (downhill), snowboarding, squash, swimming and diving, tennis, weight lifting, weight training, wrestling, yoga. 3 athletic trainers.

Computers Computers are regularly used in architecture, drawing and design, English, foreign language, graphic arts, graphic design, history, information technology, mathematics, media production, science, video film production, writing classes. Computer network features include on-campus library services, online commercial services, Internet access, Internet filtering or blocking technology. Campus intranet, student e-mail accounts, and computer access in designated common areas are available to students. The school has a published electronic and media policy.

Contact Nancy Klein, Administrative. 800-462-5247. Fax: 908-362-7975. E-mail: admissions@blair.edu. Web site: www.blair.edu

See Display below and Close-Up on page 554.

THE BLAKE SCHOOL

110 Blake Road South
Hopkins, Minnesota 55343

Head of School: Dr. Anne E. Stavney

General Information Coeducational day college-preparatory school. Grades PK–12. Founded: 1900. Setting: urban. Nearest major city is Minneapolis. 5-acre campus. 1 building on campus. Approved or accredited by Independent Schools Association of the Central States. Member of National Association of Independent Schools. Endowment: $52 million. Total enrollment: 1,372. Upper school average class size: 16. Upper school faculty-student ratio: 1:8. There are 176 required school days per year for Upper School students. Upper School students typically attend 5 days per week. The average school day consists of 7 hours and 30 minutes.

Upper School Student Profile Grade 9: 130 students (66 boys, 64 girls); Grade 10: 134 students (68 boys, 66 girls); Grade 11: 136 students (71 boys, 65 girls); Grade 12: 129 students (63 boys, 66 girls).

Faculty School total: 136. In upper school: 30 men, 24 women; 36 have advanced degrees.

Subjects Offered Advanced chemistry, African-American literature, algebra, American history, American literature, art, Asian studies, astronomy, band, biology, biology-AP, calculus, calculus-AP, ceramics, chemistry, chemistry-AP, Chinese, choir, chorus, communication arts, communications, computer math, creative writing, debate, design, drama, drawing, economics, English, English literature, English-AP, ethics, European history, European history-AP, fine arts, French, French language-AP, French literature-AP, geology, geometry, German-AP, government/civics, history, instrumental music, jazz ensemble, journalism, Latin, mathematics, multicultural studies, music, painting, performing arts, photography, physical education, physics, physics-AP, policy and value, political science, printmaking, psychology, religion, science, sculpture, senior project, social psychology, social studies, Spanish, Spanish language-AP, speech, statistics, statistics-AP, studio art, studio art-AP, theater, theater arts, trigonometry, visual and performing arts, vocal ensemble, women's studies, world cultures, world history, world literature, writing.

Graduation Requirements Arts and fine arts (art, music, dance, drama), communications, English, foreign language, mathematics, physical education (includes health), science, social studies (includes history), assembly speech.

Special Academic Programs 14 Advanced Placement exams for which test preparation is offered; honors section; term-away projects; study at local college for college credit; study abroad.

College Admission Counseling 133 students graduated in 2012; 128 went to college, including Boston College; Colby College; Dartmouth College; Northwestern University; Wellesley College. Other: 1 entered military service, 4 had other specific plans. Median SAT critical reading: 650, median SAT math: 650, median SAT writing:

650, median combined SAT: 1950, median composite ACT: 29. 68% scored over 600 on SAT critical reading, 64% scored over 600 on SAT math, 69% scored over 600 on SAT writing, 75% scored over 26 on composite ACT.
Student Life Upper grades have specified standards of dress, student council, honor system. Discipline rests primarily with faculty.
Summer Programs Remediation, enrichment, advancement, sports programs offered; session focuses on broad-based program including academics, arts, and sports; held both on and off campus; held at local lakes and beaches, museums, other locations; accepts boys and girls; open to students from other schools. 250 students usually enrolled. 2013 schedule: June 24 to August 9.
Tuition and Aid Day student tuition: $23,525. Tuition installment plan (local bank-arranged plan). Need-based scholarship grants, need-based loans, academic year low-interest loans, tuition remission for children of faculty available. In 2012–13, 20% of upper-school students received aid. Total amount of financial aid awarded in 2012–13: $1,912,893.
Admissions Traditional secondary-level entrance grade is 9. For fall 2012, 90 students applied for upper-level admission, 59 were accepted, 34 enrolled. ERB or WISC/Woodcock-Johnson required. Deadline for receipt of application materials: January 31. Application fee required: $100. On-campus interview required.
Athletics Interscholastic: alpine skiing (boys, girls), baseball (b), basketball (b,g), cross-country running (b,g), diving (b,g), football (b), golf (b,g), ice hockey (b,g), lacrosse (b,g), skiing (cross-country) (b,g), skiing (downhill) (b,g), soccer (b,g), softball (g), swimming and diving (b,g); coed interscholastic: fencing. 1 PE instructor, 45 coaches, 1 athletic trainer.
Computers Computers are regularly used in all classes. Computer network features include on-campus library services, online commercial services, Internet access, wireless campus network, Internet filtering or blocking technology, laptops. Campus intranet, student e-mail accounts, and computer access in designated common areas are available to students. Students grades are available online. The school has a published electronic and media policy.
Contact Bryan Fleming, Director of Admissions. 952-988-3420. Fax: 952-988-3455. E-mail: bfleming@blakeschool.org. Web site: www.blakeschool.org

BLANCHET SCHOOL

4373 Market Street NE
Salem, Oregon 97305

Head of School: Mr. Anthony Guevara

General Information Coeducational day college-preparatory, arts, and religious studies school, affiliated with Roman Catholic Church. Grades 6–12. Founded: 1995. Setting: suburban. 22-acre campus. 2 buildings on campus. Approved or accredited by National Catholic Education Association, Northwest Accreditation Commission, and Oregon Department of Education. Endowment: $265,400. Total enrollment: 363. Upper school average class size: 18. Upper school faculty-student ratio: 1:15. There are 175 required school days per year for Upper School students. Upper School students typically attend 5 days per week. The average school day consists of 7 hours.
Upper School Student Profile Grade 9: 59 students (30 boys, 29 girls); Grade 10: 58 students (32 boys, 26 girls); Grade 11: 60 students (30 boys, 30 girls); Grade 12: 70 students (34 boys, 36 girls). 70% of students are Roman Catholic.
Faculty School total: 25. In upper school: 8 men, 17 women; 21 have advanced degrees.
Subjects Offered Advanced Placement courses, algebra, American government, American history-AP, American literature, anatomy, anatomy and physiology, art, art education, band, Bible studies, biology, calculus, campus ministry, career and personal planning, Catholic belief and practice, chemistry, chemistry-AP, choir, civics, college counseling, college placement, comparative religion, composition, critical thinking, critical writing, debate, digital photography, drama, economics, economics and history, English literature, English literature and composition-AP, first aid, fitness, French, geometry, global studies, government, great books, health, health and safety, health and wellness, health education, history of the Catholic Church, history-AP, lab science, literature and composition-AP, mathematics, music, personal finance, physical education, physical fitness, physical science, physics, pre-algebra, pre-calculus, psychology, publications, religion, religion and culture, SAT/ACT preparation, sociology, Spanish, speech and debate, U.S. government, U.S. history, U.S. history-AP, weight training, world history, world religions, World War II.
Graduation Requirements Applied arts, arts and fine arts (art, music, dance, drama), electives, English, foreign language, mathematics, physical education (includes health), religion (includes Bible studies and theology), science, social studies (includes history), 20 hours of community service for each year in attendance.
Special Academic Programs 2 Advanced Placement exams for which test preparation is offered; honors section; study at local college for college credit; special instructional classes for deaf students; ESL (6 students enrolled).
College Admission Counseling 65 students graduated in 2012; 63 went to college, including Chemeketa Community College; Gonzaga University; Oregon State University; University of Oregon; University of Portland; Willamette University. Other: 1 went to work, 1 entered military service. Mean SAT critical reading: 523, mean SAT math: 576, mean SAT writing: 523, mean composite ACT: 26.
Student Life Upper grades have specified standards of dress, student council. Discipline rests primarily with faculty. Attendance at religious services is required.
Summer Programs Remediation, enrichment, sports programs offered; session focuses on preparation for the next academic year, athletic training; held on campus; accepts boys and girls; open to students from other schools. 75 students usually enrolled. 2013 schedule: June 13 to August 17.
Tuition and Aid Day student tuition: $7165. Tuition installment plan (FACTS Tuition Payment Plan). Tuition reduction for siblings, merit scholarship grants, need-based scholarship grants available. In 2012–13, 35% of upper-school students received aid; total upper-school merit-scholarship money awarded: $8500. Total amount of financial aid awarded in 2012–13: $240,000.
Admissions Traditional secondary-level entrance grade is 9. For fall 2012, 92 students applied for upper-level admission, 84 were accepted, 83 enrolled. Math Placement Exam required. Deadline for receipt of application materials: none. Application fee required: $100. Interview recommended.
Athletics Interscholastic: baseball (boys), basketball (b,g), cheering (g), cross-country running (b,g), fencing (b,g), football (b), golf (b,g), physical fitness (b,g), soccer (b,g), softball (g), swimming and diving (b,g), tennis (b,g), track and field (b,g), volleyball (g), weight training (b,g); intramural: weight training (b,g). 4 PE instructors, 60 coaches.
Computers Computers are regularly used in business, photography, science, social studies classes. Computer network features include online commercial services, Internet access, wireless campus network, Internet filtering or blocking technology. Computer access in designated common areas is available to students. Students grades are available online. The school has a published electronic and media policy.
Contact Mrs. Cathy McClaughry, Admissions Office. 503-485-4491. Fax: 503-399-1259. E-mail: cathy@blanchetcatholicschool.com. Web site: www.blanchetcatholicschool.com

BLESSED SACRAMENT HUGENOT

2501 Academy Road
Powhatan, Virginia 23139

Head of School: Dr. Tracy Bonday-deLeon

General Information Coeducational day college-preparatory school, affiliated with Roman Catholic Church. Grades PS–12. Founded: 1954. Setting: rural. Nearest major city is Richmond. 46-acre campus. 5 buildings on campus. Approved or accredited by National Catholic Education Association, Southern Association of Colleges and Schools, and Virginia Department of Education. Total enrollment: 337. Upper school average class size: 120. Upper school faculty-student ratio: 1:6. There are 180 required school days per year for Upper School students. Upper School students typically attend 5 days per week. The average school day consists of 6 hours and 30 minutes.
Upper School Student Profile 35% of students are Roman Catholic.
Faculty School total: 36. In upper school: 6 men, 14 women; 12 have advanced degrees.
Subjects Offered Advanced math, Advanced Placement courses, algebra, American government, American history, American history-AP, American literature-AP, art, athletics, baseball, basketball, biology, calculus, calculus-AP, Central and Eastern European history, cheerleading, chemistry, Christian education, college admission preparation, college awareness, college counseling, college planning, college writing, community service, conceptual physics, drama, drama performance, English, English-AP, European history, foreign language, geography, geometry, government-AP, history of the Catholic Church, history-AP, honors algebra, honors English, honors geometry, honors U.S. history, honors world history, Latin, modern European history, physical education, religious education, SAT preparation, Spanish, student government, swimming, tennis, theology, trigonometry, U.S. and Virginia government, U.S. and Virginia government-AP, U.S. history-AP, world history.
Graduation Requirements Admission to a 4-year Institution, Community Service Hours.
Special Academic Programs Advanced Placement exam preparation; honors section.
College Admission Counseling 33 students graduated in 2011; all went to college, including Hampden-Sydney College; Longwood University; Radford University; University of Virginia; Virginia Polytechnic Institute and State University.
Student Life Upper grades have uniform requirement, student council, honor system. Discipline rests equally with students and faculty. Attendance at religious services is required.
Tuition and Aid Day student tuition: $10,725. Tuition installment plan (FACTS Tuition Payment Plan). Tuition reduction for siblings, need-based scholarship grants available. In 2011–12, 15% of upper-school students received aid. Total amount of financial aid awarded in 2011–12: $175,000.
Admissions Traditional secondary-level entrance grade is 9. For fall 2011, 25 students applied for upper-level admission, 20 were accepted, 16 enrolled. Deadline for receipt of application materials: none. Application fee required: $50. Interview required.
Athletics Interscholastic: baseball (boys), basketball (b,g), football (b), softball (g), volleyball (g); intramural: basketball (b,g), football (b), softball (g), volleyball (g); coed interscholastic: cheering, cross-country running, golf, soccer, swimming and diving, tennis; coed intramural: cross-country running, soccer, swimming and diving, tennis. 2 PE instructors, 20 coaches, 1 athletic trainer.

Computers Computer network features include Internet access, Internet filtering or blocking technology. Campus intranet is available to students. Students grades are available online. The school has a published electronic and media policy.
Contact Mrs. Christy M. Polster, Director of Admissions. 804-598-4211. Fax: 804-598-1053. E-mail: cpolster@bshknights.org. Web site: www.bshknights.org

BLESSED TRINITY HIGH SCHOOL

11320 Woodstock Road
Roswell, Georgia 30075

Head of School: Mr. Frank Moore

General Information Coeducational day college-preparatory and religious studies school, affiliated with Roman Catholic Church. Grades 9–12. Founded: 2000. Setting: suburban. Nearest major city is Atlanta. 68-acre campus. 2 buildings on campus. Approved or accredited by Georgia Independent School Association, Southern Association of Colleges and Schools, and Georgia Department of Education. Member of National Association of Independent Schools and Secondary School Admission Test Board. Upper school average class size: 20. Upper school faculty-student ratio: 1:14. Upper School students typically attend 5 days per week. The average school day consists of 6 hours.
Upper School Student Profile 87% of students are Roman Catholic.
Faculty School total: 80. In upper school: 40 men, 40 women; 45 have advanced degrees.
Graduation Requirements American government, American history, American literature, ancient world history, theology.
Special Academic Programs 23 Advanced Placement exams for which test preparation is offered.
College Admission Counseling 227 students graduated in 2012; all went to college, including Auburn University; Georgia College & State University; Georgia Institute of Technology; Georgia Southern University; The University of Alabama; University of Georgia.
Student Life Upper grades have uniform requirement, student council. Discipline rests primarily with faculty. Attendance at religious services is required.
Tuition and Aid Day student tuition: $11,100. Tuition installment plan (FACTS Tuition Payment Plan). Need-based scholarship grants available. In 2012–13, 18% of upper-school students received aid.
Admissions Traditional secondary-level entrance grade is 9. SSAT required. Deadline for receipt of application materials: February 1. Application fee required: $100.
Athletics Interscholastic: baseball (boys), basketball (b,g), cheering (g), cross-country running (b,g), dance (b,g), dance team (g), football (b), golf (b,g), lacrosse (b,g), soccer (b,g), softball (g), strength & conditioning (b,g), swimming and diving (b,g), tennis (b,g), track and field (b,g), volleyball (g), wrestling (b). 5 PE instructors, 2 athletic trainers.
Contact Mr. Brian Marks, Director of Admissions. 678-277-0983 Ext. 502. Fax: 678-277-9756. E-mail: bmarks@btcatholic.org. Web site: www.btcatholic.org

BLUE MOUNTAIN ACADEMY

2363 Mountain Road
Hamburg, Pennsylvania 19526

Head of School: Mr. W. Craig Ziesmer

General Information Coeducational boarding and day college-preparatory, religious studies, leadership, and aviation school, affiliated with Seventh-day Adventists. Grades 9–12. Founded: 1955. Setting: rural. Students are housed in single-sex dormitories. 735-acre campus. 6 buildings on campus. Approved or accredited by Board of Regents, General Conference of Seventh-day Adventists and Middle States Association of Colleges and Schools. Total enrollment: 158. Upper school average class size: 22. Upper school faculty-student ratio: 1:9. There are 180 required school days per year for Upper School students. Upper School students typically attend 5 days per week. The average school day consists of 6 hours and 30 minutes.
Upper School Student Profile Grade 9: 27 students (12 boys, 15 girls); Grade 10: 41 students (17 boys, 24 girls); Grade 11: 39 students (23 boys, 16 girls); Grade 12: 51 students (30 boys, 21 girls). 81% of students are boarding students. 58% are state residents. 9 states are represented in upper school student body. 5% are international students. International students from Bermuda, Canada, China, Malaysia, Mexico, and Republic of Korea; 4 other countries represented in student body. 95% of students are Seventh-day Adventists.
Faculty School total: 17. In upper school: 12 men, 5 women; 12 have advanced degrees; all reside on campus.
Subjects Offered Accounting, Advanced Placement courses, algebra, anatomy and physiology, art, auto mechanics, band, bell choir, Bible, biology, business mathematics, chemistry, chemistry-AP, choir, computer applications, desktop publishing, digital photography, English, English literature and composition-AP, flight instruction, French, geometry, golf, gymnastics, health, home economics, honors English, honors world history, leadership, life science, music appreciation, music theory, organ, physical education, physics, piano, pre-algebra, pre-calculus, psychology, Spanish, U.S. government, U.S. history, U.S. history-AP, Western civilization, world history.
Graduation Requirements Algebra, arts, Bible, biology, computer applications, electives, English, foreign language, mathematics, physical education (includes health), science, social sciences, U.S. government, U.S. history, work-study, work study credit per semester enrolled.
Special Academic Programs 3 Advanced Placement exams for which test preparation is offered; honors section; accelerated programs; study at local college for college credit; academic accommodation for the musically talented; remedial reading and/or remedial writing; remedial math; programs in English, mathematics, general development for dyslexic students.
College Admission Counseling 66 students graduated in 2011; 60 went to college, including Andrews University; Southern Adventist University; Walla Walla University; Washington Adventist University. Mean SAT critical reading: 500, mean SAT math: 463, mean SAT writing: 500, mean composite ACT: 21.
Student Life Upper grades have specified standards of dress, student council, honor system. Discipline rests primarily with faculty. Attendance at religious services is required.
Tuition and Aid Day student tuition: $10,870; 7-day tuition and room/board: $17,510. Tuition installment plan (monthly payment plans). Tuition reduction for siblings, need-based scholarship grants, paying campus jobs available. In 2011–12, 45% of upper-school students received aid. Total amount of financial aid awarded in 2011–12: $287,000.
Admissions Traditional secondary-level entrance grade is 9. Math Placement Exam required. Deadline for receipt of application materials: none. Application fee required: $20. Interview recommended.
Athletics Intramural: basketball (boys, girls), flag football (b,g), soccer (b,g), softball (b,g), volleyball (b,g); coed intramural: basketball, flag football, gymnastics, soccer, softball, volleyball. 1 PE instructor.
Computers Computers are regularly used in desktop publishing, history, keyboarding, mathematics, photography, psychology, religion, science, yearbook classes. Computer network features include on-campus library services, Internet access, Internet filtering or blocking technology. Student e-mail accounts and computer access in designated common areas are available to students. Students grades are available online. The school has a published electronic and media policy.
Contact Mrs. Diana Engen, Registrar. 484-662-7000. Fax: 610-562-8050. E-mail: dengen@bma.us. Web site: www.bma.us

BLUEPRINT EDUCATION

5651 West Talavi Boulevard
Suite 170
Glendale, Arizona 85306

Head of School: Doug Covey

General Information Distance learning only college-preparatory, general academic, technology, and distance learning school. Distance learning grades 7–12. Founded: 1969. Approved or accredited by CITA (Commission on International and Trans-Regional Accreditation), North Central Association of Colleges and Schools, and Arizona Department of Education.
Faculty School total: 4. In upper school: 1 man, 3 women; all have advanced degrees.
Subjects Offered Algebra, American government, American history, art, art history, auto mechanics, biology, British literature, calculus, career experience, career exploration, career planning, careers, chemistry, child development, computer applications, computer education, earth science, economics, English, English composition, entrepreneurship, foreign language, geometry, government, health and wellness, health education, independent study, interpersonal skills, mathematics, parenting, personal development, physical education, physical fitness, physics, pre-algebra, psychology, psychology-AP, reading, remedial/makeup course work, service learning/internship, sociology, Spanish, speech, speech communications, statistics, travel, trigonometry, U.S. government, wellness, wilderness education, work experience, world geography, world history.
Graduation Requirements Arts and fine arts (art, music, dance, drama), computers, economics, English, foreign language, geography, health, mathematics, science, social studies (includes history), speech.
Special Academic Programs 1 Advanced Placement exam for which test preparation is offered; honors section; accelerated programs; independent study; academic accommodation for the musically talented and the artistically talented; remedial reading and/or remedial writing; remedial math.
College Admission Counseling Colleges students went to include Arizona State University; Northern Arizona University; Pima Community College; The University of Arizona.
Student Life Upper grades have honor system.
Summer Programs Remediation, advancement programs offered; session focuses on remediation and advancement; held off campus; held at various locations for independent study; accepts boys and girls; open to students from other schools.
Tuition and Aid Need-based scholarship grants available.
Admissions Deadline for receipt of application materials: none. Application fee required: $39.
Computers Computers are regularly used in all academic classes. Computer resources include Internet access. Students grades are available online. The school has a published electronic and media policy.

Contact Brenda Baer, Distance Learning Director. 800-426-4952 Ext. 4834. Fax: 602-943-9700. E-mail: brendab@blueprinteducation.org. Web site: www.blueprinteducation.org

THE BLUE RIDGE SCHOOL

273 Mayo Drive
St. George, Virginia 22935

Head of School: Dr. John R. O'Reilly

General Information Boys' boarding college-preparatory, general academic, arts, business, and technology school, affiliated with Episcopal Church; primarily serves underachievers. Grades 9–12. Founded: 1909. Setting: rural. Nearest major city is Charlottesville. Students are housed in single-sex dormitories. 750-acre campus. 11 buildings on campus. Approved or accredited by National Association of Episcopal Schools, Southern Association of Colleges and Schools, The Association of Boarding Schools, Virginia Association of Independent Schools, and Virginia Department of Education. Member of National Association of Independent Schools and Secondary School Admission Test Board. Endowment: $12 million. Total enrollment: 195. Upper school average class size: 8. Upper school faculty-student ratio: 1:6. There are 180 required school days per year for Upper School students. Upper School students typically attend 6 days per week. The average school day consists of 6 hours.

Upper School Student Profile Grade 9: 26 students (26 boys); Grade 10: 57 students (57 boys); Grade 11: 47 students (47 boys); Grade 12: 65 students (65 boys). 100% of students are boarding students. 25% are state residents. 27 states are represented in upper school student body. 35% are international students. International students from Canada, China, Ghana, Nigeria, Republic of Korea, and Taiwan; 12 other countries represented in student body.

Faculty School total: 35. In upper school: 25 men, 7 women; 18 have advanced degrees; 27 reside on campus.

Subjects Offered Algebra, American history, American literature, anatomy, anatomy and physiology, art, astronomy, biology, calculus, chemistry, choir, decision making skills, discrete mathematics, drama, economics, English, environmental science, ESL, European history, French, geometry, guitar, health, honors English, honors geometry, honors U.S. history, integrated science, keyboarding, leadership, marketing, mathematics, music, music history, outdoor education, physics, pre-algebra, precalculus, Spanish, trigonometry, U.S. history, world history, world literature, writing, yearbook.

Graduation Requirements Algebra, American history, American literature, biology, decision making skills, English, foreign language, geometry, leadership, mathematics, physical education (includes health), science, social studies (includes history), three years of a single foreign language.

Special Academic Programs Honors section; independent study; study at local college for college credit; remedial reading and/or remedial writing; remedial math; programs in English, general development for dyslexic students; ESL (20 students enrolled).

College Admission Counseling 60 students graduated in 2011; all went to college, including Emory University; Franklin & Marshall College; Hampden-Sydney College; Kenyon College; The Johns Hopkins University; University of California, Berkeley.

Student Life Upper grades have specified standards of dress, student council, honor system. Discipline rests primarily with faculty. Attendance at religious services is required.

Tuition and Aid 7-day tuition and room/board: $38,500. Guaranteed tuition plan. Tuition installment plan (monthly payment plans). Merit scholarship grants, need-based scholarship grants, paying campus jobs available. In 2011–12, 45% of upper-school students received aid; total upper-school merit-scholarship money awarded: $85,000. Total amount of financial aid awarded in 2011–12: $1,700,000.

Admissions For fall 2011, 313 students applied for upper-level admission, 138 were accepted, 88 enrolled. Deadline for receipt of application materials: none. Application fee required: $50. Interview required.

Athletics Interscholastic: baseball, basketball, cross-country running, football, golf, indoor soccer, lacrosse, mountain biking, soccer, table tennis, tennis, track and field, volleyball, wrestling; intramural: alpine skiing, aquatics, backpacking, bicycling, canoeing/kayaking, climbing, cooperative games, fishing, fitness, Frisbee, hiking/backpacking, kayaking, mountain biking, mountaineering, outdoor activities, outdoor adventure, outdoor education, outdoor recreation, outdoor skills, outdoors, paint ball, physical fitness, physical training, rafting, rappelling, rock climbing, ropes courses, skiing (downhill), snowboarding, soccer, strength & conditioning, tennis, ultimate Frisbee, wall climbing, weight lifting, weight training, wilderness, wilderness survival. 2 coaches, 2 athletic trainers.

Computers Computers are regularly used in business studies, English, ESL, foreign language, mathematics, science, study skills, word processing, writing, yearbook classes. Computer network features include on-campus library services, online commercial services, Internet access, wireless campus network, Internet filtering or blocking technology. Campus intranet, student e-mail accounts, and computer access in designated common areas are available to students. The school has a published electronic and media policy.

Contact Mr. Donald Smith, Assistant Headmaster for Enrollment and Marketing. 434-985-2811. Fax: 434-992-0536. E-mail: donsmith@blueridgeschool.com. Web site: www.blueridgeschool.com

THE BOLLES SCHOOL

7400 San Jose Boulevard
Jacksonville, Florida 32217-3499

Head of School: Brian M. Johnson

General Information Coeducational boarding and day college-preparatory and arts school. Boarding grades 7–PG, day grades PK–PG. Founded: 1933. Setting: suburban. Students are housed in single-sex dormitories. 52-acre campus. 12 buildings on campus. Approved or accredited by Florida Council of Independent Schools, Southern Association of Colleges and Schools, Southern Association of Independent Schools, The Association of Boarding Schools, and Florida Department of Education. Member of National Association of Independent Schools and Secondary School Admission Test Board. Endowment: $10.7 million. Total enrollment: 1,648. Upper school average class size: 17. Upper school faculty-student ratio: 1:10. There are 175 required school days per year for Upper School students. Upper School students typically attend 5 days per week. The average school day consists of 6 hours.

Upper School Student Profile Grade 9: 183 students (100 boys, 83 girls); Grade 10: 196 students (113 boys, 83 girls); Grade 11: 195 students (101 boys, 94 girls); Grade 12: 193 students (112 boys, 81 girls). 10% of students are boarding students. 92% are state residents. 8 states are represented in upper school student body. 8% are international students. International students from Brazil, China, Colombia, Democratic People's Republic of Korea, Germany, and Mexico; 20 other countries represented in student body.

Faculty School total: 130. In upper school: 40 men, 51 women; 70 have advanced degrees; 9 reside on campus.

Subjects Offered Acting, algebra, American Civil War, American government, American history, American literature, anatomy, art, art history, art history-AP, art-AP, band, biology, biology-AP, British literature, calculus, calculus-AP, ceramics, chemistry, chemistry-AP, Chinese, chorus, comparative government and politics-AP, composition, computer applications, computer science, computer science-AP, contemporary history, creative writing, dance, data analysis, design, directing, drama, drawing, driver education, earth science, ecology, economics, English, English literature-AP, environmental science, ESL, European history, fine arts, fitness, French, French-AP, geography, geometry, German, government/civics, health, history, history-AP, humanities, Japanese, journalism, Latin, Latin-AP, life management skills, life skills, literature, marine science, mathematics, Middle Eastern history, modern European history-AP, multimedia, music, mythology, neurobiology, painting, performing arts, photography, physical education, physics, physics-AP, portfolio art, pre-algebra, pre-calculus, programming, psychology, public speaking, publications, science, sculpture, social sciences, social studies, Spanish, Spanish-AP, statistics, statistics-AP, studio art, theater, U.S. government and politics-AP, visual arts, Web site design, weight training, world cultures, world history.

Graduation Requirements Arts and fine arts (art, music, dance, drama), English, foreign language, mathematics, physical education (includes health), science, social studies (includes history).

Special Academic Programs Advanced Placement exam preparation; honors section; independent study; term-away projects; study at local college for college credit; ESL (45 students enrolled).

College Admission Counseling 200 students graduated in 2012; 192 went to college, including Florida State University; Tallahassee Community College; The University of Alabama; University of Central Florida; University of Florida; University of North Florida. Other: 2 entered a postgraduate year, 6 had other specific plans. 50% scored over 600 on SAT critical reading, 50% scored over 600 on SAT math, 49% scored over 600 on SAT writing, 47% scored over 1800 on combined SAT, 50% scored over 26 on composite ACT.

Student Life Upper grades have specified standards of dress, student council, honor system. Discipline rests primarily with faculty.

Summer Programs Enrichment, ESL, art/fine arts, computer instruction programs offered; held on campus; accepts boys and girls; open to students from other schools. 150 students usually enrolled. 2013 schedule: June 6 to July 22.

Tuition and Aid Day student tuition: $20,280; 7-day tuition and room/board: $41,450. Tuition installment plan (major increment payment plan, 10-month plan, June payment plan). Need-based scholarship grants, faculty tuition remission available. In 2012–13, 22% of upper-school students received aid. Total amount of financial aid awarded in 2012–13: $3,000,000.

Admissions Traditional secondary-level entrance grade is 9. For fall 2012, 378 students applied for upper-level admission, 164 were accepted, 94 enrolled. ISEE required. Deadline for receipt of application materials: none. Application fee required: $45. Interview required.

Athletics Interscholastic: baseball (boys), basketball (b,g), cheering (g), crew (b,g), cross-country running (b,g), dance (b,g), diving (b,g), football (b), golf (b,g), lacrosse (b,g), soccer (b,g), softball (g), swimming and diving (b,g), tennis (b,g), track and field (b,g), volleyball (g), weight lifting (b), wrestling (b). 2 PE instructors, 5 coaches, 1 athletic trainer.

Computers Computers are regularly used in all academic classes. Computer network features include on-campus library services, online commercial services, Internet access, wireless campus network, Internet filtering or blocking technology. Computer access in designated common areas is available to students. Students grades are available online. The school has a published electronic and media policy.

Contact Mark I. Frampton, Director of Upper School and Boarding Admission. 904-256-5032. Fax: 904-739-9929. E-mail: framptonm@bolles.org. Web site: www.bolles.org

See Display below and Close-Up on page 556.

BOSTON TRINITY ACADEMY

17 Hale Street
Boston, Massachusetts 02136

Head of School: Mr. Frank Guerra

General Information Coeducational day college-preparatory school, affiliated with Christian faith. Grades 6–12. Founded: 2002. Setting: urban. 5-acre campus. 1 building on campus. Approved or accredited by Association of Independent Schools in New England, New England Association of Schools and Colleges, and Massachusetts Department of Education. Member of National Association of Independent Schools and Secondary School Admission Test Board. Total enrollment: 213. Upper school average class size: 14. Upper school faculty-student ratio: 1:8. There are 169 required school days per year for Upper School students. Upper School students typically attend 5 days per week. The average school day consists of 6 hours and 30 minutes.

Upper School Student Profile 70% of students are Christian faith.

Faculty School total: 29. In upper school: 13 men, 16 women; 18 have advanced degrees.

Special Academic Programs 9 Advanced Placement exams for which test preparation is offered; ESL (19 students enrolled).

College Admission Counseling 39 students graduated in 2012; 38 went to college. Other: 1 had other specific plans.

Student Life Upper grades have uniform requirement, student council, honor system. Discipline rests primarily with faculty. Attendance at religious services is required.

Summer Programs Remediation, enrichment, ESL, art/fine arts programs offered; held on campus; accepts boys and girls; open to students from other schools. Application deadline: none.

Tuition and Aid Day student tuition: $15,200. Tuition installment plan (FACTS Tuition Payment Plan). Need-based scholarship grants available. In 2012–13, 61% of upper-school students received aid. Total amount of financial aid awarded in 2012–13: $1,223,000.

Admissions Traditional secondary-level entrance grade is 9. ISEE or SSAT required. Deadline for receipt of application materials: January 31. Application fee required: $50. Interview required.

Athletics Interscholastic: baseball (boys), basketball (b,g), cross-country running (b,g), lacrosse (b,g), soccer (b,g), tennis (b,g), wrestling (b); intramural: physical fitness (b,g), table tennis (b,g).

Computers Computer network features include on-campus library services, Internet access, wireless campus network, Internet filtering or blocking technology. Campus intranet and computer access in designated common areas are available to students. Students grades are available online. The school has a published electronic and media policy.

Contact Mrs. Elaine Carroll, Associate Director of Admission. 617-364-3700 Ext. 219. Fax: 617-364-3800. E-mail: ecarroll@bostontrinity.org. Web site: www.bostontrinity.org

BOSTON UNIVERSITY ACADEMY

One University Road
Boston, Massachusetts 02215

Head of School: Mr. James Berkman

General Information Coeducational day college-preparatory and arts school. Grades 9–12. Founded: 1993. Setting: urban. 132-acre campus. 1 building on campus. Approved or accredited by Association of Independent Schools in New England, New England Association of Schools and Colleges, and Massachusetts Department of Education. Member of National Association of Independent Schools and Secondary School Admission Test Board. Total enrollment: 167. Upper school average class size: 12. Upper school faculty-student ratio: 1:8. There are 164 required school days per year for Upper School students. Upper School students typically attend 5 days per week. The average school day consists of 7 hours.

Upper School Student Profile Grade 9: 49 students (28 boys, 21 girls); Grade 10: 42 students (22 boys, 20 girls); Grade 11: 38 students (22 boys, 16 girls); Grade 12: 38 students (19 boys, 19 girls).

Faculty School total: 23. In upper school: 12 men, 11 women; 17 have advanced degrees.

Subjects Offered Advanced math, African American studies, algebra, American history, American literature, ancient history, anthropology, Arabic, archaeology, art, art history, astronomy, biochemistry, biology, calculus, chemistry, Chinese, classical studies, college counseling, community service, computer programming, drama, English, English literature, European history, French, geometry, German, Greek, Hebrew, history, Italian, Japanese, Latin, music, physical education, physics, robotics,

Russian, sculpture, senior project, Spanish, statistics, theater, trigonometry, women's studies, writing.

Graduation Requirements Arts and fine arts (art, music, dance, drama), chemistry, English, Greek, history, Latin, mathematics, physical education (includes health), physics, two semester senior thesis project, coursework at Boston University. Community service is required.

Special Academic Programs Honors section; accelerated programs; independent study; study at local college for college credit; academic accommodation for the gifted.

College Admission Counseling 39 students graduated in 2012; 37 went to college, including Boston University; Brandeis University; Case Western Reserve University; Stanford University; University of Massachusetts Amherst; University of Pennsylvania. Other: 2 had other specific plans. Mean SAT critical reading: 685, mean SAT math: 698, mean SAT writing: 681, mean combined SAT: 2064.

Student Life Upper grades have student council, honor system. Discipline rests equally with students and faculty.

Tuition and Aid Day student tuition: $33,574. Tuition installment plan (Insured Tuition Payment Plan, Academic Management Services Plan, monthly payment plans). Need-based scholarship grants available. In 2012–13, 35% of upper-school students received aid. Total amount of financial aid awarded in 2012–13: $1,175,095.

Admissions Traditional secondary-level entrance grade is 9. For fall 2012, 177 students applied for upper-level admission, 84 were accepted, 51 enrolled. SSAT required. Deadline for receipt of application materials: January 31. Application fee required: $50. On-campus interview required.

Athletics Interscholastic: basketball (boys, girls), crew (b,g); intramural: volleyball (g); coed interscholastic: cross-country running, fencing, soccer, tennis, ultimate Frisbee; coed intramural: climbing, dance, hiking/backpacking, sailing, softball, volleyball. 10 PE instructors, 7 coaches.

Computers Computers are regularly used in art, English, foreign language, history, mathematics, science classes. Computer network features include on-campus library services, online commercial services, Internet access, Internet filtering or blocking technology, internal electronic bulletin board system. Campus intranet and student e-mail accounts are available to students. Students grades are available online. The school has a published electronic and media policy.

Contact Ms. Nicole White, Admission Coordinator. 617-358-2493. Fax: 617-353-8999. E-mail: nicole_white@buacademy.org. Web site: www.buacademy.org

BOYLAN CENTRAL CATHOLIC HIGH SCHOOL

4000 Saint Francis Drive
Rockford, Illinois 61103-1699

Head of School: Rev. Paul Lipinski

General Information Coeducational day and distance learning college-preparatory, general academic, arts, business, vocational, religious studies, bilingual studies, and technology school, affiliated with Roman Catholic Church. Grades 9–12. Distance learning grades 9–12. Founded: 1960. Setting: urban. Nearest major city is Chicago. 60-acre campus. 3 buildings on campus. Approved or accredited by North Central Association of Colleges and Schools and Illinois Department of Education. Endowment: $3 million. Total enrollment: 1,152. Upper school average class size: 24. Upper school faculty-student ratio: 1:13. There are 176 required school days per year for Upper School students. Upper School students typically attend 5 days per week. The average school day consists of 7 hours.

Upper School Student Profile Grade 9: 287 students (142 boys, 145 girls); Grade 10: 280 students (146 boys, 134 girls); Grade 11: 272 students (140 boys, 132 girls); Grade 12: 313 students (159 boys, 154 girls). 87% of students are Roman Catholic.

Faculty School total: 86. In upper school: 33 men, 53 women; 62 have advanced degrees.

Subjects Offered 20th century history, 3-dimensional art, accounting, ACT preparation, acting, advanced computer applications, Advanced Placement courses, advanced studio art-AP, algebra, American history, American history-AP, American literature-AP, analysis and differential calculus, analytic geometry, anatomy and physiology, architectural drawing, architecture, art, art history, art history-AP, art-AP, athletics, auto mechanics, band, biology, bookkeeping, botany, British literature, British literature (honors), broadcast journalism, broadcasting, business, business education, business law, calculus, calculus-AP, career education, career exploration, career planning, Catholic belief and practice, cheerleading, chemistry, chemistry-AP, Chinese, choir, chorus, Christian and Hebrew scripture, Christian doctrine, Christian ethics, church history, college counseling, communications, comparative religion, composition-AP, computer multimedia, computer-aided design, concert band, concert choir, consumer economics, consumer education, consumer law, consumer mathematics, contemporary history, contemporary issues, contemporary studies, creative writing, critical thinking, culinary arts, debate, desktop publishing, drafting, drama, dramatic arts, earth science, economics-AP, English, English language-AP, English literature-AP, English/composition-AP, environmental science, European history, European history-AP, family and consumer science, family living, fashion, fiction, finite math, foods, French, French as a second language, French literature-AP, French-AP, freshman foundations, general math, geography, geometry, German, government, government-AP, graphics, guitar, health, health education, history of music, illustration, industrial technology, information processing, integrated science, jazz band, keyboarding, library assistant, marketing, music appreciation, music composition, music history, music technology, music theory, photo shop, physical science, physics, physics-AP, pre-algebra, pre-calculus, psychology, psychology-AP, religion, senior composition, Spanish, statistics, strings, studio art, swimming, technological applications, technology/design, trigonometry, U.S. history, vocal music, Web authoring, Web site design, wood lab, woodworking, world geography, world history, world literature, writing, yearbook, zoology.

Graduation Requirements Consumer education, English, mathematics, physical education (includes health), religious studies, science, social studies (includes history), fine and applied arts, community service.

Special Academic Programs 12 Advanced Placement exams for which test preparation is offered; honors section; independent study; academic accommodation for the gifted, the musically talented, and the artistically talented; remedial reading and/or remedial writing; remedial math; programs in general development for dyslexic students; special instructional classes for deaf students, blind students.

College Admission Counseling 295 students graduated in 2011; 284 went to college, including Illinois State University; Loyola University Chicago; Marquette University; Northern Illinois University; The University of Iowa; University of Illinois at Urbana–Champaign. Other: 9 went to work, 2 entered military service. 40% scored over 26 on composite ACT.

Student Life Upper grades have uniform requirement, student council. Discipline rests primarily with faculty. Attendance at religious services is required.

Tuition and Aid Day student tuition: $5100. Tuition installment plan (monthly payment plans, individually arranged payment plans, full-year or semester payment plan). Tuition reduction for siblings, need-based scholarship grants, paying campus jobs available. In 2011–12, 100% of upper-school students received aid. Total amount of financial aid awarded in 2011–12: $425,000.

Admissions Traditional secondary-level entrance grade is 9. For fall 2011, 300 students applied for upper-level admission, 300 were accepted, 287 enrolled. ETS HSPT (closed) required. Deadline for receipt of application materials: none. Application fee required: $100. Interview required.

Athletics Interscholastic: aerobics/dance (girls), baseball (b), basketball (b,g), bowling (b,g), cheering (g), cross-country running (b,g), dance team (g), diving (b,g), fishing (b,g), football (b), golf (b,g), ice hockey (b), soccer (b,g), softball (g), swimming and diving (b,g), tennis (b,g), track and field (b,g), volleyball (g), wrestling (b); intramural: aerobics (g), archery (b,g), fitness (b,g), golf (b,g), outdoor education (b,g), physical fitness (b,g), physical training (b,g), rowing (b,g), running (b,g), strength & conditioning (b,g), track and field (b,g), volleyball (b,g), weight training (b,g); coed intramural: dance. 6 PE instructors, 4 coaches, 2 athletic trainers.

Computers Computers are regularly used in all academic, architecture, business applications, computer applications, desktop publishing, drawing and design, keyboarding, music technology, photography, publications, technical drawing, technology, video film production, Web site design, word processing, yearbook classes. Computer network features include on-campus library services, online commercial services, Internet access, wireless campus network, Internet filtering or blocking technology. Campus intranet, student e-mail accounts, and computer access in designated common areas are available to students. Students grades are available online. The school has a published electronic and media policy.

Contact Mr. Dennis Hiemenz, Assistant Principal. 815-877-0531 Ext. 227. Fax: 815-877-2544. E-mail: dhiemenz@boylan.org. Web site: www.boylan.org

BRADENTON CHRISTIAN SCHOOL

3304 43rd Street West
Bradenton, Florida 34209

Head of School: Mr. Dan van der Kooy

General Information Coeducational day college-preparatory, arts, business, religious studies, and technology school, affiliated with Christian faith. Grades PK–12. Founded: 1960. Setting: suburban. Nearest major city is Tampa. 24-acre campus. 5 buildings on campus. Approved or accredited by Christian Schools International, Christian Schools of Florida, Southern Association of Colleges and Schools, and Florida Department of Education. Member of National Association of Independent Schools. Total enrollment: 542. Upper school average class size: 18. Upper school faculty-student ratio: 1:14. Upper School students typically attend 5 days per week. The average school day consists of 7 hours.

Upper School Student Profile 100% of students are Christian faith.

Faculty School total: 51. In upper school: 13 men, 9 women; 12 have advanced degrees.

Graduation Requirements 3 1/2 credits of Bible.

Special Academic Programs Advanced Placement exam preparation; honors section; study at local college for college credit.

College Admission Counseling 39 went to college, including University of South Florida. Mean SAT critical reading: 565, mean SAT math: 545, mean composite ACT: 25. 43% scored over 600 on SAT critical reading, 25% scored over 600 on SAT math.

Student Life Upper grades have specified standards of dress, student council, honor system. Discipline rests primarily with faculty. Attendance at religious services is required.

Tuition and Aid Day student tuition: $9990. Tuition installment plan (monthly payment plans, individually arranged payment plans). Tuition reduction for siblings, need-based scholarship grants available.
Admissions Traditional secondary-level entrance grade is 9. Academic Profile Tests or Woodcock-Johnson required. Deadline for receipt of application materials: none. Application fee required: $200. On-campus interview required.
Athletics Interscholastic: baseball (boys), basketball (b,g), cheering (b,g), football (b), soccer (b,g), softball (g), swimming and diving (g), tennis (b,g), track and field (b,g), volleyball (g); intramural: dance (g), flag football (b), touch football (b); coed interscholastic: golf, physical fitness; coed intramural: kickball. 2 PE instructors, 25 coaches.
Computers Computers are regularly used in art, Bible studies, business, business applications, business skills, career exploration, Christian doctrine, creative writing, design, desktop publishing, ESL, drawing and design, economics, English, ethics, foreign language classes. Computer network features include on-campus library services, Internet access, wireless campus network, Internet filtering or blocking technology. Student e-mail accounts and computer access in designated common areas are available to students. Students grades are available online. The school has a published electronic and media policy.
Contact Darcy Leahy, Director of Admissions. 941-792-5454 Ext. 104. Fax: 941-795-7190. E-mail: dleahy@bcspanthers.org. Web site: www.bcspanthers.org

BRANKSOME HALL

10 Elm Avenue
Toronto, Ontario M4W 1N4, Canada

Head of School: Karen Murton

General Information Girls' boarding and day college-preparatory and arts school. Boarding grades 8–12, day grades JK–12. Founded: 1903. Setting: urban. Students are housed in single-sex dormitories. 13-acre campus. 6 buildings on campus. Approved or accredited by Canadian Association of Independent Schools, Canadian Educational Standards Institute, International Baccalaureate Organization, Ontario Ministry of Education, The Association of Boarding Schools, and Ontario Department of Education. Affiliate member of National Association of Independent Schools; member of Secondary School Admission Test Board. Language of instruction: English. Endowment: CAN$13 million. Total enrollment: 880. Upper school average class size: 18. Upper school faculty-student ratio: 1:9. There are 180 required school days per year for Upper School students. Upper School students typically attend 5 days per week. The average school day consists of 8 hours.
Upper School Student Profile Grade 9: 107 students (107 girls); Grade 10: 121 students (121 girls); Grade 11: 115 students (115 girls); Grade 12: 119 students (119 girls). 16% of students are boarding students. 1% are province residents. 3 provinces are represented in upper school student body. 90% are international students. International students from China, Democratic People's Republic of Korea, Germany, Kenya, Saint Kitts and Nevis, and Taiwan; 12 other countries represented in student body.
Faculty School total: 115. In upper school: 15 men, 70 women; 40 have advanced degrees; 3 reside on campus.
Subjects Offered Accounting, acting, advanced math, algebra, all academic, American history, American literature, ancient history, ancient world history, Arabic, art, art and culture, art history, arts, athletics, band, biology, British history, British literature, business, calculus, Canadian geography, Canadian history, Canadian law, Canadian literature, Cantonese, career and personal planning, career exploration, career/college preparation, chemistry, Chinese, Chinese studies, classical civilization, classical Greek literature, computer multimedia, computer programming, computer science, critical thinking, critical writing, drama, drawing, economics, economics and history, English, English literature, environmental science, environmental systems, ethics, European history, European literature, expository writing, film studies, fine arts, food science, French, French studies, geography, geometry, German, government/civics, health, history, home economics, independent study, interdisciplinary studies, Latin, Mandarin, mathematics, music, physical education, physics, science, social sciences, social studies, Spanish, theater, theory of knowledge, trigonometry, typing, vocal ensemble, vocal music, world affairs, world arts, world civilizations, world cultures, world geography, world governments, world history, world issues, world literature, world religions, world studies, writing, writing workshop, yearbook.
Graduation Requirements Arts and fine arts (art, music, dance, drama), business skills (includes word processing), English, International Baccalaureate courses, language, mathematics, physical education (includes health), science, social sciences, social studies (includes history), IB diploma or certificate requirements.
Special Academic Programs International Baccalaureate program; honors section; academic accommodation for the gifted, the musically talented, and the artistically talented; ESL (20 students enrolled).
College Admission Counseling 112 students graduated in 2011; 111 went to college, including Dalhousie University; McGill University; Queen's University at Kingston; The University of British Columbia; The University of Western Ontario; University of Toronto. Other: 1 had other specific plans.
Student Life Upper grades have uniform requirement, student council, honor system. Discipline rests primarily with faculty.
Tuition and Aid Day student tuition: CAN$26,265; 7-day tuition and room/board: CAN$49,000. Tuition installment plan (monthly payment plans, tri-annual payment, early payment option ($500 savings)). Bursaries, merit scholarship grants available. In 2011–12, 10% of upper-school students received aid; total upper-school merit-scholarship money awarded: CAN$12,500. Total amount of financial aid awarded in 2011–12: CAN$650,000.
Admissions Traditional secondary-level entrance grade is 9. For fall 2011, 350 students applied for upper-level admission, 220 were accepted, 170 enrolled. SSAT required. Deadline for receipt of application materials: December 16. Application fee required: CAN$200. Interview required.
Athletics Interscholastic: alpine skiing, aquatics, badminton, baseball, basketball, crew, cross-country running, field hockey, golf, hockey, ice hockey, indoor track, indoor track & field, rowing, rugby, skiing (downhill), soccer, softball, swimming and diving, synchronized swimming, tennis, track and field, volleyball; intramural: aerobics, aerobics/dance, aquatics, badminton, ball hockey, ballet, baseball, basketball, cheering, climbing, cooperative games, cross-country running, dance, dance squad, field hockey, fitness, gymnastics, outdoor activities, paddle tennis, physical fitness, physical training, rugby, soccer, softball, squash, strength & conditioning, swimming and diving, table tennis, tennis, track and field, volleyball, yoga. 6 PE instructors, 2 coaches, 1 athletic trainer.
Computers Computers are regularly used in art, geography, mathematics, music, science classes. Computer network features include on-campus library services, Internet access, wireless campus network, Internet filtering or blocking technology. Campus intranet, student e-mail accounts, and computer access in designated common areas are available to students. The school has a published electronic and media policy.
Contact Kimberly Carter, Associate Director of Admissions. 416-920-9741. Fax: 416-920-5390. E-mail: admissions@branksome.on.ca. Web site: www.branksome.on.ca

THE BREARLEY SCHOOL

610 East 83rd Street
New York, New York 10028

Head of School: Mrs. Jane Foley. Fried

General Information Girls' day college-preparatory school. Grades K–12. Founded: 1884. Setting: urban. 2 buildings on campus. Approved or accredited by New York State Association of Independent Schools. Member of National Association of Independent Schools. Endowment: $107 million. Total enrollment: 688. Upper school average class size: 12. Upper school faculty-student ratio: 1:6. There are 169 required school days per year for Upper School students. Upper School students typically attend 5 days per week. The average school day consists of 7 hours.
Upper School Student Profile Grade 9: 56 students (56 girls); Grade 10: 54 students (54 girls); Grade 11: 57 students (57 girls); Grade 12: 47 students (47 girls).
Faculty School total: 134. In upper school: 21 men, 53 women; 56 have advanced degrees.
Subjects Offered 20th century world history, advanced biology, advanced chemistry, African history, algebra, American history, American literature, applied music, art, art history, biology, calculus, calculus-AP, chamber groups, chemistry, computer science, critical writing, drama, drama performance, drawing, English, English literature, environmental science, equality and freedom, expository writing, fiction, finite math, French, French studies, geometry, history, history of China and Japan, Homeric Greek, independent study, Latin, Mandarin, mathematics, modern European history, multimedia design, music, music history, oil painting, painting, physical education, physics, political thought, pre-calculus, senior project, Shakespeare, Spanish, Spanish literature, statistics, trigonometry, vocal music, water color painting, Web site design, world history.
Graduation Requirements Arts and fine arts (art, music, dance, drama), English, foreign language, history, mathematics, physical education (includes health), science.
Special Academic Programs 12 Advanced Placement exams for which test preparation is offered; independent study; term-away projects; study abroad.
College Admission Counseling 46 students graduated in 2012; all went to college, including Columbia University; Dartmouth College; Harvard University; Princeton University; University of Pennsylvania. Median SAT critical reading: 730, median SAT math: 690. 99% scored over 600 on SAT critical reading, 92% scored over 600 on SAT math.
Student Life Upper grades have specified standards of dress, student council. Discipline rests equally with students and faculty.
Summer Programs Advancement, sports, art/fine arts, computer instruction programs offered; session focuses on enrichment in arts and sports; held both on and off campus; held at Randalkls Island, ASphalt Green; accepts boys and girls; open to students from other schools.
Tuition and Aid Day student tuition: $36,800. Tuition installment plan (Key Tuition Payment Plan, individually arranged payment plans). Need-based scholarship grants, need-based loans available. In 2012–13, 22% of upper-school students received aid. Total amount of financial aid awarded in 2012–13: $4,245,080.
Admissions Traditional secondary-level entrance grade is 9. For fall 2012, 121 students applied for upper-level admission, 21 were accepted, 13 enrolled. ISEE and school's own exam required. Deadline for receipt of application materials: December 1. Application fee required: $60. On-campus interview required.
Athletics Interscholastic: aquatics, badminton, basketball, cross-country running, field hockey, gymnastics, lacrosse, soccer, softball, squash, swimming and diving,

tennis, track and field, volleyball; intramural: aquatics, badminton, basketball, cooperative games, dance, dance team, field hockey, fitness, gymnastics, jogging, lacrosse, modern dance, outdoor adventure, physical fitness, soccer, softball, strength & conditioning, swimming and diving, tai chi, team handball, track and field, volleyball, yoga. 12 PE instructors, 3 coaches, 2 athletic trainers.

Computers Computers are regularly used in classics, computer applications, foreign language, history, mathematics, multimedia, music, photography, science, theater arts, Web site design classes. Computer network features include on-campus library services, Internet access, wireless campus network, Internet filtering or blocking technology, Britannica Online, EBSCO, SIRS Researcher, ProQuest, JSTOR, ArtStor, AtomicLearning.com (software tutorials), a file server. Student e-mail accounts and computer access in designated common areas are available to students. The school has a published electronic and media policy.

Contact Ms. Joan Kaplan, Director of Middle and Upper School Admission. 212-744-8582. Fax: 212-472-8020. E-mail: admission@brearley.org. Web site: www.brearley.org

BRECK SCHOOL

123 Ottawa Avenue North
Minneapolis, Minnesota 55422

Head of School: Edward Kim

General Information Coeducational day college-preparatory, arts, and religious studies school, affiliated with Episcopal Church. Grades PK–12. Founded: 1886. Setting: suburban. 53-acre campus. 1 building on campus. Approved or accredited by Independent Schools Association of the Central States. Member of National Association of Independent Schools and Secondary School Admission Test Board. Endowment: $49 million. Total enrollment: 1,127. Upper school average class size: 16. Upper school faculty-student ratio: 1:11.

Upper School Student Profile 10% of students are members of Episcopal Church.

Faculty School total: 145. In upper school: 12 men, 17 women; 22 have advanced degrees.

Subjects Offered Algebra, American history, American literature, art, astronomy, biology, calculus, ceramics, chemistry, Chinese, chorus, community service, computer math, computer programming, creative writing, dance, drama, ecology, economics, English, English literature, environmental science, ethics, European history, expository writing, fine arts, French, geometry, health, history, mathematics, music, orchestra, physical education, physics, religion, science, social studies, Spanish, statistics, theater, theology, trigonometry, world history, world literature, writing.

Graduation Requirements Arts and fine arts (art, music, dance, drama), English, foreign language, mathematics, physical education (includes health), religion (includes Bible studies and theology), science, social studies (includes history), senior speech, May Program. Community service is required.

Special Academic Programs Advanced Placement exam preparation; honors section; independent study; term-away projects; academic accommodation for the gifted, the musically talented, and the artistically talented.

College Admission Counseling 94 students graduated in 2012; all went to college, including Boston College; Colby College; Miami University; Middlebury College; University of Denver; University of Minnesota, Twin Cities Campus. Mean SAT critical reading: 634, mean SAT math: 626, mean SAT writing: 644, mean combined SAT: 1904, mean composite ACT: 27.

Student Life Upper grades have specified standards of dress, student council, honor system. Discipline rests equally with students and faculty. Attendance at religious services is required.

Tuition and Aid Day student tuition: $24,995. Tuition installment plan (Key Tuition Payment Plan). Need-based scholarship grants available. In 2012–13, 23% of upper-school students received aid.

Admissions Traditional secondary-level entrance grade is 9. CTP III required. Deadline for receipt of application materials: February 1. Application fee required: $75. On-campus interview required.

Athletics Interscholastic: alpine skiing (boys, girls), baseball (b), basketball (b,g), cross-country running (b,g), diving (b,g), football (b), golf (b,g), gymnastics (g), ice hockey (b,g), lacrosse (b,g), nordic skiing (b,g), skiing (cross-country) (b,g), skiing (downhill) (b,g), soccer (b,g), softball (g), swimming and diving (b,g), tennis (b,g), track and field (b,g), volleyball (g). 6 PE instructors, 82 coaches, 1 athletic trainer.

Computers Computers are regularly used in all classes. Computer network features include on-campus library services, online commercial services, Internet access, wireless campus network, Internet filtering or blocking technology, multimedia imaging, video presentation, student laptop program. Campus intranet and student e-mail accounts are available to students. The school has a published electronic and media policy.

Contact Scott D. Wade, Director of Admissions. 763-381-8200. Fax: 763-381-8288. E-mail: scott.wade@breckschool.org. Web site: www.breckschool.org

BRENTWOOD COLLEGE SCHOOL

2735 Mount Baker Road
Mill Bay, British Columbia V0R 2P1, Canada

Head of School: Mr. Bud Patel

General Information Coeducational boarding and day college-preparatory, arts, and athletics, leadership, and citizenship school school. Grades 9–12. Founded: 1923. Setting: rural. Nearest major city is Victoria, Canada. Students are housed in single-sex dormitories. 49-acre campus. 16 buildings on campus. Approved or accredited by British Columbia Independent Schools Association, Canadian Association of Independent Schools, The Association of Boarding Schools, Western Boarding Schools Association, and British Columbia Department of Education. Affiliate member of National Association of Independent Schools. Language of instruction: English. Total enrollment: 435. Upper school average class size: 16. Upper school faculty-student ratio: 1:9.

Upper School Student Profile Grade 9: 83 students (53 boys, 30 girls); Grade 10: 115 students (61 boys, 54 girls); Grade 11: 124 students (62 boys, 62 girls); Grade 12: 113 students (62 boys, 51 girls). 81% of students are boarding students. 58% are province residents. 20 provinces are represented in upper school student body. 27% are international students. International students from Germany, Hong Kong, Mexico, Republic of Korea, Saudi Arabia, and United States; 12 other countries represented in student body.

Faculty School total: 50. In upper school: 24 men, 17 women; 13 have advanced degrees; 30 reside on campus.

Subjects Offered Advanced Placement courses, algebra, art history-AP, athletics, audio visual/media, band, basketball, biology, biology-AP, business, calculus, calculus-AP, Canadian geography, Canadian history, Canadian law, career and personal planning, ceramics, chemistry, chemistry-AP, choir, choreography, computer graphics, computer science, dance, dance performance, debate, design, drafting, drama, dramatic arts, drawing, economics, economics-AP, English, English literature, English literature-AP, French, French language-AP, geography, geometry, golf, government and politics-AP, health and wellness, history, human geography - AP, information technology, instrumental music, international studies, jazz band, jazz ensemble, marketing, mathematics, musical productions, musical theater, orchestra, outdoor education, painting, photography, physics, physics-AP, pottery, psychology, psychology-AP, public speaking, science, sculpture, sex education, social studies, Spanish, Spanish-AP, stagecraft, technical theater, tennis, theater design and production, video film production, visual and performing arts, vocal jazz, volleyball, yearbook.

Graduation Requirements Arts and fine arts (art, music, dance, drama), career and personal planning, English, foreign language, mathematics, physical education (includes health), science, social studies (includes history).

Special Academic Programs Advanced Placement exam preparation.

College Admission Counseling 112 students graduated in 2012; all went to college, including Duke University; McGill University; Queen's University at Kingston; The University of British Columbia; University of California, Berkeley; University of California, Los Angeles.

Student Life Upper grades have uniform requirement, student council, honor system. Discipline rests primarily with faculty.

Tuition and Aid Day student tuition: CAN$18,300; 7-day tuition and room/board: CAN$39,900–CAN$51,500. Tuition installment plan (The Tuition Plan). Tuition reduction for siblings available.

Admissions Traditional secondary-level entrance grade is 9. Henmon-Nelson or SSAT required. Deadline for receipt of application materials: none. Application fee required: CAN$2500. Interview required.

Athletics Interscholastic: basketball (boys, girls), crew (b,g), cross-country running (b,g), field hockey (g), hockey (g), rowing (b,g), rugby (b,g), running (b,g), soccer (b,g), squash (b,g), tennis (b,g), volleyball (g); intramural: crew (b,g), cross-country running (b,g), field hockey (g), indoor hockey (g), soccer (b,g), squash (b,g), tennis (b,g), track and field (b,g), volleyball (g), weight training (g); coed interscholastic: badminton, ballet, canoeing/kayaking, fitness, golf, ice hockey, judo, kayaking, modern dance, ocean paddling, outdoor activities, rock climbing, sailing; coed intramural: aerobics, aerobics/dance, badminton, canoeing/kayaking, cooperative games, dance, fitness, floor hockey, hiking/backpacking, indoor soccer, kayaking, outdoor activities, physical fitness, physical training, rowing, rugby, running, skiing (downhill), snowboarding, strength & conditioning, table tennis, touch football, weight lifting, weight training. 6 PE instructors, 36 coaches.

Computers Computers are regularly used in photojournalism, video film production classes. Computer network features include on-campus library services, Internet access, wireless campus network, Internet filtering or blocking technology. Campus intranet and student e-mail accounts are available to students. The school has a published electronic and media policy.

Contact Mr. Clayton Johnston, Director of Admissions. 250-743-5521. Fax: 250-743-2911. E-mail: admissions@brentwood.bc.ca. Web site: www.brentwood.bc.ca

BRENTWOOD SCHOOL

100 South Barrington Place
Los Angeles, California 90049

Head of School: Dr. Michael Riera

General Information Coeducational day college-preparatory school. Grades K–12. Founded: 1972. Setting: suburban. 30-acre campus. 12 buildings on campus. Approved or accredited by California Association of Independent Schools and Western Association of Schools and Colleges. Member of National Association of Independent Schools and Secondary School Admission Test Board. Endowment: $7 million. Total enrollment: 990. Upper school average class size: 17. Upper school faculty-student ratio: 1:7. Upper School students typically attend 5 days per week. The average school day consists of 8 hours.

Upper School Student Profile Grade 9: 121 students (60 boys, 61 girls); Grade 10: 123 students (62 boys, 61 girls); Grade 11: 111 students (61 boys, 50 girls); Grade 12: 108 students (56 boys, 52 girls).

Faculty School total: 125. In upper school: 45 men, 49 women; 70 have advanced degrees.

Subjects Offered Acting, Advanced Placement courses, advanced studio art-AP, algebra, American history, American literature, Ancient Greek, anthropology, art, art history, art history-AP, art-AP, astronomy, biology, biology-AP, calculus, calculus-AP, ceramics, chemistry, chemistry-AP, Chinese, choir, choral music, chorus, community service, comparative government and politics-AP, computer programming, computer programming-AP, computer science, computer science-AP, concert choir, creative writing, dance, digital photography, directing, drama, drawing, ecology, economics, economics-AP, English, English literature, environmental science-AP, European history, filmmaking, fine arts, French, French-AP, geometry, global studies, government and politics-AP, government-AP, history, honors algebra, honors English, honors geometry, human development, human geography - AP, Japanese, jazz band, jazz dance, journalism, language-AP, Latin, Latin-AP, literature-AP, math analysis, mathematics, music, music theater, music theory-AP, orchestra, organic chemistry, philosophy, photography, physical education, physics, physics-AP, probability and statistics, robotics, science, senior seminar, senior thesis, social sciences, social studies, Spanish, Spanish-AP, speech, speech and debate, stagecraft, stained glass, statistics-AP, studio art-AP, theater, U.S. government and politics-AP, U.S. history-AP, video, word processing, world history, world literature.

Graduation Requirements Arts and fine arts (art, music, dance, drama), English, foreign language, mathematics, physical education (includes health), science, senior seminar, social sciences, social studies (includes history). Community service is required.

Special Academic Programs 26 Advanced Placement exams for which test preparation is offered; honors section; independent study; study at local college for college credit; academic accommodation for the gifted and the artistically talented.

College Admission Counseling 115 students graduated in 2011; 114 went to college, including Brown University; Stanford University; The Johns Hopkins University; University of Pennsylvania; University of Southern California. Mean SAT critical reading: 660, mean SAT math: 670, mean SAT writing: 680, mean combined SAT: 2010.

Student Life Upper grades have specified standards of dress, student council, honor system. Discipline rests primarily with faculty.

Tuition and Aid Day student tuition: $31,250. Tuition installment plan (Insured Tuition Payment Plan, monthly payment plans, individually arranged payment plans). Need-based scholarship grants available. In 2011–12, 16% of upper-school students received aid. Total amount of financial aid awarded in 2011–12: $3,500,000.

Admissions Traditional secondary-level entrance grade is 9. For fall 2011, 171 students applied for upper-level admission, 25 were accepted, 20 enrolled. ISEE required. Deadline for receipt of application materials: January 13. Application fee required: $100. On-campus interview required.

Athletics Interscholastic: baseball (boys), basketball (b,g), cheering (g), cross-country running (b,g), dance squad (g), dance team (g), football (b), independent competitive sports (b,g), lacrosse (b,g), soccer (b,g), softball (g), swimming and diving (b,g), tennis (b,g), track and field (b,g), volleyball (b,g), water polo (b), wrestling (b); intramural: modern dance (g), ultimate Frisbee (b); coed interscholastic: dance, diving, drill team, equestrian sports, fencing, football, golf, swimming and diving, water polo; coed intramural: bicycling, fitness, Frisbee, jogging, mountain biking, outdoor activities, physical fitness, physical training, running, sailing, surfing, table tennis, ultimate Frisbee, weight lifting, weight training, wilderness, yoga. 6 PE instructors, 40 coaches, 2 athletic trainers.

Computers Computers are regularly used in college planning, computer applications, desktop publishing, digital applications, foreign language, graphic design, introduction to technology, journalism, literary magazine, mathematics, media arts, media production, photojournalism, programming, publications, research skills, science, technical drawing, technology, video film production, Web site design classes. Computer network features include on-campus library services, online commercial services, Internet access, wireless campus network, Internet filtering or blocking technology, Schoology (learning management system). Campus intranet, student e-mail accounts, and computer access in designated common areas are available to students. Students grades are available online. The school has a published electronic and media policy.

Contact Ms. Colleen Ward, Admissions Assistant. 310-889-2657. Fax: 310-476-4087. E-mail: cward@bwscampus.com. Web site: www.bwscampus.com

BREWSTER ACADEMY

80 Academy Drive
Wolfeboro, New Hampshire 03894

Head of School: Dr. Michael E. Cooper

General Information Coeducational boarding and day college-preparatory, arts, and technology school. Grades 9–PG. Founded: 1820. Setting: small town. Nearest major city is Boston, MA. Students are housed in single-sex dormitories. 91-acre campus. 39 buildings on campus. Approved or accredited by Independent Schools of Northern New England, New England Association of Schools and Colleges, and The Association of Boarding Schools. Member of National Association of Independent Schools and Secondary School Admission Test Board. Endowment: $8.4 million. Total enrollment: 364. Upper school average class size: 12. Upper school faculty-student ratio: 1:6. There are 165 required school days per year for Upper School students. Upper School students typically attend 6 days per week. The average school day consists of 6 hours.

Upper School Student Profile Grade 9: 54 students (20 boys, 34 girls); Grade 10: 95 students (56 boys, 39 girls); Grade 11: 97 students (58 boys, 39 girls); Grade 12: 102 students (54 boys, 48 girls); Postgraduate: 16 students (14 boys, 2 girls). 80% of students are boarding students. 26% are state residents. 32 states are represented in upper school student body. 23% are international students. International students from Bermuda, Canada, China, Japan, Republic of Korea, and Taiwan; 11 other countries represented in student body.

Faculty School total: 62. In upper school: 33 men, 29 women; 34 have advanced degrees; 54 reside on campus.

Subjects Offered 3-dimensional design, acting, algebra, art, art history, astronomy, biology, biology-AP, calculus, calculus-AP, chemistry, chorus, community service, computer graphics, creative writing, dance, dance performance, digital photography, drama, driver education, ecology, environmental systems, economics, English, English language and composition-AP, English literature, English literature-AP, environmental science, ESL, filmmaking, French, geometry, jazz band, journalism, macroeconomics-AP, mathematics, media arts, music, music history, music technology, music theory, orchestra, physics, physics-AP, pottery, science, Spanish, statistics-AP, studio art, theater, U.S. history, U.S. history-AP, Web authoring, Web site design, wind ensemble, world history, writing.

Graduation Requirements English, foreign language, mathematics, science, social studies (includes history).

Special Academic Programs 9 Advanced Placement exams for which test preparation is offered; honors section; programs in English, mathematics, general development for dyslexic students; ESL (20 students enrolled).

College Admission Counseling 117 students graduated in 2011; 114 went to college, including Boston University; Hobart and William Smith Colleges; New York University; Northeastern University; Saint Michael's College; Susquehanna University. Other: 3 entered a postgraduate year. Median SAT critical reading: 500, median SAT math: 530, median SAT writing: 500, median combined SAT: 1560, median composite ACT: 22. 19% scored over 600 on SAT critical reading, 29% scored over 600 on SAT math, 15% scored over 600 on SAT writing, 17% scored over 1800 on combined SAT, 21% scored over 26 on composite ACT.

Student Life Upper grades have specified standards of dress, student council, honor system. Discipline rests primarily with faculty.

Tuition and Aid Day student tuition: $27,985; 7-day tuition and room/board: $45,540. Tuition installment plan (FACTS Tuition Payment Plan, monthly payment plans). Need-based scholarship grants available. In 2011–12, 27% of upper-school students received aid. Total amount of financial aid awarded in 2011–12: $2,700,000.

Admissions Traditional secondary-level entrance grade is 9. For fall 2011, 531 students applied for upper-level admission, 297 were accepted, 146 enrolled. SSAT required. Deadline for receipt of application materials: February 1. Application fee required: $50. On-campus interview required.

Athletics Interscholastic: alpine skiing (boys, girls), baseball (b), basketball (b,g), crew (b,g), cross-country running (b,g), field hockey (g), ice hockey (b,g), lacrosse (b,g), running (b,g), skiing (downhill) (b,g), soccer (b,g), softball (g), tennis (b,g); coed interscholastic: golf, sailing, snowboarding; coed intramural: aerobics, alpine skiing, climbing, croquet, dance, equestrian sports, fitness, indoor soccer, outdoor skills, rock climbing, sailing, skiing (downhill), snowboarding, strength & conditioning, table tennis, tennis, touch football, ultimate Frisbee, wall climbing, weight training, yoga. 2 athletic trainers.

Computers Computers are regularly used in all classes. Computer network features include on-campus library services, online commercial services, Internet access, Internet filtering or blocking technology. Campus intranet, student e-mail accounts, and computer access in designated common areas are available to students. Students grades are available online. The school has a published electronic and media policy.

Contact Mary Roetger, Admission Coordinator. 603-569-7200. Fax: 603-569-7272. E-mail: mary_roetger@brewsteracademy.org. Web site: www.brewsteracademy.org

BRIARCREST CHRISTIAN HIGH SCHOOL

76 S. Houston Levee Road
Eads, Tennessee 38028

Head of School: Mr. Eric Sullivan

General Information Coeducational day college-preparatory, arts, religious studies, and technology school, affiliated with Christian faith. Grades 9–12. Founded: 1973. Setting: suburban. Nearest major city is Memphis. 100-acre campus. 1 building on campus. Approved or accredited by Association of Christian Schools International, Southern Association of Colleges and Schools, Southern Association of Independent Schools, and Tennessee Association of Independent Schools. Member of National Association of Independent Schools. Total enrollment: 1,649. Upper school average class size: 18. Upper school faculty-student ratio: 1:14. There are 176 required school days per year for Upper School students. Upper School students typically attend 5 days per week. The average school day consists of 7 hours and 30 minutes.

Upper School Student Profile Grade 9: 136 students (78 boys, 58 girls); Grade 10: 135 students (66 boys, 69 girls); Grade 11: 132 students (69 boys, 63 girls); Grade 12: 149 students (65 boys, 84 girls). 91% of students are Christian.

Faculty School total: 44. In upper school: 19 men, 25 women; 26 have advanced degrees.

Subjects Offered Algebra, American history, American literature, anatomy, art, Bible studies, biology, business, calculus, chemistry, computer math, computer programming, computer science, creative writing, drama, driver education, English, English literature, environmental science, European history, expository writing, French, geography, geometry, government/civics, grammar, health, history, Latin, mathematics, music, physical education, physics, physiology, psychology, religion, science, social sciences, social studies, sociology, Spanish, speech, theater, trigonometry, typing, world history, writing.

Graduation Requirements Arts and fine arts (art, music, dance, drama), business skills (includes word processing), English, foreign language, mathematics, physical education (includes health), religion (includes Bible studies and theology), science, social sciences, social studies (includes history).

Special Academic Programs Advanced Placement exam preparation; honors section; study at local college for college credit; academic accommodation for the gifted, the musically talented, and the artistically talented; programs in English, mathematics, general development for dyslexic students.

College Admission Counseling 163 students graduated in 2012; 160 went to college, including Mississippi State University; The University of Tennessee; The University of Tennessee at Chattanooga; University of Arkansas; University of Memphis; University of Mississippi. Other: 2 went to work, 1 entered military service. Median composite ACT: 24. 31% scored over 26 on composite ACT.

Student Life Upper grades have uniform requirement, student council, honor system. Discipline rests primarily with faculty. Attendance at religious services is required.

Tuition and Aid Day student tuition: $12,895. Tuition installment plan (Insured Tuition Payment Plan, monthly payment plans, individually arranged payment plans, 2-payment plan). Tuition reduction for siblings, need-based tuition assistance available. In 2012–13, 12% of upper-school students received aid.

Admissions Traditional secondary-level entrance grade is 9. ISEE required. Deadline for receipt of application materials: none. Application fee required: $50. On-campus interview required.

Athletics Interscholastic: baseball (boys), basketball (b,g), cheering (g), cross-country running (b,g), drill team (g), football (b), golf (b,g), lacrosse (b,g), pom squad (g), soccer (b,g), softball (g), strength & conditioning (b), swimming and diving (b,g), tennis (b,g), track and field (b,g), trap and skeet (b,g), volleyball (g), weight lifting (b), wrestling (b); coed interscholastic: bowling, cross-country running, swimming and diving. 2 PE instructors.

Computers Computers are regularly used in accounting, art, English, history, journalism, keyboarding, lab/keyboard, language development, mathematics, newspaper, science, social sciences, social studies, Spanish, speech, yearbook classes. Computer network features include on-campus library services, Internet access, wireless campus network, Internet filtering or blocking technology. Campus intranet, student e-mail accounts, and computer access in designated common areas are available to students. Students grades are available online. The school has a published electronic and media policy.

Contact Mrs. Claire Foster, Admissions Coordinator. 901-765-4605. Fax: 901-765-4614. E-mail: cofoster@briarcrest.com. Web site: www.briarcrest.com

BRIARWOOD CHRISTIAN HIGH SCHOOL

6255 Cahaba Valley Road
Birmingham, Alabama 35242

Head of School: Dr. Barrett Mosbacker

General Information Coeducational day college-preparatory, arts, and religious studies school, affiliated with Presbyterian Church in America. Grades K4–12. Founded: 1964. Setting: suburban. 85-acre campus. 5 buildings on campus. Approved or accredited by Association of Christian Schools International, Southern Association of Colleges and Schools, and Alabama Department of Education. Endowment: $500,000. Total enrollment: 1,967. Upper school average class size: 23. Upper school faculty-student ratio: 1:23. There are 177 required school days per year for Upper School students. Upper School students typically attend 5 days per week. The average school day consists of 6 hours and 10 minutes.

Upper School Student Profile Grade 9: 149 students (74 boys, 75 girls); Grade 10: 144 students (73 boys, 71 girls); Grade 11: 147 students (82 boys, 65 girls); Grade 12: 148 students (89 boys, 59 girls). 30% of students are Presbyterian Church in America.

Faculty School total: 125. In upper school: 30 men, 25 women; 35 have advanced degrees.

Subjects Offered Accounting, algebra, American history, American literature, art, band, Bible studies, biology, calculus, chemistry, community service, computer science, creative writing, debate, drama, driver education, economics, English, English literature, ethics, European history, French, geometry, government, grammar, health, history, mathematics, music, philosophy, photo shop, physical education, physics, psychology, religion, science, social sciences, social studies, Spanish, speech, trigonometry, world history, world literature.

Graduation Requirements 20th century history, business skills (includes word processing), computer science, English, foreign language, mathematics, physical education (includes health), religion (includes Bible studies and theology), science, social sciences, social studies (includes history). Community service is required.

Special Academic Programs Advanced Placement exam preparation; honors section; academic accommodation for the gifted; special instructional classes for students with learning disabilities, Attention Deficit Disorder.

College Admission Counseling 148 students graduated in 2012; 147 went to college, including Auburn University; Birmingham-Southern College; Samford University; The University of Alabama; Troy University; University of Mississippi. Other: 1 went to work. Mean combined SAT: 1183, mean composite ACT: 26.

Student Life Upper grades have specified standards of dress, student council. Discipline rests primarily with faculty. Attendance at religious services is required.

Summer Programs Remediation, advancement programs offered; session focuses on social studies and mathematics; held on campus; accepts boys and girls; not open to students from other schools. 50 students usually enrolled. 2013 schedule: June 11 to July 28. Application deadline: March 1.

Tuition and Aid Day student tuition: $6600. Tuition installment plan (monthly payment plans). Tuition reduction for siblings available. In 2012–13, 3% of upper-school students received aid. Total amount of financial aid awarded in 2012–13: $5000.

Admissions Traditional secondary-level entrance grade is 9. For fall 2012, 86 students applied for upper-level admission, 49 were accepted, 43 enrolled. SSAT required. Deadline for receipt of application materials: none. Application fee required: $75. On-campus interview required.

Athletics Interscholastic: baseball (boys), basketball (b,g), cheering (g), cross-country running (b,g), dance team (g), football (b), golf (b,g), indoor track (b,g), indoor track & field (b,g), outdoor activities (b,g), physical fitness (b,g), soccer (b,g), softball (g), strength & conditioning (b), swimming and diving (b,g), tennis (b,g), track and field (b,g), volleyball (g). 5 PE instructors, 15 coaches, 1 athletic trainer.

Computers Computers are regularly used in computer applications classes. Computer network features include on-campus library services, online commercial services, Internet access. Students grades are available online.

Contact Mrs. Kelly McCarthy Mooney, Director of Admissions. 205-776-5812. Fax: 205-776-5816. E-mail: kmooney@bcsk12.org. Web site: www.bcsk12.org

BRIDGEMONT HIGH SCHOOL

444 East Market Street
Daly City, California 94014

Head of School: Mr. Peter Tropper

General Information Coeducational day college-preparatory, arts, religious studies, and technology school, affiliated with Christian faith. Grades 9–12. Founded: 1973. Setting: urban. Nearest major city is San Francisco. 1-acre campus. 3 buildings on campus. Approved or accredited by Association of Christian Schools International and Western Association of Schools and Colleges. Total enrollment: 40. Upper school average class size: 10. Upper school faculty-student ratio: 1:4. There are 176 required school days per year for Upper School students. Upper School students typically attend 5 days per week. The average school day consists of 6 hours and 25 minutes.

Upper School Student Profile Grade 9: 9 students (3 boys, 6 girls); Grade 10: 7 students (2 boys, 5 girls); Grade 11: 12 students (5 boys, 7 girls); Grade 12: 12 students (6 boys, 6 girls). 50% of students are Christian faith.

Faculty School total: 10. In upper school: 6 men, 3 women; 2 have advanced degrees.

Subjects Offered Advanced math, algebra, American history, American literature, art, arts, Bible studies, biology, calculus, chemistry, creative writing, drama, earth science, economics, English, English literature, European history, expository writing, fine arts, French, French as a second language, geography, geometry, government/civics, grammar, health, history, mathematics, music, physical education, physics, religion, science, social sciences, social studies, Spanish, study skills, theater, trigonometry, U.S. history, world history, world literature, writing, yearbook.

Graduation Requirements Arts and fine arts (art, music, dance, drama), English, foreign language, mathematics, physical education (includes health), religion (includes Bible studies and theology), science, social sciences, social studies (includes history), field studies.

Special Academic Programs Independent study.

College Admission Counseling 15 students graduated in 2011; all went to college, including California State University, Los Angeles; City College of San Francisco; San Francisco State University; San Jose State University; University of California, Davis; University of California, Irvine.
Student Life Upper grades have specified standards of dress, student council, honor system. Discipline rests primarily with faculty. Attendance at religious services is required.
Tuition and Aid Day student tuition: $10,800. Tuition installment plan (FACTS Tuition Payment Plan, monthly payment plans, Tuition Management Systems Plan). Tuition reduction for siblings, need-based scholarship grants available. In 2011–12, 90% of upper-school students received aid. Total amount of financial aid awarded in 2011–12: $108,660.
Admissions Traditional secondary-level entrance grade is 9. For fall 2011, 12 students applied for upper-level admission, 10 were accepted, 9 enrolled. Essay, math and English placement tests and writing sample required. Deadline for receipt of application materials: none. Application fee required: $60. On-campus interview required.
Athletics Interscholastic: baseball (boys, girls), basketball (b,g), flag football (b), soccer (b), softball (g), volleyball (g); intramural: basketball (b,g), flag football (b,g), weight lifting (b); coed intramural: flag football, floor hockey, football, judo, jump rope, physical training, volleyball. 1 PE instructor, 4 coaches.
Computers Computers are regularly used in yearbook classes. Computer resources include Internet access, wireless campus network, Internet filtering or blocking technology, independent study courses through Acellus and NovelStar. Computer access in designated common areas is available to students. Students grades are available online.
Contact Ms. Janelle Tropper, Director of Student Development. 650-746-2522. Fax: 650-746-2529. E-mail: admissions@bridgemont.org. Web site: www.bridgemont.org

BRIDGES ACADEMY

Studio City, California
See Special Needs Schools section.

BRIMMER AND MAY SCHOOL

69 Middlesex Road
Chestnut Hill, Massachusetts 02467

Head of School: Judy Guild

General Information Coeducational day college-preparatory, arts, technology, Creative Arts Diploma Program, and Global Studies Diploma Program school. Grades PK–12. Founded: 1880. Setting: suburban. Nearest major city is Boston. 7-acre campus. 7 buildings on campus. Approved or accredited by Association of Independent Schools in New England and New England Association of Schools and Colleges. Member of National Association of Independent Schools and Secondary School Admission Test Board. Total enrollment: 398. Upper school average class size: 12. Upper school faculty-student ratio: 1:6. There are 175 required school days per year for Upper School students. Upper School students typically attend 5 days per week. The average school day consists of 7 hours and 10 minutes.
Upper School Student Profile Grade 9: 31 students (15 boys, 16 girls); Grade 10: 33 students (18 boys, 15 girls); Grade 11: 38 students (17 boys, 21 girls); Grade 12: 32 students (18 boys, 14 girls).
Faculty School total: 68. In upper school: 15 men, 19 women; 24 have advanced degrees.
Subjects Offered Acting, adolescent issues, Advanced Placement courses, advanced studio art-AP, algebra, American history, American literature, art, biology, biology-AP, calculus, ceramics, chamber groups, chemistry, chorus, college counseling, community service, computer education, creative arts, creative writing, desktop publishing, drama, economics, economics-AP, English, English literature, English literature-AP, ESL, European history, expository writing, fine arts, French, geometry, grammar, health, health education, history, humanities, Internet research, mathematics, music, music theory, newspaper, participation in sports, performing arts, photography, physical education, physical science, physics, psychology, social studies, Spanish, theater, trigonometry, typing, U.S. history, video film production, world history, world literature, writing, yearbook.
Graduation Requirements Creative arts, English, foreign language, history, mathematics, physical education (includes health), science, technology, Senior Independent project, senior thesis defense, Creative Art Diploma Program (optional). Community service is required.
Special Academic Programs 14 Advanced Placement exams for which test preparation is offered; honors section; independent study; study at local college for college credit; ESL (13 students enrolled).
College Admission Counseling 32 students graduated in 2012; all went to college, including Brown University; Connecticut College; Hobart and William Smith Colleges; Syracuse University; Wellesley College.
Student Life Upper grades have specified standards of dress, student council, honor system. Discipline rests equally with students and faculty.
Tuition and Aid Day student tuition: $38,600. Tuition installment plan (monthly payment plans, Tuition Management Systems). Need-based scholarship grants available. In 2012–13, 42% of upper-school students received aid. Total amount of financial aid awarded in 2012–13: $1,474,565.
Admissions Traditional secondary-level entrance grade is 9. For fall 2012, 142 students applied for upper-level admission, 64 were accepted, 22 enrolled. ISEE, SSAT or TOEFL or SLEP required. Deadline for receipt of application materials: January 18. Application fee required: $50. On-campus interview required.
Athletics Interscholastic: baseball (boys), basketball (b,g), field hockey (g), lacrosse (b,g), soccer (b,g), softball (g), tennis (b,g); coed interscholastic: cross-country running, curling, golf; coed intramural: alpine skiing, fitness, outdoor education, physical fitness, skiing (downhill), snowboarding, strength & conditioning, tennis, weight training. 3 PE instructors, 20 coaches, 2 athletic trainers.
Computers Computers are regularly used in architecture, desktop publishing, foreign language, graphic design, humanities, journalism, media production, technology, typing, video film production, Web site design, yearbook classes. Computer network features include on-campus library services, online commercial services, Internet access, wireless campus network, Internet filtering or blocking technology. Campus intranet, student e-mail accounts, and computer access in designated common areas are available to students. Students grades are available online. The school has a published electronic and media policy.
Contact Myra Korin, Admissions Coordinator. 617-738-8695. Fax: 617-734-5147. E-mail: admissions@brimmer.org. Web site: www.brimmerandmay.org

THE BRITISH SCHOOL OF BOSTON

416 Pond Street
Boston, Massachusetts 02130

Head of School: Mr. Paul Wiseman

General Information Coeducational day college-preparatory school. Grades PK–12. Founded: 2000. Setting: suburban. 40-acre campus. 2 buildings on campus. Approved or accredited by Council of International Schools and Massachusetts Department of Education. Candidate for accreditation by New England Association of Schools and Colleges. Total enrollment: 383. Upper school average class size: 12. Upper school faculty-student ratio: 1:3. There are 180 required school days per year for Upper School students. Upper School students typically attend 5 days per week. The average school day consists of 7 hours.
Faculty School total: 63. In upper school: 8 men, 11 women.
Subjects Offered International Baccalaureate courses.
Graduation Requirements International Baccalaureate courses.
Special Academic Programs International Baccalaureate program; academic accommodation for the gifted; ESL (7 students enrolled).
Student Life Upper grades have specified standards of dress, student council, honor system. Discipline rests equally with students and faculty.
Tuition and Aid Day student tuition: $28,700. Tuition reduction for siblings, merit scholarship grants available.
Admissions Traditional secondary-level entrance grade is 9. SSAT required. Deadline for receipt of application materials: February 1. Application fee required: $150. Interview required.
Athletics Interscholastic: basketball (boys, girls), cross-country running (b,g), independent competitive sports (b), soccer (b,g), swimming and diving (b,g), tennis (b,g); intramural: basketball (b,g); coed interscholastic: curling, rugby, soccer; coed intramural: alpine skiing, backpacking, combined training, cross-country running, fitness, golf, hiking/backpacking, life saving, outdoor activities, outdoor education, outdoors, sailing, strength & conditioning. 2 PE instructors.
Computers Computers are regularly used in all classes. Computer network features include Internet access, wireless campus network. Computer access in designated common areas is available to students. Students grades are available online. The school has a published electronic and media policy.
Contact Ms. Lisa van Horne, Director of Admissions. 617-522-2261 Ext. 41. Fax: 617-522-0385. E-mail: l.vanhorne@wclschools.org. Web site: www.britishschoolofboston.org/

BROCKWOOD PARK SCHOOL

Brockwood Park
Bramdean
Hampshire
Alresford SO24 0LQ, United Kingdom

Head of School: Mr. Bill Taylor

General Information Coeducational boarding college-preparatory, general academic, arts, business, vocational, religious studies, bilingual studies, and technology school. Ungraded, ages 14–19. Founded: 1969. Setting: rural. Nearest major city is Winchester, United Kingdom. Students are housed in individual rooms, single-sex compound. 40-acre campus. 8 buildings on campus. Approved or accredited by Office for Standards in Education (OFSTED). Language of instruction: English. Total enrollment: 65. Upper school average class size: 7. Upper school faculty-student ratio: 1:7. Upper School students typically attend 5 days per week. The average school day consists of 8 hours.
Upper School Student Profile 100% of students are boarding students. 75% are international students. International students from France, Germany, Italy, Netherlands, Spain, and United States; 10 other countries represented in student body.

Faculty School total: 30. In upper school: 12 men, 18 women; all reside on campus.
Subjects Offered Advanced biology, advanced chemistry, advanced math, area studies, art, band, biology, body human, bookbinding, business studies, career and personal planning, career education, carpentry, cartooning/animation, chamber groups, chemistry, choir, choral music, cinematography, classical music, communication skills, computers, design, desktop publishing, diversity studies, drama, drama performance, drama workshop, English, English literature, environmental education, ESL, ethics, ethics and responsibility, fabric arts, filmmaking, fine arts, folk dance, food and nutrition, French, gardening, gender issues, geography, graphic design, history, mathematics, music, physics, pottery, psychology, science, social studies, Spanish, statistics.
Graduation Requirements Graduation requirements determined on an individual basis.
Special Academic Programs Independent study; term-away projects; study abroad; academic accommodation for the gifted, the musically talented, and the artistically talented; remedial reading and/or remedial writing; remedial math; programs in English, mathematics, general development for dyslexic students; special instructional classes for deaf students, blind students; ESL (30 students enrolled).
College Admission Counseling 29 students graduated in 2012; 25 went to college, including University of London. Other: 2 went to work, 2 had other specific plans.
Student Life Upper grades have specified standards of dress, student council. Discipline rests equally with students and faculty.
Tuition and Aid 7-day tuition and room/board: £17,960. Tuition installment plan (individually arranged payment plans). Bursaries available. In 2012–13, 10% of upper-school students received aid.
Admissions Traditional secondary-level entrance age is 14. 3-R Achievement Test, any standardized test or ESL required. Deadline for receipt of application materials: none. Application fee required: £20. On-campus interview required.
Athletics 1 coach, 2 athletic trainers.
Computers Computer network features include Internet access, Internet filtering or blocking technology.
Contact Mrs. Victoria Lewin, Admissions Officer. 44-1962 771744. Fax: 44-1962 771875. E-mail: enquiry@brockwood.org.uk. Web site: www.brockwood.org.uk

THE BROOK HILL SCHOOL

1051 N. Houston
Bullard, Texas 75757

Head of School: Rod Fletcher

General Information Coeducational boarding and day college-preparatory and arts school, affiliated with Christian faith. Boarding grades 8–12, day grades PK–12. Founded: 1997. Setting: small town. Nearest major city is Tyler. Students are housed in single-sex houses for 16 to 20 students. 200-acre campus. 8 buildings on campus. Approved or accredited by Association of Christian Schools International, Southern Association of Colleges and Schools, The Association of Boarding Schools, and The College Board. Endowment: $1 million. Total enrollment: 519. Upper school average class size: 18. Upper school faculty-student ratio: 1:9. There are 176 required school days per year for Upper School students. Upper School students typically attend 5 days per week. The average school day consists of 6 hours and 30 minutes.
Upper School Student Profile Grade 9: 48 students (22 boys, 26 girls); Grade 10: 53 students (30 boys, 23 girls); Grade 11: 51 students (28 boys, 23 girls); Grade 12: 39 students (26 boys, 13 girls). 20% of students are boarding students. 83% are state residents. 4 states are represented in upper school student body. 17% are international students. International students from China, Nigeria, Saudi Arabia, South Africa, Thailand, and Viet Nam; 1 other country represented in student body. 70% of students are Christian faith.
Faculty School total: 44. In upper school: 14 men, 17 women; 19 have advanced degrees; 3 reside on campus.
Subjects Offered ACT preparation, advanced chemistry, advanced math, Advanced Placement courses, algebra, American government, American history-AP, American literature-AP, analysis and differential calculus, anatomy and physiology, ancient history, ancient world history, art, athletics, baseball, basketball, Bible as literature, Bible studies, biology, British literature, British literature-AP, calculus, calculus-AP, career/college preparation, chemistry, chemistry-AP, choir, choral music, Christian ethics, Christian studies, civics/free enterprise, classics, college admission preparation, college awareness, college writing, communication skills, community service, comparative religion, composition, composition-AP, computer applications, computer education, conceptual physics, concert choir, creation science, drama, drama performance, dramatic arts, drawing, economics, economics-AP, English, English composition, English language and composition-AP, English language-AP, English literature, English literature and composition-AP, English literature-AP, English/composition-AP, ensembles, environmental science, epic literature, ESL, European history, European history-AP, European literature, fine arts, foreign language, four units of summer reading, French, French as a second language, geometry, government, government and politics-AP, government-AP, great books, health, history-AP, honors algebra, honors English, honors geometry, human biology, lab science, Latin, leadership and service, literary genres, literature and composition-AP, logic, logic, rhetoric, and debate, mathematics-AP, modern European history-AP, modern languages, orchestra, painting, physical education, physics, pre-calculus, public speaking, rhetoric, SAT preparation, SAT/ACT preparation, senior project, Spanish, speech communications, stagecraft, strings, student government, student publications, theater arts, TOEFL preparation, U.S. government and politics, U.S. government and politics-AP, U.S. history, U.S. history-AP, volleyball, yearbook.
Graduation Requirements Arts and fine arts (art, music, dance, drama), Bible, college admission preparation, economics, electives, English, foreign language, government, history, lab science, leadership, mathematics, physical education (includes health). Community service is required.
Special Academic Programs 12 Advanced Placement exams for which test preparation is offered; honors section; study at local college for college credit; ESL (3 students enrolled).
College Admission Counseling 50 students graduated in 2012; all went to college, including Baylor University; Texas A&M University; Texas Tech University; The University of Texas at Austin; University of Mississippi; Wheaton College. Mean SAT critical reading: 561, mean SAT math: 572, mean SAT writing: 552, mean composite ACT: 23.
Student Life Upper grades have uniform requirement, student council, honor system. Discipline rests primarily with faculty. Attendance at religious services is required.
Summer Programs Enrichment, advancement, ESL, sports, art/fine arts programs offered; session focuses on enrichment; held on campus; accepts boys and girls; open to students from other schools. 125 students usually enrolled. 2013 schedule: June 1 to August 10. Application deadline: none.
Tuition and Aid Day student tuition: $9570; 7-day tuition and room/board: $34,285. Tuition installment plan (FACTS Tuition Payment Plan, individually arranged payment plans). Tuition reduction for siblings, need-based scholarship grants available. In 2012–13, 40% of upper-school students received aid. Total amount of financial aid awarded in 2012–13: $400,000.
Admissions Traditional secondary-level entrance grade is 10. For fall 2012, 89 students applied for upper-level admission, 33 were accepted, 30 enrolled. International English Language Test, Iowa Test, CTBS, or TAP, Iowa Tests of Basic Skills, SSAT, Stanford Achievement Test, Otis-Lennon School Ability Test, TOEFL or TOEFL or SLEP required. Deadline for receipt of application materials: none. Application fee required: $75. Interview recommended.
Athletics Interscholastic: baseball (boys, girls), basketball (b,g), cheering (g), cross-country running (b,g), dance squad (g), football (b), golf (b,g), independent competitive sports (b,g), physical fitness (b,g), physical training (b,g), soccer (b,g), softball (g), strength & conditioning (b,g), swimming and diving (b,g), tennis (b,g), track and field (b,g), volleyball (g), weight training (b,g); intramural: baseball (b,g), basketball (b,g), flag football (b,g), Frisbee (b,g); coed interscholastic: cheering, tennis; coed intramural: flag football. 1 PE instructor, 2 coaches, 1 athletic trainer.
Computers Computers are regularly used in all classes. Computer network features include on-campus library services, Internet access, wireless campus network, Internet filtering or blocking technology. Computer access in designated common areas is available to students. Students grades are available online. The school has a published electronic and media policy.
Contact Mr. Landry Humphries, Associate Director of Admissions, Boarding. 903-894-5000 Ext. 1042. Fax: 903-894-6332. E-mail: Landry.humphries@brookhill.org. Web site: www.brookhill.org/

BROOKS SCHOOL

1160 Great Pond Road
North Andover, Massachusetts 01845-1298

Head of School: Mr. John R. Packard

General Information Coeducational boarding and day college-preparatory school, affiliated with Episcopal Church. Grades 9–12. Founded: 1926. Setting: suburban. Nearest major city is Boston. Students are housed in single-sex dormitories. 251-acre campus. 39 buildings on campus. Approved or accredited by Association of Independent Schools in New England, National Association of Episcopal Schools, New England Association of Schools and Colleges, The Association of Boarding Schools, and Massachusetts Department of Education. Member of National Association of Independent Schools and Secondary School Admission Test Board. Endowment: $65.6 million. Total enrollment: 370. Upper school average class size: 12. Upper school faculty-student ratio: 1:5. There are 180 required school days per year for Upper School students. Upper School students typically attend 5 days per week. The average school day consists of 7 hours.
Upper School Student Profile Grade 9: 68 students (35 boys, 33 girls); Grade 10: 100 students (57 boys, 43 girls); Grade 11: 102 students (53 boys, 49 girls); Grade 12: 100 students (58 boys, 42 girls). 68% of students are boarding students. 64% are state residents. 23 states are represented in upper school student body. 11% are international students. International students from Canada, China, Egypt, Hong Kong, Japan, and Republic of Korea; 5 other countries represented in student body.
Faculty School total: 87. In upper school: 44 men, 43 women; 65 have advanced degrees; 47 reside on campus.
Subjects Offered Algebra, American history, American history-AP, American literature, art history, art history-AP, astronomy, Bible studies, biology, biology-AP, calculus, calculus-AP, ceramics, chemistry, chemistry-AP, Chinese, chorus, computer math, creative writing, drama, driver education, earth science, English, English literature, English-AP, environmental science-AP, ethics, European history, expository

writing, film, fine arts, French, French language-AP, French literature-AP, French-AP, geometry, government and politics-AP, grammar, Greek, health, history, history-AP, honors algebra, honors geometry, honors world history, integrated arts, journalism, Latin, Latin-AP, life skills, Mandarin, mathematics, Middle East, music, music theory, painting, photography, physics, physics-AP, playwriting, poetry, psychology, public speaking, religion, rhetoric, robotics, senior project, senior seminar, Southern literature, Spanish, Spanish language-AP, Spanish literature, Spanish literature-AP, Spanish-AP, statistics, studio art, theater, theater design and production, theology, trigonometry, U.S. government and politics-AP, visual arts, world history, world history-AP, world literature, writing.

Graduation Requirements Arts and fine arts (art, music, dance, drama), English, foreign language, health, history, mathematics, religion (includes Bible studies and theology), science. Community service is required.

Special Academic Programs 14 Advanced Placement exams for which test preparation is offered; honors section; independent study; term-away projects; study abroad.

College Admission Counseling 91 students graduated in 2012; all went to college, including Boston University; Bowdoin College; Connecticut College; Massachusetts Institute of Technology; Tufts University; Tulane University. Mean SAT critical reading: 592, mean SAT math: 619, mean SAT writing: 606, mean combined SAT: 1818, mean composite ACT: 26.

Student Life Upper grades have specified standards of dress, student council. Discipline rests primarily with faculty. Attendance at religious services is required.

Summer Programs Enrichment, advancement, sports, computer instruction programs offered; session focuses on English, mathematics, and SAT preparation; held on campus; accepts boys and girls; open to students from other schools. 70 students usually enrolled. 2013 schedule: June 28 to August 20. Application deadline: none.

Tuition and Aid Day student tuition: $37,180; 7-day tuition and room/board: $49,365. Tuition installment plan (Academic Management Services Plan, individually arranged payment plans). Need-based scholarship grants available. In 2012–13, 22% of upper-school students received aid. Total amount of financial aid awarded in 2012–13: $2,600,000.

Admissions Traditional secondary-level entrance grade is 9. For fall 2012, 1,024 students applied for upper-level admission, 240 were accepted, 99 enrolled. ISEE, SSAT, ERB, PSAT, SAT, PLAN or ACT or TOEFL required. Deadline for receipt of application materials: February 1. Application fee required: $50. Interview required.

Athletics Interscholastic: baseball (boys), basketball (b,g), crew (b,g), cross-country running (b,g), field hockey (g), football (b), golf (b,g), hockey (b,g), ice hockey (b,g), lacrosse (b,g), soccer (b,g), softball (g), squash (b,g), tennis (b,g), wrestling (b); coed intramural: dance, fitness, sailing, skiing (downhill). 1 athletic trainer.

Computers Computers are regularly used in all academic classes. Computer network features include on-campus library services, online commercial services, Internet access, wireless campus network, Internet filtering or blocking technology. Campus intranet, student e-mail accounts, and computer access in designated common areas are available to students. Students grades are available online. The school has a published electronic and media policy.

Contact Mr. Andrew C. Hirt, Director of Admission. 978-725-6272. Fax: 978-725-6298. E-mail: admission@brooksschool.org. Web site: www.brooksschool.org

BROOKSTONE SCHOOL

440 Bradley Park Drive
Columbus, Georgia 31904

Head of School: Brian D. Kennerly

General Information Coeducational day college-preparatory school. Grades PK–12. Founded: 1951. Setting: suburban. Nearest major city is Atlanta. 112-acre campus. 11 buildings on campus. Approved or accredited by Georgia Independent School Association, Southern Association of Colleges and Schools, Southern Association of Independent Schools, and Georgia Department of Education. Member of National Association of Independent Schools. Endowment: $20.4 million. Total enrollment: 799. Upper school average class size: 14. Upper school faculty-student ratio: 1:10. There are 176 required school days per year for Upper School students. Upper School students typically attend 5 days per week. The average school day consists of 5 hours and 20 minutes.

Upper School Student Profile Grade 9: 82 students (42 boys, 40 girls); Grade 10: 84 students (43 boys, 41 girls); Grade 11: 74 students (40 boys, 34 girls); Grade 12: 67 students (34 boys, 33 girls).

Faculty School total: 82. In upper school: 13 men, 16 women; 23 have advanced degrees.

Subjects Offered Advanced computer applications, Advanced Placement courses, algebra, American Civil War, American government, American history, American history-AP, American literature, anatomy and physiology, art, art-AP, band, biology, biology-AP, calculus, calculus-AP, chemistry, chemistry-AP, choral music, chorus, Civil War, communications, comparative government and politics-AP, comparative religion, computer applications, computer multimedia, computer programming, computer science, computers, concert band, concert choir, constitutional law, creative writing, drama, ecology, economics, economics-AP, English, English composition, English literature, English literature and composition-AP, European history, European history-AP, fine arts, French, French language-AP, French-AP, geometry, government and politics-AP, graphic design, health, history-AP, honors algebra, honors English, honors geometry, human geography - AP, humanities, Latin, Latin-AP, law, literature-AP, macro/microeconomics-AP, marine biology, mathematics, mythology, neuroanatomy, ornithology, physical education, physics, pre-calculus, psychology, science, social sciences, social studies, Spanish, Spanish language-AP, Spanish-AP, statistics, statistics-AP, studio art-AP, theater, trigonometry, U.S. government, U.S. government and politics-AP, U.S. history, U.S. history-AP, weight training, world history, yearbook, zoology.

Graduation Requirements Algebra, American government, American history, arts and fine arts (art, music, dance, drama), biology, chemistry, computer science, economics, electives, English, foreign language, geometry, mathematics, physical education (includes health), science, social sciences, social studies (includes history), world history, senior year speech.

Special Academic Programs 18 Advanced Placement exams for which test preparation is offered; honors section.

College Admission Counseling 49 students graduated in 2012; all went to college, including Auburn University; Georgia Institute of Technology; Georgia Southern University; The University of Alabama; University of Georgia; University of Mississippi. Mean SAT critical reading: 582, mean SAT math: 594, mean SAT writing: 610, mean combined SAT: 1786, mean composite ACT: 25. 47% scored over 600 on SAT critical reading, 47% scored over 600 on SAT math, 49% scored over 600 on SAT writing, 45% scored over 1800 on combined SAT, 46% scored over 26 on composite ACT.

Student Life Upper grades have specified standards of dress, student council, honor system. Discipline rests equally with students and faculty.

Tuition and Aid Day student tuition: $14,545. Tuition installment plan (monthly payment plans, individually arranged payment plans, 3 payments in months July, September and November (no interest)). Tuition reduction for siblings, merit scholarship grants, need-based scholarship grants, need-based loans, middle-income loans available. In 2012–13, 37% of upper-school students received aid; total upper-school merit-scholarship money awarded: $427,145. Total amount of financial aid awarded in 2012–13: $812,545.

Admissions Traditional secondary-level entrance grade is 9. For fall 2012, 68 students applied for upper-level admission, 56 were accepted, 31 enrolled. Otis-Lennon IQ Test or SSAT, ERB, PSAT, SAT, PLAN or ACT required. Deadline for receipt of application materials: none. Application fee required: $50. Interview required.

Athletics Interscholastic: baseball (boys), basketball (b,g), cheering (g), cross-country running (b,g), football (b), golf (b,g), soccer (b,g), softball (g), tennis (b,g), track and field (b,g), volleyball (g), wrestling (b); intramural: basketball (b,g). 6 PE instructors.

Computers Computers are regularly used in college planning, computer applications, creative writing, English, foreign language, French, geography, graphic arts, graphic design, history, human geography - AP, information technology, mathematics, media production, programming, publications, science, social studies, Spanish, video film production, Web site design, yearbook classes. Computer network features include on-campus library services, online commercial services, Internet access, wireless campus network, Internet filtering or blocking technology. Campus intranet and student e-mail accounts are available to students. Students grades are available online. The school has a published electronic and media policy.

Contact Mary S. Snyder, Enrollment Director. 706-324-1392. Fax: 706-571-0178. E-mail: msnyder@brookstoneschool.org. Web site: www.brookstoneschool.org

BROPHY COLLEGE PREPARATORY

4701 North Central Avenue
Phoenix, Arizona 85012-1797

Head of School: Mr. Robert E. Ryan III

General Information Boys' day college-preparatory, arts, religious studies, and technology school, affiliated with Roman Catholic Church (Jesuit order). Grades 6–12. Founded: 1928. Setting: urban. 38-acre campus. 8 buildings on campus. Approved or accredited by Jesuit Secondary Education Association, National Catholic Education Association, and Western Catholic Education Association. Endowment: $19 million. Total enrollment: 1,348. Upper school average class size: 24. Upper school faculty-student ratio: 1:15. There are 180 required school days per year for Upper School students. Upper School students typically attend 5 days per week. The average school day consists of 6 hours and 40 minutes.

Upper School Student Profile Grade 9: 340 students (340 boys); Grade 10: 333 students (333 boys); Grade 11: 307 students (307 boys); Grade 12: 311 students (311 boys). 64% of students are Roman Catholic Church (Jesuit order).

Faculty School total: 94. In upper school: 67 men, 21 women; 76 have advanced degrees.

Subjects Offered Advanced Placement courses, advanced studio art-AP, algebra, American history, American literature, anatomy, art, Bible studies, biology, business, calculus, chemistry, community service, computer math, computer programming, computer science, creative writing, drama, earth science, economics, engineering, English, English literature, ethics, European history, expository writing, fine arts, French, geography, geometry, government/civics, health, history, Latin, mathematics, mechanical drawing, music, physical education, physics, probability and statistics, psychology, religion, science, social sciences, social studies, sociology, Spanish, speech, theater, theology, trigonometry, video film production, world history, world literature.

Graduation Requirements Arts and fine arts (art, music, dance, drama), English, foreign language, mathematics, physical education (includes health), religion (includes Bible studies and theology), science, social studies (includes history). Community service is required.

Special Academic Programs Advanced Placement exam preparation; honors section; study at local college for college credit; study abroad.

College Admission Counseling 301 students graduated in 2012; all went to college, including Arizona State University; Gonzaga University; Loyola Marymount University; Northern Arizona University; Santa Clara University; The University of Arizona. Median SAT critical reading: 586, median SAT math: 598, median SAT writing: 574, median combined SAT: 1758, median composite ACT: 26.

Student Life Upper grades have specified standards of dress, student council, honor system. Discipline rests primarily with faculty. Attendance at religious services is required.

Summer Programs Enrichment, advancement, sports, art/fine arts, computer instruction programs offered; session focuses on academic skills and sports; held both on and off campus; held at Manresa Retreat (Sedona, AZ), Brophy East Campus, and Brophy Sports Campus; accepts boys and girls; open to students from other schools. 1,300 students usually enrolled. 2013 schedule: June 3 to July 3. Application deadline: May 31.

Tuition and Aid Day student tuition: $13,200. Tuition installment plan (The Tuition Plan, monthly payment plans, individually arranged payment plans). Need-based scholarship grants, paying campus jobs available. In 2012–13, 29% of upper-school students received aid. Total amount of financial aid awarded in 2012–13: $2,098,895.

Admissions Traditional secondary-level entrance grade is 9. For fall 2012, 578 students applied for upper-level admission, 383 were accepted, 340 enrolled. STS required. Deadline for receipt of application materials: February 1. Application fee required: $50. On-campus interview required.

Athletics Interscholastic: aquatics, baseball, basketball, cross-country running, diving, flagball, football, golf, ice hockey, lacrosse, soccer, swimming and diving, tennis, track and field, volleyball, wrestling; intramural: aquatics, badminton, baseball, basketball, bicycling, bowling, cheering, climbing, crew, cricket, fishing, fitness, flag football, Frisbee, golf, handball, hockey, ice hockey, lacrosse, mountain biking, outdoor activities, physical fitness, physical training, rock climbing, skiing (downhill), softball, strength & conditioning, table tennis, touch football, ultimate Frisbee, volleyball, wall climbing, water polo, weight lifting, weight training. 2 PE instructors, 15 coaches, 2 athletic trainers.

Computers Computers are regularly used in all academic classes. Computer network features include on-campus library services, online commercial services, Internet access, wireless campus network, Blackboard, computer tablets, iPads. Student e-mail accounts are available to students. Students grades are available online. The school has a published electronic and media policy.

Contact Ms. Shelly Scheuring, Assistant to Director of Admissions. 602-264-5291 Ext. 6233. Fax: 602-234-1669. E-mail: sscheuring@brophyprep.org. Web site: www.brophyprep.org/

BROTHER RICE HIGH SCHOOL

7101 Lahser Road
Bloomfield Hills, Michigan 48301

Head of School: Mr. John Birney

General Information Boys' day college-preparatory, arts, business, religious studies, and technology school, affiliated with Roman Catholic Church. Grades 9–12. Founded: 1960. Setting: suburban. Nearest major city is Detroit. 20-acre campus. 1 building on campus. Approved or accredited by North Central Association of Colleges and Schools and Michigan Department of Education. Endowment: $2 million. Total enrollment: 675. Upper school average class size: 22. Upper school faculty-student ratio: 1:13. Upper School students typically attend 5 days per week. The average school day consists of 6 hours and 51 minutes.

Upper School Student Profile Grade 9: 163 students (163 boys); Grade 10: 182 students (182 boys); Grade 11: 161 students (161 boys); Grade 12: 163 students (163 boys). 75% of students are Roman Catholic.

Faculty School total: 60. In upper school: 32 men, 10 women; 36 have advanced degrees.

Subjects Offered 20th century world history, accounting, algebra, American government, anatomy, anthropology, architectural drawing, art, band, biology, biology-AP, business law, calculus, calculus-AP, chemistry, Chinese, choir, church history, computer science, computer science-AP, computers, concert band, creative writing, death and loss, debate, drama, earth science, economics, electronics, engineering, English, English composition, English language-AP, ensembles, European history, family living, forensics, French, French-AP, geometry, German, global science, health, jazz band, Latin, library science, literature, mathematics, mechanical drawing, music, music history, music theory, organic chemistry, photography, photojournalism, physical education, physics, physiology, pre-calculus, probability and statistics, psychology, social justice, Spanish, Spanish-AP, speech, studio art-AP, theology, trigonometry, U.S. government and politics-AP, U.S. history, U.S. history-AP, Western civilization, world geography, world religions.

Graduation Requirements Computer science, electives, English, foreign language, mathematics, physical education (includes health), science, social studies (includes history), speech, theology.

Special Academic Programs Advanced Placement exam preparation; honors section; remedial reading and/or remedial writing; remedial math.

College Admission Counseling 145 students graduated in 2012; 144 went to college, including Central Michigan University; Michigan State University; University of Michigan. Other: 1 entered military service. Median combined SAT: 1838, median composite ACT: 25.

Student Life Upper grades have specified standards of dress, student council, honor system. Discipline rests primarily with faculty. Attendance at religious services is required.

Summer Programs Remediation, enrichment, art/fine arts programs offered; session focuses on camps and enrichment; held on campus; accepts boys and girls; open to students from other schools. 550 students usually enrolled. 2013 schedule: June to August.

Tuition and Aid Day student tuition: $11,050. Tuition installment plan (The Tuition Plan, monthly payment plans, individually arranged payment plans). Tuition reduction for siblings, merit scholarship grants, need-based scholarship grants available. In 2012–13, 40% of upper-school students received aid; total upper-school merit-scholarship money awarded: $600,000. Total amount of financial aid awarded in 2012–13: $900,000.

Admissions Traditional secondary-level entrance grade is 9. For fall 2012, 425 students applied for upper-level admission, 295 were accepted, 163 enrolled. SAS, STS-HSPT required. Deadline for receipt of application materials: none. No application fee required. Interview required.

Athletics Interscholastic: alpine skiing, baseball, basketball, bowling, cross-country running, diving, football, golf, hockey, ice hockey, lacrosse, skiing (downhill), soccer, swimming and diving, tennis, track and field, wrestling; intramural: basketball, bowling, drill team, fitness, football, golf, ice hockey, paint ball, rugby, skiing (downhill), snowboarding, strength & conditioning, touch football, ultimate Frisbee, winter (indoor) track. 50 coaches, 1 athletic trainer.

Computers Computer resources include online commercial services, Internet access. The school has a published electronic and media policy.

Contact Mr. David D. Sofran, Director of Admissions. 248-833-2022. Fax: 248-833-2011. E-mail: sofran@brrice.edu. Web site: www.brrice.edu

THE BROWNING SCHOOL

52 East 62nd Street
New York, New York 10065

Head of School: Stephen M. Clement III

General Information Boys' day college-preparatory school. Grades K–12. Founded: 1888. Setting: urban. 2 buildings on campus. Approved or accredited by New York State Association of Independent Schools. Member of National Association of Independent Schools and Secondary School Admission Test Board. Endowment: $30 million. Total enrollment: 408. Upper school average class size: 15. Upper school faculty-student ratio: 1:4. Upper School students typically attend 5 days per week. The average school day consists of 6 hours and 54 minutes.

Upper School Student Profile Grade 9: 28 students (28 boys); Grade 10: 30 students (30 boys); Grade 11: 27 students (27 boys); Grade 12: 28 students (28 boys).

Faculty School total: 59. In upper school: 21 men, 13 women; 33 have advanced degrees.

Subjects Offered Adolescent issues, advanced biology, advanced chemistry, advanced math, Advanced Placement courses, advanced studio art-AP, African drumming, algebra, American history, American history-AP, American literature, American literature-AP, anatomy and physiology, Ancient Greek, ancient world history, applied arts, applied music, art, art history, athletics, baseball, basketball, bell choir, biology, biology-AP, calculus, calculus-AP, ceramics, chemistry, chemistry-AP, chorus, college admission preparation, computer math, computer music, computer programming, computer science, drama, dramatic arts, English, English literature, English-AP, environmental science, environmental studies, ethics, European history, European history-AP, expository writing, fencing, filmmaking, fine arts, French, French language-AP, general science, geography, geometry, golf, government/civics, grammar, Greek, handbells, health, history, instruments, jazz ensemble, language arts, Latin, Latin-AP, mathematics, medieval/Renaissance history, mentorship program, model United Nations, music, peer counseling, philosophy, physical education, physics, physics-AP, political science, public speaking, science, senior project, social sciences, social studies, Spanish, Spanish language-AP, squash, statistics, technology, tennis, theater, track and field, trigonometry, U.S. history-AP, video film production, visual arts, wrestling, yearbook.

Graduation Requirements Arts and fine arts (art, music, dance, drama), computer science, English, foreign language, mathematics, physical education (includes health), public speaking, science, social sciences, social studies (includes history), senior community service project.

Special Academic Programs Advanced Placement exam preparation; honors section; independent study; academic accommodation for the gifted and the musically talented.

College Admission Counseling 25 students graduated in 2011; all went to college, including Cornell University; Dartmouth College; Georgetown University; University of Virginia; Williams College; Yale University. Median SAT critical reading: 636, median SAT math: 654, median SAT writing: 664, median combined SAT: 1954, median composite ACT: 27. 71% scored over 600 on SAT critical reading, 71% scored over 600 on SAT math, 83% scored over 600 on SAT writing, 75% scored over 1800 on combined SAT, 57% scored over 26 on composite ACT.

Student Life Upper grades have specified standards of dress, student council, honor system. Discipline rests primarily with faculty.

Tuition and Aid Day student tuition: $38,280. Tuition installment plan (Key Tuition Payment Plan). Need-based scholarship grants available. In 2011–12, 32% of upper-school students received aid. Total amount of financial aid awarded in 2011–12: $953,900.

Admissions Traditional secondary-level entrance grade is 9. For fall 2011, 72 students applied for upper-level admission, 26 were accepted, 9 enrolled. ERB, ISEE and SSAT required. Deadline for receipt of application materials: January 15. Application fee required: $50. On-campus interview required.

Athletics Interscholastic: baseball, basketball, soccer, tennis; intramural: basketball, cross-country running, ice hockey, soccer, softball, tai chi; coed intramural: fencing. 4 PE instructors, 6 coaches.

Computers Computers are regularly used in English, foreign language, history, mathematics, music technology, science, video film production classes. Computer network features include on-campus library services, online commercial services, Internet access, wireless campus network. Student e-mail accounts are available to students. The school has a published electronic and media policy.

Contact Liane Pei, Director of Admissions. 212-838-6280. Fax: 212-355-5602. E-mail: lpei@browning.edu. Web site: www.browning.edu

BRUNSWICK SCHOOL

100 Maher Avenue
Greenwich, Connecticut 06830

Head of School: Thomas W. Philip

General Information Boys' day college-preparatory school. Grades PK–12. Founded: 1902. Setting: suburban. Nearest major city is New York, NY. 118-acre campus. 4 buildings on campus. Approved or accredited by New England Association of Schools and Colleges and Connecticut Department of Education. Member of National Association of Independent Schools. Endowment: $85 million. Total enrollment: 939. Upper school average class size: 15. Upper school faculty-student ratio: 1:5. The average school day consists of 9 hours and 30 minutes.

Upper School Student Profile Grade 9: 87 students (87 boys); Grade 10: 92 students (92 boys); Grade 11: 89 students (89 boys); Grade 12: 89 students (89 boys).

Faculty School total: 171. In upper school: 42 men, 14 women; 46 have advanced degrees.

Subjects Offered 20th century history, 3-dimensional design, acting, advanced chemistry, African-American literature, algebra, American history, American history-AP, American literature, anthropology, Arabic, architecture, art, art history, art history-AP, astronomy, biology, biology-AP, calculus, calculus-AP, ceramics, chemistry, chemistry-AP, Chinese, choir, community service, computer graphics, computer programming, computer programming-AP, creative writing, digital art, digital music, drama, earth science, economics, economics-AP, English, environmental science-AP, ethics, European history, European history-AP, film and literature, fine arts, French, French language-AP, French literature-AP, geometry, government-AP, Greek, Greek culture, health, history, honors algebra, honors geometry, human geography - AP, Italian, Japanese history, jazz, jazz band, jazz ensemble, Latin, Latin American literature, Latin-AP, mathematics, media studies, microeconomics, military history, music, oceanography, philosophy, photography, physical education, physics, physics-AP, poetry, pre-calculus, psychology, psychology-AP, science, senior seminar, Shakespeare, short story, social studies, Spanish, Spanish language-AP, Spanish literature-AP, speech and debate, statistics-AP, studio art, studio art-AP, theater, trigonometry, U.S. government and politics-AP, U.S. history-AP, world cultures, world history-AP, writing.

Graduation Requirements Arts and fine arts (art, music, dance, drama), English, foreign language, mathematics, physical education (includes health), science, social studies (includes history). Community service is required.

Special Academic Programs Advanced Placement exam preparation; honors section; independent study; term-away projects; academic accommodation for the gifted, the musically talented, and the artistically talented.

College Admission Counseling 81 students graduated in 2011; all went to college, including Cornell University; Dartmouth College; Duke University; Georgetown University; University of Virginia; Yale University. Mean SAT critical reading: 660, mean SAT math: 665, mean SAT writing: 670, mean combined SAT: 1985. 75% scored over 600 on SAT critical reading, 87% scored over 600 on SAT math, 88% scored over 600 on SAT writing, 85% scored over 1800 on combined SAT.

Student Life Upper grades have specified standards of dress, student council, honor system. Discipline rests equally with students and faculty.

Tuition and Aid Day student tuition: $34,500. Tuition installment plan (Key Tuition Payment Plan, monthly payment plans). Need-based scholarship grants available. In 2011–12, 11% of upper-school students received aid. Total amount of financial aid awarded in 2011–12: $1,250,000.

Admissions Traditional secondary-level entrance grade is 9. For fall 2011, 162 students applied for upper-level admission, 38 were accepted, 33 enrolled. ISEE, PSAT or SSAT required. Deadline for receipt of application materials: December 15. Application fee required: $75. On-campus interview required.

Athletics Interscholastic: baseball, basketball, crew, cross-country running, fencing, fitness, football, golf, ice hockey, lacrosse, sailing, soccer, squash, tennis, track and field, water polo, wrestling; intramural: basketball, softball, squash, touch football, ultimate Frisbee. 4 PE instructors, 2 athletic trainers.

Computers Computers are regularly used in career technology classes. Computer network features include online commercial services, Internet access, wireless campus network, Internet filtering or blocking technology. Campus intranet and student e-mail accounts are available to students. The school has a published electronic and media policy.

Contact Stephen Garnett, Director, Upper School Admission. 203-625-5842. Fax: 203-625-5863. E-mail: sgarnett@brunswickschool.org. Web site: www.brunswickschool.org

THE BRYN MAWR SCHOOL FOR GIRLS

109 West Melrose Avenue
Baltimore, Maryland 21210

Head of School: Maureen E. Walsh

General Information Coeducational day (boys' only in lower grades) college-preparatory and arts school. Boys grade PK, girls grades PK–12. Founded: 1885. Setting: suburban. 26-acre campus. 9 buildings on campus. Approved or accredited by Association of Independent Maryland Schools and Maryland Department of Education. Member of National Association of Independent Schools. Endowment: $26.6 million. Total enrollment: 700. Upper school average class size: 14. Upper school faculty-student ratio: 1:6. There are 180 required school days per year for Upper School students. Upper School students typically attend 5 days per week. The average school day consists of 7 hours.

Upper School Student Profile Grade 9: 76 students (76 girls); Grade 10: 70 students (70 girls); Grade 11: 71 students (71 girls); Grade 12: 73 students (73 girls).

Faculty School total: 144. In upper school: 14 men, 37 women; 24 have advanced degrees.

Subjects Offered Accounting, acting, African studies, African-American history, African-American literature, algebra, American history, American literature, anatomy, anatomy and physiology, Arabic, architectural drawing, art, art history, art history-AP, astronomy, biology, biology-AP, British literature, calculus, ceramics, chemistry, chemistry-AP, Chinese, comparative religion, computer programming, computer science, computer science-AP, creative writing, dance, design, digital art, digital photography, drama, drawing, ecology, economics, emerging technology, English, English literature, English-AP, environmental science-AP, ethics, European history, fine arts, forensics, French, French literature-AP, genetics, geography, geology, geometry, German, grammar, Greek, health, Holocaust studies, Irish literature, Latin, Latin American history, mathematics, mechanical drawing, moral theology, music, music theory, mythology, Native American studies, orchestra, painting, personal finance, photography, physical education, physics, physics-AP, poetry, pre-calculus, public speaking, rite of passage, Russian, science, Shakespearean histories, short story, social studies, Spanish, statistics, strings, technology, theater, trigonometry, U.S. government and politics-AP, U.S. history, U.S. history-AP, urban studies, Vietnam War, world history, world history-AP, world literature, World War I, World War II, writing.

Graduation Requirements Arts and fine arts (art, music, dance, drama), emerging technology, English, foreign language, history, mathematics, physical education (includes health), public speaking, science, 50 hours of community service, convocation speech.

Special Academic Programs Advanced Placement exam preparation; honors section; independent study; term-away projects; study abroad; academic accommodation for the gifted, the musically talented, and the artistically talented.

College Admission Counseling 75 students graduated in 2012; all went to college, including Kenyon College; The Johns Hopkins University; Tulane University; University of Chicago; University of Maryland, College Park; Yale University. Median SAT critical reading: 640, median SAT math: 630, median SAT writing: 650, median combined SAT: 1920, median composite ACT: 28. 74.3% scored over 600 on SAT critical reading, 75.7% scored over 600 on SAT math, 83.8% scored over 600 on SAT writing, 77% scored over 1800 on combined SAT, 79.2% scored over 26 on composite ACT.

Student Life Upper grades have uniform requirement, student council, honor system. Discipline rests equally with students and faculty.

Summer Programs Enrichment, sports, art/fine arts programs offered; session focuses on arts, crafts, language, culture, and sports; held on campus; accepts boys and girls; open to students from other schools. 665 students usually enrolled. 2013 schedule: June 17 to August 16. Application deadline: none.

Tuition and Aid Day student tuition: $25,490. Tuition installment plan (FACTS Tuition Payment Plan, individually arranged payment plans, Tuition Management Services, Semi-monthly Payroll Deduction (for employees only)). Need-based scholarship grants, need-based loans, middle-income loans available. In 2012–13, 31% of upper-school students received aid. Total amount of financial aid awarded in 2012–13: $1,300,000.

Admissions Traditional secondary-level entrance grade is 9. For fall 2012, 111 students applied for upper-level admission, 58 were accepted, 23 enrolled. ISEE required. Deadline for receipt of application materials: December 14. Application fee required: $60. On-campus interview required.

Athletics Interscholastic: badminton, ballet, basketball, crew, cross-country running, dance, field hockey, hockey, indoor soccer, indoor track & field, lacrosse, rowing, running, soccer, softball, squash, tennis, track and field, volleyball, winter (indoor) track, winter soccer; intramural: aerobics, aerobics/dance, aerobics/Nautilus, archery, badminton, ball hockey, basketball, bowling, cooperative games, croquet, cross-country running, dance, fitness, flag football, floor hockey, ice hockey, jogging, outdoor activities, physical training, pillo polo, ropes courses, running, strength & conditioning, tennis, touch football, weight training. 5 PE instructors, 27 coaches, 1 athletic trainer.

Computers Computers are regularly used in all academic, animation, art, computer applications, Web site design classes. Computer network features include on-campus library services, online commercial services, Internet access, off-campus email. Campus intranet and student e-mail accounts are available to students. Students grades are available online. The school has a published electronic and media policy.

Contact Talia Titus, Director of Admission and Financial Aid. 410-323-8800 Ext. 1237. Fax: 410-435-4678. E-mail: titust@brynmawrschool.org. Web site: www.brynmawrschool.org

BUFFALO ACADEMY OF THE SACRED HEART

3860 Main Street
Buffalo, New York 14226-3398

Head of School: Ms. Jennifer M. Demert, Esq.

General Information Girls' day college-preparatory, arts, religious studies, technology, and music school, affiliated with Roman Catholic Church. Grades 9–12. Founded: 1877. Setting: suburban. 2-acre campus. 2 buildings on campus. Approved or accredited by Middle States Association of Colleges and Schools, New York State Board of Regents, and New York Department of Education. Total enrollment: 407. Upper school average class size: 20. Upper school faculty-student ratio: 1:10. Upper School students typically attend 5 days per week. The average school day consists of 7 hours.

Upper School Student Profile Grade 9: 110 students (110 girls); Grade 10: 106 students (106 girls); Grade 11: 100 students (100 girls); Grade 12: 91 students (91 girls). 87% of students are Roman Catholic.

Faculty School total: 41. In upper school: 9 men, 32 women; 31 have advanced degrees.

Subjects Offered Advanced Placement courses, aerobics, algebra, American history, American literature, art, biology, business, business skills, calculus, chemistry, Chinese, community service, computer math, computer programming, computer science, creative writing, desktop publishing, drama, driver education, earth science, economics, English, English literature, environmental science, European history, fine arts, French, geography, geometry, government/civics, grammar, health, history, home economics, instrumental music, journalism, Latin, mathematics, music, physical education, physics, psychology, religion, science, social studies, sociology, Spanish, theater, theology, vocal music, world history.

Graduation Requirements Arts and fine arts (art, music, dance, drama), business skills (includes word processing), computer science, English, foreign language, mathematics, physical education (includes health), religion (includes Bible studies and theology), science, social studies (includes history), 20 hours of community service per year, 4 years of leadership studies. Community service is required.

Special Academic Programs 13 Advanced Placement exams for which test preparation is offered; honors section; accelerated programs; study at local college for college credit; academic accommodation for the gifted, the musically talented, and the artistically talented; remedial math.

College Admission Counseling 90 students graduated in 2012; 89 went to college, including Boston College; Canisius College; St. Bonaventure University; State University of New York College at Geneseo; Syracuse University; University at Buffalo, the State University of New York. Other: 1 had other specific plans. Median SAT critical reading: 567, median SAT math: 550, median SAT writing: 569.

Student Life Upper grades have uniform requirement, student council, honor system. Discipline rests primarily with faculty. Attendance at religious services is required.

Summer Programs Sports, art/fine arts, computer instruction programs offered; session focuses on sports, arts; held on campus; accepts girls; open to students from other schools. 100 students usually enrolled. 2013 schedule: June 27 to July 29. Application deadline: June 24.

Tuition and Aid Day student tuition: $9565. Tuition installment plan (FACTS Tuition Payment Plan). Tuition reduction for siblings, merit scholarship grants, need-based scholarship grants, paying campus jobs, discounts for children of employees, emergency tuition assistance available. In 2012–13, 31% of upper-school students received aid. Total amount of financial aid awarded in 2012–13: $275,000.

Admissions Traditional secondary-level entrance grade is 9. For fall 2012, 155 students applied for upper-level admission, 135 were accepted, 110 enrolled. High School Placement Test required. Deadline for receipt of application materials: none. Application fee required: $20. Interview recommended.

Athletics Interscholastic: basketball, bowling, cheering, crew, cross-country running, dance, field hockey, fitness walking, golf, ice hockey, indoor track & field, lacrosse, rowing, running, sailing, soccer, softball, swimming and diving, tennis, track and field, volleyball; intramural: crew, drill team, jogging, skiing (downhill), yoga. 2 PE instructors, 9 coaches.

Computers Computers are regularly used in business applications, English, foreign language, mathematics, music, science classes. Computer network features include on-campus library services, online commercial services, Internet access, wireless campus network, Internet filtering or blocking technology. Student e-mail accounts are available to students. Students grades are available online. The school has a published electronic and media policy.

Contact Ms. Mary Ganey Cochrane, Director of Admissions. 716-834-2101 Ext. 311. Fax: 716-834-2944. E-mail: mcochrane@sacredheartacademy.org. Web site: www.sacredheartacademy.org

BULLOCH ACADEMY

873 Westside Road
Statesboro, Georgia 30458

Head of School: Mrs. Leisa Houghton

General Information Coeducational day college-preparatory, arts, and technology school, affiliated with Protestant faith, Baptist Church. Grades PK–12. Founded: 1971. Setting: small town. Nearest major city is Savannah. 35-acre campus. 4 buildings on campus. Approved or accredited by Georgia Accrediting Commission, Georgia Independent School Association, Southern Association of Colleges and Schools, and Southern Association of Independent Schools. Member of National Association of Independent Schools. Total enrollment: 498. Upper school average class size: 17. Upper school faculty-student ratio: 1:17. There are 180 required school days per year for Upper School students. Upper School students typically attend 5 days per week. The average school day consists of 8 hours.

Upper School Student Profile Grade 9: 35 students (19 boys, 16 girls); Grade 10: 36 students (20 boys, 16 girls); Grade 11: 42 students (19 boys, 23 girls); Grade 12: 45 students (20 boys, 25 girls). 90% of students are Protestant, Baptist.

Faculty School total: 31. In upper school: 4 men, 11 women; 4 have advanced degrees.

Subjects Offered Advanced Placement courses, American government, American history, anatomy and physiology, art, art education, biology, calculus, chemistry, computer applications, computer science, earth science, economics, economics and history, English, ethics, geometry, government, government-AP, government/civics, health education, journalism, language and composition, language arts, literature-AP, mathematics-AP, music, performing arts, physical education, physics, pre-algebra, pre-calculus, research skills, science, social sciences, Spanish, speech and debate, technology, U.S. government and politics-AP, U.S. history, Web site design, world geography, world history.

Graduation Requirements Computer science, English, foreign language, mathematics, physical education (includes health), science, social sciences, social studies (includes history).

Special Academic Programs 6 Advanced Placement exams for which test preparation is offered; honors section; independent study; study at local college for college credit; academic accommodation for the gifted, the musically talented, and the artistically talented.

College Admission Counseling 30 students graduated in 2012; 29 went to college, including Furman University; Georgia Institute of Technology; Georgia Southern University; The University of Alabama; University of Georgia; University of Oklahoma. Other: 1 went to work. Median SAT critical reading: 518, median SAT math: 530, median SAT writing: 508, median combined SAT: 1556, median composite ACT: 20.

Student Life Upper grades have specified standards of dress, student council, honor system. Discipline rests primarily with faculty.

Tuition and Aid Day student tuition: $6710. Tuition installment plan (monthly payment plans, individually arranged payment plans). Tuition reduction for siblings, need-based scholarship grants, tuition assistance available. In 2012–13, 10% of upper-school students received aid. Total amount of financial aid awarded in 2012–13: $50,000.

Admissions Traditional secondary-level entrance grade is 9. For fall 2012, 25 students applied for upper-level admission, 24 were accepted, 24 enrolled. Any standardized test required. Deadline for receipt of application materials: none. Application fee required: $375. Interview recommended.

Athletics Interscholastic: baseball (boys), basketball (b,g), cheering (g), cross-country running (b,g), dance team (g), football (b), golf (b,g), physical fitness (b,g), running (b,g), soccer (b,g), softball (g), strength & conditioning (b,g), tennis (b,g), track and field (b,g), weight lifting (b,g), weight training (b,g), wrestling (b); intramural: cheering (g), cross-country running (b,g), football (b), physical fitness (b,g); coed interscholastic: physical fitness; coed intramural: basketball, football, physical fitness. 3 PE instructors, 7 coaches, 3 athletic trainers.

Computers Computers are regularly used in art, career education, career exploration, computer applications, creative writing, desktop publishing, economics, geography, history, independent study, keyboarding, technology classes. Computer network features include on-campus library services, online commercial services, Internet access, wireless campus network, Internet filtering or blocking technology. Student e-mail accounts are available to students. Students grades are available online. The school has a published electronic and media policy.

Contact Mr. Leisa Houghton, Head of School. 912-764-6297. Fax: 912-764-3165. E-mail: lhoughton@bullochacademy.com. Web site: www.bullochacademy.com

BURR AND BURTON ACADEMY

57 Seminary Avenue

Manchester, Vermont 05254

Head of School: Mr. Mark Tashjian

General Information Coeducational boarding and day college-preparatory, general academic, arts, and technology school. Grades 9–12. Founded: 1829. Setting: small town. Nearest major city is Albany, NY. Students are housed in single-sex dormitories and homes of host families. 29-acre campus. 7 buildings on campus. Approved or accredited by New England Association of Schools and Colleges and Vermont Department of Education. Member of National Association of Independent Schools. Total enrollment: 680. Upper school average class size: 19. Upper school faculty-student ratio: 1:12. There are 175 required school days per year for Upper School students. Upper School students typically attend 5 days per week. The average school day consists of 6 hours and 40 minutes.

Upper School Student Profile Grade 9: 145 students (66 boys, 79 girls); Grade 10: 201 students (103 boys, 98 girls); Grade 11: 172 students (82 boys, 90 girls); Grade 12: 160 students (85 boys, 75 girls). 8% are international students.

Faculty School total: 60. In upper school: 35 men, 25 women; 30 have advanced degrees.

Subjects Offered Algebra, American history, American literature, anatomy, art, art history, biology, business, calculus, chemistry, computer math, computer programming, computer science, drafting, drama, driver education, earth science, ecology, English, English literature, environmental science, expository writing, French, geometry, German, government/civics, health, history, industrial arts, mathematics, music, photography, physical education, physics, psychology, science, social studies, Spanish, theater, trigonometry, typing, world history, world literature.

Graduation Requirements Arts, computer literacy, English, mathematics, physical education (includes health), science, social studies (includes history), U.S. history. Community service is required.

Special Academic Programs 14 Advanced Placement exams for which test preparation is offered; honors section; independent study; term-away projects; study abroad; remedial reading and/or remedial writing; remedial math; programs in English, mathematics, general development for dyslexic students; special instructional classes for deaf students, blind students; ESL (20 students enrolled).

College Admission Counseling 164 students graduated in 2012; 134 went to college, including Michigan State University; University of Vermont. Other: 16 went to work, 3 entered military service, 11 had other specific plans.

Student Life Upper grades have specified standards of dress, student council. Discipline rests primarily with faculty.

Tuition and Aid Day student tuition: $15,475; 7-day tuition and room/board: $38,800. Tuition installment plan (individually arranged payment plans). Financial aid available to upper-school students. In 2012–13, 2% of upper-school students received aid.

Admissions Traditional secondary-level entrance grade is 9. School's own test, SLEP for foreign students and TOEFL or SLEP required. Deadline for receipt of application materials: none. No application fee required. Interview required.

Athletics Interscholastic: alpine skiing (boys, girls), baseball (b), basketball (b,g), cross-country running (b,g), dance team (g), field hockey (g), football (b), golf (b,g), hockey (b,g), ice hockey (b,g), lacrosse (b,g), nordic skiing (b,g), skiing (cross-country) (b,g), skiing (downhill) (b,g), snowboarding (b,g), soccer (b,g), softball (g), tennis (b,g), track and field (b,g); coed intramural: equestrian sports, floor hockey, outdoor adventure, outdoor education, volleyball, weight training. 3 PE instructors.

Computers Computers are regularly used in drafting, drawing and design, English, foreign language, graphic design, history, information technology, mathematics, science, video film production, Web site design, yearbook classes. Computer network features include on-campus library services, online commercial services, Internet access, wireless campus network, Internet filtering or blocking technology. Campus intranet, student e-mail accounts, and computer access in designated common areas are available to students.

Contact Mr. Philip G. Anton, Director of Admission and School Counseling. 802-362-1775 Ext. 125. Fax: 802-362-0574. E-mail: panton@burrburton.org. Web site: www.burrburton.org

BUTTE CENTRAL CATHOLIC HIGH SCHOOL

9 South Idaho Street

Butte, Montana 59701

Head of School: Mr. Timothy Norbeck

General Information Boys' boarding and coeducational day college-preparatory, arts, business, vocational, religious studies, and technology school, affiliated with Roman Catholic Church. Boarding boys grades 9–12, day boys grades 9–12, day girls grades 9–12. Founded: 1892. Setting: small town. Nearest major city is Bozeman. 6-acre campus. 1 building on campus. Approved or accredited by National Catholic Education Association, Northwest Accreditation Commission, Western Catholic Education Association, and Montana Department of Education. Endowment: $300,000. Total enrollment: 134. Upper school average class size: 17. Upper school faculty-student ratio: 1:12. There are 180 required school days per year for Upper School students. Upper School students typically attend 5 days per week. The average school day consists of 7 hours.

Upper School Student Profile Grade 9: 38 students (15 boys, 23 girls); Grade 10: 31 students (22 boys, 9 girls); Grade 11: 31 students (19 boys, 12 girls); Grade 12: 34 students (16 boys, 18 girls). 10% of students are boarding students. 90% are state residents. 1 state is represented in upper school student body. 10% are international students. International students from Brazil, China, Portugal, and Taiwan. 85% of students are Roman Catholic.

Faculty School total: 12. In upper school: 5 men, 7 women; 3 have advanced degrees.

Subjects Offered Accounting, advanced math, Advanced Placement courses, algebra, American literature-AP, animal behavior, art, athletic training, biology, calculus, calculus-AP, career education, chemistry, choir, college counseling, college placement, college planning, college writing, community service, computer science, computers, debate, desktop publishing, drama, English, English literature and composition-AP, foreign language, French, French as a second language, geometry, government/civics, health, history, honors algebra, honors English, honors geometry, human biology, integrated mathematics, keyboarding, mathematics, model United Nations, physical education, physics, pre-calculus, public speaking, reading, religion, science, social studies, Spanish, student government, trigonometry, Web site design, weightlifting, world history, writing, yearbook.

Graduation Requirements American government, American history, arts and fine arts (art, music, dance, drama), electives, English, foreign language, global studies, health education, keyboarding, mathematics, physical education (includes health), religion (includes Bible studies and theology), science, social studies (includes history), writing. Community service is required.

Special Academic Programs 2 Advanced Placement exams for which test preparation is offered; honors section; independent study; study at local college for college credit; remedial reading and/or remedial writing; remedial math.

College Admission Counseling 28 students graduated in 2012; 26 went to college, including Carroll University; Division of Technology of Montana Tech of The University of Montana; Gonzaga University; Montana State University; The University of Montana Western. Other: 2 went to work. Median composite ACT: 20. 7% scored over 26 on composite ACT.

Student Life Upper grades have specified standards of dress, student council, honor system. Discipline rests primarily with faculty. Attendance at religious services is required.

Tuition and Aid Day student tuition: $4000–$7000; 7-day tuition and room/board: $10,000–$15,000. Guaranteed tuition plan. Tuition installment plan (FACTS Tuition Payment Plan, monthly payment plans, individually arranged payment plans). Tuition reduction for siblings, need-based scholarship grants available. In 2012–13, 25% of upper-school students received aid. Total amount of financial aid awarded in 2012–13: $68,000.

Admissions Traditional secondary-level entrance grade is 9. Admissions testing required. Deadline for receipt of application materials: none. Application fee required: $150. Interview required.

Athletics Interscholastic: basketball (boys, girls), cheering (g), cross-country running (b,g), football (b), golf (b,g), softball (g), strength & conditioning (b,g), tennis (b,g), track and field (b,g), volleyball (g), wrestling (b). 1 PE instructor, 30 coaches, 1 athletic trainer.

Computers Computers are regularly used in all academic classes. Computer network features include on-campus library services, Internet access, Internet filtering or blocking technology. The school has a published electronic and media policy.

Contact Mr. Timothy Norbeck, Principal. 406-782-6761. Fax: 406-723-3873. E-mail: tim.norbeck@buttecentralschools.org. Web site: www.buttecentralschools.org

BUXTON SCHOOL

291 South Street

Williamstown, Massachusetts 01267

Head of School: C. William Bennett and Peter Smith '74

General Information Coeducational boarding and day college-preparatory and arts school. Grades 9–12. Founded: 1928. Setting: small town. Nearest major city is Boston. Students are housed in single-sex dormitories. 150-acre campus. 20 buildings on campus. Approved or accredited by Association of Independent Schools in New England, New England Association of Schools and Colleges, The Association of

Boarding Schools, and Massachusetts Department of Education. Member of National Association of Independent Schools and Secondary School Admission Test Board. Endowment: $1.9 million. Total enrollment: 90. Upper school average class size: 9. Upper school faculty-student ratio: 1:4. There are 221 required school days per year for Upper School students. Upper School students typically attend 5 days per week. The average school day consists of 5 hours and 15 minutes.
Upper School Student Profile Grade 9: 16 students (6 boys, 10 girls); Grade 10: 24 students (11 boys, 13 girls); Grade 11: 27 students (16 boys, 11 girls); Grade 12: 23 students (11 boys, 12 girls). 90% of students are boarding students. 14% are state residents. 11 states are represented in upper school student body. 25% are international students. International students from Bermuda, China, Japan, Mexico, Rwanda, and Venezuela; 2 other countries represented in student body.
Faculty School total: 22. In upper school: 12 men, 10 women; 5 have advanced degrees; 14 reside on campus.
Subjects Offered Advanced math, African dance, African drumming, African studies, algebra, American history, American literature, anatomy and physiology, anthropology, architecture, astronomy, biology, British literature, calculus, cell biology, ceramics, chemistry, costumes and make-up, creative writing, critical writing, dance performance, drama, drama performance, drawing, economics, English, English literature, ensembles, ESL, European history, expository writing, fiction, film history, French, geometry, grammar, history, improvisation, independent study, instruments, lab science, linear algebra, literary genres, literature, Mandarin, marine biology, music, music composition, music performance, music theory, oceanography, painting, performing arts, philosophy, photography, physics, poetry, pre-calculus, printmaking, psychology, set design, social sciences, Spanish, studio art, technical theater, TOEFL preparation, trigonometry, video film production, voice, writing workshop.
Graduation Requirements American history, English, foreign language, lab science, mathematics, social sciences.
Special Academic Programs Honors section; academic accommodation for the gifted, the musically talented, and the artistically talented; ESL (17 students enrolled).
College Admission Counseling 30 students graduated in 2012; 26 went to college, including Bard College; Barnard College; Bennington College; Guilford College; Oberlin College; Williams College. Other: 4 had other specific plans.
Student Life Discipline rests primarily with faculty.
Tuition and Aid Day student tuition: $29,000; 7-day tuition and room/board: $47,500. Tuition installment plan (individually arranged payment plans, Tuition Management Systems). Need-based scholarship grants, need-based loans with limited in-house financing available. In 2012–13, 49% of upper-school students received aid. Total amount of financial aid awarded in 2012–13: $1,300,000.
Admissions Traditional secondary-level entrance grade is 9. SSAT or TOEFL or SLEP required. Deadline for receipt of application materials: February 1. Application fee required: $50. Interview required.
Athletics Interscholastic: soccer (boys, girls); intramural: soccer (b,g); coed interscholastic: basketball, ultimate Frisbee; coed intramural: ballet, bicycling, dance, hiking/backpacking, horseback riding, ice skating, indoor soccer, jogging, martial arts, mountain biking, outdoor activities, physical training, running, skateboarding, skiing (downhill), snowboarding, soccer, squash, table tennis, tennis, ultimate Frisbee, weight lifting, yoga.
Computers Computers are regularly used in architecture, economics, ESL, French, history, language development, mathematics, media production, multimedia, music, photography, psychology, science, Spanish, video film production, writing, yearbook classes. Computer network features include Internet access, wireless campus network, Internet filtering or blocking technology. Campus intranet and computer access in designated common areas are available to students. The school has a published electronic and media policy.
Contact Admissions Office. 413-458-3919. Fax: 413-458-9428. E-mail: Admissions@BuxtonSchool.org. Web site: www.BuxtonSchool.org

THE BYRNES SCHOOLS

1201 East Ashby Road
Florence, South Carolina 29506

Head of School: Mr. John W. Colby Jr.

General Information Coeducational day college-preparatory school. Grades PK–12. Founded: 1966. Setting: small town. 16-acre campus. 3 buildings on campus. Approved or accredited by South Carolina Independent School Association and Southern Association of Independent Schools. Candidate for accreditation by Southern Association of Colleges and Schools. Endowment: $25,000. Total enrollment: 192. Upper school average class size: 13. Upper school faculty-student ratio: 1:9. There are 175 required school days per year for Upper School students. Upper School students typically attend 5 days per week. The average school day consists of 6 hours and 50 minutes.
Upper School Student Profile Grade 9: 12 students (5 boys, 7 girls); Grade 10: 15 students (10 boys, 5 girls); Grade 11: 16 students (10 boys, 6 girls); Grade 12: 21 students (10 boys, 11 girls).
Faculty School total: 28. In upper school: 5 men, 6 women; 5 have advanced degrees.
Subjects Offered Advanced Placement courses, algebra, American history, biology, biology-AP, calculus-AP, chemistry, computer science, earth science, economics, English, English-AP, environmental science, geography, geometry, government/civics, history-AP, mathematics, physical education, physics, science, social studies, Spanish, world history.
Graduation Requirements English, foreign language, mathematics, physical education (includes health), science, social studies (includes history).
Special Academic Programs Advanced Placement exam preparation; honors section; academic accommodation for the gifted.
College Admission Counseling 13 students graduated in 2011; all went to college, including Clemson University; Francis Marion University; Sewanee: The University of the South; University of South Carolina.
Student Life Upper grades have specified standards of dress, student council, honor system. Discipline rests primarily with faculty.
Tuition and Aid Day student tuition: $7100. Tuition installment plan (Insured Tuition Payment Plan, monthly payment plans). Need-based scholarship grants available. In 2011–12, 15% of upper-school students received aid. Total amount of financial aid awarded in 2011–12: $25,000.
Admissions Traditional secondary-level entrance grade is 9. For fall 2011, 2 students applied for upper-level admission, 2 were accepted, 2 enrolled. Metropolitan Achievement Test or Stanford Achievement Test required. Deadline for receipt of application materials: none. Application fee required: $50. On-campus interview required.
Athletics Interscholastic: baseball (boys), basketball (b,g), cheering (g), football (b), golf (b,g), soccer (b,g), softball (g), volleyball (g); intramural: aerobics/dance (g), strength & conditioning (b,g), weight lifting (b,g), weight training (b,g); coed interscholastic: cross-country running; coed intramural: tennis. 1 PE instructor, 1 athletic trainer.
Computers Computers are regularly used in mathematics, yearbook classes. Computer network features include Internet access. Students grades are available online. The school has a published electronic and media policy.
Contact Mr. John W. Colby Jr., Headmaster. 843-622-0131 Ext. 116. Fax: 843-669-2466. E-mail: JColby@byrnesschools.org. Web site: www.byrnesschools.org

CALGARY ACADEMY COLLEGIATE

1677 93rd St Sw
Calgary, Alberta T3H 0R3, Canada

Head of School: Ms. Kim McLean

General Information Coeducational day college-preparatory, arts, and technology school; primarily serves students with learning disabilities, individuals with Attention Deficit Disorder, and dyslexic students. Grades 6–12. Founded: 1981. Setting: suburban. 17-acre campus. 3 buildings on campus. Approved or accredited by Association of Independent Schools and Colleges of Alberta and Alberta Department of Education. Language of instruction: English. Endowment: CAN$3 million. Total enrollment: 176. Upper school average class size: 17. Upper school faculty-student ratio: 1:8. There are 188 required school days per year for Upper School students. Upper School students typically attend 5 days per week. The average school day consists of 6 hours and 10 minutes.
Upper School Student Profile Grade 10: 30 students (20 boys, 10 girls); Grade 11: 30 students (19 boys, 11 girls); Grade 12: 35 students (21 boys, 14 girls).
Faculty School total: 25. In upper school: 10 men, 15 women; 10 have advanced degrees.
Subjects Offered Art history, athletics, band, biology, calculus, career and personal planning, character education, chemistry, computer animation, computer multimedia, drama, English composition, English literature, grammar, language arts, mathematics, outdoor education, physical education, physics, psychology, social studies, sociology, Spanish, study skills.
Graduation Requirements Biology, chemistry, English, mathematics, physics, social studies (includes history).
Special Academic Programs International Baccalaureate program; 1 Advanced Placement exam for which test preparation is offered.
College Admission Counseling 39 students graduated in 2011; 36 went to college, including Mount Royal University; University of Alberta; University of Calgary; University of Lethbridge. Other: 3 went to work.
Student Life Upper grades have specified standards of dress, student council, honor system. Discipline rests primarily with faculty.
Tuition and Aid Day student tuition: CAN$9500. Tuition installment plan (monthly payment plans, individually arranged payment plans). Bursaries available. In 2011–12, 5% of upper-school students received aid. Total amount of financial aid awarded in 2011–12: CAN$300,000.
Admissions Traditional secondary-level entrance grade is 10. For fall 2011, 50 students applied for upper-level admission, 30 were accepted, 20 enrolled. Achievement tests, Wechsler Individual Achievement Test or Wechsler Intelligence Scale for Children III required. Deadline for receipt of application materials: none. Application fee required: CAN$1500. On-campus interview required.
Athletics Interscholastic: badminton (boys, girls), ball hockey (b), basketball (b,g), cross-country running (b,g), golf (b,g), handball (b,g), track and field (b,g), volleyball (b,g), wrestling (b,g); intramural: ice hockey (b,g); coed interscholastic: badminton, curling, soccer; coed intramural: outdoor recreation, triathlon. 6 PE instructors, 30 coaches.
Computers Computers are regularly used in all academic classes. Computer network features include on-campus library services, Internet access, wireless campus network, Internet filtering or blocking technology. Computer access in designated common areas

is available to students. Students grades are available online. The school has a published electronic and media policy.

Contact Ms. Joanne Endacott, Director of Admissions. 403-686-6444 Ext. 236. Fax: 403-686-3427. E-mail: jendacott@calgaryacademy.com. Web site:

CALVARY CHAPEL HIGH SCHOOL

12808 Woodruff Avenue
Downey, California 90242

Head of School: Pastor Yuri Escandon

General Information Coeducational day college-preparatory, arts, business, religious studies, and technology school, affiliated with Christian faith. Grades K–12. Founded: 1978. Setting: suburban. Nearest major city is Los Angeles. 16-acre campus. 1 building on campus. Approved or accredited by Western Association of Schools and Colleges and California Department of Education. Total enrollment: 683. Upper school average class size: 19. Upper school faculty-student ratio: 1:19. There are 174 required school days per year for Upper School students. Upper School students typically attend 5 days per week. The average school day consists of 6 hours and 6 minutes.

Upper School Student Profile 100% of students are Christian faith.

Faculty School total: 35. In upper school: 18 men, 17 women; 5 have advanced degrees.

Subjects Offered Algebra, anatomy, art, arts, band, Bible studies, biology, calculus-AP, chemistry, choir, community service, computer science, creative writing, current events, drama, earth science, economics, English, ethics, fine arts, geometry, government, health, humanities, mathematics, media, music appreciation, physical education, physical science, physics, physiology, pre-calculus, religion, science, social studies, sociology, Spanish, speech, U.S. history, world history.

Graduation Requirements American sign language, anatomy and physiology, art-AP, computers.

Special Academic Programs Advanced Placement exam preparation; honors section; independent study; study at local college for college credit.

College Admission Counseling 92 students graduated in 2011; 90 went to college, including Azusa Pacific University; Biola University; California State University, Fullerton; California State University, Long Beach; Chapman University; Vanguard University of Southern California. Other: 1 entered military service, 1 had other specific plans. Mean SAT critical reading: 491, mean SAT math: 444, mean SAT writing: 484.

Student Life Upper grades have specified standards of dress, student council, honor system. Discipline rests primarily with faculty. Attendance at religious services is required.

Tuition and Aid Day student tuition: $8250. Guaranteed tuition plan. Tuition installment plan (monthly payment plans). Tuition reduction for siblings, need-based scholarship grants available. In 2011–12, 15% of upper-school students received aid.

Admissions Traditional secondary-level entrance grade is 9. Admissions testing required. Deadline for receipt of application materials: none. Application fee required: $125. Interview required.

Athletics Interscholastic: aquatics (boys, girls), baseball (b), basketball (b,g), cheering (g), cross-country running (b,g), football (b), outdoor activities (b,g), physical fitness (b,g), soccer (b,g), softball (g), strength & conditioning (b,g), swimming and diving (b,g), track and field (b,g), volleyball (b,g), weight training (b,g), wrestling (b); coed interscholastic: aquatics, swimming and diving. 4 PE instructors, 25 coaches, 1 athletic trainer.

Computers Computers are regularly used in all academic classes. Computer resources include on-campus library services, Internet access, Internet filtering or blocking technology. Computer access in designated common areas is available to students. Students grades are available online. The school has a published electronic and media policy.

Contact Diane Kirkhuff, Office/Admissions. 562-803-4076 Ext. 302. Fax: 562-803-1292. E-mail: dkirkhuff@calvarydowney.org. Web site: cccsdowney.org

CALVARY CHRISTIAN SCHOOL

5955 Taylor Mill Road
Covington, Kentucky 41015

Head of School: Dr. Bill Dickens

General Information Coeducational day college-preparatory, arts, religious studies, and technology school, affiliated with Baptist Church. Grades K4–12. Founded: 1974. Setting: suburban. Nearest major city is Cincinnati, OH. 64-acre campus. 1 building on campus. Approved or accredited by Association of Christian Schools International, CITA (Commission on International and Trans-Regional Accreditation), Southern Association of Colleges and Schools, and Kentucky Department of Education. Total enrollment: 359. Upper school average class size: 17. Upper school faculty-student ratio: 1:8. There are 177 required school days per year for Upper School students. Upper School students typically attend 5 days per week. The average school day consists of 7 hours.

Upper School Student Profile Grade 9: 26 students (12 boys, 14 girls); Grade 10: 32 students (11 boys, 21 girls); Grade 11: 22 students (12 boys, 10 girls); Grade 12: 28 students (12 boys, 16 girls). 30% of students are Baptist.

Faculty School total: 30. In upper school: 9 men, 11 women; 6 have advanced degrees.

Subjects Offered Advanced math, algebra, American history-AP, American literature-AP, Ancient Greek, ancient history, art, art appreciation, Bible, biology, calculus, chemistry, chemistry-AP, choir, chorus, Christian doctrine, Christian ethics, communication arts, computer applications, computer multimedia, computer science, concert band, concert choir, consumer mathematics, creative writing, cultural geography, drama, drama performance, earth science, economics, English, English composition, English language and composition-AP, English language-AP, English literature, English literature and composition-AP, English literature-AP, English-AP, ethics, European history-AP, fitness, food and nutrition, general math, general science, geography, geometry, government-AP, grammar, health education, home economics, honors algebra, independent study, journalism, Kentucky history, keyboarding, lab science, language arts, library assistant, literature-AP, logic, music theory, newspaper, physical education, physical science, physics-AP, pre-algebra, pre-calculus, rhetoric, Spanish, Spanish-AP, speech and debate, state history, student government, student publications, student teaching, U.S. government, U.S. government and politics-AP, U.S. history, U.S. history-AP, world governments, world history, yearbook.

Graduation Requirements Algebra, art appreciation, Bible, biology, chemistry, Christian doctrine, church history, civics, economics, English, English composition, English literature, European history, foreign language, geometry, health, physical science, U.S. government, U.S. history, world history, 4 years of high school Bible required for graduation.

Special Academic Programs Advanced Placement exam preparation; honors section; independent study; study at local college for college credit.

College Admission Counseling 26 students graduated in 2012; 25 went to college, including Eastern Kentucky University; Northern Kentucky University; University of Cincinnati; University of Kentucky; University of Louisville. Other: 1 went to work. Median composite ACT: 27. 25% scored over 26 on composite ACT.

Student Life Upper grades have uniform requirement, student council. Discipline rests primarily with faculty. Attendance at religious services is required.

Tuition and Aid Day student tuition: $6050. Tuition installment plan (FACTS Tuition Payment Plan, monthly payment plans, individually arranged payment plans). Tuition reduction for siblings, need-based scholarship grants, paying campus jobs available. In 2012–13, 9% of upper-school students received aid. Total amount of financial aid awarded in 2012–13: $23,000.

Admissions Traditional secondary-level entrance grade is 9. For fall 2012, 14 students applied for upper-level admission, 14 were accepted, 14 enrolled. Terra Nova-CTB required. Deadline for receipt of application materials: none. Application fee required: $285. Interview required.

Athletics Interscholastic: baseball (boys), basketball (b,g), bowling (b,g), cheering (g), cross-country running (b,g), diving (b,g), golf (b), physical fitness (b,g), soccer (b,g), softball (g), swimming and diving (b,g), tennis (b,g), track and field (b,g), volleyball (g), weight lifting (b), weight training (b); intramural: indoor soccer (b,g), martial arts (b,g), skiing (downhill) (b,g), strength & conditioning (b,g), weight training (b); coed intramural: bowling, gymnastics, physical fitness, running. 2 PE instructors, 15 coaches.

Computers Computers are regularly used in architecture, art, computer applications, design, desktop publishing, drafting, graphics, information technology, journalism, keyboarding, lab/keyboard, library, photography, photojournalism, science, Spanish, technical drawing, Web site design, yearbook classes. Computer network features include on-campus library services, Internet access, wireless campus network, Internet filtering or blocking technology. Campus intranet is available to students. Students grades are available online. The school has a published electronic and media policy.

Contact Mrs. Laurie Switzer, Registrar. 859-356-9201. Fax: 859-359-8962. E-mail: laurie.switzer@ccsky.org. Web site: www.ccsky.org

CALVERT HALL COLLEGE HIGH SCHOOL

8102 LaSalle Road
Baltimore, Maryland 21286

Head of School: Br. Thomas Zoppo, FSC

General Information Boys' day college-preparatory, arts, religious studies, and technology school, affiliated with Roman Catholic Church. Grades 9–12. Founded: 1845. Setting: suburban. 32-acre campus. 6 buildings on campus. Approved or accredited by Christian Brothers Association, Middle States Association of Colleges and Schools, National Catholic Education Association, and Maryland Department of Education. Endowment: $7.8 million. Total enrollment: 1,188. Upper school average class size: 21. Upper school faculty-student ratio: 1:12. There are 174 required school days per year for Upper School students. Upper School students typically attend 5 days per week. The average school day consists of 6 hours and 20 minutes.

Upper School Student Profile Grade 9: 313 students (313 boys); Grade 10: 308 students (308 boys); Grade 11: 278 students (278 boys); Grade 12: 289 students (289 boys). 71% of students are Roman Catholic.

Faculty School total: 100. In upper school: 71 men, 26 women; 72 have advanced degrees.

Subjects Offered Algebra, American history, American literature, art, art history, band, Bible studies, biology, business, business skills, calculus, chemistry, chorus, computer programming, computer science, creative writing, drama, earth science, economics, engineering, English, English literature, ethics, European history, fine arts, French, geography, geometry, German, government/civics, graphic arts, history, journalism, Latin, leadership, mathematics, music, painting, philosophy, physical education, physics, psychology, religion, science, sculpture, social sciences, social studies, Spanish, speech, statistics, theater, theology, typing, world history, world literature, writing.

Graduation Requirements Arts and fine arts (art, music, dance, drama), English, foreign language, mathematics, physical education (includes health), religion (includes Bible studies and theology), science, social sciences, social studies (includes history).

Special Academic Programs 22 Advanced Placement exams for which test preparation is offered; honors section; academic accommodation for the gifted, the musically talented, and the artistically talented; programs in English, mathematics, general development for dyslexic students.

College Admission Counseling 297 students graduated in 2012; 290 went to college, including Loyola University Maryland; Stevenson University; Towson University; University of Maryland, Baltimore County; University of Maryland, College Park. Other: 1 went to work, 2 entered military service. Median SAT critical reading: 555, median SAT math: 558, median SAT writing: 538.

Student Life Upper grades have specified standards of dress, student council, honor system. Discipline rests primarily with faculty. Attendance at religious services is required.

Summer Programs Remediation, enrichment, sports, art/fine arts, computer instruction programs offered; session focuses on remediation and make-up courses; held on campus; accepts boys and girls; open to students from other schools. 250 students usually enrolled. 2013 schedule: June 24 to July 26. Application deadline: June 15.

Tuition and Aid Day student tuition: $12,500. Tuition installment plan (monthly payment plans, individually arranged payment plans). Merit scholarship grants, need-based scholarship grants available. In 2012–13, 53% of upper-school students received aid; total upper-school merit-scholarship money awarded: $711,000. Total amount of financial aid awarded in 2012–13: $2,582,782.

Admissions Traditional secondary-level entrance grade is 9. For fall 2012, 652 students applied for upper-level admission, 564 were accepted, 313 enrolled. High School Placement Test (closed version) from Scholastic Testing Service required. Deadline for receipt of application materials: none. Application fee required: $25.

Athletics Interscholastic: aquatics, baseball, basketball, cross-country running, football, golf, hockey, ice hockey, indoor track & field, lacrosse, rugby, soccer, squash, swimming and diving, tennis, track and field, volleyball, water polo, winter (indoor) track, wrestling; intramural: basketball, bicycling, billiards, bocce, bowling, fitness, flag football, freestyle skiing, martial arts, outdoor adventure, rock climbing, rugby, sailing, skiing (downhill), table tennis, ultimate Frisbee, weight lifting. 2 PE instructors, 12 coaches, 1 athletic trainer.

Computers Computers are regularly used in accounting, business, college planning, computer applications, digital applications, economics, English, foreign language, graphic design, history, independent study, journalism, keyboarding, library, literary magazine, mathematics, music, programming, religion, SAT preparation, science, social sciences, stock market, video film production, writing, yearbook classes. Computer network features include on-campus library services, Internet access, wireless campus network, Internet filtering or blocking technology. Campus intranet, student e-mail accounts, and computer access in designated common areas are available to students. Students grades are available online. The school has a published electronic and media policy.

Contact Chris Bengel, Director of Admissions. 410-825-4266 Ext. 126. Fax: 410-825-6826. E-mail: bengelc@calverthall.com. Web site: www.calverthall.com

THE CALVERTON SCHOOL

300 Calverton School Road
Huntingtown, Maryland 20639

Head of School: Mr. Daniel Hildebrand

General Information Coeducational day college-preparatory, arts, and technology school. Grades PS–12. Founded: 1967. Setting: rural. Nearest major city is Annapolis. 159-acre campus. 3 buildings on campus. Approved or accredited by Association of Independent Maryland Schools, The College Board, and Maryland Department of Education. Member of National Association of Independent Schools. Total enrollment: 416. Upper school average class size: 18. The average school day consists of 7 hours and 20 minutes.

Faculty School total: 49.

Subjects Offered Advanced Placement courses, algebra, American history, American literature, art, art history, biology, calculus, chemistry, Chesapeake Bay studies, chorus, creative writing, drama, economics, English, English literature, environmental science, European civilization, fine arts, French, French-AP, geometry, government/civics, health, humanities, journalism, literature, mathematics, physical education, physics, pre-calculus, public speaking, publications, SAT/ACT preparation, science, social studies, Spanish, Spanish-AP, studio art-AP, theater, trigonometry, U.S. history, U.S. history-AP, visual and performing arts, world civilizations, world history, world literature, yearbook.

Graduation Requirements Algebra, arts and fine arts (art, music, dance, drama), biology, chemistry, English, English composition, English literature, foreign language, geometry, mathematics, physical education (includes health), physics, science, social studies (includes history), trigonometry, U.S. history, world history.

Special Academic Programs Advanced Placement exam preparation; honors section; independent study; ESL (10 students enrolled).

College Admission Counseling 44 students graduated in 2011; all went to college. Median SAT critical reading: 562, median SAT math: 570, median SAT writing: 475, median combined SAT: 1600, median composite ACT: 25. 29% scored over 600 on SAT critical reading, 29% scored over 600 on SAT math, 22% scored over 600 on SAT writing, 14% scored over 1800 on combined SAT, 40% scored over 26 on composite ACT.

Student Life Upper grades have uniform requirement, student council, honor system. Discipline rests equally with students and faculty.

Tuition and Aid Day student tuition: $18,308. Tuition installment plan (Insured Tuition Payment Plan, FACTS Tuition Payment Plan, monthly payment plans, individually arranged payment plans). Need-based scholarship grants available.

Admissions Traditional secondary-level entrance grade is 9. Admissions testing required. Deadline for receipt of application materials: none. Application fee required: $100. On-campus interview required.

Athletics Interscholastic: basketball (boys, girls), cross-country running (b,g), lacrosse (b,g), soccer (b,g); coed interscholastic: field hockey, golf, tennis; coed intramural: basketball. 3 PE instructors, 10 coaches.

Computers Computers are regularly used in all academic classes. Computer network features include on-campus library services, online commercial services, Internet access, Internet filtering or blocking technology, research services and encyclopedia research programs. Student e-mail accounts are available to students.

Contact Mrs. Julie M. Simpson, Director of Admission. 888-678-0216 Ext. 1108. Fax: 410-535-6169. E-mail: jsimpson@CalvertonSchool.org. Web site: www.CalvertonSchool.org

CALVIN CHRISTIAN HIGH SCHOOL

2000 North Broadway
Escondido, California 92026

Head of School: Mr. Terry D. Kok

General Information Coeducational day college-preparatory, arts, and religious studies school, affiliated with Reformed Church, Presbyterian Church. Grades PK–12. Founded: 1980. Setting: suburban. Nearest major city is San Diego. 24-acre campus. 2 buildings on campus. Approved or accredited by Christian Schools International, Western Association of Schools and Colleges, and California Department of Education. Endowment: $830,000. Total enrollment: 491. Upper school average class size: 18. Upper school faculty-student ratio: 1:17. There are 175 required school days per year for Upper School students. Upper School students typically attend 5 days per week. The average school day consists of 6 hours and 25 minutes.

Upper School Student Profile Grade 9: 51 students (27 boys, 24 girls); Grade 10: 44 students (28 boys, 16 girls); Grade 11: 43 students (24 boys, 19 girls); Grade 12: 24 students (11 boys, 13 girls). 35% of students are Reformed, Presbyterian.

Faculty School total: 15. In upper school: 8 men, 7 women; 8 have advanced degrees.

Subjects Offered Advanced Placement courses, algebra, American government, art, band, Bible, biology, biology-AP, business mathematics, calculus-AP, chemistry, choir, Christian doctrine, Christian ethics, Christian studies, church history, computer applications, computer programming, computers, dramatic arts, economics, electives, English, English literature-AP, geometry, health, instrumental music, intro to computers, media, modern history, photography, physical education, physical science, physics, pre-calculus, psychology, robotics, Spanish, Spanish-AP, speech, U.S. history, U.S. history-AP, world history, World War II, yearbook.

Graduation Requirements Advanced Placement courses, arts and fine arts (art, music, dance, drama), English, foreign language, mathematics, media, physical education (includes health), religion (includes Bible studies and theology), science, social studies (includes history), technology, service-learning requirements.

Special Academic Programs 6 Advanced Placement exams for which test preparation is offered; remedial reading and/or remedial writing.

College Admission Counseling 31 students graduated in 2012; all went to college, including California State University, San Marcos; Calvin College; Dordt College; Point Loma Nazarene University; Trinity Christian College; University of California, San Diego. Mean SAT critical reading: 568, mean SAT math: 570, mean SAT writing: 549, mean composite ACT: 24. 43% scored over 600 on SAT critical reading, 36% scored over 600 on SAT math, 29% scored over 600 on SAT writing.

Student Life Upper grades have specified standards of dress, student council, honor system. Discipline rests primarily with faculty. Attendance at religious services is required.

Summer Programs Remediation, advancement, sports programs offered; session focuses on Bible courses and/or athletics; held on campus; accepts boys and girls; open to students from other schools. 60 students usually enrolled. 2013 schedule: June 10 to July 19. Application deadline: May 31.

Tuition and Aid Day student tuition: $8834. Tuition installment plan (monthly payment plans, individually arranged payment plans). Need-based scholarship grants, need-based loans available. In 2012–13, 30% of upper-school students received aid. Total amount of financial aid awarded in 2012–13: $228,000.

Admissions Traditional secondary-level entrance grade is 9. For fall 2012, 31 students applied for upper-level admission, 29 were accepted, 24 enrolled. Deadline for receipt of application materials: none. Application fee required: $300. Interview required.

Athletics Interscholastic: baseball (boys), basketball (b,g), cross-country running (b,g), football (b), soccer (b,g), softball (g), track and field (b,g), volleyball (g); coed interscholastic: golf, in-line hockey; coed intramural: weight training. 2 PE instructors, 16 coaches.

Computers Computers are regularly used in computer applications, keyboarding, photography, programming, science, yearbook classes. Computer network features include on-campus library services, Internet access, wireless campus network, Internet filtering or blocking technology. Student e-mail accounts are available to students. Students grades are available online. The school has a published electronic and media policy.

Contact Mr. Frank Steidl, Principal. 760-489-6430. Fax: 760-489-7055. E-mail: franksteidl@calvinchristianescondido.org. Web site: www.calvinchristianescondido.org

THE CAMBRIDGE SCHOOL OF WESTON

45 Georgian Road
Weston, Massachusetts 02493

Head of School: Jane Moulding

General Information Coeducational boarding and day college-preparatory and arts school. Grades 9–PG. Founded: 1886. Setting: suburban. Nearest major city is Boston. Students are housed in single-sex dormitories. 65-acre campus. 25 buildings on campus. Approved or accredited by Association of Independent Schools in New England, New England Association of Schools and Colleges, The Association of Boarding Schools, and The College Board. Member of National Association of Independent Schools and Secondary School Admission Test Board. Endowment: $7.8 million. Total enrollment: 339. Upper school average class size: 14. Upper school faculty-student ratio: 1:6. There are 160 required school days per year for Upper School students. Upper School students typically attend 5 days per week.

Upper School Student Profile Grade 9: 80 students (34 boys, 46 girls); Grade 10: 81 students (34 boys, 47 girls); Grade 11: 88 students (42 boys, 46 girls); Grade 12: 90 students (37 boys, 53 girls). 25% of students are boarding students. 81% are state residents. 12 states are represented in upper school student body. 12% are international students. International students from China, Hong Kong, Republic of Korea, Taiwan, Thailand, and United Kingdom; 5 other countries represented in student body.

Subjects Offered 20th century physics, 3-dimensional art, acting, Advanced Placement courses, aerospace science, African dance, African history, African literature, African studies, African-American history, African-American literature, African-American studies, algebra, American Civil War, American democracy, American history, American literature, American sign language, analytic geometry, anatomy, anatomy and physiology, animal behavior, animal science, art, art and culture, art history, Asian literature, athletics, backpacking, ballet, ballet technique, baseball, basketball, Bible as literature, biology, botany, calculus, calculus-AP, cell biology, ceramics, chemistry, child development, Chinese history, choir, choreography, chorus, Civil War, collage and assemblage, community service, computer animation, computer math, computer programming, computer science, computer skills, constitutional history of U.S., creative writing, dance, death and loss, digital art, digital photography, discrete mathematics, drama, drama performance, drawing, driver education, earth science, ecology, economics, electronic music, English, English composition, English literature, environmental science, environmental systems, ethics, ethnic literature, European history, European literature, expository writing, fashion, field ecology, film history, film studies, filmmaking, fine arts, foods, French, geography, geometry, government/civics, grammar, great books, Harlem Renaissance, health, health and wellness, history, history of ideas, history of music, history of science, independent study, interdisciplinary studies, Islamic history, Japanese history, jazz, jazz dance, jazz ensemble, jewelry making, journalism, keyboarding, Latin, Latin American history, Latin American literature, leadership education training, literature by women, logic, Mandarin, marine biology, martial arts, mathematical modeling, mathematics, Middle East, model United Nations, music, music theory, musical theater, musicianship, mythology, ornithology, painting, philosophy, photography, physical education, physics, physiology, playwriting, poetry, pre-calculus, printmaking, psychology, religion, Roman civilization, science, sculpture, senior project, set design, Shakespeare, short story, social studies, sociology, Spanish, sports nutrition, stagecraft, statistics, the Presidency, theater, trigonometry, U.S. constitutional history, U.S. history, Vietnam War, weight training, wilderness education, wilderness experience, woodworking, world history, world literature, World War II, writing, yearbook, zoology.

Graduation Requirements Arts and fine arts (art, music, dance, drama), English, foreign language, health education, history, mathematics, performing arts, physical education (includes health), science, senior project. Community service is required.

Special Academic Programs Advanced Placement exam preparation; independent study; term-away projects; study abroad.

College Admission Counseling 92 students graduated in 2011; 91 went to college, including Clark University; Oberlin College; Rhode Island School of Design; Skidmore College; Smith College; The George Washington University. Other: 1 had other specific plans. 69% scored over 600 on SAT critical reading, 72% scored over 600 on SAT math, 77% scored over 600 on SAT writing.

Student Life Upper grades have student council. Discipline rests equally with students and faculty.

Tuition and Aid Day student tuition: $36,400; 7-day tuition and room/board: $47,900. Tuition installment plan (Insured Tuition Payment Plan, Academic Management Services Plan, monthly payment plans, individually arranged payment plans). Tuition reduction for siblings, need-based scholarship grants, paying campus jobs available. In 2011–12, 27% of upper-school students received aid. Total amount of financial aid awarded in 2011–12: $2,598,100.

Admissions Traditional secondary-level entrance grade is 9. For fall 2011, 350 students applied for upper-level admission, 198 were accepted, 89 enrolled. ISEE, PSAT, SAT, SSAT or TOEFL required. Deadline for receipt of application materials: February 1. Application fee required: $50. Interview required.

Athletics Interscholastic: basketball (boys, girls), field hockey (g), lacrosse (g), soccer (b,g); coed interscholastic: baseball, cross-country running, Frisbee, running, tennis, ultimate Frisbee; coed intramural: alpine skiing, backpacking, ballet, bicycling, canoeing/kayaking, climbing, dance, dance team, fencing, fitness, Frisbee, golf, hiking/backpacking, indoor soccer, kayaking, martial arts, modern dance, nordic skiing, outdoor activities, physical fitness, physical training, rafting, rock climbing, running, skateboarding, skiing (downhill), snowboarding, snowshoeing, soccer, strength & conditioning, table tennis, tai chi, tennis, triathlon, ultimate Frisbee, volleyball, weight training, wilderness, yoga.

Computers Computers are regularly used in art, college planning, English, ESL, ethics, French, graphic design, history, humanities, independent study, journalism, keyboarding, Latin, library, literary magazine, mathematics, music, newspaper, photography, programming, psychology, publications, science, Spanish, word processing, writing, yearbook classes. Computer network features include on-campus library services, online commercial services, Internet access, wireless campus network, Internet filtering or blocking technology, laptops available for use in-class. Student e-mail accounts and computer access in designated common areas are available to students. Students grades are available online.

Contact Trish Saunders, Director of Admissions. 781-642-8650. Fax: 781-398-8344. E-mail: admissions@csw.org. Web site: www.csw.org

CAMPBELL HALL (EPISCOPAL)

4533 Laurel Canyon Boulevard
North Hollywood, California 91607

Head of School: Rev. Julian Bull

General Information Coeducational day college-preparatory, arts, and technology school, affiliated with Episcopal Church. Grades K–12. Founded: 1944. Setting: suburban. Nearest major city is Los Angeles. 15-acre campus. 12 buildings on campus. Approved or accredited by California Association of Independent Schools, The College Board, Western Association of Schools and Colleges, and California Department of Education. Member of National Association of Independent Schools. Endowment: $5 million. Total enrollment: 1,085. Upper school average class size: 15. Upper school faculty-student ratio: 1:8. There are 140 required school days per year for Upper School students. Upper School students typically attend 5 days per week. The average school day consists of 7 hours and 15 minutes.

Upper School Student Profile Grade 9: 128 students (64 boys, 64 girls); Grade 10: 134 students (64 boys, 70 girls); Grade 11: 132 students (58 boys, 74 girls); Grade 12: 137 students (66 boys, 71 girls). 7% of students are members of Episcopal Church.

Faculty School total: 110. In upper school: 23 men, 32 women; 30 have advanced degrees.

Subjects Offered Algebra, American history, American literature, American studies, ancient history, art, art history, astronomy, band, biology, calculus, ceramics, chemistry, Chinese, community service, computer programming, computer science, creative writing, dance, drama, drawing, earth science, ecology, economics, English, English literature, environmental science, ethics, European history, filmmaking, fine arts, French, geography, geometry, government/civics, history, human development, humanities, instrumental music, Japanese, law, mathematics, music, orchestra, painting, philosophy, photography, physical education, physics, physiology, pre-calculus, printmaking, psychology, science, sculpture, senior seminar, social studies, sociology, Spanish, speech, statistics, theater, theater arts, trigonometry, voice, yearbook.

Graduation Requirements Arts and fine arts (art, music, dance, drama), computer science, English, foreign language, mathematics, physical education (includes health), science, social studies (includes history). Community service is required.

Special Academic Programs Advanced Placement exam preparation; honors section; independent study; study at local college for college credit.

College Admission Counseling 128 students graduated in 2011; all went to college, including Boston University; New York University; Syracuse University; University of California, Berkeley; University of California, Los Angeles; University of Southern California.

Student Life Upper grades have uniform requirement, student council, honor system. Discipline rests equally with students and faculty. Attendance at religious services is required.

Tuition and Aid Day student tuition: $28,310. Tuition installment plan (Insured Tuition Payment Plan, monthly payment plans, individually arranged payment plans). Need-based scholarship grants, Episcopal Credit Union tuition loans available. In 2011–12, 25% of upper-school students received aid. Total amount of financial aid awarded in 2011–12: $4,000,000.

Admissions Traditional secondary-level entrance grade is 9. ISEE required. Deadline for receipt of application materials: January 27. Application fee required: $125. Interview required.

Athletics Interscholastic: aerobics/dance (boys, girls), ballet (b,g), baseball (b), basketball (b,g), cheering (b,g), cross-country running (b,g), dance (b,g), dance squad (b,g), equestrian sports (b,g), flag football (b,g), football (b), golf (b,g), horseback riding (b,g), modern dance (b,g), soccer (b,g), softball (g), tennis (b,g), track and field (b,g), volleyball (b,g); intramural: weight lifting (b,g); coed interscholastic: aerobics/dance, ballet, cheering, cross-country running, dance, dance squad, golf, horseback riding, modern dance, track and field. 5 PE instructors, 13 coaches, 2 athletic trainers.

Computers Computers are regularly used in art, English, foreign language, history, humanities, mathematics, science, theater arts classes. Computer network features include on-campus library services, online commercial services, Internet access, wireless campus network, Internet filtering or blocking technology. Campus intranet, student e-mail accounts, and computer access in designated common areas are available to students. The school has a published electronic and media policy.

Contact Ms. Alice Fleming, Director of Admissions. 818-980-7280. Fax: 818-762-3269. Web site: www.campbellhall.org

See Display below and Close-Up on page 558.

CAMPHILL SPECIAL SCHOOL

Glenmoore, Pennsylvania

See Special Needs Schools section.

CANNON SCHOOL

5801 Poplar Tent Road
Concord, North Carolina 28027

Head of School: Mr. Matthew Gossage

General Information Coeducational day college-preparatory school. Grades PK–12. Founded: 1969. Setting: suburban. Nearest major city is Charlotte. 65-acre campus. 3 buildings on campus. Approved or accredited by Southern Association of Colleges and Schools, Southern Association of Independent Schools, and North Carolina Department of Education. Member of National Association of Independent Schools. Endowment: $2.8 million. Total enrollment: 905. Upper school average class size: 17. Upper school faculty-student ratio: 1:9.

Faculty School total: 97. In upper school: 18 men, 28 women; 27 have advanced degrees.

Subjects Offered Acting, advanced math, algebra, American history, American history-AP, American literature, anatomy and physiology, biology, biology-AP, British literature, calculus-AP, character education, chemistry, chemistry-AP, Chinese, chorus, college counseling, computer programming-AP, creative writing, dance, directing, discrete mathematics, drawing, English, English language-AP, English literature-AP, environmental science-AP, ethics, film and literature, film history, finance, French, French-AP, functions, geometry, jazz band, law and the legal system, marine science, mathematical modeling, painting, physics, physics-AP, playwriting, poetry, pre-calculus, psychology-AP, publications, sculpture, senior project, Spanish, Spanish language-AP, statistics-AP, strings, studio art-AP, theater design and production, trigonometry, U.S. government and politics-AP, visual arts, weight training, wind ensemble, world history, world literature, world religions, yearbook.

Graduation Requirements Arts and fine arts (art, music, dance, drama), biology, chemistry, computer literacy, English, foreign language, history, mathematics, physical education (includes health), science, senior project, trigonometry, U.S. history. Community service is required.

Special Academic Programs Advanced Placement exam preparation; honors section; independent study.

College Admission Counseling 87 students graduated in 2012; all went to college, including Appalachian State University; Clemson University; Emory University; Furman University; North Carolina State University; The University of North Carolina at Chapel Hill. Mean SAT critical reading: 610, mean SAT math: 624, mean SAT writing: 623, mean combined SAT: 1857, mean composite ACT: 27.

Student Life Upper grades have specified standards of dress, student council, honor system. Discipline rests equally with students and faculty.

Summer Programs Enrichment, sports, art/fine arts, computer instruction programs offered; held on campus; accepts boys and girls; open to students from other schools. 2013 schedule: June 11 to July 27.

Tuition and Aid Day student tuition: $18,170. Tuition installment plan (Insured Tuition Payment Plan, monthly payment plans). Need-based scholarship grants available. In 2012–13, 10% of upper-school students received aid. Total amount of financial aid awarded in 2012–13: $310,000.

Admissions Traditional secondary-level entrance grade is 9. For fall 2012, 79 students applied for upper-level admission, 33 were accepted, 24 enrolled. Admissions testing and ISEE required. Deadline for receipt of application materials: none. Application fee required: $90. On-campus interview required.

Athletics Interscholastic: baseball (boys), basketball (b,g), cheering (g), cross-country running (b,g), dance (g), dance team (g), football (b), golf (b,g), lacrosse (b), physical fitness (b,g), running (b,g), soccer (b,g), softball (g), strength & conditioning (b,g), swimming and diving (b,g), tennis (b,g), track and field (b,g), volleyball (g), weight training (b,g); coed interscholastic: fitness, golf, running, strength & conditioning, track and field, weight training; coed intramural: yoga. 6 PE instructors, 28 coaches, 1 athletic trainer.

Computers Computers are regularly used in all academic, art, music classes. Computer network features include on-campus library services, online commercial services, Internet access, wireless campus network, Internet filtering or blocking technology, productivity software. Campus intranet, student e-mail accounts, and computer access in designated common areas are available to students. Students grades are available online. The school has a published electronic and media policy.

Contact Mr. William D. Diskin, Director of Admission. 704-721-7164. Fax: 704-788-7779. E-mail: wdiskin@cannonschool.org. Web site: www.cannonschool.org

THE CANTERBURY EPISCOPAL SCHOOL

1708 North Westmoreland Road
DeSoto, Texas 75115

Head of School: Mr. Sandy Doerge

General Information Coeducational day college-preparatory school, affiliated with Episcopal Church. Grades K–12. Founded: 1992. Setting: suburban. Nearest major city is Dallas. 36-acre campus. 2 buildings on campus. Approved or accredited by Southwest Association of Episcopal Schools, Tennessee Association of Independent Schools, and Texas Department of Education. Member of National Association of Independent Schools. Total enrollment: 251. Upper school average class size: 11. Upper school faculty-student ratio: 1:11. There are 173 required school days per year for Upper School students. Upper School students typically attend 5 days per week. The average school day consists of 6 hours and 50 minutes.

Upper School Student Profile Grade 9: 28 students (16 boys, 12 girls); Grade 10: 20 students (11 boys, 9 girls); Grade 11: 22 students (15 boys, 7 girls); Grade 12: 10 students (1 boy, 9 girls). 5% of students are members of Episcopal Church.

Faculty School total: 36. In upper school: 8 men, 11 women; 9 have advanced degrees.

Subjects Offered 1 1/2 elective credits, advanced chemistry, Advanced Placement courses, algebra, American government, American literature, anatomy and physiology, art history-AP, athletics, basketball, biology, biology-AP, calculus, calculus-AP, cheerleading, chemistry, chemistry-AP, college counseling, comparative religion, computer applications, debate, economics, English composition, English language and composition-AP, English literature, English literature and composition-AP, environmental science-AP, European history-AP, fine arts, foreign language, geometry, government, health, math applications, music, personal money management, physics-AP, psychology-AP, Spanish, speech, studio art, theology, U.S. history, U.S. history-AP, visual and performing arts, world geography, world history, yearbook.

Graduation Requirements 1 1/2 elective credits, algebra, anatomy and physiology, arts and fine arts (art, music, dance, drama), biology, calculus, chemistry, computer applications, economics, English, English composition, English language and composition-AP, English literature, European history, foreign language, geometry, government, health, math applications, physical education (includes health), physics, precalculus, religion (includes Bible studies and theology), speech, trigonometry, U.S. history, world geography, Senior Thesis in English IV.

Special Academic Programs 9 Advanced Placement exams for which test preparation is offered; honors section; independent study; study at local college for college credit.

College Admission Counseling 23 students graduated in 2012; all went to college. Median SAT critical reading: 574, median SAT math: 553, median SAT writing: 574, median combined SAT: 1686, median composite ACT: 25. 35% scored over 600 on SAT critical reading, 18% scored over 600 on SAT math, 41% scored over 600 on SAT writing, 29% scored over 1800 on combined SAT, 33% scored over 26 on composite ACT.

Student Life Upper grades have uniform requirement, student council, honor system. Discipline rests primarily with faculty. Attendance at religious services is required.

Summer Programs Enrichment, sports programs offered; session focuses on providing programs based on the needs of our student population; held on campus; accepts boys and girls; open to students from other schools. 80 students usually enrolled. 2013 schedule: June 3 to August 12. Application deadline: May 10.

Tuition and Aid Day student tuition: $14,932. Tuition installment plan (FACTS Tuition Payment Plan, individually arranged payment plans). Tuition reduction for siblings, need-based scholarship grants available. In 2012–13, 45% of upper-school students received aid.

Admissions Traditional secondary-level entrance grade is 9. For fall 2012, 15 students applied for upper-level admission, 12 were accepted, 9 enrolled. OLSAT, Stanford Achievement Test required. Deadline for receipt of application materials: none. Application fee required: $150. Interview required.

Athletics Interscholastic: baseball (boys), basketball (b,g), cheering (g), golf (b), softball (g), volleyball (g); intramural: flag football (b); coed interscholastic: soccer, swimming and diving, tennis, track and field. 1 PE instructor, 1 coach, 1 athletic trainer.

Computers Computers are regularly used in computer applications, yearbook classes. Computer resources include Internet access, Internet filtering or blocking technology. Computer access in designated common areas is available to students. Students grades are available online.

Contact Mrs. Libby Conder, Director of Admissions and Development. 972-572-7200 Ext. 106. Fax: 972-572-2470. E-mail: ConderL@TheCanterburySchool.org. Web site: www.thecanterburyschool.org/

CANTERBURY SCHOOL

8141 College Parkway
Fort Myers, Florida 33919

Head of School: Mr. John Anthony (Tony) Paulus II

General Information Coeducational day college-preparatory and liberal arts school. Grades PK–12. Founded: 1964. Setting: suburban. Nearest major city is Fort Myers-Sarasota. 33-acre campus. 7 buildings on campus. Approved or accredited by Council of Accreditation and School Improvement, Florida Council of Independent Schools, Southern Association of Colleges and Schools, Southern Association of Independent Schools, The College Board, and Florida Department of Education. Member of National Association of Independent Schools and Secondary School Admission Test Board. Endowment: $7.1 million. Total enrollment: 580. Upper school average class size: 18. Upper school faculty-student ratio: 1:10. There are 181 required school days per year for Upper School students. Upper School students typically attend 5 days per week. The average school day consists of 7 hours and 10 minutes.

Upper School Student Profile Grade 9: 62 students (36 boys, 26 girls); Grade 10: 54 students (23 boys, 31 girls); Grade 11: 46 students (21 boys, 25 girls); Grade 12: 37 students (18 boys, 19 girls).

Faculty School total: 95. In upper school: 21 men, 19 women; 22 have advanced degrees.

Subjects Offered Advanced Placement courses, algebra, American history, American history-AP, American literature, anatomy, art, art history, biology, biology-AP, British literature, calculus, calculus-AP, ceramics, chemistry, chemistry-AP, comparative government and politics-AP, computer programming, constitutional law, creative writing, critical writing, drama, earth science, ecology, economics, English, English literature, English literature-AP, environmental science-AP, European history, fine arts, French, French language-AP, geography, geometry, government-AP, government/civics, grammar, health, history, Latin, leadership, macroeconomics-AP, marine biology, mathematics, music, nationalism and ethnic conflict, photography, physical education, physics, physics-AP, physiology, SAT preparation, science, social studies, sociology, Spanish, Spanish language-AP, speech, statistics, theater, U.S. government and politics-AP, U.S. history, United Nations and international issues, world history, world literature, writing, yearbook.

Graduation Requirements Arts and fine arts (art, music, dance, drama), English, foreign language, mathematics, physical education (includes health), science, social studies (includes history), speech. Community service is required.

Special Academic Programs 15 Advanced Placement exams for which test preparation is offered; independent study; study at local college for college credit.

College Admission Counseling 37 students graduated in 2012; all went to college, including Boston College; Harvard University; University of Florida; University of Miami; University of Pennsylvania; University of South Florida. Mean SAT critical reading: 630, mean SAT math: 620, mean SAT writing: 630, mean combined SAT: 1850, mean composite ACT: 27.

Student Life Upper grades have specified standards of dress, student council, honor system. Discipline rests primarily with faculty.

Summer Programs Remediation, enrichment, advancement, sports, art/fine arts programs offered; session focuses on academic enrichment; held on campus; accepts boys and girls; open to students from other schools. 125 students usually enrolled. 2013 schedule: June 14 to July 30. Application deadline: none.

Tuition and Aid Day student tuition: $18,550. Tuition installment plan (Insured Tuition Payment Plan, monthly payment plans, individually arranged payment plans, quarterly payment plan). Merit scholarship grants, need-based scholarship grants available. In 2012–13, 25% of upper-school students received aid; total upper-school merit-scholarship money awarded: $274,100. Total amount of financial aid awarded in 2012–13: $782,050.

Admissions Traditional secondary-level entrance grade is 9. For fall 2012, 35 students applied for upper-level admission, 24 were accepted, 17 enrolled. ERB CTP IV or SSAT required. Deadline for receipt of application materials: none. Application fee required: $75. Interview required.

Athletics Interscholastic: baseball (boys), basketball (b,g), cheering (g), football (b), lacrosse (b,g), soccer (b,g), volleyball (g), winter soccer (b,g); intramural: volleyball (b); coed interscholastic: cross-country running, golf, swimming and diving, tennis, track and field. 6 PE instructors, 26 coaches.

Computers Computers are regularly used in art, college planning, English, foreign language, French, history, independent study, journalism, Latin, library, mathematics, science, social sciences, Spanish, speech, theater arts, yearbook classes. Computer network features include on-campus library services, Internet access, wireless campus network, Internet filtering or blocking technology. Campus intranet, student e-mail accounts, and computer access in designated common areas are available to students.

Students grades are available online. The school has a published electronic and media policy.

Contact Ms. Julie A. Peters, Director of Admission. 239-415-8945. Fax: 239-481-8339. E-mail: jpeters@canterburyfortmyers.org. Web site: www.canterburyfortmyers.org

See Display below and Close-Up on page 560.

THE CANTERBURY SCHOOL OF FLORIDA

990 62nd Avenue NE
St. Petersburg, Florida 33702

Head of School: Mr. Mac H. Hall

General Information Coeducational day college-preparatory, arts, and marine studies, international program school, affiliated with Episcopal Church. Grades PK–12. Founded: 1968. Setting: suburban. 20-acre campus. 5 buildings on campus. Approved or accredited by Florida Council of Independent Schools, The College Board, and Florida Department of Education. Member of National Association of Independent Schools. Endowment: $90,000. Total enrollment: 433. Upper school average class size: 15. Upper school faculty-student ratio: 1:7. There are 180 required school days per year for Upper School students. Upper School students typically attend 5 days per week. The average school day consists of 7 hours and 23 minutes.

Upper School Student Profile Grade 9: 41 students (18 boys, 23 girls); Grade 10: 39 students (26 boys, 13 girls); Grade 11: 49 students (23 boys, 26 girls); Grade 12: 36 students (13 boys, 23 girls). 5% of students are members of Episcopal Church.

Faculty School total: 56. In upper school: 8 men, 21 women; 23 have advanced degrees.

Subjects Offered 20th century world history, advanced computer applications, Advanced Placement courses, advanced studio art-AP, algebra, American government, American history-AP, American literature, anatomy, Ancient Greek, ancient world history, art, art history, art history-AP, astronomy, athletics, band, Basic programming, biology, biology-AP, British literature, British literature (honors), calculus, calculus-AP, career exploration, ceramics, character education, chemistry, chemistry-AP, choir, choral music, chorus, classical language, classical studies, college counseling, college placement, communication skills, community service, comparative government and politics-AP, competitive science projects, computer multimedia, computer science, computer science-AP, computer skills, contemporary issues, creative writing, critical thinking, dance, dance performance, digital imaging, drama, earth science, economics, economics-AP, English, English composition, English language and composition-AP, English literature, English literature and composition-AP, English literature-AP, environmental science, environmental science-AP, environmental studies, ethics, European history, expository writing, film studies, fine arts, finite math, foreign language, French, French-AP, freshman seminar, geography, geometry, golf, government and politics-AP, government/civics, grammar, Greek culture, guitar, health, history, history of music, history-AP, honors algebra, honors geometry, honors U.S. history, honors world history, human geography - AP, independent living, interdisciplinary studies, journalism, keyboarding, Latin, Latin-AP, leadership, leadership and service, library, library research, library skills, life management skills, life science, life skills, macro/microeconomics-AP, macroeconomics-AP, Mandarin, marine biology, marine ecology, marine science, marine studies, mathematics, mathematics-AP, mechanical drawing, mentorship program, modern world history, multimedia, music, musical productions, musical theater, oceanography, outdoor education, personal and social education, personal fitness, photojournalism, physical education, physical science, physics, physics-AP, play production, portfolio art, pottery, prayer/spirituality, pre-algebra, pre-calculus, pre-college orientation, psychology, psychology-AP, reading/study skills, robotics, SAT preparation, SAT/ACT preparation, science, senior composition, senior seminar, senior thesis, Shakespeare, social sciences, social studies, Spanish, Spanish language-AP, Spanish literature-AP, Spanish-AP, speech, speech and debate, sports conditioning, stagecraft, statistics-AP, student government, student publications, student teaching, studio art-AP, swimming, technical theater, tennis, theater arts, theater design and production, theater history, theater production, track and field, typing, U.S. history, U.S. history-AP, values and decisions, visual and performing arts, volleyball, weight fitness, weight training, Western philosophy, world history, world literature, world religions, yearbook, yoga.

Graduation Requirements Arts and fine arts (art, music, dance, drama), career/college preparation, electives, English, ethics, foreign language, history, mathematics, physical education (includes health), research, science, senior seminar, writing, research and writing, miniterms, character education. Community service is required.

Special Academic Programs 23 Advanced Placement exams for which test preparation is offered; honors section; independent study; term-away projects; study at local college for college credit; study abroad.

College Admission Counseling 33 students graduated in 2012; all went to college, including Columbia University; Savannah College of Art and Design; Southern Methodist University; University of Florida; Washington and Lee University. Median combined SAT: 1660, median composite ACT: 23.

Student Life Upper grades have specified standards of dress, student council, honor system. Discipline rests equally with students and faculty.

Summer Programs Remediation, enrichment, advancement, sports, art/fine arts, computer instruction programs offered; session focuses on multi-discipline skills and abilities; held on campus; accepts boys and girls; open to students from other schools. 50 students usually enrolled. 2013 schedule: June 8 to August 7. Application deadline: March 15.

Tuition and Aid Day student tuition: $16,500–$17,100. Tuition installment plan (Insured Tuition Payment Plan, monthly payment plans, individually arranged payment plans). Tuition reduction for siblings, need-based scholarship grants available. In 2012–13, 20% of upper-school students received aid. Total amount of financial aid awarded in 2012–13: $588,000.

Admissions Traditional secondary-level entrance grade is 9. For fall 2012, 50 students applied for upper-level admission, 32 were accepted, 25 enrolled. 3-R Achievement Test, any standardized test, ERB, SSAT or TOEFL required. Deadline for receipt of application materials: none. Application fee required: $75. On-campus interview required.

Athletics Interscholastic: baseball (boys), basketball (b,g), cross-country running (b,g), dance (g), dance team (g), diving (b,g), football (b), golf (b,g), soccer (b,g), softball (g), swimming and diving (b,g), tennis (b,g), track and field (b,g), volleyball (g); intramural: yoga (g); coed interscholastic: cheering, soccer; coed intramural: canoeing/kayaking, fitness, flag football, floor hockey, hiking/backpacking, kayaking, kickball, modern dance, outdoor activities, outdoor adventure, outdoor education, paddle tennis, physical fitness, ropes courses, running, scuba diving, strength & conditioning, ultimate Frisbee, weight training. 2 PE instructors, 21 coaches, 1 athletic trainer.

Computers Computers are regularly used in all academic classes. Computer network features include on-campus library services, online commercial services, Internet access, wireless campus network, Internet filtering or blocking technology, iPad program for grades 3, 4 and 6 (each child receives an iPad). Computer access in designated common areas is available to students. Students grades are available online. The school has a published electronic and media policy.

Contact Mrs. Michelle Robinson, Director of Admission. 727-521-5903. Fax: 727-525-2545. E-mail: mrobinson@canterbury-fl.org. Web site: www.canterburyflorida.org

CANTON ACADEMY

Post Office Box 116
One Nancy Drive
Canton, Mississippi 39046

Head of School: Mr. Phil Hannon

General Information Coeducational day college-preparatory, arts, and religious studies school; primarily serves individuals with Attention Deficit Disorder and dyslexic students. Grades 6–12. Founded: 1965. Setting: small town. Nearest major city is Jackson. 1 building on campus. Approved or accredited by Mississippi Private School Association, Southern Association of Independent Schools, and Mississippi Department of Education. Total enrollment: 333. Upper school average class size: 17. Upper school faculty-student ratio: 1:17. There are 175 required school days per year for Upper School students. Upper School students typically attend 5 days per week. The average school day consists of 7 hours and 20 minutes.

Faculty School total: 60. In upper school: 6 men, 7 women.

Graduation Requirements Accounting, advanced biology, community service hours.

Special Academic Programs Honors section; independent study; study at local college for college credit; academic accommodation for the gifted; remedial reading and/or remedial writing; remedial math; programs in English, mathematics for dyslexic students.

College Admission Counseling 32 students graduated in 2012; all went to college, including Delta State University; Millsaps College; Mississippi College; Mississippi State University; University of Mississippi; University of Southern Mississippi.

Student Life Upper grades have specified standards of dress, student council, honor system. Discipline rests primarily with faculty. Attendance at religious services is required.

Summer Programs Remediation programs offered; session focuses on remediation make-up, advancement; held on campus; accepts boys and girls; open to students from other schools. 25 students usually enrolled. 2013 schedule: May 25 to July 31. Application deadline: May 15.

Tuition and Aid Tuition installment plan (monthly payment plans, individually arranged payment plans). Tuition reduction for siblings, need-based scholarship grants, paying campus jobs available. In 2012–13, 18% of upper-school students received aid. Total amount of financial aid awarded in 2012–13: $64,000.

Admissions Traditional secondary-level entrance grade is 10. For fall 2012, 15 students applied for upper-level admission, 13 were accepted, 13 enrolled. Comprehensive Test of Basic Skills required. Deadline for receipt of application materials: January 26. Application fee required: $35. Interview recommended.

Athletics Interscholastic: aerobics/dance (girls), archery (b,g), baseball (b,g), basketball (b,g), cheering (g), combined training (b,g), cross-country running (b,g), dance team (g), equestrian sports (b,g), football (b), golf (b), horseback riding (b,g), jogging (b,g), power lifting (b), running (b,g), soccer (b,g), softball (g), swimming and diving (b,g), tennis (b,g), track and field (b,g), weight training (b,g). 2 PE instructors, 8 coaches, 2 athletic trainers.

Computers Computer resources include Internet access. Campus intranet and student e-mail accounts are available to students. Students grades are available online. The school has a published electronic and media policy.

Contact Ms. Laura Pitre, Admissions. 601-859-5231. Fax: 601-859-5232. E-mail: lpitre@cantonacademy.org. Web site: www.cantonacademy.org

CANYONVILLE CHRISTIAN ACADEMY

PO Box 1100
Canyonville, Oregon 97417-1100

Head of School: Mrs. Cathy Lovato

General Information Coeducational boarding and day college-preparatory, general academic, religious studies, and English for Speakers of Other Languages school, affiliated with Christian faith. Grades 9–12. Founded: 1924. Setting: rural. Nearest major city is Medford. Students are housed in single-sex dormitories. 10-acre campus. 11 buildings on campus. Approved or accredited by Association of Christian Schools International, Northwest Accreditation Commission, The Association of Boarding Schools, and Oregon Department of Education. Upper school average class size: 20. Upper school faculty-student ratio: 1:9. There are 180 required school days per year for Upper School students. Upper School students typically attend 5 days per week. The average school day consists of 7 hours.

Upper School Student Profile Grade 9: 13 students (8 boys, 5 girls); Grade 10: 33 students (16 boys, 17 girls); Grade 11: 43 students (27 boys, 16 girls); Grade 12: 35 students (25 boys, 10 girls). 90% of students are boarding students. 10% are state residents. 4 states are represented in upper school student body. 85% are international students. International students from China, Colombia, Hong Kong, Russian Federation, Rwanda, and Taiwan; 6 other countries represented in student body. 70% of students are Christian faith.

Faculty School total: 14. In upper school: 6 men, 8 women; 3 have advanced degrees; 4 reside on campus.

Subjects Offered Advanced Placement courses, aerobics, algebra, American culture, American history, art, Bible, biology, calculus, calculus-AP, career/college preparation, chemistry, choir, Christian doctrine, composition, computer education, computer technologies, computers, consumer economics, desktop publishing, digital art, economics, English, English literature, ESL, foreign language, French as a second language, general science, government, grammar, health, integrative seminar, keyboarding, language and composition, library assistant, Life of Christ, mathematics, New Testament, physical education, physical science, physics, pre-calculus, religious education, Spanish, speech and debate, theology, U.S. government, U.S. history, United States government-AP, world history.

Graduation Requirements 1 1/2 elective credits, algebra, arts and fine arts (art, music, dance, drama), Bible, biology, economics, English, foreign language, government, health and wellness, mathematics, physical education (includes health), physical science, speech and debate, U.S. history, world history.

Special Academic Programs Advanced Placement exam preparation; honors section; accelerated programs; independent study; study at local college for college credit; ESL (50 students enrolled).

College Admission Counseling 30 students graduated in 2012; 25 went to college, including Oregon State University; Sarah Lawrence College; University of Illinois at Urbana–Champaign; University of Oregon; Washington State University. Other: 1 entered military service, 2 had other specific plans. Mean SAT critical reading: 421, mean SAT math: 571, mean SAT writing: 411, mean combined SAT: 1403.

Student Life Upper grades have specified standards of dress, student council, honor system. Discipline rests primarily with faculty. Attendance at religious services is required.

Tuition and Aid Day student tuition: $4600; 7-day tuition and room/board: $24,500. Tuition installment plan (monthly payment plans, individually arranged payment plans). Tuition reduction for siblings, merit scholarship grants, need-based scholarship grants, paying campus jobs available. In 2012–13, 15% of upper-school students received aid. Total amount of financial aid awarded in 2012–13: $390,000.

Admissions Traditional secondary-level entrance grade is 9. TOEFL or SLEP required. Deadline for receipt of application materials: none. Application fee required: $100. Interview recommended.

Athletics Interscholastic: basketball (boys, girls), cheering (g), cross-country running (b,g), soccer (b), tennis (b,g), track and field (b,g), volleyball (g); intramural: aerobics (g), soccer (b); coed interscholastic: soccer, tennis; coed intramural: badminton, basketball, billiards, table tennis, tennis, volleyball. 3 PE instructors, 9 coaches.

Computers Computers are regularly used in business applications, drawing and design, technology, yearbook classes. Computer network features include Internet access, wireless campus network, Internet filtering or blocking technology. Student e-mail accounts and computer access in designated common areas are available to students. Students grades are available online.

Contact Mr. Ed Lovato, Director of Admissions. 541-839-4401. Fax: 541-839-6228. E-mail: admissions@canyonville.net. Web site: www.canyonville.net

CAPE COD ACADEMY

50 Osterville-West Barnstable Road
Osterville, Massachusetts 02655

Head of School: Mr. Philip Petru

General Information Coeducational day college-preparatory, arts, and technology school. Grades PK–12. Founded: 1976. Setting: small town. Nearest major city is Boston. 47-acre campus. 5 buildings on campus. Approved or accredited by Association of Independent Schools in New England and New England Association of Schools and Colleges. Member of National Association of Independent Schools and Secondary

School Admission Test Board. Endowment: $2.2 million. Total enrollment: 317. Upper school average class size: 13. Upper school faculty-student ratio: 1:4. There are 172 required school days per year for Upper School students. Upper School students typically attend 5 days per week. The average school day consists of 6 hours and 30 minutes.

Upper School Student Profile Grade 9: 25 students (12 boys, 13 girls); Grade 10: 30 students (14 boys, 16 girls); Grade 11: 56 students (30 boys, 26 girls); Grade 12: 44 students (25 boys, 19 girls).

Faculty School total: 52. In upper school: 19 men, 20 women; 28 have advanced degrees.

Subjects Offered Advanced biology, advanced chemistry, advanced math, Advanced Placement courses, advanced studio art-AP, algebra, American history, American literature, art, art history, art history-AP, art-AP, biology, calculus, calculus-AP, ceramics, chemistry, chemistry-AP, community service, computer math, computer programming, computer science, digital photography, drama, earth science, English, English literature, English-AP, environmental science, ethics, European history, expository writing, fine arts, French, French-AP, geography, geometry, health, history, history-AP, honors algebra, honors geometry, Latin, mathematics, music, music composition, music history, music theory, philosophy, photography, physical education, physics, SAT preparation, science, senior internship, social sciences, social studies, Spanish, Spanish-AP, statistics-AP, studio art-AP, theater, trigonometry, world history, world literature.

Graduation Requirements Arts and fine arts (art, music, dance, drama), computer science, English, foreign language, history, independent study, mathematics, physical education (includes health), science. Community service is required.

Special Academic Programs 10 Advanced Placement exams for which test preparation is offered; honors section; independent study; term-away projects; study abroad.

College Admission Counseling 27 students graduated in 2012; all went to college, including Boston College; Boston University; Roger Williams University; University of Massachusetts Amherst; University of Pennsylvania; Wheaton College. Mean SAT critical reading: 600, mean SAT math: 620.

Student Life Upper grades have specified standards of dress, student council, honor system. Discipline rests primarily with faculty.

Tuition and Aid Day student tuition: $20,180–$24,320. Tuition installment plan (Academic Management Services Plan, SMART Tuition Payment Plan, monthly payment plans, individually arranged payment plans). Need-based scholarship grants available. In 2012–13, 40% of upper-school students received aid. Total amount of financial aid awarded in 2012–13: $1,600,000.

Admissions Traditional secondary-level entrance grade is 9. ISEE or SSAT required. Deadline for receipt of application materials: February 1. Application fee required: $95. On-campus interview required.

Athletics Interscholastic: baseball (boys), basketball (b,g), lacrosse (b,g), soccer (b,g), tennis (b,g); coed interscholastic: cross-country running, golf, ice hockey, sailing; coed intramural: aerobics, aerobics/Nautilus, archery, basketball, combined training, fitness, floor hockey, physical training, sailing, soccer, strength & conditioning, weight training. 1 PE instructor, 11 coaches, 1 athletic trainer.

Computers Computers are regularly used in all academic classes. Computer network features include on-campus library services, online commercial services, Internet access, wireless campus network, Internet filtering or blocking technology. Campus intranet, student e-mail accounts, and computer access in designated common areas are available to students. Students grades are available online. The school has a published electronic and media policy.

Contact Laurie Wyndham, Director of Admissions. 508-428-5400 Ext. 226. Fax: 508-428-0701. E-mail: lwyndham@capecodacademy.org. Web site: www.capecodacademy.org

CAPE FEAR ACADEMY

3900 South College Road
Wilmington, North Carolina 28412

Head of School: Mr. Donald Berger

General Information Coeducational day college-preparatory and arts school. Grades PK–12. Founded: 1967. Setting: suburban. 27-acre campus. 4 buildings on campus. Approved or accredited by Southern Association of Colleges and Schools, Southern Association of Independent Schools, and North Carolina Department of Education. Member of National Association of Independent Schools. Endowment: $637,600. Total enrollment: 601. Upper school average class size: 17. Upper school faculty-student ratio: 1:8. There are 177 required school days per year for Upper School students. Upper School students typically attend 5 days per week. The average school day consists of 7 hours and 20 minutes.

Upper School Student Profile Grade 9: 58 students (27 boys, 31 girls); Grade 10: 55 students (24 boys, 31 girls); Grade 11: 60 students (26 boys, 34 girls); Grade 12: 65 students (33 boys, 32 girls).

Faculty School total: 76. In upper school: 13 men, 17 women; 15 have advanced degrees.

Subjects Offered 3-dimensional art, Advanced Placement courses, algebra, American history, American history-AP, American literature, analysis, art, art history, band, biology, biology-AP, British literature, calculus-AP, chemistry, choral music, comparative government and politics-AP, computer science, conceptual physics, critical studies in film, discrete mathematics, drama, earth and space science, English, English language-AP, English literature, English literature-AP, environmental science, environmental science-AP, European history, European history-AP, film studies, finance, fine arts, fitness, geometry, global studies, government and politics-AP, government-AP, history, honors geometry, human anatomy, independent study, journalism, language, literature, marine science, mathematics, music, music theory-AP, musical theater, newspaper, organizational studies, photography, physical education, physics, pre-calculus, psychology, publications, religion, SAT preparation, science, sculpture, social studies, Spanish, student publications, theater, video film production, vocal ensemble, weight training, world history.

Graduation Requirements Arts and fine arts (art, music, dance, drama), biology, English, foreign language, mathematics, physical education (includes health), science, social studies (includes history), U.S. government, U.S. history, 72 hours of community service over 4 years. Community service is required.

Special Academic Programs 11 Advanced Placement exams for which test preparation is offered; honors section; independent study; study at local college for college credit; study abroad.

College Admission Counseling 56 students graduated in 2012; all went to college, including East Carolina University; North Carolina State University; The University of North Carolina at Chapel Hill; The University of North Carolina Wilmington. Mean combined SAT: 1742, mean composite ACT: 26.

Student Life Upper grades have specified standards of dress, student council, honor system. Discipline rests primarily with faculty.

Summer Programs Enrichment, sports, art/fine arts programs offered; session focuses on enrichment and sports; held on campus; accepts boys and girls; open to students from other schools. 250 students usually enrolled. 2013 schedule: June 11 to August 10. Application deadline: none.

Tuition and Aid Day student tuition: $14,720. Tuition installment plan (Insured Tuition Payment Plan, FACTS Tuition Payment Plan, monthly payment plans). Merit scholarship grants, need-based scholarship grants available. In 2012–13, 25% of upper-school students received aid; total upper-school merit-scholarship money awarded: $3500. Total amount of financial aid awarded in 2012–13: $320,000.

Admissions Traditional secondary-level entrance grade is 9. ERB, ISEE, PSAT or SAT or SSAT required. Deadline for receipt of application materials: none. Application fee required: $75. On-campus interview recommended.

Athletics Interscholastic: basketball (boys, girls), cheering (g), field hockey (g), lacrosse (b,g), soccer (b,g), tennis (b,g), volleyball (g); coed interscholastic: cross-country running, golf, outdoor education, outdoor recreation, surfing, swimming and diving. 2 PE instructors, 11 coaches, 1 athletic trainer.

Computers Computers are regularly used in all academic classes. Computer network features include on-campus library services, online commercial services, Internet access, wireless campus network, Internet filtering or blocking technology. Campus intranet, student e-mail accounts, and computer access in designated common areas are available to students. Students grades are available online. The school has a published electronic and media policy.

Contact Mrs. Carla Whitwell, Director of Admission. 910-791-0287 Ext. 1015. Fax: 910-791-0290. E-mail: cwhitwell@capefearacademy.org. Web site: www.capefearacademy.org

CAPE HENRY COLLEGIATE SCHOOL

1320 Mill Dam Road
Virginia Beach, Virginia 23454-2306

Head of School: Dr. John P. Lewis

General Information Coeducational day college-preparatory, arts, technology, and global education school. Grades PK–12. Founded: 1924. Setting: suburban. 30-acre campus. 9 buildings on campus. Approved or accredited by Southern Association of Independent Schools and Virginia Association of Independent Schools. Member of National Association of Independent Schools. Endowment: $6 million. Total enrollment: 835. Upper school average class size: 14. Upper school faculty-student ratio: 1:10. There are 176 required school days per year for Upper School students. Upper School students typically attend 5 days per week. The average school day consists of 7 hours and 20 minutes.

Upper School Student Profile Grade 9: 86 students (38 boys, 48 girls); Grade 10: 104 students (60 boys, 44 girls); Grade 11: 87 students (44 boys, 43 girls); Grade 12: 94 students (55 boys, 39 girls).

Faculty School total: 107. In upper school: 19 men, 23 women; 28 have advanced degrees.

Subjects Offered Algebra, American history, American literature, art, art history, biology, botany, business skills, calculus, ceramics, chemistry, community service, computer programming, computer science, creative writing, drama, driver education, earth science, ecology, economics, English, English literature, environmental science, European history, expository writing, fine arts, French, geography, geology, geometry, government/civics, health, history, journalism, Latin, law, marine biology, mathematics, music, oceanography, photography, physical education, physics, science, social sciences, social studies, sociology, Spanish, speech, statistics, theater, trigonometry, world history, world literature, writing.

Graduation Requirements Arts and fine arts (art, music, dance, drama), computer science, English, foreign language, mathematics, physical education (includes health), science, social sciences, social studies (includes history). Community service is required.

Special Academic Programs Advanced Placement exam preparation; honors section; independent study; academic accommodation for the gifted, the musically talented, and the artistically talented; ESL (10 students enrolled).

College Admission Counseling 96 students graduated in 2012; 69 went to college, including Hampden-Sydney College; James Madison University; The College of William and Mary; University of Virginia; Virginia Polytechnic Institute and State University; Washington and Lee University.

Student Life Upper grades have specified standards of dress, student council, honor system. Discipline rests equally with students and faculty.

Summer Programs Enrichment, advancement, ESL, sports, art/fine arts, computer instruction programs offered; session focuses on academics and enrichment; held on campus; accepts boys and girls; open to students from other schools. 1,200 students usually enrolled. 2013 schedule: June 8 to August 14. Application deadline: none.

Tuition and Aid Day student tuition: $17,995. Tuition installment plan (The Tuition Plan, Insured Tuition Payment Plan, monthly payment plans, individually arranged payment plans, 3-payment plan). Merit scholarship grants, need-based scholarship grants available. In 2012–13, 20% of upper-school students received aid.

Admissions Traditional secondary-level entrance grade is 9. For fall 2012, 99 students applied for upper-level admission, 77 were accepted, 54 enrolled. Brigance Test of Basic Skills, ERB CTP, ISEE or writing sample required. Deadline for receipt of application materials: February 15. Application fee required: $50. On-campus interview required.

Athletics Interscholastic: baseball (boys), basketball (b,g), crew (b,g), cross-country running (b,g), field hockey (g), golf (b,g), lacrosse (b,g), soccer (b,g), softball (g), tennis (b,g), volleyball (b,g), wrestling (b); intramural: baseball (b), basketball (b,g), crew (b,g), cross-country running (b,g), field hockey (g), floor hockey (b,g), wrestling (b); coed interscholastic: cheering, swimming and diving, track and field; coed intramural: aerobics, aerobics/dance, aerobics/Nautilus, archery, backpacking, badminton, ballet, cheering, dance, fishing, fitness, fitness walking, golf, hiking/backpacking, jogging, kayaking, lacrosse, modern dance, ocean paddling, outdoor activities, outdoor adventure, physical fitness, physical training, skiing (downhill), snowboarding, soccer, strength & conditioning, surfing, swimming and diving, table tennis, tennis, volleyball, weight lifting, weight training, wilderness, yoga. 3 PE instructors, 25 coaches, 1 athletic trainer.

Computers Computers are regularly used in computer applications, desktop publishing, graphic arts, information technology, literary magazine, newspaper, publications, technology, video film production, Web site design, word processing, yearbook classes. Computer network features include on-campus library services, online commercial services, Internet access, wireless campus network, Internet filtering or blocking technology. Student e-mail accounts and computer access in designated common areas are available to students. Students grades are available online. The school has a published electronic and media policy.

Contact Mrs. Angie Finley, Admissions Associate. 757-963-8234. Fax: 757-481-9194. E-mail: angiefinley@capehenry.org. Web site: www.capehenrycollegiate.org

CAPISTRANO VALLEY CHRISTIAN SCHOOLS

32032 Del Obispo Street
San Juan Capistrano, California 92675

Head of School: Dr. Ron Sipus

General Information Coeducational day college-preparatory, arts, business, vocational, religious studies, bilingual studies, and technology school, affiliated with Christian faith. Grades JK–12. Founded: 1972. Setting: suburban. 8-acre campus. 2 buildings on campus. Approved or accredited by Association of Christian Schools International, Western Association of Schools and Colleges, and California Department of Education. Total enrollment: 456. Upper school average class size: 18. Upper school faculty-student ratio: 1:13. There are 180 required school days per year for Upper School students. Upper School students typically attend 5 days per week. The average school day consists of 6 hours.

Upper School Student Profile Grade 9: 41 students (26 boys, 15 girls); Grade 10: 39 students (19 boys, 20 girls); Grade 11: 56 students (28 boys, 28 girls); Grade 12: 56 students (29 boys, 27 girls). 80% of students are Christian faith.

Faculty School total: 50. In upper school: 15 men, 18 women; 9 have advanced degrees.

Subjects Offered ACT preparation, advanced biology, advanced chemistry, advanced computer applications, advanced math, Advanced Placement courses, advanced TOEFL/grammar, algebra, American government, American history, American history-AP, American literature, American literature-AP, anatomy, art, ASB Leadership, athletic training, athletics, Bible, Bible studies, biology, biology-AP, business, business applications, business communications, business education, business law, business skills, business studies, calculus, calculus-AP, career planning, chemistry, Chinese, choir, chorus, Christian doctrine, Christian ethics, Christian scripture, Christian studies, Christian testament, Christianity, church history, college admission preparation, college counseling, college placement, college planning, comparative government and politics-AP, competitive science projects, composition, composition-AP, computer animation, computer applications, computer education, computer information systems, computer literacy, computer multimedia, computer skills, computer technologies, dance, desktop publishing, drama performance, economics, English, English literature-AP, English-AP, ESL, European history, geometry, government, graphic design, health, history, honors algebra, honors English, independent study, Internet, intro to computers, journalism, keyboarding, kinesiology, lab science, leadership, physical education, physical science, physics, public speaking, research skills, Spanish, sports medicine, sports nutrition, statistics-AP, student government, TOEFL preparation, U.S. government and politics-AP, U.S. history-AP, Web site design, world cultures, yearbook.

Graduation Requirements Algebra, American government, American history, American literature, arts and fine arts (art, music, dance, drama), Bible, biology, composition, computer skills, economics, electives, English, European history, foreign language, freshman foundations, geometry, physical education (includes health), research skills, speech, graduation requirements meet UC and CSU entrance requirements.

Special Academic Programs 9 Advanced Placement exams for which test preparation is offered; honors section; independent study; special instructional classes for Oportunity School Program; ESL (24 students enrolled).

College Admission Counseling 40 students graduated in 2012; 37 went to college, including Azusa Pacific University; Biola University; Point Loma Nazarene University; University of California, Berkeley; University of California, Irvine; Westmont College. Other: 2 went to work, 1 had other specific plans. Median SAT critical reading: 537, median SAT math: 619, median SAT writing: 559, median combined SAT: 1715.

Student Life Upper grades have uniform requirement, student council, honor system. Discipline rests primarily with faculty. Attendance at religious services is required.

Summer Programs Remediation, enrichment, advancement, sports, art/fine arts programs offered; session focuses on credit recovery; held on campus; accepts boys and girls; open to students from other schools. 35 students usually enrolled. 2013 schedule: July 11 to August 5. Application deadline: May 1.

Tuition and Aid Day student tuition: $11,890. Guaranteed tuition plan. Tuition installment plan (FACTS Tuition Payment Plan, monthly payment plans, individually arranged payment plans, Payroll deductions). Tuition reduction for siblings, need-based scholarship grants available. In 2012–13, 30% of upper-school students received aid. Total amount of financial aid awarded in 2012–13: $250,000.

Admissions Traditional secondary-level entrance grade is 9. For fall 2012, 50 students applied for upper-level admission, 46 were accepted, 46 enrolled. Admissions testing, ESOL English Proficiency Test, High School Placement Test, Stanford Test of Academic Skills or TOEFL required. Deadline for receipt of application materials: none. Application fee required: $100. On-campus interview required.

Athletics Interscholastic: baseball (boys), basketball (b,g), cheering (g), cross-country running (b,g), football (b), soccer (b,g), softball (g), tennis (g), volleyball (b,g); coed interscholastic: equestrian sports, golf, physical training, strength & conditioning, weight training. 2 PE instructors, 13 coaches, 2 athletic trainers.

Computers Computers are regularly used in all academic, Bible studies, data processing, design, journalism, yearbook classes. Computer network features include on-campus library services, Internet access, wireless campus network, Internet filtering or blocking technology, 1 to 1 tablet PC program. Campus intranet, student e-mail accounts, and computer access in designated common areas are available to students. Students grades are available online. The school has a published electronic and media policy.

Contact Jo Beveridge, Director of Admissions/Development. 949-493-5683 Ext. 109. Fax: 949-493-6057. E-mail: jbeveridge@cvcs.org. Web site: www.cvcs.org

CARDIGAN MOUNTAIN SCHOOL

Canaan, New Hampshire
See Junior Boarding Schools section.

CARDINAL GIBBONS HIGH SCHOOL

1401 Edwards Mill Road
Raleigh, North Carolina 27607

Head of School: Mr. Jason Curtis

General Information Coeducational day college-preparatory, arts, business, religious studies, and technology school, affiliated with Roman Catholic Church. Grades 9–12. Founded: 1909. Setting: suburban. 36-acre campus. 1 building on campus. Approved or accredited by Southern Association of Colleges and Schools and Southern Association of Independent Schools. Endowment: $750,000. Total enrollment: 1,192. Upper school average class size: 14. Upper school faculty-student ratio: 1:14. Upper School students typically attend 5 days per week. The average school day consists of 7 hours.

Upper School Student Profile Grade 9: 322 students (165 boys, 157 girls); Grade 10: 320 students (154 boys, 166 girls); Grade 11: 307 students (163 boys, 144 girls); Grade 12: 313 students (169 boys, 144 girls). 86% of students are Roman Catholic.

Faculty School total: 95. In upper school: 40 men, 55 women; 60 have advanced degrees.

Special Academic Programs Advanced Placement exam preparation; honors section; accelerated programs; independent study.

College Admission Counseling 286 students graduated in 2012; 285 went to college, including Appalachian State University; University of Notre Dame. Other: 1 had other specific plans.

Student Life Upper grades have uniform requirement, student council. Discipline rests primarily with faculty. Attendance at religious services is required.

Summer Programs Sports, art/fine arts programs offered; session focuses on sports; held on campus; accepts boys and girls; open to students from other schools. 2013 schedule: June to August.

Tuition and Aid Day student tuition: $9120–$12,880. Tuition installment plan (FACTS Tuition Payment Plan). Need-based scholarship grants available.

Admissions Traditional secondary-level entrance grade is 9. Application fee required: $75. On-campus interview required.

Athletics Interscholastic: aerobics/dance (boys, girls), baseball (b,g), basketball (b,g), cheering (g), cross-country running (b,g), dance (g), dance squad (g), dance team (g), football (b), golf (b,g), kickball (b,g), lacrosse (b,g), modern dance (g), mountain biking (b,g), outdoor education (b,g), roller hockey (b), soccer (b,g), softball (g), strength & conditioning (b), surfing (b,g), swimming and diving (b,g), tennis (b,g), track and field (b,g), ultimate Frisbee (b,g), volleyball (g), weight lifting (b,g), weight training (g), wrestling (b).

Computers Computer network features include Internet access, wireless campus network, Internet filtering or blocking technology. Campus intranet, student e-mail accounts, and computer access in designated common areas are available to students.

Contact Mrs. Marianne McCarty, Admissions Director. 919-834-1625 Ext. 209. Fax: 919-834-9771. E-mail: mmccarty@cghsnc.org. Web site: www.cghsnc.org

CARDINAL MOONEY CATHOLIC COLLEGE PREPARATORY HIGH SCHOOL

660 South Water Street
Marine City, Michigan 48039

Head of School: Ms. Celeste Conflitti

General Information Coeducational day college-preparatory school, affiliated with Roman Catholic Church. Grades 9–12. Founded: 1977. Setting: small town. Nearest major city is Mount Clemens. 1-acre campus. 1 building on campus. Approved or accredited by North Central Association of Colleges and Schools and Michigan Department of Education. Total enrollment: 180. Upper school average class size: 22. Upper school faculty-student ratio: 1:10. There are 186 required school days per year for Upper School students. Upper School students typically attend 5 days per week. The average school day consists of 6 hours and 25 minutes.

Upper School Student Profile Grade 9: 44 students (16 boys, 28 girls); Grade 10: 45 students (20 boys, 25 girls); Grade 11: 45 students (22 boys, 23 girls); Grade 12: 44 students (18 boys, 26 girls). 90% of students are Roman Catholic.

Faculty School total: 20. In upper school: 5 men, 13 women; 10 have advanced degrees.

Subjects Offered Advanced Placement courses, algebra, American literature, anatomy, art, biology, calculus, Catholic belief and practice, chemistry, choir, computer applications, computer skills, drama, economics, English, fiction, French, French language-AP, geography, geometry, government, government-AP, health, humanities, Italian, library science, moral and social development, mythology, physical education, physical science, physics, poetry, pre-calculus, Spanish, Spanish language-AP, statistics, study skills, U.S. history, U.S. history-AP, world history, world literature, yearbook.

Special Academic Programs 6 Advanced Placement exams for which test preparation is offered; honors section.

College Admission Counseling 49 students graduated in 2011; 47 went to college, including Central Michigan University; Grand Valley State University; Michigan State University; Oakland University; University of Detroit Mercy; University of Michigan. Other: 2 entered military service.

Student Life Upper grades have uniform requirement, student council, honor system. Discipline rests primarily with faculty. Attendance at religious services is required.

Tuition and Aid Tuition installment plan (monthly payment plans). Tuition reduction for siblings available.

Admissions Traditional secondary-level entrance grade is 9. For fall 2011, 48 students applied for upper-level admission, 48 were accepted, 48 enrolled. High School Placement Test required. Deadline for receipt of application materials: none. Application fee required: $250. Interview required.

Athletics Interscholastic: baseball (boys), basketball (b,g), bowling (b,g), cheering (g), cross-country running (b,g), equestrian sports (b,g), football (b), golf (b), soccer (b,g), softball (g), volleyball (g); coed interscholastic: cross-country running, track and field. 2 PE instructors, 6 coaches.

Computers Computers are regularly used in all academic, computer applications, data processing, desktop publishing, graphic design, library science, word processing, yearbook classes. Computer network features include on-campus library services, Internet access, Internet filtering or blocking technology. Computer access in designated common areas is available to students. Students grades are available online. The school has a published electronic and media policy.

Contact Ms. Celeste Conflitti, Principal. 810-765-8825 Ext. 14. Fax: 810-765-7164. E-mail: principal@cardinalmooneycatholic.com. Web site:

CARDINAL MOONEY CATHOLIC HIGH SCHOOL

4171 Fruitville Road
Sarasota, Florida 34232

Head of School: Mr. Stephen J. Christie

General Information Coeducational day college-preparatory, arts, and religious studies school, affiliated with Roman Catholic Church. Grades 9–12. Founded: 1959. Setting: suburban. Nearest major city is Tampa. 36-acre campus. 7 buildings on campus. Approved or accredited by Southern Association of Colleges and Schools. Endowment: $1.8 million. Total enrollment: 467. Upper school average class size: 18. Upper school faculty-student ratio: 1:13. There are 180 required school days per year for Upper School students. Upper School students typically attend 5 days per week. The average school day consists of 6 hours and 35 minutes.

Upper School Student Profile Grade 9: 91 students (46 boys, 45 girls); Grade 10: 132 students (57 boys, 75 girls); Grade 11: 119 students (72 boys, 47 girls); Grade 12: 125 students (74 boys, 51 girls). 80% of students are Roman Catholic.

Faculty School total: 45. In upper school: 20 men, 25 women; 25 have advanced degrees.

Subjects Offered Algebra, American government, American history, anatomy, art, biology, business, calculus, ceramics, chemistry, chorus, Christian and Hebrew scripture, community service, computer applications, computer graphics, contemporary history, creative writing, drama, earth science, economics, economics and history, English, English literature, environmental science, fine arts, French, geometry, guitar, health, history, instrumental music, integrated mathematics, journalism, keyboarding, learning strategies, marine biology, mathematics, music, physical education, physics, psychology, science, social justice, social studies, sociology, Spanish, speech, theology, trigonometry, U.S. government and politics-AP, world history, world literature, world religions.

Graduation Requirements Arts and fine arts (art, music, dance, drama), electives, English, foreign language, mathematics, musical theater, physical education (includes health), religion (includes Bible studies and theology), science, social sciences, social studies (includes history), 100 hours of community service.

Special Academic Programs 8 Advanced Placement exams for which test preparation is offered; honors section; academic accommodation for the musically talented and the artistically talented.

College Admission Counseling 147 students graduated in 2012; all went to college, including Florida Gulf Coast University; Florida State University; University of Central Florida; University of Florida; University of North Florida; University of South Florida. Median SAT critical reading: 510, median SAT math: 520, median SAT writing: 518, median composite ACT: 22. 31% scored over 600 on SAT critical reading, 41% scored over 600 on SAT math, 35% scored over 600 on SAT writing, 38% scored over 26 on composite ACT.

Student Life Upper grades have specified standards of dress, student council. Discipline rests primarily with faculty. Attendance at religious services is required.

Summer Programs Advancement, sports programs offered; session focuses on math advancement/athletic camps; held on campus; accepts boys and girls; open to students from other schools. 250 students usually enrolled. 2013 schedule: June 10 to June 30. Application deadline: June 1.

Tuition and Aid Tuition installment plan (monthly payment plans, semester payment plan). Tuition reduction for siblings, merit scholarship grants, need-based scholarship grants, paying campus jobs available. In 2012–13, 25% of upper-school students received aid. Total amount of financial aid awarded in 2012–13: $200,000.

Admissions Traditional secondary-level entrance grade is 9. For fall 2012, 180 students applied for upper-level admission, 180 were accepted, 133 enrolled. Placement test or STS required. Deadline for receipt of application materials: none. No application fee required. On-campus interview required.

Athletics Interscholastic: baseball (boys), basketball (b,g), cheering (g), cross-country running (b,g), dance team (g), diving (b,g), football (b,g), golf (b,g), lacrosse (b,g), modern dance (g), soccer (b,g), softball (g), strength & conditioning (b,g), swimming and diving (b,g), track and field (b,g), volleyball (g), weight lifting (b,g), weight training (b,g); intramural: basketball (b,g), volleyball (b,g); coed intramural: volleyball. 4 PE instructors, 66 coaches, 1 athletic trainer.

Computers Computers are regularly used in art, computer applications, English, mathematics, science classes. Computer network features include on-campus library services, online commercial services, Internet access, wireless campus network. Students grades are available online. The school has a published electronic and media policy.

Contact Mrs. Joanne Mades, Registrar. 941-371-4917. Fax: 941-371-6924. E-mail: jmades@cmhs-sarasota.org. Web site: www.cmhs-sarasota.org

CARDINAL NEWMAN HIGH SCHOOL

512 Spencer Drive
West Palm Beach, Florida 33409-3699

Head of School: Fr. David W. Carr

General Information Coeducational day college-preparatory and International Baccalaureate school, affiliated with Roman Catholic Church. Grades 9–12. Founded: 1961. Setting: suburban. Nearest major city is Miami. 50-acre campus. 5 buildings on campus. Approved or accredited by National Catholic Education Association, Southern Association of Colleges and Schools, and Florida Department of Education. Total enrollment: 517. Upper school average class size: 25. Upper school faculty-student ratio: 1:25. There are 180 required school days per year for Upper School students. Upper School students typically attend 5 days per week. The average school day consists of 6 hours and 40 minutes.

Upper School Student Profile Grade 9: 131 students (65 boys, 66 girls); Grade 10: 116 students (59 boys, 57 girls); Grade 11: 149 students (66 boys, 83 girls); Grade 12: 121 students (49 boys, 72 girls). 80% of students are Roman Catholic.

Faculty School total: 42. In upper school: 16 men, 26 women; 28 have advanced degrees.

Subjects Offered Algebra, American government, American history, American literature, anatomy and physiology, art, band, Bible studies, biology, biology-AP, calculus, calculus-AP, chemistry, chorus, church history, computer applications, computer science, desktop publishing, drama, economics, English, English literature, English-AP, ethics, European history, fine arts, French, French-AP, geometry, government/civics, health, history, honors algebra, honors English, honors geometry, integrated science, International Baccalaureate courses, journalism, leadership, marine biology, mathematics, physical education, physics, political science, pre-calculus, probability and statistics, religion, social justice, social studies, Spanish, speech, world history, world literature, writing, yearbook.

Graduation Requirements Arts and fine arts (art, music, dance, drama), English, foreign language, mathematics, physical education (includes health), religion (includes Bible studies and theology), science, social studies (includes history), 100-hour community service requirement.

Special Academic Programs International Baccalaureate program; Advanced Placement exam preparation; honors section; study at local college for college credit; academic accommodation for the gifted; remedial reading and/or remedial writing; remedial math.

College Admission Counseling 149 students graduated in 2012; 147 went to college, including Florida Atlantic University; Florida Gulf Coast University; Florida State University; Palm Beach State College; University of Central Florida; University of Florida. Other: 1 entered military service, 1 had other specific plans.

Student Life Upper grades have uniform requirement, student council, honor system. Discipline rests primarily with faculty. Attendance at religious services is required.

Summer Programs Remediation, enrichment, sports programs offered; session focuses on freshman preparation; held on campus; accepts boys and girls; not open to students from other schools. 75 students usually enrolled. 2013 schedule: June 15 to June 30.

Tuition and Aid Day student tuition: $9859–$10,850. Tuition installment plan (FACTS Tuition Payment Plan). Need-based scholarship grants available. In 2012–13, 18% of upper-school students received aid.

Admissions Traditional secondary-level entrance grade is 9. STS required. Deadline for receipt of application materials: none. Application fee required: $50. On-campus interview recommended.

Athletics Interscholastic: baseball (boys), basketball (b,g), bowling (b,g), cheering (g), cross-country running (b,g), dance team (g), diving (b,g), football (b), golf (b,g), lacrosse (b,g), physical fitness (b,g), soccer (b,g), softball (g), swimming and diving (b,g), tennis (b,g), track and field (b,g), volleyball (g), wrestling (b). 2 PE instructors, 1 athletic trainer.

Computers Computers are regularly used in all academic, Bible studies, yearbook classes. Computer network features include on-campus library services, online commercial services, Internet access, wireless campus network, Internet filtering or blocking technology. Students grades are available online. The school has a published electronic and media policy.

Contact Mrs. Jan Joy, Admissions Coordinator. 561-242-2268. Fax: 561-683-7307. E-mail: jjoy@cardinalnewman.com. Web site: www.cardinalnewman.com

CARDINAL O'HARA HIGH SCHOOL

1701 South Sproul Road
Springfield, Pennsylvania 19064-1199

Head of School: Mrs. Marie Rogai

General Information Coeducational day college-preparatory school, affiliated with Roman Catholic Church. Grades 9–12. Founded: 1963. Setting: suburban. Nearest major city is Philadelphia. 1 building on campus. Approved or accredited by Pennsylvania Department of Education. Upper school average class size: 30. Upper school faculty-student ratio: 1:21. There are 180 required school days per year for Upper School students. Upper School students typically attend 5 days per week. The average school day consists of 6 hours and 35 minutes.

Upper School Student Profile Grade 9: 287 students (125 boys, 162 girls); Grade 10: 332 students (140 boys, 192 girls); Grade 11: 362 students (156 boys, 206 girls); Grade 12: 308 students (134 boys, 174 girls). 83% of students are Roman Catholic.

Faculty School total: 76. In upper school: 42 men, 34 women; 31 have advanced degrees.

Special Academic Programs Advanced Placement exam preparation; academic accommodation for the musically talented.

Student Life Upper grades have uniform requirement, student council, honor system. Discipline rests primarily with faculty. Attendance at religious services is required.

Summer Programs Enrichment programs offered; held on campus; accepts boys and girls; not open to students from other schools. 75 students usually enrolled.

Tuition and Aid Day student tuition: $5600. Tuition installment plan (monthly payment plans). Need-based scholarship grants available.

Admissions Traditional secondary-level entrance grade is 9. Application fee required: $250.

Athletics Interscholastic: baseball (boys), basketball (b,g), bowling (b,g), cheering (g), cross-country running (b,g), field hockey (g), football (b), Frisbee (b,g), golf (b), ice hockey (b), indoor track (b,g), indoor track & field (b,g), lacrosse (b,g), rugby (b), soccer (b,g), softball (g), tennis (b,g), track and field (b,g), ultimate Frisbee (b,g), volleyball (g), wrestling (b).

Computers Computer resources include on-campus library services, Internet access, wireless campus network, Internet filtering or blocking technology. Students grades are available online. The school has a published electronic and media policy.

Contact Mrs. Patti Arnold, Admissions Director. 610-544-3800 Ext. 70. Fax: 610-544-1189. E-mail: pattiarnold@cohs.com. Web site: www.cohs.com

CARLISLE SCHOOL

300 Carlisle Road
Axton, Virginia 24054

Head of School: Dr. Barry M. Dorsey

General Information Coeducational boarding and day college-preparatory, International Baccalaureate (IB), and IB Middle Years program and Primary Years program school. Boarding grades 9–12, day grades PK–12. Founded: 1968. Setting: rural. Nearest major city is Danville. Students are housed in single-sex dormitories. 50-acre campus. 5 buildings on campus. Approved or accredited by International Baccalaureate Organization, Southern Association of Colleges and Schools, Virginia Association of Independent Schools, and Virginia Department of Education. Member of National Association of Independent Schools. Endowment: $1.5 million. Total enrollment: 549. Upper school average class size: 15. Upper school faculty-student ratio: 1:7. There are 176 required school days per year for Upper School students. Upper School students typically attend 5 days per week. The average school day consists of 6 hours and 45 minutes.

Upper School Student Profile Grade 9: 32 students (19 boys, 13 girls); Grade 10: 41 students (22 boys, 19 girls); Grade 11: 38 students (22 boys, 16 girls); Grade 12: 44 students (16 boys, 28 girls). 24% of students are boarding students. 74% are state residents. 2 states are represented in upper school student body. 24% are international students. International students from Australia, China, Finland, Japan, Mexico, and Republic of Korea.

Faculty School total: 30. In upper school: 7 men, 18 women; 11 have advanced degrees; 3 reside on campus.

Subjects Offered Advanced computer applications, advanced math, Advanced Placement courses, algebra, American government, American history, American history-AP, American literature, art, arts, band, biology, biology-AP, calculus, calculus-AP, chemistry, chemistry-AP, choir, composition-AP, computer information systems, computer programming, computer science, computer science-AP, concert band, creative dance, creative drama, creative writing, dance, drama, earth science, economics, economics-AP, English, English language and composition-AP, English literature, English literature and composition-AP, English literature-AP, ESL, film studies, fine arts, geometry, government, government/civics, health, health and wellness, history, history of the Americas, honors algebra, honors English, honors geometry, HTML design, independent study, International Baccalaureate courses, intro to computers, jazz band, jazz ensemble, journalism, lab science, madrigals, mathematics, mathematics-AP, music, physical education, physics, play production, pre-algebra, pre-calculus, psychology, psychology-AP, publications, robotics, science, senior project, social studies, Spanish, statistics, statistics-AP, studio art, theater, theory of knowledge, U.S. government and politics-AP, U.S. history-AP, wind ensemble, world civilizations, world history, world history-AP, world wide web design, yearbook.

Graduation Requirements Advanced math, algebra, arts and fine arts (art, music, dance, drama), computer science, electives, English, foreign language, mathematics, physical education (includes health), science, social studies (includes history), U.S. and Virginia history, U.S. government, community and service, senior project, IB MYP Personal Project.

Special Academic Programs International Baccalaureate program; Advanced Placement exam preparation; honors section; independent study; term-away projects; study at local college for college credit; ESL (17 students enrolled).

College Admission Counseling 49 students graduated in 2012; all went to college, including Lynchburg College; The College of William and Mary; The University of North Carolina at Chapel Hill; The University of North Carolina at Greensboro; University of Virginia; Virginia Commonwealth University. Median SAT critical reading: 546, median SAT math: 540, median SAT writing: 526. 33% scored over 600 on SAT critical reading, 37% scored over 600 on SAT math, 33% scored over 600 on SAT writing.

Student Life Upper grades have specified standards of dress, student council, honor system. Discipline rests equally with students and faculty.

Summer Programs Remediation, enrichment, advancement, ESL, sports, art/fine arts, computer instruction programs offered; session focuses on enrichment, academics, sports, fun; held on campus; accepts boys and girls; open to students from other schools. 60 students usually enrolled. 2013 schedule: June 15 to August 15. Application deadline: June 1.

Tuition and Aid Day student tuition: $9575; 7-day tuition and room/board: $35,000. Tuition installment plan (Insured Tuition Payment Plan, FACTS Tuition Payment Plan). Need-based scholarship grants available. In 2012–13, 50% of upper-school students received aid. Total amount of financial aid awarded in 2012–13: $250,000.

Admissions Traditional secondary-level entrance grade is 9. Nelson-Denny Reading Test, Woodcock-Johnson or writing sample required. Deadline for receipt of application materials: none. Application fee required: $50. On-campus interview required.

Athletics Interscholastic: basketball (boys, girls), cheering (g), field hockey (g), soccer (b,g), softball (g), tennis (b,g), volleyball (g); intramural: basketball (b,g), cheering (g), softball (g); coed interscholastic: baseball, cross-country running, dance, fencing, golf; coed intramural: aerobics/Nautilus, archery, basketball, Frisbee, table tennis, weight lifting. 2 PE instructors, 12 coaches.

Computers Computers are regularly used in all academic classes. Computer network features include on-campus library services, online commercial services, Internet access, wireless campus network, Internet filtering or blocking technology. Campus intranet and computer access in designated common areas are available to students. Students grades are available online. The school has a published electronic and media policy.

Contact Mrs. Jenna Martin, Assistant Director of Admissions. 276-632-7288 Ext. 221. Fax: 276-632-9545. E-mail: jmartin@carlisleschool.org. Web site: www.carlisleschool.org

CAROLINA DAY SCHOOL

1345 Hendersonville Road
Asheville, North Carolina 28803

Head of School: Thomas F. H. Trigg

General Information Coeducational day college-preparatory school. Grades PK–12. Founded: 1987. Setting: suburban. 60-acre campus. 9 buildings on campus. Approved or accredited by Southern Association of Colleges and Schools, Southern Association of Independent Schools, and North Carolina Department of Education. Member of National Association of Independent Schools. Endowment: $3.4 million. Total enrollment: 610. Upper school average class size: 12. Upper school faculty-student ratio: 1:6. There are 180 required school days per year for Upper School students. Upper School students typically attend 5 days per week. The average school day consists of 6 hours and 25 minutes.

Upper School Student Profile Grade 9: 44 students (18 boys, 26 girls); Grade 10: 45 students (28 boys, 17 girls); Grade 11: 37 students (19 boys, 18 girls); Grade 12: 44 students (19 boys, 25 girls).

Faculty School total: 114. In upper school: 11 men, 12 women; 17 have advanced degrees.

Subjects Offered 3-dimensional art, 3-dimensional design, acting, advanced biology, advanced chemistry, advanced studio art-AP, algebra, American literature, art history, art history-AP, biology, biology-AP, calculus, calculus-AP, ceramics, chemistry, chemistry-AP, chorus, CPR, creative writing, debate, ecology, English language and composition-AP, English literature, environmental science-AP, European history-AP, fiction, French, geometry, global studies, history, industrial arts, language and composition, linear algebra, linguistics, literature, literature and composition-AP, martial arts, music theory, music theory-AP, photography, physical education, physics, physics-AP, pre-calculus, psychology-AP, reading/study skills, research, science, Spanish, Spanish-AP, speech, statistics-AP, studio art, theater, U.S. government and politics-AP, U.S. history, U.S. history-AP, world literature.

Graduation Requirements Algebra, arts and fine arts (art, music, dance, drama), biology, chemistry, electives, English, geometry, global studies, modern languages, physical education (includes health), public speaking, social studies (includes history), U.S. history, CPR/First Aid (non-credit class).

Special Academic Programs 14 Advanced Placement exams for which test preparation is offered; honors section; independent study.

College Admission Counseling 54 students graduated in 2012; 52 went to college, including Amherst College; Duke University; High Point University; The University of North Carolina at Asheville; The University of North Carolina Wilmington; University of South Carolina. Other: 2 had other specific plans. Median SAT critical reading: 570, median SAT math: 600, median SAT writing: 560, median combined SAT: 1740, median composite ACT: 26.

Student Life Upper grades have specified standards of dress, student council, honor system. Discipline rests equally with students and faculty.

Summer Programs Enrichment, sports, art/fine arts, computer instruction programs offered; session focuses on recreation and enrichment; held on campus; accepts boys and girls; open to students from other schools. 180 students usually enrolled. 2013 schedule: June 18 to August 9.

Tuition and Aid Day student tuition: $19,500–$20,700. Tuition installment plan (Insured Tuition Payment Plan, FACTS Tuition Payment Plan, monthly payment plans, individually arranged payment plans, 1-payment plan or 2-installments plan (August and January)). Merit scholarship grants, need-based scholarship grants available. In 2012–13, 47% of upper-school students received aid; total upper-school merit-scholarship money awarded: $152,459. Total amount of financial aid awarded in 2012–13: $553,447.

Admissions Traditional secondary-level entrance grade is 9. For fall 2012, 33 students applied for upper-level admission, 23 were accepted, 16 enrolled. ERB, ISEE, PSAT or SAT or SSAT required. Deadline for receipt of application materials: none. Application fee required: $100. On-campus interview required.

Athletics Interscholastic: baseball (boys), basketball (b,g), cross-country running (b,g), field hockey (g), swimming and diving (b,g), tennis (b,g), track and field (b,g), volleyball (g); coed interscholastic: golf; coed intramural: basketball, lacrosse, skiing (downhill), snowboarding, table tennis. 2 PE instructors, 11 coaches, 1 athletic trainer.

Computers Computers are regularly used in all academic classes. Computer network features include on-campus library services, online commercial services, Internet access, wireless campus network, Internet filtering or blocking technology. Campus intranet, student e-mail accounts, and computer access in designated common areas are available to students. The school has a published electronic and media policy.

Contact Michelle Nailen, Assistant Director of Admissions. 828-274-0757 Ext. 318. Fax: 828-274-0756. E-mail: mnailen@carolinaday.org. Web site: www.carolinaday.org

CARONDELET HIGH SCHOOL

1133 Winton Drive
Concord, California 94518

Head of School: Nancy Libby

General Information Girls' day college-preparatory, arts, religious studies, and technology school, affiliated with Roman Catholic Church. Grades 9–12. Founded: 1965. Setting: suburban. Nearest major city is Oakland. 9-acre campus. 5 buildings on campus. Approved or accredited by Western Association of Schools and Colleges. Total enrollment: 800. Upper school average class size: 30. Upper school faculty-student ratio: 1:15. Upper School students typically attend 5 days per week. The average school day consists of 7 hours and 30 minutes.

Upper School Student Profile Grade 9: 200 students (200 girls); Grade 10: 200 students (200 girls); Grade 11: 200 students (200 girls); Grade 12: 200 students (200 girls). 90% of students are Roman Catholic.

Faculty School total: 65. In upper school: 13 men, 48 women; 30 have advanced degrees.

Subjects Offered Algebra, American studies, animation, architectural drawing, art, band, biology, calculus, calculus-AP, cartooning/animation, chemistry, chorus, church history, civics, community service, computer applications, concert band, concert choir, creative writing, criminal justice, dance, design, drafting, drawing, economics, English, English-AP, ethics, finite math, fitness, French, geometry, government-AP, health, honors algebra, honors English, honors geometry, Italian, jazz band, journalism, Latin, marching band, marine biology, music history, music theory, musical theater, orchestra, painting, physical education, physics, physics-AP, physiology, pre-algebra, pre-calculus, psychology, psychology-AP, relationships, sculpture, Spanish, Spanish-AP, sports medicine, statistics, studio art-AP, technical drawing, transition mathematics, U.S. history, U.S. history-AP, water color painting, Web site design, women's health, world arts, world civilizations, world religions, writing, yearbook.

Graduation Requirements Computer literacy, English, mathematics, modern languages, physical education (includes health), religious studies, science, social studies (includes history), visual and performing arts.

Special Academic Programs 12 Advanced Placement exams for which test preparation is offered; honors section; independent study; academic accommodation for the gifted.

College Admission Counseling 199 students graduated in 2012; all went to college, including California Polytechnic State University, San Luis Obispo; California State University, Chico; University of California, Berkeley. Mean SAT critical reading: 548, mean SAT math: 538, mean SAT writing: 556, mean composite ACT: 24.

Student Life Upper grades have uniform requirement, honor system. Discipline rests primarily with faculty. Attendance at religious services is required.

Tuition and Aid Day student tuition: $14,300. Tuition installment plan (SMART Tuition Payment Plan, monthly payment plans, prepayment plan, semester or quarterly payment plans). Need-based scholarship grants available. In 2012–13, 25% of upper-school students received aid. Total amount of financial aid awarded in 2012–13: $1,300,000.

Admissions Traditional secondary-level entrance grade is 9. For fall 2012, 380 students applied for upper-level admission, 240 were accepted, 220 enrolled. High School Placement Test required. Deadline for receipt of application materials: December 3. Application fee required: $100. On-campus interview recommended.

Athletics Interscholastic: aquatics, basketball, cheering, combined training, cross-country running, dance squad, dance team, diving, golf, lacrosse, soccer, softball, swimming and diving, tennis, volleyball, water polo; intramural: badminton, basketball, broomball, flag football, physical fitness, physical training, touch football, volleyball. 3 PE instructors, 40 coaches, 1 athletic trainer.

Computers Computers are regularly used in computer applications classes. Computer network features include on-campus library services, Internet access, wireless campus network, Internet filtering or blocking technology. Student e-mail accounts are available to students. Students grades are available online. The school has a published electronic and media policy.

Contact Ms. Kathy Harris, Director of Admissions. 925-686-5353 Ext. 161. Fax: 925-671-9429. E-mail: kharris@carondeleths.org. Web site: www.carondelet.net

CARROLLTON CHRISTIAN ACADEMY

2205 East Hebron Parkway
Carrollton, Texas 75010

Head of School: Dr. Alex Ward

General Information Coeducational day college-preparatory, arts, religious studies, and technology school, affiliated with United Methodist Church. Grades PK–12. Founded: 1980. Setting: suburban. Nearest major city is Dallas/Fort Worth. 25-acre campus. 1 building on campus. Approved or accredited by Southern Association of Colleges and Schools, University Senate of United Methodist Church, and Texas Department of Education. Language of instruction: Spanish. Total enrollment: 375. Upper school average class size: 20.

Student Life Upper grades have uniform requirement, student council, honor system. Discipline rests primarily with faculty.

Tuition and Aid Tuition installment plan (FACTS Tuition Payment Plan). Tuition reduction for siblings, need-based scholarship grants available.

Admissions Stanford Achievement Test required. Application fee required. Interview required.

Athletics Interscholastic: baseball (boys), basketball (b,g), cheering (g), cross-country running (b,g), dance team (g), football (b), golf (b,g), soccer (b,g), softball (g), strength & conditioning (b,g), tennis (b,g), track and field (b,g), volleyball (g), winter soccer (b,g).

Contact Ms. Jane Funk, Admissions Coordinator. . 972-242-6688 Ext. 1360. Fax: 469-568-1396. E-mail: jane.funk@ccasaints.org. Web site: www.ccasaints.org

CARROLLTON SCHOOL OF THE SACRED HEART

3747 Main Highway
Miami, Florida 33133

Head of School: Sr. Suzanne Cooke

General Information Girls' day college-preparatory, arts, religious studies, bilingual studies, and technology school, affiliated with Roman Catholic Church. Grades PK–12. Founded: 1961. Setting: urban. 17-acre campus. 5 buildings on campus. Approved or accredited by Florida Council of Independent Schools, Network of Sacred Heart Schools, and Southern Association of Colleges and Schools. Member of National Association of Independent Schools and Secondary School Admission Test Board. Endowment: $2 million. Total enrollment: 800. Upper school average class size: 16. Upper school faculty-student ratio: 1:9.

Upper School Student Profile 87% of students are Roman Catholic.

Faculty School total: 74. In upper school: 9 men, 24 women; 20 have advanced degrees.

Subjects Offered Algebra, American history, American literature, anatomy and physiology, art, art history, Bible studies, biology, British literature, calculus, chemistry, computer science, debate, drama, earth systems analysis, economics, English, English literature, environmental science, ethics, expository writing, fine arts, French, general science, geometry, government/civics, grammar, health, history, humanities, journalism, mathematics, music, photography, physical education, physical science, physics, pre-calculus, psychology, religion, science, scripture, social sciences, social studies, Spanish, speech, theater, trigonometry, vocal ensemble, world history, world literature.

Graduation Requirements Arts and fine arts (art, music, dance, drama), computer science, English, foreign language, mathematics, physical education (includes health), religion (includes Bible studies and theology), science, social studies (includes history). Community service is required.

Special Academic Programs International Baccalaureate program; Advanced Placement exam preparation; honors section; independent study; study at local college for college credit; domestic exchange program; study abroad.

College Admission Counseling 66 students graduated in 2011; all went to college, including Boston College; Massachusetts Institute of Technology; Northwestern University; University of Miami; Vanderbilt University. Median SAT math: 590, median composite ACT: 24. Mean SAT critical reading: 590. 51% scored over 600 on SAT critical reading, 47% scored over 600 on SAT math, 30% scored over 26 on composite ACT.

Student Life Upper grades have uniform requirement, student council, honor system. Discipline rests primarily with faculty. Attendance at religious services is required.

Tuition and Aid Day student tuition: $23,150. Tuition installment plan (Insured Tuition Payment Plan, monthly payment plans). Merit scholarship grants, need-based scholarship grants available. In 2011–12, 25% of upper-school students received aid; total upper-school merit-scholarship money awarded: $45,000. Total amount of financial aid awarded in 2011–12: $920,000.

Admissions Traditional secondary-level entrance grade is 9. For fall 2011, 132 students applied for upper-level admission, 37 were accepted, 30 enrolled. Admissions testing or ISEE required. Deadline for receipt of application materials: February 1. Application fee required: $50. On-campus interview required.

Athletics Interscholastic: aquatics, basketball, crew, cross-country running, golf, sailing, soccer, softball, swimming and diving, tennis, track and field, volleyball, water polo, winter soccer. 4 PE instructors, 8 coaches.

Computers Computers are regularly used in all academic classes. Computer network features include on-campus library services, online commercial services, Internet access, wireless campus network, Internet filtering or blocking technology, laptop program. Student e-mail accounts are available to students. The school has a published electronic and media policy.

Contact Ms. Ana J. Roye, Director of Admission and Financial Aid. 305-446-5673 Ext. 1224. Fax: 305-446-4160. E-mail: aroye@carrollton.org. Web site: www.carrollton.org

CASCADES ACADEMY OF CENTRAL OREGON

2150 NE Studio Road
Suite 2
Bend, Oregon 97701

Head of School: Blair Jenkins

General Information Distance learning only college-preparatory and experiential education school. Distance learning grades K–12. Founded: 2003. Setting: suburban. 1 building on campus. Approved or accredited by Northwest Accreditation Commission, Pacific Northwest Association of Independent Schools, and Oregon Department of Education. Total enrollment: 143. Upper school average class size: 10. Upper school faculty-student ratio: 1:6. There are 168 required school days per year for Upper School students. Upper School students typically attend 5 days per week. The average school day consists of 7 hours and 15 minutes.

Upper School Student Profile Grade 9: 13 students (5 boys, 8 girls); Grade 10: 3 students (2 boys, 1 girl); Grade 11: 6 students (5 boys, 1 girl); Grade 12: 1 student (1 boy).

Faculty School total: 21. In upper school: 1 man, 3 women; 3 have advanced degrees.

Graduation Requirements Internship.

College Admission Counseling 6 students graduated in 2012; all went to college, including Rensselaer Polytechnic Institute; University of Oregon; Willamette University.

Student Life Upper grades have honor system. Discipline rests primarily with faculty.

Tuition and Aid Day student tuition: $10,950. Tuition installment plan (monthly payment plans, individually arranged payment plans). Merit scholarship grants, need-based scholarship grants available. In 2012–13, 48% of upper-school students received aid.

Admissions Traditional secondary-level entrance grade is 9. For fall 2012, 7 students applied for upper-level admission, 6 were accepted, 5 enrolled. Deadline for receipt of application materials: none. Application fee required: $50. On-campus interview required.

Computers Computer network features include Internet access, wireless campus network, Internet filtering or blocking technology. Student e-mail accounts and computer access in designated common areas are available to students. Students grades are available online. The school has a published electronic and media policy.

Contact 541-382-0699. Fax: 541-382-0225. Web site: www.cascadesacademy.org/

CASCADILLA SCHOOL

116 Summit Street
Ithaca, New York 14850

Head of School: Patricia T. Kendall

General Information Coeducational boarding and day college-preparatory, arts, bilingual studies, English/language arts (The Cascadilla Seminar/Cornell Univ.), and mathematics school. Grades 9–PG. Founded: 1870. Setting: urban. Nearest major city is Syracuse. Students are housed in single-sex dormitories. 2-acre campus. 3 buildings on campus. Approved or accredited by New York State Board of Regents, New York State University, The College Board, US Department of State, and New York Department of Education. Endowment: $1.2 million. Total enrollment: 50. Upper school average class size: 7. Upper school faculty-student ratio: 1:6. There are 185 required school days per year for Upper School students. Upper School students typically attend 5 days per week. The average school day consists of 7 hours and 40 minutes.

Upper School Student Profile Grade 9: 10 students (5 boys, 5 girls); Grade 10: 14 students (8 boys, 6 girls); Grade 11: 13 students (7 boys, 6 girls); Grade 12: 13 students (6 boys, 7 girls). 30% of students are boarding students. 70% are state residents. 4 states are represented in upper school student body. 30% are international students. International students from Angola, China, Republic of Korea, Saudi Arabia, Turkey, and United States; 3 other countries represented in student body.

Faculty School total: 16. In upper school: 7 men, 9 women; 15 have advanced degrees; 4 reside on campus.

Subjects Offered Advanced chemistry, Advanced Placement courses, advanced TOEFL/grammar, African literature, algebra, alternative physical education, American history, American literature, anatomy and physiology, art, biochemistry, biology, biology-AP, calculus, calculus-AP, career/college preparation, chemistry, chemistry-AP, college admission preparation, college awareness, college counseling, college placement, college planning, college writing, computer programming, computer science, creative writing, decision making skills, earth science, economics, English, English as a foreign language, English composition, English literature, English literature and composition-AP, English literature-AP, environmental education, environmental science, ESL, ethics, European history, expository writing, fabric arts, French, French as a second language, geometry, government/civics, health, health and wellness, health education, history, honors algebra, honors English, honors geometry, honors U.S. history, honors world history, lab science, Latin, leadership, mathematics, philosophy, photography, physical education, physics, psychology, public speaking, reading, reading/study skills, SAT preparation, SAT/ACT preparation, science, Shakespeare, social studies, Spanish, trigonometry, typing, video film production, world history, world history-AP, world literature, writing.

Graduation Requirements Alternative physical education, arts, arts and fine arts (art, music, dance, drama), computer science, current events, debate, economics, economics and history, English, European history, foreign language, government, health education, international affairs, mathematics, physical education (includes health), political science, public speaking, research, research and reference, research seminar, science, senior seminar, social studies (includes history), study skills, U.S. government and politics, English V-The Cascadilla Seminar (for college research preparation). Community service is required.

Special Academic Programs 5 Advanced Placement exams for which test preparation is offered; honors section; accelerated programs; independent study; term-away projects; study at local college for college credit; academic accommodation for the gifted, the musically talented, and the artistically talented; remedial reading and/or remedial writing; remedial math; programs in English, mathematics for dyslexic students; special instructional classes for students with learning disabilities and Attention Deficit Disorder; ESL (26 students enrolled).

College Admission Counseling 15 students graduated in 2012; 14 went to college, including Columbia University; Cornell University; Hamilton College; Michigan State University; University of California, San Diego; University of Illinois at Urbana–Champaign. Other: 1 had other specific plans. Median SAT critical reading: 600, median SAT math: 650, median SAT writing: 550. 50% scored over 600 on SAT critical reading, 50% scored over 600 on SAT math, 15% scored over 600 on SAT writing.

Student Life Upper grades have specified standards of dress, student council, honor system. Discipline rests equally with students and faculty.

Summer Programs Remediation, enrichment, advancement, ESL, art/fine arts programs offered; session focuses on academics; held on campus; accepts boys and girls; open to students from other schools. 40 students usually enrolled. 2013 schedule: July 1 to August 17. Application deadline: June 30.

Tuition and Aid Day student tuition: $14,000; 7-day tuition and room/board: $35,000. Tuition installment plan (monthly payment plans, individually arranged payment plans). Tuition reduction for siblings, merit scholarship grants, need-based scholarship grants available. In 2012–13, 40% of upper-school students received aid; total upper-school merit-scholarship money awarded: $50,000. Total amount of financial aid awarded in 2012–13: $60,000.

Admissions Traditional secondary-level entrance grade is 10. For fall 2012, 55 students applied for upper-level admission, 30 were accepted, 15 enrolled. English Composition Test for ESL students, English entrance exam, English for Non-native Speakers, English language, English proficiency, High School Placement Test, math and English placement tests, mathematics proficiency exam, non-standardized placement tests, Reading for Understanding, school's own exam, skills for ESL students or writing sample required. Deadline for receipt of application materials: none. Application fee required: $75. Interview recommended.

Athletics Interscholastic: crew (boys, girls), modern dance (g); intramural: crew (b,g), fencing (b), independent competitive sports (b,g), rowing (b,g), sailing (b,g), skiing (cross-country) (b,g), skiing (downhill) (b,g), soccer (b,g), tennis (b,g); coed interscholastic: aerobics, aerobics/Nautilus, alpine skiing, aquatics, backpacking, badminton, ballet, basketball, billiards, blading, bowling, climbing, combined training, fencing, fitness, fitness walking, Frisbee, hiking/backpacking, jogging, kayaking, nordic skiing, outdoor activities, outdoor adventure, outdoor education, physical fitness, physical training, swimming and diving, table tennis, weight lifting, yoga; coed intramural: aerobics, aerobics/dance, badminton, basketball, blading, bowling, horseback riding, independent competitive sports, jogging, Nautilus, nordic skiing, outdoor activities, outdoor adventure, physical fitness, physical training, pillo polo, racquetball, rowing, sailboarding, skiing (cross-country), skiing (downhill), snowboarding, strength & conditioning, tennis, volleyball, walking, wall climbing, windsurfing. 3 PE instructors.

Computers Computers are regularly used in career exploration, college planning, creative writing, desktop publishing, desktop publishing, ESL, ESL, French as a second language, literary magazine, mathematics, media arts, newspaper, photography, publishing, research skills, SAT preparation, senior seminar, Spanish, stock market, theater, theater arts, video film production, Web site design, word processing, writing, writing, yearbook classes. Computer network features include on-campus library services, online commercial services, Internet access, wireless campus network, Internet filtering or blocking technology. Student e-mail accounts and computer access in designated common areas are available to students. Students grades are available online.

Contact Donna W. Collins, Administrative Assistant. 607-272-3110. Fax: 607-272-0747. E-mail: admissions@cascadillaschool.org. Web site: www.cascadillaschool.org

CASTILLEJA SCHOOL

1310 Bryant Street
Palo Alto, California 94301

Head of School: Nanci Z. Kauffman

General Information Girls' day college-preparatory, arts, and technology school. Grades 6–12. Founded: 1907. Setting: suburban. Nearest major city is San Francisco/San Jose. 5-acre campus. 7 buildings on campus. Approved or accredited by California Association of Independent Schools, National Council for Private School Accreditation, and Western Association of Schools and Colleges. Member of National Association of Independent Schools and Secondary School Admission Test Board. Endowment: $35 million. Total enrollment: 451. Upper school average class size: 14. Upper school faculty-student ratio: 1:6. Upper School students typically attend 5 days per week. The average school day consists of 7 hours.

Upper School Student Profile Grade 9: 68 students (68 girls); Grade 10: 64 students (64 girls); Grade 11: 63 students (63 girls); Grade 12: 63 students (63 girls).

Faculty School total: 75. In upper school: 12 men, 34 women; 40 have advanced degrees.

Subjects Offered Advanced Placement courses, African studies, algebra, American history, American literature, art, art history, biology, calculus, ceramics, chemistry, computer math, computer science, creative writing, drama, economics, English, English literature, environmental science, European history, expository writing, fine arts, French, geometry, global issues, government/civics, grammar, health, history, journalism, Latin, marine biology, mathematics, music, philosophy, physical education, physics, psychology, Russian history, science, social studies, Spanish, speech, statistics, theater, trigonometry, world history, writing.

Graduation Requirements Arts and fine arts (art, music, dance, drama), English, foreign language, health and wellness, mathematics, science, social studies (includes history).

Special Academic Programs 13 Advanced Placement exams for which test preparation is offered; honors section; independent study; academic accommodation for the gifted.

College Admission Counseling 52 students graduated in 2012; 51 went to college, including Brown University; Colgate University; Harvard University; Stanford University; Tufts University; University of Southern California. Other: 1 entered a postgraduate year. Mean SAT critical reading: 706, mean SAT math: 693, mean SAT writing: 731.

Student Life Upper grades have uniform requirement, student council, honor system. Discipline rests equally with students and faculty.

Tuition and Aid Day student tuition: $35,750. Tuition installment plan (monthly payment plans, individually arranged payment plans). Need-based scholarship grants available. In 2012–13, 20% of upper-school students received aid. Total amount of financial aid awarded in 2012–13: $2,200,000.

Admissions Traditional secondary-level entrance grade is 9. For fall 2012, 131 students applied for upper-level admission, 19 were accepted, 15 enrolled. ISEE, SSAT or TOEFL required. Deadline for receipt of application materials: January 17. Application fee required: $75. On-campus interview required.

Athletics Interscholastic: basketball, cross-country running, golf, lacrosse, soccer, softball, swimming and diving, tennis, track and field, volleyball, water polo; intramural: climbing, fitness, rock climbing. 6 PE instructors, 15 coaches, 1 athletic trainer.

Computers Computers are regularly used in art, English, foreign language, history, mathematics, science classes. Computer network features include on-campus library services, online commercial services, Internet access, wireless campus network, Internet filtering or blocking technology, one to one laptop program. Campus intranet and student e-mail accounts are available to students. Students grades are available online. The school has a published electronic and media policy.

Contact Jill V.W. Lee, Director of Admission. 650-470-7731. Fax: 650-326-8036. E-mail: jlee@castilleja.org. Web site: www.castilleja.org

CATHEDRAL HIGH SCHOOL

5225 East 56th Street
Indianapolis, Indiana 46226

Head of School: Mr. Stephen J. Helmich

General Information Coeducational day college-preparatory, arts, religious studies, technology, International Baccalaureate, and AP/honors school, affiliated with Roman Catholic Church. Grades 9–12. Founded: 1918. Setting: urban. 40-acre campus. 5 buildings on campus. Approved or accredited by Independent Schools Association of the Central States, National Catholic Education Association, National Council for Private School Accreditation, North Central Association of Colleges and Schools, and

Indiana Department of Education. Endowment: $4 million. Total enrollment: 1,255. Upper school average class size: 19. Upper school faculty-student ratio: 1:13. There are 185 required school days per year for Upper School students. Upper School students typically attend 5 days per week. The average school day consists of 7 hours and 40 minutes.

Upper School Student Profile Grade 9: 349 students (178 boys, 171 girls); Grade 10: 314 students (156 boys, 158 girls); Grade 11: 298 students (155 boys, 143 girls); Grade 12: 295 students (162 boys, 133 girls). 75% of students are Roman Catholic.

Faculty School total: 100. In upper school: 47 men, 53 women; 54 have advanced degrees.

Subjects Offered Advanced biology, advanced chemistry, advanced math, Advanced Placement courses, algebra, American history, American history-AP, American literature-AP, American studies, anatomy, anatomy and physiology, art and culture, art history, arts, Bible, Bible studies, biology, botany, business, business communications, business education, business law, calculus, calculus-AP, career and personal planning, Catholic belief and practice, ceramics, chemistry, chemistry-AP, choir, choral music, chorus, Christianity, civics, civil war history, college counseling, composition-AP, computer science, debate, drama, driver education, earth science, economics, economics-AP, English, English literature, English literature and composition-AP, English literature-AP, English-AP, English/composition-AP, environmental science, fine arts, French, French language-AP, geography, geology, geometry, German, German-AP, government and politics-AP, government-AP, history, history-AP, independent study, journalism, lab science, language development, Latin, life science, macro/microeconomics-AP, mathematics, mathematics-AP, microbiology, music, music appreciation, news writing, newspaper, organic chemistry, photography, photojournalism, physical education, physical fitness, physics, physiology, psychology, religion, SAT/ACT preparation, science, social sciences, social studies, sociology, Spanish, speech, textiles, theater, theater design and production, theater production, theory of knowledge, trigonometry, U.S. government and politics-AP, U.S. history, U.S. history-AP, vocal music, world history, world literature.

Graduation Requirements Arts and fine arts (art, music, dance, drama), biology, composition, economics, English, foreign language, government, mathematics, modern world history, physical education (includes health), religious studies, science, social studies (includes history), speech and debate, technology, U.S. history, 30 hours annually of community service.

Special Academic Programs International Baccalaureate program; Advanced Placement exam preparation; honors section; independent study; academic accommodation for the gifted, the musically talented, and the artistically talented; remedial reading and/or remedial writing; remedial math; programs in English, mathematics for dyslexic students; special instructional classes for deaf students, blind students, students with learning disabilities, Attention Deficit Disorder, and dyslexia.

College Admission Counseling 314 students graduated in 2012; 312 went to college, including Ball State University; Indiana University Bloomington; Loyola University Chicago; Purdue University; University of Dayton; Xavier University. Other: 2 entered military service. Mean SAT critical reading: 541, mean SAT math: 548, mean SAT writing: 536, mean composite ACT: 25.

Student Life Upper grades have uniform requirement, student council, honor system. Discipline rests primarily with faculty. Attendance at religious services is required.

Summer Programs Remediation, enrichment, advancement, sports, art/fine arts, computer instruction programs offered; session focuses on advancement; held on campus; accepts boys and girls; not open to students from other schools. 500 students usually enrolled. 2013 schedule: June 3 to June 28. Application deadline: June 1.

Tuition and Aid Day student tuition: $11,750. Tuition installment plan (Key Tuition Payment Plan, monthly payment plans). Merit scholarship grants, need-based scholarship grants, paying campus jobs available. In 2012–13, 42% of upper-school students received aid; total upper-school merit-scholarship money awarded: $566,000. Total amount of financial aid awarded in 2012–13: $2,300,000.

Admissions Traditional secondary-level entrance grade is 9. For fall 2012, 627 students applied for upper-level admission, 491 were accepted, 349 enrolled. High School Placement Test and High School Placement Test (closed version) from Scholastic Testing Service required. Deadline for receipt of application materials: none. No application fee required. On-campus interview required.

Athletics Interscholastic: baseball (boys), basketball (b,g), cheering (g), cross-country running (b,g), football (b), golf (b,g), soccer (b,g), softball (g), swimming and diving (b,g), tennis (b,g), track and field (b,g), volleyball (g), wrestling (b); intramural: dance squad (g), dance team (g), field hockey (g), kickball (g), lacrosse (b,g), rugby (b,g), volleyball (b), weight lifting (b,g); coed interscholastic: bowling, diving, ice hockey; coed intramural: badminton, bicycling, crew, fencing, Frisbee, martial arts, skiing (downhill), ultimate Frisbee. 6 PE instructors, 1 athletic trainer.

Computers Computers are regularly used in business, business skills, creative writing, desktop publishing, English, foreign language, history, information technology, journalism, mathematics, newspaper, photography, photojournalism, SAT preparation, science, writing, writing, yearbook classes. Computer network features include on-campus library services, online commercial services, Internet access, wireless campus network, Internet filtering or blocking technology. Student e-mail accounts are available to students. Students grades are available online. The school has a published electronic and media policy.

Contact Mr. Duane Emery, Vice President for Enrollment Management. 317-968-7360. Fax: 317-968-7395. E-mail: demery@gocathedral.com. Web site: www.cathedral-irish.org/

CATHEDRAL HIGH SCHOOL

350 East 56th Street
New York, New York 10022-4199

Head of School: Ms. Maria Spagnuolo

General Information Girls' day college-preparatory, arts, business, religious studies, and technology school, affiliated with Roman Catholic Church. Grades 9–12. Founded: 1905. Setting: urban. 1 building on campus. Approved or accredited by Middle States Association of Colleges and Schools, National Catholic Education Association, New York Department of Education, New York State Board of Regents, The College Board, and New York Department of Education. Total enrollment: 600. Upper school average class size: 35. Upper school faculty-student ratio: 1:17. The average school day consists of 7 hours.

Upper School Student Profile 75% of students are Roman Catholic.

Subjects Offered Advanced Placement courses, algebra, art, band, biology, biology-AP, business law, business skills, business studies, calculus, calculus-AP, campus ministry, career education internship, career exploration, Catholic belief and practice, chemistry, chemistry-AP, choir, chorus, Christian doctrine, college admission preparation, college counseling, computer education, computer graphics, computers, constitutional history of U.S., crafts, drama, earth science, economics, electives, English composition, English literature, English-AP, English/composition-AP, fashion, fitness, foreign language, French, general math, geometry, government, guidance, health, health education, honors algebra, honors English, honors geometry, honors U.S. history, honors world history, HTML design, integrated mathematics, internship, lab science, law and the legal system, literature, mathematics-AP, physics, physics-AP, physiology, portfolio art, pre-algebra, pre-calculus, psychology, psychology-AP, religion, science, social education, sociology, Spanish literature, Spanish-AP, studio art, U.S. government, U.S. history, U.S. history-AP, world history, world wide web design.

Graduation Requirements Art, electives, English, foreign language, mathematics, music, physical education (includes health), religion (includes Bible studies and theology), science, social studies (includes history), New York State Regents.

Special Academic Programs 7 Advanced Placement exams for which test preparation is offered; honors section; remedial reading and/or remedial writing; remedial math.

Student Life Upper grades have uniform requirement, student council, honor system. Discipline rests primarily with faculty. Attendance at religious services is required.

Tuition and Aid Day student tuition: $6590. Tuition installment plan (monthly payment plans). Tuition reduction for siblings, merit scholarship grants, need-based scholarship grants available.

Admissions Traditional secondary-level entrance grade is 9. Catholic High School Entrance Examination required. Deadline for receipt of application materials: none. No application fee required.

Athletics Interscholastic: basketball, soccer, softball, volleyball; intramural: basketball, swimming and diving. 1 PE instructor, 3 coaches.

Computers Computers are regularly used in all academic classes. Computer network features include on-campus library services, Internet access, Internet filtering or blocking technology. Campus intranet, student e-mail accounts, and computer access in designated common areas are available to students. Students grades are available online.

Contact Mrs. Johanna Velez, Director of Recruitment. 212-688-1545 Ext. 224. Fax: 212-754-2024. E-mail: jcastex@cathedralhs.org. Web site: www.cathedralhs.org

CATHEDRAL PREPARATORY SCHOOL

225 West 9th Street
Erie, Pennsylvania 16501

Head of School: Rev. Scott William Jabo

General Information Boys' day college-preparatory, arts, religious studies, and technology school, affiliated with Roman Catholic Church. Grades 9–12. Founded: 1921. Setting: urban. 16-acre campus. 1 building on campus. Approved or accredited by Middle States Association of Colleges and Schools and Pennsylvania Department of Education. Endowment: $31 million. Total enrollment: 581. Upper school average class size: 22. Upper school faculty-student ratio: 1:13. There are 180 required school days per year for Upper School students. Upper School students typically attend 5 days per week. The average school day consists of 6 hours and 47 minutes.

Upper School Student Profile Grade 9: 153 students (153 boys); Grade 10: 134 students (134 boys); Grade 11: 151 students (151 boys); Grade 12: 143 students (143 boys). 85% of students are Roman Catholic.

Faculty School total: 48. In upper school: 35 men, 13 women; 23 have advanced degrees.

Subjects Offered Aerospace science, algebra, American history, American history-AP, anatomy and physiology, aviation, Basic programming, biology, biology-AP, calculus, ceramics, chemistry, chemistry-AP, church history, computer literacy, computer programming, creative writing, critical thinking, death and loss, debate, desktop publishing, discrete mathematics, drawing, driver education, English, expository writing, finance, first aid, flight instruction, French, geometry, German, health, history of the Catholic Church, history-AP, human anatomy, integrated science, interpersonal skills, introduction to theater, jazz band, keyboarding, Latin, leadership, Mandarin, mechanical drawing, men's studies, Microsoft, moral theology, newspaper, physical education, physics, pre-calculus, probability and statistics, public speaking, reading, ROTC, sexuality, social justice, Spanish, studio art, theater, trigonometry, U.S. government and politics-AP, video communication, video film production, Vietnam War, world geography, world history, writing, yearbook.

Graduation Requirements American government, biology, chemistry, economics, English, English composition, English literature, geography, government, language, mathematics, physical education (includes health), physics, psychology, social studies (includes history), theology, U.S. government, 100 hours of community service (school, church and community).

Special Academic Programs 13 Advanced Placement exams for which test preparation is offered; honors section; study at local college for college credit.

College Admission Counseling 115 students graduated in 2012; 111 went to college, including Edinboro University of Pennsylvania; Gannon University; John Carroll University; Penn State Erie, The Behrend College; Penn State University Park; University of Pittsburgh. Other: 4 went to work.

Student Life Upper grades have uniform requirement, student council, honor system. Discipline rests primarily with faculty. Attendance at religious services is required.

Summer Programs Remediation, enrichment, advancement, sports programs offered; session focuses on academics; held both on and off campus; held at athletic fields; accepts boys and girls; open to students from other schools. 50 students usually enrolled. 2013 schedule: June 17 to July 12. Application deadline: June 14.

Tuition and Aid Day student tuition: $7345. Tuition installment plan (FACTS Tuition Payment Plan). Tuition reduction for siblings, merit scholarship grants, need-based scholarship grants available. In 2012–13, 51% of upper-school students received aid; total upper-school merit-scholarship money awarded: $10,000. Total amount of financial aid awarded in 2012–13: $550,000.

Admissions Traditional secondary-level entrance grade is 9. For fall 2012, 212 students applied for upper-level admission, 195 were accepted, 153 enrolled. High School Placement Test required. Deadline for receipt of application materials: March 1. No application fee required. Interview recommended.

Athletics Interscholastic: baseball, basketball, cross-country running, football, golf, hockey, independent competitive sports, JROTC drill, lacrosse, outdoor recreation, power lifting, skiing (cross-country), skiing (downhill), soccer, swimming and diving, tennis, track and field, water polo, weight lifting, weight training, wrestling; intramural: bowling, table tennis, weight lifting. 2 PE instructors, 1 athletic trainer.

Computers Computers are regularly used in all academic classes. Computer network features include on-campus library services, Internet access, wireless campus network, Internet filtering or blocking technology, all students receive an Apple iPad upon admission. Campus intranet and student e-mail accounts are available to students. Students grades are available online. The school has a published electronic and media policy.

Contact Mr. Timothy Dougherty, Director of Admissions. 814-453-7737 Ext. 2242. Fax: 814-455-5462. E-mail: Timothy.Dougherty@prep-villa.com. Web site: www.prep-villa.com

CATHOLIC CENTRAL HIGH SCHOOL

625 Seventh Avenue
Troy, New York 12182-2595

Head of School: Mr. Christopher Bott

General Information Coeducational day college-preparatory, arts, business, and religious studies school, affiliated with Roman Catholic Church. Grades 7–12. Founded: 1924. Setting: suburban. 4-acre campus. 2 buildings on campus. Approved or accredited by National Catholic Education Association and New York State Board of Regents. Endowment: $50,000. Total enrollment: 520. Upper school average class size: 16. Upper school faculty-student ratio: 1:12. There are 168 required school days per year for Upper School students. Upper School students typically attend 5 days per week. The average school day consists of 6 hours and 21 minutes.

Upper School Student Profile Grade 9: 102 students (47 boys, 55 girls); Grade 10: 101 students (46 boys, 55 girls); Grade 11: 96 students (33 boys, 63 girls); Grade 12: 110 students (46 boys, 64 girls). 85% of students are Roman Catholic.

Faculty School total: 39. In upper school: 15 men, 22 women; 28 have advanced degrees.

Subjects Offered Accounting, algebra, anatomy and physiology, art, astronomy, band, biology, business communications, business law, calculus, Catholic belief and practice, chemistry, chorus, computer art, computer programming, computer science, drama, drawing and design, driver education, earth science, economics, English, English language-AP, global studies, government, health, history, honors English, honors U.S. history, Internet, keyboarding, library skills, mathematics, physics, pre-calculus, printmaking, religion, social studies, Spanish, U.S. history.

Graduation Requirements Art, English, mathematics, physical education (includes health), science, social studies (includes history), theology.

Special Academic Programs Advanced Placement exam preparation; remedial reading and/or remedial writing; remedial math; ESL (12 students enrolled).

College Admission Counseling 108 students graduated in 2012; 107 went to college, including Rensselaer Polytechnic Institute; Siena College; State University of New York at New Paltz; State University of New York College at Geneseo; University at Albany, State University of New York. Other: 1 went to work.

Student Life Upper grades have uniform requirement, student council. Discipline rests primarily with faculty. Attendance at religious services is required.

Tuition and Aid Day student tuition: $5900. Tuition installment plan (FACTS Tuition Payment Plan). Need-based scholarship grants, paying campus jobs available. In 2012–13, 26% of upper-school students received aid. Total amount of financial aid awarded in 2012–13: $15,000.

Admissions Traditional secondary-level entrance grade is 9. Scholastic Testing Service High School Placement Test required. Deadline for receipt of application materials: none. Application fee required: $100. Interview recommended.

Athletics Interscholastic: baseball (boys), basketball (b,g), bowling (b,g), cross-country running (b,g), dance squad (g), football (b), golf (b), indoor track & field (b,g), soccer (b,g), softball (g), tennis (b,g), track and field (b,g), volleyball (g); intramural: figure skating (g), lacrosse (g); coed interscholastic: cheering; coed intramural: Frisbee. 2 PE instructors, 8 coaches, 1 athletic trainer.

Computers Computers are regularly used in accounting, art, business applications, graphic design, programming classes. Computer network features include on-campus library services, Internet access, Internet filtering or blocking technology.

Contact Mrs. Teresa Mainello, Publicity Director. 518-235-7100 Ext. 224. Fax: 518-237-1796. E-mail: tmainello@cchstroy.org. Web site: www.cchstroy.org

CATHOLIC CENTRAL HIGH SCHOOL

148 McHenry Street
Burlington, Wisconsin 53105

Head of School: Mr. Eric Henderson

General Information Coeducational day college-preparatory, arts, business, religious studies, bilingual studies, and technology school, affiliated with Roman Catholic Church. Grades 9–12. Founded: 1924. Setting: small town. Nearest major city is Milwaukee. 25-acre campus. 2 buildings on campus. Approved or accredited by North Central Association of Colleges and Schools and Wisconsin Department of Education. Endowment: $1 million. Total enrollment: 168. Upper school average class size: 14. Upper school faculty-student ratio: 1:9. There are 180 required school days per year for Upper School students. Upper School students typically attend 5 days per week. The average school day consists of 7 hours.

Upper School Student Profile Grade 9: 51 students (23 boys, 28 girls); Grade 10: 48 students (19 boys, 29 girls); Grade 11: 33 students (19 boys, 14 girls); Grade 12: 36 students (21 boys, 15 girls). 86% of students are Roman Catholic.

Faculty School total: 19. In upper school: 9 men, 10 women; 9 have advanced degrees.

Subjects Offered 20th century history, 3-dimensional art, 3-dimensional design, accounting, advanced biology, advanced chemistry, advanced computer applications, advanced math, Advanced Placement courses, African-American history, algebra, American government, American history, American literature, American literature-AP, analytic geometry, anatomy, anatomy and physiology, animation, Arabic, art, band, Bible, Bible studies, biology, biotechnology, botany, business, business education, business technology, calculus, calculus-AP, cartooning/animation, Catholic belief and practice, ceramics, chemistry, Chinese, choir, church history, college admission preparation, college planning, composition, composition-AP, computer animation, computer graphics, computer skills, consumer education, digital photography, diversity studies, drawing, earth science, economics, English, English literature-AP, environmental science, finance, forensics, French, geography, geometry, government, health, history of religion, history of the Catholic Church, human anatomy, human biology, integrated science, intro to computers, Italian, journalism, marketing, mathematics-AP, music theory, New Testament, painting, personal finance, personal fitness, photography, physical fitness, physics, physiology, pre-calculus, probability and statistics, psychology, psychology-AP, religion, religious studies, skills for success, social justice, sociology, Spanish, speech, statistics, study skills, theology, trigonometry, U.S. history, video and animation, world religions, zoology.

Graduation Requirements 20th century history, American government, health, personal finance, physical education (includes health), religious education, speech.

Special Academic Programs 3 Advanced Placement exams for which test preparation is offered; honors section; independent study; study at local college for college credit; study abroad; academic accommodation for the gifted and the artistically talented.

College Admission Counseling 24 students graduated in 2012; 22 went to college, including Marquette University; St. Norbert College; The University of Iowa; University of Wisconsin–La Crosse; University of Wisconsin–Madison. Other: 2 went to work. Median composite ACT: 24. 8% scored over 26 on composite ACT.

Student Life Upper grades have specified standards of dress, student council, honor system. Discipline rests primarily with faculty. Attendance at religious services is required.

Summer Programs Sports programs offered; session focuses on basketball; held on campus; accepts boys and girls; open to students from other schools. 150 students usually enrolled. 2013 schedule: June 15 to July 31. Application deadline: June 15.

Tuition and Aid Day student tuition: $6950–$7600. Tuition installment plan (FACTS Tuition Payment Plan, individually arranged payment plans). Tuition reduction for siblings, need-based scholarship grants available. In 2012–13, 55% of upper-school students received aid. Total amount of financial aid awarded in 2012–13: $130,000.

Admissions Traditional secondary-level entrance grade is 9. For fall 2012, 171 students applied for upper-level admission, 171 were accepted, 168 enrolled. ACT-Explore required. Deadline for receipt of application materials: none. Application fee required: $200. On-campus interview required.

Athletics Interscholastic: baseball (boys), basketball (b,g), dance team (g), football (b), golf (b), softball (g), tennis (g), volleyball (g), wrestling (b); coed interscholastic: bowling, cheering, cross-country running, fitness, gymnastics, physical fitness, track and field; coed intramural: bicycling, dance, dance squad, strength & conditioning, table tennis, ultimate Frisbee, weight training. 1 PE instructor, 31 coaches, 1 athletic trainer.

Computers Computers are regularly used in accounting, business, economics, graphic design, journalism, multimedia, newspaper, photography, typing, video film production, Web site design, writing classes. Computer network features include Internet access, wireless campus network, Internet filtering or blocking technology. Student e-mail accounts and computer access in designated common areas are available to students. Students grades are available online. The school has a published electronic and media policy.

Contact Mr. Kyle Scott, Admissions Director. 262-763-1510 Ext. 225. Fax: 262-763-1509. E-mail: kscott@cchsnet.org. Web site: www.cchsnet.org

THE CATHOLIC HIGH SCHOOL OF BALTIMORE

2800 Edison Highway
Baltimore, Maryland 21213

Head of School: Dr. Barbara D. Nazelrod

General Information Girls' day and distance learning college-preparatory, general academic, arts, religious studies, and technology school, affiliated with Roman Catholic Church. Grades 9–12. Distance learning grades 9–12. Founded: 1939. Setting: urban. 6-acre campus. 1 building on campus. Approved or accredited by Association of Independent Maryland Schools, Middle States Association of Colleges and Schools, National Catholic Education Association, and Maryland Department of Education. Endowment: $3 million. Total enrollment: 299. Upper school average class size: 17. Upper school faculty-student ratio: 1:12. There are 175 required school days per year for Upper School students. Upper School students typically attend 5 days per week. The average school day consists of 6 hours and 45 minutes.

Upper School Student Profile Grade 9: 95 students (95 girls); Grade 10: 86 students (86 girls); Grade 11: 60 students (60 girls); Grade 12: 58 students (58 girls). 79% of students are Roman Catholic.

Faculty School total: 33. In upper school: 11 men, 16 women; 20 have advanced degrees.

Subjects Offered Algebra, American history, American literature, anatomy, art, band, biology, calculus, chemistry, community service, computer programming, computer science, creative writing, dance, drama, earth science, English, English literature, expository writing, fine arts, French, geometry, government/civics, grammar, health, history, instrumental music, journalism, keyboarding, literature, mathematics, music, photography, physical education, physics, physiology, psychology, reading, religion, science, social studies, Spanish, speech, study skills, technology, theater, theology, Web site design, world history, world literature.

Graduation Requirements Arts and fine arts (art, music, dance, drama), computer science, English, foreign language, mathematics, physical education (includes health), science, social studies (includes history), theology. Community service is required.

Special Academic Programs Advanced Placement exam preparation; honors section; independent study; study at local college for college credit; remedial reading and/or remedial writing; remedial math; programs in English, mathematics, general development for dyslexic students.

College Admission Counseling 97 students graduated in 2012; 95 went to college, including Salisbury University; Stevenson University; Towson University. Other: 2 went to work. Median SAT critical reading: 500, median SAT math: 445, median SAT writing: 510.

Student Life Upper grades have uniform requirement, student council, honor system. Discipline rests primarily with faculty. Attendance at religious services is required.

Summer Programs Enrichment, sports, art/fine arts, computer instruction programs offered; session focuses on enrichment; held both on and off campus; held at sports field; accepts girls; not open to students from other schools. 100 students usually enrolled. 2013 schedule: June 18 to July 23. Application deadline: none.

Tuition and Aid Day student tuition: $11,000. Guaranteed tuition plan. Tuition installment plan (Insured Tuition Payment Plan, FACTS Tuition Payment Plan, biannual payment plan, annual payment plan). Tuition reduction for siblings, merit scholarship grants, need-based scholarship grants available. In 2012–13, 75% of upper-school students received aid; total upper-school merit-scholarship money awarded: $326,750. Total amount of financial aid awarded in 2012–13: $523,116.

Admissions Traditional secondary-level entrance grade is 9. For fall 2012, 230 students applied for upper-level admission, 207 were accepted, 101 enrolled. High School Placement Test required. Deadline for receipt of application materials: December 19. Application fee required: $40. On-campus interview required.

Athletics Interscholastic: basketball, cheering, cross-country running, dance team, field hockey, golf, indoor track & field, lacrosse, soccer, softball, swimming and diving, tennis, track and field, volleyball; intramural: aerobics, aerobics/dance, cooperative games. 1 PE instructor, 20 coaches, 1 athletic trainer.

Computers Computers are regularly used in art, English, foreign language, history, mathematics, music, science, theology classes. Computer network features include on-campus library services, online commercial services, Internet access, wireless campus network, Internet filtering or blocking technology. Campus intranet and student e-mail accounts are available to students. Students grades are available online. The school has a published electronic and media policy.

Contact Ms. Michelle Illar, Assistant Director of Enrollment. 410-732-6200 Ext. 213. Fax: 410-732-7639. E-mail: millar@thecatholichighschool.org. Web site: www.thecatholichighschool.org

THE CATLIN GABEL SCHOOL

8825 SW Barnes Road
Portland, Oregon 97225

Head of School: Dr. Lark P. Palma

General Information Coeducational day college-preparatory, arts, technology, and sciences school. Grades PK–12. Founded: 1957. Setting: suburban. 60-acre campus. 13 buildings on campus. Approved or accredited by Northwest Accreditation Commission and Pacific Northwest Association of Independent Schools. Member of National Association of Independent Schools and Secondary School Admission Test Board. Endowment: $19.5 million. Total enrollment: 753. Upper school average class size: 15. Upper school faculty-student ratio: 1:8. There are 170 required school days per year for Upper School students. Upper School students typically attend 5 days per week. The average school day consists of 7 hours and 10 minutes.

Upper School Student Profile Grade 6: 56 students (27 boys, 29 girls); Grade 7: 64 students (30 boys, 34 girls); Grade 8: 65 students (29 boys, 36 girls); Grade 9: 79 students (39 boys, 40 girls); Grade 10: 77 students (40 boys, 37 girls); Grade 11: 76 students (44 boys, 32 girls); Grade 12: 77 students (38 boys, 39 girls).

Faculty School total: 92. In upper school: 28 men, 22 women; 34 have advanced degrees.

Subjects Offered Acting, advanced chemistry, advanced computer applications, advanced math, algebra, American democracy, American history, American literature, ancient world history, applied music, art, art history, arts, astronomy, athletics, baseball, Basic programming, basketball, biology, bookmaking, bowling, calculus, ceramics, chemistry, Chinese, choir, college admission preparation, college counseling, comedy, computer art, computer graphics, computer programming, computer resources, computer science, computer skills, computer studies, concert choir, creative writing, critical studies in film, critical thinking, debate, digital imaging, digital photography, drama, drama performance, dramatic arts, drawing and design, driver education, ecology, economics, English, English literature, ensembles, ethics and responsibility, European history, expository writing, fiber arts, film studies, fine arts, foreign language, foreign policy, French, geometry, golf, government/civics, graphic arts, graphic design, health, history, human sexuality, Japanese, jazz band, mathematics, model United Nations, music, musical productions, ornithology, outdoor education, peer counseling, performing arts, photo shop, photography, physical education, physical fitness, physics, playwriting and directing, pre-calculus, probability and statistics, robotics, science, set design, Shakespeare, social studies, Spanish, Spanish literature, speech and debate, stage design, stagecraft, statistics, strings, studio art, study skills, technical theater, tennis, theater, theater arts, theater design and production, track and field, trigonometry, U.S. history, visual and performing arts, vocal ensemble, voice, voice ensemble, volleyball, weight fitness, weight training, woodworking, world affairs, world history, world literature, world wide web design, writing, writing workshop, yearbook.

Graduation Requirements Arts and fine arts (art, music, dance, drama), English, foreign language, mathematics, physical education (includes health), science, social studies (includes history). Community service is required.

Special Academic Programs Honors section; independent study; term-away projects; study at local college for college credit; study abroad; academic accommodation for the gifted, the musically talented, and the artistically talented; special instructional classes for deaf students.

College Admission Counseling 77 students graduated in 2012; all went to college, including Stanford University. Mean SAT critical reading: 655, mean SAT math: 644, mean SAT writing: 644, mean combined SAT: 1943, mean composite ACT: 29. 89% scored over 600 on SAT critical reading, 87% scored over 600 on SAT math, 80% scored over 600 on SAT writing, 86% scored over 1800 on combined SAT, 96% scored over 26 on composite ACT.

Student Life Upper grades have student council, honor system. Discipline rests equally with students and faculty.

Summer Programs Enrichment, art/fine arts, computer instruction programs offered; session focuses on arts and enrichment; held both on and off campus; held at various outdoor areas—hiking, climbing, etc.; accepts boys and girls; open to students from other schools. 85 students usually enrolled. 2013 schedule: June 24 to August 2.

Tuition and Aid Day student tuition: $24,750. Tuition installment plan (Insured Tuition Payment Plan, monthly payment plans, individually arranged payment plans).

Merit scholarship grants, need-based scholarship grants available. In 2012–13, 29% of upper-school students received aid. Total amount of financial aid awarded in 2012–13: $2,900,000.

Admissions Traditional secondary-level entrance grade is 9. For fall 2012, 64 students applied for upper-level admission, 50 were accepted, 29 enrolled. SSAT required. Deadline for receipt of application materials: February 4. Application fee required: $75. Interview required.

Athletics Interscholastic: baseball (boys, girls), basketball (b,g), cross-country running (b,g), golf (b,g), racquetball (b,g), soccer (b,g), tennis (b,g), track and field (b,g), volleyball (g); coed interscholastic: racquetball; coed intramural: alpine skiing, backpacking, bicycling, bowling, canoeing/kayaking, climbing, fishing, fitness, Frisbee, hiking/backpacking, jogging, kayaking, mountain biking, mountaineering, nordic skiing, ocean paddling, outdoor activities, outdoor adventure, outdoor education, outdoor recreation, outdoors, physical fitness, physical training, rafting, rock climbing, ropes courses, running, skiing (cross-country), skiing (downhill), snowshoeing, strength & conditioning, telemark skiing, ultimate Frisbee, walking, wall climbing, weight lifting, weight training, wilderness, wilderness survival, yoga. 6 PE instructors, 20 coaches.

Computers Computers are regularly used in animation, art, English, foreign language, graphic design, mathematics, science, theater, writing classes. Computer network features include on-campus library services, online commercial services, Internet access, wireless campus network, laptop requirement for all upper school students, videoconferencing, SmartBoards. Campus intranet and student e-mail accounts are available to students. The school has a published electronic and media policy.

Contact Ms. Sara Nordhoff, Director of Admission and Financial Aid. 503-297-1894 Ext. 345. Fax: 503-297-0139. E-mail: nordhoffs@catlin.edu. Web site: www.catlin.edu

CENTRAL ALBERTA CHRISTIAN HIGH SCHOOL

22 Eagle Road
Lacombe, Alberta T4L 1G7, Canada

Head of School: Mr. Mel Brandsma

General Information Coeducational day college-preparatory, general academic, religious studies, and bilingual studies school, affiliated with Christian Reformed Church. Grades 10–12. Founded: 1989. Setting: rural. Nearest major city is Red Deer, Canada. 1 building on campus. Approved or accredited by Christian Schools International and Alberta Department of Education. Language of instruction: English. Total enrollment: 108. Upper school average class size: 108. Upper school faculty-student ratio: 1:13. Upper School students typically attend 5 days per week. The average school day consists of 6 hours and 25 minutes.

Upper School Student Profile Grade 10: 29 students (14 boys, 15 girls); Grade 11: 39 students (18 boys, 21 girls); Grade 12: 40 students (21 boys, 19 girls). 75% of students are members of Christian Reformed Church.

Faculty School total: 9. In upper school: 4 men, 4 women; 1 has an advanced degree.

Subjects Offered Accounting, agriculture, all academic, art, career education, Christian ethics, computer education, drafting, foods, French as a second language, photography, physical education, work experience.

Graduation Requirements All academic, French.

College Admission Counseling 34 students graduated in 2012; they went to Redeemer University College.

Student Life Upper grades have student council, honor system. Discipline rests primarily with faculty.

Tuition and Aid Day student tuition: CAN$5150. Tuition installment plan (monthly payment plans, individually arranged payment plans). Tuition reduction for siblings available.

Admissions Traditional secondary-level entrance grade is 10. Deadline for receipt of application materials: none. No application fee required. Interview recommended.

Athletics Coed Interscholastic: badminton, basketball, bowling, climbing, cross-country running, fitness, ice skating, jogging, outdoor activities, physical fitness, physical training, running, soccer, softball, swimming and diving, track and field, volleyball, wall climbing, weight training, whiffle ball; coed intramural: basketball, broomball, cooperative games. 1 PE instructor, 1 coach.

Computers Computers are regularly used in all classes. Computer network features include Internet access, wireless campus network, Internet filtering or blocking technology. Campus intranet is available to students.

Contact Office. 403-782-4535. Fax: 403-782-5425. E-mail: office@cachs.ca. Web site: www.cachs.ca/

CENTRAL CATHOLIC HIGH SCHOOL

200 South Carpenter Road
Modesto, California 95351

Head of School: Jim Pecchenino

General Information Coeducational day college-preparatory, arts, religious studies, and bilingual studies school, affiliated with Roman Catholic Church. Grades 9–12. Founded: 1966. Setting: urban. Nearest major city is Sacramento. 21-acre campus. 13 buildings on campus. Approved or accredited by National Catholic Education Association, Western Association of Schools and Colleges, and Western Catholic Education Association. Endowment: $2.1 million. Total enrollment: 389. Upper school average class size: 22. Upper school faculty-student ratio: 1:14. There are 180 required school days per year for Upper School students. Upper School students typically attend 5 days per week. The average school day consists of 6 hours and 50 minutes.

Upper School Student Profile Grade 9: 94 students (66 boys, 28 girls); Grade 10: 96 students (55 boys, 41 girls); Grade 11: 100 students (52 boys, 48 girls); Grade 12: 99 students (51 boys, 48 girls). 81% of students are Roman Catholic.

Faculty School total: 29. In upper school: 8 men, 21 women; 11 have advanced degrees.

Subjects Offered Algebra, American history, American literature, art, Bible studies, biology, broadcast journalism, calculus, chemistry, dance, drama, drawing and design, economics, English, English literature, environmental science, ethics, European history, geometry, government/civics, health, mathematics, music, physical education, physical science, physics, pre-calculus, Spanish, speech, theology, vocal ensemble, world history, world literature, yearbook.

Graduation Requirements Arts and fine arts (art, music, dance, drama), English, mathematics, physical education (includes health), religion (includes Bible studies and theology), science, social studies (includes history), speech, 100 Christian service hours.

Special Academic Programs Advanced Placement exam preparation; honors section; study at local college for college credit; remedial reading and/or remedial writing; remedial math; programs in English, mathematics, general development for dyslexic students.

College Admission Counseling 102 students graduated in 2012; 101 went to college, including California Polytechnic State University, San Luis Obispo; California State University, Stanislaus; Saint Mary's College of California; University of California, Berkeley; University of California, Davis; University of California, Los Angeles. Other: 1 entered a postgraduate year. Median SAT critical reading: 520, median SAT math: 500, median SAT writing: 500, median combined SAT: 820. 31.7% scored over 600 on SAT critical reading, 26.8% scored over 600 on SAT math, 20.7% scored over 600 on SAT writing, 28% scored over 1800 on combined SAT.

Student Life Upper grades have specified standards of dress, student council. Discipline rests primarily with faculty. Attendance at religious services is required.

Summer Programs Remediation programs offered; session focuses on remediation and SAT Prep; held on campus; accepts boys and girls; open to students from other schools. 109 students usually enrolled. 2013 schedule: June 4 to July 6. Application deadline: May 11.

Tuition and Aid Day student tuition: $8995–$9378. Tuition installment plan (FACTS Tuition Payment Plan, monthly payment plans, individually arranged payment plans, quarterly and semiannual payment plans). Tuition reduction for siblings, merit scholarship grants, need-based scholarship grants, paying campus jobs available. In 2012–13, 34% of upper-school students received aid; total upper-school merit-scholarship money awarded: $13,400. Total amount of financial aid awarded in 2012–13: $392,671.

Admissions Traditional secondary-level entrance grade is 9. For fall 2012, 123 students applied for upper-level admission, 94 were accepted, 94 enrolled. Otis-Lennon School Ability Test required. Deadline for receipt of application materials: none. Application fee required: $45. On-campus interview required.

Athletics Interscholastic: baseball (boys), basketball (b,g), cross-country running (b,g), football (b), golf (b,g), soccer (b,g), softball (g), tennis (b,g), track and field (b,g), volleyball (g), water polo (b,g), wrestling (b,g); intramural: cheering (g); coed interscholastic: swimming and diving; coed intramural: dance. 1 PE instructor, 91 coaches.

Computers Computers are regularly used in literacy, yearbook classes. Computer network features include on-campus library services, Internet access, Internet filtering or blocking technology. Computer access in designated common areas is available to students. Students grades are available online. The school has a published electronic and media policy.

Contact Jodi Tybor, Admissions Coordinator/Registrar. 209-524-9611 Ext. 104. Fax: 209-524-4913. E-mail: tybor@cchsca.org. Web site: www.cchsca.org

CENTRAL CATHOLIC HIGH SCHOOL

300 Hampshire Street
Lawrence, Massachusetts 01841

Head of School: Mrs. Doreen A. Keller

General Information Coeducational day college-preparatory, arts, business, religious studies, and technology school, affiliated with Roman Catholic Church. Grades 9–12. Founded: 1935. Setting: urban. Nearest major city is Boston. 1 building on campus. Approved or accredited by Commission on Independent Schools, New England Association of Schools and Colleges, and Massachusetts Department of Education. Member of National Association of Independent Schools. Total enrollment: 1,340. Upper school average class size: 25. Upper school faculty-student ratio: 1:24. There are 165 required school days per year for Upper School students. Upper School students typically attend 5 days per week. The average school day consists of 6 hours and 15 minutes.

Upper School Student Profile Grade 9: 375 students (186 boys, 189 girls); Grade 10: 331 students (182 boys, 149 girls); Grade 11: 317 students (160 boys, 157

girls); Grade 12: 317 students (159 boys, 158 girls). 80% of students are Roman Catholic.
Faculty School total: 101. In upper school: 40 men, 41 women; 59 have advanced degrees.
Subjects Offered Art, arts, computer science, English, fine arts, French, health, mathematics, physical education, religion, science, social studies, Spanish.
Graduation Requirements Arts and fine arts (art, music, dance, drama), computer science, English, foreign language, mathematics, religion (includes Bible studies and theology), science, social studies (includes history).
Special Academic Programs International Baccalaureate program; Advanced Placement exam preparation; honors section; study at local college for college credit.
College Admission Counseling 323 students graduated in 2012; 315 went to college. Other: 2 went to work, 3 entered military service.
Student Life Upper grades have uniform requirement, student council, honor system. Discipline rests primarily with faculty. Attendance at religious services is required.
Tuition and Aid Day student tuition: $11,300. Tuition installment plan (FACTS Tuition Payment Plan, monthly payment plans). Merit scholarship grants, need-based scholarship grants available.
Admissions Archdiocese of Boston High School entrance exam provided by STS, High School Placement Test and High School Placement Test (closed version) from Scholastic Testing Service required. Deadline for receipt of application materials: none. No application fee required. Interview required.
Athletics Interscholastic: baseball (boys), basketball (b,g), bowling (b,g), cheering (g), cross-country running (b,g), dance squad (b,g), diving (b,g), field hockey (g), figure skating (g), fishing (b,g), football (b), golf (b), gymnastics (g), hockey (b), ice hockey (b), ice skating (g), indoor hockey (g), indoor track (b,g), indoor track & field (b,g), lacrosse (b,g), martial arts (b,g), modern dance (b,g), soccer (b,g), softball (g), swimming and diving (b,g), tennis (b,g), track and field (b,g), volleyball (b,g), wall climbing (b,g), winter (indoor) track (b,g), wrestling (b); intramural: basketball (b,g); coed interscholastic: dance team. 3 PE instructors, 80 coaches, 1 athletic trainer.
Computers Computer network features include on-campus library services, Internet access, wireless campus network, Internet filtering or blocking technology. Campus intranet, student e-mail accounts, and computer access in designated common areas are available to students. The school has a published electronic and media policy.
Contact Mr. Thomas Sipsey, Assistant Director of Admissions. 978-682-0260 Ext. 623. Fax: 978-685-2707. E-mail: tsipsey@centralcatholic.net. Web site: www.centralcatholic.net

CENTRAL CATHOLIC HIGH SCHOOL

1403 North St. Mary's Street
San Antonio, Texas 78215-1785

Head of School: Rev. Richard G.T. Wosman, S.M.

General Information Boys' day college-preparatory school, affiliated with Roman Catholic Church. Grades 9–12. Founded: 1852. Setting: urban. 10-acre campus. 2 buildings on campus. Approved or accredited by National Catholic Education Association, Southern Association of Colleges and Schools, Texas Catholic Conference, and Texas Department of Education. Endowment: $1 million. Total enrollment: 558. Upper school average class size: 23. Upper school faculty-student ratio: 1:20. There are 180 required school days per year for Upper School students. Upper School students typically attend 5 days per week. The average school day consists of 6 hours and 30 minutes.
Upper School Student Profile Grade 9: 148 students (148 boys); Grade 10: 139 students (139 boys); Grade 11: 136 students (136 boys); Grade 12: 136 students (136 boys). 90% of students are Roman Catholic.
Faculty School total: 46. In upper school: 33 men, 13 women; 23 have advanced degrees.
Subjects Offered Algebra, American government, American history-AP, anatomy, art, biology, calculus-AP, ceramics, chemistry, chemistry-AP, chorus, Christian and Hebrew scripture, church history, community service, computer science, concert band, economics, English, English language and composition-AP, English language-AP, English literature and composition-AP, English literature-AP, environmental science, fine arts, geometry, health, honors algebra, honors English, honors geometry, honors world history, humanities, information technology, jazz band, journalism, JROTC, languages, Latin, marching band, physics, pre-calculus, probability and statistics, psychology, religion, science, social studies, Spanish, Spanish literature-AP, speech, trigonometry, world geography, world history.
Graduation Requirements Algebra, American government, American history, arts and fine arts (art, music, dance, drama), biology, chemistry, Christian and Hebrew scripture, Christian doctrine, computer information systems, computer science, economics, English, foreign language, geometry, health, JROTC, moral reasoning, religion (includes Bible studies and theology), religious education, social justice, speech, trigonometry, world civilizations, world geography, world history, world religions, different requirements for Marianist Honors Diploma. Community service is required.
Special Academic Programs 6 Advanced Placement exams for which test preparation is offered; honors section; independent study; study at local college for college credit; study abroad.
College Admission Counseling 106 students graduated in 2012; 105 went to college, including Saint Mary's University; Texas A&M University; Texas Tech University; The University of Texas at Austin; The University of Texas at San Antonio; University of the Incarnate Word. Other: 1 entered military service. Mean SAT critical reading: 541, mean SAT math: 537, mean SAT writing: 528, mean combined SAT: 1606, mean composite ACT: 25.
Student Life Upper grades have specified standards of dress, student council, honor system. Discipline rests primarily with faculty. Attendance at religious services is required.
Summer Programs Remediation, enrichment, advancement, sports, computer instruction programs offered; session focuses on enrichment and make-up courses, sports; held on campus; accepts boys and girls; open to students from other schools. 225 students usually enrolled. 2013 schedule: June 11 to July 20. Application deadline: none.
Tuition and Aid Day student tuition: $1040. Tuition installment plan (FACTS Tuition Payment Plan, monthly payment plans, individually arranged payment plans, semester payment plan, Tuition Management Systems). Tuition reduction for siblings, merit scholarship grants, need-based scholarship grants, paying campus jobs available. In 2012–13, 45% of upper-school students received aid; total upper-school merit-scholarship money awarded: $54,000. Total amount of financial aid awarded in 2012–13: $717,000.
Admissions Traditional secondary-level entrance grade is 9. Essay, Scholastic Testing Service High School Placement Test and writing sample required. Deadline for receipt of application materials: none. No application fee required. On-campus interview recommended.
Athletics Interscholastic: baseball, basketball, cheering (g), cross-country running, drill team, football, golf, JROTC drill, lacrosse, physical training, riflery, soccer, strength & conditioning, swimming and diving, tennis, track and field, weight training; intramural: basketball, bowling, football, softball, strength & conditioning, swimming and diving, volleyball. 1 PE instructor, 21 coaches, 1 athletic trainer.
Computers Computers are regularly used in college planning, computer applications, drawing and design, engineering, English, information technology, journalism, newspaper, science, yearbook classes. Computer network features include on-campus library services, Internet access, Internet filtering or blocking technology, access to other libraries through Texas Library Connection. Students grades are available online. The school has a published electronic and media policy.
Contact Mrs. Veronica Beck, Director of Admissions and Tuition Assistance. 210-225-6794 Ext. 209. Fax: 210-227-9353. E-mail: admissions@cchs-satx.org. Web site: www.cchs-satx.org

CHADWICK SCHOOL

26800 South Academy Drive
Palos Verdes Peninsula, California 90274

Head of School: Frederick T. Hill

General Information Coeducational day college-preparatory, arts, and technology school. Grades K–12. Founded: 1935. Setting: suburban. Nearest major city is Los Angeles. 45-acre campus. 5 buildings on campus. Approved or accredited by Association for Experiential Education, California Association of Independent Schools, The College Board, Western Association of Schools and Colleges, and California Department of Education. Member of National Association of Independent Schools. Endowment: $20 million. Total enrollment: 830. Upper school average class size: 17. Upper school faculty-student ratio: 1:6. There are 167 required school days per year for Upper School students. Upper School students typically attend 5 days per week. The average school day consists of 7 hours and 45 minutes.
Upper School Student Profile Grade 9: 91 students (41 boys, 50 girls); Grade 10: 87 students (37 boys, 50 girls); Grade 11: 85 students (41 boys, 44 girls); Grade 12: 94 students (42 boys, 52 girls).
Faculty School total: 71. In upper school: 26 men, 45 women; 50 have advanced degrees.
Subjects Offered 3-dimensional art, Advanced Placement courses, African history, algebra, American history, American literature, American studies, art, art history-AP, art-AP, Asian history, biology, calculus, calculus-AP, ceramics, chemistry, chemistry-AP, choral music, comparative government and politics-AP, computer math, computer programming, computer science-AP, constitutional law, creative writing, dance, drama, economics, English, English literature, English literature-AP, environmental science, environmental science-AP, European history, expository writing, fine arts, forensics, French, French-AP, geometry, grammar, health, history, honors algebra, honors geometry, instrumental music, integrated science, Latin, Latin American history, Latin American studies, life science, Mandarin, marine biology, mathematics, Middle East, Middle Eastern history, music, music theory-AP, outdoor education, photography, physical education, physics, pre-calculus, probability, robotics, science, social studies, South African history, Spanish, Spanish-AP, speech, statistics, statistics-AP, theater, trigonometry, U.S. history-AP, wilderness education, world history, world literature, writing, yearbook.
Graduation Requirements Arts and fine arts (art, music, dance, drama), English, foreign language, history, mathematics, outdoor education, performing arts, physical education (includes health), science.
Special Academic Programs Advanced Placement exam preparation; honors section; independent study; term-away projects; study abroad; academic accommodation for the gifted, the musically talented, and the artistically talented.

College Admission Counseling 95 students graduated in 2012; all went to college, including Amherst College; Duke University; Loyola Marymount University; New York University; University of Southern California; Washington University in St. Louis. Mean SAT critical reading: 653, mean SAT math: 681, mean SAT writing: 680, mean combined SAT: 2014.
Student Life Upper grades have specified standards of dress, student council, honor system. Discipline rests equally with students and faculty.
Summer Programs Sports, art/fine arts, computer instruction programs offered; session focuses on visual and performing arts, academics, athletics, enrichment; held on campus; accepts boys and girls; open to students from other schools. 500 students usually enrolled. 2013 schedule: June 24 to July 26. Application deadline: April.
Tuition and Aid Day student tuition: $28,770. Tuition installment plan (Key Tuition Payment Plan, individually arranged payment plans). Need-based scholarship grants, paying campus jobs, Malone Scholarship (need/merit-based), MacFarlane Scholarship (need/merit-based) available. In 2012–13, 18% of upper-school students received aid. Total amount of financial aid awarded in 2012–13: $1,750,500.
Admissions Traditional secondary-level entrance grade is 9. ISEE required. Deadline for receipt of application materials: January 17. Application fee required: $125. On-campus interview required.
Athletics Interscholastic: baseball (boys), basketball (b,g), cheering (g), cross-country running (b,g), diving (b,g), football (b), golf (b,g), lacrosse (b,g), soccer (b,g), softball (g), swimming and diving (b,g), tennis (b,g), track and field (b,g), volleyball (b,g), water polo (b,g); intramural: aerobics/dance (g), dance (g), horseback riding (g); coed interscholastic: cheering, equestrian sports; coed intramural: fencing. 11 coaches, 3 athletic trainers.
Computers Computers are regularly used in art, college planning, computer applications, creative writing, drawing and design, economics, engineering, English, foreign language, geography, graphic arts, health, history, humanities, journalism, mathematics, music, newspaper, photography, photojournalism, programming, publications, research skills, science, social studies, theater arts, Web site design, wilderness education, writing, yearbook classes. Computer network features include on-campus library services, Internet access, wireless campus network, Internet filtering or blocking technology. Campus intranet, student e-mail accounts, and computer access in designated common areas are available to students. Students grades are available online. The school has a published electronic and media policy.
Contact Admission Manager. 310-377-1543 Ext. 4025. Fax: 310-377-0380. E-mail: admissions@chadwickschool.org. Web site: www.chadwickschool.org

CHAMBERLAIN-HUNT ACADEMY

124 McComb Avenue
Port Gibson, Mississippi 39150

Head of School: Col. Jack Gardner West

General Information Boys' boarding and coeducational day college-preparatory, arts, religious studies, and military school, affiliated with Presbyterian Church, Reformed Church. Boarding boys grades 7–12, day boys grades 7–12, day girls grades 7–12. Founded: 1879. Setting: small town. Nearest major city is Vicksburg. Students are housed in single-sex dormitories. 230-acre campus. 11 buildings on campus. Approved or accredited by Assocaition of Classical Christian Schools, Mississippi Private School Association, Southern Association of Colleges and Schools, and Mississippi Department of Education. Endowment: $29 million. Total enrollment: 90. Upper school average class size: 5. Upper school faculty-student ratio: 1:5. There are 180 required school days per year for Upper School students. Upper School students typically attend 5 days per week. The average school day consists of 7 hours and 45 minutes.
Upper School Student Profile Grade 10: 19 students (19 boys); Grade 11: 25 students (25 boys); Grade 12: 17 students (17 boys). 95% of students are boarding students. 27% are state residents. 20 states are represented in upper school student body. 2% are international students. International students from Costa Rica, India, Kenya, Singapore, and Venezuela. 16% of students are Presbyterian, Reformed.
Faculty School total: 19. In upper school: 12 men, 2 women; 11 have advanced degrees; 11 reside on campus.
Subjects Offered ACT preparation, advanced math, Advanced Placement courses, algebra, American Civil War, American government, American history, American literature-AP, ancient history, art, Bible, biology, British literature, business, calculus, chemistry, choir, Christian doctrine, Christian ethics, church history, classical Greek literature, computer programming, computer skills, CPR, earth science, economics, English, English literature, English literature-AP, ethics, French, geometry, government, keyboarding, Latin, logic, men's studies, military history, physics, pre-algebra, rhetoric, Spanish, theology, U.S. government, U.S. history, vocal ensemble, wilderness experience, world history, world wide web design.
Graduation Requirements Algebra, American literature, anatomy and physiology, Bible, biology, British literature, chemistry, classical Greek literature, economics, electives, geometry, intro to computers, languages, medieval literature, rhetoric, state history, Talmud, U.S. government, U.S. history, world geography, world history, oral comprehensive exams, senior speech, worldview class.
Special Academic Programs International Baccalaureate program; honors section; accelerated programs; independent study; academic accommodation for the gifted, the musically talented, and the artistically talented; remedial reading and/or remedial writing; remedial math; ESL.
College Admission Counseling 10 students graduated in 2012; 7 went to college, including Auburn University; Hinds Community College; Louisiana State University and Agricultural and Mechanical College; Mississippi College; Palm Beach Atlantic University; University of the Ozarks. Other: 2 went to work, 1 entered military service. Median composite ACT: 22. 20% scored over 26 on composite ACT.
Student Life Upper grades have uniform requirement, student council, honor system. Discipline rests primarily with faculty. Attendance at religious services is required.
Summer Programs Remediation, enrichment, advancement, ESL, sports, rigorous outdoor training programs offered; session focuses on remediation and advancement courses along with weekend activities such as rafting, paintball, and ropes course; held both on and off campus; held at Kayaking and professional sporting events; accepts boys; open to students from other schools. 55 students usually enrolled. 2013 schedule: June 3 to June 29. Application deadline: May 31.
Tuition and Aid Day student tuition: $14,500; 7-day tuition and room/board: $25,000. Guaranteed tuition plan. Tuition installment plan (The Tuition Plan, monthly payment plans, individually arranged payment plans). Tuition reduction for siblings, merit scholarship grants, need-based scholarship grants available. In 2012–13, 33% of upper-school students received aid; total upper-school merit-scholarship money awarded: $10,000. Total amount of financial aid awarded in 2012–13: $250,000.
Admissions Traditional secondary-level entrance grade is 10. For fall 2012, 39 students applied for upper-level admission, 35 were accepted, 30 enrolled. Math and English placement tests required. Deadline for receipt of application materials: none. Application fee required: $50. Interview required.
Athletics Interscholastic: basketball, cross-country running, football, golf, independent competitive sports, soccer, track and field, winter soccer; intramural: archery, baseball, basketball, canoeing/kayaking, climbing, cross-country running, field hockey, fishing, fitness, flag football, jogging, life saving, marksmanship, outdoor activities, outdoor adventure, outdoor education, outdoor recreation, outdoor skills, paint ball, physical fitness, physical training, pistol, rappelling, riflery, rock climbing, ropes courses, running, soccer, softball, strength & conditioning, table tennis, tennis, track and field, volleyball, wall climbing, weight lifting, weight training, wilderness, wilderness survival, wildernessways. 6 PE instructors, 4 coaches, 1 athletic trainer.
Computers Computers are regularly used in library skills, programming, typing, Web site design classes. Computer network features include on-campus library services, online commercial services, Internet access, wireless campus network, Internet filtering or blocking technology. Students grades are available online. The school has a published electronic and media policy.
Contact Mr. Wesley McClure, Admissions Counselor. 601-437-8855 Ext. 225. Fax: 601-437-3212. E-mail: wes.mcclure@chamberlain-hunt.com. Web site: www.chamberlain-hunt.com/

CHAMINADE COLLEGE PREPARATORY

7500 Chaminade Avenue
West Hills, California 91304

Head of School: Br. Thomas Fahy

General Information Coeducational day college-preparatory, arts, business, religious studies, and technology school, affiliated with Roman Catholic Church. Grades 9–12. Founded: 1952. Setting: suburban. Nearest major city is Los Angeles. 21-acre campus. 15 buildings on campus. Approved or accredited by Western Association of Schools and Colleges, Western Catholic Education Association, and California Department of Education. Endowment: $5.3 million. Total enrollment: 2,028. Upper school average class size: 27. Upper school faculty-student ratio: 1:16. There are 180 required school days per year for Upper School students. Upper School students typically attend 5 days per week. The average school day consists of 6 hours and 25 minutes.
Upper School Student Profile Grade 9: 344 students (176 boys, 168 girls); Grade 10: 317 students (161 boys, 156 girls); Grade 11: 344 students (189 boys, 155 girls); Grade 12: 315 students (162 boys, 153 girls). 50% of students are Roman Catholic.
Faculty School total: 88. In upper school: 36 men, 51 women; 55 have advanced degrees.
Subjects Offered Algebra, American history, American literature, anatomy, art, art history, athletic training, band, baseball, basketball, biology, biology-AP, British literature, British literature (honors), calculus, calculus-AP, chemistry, chemistry-AP, Chinese, Christian and Hebrew scripture, community service, comparative government and politics-AP, composition, computer programming, computer programming-AP, computer science, creative writing, dance, dance performance, debate, drama, drawing, driver education, economics, economics and history, English, English language-AP, English literature and composition-AP, environmental science-AP, ethics, European history, expository writing, film studies, finance, fine arts, finite math, French, French language-AP, French literature-AP, geography, geometry, government-AP, government/civics, guitar, jazz ensemble, journalism, Latin, Latin-AP, literature and composition-AP, macroeconomics-AP, marching band, mathematics, microeconomics-AP, modern European history-AP, music, music appreciation, music performance, physical education, physical science, physics, physics-AP, physiology, play/screen writing, probability and statistics, psychology, psychology-AP, religion, science, science fiction, scripture, Shakespeare, social studies, Spanish, Spanish language-AP, Spanish literature-AP, speech, speech and debate, sports medicine, statistics-AP, studio art, theater,

trigonometry, U.S. government, U.S. history, U.S. history-AP, United States government-AP, visual and performing arts, visual arts, Western philosophy, Western religions, women's studies, world history, world history-AP, world literature, writing.

Graduation Requirements Arts and fine arts (art, music, dance, drama), college writing, computer science, English, foreign language, mathematics, physical education (includes health), religious studies, science, social studies (includes history), speech. Community service is required.

Special Academic Programs Advanced Placement exam preparation; honors section.

College Admission Counseling 313 students graduated in 2012; 307 went to college, including California State University, Northridge; California State University Channel Islands; Loyola Marymount University; The University of Arizona; University of San Francisco; University of Southern California. Other: 1 entered military service, 5 had other specific plans. Mean SAT critical reading: 566, mean SAT math: 562, mean SAT writing: 568, mean combined SAT: 1696, mean composite ACT: 25. 38% scored over 600 on SAT critical reading, 38% scored over 600 on SAT math, 41% scored over 600 on SAT writing, 39% scored over 1800 on combined SAT, 39% scored over 26 on composite ACT.

Student Life Upper grades have uniform requirement, student council, honor system. Discipline rests primarily with faculty. Attendance at religious services is required.

Summer Programs Remediation, enrichment, advancement, sports, art/fine arts, computer instruction programs offered; session focuses on remediation; held on campus; accepts boys and girls; open to students from other schools. 450 students usually enrolled. 2013 schedule: June 10 to July 19. Application deadline: none.

Tuition and Aid Day student tuition: $12,925. Tuition installment plan (monthly payment plans, 2-payment plan, discounted one-payment plan). Merit scholarship grants, need-based scholarship grants available. In 2012–13, 28% of upper-school students received aid; total upper-school merit-scholarship money awarded: $20,000. Total amount of financial aid awarded in 2012–13: $2,383,381.

Admissions Traditional secondary-level entrance grade is 9. For fall 2012, 372 students applied for upper-level admission, 298 were accepted, 205 enrolled. Non-standardized placement tests required. Deadline for receipt of application materials: January 11. Application fee required: $100. On-campus interview required.

Athletics Interscholastic: aquatics (boys, girls), baseball (b), basketball (b,g), cross-country running (b,g), equestrian sports (b,g), fencing (b,g), field hockey (g), football (b), golf (b,g), lacrosse (b,g), soccer (b,g), softball (g), strength & conditioning (b,g), swimming and diving (b,g), tennis (b,g), track and field (b,g), volleyball (b,g), weight training (b,g), wrestling (b); coed interscholastic: cheering, dance, equestrian sports, physical fitness, strength & conditioning, weight training; coed intramural: dance team, hiking/backpacking, table tennis. 5 PE instructors, 85 coaches, 2 athletic trainers.

Computers Computers are regularly used in creative writing, data processing, information technology, introduction to technology, literary magazine, news writing, newspaper, photojournalism, writing, writing, yearbook classes. Computer network features include on-campus library services, online commercial services, Internet access, wireless campus network, Internet filtering or blocking technology, laptops are issued to students in grades 9-12, Blackboard online learning system, Dyno. Student e-mail accounts are available to students. Students grades are available online. The school has a published electronic and media policy.

Contact Mrs. Yolanda Uramoto, Assistant to Admissions and Registrar. 818-347-8300 Ext. 355. Fax: 818-348-8374. E-mail: yuramoto@chaminade.org. Web site: www.chaminade.org

CHAMINADE COLLEGE PREPARATORY SCHOOL

425 South Lindbergh Boulevard
St. Louis, Missouri 63131-2799

Head of School: Rev. Ralph A. Siefert, SM

General Information Boys' boarding and day college-preparatory, arts, business, religious studies, bilingual studies, and technology school, affiliated with Roman Catholic Church. Grades 6–12. Founded: 1910. Setting: suburban. Students are housed in single-sex dormitories. 55-acre campus. 12 buildings on campus. Approved or accredited by Independent Schools Association of the Central States, Midwest Association of Boarding Schools, National Catholic Education Association, North Central Association of Colleges and Schools, The Association of Boarding Schools, The College Board, and Missouri Department of Education. Member of National Association of Independent Schools and Secondary School Admission Test Board. Endowment: $11 million. Total enrollment: 775. Upper school average class size: 17. Upper school faculty-student ratio: 1:10. There are 174 required school days per year for Upper School students. Upper School students typically attend 5 days per week. The average school day consists of 7 hours.

Upper School Student Profile Grade 9: 134 students (134 boys); Grade 10: 131 students (131 boys); Grade 11: 117 students (117 boys); Grade 12: 117 students (117 boys). 8% of students are boarding students. 92% are state residents. 3 states are represented in upper school student body. 8% are international students. International students from China, Japan, Mexico, Republic of Korea, Taiwan, and Viet Nam; 3 other countries represented in student body. 81% of students are Roman Catholic.

Faculty School total: 89. In upper school: 68 men, 16 women; 67 have advanced degrees; 6 reside on campus.

Subjects Offered Accounting, algebra, American government, American history, American history-AP, American literature, anatomy and physiology, architecture, art, art history, band, Bible studies, biology, biology-AP, botany, broadcasting, business, business law, business skills, calculus, calculus-AP, campus ministry, Catholic belief and practice, chemistry, chemistry-AP, Chinese, church history, civics, communication skills, communications, community service, comparative government and politics-AP, comparative political systems-AP, computer literacy, computer processing, computer programming, computer programming-AP, computer science, computer science-AP, concert band, creative writing, drama, dramatic arts, earth science, ecology, economics, economics-AP, engineering, English, English composition, English literature, English literature-AP, English/composition-AP, ESL, European history, European history-AP, expository writing, fine arts, French, French-AP, geography, geology, geometry, government/civics, grammar, health, history, industrial arts, keyboarding, Latin, Latin-AP, mathematics, music theory-AP, physical education, physics, physics-AP, psychology, psychology-AP, religion, science, social studies, sociology, Spanish, Spanish-AP, speech, statistics, statistics-AP, studio art-AP, theater, theology, trigonometry, weight training, world affairs, world history, world literature, writing.

Graduation Requirements Arts and fine arts (art, music, dance, drama), computer science, English, foreign language, mathematics, physical education (includes health), practical arts, religion (includes Bible studies and theology), science, social studies (includes history). Community service is required.

Special Academic Programs 23 Advanced Placement exams for which test preparation is offered; honors section; study at local college for college credit; academic accommodation for the gifted; ESL (32 students enrolled).

College Admission Counseling 118 students graduated in 2012; 117 went to college, including Purdue University; Saint Louis University; University of Dayton; University of Illinois at Urbana–Champaign; University of Missouri; Vanderbilt University. Other: 1 entered military service. Mean composite ACT: 26. 42% scored over 26 on composite ACT.

Student Life Upper grades have specified standards of dress, honor system. Discipline rests primarily with faculty. Attendance at religious services is required.

Summer Programs Enrichment, sports, art/fine arts programs offered; held on campus; accepts boys; open to students from other schools. 500 students usually enrolled. 2013 schedule: June to July.

Tuition and Aid Day student tuition: $15,765; 5-day tuition and room/board: $31,991; 7-day tuition and room/board: $33,091. Tuition installment plan (FACTS Tuition Payment Plan). Merit scholarship grants, need-based scholarship grants, paying campus jobs available. In 2012–13, 32% of upper-school students received aid; total upper-school merit-scholarship money awarded: $95,000. Total amount of financial aid awarded in 2012–13: $1,600,000.

Admissions Traditional secondary-level entrance grade is 9. For fall 2012, 78 students applied for upper-level admission, 66 were accepted, 53 enrolled. SSAT required. Deadline for receipt of application materials: none. Application fee required: $50. Interview required.

Athletics Interscholastic: baseball, basketball, bowling, cross-country running, football, golf, ice hockey, lacrosse, racquetball, soccer, swimming and diving, tennis, track and field, ultimate Frisbee, volleyball, water polo, wrestling; intramural: in-line hockey, rugby, table tennis, weight training. 5 PE instructors, 30 coaches, 1 athletic trainer.

Computers Computers are regularly used in all academic classes. Computer network features include on-campus library services, online commercial services, Internet access, wireless campus network, Internet filtering or blocking technology. Campus intranet and student e-mail accounts are available to students. Students grades are available online. The school has a published electronic and media policy.

Contact Ms. Dianne Dunning-Gill, Associate Director of Admissions. 314-692-6640. Fax: 314-993-5732. E-mail: ddunning-gill@chaminade-stl.com. Web site: www.chaminade-stl.org

CHAMINADE-MADONNA COLLEGE PREPARATORY

500 Chaminade Drive
Hollywood, Florida 33021-5800

Head of School: Fr. Larry Doersching, SM

General Information Coeducational day college-preparatory, arts, business, and religious studies school, affiliated with Roman Catholic Church. Grades 9–12. Founded: 1960. Setting: suburban. Nearest major city is Fort Lauderdale. 13-acre campus. 10 buildings on campus. Approved or accredited by Southern Association of Colleges and Schools and Florida Department of Education. Total enrollment: 594. Upper school average class size: 26. Upper school faculty-student ratio: 1:19. There are 180 required school days per year for Upper School students. Upper School students typically attend 5 days per week. The average school day consists of 6 hours and 45 minutes.

Upper School Student Profile Grade 9: 147 students (92 boys, 55 girls); Grade 10: 154 students (83 boys, 71 girls); Grade 11: 143 students (94 boys, 49 girls); Grade 12: 150 students (85 boys, 65 girls). 70% of students are Roman Catholic.

Faculty School total: 48. In upper school: 23 men, 24 women.

Subjects Offered Advanced chemistry, advanced computer applications, advanced math, advanced studio art-AP, algebra, American history, American literature, anatomy, art, art history, band, biology, business skills, calculus, ceramics, chemistry, choir, community service, computer applications, creative writing, design, directing, drama, economics, English, fine arts, French, geography, geometry, government/civics, health, history, international relations, journalism, keyboarding, marine biology, mathematics, music, philosophy, physical education, physics, physiology, play production, practical arts, pre-calculus, psychology, reading, religion, science, Shakespeare, social studies, sociology, Spanish, speech, stagecraft, theater, trigonometry, word processing, world history, writing, yearbook.

Graduation Requirements Arts and fine arts (art, music, dance, drama), business skills (includes word processing), English, foreign language, mathematics, physical education (includes health), practical arts, religion (includes Bible studies and theology), science, social studies (includes history), 80 community service hours.

Special Academic Programs 10 Advanced Placement exams for which test preparation is offered; honors section; study at local college for college credit; academic accommodation for the gifted, the musically talented, and the artistically talented; remedial reading and/or remedial writing; remedial math; programs in general development for dyslexic students; special instructional classes for students with learning disabilities, Attention Deficit Disorder, and dyslexia.

College Admission Counseling 156 students graduated in 2011; all went to college, including Florida Atlantic University; Florida International University; Florida State University; University of Central Florida; University of Florida; University of Miami. Mean SAT critical reading: 512, mean SAT math: 504, mean composite ACT: 20.

Student Life Upper grades have uniform requirement, student council, honor system. Discipline rests primarily with faculty. Attendance at religious services is required.

Tuition and Aid Day student tuition: $9700. Tuition installment plan (FACTS Tuition Payment Plan). Tuition reduction for siblings, need-based scholarship grants available. In 2011–12, 33% of upper-school students received aid. Total amount of financial aid awarded in 2011–12: $400,000.

Admissions Traditional secondary-level entrance grade is 9. For fall 2011, 250 students applied for upper-level admission, 200 were accepted, 147 enrolled. High School Placement Test (closed version) from Scholastic Testing Service required. Deadline for receipt of application materials: January 20. Application fee required: $50. Interview required.

Athletics Interscholastic: baseball (boys), basketball (b,g), cheering (g), cross-country running (b,g), dance (g), dance team (g), flag football (g), football (b), golf (b,g), hockey (b,g), ice hockey (b,g), lacrosse (g), soccer (b,g), swimming and diving (b,g), track and field (b,g), volleyball (b,g), wrestling (b); intramural: aerobics/dance (g), danceline (g), football (b,g). 2 PE instructors, 1 athletic trainer.

Computers Computers are regularly used in English, mathematics, reading classes. Computer resources include on-campus library services, online commercial services, Internet access. The school has a published electronic and media policy.

Contact Mrs. Carol Manzella, Admissions Coordinator. 954-989-5150 Ext. 136. Fax: 954-983-4663. E-mail: cmanzella@cmlions.org. Web site: www.cmlions.org

CHAPEL HILL–CHAUNCY HALL SCHOOL

785 Beaver Street
Waltham, Massachusetts 02452

Head of School: Mr. Lance Conrad

General Information Coeducational boarding and day college-preparatory and arts school. Grades 9–PG. Founded: 1828. Setting: suburban. Nearest major city is Boston. Students are housed in single-sex dormitories. 40-acre campus. 11 buildings on campus. Approved or accredited by New England Association of Schools and Colleges and Massachusetts Department of Education. Member of National Association of Independent Schools and Secondary School Admission Test Board. Endowment: $1.8 million. Total enrollment: 165. Upper school average class size: 11. Upper school faculty-student ratio: 1:6. Upper School students typically attend 5 days per week. The average school day consists of 7 hours.

Upper School Student Profile Grade 9: 25 students (12 boys, 13 girls); Grade 10: 41 students (21 boys, 20 girls); Grade 11: 36 students (24 boys, 12 girls); Grade 12: 47 students (24 boys, 23 girls). 45% of students are boarding students. 65% are state residents. 7 states are represented in upper school student body. 25% are international students. International students from China, Japan, Kazakhstan, Republic of Korea, Taiwan, and Viet Nam; 6 other countries represented in student body.

Faculty School total: 35. In upper school: 14 men, 16 women; 20 have advanced degrees; 20 reside on campus.

Subjects Offered 20th century history, 3-dimensional design, acting, adolescent issues, advanced biology, advanced chemistry, advanced studio art-AP, algebra, American history, American literature, anatomy and physiology, art, biology, calculus, ceramics, chamber groups, chemistry, chorus, comparative religion, creative writing, drama, economics, English, English literature, English-AP, ESL, European history, fine arts, geography, geometry, government/civics, grammar, health, history, journalism, Mandarin, mathematics, music, music theory, photography, physical education, physics, psychology, science, social studies, Spanish, theater, world history, world literature, writing.

Graduation Requirements Arts and fine arts (art, music, dance, drama), English, foreign language, mathematics, physical education (includes health), science, social studies (includes history), senior presentations, earn Charger Points for service. Community service is required.

Special Academic Programs Advanced Placement exam preparation; honors section; independent study; programs in general development for dyslexic students; special instructional classes for students with mild to moderate learning disabilities; ESL (12 students enrolled).

College Admission Counseling 48 students graduated in 2011; all went to college, including Clark University; Curry College; Drew University; Roger Williams University; University of Illinois at Urbana–Champaign; Wheaton College. Mean SAT critical reading: 520, mean SAT math: 540, mean SAT writing: 530.

Student Life Upper grades have student council. Discipline rests equally with students and faculty.

Tuition and Aid Day student tuition: $33,900; 7-day tuition and room/board: $46,000. Tuition installment plan (Key Tuition Payment Plan, monthly payment plans, individually arranged payment plans). Need-based scholarship grants available. In 2011–12, 22% of upper-school students received aid. Total amount of financial aid awarded in 2011–12: $850,000.

Admissions Traditional secondary-level entrance grade is 9. For fall 2011, 221 students applied for upper-level admission, 121 were accepted, 56 enrolled. SSAT or WISC III, TOEFL or SLEP or WISC or WAIS required. Deadline for receipt of application materials: February 1. Application fee required: $50. Interview required.

Athletics Interscholastic: baseball (boys), basketball (b,g), lacrosse (b,g), soccer (b,g), softball (g), volleyball (g), wrestling (b); coed interscholastic: climbing, combined training, cross-country running, fitness, Frisbee, golf, rock climbing, ropes courses, ultimate Frisbee; coed intramural: aerobics/dance, cooperative games, dance team, fitness, outdoor education, physical fitness, racquetball, rock climbing, ropes courses, swimming and diving, yoga. 1 PE instructor, 1 athletic trainer.

Computers Computers are regularly used in art, English, history, mathematics, multimedia, newspaper, yearbook classes. Computer network features include on-campus library services, online commercial services, Internet access, wireless campus network, Internet filtering or blocking technology. Campus intranet, student e-mail accounts, and computer access in designated common areas are available to students. Students grades are available online. The school has a published electronic and media policy.

Contact Ms. Lauren Lewis, Admissions Administrative Assistant. 781-314-0800. Fax: 781-894-5205. E-mail: llewis@chch.org. Web site: www.chch.org

CHARLOTTE CHRISTIAN SCHOOL

7301 Sardis Road
Charlotte, North Carolina 28270

Head of School: Mr. Barry Giller

General Information Coeducational day college-preparatory and arts school, affiliated with Christian faith. Grades JK–12. Founded: 1950. Setting: suburban. 55-acre campus. 4 buildings on campus. Approved or accredited by Association of Christian Schools International, Southern Association of Colleges and Schools, Southern Association of Independent Schools, and North Carolina Department of Education. Total enrollment: 1,018. Upper school average class size: 20. Upper school faculty-student ratio: 1:11. There are 172 required school days per year for Upper School students. Upper School students typically attend 5 days per week. The average school day consists of 7 hours.

Upper School Student Profile Grade 9: 94 students (61 boys, 33 girls); Grade 10: 89 students (54 boys, 35 girls); Grade 11: 84 students (48 boys, 36 girls); Grade 12: 93 students (42 boys, 51 girls). 100% of students are Christian faith.

Faculty School total: 121. In upper school: 18 men, 18 women; 14 have advanced degrees.

Subjects Offered Accounting, acting, advanced studio art-AP, algebra, American culture, American government, American literature, anatomy and physiology, art, art history-AP, athletic training, band, biology, biology-AP, British literature, business, business law, calculus-AP, chamber groups, chemistry, choir, choreography, Christian doctrine, Christian education, Christian ethics, church history, civil war history, computer applications, computer science-AP, computer-aided design, economics, English literature, environmental science-AP, European history-AP, French, French-AP, geometry, German, graphic arts, graphic design, health and wellness, language-AP, Latin, leadership, learning strategies, Life of Christ, literature and composition-AP, marketing, math applications, music composition, music theory-AP, newspaper, painting, photography, physical education, physical science, physics, physics-AP, pre-calculus, psychology, public speaking, research skills, SAT preparation, sign language, Spanish, Spanish-AP, speech and debate, sports medicine, stage design, statistics-AP, studio art-AP, theater, theater design and production, trigonometry, U.S. government and politics-AP, U.S. history, U.S. history-AP, video film production, voice, voice and diction, Web site design, weight training, wind ensemble, world civilizations, world literature, World War II, yearbook.

Graduation Requirements Arts and fine arts (art, music, dance, drama), Bible studies, English, foreign language, mathematics, physical education (includes health), SAT preparation, science, social studies (includes history), speech, service hours.

Special Academic Programs Advanced Placement exam preparation; honors section; study at local college for college credit.

College Admission Counseling 93 students graduated in 2011; 92 went to college, including Appalachian State University; Furman University; North Carolina

State University; The University of North Carolina at Chapel Hill; University of South Carolina; Wake Forest University. Other: 1 had other specific plans.

Student Life Upper grades have specified standards of dress, student council, honor system. Discipline rests primarily with faculty. Attendance at religious services is required.

Tuition and Aid Day student tuition: $11,240–$16,125. Tuition installment plan (The Tuition Plan, Insured Tuition Payment Plan, monthly payment plans, individually arranged payment plans). Tuition reduction for siblings, need-based scholarship grants available. In 2011–12, 20% of upper-school students received aid. Total amount of financial aid awarded in 2011–12: $389,150.

Admissions Traditional secondary-level entrance grade is 9. Admissions testing, ISEE, Wechsler Intelligence Scale for Children III or Woodcock-Johnson required. Deadline for receipt of application materials: none. Application fee required: $90. On-campus interview required.

Athletics Interscholastic: baseball (boys), basketball (b,g), cheering (g), cross-country running (b,g), dance (g), football (b), golf (b), indoor track (b,g), lacrosse (b), soccer (b,g), softball (g), swimming and diving (b,g), tennis (b,g), track and field (b,g), volleyball (g), wrestling (b); intramural: basketball (b,g), cheering (g), jogging (g), lacrosse (b), volleyball (g); coed interscholastic: physical fitness, physical training, strength & conditioning, weight training; coed intramural: basketball, fencing, soccer, tennis, weight training. 2 PE instructors, 25 coaches, 1 athletic trainer.

Computers Computers are regularly used in computer applications, journalism, keyboarding, photography, publications, yearbook classes. Computer network features include on-campus library services, Internet access, wireless campus network, Internet filtering or blocking technology, NewsBank InfoWeb. Students grades are available online. The school has a published electronic and media policy.

Contact Mrs. Cathie Broocks, Director of Admissions. 704-366-5657. Fax: 704-366-5678. E-mail: cathie.broocks@charchrist.com. Web site: www.charlottechristian.com

CHARLOTTE COUNTRY DAY SCHOOL

1440 Carmel Road
Charlotte, North Carolina 28226

Head of School: Mr. Mark Reed

General Information Coeducational day college-preparatory school. Grades JK–12. Founded: 1941. Setting: suburban. 60-acre campus. 10 buildings on campus. Approved or accredited by Southern Association of Colleges and Schools, Southern Association of Independent Schools, and North Carolina Department of Education. Member of National Association of Independent Schools and Secondary School Admission Test Board. Endowment: $28 million. Total enrollment: 1,622. Upper school average class size: 12. Upper school faculty-student ratio: 1:12. There are 170 required school days per year for Upper School students. Upper School students typically attend 5 days per week. The average school day consists of 7 hours and 15 minutes.

Upper School Student Profile Grade 9: 120 students (59 boys, 61 girls); Grade 10: 126 students (64 boys, 62 girls); Grade 11: 126 students (67 boys, 59 girls); Grade 12: 116 students (61 boys, 55 girls).

Faculty School total: 216. In upper school: 31 men, 35 women; 47 have advanced degrees.

Subjects Offered Algebra, American history, American history-AP, anatomy, art, art history-AP, astronomy, biology, biology-AP, biotechnology, calculus-AP, ceramics, chemistry, chemistry-AP, Chinese, computer graphics, computer science, computer science-AP, creative writing, dance, debate, discrete mathematics, drama, ecology, economics, English, English literature, English-AP, environmental science-AP, ESL, European history, European history-AP, French, French-AP, geography, geometry, German, German-AP, Japanese, journalism, Latin, Latin-AP, library studies, music, novels, photography, physical education, physics, physics-AP, physiology, poetry, political science, pre-calculus, probability and statistics, psychology-AP, sculpture, Shakespeare, short story, Spanish, Spanish-AP, studio art-AP, theater, theory of knowledge, trigonometry, visual arts, yearbook.

Graduation Requirements Arts and fine arts (art, music, dance, drama), computer science, English, foreign language, mathematics, physical education (includes health), science, social sciences, social studies (includes history). Community service is required.

Special Academic Programs International Baccalaureate program; honors section; independent study; term-away projects; study abroad; academic accommodation for the gifted; ESL (14 students enrolled).

College Admission Counseling 116 students graduated in 2012; all went to college, including Duke University; North Carolina State University; The University of North Carolina at Chapel Hill; University of Georgia; University of South Carolina. Median SAT critical reading: 605, median SAT math: 640, median SAT writing: 620, median combined SAT: 1870, median composite ACT: 27. 52% scored over 600 on SAT critical reading, 64% scored over 600 on SAT math, 54% scored over 600 on SAT writing, 57% scored over 1800 on combined SAT, 67% scored over 26 on composite ACT.

Student Life Upper grades have specified standards of dress, student council, honor system. Discipline rests primarily with faculty.

Summer Programs Remediation, enrichment, advancement, ESL, sports, art/fine arts, computer instruction programs offered; session focuses on enrichment classes, academic courses, and sports camps; held on campus; accepts boys and girls; open to students from other schools. 200 students usually enrolled. 2013 schedule: June 10 to July 26. Application deadline: none.

Tuition and Aid Day student tuition: $21,125. Tuition installment plan (The Tuition Plan, Insured Tuition Payment Plan, monthly payment plans). Need-based scholarship grants available. In 2012–13, 18% of upper-school students received aid. Total amount of financial aid awarded in 2012–13: $1,353,765.

Admissions Traditional secondary-level entrance grade is 9. For fall 2012, 105 students applied for upper-level admission, 66 were accepted, 46 enrolled. CTP III, ERB or ISEE required. Deadline for receipt of application materials: January 15. Application fee required: $90. On-campus interview required.

Athletics Interscholastic: baseball (boys), basketball (b,g), cheering (g), crew (g), cross-country running (b,g), dance (g), dance team (g), field hockey (g), fitness (b,g), football (b), golf (b,g), lacrosse (b,g), soccer (b,g), softball (g), strength & conditioning (b,g), swimming and diving (b,g), tennis (b,g), track and field (b,g), volleyball (g), weight training (b,g), wrestling (b). 1 PE instructor, 38 coaches, 3 athletic trainers.

Computers Computers are regularly used in art, computer applications, English, foreign language, mathematics, photography, science, yearbook classes. Computer network features include on-campus library services, Internet access, wireless campus network, Internet filtering or blocking technology. Campus intranet and student e-mail accounts are available to students. Students grades are available online. The school has a published electronic and media policy.

Contact Nancy R. Ehringhaus, Director of Admissions. 704-943-4530 Ext. 4531. Fax: 704-943-4536. E-mail: nancy.ehringhaus@charlottecountryday.org. Web site: www.charlottecountryday.org

CHARLOTTE LATIN SCHOOL

9502 Providence Road
Charlotte, North Carolina 28277-8695

Head of School: Mr. Arch N. McIntosh Jr.

General Information Coeducational day college-preparatory school. Grades K–12. Founded: 1970. Setting: suburban. 122-acre campus. 7 buildings on campus. Approved or accredited by Southern Association of Colleges and Schools, Southern Association of Independent Schools, and North Carolina Department of Education. Member of National Association of Independent Schools and Secondary School Admission Test Board. Endowment: $28.3 million. Total enrollment: 1,402. Upper school average class size: 16. Upper school faculty-student ratio: 1:8. There are 173 required school days per year for Upper School students. Upper School students typically attend 5 days per week. The average school day consists of 7 hours and 5 minutes.

Upper School Student Profile Grade 9: 119 students (57 boys, 62 girls); Grade 10: 131 students (67 boys, 64 girls); Grade 11: 122 students (63 boys, 59 girls); Grade 12: 123 students (58 boys, 65 girls).

Faculty School total: 185. In upper school: 34 men, 28 women; 41 have advanced degrees.

Subjects Offered 20th century American writers, 20th century history, 20th century physics, 20th century world history, 3-dimensional art, acting, advanced chemistry, Advanced Placement courses, algebra, American culture, American government, American history, American history-AP, American literature, anatomy, anatomy and physiology, art, biology, biology-AP, British literature, calculus, calculus-AP, ceramics, chemistry, chemistry-AP, college counseling, computer applications, computer math, computer programming, computer science, computer science-AP, conceptual physics, concert band, concert choir, creative writing, debate, discrete mathematics, drama, dramatic arts, earth science, ecology, economics, economics and history, engineering, English, English literature, English-AP, environmental science, European history, European history-AP, expository writing, finite math, French, French-AP, geography, geology, geometry, government/civics, grammar, Greek, health, history, Holocaust and other genocides, honors algebra, honors English, honors geometry, human rights, international relations, international studies, journalism, Latin, Latin-AP, leadership and service, mathematics, media literacy, music, music theory, music theory-AP, physical education, physics, physics-AP, pre-calculus, programming, psychology, science, social studies, Southern literature, Spanish, Spanish language-AP, Spanish-AP, speech, sports medicine, statistics-AP, studio art, technical theater, theater, trigonometry, U.S. government and politics-AP, Web site design, world history, world literature, world religions, writing, yearbook.

Graduation Requirements Electives, English, foreign language, history, mathematics, physical education (includes health), science.

Special Academic Programs 14 Advanced Placement exams for which test preparation is offered; honors section; study abroad; academic accommodation for the gifted.

College Admission Counseling 118 students graduated in 2012; 114 went to college, including Clemson University; The University of North Carolina at Chapel Hill; University of Georgia; Vanderbilt University; Wake Forest University. 67% scored over 600 on SAT critical reading, 81% scored over 600 on SAT math, 72% scored over 600 on SAT writing, 75% scored over 1800 on combined SAT, 76% scored over 26 on composite ACT.

Student Life Upper grades have specified standards of dress, student council, honor system. Discipline rests primarily with faculty.

Summer Programs Enrichment, sports, art/fine arts, computer instruction programs offered; session focuses on enrichment, sports camps; held both on and off campus; held at N.C. coast (offered for Charlotte Latin students only); accepts boys and girls; open to students from other schools. 850 students usually enrolled. 2013 schedule: June 11 to July 27. Application deadline: none.

Tuition and Aid Day student tuition: $19,650. Tuition installment plan (monthly payment plans, individually arranged payment plans). Merit scholarship grants, need-based scholarship grants available. In 2012–13, 14% of upper-school students received aid; total upper-school merit-scholarship money awarded: $214,440. Total amount of financial aid awarded in 2012–13: $827,525.

Admissions Traditional secondary-level entrance grade is 9. For fall 2012, 101 students applied for upper-level admission, 47 were accepted, 27 enrolled. ERB, ISEE, Wechsler Intelligence Scale for Children III or Woodcock-Johnson required. Deadline for receipt of application materials: none. Application fee required: $90. On-campus interview required.

Athletics Interscholastic: aquatics (boys, girls), baseball (b), basketball (b,g), cross-country running (b,g), dance team (g), field hockey (g), football (b), golf (b,g), independent competitive sports (b,g), indoor track (b,g), lacrosse (b,g), soccer (b,g), softball (g), swimming and diving (b,g), tennis (b,g), track and field (b,g), volleyball (g), wrestling (b); intramural: basketball (b,g), outdoor activities (b,g); coed interscholastic: ultimate Frisbee; coed intramural: outdoor activities. 5 PE instructors, 67 coaches, 3 athletic trainers.

Computers Computers are regularly used in all academic classes. Computer network features include on-campus library services, online commercial services, Internet access, wireless campus network, Internet filtering or blocking technology. Computer access in designated common areas is available to students. The school has a published electronic and media policy.

Contact Mr. Peter C. Egan, Director of Admissions. 704-846-7207. Fax: 704-847-8776. E-mail: pegan@charlottelatin.org. Web site: www.charlottelatin.org

See Display below and Close-Up on page 562.

CHASE COLLEGIATE SCHOOL

565 Chase Parkway
Waterbury, Connecticut 06708-3394

Head of School: John D. Fixx

General Information Coeducational day college-preparatory and arts school. Grades PK–12. Founded: 1865. Setting: suburban. 47-acre campus. 8 buildings on campus. Approved or accredited by Connecticut Association of Independent Schools, New England Association of Schools and Colleges, and Connecticut Department of Education. Member of National Association of Independent Schools and Secondary School Admission Test Board. Endowment: $11 million. Total enrollment: 440. Upper school average class size: 11. Upper school faculty-student ratio: 1:6. There are 173 required school days per year for Upper School students. Upper School students typically attend 5 days per week. The average school day consists of 6 hours and 45 minutes.

Upper School Student Profile Grade 9: 43 students (20 boys, 23 girls); Grade 10: 52 students (25 boys, 27 girls); Grade 11: 55 students (29 boys, 26 girls); Grade 12: 44 students (24 boys, 20 girls).

Faculty School total: 54. In upper school: 18 men, 13 women; 25 have advanced degrees.

Subjects Offered 20th century American writers, 20th century history, 3-dimensional art, acting, Advanced Placement courses, African-American literature, algebra, American foreign policy, ancient world history, animation, archaeology, art, art history-AP, astronomy, band, biology, biology-AP, calculus, calculus-AP, ceramics, chamber groups, chemistry, chemistry-AP, China/Japan history, chorus, classical Greek literature, classical language, college writing, computer animation, computer graphics, computer programming, computer science-AP, concert band, concert bell choir, current events, digital photography, directing, drama, drawing, ecology, economics, economics-AP, English, English language-AP, English literature and composition-AP, environmental science, environmental science-AP, ethics, film studies, filmmaking, fine arts, foreign policy, French, French language-AP, French literature-AP, freshman seminar, geometry, Greek, handbells, health and wellness, history of China and Japan, honors algebra, honors geometry, humanities, independent study, introduction to theater, jazz band, jazz ensemble, journalism, Latin, Latin-AP, macro/microeconomics-AP, model United Nations, modern European history, music, music technology, natural history, oceanography, oil painting, photography, physics, physics-AP, play production, playwriting and directing, pre-calculus, probability and statistics, public speaking, sculpture, senior project, society and culture, socioeconomic problems, sociology, Spanish, Spanish literature-AP, Spanish-AP, statistics, technical theater, technology, theater, U.S. government and politics-AP, U.S. history, U.S. history-AP, visual arts, water color painting, Web site design, woodworking, world cultures, world history-AP, yearbook.

Graduation Requirements Arts and fine arts (art, music, dance, drama), athletics, computer literacy, electives, English, ethics, foreign language, history, lab science, mathematics, music appreciation, psychology, public speaking, science, technology, theater arts, senior speech.

Special Academic Programs 19 Advanced Placement exams for which test preparation is offered; honors section; accelerated programs; independent study; study abroad; academic accommodation for the gifted.

College Admission Counseling 45 students graduated in 2012; all went to college, including Boston University; Fairfield University; High Point University; Northeastern University; Providence College; University of Connecticut. Mean SAT critical reading: 612, mean SAT math: 573, mean SAT writing: 598, mean combined SAT: 1783.

Student Life Upper grades have specified standards of dress, student council, honor system. Discipline rests equally with students and faculty.

Summer Programs Enrichment, advancement, sports, art/fine arts, computer instruction programs offered; session focuses on enrichment and advancement; held on campus; accepts boys and girls; open to students from other schools. 500 students usually enrolled. 2013 schedule: June to July. Application deadline: none.

Tuition and Aid Day student tuition: $32,425. Tuition installment plan (monthly payment plans). Merit scholarship grants, need-based scholarship grants, Founders' Scholarships (for students entering 9th grade) available. In 2012–13, 50% of upper-school students received aid; total upper-school merit-scholarship money awarded: $388,000. Total amount of financial aid awarded in 2012–13: $2,500,000.

Admissions Traditional secondary-level entrance grade is 9. For fall 2012, 121 students applied for upper-level admission, 88 were accepted, 31 enrolled. SSAT required. Deadline for receipt of application materials: none. Application fee required: $60. On-campus interview required.

Athletics Interscholastic: baseball (boys), basketball (b,g), cross-country running (b,g), independent competitive sports (b,g), lacrosse (b,g), soccer (b,g), softball (g), tennis (b,g), volleyball (g), wrestling (b,g); intramural: ice hockey (b,g), strength & conditioning (b,g); coed interscholastic: crew, Frisbee, golf, independent competitive sports, swimming and diving, ultimate Frisbee, wrestling; coed intramural: aerobics/dance, aerobics/Nautilus, curling, dance, equestrian sports, figure skating, fitness, ice skating, modern dance, outdoor education, physical fitness, skiing (downhill), snowboarding, weight training. 4 PE instructors, 12 coaches, 1 athletic trainer.

Computers Computers are regularly used in art, creative writing, English, foreign language, history, humanities, library, literary magazine, mathematics, music, newspaper, photography, research skills, SAT preparation, science, social sciences, study skills, technology, yearbook classes. Computer network features include on-campus library services, online commercial services, Internet access, wireless campus network, Internet filtering or blocking technology. Campus intranet, student e-mail accounts, and computer access in designated common areas are available to students. Students grades are available online. The school has a published electronic and media policy.

Contact Melissa Medeiros, Director of Admission. 203-236-9560. Fax: 203-236-9503. E-mail: mmedeiros@chasemail.org. Web site: www.chasecollegiate.org

CHATHAM ACADEMY

Savannah, Georgia

See Special Needs Schools section.

CHATHAM HALL

800 Chatham Hall Circle
Chatham, Virginia 24531

Head of School: Dr. Gary J. Fountain

General Information Girls' boarding and day college-preparatory and arts school, affiliated with Episcopal Church. Grades 9–12. Founded: 1894. Setting: small town. Nearest major city is Greensboro, NC. Students are housed in single-sex dormitories. 362-acre campus. 9 buildings on campus. Approved or accredited by National Association of Episcopal Schools, Southern Association of Colleges and Schools, The Association of Boarding Schools, and Virginia Association of Independent Schools. Member of Secondary School Admission Test Board. Endowment: $20 million. Total enrollment: 140. Upper school average class size: 8. Upper school faculty-student ratio: 1:7.

Upper School Student Profile 82% of students are boarding students. 34% are state residents. 20 states are represented in upper school student body. 14% are international students. International students from Bermuda, China, Costa Rica, Germany, Republic of Korea, and Taiwan; 12 other countries represented in student body. 20% of students are members of Episcopal Church.

Faculty School total: 34. In upper school: 11 men, 23 women; 19 have advanced degrees; 29 reside on campus.

Subjects Offered Algebra, American history-AP, American literature, art, art history, biology, biology-AP, calculus, calculus-AP, ceramics, chemistry, chemistry-AP, choir, college counseling, computer art, creative writing, dance, DNA science lab, drama, drama performance, earth science, economics, English, English language-AP, English literature, English-AP, ESL, ethics, European history, European history-AP, fine arts, French, French-AP, general science, geography, geometry, history, instrumental music, journalism, Latin, mathematics, medieval/Renaissance history, model United Nations, modern European history, modern European history-AP, music, music composition, music theory, music theory-AP, photography, physical education, physics, pre-calculus, psychology, religion, robotics, SAT/ACT preparation, science, service learning/internship, social studies, Spanish, Spanish-AP, studio art-AP, swimming, theater design and production, trigonometry, U.S. government and politics, U.S. history, veterinary science, Western civilization, world history, writing workshop, yearbook.

Graduation Requirements Arts and fine arts (art, music, dance, drama), English, ethics, foreign language, mathematics, physical education (includes health), religion (includes Bible studies and theology), science, social studies (includes history).

Special Academic Programs 13 Advanced Placement exams for which test preparation is offered; honors section; independent study; study abroad; academic accommodation for the gifted, the musically talented, and the artistically talented; ESL (3 students enrolled).

College Admission Counseling 38 students graduated in 2011; all went to college, including Cornell University; Dartmouth College; Duke University; Georgetown University; University of Virginia; Vanderbilt University. Median SAT critical reading: 605, median SAT math: 600. 61% scored over 600 on SAT critical reading, 55% scored over 600 on SAT math.

Student Life Upper grades have specified standards of dress, student council, honor system. Discipline rests equally with students and faculty. Attendance at religious services is required.

Tuition and Aid Day student tuition: $16,500; 7-day tuition and room/board: $38,000. Tuition installment plan (Key Tuition Payment Plan, increments of 45%, 30%, and 20% due July 1, September 1, and December 1 respectively). Merit scholarship grants, need-based scholarship grants available.

Admissions Traditional secondary-level entrance grade is 9. For fall 2011, 114 students applied for upper-level admission, 89 were accepted, 49 enrolled. ISEE, PSAT or SAT, SSAT or TOEFL required. Deadline for receipt of application materials: February 1. Application fee required: $50. Interview required.

Athletics Interscholastic: aquatics, basketball, cross-country running, diving, equestrian sports, field hockey, fitness, golf, horseback riding, soccer, swimming and diving, tennis, volleyball; intramural: aerobics, aquatics, ballet, basketball, dance, diving, equestrian sports, field hockey, fitness, horseback riding, lacrosse, modern dance, soccer, softball, swimming and diving, tennis, volleyball. 2 PE instructors, 3 coaches, 1 athletic trainer.

Computers Computers are regularly used in art, English, foreign language, graphic design, history, independent study, journalism, literary magazine, mathematics, music, newspaper, photography, science, yearbook classes. Computer network features include on-campus library services, online commercial services, Internet access, Internet filtering or blocking technology. Campus intranet, student e-mail accounts, and computer access in designated common areas are available to students. The school has a published electronic and media policy.

Contact Vicki Wright, Director of Admission and Financial Aid. 434-432-5613. Fax: 434-432-1002. E-mail: vwright@chathamhall.org. Web site: www.chathamhall.org

CHATTANOOGA CHRISTIAN SCHOOL

3354 Charger Drive
Chattanooga, Tennessee 37409

Head of School: Mr. Chad Dirkse

General Information Coeducational day college-preparatory, arts, religious studies, technology, college-level (AP) courses, and dual enrollment courses school, affiliated with Christian faith. Grades K–12. Founded: 1970. Setting: urban. Nearest major city is Atlanta, GA. 60-acre campus. 6 buildings on campus. Approved or accredited by Christian Schools International, Southern Association of Colleges and Schools, and Tennessee Department of Education. Endowment: $10 million. Total enrollment: 1,156. Upper school average class size: 20. Upper school faculty-student ratio: 1:17. There are 175 required school days per year for Upper School students. Upper School students typically attend 5 days per week. The average school day consists of 7 hours.

Upper School Student Profile Grade 9: 117 students (59 boys, 58 girls); Grade 10: 111 students (55 boys, 56 girls); Grade 11: 111 students (44 boys, 67 girls); Grade 12: 104 students (48 boys, 56 girls). 100% of students are Christian faith.

Faculty School total: 104. In upper school: 28 men, 21 women; 19 have advanced degrees.

Subjects Offered Advanced biology, advanced chemistry, advanced studio art-AP, algebra, American government, American history, American literature, anatomy, ancient history, art, art and culture, art appreciation, art history, art-AP, astronomy, band, Bible, Bible studies, biology, biology-AP, calculus, calculus-AP, chemistry, choir, civil rights, community service, computer applications, computer programming, computer-aided design, concert band, concert choir, creative writing, current events, dance, drama, drama performance, earth science, Eastern world civilizations, economics, English, English literature, English-AP, entrepreneurship, environmental science, environmental studies, ethics, European history, European history-AP, fine arts, foreign language, French, geometry, German, government, health, honors geometry, industrial arts, introduction to theater, Latin, leadership education training, life science, mathematics, mathematics-AP, mechanical drawing, Microsoft, modern dance, modern European history-AP, music, music theory, New Testament, personal finance, physical education, physical science, physics, physics-AP, physiology, psychology, religion, science, shop, Spanish, statistics-AP, studio art-AP, theater, trigonometry, U.S. history-AP, Web site design, weight training, wellness, world literature, writing.

Graduation Requirements Arts and fine arts (art, music, dance, drama), computer science, English, foreign language, mathematics, physical education (includes health), religion (includes Bible studies and theology), science, social sciences, social studies (includes history). Community service is required.

Special Academic Programs Advanced Placement exam preparation; honors section; independent study; study at local college for college credit; academic accommodation for the gifted and the artistically talented; remedial reading and/or remedial writing; remedial math.

College Admission Counseling 104 students graduated in 2012; 98 went to college, including Chattanooga State Community College; Covenant College; Samford University; Tennessee Technological University; The University of Tennessee; The University of Tennessee at Chattanooga. Other: 1 went to work, 2 entered military service, 3 had other specific plans. Mean SAT critical reading: 560, mean SAT math: 536, mean SAT writing: 542, mean combined SAT: 1639, mean composite ACT: 24. 32% scored over 600 on SAT critical reading, 24% scored over 600 on SAT math, 29% scored over 600 on SAT writing, 26% scored over 1800 on combined SAT, 35% scored over 26 on composite ACT.

Student Life Upper grades have specified standards of dress, student council, honor system. Discipline rests primarily with faculty. Attendance at religious services is required.

Summer Programs Remediation, enrichment, sports, art/fine arts programs offered; session focuses on sports camps and arts camps; held on campus; accepts boys and girls; open to students from other schools. 100 students usually enrolled. 2013 schedule: June 4 to June 29. Application deadline: May 31.

Tuition and Aid Day student tuition: $9059. Tuition installment plan (monthly payment plans, individually arranged payment plans). Tuition reduction for siblings, need-based scholarship grants, paying campus jobs available. In 2012–13, 20% of upper-school students received aid. Total amount of financial aid awarded in 2012–13: $400,941.

Admissions Traditional secondary-level entrance grade is 9. For fall 2012, 177 students applied for upper-level admission, 148 were accepted, 109 enrolled. Deadline for receipt of application materials: none. Application fee required: $100. Interview required.

Athletics Interscholastic: baseball (boys), basketball (b,g), bowling (b,g), cheering (g), cross-country running (b,g), football (b), golf (b,g), soccer (b,g), softball (g), strength & conditioning (b,g), tennis (b,g), track and field (b,g), volleyball (g), weight lifting (b,g), weight training (b,g), wrestling (b); intramural: basketball (b,g); coed intramural: aerobics/dance, swimming and diving. 4 PE instructors, 15 coaches, 2 athletic trainers.

Computers Computers are regularly used in all academic, drawing and design, English, foreign language, history, lab/keyboard, library, mathematics, psychology, science, technology classes. Computer network features include on-campus library services, Internet access, wireless campus network, Internet filtering or blocking technology. Students grades are available online. The school has a published electronic and media policy.

Contact Mrs. Debbie Grisham, Admission Director. 423-265-6411 Ext. 209. Fax: 423-756-4044. E-mail: dgrisham@ccsk12.com. Web site: www.ccsk12.com

CHELSEA SCHOOL

Silver Spring, Maryland

See Special Needs Schools section.

CHESHIRE ACADEMY

10 Main Street
Cheshire, Connecticut 06410

Head of School: Douglas G. Rogers

General Information Coeducational boarding and day college-preparatory and bilingual studies school. Boarding grades 9–PG, day grades 8–PG. Founded: 1794. Setting: small town. Nearest major city is New Haven. Students are housed in single-sex dormitories. 104-acre campus. 24 buildings on campus. Approved or accredited by Connecticut Association of Independent Schools, International Baccalaureate Organization, New England Association of Schools and Colleges, and The Association of Boarding Schools. Member of National Association of Independent Schools and Secondary School Admission Test Board. Endowment: $8 million. Total enrollment: 355. Upper school average class size: 12. Upper school faculty-student ratio: 1:7. There are 171 required school days per year for Upper School students. Upper School students typically attend 5 days per week.

Upper School Student Profile Grade 9: 41 students (20 boys, 21 girls); Grade 10: 84 students (53 boys, 31 girls); Grade 11: 94 students (52 boys, 42 girls); Grade 12: 93 students (53 boys, 40 girls); Postgraduate: 13 students (13 boys). 62% of students are boarding students. 46% are state residents. 14 states are represented in upper school student body. 40% are international students. International students from China, Democratic People's Republic of Korea, Jamaica, and Taiwan; 8 other countries represented in student body.

Faculty School total: 70. In upper school: 26 men, 41 women; 47 have advanced degrees; 47 reside on campus.

Subjects Offered Acting, Advanced Placement courses, algebra, American Civil War, American government, American history, American literature, anatomy, art, art history, Asian studies, biology, calculus, ceramics, chemistry, Chinese, community service, computer programming, computer science, creative writing, digital imaging, drama, earth science, ecology, economics, English, English literature, environmental science, ESL, European history, expository writing, fine arts, French, geography, geometry, government/civics, grammar, health, history, International Baccalaureate courses, Latin American studies, mathematics, music, photography, physical education, physics, physiology, psychology, reading, science, social sciences, social studies, Spanish, speech, statistics, theater, Vietnam, world history, world literature, writing.

Graduation Requirements Arts and fine arts (art, music, dance, drama), computer science, electives, English, foreign language, mathematics, science, social sciences, social studies (includes history), senior speech, 10 hours of community service, Discover Week program.

Special Academic Programs International Baccalaureate program; Advanced Placement exam preparation; honors section; independent study; study abroad; academic accommodation for the musically talented and the artistically talented; remedial reading and/or remedial writing; remedial math; programs in English, mathematics, general development for dyslexic students; ESL (45 students enrolled).

College Admission Counseling 90 students graduated in 2011; all went to college, including Carnegie Mellon University; Furman University; Gettysburg College; School of the Art Institute of Chicago; University of Washington.

Student Life Upper grades have specified standards of dress, student council, honor system. Discipline rests primarily with faculty.

Tuition and Aid Day student tuition: $32,360; 7-day tuition and room/board: $45,385. Tuition installment plan (Key Tuition Payment Plan, monthly payment plans). Merit scholarship grants, need-based scholarship grants, need-based loans available. In 2011–12, 30% of upper-school students received aid; total upper-school merit-scholarship money awarded: $120,000. Total amount of financial aid awarded in 2011–12: $2,000,000.

Admissions Traditional secondary-level entrance grade is 9. ACT, ISEE, PSAT, SAT, SSAT or TOEFL required. Deadline for receipt of application materials: February 1. Application fee required: $50. Interview required.

Athletics Interscholastic: baseball (boys), basketball (b,g), cross-country running (b,g), field hockey (g), football (b), lacrosse (b,g), soccer (b,g), softball (g), swimming and diving (b,g), tennis (b,g), track and field (b,g), volleyball (g), wrestling (b); coed interscholastic: archery, fencing, golf, ultimate Frisbee; coed intramural: fitness, indoor soccer, ropes courses, skiing (downhill), weight training. 1 PE instructor, 9 coaches, 2 athletic trainers.

Computers Computers are regularly used in art, classics, college planning, computer applications, creative writing, design, English, foreign language, mathematics, science classes. Computer network features include on-campus library services, online commercial services, Internet access, wireless campus network, Internet filtering or blocking technology. Campus intranet, student e-mail accounts, and computer access in designated common areas are available to students. The school has a published electronic and media policy.

Contact Gayle Holt, Associate Director of Admission. 203-272-5396 Ext. 455. Fax: 203-250-7209. E-mail: gayle.holt@cheshireacademy.org. Web site: www.cheshireacademy.org

CHEVERUS HIGH SCHOOL

267 Ocean Avenue
Portland, Maine 04103

Head of School: Mr. John H.R. Mullen

General Information Coeducational day college-preparatory, religious studies, technology, Honors, and AP courses school, affiliated with Roman Catholic Church (Jesuit order). Grades 9–12. Founded: 1917. Setting: suburban. 32-acre campus. 2 buildings on campus. Approved or accredited by Association of Independent Schools in New England, Independent Schools of Northern New England, Jesuit Secondary Education Association, New England Association of Schools and Colleges, The College Board, and Maine Department of Education. Endowment: $3 million. Total enrollment: 504. Upper school average class size: 22. Upper school faculty-student ratio: 1:12. There are 173 required school days per year for Upper School students. Upper School students typically attend 5 days per week. The average school day consists of 6 hours and 30 minutes.

Upper School Student Profile Grade 9: 120 students (77 boys, 43 girls); Grade 10: 133 students (83 boys, 50 girls); Grade 11: 128 students (63 boys, 65 girls); Grade 12: 123 students (75 boys, 48 girls). 65% of students are Roman Catholic Church (Jesuit order).

Faculty School total: 50. In upper school: 26 men, 20 women; 28 have advanced degrees.

Subjects Offered Advanced Placement courses, algebra, American history, art, biology, calculus, chemistry, college counseling, creative writing, economics, English, European history, fine arts, French, geography, geometry, government/civics, history, journalism, Latin, library skills, mathematics, music, physics, religion, science, social studies, Spanish, statistics, trigonometry, world history, yearbook.

Graduation Requirements Arts and fine arts (art, music, dance, drama), computer science, English, foreign language, health, mathematics, science, social studies (includes history), theology, all seniors are required to fill a community service requirement. Community service is required.

Special Academic Programs Advanced Placement exam preparation; honors section; study at local college for college credit; programs in general development for dyslexic students.

College Admission Counseling 119 students graduated in 2012; 113 went to college, including Endicott College; Maine Maritime Academy; Saint Anselm College; Stonehill College; University of Maine; University of Southern Maine. Other: 1 had other specific plans. Median SAT critical reading: 555, median SAT math: 573, median SAT writing: 549.
Student Life Upper grades have specified standards of dress, student council, honor system. Discipline rests primarily with faculty. Attendance at religious services is required.
Summer Programs Enrichment, sports programs offered; session focuses on enrichment; held on campus; accepts boys and girls; open to students from other schools. 65 students usually enrolled. 2013 schedule: June 21 to August 8. Application deadline: June 1.
Tuition and Aid Day student tuition: $15,835. Tuition installment plan (FACTS Tuition Payment Plan, monthly payment plans, individually arranged payment plans). Tuition reduction for siblings, merit scholarship grants, need-based scholarship grants, paying campus jobs available. In 2012–13, 66% of upper-school students received aid; total upper-school merit-scholarship money awarded: $12,500. Total amount of financial aid awarded in 2012–13: $1,919,108.
Admissions Traditional secondary-level entrance grade is 9. For fall 2012, 193 students applied for upper-level admission, 173 were accepted, 143 enrolled. English language and Math Placement Exam required. Deadline for receipt of application materials: none. Application fee required: $50. On-campus interview required.
Athletics Interscholastic: baseball (boys), basketball (b,g), cross-country running (b,g), diving (b,g), field hockey (g), football (b), golf (b,g), ice hockey (b,g), indoor track & field (b,g), lacrosse (b,g), sailing (b,g), skiing (downhill) (b,g), soccer (b,g), softball (g), swimming and diving (b,g), tennis (b,g), track and field (b,g), volleyball (g), winter (indoor) track (b,g), wrestling (b); intramural: basketball (b,g), flag football (b,g); coed interscholastic: alpine skiing, outdoor adventure; coed intramural: basketball, bicycling, flag football, hiking/backpacking, table tennis, volleyball. 82 coaches, 2 athletic trainers.
Computers Computers are regularly used in creative writing, economics, history, information technology, journalism, mathematics, SAT preparation, science, word processing, yearbook classes. Computer network features include on-campus library services, online commercial services, Internet access, wireless campus network. Student e-mail accounts and computer access in designated common areas are available to students. Students grades are available online. The school has a published electronic and media policy.
Contact Ms. Kate Luke-Jenkins, Admissions Assistant. 207-774-6238 Ext. 35. Fax: 207-321-0004. E-mail: luke-jenkins@cheverus.org. Web site: www.cheverus.org

THE CHICAGO ACADEMY FOR THE ARTS

1010 West Chicago Avenue
Chicago, Illinois 60642

Head of School: Ms. Pamela Jordan

General Information Coeducational day college-preparatory and arts school. Grades 9–12. Founded: 1981. Setting: urban. 1-acre campus. 1 building on campus. Approved or accredited by Independent Schools Association of the Central States, North Central Association of Colleges and Schools, and Illinois Department of Education. Member of National Association of Independent Schools. Upper school average class size: 15. Upper school faculty-student ratio: 1:15. There are 163 required school days per year for Upper School students. Upper School students typically attend 5 days per week. The average school day consists of 8 hours.
Faculty School total: 43. In upper school: 21 men, 21 women; 21 have advanced degrees.
Subjects Offered Algebra, American history, anatomy, art history, arts, biology, calculus, chemistry, consumer law, creative writing, dance, drama, English, film, fine arts, French, geometry, historical foundations for arts, humanities, mathematics, music, physics, science, social sciences, Spanish, speech, theater.
Graduation Requirements Arts and fine arts (art, music, dance, drama), English, foreign language, mathematics, science, social sciences, U.S. history, requirements vary according to arts discipline.
Special Academic Programs Advanced Placement exam preparation; honors section; academic accommodation for the musically talented and the artistically talented; programs in general development for dyslexic students.
College Admission Counseling 33 students graduated in 2012; all went to college, including New England Conservatory of Music; New York University; Rhode Island School of Design; School of the Art Institute of Chicago; The Juilliard School; University of Chicago.
Student Life Upper grades have student council, honor system. Discipline rests equally with students and faculty.
Tuition and Aid Day student tuition: $22,105. Tuition installment plan (FACTS Tuition Payment Plan, monthly payment plans). Merit scholarship grants, need-based scholarship grants available. In 2012–13, 48% of upper-school students received aid.
Admissions Traditional secondary-level entrance grade is 9. For fall 2012, 137 students applied for upper-level admission, 67 were accepted, 41 enrolled. ISEE required. Deadline for receipt of application materials: December 3. Application fee required: $65. On-campus interview required.
Computers Computers are regularly used in English, historical foundations for arts classes. Computer resources include online commercial services, Internet access, graphic design and production.
Contact Ms. Mollie Kolosky, Admissions Assistant. 312-421-0202 Ext. 21. Fax: 312-421-3816. E-mail: mkolosky@chicagoartsacademy.org. Web site: www.chicagoartsacademy.org

CHICAGO WALDORF SCHOOL

1300 West Loyola Avenue
Chicago, Illinois 60626

Head of School: Mr. Leukos Goodwin

General Information Coeducational day college-preparatory, arts, vocational, service learning, and arts integrated school. Grades 1–12. Founded: 1974. Setting: urban. 2 buildings on campus. Approved or accredited by Association of Waldorf Schools of North America, Independent Schools Association of the Central States, and Illinois Department of Education. Member of National Association of Independent Schools. Total enrollment: 279. Upper school average class size: 25. There are 166 required school days per year for Upper School students. Upper School students typically attend 5 days per week. The average school day consists of 7 hours and 30 minutes.
Upper School Student Profile Grade 9: 26 students (14 boys, 12 girls); Grade 10: 19 students (11 boys, 8 girls); Grade 11: 15 students (8 boys, 7 girls); Grade 12: 11 students (1 boy, 10 girls).
Faculty School total: 50. In upper school: 12 men, 12 women.
Subjects Offered All academic.
Special Academic Programs Independent study; study abroad.
College Admission Counseling 21 students graduated in 2012; all went to college, including DePaul University; Grinnell College; Knox College; Skidmore College; University of Illinois at Urbana–Champaign; Vassar College.
Student Life Upper grades have specified standards of dress, student council. Discipline rests primarily with faculty.
Tuition and Aid Day student tuition: $17,480. Tuition installment plan (SMART Tuition Payment Plan, monthly payment plans, individually arranged payment plans). Tuition reduction for siblings, need-based scholarship grants available. In 2012–13, 55% of upper-school students received aid. Total amount of financial aid awarded in 2012–13: $361,783.
Admissions Traditional secondary-level entrance grade is 9. For fall 2012, 18 students applied for upper-level admission, 13 were accepted, 9 enrolled. Deadline for receipt of application materials: none. Application fee required: $75. Interview required.
Athletics Interscholastic: basketball (boys, girls), soccer (b,g), touch football (b), volleyball (b,g); coed interscholastic: Circus, cross-country running. 2 PE instructors, 4 coaches.
Computers Computers are regularly used in all academic classes. Computer network features include Internet access, wireless campus network. The school has a published electronic and media policy.
Contact Ms. Lisa Payton, Admissions Director. 773-465-2371. Fax: 773-465-6648. E-mail: lpayton@chicagowaldorf.org. Web site: www.chicagowaldorf.org/

CHILDREN'S CREATIVE AND PERFORMING ARTS ACADEMY OF SAN DIEGO

3051 El Cajon Boulevard
San Diego, California 92104

Head of School: Mrs. Janet M. Cherif

General Information Coeducational boarding and day college-preparatory and arts school. Boarding grades 6–12, day grades K–12. Founded: 1981. Setting: urban. Students are housed in homestay families. 1-acre campus. 1 building on campus. Approved or accredited by Western Association of Schools and Colleges and California Department of Education. Total enrollment: 265. Upper school average class size: 16. Upper school faculty-student ratio: 1:15. There are 186 required school days per year for Upper School students. Upper School students typically attend 5 days per week. The average school day consists of 7 hours and 30 minutes.
Upper School Student Profile Grade 9: 31 students (11 boys, 20 girls); Grade 10: 28 students (12 boys, 16 girls); Grade 11: 28 students (13 boys, 15 girls); Grade 12: 28 students (15 boys, 13 girls). 20% of students are boarding students. 80% are state residents. 1 state is represented in upper school student body. 20% are international students. International students from China, Mexico, Republic of Korea, Taiwan, Thailand, and Viet Nam; 3 other countries represented in student body.
Faculty School total: 30. In upper school: 3 men, 14 women; 10 have advanced degrees.
Subjects Offered 3-dimensional art, 3-dimensional design, accounting, algebra, American government, anatomy and physiology, art, art history, art history-AP, art-AP, audition methods, ballet, band, biology, business skills, calculus, calculus-AP, ceramics, chamber groups, cheerleading, chemistry, Chinese, choir, choreography, chorus, communications, comparative government and politics-AP, computer applications, computer literacy, computer programming-AP, concert band, concert choir, creative writing,

dance performance, digital photography, drama, drama performance, earth science, ecology, English, English literature-AP, English-AP, English/composition-AP, ensembles, environmental science-AP, ESL, European history-AP, film, fitness, French, French language-AP, French literature-AP, geometry, government and politics-AP, government/civics, government/civics-AP, graphic design, gymnastics, health, history of music, history-AP, honors algebra, honors English, honors geometry, honors U.S. history, honors world history, HTML design, human anatomy, humanities, instrumental music, Japanese, jazz band, jazz dance, jazz ensemble, journalism, Latin, library studies, mathematics, mathematics-AP, modern dance, music history, music performance, music theory-AP, orchestra, performing arts, physical education, physics, physics-AP, playwriting and directing, political science, portfolio art, pottery, pre-algebra, pre-calculus, psychology, reading/study skills, SAT preparation, SAT/ACT preparation, science, senior seminar, social sciences, social studies, Spanish, Spanish language-AP, Spanish literature-AP, speech, sports, stage design, statistics, studio art-AP, tap dance, tennis, theater design and production, TOEFL preparation, track and field, trigonometry, U.S. government and politics-AP, U.S. history, U.S. history-AP, vocal ensemble, vocal jazz, voice ensemble, volleyball, Web site design, Western civilization, world history, world history-AP, writing, writing workshop, yearbook.

Graduation Requirements Algebra, arts, biology, business skills (includes word processing), chemistry, choir, chorus, computer applications, computer skills, English, English composition, English literature, foreign language, government/civics, history, mathematics, modern world history, music, physical education (includes health), physics, science, social sciences, Spanish, sports, trigonometry, U.S. government, U.S. history, visual and performing arts, senior recital or project, 30 hours of community service per year of attendance. Community service is required.

Special Academic Programs 14 Advanced Placement exams for which test preparation is offered; honors section; accelerated programs; independent study; study at local college for college credit; academic accommodation for the gifted, the musically talented, and the artistically talented; remedial reading and/or remedial writing; remedial math; ESL (15 students enrolled).

College Admission Counseling 15 students graduated in 2012; all went to college, including San Diego State University; The George Washington University; The University of Texas at Austin; University of California, Berkeley; University of California, Davis; University of California, San Diego. Median SAT critical reading: 627, median SAT math: 677, median SAT writing: 590, median combined SAT: 1894. 50% scored over 600 on SAT critical reading, 50% scored over 600 on SAT math, 45% scored over 600 on SAT writing, 45% scored over 1800 on combined SAT.

Student Life Upper grades have uniform requirement, student council, honor system. Discipline rests primarily with faculty.

Summer Programs Remediation, enrichment, advancement, ESL, art/fine arts, computer instruction programs offered; session focuses on advancement and ESL; held on campus; accepts boys and girls; open to students from other schools. 40 students usually enrolled. 2013 schedule: June 21 to August 13. Application deadline: none.

Tuition and Aid Day student tuition: $9750; 7-day tuition and room/board: $17,900. Tuition installment plan (individually arranged payment plans, Pay by semester). Tuition reduction for siblings, merit scholarship grants, need-based scholarship grants, paying campus jobs, music scholarships available. In 2012–13, 20% of upper-school students received aid; total upper-school merit-scholarship money awarded: $10,000. Total amount of financial aid awarded in 2012–13: $25,000.

Admissions Admissions testing, any standardized test, audition, math and English placement tests, Math Placement Exam or writing sample required. Deadline for receipt of application materials: none. Application fee required: $300. Interview recommended.

Athletics Interscholastic: baseball (boys, girls), basketball (b,g), cross-country running (b,g), flag football (b), gymnastics (g), indoor soccer (b,g), soccer (b,g), softball (g), track and field (b,g), volleyball (b,g); intramural: aerobics/dance (b,g), badminton (b,g), ballet (b,g), baseball (b,g), basketball (b,g), bowling (b,g), cheering (g), dance (b,g), dance squad (b,g), dance team (b,g), fitness (b,g), flag football (b,g), gymnastics (b,g), hiking/backpacking (b,g), horseback riding (b,g), indoor soccer (b,g), jump rope (b,g), modern dance (b,g), outdoor activities (b,g), outdoor education (b,g), physical fitness (b,g), soccer (b,g), softball (b,g), surfing (b,g), swimming and diving (b,g), table tennis (b,g), tennis (b,g), track and field (b,g), volleyball (b,g); coed interscholastic: indoor soccer; coed intramural: aerobics/dance, badminton, ballet, baseball, bowling, dance, dance squad, dance team, fitness, flag football, hiking/backpacking, indoor soccer, jump rope, modern dance, outdoor activities, outdoor education, physical fitness, softball, surfing, swimming and diving, table tennis, track and field. 2 PE instructors, 2 coaches.

Computers Computers are regularly used in architecture, business skills, commercial art, creative writing, data processing, desktop publishing, drawing and design, journalism, keyboarding, media arts, music, programming, SAT preparation, typing, video film production, Web site design, word processing, yearbook classes. Computer network features include Internet access, college credit classes online.

Contact Karen Peterson, Admissions Department. 619-584-2454. Fax: 619-584-2422. E-mail: jmcherif@yahoo.com. Web site: www.ccpaasd.com

CHINESE CHRISTIAN SCHOOLS

1501 Harbor Bay Parkway
Alameda, California 94502

Head of School: Mr. Robin S. Hom

General Information Coeducational day college-preparatory and religious studies school, affiliated with Bible Fellowship Church, Evangelical/Fundamental faith. Grades K–12. Founded: 1979. Setting: suburban. Nearest major city is Oakland. 10-acre campus. 3 buildings on campus. Approved or accredited by Association of Christian Schools International, The College Board, US Department of State, Western Association of Schools and Colleges, and California Department of Education. Endowment: $14,000. Total enrollment: 640. Upper school average class size: 20. Upper school faculty-student ratio: 1:8. There are 173 required school days per year for Upper School students. Upper School students typically attend 5 days per week. The average school day consists of 6 hours and 50 minutes.

Upper School Student Profile Grade 9: 49 students (16 boys, 33 girls); Grade 10: 50 students (26 boys, 24 girls); Grade 11: 55 students (22 boys, 33 girls); Grade 12: 69 students (41 boys, 28 girls). 20% of students are Bible Fellowship Church, Evangelical/Fundamental faith.

Faculty School total: 40. In upper school: 15 men, 20 women; 12 have advanced degrees.

Subjects Offered Advanced computer applications, Advanced Placement courses, aerobics, algebra, American government, American history, American history-AP, American literature, American literature-AP, applied music, art, art-AP, audio visual/media, Basic programming, basketball, Bible, Bible studies, biology, biology-AP, British literature, calculus, calculus-AP, career/college preparation, chemistry, Chinese, Chinese studies, choir, choral music, Christian doctrine, Christian ethics, Christian studies, civics, civics/free enterprise, college counseling, college placement, college planning, communications, community service, comparative religion, computer applications, computer graphics, computer science, computer science-AP, CPR, debate, drama, driver education, economics, economics-AP, electives, English, English language-AP, English literature, English literature-AP, ESL, European history-AP, first aid, foreign language, general science, geometry, government, government and politics-AP, government-AP, graphic arts, honors English, intro to computers, language arts, leadership and service, learning strategies, library assistant, literature and composition-AP, literature-AP, macro/microeconomics-AP, Mandarin, marching band, marine science, martial arts, mathematics-AP, microeconomics, microeconomics-AP, music, newspaper, participation in sports, physical education, physics, physics-AP, pre-algebra, pre-calculus, probability and statistics, psychology-AP, public speaking, religious education, religious studies, ROTC (for boys), SAT preparation, SAT/ACT preparation, science, science research, Spanish, speech, speech and debate, speech communications, sports, state history, statistics, student government, theater, theater arts, trigonometry, U.S. government, U.S. government and politics-AP, U.S. history, U.S. history-AP, visual and performing arts, volleyball, Web authoring, world history, world wide web design, yearbook.

Graduation Requirements Algebra, American government, American history, Bible, Chinese, CPR, driver education, economics, English, first aid, foreign language, geometry, history, lab science, Life of Christ, mathematics, physical education (includes health), physics, pre-algebra, science, visual and performing arts, world history, Mandarin I or Chinese Culture class.

Special Academic Programs 13 Advanced Placement exams for which test preparation is offered; honors section; term-away projects; study at local college for college credit; study abroad; academic accommodation for the gifted; remedial reading and/or remedial writing; ESL (30 students enrolled).

College Admission Counseling 50 students graduated in 2012; all went to college, including University of California, Berkeley; University of California, Davis; University of California, Irvine; University of California, Riverside; University of California, San Diego; University of the Pacific. Mean SAT critical reading: 563, mean SAT math: 622, mean SAT writing: 558, mean combined SAT: 1743. 43% scored over 600 on SAT critical reading, 59% scored over 600 on SAT math, 39% scored over 600 on SAT writing, 38% scored over 1800 on combined SAT.

Student Life Upper grades have uniform requirement, student council. Discipline rests primarily with faculty. Attendance at religious services is required.

Summer Programs Remediation, enrichment, advancement, ESL, sports programs offered; session focuses on academic enrichment or remediation; held on campus; accepts boys and girls; open to students from other schools. 270 students usually enrolled. 2013 schedule: June 19 to July 19. Application deadline: May 15.

Tuition and Aid Day student tuition: $7500–$9700. Tuition installment plan (monthly payment plans, individually arranged payment plans, eTuition automatic electronic deposit). Tuition reduction for siblings, merit scholarship grants, need-based scholarship grants, paying campus jobs, tuition reduction for staff children, tuition reduction for children of full-time Christian ministers of like faith available. In 2012–13, 10% of upper-school students received aid; total upper-school merit-scholarship money awarded: $10,000. Total amount of financial aid awarded in 2012–13: $120,000.

Admissions Traditional secondary-level entrance grade is 9. For fall 2012, 53 students applied for upper-level admission, 51 were accepted, 49 enrolled. Achievement/Aptitude/Writing, admissions testing, California Achievement Test, CTBS (or similar from their school), Math Placement Exam, Stanford Achievement Test or writing sample required. Deadline for receipt of application materials: none. No application fee required. Interview required.

Athletics Interscholastic: badminton (boys, girls), baseball (b), basketball (b,g), cross-country running (b,g), drill team (b,g), golf (b,g), JROTC drill (b,g), soccer (b,g), tennis (b,g), track and field (b,g), volleyball (b,g); intramural: basketball (b,g), drill team (b,g), martial arts (b,g), outdoor education (b,g), outdoor recreation (b,g), soccer (b,g), softball (b,g), street hockey (b,g), table tennis (b,g), volleyball (b,g); coed interscholastic: badminton, golf, swimming and diving; coed intramural: outdoor education, outdoor recreation, softball, table tennis, volleyball. 2 PE instructors, 1 coach.

Computers Computers are regularly used in lab/keyboard, programming, science, senior seminar, Web site design classes. Computer network features include on-campus library services, Internet access, wireless campus network, Internet filtering or blocking technology. Student e-mail accounts are available to students. Students grades are available online. The school has a published electronic and media policy.

Contact Mrs. Cindy Loh, Admissions Director. 510-351-4957 Ext. 210. Fax: 510-351-1789. E-mail: CindyLoh@ccs-rams.org. Web site: www.ccs-rams.org

CHOATE ROSEMARY HALL

333 Christian Street
Wallingford, Connecticut 06492-3800

Head of School: Alex D. Curtis, PhD

General Information Coeducational boarding and day college-preparatory school. Grades 9–PG. Founded: 1890. Setting: small town. Nearest major city is New Haven. Students are housed in single-sex dormitories. 458-acre campus. 121 buildings on campus. Approved or accredited by Connecticut Association of Independent Schools, New England Association of Schools and Colleges, The Association of Boarding Schools, and Connecticut Department of Education. Member of National Association of Independent Schools and Secondary School Admission Test Board. Endowment: $283 million. Total enrollment: 864. Upper school average class size: 12. Upper school faculty-student ratio: 1:6. There are 166 required school days per year for Upper School students. Upper School students typically attend 5 days per week. The average school day consists of 5 hours.

Upper School Student Profile Grade 9: 143 students (70 boys, 73 girls); Grade 10: 230 students (118 boys, 112 girls); Grade 11: 228 students (113 boys, 115 girls); Grade 12: 240 students (119 boys, 121 girls); Postgraduate: 23 students (17 boys, 6 girls). 74% of students are boarding students. 41% are state residents. 37 states are represented in upper school student body. 15% are international students. International students from Canada, China, Hong Kong, Republic of Korea, Saudi Arabia, and Thailand; 38 other countries represented in student body.

Faculty School total: 139. In upper school: 72 men, 59 women; 125 have advanced degrees; 110 reside on campus.

Subjects Offered Algebra, American history, American literature, anatomy, Arabic, architecture, art, astronomy, biology, British history, calculus, calculus-AP, ceramics, chemistry, chemistry-AP, child development, Chinese, computer programming, computer science, computer science-AP, creative writing, dance, drama, ecology, economics, English, English literature, environmental science, environmental science-AP, European history-AP, fine arts, French, French language-AP, French studies, geometry, government and politics-AP, history, history-AP, Holocaust, interdisciplinary studies, international studies, Italian, language, Latin, Latin-AP, linear algebra, macroeconomics-AP, marine biology, mathematics, microbiology, microeconomics-AP, music, music composition, music history, music performance, music technology, music theater, music theory-AP, musical productions, musical theater, musical theater dance, musicianship, philosophy, photography, physics, physics-AP, psychology, psychology-AP, public speaking, religion, Spanish, Spanish language-AP, Spanish literature, Spanish literature-AP, Spanish-AP, statistics, statistics-AP, studio art, theater, trigonometry, U.S. history, U.S. history-AP, visual arts, world history, world literature, world religions, world studies, wrestling, writing, writing, writing workshop.

Graduation Requirements Art, English, foreign language, global studies, history, mathematics, philosophy, physical education (includes health), science, 30 hours of community service.

Special Academic Programs 25 Advanced Placement exams for which test preparation is offered; honors section; independent study; term-away projects; study abroad; academic accommodation for the gifted, the musically talented, and the artistically talented.

College Admission Counseling 240 students graduated in 2012; 235 went to college, including Boston University; Columbia University; Georgetown University; New York University; Wesleyan University; Yale University. Other: 1 entered a postgraduate year, 4 had other specific plans. Mean SAT critical reading: 664, mean SAT math: 674, mean SAT writing: 680, mean combined SAT: 2018, mean composite ACT: 29.

Student Life Upper grades have specified standards of dress, student council, honor system. Discipline rests primarily with faculty.

Summer Programs Enrichment, advancement, ESL, sports, art/fine arts programs offered; session focuses on academic growth and enrichment; held both on and off campus; held at China, France, Jordan, and Spain; accepts boys and girls; open to students from other schools. 575 students usually enrolled. 2013 schedule: June 23 to July 26. Application deadline: May 1.

Tuition and Aid Day student tuition: $37,000; 7-day tuition and room/board: $48,000. Tuition installment plan (Smart Tuition Payment Plan). Need-based scholarship grants, need-based loans available. In 2012–13, 33% of upper-school students received aid. Total amount of financial aid awarded in 2012–13: $10,000,000.

Admissions Traditional secondary-level entrance grade is 9. For fall 2012, 2,018 students applied for upper-level admission, 447 were accepted, 269 enrolled. ACT, ISEE, PSAT or SAT for applicants to grade 11 and 12, SSAT or TOEFL required. Deadline for receipt of application materials: January 10. Application fee required: $60. Interview required.

Athletics Interscholastic: baseball (boys), basketball (b,g), crew (b,g), cross-country running (b,g), diving (b,g), field hockey (g), football (b), golf (b,g), ice hockey (b,g), lacrosse (b,g), soccer (b,g), softball (g), squash (b,g), swimming and diving (b,g), tennis (b,g), track and field (b,g), volleyball (b,g), water polo (b,g); intramural: crew (b,g), squash (b,g); coed interscholastic: archery, ultimate Frisbee, wrestling; coed intramural: aerobics, aerobics/dance, aerobics/Nautilus, ballet, basketball, dance, dance squad, fitness, martial arts, modern dance, Nautilus, outdoor activities, physical fitness, physical training, rock climbing, running, soccer, softball, strength & conditioning, swimming and diving, tennis, ultimate Frisbee, volleyball, wall climbing, weight training, winter (indoor) track, yoga. 10 coaches, 3 athletic trainers.

Computers Computers are regularly used in all academic, art, college planning, computer applications, desktop publishing, drawing and design, graphic design, information technology, library skills, literary magazine, media production, music, newspaper, photography, programming, stock market, study skills, theater arts, video film production, word processing, yearbook classes. Computer network features include on-campus library services, online commercial services, Internet access, wireless campus network, Internet filtering or blocking technology. Campus intranet, student e-mail accounts, and computer access in designated common areas are available to students. Students grades are available online. The school has a published electronic and media policy.

Contact Raymond M. Diffley III, Director of Admission. 203-697-2239. Fax: 203-697-2629. E-mail: admission@choate.edu. Web site: www.choate.edu

CHRISTA MCAULIFFE ACADEMY SCHOOL OF ARTS AND SCIENCES

5200 SW Meadows Road, Ste 150
Lake Oswego, Oregon 97035

Head of School: Christopher M. Geis

General Information Coeducational day and distance learning college-preparatory, general academic, arts, vocational, technology, and advanced placement, honors, credit recovery school. Grades K–12. Distance learning grades K–12. Founded: 2009. Setting: small town. Nearest major city is Portland. 1 building on campus. Approved or accredited by CITA (Commission on International and Trans-Regional Accreditation), Northwest Accreditation Commission, and Oregon Department of Education. Total enrollment: 108. Upper school average class size: 25. Upper school faculty-student ratio: 1:25. There are 195 required school days per year for Upper School students. Upper School students typically attend 5 days per week. The average school day consists of 5 hours.

Faculty School total: 18. In upper school: 1 man, 12 women; 4 have advanced degrees.

Subjects Offered ACT preparation, alternative physical education, American government, American history, American literature, American sign language, art, art appreciation, art history, astronomy, Bible studies, British literature, British literature (honors), career education, chemistry, child development, Chinese, civics, computer literacy, economics, electives, English, English composition, environmental science, foreign language, forensics, French, geography, geometry, German, government, health, Japanese, keyboarding, Latin, mathematics, music, occupational education, physical education, science, social studies, standard curriculum, technology.

Graduation Requirements Art, career exploration, computer applications, English, mathematics, music, pre-vocational education, science, social studies (includes history).

Special Academic Programs Advanced Placement exam preparation; honors section; accelerated programs; independent study; academic accommodation for the gifted, the musically talented, and the artistically talented; remedial reading and/or remedial writing; remedial math; programs in general development for dyslexic students.

College Admission Counseling 20 students graduated in 2012; 12 went to college, including Florida State University; Massachusetts Institute of Technology; Penn State University Park; University of Illinois at Chicago; University of Washington; Washington State University.

Student Life Upper grades have student council, honor system. Discipline rests equally with students and faculty.

Summer Programs Remediation, enrichment, advancement, computer instruction programs offered; session focuses on make-up and advancement; held both on and off campus; held at students' homes; accepts boys and girls; open to students from other schools. 40 students usually enrolled. 2013 schedule: July 1 to August 31. Application deadline: none.

Tuition and Aid Day student tuition: $5295. Guaranteed tuition plan. Tuition installment plan (monthly payment plans, individually arranged payment plans). Tuition reduction for siblings available.

Admissions Traditional secondary-level entrance grade is 9. Achievement/Aptitude/Writing required. Deadline for receipt of application materials: none. Application fee required: $250.
Computers Computer resources include Internet access. The school has a published electronic and media policy.
Contact Kimberly Fowler, Director of Administrative Services. 888-832-9437 Ext. 3. Fax: 866-920-1619. E-mail: kfowler@personalizededucation.org. Web site: www.personalizededucation.org/schools/sas

CHRIST CHURCH EPISCOPAL SCHOOL

245 Cavalier Drive
Greenville, South Carolina 29607

Head of School: Dr. Leonard Kupersmith

General Information Coeducational day college-preparatory, arts, religious studies, and technology school, affiliated with Episcopal Church. Grades K–12. Founded: 1959. Setting: suburban. Nearest major city is Charlotte, NC. 72-acre campus. 8 buildings on campus. Approved or accredited by International Baccalaureate Organization, National Association of Episcopal Schools, South Carolina Independent School Association, Southern Association of Colleges and Schools, Southern Association of Independent Schools, and The College Board. Member of National Association of Independent Schools. Endowment: $12.3 million. Total enrollment: 1,095. Upper school average class size: 12. Upper school faculty-student ratio: 1:9. There are 175 required school days per year for Upper School students. Upper School students typically attend 5 days per week. The average school day consists of 7 hours.
Upper School Student Profile 28% of students are members of Episcopal Church.
Faculty School total: 118. In upper school: 20 men, 22 women; 31 have advanced degrees.
Subjects Offered Algebra, Ancient Greek, ancient history, archaeology, art, art-AP, Bible studies, biology, biology-AP, calculus, calculus-AP, ceramics, chemistry, chemistry-AP, China/Japan history, comparative government and politics-AP, computer applications, computer graphics, computer programming, computer science, computer science-AP, contemporary issues, creative writing, digital applications, digital photography, economics, English, environmental science, environmental science-AP, environmental systems, ESL, ethics, European history, European history-AP, film appreciation, French, French-AP, geometry, German, government and politics-AP, government/civics, graphic arts, honors English, instrumental music, International Baccalaureate courses, journalism, Latin, Latin-AP, literature-AP, Mandarin, mathematics, military history, modern European history, music, music history, music theory, music theory-AP, physical education, physical fitness, physics, physics-AP, pre-calculus, probability and statistics, psychology, psychology-AP, religion, sculpture, senior thesis, service learning/internship, Southern literature, Spanish, Spanish-AP, sports conditioning, statistics, statistics-AP, theater, theater design and production, theology, theory of knowledge, U.S. history, U.S. history-AP, video communication, visual and performing arts, visual arts, voice, voice ensemble, Web authoring, world religions, World War II, yearbook.
Graduation Requirements American history, arts and fine arts (art, music, dance, drama), electives, English, foreign language, mathematics, physical education (includes health), religion (includes Bible studies and theology), science, senior thesis, service learning/internship, extended essay (for IB diploma candidates), sophomore project (all students), senior thesis (for non-IB diploma candidates).
Special Academic Programs International Baccalaureate program; honors section; independent study; academic accommodation for the gifted; remedial reading and/or remedial writing; remedial math; ESL (1 student enrolled).
College Admission Counseling 70 students graduated in 2012; all went to college, including Clemson University; College of Charleston; Furman University; University of South Carolina; Washington and Lee University; Wofford College. Mean SAT critical reading: 604, mean SAT math: 597, mean SAT writing: 602, mean combined SAT: 1803, mean composite ACT: 26.
Student Life Upper grades have specified standards of dress, student council, honor system. Discipline rests equally with students and faculty. Attendance at religious services is required.
Summer Programs Enrichment, advancement, sports programs offered; session focuses on enrichment, athletics, academics; held both on and off campus; held at field trips to other locations; accepts boys and girls; open to students from other schools. 73 students usually enrolled. 2013 schedule: June 3 to August 9.
Tuition and Aid Day student tuition: $16,920. Tuition installment plan (Insured Tuition Payment Plan, FACTS Tuition Payment Plan, monthly payment plans). Merit scholarship grants, need-based scholarship grants available. In 2012–13, 23% of upper-school students received aid; total upper-school merit-scholarship money awarded: $188,431. Total amount of financial aid awarded in 2012–13: $482,208.
Admissions Traditional secondary-level entrance grade is 9. For fall 2012, 51 students applied for upper-level admission, 38 were accepted, 31 enrolled. PSAT required. Deadline for receipt of application materials: December 3. Application fee required: $150. On-campus interview required.
Athletics Interscholastic: baseball (boys), basketball (b,g), cheering (g), cross-country running (b,g), dance team (g), field hockey (g), football (b), golf (b,g), lacrosse (b,g), soccer (b,g), softball (g), swimming and diving (b,g), tennis (b,g), track and field (b,g), volleyball (g), wrestling (b); intramural: dance team (g). 2 PE instructors, 54 coaches, 1 athletic trainer.
Computers Computers are regularly used in all academic classes. Computer network features include on-campus library services, online commercial services, Internet access, wireless campus network, Internet filtering or blocking technology, classroom computers, 6th grade 1 to 1 iPad program. Computer access in designated common areas is available to students. Students grades are available online. The school has a published electronic and media policy.
Contact Mrs. Kathy Jones, Director of Admission. 864-299-1522 Ext. 1208. Fax: 864-299-8861. E-mail: jonesk@cces.org. Web site: www.cces.org

CHRISTCHURCH SCHOOL

49 Seahorse Lane
Christchurch, Virginia 23031

Head of School: Mr. John E. Byers

General Information Coeducational boarding and day college-preparatory, marine and environmental sciences, and ESL school, affiliated with Episcopal Church. Grades 9–12. Founded: 1921. Setting: rural. Nearest major city is Richmond. Students are housed in single-sex dormitories. 125-acre campus. 14 buildings on campus. Approved or accredited by National Association of Episcopal Schools, The Association of Boarding Schools, The College Board, Virginia Association of Independent Schools, and Virginia Department of Education. Member of National Association of Independent Schools and Secondary School Admission Test Board. Endowment: $3 million. Total enrollment: 221. Upper school average class size: 12. Upper school faculty-student ratio: 1:6. There are 165 required school days per year for Upper School students. Upper School students typically attend 5 days per week. The average school day consists of 9 hours.
Upper School Student Profile Grade 9: 30 students (18 boys, 12 girls); Grade 10: 62 students (47 boys, 15 girls); Grade 11: 72 students (52 boys, 20 girls); Grade 12: 57 students (54 boys, 3 girls). 60% of students are boarding students. 65% are state residents. 14 states are represented in upper school student body. 21% are international students. International students from Bahamas, China, Germany, Ghana, Guatemala, and Republic of Korea; 5 other countries represented in student body. 17% of students are members of Episcopal Church.
Faculty School total: 42. In upper school: 27 men, 15 women; 26 have advanced degrees; 25 reside on campus.
Subjects Offered Advanced biology, advanced chemistry, algebra, ancient world history, art, biology, calculus, chemistry, Chesapeake Bay studies, Chinese, computer art, computer-aided design, conceptual physics, digital art, drawing and design, economics, English, English language and composition-AP, English literature and composition-AP, environmental science, environmental science-AP, ESL, fine arts, finite math, geography, geometry, health and wellness, honors U.S. history, honors world history, marine biology, modern world history, Native American history, physical education, physics, pre-calculus, probability and statistics, SAT/ACT preparation, Spanish, Spanish-AP, technology/design, theology, U.S. government, U.S. government and politics-AP, U.S. history, U.S. history-AP, world geography, world history.
Graduation Requirements Arts and fine arts (art, music, dance, drama), English, foreign language, health and wellness, mathematics, physical education (includes health), religion (includes Bible studies and theology), science, social studies (includes history), theology, Great Journeys Integrated Work.
Special Academic Programs 11 Advanced Placement exams for which test preparation is offered; honors section; independent study; academic accommodation for the gifted; ESL (18 students enrolled).
College Admission Counseling 58 students graduated in 2012; all went to college, including James Madison University; Randolph-Macon College; Roanoke College; University of Mary Washington; University of Virginia; Virginia Polytechnic Institute and State University. Mean SAT critical reading: 521, mean SAT math: 554, mean SAT writing: 516, mean combined SAT: 1591. 25% scored over 600 on SAT critical reading, 25% scored over 600 on SAT math.
Student Life Upper grades have specified standards of dress, student council, honor system. Discipline rests equally with students and faculty. Attendance at religious services is required.
Summer Programs Enrichment, sports programs offered; session focuses on marine and environmental science, sailing, camping, fishing; held on campus; accepts boys and girls; open to students from other schools. 75 students usually enrolled. 2013 schedule: June 21 to July 21. Application deadline: none.
Tuition and Aid Day student tuition: $18,700; 7-day tuition and room/board: $43,900. Tuition installment plan (monthly payment plans, individually arranged payment plans, 10 month plan, 1st payment due 6/15, 4-payment plan, first payment due 6/15, 2-payment plan, first payment due 6/15). Need-based scholarship grants available. In 2012–13, 46% of upper-school students received aid. Total amount of financial aid awarded in 2012–13: $1,957,070.
Admissions Traditional secondary-level entrance grade is 9. For fall 2012, 228 students applied for upper-level admission, 169 were accepted, 78 enrolled. PSAT or SAT, SSAT, TOEFL or WISC/Woodcock-Johnson required. Deadline for receipt of application materials: none. Application fee required: $50. Interview required.
Athletics Interscholastic: baseball (boys), basketball (b,g), crew (b,g), field hockey (g), football (b), golf (b), lacrosse (b), sailing (b,g), soccer (b,g), tennis (b,g), volleyball

(g); intramural: basketball (b), weight training (b,g); coed interscholastic: cross-country running, golf, sailing; coed intramural: backpacking, canoeing/kayaking, fishing, fitness, fly fishing, Frisbee, hiking/backpacking, indoor soccer, kayaking, mountain biking, outdoor activities, outdoor adventure, outdoor education, outdoor recreation, outdoor skills, outdoors, paint ball, physical training, rock climbing, sailing, skateboarding, skeet shooting, snowboarding, soccer, strength & conditioning, tennis, winter soccer. 1 athletic trainer.

Computers Computers are regularly used in all academic classes. Computer network features include on-campus library services, online commercial services, Internet access, wireless campus network, Internet filtering or blocking technology. Campus intranet, student e-mail accounts, and computer access in designated common areas are available to students. Students grades are available online. The school has a published electronic and media policy.

Contact Mr. Lawrence J. Jensen, Director of Admission. 804-758-2306. Fax: 804-758-0721. E-mail: admission@christchurchschool.org. Web site: www.christchurchschool.org

CHRISTIAN ACADEMY OF KNOXVILLE

529 Academy Way
Knoxville, Tennessee 37923

Head of School: Mr. Scott Sandie

General Information Coeducational day college-preparatory, arts, religious studies, and technology school, affiliated with Christian faith. Grades PK–12. Founded: 1977. Setting: suburban. 77-acre campus. 1 building on campus. Approved or accredited by Association of Christian Schools International, Southern Association of Colleges and Schools, Tennessee Association of Independent Schools, and Tennessee Department of Education. Total enrollment: 1,158. Upper school average class size: 20. Upper school faculty-student ratio: 1:17. There are 180 required school days per year for Upper School students. Upper School students typically attend 5 days per week. The average school day consists of 7 hours and 25 minutes.

Upper School Student Profile 100% of students are Christian faith.

Faculty School total: 98. In upper school: 15 men, 20 women; 26 have advanced degrees.

Subjects Offered U.S. government and politics-AP.

Student Life Upper grades have specified standards of dress, student council, honor system. Discipline rests primarily with faculty. Attendance at religious services is required.

Summer Programs Remediation, art/fine arts programs offered; held on campus; accepts boys and girls; not open to students from other schools. 2013 schedule: June 1 to August 1.

Tuition and Aid Guaranteed tuition plan. Tuition installment plan (The Tuition Plan, monthly payment plans). Need-based scholarship grants available.

Admissions Traditional secondary-level entrance grade is 9. Admissions testing required. Application fee required: $250. On-campus interview required.

Athletics Interscholastic: baseball (boys), cheering (g), dance team (g), football (b), softball (g), volleyball (g), wrestling (b); coed interscholastic: aquatics, basketball, cross-country running, golf, hiking/backpacking, soccer, strength & conditioning, swimming and diving. 4 PE instructors, 14 coaches, 5 athletic trainers.

Computers Computer resources include on-campus library services, Internet access, wireless campus network, Internet filtering or blocking technology. Campus intranet, student e-mail accounts, and computer access in designated common areas are available to students. Students grades are available online. The school has a published electronic and media policy.

Contact Mrs. Amy Williams, Admissions Director. 865-690-4721 Ext. 190. Fax: 865-690-4752. E-mail: awilliams@cakmail.org. Web site:

CHRISTIAN BROTHERS ACADEMY

850 Newman Springs Road
Lincroft, New Jersey 07738

Head of School: Mr. Peter Santanello

General Information Boys' day college-preparatory school, affiliated with Roman Catholic Church. Grades 9–12. Founded: 1959. Setting: suburban. Nearest major city is New York, NY. 157-acre campus. 3 buildings on campus. Approved or accredited by Middle States Association of Colleges and Schools. Total enrollment: 997. Upper school average class size: 18. Upper school faculty-student ratio: 1:15. There are 180 required school days per year for Upper School students. Upper School students typically attend 5 days per week. The average school day consists of 6 hours and 15 minutes.

Upper School Student Profile Grade 9: 301 students (301 boys); Grade 10: 247 students (247 boys); Grade 11: 227 students (227 boys); Grade 12: 222 students (222 boys). 80% of students are Roman Catholic.

Faculty School total: 69. In upper school: 47 men, 22 women; 41 have advanced degrees.

Subjects Offered 20th century history, algebra, American government, American history, anatomy and physiology, Arabic, Bible studies, biology, biology-AP, business, business skills, calculus, calculus-AP, chemistry, chemistry-AP, computer science, computer science-AP, creative writing, driver education, economics, economics-AP, English, English language-AP, English literature-AP, environmental science, environmental science-AP, European history, European history-AP, French, French-AP, geometry, health, history, honors algebra, honors English, honors geometry, honors U.S. history, journalism, Latin, Latin-AP, linear algebra, mathematics, physical education, physics, physics-AP, psychology, psychology-AP, religion, science, social sciences, social studies, Spanish, Spanish-AP, theology, trigonometry, U.S. history, world history, world literature, writing.

Graduation Requirements Business skills (includes word processing), computer science, English, foreign language, mathematics, physical education (includes health), religion (includes Bible studies and theology), science, social sciences, social studies (includes history).

Special Academic Programs Advanced Placement exam preparation; honors section.

College Admission Counseling 220 students graduated in 2012; 218 went to college, including Boston College; Fordham University; La Salle University; Rutgers, The State University of New Jersey, New Brunswick; Saint Joseph's University; Villanova University. Other: 2 had other specific plans. Median SAT critical reading: 590, median SAT math: 620, median SAT writing: 600, median combined SAT: 1810.

Student Life Upper grades have specified standards of dress, student council. Discipline rests primarily with faculty. Attendance at religious services is required.

Tuition and Aid Day student tuition: $13,650. Tuition installment plan (Academic Management Services Plan, individually arranged payment plans). Merit scholarship grants, need-based scholarship grants available. In 2012–13, 19% of upper-school students received aid; total upper-school merit-scholarship money awarded: $300,000. Total amount of financial aid awarded in 2012–13: $994,100.

Admissions Traditional secondary-level entrance grade is 9. For fall 2012, 530 students applied for upper-level admission, 350 were accepted, 301 enrolled. School's own test required. Deadline for receipt of application materials: none. Application fee required: $75.

Athletics Interscholastic: baseball, basketball, bowling, cross-country running, golf, ice hockey, lacrosse, soccer, swimming and diving, tennis, track and field, winter (indoor) track, wrestling; intramural: baseball, basketball, bowling, Frisbee, soccer, tennis, volleyball. 3 PE instructors, 21 coaches, 1 athletic trainer.

Computers Computers are regularly used in mathematics, science classes. Computer network features include on-campus library services, Internet access.

Contact Mr. Peter Santanello, Principal. 732-747-1959 Ext. 100. Fax: 732-747-1643. Web site: www.cbalincroftnj.org

CHRISTIAN BROTHERS ACADEMY

6245 Randall Road
Syracuse, New York 13214

Head of School: Br. Joseph Jozwiak, FSC

General Information Coeducational day college-preparatory and religious studies school, affiliated with Roman Catholic Church. Grades 7–12. Founded: 1900. Setting: suburban. 40-acre campus. 1 building on campus. Approved or accredited by Christian Brothers Association, Middle States Association of Colleges and Schools, and New York State Board of Regents. Endowment: $800,000. Total enrollment: 750. Upper school average class size: 25.

Upper School Student Profile 85% of students are Roman Catholic.

Faculty School total: 62. In upper school: 32 men, 30 women; 58 have advanced degrees.

Subjects Offered Advanced Placement courses, American history, American literature, art, biology, business, calculus, chemistry, chemistry-AP, earth science, economics, English, English literature, European history, expository writing, fine arts, French, government/civics, grammar, health, history, mathematics, music, physical education, physics, pre-calculus, psychology, religion, science, social sciences, social studies, Spanish, theology, world history, world literature.

Graduation Requirements Arts and fine arts (art, music, dance, drama), English, foreign language, mathematics, physical education (includes health), religion (includes Bible studies and theology), science, social sciences, social studies (includes history), community service for seniors.

Special Academic Programs Advanced Placement exam preparation; honors section.

College Admission Counseling 122 students graduated in 2012; 121 went to college, including Le Moyne College; Loyola University Maryland; New York University; Saint Joseph's University; Syracuse University. Other: 1 entered a postgraduate year. Mean SAT critical reading: 579, mean SAT math: 581, mean composite ACT: 26.

Student Life Upper grades have specified standards of dress, student council. Discipline rests primarily with faculty. Attendance at religious services is required.

Tuition and Aid Day student tuition: $8650. Tuition installment plan (SMART Tuition Payment Plan, individually arranged payment plans). Merit scholarship grants, need-based scholarship grants available. In 2012–13, 95% of upper-school students received aid; total upper-school merit-scholarship money awarded: $650,000.

Admissions Traditional secondary-level entrance grade is 9. For fall 2012, 50 students applied for upper-level admission, 38 were accepted, 38 enrolled. Admissions testing required. Deadline for receipt of application materials: February 1. Application fee required: $40. Interview recommended.

Athletics Interscholastic: baseball (boys), basketball (b,g), cheering (g), cross-country running (b,g), diving (b,g), football (b), golf (b,g), gymnastics (b), ice hockey (b), lacrosse (b,g), soccer (b,g), softball (g), swimming and diving (b,g), tennis (b,g), track and field (b,g), volleyball (g), wrestling (b); coed interscholastic: bowling. 3 PE instructors, 1 athletic trainer.
Computers Computer network features include on-campus library services, Internet access, Internet filtering or blocking technology. Students grades are available online. The school has a published electronic and media policy.
Contact Mr. Mark Person, Assistant Principal for Student Affairs. 315-446-5960 Ext. 1227. Fax: 315-446-3393. E-mail: mperson@cbasyracuse.org. Web site: www.cbasyracuse.org

CHRISTIAN CENTRAL ACADEMY

39 Academy Street
Williamsville, New York 14221

Head of School: Mrs. Nurline Lawrence

General Information Coeducational day college-preparatory, arts, and religious studies school, affiliated with Christian faith. Grades K–12. Founded: 1949. Setting: suburban. Nearest major city is Buffalo. 5-acre campus. 4 buildings on campus. Approved or accredited by Association of Christian Schools International, Middle States Association of Colleges and Schools, New York State Association of Independent Schools, New York State Board of Regents, and New York Department of Education. Member of Secondary School Admission Test Board. Endowment: $690,000. Total enrollment: 370. Upper school average class size: 20. Upper school faculty-student ratio: 1:10. There are 180 required school days per year for Upper School students. Upper School students typically attend 5 days per week. The average school day consists of 6 hours and 30 minutes.
Upper School Student Profile Grade 9: 29 students (17 boys, 12 girls); Grade 10: 29 students (11 boys, 18 girls); Grade 11: 21 students (12 boys, 9 girls); Grade 12: 24 students (7 boys, 17 girls). 100% of students are Christian faith.
Faculty School total: 39. In upper school: 5 men, 13 women; 9 have advanced degrees.
Subjects Offered Advanced computer applications, advertising design, algebra, art, band, Bible, biology, biology-AP, business mathematics, calculus-AP, career/college preparation, chemistry, chorus, communications, computer skills, drawing, driver education, earth science, economics, English, English language-AP, English literature-AP, European history-AP, geometry, global studies, government, health, honors English, independent study, journalism, mathematics, music, music theory, orchestra, painting, physical education, physics, physics-AP, pre-calculus, Spanish, studio art, trigonometry, U.S. history, U.S. history-AP, yearbook.
Graduation Requirements Algebra, American government, American history, American literature, arts and fine arts (art, music, dance, drama), Bible, biology, chemistry, earth science, economics, English, geometry, global studies, keyboarding, physical education (includes health), physics, pre-calculus, Spanish, trigonometry, writing, community service hours for all four years, completion of standardized NYS Regents exams, honors and high honors diplomas have more rigorous requirements.
Special Academic Programs 7 Advanced Placement exams for which test preparation is offered; honors section; independent study.
College Admission Counseling 35 students graduated in 2012; 34 went to college, including Buffalo State College, State University of New York; Canisius College; Houghton College; Liberty University; University at Buffalo, the State University of New York. Other: 1 entered military service. Median SAT critical reading: 570, median SAT math: 565, median SAT writing: 565, median combined SAT: 1705. 31% scored over 600 on SAT critical reading, 25% scored over 600 on SAT math, 34% scored over 600 on SAT writing, 28% scored over 1800 on combined SAT.
Student Life Upper grades have specified standards of dress, student council, honor system. Discipline rests primarily with faculty. Attendance at religious services is required.
Summer Programs Sports programs offered; session focuses on basketball camp, soccer camp; held on campus; accepts boys and girls; open to students from other schools. 45 students usually enrolled. 2013 schedule: July 1 to July 1. Application deadline: June 1.
Tuition and Aid Day student tuition: $7926. Tuition installment plan (FACTS Tuition Payment Plan, monthly payment plans, prepayment discount plans, multiple-student discounts, pastors/full-time Christian service discounts). Tuition reduction for siblings, merit scholarship grants, need-based scholarship grants available. In 2012–13, 22% of upper-school students received aid; total upper-school merit-scholarship money awarded: $4000. Total amount of financial aid awarded in 2012–13: $51,527.
Admissions Traditional secondary-level entrance grade is 9. For fall 2012, 19 students applied for upper-level admission, 17 were accepted, 15 enrolled. Admissions testing, Brigance Test of Basic Skills, essay, Iowa Subtests, school's own test or writing sample required. Deadline for receipt of application materials: none. Application fee required: $50. Interview recommended.
Athletics Interscholastic: baseball (boys), basketball (b,g), bowling (b), cheering (g), cross-country running (b,g), flag football (b), soccer (b,g), softball (g); intramural: basketball (b,g), physical fitness (b,g), soccer (b,g); coed interscholastic: cross-country running, soccer; coed intramural: basketball, track and field, volleyball. 2 PE instructors, 17 coaches.
Computers Computers are regularly used in college planning, computer applications, desktop publishing, drawing and design, English, journalism, library skills, photojournalism, yearbook classes. Computer resources include on-campus library services, Internet access, Internet filtering or blocking technology, teacher-guided use of programs in various subject areas. Computer access in designated common areas is available to students. The school has a published electronic and media policy.
Contact Deborah L. White, Director of Admissions. 716-634-4821 Ext. 107. Fax: 716-634-5851. E-mail: dwhitecca@gmail.com. Web site: www.christianca.com

CHRISTIAN HOME AND BIBLE SCHOOL

301 West 13th Avenue
Mount Dora, Florida 32757

Head of School: Patrick Todd

General Information Coeducational day college-preparatory, general academic, arts, religious studies, and technology school, affiliated with Church of Christ. Grades PK–12. Founded: 1945. Setting: small town. Nearest major city is Orlando. 70-acre campus. 9 buildings on campus. Approved or accredited by National Christian School Association, Southern Association of Colleges and Schools, and Florida Department of Education. Total enrollment: 533. Upper school average class size: 21. Upper school faculty-student ratio: 1:15. There are 180 required school days per year for Upper School students. Upper School students typically attend 5 days per week. The average school day consists of 6 hours and 30 minutes.
Upper School Student Profile Grade 6: 40 students (22 boys, 18 girls); Grade 7: 40 students (22 boys, 18 girls); Grade 8: 54 students (20 boys, 34 girls); Grade 9: 37 students (22 boys, 15 girls); Grade 10: 58 students (32 boys, 26 girls); Grade 11: 42 students (30 boys, 12 girls); Grade 12: 47 students (27 boys, 20 girls). 20% of students are members of Church of Christ.
Faculty School total: 45. In upper school: 11 men, 14 women; 12 have advanced degrees.
Subjects Offered Algebra, American government, American history, anatomy and physiology, art, band, Bible, biology, calculus-AP, ceramics, chemistry, computer applications, computer skills, consumer mathematics, drama, drawing, economics, English, English literature-AP, European history, geography, geometry, government, health, honors algebra, honors English, honors geometry, honors world history, intro to computers, jazz band, journalism, life management skills, life skills, math applications, Microsoft, painting, personal fitness, photography, physical education, physical science, physics, pre-algebra, pre-calculus, probability and statistics, psychology, sculpture, sign language, Spanish, speech, state history, student publications, technology/design, television, theater, theater production, trigonometry, video communication, video film production, visual and performing arts, Web site design, weight training, word processing, world history.
Graduation Requirements Advanced math, algebra, American government, American history, arts and fine arts (art, music, dance, drama), Bible, biology, chemistry, economics, electives, English, foreign language, keyboarding, lab science, life skills, physical education (includes health), physical science, world history, 80 hours of community service.
Special Academic Programs 4 Advanced Placement exams for which test preparation is offered; honors section; independent study; study at local college for college credit.
College Admission Counseling 47 students graduated in 2011; 45 went to college, including Florida State University; Harding University; Lipscomb University; University of Central Florida; University of Florida; University of South Florida. Other: 2 went to work. Median SAT critical reading: 600, median SAT math: 580, median SAT writing: 540, median combined SAT: 1640, median composite ACT: 22. 47.6% scored over 600 on SAT critical reading, 42.8% scored over 600 on SAT math, 28.5% scored over 600 on SAT writing, 38% scored over 1800 on combined SAT, 20.3% scored over 26 on composite ACT.
Student Life Upper grades have specified standards of dress, student council. Discipline rests primarily with faculty. Attendance at religious services is required.
Tuition and Aid Day student tuition: $8044. Tuition installment plan (monthly payment plans). Tuition reduction for siblings, need-based scholarship grants, discount for members of the Churches of Christ available. In 2011–12, 17% of upper-school students received aid.
Admissions Traditional secondary-level entrance grade is 9. For fall 2011, 160 students applied for upper-level admission, 138 were accepted, 138 enrolled. Any standardized test required. Deadline for receipt of application materials: none. Application fee required: $100. On-campus interview required.
Athletics Interscholastic: baseball (boys), basketball (b,g), bowling (b,g), cheering (g), cross-country running (b,g), fitness (b,g), football (b), golf (b,g), physical fitness (b,g), physical training (b,g), softball (g), tennis (b,g), track and field (b,g), volleyball (g), weight training (b,g). 3 coaches.
Computers Computers are regularly used in independent study, journalism, library, mathematics, publications, reading, video film production, Web site design, yearbook classes. Computer network features include on-campus library services, Internet access, wireless campus network, Internet filtering or blocking technology, Net Classroom communication for students and parents, Desk Top Monitoring and manage software, Accelerated Reader Access. Computer access in designated common areas is available

to students. Students grades are available online. The school has a published electronic and media policy.

Contact Natalie Yawn, Admissions Director. 352-383-2155 Ext. 261. Fax: 352-383-0098. E-mail: natalie.yawn@chbs.org. Web site: www.chbs.org

CHRISTOPHER COLUMBUS HIGH SCHOOL

3000 Southwest 87th Avenue
Miami, Florida 33165-3293

Head of School: Br. Michael Brady, FMS

General Information Boys' day college-preparatory school, affiliated with Roman Catholic Church. Grades 9–12. Founded: 1958. Setting: suburban. 19-acre campus. 10 buildings on campus. Approved or accredited by National Catholic Education Association, Southern Association of Colleges and Schools, and Florida Department of Education. Total enrollment: 1,357. Upper school average class size: 25. Upper school faculty-student ratio: 1:17. There are 180 required school days per year for Upper School students. Upper School students typically attend 5 days per week. The average school day consists of 6 hours and 25 minutes.

Upper School Student Profile Grade 9: 347 students (347 boys); Grade 10: 363 students (363 boys); Grade 11: 302 students (302 boys); Grade 12: 345 students (345 boys). 95% of students are Roman Catholic.

Faculty School total: 82. In upper school: 56 men, 26 women; 35 have advanced degrees.

Subjects Offered 3-dimensional art, accounting, acting, advanced biology, advanced chemistry, advanced computer applications, advanced math, Advanced Placement courses, algebra, American government, American history, American history-AP, American literature, analysis, anatomy, ancient world history, architectural drawing, art, athletic training, athletics, band, Basic programming, Bible, biology, biology-AP, British literature (honors), business law, business skills, calculus, calculus-AP, campus ministry, Catholic belief and practice, chemistry, chemistry-AP, Christian and Hebrew scripture, Christian doctrine, Christian ethics, church history, college counseling, composition-AP, computer applications, computer information systems, computer programming, computer science, computer science-AP, computer-aided design, contemporary history, debate, drama, economics, economics-AP, English, English language and composition-AP, English literature, English literature-AP, English-AP, ethics, European history, European history-AP, French, French language-AP, French-AP, geometry, global studies, government, government and politics-AP, health, history of the Catholic Church, Holocaust studies, keyboarding, library assistant, marine biology, physical education, physical fitness, physics, physics-AP, pre-algebra, pre-calculus, psychology, Spanish, Spanish language-AP, Spanish literature, Spanish literature-AP, speech, U.S. government, U.S. government and politics, U.S. government and politics-AP, U.S. history, U.S. history-AP, Vietnam War, word processing, world governments, yearbook.

Graduation Requirements Algebra, arts and fine arts (art, music, dance, drama), computer applications, English, lab science, language, mathematics, personal fitness, physical education (includes health), practical arts, religion (includes Bible studies and theology), science, social studies (includes history), students must earn a Florida scale GPA of 2.0, students must complete 75 hours of community service during their four years of high school.

Special Academic Programs Advanced Placement exam preparation; honors section; study at local college for college credit; academic accommodation for the gifted; remedial reading and/or remedial writing.

College Admission Counseling Colleges students went to include Florida International University; The University of Alabama; University of Florida; University of Miami; University of Notre Dame; University of Pennsylvania.

Student Life Upper grades have uniform requirement, student council, honor system. Discipline rests primarily with faculty. Attendance at religious services is required.

Summer Programs Remediation, enrichment programs offered; session focuses on enrichment, remediation, and study skills; held on campus; accepts boys; not open to students from other schools. 154 students usually enrolled. 2013 schedule: June 11 to June 29. Application deadline: January 18.

Tuition and Aid Tuition installment plan (monthly payment plans, individually arranged payment plans). Bursaries available.

Admissions Traditional secondary-level entrance grade is 9. For fall 2012, 494 students applied for upper-level admission, 347 were accepted, 347 enrolled. High School Placement Test required. Deadline for receipt of application materials: none. Application fee required: $50. Interview required.

Athletics Interscholastic: baseball, basketball, bowling, cross-country running, football, golf, lacrosse, soccer, swimming and diving, tennis, track and field, volleyball, water polo, wrestling; intramural: basketball, flag football, power lifting, roller hockey, weight training. 2 PE instructors, 25 coaches, 2 athletic trainers.

Computers Computers are regularly used in architecture, computer applications, history, journalism, keyboarding, media production, science, yearbook classes. Computer network features include on-campus library services, online commercial services, Internet access, wireless campus network, Internet filtering or blocking technology. Campus intranet and computer access in designated common areas are available to students. Students grades are available online. The school has a published electronic and media policy.

Contact Mrs. Rebecca Rafuls, Registrar. 305-223-5650 Ext. 2239. Fax: 305-559-4306. E-mail: rrafuls@columbushs.com. Web site: www.columbushs.com

CHRISTOPHER DOCK MENNONITE HIGH SCHOOL

1000 Forty Foot Road
Lansdale, Pennsylvania 19446

Head of School: Dr. Conrad Swartzentruber

General Information Coeducational boarding and day college-preparatory, general academic, arts, vocational, religious studies, and technology school, affiliated with Christian faith, Mennonite Church. Grades 9–12. Founded: 1954. Setting: suburban. Nearest major city is Philadelphia. Students are housed in homes. 75-acre campus. 6 buildings on campus. Approved or accredited by Mennonite Education Agency, Mennonite Schools Council, Middle States Association of Colleges and Schools, and Pennsylvania Department of Education. Endowment: $2.2 million. Total enrollment: 343. Upper school average class size: 21. Upper school faculty-student ratio: 1:11. There are 182 required school days per year for Upper School students. Upper School students typically attend 5 days per week. The average school day consists of 6 hours and 55 minutes.

Upper School Student Profile Grade 9: 73 students (44 boys, 29 girls); Grade 10: 83 students (34 boys, 49 girls); Grade 11: 105 students (51 boys, 54 girls); Grade 12: 86 students (42 boys, 44 girls). 2% of students are boarding students. 89% are state residents. 2 states are represented in upper school student body. 11% are international students. International students from China, Colombia, and Republic of Korea. 49% of students are Christian, Mennonite.

Faculty School total: 33. In upper school: 19 men, 14 women; 24 have advanced degrees.

Subjects Offered Accounting, advanced biology, advanced chemistry, advanced math, Advanced Placement courses, algebra, all , American government, American history, American literature, anatomy, anatomy and physiology, art, art history, arts, arts appreciation, athletic training, athletics, Basic programming, Bible, Bible studies, biology, British literature, business, business mathematics, business skills, calculus, calculus-AP, career education internship, career technology, ceramics, chemistry, child development, choir, choral music, chorus, Christian and Hebrew scripture, Christian doctrine, Christian education, Christian ethics, Christian scripture, Christian studies, Christian testament, Christianity, church history, communication skills, communications, composition-AP, computer graphics, computer information systems, computer literacy, computer programming, computer science, computer skills, computer technologies, computers, concert choir, consumer economics, creative writing, design, digital art, digital imaging, digital music, digital photography, drama, driver education, early childhood, earth science, ecology, environmental systems, economics, economics and history, economics-AP, English, English language and composition-AP, English literature, environmental science, European history, family and consumer science, family living, family studies, fine arts, food science, foreign language, forensics, genetics, geography, geology, geometry, global studies, government-AP, government/civics, grammar, graphic design, guitar, health, health and wellness, health education, history, honors English, honors geometry, instrumental music, instruments, international foods, jazz band, journalism, keyboarding, language and composition, Life of Christ, life saving, life science, mathematics, mathematics-AP, music, New Testament, oral communications, parent/child development, peace and justice, peace education, peace studies, personal finance, photography, physical education, physics, religion, religion and culture, religious education, religious studies, research and reference, rhetoric, science, science research, scripture, sculpture, senior internship, service learning/internship, social sciences, social studies, Spanish, Spanish language-AP, Spanish literature-AP, Spanish-AP, speech, speech communications, sports team management, stage and body movement, statistics, student government, student publications, theater, trigonometry, U.S. government, U.S. history, U.S. literature, Vietnam, vocal ensemble, vocal music, vocational skills, vocational-technical courses, Web site design, word processing, work-study, world cultures, world history, world literature.

Graduation Requirements Arts and fine arts (art, music, dance, drama), business skills (includes word processing), computer science, English, family and consumer science, mathematics, physical education (includes health), religion (includes Bible studies and theology), science, social sciences, social studies (includes history), three-day urban experience, senior independent study/service experience (one week), senior presentation.

Special Academic Programs 16 Advanced Placement exams for which test preparation is offered; honors section; term-away projects; study at local college for college credit; remedial reading and/or remedial writing; programs in English for dyslexic students.

College Admission Counseling 112 students graduated in 2012; 105 went to college, including Eastern Mennonite University; Eastern University; Messiah College; Montgomery County Community College; Penn State University Park. Other: 7 had other specific plans. Mean SAT critical reading: 531, mean SAT math: 560, mean SAT writing: 531, mean combined SAT: 1622. 28% scored over 600 on SAT critical reading, 45% scored over 600 on SAT math, 27% scored over 600 on SAT writing, 33% scored over 1800 on combined SAT.

Student Life Upper grades have specified standards of dress, student council, honor system. Discipline rests primarily with faculty. Attendance at religious services is required.

Tuition and Aid Day student tuition: $14,585. Tuition installment plan (monthly payment plans). Tuition reduction for siblings, need-based scholarship grants available. In 2012–13, 27% of upper-school students received aid. Total amount of financial aid awarded in 2012–13: $533,185.

Admissions Traditional secondary-level entrance grade is 9. For fall 2012, 136 students applied for upper-level admission, 131 were accepted, 100 enrolled. Deadline for receipt of application materials: none. Application fee required: $50. Interview required.

Athletics Interscholastic: baseball (boys), basketball (b,g), bowling (b,g), cheering (g), cross-country running (b,g), field hockey (g), golf (b), soccer (b,g), softball (g), tennis (b,g), track and field (b,g), volleyball (b,g); coed interscholastic: bowling, track and field. 3 PE instructors, 37 coaches, 1 athletic trainer.

Computers Computers are regularly used in accounting, art, computer applications, design, digital applications, graphic design, journalism, keyboarding, lab/keyboard, library, library skills, mathematics, music, music technology, programming, research skills, SAT preparation, science, technology, Web site design, word processing, yearbook classes. Computer network features include on-campus library services, online commercial services, Internet access, wireless campus network, Internet filtering or blocking technology, PowerSchool, WinSNAP. Computer access in designated common areas is available to students. Students grades are available online. The school has a published electronic and media policy.

Contact Doug Hackman, Admissions Director. 215-362-2675 Ext. 106. Fax: 215-362-2943. E-mail: dhackman@dockhs.org. Web site: www.dockhs.org

CHRYSALIS SCHOOL

14241 North East Woodinville-Duvall Road
PMB 243
Woodinville, Washington 98072

Head of School: Karen Fogle

General Information Coeducational day college-preparatory, general academic, arts, and technology school. Grades 1–12. Founded: 1983. Setting: suburban. Nearest major city is Seattle. 1 building on campus. Approved or accredited by Northwest Accreditation Commission, and Washington Department of Education. Total enrollment: 165. Upper school average class size: 8. Upper school faculty-student ratio: 1:4. Upper School students typically attend 4 days per week. The average school day consists of 5 hours.

Upper School Student Profile Grade 9: 19 students (11 boys, 8 girls); Grade 10: 28 students (18 boys, 10 girls); Grade 11: 41 students (31 boys, 10 girls); Grade 12: 29 students (19 boys, 10 girls).

Faculty School total: 29. In upper school: 11 men, 17 women; 28 have advanced degrees.

Subjects Offered Advanced biology, advanced chemistry, advanced computer applications, advanced math, art, audio visual/media, career planning, college counseling, computer technologies, drama, English, filmmaking, French, geography, German, graphics, history, Japanese, mathematics, physical education, SAT preparation, science, social sciences, Spanish.

Graduation Requirements Career and personal planning, computer literacy, English, foreign language, history, mathematics, physical education (includes health), science, portfolio.

Special Academic Programs Honors section; accelerated programs; study at local college for college credit; academic accommodation for the gifted; programs in English, mathematics, general development for dyslexic students; special instructional classes for students with learning disabilities.

College Admission Counseling 35 students graduated in 2012; 30 went to college, including Bellevue College; Central Washington University; University of Washington; Washington State University; Western Washington University. Other: 2 went to work, 1 entered military service, 2 had other specific plans.

Student Life Upper grades have specified standards of dress, honor system. Discipline rests primarily with faculty.

Summer Programs Remediation, enrichment, advancement, computer instruction programs offered; session focuses on enrichment; held on campus; accepts boys and girls; open to students from other schools. 35 students usually enrolled. 2013 schedule: July 10 to August 23. Application deadline: June 1.

Tuition and Aid Tuition installment plan (monthly payment plans).

Admissions Traditional secondary-level entrance grade is 9. For fall 2012, 100 students applied for upper-level admission, 60 were accepted, 60 enrolled. Deadline for receipt of application materials: none. Application fee required: $750. On-campus interview required.

Computers Computers are regularly used in computer applications, English, foreign language, graphic arts, history, information technology, introduction to technology, keyboarding, mathematics, media, science, video film production, Web site design, word processing, yearbook classes. Computer resources include on-campus library services, online commercial services, Internet access, Internet filtering or blocking technology. Computer access in designated common areas is available to students.

Contact Wanda Metcalfe, Director of Student Services. 425-481-2228. Fax: 425-486-8107. E-mail: wanda@chrysalis-school.com. Web site: www.chrysalis-school.com

THE CHURCH FARM SCHOOL

1001 East Lincoln Highway
Exton, Pennsylvania 19341

Head of School: Rev. Edmund K. Sherrill II

General Information Boys' boarding and day college-preparatory, arts, and technology school, affiliated with Episcopal Church. Grades 7–12. Founded: 1918. Setting: suburban. Nearest major city is Philadelphia. Students are housed in single-sex dormitories. 150-acre campus. 19 buildings on campus. Approved or accredited by Middle States Association of Colleges and Schools, National Association of Episcopal Schools, The Association of Boarding Schools, and Pennsylvania Department of Education. Member of National Association of Independent Schools and Secondary School Admission Test Board. Endowment: $135 million. Total enrollment: 193. Upper school average class size: 12. Upper school faculty-student ratio: 1:6. There are 180 required school days per year for Upper School students. Upper School students typically attend 5 days per week. The average school day consists of 7 hours and 5 minutes.

Upper School Student Profile Grade 9: 42 students (42 boys); Grade 10: 47 students (47 boys); Grade 11: 40 students (40 boys); Grade 12: 33 students (33 boys). 90% of students are boarding students. 35% are state residents. 15 states are represented in upper school student body. 16% are international students. International students from British Virgin Islands, China, Mexico, Nigeria, Republic of Korea, and Thailand; 4 other countries represented in student body. 10% of students are members of Episcopal Church.

Faculty School total: 33. In upper school: 22 men, 11 women; 17 have advanced degrees; 24 reside on campus.

Subjects Offered 20th century history, 3-dimensional design, African-American history, algebra, American government, American history, American history-AP, American literature, American studies, anatomy and physiology, art, art history, biology, biology-AP, British literature, calculus-AP, ceramics, chemistry, chemistry-AP, choir, choral music, clayworking, college writing, composition, computer science, construction, creative writing, design, drama, driver education, earth science, ecology, economics, English, English-AP, environmental science, ethics, European history, expository writing, film and literature, fine arts, French, geometry, government/civics, grammar, health, history, history of jazz, industrial arts, instrumental music, journalism, leadership, mathematics, medieval history, music, music history, music technology, musicianship, mythology, photography, physical education, physics, poetry, pre-calculus, psychology, public speaking, Russian history, science, Shakespeare, Shakespearean histories, social studies, sociology, Spanish, speech, statistics, technology, theater, trigonometry, Vietnam history, Vietnam War, weaving, Web site design, woodworking, world history, world literature, world religions, World War II, writing.

Graduation Requirements Arts and fine arts (art, music, dance, drama), English, foreign language, mathematics, physical education (includes health), religion (includes Bible studies and theology), science, social studies (includes history), technology, Challenge of Required Experience (combination of community service and outdoor educational experience).

Special Academic Programs 5 Advanced Placement exams for which test preparation is offered; honors section; accelerated programs; independent study; study at local college for college credit; study abroad; academic accommodation for the gifted, the musically talented, and the artistically talented.

College Admission Counseling 35 students graduated in 2012; 32 went to college, including Bard College; Brandeis University; Emory University; Northwestern University; University of California, San Diego; University of Southern California. Other: 1 went to work, 2 had other specific plans. Median SAT critical reading: 540, median SAT math: 570, median SAT writing: 520, median combined SAT: 1660. 29% scored over 600 on SAT critical reading, 43% scored over 600 on SAT math, 29% scored over 600 on SAT writing, 30% scored over 1800 on combined SAT.

Student Life Upper grades have specified standards of dress, student council, honor system. Discipline rests primarily with faculty. Attendance at religious services is required.

Tuition and Aid Day student tuition: $17,172; 5-day tuition and room/board: $30,000; 7-day tuition and room/board: $30,000. Tuition installment plan (monthly payment plans, individually arranged payment plans). Tuition reduction for siblings, need-based scholarship grants, paying campus jobs available. In 2012–13, 90% of upper-school students received aid. Total amount of financial aid awarded in 2012–13: $3,881,717.

Admissions Traditional secondary-level entrance grade is 9. For fall 2012, 264 students applied for upper-level admission, 94 were accepted, 60 enrolled. 3-R Achievement Test, ISEE, SSAT or TOEFL required. Deadline for receipt of application materials: none. Application fee required: $25. Interview required.

Athletics Interscholastic: baseball, basketball, cross-country running, golf, indoor track, soccer, tennis, track and field, wrestling; intramural: fitness, floor hockey, indoor soccer, physical fitness, strength & conditioning, touch football, weight lifting. 2 coaches, 1 athletic trainer.

Computers Computers are regularly used in art, English, foreign language, history, mathematics, music, science, technology classes. Computer network features include on-campus library services, online commercial services, Internet access, wireless campus network, Internet filtering or blocking technology, 1:1 MacBook program. Campus intranet and student e-mail accounts are available to students. Students grades are available online. The school has a published electronic and media policy.

Contact Mr. Bart Bronk, Director of Admissions. 610-363-5346. Fax: 610-280-6746. E-mail: bbronk@gocfs.net. Web site: www.gocfs.net

CINCINNATI COUNTRY DAY SCHOOL

6905 Given Road
Cincinnati, Ohio 45243-2898

Head of School: Dr. Robert P. Macrae

General Information Coeducational day college-preparatory, arts, and technology school. Grades PK–12. Founded: 1926. Setting: suburban. 62-acre campus. 8 buildings on campus. Approved or accredited by Independent Schools Association of the Central States and Ohio Department of Education. Member of National Association of Independent Schools and Secondary School Admission Test Board. Endowment: $18 million. Total enrollment: 830. Upper school average class size: 15. Upper school faculty-student ratio: 1:9. There are 180 required school days per year for Upper School students. Upper School students typically attend 5 days per week. The average school day consists of 7 hours.

Upper School Student Profile Grade 9: 72 students (33 boys, 39 girls); Grade 10: 78 students (38 boys, 40 girls); Grade 11: 65 students (32 boys, 33 girls); Grade 12: 57 students (25 boys, 32 girls).

Faculty School total: 110. In upper school: 24 men, 16 women; 32 have advanced degrees.

Subjects Offered Acting, algebra, American history, American history-AP, American literature, analysis, art, art history, biology, biology-AP, calculus, calculus-AP, ceramics, chemistry, chemistry-AP, choir, computer graphics, computer programming, computer science, CPR, creative writing, dance, drama, earth science, English, English literature, European history, fine arts, French, French language-AP, French literature-AP, genetics, geometry, health, humanities, music, photography, physical education, physics, psychology, public speaking, Spanish, Spanish language-AP, Spanish literature-AP, speech, statistics, theater, trigonometry, world history.

Graduation Requirements Arts and fine arts (art, music, dance, drama), computer science, English, foreign language, history, mathematics, physical education (includes health), science, senior project. Community service is required.

Special Academic Programs Advanced Placement exam preparation; honors section; independent study; study abroad.

College Admission Counseling 70 students graduated in 2012; all went to college, including Denison University; Indiana University Bloomington; The Ohio State University; Vanderbilt University; Williams College. Mean SAT critical reading: 630, mean SAT math: 630, mean SAT writing: 640, mean combined SAT: 1900, mean composite ACT: 27.

Student Life Upper grades have specified standards of dress, student council, honor system. Discipline rests equally with students and faculty.

Summer Programs Remediation, enrichment, advancement, sports, art/fine arts, computer instruction programs offered; session focuses on camps and academic programs; held on campus; accepts boys and girls; open to students from other schools. 500 students usually enrolled. 2013 schedule: June 18 to August 10. Application deadline: May 31.

Tuition and Aid Day student tuition: $21,920. Tuition installment plan (Insured Tuition Payment Plan, FACTS Tuition Payment Plan, monthly payment plans, individually arranged payment plans). Merit scholarship grants, need-based scholarship grants, parent loans, Sallie Mae loans available. In 2012–13, 40% of upper-school students received aid; total upper-school merit-scholarship money awarded: $520,000. Total amount of financial aid awarded in 2012–13: $1,400,000.

Admissions Traditional secondary-level entrance grade is 9. For fall 2012, 63 students applied for upper-level admission, 41 were accepted, 28 enrolled. ISEE, Otis-Lennon Ability or Stanford Achievement Test or SSAT, ERB, PSAT, SAT, PLAN or ACT required. Deadline for receipt of application materials: February 15. Application fee required: $25. Interview recommended.

Athletics Interscholastic: baseball (boys), basketball (b,g), crew (b,g), cross-country running (b,g), football (b), golf (b,g), gymnastics (g), lacrosse (b,g), softball (g), swimming and diving (b,g), tennis (b,g), track and field (b,g); intramural: dance team (g); coed interscholastic: crew, dance squad. 4 PE instructors, 1 athletic trainer.

Computers Computers are regularly used in all academic classes. Computer network features include on-campus library services, online commercial services, Internet access, wireless campus network, Internet filtering or blocking technology. Campus intranet, student e-mail accounts, and computer access in designated common areas are available to students. Students grades are available online. The school has a published electronic and media policy.

Contact Mr. Aaron B. Kellenberger, Director of Admission. 513-979-0220. Fax: 513-527-7614. E-mail: kellenbea@countryday.net. Web site: www.countryday.net

CISTERCIAN PREPARATORY SCHOOL

3660 Cistercian Road
Irving, Texas 75039

Head of School: Fr. Paul McCormick

General Information Boys' day college-preparatory, arts, and religious studies school, affiliated with Roman Catholic Church. Grades 5–12. Founded: 1962. Setting: suburban. Nearest major city is Dallas. 80-acre campus. 7 buildings on campus. Approved or accredited by Independent Schools Association of the Southwest, Texas Catholic Conference, and Texas Department of Education. Member of National Association of Independent Schools. Endowment: $7.1 million. Total enrollment: 348. Upper school average class size: 22. Upper school faculty-student ratio: 1:7. There are 180 required school days per year for Upper School students. Upper School students typically attend 5 days per week. The average school day consists of 8 hours.

Upper School Student Profile Grade 9: 48 students (48 boys); Grade 10: 43 students (43 boys); Grade 11: 43 students (43 boys); Grade 12: 41 students (41 boys). 82% of students are Roman Catholic.

Faculty School total: 52. In upper school: 27 men, 6 women; 29 have advanced degrees.

Subjects Offered Advanced biology, advanced chemistry, algebra, American history, American literature, art, athletics, baseball, basketball, biology, calculus, chemistry, computer science, creative writing, digital applications, drama, earth science, ecology, economics, English, English composition, English literature, epic literature, ethics, European history, expository writing, fine arts, French, geometry, government/civics, grammar, health, history, history of the Catholic Church, Latin, modern world history, music, performing arts, photography, physical education, physics, pre-algebra, pre-calculus, religion, science, senior project, social studies, Spanish, speech, studio art, swimming, tennis, Texas history, theology, trigonometry, world history, world literature.

Graduation Requirements Arts and fine arts (art, music, dance, drama), electives, English, foreign language, mathematics, physical education (includes health), science, senior project, social studies (includes history), theology, completion of an independent senior project during fourth quarter of senior year.

Special Academic Programs 18 Advanced Placement exams for which test preparation is offered; independent study; study at local college for college credit.

College Admission Counseling 48 students graduated in 2012; 47 went to college, including Southern Methodist University; Stanford University; Texas A&M University; Texas Christian University; University of Dallas; Vanderbilt University. Other: 1 had other specific plans. Median SAT critical reading: 690, median SAT math: 700, median SAT writing: 690, median combined SAT: 2110, median composite ACT: 32. 92% scored over 600 on SAT critical reading, 90% scored over 600 on SAT math, 85% scored over 600 on SAT writing, 90% scored over 1800 on combined SAT, 97% scored over 26 on composite ACT.

Student Life Upper grades have uniform requirement, student council. Discipline rests primarily with faculty. Attendance at religious services is required.

Summer Programs Remediation, enrichment, sports, art/fine arts, computer instruction programs offered; session focuses on remediation and enrichment in mathematics and English, arts and fine arts, computers, and sports camp; held on campus; accepts boys; open to students from other schools. 125 students usually enrolled. 2013 schedule: June 10 to July 3. Application deadline: May 31.

Tuition and Aid Day student tuition: $15,500–$16,800. Tuition installment plan (FACTS Tuition Payment Plan). Need-based scholarship grants available. In 2012–13, 16% of upper-school students received aid. Total amount of financial aid awarded in 2012–13: $599,400.

Admissions Traditional secondary-level entrance grade is 9. For fall 2012, 51 students applied for upper-level admission, 3 were accepted, 3 enrolled. English language, High School Placement Test, Iowa Tests of Basic Skills, ITBS achievement test, Kuhlmann-Anderson, mathematics proficiency exam or writing sample required. Deadline for receipt of application materials: January 19. Application fee required: $100.

Athletics Interscholastic: baseball, basketball, cross-country running, football, physical training, soccer, swimming and diving, tennis, track and field; intramural: basketball, physical training, soccer, strength & conditioning, ultimate Frisbee, volleyball, weight lifting, weight training. 5 coaches, 1 athletic trainer.

Computers Computers are regularly used in college planning, computer applications, digital applications, library, literary magazine, newspaper, photography, programming, publications, yearbook classes. Computer network features include on-campus library services, Internet access, Internet filtering or blocking technology, online college applications, numerous online databases, reference sources, Moodle. Student e-mail accounts and computer access in designated common areas are available to students. The school has a published electronic and media policy.

Contact Mrs. Lisa Richard, Assistant to Headmaster. 469-499-5402. Fax: 469-499-5440. E-mail: lrichard@cistercian.org. Web site: www.cistercian.org

CLARKSVILLE ACADEMY

710 North Second Street
Clarksville, Tennessee 37040-2998

Head of School: Mrs. Kay D. Drew

General Information Coeducational day college-preparatory and 1:1 Apple Program school. Grades PK–12. Founded: 1970. Setting: urban. 31-acre campus. 7 buildings on campus. Approved or accredited by Southern Association of Colleges and Schools and Tennessee Department of Education. Member of National Association of Independent Schools. Endowment: $1 million. Total enrollment: 566. Upper school average class size: 15. Upper school faculty-student ratio: 1:7. There are 175 required school days per year for Upper School students. Upper School students typically attend 5 days per week. The average school day consists of 7 hours.

Upper School Student Profile Grade 9: 51 students (23 boys, 28 girls); Grade 10: 39 students (21 boys, 18 girls); Grade 11: 44 students (25 boys, 19 girls); Grade 12: 56 students (34 boys, 22 girls).
Faculty School total: 56. In upper school: 9 men, 18 women; 19 have advanced degrees.
Subjects Offered ACT preparation, American history, anatomy and physiology, art, art appreciation, art history, Bible as literature, biology, biology-AP, broadcasting, calculus, calculus-AP, ceramics, chemistry, chemistry-AP, choir, chorus, college writing, computer education, computer science, debate, drama, driver education, ecology, economics, economics and history, English language and composition-AP, English literature and composition-AP, fitness, geography, geometry, German, government, graphic design, health, health education, honors algebra, honors English, honors geometry, honors U.S. history, honors world history, Latin, leadership, marketing, media arts, modern history, music, music theory-AP, mythology, personal finance, physical education, physical fitness, physics, physics-AP, physiology, piano, political science, precalculus, sculpture, Spanish, speech, statistics, statistics-AP, studio art, study skills, trigonometry, U.S. history, U.S. history-AP, weight training, wellness, women's health, world history, writing, yearbook.
Graduation Requirements 24 credit, 4 years of high school math required.
Special Academic Programs 8 Advanced Placement exams for which test preparation is offered; honors section; independent study; study at local college for college credit.
College Admission Counseling 51 students graduated in 2012; all went to college, including Austin Peay State University; Lipscomb University; The University of Tennessee; The University of Tennessee at Chattanooga; Western Kentucky University.
Student Life Upper grades have specified standards of dress, student council, honor system. Discipline rests primarily with faculty.
Summer Programs Remediation, enrichment, sports, art/fine arts, computer instruction programs offered; session focuses on enrichment and remediation; held both on and off campus; held at sports complex; accepts boys and girls; open to students from other schools. 2013 schedule: June 1 to August 13. Application deadline: May 20.
Tuition and Aid Tuition installment plan (monthly payment plans). Tuition reduction for siblings, paying campus jobs available.
Admissions Otis-Lennon School Ability Test required. Deadline for receipt of application materials: none. Application fee required: $75. On-campus interview required.
Athletics Interscholastic: baseball (boys), basketball (b,g), cheering (g), dance team (g), football (b), soccer (b,g), softball (g), volleyball (g); coed interscholastic: bowling, cross-country running, golf, tennis. 15 coaches, 1 athletic trainer.
Computers Computers are regularly used in art classes. Computer network features include on-campus library services, Internet access, wireless campus network, Internet filtering or blocking technology, 1:1 Apple MacBook program, 1:1 Apple iPad program. Campus intranet, student e-mail accounts, and computer access in designated common areas are available to students. Students grades are available online. The school has a published electronic and media policy.
Contact Mrs. Angie Henson, Business Office and Admissions. 931-647-6311. Fax: 931-906-0610. E-mail: ahenson@clarksvilleacademy.com. Web site: www.clarksvilleacademy.com

CLEARWATER CENTRAL CATHOLIC HIGH SCHOOL

2750 Haines Bayshore Road
Clearwater, Florida 33760

Head of School: Dr. John A. Venturella

General Information Coeducational day college-preparatory, arts, religious studies, technology, and International Baccalaureate diploma programme school, affiliated with Roman Catholic Church. Grades 9–12. Founded: 1962. Setting: suburban. Nearest major city is Tampa. 40-acre campus. 7 buildings on campus. Approved or accredited by International Baccalaureate Organization, National Catholic Education Association, Southern Association of Colleges and Schools, The College Board, and Florida Department of Education. Upper school average class size: 25. Upper school faculty-student ratio: 1:16. There are 190 required school days per year for Upper School students. Upper School students typically attend 5 days per week. The average school day consists of 6 hours and 13 minutes.
Upper School Student Profile 80% of students are Roman Catholic.
Faculty School total: 41. In upper school: 14 men, 27 women; 32 have advanced degrees.
Subjects Offered Acting, advanced chemistry, Advanced Placement courses, aerobics, algebra, American government, American history, American history-AP, American literature, American literature-AP, American sign language, anatomy, architecture, Bible studies, biology, biology-AP, British literature, British literature (honors), calculus, calculus-AP, campus ministry, chemistry, chemistry-AP, choral music, chorus, church history, composition, computer processing, creative writing, desktop publishing, discrete mathematics, drama, drawing, drawing and design, ecology, economics, English, English literature and composition-AP, foreign language, French, general science, geometry, health, honors algebra, honors English, honors geometry, honors U.S. history, honors world history, information technology, journalism, keyboarding, language arts, law, law studies, leadership, learning strategies, life management skills, marine biology, music appreciation, oral communications, painting, personal fitness, philosophy, physical education, physics, pre-algebra, probability and statistics, psychology, sociology, Spanish, Spanish language-AP, speech, speech and debate, theater, theology, trigonometry, U.S. government, U.S. government and politics-AP, U.S. history, U.S. history-AP, video, volleyball, Web site design, wellness, world history.
Graduation Requirements Algebra, biology, ceramics, chemistry, comparative government and politics-AP, economics, English, general science, geometry, global studies, physical education (includes health), physical fitness, physical science, physics, Spanish, theology, U.S. government, U.S. history, United States government-AP, visual and performing arts, world geography, world history, world religions, yearbook.
Special Academic Programs International Baccalaureate program; Advanced Placement exam preparation; honors section; study at local college for college credit; programs in English, mathematics, general development for dyslexic students.
College Admission Counseling 130 students graduated in 2011; all went to college, including Florida State University; University of Central Florida; University of Florida; University of South Florida.
Student Life Upper grades have uniform requirement, student council, honor system. Discipline rests primarily with faculty. Attendance at religious services is required.
Tuition and Aid Day student tuition: $9800–$11,775. Tuition installment plan (SMART Tuition Payment Plan). Tuition reduction for siblings, merit scholarship grants, need-based scholarship grants available. In 2011–12, 20% of upper-school students received aid.
Admissions Traditional secondary-level entrance grade is 9. For fall 2011, 230 students applied for upper-level admission, 200 were accepted, 170 enrolled. Explore required. Deadline for receipt of application materials: none. Application fee required: $100. Interview recommended.
Athletics Interscholastic: baseball (boys), basketball (b,g), cheering (g), cross-country running (b,g), diving (b,g), football (b), golf (b,g), physical fitness (b,g), running (b,g), soccer (b,g), softball (g), swimming and diving (b,g), tennis (b,g), track and field (b,g), volleyball (g), weight lifting (b,g), weight training (b,g), winter soccer (b,g), wrestling (b). 1 PE instructor, 43 coaches, 1 athletic trainer.
Computers Computer network features include on-campus library services, online commercial services, Internet access. The school has a published electronic and media policy.
Contact Mrs. Helen Lambert, Director of Admissions. 727-531-1449 Ext. 304. Fax: 727-451-0003. E-mail: hlambert@ccchs.org. Web site: www.ccchs.org

COLEGIO BOLIVAR

Calle 5 # 122-21 Via a Pance
Cali, Colombia

Head of School: Dr. Joseph Nagy

General Information Coeducational day college-preparatory, bilingual studies, and technology school. Grades PK–12. Founded: 1947. Setting: suburban. 14-hectare campus. 7 buildings on campus. Approved or accredited by Association of American Schools in South America, Colombian Ministry of Education, and Southern Association of Colleges and Schools. Languages of instruction: English and Spanish. Total enrollment: 1,228. Upper school average class size: 18. Upper school faculty-student ratio: 1:9. There are 180 required school days per year for Upper School students. The average school day consists of 7 hours.
Upper School Student Profile Grade 9: 104 students (56 boys, 48 girls); Grade 10: 91 students (39 boys, 52 girls); Grade 11: 97 students (46 boys, 51 girls); Grade 12: 86 students (37 boys, 49 girls).
Faculty School total: 156. In upper school: 19 men, 18 women; 21 have advanced degrees.
Subjects Offered Advanced chemistry, Advanced Placement courses, algebra, American history, American literature, art, art history, biology, business, calculus, chemistry, computer science, dance, drama, English, English literature, environmental science, ESL, ethics, French, geology, government/civics, graphic design, history, journalism, mathematics, music, philosophy, photography, physical education, physics, programming, psychology, religion, robotics, social studies, Spanish, theater, trigonometry, world literature.
Graduation Requirements Algebra, American history, American literature, art, biology, calculus, chemistry, computer education, economics, electives, geography, geometry, history of the Americas, music, physical education (includes health), physics, political science, pre-calculus, senior project, Spanish, Spanish literature, trigonometry, world history, world literature, writing, social service hours, senior project.
Special Academic Programs Advanced Placement exam preparation; independent study; remedial reading and/or remedial writing; ESL.
College Admission Counseling 82 students graduated in 2012; 72 went to college, including Bentley University; DePaul University; Loras College; The University of Montana Western; University of Central Florida; University of Pittsburgh. Other: 10 had other specific plans. Median combined SAT: 1550. Mean SAT critical reading: 510, mean SAT math: 540, mean SAT writing: 510. 22% scored over 600 on SAT critical reading, 28% scored over 600 on SAT math, 18% scored over 600 on SAT writing, 15% scored over 1800 on combined SAT.
Student Life Upper grades have specified standards of dress, student council, honor system. Discipline rests equally with students and faculty.

Tuition and Aid Day student tuition: 16,074,832 Colombian pesos–22,859,796 Colombian pesos. Tuition installment plan (monthly payment plans, annual payment plan). Need-based scholarship grants available.
Admissions Traditional secondary-level entrance grade is 9. School's own exam required. Deadline for receipt of application materials: none. Application fee required: 80,000 Colombian pesos. On-campus interview required.
Athletics Interscholastic: aerobics/dance (girls), baseball (b), basketball (b,g), dance (g), equestrian sports (b,g), gymnastics (b,g), horseback riding (b,g), running (b,g), soccer (b,g), swimming and diving (b,g), track and field (b,g), volleyball (b,g); intramural: gymnastics (b,g), soccer (b,g), softball (b), swimming and diving (b,g), track and field (b,g), volleyball (b,g). 10 PE instructors, 23 coaches.
Computers Computers are regularly used in graphic design, photography, Web site design, yearbook classes. Computer network features include Internet access, Internet filtering or blocking technology. The school has a published electronic and media policy.
Contact Mrs. Patricia Nasser, Admissions Assistant. 57-2-485-5050 Ext. 274. Fax: 57-2-555-2041. E-mail: pnasser@colegiobolivar.edu.co. Web site: www.colegiobolivar.edu.co

COLEGIO NUEVA GRANADA

Carrera 2E #70-20
Bogota, Colombia

Head of School: Dr. Eric H. Habegger

General Information Coeducational day college-preparatory, Colombian Bachillerato, and Advanced Placement school, affiliated with Roman Catholic Church, Jewish faith. Grades PK–12. Founded: 1938. Setting: urban. 10-hectare campus. 2 buildings on campus. Approved or accredited by Southern Association of Colleges and Schools. Languages of instruction: English and Spanish. Total enrollment: 1,801. Upper school average class size: 23. Upper school faculty-student ratio: 1:22. There are 183 required school days per year for Upper School students. Upper School students typically attend 5 days per week. The average school day consists of 7 hours.
Upper School Student Profile Grade 9: 160 students (77 boys, 83 girls); Grade 10: 127 students (58 boys, 69 girls); Grade 11: 119 students (61 boys, 58 girls); Grade 12: 121 students (64 boys, 57 girls).
Faculty School total: 233. In upper school: 28 men, 35 women; 27 have advanced degrees.
Subjects Offered Art, art history-AP, basketball, biology, biology-AP, calculus, chemistry, crafts, dance performance, drama, drawing, economics-AP, English, English-AP, ESL, ethics, European history-AP, French, graphic design, human geography - AP, macroeconomics-AP, Mandarin, mathematics, model United Nations, music, philosophy, photography, physical education, physics, pre-calculus, religion, science, sex education, social studies, Spanish, Spanish language-AP, studio art-AP, theater, U.S. history, U.S. history-AP, volleyball, weight training, world history, world history-AP.
Graduation Requirements Arts and fine arts (art, music, dance, drama), computer education, electives, English, foreign language, mathematics, physical education (includes health), science, social studies (includes history), senior independent project.
Special Academic Programs Advanced Placement exam preparation; honors section; independent study; academic accommodation for the gifted; programs in English, mathematics, general development for dyslexic students; special instructional classes for students with learning disabilities, students with emotional and behavioral problems, Attention Deficit Disorder; ESL (8 students enrolled).
College Admission Counseling 114 students graduated in 2011; 90 went to college, including Florida International University; Massachusetts Institute of Technology; Northeastern University; Penn State University Park; University of Miami; University of Pennsylvania. Other: 1 went to work, 23 had other specific plans. Median SAT critical reading: 470, median SAT math: 500, median SAT writing: 490, median combined SAT: 1470.
Student Life Upper grades have uniform requirement, student council, honor system. Discipline rests equally with students and faculty.
Tuition and Aid Day student tuition: 15,100,000 Colombian pesos–24,100,000 Colombian pesos. Tuition installment plan (5-installment plan, yearly). Need-based scholarship grants available.
Admissions For fall 2011, 50 students applied for upper-level admission, 38 were accepted, 38 enrolled. Academic Profile Tests, admissions testing, Reading for Understanding and writing sample required. Deadline for receipt of application materials: none. Application fee required: $85. On-campus interview required.
Athletics Interscholastic: aerobics/dance (girls), baseball (b), basketball (b,g), gymnastics (b,g), soccer (b,g), table tennis (b,g), volleyball (b,g); intramural: basketball (b,g), soccer (b,g), table tennis (b,g), volleyball (b,g), weight training (b,g); coed interscholastic: gymnastics; coed intramural: basketball, soccer, table tennis, volleyball, weight training. 5 PE instructors, 25 coaches.
Computers Computers are regularly used in desktop publishing, ESL, introduction to technology, mathematics, science, technology, video film production, Web site design classes. Computer network features include on-campus library services, Internet access, wireless campus network, Internet filtering or blocking technology, Sharepoint, SDS. Campus intranet, student e-mail accounts, and computer access in designated common areas are available to students. Students grades are available online.
Contact Laura De Brigard, Director of Admissions. 57-1-359-9344. Fax: 57-1-211-3720. E-mail: lbrigard@cng.edu. Web site: www.cng.edu

COLEGIO SAN JOSE

PO Box 21300
San Juan, Puerto Rico 00928-1300

Head of School: Br. Francisco T. Gonzalez, DMD

General Information Boys' day college-preparatory, arts, business, religious studies, bilingual studies, technology, science, anatomy, and marine biology, and psychology, humanities, health, economy, political science school, affiliated with Roman Catholic Church. Grades 7–12. Founded: 1938. Setting: urban. 6-acre campus. 1 building on campus. Approved or accredited by Middle States Association of Colleges and Schools, National Catholic Education Association, The College Board, and Puerto Rico Department of Education. Languages of instruction: English and Spanish. Endowment: $230,000. Total enrollment: 502. Upper school average class size: 23. Upper School students typically attend 5 days per week. The average school day consists of 6 hours and 50 minutes.
Upper School Student Profile Grade 9: 65 students (65 boys); Grade 10: 98 students (98 boys); Grade 11: 108 students (108 boys); Grade 12: 74 students (74 boys). 90% of students are Roman Catholic.
Faculty School total: 44. In upper school: 24 men, 20 women; 24 have advanced degrees.
Subjects Offered Accounting, algebra, American history, American literature, anatomy, art, art history, biology, biology-AP, broadcasting, business skills, calculus, chemistry, choir, Christian ethics, computer education, computer science, ecology, English, English literature, ethics, European history, French, French as a second language, geography, geometry, government/civics, grammar, health, history, instrumental music, keyboarding, marine biology, mathematics, music, physical education, physics, pre-calculus, psychology, religion, science, social studies, Spanish, world history.
Graduation Requirements Business skills (includes word processing), computer science, English, foreign language, history, mathematics, physical education (includes health), religion (includes Bible studies and theology), science, social studies (includes history), Spanish, 40 hours of Christian community service.
Special Academic Programs International Baccalaureate program; Advanced Placement exam preparation; honors section.
College Admission Counseling 78 students graduated in 2012; all went to college, including University of Dayton; University of Puerto Rico, Mayagüez Campus; University of Puerto Rico, Río Piedras.
Student Life Upper grades have uniform requirement, student council, honor system. Discipline rests equally with students and faculty. Attendance at religious services is required.
Summer Programs Remediation programs offered; session focuses on remediation/make-up; held on campus; accepts boys and girls; open to students from other schools. 150 students usually enrolled. 2013 schedule: June 1 to June 30. Application deadline: May 31.
Tuition and Aid Day student tuition: $7050. Tuition installment plan (The Tuition Plan, individually arranged payment plans). Need-based scholarship grants available. In 2012–13, 13% of upper-school students received aid. Total amount of financial aid awarded in 2012–13: $230,000.
Admissions Traditional secondary-level entrance grade is 9. Catholic High School Entrance Examination required. Deadline for receipt of application materials: February 28. Application fee required: $10. On-campus interview required.
Athletics Interscholastic: baseball, basketball, bowling, cross-country running, fitness, golf, indoor soccer, physical fitness, soccer, swimming and diving, tennis, track and field, volleyball; intramural: cross-country running, indoor soccer, soccer, swimming and diving, tennis, track and field, volleyball. 3 PE instructors, 6 coaches, 1 athletic trainer.
Computers Computers are regularly used in accounting, art, data processing, English, foreign language, keyboarding, mathematics, music, psychology, science, Spanish, yearbook classes. Computer network features include on-campus library services, Internet access, wireless campus network, Internet filtering or blocking technology, Edline, Rediker. Campus intranet and student e-mail accounts are available to students. Students grades are available online. The school has a published electronic and media policy.
Contact Sra. María Guzmán de Caro, Guidance Advisor. 787-751-8177 Ext. 229. Fax: 866-955-7646. E-mail: mguzman@csj-rpi.org. Web site: www.csj-rpi.org

COLE VALLEY CHRISTIAN HIGH SCHOOL

200 East Carlton Avenue
Meridian, Idaho 83642

Head of School: Mr. Bradley Carr

General Information Coeducational day college-preparatory, general academic, arts, religious studies, and bilingual studies school, affiliated with Christian faith. Grades PK–12. Founded: 1990. Setting: suburban. Nearest major city is Boise. 5-acre campus. 2 buildings on campus. Approved or accredited by Association of Christian Schools International and Idaho Department of Education. Total enrollment: 801. Upper school average class size: 20. Upper school faculty-student ratio: 1:10. There are 180 required school days per year for Upper School students. Upper School students typically attend 5 days per week. The average school day consists of 5 hours and 50 minutes.

Upper School Student Profile 95% of students are Christian.

Faculty School total: 25. In upper school: 13 men, 12 women; 5 have advanced degrees.

Subjects Offered 20th century history, acting, algebra, American government, American literature, art, Bible, biology, British literature, business mathematics, calculus-AP, chemistry, choral music, computer literacy, ecology, economics, English, English literature, French, geometry, honors English, physical education, physical science, physics, pre-algebra, pre-calculus, Spanish, speech, U.S. history, world history, yearbook.

Graduation Requirements 20th century history, American government, economics, English, mathematics, physical education (includes health), religion (includes Bible studies and theology), science, social studies (includes history), speech, Bible classes.

Special Academic Programs Advanced Placement exam preparation; honors section; independent study; study at local college for college credit.

College Admission Counseling 55 students graduated in 2012; 49 went to college, including American River College; Boise State University; Northwest Nazarene University; The College of Idaho; University of Idaho. Other: 4 went to work, 2 entered military service.

Student Life Upper grades have specified standards of dress, student council, honor system. Discipline rests primarily with faculty. Attendance at religious services is required.

Tuition and Aid Day student tuition: $6000. Tuition installment plan (monthly payment plans, individually arranged payment plans). Tuition reduction for siblings, need-based scholarship grants available. In 2012–13, 20% of upper-school students received aid.

Admissions Traditional secondary-level entrance grade is 9. Deadline for receipt of application materials: none. Application fee required: $125. Interview required.

Athletics Interscholastic: basketball (boys, girls), cheering (g), cross-country running (b,g), football (b), track and field (b,g), volleyball (g), wrestling (b); intramural: skiing (cross-country) (b,g), skiing (downhill) (b,g), snowboarding (b,g). 3 PE instructors, 12 coaches.

Computers Computers are regularly used in all academic classes. Computer network features include on-campus library services, Internet access, Internet filtering or blocking technology. Student e-mail accounts are available to students. Students grades are available online.

Contact Mrs. Robin Didriksen, Administrative Assistant to the Guidance Counselor/Registrar. 208-947-1212. Fax: 208-898-9016. E-mail: rdidriksen@cvcsonline.org. Web site: colevalleychristian.org

COLLEGEDALE ACADEMY

PO Box 628
4855 College Drive East
Collegedale, Tennessee 37315

Head of School: Mr. Murray J. Cooper

General Information Coeducational day college-preparatory and arts school, affiliated with Seventh-day Adventists. Grades 9–12. Founded: 1892. Setting: small town. Nearest major city is Chattanooga. 20-acre campus. 3 buildings on campus. Approved or accredited by Southern Association of Colleges and Schools and Tennessee Department of Education. Endowment: $496,487. Total enrollment: 361. Upper school average class size: 25. Upper school faculty-student ratio: 1:18. There are 180 required school days per year for Upper School students. Upper School students typically attend 5 days per week. The average school day consists of 7 hours.

Upper School Student Profile Grade 9: 98 students (47 boys, 51 girls); Grade 10: 86 students (39 boys, 47 girls); Grade 11: 90 students (51 boys, 39 girls); Grade 12: 89 students (48 boys, 41 girls). 98% of students are Seventh-day Adventists.

Faculty School total: 39. In upper school: 19 men, 17 women; 22 have advanced degrees.

Subjects Offered Algebra, American history, American literature, anatomy, art, art appreciation, Bible studies, biology, calculus-AP, chemistry, choir, composition, computer skills, concert band, digital imaging, drawing, earth science, economics, English, English literature, environmental science, fine arts, French, geometry, government/civics, gymnastics, health and wellness, history, home economics, journalism, mathematics, music, music appreciation, personal fitness, physical education, physical science, physics, physiology, pre-calculus, religion, social studies, Spanish, woodworking, world history, yearbook.

Graduation Requirements Arts and fine arts (art, music, dance, drama), computer science, English, foreign language, mathematics, physical education (includes health), religion (includes Bible studies and theology), science, social studies (includes history).

Special Academic Programs 1 Advanced Placement exam for which test preparation is offered; accelerated programs; study at local college for college credit.

College Admission Counseling 89 students graduated in 2011; 85 went to college, including Chattanooga State Community College; Cleveland State University; Southern Adventist University; The University of Tennessee at Chattanooga. Other: 3 went to work, 1 entered military service. 24.5% scored over 26 on composite ACT.

Student Life Upper grades have uniform requirement, student council, honor system. Discipline rests primarily with faculty. Attendance at religious services is required.

Tuition and Aid Day student tuition: $8760. Tuition installment plan (monthly payment plans). Need-based scholarship grants available. In 2011–12, 20% of upper-school students received aid. Total amount of financial aid awarded in 2011–12: $55,000.

Admissions Traditional secondary-level entrance grade is 9. Mathematics proficiency exam required. Deadline for receipt of application materials: August 1. Application fee required: $125. On-campus interview required.

Athletics Interscholastic: cross-country running (boys, girls), golf (b), tennis (b,g); intramural: basketball (b,g), soccer (b,g), track and field (b,g), volleyball (b,g); coed intramural: flag football, gymnastics, hiking/backpacking, paddle tennis, volleyball. 1 PE instructor, 2 coaches.

Computers Computers are regularly used in business applications, computer applications, digital applications, English, library, publications, yearbook classes. Computer network features include on-campus library services, Internet access, wireless campus network, Internet filtering or blocking technology. Student e-mail accounts and computer access in designated common areas are available to students. Students grades are available online. The school has a published electronic and media policy.

Contact Miss Kerre Conerly, Registrar. 423-396-2124 Ext. 415. Fax: 423-396-3363. E-mail: kconerly@collegedaleacademy.com. Web site: www.collegedaleacademy.com

COLLEGIATE SCHOOL

260 West 78th Street
New York, New York 10024

Head of School: Dr. Lee M. Levison

General Information Boys' day college-preparatory and arts school. Grades K–12. Founded: 1628. Setting: urban. 4 buildings on campus. Approved or accredited by New York State Association of Independent Schools. Member of National Association of Independent Schools. Endowment: $70 million. Total enrollment: 648. Upper school average class size: 14. Upper school faculty-student ratio: 1:4. There are 164 required school days per year for Upper School students. Upper School students typically attend 5 days per week. The average school day consists of 6 hours and 45 minutes.

Upper School Student Profile Grade 9: 59 students (59 boys); Grade 10: 59 students (59 boys); Grade 11: 56 students (56 boys); Grade 12: 55 students (55 boys).

Faculty School total: 111. In upper school: 39 men, 22 women; 56 have advanced degrees.

Subjects Offered African drumming, African history, algebra, American history, Ancient Greek, applied music, architecture, art, art appreciation, art history, Asian history, athletics, biology, calculus, ceramics, chemistry, Chinese, chorus, contemporary issues in science, digital photography, drama, dramatic arts, drawing, drawing and design, East Asian history, economics, English, environmental science, European history, film, film appreciation, film studies, foreign policy, French, geometry, health and wellness, history, Latin, Latin American history, linear algebra, literature, logic, Mandarin, mathematics, Middle Eastern history, music, music composition, music theory, orchestra, painting, philosophy, photography, physical education, physics, play production, poetry, pre-calculus, religion, sculpture, senior project, Shakespeare, social studies, Spanish, technical theater, theater, U.S. history, Web site design, world history, world literature, world religions.

Graduation Requirements Drama, English, foreign language, history, mathematics, music, physical education (includes health), religion (includes Bible studies and theology), science, visual arts. Community service is required.

Special Academic Programs 15 Advanced Placement exams for which test preparation is offered; honors section; independent study; term-away projects; study abroad.

College Admission Counseling 55 students graduated in 2011; all went to college, including Brown University; Dartmouth College; University of Pennsylvania; Williams College; Yale University.

Student Life Upper grades have specified standards of dress, student council, honor system. Discipline rests equally with students and faculty.

Tuition and Aid Day student tuition: $37,500. Tuition installment plan (SMART Tuition Payment Plan). Need-based scholarship grants available. In 2011–12, 22% of upper-school students received aid. Total amount of financial aid awarded in 2011–12: $1,630,000.

Admissions Traditional secondary-level entrance grade is 9. ERB or ISEE required. Deadline for receipt of application materials: December 1. Application fee required: $50. On-campus interview required.

Athletics Interscholastic: baseball, basketball, cross-country running, indoor track & field, lacrosse, soccer, tennis, track and field, winter (indoor) track, wrestling; intramural: physical fitness, weight training, yoga. 3 PE instructors, 8 coaches, 2 athletic trainers.

Computers Computers are regularly used in all academic classes. Computer network features include on-campus library services, online commercial services, Internet access, wireless campus network, Internet filtering or blocking technology. Campus intranet, student e-mail accounts, and computer access in designated common areas are available to students. The school has a published electronic and media policy.

Contact Joanne P. Heyman, Director of Admissions and Financial Aid. 212-812-8552. Fax: 212-812-8547. E-mail: jheyman@collegiateschool.org. Web site: www.collegiateschool.org

THE COLLEGIATE SCHOOL

103 North Mooreland Road
Richmond, Virginia 23229

Head of School: Keith A. Evans

General Information Coeducational day college-preparatory, arts, and technology school. Grades K–12. Founded: 1915. Setting: suburban. 211-acre campus. 13 buildings on campus. Approved or accredited by Southern Association of Colleges and Schools and Virginia Department of Education. Member of National Association of Independent Schools and Secondary School Admission Test Board. Endowment: $45.4 million. Total enrollment: 1,602. Upper school average class size: 15. Upper school faculty-student ratio: 1:15. There are 174 required school days per year for Upper School students. Upper School students typically attend 5 days per week. The average school day consists of 7 hours.

Upper School Student Profile Grade 9: 133 students (66 boys, 67 girls); Grade 10: 139 students (71 boys, 68 girls); Grade 11: 124 students (61 boys, 63 girls); Grade 12: 125 students (62 boys, 63 girls).

Faculty School total: 193. In upper school: 31 men, 39 women; 46 have advanced degrees.

Subjects Offered 20th century history, acting, advanced chemistry, African studies, algebra, American Civil War, American history, American history-AP, American literature, art, Asian literature, Bible as literature, biology, biology-AP, calculus-AP, ceramics, chemistry, chemistry-AP, community service, computer applications, creative writing, drama, driver education, earth science, economics, economics-AP, English, English literature, ethics, European history, film and literature, fine arts, French, French-AP, geometry, government and politics-AP, government/civics, health, journalism, Latin, music, photography, physics, physics-AP, religion, robotics, Russian literature, senior project, senior seminar, Spanish, Spanish language-AP, statistics, theater, trigonometry, world history, World War II.

Graduation Requirements Arts and fine arts (art, music, dance, drama), English, ethics, foreign language, government, history, mathematics, physical education (includes health), religion (includes Bible studies and theology), science, sports, senior speech. Community service is required.

Special Academic Programs 16 Advanced Placement exams for which test preparation is offered; honors section; independent study; study at local college for college credit; programs in general development for dyslexic students.

College Admission Counseling 125 students graduated in 2012; all went to college, including Elon University; James Madison University; The College of William and Mary; University of South Carolina; University of Virginia; Virginia Polytechnic Institute and State University.

Student Life Upper grades have specified standards of dress, student council, honor system. Discipline rests equally with students and faculty.

Summer Programs Remediation, enrichment, advancement, sports, art/fine arts, computer instruction programs offered; session focuses on advancement, remediation, sports; held both on and off campus; held at various locations in metro Richmond; accepts boys and girls; open to students from other schools. 1,225 students usually enrolled. 2013 schedule: June 11 to August 3. Application deadline: none.

Tuition and Aid Day student tuition: $20,690. Tuition installment plan (Insured Tuition Payment Plan, monthly payment plans). Need-based scholarship grants available.

Admissions Traditional secondary-level entrance grade is 9. For fall 2012, 108 students applied for upper-level admission, 44 were accepted, 25 enrolled. PSAT and SAT for applicants to grade 11 and 12, SSAT or writing sample required. Deadline for receipt of application materials: none. Application fee required: $50. Interview required.

Athletics Interscholastic: baseball (boys), basketball (b,g), cross-country running (b,g), diving (b,g), field hockey (g), football (b), indoor track & field (b,g), lacrosse (b,g), soccer (b,g), softball (g), swimming and diving (b,g), tennis (b,g), track and field (b,g), volleyball (g), winter (indoor) track (b,g), wrestling (b); coed interscholastic: golf, indoor soccer; coed intramural: combined training, dance, dance squad, dance team, fitness, modern dance. 3 PE instructors, 50 coaches, 2 athletic trainers.

Computers Computers are regularly used in all academic classes. Computer network features include on-campus library services, Internet access, wireless campus network, Internet filtering or blocking technology. Student e-mail accounts are available to students. The school has a published electronic and media policy.

Contact Amanda L. Surgner, Vice President for Advancement. 804-741-9722. Fax: 804-741-9128. E-mail: asurgner@collegiate-va.org. Web site: www.collegiate-va.org/

THE COLORADO SPRINGS SCHOOL

21 Broadmoor Avenue
Colorado Springs, Colorado 80906

Head of School: Mr. Kevin Reel

General Information Coeducational day college-preparatory, arts, experiential learning, and global perspectives school. Grades PK–12. Founded: 1962. Setting: suburban. 30-acre campus. 6 buildings on campus. Approved or accredited by Association of Colorado Independent Schools. Member of National Association of Independent Schools, Secondary School Admission Test Board, and National Association for College Admission Counseling. Endowment: $3.1 million. Total enrollment: 302. Upper school average class size: 16. Upper school faculty-student ratio: 1:6. There are 160 required school days per year for Upper School students. Upper School students typically attend 5 days per week. The average school day consists of 6 hours and 30 minutes.

Upper School Student Profile Grade 9: 22 students (12 boys, 10 girls); Grade 10: 26 students (9 boys, 17 girls); Grade 11: 25 students (19 boys, 6 girls); Grade 12: 31 students (11 boys, 20 girls).

Faculty School total: 46. In upper school: 11 men, 13 women; 18 have advanced degrees.

Subjects Offered 20th century history, 3-dimensional art, 3-dimensional design, ACT preparation, acting, adolescent issues, advanced chemistry, advanced math, Advanced Placement courses, advanced studio art-AP, African history, African studies, algebra, American government, American history, American history-AP, American literature, American literature-AP, American studies, analysis and differential calculus, anatomy and physiology, art history, art-AP, athletics, band, biology, biology-AP, botany, British literature-AP, calculus, calculus-AP, career education internship, career/college preparation, ceramics, chemistry, choir, choral music, clayworking, college admission preparation, college counseling, community service, comparative government and politics, comparative government and politics-AP, composition, computer applications, concert band, costumes and make-up, creative arts, digital art, digital photography, directing, discrete mathematics, drama, drawing, economics, economics-AP, English, English literature, English literature and composition-AP, English literature-AP, environmental science, environmental science-AP, environmental studies, equality and freedom, ethics, European history-AP, European literature, experiential education, filmmaking, fine arts, French, French language-AP, French literature-AP, French-AP, functions, gardening, geography, geology, geometry, glassblowing, global studies, government and politics-AP, grammar, health and wellness, history, history-AP, Latin American history, literature, macro/microeconomics-AP, microeconomics, music, music appreciation, musical productions, painting, philosophy, photography, photojournalism, physical education, physics, physics-AP, playwriting, post-calculus, pottery, pre-algebra, pre-calculus, printmaking, SAT/ACT preparation, science, sculpture, Spanish, Spanish literature, Spanish literature-AP, speech, statistics, statistics-AP, stone carving, studio art, studio art-AP, textiles, theater, theater arts, theater production, trigonometry, U.S. history, U.S. history-AP, welding, Western civilization, world geography, world history, world literature, writing, writing workshop, yearbook.

Graduation Requirements Arts and fine arts (art, music, dance, drama), athletics, college admission preparation, English, experiential education, foreign language, mathematics, science, social studies (includes history), speech and oral interpretations, experience-centered seminar each year, college overview course, 24 hours of community service per each year of high school.

Special Academic Programs Advanced Placement exam preparation; honors section; independent study; term-away projects; academic accommodation for the gifted; programs in general development for dyslexic students; special instructional classes for deaf students.

College Admission Counseling 30 students graduated in 2012; all went to college, including Vanderbilt University. Mean combined SAT: 1952, mean composite ACT: 27.

Student Life Upper grades have specified standards of dress, student council, honor system. Discipline rests equally with students and faculty.

Summer Programs Enrichment, advancement, sports, art/fine arts, computer instruction programs offered; session focuses on summer camp; held both on and off campus; held at various field trip locations; accepts boys and girls; open to students from other schools. 90 students usually enrolled. 2013 schedule: August 22 to May 23. Application deadline: none.

Tuition and Aid Day student tuition: $18,275. Tuition installment plan (Insured Tuition Payment Plan, monthly payment plans, individually arranged payment plans). Merit scholarship grants, need-based scholarship grants available. In 2012–13, 51% of upper-school students received aid; total upper-school merit-scholarship money awarded: $54,237. Total amount of financial aid awarded in 2012–13: $224,825.

Admissions Traditional secondary-level entrance grade is 9. For fall 2012, 16 students applied for upper-level admission, 14 were accepted, 12 enrolled. Otis-Lennon School Ability Test or SLEP for foreign students required. Deadline for receipt of application materials: none. Application fee required: $50. Interview required.

Athletics Interscholastic: basketball (boys, girls), cross-country running (b,g), golf (b), ice hockey (b), lacrosse (b), soccer (b,g), tennis (b,g), volleyball (g); intramural: archery (b,g), climbing (b,g), physical fitness (b,g), physical training (b,g); coed intramural: fly fishing, golf, mountaineering, outdoor activities, outdoor education, paddle tennis, rock climbing, skiing (cross-country), skiing (downhill), wilderness, yoga. 2 PE instructors, 8 coaches.

Computers Computer network features include on-campus library services, online commercial services, Internet access, wireless campus network, Internet filtering or blocking technology. Campus intranet, student e-mail accounts, and computer access in designated common areas are available to students. Students grades are available online. The school has a published electronic and media policy.

Contact Mrs. Nori Madrigal, Director of Admission and Financial Assistance. 719-475-9747 Ext. 524. Fax: 719-475-9864. E-mail: nmadrigal@css.org. Web site: www.css.org

COLUMBIA ACADEMY

1101 West 7th Street
Columbia, Tennessee 38401

Head of School: Dr. James Thomas

General Information Coeducational day college-preparatory, arts, business, religious studies, and technology school, affiliated with Church of Christ. Grades K–12. Founded: 1978. Setting: small town. Nearest major city is Nashville. 67-acre campus. 6 buildings on campus. Approved or accredited by National Christian School Association, Southern Association of Colleges and Schools, and Tennessee Department of Education. Endowment: $1.4 million. Total enrollment: 623. Upper school average class size: 17. Upper school faculty-student ratio: 1:10. There are 175 required school days per year for Upper School students. Upper School students typically attend 5 days per week. The average school day consists of 7 hours.

Upper School Student Profile Grade 7: 53 students (32 boys, 21 girls); Grade 8: 44 students (19 boys, 25 girls); Grade 9: 43 students (24 boys, 19 girls); Grade 10: 49 students (22 boys, 27 girls); Grade 11: 43 students (25 boys, 18 girls); Grade 12: 29 students (14 boys, 15 girls). 60% of students are members of Church of Christ.

Faculty School total: 56. In upper school: 12 men, 15 women; 14 have advanced degrees.

Subjects Offered Accounting, advanced math, algebra, American history, American literature, anatomy and physiology, art, band, Bible, biology, British literature, calculus, chemistry, chorus, computer applications, drama, economics, English, English literature and composition-AP, environmental science, fine arts, geometry, government/civics, grammar, health, keyboarding, math review, music, personal finance, physical education, physics, pre-calculus, psychology, religion, Spanish, speech, U.S. history-AP, world geography, world history.

Graduation Requirements Arts and fine arts (art, music, dance, drama), computer applications, economics, electives, English, foreign language, mathematics, physical education (includes health), religion (includes Bible studies and theology), science, social sciences, social studies (includes history), speech, four hours of approved service required for each quarter enrolled.

Special Academic Programs Advanced Placement exam preparation; honors section; independent study; study at local college for college credit.

College Admission Counseling 51 students graduated in 2012; 49 went to college, including Columbia State Community College; Freed-Hardeman University; Harding University; Lipscomb University; Tennessee Technological University; The University of Tennessee. Other: 2 went to work. Median composite ACT: 23. 25% scored over 26 on composite ACT.

Student Life Upper grades have specified standards of dress, student council, honor system. Discipline rests primarily with faculty.

Summer Programs Remediation programs offered; session focuses on make-up or credit recovery for failing grades during the semesters; held on campus; accepts boys and girls; not open to students from other schools. 5 students usually enrolled. 2013 schedule: May 29. Application deadline: May 11.

Tuition and Aid Day student tuition: $6380. Tuition installment plan (monthly payment plans, individually arranged payment plans). Tuition reduction for siblings, need-based scholarship grants, paying campus jobs available. In 2012–13, 9% of upper-school students received aid. Total amount of financial aid awarded in 2012–13: $36,750.

Admissions Traditional secondary-level entrance grade is 9. For fall 2012, 31 students applied for upper-level admission, 29 were accepted, 29 enrolled. Otis-Lennon School Ability Test required. Deadline for receipt of application materials: none. Application fee required: $50. On-campus interview recommended.

Athletics Interscholastic: baseball (boys), basketball (b,g), cheering (g), football (b), golf (b,g), soccer (b,g), softball (g), strength & conditioning (b), tennis (b,g), trap and skeet (b,g), volleyball (g); intramural: flag football (g); coed interscholastic: bowling, cross-country running, marksmanship. 1 PE instructor, 1 coach.

Computers Computers are regularly used in accounting, all academic, computer applications, keyboarding, library, yearbook classes. Computer network features include on-campus library services, Internet access, wireless campus network, students in grades 7-12 are issued iPads. Campus intranet and student e-mail accounts are available to students. Students grades are available online. The school has a published electronic and media policy.

Contact Mrs. Emily Lansdell, Director of Admissions. 931-398-5355. Fax: 931-380-8506. E-mail: emily.lansdell@cabulldogs.org. Web site: www.columbia-academy.net

COLUMBIA INTERNATIONAL COLLEGE OF CANADA

1003 Main Street West
Hamilton, Ontario L8S 4P3, Canada

Head of School: Mr. Ron Rambarran

General Information Coeducational boarding and day college-preparatory, general academic, arts, business, technology, Science, and Mathematics school. Grades 7–12. Founded: 1979. Setting: urban. Nearest major city is Toronto, Canada. Students are housed in single-sex dormitories. 12-acre campus. 3 buildings on campus. Approved or accredited by Ontario Ministry of Education and Ontario Department of Education. Language of instruction: English. Endowment: CAN$1 million. Total enrollment: 1,622. Upper school average class size: 20. Upper school faculty-student ratio: 1:20. There are 208 required school days per year for Upper School students. Upper School students typically attend 5 days per week. The average school day consists of 7 hours and 15 minutes.

Upper School Student Profile Grade 7: 44 students (22 boys, 22 girls); Grade 8: 60 students (30 boys, 30 girls); Grade 9: 96 students (48 boys, 48 girls); Grade 10: 214 students (130 boys, 84 girls); Grade 11: 321 students (206 boys, 115 girls); Grade 12: 887 students (499 boys, 388 girls). 80% of students are boarding students. 5% are province residents. 5 provinces are represented in upper school student body. 95% are international students. International students from China, Indonesia, Mexico, Nigeria, Russian Federation, and Viet Nam; 70 other countries represented in student body.

Faculty School total: 93. In upper school: 38 men, 55 women; 32 have advanced degrees.

Subjects Offered 20th century world history, accounting, advanced TOEFL/grammar, algebra, analytic geometry, anthropology, applied arts, art, band, biology, business, calculus, calculus-AP, Canadian geography, Canadian history, career education, chemistry, Chinese, choir, civics, computer programming, computer science, computer technologies, dance, discrete mathematics, dramatic arts, economics, English, English composition, English literature, ESL, family studies, food and nutrition, French, French as a second language, general business, general math, general science, geography, geometry, history, intro to computers, kinesiology, Korean, lab science, language arts, law, leadership, life skills, Mandarin, marketing, math applications, mathematics, mathematics-AP, music, physical education, physics, psychology, society challenge and change, sociology, Spanish, visual arts.

Graduation Requirements Arts, business, English, mathematics, science, social studies (includes history), Community Volunteer Hours, Ontario Secondary School Literacy Test.

Special Academic Programs 4 Advanced Placement exams for which test preparation is offered; accelerated programs; study at local college for college credit; academic accommodation for the gifted; ESL (316 students enrolled).

College Admission Counseling 770 students graduated in 2011; all went to college, including McMaster University; The University of Western Ontario; University of Alberta; University of Toronto; University of Waterloo; York University.

Student Life Upper grades have uniform requirement, student council. Discipline rests primarily with faculty.

Tuition and Aid Day student tuition: CAN$12,516–CAN$20,446; 7-day tuition and room/board: CAN$18,621–CAN$33,046. Tuition reduction for siblings, merit scholarship grants, tuition reduction for Canadian citizens and permanent residents available. Total upper-school merit-scholarship money awarded for 2011–12: CAN$45,000.

Admissions Traditional secondary-level entrance grade is 11. For fall 2011, 1,800 students applied for upper-level admission, 1,100 were accepted, 1,046 enrolled. Math Placement Exam and SLEP required. Deadline for receipt of application materials: none. Application fee required: CAN$200. Interview recommended.

Athletics Interscholastic: badminton (boys, girls), basketball (b), indoor soccer (b), soccer (b); intramural: aerobics (g), aquatics (b,g), badminton (b,g), ball hockey (b,g), basketball (b,g), cheering (g), fitness (b,g), floor hockey (b), football (b), indoor soccer (b,g), martial arts (b), outdoor activities (b,g), soccer (b,g), squash (b), strength & conditioning (b), swimming and diving (b,g), table tennis (b,g), volleyball (b,g), weight training (b,g); coed interscholastic: badminton, indoor track & field; coed intramural: aquatics, badminton, ball hockey, canoeing/kayaking, cooperative games, cross-country running, floor hockey, golf, hiking/backpacking, ice skating, in-line skating, indoor track & field, jogging, kayaking, martial arts, outdoor activities, physical fitness, physical training, roller blading, ropes courses, running, self defense, skiing (cross-country), snowshoeing, squash, strength & conditioning, swimming and diving, table tennis, volleyball, wallyball, weight training, wilderness, wilderness survival, winter walking, yoga. 3 PE instructors, 4 coaches.

Computers Computers are regularly used in accounting, business, business applications, career education, economics, English, ESL, geography, information technology, music, SAT preparation, science classes. Computer network features include Internet access, wireless campus network. Computer access in designated common areas is available to students. Students grades are available online.

Contact Ms. Marina Rosas, Admissions Officer. 905-572-7883 Ext. 2835. Fax: 905-572-9332. E-mail: admissions02@cic-totalcare.com. Web site: www.cic-TotalCare.com

COLUMBIA INTERNATIONAL SCHOOL

153 Matsugo

Tokorozawa, Saitama 359-0027, Japan

Head of School: Mr. Barrie McCliggott

General Information Coeducational boarding and day and distance learning college-preparatory, business, bilingual studies, and technology school. Boarding grades 7–12, day grades 1–12. Distance learning grade X. Founded: 1988. Setting: suburban. Nearest major city is Tokyo, Japan. Students are housed in coed dormitories. 2-acre campus. 3 buildings on campus. Approved or accredited by Ontario Ministry of Education, Western Association of Schools and Colleges, and state department of education. Language of instruction: English. Endowment: ¥100 million. Total enrollment: 278. Upper school average class size: 14. Upper school faculty-student ratio: 1:12. There are 180 required school days per year for Upper School students. Upper School students typically attend 5 days per week. The average school day consists of 5 hours and 30 minutes.

Upper School Student Profile Grade 10: 25 students (13 boys, 12 girls); Grade 11: 23 students (10 boys, 13 girls); Grade 12: 25 students (14 boys, 11 girls). 5% of students are boarding students. 10% are international students. International students from Canada, China, Philippines, Republic of Korea, United Kingdom, and United States; 10 other countries represented in student body.

Faculty School total: 24. In upper school: 12 men, 2 women; 7 have advanced degrees; 4 reside on campus.

Subjects Offered 1 1/2 elective credits, 20th century world history, advanced TOEFL/grammar, algebra, ancient world history, art, Asian history, biology, business, calculus, Canadian geography, Canadian history, chemistry, communications, community service, computer science, computers, economics, English, ESL, foreign language, geography, geometry, global issues, history, Internet, keyboarding, literacy, mathematics, media studies, physical education, reading, TOEFL preparation, world issues, yearbook.

Graduation Requirements 20th century history, arts, Asian history, biology, chemistry, economics, English, geography, humanities, law, mathematics, physical education (includes health), science, social sciences, Ontario Literacy Test, 40 hours of community involvement activities.

Special Academic Programs Advanced Placement exam preparation; honors section; accelerated programs; independent study; study abroad; remedial reading and/or remedial writing; remedial math; ESL (70 students enrolled).

College Admission Counseling 21 students graduated in 2012; 19 went to college, including Queen's University at Kingston; Temple University; The University of British Columbia; University of Saskatchewan; University of Victoria; Western Michigan University. Other: 2 had other specific plans.

Student Life Upper grades have uniform requirement, student council, honor system. Discipline rests primarily with faculty.

Summer Programs Remediation, enrichment, advancement, ESL, sports, art/fine arts, computer instruction programs offered; session focuses on ESL, computers, science, and art; held both on and off campus; held at Tokyo, Japan, Edmonton, Canada, and Gold Coast, Australia; accepts boys and girls; open to students from other schools. 350 students usually enrolled. 2013 schedule: July 5 to August 31. Application deadline: June 30.

Tuition and Aid Day student tuition: ¥1,575,000; 7-day tuition and room/board: ¥2,805,000. Tuition installment plan (individually arranged payment plans, term payment plans). Tuition reduction for siblings, merit scholarship grants available. In 2012–13, 5% of upper-school students received aid; total upper-school merit-scholarship money awarded: ¥2,735,000. Total amount of financial aid awarded in 2012–13: ¥3,360,000.

Admissions Traditional secondary-level entrance grade is 10. For fall 2012, 53 students applied for upper-level admission, 30 were accepted, 26 enrolled. Any standardized test required. Deadline for receipt of application materials: none. Application fee required: ¥25,000. Interview required.

Athletics Coed Interscholastic: basketball, dance, football, soccer; coed intramural: aerobics, alpine skiing, artistic gym, badminton, ball hockey, baseball, bicycling, bowling, climbing, cooperative games, dance team, field hockey, fitness, flag football, floor hockey, freestyle skiing, Frisbee, golf, hiking/backpacking, hockey, horseback riding, indoor hockey, indoor soccer, juggling, kickball, life saving, mountain biking, outdoor activities, physical fitness, power lifting, rock climbing, self defense, ski jumping, skiing (downhill), snowboarding, softball, table tennis, team handball, tennis, volleyball, wall climbing, weight lifting, weight training, yoga. 2 PE instructors.

Computers Computers are regularly used in all classes. Computer network features include Internet access, wireless campus network, Internet filtering or blocking technology, repair service. Campus intranet and student e-mail accounts are available to students. The school has a published electronic and media policy.

Contact Mr. Christopher Holland, Administrator. 81-4-2946-1911. Fax: 81-4-2946-1955. E-mail: holland@columbia-ca.co.jp. Web site: www.columbia-ca.co.jp

THE COLUMBUS ACADEMY

4300 Cherry Bottom Road

Gahanna, Ohio 43230

Head of School: John M. Mackenzie

General Information Coeducational day college-preparatory school. Grades PK–12. Founded: 1911. Setting: suburban. Nearest major city is Columbus. 233-acre campus. 16 buildings on campus. Approved or accredited by Independent Schools Association of the Central States and Ohio Department of Education. Member of National Association of Independent Schools and Secondary School Admission Test Board. Endowment: $23.5 million. Total enrollment: 1,077. Upper school average class size: 14. Upper school faculty-student ratio: 1:8. The average school day consists of 7 hours and 5 minutes.

Upper School Student Profile Grade 9: 95 students (44 boys, 51 girls); Grade 10: 96 students (54 boys, 42 girls); Grade 11: 82 students (41 boys, 41 girls); Grade 12: 87 students (44 boys, 43 girls).

Faculty School total: 135. In upper school: 27 men, 22 women; 37 have advanced degrees.

Subjects Offered Advanced chemistry, advanced computer applications, advanced math, Advanced Placement courses, advanced studio art-AP, algebra, American history, American history-AP, American literature, analysis and differential calculus, art history, biology, biology-AP, British literature, calculus, calculus-AP, career/college preparation, ceramics, chemistry, chemistry-AP, China/Japan history, Chinese, choir, choral music, chorus, college counseling, comparative government and politics-AP, comparative political systems-AP, computer applications, computer education, computer programming-AP, computer science, computer science-AP, concert band, concert choir, creative writing, drawing and design, economics, economics-AP, English, European history, European history-AP, fine arts, French, French-AP, geology, geometry, government and politics-AP, government-AP, health education, history of China and Japan, instrumental music, Latin, Latin-AP, military history, photography, physical education, physics, physics-AP, pre-calculus, senior career experience, South African history, Spanish, Spanish language-AP, Spanish literature-AP, speech, statistics-AP, strings, theater, trigonometry, U.S. government and politics-AP, U.S. history-AP, United States government-AP, weight training, world history, world religions.

Graduation Requirements Arts and fine arts (art, music, dance, drama), English, foreign language, mathematics, science, social studies (includes history), formal speech delivered to the students and faculty of the upper school during junior year, community service requirement.

Special Academic Programs 23 Advanced Placement exams for which test preparation is offered; honors section; independent study; academic accommodation for the gifted.

College Admission Counseling 93 students graduated in 2011; all went to college, including Kenyon College; Miami University; Northwestern University; The Ohio State University; University of Chicago; University of Richmond. Median SAT critical reading: 640, median SAT math: 670, median SAT writing: 650, median combined SAT: 1970, median composite ACT: 27. 74% scored over 600 on SAT critical reading, 78% scored over 600 on SAT math, 78% scored over 600 on SAT writing, 78% scored over 1800 on combined SAT, 74% scored over 26 on composite ACT.

Student Life Upper grades have specified standards of dress, student council. Discipline rests equally with students and faculty.

Tuition and Aid Day student tuition: $20,200. Tuition installment plan (The Tuition Plan, Academic Management Services Plan, Tuition Management Systems Plan). Merit scholarship grants, need-based scholarship grants available. In 2011–12, 18% of upper-school students received aid. Total amount of financial aid awarded in 2011–12: $979,150.

Admissions Traditional secondary-level entrance grade is 9. For fall 2011, 57 students applied for upper-level admission, 34 were accepted, 29 enrolled. ISEE or SSAT required. Deadline for receipt of application materials: February 10. Application fee required: $50. On-campus interview required.

Athletics Interscholastic: baseball (boys), basketball (b,g), bowling (b,g), cross-country running (b,g), diving (b,g), field hockey (g), football (b), lacrosse (b,g), soccer (b,g), swimming and diving (b,g), tennis (b,g), track and field (b,g), volleyball (g), wrestling (b); coed intramural: bicycling. 3 PE instructors, 2 athletic trainers.

Computers Computers are regularly used in college planning, current events, economics, English, foreign language, humanities, journalism, Latin, learning cognition, library skills, mathematics, media production, multimedia, music, photography, publications, reading, research skills, SAT preparation, science, technology, theater, writing, yearbook classes. Computer network features include on-campus library services, online commercial services, Internet access, wireless campus network. Campus intranet, student e-mail accounts, and computer access in designated common areas are available to students. The school has a published electronic and media policy.

Contact John Wuorinen, Director of Admissions and Financial Aid. 614-509-2220. Fax: 614-475-0396. E-mail: admissions@columbusacademy.org. Web site: www.ColumbusAcademy.org

COLUMBUS SCHOOL FOR GIRLS

56 South Columbia Avenue
Columbus, Ohio 43209

Head of School: Mrs. Elizabeth M. Lee

General Information Girls' day college-preparatory, arts, and technology school. Grades PK–12. Founded: 1898. Setting: urban. 80-acre campus. 1 building on campus. Approved or accredited by Independent Schools Association of the Central States and Ohio Association of Independent Schools. Member of National Association of Independent Schools. Endowment: $21.8 million. Total enrollment: 573. Upper school average class size: 13. Upper school faculty-student ratio: 1:9. There are 180 required school days per year for Upper School students. Upper School students typically attend 5 days per week. The average school day consists of 6 hours and 45 minutes.

Upper School Student Profile Grade 9: 56 students (56 girls); Grade 10: 45 students (45 girls); Grade 11: 50 students (50 girls); Grade 12: 60 students (60 girls).

Faculty School total: 77. In upper school: 7 men, 19 women; 21 have advanced degrees.

Subjects Offered Acting, Advanced Placement courses, algebra, American literature, astronomy, band, biology, biology-AP, British literature, calculus, calculus-AP, ceramics, chemistry, chemistry-AP, civics, college admission preparation, comparative government and politics-AP, computer science, concert choir, digital photography, discrete mathematics, drawing, economics, English, English language and composition-AP, English literature and composition-AP, European history-AP, fine arts, geometry, German, health, lab science, Latin, Latin-AP, Mandarin, modern European history-AP, music theory-AP, newspaper, philosophy, photography, physical education, physics, physics-AP, pre-calculus, public speaking, robotics, senior seminar, Spanish, Spanish language-AP, statistics, strings, studio art-AP, theater, trigonometry, U.S. government and politics-AP, U.S. history, visual arts, vocal ensemble, world history, world literature, world religions, yearbook.

Graduation Requirements Algebra, arts and fine arts (art, music, dance, drama), biology, civics, college planning, computer science, electives, English, foreign language, geometry, history, lab science, mathematics, physical education (includes health), public speaking, science, technology, U.S. history, world history, Senior May program, service hours, self defense/water safety.

Special Academic Programs Advanced Placement exam preparation; honors section; independent study; study at local college for college credit.

College Admission Counseling 50 students graduated in 2012; all went to college, including Miami University; New York University; The College of Wooster; The Ohio State University; University of Kentucky; University of Richmond. Mean SAT critical reading: 639, mean SAT math: 605, mean SAT writing: 644, mean combined SAT: 1888, mean composite ACT: 28.

Student Life Upper grades have uniform requirement, student council, honor system. Discipline rests primarily with faculty.

Summer Programs Remediation, enrichment, advancement, sports, art/fine arts, rigorous outdoor training, computer instruction programs offered; session focuses on academic areas; held both on and off campus; held at various sites in community and CSG's Kirk Athletic Campus; accepts boys and girls; open to students from other schools. 600 students usually enrolled. 2013 schedule: June 10 to August 9. Application deadline: none.

Tuition and Aid Day student tuition: $19,500–$20,500. Tuition installment plan (Tuition Management Systems Plan). Tuition reduction for siblings, need-based scholarship grants, tuition reduction for three or more siblings available. In 2012–13, 33% of upper-school students received aid. Total amount of financial aid awarded in 2012–13: $757,230.

Admissions Traditional secondary-level entrance grade is 9. For fall 2012, 36 students applied for upper-level admission, 27 were accepted, 18 enrolled. CTP, ISEE or school's own test required. Deadline for receipt of application materials: February 15. Application fee required: $50. On-campus interview required.

Athletics Interscholastic: aquatics, basketball, cross-country running, diving, field hockey, golf, indoor track & field, lacrosse, running, soccer, swimming and diving, tennis, track and field, volleyball, winter (indoor) track; intramural: aquatics, badminton, basketball, bocce, climbing, cooperative games, cricket, field hockey, fitness, fitness walking, flag football, floor hockey, Frisbee, golf, indoor hockey, indoor soccer, indoor track, jogging, kickball, lacrosse, martial arts, physical fitness, physical training, rugby, running, self defense, soccer, softball, strength & conditioning, swimming and diving, synchronized swimming, table tennis, tennis, track and field, ultimate Frisbee, volleyball, walking, weight training, winter soccer, yoga. 4 PE instructors, 25 coaches, 1 athletic trainer.

Computers Computers are regularly used in art, English, foreign language, freshman foundations, health, history, mathematics, music, publications, science, technology, theater, yearbook classes. Computer network features include on-campus library services, online commercial services, Internet access, wireless campus network, Internet filtering or blocking technology. Campus intranet, student e-mail accounts, and computer access in designated common areas are available to students. Students grades are available online. The school has a published electronic and media policy.

Contact Jenni Biehn, Director of Admission and Financial Aid. 614-252-0781 Ext. 104. Fax: 614-252-0571. E-mail: jbiehn@columbusschoolforgirls.org. Web site: www.columbusschoolforgirls.org

COMMONWEALTH PARKVILLE SCHOOL

PO Box 70177
San Juan, Puerto Rico 00936-8177

Head of School: Mr. F. Richard Marracino

General Information Coeducational day college-preparatory, arts, and technology school. Grades PS–12. Founded: 1952. Setting: urban. 1-acre campus. 1 building on campus. Approved or accredited by Middle States Association of Colleges and Schools and Puerto Rico Department of Education. Member of National Association of Independent Schools. Endowment: $502,005. Total enrollment: 672. Upper school average class size: 13. Upper school faculty-student ratio: 1:7. There are 180 required school days per year for Upper School students. Upper School students typically attend 5 days per week. The average school day consists of 5 hours and 8 minutes.

Upper School Student Profile Grade 9: 41 students (20 boys, 21 girls); Grade 10: 38 students (19 boys, 19 girls); Grade 11: 41 students (19 boys, 22 girls); Grade 12: 54 students (36 boys, 18 girls).

Faculty School total: 27. In upper school: 11 men, 16 women; 13 have advanced degrees.

Subjects Offered 3-dimensional art, Advanced Placement courses, algebra, American history, American literature, American literature-AP, art, art history-AP, band, biology, business mathematics, calculus, ceramics, chemistry, chemistry-AP, civics, computer science, computer technologies, creative writing, drama, drawing, ecology, English, English language and composition-AP, English literature, ethics, European history, forensics, French, geometry, health, journalism, mathematics, modern world history, music, music appreciation, music history, painting, physical education, physics, play production, pre-calculus, sculpture, Spanish, Spanish-AP, stained glass, theater, trigonometry, world history.

Graduation Requirements Art, computer science, English, ethics, health, mathematics, music, physical education (includes health), Puerto Rican history, science, social studies (includes history), Spanish, community service hours.

Special Academic Programs 8 Advanced Placement exams for which test preparation is offered; honors section; independent study; domestic exchange program (with The Network Program Schools); study abroad; programs in English, mathematics, general development for dyslexic students; special instructional classes for students with mild learning disabilities and Attention Deficit Disorder.

College Admission Counseling 46 students graduated in 2012; all went to college, including Bentley University; Boston College; Massachusetts Institute of Technology; New York University; Syracuse University; University of Puerto Rico, Río Piedras. Mean SAT critical reading: 560, mean SAT math: 570, mean SAT writing: 575.

Student Life Upper grades have uniform requirement, student council, honor system. Discipline rests primarily with faculty.

Summer Programs Remediation, enrichment, ESL, sports, art/fine arts, computer instruction programs offered; session focuses on improving grades on previously taken courses; held on campus; accepts boys and girls; open to students from other schools. 90 students usually enrolled. 2013 schedule: June 1 to June 30. Application deadline: June 1.

Tuition and Aid Day student tuition: $10,350–$12,810. Tuition installment plan (monthly payment plans, individually arranged payment plans, annual and semester payment plans). Tuition reduction for siblings, merit scholarship grants, need-based scholarship grants available. In 2012–13, 12% of upper-school students received aid; total upper-school merit-scholarship money awarded: $47,818. Total amount of financial aid awarded in 2012–13: $82,318.

Admissions Traditional secondary-level entrance grade is 9. For fall 2012, 34 students applied for upper-level admission, 32 were accepted, 26 enrolled. Math and English placement tests, Stanford Achievement Test and writing sample required. Deadline for receipt of application materials: none. Application fee required: $85. Interview required.

Athletics Interscholastic: baseball (boys), basketball (b), bowling (b,g), cross-country running (b,g), fitness (b,g), football (b), indoor soccer (b,g), physical fitness (b,g), soccer (b,g), softball (g), table tennis (b,g), tennis (b,g), track and field (b,g), volleyball (b,g), weight training (b,g); intramural: soccer (b,g), softball (b,g), volleyball (b,g); coed interscholastic: swimming and diving; coed intramural: badminton, basketball, cooperative games, field hockey, fitness, flag football, Frisbee, indoor soccer, jogging, outdoor activities, outdoor education, outdoor recreation, physical fitness, physical training, soccer, softball, strength & conditioning, table tennis, tennis, track and field, volleyball, walking. 3 PE instructors, 9 coaches.

Computers Computers are regularly used in all academic, music, yearbook classes. Computer network features include on-campus library services, Internet access, wireless campus network, Internet filtering or blocking technology. Campus intranet, student e-mail accounts, and computer access in designated common areas are available to students. Students grades are available online. The school has a published electronic and media policy.

Contact Mrs. Jo-Ann Aranguren, Director of Admissions and Alumni. 787-765-4411 Ext. 232. Fax: 787-764-3809. E-mail: jaranguren@cpspr.org. Web site: www.cpspr.org

COMMONWEALTH SCHOOL

151 Commonwealth Avenue
Boston, Massachusetts 02116

Head of School: Mr. William D. Wharton

General Information Coeducational day college-preparatory school. Grades 9–12. Founded: 1957. Setting: urban. 1 building on campus. Approved or accredited by Association of Independent Schools in New England, New England Association of Schools and Colleges, and Massachusetts Department of Education. Member of National Association of Independent Schools and Secondary School Admission Test Board. Endowment: $14 million. Total enrollment: 149. Upper school average class size: 12. Upper school faculty-student ratio: 1:5. Upper School students typically attend 5 days per week. The average school day consists of 6 hours and 30 minutes.

Upper School Student Profile Grade 9: 39 students (18 boys, 21 girls); Grade 10: 36 students (15 boys, 21 girls); Grade 11: 37 students (23 boys, 14 girls); Grade 12: 37 students (19 boys, 18 girls).

Faculty School total: 36. In upper school: 14 men, 19 women; 26 have advanced degrees.

Subjects Offered 20th century American writers, 20th century history, acting, advanced biology, advanced chemistry, advanced computer applications, advanced math, Advanced Placement courses, African-American literature, algebra, American history, American history-AP, American literature, analysis and differential calculus, analysis of data, analytic geometry, ancient history, ancient world history, art, art history, biology, biology-AP, calculus, calculus-AP, ceramics, chamber groups, chemistry, chemistry-AP, choral music, chorus, classics, college counseling, community service, computer programming, computer science, constitutional law, creative writing, current events, dance, drama, drawing, economics, economics-AP, English, English literature, English-AP, environmental science, environmental studies, ethics, European history, European history-AP, expository writing, film series, film studies, fine arts, foreign language, French, French language-AP, French literature-AP, French studies, French-AP, geometry, Greek, health and safety, Hispanic literature, history of the Americas, history-AP, honors algebra, honors English, honors geometry, honors U.S. history, Japanese history, jazz, jazz band, jazz ensemble, jazz theory, Latin, Latin American history, Latin-AP, mathematics, mathematics-AP, medieval history, medieval/Renaissance history, modern European history-AP, music, music theory, music theory-AP, orchestra, organic chemistry, painting, performing arts, philosophy, photography, physical education, physics, physics-AP, poetry, pottery, pre-calculus, printmaking, probability and statistics, psychology, Russian literature, science, short story, society, politics and law, Spanish, Spanish language-AP, Spanish literature, Spanish literature-AP, Spanish-AP, studio art, tap dance, theater, U.S. history-AP, visual and performing arts, visual arts, vocal music, voice, voice ensemble, writing.

Graduation Requirements Algebra, ancient history, art, biology, calculus, chemistry, English, ethics, foreign language, geometry, medieval history, physical education (includes health), physics, U.S. history, City of Boston course, completion of a one- to three-week project each year (with report), Health and Community. Community service is required.

Special Academic Programs Advanced Placement exam preparation; honors section; independent study; term-away projects; study abroad; academic accommodation for the gifted, the musically talented, and the artistically talented.

College Admission Counseling 37 students graduated in 2011; 36 went to college, including Brown University; Haverford College; Reed College; Smith College; University of Chicago. Other: 1 had other specific plans. Median SAT critical reading: 740, median SAT math: 740, median SAT writing: 720.

Student Life Discipline rests primarily with faculty.

Tuition and Aid Day student tuition: $33,080. Tuition installment plan (Key Tuition Payment Plan). Need-based scholarship grants, need-based loans available. In 2011–12, 34% of upper-school students received aid. Total amount of financial aid awarded in 2011–12: $1,108,002.

Admissions Traditional secondary-level entrance grade is 9. For fall 2011, 184 students applied for upper-level admission, 77 were accepted, 42 enrolled. ISEE or SSAT required. Deadline for receipt of application materials: February 1. Application fee required: $50. On-campus interview required.

Athletics Interscholastic: basketball (boys, girls), independent competitive sports (b,g), soccer (b,g); coed interscholastic: baseball, cross-country running, fencing, squash, ultimate Frisbee; coed intramural: aerobics/Nautilus, ballet, cross-country running, dance, fencing, fitness, martial arts, sailing, squash, tai chi, yoga. 12 coaches.

Computers Computers are regularly used in computer applications, photography, programming classes. Computer network features include on-campus library services, online commercial services, Internet access, wireless campus network, Internet filtering or blocking technology. Campus intranet, student e-mail accounts, and computer access in designated common areas are available to students. The school has a published electronic and media policy.

Contact Ms. Robyn Gibson, Assistant Director of Admissions. 617-266-7525. Fax: 617-266-5769. E-mail: admissions@commschool.org. Web site: www.commschool.org

COMMUNITY CHRISTIAN ACADEMY

11875 Taylor Mill Road
Independence, Kentucky 41051

Head of School: Tara Montez Bates

General Information Coeducational day college-preparatory and religious studies school, affiliated with Pentecostal Church. Grades PS–12. Founded: 1983. Setting: rural. Nearest major city is Cincinnati, OH. 112-acre campus. 2 buildings on campus. Approved or accredited by International Christian Accrediting Association and Kentucky Department of Education. Total enrollment: 268. Upper school average class size: 15. Upper school faculty-student ratio: 1:15. There are 175 required school days per year for Upper School students. Upper School students typically attend 5 days per week. The average school day consists of 6 hours.

Upper School Student Profile Grade 9: 20 students (9 boys, 11 girls); Grade 10: 11 students (5 boys, 6 girls); Grade 11: 10 students (7 boys, 3 girls); Grade 12: 20 students (11 boys, 9 girls). 50% of students are Pentecostal.

Faculty School total: 14. In upper school: 1 man, 5 women; 2 have advanced degrees.

Subjects Offered Advanced biology, advanced math, algebra, American history, art appreciation, Bible, biology, business skills, calculus, chemistry, choral music, computer applications, cultural geography, English, geography, health, integrated science, life skills, literature, pre-algebra, pre-calculus, Spanish.

Graduation Requirements Bible, electives, English, foreign language, mathematics, physical education (includes health), science, social studies (includes history), statistics, visual and performing arts.

College Admission Counseling 15 students graduated in 2012; 12 went to college, including Cincinnati State Technical and Community College; Northern Kentucky University; University of Cincinnati. Other: 2 went to work, 1 entered military service. Mean composite ACT: 21. 20% scored over 26 on composite ACT.

Student Life Upper grades have uniform requirement, student council, honor system. Discipline rests primarily with faculty. Attendance at religious services is required.

Tuition and Aid Day student tuition: $3349. Guaranteed tuition plan. Tuition installment plan (The Tuition Plan, monthly payment plans). Financial aid available to upper-school students. In 2012–13, 5% of upper-school students received aid. Total amount of financial aid awarded in 2012–13: $9000.

Admissions Traditional secondary-level entrance grade is 9. For fall 2012, 20 students applied for upper-level admission, 15 were accepted, 15 enrolled. Admissions testing required. Deadline for receipt of application materials: none. Application fee required: $50. Interview required.

Athletics Interscholastic: baseball (boys), basketball (b,g), cheering (g), golf (b), volleyball (g); coed interscholastic: archery. 2 PE instructors, 13 coaches.

Computers Computers are regularly used in foreign language classes. Computer network features include Internet access.

Contact Edie Carkeek, Secretary. 859-356-7990 Ext. 112. Fax: 859-356-7991. E-mail: edie.carkeek@ccaky.org. Web site: www.ccaky.org

THE COMMUNITY SCHOOL OF NAPLES

13275 Livingston Road
Naples, Florida 34109

Head of School: Mr. Dennis H. Grubbs

General Information Coeducational day college-preparatory and arts school. Grades PK–12. Founded: 1982. Setting: suburban. Nearest major city is Miami. 77-acre campus. 4 buildings on campus. Approved or accredited by Florida Council of Independent Schools. Member of National Association of Independent Schools and Secondary School Admission Test Board. Endowment: $9.4 million. Total enrollment: 706. Upper school average class size: 12. Upper school faculty-student ratio: 1:8. There are 172 required school days per year for Upper School students. Upper School students typically attend 5 days per week. The average school day consists of 6 hours.

Upper School Student Profile Grade 9: 76 students (29 boys, 47 girls); Grade 10: 84 students (50 boys, 34 girls); Grade 11: 69 students (27 boys, 42 girls); Grade 12: 57 students (34 boys, 23 girls).

Faculty School total: 90. In upper school: 19 men, 23 women; 27 have advanced degrees.

Subjects Offered 3-dimensional art, 3-dimensional design, advanced computer applications, advanced math, Advanced Placement courses, advanced studio art-AP, algebra, American government, American history, American literature, American literature-AP, American sign language, anatomy and physiology, art, art history, art history-AP, art-AP, band, biology, biology-AP, biotechnology, calculus, calculus-AP, chemistry, chemistry-AP, chorus, clayworking, comparative government and politics-AP, composition, composition-AP, computer graphics, computer programming, computer programming-AP, computer science, computer science-AP, creative writing, digital photography, drama performance, dramatic arts, drawing, drawing and design, economics, economics-AP, electives, English, English composition, English language and composition-AP, English language-AP, English literature, English literature and composition-AP, English literature-AP, English-AP, English/composition-AP, environmental science, environmental science-AP, fine arts, French, French language-AP, French literature-AP, French-AP, geometry, government, government and politics-AP, government-AP, government/civics, government/civics-AP, graphic design, health, history, history-AP, honors algebra, honors English, honors geometry, honors U.S. history, honors world history, human geography - AP, jazz band, Latin, literature, literature and composition-AP, literature-AP, macro/microeconomics-AP, macroeconomics-AP, marine biology, marine science, mathematics, mathematics-AP, microeconomics, microeconomics-AP, modern European history-AP, music, music theory-AP, oceanography, painting, performing arts, personal fitness, photography, physical education, physical fitness, physics, physics-AP, portfolio art, pre-algebra, pre-calculus, psychology, psychology-AP, robotics, science, senior project, Spanish, Spanish language-AP, Spanish literature-AP, Spanish-AP, statistics-AP, strings, studio art-AP, theater, U.S. government and politics, U.S. government and politics-AP, U.S. history, U.S. history-AP, United States government-AP, visual and performing arts, visual arts, vocal music, Web site design, world history, world history-AP, world literature.

Graduation Requirements Arts and fine arts (art, music, dance, drama), computer science, electives, English, foreign language, history, mathematics, physical education (includes health), science, community service hours (20 per year).

Special Academic Programs 26 Advanced Placement exams for which test preparation is offered; honors section; independent study; study at local college for college credit; study abroad.

College Admission Counseling 72 students graduated in 2012; all went to college, including Florida State University; Georgetown University; The University of North Carolina at Chapel Hill; University of Florida; University of Miami; Vanderbilt University. Median SAT critical reading: 600, median SAT math: 635, median SAT writing: 600, median combined SAT: 1825, median composite ACT: 27. 47% scored over 600 on SAT critical reading, 65% scored over 600 on SAT math, 49% scored over 600 on SAT writing, 53% scored over 1800 on combined SAT, 51% scored over 26 on composite ACT.

Student Life Upper grades have specified standards of dress, student council, honor system. Discipline rests equally with students and faculty.

Summer Programs Remediation, enrichment, sports, art/fine arts programs offered; session focuses on mathematics, English, and SAT preparation, sports; held on campus; accepts boys and girls; open to students from other schools. 75 students usually enrolled. 2013 schedule: June 10 to August 18. Application deadline: June 1.

Tuition and Aid Day student tuition: $23,050. Tuition installment plan (Insured Tuition Payment Plan, monthly payment plans, individually arranged payment plans). Merit scholarship grants, need-based scholarship grants available. In 2012–13, 31% of upper-school students received aid; total upper-school merit-scholarship money awarded: $55,000. Total amount of financial aid awarded in 2012–13: $1,042,686.

Admissions Traditional secondary-level entrance grade is 9. For fall 2012, 65 students applied for upper-level admission, 50 were accepted, 34 enrolled. School's own exam or SSAT required. Deadline for receipt of application materials: February 1. Application fee required: $100. On-campus interview required.

Athletics Interscholastic: baseball (boys), basketball (b,g), cross-country running (b,g), diving (b,g), football (b), golf (b,g), lacrosse (b,g), soccer (b,g), softball (g), swimming and diving (b,g), tennis (b,g), track and field (b,g), volleyball (g), winter soccer (b,g); intramural: cross-country running (g), football (b); coed intramural: cheering, rock climbing, sailing, weight training. 4 PE instructors, 67 coaches, 1 athletic trainer.

Computers Computers are regularly used in art, computer applications, creative writing, design, desktop publishing, digital applications, English, foreign language, history, mathematics, music, science, Web site design, writing, writing, yearbook classes. Computer network features include on-campus library services, online commercial services, Internet access, wireless campus network, Internet filtering or blocking technology. Campus intranet, student e-mail accounts, and computer access in designated common areas are available to students. The school has a published electronic and media policy.

Contact Mr. Scott Vasey, Director of Admissions. 239-597-7575 Ext. 205. Fax: 239-598-2973. E-mail: Svasey@communityschoolnaples.org. Web site: www.communityschoolnaples.org

THE CONCEPT SCHOOL

1120 E. Street Rd
PO Box 54
Westtown, Pennsylvania 19395

Head of School: Mr. James Symonds

General Information Coeducational day college-preparatory, general academic, arts, technology, and The Arts school. Grades 5–12. Founded: 1972. Setting: suburban. Nearest major city is Philadelphia. 10-acre campus. 1 building on campus. Approved or accredited by Pennsylvania Department of Education. Endowment: $250,000. Total enrollment: 19. Upper school average class size: 5. Upper school faculty-student ratio: 1:4. There are 180 required school days per year for Upper School students. Upper School students typically attend 5 days per week. The average school day consists of 6 hours and 30 minutes.

Upper School Student Profile Grade 9: 1 student (1 boy); Grade 10: 2 students (2 boys); Grade 11: 7 students (6 boys, 1 girl); Grade 12: 3 students (3 boys).

Faculty School total: 6. In upper school: 2 men, 4 women; 3 have advanced degrees.

Subjects Offered 20th century world history, acting, algebra, American history, art, biology, career and personal planning, chemistry, computer graphics, consumer mathematics, cultural arts, earth science, economics, English, environmental science, fine arts, foreign language, general science, geometry, government, government/civics, health, history, human development, independent study, keyboarding, lab science, language arts, mathematics, physical education, physics, physiology, pre-algebra, pre-calculus, science, Shakespeare, social sciences, social studies, trigonometry, U.S. government, visual arts.

Graduation Requirements Arts and fine arts (art, music, dance, drama), computer science, English, mathematics, physical education (includes health), science, social sciences, social studies (includes history).

Special Academic Programs Accelerated programs; independent study; academic accommodation for the gifted and the artistically talented; remedial reading and/or remedial writing; remedial math; programs in English, mathematics, general development for dyslexic students; special instructional classes for deaf students.

College Admission Counseling 9 students graduated in 2012; 7 went to college, including Ithaca College; Neumann University; Pennsylvania State University System; West Chester University of Pennsylvania. Other: 1 went to work, 1 had other specific plans. Mean SAT critical reading: 510, mean SAT math: 490, mean SAT writing: 480, mean combined SAT: 495.

Student Life Upper grades have specified standards of dress, honor system. Discipline rests primarily with faculty.

Tuition and Aid Day student tuition: $18,750. Tuition installment plan (monthly payment plans). Tuition reduction for siblings available.

Admissions Traditional secondary-level entrance grade is 9. For fall 2012, 2 students applied for upper-level admission, 1 was accepted. Stanford Binet, Wechsler Individual Achievement Test or WISC or WAIS required. Deadline for receipt of application materials: none. Application fee required: $75. On-campus interview required.

Athletics Coed Intramural: aerobics, basketball, bowling, ice skating, in-line skating, physical fitness, physical training, roller skating, skiing (downhill), snowboarding, yoga. 1 PE instructor.

Computers Computers are regularly used in all academic classes. Computer network features include on-campus library services, Internet access, wireless campus network, Internet filtering or blocking technology, all students are issued Chrome Books. Campus intranet and student e-mail accounts are available to students. The school has a published electronic and media policy.

Contact Mrs. Carol McAdam, School Secretary. 610-399-1135. Fax: 610-399-0767. E-mail: cmcadam@theconceptschool.org. Web site: www.theconceptschool.org

CONCORD ACADEMY

166 Main Street
Concord, Massachusetts 01742

Head of School: Rick Hardy

General Information Coeducational boarding and day college-preparatory and arts school. Grades 9–12. Founded: 1922. Setting: suburban. Nearest major city is Boston. Students are housed in single-sex dormitories. 39-acre campus. 29 buildings on campus. Approved or accredited by New England Association of Schools and Colleges, The Association of Boarding Schools, and Massachusetts Department of Education. Member of National Association of Independent Schools and Secondary School Admission Test Board. Endowment: $51 million. Total enrollment: 370. Upper school average class size: 12. Upper school faculty-student ratio: 1:6. Upper School students typically attend 5 days per week. The average school day consists of 6 hours and 30 minutes.

Upper School Student Profile Grade 9: 84 students (47 boys, 37 girls); Grade 10: 92 students (48 boys, 44 girls); Grade 11: 99 students (53 boys, 46 girls); Grade 12: 95 students (49 boys, 46 girls). 42% of students are boarding students. 33% are state residents. 19 states are represented in upper school student body. 10% are international students. International students from Canada, China, Indonesia, Republic of Korea, Taiwan, and Thailand; 4 other countries represented in student body.

Faculty School total: 62. In upper school: 27 men, 35 women; 49 have advanced degrees; 26 reside on campus.

Subjects Offered 20th century American writers, 3-dimensional art, advanced chemistry, advanced math, African history, African-American literature, algebra, American history, American literature, ancient history, ancient world history, anthropology, applied music, architecture, art, art history, Asian history, astronomy, astrophysics, batik, Bible as literature, biochemistry, biology, bookmaking, British literature, calculus, ceramics, chamber groups, chemistry, Chinese history, choreography, chorus, classical civilization, classical Greek literature, classical language, computer multimedia, computer programming, computer science, computer studies, creative writing, critical studies in film, dance, dance performance, digital imaging, directing, drama, drama performance, drawing, earth science, economics, English, English literature, environmental science, environmental studies, European history, experimental science, expository writing, fiber arts, fiction, film, film history, filmmaking, forensics, French, freshman seminar, geology, geometry, German, German literature, guitar, health and wellness, history, history of China and Japan, history of music, Holocaust, HTML design, improvisation, instruments, introduction to digital multitrack recording techniques, Irish literature, Islamic history, jazz ensemble, journalism, Latin, Latin American history, Latin American literature, life management skills, literature seminar, math analysis, mathematics, medieval/Renaissance history, Middle East, Middle Eastern history, model United Nations, modern dance, modern European history, modern languages, music, music composition, music history, music technology, music theory, musical productions, neuroscience, newspaper, novels, oceanography, orchestra, painting, performing arts, philosophy, photography, physical education, physics, piano, play/screen writing, poetry, post-calculus, pre-calculus, printmaking, probability and statistics, Roman civilization, science, science fiction, sculpture, senior project, sex education, Shakespeare, Spanish, Spanish literature, statistics, student publications, studio art, technical theater, theater, theater design and production, theater history, trigonometry, U.S. history, urban studies, visual arts, voice, Web site design, wind ensemble, writing.

Graduation Requirements Computer science, English, foreign language, history, mathematics, performing arts, physical education (includes health), science, visual arts.

Special Academic Programs Honors section; independent study; term-away projects; study abroad; academic accommodation for the gifted, the musically talented, and the artistically talented.

College Admission Counseling 97 students graduated in 2012; all went to college, including Barnard College; Brown University; Carleton College; Columbia College; New York University; Tufts University. Mean SAT critical reading: 688, mean SAT math: 677, mean SAT writing: 685, mean combined SAT: 2050.

Student Life Upper grades have student council, honor system. Discipline rests equally with students and faculty.

Tuition and Aid Day student tuition: $40,500; 7-day tuition and room/board: $50,075. Tuition installment plan (Key Tuition Payment Plan, monthly payment plans). Need-based scholarship grants, need-based loans available. In 2012–13, 24% of upper-school students received aid. Total amount of financial aid awarded in 2012–13: $3,468,400.

Admissions Traditional secondary-level entrance grade is 9. For fall 2012, 766 students applied for upper-level admission, 247 were accepted, 108 enrolled. ISEE, SSAT or TOEFL required. Deadline for receipt of application materials: January 15. Application fee required: $50. Interview recommended.

Athletics Interscholastic: baseball (boys), basketball (b,g), cross-country running (b,g), field hockey (g), lacrosse (g), skiing (downhill) (b,g), soccer (b,g), squash (g), tennis (b,g), volleyball (g), wrestling (b); intramural: softball (g), squash (b); coed interscholastic: alpine skiing, golf, lacrosse, ultimate Frisbee; coed intramural: aerobics, aerobics/dance, ballet, canoeing/kayaking, combined training, cross-country running, dance, fencing, fitness, jogging, martial arts, modern dance, outdoor activities, physical fitness, physical training, sailing, self defense, skiing (downhill), strength & conditioning, track and field, ultimate Frisbee, weight training, yoga. 8 PE instructors, 35 coaches, 2 athletic trainers.

Computers Computers are regularly used in English, foreign language, history, library skills, mathematics, music, newspaper, science, social studies, technology, video film production, Web site design, yearbook classes. Computer network features include on-campus library services, online commercial services, Internet access, wireless campus network, Internet filtering or blocking technology. Campus intranet, student e-mail accounts, and computer access in designated common areas are available to students. Students grades are available online. The school has a published electronic and media policy.

Contact Marie D. Myers, Director of Admissions. 978-402-2250. Fax: 978-402-2345. E-mail: admissions@concordacademy.org. Web site: www.concordacademy.org

CONCORDIA LUTHERAN HIGH SCHOOL

1601 Saint Joe River Drive
Fort Wayne, Indiana 46805

Head of School: Mr. Terry Breininger

General Information Coeducational day college-preparatory and religious studies school, affiliated with Lutheran Church–Missouri Synod. Grades 9–12. Founded: 1935. Setting: urban. Nearest major city is Indianapolis. 3 buildings on campus. Approved or accredited by National Lutheran School Accreditation, North Central Association of Colleges and Schools, and Indiana Department of Education. Total enrollment: 691. Upper school average class size: 23. Upper school faculty-student ratio: 1:17. There are 180 required school days per year for Upper School students. Upper School students typically attend 5 days per week. The average school day consists of 7 hours and 5 minutes.

Upper School Student Profile Grade 9: 175 students (83 boys, 92 girls); Grade 10: 186 students (98 boys, 88 girls); Grade 11: 160 students (85 boys, 75 girls); Grade 12: 170 students (82 boys, 88 girls). 80% of students are Lutheran Church–Missouri Synod.

Faculty School total: 43. In upper school: 22 men, 21 women; 25 have advanced degrees.

Subjects Offered 3-dimensional art, Advanced Placement courses, algebra, American history, American literature, art, band, Bible studies, biology, biology-AP, broadcasting, business, calculus, calculus-AP, ceramics, chemistry, chemistry-AP, choir, computer science, creative writing, discrete mathematics, driver education, earth science, economics, English, English literature, English literature and composition-AP, entrepreneurship, environmental science, ethics, expository writing, family and consumer science, food and nutrition, French, geography, geometry, German, government/civics, grammar, health, health and safety, history, home economics, honors algebra, honors English, honors geometry, internship, journalism, JROTC, JROTC or LEAD (Leadership Education and Development), keyboarding, Latin, marching band, mathematics, media arts, media communications, microeconomics-AP, music, newspaper, painting, physical education, physics, physics-AP, psychology, religion, science, social sciences, social studies, sociology, Spanish, speech, statistics-AP, theater, theater arts, theology, typing, U.S. government, U.S. history, U.S. history-AP, video film production, weight training, world history, world literature, writing, yearbook.

Graduation Requirements English, foreign language, mathematics, physical education (includes health), religion (includes Bible studies and theology), science, social sciences, social studies (includes history). Community service is required.

Special Academic Programs Advanced Placement exam preparation; honors section; independent study; study at local college for college credit; programs in English, mathematics, general development for dyslexic students.

College Admission Counseling 148 students graduated in 2012; 139 went to college, including Ball State University; Indiana University–Purdue University Fort Wayne; Indiana University Bloomington; Purdue University; Valparaiso University. Other: 6 went to work, 3 entered military service. Mean SAT critical reading: 525, mean SAT math: 558, mean SAT writing: 517, mean composite ACT: 24.

Student Life Upper grades have uniform requirement, student council. Discipline rests primarily with faculty. Attendance at religious services is required.

Summer Programs Remediation, advancement, sports, art/fine arts programs offered; session focuses on summer classes, drivers education, summer conditioning and sports camps; held both on and off campus; held at various locations based on sport; accepts boys and girls; open to students from other schools. 700 students usually enrolled.

Tuition and Aid Day student tuition: $6975–$8425. Tuition installment plan (FACTS Tuition Payment Plan, monthly payment plans, individually arranged payment plans, Bank loan). Tuition reduction for siblings, merit scholarship grants, need-based scholarship grants available.

Admissions Traditional secondary-level entrance grade is 9. Deadline for receipt of application materials: none. Application fee required: $35. On-campus interview recommended.

Athletics Interscholastic: baseball (boys), basketball (b,g), cheering (g), cross-country running (b,g), dance team (g), diving (b,g), football (b), golf (b,g), gymnastics (g), soccer (b,g), softball (g), swimming and diving (b,g), tennis (b,g), track and field (b,g), volleyball (g), wrestling (b); coed interscholastic: bowling, crew, JROTC drill, lacrosse, rappelling, riflery; coed intramural: volleyball. 3 PE instructors, 70 coaches, 2 athletic trainers.

Computers Computers are regularly used in all academic, newspaper, religion, yearbook classes. Computer resources include on-campus library services, online commercial services, Internet access, wireless campus network, Internet filtering or blocking technology. Student e-mail accounts and computer access in designated common areas are available to students. Students grades are available online.

Contact Mrs. Krista Friend, Enrollment Manager. 260-483-1102. Fax: 260-471-0180. E-mail: kfriend@clhscadets.com. Web site: www.clhscadets.com

CONCORDIA PREPARATORY SCHOOL

12723 S Park Ave
Riverton, Utah 84065

Head of School: Mr. Darren Morrison

General Information Coeducational day and distance learning college-preparatory, general academic, and religious studies school, affiliated with Lutheran Church. Grades 9–12. Distance learning grades 10–12. Founded: 1984. Setting: suburban. 10-acre campus. 1 building on campus. Approved or accredited by National Lutheran School Accreditation, Northwest Accreditation Commission, and Utah Department of Education. Total enrollment: 58. Upper school average class size: 10. Upper school faculty-student ratio: 1:3. There are 180 required school days per year for Upper School students. Upper School students typically attend 5 days per week. The average school day consists of 6 hours and 45 minutes.

Upper School Student Profile Grade 9: 9 students (6 boys, 3 girls); Grade 10: 7 students (5 boys, 2 girls); Grade 11: 7 students (3 boys, 4 girls); Grade 12: 8 students (3 boys, 5 girls). 25% of students are Lutheran.

Faculty School total: 9. In upper school: 4 men, 5 women; 5 have advanced degrees.

Subjects Offered Advanced biology, advanced chemistry, advanced computer applications, advanced math, Advanced Placement courses, algebra, American history, American literature, art, band, bell choir, Bible studies, biology, calculus, chemistry, chorus, computer science, drama, English, general science, geography, geometry, government/civics, health, journalism, keyboarding, literature, mathematics, novels, physical education, physics, psychology, religion, science, social sciences, sociology, Spanish, speech, vocal music, word processing, world history, world literature.

Graduation Requirements Arts and fine arts (art, music, dance, drama), business skills (includes word processing), computer science, English, mathematics, physical education (includes health), religion (includes Bible studies and theology), science, social sciences.

Special Academic Programs Advanced Placement exam preparation; honors section; accelerated programs; independent study; study at local college for college credit; academic accommodation for the gifted; remedial reading and/or remedial writing.

College Admission Counseling 10 students graduated in 2012; all went to college, including Concordia College; Salt Lake Community College; Southern Utah University; University of Utah; Utah State University; Westminster College. Median composite ACT: 24. 23% scored over 26 on composite ACT.
Student Life Upper grades have uniform requirement, student council, honor system. Discipline rests equally with students and faculty. Attendance at religious services is required.
Tuition and Aid Day student tuition: $9000. Tuition installment plan (SMART Tuition Payment Plan). Tuition reduction for siblings, merit scholarship grants, need-based scholarship grants available. In 2012–13, 40% of upper-school students received aid; total upper-school merit-scholarship money awarded: $16,000. Total amount of financial aid awarded in 2012–13: $33,700.
Admissions Traditional secondary-level entrance grade is 9. For fall 2012, 35 students applied for upper-level admission, 33 were accepted, 32 enrolled. School placement exam, SLEP for foreign students, TOEFL or SLEP or writing sample required. Deadline for receipt of application materials: none. Application fee required: $250. Interview required.
Athletics Interscholastic: baseball (boys), basketball (b,g), cross-country running (b,g), golf (b,g), soccer (b,g), swimming and diving (b,g), track and field (b,g), volleyball (g); coed interscholastic: cross-country running, golf, swimming and diving, track and field; coed intramural: badminton, basketball, cross-country running, fencing, golf, outdoors, physical fitness, physical training, soccer, track and field, volleyball, weight training. 3 coaches.
Computers Computers are regularly used in all classes. Computer network features include online commercial services, Internet access, wireless campus network, Internet filtering or blocking technology. Campus intranet, student e-mail accounts, and computer access in designated common areas are available to students. Students grades are available online. The school has a published electronic and media policy.
Contact Mrs. Tia Donohoe, Director of Admissions. 801-878-1515. Fax: 801-878-1730. E-mail: tdonohoe@concordiautah.org. Web site: concordiautah.org

CONTRA COSTA CHRISTIAN HIGH SCHOOL

2721 Larkey Lane
Walnut Creek, California 94596

Head of School: Mr. Darren Price

General Information Coeducational day and distance learning college-preparatory and religious studies school. Grades PK–12. Distance learning grades K–12. Founded: 1978. Setting: suburban. 2 buildings on campus. Approved or accredited by Western Association of Schools and Colleges and California Department of Education. Total enrollment: 230. Upper school average class size: 15. Upper school faculty-student ratio: 1:10. Upper School students typically attend 5 days per week. The average school day consists of 7 hours.
Upper School Student Profile Grade 9: 16 students (8 boys, 8 girls); Grade 10: 19 students (8 boys, 11 girls); Grade 11: 22 students (12 boys, 10 girls); Grade 12: 29 students (16 boys, 13 girls).
Faculty In upper school: 4 men, 6 women.
Subjects Offered Advanced Placement courses, algebra, art history, band, biology, chemistry, choir, computer applications, drama, economics, English composition, English literature, geometry, human anatomy, music appreciation, physics, pre-calculus, religious studies, Spanish, U.S. government and politics, U.S. history, visual arts, world history.
Graduation Requirements Community service is required.
Special Academic Programs 4 Advanced Placement exams for which test preparation is offered; ESL (15 students enrolled).
College Admission Counseling 28 students graduated in 2012.
Student Life Upper grades have specified standards of dress. Discipline rests primarily with faculty. Attendance at religious services is required.
Tuition and Aid Tuition installment plan (FACTS Tuition Payment Plan).
Athletics Interscholastic: aquatics (boys, girls), basketball (b,g), cross-country running (b,g), soccer (b,g), volleyball (b,g). 2 PE instructors, 12 coaches.
Computers Computers are regularly used in accounting, aerospace science, all academic, animation, architecture, art, aviation, basic skills, Bible studies, business, business applications, business education, business skills, business studies, cabinet making, career education, career exploration, career technology, Christian doctrine, classics, college planning, commercial art, computer applications, construction, creative writing, current events, dance, data processing, design, desktop publishing, desktop publishing, ESL, digital applications, drafting, drawing and design, economics, engineering, English, ESL, ethics, foreign language, French, French as a second language, freshman foundations, geography, graphic arts, graphic design, graphics, health, historical foundations for arts, history, human geography - AP, humanities, independent study, industrial technology, information technology, introduction to technology, journalism, JROTC, keyboarding, lab/keyboard, language development, Latin, learning cognition, library, library science, library skills, life skills, literacy, literary magazine, mathematics, media, media arts, media production, media services, mentorship program, multimedia, music, music technology, news writing, newspaper, NJROTC, occupational education, philosophy, photography, photojournalism, programming, psychology, publications, publishing, reading, religion, religious studies, remedial study skills, research skills, SAT preparation, science, senior seminar, social sciences, social studies, Spanish, speech, stock market, study skills, technical drawing, technology, theater, theater arts, theology, typing, video film production, vocational-technical courses, Web site design, wilderness education, woodworking, word processing, writing, writing, yearbook classes. Computer network features include wireless campus network, Internet filtering or blocking technology. Student e-mail accounts and computer access in designated common areas are available to students. Students grades are available online. The school has a published electronic and media policy.
Contact Ms. Lisa Asher. 925-934-4964. E-mail: lasher@cccss.org. Web site: www.cccss.org

CONVENT OF THE SACRED HEART

1177 King Street
Greenwich, Connecticut 06831

Head of School: Mrs. Pamela Juan Hayes

General Information Girls' day and distance learning college-preparatory, arts, religious studies, and technology school, affiliated with Roman Catholic Church. Grades PS–12. Distance learning grades 9–12. Founded: 1848. Setting: suburban. Nearest major city is New York, NY. 118-acre campus. 10 buildings on campus. Approved or accredited by Network of Sacred Heart Schools, New England Association of Schools and Colleges, and Connecticut Department of Education. Member of National Association of Independent Schools and Secondary School Admission Test Board. Endowment: $22.8 million. Total enrollment: 776. Upper school average class size: 13. Upper school faculty-student ratio: 1:7. There are 163 required school days per year for Upper School students. Upper School students typically attend 5 days per week. The average school day consists of 7 hours and 15 minutes.
Upper School Student Profile Grade 6: 76 students (76 girls); Grade 7: 72 students (72 girls); Grade 8: 74 students (74 girls); Grade 9: 77 students (77 girls); Grade 10: 78 students (78 girls); Grade 11: 63 students (63 girls); Grade 12: 82 students (82 girls). 70% of students are Roman Catholic.
Faculty School total: 122. In upper school: 12 men, 38 women; 45 have advanced degrees.
Subjects Offered 20th century world history, advanced biology, advanced chemistry, advanced math, Advanced Placement courses, advanced studio art-AP, algebra, American literature, American literature-AP, Arabic, biology, biology-AP, broadcast journalism, calculus, calculus-AP, Catholic belief and practice, chemistry, chemistry-AP, Chinese, choir, choral music, Christian and Hebrew scripture, Christian education, Christian ethics, Christianity, college counseling, community service, comparative government and politics-AP, concert bell choir, design, drama, drawing, English language and composition-AP, English literature, English literature and composition-AP, environmental science-AP, ethics, European history, European history-AP, fine arts, French, French language-AP, geometry, health, honors algebra, honors geometry, honors U.S. history, HTML design, instrumental music, journalism, Latin, literary magazine, photography, physical education, physics, physics-AP, pre-calculus, SAT/ACT preparation, Spanish, Spanish language-AP, Spanish literature-AP, statistics, theology, trigonometry, U.S. history, U.S. history-AP, world cultures, world literature.
Graduation Requirements Arts and fine arts (art, music, dance, drama), electives, English, foreign language, mathematics, physical education (includes health), religion (includes Bible studies and theology), science, social studies (includes history). Community service is required.
Special Academic Programs 17 Advanced Placement exams for which test preparation is offered; honors section; independent study; term-away projects; study at local college for college credit; domestic exchange program (with Network of Sacred Heart Schools); study abroad; academic accommodation for the gifted and the artistically talented.
College Admission Counseling 61 students graduated in 2012; all went to college, including College of the Holy Cross; Columbia University; Dartmouth College; Villanova University; Wake Forest University; Yale University.
Student Life Upper grades have uniform requirement, student council, honor system. Discipline rests primarily with faculty. Attendance at religious services is required.
Summer Programs Enrichment programs offered; session focuses on Enrichment; held on campus; accepts girls; not open to students from other schools. 2013 schedule: June to June.
Tuition and Aid Day student tuition: $34,500. Tuition installment plan (Sallie May Payment Plan). Need-based scholarship grants available. In 2012–13, 23% of upper-school students received aid. Total amount of financial aid awarded in 2012–13: $1,679,200.
Admissions Traditional secondary-level entrance grade is 9. ISEE or SSAT required. Deadline for receipt of application materials: February 1. Application fee required: $50. On-campus interview required.
Athletics Interscholastic: basketball (girls), cooperative games (g), crew (g), cross-country running (g), dance (g), diving (g), field hockey (g), fitness (g), golf (g), jogging (g), lacrosse (g), physical fitness (g), running (g), soccer (g), softball (g), squash (g), swimming and diving (g), tennis (g), volleyball (g); intramural: equestrian sports (g), fitness (g), independent competitive sports (g), physical training (g), strength & conditioning (g). 4 PE instructors, 34 coaches, 1 athletic trainer.
Computers Computers are regularly used in all academic classes. Computer network features include on-campus library services, online commercial services, Internet access, wireless campus network, Internet filtering or blocking technology, course

selection online; grades online; CSH is a member of the Online School for Girls, laptops mandatory for students in grades 6 to 12. Campus intranet, student e-mail accounts, and computer access in designated common areas are available to students. The school has a published electronic and media policy.

Contact Mrs. Catherine Cullinane, Director of Admission. 203-532-3534. Fax: 203-532-3301. E-mail: admission@cshgreenwich.org. Web site: www.cshgreenwich.org

See Display on this page and Close-Up on page 564.

CONVENT OF THE SACRED HEART

1 East 91st Street
New York, New York 10128-0689

Head of School: Dr. Joseph J. Ciancaglini

General Information Girls' day college-preparatory, arts, religious studies, bilingual studies, and technology school, affiliated with Roman Catholic Church. Grades PK–12. Founded: 1881. Setting: urban. 2 buildings on campus. Approved or accredited by Network of Sacred Heart Schools, New York State Association of Independent Schools, and New York Department of Education. Member of National Association of Independent Schools and Secondary School Admission Test Board. Endowment: $33.8 million. Total enrollment: 698. Upper school average class size: 14. Upper school faculty-student ratio: 1:10.

Upper School Student Profile Grade 9: 56 students (56 girls); Grade 10: 57 students (57 girls); Grade 11: 45 students (45 girls); Grade 12: 50 students (50 girls). 65% of students are Roman Catholic.

Faculty School total: 110. In upper school: 10 men, 30 women; 38 have advanced degrees.

Subjects Offered Advanced studio art-AP, algebra, American history, American literature, art, audio visual/media, biology, biology-AP, calculus, calculus-AP, campus ministry, ceramics, chemistry, chemistry-AP, chorus, computer applications, computer multimedia, creative writing, dance, desktop publishing, digital photography, drama, earth science, East European studies, English, English literature, English literature-AP, environmental science, ethics, European history, expository writing, film history, fine arts, finite math, forensics, French, French-AP, functions, geography, geometry, government/civics, handbells, health, history, journalism, Latin, madrigals, mathematics, model United Nations, multicultural literature, multimedia design, music, musical theater, performing arts, photography, physical education, physical science, physics, physics-AP, portfolio art, pottery, pre-calculus, religion, science, science research, social studies, Spanish, Spanish-AP, speech, statistics, statistics-AP, theater, theology, trigonometry, U.S. history-AP, visual arts, women's literature, world history, world issues, world literature, world religions, writing.

Graduation Requirements Arts and fine arts (art, music, dance, drama), computer science, English, foreign language, mathematics, physical education (includes health), religion (includes Bible studies and theology), science, social studies (includes history).

Special Academic Programs 18 Advanced Placement exams for which test preparation is offered; honors section; independent study; term-away projects; domestic exchange program (with Network of Sacred Heart Schools); study abroad.

College Admission Counseling 48 students graduated in 2012; all went to college, including Boston College; Georgetown University; Lehigh University; New York University; The George Washington University; University of Pennsylvania.

Student Life Upper grades have uniform requirement, student council. Discipline rests primarily with faculty. Attendance at religious services is required.

Summer Programs Sports, art/fine arts, computer instruction programs offered; session focuses on visual and performing arts; held on campus; accepts boys and girls; open to students from other schools. 200 students usually enrolled. 2013 schedule: June 30 to July 25. Application deadline: April 15.

Tuition and Aid Day student tuition: $39,265. Tuition installment plan (monthly payment plans). Need-based scholarship grants available. In 2012–13, 37% of upper-school students received aid. Total amount of financial aid awarded in 2012–13: $1,800,000.

Admissions Traditional secondary-level entrance grade is 9. For fall 2012, 200 students applied for upper-level admission, 35 were accepted, 16 enrolled. ERB or ISEE required. Deadline for receipt of application materials: December 1. Application fee required: $65. On-campus interview required.

Athletics Interscholastic: basketball, cross-country running, indoor track & field, lacrosse, soccer, softball, swimming and diving, tennis, track and field, volleyball, winter (indoor) track; intramural: aerobics/dance, aquatics, ballet, basketball, dance, fitness, gymnastics, jogging, physical training, roller blading, running, soccer, softball, swimming and diving, tennis, volleyball, weight lifting, weight training. 8 PE instructors, 8 coaches, 1 athletic trainer.

Computers Computers are regularly used in all academic classes. Computer network features include on-campus library services, online commercial services, Internet access, wireless campus network, Internet filtering or blocking technology. Campus intranet, student e-mail accounts, and computer access in designated common areas are available to students. The school has a published electronic and media policy.

Contact Amanda Rosenthal, Admissions Office Coordinator. 212-722-4745 Ext. 105. Fax: 212-996-1784. E-mail: arosenthal@cshnyc.org. Web site: www.cshnyc.org

COPENHAGEN INTERNATIONAL SCHOOL

Hellerupvej 22
2900 Hellerup, Denmark

Head of School: Walter Plotkin

General Information Coeducational day college-preparatory school. Grades 6–12. Founded: 1963. Setting: suburban. Nearest major city is Copenhagen, Denmark. 1-hectare campus. 2 buildings on campus. Approved or accredited by New England Association of Schools and Colleges. Member of European Council of International Schools. Language of instruction: English. Total enrollment: 602. Upper school average class size: 12. Upper school faculty-student ratio: 1:7. There are 185 required school days per year for Upper School students. Upper School students typically attend 5 days per week. The average school day consists of 7 hours and 10 minutes.

Upper School Student Profile Grade 6: 41 students (22 boys, 19 girls); Grade 7: 46 students (19 boys, 27 girls); Grade 8: 39 students (20 boys, 19 girls); Grade 9: 44 students (21 boys, 23 girls); Grade 10: 44 students (21 boys, 23 girls); Grade 11: 54 students (31 boys, 23 girls); Grade 12: 40 students (21 boys, 19 girls).

Faculty School total: 90. In upper school: 27 men, 23 women; 35 have advanced degrees.

Subjects Offered Anthropology, art, biology, chemistry, computer programming, Danish, English, English literature, ESL, European history, French, German, history, International Baccalaureate courses, mathematics, music, physics, science, social sciences, social studies, theory of knowledge.

Special Academic Programs International Baccalaureate program; special instructional classes for students with mild learning disabilities and dyslexia; ESL (4 students enrolled).

College Admission Counseling 47 students graduated in 2011; 40 went to college, including Harvard University; The University of North Carolina at Chapel Hill; Vanderbilt University. Other: 7 had other specific plans.

Student Life Upper grades have student council, honor system. Discipline rests equally with students and faculty.

Tuition and Aid Day student tuition: 114,000 Danish kroner. Tuition installment plan (monthly payment plans, individually arranged payment plans). Need-based scholarship grants available. In 2011–12, 15% of upper-school students received aid. Total amount of financial aid awarded in 2011–12: 4,000,000 Danish kroner.

Admissions Traditional secondary-level entrance grade is 11. For fall 2011, 59 students applied for upper-level admission, 57 were accepted, 56 enrolled. English for Non-native Speakers, math and English placement tests and writing sample required. Deadline for receipt of application materials: none. Application fee required: 25,000 Danish kroner. On-campus interview required.

Athletics Interscholastic: basketball (boys, girls), scooter football (b,g), soccer (b,g), softball (b,g), swimming and diving (b,g). 3 PE instructors, 3 coaches.

Computers Computers are regularly used in English, geography, history, humanities, information technology, lab/keyboard, library, mathematics, media arts, programming classes. Computer network features include on-campus library services, online commercial services, Internet access, wireless campus network, Internet filtering or blocking technology. Student e-mail accounts are available to students.

Contact Thomas Martin Nielsen, Admissions Officer. 45-39-46-33-00 Ext. 315. Fax: 45-39-61-22-30. E-mail: admission@cis.dk. Web site: www.cis-edu.dk

COPPER CANYON ACADEMY

Rimrock, Arizona
See Special Needs Schools section.

COTTER SCHOOLS

1115 West Broadway
Winona, Minnesota 55987-1399

Head of School: Sr. Judith Schaefer, OP

General Information Coeducational boarding and day college-preparatory, general academic, arts, religious studies, technology, and ESL school, affiliated with Roman Catholic Church. Boarding grades 9–12, day grades 7–12. Founded: 1911. Setting: small town. Nearest major city is Minneapolis. Students are housed in single-sex by floor dormitories. 75-acre campus. 7 buildings on campus. Approved or accredited by Midwest Association of Boarding Schools, National Catholic Education Association, North Central Association of Colleges and Schools, The Association of Boarding Schools, and Minnesota Department of Education. Endowment: $15 million. Total enrollment: 380. Upper school average class size: 18. Upper school faculty-student ratio: 1:11. There are 176 required school days per year for Upper School students. Upper School students typically attend 5 days per week. The average school day consists of 5 hours and 55 minutes.

Upper School Student Profile Grade 9: 58 students (31 boys, 27 girls); Grade 10: 88 students (46 boys, 42 girls); Grade 11: 78 students (40 boys, 38 girls); Grade 12: 74 students (41 boys, 33 girls). 31% of students are boarding students. 65% are state residents. 4 states are represented in upper school student body. 30% are international students. International students from China, Japan, Mexico, Republic of Korea, Taiwan, and Viet Nam; 7 other countries represented in student body. 66% of students are Roman Catholic.

Faculty School total: 38. In upper school: 18 men, 20 women; 32 have advanced degrees; 3 reside on campus.

Subjects Offered Algebra, American history, anatomy, art, band, Bible, biology, calculus, calculus-AP, campus ministry, chemistry, chorus, Christian and Hebrew scripture, Christian ethics, community service, computer science, death and loss, economics, English, environmental science, ESL, German, health, Hebrew scripture, honors English, learning lab, linear algebra, literature and composition-AP, math analysis, mathematics, media, painting, physical education, physical science, physics, psychology, science, Spanish, statistics, U.S. history, U.S. history-AP, visual arts, world geography, world religions.

Graduation Requirements English, foreign language, mathematics, performing arts, physical education (includes health), religion (includes Bible studies and theology), science, social studies (includes history), visual arts, 80 hours of community service.

Special Academic Programs Honors section; accelerated programs; independent study; term-away projects; study at local college for college credit; study abroad; academic accommodation for the gifted, the musically talented, and the artistically talented; remedial reading and/or remedial writing; remedial math; programs in English, mathematics for dyslexic students; ESL (25 students enrolled).

College Admission Counseling 80 students graduated in 2012; 78 went to college, including Saint John's University; Saint Mary's University of Minnesota; University of Illinois at Urbana–Champaign; University of Minnesota, Twin Cities Campus; University of St. Thomas; University of Wisconsin–Madison. Other: 1 went to work, 1 entered military service. Median composite ACT: 24. 50% scored over 26 on composite ACT.

Student Life Upper grades have specified standards of dress, student council. Discipline rests primarily with faculty. Attendance at religious services is required.

Summer Programs Remediation, enrichment, advancement, sports, art/fine arts programs offered; held on campus; accepts boys and girls; open to students from other schools. 150 students usually enrolled. 2013 schedule: June 5 to July 7.

Tuition and Aid Day student tuition: $6075; 5-day tuition and room/board: $24,850; 7-day tuition and room/board: $30,700. Tuition installment plan (monthly payment plans, individually arranged payment plans). Tuition reduction for siblings, merit scholarship grants, need-based scholarship grants available. In 2012–13, 60% of upper-school students received aid.

Admissions Traditional secondary-level entrance grade is 9. For fall 2012, 78 students applied for upper-level admission, 56 were accepted, 42 enrolled. SLEP for foreign students or TOEFL required. Deadline for receipt of application materials: none. Application fee required: $50. Interview required.

Athletics Interscholastic: aerobics/dance (girls), baseball (b), basketball (b,g), cheering (g), cross-country running (b,g), dance (g), dance team (g), danceline (g), football (b), golf (b,g), gymnastics (g), hockey (b,g), ice hockey (b,g), skiing (cross-country) (b,g), soccer (b,g), softball (g), swimming and diving (b,g), tennis (b,g), track and field (b,g), volleyball (g), weight lifting (b,g), weight training (b,g), wrestling (b); intramural: basketball (b,g), indoor soccer (b), skiing (downhill) (b,g), snowboarding (b,g), yoga (b,g); coed interscholastic: weight lifting, weight training; coed intramural: badminton, basketball, canoeing/kayaking, indoor soccer, skiing (downhill), snowboarding, yoga. 2 PE instructors, 66 coaches, 1 athletic trainer.

Computers Computers are regularly used in art, freshman foundations, graphic arts, graphic design, introduction to technology, journalism, photography, technology, video film production classes. Computer network features include on-campus library services, Internet access, wireless campus network, Internet filtering or blocking technology. Campus intranet, student e-mail accounts, and computer access in designated common areas are available to students. Students grades are available online. The school has a published electronic and media policy.

Contact Mr. Will Gibson, Director of Admissions and Resident Life. 507-453-5403. Fax: 507-453-5013. E-mail: wgibson@cotterschools.org. Web site: www.cotterschools.org

THE COUNTRY DAY SCHOOL

13415 Dufferin Street
King City, Ontario L7B 1K5, Canada

Head of School: Mr. John Liggett

General Information Coeducational day college-preparatory, arts, business, and technology school. Grades JK–12. Founded: 1972. Setting: rural. Nearest major city is Toronto, Canada. 100-acre campus. 2 buildings on campus. Approved or accredited by Canadian Association of Independent Schools, Canadian Educational Standards Institute, Conference of Independent Schools of Ontario, and Ontario Department of Education. Affiliate member of National Association of Independent Schools. Language of instruction: English. Total enrollment: 720. Upper school average class size: 17. Upper school faculty-student ratio: 1:9. Upper School students typically attend 5 days per week. The average school day consists of 6 hours.

Upper School Student Profile Grade 9: 80 students (40 boys, 40 girls); Grade 10: 80 students (40 boys, 40 girls); Grade 11: 80 students (40 boys, 40 girls); Grade 12: 80 students (40 boys, 40 girls).

Faculty School total: 81. In upper school: 28 men, 20 women.

Subjects Offered Advanced chemistry, advanced computer applications, advanced math, algebra, American history, anatomy and physiology, ancient history, ancient/medieval philosophy, art and culture, art history, athletics, band, biology, business studies, Canadian geography, Canadian history, Canadian literature, career education, career/college preparation, choir, comparative politics, computer programming, creative writing, English, environmental geography, European history, French, government/civics, history, languages, mathematics, modern Western civilization, performing arts, philosophy, physical education, physics, politics, science, society, world history.
Graduation Requirements Ministry Grade 10 Literacy Test (Government of Ontario).
Special Academic Programs Advanced Placement exam preparation; study abroad.
College Admission Counseling 79 students graduated in 2012; all went to college, including McGill University; McMaster University; Queen's University at Kingston; The University of Western Ontario; University of Toronto; Wilfrid Laurier University.
Student Life Upper grades have uniform requirement, student council, honor system. Discipline rests primarily with faculty.
Summer Programs Advancement, sports, art/fine arts programs offered; session focuses on advancement; held both on and off campus; held at Costa Rica, England, and Galapagos Islands; accepts boys and girls; open to students from other schools. 20 students usually enrolled. 2013 schedule: July 2 to July 31. Application deadline: March 1.
Tuition and Aid Day student tuition: CAN$23,850. Bursaries available.
Admissions Traditional secondary-level entrance grade is 9. For fall 2012, 97 students applied for upper-level admission, 58 were accepted, 37 enrolled. CAT 5 or SSAT required. Deadline for receipt of application materials: none. Application fee required: CAN$125. On-campus interview required.
Athletics Interscholastic: baseball (girls), basketball (b,g), cross-country running (b,g), golf (b,g), hockey (b,g), ice hockey (b,g), rugby (b,g), running (b,g), soccer (b,g), softball (b,g), tennis (b,g), track and field (b,g), volleyball (b,g); intramural: badminton (b,g), basketball (b,g), bowling (b,g), ice hockey (b), ice skating (b,g), physical fitness (b,g), skiing (downhill) (b,g), snowboarding (b,g), soccer (b,g), softball (b,g), volleyball (b,g); coed interscholastic: skiing (cross-country); coed intramural: curling, Frisbee, nordic skiing, physical fitness, physical training, rock climbing, strength & conditioning, swimming and diving, table tennis, weight training, yoga. 5 PE instructors.
Computers Computers are regularly used in accounting, business, career education, English, geography, history, mathematics, media, music, writing, yearbook classes. Computer network features include on-campus library services, Internet access, wireless campus network, Internet filtering or blocking technology, access to online library resources from home, access to homework online via Blackboard Software. Campus intranet is available to students.
Contact Mr. David Huckvale, Director of Admission. 905-833-1220. Fax: 905-833-1350. E-mail: admissions@cds.on.ca. Web site: www.cds.on.ca/

COUNTRY DAY SCHOOL OF THE SACRED HEART

480 Bryn Mawr Avenue
Bryn Mawr, Pennsylvania 19010

Head of School: Sr. Matthew Anita MacDonald, SSJ

General Information Girls' day college-preparatory, arts, religious studies, and technology school, affiliated with Roman Catholic Church. Grades PK–12. Founded: 1865. Setting: suburban. Nearest major city is Philadelphia. 16-acre campus. 3 buildings on campus. Approved or accredited by Middle States Association of Colleges and Schools, Network of Sacred Heart Schools, and Pennsylvania Department of Education. Member of National Association of Independent Schools. Total enrollment: 307. Upper school average class size: 15. Upper school faculty-student ratio: 1:8. There are 180 required school days per year for Upper School students. The average school day consists of 7 hours.
Upper School Student Profile Grade 9: 41 students (41 girls); Grade 10: 48 students (48 girls); Grade 11: 40 students (40 girls); Grade 12: 36 students (36 girls). 75% of students are Roman Catholic.
Faculty School total: 44. In upper school: 4 men, 30 women; 21 have advanced degrees.
Subjects Offered Algebra, American history, American history-AP, American literature, art, arts, Bible studies, biology, calculus, chemistry, composition, computer science, economics, English, English literature, environmental science, ethics, European history, film, fine arts, French, geometry, government/civics, health, Latin, mathematics, media studies, physical education, physics, pre-calculus, religion, science, social sciences, social studies, Spanish, trigonometry, word processing, world history, world literature.
Graduation Requirements Arts and fine arts (art, music, dance, drama), English, foreign language, mathematics, physical education (includes health), religion (includes Bible studies and theology), science, social studies (includes history), two weeks of senior independent study with a working professional, 25 hours of community service per year.
Special Academic Programs 7 Advanced Placement exams for which test preparation is offered; honors section; independent study; term-away projects; study at local college for college credit; domestic exchange program (with Network of Sacred Heart Schools); study abroad; academic accommodation for the musically talented.
College Admission Counseling 49 students graduated in 2012; all went to college, including Drexel University; Fordham University; Georgetown University; Saint Joseph's University; The Catholic University of America; University of Pittsburgh. Mean SAT critical reading: 620, mean SAT math: 580, mean SAT writing: 650. 45% scored over 600 on SAT critical reading, 40% scored over 600 on SAT math, 50% scored over 600 on SAT writing.
Student Life Upper grades have uniform requirement, student council. Discipline rests equally with students and faculty. Attendance at religious services is required.
Tuition and Aid Day student tuition: $16,400. Tuition installment plan (SMART Tuition Payment Plan). Tuition reduction for siblings, merit scholarship grants, need-based scholarship grants available. In 2012–13, 72% of upper-school students received aid; total upper-school merit-scholarship money awarded: $415,900. Total amount of financial aid awarded in 2012–13: $424,500.
Admissions Traditional secondary-level entrance grade is 9. For fall 2012, 90 students applied for upper-level admission, 65 were accepted, 32 enrolled. High School Placement Test required. Deadline for receipt of application materials: none. Application fee required: $35. Interview required.
Athletics Interscholastic: basketball, crew, cross-country running, field hockey, golf, lacrosse, softball, tennis, track and field, volleyball; intramural: fitness walking. 2 PE instructors, 12 coaches, 1 athletic trainer.
Computers Computers are regularly used in English, foreign language, history, mathematics, science, technology classes. Computer network features include on-campus library services, online commercial services, Internet access, wireless campus network. Student e-mail accounts are available to students. Students grades are available online. The school has a published electronic and media policy.
Contact Mrs. Mary Lee FitzPatrick, Director of Admissions. 610-527-3915 Ext. 214. Fax: 610-527-0942. E-mail: mfitzpatrick@cdssh.org. Web site: www.cdssh.org

COVENANT CANADIAN REFORMED SCHOOL

3030 TWP Road 615A
PO Box 67
Neerlandia, Alberta T0G 1R0, Canada

Head of School: Mr. James Meinen

General Information Coeducational day college-preparatory, general academic, business, religious studies, and technology school, affiliated with Reformed Church. Grades K–12. Founded: 1977. Setting: rural. Nearest major city is Edmonton, Canada. 5-acre campus. 2 buildings on campus. Approved or accredited by Association of Independent Schools and Colleges of Alberta and Alberta Department of Education. Language of instruction: English. Total enrollment: 188. Upper school average class size: 10. Upper school faculty-student ratio: 1:10. There are 167 required school days per year for Upper School students. Upper School students typically attend 4 days per week. The average school day consists of 6 hours and 10 minutes.
Upper School Student Profile Grade 10: 9 students (6 boys, 3 girls); Grade 11: 11 students (2 boys, 9 girls); Grade 12: 8 students (3 boys, 5 girls). 100% of students are Reformed.
Faculty School total: 16. In upper school: 6 men, 3 women.
Subjects Offered Accounting, architectural drawing, Bible studies, biology, Canadian geography, career and personal planning, career technology, chemistry, child development, Christian education, computer information systems, computer skills, computer studies, consumer law, desktop publishing, digital photography, drama, drawing and design, early childhood, electronic publishing, English, ESL, French as a second language, geology, health education, history, HTML design, information processing, intro to computers, introduction to technology, keyboarding, mathematics, physical education, physics, prayer/spirituality, religious studies, science, sewing, social studies, theology and the arts, Web site design, Western religions, work experience, world geography, world religions, yearbook.
Graduation Requirements Must pass religious studies courses offered in grades 10, 11, and 12 for the years the student attended.
Special Academic Programs Independent study; remedial reading and/or remedial writing; remedial math.
College Admission Counseling 7 students graduated in 2011; 4 went to college, including University of Alberta; University of Calgary; University of Lethbridge. Other: 3 went to work.
Student Life Upper grades have specified standards of dress, student council. Discipline rests primarily with faculty.
Tuition and Aid Day student tuition: CAN$6000. Tuition installment plan (monthly payment plans, individually arranged payment plans). Tuition rates per family available.
Admissions Traditional secondary-level entrance grade is 10. Achievement tests or CTBS or ERB required. Deadline for receipt of application materials: none. No application fee required. Interview required.
Athletics Interscholastic: track and field (boys, girls), volleyball (b,g); coed intramural: badminton, ball hockey, baseball, basketball, flag football, floor hockey, football, Frisbee, hockey, ice hockey, indoor hockey, indoor soccer, lacrosse, soccer, softball, volleyball. 4 PE instructors, 6 coaches.
Computers Computers are regularly used in all classes. Computer network features include on-campus library services, Internet access, Internet filtering or blocking tech-

nology. Computer access in designated common areas is available to students. The school has a published electronic and media policy.

Contact Mr. James Meinen, Principal. 780-674-4774. Fax: 780-401-3295. E-mail: principal@covenantschool.ca. Web site:

COVINGTON CATHOLIC HIGH SCHOOL

1600 Dixie Highway
Park Hills, Kentucky 41011

Head of School: Mr. Robert Rowe

General Information Boys' day college-preparatory, arts, business, religious studies, bilingual studies, and technology school, affiliated with Roman Catholic Church. Grades 9–12. Founded: 1925. Setting: suburban. Nearest major city is Cincinnati, OH. 4 buildings on campus. Approved or accredited by Southern Association of Colleges and Schools and Kentucky Department of Education. Total enrollment: 502. Upper school faculty-student ratio: 1:14. Upper School students typically attend 5 days per week. The average school day consists of 6 hours and 40 minutes.

Upper School Student Profile Grade 9: 133 students (133 boys); Grade 10: 126 students (126 boys); Grade 11: 120 students (120 boys); Grade 12: 115 students (115 boys).

Faculty School total: 37. In upper school: 31 men, 5 women; 21 have advanced degrees.

Subjects Offered Algebra, American government, American history, American history-AP, anatomy and physiology, art, biology, business law, calculus-AP, career exploration, chemistry, chemistry-AP, chorus, church history, computer applications, computer programming, computer science, computer science-AP, computer-aided design, creative writing, current events, drama, economics, English, film, geometry, German, graphic design, health, journalism, Latin, modern European history, music appreciation, orchestra, personal finance, physical education, physical science, physics, pre-algebra, pre-calculus, probability and statistics, psychology, psychology-AP, reading, scripture, social justice, sociology, Spanish, Spanish-AP, speech, theology, Web site design, wood processing, world civilizations, world geography, world history-AP, writing workshop.

Graduation Requirements Arts and fine arts (art, music, dance, drama), electives, English, mathematics, physical education (includes health), science, social studies (includes history), community service requirement.

Special Academic Programs 10 Advanced Placement exams for which test preparation is offered; honors section; study at local college for college credit.

College Admission Counseling 127 students graduated in 2011; 124 went to college, including Bellarmine University; Miami University; University of Dayton; University of Kentucky; University of Louisville; Xavier University. Other: 2 went to work, 1 entered military service. Mean composite ACT: 25.

Student Life Upper grades have specified standards of dress, student council. Discipline rests primarily with faculty. Attendance at religious services is required.

Tuition and Aid Day student tuition: $5985–$6590. Tuition installment plan (monthly payment plans). Tuition reduction for siblings, merit scholarship grants, paying campus jobs available.

Admissions Traditional secondary-level entrance grade is 9. High School Placement Test required. Deadline for receipt of application materials: none. No application fee required.

Athletics Interscholastic: baseball, basketball, bowling, football, golf, soccer, swimming and diving, tennis, track and field; intramural: basketball, bicycling, fishing, Frisbee, lacrosse, skiing (downhill), ultimate Frisbee, whiffle ball. 1 PE instructor.

Computers Computers are regularly used in all academic classes. Computer network features include Internet access, wireless campus network, Internet filtering or blocking technology. Student e-mail accounts are available to students. Students grades are available online.

Contact Mr. Tony Barczak, Freshman/Sophomore Counselor. 859-491-2247 Ext. 2257. Fax: 859-448-2242. E-mail: tbarczak@covcath.org. Web site: www.covcath.org/

CRANBROOK SCHOOLS

39221 Woodward Avenue
PO Box 801
Bloomfield Hills, Michigan 48303-0801

General Information Coeducational boarding and day college-preparatory and arts school. Boarding grades 9–12, day grades PK–12. Founded: 1922. Setting: suburban. Nearest major city is Detroit. Students are housed in single-sex dormitories. 315-acre campus. 10 buildings on campus. Approved or accredited by Independent Schools Association of the Central States, Midwest Association of Boarding Schools, The Association of Boarding Schools, The College Board, and Michigan Department of Education. Member of National Association of Independent Schools and Secondary School Admission Test Board. Endowment: $218 million. Total enrollment: 1,636. Upper school average class size: 16. Upper school faculty-student ratio: 1:8. There are 164 required school days per year for Upper School students. Upper School students typically attend 5 days per week. The average school day consists of 5 hours and 15 minutes.

See Display below and Close-Up on page 566.

CRAWFORD ADVENTIST ACADEMY

531 Finch Avenue West
Willowdale, Ontario M2R 3X2, Canada

Head of School: Mr. Norman Brown

General Information Coeducational day college-preparatory, arts, business, religious studies, bilingual studies, and technology school, affiliated with Seventh-day Adventist Church. Grades JK–12. Founded: 1954. Setting: urban. Nearest major city is Toronto, Canada. 5-acre campus. 1 building on campus. Approved or accredited by National Council for Private School Accreditation, Ontario Ministry of Education, and Ontario Department of Education. Language of instruction: English. Total enrollment: 354. Upper school average class size: 25. Upper school faculty-student ratio: 1:16. There are 196 required school days per year for Upper School students. Upper School students typically attend 5 days per week. The average school day consists of 7 hours.

Upper School Student Profile Grade 9: 32 students (18 boys, 14 girls); Grade 10: 35 students (16 boys, 19 girls); Grade 11: 39 students (19 boys, 20 girls); Grade 12: 43 students (21 boys, 22 girls). 90% of students are Seventh-day Adventists.

Faculty School total: 18. In upper school: 11 men, 6 women; 11 have advanced degrees.

Subjects Offered Advanced computer applications, band, Bible, biology, business, business technology, calculus, Canadian geography, Canadian history, chemistry, choir, civics, community service, computer applications, computer information systems, drama, dramatic arts, earth and space science, English, English composition, French, French as a second language, geography, guidance, independent study, information technology, marketing, mathematics, physical education, physics, religion, science, writing, yearbook.

Special Academic Programs 3 Advanced Placement exams for which test preparation is offered; remedial reading and/or remedial writing; programs in English for dyslexic students; ESL.

College Admission Counseling 32 students graduated in 2012; 4 went to college, including Andrews University; Oakwood University; Ryerson University; University of Toronto; University of Waterloo; York University. Other: 28 entered a postgraduate year. Median composite ACT: 20. 22% scored over 26 on composite ACT.

Student Life Upper grades have uniform requirement, student council, honor system. Discipline rests primarily with faculty. Attendance at religious services is required.

Tuition and Aid Day student tuition: CAN$8500. Guaranteed tuition plan. Tuition installment plan (monthly payment plans, individually arranged payment plans). Tuition reduction for siblings, need-based scholarship grants, paying campus jobs available. In 2012–13, 20% of upper-school students received aid. Total amount of financial aid awarded in 2012–13: CAN$35,000.

Admissions Traditional secondary-level entrance grade is 11. For fall 2012, 15 students applied for upper-level admission, 10 were accepted, 10 enrolled. CAT, CAT 2, CCAT, CTBS (or similar from their school) or Learn Aid Aptitude Test required. Deadline for receipt of application materials: none. Application fee required: CAN$50. On-campus interview required.

Athletics Interscholastic: basketball (boys, girls), weight lifting (b,g); intramural: basketball (b,g); coed interscholastic: cooperative games, outdoor recreation; coed intramural: basketball, flag football, floor hockey, indoor soccer, outdoor education, outdoor recreation, physical fitness, physical training, snowboarding, soccer, volleyball. 1 PE instructor, 1 coach.

Computers Computers are regularly used in accounting, business, computer applications, yearbook classes. Computer network features include Internet access, wireless campus network, Internet filtering or blocking technology. Student e-mail accounts and computer access in designated common areas are available to students. Students grades are available online. The school has a published electronic and media policy.

Contact Mr. Andrew Mark Thomas, Principal, 9-12. 416-633-0090 Ext. 223. Fax: 416-633-0467. E-mail: athomas@caasda.com. Web site:

CRESPI CARMELITE HIGH SCHOOL

5031 Alonzo Avenue
Encino, California 91316-3699

Head of School: Fr. Paul Henson, OCARM

General Information Boys' day college-preparatory, arts, and religious studies school, affiliated with Roman Catholic Church. Grades 9–12. Founded: 1959. Setting: suburban. Nearest major city is Los Angeles. 3-acre campus. 3 buildings on campus. Approved or accredited by Western Association of Schools and Colleges, Western Catholic Education Association, and California Department of Education. Total enrollment: 565. Upper school average class size: 23. Upper school faculty-student ratio: 1:14. There are 182 required school days per year for Upper School students. Upper School students typically attend 5 days per week. The average school day consists of 6 hours.

Upper School Student Profile Grade 9: 155 students (155 boys); Grade 10: 134 students (134 boys); Grade 11: 149 students (149 boys); Grade 12: 128 students (128 boys). 59% of students are Roman Catholic.

Faculty School total: 37. In upper school: 33 men, 4 women; 29 have advanced degrees.

Subjects Offered Advanced Placement courses, advanced studio art-AP, algebra, American history-AP, American literature-AP, anatomy and physiology, Ancient Greek, ancient world history, applied music, ASB Leadership, astronomy, athletic training, audio visual/media, baseball, Basic programming, basketball, biology, biology-AP, British literature, British literature-AP, business mathematics, calculus, calculus-AP, chemistry, Christian scripture, church history, classical Greek literature, computer graphics, constitutional law, drama performance, driver education, earth science, economics and history, economics-AP, English composition, English literature and composition-AP, environmental science, ethics, European history-AP, film studies, French language-AP, French-AP, geometry, golf, government, government and politics-AP, Greek, Greek culture, health, history of the Catholic Church, Holocaust, Holocaust studies, honors English, honors geometry, international studies, journalism, language and composition, Latin-AP, law, media arts, men's studies, model United Nations, moral and social development, music appreciation, music composition, photography, physical science, physics-AP, prayer/spirituality, pre-calculus, probability and statistics, psychology, Shakespeare, social justice, Spanish, Spanish language-AP, Spanish literature-AP, Spanish-AP, speech, sports, sports conditioning, statistics-AP, student government, student publications, U.S. history, U.S. history-AP, video film production, Vietnam War, visual arts, Web site design, weight training, Western civilization, Western religions, world cultures, world geography, world religions, yearbook, zoology.

Graduation Requirements Arts and fine arts (art, music, dance, drama), English, foreign language, mathematics, physical education (includes health), religion (includes Bible studies and theology), science, social sciences, social studies (includes history). Community service is required.

Special Academic Programs 13 Advanced Placement exams for which test preparation is offered; honors section.

College Admission Counseling 129 students graduated in 2012; 122 went to college, including California Polytechnic State University, San Luis Obispo; California State University, Northridge; University of California, Los Angeles; University of California, Santa Barbara; University of San Diego. Other: 1 entered military service, 6 had other specific plans. Mean SAT critical reading: 530, mean SAT math: 540, mean SAT writing: 534.

Student Life Upper grades have specified standards of dress, student council, honor system. Discipline rests primarily with faculty. Attendance at religious services is required.

Summer Programs Remediation, enrichment, advancement, sports, art/fine arts programs offered; session focuses on remediation and/or enrichment in math, science, language, and social studies; held on campus; accepts boys and girls; open to students from other schools. 250 students usually enrolled. 2013 schedule: June 24 to July 26. Application deadline: June 21.

Tuition and Aid Day student tuition: $12,000. Tuition installment plan (SMART Tuition Payment Plan, Tuition Management Systems Plan). Merit scholarship grants, need-based scholarship grants available. In 2012–13, 32% of upper-school students received aid; total upper-school merit-scholarship money awarded: $48,600.

Admissions Traditional secondary-level entrance grade is 9. For fall 2012, 295 students applied for upper-level admission, 286 were accepted, 173 enrolled. High School Placement Test required. Deadline for receipt of application materials: January 25. Application fee required: $125. On-campus interview required.

Athletics Interscholastic: aquatics, baseball, basketball, cross-country running, football, golf, lacrosse, soccer, swimming and diving, tennis, track and field, volleyball, water polo, wrestling; intramural: basketball, floor hockey, Frisbee, table tennis. 4 PE instructors, 2 athletic trainers.

Computers Computers are regularly used in business applications, business studies, economics, English, foreign language, history, mathematics, media production, science, video film production, yearbook classes. Computer network features include on-campus library services, online commercial services, Internet access, wireless campus network. Students grades are available online. The school has a published electronic and media policy.

Contact Ms. Michele Enich, Assistant Admissions Director. 818-345-1672 Ext. 329. Fax: 818-705-0209. E-mail: menich@crespi.org. Web site: www.crespi.org

CROSSPOINT ACADEMY

4012 Chico Way NW
Bremerton, Washington 98312-1397

Head of School: Mr. Nick Sweeney

General Information Coeducational day college-preparatory, arts, religious studies, and technology school, affiliated with Christian faith. Grades K–12. Founded: 1991. Setting: small town. Nearest major city is Silverdale. 7-acre campus. 7 buildings on campus. Approved or accredited by Washington Department of Education. Member of National Association of Independent Schools. Total enrollment: 253. Upper school average class size: 24. Upper school faculty-student ratio: 1:8. There are 171 required school days per year for Upper School students. Upper School students typically attend 5 days per week. The average school day consists of 6 hours and 45 minutes.

Upper School Student Profile 70% of students are Christian faith.

Faculty School total: 30. In upper school: 6 men, 10 women; 8 have advanced degrees.

Subjects Offered Algebra, American literature, art, band, Bible, biology, calculus-AP, chemistry, choir, computer animation, computers, creative writing, desktop publishing, digital photography, drama, drama performance, earth science, English, geography, geometry, health, introduction to theater, keyboarding, leadership, life science, life skills, physical fitness, physical science, physics, practical living, pre-algebra, pre-calculus, programming, religion, science, senior project, Spanish, speech, student government, technology, U.S. government and politics-AP, U.S. history, U.S. history-AP, video, vocal ensemble, Washington State and Northwest History, weight training, world history, world literature, world religions, world wide web design, yearbook.

Graduation Requirements Arts and fine arts (art, music, dance, drama), Bible, computer science, English, foreign language, mathematics, physical education (includes health), practical living, science, social studies (includes history), speech.

Special Academic Programs Honors section; study at local college for college credit.

College Admission Counseling 23 students graduated in 2012; all went to college, including Baylor University; Central Washington University; Georgia Institute of Technology; Olympic College; Seattle Pacific University; University of Washington. Mean SAT critical reading: 578, mean SAT math: 569, mean SAT writing: 557, mean combined SAT: 1704, mean composite ACT: 24. 36% scored over 600 on SAT critical reading, 24% scored over 600 on SAT math, 36% scored over 600 on SAT writing, 36% scored over 1800 on combined SAT, 14% scored over 26 on composite ACT.

Student Life Upper grades have specified standards of dress, student council, honor system. Discipline rests primarily with faculty. Attendance at religious services is required.

Tuition and Aid Day student tuition: $9430. Tuition installment plan (monthly payment plans, prepayment discount plan, active military discount, Pastor, church employee, and Christian school employee discounts). Tuition reduction for siblings, need-based scholarship grants available. In 2012–13, 28% of upper-school students received aid. Total amount of financial aid awarded in 2012–13: $171,000.

Admissions Traditional secondary-level entrance grade is 9. Comprehensive educational evaluation required. Deadline for receipt of application materials: none. Application fee required: $50. Interview required.

Athletics Interscholastic: basketball (boys, girls), cross-country running (b,g), golf (b), soccer (b,g), softball (g), track and field (b,g), volleyball (g), weight training (b,g). 2 PE instructors, 8 coaches.

Computers Computers are regularly used in animation, computer applications, desktop publishing, digital applications, graphics, keyboarding, photography, publications, technology, video film production, Web site design, yearbook classes. Computer network features include Internet access, wireless campus network, Internet filtering or blocking technology. Student e-mail accounts are available to students. Students grades are available online. The school has a published electronic and media policy.

Contact Ms. Sherri M. Miller, Admissions and Marketing Coordinator. 360-377-7700 Ext. 5004. Fax: 360-377-7795. E-mail: sherri.miller@gatewaychristianschools.org. Web site: www.gatewaychristianschools.org/

CROSSROADS SCHOOL FOR ARTS & SCIENCES

1714 21st Street
Santa Monica, California 90404-3917

Head of School: Mr. Bob Riddle

General Information Coeducational day college-preparatory, arts, and technology school. Grades K–12. Founded: 1971. Setting: urban. Nearest major city is Los Angeles. 3-acre campus. 19 buildings on campus. Approved or accredited by Western Association of Schools and Colleges and California Department of Education. Member of National Association of Independent Schools. Endowment: $15.6 million. Total enrollment: 1,154. Upper school average class size: 15. Upper school faculty-student ratio: 1:11. There are 164 required school days per year for Upper School students. Upper School students typically attend 5 days per week. The average school day consists of 7 hours.

Upper School Student Profile Grade 9: 132 students (66 boys, 66 girls); Grade 10: 121 students (63 boys, 58 girls); Grade 11: 123 students (55 boys, 68 girls); Grade 12: 130 students (60 boys, 70 girls).

Faculty School total: 160. In upper school: 39 men, 42 women; 40 have advanced degrees.

Subjects Offered Algebra, American history, American studies, art history, biology, calculus, ceramics, chemistry, community service, computer programming, computer science, creative writing, critical studies in film, cultural arts, dance, earth and space science, English, environmental education, film studies, French, gender issues, geometry, graphic design, great books, Greek, human development, Japanese, jazz ensemble, jazz theory, journalism, Latin, marine biology, marine ecology, music appreciation, music theory, orchestra, photography, physical education, physics, physiology, pre-calculus, sculpture, Spanish, statistics, studio art, theater, trigonometry, video film production, world civilizations, yoga.

Graduation Requirements Arts and fine arts (art, music, dance, drama), English, foreign language, human development, mathematics, physical education (includes health), science, social studies (includes history). Community service is required.

Special Academic Programs Honors section; term-away projects; academic accommodation for the gifted, the musically talented, and the artistically talented.

College Admission Counseling 118 students graduated in 2012; 115 went to college, including Bard College; Columbia University; New York University; University of California, Santa Cruz; University of Michigan; University of Southern California. Mean SAT critical reading: 656, mean SAT math: 622, mean SAT writing: 675, mean combined SAT: 1953, mean composite ACT: 27.

Student Life Upper grades have student council. Discipline rests primarily with faculty.

Summer Programs Remediation, enrichment, advancement, sports, art/fine arts, computer instruction programs offered; session focuses on enrichment, academics, day care; held on campus; accepts boys and girls; open to students from other schools. 1,000 students usually enrolled. 2013 schedule: June 24 to August 6. Application deadline: none.

Tuition and Aid Day student tuition: $31,900. Tuition installment plan (individually arranged payment plans, In-House only - 2 payment plan for full pay students and 10, payment plan exclusively for financial aid students only). Merit scholarship grants, need-based scholarship grants, tuition reduction fund, need-based financial aid, merit-based scholarships for Elizabeth Mandell Music Institute only available. In 2012–13, 44% of upper-school students received aid; total upper-school merit-scholarship money awarded: $50,000. Total amount of financial aid awarded in 2012–13: $3,114,960.

Admissions Traditional secondary-level entrance grade is 9. For fall 2012, 178 students applied for upper-level admission, 73 were accepted, 48 enrolled. ISEE or PSAT required. Deadline for receipt of application materials: December 5. Application fee required: $130. On-campus interview required.

Athletics Interscholastic: baseball (boys), basketball (b,g), cross-country running (b,g), soccer (b,g), softball (g), tennis (b,g), track and field (b,g), volleyball (b,g); coed interscholastic: flag football, golf, swimming and diving; coed intramural: canoeing/kayaking, climbing, hiking/backpacking, kayaking, outdoor activities, outdoor education, rock climbing, ropes courses, snowshoeing, table tennis. 10 PE instructors, 29 coaches, 1 athletic trainer.

Computers Computers are regularly used in college planning, creative writing, foreign language, graphic design, journalism, Latin, mathematics, music, newspaper, programming, science classes. Computer network features include on-campus library services, online commercial services, Internet access, wireless campus network. Student e-mail accounts and computer access in designated common areas are available to students. Students grades are available online. The school has a published electronic and media policy.

Contact Celia Lee, Director of Admissions. 310-829-7391 Ext. 104. Fax: 310-392-9011. E-mail: clee@xrds.org. Web site: www.xrds.org

CRYSTAL SPRINGS UPLANDS SCHOOL

400 Uplands Drive
Hillsborough, California 94010

Head of School: Ms. Amy Richards

General Information Coeducational day college-preparatory school. Grades 6–12. Founded: 1952. Setting: suburban. Nearest major city is San Francisco. 10-acre campus. 4 buildings on campus. Approved or accredited by California Association of Independent Schools, Western Association of Schools and Colleges, and California Department of Education. Member of National Association of Independent Schools and Secondary School Admission Test Board. Endowment: $15 million. Total enrollment: 350. Upper school average class size: 14. Upper school faculty-student ratio: 1:9. Upper School students typically attend 5 days per week.

Faculty School total: 44. In upper school: 18 men, 26 women; 24 have advanced degrees.

Subjects Offered Acting, advanced computer applications, algebra, American history, American literature, art, art-AP, astronomy, biology, calculus, ceramics, chamber groups, chemistry, chorus, comparative cultures, computer math, computer programming, computer science, concert bell choir, creative writing, dance, dance performance, drama, English, English literature, ensembles, European history, fine arts, French, geometry, graphic design, health, history, mathematics, multicultural literature, music, photography, physical education, physics, poetry, post-calculus, pre-calculus, science, Shakespeare, Spanish, statistics, theater, video film production, wellness, world history, world literature, writing.

Graduation Requirements Arts and fine arts (art, music, dance, drama), English, foreign language, history, mathematics, physical education (includes health), science, senior project.

Special Academic Programs Honors section; term-away projects; domestic exchange program; study abroad.

College Admission Counseling 61 students graduated in 2012; all went to college, including Stanford University; University of California, Los Angeles; University of California, San Diego; University of Pennsylvania; University of Southern California. Mean SAT critical reading: 674, mean SAT math: 703, mean SAT writing: 688, mean combined SAT: 2067, mean composite ACT: 29.

Student Life Upper grades have specified standards of dress, student council, honor system. Discipline rests equally with students and faculty.

Tuition and Aid Day student tuition: $35,700. Tuition installment plan (Insured Tuition Payment Plan, monthly payment plans, Tuition Management Systems Plan). Need-based scholarship grants available. In 2012–13, 22% of upper-school students received aid. Total amount of financial aid awarded in 2012–13: $2,200,000.

Admissions Traditional secondary-level entrance grade is 9. ISEE or SSAT required. Deadline for receipt of application materials: January 17. Application fee required: $85. On-campus interview required.

Athletics Interscholastic: baseball (boys), basketball (b,g), cross-country running (b,g), football (b), soccer (b,g), softball (g), swimming and diving (b,g), tennis (b,g), track and field (b,g), volleyball (g); coed interscholastic: badminton, dance, golf, running, strength & conditioning; coed intramural: dance, fitness, Frisbee, hiking/backpacking, outdoors, rock climbing, table tennis, ultimate Frisbee, weight lifting, weight training. 3 PE instructors, 14 coaches, 1 athletic trainer.

Computers Computers are regularly used in all academic classes. Computer network features include on-campus library services, online commercial services, Internet access, wireless campus network, Internet filtering or blocking technology. Campus intranet, student e-mail accounts, and computer access in designated common areas are available to students. Students grades are available online. The school has a published electronic and media policy.

Contact Aaron Whitmore, Director of Admission. 650-342-4175 Ext. 1517. Fax: 650-342-7611. E-mail: admission@csus.org. Web site: www.csus.org

THE CULVER ACADEMIES

1300 Academy Road
Culver, Indiana 46511

Head of School: Mr. John N. Buxton

General Information Coeducational boarding and day college-preparatory and arts school. Grades 9–PG. Founded: 1894. Setting: small town. Nearest major city is South Bend. Students are housed in single-sex dormitories. 1,700-acre campus. 38 buildings on campus. Approved or accredited by Independent Schools Association of the Central States, North Central Association of Colleges and Schools, and Indiana Department of Education. Member of National Association of Independent Schools and Secondary School Admission Test Board. Endowment: $285 million. Total enrollment: 802. Upper school average class size: 13. Upper school faculty-student ratio: 1:9. There are 185 required school days per year for Upper School students. Upper School students typically attend 5 days per week. The average school day consists of 6 hours.

Upper School Student Profile Grade 9: 150 students (86 boys, 64 girls); Grade 10: 215 students (123 boys, 92 girls); Grade 11: 225 students (118 boys, 107 girls); Grade 12: 212 students (121 boys, 91 girls). 92% of students are boarding students. 30% are state residents. 41 states are represented in upper school student body. 32% are international students. International students from Canada, China, Mexico, Republic of Korea, Saudi Arabia, and Taiwan; 26 other countries represented in student body.

Faculty School total: 97. In upper school: 53 men, 44 women; 83 have advanced degrees; 16 reside on campus.

Subjects Offered Acting, advanced math, African-American history, algebra, American government, American history, American history-AP, American literature, anatomy, anatomy and physiology, art, art history, arts, ballet, Basic programming, biology, biology-AP, calculus, calculus-AP, career/college preparation, ceramics, character education, chemistry, chemistry-AP, Chinese, choir, church history, college admission preparation, college placement, college planning, comparative government and politics-AP, comparative religion, computer math, computer programming, computer science, computer science-AP, dance, drama, dramatic arts, driver education, economics, economics-AP, English, English language-AP, English literature, entrepreneurship, equestrian sports, equine science, equitation, ESL, ethics and responsibility, European history, film studies, fine arts, fitness, French, French-AP, geology, geometry, German, German literature, German-AP, global studies, government, government-AP, government/civics, health and wellness, honors English, honors geometry, humanities, instrumental music, integrated mathematics, integrated science, jazz band, Latin, Latin-AP, leadership, library research, macro/microeconomics-AP, mathematics, mentorship program, music, music theory, music theory-AP, photography, physical education, physics, physics-AP, physiology, piano, play production, pottery, pre-algebra, pre-calculus, science, science research, Shakespeare, social studies, Spanish, Spanish language-AP, Spanish-AP, speech, statistics-AP, strings, theater, trigonometry, U.S. government and politics-AP, U.S. history-AP, world history, world religions.

Graduation Requirements Arts and fine arts (art, music, dance, drama), English, foreign language, health education, history, leadership, mathematics, science, senior community service project.

Special Academic Programs 21 Advanced Placement exams for which test preparation is offered; honors section; academic accommodation for the gifted, the musically talented, and the artistically talented; ESL (24 students enrolled).

College Admission Counseling 204 students graduated in 2011; 197 went to college, including Indiana University Bloomington; Purdue University; Southern Methodist University; The University of North Carolina at Chapel Hill; Vanderbilt University. Other: 1 entered military service, 4 entered a postgraduate year, 2 had other specific plans.

Student Life Upper grades have uniform requirement, student council, honor system. Discipline rests equally with students and faculty. Attendance at religious services is required.

Tuition and Aid Day student tuition: $28,000; 7-day tuition and room/board: $38,000. Guaranteed tuition plan. Tuition installment plan (Key Tuition Payment Plan). Merit scholarship grants, need-based scholarship grants available. In 2011–12, 46% of upper-school students received aid; total upper-school merit-scholarship money awarded: $7,850,000. Total amount of financial aid awarded in 2011–12: $8,900,000.

Admissions Traditional secondary-level entrance grade is 9. For fall 2011, 2,500 students applied for upper-level admission, 528 were accepted, 261 enrolled. SSAT or TOEFL required. Deadline for receipt of application materials: June 1. Application fee required: $30. Interview required.

Athletics Interscholastic: baseball (boys), basketball (b,g), cheering (g), crew (b,g), cross-country running (b,g), diving (b,g), equestrian sports (b,g), fencing (b,g), football (b), golf (b,g), hockey (b,g), horseback riding (b,g), ice hockey (b,g), indoor hockey (b,g), indoor track & field (b,g), lacrosse (b,g), polo (b,g), rugby (b,g), soccer (b,g), softball (g), swimming and diving (b,g), tennis (b,g), track and field (b,g), volleyball (g), winter (indoor) track (b,g), wrestling (b,g); intramural: aerobics (b,g), basketball (b,g), dance (b,g), dance squad (g), dance team (g), danceline (g), drill team (b,g), flag football (b,g), ice hockey (b,g), indoor soccer (b,g), marksmanship (b,g), modern dance (b,g), paint ball (b,g), racquetball (b,g), soccer (b,g); coed interscholastic: dressage, sailing, trap and skeet; coed intramural: aerobics, aerobics/dance, aerobics/Nautilus, alpine skiing, aquatics, archery, backpacking, badminton, ballet, broomball, climbing, combined training, cooperative games, cross-country running, figure skating, fitness, fitness walking, Frisbee, handball, hiking/backpacking, horseback riding, ice skating, independent competitive sports, indoor track, indoor track & field, jogging, life saving, Nautilus, outdoor activities, outdoor adventure, outdoor education, outdoor recreation, outdoor skills, outdoors, physical fitness, physical training, power lifting, project adventure, ropes courses, rowing, running, scuba diving, skeet shooting, skiing (downhill), snowboarding, strength & conditioning, swimming and diving, table tennis, tai chi, ultimate Frisbee, volleyball, walking, wall climbing, weight lifting, weight training, wilderness, yoga. 8 PE instructors, 4 athletic trainers.

Computers Computers are regularly used in all classes. Computer network features include on-campus library services, online commercial services, Internet access, wireless campus network, Internet filtering or blocking technology, each student is issued a laptop. Campus intranet, student e-mail accounts, and computer access in designated common areas are available to students. Students grades are available online. The school has a published electronic and media policy.

Contact Mr. Michael Turnbull, Director of Admissions. 574-842-7100. Fax: 574-842-8066. E-mail: turnbul@culver.org. Web site: culver.org

CURREY INGRAM ACADEMY

6544 Murray Lane
Brentwood, Tennessee 37027

Head of School: Ms. Kathleen G. Rayburn

General Information Coeducational day college-preparatory, arts, technology, ethics and character education, and service learning school; primarily serves students with learning disabilities, individuals with Attention Deficit Disorder, dyslexic students, non-verbal learning disabilities, and speech and language disabilities. Grades K–12. Founded: 1968. Setting: suburban. Nearest major city is Nashville. 83-acre campus. 2 buildings on campus. Approved or accredited by Council of Accreditation and School Improvement, Southern Association of Colleges and Schools, Southern Association of Independent Schools, and Tennessee Department of Education. Member of National Association of Independent Schools. Total enrollment: 299. Upper school average class size: 7. Upper school faculty-student ratio: 1:4. There are 175 required school days per year for Upper School students. Upper School students typically attend 5 days per week. The average school day consists of 7 hours and 30 minutes.

Faculty School total: 120.

Subjects Offered Algebra, American government, art, basic language skills, biology, British literature, character education, chemistry, cinematography, college admission preparation, college awareness, college counseling, college planning, community service, digital music, digital photography, drama performance, earth science, economics, electives, English composition, English literature, environmental science, ethics and responsibility, government, health, history, integrated technology fundamentals, learning strategies, life skills, literature, modern world history, music, newspaper, physical education, physics, pragmatics, pre-calculus, reading/study skills, social studies, sports, studio art, technology, video film production, vocal music, writing, writing workshop, yearbook.

Graduation Requirements Arts and fine arts (art, music, dance, drama), electives, English, ethics, foreign language, mathematics, physical education (includes health), science, social studies (includes history), students who need remediation in reading/writing take reading/writing workshop instead of foreign language, seniors must complete Service Learning credit plus 30 hours of community service.

Special Academic Programs Honors section; independent study; academic accommodation for the gifted, the musically talented, and the artistically talented; remedial reading and/or remedial writing; programs in English, mathematics, general development for dyslexic students.

College Admission Counseling 17 students graduated in 2012; all went to college, including Abilene Christian University.

Student Life Upper grades have uniform requirement, student council, honor system. Discipline rests primarily with faculty.

Summer Programs Enrichment, art/fine arts programs offered; session focuses on camp for theatre and music; held on campus; accepts boys and girls; open to students from other schools. 2013 schedule: June.

Tuition and Aid Day student tuition: $33,070–$36,690. Tuition installment plan (Insured Tuition Payment Plan, monthly payment plans). Need-based scholarship grants available. In 2012–13, 35% of upper-school students received aid. Total amount of financial aid awarded in 2012–13: $1,500,000.

Admissions Traditional secondary-level entrance grade is 9. Psychoeducational evaluation required. Deadline for receipt of application materials: none. Application fee required: $250. Interview required.

Athletics Interscholastic: basketball (boys, girls), cheering (g), cross-country running (b,g), football (b), golf (b,g), volleyball (g); intramural: fitness (b,g); coed interscholastic: soccer.

Computers Computers are regularly used in all academic classes. Computer network features include on-campus library services, Internet access, wireless campus network, Internet filtering or blocking technology, iPods for instructional use in classrooms, 1:1 laptop program, assistive technology. Students grades are available online. The school has a published electronic and media policy.

Contact Ms. Amber Mogg, Director of Admission. 615-507-3173 Ext. 244. Fax: 615-507-3170. E-mail: amber.mogg@curreyingram.org. Web site: www.curreyingram.org

CUSHING ACADEMY

39 School Street
PO Box 8000
Ashburnham, Massachusetts 01430-8000

Head of School: Dr. James Tracy

General Information Coeducational boarding and day college-preparatory, arts, and technology school. Grades 9–PG. Founded: 1865. Setting: small town. Nearest major city is Boston. Students are housed in single-sex dormitories. 162-acre campus. 31 buildings on campus. Approved or accredited by Association of Independent Schools in New England, New England Association of Schools and Colleges, and Massachusetts Department of Education. Member of National Association of Independent Schools and Secondary School Admission Test Board. Endowment: $29.2 million. Total enrollment: 445. Upper school average class size: 12. Upper school faculty-student ratio: 1:8. There are 152 required school days per year for Upper School students. Upper School students typically attend 5 days per week. The average school day consists of 7 hours.

Upper School Student Profile Grade 9: 65 students (41 boys, 24 girls); Grade 10: 107 students (67 boys, 40 girls); Grade 11: 140 students (71 boys, 69 girls); Grade 12: 110 students (70 boys, 40 girls); Postgraduate: 23 students (20 boys, 3 girls). 85% of students are boarding students. 31% are state residents. 28 states are represented in upper school student body. 30% are international students. International students from China, Germany, Mexico, Republic of Korea, Saudi Arabia, and Taiwan; 30 other countries represented in student body.

Faculty School total: 64. In upper school: 27 men, 37 women; 37 have advanced degrees; 47 reside on campus.

Subjects Offered Advanced biology, advanced math, Advanced Placement courses, aerobics, algebra, American government, American history, American literature, American literature-AP, anatomy, anatomy and physiology, architectural drawing, art, art history, athletic training, bioethics, biology, biology-AP, calculus, calculus-AP, career education internship, chemistry, chemistry-AP, Chinese, chorus, Civil War, community service, computer programming, computer science, creative arts, creative drama, creative writing, dance, developmental language skills, digital photography, discrete mathematics, drafting, drama, drawing, driver education, earth and space science, ecology, ecology, environmental systems, economics, economics and history, economics-AP, English, English literature, environmental science, ESL, ethics, European history, expository writing, fine arts, French, geometry, government/civics, grammar, graphic arts, health, health and wellness, history, honors algebra, honors English, honors geometry, honors U.S. history, honors world history, Latin, Latin-AP, Mandarin, marine biology, mathematics, mechanical drawing, music, music history, music theory, musical theater, photography, physics, physiology, pre-calculus, probability and statistics, psychology, SAT preparation, science, social studies, sociology, Spanish, Spanish-AP, speech, stagecraft, statistics-AP, student government, technology, The 20th Century, theater, theater history, trigonometry, U.S. government and politics-AP, U.S. history, United Nations and international issues, Vietnam War, visual arts, vocal music, wind instruments, world history, world literature, World-Wide-Web publishing, writing.

Graduation Requirements English, foreign language, health and wellness, mathematics, science, social studies (includes history).

Special Academic Programs 14 Advanced Placement exams for which test preparation is offered; honors section; independent study; term-away projects; academic accommodation for the gifted, the musically talented, and the artistically talented; remedial reading and/or remedial writing; remedial math; programs in English, mathematics, general development for dyslexic students; ESL (75 students enrolled).

College Admission Counseling 150 students graduated in 2011; 147 went to college, including Boston University; Northeastern University; Purdue University; Suffolk University; Syracuse University; University of New Hampshire. Other: 1 entered military service, 2 had other specific plans.

Student Life Upper grades have specified standards of dress, student council, honor system. Discipline rests primarily with faculty.

Tuition and Aid Day student tuition: $34,900; 7-day tuition and room/board: $49,600. Tuition installment plan (Academic Management Services Plan, monthly payment plans). Merit scholarship grants, need-based scholarship grants available. In 2011–12, 26% of upper-school students received aid; total upper-school merit-scholarship money awarded: $100,000. Total amount of financial aid awarded in 2011–12: $3,200,000.

Admissions Traditional secondary-level entrance grade is 9. For fall 2011, 804 students applied for upper-level admission, 505 were accepted, 185 enrolled. ACT, PSAT, SAT, SLEP, SSAT or TOEFL required. Deadline for receipt of application materials: February 1. Application fee required: $50. Interview required.

Athletics Interscholastic: baseball (boys), basketball (b,g), field hockey (g), football (b), hockey (b,g), ice hockey (b,g), lacrosse (b,g), running (b,g), skiing (downhill) (b,g), soccer (b,g), softball (g), tennis (b,g), track and field (b,g), volleyball (g); intramural: flag football (b); coed interscholastic: alpine skiing, cross-country running, golf, running; coed intramural: aerobics, aerobics/dance, alpine skiing, dance, equestrian sports, figure skating, fitness, horseback riding, ice hockey, ice skating, independent competitive sports, martial arts, modern dance, outdoor adventure, outdoor education, outdoor recreation, outdoor skills, physical fitness, physical training, ropes courses, skiing (downhill), snowboarding, strength & conditioning, wall climbing, weight training. 2 coaches, 2 athletic trainers.

Computers Computers are regularly used in all academic classes. Computer network features include on-campus library services, online commercial services, Internet access, wireless campus network, Internet filtering or blocking technology, CushNet (on-campus network), Cushing-designed iClass interactive tables, Digital Library. Campus intranet, student e-mail accounts, and computer access in designated common areas are available to students. Students grades are available online. The school has a published electronic and media policy.

Contact Mrs. Deborah A. Gustafson, Co-Director of Admissions. 978-827-7300. Fax: 978-827-6253. E-mail: admissions@cushing.org. Web site: www.cushing.org

See Display on next page, Close-Up on page 568, and Summer Program Close-Up on page 704.

DAKAR ACADEMY

Rue des Peres Maristes, #69
Dakar, Senegal

Head of School: Joseph M. Rosa

General Information Coeducational boarding and day college-preparatory and general academic school, affiliated with Christian faith. Boarding grades 6–12, day grades K–12. Founded: 1961. Setting: suburban. Students are housed in single-sex dormitories. 6-acre campus. 5 buildings on campus. Approved or accredited by Association of Christian Schools International. Language of instruction: English. Upper school average class size: 20. Upper school faculty-student ratio: 1:6. There are 174 required school days per year for Upper School students. Upper School students typically attend 5 days per week. The average school day consists of 7 hours and 15 minutes.

Upper School Student Profile Grade 6: 10 students (4 boys, 6 girls); Grade 7: 17 students (8 boys, 9 girls); Grade 8: 20 students (8 boys, 12 girls); Grade 9: 15 students (10 boys, 5 girls); Grade 10: 24 students (12 boys, 12 girls); Grade 11: 28 students (20 boys, 8 girls); Grade 12: 36 students (23 boys, 13 girls). 46% of students are boarding students. 75% of students are Christian faith.

Faculty School total: 36. In upper school: 10 men, 14 women; 11 reside on campus.

Special Academic Programs Advanced Placement exam preparation; honors section; accelerated programs; independent study.

College Admission Counseling 42 students graduated in 2012.

Student Life Upper grades have specified standards of dress, honor system. Discipline rests primarily with faculty. Attendance at religious services is required.

Admissions For fall 2012, 24 students applied for upper-level admission, 21 were accepted, 18 enrolled. Deadline for receipt of application materials: none. Application fee required: $300.

Athletics Interscholastic: basketball (boys, girls), soccer (b,g), softball (b), volleyball (b,g); intramural: basketball (b,g), handball (b,g), soccer (b,g), softball (b), volleyball (b,g); coed interscholastic: softball; coed intramural: ultimate Frisbee.

Contact Office Manager. 221-33 832 0682. Fax: 221-33 832 1721. E-mail: office@dakar-academy.org. Web site: www.dakar-academy.org

DALLAS CHRISTIAN SCHOOL

1515 Republic Parkway
Mesquite, Texas 75150

Head of School: Mr. Chris King

General Information Coeducational day college-preparatory and religious studies school, affiliated with Church of Christ. Grades PK–12. Founded: 1957. Setting: suburban. Nearest major city is Dallas. 60-acre campus. 7 buildings on campus. Approved or accredited by National Christian School Association, Southern Association of Colleges and Schools, and Texas Department of Education. Total enrollment: 585. Upper school average class size: 25. Upper school faculty-student ratio: 1:12. There are 178 required school days per year for Upper School students. Upper School students typically attend 5 days per week. The average school day consists of 7 hours and 15 minutes.

Upper School Student Profile Grade 6: 45 students (20 boys, 25 girls); Grade 7: 43 students (16 boys, 27 girls); Grade 8: 53 students (31 boys, 22 girls); Grade 9: 51

students (29 boys, 22 girls); Grade 10: 51 students (19 boys, 32 girls); Grade 11: 57 students (31 boys, 26 girls); Grade 12: 63 students (43 boys, 20 girls). 36% of students are members of Church of Christ.

Faculty School total: 56. In upper school: 13 men, 17 women; 14 have advanced degrees.

Subjects Offered Algebra, American history, American literature, art, band, Bible studies, biology, calculus, cheerleading, chemistry, chorus, computer math, computer science, creative writing, drama, economics, English, English literature, fine arts, French, geography, geometry, government/civics, health, history, humanities, journalism, mathematics, newspaper, physical education, physics, religion, science, sign language, social studies, Spanish, speech, speech origins of English, theater, world history, world literature, yearbook.

Graduation Requirements Arts and fine arts (art, music, dance, drama), computer science, English, foreign language, mathematics, physical education (includes health), religion (includes Bible studies and theology), science, social studies (includes history), speech origins of English, seniors must take SAT or ACT.

Special Academic Programs Study at local college for college credit.

College Admission Counseling 71 students graduated in 2012; 70 went to college, including Abilene Christian University; Austin College; Baylor University; Dallas Baptist University; Pepperdine University; Texas A&M University.

Student Life Upper grades have uniform requirement, student council, honor system. Discipline rests primarily with faculty. Attendance at religious services is required.

Tuition and Aid Day student tuition: $12,450. Tuition installment plan (FACTS Tuition Payment Plan). Tuition reduction for siblings, need-based scholarship grants available. In 2012–13, 18% of upper-school students received aid. Total amount of financial aid awarded in 2012–13: $180,000.

Admissions ERB IF, ERB Mathematics, ERB Reading and Math and Woodcock-Johnson Revised Achievement Test required. Deadline for receipt of application materials: none. Application fee required: $400. On-campus interview required.

Athletics Interscholastic: baseball (boys), basketball (b,g), cheering (g), cross-country running (b,g), drill team (g), football (b), golf (b,g), soccer (b,g), softball (g), tennis (b,g), track and field (b,g), volleyball (g). 2 PE instructors.

Computers Computers are regularly used in computer applications, newspaper, Web site design, yearbook classes. Computer network features include on-campus library services, Internet access, Internet filtering or blocking technology. Student e-mail accounts are available to students. Students grades are available online.

Contact Mrs. Katie Neuroth, Admissions Assistant. 972-270-5495 Ext. 266. Fax: 972-686-9436. E-mail: kneuroth@dallaschristian.com. Web site: www.dallaschristian.com

THE DALTON SCHOOL

108 East 89th Street
New York, New York 10128-1599

Head of School: Ellen C. Stein

General Information Coeducational day college-preparatory and arts school. Grades K–12. Founded: 1919. Setting: urban. 2 buildings on campus. Approved or accredited by New York State Association of Independent Schools. Member of National Association of Independent Schools and Secondary School Admission Test Board. Endowment: $65 million. Total enrollment: 1,311. Upper school average class size: 15. Upper school faculty-student ratio: 1:7.

Upper School Student Profile Grade 9: 116 students (59 boys, 57 girls); Grade 10: 119 students (61 boys, 58 girls); Grade 11: 117 students (59 boys, 58 girls); Grade 12: 109 students (52 boys, 57 girls).

Faculty School total: 203. In upper school: 60 men, 61 women; 58 have advanced degrees.

Subjects Offered Algebra, American history, American legal systems, American literature, architecture, art, art history, Asian literature, astronomy, biology, calculus, ceramics, chemistry, community service, computer programming, computer science, dance, earth science, ecology, economics, English, English literature, environmental science, ethics, European history, fine arts, French, geometry, government/civics, health, history, Latin, law, mathematics, music, philosophy, photography, physical education, physics, Russian literature, science, social studies, Spanish, theater, trigonometry, world history, world literature.

Graduation Requirements Arts and fine arts (art, music, dance, drama), computer science, English, foreign language, history, mathematics, physical education (includes health), science. Community service is required.

Special Academic Programs Advanced Placement exam preparation; honors section; independent study; study at local college for college credit.

College Admission Counseling 100 students graduated in 2011; all went to college, including Brown University; Cornell University; Harvard University; The George Washington University; University of Pennsylvania; Yale University. Median SAT critical reading: 690, median SAT math: 680, median SAT writing: 720.

Student Life Upper grades have student council. Discipline rests equally with students and faculty.

Tuition and Aid Day student tuition: $36,970. Tuition installment plan (FACTS Tuition Payment Plan, 2-payment plan). Need-based scholarship grants available. In 2011–12, 24% of upper-school students received aid. Total amount of financial aid awarded in 2011–12: $2,938,600.

Admissions Traditional secondary-level entrance grade is 9. For fall 2011, 394 students applied for upper-level admission, 50 were accepted, 30 enrolled. ISEE or SSAT required. Deadline for receipt of application materials: November 11. Application fee required: $60. On-campus interview required.

Athletics Interscholastic: baseball (boys), basketball (b,g), lacrosse (b,g), soccer (b,g), softball (g), tennis (b,g), track and field (b,g), wrestling (b); intramural: baseball (b), basketball (b,g); coed interscholastic: cross-country running, football, swimming and diving, volleyball; coed intramural: cheering, dance, football, modern dance, ultimate Frisbee. 10 PE instructors, 14 coaches, 1 athletic trainer.

Computers Computers are regularly used in English, foreign language, mathematics, science classes. Computer network features include on-campus library services, online commercial services, Internet access, wireless campus network, Internet filtering or blocking technology. Campus intranet, student e-mail accounts, and computer access in designated common areas are available to students.

Contact Jacqueline Katz, Associate Director, Middle and High School Admissions. 212-423-5262. Fax: 212-423-5259. E-mail: admissionsmshs@dalton.org. Web site: www.dalton.org

DAMIEN HIGH SCHOOL

2280 Damien Avenue
La Verne, California 91750

Head of School: Rev. Peadar Cronin

General Information Boys' day college-preparatory school, affiliated with Roman Catholic Church. Grades 9–12. Founded: 1959. Setting: suburban. Nearest major city is Los Angeles. 28-acre campus. 9 buildings on campus. Approved or accredited by Western Association of Schools and Colleges, Western Catholic Education Association, and California Department of Education. Member of National Association of Independent Schools. Endowment: $2 million. Total enrollment: 922. Upper school average class size: 22. Upper school faculty-student ratio: 1:20. There are 180 required school days per year for Upper School students. Upper School students typically attend 5 days per week. The average school day consists of 7 hours.

Upper School Student Profile Grade 9: 251 students (251 boys); Grade 10: 235 students (235 boys); Grade 11: 216 students (216 boys); Grade 12: 220 students (220 boys). 75% of students are Roman Catholic.

Faculty School total: 60. In upper school: 50 men, 10 women; 55 have advanced degrees.

Subjects Offered Advanced Placement courses, algebra, American history, art history, biology, chemistry, choir, computer applications, debate, economics, English composition, English literature, French, German, government, health, history, mathematics, music, physics, pre-calculus, Spanish, theater arts, theology, U.S. government and politics, U.S. history, visual arts, Western civilization, world history.

Special Academic Programs 18 Advanced Placement exams for which test preparation is offered; honors section; accelerated programs; independent study; study at local college for college credit; study abroad; remedial reading and/or remedial writing; remedial math.

College Admission Counseling 234 students graduated in 2012; 230 went to college, including California State University, Fullerton; California State University, Monterey Bay. Other: 4 entered military service. Median SAT critical reading: 480, median SAT math: 540. 40% scored over 600 on SAT critical reading, 50% scored over 600 on SAT math.

Student Life Upper grades have uniform requirement, student council. Discipline rests primarily with faculty.

Summer Programs Remediation, enrichment, advancement, sports, art/fine arts, computer instruction programs offered; session focuses on academics; held on campus; accepts boys and girls; open to students from other schools. 600 students usually enrolled. 2013 schedule: June 18 to July 20. Application deadline: June 1.

Tuition and Aid Day student tuition: $7600. Guaranteed tuition plan. Tuition installment plan (The Tuition Plan, FACTS Tuition Payment Plan). Tuition reduction for siblings, merit scholarship grants, need-based scholarship grants available. In 2012–13, 25% of upper-school students received aid; total upper-school merit-scholarship money awarded: $600,000. Total amount of financial aid awarded in 2012–13: $600,000.

Admissions Traditional secondary-level entrance grade is 9. For fall 2012, 305 students applied for upper-level admission, 305 were accepted, 252 enrolled. Scholastic Testing Service required. Deadline for receipt of application materials: none. Application fee required: $75. Interview required.

Athletics Interscholastic: baseball, basketball, billiards, bowling, cross-country running, diving, field hockey, fishing, football, golf, hockey, ice hockey, in-line hockey, indoor hockey, lacrosse, physical fitness, racquetball, roller hockey, running, soccer, surfing, swimming and diving, tennis, track and field, water polo, weight lifting, wrestling. 1 PE instructor, 30 coaches, 2 athletic trainers.

Computers Computer network features include on-campus library services, online commercial services, Internet access. Students grades are available online. The school has a published electronic and media policy.

Contact Mrs. Christina Provenzano, Admissions Coordinator. 909-596-1946 Ext. 247. Fax: 909-596-6112. E-mail: christina@damien-hs.edu. Web site: www.damien-hs.edu

DANA HALL SCHOOL

45 Dana Road
Wellesley, Massachusetts 02482

Head of School: Ms. Caroline Erisman, JD

General Information Girls' boarding and day college-preparatory and Forum-Life Skills school. Boarding grades 9–12, day grades 6–12. Founded: 1881. Setting: suburban. Nearest major city is Boston. Students are housed in single-sex dormitories. 55-acre campus. 34 buildings on campus. Approved or accredited by Association of Independent Schools in New England, Massachusetts Department of Education, New England Association of Schools and Colleges, The Association of Boarding Schools, and Massachusetts Department of Education. Member of National Association of Independent Schools and Secondary School Admission Test Board. Endowment: $29 million. Total enrollment: 475. Upper school average class size: 12. Upper school faculty-student ratio: 1:9. There are 180 required school days per year for Upper School students. Upper School students typically attend 5 days per week. The average school day consists of 7 hours and 30 minutes.

Upper School Student Profile Grade 9: 84 students (84 girls); Grade 10: 86 students (86 girls); Grade 11: 98 students (98 girls); Grade 12: 88 students (88 girls). 40% of students are boarding students. 90% are state residents. 15 states are represented in upper school student body. 25% are international students. International students from China, Hong Kong, Mexico, Republic of Korea, Taiwan, and Thailand; 14 other countries represented in student body.

Faculty School total: 64. In upper school: 18 men, 33 women; 39 have advanced degrees; 36 reside on campus.

Subjects Offered 20th century history, acting, African history, African studies, algebra, American history, American literature, architecture, art, art history, art-AP, astronomy, biology, calculus, ceramics, chemistry, chorus, community service, computer programming, computer science, computer science-AP, creative writing, dance, dance performance, drama, drama workshop, drawing, East Asian history, economics, electives, English, English composition, English language and composition-AP, English/composition-AP, European history, European history-AP, fitness, French, French language-AP, French literature-AP, freshman foundations, geometry, government, government/civics, health, journalism, Latin, Latin American history, Latin-AP, leadership education training, library, Mandarin, marine biology, mathematics-AP, Middle Eastern history, music, music composition, music performance, music theory, photography, physics, physics-AP, public speaking, Russian studies, Spanish, Spanish-AP, statistics-AP, trigonometry, U.S. history-AP, U.S. literature, weight training, Western civilization, women in the classical world.

Graduation Requirements American history, area studies, computer science, English, fitness, foreign language, mathematics, performing arts, science, social studies (includes history), visual arts, 20 hours of community service.

Special Academic Programs 17 Advanced Placement exams for which test preparation is offered; honors section; independent study; term-away projects; study abroad.

College Admission Counseling 90 students graduated in 2012; all went to college, including New York University; Syracuse University; Tufts University; Tulane University; University of Richmond; Wellesley College. Mean SAT critical reading: 613, mean SAT math: 639, mean SAT writing: 633, mean combined SAT: 1885, mean composite ACT: 28.

Student Life Upper grades have specified standards of dress, student council, honor system. Discipline rests equally with students and faculty.

Summer Programs Enrichment programs offered; session focuses on leadership training and confidence building for girls entering high school; held on campus; accepts girls; open to students from other schools. 40 students usually enrolled. 2013 schedule: June 23 to June 30. Application deadline: none.

Tuition and Aid Day student tuition: $39,266; 7-day tuition and room/board: $52,131. Tuition installment plan (monthly payment plans, K-12 Family Education Loan, AchieverLoan). Need-based scholarship grants, need-based loans available. In 2012–13, 20% of upper-school students received aid. Total amount of financial aid awarded in 2012–13: $3,395,219.

Admissions Traditional secondary-level entrance grade is 9. For fall 2012, 555 students applied for upper-level admission, 260 were accepted, 116 enrolled. ISEE, SSAT or TOEFL required. Deadline for receipt of application materials: January 15. Application fee required: $50. Interview required.

Athletics Interscholastic: basketball, cross-country running, equestrian sports, fencing, field hockey, golf, horseback riding, ice hockey, lacrosse, modern dance, soccer, softball, squash, swimming and diving, tennis, volleyball; intramural: aerobics, aerobics/dance, aquatics, ballet, crew, dance, equestrian sports, fitness, Frisbee, golf, hiking/backpacking, horseback riding, indoor track, life saving, martial arts, modern dance, Nautilus, outdoor activities, physical fitness, physical training, rock climbing, scuba diving, self defense, skiing (downhill), squash, strength & conditioning, swimming and diving, tennis, ultimate Frisbee, weight lifting, weight training, yoga. 5 PE instructors, 20 coaches, 1 athletic trainer.

Computers Computers are regularly used in art, English, French, history, Latin, mathematics, science, Spanish, Web site design, yearbook classes. Computer network features include on-campus library services, online commercial services, Internet access, wireless campus network, Internet filtering or blocking technology. Campus intranet, student e-mail accounts, and computer access in designated common areas are available to students.

Contact Mrs. Brenda Dowdell, Admission Office Manager. 781-235-3010 Ext. 2531. Fax: 781-239-1383. E-mail: admission@danahall.org. Web site: www.danahall.org

DARLINGTON SCHOOL

1014 Cave Spring Road
Rome, Georgia 30161

Head of School: Thomas C. Whitworth III

General Information Coeducational boarding and day college-preparatory, arts, and technology school. Boarding grades 9–PG, day grades PK–PG. Founded: 1905. Setting: small town. Nearest major city is Atlanta. Students are housed in single-sex dormitories. 500-acre campus. 15 buildings on campus. Approved or accredited by Georgia Independent School Association, Southern Association of Colleges and Schools, Southern Association of Independent Schools, The Association of Boarding Schools, The College Board, and Georgia Department of Education. Member of National Association of Independent Schools and Secondary School Admission Test Board. Endowment: $29.2 million. Total enrollment: 848. Upper school average class size: 13. Upper school faculty-student ratio: 1:13. There are 176 required school days per year for Upper School students. Upper School students typically attend 5 days per week. The average school day consists of 7 hours and 30 minutes.

Upper School Student Profile Grade 9: 98 students (57 boys, 41 girls); Grade 10: 111 students (59 boys, 52 girls); Grade 11: 138 students (78 boys, 60 girls); Grade 12: 130 students (69 boys, 61 girls). 38% of students are boarding students. 72% are state residents. 22 states are represented in upper school student body. 31% are international students. International students from Bahamas, Bermuda, China, Germany, Mexico, and Republic of Korea; 16 other countries represented in student body.

Faculty School total: 98. In upper school: 45 men, 53 women; 47 have advanced degrees; 57 reside on campus.

Subjects Offered Advanced biology, advanced chemistry, Advanced Placement courses, advanced studio art-AP, algebra, ancient world history, art, art history, art history-AP, band, biology, biology-AP, calculus, calculus-AP, chemistry, chemistry-AP, choir, chorus, college counseling, computer programming, computer science, concert choir, creative writing, drama, drawing, economics, economics-AP, English, English language and composition-AP, English language-AP, English literature, English literature-AP, English-AP, ensembles, environmental science, environmental science-AP, ESL, fine arts, French, geometry, government-AP, graphic arts, graphic design, health, honors algebra, honors English, honors geometry, honors world history, humanities, jazz ensemble, journalism, lab science, macro/microeconomics-AP, macroeconomics-AP, modern European history-AP, music, music theory-AP, musical theater, newspaper, personal fitness, physical education, physics, physics-AP, pre-calculus, probability and statistics, psychology-AP, robotics, Spanish, Spanish language-AP, Spanish literature-AP, Spanish-AP, statistics-AP, studio art-AP, trigonometry, U.S. history, U.S. history-AP, video, video film production, vocal ensemble, wind ensemble, world cultures, world history, world history-AP, yearbook.

Graduation Requirements Arts and fine arts (art, music, dance, drama), English, foreign language, information technology, mathematics, physical education (includes health), science, social studies (includes history), community service/servant leadership program, after school activity.

Special Academic Programs 21 Advanced Placement exams for which test preparation is offered; honors section; academic accommodation for the musically talented; ESL (18 students enrolled).

College Admission Counseling 135 students graduated in 2012; all went to college, including Furman University; Georgia Institute of Technology; The University of Alabama; University of Georgia; University of Mississippi; University of Washington. Median SAT critical reading: 547, median SAT math: 574, median SAT writing: 557, median combined SAT: 1678.

Student Life Upper grades have uniform requirement, student council, honor system. Discipline rests equally with students and faculty.

Summer Programs Enrichment, ESL, sports, art/fine arts, computer instruction programs offered; session focuses on academic enrichment and specialized sports camps for all ages; held on campus; accepts boys and girls; open to students from other schools. 3,500 students usually enrolled. 2013 schedule: June 2 to August 5. Application deadline: none.

Tuition and Aid Day student tuition: $18,200; 7-day tuition and room/board: $42,300–$47,300. Tuition installment plan (FACTS Tuition Payment Plan, monthly payment plans, individually arranged payment plans). Merit scholarship grants, need-based scholarship grants available. In 2012–13, 44% of upper-school students received aid; total upper-school merit-scholarship money awarded: $486,600. Total amount of financial aid awarded in 2012–13: $3,405,880.

Admissions Traditional secondary-level entrance grade is 9. For fall 2012, 265 students applied for upper-level admission, 195 were accepted, 113 enrolled. PSAT and SAT for applicants to grade 11 and 12, SSAT or WISC III or TOEFL required. Deadline for receipt of application materials: February 1. Application fee required: $50. Interview required.

Athletics Interscholastic: baseball (boys), basketball (b,g), cheering (g), crew (b,g), cross-country running (b,g), diving (b,g), football (b), golf (b,g), lacrosse (b,g), rowing (b,g), soccer (b,g), softball (g), swimming and diving (b,g), tennis (b,g), track and field (b,g), volleyball (g), wrestling (b); intramural: aerobics/dance (g), aquatics (b,g), basketball (b,g), cheering (g), dance squad (g), fitness (b,g), flag football (b,g), flagball (b,g), running (b,g), tennis (b,g), volleyball (b,g); coed intramural: aerobics, fishing, fly fishing, Frisbee, independent competitive sports, outdoor activities, outdoor education, outdoor recreation, physical fitness, physical training, skeet shooting, soccer, speleology, strength & conditioning, table tennis, ultimate Frisbee, water volleyball, weight lifting, weight training. 2 PE instructors, 11 coaches, 2 athletic trainers.

Computers Computers are regularly used in computer applications, English, foreign language, history, mathematics, science, Web site design classes. Computer network features include on-campus library services, Internet access, wireless campus network, Internet filtering or blocking technology. Campus intranet, student e-mail accounts, and computer access in designated common areas are available to students. Students grades are available online. The school has a published electronic and media policy.

Contact Mrs. Kila McCann, Director of Boarding Admission. 706-236-0447. Fax: 706-232-3600. E-mail: kmccann@darlingtonschool.org. Web site: www.darlingtonschool.org

DARROW SCHOOL

110 Darrow Road
New Lebanon, New York 12125

Head of School: Mrs. Nancy Wolf

General Information Coeducational boarding and day college-preparatory, arts, hands-on learning, and sustainability school. Grades 9–12. Founded: 1932. Setting: rural. Nearest major city is Pittsfield, MA. Students are housed in single-sex dormitories. 365-acre campus. 26 buildings on campus. Approved or accredited by Middle States Association of Colleges and Schools, New York State Association of Independent Schools, The Association of Boarding Schools, and New York Department of Education. Member of National Association of Independent Schools and Secondary School Admission Test Board. Endowment: $2.5 million. Upper school average class size: 9. Upper school faculty-student ratio: 1:4. There are 220 required school days per year for Upper School students. Upper School students typically attend 6 days per week. The average school day consists of 6 hours.

Upper School Student Profile 80% of students are boarding students. 52% are state residents. 13 states are represented in upper school student body. 25% are international students. International students from China, Ghana, Jamaica, Japan, Republic of Korea, and Russian Federation; 5 other countries represented in student body.

Faculty School total: 33. In upper school: 17 men, 16 women; 15 have advanced degrees; 30 reside on campus.

Subjects Offered 3-dimensional art, advanced math, African-American literature, algebra, American literature, art, art history, athletics, biology, calculus, ceramics, chemistry, civil rights, clayworking, computer graphics, creative writing, critical writing, culinary arts, design, digital art, drama, drawing, drawing and design, ecology, economics, English, English literature, ensembles, environmental education, environmental science, environmental studies, ESL, ethics, experiential education, fine arts, French, geometry, health and wellness, history, independent study, Latin American literature, leadership, literature, mathematics, microeconomics, multicultural studies, music appreciation, music theory, oil painting, ornithology, photo shop, photography, physics, play production, poetry, portfolio art, pottery, pre-calculus, reading/study skills, Russian literature, science, social studies, Spanish, Spanish literature, sports, studio art, study skills, theater, U.S. history, Western civilization, women's literature, woodworking, writing, yearbook.

Graduation Requirements Arts, arts and fine arts (art, music, dance, drama), electives, English, foreign language, history, mathematics, physical education (includes health), science.

Special Academic Programs Advanced Placement exam preparation; independent study; term-away projects; academic accommodation for the musically talented and the artistically talented; ESL (10 students enrolled).

College Admission Counseling 30 students graduated in 2012; 29 went to college, including Brandeis University; Clarkson University; Hartwick College; Hobart and William Smith Colleges; Suffolk University; Wheaton College. Other: 1 went to work.

Student Life Upper grades have specified standards of dress, student council. Discipline rests equally with students and faculty.

Summer Programs ESL programs offered; session focuses on ESOL; held on campus; accepts boys and girls; not open to students from other schools. 8 students usually enrolled. 2013 schedule: August 15 to August 30.

Tuition and Aid Day student tuition: $28,300; 7-day tuition and room/board: $49,600. Tuition installment plan (Academic Management Services Plan, SMART Tuition Payment Plan, individually arranged payment plans). Need-based scholarship grants available. In 2012–13, 32% of upper-school students received aid. Total amount of financial aid awarded in 2012–13: $950,000.

Admissions Traditional secondary-level entrance grade is 9. For fall 2012, 170 students applied for upper-level admission, 109 were accepted, 52 enrolled. SLEP for foreign students or TOEFL or SLEP required. Deadline for receipt of application materials: none. Application fee required: $50. On-campus interview required.

Athletics Interscholastic: baseball (boys), basketball (b,g), cross-country running (b,g), soccer (b,g), softball (g), tennis (b,g); coed interscholastic: cross-country running, Frisbee, lacrosse, tennis, ultimate Frisbee; coed intramural: alpine skiing, dance, equestrian sports, fitness, freestyle skiing, hiking/backpacking, horseback riding, outdoor activities, outdoor education, physical fitness, rock climbing, skiing (cross-country), skiing (downhill), snowboarding, telemark skiing, weight lifting, yoga.

Computers Computers are regularly used in graphic design, photography, video film production classes. Computer network features include on-campus library services, Internet access, wireless campus network, Internet filtering or blocking technology. Campus intranet, student e-mail accounts, and computer access in designated common areas are available to students. The school has a published electronic and media policy.

Contact Ms. Jamie Hicks-Furgang, Director of Admission. 518-794-6008. Fax: 518-794-7065. E-mail: hicksj@darrowschool.org. Web site: www.darrowschool.org

DAVIDSON ACADEMY

1414 Old Hickory Boulevard
Nashville, Tennessee 37207-1098

Head of School: Dr. Bill Chaney

General Information Coeducational day college-preparatory, arts, religious studies, technology, and science, mathematics school, affiliated with Christian faith. Grades PK–12. Founded: 1980. Setting: suburban. 67-acre campus. 1 building on campus. Approved or accredited by Association of Christian Schools International, Southern Association of Colleges and Schools, and Tennessee Department of Education. Endowment: $25,000. Upper school average class size: 17. There are 180 required school days per year for Upper School students. Upper School students typically attend 5 days per week.

Upper School Student Profile 99.9% of students are Christian faith.

Subjects Offered 3-dimensional art, ACT preparation, advanced math, Advanced Placement courses, algebra, American government, American history, American history-AP, art, art appreciation, audio visual/media, band, Bible, Bible studies, biology, calculus, calculus-AP, cheerleading, chemistry, choral music, chorus, church history, college admission preparation, college counseling, college placement, composition-AP, computer applications, computer skills, conceptual physics, concert band, concert choir, consumer economics, creative writing, drama, drama performance, dramatic arts, earth science, economics, English, English literature-AP, English-AP, English/composition-AP, European history-AP, film and new technologies, geography, geometry, government-AP, health and wellness, history, honors algebra, honors English, honors geometry, human anatomy, independent study, Latin, leadership and service, Life of Christ, literature, marching band, mathematics, mathematics-AP, music, musical productions, New Testament, newspaper, physical education, physical fitness, physical science, physics, physics-AP, poetry, pre-algebra, pre-calculus, pre-college orientation, probability and statistics, psychology, reading, religious studies, science, senior project, Spanish, speech, speech communications, trigonometry, U.S. history, U.S. history-AP, video film production, wellness, world geography, world history, writing, yearbook.

Graduation Requirements Algebra, art, biology, calculus, chemistry, computer technologies, drama, economics, electives, English, English composition, English literature, foreign language, geometry, government, literature, physical science, physics, senior project, trigonometry, U.S. history, wellness, world history, senior math topics, Old Testament, New Testament.

Special Academic Programs Advanced Placement exam preparation; honors section; independent study; study at local college for college credit; programs in general development for dyslexic students.

College Admission Counseling 54 students graduated in 2012; all went to college, including Belmont University; The University of Tennessee.

Student Life Upper grades have uniform requirement, student council, honor system. Discipline rests primarily with faculty.

Summer Programs Enrichment, advancement, sports, art/fine arts programs offered; session focuses on physical and mental growth through a caring, Christian, and learning-enriched environment; held on campus; accepts boys and girls; open to students from other schools. 250 students usually enrolled. 2013 schedule: May 30 to July 30. Application deadline: April 15.

Tuition and Aid Day student tuition: $8940. Tuition installment plan (monthly payment plans, individually arranged payment plans). Tuition reduction for siblings, need-based scholarship grants, need-based financial aid, tuition reduction for children of faculty and staff available. In 2012–13, 10% of upper-school students received aid.

Admissions Traditional secondary-level entrance grade is 9. Admissions testing, any standardized test and WRAT required. Deadline for receipt of application materials: none. Application fee required: $125.

Athletics Interscholastic: baseball (boys), basketball (b,g), cheering (g), cross-country running (b,g), dance team (g), football (b), golf (b,g), soccer (b,g), softball (g), tennis (b,g), track and field (b,g), volleyball (g); intramural: ballet (g), dance (g), weight training (b); coed interscholastic: bowling. 1 athletic trainer.

Computers Computers are regularly used in computer applications, English, graphic arts, history, mathematics, media production, newspaper, yearbook classes. Computer network features include on-campus library services, Internet access, wireless campus network, Internet filtering or blocking technology, RenWeb, Accelerated Reader, CollegeView. Computer access in designated common areas is available to students. Students grades are available online.

Contact Mr. Jason McGehee, Admission Counselor. 615-860-5317. Fax: 615-860-7631. E-mail: jason.mcgehee@davidsonacademy.com. Web site: www.davidsonacademy.com

DEERFIELD ACADEMY

7 Boyden Lane
Deerfield, Massachusetts 01342

Head of School: Dr. Margarita O'Byrne Curtis

General Information Coeducational boarding and day college-preparatory school. Grades 9–PG. Founded: 1797. Setting: rural. Nearest major city is Hartford, CT. Students are housed in single-sex dormitories. 280-acre campus. 81 buildings on campus. Approved or accredited by Association of Independent Schools in New England, National Independent Private Schools Association, New England Association of Schools and Colleges, and Massachusetts Department of Education. Member of National Association of Independent Schools and Secondary School Admission Test Board. Endowment: $398 million. Total enrollment: 630. Upper school average class size: 12. Upper school faculty-student ratio: 1:6. There are 150 required school days per year for Upper School students. Upper School students typically attend 5 days per week. The average school day consists of 5 hours and 25 minutes.

Upper School Student Profile Grade 9: 101 students (52 boys, 49 girls); Grade 10: 150 students (73 boys, 77 girls); Grade 11: 180 students (86 boys, 94 girls); Grade 12: 179 students (90 boys, 89 girls); Postgraduate: 20 students (18 boys, 2 girls). 88% of students are boarding students. 23% are state residents. 39 states are represented in upper school student body. 16% are international students. International students from Canada, China, Jamaica, Republic of Korea, Singapore, and Thailand; 25 other countries represented in student body.

Faculty School total: 124. In upper school: 67 men, 57 women; 89 have advanced degrees; 115 reside on campus.

Subjects Offered Advanced chemistry, advanced computer applications, advanced math, advanced studio art-AP, algebra, American government, American history-AP, American studies, analytic geometry, anatomy, applied arts, applied music, Arabic, architectural drawing, architecture, art, art history, art history-AP, Asian history, Asian literature, Asian studies, astronomy, Basic programming, biochemistry, biology, biology-AP, Black history, calculus, calculus-AP, chemistry, chemistry-AP, Chinese, computer applications, computer math, computer programming, computer science, computer science-AP, concert band, creative writing, dance, dance performance, discrete mathematics, drama, drama performance, drama workshop, drawing and design, earth science, Eastern religion and philosophy, economics, economics-AP, English, English literature, English literature-AP, English-AP, environmental science, ethics, European history, expository writing, fine arts, French, geology, geometry, Greek, health, health education, history, instrumental music, journalism, Latin, literature, mathematics, modern European history, music, philosophy, photography, physics, physics-AP, physiology, probability and statistics, religion, science, social studies, Spanish, Spanish literature, studio art, studio art-AP, theater, theater arts, trigonometry, U.S. history, U.S. literature, video, vocal music, Western civilization, world civilizations, world governments, world history, world literature, world religions, writing.

Graduation Requirements Arts and fine arts (art, music, dance, drama), English, foreign language, history, mathematics, philosophy, science.

Special Academic Programs Advanced Placement exam preparation; honors section; independent study; term-away projects; study abroad; academic accommodation for the gifted, the musically talented, and the artistically talented; ESL (6 students enrolled).

College Admission Counseling 197 students graduated in 2012; 190 went to college, including Brown University; Dartmouth College; Georgetown University; Harvard University; Middlebury College; Yale University. Other: 7 had other specific plans. Mean SAT critical reading: 653, mean SAT math: 662, mean SAT writing: 661.

Student Life Upper grades have specified standards of dress, student council, honor system. Discipline rests equally with students and faculty.

Tuition and Aid Day student tuition: $34,050; 7-day tuition and room/board: $47,500. Tuition installment plan (Educational Data Systems, Inc.). Need-based scholarship grants available. In 2012–13, 35% of upper-school students received aid. Total amount of financial aid awarded in 2012–13: $7,300,000.

Admissions Traditional secondary-level entrance grade is 9. For fall 2012, 2,378 students applied for upper-level admission, 324 were accepted, 208 enrolled. ACT, ISEE, PSAT, SAT, SSAT or TOEFL required. Deadline for receipt of application materials: January 15. Application fee required: $60. Interview required.

Athletics Interscholastic: alpine skiing (boys, girls), baseball (b), basketball (b,g), crew (b,g), cross-country running (b,g), diving (b,g), field hockey (g), football (b), golf (b), ice hockey (b,g), lacrosse (b,g), rowing (b,g), skiing (downhill) (b,g), soccer (b,g), softball (g), squash (b,g), swimming and diving (b,g), tennis (b,g), track and field (b,g), volleyball (g), water polo (b,g), wrestling (b); intramural: dance (b,g), fitness (b,g), modern dance (b,g); coed interscholastic: bicycling, diving, golf, indoor track & field, swimming and diving; coed intramural: aerobics/dance, aerobics/Nautilus, alpine skiing, aquatics, ballet, canoeing/kayaking, combined training, dance, dance team, fitness, hiking/backpacking, life saving, modern dance, nordic skiing, outdoor recreation, outdoor skills, paddle tennis, sailing, skiing (cross-country), skiing (downhill), snowboarding, soccer, squash, strength & conditioning, swimming and diving, tennis, volleyball, weight lifting, weight training. 1 coach, 2 athletic trainers.

Computers Computers are regularly used in architecture, mathematics, programming, science classes. Computer network features include on-campus library services, online commercial services, Internet access, wireless campus network, Internet filtering or blocking technology. Campus intranet, student e-mail accounts, and computer access in designated common areas are available to students. Students grades are available online. The school has a published electronic and media policy.

Contact Patricia L. Gimbel, Dean of Admission and Financial Aid. 413-774-1400. Fax: 413-772-1100. E-mail: admission@deerfield.edu. Web site: www.deerfield.edu

See Display on this page and Close-Up on page 570.

DEERFIELD-WINDSOR SCHOOL

2500 Nottingham Way
Albany, Georgia 31707

Head of School: Mr. David L. Davies

General Information Coeducational day college-preparatory, arts, and technology school; primarily serves students with learning disabilities and individuals with Attention Deficit Disorder. Grades PK–12. Founded: 1964. Setting: suburban. Nearest major city is Atlanta. 24-acre campus. 1 building on campus. Approved or accredited by Southern Association of Colleges and Schools, Southern Association of Independent Schools, and Georgia Department of Education. Member of National Association of Independent Schools. Endowment: $1 million. Total enrollment: 836. Upper school average class size: 18. Upper school faculty-student ratio: 1:18. There are 180 required school days per year for Upper School students. Upper School students typically attend 5 days per week. The average school day consists of 6 hours and 25 minutes.

Upper School Student Profile Grade 9: 61 students (35 boys, 26 girls); Grade 10: 68 students (33 boys, 35 girls); Grade 11: 61 students (28 boys, 33 girls); Grade 12: 71 students (39 boys, 32 girls).

Faculty School total: 56. In upper school: 9 men, 28 women; 22 have advanced degrees.

Subjects Offered Advanced studio art-AP, algebra, American history, American literature, art, art history, biology, calculus, chemistry, creative writing, drama, earth science, economics, English, English literature, environmental science, expository writing, French, geometry, government/civics, grammar, health, history, Latin, mathematics, music, physical education, physics, physiology, psychology, science, social sciences, social studies, Spanish, speech, theater, trigonometry, world history, world literature, writing, yearbook.

Graduation Requirements All academic, 55 volunteer hours of community service.

Special Academic Programs 10 Advanced Placement exams for which test preparation is offered; honors section; independent study; study at local college for college credit; academic accommodation for the gifted, the musically talented, and the artistically talented; remedial reading and/or remedial writing; remedial math; programs in general development for dyslexic students.

College Admission Counseling 68 students graduated in 2011; all went to college, including Auburn University; Georgia Institute of Technology; Georgia Southern University; University of Georgia; Valdosta State University. Mean SAT critical reading: 576, mean SAT math: 527, mean SAT writing: 587, mean combined SAT: 1690.

Student Life Upper grades have specified standards of dress, student council, honor system. Discipline rests primarily with faculty.

Tuition and Aid Day student tuition: $9800. Tuition installment plan (Insured Tuition Payment Plan, monthly payment plans, individually arranged payment plans, quarterly and semi-annual payment plans). Tuition reduction for siblings, merit scholarship grants, need-based scholarship grants, need-based tuition reduction available. In 2011–12, 7% of upper-school students received aid; total upper-school merit-scholarship money awarded: $25,200. Total amount of financial aid awarded in 2011–12: $350,000.

Admissions Traditional secondary-level entrance grade is 9. For fall 2011, 36 students applied for upper-level admission, 21 were accepted, 18 enrolled. ERB verbal, ERB math and Otis-Lennon Mental Ability Test required. Deadline for receipt of application materials: none. Application fee required: $50. On-campus interview recommended.

Athletics Interscholastic: aquatics (boys, girls), baseball (b), basketball (b,g), cross-country running (b,g), football (b), golf (b), running (b,g), soccer (b,g), softball (g), strength & conditioning (b,g), swimming and diving (b,g), tennis (b,g), track and field (b,g), wrestling (b); intramural: basketball (b,g), cheering (b,g), danceline (b,g), football (b), soccer (b,g), weight lifting (b,g); coed intramural: badminton. 5 PE instructors, 9 coaches, 1 athletic trainer.

Computers Computers are regularly used in mathematics, yearbook classes. Computer network features include on-campus library services, Internet access, wireless campus network. Student e-mail accounts and computer access in designated common areas are available to students. Students grades are available online.

Contact Mrs. DeeDee R. Willcox, College Counselor. 912-435-1301 Ext. 256. Fax: 912-888-6085. E-mail: deedee.willcox@deerfieldwindsor.com. Web site: www.deerfieldwindsor.com

DE LA SALLE HIGH SCHOOL

1130 Winton Drive
Concord, California 94518-3528

Head of School: Br. Robert J. Wickman, FSC

General Information Boys' day college-preparatory, arts, and religious studies school, affiliated with Roman Catholic Church. Grades 9–12. Founded: 1965. Setting: suburban. Nearest major city is Oakland. 25-acre campus. 11 buildings on campus. Approved or accredited by Western Association of Schools and Colleges and Western Catholic Education Association. Endowment: $3.7 million. Total enrollment: 1,021. Upper school average class size: 30. Upper school faculty-student ratio: 1:28. There are 172 required school days per year for Upper School students. Upper School students typically attend 5 days per week. The average school day consists of 6 hours and 5 minutes.

Upper School Student Profile Grade 9: 267 students (267 boys); Grade 10: 254 students (254 boys); Grade 11: 249 students (249 boys); Grade 12: 251 students (251 boys). 80% of students are Roman Catholic.

Faculty School total: 73. In upper school: 50 men, 23 women; 41 have advanced degrees.

Subjects Offered Advanced studio art-AP, algebra, American history, anatomy, art, band, Bible studies, biology, calculus, chemistry, chorus, design, drafting, drawing, economics, English, English-AP, ethics, fine arts, first aid, French, geometry, government/civics, health, history, Italian, jazz, Latin, literature, marine biology, mathematics, music theory, painting, physical education, physics, physiology, pre-calculus, psychology, religion, science, sculpture, social studies, Spanish, Spanish-AP, sports medicine, statistics, statistics-AP, trigonometry, world history, world religions, writing.

Graduation Requirements Arts and fine arts (art, music, dance, drama), English, foreign language, mathematics, physical education (includes health), religion (includes Bible studies and theology), science, social studies (includes history).

Special Academic Programs Advanced Placement exam preparation; honors section; independent study; remedial math.

College Admission Counseling 253 students graduated in 2012; 249 went to college, including California Polytechnic State University, San Luis Obispo; California State University, Chico; Saint Mary's College of California; Santa Clara University; University of California, Berkeley; University of California, Santa Cruz. Other: 1 went to work, 2 entered a postgraduate year, 1 had other specific plans. Mean SAT critical reading: 564, mean SAT math: 580, mean SAT writing: 549, mean combined SAT: 1687, mean composite ACT: 25. 31% scored over 600 on SAT critical reading, 39% scored over 600 on SAT math, 25% scored over 600 on SAT writing, 33% scored over 1800 on combined SAT, 40% scored over 26 on composite ACT.

Student Life Upper grades have specified standards of dress, student council, honor system. Discipline rests primarily with faculty. Attendance at religious services is required.

Summer Programs Remediation programs offered; session focuses on remediation for incoming and/or conditionally accepted freshmen only; held on campus; accepts boys; not open to students from other schools. 40 students usually enrolled. 2013 schedule: June 10 to July 5. Application deadline: May 30.

Tuition and Aid Day student tuition: $14,750. Tuition installment plan (10-month). Need-based grants available. In 2012–13, 30% of upper-school students received aid.

Admissions Traditional secondary-level entrance grade is 9. For fall 2012, 460 students applied for upper-level admission, 267 were accepted, 267 enrolled. High School Placement Test required. Deadline for receipt of application materials: November 30. Application fee required: $75. On-campus interview required.

Athletics Interscholastic: baseball, basketball, cross-country running, diving, football, golf, lacrosse, rugby, soccer, swimming and diving, tennis, track and field, volleyball, water polo, wrestling; intramural: bowling, flag football, floor hockey, football, ultimate Frisbee. 3 PE instructors, 85 coaches, 3 athletic trainers.

Computers Computers are regularly used in animation, Web site design, yearbook classes. Computer network features include on-campus library services, Internet access, wireless campus network, Internet filtering or blocking technology. Student e-mail accounts and computer access in designated common areas are available to students. Students grades are available online. The school has a published electronic and media policy.

Contact Mr. Joseph Grantham, Director of Admissions. 925-288-8102. Fax: 925-686-3474. E-mail: granthamj@dlshs.org. Web site: www.dlshs.org

DE LA SALLE NORTH CATHOLIC HIGH SCHOOL

7528 N. Fenwick Avenue
Portland, Oregon 97217

Head of School: Mr. Tim Joy

General Information Coeducational day college-preparatory and business school, affiliated with Roman Catholic Church. Grades 9–12. Founded: 2000. Setting: urban. 1 building on campus. Approved or accredited by Northwest Accreditation Commission and Oregon Department of Education. Total enrollment: 322. Upper school average class size: 81. Upper school faculty-student ratio: 1:17. There are 180 required school days per year for Upper School students. Upper School students typically attend 4 days per week. The average school day consists of 7 hours and 30 minutes.

Upper School Student Profile Grade 9: 80 students (36 boys, 44 girls); Grade 10: 79 students (35 boys, 44 girls); Grade 11: 80 students (36 boys, 44 girls); Grade 12: 79 students (35 boys, 44 girls). 40% of students are Roman Catholic.

Faculty School total: 19. In upper school: 10 men, 9 women; 16 have advanced degrees.

Special Academic Programs 2 Advanced Placement exams for which test preparation is offered; honors section; independent study; remedial reading and/or remedial writing; remedial math.

College Admission Counseling 46 students graduated in 2012; 44 went to college, including College of Saint Benedict; Georgetown University; Oregon State University; Pacific University; Portland Community College. Other: 1 went to work, 1 entered military service.

Student Life Upper grades have uniform requirement, student council, honor system. Discipline rests primarily with faculty. Attendance at religious services is required.

Tuition and Aid Day student tuition: $2995. Tuition installment plan (FACTS Tuition Payment Plan, monthly payment plans, individually arranged payment plans). Need-based scholarship grants, paying campus jobs available. In 2012–13, 83% of upper-school students received aid.

Admissions Traditional secondary-level entrance grade is 9. School placement exam required. Deadline for receipt of application materials: none. No application fee required. On-campus interview required.

Computers Computer network features include on-campus library services, Internet access, wireless campus network, Internet filtering or blocking technology. Campus intranet, student e-mail accounts, and computer access in designated common areas are available to students. Students grades are available online. The school has a published electronic and media policy.

Contact Mariana Parra, Admissions Assistant. 503-285-9385 Ext. 135. Fax: 503-285-9546. E-mail: mparra@dlsnc.org. Web site: www.delasallenorth.org/

DELBARTON SCHOOL

230 Mendham Road
Morristown, New Jersey 07960

Head of School: Br. Paul Diveny, OSB

General Information Boys' day college-preparatory, arts, religious studies, and technology school, affiliated with Roman Catholic Church. Grades 7–12. Founded: 1939. Setting: suburban. Nearest major city is New York, NY. 200-acre campus. 7 buildings on campus. Approved or accredited by Middle States Association of Colleges and Schools, National Catholic Education Association, New Jersey Association of Independent Schools, and New Jersey Department of Education. Member of National Association of Independent Schools and Secondary School Admission Test Board. Endowment: $26 million. Total enrollment: 554. Upper school average class size: 15. Upper school faculty-student ratio: 1:10. There are 160 required school days per year for Upper School students. Upper School students typically attend 5 days per week. The average school day consists of 6 hours and 15 minutes.

Upper School Student Profile Grade 9: 119 students (119 boys); Grade 10: 120 students (120 boys); Grade 11: 131 students (131 boys); Grade 12: 117 students (117 boys). 82% of students are Roman Catholic.

Faculty School total: 87. In upper school: 72 men, 14 women; 57 have advanced degrees.

Subjects Offered Accounting, advanced chemistry, algebra, American history, American literature, art, art history, astronomy, biology, calculus, chemistry, computer math, computer programming, computer science, creative writing, driver education, economics, English, English literature, environmental science, ethics, European history, fine arts, French, geography, geometry, German, grammar, health, history, international relations, Latin, mathematics, music, philosophy, physical education, physics, religion, Russian, social studies, Spanish, speech, trigonometry, world history.

Graduation Requirements Arts and fine arts (art, music, dance, drama), computer science, English, foreign language, mathematics, physical education (includes health), religion (includes Bible studies and theology), science, social studies (includes history), speech.

Special Academic Programs Advanced Placement exam preparation; independent study.

College Admission Counseling 119 students graduated in 2012; all went to college, including Boston College; Columbia University; Georgetown University; Loyola University Maryland; Princeton University; Villanova University.

Student Life Upper grades have specified standards of dress, student council, honor system. Discipline rests primarily with faculty. Attendance at religious services is required.

Summer Programs Enrichment, advancement, sports, computer instruction programs offered; session focuses on summer school (coed) and summer sports (boys); held on campus; accepts boys and girls; open to students from other schools. 1,200 students usually enrolled. 2013 schedule: June 26 to August 2. Application deadline: June 1.

Tuition and Aid Day student tuition: $30,200. Tuition installment plan (monthly payment plans, individually arranged payment plans). Need-based scholarship grants available. In 2012–13, 17% of upper-school students received aid. Total amount of financial aid awarded in 2012–13: $1,600,000.

Admissions Traditional secondary-level entrance grade is 9. For fall 2012, 286 students applied for upper-level admission, 113 were accepted, 87 enrolled. Stanford Achievement Test, Otis-Lennon School Ability Test, school's own exam required. Deadline for receipt of application materials: November 28. Application fee required: $65. On-campus interview required.

Athletics Interscholastic: baseball, basketball, bowling, cross-country running, football, golf, ice hockey, indoor track, lacrosse, soccer, squash, swimming and diving, tennis, track and field, winter (indoor) track, wrestling; intramural: bicycling, combined training, fitness, flag football, Frisbee, independent competitive sports, mountain biking, skiing (downhill), strength & conditioning, ultimate Frisbee, weight lifting, weight training. 3 PE instructors, 2 athletic trainers.

Computers Computers are regularly used in computer applications, music, science, word processing classes. Computer network features include on-campus library services, online commercial services, Internet access, wireless campus network. Student e-mail accounts are available to students. Students grades are available online.

Contact Mrs. Connie Curnow, Administrative Assistant, Office of Admissions. 973-538-3231 Ext. 3019. Fax: 973-538-8836. E-mail: ccurnow@delbarton.org. Web site: www.delbarton.org

See Display below and Close-Up on page 572.

DEMATHA CATHOLIC HIGH SCHOOL

4313 Madison Street
Hyattsville, Maryland 20781

Head of School: Daniel J. McMahon, PhD

General Information Boys' day college-preparatory, arts, business, religious studies, technology, and music (instrumental and choral) school, affiliated with Roman Catholic Church. Grades 9–12. Founded: 1946. Setting: suburban. Nearest major city is Washington, DC. 6-acre campus. 5 buildings on campus. Approved or accredited by Middle States Association of Colleges and Schools, National Catholic Education Association, and Maryland Department of Education. Total enrollment: 884. Upper school average class size: 22. Upper school faculty-student ratio: 1:13. There are 177 required school days per year for Upper School students. Upper School students typically attend 5 days per week. The average school day consists of 6 hours.

Upper School Student Profile Grade 9: 229 students (229 boys); Grade 10: 233 students (233 boys); Grade 11: 236 students (236 boys); Grade 12: 186 students (186 boys). 59% of students are Roman Catholic.

Faculty School total: 67. In upper school: 53 men, 14 women; 43 have advanced degrees.

Subjects Offered Accounting, Advanced Placement courses, algebra, American government, American history, American history-AP, anatomy and physiology, art, art history, art-AP, astronomy, band, biology, biology-AP, British literature, British literature-AP, business, business law, calculus, calculus-AP, campus ministry, chemistry, chemistry-AP, Chinese, choral music, chorus, Christian ethics, church history, college admission preparation, community service, computer applications, computer programming, computer science, computer science-AP, computer skills, computer studies, contemporary art, digital photography, English, English composition, English literature, environmental science, film studies, French, French language-AP, geology, geometry, German, German-AP, government, government-AP, Greek, health, health education, history, history of religion, history of rock and roll, honors algebra, honors English, honors geometry, honors U.S. history, honors world history, instrumental music, jazz, journalism, Latin, Latin American studies, Latin-AP, literature-AP, mathematics, modern languages, music, music performance, mythology, newspaper, photography, photojournalism, physical education, physical science, physics, physics-AP, pre-calculus, psychology, SAT preparation, science, science research, social studies, Spanish, Spanish-AP, speech, sports medicine, statistics, studio art, studio art-AP, study skills, symphonic band, theology, trigonometry, U.S. government, U.S. government and politics-AP, U.S. history, U.S. literature, vocal music, world history, writing, yearbook.

Graduation Requirements Arts, computer science, English, foreign language, mathematics, physical education (includes health), science, social studies (includes history), theology, 55 hours of Christian service, service reflection paper.

Special Academic Programs Advanced Placement exam preparation; honors section; independent study; academic accommodation for the gifted, the musically talented, and the artistically talented; remedial reading and/or remedial writing.

College Admission Counseling 200 students graduated in 2012; 196 went to college, including Howard University; Salisbury University; The Catholic University of America; Towson University; University of Maryland, Baltimore County; University of Maryland, College Park. Other: 4 went to work. Mean SAT critical reading: 530, mean SAT math: 530, mean SAT writing: 506. 26% scored over 600 on SAT critical reading, 26% scored over 600 on SAT math, 15% scored over 600 on SAT writing.

Student Life Upper grades have uniform requirement, student council, honor system. Discipline rests primarily with faculty. Attendance at religious services is required.

Summer Programs Remediation, enrichment, sports, art/fine arts, computer instruction programs offered; session focuses on remediation/enrichment; held on campus; accepts boys and girls; open to students from other schools. 400 students usually enrolled. 2013 schedule: June 24 to July 26. Application deadline: June 19.

Tuition and Aid Day student tuition: $13,950. Tuition installment plan (FACTS Tuition Payment Plan). Tuition reduction for siblings, merit scholarship grants, need-based scholarship grants, paying campus jobs available. In 2012–13, 54% of upper-school students received aid; total upper-school merit-scholarship money awarded: $479,700. Total amount of financial aid awarded in 2012–13: $1,279,120.

Admissions Traditional secondary-level entrance grade is 9. For fall 2012, 548 students applied for upper-level admission, 425 were accepted, 229 enrolled. Archdiocese

of Washington Entrance Exam, High School Placement Test or High School Placement Test (closed version) from Scholastic Testing Service required. Deadline for receipt of application materials: December 15. Application fee required: $50.
Athletics Interscholastic: baseball, basketball, crew, cross-country running, diving, football, golf, hockey, ice hockey, indoor track, indoor track & field, lacrosse, rugby, soccer, swimming and diving, tennis, track and field, ultimate Frisbee, water polo, winter (indoor) track, wrestling; intramural: basketball, paddle tennis, strength & conditioning, table tennis. 2 PE instructors, 1 coach, 2 athletic trainers.
Computers Computers are regularly used in computer applications, digital applications, English, independent study, lab/keyboard, library, newspaper, publishing, science, technology, Web site design, word processing, yearbook classes. Computer network features include on-campus library services, Internet access, wireless campus network, Internet filtering or blocking technology, ProQuest, SIRS, World Book. Computer access in designated common areas is available to students. Students grades are available online. The school has a published electronic and media policy.
Contact Mrs. Christine Thomas, Assistant Director of Admissions. 240-764-2210. Fax: 240-764-2277. E-mail: cthomas@dematha.org. Web site: www.dematha.org

DENVER ACADEMY

Denver, Colorado
See Special Needs Schools section.

DENVER CHRISTIAN HIGH SCHOOL

2135 South Pearl Street
Denver, Colorado 80210

Head of School: Mr. Steve Kortenhoeven

General Information Coeducational day college-preparatory, general academic, arts, business, religious studies, bilingual studies, and technology school, affiliated with Christian Reformed Church. Grades 9–12. Founded: 1950. Setting: urban. 4-acre campus. 1 building on campus. Approved or accredited by Association of Christian Schools International, Christian Schools International, North Central Association of Colleges and Schools, and Colorado Department of Education. Endowment: $1.5 million. Total enrollment: 150. Upper school average class size: 20. Upper school faculty-student ratio: 1:19. There are 181 required school days per year for Upper School students. Upper School students typically attend 5 days per week. The average school day consists of 6 hours and 45 minutes.
Upper School Student Profile Grade 9: 43 students (19 boys, 24 girls); Grade 10: 33 students (19 boys, 14 girls); Grade 11: 31 students (17 boys, 14 girls); Grade 12: 43 students (21 boys, 22 girls). 20% of students are members of Christian Reformed Church.
Faculty School total: 17. In upper school: 8 men, 9 women; 16 have advanced degrees.
Subjects Offered Acting, advanced chemistry, advanced computer applications, advanced math, algebra, American government, American history, American literature, art, band, Bible, biology, British literature, calculus, chamber groups, chemistry, choir, Christian doctrine, Christian scripture, church history, composition, computer applications, concert band, concert choir, consumer economics, drama, driver education, earth science, European history, general math, government, grammar, health, introduction to literature, jazz band, keyboarding, personal fitness, physical education, physical fitness, physics, poetry, pre-algebra, pre-calculus, psychology, research, senior seminar, Shakespeare, Spanish, speech, studio art, symphonic band, the Web, trigonometry, U.S. government, U.S. history, Web site design, weight fitness, Western civilization, world geography, world history, yearbook.
Graduation Requirements Bible studies, veterinary science.
Special Academic Programs Honors section; independent study; special instructional classes for deaf students.
College Admission Counseling 48 students graduated in 2012; 44 went to college, including Azusa Pacific University; Calvin College; Colorado State University; Dordt College; University of Northern Colorado. Other: 4 had other specific plans. Mean SAT critical reading: 560, mean SAT math: 545, mean composite ACT: 24.
Student Life Upper grades have specified standards of dress, student council. Discipline rests primarily with faculty. Attendance at religious services is required.
Tuition and Aid Day student tuition: $9850. Tuition installment plan (FACTS Tuition Payment Plan, monthly payment plans). Tuition reduction for siblings, merit scholarship grants, need-based scholarship grants available. In 2012–13, 45% of upper-school students received aid. Total amount of financial aid awarded in 2012–13: $40,000.
Admissions Traditional secondary-level entrance grade is 9. For fall 2012, 36 students applied for upper-level admission, 34 were accepted, 34 enrolled. WISC-III and Woodcock-Johnson, WISC/Woodcock-Johnson or Woodcock-Johnson Educational Evaluation, WISC III required. Deadline for receipt of application materials: none. Application fee required: $260. Interview required.
Athletics Interscholastic: baseball (boys), basketball (b,g), cheering (g), cross-country running (b,g), football (b), golf (b), soccer (b,g), track and field (b,g), volleyball (g); coed interscholastic: physical training, strength & conditioning. 1 PE instructor, 25 coaches.
Computers Computer network features include on-campus library services, Internet access, wireless campus network, Internet filtering or blocking technology. Student e-mail accounts are available to students. Students grades are available online. The school has a published electronic and media policy.
Contact Mrs. Sandie Posthumus, Administrative Assistant. 303-733-1804 Ext. 110. Fax: 303-733-7734. E-mail: sposthumus@denverchristian.org. Web site: www.denver-christian.org/

DEPAUL CATHOLIC HIGH SCHOOL

1512 Alps Road
Wayne, New Jersey 07470

Head of School: Fr. Mike Donovan

General Information Coeducational day college-preparatory, arts, religious studies, and technology school, affiliated with Roman Catholic Church. Grades 9–12. Founded: 1956. Setting: suburban. Nearest major city is New York, NY. 5-acre campus. 2 buildings on campus. Approved or accredited by National Catholic Education Association and New Jersey Department of Education. Upper school average class size: 22. Upper school faculty-student ratio: 1:19. There are 185 required school days per year for Upper School students. Upper School students typically attend 5 days per week. The average school day consists of 7 hours.
Upper School Student Profile 90% of students are Roman Catholic.
Faculty School total: 65. In upper school: 25 men, 40 women; 40 have advanced degrees.
Special Academic Programs International Baccalaureate program; Advanced Placement exam preparation; honors section; accelerated programs; remedial reading and/or remedial writing; remedial math; programs in general development for dyslexic students; special instructional classes for deaf students, blind students.
College Admission Counseling 195 students graduated in 2011; all went to college.
Student Life Upper grades have uniform requirement, student council, honor system. Discipline rests equally with students and faculty. Attendance at religious services is required.
Tuition and Aid Day student tuition: $10,300. Tuition installment plan (SMART Tuition Payment Plan, monthly payment plans, individually arranged payment plans). Tuition reduction for siblings, merit scholarship grants, need-based scholarship grants available.
Admissions Deadline for receipt of application materials: none. No application fee required. Interview recommended.
Athletics Interscholastic: baseball (boys), basketball (b,g), cheering (g), cross-country running (b,g), dance (g), dance squad (g), dance team (g), danceline (g), figure skating (g), football (b), gymnastics (g), ice skating (g), independent competitive sports (b,g), indoor track (b,g), indoor track & field (b,g), lacrosse (b,g), modern dance (g), soccer (b,g), softball (b), swimming and diving (b,g), tennis (b,g), track and field (b,g), volleyball (b,g), weight lifting (b,g), weight training (b,g), winter (indoor) track (b,g), wrestling (b); intramural: aerobics/dance (g), equestrian sports (g), strength & conditioning (b,g); coed interscholastic: alpine skiing, bowling, drill team, golf, ice hockey, skiing (downhill); coed intramural: backpacking, hiking/backpacking. 5 PE instructors, 40 coaches, 1 athletic trainer.
Computers Computer network features include on-campus library services, Internet access, wireless campus network, Internet filtering or blocking technology. Campus intranet, student e-mail accounts, and computer access in designated common areas are available to students. Students grades are available online. The school has a published electronic and media policy.
Contact Mr. John W. Merritt, Director of Admissions. 973-694-3702 Ext. 410. Fax: 973-694-3525. E-mail: merrittj@dpchs.org. Web site: www.depaulcatholic.org

THE DERRYFIELD SCHOOL

2108 River Road
Manchester, New Hampshire 03104-1302

Head of School: Mrs. Mary Halpin Carter, PhD

General Information Coeducational day college-preparatory school. Grades 6–12. Founded: 1964. Setting: suburban. Nearest major city is Boston, MA. 84-acre campus. 3 buildings on campus. Approved or accredited by Association of Independent Schools in New England, Independent Schools of Northern New England, New England Association of Schools and Colleges, and New Hampshire Department of Education. Member of National Association of Independent Schools and Secondary School Admission Test Board. Endowment: $5 million. Total enrollment: 363. Upper school average class size: 14. Upper school faculty-student ratio: 1:8. There are 159 required school days per year for Upper School students. Upper School students typically attend 5 days per week. The average school day consists of 6 hours and 45 minutes.
Upper School Student Profile Grade 9: 61 students (24 boys, 37 girls); Grade 10: 68 students (32 boys, 36 girls); Grade 11: 64 students (30 boys, 34 girls); Grade 12: 56 students (33 boys, 23 girls).
Faculty School total: 43. In upper school: 15 men, 12 women; 16 have advanced degrees.

Subjects Offered 20th century history, 3-dimensional art, algebra, American literature, anatomy and physiology, ancient world history, art, biology, British literature, calculus, calculus-AP, chemistry, chemistry-AP, China/Japan history, Chinese, chorus, computer science, contemporary issues, creative writing, drafting, drama, driver education, earth science, economics, economics and history, engineering, English, English composition, English literature, English-AP, European history, expository writing, film, fine arts, freshman foundations, geography, geometry, global issues, government/civics, graphics, Greek, health, history, Holocaust, independent study, Latin, Latin-AP, mathematics, media, music, music theory, mythology, organic chemistry, philosophy, physical education, physics, physics-AP, pre-calculus, public speaking, robotics, science, sculpture, senior project, social studies, Spanish, Spanish language-AP, speech, statistics, statistics-AP, studio art, theater, trigonometry, U.S. history-AP, Western civilization, world history, world literature, writing.

Graduation Requirements Arts and fine arts (art, music, dance, drama), athletics, English, foreign language, health and wellness, history, mathematics, science.

Special Academic Programs Advanced Placement exam preparation; honors section; independent study; term-away projects.

College Admission Counseling 64 students graduated in 2012; all went to college, including Bates College; Boston University; Northeastern University; Rochester Institute of Technology; The University of Tampa; University of New Hampshire. Mean SAT critical reading: 633, mean SAT math: 611, mean SAT writing: 625, mean combined SAT: 1244, mean composite ACT: 26.

Student Life Upper grades have specified standards of dress, student council. Discipline rests equally with students and faculty.

Summer Programs Art/fine arts programs offered; session focuses on theater camp; held on campus; accepts boys and girls; open to students from other schools. 150 students usually enrolled. 2013 schedule: July to August. Application deadline: June.

Tuition and Aid Day student tuition: $27,730. Tuition installment plan (The Tuition Plan, FACTS Tuition Payment Plan). Merit scholarship grants, need-based scholarship grants, Malone Family Foundation grants available. In 2012–13, 26% of upper-school students received aid; total upper-school merit-scholarship money awarded: $62,000. Total amount of financial aid awarded in 2012–13: $1,527,520.

Admissions Traditional secondary-level entrance grade is 9. SSAT required. Deadline for receipt of application materials: February 1. Application fee required: $50. On-campus interview required.

Athletics Interscholastic: alpine skiing (boys, girls), baseball (b), basketball (b,g), crew (b,g), cross-country running (b,g), diving (b), field hockey (g), independent competitive sports (b,g), lacrosse (b,g), skiing (cross-country) (b,g), skiing (downhill) (b,g), soccer (b,g), softball (g), tennis (b,g); coed interscholastic: equestrian sports, golf, swimming and diving; coed intramural: aerobics, aerobics/dance, cooperative games, flag football, physical training, ropes courses, strength & conditioning, weight training, yoga. 1 PE instructor, 10 coaches, 1 athletic trainer.

Computers Computers are regularly used in all academic, college planning classes. Computer network features include on-campus library services, online commercial services, Internet access, wireless campus network, online computer linked to New Hampshire State Library. Student e-mail accounts and computer access in designated common areas are available to students. Students grades are available online. The school has a published electronic and media policy.

Contact Ms. Allison Price, Director of Admission and Financial Aid. 603-669-4524 Ext. 6201. Fax: 603-641-9521. E-mail: aprice@derryfield.org. Web site: www.derryfield.org

See Display below and Close-Up on page 574.

DEVON PREPARATORY SCHOOL

363 North Valley Forge Road
Devon, Pennsylvania 19333-1299

Head of School: Rev. James J. Shea, Sch.P

General Information Boys' day college-preparatory and religious studies school, affiliated with Roman Catholic Church. Grades 6–12. Founded: 1956. Setting: suburban. Nearest major city is Philadelphia. 20-acre campus. 7 buildings on campus. Approved or accredited by Middle States Association of Colleges and Schools, National Catholic Education Association, and Pennsylvania Department of Education. Member of National Association of Independent Schools. Endowment: $600,000. Total enrollment: 260. Upper school average class size: 15. Upper school faculty-student ratio: 1:10. There are 180 required school days per year for Upper School students. Upper School students typically attend 5 days per week. The average school day consists of 6 hours.

Upper School Student Profile Grade 9: 59 students (59 boys); Grade 10: 56 students (56 boys); Grade 11: 43 students (43 boys); Grade 12: 39 students (39 boys). 84% of students are Roman Catholic.

Faculty School total: 32. In upper school: 23 men, 9 women; 15 have advanced degrees.

Subjects Offered Accounting, ACT preparation, Advanced Placement courses, algebra, American history, American literature, anatomy and physiology, art, biology, biology-AP, British literature, calculus, calculus-AP, chemistry, chemistry-AP, community service, computer science, computer science-AP, economics, English, environmental science, environmental science-AP, European history, forensics, French, French language-AP, geography, geometry, German, German-AP, health, human geography - AP, language-AP, Latin, literature and composition-AP, mathematics, modern European history, music, physical education, physics, physics-AP, political science, pre-calculus, religion, science, social studies, Spanish, Spanish-AP, trigonometry, U.S. history-AP, world cultures, world literature.

Graduation Requirements Computer science, English, foreign language, geography, Latin, mathematics, physical education (includes health), political science, religion (includes Bible studies and theology), science, social studies (includes history). Community service is required.
Special Academic Programs 18 Advanced Placement exams for which test preparation is offered.
College Admission Counseling 49 students graduated in 2012; all went to college, including Drexel University; La Salle University; Loyola University Maryland; Penn State University Park; Saint Joseph's University; University of Delaware. Median SAT critical reading: 625, median SAT math: 634, median SAT writing: 615, median combined SAT: 1874.
Student Life Upper grades have specified standards of dress, student council. Discipline rests primarily with faculty. Attendance at religious services is required.
Tuition and Aid Day student tuition: $19,800. Tuition installment plan (monthly payment plans). Tuition reduction for siblings, merit scholarship grants, need-based scholarship grants available. In 2012–13, 65% of upper-school students received aid; total upper-school merit-scholarship money awarded: $660,000. Total amount of financial aid awarded in 2012–13: $1,030,000.
Admissions Traditional secondary-level entrance grade is 9. For fall 2012, 200 students applied for upper-level admission, 75 were accepted, 32 enrolled. Math and English placement tests required. Deadline for receipt of application materials: none. Application fee required: $50. On-campus interview recommended.
Athletics Interscholastic: baseball, basketball, cross-country running, golf, indoor track & field, lacrosse, soccer, swimming and diving, tennis, track and field. 2 PE instructors, 9 coaches, 1 athletic trainer.
Computers Computers are regularly used in all academic, newspaper, technology, writing, yearbook classes. Computer network features include on-campus library services, Internet access, wireless campus network, Internet filtering or blocking technology. Student e-mail accounts and computer access in designated common areas are available to students. Students grades are available online. The school has a published electronic and media policy.
Contact Mr. Patrick Kane, Director of Admissions. 610-688-7337 Ext. 129. Fax: 610-688-2409. E-mail: pkane@devonprep.com. Web site: www.devonprep.com

DEXTER SCHOOL

20 Newton Street
Brookline, Massachusetts 02445

Head of School: Mr. Todd A. Vincent

General Information Boys' day college-preparatory and arts school. Grades 1–12. Founded: 1926. Setting: suburban. Nearest major city is Boston. 36-acre campus. 4 buildings on campus. Approved or accredited by Association of Independent Schools in New England and Massachusetts Department of Education. Candidate for accreditation by New England Association of Schools and Colleges. Member of Secondary School Admission Test Board. Endowment: $24 million. Total enrollment: 415. Upper school average class size: 16. Upper school faculty-student ratio: 1:7. There are 172 required school days per year for Upper School students. Upper School students typically attend 5 days per week. The average school day consists of 6 hours and 45 minutes.
Upper School Student Profile Grade 9: 25 students (25 boys); Grade 10: 37 students (37 boys); Grade 11: 43 students (43 boys); Grade 12: 40 students (40 boys).
Faculty School total: 110. In upper school: 26 men, 23 women; 31 have advanced degrees.
Subjects Offered Acting, advanced studio art-AP, algebra, American government, American history-AP, American literature, American literature-AP, analysis and differential calculus, Ancient Greek, ancient history, art, art history, art history-AP, art-AP, astronomy, biology, biology-AP, British literature, British literature-AP, calculus, calculus-AP, Central and Eastern European history, ceramics, character education, chemistry, chemistry-AP, Chinese history, choral music, community service, computer graphics, computer music, conceptual physics, constitutional law, digital photography, drama workshop, earth and space science, economics, electronic music, engineering, English, English language-AP, English literature-AP, environmental science, ethics, European history, European history-AP, European literature, Far Eastern history, French, French language-AP, French literature-AP, French-AP, geometry, grammar, graphic arts, history of China and Japan, history of England, history of music, honors algebra, honors English, honors geometry, honors U.S. history, independent study, instrumental music, jazz ensemble, Latin, Latin-AP, marine biology, medieval history, Middle Eastern history, modern European history, music, music composition, music history, music technology, music theory, music theory-AP, music-AP, photography, physics, physics-AP, probability and statistics, public speaking, robotics, Russian history, SAT preparation, Spanish, Spanish language-AP, Spanish literature-AP, Spanish-AP, statistics, studio art, studio art-AP, U.S. history, U.S. history-AP, vocal music, woodworking, writing workshop.
Special Academic Programs 11 Advanced Placement exams for which test preparation is offered; honors section; independent study.
College Admission Counseling 40 students graduated in 2012; 39 went to college, including Berklee College of Music; Boston College; Bowdoin College; Dartmouth College; Harvard University; Trinity College. Other: 1 entered a postgraduate year.
Student Life Upper grades have specified standards of dress, student council, honor system. Discipline rests equally with students and faculty. Attendance at religious services is required.
Tuition and Aid Day student tuition: $39,995. Tuition installment plan (monthly payment plans). Need-based scholarship grants available. In 2012–13, 29% of upper-school students received aid. Total amount of financial aid awarded in 2012–13: $3,000,000.
Admissions Traditional secondary-level entrance grade is 9. For fall 2012, 71 students applied for upper-level admission, 38 were accepted, 15 enrolled. ISEE, PSAT and SAT for applicants to grade 11 and 12 or SSAT required. Deadline for receipt of application materials: February 1. Application fee required: $50. Interview required.
Athletics Interscholastic: baseball, basketball, crew, cross-country running, curling, fitness, football, golf, ice hockey, lacrosse, rowing, soccer, squash, strength & conditioning, swimming and diving, tennis. 6 coaches, 2 athletic trainers.
Computers Computers are regularly used in all classes. Computer network features include on-campus library services, online commercial services, Internet access, wireless campus network, Internet filtering or blocking technology, one to one laptop program. Campus intranet and student e-mail accounts are available to students. The school has a published electronic and media policy.
Contact Mrs. Jennifer DaPonte, Admissions Office Manager. 617-454-2721. Fax: 617-928-7691. E-mail: admissions@dexter.org. Web site: www.dexter.org

DOANE STUART SCHOOL

199 Washington Avenue
Rensselaer, New York 12144

Head of School: Mrs. Lisa F. Brown

General Information Coeducational day college-preparatory, arts, religious studies, Irish and peace studies, and bioethics school, affiliated with Episcopal Church. Grades N–12. Founded: 1852. Setting: urban. Nearest major city is Albany. 27-acre campus. 3 buildings on campus. Approved or accredited by National Association of Episcopal Schools and New York Department of Education. Member of National Association of Independent Schools. Endowment: $1 million. Total enrollment: 302. Upper school average class size: 14. Upper school faculty-student ratio: 1:7. Upper School students typically attend 5 days per week. The average school day consists of 7 hours and 30 minutes.
Upper School Student Profile Grade 9: 36 students (15 boys, 21 girls); Grade 10: 49 students (23 boys, 26 girls); Grade 11: 36 students (18 boys, 18 girls); Grade 12: 33 students (13 boys, 20 girls). 10% of students are members of Episcopal Church.
Faculty School total: 50. In upper school: 13 men, 10 women; 13 have advanced degrees.
Subjects Offered 3-dimensional art, 3-dimensional design, accounting, advanced biology, advanced chemistry, advanced math, advanced studio art-AP, African-American literature, algebra, American history, American literature, art, bioethics, biology, Buddhism, calculus, campus ministry, ceramics, chemistry, choral music, college admission preparation, college counseling, college placement, college planning, college writing, community service, computer science, creative writing, earth science, economics, English, English literature, environmental science, ethics, fencing, fine arts, French, geometry, government/civics, health, history, independent study, instrumental music, instruments, international studies, internship, Irish literature, Irish studies, jazz band, jazz ensemble, journalism, literature, mathematics, mechanical drawing, media arts, medieval/Renaissance history, mentorship program, microeconomics, Middle Eastern history, music, music composition, music performance, music theory, newspaper, oil painting, opera, oral communications, oral expression, organ, painting, peace and justice, peace education, peace studies, performing arts, photography, physical education, physical fitness, physical science, physics, play production, play/screen writing, playwriting, playwriting and directing, poetry, policy and value, political economy, political science, politics, portfolio art, portfolio writing, pre-algebra, pre-calculus, psychology, psychology-AP, public service, public speaking, religion, SAT preparation, science, senior humanities, senior seminar, Shakespeare, social studies, Spanish, theater, trigonometry, world history, writing.
Special Academic Programs 30 Advanced Placement exams for which test preparation is offered; independent study; term-away projects; study at local college for college credit; domestic exchange program; study abroad; academic accommodation for the gifted, the musically talented, and the artistically talented.
College Admission Counseling 29 students graduated in 2012; all went to college, including Emory University; Northwestern University; The Juilliard School; Tufts University; University of California, Berkeley; Vassar College.
Student Life Upper grades have uniform requirement, student council. Discipline rests primarily with faculty. Attendance at religious services is required.
Tuition and Aid Day student tuition: $20,105–$22,255. Tuition installment plan (Academic Management Services Plan). Need-based scholarship grants available. In 2012–13, 50% of upper-school students received aid. Total amount of financial aid awarded in 2012–13: $844,207.
Admissions Traditional secondary-level entrance grade is 9. For fall 2012, 121 students applied for upper-level admission, 70 were accepted, 40 enrolled. School's own test required. Deadline for receipt of application materials: none. Application fee required: $75. On-campus interview required.

Athletics Interscholastic: baseball (boys), basketball (b,g), crew (b,g), soccer (b,g), softball (g), volleyball (g); intramural: backpacking (b,g), independent competitive sports (b,g); coed interscholastic: crew, cross-country running, independent competitive sports, tennis; coed intramural: backpacking, crew, cross-country running, fencing, Frisbee, hiking/backpacking, independent competitive sports, jogging, outdoor adventure, outdoors, physical fitness, sailing, soccer, strength & conditioning, tai chi, ultimate Frisbee, walking, yoga. 2 PE instructors, 8 coaches.

Computers Computers are regularly used in accounting, architecture, art, basic skills, business, career exploration, college planning, creative writing, current events, data processing, desktop publishing, drawing and design, economics, English, ethics, foreign language, freshman foundations, geography, graphic arts, graphic design, graphics, health, historical foundations for arts, history, humanities, independent study, introduction to technology, journalism, keyboarding, language development, learning cognition, library science, library skills, literary magazine, mathematics, media arts, media production, mentorship program, multimedia, music, music technology, news writing, newspaper, philosophy, photography, programming, psychology, publications, publishing, reading, religion, religious studies, remedial study skills, research skills, SAT preparation, science, senior seminar, social sciences, social studies, study skills, technology, theater, theater arts, video film production, Web site design, writing, writing, yearbook classes. Computer resources include on-campus library services, online commercial services, Internet access, wireless campus network. Computer access in designated common areas is available to students. The school has a published electronic and media policy.

Contact Mr. Michael Green, Director of Admission. 518-465-5222 Ext. 241. Fax: 518-465-5230. E-mail: mgreen@doanestuart.org. Web site: www.doanestuart.org

THE DR. MIRIAM AND SHELDON G. ADELSON EDUCATIONAL CAMPUS, THE ADELSON UPPER SCHOOL

9700 West Hillpoint Road
Las Vegas, Nevada 89134

Head of School: Mr. Paul Schiffman

General Information Coeducational day college-preparatory, arts, religious studies, and bilingual studies school, affiliated with Jewish faith. Grades PS–12. Founded: 1979. Setting: suburban. 30-acre campus. 1 building on campus. Approved or accredited by Pacific Northwest Association of Independent Schools and Nevada Department of Education. Member of National Association of Independent Schools. Languages of instruction: English and Hebrew. Total enrollment: 482. Upper school average class size: 16. Upper school faculty-student ratio: 1:10. There are 185 required school days per year for Upper School students. Upper School students typically attend 5 days per week. The average school day consists of 8 hours and 15 minutes.

Upper School Student Profile Grade 6: 33 students (19 boys, 14 girls); Grade 7: 35 students (19 boys, 16 girls); Grade 8: 21 students (11 boys, 10 girls); Grade 9: 26 students (12 boys, 14 girls); Grade 10: 24 students (12 boys, 12 girls); Grade 11: 21 students (4 boys, 17 girls); Grade 12: 17 students (7 boys, 10 girls). 80% of students are Jewish.

Faculty School total: 20. In upper school: 8 men, 12 women; all have advanced degrees.

Graduation Requirements Jewish studies.

College Admission Counseling 24 students graduated in 2011; all went to college.

Student Life Upper grades have uniform requirement, student council, honor system. Discipline rests primarily with faculty. Attendance at religious services is required.

Tuition and Aid Tuition reduction for siblings, need-based scholarship grants available. In 2011–12, 30% of upper-school students received aid.

Admissions ERB (CTP-Verbal, Quantitative) required. Deadline for receipt of application materials: none. Application fee required: $100. Interview required.

Athletics Interscholastic: aerobics/dance (girls), baseball (b), basketball (b,g), cross-country running (b,g), dance (b,g), dance team (b,g), soccer (b,g), swimming and diving (b,g), tennis (b,g), volleyball (b,g). 10 coaches.

Contact 702-255-4500. Fax: 702-255-7232. Web site: www.adelsoncampus.org

DOMINICAN ACADEMY

44 East 68th Street
New York, New York 10065

Head of School: Sr. Barbara Kane, OP

General Information Girls' day college-preparatory, arts, religious studies, and technology school, affiliated with Roman Catholic Church. Grades 9–12. Founded: 1897. Setting: urban. 1 building on campus. Approved or accredited by Middle States Association of Colleges and Schools, National Catholic Education Association, New York State Board of Regents, and New York Department of Education. Member of National Association of Independent Schools and Secondary School Admission Test Board. Total enrollment: 209. Upper school average class size: 20. Upper school faculty-student ratio: 1:8. There are 180 required school days per year for Upper School students. Upper School students typically attend 5 days per week. The average school day consists of 6 hours and 30 minutes.

Upper School Student Profile Grade 9: 56 students (56 girls); Grade 10: 39 students (39 girls); Grade 11: 59 students (59 girls); Grade 12: 55 students (55 girls). 85% of students are Roman Catholic.

Faculty School total: 26. In upper school: 5 men, 21 women; 20 have advanced degrees.

Subjects Offered Algebra, American history, American history-AP, American literature, art history-AP, biology, biology-AP, calculus, calculus-AP, chemistry, chemistry-AP, Chinese, chorus, communications, computer science, creative writing, dance, debate, drama, economics, economics-AP, English, English literature, English-AP, European history-AP, forensics, French, French-AP, geometry, global studies, government and politics-AP, government/civics, health, history, Latin, Latin-AP, library studies, logic, mathematics, music, music theory, physical education, physics, physics-AP, pre-calculus, psychology, religion, science, social studies, Spanish, Spanish-AP, world history.

Graduation Requirements Alternative physical education, arts and fine arts (art, music, dance, drama), English, foreign language, Latin, mathematics, religion (includes Bible studies and theology), science, social studies (includes history).

Special Academic Programs 11 Advanced Placement exams for which test preparation is offered; honors section.

College Admission Counseling 67 students graduated in 2012; all went to college, including Barnard College; Binghamton University, State University of New York; Boston University; Cornell University; Fordham University; St. John's University.

Student Life Upper grades have uniform requirement, student council. Discipline rests primarily with faculty. Attendance at religious services is required.

Summer Programs Remediation, enrichment, advancement programs offered; session focuses on integrated Algebra Regents prep; held on campus; accepts girls; open to students from other schools. 15 students usually enrolled. 2013 schedule: June 24 to August 17. Application deadline: May 15.

Tuition and Aid Day student tuition: $11,750. Tuition installment plan (FACTS Tuition Payment Plan, individually arranged payment plans, quarterly payment plan, semester payment plan). Tuition reduction for siblings, merit scholarship grants, need-based scholarship grants, paying campus jobs available. In 2012–13, 33% of upper-school students received aid; total upper-school merit-scholarship money awarded: $45,000.

Admissions Traditional secondary-level entrance grade is 9. For fall 2012, 352 students applied for upper-level admission, 228 were accepted, 56 enrolled. Catholic High School Entrance Examination required. Deadline for receipt of application materials: December 20. No application fee required.

Athletics Interscholastic: basketball, cross-country running, soccer, softball, tennis, track and field, volleyball; intramural: billiards, dance, soccer, track and field, volleyball. 1 PE instructor.

Computers Computers are regularly used in economics, health, history, Latin, library science, library studies, mathematics, religious studies, science, technology classes. Computer network features include on-campus library services, online commercial services, Internet access, wireless campus network, Internet filtering or blocking technology, T1 fiber optic network. Campus intranet, student e-mail accounts, and computer access in designated common areas are available to students. The school has a published electronic and media policy.

Contact Mrs. Jo Ann Fannon, Associate Director of Admissions. 212-744-0195 Ext. 31. Fax: 212-744-0375. E-mail: jfannon@dominicanacademy.org. Web site: www.dominicanacademy.org

DONELSON CHRISTIAN ACADEMY

300 Danyacrest Drive
Nashville, Tennessee 37214

Head of School: Mr. Keith M. Singer

General Information Coeducational day college-preparatory, arts, religious studies, and technology school, affiliated with Christian faith. Grades K4–12. Founded: 1971. Setting: suburban. 50-acre campus. 1 building on campus. Approved or accredited by Association of Christian Schools International, Southern Association of Colleges and Schools, Tennessee Association of Independent Schools, and Tennessee Department of Education. Endowment: $78,000. Total enrollment: 735. Upper school average class size: 16. Upper school faculty-student ratio: 1:16. There are 175 required school days per year for Upper School students. Upper School students typically attend 5 days per week. The average school day consists of 6 hours and 50 minutes.

Upper School Student Profile Grade 9: 45 students (26 boys, 19 girls); Grade 10: 63 students (30 boys, 33 girls); Grade 11: 65 students (32 boys, 33 girls); Grade 12: 64 students (29 boys, 35 girls). 95% of students are Christian faith.

Faculty School total: 66. In upper school: 16 men, 23 women; 17 have advanced degrees.

Subjects Offered Advanced Placement courses, algebra, American history, American history-AP, American literature, American literature-AP, anatomy, art, athletic training, Bible studies, biology, biology-AP, business, business skills, calculus, calculus-AP, chemistry, chemistry-AP, Chinese, choir, community service, computer science, creative writing, drama, earth science, ecology, economics, English, English language and composition-AP, English literature, English literature and composition-AP, environmental science, ESL, European history-AP, fine arts, French, geography, geometry, government/civics, grammar, health, history, honors algebra, honors English, honors geometry, honors U.S. history, journalism, keyboarding, Latin, Latin-AP, mathematics, music, personal finance, physical education, physics, physiology, psychology, religion, science, social sciences, social studies, sociology, Spanish, speech, theater, U.S. history-AP, world history, world literature, yearbook.

Graduation Requirements Arts and fine arts (art, music, dance, drama), Bible, chemistry, electives, English, foreign language, mathematics, physical education (includes health), science, social sciences, social studies (includes history), wellness, senior service (community service for 12th grade students).

Special Academic Programs 6 Advanced Placement exams for which test preparation is offered; honors section; independent study; study at local college for college credit; academic accommodation for the gifted; ESL (8 students enrolled).

College Admission Counseling 74 students graduated in 2012; 72 went to college, including Lipscomb University; Middle Tennessee State University; Tennessee Technological University; The University of Tennessee System; Union University; Western Kentucky University. Other: 2 went to work. Median SAT critical reading: 600, median SAT math: 650, median SAT writing: 550, median combined SAT: 1830, median composite ACT: 23. 40% scored over 600 on SAT critical reading, 60% scored over 600 on SAT math, 25% scored over 600 on SAT writing, 60% scored over 1800 on combined SAT, 21% scored over 26 on composite ACT.

Student Life Upper grades have uniform requirement, student council, honor system. Discipline rests primarily with faculty. Attendance at religious services is required.

Summer Programs Sports programs offered; session focuses on skill development; held on campus; accepts boys and girls; not open to students from other schools. 230 students usually enrolled. 2013 schedule: June 1 to August 1. Application deadline: none.

Tuition and Aid Day student tuition: $9995. Tuition installment plan (FACTS Tuition Payment Plan). Need-based scholarship grants available. In 2012–13, 35% of upper-school students received aid. Total amount of financial aid awarded in 2012–13: $125,757.

Admissions Traditional secondary-level entrance grade is 9. For fall 2012, 53 students applied for upper-level admission, 38 were accepted, 26 enrolled. Admissions testing required. Deadline for receipt of application materials: none. Application fee required: $40. On-campus interview required.

Athletics Interscholastic: baseball (boys), basketball (b,g), bowling (b,g), cheering (g), cross-country running (b,g), football (b), golf (b,g), soccer (b,g), softball (g), tennis (b,g), track and field (b,g), volleyball (g), wrestling (b); intramural: basketball (b,g), football (b); coed interscholastic: fitness, physical fitness, swimming and diving, weight training; coed intramural: fitness, rappelling. 1 PE instructor, 2 coaches, 1 athletic trainer.

Computers Computers are regularly used in all academic, career exploration, college planning, creative writing, English, French, history, journalism, library, mathematics, newspaper, science, social sciences, Spanish, technology, yearbook classes. Computer network features include on-campus library services, Internet access, wireless campus network, Internet filtering or blocking technology. Campus intranet and student e-mail accounts are available to students. Students grades are available online. The school has a published electronic and media policy.

Contact Mrs. Nicole Schierling, Assistant to Development. 615-577-1215. Fax: 615-883-2998. E-mail: nschierling@dcawildcats.org. Web site: www.dcawildcats.org

DONNA KLEIN JEWISH ACADEMY

9801 Donna Klein Boulevard
Boca Raton, Florida 33428-1524

Head of School: Helena Levine

General Information Coeducational day college-preparatory, arts, religious studies, and bilingual studies school, affiliated with Jewish faith. Grades PK–12. Founded: 1979. Setting: suburban. 32-acre campus. 1 building on campus. Approved or accredited by Florida Council of Independent Schools, Southern Association of Colleges and Schools, and Florida Department of Education. Member of National Association of Independent Schools. Languages of instruction: English and Hebrew. Upper school average class size: 15. Upper school faculty-student ratio: 1:6. There are 172 required school days per year for Upper School students. Upper School students typically attend 5 days per week. The average school day consists of 7 hours and 30 minutes.

Upper School Student Profile Grade 9: 49 students (22 boys, 27 girls); Grade 10: 41 students (18 boys, 23 girls); Grade 11: 26 students (12 boys, 14 girls); Grade 12: 23 students (6 boys, 17 girls). 100% of students are Jewish.

Faculty School total: 24. In upper school: 11 men, 13 women; 11 have advanced degrees.

Subjects Offered Advanced biology, advanced chemistry, advanced math, Advanced Placement courses, advanced studio art-AP, anatomy and physiology, art, band, basketball, Bible studies, biology, calculus, calculus-AP, chemistry, college counseling, computer programming, computer skills, computer tools, dance, debate, drama, economics, English, English language and composition-AP, English literature and composition-AP, environmental science, environmental science-AP, French studies, geometry, government, government-AP, guidance, health, Hebrew, honors English, honors geometry, honors U.S. history, honors world history, Jewish history, journalism, Judaic studies, literature and composition-AP, model United Nations, physical education, pre-calculus, psychology-AP, SAT/ACT preparation, softball, Spanish, statistics, statistics-AP, student government, studio art-AP, theater production, U.S. government and politics, U.S. history-AP, visual arts, volleyball, world history, world history-AP, writing, yearbook.

Graduation Requirements Electives, English, foreign language, history, Judaic studies, mathematics, physical education (includes health), science, writing, completion of 225 hours of community service.

Special Academic Programs 15 Advanced Placement exams for which test preparation is offered; honors section; independent study; study at local college for college credit; study abroad.

College Admission Counseling 25 students graduated in 2012; 23 went to college, including Boston University; Florida Atlantic University; Florida State University; University of Central Florida; University of Florida; University of Miami. Other: 2 went to work. Median combined SAT: 1090, median composite ACT: 25.

Student Life Upper grades have specified standards of dress, student council, honor system. Discipline rests primarily with faculty. Attendance at religious services is required.

Tuition and Aid Tuition installment plan (Key Tuition Payment Plan, monthly payment plans, individually arranged payment plans). Need-based scholarship grants available. In 2012–13, 52% of upper-school students received aid.

Admissions Traditional secondary-level entrance grade is 9. For fall 2012, 30 students applied for upper-level admission, 14 were accepted, 14 enrolled. SSAT required. Deadline for receipt of application materials: none. Application fee required: $100. On-campus interview required.

Athletics Interscholastic: baseball (boys), basketball (b,g), dance team (g), golf (b), soccer (b,g), softball (g), volleyball (g); coed interscholastic: cross-country running, tennis; coed intramural: dance team, fitness, scuba diving, self defense, swimming and diving, tennis, weight lifting, weight training. 1 PE instructor, 6 coaches.

Computers Computers are regularly used in all classes. Computer network features include Internet access, wireless campus network, Internet filtering or blocking technology. Campus intranet and student e-mail accounts are available to students. Students grades are available online. The school has a published electronic and media policy.

Contact Mrs. Jodi Orshan, Assistant Director of Admissions, High School. 561-558-2583. Fax: 561-558-2581. E-mail: orshanj@dkja.org. Web site: www.dkja.org

DOWLING CATHOLIC HIGH SCHOOL

1400 Buffalo Road
West Des Moines, Iowa 50265

Head of School: Dr. Jerry M. Deegan

General Information Coeducational day college-preparatory, general academic, arts, business, religious studies, bilingual studies, technology, performing arts, and Advanced Placement school, affiliated with Roman Catholic Church. Grades 9–12. Founded: 1918. Setting: suburban. 60-acre campus. 1 building on campus. Approved or accredited by North Central Association of Colleges and Schools and Iowa Department of Education. Endowment: $9 million. Total enrollment: 1,400. Upper school average class size: 25. Upper school faculty-student ratio: 1:18.

Upper School Student Profile 95% of students are Roman Catholic.

Faculty School total: 79. In upper school: 39 men, 40 women; 40 have advanced degrees.

Subjects Offered 20th century world history, accounting, ACT preparation, acting, advanced chemistry, advanced computer applications, advanced math, Advanced Placement courses, advertising design, algebra, American government, American history, American history-AP, American literature, American literature-AP, applied arts, aquatics, art, art history, athletics, band, baseball, Basic programming, biology, biology-AP, brass choir, British literature, business, business communications, business law, calculus, calculus-AP, career and personal planning, career planning, career/college preparation, ceramics, chamber groups, cheerleading, chemistry, chemistry-AP, choir, choral music, chorus, church history, college counseling, college planning, composition, composition-AP, computer applications, computer information systems, computer processing, computer programming, computers, concert band, concert choir, creative writing, digital photography, drama, economics, economics-AP, engineering, English, English composition, English language and composition-AP, English literature, environmental science, European history, European history-AP, finance, fine arts, foreign language, French, general business, general science, geography, geometry, German, government, government-AP, health, health education, history, history-AP, honors algebra, honors English, honors geometry, honors U.S. history, honors world history, humanities, information processing, integrated mathematics, jazz band, journalism, keyboarding, Latin, life saving, literature, literature-AP, marching band, metalworking, modern European history, newspaper, painting, personal finance, physical education, physics, physics-AP, play production, poetry, pottery, pre-algebra, pre-calculus, probability and statistics, programming, religion, SAT/ACT preparation, scuba diving, social justice, sociology, Spanish, Spanish language-AP, speech and debate, swimming, tennis, theater production, theology, U.S. government, U.S. government and politics-AP, U.S. history, U.S. history-AP, visual arts, vocal jazz, weight training, world religions, yearbook.

Graduation Requirements Arts, business, electives, English, mathematics, reading, science, social studies (includes history), theology, Reading Across the Curriculum (RAC), 10 service hours per semester/20 per year, 10.5 credits of electives. Community service is required.

Special Academic Programs Advanced Placement exam preparation; honors section; accelerated programs; independent study; study at local college for college credit; academic accommodation for the gifted, the musically talented, and the artistically talented; remedial reading and/or remedial writing; remedial math; special instructional classes for blind students.

College Admission Counseling 327 students graduated in 2012; 320 went to college, including Creighton University; Iowa State University of Science and Technology; Loras College; The University of Iowa; University of Northern Iowa. Other: 1 went to work, 1 entered military service. Median SAT critical reading: 663, median SAT math: 640, median SAT writing: 623, median combined SAT: 648, median composite ACT: 24.

Student Life Upper grades have uniform requirement, student council, honor system. Discipline rests primarily with faculty. Attendance at religious services is required.

Summer Programs Enrichment, advancement, sports, art/fine arts, computer instruction programs offered; session focuses on advancement for the purpose of freeing up a slot in the schedule to take an elective; held on campus; accepts boys and girls; not open to students from other schools. 250 students usually enrolled. 2013 schedule: June 3 to July 1.

Tuition and Aid Day student tuition: $6368. Tuition installment plan (monthly payment plans, individually arranged payment plans). Need-based scholarship grants, paying campus jobs available. In 2012–13, 46% of upper-school students received aid. Total amount of financial aid awarded in 2012–13: $1,000,000.

Admissions Traditional secondary-level entrance grade is 9. Placement test required. Deadline for receipt of application materials: none. Application fee required: $95.

Athletics Interscholastic: aerobics/dance (girls), aquatics (b,g), baseball (b), basketball (b,g), bowling (b,g), cheering (g), cross-country running (b,g), dance team (b,g), diving (g), drill team (g), football (b), golf (b,g), hockey (b), soccer (b,g), softball (g), swimming and diving (b,g), tennis (b,g), track and field (b,g), volleyball (g), wrestling (b); coed interscholastic: cheering; coed intramural: ultimate Frisbee.

Computers Computers are regularly used in keyboarding classes. Computer network features include on-campus library services, Internet access, wireless campus network, Internet filtering or blocking technology. Computer access in designated common areas is available to students. Students grades are available online.

Contact Mrs. Monique Flores, Admissions Assistant. 515-222-1047. Fax: 515-222-1056. E-mail: mflores@dowlingcatholic.org. Web site: www.dowlingcatholic.org

DUBLIN CHRISTIAN ACADEMY

106 Page Road
Dublin, New Hampshire 03444

Head of School: Mr. Kevin E. Moody

General Information Coeducational boarding and day college-preparatory, arts, business, and religious studies school, affiliated with Christian faith, Christian faith. Boarding grades 7–12, day grades K–12. Founded: 1964. Setting: rural. Nearest major city is Boston, MA. Students are housed in single-sex dormitories. 200-acre campus. 5 buildings on campus. Approved or accredited by American Association of Christian Schools and New Hampshire Department of Education. Total enrollment: 88. Upper school average class size: 15. Upper school faculty-student ratio: 1:8. There are 170 required school days per year for Upper School students. Upper School students typically attend 5 days per week. The average school day consists of 5 hours and 45 minutes.

Upper School Student Profile Grade 9: 10 students (5 boys, 5 girls); Grade 10: 15 students (9 boys, 6 girls); Grade 11: 7 students (2 boys, 5 girls); Grade 12: 18 students (8 boys, 10 girls). 33% of students are boarding students. 57% are state residents. 5 states are represented in upper school student body. 25% are international students. International students from China and Republic of Korea. 80% of students are Christian faith, Christian.

Faculty School total: 22. In upper school: 7 men, 7 women; 7 have advanced degrees; 17 reside on campus.

Subjects Offered Accounting, algebra, art, Bible studies, biology, business, calculus, ceramics, chemistry, chorus, computer literacy, consumer mathematics, economics, English, geometry, history, home economics, instrumental music, law, mathematics, music, physics, piano, religion, science, social studies, Spanish, speech, studio art, study skills, U.S. history, voice, word processing, world history.

Graduation Requirements English, foreign language, mathematics, religion (includes Bible studies and theology), science, social studies (includes history), speech.

Special Academic Programs Advanced Placement exam preparation; academic accommodation for the musically talented and the artistically talented; remedial reading and/or remedial writing; remedial math.

College Admission Counseling 16 students graduated in 2012; 14 went to college, including Bob Jones University; Clearwater Christian College; Grove City College; Johnson & Wales University; Liberty University; The Master's College and Seminary. Other: 2 entered military service. Mean SAT critical reading: 620, mean SAT math: 560, mean SAT writing: 510, mean composite ACT: 23.

Student Life Upper grades have uniform requirement, student council, honor system. Discipline rests primarily with faculty. Attendance at religious services is required.

Tuition and Aid Day student tuition: $6500; 7-day tuition and room/board: $12,500. Tuition installment plan (FACTS Tuition Payment Plan). Need-based scholarship grants available. In 2012–13, 20% of upper-school students received aid. Total amount of financial aid awarded in 2012–13: $45,000.

Admissions Traditional secondary-level entrance grade is 9. SLEP for foreign students or Stanford Diagnostic Test required. Deadline for receipt of application materials: June 1. Application fee required: $35. Interview recommended.

Athletics Interscholastic: basketball (boys, girls), soccer (b), volleyball (g); intramural: cheering (g), flag football (b); coed intramural: alpine skiing, ice skating, snowboarding, softball, table tennis. 1 PE instructor, 4 coaches.

Computers Computers are regularly used in accounting, business, English, foreign language, history, mathematics, music, science classes. Computer network features include on-campus library services, Internet access, Internet filtering or blocking technology.

Contact Mrs. Jenn Lawton, Admissions Secretary. 603-563-8505. Fax: 603-563-8008. E-mail: jlawton@dublinchristian.org. Web site: www.dublinchristian.org

DUBLIN SCHOOL

Box 522
18 Lehmann Way
Dublin, New Hampshire 03444-0522

Head of School: Bradford D. Bates

General Information Coeducational boarding and day college-preparatory, arts, and technology school; primarily serves students with learning disabilities and individuals with Attention Deficit Disorder. Grades 9–12. Founded: 1935. Setting: rural. Nearest major city is Boston, MA. Students are housed in single-sex dormitories. 300-acre campus. 22 buildings on campus. Approved or accredited by Independent Schools of Northern New England, New England Association of Schools and Colleges, and The Association of Boarding Schools. Member of National Association of Independent Schools and Secondary School Admission Test Board. Endowment: $2.2 million. Total enrollment: 140. Upper school average class size: 8. Upper school faculty-student ratio: 1:4. Upper School students typically attend 5 days per week. The average school day consists of 4 hours and 30 minutes.

Upper School Student Profile Grade 9: 26 students (16 boys, 10 girls); Grade 10: 31 students (19 boys, 12 girls); Grade 11: 39 students (22 boys, 17 girls); Grade 12: 44 students (22 boys, 22 girls). 75% of students are boarding students. 30% are state residents. 16 states are represented in upper school student body. 28% are international students. International students from China, Egypt, France, Republic of Korea, Russian Federation, and Spain; 8 other countries represented in student body.

Faculty School total: 42. In upper school: 15 men, 20 women; 35 have advanced degrees; 28 reside on campus.

Subjects Offered Acting, advanced biology, advanced math, algebra, American foreign policy, American literature, anatomy and physiology, ancient world history, art, arts, biology, biology-AP, calculus, calculus-AP, carpentry, ceramics, chemistry, choir, chorus, college counseling, college placement, community service, computer education, computer literacy, computer programming, costumes and make-up, creative arts, creative dance, creative drama, cultural arts, dance performance, digital music, drama, drama performance, dramatic arts, drawing and design, electronic music, English, English composition, English literature, ESL, European civilization, European history, film history, fine arts, foreign policy, French, geology, geometry, guitar, honors U.S. history, instrumental music, Latin, library research, library skills, literature, marine biology, mathematics, modern dance, modern European history, music, music composition, music performance, music technology, music theory, musical productions, musical theater, musical theater dance, painting, personal and social education, personal development, philosophy, photography, physics, poetry, pre-calculus, psychology, research, science, senior project, Shakespeare, social studies, Spanish, stagecraft, statistics, student government, studio art, study skills, theater, theater arts, U.S. government and politics, U.S. history, U.S. history-AP, video film production, vocal ensemble, voice, voice ensemble, Web site design, weight training, white-water trips, wilderness experience, women's studies, woodworking, world literature, writing, writing workshop, yearbook.

Graduation Requirements Art, computer skills, English, general science, history, languages, mathematics, Senior Presentation, graduation requirements for honors diploma different.

Special Academic Programs 12 Advanced Placement exams for which test preparation is offered; honors section; independent study; term-away projects; study at local college for college credit; domestic exchange program (with The Network Program Schools); academic accommodation for the gifted; programs in general development for dyslexic students; ESL (10 students enrolled).

College Admission Counseling 35 students graduated in 2012; all went to college, including Barnard College; New York University; Smith College; University of New Hampshire; University of Pennsylvania; University of Washington. Median SAT critical reading: 480, median SAT math: 605, median SAT writing: 525, median combined SAT: 1610, median composite ACT: 24.

Student Life Upper grades have specified standards of dress, student council, honor system. Discipline rests equally with students and faculty.

Tuition and Aid Day student tuition: $28,000; 7-day tuition and room/board: $48,200. Tuition installment plan (monthly payment plans). Need-based scholarship grants, loans and payment plans are through a third party available. In 2012–13, 32% of upper-school students received aid. Total amount of financial aid awarded in 2012–13: $1,200,000.

Admissions Traditional secondary-level entrance grade is 9. For fall 2012, 143 students applied for upper-level admission, 97 were accepted, 48 enrolled. SSAT, SSAT, ERB, PSAT, SAT, PLAN or ACT or TOEFL or SLEP required. Deadline for receipt of application materials: January 31. Application fee required: $50. Interview required.

Athletics Interscholastic: basketball (boys, girls), crew (b,g), cross-country running (b,g), lacrosse (b,g), mountain biking (b), nordic skiing (b,g), rowing (b,g), running (b,g), sailing (b,g), skiing (cross-country) (b,g), skiing (downhill) (b,g), snowboarding (b,g), soccer (b,g), tennis (b,g); coed interscholastic: aerobics/dance, alpine skiing, ballet, crew, cross-country running, dance, dance team, equestrian sports, golf, modern dance, mountain biking, nordic skiing, rowing, running, sailing, skiing (cross-country), skiing (downhill), snowboarding; coed intramural: aerobics/dance, alpine skiing, archery, backpacking, badminton, basketball, biathlon, bicycling, billiards, bowling, canoeing/kayaking, climbing, cooperative games, equestrian sports, fencing, fishing, fitness, flag football, flagball, fly fishing, freestyle skiing, Frisbee, golf, hiking/backpacking, horseback riding, ice hockey, indoor soccer, kayaking, martial arts, outdoor activities, outdoor adventure, outdoor education, outdoor recreation, paddle tennis, physical fitness, physical training, rafting, rock climbing, ropes courses, rowing, sailing, skateboarding, skiing (cross-country), skiing (downhill), snowshoeing, softball, strength & conditioning, table tennis, telemark skiing, tennis, ultimate Frisbee, volleyball, wall climbing, weight lifting, weight training, whiffle ball, wrestling, yoga. 20 coaches, 1 athletic trainer.

Computers Computers are regularly used in all academic classes. Computer network features include on-campus library services, online commercial services, Internet access, wireless campus network, Internet filtering or blocking technology. Campus intranet and student e-mail accounts are available to students. The school has a published electronic and media policy.

Contact Jill Hutchins, Director of Admission and Financial Aid. 603-563-1233. Fax: 603-563-8671. E-mail: admission@dublinschool.org. Web site: www.dublinschool.org/

DUBOIS CENTRAL CATHOLIC HIGH SCHOOL/ MIDDLE SCHOOL

PO Box 567
200 Central Christian Road
DuBois, Pennsylvania 15801

Head of School: Mrs. Dawn Bressler

General Information Coeducational day college-preparatory and general academic school, affiliated with Roman Catholic Church. Grades 6–12. Founded: 1961. Setting: small town. Nearest major city is Pittsburgh. 51-acre campus. 1 building on campus. Approved or accredited by Middle States Association of Colleges and Schools, National Catholic Education Association, Western Catholic Education Association, and Pennsylvania Department of Education. Endowment: $500,000. Total enrollment: 241. Upper school average class size: 20. Upper school faculty-student ratio: 1:14. There are 180 required school days per year for Upper School students. Upper School students typically attend 5 days per week. The average school day consists of 6 hours and 20 minutes.

Upper School Student Profile Grade 9: 35 students (18 boys, 17 girls); Grade 10: 39 students (12 boys, 27 girls); Grade 11: 42 students (22 boys, 20 girls); Grade 12: 45 students (17 boys, 28 girls). 86% of students are Roman Catholic.

Faculty School total: 30. In upper school: 9 men, 21 women; 13 have advanced degrees.

Subjects Offered 20th century American writers, 20th century history, 20th century physics, 20th century world history, 3-dimensional art, accounting, advanced biology, advanced chemistry, advanced computer applications, advanced math, Advanced Placement courses, algebra, American government, American history, American legal systems, American literature, analysis and differential calculus, anatomy and physiology, ancient world history, biology, biology-AP, British literature, calculus, calculus-AP, calligraphy, career and personal planning, career planning, career/college preparation, Catholic belief and practice, chemistry, chemistry-AP, Christian doctrine, Christian ethics, Christian scripture, Christian testament, civil war history, college admission preparation, college counseling, college placement, college planning, college writing, communications, computer applications, computer graphics, constitutional law, contemporary art, creative drama, creative writing, critical writing, debate, digital applications, digital imaging, drama, drama performance, driver education, earth science, ecology, ecology, environmental systems, economics, electives, English, English composition, English literature, English/composition-AP, environmental education, ethics and responsibility, expository writing, fitness, foreign language, forensics, French, general math, general science, geography, geometry, German, government, grammar, graphic arts, graphic design, guidance, health and wellness, health education, history of the Catholic Church, honors algebra, honors English, honors geometry, humanities, information technology, Internet, Internet research, journalism, keyboarding, lab science, language and composition, language arts, law, leadership and service, library, library assistant, library science, library skills, life management skills, Life of Christ, literature, marketing, mathematics, media communications, medieval/Renaissance history, methods of research, Microsoft, minority studies, moral and social development, moral theology, multicultural literature, music, music appreciation, music composition, music performance, music theater, musical productions, musical theater dance, mythology, Native American history, nature study, New Testament, news writing, newspaper, nutrition, oral communications, participation in sports, peer ministry, performing arts, personal fitness, philosophy, physical education, physical fitness, physical science, physics, piano, poetry, political systems, prayer/spirituality, pre-algebra, pre-calculus, probability and statistics, psychology, public speaking, publications, reading, reading/study skills, religion and culture, research, research seminar, research skills, Roman culture, SAT preparation, science, science and technology, science project, science research, scripture, senior career experience, senior humanities, senior project, senior seminar, Shakespeare, Shakespearean histories, short story, skills for success, social issues, social justice, sociology, sophomore skills, Spanish, speech, speech and debate, speech communications, sports, standard curriculum, student government, student publications, student teaching, study skills, substance abuse, technology, telecommunications and the Internet, theater, trigonometry, U.S. government, U.S. history, U.S. literature, values and decisions, visual and performing arts, vocal ensemble, Web site design, wellness, Western religions, word processing, world cultures, world history, world literature, world religions, writing, writing workshop, yearbook.

Graduation Requirements Seniors must take an exit exam, service hours are mandated for each grade level from 6th through 12th.

Special Academic Programs International Baccalaureate program; honors section; independent study; study at local college for college credit.

College Admission Counseling 44 students graduated in 2012; 41 went to college, including Gannon University; Penn State University Park. Other: 1 entered military service, 2 had other specific plans.

Student Life Upper grades have uniform requirement, student council. Discipline rests primarily with faculty.

Tuition and Aid Tuition installment plan (FACTS Tuition Payment Plan, monthly payment plans, individually arranged payment plans). Tuition reduction for siblings, merit scholarship grants, need-based scholarship grants, Rotary Rebate Program uses 'scrips' both national and local, tuition aid based on criteria selected by the donor (certain parish, town, etc) available. In 2012–13, 46% of upper-school students received aid; total upper-school merit-scholarship money awarded: $448,000. Total amount of financial aid awarded in 2012–13: $448,000.

Admissions Traditional secondary-level entrance grade is 9. For fall 2012, 26 students applied for upper-level admission, 26 were accepted, 26 enrolled. ACT-Explore, Math Placement Exam, school's own exam or writing sample required. Application fee required: $25. On-campus interview required.

Athletics 2 PE instructors, 17 coaches.

Computers Computer network features include on-campus library services, Internet access, wireless campus network, Internet filtering or blocking technology, personal laptops or notebooks mandated in 2011-12 for all 8th, 9th, and 10th graders, soon all students in grades 6th through 12th will be required for curricular instruction. Campus intranet, student e-mail accounts, and computer access in designated common areas are available to students. Students grades are available online. The school has a published electronic and media policy.

Contact Mrs. Joyce Taylor, Director of Development. 814-371-3060 Ext. 606. Fax: 814-371-3215. E-mail: jtaylor@duboiscatholic.com. Web site: www.duboiscatholic.com

DUCHESNE ACADEMY OF THE SACRED HEART

10202 Memorial Drive
Houston, Texas 77024

Head of School: Ms. Patricia Swenson

General Information Girls' day college-preparatory, arts, religious studies, and technology school, affiliated with Roman Catholic Church. Grades PK–12. Founded: 1960. Setting: suburban. 14-acre campus. 2 buildings on campus. Approved or accredited by Independent Schools Association of the Southwest, National Catholic Education Association, Network of Sacred Heart Schools, Texas Catholic Conference, Texas Education Agency, and Texas Department of Education. Endowment: $7 million. Total enrollment: 681. Upper school average class size: 14. Upper school faculty-student ratio: 1:7. There are 180 required school days per year for Upper School students. Upper School students typically attend 5 days per week. The average school day consists of 7 hours and 25 minutes.

Upper School Student Profile Grade 9: 66 students (66 girls); Grade 10: 43 students (43 girls); Grade 11: 57 students (57 girls); Grade 12: 63 students (63 girls). 64% of students are Roman Catholic.

Faculty School total: 93. In upper school: 2 men, 36 women; 28 have advanced degrees.

Subjects Offered Algebra, American literature, art history, arts, band, Bible studies, bioethics, biology, British literature, calculus, calculus-AP, ceramics, chemistry, chemistry-AP, community service, composition, computer graphics, computer programming, creative writing, desktop publishing, drawing, economics, English, English literature, European history, fine arts, French, French-AP, geometry, government/civics, health, human sexuality, Internet, Latin, mathematics, music, photography, physical education, physical fitness, physics, prayer/spirituality, pre-calculus, psychology, religious studies, science, scripture, sexuality, Shakespeare, social justice, social studies, Spanish, Spanish-AP, speech, statistics, statistics-AP, studio art, theater, theater production, theology, U.S. government and politics-AP, U.S. history, U.S. history-AP, Western literature, women's studies, world history, world literature, world religions, writing.

Graduation Requirements Arts and fine arts (art, music, dance, drama), computer science, English, foreign language, history, mathematics, physical education (includes health), religion (includes Bible studies and theology), science, completion of social awareness program. Community service is required.

Special Academic Programs 15 Advanced Placement exams for which test preparation is offered; honors section; independent study; domestic exchange program (with Network of Sacred Heart Schools); academic accommodation for the musically talented and the artistically talented.

College Admission Counseling 67 students graduated in 2012; all went to college, including Georgia Institute of Technology; Purdue University; Rice University; Texas A&M University; The University of Texas at Austin. Median SAT critical reading: 600, median SAT math: 585, median SAT writing: 640, median combined SAT: 1845, median composite ACT: 27. 61% scored over 600 on SAT critical reading, 48% scored over 600 on SAT math, 78% scored over 600 on SAT writing, 59% scored over 1800 on combined SAT, 54% scored over 26 on composite ACT.

Student Life Upper grades have uniform requirement, student council, honor system. Discipline rests primarily with faculty. Attendance at religious services is required.

Summer Programs Enrichment, art/fine arts, computer instruction programs offered; session focuses on high school credit, and math review, enrichment; held on campus; accepts boys and girls; open to students from other schools. 225 students usually enrolled. 2013 schedule: June 7 to July 23.

Tuition and Aid Tuition installment plan (monthly payment plans). Merit scholarship grants, need-based scholarship grants available. In 2012–13, 21% of upper-school students received aid; total upper-school merit-scholarship money awarded: $46,300. Total amount of financial aid awarded in 2012–13: $641,530.

Admissions Traditional secondary-level entrance grade is 9. For fall 2012, 104 students applied for upper-level admission, 79 were accepted, 30 enrolled. ISEE required. Deadline for receipt of application materials: January 15. Application fee required: $80. On-campus interview required.

Athletics Interscholastic: basketball, combined training, cross-country running, dance team, diving, field hockey, golf, soccer, softball, swimming and diving, tennis, track and field, volleyball, winter soccer. 5 PE instructors, 25 coaches, 2 athletic trainers.

Computers Computers are regularly used in all academic classes. Computer network features include on-campus library services, online commercial services, Internet access, wireless campus network, Internet filtering or blocking technology. Student e-mail accounts are available to students. Students grades are available online. The school has a published electronic and media policy.

Contact Mrs. Beth Lowry Speck, Director of Admission. 713-468-8211 Ext. 133. Fax: 713-465-9809. E-mail: beth.speck@duchesne.org. Web site: www.duchesne.org

DURHAM ACADEMY

3601 Ridge Road
Durham, North Carolina 27705

Head of School: Mr. Edward Costello

General Information Coeducational day college-preparatory, arts, and technology school. Grades PK–12. Founded: 1933. Setting: suburban. 75-acre campus. 11 buildings on campus. Approved or accredited by North Carolina Association of Independent Schools, Southern Association of Colleges and Schools, Southern Association of Independent Schools, and North Carolina Department of Education. Member of National Association of Independent Schools and Secondary School Admission Test Board. Endowment: $9.6 million. Total enrollment: 1,165. Upper school average class size: 15. Upper school faculty-student ratio: 1:12. There are 179 required school days per year for Upper School students. Upper School students typically attend 5 days per week. The average school day consists of 6 hours.

Upper School Student Profile Grade 9: 80 students (38 boys, 42 girls); Grade 10: 95 students (39 boys, 56 girls); Grade 11: 101 students (49 boys, 52 girls); Grade 12: 102 students (49 boys, 53 girls).

Faculty School total: 196. In upper school: 25 men, 30 women; 40 have advanced degrees.

Subjects Offered 3-dimensional art, accounting, acting, advanced biology, advanced chemistry, advanced computer applications, advanced math, Advanced Placement courses, advanced studio art-AP, algebra, American history, American literature, art, art history, art history-AP, astronomy, biology, calculus, ceramics, chemistry, chemistry-AP, Chinese, chorus, community service, computer graphics, computer programming, computer science, computer science-AP, concert band, creative writing, dance, drama, ecology, economics, engineering, English, English literature, environmental science, fine arts, finite math, forensics, French, French language-AP, French-AP, geometry, German, history, Latin, mathematics, music, outdoor education, physical education, physics, psychology, robotics, science, social studies, Spanish, statistics, theater, U.S. history-AP.

Graduation Requirements Arts and fine arts (art, music, dance, drama), computer science, English, foreign language, mathematics, outdoor education, physical education (includes health), science, senior project, social studies (includes history), community service hours required for graduation, senior project required for graduation.

Special Academic Programs Advanced Placement exam preparation; honors section; independent study; special instructional classes for students with learning disabilities and Attention Deficit Disorder.

College Admission Counseling 91 students graduated in 2012; 88 went to college, including Duke University; Harvard University; North Carolina State University; Princeton University; The University of North Carolina at Chapel Hill; Wake Forest University. Other: 1 entered a postgraduate year, 2 had other specific plans. Mean SAT critical reading: 672, mean SAT math: 676, mean SAT writing: 684.

Student Life Upper grades have specified standards of dress, student council, honor system. Discipline rests equally with students and faculty.

Summer Programs Remediation, enrichment, sports, art/fine arts, computer instruction programs offered; session focuses on academic enrichment, non-academic activities; held on campus; accepts boys and girls; open to students from other schools. 600 students usually enrolled. 2013 schedule: June 10 to July 26. Application deadline: none.

Tuition and Aid Day student tuition: $20,780. Tuition installment plan (Insured Tuition Payment Plan, SMART Tuition Payment Plan). Need-based scholarship grants available. In 2012–13, 14% of upper-school students received aid. Total amount of financial aid awarded in 2012–13: $916,540.

Admissions Traditional secondary-level entrance grade is 9. For fall 2012, 85 students applied for upper-level admission, 46 were accepted, 36 enrolled. ISEE required. Deadline for receipt of application materials: January 18. Application fee required: $55. Interview required.

Athletics Interscholastic: aquatics (boys, girls), baseball (b), basketball (b,g), cross-country running (b,g), dance team (g), field hockey (g), golf (b,g), lacrosse (b,g), soccer (b,g), softball (g), swimming and diving (b,g), tennis (b,g), track and field (b,g), volleyball (g), weight training (b,g); coed interscholastic: outdoor adventure, outdoor education, ultimate Frisbee, weight training; coed intramural: indoor soccer, judo, martial arts, modern dance, physical fitness, physical training, winter soccer. 1 PE instructor, 6 coaches, 1 athletic trainer.

Computers Computers are regularly used in all academic, animation, computer applications, graphic arts, graphic design, introduction to technology, video film production, Web site design classes. Computer network features include on-campus library services, online commercial services, Internet access, wireless campus network, Internet filtering or blocking technology. Student e-mail accounts and computer access in designated common areas are available to students. Students grades are available online. The school has a published electronic and media policy.

Contact Ms. S. Victoria Muradi, Director of Admission and Financial Aid. 919-493-5787. Fax: 919-489-4893. E-mail: admissions@da.org. Web site: www.da.org

EAGLEBROOK SCHOOL

Deerfield, Massachusetts

See Junior Boarding Schools section.

EAGLE HILL SCHOOL

Greenwich, Connecticut

See Special Needs Schools section.

EAGLE HILL SCHOOL

Hardwick, Massachusetts

See Special Needs Schools section.

EASTERN MENNONITE HIGH SCHOOL

801 Parkwood Drive
Harrisonburg, Virginia 22802

Head of School: Mr. Paul G. Leaman

General Information Coeducational day college-preparatory, general academic, arts, and religious studies school, affiliated with Mennonite Church. Grades K–12. Founded: 1917. Setting: small town. Nearest major city is Washington, DC. 24-acre campus. 1 building on campus. Approved or accredited by Southern Association of Colleges and Schools, Virginia Association of Independent Schools, and Virginia Department of Education. Endowment: $3 million. Total enrollment: 385. Upper school average class size: 20. Upper school faculty-student ratio: 1:10. Upper School students typically attend 5 days per week. The average school day consists of 7 hours.

Upper School Student Profile Grade 9: 44 students (24 boys, 20 girls); Grade 10: 55 students (31 boys, 24 girls); Grade 11: 56 students (25 boys, 31 girls); Grade 12: 49 students (21 boys, 28 girls). 60% of students are Mennonite.

Faculty School total: 50. In upper school: 21 men, 14 women; 24 have advanced degrees.

Subjects Offered Acting, advanced math, algebra, American government, American history, American literature, analysis, applied music, art, art history, band, bell choir, Bible studies, biology, British literature, British literature (honors), business, business skills, ceramics, chemistry, Chinese, Chinese studies, choir, choral music, chorus, Christian and Hebrew scripture, Christian doctrine, Christian ethics, Christian studies, Christian testament, Christianity, church history, community service, computer education, computer science, concert choir, consumer mathematics, creative writing, desktop publishing, drama, drawing, driver education, earth science, economics, engineering, English, English composition, English literature, family and consumer science, fiction, fine arts, food and nutrition, food science, French, general science, geography, geometry, government, grammar, guitar, handbells, health, health education, history, home economics, honors English, human development, industrial arts, industrial technology, instrumental music, interior design, keyboarding, Latin, mathematics, mechanical drawing, music, music composition, music theory, novels, oil painting, orchestra, outdoor education, painting, photography, physical education, physical science, physics, poetry, pottery, pre-algebra, religion, religious education, research skills, science, sculpture, sewing, shop, social sciences, social studies, sociology, Spanish, speech, speech communications, stained glass, study skills, theater, typing, U.S. government, U.S. history, vocal music, voice, water color painting, woodworking, world cultures, world history, writing.

Graduation Requirements Arts and fine arts (art, music, dance, drama), electives, English, foreign language, history, home economics, keyboarding, mathematics, physical education (includes health), religion (includes Bible studies and theology), science, social studies (includes history), technical arts.

Special Academic Programs Advanced Placement exam preparation; independent study; term-away projects; study at local college for college credit; study abroad; academic accommodation for the gifted; remedial reading and/or remedial writing; remedial math; ESL (10 students enrolled).

College Admission Counseling 49 students graduated in 2012; 44 went to college, including Eastern Mennonite University; James Madison University; New York University. Other: 2 went to work, 3 had other specific plans. Median SAT math: 590, median combined SAT: 1710. Mean SAT critical reading: 590, mean SAT writing: 565. 47% scored over 600 on SAT critical reading, 43% scored over 600 on SAT math, 35% scored over 600 on SAT writing, 37% scored over 1800 on combined SAT.

Student Life Upper grades have specified standards of dress, student council. Discipline rests primarily with faculty. Attendance at religious services is required.

Tuition and Aid Day student tuition: $5494–$11,787. Tuition installment plan (monthly payment plans, individually arranged payment plans). Need-based scholarship grants available. In 2012–13, 19% of upper-school students received aid. Total amount of financial aid awarded in 2012–13: $129,736.

Admissions Traditional secondary-level entrance grade is 9. For fall 2012, 33 students applied for upper-level admission, 30 were accepted, 27 enrolled. Any standardized test required. Deadline for receipt of application materials: April 15. Application fee required: $50. Interview recommended.

Athletics Interscholastic: basketball (boys, girls), cheering (g), cross-country running (b,g), golf (b), soccer (b,g), softball (g), tennis (b,g), track and field (b,g), volleyball (g); intramural: baseball (b), basketball (b,g), soccer (g), wrestling (b); coed interscholastic: baseball; coed intramural: volleyball. 3 PE instructors, 9 coaches, 2 athletic trainers.

Computers Computers are regularly used in business skills, foreign language, French, graphic design, industrial technology, library, literary magazine, mathematics, music, publications, research skills, science, social sciences, social studies, Web site design, word processing, yearbook classes. Computer resources include on-campus library services, Internet access, wireless campus network, Internet filtering or blocking technology. Campus intranet, student e-mail accounts, and computer access in designated common areas are available to students. Students grades are available online.

Contact Mrs. Kate Bergy, Admissions Counselor. 540-236-6021. Fax: 540-236-6028. E-mail: bergeyk@emhs.net. Web site: www.emhs.net

EASTSIDE CATHOLIC SCHOOL

232 228th Avenue SE
Sammamish, Washington 98074

Head of School: Sr. Mary E. Tracy

General Information Coeducational day college-preparatory, arts, business, religious studies, and technology school, affiliated with Roman Catholic Church. Grades 6–12. Founded: 1980. Setting: suburban. 50-acre campus. 2 buildings on campus. Approved or accredited by National Catholic Education Association, Northwest Accreditation Commission, Pacific Northwest Association of Independent Schools, and Washington Department of Education. Upper school average class size: 20. Upper school faculty-student ratio: 1:13. There are 180 required school days per year for Upper School students. The average school day consists of 7 hours.

Upper School Student Profile 60% of students are Roman Catholic.

Faculty School total: 65. In upper school: 22 men, 30 women; 38 have advanced degrees.

Subjects Offered Advanced Placement courses, algebra, American government, American history, American literature, anatomy and physiology, art, ASB Leadership, athletic training, band, biology, biology-AP, British literature, calculus, calculus-AP, campus ministry, Catholic belief and practice, ceramics, chemistry, chemistry-AP, choir, church history, community service, computers, contemporary issues, creative writing, debate, digital photography, drama, drawing, economics, English, English literature, environmental science-AP, French, French-AP, geometry, government and politics-AP, graphic design, health, history, honors algebra, honors English, honors geometry, honors U.S. history, honors world history, journalism, law, literature and composition-AP, math analysis, music, music theory-AP, painting, performing arts, physical education, physics, physics-AP, religious education, social justice, Spanish, Spanish-AP, speech and debate, statistics-AP, studio art, studio art-AP, theology, trigonometry, U.S. history-AP, Web site design, world history, world history-AP, yearbook.

Graduation Requirements Arts and fine arts (art, music, dance, drama), business education, English, foreign language, health, history, information technology, lab science, mathematics, physical education (includes health), science, social sciences, theology, 100 hours of community service (over 4 years).

Special Academic Programs Advanced Placement exam preparation; honors section; study at local college for college credit; academic accommodation for the gifted; programs in English, mathematics, general development for dyslexic students.

College Admission Counseling 144 students graduated in 2011; 142 went to college, including Gonzaga University; Santa Clara University; University of Colorado Boulder; University of Portland; University of Washington; Washington State University. Other: 1 entered a postgraduate year, 1 had other specific plans.

Student Life Upper grades have specified standards of dress, student council, honor system. Discipline rests primarily with faculty. Attendance at religious services is required.

Tuition and Aid Day student tuition: $17,260. Tuition installment plan (monthly payment plans). Tuition reduction for siblings, merit scholarship grants, need-based scholarship grants available.

Admissions Traditional secondary-level entrance grade is 9. ISEE required. Deadline for receipt of application materials: January 12. Application fee required: $25. Interview recommended.

Athletics Interscholastic: baseball (boys), basketball (b,g), cheering (g), cross-country running (b,g), drill team (g), football (b), golf (b,g), lacrosse (b,g), soccer (b,g), softball (g), swimming and diving (b,g), tennis (b,g), track and field (b,g), volleyball (g), wrestling (b); coed interscholastic: Special Olympics; coed intramural: strength & conditioning, weight lifting, weight training. 2 PE instructors, 43 coaches, 1 athletic trainer.

Computers Computers are regularly used in business education, digital applications, graphic design, technology, Web site design, yearbook classes. Computer network features include on-campus library services, online commercial services, Internet access, wireless campus network, Internet filtering or blocking technology. Students grades are available online.

Contact Sarah Dahleen, Director of Admissions. 425-295-3017. Fax: 425-392-5160. E-mail: sdahleen@eastsidecatholic.org. Web site: www.eastsidecatholic.org

EATON ACADEMY

1000 Old Roswell Lakes Parkway
Roswell, Georgia 30076

Head of School: Ms. Bridgit Eaton-Partalis

General Information Coeducational day and distance learning college-preparatory school. Grades K–12. Distance learning grades 5–12. Founded: 1995. Setting: suburban. Nearest major city is Atlanta. 12-acre campus. 1 building on campus. Approved or accredited by Georgia Accrediting Commission, Southern Association of Colleges and Schools, Southern Association of Independent Schools, and Georgia Department of Education. Total enrollment: 80. Upper school average class size: 5. Upper school faculty-student ratio: 1:5. There are 180 required school days per year for Upper School students. Upper School students typically attend 5 days per week. The average school day consists of 6 hours and 45 minutes.

Upper School Student Profile Grade 9: 8 students (7 boys, 1 girl); Grade 10: 8 students (6 boys, 2 girls); Grade 11: 8 students (8 boys); Grade 12: 8 students (6 boys, 2 girls).

Faculty School total: 33. In upper school: 3 men, 6 women; 6 have advanced degrees.

Subjects Offered All academic.

Graduation Requirements All academic.

Special Academic Programs Honors section; accelerated programs; independent study; academic accommodation for the gifted, the musically talented, and the artistically talented; remedial reading and/or remedial writing; remedial math; special instructional classes for deaf students.

College Admission Counseling 22 students graduated in 2012; all went to college, including Georgia College & State University; Georgia Institute of Technology; Georgia Perimeter College; Georgia Southern University; Kennesaw State University; University of Georgia.

Student Life Upper grades have specified standards of dress. Discipline rests primarily with faculty.

Summer Programs Remediation, enrichment, advancement, ESL, sports, art/fine arts, computer instruction programs offered; session focuses on academic acceleration and remediation; held both on and off campus; held at local sports facilities; accepts boys and girls; open to students from other schools. 35 students usually enrolled. 2013 schedule: June 3 to July 26. Application deadline: none.

Tuition and Aid Day student tuition: $19,400.

Admissions For fall 2012, 50 students applied for upper-level admission, 25 were accepted, 20 enrolled. Deadline for receipt of application materials: none. Application fee required: $250. Interview required.

Athletics Coed Intramural: aquatics, artistic gym, basketball, bowling, canoeing/kayaking, crew, cross-country running, equestrian sports, field hockey, fitness walking, flag football, floor hockey, Frisbee, golf, gymnastics, hockey, horseback riding, ice hockey, ice skating, jogging, kayaking, martial arts, modern dance, outdoor activities, physical fitness, racquetball, rock climbing, ropes courses, running, scuba diving, strength & conditioning, tennis, volleyball, weight training. 2 PE instructors.
Computers Computers are regularly used in all academic classes. Computer network features include Internet access, wireless campus network, Internet filtering or blocking technology. Student e-mail accounts are available to students. Students grades are available online. The school has a published electronic and media policy.
Contact 770-645-2673. Fax: 770-645-2711. Web site: www.eatonacademy.org

EDGEWOOD ACADEMY

5475 Elmore Road
PO Box 160
Elmore, Alabama 36025

Head of School: Mr. Clint Welch

General Information Coeducational day college-preparatory, arts, business, religious studies, bilingual studies, and technology school. Grades K–12. Founded: 1967. Setting: small town. Nearest major city is Montgomery. 30-acre campus. 4 buildings on campus. Approved or accredited by National Independent Private Schools Association, Southern Association of Colleges and Schools, and Alabama Department of Education. Total enrollment: 275. Upper school average class size: 18. Upper school faculty-student ratio: 1:14. There are 177 required school days per year for Upper School students. Upper School students typically attend 5 days per week. The average school day consists of 5 hours and 45 minutes.
Upper School Student Profile Grade 9: 19 students (11 boys, 8 girls); Grade 10: 26 students (15 boys, 11 girls); Grade 11: 19 students (12 boys, 7 girls); Grade 12: 35 students (23 boys, 12 girls).
Faculty School total: 20. In upper school: 3 men, 6 women; 7 have advanced degrees.
Graduation Requirements Advanced diploma requires 100 hours of community service, standard diplomas requires 50 hours of community service.
Special Academic Programs Advanced Placement exam preparation; study at local college for college credit.
College Admission Counseling 18 students graduated in 2012; they went to Auburn University Montgomery. Median composite ACT: 25.
Student Life Upper grades have specified standards of dress, student council.
Summer Programs Session focuses on driver education; held both on and off campus; held at on the road/street/highway; accepts boys and girls; open to students from other schools. 15 students usually enrolled. 2013 schedule: June to July. Application deadline: May.
Tuition and Aid Day student tuition: $5700. Tuition installment plan (SMART Tuition Payment Plan). Tuition reduction for siblings available.
Admissions Admissions testing required. Deadline for receipt of application materials: none. No application fee required. Interview required.
Athletics Interscholastic: baseball (boys), basketball (b,g), cheering (g), football (b), physical fitness (b,g), physical training (b,g), softball (g), volleyball (g), weight lifting (b), weight training (b,g); coed interscholastic: fishing, track and field. 2 PE instructors, 4 coaches.
Computers Computers are regularly used in yearbook classes. Computer network features include on-campus library services, Internet access, wireless campus network, Internet filtering or blocking technology. Students grades are available online. The school has a published electronic and media policy.
Contact 334-567-5102. Fax: 334-567-8316. Web site: www.edgewoodacademy.org/pages/Edgewood_Academy

EDISON SCHOOL

Box 2, Site 11, RR2
Okotoks, Alberta T1S 1A2, Canada

Head of School: Mrs. Beth Chernoff

General Information Coeducational day college-preparatory and general academic school. Grades K–12. Founded: 1993. Setting: small town. Nearest major city is Calgary, Canada. 5-acre campus. 3 buildings on campus. Approved or accredited by Association of Independent Schools and Colleges of Alberta and Alberta Department of Education. Languages of instruction: English, French and Spanish. Total enrollment: 198. Upper school average class size: 12. Upper school faculty-student ratio: 1:12. There are 185 required school days per year for Upper School students. Upper School students typically attend 5 days per week. The average school day consists of 6 hours and 15 minutes.
Upper School Student Profile Grade 9: 12 students (6 boys, 6 girls); Grade 10: 12 students (6 boys, 6 girls); Grade 11: 12 students (6 boys, 6 girls); Grade 12: 12 students (6 boys, 6 girls).
Faculty School total: 18. In upper school: 5 men, 1 woman; 4 have advanced degrees.
Subjects Offered Advanced Placement courses, art, biology, chemistry, English, French, mathematics, physical education, physics, science, social studies, Spanish, standard curriculum.
Graduation Requirements Alberta Learning requirements.
Special Academic Programs Advanced Placement exam preparation; accelerated programs; independent study; study at local college for college credit; academic accommodation for the gifted.
College Admission Counseling 8 students graduated in 2011; 7 went to college, including The University of British Columbia; University of Alberta; University of Calgary; University of Waterloo. Other: 1 went to work. Median composite ACT: 26. 58% scored over 26 on composite ACT.
Student Life Upper grades have uniform requirement, student council, honor system. Discipline rests primarily with faculty.
Tuition and Aid Day student tuition: CAN$7000. Tuition installment plan (monthly payment plans). Tuition reduction for siblings available.
Admissions Traditional secondary-level entrance grade is 9. For fall 2011, 20 students applied for upper-level admission, 4 were accepted, 4 enrolled. Achievement tests or admissions testing required. Deadline for receipt of application materials: none. No application fee required. On-campus interview required.
Athletics Interscholastic: badminton (boys, girls), basketball (b,g), cross-country running (b,g); intramural: badminton (b,g), basketball (b,g), cross-country running (b,g); coed interscholastic: badminton, flag football; coed intramural: badminton, flag football, outdoor education. 1 PE instructor, 1 coach.
Computers Computers are regularly used in all classes. Computer resources include Internet access. Computer access in designated common areas is available to students.
Contact Mrs. Beth Chernoff, Headmistress. 403-938-7670. Fax: 403-938-7224. E-mail: office@edisonschool.ca. Web site: www.edisonschool.ca

EDMUND BURKE SCHOOL

4101 Connecticut Avenue NW
Washington, District of Columbia 20008

Head of School: Andrew Slater

General Information Coeducational day college-preparatory and arts school. Grades 6–12. Founded: 1968. Setting: urban. 2 buildings on campus. Approved or accredited by Association of Independent Schools of Greater Washington, Middle States Association of Colleges and Schools, and District of Columbia Department of Education. Member of National Association of Independent Schools and Secondary School Admission Test Board. Endowment: $829,556. Total enrollment: 297. Upper school average class size: 12. Upper school faculty-student ratio: 1:6. There are 180 required school days per year for Upper School students. Upper School students typically attend 5 days per week. The average school day consists of 5 hours.
Upper School Student Profile Grade 9: 42 students (19 boys, 23 girls); Grade 10: 52 students (29 boys, 23 girls); Grade 11: 53 students (30 boys, 23 girls); Grade 12: 60 students (29 boys, 31 girls).
Faculty School total: 50. In upper school: 19 men, 19 women; 25 have advanced degrees.
Subjects Offered African-American literature, algebra, American history, American literature, anatomy, anthropology, biology, calculus, ceramics, chemistry, computer science, creative writing, economics, English, English literature, European history, French, geography, geometry, health, history, journalism, Latin, linguistics, music, performing arts, philosophy, photography, physical education, physics, senior seminar, Spanish, theater, trigonometry, values and decisions, visual arts, women's studies, world history, writing.
Graduation Requirements English, foreign language, history, mathematics, physical education (includes health), science, social sciences, values and decisions, visual and performing arts, senior research seminar. Community service is required.
Special Academic Programs Advanced Placement exam preparation; independent study; term-away projects.
College Admission Counseling 65 students graduated in 2012; all went to college, including New York University; University of New Hampshire; University of Pittsburgh; University of Rhode Island; Wesleyan University. Median SAT critical reading: 651, median SAT math: 641, median SAT writing: 648.
Student Life Upper grades have student council, honor system. Discipline rests primarily with faculty.
Summer Programs Remediation, enrichment, advancement, ESL, art/fine arts, computer instruction programs offered; session focuses on academic programs and visual arts; held on campus; accepts boys and girls; open to students from other schools. 50 students usually enrolled. 2013 schedule: June 20 to August 21. Application deadline: none.
Tuition and Aid Day student tuition: $31,820. Tuition installment plan (The Tuition Plan, Insured Tuition Payment Plan, Academic Management Services Plan, individually arranged payment plans). Need-based scholarship grants available. In 2012–13, 29% of upper-school students received aid. Total amount of financial aid awarded in 2012–13: $978,185.
Admissions Traditional secondary-level entrance grade is 9. For fall 2012, 130 students applied for upper-level admission, 86 were accepted, 45 enrolled. ISEE or SSAT required. Deadline for receipt of application materials: January 7. Application fee required: $60. Interview required.
Athletics Interscholastic: aquatics (boys, girls), basketball (b,g), cross-country running (b,g), golf (b,g), soccer (b,g), softball (g), swimming and diving (g), track and field (b,g), volleyball (b,g), wrestling (b,g); intramural: dance team (b,g), Frisbee (b,g),

martial arts (b,g), physical fitness (b,g), weight lifting (b,g); coed interscholastic: swimming and diving; coed intramural: indoor soccer, jogging. 2 PE instructors, 2 coaches.

Computers Computers are regularly used in creative writing, English, foreign language, French, graphic arts, history, journalism, mathematics, science classes. Computer network features include on-campus library services, online commercial services, Internet access. Students grades are available online. The school has a published electronic and media policy.

Contact Admissions Office. 202-362-8882 Ext. 670. Fax: 202-362-1914. E-mail: admissions@burkeschool.org. Web site: www.burkeschool.org

ELDORADO EMERSON PRIVATE SCHOOL

4100 East Walnut Street
Orange, California 92869

Head of School: Dr. Glory Ludwick

General Information Coeducational day college-preparatory, general academic, and arts school. Grades K–12. Founded: 1958. Setting: suburban. Nearest major city is Los Angeles. Students are housed in homes of host families. 5-acre campus. 8 buildings on campus. Approved or accredited by Western Association of Schools and Colleges and California Department of Education. Total enrollment: 150. Upper school average class size: 18. Upper school faculty-student ratio: 1:18. There are 180 required school days per year for Upper School students. Upper School students typically attend 5 days per week. The average school day consists of 6 hours.

Upper School Student Profile Grade 7: 7 students (3 boys, 4 girls); Grade 8: 6 students (3 boys, 3 girls); Grade 9: 7 students (3 boys, 4 girls); Grade 10: 17 students (7 boys, 10 girls); Grade 11: 17 students (6 boys, 11 girls); Grade 12: 25 students (9 boys, 16 girls).

Faculty School total: 25. In upper school: 7 men, 6 women; 11 have advanced degrees.

Subjects Offered Acting, advanced chemistry, advanced math, advanced TOEFL/grammar, algebra, American government, American history-AP, analysis and differential calculus, anatomy, ancient world history, applied arts, applied music, Arabic, art, art and culture, art appreciation, art education, art history, Basic programming, biology, biology-AP, calculus, calculus-AP, cell biology, ceramics, chemistry, chemistry-AP, Chinese, civil war history, classical civilization, classical Greek literature, classical music, classics, clayworking, computer processing, computer programming, computer skills, concert band, contemporary art, contemporary history, creative drama, creative writing, cultural geography, current events, current history, drama workshop, drawing, earth science, economics and history, Egyptian history, English, English literature, ESL, fine arts, gardening, general math, geography, geometry, grammar, jazz band, keyboarding, library skills, Mandarin, math analysis, physics, physics-AP, pre-algebra, precalculus, reading, SAT preparation, science, Shakespeare, Spanish, TOEFL preparation, U.S. government and politics-AP, U.S. history, world history.

Graduation Requirements Art, English, foreign language, mathematics, music, physical education (includes health), science, social studies (includes history). Community service is required.

Special Academic Programs Advanced Placement exam preparation; honors section; accelerated programs; independent study; study at local college for college credit; academic accommodation for the gifted, the musically talented, and the artistically talented; ESL (50 students enrolled).

College Admission Counseling 25 students graduated in 2012; they went to California State University, Fullerton; Chapman University; Occidental College; Purdue University; The Johns Hopkins University; University of California, Santa Cruz.

Student Life Upper grades have specified standards of dress, honor system. Discipline rests equally with students and faculty.

Tuition and Aid Day student tuition: $12,150; 7-day tuition and room/board: $20,000–$30,000. Tuition installment plan (monthly payment plans, individually arranged payment plans). Tuition reduction for siblings, need-based scholarship grants available. In 2012–13, 10% of upper-school students received aid. Total amount of financial aid awarded in 2012–13: $50,000.

Admissions Traditional secondary-level entrance grade is 10. For fall 2012, 95 students applied for upper-level admission, 70 were accepted, 70 enrolled. Achievement tests or any standardized test required. Deadline for receipt of application materials: none. Application fee required: $250. Interview required.

Athletics Interscholastic: baseball (boys), flag football (b), soccer (b); coed interscholastic: baseball, cross-country running, fitness, flag football, physical fitness, physical training, soccer. 1 PE instructor, 4 coaches.

Computers Computers are regularly used in desktop publishing, graphic design, keyboarding, Web site design, word processing, yearbook classes. Computer resources include Internet access, Internet filtering or blocking technology.

Contact Mrs. Venessa Marquez, Administration. 714-633-4774. Fax: 714-744-3304. E-mail: mbently@eldoradoemerson.org. Web site: www.eldorado-emerson.org

ELGIN ACADEMY

350 Park Street
Elgin, Illinois 60120

Head of School: Mr. Seth L. Hanford

General Information Coeducational day college-preparatory, arts, and technology school. Grades PS–12. Founded: 1839. Setting: suburban. Nearest major city is Chicago. 20-acre campus. 8 buildings on campus. Approved or accredited by Independent Schools Association of the Central States. Member of National Association of Independent Schools and Secondary School Admission Test Board. Endowment: $10 million. Total enrollment: 432. Upper school average class size: 12. Upper school faculty-student ratio: 1:5. There are 183 required school days per year for Upper School students. Upper School students typically attend 5 days per week. The average school day consists of 6 hours and 30 minutes.

Upper School Student Profile Grade 9: 39 students (15 boys, 24 girls); Grade 10: 29 students (16 boys, 13 girls); Grade 11: 35 students (13 boys, 22 girls); Grade 12: 41 students (18 boys, 23 girls).

Subjects Offered Algebra, American history, American literature, anatomy and physiology, art, art history, biology, calculus, ceramics, chemistry, computer programming, computer science, creative writing, drama, English, English literature, environmental science, European history, expository writing, fine arts, finite math, French, geometry, government/civics, grammar, history, Latin, Latin-AP, mathematics, music, painting, photography, physical education, psychology, psychology-AP, science, social studies, Spanish, statistics, theater, trigonometry, world history, world literature, writing.

Graduation Requirements 20th century history, arts and fine arts (art, music, dance, drama), English, foreign language, mathematics, science, social studies (includes history).

Special Academic Programs 16 Advanced Placement exams for which test preparation is offered; honors section; independent study.

College Admission Counseling 29 students graduated in 2012; all went to college, including Brown University; Grinnell College; Miami University; Michigan State University; The George Washington University; University of Wisconsin–Madison. Median SAT critical reading: 650, median SAT math: 600, median SAT writing: 650, median combined SAT: 1910, median composite ACT: 27.

Student Life Upper grades have specified standards of dress, student council, honor system. Discipline rests primarily with faculty.

Summer Programs Enrichment, sports, art/fine arts programs offered; session focuses on college prep work, academics, athletics, art, music; held on campus; accepts boys and girls; open to students from other schools. 2013 schedule: June 1 to August 30.

Tuition and Aid Day student tuition: $17,725. Tuition installment plan (FACTS Tuition Payment Plan, 10-month payment plan). Tuition reduction for siblings, merit scholarship grants, need-based scholarship grants available. In 2012–13, 40% of upper-school students received aid; total upper-school merit-scholarship money awarded: $15,000.

Admissions Traditional secondary-level entrance grade is 9. ERB - verbal abilities, reading comprehension, quantitative abilities (level F, form 1) required. Deadline for receipt of application materials: none. Application fee required: $50. Interview required.

Athletics Interscholastic: field hockey (girls), golf (b); coed interscholastic: basketball, cross-country running, outdoors, soccer, tennis, track and field, volleyball, wilderness, wilderness survival; coed intramural: backpacking, canoeing/kayaking. 2 PE instructors.

Computers Computers are regularly used in art, English, foreign language, mathematics, science, social studies classes. Computer network features include on-campus library services, online commercial services, Internet access, wireless campus network. Campus intranet is available to students. Students grades are available online. The school has a published electronic and media policy.

Contact Mr. Shannon D. Howell, Assistant Head of School for Institutional Advancement. 847-695-0303. Fax: 847-695-5017. E-mail: showell@elginacademy.org. Web site: www.elginacademy.org

See Display on next page and Close-Up on page 576.

ELIZABETH SETON HIGH SCHOOL

5715 Emerson Street
Bladensburg, Maryland 20710-1844

Head of School: Sr. Ellen Marie Hagar

General Information Girls' day college-preparatory, arts, religious studies, bilingual studies, technology, visual arts, and music school, affiliated with Roman Catholic Church. Grades 9–12. Founded: 1959. Setting: suburban. Nearest major city is Washington, DC. 24-acre campus. 2 buildings on campus. Approved or accredited by Middle States Association of Colleges and Schools, National Catholic Education Association, and Maryland Department of Education. Total enrollment: 575. Upper school average class size: 17. Upper school faculty-student ratio: 1:13. There are 180 required school days per year for Upper School students. Upper School students typically attend 5 days per week. The average school day consists of 6 hours and 30 minutes.

Upper School Student Profile Grade 9: 166 students (166 girls); Grade 10: 122 students (122 girls); Grade 11: 149 students (149 girls); Grade 12: 147 students (147 girls). 60% of students are Roman Catholic.

Faculty School total: 59. In upper school: 4 men, 55 women; 35 have advanced degrees.

Subjects Offered Accounting, advanced chemistry, advanced math, algebra, American history, American history-AP, American literature, analytic geometry, anatomy, art, art-AP, bioethics, biology, business, calculus, calculus-AP, ceramics, chemistry, choir, chorus, Christian and Hebrew scripture, Christianity, church history, community service, computer multimedia, computer programming, computer science, desktop publishing, earth science, economics, English, English literature, English literature and composition-AP, English literature-AP, environmental science, ethics, European history, film and literature, fine arts, French, geography, geometry, government-AP, government/civics, grammar, health, history, home economics, honors algebra, honors English, honors geometry, journalism, keyboarding, Latin, mathematics, music, newspaper, philosophy, photography, physical education, physics, physiology, pre-calculus, probability and statistics, psychology, psychology-AP, religion, science, social studies, sociology, Spanish, speech, symphonic band, theology, trigonometry, U.S. government and politics-AP, Web site design, world history, world literature, writing.

Graduation Requirements 1 1/2 elective credits, arts and fine arts (art, music, dance, drama), English, foreign language, health education, mathematics, physical education (includes health), religion (includes Bible studies and theology), science, social studies (includes history), technology. Community service is required.

Special Academic Programs Advanced Placement exam preparation; honors section; independent study; academic accommodation for the gifted, the musically talented, and the artistically talented; programs in general development for dyslexic students; special instructional classes for students with mild learning disabilities, organizational deficiencies, Attention Deficit Disorder, and dyslexia.

College Admission Counseling 179 students graduated in 2012; all went to college, including Frostburg State University; Salisbury University; Temple University; Towson University; University of Maryland, Baltimore County; University of Maryland, College Park. Mean SAT critical reading: 533, mean SAT math: 502, mean SAT writing: 550.

Student Life Upper grades have uniform requirement, student council, honor system. Discipline rests equally with students and faculty. Attendance at religious services is required.

Summer Programs Remediation, enrichment, sports, art/fine arts, computer instruction programs offered; held on campus; accepts girls; open to students from other schools. 2013 schedule: June to August.

Tuition and Aid Day student tuition: $11,200. Tuition installment plan (FACTS Tuition Payment Plan, monthly payment plans, individually arranged payment plans, quarterly payment plan). Tuition reduction for siblings, merit scholarship grants, need-based scholarship grants, paying campus jobs available. In 2012–13, 40% of upper-school students received aid; total upper-school merit-scholarship money awarded: $104,000. Total amount of financial aid awarded in 2012–13: $500,000.

Admissions Traditional secondary-level entrance grade is 9. High School Placement Test required. Deadline for receipt of application materials: December 6. Application fee required: $50. On-campus interview required.

Athletics Interscholastic: basketball, cheering, crew, cross-country running, dance squad, dance team, equestrian sports, field hockey, golf, horseback riding, indoor track, lacrosse, modern dance, pom squad, rowing, running, soccer, softball, swimming and diving, tennis, volleyball, winter (indoor) track; intramural: aerobics, aerobics/dance, aerobics/Nautilus, combined training, cooperative games, cross-country running, dance, fitness, fitness walking, flag football, martial arts, ocean paddling, outdoor recreation, physical fitness, strength & conditioning, walking, weight training. 5 PE instructors, 32 coaches, 1 athletic trainer.

Computers Computers are regularly used in computer applications, desktop publishing, English, graphic design, independent study, keyboarding, lab/keyboard, literary magazine, multimedia, photojournalism, programming, research skills, science, typing, Web site design, word processing, yearbook classes. Computer network features include on-campus library services, online commercial services, Internet access, wireless campus network, Internet filtering or blocking technology. Campus intranet and student e-mail accounts are available to students. Students grades are available online. The school has a published electronic and media policy.

Contact Ms. Melissa Davey, Director of Admissions. 301-864-4532 Ext. 7115. Fax: 301-864-8946. E-mail: mdavey@setonhs.org. Web site: www.setonhs.org

THE ELLIS SCHOOL

6425 Fifth Avenue
Pittsburgh, Pennsylvania 15206

Head of School: Mrs. A. Randol Benedict

General Information Girls' day college-preparatory and arts school. Grades PK–12. Founded: 1916. Setting: urban. 8-acre campus. 9 buildings on campus. Approved or accredited by Pennsylvania Association of Independent Schools and Pennsylvania Department of Education. Member of National Association of Independent Schools. Total enrollment: 448. Upper school average class size: 10. Upper school faculty-student ratio: 1:6. There are 167 required school days per year for Upper School students. Upper School students typically attend 5 days per week. The average school day consists of 6 hours.

Upper School Student Profile Grade 9: 31 students (31 girls); Grade 10: 60 students (60 girls); Grade 11: 43 students (43 girls); Grade 12: 43 students (43 girls).

Faculty School total: 78. In upper school: 10 men, 25 women; 23 have advanced degrees.
Subjects Offered Algebra, American history, American literature, anthropology, art, art history, biology, calculus, ceramics, chemistry, computer science, creative writing, dance, drama, English, English literature, European history, expository writing, fine arts, French, geometry, government/civics, health, history, journalism, Latin, linear algebra, mathematics, music, photography, physical education, physics, social studies, Spanish, speech, statistics, theater, trigonometry, world history, world literature, writing.
Graduation Requirements Arts and fine arts (art, music, dance, drama), computer literacy, English, first aid, foreign language, health education, mathematics, physical education (includes health), science, social studies (includes history), completion of three-week mini-course program (grades 9-11), senior projects.
Special Academic Programs Advanced Placement exam preparation; honors section; independent study; term-away projects; academic accommodation for the gifted.
College Admission Counseling 34 students graduated in 2011; all went to college, including Brown University; Davidson College; Harvard University; Indiana University of Pennsylvania; Northwestern University; University of Rochester. Mean SAT critical reading: 637, mean SAT math: 632, mean SAT writing: 635, mean combined SAT: 1902. 67% scored over 600 on SAT critical reading, 71% scored over 600 on SAT math, 71% scored over 600 on SAT writing, 76% scored over 1800 on combined SAT, 74% scored over 26 on composite ACT.
Student Life Upper grades have uniform requirement, student council, honor system. Discipline rests primarily with faculty.
Tuition and Aid Day student tuition: $20,500. Tuition installment plan (FACTS Tuition Payment Plan, 10-month payment plan; two-payment plan). Need-based financial aid available. In 2011–12, 31% of upper-school students received aid. Total amount of financial aid awarded in 2011–12: $968,120.
Admissions Traditional secondary-level entrance grade is 9. For fall 2011, 44 students applied for upper-level admission, 31 were accepted, 15 enrolled. ISEE required. Deadline for receipt of application materials: none. Application fee required: $50. Interview required.
Athletics Interscholastic: basketball, crew, cross-country running, field hockey, gymnastics, lacrosse, soccer, softball, swimming and diving, tennis; intramural: crew, field hockey, lacrosse. 3 PE instructors, 4 coaches, 1 athletic trainer.
Computers Computers are regularly used in all classes. Computer network features include on-campus library services, online commercial services, Internet access, wireless campus network, Internet filtering or blocking technology. Student e-mail accounts are available to students. The school has a published electronic and media policy.
Contact Sara I. Leone, Director of Admissions. 412-661-4880. Fax: 412-661-7634. E-mail: admissions@theellisschool.org. Web site: www.theellisschool.org

ELYRIA CATHOLIC HIGH SCHOOL

725 Gulf Road
Elyria, Ohio 44035-3697

Head of School: Mrs. Amy Butler

General Information Coeducational day college-preparatory, arts, business, and religious studies school, affiliated with Roman Catholic Church. Grades 9–12. Founded: 1948. Setting: suburban. Nearest major city is Cleveland. 16-acre campus. 1 building on campus. Approved or accredited by North Central Association of Colleges and Schools and Ohio Department of Education. Endowment: $3 million. Total enrollment: 486. Upper school average class size: 24. Upper school faculty-student ratio: 1:14. There are 180 required school days per year for Upper School students. Upper School students typically attend 5 days per week. The average school day consists of 6 hours and 42 minutes.
Upper School Student Profile Grade 9: 131 students (67 boys, 64 girls); Grade 10: 94 students (48 boys, 46 girls); Grade 11: 121 students (67 boys, 54 girls); Grade 12: 101 students (51 boys, 50 girls). 90% of students are Roman Catholic.
Faculty School total: 40. In upper school: 18 men, 15 women; 19 have advanced degrees.
Subjects Offered Accounting, advanced math, algebra, American government, American history, American history-AP, analysis of data, anatomy and physiology, art, band, biology, business, calculus, calculus-AP, campus ministry, Catholic belief and practice, chamber groups, chemistry, child development, choir, Christian and Hebrew scripture, Christian doctrine, Christian ethics, church history, computer applications, concert band, concert choir, current events, data analysis, drama, drama performance, earth science, English, fine arts, food and nutrition, French, French language-AP, geometry, German, health, history, honors English, industrial arts, introduction to theater, journalism, leadership, life issues, marching band, music appreciation, parent/child development, peer ministry, physical fitness, physics, prayer/spirituality, pre-calculus, psychology, reading/study skills, social justice, Spanish, Spanish language-AP, theater, world religions, yearbook.
Graduation Requirements Arts and fine arts (art, music, dance, drama), computers, English, mathematics, physical education (includes health), religion (includes Bible studies and theology), science, social studies (includes history), school and community service hours, Ohio Proficiency Test.
Special Academic Programs Advanced Placement exam preparation; honors section; study at local college for college credit; remedial reading and/or remedial writing; remedial math; special instructional classes for students with learning disabilities and Attention Deficit Disorder.
College Admission Counseling 105 students graduated in 2012; 103 went to college. Other: 2 entered military service. Mean SAT critical reading: 570, mean SAT math: 557.
Student Life Upper grades have specified standards of dress, student council, honor system. Discipline rests primarily with faculty. Attendance at religious services is required.
Summer Programs Sports programs offered; session focuses on sports; held on campus; accepts boys and girls; open to students from other schools.
Tuition and Aid Day student tuition: $7050. Tuition installment plan (monthly payment plans). Tuition reduction for siblings, merit scholarship grants, need-based scholarship grants, paying campus jobs available. In 2012–13, 24% of upper-school students received aid; total upper-school merit-scholarship money awarded: $20,000. Total amount of financial aid awarded in 2012–13: $200,000.
Admissions Traditional secondary-level entrance grade is 9. For fall 2012, 152 students applied for upper-level admission, 139 were accepted, 131 enrolled. High School Placement Test (closed version) from Scholastic Testing Service required. Deadline for receipt of application materials: January 14. No application fee required. Interview recommended.
Athletics Interscholastic: baseball (boys), basketball (b,g), cross-country running (b,g), football (b), golf (b), ice hockey (b), rugby (b), soccer (b,g), softball (g), tennis (b,g), volleyball (g), wrestling (b); coed interscholastic: bowling, cheering, swimming and diving, track and field. 2 PE instructors, 47 coaches, 1 athletic trainer.
Computers Computers are regularly used in business studies, journalism, newspaper, typing, word processing, yearbook classes. Computer network features include on-campus library services, Internet access, Internet filtering or blocking technology. Students grades are available online. The school has a published electronic and media policy.
Contact Mr. Michael Polevacik, Director of Admissions. 440-365-1821 Ext. 16. Fax: 440-365-7536. E-mail: polevacik@elyriacatholic.com. Web site: www.elyriacatholic.com

EMMA WILLARD SCHOOL

285 Pawling Avenue
Troy, New York 12180

Head of School: Ms. Trudy E. Hall

General Information Girls' boarding and day college-preparatory and arts school. Grades 9–PG. Founded: 1814. Setting: suburban. Nearest major city is Albany. Students are housed in single-sex dormitories. 137-acre campus. 23 buildings on campus. Approved or accredited by The Association of Boarding Schools and New York Department of Education. Member of National Association of Independent Schools and Secondary School Admission Test Board. Endowment: $86.1 million. Total enrollment: 329. Upper school average class size: 12. Upper school faculty-student ratio: 1:6. There are 167 required school days per year for Upper School students. Upper School students typically attend 5 days per week. The average school day consists of 7 hours and 20 minutes.
Upper School Student Profile Grade 9: 77 students (77 girls); Grade 10: 73 students (73 girls); Grade 11: 89 students (89 girls); Grade 12: 89 students (89 girls); Postgraduate: 3 students (3 girls). 63% of students are boarding students. 53% are state residents. 22 states are represented in upper school student body. 27% are international students. International students from China, Hong Kong, Japan, Mexico, Republic of Korea, and Taiwan; 22 other countries represented in student body.
Faculty School total: 60. In upper school: 13 men, 46 women; 39 have advanced degrees; 43 reside on campus.
Subjects Offered Advanced Placement courses, advanced studio art-AP, algebra, American history, American literature, ancient world history, art, art history, art history-AP, art-AP, ballet, bioethics, biology, biology-AP, calculus, calculus-AP, ceramics, chemistry, chemistry-AP, chorus, comparative government and politics-AP, computer programming, computer science, computer science-AP, conceptual physics, creative writing, dance, digital imaging, drama, drawing and design, economics, English, English literature, English literature and composition-AP, ESL, European history, expository writing, fiber arts, fine arts, forensics, French, French language-AP, geometry, government and politics-AP, government-AP, government/civics, health and wellness, history, internship, Latin, Latin-AP, mathematics, medieval/Renaissance history, music, neuroscience, orchestra, photography, physical education, physics, physics-AP, poetry, practicum, pre-calculus, SAT preparation, science, social sciences, Spanish, Spanish language-AP, Spanish-AP, statistics, statistics-AP, studio art-AP, theater, trigonometry, U.S. history-AP, weaving, world history, world literature.
Graduation Requirements Arts and fine arts (art, music, dance, drama), computer science, English, foreign language, mathematics, physical education (includes health), science, social studies (includes history). Community service is required.
Special Academic Programs 14 Advanced Placement exams for which test preparation is offered; independent study; term-away projects; domestic exchange program (with The Masters School); study abroad; academic accommodation for the gifted, the musically talented, and the artistically talented.

College Admission Counseling 84 students graduated in 2012; 82 went to college, including Cornell University; Hamilton College; Ithaca College; New York University; St. Lawrence University; Wellesley College. Other: 2 had other specific plans. Median SAT critical reading: 630, median SAT math: 630, median SAT writing: 650, median combined SAT: 1930, median composite ACT: 24. 58% scored over 600 on SAT critical reading, 61% scored over 600 on SAT math, 67% scored over 600 on SAT writing, 67% scored over 1800 on combined SAT, 32% scored over 26 on composite ACT.

Student Life Upper grades have specified standards of dress, student council, honor system. Discipline rests equally with students and faculty.

Summer Programs ESL programs offered; session focuses on English language immersion; held on campus; accepts girls; open to students from other schools. 25 students usually enrolled. 2013 schedule: July 20 to August 17. Application deadline: June 1.

Tuition and Aid Day student tuition: $29,690; 7-day tuition and room/board: $48,480. Tuition installment plan (Key Tuition Payment Plan, monthly payment plans). Merit scholarship grants, need-based scholarship grants, Davis Scholars Program, Day Student /Capital District Scholarships available. In 2012–13, 54% of upper-school students received aid; total upper-school merit-scholarship money awarded: $44,535. Total amount of financial aid awarded in 2012–13: $4,408,666.

Admissions Traditional secondary-level entrance grade is 9. For fall 2012, 467 students applied for upper-level admission, 167 were accepted, 112 enrolled. ISEE, PSAT, SAT, or ACT for applicants to grade 11 and 12, psychoeducational evaluation, SSAT or TOEFL required. Deadline for receipt of application materials: February 1. Application fee required: $50. Interview required.

Athletics Interscholastic: aquatics, basketball, crew, cross-country running, diving, field hockey, lacrosse, rowing, soccer, softball, swimming and diving, tennis, track and field, volleyball; intramural: aerobics, aerobics/dance, ballet, basketball, dance, fencing, fitness, fitness walking, floor hockey, hiking/backpacking, jogging, martial arts, modern dance, outdoor activities, physical fitness, physical training, riflery, running, skiing (downhill), snowboarding, soccer, softball, strength & conditioning, swimming and diving, tennis, ultimate Frisbee, volleyball, water polo, weight training. 3 PE instructors, 3 coaches, 1 athletic trainer.

Computers Computers are regularly used in all classes. Computer network features include on-campus library services, online commercial services, Internet access, wireless campus network, Internet filtering or blocking technology. Campus intranet, student e-mail accounts, and computer access in designated common areas are available to students. Students grades are available online. The school has a published electronic and media policy.

Contact Ms. Sharon Busone, Officer Manager. 518-883-1327. Fax: 518-883-1805. E-mail: sbusone@emmawillard.org. Web site: www.emmawillard.org

See Display below, Close-Up on page 578, and Summer Program Close-Up on 706.

THE ENGLISH COLLEGE IN PRAGUE

Sokolovska 320
Prague 190 00, Czech Republic

Head of School: Mr. Mark A. Waldron

General Information Coeducational day college-preparatory and arts school. Grades 8–13. Founded: 1994. Setting: urban. 1-acre campus. 2 buildings on campus. Approved or accredited by Department of Education and Employment, United Kingdom, Headmasters' Conference, Independent Schools Council (UK), and International Baccalaureate Organization. Language of instruction: English. Total enrollment: 360. Upper school average class size: 13. Upper school faculty-student ratio: 1:11. The average school day consists of 7 hours and 30 minutes.

Faculty School total: 40. In upper school: 22 men, 18 women.

Subjects Offered Independent study, International Baccalaureate courses.

Graduation Requirements International Baccalaureate courses, Czech maturita for Czech students.

Special Academic Programs International Baccalaureate program; independent study; academic accommodation for the gifted, the musically talented, and the artistically talented; programs in English for dyslexic students; ESL (30 students enrolled).

College Admission Counseling 67 students graduated in 2012; 64 went to college. Other: 1 went to work, 2 had other specific plans.

Student Life Upper grades have student council, honor system. Discipline rests primarily with faculty.

Summer Programs ESL programs offered; session focuses on English preparation for new students; held on campus; accepts boys and girls; not open to students from other schools. 60 students usually enrolled.

Tuition and Aid Tuition reduction for siblings, bursaries, merit scholarship grants, need-based scholarship grants available. In 2012–13, 30% of upper-school students received aid.

Admissions Traditional secondary-level entrance grade is 12. For fall 2012, 15 students applied for upper-level admission, 6 were accepted, 6 enrolled. English entrance exam and mathematics proficiency exam required. Deadline for receipt of application materials: May 1. Application fee required: 500 Czech korun. Interview required.

Athletics 2 PE instructors.

Computers Computers are regularly used in all academic classes. Computer network features include on-campus library services, online commercial services, Internet access, wireless campus network, Internet filtering or blocking technology. Campus intranet, student e-mail accounts, and computer access in designated common areas are available to students. Students grades are available online.

Contact Mrs. Iva Rozkosna, Admissions Registrar. 420-283893113. Fax: 420-283890118. E-mail: office@englishcollege.cz. Web site: www.englishcollege.cz

THE EPISCOPAL ACADEMY

1785 Bishop White Drive
Newtown Square, Pennsylvania 19073

General Information Coeducational day college-preparatory, arts, religious studies, and technology school, affiliated with Episcopal Church. Grades PK–12. Founded: 1785. Setting: suburban. Nearest major city is Philadelphia. 123-acre campus. 12 buildings on campus. Approved or accredited by Middle States Association of Colleges and Schools, Pennsylvania Association of Independent Schools, and Pennsylvania Department of Education. Member of National Association of Independent Schools and Secondary School Admission Test Board. Endowment: $16.5 million. Total enrollment: 1,223. Upper school average class size: 13. Upper school faculty-student ratio: 1:7. There are 172 required school days per year for Upper School students. Upper School students typically attend 5 days per week. The average school day consists of 9 hours and 30 minutes.

See Display below and Close-Up on page 580.

EPISCOPAL COLLEGIATE SCHOOL

Jackson T. Stephens Campus
1701 Cantrell Road
Little Rock, Arkansas 72201

Head of School: Mr. Steve Hickman

General Information Coeducational day college-preparatory, arts, and technology school, affiliated with Episcopal Church. Grades PK–12. Founded: 2000. Setting: suburban. Nearest major city is Memphis, TN. 34-acre campus. 3 buildings on campus. Approved or accredited by National Association of Episcopal Schools and Southwest Association of Episcopal Schools. Member of National Association of Independent Schools. Endowment: $40 million. Total enrollment: 763. Upper school average class size: 15. Upper school faculty-student ratio: 1:10. There are 179 required school days per year for Upper School students. Upper School students typically attend 5 days per week. The average school day consists of 7 hours and 30 minutes.

Upper School Student Profile Grade 9: 62 students (28 boys, 34 girls); Grade 10: 51 students (27 boys, 24 girls); Grade 11: 62 students (30 boys, 32 girls); Grade 12: 53 students (19 boys, 34 girls). 20% of students are members of Episcopal Church.

Faculty School total: 96. In upper school: 15 men, 25 women; 33 have advanced degrees.

Graduation Requirements Senior chapel talk.

Special Academic Programs 16 Advanced Placement exams for which test preparation is offered; honors section; independent study.

College Admission Counseling 43 students graduated in 2012; all went to college, including Hendrix College; Rhodes College; Sewanee: The University of the South; The University of Texas at Austin; Tulane University; University of Arkansas. Mean SAT critical reading: 637, mean SAT math: 610, mean SAT writing: 633, mean combined SAT: 1879, mean composite ACT: 27. 66% scored over 600 on SAT critical reading, 47% scored over 600 on SAT math, 63% scored over 600 on SAT writing, 63% scored over 1800 on combined SAT, 43% scored over 26 on composite ACT.

Student Life Upper grades have uniform requirement, student council, honor system. Discipline rests primarily with faculty. Attendance at religious services is required.

Summer Programs Enrichment, sports, art/fine arts, computer instruction programs offered; session focuses on enrichment; held on campus; accepts boys and girls; open to students from other schools. 150 students usually enrolled. 2013 schedule: June 1 to July 31. Application deadline: May 30.

Tuition and Aid Day student tuition: $10,700. Tuition installment plan (FACTS Tuition Payment Plan). Need-based scholarship grants available. In 2012–13, 20% of upper-school students received aid. Total amount of financial aid awarded in 2012–13: $440,000.

Admissions Traditional secondary-level entrance grade is 9. For fall 2012, 28 students applied for upper-level admission, 20 were accepted, 16 enrolled. Stanford 9 required. Deadline for receipt of application materials: none. Application fee required: $50. Interview required.

Athletics Interscholastic: baseball (boys), basketball (b,g), cross-country running (b,g), fishing (b,g), fitness (b,g), football (b), golf (b,g), physical fitness (b,g), physical training (b,g), soccer (b,g), tennis (b,g), track and field (b,g), volleyball (g), weight training (b,g), wrestling (b,g); coed interscholastic: cheering. 3 PE instructors, 8 coaches, 2 athletic trainers.

Computers Computers are regularly used in all academic classes. Computer network features include on-campus library services, online commercial services, Internet access, wireless campus network, Internet filtering or blocking technology. Campus intranet, student e-mail accounts, and computer access in designated common areas are available to students. Students grades are available online. The school has a published electronic and media policy.

Contact Ms. Ashley Honeywell, Director of Admission. 501-372-1194 Ext. 2406. Fax: 501-372-2160. E-mail: ahoneywell@episcopalcollegiate.org. Web site: www.episcopalcollegiate.org

EPISCOPAL HIGH SCHOOL

4650 Bissonnet
Bellaire, Texas 77401

Head of School: Mr. C. Edward Smith

General Information Coeducational day college-preparatory, arts, religious studies, and technology school, affiliated with Episcopal Church. Grades 9–12. Founded: 1984. Setting: urban. Nearest major city is Houston. 35-acre campus. 7 buildings on campus. Approved or accredited by Independent Schools Association of the Southwest, National Association of Episcopal Schools, and Texas Department of Education. Member of National Association of Independent Schools and Secondary School Admission Test Board. Total enrollment: 673. Upper school average class size: 15. Upper school faculty-student ratio: 1:9. Upper School students typically attend 5 days per week. The average school day consists of 8 hours.

Upper School Student Profile Grade 9: 164 students (94 boys, 70 girls); Grade 10: 166 students (80 boys, 86 girls); Grade 11: 172 students (76 boys, 96 girls); Grade 12: 171 students (81 boys, 90 girls). 22.9% of students are members of Episcopal Church.

Faculty School total: 95. In upper school: 41 men, 54 women; 57 have advanced degrees.

Subjects Offered Acting, algebra, anatomy, ancient history, art appreciation, art history, band, Bible studies, biology, biology-AP, calculus-AP, ceramics, chemistry, choir, civil rights, dance, debate, design, drawing, English, English-AP, ethics, European history, French, French-AP, geography, geology, geometry, government, government-AP, graphic design, health, history of science, instrumental music, journalism, Latin, Latin American studies, music theory, newspaper, oceanography, orchestra, painting, photography, physical education, physics, physics-AP, physiology, pre-calculus, sculpture, Spanish, Spanish-AP, speech, stagecraft, statistics, theater, theology, U.S. history, U.S. history-AP, video film production, Vietnam War, world religions, World War II, writing, yearbook.

Graduation Requirements Arts and fine arts (art, music, dance, drama), English, foreign language, mathematics, physical education (includes health), religion (includes Bible studies and theology), religious studies, science, social studies (includes history).

Special Academic Programs 14 Advanced Placement exams for which test preparation is offered; honors section; independent study; study at local college for college credit.

College Admission Counseling 171 students graduated in 2012; all went to college, including Southern Methodist University; Texas Christian University; The University of Texas at Austin; Washington and Lee University. Mean SAT critical reading: 608, mean SAT math: 617, mean SAT writing: 610, mean combined SAT: 2010.

Student Life Upper grades have uniform requirement, student council, honor system. Discipline rests equally with students and faculty. Attendance at religious services is required.

Summer Programs Remediation, enrichment, advancement, art/fine arts programs offered; session focuses on remediation, advancement, enrichment; held on campus; accepts boys and girls; open to students from other schools. 250 students usually enrolled. 2013 schedule: June 3 to July 14. Application deadline: May 10.

Tuition and Aid Day student tuition: $22,880. Tuition installment plan (Insured Tuition Payment Plan, SMART Tuition Payment Plan, monthly payment plans). Need-based scholarship grants, middle-income loans available. In 2012–13, 19% of upper-school students received aid. Total amount of financial aid awarded in 2012–13: $1,700,000.

Admissions Traditional secondary-level entrance grade is 9. For fall 2012, 617 students applied for upper-level admission, 412 were accepted, 182 enrolled. ISEE and Otis-Lennon Ability or Stanford Achievement Test required. Deadline for receipt of application materials: January 7. Application fee required: $75. On-campus interview required.

Athletics Interscholastic: ballet (boys, girls), baseball (b), basketball (b,g), cheering (b,g), cross-country running (b,g), dance (b,g), drill team (g), field hockey (b,g), fitness (b,g), football (b), golf (b,g), lacrosse (b,g), physical fitness (b,g), running (b,g), soccer (b,g), softball (g), strength & conditioning (b,g), swimming and diving (b,g), tennis (b,g), track and field (b,g), volleyball (b,g), weight training (b,g), wrestling (b). 7 PE instructors, 8 coaches, 1 athletic trainer.

Computers Computers are regularly used in art, English, foreign language, history, mathematics, music, religion, science classes. Computer network features include on-campus library services, online commercial services, Internet access, wireless campus network, CollegeView. Student e-mail accounts are available to students. Students grades are available online. The school has a published electronic and media policy.

Contact Audrey Koehler, Director of Admission. 713-512-3400. Fax: 713-512-3603. E-mail: kpiper@ehshouston.org. Web site: www.ehshouston.org/

EPISCOPAL HIGH SCHOOL

1200 North Quaker Lane
Alexandria, Virginia 22302

Head of School: Mr. F. Robertson Hershey

General Information Coeducational boarding college-preparatory, arts, religious studies, and technology school, affiliated with Episcopal Church. Grades 9–12. Founded: 1839. Setting: urban. Nearest major city is Washington, DC. Students are housed in single-sex dormitories. 130-acre campus. 26 buildings on campus. Approved or accredited by Association of Independent Schools of Greater Washington, National Association of Episcopal Schools, Southern Association of Colleges and Schools, and Virginia Department of Education. Member of National Association of Independent Schools and Secondary School Admission Test Board. Endowment: $167 million. Total enrollment: 435. Upper school average class size: 12. Upper school faculty-student ratio: 1:6.

Upper School Student Profile Grade 9: 100 students (49 boys, 51 girls); Grade 10: 125 students (59 boys, 66 girls); Grade 11: 124 students (69 boys, 55 girls); Grade 12: 100 students (48 boys, 52 girls). 100% of students are boarding students. 35% are state residents. 27 states are represented in upper school student body. 7% are international students. International students from China, Republic of Korea, Saudi Arabia, Thailand, United Kingdom, and Zimbabwe; 12 other countries represented in student body. 40% of students are members of Episcopal Church.

Faculty School total: 68. In upper school: 42 men, 26 women; 61 have advanced degrees; 54 reside on campus.

Subjects Offered 3-dimensional art, 3-dimensional design, advanced chemistry, advanced math, Advanced Placement courses, advanced studio art-AP, algebra, American history, American literature, art, art history, art-AP, astronomy, biology, biology-AP, calculus, calculus-AP, ceramics, chemistry, chemistry-AP, Chinese, choir, composition-AP, computer programming, computer programming-AP, computer science, computer science-AP, creative writing, dance, drama, economics, economics-AP, English, English literature, English literature and composition-AP, English literature-AP, English-AP, English/composition-AP, environmental science, environmental science-AP, ethics, European history, European history-AP, fine arts, forensics, French, French language-AP, French literature-AP, geometry, German, German-AP, government-AP, government/civics, Greek, history, honors algebra, honors English, honors geometry, honors U.S. history, honors world history, international relations, Latin, Latin-AP, mathematics, microeconomics-AP, Middle Eastern history, modern European history-AP, music, music theory-AP, photography, physical education, physics, physics-AP, pre-calculus, psychology-AP, religion, science, senior internship, Shakespeare, social sciences, social studies, Spanish, Spanish literature-AP, statistics-AP, theater, theology, trigonometry, U.S. history-AP, world history, world history-AP, writing.

Graduation Requirements Arts and fine arts (art, music, dance, drama), computer studies, English, foreign language, mathematics, physical education (includes health), science, social studies (includes history), theology.

Special Academic Programs Advanced Placement exam preparation; honors section; independent study; term-away projects; study abroad; academic accommodation for the gifted, the musically talented, and the artistically talented.

College Admission Counseling 111 students graduated in 2012; all went to college, including The University of North Carolina at Chapel Hill; University of Virginia; Washington and Lee University. 64% scored over 600 on SAT critical reading, 68% scored over 600 on SAT math, 71% scored over 600 on SAT writing.

Student Life Upper grades have specified standards of dress, student council, honor system. Discipline rests primarily with faculty. Attendance at religious services is required.

Summer Programs Enrichment, advancement, sports, art/fine arts programs offered; session focuses on academic enrichment and athletic skills; held on campus; accepts boys and girls; open to students from other schools.

Tuition and Aid 7-day tuition and room/board: $46,600. Tuition installment plan (Insured Tuition Payment Plan, monthly payment plans). Merit scholarship grants, need-based scholarship grants, paying campus jobs available. In 2012–13, 30% of upper-school students received aid; total upper-school merit-scholarship money awarded: $145,000. Total amount of financial aid awarded in 2012–13: $4,400,000.

Admissions Traditional secondary-level entrance grade is 9. For fall 2012, 634 students applied for upper-level admission, 246 were accepted, 147 enrolled. ISEE, PSAT or SAT or SSAT required. Deadline for receipt of application materials: January 15. Application fee required: $60. Interview required.

Athletics Interscholastic: baseball (boys), basketball (b,g), crew (g), cross-country running (b,g), field hockey (g), football (b), golf (b), indoor track (b,g), indoor track & field (b,g), lacrosse (b,g), modern dance (g), rowing (g), soccer (b,g), softball (g), squash (b,g), tennis (b,g), track and field (b,g), volleyball (g), winter (indoor) track (b,g), wrestling (b); intramural: soccer (b), strength & conditioning (b,g); coed interscholastic: aerobics, aerobics/dance, aerobics/Nautilus, backpacking, ballet, canoeing/kayaking, climbing, dance, fitness, hiking/backpacking, kayaking, outdoor activities, outdoor adventure, outdoor education, outdoor recreation, outdoors, physical fitness, physical training, rock climbing, strength & conditioning, weight lifting, weight training; coed intramural: ballet, fitness, modern dance, outdoor activities, physical fitness, physical training, power lifting, wall climbing, weight lifting, weight training. 4 coaches, 2 athletic trainers.

Computers Computers are regularly used in all academic classes. Computer network features include on-campus library services, online commercial services, Internet access, wireless campus network, Internet filtering or blocking technology. Campus intranet and student e-mail accounts are available to students. Students grades are available online. The school has a published electronic and media policy.

Contact Mr. Scott Conklin, Director of Admission. 703-933-4062. Fax: 703-933-3016. E-mail: admissions@episcopalhighschool.org. Web site: www.episcopalhighschool.org

EPISCOPAL HIGH SCHOOL OF JACKSONVILLE

Episcopal School of Jacksonville
4455 Atlantic Boulevard
Jacksonville, Florida 32207

Head of School: Charles F. Zimmer

General Information Coeducational day college-preparatory, arts, religious studies, and technology school, affiliated with Episcopal Church. Grades 6–12. Founded: 1966. Setting: urban. 88-acre campus. 25 buildings on campus. Approved or accredited by Florida Council of Independent Schools, National Association of Episcopal Schools, Southern Association of Colleges and Schools, and Southern Association of Independent Schools. Member of National Association of Independent Schools. Endowment: $15.4 million. Total enrollment: 857. Upper school average class size: 17. Upper school faculty-student ratio: 1:10. There are 175 required school days per year for Upper School students. Upper School students typically attend 5 days per week. The average school day consists of 6 hours and 50 minutes.

Upper School Student Profile Grade 9: 140 students (76 boys, 64 girls); Grade 10: 142 students (73 boys, 69 girls); Grade 11: 140 students (73 boys, 67 girls); Grade 12: 144 students (77 boys, 67 girls). 33% of students are members of Episcopal Church.

Faculty School total: 93. In upper school: 35 men, 58 women; 53 have advanced degrees.

Subjects Offered Advanced studio art-AP, algebra, American history, American history-AP, American literature, ancient history, art, art history, art history-AP, band, Basic programming, biology, biology-AP, calculus, calculus-AP, ceramics, chemistry, chemistry-AP, Chinese, computer programming, computer science, computer science-AP, dance, drama, earth science, economics, electronic publishing, English, English language and composition-AP, English literature and composition-AP, English/composition-AP, environmental science-AP, European history-AP, fine arts, French, French language-AP, geography, geometry, German, German-AP, government and politics-AP, government/civics, health, history, journalism, Latin, Latin-AP, marine biology, mathematics, music, music history, music theory, music theory-AP, photography, physical education, physics, physics-AP, public speaking, religion, religious studies, science, social studies, Spanish, Spanish language-AP, statistics, statistics-AP, studio art-AP, technical theater, theater, theology, trigonometry, U.S. government and politics-AP, U.S. history-AP, world history, writing, yearbook.

Graduation Requirements Arts and fine arts (art, music, dance, drama), computer science, English, foreign language, leadership, library skills, mathematics, physical education (includes health), religion (includes Bible studies and theology), science, social studies (includes history), 75 community service hours. Community service is required.

Special Academic Programs Advanced Placement exam preparation; honors section; independent study; study abroad; academic accommodation for the gifted.

College Admission Counseling 156 students graduated in 2012; all went to college, including Florida State University; University of Florida; University of North Florida. Median SAT critical reading: 579, median SAT math: 584, median SAT writing: 567, median combined SAT: 1729, median composite ACT: 26.

Student Life Upper grades have uniform requirement, student council, honor system. Discipline rests equally with students and faculty. Attendance at religious services is required.

Summer Programs Remediation, enrichment, advancement, sports, art/fine arts, rigorous outdoor training, computer instruction programs offered; session focuses on academics, athletics, fine arts, specialty programs; held both on and off campus; held at beach for fishing camp, paint ball facility, ice skating facility, golf course; accepts boys and girls; open to students from other schools. 500 students usually enrolled. 2013 schedule: May 27 to August 5. Application deadline: May 26.

Tuition and Aid Day student tuition: $18,500. Tuition installment plan (Insured Tuition Payment Plan, monthly payment plans). Need-based scholarship grants available. In 2012–13, 23% of upper-school students received aid. Total amount of financial aid awarded in 2012–13: $2,000,000.

Admissions Traditional secondary-level entrance grade is 9. For fall 2012, 89 students applied for upper-level admission, 58 were accepted, 38 enrolled. ISEE required. Deadline for receipt of application materials: January 11. Application fee required: $50. On-campus interview required.

Athletics Interscholastic: baseball (boys), basketball (b,g), crew (b,g), cross-country running (b,g), football (b), golf (b,g), lacrosse (b,g), modern dance (b,g), soccer (b,g), softball (g), swimming and diving (b,g), tennis (b,g), track and field (b,g), volleyball (g), weight lifting (b), weight training (b), wrestling (b); intramural: dance (g); coed interscholastic: cheering, dance, dance squad, dance team, wrestling; coed intramural: fencing. 7 PE instructors, 100 coaches, 4 athletic trainers.

Computers Computers are regularly used in all classes. Computer network features include on-campus library services, online commercial services, Internet access, wireless campus network, Internet filtering or blocking technology, Senior Systems: My BackPack online grading and student accounts, online parent portals, RSS feeds. Campus intranet, student e-mail accounts, and computer access in designated common areas are available to students. Students grades are available online. The school has a published electronic and media policy.

Contact Peggy P. Fox, Director of Admissions. 904-396-7104. Fax: 904-396-0981. E-mail: foxp@episcopalhigh.org. Web site: www.episcopalhigh.org

ESCOLA AMERICANA DE CAMPINAS

Rua Cajamar, 35
Ch?ra da Barra
Campinas-SP 13090-860, Brazil

Head of School: Stephen A. Herrera

General Information Coeducational day college-preparatory, arts, bilingual studies, and technology school. Grades PK–12. Founded: 1956. Setting: urban. Nearest major city is S?Paulo, Brazil. 4-acre campus. 4 buildings on campus. Approved or accredited by Association of American Schools in South America and Southern Association of Colleges and Schools. Affiliate member of National Association of Independent Schools; member of European Council of International Schools. Languages of instruction: English and Portuguese. Endowment: $350,000. Total enrollment: 300. Upper school average class size: 20. Upper school faculty-student ratio: 1:7.

Upper School Student Profile Grade 6: 46 students (26 boys, 20 girls); Grade 7: 39 students (15 boys, 24 girls); Grade 8: 53 students (28 boys, 25 girls); Grade 9: 42 students (19 boys, 23 girls); Grade 10: 41 students (19 boys, 22 girls); Grade 11: 45 students (21 boys, 24 girls); Grade 12: 34 students (17 boys, 17 girls).

Faculty School total: 76. In upper school: 11 men, 24 women; 30 have advanced degrees.

Subjects Offered Algebra, American history, American literature, art, biology, calculus, chemistry, computer science, creative writing, drama, economics, English, English literature, fine arts, geography, geometry, government/civics, grammar, history, journalism, mathematics, music, physical education, physics, Portuguese, psychology, science, social studies, speech, trigonometry, world history, world literature, writing.

Graduation Requirements Arts and fine arts (art, music, dance, drama), computer science, English, foreign language, mathematics, physical education (includes health), science, social studies (includes history). Community service is required.

Special Academic Programs Advanced Placement exam preparation; honors section; term-away projects; study at local college for college credit; study abroad; special instructional classes for students with mild learning differences; ESL (5 students enrolled).

College Admission Counseling 17 students graduated in 2012; 16 went to college, including Emerson College; Northwestern University; Southwestern University; The University of Tampa. Other: 1 entered a postgraduate year. Median SAT critical reading: 610, median SAT math: 640, median SAT writing: 540, median combined SAT: 1790.

Student Life Upper grades have student council, honor system. Discipline rests equally with students and faculty.

Tuition and Aid Day student tuition: 57,594 Brazilian reals. Tuition installment plan (monthly payment plans). Need-based scholarship grants available. In 2012–13, 10% of upper-school students received aid. Total amount of financial aid awarded in 2012–13: $51,000.

Admissions Traditional secondary-level entrance grade is 9. For fall 2012, 57 students applied for upper-level admission, 33 were accepted, 28 enrolled. Admissions testing, English Composition Test for ESL students, ERB CTP IV, Iowa Test, CTBS, or TAP, SAT and writing sample required. Deadline for receipt of application materials: September 3. No application fee required. On-campus interview required.

Athletics Interscholastic: basketball (boys, girls), canoeing/kayaking (g), cheering (g), indoor soccer (b,g), soccer (b,g), volleyball (g); intramural: ballet (g), basketball (b,g), canoeing/kayaking (g), cheering (g), climbing (b,g), indoor soccer (b,g), soccer (b,g); coed intramural: aerobics, baseball, basketball, climbing, cooperative games, fitness, flag football, Frisbee, gymnastics, handball, indoor soccer, jogging, judo, kickball, martial arts, physical fitness, self defense, soccer, softball, strength & conditioning, table tennis, track and field, ultimate Frisbee, volleyball. 6 PE instructors, 11 coaches.

Computers Computers are regularly used in art, English, history, independent study, mathematics, science, yearbook classes. Computer network features include on-campus library services, online commercial services, Internet access. Campus intranet is available to students.

Contact Davi Sanchez, High School Principal. 55-19-2102-1006. Fax: 55-19-2102-1016. E-mail: davi.sanchez@eac.com.br. Web site: www.eac.com.br

THE ETHEL WALKER SCHOOL

230 Bushy Hill Road
Simsbury, Connecticut 06070

Head of School: Mrs. Elizabeth Cromwell Speers

General Information Girls' boarding and day college-preparatory and arts school. Boarding grades 9–12, day grades 6–12. Founded: 1911. Setting: suburban. Nearest major city is Hartford. Students are housed in single-sex dormitories. 300-acre campus. 9 buildings on campus. Approved or accredited by Connecticut Association of Independent Schools, New England Association of Schools and Colleges, The Association of Boarding Schools, and Connecticut Department of Education. Member of National Association of Independent Schools and Secondary School Admission Test Board. Endowment: $15.9 million. Total enrollment: 260. Upper school average class size: 12. Upper school faculty-student ratio: 1:6. There are 180 required school days per year for Upper School students. Upper School students typically attend 5 days per week. The average school day consists of 7 hours.

Upper School Student Profile Grade 9: 42 students (42 girls); Grade 10: 63 students (63 girls); Grade 11: 64 students (64 girls); Grade 12: 52 students (52 girls). 62% of students are boarding students. 43% are state residents. 23 states are represented in upper school student body. 19% are international students. International students from Afghanistan, China, Germany, Republic of Korea, Somalia, and Spain; 9 other countries represented in student body.

Faculty School total: 45. In upper school: 12 men, 31 women; 27 have advanced degrees; 30 reside on campus.

Subjects Offered 3-dimensional art, acting, advanced studio art-AP, African history, African literature, African studies, algebra, American government, American history, American history-AP, American literature, anatomy and physiology, Ancient Greek, ancient world history, art, art history, art-AP, Asian history, astronomy, bell choir, biology, biology-AP, calculus, calculus-AP, Caribbean history, ceramics, chemistry, chemistry-AP, Chinese, choir, choral music, choreography, civil rights, computer literacy, computer science, computer science-AP, conceptual physics, concert bell choir, concert choir, creative writing, digital photography, directing, diversity studies, drama, drama performance, dramatic arts, drawing, drawing and design, East Asian history, economics, economics-AP, English, English composition, English literature, English literature and composition-AP, English literature-AP, environmental science, environmental science-AP, environmental studies, equine science, ethics, European history, European history-AP, fiber arts, fiction, fine arts, forensics, French language-AP, geography, geometry, graphic design, health and wellness, history, history-AP, honors algebra, honors English, honors geometry, honors U.S. history, honors world history, independent study, instrumental music, Islamic studies, justice seminar, Latin, Latin American history, Latin-AP, leadership, macro/microeconomics-AP, Mandarin, Middle Eastern history, modern civilization, modern European history, modern European history-AP, music, music theory, musical theater, mythology, newspaper, painting, peace and justice, philosophy of government, photography, physics, physics-AP, playwriting, poetry, pre-calculus, psychology, psychology-AP, public speaking, religion and culture, Russian studies, sculpture, senior project, set design, Shakespeare, social justice, Spanish, Spanish language-AP, Spanish literature-AP, statistics-AP, student publications, studio art-AP, the Web, theater, trigonometry, U.S. history, U.S. history-AP, visual and performing arts, voice, Western civilization, women in literature, women's health, world history, world literature, world religions, writing, yearbook.

Graduation Requirements Arts and fine arts (art, music, dance, drama), English, ethics, foreign language, history, leadership, mathematics, performing arts, science, women's health, Junior/Senior project, community service hours. Community service is required.

Special Academic Programs 19 Advanced Placement exams for which test preparation is offered; honors section; independent study; term-away projects; study at local college for college credit; study abroad; academic accommodation for the gifted, the musically talented, and the artistically talented; ESL (12 students enrolled).

College Admission Counseling 41 students graduated in 2012; 39 went to college, including Barnard College; Bates College; Boston University; Carnegie Mellon University; Colgate University; Harvard University. Other: 2 entered a postgraduate year. Mean SAT critical reading: 545, mean SAT math: 552, mean SAT writing: 579, mean composite ACT: 24.

Student Life Upper grades have specified standards of dress, student council, honor system. Discipline rests equally with students and faculty.

Summer Programs Sports, art/fine arts programs offered; held on campus; accepts boys and girls; open to students from other schools. 2013 schedule: June to August. Application deadline: May.

Tuition and Aid Day student tuition: $36,350; 7-day tuition and room/board: $49,925. Tuition installment plan (monthly payment plans, individually arranged payment plans, 1-, 2-, and 10-payment plans). Need-based scholarship grants available. In 2012–13, 42% of upper-school students received aid. Total amount of financial aid awarded in 2012–13: $3,058,789.

Admissions Traditional secondary-level entrance grade is 9. For fall 2012, 321 students applied for upper-level admission, 171 were accepted, 88 enrolled. SSAT and TOEFL required. Deadline for receipt of application materials: February 1. Application fee required: $60. Interview required.

Athletics Interscholastic: alpine skiing, basketball, dance, dressage, equestrian sports, field hockey, golf, horseback riding, independent competitive sports, lacrosse, modern dance, nordic skiing, skiing (downhill), soccer, softball, squash, swimming and diving, tennis, volleyball; intramural: ballet, climbing, combined training, cross-country running, dance, dance team, equestrian sports, fitness, hiking/backpacking, jogging, kayaking, mountain biking, mountaineering, Nautilus, outdoor activities, outdoor adventure, physical fitness, physical training, rock climbing, ropes courses, running, strength & conditioning, wall climbing, weight lifting, weight training, yoga. 5 coaches, 1 athletic trainer.

Computers Computer network features include on-campus library services, online commercial services, Internet access, wireless campus network, Internet filtering or blocking technology. Student e-mail accounts and computer access in designated common areas are available to students. Students grades are available online. The school has a published electronic and media policy.

Contact Ms. Missy Shea, Director of Admission. 860-408-4200. Fax: 860-408-4201. E-mail: mshea@ethelwalker.org. Web site: www.ethelwalker.org

EXCEL CHRISTIAN ACADEMY

325 Old Mill Road
Cartersville, Georgia 30120

Head of School: Dr. Davis Nelson

General Information Coeducational day college-preparatory school, affiliated with Christian faith. Grades K–12. Founded: 1993. Setting: suburban. 15-acre campus. 3 buildings on campus. Approved or accredited by Association of Christian Schools International, Southern Association of Colleges and Schools, and Georgia Department of Education. Total enrollment: 297. Upper school average class size: 20. Upper school faculty-student ratio: 1:18. There are 177 required school days per year for Upper School students. Upper School students typically attend 5 days per week. The average school day consists of 7 hours and 25 minutes.

Upper School Student Profile Grade 9: 21 students (9 boys, 12 girls); Grade 10: 30 students (13 boys, 17 girls); Grade 11: 26 students (16 boys, 10 girls); Grade 12: 24 students (9 boys, 15 girls). 99% of students are Christian.

Faculty School total: 29. In upper school: 10 men, 10 women; 10 have advanced degrees.

Subjects Offered Algebra, American government, anatomy, art, band, Bible, British literature, broadcast journalism, business education, calculus-AP, chemistry, choir, chorus, computer applications, concert band, dance, drama, earth science, electives, English, English literature, foreign language, government, health, history, life science, literature, mathematics, music, personal fitness, physical education, physical science, physics, pre-algebra, psychology, reading, science, social studies, Spanish, trigonometry, U.S. government, U.S. history, U.S. history-AP, world geography, world history.

Graduation Requirements Advanced Placement courses, Bible, computer technologies, electives, English, foreign language, history, mathematics, physical education (includes health), science.

Special Academic Programs 2 Advanced Placement exams for which test preparation is offered; honors section; study at local college for college credit.

College Admission Counseling 18 students graduated in 2011; 17 went to college, including Georgia Institute of Technology; Kennesaw State University; Truett-McConnell College; Valdosta State University. Other: 1 had other specific plans. Median SAT critical reading: 480, median SAT math: 490, median SAT writing: 470. Mean combined SAT: 1481. 11% scored over 600 on SAT critical reading, 17% scored over 600 on SAT math, 17% scored over 600 on SAT writing, 17% scored over 1800 on combined SAT.

Student Life Upper grades have uniform requirement, student council, honor system. Discipline rests primarily with faculty.

Tuition and Aid Day student tuition: $8640. Tuition installment plan (monthly payment plans). Need-based scholarship grants available.

Admissions Traditional secondary-level entrance grade is 9. For fall 2011, 21 students applied for upper-level admission, 21 were accepted, 17 enrolled. Any standardized test required. Deadline for receipt of application materials: none. Application fee required: $100. Interview required.

Athletics Interscholastic: baseball (boys), basketball (b,g), cheering (g), cross-country running (b,g), softball (g); intramural: football (b); coed interscholastic: soccer. 2 PE instructors, 4 coaches.

Computers Computers are regularly used in business applications, computer applications, newspaper, yearbook classes. Computer network features include Internet access, wireless campus network, Internet filtering or blocking technology. Computer access in designated common areas is available to students. Students grades are available online. The school has a published electronic and media policy.

Contact Mrs. Krista K. Keefe, Counselor. 770-382-9488. Fax: 770-606-9884. E-mail: kkeefe@excelacademy.cc. Web site: www.excelacademy.cc

EXPLORATIONS ACADEMY

PO Box 3014
Bellingham, Washington 98227

Head of School: Daniel Kirkpatrick

General Information Coeducational day college-preparatory, experiential education, and international field study expeditions school. Ungraded, ages 11–18.

Founded: 1995. Setting: urban. Nearest major city is Vancouver, BC, Canada. 1-acre campus. 1 building on campus. Approved or accredited by Northwest Accreditation Commission, Pacific Northwest Association of Independent Schools, and Washington Department of Education. Total enrollment: 33. Upper school average class size: 9. Upper school faculty-student ratio: 1:7. There are 177 required school days per year for Upper School students. Upper School students typically attend 5 days per week. The average school day consists of 6 hours.

Faculty School total: 10. In upper school: 5 men, 5 women; 6 have advanced degrees.

Subjects Offered Agriculture, American literature, anatomy and physiology, anthropology, archaeology, art, boat building, botany, calculus, carpentry, chemistry, Chinese, computer graphics, computer programming, conflict resolution, construction, creative writing, desktop publishing, drawing, earth science, ecology, environmental science, first aid, gardening, gender issues, geology, government, health, horticulture, human relations, journalism, Latin American studies, leadership, marine biology, media, meteorology, microbiology, music, music history, painting, philosophy, photography, physical education, physics, poetry, political science, psychology, sculpture, sexuality, short story, Spanish, technology, theater design and production, video film production, world cultures, world geography, world history, world literature, writing.

Graduation Requirements Arts and fine arts (art, music, dance, drama), computer science, English, foreign language, human relations, lab science, mathematics, occupational education, physical education (includes health), science, social sciences, social studies (includes history), U.S. government and politics, Washington State and Northwest History, world history, one term of self-designed interdisciplinary studies, one month-long international study/service expedition. Community service is required.

Special Academic Programs Advanced Placement exam preparation; honors section; accelerated programs; independent study; term-away projects; academic accommodation for the gifted.

College Admission Counseling 1 student graduated in 2012 and went to The Evergreen State College; University of Washington; Western Washington University.

Student Life Upper grades have honor system. Discipline rests primarily with faculty.

Summer Programs Enrichment, advancement, art/fine arts, rigorous outdoor training programs offered; session focuses on experiential learning; held both on and off campus; held at local urban and wilderness areas; accepts boys and girls; open to students from other schools. 12 students usually enrolled. 2013 schedule: July 8 to August 16. Application deadline: none.

Tuition and Aid Day student tuition: $12,700. Tuition installment plan (monthly payment plans, individually arranged payment plans, school's own payment plan). Merit scholarship grants, need-based scholarship grants, need-based loans, low-interest loans with deferred payment available. In 2012–13, 48% of upper-school students received aid; total upper-school merit-scholarship money awarded: $35,000. Total amount of financial aid awarded in 2012–13: $140,000.

Admissions Traditional secondary-level entrance age is 14. For fall 2012, 35 students applied for upper-level admission, 33 were accepted, 33 enrolled. Non-standardized placement tests required. Deadline for receipt of application materials: none. Application fee required: $50. Interview required.

Computers Computers are regularly used in animation, art, English, French, graphics, mathematics, media production, publications, SAT preparation, science, writing, yearbook classes. Computer network features include online commercial services, Internet access, wireless campus network. Computer access in designated common areas is available to students. The school has a published electronic and media policy.

Contact Allison Roberts, Registrar. 360-671-8085. Fax: 360-671-2521. E-mail: info@explorationsacademy.org. Web site: www.ExplorationsAcademy.org

EZELL-HARDING CHRISTIAN SCHOOL

574 Bell Road
Antioch, Tennessee 37013

Head of School: Mrs. Belvia Pruitt

General Information Coeducational day college-preparatory and religious studies school, affiliated with Church of Christ. Grades K–12. Founded: 1973. Setting: suburban. Nearest major city is Nashville. 30-acre campus. 1 building on campus. Approved or accredited by National Christian School Association, Southern Association of Colleges and Schools, and Tennessee Association of Independent Schools. Endowment: $100,000. Total enrollment: 648. Upper school average class size: 19. Upper school faculty-student ratio: 1:12. There are 176 required school days per year for Upper School students. Upper School students typically attend 5 days per week. The average school day consists of 7 hours.

Upper School Student Profile Grade 9: 62 students (33 boys, 29 girls); Grade 10: 50 students (27 boys, 23 girls); Grade 11: 52 students (18 boys, 34 girls); Grade 12: 62 students (32 boys, 30 girls). 40% of students are members of Church of Christ.

Faculty School total: 70. In upper school: 9 men, 10 women; 10 have advanced degrees.

Subjects Offered ACT preparation, advanced math, Advanced Placement courses, algebra, American history, American history-AP, anatomy and physiology, art, band, Bible, biology, broadcasting, calculus, calculus-AP, chemistry, chorus, economics, English literature and composition-AP, European history, European history-AP, fitness, geography, geometry, government, grammar, keyboarding, microcomputer technology applications, physical science, psychology, sociology, Spanish, statistics-AP, trigonometry, weight training, wellness, world history.

Graduation Requirements American history, Bible, computers, economics, English, government, mathematics, physical education (includes health), science, wellness, world history.

Special Academic Programs 5 Advanced Placement exams for which test preparation is offered; honors section; study at local college for college credit; remedial math.

College Admission Counseling 49 students graduated in 2012; 44 went to college, including Austin Peay State University; Harding University; Lipscomb University; Middle Tennessee State University; Tennessee Technological University; The University of Tennessee. Other: 1 went to work, 1 entered a postgraduate year, 3 had other specific plans. Median composite ACT: 25. 43% scored over 26 on composite ACT.

Student Life Upper grades have uniform requirement, student council. Discipline rests primarily with faculty.

Tuition and Aid Day student tuition: $6750. Tuition installment plan (The Tuition Plan, monthly payment plans). Need-based scholarship grants, paying campus jobs available.

Admissions Traditional secondary-level entrance grade is 9. For fall 2012, 29 students applied for upper-level admission, 25 were accepted, 24 enrolled. Deadline for receipt of application materials: none. Application fee required: $50. Interview recommended.

Athletics Interscholastic: baseball (boys), basketball (b,g), bowling (b,g), cheering (g), cross-country running (b,g), drill team (g), football (b), golf (b,g), hockey (b), soccer (b,g), softball (g), tennis (b,g), track and field (b,g), volleyball (g), weight training (b,g). 2 PE instructors, 6 coaches, 1 athletic trainer.

Computers Computers are regularly used in all academic classes. Computer network features include on-campus library services, Internet access, wireless campus network, Internet filtering or blocking technology. Student e-mail accounts are available to students. Students grades are available online. The school has a published electronic and media policy.

Contact Mr. Reggie Grimes, Admissions Officer. 615-367-0532 Ext. 109. Fax: 615-399-8747. E-mail: rgrimes@ezellharding.com. Web site: www.ezellharding.com

FAIRFIELD COLLEGE PREPARATORY SCHOOL

1073 North Benson Road
Fairfield, Connecticut 06824-5157

Head of School: Rev. John J. Hanwell, SJ

General Information Boys' day college-preparatory, arts, religious studies, and technology school, affiliated with Roman Catholic Church. Grades 9–12. Founded: 1942. Setting: suburban. Nearest major city is Bridgeport. 220-acre campus. 4 buildings on campus. Approved or accredited by Connecticut Association of Independent Schools, Jesuit Secondary Education Association, New England Association of Schools and Colleges, and Connecticut Department of Education. Member of National Association of Independent Schools. Endowment: $16 million. Total enrollment: 896. Upper school average class size: 22. Upper school faculty-student ratio: 1:18. There are 182 required school days per year for Upper School students. Upper School students typically attend 5 days per week. The average school day consists of 5 hours and 50 minutes.

Upper School Student Profile Grade 9: 235 students (235 boys); Grade 10: 235 students (235 boys); Grade 11: 225 students (225 boys); Grade 12: 201 students (201 boys). 71% of students are Roman Catholic.

Faculty School total: 55. In upper school: 34 men, 21 women; 48 have advanced degrees.

Subjects Offered Advanced Placement courses, algebra, American history, American history-AP, American literature, American literature-AP, art, Asian studies, band, biology, biology-AP, British literature-AP, calculus, calculus-AP, career exploration, chemistry, choir, chorus, college admission preparation, college planning, community service, computer literacy, computer programming, computer science, constitutional law, creative writing, drama, drama workshop, drawing and design, driver education, economics, English, English literature, English literature-AP, English-AP, environmental science, European history, fine arts, French, French language-AP, French literature-AP, French-AP, geometry, graphics, guidance, history, honors algebra, honors English, honors geometry, honors U.S. history, journalism, language and composition, language arts, language structure, Latin, Latin-AP, mathematics, Middle East, moral theology, music, physics, physics-AP, pre-calculus, religion, SAT preparation, science, social justice, social studies, sociology, Spanish, Spanish language-AP, Spanish-AP, studio art, theater, theology, trigonometry, U.S. history-AP, United States government-AP, Web site design, Western civilization, word processing, world history, world literature, world religions, world wide web design, World-Wide-Web publishing.

Graduation Requirements Arts and fine arts (art, music, dance, drama), computer science, English, foreign language, mathematics, religion (includes Bible studies and theology), science, social studies (includes history), senior comprehensive exercises. Community service is required.

Special Academic Programs Advanced Placement exam preparation; honors section; study at local college for college credit.

College Admission Counseling 226 students graduated in 2012; 218 went to college, including Boston College; College of the Holy Cross; Fordham University; Georgetown University; Loyola University Maryland; University of Connecticut. Other: 1 entered military service, 5 entered a postgraduate year, 2 had other specific plans. Mean SAT critical reading: 590, mean SAT math: 596, mean SAT writing: 589, mean combined SAT: 1775.

Student Life Upper grades have specified standards of dress, student council. Discipline rests primarily with faculty. Attendance at religious services is required.

Summer Programs Remediation, enrichment, sports, computer instruction programs offered; session focuses on enrichment; held on campus; accepts boys and girls; open to students from other schools. 160 students usually enrolled. 2013 schedule: June 24 to July 19.

Tuition and Aid Day student tuition: $17,000. Tuition installment plan (monthly payment plans). Need-based scholarship grants available. In 2012–13, 28% of upper-school students received aid. Total amount of financial aid awarded in 2012–13: $2,100,000.

Admissions Traditional secondary-level entrance grade is 9. For fall 2012, 507 students applied for upper-level admission, 235 enrolled. High School Placement Test required. Deadline for receipt of application materials: December 1. Application fee required: $60.

Athletics Interscholastic: alpine skiing, baseball, basketball, bowling, crew, cross-country running, diving, fencing, flag football, football, golf, ice hockey, indoor track & field, lacrosse, rugby, sailing, skiing (downhill), soccer, strength & conditioning, swimming and diving, tennis, track and field, weight training, winter (indoor) track, wrestling; intramural: basketball, bicycling, fitness, mountain biking, Nautilus, power lifting, skiing (downhill), strength & conditioning, table tennis, weight lifting. 33 coaches, 2 athletic trainers.

Computers Computers are regularly used in art, English, foreign language, history, mathematics, science, technology, theology classes. Computer network features include on-campus library services, online commercial services, Internet access, Internet filtering or blocking technology. Student e-mail accounts are available to students. Students grades are available online. The school has a published electronic and media policy.

Contact Mrs. Colleen H. Adams, Director of Communications. 203-254-4200 Ext. 2487. Fax: 203-254-4071. E-mail: cadams@fairfieldprep.org. Web site: www.fairfieldprep.org

FAIRHILL SCHOOL

Dallas, Texas

See Special Needs Schools section.

FAITH CHRISTIAN HIGH SCHOOL

3105 Colusa Highway
Yuba City, California 95993

Head of School: Mr. Stephen Finlay

General Information Coeducational day college-preparatory, arts, religious studies, and technology school, affiliated with Christian faith. Grades 9–12. Founded: 1975. Setting: small town. Nearest major city is Sacramento. 10-acre campus. 4 buildings on campus. Approved or accredited by Association of Christian Schools International, Western Association of Schools and Colleges, and California Department of Education. Total enrollment: 100. Upper school average class size: 25. Upper school faculty-student ratio: 1:12. There are 175 required school days per year for Upper School students. Upper School students typically attend 5 days per week. The average school day consists of 5 hours and 30 minutes.

Upper School Student Profile Grade 9: 20 students (10 boys, 10 girls); Grade 10: 26 students (13 boys, 13 girls); Grade 11: 29 students (13 boys, 16 girls); Grade 12: 25 students (13 boys, 12 girls). 99% of students are Christian.

Faculty School total: 16. In upper school: 10 men, 6 women; 4 have advanced degrees.

Subjects Offered Algebra, arts, Bible, biology, biology-AP, British literature, calculus-AP, chemistry, civics, computer science, computer studies, concert band, drama, economics, English, English composition, English literature, English-AP, geography, geometry, government, health, honors English, physical education, physical science, pre-calculus, senior project, Spanish, U.S. history, world geography, world history, yearbook.

Graduation Requirements Algebra, Bible, biology, civics, economics, English, geometry, health, physical science, senior project, U.S. history, world geography, world history.

Special Academic Programs Advanced Placement exam preparation; study at local college for college credit.

College Admission Counseling 26 students graduated in 2012; 23 went to college, including Azusa Pacific University; Point Loma Nazarene University; Simpson University; University of California, Davis; University of Nevada, Reno; University of the Pacific. Other: 1 entered military service, 2 had other specific plans. Median SAT critical reading: 580, median SAT math: 540, median SAT writing: 550, median combined SAT: 1640, median composite ACT: 20. 30% scored over 600 on SAT critical reading, 20% scored over 600 on SAT math, 30% scored over 600 on SAT writing, 30% scored over 1800 on combined SAT, 25% scored over 26 on composite ACT.

Student Life Upper grades have specified standards of dress, student council, honor system. Discipline rests primarily with faculty. Attendance at religious services is required.

Tuition and Aid Day student tuition: $7460. Tuition installment plan (monthly payment plans). Tuition reduction for siblings, need-based scholarship grants available. In 2012–13, 20% of upper-school students received aid. Total amount of financial aid awarded in 2012–13: $50,000.

Admissions Traditional secondary-level entrance grade is 9. For fall 2012, 18 students applied for upper-level admission, 17 were accepted, 17 enrolled. Achievement tests required. Deadline for receipt of application materials: none. Application fee required: $50. Interview required.

Athletics Interscholastic: baseball (boys), basketball (b,g), cheering (g), cross-country running (b,g), soccer (b,g), volleyball (g); coed interscholastic: golf. 1 PE instructor, 8 coaches.

Computers Computers are regularly used in all academic classes. Computer network features include on-campus library services, Internet access, Internet filtering or blocking technology. Students grades are available online. The school has a published electronic and media policy.

Contact Mrs. Sue Shorey, Secretary. 530-674-5474. Fax: 530-674-0194. E-mail: sshorey@fcs-k12.org. Web site: www.fcs-k12.org

FAITH LUTHERAN HIGH SCHOOL

2015 South Hualapai Way
Las Vegas, Nevada 89117-6949

Head of School: Dr. Steve J. Buuck

General Information Coeducational day college-preparatory and religious studies school, affiliated with Lutheran Church–Missouri Synod, Evangelical Lutheran Church in America. Grades 6–12. Founded: 1979. Setting: suburban. 39-acre campus. 4 buildings on campus. Approved or accredited by Lutheran School Accreditation Commission, National Lutheran School Accreditation, Northwest Accreditation Commission, and Nevada Department of Education. Endowment: $1 million. Total enrollment: 1,390. Upper school average class size: 25. Upper school faculty-student ratio: 1:17. There are 180 required school days per year for Upper School students. Upper School students typically attend 5 days per week. The average school day consists of 7 hours.

Upper School Student Profile 24% of students are Lutheran Church–Missouri Synod, Evangelical Lutheran Church in America.

Faculty School total: 92. In upper school: 32 men, 54 women; 48 have advanced degrees.

Subjects Offered Algebra, American history, art, biology, chemistry, computer science, earth science, English, fine arts, fitness, geometry, German, health, mathematics, music, physical education, physical science, religion, SAT/ACT preparation, science, social studies, Spanish.

Graduation Requirements American history, arts and fine arts (art, music, dance, drama), computer science, English, foreign language, mathematics, physical education (includes health), religion (includes Bible studies and theology), science, social studies (includes history).

Special Academic Programs 7 Advanced Placement exams for which test preparation is offered; honors section; independent study; study at local college for college credit; academic accommodation for the musically talented.

College Admission Counseling 142 students graduated in 2012; 138 went to college, including Concordia University; University of Nevada, Las Vegas; University of Nevada, Reno. Other: 1 entered military service, 3 had other specific plans. Median SAT critical reading: 540, median SAT math: 520, median SAT writing: 510, median combined SAT: 1570, median composite ACT: 23. 25% scored over 600 on SAT critical reading, 25% scored over 600 on SAT math, 20% scored over 600 on SAT writing, 23% scored over 1800 on combined SAT, 30% scored over 26 on composite ACT.

Student Life Upper grades have uniform requirement, student council. Discipline rests primarily with faculty. Attendance at religious services is required.

Tuition and Aid Day student tuition: $9700. Tuition installment plan (monthly payment plans, individually arranged payment plans). Tuition reduction for siblings, need-based scholarship grants available. In 2012–13, 12% of upper-school students received aid. Total amount of financial aid awarded in 2012–13: $461,000.

Admissions Traditional secondary-level entrance grade is 9. For fall 2012, 110 students applied for upper-level admission, 100 were accepted, 80 enrolled. High School Placement Test and Stanford 9 required. Deadline for receipt of application materials: none. Application fee required: $350. On-campus interview required.

Athletics Interscholastic: aerobics/dance (girls), aquatics (b,g), baseball (b), basketball (b,g), cheering (g), cross-country running (b,g), dance team (g), football (b), golf (b,g), lacrosse (b,g), soccer (b,g), softball (g), swimming and diving (b,g), tennis (b,g), track and field (b,g), volleyball (g), wrestling (b); intramural: strength & conditioning (b,g), weight training (b,g); coed interscholastic: strength & conditioning; coed intramural: skiing (downhill), snowboarding, ultimate Frisbee. 7 PE instructors, 26 coaches.

Computers Computers are regularly used in keyboarding, yearbook classes. Computer network features include on-campus library services, online commercial services, Internet access, wireless campus network, Internet filtering or blocking technology.

Student e-mail accounts and computer access in designated common areas are available to students. Students grades are available online. The school has a published electronic and media policy.

Contact Mr. Joel Arnold, Director of Admissions. 702-804-4413. Fax: 702-562-7728. E-mail: arnoldj@flhsemail.org. Web site: www.faithlutheranlv.org

FALMOUTH ACADEMY

7 Highfield Drive
Falmouth, Massachusetts 02540

Head of School: Mr. David C. Faus

General Information Coeducational day college-preparatory and arts school. Grades 7–12. Founded: 1976. Setting: small town. Nearest major city is Boston. 34-acre campus. 2 buildings on campus. Approved or accredited by Association of Independent Schools in New England and New England Association of Schools and Colleges. Member of National Association of Independent Schools and Secondary School Admission Test Board. Endowment: $4 million. Total enrollment: 186. Upper school average class size: 12. Upper school faculty-student ratio: 1:4. There are 165 required school days per year for Upper School students. Upper School students typically attend 5 days per week. The average school day consists of 6 hours and 20 minutes.

Upper School Student Profile Grade 9: 32 students (18 boys, 14 girls); Grade 10: 34 students (15 boys, 19 girls); Grade 11: 22 students (10 boys, 12 girls); Grade 12: 28 students (10 boys, 18 girls).

Faculty School total: 35. In upper school: 14 men, 20 women; 26 have advanced degrees.

Subjects Offered Algebra, American history, American literature, art, biology, calculus, ceramics, chemistry, creative writing, drama, earth science, ecology, English, English literature, environmental science, European history, expository writing, fine arts, French, geography, geology, geometry, German, grammar, health, history, journalism, mathematics, music, photography, physical education, physics, science, sculpture, social studies, statistics, theater, trigonometry, woodworking, world history, world literature, writing.

Graduation Requirements Arts and fine arts (art, music, dance, drama), English, foreign language, history, mathematics, science.

Special Academic Programs 5 Advanced Placement exams for which test preparation is offered; independent study; term-away projects; study abroad; ESL (4 students enrolled).

College Admission Counseling 31 students graduated in 2012; all went to college, including Union College; University of Massachusetts Amherst; University of Pennsylvania. Mean SAT critical reading: 676, mean SAT math: 595, mean SAT writing: 604.

Student Life Upper grades have specified standards of dress, student council, honor system. Discipline rests primarily with faculty.

Summer Programs Enrichment, art/fine arts programs offered; session focuses on arts enrichment; held on campus; accepts boys and girls; open to students from other schools. 150 students usually enrolled. 2013 schedule: July 1 to August 15.

Tuition and Aid Day student tuition: $24,860. Merit scholarship grants, need-based scholarship grants, need-based loans available. In 2012–13, 45% of upper-school students received aid; total upper-school merit-scholarship money awarded: $6000. Total amount of financial aid awarded in 2012–13: $750,000.

Admissions Traditional secondary-level entrance grade is 9. For fall 2012, 32 students applied for upper-level admission, 29 were accepted, 19 enrolled. SSAT required. Deadline for receipt of application materials: March 1. Application fee required: $50. On-campus interview required.

Athletics Interscholastic: basketball (boys, girls), lacrosse (b,g), soccer (b,g). 1 PE instructor.

Computers Computers are regularly used in design, English, mathematics, science classes. Computer resources include on-campus library services, Internet access, Internet filtering or blocking technology. The school has a published electronic and media policy.

Contact Mr. Michael J. Earley, Assistant Headmaster/Director of Admissions. 508-457-9696 Ext. 224. Fax: 508-457-4112. E-mail: mearley@falmouthacademy.org. Web site: www.falmouthacademy.org

THE FAMILY FOUNDATION SCHOOL

Hancock, New York
See Special Needs Schools section.

FATHER LOPEZ HIGH SCHOOL

3918 LPGA Boulevard
Daytona Beach, Florida 32124

Head of School: Dr. Michael J. Coury

General Information Coeducational day college-preparatory and religious studies school, affiliated with Roman Catholic Church. Grades 9–12. Founded: 1959. Setting: urban. 90-acre campus. 9 buildings on campus. Approved or accredited by National Catholic Education Association, Southern Association of Colleges and Schools, and Florida Department of Education. Total enrollment: 407. Upper school average class size: 18. Upper school faculty-student ratio: 1:13. There are 181 required school days per year for Upper School students. Upper School students typically attend 5 days per week. The average school day consists of 6 hours and 20 minutes.

Upper School Student Profile Grade 9: 110 students (67 boys, 43 girls); Grade 10: 125 students (70 boys, 55 girls); Grade 11: 79 students (44 boys, 35 girls); Grade 12: 93 students (44 boys, 49 girls). 62% of students are Roman Catholic.

Faculty School total: 31. In upper school: 10 men, 21 women; 12 have advanced degrees.

Subjects Offered Advanced biology, advanced chemistry, advanced math, Advanced Placement courses, aerobics, algebra, American history, American history-AP, American literature, anatomy and physiology, applied skills, art, audio visual/media, biology, biology-AP, British literature, calculus, calculus-AP, Catholic belief and practice, chemistry, Chinese, Christian and Hebrew scripture, church history, classical Greek literature, computer applications, computer art, computer graphics, consumer mathematics, culinary arts, dance, dance performance, death and loss, design, digital photography, drama, drama performance, drawing, economics, English, English as a foreign language, English literature, English literature and composition-AP, film, film and literature, filmmaking, French, geometry, government, graphic design, health education, honors algebra, honors English, honors geometry, honors U.S. history, honors world history, human geography - AP, Latin, marine science, moral and social development, philosophy, photography, physical education, physical science, physics, precalculus, psychology, psychology-AP, social justice, sociology, Spanish, speech, statistics, statistics-AP, studio art-AP, television, tennis, theology, trigonometry, U.S. government and politics-AP, U.S. history, U.S. history-AP, video film production, Web authoring, Web site design, weight training, weightlifting, world geography, world history, world history-AP, world religions, writing, yearbook.

Graduation Requirements Algebra, American history, American literature, arts and fine arts (art, music, dance, drama), biology, British literature, chemistry, economics, electives, English, English literature, foreign language, geometry, health and wellness, physical education (includes health), physics, theology, U.S. government, world history, 100 hours of community service.

Special Academic Programs 9 Advanced Placement exams for which test preparation is offered; honors section; study at local college for college credit; ESL (23 students enrolled).

College Admission Counseling 67 students graduated in 2012; 66 went to college, including Embry-Riddle Aeronautical University–Daytona; Florida State University; Stetson University; University of Central Florida; University of South Florida. Other: 1 entered a postgraduate year. Mean SAT critical reading: 498, mean SAT math: 504, mean SAT writing: 499, mean composite ACT: 22. 18% scored over 26 on composite ACT.

Student Life Upper grades have uniform requirement, student council, honor system. Discipline rests primarily with faculty. Attendance at religious services is required.

Tuition and Aid Day student tuition: $9800. Tuition installment plan (FACTS Tuition Payment Plan). Tuition reduction for siblings, merit scholarship grants, need-based scholarship grants, tiered tuition rate based on income available. In 2012–13, 49% of upper-school students received aid. Total amount of financial aid awarded in 2012–13: $1,275,284.

Admissions Traditional secondary-level entrance grade is 9. For fall 2012, 171 students applied for upper-level admission, 162 were accepted, 143 enrolled. High School Placement Test required. Deadline for receipt of application materials: none. Application fee required: $50. Interview required.

Athletics Interscholastic: baseball (boys), basketball (b,g), cross-country running (b,g), flag football (g), football (b), golf (b,g), lacrosse (b), softball (g), swimming and diving (b,g), tennis (b,g), track and field (b,g), volleyball (g), weight lifting (b), winter soccer (b,g); coed intramural: cheering, dance team, pom squad, soccer, table tennis, tennis, weight lifting, weight training. 2 PE instructors, 40 coaches, 1 athletic trainer.

Computers Computers are regularly used in all academic, art, computer applications, graphic design, media production, photography, video film production, yearbook classes. Computer network features include Internet access, wireless campus network, Internet filtering or blocking technology. Student e-mail accounts and computer access in designated common areas are available to students. Students grades are available online. The school has a published electronic and media policy.

Contact Mrs. Carmen Rivera, Admissions Coordinator. 386-253-5213 Ext. 325. Fax: 386-252-6101. E-mail: crivera@fatherlopez.org. Web site: www.fatherlopez.org

FATHER RYAN HIGH SCHOOL

700 Norwood Drive
Nashville, Tennessee 37204

Head of School: Mr. Jim McIntyre

General Information Coeducational day college-preparatory, arts, and religious studies school, affiliated with Roman Catholic Church. Grades 9–12. Founded: 1925. Setting: suburban. 40-acre campus. 9 buildings on campus. Approved or accredited by National Catholic Education Association, Southern Association of Colleges and Schools, Southern Association of Independent Schools, Tennessee Association of Independent Schools, and The College Board. Endowment: $5 million. Total enrollment: 948. Upper school average class size: 20. Upper school faculty-student ratio: 1:12.

There are 180 required school days per year for Upper School students. Upper School students typically attend 5 days per week. The average school day consists of 7 hours and 10 minutes.

Upper School Student Profile Grade 9: 254 students (149 boys, 105 girls); Grade 10: 240 students (141 boys, 99 girls); Grade 11: 227 students (134 boys, 93 girls); Grade 12: 227 students (132 boys, 95 girls). 90% of students are Roman Catholic.

Faculty School total: 84. In upper school: 42 men, 40 women; 46 have advanced degrees.

Subjects Offered 3-dimensional design, Advanced Placement courses, aerobics, algebra, American government, American history, American history-AP, American literature, anatomy, art, art history, art-AP, Bible studies, biology, British literature, calculus, calculus-AP, Catholic belief and practice, chemistry, chemistry-AP, Chinese, Chinese studies, chorus, church history, college counseling, college planning, college writing, computer programming, computer science, computer studies, dance, dance performance, drama, drama performance, driver education, economics, English, English literature, English-AP, European history, European history-AP, film studies, French, French-AP, geography, geometry, government-AP, government/civics, grammar, health, history, honors geometry, honors U.S. history, journalism, Latin, mathematics, music, physical education, physics, physics-AP, physiology, psychology, psychology-AP, religion, SAT preparation, science, Shakespeare, social studies, Spanish, Spanish-AP, speech, statistics-AP, theater, theater production, theology, trigonometry, U.S. government and politics-AP, Web site design, wind ensemble, world history, world literature, world religions, writing.

Graduation Requirements Arts and fine arts (art, music, dance, drama), computer science, English, foreign language, health education, mathematics, physical education (includes health), religion (includes Bible studies and theology), science, social studies (includes history), service hours required each year.

Special Academic Programs 27 Advanced Placement exams for which test preparation is offered; honors section; academic accommodation for the gifted, the musically talented, and the artistically talented; programs in English, mathematics for dyslexic students.

College Admission Counseling 211 students graduated in 2012; all went to college, including Belmont University; Middle Tennessee State University; Tennessee Technological University; The University of Tennessee; Western Kentucky University. Median SAT critical reading: 553, median SAT math: 524, median composite ACT: 24. 20% scored over 26 on composite ACT.

Student Life Upper grades have uniform requirement, student council. Discipline rests primarily with faculty. Attendance at religious services is required.

Summer Programs Remediation, enrichment, advancement, sports, art/fine arts, computer instruction programs offered; held on campus; accepts boys and girls; open to students from other schools. 240 students usually enrolled. 2013 schedule: June 1 to June 30. Application deadline: none.

Tuition and Aid Day student tuition: $11,440. Tuition installment plan (FACTS Tuition Payment Plan, individually arranged payment plans). Tuition reduction for siblings, need-based scholarship grants available. In 2012–13, 13% of upper-school students received aid. Total amount of financial aid awarded in 2012–13: $550,000.

Admissions Traditional secondary-level entrance grade is 9. For fall 2012, 347 students applied for upper-level admission, 278 were accepted, 251 enrolled. High School Placement Test required. Deadline for receipt of application materials: none. Application fee required: $80. On-campus interview required.

Athletics Interscholastic: aquatics (boys, girls), baseball (b), basketball (b,g), bowling (b,g), cheering (g), cross-country running (b,g), dance (b,g), dance squad (b), dance team (g), diving (b,g), football (b), golf (b,g), ice hockey (b), lacrosse (b,g), modern dance (g), power lifting (b), soccer (b,g), softball (g), Special Olympics (b,g), strength & conditioning (b,g), swimming and diving (b,g), tennis (b,g), track and field (b,g), volleyball (g), weight lifting (b,g), weight training (b,g), wrestling (b); intramural: fishing (b,g), indoor soccer (b,g), physical fitness (b,g). 1 athletic trainer.

Computers Computers are regularly used in all classes. Computer network features include on-campus library services, online commercial services, Internet access, wireless campus network, Internet filtering or blocking technology. Computer access in designated common areas is available to students. Students grades are available online. The school has a published electronic and media policy.

Contact Ms. Kate Goetzinger, Director of Admissions. 615-383-4200. Fax: 615-783-0264. E-mail: goetzinferk@fatherryan.org. Web site: www.fatherryan.org

FAYETTEVILLE ACADEMY

3200 Cliffdale Road
Fayetteville, North Carolina 28303

Head of School: Mr. Ray J. Quesnel

General Information Coeducational day college-preparatory, arts, and technology school. Grades PK–12. Founded: 1970. Setting: suburban. 30-acre campus. 10 buildings on campus. Approved or accredited by North Carolina Association of Independent Schools, Southern Association of Colleges and Schools, Southern Association of Independent Schools, The College Board, and North Carolina Department of Education. Member of National Association of Independent Schools. Endowment: $351,275. Total enrollment: 378. Upper school average class size: 14. Upper school faculty-student ratio: 1:14. There are 175 required school days per year for Upper School students. Upper School students typically attend 5 days per week. The average school day consists of 6 hours and 55 minutes.

Upper School Student Profile Grade 9: 32 students (16 boys, 16 girls); Grade 10: 39 students (20 boys, 19 girls); Grade 11: 32 students (16 boys, 16 girls); Grade 12: 34 students (15 boys, 19 girls).

Faculty School total: 62. In upper school: 4 men, 14 women; 11 have advanced degrees.

Subjects Offered Algebra, American history, American literature, anatomy, art, band, biology, biology-AP, calculus, calculus-AP, chemistry, chemistry-AP, chorus, communications, ecology, English, English language and composition-AP, English literature, English literature-AP, European history, European history-AP, geography, geometry, government/civics, history, honors geometry, mathematics, music, physical education, physics, physiology, pre-calculus, psychology, science, social studies, Spanish, Spanish-AP, statistics-AP, trigonometry, typing, U.S. history-AP, weight training, world history, world history-AP, yearbook.

Graduation Requirements Arts and fine arts (art, music, dance, drama), English, foreign language, history, lab science, mathematics, physical education (includes health), senior projects.

Special Academic Programs Advanced Placement exam preparation; honors section; independent study.

College Admission Counseling 41 students graduated in 2012; all went to college, including East Carolina University; North Carolina State University; The University of North Carolina at Chapel Hill; The University of North Carolina at Charlotte; The University of North Carolina at Greensboro; The University of North Carolina Wilmington. Mean SAT critical reading: 560, mean SAT math: 560, mean SAT writing: 570, mean combined SAT: 1690, mean composite ACT: 25.

Student Life Upper grades have specified standards of dress, student council, honor system. Discipline rests primarily with faculty.

Summer Programs Enrichment, sports, art/fine arts, computer instruction programs offered; session focuses on enrichment; held on campus; accepts boys and girls; open to students from other schools. 200 students usually enrolled. 2013 schedule: June 7 to August 1.

Tuition and Aid Day student tuition: $13,389. Tuition installment plan (monthly payment plans, payment in full, 3-payment plan). Need-based scholarship grants available. In 2012–13, 29% of upper-school students received aid. Total amount of financial aid awarded in 2012–13: $514,750.

Admissions Traditional secondary-level entrance grade is 9. For fall 2012, 26 students applied for upper-level admission, 23 were accepted, 20 enrolled. ERB, SSAT and TOEFL or SLEP required. Deadline for receipt of application materials: none. Application fee required: $75. On-campus interview recommended.

Athletics Interscholastic: baseball (boys), basketball (b,g), cheering (g), cross-country running (b,g), soccer (b,g), softball (g), tennis (b,g), track and field (b,g), volleyball (g); intramural: weight training (g); coed interscholastic: golf, swimming and diving. 4 PE instructors, 10 coaches, 1 athletic trainer.

Computers Computers are regularly used in all classes. Computer network features include on-campus library services, online commercial services, Internet access, wireless campus network. Computer access in designated common areas is available to students. Students grades are available online. The school has a published electronic and media policy.

Contact Ms. Barbara E. Lambert, Director of Admissions. 910-868-5131 Ext. 3311. Fax: 910-868-7351. E-mail: blambert@fayettevilleacademy.com. Web site: www.fayettevilleacademy.com

FAY SCHOOL

Southborough, Massachusetts
See Junior Boarding Schools section.

THE FESSENDEN SCHOOL

West Newton, Massachusetts
See Junior Boarding Schools section.

THE FIRST ACADEMY

2667 Bruton Boulevard
Orlando, Florida 32805

Head of School: Dr. Steve D. Whitaker

General Information Coeducational day college-preparatory, arts, religious studies, and technology school, affiliated with Christian faith. Grades K4–12. Founded: 1986. Setting: suburban. 140-acre campus. 1 building on campus. Approved or accredited by Association of Christian Schools International, Association of Independent Schools of Florida, Southern Association of Colleges and Schools, Southern Association of Independent Schools, and Florida Department of Education. Endowment: $2.5 million. Total enrollment: 989. Upper school average class size: 17. Upper school faculty-student ratio: 1:17. There are 180 required school days per year for Upper School students. Upper School students typically attend 5 days per week. The average school day consists of 6 hours and 30 minutes.

Upper School Student Profile Grade 9: 110 students (47 boys, 63 girls); Grade 10: 103 students (61 boys, 42 girls); Grade 11: 99 students (51 boys, 48 girls); Grade 12: 86 students (43 boys, 43 girls). 100% of students are Christian.
Faculty School total: 85. In upper school: 14 men, 15 women; 14 have advanced degrees.
Subjects Offered Advanced chemistry, advanced computer applications, advanced math, Advanced Placement courses, advanced studio art-AP, algebra, American government, American history, American history-AP, American literature, American literature-AP, analytic geometry, anatomy, ancient world history, art, art-AP, athletics, audio visual/media, band, Bible, Bible studies, biology, biology-AP, broadcasting, calculus, calculus-AP, chemistry, chemistry-AP, choir, Christian doctrine, Christian ethics, Christian testament, comparative government and politics, composition, computer programming, computer science, creative writing, drama, economics, economics and history, electives, English, English composition, English literature, English literature-AP, English-AP, ethics, European history, European history-AP, expository writing, fine arts, genetics, geometry, government, grammar, health, history, history-AP, honors algebra, honors English, honors geometry, honors U.S. history, honors world history, integrated mathematics, journalism, keyboarding, Latin, life skills, literature, literature-AP, marine biology, mathematics, media communications, music, newspaper, physical education, physical science, physics, politics, pottery, pre-algebra, pre-calculus, religion, SAT/ACT preparation, science, social sciences, social studies, Spanish, Spanish-AP, speech, speech and debate, theater, trigonometry, U.S. government, U.S. government and politics-AP, world history, world history-AP, world literature, writing, yearbook.
Graduation Requirements Arts and fine arts (art, music, dance, drama), computer science, English, foreign language, mathematics, physical education (includes health), religion (includes Bible studies and theology), science, social sciences, social studies (includes history).
Special Academic Programs Advanced Placement exam preparation; honors section; study at local college for college credit.
College Admission Counseling 80 students graduated in 2012; all went to college, including Clemson University; Florida State University; Liberty University; Samford University; University of Central Florida; University of Florida.
Student Life Upper grades have uniform requirement, student council, honor system. Discipline rests primarily with faculty. Attendance at religious services is required.
Summer Programs Enrichment, advancement, sports, art/fine arts programs offered; session focuses on academics and athletic camps; held on campus; accepts boys and girls; open to students from other schools. 200 students usually enrolled. 2013 schedule: June 1 to July 31. Application deadline: March 1.
Tuition and Aid Day student tuition: $14,000. Tuition installment plan (SMART Tuition Payment Plan). Need-based scholarship grants available.
Admissions Traditional secondary-level entrance grade is 9. Stanford Achievement Test, Otis-Lennon School Ability Test required. Deadline for receipt of application materials: none. Application fee required: $125. On-campus interview required.
Athletics Interscholastic: baseball (boys), basketball (b,g), cheering (g), cross-country running (b,g), diving (b,g), flag football (b), football (b), golf (b,g), lacrosse (b), physical fitness (b,g), physical training (b,g), power lifting (b), running (b,g), soccer (b,g), softball (g), strength & conditioning (b,g), swimming and diving (b,g), tennis (b,g), track and field (b,g), volleyball (g), weight lifting (b), wrestling (b). 6 PE instructors, 18 coaches, 1 athletic trainer.
Computers Computers are regularly used in art, computer applications, English, foreign language, history, journalism, keyboarding, library, library skills, mathematics, media production, science, yearbook classes. Computer network features include on-campus library services, Internet access, wireless campus network, Internet filtering or blocking technology. Campus intranet and student e-mail accounts are available to students. Students grades are available online. The school has a published electronic and media policy.
Contact Shannon Word, Admissions Coordinator. 407-206-8818. Fax: 407-206-8700. E-mail: ShannonWord@thefirstacademy.org. Web site: www.TheFirstAcademy.org

FIRST BAPTIST ACADEMY

PO Box 868
Dallas, Texas 75221

Head of School: Mr. Brian Littlefield

General Information Coeducational day college-preparatory, arts, religious studies, and technology school, affiliated with Baptist Church, Southern Baptist Convention. Grades PK–12. Founded: 1972. Setting: urban. 1 building on campus. Approved or accredited by Accreditation Commission of the Texas Association of Baptist Schools, Association of Christian Schools International, Southern Association of Colleges and Schools, Texas Private School Accreditation Commission, and Texas Department of Education. Endowment: $1 million. Total enrollment: 239. Upper school average class size: 15. Upper school faculty-student ratio: 1:8. There are 176 required school days per year for Upper School students. Upper School students typically attend 5 days per week. The average school day consists of 7 hours.
Upper School Student Profile 50% of students are Baptist, Southern Baptist Convention.
Faculty School total: 49. In upper school: 12 men, 16 women; 11 have advanced degrees.
Subjects Offered Algebra, American history, architecture, Bible, biology, calculus, calculus-AP, chemistry, choir, computer skills, concert band, desktop publishing, drawing, economics, English, English literature-AP, English-AP, fine arts, geometry, government-AP, health, history, math analysis, photography, physics, pre-calculus, Spanish, speech and debate, theater arts, world history.
Graduation Requirements Algebra, American history, arts and fine arts (art, music, dance, drama), Basic programming, Bible studies, biology, chemistry, economics, electives, English, foreign language, government, history, keyboarding, mathematics, physical education (includes health), physics, science, U.S. history, world geography, service hours are required for graduation. Community service is required.
Special Academic Programs 4 Advanced Placement exams for which test preparation is offered; honors section.
College Admission Counseling 40 students graduated in 2012; 39 went to college, including Baylor University; Texas A&M University; Texas Tech University; The University of Texas at Austin; University of Mississippi; University of Oklahoma.
Student Life Upper grades have uniform requirement, student council, honor system. Discipline rests primarily with faculty. Attendance at religious services is required.
Tuition and Aid Day student tuition: $13,015. Tuition installment plan (FACTS Tuition Payment Plan). Need-based scholarship grants available. In 2012–13, 22% of upper-school students received aid.
Admissions Traditional secondary-level entrance grade is 9. ERB (grade level), ISEE or Stanford Achievement Test required. Deadline for receipt of application materials: none. Application fee required: $75. Interview required.
Athletics Interscholastic: aquatics (boys, girls), baseball (b), basketball (b,g), cheering (g), diving (b,g), football (b), golf (b,g), softball (g), strength & conditioning (b,g), swimming and diving (b,g), tennis (b,g), track and field (b,g), volleyball (g), wrestling (b). 1 PE instructor, 25 coaches.
Computers Computers are regularly used in computer applications, desktop publishing, yearbook classes. Computer resources include on-campus library services, Internet access. Students grades are available online. The school has a published electronic and media policy.
Contact Elizabeth Gore, Director of Admissions and Marketing. 214-969-7861. Fax: 214-969-7797. E-mail: egore@firstdallas.org. Web site: www.fbacademy.com

FIRST PRESBYTERIAN DAY SCHOOL

5671 Calvin Drive
Macon, Georgia 31210

Head of School: Mr. Gregg E. Thompson

General Information Coeducational day college-preparatory, arts, and religious studies school, affiliated with Christian faith, Presbyterian Church in America. Grades PK–12. Founded: 1970. Setting: suburban. Nearest major city is Atlanta. 104-acre campus. 7 buildings on campus. Approved or accredited by Christian Schools International, Georgia Independent School Association, Southern Association of Colleges and Schools, Southern Association of Independent Schools, and Georgia Department of Education. Endowment: $3.1 million. Total enrollment: 949. Upper school average class size: 18. Upper school faculty-student ratio: 1:12. There are 180 required school days per year for Upper School students. Upper School students typically attend 5 days per week. The average school day consists of 7 hours.
Upper School Student Profile Grade 9: 84 students (41 boys, 43 girls); Grade 10: 78 students (40 boys, 38 girls); Grade 11: 81 students (41 boys, 40 girls); Grade 12: 83 students (42 boys, 41 girls). 89% of students are Christian, Presbyterian Church in America.
Faculty School total: 73. In upper school: 27 men, 39 women; 47 have advanced degrees.
Subjects Offered 3-dimensional design, accounting, advanced biology, advanced chemistry, Advanced Placement courses, advanced studio art-AP, algebra, American literature, anatomy and physiology, art, art appreciation, art-AP, band, Bible, biology, biology-AP, British literature, calculus-AP, chemistry, chorus, comparative religion, computer applications, debate, economics, English, English language and composition-AP, English literature and composition-AP, family living, French, geometry, government, government-AP, honors algebra, honors English, honors geometry, journalism, Latin, Latin-AP, logic, model United Nations, modern European history, music appreciation, physical science, physics, physics-AP, pre-calculus, psychology, Spanish, statistics, studio art-AP, theater, U.S. government and politics-AP, U.S. history, U.S. history-AP, world history.
Graduation Requirements Arts and fine arts (art, music, dance, drama), Bible, computer skills, electives, English, foreign language, mathematics, physical education (includes health), science, social studies (includes history), service to distressed populations.
Special Academic Programs 12 Advanced Placement exams for which test preparation is offered; honors section; ESL (4 students enrolled).
College Admission Counseling 86 students graduated in 2012; all went to college, including Auburn University; Georgia College & State University; Georgia Institute of Technology; Mercer University; Samford University; University of Georgia. 35% scored over 600 on SAT critical reading, 47% scored over 600 on SAT math, 38% scored over 600 on SAT writing, 43% scored over 1800 on combined SAT.
Student Life Upper grades have uniform requirement, student council, honor system. Discipline rests primarily with faculty. Attendance at religious services is required.

Summer Programs Remediation, enrichment, sports, art/fine arts programs offered; session focuses on reading and study skills, mathematics enrichment, science, sports; held on campus; accepts boys and girls; open to students from other schools. 200 students usually enrolled. 2013 schedule: June 10 to July 30. Application deadline: May 15.

Tuition and Aid Day student tuition: $12,100. Tuition installment plan (monthly payment plans). Tuition reduction for siblings, merit scholarship grants, need-based scholarship grants available. In 2012–13, 33% of upper-school students received aid; total upper-school merit-scholarship money awarded: $28,000. Total amount of financial aid awarded in 2012–13: $874,000.

Admissions Traditional secondary-level entrance grade is 9. CTP, Math Placement Exam or writing sample required. Deadline for receipt of application materials: February 1. Application fee required: $50. Interview recommended.

Athletics Interscholastic: baseball (boys), basketball (b,g), cheering (g), cross-country running (b,g), dance team (g), football (b), golf (b,g), soccer (b,g), softball (g), swimming and diving (b,g), tennis (b,g), track and field (b,g), volleyball (g), wrestling (b,g); intramural: football (b), indoor soccer (b,g), soccer (b,g), strength & conditioning (b,g), weight training (b,g). 3 PE instructors, 5 coaches, 1 athletic trainer.

Computers Computers are regularly used in all classes. Computer network features include on-campus library services, online commercial services, Internet access, wireless campus network, Internet filtering or blocking technology. Campus intranet and computer access in designated common areas are available to students. Students grades are available online. The school has a published electronic and media policy.

Contact Mrs. Cheri Frame, Director of Admissions. 478-477-6505 Ext. 107. Fax: 478-477-2804. E-mail: admissions@fpdmacon.org. Web site: www.fpdmacon.org

FISHBURNE MILITARY SCHOOL

225 South Wayne Avenue
Waynesboro, Virginia 22980

Head of School: Col. Gary R. Morrison

General Information Boys' boarding and day college-preparatory, Army Junior ROTC, and military school. Grades 7–PG. Founded: 1879. Setting: small town. Nearest major city is Washington, DC. Students are housed in single-sex dormitories. 10-acre campus. 4 buildings on campus. Approved or accredited by Southern Association of Colleges and Schools, Virginia Association of Independent Schools, and Virginia Department of Education. Endowment: $1.3 million. Total enrollment: 170. Upper school average class size: 9. Upper school faculty-student ratio: 1:9.

Upper School Student Profile Grade 9: 35 students (35 boys); Grade 10: 45 students (45 boys); Grade 11: 50 students (50 boys); Grade 12: 45 students (45 boys); Postgraduate: 15 students (15 boys). 90% of students are boarding students. 17 states are represented in upper school student body. 5% are international students. International students from Aruba, Mexico, Republic of Korea, Russian Federation, Saudi Arabia, and Taiwan; 5 other countries represented in student body.

Faculty School total: 20. In upper school: 14 men, 6 women; 5 have advanced degrees; 6 reside on campus.

Subjects Offered Algebra, American history, American literature, biology, calculus, chemistry, computer programming, computer science, computer technologies, creative writing, driver education, earth science, English, English literature, environmental science, French, geography, geology, geometry, government/civics, grammar, health, history, JROTC, mathematics, military science, music, physical education, physics, science, social studies, Spanish, speech, trigonometry, world history.

Graduation Requirements Computer science, English, foreign language, JROTC, mathematics, physical education (includes health), science, social studies (includes history).

Special Academic Programs Advanced Placement exam preparation; honors section; study at local college for college credit; remedial reading and/or remedial writing; remedial math.

College Admission Counseling 47 students graduated in 2012; all went to college, including Miami University; Penn State University Park; United States Military Academy; University of Virginia; Virginia Military Institute; Virginia Polytechnic Institute and State University. Median SAT critical reading: 470, median SAT math: 530, median SAT writing: 540, median combined SAT: 1535. 4.5% scored over 600 on SAT critical reading, 11.4% scored over 600 on SAT math, 4.5% scored over 600 on SAT writing, 2.3% scored over 1800 on combined SAT.

Student Life Upper grades have uniform requirement, student council, honor system. Discipline rests equally with students and faculty.

Tuition and Aid Tuition reduction for siblings, need-based scholarship grants available.

Admissions Traditional secondary-level entrance grade is 10. For fall 2012, 200 students applied for upper-level admission, 180 were accepted, 65 enrolled. Deadline for receipt of application materials: none. Application fee required: $50. Interview required.

Athletics Interscholastic: aquatics, baseball, basketball, canoeing/kayaking, cooperative games, cross-country running, drill team, football, JROTC drill, marksmanship, wrestling; intramural: baseball, basketball, fitness. 1 PE instructor, 15 coaches, 1 athletic trainer.

Computers Computers are regularly used in English, foreign language, history, mathematics, science classes. Computer network features include on-campus library services, Internet access, Internet filtering or blocking technology. Campus intranet and student e-mail accounts are available to students. The school has a published electronic and media policy.

Contact Mr. Cedrick Broadhurst, Director of Admissions. 800-946-7773. Fax: 540-946-7738. E-mail: cbroadhurst@fishburne.org. Web site: www.fishburne.org

FLINT HILL SCHOOL

3320 Jermantown Road
Oakton, Virginia 22124

Head of School: Mr. John Thomas

General Information Coeducational day college-preparatory, arts, technology, and athletics, community service school. Grades JK–12. Founded: 1956. Setting: suburban. Nearest major city is Washington, DC. 45-acre campus. 1 building on campus. Approved or accredited by Virginia Association of Independent Schools and Virginia Department of Education. Member of National Association of Independent Schools and Secondary School Admission Test Board. Endowment: $1.9 million. Total enrollment: 1,099. Upper school average class size: 12. Upper school faculty-student ratio: 1:7. There are 168 required school days per year for Upper School students. Upper School students typically attend 5 days per week. The average school day consists of 6 hours and 30 minutes.

Upper School Student Profile Grade 9: 129 students (65 boys, 64 girls); Grade 10: 135 students (69 boys, 66 girls); Grade 11: 124 students (63 boys, 61 girls); Grade 12: 125 students (75 boys, 50 girls).

Faculty School total: 163. In upper school: 28 men, 44 women; 52 have advanced degrees.

Subjects Offered 20th century history, advanced chemistry, algebra, anatomy, art, ballet, biology, biology-AP, British literature, calculus, calculus-AP, ceramics, chemistry, chemistry-AP, Chinese, choir, choral music, chorus, civil rights, community service, computer animation, computer graphics, computer programming, computer science-AP, concert band, concert choir, creative writing, digital imaging, discrete mathematics, drama, drawing, drawing and design, earth science, economics-AP, English, English literature, English literature and composition-AP, English-AP, environmental science, environmental science-AP, environmental studies, European civilization, European history, fine arts, French, French language-AP, French literature-AP, geometry, government-AP, history, history of music, honors English, improvisation, jazz band, jazz dance, Latin, Latin American studies, Latin-AP, macro/microeconomics-AP, marine science, modern European history-AP, music, music history, music theory, music theory-AP, orchestra, ornithology, photography, physical education, physics, physics-AP, physiology, playwriting, pre-calculus, psychology, psychology-AP, science, sculpture, senior project, Shakespeare, short story, Spanish, Spanish-AP, statistics-AP, studio art, study skills, symphonic band, theater, trigonometry, U.S. history, U.S. history-AP, world religions.

Graduation Requirements Arts and fine arts (art, music, dance, drama), athletics, English, foreign language, history, mathematics, physical education (includes health), science, senior project. Community service is required.

Special Academic Programs 23 Advanced Placement exams for which test preparation is offered; honors section; academic accommodation for the musically talented and the artistically talented.

College Admission Counseling 119 students graduated in 2012; 116 went to college, including Christopher Newport University; James Madison University; The College of William and Mary; University of Colorado Boulder; University of Virginia; Virginia Polytechnic Institute and State University. Other: 1 entered military service, 1 entered a postgraduate year, 1 had other specific plans. Median SAT critical reading: 590, median SAT math: 610, median SAT writing: 590, median combined SAT: 1790, median composite ACT: 26. 48% scored over 600 on SAT critical reading, 60% scored over 600 on SAT math, 52% scored over 600 on SAT writing, 54% scored over 1800 on combined SAT, 55% scored over 26 on composite ACT.

Student Life Upper grades have specified standards of dress, student council, honor system. Discipline rests primarily with faculty.

Summer Programs Remediation, enrichment, advancement, ESL, sports, art/fine arts, rigorous outdoor training, computer instruction programs offered; session focuses on academics, arts, enrichment, travel, athletics, and service; held both on and off campus; held at various domestic and international locations; accepts boys and girls; open to students from other schools. 815 students usually enrolled. 2013 schedule: June 24 to August 2. Application deadline: none.

Tuition and Aid Day student tuition: $30,950. Tuition installment plan (Insured Tuition Payment Plan, FACTS Tuition Payment Plan, monthly payment plans, one payment, two payments, or ten payments). Need-based scholarship grants available. In 2012–13, 19% of upper-school students received aid. Total amount of financial aid awarded in 2012–13: $2,027,705.

Admissions Traditional secondary-level entrance grade is 9. For fall 2012, 269 students applied for upper-level admission, 145 were accepted, 73 enrolled. ISEE, PSAT, SAT or SSAT required. Deadline for receipt of application materials: January 16. Application fee required: $50. On-campus interview required.

Athletics Interscholastic: aerobics/dance (girls), baseball (b), basketball (b,g), cross-country running (b,g), dance (g), dance team (g), diving (b,g), football (b), lacrosse (b,g), self defense (g), soccer (b,g), softball (g), swimming and diving (b,g), tennis (b,g), track and field (b,g), volleyball (g); coed interscholastic: golf, hockey, ice hockey, independent competitive sports, physical fitness, running, strength & conditioning, yoga; coed intramural: aerobics/dance, canoeing/kayaking, climbing, dance, fitness, modern dance, mountaineering, outdoor activities, outdoor education, physical fitness, physical training, strength & conditioning, wall climbing, weight training, winter soccer. 16 coaches, 2 athletic trainers.

Computers Computers are regularly used in all academic classes. Computer network features include on-campus library services, online commercial services, Internet access, wireless campus network, Internet filtering or blocking technology. Campus intranet, student e-mail accounts, and computer access in designated common areas are available to students. Students grades are available online. The school has a published electronic and media policy.

Contact Mr. Chris Pryor, Director of Admission. 703-584-2300. Fax: 703-242-0718. E-mail: cpryor@flinthill.org. Web site: www.flinthill.org

FLINTRIDGE PREPARATORY SCHOOL

4543 Crown Avenue
La Canada Flintridge, California 91011

Head of School: Mr. Peter H. Bachmann

General Information Coeducational day college-preparatory school. Grades 7–12. Founded: 1933. Setting: suburban. Nearest major city is Los Angeles. 7-acre campus. 8 buildings on campus. Approved or accredited by California Association of Independent Schools, The College Board, and Western Association of Schools and Colleges. Member of National Association of Independent Schools. Total enrollment: 500. Upper school average class size: 12. Upper school faculty-student ratio: 1:13. Upper School students typically attend 5 days per week. The average school day consists of 6 hours and 20 minutes.

Upper School Student Profile Grade 9: 100 students (47 boys, 53 girls); Grade 10: 101 students (51 boys, 50 girls); Grade 11: 102 students (49 boys, 53 girls); Grade 12: 96 students (46 boys, 50 girls).

Faculty School total: 66. In upper school: 35 men, 31 women; 48 have advanced degrees.

Subjects Offered African history, algebra, American history, American history-AP, American literature, American politics in film, analysis and differential calculus, art, art history, art history-AP, art-AP, Basic programming, biology, biology-AP, British literature-AP, business applications, calculus, calculus-AP, career/college preparation, ceramics, chemistry, chemistry-AP, choral music, computer literacy, computer math, computer programming, computer science, creative writing, dance, drama, driver education, earth science, economics, English, English literature, environmental studies, European history, expository writing, fine arts, French, French language-AP, geography, geometry, government-AP, government/civics, grammar, great books, history, jazz band, Latin, mathematics, music, photography, physical education, physics, physiology, psychology, science, social studies, Spanish, Spanish literature-AP, Spanish-AP, statistics, theater, trigonometry, world history, world literature, writing.

Graduation Requirements Arts and fine arts (art, music, dance, drama), English, foreign language, mathematics, science, social studies (includes history), community service.

Special Academic Programs 20 Advanced Placement exams for which test preparation is offered; honors section; independent study; study abroad; academic accommodation for the gifted, the musically talented, and the artistically talented.

College Admission Counseling 96 students graduated in 2012; all went to college, including Loyola Marymount University; New York University; University of California, Berkeley; University of California, Los Angeles; University of Southern California. Median SAT critical reading: 680, median SAT math: 720, median SAT writing: 740.

Student Life Upper grades have specified standards of dress, student council, honor system. Discipline rests equally with students and faculty.

Summer Programs Remediation, enrichment, advancement, sports, art/fine arts, rigorous outdoor training, computer instruction programs offered; session focuses on academic enrichment/advancement, fine arts, and athletics; held on campus; accepts boys and girls; open to students from other schools. 300 students usually enrolled. 2013 schedule: June 23 to August 1. Application deadline: June 23.

Tuition and Aid Day student tuition: $29,000. Tuition installment plan (Tuition Management Systems). Need-based scholarship grants available. In 2012–13, 29% of upper-school students received aid.

Admissions Traditional secondary-level entrance grade is 9. ISEE required. Deadline for receipt of application materials: January 18. Application fee required: $90. On-campus interview required.

Athletics Interscholastic: aquatics (boys, girls), baseball (b), basketball (b,g), cheering (g), cross-country running (b,g), diving (b,g), football (b), soccer (b,g), softball (g), swimming and diving (b,g), tennis (b,g), track and field (b,g), volleyball (b,g), water polo (b,g), winter soccer (b,g); coed interscholastic: equestrian sports, golf. 4 PE instructors, 41 coaches, 1 athletic trainer.

Computers Computers are regularly used in all academic, foreign language, mathematics, photography, science classes. Computer network features include on-campus library services, online commercial services, Internet access, wireless campus network. Campus intranet, student e-mail accounts, and computer access in designated common areas are available to students. The school has a published electronic and media policy.

Contact Ms. Dana Valentino, Admissions Assistant. 818-949-5514. Fax: 818-952-6247. E-mail: dvalentino@flintridgeprep.org. Web site: www.flintridgeprep.org

FLINT RIVER ACADEMY

11556 East Highway 85
Woodbury, Georgia 30293

Head of School: Mrs. Michele Purvis

General Information Coeducational day college-preparatory, arts, and technology school. Grades PK–12. Founded: 1967. Setting: rural. Nearest major city is Atlanta. 8-acre campus. 1 building on campus. Approved or accredited by Georgia Accrediting Commission and Southern Association of Colleges and Schools. Total enrollment: 312. Upper school average class size: 18. Upper school faculty-student ratio: 1:14. There are 180 required school days per year for Upper School students. Upper School students typically attend 5 days per week. The average school day consists of 6 hours and 23 minutes.

Upper School Student Profile Grade 9: 28 students (16 boys, 12 girls); Grade 10: 21 students (13 boys, 8 girls); Grade 11: 24 students (14 boys, 10 girls); Grade 12: 18 students (9 boys, 9 girls).

Faculty School total: 45. In upper school: 2 men, 12 women; 10 have advanced degrees.

Subjects Offered Algebra, American history, American literature, art, biology, calculus, chemistry, creative writing, drama, earth science, economics, English, fine arts, geography, geometry, government/civics, grammar, health, history, mathematics, music, physical education, physics, physiology, science, social studies, Spanish, theater, trigonometry, typing, world history, world literature.

Graduation Requirements Arts and fine arts (art, music, dance, drama), business skills (includes word processing), computer science, English, foreign language, mathematics, physical education (includes health), science, social sciences, social studies (includes history).

Special Academic Programs Advanced Placement exam preparation; honors section; study at local college for college credit; academic accommodation for the musically talented and the artistically talented; remedial math.

College Admission Counseling 28 students graduated in 2012; all went to college, including Columbus State University; Georgia Institute of Technology; Georgia Southern University; Kennesaw State University; University of Georgia; Valdosta State University. Median SAT critical reading: 210, median SAT math: 527, median SAT writing: 513, median combined SAT: 1544, median composite ACT: 20.

Student Life Upper grades have specified standards of dress, student council, honor system. Discipline rests primarily with faculty.

Tuition and Aid Day student tuition: $6555. Tuition installment plan (monthly payment plans). Tuition reduction for third sibling available.

Admissions Traditional secondary-level entrance grade is 9. For fall 2012, 4 students applied for upper-level admission, 4 were accepted, 4 enrolled. ACT-Explore required. Deadline for receipt of application materials: none. Application fee required: $50. On-campus interview required.

Athletics Interscholastic: baseball (boys), basketball (b,g), cheering (g), cross-country running (b,g), football (b), golf (b,g), softball (g), tennis (b,g), track and field (b,g); intramural: baseball (b), basketball (b,g), cheering (g), dance team (g), golf (g), soccer (b), softball (g), tennis (b,g), volleyball (b,g), weight lifting (b,g), weight training (b); coed intramural: ropes courses. 2 PE instructors, 2 coaches.

Computers Computer network features include on-campus library services, Internet access.

Contact Ms. Ida Ann Dunn, Guidance Counselor. 706-553-2541. Fax: 706-553-9777. E-mail: counselor@flintriveracademy.com. Web site: www.flintriveracademy.com

FONTBONNE HALL ACADEMY

9901 Shore Road
Brooklyn, New York 11209

Head of School: Sr. Dolores F. Crepeau, CSJ

General Information Girls' day college-preparatory, arts, religious studies, and technology school, affiliated with Roman Catholic Church. Grades 9–12. Founded: 1937. Setting: urban. Nearest major city is New York. 5 buildings on campus. Approved or accredited by Middle States Association of Colleges and Schools, New York State Board of Regents, and New York Department of Education. Total enrollment: 486. Upper school average class size: 18. Upper school faculty-student ratio: 1:13. There are 180 required school days per year for Upper School students. Upper School students typically attend 5 days per week. The average school day consists of 6 hours and 30 minutes.

Upper School Student Profile Grade 9: 101 students (101 girls); Grade 10: 132 students (132 girls); Grade 11: 125 students (125 girls); Grade 12: 128 students (128 girls). 90% of students are Roman Catholic.

Faculty School total: 39. In upper school: 3 men, 36 women; 37 have advanced degrees.

Subjects Offered Advanced chemistry, algebra, American literature-AP, anatomy and physiology, anthropology, art, biology-AP, calculus, calculus-AP, chemistry, chorus, computer multimedia, computers, earth science, economics, English, forensics, genetics, government, health, history-AP, Italian, Latin, marine science, mathematics, music, photography, physical education, physics, religion, Spanish, Spanish language-AP, U.S. history, world geography, world history.

Graduation Requirements Algebra, American government, American history, American literature, art, biology, British literature, chemistry, college counseling, college writing, computer applications, economics, electives, English, European civilization, foreign language, geometry, government, guidance, Internet research, lab science, music, physical education (includes health), religion (includes Bible studies and theology), science, world civilizations, Board of Regents requirements, 60 hours of service.

Special Academic Programs Advanced Placement exam preparation; honors section; study at local college for college credit.

College Admission Counseling 132 students graduated in 2012; all went to college, including Columbia University; Fordham University; Georgetown University; Manhattan College; New York University; The Catholic University of America. Median SAT critical reading: 560, median SAT math: 550, median SAT writing: 640, median combined SAT: 1750.

Student Life Upper grades have uniform requirement, student council. Discipline rests primarily with faculty. Attendance at religious services is required.

Summer Programs Sports programs offered; session focuses on sports clinics; held on campus; accepts girls; open to students from other schools. 50 students usually enrolled. 2013 schedule: August 1 to August 12. Application deadline: June 27.

Tuition and Aid Day student tuition: $8100. Tuition installment plan (monthly payment plans, 3 payments per year). Tuition reduction for siblings, merit scholarship grants, Service Scholarships available. In 2012–13, 20% of upper-school students received aid; total upper-school merit-scholarship money awarded: $100,000. Total amount of financial aid awarded in 2012–13: $121,500.

Admissions Traditional secondary-level entrance grade is 9. For fall 2012, 437 students applied for upper-level admission, 356 were accepted, 214 enrolled. Diocesan Entrance Exam required. Deadline for receipt of application materials: February 4. Application fee required: $250.

Athletics Interscholastic: aquatics, baseball, basketball, cheering, cross-country running, dance, dance squad, drill team, fishing, golf, running, soccer, softball, swimming and diving, tennis, track and field, volleyball. 2 PE instructors, 23 coaches.

Computers Computers are regularly used in all academic classes. Computer network features include on-campus library services, Internet access, wireless campus network, Internet filtering or blocking technology. Campus intranet and computer access in designated common areas are available to students. The school has a published electronic and media policy.

Contact Sr. Dolores F. Crepeau, CSJ, Principal. 718-748-2244. Fax: 718-745-3841. E-mail: crepeau@fontbonne.org. Web site: www.fontbonne.org

FOOTHILLS ACADEMY

Calgary, Alberta, Canada

See Special Needs Schools section.

FORDHAM PREPARATORY SCHOOL

East Fordham Road
Bronx, New York 10458-5175

Head of School: Rev. Kenneth J. Boller, SJ

General Information Boys' day college-preparatory school, affiliated with Roman Catholic Church. Grades 9–12. Founded: 1841. Setting: urban. Nearest major city is New York. 5-acre campus. 2 buildings on campus. Approved or accredited by Jesuit Secondary Education Association, Middle States Association of Colleges and Schools, National Catholic Education Association, and New York Department of Education. Endowment: $1.8 million. Total enrollment: 955. Upper school average class size: 24. Upper school faculty-student ratio: 1:11.

Upper School Student Profile Grade 9: 215 students (215 boys); Grade 10: 260 students (260 boys); Grade 11: 238 students (238 boys); Grade 12: 242 students (242 boys). 75% of students are Roman Catholic.

Faculty School total: 86. In upper school: 62 men, 24 women; 77 have advanced degrees.

Subjects Offered Advanced chemistry, algebra, American Civil War, American history, American history-AP, American literature, Ancient Greek, architectural drawing, art history-AP, biochemistry, biology, biology-AP, British literature, calculus, calculus-AP, chemistry, chemistry-AP, Chinese, computer graphics, computer programming, constitutional history of U.S., creative writing, economics, emerging technology, English, English language and composition-AP, English literature-AP, European history-AP, finite math, forensics, French, geometry, German, global studies, government and politics-AP, health, Italian, Latin, Latin-AP, macroeconomics-AP, media communications, modern history, modern world history, music, physical education, physics, physics-AP, poetry, pre-calculus, religious studies, science research, short story, Spanish, Spanish language-AP, Spanish literature-AP, statistics-AP, studio art, studio art-AP, trigonometry, world history-AP.

Graduation Requirements Arts and fine arts (art, music, dance, drama), English, foreign language, mathematics, physical education (includes health), religious studies, science, social studies (includes history), senior service project.

Special Academic Programs Advanced Placement exam preparation; honors section; study at local college for college credit.

College Admission Counseling 251 students graduated in 2012; 246 went to college, including Binghamton University, State University of New York; College of the Holy Cross; Fordham University; Manhattan College; Providence College; Villanova University. Other: 1 entered military service, 4 had other specific plans. Mean SAT critical reading: 593, mean SAT math: 592, mean SAT writing: 591.

Student Life Upper grades have specified standards of dress. Discipline rests primarily with faculty. Attendance at religious services is required.

Tuition and Aid Day student tuition: $16,720. Tuition installment plan (monthly payment plans). Merit scholarship grants, need-based scholarship grants available. In 2012–13, 35% of upper-school students received aid; total upper-school merit-scholarship money awarded: $400,000. Total amount of financial aid awarded in 2012–13: $2,200,000.

Admissions Traditional secondary-level entrance grade is 9. For fall 2012, 1,122 students applied for upper-level admission, 534 were accepted, 215 enrolled. Cooperative Entrance Exam (McGraw-Hill), Diocesan Entrance Exam, ISEE, SSAT or STS required. Deadline for receipt of application materials: December 15. No application fee required.

Athletics Interscholastic: baseball, basketball, bowling, crew, cross-country running, diving, football, golf, ice hockey, indoor track, lacrosse, rugby, soccer, swimming and diving, tennis, track and field, volleyball, winter (indoor) track, wrestling; intramural: basketball, fitness, Frisbee, rock climbing, weight training. 2 PE instructors, 16 coaches.

Computers Computers are regularly used in English, foreign language, history, mathematics, science classes. Computer network features include on-campus library services, online commercial services, Internet access, wireless campus network, Internet filtering or blocking technology, Rosetta Stone. Student e-mail accounts are available to students. The school has a published electronic and media policy.

Contact Christopher D. Lauber, Director of Admissions. 718-584-8367. Fax: 718-367-7598. E-mail: lauberc@fordhamprep.org. Web site: www.fordhamprep.org

FOREST LAKE ACADEMY

500 Education Loop
Apopka, Florida 32703

Head of School: Mr. David Denton

General Information Coeducational boarding and day and distance learning college-preparatory, arts, religious studies, and bilingual studies school, affiliated with Seventh-day Adventists. Grades 9–12. Distance learning grades 9–12. Founded: 1918. Setting: suburban. Nearest major city is Orlando. Students are housed in single-sex dormitories. 6 buildings on campus. Approved or accredited by CITA (Commission on International and Trans-Regional Accreditation), Middle States Association of Colleges and Schools, National Council for Private School Accreditation, and Florida Department of Education. Total enrollment: 389. Upper school average class size: 22. Upper school faculty-student ratio: 1:12. There are 179 required school days per year for Upper School students. Upper School students typically attend 5 days per week. The average school day consists of 6 hours.

Upper School Student Profile Grade 9: 85 students (49 boys, 36 girls); Grade 10: 98 students (48 boys, 50 girls); Grade 11: 112 students (57 boys, 55 girls); Grade 12: 94 students (45 boys, 49 girls). 8% of students are boarding students. 84% are state residents. 13 states are represented in upper school student body. 1% are international students. International students from Argentina, Bermuda, and China. 95% of students are Seventh-day Adventists.

Faculty School total: 32. In upper school: 20 men, 12 women; 15 have advanced degrees; 4 reside on campus.

Subjects Offered Algebra, American government, American literature, art, band, bell choir, Bible studies, biology, calculus, chemistry, choir, church history, computer applications, desktop publishing, digital photography, economics, English, environmental science, geometry, health, honors algebra, honors English, honors geometry, honors world history, integrated mathematics, life management skills, physical science, physics, play production, pre-calculus, psychology, SAT preparation, senior project, Spanish, statistics, strings, swimming, tennis, U.S. history, video film production, world geography, world history, world literature, writing, yearbook.

Graduation Requirements Algebra, American government, American literature, arts and fine arts (art, music, dance, drama), Bible studies, biology, chemistry, computer applications, computer science, economics, English, environmental science, fitness, foreign language, geometry, health education, life management skills, physical education (includes health), physical science, pre-calculus, religion (includes Bible studies and theology), science, social studies (includes history), Spanish, statistics, U.S. history, world history, world literature, writing, 20 hours of community service activity for each year enrolled.

Special Academic Programs Honors section; study at local college for college credit.

College Admission Counseling 94 students graduated in 2012; they went to Adventist University of Health Sciences; Andrews University; Oakwood University;

Seminole State College of Florida; Southern Adventist University; University of Central Florida.

Student Life Upper grades have uniform requirement, student council, honor system. Discipline rests primarily with faculty.

Tuition and Aid Day student tuition: $11,370; 7-day tuition and room/board: $22,350. Tuition installment plan (FACTS Tuition Payment Plan, monthly payment plans, individually arranged payment plans). Merit scholarship grants, need-based scholarship grants, paying campus jobs available. In 2012–13, 37% of upper-school students received aid; total upper-school merit-scholarship money awarded: $75,000. Total amount of financial aid awarded in 2012–13: $347,000.

Admissions Traditional secondary-level entrance grade is 9. For fall 2012, 425 students applied for upper-level admission, 415 were accepted, 389 enrolled. Deadline for receipt of application materials: none. Application fee required: $60. Interview recommended.

Athletics Interscholastic: basketball (boys, girls), golf (b), volleyball (g); intramural: golf (b); coed interscholastic: aquatics, life saving, physical fitness, strength & conditioning, tennis; coed intramural: basketball, flag football, floor hockey, indoor hockey, indoor soccer, soccer, tennis, volleyball. 2 PE instructors, 1 coach.

Computers Computers are regularly used in computer applications, desktop publishing, photography, Web site design, writing, yearbook classes. Computer resources include Internet access, wireless campus network, Internet filtering or blocking technology, financial aid and grant search programs for college. Campus intranet, student e-mail accounts, and computer access in designated common areas are available to students. Students grades are available online. The school has a published electronic and media policy.

Contact Mrs. Claudia Dure C. Osorio, Director of Student Records. 407-862-8411 Ext. 743. Fax: 407-862-7050. E-mail: osorioc@forestlake.org. Web site: www.forestlakeacademy.org

FORSYTH COUNTRY DAY SCHOOL

5501 Shallowford Road
PO Box 549
Lewisville, North Carolina 27023-0549

Head of School: Mrs. Joyce Henson

General Information Coeducational day college-preparatory school. Grades PK–12. Founded: 1970. Setting: suburban. Nearest major city is Winston-Salem. 80-acre campus. 7 buildings on campus. Approved or accredited by Southern Association of Colleges and Schools, Southern Association of Independent Schools, The College Board, and North Carolina Department of Education. Member of National Association of Independent Schools. Endowment: $13 million. Total enrollment: 776. Upper school average class size: 15. Upper school faculty-student ratio: 1:12. There are 175 required school days per year for Upper School students. Upper School students typically attend 5 days per week. The average school day consists of 5 hours and 45 minutes.

Upper School Student Profile Grade 9: 70 students (41 boys, 29 girls); Grade 10: 80 students (44 boys, 36 girls); Grade 11: 92 students (55 boys, 37 girls); Grade 12: 77 students (44 boys, 33 girls).

Faculty School total: 175. In upper school: 18 men, 29 women; 24 have advanced degrees.

Subjects Offered Advanced Placement courses, advanced studio art-AP, algebra, American history, American history-AP, American literature, art, astronomy, biology, calculus, calculus-AP, ceramics, chemistry, Chinese studies, community service, computer math, computer programming, computer science, creative writing, digital art, drama, English, English literature, European history, fine arts, foreign policy, French, freshman seminar, geometry, grammar, health, history, history of science, humanities, international relations, Japanese studies, journalism, Latin, Mandarin, mathematics, Middle Eastern history, music, photography, physical education, physics, psychology, SAT/ACT preparation, science, social studies, Spanish, statistics-AP, theater, yearbook.

Graduation Requirements Arts and fine arts (art, music, dance, drama), English, foreign language, history, mathematics, physical education (includes health), physical fitness, science. Community service is required.

Special Academic Programs 18 Advanced Placement exams for which test preparation is offered; honors section; academic accommodation for the gifted; programs in English, general development for dyslexic students; ESL (2 students enrolled).

College Admission Counseling 106 students graduated in 2012; all went to college, including Duke University; Elon University; North Carolina State University; The University of North Carolina at Chapel Hill; The University of North Carolina Wilmington; Wake Forest University. Median SAT critical reading: 600, median SAT math: 615. 70% scored over 600 on SAT critical reading, 68% scored over 600 on SAT math.

Student Life Upper grades have specified standards of dress, student council, honor system. Discipline rests equally with students and faculty.

Summer Programs Enrichment programs offered; session focuses on leadership training; held both on and off campus; held at various businesses and offices throughout the community; accepts boys and girls; open to students from other schools. 50 students usually enrolled. 2013 schedule: June 15 to July 31.

Tuition and Aid Day student tuition: $19,910. Tuition installment plan (Insured Tuition Payment Plan, monthly payment plans, individually arranged payment plans). Need-based scholarship grants available. In 2012–13, 23% of upper-school students received aid. Total amount of financial aid awarded in 2012–13: $846,329.

Admissions Traditional secondary-level entrance grade is 9. For fall 2012, 61 students applied for upper-level admission, 51 were accepted, 41 enrolled. ERB CTP IV, WRAT and writing sample required. Deadline for receipt of application materials: none. Application fee required: $100. On-campus interview recommended.

Athletics Interscholastic: baseball (boys), basketball (b,g), cheering (g), cross-country running (b,g), field hockey (g), football (b), golf (b,g), lacrosse (b,g), physical fitness (b,g), soccer (b,g), softball (g), tennis (b,g), track and field (b,g), volleyball (g), wrestling (b); coed interscholastic: swimming and diving; coed intramural: sailing. 4 PE instructors, 4 coaches, 2 athletic trainers.

Computers Computers are regularly used in art, English, foreign language, history, mathematics, music, science classes. Computer network features include on-campus library services, online commercial services, Internet access, wireless campus network, Internet filtering or blocking technology. Campus intranet, student e-mail accounts, and computer access in designated common areas are available to students. Students grades are available online. The school has a published electronic and media policy.

Contact Cindy C. Kluttz, Director of Admission. 336-945-3151 Ext. 340. Fax: 336-945-2907. E-mail: cindykluttz@fcds.org. Web site: www.fcds.org

FORT LAUDERDALE PREPARATORY SCHOOL

3275 West Oakland Park Boulevard
Fort Lauderdale, Florida 33311

Head of School: Dr. Lawrence Berkowitz

General Information Coeducational day college-preparatory, general academic, arts, and technology school. Grades PK–12. Founded: 1986. Setting: urban. 5-acre campus. 1 building on campus. Approved or accredited by CITA (Commission on International and Trans-Regional Accreditation), National Council for Private School Accreditation, National Independent Private Schools Association, Southern Association of Colleges and Schools, and Florida Department of Education. Member of National Association of Independent Schools and European Council of International Schools. Languages of instruction: English and Spanish. Total enrollment: 195. Upper school average class size: 16. Upper school faculty-student ratio: 1:8. There are 177 required school days per year for Upper School students. Upper School students typically attend 5 days per week. The average school day consists of 7 hours.

Upper School Student Profile Grade 7: 18 students (8 boys, 10 girls); Grade 8: 17 students (9 boys, 8 girls); Grade 9: 17 students (8 boys, 9 girls); Grade 10: 17 students (7 boys, 10 girls); Grade 11: 15 students (7 boys, 8 girls); Grade 12: 16 students (8 boys, 8 girls).

Faculty School total: 28. In upper school: 11 men, 10 women; 9 have advanced degrees.

Subjects Offered Accounting, ACT preparation, advanced chemistry, advanced computer applications, advanced math, Advanced Placement courses, advanced studio art-AP, advanced TOEFL/grammar, algebra, American government, American history, American history-AP, American literature, American literature-AP, art, art appreciation, art history, art history-AP, art-AP, automated accounting, Basic programming, biology, biology-AP, bookkeeping, British literature, British literature (honors), business applications, business education, business mathematics, calculus, calculus-AP, career education, career/college preparation, character education, chemistry, chemistry-AP, U.S. government and politics-AP.

Special Academic Programs International Baccalaureate program; Advanced Placement exam preparation; honors section; accelerated programs; independent study; study at local college for college credit; academic accommodation for the gifted; remedial reading and/or remedial writing; remedial math; programs in English, mathematics, general development for dyslexic students; ESL (17 students enrolled).

College Admission Counseling 18 students graduated in 2011; 16 went to college, including Florida Atlantic University; Florida State University; Hunter College of the City University of New York; University of Florida; University of Miami; University of South Florida. Other: 1 went to work, 1 entered military service.

Student Life Upper grades have uniform requirement, student council, honor system. Discipline rests primarily with faculty.

Tuition and Aid Day student tuition: $12,500. Tuition installment plan (monthly payment plans, individually arranged payment plans). Tuition reduction for siblings, merit scholarship grants, need-based scholarship grants available. In 2011–12, 50% of upper-school students received aid; total upper-school merit-scholarship money awarded: $200,000. Total amount of financial aid awarded in 2011–12: $1,000,000.

Admissions Traditional secondary-level entrance grade is 7. For fall 2011, 92 students applied for upper-level admission, 51 were accepted, 39 enrolled. Admissions testing, High School Placement Test, math and English placement tests, Math Placement Exam, school's own exam, standardized test scores, Stanford Achievement Test, TOEFL or writing sample required. Deadline for receipt of application materials: none. Application fee required: $50. Interview recommended.

Athletics 2 PE instructors.

Computers Computers are regularly used in all academic classes. Computer network features include on-campus library services, Internet access, wireless campus network, Internet filtering or blocking technology. Campus intranet is available to students. The school has a published electronic and media policy.

Contact Jonathan A. Lonstein, Director of Admissions. 954-485-7500. Fax: 954-485-1732. E-mail: admissions@flps.com. Web site: www.flps.com/

FORT WORTH CHRISTIAN SCHOOL

6200 Holiday Lane
North Richland Hills, Texas 76180

Head of School: Mr. Kelly Moore

General Information Coeducational day college-preparatory, arts, religious studies, and technology school, affiliated with Christian faith, Christian faith. Grades PK–12. Founded: 1958. Setting: suburban. 40-acre campus. 6 buildings on campus. Approved or accredited by National Christian School Association, Southern Association of Colleges and Schools, Texas Private School Accreditation Commission, and Texas Department of Education. Endowment: $600,000. Total enrollment: 870. Upper school average class size: 17. Upper school faculty-student ratio: 1:14. There are 175 required school days per year for Upper School students. Upper School students typically attend 5 days per week. The average school day consists of 6 hours and 40 minutes.

Upper School Student Profile Grade 9: 90 students (49 boys, 41 girls); Grade 10: 84 students (43 boys, 41 girls); Grade 11: 94 students (47 boys, 47 girls); Grade 12: 95 students (53 boys, 42 girls). 80% of students are Christian faith, Christian.

Faculty School total: 108. In upper school: 12 men, 21 women; 12 have advanced degrees.

Subjects Offered Advanced Placement courses, African drumming, algebra, anatomy and physiology, art, band, Bible studies, biology, biology-AP, calculus, calculus-AP, chemistry, chemistry-AP, chorus, computer applications, computer information systems, computer science-AP, drama, economics, economics and history, economics-AP, English, English language and composition-AP, English literature and composition-AP, ethics, family studies, geometry, golf, government, government/civics, Latin, physical education, physics, pre-calculus, robotics, SAT/ACT preparation, Spanish, strings, theater arts, U.S. history, U.S. history-AP, video, world geography, world history, world history-AP, yearbook.

Graduation Requirements Arts and fine arts (art, music, dance, drama), business skills (includes word processing), computer science, electives, English, foreign language, mathematics, physical education (includes health), religion (includes Bible studies and theology), science, social sciences, social studies (includes history), world geography, community service hours.

Special Academic Programs Advanced Placement exam preparation; honors section; independent study; study at local college for college credit.

College Admission Counseling 104 students graduated in 2012; all went to college, including Abilene Christian University; Baylor University; Harding University; Texas A&M University; Texas Christian University; University of North Texas. Mean SAT critical reading: 537, mean SAT math: 543, mean SAT writing: 520, mean combined SAT: 1600, mean composite ACT: 24. 49% scored over 600 on SAT critical reading, 59% scored over 600 on SAT math, 46% scored over 600 on SAT writing, 21% scored over 1800 on combined SAT, 37% scored over 26 on composite ACT.

Student Life Upper grades have uniform requirement, student council, honor system. Discipline rests primarily with faculty. Attendance at religious services is required.

Tuition and Aid Day student tuition: $11,600. Tuition installment plan (FACTS Tuition Payment Plan, monthly payment plans). Tuition reduction for siblings, need-based scholarship grants, tuition reduction for children of faculty and staff available. In 2012–13, 13% of upper-school students received aid. Total amount of financial aid awarded in 2012–13: $111,000.

Admissions Traditional secondary-level entrance grade is 9. For fall 2012, 58 students applied for upper-level admission, 52 were accepted, 52 enrolled. Wechsler Individual Achievement Test required. Deadline for receipt of application materials: none. No application fee required. On-campus interview required.

Athletics Interscholastic: baseball (boys), basketball (b,g), cheering (g), cross-country running (b,g), football (b), golf (b,g), physical fitness (b,g), physical training (b,g), rodeo (b,g), running (b,g), soccer (b,g), softball (g), strength & conditioning (b,g), tennis (b,g), track and field (b,g), volleyball (g). 8 coaches, 1 athletic trainer.

Computers Computers are regularly used in computer applications, desktop publishing, independent study, media production, newspaper, technology, word processing, yearbook classes. Computer network features include on-campus library services, Internet access, wireless campus network, Internet filtering or blocking technology, online courses. Student e-mail accounts and computer access in designated common areas are available to students. Students grades are available online. The school has a published electronic and media policy.

Contact Mrs. Shirley Atkinson, Director of Admissions. 817-520-6561. Fax: 817-281-7063. E-mail: satkinson@fwc.org. Web site: www.fwc.org

FORT WORTH COUNTRY DAY SCHOOL

4200 Country Day Lane
Fort Worth, Texas 76109-4299

Head of School: Evan D. Peterson

General Information Coeducational day college-preparatory, arts, and technology school. Grades K–12. Founded: 1962. Setting: suburban. 100-acre campus. 13 buildings on campus. Approved or accredited by Independent Schools Association of the Southwest. Member of National Association of Independent Schools. Endowment: $42 million. Total enrollment: 1,110. Upper school average class size: 14. Upper school faculty-student ratio: 1:10. There are 174 required school days per year for Upper School students. Upper School students typically attend 5 days per week. The average school day consists of 8 hours.

Upper School Student Profile Grade 9: 90 students (46 boys, 44 girls); Grade 10: 104 students (50 boys, 54 girls); Grade 11: 110 students (53 boys, 57 girls); Grade 12: 99 students (50 boys, 49 girls).

Faculty School total: 137. In upper school: 16 men, 21 women; 12 have advanced degrees.

Subjects Offered 3-dimensional art, algebra, American history, American literature, art, art history, biology, calculus, ceramics, chemistry, comparative religion, computer math, computer programming, computer science, computer technologies, creative writing, dance, drama, earth science, ecology, economics, English, English literature, European history, fine arts, French, geography, geology, geometry, government/civics, health, history, journalism, Latin, mathematics, modern problems, music, music history, photography, physical education, physics, psychology, science, social studies, Spanish, technology, theater, trigonometry, word processing, world history, writing.

Graduation Requirements Algebra, American government, arts and fine arts (art, music, dance, drama), biology, English, foreign language, lab science, mathematics, physical education (includes health), science, social studies (includes history), participation in athletics, completion of a two year College Counseling Course. Community service is required.

Special Academic Programs 22 Advanced Placement exams for which test preparation is offered; study at local college for college credit; academic accommodation for the gifted, the musically talented, and the artistically talented.

College Admission Counseling 96 students graduated in 2012; all went to college, including Southern Methodist University; Texas A&M University; Texas Christian University; The University of Texas at Austin; University of Georgia; University of Oklahoma.

Student Life Upper grades have uniform requirement, student council, honor system. Discipline rests equally with students and faculty.

Summer Programs Remediation, enrichment, sports, art/fine arts programs offered; session focuses on athletics and enrichment; held both on and off campus; held at local golf course (for enrichment golf and golf team practice); accepts boys and girls; open to students from other schools. 300 students usually enrolled. 2013 schedule: June 1 to July 31. Application deadline: May 30.

Tuition and Aid Day student tuition: $19,505. Tuition installment plan (monthly payment plans, individually arranged payment plans). Merit scholarship grants, need-based scholarship grants, Malone Scholars Program, Betty Reese Memorial, Vicki and Edward P. Bass Scholarship, Reilly Breakthrough Scholarship, Joey Pollard Memorial Scholarship, Joann Chandler Thompson Memorial Scholarship available. In 2012–13, 22% of upper-school students received aid; total upper-school merit-scholarship money awarded: $176,482. Total amount of financial aid awarded in 2012–13: $980,225.

Admissions Traditional secondary-level entrance grade is 9. For fall 2012, 65 students applied for upper-level admission, 38 were accepted, 27 enrolled. ERB or ISEE required. Deadline for receipt of application materials: March 3. Application fee required: $75. Interview required.

Athletics Interscholastic: ballet (boys, girls), baseball (b), basketball (b,g), cheering (g), field hockey (g), football (b), lacrosse (b), track and field (b,g), volleyball (b,g), winter soccer (b,g), wrestling (b); intramural: lacrosse (b); coed interscholastic: ballet, cross-country running, dance, dance team, fitness, golf, independent competitive sports, outdoor education, outdoor recreation, physical fitness, physical training, ropes courses, strength & conditioning, swimming and diving, tennis, weight training. 12 PE instructors, 45 coaches, 2 athletic trainers.

Computers Computers are regularly used in architecture, college planning, computer applications, creative writing, desktop publishing, English, foreign language, history, humanities, introduction to technology, journalism, library skills, life skills, mathematics, music, newspaper, publications, reading, science, Web site design, writing, yearbook classes. Computer network features include on-campus library services, online commercial services, Internet access, wireless campus network, Internet filtering or blocking technology. Campus intranet, student e-mail accounts, and computer access in designated common areas are available to students. Students grades are available online. The school has a published electronic and media policy.

Contact Yolanda Espinoza, Admission Associate. 817-302-3209. Fax: 817-377-3425. E-mail: yolanda.espinoza@fwcd.org. Web site: www.fwcd.org

FOUNDATION ACADEMY

15304 Tilden Road
Winter Garden, Florida 34787

Head of School: Mr. Shawn Minks

General Information Coeducational day college-preparatory, general academic, and arts school, affiliated with Baptist Church. Grades 6–12. Founded: 1958. Setting: suburban. Nearest major city is Orlando. 75-acre campus. 3 buildings on campus. Approved or accredited by Association of Christian Schools International and Southern Association of Colleges and Schools. Total enrollment: 496. Upper school average class size: 16. Upper school faculty-student ratio: 1:14. There are 180 required school days per year for Upper School students. Upper School students typically attend 5 days per week. The average school day consists of 6 hours and 20 minutes.

Upper School Student Profile Grade 9: 31 students (12 boys, 19 girls); Grade 10: 36 students (16 boys, 20 girls); Grade 11: 32 students (22 boys, 10 girls); Grade 12: 31 students (24 boys, 7 girls). 20% of students are Baptist.

Faculty School total: 30. In upper school: 10 men, 19 women; 11 have advanced degrees.

Subjects Offered Advanced math, Advanced Placement courses, algebra, American government, American literature, anatomy and physiology, art, band, Bible, biology, biology-AP, business law, business mathematics, calculus, calculus-AP, career/college preparation, chemistry, choir, Christian education, college admission preparation, communication skills, computer processing, drama, ecology, economics and history, English, English composition, English language-AP, English literature, English literature-AP, geometry, government, health and wellness, health education, history-AP, honors algebra, honors English, honors geometry, honors U.S. history, honors world history, human anatomy, human biology, journalism, life science, marine biology, personal fitness, physical education, physical fitness, pre-algebra, pre-calculus, SAT preparation, SAT/ACT preparation, science, science project, Spanish, speech, speech and debate, speech communications, sports conditioning, studio art-AP, U.S. government and politics-AP, U.S. history, weight training, weightlifting, yearbook.

Graduation Requirements Algebra, American government, American history, American literature, anatomy and physiology, art, arts and fine arts (art, music, dance, drama), Bible, Bible studies, biology, chemistry, college admission preparation, economics and history, English, English composition, English literature, geography, geometry, government, health and wellness, history, human anatomy, languages, pre-calculus, SAT preparation, science, U.S. history, 4 credits of Bible.

Special Academic Programs Advanced Placement exam preparation; honors section; independent study; study at local college for college credit; remedial reading and/or remedial writing; remedial math; programs in English, mathematics for dyslexic students; special instructional classes for deaf students.

College Admission Counseling 29 students graduated in 2012; 28 went to college, including Cornell University; Florida Gulf Coast University; Florida State University; University of Central Florida; University of Florida; Valencia College. Other: 1 entered military service.

Student Life Upper grades have uniform requirement, student council. Discipline rests primarily with faculty. Attendance at religious services is required.

Summer Programs Remediation, enrichment, sports, art/fine arts programs offered; session focuses on sports camps, art, drama, academic; held on campus; accepts boys and girls; open to students from other schools. 100 students usually enrolled. 2013 schedule: June 1 to July 31.

Tuition and Aid Day student tuition: $10,143–$10,571. Guaranteed tuition plan. Tuition installment plan (SMART Tuition Payment Plan). Tuition reduction for siblings, need-based scholarship grants available. In 2012–13, 10% of upper-school students received aid. Total amount of financial aid awarded in 2012–13: $300,000.

Admissions Traditional secondary-level entrance grade is 9. For fall 2012, 76 students applied for upper-level admission, 57 were accepted, 49 enrolled. Admissions testing, Gates MacGinite Reading Tests, Math Placement Exam and Wide Range Achievement Test required. Deadline for receipt of application materials: none. Application fee required: $150. Interview required.

Athletics Interscholastic: baseball (boys), basketball (b,g), bowling (b,g), cheering (g), cross-country running (b,g), football (b), golf (b), soccer (b,g), softball (g), tennis (b,g), track and field (b,g), volleyball (g). 2 PE instructors, 2 athletic trainers.

Computers Computers are regularly used in career exploration, college planning, computer applications, economics, English, geography, health, history, independent study, keyboarding, library skills, mathematics, music, SAT preparation, word processing, writing, yearbook classes. Computer network features include on-campus library services, Internet access, wireless campus network, Internet filtering or blocking technology. Campus intranet and student e-mail accounts are available to students. Students grades are available online.

Contact Mrs. Stephanie Baysinger, Student Advisor. 407-877-2744 Ext. 259. Fax: 407-877-1985. E-mail: sbaysinger@foundationacademy.net. Web site: www.foundationacademy.net

FOUNTAIN VALLEY SCHOOL OF COLORADO

6155 Fountain Valley School Road
Colorado Springs, Colorado 80911

Head of School: Craig W. Larimer Jr.

General Information Coeducational boarding and day college-preparatory, arts, and technology school. Grades 9–12. Founded: 1930. Setting: suburban. Students are housed in single-sex dormitories. 1,100-acre campus. 42 buildings on campus. Approved or accredited by Association of Colorado Independent Schools, The Association of Boarding Schools, and Colorado Department of Education. Member of National Association of Independent Schools and Secondary School Admission Test Board. Endowment: $34 million. Total enrollment: 23,624. Upper school average class size: 12. Upper school faculty-student ratio: 1:5. Upper School students typically attend 5 days per week. The average school day consists of 9 hours and 15 minutes.

Upper School Student Profile Grade 9: 46 students (24 boys, 22 girls); Grade 10: 69 students (36 boys, 33 girls); Grade 11: 67 students (29 boys, 38 girls); Grade 12: 54 students (22 boys, 32 girls). 69% of students are boarding students. 52% are state residents. 26 states are represented in upper school student body. 24% are international students. International students from China, Germany, Japan, Mexico, Republic of Korea, and Taiwan; 10 other countries represented in student body.

Faculty School total: 43. In upper school: 20 men, 12 women; 25 have advanced degrees; 23 reside on campus.

Subjects Offered 3-dimensional art, 3-dimensional design, ACT preparation, advanced chemistry, Advanced Placement courses, advanced studio art-AP, algebra, American history, American history-AP, American literature, band, biology, biology-AP, British literature, calculus, calculus-AP, ceramics, chamber groups, chemistry, chemistry-AP, college counseling, Colorado ecology, composition, computer applications, computer multimedia, computer programming, creative writing, drama, English, English literature and composition-AP, environmental science-AP, ESL, fiction, film and literature, French, French language-AP, geology, geometry, honors algebra, honors English, honors geometry, instrumental music, jewelry making, literature, Mandarin, music theory, musical productions, outdoor education, photography, physics, physics-AP, pre-calculus, probability and statistics, robotics, senior project, senior seminar, Shakespeare, Shakespearean histories, short story, Spanish, Spanish language-AP, statistics-AP, strings, student government, student publications, studio art, studio art-AP, U.S. government and politics-AP, visual and performing arts, vocal ensemble, wilderness education, wind ensemble, world history, world history-AP, world literature, writing.

Graduation Requirements Arts and fine arts (art, music, dance, drama), computer science, English, foreign language, mathematics, physical education (includes health), science, social studies (includes history), senior seminar. Community service is required.

Special Academic Programs 20 Advanced Placement exams for which test preparation is offered; honors section; independent study; academic accommodation for the gifted, the musically talented, and the artistically talented; ESL (17 students enrolled).

College Admission Counseling 62 students graduated in 2012; 61 went to college, including American University; Colorado State University; Santa Clara University; The University of Alabama; University of Colorado Boulder; University of Denver. Other: 1 had other specific plans. Median SAT critical reading: 560, median SAT math: 635, median SAT writing: 590, median composite ACT: 25.

Student Life Upper grades have specified standards of dress, student council, honor system. Discipline rests equally with students and faculty.

Summer Programs Enrichment, ESL, sports, computer instruction programs offered; session focuses on outdoor education, natural sciences, leadership, sports camps, international student enrichment; held both on and off campus; held at FVS' 40-acre Mountain Campus and surrounding Mount Princeton region; accepts boys and girls; open to students from other schools. 100 students usually enrolled. 2013 schedule: June 5 to August 15. Application deadline: none.

Tuition and Aid Day student tuition: $25,100; 7-day tuition and room/board: $46,300. Tuition installment plan (Key Tuition Payment Plan, monthly payment plans, individually arranged payment plans). Merit scholarship grants, need-based scholarship grants available. In 2012–13, 41% of upper-school students received aid. Total amount of financial aid awarded in 2012–13: $2,180,000.

Admissions Traditional secondary-level entrance grade is 9. For fall 2012, 225 students applied for upper-level admission, 148 were accepted, 85 enrolled. SSAT or TOEFL required. Deadline for receipt of application materials: February 1. Application fee required: $50. Interview required.

Athletics Interscholastic: basketball (boys, girls), cross-country running (b,g), diving (g), hockey (b), ice hockey (b), lacrosse (b,g), soccer (b,g), swimming and diving (g), tennis (b,g), track and field (b,g), volleyball (b,g); coed interscholastic: climbing, equestrian sports, golf, horseback riding, independent competitive sports, mountain biking, rock climbing, rodeo, skiing (downhill), snowboarding, telemark skiing, wall climbing; coed intramural: aerobics/dance, alpine skiing, backpacking, climbing, dance, equestrian sports, fitness, Frisbee, hiking/backpacking, horseback riding, modern dance, mountain biking, mountaineering, outdoor activities, outdoor adventure, outdoor education, outdoor recreation, outdoor skills, physical fitness, rock climbing, skiing (downhill), snowboarding, strength & conditioning, table tennis, telemark skiing, tennis, ultimate Frisbee, wall climbing, weight training, wilderness. 2 coaches, 1 athletic trainer.

Computers Computers are regularly used in all academic, college planning, multimedia, news writing, newspaper, photography, publications, Web site design, yearbook classes. Computer network features include on-campus library services, online commercial services, Internet access, wireless campus network, Internet filtering or blocking technology. Campus intranet, student e-mail accounts, and computer access in designated common areas are available to students. Students grades are available online. The school has a published electronic and media policy.

Contact Mr. Randy Roach, Director of Admission. 719-390-7035 Ext. 251. Fax: 719-390-7762. E-mail: admission@fvs.edu. Web site: www.fvs.edu

FOWLERS ACADEMY

PO Box 921
Guaynabo, Puerto Rico 00970-0921

Head of School: Mrs. Nancy Santana

General Information Coeducational day general academic, arts, religious studies, music, and graphic art design school, affiliated with Christian faith; primarily serves underachievers. Grades 7–12. Founded: 1986. Setting: suburban. 2-acre campus. 2 buildings on campus. Approved or accredited by Comisión Acreditadora de Instituciones Educativas, The College Board, and Puerto Rico Department of Education. Languages of instruction: English and Spanish. Total enrollment: 68. Upper school average class size: 15. Upper school faculty-student ratio: 1:15. Upper School students typically attend 5 days per week. The average school day consists of 6 hours and 50 minutes.

Upper School Student Profile Grade 9: 9 students (5 boys, 4 girls); Grade 10: 14 students (10 boys, 4 girls); Grade 11: 13 students (9 boys, 4 girls); Grade 12: 16 students (14 boys, 2 girls).

Faculty School total: 7. In upper school: 5 men, 2 women; 3 have advanced degrees.

Subjects Offered Algebra, American history, ancient world history, art, athletics, basketball, Bible, character education, chemistry, Christian education, Christian ethics, Christian scripture, computer applications, computer art, computer education, computer graphics, computer literacy, computer skills, drama, drawing, earth science, electives, English, film appreciation, geometry, history, instrumental music, keyboarding, leadership, leadership and service, martial arts, mathematics, music, physical education, physics, pre-algebra, pre-college orientation, Puerto Rican history, science, sex education, Spanish, Spanish literature, theater, U.S. history, world history.

Graduation Requirements Algebra, ancient world history, biology, chemistry, Christian education, electives, English, geometry, physical education (includes health), physical science, physics, pre-college orientation, Puerto Rican history, Spanish, U.S. history, world history.

Special Academic Programs Accelerated programs; special instructional classes for students with ADD and LD.

College Admission Counseling 14 students graduated in 2011; 12 went to college, including University of Puerto Rico, Río Piedras; University of Puerto Rico at Carolina. Other: 2 had other specific plans.

Student Life Upper grades have uniform requirement, student council, honor system. Discipline rests primarily with faculty.

Tuition and Aid Day student tuition: $5900. Tuition installment plan (monthly payment plans, individually arranged payment plans). Tuition reduction for siblings, need-based scholarship grants available. In 2011–12, 5% of upper-school students received aid. Total amount of financial aid awarded in 2011–12: $5000.

Admissions Traditional secondary-level entrance grade is 9. For fall 2011, 21 students applied for upper-level admission, 19 were accepted, 19 enrolled. Psychoeducational evaluation required. Deadline for receipt of application materials: none. No application fee required. On-campus interview required.

Athletics Interscholastic: basketball (boys); intramural: basketball (b); coed interscholastic: archery, physical fitness; coed intramural: archery, fitness, physical fitness, soccer, table tennis, volleyball. 1 PE instructor.

Computers Computers are regularly used in English, graphic arts, graphic design, keyboarding, mathematics, religious studies, science, Spanish classes. Computer resources include Internet access, Internet filtering or blocking technology. Computer access in designated common areas is available to students.

Contact Mr. Lynette Montes, Registrar. 787-787-1350. Fax: 787-789-0055. E-mail: fowlersacademy@gmail.com. Web site:

FOXCROFT SCHOOL

22407 Foxhound Lane
P.O. Box 5555
Middleburg, Virginia 20118

Head of School: Mary Louise Leipheimer

General Information Girls' boarding and day college-preparatory school. Grades 9–12. Founded: 1914. Setting: rural. Nearest major city is Washington, DC. Students are housed in single-sex dormitories. 500-acre campus. 32 buildings on campus. Approved or accredited by The Association of Boarding Schools, Virginia Association of Independent Schools, and Virginia Department of Education. Member of National Association of Independent Schools and Secondary School Admission Test Board. Endowment: $22.8 million. Total enrollment: 160. Upper school average class size: 12. Upper school faculty-student ratio: 1:7. There are 160 required school days per year for Upper School students. Upper School students typically attend 5 days per week. The average school day consists of 7 hours and 15 minutes.

Upper School Student Profile Grade 9: 41 students (41 girls); Grade 10: 36 students (36 girls); Grade 11: 45 students (45 girls); Grade 12: 38 students (38 girls). 67% of students are boarding students. 49% are state residents. 21 states are represented in upper school student body. 18% are international students. International students from China, India, Mexico, Nigeria, Republic of Korea, and Spain; 1 other country represented in student body.

Faculty School total: 22. In upper school: 5 men, 17 women; 17 have advanced degrees; 16 reside on campus.

Subjects Offered 3-dimensional art, acting, advanced chemistry, algebra, American literature, anatomy and physiology, ancient world history, architecture, art, art history, astronomy, biology, British literature, calculus, calculus-AP, cell biology, ceramics, chemistry, chemistry-AP, choir, chorus, college counseling, community service, comparative religion, computer graphics, computer science, conceptual physics, constitutional law, creative dance, creative drama, creative writing, current events, dance, debate, digital photography, discrete mathematics, drama, drawing and design, economics, economics-AP, electives, English, English composition, English literature, English literature-AP, environmental science, European civilization, European history, European literature, expository writing, fine arts, fitness, French, French language-AP, general science, geology, geometry, grammar, health education, history, human anatomy, independent study, leadership, library, macroeconomics-AP, mathematics, microbiology, music, music theory, music theory-AP, painting, performing arts, photography, physical education, physics, piano, poetry, pottery, pre-calculus, probability and statistics, production, public speaking, SAT preparation, sculpture, senior project, social studies, Spanish, Spanish language-AP, Spanish literature, Spanish literature-AP, studio art, studio art-AP, technology, The 20th Century, trigonometry, U.S. history, U.S. history-AP, vocal ensemble, world cultures, world literature, writing, yearbook, yoga.

Graduation Requirements Arts and fine arts (art, music, dance, drama), English, foreign language, history, mathematics, physical education (includes health), science, senior thesis if student is not enrolled in AP English.

Special Academic Programs 11 Advanced Placement exams for which test preparation is offered; independent study; term-away projects; study abroad; academic accommodation for the gifted, the musically talented, and the artistically talented.

College Admission Counseling 37 students graduated in 2012; all went to college, including College of Charleston; Columbia University; Connecticut College; Gettysburg College; Lynchburg College; Middlebury College.

Student Life Upper grades have specified standards of dress, student council, honor system. Discipline rests equally with students and faculty.

Summer Programs Sports, art/fine arts programs offered; session focuses on traditional summer camp activities; held on campus; accepts boys and girls. 100 students usually enrolled. 2013 schedule: July 9 to August 10.

Tuition and Aid Day student tuition: $38,500; 7-day tuition and room/board: $47,500. Tuition installment plan (Insured Tuition Payment Plan, Tuition Management Systems Plan (Monthly Payment Plan)). Merit scholarship grants, need-based scholarship grants, merit-based scholarship grants are offered to prospective 9th grade students available. In 2012–13, 30% of upper-school students received aid; total upper-school merit-scholarship money awarded: $31,000. Total amount of financial aid awarded in 2012–13: $1,200,000.

Admissions Traditional secondary-level entrance grade is 9. For fall 2012, 171 students applied for upper-level admission, 111 were accepted, 56 enrolled. SSAT or TOEFL required. Deadline for receipt of application materials: February 1. Application fee required: $50. Interview required.

Athletics Interscholastic: basketball, cross-country running, dressage, equestrian sports, field hockey, horseback riding, lacrosse, running, soccer, softball, tennis, volleyball; intramural: aerobics, aerobics/dance, basketball, climbing, combined training, dance, dance team, dressage, equestrian sports, field hockey, fitness, horseback riding, indoor soccer, indoor track, lacrosse, modern dance, outdoor activities, physical fitness, physical training, rock climbing, ropes courses, running, squash, strength & conditioning, swimming and diving, tennis, volleyball, walking, weight lifting, weight training, yoga. 3 coaches, 1 athletic trainer.

Computers Computers are regularly used in all classes. Computer resources include on-campus library services, online commercial services, Internet access, wireless campus network, Internet filtering or blocking technology. Campus intranet, student e-mail accounts, and computer access in designated common areas are available to students. The school has a published electronic and media policy.

Contact Gina B. Finn, Director of Admission and Financial Aid. 540-687-4340. Fax: 540-687-3627. E-mail: gina.finn@foxcroft.org. Web site: www.foxcroft.org

FOX VALLEY LUTHERAN HIGH SCHOOL

5300 North Meade Street
Appleton, Wisconsin 54913-8383

Head of School: Mr. Paul Hartwig

General Information Coeducational day college-preparatory, general academic, arts, business, vocational, religious studies, and technology school, affiliated with Wisconsin Evangelical Lutheran Synod. Grades 9–12. Founded: 1953. Setting: suburban. 63-acre campus. 1 building on campus. Approved or accredited by National Council for Private School Accreditation and Wisconsin Department of Education. Endowment: $4.1 million. Total enrollment: 542. Upper school average class size: 22. Upper school faculty-student ratio: 1:14. There are 180 required school days per year for Upper School students. Upper School students typically attend 5 days per week. The average school day consists of 6 hours and 30 minutes.

Upper School Student Profile Grade 9: 121 students (62 boys, 59 girls); Grade 10: 144 students (74 boys, 70 girls); Grade 11: 135 students (59 boys, 76 girls); Grade 12: 142 students (74 boys, 68 girls). 85% of students are Wisconsin Evangelical Lutheran Synod.

Faculty School total: 42. In upper school: 28 men, 14 women; 18 have advanced degrees.

Subjects Offered Accounting, advanced chemistry, advanced computer applications, advanced math, algebra, American government, American history, American literature, art, athletics, band, basic language skills, Basic programming, Bible, Bible studies, biology, British literature, British literature (honors), British literature-AP, business, business law, calculus, calculus-AP, choir, Christian doctrine, church history, communication skills, comparative religion, composition, computer applications, computer programming, computer skills, computer-aided design, concert band, concert choir, construction, critical writing, digital applications, digital photography, earth science, economics, economics-AP, engineering, English, English composition, foods, general science, geometry, German, government, graphic arts, health and wellness, honors English, keyboarding, language and composition, Latin, Life of Christ, modern Western civilization, modern world history, personal fitness, physical fitness, physics, piano, psychology, reading/study skills, religion, remedial/makeup course work, sewing, Spanish, statistics, symphonic band, woodworking, world geography, world history.

Graduation Requirements 1 1/2 elective credits, arts and fine arts (art, music, dance, drama), English, mathematics, physical education (includes health), religion (includes Bible studies and theology), science.

Special Academic Programs 1 Advanced Placement exam for which test preparation is offered; honors section; accelerated programs; study at local college for college credit; academic accommodation for the gifted; remedial reading and/or remedial writing; remedial math.

College Admission Counseling 154 students graduated in 2012; 144 went to college, including Martin Luther College; University of Wisconsin–Fox Valley; University of Wisconsin–Madison; University of Wisconsin–Oshkosh. Other: 4 went to work, 2 entered military service, 1 had other specific plans. Median composite ACT: 24.

Student Life Upper grades have specified standards of dress, student council, honor system. Discipline rests primarily with faculty. Attendance at religious services is required.

Summer Programs Remediation, advancement programs offered; session focuses on alleviate school year schedule conflicts; held on campus; accepts boys and girls; not open to students from other schools. 30 students usually enrolled. 2013 schedule: June 1 to August 7. Application deadline: April 30.

Tuition and Aid Day student tuition: $5100–$7700. Tuition installment plan (FACTS Tuition Payment Plan). Tuition reduction for siblings, need-based scholarship grants available. In 2012–13, 25% of upper-school students received aid. Total amount of financial aid awarded in 2012–13: $325,000.

Admissions Traditional secondary-level entrance grade is 9. ACT-Explore or Explore required. Deadline for receipt of application materials: none. Application fee required: $25. Interview required.

Athletics Interscholastic: baseball (boys), basketball (b,g), cheering (g), cross-country running (b,g), dance team (g), football (b), golf (b,g), hockey (b,g), ice hockey (b,g), soccer (b,g), softball (g), track and field (b,g), volleyball (g), wrestling (b). 2 PE instructors, 1 athletic trainer.

Computers Computers are regularly used in business, current events, drafting, economics, engineering, English, foreign language, graphic arts, keyboarding, science classes. Computer network features include on-campus library services, Internet access, Internet filtering or blocking technology. Campus intranet and student e-mail accounts are available to students. Students grades are available online. The school has a published electronic and media policy.

Contact Mrs. Heather Knoll, Guidance Assistant. 920-739-4441. Fax: 920-739-4418. E-mail: hknoll@fvlhs.org. Web site: www.fvlhs.org

FREDERICA ACADEMY

200 Murray Way
St. Simons Island, Georgia 31522

Head of School: Mr. Greg F. Griffeth

General Information Coeducational day college-preparatory, arts, and technology school. Grades PK–12. Founded: 1970. Setting: small town. Nearest major city is Jacksonville, FL. 40-acre campus. 7 buildings on campus. Approved or accredited by Georgia Independent School Association, Southern Association of Colleges and Schools, and Georgia Department of Education. Member of National Association of Independent Schools. Endowment: $2 million. Total enrollment: 412. Upper school average class size: 18. Upper school faculty-student ratio: 1:9. There are 180 required school days per year for Upper School students. Upper School students typically attend 5 days per week. The average school day consists of 8 hours and 5 minutes.

Upper School Student Profile Grade 9: 36 students (20 boys, 16 girls); Grade 10: 40 students (20 boys, 20 girls); Grade 11: 41 students (23 boys, 18 girls); Grade 12: 29 students (14 boys, 15 girls).

Faculty School total: 50. In upper school: 8 men, 9 women; 10 have advanced degrees.

Subjects Offered Algebra, American history, American literature, anatomy, ancient history, art, biology, biology-AP, calculus-AP, chemistry, choral music, computer applications, drama, economics, English, English literature, environmental science, geometry, government/civics, grammar, keyboarding, literature-AP, photography, physical education, physical science, physics, pre-calculus, psychology, public speaking, science, Spanish, U.S. history-AP, world history, world literature, writing, yearbook.

Graduation Requirements Algebra, American government, American history, arts and fine arts (art, music, dance, drama), biology, chemistry, computer applications, economics, English literature, foreign language, geometry, physical education (includes health), world history.

Special Academic Programs Advanced Placement exam preparation; honors section.

College Admission Counseling 23 students graduated in 2012; all went to college, including Georgia Institute of Technology; Georgia Southern University; University of Georgia. Mean SAT critical reading: 591, mean SAT math: 583, mean SAT writing: 584, mean combined SAT: 1758.

Student Life Upper grades have specified standards of dress, student council, honor system. Discipline rests primarily with faculty.

Summer Programs Enrichment, sports, art/fine arts, computer instruction programs offered; session focuses on enrichment; held on campus; accepts boys and girls; open to students from other schools. 200 students usually enrolled. 2013 schedule: June 15 to August 1. Application deadline: May 2.

Tuition and Aid Day student tuition: $15,900. Tuition installment plan (The Tuition Plan, Insured Tuition Payment Plan). Need-based scholarship grants, local bank financing available. In 2012–13, 30% of upper-school students received aid. Total amount of financial aid awarded in 2012–13: $500,000.

Admissions Traditional secondary-level entrance grade is 9. Admissions testing, any standardized test, Cognitive Abilities Test, OLSAT/Stanford and writing sample required. Deadline for receipt of application materials: none. Application fee required: $75. On-campus interview required.

Athletics Interscholastic: aquatics (boys, girls), baseball (b), basketball (b,g), cheering (g), cross-country running (b,g), equestrian sports (b,g), fitness (b,g), football (b), golf (b,g), lacrosse (b), outdoor education (b,g), physical fitness (b,g), sailing (b,g), soccer (b,g), tennis (b,g), track and field (b,g), volleyball (g), weight training (b,g); coed interscholastic: cross-country running, fitness, golf, sailing, swimming and diving. 2 PE instructors, 5 coaches, 1 athletic trainer.

Computers Computers are regularly used in all academic, English, library skills, photography, yearbook classes. Computer network features include on-campus library services, online commercial services, Internet access, wireless campus network, Internet filtering or blocking technology. Campus intranet and student e-mail accounts are available to students. Students grades are available online. The school has a published electronic and media policy.

Contact Mrs. Julie J. Ackerman, Director of Admission. 912-638-9981 Ext. 106. Fax: 912-638-1442. E-mail: julieackerman@fredericaacademy.org. Web site: www.fredericaacademy.org

FREEMAN ACADEMY

748 South Main Street
PO Box 1000
Freeman, South Dakota 57029

Head of School: Ms. Pam Tieszen

General Information Coeducational boarding and day college-preparatory, arts, and religious studies school, affiliated with Mennonite Church. Boarding grades 9–12, day grades 5–12. Founded: 1900. Setting: rural. Nearest major city is Sioux Falls. Students are housed in coed dormitories and host family homes. 80-acre campus. 6 buildings on campus. Approved or accredited by Mennonite Schools Council, North Central Association of Colleges and Schools, and South Dakota Department of Education. Endowment: $450,000. Total enrollment: 79. Upper school average class size: 1. Upper school faculty-student ratio: 1:5. There are 180 required school days per year for Upper School students. Upper School students typically attend 5 days per week. The average school day consists of 8 hours.

Upper School Student Profile Grade 9: 8 students (4 boys, 4 girls); Grade 10: 11 students (5 boys, 6 girls); Grade 11: 12 students (6 boys, 6 girls); Grade 12: 15 students (8 boys, 7 girls). 17% of students are boarding students. 83% are state residents. 2 states are represented in upper school student body. 19% are international students. International students from China, Gambia, Paraguay, Republic of Korea, and Thailand. 55% of students are Mennonite.

Faculty School total: 10. In upper school: 4 men, 6 women; 3 have advanced degrees.

Subjects Offered Computer science, English, fine arts, humanities, mathematics, music, religion, science, social sciences.

Graduation Requirements Arts and fine arts (art, music, dance, drama), computer science, English, foreign language, mathematics, religion (includes Bible studies and theology), science, social studies (includes history), humanities.

Special Academic Programs Independent study; academic accommodation for the musically talented and the artistically talented.

College Admission Counseling 9 students graduated in 2012; 8 went to college, including Bethel College; Bluffton University; Goshen College; Hesston College; University of Sioux Falls. Other: 1 entered military service. Median composite ACT: 23. 14% scored over 26 on composite ACT.

Student Life Upper grades have specified standards of dress, honor system. Discipline rests primarily with faculty. Attendance at religious services is required.

Tuition and Aid Day student tuition: $6135; 7-day tuition and room/board: $19,550. Tuition installment plan (FACTS Tuition Payment Plan, monthly payment plans, individually arranged payment plans, semester payment plan). Tuition reduction for siblings, merit scholarship grants, need-based scholarship grants available. In 2012–13, 28% of upper-school students received aid; total upper-school merit-scholarship money awarded: $500. Total amount of financial aid awarded in 2012–13: $38,000.

Admissions Traditional secondary-level entrance grade is 9. For fall 2012, 10 students applied for upper-level admission, 8 were accepted, 8 enrolled. Secondary Level English Proficiency required. Deadline for receipt of application materials: none. No application fee required. Interview recommended.

Athletics Interscholastic: basketball (boys, girls), cheering (g), cross-country running (b,g), golf (b,g), soccer (b,g), track and field (b,g), volleyball (g); coed interscholastic: soccer. 4 coaches.

Computers Computers are regularly used in English, keyboarding, mathematics, religion, science, social studies, speech, yearbook classes. Computer network features include on-campus library services, Internet access, wireless campus network, Internet filtering or blocking technology. Student e-mail accounts and computer access in designated common areas are available to students. Students grades are available online. The school has a published electronic and media policy.

Contact Ms. Bonnie Young, Enrollment Director. 605-925-4237 Ext. 225. Fax: 605-925-4271. E-mail: byoung@freemanacademy.org. Web site: www.freemanacademy.org

FRENCH-AMERICAN SCHOOL OF NEW YORK

525 Fenimore Road
Mamaroneck, New York 10543

Head of School: Mr. Jo?Peinado

General Information Coeducational day college-preparatory and bilingual studies school. Grades N–12. Founded: 1980. Setting: suburban. Nearest major city is White Plains. 1 building on campus. Approved or accredited by Middle States Association of Colleges and Schools, New York State Association of Independent Schools, and New York Department of Education. Member of National Association of Independent Schools. Languages of instruction: English and French. Total enrollment: 848. Upper school average class size: 17. Upper school faculty-student ratio: 1:7. There are 168 required school days per year for Upper School students. Upper School students typically attend 5 days per week. The average school day consists of 7 hours and 45 minutes.

Upper School Student Profile Grade 9: 37 students (21 boys, 16 girls); Grade 10: 53 students (21 boys, 32 girls); Grade 11: 52 students (22 boys, 30 girls); Grade 12: 44 students (16 boys, 28 girls).

Faculty School total: 118. In upper school: 20 men, 40 women; 33 have advanced degrees.

Subjects Offered Algebra, American history, American literature, art, biology, choir, civics, computer applications, computer multimedia, current events, earth science, ecology, economics, English, ESL, European history, expository writing, French, French language-AP, French literature-AP, French studies, geometry, German, government, health, Latin, mathematics, multimedia, music, newspaper, philosophy, physical education, physics, physics-AP, public speaking, science, social studies, Spanish, Spanish language-AP, world history, world literature, writing, yearbook.

Graduation Requirements 20th century history, algebra, American history, biology, calculus, chemistry, civics, computer studies, current events, English, European history, foreign language, French, geography, geology, geometry, mathematics, music, philosophy, physical education (includes health), physics, pre-algebra, pre-calculus, research seminar, social studies (includes history). Community service is required.

Special Academic Programs Advanced Placement exam preparation; honors section; ESL (35 students enrolled).

College Admission Counseling 36 students graduated in 2012; all went to college, including Boston University; McGill University; New York University. Mean SAT critical reading: 624, mean SAT math: 654, mean SAT writing: 630.

Student Life Upper grades have specified standards of dress, student council. Discipline rests primarily with faculty.

Tuition and Aid Day student tuition: $22,800–$26,300. Tuition installment plan (Academic Management Services Plan). Need-based scholarship grants available. In 2012–13, 5% of upper-school students received aid. Total amount of financial aid awarded in 2012–13: $138,499.

Admissions Traditional secondary-level entrance grade is 9. For fall 2012, 324 students applied for upper-level admission, 207 were accepted, 145 enrolled. English, French, and math proficiency required. Deadline for receipt of application materials: none. Application fee required: $150. Interview recommended.

Athletics Interscholastic: baseball (boys), basketball (b,g), cross-country running (b,g), rugby (b,g), soccer (b,g), softball (g), tennis (b,g); coed intramural: fencing. 3 PE instructors, 3 coaches.

Computers Computers are regularly used in art, English, foreign language, French, history, mathematics, music, publications, science classes. Computer network features include on-campus library services, Internet access, Internet filtering or blocking technology, laptop use (in certain classes). Student e-mail accounts are available to students. The school has a published electronic and media policy.

Contact Mr. Antoine Agopian, Director of Admissions. 914-250-0400. Fax: 914-940-2214. E-mail: aagopian@fasny.org. Web site: www.fasny.org

FRESNO CHRISTIAN SCHOOLS

7280 North Cedar Avenue
Fresno, California 93720

Head of School: Mrs. Debbie Siebert

General Information Coeducational day college-preparatory, arts, religious studies, and technology school, affiliated with Protestant-Evangelical faith. Grades K–12. Founded: 1977. Setting: suburban. 27-acre campus. 4 buildings on campus. Approved or accredited by Association of Christian Schools International, Western Association of Schools and Colleges, and California Department of Education. Endowment: $161,867. Total enrollment: 512. Upper school average class size: 28. Upper school faculty-student ratio: 1:12. There are 176 required school days per year for Upper School students. Upper School students typically attend 5 days per week. The average school day consists of 5 hours and 50 minutes.

Upper School Student Profile Grade 9: 53 students (25 boys, 28 girls); Grade 10: 45 students (19 boys, 26 girls); Grade 11: 48 students (24 boys, 24 girls); Grade 12: 40 students (16 boys, 24 girls). 90% of students are Protestant-Evangelical faith.

Faculty School total: 26. In upper school: 8 men, 8 women; 5 have advanced degrees.

Subjects Offered Advanced Placement courses, algebra, alternative physical education, American government, American history, American history-AP, art, athletics, band, baseball, basketball, Bible, Bible studies, biology, British literature, calculus-AP, cheerleading, chemistry, Chinese, choir, choral music, Christian education, civics, composition-AP, computer applications, computer graphics, concert band, concert choir, drama, drama performance, economics, economics and history, English, English language and composition-AP, English literature and composition-AP, English-AP, ensembles, geometry, golf, home economics, honors algebra, honors English, honors geometry, humanities, jazz band, journalism, leadership, marching band, mathematics, mathematics-AP, physical education, physical science, physics, pre-calculus, softball, Spanish, sports, statistics-AP, student government, tennis, track and field, trigonometry, U.S. history, video film production, vocal music, volleyball, woodworking, work experience, world history, yearbook.

Graduation Requirements Arts and fine arts (art, music, dance, drama), electives, English, mathematics, physical education (includes health), religion (includes Bible studies and theology), science, social studies (includes history), 4 years of Biblical Studies classes.

Special Academic Programs 5 Advanced Placement exams for which test preparation is offered; honors section; independent study; study at local college for college credit; remedial reading and/or remedial writing; remedial math; special instructional classes for students with learning disabilities.

College Admission Counseling 54 students graduated in 2012; 49 went to college, including Arizona State University; Biola University; California Polytechnic State University, San Luis Obispo; California State University, Fresno; Fresno City College; Whitworth University. Other: 1 entered military service, 4 had other specific plans. Mean SAT critical reading: 553, mean SAT math: 543, mean SAT writing: 533, mean combined SAT: 1538.

Student Life Upper grades have specified standards of dress, student council, honor system. Discipline rests primarily with faculty. Attendance at religious services is required.

Tuition and Aid Day student tuition: $8275. Tuition installment plan (monthly payment plans, individually arranged payment plans). Tuition reduction for siblings, merit scholarship grants, need-based scholarship grants available. In 2012–13, 24% of upper-school students received aid; total upper-school merit-scholarship money awarded: $2000. Total amount of financial aid awarded in 2012–13: $148,074.

Admissions Stanford Achievement Test required. Deadline for receipt of application materials: none. Application fee required: $100. Interview required.

Athletics Interscholastic: baseball (boys), basketball (b,g), cheering (g), cross-country running (b,g), drill team (g), football (b), soccer (b,g), softball (g), strength & conditioning (b,g), tennis (b,g), track and field (b,g), volleyball (g), weight training (b,g); coed interscholastic: golf, physical training; coed intramural: badminton, basketball, outdoor recreation, volleyball. 1 PE instructor, 16 coaches.

Computers Computers are regularly used in media production, publications, yearbook classes. Computer network features include on-campus library services, online commercial services, Internet access, wireless campus network, Internet filtering or blocking technology. Computer access in designated common areas is available to students. Students grades are available online. The school has a published electronic and media policy.

Contact Mrs. Kerry Roberts, Registrar. 559-299-1695 Ext. 102. Fax: 559-299-1051. E-mail: kroberts@fresnochristian.com. Web site: www.fresnochristian.com

FRIENDS ACADEMY

270 Duck Pond Road
Locust Valley, New York 11560

Head of School: William Morris

General Information Coeducational day college-preparatory school, affiliated with Society of Friends. Grades N–12. Founded: 1876. Setting: suburban. Nearest major city is New York. 65-acre campus. 8 buildings on campus. Approved or accredited by New York State Association of Independent Schools and New York Department of Education. Member of National Association of Independent Schools and

Secondary School Admission Test Board. Endowment: $30 million. Total enrollment: 775. Upper school average class size: 15. Upper school faculty-student ratio: 1:8. There are 165 required school days per year for Upper School students. Upper School students typically attend 5 days per week. The average school day consists of 7 hours.

Upper School Student Profile Grade 9: 93 students (42 boys, 51 girls); Grade 10: 96 students (38 boys, 58 girls); Grade 11: 85 students (45 boys, 40 girls); Grade 12: 97 students (42 boys, 55 girls). 1% of students are members of Society of Friends.

Faculty School total: 98. In upper school: 21 men, 27 women; 40 have advanced degrees.

Subjects Offered Advanced Placement courses, African studies, algebra, American history, American literature, art, art history, Bible studies, biology, calculus, ceramics, chemistry, community service, computer literacy, computer programming, computer science, creative writing, drama, driver education, English, English literature, environmental science, ethics, European history, expository writing, fine arts, French, geography, geometry, grammar, Greek, health, history, Italian, Latin, logic, mathematics, mechanical drawing, music, outdoor education, photography, physical education, physics, psychology, religion, science, social sciences, social studies, Spanish, speech, theater, trigonometry, Western civilization, world literature, writing.

Graduation Requirements Arts and fine arts (art, music, dance, drama), computer literacy, English, foreign language, mathematics, outdoor education, physical education (includes health), religion (includes Bible studies and theology), science, social sciences, social studies (includes history), speech, participation in on-campus work crew program, independent service program. Community service is required.

Special Academic Programs 18 Advanced Placement exams for which test preparation is offered; honors section; independent study; remedial reading and/or remedial writing; remedial math.

College Admission Counseling 101 students graduated in 2012; all went to college, including Dartmouth College; Duke University; New York University; Syracuse University; University of Pennsylvania; Villanova University.

Student Life Upper grades have specified standards of dress, student council. Discipline rests primarily with faculty. Attendance at religious services is required.

Summer Programs Art/fine arts programs offered; session focuses on arts and sports; held both on and off campus; held at off-campus for golf, sailing and riding. and Off campus field trips; accepts boys and girls; open to students from other schools. 250 students usually enrolled. 2013 schedule: June 24 to August 16.

Tuition and Aid Day student tuition: $28,300. Tuition installment plan (Insured Tuition Payment Plan, monthly payment plans). Need-based scholarship grants, Quaker grants, tuition remission for children of faculty and staff available. In 2012–13, 20% of upper-school students received aid. Total amount of financial aid awarded in 2012–13: $1,664,000.

Admissions Traditional secondary-level entrance grade is 9. For fall 2012, 142 students applied for upper-level admission, 61 were accepted, 43 enrolled. SSAT required. Deadline for receipt of application materials: January 15. Application fee required: $55. Interview required.

Athletics Interscholastic: baseball (boys), basketball (b,g), crew (b,g), cross-country running (b,g), field hockey (g), fitness (b,g), football (b), golf (b,g), ice hockey (b), indoor track & field (b,g), lacrosse (b,g), soccer (b,g), softball (g), tennis (b,g), track and field (b,g), winter (indoor) track (b,g); coed intramural: dance, volleyball. 7 PE instructors, 1 athletic trainer.

Computers Computers are regularly used in English, mathematics, science, technology classes. Computer network features include on-campus library services, online commercial services, Internet access, wireless campus network, Internet filtering or blocking technology, 6th and 7th graders use an iPad in school. Campus intranet, student e-mail accounts, and computer access in designated common areas are available to students. Students grades are available online. The school has a published electronic and media policy.

Contact Joanna Kim, Admissions Assistant. 516-393-4244. Fax: 516-465-1718. E-mail: joanna_kim@fa.org. Web site: www.fa.org

FRIENDS' CENTRAL SCHOOL

1101 City Avenue
Wynnewood, Pennsylvania 19096

Head of School: Craig N. Sellers

General Information Coeducational day college-preparatory school, affiliated with Society of Friends. Grades N–12. Founded: 1845. Setting: suburban. Nearest major city is Philadelphia. 23-acre campus. 7 buildings on campus. Approved or accredited by Pennsylvania Association of Independent Schools and Pennsylvania Department of Education. Member of National Association of Independent Schools and Secondary School Admission Test Board. Endowment: $22 million. Total enrollment: 832. Upper school average class size: 18. Upper school faculty-student ratio: 1:8. There are 170 required school days per year for Upper School students. Upper School students typically attend 5 days per week. The average school day consists of 6 hours and 40 minutes.

Upper School Student Profile Grade 9: 99 students (49 boys, 50 girls); Grade 10: 93 students (46 boys, 47 girls); Grade 11: 95 students (50 boys, 45 girls); Grade 12: 105 students (51 boys, 54 girls). 3% of students are members of Society of Friends.

Faculty School total: 130. In upper school: 26 men, 26 women; 38 have advanced degrees.

Subjects Offered Advanced biology, advanced chemistry, advanced math, algebra, American history, American literature, Bible, biology, calculus, ceramics, chemistry, chorus, computer applications, computer programming, conflict resolution, drama, English, French, geometry, instrumental music, Latin, life skills, media studies, modern European history, music history, music theory, philosophy, photography, physical education, physical science, physics, pre-calculus, psychology, sexuality, Spanish, studio art, study skills, Western literature, women in world history, woodworking, world history, writing workshop.

Graduation Requirements Arts and fine arts (art, music, dance, drama), English, foreign language, mathematics, science, service learning/internship, U.S. history, world cultures.

Special Academic Programs Honors section; independent study; term-away projects.

College Admission Counseling 97 students graduated in 2012; all went to college, including Bryn Mawr College; Drexel University; Syracuse University; The George Washington University; University of Pennsylvania; Yale University. Mean SAT critical reading: 669, mean SAT math: 649, mean SAT writing: 666.

Student Life Upper grades have specified standards of dress, student council. Discipline rests primarily with faculty. Attendance at religious services is required.

Summer Programs Remediation, advancement programs offered; held on campus; accepts boys and girls; open to students from other schools. 37 students usually enrolled. 2013 schedule: June 27 to August 5.

Tuition and Aid Day student tuition: $13,500–$27,950. Tuition installment plan (monthly payment plans, Higher Education Service, Inc). Need-based scholarship grants available. In 2012–13, 32% of upper-school students received aid. Total amount of financial aid awarded in 2012–13: $3,515,676.

Admissions Traditional secondary-level entrance grade is 9. For fall 2012, 134 students applied for upper-level admission, 65 were accepted, 31 enrolled. ISEE, SSAT or Wechsler Intelligence Scale for Children required. Deadline for receipt of application materials: January 15. Application fee required: $50. On-campus interview required.

Athletics Interscholastic: aquatics (boys, girls), baseball (b), basketball (b,g), cross-country running (b,g), field hockey (g), indoor track (b,g), lacrosse (b,g), soccer (b,g), softball (g), tennis (b,g), track and field (b,g), winter (indoor) track (b,g), wrestling (b,g); coed interscholastic: golf, squash, water polo; coed intramural: aerobics, aerobics/dance, aerobics/Nautilus, cheering, dance, fitness, flag football, life saving, table tennis. 8 PE instructors, 10 coaches, 1 athletic trainer.

Computers Computers are regularly used in college planning, foreign language, French, health, information technology, introduction to technology, Latin, mathematics, publishing, science, Spanish, technology, Web site design, yearbook classes. Computer network features include on-campus library services, online commercial services, Internet access, wireless campus network, Internet filtering or blocking technology, Intranet collaboration. Campus intranet and student e-mail accounts are available to students. The school has a published electronic and media policy.

Contact Cynthia Harris, Interim Director of Admission. 610-645-5032. Fax: 610-658-5644. E-mail: admission@friendscentral.org. Web site: www.friendscentral.org

FRONT RANGE CHRISTIAN HIGH SCHOOL

6637 West Ottawa Avenue
Littleton, Colorado 80128

Head of School: David Cooper

General Information Coeducational day college-preparatory, general academic, arts, business, vocational, religious studies, bilingual studies, technology, and science, math, language arts, media, Spanish school, affiliated with Christian faith. Grades PK–12. Founded: 1994. Setting: suburban. Nearest major city is Denver. 20-acre campus. 3 buildings on campus. Approved or accredited by Association of Christian Schools International, North Central Association of Colleges and Schools, and Colorado Department of Education. Total enrollment: 391. Upper school average class size: 25. Upper school faculty-student ratio: 1:7. There are 175 required school days per year for Upper School students. Upper School students typically attend 5 days per week. The average school day consists of 6 hours and 30 minutes.

Upper School Student Profile Grade 9: 40 students (20 boys, 20 girls); Grade 10: 33 students (17 boys, 16 girls); Grade 11: 41 students (19 boys, 22 girls); Grade 12: 46 students (26 boys, 20 girls). 100% of students are Christian faith.

Faculty School total: 41. In upper school: 12 men, 16 women; 11 have advanced degrees.

Subjects Offered ACT preparation, acting, advanced biology, advanced math, Advanced Placement courses, algebra, American history, American literature, anatomy and physiology, ancient world history, art, athletics, band, baseball, basketball, Bible, biology, British literature, calculus, career/college preparation, cheerleading, chemistry, choir, Christian doctrine, Christian scripture, composition, dance, drama, drama performance, earth science, electives, foreign language, forensics, geometry, golf, grammar, guitar, health education, home economics, junior and senior seminars, lab science, language arts, leadership and service, Life of Christ, music, musical productions, participation in sports, performing arts, photography, photojournalism, physical education, physical fitness, physics, pre-calculus, psychology, Spanish, speech, sports, statistics, trigonometry, video film production, vocal ensemble, volleyball, yearbook.

Graduation Requirements Algebra, career planning, college planning, history, language arts, science, Spanish, speech, participation in annual Spring Practicum, participation in monthly service projects (called Go! Wednesdays).

Special Academic Programs 4 Advanced Placement exams for which test preparation is offered; honors section; study at local college for college credit; academic accommodation for the gifted; remedial reading and/or remedial writing; remedial math; programs in English, mathematics, general development for dyslexic students; special instructional classes for deaf students, blind students.

College Admission Counseling 34 students graduated in 2012; 32 went to college, including Colorado Christian University; Colorado State University; Fort Lewis College. Other: 1 went to work, 1 had other specific plans. Median composite ACT: 23. 35% scored over 26 on composite ACT.

Student Life Upper grades have specified standards of dress, student council, honor system. Discipline rests primarily with faculty. Attendance at religious services is required.

Tuition and Aid Day student tuition: $8750. Tuition installment plan (FACTS Tuition Payment Plan, monthly payment plans). Need-based scholarship grants, employee discounts for parents with students who attend available. In 2012–13, 16% of upper-school students received aid. Total amount of financial aid awarded in 2012–13: $118,822.

Admissions Traditional secondary-level entrance grade is 9. For fall 2012, 28 students applied for upper-level admission, 26 were accepted, 24 enrolled. English proficiency, essay and Math Placement Exam required. Deadline for receipt of application materials: April 1. Application fee required: $50. Interview required.

Athletics Interscholastic: baseball (boys), basketball (b,g), cheering (g), football (b), golf (b), soccer (g), volleyball (g); intramural: basketball (b,g), volleyball (g); coed interscholastic: cross-country running, track and field; coed intramural: aerobics, climbing, dance, martial arts, mountain biking, physical fitness, rock climbing, snowboarding, weight training. 1 PE instructor, 28 coaches.

Computers Computers are regularly used in all academic, basic skills, computer applications, data processing, introduction to technology, media arts, multimedia, yearbook classes. Computer network features include Internet access, wireless campus network, Internet filtering or blocking technology, RenWeb Parents access, 1 to 1 iPad program, My Big Campus access. Student e-mail accounts and computer access in designated common areas are available to students. Students grades are available online. The school has a published electronic and media policy.

Contact Sara Ogdon, Admissions Coordinator. 303-531-4541. Fax: 720-922-3296. E-mail: admissions@frcs.org. Web site: www.frcs.org

THE FROSTIG SCHOOL

Pasadena, California

See Special Needs Schools section.

FRYEBURG ACADEMY

745 Main Street
Fryeburg, Maine 04037-1329

Head of School: Mr. Daniel G. Lee Jr.

General Information Coeducational boarding and day college-preparatory, general academic, arts, and technology school. Grades 9–PG. Founded: 1792. Setting: small town. Nearest major city is Portland. Students are housed in single-sex dormitories. 35-acre campus. 17 buildings on campus. Approved or accredited by Association of Independent Schools in New England, Independent Schools of Northern New England, New England Association of Schools and Colleges, The Association of Boarding Schools, The College Board, and Maine Department of Education. Member of National Association of Independent Schools and Secondary School Admission Test Board. Endowment: $23 million. Total enrollment: 681. Upper school average class size: 15. Upper school faculty-student ratio: 1:10. There are 170 required school days per year for Upper School students. Upper School students typically attend 5 days per week. The average school day consists of 6 hours and 30 minutes.

Upper School Student Profile Grade 9: 145 students (73 boys, 72 girls); Grade 10: 151 students (76 boys, 75 girls); Grade 11: 159 students (83 boys, 76 girls); Grade 12: 184 students (96 boys, 88 girls). 20% of students are boarding students. 83% are state residents. 9 states are represented in upper school student body. 14% are international students. International students from China, Democratic People's Republic of Korea, Germany, Spain, United States, and Viet Nam; 15 other countries represented in student body.

Faculty School total: 67. In upper school: 35 men, 32 women; 27 have advanced degrees; 25 reside on campus.

Subjects Offered Algebra, American literature, anatomy, art, art history, biology, botany, business, calculus, chemistry, computer math, computer programming, computer science, creative writing, drafting, drama, driver education, earth science, ecology, economics, English, English literature, ethics, European history, expository writing, fine arts, French, geography, geometry, government/civics, grammar, health, history, industrial arts, journalism, Latin, linear algebra, marine biology, mathematics, mechanical drawing, music, photography, physical education, physics, physiology, psychology, science, social studies, sociology, Spanish, speech, theater, trigonometry, typing, world history, world literature, writing.

Graduation Requirements Arts and fine arts (art, music, dance, drama), computer science, English, foreign language, mathematics, physical education (includes health), science, social studies (includes history). Community service is required.

Special Academic Programs 14 Advanced Placement exams for which test preparation is offered; honors section; independent study; study at local college for college credit; academic accommodation for the musically talented; remedial reading and/or remedial writing; remedial math; programs in English, mathematics, general development for dyslexic students; special instructional classes for students with learning disabilities, Attention Deficit Disorder, and dyslexia; ESL (45 students enrolled).

College Admission Counseling 191 students graduated in 2012; 153 went to college, including Boston University; Colby College; Massachusetts Institute of Technology; Northeastern University; University of Maine; University of New Hampshire. Other: 29 went to work, 3 entered military service, 1 entered a postgraduate year, 5 had other specific plans.

Student Life Upper grades have specified standards of dress, student council. Discipline rests primarily with faculty.

Tuition and Aid Day student tuition: $20,200; 5-day tuition and room/board: $32,700; 7-day tuition and room/board: $42,300. Tuition installment plan (monthly payment plans, individually arranged payment plans). Need-based scholarship grants available. In 2012–13, 42% of upper-school students received aid. Total amount of financial aid awarded in 2012–13: $1,800,000.

Admissions Traditional secondary-level entrance grade is 10. For fall 2012, 175 students applied for upper-level admission, 137 were accepted, 52 enrolled. Writing sample required. Deadline for receipt of application materials: February 1. Application fee required: $50. Interview required.

Athletics Interscholastic: baseball (boys), basketball (b,g), cross-country running (b,g), field hockey (g), football (b), golf (b), hockey (b,g), ice hockey (b), lacrosse (b,g), skiing (cross-country) (b,g), skiing (downhill) (b,g), soccer (b,g), softball (g), tennis (b,g), track and field (b,g), wrestling (b); intramural: ice hockey (g), strength & conditioning (b,g), table tennis (b,g); coed interscholastic: alpine skiing, cheering, mountain biking, nordic skiing; coed intramural: alpine skiing, archery, backpacking, badminton, ball hockey, basketball, bicycling, billiards, bowling, canoeing/kayaking, climbing, figure skating, fishing, fitness, fitness walking, flag football, floor hockey, fly fishing, freestyle skiing, Frisbee, golf, hiking/backpacking, ice skating, jogging, kayaking, mountain biking, mountaineering, paint ball, physical fitness, physical training, pistol, rock climbing, roller blading, skiing (downhill), snowboarding, snowshoeing, swimming and diving, table tennis, tai chi, telemark skiing, tennis, ultimate Frisbee, volleyball, walking, wall climbing, weight lifting, whiffle ball, winter walking. 2 PE instructors, 3 coaches, 1 athletic trainer.

Computers Computers are regularly used in all classes. Computer network features include on-campus library services, Internet access, wireless campus network. Computer access in designated common areas is available to students. The school has a published electronic and media policy.

Contact Stephanie S. Morin, Director of Enrollment Management and Marketing. 207-935-2013. Fax: 207-935-4292. E-mail: smorin@fryeburgacademy.org. Web site: www.fryeburgacademy.org

FUQUA SCHOOL

605 Fuqua Drive
PO Drawer 328
Farmville, Virginia 23901

Head of School: Ms. Ruth S. Murphy

General Information Coeducational day college-preparatory, arts, and business school. Grades PK–12. Founded: 1959. Setting: small town. Nearest major city is Richmond. 60-acre campus. 19 buildings on campus. Approved or accredited by Southern Association of Colleges and Schools and Virginia Department of Education. Member of Secondary School Admission Test Board. Endowment: $5.1 million. Total enrollment: 431. Upper school average class size: 16. Upper school faculty-student ratio: 1:16. There are 180 required school days per year for Upper School students. Upper School students typically attend 5 days per week. The average school day consists of 6 hours.

Upper School Student Profile Grade 9: 37 students (16 boys, 21 girls); Grade 10: 36 students (20 boys, 16 girls); Grade 11: 32 students (19 boys, 13 girls); Grade 12: 40 students (18 boys, 22 girls).

Faculty School total: 42. In upper school: 7 men, 12 women; 6 have advanced degrees.

Subjects Offered Agriculture, algebra, art, band, biology-AP, calculus-AP, chemistry, chemistry-AP, communications, composition, computer information systems, driver education, economics, English composition, English literature-AP, English-AP, environmental science, environmental studies, ethics, fitness, general business, geometry, government-AP, grammar, health, history-AP, industrial technology, personal finance, physics, pre-calculus, psychology, Spanish, theater, U.S. government, U.S. history-AP, United States government-AP, weight training, yearbook, zoology.

Graduation Requirements Arts and fine arts (art, music, dance, drama), communications, composition, computer information systems, driver education, English, fitness, foreign language, grammar, health education, mathematics, physical education (includes health), science, social studies (includes history). Community service is required.

Special Academic Programs Advanced Placement exam preparation; honors section; accelerated programs; independent study; study at local college for college credit.

College Admission Counseling 41 students graduated in 2011; all went to college, including James Madison University; Longwood University; Lynchburg College; University of Virginia; Virginia Polytechnic Institute and State University; Washington and Lee University. Median SAT critical reading: 570, median SAT math: 540, median SAT writing: 550, median composite ACT: 26. 42% scored over 600 on SAT critical reading, 41% scored over 600 on SAT math, 40% scored over 600 on SAT writing, 57% scored over 26 on composite ACT.

Student Life Upper grades have specified standards of dress, student council, honor system. Discipline rests primarily with faculty.

Tuition and Aid Day student tuition: $7325. Tuition installment plan (The Tuition Plan, Insured Tuition Payment Plan, monthly payment plans, individually arranged payment plans). Tuition reduction for siblings, merit scholarship grants, need-based scholarship grants available. In 2011–12, 44% of upper-school students received aid; total upper-school merit-scholarship money awarded: $7000. Total amount of financial aid awarded in 2011–12: $44,000.

Admissions Traditional secondary-level entrance grade is 9. For fall 2011, 9 students applied for upper-level admission, 9 were accepted, 9 enrolled. Placement test required. Deadline for receipt of application materials: none. Application fee required: $100. On-campus interview required.

Athletics Interscholastic: baseball (boys), basketball (b,g), cheering (g), football (b), softball (g), tennis (g), volleyball (g); intramural: lacrosse (b); coed interscholastic: cross-country running, golf, soccer, swimming and diving, track and field; coed intramural: basketball. 2 PE instructors, 38 coaches, 1 athletic trainer.

Computers Computer network features include on-campus library services, online commercial services, Internet access, wireless campus network, Internet filtering or blocking technology, video editing software, CD-ROM +RW and DVD +RW. Student e-mail accounts and computer access in designated common areas are available to students. The school has a published electronic and media policy.

Contact Mrs. Christy M. Murphy, Director of Admissions and Development. 434-392-4131 Ext. 273. Fax: 434-392-5062. E-mail: murphycm@fuquaschool.com. Web site: www.fuquaschool.com

GABRIEL RICHARD CATHOLIC HIGH SCHOOL

15325 Pennsylvania Road
Riverview, Michigan 48193

Head of School: Mr. Joseph J. Whalen

General Information Coeducational day college-preparatory school, affiliated with Roman Catholic Church. Grades 9–12. Founded: 1965. Setting: suburban. Nearest major city is Detroit. 23-acre campus. 1 building on campus. Approved or accredited by Michigan Association of Non-Public Schools, North Central Association of Colleges and Schools, and Michigan Department of Education. Total enrollment: 309. Upper school average class size: 17. Upper school faculty-student ratio: 1:17. There are 180 required school days per year for Upper School students. Upper School students typically attend 5 days per week. The average school day consists of 7 hours and 5 minutes.

Upper School Student Profile Grade 9: 76 students (44 boys, 32 girls); Grade 10: 63 students (32 boys, 31 girls); Grade 11: 84 students (42 boys, 42 girls); Grade 12: 86 students (30 boys, 56 girls); Postgraduate: 310 students (148 boys, 162 girls). 90% of students are Roman Catholic.

Faculty School total: 19. In upper school: 4 men, 15 women; 13 have advanced degrees.

Subjects Offered 1 1/2 elective credits, 20th century American writers, 20th century history, 20th century world history, accounting, acting, advanced chemistry, advanced math, Advanced Placement courses, advanced studio art-AP, algebra, American Civil War, American democracy, American government, American history, American history-AP, American literature, American literature-AP, anatomy, anatomy and physiology, ancient history, ancient world history, animal science, art, band, basic language skills, biology, biology-AP, British literature (honors), business law, calculus, calculus-AP, campus ministry, Catholic belief and practice, ceramics, chemistry, chemistry-AP, Christian doctrine, Christian education, Christian scripture, Christian testament, Christianity, church history, Civil War, civil war history, clayworking, college planning, communications, comparative politics, comparative religion, constitutional history of U.S., constitutional law, digital art, digital photography, drama, drawing, earth science, economics, English literature, English-AP, environmental science, European history-AP, family living, forensics, French, general science, geography, geometry, government, government-AP, health, history, history of the Catholic Church, history-AP, honors algebra, honors English, human anatomy, humanities, lab science, logic, New Testament, participation in sports, peace and justice, peer ministry, photography, physical fitness, physics, physics-AP, portfolio art, psychology-AP, publications, research, senior composition, sociology, Spanish, speech, sports, studio art-AP, theater arts, U.S. government and politics-AP, U.S. history, U.S. history-AP, United States government-AP, weight training, zoology.

Graduation Requirements Arts and fine arts (art, music, dance, drama), English, mathematics, physical education (includes health), science, social studies (includes history), speech, theology.

Special Academic Programs Advanced Placement exam preparation; honors section; independent study.

College Admission Counseling 85 students graduated in 2012; all went to college. Median composite ACT: 24. 32% scored over 26 on composite ACT.

Student Life Upper grades have uniform requirement, student council, honor system. Discipline rests primarily with faculty. Attendance at religious services is required.

Tuition and Aid Tuition installment plan (The Tuition Plan, Academic Management Services Plan). Tuition reduction for siblings, merit scholarship grants, need-based scholarship grants available.

Admissions Traditional secondary-level entrance grade is 9. For fall 2012, 79 students applied for upper-level admission, 79 were accepted, 79 enrolled. High School Placement Test required. Deadline for receipt of application materials: none. Application fee required: $100. Interview required.

Athletics Interscholastic: baseball (boys), basketball (b,g), cheering (g), cross-country running (b,g), football (b), ice hockey (b), pom squad (g), soccer (b,g), softball (g), tennis (b,g), track and field (b,g), volleyball (g), wrestling (b); coed interscholastic: bowling, equestrian sports, figure skating, golf. 1 PE instructor.

Computers Computers are regularly used in digital applications, research skills, speech classes. Computer network features include on-campus library services, Internet access, Internet filtering or blocking technology. Computer access in designated common areas is available to students. Students grades are available online.

Contact Mr. Joseph J. Whalen, Principal. 734-284-1875. Fax: 734-284-9304. E-mail: whalenj@gabrielrichard.org. Web site: www.gabrielrichard.org

THE GALLOWAY SCHOOL

215 West Wieuca Road NW
Atlanta, Georgia 30342

Head of School: Mrs. Suzanna Jemsby

General Information Coeducational day college-preparatory, arts, and technology school. Grades P3–12. Founded: 1969. Setting: suburban. 8.2-acre campus. 4 buildings on campus. Approved or accredited by Academy of Orton-Gillingham Practitioners and Educators, Georgia Independent School Association, Southern Association of Colleges and Schools, Southern Association of Independent Schools, and Georgia Department of Education. Member of National Association of Independent Schools and Secondary School Admission Test Board. Endowment: $7.5 million. Total enrollment: 747. Upper school average class size: 12. Upper school faculty-student ratio: 1:9.

Faculty In upper school: 12 men, 15 women.

Subjects Offered 20th century American writers, 20th century history, 20th century world history, 3-dimensional design, acting, advanced biology, advanced chemistry, advanced computer applications, advanced math, Advanced Placement courses, advanced studio art-AP, algebra, American Civil War, American culture, American government, American history, American history-AP, American literature, American literature-AP, analytic geometry, animation, art history, audio visual/media, band, biology, biology-AP, British literature, British literature-AP, calculus, calculus-AP, ceramics, chemistry, chemistry-AP, chorus, comparative government and politics-AP, composition-AP, computer animation, computer applications, computer graphics, concert band, desktop publishing, digital art, digital music, digital photography, drama, economics, electives, English, English-AP, filmmaking, fine arts, French, geometry, guidance, history, integrated physics, language arts, Latin, library, mathematics, music, physical education, physical science, political science, pre-calculus, public speaking, science, senior composition, social studies, Spanish, technology, U.S. government and politics-AP, visual arts, world geography, world history, world literature.

Graduation Requirements Arts and fine arts (art, music, dance, drama), computers, electives, English, foreign language, health and wellness, mathematics, science, social studies (includes history).

Special Academic Programs Advanced Placement exam preparation; accelerated programs; independent study; term-away projects; study at local college for college credit; academic accommodation for the gifted, the musically talented, and the artistically talented.

College Admission Counseling 62 students graduated in 2012; all went to college, including Emory University; Emory University, Oxford College; Georgia Institute of Technology; Tulane University; University of Georgia.

Student Life Upper grades have student council, honor system. Discipline rests primarily with faculty.

Summer Programs Remediation, enrichment, advancement, sports, art/fine arts programs offered; held both on and off campus; held at Athletics Complex; accepts boys and girls; open to students from other schools. 55 students usually enrolled. 2013 schedule: June 10 to July 26. Application deadline: June 3.

Tuition and Aid Day student tuition: $21,370. Tuition installment plan (FACTS Tuition Payment Plan, 50/50). Need-based scholarship grants available. In 2012–13, 28% of upper-school students received aid. Total amount of financial aid awarded in 2012–13: $1,134,000.

Admissions Traditional secondary-level entrance grade is 9. Admissions testing and SSAT required. Deadline for receipt of application materials: February 4. Application fee required: $100. On-campus interview required.

Athletics Interscholastic: basketball (boys, girls), golf (b,g), soccer (b,g), softball (g), swimming and diving (b,g), tennis (b,g), volleyball (g); intramural: dance team (g); coed interscholastic: cross-country running, outdoor adventure, running, track and field, ultimate Frisbee. 1 PE instructor, 4 coaches, 1 athletic trainer.

Computers Computers are regularly used in art, desktop publishing, drawing and design, English, graphic arts, information technology, introduction to technology, journalism, keyboarding, literary magazine, mathematics, multimedia, music, newspaper, photography, publishing, research skills, science, technology, theater, Web site design, yearbook classes. Computer network features include on-campus library services, online commercial services, Internet access, wireless campus network, Internet filtering or blocking technology, print sharing. Campus intranet, student e-mail accounts, and computer access in designated common areas are available to students. Students grades are available online. The school has a published electronic and media policy.

Contact Polly Williams, Director of Admissions. 404-252-8389. Fax: 404-252-7770. E-mail: pwilliams@gallowayschool.org. Web site: www.gallowayschool.org

GANN ACADEMY (THE NEW JEWISH HIGH SCHOOL OF GREATER BOSTON)

333 Forest Street
Waltham, Massachusetts 02452

Head of School: Rabbi Marc A. Baker

General Information Coeducational day college-preparatory, arts, and religious studies school, affiliated with Jewish faith. Grades 9–12. Founded: 1997. Setting: suburban. Nearest major city is Boston. 20-acre campus. 2 buildings on campus. Approved or accredited by New England Association of Schools and Colleges and Massachusetts Department of Education. Member of National Association of Independent Schools. Total enrollment: 311. Upper school average class size: 14. Upper school faculty-student ratio: 1:5. There are 165 required school days per year for Upper School students. Upper School students typically attend 5 days per week. The average school day consists of 8 hours.

Upper School Student Profile Grade 9: 67 students (36 boys, 31 girls); Grade 10: 89 students (38 boys, 51 girls); Grade 11: 92 students (45 boys, 47 girls); Grade 12: 63 students (27 boys, 36 girls). 100% of students are Jewish.

Faculty School total: 73. In upper school: 28 men, 45 women; 52 have advanced degrees.

Subjects Offered Advanced Placement courses, algebra, American history-AP, American literature-AP, art history, arts, Bible as literature, biology, calculus, calculus-AP, chemistry, creative arts, creative writing, drama, English, French, geometry, health and wellness, Hebrew, history, Holocaust, Jewish history, Judaic studies, Mandarin, modern dance, music, photography, physics, pre-calculus, Rabbinic literature, robotics, Spanish.

Graduation Requirements Arts, athletics, Bible as literature, English, health, Hebrew, history, mathematics, Rabbinic literature, science, Jewish Thought, electives.

Special Academic Programs Advanced Placement exam preparation; study abroad.

College Admission Counseling 85 students graduated in 2012; 74 went to college, including Harvard University; Syracuse University; University of Maryland, Baltimore County; University of Massachusetts Amherst; University of Rochester; Washington University in St. Louis. Other: 11 had other specific plans. Mean SAT critical reading: 651, mean SAT math: 636, mean SAT writing: 663, mean combined SAT: 1950, mean composite ACT: 27.

Student Life Upper grades have specified standards of dress, student council, honor system. Discipline rests primarily with faculty. Attendance at religious services is required.

Tuition and Aid Day student tuition: $32,350. Tuition installment plan (FACTS Tuition Payment Plan). Need-based scholarship grants available. In 2012–13, 41% of upper-school students received aid.

Admissions Traditional secondary-level entrance grade is 9. For fall 2012, 115 students applied for upper-level admission, 107 were accepted, 76 enrolled. SSAT required. Deadline for receipt of application materials: January 31. Application fee required: $100. On-campus interview required.

Athletics Interscholastic: baseball (boys), basketball (b,g), cross-country running (b,g), lacrosse (b,g), soccer (b,g), softball (g), tennis (b,g); intramural: basketball (b,g), tennis (b,g); coed interscholastic: juggling, ultimate Frisbee; coed intramural: fitness, golf, modern dance, table tennis, yoga. 26 coaches, 1 athletic trainer.

Computers Computer network features include on-campus library services, Internet access, wireless campus network, Internet filtering or blocking technology, computer lab. Campus intranet, student e-mail accounts, and computer access in designated common areas are available to students. Students grades are available online. The school has a published electronic and media policy.

Contact Efraim Yudewitz, Director of Admissions. 781-642-6800 Ext. 101. Fax: 781-642-6805. E-mail: eyudewitz@gannacademy.org. Web site: www.gannacademy.org/

GARCES MEMORIAL HIGH SCHOOL

2800 Loma Linda Drive
Bakersfield, California 93305

Head of School: Mrs. Kathleen B. Bears

General Information Coeducational day college-preparatory school, affiliated with Roman Catholic Church. Grades 9–12. Founded: 1947. Setting: suburban. Nearest major city is Los Angeles. 32-acre campus. 16 buildings on campus. Approved or accredited by Western Association of Schools and Colleges and Western Catholic Education Association. Endowment: $460,000. Total enrollment: 622. Upper school average class size: 25. Upper school faculty-student ratio: 1:28. There are 180 required school days per year for Upper School students. Upper School students typically attend 5 days per week. The average school day consists of 6 hours.

Upper School Student Profile Grade 9: 169 students (86 boys, 83 girls); Grade 10: 139 students (68 boys, 71 girls); Grade 11: 150 students (75 boys, 75 girls); Grade 12: 164 students (80 boys, 84 girls). 75% of students are Roman Catholic.

Faculty School total: 41. In upper school: 20 men, 21 women; 24 have advanced degrees.

Subjects Offered Algebra, American history, American literature, anatomy, art, biology, calculus, chemistry, community service, computer science, creative writing, drama, driver education, economics, English, English literature, ethics, fine arts, French, geography, geometry, government/civics, graphic arts, health, history, journalism, mathematics, music, physical education, physics, physiology, psychology, religion, science, social studies, Spanish, theater, world history, world literature.

Graduation Requirements Arts and fine arts (art, music, dance, drama), computer literacy, English, foreign language, health education, mathematics, physical education (includes health), religion (includes Bible studies and theology), science, social studies (includes history), 60 hours of community service.

Special Academic Programs Advanced Placement exam preparation; honors section; study at local college for college credit.

College Admission Counseling 149 students graduated in 2011; all went to college, including Bakersfield College; California Polytechnic State University, San Luis Obispo; California State University, Bakersfield; Texas Christian University; University of California, Santa Barbara; University of California, Santa Cruz. Mean SAT critical reading: 538, mean SAT math: 525, mean SAT writing: 529, mean composite ACT: 24. 15.3% scored over 600 on SAT critical reading, 16.9% scored over 600 on SAT math.

Student Life Upper grades have uniform requirement, student council. Discipline rests primarily with faculty. Attendance at religious services is required.

Tuition and Aid Day student tuition: $7500–$8500. Tuition installment plan (monthly payment plans, individually arranged payment plans). Merit scholarship grants, need-based scholarship grants available. In 2011–12, 32% of upper-school students received aid; total upper-school merit-scholarship money awarded: $9035. Total amount of financial aid awarded in 2011–12: $312,000.

Admissions Traditional secondary-level entrance grade is 9. For fall 2011, 185 students applied for upper-level admission, 175 were accepted, 162 enrolled. CTBS/4 required. Deadline for receipt of application materials: January 31. Application fee required: $75. Interview required.

Athletics Interscholastic: baseball (boys), basketball (b,g), cheering (g), cross-country running (b,g), dance squad (g), dance team (g), diving (b,g), football (b), golf (b,g), soccer (b,g), softball (g), swimming and diving (b,g), tennis (b,g), track and field (b,g), volleyball (g), water polo (b,g), weight training (b); intramural: baseball (b), basketball (b,g), volleyball (b,g); coed intramural: basketball, volleyball. 3 PE instructors, 28 coaches, 1 athletic trainer.

Computers Computers are regularly used in graphic arts, journalism, keyboarding classes. Computer resources include Internet access.

Contact Mrs. Joan M. Richardson, Registrar. 661-327-2578 Ext. 109. Fax: 661-327-5427. E-mail: jrichardson@garces.org. Web site: www.garces.org

GARRISON FOREST SCHOOL

300 Garrison Forest Road
Owings Mills, Maryland 21117

Head of School: Mr. G. Peter O'Neill Jr.

General Information Girls' boarding and day (coeducational in lower grades) college-preparatory, arts, technology, Women in Science & Engineering (WISE), and The James Center at Garrison Forest School school. Boarding girls grades 8–12, day boys grades N–PK, day girls grades N–12. Founded: 1910. Setting: suburban. Nearest major city is Baltimore. Students are housed in single-sex dormitories. 110-acre campus. 18 buildings on campus. Approved or accredited by Association of Independent Maryland Schools, Middle States Association of Colleges and Schools, The Association of Boarding Schools, and Maryland Department of Education. Member of National Association of Independent Schools and Secondary School Admission Test Board. Endowment: $37 million. Total enrollment: 652. Upper school average class size: 14. Upper school faculty-student ratio: 1:9. There are 176 required school days per year for Upper School students. Upper School students typically attend 5 days per week. The average school day consists of 7 hours.

Upper School Student Profile Grade 9: 78 students (78 girls); Grade 10: 73 students (73 girls); Grade 11: 75 students (75 girls); Grade 12: 73 students (73 girls). 25%

of students are boarding students. 70% are state residents. 7 states are represented in upper school student body. 12% are international students. International students from Bahamas, China, Mauritius, Mexico, Republic of Korea, and Taiwan.

Faculty School total: 104. In upper school: 6 men, 36 women; 39 have advanced degrees; 20 reside on campus.

Subjects Offered 3-dimensional art, 3-dimensional design, advanced chemistry, advanced math, algebra, American foreign policy, American government, American history, American history-AP, American literature, anatomy, ancient world history, animation, applied music, art, art history, art history-AP, arts and crafts, biology, calculus, calculus-AP, ceramics, chemistry, chemistry-AP, Chinese, Chinese studies, choral music, college counseling, college placement, college planning, computer science, computer skills, creative writing, dance, decision making skills, design, desktop publishing, digital applications, digital art, digital imaging, digital photography, drama, drawing, ecology, English, English composition, English literature, English-AP, environmental science-AP, environmental studies, equestrian sports, equine science, equitation, ESL, ethics, film studies, filmmaking, fine arts, French, French language-AP, French-AP, geometry, health and safety, health and wellness, history-AP, jewelry making, Latin, Latin-AP, leadership and service, life skills, mathematics, music, musical productions, painting, peace studies, peer counseling, philosophy, photography, physical education, physics, physics-AP, play production, portfolio art, pre-calculus, public policy, public policy issues and action, public service, public speaking, publications, science, science project, science research, sculpture, social justice, Spanish, Spanish language-AP, Spanish-AP, sports, stage design, statistics, student government, study skills, technological applications, technology, technology/design, theater, trigonometry, U.S. history-AP, values and decisions, voice ensemble, world history, writing, yearbook.

Graduation Requirements Arts and fine arts (art, music, dance, drama), decision making skills, English, foreign language, mathematics, physical education (includes health), science, social studies (includes history).

Special Academic Programs 12 Advanced Placement exams for which test preparation is offered; honors section; independent study; term-away projects; academic accommodation for the gifted, the musically talented, and the artistically talented; ESL (10 students enrolled).

College Admission Counseling 68 students graduated in 2012; all went to college, including Clemson University; Columbia University; Rensselaer Polytechnic Institute; University of Maryland, College Park; University of South Carolina; University of Virginia. 50% scored over 600 on SAT critical reading, 50% scored over 600 on SAT math, 50% scored over 600 on SAT writing.

Student Life Upper grades have uniform requirement, student council, honor system. Discipline rests equally with students and faculty.

Summer Programs Sports, art/fine arts programs offered; session focuses on extracurricular activities and young children; held on campus; accepts boys and girls; open to students from other schools. 400 students usually enrolled. 2013 schedule: June 13 to August 5. Application deadline: June 1.

Tuition and Aid Day student tuition: $25,130; 7-day tuition and room/board: $45,945. Tuition installment plan (FACTS Tuition Payment Plan). Need-based scholarship grants available. In 2012–13, 32% of upper-school students received aid. Total amount of financial aid awarded in 2012–13: $3,000,000.

Admissions Traditional secondary-level entrance grade is 9. For fall 2012, 161 students applied for upper-level admission, 83 were accepted, 43 enrolled. Admissions testing, ISEE, SSAT, TOEFL or WISC-R or WISC-III required. Deadline for receipt of application materials: December 14. Application fee required: $50. Interview required.

Athletics Interscholastic: badminton, basketball, cross-country running, equestrian sports, field hockey, golf, horseback riding, indoor soccer, indoor track, lacrosse, polo, soccer, softball, tennis, winter (indoor) track, winter soccer; intramural: aerobics, aerobics/dance, bowling, dance, fitness, horseback riding, modern dance, physical fitness, squash, strength & conditioning, swimming and diving, volleyball, yoga. 5 PE instructors, 12 coaches, 1 athletic trainer.

Computers Computers are regularly used in animation, art, college planning, design, desktop publishing, digital applications, English, ESL, foreign language, French, history, humanities, literary magazine, mathematics, newspaper, photography, publications, science, Spanish, study skills, technology, word processing, writing, yearbook classes. Computer network features include on-campus library services, Internet access, wireless campus network, Internet filtering or blocking technology, Moodle. Student e-mail accounts and computer access in designated common areas are available to students. Students grades are available online. The school has a published electronic and media policy.

Contact Mrs. Leslie D. Tinati, Director of Admission and Financial Aid. 410-559-3111. Fax: 410-363-8441. E-mail: gfsinfo@gfs.org. Web site: www.gfs.org

GASTON DAY SCHOOL

2001 Gaston Day School Road
Gastonia, North Carolina 28056

Head of School: Dr. Richard E. Rankin

General Information Coeducational day college-preparatory and arts school. Grades PS–12. Founded: 1967. Setting: suburban. Nearest major city is Charlotte. 60-acre campus. 4 buildings on campus. Approved or accredited by Southern Association of Colleges and Schools, Southern Association of Independent Schools, and North Carolina Department of Education. Member of National Association of Independent Schools. Endowment: $1.9 million. Total enrollment: 495. Upper school average class size: 12. Upper school faculty-student ratio: 1:7. There are 180 required school days per year for Upper School students. Upper School students typically attend 5 days per week. The average school day consists of 7 hours and 15 minutes.

Upper School Student Profile Grade 9: 30 students (11 boys, 19 girls); Grade 10: 44 students (19 boys, 25 girls); Grade 11: 39 students (22 boys, 17 girls); Grade 12: 32 students (13 boys, 19 girls).

Faculty School total: 58. In upper school: 7 men, 15 women; 9 have advanced degrees.

Subjects Offered Advanced chemistry, Advanced Placement courses, advanced studio art-AP, algebra, American history-AP, American literature, anatomy and physiology, art, band, biology, biology-AP, British literature, British literature (honors), calculus-AP, chemistry, chemistry-AP, choral music, chorus, creative writing, drama, English language and composition-AP, English language-AP, English literature and composition-AP, environmental science, environmental science-AP, film and literature, fine arts, French, general science, geometry, government/civics, honors algebra, honors English, honors geometry, honors U.S. history, honors world history, jazz band, journalism, learning lab, physics, pre-calculus, senior internship, Spanish, Spanish-AP, statistics-AP, student government, studio art-AP, study skills, U.S. government, U.S. history, U.S. history-AP, United States government-AP, visual arts, weight training, world literature, yearbook.

Graduation Requirements Arts and fine arts (art, music, dance, drama), electives, English, foreign language, mathematics, physical education (includes health), science, social studies (includes history), 25 hours of community service per year, seniors must complete a senior project.

Special Academic Programs Advanced Placement exam preparation; honors section; independent study; academic accommodation for the gifted.

College Admission Counseling 33 students graduated in 2012; all went to college, including Appalachian State University; Clemson University; Furman University; Indiana University Bloomington; The George Washington University; The University of North Carolina at Chapel Hill. Mean SAT critical reading: 603, mean SAT math: 618, mean SAT writing: 623, mean combined SAT: 1844, mean composite ACT: 26.

Student Life Upper grades have specified standards of dress, student council, honor system. Discipline rests primarily with faculty.

Summer Programs Remediation, enrichment, advancement, sports, art/fine arts programs offered; session focuses on academic enrichment, advancement in sports and arts; held on campus; accepts boys and girls; open to students from other schools. 200 students usually enrolled. 2013 schedule: June to August.

Tuition and Aid Day student tuition: $13,640. Tuition installment plan (monthly payment plans, individually arranged payment plans). Merit scholarship grants, need-based scholarship grants available. In 2012–13, 54% of upper-school students received aid; total upper-school merit-scholarship money awarded: $159,150. Total amount of financial aid awarded in 2012–13: $256,070.

Admissions Traditional secondary-level entrance grade is 9. For fall 2012, 55 students applied for upper-level admission, 33 were accepted, 27 enrolled. ISEE required. Deadline for receipt of application materials: none. Application fee required: $50. On-campus interview required.

Athletics Interscholastic: baseball (boys), basketball (b,g), cheering (g), cross-country running (b,g), golf (b), soccer (b,g), swimming and diving (b,g), tennis (b,g), track and field (b,g), volleyball (g); intramural: fitness (b,g), physical fitness (b,g), physical training (b,g), strength & conditioning (b,g), weight lifting (b,g), weight training (b,g). 2 PE instructors, 27 coaches, 1 athletic trainer.

Computers Computers are regularly used in art, English, foreign language, history, journalism, mathematics, newspaper, science, yearbook classes. Computer network features include on-campus library services, online commercial services, Internet access, wireless campus network, Internet filtering or blocking technology. Student e-mail accounts and computer access in designated common areas are available to students. Students grades are available online. The school has a published electronic and media policy.

Contact Mrs. Martha Jayne Rhyne, Director of Admission. 704-864-7744 Ext. 174. Fax: 704-865-3813. E-mail: mrhyne@gastonday.org. Web site: www.gastonday.org

GATEWAY SCHOOL

Arlington, Texas
See Special Needs Schools section.

THE GENEVA SCHOOL

2025 State Road 436
Winter Park, Florida 32792

Head of School: Rev. Robert Forrest Ingram

General Information Coeducational day college-preparatory, arts, and religious studies school, affiliated with Christian faith. Grades K4–12. Founded: 1993. Setting: suburban. Nearest major city is Orlando. 3-acre campus. 1 building on campus. Approved or accredited by Florida Council of Independent Schools. Total enrollment: 454. Upper school average class size: 18. Upper school faculty-student ratio: 1:9. There are 174 required school days per year for Upper School students. Upper School students typically attend 5 days per week. The average school day consists of 6 hours and 45 minutes.

Upper School Student Profile 95% of students are Christian faith.

Faculty School total: 53. In upper school: 17 men, 12 women; 19 have advanced degrees.

Subjects Offered Advanced Placement courses, advanced studio art-AP, aesthetics, algebra, American government, anatomy and physiology, Ancient Greek, ancient world history, art, Bible, biology, British literature (honors), calculus, calculus-AP, chemistry, chemistry-AP, choir, choral music, Christian ethics, classical Greek literature, classics, comparative religion, critical thinking, critical writing, debate, drama, earth science, economics, English language and composition-AP, English literature and composition-AP, ethics, European history, foreign language, French, French-AP, history, honors algebra, honors English, honors geometry, honors U.S. history, honors world history, independent study, instrumental music, Irish literature, journalism, Latin, life management skills, mathematics, medieval literature, music appreciation, oral communications, philosophy, photography, photojournalism, physical education, physical fitness, physical science, physics, physics-AP, pre-algebra, pre-calculus, reading/study skills, rhetoric, science, senior thesis, Shakespeare, Spanish, speech and debate, studio art-AP, theater, theater arts, trigonometry, U.S. history, U.S. history-AP, world history, yearbook.

Graduation Requirements Arts and fine arts (art, music, dance, drama), athletics, Bible, electives, English, foreign language, history, mathematics, rhetoric, science, classics.

Special Academic Programs 12 Advanced Placement exams for which test preparation is offered; honors section; independent study; study at local college for college credit; academic accommodation for the gifted, the musically talented, and the artistically talented.

College Admission Counseling 10 students graduated in 2011; 9 went to college, including Auburn University; Furman University; Rollins College; The University of Alabama; University of Central Florida; University of Florida. Other: 1 had other specific plans. Median SAT critical reading: 625, median SAT math: 581, median SAT writing: 593, median combined SAT: 1830, median composite ACT: 26.

Student Life Upper grades have uniform requirement, student council, honor system. Discipline rests primarily with faculty. Attendance at religious services is required.

Tuition and Aid Day student tuition: $11,590. Tuition installment plan (The Tuition Plan, monthly payment plans). Need-based scholarship grants available. In 2011–12, 30% of upper-school students received aid.

Admissions Traditional secondary-level entrance grade is 9. For fall 2011, 64 students applied for upper-level admission, 25 were accepted, 24 enrolled. ISEE required. Deadline for receipt of application materials: none. Application fee required: $100. Interview required.

Athletics Interscholastic: baseball (boys), basketball (b,g), cross-country running (b,g), flag football (b), soccer (b,g), softball (g), tennis (b,g), volleyball (g); coed interscholastic: golf. 3 PE instructors, 10 coaches, 1 athletic trainer.

Computers Computers are regularly used in all academic, college planning, journalism, photography, yearbook classes. Computer network features include on-campus library services, Internet access, wireless campus network, Internet filtering or blocking technology. Students grades are available online. The school has a published electronic and media policy.

Contact Mrs. Patti Rader, Director of Admission. 407-332-6363 Ext. 204. Fax: 407-332-1664. E-mail: pnrader@genevaschool.org. Web site: www.genevaschool.org

GEORGE STEVENS ACADEMY

23 Union Street
Blue Hill, Maine 04614

Head of School: Mr. Paul Perkinson

General Information Coeducational boarding and day college-preparatory and general academic school. Grades 9–12. Founded: 1803. Setting: small town. Nearest major city is Bangor. Students are housed in single-sex dormitories and host family homes. 20-acre campus. 6 buildings on campus. Approved or accredited by Independent Schools of Northern New England, New England Association of Schools and Colleges, The College Board, and Maine Department of Education. Member of Secondary School Admission Test Board. Endowment: $7 million. Total enrollment: 313. Upper school average class size: 15. Upper school faculty-student ratio: 1:10. There are 180 required school days per year for Upper School students. Upper School students typically attend 5 days per week. The average school day consists of 6 hours and 30 minutes.

Upper School Student Profile Grade 9: 78 students (35 boys, 43 girls); Grade 10: 84 students (42 boys, 42 girls); Grade 11: 69 students (46 boys, 23 girls); Grade 12: 82 students (42 boys, 40 girls). 8% of students are boarding students. 86% are state residents. 2 states are represented in upper school student body. 14% are international students. International students from Australia, China, France, Italy, Japan, and Republic of Korea.

Faculty School total: 34. In upper school: 17 men, 17 women; 18 have advanced degrees; 2 reside on campus.

Subjects Offered 20th century history, 3-dimensional design, advanced chemistry, advanced math, Advanced Placement courses, algebra, American literature, American literature-AP, art, art history, art-AP, arts and crafts, band, biology, British literature (honors), business mathematics, calculus-AP, carpentry, chamber groups, chemistry, computer applications, computer literacy, creative writing, critical thinking, desktop publishing, developmental language skills, drafting, drawing, driver education, earth science, electives, English, English-AP, environmental science, environmental science-AP, ESL, European history, fine arts, foreign language, forensics, French, general math, general science, geometry, German, health education, history, history-AP, honors algebra, honors English, honors geometry, honors U.S. history, human geography - AP, humanities, independent study, industrial arts, industrial technology, instrumental music, internship, jazz band, jazz ensemble, lab science, languages, Latin, literature, literature-AP, marine science, mathematics, mathematics-AP, mechanics, model United Nations, modern history, modern languages, modern problems, music, music theory, musical productions, mythology, personal fitness, photo shop, photography, physical education, physics, pre-algebra, pre-calculus, printmaking, psychology, reading/study skills, remedial study skills, science, senior project, shop, small engine repair, social issues, social sciences, Spanish, speech and debate, sports, statistics-AP, street law, student government, technology/design, TOEFL preparation, transportation technology, U.S. history, U.S. history-AP, Western civilization, wilderness education, woodworking, work-study, World-Wide-Web publishing, writing.

Graduation Requirements Arts and fine arts (art, music, dance, drama), electives, English, foreign language, history, mathematics, physical education (includes health), science, social sciences, U.S. history, senior debate.

Special Academic Programs Advanced Placement exam preparation; honors section; accelerated programs; independent study; term-away projects; study at local college for college credit; study abroad; academic accommodation for the gifted, the musically talented, and the artistically talented; remedial reading and/or remedial writing; remedial math; special instructional classes for deaf students, blind students; ESL (24 students enrolled).

College Admission Counseling 60 students graduated in 2012; 58 went to college, including Bowdoin College; Maine Maritime Academy; Simmons College; University of Maine; University of Southern Maine; University of Vermont. Other: 1 went to work, 1 entered military service. Mean SAT critical reading: 499, mean SAT math: 526, mean SAT writing: 508.

Student Life Upper grades have student council. Discipline rests primarily with faculty.

Summer Programs Remediation, enrichment, ESL, sports, art/fine arts programs offered; session focuses on ESL; held on campus; accepts boys and girls; open to students from other schools. 15 students usually enrolled. 2013 schedule: August 1 to August 26. Application deadline: May 15.

Tuition and Aid 7-day tuition and room/board: $37,400. Tuition installment plan (monthly payment plans, individually arranged payment plans). Need-based scholarship grants available. In 2012–13, 1% of upper-school students received aid.

Admissions Traditional secondary-level entrance grade is 9. International English Language Test, SSAT or TOEFL or SLEP required. Deadline for receipt of application materials: March 1. Application fee required: $75. Interview required.

Athletics Interscholastic: baseball (boys), basketball (b,g), cheering (b,g), cross-country running (b,g), golf (b,g), independent competitive sports (b,g), running (b,g), sailing (b,g), soccer (b,g), softball (g), swimming and diving (b,g), tennis (b,g), track and field (b,g), wrestling (b); coed intramural: backpacking, bocce, canoeing/kayaking, croquet, dance, dance team, fitness, fitness walking, flag football, floor hockey, Frisbee, hiking/backpacking, jogging, kayaking, modern dance, ocean paddling, outdoor activities, outdoor adventure, outdoor education, outdoor recreation, outdoor skills, paddle tennis, physical fitness, physical training, running, sailing, skateboarding, skiing (cross-country), skiing (downhill), snowboarding, snowshoeing, strength & conditioning, table tennis, ultimate Frisbee, volleyball, walking, weight lifting, weight training, wilderness, winter walking, yoga. 2 PE instructors, 26 coaches.

Computers Computers are regularly used in all academic, business skills, computer applications, creative writing, design, desktop publishing, drafting, English, foreign language, graphic design, photography, Web site design classes. Computer network features include on-campus library services, online commercial services, Internet access, wireless campus network, Internet filtering or blocking technology. Student e-mail accounts and computer access in designated common areas are available to students. Students grades are available online. The school has a published electronic and media policy.

Contact Mrs. Libby Chamberlain, Director of Admissions. 207-374-2808 Ext. 134. Fax: 207-374-2982. E-mail: l.chamberlain@georgestevens.org. Web site: www.georgestevensacademy.org

GEORGETOWN DAY SCHOOL

4200 Davenport Street NW
Washington, District of Columbia 20016

Head of School: Russell Shaw

General Information Coeducational day college-preparatory, arts, and athletics school. Grades PK–12. Founded: 1945. Setting: urban. 6-acre campus. 1 building on campus. Approved or accredited by Association of Independent Maryland Schools, Middle States Association of Colleges and Schools, and District of Columbia Department of Education. Member of National Association of Independent Schools and Secondary School Admission Test Board. Endowment: $7.5 million. Total enrollment:

1,075. Upper school average class size: 15. Upper school faculty-student ratio: 1:7. There are 170 required school days per year for Upper School students. Upper School students typically attend 5 days per week. The average school day consists of 10 hours.
Upper School Student Profile Grade 9: 114 students (55 boys, 59 girls); Grade 10: 117 students (63 boys, 54 girls); Grade 11: 114 students (56 boys, 58 girls); Grade 12: 113 students (56 boys, 57 girls).
Faculty School total: 160. In upper school: 30 men, 40 women; 50 have advanced degrees.
Subjects Offered Algebra, American history, American literature, anthropology, art, art history, astronomy, biology, calculus, ceramics, chemistry, community service, computer science, creative writing, dance, drama, driver education, economics, English, environmental science-AP, European history, fine arts, French, geometry, government/civics, history, Latin, law, linear algebra, mathematics, music, photography, physical education, physics, psychology, science, social studies, Spanish, statistics-AP, theater, trigonometry, world history.
Graduation Requirements Arts and fine arts (art, music, dance, drama), English, foreign language, literature, mathematics, physical education (includes health), science, social studies (includes history). Community service is required.
Special Academic Programs 20 Advanced Placement exams for which test preparation is offered; honors section; independent study.
College Admission Counseling Colleges students went to include Brown University; Duke University; Harvard University; Stanford University; Wesleyan University; Yale University.
Student Life Upper grades have student council, honor system. Discipline rests primarily with faculty.
Summer Programs Enrichment programs offered; session focuses on based on interest; held on campus; accepts boys and girls; open to students from other schools. 120 students usually enrolled. 2013 schedule: June to August.
Tuition and Aid Day student tuition: $29,990–$34,325. Tuition installment plan (Insured Tuition Payment Plan, Academic Management Services Plan, monthly payment plans). Need-based scholarship grants available. In 2012–13, 20% of upper-school students received aid. Total amount of financial aid awarded in 2012–13: $1,000,000.
Admissions Traditional secondary-level entrance grade is 9. For fall 2012, 240 students applied for upper-level admission, 80 were accepted, 58 enrolled. ISEE or SSAT required. Deadline for receipt of application materials: January 7. Application fee required: $65. On-campus interview required.
Athletics Interscholastic: baseball (boys), basketball (b,g), crew (b,g), cross-country running (b,g), lacrosse (b,g); intramural: indoor soccer (b,g); coed interscholastic: golf, swimming and diving; coed intramural: flag football. 5 PE instructors, 6 coaches, 1 athletic trainer.
Computers Computers are regularly used in art, English, foreign language, history, mathematics, music, science classes. Computer network features include on-campus library services, online commercial services, Internet access, wireless campus network. Student e-mail accounts are available to students. The school has a published electronic and media policy.
Contact Vincent W. Rowe Jr., Director of Enrollment Management and Financial Aid. 202-274-3210. Fax: 202-274-3211. E-mail: vrowe@gds.org. Web site: www.gds.org

GEORGETOWN PREPARATORY SCHOOL

10900 Rockville Pike
North Bethesda, Maryland 20852-3299

Head of School: Mr. Jeff Jones

General Information Boys' boarding and day college-preparatory, arts, religious studies, and technology school, affiliated with Roman Catholic Church. Grades 9–12. Founded: 1789. Setting: suburban. Nearest major city is Washington, DC. Students are housed in single-sex dormitories. 92-acre campus. 8 buildings on campus. Approved or accredited by Jesuit Secondary Education Association, Middle States Association of Colleges and Schools, National Catholic Education Association, The Association of Boarding Schools, and Maryland Department of Education. Member of National Association of Independent Schools and Secondary School Admission Test Board. Endowment: $20 million. Total enrollment: 490. Upper school average class size: 16. Upper school faculty-student ratio: 1:8. Upper School students typically attend 5 days per week. The average school day consists of 6 hours and 30 minutes.
Upper School Student Profile Grade 9: 127 students (127 boys); Grade 10: 122 students (122 boys); Grade 11: 130 students (130 boys); Grade 12: 111 students (111 boys). 20% of students are boarding students. 60% are state residents. 16 states are represented in upper school student body. 30% are international students. International students from China, Indonesia, Mexico, Republic of Korea, Saudi Arabia, and Taiwan; 22 other countries represented in student body. 70% of students are Roman Catholic.
Faculty School total: 58. In upper school: 36 men, 22 women; 53 have advanced degrees; 18 reside on campus.
Subjects Offered Algebra, American history, American literature, art, art history, Bible studies, biology, calculus, chemistry, computer programming, computer science, drama, driver education, economics, English, English literature, ESL, ethics, European history, fine arts, French, geometry, German, government/civics, history, journalism, Latin, mathematics, music, philosophy, physical education, physics, psychology, religion, science, social studies, Spanish, speech, stained glass, theater, theology, trigonometry, world history, world literature.
Graduation Requirements Arts and fine arts (art, music, dance, drama), classics, English, foreign language, mathematics, music theory, religion (includes Bible studies and theology), science, social studies (includes history), two years of Latin. Community service is required.
Special Academic Programs 24 Advanced Placement exams for which test preparation is offered; honors section; independent study; term-away projects; study abroad; academic accommodation for the gifted; ESL (14 students enrolled).
College Admission Counseling 118 students graduated in 2012; all went to college, including Boston College; Georgetown University; Stanford University; University of Notre Dame; University of Pennsylvania; University of Virginia. Mean SAT critical reading: 670, mean SAT math: 643, mean SAT writing: 637, mean combined SAT: 1950, mean composite ACT: 27.
Student Life Upper grades have specified standards of dress, student council. Discipline rests primarily with faculty. Attendance at religious services is required.
Summer Programs Remediation, enrichment, advancement, ESL, sports programs offered; session focuses on ESL; held on campus; accepts boys and girls; open to students from other schools. 75 students usually enrolled. 2013 schedule: June 28 to August 6. Application deadline: March 1.
Tuition and Aid Day student tuition: $29,625; 7-day tuition and room/board: $50,465. Tuition installment plan (FACTS Tuition Payment Plan). Need-based scholarship grants, middle-income loans available. In 2012–13, 25% of upper-school students received aid. Total amount of financial aid awarded in 2012–13: $2,000,000.
Admissions Traditional secondary-level entrance grade is 9. For fall 2012, 405 students applied for upper-level admission, 165 were accepted, 138 enrolled. SSAT required. Deadline for receipt of application materials: January 10. Application fee required: $100. Interview required.
Athletics Interscholastic: baseball, basketball, cross-country running, diving, fencing, football, golf, ice hockey, indoor soccer, indoor track & field, lacrosse, rugby, running, soccer, swimming and diving, tennis, track and field, winter (indoor) track, wrestling; intramural: basketball, canoeing/kayaking, fitness, flag football, floor hockey, Frisbee, hiking/backpacking, ice skating, indoor hockey, kayaking, life saving, martial arts, mountain biking, Nautilus, ocean paddling, paddle tennis, paint ball, physical fitness, physical training, power lifting, racquetball, rappelling, rock climbing, ropes courses, scuba diving, skiing (downhill), snowboarding, soccer, softball, strength & conditioning, table tennis, tennis, ultimate Frisbee, volleyball, weight training. 16 coaches, 3 athletic trainers.
Computers Computers are regularly used in art, classics, data processing, English, French, history, Latin, mathematics, music, religious studies, science, Spanish, writing classes. Computer network features include on-campus library services, online commercial services, Internet access, wireless campus network, Internet filtering or blocking technology. Campus intranet, student e-mail accounts, and computer access in designated common areas are available to students. Students grades are available online. The school has a published electronic and media policy.
Contact Mr. Brian J. Gilbert, Dean of Admissions. 301-214-1215. Fax: 301-493-6128. E-mail: admissions@gprep.org. Web site: www.gprep.org

GEORGETOWN VISITATION PREPARATORY SCHOOL

1524 35th Street NW
Washington, District of Columbia 20007

Head of School: Daniel M. Kerns Jr.

General Information Girls' day college-preparatory school, affiliated with Roman Catholic Church. Grades 9–12. Founded: 1799. Setting: urban. 23-acre campus. 7 buildings on campus. Approved or accredited by Association of Independent Schools of Greater Washington, Middle States Association of Colleges and Schools, National Catholic Education Association, National Independent Private Schools Association, and District of Columbia Department of Education. Member of National Association of Independent Schools. Endowment: $16.7 million. Total enrollment: 490. Upper school average class size: 15. Upper school faculty-student ratio: 1:10. There are 181 required school days per year for Upper School students. Upper School students typically attend 5 days per week. The average school day consists of 5 hours and 30 minutes.
Upper School Student Profile Grade 9: 118 students (118 girls); Grade 10: 126 students (126 girls); Grade 11: 125 students (125 girls); Grade 12: 121 students (121 girls). 93% of students are Roman Catholic.
Faculty School total: 54. In upper school: 12 men, 42 women; 39 have advanced degrees.
Subjects Offered Advanced Placement courses, advanced studio art-AP, algebra, American history, American literature, anthropology, art, art history, art history-AP, Bible studies, biology, biology-AP, calculus, calculus-AP, chemistry, comparative political systems-AP, computer programming, computer science, creative writing, dance, English, English language and composition-AP, English literature, English literature and composition-AP, environmental science, environmental science-AP, ethics, European history, European history-AP, expository writing, fine arts, French, French-AP, geography, geometry, government-AP, government/civics, health, history, Latin, mathematics, music, philosophy, physical education, physics, psychology, psychology-

AP, religion, science, social sciences, social studies, Spanish, speech, theology, trigonometry, U.S. government and politics-AP, U.S. history-AP, world history.

Graduation Requirements Arts and fine arts (art, music, dance, drama), English, foreign language, mathematics, physical education (includes health), religion (includes Bible studies and theology), science, social sciences, social studies (includes history), 80 hours of community service.

Special Academic Programs Advanced Placement exam preparation; honors section; independent study; study at local college for college credit.

College Admission Counseling 122 students graduated in 2012; all went to college, including Boston College; Georgetown University; Princeton University; University of Notre Dame; University of Virginia. Mean SAT critical reading: 651, mean SAT math: 626.

Student Life Upper grades have uniform requirement, student council, honor system. Discipline rests primarily with faculty. Attendance at religious services is required.

Summer Programs Remediation, enrichment, sports, art/fine arts, computer instruction programs offered; held on campus; accepts girls; not open to students from other schools. 100 students usually enrolled. 2013 schedule: June to July. Application deadline: April.

Tuition and Aid Day student tuition: $24,500. Tuition installment plan (FACTS Tuition Payment Plan, individually arranged payment plans). Merit scholarship grants, need-based scholarship grants available. In 2012–13, 25% of upper-school students received aid; total upper-school merit-scholarship money awarded: $55,000. Total amount of financial aid awarded in 2012–13: $1,700,000.

Admissions Traditional secondary-level entrance grade is 9. For fall 2012, 430 students applied for upper-level admission, 160 were accepted, 118 enrolled. High School Placement Test or High School Placement Test (closed version) from Scholastic Testing Service required. Deadline for receipt of application materials: December 5. Application fee required: $50. On-campus interview required.

Athletics Interscholastic: aerobics/dance, basketball, crew, cross-country running, dance, diving, field hockey, fitness, indoor track, lacrosse, soccer, softball, swimming and diving, tennis, track and field, volleyball; intramural: cheering, flag football, strength & conditioning. 4 PE instructors, 23 coaches, 1 athletic trainer.

Computers Computers are regularly used in all academic, art, English, French, history, mathematics, religion, science, Spanish classes. Computer network features include on-campus library services, online commercial services, Internet access, wireless campus network, Internet filtering or blocking technology. Campus intranet and student e-mail accounts are available to students.

Contact Janet Keller, Director of Admissions. 202-337-3350 Ext. 2241. Fax: 202-333-3522. E-mail: jkeller@visi.org. Web site: www.visi.org

GEORGE WALTON ACADEMY

One Bulldog Drive
Monroe, Georgia 30655

Head of School: Mr. William M. Nicholson

General Information Coeducational day college-preparatory, arts, and technology school. Grades K4–12. Founded: 1969. Setting: small town. Nearest major city is Atlanta. 54-acre campus. 8 buildings on campus. Approved or accredited by Georgia Independent School Association, Southern Association of Colleges and Schools, and Georgia Department of Education. Total enrollment: 878. Upper school average class size: 17. Upper school faculty-student ratio: 1:12. There are 180 required school days per year for Upper School students. Upper School students typically attend 5 days per week. The average school day consists of 6 hours and 45 minutes.

Upper School Student Profile Grade 9: 75 students (45 boys, 30 girls); Grade 10: 71 students (36 boys, 35 girls); Grade 11: 92 students (44 boys, 48 girls); Grade 12: 78 students (41 boys, 37 girls).

Faculty School total: 83. In upper school: 15 men, 38 women; 20 have advanced degrees.

Subjects Offered Algebra, American history, American literature, anatomy, art, art history, Bible studies, biology, calculus, chemistry, creative writing, drama, economics, English, English literature, environmental science, European history, fine arts, geography, geometry, government/civics, grammar, health, history, journalism, Latin, mathematics, music, photography, physical education, physics, psychology, science, social sciences, social studies, sociology, Spanish, trigonometry, world history, world literature, writing.

Graduation Requirements Arts and fine arts (art, music, dance, drama), composition, English, foreign language, mathematics, physical education (includes health), science, social sciences, social studies (includes history), all students must be accepted to a college or university to graduate.

Special Academic Programs 11 Advanced Placement exams for which test preparation is offered; honors section; academic accommodation for the musically talented and the artistically talented.

College Admission Counseling 80 students graduated in 2012; all went to college, including Georgia College & State University; Georgia Institute of Technology; Georgia Southern University; Georgia State University; North Georgia College & State University; University of Georgia.

Student Life Upper grades have uniform requirement, student council, honor system. Discipline rests primarily with faculty.

Summer Programs Enrichment, sports, art/fine arts programs offered; session focuses on academic and athletic enrichment; held on campus; accepts boys and girls; open to students from other schools. 500 students usually enrolled. 2013 schedule: May 29 to July 31.

Tuition and Aid Day student tuition: $8500. Tuition installment plan (monthly payment plans). Tuition reduction for siblings, need-based scholarship grants available. In 2012–13, 1% of upper-school students received aid.

Admissions Traditional secondary-level entrance grade is 9. ACT, CAT 5, CTBS, Stanford Achievement Test, any other standardized test, Otis-Lennon, Stanford Achievement Test, PSAT or SAT required. Deadline for receipt of application materials: none. Application fee required: $150. On-campus interview required.

Athletics Interscholastic: aquatics (boys, girls), baseball (b), basketball (b,g), cheering (g), cross-country running (b,g), dance squad (g), drill team (g), football (b), golf (b), physical fitness (b,g), soccer (b,g), softball (g), swimming and diving (b,g), tennis (b,g), track and field (b,g), volleyball (g), weight lifting (b), weight training (b,g), wrestling (b). 3 PE instructors, 8 coaches.

Computers Computers are regularly used in all academic classes. Computer network features include on-campus library services, online commercial services, Internet access, wireless campus network, Internet filtering or blocking technology. Computer access in designated common areas is available to students. Students grades are available online. The school has a published electronic and media policy.

Contact Ms. Chris Stancil, Director of Admissions. 770-207-5172 Ext. 234. Fax: 770-267-4023. E-mail: cstancil@gwa.com. Web site: www.gwa.com

GERMANTOWN FRIENDS SCHOOL

31 West Coulter Street
Philadelphia, Pennsylvania 19144

Head of School: Richard L. Wade

General Information Coeducational day college-preparatory, arts, and technology school, affiliated with Society of Friends. Grades K–12. Founded: 1845. Setting: urban. 21-acre campus. 21 buildings on campus. Approved or accredited by Friends Council on Education, Middle States Association of Colleges and Schools, National Independent Private Schools Association, and Pennsylvania Association of Independent Schools. Member of National Association of Independent Schools and Secondary School Admission Test Board. Endowment: $22 million. Total enrollment: 861. Upper school average class size: 18. Upper school faculty-student ratio: 1:9. There are 172 required school days per year for Upper School students. Upper School students typically attend 5 days per week. The average school day consists of 6 hours and 25 minutes.

Upper School Student Profile Grade 9: 88 students (44 boys, 44 girls); Grade 10: 94 students (40 boys, 54 girls); Grade 11: 88 students (39 boys, 49 girls); Grade 12: 83 students (50 boys, 33 girls). 6.3% of students are members of Society of Friends.

Faculty School total: 136. In upper school: 28 men, 30 women; 44 have advanced degrees.

Subjects Offered 3-dimensional art, advanced chemistry, advanced math, algebra, American history, ancient history, art, art history, biology, calculus, chemistry, choir, chorus, comparative cultures, computer applications, computer programming, creative writing, drama, dramatic arts, drawing, English, environmental education, environmental science, European history, French, geometry, Greek, health, human sexuality, independent study, instrumental music, jazz ensemble, Latin, Latin History, madrigals, mathematics, music, music theory, orchestra, painting, philosophy, photography, physical education, physics, pre-calculus, science, social studies, Spanish, sports, stagecraft, statistics, studio art, theater, trigonometry, vocal music.

Graduation Requirements English, foreign language, history, lab science, mathematics, music, physical education (includes health), month-long off-campus independent project.

Special Academic Programs Honors section; independent study; term-away projects; domestic exchange program (with The Network Program Schools, The Catlin Gabel School); study abroad; academic accommodation for the gifted, the musically talented, and the artistically talented; ESL (3 students enrolled).

College Admission Counseling 76 students graduated in 2012; all went to college, including Brown University; College of Charleston; Drexel University; Massachusetts Institute of Technology; University of Pennsylvania; Yale University. Mean SAT critical reading: 648, mean SAT math: 634, mean SAT writing: 629. 78% scored over 600 on SAT critical reading, 70% scored over 600 on SAT math, 69% scored over 600 on SAT writing.

Student Life Upper grades have student council. Discipline rests primarily with faculty. Attendance at religious services is required.

Summer Programs Enrichment programs offered; session focuses on partnership of public and private school, studying water as both environmental and social justice issues; held both on and off campus; held at various locations around Philadelphia; accepts boys and girls; open to students from other schools. 36 students usually enrolled. 2013 schedule: June 10 to August 26. Application deadline: June 1.

Tuition and Aid Day student tuition: $28,450. Tuition installment plan (Academic Management Services Plan, Key Tuition Payment Plan, FACTS Tuition Payment Plan, individually arranged payment plans). Need-based scholarship grants available. In 2012–13, 29% of upper-school students received aid. Total amount of financial aid awarded in 2012–13: $1,992,162.

Admissions Traditional secondary-level entrance grade is 9. For fall 2012, 100 students applied for upper-level admission, 66 were accepted, 31 enrolled. ISEE or SSAT required. Deadline for receipt of application materials: December 7. Application fee required: $40. On-campus interview required.

Athletics Interscholastic: baseball (boys), basketball (b,g), cross-country running (b,g), field hockey (g), indoor track & field (b,g), lacrosse (g), soccer (b,g), softball (g), squash (b,g), tennis (b,g), track and field (b,g), wrestling (b); intramural: flag football (b); coed intramural: physical training, strength & conditioning, weight training. 7 PE instructors, 37 coaches, 2 athletic trainers.

Computers Computers are regularly used in art, English, foreign language, history, mathematics, music, photography, publications, science classes. Computer network features include on-campus library services, online commercial services, Internet access, wireless campus network, Internet filtering or blocking technology. Campus intranet, student e-mail accounts, and computer access in designated common areas are available to students.

Contact Laura Sharpless Myran, Director, Enrollment and Financial Aid. 215-951-2346. Fax: 215-951-2370. E-mail: lauram@gfsnet.org. Web site: www.germantownfriends.org

GILL ST. BERNARD'S SCHOOL

PO Box 604
St. Bernard's Road
Gladstone, New Jersey 07934

Head of School: Mr. S.A. Rowell

General Information Coeducational day college-preparatory school. Grades PK–12. Founded: 1900. Setting: small town. Nearest major city is New York, NY. 72-acre campus. 15 buildings on campus. Approved or accredited by Middle States Association of Colleges and Schools and New Jersey Association of Independent Schools. Member of National Association of Independent Schools and Secondary School Admission Test Board. Endowment: $7 million. Total enrollment: 695. Upper school average class size: 16. Upper school faculty-student ratio: 1:15. There are 175 required school days per year for Upper School students. Upper School students typically attend 5 days per week. The average school day consists of 7 hours.

Faculty School total: 99. In upper school: 22 men, 24 women; 27 have advanced degrees.

Subjects Offered 20th century world history, 3-dimensional art, advanced chemistry, advanced computer applications, advanced math, Advanced Placement courses, algebra, American democracy, American history, American history-AP, American literature, analysis and differential calculus, analytic geometry, art, astronomy, biology, biology-AP, British literature, British literature (honors), calculus, calculus-AP, chemistry, chemistry-AP, chorus, college counseling, comparative cultures, computer science, computer science-AP, contemporary issues, creative writing, earth science, economics, English, English literature, English literature-AP, environmental science, environmental science-AP, European history, European history-AP, fine arts, forensics, French, gender issues, geography, geometry, government/civics, health, history, honors English, human geography - AP, independent study, international relations, Latin, Latin American literature, literature, mathematics, music, oceanography, philosophy, photography, physical education, physics, portfolio art, psychology, science, social studies, Spanish, Spanish-AP, technology, theater, U.S. government and politics-AP, United States government-AP, woodworking, world history, world literature.

Graduation Requirements Arts and fine arts (art, music, dance, drama), English, foreign language, history, mathematics, science, The Unit: an intensive 2-week course each year of Upper School.

Special Academic Programs 15 Advanced Placement exams for which test preparation is offered; honors section; independent study; study abroad.

College Admission Counseling 75 students graduated in 2011; all went to college, including Boston College; Furman University; New York University; The George Washington University; Vanderbilt University; Villanova University. 65% scored over 600 on SAT critical reading, 65% scored over 600 on SAT math, 70% scored over 600 on SAT writing.

Student Life Upper grades have specified standards of dress, student council, honor system. Discipline rests primarily with faculty.

Tuition and Aid Day student tuition: $29,400. Tuition installment plan (The Tuition Plan, Insured Tuition Payment Plan). Merit scholarship grants, need-based scholarship grants available. In 2011–12, 12% of upper-school students received aid; total upper-school merit-scholarship money awarded: $40,000. Total amount of financial aid awarded in 2011–12: $1,200,000.

Admissions Traditional secondary-level entrance grade is 9. For fall 2011, 263 students applied for upper-level admission, 164 were accepted, 112 enrolled. ISEE or SSAT required. Deadline for receipt of application materials: January 25. Application fee required: $75. On-campus interview required.

Athletics Interscholastic: baseball (boys), basketball (b,g), cheering (g), cross-country running (b,g), fencing (b,g), ice hockey (b), indoor track & field (b,g), lacrosse (b,g), soccer (b,g), softball (g), tennis (b,g), track and field (b,g), winter (indoor) track (b,g); intramural: skiing (downhill) (b,g), strength & conditioning (b,g); coed interscholastic: golf, swimming and diving; coed intramural: backpacking, hiking/backpacking, outdoor adventure, outdoor recreation, physical fitness, physical training. 6 PE instructors, 37 coaches, 1 athletic trainer.

Computers Computers are regularly used in art, computer applications, design, desktop publishing, graphic arts, graphic design, independent study, information technology, introduction to technology, journalism, library, library skills, literary magazine, multimedia, news writing, newspaper, photography, programming, research skills, science, technology, Web site design, yearbook classes. Computer network features include on-campus library services, online commercial services, Internet access, wireless campus network, Internet filtering or blocking technology. Campus intranet and computer access in designated common areas are available to students. The school has a published electronic and media policy.

Contact Mrs. Ann Marie Blackman, Admission Office Manager. 908-234-1611 Ext. 245. Fax: 908-234-1712. E-mail: ablackman@gsbschool.org. Web site: www.gsbschool.org

GILMAN SCHOOL

5407 Roland Avenue
Baltimore, Maryland 21210

Head of School: Mr. John E. Schmick

General Information Boys' day college-preparatory school. Grades K–12. Founded: 1897. Setting: suburban. 68-acre campus. 6 buildings on campus. Approved or accredited by Association of Independent Maryland Schools, Middle States Association of Colleges and Schools, and Maryland Department of Education. Member of National Association of Independent Schools and Secondary School Admission Test Board. Endowment: $83.5 million. Total enrollment: 1,034. Upper school average class size: 16. Upper school faculty-student ratio: 1:8. There are 172 required school days per year for Upper School students. Upper School students typically attend 5 days per week. The average school day consists of 9 hours.

Upper School Student Profile Grade 9: 117 students (117 boys); Grade 10: 116 students (116 boys); Grade 11: 117 students (117 boys); Grade 12: 115 students (115 boys).

Faculty School total: 145. In upper school: 58 men, 8 women; 50 have advanced degrees.

Subjects Offered Algebra, American history, American literature, anatomy, Arabic, art, art history, biology, calculus, chemistry, Chinese, community service, computer math, computer programming, computer science, creative writing, drafting, drama, ecology, economics, English, English literature, environmental science, European history, expository writing, fine arts, French, geometry, German, government/civics, Greek, history, industrial arts, Latin, mathematics, mechanical drawing, music, photography, physical education, physics, physiology, religion, Russian, science, social studies, Spanish, speech, statistics, theater, trigonometry, writing.

Graduation Requirements Art history, athletics, English, foreign language, history, mathematics, music appreciation, religion (includes Bible studies and theology), science, senior project.

Special Academic Programs 30 Advanced Placement exams for which test preparation is offered; honors section; independent study; term-away projects; academic accommodation for the gifted, the musically talented, and the artistically talented.

College Admission Counseling 106 students graduated in 2012; all went to college, including Dickinson College; Princeton University; University of Maryland, Baltimore County; University of Maryland, College Park; University of Virginia; Yale University. Mean SAT critical reading: 638, mean SAT math: 660, mean SAT writing: 637.

Student Life Upper grades have specified standards of dress, student council, honor system. Discipline rests primarily with faculty.

Summer Programs Remediation, enrichment, advancement, sports, art/fine arts, rigorous outdoor training programs offered; session focuses on remediation and enrichment; held on campus; accepts boys and girls; open to students from other schools. 250 students usually enrolled. 2013 schedule: June 18 to July 18. Application deadline: June 18.

Tuition and Aid Day student tuition: $25,400. Tuition installment plan (Insured Tuition Payment Plan, FACTS Tuition Payment Plan, monthly payment plans). Need-based scholarship grants, need-based loans available. In 2012–13, 25% of upper-school students received aid. Total amount of financial aid awarded in 2012–13: $1,839,100.

Admissions Traditional secondary-level entrance grade is 9. For fall 2012, 140 students applied for upper-level admission, 52 were accepted, 40 enrolled. ISEE required. Deadline for receipt of application materials: December 21. Application fee required: $50. On-campus interview required.

Athletics Interscholastic: baseball, basketball, cross-country running, football, golf, ice hockey, indoor track, lacrosse, soccer, squash, swimming and diving, tennis, track and field, volleyball, water polo, winter (indoor) track, wrestling; intramural: basketball, bicycling, cross-country running, fitness, flag football, Frisbee, golf, physical fitness, rugby, table tennis, tennis, touch football, weight lifting. 3 PE instructors, 2 athletic trainers.

Computers Computers are regularly used in all academic, computer applications, design, digital applications classes. Computer network features include on-campus library services, Internet access, wireless campus network, Internet filtering or blocking technology. Campus intranet, student e-mail accounts, and computer access in desig-

nated common areas are available to students. Students grades are available online. The school has a published electronic and media policy.
Contact Danielle Moran, Admissions Assistant. 410-323-7169. Fax: 410-864-2825. E-mail: dmoran@gilman.edu. Web site: www.gilman.edu

GILMOUR ACADEMY

34001 Cedar Road
Gates Mills, Ohio 44040-9356

Head of School: Br. Robert E. Lavelle, CSC

General Information Coeducational boarding and day and distance learning college-preparatory, arts, religious studies, and technology school, affiliated with Roman Catholic Church. Boarding grades 7–12, day grades PK–12. Distance learning grades 9–12. Founded: 1946. Setting: suburban. Nearest major city is Cleveland. Students are housed in coed dormitories and boys' wing and girls' wing dormitory. 144-acre campus. 15 buildings on campus. Approved or accredited by Independent Schools Association of the Central States, Midwest Association of Boarding Schools, National Catholic Education Association, North Central Association of Colleges and Schools, The Association of Boarding Schools, and Ohio Department of Education. Member of National Association of Independent Schools and Secondary School Admission Test Board. Endowment: $30 million. Total enrollment: 689. Upper school average class size: 14. Upper school faculty-student ratio: 1:9. Upper School students typically attend 5 days per week. The average school day consists of 7 hours and 20 minutes.
Upper School Student Profile Grade 9: 103 students (54 boys, 49 girls); Grade 10: 102 students (54 boys, 48 girls); Grade 11: 116 students (66 boys, 50 girls); Grade 12: 110 students (57 boys, 53 girls); Postgraduate: 1 student (1 boy). 13% of students are boarding students. 88% are state residents. 16 states are represented in upper school student body. 8% are international students. International students from Canada, China, and Republic of Korea; 1 other country represented in student body. 75% of students are Roman Catholic.
Faculty School total: 77. In upper school: 43 men, 34 women; 57 have advanced degrees; 4 reside on campus.
Subjects Offered Advanced Placement courses, advanced studio art-AP, algebra, American government, American history, American literature, art, band, Bible, biology, biology-AP, British literature, broadcast journalism, calculus, calculus-AP, ceramics, chemistry, chemistry-AP, chorus, community service, computer programming, computer science, computer science-AP, creative writing, drama, drawing, economics, English, English literature, English-AP, ensembles, ethics, European history, European history-AP, fine arts, French, French language-AP, French-AP, geometry, geometry with art applications, government, government-AP, government/civics, health, history, history of rock and roll, independent study, jazz ensemble, journalism, Latin, Latin-AP, law, leadership, mathematics, mathematics-AP, model United Nations, modern European history-AP, music, musical productions, oil painting, painting, photography, physical education, physical fitness, physics, physics-AP, pre-algebra, pre-calculus, religion, religious studies, SAT/ACT preparation, science, social studies, Spanish, Spanish language-AP, speech, speech and debate, statistics-AP, student government, student publications, studio art, studio art-AP, swimming, theater, trigonometry, U.S. history, U.S. history-AP, weight training, work-study, world history, writing, writing workshop, yearbook.
Graduation Requirements Arts and fine arts (art, music, dance, drama), English, foreign language, mathematics, physical education (includes health), religion (includes Bible studies and theology), science, social studies (includes history), speech, senior project. Community service is required.
Special Academic Programs Advanced Placement exam preparation; accelerated programs; independent study; study at local college for college credit; academic accommodation for the gifted, the musically talented, and the artistically talented.
College Admission Counseling 114 students graduated in 2012; 110 went to college, including Boston College; Case Western Reserve University; John Carroll University; Loyola University Chicago; Miami University; University of Dayton. Other: 4 had other specific plans. Mean SAT critical reading: 566, mean SAT math: 574, mean SAT writing: 564, mean combined SAT: 1704, mean composite ACT: 24.
Student Life Upper grades have specified standards of dress, student council, honor system. Discipline rests equally with students and faculty. Attendance at religious services is required.
Summer Programs Enrichment, advancement, sports programs offered; session focuses on athletics and other opportunities available; held both on and off campus; held at some universities; accepts boys and girls; open to students from other schools. 100 students usually enrolled. 2013 schedule: June to July. Application deadline: none.
Tuition and Aid Day student tuition: $10,160–$23,180; 7-day tuition and room/board: $38,895. Tuition installment plan (monthly payment plans, Tuition Management Systems). Tuition reduction for siblings, merit scholarship grants, need-based scholarship grants, need-based loans, paying campus jobs, endowed scholarships with criteria specified by donors available. In 2012–13, 50% of upper-school students received aid; total upper-school merit-scholarship money awarded: $95,000. Total amount of financial aid awarded in 2012–13: $3,500,000.
Admissions Traditional secondary-level entrance grade is 9. For fall 2012, 240 students applied for upper-level admission, 205 were accepted, 99 enrolled. ACT, ACT-Explore, ISEE, PSAT, SAT, SSAT or TOEFL required. Deadline for receipt of application materials: none. Application fee required: $35. Interview required.
Athletics Interscholastic: baseball (boys), basketball (b,g), cross-country running (b,g), football (b), gymnastics (g), hockey (b,g), ice hockey (b,g), lacrosse (b,g), running (b,g), soccer (b,g), softball (g), swimming and diving (b,g), tennis (b,g), track and field (b,g), volleyball (g), winter soccer (b,g); intramural: cheering (g), indoor soccer (b,g); coed interscholastic: figure skating, golf, indoor track, indoor track & field, winter (indoor) track; coed intramural: aerobics, alpine skiing, aquatics, basketball, bowling, broomball, figure skating, fitness, golf, ice skating, indoor track, paddle tennis, physical fitness, physical training, skiing (downhill), snowboarding, soccer, strength & conditioning, swimming and diving, tennis, volleyball, weight training, winter (indoor) track, winter soccer. 9 coaches, 3 athletic trainers.
Computers Computers are regularly used in all academic classes. Computer network features include on-campus library services, online commercial services, Internet access, wireless campus network, Internet filtering or blocking technology. Campus intranet, student e-mail accounts, and computer access in designated common areas are available to students. Students grades are available online. The school has a published electronic and media policy.
Contact Mr. Steve M. Scheidt, Director of Middle and Upper School Admissions. 440-473-8050. Fax: 440-473-8010. E-mail: admissions@gilmour.org. Web site: www.gilmour.org

GIRLS PREPARATORY SCHOOL

205 Island Avenue
Chattanooga, Tennessee 37405

Head of School: Mr. Stanley R. Tucker Jr.

General Information Girls' day college-preparatory, arts, and technology school. Grades 6–12. Founded: 1906. Setting: suburban. Nearest major city is Atlanta, GA. 55-acre campus. 8 buildings on campus. Approved or accredited by Southern Association of Colleges and Schools and Southern Association of Independent Schools. Member of National Association of Independent Schools. Endowment: $25.3 million. Total enrollment: 590. Upper school average class size: 16. Upper school faculty-student ratio: 1:8. There are 180 required school days per year for Upper School students. Upper School students typically attend 5 days per week. The average school day consists of 7 hours.
Upper School Student Profile Grade 9: 87 students (87 girls); Grade 10: 73 students (73 girls); Grade 11: 96 students (96 girls); Grade 12: 89 students (89 girls).
Faculty School total: 73. In upper school: 10 men, 33 women; 29 have advanced degrees.
Subjects Offered Advanced Placement courses, algebra, American history, American literature, art, art history, Basic programming, Bible studies, biology, calculus, chemistry, Chinese, choral music, computer science, dance, drama, engineering, English, English literature, environmental science, European history, fine arts, forensics, French, geometry, government/civics, graphic design, history, Latin, mathematics, modern civilization, music, physics, pottery, pre-calculus, public speaking, religion, science, Spanish, statistics, trigonometry, world history.
Graduation Requirements Arts and fine arts (art, music, dance, drama), electives, English, foreign language, history, mathematics, physical education (includes health), religion (includes Bible studies and theology), science.
Special Academic Programs 21 Advanced Placement exams for which test preparation is offered; honors section; independent study.
College Admission Counseling 97 students graduated in 2012; 96 went to college, including Auburn University; Samford University; Sewanee: The University of the South; The University of Tennessee; The University of Tennessee at Chattanooga; University of Georgia. Other: 1 had other specific plans. Median SAT critical reading: 560, median SAT math: 580, median SAT writing: 580, median combined SAT: 1730, median composite ACT: 27. 34% scored over 600 on SAT critical reading, 46% scored over 600 on SAT math, 44% scored over 600 on SAT writing, 42% scored over 1800 on combined SAT, 61% scored over 26 on composite ACT.
Student Life Upper grades have uniform requirement, student council, honor system. Discipline rests primarily with faculty.
Summer Programs Remediation, enrichment, advancement, sports, art/fine arts, computer instruction programs offered; session focuses on summer fun and enrichment; held both on and off campus; held at Lupton Athletic fields and yacht club in Hixson, various locations throughout town, and Nantahala River Gorge; accepts boys and girls; open to students from other schools. 450 students usually enrolled. 2013 schedule: June 3 to July 19. Application deadline: June 1.
Tuition and Aid Day student tuition: $20,020. Tuition installment plan (Insured Tuition Payment Plan, FACTS Tuition Payment Plan, monthly payment plans, individually arranged payment plans, 60%/40% and 100% payment plans). Merit scholarship grants, need-based scholarship grants available. In 2012–13, 41% of upper-school students received aid; total upper-school merit-scholarship money awarded: $41,140. Total amount of financial aid awarded in 2012–13: $1,388,888.
Admissions Traditional secondary-level entrance grade is 9. For fall 2012, 57 students applied for upper-level admission, 34 were accepted, 22 enrolled. Admissions testing, mathematics proficiency exam, Otis-Lennon School Ability Test and Reading for Understanding required. Deadline for receipt of application materials: none. Application fee required: $75. Interview recommended.
Athletics Interscholastic: basketball, bowling, cheering, crew, cross-country running, diving, golf, lacrosse, rowing, soccer, softball, swimming and diving, tennis, track and

field, volleyball; intramural: backpacking, bicycling, canoeing/kayaking, climbing, dance, dance squad, fitness, fitness walking, Frisbee, hiking/backpacking, jogging, kayaking, life saving, modern dance, mountain biking, outdoor activities, outdoor education, outdoor skills, paddle tennis, physical fitness, rafting, rock climbing, running, self defense, strength & conditioning, ultimate Frisbee, walking, weight training, wilderness, yoga; coed interscholastic: cheering. 6 PE instructors, 24 coaches, 1 athletic trainer.

Computers Computers are regularly used in all academic classes. Computer network features include on-campus library services, online commercial services, Internet access, wireless campus network, Internet filtering or blocking technology, network printing, scanning. Campus intranet and student e-mail accounts are available to students. Students grades are available online. The school has a published electronic and media policy.

Contact Debbie Bohner Young, Director of Admissions. 423-634-7647. Fax: 423-634-7643. E-mail: dyoung@gps.edu. Web site: www.gps.edu

GLADES DAY SCHOOL

400 Gator Boulevard
Belle Glade, Florida 33430

Head of School: Dr. Robert Egley

General Information Coeducational day college-preparatory, general academic, vocational, and agriscience school. Grades PK–12. Founded: 1965. Setting: small town. Nearest major city is West Palm Beach. 21-acre campus. 4 buildings on campus. Approved or accredited by Florida Council of Independent Schools. Total enrollment: 339. Upper school average class size: 20. Upper school faculty-student ratio: 1:15. There are 180 required school days per year for Upper School students. Upper School students typically attend 5 days per week. The average school day consists of 6 hours and 35 minutes.

Upper School Student Profile Grade 9: 27 students (20 boys, 7 girls); Grade 10: 35 students (25 boys, 10 girls); Grade 11: 35 students (21 boys, 14 girls); Grade 12: 47 students (24 boys, 23 girls).

Faculty School total: 28. In upper school: 10 men, 9 women; 5 have advanced degrees.

Subjects Offered Agriculture, algebra, American government, American history, American literature, anatomy, ancient history, art, Bible studies, biology, calculus, calculus-AP, chemistry, computer applications, computer skills, computer technologies, earth science, economics, English, English language and composition-AP, English literature, English literature and composition-AP, European history, general math, geometry, government and politics-AP, grammar, health, health education, human geography - AP, journalism, keyboarding, literature and composition-AP, macro/microeconomics-AP, macroeconomics-AP, modern world history, music performance, physical education, pre-calculus, SAT/ACT preparation, Spanish, Spanish-AP, trigonometry, U.S. government and politics-AP, U.S. history, U.S. history-AP, weightlifting, world geography, world history, world history-AP, yearbook.

Graduation Requirements Algebra, American government, American literature, anatomy, ancient world history, arts and fine arts (art, music, dance, drama), biology, calculus, chemistry, computer applications, economics, English, English composition, English literature, geometry, health education, keyboarding, macroeconomics-AP, marine biology, modern world history, physical education (includes health), physical fitness, physical science, physics, pre-calculus, Spanish, U.S. history, world history.

Special Academic Programs 10 Advanced Placement exams for which test preparation is offered; honors section; independent study; study at local college for college credit; programs in general development for dyslexic students.

College Admission Counseling 40 students graduated in 2012; 37 went to college, including Florida Gulf Coast University; Florida State University; Palm Beach State College; Santa Fe College; University of Central Florida; University of Florida. Other: 3 went to work.

Student Life Upper grades have uniform requirement, student council, honor system. Discipline rests primarily with faculty.

Summer Programs Remediation programs offered; session focuses on remediation; held on campus; accepts boys and girls; not open to students from other schools. 7 students usually enrolled. 2013 schedule: June 7 to July 15. Application deadline: June 4.

Tuition and Aid Day student tuition: $6900–$7650. Tuition installment plan (FACTS Tuition Payment Plan, monthly payment plans, individually arranged payment plans). Tuition reduction for siblings, need-based scholarship grants available. In 2012–13, 10% of upper-school students received aid.

Admissions Traditional secondary-level entrance grade is 9. For fall 2012, 30 students applied for upper-level admission, 25 were accepted, 25 enrolled. Deadline for receipt of application materials: none. Application fee required: $400. On-campus interview required.

Athletics Interscholastic: baseball (boys), basketball (b,g), cheering (g), cross-country running (b,g), football (b), soccer (b,g), softball (g), track and field (b,g), volleyball (g); intramural: strength & conditioning (b,g), weight training (b,g). 3 PE instructors, 2 coaches.

Computers Computers are regularly used in English, journalism, science, Spanish, Web site design, word processing, yearbook classes. Computer network features include on-campus library services, Internet access, wireless campus network. Campus intranet and student e-mail accounts are available to students. Students grades are available online. The school has a published electronic and media policy.

Contact Mrs. Jamie Redish, High School Secretary. 561-996-6769 Ext. 10. Fax: 561-992-9274. E-mail: jredish@gladesdayschool.com. Web site: www.gladesdayschool.com

GLEN EDEN SCHOOL

Vancouver, British Columbia, Canada

See Special Needs Schools section.

GLENELG COUNTRY SCHOOL

12793 Folly Quarter Road
Ellicott City, Maryland 21042

Head of School: Mr. Gregory J. Ventre

General Information Coeducational day college-preparatory, arts, and technology school. Grades PK–12. Founded: 1954. Setting: suburban. Nearest major city is Baltimore. 87-acre campus. 1 building on campus. Approved or accredited by Association of Independent Maryland Schools, Middle States Association of Colleges and Schools, and Maryland Department of Education. Member of National Association of Independent Schools. Endowment: $900,000. Total enrollment: 768. Upper school average class size: 15. Upper school faculty-student ratio: 1:6. There are 175 required school days per year for Upper School students. Upper School students typically attend 5 days per week. The average school day consists of 7 hours.

Upper School Student Profile Grade 9: 61 students (31 boys, 30 girls); Grade 10: 70 students (35 boys, 35 girls); Grade 11: 69 students (39 boys, 30 girls); Grade 12: 81 students (41 boys, 40 girls).

Faculty School total: 131. In upper school: 26 men, 21 women; 37 have advanced degrees.

Subjects Offered Algebra, American history, American literature, art, art history, biology, biology-AP, calculus, calculus-AP, chemistry, chemistry-AP, Chinese, chorus, computer science, creative writing, drama, English, English literature, English-AP, European history, expository writing, French, French-AP, geometry, history, humanities, integrative seminar, Latin, Latin-AP, mathematics, photography, physical education, physical science, physics, physics-AP, pre-calculus, psychology, publications, science, social studies, Spanish, Spanish-AP, statistics, studio art, theater, trigonometry, world affairs.

Graduation Requirements Civics, English, foreign language, integrative seminar, mathematics, physical education (includes health), science, social studies (includes history), participation in Civic Leadership Program, 25 hours of community service per year.

Special Academic Programs 17 Advanced Placement exams for which test preparation is offered; honors section; independent study; academic accommodation for the gifted.

College Admission Counseling 66 students graduated in 2012; all went to college, including University of Maryland, College Park; University of South Carolina; Wake Forest University. Mean SAT critical reading: 600, mean SAT math: 620, mean SAT writing: 600, mean combined SAT: 1820. 51% scored over 600 on SAT critical reading, 53% scored over 600 on SAT math, 56% scored over 600 on SAT writing, 57% scored over 1800 on combined SAT.

Student Life Upper grades have uniform requirement, student council, honor system. Discipline rests equally with students and faculty.

Summer Programs Sports programs offered; session focuses on athletics and CIT (Counselor-In-Training) programs; held on campus; accepts boys and girls; open to students from other schools. 300 students usually enrolled. 2013 schedule: June 18 to July 27. Application deadline: May 31.

Tuition and Aid Day student tuition: $24,170. Tuition installment plan (monthly payment plans, individually arranged payment plans, 2-payment plan). Merit scholarship grants, need-based scholarship grants available. In 2012–13, 40% of upper-school students received aid; total upper-school merit-scholarship money awarded: $150,000. Total amount of financial aid awarded in 2012–13: $1,850,000.

Admissions Traditional secondary-level entrance grade is 9. For fall 2012, 74 students applied for upper-level admission, 55 were accepted, 31 enrolled. ISEE or SSAT required. Deadline for receipt of application materials: January 15. Application fee required: $75. On-campus interview required.

Athletics Interscholastic: baseball (boys), basketball (b,g), cross-country running (b,g), field hockey (g), golf (b,g), ice hockey (b), indoor soccer (g), indoor track (b,g), lacrosse (b,g), soccer (b,g), tennis (b,g), volleyball (g), winter soccer (g), wrestling (b); coed interscholastic: golf, ice hockey, strength & conditioning; coed intramural: aerobics, aerobics/dance, dance, fitness, flag football, Frisbee, physical fitness, physical training, skiing (downhill), strength & conditioning, ultimate Frisbee, weight training, yoga. 5 PE instructors, 12 coaches, 1 athletic trainer.

Computers Computers are regularly used in all academic classes. Computer network features include on-campus library services, Internet access, wireless campus network. Campus intranet, student e-mail accounts, and computer access in designated common areas are available to students. Students grades are available online. The school has a published electronic and media policy.

Contact Mrs. Karen K. Wootton, Director of Admission and Financial Aid. 410-531-7346 Ext. 2203. Fax: 410-531-7363. E-mail: wootton@glenelg.org. Web site: www.glenelg.org

THE GLENHOLME SCHOOL, DEVEREUX CONNECTICUT

Washington, Connecticut
See Special Needs Schools section.

GLENLYON NORFOLK SCHOOL

801 Bank Street
Victoria, British Columbia V8S 4A8, Canada

Head of School: Mr. Simon Bruce-Lockhart

General Information Coeducational day college-preparatory, arts, technology, and International Baccalaureate school. Grades JK–12. Founded: 1913. Setting: urban. 6-acre campus. 5 buildings on campus. Approved or accredited by International Baccalaureate Organization and British Columbia Department of Education. Affiliate member of National Association of Independent Schools. Language of instruction: English. Endowment: CAN$800,000. Total enrollment: 691. Upper school average class size: 18. Upper school faculty-student ratio: 1:10. There are 180 required school days per year for Upper School students. Upper School students typically attend 5 days per week. The average school day consists of 6 hours.

Upper School Student Profile Grade 9: 85 students (44 boys, 41 girls); Grade 10: 63 students (31 boys, 32 girls); Grade 11: 58 students (19 boys, 39 girls); Grade 12: 67 students (24 boys, 43 girls).

Faculty School total: 90. In upper school: 20 men, 21 women; 13 have advanced degrees.

Subjects Offered 20th century world history, art, band, biology, calculus, chemistry, choir, community service, comparative civilizations, concert band, creative writing, debate, directing, drama, English, English literature, European history, European literature, fine arts, French, geography, history, information technology, International Baccalaureate courses, jazz band, journalism, life skills, mathematics, music, newspaper, peer counseling, physical education, physics, public speaking, science, social studies, Spanish, stagecraft, theater arts, theory of knowledge, vocal jazz, world history, world literature, writing, yearbook.

Graduation Requirements Arts and fine arts (art, music, dance, drama), career planning, English, foreign language, information technology, mathematics, physical education (includes health), science, social studies (includes history). Community service is required.

Special Academic Programs International Baccalaureate program; honors section; term-away projects; ESL (10 students enrolled).

College Admission Counseling 58 students graduated in 2011; 52 went to college, including McGill University; The University of British Columbia; University of Calgary; University of Toronto; University of Victoria. Other: 6 went to work.

Student Life Upper grades have uniform requirement, student council, honor system. Discipline rests primarily with faculty.

Tuition and Aid Day student tuition: CAN$13,575–CAN$16,785. Guaranteed tuition plan. Tuition installment plan (monthly payment plans, individually arranged payment plans). Tuition reduction for siblings, bursaries, merit scholarship grants, tuition allowances for children of staff available. In 2011–12, 20% of upper-school students received aid; total upper-school merit-scholarship money awarded: CAN$23,050. Total amount of financial aid awarded in 2011–12: CAN$129,895.

Admissions Traditional secondary-level entrance grade is 9. SAT, SLEP, SSAT or writing sample required. Deadline for receipt of application materials: none. Application fee required: CAN$185. Interview recommended.

Athletics Interscholastic: backpacking (boys, girls), badminton (b,g), basketball (b,g), canoeing/kayaking (b,g), climbing (b,g), crew (b,g), cross-country running (b,g), field hockey (g), fitness (b,g), kayaking (b,g), rock climbing (b,g), rowing (b,g), rugby (b), soccer (b,g), squash (b,g), swimming and diving (b,g), tennis (b,g), track and field (b,g), volleyball (g); intramural: badminton (b,g), ball hockey (b), basketball (b,g), floor hockey (b), outdoor education (b,g), outdoor recreation (b,g), outdoor skills (b,g), swimming and diving (b,g), track and field (b,g), ultimate Frisbee (b,g); coed interscholastic: backpacking, badminton, canoeing/kayaking, crew, cross-country running, fitness, golf, kayaking, sailing, tennis; coed intramural: badminton, basketball, outdoor education, outdoor recreation, outdoor skills, swimming and diving, track and field, ultimate Frisbee. 4 PE instructors, 12 coaches.

Computers Computers are regularly used in all classes. Computer network features include on-campus library services, Internet access, wireless campus network, Internet filtering or blocking technology. Campus intranet and student e-mail accounts are available to students. The school has a published electronic and media policy.

Contact Ms. Andrea Hughes, Admissions Associate. 250-370-6801. Fax: 250-370-6811. E-mail: admissions@mygns.ca. Web site: www.glenlyonnorfolk.bc.ca

GONZAGA COLLEGE HIGH SCHOOL

19 Eye Street NW
Washington, District of Columbia 20001

Head of School: Rev. Vincent Conti, SJ

General Information Boys' day college-preparatory, arts, religious studies, and technology school, affiliated with Roman Catholic Church. Grades 9–12. Founded: 1821. Setting: urban. 1-acre campus. 9 buildings on campus. Approved or accredited by Association of Independent Schools of Greater Washington, Jesuit Secondary Education Association, Middle States Association of Colleges and Schools, and District of Columbia Department of Education. Member of National Association of Independent Schools. Endowment: $9.1 million. Total enrollment: 958. Upper school average class size: 26. Upper school faculty-student ratio: 1:15. There are 166 required school days per year for Upper School students. Upper School students typically attend 5 days per week. The average school day consists of 6 hours and 35 minutes.

Upper School Student Profile Grade 9: 242 students (242 boys); Grade 10: 236 students (236 boys); Grade 11: 245 students (245 boys); Grade 12: 235 students (235 boys). 85% of students are Roman Catholic.

Faculty School total: 66. In upper school: 50 men, 16 women; 60 have advanced degrees.

Subjects Offered Advanced Placement courses, African-American literature, algebra, American history, American literature, applied music, art, band, biology, broadcasting, calculus, calculus-AP, Catholic belief and practice, chemistry, chemistry-AP, Chinese, choir, choral music, Christian and Hebrew scripture, Christian ethics, Christian scripture, communications, community service, computer applications, computer math, computer programming, computer science, concert band, concert choir, creative writing, driver education, earth science, economics, economics-AP, English, English literature, English literature and composition-AP, English literature-AP, English-AP, environmental science-AP, ethics, ethics and responsibility, European history, European history-AP, expository writing, film appreciation, film studies, fine arts, French, French-AP, functions, geometry, government, government/civics, grammar, Greek, health, health education, history, honors algebra, honors English, honors geometry, human geography - AP, independent study, Irish literature, jazz ensemble, Latin, Latin-AP, mathematics, media communications, music, musicianship, philosophy, photography, physical education, physics, physics-AP, piano, poetry, political science, political systems, psychology, psychology-AP, religion, Russian history, Russian studies, science, social justice, social sciences, social studies, Spanish, Spanish-AP, statistics, statistics-AP, studio art-AP, symphonic band, theology, trigonometry, U.S. government and politics-AP, Web site design, world history, world literature.

Graduation Requirements Arts and fine arts (art, music, dance, drama), English, ethics, foreign language, mathematics, physical education (includes health), religion (includes Bible studies and theology), science, social justice, social sciences, social studies (includes history). Community service is required.

Special Academic Programs Advanced Placement exam preparation; honors section.

College Admission Counseling 235 students graduated in 2012; all went to college, including Boston College; Georgetown University; James Madison University; University of Maryland, College Park; University of Virginia; Virginia Polytechnic Institute and State University.

Student Life Upper grades have specified standards of dress, student council, honor system. Discipline rests primarily with faculty. Attendance at religious services is required.

Summer Programs Remediation, enrichment programs offered; session focuses on new student remediation, enrichment, and SAT preparation; held on campus; accepts boys and girls; open to students from other schools. 200 students usually enrolled. 2013 schedule: June 25 to July 20. Application deadline: June 1.

Tuition and Aid Day student tuition: $18,550. Tuition installment plan (Insured Tuition Payment Plan, monthly payment plans). Merit scholarship grants, need-based scholarship grants available. In 2012–13, 33% of upper-school students received aid; total upper-school merit-scholarship money awarded: $100,000. Total amount of financial aid awarded in 2012–13: $2,210,000.

Admissions Traditional secondary-level entrance grade is 9. For fall 2012, 700 students applied for upper-level admission, 300 were accepted, 242 enrolled. High School Placement Test (closed version) from Scholastic Testing Service required. Deadline for receipt of application materials: December 10. Application fee required: $35.

Athletics Interscholastic: baseball, basketball, crew, cross-country running, diving, football, golf, ice hockey, indoor track & field, lacrosse, rugby, soccer, squash, swimming and diving, tennis, track and field, water polo, winter (indoor) track, wrestling; intramural: basketball, bowling, fencing, fishing, football, Frisbee, hiking/backpacking, martial arts, physical training, skiing (downhill), softball, strength & conditioning, table tennis, volleyball, weight lifting, whiffle ball. 2 PE instructors, 30 coaches, 3 athletic trainers.

Computers Computer network features include on-campus library services, Internet access. Student e-mail accounts are available to students. Students grades are available online.

Contact Mr. Andrew C. Battaile, Director of Admission. 202-336-7101. Fax: 202-454-1188. E-mail: abattaile@gonzaga.org. Web site: www.gonzaga.org

GONZAGA PREPARATORY SCHOOL

1224 East Euclid Avenue

Spokane, Washington 99207-2899

Head of School: Rev. Fr. Kevin Gerard Connell, SJ

General Information Coeducational day college-preparatory, general academic, and religious studies school, affiliated with Roman Catholic Church (Jesuit order). Grades 9–12. Founded: 1887. Setting: urban. 20-acre campus. 4 buildings on campus. Approved or accredited by Northwest Accreditation Commission and Washington Department of Education. Endowment: $10 million. Total enrollment: 902. Upper school average class size: 19. Upper school faculty-student ratio: 1:14. There are 180 required school days per year for Upper School students. Upper School students typically attend 5 days per week. The average school day consists of 6 hours and 30 minutes.

Upper School Student Profile Grade 9: 222 students (116 boys, 106 girls); Grade 10: 216 students (104 boys, 112 girls); Grade 11: 223 students (121 boys, 102 girls); Grade 12: 241 students (119 boys, 122 girls). 70% of students are Roman Catholic Church (Jesuit order).

Faculty School total: 66. In upper school: 43 men, 23 women; 55 have advanced degrees.

Subjects Offered Algebra, American history, American literature, art, Bible studies, biology, calculus, ceramics, chemistry, computer programming, computer science, drama, earth science, English, English literature, environmental science, European history, fine arts, French, geography, geometry, government/civics, grammar, Greek, health, history, home economics, journalism, keyboarding, Latin, mathematics, music, philosophy, photography, physical education, physics, psychology, religion, science, single survival, social studies, Spanish, theater, theology, trigonometry, world history, world literature, writing, zoology.

Graduation Requirements Arts and fine arts (art, music, dance, drama), English, foreign language, mathematics, occupational education, physical education (includes health), religion (includes Bible studies and theology), science, social studies (includes history). Community service is required.

Special Academic Programs 13 Advanced Placement exams for which test preparation is offered; honors section; independent study; study at local college for college credit; academic accommodation for the gifted; remedial reading and/or remedial writing; remedial math; programs in English for dyslexic students; special instructional classes for deaf students, blind students; ESL (11 students enrolled).

College Admission Counseling 217 students graduated in 2011; 215 went to college, including Gonzaga University; Seattle University; University of Portland; University of Washington; Washington State University; Western Washington University. Other: 1 went to work, 1 entered military service. Median SAT critical reading: 552, median SAT math: 544, median SAT writing: 526, median composite ACT: 24. 32% scored over 600 on SAT critical reading, 29% scored over 600 on SAT math, 24% scored over 600 on SAT writing.

Student Life Upper grades have specified standards of dress, student council. Discipline rests primarily with faculty. Attendance at religious services is required.

Tuition and Aid Day student tuition: $9800. Tuition installment plan (monthly payment plans, individually arranged payment plans). Tuition reduction for siblings, merit scholarship grants, need-based scholarship grants, Fair Share Tuition Program available. In 2011–12, 60% of upper-school students received aid; total upper-school merit-scholarship money awarded: $5000. Total amount of financial aid awarded in 2011–12: $2,000,000.

Admissions Traditional secondary-level entrance grade is 9. Explore required. Deadline for receipt of application materials: December 3. Application fee required: $25.

Athletics Interscholastic: baseball (boys), basketball (b,g), cheering (g), cross-country running (b,g), dance team (g), football (b), golf (b,g), ice hockey (b), lacrosse (b,g), soccer (b,g), softball (g), tennis (b,g), track and field (b,g), volleyball (g), wrestling (b); intramural: lacrosse (b,g); coed interscholastic: aerobics/dance, dance, strength & conditioning; coed intramural: aerobics/dance, bowling, dance, dance squad, dance team, rock climbing, tennis, wall climbing, weight lifting, yoga. 2 PE instructors, 44 coaches, 1 athletic trainer.

Computers Computers are regularly used in Christian doctrine, computer applications, English, ethics, foreign language, French, health, history, Latin, mathematics, occupational education, photography, psychology, religious studies, remedial study skills, research skills, SAT preparation, science, social sciences, Spanish, speech, study skills, theater, theology, writing, yearbook classes. Computer network features include on-campus library services, online commercial services, Internet access, wireless campus network, Internet filtering or blocking technology. Computer access in designated common areas is available to students. Students grades are available online. The school has a published electronic and media policy.

Contact Mr. Derek Duchesne, Academic Vice Principal. 509-483-8511 Ext. 414. Fax: 509-483-3124. E-mail: dduchesne@gprep.com. Web site: www.gprep.com

GOULD ACADEMY

PO Box 860

39 Church Street

Bethel, Maine 04217

Head of School: Matthew C. Ruby

General Information Coeducational boarding and day college-preparatory, arts, and technology school. Grades 9–PG. Founded: 1836. Setting: small town. Nearest major city is Portland. Students are housed in single-sex dormitories. 456-acre campus. 30 buildings on campus. Approved or accredited by Association of Independent Schools in New England, Independent Schools of Northern New England, New England Association of Schools and Colleges, The Association of Boarding Schools, and Maine Department of Education. Member of National Association of Independent Schools and Secondary School Admission Test Board. Endowment: $9.5 million. Total enrollment: 232. Upper school average class size: 12. Upper school faculty-student ratio: 1:6. There are 175 required school days per year for Upper School students. Upper School students typically attend 5 days per week.

Upper School Student Profile Grade 9: 44 students (22 boys, 22 girls); Grade 10: 50 students (31 boys, 19 girls); Grade 11: 57 students (37 boys, 20 girls); Grade 12: 78 students (51 boys, 27 girls); Grade 13: 3 students (2 boys, 1 girl); Postgraduate: 4 students (4 boys). 71% of students are boarding students. 42% are state residents. 22 states are represented in upper school student body. 20% are international students. International students from China, Germany, Japan, Republic of Korea, Spain, and Taiwan; 2 other countries represented in student body.

Faculty School total: 44. In upper school: 23 men, 21 women; 25 have advanced degrees; 32 reside on campus.

Subjects Offered Acting, Advanced Placement courses, African-American literature, algebra, American foreign policy, American history, American literature, American literature-AP, analytic geometry, art, art history, athletic training, band, bioethics, DNA and culture, biology, biology-AP, British literature, British literature (honors), British literature-AP, calculus, calculus-AP, celestial navigation, ceramics, chemistry, chemistry-AP, chorus, Civil War, clayworking, college placement, computer information systems, computer music, computer programming, computer science, computers, conceptual physics, creative writing, debate, design, digital music, drama, drawing, earth science, Eastern religion and philosophy, ecology, economics, electives, electronic music, electronics, English, environmental science, environmental science-AP, ESL, European history, expository writing, foreign policy, French, geography, geometry, government and politics-AP, history, history-AP, honors algebra, honors English, honors world history, introduction to digital multitrack recording techniques, jazz band, jewelry making, Latin, learning strategies, literature by women, mathematics, music, music appreciation, music theory, musicianship, navigation, painting, philosophy, photography, physics, pottery, pre-calculus, printmaking, robotics, science, sculpture, Shakespeare, social studies, software design, Spanish, theater, U.S. government and politics-AP, video film production, women's literature, world history, writing.

Graduation Requirements English, foreign language, mathematics, physical education (includes health), science, social studies (includes history).

Special Academic Programs Advanced Placement exam preparation; honors section; independent study; academic accommodation for the gifted, the musically talented, and the artistically talented; ESL (25 students enrolled).

College Admission Counseling 61 students graduated in 2012; all went to college, including Bentley University; Lewis & Clark College; Rochester Institute of Technology; Saint Michael's College; University of Illinois at Urbana–Champaign; University of Vermont.

Student Life Upper grades have specified standards of dress, student council, honor system. Discipline rests equally with students and faculty.

Tuition and Aid Day student tuition: $29,250; 7-day tuition and room/board: $49,600. Tuition installment plan (individually arranged payment plans, full payment by August 15, 2/3 payment by August 12, 1/3 by December 1). Need-based scholarship grants, need-based loans available. In 2012–13, 38% of upper-school students received aid. Total amount of financial aid awarded in 2012–13: $1,355,000.

Admissions Traditional secondary-level entrance grade is 9. For fall 2012, 216 students applied for upper-level admission, 184 were accepted, 90 enrolled. SSAT required. Deadline for receipt of application materials: February 1. Application fee required: $50. Interview required.

Athletics Interscholastic: alpine skiing (boys, girls), baseball (b), basketball (b,g), bicycling (b,g), cross-country running (b,g), field hockey (g), freestyle skiing (b,g); coed interscholastic: climbing, dance, dressage, equestrian sports, golf; coed intramural: golf. 11 coaches, 1 athletic trainer.

Computers Computers are regularly used in English, foreign language, history, mathematics, music, science, technology classes. Computer network features include on-campus library services, Internet access, wireless campus network. Student e-mail accounts are available to students. Students grades are available online. The school has a published electronic and media policy.

Contact Todd Ormiston, Director of Admission. 207-824-7777. Fax: 207-824-2926. E-mail: todd.ormiston@gouldacademy.org. Web site: www.gouldacademy.org

THE GOVERNOR FRENCH ACADEMY

219 West Main Street
Belleville, Illinois 62220-1537

Head of School: Mr. Phillip E. Paeltz

General Information Coeducational boarding and day college-preparatory and bilingual studies school. Boarding grades 9–12, day grades K–12. Founded: 1983. Setting: urban. Nearest major city is St. Louis, MO. Students are housed in homes of local families. 3 buildings on campus. Approved or accredited by CITA (Commission on International and Trans-Regional Accreditation), North Central Association of Colleges and Schools, and Illinois Department of Education. Endowment: $100,000. Total enrollment: 164. Upper school average class size: 15. Upper school faculty-student ratio: 1:6. There are 176 required school days per year for Upper School students. Upper School students typically attend 5 days per week. The average school day consists of 7 hours and 15 minutes.

Upper School Student Profile Grade 9: 8 students (3 boys, 5 girls); Grade 10: 12 students (7 boys, 5 girls); Grade 11: 12 students (7 boys, 5 girls); Grade 12: 12 students (4 boys, 8 girls). 1% of students are boarding students. 95% are state residents. 1 state is represented in upper school student body. 1% are international students. International students from China, Republic of Korea, and Taiwan.

Faculty School total: 14. In upper school: 3 men, 3 women; 3 have advanced degrees.

Subjects Offered Algebra, American history, American literature, biology, calculus, chemistry, creative writing, earth science, ecology, economics, English, English literature, environmental science, European history, expository writing, geography, geometry, government/civics, grammar, history, mathematics, physical education, physics, science, social sciences, social studies, theater arts, trigonometry, world history, world literature.

Graduation Requirements English, foreign language, mathematics, physical education (includes health), science, social sciences, vote of faculty.

Special Academic Programs 6 Advanced Placement exams for which test preparation is offered; accelerated programs; independent study; academic accommodation for the gifted and the artistically talented; programs in English for dyslexic students; ESL (2 students enrolled).

College Admission Counseling 8 students graduated in 2012; all went to college, including Saint Louis University; Southern Illinois University Edwardsville; The University of Tampa; Trinity College; University of Illinois at Urbana–Champaign. Median composite ACT: 25. 41.7% scored over 26 on composite ACT.

Student Life Upper grades have uniform requirement, honor system. Discipline rests primarily with faculty.

Summer Programs Remediation, enrichment, advancement programs offered; session focuses on academics; held on campus; accepts boys and girls; open to students from other schools. 30 students usually enrolled. 2013 schedule: June 17 to July 26. Application deadline: none.

Tuition and Aid Day student tuition: $5950; 7-day tuition and room/board: $22,200. Tuition installment plan (monthly payment plans). Tuition reduction for siblings available.

Admissions Traditional secondary-level entrance grade is 9. For fall 2012, 10 students applied for upper-level admission, 9 were accepted, 4 enrolled. School placement exam required. Deadline for receipt of application materials: none. No application fee required. Interview required.

Athletics Interscholastic: martial arts (boys, girls), volleyball (b,g); intramural: basketball (b), martial arts (b,g); coed interscholastic: basketball, soccer; coed intramural: independent competitive sports, softball.

Computers Computers are regularly used in computer applications, science, yearbook classes. Computer network features include Internet access, wireless campus network, Internet filtering or blocking technology. Computer access in designated common areas is available to students. The school has a published electronic and media policy.

Contact Ms. Carol S. Wilson, Director of Admissions. 618-233-7542. Fax: 618-233-0541. E-mail: admiss@governorfrench.com. Web site: www.governorfrench.com

GRACE BAPTIST ACADEMY

7815 Shallowford Road
Chattanooga, Tennessee 37421

Head of School: Dr. William Summers

General Information Coeducational day college-preparatory and religious studies school, affiliated with Baptist Church. Grades K4–12. Founded: 1985. Setting: suburban. 2 buildings on campus. Approved or accredited by Association of Christian Schools International, Southern Association of Colleges and Schools, and Tennessee Department of Education. Total enrollment: 572. Upper school average class size: 18. Upper school faculty-student ratio: 1:12. Upper School students typically attend 5 days per week. The average school day consists of 7 hours.

Upper School Student Profile Grade 9: 41 students (23 boys, 18 girls); Grade 10: 45 students (18 boys, 27 girls); Grade 11: 49 students (20 boys, 29 girls); Grade 12: 38 students (17 boys, 21 girls). 75% of students are Baptist.

Faculty School total: 47. In upper school: 14 men, 11 women; 5 have advanced degrees.

Subjects Offered Algebra, American government, American history, American literature, ancient world history, art, band, Bible, Bible studies, biology, biology-AP, calculus, chemistry, choir, Christian doctrine, Christian ethics, Christian testament, computer applications, drama performance, dramatic arts, economics, English, English composition, English literature, environmental studies, fitness, general math, general science, geometry, global studies, health, health and safety, honors English, honors world history, keyboarding, language arts, Life of Christ, mathematics, music, New Testament, physical education, physics, pre-algebra, pre-calculus, SAT/ACT preparation, Spanish, speech, state history, study skills, U.S. government and politics, U.S. history, weight training, weightlifting, world geography, yearbook.

Graduation Requirements Algebra, Bible, biology, chemistry, economics, English, English literature, geometry, global studies, physical education (includes health), senior project, Spanish, speech, trigonometry, U.S. government, U.S. history, visual and performing arts, world geography.

Special Academic Programs 2 Advanced Placement exams for which test preparation is offered; honors section; study at local college for college credit.

College Admission Counseling 46 students graduated in 2012; 44 went to college, including Chattanooga State Community College; Tennessee Technological University; The University of Tennessee; The University of Tennessee at Chattanooga. Other: 2 entered military service. Mean composite ACT: 23.

Student Life Upper grades have uniform requirement, student council, honor system. Discipline rests primarily with faculty. Attendance at religious services is required.

Summer Programs Remediation programs offered; session focuses on credit recovery; held on campus; accepts boys and girls; open to students from other schools. 45 students usually enrolled. 2013 schedule: June 17 to July 19. Application deadline: June 5.

Tuition and Aid Tuition installment plan (FACTS Tuition Payment Plan, monthly payment plans, individually arranged payment plans, bank draft). Tuition reduction for siblings, need-based scholarship grants available. In 2012–13, 5% of upper-school students received aid.

Admissions Traditional secondary-level entrance grade is 9. For fall 2012, 26 students applied for upper-level admission, 25 were accepted, 25 enrolled. Latest standardized score from previous school required. Deadline for receipt of application materials: none. Application fee required: $300. On-campus interview required.

Athletics Interscholastic: baseball (boys), basketball (b,g), cheering (g), cross-country running (b,g), football (b), soccer (b,g), softball (g), tennis (b,g), track and field (b,g), volleyball (g), weight training (b,g); intramural: physical training (b,g), strength & conditioning (b,g), weight lifting (b), weight training (b); coed interscholastic: archery, golf. 2 PE instructors, 5 coaches, 1 athletic trainer.

Computers Computers are regularly used in career education, career exploration, college planning, computer applications, keyboarding, mathematics, senior seminar, yearbook classes. Computer network features include on-campus library services, Internet access, Internet filtering or blocking technology. Student e-mail accounts and computer access in designated common areas are available to students. Students grades are available online.

Contact Mrs. Kristi Dolan, Admissions Director. 423-892-8222 Ext. 115. Fax: 423-892-1194. E-mail: kdolan@mygracechatt.org. Web site: www.gracechatt.org

GRACE BRETHREN SCHOOL

1350 Cherry Avenue
Simi Valley, California 93065

Head of School: Mr. John Hynes

General Information Coeducational day college-preparatory, arts, vocational, religious studies, and bilingual studies school, affiliated with Brethren Church, Christian faith. Grades PS–12. Founded: 1979. Setting: suburban. Nearest major city is Los Angeles. 12-acre campus. 9 buildings on campus. Approved or accredited by Association of Christian Schools International, Western Association of Schools and Colleges, and California Department of Education. Total enrollment: 840. Upper school average class size: 20. Upper school faculty-student ratio: 1:11.

Upper School Student Profile 90% of students are Brethren, Christian.

Faculty School total: 36. In upper school: 18 men, 18 women; 15 have advanced degrees.

Subjects Offered Accounting, Advanced Placement courses, algebra, American literature, American literature-AP, anatomy and physiology, ancient world history, art, ASB Leadership, athletic training, band, baseball, basketball, Bible, Bible studies, biology, British literature, British literature-AP, career/college preparation, cheerleading, chemistry, choir, college counseling, computer graphics, computer music, computer tools, concert choir, critical thinking, critical writing, digital photography, drama, drama performance, environmental science, film studies, forensics, geometry, government and politics-AP, health, home economics, jazz ensemble, New Testament, photography, physical education, physics, physics-AP, pre-algebra, pre-calculus, set design, softball, Spanish, Spanish language-AP, speech, stage design, statistics, statistics-AP, technical theater, U.S. government and politics, U.S. government and politics-AP, U.S. history, U.S. history-AP, visual and performing arts, volleyball, world cultures, world geography, world history, yearbook.

Graduation Requirements Bible studies, electives, English, foreign language, mathematics, physical education (includes health), science, social studies (includes history), visual and performing arts.

Special Academic Programs Advanced Placement exam preparation; honors section; independent study; study at local college for college credit; remedial math.

College Admission Counseling 55 students graduated in 2012; 53 went to college, including California State University, Northridge; Moorpark College; The Master's College and Seminary; University of California, Los Angeles; Westmont College. Other: 2 entered a postgraduate year. Median combined SAT: 1480. 15% scored over 1800 on combined SAT.

Student Life Upper grades have uniform requirement, student council, honor system. Discipline rests primarily with faculty. Attendance at religious services is required.

Summer Programs Remediation, advancement programs offered; session focuses on remediation; held on campus; accepts boys and girls; open to students from other schools. 45 students usually enrolled.

Tuition and Aid Day student tuition: $8376. Guaranteed tuition plan. Tuition installment plan (monthly payment plans). Tuition reduction for siblings, need-based scholarship grants available. In 2012–13, 5% of upper-school students received aid.

Admissions Traditional secondary-level entrance grade is 9. For fall 2012, 71 students applied for upper-level admission, 68 were accepted, 64 enrolled. Math Placement Exam, Stanford Achievement Test and writing sample required. Deadline for receipt of application materials: none. Application fee required: $385. On-campus interview required.

Athletics Interscholastic: aquatics (boys, girls), baseball (b), basketball (b,g), cheering (g), cross-country running (b,g), equestrian sports (b,g), flag football (b), football (b), golf (b,g), physical training (b,g), soccer (b,g), softball (g), strength & conditioning (b,g), swimming and diving (b,g), track and field (b,g), volleyball (g), weight training (b). 4 PE instructors, 16 coaches, 1 athletic trainer.

Computers Computers are regularly used in art, graphic arts, library, newspaper, photography, photojournalism, science, study skills, video film production, writing, yearbook classes. Computer network features include on-campus library services, Internet access, wireless campus network, Internet filtering or blocking technology. Computer access in designated common areas is available to students. Students grades are available online. The school has a published electronic and media policy.

Contact Mrs. Sheri Herr, Registrar. 805-522-4667 Ext. 2033. Fax: 805-522-5617. E-mail: sherr@gracebrethren.com. Web site: www.gracebrethrenschools.com

GRACE CHRISTIAN SCHOOL

12407 Pintail Street
Anchorage, Alaska 99516

Head of School: Mr. Nathan Davis

General Information Coeducational day college-preparatory, arts, religious studies, and technology school, affiliated with Christian faith. Grades K–12. Founded: 1980. Setting: urban. 7-acre campus. 1 building on campus. Approved or accredited by American Association of Christian Schools, Association of Christian Schools International, and Northwest Accreditation Commission. Total enrollment: 617. Upper school average class size: 17. Upper school faculty-student ratio: 1:15. There are 180 required school days per year for Upper School students. Upper School students typically attend 5 days per week. The average school day consists of 6 hours and 50 minutes.

Upper School Student Profile Grade 7: 57 students (28 boys, 29 girls); Grade 8: 51 students (23 boys, 28 girls); Grade 9: 48 students (26 boys, 22 girls); Grade 10: 58 students (25 boys, 33 girls); Grade 11: 56 students (30 boys, 26 girls); Grade 12: 50 students (25 boys, 25 girls). 99% of students are Christian faith.

Faculty School total: 45. In upper school: 13 men, 15 women; 14 have advanced degrees.

Subjects Offered Algebra, American government, American history, art, Bible, biology, biology-AP, calculus-AP, chemistry, chemistry-AP, choir, computer skills, computer technologies, drama, economics, English, English language and composition-AP, English literature and composition-AP, English literature-AP, English/composition-AP, film, fine arts, geometry, health, leadership and service, literature, media, music theory-AP, physical education, physical science, physics, psychology, publications, science, social studies, Spanish, speech, trigonometry, U.S. history, weightlifting, world history, yearbook.

Graduation Requirements Algebra, American government, American literature, biology, British literature, consumer economics, electives, English composition, English literature, geometry, literary genres, literature, physical education (includes health), physical science, practical arts, U.S. history, world history, one year of Bible for every year attending, Old Testament survey in 9th grade, 10th Grade—New Testament survey, 11th Grade—Life and Times of Christ/Marriage and Family, 12th grade—Defending Your Faith/Understanding the Times.

Special Academic Programs Advanced Placement exam preparation.

College Admission Counseling 50 students graduated in 2012; 45 went to college, including Corban University; George Fox University; The Master's College and Seminary; University of Alaska Anchorage; University of Alaska Fairbanks. Other: 5 went to work. Mean SAT critical reading: 577, mean SAT math: 536, mean SAT writing: 544, mean combined SAT: 1657, mean composite ACT: 23.

Student Life Upper grades have specified standards of dress, student council, honor system. Discipline rests primarily with faculty. Attendance at religious services is required.

Summer Programs Enrichment programs offered; session focuses on science/forensics; held on campus; accepts boys and girls; open to students from other schools. 30 students usually enrolled. 2013 schedule: June 10 to June 14.

Tuition and Aid Day student tuition: $7750. Tuition installment plan (monthly payment plans, individually arranged payment plans). Tuition reduction for siblings, need-based scholarship grants available. In 2012–13, 15% of upper-school students received aid. Total amount of financial aid awarded in 2012–13: $200,000.

Admissions Traditional secondary-level entrance grade is 9. For fall 2012, 36 students applied for upper-level admission, 34 were accepted, 34 enrolled. Math and English placement tests, school's own exam or Stanford Achievement Test required. Deadline for receipt of application materials: none. Application fee required: $50. Interview required.

Athletics Interscholastic: basketball (boys, girls), cheering (g), cross-country running (b,g), skiing (cross-country) (b,g), soccer (b,g), track and field (b,g), volleyball (g), wrestling (b). 2 PE instructors, 15 coaches.

Computers Computers are regularly used in career exploration, computer applications, media, publications, technology, video film production, yearbook classes. Computer network features include on-campus library services, online commercial services, Internet access, wireless campus network, Internet filtering or blocking technology. Students grades are available online.

Contact Carrie Schliesing, Admissions. 907-345-4814. Fax: 907-644-2260. E-mail: admissions@gracechristianalaska.org. Web site: www.gracechristianalaska.org

THE GRAUER SCHOOL

1500 South El Camino Real
Encinitas, California 92024

Head of School: Dr. Stuart Robert Grauer

General Information Coeducational day college-preparatory, arts, technology, and all students graduate with Distinction in a subject school. Grades 6–12. Founded: 1991. Setting: suburban. Nearest major city is San Diego. 5-acre campus. 6 buildings on campus. Approved or accredited by California Association of Independent Schools, Western Association of Schools and Colleges, and California Department of Education. Endowment: $150,000. Total enrollment: 160. Upper school average class size: 12. Upper school faculty-student ratio: 1:6. There are 178 required school days per year for Upper School students. Upper School students typically attend 5 days per week. The average school day consists of 6 hours and 30 minutes.

Upper School Student Profile Grade 9: 24 students (15 boys, 9 girls); Grade 10: 24 students (15 boys, 9 girls); Grade 11: 18 students (10 boys, 8 girls); Grade 12: 22 students (10 boys, 12 girls).

Faculty School total: 30. In upper school: 11 men, 15 women; 22 have advanced degrees.

Subjects Offered ACT preparation, advanced biology, advanced chemistry, advanced math, advanced TOEFL/grammar, algebra, alternative physical education, American government, American history, anatomy and physiology, ancient history, applied music, art, art appreciation, art history, art history-AP, ASB Leadership, athletic training, audio visual/media, backpacking, baseball, basketball, bell choir, biology, business mathematics, calculus, character education, chemistry, Chinese, choir, civics, classical music, college admission preparation, college planning, community service, computer applications, computer education, computer multimedia, computers, creative writing, culinary arts, drama, dramatic arts, earth and space science, economics, English literature, environmental education, ESL, ESL, experiential education, fencing, film studies, filmmaking, fitness, French, gardening, geography, geometry, global studies, health, high adventure outdoor program, honors algebra, honors English, honors geometry, honors U.S. history, honors world history, Japanese, keyboarding, Latin, leadership and service, marine science, multimedia, music, music appreciation, music performance, outdoor education, peace studies, personal fitness, photo shop, photography, physical education, physics, pre-algebra, pre-calculus, religion, religion and culture, robotics, SAT preparation, Spanish, speech and debate, studio art, study skills, surfing, tennis, theater arts, trigonometry, U.S. government, U.S. history, U.S. literature, world geography, world history, world religions.

Graduation Requirements Algebra, American history, art, biology, chemistry, college admission preparation, computer applications, computer skills, economics, English, experiential education, foreign language, French, geometry, life science, marine science, mathematics, non-Western literature, outdoor education, physical education (includes health), physical science, physics, science, senior project, social studies (includes history), studio art, U.S. government, U.S. history, U.S. literature, Western civilization, Western literature, wilderness education, world geography, world history, world literature, world religions, expeditionary learning in the field and 50 hours community service, all students graduate with distinction in a subject of their choice.

Special Academic Programs Advanced Placement exam preparation; honors section; independent study; study abroad; academic accommodation for the gifted, the musically talented, and the artistically talented; remedial math; special instructional classes for deaf students; ESL (7 students enrolled).

College Admission Counseling 20 students graduated in 2012; all went to college, including Loyola University New Orleans; Sarah Lawrence College; University of California, Berkeley; University of San Francisco; University of Southern California; Vassar College. 60% scored over 600 on SAT critical reading, 60% scored over 600 on SAT math, 60% scored over 600 on SAT writing.

Student Life Upper grades have specified standards of dress, student council, honor system. Discipline rests equally with students and faculty.

Summer Programs Remediation, enrichment, advancement, ESL, sports, art/fine arts, rigorous outdoor training, computer instruction programs offered; session focuses on academics and enrichment; held on campus; accepts boys and girls; open to students from other schools. 60 students usually enrolled. 2013 schedule: June 24 to August 2. Application deadline: June 1.

Tuition and Aid Day student tuition: $20,000. Tuition installment plan (individually arranged payment plans, 3 payment plans). Tuition reduction for siblings, need-based scholarship grants available. In 2012–13, 10% of upper-school students received aid. Total amount of financial aid awarded in 2012–13: $70,000.

Admissions Traditional secondary-level entrance grade is 9. For fall 2012, 35 students applied for upper-level admission, 23 were accepted, 19 enrolled. Admissions testing, any standardized test and writing sample required. Deadline for receipt of application materials: March 1. Application fee required: $100. Interview required.

Athletics Interscholastic: tennis (boys, girls); intramural: baseball (b), basketball (b,g), football (b), soccer (b,g), triathlon (b,g), volleyball (b,g); coed interscholastic: aerobics/dance, archery, badminton, baseball, basketball, billiards, canoeing/kayaking, climbing, combined training, cooperative games, cross-country running, dance, fitness, fitness walking, flag football, Frisbee, hiking/backpacking, jogging, jump rope, kayaking, kickball, martial arts, outdoor activities, outdoor adventure, outdoor education, outdoor recreation, outdoor skills, outdoors, physical fitness, physical training, rafting, rock climbing, roller skating, running, self defense, soccer, softball, strength & conditioning, surfing, table tennis, tennis, track and field, ultimate Frisbee, volleyball, walking, weight training, yoga; coed intramural: cross-country running, dressage, equestrian sports, flag football, golf, independent competitive sports, running, sailing, soccer, surfing, tennis, track and field, triathlon. 5 PE instructors, 5 coaches.

Computers Computers are regularly used in English, ESL, foreign language, graphic arts, journalism, keyboarding, multimedia, photography, programming, SAT preparation, video film production, yearbook classes. Computer network features include Internet access, wireless campus network, Internet filtering or blocking technology, online text books, online portfolios, all students required to have computers. "Loaner" computers are available. Campus intranet, student e-mail accounts, and computer access in designated common areas are available to students. Students grades are available online. The school has a published electronic and media policy.

Contact Mrs. Elizabeth Braymen, JD, Admissions Director. 760-274-2116. Fax: 760-944-6784. E-mail: admissions@grauerschool.com. Web site: www.grauerschool.com

GREAT LAKES CHRISTIAN HIGH SCHOOL

4875 King Street
Beamsville, Ontario L0R 1B6, Canada

Head of School: Mr. Don Rose

General Information Coeducational boarding and day college-preparatory, general academic, arts, and religious studies school, affiliated with Church of Christ. Grades 9–12. Founded: 1952. Setting: small town. Nearest major city is Hamilton, Canada. Students are housed in single-sex dormitories. 15-acre campus. 6 buildings on campus. Approved or accredited by Ontario Ministry of Education and Ontario Department of Education. Language of instruction: English. Endowment: CAN$500,000. Total enrollment: 94. Upper school average class size: 22. Upper school faculty-student ratio: 1:10. There are 180 required school days per year for Upper School students. Upper School students typically attend 5 days per week. The average school day consists of 6 hours and 10 minutes.

Upper School Student Profile Grade 9: 18 students (10 boys, 8 girls); Grade 10: 22 students (10 boys, 12 girls); Grade 11: 25 students (11 boys, 14 girls); Grade 12: 33 students (19 boys, 14 girls). 60% of students are boarding students. 55% are province residents. 5 provinces are represented in upper school student body. 40% are international students. International students from China, Hong Kong, Republic of Korea, Taiwan, Thailand, and United States; 3 other countries represented in student body. 40% of students are members of Church of Christ.

Faculty School total: 11. In upper school: 8 men, 3 women; 5 have advanced degrees; 2 reside on campus.

Subjects Offered 20th century world history, accounting, algebra, arts appreciation, Bible, biology, calculus, career and personal planning, chemistry, computer science, computer technologies, dramatic arts, economics, English, English composition, English language and composition-AP, English literature, English-AP, ESL, family studies, finite math, French, geography, history, mathematics, mathematics-AP, media, music, music composition, physical education, physics, society, technology, world issues.

Graduation Requirements 20th century history, advanced math, art, Bible, business, Canadian geography, Canadian history, Canadian literature, career planning, civics, computer information systems, conceptual physics, critical thinking, current events, economics, English, English composition, English literature, French as a second language, geography, mathematics, physical education (includes health), science, society challenge and change, world geography, world history.

Special Academic Programs Independent study; ESL (18 students enrolled).

College Admission Counseling 26 students graduated in 2012; 17 went to college, including Carleton University; McMaster University; University of Ottawa; University of Toronto; Wilfrid Laurier University; York University. Other: 6 went to work, 1 entered military service.

Student Life Upper grades have uniform requirement, student council. Discipline rests primarily with faculty. Attendance at religious services is required.

Summer Programs Enrichment programs offered; session focuses on skill levels improvement; held on campus; accepts boys and girls; not open to students from other schools. 2013 schedule: June 25 to August 24. Application deadline: May 11.

Tuition and Aid Day student tuition: CAN$8800; 5-day tuition and room/board: CAN$13,400; 7-day tuition and room/board: CAN$15,200. Tuition installment plan (monthly payment plans, individually arranged payment plans). Tuition reduction for siblings, bursaries, merit scholarship grants, need-based scholarship grants, need-based loans, middle-income loans, paying campus jobs available. In 2012–13, 45% of upper-school students received aid; total upper-school merit-scholarship money awarded: CAN$8000. Total amount of financial aid awarded in 2012–13: CAN$150,000.

Admissions Traditional secondary-level entrance grade is 9. For fall 2012, 130 students applied for upper-level admission, 115 were accepted, 95 enrolled. CAT or SLEP required. Deadline for receipt of application materials: none. Application fee required: CAN$100. Interview recommended.

Athletics Interscholastic: badminton (boys, girls), basketball (b,g), cross-country running (b,g), golf (b), hockey (b,g), ice hockey (b,g), soccer (b,g), tennis (b,g), track and field (b,g), volleyball (b,g); intramural: aerobics (g), badminton (b,g), basketball (b,g), cooperative games (b,g), fitness (b,g), ice hockey (b,g), volleyball (b,g); coed interscholastic: badminton, indoor hockey, indoor soccer, netball, tennis; coed intramural: badminton, ball hockey, baseball, basketball, cooperative games, floor hockey, hockey, volleyball. 2 PE instructors, 2 coaches.

Computers Computers are regularly used in accounting, business, music, technology, typing classes. Computer network features include on-campus library services, Internet access, Internet filtering or blocking technology, grades are available online to parents. Campus intranet and computer access in designated common areas are available to students. Students grades are available online.

Contact Mrs. Sandy McBay, Admissions Liaison. 905-563-5374 Ext. 230. Fax: 905-563-0818. E-mail: study@glchs.on.ca. Web site: www.glchs.on.ca

GREENFIELD SCHOOL

PO Box 3525
Wilson, North Carolina 27895-3525

Head of School: Dr. Vincent M. Janney

General Information Coeducational day and distance learning college-preparatory school. Grades PS–12. Distance learning grades 11–12. Founded: 1969. Setting: small town. Nearest major city is Raleigh. 61-acre campus. 9 buildings on campus. Approved or accredited by Southern Association of Colleges and Schools and North Carolina Department of Education. Member of National Association of Independent Schools. Total enrollment: 307. Upper school average class size: 19. Upper school faculty-student ratio: 1:3. There are 180 required school days per year for Upper School students. Upper School students typically attend 5 days per week. The average school day consists of 6 hours and 45 minutes.

Upper School Student Profile Grade 9: 18 students (7 boys, 11 girls); Grade 10: 19 students (7 boys, 12 girls); Grade 11: 20 students (10 boys, 10 girls); Grade 12: 15 students (12 boys, 3 girls).

Faculty School total: 56. In upper school: 9 men, 15 women; 13 have advanced degrees.

Subjects Offered Advanced computer applications, advanced math, Advanced Placement courses, algebra, American history, American literature, ancient world history, art, athletics, biology, British literature, calculus, calculus-AP, chemistry, chorus, college awareness, community service, computer applications, computer education, computer graphics, computer information systems, computer math, computer multimedia, computer processing, computer programming, computer programming-AP, computer science, computer skills, computer technologies, desktop publishing, drama, earth science, economics, electives, English, English literature, fine arts, foreign language, geography, geometry, government/civics, grammar, health, history, honors algebra, honors English, honors geometry, honors world history, keyboarding, language arts, mathematics, music, physical education, physical science, physics, pre-algebra, pre-calculus, SAT preparation, science, social studies, Spanish, sports conditioning, trigonometry, Web site design, world geography, world history, writing, yearbook.

Graduation Requirements Arts and fine arts (art, music, dance, drama), computer science, English, foreign language, mathematics, physical education (includes health), science, social studies (includes history). Community service is required.

Special Academic Programs 5 Advanced Placement exams for which test preparation is offered; honors section; independent study; academic accommodation for the gifted; remedial reading and/or remedial writing; remedial math; programs in English, general development for dyslexic students.

College Admission Counseling 19 students graduated in 2011; all went to college, including Agnes Scott College; East Carolina University; Meredith College; North Carolina State University; The University of North Carolina at Chapel Hill; University of Kentucky. Median SAT critical reading: 520, median SAT math: 510, median SAT writing: 500, median combined SAT: 1540, median composite ACT: 23. 18% scored over 600 on SAT critical reading, 24% scored over 600 on SAT math, 29%

scored over 600 on SAT writing, 24% scored over 1800 on combined SAT, 38% scored over 26 on composite ACT.

Student Life Upper grades have specified standards of dress, student council, honor system. Discipline rests primarily with faculty.

Tuition and Aid Day student tuition: $8730. Tuition installment plan (monthly payment plans). Tuition reduction for siblings, merit scholarship grants, need-based scholarship grants available.

Admissions Traditional secondary-level entrance grade is 9. For fall 2011, 15 students applied for upper-level admission, 12 were accepted, 7 enrolled. Brigance Test of Basic Skills, Comprehensive Test of Basic Skills or CTP III required. Deadline for receipt of application materials: none. Application fee required: $100. On-campus interview required.

Athletics Interscholastic: baseball (boys), basketball (b,g), cheering (g), soccer (b,g), tennis (b,g), volleyball (g); coed interscholastic: golf. 3 PE instructors, 11 coaches.

Computers Computers are regularly used in all academic classes. Computer resources include on-campus library services, Internet access, wireless campus network, Internet filtering or blocking technology. Computer access in designated common areas is available to students. The school has a published electronic and media policy.

Contact Diane Oliphant Hamilton, Director of Admissions and Community Relations. 252-237-8046. Fax: 252-237-1825. E-mail: hamiltond@greenfieldschool.org. Web site: www.greenfieldschool.org

GREENHILL SCHOOL

4141 Spring Valley Road
Addison, Texas 75001

Head of School: Scott A. Griggs

General Information Coeducational day college-preparatory school. Grades PK–12. Founded: 1950. Setting: suburban. Nearest major city is Dallas. 78-acre campus. 8 buildings on campus. Approved or accredited by Independent Schools Association of the Southwest, Texas Education Agency, and Texas Department of Education. Member of National Association of Independent Schools and Secondary School Admission Test Board. Endowment: $27.7 million. Total enrollment: 1,279. Upper school average class size: 16. Upper school faculty-student ratio: 1:7. Upper School students typically attend 5 days per week. The average school day consists of 7 hours and 45 minutes.

Upper School Student Profile Grade 9: 118 students (59 boys, 59 girls); Grade 10: 118 students (59 boys, 59 girls); Grade 11: 117 students (59 boys, 58 girls); Grade 12: 115 students (55 boys, 60 girls).

Faculty School total: 171. In upper school: 39 men, 29 women; 50 have advanced degrees.

Subjects Offered Algebra, American history, American literature, art, art history, biology, calculus, ceramics, chemistry, Chinese, computer programming, computer science, creative writing, dance, drama, ecology, economics, English, English literature, European history, fine arts, French, geometry, government/civics, health, history, journalism, Latin, mathematics, music, philosophy, photography, physical education, physics, science, social studies, Spanish, speech, theater, trigonometry.

Graduation Requirements Arts and fine arts (art, music, dance, drama), classical language, computer studies, English, history, mathematics, modern languages, physical education (includes health), public speaking, science. Community service is required.

Special Academic Programs Advanced Placement exam preparation; honors section; independent study; term-away projects.

College Admission Counseling 118 students graduated in 2012; all went to college, including New York University; Rice University; Southern Methodist University; The University of Texas at Austin; University of Southern California; Washington University in St. Louis. Median SAT critical reading: 670, median SAT math: 660, median SAT writing: 650, median combined SAT: 1990, median composite ACT: 30. 79% scored over 600 on SAT critical reading, 73% scored over 600 on SAT math, 73% scored over 600 on SAT writing, 77% scored over 1800 on combined SAT, 92% scored over 26 on composite ACT.

Student Life Upper grades have specified standards of dress, student council, honor system. Discipline rests primarily with faculty.

Summer Programs Enrichment, sports, art/fine arts, computer instruction programs offered; session focuses on enrichment and sports; held on campus; accepts boys and girls; open to students from other schools. 1,300 students usually enrolled. 2013 schedule: June 3 to August 9. Application deadline: none.

Tuition and Aid Day student tuition: $23,900. Need-based scholarship grants available. In 2012–13, 21% of upper-school students received aid. Total amount of financial aid awarded in 2012–13: $1,513,400.

Admissions Traditional secondary-level entrance grade is 9. For fall 2012, 184 students applied for upper-level admission, 60 were accepted, 44 enrolled. ISEE required. Deadline for receipt of application materials: January 18. Application fee required: $175. Interview required.

Athletics Interscholastic: aquatics (boys, girls), baseball (b), basketball (b,g), cross-country running (b,g), field hockey (g), football (b), golf (b,g), lacrosse (b,g), running (b,g), soccer (b,g), softball (g), swimming and diving (b,g), tennis (b,g), track and field (b,g), volleyball (b,g), winter soccer (b,g); intramural: baseball (b), basketball (b,g), field hockey (g), fitness (b,g), football (b), lacrosse (b,g), physical fitness (b,g), running (b,g), soccer (b,g), softball (g), strength & conditioning (b,g), swimming and diving (b,g), tennis (b,g), track and field (b,g), volleyball (b,g), weight lifting (b,g), winter soccer (b,g); coed interscholastic: cheering; coed intramural: aquatics, ballet, cross-country running, dance, fitness, Frisbee, golf, physical fitness, running, soccer, strength & conditioning, swimming and diving, table tennis, tai chi, tennis, track and field, ultimate Frisbee, volleyball, weight lifting, weight training, winter soccer, yoga. 15 PE instructors, 4 athletic trainers.

Computers Computers are regularly used in computer applications, digital applications, independent study, programming, video film production, Web site design classes. Computer network features include on-campus library services, online commercial services, Internet access, wireless campus network, Internet filtering or blocking technology. Campus intranet, student e-mail accounts, and computer access in designated common areas are available to students. Students grades are available online. The school has a published electronic and media policy.

Contact Angela H. Woodson, Director of Admission. 972-628-5910. Fax: 972-404-8217. E-mail: admission@greenhill.org. Web site: www.greenhill.org

GREENHILLS SCHOOL

850 Greenhills Drive
Ann Arbor, Michigan 48105

Head of School: Carl J. Pelofsky

General Information Coeducational day college-preparatory and arts school. Grades 6–12. Founded: 1968. Setting: suburban. Nearest major city is Detroit. 30-acre campus. 1 building on campus. Approved or accredited by Independent Schools Association of the Central States and Michigan Department of Education. Member of National Association of Independent Schools and Secondary School Admission Test Board. Endowment: $7 million. Total enrollment: 556. Upper school average class size: 16. Upper school faculty-student ratio: 1:8. There are 165 required school days per year for Upper School students. Upper School students typically attend 5 days per week. The average school day consists of 7 hours.

Upper School Student Profile Grade 9: 75 students (40 boys, 35 girls); Grade 10: 87 students (42 boys, 45 girls); Grade 11: 78 students (34 boys, 44 girls); Grade 12: 81 students (44 boys, 37 girls).

Faculty School total: 67. In upper school: 21 men, 30 women; 41 have advanced degrees.

Subjects Offered 3-dimensional art, advanced chemistry, Advanced Placement courses, African-American literature, algebra, American history, American literature, ancient history, art, astronomy, biology, calculus, calculus-AP, ceramics, chemistry, Chinese, Chinese studies, chorus, community service, creative writing, discrete mathematics, drama, drawing, economics, economics and history, English, English literature, ethics, European history, expository writing, fine arts, French, geometry, government, health, history, jazz, journalism, Latin, mathematics, music, orchestra, painting, photography, physical education, physical science, physics, science, social studies, Spanish, theater, trigonometry, world history, world literature, writing.

Graduation Requirements Arts and fine arts (art, music, dance, drama), English, foreign language, mathematics, physical education (includes health), science, social studies (includes history), senior project. Community service is required.

Special Academic Programs Advanced Placement exam preparation; honors section; independent study; programs in English, mathematics for dyslexic students; special instructional classes for blind students.

College Admission Counseling 90 students graduated in 2012; all went to college, including Kalamazoo College; Michigan State University; The Johns Hopkins University; University of Michigan; University of Pennsylvania; Washington University in St. Louis. Mean SAT critical reading: 654, mean SAT math: 660, mean SAT writing: 653, mean combined SAT: 1967, mean composite ACT: 29.

Student Life Upper grades have specified standards of dress, student council, honor system. Discipline rests equally with students and faculty.

Summer Programs Enrichment, sports, art/fine arts, rigorous outdoor training programs offered; session focuses on enrichment, academics, travel; held on campus; accepts boys and girls; open to students from other schools. 30 students usually enrolled. 2013 schedule: July 1 to July 30. Application deadline: none.

Tuition and Aid Day student tuition: $19,680. Tuition installment plan (FACTS Tuition Payment Plan, monthly payment plans). Need-based scholarship grants available. In 2012–13, 19% of upper-school students received aid. Total amount of financial aid awarded in 2012–13: $1,000,000.

Admissions Traditional secondary-level entrance grade is 9. For fall 2012, 71 students applied for upper-level admission, 57 were accepted, 40 enrolled. SSAT or TOEFL required. Deadline for receipt of application materials: none. Application fee required: $50. Interview required.

Athletics Interscholastic: baseball (boys), basketball (b,g), cross-country running (b,g), field hockey (g), golf (b,g), soccer (b,g), softball (g), tennis (b,g), track and field (b,g), volleyball (g); intramural: basketball (b,g), cross-country running (b,g), field hockey (g), soccer (b,g); coed interscholastic: equestrian sports, swimming and diving; coed intramural: hiking/backpacking, outdoor activities, outdoor education. 3 PE instructors, 36 coaches, 1 athletic trainer.

Computers Computers are regularly used in all academic classes. Computer network features include on-campus library services, online commercial services, Internet access, wireless campus network, Internet filtering or blocking technology. Campus intranet, student e-mail accounts, and computer access in designated common areas are

available to students. Students grades are available online. The school has a published electronic and media policy.
Contact Betsy Ellsworth, Director of Admission and Financial Aid. 734-205-4061. Fax: 734-205-4056. E-mail: admission@greenhillsschool.org. Web site: www.greenhillsschool.org

GREENSBORO DAY SCHOOL

5401 Lawndale Drive
Greensboro, North Carolina 27455

Head of School: Mr. Mark C. Hale

General Information Coeducational day college-preparatory, arts, and technology school. Grades K–12. Founded: 1970. Setting: suburban. 65-acre campus. 10 buildings on campus. Approved or accredited by North Carolina Association of Independent Schools and Southern Association of Colleges and Schools. Member of National Association of Independent Schools. Total enrollment: 904. Upper school average class size: 16. Upper school faculty-student ratio: 1:13. There are 182 required school days per year for Upper School students. Upper School students typically attend 5 days per week. The average school day consists of 6 hours and 15 minutes.
Upper School Student Profile Grade 9: 86 students (39 boys, 47 girls); Grade 10: 90 students (42 boys, 48 girls); Grade 11: 95 students (51 boys, 44 girls); Grade 12: 86 students (45 boys, 41 girls).
Faculty School total: 120. In upper school: 24 men, 26 women.
Subjects Offered Algebra, American government, American history, American literature, art, art appreciation, biology, biology-AP, calculus, calculus-AP, chemistry, chorus, college admission preparation, college counseling, college placement, computer programming, computer science-AP, creative writing, drama, economics, English, English language-AP, English literature, ESL, European history, European history-AP, fine arts, French, French language-AP, French literature-AP, geometry, government/civics, health, history, journalism, Latin, Latin-AP, mathematics, music, photography, physical education, physics, physics-AP, psychology, SAT preparation, science, social studies, Spanish, Spanish language-AP, Spanish literature-AP, sports medicine, statistics-AP, theater, trigonometry, U.S. history-AP, world history, writing, yearbook.
Graduation Requirements Arts and fine arts (art, music, dance, drama), English, foreign language, mathematics, physical education (includes health), science, social studies (includes history), senior project (four-week internship).
Special Academic Programs 11 Advanced Placement exams for which test preparation is offered; honors section; independent study; term-away projects; study abroad; academic accommodation for the gifted and the artistically talented; special instructional classes for students with learning disabilities and Attention Deficit Disorder; ESL (8 students enrolled).
College Admission Counseling 80 students graduated in 2011; all went to college, including Duke University; Elon University; The University of North Carolina at Chapel Hill; The University of North Carolina Wilmington; Wake Forest University. Median SAT critical reading: 610, median SAT math: 650, median SAT writing: 650.
Student Life Upper grades have specified standards of dress, student council, honor system. Discipline rests equally with students and faculty.
Tuition and Aid Day student tuition: $8200–$18,980. Tuition installment plan (FACTS Tuition Payment Plan, monthly payment plans, individually arranged payment plans). Need-based scholarship grants available.
Admissions Traditional secondary-level entrance grade is 9. ERB (CTP-Verbal, Quantitative) required. Deadline for receipt of application materials: none. Application fee required: $50. On-campus interview required.
Athletics Interscholastic: baseball (boys), basketball (b,g), cheering (g), cross-country running (b,g), field hockey (g), lacrosse (b,g), soccer (b,g), swimming and diving (b,g), tennis (b,g), track and field (b,g), volleyball (g), wrestling (b); intramural: weight lifting (b,g); coed interscholastic: aquatics, golf; coed intramural: backpacking, badminton, basketball, ropes courses. 11 PE instructors, 20 coaches, 2 athletic trainers.
Computers Computers are regularly used in yearbook classes. Computer network features include on-campus library services, online commercial services, Internet access, wireless campus network, Internet filtering or blocking technology. Student e-mail accounts are available to students. Students grades are available online. The school has a published electronic and media policy.
Contact Robin Schenck, Director of Admission and Financial Aid. 336-288-8590 Ext. 106. Fax: 336-282-2905. E-mail: robinschenck@greensboroday.org. Web site: www.greensboroday.org

GREENWICH ACADEMY

200 North Maple Avenue
Greenwich, Connecticut 06830-4799

Head of School: Molly H. King

General Information Girls' day college-preparatory and arts school. Grades PK–12. Founded: 1827. Setting: suburban. Nearest major city is New York, NY. 39-acre campus. 6 buildings on campus. Approved or accredited by New England Association of Schools and Colleges and Connecticut Department of Education. Member of National Association of Independent Schools and Secondary School Admission Test Board. Endowment: $61.9 million. Total enrollment: 805. Upper school average class size: 13. Upper school faculty-student ratio: 1:6. There are 164 required school days per year for Upper School students. Upper School students typically attend 5 days per week. The average school day consists of 5 hours.
Upper School Student Profile Grade 9: 83 students (83 girls); Grade 10: 85 students (85 girls); Grade 11: 91 students (91 girls); Grade 12: 89 students (89 girls).
Faculty School total: 139. In upper school: 29 men, 109 women; 41 have advanced degrees.
Subjects Offered Advanced Placement courses, advanced studio art-AP, African-American literature, algebra, American history, American history-AP, American literature, ancient history, Arabic, architecture, art, art history, art history-AP, art-AP, astronomy, biochemistry, biology, biology-AP, calculus, calculus-AP, ceramics, chemistry, chemistry-AP, Chinese, classics, computer science, creative writing, dance, dance performance, drama, drama performance, earth science, ecology, economics, economics-AP, English, English literature, environmental science, European history, European history-AP, expository writing, film, film and literature, fine arts, foreign language, French, French language-AP, French literature-AP, French-AP, geology, geometry, government and politics-AP, government/civics, health, history, history-AP, honors algebra, honors geometry, independent study, Italian, Latin, Latin-AP, mathematics, mathematics-AP, medieval history, microeconomics, microeconomics-AP, music, music performance, music theory-AP, oceanography, physical education, physics, pre-calculus, psychology, science, senior project, Spanish, Spanish-AP, speech, statistics, studio art-AP, theater, trigonometry, world history, world literature.
Graduation Requirements Arts and fine arts (art, music, dance, drama), English, foreign language, mathematics, physical education (includes health), science, social studies (includes history). Community service is required.
Special Academic Programs 26 Advanced Placement exams for which test preparation is offered; honors section; independent study; term-away projects; study abroad.
College Admission Counseling 77 students graduated in 2011; all went to college, including Boston College; Bowdoin College; New York University; Princeton University; Stanford University; Yale University. Mean SAT critical reading: 675, mean SAT math: 664, mean SAT writing: 700, mean combined SAT: 1900, mean composite ACT: 29. 84% scored over 600 on SAT critical reading, 82% scored over 600 on SAT math, 94% scored over 600 on SAT writing, 91% scored over 1800 on combined SAT, 91% scored over 26 on composite ACT.
Student Life Upper grades have uniform requirement, student council, honor system. Discipline rests equally with students and faculty.
Tuition and Aid Day student tuition: $35,400. Tuition installment plan (Academic Management Services Plan, monthly payment plans). Need-based scholarship grants, middle-income loans, PLITT Loans, tuition reduction for children of faculty and staff available. In 2011–12, 20% of upper-school students received aid. Total amount of financial aid awarded in 2011–12: $1,351,850.
Admissions Traditional secondary-level entrance grade is 9. For fall 2011, 105 students applied for upper-level admission, 50 were accepted, 36 enrolled. ERB, ISEE or SSAT required. Deadline for receipt of application materials: December 15. Application fee required: $75. On-campus interview required.
Athletics Interscholastic: basketball, crew, cross-country running, dance, dance team, fencing, field hockey, golf, hockey, ice hockey, independent competitive sports, lacrosse, sailing, soccer, softball, squash, swimming and diving, tennis, volleyball; intramural: aerobics, aerobics/Nautilus, basketball, cooperative games, crew, dance, fitness, floor hockey, Frisbee, independent competitive sports, lacrosse, modern dance, Nautilus, physical fitness, physical training, running, self defense, soccer, strength & conditioning, tennis, volleyball, weight lifting, yoga. 7 PE instructors, 54 coaches, 1 athletic trainer.
Computers Computers are regularly used in art, English, foreign language, history, humanities, mathematics, music, science classes. Computer network features include on-campus library services, online commercial services, Internet access, wireless campus network, Internet filtering or blocking technology. Campus intranet and student e-mail accounts are available to students. The school has a published electronic and media policy.
Contact Irene Mann, Admission Associate, Registrar. 203-625-8990. Fax: 203-625-8912. E-mail: imann@greenwichacademy.org. Web site: www.greenwichacademy.org

THE GREENWOOD SCHOOL

Putney, Vermont
See Junior Boarding Schools section.

GRIER SCHOOL

PO Box 308
Tyrone, Pennsylvania 16686-0308

Head of School: Mrs. Gina Borst

General Information Girls' boarding and day college-preparatory, arts, and business school. Boarding grades 7–PG, day grades 7–12. Founded: 1853. Setting: rural. Nearest major city is Pittsburgh. Students are housed in single-sex dormitories. 320-acre campus. 4 buildings on campus. Approved or accredited by Middle States Association of Colleges and Schools, Pennsylvania Association of Independent Schools, and The Association of Boarding Schools. Member of National Association of Independent

Schools and Secondary School Admission Test Board. Endowment: $16 million. Total enrollment: 290. Upper school average class size: 10. Upper school faculty-student ratio: 1:7. There are 160 required school days per year for Upper School students. Upper School students typically attend 5 days per week. The average school day consists of 7 hours.

Upper School Student Profile Grade 9: 57 students (57 girls); Grade 10: 77 students (77 girls); Grade 11: 70 students (70 girls); Grade 12: 48 students (48 girls). 87% of students are boarding students. 12% are state residents. 22 states are represented in upper school student body. 50% are international students. International students from China, Germany, Mexico, Republic of Korea, Russian Federation, and Viet Nam; 7 other countries represented in student body.

Faculty School total: 60. In upper school: 18 men, 42 women; 34 have advanced degrees; 18 reside on campus.

Subjects Offered 3-dimensional art, acting, advanced biology, advanced chemistry, advanced studio art-AP, advanced TOEFL/grammar, algebra, American history, American history-AP, American literature, anatomy, art, art history, art history-AP, art-AP, ballet, ballet technique, batik, biology, biology-AP, British literature, British literature (honors), Broadway dance, calculus, calculus-AP, ceramics, chemistry, chemistry-AP, Chinese, choir, choral music, choreography, civics, community service, comparative religion, computer graphics, computer math, computer programming, computer-aided design, costumes and make-up, creative writing, criminology, current events, dance, desktop publishing, digital art, digital photography, directing, drama, drama performance, dramatic arts, drawing, earth science, ecology, economics, economics-AP, English, English as a foreign language, English literature, English literature and composition-AP, English literature-AP, environmental science, environmental science-AP, equine science, ESL, European history, European history-AP, fabric arts, fashion, fiber arts, filmmaking, finance, fine arts, French, French language-AP, French-AP, geography, geometry, government, government/civics, graphic arts, guitar, health, health and wellness, history, honors algebra, honors English, honors geometry, honors U.S. history, honors world history, human anatomy, human biology, instrumental music, international relations, jazz band, jazz dance, journalism, linguistics, macro/microeconomics-AP, macroeconomics-AP, marine biology, mathematics, microeconomics-AP, model United Nations, modern dance, music, music technology, music theater, music theory, musical theater, musical theater dance, newspaper, oil painting, painting, personal finance, philosophy, photography, physical education, physics, physics-AP, physiology, piano, portfolio art, pre-algebra, pre-calculus, printmaking, probability and statistics, psychology, science, scuba diving, social studies, Spanish, Spanish language-AP, stagecraft, statistics-AP, studio art-AP, symphonic band, tap dance, theater, TOEFL preparation, trigonometry, typing, video film production, vocal ensemble, voice, weaving, women's studies, world history, world literature, writing, writing, writing workshop, yearbook.

Graduation Requirements Arts and fine arts (art, music, dance, drama), computer science, English, foreign language, mathematics, physical education (includes health), science, social sciences, social studies (includes history).

Special Academic Programs 17 Advanced Placement exams for which test preparation is offered; honors section; independent study; study abroad; academic accommodation for the gifted, the musically talented, and the artistically talented; remedial reading and/or remedial writing; remedial math; programs in English, general development for dyslexic students; special instructional classes for students with learning disabilities, Attention Deficit Disorder, and dyslexia; ESL (68 students enrolled).

College Admission Counseling 48 students graduated in 2012; all went to college, including Bryn Mawr College; Penn State University Park; Purdue University; University of California, Berkeley; University of California, Los Angeles. Median SAT critical reading: 600, median SAT math: 640. 25% scored over 600 on SAT critical reading, 20% scored over 600 on SAT math.

Student Life Upper grades have specified standards of dress, student council, honor system. Discipline rests primarily with faculty.

Summer Programs Enrichment, ESL, sports, art/fine arts programs offered; session focuses on recreation and ESL; held on campus; accepts girls; open to students from other schools. 25 students usually enrolled. 2013 schedule: June 16 to September 7. Application deadline: none.

Tuition and Aid Day student tuition: $22,500; 7-day tuition and room/board: $46,800. Tuition installment plan (individually arranged payment plans). Tuition reduction for siblings, merit scholarship grants, need-based scholarship grants, need-based loans, paying campus jobs available. In 2012–13, 45% of upper-school students received aid; total upper-school merit-scholarship money awarded: $540,000. Total amount of financial aid awarded in 2012–13: $1,940,000.

Admissions Traditional secondary-level entrance grade is 9. For fall 2012, 200 students applied for upper-level admission, 150 were accepted, 102 enrolled. SSAT or WISC III required. Deadline for receipt of application materials: none. Application fee required: $50. Interview recommended.

Athletics Interscholastic: basketball, dance team, drill team, equestrian sports, martial arts, skiing (downhill), soccer, tennis, volleyball; intramural: aerobics, aerobics/dance, alpine skiing, aquatics, archery, badminton, ballet, basketball, bicycling, bowling, canoeing/kayaking, cheering, dance, dance team, equestrian sports, fencing, figure skating, fitness, fitness walking, fly fishing, gymnastics, hiking/backpacking, horseback riding, jogging, martial arts, modern dance, mountain biking, nordic skiing, ropes courses, scuba diving, skiing (cross-country), skiing (downhill), soccer, swimming and diving, tennis, volleyball, walking, weight training, yoga. 3 PE instructors, 3 coaches, 3 athletic trainers.

Computers Computers are regularly used in creative writing, English, foreign language, graphic arts, mathematics, music technology, newspaper, science, yearbook classes. Computer network features include on-campus library services, online commercial services, Internet access, wireless campus network, Internet filtering or blocking technology. Campus intranet and student e-mail accounts are available to students. The school has a published electronic and media policy.

Contact Mr. Andrew M. Wilson, Headmaster/Director of Admissions. 814-684-3000 Ext. 106. Fax: 814-684-2177. E-mail: admissions@grier.org. Web site: www.grier.org

See Display on previous page, Close-Up on page 582, and Summer Program Close-Up on page 710.

GRIGGS INTERNATIONAL ACADEMY

12501 Old Columbia Pike
Silver Spring, Maryland 20904-6600

General Information Coeducational day and distance learning college-preparatory, general academic, and religious studies school, affiliated with Seventh-day Adventist Church. Grades PK–PG. Distance learning grades K–12. Founded: 1909. Setting: suburban. Nearest major city is Washington, DC. 1 building on campus. Approved or accredited by Board of Regents, General Conference of Seventh-day Adventists, CITA (Commission on International and Trans-Regional Accreditation), Distance Education and Training Council, Middle States Association of Colleges and Schools, and Maryland Department of Education. Total enrollment: 728.

See Display below and Close-Up on page 584.

GROTON SCHOOL

Box 991
Farmers Row
Groton, Massachusetts 01450

Head of School: Richard B. Commons

General Information Coeducational boarding and day college-preparatory, arts, and religious studies school, affiliated with Episcopal Church. Grades 8–12. Founded: 1884. Setting: rural. Nearest major city is Boston. Students are housed in single-sex dormitories. 410-acre campus. 17 buildings on campus. Approved or accredited by Association of Independent Schools in New England, New England Association of Schools and Colleges, and The Association of Boarding Schools. Member of National Association of Independent Schools and Secondary School Admission Test Board. Endowment: $265.6 million. Total enrollment: 370. Upper school average class size: 13. Upper school faculty-student ratio: 1:7. There are 182 required school days per year for Upper School students. Upper School students typically attend 6 days per week. The average school day consists of 6 hours and 30 minutes.

Upper School Student Profile Grade 8: 26 students (13 boys, 13 girls); Grade 9: 78 students (41 boys, 37 girls); Grade 10: 85 students (44 boys, 41 girls); Grade 11: 86 students (43 boys, 43 girls); Grade 12: 95 students (49 boys, 46 girls). 86% of students are boarding students. 27% are state residents. 31 states are represented in upper school student body. 13% are international students. International students from Bermuda, Canada, China, France, Republic of Korea, and United Arab Emirates; 4 other countries represented in student body.

Faculty School total: 52. In upper school: 30 men, 22 women; 45 have advanced degrees; all reside on campus.

Subjects Offered Advanced chemistry, advanced math, algebra, American literature, American literature-AP, analytic geometry, Ancient Greek, ancient world history, archaeology, art, art history, art history-AP, Bible studies, biology, biology-AP, botany, Buddhism, calculus, calculus-AP, cell biology, Central and Eastern European history, ceramics, chemistry, chemistry-AP, Chinese, choir, choral music, civil rights, Civil War, civil war history, classical Greek literature, classical language, classics, composition, composition-AP, creative writing, dance, discrete mathematics, drawing, earth science, ecology, environmental systems, economics, English, English composition, English-AP, environmental science, environmental science-AP, environmental studies, ethics, ethics and responsibility, European history, European history-AP, expository writing, fine arts, fractal geometry, French, French language-AP, French literature-AP, geography, geometry, government, grammar, Greek, health, history, Holocaust, honors algebra, honors English, honors geometry, honors U.S. history, honors world history, independent study, lab science, language-AP, Latin, Latin-AP, linear algebra, literature, literature and composition-AP, mathematics, mathematics-AP, modern European history, modern European history-AP, modern history, modern languages, modern world history, music, music history, music theory, organic biochemistry, painting, philosophy, photo shop, photography, physical science, physics, physics-AP, pre-algebra, pre-calculus, psychology, religion, religious education, religious studies, science, Shakespeare, social sciences, Spanish, Spanish language-AP, Spanish literature, Spanish literature-AP, sports medicine, statistics, studio art, studio art-AP, theology, trigonometry, U.S. constitutional history, U.S. government, U.S. government and politics, U.S. government and politics-AP, U.S. history, U.S. history-AP, vocal music, Western civilization, wood lab, woodworking, world history, world history-AP, writing.

Graduation Requirements Arts and fine arts (art, music, dance, drama), classical language, English, foreign language, mathematics, religious studies, science, social studies (includes history).

Special Academic Programs 13 Advanced Placement exams for which test preparation is offered; honors section; independent study; study abroad; academic accommodation for the gifted, the musically talented, and the artistically talented.

College Admission Counseling Colleges students went to include Georgetown University; Harvard University; Northwestern University; Stanford University; Tufts University; University of Virginia. Median SAT critical reading: 700, median SAT math: 700, median SAT writing: 710, median combined SAT: 2100, median composite ACT: 28. 92% scored over 600 on SAT critical reading, 95% scored over 600 on SAT math, 96% scored over 600 on SAT writing, 99% scored over 1800 on combined SAT, 78% scored over 26 on composite ACT.

Student Life Upper grades have specified standards of dress, student council, honor system. Discipline rests equally with students and faculty. Attendance at religious services is required.

Tuition and Aid Day student tuition: $38,420; 7-day tuition and room/board: $49,810. Tuition installment plan (Insured Tuition Payment Plan, Key Tuition Payment Plan, monthly payment plans, individually arranged payment plans). Need-based scholarship grants, Key Education Resources available. In 2011–12, 37% of upper-school students received aid. Total amount of financial aid awarded in 2011–12: $4,900,000.

Admissions Traditional secondary-level entrance grade is 9. For fall 2011, 1,120 students applied for upper-level admission, 138 were accepted, 92 enrolled. ISEE, SSAT or TOEFL required. Deadline for receipt of application materials: January 15. Application fee required: $50. Interview required.

Athletics Interscholastic: baseball (boys), basketball (b,g), crew (b,g), cross-country running (b,g), field hockey (g), Fives (b,g), football (b), hockey (b,g), ice hockey (b,g), lacrosse (b,g), rowing (b,g), soccer (b,g), squash (b,g), tennis (b,g); intramural: physical training (b,g), self defense (g), weight training (b,g); coed intramural: aerobics/dance, alpine skiing, dance, fitness, Fives, Frisbee, golf, ice skating, modern dance, nordic skiing, outdoor activities, running, skeet shooting, skiing (cross-country), skiing (downhill), snowboarding, strength & conditioning, swimming and diving, track and field, trap and skeet, ultimate Frisbee, yoga. 2 coaches, 1 athletic trainer.

Computers Computers are regularly used in all academic classes. Computer network features include on-campus library services, Internet access, wireless campus network, Internet filtering or blocking technology, campus-wide wireless environment. Campus intranet and student e-mail accounts are available to students. The school has a published electronic and media policy.

Contact Mr. Ian Gracey, Director of Admission. 978-448-7510. Fax: 978-448-9623. E-mail: igracey@groton.org. Web site: www.groton.org

GUAMANI PRIVATE SCHOOL

PO Box 3000
Guayama, Puerto Rico 00785

Head of School: Mr. Eduardo Delgado

General Information Coeducational day college-preparatory and bilingual studies school. Grades 1–12. Founded: 1914. Setting: urban. Nearest major city is Caguas. 1-acre campus. 1 building on campus. Approved or accredited by Middle States Association of Colleges and Schools, National Catholic Education Association, and Puerto Rico Department of Education. Languages of instruction: English and Spanish. Total enrollment: 606. Upper school average class size: 20. Upper school faculty-student ratio: 1:13.

Faculty School total: 32. In upper school: 10 men, 10 women; 3 have advanced degrees.

Subjects Offered Advanced math, Advanced Placement courses, algebra, American government, American history, analysis and differential calculus, chemistry, civics, pre-algebra, pre-calculus, science project, science research, social sciences, social studies, sociology, Spanish, Spanish language-AP, U.S. literature, visual arts, world geography, world history.

Graduation Requirements Mathematics, science, social sciences, Spanish, acceptance into a college or university. Community service is required.

Special Academic Programs Advanced Placement exam preparation; honors section; independent study.

College Admission Counseling 23 students graduated in 2012; they went to Embry-Riddle Aeronautical University–Daytona; Syracuse University; University of Puerto Rico, Cayey University College; University of Puerto Rico, Mayagüez Campus; University of Puerto Rico, Río Piedras. Other: 23 entered a postgraduate year.

Student Life Upper grades have uniform requirement, student council, honor system. Discipline rests primarily with faculty.

Summer Programs Remediation, ESL programs offered; held on campus; accepts boys and girls; open to students from other schools. 30 students usually enrolled. 2013 schedule: June 1 to June 30. Application deadline: May 27.

Admissions Traditional secondary-level entrance grade is 9. For fall 2012, 30 students applied for upper-level admission, 21 were accepted, 20 enrolled. School's own test or Test of Achievement and Proficiency required. Deadline for receipt of application materials: none. Application fee required: $30. Interview required.

Athletics Interscholastic: aerobics/dance (girls), basketball (b,g), cheering (g), dance squad (g), volleyball (b,g); coed interscholastic: dance team. 3 PE instructors, 2 coaches.

Computers Computers are regularly used in aviation, English, mathematics, science, social sciences, Spanish, word processing classes. Computer resources include on-campus library services, Internet access, wireless campus network, Internet filtering or blocking technology. The school has a published electronic and media policy.

Contact Mrs. Digna Torres, Secretary. 787-864-6880. Fax: 787-866-4947. Web site: www.guamani.com

THE GUNSTON SCHOOL

911 Gunston Road
PO Box 200
Centreville, Maryland 21617

Head of School: Mr. John A. Lewis, IV

General Information Coeducational day college-preparatory, arts, and technology school. Grades 9–12. Founded: 1911. Setting: rural. Nearest major city is Annapolis. 32-acre campus. 4 buildings on campus. Approved or accredited by Association of Independent Maryland Schools, Middle States Association of Colleges and Schools, and Maryland Department of Education. Member of National Association of Independent Schools and Secondary School Admission Test Board. Endowment: $1 million. Total enrollment: 148. Upper school average class size: 10. Upper school faculty-student ratio: 1:6. There are 170 required school days per year for Upper School students. Upper School students typically attend 5 days per week. The average school day consists of 8 hours.

Upper School Student Profile Grade 9: 36 students (13 boys, 23 girls); Grade 10: 43 students (26 boys, 17 girls); Grade 11: 38 students (16 boys, 22 girls); Grade 12: 31 students (19 boys, 12 girls).

Faculty School total: 23. In upper school: 12 men, 11 women; 14 have advanced degrees.

Subjects Offered Advanced biology, advanced chemistry, advanced math, Advanced Placement courses, advanced studio art-AP, algebra, American government, American history, American literature, anatomy and physiology, ancient history, applied arts, art, art history, art history-AP, biology, biology-AP, British literature, British literature (honors), calculus, calculus-AP, calligraphy, ceramics, chemistry, chemistry-AP, Chesapeake Bay studies, Chinese literature, chorus, college counseling, college placement, college planning, community service, computer applications, computer science, digital photography, drama performance, economics, English, English as a foreign language, English literature, environmental science, environmental science-AP, ethical decision making, ethics, European history-AP, fine arts, fitness, freshman seminar, geometry, golf, government, government-AP, government/civics, health, health and wellness, history, history-AP, honors algebra, honors English, honors geometry, ideas, lab science, Latin, Latin-AP, mathematics, mathematics-AP, medieval history, Microsoft, music, music appreciation, music composition, music theory, painting, performing arts, photography, physics, physics-AP, play production, poetry, pottery, pre-calculus, pre-college orientation, printmaking, psychology, SAT preparation, SAT/ACT preparation, science, sculpture, senior internship, senior project, senior thesis, short story, silk screening, Spanish, Spanish-AP, sports, studio art, studio art-AP, swimming, tennis, trigonometry, U.S. government, U.S. government and politics-AP, U.S. history, U.S. history-AP, weight training, wellness, woodworking, world history, writing workshop.

Graduation Requirements Arts and fine arts (art, music, dance, drama), athletics, computer science, English, foreign language, history, mathematics, science, social sciences. Community service is required.

Special Academic Programs Advanced Placement exam preparation; honors section; independent study; term-away projects; study at local college for college credit; study abroad; academic accommodation for the gifted, the musically talented, and the artistically talented; ESL (27 students enrolled).

College Admission Counseling 35 students graduated in 2012; all went to college, including Dickinson College; Lehigh University; St. Mary's College of Maryland; University of Maryland, College Park; Virginia Polytechnic Institute and State University; Washington College. Mean SAT critical reading: 575, mean SAT math: 528, mean SAT writing: 546, mean combined SAT: 1649.

Student Life Upper grades have specified standards of dress, student council, honor system. Discipline rests primarily with faculty.

Summer Programs Enrichment, advancement, sports, computer instruction programs offered; session focuses on student activities for ages 6-18; held on campus; accepts boys and girls; open to students from other schools. 75 students usually enrolled. 2013 schedule: June 17 to August 22. Application deadline: none.

Tuition and Aid Day student tuition: $21,950. Tuition installment plan (monthly payment plans, individually arranged payment plans, Sallie Mae, Tuition Management Solutions). Merit scholarship grants, need-based scholarship grants available. In 2012–13, 50% of upper-school students received aid; total upper-school merit-scholarship money awarded: $10,000. Total amount of financial aid awarded in 2012–13: $860,000.

Admissions Traditional secondary-level entrance grade is 9. For fall 2012, 90 students applied for upper-level admission, 86 were accepted, 55 enrolled. ISEE or SSAT required. Deadline for receipt of application materials: February 1. Application fee required: $50. On-campus interview required.

Athletics Interscholastic: basketball (boys, girls), field hockey (g), lacrosse (b,g), soccer (b,g), tennis (b,g); intramural: independent competitive sports (b,g), tennis (b,g); coed interscholastic: crew, golf, sailing, tennis; coed intramural: badminton, equestrian sports, fitness, horseback riding, independent competitive sports, strength & conditioning, swimming and diving, tennis, weight training. 4 coaches.

Computers Computers are regularly used in English, foreign language, history, mathematics, science classes. Computer network features include on-campus library services, Internet access, wireless campus network, Internet filtering or blocking technology. Campus intranet, student e-mail accounts, and computer access in designated common areas are available to students.

Contact David Henry, Director of Admission and Financial Aid. 410-758-0620. Fax: 410-758-0628. E-mail: dhenry@gunston.org. Web site: www.gunston.org

HACKLEY SCHOOL

293 Benedict Avenue
Tarrytown, New York 10591

Head of School: Mr. Walter C. Johnson

General Information Coeducational boarding and day college-preparatory, arts, technology, and liberal arts, math and science school. Boarding grades 9–12, day grades K–12. Founded: 1899. Setting: suburban. Nearest major city is New York. Students are housed in single-sex dormitories. 285-acre campus. 15 buildings on campus. Approved or accredited by Middle States Association of Colleges and Schools, New York State Association of Independent Schools, New York State Board of Regents, and The Association of Boarding Schools. Member of National Association of Independent Schools and Secondary School Admission Test Board. Endowment: $28 million. Total enrollment: 842. Upper school average class size: 15. Upper school faculty-student ratio: 1:6. There are 169 required school days per year for Upper School students. Upper School students typically attend 5 days per week. The average school day consists of 7 hours.

Upper School Student Profile Grade 9: 102 students (59 boys, 43 girls); Grade 10: 101 students (49 boys, 52 girls); Grade 11: 98 students (48 boys, 50 girls); Grade 12: 90 students (45 boys, 45 girls). 3% of students are boarding students. 96% are state residents. 3 states are represented in upper school student body.

Faculty School total: 128. In upper school: 30 men, 34 women; 53 have advanced degrees; 43 reside on campus.

Subjects Offered 20th century world history, 3-dimensional art, acting, algebra, American history, American literature, ancient history, anthropology, architectural drawing, art, art history-AP, biology, biology-AP, British literature, calculus-AP, ceramics, chemistry, chemistry-AP, Chinese, chorus, computer graphics, computer programming, computer science, computer science-AP, concert band, contemporary issues, creative writing, driver education, ecology, economics, electronic publishing, English, environmental science-AP, European history, fine arts, finite math, French, French language-AP, French literature-AP, geometry, Greek, history, Italian, Latin, Latin-AP, marine biology, mathematics, modern European history, music, music theory, music theory-AP, orchestra, organic chemistry, performing arts, photography, physical education, physics, physics-AP, pre-calculus, science, Spanish, Spanish language-AP, Spanish literature-AP, statistics-AP, studio art-AP, trigonometry, U.S. government and politics-AP, world history.

Graduation Requirements Arts and fine arts (art, music, dance, drama), English, foreign language, history, mathematics, physical education (includes health), science.

Special Academic Programs 21 Advanced Placement exams for which test preparation is offered; honors section; independent study.

College Admission Counseling 96 students graduated in 2011; 95 went to college, including Colgate University; Columbia University; Cornell University; University of Michigan; University of Pennsylvania; Vanderbilt University. Median SAT critical reading: 670, median SAT math: 690, median SAT writing: 700, median combined SAT: 2080. 90% scored over 600 on SAT critical reading, 88% scored over 600 on SAT math, 90% scored over 600 on SAT writing, 90% scored over 1800 on combined SAT.

Student Life Upper grades have specified standards of dress, student council. Discipline rests primarily with faculty.

Tuition and Aid Day student tuition: $35,700; 5-day tuition and room/board: $46,800. Tuition installment plan (Insured Tuition Payment Plan, Academic Management Services Plan, Key Tuition Payment Plan, monthly payment plans). Need-based scholarship grants, need-based loans available. In 2011–12, 15% of upper-school students received aid. Total amount of financial aid awarded in 2011–12: $3,500,000.

Admissions Traditional secondary-level entrance grade is 9. For fall 2011, 217 students applied for upper-level admission, 96 were accepted, 51 enrolled. ERB, ISEE or SSAT required. Deadline for receipt of application materials: January 14. Application fee required: $65. On-campus interview required.

Athletics Interscholastic: baseball (boys), basketball (b,g), field hockey (g), football (b), golf (b,g), lacrosse (b,g), soccer (b,g), softball (g), squash (b,g), tennis (b,g), wrestling (b); intramural: squash (b,g); coed interscholastic: cross-country running, fencing, indoor track, strength & conditioning, swimming and diving, track and field; coed intramural: aerobics, aerobics/Nautilus, canoeing/kayaking, climbing, cooperative games, fencing, fitness, Frisbee, golf, kayaking, life saving, martial arts, outdoor education, outdoor recreation, physical fitness, physical training, ropes courses, scuba diving, weight training, yoga. 6 PE instructors, 9 coaches, 1 athletic trainer.

Computers Computers are regularly used in computer applications, desktop publishing, drawing and design, graphic arts, independent study, keyboarding, literary magazine, music, newspaper, photography, programming, Web site design, yearbook classes. Computer network features include on-campus library services, online commercial services, Internet access, wireless campus network, laptop loaner program. Campus intranet and computer access in designated common areas are available to students.

Contact Mrs. Lynn Hooley, Admissions Associate. 914-366-2642. Fax: 914-366-2636. E-mail: lhooley@hackleyschool.org. Web site: www.hackleyschool.org

HAMDEN HALL COUNTRY DAY SCHOOL

1108 Whitney Avenue
Hamden, Connecticut 06517

Head of School: Mr. Robert J. Izzo

General Information Coeducational day college-preparatory school. Grades PS–12. Founded: 1912. Setting: suburban. Nearest major city is New Haven. 42-acre campus. 8 buildings on campus. Approved or accredited by Connecticut Association of Independent Schools, New England Association of Schools and Colleges, and Connecticut Department of Education. Member of National Association of Independent Schools and Secondary School Admission Test Board. Endowment: $8.2 million. Total enrollment: 545. Upper school average class size: 13. Upper school faculty-student ratio: 1:8. There are 165 required school days per year for Upper School students. Upper School students typically attend 5 days per week. The average school day consists of 4 hours and 45 minutes.

Upper School Student Profile Grade 9: 64 students (37 boys, 27 girls); Grade 10: 54 students (33 boys, 21 girls); Grade 11: 62 students (34 boys, 28 girls); Grade 12: 82 students (46 boys, 36 girls).

Faculty School total: 80. In upper school: 22 men, 21 women; 31 have advanced degrees.

Subjects Offered African-American history, algebra, American literature, anatomy, art history, astronomy, biology, British literature, calculus, ceramics, chamber groups, chemistry, chorus, computer graphics, computer multimedia, computer programming, computer science, constitutional law, creative writing, digital photography, drama, drawing, electronics, English language and composition-AP, European history-AP, expository writing, French, genetics, geology, geometry, improvisation, independent study, jazz, Latin, life science, Mandarin, marine biology, meteorology, multimedia design, music appreciation, music history, music theory, oceanography, painting, peer counseling, performing arts, physiology, playwriting, poetry, printmaking, sculpture, Spanish, speech, statistics, theater, trigonometry, U.S. history, video film production, Western civilization, women in literature, world history, world literature, zoology.

Graduation Requirements Arts and fine arts (art, music, dance, drama), computer science, English, foreign language, mathematics, physical education (includes health), science, social studies (includes history), participation in 2 athletic seasons each year.

Special Academic Programs Advanced Placement exam preparation; honors section; independent study; term-away projects; academic accommodation for the gifted.

College Admission Counseling 70 students graduated in 2011; all went to college, including Boston College; Brown University; Emory University; Lehigh University; Princeton University; University of Michigan. Median SAT critical reading: 600, median SAT math: 600, median SAT writing: 600, median combined SAT: 1800, median composite ACT: 26.

Student Life Upper grades have specified standards of dress, student council, honor system. Discipline rests equally with students and faculty.

Tuition and Aid Day student tuition: $29,990. Tuition installment plan (monthly payment plans, Tuition Management Services). Need-based scholarship grants, need-based loans, paying campus jobs, Key Education Resources available. In 2011–12, 30% of upper-school students received aid. Total amount of financial aid awarded in 2011–12: $1,600,000.

Admissions Traditional secondary-level entrance grade is 9. For fall 2011, 128 students applied for upper-level admission, 80 were accepted, 33 enrolled. ISEE or SSAT required. Deadline for receipt of application materials: January 15. Application fee required: $50. Interview required.

Athletics Interscholastic: baseball (boys), basketball (b,g), field hockey (g), football (b), ice hockey (b), lacrosse (b,g), soccer (b,g), softball (g), tennis (b,g), volleyball (g), wrestling (b); coed interscholastic: cross-country running, golf, outdoors, physical fitness, swimming and diving; coed intramural: outdoors, physical fitness, running, weight training. 3 PE instructors, 15 coaches, 1 athletic trainer.

Computers Computers are regularly used in all academic, art, digital applications, graphic arts, graphic design, information technology, video film production, yearbook classes. Computer network features include on-campus library services, Internet access, wireless campus network, Internet filtering or blocking technology. Student e-mail accounts are available to students. The school has a published electronic and media policy.

Contact Janet B. Izzo, Director of Admissions. 203-752-2610. Fax: 203-752-2611. E-mail: jizzo@hamdenhall.org. Web site: www.hamdenhall.org

HAMPSHIRE COUNTRY SCHOOL

Rindge, New Hampshire

See Junior Boarding Schools section.

HAMPTON ROADS ACADEMY

739 Academy Lane
Newport News, Virginia 23602

Head of School: Mr. Peter Mertz

General Information Coeducational day college-preparatory school. Grades PK–12. Founded: 1959. Setting: suburban. 53-acre campus. 4 buildings on campus. Approved or accredited by Virginia Association of Independent Schools and Virginia Department of Education. Member of National Association of Independent Schools. Total enrollment: 589. Upper school average class size: 16. Upper school faculty-student ratio: 1:10. Upper School students typically attend 5 days per week. The average school day consists of 6 hours and 30 minutes.

Faculty School total: 70. In upper school: 13 men, 17 women; 19 have advanced degrees.

Subjects Offered African studies, algebra, American history, American literature, anatomy, art, biology, calculus, ceramics, chemistry, creative writing, drama, driver education, earth science, economics, English, English literature, European history, expository writing, fine arts, French, geography, geometry, government/civics, grammar, health, history, Latin, mathematics, music, photography, physical education, physics, physiology, science, social studies, Spanish, speech, statistics, theater, trigonometry, typing, world history, world literature, writing.

Graduation Requirements Arts and fine arts (art, music, dance, drama), English, foreign language, mathematics, physical education (includes health), science, social studies (includes history), community service. Community service is required.

Special Academic Programs 19 Advanced Placement exams for which test preparation is offered; honors section; independent study.

College Admission Counseling 71 students graduated in 2011; all went to college, including Hampden-Sydney College; James Madison University; The College of William and Mary; University of Virginia; Virginia Polytechnic Institute and State University. Median SAT critical reading: 600, median SAT math: 600, median SAT writing: 600, median combined SAT: 1800, median composite ACT: 22. 60% scored over 600 on SAT critical reading, 54% scored over 600 on SAT math, 56% scored over 600 on SAT writing, 57% scored over 1800 on combined SAT, 36% scored over 26 on composite ACT.

Student Life Upper grades have specified standards of dress, student council, honor system. Discipline rests primarily with faculty.

Tuition and Aid Day student tuition: $14,800. Tuition installment plan (SMART Tuition Payment Plan). Need-based scholarship grants available. In 2011–12, 18% of upper-school students received aid. Total amount of financial aid awarded in 2011–12: $800,000.

Admissions Traditional secondary-level entrance grade is 9. For fall 2011, 43 students applied for upper-level admission, 37 were accepted, 29 enrolled. ERB, school's own test and writing sample required. Deadline for receipt of application materials: none. Application fee required: $125. On-campus interview required.

Athletics Interscholastic: baseball (boys), basketball (b,g), cheering (g), cross-country running (b,g), field hockey (g), football (b), golf (b,g), lacrosse (b), physical training (b,g), sailing (b,g), soccer (b,g), softball (g), swimming and diving (b,g), tennis (b,g), track and field (b,g), volleyball (g), weight training (b,g); coed interscholastic: aquatics; coed intramural: equestrian sports, fitness, physical fitness, physical training, ropes courses, strength & conditioning, ultimate Frisbee, weight training. 3 PE instructors, 44 coaches, 1 athletic trainer.

Computers Computers are regularly used in English, mathematics, music, science, writing, yearbook classes. Computer network features include on-campus library services, online commercial services, Internet access, wireless campus network, Internet filtering or blocking technology. Student e-mail accounts are available to students. Students grades are available online. The school has a published electronic and media policy.

Contact Rebecca Bresee, Director of Admission. 757-884-9148. Fax: 757-884-9137. E-mail: RBrese@hra.org. Web site: www.hra.org

HARDING ACADEMY

1100 Cherry Road
Memphis, Tennessee 38117

Head of School: Mr. Allen Gillespie

General Information Coeducational day college-preparatory, arts, and religious studies school, affiliated with Christian faith. Grades PS–12. Founded: 1952. Setting: urban. 28-acre campus. 3 buildings on campus. Approved or accredited by National Christian School Association, Southern Association of Colleges and Schools, and Tennessee Department of Education. Endowment: $2 million. Total enrollment: 1,222. Upper school average class size: 19. Upper school faculty-student ratio: 1:13. There are 175 required school days per year for Upper School students. Upper School students typically attend 5 days per week. The average school day consists of 6 hours and 45 minutes.

Upper School Student Profile Grade 7: 82 students (38 boys, 44 girls); Grade 8: 93 students (48 boys, 45 girls); Grade 9: 84 students (37 boys, 47 girls); Grade 10: 75 students (37 boys, 38 girls); Grade 11: 100 students (54 boys, 46 girls); Grade 12: 100 students (52 boys, 48 girls). 47% of students are Christian.

Faculty School total: 45. In upper school: 18 men, 27 women; 23 have advanced degrees.

Subjects Offered Accounting, algebra, American government, American history, American history-AP, American literature, art, art-AP, band, Bible, biology, biology-AP, British literature, calculus-AP, chemistry, chorus, computer applications, concert band, drama, earth science, English, English language and composition-AP, English literature and composition-AP, etymology, French, geography, geometry, grammar, humanities, journalism, keyboarding, physical fitness, Spanish, Spanish language-AP, speech, statistics, world history.

Graduation Requirements Algebra, American government, American history, American literature, arts and fine arts (art, music, dance, drama), Bible, biology, British literature, English, fitness, foreign language, geometry, speech, world history.

Special Academic Programs 8 Advanced Placement exams for which test preparation is offered; honors section.

College Admission Counseling 64 students graduated in 2011; 63 went to college, including Harding University; Lipscomb University; The University of Tennessee; The University of Tennessee at Chattanooga; University of Memphis. Other: 1 entered military service. Mean SAT critical reading: 534, mean SAT math: 499, mean SAT writing: 540, mean composite ACT: 24.

Student Life Upper grades have uniform requirement, student council, honor system. Discipline rests primarily with faculty. Attendance at religious services is required.

Tuition and Aid Day student tuition: $9795–$10,795. Tuition installment plan (monthly payment plans, individually arranged payment plans). Tuition reduction for siblings, need-based scholarship grants available. In 2011–12, 18% of upper-school students received aid. Total amount of financial aid awarded in 2011–12: $191,824.

Admissions Traditional secondary-level entrance grade is 7. For fall 2011, 74 students applied for upper-level admission, 62 were accepted, 56 enrolled. Metropolitan Achievement Short Form and Otis-Lennon School Ability Test required. Deadline for receipt of application materials: none. Application fee required: $50. Interview required.

Athletics Interscholastic: baseball (boys), basketball (b,g), bowling (b,g), cheering (g), cross-country running (b,g), fitness (b,g), football (b), golf (b,g), soccer (b,g), softball (g), tennis (b,g), track and field (b,g), volleyball (g). 2 PE instructors, 45 coaches, 1 athletic trainer.

Computers Computers are regularly used in accounting, keyboarding classes. Computer network features include on-campus library services, online commercial services, Internet access. Students grades are available online. The school has a published electronic and media policy.

Contact Mrs. Karen Sills, Administrative Assistant in Admissions. 901-767-4494 Ext. 113. Fax: 901-763-4949. E-mail: sills.karen@hardinglions.org. Web site: www.hardinglions.org

HARGRAVE MILITARY ACADEMY

200 Military Drive
Chatham, Virginia 24531

Head of School: Brig. Gen. Don Broome, USA (Ret.)

General Information Boys' boarding and day college-preparatory, general academic, arts, religious studies, technology, academic post-graduate, leadership and ethics, and military school, affiliated with Baptist General Association of Virginia. Grades 7–PG. Founded: 1909. Setting: small town. Nearest major city is Danville. Students are housed in single-sex dormitories. 214-acre campus. 13 buildings on campus. Approved or accredited by Southern Association of Colleges and Schools, The Association of Boarding Schools, and Virginia Association of Independent Schools. Member of National Association of Independent Schools. Endowment: $3.5 million. Total enrollment: 310. Upper school average class size: 11. Upper school faculty-student ratio: 1:12. Upper School students typically attend 5 days per week.

Upper School Student Profile 24 states are represented in upper school student body. 20% of students are Baptist General Association of Virginia.

Faculty In upper school: 18 men, 12 women; 30 have advanced degrees; 12 reside on campus.

Subjects Offered Advanced biology, advanced chemistry, advanced math, Advanced Placement courses, algebra, American government, American history, American literature, art, astronomy, Bible studies, biology, calculus, chemistry, creative writing, debate, English, English literature, environmental science, ESL, geometry, government/civics, health, history, journalism, leadership, leadership and service, leadership education training, Mandarin, mathematics, media production, physical education, physics, psychology, reading, religion, SAT/ACT preparation, science, social studies, sociology, Spanish, speech, study skills, TOEFL preparation, trigonometry.

Graduation Requirements English, foreign language, mathematics, physical education (includes health), religion (includes Bible studies and theology), science, social studies (includes history).

Special Academic Programs Advanced Placement exam preparation; honors section; independent study; study at local college for college credit; remedial reading and/or remedial writing; remedial math; programs in general development for dyslexic students; special instructional classes for students with Attention Deficit Disorder; ESL (8 students enrolled).

College Admission Counseling 63 students graduated in 2012; 59 went to college, including Hampden-Sydney College; The University of North Carolina at

Charlotte; United States Military Academy; Virginia Military Institute; Virginia Polytechnic Institute and State University.

Student Life Upper grades have uniform requirement, student council, honor system. Discipline rests equally with students and faculty. Attendance at religious services is required.

Summer Programs Remediation, enrichment, advancement, ESL, sports, rigorous outdoor training, computer instruction programs offered; session focuses on academics/sports camps; held on campus; accepts boys; open to students from other schools. 140 students usually enrolled. 2013 schedule: June 30 to July 28. Application deadline: June 29.

Tuition and Aid Day student tuition: $12,900; 5-day tuition and room/board: $29,900; 7-day tuition and room/board: $28,600. Guaranteed tuition plan. Tuition installment plan (monthly payment plans, individually arranged payment plans). Tuition reduction for siblings, merit scholarship grants, need-based scholarship grants, need-based loans, Sallie Mae available. In 2012–13, 32% of upper-school students received aid; total upper-school merit-scholarship money awarded: $52,000. Total amount of financial aid awarded in 2012–13: $525,000.

Admissions Traditional secondary-level entrance grade is 10. Math and English placement tests required. Deadline for receipt of application materials: none. Application fee required: $75. Interview recommended.

Athletics Interscholastic: aquatics, baseball, basketball, cross-country running, football, golf, independent competitive sports, lacrosse, marksmanship, riflery, soccer, swimming and diving, tennis, wrestling; intramural: aquatics, backpacking, billiards, canoeing/kayaking, climbing, cross-country running, drill team, fishing, fitness, fitness walking, hiking/backpacking, independent competitive sports, jogging, jump rope, kayaking, lacrosse, life saving, marksmanship, mountaineering, Nautilus, outdoor activities, outdoor adventure, outdoor recreation, paint ball, physical fitness, physical training, rappelling, riflery, rock climbing, ropes courses, running, scuba diving, skeet shooting, skiing (downhill), strength & conditioning, swimming and diving, table tennis, tennis, trap and skeet, walking, water polo, weight lifting, weight training. 1 PE instructor, 10 coaches, 1 athletic trainer.

Computers Computers are regularly used in all academic classes. Computer network features include on-campus library services, online commercial services, Internet access, wireless campus network, Internet filtering or blocking technology. Campus intranet, student e-mail accounts, and computer access in designated common areas are available to students. Students grades are available online. The school has a published electronic and media policy.

Contact Mrs. Amy Walker, Director of Admissions. 434-432-2481 Ext. 2130. Fax: 434-432-3129. E-mail: admissions@hargrave.edu. Web site: www.hargrave.edu

THE HARKER SCHOOL

500 Saratoga Avenue
San Jose, California 95129

Head of School: Christopher Nikoloff

General Information Coeducational day college-preparatory, arts, technology, and gifted students school. Grades K–12. Founded: 1893. Setting: urban. 16-acre campus. 7 buildings on campus. Approved or accredited by California Association of Independent Schools, Western Association of Schools and Colleges, and California Department of Education. Member of National Association of Independent Schools. Total enrollment: 1,819. Upper school average class size: 18. Upper school faculty-student ratio: 1:10. Upper School students typically attend 5 days per week.

Upper School Student Profile Grade 9: 190 students (88 boys, 102 girls); Grade 10: 187 students (99 boys, 88 girls); Grade 11: 175 students (99 boys, 76 girls); Grade 12: 175 students (85 boys, 90 girls).

Faculty School total: 187. In upper school: 40 men, 51 women; 80 have advanced degrees.

Subjects Offered 20th century American writers, acting, advanced math, algebra, American literature, anatomy and physiology, architecture, art history, art history-AP, Asian history, astronomy, baseball, basketball, biology, biology-AP, biotechnology, British literature, British literature (honors), calculus-AP, ceramics, cheerleading, chemistry, chemistry-AP, choreography, classical studies, college counseling, community service, computer science-AP, dance, dance performance, debate, discrete mathematics, drawing, ecology, economics, electronics, engineering, English literature and composition-AP, English literature-AP, environmental science-AP, ethics, European history-AP, evolution, expository writing, film and literature, fitness, forensics, French, French language-AP, French literature-AP, geometry, golf, graphic arts, great books, history of dance, Holocaust seminar, honors algebra, honors geometry, human geography - AP, Japanese, Japanese literature, jazz band, journalism, Latin, Latin-AP, linear algebra, literary magazine, macro/microeconomics-AP, macroeconomics-AP, Mandarin, medieval literature, mentorship program, music appreciation, music theory-AP, newspaper, orchestra, organic chemistry, painting, photography, physics, physics-AP, play production, poetry, political thought, pre-calculus, programming, psychology, psychology-AP, public policy, public speaking, research, robotics, scene study, sculpture, Shakespeare, softball, Spanish, Spanish language-AP, Spanish literature-AP, statistics, statistics-AP, stone carving, student government, studio art-AP, study skills, swimming, technical theater, tennis, theater arts, theater history, track and field, trigonometry, U.S. government and politics-AP, U.S. history, U.S. history-AP, video and animation, visual arts, vocal ensemble, volleyball, water polo, weight training, Western philosophy, world history, world history-AP, world religions, wrestling, yearbook, yoga.

Graduation Requirements Arts and fine arts (art, music, dance, drama), biology, chemistry, computer science, English, foreign language, mathematics, physical education (includes health), physics, public speaking, U.S. history, world history, 30 total hours of community service, one year arts survey theater, dance, music or visual arts).

Special Academic Programs Advanced Placement exam preparation; honors section; independent study; academic accommodation for the gifted.

College Admission Counseling 172 students graduated in 2012; all went to college, including Duke University; Santa Clara University; Stanford University; University of California, Berkeley; University of California, San Diego; University of Southern California. Mean SAT critical reading: 708, mean SAT math: 735, mean SAT writing: 731.

Student Life Upper grades have specified standards of dress, student council, honor system. Discipline rests primarily with faculty.

Summer Programs Enrichment, advancement, sports programs offered; session focuses on academics, sports, enrichment, research; held both on and off campus; held at abroad for upper school research & language students and field trips to local historical and cultural sites; accepts boys and girls; open to students from other schools. 1,200 students usually enrolled. 2013 schedule: June 21 to August 9.

Tuition and Aid Day student tuition: $37,000. Need-based scholarship grants, need-based loans available. In 2012–13, 10% of upper-school students received aid.

Admissions Traditional secondary-level entrance grade is 9. ERB CTP IV, essay, ISEE or SSAT required. Deadline for receipt of application materials: January 17. Application fee required: $100. Interview required.

Athletics Interscholastic: baseball (boys), basketball (b,g), cross-country running (b,g), football (b), golf (b,g), lacrosse (g), soccer (b,g), softball (g), swimming and diving (b,g), tennis (b,g), track and field (b,g), volleyball (b,g), water polo (b,g); coed interscholastic: cheering, wrestling; coed intramural: aerobics/dance, dance, fencing, fitness, physical fitness, tennis, yoga. 4 PE instructors, 50 coaches, 1 athletic trainer.

Computers Computers are regularly used in all academic, college planning, graphic arts, newspaper, yearbook classes. Computer network features include on-campus library services, online commercial services, Internet access, wireless campus network, Internet filtering or blocking technology, ProQuest, Gale Group, InfoTrac, Facts On File. Campus intranet and student e-mail accounts are available to students. The school has a published electronic and media policy.

Contact Christianne Marra, Assistant to the Director of Admission. 408-249-2510. Fax: 408-984-2325. E-mail: ChristianneM@harker.org. Web site: www.harker.org

THE HARLEY SCHOOL

1981 Clover Street
Rochester, New York 14618

Head of School: Ms. Valerie Myntti

General Information Coeducational day college-preparatory and arts school. Grades N–12. Founded: 1917. Setting: suburban. 25-acre campus. 3 buildings on campus. Approved or accredited by National Independent Private Schools Association and New York State Association of Independent Schools. Member of National Association of Independent Schools. Endowment: $9.2 million. Total enrollment: 513. Upper school average class size: 7. Upper school faculty-student ratio: 1:7. There are 180 required school days per year for Upper School students. Upper School students typically attend 5 days per week. The average school day consists of 6 hours and 50 minutes.

Upper School Student Profile Grade 9: 43 students (19 boys, 24 girls); Grade 10: 41 students (16 boys, 25 girls); Grade 11: 46 students (24 boys, 22 girls); Grade 12: 13 students (11 boys, 2 girls).

Faculty School total: 90. In upper school: 14 men, 14 women; 28 have advanced degrees.

Subjects Offered 3-dimensional art, Advanced Placement courses, algebra, American history, anthropology, art, art history, art-AP, band, biology, calculus, calculus-AP, ceramics, chamber groups, chemistry, Chinese, choir, chorus, community service, comparative government and politics-AP, computer graphics, computer math, computer programming, computer science, creative writing, debate, desktop publishing, drama, drawing, driver education, economics-AP, English, English language and composition-AP, English literature, environmental science, ethics, European history, expository writing, film, fine arts, foreign language, French, gardening, geometry, graphic arts, Greek, health, jazz band, language-AP, Latin, mathematics, multimedia, music, music theory, orchestra, organic gardening, outdoor education, photography, physical education, physics, psychology, SAT preparation, science, Shakespeare, social studies, Spanish, speech, student government, study skills, theater, theater arts, theater production, U.S. history-AP, voice, world history, writing, yoga.

Graduation Requirements Arts and fine arts (art, music, dance, drama), computer science, English, foreign language, internship, mathematics, physical education (includes health), science, social studies (includes history), participation in team sports, community service. Community service is required.

Special Academic Programs 17 Advanced Placement exams for which test preparation is offered.

College Admission Counseling 46 students graduated in 2012; all went to college, including Cornell University; Hobart and William Smith Colleges; Rochester

Institute of Technology; University of Rochester; Vassar College; Yale University. Mean SAT critical reading: 615, mean SAT math: 618, mean SAT writing: 601.

Student Life Upper grades have student council, honor system. Discipline rests primarily with faculty.

Summer Programs Remediation, enrichment, sports, art/fine arts, computer instruction programs offered; session focuses on day camp, outdoor skills, swimming, tennis, writing, college prep; held both on and off campus; held at field house, classrooms, grounds, field trips; accepts boys and girls; open to students from other schools. 150 students usually enrolled. 2013 schedule: June 10 to August 2. Application deadline: May.

Tuition and Aid Day student tuition: $19,800–$21,470. Tuition installment plan (Insured Tuition Payment Plan, monthly payment plans, 2-payment plan, prepaid discount plan). Tuition reduction for siblings, need-based scholarship grants available. In 2012–13, 36% of upper-school students received aid.

Admissions Traditional secondary-level entrance grade is 9. For fall 2012, 20 students applied for upper-level admission, 18 were accepted, 18 enrolled. Essay and Math Placement Exam required. Deadline for receipt of application materials: none. Application fee required: $50. On-campus interview required.

Athletics Interscholastic: baseball (boys), basketball (b,g), bowling (b,g), golf (b), skiing (downhill) (b,g), soccer (b,g), softball (b,g), swimming and diving (b,g), tennis (b,g), track and field (b,g), volleyball (b,g); coed interscholastic: cross-country running, outdoor education, running, yoga. 3 PE instructors, 11 coaches.

Computers Computers are regularly used in all academic, art classes. Computer network features include Internet access, wireless campus network. The school has a published electronic and media policy.

Contact Mrs. Ivone Foisy, Director of Admissions. 585-442-1770. Fax: 585-442-5758. E-mail: ifoisy@harleyschool.org. Web site: www.harleyschool.org

HARRELLS CHRISTIAN ACADEMY

360 Tomahawk Highway
PO Box 88
Harrells, North Carolina 28444

Head of School: Mr. Marcus P. Skipper

General Information Coeducational day college-preparatory school, affiliated with Christian faith. Grades K–12. Founded: 1969. Setting: rural. Nearest major city is Wilmington. 32-acre campus. 7 buildings on campus. Approved or accredited by North Carolina Association of Independent Schools, Southern Association of Colleges and Schools, Southern Association of Independent Schools, and North Carolina Department of Education. Total enrollment: 404. Upper school average class size: 12. Upper school faculty-student ratio: 1:9. There are 178 required school days per year for Upper School students. Upper School students typically attend 5 days per week. The average school day consists of 6 hours and 16 minutes.

Upper School Student Profile Grade 9: 36 students (16 boys, 20 girls); Grade 10: 42 students (26 boys, 16 girls); Grade 11: 35 students (20 boys, 15 girls); Grade 12: 33 students (21 boys, 12 girls). 96% of students are Christian.

Faculty School total: 15. In upper school: 4 men, 11 women; 5 have advanced degrees.

Subjects Offered Algebra, animal science, art, art education, biology, biology-AP, calculus, ceramics, chemistry, chemistry-AP, computer art, earth science, English, English language and composition-AP, English literature, English literature and composition-AP, French, government/civics, history, journalism, mathematics, painting, photography, physical education, physical science, religion, social studies, Spanish, U.S. history-AP, weightlifting, world history-AP, yearbook.

Graduation Requirements Biology, computer applications, electives, English, environmental science, foreign language, mathematics, physical education (includes health), physical science, religious studies, social studies (includes history).

Special Academic Programs 4 Advanced Placement exams for which test preparation is offered; honors section; study at local college for college credit; programs in English, mathematics, general development for dyslexic students.

College Admission Counseling 36 students graduated in 2012; 33 went to college, including East Carolina University; Meredith College; North Carolina State University; The University of North Carolina at Chapel Hill; The University of North Carolina Wilmington. Other: 1 went to work, 2 had other specific plans. Median SAT critical reading: 470, median SAT math: 480, median SAT writing: 490, median combined SAT: 1440, median composite ACT: 21. 15% scored over 600 on SAT critical reading, 9% scored over 600 on SAT math, 9% scored over 600 on SAT writing, 13% scored over 1800 on combined SAT, 1% scored over 26 on composite ACT.

Student Life Upper grades have specified standards of dress, honor system. Discipline rests primarily with faculty. Attendance at religious services is required.

Tuition and Aid Day student tuition: $7950. Tuition installment plan (monthly payment plans, individually arranged payment plans). Tuition reduction for siblings, need-based scholarship grants available. In 2012–13, 10% of upper-school students received aid. Total amount of financial aid awarded in 2012–13: $62,500.

Admissions Traditional secondary-level entrance grade is 9. For fall 2012, 11 students applied for upper-level admission, 11 were accepted, 10 enrolled. Admissions testing or Stanford Achievement Test required. Deadline for receipt of application materials: none. Application fee required: $35. On-campus interview required.

Athletics Interscholastic: baseball (boys), basketball (b,g), cheering (g), football (b), soccer (b,g), softball (g), tennis (g), volleyball (g); coed interscholastic: golf. 1 PE instructor, 1 coach.

Computers Computers are regularly used in art, computer applications, English, journalism, yearbook classes. Computer resources include Internet access, wireless campus network, Internet filtering or blocking technology. Students grades are available online. The school has a published electronic and media policy.

Contact Mrs. Susan Frederick, Administrative Assistant. 910-532-4575 Ext. 221. Fax: 910-532-2958. E-mail: sfrederick@harrellsca.org. Web site: www.harrellschristianacademy.com

THE HARRISBURG ACADEMY

10 Erford Road
Wormleysburg, Pennsylvania 17043

Head of School: Dr. James Newman

General Information Coeducational day college-preparatory and arts school. Grades PS–12. Founded: 1784. Setting: suburban. Nearest major city is Harrisburg. 23-acre campus. 1 building on campus. Approved or accredited by International Baccalaureate Organization, Middle States Association of Colleges and Schools, Pennsylvania Association of Independent Schools, and Pennsylvania Department of Education. Member of National Association of Independent Schools. Endowment: $5 million. Total enrollment: 400. Upper school average class size: 10. Upper school faculty-student ratio: 1:8. There are 172 required school days per year for Upper School students. Upper School students typically attend 5 days per week. The average school day consists of 7 hours.

Upper School Student Profile Grade 6: 28 students (14 boys, 14 girls); Grade 7: 28 students (18 boys, 10 girls); Grade 8: 20 students (10 boys, 10 girls); Grade 9: 20 students (10 boys, 10 girls); Grade 10: 22 students (12 boys, 10 girls); Grade 11: 25 students (15 boys, 10 girls); Grade 12: 23 students (10 boys, 13 girls).

Faculty School total: 55. In upper school: 8 men, 13 women; 9 have advanced degrees.

Subjects Offered Advanced Placement courses, algebra, American history, American literature, art, biology, calculus, ceramics, chemistry, computer science, creative writing, drama, economics, English, English literature, environmental science, European history, expository writing, fine arts, French, geography, geometry, grammar, health, history, International Baccalaureate courses, Latin, mathematics, music, philosophy, physical education, physics, science, social studies, Spanish, world history, world literature, writing.

Graduation Requirements Algebra, arts and fine arts (art, music, dance, drama), college planning, English, foreign language, geometry, physical education (includes health), public speaking, science, social studies (includes history). Community service is required.

Special Academic Programs International Baccalaureate program; Advanced Placement exam preparation; independent study.

College Admission Counseling 32 students graduated in 2012; all went to college, including American University; Dickinson College; Drexel University; Franklin & Marshall College; Penn State University Park; University of Pittsburgh. 50% scored over 600 on SAT critical reading, 50% scored over 600 on SAT math.

Student Life Upper grades have specified standards of dress, student council, honor system. Discipline rests primarily with faculty.

Summer Programs Enrichment, art/fine arts programs offered; session focuses on enrichment; held on campus; accepts boys and girls; open to students from other schools. 2013 schedule: July 1 to August 10.

Tuition and Aid Day student tuition: $16,880. Tuition installment plan (Insured Tuition Payment Plan, monthly payment plans, individually arranged payment plans, need-based financial aid and merit scholarship programs). Tuition reduction for siblings, merit scholarship grants, need-based scholarship grants available. In 2012–13, 30% of upper-school students received aid; total upper-school merit-scholarship money awarded: $40,000. Total amount of financial aid awarded in 2012–13: $400,000.

Admissions Traditional secondary-level entrance grade is 9. For fall 2012, 14 students applied for upper-level admission, 10 were accepted, 8 enrolled. Admissions testing or TOEFL or SLEP required. Deadline for receipt of application materials: none. Application fee required: $75. Interview required.

Athletics Interscholastic: basketball (boys, girls), golf (b,g), lacrosse (b), soccer (b,g), swimming and diving (b,g), tennis (b,g); coed interscholastic: golf; coed intramural: cross-country running, skiing (downhill). 3 PE instructors, 18 coaches, 1 athletic trainer.

Computers Computers are regularly used in art, English, foreign language, graphic design, library, mathematics, music, science classes. Computer network features include on-campus library services, Internet access, wireless campus network, Internet filtering or blocking technology. Campus intranet and student e-mail accounts are available to students. Students grades are available online. The school has a published electronic and media policy.

Contact Mrs. Jessica Warren, Director of Admissions and Marketing. 717-763-7811 Ext. 313. Fax: 717-975-0894. E-mail: warren.j@harrisburgacademy.org. Web site: www.harrisburgacademy.org

HARVARD-WESTLAKE SCHOOL

3700 Coldwater Canyon
Studio City, California 91604

Head of School: Thomas C. Hudnut

General Information Coeducational day college-preparatory school, affiliated with Episcopal Church. Grades 7–12. Founded: 1989. Setting: urban. Nearest major city is Los Angeles. 26-acre campus. 12 buildings on campus. Approved or accredited by Western Association of Schools and Colleges. Member of National Association of Independent Schools. Endowment: $47.1 million. Total enrollment: 1,605. Upper school average class size: 16. Upper school faculty-student ratio: 1:8. Upper School students typically attend 5 days per week. The average school day consists of 6 hours and 35 minutes.

Upper School Student Profile Grade 9: 299 students (158 boys, 141 girls); Grade 10: 295 students (154 boys, 141 girls); Grade 11: 297 students (160 boys, 137 girls); Grade 12: 287 students (147 boys, 140 girls).

Faculty School total: 122. In upper school: 72 men, 50 women; 85 have advanced degrees.

Subjects Offered 3-dimensional art, advanced studio art-AP, algebra, American history, American literature, American literature-AP, anatomy, architecture, art, art history, art history-AP, Asian studies, astronomy, biology, biology-AP, calculus, calculus-AP, ceramics, chemistry, chemistry-AP, Chinese, choreography, chorus, classics, community service, comparative government and politics-AP, computer animation, computer programming, computer science, computer science-AP, creative writing, dance, drama, drawing, economics, economics-AP, electronics, English, English language and composition-AP, English literature, English literature-AP, environmental science, environmental science-AP, European history, expository writing, film, film studies, fine arts, French, French language-AP, French literature-AP, geography, geology, geometry, government and politics-AP, government/civics, grammar, health, human development, human geography - AP, Japanese, jazz, journalism, Latin, Latin-AP, logic, macro/microeconomics-AP, Mandarin, mathematics, music, music history, music theory-AP, oceanography, orchestra, painting, photography, physical education, physics, physics-AP, physiology, political science, pre-calculus, psychology, Russian, science, senior project, Shakespeare, social studies, Spanish, Spanish language-AP, Spanish literature-AP, statistics, statistics-AP, studio art-AP, technical theater, theater, trigonometry, U.S. government and politics-AP, U.S. history-AP, video, women's studies, world history, world history-AP, world literature, yearbook, zoology.

Graduation Requirements English, foreign language, history, human development, mathematics, performing arts, physical education (includes health), science, visual arts. Community service is required.

Special Academic Programs 30 Advanced Placement exams for which test preparation is offered; honors section; independent study; term-away projects; study abroad; academic accommodation for the gifted, the musically talented, and the artistically talented.

College Admission Counseling 292 students graduated in 2012; 289 went to college, including Cornell University; New York University; Stanford University; University of Chicago; University of Michigan; University of Southern California. Other: 3 had other specific plans. Mean SAT critical reading: 693, mean SAT math: 702, mean SAT writing: 718. 90% scored over 600 on SAT critical reading, 91% scored over 600 on SAT math.

Student Life Upper grades have specified standards of dress, student council, honor system. Discipline rests primarily with faculty.

Summer Programs Enrichment, sports, art/fine arts, rigorous outdoor training, computer instruction programs offered; session focuses on enrichment and sports; held on campus; accepts boys and girls; open to students from other schools. 500 students usually enrolled. 2013 schedule: June 10 to August 9. Application deadline: none.

Tuition and Aid Day student tuition: $31,350. Tuition installment plan (monthly payment plans, semi-annual payment plan, triennial payment plan). Need-based scholarship grants, short-term loans (payable by end of year in which loan is made) available. In 2012–13, 18% of upper-school students received aid. Total amount of financial aid awarded in 2012–13: $8,069,000.

Admissions Traditional secondary-level entrance grade is 9. For fall 2012, 536 students applied for upper-level admission, 124 were accepted, 86 enrolled. ISEE required. Deadline for receipt of application materials: January 18. Application fee required: $200. On-campus interview required.

Athletics Interscholastic: baseball (boys), basketball (b,g), cross-country running (b,g), field hockey (g), football (b), golf (b,g), gymnastics (g), lacrosse (b), soccer (b,g), softball (g), swimming and diving (b,g), tennis (b,g), track and field (b,g), volleyball (b,g), water polo (b,g), wrestling (b); coed interscholastic: diving, equestrian sports, fencing, martial arts; coed intramural: badminton. 6 PE instructors, 32 coaches, 3 athletic trainers.

Computers Computers are regularly used in art, English, foreign language, history, mathematics, music, science classes. Computer resources include on-campus library services, Internet access, wireless campus network, music composition and editing, foreign language lab, science lab. Campus intranet, student e-mail accounts, and computer access in designated common areas are available to students. Students grades are available online.

Contact Elizabeth Gregory, Director of Admission. 310-274-7281. Fax: 310-288-3212. E-mail: egregory@hw.com. Web site: www.hw.com

THE HARVEY SCHOOL

260 Jay Street
Katonah, New York 10536

Head of School: Mr. Barry W. Fenstermacher

General Information Coeducational boarding and day and distance learning college-preparatory school. Boarding grades 9–12, day grades 6–12. Distance learning grades 6–12. Founded: 1916. Setting: suburban. Students are housed in single-sex dormitories. 125-acre campus. 14 buildings on campus. Approved or accredited by New York State Association of Independent Schools. Member of National Association of Independent Schools. Endowment: $2 million. Total enrollment: 334. Upper school average class size: 11. Upper school faculty-student ratio: 1:6. There are 165 required school days per year for Upper School students. Upper School students typically attend 5 days per week. The average school day consists of 8 hours and 50 minutes.

Upper School Student Profile Grade 9: 51 students (27 boys, 24 girls); Grade 10: 67 students (39 boys, 28 girls); Grade 11: 75 students (43 boys, 32 girls); Grade 12: 55 students (31 boys, 24 girls). 11% of students are boarding students. 75% are state residents. 3 states are represented in upper school student body.

Faculty School total: 56. In upper school: 27 men, 19 women; 34 have advanced degrees; 24 reside on campus.

Subjects Offered Algebra, American history, American literature, art, art history, biology, calculus, ceramics, chemistry, composition-AP, computer programming-AP, creative writing, drama, English, English literature, European history, expository writing, fine arts, French, general science, geology, geometry, government/civics, grammar, Greek, history, Japanese, Latin, mathematics, music, photography, physics, religion, science, social studies, Spanish, theater, trigonometry, world history, writing.

Graduation Requirements Arts and fine arts (art, music, dance, drama), computer literacy, English, foreign language, mathematics, science, social sciences, social studies (includes history).

Special Academic Programs 10 Advanced Placement exams for which test preparation is offered; honors section; independent study.

College Admission Counseling 63 students graduated in 2012; all went to college, including Barnard College; Bentley University; Cornell University; University of Connecticut; Villanova University.

Student Life Upper grades have specified standards of dress, student council. Discipline rests primarily with faculty.

Summer Programs Remediation, advancement programs offered; session focuses on online academic course; held both on and off campus; held at via distance learning; accepts boys and girls; open to students from other schools. 2013 schedule: June 20 to August 10. Application deadline: May 1.

Tuition and Aid Day student tuition: $31,250–$33,250; 5-day tuition and room/board: $40,250–$41,250. Tuition installment plan (FACTS Tuition Payment Plan, individually arranged payment plans). Need-based scholarship grants available. In 2012–13, 28% of upper-school students received aid. Total amount of financial aid awarded in 2012–13: $2,088,000.

Admissions Traditional secondary-level entrance grade is 9. For fall 2012, 134 students applied for upper-level admission, 94 were accepted, 59 enrolled. Deadline for receipt of application materials: none. Application fee required: $50. Interview required.

Athletics Interscholastic: baseball (boys), basketball (b,g), football (b), ice hockey (b), lacrosse (b,g), rugby (b), soccer (b,g), softball (g), volleyball (g); coed interscholastic: cross-country running, tennis, weight lifting; coed intramural: aerobics, dance, figure skating, fitness, fitness walking, Frisbee, golf, modern dance, strength & conditioning, tai chi, yoga. 1 athletic trainer.

Computers Computers are regularly used in English, foreign language, history, mathematics, science classes. Computer resources include on-campus library services, online commercial services, Internet access. The school has a published electronic and media policy.

Contact Mr. William Porter, Director of Admissions. 914-232-3161 Ext. 113. Fax: 914-232-6034. E-mail: wporter@harveyschool.org. Web site: www.harveyschool.org

THE HAVERFORD SCHOOL

450 Lancaster Avenue
Haverford, Pennsylvania 19041

Head of School: Dr. Joseph T. Cox

General Information Boys' day college-preparatory and arts school. Grades PK–12. Founded: 1884. Setting: suburban. Nearest major city is Philadelphia. 32-acre campus. 7 buildings on campus. Approved or accredited by Middle States Association of Colleges and Schools, Pennsylvania Association of Independent Schools, and Pennsylvania Department of Education. Member of National Association of Independent Schools and Secondary School Admission Test Board. Endowment: $40 million. Total enrollment: 991. Upper school average class size: 16. Upper school faculty-student ratio: 1:7. Upper School students typically attend 5 days per week.

Upper School Student Profile Grade 9: 121 students (121 boys); Grade 10: 106 students (106 boys); Grade 11: 103 students (103 boys); Grade 12: 88 students (88 boys).

Faculty School total: 117. In upper school: 36 men, 11 women; 31 have advanced degrees.

Subjects Offered Algebra, American history, American literature, animal behavior, art, astronomy, biology, calculus, ceramics, chemistry, Chinese, Chinese studies, drama, ecology, economics, economics and history, English, English literature, European history, fine arts, French, geology, geometry, German, government/civics, history, Latin, mathematics, music, photography, physical education, physics, physiology, science, social studies, Spanish, statistics, theater, trigonometry, world affairs, world history, world literature.

Graduation Requirements Arts and fine arts (art, music, dance, drama), English, foreign language, mathematics, physical education (includes health), science, social studies (includes history).

Special Academic Programs Honors section; independent study; term-away projects; academic accommodation for the gifted; remedial reading and/or remedial writing; remedial math.

College Admission Counseling 96 students graduated in 2011; 94 went to college, including Cornell University; Franklin & Marshall College; Penn State University Park; Princeton University; University of Pennsylvania; University of Pittsburgh. Other: 1 entered a postgraduate year, 1 had other specific plans. Mean SAT critical reading: 630, mean SAT math: 640, mean SAT writing: 640, mean combined SAT: 1910, mean composite ACT: 26. 41% scored over 600 on SAT critical reading, 48% scored over 600 on SAT math, 42% scored over 600 on SAT writing.

Student Life Upper grades have specified standards of dress, student council, honor system. Discipline rests equally with students and faculty.

Tuition and Aid Day student tuition: $31,800. Tuition installment plan (Insured Tuition Payment Plan, monthly payment plans, individually arranged payment plans). Merit scholarship grants, need-based scholarship grants available. In 2011–12, 32% of upper-school students received aid; total upper-school merit-scholarship money awarded: $20,000. Total amount of financial aid awarded in 2011–12: $2,614,756.

Admissions Traditional secondary-level entrance grade is 9. For fall 2011, 183 students applied for upper-level admission, 73 were accepted, 52 enrolled. ISEE, SSAT or Wechsler Intelligence Scale for Children required. Deadline for receipt of application materials: none. Application fee required: $50. Interview required.

Athletics Interscholastic: aquatics, baseball, basketball, crew, cross-country running, football, golf, ice hockey, indoor track, lacrosse, rowing, soccer, squash, swimming and diving, tennis, track and field, water polo, winter (indoor) track, wrestling; intramural: fitness, physical fitness, physical training, soccer, strength & conditioning, weight training. 6 PE instructors, 2 coaches, 2 athletic trainers.

Computers Computers are regularly used in art, English, history, mathematics, music, science classes. Computer network features include on-campus library services, online commercial services, Internet access. Computer access in designated common areas is available to students. Students grades are available online. The school has a published electronic and media policy.

Contact Mr. Henry D. Fairfax, Director of Admissions. 610-642-3020 Ext. 1923. Fax: 610-642-8724. E-mail: hfairfax@haverford.org. Web site: www.haverford.org

HAWAIIAN MISSION ACADEMY

1438 Pensacola Street
Honolulu, Hawaii 96822

Head of School: Mr. Hugh P. Winn

General Information Coeducational boarding and day college-preparatory, general academic, arts, business, religious studies, bilingual studies, and technology school, affiliated with Seventh-day Adventist Church. Grades 9–12. Founded: 1895. Setting: urban. Students are housed in single-sex by floor dormitories. 4-acre campus. 4 buildings on campus. Approved or accredited by The Hawaii Council of Private Schools, Western Association of Schools and Colleges, and Hawaii Department of Education. Total enrollment: 118. Upper school average class size: 25. Upper school faculty-student ratio: 1:15. The average school day consists of 6 hours and 50 minutes.

Upper School Student Profile Grade 9: 30 students (16 boys, 14 girls); Grade 10: 34 students (20 boys, 14 girls); Grade 11: 34 students (20 boys, 14 girls); Grade 12: 22 students (8 boys, 14 girls). 20% of students are boarding students. 46% are state residents. 3 states are represented in upper school student body. 50% are international students. International students from China, Hong Kong, Japan, Macao, Republic of Korea, and Taiwan. 80% of students are Seventh-day Adventists.

Faculty School total: 13. In upper school: 8 men, 5 women; 9 have advanced degrees; 2 reside on campus.

Subjects Offered Algebra, anatomy and physiology, art, Bible, biology, business, business education, business skills, calculus, chemistry, choir, Christianity, community service, computer literacy, computer science, conceptual physics, concert choir, desktop publishing, digital art, economics, electives, English, English literature, ESL, family and consumer science, family living, general science, geometry, grammar, Hawaiian history, health, independent living, interactive media, journalism, keyboarding, lab science, library, Microsoft, personal finance, physical education, pre-algebra, pre-calculus, Spanish, student government, student publications, U.S. government, U.S. history, video film production, weight training, work experience, work-study, world history, yearbook.

Graduation Requirements Algebra, arts and fine arts (art, music, dance, drama), biology, chemistry, computer literacy, English, foreign language, geometry, Hawaiian history, keyboarding, physical education (includes health), physics, practical arts, religion (includes Bible studies and theology), social studies (includes history), U.S. government, work experience, world history, 25 hours of community service per year, 100 hours of work experience throughout the 4 years combined.

Special Academic Programs Honors section; ESL (8 students enrolled).

College Admission Counseling 33 students graduated in 2011; 30 went to college, including Kapiolani Community College; La Sierra University; Pacific Union College; University of Hawaii at Hilo; University of Hawaii at Manoa. Other: 3 had other specific plans. Mean SAT critical reading: 505, mean SAT math: 535.

Student Life Upper grades have uniform requirement, student council. Discipline rests primarily with faculty.

Tuition and Aid Day student tuition: $10,510; 7-day tuition and room/board: $9500. Tuition installment plan (Insured Tuition Payment Plan, monthly payment plans, individually arranged payment plans). Tuition reduction for siblings, need-based scholarship grants, paying campus jobs available. In 2011–12, 25% of upper-school students received aid.

Admissions Placement test and TOEFL required. Deadline for receipt of application materials: none. Application fee required: $25. Interview recommended.

Athletics Interscholastic: basketball (boys, girls), golf (b,g), volleyball (b,g). 3 PE instructors, 6 coaches.

Computers Computers are regularly used in desktop publishing, economics, graphic arts, journalism, keyboarding, media production, newspaper, publications, science, video film production, word processing, yearbook classes. Computer network features include on-campus library services, Internet access, wireless campus network. Students grades are available online.

Contact Mrs. Nenny Safotu, Registrar. 808-536-2207 Ext. 202. Fax: 808-524-3294. E-mail: registrar@hawaiianmissionacademy.org. Web site: www.hawaiianmissionacademy.org

HAWAII BAPTIST ACADEMY

2429 Pali Highway
Honolulu, Hawaii 96817

Head of School: Richard Bento

General Information Coeducational day college-preparatory and Christian education school, affiliated with Southern Baptist Convention. Grades K–12. Founded: 1949. Setting: urban. 13-acre campus. 6 buildings on campus. Approved or accredited by Association of Christian Schools International and Western Association of Schools and Colleges. Member of National Association of Independent Schools and Secondary School Admission Test Board. Endowment: $4.6 million. Total enrollment: 1,138. Upper school average class size: 17. Upper school faculty-student ratio: 1:17. There are 176 required school days per year for Upper School students. Upper School students typically attend 5 days per week. The average school day consists of 6 hours.

Upper School Student Profile Grade 9: 119 students (48 boys, 71 girls); Grade 10: 120 students (54 boys, 66 girls); Grade 11: 122 students (64 boys, 58 girls); Grade 12: 113 students (52 boys, 61 girls). 11% of students are Southern Baptist Convention.

Faculty School total: 89. In upper school: 20 men, 24 women; 20 have advanced degrees.

Subjects Offered Advanced Placement courses, algebra, American history, American literature, ancient world history, art, Bible studies, biology, biology-AP, British literature, calculus-AP, chemistry, chemistry-AP, Chinese, Christian education, Christian ethics, Christian studies, communication skills, computer applications, concert band, digital photography, discrete mathematics, drafting, drama, drama performance, drawing, economics, English, English language and composition-AP, English literature, English literature-AP, environmental science, film, film history, fine arts, forensics, French, geometry, handbells, Japanese, journalism, mathematics, modern world history, music theory-AP, oceanography, physical education, physics, physics-AP, political science, pre-calculus, psychology, psychology-AP, religion, science, social studies, Spanish, speech, statistics, statistics-AP, trigonometry, U.S. history-AP, world history, world literature, writing.

Graduation Requirements Algebra, ancient history, arts and fine arts (art, music, dance, drama), Bible studies, biology, communication skills, computer applications, economics, English, foreign language, mathematics, physical education (includes health), political science, science, social studies (includes history), U.S. history, world history.

Special Academic Programs Advanced Placement exam preparation; independent study.

College Admission Counseling 109 students graduated in 2012; all went to college, including Northern Arizona University; Santa Clara University; Seattle Pacific University; University of Hawaii at Manoa; University of Portland; Washington State University. Mean SAT critical reading: 543, mean SAT math: 600, mean SAT writing: 542, mean composite ACT: 25.

Student Life Upper grades have uniform requirement, student council. Discipline rests primarily with faculty. Attendance at religious services is required.

Summer Programs Remediation, enrichment, sports, art/fine arts, computer instruction programs offered; session focuses on academic/social preparation for entrance to regular school, instruction/remediation, and personal growth; held both on and off campus; held at various recreation sites; accepts boys and girls; open to students from other schools. 275 students usually enrolled. 2013 schedule: June 10 to July 5. Application deadline: April 15.

Tuition and Aid Day student tuition: $13,300. Guaranteed tuition plan. Tuition installment plan (Insured Tuition Payment Plan, monthly payment plans). Need-based scholarship grants available. In 2012–13, 16% of upper-school students received aid. Total amount of financial aid awarded in 2012–13: $283,240.

Admissions Traditional secondary-level entrance grade is 9. For fall 2012, 60 students applied for upper-level admission, 37 were accepted, 21 enrolled. Achievement tests and SSAT required. Deadline for receipt of application materials: January 31. Application fee required: $75. On-campus interview required.

Athletics Interscholastic: aquatics (boys, girls), baseball (b), basketball (b,g), bowling (b,g), canoeing/kayaking (b,g), cheering (g), cross-country running (b,g), diving (b,g), football (b), golf (b,g), judo (b,g), kayaking (b,g), riflery (b,g), soccer (b,g), softball (g), swimming and diving (b,g), tennis (b,g), track and field (b,g), volleyball (b,g), water polo (b,g), wrestling (b,g); coed interscholastic: canoeing/kayaking, cheering, golf, sailing. 3 PE instructors, 30 coaches, 2 athletic trainers.

Computers Computers are regularly used in college planning, digital applications, graphic design, journalism, keyboarding, media production, newspaper, video film production, word processing, yearbook classes. Computer resources include Internet access, Internet filtering or blocking technology. Student e-mail accounts and computer access in designated common areas are available to students. Students grades are available online. The school has a published electronic and media policy.

Contact Mrs. Katherine Lee, Director of Admissions. 808-595-7585. Fax: 808-564-0332. E-mail: klee@hba.net. Web site: www.hba.net

HAWKEN SCHOOL

12465 County Line Road
PO Box 8002
Gates Mills, Ohio 44040-8002

Head of School: D. Scott Looney

General Information Coeducational day college-preparatory, arts, business, STEMM (Science, Technology, Engineering, Math, Medicine), and Experiential and Service Learning school. Grades PS–12. Founded: 1915. Setting: suburban. Nearest major city is Cleveland. 325-acre campus. 5 buildings on campus. Approved or accredited by Ohio Association of Independent Schools and Ohio Department of Education. Member of National Association of Independent Schools. Endowment: $43.6 million. Total enrollment: 972. Upper school average class size: 15. Upper school faculty-student ratio: 1:9. There are 176 required school days per year for Upper School students. Upper School students typically attend 5 days per week. The average school day consists of 5 hours and 54 minutes.

Upper School Student Profile Grade 9: 119 students (61 boys, 58 girls); Grade 10: 101 students (53 boys, 48 girls); Grade 11: 109 students (57 boys, 52 girls); Grade 12: 95 students (51 boys, 44 girls).

Faculty School total: 143. In upper school: 29 men, 31 women; 43 have advanced degrees.

Subjects Offered 20th century world history, accounting, acting, advanced chemistry, advanced math, Advanced Placement courses, advanced studio art-AP, African-American literature, algebra, American Civil War, American history, American history-AP, American literature, animal science, art, art appreciation, art history, band, Bible as literature, biology, business, calculus, calculus-AP, ceramics, chemistry, chemistry-AP, Chinese, choir, choral music, chorus, Civil War, classical Greek literature, creative dance, creative writing, dance, dance performance, drama, drawing, ecology, economics, economics and history, engineering, English, English literature, English-AP, entrepreneurship, environmental science-AP, ethics, European history, experiential education, field ecology, film, film studies, fine arts, first aid, French, French studies, French-AP, geography, geometry, government/civics, graphic design, health, history, Holocaust and other genocides, humanities, improvisation, Latin, Latin-AP, mathematics, mathematics-AP, music, music theory, outdoor education, painting, performing arts, philosophy, photography, physical education, physics, physics-AP, physiology, poetry, probability and statistics, science, science research, sculpture, senior project, service learning/internship, social sciences, social studies, Spanish, Spanish literature-AP, speech, statistics-AP, strings, studio art-AP, swimming, theater, theater arts, theater design and production, theater production, trigonometry, U.S. history, U.S. history-AP, world history, world literature, World War I, World War II, writing.

Graduation Requirements Arts and fine arts (art, music, dance, drama), computer science, English, foreign language, history, mathematics, physical education (includes health), science. Community service is required.

Special Academic Programs 16 Advanced Placement exams for which test preparation is offered; honors section; accelerated programs; independent study; term-away projects; study abroad.

College Admission Counseling 113 students graduated in 2012; all went to college, including Brown University; Case Western Reserve University; Chicago State University; Southern Methodist University; The Ohio State University; Washington University in St. Louis. Median SAT critical reading: 630, median SAT math: 640, median SAT writing: 620, median combined SAT: 1910, median composite ACT: 28. 58% scored over 600 on SAT critical reading, 69% scored over 600 on SAT math, 61% scored over 600 on SAT writing, 64% scored over 1800 on combined SAT, 70% scored over 26 on composite ACT.

Student Life Upper grades have specified standards of dress, student council, honor system. Discipline rests equally with students and faculty.

Summer Programs Remediation, enrichment, advancement, computer instruction programs offered; session focuses on credit, review, preview and enrichment in English, math, computer studies, and health; held on campus; accepts boys and girls; open to students from other schools. 133 students usually enrolled. 2013 schedule: June 10 to August 9. Application deadline: none.

Tuition and Aid Day student tuition: $23,115–$25,570. Tuition installment plan (Key Tuition Payment Plan, individually arranged payment plans, installment payment plan (60 percent by 8/15 and 40 percent by 1/15), AchieverLoans (Key Education Resources)). Merit scholarship grants, need-based scholarship grants, need-based loans available. In 2012–13, 37% of upper-school students received aid; total upper-school merit-scholarship money awarded: $162,000. Total amount of financial aid awarded in 2012–13: $5,102,962.

Admissions Traditional secondary-level entrance grade is 9. For fall 2012, 128 students applied for upper-level admission, 91 were accepted, 52 enrolled. ISEE required. Deadline for receipt of application materials: December 19. Application fee required: $25. On-campus interview required.

Athletics Interscholastic: baseball (boys), basketball (b,g), cross-country running (b,g), diving (b,g), field hockey (g), football (b), golf (b,g), lacrosse (b,g), soccer (b,g), softball (g), swimming and diving (b,g), tennis (b,g), track and field (b,g), wrestling (b); intramural: basketball (b); coed intramural: dance, life saving, outdoor skills. 3 PE instructors, 33 coaches, 1 athletic trainer.

Computers Computers are regularly used in all classes. Computer network features include on-campus library services, Internet access, wireless campus network, Internet filtering or blocking technology. Campus intranet and student e-mail accounts are available to students. Students grades are available online. The school has a published electronic and media policy.

Contact Heather Willis Daly, Director of Admission and Financial Assistance. 440-423-2955. Fax: 440-423-2994. E-mail: hdaly@hawken.edu. Web site: www.hawken.edu/

HAWTHORNE CHRISTIAN ACADEMY

2000 Route 208
Hawthorne, New Jersey 07506

Head of School: Mr. Donald J. Klingen

General Information Coeducational day college-preparatory, arts, religious studies, technology, music, and missions school, affiliated with Christian faith, Christian faith. Grades PS–12. Founded: 1981. Setting: suburban. Nearest major city is New York, NY. 22-acre campus. 4 buildings on campus. Approved or accredited by Association of Christian Schools International, Middle States Association of Colleges and Schools, and New Jersey Department of Education. Total enrollment: 496. Upper school average class size: 21. Upper school faculty-student ratio: 1:7. There are 180 required school days per year for Upper School students. Upper School students typically attend 5 days per week. The average school day consists of 6 hours and 40 minutes.

Upper School Student Profile Grade 9: 30 students (15 boys, 15 girls); Grade 10: 46 students (21 boys, 25 girls); Grade 11: 37 students (22 boys, 15 girls); Grade 12: 33 students (17 boys, 16 girls). 100% of students are Christian faith, Christian.

Faculty School total: 60. In upper school: 9 men, 15 women; 6 have advanced degrees.

Subjects Offered Accounting, advanced computer applications, Advanced Placement courses, algebra, anatomy and physiology, art and culture, band, Basic programming, bell choir, Bible, biology, biology-AP, business applications, calculus, calculus-AP, chemistry, choir, choral music, chorus, Christian ethics, composition, computer information systems, computer programming, computers, contemporary issues, creative writing, current events, drama, electives, English literature, English literature-AP, ensembles, foreign language, geometry, government, guidance, handbells, health, information technology, instrumental music, instruments, intro to computers, law, mathematics, music, music history, music theory, physical education, physical science, physics, politics, pre-calculus, psychology, Spanish, Spanish-AP, studio art, U.S. government, U.S. government and politics-AP, U.S. history-AP, video, visual arts, voice, Web site design, world history, yearbook.

Graduation Requirements Algebra, Bible, biology, chemistry, English literature, English literature-AP, geometry, intro to computers, mathematics, physical education (includes health), physical science, pre-calculus, Spanish, U.S. government, U.S. history, U.S. history-AP, world history, Christian service hours, Apologetics and Current Issues, specified number of Academic Elective Courses.

Special Academic Programs 4 Advanced Placement exams for which test preparation is offered.

College Admission Counseling 33 students graduated in 2012; all went to college, including Liberty University; Montclair State University; Nyack College; Rutgers, The State University of New Jersey, New Brunswick. Mean SAT critical reading: 585, mean SAT math: 541, mean SAT writing: 578, mean combined SAT: 1126.

Student Life Upper grades have specified standards of dress, student council. Discipline rests primarily with faculty. Attendance at religious services is required.

Tuition and Aid Day student tuition: $10,640. Tuition installment plan (monthly payment plans). Tuition reduction for siblings, merit scholarship grants, need-based scholarship grants, pastoral discounts, teacher/employee discounts available. In 2012–

13, 29% of upper-school students received aid; total upper-school merit-scholarship money awarded: $20,000. Total amount of financial aid awarded in 2012–13: $74,440.

Admissions Traditional secondary-level entrance grade is 9. Admissions testing, Otis-Lennon School Ability Test or WRAT required. Deadline for receipt of application materials: none. Application fee required: $100. On-campus interview required.

Athletics Interscholastic: baseball (boys), basketball (b,g), soccer (b,g), softball (g), volleyball (g); coed interscholastic: bowling, cross-country running, golf, track and field; coed intramural: strength & conditioning. 2 PE instructors.

Computers Computers are regularly used in business applications, computer applications, information technology, introduction to technology, lab/keyboard, library, technology, Web site design, yearbook classes. Computer network features include on-campus library services, Internet access, Internet filtering or blocking technology. Campus intranet is available to students. Students grades are available online. The school has a published electronic and media policy.

Contact Mrs. Judith De Boer, Admissions Coordinator. 973-423-3331 Ext. 261. Fax: 973-238-1718. E-mail: jdeboer@hca.org. Web site: www.hca.org/

HEAD-ROYCE SCHOOL

4315 Lincoln Avenue
Oakland, California 94602

Head of School: Robert Lake

General Information Coeducational day college-preparatory, arts, technology, and STEM, robotics, Global Online Academy school. Grades K–12. Founded: 1887. Setting: urban. 14-acre campus. 8 buildings on campus. Approved or accredited by Western Association of Schools and Colleges and California Department of Education. Member of National Association of Independent Schools. Endowment: $15 million. Total enrollment: 876. Upper school average class size: 16. Upper school faculty-student ratio: 1:9. There are 175 required school days per year for Upper School students. Upper School students typically attend 5 days per week. The average school day consists of 7 hours.

Upper School Student Profile Grade 9: 101 students (42 boys, 59 girls); Grade 10: 87 students (46 boys, 41 girls); Grade 11: 89 students (49 boys, 40 girls); Grade 12: 78 students (41 boys, 37 girls).

Faculty School total: 95. In upper school: 24 men, 19 women; 29 have advanced degrees.

Subjects Offered Algebra, American history, American literature, art, art history, astronomy, biology, calculus, ceramics, chemistry, Chinese, community service, computer programming, computer science, creative writing, debate, drama, ecology, English, English literature, European history, expository writing, fine arts, French, geometry, graphic arts, health, history, journalism, Latin, marine biology, mathematics, music, neurobiology, photography, physical education, physics, psychology, science, social studies, Spanish, theater, trigonometry, typing, video, world history, world literature, writing.

Graduation Requirements Art history, arts and fine arts (art, music, dance, drama), computer science, English, foreign language, mathematics, physical education (includes health), science, social studies (includes history), 40 hours of community service.

Special Academic Programs 24 Advanced Placement exams for which test preparation is offered; honors section; independent study; term-away projects; study at local college for college credit; study abroad; academic accommodation for the gifted, the musically talented, and the artistically talented.

College Admission Counseling 82 students graduated in 2012; all went to college, including Princeton University; Stanford University; University of California, Davis; University of California, Los Angeles; University of Michigan; University of Pennsylvania. Mean SAT critical reading: 691, mean SAT math: 689, mean SAT writing: 712.

Student Life Upper grades have specified standards of dress, student council, honor system. Discipline rests primarily with faculty.

Summer Programs Remediation, enrichment, advancement programs offered; session focuses on sports and enrichment; held on campus; accepts boys and girls; open to students from other schools. 800 students usually enrolled. 2013 schedule: June 17 to July 26. Application deadline: February.

Tuition and Aid Day student tuition: $31,475. Tuition installment plan (SMART Tuition Payment Plan, monthly payment plans). Need-based scholarship grants, paying campus jobs, tuition remission for children of faculty and staff available. In 2012–13, 30% of upper-school students received aid. Total amount of financial aid awarded in 2012–13: $2,062,725.

Admissions Traditional secondary-level entrance grade is 9. For fall 2012, 217 students applied for upper-level admission, 120 were accepted, 45 enrolled. ISEE or SSAT required. Deadline for receipt of application materials: January 17. Application fee required: $100. On-campus interview required.

Athletics Interscholastic: baseball (boys), basketball (b,g), cross-country running (b,g), dance squad (g), golf (b,g), lacrosse (b), modern dance (g), outdoor education (b,g), physical fitness (b,g), soccer (b,g), softball (g), strength & conditioning (b,g), swimming and diving (b,g), tennis (b,g), volleyball (b,g), weight lifting (b,g), weight training (b,g); coed interscholastic: cross-country running, golf, outdoor education, physical fitness, strength & conditioning, swimming and diving; coed intramural: bicycling, dance, ultimate Frisbee. 6 PE instructors, 39 coaches.

Computers Computers are regularly used in all academic, English, graphics, mathematics, science, yearbook classes. Computer network features include on-campus library services, online commercial services, Internet access, wireless campus network, laptop carts, Smartboards, iPad carts. Student e-mail accounts and computer access in designated common areas are available to students. Students grades are available online. The school has a published electronic and media policy.

Contact Mrs. Catherine Epstein, Director of Admissions and Financial Aid. 510-531-1300. Fax: 510-530-8329. E-mail: cepstein@headroyce.org. Web site: www.headroyce.org

HEBREW ACADEMY

14401 Willow Lane
Huntington Beach, California 92647

Head of School: Dr. Megan Carlson

General Information Coeducational day college-preparatory, general academic, religious studies, and technology school, affiliated with Jewish faith. Boys grades N–8, girls grades N–12. Founded: 1969. Setting: suburban. 11-acre campus. 11 buildings on campus. Approved or accredited by Accrediting Commission for Schools and Western Association of Schools and Colleges. Total enrollment: 259. Upper school average class size: 10. Upper school faculty-student ratio: 1:4. There are 175 required school days per year for Upper School students. Upper School students typically attend 5 days per week. The average school day consists of 7 hours and 30 minutes.

Upper School Student Profile Grade 9: 6 students (6 girls); Grade 10: 11 students (11 girls); Grade 11: 4 students (4 girls). 100% of students are Jewish.

Faculty School total: 41. In upper school: 6 men, 12 women; 2 have advanced degrees.

Subjects Offered Algebra, American history, American literature, art history, biology, earth science, economics, English, English literature, geography, government/civics, grammar, Hebrew, history, mathematics, physical education, physics, physiology, psychology, religion, science, social sciences, social studies, theology, world cultures, world history, writing.

Graduation Requirements Computer science, English, foreign language, mathematics, physical education (includes health), religion (includes Bible studies and theology), science, social sciences, social studies (includes history).

Special Academic Programs International Baccalaureate program; 5 Advanced Placement exams for which test preparation is offered; honors section; independent study; remedial reading and/or remedial writing; remedial math; programs in general development for dyslexic students.

College Admission Counseling 1 student graduated in 2012 and went to Yeshiva University.

Student Life Upper grades have uniform requirement, student council. Discipline rests primarily with faculty. Attendance at religious services is required.

Tuition and Aid Day student tuition: $13,000. Guaranteed tuition plan. Tuition installment plan (monthly payment plans, individually arranged payment plans). Tuition reduction for siblings, need-based scholarship grants available. In 2012–13, 30% of upper-school students received aid. Total amount of financial aid awarded in 2012–13: $30,000.

Admissions Deadline for receipt of application materials: none. Application fee required: $100. On-campus interview required.

Athletics Interscholastic: aerobics/dance, aerobics/Nautilus, aquatics (b), archery (b), badminton, baseball (b), basketball (b), dance, jogging (b), physical fitness (b), soccer (b), softball (b), swimming and diving (b), volleyball. 1 PE instructor.

Computers Computers are regularly used in English, foreign language, science, technology classes. Computer network features include on-campus library services, online commercial services, Internet access, multimedia, including laser disks, digital cameras. Computer access in designated common areas is available to students.

Contact Mrs. Alex Greenberg, Director of Admissions. 714-898-0051 Ext. 284. Fax: 714-898-0633. E-mail: agreenberg@hacds.org. Web site: www.hebrewacademyhb.com

HEBREW ACADEMY OF THE FIVE TOWNS & ROCKAWAY

635 Central Avenue
Cedarhurst, New York 11516

Head of School: Ms. Naomi Lippman

General Information Coeducational day college-preparatory, arts, business, and religious studies school, affiliated with Jewish faith. Grades 9–12. Founded: 1978. Setting: suburban. Nearest major city is New York. 1 building on campus. Approved or accredited by Middle States Association of Colleges and Schools, The College Board, and New York Department of Education. Languages of instruction: English and Hebrew. Total enrollment: 388. Upper school average class size: 20. The average school day consists of 9 hours and 15 minutes.

Upper School Student Profile 100% of students are Jewish.

Faculty School total: 60.

Subjects Offered Advanced Placement courses, arts, English, fine arts, foreign language, Jewish studies, Judaic studies, mathematics, physical education, religion, science, social sciences, social studies.

Graduation Requirements Arts and fine arts (art, music, dance, drama), English, foreign language, Judaic studies, mathematics, physical education (includes health), religion (includes Bible studies and theology), science, social sciences, social studies (includes history).

Special Academic Programs 11 Advanced Placement exams for which test preparation is offered; honors section; independent study; study abroad; academic accommodation for the artistically talented.

College Admission Counseling 95 students graduated in 2012; all went to college, including Binghamton University, State University of New York; Columbia University; New York University; Queens College of the City University of New York; University of Maryland, College Park; Yeshiva University. Median SAT critical reading: 590, median SAT math: 610, median SAT writing: 570. 48% scored over 600 on SAT critical reading, 56% scored over 600 on SAT math, 41% scored over 600 on SAT writing.

Student Life Upper grades have specified standards of dress, student council, honor system. Discipline rests primarily with faculty. Attendance at religious services is required.

Tuition and Aid Tuition installment plan (monthly payment plans, individually arranged payment plans). Need-based scholarship grants available.

Admissions Traditional secondary-level entrance grade is 9. Board of Jewish Education Entrance Exam required. Deadline for receipt of application materials: March 15. Application fee required. On-campus interview required.

Athletics Interscholastic: baseball (boys, girls), basketball (b,g), field hockey (b), softball (b,g), tennis (b,g), volleyball (g); coed intramural: skiing (downhill). 2 PE instructors, 8 coaches.

Computers Computers are regularly used in computer applications classes. Computer resources include on-campus library services, online commercial services, Internet access, Internet filtering or blocking technology. Student e-mail accounts are available to students. The school has a published electronic and media policy.

Contact Ms. Naomi Lippman, Principal, General Studies. 516-569-3807. Fax: 516-374-5761. Web site: www.haftr.org

HERITAGE CHRISTIAN ACADEMY

2003 McKnight Boulevard NE
Calgary, Alberta T2E 6L2, Canada

Head of School: Mr. Ryan Brennan

General Information Coeducational day college-preparatory, general academic, arts, religious studies, bilingual studies, and technology school, affiliated with Christian faith, Evangelical faith. Grades K–12. Founded: 1979. Setting: urban. 10-acre campus. 1 building on campus. Approved or accredited by Association of Christian Schools International, Association of Independent Schools and Colleges of Alberta, and Alberta Department of Education. Language of instruction: English. Total enrollment: 568. Upper school average class size: 27. Upper school faculty-student ratio: 1:9. There are 184 required school days per year for Upper School students. Upper School students typically attend 5 days per week. The average school day consists of 6 hours and 55 minutes.

Upper School Student Profile Grade 10: 51 students (21 boys, 30 girls); Grade 11: 40 students (25 boys, 15 girls); Grade 12: 30 students (13 boys, 17 girls). 100% of students are Christian, members of Evangelical faith.

Faculty School total: 34. In upper school: 6 men, 7 women; 2 have advanced degrees.

Subjects Offered Art, band, Bible, biology, career and personal planning, chemistry, choir, choral music, Christian education, computer applications, computer multimedia, creative writing, English, essential learning systems, French as a second language, health, language arts, mathematics, physical education, physics, psychology, religious studies, science, sewing, social studies, sports medicine, work experience.

Graduation Requirements Career and personal planning, English, mathematics, physical education (includes health), religious studies, science, social studies (includes history).

Special Academic Programs Independent study; remedial reading and/or remedial writing; remedial math; special instructional classes for deaf students, students with dyslexia addressed through IPPs and classroom accommodations.

College Admission Counseling 28 students graduated in 2012; 22 went to college, including Mount Royal University; The University of British Columbia; University of Alberta; University of Calgary; University of Lethbridge. Other: 5 went to work, 1 had other specific plans.

Student Life Upper grades have uniform requirement, student council, honor system. Discipline rests primarily with faculty. Attendance at religious services is required.

Tuition and Aid Day student tuition: CAN$3030. Tuition installment plan (monthly payment plans, individually arranged payment plans). Tuition reduction for siblings available.

Admissions Traditional secondary-level entrance grade is 10. For fall 2012, 6 students applied for upper-level admission, 6 were accepted, 6 enrolled. CTBS (or similar from their school) required. Deadline for receipt of application materials: none. Application fee required: CAN$100. Interview required.

Athletics Interscholastic: basketball (boys, girls), cross-country running (b,g), golf (b,g), track and field (b,g), volleyball (b,g), wrestling (b,g); coed interscholastic: floor hockey, track and field; coed intramural: basketball, climbing, floor hockey, indoor soccer, indoor track & field, outdoor activities, physical fitness, project adventure, soccer, touch football, track and field, volleyball, wall climbing. 1 PE instructor.

Computers Computers are regularly used in animation, Bible studies, career education, data processing, English, graphics, information technology, keyboarding, mathematics, multimedia, photography, science, social studies classes. Computer network features include Internet access, Internet filtering or blocking technology. Student e-mail accounts are available to students. The school has a published electronic and media policy.

Contact Office. 403-219-3201. Fax: 403-219-3210. E-mail: heritage_info@pallisersd.ab.ca. Web site: www.hcacalgary.com

HERITAGE CHRISTIAN SCHOOL

9825 Woodley Avenue
North Hills, California 91343

Head of School: Mr. Lance Haliday

General Information Coeducational day college-preparatory, arts, religious studies, and technology school, affiliated with Christian faith. Grades 7–12. Founded: 1962. Setting: suburban. Nearest major city is Los Angeles. 11-acre campus. 5 buildings on campus. Approved or accredited by Association of Christian Schools International and Western Association of Schools and Colleges. Total enrollment: 911. Upper school average class size: 30. Upper school faculty-student ratio: 1:22. There are 180 required school days per year for Upper School students. Upper School students typically attend 5 days per week. The average school day consists of 6 hours and 45 minutes.

Upper School Student Profile Grade 9: 157 students (86 boys, 71 girls); Grade 10: 181 students (80 boys, 101 girls); Grade 11: 166 students (88 boys, 78 girls); Grade 12: 193 students (90 boys, 103 girls).

Faculty School total: 44. In upper school: 17 men, 20 women; 32 have advanced degrees.

Subjects Offered 3-dimensional design, advanced computer applications, algebra, American history, American literature, analysis and differential calculus, anatomy and physiology, art, ASB Leadership, band, Bible studies, biology, biology-AP, calculus-AP, ceramics, chemistry, choir, choral music, Christian doctrine, Christian education, Christian ethics, computer applications, computer education, computer graphics, computer programming, computer science, computer skills, computer technologies, digital photography, drama, drama performance, earth science, economics, English, English literature, English-AP, expository writing, fine arts, French, French-AP, geography, geometry, government/civics, HTML design, intro to computers, jazz band, journalism, keyboarding, mathematics, music, photography, physical education, physics, physics-AP, practical arts, pre-calculus, psychology, psychology-AP, religion, science, social studies, Spanish, Spanish-AP, statistics, statistics-AP, studio art, theater arts, trigonometry, typing, U.S. history-AP, world history.

Graduation Requirements Arts and fine arts (art, music, dance, drama), English, foreign language, mathematics, physical education (includes health), practical arts, religion (includes Bible studies and theology), science, social studies (includes history).

Special Academic Programs Advanced Placement exam preparation; honors section; ESL (13 students enrolled).

College Admission Counseling 105 students graduated in 2012; 102 went to college, including Arizona State University; California State University, Northridge; The Master's College and Seminary; University of California, Los Angeles; University of Southern California. Other: 2 went to work, 1 entered military service. Median SAT critical reading: 570, median SAT math: 565, median SAT writing: 550, median combined SAT: 1650, median composite ACT: 25. 33.5% scored over 600 on SAT critical reading, 31.3% scored over 600 on SAT math, 33% scored over 600 on SAT writing, 3% scored over 1800 on combined SAT, 26.8% scored over 26 on composite ACT.

Student Life Upper grades have uniform requirement, student council, honor system. Discipline rests primarily with faculty. Attendance at religious services is required.

Summer Programs Remediation, advancement, sports, computer instruction programs offered; session focuses on remediation and enrichment; held both on and off campus; held at Internet-based learning can be done from any computer; accepts boys and girls; open to students from other schools. 350 students usually enrolled. 2013 schedule: June 1 to July 30.

Tuition and Aid Day student tuition: $8250. Tuition installment plan (FACTS Tuition Payment Plan, monthly payment plans, 2-semester payment plan, annual payment plan). Need-based scholarship grants available. In 2012–13, 30% of upper-school students received aid. Total amount of financial aid awarded in 2012–13: $820,000.

Admissions Traditional secondary-level entrance grade is 9. For fall 2012, 163 students applied for upper-level admission, 160 were accepted, 136 enrolled. QUIC required. Deadline for receipt of application materials: August 1. Application fee required: $100. On-campus interview required.

Athletics Interscholastic: baseball (boys), basketball (b,g), cheering (g), cross-country running (b,g), football (b), golf (b), soccer (b,g), softball (g), tennis (g), track and field (b,g), volleyball (b,g). 2 PE instructors, 36 coaches.

Computers Computers are regularly used in animation, business applications, career technology, graphic design, graphics, introduction to technology, keyboarding, lab/keyboard, programming, technology, typing, Web site design, word processing classes. Computer network features include on-campus library services, Internet access, Internet filtering or blocking technology. The school has a published electronic and media policy.

Contact Mrs. Penny Lade, South Campus Registrar. 818-894-5742 Ext. 324. Fax: 818-892-5018. E-mail: plade@heritage-schools.org. Web site: www.heritage-schools.org

HERITAGE CHRISTIAN SCHOOL

2850 Fourth Avenue
PO Box 400
Jordan, Ontario L0R 1S0, Canada

Head of School: Mr. A. Ben Harsevoort

General Information Coeducational day college-preparatory, general academic, arts, and religious studies school, affiliated with Reformed Church. Grades K–12. Founded: 1992. Setting: rural. Nearest major city is St. Catharines, Canada. 26-acre campus. 1 building on campus. Approved or accredited by Ontario Department of Education. Language of instruction: English. Total enrollment: 610. Upper school average class size: 50. Upper school faculty-student ratio: 1:15. There are 185 required school days per year for Upper School students. Upper School students typically attend 5 days per week. The average school day consists of 5 hours.

Upper School Student Profile Grade 9: 31 students (21 boys, 10 girls); Grade 10: 49 students (23 boys, 26 girls); Grade 11: 41 students (20 boys, 21 girls); Grade 12: 43 students (22 boys, 21 girls). 95% of students are Reformed.

Faculty School total: 35. In upper school: 11 men, 4 women; 4 have advanced degrees.

Subjects Offered 20th century American writers, 20th century physics, 20th century world history, advanced chemistry, advanced math, algebra, analysis and differential calculus, art, Bible, biology, bookkeeping, British literature, business mathematics, business studies, calculus, Canadian geography, Canadian history, Canadian law, Canadian literature, career education, chemistry, choral music, Christian and Hebrew scripture, Christian doctrine, Christian education, Christian ethics, Christian studies, Christian testament, Christianity, church history, civics, classical civilization, computer education, computer programming, computer skills, consumer mathematics, creative writing, culinary arts, drafting, English, English composition, English literature, entrepreneurship, environmental education, ethics, European civilization, European history, family studies, finite math, foods, foundations of civilization, French as a second language, general math, geography, geometry, grammar, health, history, honors algebra, honors English, honors geometry, honors world history, humanities, independent living, keyboarding, language and composition, language arts, law and the legal system, life science, literature, marketing, mathematics, media literacy, modern civilization, modern European history, modern Western civilization, music, music appreciation, novels, personal finance, physical education, physics, practicum, public speaking, religion and culture, religious education, religious studies, Shakespeare, society challenge and change, speech communications, technical drawing, vocal music, word processing, world civilizations, world literature, writing.

Graduation Requirements Ontario Secondary School Diploma requirements.

Special Academic Programs Remedial reading and/or remedial writing; remedial math.

College Admission Counseling 38 students graduated in 2012; 30 went to college, including Calvin College; Covenant College. Other: 8 went to work.

Student Life Upper grades have uniform requirement, student council. Discipline rests primarily with faculty. Attendance at religious services is required.

Tuition and Aid Day student tuition: CAN$12,500. Tuition installment plan (monthly payment plans).

Admissions Traditional secondary-level entrance grade is 9. Deadline for receipt of application materials: none. No application fee required. On-campus interview required.

Athletics Interscholastic: badminton (boys, girls), basketball (b,g), ice hockey (b), soccer (b,g), volleyball (b,g). 3 coaches.

Computers Computers are regularly used in accounting, business, economics, information technology, keyboarding, mathematics, newspaper, typing, yearbook classes. The school has a published electronic and media policy.

Contact Mrs. Mariam Sinke, Administrative Assistant. 905-562-7303 Ext. 221. Fax: 905-562-0020. E-mail: heritage@hcsjordan.ca. Web site: www.hcsjordan.ca

THE HERITAGE SCHOOL

2093 Highway 29 North
Newnan, Georgia 30263

Head of School: Judith Griffith

General Information Coeducational day college-preparatory, arts, and technology school. Grades PK–12. Founded: 1970. Setting: suburban. Nearest major city is Atlanta. 62-acre campus. 13 buildings on campus. Approved or accredited by Georgia Independent School Association, Southern Association of Colleges and Schools, Southern Association of Independent Schools, and Georgia Department of Education. Member of National Association of Independent Schools. Endowment: $1.1 million. Total enrollment: 428. Upper school average class size: 18. Upper school faculty-student ratio: 1:8. There are 180 required school days per year for Upper School students. Upper School students typically attend 5 days per week. The average school day consists of 6 hours and 30 minutes.

Upper School Student Profile Grade 9: 38 students (22 boys, 16 girls); Grade 10: 48 students (24 boys, 24 girls); Grade 11: 37 students (26 boys, 11 girls); Grade 12: 43 students (28 boys, 15 girls).

Faculty School total: 50. In upper school: 5 men, 18 women; 7 have advanced degrees.

Subjects Offered Advanced studio art-AP, algebra, American government, American history, American history-AP, American literature, art, art history, art-AP, biology, biology-AP, calculus, calculus-AP, chemistry, chemistry-AP, Chinese, college admission preparation, composition-AP, computer applications, digital photography, drama, economics, English, English language and composition-AP, English literature, English literature and composition-AP, environmental science, environmental science-AP, European history-AP, film appreciation, fitness, French, French language-AP, French-AP, gardening, geometry, government-AP, graphic arts, health, history, integrated science, language-AP, Latin, mathematics, music, music theory-AP, physical education, physical science, physics-AP, pre-calculus, psychology, psychology-AP, public speaking, Spanish, Spanish-AP, statistics-AP, strings, studio art-AP, U.S. history-AP, video film production, world history, world literature, writing workshop.

Graduation Requirements Arts and fine arts (art, music, dance, drama), computer science, electives, English, foreign language, mathematics, physical education (includes health), public speaking, science, social studies (includes history).

Special Academic Programs 16 Advanced Placement exams for which test preparation is offered; independent study.

College Admission Counseling 43 students graduated in 2012; all went to college, including Auburn University; Georgia Institute of Technology; Georgia Southern University; Kennesaw State University; University of Georgia; University of West Georgia. Mean SAT critical reading: 560, mean SAT math: 585, mean SAT writing: 550, mean combined SAT: 1695, mean composite ACT: 26.

Student Life Upper grades have specified standards of dress, student council, honor system. Discipline rests primarily with faculty.

Tuition and Aid Day student tuition: $7205–$13,640. Tuition installment plan (monthly payment plans). Tuition reduction for siblings, need-based scholarship grants available. In 2012–13, 30% of upper-school students received aid. Total amount of financial aid awarded in 2012–13: $367,651.

Admissions Traditional secondary-level entrance grade is 9. For fall 2012, 30 students applied for upper-level admission, 24 were accepted, 15 enrolled. Otis-Lennon School Ability Test required. Deadline for receipt of application materials: none. Application fee required: $50. On-campus interview required.

Athletics Interscholastic: aerobics/dance (girls), baseball (b), basketball (b,g), cheering (g), cross-country running (b,g), football (b), golf (b,g), soccer (b,g), softball (g), swimming and diving (b,g), tennis (b,g), track and field (b,g), volleyball (g), weight training (b,g); intramural: cheering (g), football (b); coed interscholastic: physical fitness, skeet shooting; coed intramural: backpacking, basketball, canoeing/kayaking, climbing, equestrian sports, flag football, hiking/backpacking, horseback riding, kayaking, mountaineering, outdoor adventure, outdoor education, ropes courses, wilderness survival. 3 PE instructors, 1 athletic trainer.

Computers Computers are regularly used in college planning, creative writing, English, foreign language, publications, science, yearbook classes. Computer network features include on-campus library services, online commercial services, Internet access, wireless campus network, Internet filtering or blocking technology. Campus intranet, student e-mail accounts, and computer access in designated common areas are available to students. Students grades are available online. The school has a published electronic and media policy.

Contact Amy Riley, Director of Admission and Marketing. 678-423-5393. Fax: 770-253-4850. E-mail: ariley@heritagehawks.org. Web site: www.heritagehawks.org

THE HEWITT SCHOOL

45 East 75th Street
New York, New York 10021

Head of School: Ms. Joan Z. Lonergan

General Information Girls' day college-preparatory school. Grades K–12. Founded: 1920. Setting: urban. 1 building on campus. Approved or accredited by Middle States Association of Colleges and Schools, National Independent Private Schools Association, New York State Association of Independent Schools, and New York Department of Education. Member of National Association of Independent Schools and Secondary School Admission Test Board. Total enrollment: 520. Upper school average class size: 15. Upper school faculty-student ratio: 1:7. Upper School students typically attend 5 days per week. The average school day consists of 7 hours.

Upper School Student Profile Grade 9: 26 students (26 girls); Grade 10: 30 students (30 girls); Grade 11: 30 students (30 girls); Grade 12: 29 students (29 girls).

Faculty School total: 82. In upper school: 14 men, 16 women; 24 have advanced degrees.

Subjects Offered Algebra, American history, American literature, anatomy and physiology, art, biology, calculus, chemistry, computers, drama, earth science, English, English literature, European history, fine arts, French, genetics, geometry, history, Latin, mathematics, music, photography, physical education, physics, pre-calculus, science, Spanish, world history.
Graduation Requirements Creative arts, English, foreign language, history, mathematics, physical education (includes health), science, technology.
Special Academic Programs Advanced Placement exam preparation; honors section; independent study; term-away projects; study abroad.
College Admission Counseling 24 students graduated in 2012; all went to college, including Bard College; Barnard College; Bates College; Syracuse University; University of Michigan; University of Pennsylvania.
Student Life Upper grades have uniform requirement, student council. Discipline rests primarily with faculty.
Tuition and Aid Day student tuition: $38,550. Guaranteed tuition plan. Tuition installment plan (Insured Tuition Payment Plan, Key Tuition Payment Plan, monthly payment plans). Need-based scholarship grants available. In 2012–13, 22% of upper-school students received aid. Total amount of financial aid awarded in 2012–13: $1,394,709.
Admissions Traditional secondary-level entrance grade is 9. ERB and ISEE required. Deadline for receipt of application materials: December 1. Application fee required: $60. On-campus interview required.
Athletics Interscholastic: badminton, basketball, cross-country running, soccer, squash, swimming and diving, tennis, track and field, volleyball; intramural: badminton, basketball, crew, cross-country running, lacrosse, soccer, swimming and diving, tennis, track and field, volleyball. 4 PE instructors.
Computers Computers are regularly used in all academic, art, English, foreign language, history, humanities, mathematics, music, science classes. Computer network features include on-campus library services, online commercial services, Internet access, wireless campus network, Internet filtering or blocking technology. Campus intranet, student e-mail accounts, and computer access in designated common areas are available to students. The school has a published electronic and media policy.
Contact Ms. Jessica Acee, Director of Admissions, Middle and Upper School. 212-994-2623. Fax: 212-472-7531. E-mail: jacee@hewittschool.org. Web site: hewittschool.org

HIGHLAND HALL WALDORF SCHOOL

17100 Superior Street
Northridge, California 91325

Head of School: Lynn Kern

General Information Coeducational day college-preparatory and arts school. Grades N–12. Founded: 1955. Setting: suburban. Nearest major city is Los Angeles. 11-acre campus. 4 buildings on campus. Approved or accredited by Association of Waldorf Schools of North America and Western Association of Schools and Colleges. Total enrollment: 225. Upper school average class size: 25. Upper school faculty-student ratio: 1:6. There are 170 required school days per year for Upper School students. Upper School students typically attend 5 days per week. The average school day consists of 7 hours and 10 minutes.
Upper School Student Profile Grade 9: 16 students (5 boys, 11 girls); Grade 10: 21 students (3 boys, 18 girls); Grade 11: 21 students (10 boys, 11 girls); Grade 12: 22 students (10 boys, 12 girls).
Faculty School total: 59. In upper school: 11 men, 15 women; 3 have advanced degrees.
Subjects Offered Algebra, American history, American literature, anatomy, ancient history, architecture, art, art history, astronomy, biology, bookbinding, botany, calculus, career/college preparation, cell biology, chemistry, choral music, chorus, clayworking, conflict resolution, CPR, creative writing, drama, drawing, earth science, economics, English, English literature, ethnic studies, European history, eurythmy, expository writing, geography, geology, geometry, German, government/civics, grammar, guidance, guitar, handbells, health, history, honors U.S. history, jazz ensemble, marine biology, mathematics, metalworking, music, music history, Native American history, orchestra, painting, physical education, physics, physiology, pre-algebra, pre-calculus, SAT preparation, sculpture, sewing, social studies, Spanish, speech, stone carving, theater, trigonometry, woodworking, world history, world literature, writing, yearbook, zoology.
Graduation Requirements Ancient history, art, art history, crafts, earth science, economics, English, foreign language, government, history of music, human sexuality, mathematics, music, physical education (includes health), science, sculpture, society and culture, U.S. history, world history. Community service is required.
Special Academic Programs Independent study; study abroad.
College Admission Counseling 22 students graduated in 2012; 21 went to college, including Berklee College of Music; Lewis & Clark College; Marlboro College; Middlebury College; Sarah Lawrence College; Vassar College. Other: 1 went to work. Mean SAT critical reading: 645, mean SAT math: 550, mean composite ACT: 27. 50% scored over 600 on SAT critical reading, 60% scored over 600 on SAT math, 50% scored over 26 on composite ACT.
Student Life Upper grades have specified standards of dress, student council. Discipline rests primarily with faculty.
Tuition and Aid Day student tuition: $21,425. Tuition installment plan (Insured Tuition Payment Plan, FACTS Tuition Payment Plan, monthly payment plans). Need-based scholarship grants available. In 2012–13, 19% of upper-school students received aid. Total amount of financial aid awarded in 2012–13: $204,600.
Admissions Traditional secondary-level entrance grade is 9. For fall 2012, 28 students applied for upper-level admission, 22 were accepted, 9 enrolled. Essay, math and English placement tests and writing sample required. Deadline for receipt of application materials: January 31. Application fee required: $100. On-campus interview required.
Athletics Interscholastic: baseball (boys), basketball (b,g), softball (g), volleyball (b,g); coed interscholastic: soccer; coed intramural: golf. 2 PE instructors, 2 coaches.
Computers Computers are regularly used in library skills, newspaper, yearbook classes. Computer network features include on-campus library services, Internet access, wireless campus network.
Contact Lynn van Schilfgaarde, Enrollment Director. 818-349-1394 Ext. 211. Fax: 818-349-2390. E-mail: lvs@highlandhall.org. Web site: www.highlandhall.org

HIGHROAD ACADEMY

46641 Chilliwack Central Road
Chilliwack, British Columbia V2P 1K3, Canada

Head of School: Mr. David Shinness

General Information college-preparatory and religious studies school, affiliated with Christian faith; primarily serves students with learning disabilities, individuals with Attention Deficit Disorder, individuals with emotional and behavioral problems, and dyslexic students. Founded: 1978. Setting: small town. Nearest major city is Vancouver, Canada. 45-acre campus. 1 building on campus. Approved or accredited by British Columbia Department of Education. Language of instruction: English. Total enrollment: 392. Upper school average class size: 25. Upper school faculty-student ratio: 1:10.
Upper School Student Profile Grade 6: 33 students (16 boys, 17 girls); Grade 7: 42 students (20 boys, 22 girls); Grade 8: 29 students (21 boys, 8 girls); Grade 9: 32 students (18 boys, 14 girls); Grade 10: 32 students (17 boys, 15 girls); Grade 11: 27 students (13 boys, 14 girls); Grade 12: 32 students (10 boys, 22 girls). 100% of students are Christian.
Faculty School total: 30. In upper school: 5 men, 5 women.
Graduation Requirements Bible.
Special Academic Programs Independent study; study at local college for college credit; ESL (25 students enrolled).
College Admission Counseling 32 students graduated in 2011; 12 went to college, including The University of British Columbia. Other: 6 went to work, 8 entered a postgraduate year, 6 had other specific plans.
Student Life Upper grades have uniform requirement, student council, honor system. Discipline rests primarily with faculty. Attendance at religious services is required.
Admissions Traditional secondary-level entrance grade is 10. Deadline for receipt of application materials: none. Application fee required: CAN$100. Interview required.
Athletics 1 PE instructor, 3 coaches.
Computers Computer network features include Internet access, wireless campus network, Internet filtering or blocking technology. Computer access in designated common areas is available to students. Students grades are available online.
Contact Mrs. Denise Kraubner, Office Manager. 604-792-4680. Fax: 604-792-2465. E-mail: dkraubner@highroadacademy.com. Web site: www.highroadacademy.com

THE HILL CENTER, DURHAM ACADEMY

Durham, North Carolina
See Special Needs Schools section.

HILLCREST CHRISTIAN SCHOOL

384 Erbes Road
Thousand Oaks, California 91362

Head of School: Mr. Stephen Allen

General Information Coeducational day college-preparatory school, affiliated with Christian faith. Grades K–12. Founded: 1977. Setting: suburban. 4-acre campus. 7 buildings on campus. Approved or accredited by Association of Christian Schools International, Western Association of Schools and Colleges, and California Department of Education. Total enrollment: 288. Upper school average class size: 15. Upper school faculty-student ratio: 1:8. There are 179 required school days per year for Upper School students. Upper School students typically attend 5 days per week. The average school day consists of 6 hours and 30 minutes.
Upper School Student Profile Grade 9: 21 students (17 boys, 4 girls); Grade 10: 16 students (9 boys, 7 girls); Grade 11: 16 students (8 boys, 8 girls); Grade 12: 18 students (6 boys, 12 girls). 90% of students are Christian faith.
Faculty School total: 17. In upper school: 5 men, 7 women; 5 have advanced degrees.
Subjects Offered Algebra, American literature, anatomy and physiology, art, Bible, biology, British literature, British literature (honors), calculus, chemistry, computers, earth science, economics, film studies, French, geometry, health, Hebrew scripture, home economics, honors English, honors U.S. history, honors world history, intro-

duction to literature, keyboarding, life science, marine biology, physical education, physics, pre-algebra, pre-calculus, Spanish, trigonometry, U.S. government, U.S. history, world history, world literature, yearbook.

Graduation Requirements Algebra, American literature, Bible, biology, British literature, chemistry, economics, electives, English, foreign language, geometry, introduction to literature, mathematics, physical education (includes health), physical science, U.S. government, U.S. history, world history, world literature, 20 hours of community service each year.

Special Academic Programs 3 Advanced Placement exams for which test preparation is offered; honors section; ESL (2 students enrolled).

College Admission Counseling 6 students graduated in 2011; all went to college, including Moorpark College; Westmont College. Mean SAT critical reading: 570, mean SAT math: 590. 10% scored over 600 on SAT critical reading, 10% scored over 600 on SAT math, 20% scored over 600 on SAT writing.

Student Life Upper grades have uniform requirement, student council, honor system. Discipline rests primarily with faculty. Attendance at religious services is required.

Tuition and Aid Day student tuition: $8980. Tuition installment plan (FACTS Tuition Payment Plan). Tuition reduction for siblings, need-based scholarship grants, tuition reduction for families of full-time pastors, tuition reduction for children of faculty and staff available. In 2011–12, 8% of upper-school students received aid. Total amount of financial aid awarded in 2011–12: $20,000.

Admissions Traditional secondary-level entrance grade is 9. For fall 2011, 11 students applied for upper-level admission, 9 were accepted, 9 enrolled. Admissions testing and Stanford Diagnostic Test required. Deadline for receipt of application materials: none. Application fee required: $100. On-campus interview required.

Athletics Interscholastic: baseball (boys), basketball (b,g), cheering (g), football (b), volleyball (g); coed interscholastic: golf; coed intramural: flag football. 2 PE instructors, 4 coaches.

Computers Computers are regularly used in all classes. Computer resources include on-campus library services, Internet access, wireless campus network, Internet filtering or blocking technology, computer lab. Computer access in designated common areas is available to students. Students grades are available online. The school has a published electronic and media policy.

Contact Mrs. Gail Matheson, Office Manager. 805-497-7501 Ext. 200. Fax: 805-494-9355. E-mail: gmatheson@hillcrestcs.org. Web site: www.hillcrestcs.org

HILLCREST CHRISTIAN SCHOOL

4060 South Siwell Road
Jackson, Mississippi 39212

Head of School: Dr. Tom Prather

General Information Coeducational day college-preparatory, arts, business, religious studies, and technology school. Grades 1–12. Founded: 1971. Setting: urban. 36-acre campus. 5 buildings on campus. Approved or accredited by Association of Christian Schools International, Mississippi Private School Association, and Southern Association of Colleges and Schools. Total enrollment: 590. Upper school average class size: 15. Upper school faculty-student ratio: 1:11. There are 175 required school days per year for Upper School students. Upper School students typically attend 5 days per week. The average school day consists of 5 hours and 50 minutes.

Upper School Student Profile Grade 7: 35 students (17 boys, 18 girls); Grade 8: 53 students (29 boys, 24 girls); Grade 9: 59 students (25 boys, 34 girls); Grade 10: 31 students (13 boys, 18 girls); Grade 11: 39 students (26 boys, 13 girls); Grade 12: 39 students (17 boys, 22 girls).

Faculty School total: 63. In upper school: 12 men, 14 women; 11 have advanced degrees.

Subjects Offered Advanced biology, advanced math, Advanced Placement courses, algebra, American government, American history-AP, American literature, American literature-AP, anatomy and physiology, art, band, baseball, basketball, Bible, biology, biology-AP, British literature, business communications, calculus, chemistry, chemistry-AP, choir, choral music, comparative government and politics-AP, computer applications, computer graphics, critical writing, current events, desktop publishing, earth science, economics, electives, English, English language and composition-AP, English literature, English literature and composition-AP, geography, geometry, health, library assistant, life science, pre-algebra, reading/study skills, social studies, Spanish, sports, state history, transition mathematics, trigonometry, U.S. government, U.S. government and politics-AP, U.S. history, U.S. history-AP, world geography, world history.

Graduation Requirements Bible, electives, English, history, language, mathematics, science, must complete 10 community service hours per school year attended, must apply and be accepted to a college.

Special Academic Programs 7 Advanced Placement exams for which test preparation is offered; honors section; independent study; study at local college for college credit.

College Admission Counseling 31 students graduated in 2011; 30 went to college, including Hinds Community College; Holmes Community College; Mississippi College; Mississippi State University; University of Mississippi; University of Southern Mississippi. Other: 1 entered military service. Median composite ACT: 22. 3% scored over 26 on composite ACT.

Student Life Upper grades have uniform requirement, student council, honor system. Discipline rests primarily with faculty.

Tuition and Aid Day student tuition: $5628. Tuition installment plan (monthly payment plans). Tuition reduction for siblings, need-based scholarship grants available. In 2011–12, 8% of upper-school students received aid. Total amount of financial aid awarded in 2011–12: $42,824.

Admissions Traditional secondary-level entrance grade is 7. For fall 2011, 40 students applied for upper-level admission, 29 were accepted, 23 enrolled. Admissions testing and Stanford Achievement Test, Otis-Lennon School Ability Test required. Deadline for receipt of application materials: none. Application fee required: $50. Interview recommended.

Athletics Interscholastic: baseball (boys), basketball (b,g), cheering (g), drill team (g), football (b), golf (b), softball (g), weight lifting (b); intramural: basketball (b,g), football (b), softball (g); coed interscholastic: cross-country running, soccer, tennis; coed intramural: cross-country running, golf, tennis, track and field, weight lifting, weight training. 2 coaches.

Computers Computers are regularly used in computer applications, graphic design, yearbook classes. Computer resources include Internet access. Students grades are available online.

Contact Mrs. Melissa Jones, Director of Admissions. 601-372-0149 Ext. 300. Fax: 601-371-8061. E-mail: mjones@hillcrestchristian.org. Web site: www.hillcrestchristian.org

THE HILL SCHOOL

717 East High Street
Pottstown, Pennsylvania 19464-5791

Head of School: Mr. David R. Dougherty

General Information Coeducational boarding and day college-preparatory school, affiliated with Christian faith. Boarding grades 9–PG, day grades 9–12. Founded: 1851. Setting: small town. Nearest major city is Philadelphia. Students are housed in single-sex dormitories. 200-acre campus. 58 buildings on campus. Approved or accredited by Middle States Association of Colleges and Schools, The Association of Boarding Schools, and Pennsylvania Department of Education. Member of National Association of Independent Schools and Secondary School Admission Test Board. Endowment: $10 million. Total enrollment: 494. Upper school average class size: 13. Upper school faculty-student ratio: 1:7. Upper School students typically attend 6 days per week. The average school day consists of 5 hours and 33 minutes.

Upper School Student Profile Grade 9: 106 students (57 boys, 49 girls); Grade 10: 124 students (67 boys, 57 girls); Grade 11: 118 students (73 boys, 45 girls); Grade 12: 123 students (59 boys, 64 girls); Postgraduate: 23 students (21 boys, 2 girls). 80% of students are boarding students. 48% are state residents. 30 states are represented in upper school student body. 11% are international students. International students from China, Germany, Hong Kong, Republic of Korea, Spain, and Venezuela; 14 other countries represented in student body.

Faculty School total: 86. In upper school: 56 men, 30 women; 61 have advanced degrees; 80 reside on campus.

Subjects Offered Acting, advanced chemistry, advanced computer applications, advanced math, Advanced Placement courses, advanced studio art-AP, algebra, American Civil War, American history, American history-AP, American literature-AP, American studies, anatomy and physiology, Ancient Greek, ancient world history, art, art history, art-AP, arts, astronomy, athletic training, basic language skills, Basic programming, Bible studies, biochemistry, biology, biology-AP, boat building, botany, British literature-AP, calculus, calculus-AP, chamber groups, chemistry, chemistry-AP, Chinese, choral music, Christian ethics, Christian scripture, Christian testament, college admission preparation, college counseling, college placement, college planning, college writing, composition-AP, computer math, computer programming, computer science, computer science-AP, concert choir, creative writing, digital art, earth science, ecology, economics, economics-AP, English, English language and composition-AP, English literature, English literature and composition-AP, environmental science, European history, European history-AP, expository writing, French, French language-AP, French literature-AP, geography, geometry, German, government/civics, grammar, Greek, history, honors algebra, honors English, honors geometry, humanities, independent study, instrumental music, jazz band, journalism, lab science, Latin, Latin-AP, life issues, linear algebra, mathematics, music, oral communications, orchestra, participation in sports, photography, physics, physics-AP, pre-calculus, pre-college orientation, psychology, psychology-AP, radio broadcasting, religion, SAT/ACT preparation, science, sex education, sexuality, social studies, sociology, Spanish, speech, sports medicine, theater, theology, trigonometry, typing, U.S. history-AP, woodworking, world history, world literature.

Graduation Requirements Art, English, foreign language, mathematics, religion (includes Bible studies and theology), science, social studies (includes history).

Special Academic Programs Advanced Placement exam preparation; honors section; independent study; study abroad.

College Admission Counseling 130 students graduated in 2011; all went to college, including Brown University; Cornell University; Georgetown University; Trinity College; United States Naval Academy; University of Pennsylvania. Mean SAT critical reading: 625, mean SAT math: 633, mean SAT writing: 625, mean composite ACT: 26. 62% scored over 600 on SAT critical reading, 66% scored over 600 on SAT math, 53% scored over 26 on composite ACT.

Student Life Upper grades have specified standards of dress, student council, honor system. Discipline rests equally with students and faculty. Attendance at religious services is required.
Tuition and Aid Day student tuition: $32,800; 7-day tuition and room/board: $47,500. Tuition installment plan (Insured Tuition Payment Plan, monthly payment plans, individually arranged payment plans). Need-based scholarship grants available. In 2011–12, 38% of upper-school students received aid. Total amount of financial aid awarded in 2011–12: $4,800,000.
Admissions Traditional secondary-level entrance grade is 9. For fall 2011, 749 students applied for upper-level admission, 305 were accepted, 192 enrolled. ACT, ISEE, PSAT or SAT for applicants to grade 11 and 12, SSAT or TOEFL required. Deadline for receipt of application materials: January 31. Application fee required: $50. Interview required.
Athletics Interscholastic: baseball (boys), basketball (b,g), cross-country running (b,g), field hockey (g), football (b), ice hockey (b,g), indoor track (b,g), lacrosse (b,g), soccer (b,g), softball (g), squash (b,g), swimming and diving (b,g), tennis (b,g), water polo (b,g), winter (indoor) track (b,g), wrestling (b); coed interscholastic: diving, golf, track and field; coed intramural: aerobics, basketball, golf, martial arts, riflery, soccer, squash, strength & conditioning, tennis, volleyball, weight lifting. 2 coaches, 2 athletic trainers.
Computers Computers are regularly used in all classes. Computer network features include on-campus library services, online commercial services, Internet access, wireless campus network. Student e-mail accounts are available to students. The school has a published electronic and media policy.
Contact Mr. Thomas Eccleston, IV, Assistant Headmaster for Admission and External Affairs. 610-326-1000. Fax: 610-705-1753. E-mail: teccleston@thehill.org. Web site: www.thehill.org

See Display below and Close-Up on page 586.

HILL SCHOOL OF FORT WORTH

4817 Odessa Avenue
Fort Worth, Texas 76133-1640

Head of School: Audrey Boda-Davis

General Information Coeducational day college-preparatory, general academic, arts, and technology school; primarily serves individuals with Attention Deficit Disorder and dyslexic students. Grades 1–12. Founded: 1973. Setting: suburban. 1 building on campus. Approved or accredited by Southern Association of Colleges and Schools and Texas Department of Education. Member of National Association of Independent Schools. Total enrollment: 169. Upper school average class size: 9. Upper school faculty-student ratio: 1:9. There are 175 required school days per year for Upper School students. Upper School students typically attend 5 days per week. The average school day consists of 6 hours and 30 minutes.
Faculty School total: 29. In upper school: 6 men, 13 women.
Special Academic Programs Special instructional classes for students with learning differences.
Student Life Upper grades have uniform requirement, student council, honor system. Discipline rests primarily with faculty.
Tuition and Aid Tuition installment plan (The Tuition Plan).
Admissions Deadline for receipt of application materials: none. No application fee required. Interview required.
Athletics Interscholastic: basketball (boys, girls), football (b), track and field (b,g), volleyball (g).
Computers Computers are regularly used in all academic classes. Computer network features include on-campus library services, Internet access, wireless campus network, Internet filtering or blocking technology. Campus intranet and student e-mail accounts are available to students. Students grades are available online. The school has a published electronic and media policy.
Contact Judy King, Director of Admissions. 817-923-9482. E-mail: jking@hillschool.org. Web site: www.hillschool.org

THE HILL TOP PREPARATORY SCHOOL

Rosemont, Pennsylvania
See Special Needs Schools section.

HO'ALA SCHOOL

1067A California Avenue
Wahiawa, Hawaii 96786

Head of School: Linda Perry

General Information college-preparatory, arts, and Service Learning school; primarily serves students with learning disabilities. Founded: 1986. Setting: rural. Nearest major city is Honolulu. 1-acre campus. 1 building on campus. Approved or accredited by Western Association of Schools and Colleges and Hawaii Department of Education. Total enrollment: 65. Upper school average class size: 5. There are 182 required school days per year for Upper School students. Upper School students typically attend 5 days per week. The average school day consists of 5 hours and 30 minutes.
Faculty School total: 6. In upper school: 2 men, 4 women; 1 has an advanced degree.
Subjects Offered 1 1/2 elective credits, 20th century history, 20th century physics, 20th century world history, advanced biology, advanced chemistry, advanced computer

applications, advanced math, Advanced Placement courses, advanced studio art-AP, algebra, alternative physical education, American Civil War, American government, American history, American history-AP, American literature, American literature-AP, analytic geometry, anthropology, art, art appreciation, art education, art history, art history-AP, athletics, basketball, biology, biology-AP, bowling, calculus, calculus-AP, character education, chemistry, chemistry-AP, civics, Civil War, civil war history, college admission preparation, college awareness, college counseling, college placement, college planning, college writing, community service, composition, composition-AP, computer applications, contemporary art, creative arts, creative dance, creative drama, creative thinking, creative writing, dance, drama, drama performance, drawing, drawing and design, English, English composition, English language and composition-AP, English language-AP, English literature and composition-AP, English literature-AP, English-AP, English/composition-AP, environmental science, environmental studies, fine arts, foreign language, general science, geometry, government/civics, government/civics-AP, grammar, guidance, Hawaiian history, health, health and safety, health and wellness, health education, history, home economics, honors algebra, honors English, honors geometry, honors U.S. history, honors world history, Internet, Internet research, lab science, language, language and composition, language-AP, life management skills, life skills, marine biology, marine science, mathematics-AP, mentorship program, modern dance, modern history, painting, personal and social education, physical education, physics, physics-AP, post-calculus, pre-algebra, precalculus, pre-college orientation, SAT/ACT preparation, science, scuba diving, senior career experience, senior project, service learning/internship, sewing, social sciences, social studies, Spanish, Spanish language-AP, Spanish-AP, student government, student teaching, studio art-AP, study skills, theater arts, volleyball, world geography, world governments, world history, world history-AP, writing, yearbook.

Special Academic Programs Advanced Placement exam preparation; academic accommodation for the gifted and the artistically talented; remedial reading and/or remedial writing; remedial math; programs in general development for dyslexic students.

College Admission Counseling 4 students graduated in 2012; all went to college.

Student Life Upper grades have uniform requirement, student council, honor system. Discipline rests primarily with faculty.

Tuition and Aid Day student tuition: $9800. Tuition installment plan (monthly payment plans, individually arranged payment plans). Tuition reduction for siblings, need-based scholarship grants available. In 2012–13, 20% of upper-school students received aid. Total amount of financial aid awarded in 2012–13: $10,000.

Admissions Traditional secondary-level entrance grade is 9. For fall 2012, 2 students applied for upper-level admission. Admissions testing, High School Placement Test, school's own exam and writing sample required. Deadline for receipt of application materials: none. Application fee required: $50. Interview recommended.

Athletics Interscholastic: basketball (boys), bowling (b,g), swimming and diving (b,g), track and field (b,g); intramural: basketball (b). 5 PE instructors, 1 coach.

Computers Computers are regularly used in college planning, computer applications, English, health, history, keyboarding, lab/keyboard, mentorship program, science, Web site design, yearbook classes. Computer network features include wireless campus network. Students grades are available online.

Contact Nona Fern, Admissions Clerk. 808-621-1898. Fax: 808-622-3615. E-mail: nona@hoala.org. Web site:

THE HOCKADAY SCHOOL

11600 Welch Road
Dallas, Texas 75229-2999

Head of School: Kim Wargo

General Information Girls' boarding and day and distance learning college-preparatory, arts, and technology school. Boarding grades 8–12, day grades PK–12. Distance learning grades 3–12. Founded: 1913. Setting: suburban. Students are housed in single-sex dormitories. 85-acre campus. 12 buildings on campus. Approved or accredited by Independent Schools Association of the Southwest and The Association of Boarding Schools. Member of National Association of Independent Schools and Secondary School Admission Test Board. Endowment: $121.5 million. Total enrollment: 1,086. Upper school average class size: 15. Upper school faculty-student ratio: 1:15. There are 160 required school days per year for Upper School students. Upper School students typically attend 5 days per week. The average school day consists of 6 hours and 40 minutes.

Upper School Student Profile Grade 9: 117 students (117 girls); Grade 10: 124 students (124 girls); Grade 11: 117 students (117 girls); Grade 12: 120 students (120 girls). 15% of students are boarding students. 86% are state residents. 10 states are represented in upper school student body. 11% are international students. International students from China, Jamaica, Mexico, Nigeria, Republic of Korea, and Taiwan; 7 other countries represented in student body.

Faculty School total: 128. In upper school: 18 men, 41 women; 47 have advanced degrees; 1 resides on campus.

Subjects Offered Acting, advanced math, advanced studio art-AP, algebra, American history, American history-AP, American literature, analytic geometry, anatomy, applied arts, applied music, art history, astronomy, athletics, audio visual/media, ballet, basketball, biology, biology-AP, body human, British literature, broadcast journalism, broadcasting, Broadway dance, calculus, calculus-AP, cell biology, ceramics, chemistry, chemistry-AP, college counseling, comparative religion, computer applications, computer science, computer science-AP, concert choir, consumer economics, CPR, creative writing, current events, dance, dance performance, debate, digital art, digital imaging, digital music, digital photography, directing, discrete mathematics, drawing and design, ecology, environmental systems, economics-AP, English, English literature, English literature and composition-AP, English-AP, environmental science, environmental science-AP, ESL, ESL, fencing, fine arts, finite math, first aid, French, French language-AP, French literature-AP, genetics, geometry, guitar, health, health and wellness, honors English, humanities, information technology, interdisciplinary studies, journalism, Latin, Latin-AP, madrigals, Mandarin, microbiology, modern European history-AP, newspaper, non-Western literature, orchestra, philosophy, photography, physical education, physical fitness, physics, physics-AP, piano, pre-calculus, printmaking, probability and statistics, psychology, psychology-AP, self-defense, senior internship, set design, short story, Spanish, Spanish language-AP, Spanish literature-AP, stagecraft, studio art, studio art-AP, swimming, technology, tennis, track and field, U.S. government, U.S. history, U.S. history-AP, voice, volleyball, Web site design, wellness, world history, yearbook.

Graduation Requirements Algebra, American literature, art history, audio visual/media, biology-AP, chemistry, computer literacy, computer skills, English, English literature, geometry, history of music, information technology, languages, physical education (includes health), physics, senior project, U.S. government, U.S. history, world history, one semester of History of Art and Music, 60 hours of community service.

Special Academic Programs Advanced Placement exam preparation; honors section; independent study; term-away projects; study abroad; ESL (12 students enrolled).

College Admission Counseling 121 students graduated in 2012; all went to college, including Cornell University; Georgetown University; Harvard University; Northwestern University; Stanford University; Vanderbilt University.

Student Life Upper grades have uniform requirement, student council, honor system. Discipline rests primarily with faculty.

Summer Programs Enrichment, advancement, ESL, sports, art/fine arts, computer instruction programs offered; session focuses on enrichment; held on campus; accepts boys and girls; open to students from other schools. 900 students usually enrolled. 2013 schedule: June 10 to July 19. Application deadline: none.

Tuition and Aid Day student tuition: $23,300–$23,925; 7-day tuition and room/board: $41,499–$46,258. Need-based scholarship grants, need-based financial aid available. In 2012–13, 22% of upper-school students received aid. Total amount of financial aid awarded in 2012–13: $1,851,800.

Admissions Traditional secondary-level entrance grade is 9. For fall 2012, 204 students applied for upper-level admission, 64 were accepted, 43 enrolled. Admissions testing required. Deadline for receipt of application materials: none. Application fee required: $175. Interview required.

Athletics Interscholastic: basketball, crew, cross-country running, fencing, field hockey, golf, independent competitive sports, jogging, lacrosse, rowing, running, soccer, softball, swimming and diving, tennis, track and field, volleyball, winter soccer; intramural: aerobics, aerobics/dance, aquatics, archery, ballet, basketball, cheering, cooperative games, dance, fitness, independent competitive sports, jogging, life saving, martial arts, modern dance, outdoor skills, physical fitness, physical training, project adventure, racquetball, ropes courses, running, self defense, strength & conditioning, swimming and diving, tennis, track and field, ultimate Frisbee, volleyball, weight lifting, weight training, yoga. 13 PE instructors, 9 coaches, 3 athletic trainers.

Computers Computers are regularly used in animation, art, computer applications, creative writing, dance, engineering, English, French, health, history, humanities, information technology, introduction to technology, journalism, Latin, mathematics, media, media production, media services, multimedia, music, newspaper, photography, photojournalism, psychology, publications, publishing, science, Spanish, technology, Web site design, yearbook classes. Computer network features include on-campus library services, online commercial services, Internet access, wireless campus network, Internet filtering or blocking technology. Campus intranet, student e-mail accounts, and computer access in designated common areas are available to students. Students grades are available online. The school has a published electronic and media policy.

Contact Jen Liggitt, Director of Admission. 214-363-6311. Fax: 214-265-1649. E-mail: admissions@mail.hockaday.org. Web site: www.hockaday.org

See Display on next page and Close-Up on page 588.

HOLLAND HALL

5666 East 81st Street
Tulsa, Oklahoma 74137-2099

Head of School: Richard P. Hart

General Information Coeducational day college-preparatory, arts, religious studies, and technology school, affiliated with Episcopal Church. Grades PK–12. Founded: 1922. Setting: suburban. 162-acre campus. 5 buildings on campus. Approved or accredited by Independent Schools Association of the Southwest, National Association of Episcopal Schools, and Oklahoma Department of Education. Member of National Association of Independent Schools. Endowment: $68 million. Total enrollment: 995. Upper school average class size: 13. Upper school faculty-student ratio: 1:9. There are 172 required school days per year for Upper School students. Upper School students typically attend 5 days per week. The average school day consists of 6 hours and 52 minutes.

Upper School Student Profile Grade 6: 77 students (32 boys, 45 girls); Grade 7: 63 students (31 boys, 32 girls); Grade 8: 64 students (36 boys, 28 girls); Grade 9: 77 students (40 boys, 37 girls); Grade 10: 90 students (44 boys, 46 girls); Grade 11: 95 students (55 boys, 40 girls); Grade 12: 71 students (38 boys, 33 girls). 7% of students are members of Episcopal Church.

Faculty School total: 93. In upper school: 23 men, 19 women; 28 have advanced degrees.

Subjects Offered Algebra, American history, American studies, art, biology, calculus, calculus-AP, ceramics, chemistry, chemistry-AP, Chinese, computer programming, computer science, creative writing, dance, drama, driver education, ecology, economics, English, English literature, ethics, fine arts, French, geology, geometry, government/civics, history, Latin, mathematics, music, photography, physical education, physics, religion, science, social studies, Spanish, statistics-AP, theater, trigonometry, writing.

Graduation Requirements Arts and fine arts (art, music, dance, drama), English, foreign language, mathematics, physical education (includes health), religion (includes Bible studies and theology), science, social studies (includes history), senior intern program.

Special Academic Programs Advanced Placement exam preparation; honors section; independent study; study at local college for college credit; study abroad.

College Admission Counseling 74 students graduated in 2012; all went to college, including Oklahoma State University; Southern Methodist University; University of Oklahoma; University of Tulsa.

Student Life Upper grades have uniform requirement, student council, honor system. Discipline rests equally with students and faculty. Attendance at religious services is required.

Summer Programs Enrichment, advancement, sports, art/fine arts programs offered; session focuses on academic enrichment; held on campus; accepts boys and girls; open to students from other schools. 830 students usually enrolled. 2013 schedule: June 3 to July 26. Application deadline: June 1.

Tuition and Aid Day student tuition: $17,300. Tuition installment plan (monthly payment plans, school's own payment plan). Merit scholarship grants, need-based scholarship grants available. In 2012–13, 28% of upper-school students received aid; total upper-school merit-scholarship money awarded: $154,900. Total amount of financial aid awarded in 2012–13: $928,525.

Admissions Traditional secondary-level entrance grade is 9. Admissions testing, Brigance Test of Basic Skills and ERB required. Deadline for receipt of application materials: none. Application fee required: $25. On-campus interview required.

Athletics Interscholastic: baseball (boys), basketball (b,g), cheering (g), cross-country running (b,g), field hockey (g), football (b), golf (b,g), modern dance (b,g), soccer (b,g), softball (g), tennis (b,g), track and field (b,g), volleyball (g); intramural: aerobics (b,g), dance (b,g), modern dance (b,g), soccer (b,g); coed interscholastic: cheering, crew, modern dance, physical training, strength & conditioning; coed intramural: fitness, modern dance, physical training, soccer, weight lifting. 39 coaches, 1 athletic trainer.

Computers Computers are regularly used in English, foreign language, history, mathematics, science classes. Computer network features include on-campus library services, online commercial services, Internet access, wireless campus network, Internet filtering or blocking technology. Student e-mail accounts and computer access in designated common areas are available to students. The school has a published electronic and media policy.

Contact Olivia Martin, Interim Director of Admission and Financial Aid. 918-481-1111 Ext. 740. Fax: 918-481-1145. E-mail: omartin@hollandhall.org. Web site: www.hollandhall.org

HOLY ANGELS ACADEMY

24 Shoshone Drive
Buffalo, New York 14214-1097

Head of School: Mrs. Kathy Tedesco

General Information Girls' day college-preparatory, arts, religious studies, and technology school, affiliated with Roman Catholic Church. Grades 6–12. Founded: 1861. Setting: urban. 5-acre campus. 1 building on campus. Approved or accredited by Middle States Association of Colleges and Schools, New York State Board of Regents, and New York Department of Education. Member of Secondary School Admission Test Board. Total enrollment: 242. Upper school average class size: 18. Upper school faculty-student ratio: 1:10. Upper School students typically attend 5 days per week. The average school day consists of 6 hours and 35 minutes.

Upper School Student Profile Grade 9: 66 students (66 girls); Grade 10: 47 students (47 girls); Grade 11: 58 students (58 girls). 80% of students are Roman Catholic.

Faculty School total: 31. In upper school: 5 men, 26 women; 19 have advanced degrees.

Subjects Offered Algebra, American history, American history-AP, American literature, art, art history, Bible studies, biology, biology-AP, calculus, calculus-AP, chemistry, chorus, computer applications, computer programming, computer science, creative writing, design, digital art, drama, drawing, driver education, economics, English, English literature, English literature-AP, English/composition-AP, ESL, expository writing, fine arts, forensics, French, geometry, global studies, government and politics-AP, government/civics, grammar, health, history, instrumental music, keyboarding,

Latin, law, Mandarin, mathematics, media, music, music composition, music theory, music theory-AP, mythology, nutrition, orchestra, painting, photography, physical education, physics, physics-AP, pre-calculus, psychology, religion, science, sculpture, social studies, sociology, Spanish, statistics, statistics-AP, studio art, theater, trigonometry, world history, world history-AP, writing.

Graduation Requirements Arts and fine arts (art, music, dance, drama), computer science, English, foreign language, health, mathematics, physical education (includes health), religion (includes Bible studies and theology), science, social sciences, social studies (includes history). Community service is required.

Special Academic Programs Advanced Placement exam preparation; honors section; accelerated programs; independent study; study at local college for college credit; remedial reading and/or remedial writing; remedial math; special instructional classes for deaf students; ESL (12 students enrolled).

College Admission Counseling 54 students graduated in 2012; all went to college, including Buffalo State College, State University of New York; Canisius College; Niagara University; Rochester Institute of Technology; State University of New York College at Geneseo; University at Buffalo, the State University of New York. Mean SAT critical reading: 529, mean SAT math: 547, mean SAT writing: 541.

Student Life Upper grades have uniform requirement, student council, honor system. Discipline rests primarily with faculty. Attendance at religious services is required.

Tuition and Aid Day student tuition: $9150. Tuition installment plan (FACTS Tuition Payment Plan, individually arranged payment plans, quarterly payment plan). Tuition reduction for siblings, merit scholarship grants, need-based scholarship grants, paying campus jobs, alumnae awards, leadership awards available. In 2012–13, 75% of upper-school students received aid; total upper-school merit-scholarship money awarded: $30,000. Total amount of financial aid awarded in 2012–13: $400,000.

Admissions Traditional secondary-level entrance grade is 9. For fall 2012, 90 students applied for upper-level admission, 75 were accepted, 66 enrolled. High School Placement Test (closed version) from Scholastic Testing Service required. Deadline for receipt of application materials: none. Application fee required: $20. Interview recommended.

Athletics Interscholastic: badminton, basketball, bowling, crew, cross-country running, golf, hockey, ice hockey, lacrosse, rowing, running, soccer, softball, swimming and diving, tennis, track and field, volleyball, winter (indoor) track; intramural: aerobics, aerobics/dance, alpine skiing, dance, indoor track, skiing (downhill). 1 PE instructor, 20 coaches.

Computers Computers are regularly used in all classes. Computer network features include on-campus library services, online commercial services, Internet access, wireless campus network, Internet filtering or blocking technology, iPads. Student e-mail accounts and computer access in designated common areas are available to students. Students grades are available online. The school has a published electronic and media policy.

Contact Miss Mary Colby, Assistant Principal. 716-834-7120. Fax: 716-834-7128. E-mail: mcolby@holyangelsacademy.org. Web site: www.holyangelsacademy.org

HOLY CROSS HIGH SCHOOL

587 Oronoke Road
Waterbury, Connecticut 06708

Head of School: Mr. TimothY McDonald

General Information Coeducational day college-preparatory, arts, religious studies, and technology school, affiliated with Roman Catholic Church. Grades 9–12. Founded: 1968. Setting: suburban. 37-acre campus. 1 building on campus. Approved or accredited by National Catholic Education Association, New England Association of Schools and Colleges, and Connecticut Department of Education. Total enrollment: 630. Upper school average class size: 20. Upper school faculty-student ratio: 1:15. There are 160 required school days per year for Upper School students. Upper School students typically attend 5 days per week. The average school day consists of 6 hours.

Upper School Student Profile Grade 9: 129 students (60 boys, 69 girls); Grade 10: 156 students (83 boys, 73 girls); Grade 11: 165 students (86 boys, 79 girls); Grade 12: 177 students (97 boys, 80 girls). 85% of students are Roman Catholic.

Faculty School total: 60. In upper school: 28 men, 32 women; 37 have advanced degrees.

Subjects Offered Advanced biology, advanced math, Advanced Placement courses, advanced studio art-AP, algebra, American history, American history-AP, American literature, American literature-AP, American studies, anatomy, anatomy and physiology, art, art-AP, arts, band, Basic programming, biology, biology-AP, British literature, British literature-AP, business, business law, calculus, calculus-AP, campus ministry, Catholic belief and practice, chamber groups, chemistry, chemistry-AP, choir, computer applications, computer programming, computer science, concert band, concert choir, CPR, creative writing, drama, driver education, economics, economics and history, English, English literature, English-AP, environmental science, French, geometry, history, mathematics, music, physical education, physics, physiology, psychology, religion, science, social studies, Spanish, statistics, theater, theology, trigonometry, word processing, world history, world literature.

Graduation Requirements English, foreign language, mathematics, physical education (includes health), religion (includes Bible studies and theology), science, social studies (includes history).

Special Academic Programs Advanced Placement exam preparation; honors section; independent study; study at local college for college credit.

College Admission Counseling 196 students graduated in 2012; 187 went to college, including Central Connecticut State University; Naugatuck Valley Community College; Southern Connecticut State University; University of Connecticut; Western Connecticut State University. Other: 4 went to work, 2 entered military service, 3 entered a postgraduate year.

Student Life Upper grades have specified standards of dress, student council. Discipline rests primarily with faculty. Attendance at religious services is required.

Tuition and Aid Day student tuition: $10,750. Tuition installment plan (monthly payment plans, individually arranged payment plans, Tuition Management Systems (TMS)). Merit scholarship grants, need-based scholarship grants available. In 2012–13, 30% of upper-school students received aid; total upper-school merit-scholarship money awarded: $135,000. Total amount of financial aid awarded in 2012–13: $550,000.

Admissions Traditional secondary-level entrance grade is 9. For fall 2012, 365 students applied for upper-level admission, 321 were accepted, 130 enrolled. ETS HSPT (closed) required. Deadline for receipt of application materials: none. Application fee required: $25.

Athletics Interscholastic: baseball (boys), basketball (b,g), cheering (g), cross-country running (b,g), dance team (g), diving (b,g), football (b), golf (b,g), gymnastics (g), lacrosse (b), soccer (b,g), softball (g), swimming and diving (b,g), tennis (b,g), track and field (b,g), volleyball (g), winter (indoor) track (b,g), wrestling (b); intramural: basketball (b), skiing (downhill) (b,g), weight lifting (b); coed intramural: bowling, table tennis, ultimate Frisbee, yoga. 3 PE instructors, 22 coaches, 1 athletic trainer.

Computers Computers are regularly used in accounting, business, computer applications, creative writing, English, foreign language, French, history, mathematics, music technology, psychology, religious studies, science, social sciences, social studies, Spanish, technology, theology, Web site design, word processing, writing, writing, yearbook classes. Computer network features include on-campus library services, online commercial services, Internet access, wireless campus network. Campus intranet and computer access in designated common areas are available to students. Students grades are available online.

Contact Mrs. Jodie LaCava McGarrity, Director of Admissions. 203-757-9248. Fax: 203-757-3423. E-mail: jmcgarrity@holycrosshs-ct.com. Web site: www.holycrosshs-ct.com

HOLY CROSS HIGH SCHOOL

26-20 Francis Lewis Boulevard
Flushing, New York 11358

Head of School: Fr. Walter E. Jenkins, CSC

General Information Boys' day college-preparatory, arts, business, religious studies, and technology school, affiliated with Roman Catholic Church. Grades 9–12. Founded: 1955. Setting: urban. Nearest major city is New York. 1 building on campus. Approved or accredited by National Catholic Education Association and New York Department of Education. Upper school average class size: 29. There are 180 required school days per year for Upper School students. Upper School students typically attend 5 days per week. The average school day consists of 6 hours and 2 minutes.

Upper School Student Profile Grade 9: 240 students (240 boys); Grade 10: 230 students (230 boys); Grade 11: 220 students (220 boys); Grade 12: 210 students (210 boys). 70% of students are Roman Catholic.

Special Academic Programs Honors section; study at local college for college credit.

College Admission Counseling 212 students graduated in 2011; all went to college.

Student Life Upper grades have specified standards of dress, student council, honor system. Discipline rests primarily with faculty. Attendance at religious services is required.

Tuition and Aid Day student tuition: $8125. Tuition installment plan (SMART Tuition Payment Plan). Tuition reduction for siblings, merit scholarship grants, need-based scholarship grants available.

Admissions Traditional secondary-level entrance grade is 9. No application fee required.

Athletics Interscholastic: baseball, basketball, bowling, cross-country running, football, golf, ice hockey, indoor track, soccer, tennis, winter (indoor) track. 3 PE instructors, 35 coaches.

Computers Computer network features include on-campus library services, online commercial services, Internet access. Student e-mail accounts are available to students. Students grades are available online. The school has a published electronic and media policy.

Contact Mr. Paul Gilvary, Director of Admissions. 718-886-7250 Ext. 525. Fax: 718-886-7257. E-mail: admissions@holycrosshs.org. Web site: www.holycrosshs.org

HOLY CROSS SCHOOL

5500 Paris Avenue
New Orleans, Louisiana 70122

Head of School: Mr. Charles DiGange

General Information Boys' day college-preparatory, arts, religious studies, and technology school, affiliated with Roman Catholic Church. Grades 5–12. Founded: 1849. Setting: suburban. 20-acre campus. 5 buildings on campus. Approved or accredited by National Catholic Education Association, Southern Association of Colleges and Schools, and Louisiana Department of Education. Total enrollment: 980. Upper school average class size: 23. Upper school faculty-student ratio: 1:13. There are 184 required school days per year for Upper School students. Upper School students typically attend 5 days per week. The average school day consists of 6 hours and 35 minutes.

Upper School Student Profile Grade 8: 150 students (150 boys); Grade 9: 175 students (175 boys); Grade 10: 170 students (170 boys); Grade 11: 165 students (165 boys); Grade 12: 160 students (160 boys). 80% of students are Roman Catholic.

Faculty School total: 66. In upper school: 14 men, 40 women; 24 have advanced degrees.

Graduation Requirements Community service requirement.

Special Academic Programs 11 Advanced Placement exams for which test preparation is offered; honors section; study at local college for college credit; academic accommodation for the gifted, the musically talented, and the artistically talented.

College Admission Counseling 90 students graduated in 2012; 89 went to college, including Louisiana State University and Agricultural and Mechanical College; Loyola University New Orleans; Spring Hill College; St. Edward's University; University of Louisiana at Lafayette; University of Southern Mississippi. Other: 1 entered military service.

Student Life Upper grades have uniform requirement, student council, honor system. Discipline rests primarily with faculty. Attendance at religious services is required.

Summer Programs Remediation, enrichment programs offered; session focuses on enrichment; held on campus; accepts boys; not open to students from other schools. 75 students usually enrolled. 2013 schedule: July 14 to July 28. Application deadline: May 31.

Tuition and Aid Day student tuition: $7277. Tuition installment plan (monthly payment plans). Tuition reduction for siblings, merit scholarship grants, need-based scholarship grants, paying campus jobs available. In 2012–13, 7% of upper-school students received aid; total upper-school merit-scholarship money awarded: $50,000.

Admissions Traditional secondary-level entrance grade is 8. For fall 2012, 350 students applied for upper-level admission, 235 were accepted, 210 enrolled. ACT-Explore required. Deadline for receipt of application materials: November 16. Application fee required: $20. Interview required.

Athletics Interscholastic: baseball, basketball, bowling, cheering, cross-country running, football, golf, indoor track, indoor track & field, power lifting, soccer, swimming and diving, tennis, wrestling; intramural: baseball, basketball, bicycling, fishing, flag football, football, Frisbee, lacrosse, martial arts, physical training, skateboarding, soccer, softball, strength & conditioning, ultimate Frisbee, volleyball, weight training. 8 PE instructors, 36 coaches, 3 athletic trainers.

Computers Computer network features include on-campus library services, online commercial services, Internet access, wireless campus network, Internet filtering or blocking technology. Student e-mail accounts and computer access in designated common areas are available to students. Students grades are available online. The school has a published electronic and media policy.

Contact Mr. Brian Kitchen, Director of Admissions. 504-942-3100. Fax: 504-284-3424. E-mail: bkitchen@holycrosstigers.com. Web site: www.holycrosstigers.com

HOLY GHOST PREPARATORY SCHOOL

2429 Bristol Pike
Bensalem, Pennsylvania 19020

Head of School: Rev. Jeffrey T. Duaime, CSSP

General Information Boys' day college-preparatory, arts, and technology school, affiliated with Roman Catholic Church. Grades 9–12. Founded: 1897. Setting: suburban. Nearest major city is Philadelphia. 53-acre campus. 4 buildings on campus. Approved or accredited by Middle States Association of Colleges and Schools, National Catholic Education Association, and Pennsylvania Association of Independent Schools. Member of National Association of Independent Schools. Endowment: $2 million. Total enrollment: 480. Upper school average class size: 17. Upper school faculty-student ratio: 1:11. The average school day consists of 6 hours and 30 minutes.

Upper School Student Profile Grade 9: 106 students (106 boys); Grade 10: 124 students (124 boys); Grade 11: 127 students (127 boys); Grade 12: 123 students (123 boys). 94% of students are Roman Catholic.

Faculty School total: 50. In upper school: 32 men, 18 women; 34 have advanced degrees.

Subjects Offered 3-dimensional art, Advanced Placement courses, advanced studio art-AP, algebra, American government, American history, American history-AP, American literature, analysis, anatomy and physiology, art, Bible, biology, biology-AP, calculus, calculus-AP, campus ministry, career/college preparation, careers, ceremonies of life, chemistry, Chinese history, choral music, church history, college admission preparation, college counseling, communication arts, communication skills, computer programming-AP, computer science, computer science-AP, creative writing, drama performance, earth science, economics, English, English language and composition-AP, English literature, English literature and composition-AP, environmental science, European history, European history-AP, film, fine arts, French, French language-AP, geometry, government and politics-AP, government/civics, health, history, journalism, language-AP, Latin, Latin-AP, mathematics, modern European history-AP, music, music theory-AP, oral communications, physical education, physics, public speaking, religion, science, sexuality, social studies, Spanish, Spanish language-AP, Spanish-AP, speech, statistics, trigonometry, U.S. history-AP, United States government-AP, world cultures, world history, world history-AP, world literature, writing, yearbook.

Graduation Requirements Arts and fine arts (art, music, dance, drama), computer science, English, foreign language, mathematics, physical education (includes health), religion (includes Bible studies and theology), science, social studies (includes history), summer reading. Community service is required.

Special Academic Programs Advanced Placement exam preparation; honors section; independent study; study abroad.

College Admission Counseling 124 students graduated in 2012; all went to college, including Boston College; Duquesne University; Penn State University Park; Saint Joseph's University; University of Pennsylvania; Villanova University. Median SAT critical reading: 610, median SAT math: 640.

Student Life Upper grades have specified standards of dress, student council, honor system. Discipline rests primarily with faculty.

Summer Programs Enrichment, advancement, sports, computer instruction programs offered; session focuses on entrance exam preparation; held on campus; accepts boys and girls; open to students from other schools. 100 students usually enrolled. 2013 schedule: June 24 to July 26. Application deadline: June 15.

Tuition and Aid Day student tuition: $16,700. Tuition installment plan (monthly payment plans, quarterly and semi-annual payment plans). Merit scholarship grants, need-based scholarship grants, music scholarships, minority scholarships, art scholarships available. In 2012–13, 35% of upper-school students received aid; total upper-school merit-scholarship money awarded: $1,000,000. Total amount of financial aid awarded in 2012–13: $1,000,000.

Admissions Traditional secondary-level entrance grade is 9. For fall 2012, 398 students applied for upper-level admission, 158 were accepted, 106 enrolled. High School Placement Test (closed version) from Scholastic Testing Service required. Deadline for receipt of application materials: December 9. Application fee required: $60. On-campus interview required.

Athletics Interscholastic: baseball, basketball, bowling, cross-country running, golf, ice hockey, indoor track & field, lacrosse, soccer, Special Olympics, swimming and diving, tennis, track and field; intramural: basketball, fitness walking, flag football, football, Frisbee, soccer, street hockey, tennis, ultimate Frisbee. 10 coaches, 1 athletic trainer.

Computers Computers are regularly used in college planning, English, foreign language, mathematics, programming, publications, science, speech, yearbook classes. Computer network features include on-campus library services, online commercial services, Internet access, wireless campus network, Internet filtering or blocking technology. Student e-mail accounts are available to students.

Contact Mr. Ryan T. Abramson, Director of Admissions. 215-639-0811. Fax: 215-639-4225. E-mail: rabramson@holyghostprep.org. Web site: www.holyghostprep.org

HOLY INNOCENTS' EPISCOPAL SCHOOL

805 Mount Vernon Highway NW
Atlanta, Georgia 30327

Head of School: Mr. Eugene A. Bratek

General Information Coeducational day college-preparatory, arts, religious studies, and technology school, affiliated with Episcopal Church. Grades PS–12. Founded: 1959. Setting: suburban. 42-acre campus. 4 buildings on campus. Approved or accredited by Georgia Independent School Association, National Association of Episcopal Schools, Southern Association of Colleges and Schools, and Georgia Department of Education. Member of National Association of Independent Schools and Secondary School Admission Test Board. Endowment: $17 million. Total enrollment: 1,302. Upper school average class size: 14. Upper school faculty-student ratio: 1:7. There are 173 required school days per year for Upper School students. Upper School students typically attend 5 days per week. The average school day consists of 7 hours and 15 minutes.

Upper School Student Profile Grade 9: 119 students (64 boys, 55 girls); Grade 10: 120 students (56 boys, 64 girls); Grade 11: 105 students (53 boys, 52 girls); Grade 12: 100 students (43 boys, 57 girls). 26% of students are members of Episcopal Church.

Faculty School total: 180. In upper school: 29 men, 32 women; 45 have advanced degrees.

Subjects Offered 3-dimensional art, 3-dimensional design, advanced biology, advanced chemistry, advanced math, Advanced Placement courses, advanced studio art-AP, algebra, American government, American history, American history-AP, American literature, American literature-AP, anatomy, anatomy and physiology, ancient world history, applied music, art, art-AP, athletics, band, baseball, basketball, Bible, Bible studies, biology, biology-AP, calculus, calculus-AP, cheerleading, chemistry, chemistry-AP, choir, choral music, chorus, college counseling, college placement, community service, composition, computer animation, computer education, computer graphics, computer resources, computer science-AP, concert band, concert choir, creative writing, drama, drama performance, drawing and design, earth science, economics, electives, English, English composition, English language-AP, English literature, English literature-AP, English-AP, environmental studies, ethics, European history, European history-AP, fine arts, French, French language-AP, French-AP, geometry, golf, government, government and politics-AP, government/civics, Greek, guidance, health and wellness, history, honors algebra, honors English, honors geometry, honors U.S. history, honors world history, human geography - AP, Jewish history, Jewish studies, language arts, Latin, Latin-AP, mathematics, New Testament, orchestra, peer counseling, performing arts, personal finance, photography, physical education, physics, physics-AP, pre-calculus, psychology, religion, religious studies, SAT preparation, SAT/ACT preparation, science, science project, sex education, social studies, Spanish, Spanish language-AP, speech and debate, sports, study skills, swimming, U.S. history, U.S. history-AP, visual arts, world history, writing workshop, yearbook.

Graduation Requirements Arts and fine arts (art, music, dance, drama), electives, English, foreign language, history, mathematics, physical education (includes health), physical fitness, religion (includes Bible studies and theology), science, 15 hours of community service each year, plus additional hours for NHS students.

Special Academic Programs Advanced Placement exam preparation; honors section; term-away projects; study abroad.

College Admission Counseling 90 students graduated in 2011; all went to college, including Auburn University; Clemson University; Georgia Institute of Technology; The University of Alabama; The University of North Carolina at Chapel Hill; University of Georgia. Mean SAT critical reading: 600, mean SAT math: 610, mean SAT writing: 620, mean composite ACT: 26.

Student Life Upper grades have uniform requirement, student council, honor system. Discipline rests primarily with faculty. Attendance at religious services is required.

Tuition and Aid Day student tuition: $21,500. Tuition installment plan (Insured Tuition Payment Plan, FACTS Tuition Payment Plan, monthly payment plans). Need-based scholarship grants available. In 2011–12, 20% of upper-school students received aid. Total amount of financial aid awarded in 2011–12: $1,800,000.

Admissions Traditional secondary-level entrance grade is 9. For fall 2011, 116 students applied for upper-level admission, 59 were accepted, 33 enrolled. Essay, ISEE, mathematics proficiency exam, school's own test and SSAT required. Deadline for receipt of application materials: February 1. Application fee required: $95. Interview required.

Athletics Interscholastic: baseball (boys), basketball (b,g), cheering (g), cross-country running (b,g), equestrian sports (g), football (b), golf (b,g), lacrosse (b,g), physical fitness (b,g), physical training (b,g), soccer (b,g), softball (g), swimming and diving (b,g), tennis (b,g), track and field (b,g), volleyball (g), wrestling (b); intramural: combined training (b,g), fitness (b,g), ultimate Frisbee (b); coed intramural: combined training, fitness. 9 PE instructors, 120 coaches, 1 athletic trainer.

Computers Computers are regularly used in all academic classes. Computer network features include on-campus library services, Internet access, wireless campus network, Internet filtering or blocking technology, 1-to-1 student laptops (grades 5-12), two computer labs, and various individual classroom computers. Campus intranet and student e-mail accounts are available to students. Students grades are available online. The school has a published electronic and media policy.

Contact Mr. Chris Pomar, Director of Admissions. 404-255-4026. Fax: 404-847-1156. E-mail: chris.pomar@hies.org. Web site: www.hies.org

HOLY NAMES ACADEMY

728 21st Avenue East

Seattle, Washington 98112

Head of School: Elizabeth Swift

General Information Girls' day college-preparatory school, affiliated with Roman Catholic Church. Grades 9–12. Founded: 1880. Setting: urban. Approved or accredited by Northwest Accreditation Commission, Pacific Northwest Association of Independent Schools, and Washington Department of Education. Member of National Association of Independent Schools. Upper school average class size: 14.

Upper School Student Profile 74% of students are Roman Catholic.

Student Life Attendance at religious services is required.

Tuition and Aid Day student tuition: $12,396. Financial aid available to upper-school students. In 2011–12, 31% of upper-school students received aid. Total amount of financial aid awarded in 2011–12: $1,005,360.

Admissions MAT 7 Metropolitan Achievement Test required. Deadline for receipt of application materials: January 12. Application fee required: $25.

Contact 206-323-4272. Web site: www.holynames-sea.org

HOLYOKE CATHOLIC HIGH SCHOOL

134 Springfield Street
Chicopee, Massachusetts 01013

Head of School: Mrs. Theresa J. Kitchell

General Information Coeducational day college-preparatory and arts school, affiliated with Roman Catholic Church. Grades 9–12. Founded: 1963. Setting: small town. Nearest major city is Springfield. 3 buildings on campus. Approved or accredited by New England Association of Schools and Colleges and Massachusetts Department of Education. Total enrollment: 298. Upper school average class size: 15. Upper school faculty-student ratio: 1:10. There are 180 required school days per year for Upper School students. Upper School students typically attend 5 days per week. The average school day consists of 6 hours.

Upper School Student Profile Grade 9: 71 students (32 boys, 39 girls); Grade 10: 78 students (32 boys, 46 girls); Grade 11: 66 students (29 boys, 37 girls); Grade 12: 83 students (34 boys, 49 girls). 90% of students are Roman Catholic.

Faculty School total: 31. In upper school: 13 men, 18 women; 21 have advanced degrees.

Subjects Offered Advanced biology, advanced math, algebra, American literature, American literature-AP, art, biology, calculus, calculus-AP, Catholic belief and practice, chemistry, English, English literature, environmental science, forensics, French, geometry, Latin, literature-AP, moral theology, multimedia design, performing arts, physics, pottery, pre-calculus, psychology, social sciences, Spanish, studio art, The 20th Century, U.S. history, U.S. history-AP, vocal ensemble, Web site design, world civilizations, world history, world religions, yearbook.

Graduation Requirements Electives, English, foreign language, mathematics, religion (includes Bible studies and theology), science, social studies (includes history), U.S. literature, community service hours at each grade level, English research paper at each level, Senior Internship Program.

Special Academic Programs 5 Advanced Placement exams for which test preparation is offered; honors section; independent study; study at local college for college credit; ESL (3 students enrolled).

College Admission Counseling 71 students graduated in 2012; all went to college, including Elms College; Fairfield University; Holyoke Community College; Western New England University; Westfield State University. Median composite ACT: 24. 1% scored over 26 on composite ACT.

Student Life Upper grades have uniform requirement, student council. Discipline rests primarily with faculty. Attendance at religious services is required.

Summer Programs Enrichment programs offered; session focuses on study skills, essay writing, SAT Prep, Algebra review; held on campus; accepts boys and girls; not open to students from other schools. 25 students usually enrolled. 2013 schedule: July 30 to August 17. Application deadline: July 2.

Tuition and Aid Day student tuition: $7500. Tuition installment plan (FACTS Tuition Payment Plan). Merit scholarship grants, need-based scholarship grants available. In 2012–13, 30% of upper-school students received aid; total upper-school merit-scholarship money awarded: $1000. Total amount of financial aid awarded in 2012–13: $135,350.

Admissions Traditional secondary-level entrance grade is 9. For fall 2012, 113 students applied for upper-level admission, 107 were accepted, 73 enrolled. Scholastic Testing Service High School Placement Test required. Deadline for receipt of application materials: none. Application fee required: $100. Interview required.

Athletics Interscholastic: baseball (boys), basketball (b,g), cheering (g), cross-country running (b,g), football (b), indoor track & field (b,g), lacrosse (b,g), soccer (b,g), softball (g), winter (indoor) track (b,g); coed interscholastic: golf, hiking/backpacking, outdoor adventure, skiing (downhill), swimming and diving, tennis, unicycling; coed intramural: volleyball, weight training. 10 coaches.

Computers Computers are regularly used in multimedia classes. Computer network features include on-campus library services, Internet access, Internet filtering or blocking technology. Campus intranet and student e-mail accounts are available to students. Students grades are available online. The school has a published electronic and media policy.

Contact Mrs. Theresa Marie Zaborowski, Director of Admissions. 413-331-2480 Ext. 1132. Fax: 413-331-2708. E-mail: tzaborowski@holyokecatholichigh.org. Web site: www.holyokecatholichigh.org

HOLY SAVIOR MENARD CATHOLIC HIGH SCHOOL

4603 Coliseum Boulevard
Alexandria, Louisiana 71303

Head of School: Mr. Joel Desselle

General Information Coeducational day college-preparatory and religious studies school, affiliated with Roman Catholic Church. Grades 7–12. Founded: 1930. Setting: suburban. 5-acre campus. 5 buildings on campus. Approved or accredited by National Catholic Education Association, Southern Association of Colleges and Schools, The College Board, and Louisiana Department of Education. Total enrollment: 480. Upper school average class size: 18. Upper school faculty-student ratio: 1:12. There are 178 required school days per year for Upper School students. Upper School students typically attend 5 days per week. The average school day consists of 7 hours and 15 minutes.

Upper School Student Profile Grade 9: 88 students (48 boys, 40 girls); Grade 10: 81 students (33 boys, 48 girls); Grade 11: 65 students (24 boys, 41 girls); Grade 12: 65 students (39 boys, 26 girls). 84% of students are Roman Catholic.

Faculty School total: 38. In upper school: 14 men, 22 women; 13 have advanced degrees.

Subjects Offered Advanced math, algebra, American history, anatomy and physiology, art, athletics, biology, biology-AP, British literature, British literature (honors), calculus-AP, campus ministry, Catholic belief and practice, cheerleading, chemistry, civics/free enterprise, computer applications, computer science, digital photography, English, English composition, English literature, English literature-AP, fine arts, French, general science, geometry, health, honors algebra, honors English, honors geometry, honors U.S. history, honors world history, journalism, language arts, moral reasoning, New Testament, newspaper, philosophy, physical education, physical science, physics, pre-algebra, pre-calculus, psychology, publications, reading/study skills, religion, sociology, Spanish, world geography, world history, yearbook.

Graduation Requirements Algebra, American history, arts and fine arts (art, music, dance, drama), biology, chemistry, civics/free enterprise, computer applications, English, foreign language, geometry, physical science, religion (includes Bible studies and theology), world history, 27 credits required.

Special Academic Programs 4 Advanced Placement exams for which test preparation is offered; honors section; independent study; study at local college for college credit.

College Admission Counseling 80 students graduated in 2012; 75 went to college, including Louisiana State University and Agricultural and Mechanical College; Louisiana Tech University; Millsaps College; Northwestern State University of Louisiana; Tulane University; University of Louisiana at Lafayette. Other: 3 went to work, 2 had other specific plans. Mean composite ACT: 22. 29% scored over 26 on composite ACT.

Student Life Upper grades have uniform requirement, student council, honor system. Discipline rests primarily with faculty. Attendance at religious services is required.

Tuition and Aid Day student tuition: $5700. Tuition installment plan (FACTS Tuition Payment Plan, monthly payment plans, individually arranged payment plans). Tuition reduction for siblings, merit scholarship grants, need-based scholarship grants available. In 2012–13, 12% of upper-school students received aid; total upper-school merit-scholarship money awarded: $5000. Total amount of financial aid awarded in 2012–13: $150,000.

Admissions Traditional secondary-level entrance grade is 9. For fall 2012, 15 students applied for upper-level admission, 15 were accepted, 15 enrolled. CTBS, Stanford Achievement Test, any other standardized test required. Deadline for receipt of application materials: March 15. Application fee required: $300. On-campus interview required.

Athletics Interscholastic: baseball (boys), basketball (b,g), cheering (g), cross-country running (b,g), danceline (g), football (b), golf (b,g), power lifting (b,g), running (b,g), soccer (b,g), softball (g), tennis (b,g), track and field (b,g); intramural: paddle tennis (b,g); coed interscholastic: swimming and diving; coed intramural: paddle tennis. 3 PE instructors, 3 coaches.

Computers Computers are regularly used in computer applications, English, journalism, mathematics, photography, publications, science, Web site design classes. Computer network features include on-campus library services, Internet access, wireless campus network, Internet filtering or blocking technology. Computer access in designated common areas is available to students. Students grades are available online.

Contact Mrs. Ashley Meadows, Guidance Secretary. 318-445-8233. Fax: 318-448-8170. E-mail: ameadows@holysaviormenard.com. Web site: www.holysaviormenard.com

HOLY TRINITY DIOCESAN HIGH SCHOOL

98 Cherry Lane
Hicksville, New York 11801

Head of School: Mr. Gene Fennell

General Information Coeducational day college-preparatory school, affiliated with Roman Catholic Church. Grades 9–12. Founded: 1967. Setting: suburban. Nearest major city is New York. 1 building on campus. Approved or accredited by Middle States Association of Colleges and Schools, National Council for Private School Accreditation, New York State Board of Regents, The College Board, and New York Department of Education. Total enrollment: 1,351. Upper school average class size: 32. Upper school faculty-student ratio: 1:17. There are 180 required school days per year for Upper School students. Upper School students typically attend 5 days per week.

Upper School Student Profile Grade 9: 323 students (150 boys, 173 girls); Grade 10: 349 students (180 boys, 169 girls); Grade 11: 356 students (167 boys, 189 girls); Grade 12: 323 students (165 boys, 158 girls). 90% of students are Roman Catholic.

Faculty School total: 82. In upper school: 29 men, 53 women; 77 have advanced degrees.

Subjects Offered Accounting, advanced math, Advanced Placement courses, American government, American history, American history-AP, American literature, American literature-AP, anatomy and physiology, architectural drawing, art, band, biology, biology-AP, British literature, British literature (honors), business law, calculus, calculus-AP, campus ministry, ceramics, chemistry, chemistry-AP, chorus, Christian scripture, Christian studies, Christian testament, comparative religion, composition, concert band, criminology, critical studies in film, dance, desktop publishing, earth science, economics, English, English composition, English language and composition-AP, English literature, English literature-AP, environmental science, film, food and nutrition, French, government and politics-AP, health, honors English, honors U.S. history, honors world history, intro to computers, jazz theory, keyboarding, literature and composition-AP, mathematics, music, performing arts, physical education, physics, physics-AP, pre-calculus, public speaking, religion, Spanish, Spanish language-AP, stagecraft, statistics, theater arts, theology, U.S. government and politics, U.S. government and politics-AP, U.S. history, U.S. history-AP, world wide web design.

Graduation Requirements Arts and fine arts (art, music, dance, drama), economics, English, foreign language, mathematics, physical education (includes health), religion (includes Bible studies and theology), science, U.S. government and politics.

Special Academic Programs Advanced Placement exam preparation; honors section; study at local college for college credit.

College Admission Counseling 326 students graduated in 2012; all went to college, including Adelphi University; Hofstra University; Nassau Community College; Stony Brook University, State University of New York. Mean SAT critical reading: 501, mean SAT math: 514, mean SAT writing: 503.

Student Life Upper grades have uniform requirement, student council. Discipline rests primarily with faculty.

Tuition and Aid Day student tuition: $8495. Tuition installment plan (monthly payment plans, individually arranged payment plans, 10-month tuition plan, 3-payment plan). Need-based scholarship grants available.

Admissions Traditional secondary-level entrance grade is 9. Catholic High School Entrance Examination required. Deadline for receipt of application materials: none. Application fee required. Interview recommended.

Athletics Interscholastic: badminton (girls), baseball (b), basketball (b,g), cheering (g), cross-country running (b,g), dance team (g), football (b), golf (b), gymnastics (g), indoor track (b,g), lacrosse (b,g), soccer (b,g), softball (g), swimming and diving (b,g), tennis (b,g), track and field (b,g), volleyball (b,g), weight lifting (b), weight training (b), winter (indoor) track (b,g), wrestling (b); intramural: physical training (b), weight training (b); coed interscholastic: bowling, fitness. 6 PE instructors, 1 athletic trainer.

Computers Computers are regularly used in college planning, computer applications, desktop publishing, drawing and design, economics, English, foreign language, graphic design, history, journalism, library, music technology, newspaper, occupational education, programming, research skills, SAT preparation, science, social studies, theater, Web site design, writing, yearbook classes. Computer network features include on-campus library services, Internet access, Internet filtering or blocking technology. Student e-mail accounts and computer access in designated common areas are available to students. Students grades are available online. The school has a published electronic and media policy.

Contact Admissions. 516-433-2900. Fax: 516-433-2827. E-mail: hths98@holytrinityhs.echalk.com. Web site: www.holytrinityhs.org

HOLY TRINITY HIGH SCHOOL

1443 West Division Street
Chicago, Illinois 60642

Head of School: Mr. Timothy M. Bopp

General Information Coeducational day college-preparatory, arts, business, religious studies, bilingual studies, and technology school, affiliated with Roman Catholic Church. Grades 9–12. Founded: 1910. Setting: urban. 1 building on campus. Approved or accredited by North Central Association of Colleges and Schools and Illinois Department of Education. Total enrollment: 270. Upper school average class size: 20. Upper school faculty-student ratio: 1:12. There are 180 required school days per year for Upper School students. The average school day consists of 5 hours and 52 minutes.

Upper School Student Profile Grade 9: 63 students (35 boys, 28 girls); Grade 10: 58 students (31 boys, 27 girls); Grade 11: 79 students (49 boys, 30 girls); Grade 12: 70 students (40 boys, 30 girls). 40% of students are Roman Catholic.

Faculty School total: 28. In upper school: 12 men, 16 women; 14 have advanced degrees.

Subjects Offered Band, French.

Graduation Requirements Business, English, mathematics, modern languages, physical education (includes health), religion (includes Bible studies and theology), science, social studies (includes history), visual and performing arts.

Special Academic Programs Advanced Placement exam preparation; honors section; study at local college for college credit; remedial reading and/or remedial writing; ESL.

College Admission Counseling 65 students graduated in 2011; 64 went to college, including Brigham Young University; Knox College; Northeastern Illinois University; Northern Illinois University; Triton College; Western Illinois University. Other: 1 entered military service.

Student Life Upper grades have uniform requirement, student council, honor system. Discipline rests equally with students and faculty. Attendance at religious services is required.

Tuition and Aid Day student tuition: $6800. Tuition installment plan (monthly payment plans). Tuition reduction for siblings, merit scholarship grants, need-based scholarship grants available. In 2011–12, 95% of upper-school students received aid;

total upper-school merit-scholarship money awarded: $125,000. Total amount of financial aid awarded in 2011–12: $600,000.

Admissions Traditional secondary-level entrance grade is 9. For fall 2011, 195 students applied for upper-level admission, 176 were accepted, 84 enrolled. TerraNova required. Deadline for receipt of application materials: January 14. Application fee required: $25.

Athletics Interscholastic: baseball (boys), basketball (b,g), cross-country running (b,g), soccer (b,g), softball (g), track and field (b,g), volleyball (b,g); coed interscholastic: bowling, flag football; coed intramural: cheering, dance, dance team, fitness, physical fitness, weight lifting. 2 PE instructors, 4 coaches.

Computers Computers are regularly used in animation, business education, business skills, college planning, keyboarding classes. Computer network features include on-campus library services, Internet access, wireless campus network, Internet filtering or blocking technology. Computer access in designated common areas is available to students. The school has a published electronic and media policy.

Contact Ms. Samara Galvan, Admission Coordinator. 773-278-4212 Ext. 3025. Fax: 773-278-0144. E-mail: sglavan@holytrinity-hs.org. Web site: www.holytrinity-hs.org

HOLY TRINITY SCHOOL

11300 Bayview Avenue
Richmond Hill, Ontario L4S 1L4, Canada

Head of School: Mr. Barry Hughes

General Information Coeducational day college-preparatory, arts, and business school. Grades JK–12. Founded: 1985. Approved or accredited by Conference of Independent Schools of Ontario and Ontario Department of Education. Language of instruction: English. Total enrollment: 750. The average school day consists of 6 hours.

Upper School Student Profile Grade 9: 110 students (50 boys, 60 girls); Grade 10: 100 students (50 boys, 50 girls); Grade 11: 80 students (45 boys, 35 girls); Grade 12: 100 students (50 boys, 50 girls).

Special Academic Programs Advanced Placement exam preparation.

College Admission Counseling 90 students graduated in 2012; all went to college, including Queen's University at Kingston.

Tuition and Aid Day student tuition: CAN$21,425. Bursaries, need-based scholarship grants available.

Admissions SSAT required. Deadline for receipt of application materials: December 1. Application fee required: CAN$125. Interview required.

Athletics 4 PE instructors, 15 coaches, 1 athletic trainer.

Computers Computer network features include on-campus library services, Internet access, wireless campus network, Internet filtering or blocking technology. Campus intranet, student e-mail accounts, and computer access in designated common areas are available to students. Students grades are available online.

Contact Mrs. Mary-Lynn Seeley, Admission Assistant. 905-737-1114 Ext. 236. Fax: 905-737-5187. E-mail: mseeley@hts.on.ca. Web site: www.hts.on.ca

HOOSAC SCHOOL

PO Box 9
Hoosick, New York 12089

Head of School: Dean S. Foster

General Information Coeducational boarding and day college-preparatory and arts school, affiliated with Episcopal Church. Grades 8–PG. Founded: 1889. Setting: rural. Nearest major city is Albany. Students are housed in single-sex dormitories. 350-acre campus. 16 buildings on campus. Approved or accredited by Middle States Association of Colleges and Schools, National Association of Episcopal Schools, New York State Board of Regents, The Association of Boarding Schools, and New York Department of Education. Member of National Association of Independent Schools and Secondary School Admission Test Board. Endowment: $1.5 million. Total enrollment: 125. Upper school average class size: 8. Upper school faculty-student ratio: 1:5. Upper School students typically attend 6 days per week. The average school day consists of 6 hours and 15 minutes.

Upper School Student Profile Grade 8: 7 students (5 boys, 2 girls); Grade 9: 20 students (10 boys, 10 girls); Grade 10: 23 students (16 boys, 7 girls); Grade 11: 29 students (17 boys, 12 girls); Grade 12: 41 students (29 boys, 12 girls); Postgraduate: 5 students (5 boys). 90% of students are boarding students. 31% are state residents. 17 states are represented in upper school student body. 38% are international students. International students from Canada, China, Republic of Korea, Russian Federation, Rwanda, and Uruguay; 9 other countries represented in student body.

Faculty School total: 23. In upper school: 14 men, 9 women; 11 have advanced degrees; 15 reside on campus.

Subjects Offered Advertising design, algebra, American history, American literature, art, art history, astronomy, biology, British literature, calculus, calculus-AP, ceramics, chemistry, choral music, computer science, creative writing, criminology, dance, drama, driver education, earth science, English, English literature, English-AP, ESL, ethics, European history, expository writing, fine arts, French, French as a second language, geometry, government/civics, grammar, history, history-AP, Latin, marketing, mathematics, music, photography, physical education, physics, science, social studies, speech communications, theater, world history, world literature, writing.

Graduation Requirements Arts and fine arts (art, music, dance, drama), computer literacy, English, ethics, foreign language, mathematics, physical education (includes health), science, social studies (includes history), Ethics, public speaking.

Special Academic Programs 7 Advanced Placement exams for which test preparation is offered; honors section; accelerated programs; independent study; study at local college for college credit; academic accommodation for the musically talented and the artistically talented; remedial reading and/or remedial writing; remedial math; programs in English, mathematics, general development for dyslexic students; ESL (40 students enrolled).

College Admission Counseling 36 students graduated in 2011; all went to college, including Bentley University; Carnegie Mellon University; Cornell University; Gettysburg College; University of California, Berkeley; University of Michigan.

Student Life Upper grades have specified standards of dress, student council, honor system. Discipline rests primarily with faculty. Attendance at religious services is required.

Tuition and Aid Day student tuition: $17,000; 7-day tuition and room/board: $38,000. Tuition installment plan (Academic Management Services Plan, Key Tuition Payment Plan, monthly payment plans, individually arranged payment plans). Merit scholarship grants, need-based scholarship grants available. In 2011–12, 35% of upper-school students received aid. Total amount of financial aid awarded in 2011–12: $625,000.

Admissions Traditional secondary-level entrance grade is 9. For fall 2011, 198 students applied for upper-level admission, 108 were accepted, 56 enrolled. Deadline for receipt of application materials: none. Application fee required: $40. Interview required.

Athletics Interscholastic: baseball (boys), basketball (b,g), cross-country running (b,g), ice hockey (b), lacrosse (b,g); intramural: bicycling (b,g), flag football (b,g), floor hockey (b,g); coed intramural: aerobics/dance, alpine skiing, aquatics, backpacking, ball hockey, bowling, broomball, canoeing/kayaking, cooperative games, cross-country running, dance, deck hockey, fishing, freestyle skiing, golf, hiking/backpacking, indoor hockey, indoor soccer, life saving, mountain biking, outdoor activities, outdoor recreation, outdoor skills, physical fitness, physical training, weight training, whiffle ball, yoga. 1 PE instructor, 2 coaches.

Computers Computers are regularly used in computer applications, journalism, literary magazine, media arts, media production, multimedia, news writing, newspaper, photography, photojournalism classes. Computer network features include on-campus library services, Internet access, wireless campus network, Internet filtering or blocking technology. Campus intranet, student e-mail accounts, and computer access in designated common areas are available to students. Students grades are available online. The school has a published electronic and media policy.

Contact Mr. Michael S. Foster, Director of Admission and Residential Life. 800-822-0159. Fax: 518-686-3370. E-mail: admissions@hoosac.com. Web site: www.hoosac.com

HOPKINS SCHOOL

986 Forest Road
New Haven, Connecticut 06515

Head of School: Ms. Barbara M. Riley

General Information Coeducational day college-preparatory school. Grades 7–12. Founded: 1660. Setting: urban. Nearest major city is New York, NY. 108-acre campus. 10 buildings on campus. Approved or accredited by New England Association of Schools and Colleges and Connecticut Department of Education. Member of National Association of Independent Schools. Endowment: $68.6 million. Total enrollment: 709. Upper school average class size: 12. Upper school faculty-student ratio: 1:6. There are 170 required school days per year for Upper School students. Upper School students typically attend 5 days per week. The average school day consists of 7 hours and 30 minutes.

Upper School Student Profile Grade 9: 150 students (78 boys, 72 girls); Grade 10: 136 students (68 boys, 68 girls); Grade 11: 135 students (68 boys, 67 girls); Grade 12: 133 students (72 boys, 61 girls).

Faculty School total: 126. In upper school: 56 men, 70 women; 85 have advanced degrees.

Subjects Offered African-American history, algebra, American history, American literature, anatomy and physiology, ancient history, art, art history, art history-AP, art-AP, Asian studies, astrophysics, biochemistry, biology, biology-AP, calculus, calculus-AP, ceramics, chemistry, chemistry-AP, Chinese, chorus, classical music, computer math, computer programming, computer science, computer science-AP, creative writing, drama, earth science, economics, English, English literature, environmental science-AP, European history, expository writing, film, fine arts, forensics, French, French-AP, geometry, government/civics, Greek, history, Holocaust studies, HTML design, human geography - AP, human sexuality, Islamic history, Italian, jazz, Latin, Latin American history, Latin-AP, linear algebra, mathematics, military history, music, music theory, philosophy, photography, physics, physics-AP, politics, probability and statistics, psychology, Spanish, Spanish-AP, studio art, studio art-AP, theater, trigonometry, U.S. history-AP, urban studies, video, Web site design, woodworking, world literature, writing.

Graduation Requirements Arts and fine arts (art, music, dance, drama), English, foreign language, mathematics, physical education (includes health), science, social studies (includes history), swimming, grade 12 community service project.

Special Academic Programs Advanced Placement exam preparation; honors section; independent study; term-away projects; study abroad.

College Admission Counseling 122 students graduated in 2012; all went to college, including Georgetown University; Harvard University; Massachusetts Institute of Technology; Stanford University; University of Chicago; Yale University. Mean SAT critical reading: 694, mean SAT math: 684, mean SAT writing: 701, mean combined SAT: 2079, mean composite ACT: 30.

Student Life Upper grades have specified standards of dress, student council, honor system. Discipline rests equally with students and faculty.

Summer Programs Remediation, enrichment, advancement, sports programs offered; session focuses on middle and upper school academics and some athletics; held on campus; accepts boys and girls; open to students from other schools. 180 students usually enrolled. 2013 schedule: June 24 to August 2. Application deadline: June 17.

Tuition and Aid Day student tuition: $33,700. Tuition installment plan (Academic Management Services Plan, Key Tuition Payment Plan). Need-based scholarship grants available. In 2012–13, 19% of upper-school students received aid. Total amount of financial aid awarded in 2012–13: $2,900,000.

Admissions Traditional secondary-level entrance grade is 9. For fall 2012, 292 students applied for upper-level admission, 127 were accepted, 80 enrolled. ISEE or SSAT required. Deadline for receipt of application materials: January 15. Application fee required: $75. On-campus interview required.

Athletics Interscholastic: aquatics (boys, girls), baseball (b), basketball (b,g), crew (b,g), cross-country running (b,g), diving (b,g), fencing (b,g), field hockey (g), football (b), golf (b,g), independent competitive sports (b,g), indoor track (b,g), lacrosse (b,g), soccer (b,g), softball (g), squash (b,g), swimming and diving (b,g), tennis (b,g), track and field (b,g), volleyball (g), water polo (b,g), wrestling (b); intramural: independent competitive sports (b,g); coed interscholastic: independent competitive sports, winter (indoor) track; coed intramural: aerobics, aerobics/Nautilus, basketball, cooperative games, fencing, fitness, floor hockey, Frisbee, independent competitive sports, Nautilus, outdoor adventure, project adventure, ropes courses, running, soccer, swimming and diving, tennis, volleyball, weight lifting, weight training, wilderness, yoga. 4 coaches, 3 athletic trainers.

Computers Computers are regularly used in art, English, foreign language, history, mathematics, science classes. Computer network features include on-campus library services, Internet access, wireless campus network, Internet filtering or blocking technology. Campus intranet and student e-mail accounts are available to students. The school has a published electronic and media policy.

Contact Ms. Gena Eggert, Administrative Assistant to Director of Admissions. 203-397-1001 Ext. 211. Fax: 203-389-2249. E-mail: admissions@hopkins.edu. Web site: www.hopkins.edu

HORIZON CHRISTIAN ACADEMY JUNIOR/SENIOR HIGH SCHOOL

5331 Mt. Alifan Drive
San Diego, California 92111

Head of School: Dr. F. Chapin Marsh III

General Information college-preparatory school, affiliated with Christian faith. Founded: 1992. Approved or accredited by Association of Christian Schools International, Western Association of Schools and Colleges, and California Department of Education. Upper school average class size: 25.

College Admission Counseling Colleges students went to include Biola University.

Student Life Upper grades have uniform requirement. Discipline rests primarily with faculty.

Admissions WRAT required. Application fee required: $350. On-campus interview required.

Athletics Interscholastic: baseball (boys, girls), basketball (b,g), cheering (g), cross-country running (b,g), curling (g), flag football (b), football (b), golf (b,g), soccer (b,g), surfing (b,g), volleyball (g), wilderness (b,g).

Contact Mrs. Katie Ramirez, Director of Admissions/Registrar. . 858-244-0376. E-mail: kramirez@horizonsd.org. Web site: www.horizonsd.org/jr_sr_high_school.asp

THE HOTCHKISS SCHOOL

11 Interlaken Road
PO Box 800
Lakeville, Connecticut 06039

Head of School: Mr. Malcolm H. McKenzie

General Information Coeducational boarding and day college-preparatory school. Grades 9–PG. Founded: 1891. Setting: rural. Nearest major city is Hartford. Students are housed in single-sex dormitories. 810-acre campus. 80 buildings on campus. Approved or accredited by Connecticut Association of Independent Schools, New England Association of Schools and Colleges, The Association of Boarding Schools, and Connecticut Department of Education. Member of National Association of Independent Schools and Secondary School Admission Test Board. Endowment: $380.3 million. Total enrollment: 599. Upper school average class size: 12. Upper school faculty-student ratio: 1:6. There are 168 required school days per year for Upper School students. Upper School students typically attend 6 days per week. The average school day consists of 6 hours and 50 minutes.

Upper School Student Profile Grade 9: 103 students (48 boys, 55 girls); Grade 10: 152 students (70 boys, 82 girls); Grade 11: 166 students (80 boys, 86 girls); Grade 12: 160 students (77 boys, 83 girls); Postgraduate: 18 students (17 boys, 1 girl). 93% of students are boarding students. 19% are state residents. 40 states are represented in upper school student body. 18% are international students. International students from Canada, China, Colombia, Hong Kong, Republic of Korea, and Singapore; 21 other countries represented in student body.

Faculty School total: 115. In upper school: 63 men, 52 women; 91 have advanced degrees; 103 reside on campus.

Subjects Offered 3-dimensional design, acting, advanced math, Advanced Placement courses, advanced studio art-AP, algebra, American history, American history-AP, American literature, American studies, anatomy and physiology, Ancient Greek, ancient history, architecture, art, art history-AP, astronomy, bioethics, biology, biology-AP, calculus, calculus-AP, ceramics, chemistry, chemistry-AP, China/Japan history, Chinese, chorus, classics, college counseling, comparative government and politics-AP, computer programming, computer science, computer science-AP, conceptual physics, constitutional history of U.S., creative writing, dance, digital photography, discrete mathematics, drama, drawing, economics, economics-AP, English, English-AP, environmental science, environmental science-AP, ethics, European history, European history-AP, expository writing, fine arts, French, French language-AP, French literature-AP, geometry, German, history of music, Holocaust, humanities, independent study, jazz dance, jazz ensemble, Latin, Latin American history, Latin-AP, limnology, mathematics, music, music history, music technology, music theory, music theory-AP, musical productions, non-Western literature, orchestra, organic chemistry, philosophy, photography, physics, physics-AP, playwriting, pre-calculus, public speaking, religion, science, Spanish, Spanish language-AP, Spanish literature-AP, statistics-AP, studio art, theater, trigonometry, video, voice, world literature, writing.

Graduation Requirements American history, arts and fine arts (art, music, dance, drama), English, foreign language, mathematics, science.

Special Academic Programs Advanced Placement exam preparation; honors section; independent study; term-away projects; study abroad; academic accommodation for the gifted, the musically talented, and the artistically talented.

College Admission Counseling 170 students graduated in 2011; all went to college, including Bucknell University; Georgetown University; Harvard University; Hobart and William Smith Colleges; Princeton University; Yale University. Median SAT critical reading: 620, median SAT math: 640, median SAT writing: 630, median combined SAT: 1890, median composite ACT: 29. 61% scored over 600 on SAT critical reading, 70% scored over 600 on SAT math, 65% scored over 600 on SAT writing, 64% scored over 1800 on combined SAT, 75% scored over 26 on composite ACT.

Student Life Upper grades have specified standards of dress, student council. Discipline rests equally with students and faculty.

Tuition and Aid Day student tuition: $38,650; 7-day tuition and room/board: $45,350. Tuition installment plan (Tuition Management Systems (formerly Key Tuition Plan)). Need-based scholarship grants, need-based loans available. In 2011–12, 37% of upper-school students received aid. Total amount of financial aid awarded in 2011–12: $8,282,237.

Admissions Traditional secondary-level entrance grade is 9. For fall 2011, 1,980 students applied for upper-level admission, 322 were accepted, 187 enrolled. ACT, ISEE, PSAT, SAT, or ACT for applicants to grade 11 and 12, SSAT or TOEFL required. Deadline for receipt of application materials: January 15. Application fee required: $65. Interview required.

Athletics Interscholastic: baseball (boys), basketball (b,g), cross-country running (b,g), diving (b,g), field hockey (g), football (b), golf (b,g), ice hockey (b,g), lacrosse (b,g), soccer (b,g), softball (g), squash (b,g), swimming and diving (b,g), tennis (b,g), touch football (b), track and field (b,g), volleyball (g), water polo (b), wrestling (b); coed interscholastic: Frisbee, sailing, ultimate Frisbee; coed intramural: aerobics, aerobics/Nautilus, ballet, basketball, canoeing/kayaking, climbing, combined training, dance, drill team, fitness, fitness walking, Frisbee, golf, hiking/backpacking, ice hockey, jogging, Nautilus, outdoor education, paddle tennis, physical fitness, physical training, rock climbing, running, squash, strength & conditioning, tennis, ultimate Frisbee, volleyball, walking, wall climbing, water polo, weight lifting, yoga. 2 coaches, 2 athletic trainers.

Computers Computers are regularly used in all academic classes. Computer network features include on-campus library services, online commercial services, Internet access, wireless campus network, Internet filtering or blocking technology. Campus intranet, student e-mail accounts, and computer access in designated common areas are available to students. Students grades are available online. The school has a published electronic and media policy.

Contact Ms. Rachael N. Beare, Dean of Admission and Financial Aid. 860-435-3102. Fax: 860-435-0042. E-mail: admission@hotchkiss.org. Web site: www.hotchkiss.org

HOUGHTON ACADEMY

9790 Thayer Street
Houghton, New York 14744

Head of School: Dr. George Wiedmaier

General Information Coeducational boarding and day college-preparatory, religious studies, and ESL school, affiliated with Wesleyan Church. Boarding grades 9–PG, day grades 6–PG. Founded: 1883. Setting: rural. Nearest major city is Buffalo. Students are housed in single-sex dormitories and staff homes. 25-acre campus. 6 buildings on campus. Approved or accredited by Association of Christian Schools International, Middle States Association of Colleges and Schools, The Association of Boarding Schools, and New York Department of Education. Member of National Association of Independent Schools. Endowment: $90,000. Total enrollment: 134. Upper school average class size: 16. Upper school faculty-student ratio: 1:8. There are 177 required school days per year for Upper School students. Upper School students typically attend 5 days per week. The average school day consists of 6 hours and 30 minutes.

Upper School Student Profile Grade 9: 17 students (7 boys, 10 girls); Grade 10: 32 students (17 boys, 15 girls); Grade 11: 32 students (15 boys, 17 girls); Grade 12: 30 students (19 boys, 11 girls). 62% of students are boarding students. 43% are state residents. 1 state is represented in upper school student body. 57% are international students. International students from China, Nigeria, Republic of Korea, Taiwan, and Viet Nam; 3 other countries represented in student body. 25% of students are members of Wesleyan Church.

Faculty School total: 17. In upper school: 6 men, 10 women; 14 have advanced degrees; 3 reside on campus.

Subjects Offered Algebra, American history, American literature, art, band, Bible, Bible studies, biology, business, business skills, calculus, chemistry, chorus, community service, computer science, creative writing, desktop publishing, driver education, earth science, economics, English, English literature, environmental science, ESL, ethics, fine arts, geography, geometry, government/civics, grammar, history, international relations, mathematics, music, photography, physical education, physics, science, social sciences, social studies, Spanish, speech, trigonometry, word processing, world history, writing.

Graduation Requirements Arts and fine arts (art, music, dance, drama), Bible, electives, English, mathematics, physical education (includes health), science, social studies (includes history).

Special Academic Programs 4 Advanced Placement exams for which test preparation is offered; honors section; independent study; study at local college for college credit; ESL.

College Admission Counseling 33 students graduated in 2012; 30 went to college, including Binghamton University, State University of New York; Houghton College; Michigan State University; Stony Brook University, State University of New York; University of California, San Diego; University of Washington. Other: 1 went to work, 2 entered military service. Median SAT critical reading: 460, median SAT math: 650, median SAT writing: 485, median combined SAT: 1585, median composite ACT: 18. 10% scored over 600 on SAT critical reading, 62% scored over 600 on SAT math, 18% scored over 600 on SAT writing, 24% scored over 1800 on combined SAT.

Student Life Upper grades have specified standards of dress, student council. Discipline rests primarily with faculty. Attendance at religious services is required.

Tuition and Aid Day student tuition: $6930; 7-day tuition and room/board: $26,385. Tuition installment plan (FACTS Tuition Payment Plan). Need-based scholarship grants available. In 2012–13, 25% of upper-school students received aid. Total amount of financial aid awarded in 2012–13: $95,000.

Admissions Traditional secondary-level entrance grade is 9. For fall 2012, 150 students applied for upper-level admission, 70 were accepted, 36 enrolled. PSAT or SAT for applicants to grade 11 and 12, SLEP, SSAT or TOEFL required. Deadline for receipt of application materials: February 15. Application fee required: $50. Interview required.

Athletics Interscholastic: basketball (boys, girls), cheering (g), soccer (b), volleyball (g); intramural: badminton (b,g), basketball (b,g), floor hockey (b,g), golf (b,g), indoor soccer (b,g), paddle tennis (b,g), racquetball (b,g), skiing (downhill) (b,g), soccer (b,g), table tennis (b,g), tennis (b,g), volleyball (b,g); coed interscholastic: golf; coed intramural: badminton, ball hockey, indoor soccer, paddle tennis, skiing (downhill), softball, table tennis. 2 PE instructors, 9 coaches, 1 athletic trainer.

Computers Computers are regularly used in accounting, Bible studies, college planning, English, graphic design, keyboarding, mathematics, multimedia, SAT preparation, science, word processing, yearbook classes. Computer network features include on-campus library services, Internet access, Internet filtering or blocking technology, electronic access to Houghton College Library holdings. Computer access in designated common areas is available to students. Students grades are available online. The school has a published electronic and media policy.

Contact Mr. Ronald J. Bradbury, Director of Admissions. 585-567-8115. Fax: 585-567-8048. E-mail: admissions@houghtonacademy.org. Web site: www.houghtonacademy.org

HOUSTON LEARNING ACADEMY-NORTH HOUSTON

13029 Champions Drive
Houston, Texas 77069-3204

General Information Distance learning only college-preparatory and general academic school. Distance learning grades 9–12. Founded: 1988. Setting: urban. 1 building on campus. Approved or accredited by Southern Association of Colleges and Schools and Texas Department of Education. Upper school average class size: 15. Upper school faculty-student ratio: 1:5. There are 171 required school days per year for Upper School students. Upper School students typically attend 5 days per week. The average school day consists of 4 hours and 30 minutes.

Faculty School total: 5. In upper school: 4 men; 3 have advanced degrees.

Subjects Offered ACT preparation.

College Admission Counseling 25 students graduated in 2012; 10 went to college, including Houston Community College System. Other: 10 went to work, 1 entered military service, 3 had other specific plans.

Student Life Discipline rests primarily with faculty.

Summer Programs Remediation, advancement programs offered; session focuses on academic core classes and electives; held on campus; accepts boys and girls; open to students from other schools. 2013 schedule: June 10 to August 9. Application deadline: June 5.

Tuition and Aid Day student tuition: $6500. Tuition installment plan (The Tuition Plan).

Admissions Traditional secondary-level entrance grade is 11. For fall 2012, 50 students applied for upper-level admission, 35 were accepted, 30 enrolled. Deadline for receipt of application materials: none. Application fee required: $150. On-campus interview required.

Computers Computers are regularly used in all classes. Computer network features include Internet access, Internet filtering or blocking technology. Students grades are available online.

Contact Mrs. Lesley L. Boyer, Principal. 281-537-6433. Fax: 281-537-2361. E-mail: lesley.boyer@nlcinc.com. Web site: north.hlahighschools.com

THE HOWARD SCHOOL

Atlanta, Georgia
See Special Needs Schools section.

THE HUDSON SCHOOL

601 Park Avenue
Hoboken, New Jersey 07030

Head of School: Mrs. Suellen F. Newman

General Information Coeducational day college-preparatory, arts, and music, theater, foreign languages school. Grades 5–12. Founded: 1978. Setting: urban. Nearest major city is New York, NY. 1 building on campus. Approved or accredited by Middle States Association of Colleges and Schools, New Jersey Association of Independent Schools, and New Jersey Department of Education. Member of National Association of Independent Schools. Endowment: $2 million. Total enrollment: 185. Upper school average class size: 18. Upper school faculty-student ratio: 1:4. There are 175 required school days per year for Upper School students. Upper School students typically attend 5 days per week. The average school day consists of 8 hours.

Upper School Student Profile Grade 9: 15 students (8 boys, 7 girls); Grade 10: 25 students (12 boys, 13 girls); Grade 11: 19 students (12 boys, 7 girls); Grade 12: 26 students (9 boys, 17 girls).

Faculty School total: 50. In upper school: 12 men, 15 women; 17 have advanced degrees.

Subjects Offered African drumming, algebra, American government, American literature, anatomy and physiology, art, biology, British literature, calculus, chemistry, computer science, computer science-AP, computers, conceptual physics, contemporary issues, creative writing, English, English literature, English literature-AP, English-AP, environmental science, ethnic literature, film, French, gender issues, German, health, Japanese, Latin, learning strategies, mathematics, media studies, microbiology, music, music theory, mythology, personal finance, physical education, physics-AP, psychology, psychology-AP, social sciences, Spanish, Spanish-AP, U.S. history, U.S. history-AP, world civilizations, world literature.

Graduation Requirements American history, art, art history, computer science, English, foreign language, Latin, mathematics, music history, personal finance, physical education (includes health), science, world history. Community service is required.

Special Academic Programs Advanced Placement exam preparation; honors section; accelerated programs; independent study; study at local college for college credit; study abroad; academic accommodation for the gifted, the musically talented, and the artistically talented; remedial reading and/or remedial writing; remedial math; ESL (6 students enrolled).

College Admission Counseling 22 students graduated in 2012; all went to college, including Bard College; Boston University; Drew University; New York University; Skidmore College; The George Washington University. Median SAT critical reading: 620, median SAT math: 580, median SAT writing: 620, median combined SAT: 1770. 65% scored over 600 on SAT critical reading, 40% scored over 600 on SAT math, 65% scored over 600 on SAT writing, 45% scored over 1800 on combined SAT.

Student Life Upper grades have student council, honor system. Discipline rests primarily with faculty.

Summer Programs Art/fine arts programs offered; session focuses on theater; held on campus; accepts boys and girls; open to students from other schools. 20 students usually enrolled. 2013 schedule: July 1 to July 31. Application deadline: May 1.

Tuition and Aid Day student tuition: $17,130. Tuition installment plan (monthly payment plans, individually arranged payment plans, semiannual and annual payment plans, quarterly by special arrangement). Need-based scholarship grants available. In 2012–13, 45% of upper-school students received aid. Total amount of financial aid awarded in 2012–13: $363,025.

Admissions Traditional secondary-level entrance grade is 9. For fall 2012, 51 students applied for upper-level admission, 41 were accepted, 21 enrolled. ERB, ISEE or SSAT required. Deadline for receipt of application materials: December 15. Application fee required: $60. On-campus interview required.

Athletics Interscholastic: basketball (boys, girls), soccer (b,g), softball (g); intramural: modern dance (g); coed interscholastic: cheering, track and field; coed intramural: aerobics/dance, bowling, dance, fencing, Frisbee, outdoor education, physical fitness, ultimate Frisbee, yoga. 2 PE instructors, 4 coaches.

Computers Computers are regularly used in college planning, creative writing, desktop publishing, ESL, English, ethics, French, humanities, music, newspaper, philosophy, photography, photojournalism, programming, publications, Spanish, technology, theater, video film production, Web site design, word processing, writing, yearbook classes. Computer network features include Internet access, Internet filtering or blocking technology.

Contact Mrs. Suellen F. Newman, Director. 201-659-8335 Ext. 107. Fax: 201-222-3669. E-mail: admissions@thehudsonschool.org. Web site: www.thehudsonschool.org

HUMANEX ACADEMY

Englewood, Colorado

See Special Needs Schools section.

HUNTINGTON-SURREY SCHOOL

4804 Grover Avenue
Austin, Texas 78756

Head of School: Dr. Light Bailey German

General Information Coeducational day college-preparatory, arts, and writing, theater arts school. Grades 8–12. Founded: 1973. Setting: urban. 1 building on campus. Approved or accredited by Southern Association of Colleges and Schools and Texas Department of Education. Total enrollment: 42. Upper school average class size: 8. Upper school faculty-student ratio: 1:4. There are 160 required school days per year for Upper School students. Upper School students typically attend 5 days per week. The average school day consists of 4 hours and 45 minutes.

Upper School Student Profile Grade 9: 12 students (7 boys, 5 girls); Grade 10: 8 students (5 boys, 3 girls); Grade 11: 6 students (3 boys, 3 girls); Grade 12: 14 students (10 boys, 4 girls).

Faculty School total: 20. In upper school: 7 men, 13 women; 10 have advanced degrees.

Subjects Offered Algebra, art, biology, calculus, chemistry, college planning, comparative religion, creative drama, discrete mathematics, drama, ecology, environmental systems, English, film history, French, geometry, German, history, Latin, literature, math analysis, math review, mathematics, philosophy, physical science, physics, portfolio art, pre-algebra, pre-calculus, SAT preparation, senior science survey, social studies, Spanish, student publications, study skills, theater arts, trigonometry, U.S. history, work-study, world history, writing, yoga.

Graduation Requirements American literature, biology, British literature, economics, mathematics, science, U.S. government, U.S. history, world history, world literature, writing, senior research project, school exit examinations: assertion with proof essay exam and mathematical competency exam, senior advisory course.

Special Academic Programs Accelerated programs; academic accommodation for the gifted.

College Admission Counseling 16 students graduated in 2012; 14 went to college, including Schreiner University; St. Edward's University; Texas A&M University; Texas State University–San Marcos; The University of Texas at Austin; The University of Texas at San Antonio. Other: 2 went to work. Median SAT critical reading: 550, median SAT math: 570, median SAT writing: 450, median combined SAT: 1570. 42% scored over 600 on SAT critical reading, 42% scored over 600 on SAT math, 8% scored over 600 on SAT writing, 25% scored over 1800 on combined SAT.

Student Life Upper grades have student council, honor system. Discipline rests primarily with faculty.

Summer Programs Remediation, enrichment, advancement programs offered; session focuses on one-on-one teaching, or small classes; held on campus; accepts boys and girls; open to students from other schools. 12 students usually enrolled. 2013 schedule: June 10 to July 26. Application deadline: May 6.

Tuition and Aid Day student tuition: $1080. Tuition installment plan (monthly payment plans).

Admissions Traditional secondary-level entrance grade is 9. For fall 2012, 15 students applied for upper-level admission, 11 were accepted, 11 enrolled. Deadline for receipt of application materials: none. No application fee required. On-campus interview required.

Computers Computers are regularly used in study skills, writing classes. Computer resources include study hall computers and printers (available for student use). Computer access in designated common areas is available to students.

Contact Ms. Johni Walker-Little, Assistant Director. 512-478-4743. Fax: 512-457-0235. Web site: www.huntingtonsurrey.com

HYDE PARK BAPTIST SCHOOL

3901 Speedway
Austin, Texas 78751

Head of School: Mrs. Karen Winter

General Information Coeducational day college-preparatory, arts, religious studies, and technology school, affiliated with Baptist Church. Grades PK–12. Founded: 1968. Setting: urban. 10-acre campus. 1 building on campus. Approved or accredited by Accreditation Commission of the Texas Association of Baptist Schools, Southern Association of Colleges and Schools, Texas Education Agency, Texas Private School Accreditation Commission, and Texas Department of Education. Endowment: $236,500. Total enrollment: 568. Upper school average class size: 18. Upper school faculty-student ratio: 1:12. There are 177 required school days per year for Upper School students. Upper School students typically attend 5 days per week. The average school day consists of 7 hours and 20 minutes.

Upper School Student Profile Grade 9: 65 students (28 boys, 37 girls); Grade 10: 60 students (29 boys, 31 girls); Grade 11: 77 students (27 boys, 50 girls); Grade 12: 57 students (21 boys, 36 girls). 10% of students are Baptist.

Faculty School total: 25. In upper school: 6 men, 19 women; 4 have advanced degrees.

Subjects Offered Algebra, anatomy and physiology, art, athletics, Bible, Bible studies, biology, biology-AP, calculus, calculus-AP, cheerleading, chemistry, chemistry-AP, choir, choral music, Christian doctrine, Christian education, Christian ethics, Christian studies, college writing, communication skills, computer information systems, computer technologies, creative writing, digital photography, drama performance, earth science, economics, economics-AP, English, English language and composition-AP, English literature and composition-AP, English literature-AP, English-AP, environmental science, ESL, film and literature, French, geometry, government/civics, health, honors algebra, honors English, honors geometry, honors U.S. history, honors world history, internship, keyboarding, Latin, Latin-AP, macroeconomics-AP, marine biology, microeconomics-AP, musical productions, personal money management, physical education, physics, physics-AP, pre-algebra, pre-calculus, psychology, public speaking, SAT preparation, science, sign language, sociology, Spanish, Spanish-AP, speech, statistics-AP, study skills, theater, theater arts, U.S. government, U.S. government and politics-AP, U.S. history, U.S. history-AP, world geography, world history, writing, yearbook.

Graduation Requirements Arts and fine arts (art, music, dance, drama), Bible studies, computer science, electives, English, foreign language, mathematics, physical education (includes health), public speaking, science, social studies (includes history), 15 hours of community service per year.

Special Academic Programs Advanced Placement exam preparation; honors section; independent study; ESL (5 students enrolled).

College Admission Counseling 62 students graduated in 2012; all went to college, including Baylor University; Texas A&M University; Texas Christian University; Texas State University–San Marcos; The University of Texas at Austin. Mean SAT critical reading: 559, mean SAT math: 572, mean SAT writing: 565, mean combined SAT: 1696, mean composite ACT: 24. 36% scored over 600 on SAT critical reading, 41% scored over 600 on SAT math, 31% scored over 600 on SAT writing, 25% scored over 26 on composite ACT.

Student Life Upper grades have specified standards of dress, student council, honor system. Discipline rests primarily with faculty. Attendance at religious services is required.

Tuition and Aid Day student tuition: $12,550. Tuition installment plan (SMART Tuition Payment Plan, monthly payment plans). Tuition reduction for siblings, merit scholarship grants, need-based scholarship grants available. In 2012–13, 14% of upper-school students received aid; total upper-school merit-scholarship money awarded: $5000. Total amount of financial aid awarded in 2012–13: $95,700.

Admissions Traditional secondary-level entrance grade is 9. For fall 2012, 66 students applied for upper-level admission, 59 were accepted, 49 enrolled. ISEE required. Deadline for receipt of application materials: none. Application fee required: $150. On-campus interview required.

Athletics Interscholastic: baseball (boys), basketball (b,g), cheering (g), cross-country running (b,g), dance squad (g), dance team (g), drill team (g), football (b), golf (b,g), softball (g), strength & conditioning (b,g), tennis (b,g), track and field (b,g), volleyball (g). 1 PE instructor, 8 coaches, 1 athletic trainer.

Computers Computers are regularly used in business applications, computer applications, desktop publishing, keyboarding, multimedia, technology, Web site design, word processing, yearbook classes. Computer network features include on-campus library services, online commercial services, Internet access, wireless campus network, Internet filtering or blocking technology. Students grades are available online. The school has a published electronic and media policy.

Contact Mrs. Lisa Thomas, Director of Admissions, High School. 512-465-8333. Fax: 512-827-2020. E-mail: lthomas@hpbs.org. Web site: www.hpbs.org

HYDE SCHOOL

PO Box 237

150 Route 169

Woodstock, Connecticut 06281

Head of School: Laura Gauld

General Information Coeducational boarding and day college-preparatory and general academic school. Grades 9–12. Founded: 1996. Setting: rural. Nearest major city is Providence, RI. Students are housed in single-sex dormitories. 120-acre campus. 7 buildings on campus. Approved or accredited by Association of Independent Schools in New England, New England Association of Schools and Colleges, The Association of Boarding Schools, and Connecticut Department of Education. Member of National Association of Independent Schools. Endowment: $8 million. Total enrollment: 178. Upper school average class size: 12. Upper school faculty-student ratio: 1:12.

Upper School Student Profile Grade 9: 9 students (8 boys, 1 girl); Grade 10: 28 students (18 boys, 10 girls); Grade 11: 52 students (36 boys, 16 girls); Grade 12: 60 students (38 boys, 22 girls); Postgraduate: 2 students (2 boys). 98% of students are boarding students. 24% are state residents. 21 states are represented in upper school student body. 21% are international students. International students from Canada, China, Japan, Nigeria, and Republic of Korea.

Faculty School total: 27. In upper school: 17 men, 10 women; 11 have advanced degrees; all reside on campus.

Subjects Offered 20th century history, advanced chemistry, Advanced Placement courses, algebra, athletics, biology, calculus, calculus-AP, character education, chemistry, English, English language and composition-AP, English language-AP, English literature, environmental science-AP, ethics, geometry, global issues, independent study, media arts, physics, pre-calculus, Spanish, Spanish-AP, sports, U.S. history, U.S. history-AP, wilderness education, wilderness experience.

Graduation Requirements Electives, English, foreign language, mathematics, science, social studies (includes history), Hyde's graduation requirements embody academic achievement and character development. Character growth is determined through an intense 40-hour, evaluation process involving all members of the senior class and faculty. All students make a speech at graduation representing their principles.

Special Academic Programs 5 Advanced Placement exams for which test preparation is offered; honors section; independent study; remedial reading and/or remedial writing; remedial math; ESL (6 students enrolled).

College Admission Counseling 47 students graduated in 2011; 44 went to college, including Abilene Christian University; Northeastern University; University of California, Berkeley; University of California, Santa Barbara. Other: 1 went to work, 1 entered military service, 1 entered a postgraduate year. Median SAT critical reading: 550, median SAT math: 525, median SAT writing: 530, median combined SAT: 1605, median composite ACT: 20.

Student Life Upper grades have specified standards of dress, honor system. Discipline rests equally with students and faculty.

Tuition and Aid Day student tuition: $24,200; 5-day tuition and room/board: $46,700; 7-day tuition and room/board: $46,700. Tuition reduction for siblings, need-based scholarship grants available. In 2011–12, 25% of upper-school students received aid. Total amount of financial aid awarded in 2011–12: $258,000.

Admissions Traditional secondary-level entrance grade is 11. For fall 2011, 151 students applied for upper-level admission, 106 were accepted, 94 enrolled. Deadline for receipt of application materials: none. Application fee required: $100. Interview required.

Athletics Interscholastic: basketball (boys, girls), cross-country running (b,g), football (b), lacrosse (b,g), soccer (b,g), tennis (b,g), track and field (b,g), wrestling (b); coed interscholastic: equestrian sports, ropes courses, wrestling; coed intramural: backpacking, canoeing/kayaking, climbing, hiking/backpacking, outdoor adventure, outdoor skills, ropes courses, wilderness. 2 athletic trainers.

Computers Computer network features include on-campus library services, online commercial services, Internet access, Internet filtering or blocking technology. Student e-mail accounts are available to students. The school has a published electronic and media policy.

Contact Jason Warnick, Director of Admission. 860-963-4736. Fax: 860-928-0612. E-mail: jwarnick@hyde.edu. Web site: www.hyde.edu

HYDE SCHOOL

616 High Street

Bath, Maine 04530

Head of School: Don MacMillan

General Information Coeducational boarding and day college-preparatory and arts school. Grades 9–12. Founded: 1966. Setting: small town. Nearest major city is Portland. Students are housed in single-sex dormitories. 145-acre campus. 32 buildings on campus. Approved or accredited by Association of Independent Schools in New England, Independent Schools of Northern New England, New England Association of Schools and Colleges, and The Association of Boarding Schools. Member of National Association of Independent Schools. Endowment: $16.5 million. Total enrollment: 143. Upper school average class size: 7. Upper school faculty-student ratio: 1:6. There are 191 required school days per year for Upper School students. Upper School students typically attend 6 days per week. The average school day consists of 7 hours.

Upper School Student Profile Grade 9: 7 students (3 boys, 4 girls); Grade 10: 20 students (15 boys, 5 girls); Grade 11: 52 students (38 boys, 14 girls); Grade 12: 46 students (24 boys, 22 girls); Postgraduate: 4 students (3 boys, 1 girl). 99% of students are boarding students. 21% are state residents. 27 states are represented in upper school student body. 21% are international students. International students from Canada, China, Democratic People's Republic of Korea, Rwanda, Spain, and United Kingdom; 7 other countries represented in student body.

Faculty School total: 23. In upper school: 12 men, 7 women; 16 have advanced degrees; 21 reside on campus.

Subjects Offered 20th century history, 3-dimensional design, acting, advanced biology, advanced chemistry, advanced math, Advanced Placement courses, advanced studio art-AP, advanced TOEFL/grammar, algebra, American government, American history, American history-AP, American literature-AP, ancient history, art, backpacking, band, biology, biology-AP, calculus, calculus-AP, chemistry, chemistry-AP, Chinese, college admission preparation, college counseling, college placement, college planning, college writing, communication skills, communications, comparative government and politics, comparative government and politics-AP, composition-AP, creative writing, early childhood, economics, English, European history, geometry, government, history, music, physical education, physics-AP, pre-calculus, public policy, religion and culture, Spanish, statistics, technical theater, U.S. history, U.S. history-AP.

Graduation Requirements Electives, English, foreign language, history, mathematics, science, Hyde's graduation requirements embody academic achievement and character development. Character growth is determined through an intense 40-hour, evaluation process involving all members of the senior class and faculty. All students make a speech at graduation representing their principles.

Special Academic Programs Honors section; independent study; study at local college for college credit; academic accommodation for the gifted, the musically talented, and the artistically talented; remedial reading and/or remedial writing; remedial math; programs in English, mathematics, general development for dyslexic students; ESL (18 students enrolled).

College Admission Counseling 53 students graduated in 2011; 51 went to college, including Brandeis University; Columbia University; Cornell University; Stanford University; Tufts University; United States Military Academy. Other: 1 went to work, 1 entered military service. Mean SAT critical reading: 530, mean SAT math: 520, mean SAT writing: 520, mean combined SAT: 1570, mean composite ACT: 21. 25% scored over 600 on SAT critical reading, 17% scored over 600 on SAT math, 14% scored over 600 on SAT writing, 18% scored over 1800 on combined SAT, 16% scored over 26 on composite ACT.

Student Life Upper grades have specified standards of dress, student council, honor system. Discipline rests equally with students and faculty.

Tuition and Aid Day student tuition: $24,500; 7-day tuition and room/board: $46,200. Tuition installment plan (monthly payment plans, individually arranged payment plans). Tuition reduction for siblings, merit scholarship grants, need-based scholarship grants available. In 2011–12, 33% of upper-school students received aid. Total amount of financial aid awarded in 2011–12: $1,300,000.

Admissions Traditional secondary-level entrance grade is 9. For fall 2011, 137 students applied for upper-level admission, 83 were accepted, 68 enrolled. Deadline for receipt of application materials: none. Application fee required: $100. Interview required.

Athletics Interscholastic: basketball (boys, girls), crew (b,g), cross-country running (b,g), field hockey (g), football (b), lacrosse (b,g), rowing (b), soccer (b,g), swimming and diving (b,g), tennis (b,g), track and field (b,g), ultimate Frisbee (b); coed interscholastic: aerobics, aerobics/dance, aerobics/Nautilus, aquatics, climbing, dance, hiking/backpacking, indoor track, nordic skiing, rock climbing, ropes courses, wrestling; coed intramural: hiking/backpacking, kayaking, life saving, outdoor adventure, outdoor skills, physical fitness, physical training, project adventure, ropes courses, skateboarding, skiing (downhill), snowshoeing, strength & conditioning, ultimate Frisbee, walking, weight lifting, weight training, wilderness, wilderness survival. 8 coaches, 1 athletic trainer.

Computers Computer network features include on-campus library services, online commercial services, Internet access, wireless campus network, Internet filtering or blocking technology. Student e-mail accounts are available to students. The school has a published electronic and media policy.

Contact Wanda Smith, Admission Assistant. 207-443-7101. Fax: 207-442-9346. E-mail: wsmith@hyde.edu. Web site: www.hyde.edu

HYMAN BRAND HEBREW ACADEMY OF GREATER KANSAS CITY

5801 West 115th Street
Overland Park, Kansas 66211

Head of School: Mr. Howard Haas

General Information Coeducational day college-preparatory, general academic, and religious studies school, affiliated with Jewish faith. Grades K–12. Founded: 1966. Setting: suburban. Nearest major city is Kansas City, MO. 32-acre campus. 1 building on campus. Approved or accredited by Independent Schools Association of the Central States. Languages of instruction: English and Hebrew. Endowment: $4.3 million. Total enrollment: 228. Upper school average class size: 11. Upper school faculty-student ratio: 1:5. There are 162 required school days per year for Upper School students. Upper School students typically attend 5 days per week. The average school day consists of 7 hours and 45 minutes.

Upper School Student Profile Grade 9: 14 students (8 boys, 6 girls); Grade 10: 9 students (4 boys, 5 girls); Grade 11: 16 students (9 boys, 7 girls); Grade 12: 10 students (7 boys, 3 girls). 100% of students are Jewish.

Faculty School total: 41. In upper school: 8 men, 10 women; 14 have advanced degrees.

Subjects Offered 3-dimensional design, algebra, American government, American history, American history-AP, American literature, anatomy and physiology, art, art history, Bible studies, biology, British literature, calculus-AP, chemistry, community service, computer applications, computer science, digital art, economics, English, English language and composition-AP, English literature, English literature and composition-AP, environmental science, ethics, European history, fine arts, geometry, health, Hebrew, Hebrew scripture, Holocaust seminar, Jewish studies, model United Nations, physical education, physics, statistics-AP, Talmud, trigonometry, U.S. government and politics-AP, world history, world literature, yearbook.

Graduation Requirements Arts and fine arts (art, music, dance, drama), English, foreign language, mathematics, physical education (includes health), religion (includes Bible studies and theology), science, social studies (includes history). Community service is required.

Special Academic Programs 6 Advanced Placement exams for which test preparation is offered; honors section; independent study; study at local college for college credit; academic accommodation for the gifted.

College Admission Counseling 9 students graduated in 2012; 8 went to college, including Loyola Marymount University; Occidental College; The University of Kansas; Tulane University; University of Michigan; University of Missouri. Other: 1 entered a postgraduate year.

Student Life Upper grades have specified standards of dress, student council. Discipline rests primarily with faculty. Attendance at religious services is required.

Tuition and Aid Day student tuition: $6850. Tuition installment plan (FACTS Tuition Payment Plan). Need-based scholarship grants available. In 2012–13, 33% of upper-school students received aid. Total amount of financial aid awarded in 2012–13: $66,850.

Admissions Traditional secondary-level entrance grade is 9. For fall 2012, 1 student applied for upper-level admission, 1 was accepted, 1 enrolled. Writing sample required. Deadline for receipt of application materials: none. Application fee required: $50.

Athletics Interscholastic: basketball (boys, girls), soccer (b,g), tennis (b,g); coed interscholastic: cross-country running; coed intramural: tennis. 2 PE instructors, 6 coaches.

Computers Computers are regularly used in computer applications, desktop publishing, digital applications, economics, English, humanities, mathematics, newspaper, psychology, religious studies, science, social studies, writing, yearbook classes. Computer network features include on-campus library services, online commercial services, Internet access, wireless campus network. Student e-mail accounts and computer access in designated common areas are available to students. Students grades are available online. The school has a published electronic and media policy.

Contact Mrs. Tamara Lawson Schuster, Director of Admissions. 913-327-8135. Fax: 913-327-8180. E-mail: tschuster@hbha.edu. Web site: www.hbha.edu

IDYLLWILD ARTS ACADEMY

52500 Temecula Road
PO Box 38
Idyllwild, California 92549

Head of School: Doug Ashcraft

General Information Coeducational boarding and day college-preparatory and arts school. Grades 9–PG. Founded: 1986. Setting: rural. Nearest major city is Los Angeles. Students are housed in single-sex dormitories. 205-acre campus. 44 buildings on campus. Approved or accredited by California Association of Independent Schools, The Association of Boarding Schools, Western Association of Schools and Colleges, and California Department of Education. Member of National Association of Independent Schools and Secondary School Admission Test Board. Endowment: $3 million. Total enrollment: 295. Upper school average class size: 16. Upper school faculty-student ratio: 1:12. Upper School students typically attend 6 days per week.

Upper School Student Profile Grade 9: 39 students (16 boys, 23 girls); Grade 10: 61 students (28 boys, 33 girls); Grade 11: 77 students (37 boys, 40 girls); Grade 12: 83 students (41 boys, 42 girls); Postgraduate: 4 students (2 boys, 2 girls). 92% of students are boarding students. 38% are state residents. 35 states are represented in upper school student body. 44% are international students. International students from Australia, China, Japan, Mexico, Republic of Korea, and Taiwan; 16 other countries represented in student body.

Faculty School total: 65. In upper school: 24 men, 20 women; 30 have advanced degrees; 23 reside on campus.

Subjects Offered 3-dimensional art, 3-dimensional design, acting, advanced math, algebra, American government, American history, American literature, anatomy, art, art history, audio visual/media, audition methods, ballet, biology, Broadway dance, calculus, career/college preparation, ceramics, chemistry, choir, choral music, choreography, computer graphics, computer science, creative writing, critical studies in film, dance, digital art, directing, drama, drawing and design, economics, English, English literature, ensembles, environmental science, ESL, fiction, film and literature, film and new technologies, film appreciation, film history, film studies, filmmaking, fine arts, French, geography, geometry, government/civics, grammar, history, illustration, improvisation, jazz dance, jazz ensemble, jazz theory, mathematics, multimedia, music, music theater, music theory, musical productions, musical theater dance, orchestra, performing arts, photography, physical education, physics, play production, playwriting and directing, poetry, pottery, printmaking, science, social sciences, social studies, Spanish, tap dance, technical theater, technology/design, theater, video film production, vocal music, voice and diction, voice ensemble, world history, world literature, writing.

Graduation Requirements Art, arts and fine arts (art, music, dance, drama), English, foreign language, mathematics, performing arts, physical education (includes health), science, social sciences, social studies (includes history).

Special Academic Programs Advanced Placement exam preparation; honors section; ESL (45 students enrolled).

College Admission Counseling 68 students graduated in 2012; 66 went to college, including California Institute of the Arts; New York University; The Johns Hopkins University; The Juilliard School; University of California, Los Angeles; University of Rochester. Other: 2 went to work.

Student Life Upper grades have student council. Discipline rests equally with students and faculty.

Summer Programs ESL, art/fine arts programs offered; session focuses on visual and performing arts; held on campus; accepts boys and girls; open to students from other schools. 600 students usually enrolled. 2013 schedule: July 10 to August 19. Application deadline: none.

Tuition and Aid Day student tuition: $36,000; 7-day tuition and room/board: $52,000. Tuition installment plan (Key Tuition Payment Plan, monthly payment plans, individually arranged payment plans, school's own payment plan). Need-based scholarship grants available. In 2012–13, 68% of upper-school students received aid. Total amount of financial aid awarded in 2012–13: $5,054,332.

Admissions Traditional secondary-level entrance grade is 10. For fall 2012, 400 students applied for upper-level admission, 400 were accepted, 295 enrolled. SLEP, SSAT or TOEFL required. Deadline for receipt of application materials: none. Application fee required: $50. Interview required.

Athletics Intramural: aerobics (boys, girls); coed intramural: aerobics, aerobics/dance, aerobics/Nautilus, ballet, basketball, bicycling, billiards, bowling, climbing, combined training, cooperative games, cross-country running, dance, fencing, fitness, Frisbee, hiking/backpacking, jogging, judo, martial arts, modern dance, mountain biking, outdoor activities, outdoor adventure, outdoor education, outdoor recreation, outdoors, physical fitness, physical training, rock climbing, soccer, swimming and diving, tennis, ultimate Frisbee, volleyball, walking, weight training, yoga. 1 PE instructor.

Computers Computers are regularly used in art, design, drafting, drawing and design, English, ESL, graphic design, media production, science classes. Computer resources include on-campus library services, Internet access, wireless campus network, Internet filtering or blocking technology. Computer access in designated common areas is available to students. Students grades are available online. The school has a published electronic and media policy.

Contact Mr. Marek Pramuka, Dean of Admission and Financial Aid. 951-659-2171 Ext. 2223. Fax: 951-659-3168. E-mail: admission@idyllwildarts.org. Web site: www.idyllwildarts.org

IMMACULATA HIGH SCHOOL

600 Shawnee
Leavenworth, Kansas 66048

Head of School: Mrs. Helen C. Schwinn

General Information Coeducational day college-preparatory, arts, business, religious studies, and technology school, affiliated with Roman Catholic Church. Grades 9–12. Founded: 1924. Setting: suburban. Nearest major city is Kansas City. 2-acre campus. 1 building on campus. Approved or accredited by North Central Association of Colleges and Schools and Kansas Department of Education. Total enrollment: 122. Upper school average class size: 15. Upper school faculty-student ratio: 1:9. There are 171 required school days per year for Upper School students. Upper School students typically attend 5 days per week. The average school day consists of 7 hours and 30 minutes.

Upper School Student Profile Grade 9: 36 students (24 boys, 12 girls); Grade 10: 30 students (16 boys, 14 girls); Grade 11: 25 students (14 boys, 11 girls); Grade 12: 31 students (18 boys, 13 girls). 82% of students are Roman Catholic.

Faculty School total: 15. In upper school: 6 men, 9 women; 7 have advanced degrees.

Special Academic Programs Honors section; study at local college for college credit.

College Admission Counseling 26 students graduated in 2012; 24 went to college, including Johnson County Community College.

Student Life Upper grades have uniform requirement, student council. Discipline rests primarily with faculty. Attendance at religious services is required.

Admissions Traditional secondary-level entrance grade is 9. Achievement tests required. Deadline for receipt of application materials: none. No application fee required. Interview recommended.

Athletics Interscholastic: baseball (boys), basketball (b,g), cheering (g), dance team (g), football (b), golf (b), power lifting (b,g), soccer (b,g), softball (g), swimming and diving (b), tennis (b,g), track and field (b,g), volleyball (g), wrestling (b). 2 PE instructors, 4 coaches.

Computers Computers are regularly used in business education classes. Computer network features include Internet access, wireless campus network. Campus intranet is available to students. Students grades are available online.

Contact Paula Hyde, Academic Adviser. 913-682-3900. Fax: 913-682-9036. E-mail: phyde@archkckcs.org. Web site: www.archkckcs.org/immaculata

IMMACULATA HIGH SCHOOL

240 Mountain Avenue
Somerville, New Jersey 08876

Head of School: Sr. Mary Smith

General Information Coeducational day college-preparatory and religious studies school, affiliated with Roman Catholic Church. Grades 9–12. Founded: 1962. Setting: suburban. 19-acre campus. 3 buildings on campus. Approved or accredited by Middle States Association of Colleges and Schools, National Catholic Education Association, New South Wales Department of School Education, and New Jersey Department of Education. Total enrollment: 690. Upper school average class size: 22. Upper school faculty-student ratio: 1:13. There are 180 required school days per year for Upper School students. Upper School students typically attend 5 days per week. The average school day consists of 6 hours and 30 minutes.

Upper School Student Profile Grade 9: 148 students (73 boys, 75 girls); Grade 10: 176 students (82 boys, 94 girls); Grade 11: 183 students (99 boys, 84 girls); Grade 12: 183 students (96 boys, 87 girls). 92% of students are Roman Catholic.

Faculty School total: 71. In upper school: 20 men, 51 women; 43 have advanced degrees.

Subjects Offered Accounting, advanced chemistry, advanced math, Advanced Placement courses, algebra, American history, American literature, anatomy, ancient world history, art, art history-AP, biology, British literature, business, calculus, calculus-AP, chemistry, chemistry-AP, creative writing, drama, drawing and design, driver education, Eastern world civilizations, ecology, English-AP, environmental science, environmental studies, European history-AP, film history, foreign language, French language-AP, geometry, global issues, global studies, graphic design, health, honors algebra, honors English, honors geometry, marching band, music theory, religious education, science, social studies, speech, trigonometry, U.S. history-AP.

Graduation Requirements Algebra, American literature, biology, British literature, chemistry, driver education, foreign language, geometry, health education, physical education (includes health), physics, theology, U.S. history.

Special Academic Programs Advanced Placement exam preparation; honors section; academic accommodation for the musically talented.

College Admission Counseling 191 students graduated in 2012; 187 went to college, including Loyola University Maryland; Penn State University Park; Rutgers, The State University of New Jersey, New Brunswick; Saint Joseph's University; Seton Hall University; The University of Scranton. Other: 2 entered military service, 2 had other specific plans. Mean SAT critical reading: 532, mean SAT math: 540, mean SAT writing: 554.

Student Life Upper grades have uniform requirement. Discipline rests primarily with faculty. Attendance at religious services is required.

Tuition and Aid Day student tuition: $10,400. Tuition installment plan (FACTS Tuition Payment Plan).

Admissions Traditional secondary-level entrance grade is 9. For fall 2012, 225 students applied for upper-level admission, 175 were accepted, 148 enrolled. High School Placement Test required. Deadline for receipt of application materials: December 31. Application fee required: $150. On-campus interview required.

Athletics Interscholastic: baseball (boys), basketball (b,g), cheering (g), cross-country running (b,g), football (b), lacrosse (b,g), soccer (b,g), softball (g), tennis (b,g); coed interscholastic: bowling, golf, swimming and diving. 4 PE instructors, 50 coaches, 1 athletic trainer.

Computers Computers are regularly used in graphic design, journalism, yearbook classes. Computer network features include on-campus library services, online commercial services, Internet access. Students grades are available online.

Contact Sr. Anne Brigid Gallagher, Assistant Principal/Academic Dean. 908-722-0200 Ext. 118. Fax: 908-218-7765. E-mail: sannebrigid@immaculatahighschool.org. Web site: www.immaculatahighschool.org

IMMACULATA-LA SALLE HIGH SCHOOL

3601 South Miami Avenue
Miami, Florida 33133

Head of School: Sr. Kim Keraitis, FMA

General Information Coeducational day college-preparatory, arts, business, religious studies, and technology school, affiliated with Roman Catholic Church. Grades 9–12. Founded: 1958. Setting: urban. 13-acre campus. 7 buildings on campus. Approved or accredited by Southern Association of Colleges and Schools, The College Board, and Florida Department of Education. Endowment: $80,200. Total enrollment: 758. Upper school average class size: 24. Upper school faculty-student ratio: 1:15. There are 180 required school days per year for Upper School students. Upper School students typically attend 5 days per week. The average school day consists of 6 hours and 30 minutes.

Upper School Student Profile Grade 9: 187 students (70 boys, 117 girls); Grade 10: 203 students (73 boys, 130 girls); Grade 11: 183 students (67 boys, 116 girls); Grade 12: 185 students (52 boys, 133 girls). 95% of students are Roman Catholic.

Faculty School total: 59. In upper school: 22 men, 32 women; 22 have advanced degrees.

Subjects Offered Advanced Placement courses, African American studies, algebra, American history, American history-AP, analytic geometry, anatomy, art, automated accounting, band, Bible studies, biology, calculus, chemistry, Chinese, choral music, computer programming, computer programming-AP, computer science, desktop publishing, drama, economics, English, European history, fine arts, French, geometry, government/civics, health, history, humanities, Italian, marine biology, mathematics, music appreciation, physical education, physics, psychology, religion, science, social studies, sociology, Spanish, speech, trigonometry, U.S. government and politics-AP, world history.

Graduation Requirements Arts and fine arts (art, music, dance, drama), business skills (includes word processing), computer science, English, foreign language, mathematics, physical education (includes health), religion (includes Bible studies and theology), science, social studies (includes history), 20 hours of community service for each of the 4 years.

Special Academic Programs Advanced Placement exam preparation; honors section; independent study; study at local college for college credit; academic accommodation for the gifted.

College Admission Counseling 170 students graduated in 2011; all went to college, including Barry University; Florida International University; Florida State University; Miami Dade College; University of Central Florida; University of Miami. Mean SAT critical reading: 487, mean SAT math: 483, mean SAT writing: 488, mean combined SAT: 1458, mean composite ACT: 21. 13% scored over 600 on SAT critical reading, 11% scored over 600 on SAT math, 10% scored over 600 on SAT writing, 34% scored over 1800 on combined SAT, 18% scored over 26 on composite ACT.

Student Life Upper grades have uniform requirement, student council. Discipline rests equally with students and faculty. Attendance at religious services is required.

Tuition and Aid Day student tuition: $11,000. Tuition installment plan (FACTS Tuition Payment Plan, monthly payment plans, individually arranged payment plans). Paying campus jobs available. In 2011–12, 11% of upper-school students received aid. Total amount of financial aid awarded in 2011–12: $165,000.

Admissions Traditional secondary-level entrance grade is 9. For fall 2011, 441 students applied for upper-level admission, 282 were accepted, 233 enrolled. Catholic High School Entrance Examination or PSAT and SAT for applicants to grade 11 and 12 required. Deadline for receipt of application materials: none. Application fee required: $500. On-campus interview required.

Athletics Interscholastic: baseball (boys), basketball (b,g), bicycling (b,g), cheering (g), cross-country running (b,g), dance team (g), football (b), lacrosse (b), soccer (b,g), softball (g), swimming and diving (b,g), tennis (b,g), track and field (b,g), trap and skeet (b,g), volleyball (g), weight training (b,g), winter soccer (b,g); intramural: football (b), volleyball (g); coed interscholastic: tennis, track and field; coed intramural: aerobics/dance, bicycling, dance, dance team, mountain biking, physical fitness, sailing, table tennis, weight training. 3 PE instructors, 15 coaches, 1 athletic trainer.

Computers Computers are regularly used in business, business applications, economics, French, journalism, mathematics, programming, science, technology, word processing, yearbook classes. Computer network features include on-campus library services, Internet access. Students grades are available online.

Contact Mrs. Nancy Ramirez, Admissions Director. 305-854-2334 Ext. 130. Fax: 305-858-5971. E-mail: admissions@ilsroyals.com. Web site: www.ilsroyals.com

IMMACULATE CONCEPTION HIGH SCHOOL

258 South Main Street
Lodi, New Jersey 07644-2199

Head of School: Mr. Joseph Robert Azzolino

General Information Girls' day college-preparatory, arts, business, and religious studies school, affiliated with Roman Catholic Church. Grades 9–12. Founded: 1915. Setting: suburban. Nearest major city is Paterson. 3-acre campus. 1 building on campus. Approved or accredited by Middle States Association of Colleges and Schools, National Catholic Education Association, and New Jersey Department of Education. Total enrollment: 162. Upper school average class size: 17. Upper school faculty-student ratio: 1:10. There are 180 required school days per year for Upper School students. Upper School students typically attend 5 days per week. The average school day consists of 6 hours and 21 minutes.

Upper School Student Profile Grade 9: 45 students (45 girls); Grade 10: 39 students (39 girls); Grade 11: 40 students (40 girls); Grade 12: 38 students (38 girls). 85% of students are Roman Catholic.

Faculty School total: 16. In upper school: 3 men, 13 women.

Subjects Offered Advanced math, algebra, American government, American history, American history-AP, American literature, anatomy and physiology, art, Bible studies, biology, British literature, character education, chemistry, communications, computer graphics, computer skills, driver education, English, French, genetics, geometry, health and safety, honors algebra, honors English, honors geometry, honors U.S. history, lab science, musical productions, organic chemistry, performing arts, photography, physical education, physical science, pre-calculus, psychology, religious education, social psychology, Spanish, women in society, world cultures, writing.

Graduation Requirements English, foreign language, lab science, mathematics, physical education (includes health), religious studies, social studies (includes history). Community service is required.

Special Academic Programs 1 Advanced Placement exam for which test preparation is offered; honors section; study at local college for college credit.

College Admission Counseling 38 students graduated in 2011; 37 went to college, including Bergen Community College; Felician College; Ramapo College of New Jersey; Rutgers, The State University of New Jersey, New Brunswick; Seton Hall University; William Paterson University of New Jersey. Other: 1 had other specific plans. Mean SAT critical reading: 500, mean SAT math: 450, mean SAT writing: 520, mean combined SAT: 1470.

Student Life Upper grades have uniform requirement, student council. Discipline rests primarily with faculty. Attendance at religious services is required.

Tuition and Aid Day student tuition: $8750. Tuition installment plan (FACTS Tuition Payment Plan, annual payment plan). Tuition reduction for siblings, merit scholarship grants, need-based scholarship grants available. In 2011–12, 27% of upper-school students received aid; total upper-school merit-scholarship money awarded: $54,500. Total amount of financial aid awarded in 2011–12: $73,250.

Admissions Traditional secondary-level entrance grade is 9. For fall 2011, 251 students applied for upper-level admission, 240 were accepted, 37 enrolled. Cooperative Entrance Exam (McGraw-Hill) required. Deadline for receipt of application materials: none. No application fee required. Interview recommended.

Athletics Interscholastic: basketball, cheering, cross-country running, soccer, softball, swimming and diving, tennis, volleyball; intramural: aerobics, basketball, fitness, fitness walking, floor hockey, physical fitness, physical training, tennis, volleyball, walking. 2 PE instructors, 12 coaches, 1 athletic trainer.

Computers Computers are regularly used in graphics, newspaper, photography, word processing, yearbook classes. Computer resources include Internet access, Internet filtering or blocking technology. Computer access in designated common areas is available to students. Students grades are available online. The school has a published electronic and media policy.

Contact Mrs. Sara Simon, Director of Enrollment Management. 973-773-2665. Fax: 973-614-0893. E-mail: ssimon@ichslodi.org. Web site: www.ichslodi.org

IMMACULATE CONCEPTION SCHOOL

217 Cottage Hill Avenue
Elmhurst, Illinois 60126

Head of School: Pamela M. Levar

General Information Coeducational day college-preparatory, arts, and religious studies school, affiliated with Roman Catholic Church. Grades 9–12. Founded: 1936. Setting: suburban. Nearest major city is Chicago. 3 buildings on campus. Approved or accredited by North Central Association of Colleges and Schools and Illinois Department of Education. Member of National Association of Independent Schools. Total enrollment: 340. Upper school average class size: 18. Upper school faculty-student ratio: 1:8. There are 176 required school days per year for Upper School students. Upper School students typically attend 5 days per week. The average school day consists of 6 hours and 30 minutes.

Upper School Student Profile Grade 9: 87 students (48 boys, 39 girls); Grade 10: 76 students (32 boys, 44 girls); Grade 11: 74 students (46 boys, 28 girls); Grade 12: 77 students (38 boys, 39 girls). 89% of students are Roman Catholic.

Faculty School total: 26. In upper school: 8 men, 18 women; 15 have advanced degrees.

Subjects Offered 3-dimensional art, advanced chemistry, advanced math, algebra, American government, American history, anatomy and physiology, ancient world history, art, biology, biology-AP, British literature, business law, calculus, calculus-AP, campus ministry, career/college preparation, Catholic belief and practice, ceramics, chemistry, chemistry-AP, college counseling, computer applications, constitutional history of U.S., consumer education, current events, drawing, ecology, environmental systems, economics, English, English-AP, environmental science, fitness, foreign language, French, geometry, government/civics, health education, honors algebra, honors English, honors geometry, honors U.S. history, humanities, keyboarding, library, musical theater, newspaper, painting, physical education, physics, pre-calculus, psychology, SAT/ACT preparation, sociology, Spanish, student government, trigonometry, U.S. history-AP, yearbook.

Graduation Requirements Algebra, American government, American literature, anatomy and physiology, art, biology, British literature, Catholic belief and practice, chemistry, computer applications, constitutional history of U.S., consumer education, English, foreign language, geometry, grammar, health, history, human biology, language and composition, mathematics, physical science, political science, pre-calculus, science, theology, trigonometry, U.S. history, world history, 40 hours of Christian service, attendance at retreat.

Special Academic Programs 5 Advanced Placement exams for which test preparation is offered; honors section; study at local college for college credit.

College Admission Counseling 87 students graduated in 2012; 84 went to college, including Illinois State University; Loyola University Chicago; Marquette University; St. Norbert College; The University of Iowa; University of Illinois at Urbana–Champaign. Other: 2 went to work, 1 had other specific plans.

Student Life Upper grades have uniform requirement, student council. Discipline rests primarily with faculty. Attendance at religious services is required.

Summer Programs Sports programs offered; session focuses on sports; held both on and off campus; held at Plunkett Field; accepts boys and girls; not open to students from other schools. 150 students usually enrolled. 2013 schedule: June 15 to July 28.

Tuition and Aid Day student tuition: $9250. Tuition installment plan (SMART Tuition Payment Plan). Tuition reduction for siblings, merit scholarship grants, need-based scholarship grants, merit scholarships (for placement test top scorers), externally funded scholarships (alumni, memorials), Catholic school teacher grants (1/3 reduction) available. In 2012–13, 55% of upper-school students received aid; total upper-school merit-scholarship money awarded: $15,000. Total amount of financial aid awarded in 2012–13: $150,000.

Admissions Traditional secondary-level entrance grade is 9. High School Placement Test (closed version) from Scholastic Testing Service required. Deadline for receipt of application materials: none. No application fee required.

Athletics Interscholastic: baseball (boys), basketball (b,g), bowling (b), cheering (g), cross-country running (b,g), dance team (g), football (b), ice hockey (b), lacrosse (b), pom squad (g), soccer (g), softball (g), strength & conditioning (b,g), tennis (g), track and field (b,g), volleyball (g), weight lifting (b), weight training (b,g), wrestling (b); coed interscholastic: fishing, golf, winter (indoor) track. 2 PE instructors, 48 coaches, 2 athletic trainers.

Computers Computers are regularly used in business applications, business education, career exploration, college planning, computer applications, keyboarding, library, library skills, news writing, publications, science, stock market, yearbook classes. Computer network features include on-campus library services, online commercial services, Internet access, wireless campus network, Internet filtering or blocking technology, Edline. Student e-mail accounts and computer access in designated common areas are available to students. Students grades are available online. The school has a published electronic and media policy.

Contact Mrs. Sarah Ford, Director of Admissions. 630-530-3484. Fax: 630-530-2290. E-mail: sford@ichsknights.org. Web site: www.ichsknights.org

IMMACULATE HEART HIGH SCHOOL

625 East Magee Road
Oro Valley, Arizona 85704-7207

Head of School: Sr. Luisa Sanchez

General Information Coeducational day college-preparatory and religious studies school, affiliated with Roman Catholic Church. Grades 9–12. Founded: 1930. Setting: suburban. 5-acre campus. 2 buildings on campus. Approved or accredited by National Catholic Education Association, Western Catholic Education Association, and Arizona Department of Education. Total enrollment: 91. Upper school average class size: 10. Upper school faculty-student ratio: 1:10. There are 180 required school days per year for Upper School students. Upper School students typically attend 5 days per week. The average school day consists of 7 hours.

Upper School Student Profile Grade 9: 19 students (10 boys, 9 girls); Grade 10: 27 students (12 boys, 15 girls); Grade 11: 22 students (6 boys, 16 girls); Grade 12: 23 students (15 boys, 8 girls). 92% of students are Roman Catholic.

Faculty School total: 11. In upper school: 3 men, 8 women; 3 have advanced degrees.

Special Academic Programs International Baccalaureate program; Advanced Placement exam preparation; independent study; study at local college for college credit; ESL (3 students enrolled).

College Admission Counseling 14 students graduated in 2011; all went to college, including Arizona State University; Northern Arizona University; Pima Community College; The University of Arizona.

Student Life Upper grades have uniform requirement, student council, honor system. Discipline rests primarily with faculty. Attendance at religious services is required.

Tuition and Aid Day student tuition: $6400. Tuition installment plan (monthly payment plans). Tuition reduction for siblings, need-based scholarship grants available. In 2011–12, 45% of upper-school students received aid. Total amount of financial aid awarded in 2011–12: $121,000.

Admissions Traditional secondary-level entrance grade is 9. For fall 2011, 27 students applied for upper-level admission, 27 were accepted, 25 enrolled. Deadline for receipt of application materials: none. No application fee required. On-campus interview required.

Athletics Interscholastic: basketball (boys, girls), cheering (g), volleyball (g); coed interscholastic: bowling, cross-country running, golf, soccer, swimming and diving, tennis, track and field; coed intramural: billiards, bowling, skiing (downhill), table tennis. 1 PE instructor, 8 coaches.

Computers Computer network features include on-campus library services, Internet access, wireless campus network, Internet filtering or blocking technology, virtual high school courses for electives, homework online. Campus intranet, student e-mail accounts, and computer access in designated common areas are available to students. Students grades are available online. The school has a published electronic and media policy.

Contact Mr. Daniel Ethridge, Principal/Admissions. 520-297-2851. Fax: 520-797-7374. E-mail: danethridge@ihhschool.org. Web site: www.immaculateheartschool.com

IMMACULATE HEART HIGH SCHOOL AND MIDDLE SCHOOL

5515 Franklin Avenue
Los Angeles, California 90028-5999

Head of School: Ms. Virginia Hurst

General Information Girls' day college-preparatory school, affiliated with Roman Catholic Church. Grades 6–12. Founded: 1906. Setting: urban. 7-acre campus. 7 buildings on campus. Approved or accredited by Western Association of Schools and Colleges and California Department of Education. Upper school average class size: 22. Upper school faculty-student ratio: 1:16.

Faculty School total: 45. In upper school: 34 have advanced degrees.

Student Life Upper grades have uniform requirement, student council, honor system. Discipline rests primarily with faculty. Attendance at religious services is required.

Tuition and Aid Tuition installment plan (The Tuition Plan).

Admissions High School Placement Test or High School Placement Test (closed version) from Scholastic Testing Service required. Deadline for receipt of application materials: January 4. Application fee required: $50. On-campus interview required.

Contact Ms. Jennie Lee, Director of Admissions. 323-461-3651 Ext. 240. Fax: 323-462-0610. E-mail: jlee@immaculateheart.org. Web site: www.immaculateheart.org

INDEPENDENT SCHOOL

8317 East Douglas
Wichita, Kansas 67207

Head of School: Dr. Mary Dickerson

General Information Coeducational day college-preparatory, arts, and technology school. Grades PK–12. Founded: 1980. Setting: suburban. 22-acre campus. 2 buildings on campus. Language of instruction: Spanish. Total enrollment: 511. Upper school average class size: 15. Upper school faculty-student ratio: 1:8. There are 170 required school days per year for Upper School students. Upper School students typically attend 5 days per week. The average school day consists of 7 hours.

Faculty School total: 25. In upper school: 11 men, 14 women; 18 have advanced degrees.

Subjects Offered 3-dimensional art, advanced math, Advanced Placement courses, algebra, American government, American history, American history-AP, American literature, anatomy and physiology, art, biology, biology-AP, British literature, British literature (honors), calculus, calculus-AP, ceramics, chemistry, chemistry-AP, choir, computer applications, computer art, debate, economics, engineering, English literature-AP, film and new technologies, foreign language, forensics, geometry, health, health and wellness, Latin, music, music theory, music theory-AP, music-AP, newspaper, physics, physics-AP, psychology, psychology-AP, Spanish, Spanish-AP, statistics-AP, theater, theater arts, trigonometry, U.S. government and politics-AP, Web site design, weight training, yearbook.

Graduation Requirements Algebra, American government, American history, American literature, arts and fine arts (art, music, dance, drama), biology, British literature, chemistry, computer applications, computer literacy, English, foreign language, geography, geometry, humanities, physical education (includes health), world history, world literature, 50 hours of community service.

Special Academic Programs 14 Advanced Placement exams for which test preparation is offered; honors section; independent study; academic accommodation for the gifted, the musically talented, and the artistically talented.

College Admission Counseling 54 students graduated in 2012; all went to college, including Oklahoma State University; The University of Kansas; Trinity University; University of Tulsa. Mean SAT critical reading: 615, mean SAT math: 604, mean SAT writing: 591, mean combined SAT: 1810, mean composite ACT: 27.

Student Life Upper grades have specified standards of dress, student council, honor system. Discipline rests primarily with faculty.

Summer Programs Enrichment, advancement, sports, art/fine arts, computer instruction programs offered; held on campus; accepts boys and girls; open to students from other schools. 2013 schedule: May 20 to August 15.

Tuition and Aid Day student tuition: $10,400. Tuition installment plan (monthly payment plans, individually arranged payment plans). Need-based scholarship grants available. In 2012–13, 25% of upper-school students received aid.

Admissions Traditional secondary-level entrance grade is 9. For fall 2012, 30 students applied for upper-level admission, 26 were accepted, 24 enrolled. Admissions testing, non-standardized placement tests and Otis-Lennon Ability or Stanford Achievement Test required. Deadline for receipt of application materials: none. Application fee required: $40. Interview recommended.

Athletics Interscholastic: baseball (boys), basketball (b,g), cheering (g), cross-country running (b,g), dance team (g), football (b), golf (b,g), soccer (b,g), softball (g), strength & conditioning (b,g), swimming and diving (b,g), tennis (b,g), track and field (b,g), volleyball (g), weight training (b,g), wrestling (b); coed interscholastic: strength & conditioning, weight training. 2 PE instructors, 5 coaches, 1 athletic trainer.

Computers Computers are regularly used in art, college planning, economics, English, humanities, introduction to technology, library, literary magazine, mathematics, newspaper, photography, publications, Web site design, yearbook classes. Computer network features include on-campus library services, Internet access, wireless campus network, Internet filtering or blocking technology, homework online. Students grades are available online. The school has a published electronic and media policy.

Contact Ms. Danielle T. Dankey, Director of Admissions. 316-686-0152 Ext. 405. Fax: 316-686-3918. E-mail: danielle.dankey@theindependentschool.com. Web site: www.theindependentschool.com

INDIAN SPRINGS SCHOOL

190 Woodward Drive
Indian Springs, Alabama 35124

Head of School: Mr. Gareth Vaughan

General Information Coeducational boarding and day college-preparatory and arts school. Boarding grades 9–12, day grades 8–12. Founded: 1952. Setting: suburban. Nearest major city is Birmingham. Students are housed in single-sex dormitories. 350-acre campus. 38 buildings on campus. Approved or accredited by Southern Association of Colleges and Schools, Southern Association of Independent Schools, The Association of Boarding Schools, and Alabama Department of Education. Member of National Association of Independent Schools and Secondary School Admission Test Board. Endowment: $18 million. Total enrollment: 261. Upper school average class size: 12. Upper school faculty-student ratio: 1:7. There are 175 required school days per year for Upper School students. Upper School students typically attend 5 days per week. The average school day consists of 6 hours and 20 minutes.

Upper School Student Profile Grade 8: 30 students (15 boys, 15 girls); Grade 9: 51 students (28 boys, 23 girls); Grade 10: 57 students (29 boys, 28 girls); Grade 11: 60 students (29 boys, 31 girls); Grade 12: 63 students (29 boys, 34 girls). 32% of students are boarding students. 79% are state residents. 12 states are represented in upper school student body. 17% are international students. International students from Australia, China, Germany, Republic of Korea, Rwanda, and Spain; 13 other countries represented in student body.

Faculty School total: 43. In upper school: 20 men, 21 women; 34 have advanced degrees; 23 reside on campus.

Subjects Offered Advanced Placement courses, algebra, American history, American literature, art, art history, astronomy, athletics, biology, biology-AP, calculus, calculus-AP, ceramics, chemistry, chemistry-AP, Chinese, computer applications, computer multimedia, concert choir, constitutional law, contemporary issues, creative writing, drama, economics, economics-AP, English, English literature, English-AP, environmental science-AP, European history, expository writing, film studies, fine arts, French, French-AP, geology, geometry, government-AP, government/civics, history, jazz, jazz ensemble, keyboarding, Latin, Latin-AP, mathematics, music, painting, philosophy, photo shop, physical education, physical fitness, physics, play production, precalculus, science, Shakespeare, social studies, Spanish, Spanish-AP, statistics-AP, theater, trigonometry, U.S. government and politics-AP, world history, world literature, world religions, writing, yearbook.

Graduation Requirements Arts and fine arts (art, music, dance, drama), English, foreign language, mathematics, physical education (includes health), science, social studies (includes history), art or music history.

Special Academic Programs Advanced Placement exam preparation; independent study; academic accommodation for the gifted and the musically talented.

College Admission Counseling 73 students graduated in 2011; all went to college, including Emory University; Georgetown University; The Johns Hopkins University; The University of Alabama; University of Illinois at Urbana–Champaign. Mean SAT critical reading: 643, mean SAT math: 629, mean SAT writing: 633, mean composite ACT: 27.

Student Life Upper grades have student council, honor system. Discipline rests equally with students and faculty.

Tuition and Aid Day student tuition: $17,950; 5-day tuition and room/board: $32,000; 7-day tuition and room/board: $36,500. Tuition installment plan (FACTS Tuition Payment Plan, monthly payment plans). Need-based scholarship grants available. In 2011–12, 27% of upper-school students received aid. Total amount of financial aid awarded in 2011–12: $1,000,000.

Admissions Traditional secondary-level entrance grade is 9. For fall 2011, 205 students applied for upper-level admission, 111 were accepted, 84 enrolled. SSAT or TOEFL required. Deadline for receipt of application materials: January 31. Application fee required: $65. Interview required.

Athletics Interscholastic: baseball (boys), basketball (b,g), soccer (b,g), softball (g), tennis (b,g), volleyball (g); intramural: basketball (b,g), flag football (b), soccer (b,g); coed interscholastic: cross-country running, golf, ultimate Frisbee; coed intramural: aerobics, aerobics/Nautilus, outdoor activities, paint ball, physical fitness, strength & conditioning, table tennis, ultimate Frisbee, yoga. 2 PE instructors, 5 coaches, 1 athletic trainer.

Computers Computers are regularly used in all academic classes. Computer network features include on-campus library services, online commercial services, Internet access, wireless campus network, Internet filtering or blocking technology. Campus intranet, student e-mail accounts, and computer access in designated common areas are available to students. Students grades are available online.

Contact Mrs. Christine Copeland, Assistant Director of Admission and Financial Aid. 205-332-0582. Fax: 205-988-3797. E-mail: ccopeland@indiansprings.org. Web site: www.indiansprings.org

INSTITUTE OF NOTRE DAME

901 Aisquith Street
Baltimore, Maryland 21202-5499

Head of School: Dr. Mary L. Funke

General Information Girls' day college-preparatory, arts, business, religious studies, bilingual studies, and technology school, affiliated with Roman Catholic Church. Grades 9–12. Founded: 1847. Setting: urban. 2-acre campus. 1 building on campus. Approved or accredited by Association of Independent Maryland Schools, Middle States Association of Colleges and Schools, National Catholic Education Association, and Maryland Department of Education. Endowment: $5 million. Total enrollment: 384. Upper school average class size: 18. Upper school faculty-student ratio: 1:11. There are 180 required school days per year for Upper School students. Upper School students typically attend 5 days per week. The average school day consists of 6 hours and 20 minutes.

Upper School Student Profile Grade 9: 110 students (110 girls); Grade 10: 98 students (98 girls); Grade 11: 90 students (90 girls); Grade 12: 86 students (86 girls). 70% of students are Roman Catholic.

Faculty School total: 36. In upper school: 6 men, 30 women; 28 have advanced degrees.

Subjects Offered Accounting, algebra, American history, American literature, anatomy, art, Bible studies, biology, business, calculus, chemistry, Christianity, computer applications, computer math, computer programming, computer science, creative writing, criminal justice, dance, design, drama, drawing, driver education, earth science, engineering, English, English literature, environmental science, finance, fine arts, French, freshman seminar, geography, geology, geometry, government/civics, health, history, journalism, Latin, marine biology, mathematics, music, music history, physical education, physics, physiology, psychology, religion, science, social studies, sociology, Spanish, speech, theater, theology, trigonometry, women's studies, world history, world literature.

Graduation Requirements Arts and fine arts (art, music, dance, drama), business skills (includes word processing), computer science, English, foreign language, mathematics, physical education (includes health), religion (includes Bible studies and theology), science, social studies (includes history), 80 hours of community service.

Special Academic Programs 10 Advanced Placement exams for which test preparation is offered; honors section; accelerated programs; independent study; study at local college for college credit; academic accommodation for the gifted; remedial reading and/or remedial writing; remedial math.

College Admission Counseling 66 students graduated in 2012; all went to college, including Loyola University Maryland; Notre Dame of Maryland University; Stevenson University; Towson University; University of Maryland, Baltimore; University of Maryland, Baltimore County.

Student Life Upper grades have uniform requirement, student council, honor system. Discipline rests primarily with faculty. Attendance at religious services is required.

Summer Programs Remediation, enrichment, sports, art/fine arts, rigorous outdoor training, computer instruction programs offered; session focuses on community and incoming freshmen; held both on and off campus; held at Patterson Park, Herring Run Park, and Meadowood Regional Park; accepts girls; open to students from other schools. 150 students usually enrolled. 2013 schedule: June to July. Application deadline: none.

Tuition and Aid Day student tuition: $12,995. Tuition installment plan (monthly payment plans). Tuition reduction for siblings, merit scholarship grants, need-based scholarship grants, paying campus jobs, bank loans available. In 2012–13, 52% of upper-school students received aid; total upper-school merit-scholarship money awarded: $72,750. Total amount of financial aid awarded in 2012–13: $843,000.

Admissions Traditional secondary-level entrance grade is 9. For fall 2012, 219 students applied for upper-level admission, 110 enrolled. High School Placement Test required. Deadline for receipt of application materials: December 14. Application fee required: $30. On-campus interview required.

Athletics Interscholastic: aerobics/dance, badminton, basketball, cheering, crew, cross-country running, field hockey, golf, independent competitive sports, lacrosse, outdoor adventure, outdoors, physical training, pom squad, rowing, running, soccer, softball, strength & conditioning, swimming and diving, track and field, volleyball, winter (indoor) track, winter soccer; intramural: aerobics/dance, ballet, dance, dance squad, dance team, horseback riding, modern dance, outdoor adventure, self defense, weight training. 2 PE instructors, 27 coaches, 1 athletic trainer.

Computers Computers are regularly used in all academic classes. Computer network features include on-campus library services, online commercial services, Internet access, wireless campus network, Internet filtering or blocking technology. Campus intranet, student e-mail accounts, and computer access in designated common areas are available to students. Students grades are available online. The school has a published electronic and media policy.

Contact Mrs. Amy Hoey Conly, Director of Admissions. 410-522-7800 Ext. 220. Fax: 410-522-7810. E-mail: aconly@indofmd.org. Web site: www.indofmd.org

INTERLOCHEN ARTS ACADEMY

PO Box 199
4000 Highway M-137
Interlochen, Michigan 49643-0199

Head of School: Mr. Jeffrey S. Kimpton

General Information Coeducational boarding and day college-preparatory and arts school. Grades 9–PG. Founded: 1962. Setting: rural. Nearest major city is Traverse City. Students are housed in single-sex dormitories. 1,200-acre campus. 225 buildings on campus. Approved or accredited by North Central Association of Colleges and Schools and Michigan Department of Education. Member of National Association of Independent Schools and Secondary School Admission Test Board. Endowment: $61.7 million. Total enrollment: 471. Upper school average class size: 13. Upper school faculty-student ratio: 1:6. There are 151 required school days per year for Upper School students. Upper School students typically attend 5 days per week. The average school day consists of 6 hours and 40 minutes.

Upper School Student Profile Grade 9: 45 students (16 boys, 29 girls); Grade 10: 76 students (28 boys, 48 girls); Grade 11: 132 students (48 boys, 84 girls); Grade 12: 203 students (80 boys, 123 girls); Postgraduate: 15 students (9 boys, 6 girls). 95% of students are boarding students. 20% are state residents. 47 states are represented in upper school student body. 22% are international students. International students from Canada, China, Hong Kong, Mexico, Republic of Korea, and Taiwan; 21 other countries represented in student body.

Faculty School total: 82. In upper school: 43 men, 39 women; 74 have advanced degrees; 28 reside on campus.

Subjects Offered Algebra, American history, American literature, art, ballet, ballet technique, biology, British literature, calculus, ceramics, chamber groups, chemistry, chemistry-AP, choir, choral music, choreography, civil war history, computer math, computer science, contemporary art, creative writing, current events, dance, dance performance, drafting, drama, dramatic arts, earth science, ecology, English, English literature, environmental science, European history, expository writing, film, fine arts, French, geometry, government/civics, health, history, mathematics, music, philosophy, photography, physical education, physics, science, social studies, Spanish, speech, statistics, theater, trigonometry, world history, world literature, writing.

Graduation Requirements Arts and fine arts (art, music, dance, drama), English, mathematics, physical education (includes health), science, social studies (includes history).

Special Academic Programs Advanced Placement exam preparation; accelerated programs; independent study; term-away projects; academic accommodation for the gifted, the musically talented, and the artistically talented; ESL (41 students enrolled).

College Admission Counseling 217 students graduated in 2012; 206 went to college, including New York University; Oberlin College; University of Michigan; University of Rochester. Other: 5 entered a postgraduate year, 6 had other specific plans. Mean SAT critical reading: 586, mean SAT math: 558, mean SAT writing: 564, mean combined SAT: 1707, mean composite ACT: 25. 44% scored over 600 on SAT critical reading, 29% scored over 600 on SAT math, 33% scored over 600 on SAT writing, 32% scored over 1800 on combined SAT, 38% scored over 26 on composite ACT.

Student Life Upper grades have uniform requirement, student council, honor system. Discipline rests primarily with faculty.

Summer Programs Art/fine arts programs offered; session focuses on fine and performing arts; held on campus; accepts boys and girls; open to students from other schools. 2,500 students usually enrolled. 2013 schedule: June 22 to August 4. Application deadline: February 1.

Tuition and Aid Day student tuition: $30,580; 7-day tuition and room/board: $48,520. Tuition installment plan (monthly payment plans, individually arranged payment plans, Sallie Mae, Your Tuition Solution, PrepGate). Merit scholarship grants, need-based scholarship grants available. In 2012–13, 79% of upper-school students received aid; total upper-school merit-scholarship money awarded: $1,065,000. Total amount of financial aid awarded in 2012–13: $8,844,645.

Admissions Traditional secondary-level entrance grade is 11. For fall 2012, 1,083 students applied for upper-level admission, 582 were accepted, 471 enrolled. Achievement tests, any standardized test, audition, essay, placement test or SSAT required. Deadline for receipt of application materials: none. Application fee required: $60. Interview recommended.

Athletics 1 PE instructor.

Computers Computers are regularly used in graphic arts, mathematics, music, science, video film production classes. Computer network features include on-campus library services, online commercial services, Internet access, wireless campus network. Campus intranet and student e-mail accounts are available to students. The school has a published electronic and media policy.

Contact Jim Bekkering, Director of Admission and Financial Aid. 231-276-7472. Fax: 231-276-7464. E-mail: admission@interlochen.org. Web site: www.interlochen.org

INTERMOUNTAIN CHRISTIAN SCHOOL

6515 South Lion Lane
Salt Lake City, Utah 84121

Head of School: Dean James Kerr

General Information Coeducational day college-preparatory, general academic, arts, business, and religious studies school, affiliated with Evangelical Free Church of America, Christian faith. Grades PK–12. Founded: 1982. Setting: suburban. 6-acre campus. 1 building on campus. Approved or accredited by Association of Christian Schools International, Northwest Accreditation Commission, and Utah Department of Education. Endowment: $63,203. Total enrollment: 277. Upper school average class size: 17. Upper school faculty-student ratio: 1:8. There are 180 required school days per year for Upper School students. Upper School students typically attend 5 days per week. The average school day consists of 6 hours.

Upper School Student Profile Grade 9: 16 students (5 boys, 11 girls); Grade 10: 13 students (6 boys, 7 girls); Grade 11: 14 students (8 boys, 6 girls); Grade 12: 17 students (10 boys, 7 girls). 97% of students are members of Evangelical Free Church of America, Christian.

Faculty School total: 33. In upper school: 7 men, 7 women; 9 have advanced degrees.

Subjects Offered Advanced Placement courses, algebra, American government, American history, American literature, American literature-AP, art, athletics, baseball, basketball, bell choir, Bible, biology, calculus, career education, ceramics, chemistry, choir, chorus, Christian doctrine, church history, community service, composition, computer science, computer skills, concert band, concert bell choir, concert choir, current events, debate, drama, drama performance, economics, economics and history, electives, English, English literature-AP, environmental science-AP, European history, European literature, family and consumer science, finance, fine arts, food science, geometry, government, handbells, health, history, independent study, instrumental music, jazz band, keyboarding, leadership and service, Life of Christ, mathematics, peer ministry, physical education, physics, pre-algebra, pre-calculus, science, senior seminar, sex education, social studies, Spanish, statistics, U.S. government, U.S. history, vocal ensemble, volleyball, world geography, world history.

Graduation Requirements Arts and fine arts (art, music, dance, drama), Bible, computer science, English, finance, foreign language, mathematics, physical education (includes health), science, social studies (includes history), class trips. Community service is required.

Special Academic Programs 3 Advanced Placement exams for which test preparation is offered; honors section; study at local college for college credit.

College Admission Counseling 12 students graduated in 2012; all went to college, including Azusa Pacific University; Biola University; Corban University; University of Utah. Mean SAT critical reading: 598, mean SAT math: 628, mean SAT writing: 606, mean combined SAT: 1832, mean composite ACT: 26. 40% scored over 600 on SAT critical reading, 60% scored over 600 on SAT math, 60% scored over 600 on SAT writing, 60% scored over 1800 on combined SAT, 50% scored over 26 on composite ACT.

Student Life Upper grades have specified standards of dress, student council, honor system. Discipline rests primarily with faculty. Attendance at religious services is required.

Tuition and Aid Day student tuition: $6220. Tuition installment plan (Insured Tuition Payment Plan, monthly payment plans, discounted up-front tuition payment). Tuition reduction for siblings, need-based scholarship grants available. In 2012–13, 15% of upper-school students received aid. Total amount of financial aid awarded in 2012–13: $14,662.

Admissions Traditional secondary-level entrance grade is 9. For fall 2012, 5 students applied for upper-level admission, 5 were accepted, 5 enrolled. School's own test and TOEFL required. Deadline for receipt of application materials: none. Application fee required: $90. On-campus interview required.

Athletics Interscholastic: baseball (boys), basketball (b,g), golf (b,g), soccer (b,g), volleyball (g). 2 PE instructors, 4 coaches.

Computers Computers are regularly used in art, computer applications, technology, writing classes. Computer network features include Internet access, wireless campus network, Internet filtering or blocking technology. Computer access in designated common areas is available to students. Students grades are available online. The school has a published electronic and media policy.

Contact Eileen Rocco, Registrar. 801-942-8811. Fax: 801-942-8813. E-mail: rocco_e@slcics.org. Web site: www.slcics.org

INTERNATIONAL HIGH SCHOOL

150 Oak Street
San Francisco, California 94102

Head of School: Ms. Jane Camblin

General Information Coeducational day college-preparatory, arts, bilingual studies, and technology school. Grades PK–12. Founded: 1962. Setting: urban. 3-acre campus. 2 buildings on campus. Approved or accredited by California Association of Independent Schools, Council of International Schools, French Ministry of Education, International Baccalaureate Organization, Western Association of Schools and Colleges, and California Department of Education. Member of National Association of Independent Schools, Secondary School Admission Test Board, and European Council of International Schools. Languages of instruction: English and French. Endowment: $5.1 million. Total enrollment: 1,021. Upper school average class size: 17. Upper school faculty-student ratio: 1:10. There are 165 required school days per year for Upper School students. The average school day consists of 7 hours.

Upper School Student Profile Grade 9: 74 students (35 boys, 39 girls); Grade 10: 82 students (37 boys, 45 girls); Grade 11: 83 students (36 boys, 47 girls); Grade 12: 74 students (29 boys, 45 girls).

Faculty School total: 139. In upper school: 33 men, 30 women; 35 have advanced degrees.

Subjects Offered Advanced chemistry, advanced math, algebra, American history, American literature, art, biology, calculus, chemistry, community service, current events, drama, earth science, economics, English, English literature, environmental science, ESL, European history, fine arts, French, geography, geometry, German, government/civics, history, International Baccalaureate courses, Mandarin, mathematics, music, philosophy, physical education, physics, science, social studies, Spanish, theater, theory of knowledge, trigonometry, world history, world literature, writing.

Graduation Requirements Arts and fine arts (art, music, dance, drama), English, foreign language, International Baccalaureate courses, mathematics, physical education (includes health), science, social studies (includes history), theory of knowledge, extended essay, 150 hours of CAS.

Special Academic Programs International Baccalaureate program; honors section; independent study; term-away projects; study abroad; academic accommodation for the gifted, the musically talented, and the artistically talented; ESL (12 students enrolled).

College Admission Counseling 80 students graduated in 2012; all went to college, including Boston University; McGill University; University of California, Berkeley; University of California, Davis; University of California, Los Angeles; University of California, Santa Cruz. Mean SAT critical reading: 614, mean SAT math: 615, mean SAT writing: 614.

Student Life Upper grades have student council. Discipline rests equally with students and faculty.

Summer Programs Remediation, enrichment, advancement programs offered; session focuses on enrichment; held on campus; accepts boys and girls; open to students from other schools. 15 students usually enrolled.

Tuition and Aid Day student tuition: $32,290. Tuition installment plan (FACTS Tuition Payment Plan). Need-based scholarship grants, French bourse available. In 2012–13, 25% of upper-school students received aid. Total amount of financial aid awarded in 2012–13: $748,000.

Admissions Traditional secondary-level entrance grade is 9. For fall 2012, 316 students applied for upper-level admission, 201 were accepted, 60 enrolled. Any standardized test, SSAT or writing sample required. Deadline for receipt of application materials: January 12. Application fee required: $100. Interview required.

Athletics Interscholastic: baseball (boys, girls), basketball (b,g), football (b), soccer (b,g), volleyball (b,g); intramural: ballet (b,g), baseball (b), basketball (b,g), floor hockey (b,g), soccer (b,g), softball (g), tennis (b,g), volleyball (b,g); coed interscholastic: badminton, cross-country running, swimming and diving, tennis, track and field; coed intramural: badminton, ballet, cross-country running, fencing, flagball, golf, handball, indoor hockey, outdoor activities, outdoor adventure, physical fitness, physical training, swimming and diving, water polo, weight training. 4 PE instructors, 8 coaches, 3 athletic trainers.

Computers Computers are regularly used in all academic classes. Computer network features include on-campus library services, online commercial services, Internet access, wireless campus network, iPad program. Campus intranet, student e-mail accounts, and computer access in designated common areas are available to students. The school has a published electronic and media policy.

Contact Ms. Erin Cronin, Associate Director of Admission. 415-558-2093. Fax: 415-558-2085. E-mail: erinc@internationalsf.org. Web site: www.internationalsf.org

INTERNATIONAL SCHOOL BANGKOK

39/7 Soi Nichada Thani, Samakee Road
Pakkret 11120, Thailand

Head of School: Dr. Andrew Davies

General Information Coeducational day college-preparatory, arts, and technology school. Grades PK–12. Founded: 1951. Setting: suburban. Nearest major city is Bangkok, Thailand. 37-acre campus. 2 buildings on campus. Approved or accredited by Ministry of Education (Thailand), Western Association of Schools and Colleges, and state department of education. Affiliate member of National Association of Independent Schools; member of European Council of International Schools. Language of instruction: English. Total enrollment: 1,840. Upper school average class size: 18. Upper school faculty-student ratio: 1:10. There are 183 required school days per year for Upper School students. Upper School students typically attend 5 days per week. The average school day consists of 6 hours.

Upper School Student Profile Grade 9: 185 students (93 boys, 92 girls); Grade 10: 162 students (83 boys, 79 girls); Grade 11: 178 students (100 boys, 78 girls); Grade 12: 178 students (77 boys, 101 girls).

Faculty School total: 229. In upper school: 50 men, 42 women; 70 have advanced degrees.

Subjects Offered 3-dimensional design, algebra, American history, American literature, art, art history, biology, business, business education, business studies, calculus, calculus-AP, ceramics, chemistry, choir, computer math, computer science, concert band, creative writing, dance, drama, drawing, drawing and design, Dutch, earth science, ecology, economics, economics and history, electives, English, English literature, environmental education, environmental science, environmental studies, ESL, European history, expository writing, fine arts, French, French studies, geography, geology, geometry, German, government/civics, health, history, humanities, industrial arts, Japanese, journalism, language arts, languages, mathematics, music, performing arts, philosophy, photography, physical education, physics, psychology, reading, robotics, science, social studies, sociology, Spanish, speech, statistics, Thai, theater, theory of knowledge, trigonometry, world history, world literature, writing.

Graduation Requirements Arts and fine arts (art, music, dance, drama), English, mathematics, physical education (includes health), science, social studies (includes history), community service hours, Senior Seminar, Global Citizenship Week, Thailand and Southeast Asia course. Community service is required.

Special Academic Programs International Baccalaureate program; Advanced Placement exam preparation; ESL.

College Admission Counseling 169 students graduated in 2012; 167 went to college, including Boston University; Northeastern University; The University of British Columbia; University of California, Los Angeles; University of Illinois at Urbana–Champaign; University of Washington. Other: 1 entered military service, 1 had other specific plans.

Student Life Upper grades have uniform requirement, student council, honor system. Discipline rests primarily with faculty.

Summer Programs Remediation, enrichment, ESL, art/fine arts programs offered; held on campus; accepts boys and girls; open to students from other schools. 400 students usually enrolled. 2013 schedule: June to July. Application deadline: June 3.

Tuition and Aid Day student tuition: 773,000 Thai bahts. Tuition installment plan (individually arranged payment plans).

Admissions Math and English placement tests and school's own exam required. Deadline for receipt of application materials: none. Application fee required: 4500 Thai bahts. On-campus interview required.

Athletics Interscholastic: aquatics (boys, girls), badminton (b,g), basketball (b,g), cross-country running (b,g), dance (b,g), rugby (b,g), running (b,g), soccer (b,g), softball (b,g), swimming and diving (b,g), tennis (b,g), track and field (b,g), volleyball (b,g); intramural: aquatics (b,g), badminton (b,g), basketball (b,g), cross-country running (b,g), dance (b,g), fencing (b), rugby (b,g), running (b,g), swimming and diving (b,g), track and field (b,g), volleyball (b,g); coed interscholastic: dance team. 5 PE instructors.

Computers Computers are regularly used in all academic classes. Computer network features include on-campus library services, Internet access, wireless campus network, Internet filtering or blocking technology. Campus intranet, student e-mail accounts, and computer access in designated common areas are available to students. Students grades are available online. The school has a published electronic and media policy.

Contact Ms. Wendy Van Bramer, Admissions Director. 662-963-5800. Fax: 662-960-4103. E-mail: register@isb.ac.th. Web site: www.isb.ac.th

INTERNATIONAL SCHOOL HAMBURG

Hemmingstedter Weg 130
Hamburg 22609, Germany

Head of School: Mr. Andreas Swoboda

General Information Coeducational day college-preparatory, arts, and technology school. Grades PK–12. Founded: 1957. Setting: suburban. 3-acre campus. 1 building on campus. Approved or accredited by New England Association of Schools and Colleges. Language of instruction: English. Total enrollment: 694. Upper school average class size: 20. Upper school faculty-student ratio: 1:8. Upper School students typically attend 5 days per week.

Upper School Student Profile Grade 9: 69 students (43 boys, 26 girls); Grade 10: 51 students (29 boys, 22 girls); Grade 11: 46 students (25 boys, 21 girls); Grade 12: 47 students (22 boys, 25 girls).

Faculty School total: 85. In upper school: 47 men, 25 women; 25 have advanced degrees.

Subjects Offered Art, biology, chemistry, computer math, drama, English, ESL, European history, fine arts, French, geography, German, history, mathematics, model United Nations, music, photography, physical education, physics, science, social studies, Spanish, theater, theory of knowledge, world history.

Graduation Requirements Arts and fine arts (art, music, dance, drama), English, foreign language, mathematics, physical education (includes health), science, social studies (includes history).

Special Academic Programs International Baccalaureate program; ESL (80 students enrolled).

College Admission Counseling 50 students graduated in 2011; 45 went to college, including Columbia University; McGill University; University of Edinburgh; Yale University. Other: 1 entered military service, 3 had other specific plans.

Student Life Upper grades have student council. Discipline rests primarily with faculty.

Tuition and Aid Day student tuition: €14,250–€17,800. Tuition installment plan (2-payment plan). Financial aid available to upper-school students. In 2011–12, 1% of upper-school students received aid.

Admissions Traditional secondary-level entrance grade is 9. For fall 2011, 50 students applied for upper-level admission, 45 were accepted, 44 enrolled. ACT, CTBS, Stanford Achievement Test, any other standardized test or PSAT and SAT for applicants to grade 11 and 12 required. Deadline for receipt of application materials: none. Application fee required: €100. On-campus interview required.

Athletics Interscholastic: badminton (boys, girls), basketball (b,g), canoeing/kayaking (b,g), climbing (b,g), cross-country running (b,g), floor hockey (b,g), football (b,g), indoor hockey (b,g), indoor soccer (b,g), netball (b,g), physical training (b,g), rowing (b,g), running (b,g), sailing (b,g), soccer (b,g), tennis (b,g), track and field (b,g), volleyball (b,g); intramural: basketball (b,g), cross-country running (b,g), field hockey (b,g), football (b,g), soccer (b,g), tennis (b,g), track and field (b,g), volleyball (b,g); coed interscholastic: badminton, canoeing/kayaking, climbing, cross-country running, floor hockey, football, indoor hockey, indoor soccer, netball, running, sailing, soccer, tennis, track and field, volleyball; coed intramural: cross-country running, football, soccer, tennis, track and field, volleyball. 5 PE instructors, 4 coaches.

Computers Computers are regularly used in business studies, English, ESL, foreign language, French, geography, history, humanities, library, mathematics, music, science, Spanish, yearbook classes. Computer network features include on-campus library services, online commercial services, Internet access, wireless campus network, Internet filtering or blocking technology. Campus intranet and student e-mail accounts are available to students. Students grades are available online. The school has a published electronic and media policy.

Contact Catherine Bissonnet, Director of Admissions. 49-40-800050-133. Fax: 49-40-881-1405. E-mail: cbissonnet@ishamburg.org. Web site: www.ishamburg.org

INTERNATIONAL SCHOOL MANILA

University Parkway
Fort Bonifacio
1634 Taguig City, Philippines

Head of School: Mr. David Toze

General Information Coeducational day college-preparatory, arts, business, bilingual studies, and technology school. Grades PS–12. Founded: 1920. Setting: urban. Nearest major city is Manila, Philippines. 7-hectare campus. 1 building on campus. Approved or accredited by Council of International Schools and Western Association of Schools and Colleges. Affiliate member of National Association of Independent Schools; member of Secondary School Admission Test Board. Language of instruction: English. Total enrollment: 1,966. Upper school average class size: 16. Upper school faculty-student ratio: 1:9. There are 181 required school days per year for Upper School students.

Upper School Student Profile Grade 6: 142 students (68 boys, 74 girls); Grade 7: 156 students (80 boys, 76 girls); Grade 8: 168 students (89 boys, 79 girls); Grade 9: 188 students (98 boys, 90 girls); Grade 10: 172 students (82 boys, 90 girls); Grade 11: 188 students (86 boys, 102 girls); Grade 12: 174 students (86 boys, 88 girls).

Faculty School total: 200. In upper school: 42 men, 38 women; 35 have advanced degrees.

Subjects Offered Acting, anthropology, art, athletic training, band, Basic programming, biology, business, calculus-AP, chemistry, Chinese, choir, college admission preparation, college awareness, college counseling, college placement, college planning, computer applications, computer graphics, computer literacy, computer multimedia, computer programming, computer science, creative writing, critical writing, dance, desktop publishing, digital photography, economics, economics and history, English, environmental science, ESL, film, filmmaking, foreign language, French,

French as a second language, general science, geography, graphic design, health, health and wellness, health education, information technology, integrated mathematics, International Baccalaureate courses, international relations, Japanese, Japanese as Second Language, jazz band, leadership, math applications, math methods, mathematics, media studies, music, orchestra, parenting, peer counseling, personal fitness, Philippine culture, physical science, physics, political science, pre-calculus, programming, psychology, reading/study skills, remedial study skills, research, service learning/internship, sex education, Spanish, theater, theater arts, theory of knowledge, track and field, U.S. history, U.S. history-AP, video film production, visual and performing arts, visual arts, weight fitness, weight training, world history, world religions, writing.

Special Academic Programs International Baccalaureate program; Advanced Placement exam preparation; honors section; accelerated programs; independent study; ESL (166 students enrolled).

College Admission Counseling 166 students graduated in 2011; 161 went to college, including New York University; Penn State University Park; Purdue University; The University of British Columbia; University of California, Berkeley; University of Southern California. Other: 2 went to work, 3 had other specific plans. Mean SAT critical reading: 581, mean SAT math: 649, mean SAT writing: 603, mean combined SAT: 1832, mean composite ACT: 26.

Student Life Upper grades have uniform requirement, student council, honor system. Discipline rests equally with students and faculty.

Tuition and Aid Day student tuition: $1997–$7280. Tuition installment plan (monthly payment plans, individually arranged payment plans, quarterly payment plan). Scholarships for low-income local students available.

Admissions Traditional secondary-level entrance grade is 9. For fall 2011, 273 students applied for upper-level admission, 170 were accepted, 148 enrolled. Deadline for receipt of application materials: none. Application fee required: $200. On-campus interview recommended.

Athletics Interscholastic: badminton (boys, girls), basketball (b,g), bowling (b,g), cheering (g), cross-country running (b,g), dance (b,g), golf (b,g), gymnastics (b,g), martial arts (b,g), rugby (b,g), soccer (b,g), softball (b,g), swimming and diving (b,g), table tennis (b,g), tennis (b,g), track and field (b,g), volleyball (b,g), wall climbing (b,g); intramural: rugby (b,g), wall climbing (b,g), water polo (b,g); coed interscholastic: wall climbing; coed intramural: volleyball, wall climbing. 4 PE instructors, 10 coaches.

Computers Computers are regularly used in art, English, foreign language, history, mathematics, music, science classes. Computer network features include on-campus library services, online commercial services, Internet access, wireless campus network, Internet filtering or blocking technology. Campus intranet and student e-mail accounts are available to students. Students grades are available online. The school has a published electronic and media policy.

Contact Stephanie Hagedorn, Director of Admissions and Advancement. 63-2-840-8488. Fax: 63-2-840-8489. E-mail: admission@ismanila.org. Web site: www.ismanila.org

INTERNATIONAL SCHOOL OF AMSTERDAM

Sportlaan 45
Amstelveen 1185 TB, Netherlands

Head of School: Dr. Ed Greene

General Information Coeducational day college-preparatory, arts, bilingual studies, and technology school. Grades PS–12. Founded: 1964. Setting: suburban. Nearest major city is Amsterdam, Netherlands. 1-acre campus. 2 buildings on campus. Approved or accredited by New England Association of Schools and Colleges. Member of European Council of International Schools. Language of instruction: English. Total enrollment: 1,008. Upper school average class size: 20. Upper school faculty-student ratio: 1:5. There are 177 required school days per year for Upper School students. Upper School students typically attend 5 days per week. The average school day consists of 7 hours.

Upper School Student Profile Grade 9: 67 students (39 boys, 28 girls); Grade 10: 62 students (32 boys, 30 girls); Grade 11: 64 students (28 boys, 36 girls); Grade 12: 53 students (26 boys, 27 girls).

Faculty School total: 180. In upper school: 29 men, 42 women; 28 have advanced degrees.

Subjects Offered Addiction, advanced math, algebra, American literature, art, biology, calculus, chemistry, community service, computer programming, computer science, drama, Dutch, economics, English, English literature, ESL, European history, food science, French, geography, geometry, German, history, Japanese, mathematics, music, photography, physical education, physics, science, social sciences, social studies, Spanish, technology, theater, theory of knowledge, trigonometry, world history, world literature.

Graduation Requirements Arts, computer science, English, foreign language, mathematics, physical education (includes health), science, social sciences, social studies (includes history). Community service is required.

Special Academic Programs International Baccalaureate program; independent study; academic accommodation for the gifted, the musically talented, and the artistically talented; remedial reading and/or remedial writing; remedial math; programs in English, mathematics, general development for dyslexic students; ESL (19 students enrolled).

College Admission Counseling 48 students graduated in 2012; 38 went to college, including Austin College; Brandeis University; Suffolk University; University of Arkansas. Other: 1 entered military service, 9 had other specific plans. Median SAT critical reading: 590, median SAT math: 630, median SAT writing: 600, median combined SAT: 1770. 45% scored over 600 on SAT critical reading, 55% scored over 600 on SAT math, 55% scored over 600 on SAT writing, 45% scored over 1800 on combined SAT.

Student Life Upper grades have specified standards of dress, student council, honor system. Discipline rests primarily with faculty.

Tuition and Aid Day student tuition: €21,375–€22,050. Tuition installment plan (monthly payment plans, individually arranged payment plans).

Admissions Traditional secondary-level entrance grade is 9. For fall 2012, 69 students applied for upper-level admission, 38 were accepted, 24 enrolled. Deadline for receipt of application materials: none. No application fee required. On-campus interview required.

Athletics Interscholastic: basketball (boys, girls), soccer (b,g), softball (b,g), swimming and diving (b,g), tennis (b,g), track and field (b,g), volleyball (g); coed intramural: aerobics, aerobics/dance, badminton, basketball, cricket, fitness, handball, hockey, netball, rugby, running, soccer, softball, tennis, track and field, volleyball. 7 PE instructors, 14 coaches, 14 athletic trainers.

Computers Computers are regularly used in art, drawing and design, English, foreign language, information technology, keyboarding, library, mathematics, music, science, yearbook classes. Computer network features include on-campus library services, online commercial services, Internet access, Internet filtering or blocking technology. Campus intranet and student e-mail accounts are available to students.

Contact Julia True, Director of Admissions. 31-20-347-1111. Fax: 31-20-347-1105. E-mail: admissions@isa.nl. Web site: www.isa.nl

THE INTERNATIONAL SCHOOL OF LONDON

139 Gunnersbury Avenue
London W3 8LG, United Kingdom

Head of School: Mr. Huw Davies

General Information Coeducational day college-preparatory school. Grades K–12. Founded: 1972. Setting: urban. 2 buildings on campus. Member of European Council of International Schools. Language of instruction: English. Total enrollment: 340. Upper school average class size: 18. Upper school faculty-student ratio: 1:8. Upper School students typically attend 5 days per week.

Upper School Student Profile Grade 11: 30 students (15 boys, 15 girls); Grade 12: 30 students (15 boys, 15 girls).

Faculty School total: 67. In upper school: 15 men, 16 women; 21 have advanced degrees.

Subjects Offered Art, economics, English, French, geography, history, languages, mathematics, music, physical education, science, social sciences, Spanish, world affairs.

Graduation Requirements Foreign language, mathematics, science, social sciences. Community service is required.

Special Academic Programs International Baccalaureate program; ESL (47 students enrolled).

College Admission Counseling 22 students graduated in 2012; all went to college, including University of London; University of Oxford.

Student Life Upper grades have student council. Discipline rests primarily with faculty.

Tuition and Aid Day student tuition: £19,500.

Admissions For fall 2012, 36 students applied for upper-level admission, 30 were accepted, 30 enrolled. Deadline for receipt of application materials: July 30. Application fee required: £200. Interview recommended.

Athletics Interscholastic: basketball (boys, girls), soccer (b); intramural: badminton (b,g), softball (b,g), swimming and diving (b,g), table tennis (b,g), tennis (b,g); coed interscholastic: soccer; coed intramural: softball, swimming and diving, table tennis, tennis. 2 PE instructors, 2 coaches.

Computers Computers are regularly used in English, foreign language, mathematics, science classes. Computer network features include on-campus library services, Internet access, wireless campus network, Internet filtering or blocking technology. Student e-mail accounts are available to students. The school has a published electronic and media policy.

Contact Mr. Yoel Gordon, Director of Admissions. 20-8992-5823. Fax: 44-8993-7012. E-mail: ygordon@isllondon.org. Web site: www.isllondon.org

IONA PREPARATORY SCHOOL

255 Wilmot Road
New Rochelle, New York 10804

Head of School: Br. Thomas Leto

General Information Boys' day college-preparatory, arts, religious studies, and technology school, affiliated with Roman Catholic Church. Grades 9–12. Founded: 1916. Setting: suburban. Nearest major city is New York. 27-acre campus. 3 buildings on campus. Approved or accredited by Christian Brothers Association, Middle States Association of Colleges and Schools, National Catholic Education Association, New York State Association of Independent Schools, and New York State Board of Regents. Member of National Association of Independent Schools. Endowment: $6 million. Total enrollment: 785. Upper school average class size: 23. Upper school faculty-student ratio: 1:13. There are 180 required school days per year for Upper School students. Upper School students typically attend 5 days per week. The average school day consists of 6 hours and 30 minutes.

Upper School Student Profile Grade 9: 213 students (213 boys); Grade 10: 195 students (195 boys); Grade 11: 188 students (188 boys); Grade 12: 189 students (189 boys). 87% of students are Roman Catholic.

Faculty School total: 67. In upper school: 47 men, 18 women; 65 have advanced degrees.

Subjects Offered Accounting, Advanced Placement courses, algebra, American history, American history-AP, American literature, anatomy, art, astronomy, biology, biology-AP, British literature, calculus, chemistry, chemistry-AP, communications, community service, composition-AP, computer programming, computer science, economics, English, English literature-AP, English/composition-AP, environmental science, European history, European history-AP, European literature, fine arts, French, French as a second language, geometry, government-AP, graphic design, health, health and safety, history, Italian, Latin, media, music, painting, physical education, physics, physiology, psychology, psychology-AP, religion, science, social sciences, social studies, Spanish, trigonometry, U.S. government and politics-AP, word processing, world literature, world religions.

Graduation Requirements Art, computer science, English, foreign language, mathematics, music, physical education (includes health), religion (includes Bible studies and theology), science, social studies (includes history), 100 hours of community service.

Special Academic Programs Advanced Placement exam preparation; honors section; study at local college for college credit; study abroad; academic accommodation for the gifted.

College Admission Counseling 180 students graduated in 2012; all went to college, including Boston College; Fairfield University; Fordham University; Iona College; Loyola University Maryland. Mean SAT critical reading: 610, mean SAT math: 620. 30% scored over 600 on SAT critical reading, 39% scored over 600 on SAT math.

Student Life Upper grades have specified standards of dress, student council, honor system. Discipline rests primarily with faculty. Attendance at religious services is required.

Tuition and Aid Day student tuition: $15,300. Tuition installment plan (monthly payment plans, individually arranged payment plans, 10-payment plan, semester payment plan). Merit scholarship grants, need-based scholarship grants available. In 2012–13, 31% of upper-school students received aid; total upper-school merit-scholarship money awarded: $190,000. Total amount of financial aid awarded in 2012–13: $325,000.

Admissions Traditional secondary-level entrance grade is 9. For fall 2012, 913 students applied for upper-level admission, 560 were accepted, 213 enrolled. Admissions testing, Catholic High School Entrance Examination, ISEE, SSAT, Test of Achievement and Proficiency or writing sample required. Deadline for receipt of application materials: none. No application fee required. Interview recommended.

Athletics Interscholastic: badminton, baseball, basketball, bowling, climbing, crew, cross-country running, diving, field hockey, flag football, football, golf, ice hockey, indoor track, indoor track & field, lacrosse, paint ball, physical fitness, rock climbing, running, soccer, swimming and diving, tennis, track and field, ultimate Frisbee, volleyball, weight lifting, weight training, winter (indoor) track, wrestling; intramural: baseball, basketball, climbing, fitness, flag football, floor hockey, Frisbee, physical fitness, physical training, rock climbing, soccer, strength & conditioning, tennis, volleyball, wall climbing, weight lifting. 3 PE instructors, 40 coaches, 1 athletic trainer.

Computers Computers are regularly used in all classes. Computer network features include on-campus library services, online commercial services, Internet access, wireless campus network, Internet filtering or blocking technology. Campus intranet and student e-mail accounts are available to students. The school has a published electronic and media policy.

Contact Mrs. Judy M. Musho, Director of Admissions. 914-632-0714 Ext. 215. Fax: 914-632-9760. E-mail: jmusho@ionaprep.org. Web site: www.ionaprep.org

ISTANBUL INTERNATIONAL COMMUNITY SCHOOL

Karaagac Mahallesi, G72 Sokak, No 1/1
Buyukcekmece
Istanbul 34866, Turkey

Head of School: Mr. Peter Welch

General Information Coeducational day college-preparatory, general academic, and International Baccalaureate school. Grades 1–12. Founded: 1911. Setting: rural. 16-hectare campus. 4 buildings on campus. Approved or accredited by Council of International Schools, International Baccalaureate Organization, New England Association of Schools and Colleges, Northwest Accreditation Commission, and The College Board. Affiliate member of National Association of Independent Schools; member of European Council of International Schools. Language of instruction: English. Endowment: $7 million. Total enrollment: 555. Upper school average class size: 20. Upper school faculty-student ratio: 1:9. There are 178 required school days per year for Upper School students. Upper School students typically attend 5 days per week. The average school day consists of 5 hours and 30 minutes.

Upper School Student Profile Grade 7: 40 students (18 boys, 22 girls); Grade 8: 38 students (16 boys, 22 girls); Grade 9: 38 students (16 boys, 22 girls); Grade 10: 56 students (32 boys, 24 girls); Grade 11: 33 students (11 boys, 22 girls); Grade 12: 34 students (14 boys, 20 girls).

Faculty School total: 72. In upper school: 23 men, 20 women; 22 have advanced degrees.

Graduation Requirements International Baccalaureate courses.

Special Academic Programs International Baccalaureate program; ESL.

College Admission Counseling 44 students graduated in 2012; 42 went to college, including Columbia University; Cornell University; Georgetown University; New York University; Tufts University. Other: 2 entered military service. Mean SAT critical reading: 540, mean SAT math: 620, mean SAT writing: 660.

Student Life Upper grades have student council, honor system. Discipline rests primarily with faculty.

Tuition and Aid Day student tuition: $29,500–$34,200.

Admissions Comprehensive educational evaluation, English proficiency, school's own test or writing sample required. Application fee required: $1000. Interview required.

Athletics Interscholastic: basketball (boys, girls), cross-country running (b,g), equestrian sports (b,g), soccer (b,g), softball (b,g), volleyball (b,g); intramural: basketball (b,g), cross-country running (b,g), soccer (b,g), softball (b,g), volleyball (b,g); coed interscholastic: ballet, horseback riding, table tennis, tennis; coed intramural: tennis. 6 PE instructors, 20 coaches.

Computers Computers are regularly used in all classes. Computer network features include on-campus library services, online commercial services, Internet access, wireless campus network, Internet filtering or blocking technology, 1 to 1 laptop program in grades 6-12, 2 to 1 laptop program in grades 2-5, iPads for Preschool-Grade 1. Campus intranet and student e-mail accounts are available to students. Students grades are available online. The school has a published electronic and media policy.

Contact Mrs. Suzan Gurkan, Director of Admissions. 90-212-857-8264 Ext. 215. Fax: 90-212-857-8270. E-mail: admissions@iics.k12.tr. Web site: www.iics.k12.tr

JACK M. BARRACK HEBREW ACADEMY

272 South Bryn Mawr Avenue
Bryn Mawr, Pennsylvania 19010

Head of School: Mrs. Sharon P. Levin

General Information Coeducational day college-preparatory, arts, religious studies, and bilingual studies school, affiliated with Jewish faith. Grades 6–12. Founded: 1946. Setting: suburban. Nearest major city is Philadelphia. 35-acre campus. 2 buildings on campus. Approved or accredited by Middle States Association of Colleges and Schools and Pennsylvania Department of Education. Member of National Association of Independent Schools. Languages of instruction: English and Hebrew. Endowment: $3.1 million. Total enrollment: 274. Upper school average class size: 16. Upper school faculty-student ratio: 1:15. There are 168 required school days per year for Upper School students. Upper School students typically attend 5 days per week. The average school day consists of 7 hours.

Upper School Student Profile Grade 9: 34 students (16 boys, 18 girls); Grade 10: 62 students (32 boys, 30 girls); Grade 11: 56 students (19 boys, 37 girls); Grade 12: 53 students (20 boys, 33 girls). 100% of students are Jewish.

Faculty School total: 53. In upper school: 17 men, 36 women; 40 have advanced degrees.

Subjects Offered Algebra, American history, American literature, art, astronomy, Bible studies, biology, calculus, chemistry, community service, computer math, computer programming, computer science, creative writing, earth science, English, English literature, environmental science, environmental science-AP, ethics, European history, French, geometry, government/civics, grammar, health, Hebrew, history, Jewish studies, Latin, mathematics, music, physical education, physics, public speaking, religion, science, social studies, Spanish, trigonometry, world history, writing.

Graduation Requirements English, foreign language, mathematics, physical education (includes health), religion (includes Bible studies and theology), science, social studies (includes history), senior community service project–150 hours in the senior year.

Special Academic Programs 8 Advanced Placement exams for which test preparation is offered; accelerated programs; independent study; term-away projects; study at local college for college credit; study abroad; academic accommodation for the gifted; remedial reading and/or remedial writing; remedial math; special instructional classes for deaf students.

College Admission Counseling 50 students graduated in 2012; all went to college, including Brandeis University; New York University; University of Maryland, College Park; University of Pennsylvania; University of Pittsburgh. Median SAT critical reading: 605, median SAT math: 642, median SAT writing: 605.

Student Life Upper grades have specified standards of dress, student council, honor system. Discipline rests primarily with faculty.

Tuition and Aid Day student tuition: $26,650. Tuition installment plan (Key Tuition Payment Plan, monthly payment plans, individually arranged payment plans). Tuition reduction for siblings, merit scholarship grants, need-based scholarship grants available. Total upper-school merit-scholarship money awarded for 2012–13: $151,200. Total amount of financial aid awarded in 2012–13: $1,483,690.

Admissions Traditional secondary-level entrance grade is 9. For fall 2012, 65 students applied for upper-level admission, 59 were accepted, 49 enrolled. ISEE required. Deadline for receipt of application materials: none. Application fee required: $75. On-campus interview required.

Athletics Interscholastic: baseball (boys), basketball (b,g), soccer (b,g), softball (g), tennis (b,g), track and field (g); intramural: basketball (b,g), field hockey (b,g), golf (b,g), lacrosse (g), running (b,g), soccer (b,g), squash (g), track and field (g), volleyball (b,g); coed interscholastic: cross-country running, soccer, swimming and diving. 2 PE instructors, 17 coaches.

Computers Computers are regularly used in foreign language, French, health, history, humanities, independent study, information technology, introduction to technology, journalism, keyboarding, Latin, library, literary magazine, mathematics, media production, multimedia, news writing, newspaper, photojournalism, programming, publications, remedial study skills, research skills, SAT preparation, science, social sciences, Spanish, study skills, technology, video film production, Web site design, word processing, writing, yearbook classes. Computer network features include on-campus library services, online commercial services, Internet access, wireless campus network, Internet filtering or blocking technology. Campus intranet, student e-mail accounts, and computer access in designated common areas are available to students. Students grades are available online. The school has a published electronic and media policy.

Contact Jennifer Groen, Director of Admission and Strategic Engagement. 610-922-2350. Fax: 610-922-2301. E-mail: jgroen@jbha.org. Web site: www.jbha.org

JACKSON PREPARATORY SCHOOL

3100 Lakeland Drive
Jackson, Mississippi 39232

Head of School: Susan R. Lindsay

General Information Coeducational day college-preparatory school. Grades 6–12. Founded: 1970. Setting: urban. 74-acre campus. 6 buildings on campus. Approved or accredited by Mississippi Private School Association, Southern Association of Colleges and Schools, Southern Association of Independent Schools, and The College Board. Member of National Association of Independent Schools. Endowment: $993,373. Total enrollment: 800. Upper school average class size: 16. Upper school faculty-student ratio: 1:13. There are 176 required school days per year for Upper School students. Upper School students typically attend 5 days per week. The average school day consists of 6 hours and 45 minutes.

Upper School Student Profile Grade 10: 122 students (59 boys, 63 girls); Grade 11: 133 students (68 boys, 65 girls); Grade 12: 120 students (63 boys, 57 girls).

Faculty School total: 90. In upper school: 26 men, 49 women; 42 have advanced degrees.

Subjects Offered Accounting, advanced chemistry, Advanced Placement courses, algebra, American government, American history, American history-AP, American literature, art, Asian studies, Bible as literature, biology, biology-AP, British literature, calculus, calculus-AP, chemistry, chemistry-AP, choral music, civics, classical studies, computer science, creative writing, debate, discrete mathematics, drama, driver education, earth science, economics, English, English literature, English literature-AP, European history, film, fine arts, finite math, French, geography, geometry, government-AP, government/civics, grammar, Greek, Greek culture, history, honors algebra, honors English, honors geometry, journalism, Latin, Latin-AP, mathematics, music, physical education, physics, physics-AP, pre-algebra, pre-calculus, science, social studies, Spanish, trigonometry, U.S. government, U.S. government and politics-AP, U.S. history, U.S. history-AP, world history, world literature.

Graduation Requirements Arts and fine arts (art, music, dance, drama), computer applications, English, foreign language, mathematics, science, social studies (includes history).

Special Academic Programs Advanced Placement exam preparation; honors section; academic accommodation for the gifted, the musically talented, and the artistically talented; programs in English, mathematics, general development for dyslexic students.

College Admission Counseling 135 students graduated in 2012; all went to college, including Louisiana State University in Shreveport; Millsaps College; Mississippi College; Mississippi State University; The University of Alabama; University of Mississippi. Mean SAT critical reading: 617, mean SAT math: 621, mean SAT writing: 595, mean composite ACT: 25.

Student Life Upper grades have uniform requirement, student council, honor system. Discipline rests primarily with faculty.

Summer Programs Remediation, enrichment, art/fine arts, computer instruction programs offered; session focuses on enrichment; held on campus; accepts boys and girls; open to students from other schools. 200 students usually enrolled. 2013 schedule: June 3 to July 12. Application deadline: May 1.

Tuition and Aid Day student tuition: $12,543. Tuition installment plan (monthly payment plans). Need-based scholarship grants available. In 2012–13, 12% of upper-school students received aid. Total amount of financial aid awarded in 2012–13: $195,000.

Admissions Traditional secondary-level entrance grade is 10. For fall 2012, 16 students applied for upper-level admission, 11 were accepted, 10 enrolled. Nonstandardized placement tests and OLSAT, Stanford Achievement Test required. Deadline for receipt of application materials: none. Application fee required: $40. Interview required.

Athletics Interscholastic: baseball (boys), basketball (b,g), cheering (g), cross-country running (b,g), dance team (g), football (b), Frisbee (b), soccer (b,g), softball (g), swimming and diving (b,g), tennis (b,g), track and field (b,g), ultimate Frisbee (b), volleyball (g); intramural: basketball (b,g), Frisbee (b), soccer (b,g), volleyball (b,g); coed interscholastic: cheering, golf. 4 coaches.

Computers Computers are regularly used in all classes. Computer network features include on-campus library services, online commercial services, Internet access, Electric Library, EBSCOhost®, GaleNet, Grolier Online, NewsBank, online subscription services. The school has a published electronic and media policy.

Contact Lesley W. Morton, Director of Admission. 601-932-8106 Ext. 1. Fax: 601-936-4068. E-mail: lmorton@jacksonprep.net. Web site: www.jacksonprep.net

JEAN AND SAMUEL FRANKEL JEWISH ACADEMY OF METROPOLITAN DETROIT

6600 West Maple Road
West Bloomfield, Michigan 48322

Head of School: Rabbi Eric Grossman

General Information Boys' day college-preparatory, business, and religious studies school, affiliated with Jewish faith. Grades 9–12. Setting: suburban. Nearest major city is Detroit. Approved or accredited by Independent Schools Association of the Central States and Michigan Department of Education. Upper school average class size: 13. The average school day consists of 8 hours.

Faculty In upper school: 30 have advanced degrees.

Special Academic Programs Advanced Placement exam preparation; honors section; study abroad; academic accommodation for the gifted; remedial reading and/or remedial writing; remedial math; special instructional classes for deaf students, blind students.

College Admission Counseling 56 went to college, including Michigan State University; University of Michigan–Dearborn.

Student Life Upper grades have specified standards of dress, student council, honor system. Discipline rests primarily with faculty. Attendance at religious services is required.

Tuition and Aid Day student tuition: $21,000. Tuition reduction for siblings, need-based scholarship grants available.

Admissions Traditional secondary-level entrance grade is 9. High School Placement Test required. Deadline for receipt of application materials: January 30. Application fee required: $100. Interview required.

Athletics 2 PE instructors, 8 coaches.

Computers Computer network features include on-campus library services, online commercial services, Internet access, wireless campus network, all students are given issued an iPad. Campus intranet and student e-mail accounts are available to students. Students grades are available online. The school has a published electronic and media policy.

Contact Lisa Gilan, Director of Admissions. 248-592-5263. Fax: 248-592-0022. E-mail: lgilan@frankelja.org. Web site: www.frankelja.org/

JESUIT COLLEGE PREPARATORY SCHOOL

12345 Inwood Road
Dallas, Texas 75244

Head of School: Mr. Tom Garrison

General Information Boys' day college-preparatory school, affiliated with Roman Catholic Church (Jesuit order). Grades 9–12. Founded: 1942. Setting: suburban. 27-acre campus. 2 buildings on campus. Approved or accredited by Jesuit Secondary Education Association, National Catholic Education Association, Southern Association of Colleges and Schools, Texas Catholic Conference, and Texas Department of Education. Endowment: $25.6 million. Total enrollment: 1,072. Upper school average class size: 17. Upper school faculty-student ratio: 1:11. There are 190 required school days per year for Upper School students. Upper School students typically attend 5 days per week. The average school day consists of 6 hours.

Upper School Student Profile Grade 9: 276 students (276 boys); Grade 10: 269 students (269 boys); Grade 11: 259 students (259 boys); Grade 12: 268 students (268 boys). 80.5% of students are Roman Catholic Church (Jesuit order).

Faculty School total: 115. In upper school: 85 men, 30 women; 56 have advanced degrees.

Subjects Offered Advanced chemistry, advanced computer applications, advanced math, American literature-AP, American studies, art, art appreciation, art-AP, arts, band, Bible, biology, biology-AP, British literature, British literature-AP, calculus, calculus-AP, Catholic belief and practice, ceramics, chemistry, chemistry-AP, choir, Christian ethics, church history, civics, college counseling, community service, composition, composition-AP, computer applications, computer graphics, computer science, computer science-AP, contemporary issues, discrete mathematics, drama, drama performance, drama workshop, drawing, drawing and design, driver education, earth science, economics, economics-AP, English, English composition, English language and composition-AP, English language-AP, English literature, English literature and composition-AP, English literature-AP, English-AP, English/composition-AP, ethical decision making, European history, fine arts, French, French-AP, general science, geometry, government, government-AP, grammar, guitar, health, history, history-AP, honors algebra, honors English, honors geometry, honors U.S. history, honors world history, instrumental music, jazz band, journalism, Latin, literature and composition-AP, marching band, mathematics, mathematics-AP, microcomputer technology applications, music, music appreciation, musical productions, orchestra, peace and justice, peer ministry, performing arts, physical education, physics, physics-AP, pottery, prayer/spirituality, pre-calculus, psychology, public speaking, publications, religion, scripture, social studies, Spanish, Spanish language-AP, Spanish literature-AP, Spanish-AP, speech, speech and debate, speech and oral interpretations, statistics, student government, student publications, studio art, studio art-AP, symphonic band, theater, theology, U.S. government, U.S. government and politics-AP, U.S. history, U.S. history-AP, U.S. literature, world history, world history-AP.

Graduation Requirements Arts and fine arts (art, music, dance, drama), computer science, English, foreign language, mathematics, physical education (includes health), science, social studies (includes history), theology. Community service is required.

Special Academic Programs 18 Advanced Placement exams for which test preparation is offered; honors section; independent study; study at local college for college credit.

College Admission Counseling 248 students graduated in 2011; 246 went to college, including Saint Louis University; Southern Methodist University; Texas A&M University; Texas Christian University; The University of Alabama; The University of Texas at Austin. Other: 2 had other specific plans. Mean SAT critical reading: 598, mean SAT math: 618, mean SAT writing: 595.

Student Life Upper grades have specified standards of dress, student council, honor system. Discipline rests primarily with faculty. Attendance at religious services is required.

Tuition and Aid Day student tuition: $13,800. Tuition installment plan (FACTS Tuition Payment Plan). Merit scholarship grants, need-based scholarship grants, paying campus jobs available. In 2011–12, 25% of upper-school students received aid; total upper-school merit-scholarship money awarded: $56,000. Total amount of financial aid awarded in 2011–12: $1,233,850.

Admissions Traditional secondary-level entrance grade is 9. For fall 2011, 492 students applied for upper-level admission, 310 were accepted, 276 enrolled. ISEE required. Deadline for receipt of application materials: January 6. Application fee required: $75. Interview required.

Athletics Interscholastic: baseball, basketball, bowling, crew, cross-country running, diving, fencing, football, golf, ice hockey, lacrosse, power lifting, rugby, soccer, swimming and diving, tennis, track and field, water polo, wrestling; intramural: basketball, bicycling, broomball, flagball, floor hockey, indoor soccer, ultimate Frisbee, volleyball; coed interscholastic: cheering, drill team. 6 PE instructors, 30 coaches, 2 athletic trainers.

Computers Computers are regularly used in college planning, desktop publishing, digital applications, engineering, English, foreign language, graphic design, graphics, humanities, introduction to technology, journalism, literary magazine, mathematics, media production, multimedia, newspaper, programming, publications, science, social studies, technology, video film production, Web site design, writing, yearbook classes. Computer network features include on-campus library services, online commercial services, Internet access, wireless campus network, Internet filtering or blocking technology. Campus intranet, student e-mail accounts, and computer access in designated common areas are available to students. Students grades are available online. The school has a published electronic and media policy.

Contact Mrs. Susie Herrmann, Admissions Assistant. 972-387-8700 Ext. 453. Fax: 972-980-6707. E-mail: sherrmann@jesuitcp.org. Web site: www.jesuitcp.org

JESUIT HIGH SCHOOL OF NEW ORLEANS

4133 Banks Street
New Orleans, Louisiana 70119-6883

Head of School: Rev. Raymond R. Fitzgerald, SJ

General Information Boys' day college-preparatory school, affiliated with Roman Catholic Church. Grades 8–12. Founded: 1847. Setting: urban. Nearest major city is Baton Rouge. 8-acre campus. 3 buildings on campus. Approved or accredited by Jesuit Secondary Education Association, National Catholic Education Association, Southern Association of Colleges and Schools, and Louisiana Department of Education. Endowment: $1.2 million. Total enrollment: 1,354. Upper school average class size: 22. Upper school faculty-student ratio: 1:22. There are 180 required school days per year for Upper School students. Upper School students typically attend 5 days per week. The average school day consists of 5 hours and 30 minutes.

Upper School Student Profile Grade 9: 292 students (292 boys); Grade 10: 270 students (270 boys); Grade 11: 261 students (261 boys); Grade 12: 266 students (266 boys). 87.4% of students are Roman Catholic.

Faculty School total: 110. In upper school: 73 men, 37 women; 59 have advanced degrees.

Subjects Offered Algebra, American history, American literature, analysis, art history, arts, band, Bible studies, biology, biology-AP, calculus, calculus-AP, chemistry, chemistry-AP, Christianity, church history, civics, community service, comparative government and politics-AP, computer applications, computer literacy, computer programming, computer science, creative writing, economics, English, English literature, English literature and composition-AP, environmental science, fine arts, French, French language-AP, geography, geometry, government/civics, grammar, Greek, health, history, JROTC, Latin, Latin-AP, law, mathematics, military history, military science, music, physical education, physical science, physics, physics-AP, politics, psychology, public speaking, religion, ROTC (for boys), SAT/ACT preparation, science, scripture, social studies, sociology, Spanish, Spanish language-AP, speech, study skills, theology, trigonometry, U.S. government and politics-AP, U.S. history-AP, Western civilization, world literature, writing.

Graduation Requirements Arts and fine arts (art, music, dance, drama), computer science, English, foreign language, mathematics, physical education (includes health), religion (includes Bible studies and theology), science, social sciences, social studies (includes history), speech. Community service is required.

Special Academic Programs Advanced Placement exam preparation; honors section.

College Admission Counseling 264 students graduated in 2011; 263 went to college, including Louisiana State University and Agricultural and Mechanical College; Loyola University New Orleans; The University of Alabama; University of Louisiana at Lafayette; Xavier University of Louisiana. Other: 1 had other specific plans. Median SAT critical reading: 640, median SAT math: 640, median SAT writing: 660, median combined SAT: 1940, median composite ACT: 27. 71% scored over 600 on SAT critical reading, 73% scored over 600 on SAT math, 71% scored over 600 on SAT writing, 64% scored over 1800 on combined SAT, 64% scored over 26 on composite ACT.

Student Life Upper grades have uniform requirement, student council, honor system. Discipline rests primarily with faculty. Attendance at religious services is required.

Tuition and Aid Day student tuition: $7400. Tuition installment plan (monthly payment plans, individually arranged payment plans, monthly, quarterly as arranged with parents on an individual basis). Need-based scholarship grants, paying campus jobs available. In 2011–12, 10% of upper-school students received aid. Total amount of financial aid awarded in 2011–12: $523,900.

Admissions Traditional secondary-level entrance grade is 9. For fall 2011, 98 students applied for upper-level admission, 67 were accepted, 48 enrolled. High School Placement Test required. Deadline for receipt of application materials: January 7. Application fee required: $20.

Athletics Interscholastic: baseball, basketball, bowling, cross-country running, football, golf, in-line hockey, indoor track & field, JROTC drill, lacrosse, marksmanship, physical fitness, riflery, rugby, soccer, swimming and diving, tennis, track and field, wrestling; intramural: baseball, basketball, bicycling, bowling, cheering, flag football, football, Frisbee, golf, outdoors, paddle tennis, paint ball, touch football. 9 PE instructors, 41 coaches, 1 athletic trainer.

Computers Computers are regularly used in library skills, mathematics, reading, science, yearbook classes. Computer network features include on-campus library services, online commercial services, Internet access, Internet filtering or blocking technology. Computer access in designated common areas is available to students. The school has a published electronic and media policy.

Contact Mr. Jack S. Truxillo, Director of Admissions. 504-483-3936. Fax: 504-483-3942. E-mail: truxillo@jesuitnola.org. Web site: www.jesuitnola.org

JESUIT HIGH SCHOOL OF TAMPA

4701 North Himes Avenue
Tampa, Florida 33614-6694

Head of School: Mr. Barry Neuburger

General Information Boys' day college-preparatory school, affiliated with Roman Catholic Church. Grades 9–12. Founded: 1899. Setting: urban. 40-acre campus. 9 buildings on campus. Approved or accredited by Jesuit Secondary Education Association, National Catholic Education Association, Southern Association of Colleges and Schools, and Florida Department of Education. Total enrollment: 752. Upper school average class size: 24. Upper school faculty-student ratio: 1:13. There are 175 required school days per year for Upper School students. Upper School students typically attend 5 days per week. The average school day consists of 7 hours and 23 minutes.

Upper School Student Profile Grade 9: 208 students (208 boys); Grade 10: 188 students (188 boys); Grade 11: 180 students (180 boys); Grade 12: 176 students (176 boys). 78% of students are Roman Catholic.

Faculty School total: 60. In upper school: 45 men, 15 women; 40 have advanced degrees.

Subjects Offered Algebra, American foreign policy, American government, American history, analytic geometry, anatomy, art, biology, calculus, calculus-AP, chemistry, chemistry-AP, chorus, computer science, economics, English, English language and composition-AP, English literature and composition-AP, environmental science, ethics, European history, French, geometry, global studies, health, Latin, marine biology, math analysis, music, physical education, physics, physics-AP, physiology, pre-calculus, psychology, Spanish, Spanish language-AP, speech, studio art-AP, theology, trigonometry, U.S. government and politics-AP, U.S. history-AP, world history, world history-AP, writing.

Graduation Requirements Arts and fine arts (art, music, dance, drama), English, foreign language, mathematics, physical education (includes health), science, social studies (includes history), theology, 150 hours of community service (additional 20 hours for National Honor Society members).

Special Academic Programs 10 Advanced Placement exams for which test preparation is offered; honors section.

College Admission Counseling 160 students graduated in 2012; all went to college, including Florida Gulf Coast University; Florida State University; Georgia Institute of Technology; University of Florida; University of South Florida. Mean SAT critical reading: 590, mean SAT math: 601, mean SAT writing: 582, mean combined SAT: 1773, mean composite ACT: 26.

Student Life Upper grades have specified standards of dress, student council. Discipline rests primarily with faculty. Attendance at religious services is required.

Summer Programs Remediation programs offered; session focuses on remediation only; held on campus; accepts boys; not open to students from other schools. 50 students usually enrolled. 2013 schedule: June 18 to July 20.

Tuition and Aid Day student tuition: $12,900. Tuition installment plan (FACTS Tuition Payment Plan). Need-based scholarship grants available. In 2012–13, 25% of upper-school students received aid. Total amount of financial aid awarded in 2012–13: $1,213,590.

Admissions Traditional secondary-level entrance grade is 9. For fall 2012, 383 students applied for upper-level admission, 253 were accepted, 208 enrolled. High School Placement Test (closed version) from Scholastic Testing Service required. Deadline for receipt of application materials: January 12. Application fee required: $50.

Athletics Interscholastic: baseball, basketball, bowling, cross-country running, diving, football, golf, lacrosse, soccer, swimming and diving, tennis, track and field, wrestling; intramural: basketball, football, Frisbee, ice hockey, sailing, softball, ultimate Frisbee. 2 PE instructors, 1 athletic trainer.

Computers Computer network features include on-campus library services, online commercial services, Internet access, wireless campus network, Internet filtering or blocking technology. Campus intranet, student e-mail accounts, and computer access in designated common areas are available to students. Students grades are available online. The school has a published electronic and media policy.

Contact Mr. Steve Matesich, Director of Admissions. 813-877-5344 Ext. 509. Fax: 813-872-1853. E-mail: smatesich@jesuittampa.org. Web site: www.jesuittampa.org

JOHN BURROUGHS SCHOOL

755 South Price Road
St. Louis, Missouri 63124

Head of School: Andy Abbott

General Information Coeducational day college-preparatory school. Grades 7–12. Founded: 1923. Setting: suburban. 47-acre campus. 7 buildings on campus. Approved or accredited by Independent Schools Association of the Central States. Member of National Association of Independent Schools and Secondary School Admission Test Board. Endowment: $37.2 million. Total enrollment: 600. Upper school average class size: 13. Upper school faculty-student ratio: 1:7. There are 164 required school days per year for Upper School students. Upper School students typically attend 5 days per week. The average school day consists of 8 hours.

Upper School Student Profile Grade 9: 103 students (51 boys, 52 girls); Grade 10: 98 students (49 boys, 49 girls); Grade 11: 105 students (54 boys, 51 girls); Grade 12: 99 students (50 boys, 49 girls).

Faculty School total: 109. In upper school: 45 men, 60 women; 81 have advanced degrees.

Subjects Offered Acting, Advanced Placement courses, African American history, algebra, American history, American literature, Ancient Greek, ancient world history, applied arts, architectural drawing, art, art history, art history-AP, astronomy, bioethics, biology, biology-AP, calculus, calculus-AP, ceramics, chemistry, chemistry-AP, Chinese, choral music, chorus, classical language, community service, comparative religion, computer math, computer science, computer skills, computer-aided design, creative writing, dance, debate, drama, earth science, ecology, engineering, English, English literature, environmental science, environmental systems, expository writing, fine arts, finite math, foreign language, French, French language-AP, gardening, geology, geometry, German, global issues, global studies, Greek, Greek culture, health, history, home economics, honors English, industrial arts, jazz, jazz band, keyboarding, lab science, Latin, Latin-AP, mathematics, mechanical drawing, meteorology, model United Nations, music, orchestra, organic chemistry, personal finance, photography, physical education, physics, poetry, pre-algebra, pre-calculus, probability and statistics, psychology, public speaking, reading/study skills, religion, Russian, science, social sciences, social studies, Spanish, Spanish-AP, speech and debate, statistics, trigonometry, vocal music, word processing, world civilizations, world history, world literature, world religions, writing.

Graduation Requirements Arts and fine arts (art, music, dance, drama), English, foreign language, history, mathematics, performing arts, physical education (includes health), practical arts, science, Senior May Project, Sophomore Diversity Seminar.

Special Academic Programs 8 Advanced Placement exams for which test preparation is offered; honors section; independent study.

College Admission Counseling 98 students graduated in 2012; all went to college, including Dartmouth College; Middlebury College; New York University; Princeton University; Tulane University; Washington University in St. Louis. Median SAT critical reading: 680, median SAT math: 710, median SAT writing: 690, median combined SAT: 2080, median composite ACT: 32. 86% scored over 600 on SAT critical reading, 90% scored over 600 on SAT math, 86% scored over 600 on SAT writing, 89% scored over 1800 on combined SAT, 92% scored over 26 on composite ACT.

Student Life Upper grades have student council, honor system. Discipline rests equally with students and faculty.

Tuition and Aid Day student tuition: $22,900. Tuition installment plan (monthly payment plans). Need-based scholarship grants, need-based loans available. In 2012–13, 20% of upper-school students received aid. Total amount of financial aid awarded in 2012–13: $2,034,000.

Admissions Traditional secondary-level entrance grade is 7. Applicants for grades 9–12 are welcome as space permits. For fall 2012, 214 applied, 104 were accepted, 94 enrolled. SSAT required. Deadline for receipt of application materials: January 18. Application fee required: $40. On-campus interview required.

Athletics Interscholastic: baseball (boys), basketball (b,g), cheering (b,g), cross-country running (b,g), dance (g), dance squad (g), diving (b,g), field hockey (g), fitness (b,g), football (b), golf (b,g), ice hockey (b), independent competitive sports (b,g), lacrosse (b,g), modern dance (g), outdoor education (b,g), physical fitness (b,g), physical training (b,g), soccer (b,g), strength & conditioning (b,g), swimming and diving (b,g), tennis (b,g), track and field (b,g), volleyball (g), water polo (b), wrestling (b), yoga (b,g); coed interscholastic: cheering, dance, dance squad, ice hockey, modern dance, outdoor education, physical fitness, physical training, strength & conditioning, water polo, wrestling, yoga. 40 coaches, 1 athletic trainer.

Computers Computers are regularly used in all academic, animation, architecture, art, basic skills, cabinet making, college planning, current events, desktop publishing, drafting, drawing and design, industrial technology, keyboarding, lab/keyboard, library, library skills, media production, music, photography, photojournalism, remedial study skills, research skills, study skills, technical drawing, theater, video film production, Web site design, yearbook classes. Computer network features include on-campus library services, online commercial services, Internet access, wireless campus network, access to Google Apps, access to necessary curricular software, iPad/laptop check out from library. Campus intranet, student e-mail accounts, and computer access in designated common areas are available to students. The school has a published electronic and media policy.

Contact Caroline LaVigne, Director of Admissions and Tuition Aid. 314-993-4040. Fax: 314-567-2896. E-mail: clavigne@jburroughs.org. Web site: www.jburroughs.org

THE JOHN DEWEY ACADEMY

Great Barrington, Massachusetts

See Special Needs Schools section.

JOHN HANCOCK ACADEMY

PO Drawer E
Sparta, Georgia 31087

Head of School: Mr. Steve James

General Information Coeducational day college-preparatory, general academic, arts, religious studies, and technology school, affiliated with Baptist Church, United Methodist Church. Grades K–12. Founded: 1966. Setting: rural. Nearest major city is Macon. 1 building on campus. Approved or accredited by Georgia Accrediting Commission, Georgia Independent School Association, and Georgia Department of Education. Languages of instruction: English and Spanish. Total enrollment: 122. Upper school average class size: 8. Upper school faculty-student ratio: 1:8. There are 180 required school days per year for Upper School students. Upper School students typically attend 5 days per week. The average school day consists of 8 hours.

Upper School Student Profile Grade 9: 11 students (7 boys, 4 girls); Grade 10: 13 students (6 boys, 7 girls); Grade 11: 11 students (7 boys, 4 girls); Grade 12: 9 students (4 boys, 5 girls). 80% of students are Baptist, United Methodist Church.

Faculty School total: 15. In upper school: 3 men, 5 women; 2 have advanced degrees.

Subjects Offered Advanced math, algebra, American government, American history, American literature, anatomy, art history, Bible, biology, botany, chemistry, computer applications, data processing, earth science, economics, English, English literature, environmental science, general math, geography, geometry, government, health, history, journalism, keyboarding, language arts, physical education, physical science, physics, pre-algebra, science, social studies, Spanish, state history, statistics, trigonometry, U.S. government, U.S. history, Web site design, weight training, world geography, world history, yearbook.

Special Academic Programs International Baccalaureate program; honors section; independent study.

College Admission Counseling 7 students graduated in 2012; 4 went to college, including University of Georgia; Valdosta State University. Other: 2 went to work, 1 had other specific plans.
Student Life Upper grades have specified standards of dress, student council, honor system. Discipline rests primarily with faculty.
Summer Programs Remediation programs offered; session focuses on make-up work; held on campus; accepts boys and girls; open to students from other schools. 10 students usually enrolled. 2013 schedule: June 7 to July 7.
Tuition and Aid Day student tuition: $4400. Tuition installment plan (monthly payment plans, individually arranged payment plans). Tuition reduction for siblings available.
Admissions Traditional secondary-level entrance grade is 9. ACT, any standardized test, OLSAT, Stanford Achievement Test, Otis-Lennon Ability or Stanford Achievement Test, PSAT or SAT required. Deadline for receipt of application materials: none. Application fee required: $100. Interview required.
Athletics Interscholastic: baseball (boys), basketball (b,g), cheering (g), football (b), golf (b,g), running (b,g), softball (g), tennis (b,g), track and field (b,g), volleyball (g), weight lifting (b,g); coed interscholastic: physical fitness. 1 PE instructor, 5 coaches.
Computers Computers are regularly used in keyboarding, Web site design, yearbook classes. Computer resources include Internet access.
Contact Mrs. Kaye Smith, Secretary. 706-444-6470. Fax: 706-444-6933. E-mail: johnhancockad@bellsouth.net. Web site: www.johnhancockacademy.com/

JOHN PAUL II CATHOLIC HIGH SCHOOL

5100 Terrebone Drive
Tallahassee, Florida 32311-7848

Head of School: Sr. Ellen Cronan

General Information Coeducational day college-preparatory and religious studies school, affiliated with Roman Catholic Church. Grades 9–12. Founded: 2001. Setting: suburban. 37-acre campus. 3 buildings on campus. Approved or accredited by Academy of Orton-Gillingham Practitioners and Educators, Accreditation Commission of the Texas Association of Baptist Schools, American Association of Christian Schools, Arizona Association of Independent Schools, Association for Experiential Education, Association of American Schools in South America, Association of Christian Schools International, Association of Colorado Independent Schools, Association of Independent Maryland Schools, Association of Independent Schools and Colleges of Alberta, Association of Independent Schools in New England, Association of Independent Schools of Florida, Association of Independent Schools of Greater Washington, Southern Association of Colleges and Schools, and Florida Department of Education. Total enrollment: 119. Upper school average class size: 12. Upper school faculty-student ratio: 1:8. There are 180 required school days per year for Upper School students. Upper School students typically attend 5 days per week. The average school day consists of 7 hours.
Upper School Student Profile Grade 9: 30 students (11 boys, 19 girls); Grade 10: 20 students (8 boys, 12 girls); Grade 11: 32 students (14 boys, 18 girls); Grade 12: 37 students (22 boys, 15 girls). 83% of students are Roman Catholic.
Faculty School total: 16. In upper school: 5 men, 11 women; 14 have advanced degrees.
Subjects Offered All academic, Bible, English language and composition-AP, English literature and composition-AP, history of the Catholic Church, Latin, music, Spanish, Spanish language-AP, strings.
Graduation Requirements Algebra, American government, American history, biology, Christian doctrine, economics, English, fitness, foreign language, health.
Special Academic Programs 6 Advanced Placement exams for which test preparation is offered; honors section; study at local college for college credit.
College Admission Counseling 21 students graduated in 2011; all went to college, including Florida State University; Georgia Institute of Technology; Mount St. Mary's University; Tallahassee Community College; University of South Florida. Mean SAT critical reading: 558, mean SAT math: 544, mean SAT writing: 535. 43% scored over 600 on SAT critical reading, 57% scored over 600 on SAT math.
Student Life Upper grades have uniform requirement, student council. Discipline rests primarily with faculty. Attendance at religious services is required.
Tuition and Aid Day student tuition: $8700. Tuition installment plan (FACTS Tuition Payment Plan). Need-based scholarship grants available. In 2011–12, 17% of upper-school students received aid. Total amount of financial aid awarded in 2011–12: $40,000.
Admissions Traditional secondary-level entrance grade is 9. Explore, High School Placement Test or High School Placement Test (closed version) from Scholastic Testing Service required. Deadline for receipt of application materials: none. Application fee required: $200. On-campus interview recommended.
Athletics Interscholastic: baseball (boys), basketball (b,g), cheering (g), cross-country running (b,g), football (b), golf (b), soccer (b,g), tennis (b,g), volleyball (g). 1 PE instructor, 8 coaches, 1 athletic trainer.
Computers Computers are regularly used in drawing and design, technology classes. Computer network features include on-campus library services, Internet access, Internet filtering or blocking technology. Student e-mail accounts are available to students. Students grades are available online. The school has a published electronic and media policy.
Contact Mrs. Sharon Strohl, Office Administrator. 850-201-5744. Fax: 850-205-3299. E-mail: sstrohl@jpiichs.org. Web site: www.jpiichs.org

JOHN T. MORGAN ACADEMY

2901 West Dallas Avenue
PO Box 2650
Selma, Alabama 36702-2650

Head of School: Mr. Randy Skipper

General Information Coeducational day college-preparatory school. Grades K–12. Founded: 1965. Setting: small town. 5 buildings on campus. Approved or accredited by Southern Association of Colleges and Schools. Upper school average class size: 22. Upper school faculty-student ratio: 1:22. There are 178 required school days per year for Upper School students. Upper School students typically attend 5 days per week. The average school day consists of 6 hours.
Faculty School total: 36. In upper school: 5 men, 14 women; 4 have advanced degrees.
Subjects Offered World history.
Special Academic Programs Honors section.
College Admission Counseling 48 students graduated in 2011; all went to college, including The University of Alabama. Median composite ACT: 22.
Student Life Upper grades have uniform requirement, student council, honor system. Discipline rests primarily with faculty.
Tuition and Aid Day student tuition: $310. Tuition installment plan (monthly payment plans).
Admissions Traditional secondary-level entrance grade is 9. ACT required. Application fee required: $185. Interview required.
Athletics Interscholastic: baseball (boys), basketball (b,g), cheering (g), fitness (b,g), fitness walking (b,g), flag football (b,g), football (b), golf (b,g), physical fitness (b,g), running (b,g), scooter football (b), soccer (b,g), softball (g), strength & conditioning (b,g), tennis (b,g), track and field (b,g), volleyball (g), walking (b,g), weight lifting (b), weight training (b), whiffle ball (b,g), yoga (g); intramural: basketball (b,g), cooperative games (b,g), jogging (b,g), kickball (b,g), soccer (b,g), softball (g), tennis (b,g), touch football (b,g); coed interscholastic: golf, whiffle ball; coed intramural: cooperative games, jogging, jump rope, kickball. 2 PE instructors, 5 coaches.
Computers Computers are regularly used in computer applications classes. Computer resources include on-campus library services, Internet access, Internet filtering or blocking technology. Students grades are available online.
Contact Mrs. Tina P. Cox, Secretary. 334-375-1044. Fax: 334-875-4465. E-mail: tcox@morganacademy.com. Web site:

JOSEPHINUM ACADEMY

1501 North Oakley Boulevard
Chicago, Illinois 60622

Head of School: Mrs. Lourdes Weber

General Information Girls' day college-preparatory, arts, religious studies, and technology school, affiliated with Roman Catholic Church. Grades 9–12. Founded: 1890. Setting: urban. 2-acre campus. 1 building on campus. Approved or accredited by National Catholic Education Association, Network of Sacred Heart Schools, North Central Association of Colleges and Schools, and Illinois Department of Education. Endowment: $1.5 million. Total enrollment: 187. Upper school average class size: 18. Upper school faculty-student ratio: 1:9. There are 176 required school days per year for Upper School students. Upper School students typically attend 5 days per week. The average school day consists of 7 hours and 30 minutes.
Upper School Student Profile Grade 9: 57 students (57 girls); Grade 10: 59 students (59 girls); Grade 11: 39 students (39 girls); Grade 12: 32 students (32 girls). 50% of students are Roman Catholic.
Faculty School total: 18. In upper school: 4 men, 14 women; 11 have advanced degrees.
Subjects Offered ACT preparation, acting, advanced biology, advanced chemistry, Advanced Placement courses, algebra, American literature, applied arts, art, athletics, basketball, biology, biology-AP, business education, calculus-AP, campus ministry, Catholic belief and practice, chemistry, Christian studies, civics, college admission preparation, college awareness, college counseling, college placement, college planning, community garden, community service, computer education, constitutional history of U.S., consumer economics, consumer education, current events, drama, drama performance, electives, English, English literature-AP, English-AP, environmental science, fitness, foreign language, French, French as a second language, freshman seminar, geometry, global issues, global studies, health, health and wellness, history of the Americas, honors English, honors geometry, honors U.S. history, honors world history, Life of Christ, literature by women, modern history, moral theology, peer counseling, performing arts, physical education, physical science, physics, pre-calculus, religious studies, research seminar, senior project, senior thesis, Shakespeare, social justice, softball, Spanish, Spanish literature, Spanish-AP, speech, U.S. history, volleyball, water color painting, women's literature, women's studies, world history, world literature, world religions, world religions, writing, yearbook.

Graduation Requirements Algebra, arts and fine arts (art, music, dance, drama), biology, college admission preparation, computer science, consumer education, English, foreign language, health, mathematics, physical education (includes health), religion (includes Bible studies and theology), science, social sciences, social studies (includes history), technology, Senior Capstone Project, portfolio projects. Community service is required.
Special Academic Programs 4 Advanced Placement exams for which test preparation is offered; honors section; independent study; term-away projects; domestic exchange program (with Network of Sacred Heart Schools); study abroad; remedial reading and/or remedial writing; remedial math; ESL (5 students enrolled).
College Admission Counseling 30 students graduated in 2012; all went to college, including Carleton College; DePaul University; Grand Valley State University; Loyola University Chicago; University of Illinois at Chicago; University of Illinois at Urbana–Champaign.
Student Life Upper grades have uniform requirement, student council, honor system. Discipline rests primarily with faculty. Attendance at religious services is required.
Summer Programs Remediation, enrichment, sports, art/fine arts, computer instruction programs offered; session focuses on community service and educational advancement; held both on and off campus; held at Sacred Heart schools; accepts girls; open to students from other schools. 40 students usually enrolled.
Tuition and Aid Day student tuition: $4700. Tuition installment plan (SMART Tuition Payment Plan, monthly payment plans, individually arranged payment plans). Tuition reduction for siblings, merit scholarship grants, need-based scholarship grants available. In 2012–13, 89% of upper-school students received aid.
Admissions Traditional secondary-level entrance grade is 9. Catholic High School Entrance Examination required. Deadline for receipt of application materials: none. No application fee required. Interview recommended.
Athletics Interscholastic: basketball, soccer, softball, volleyball; intramural: fitness, football, track and field. 2 PE instructors, 5 coaches.
Computers Computers are regularly used in all academic classes. Computer network features include on-campus library services, online commercial services, Internet access, wireless campus network, Internet filtering or blocking technology, all students provided with NetBook computers or iPads. Campus intranet, student e-mail accounts, and computer access in designated common areas are available to students. Students grades are available online. The school has a published electronic and media policy.
Contact Mrs. Alex Gonzalez, Director of Admissions. 773-276-1261 Ext. 234. Fax: 773-292-3963. E-mail: alex.gonzalez@josephinum.org. Web site: www.josephinum.org

THE JOURNEYS SCHOOL OF TETON SCIENCE SCHOOL

700 Coyote Canyon Road
Jackson, Wyoming 83001

Head of School: Mr. Nate McClennen

General Information Coeducational day college-preparatory school. Grades K–12. Founded: 2001. Setting: rural. 800-acre campus. 1 building on campus. Approved or accredited by International Baccalaureate Organization, Pacific Northwest Association of Independent Schools, and Wyoming Department of Education. Member of National Association of Independent Schools. Endowment: $12 million. Total enrollment: 152. Upper school average class size: 10. Upper school faculty-student ratio: 1:7. There are 175 required school days per year for Upper School students. Upper School students typically attend 5 days per week. The average school day consists of 7 hours and 45 minutes.
Upper School Student Profile Grade 6: 13 students (10 boys, 3 girls); Grade 7: 16 students (6 boys, 10 girls); Grade 8: 12 students (5 boys, 7 girls); Grade 9: 8 students (1 boy, 7 girls); Grade 10: 12 students (7 boys, 5 girls); Grade 11: 13 students (6 boys, 7 girls); Grade 12: 9 students (9 girls).
Faculty In upper school: 8 men, 13 women; 13 have advanced degrees.
Subjects Offered International Baccalaureate courses.
Graduation Requirements International Baccalaureate courses.
Special Academic Programs International Baccalaureate program; independent study; academic accommodation for the gifted.
College Admission Counseling 8 students graduated in 2012; all went to college.
Student Life Upper grades have student council. Discipline rests equally with students and faculty.
Tuition and Aid Day student tuition: $18,900. Tuition installment plan (monthly payment plans, individually arranged payment plans). Need-based scholarship grants available. In 2012–13, 43% of upper-school students received aid. Total amount of financial aid awarded in 2012–13: $240,150.
Admissions Deadline for receipt of application materials: none. Application fee required: $50. Interview required.
Athletics Interscholastic: aerobics/dance (girls), alpine skiing (b,g), aquatics (g), baseball (b), basketball (b,g), cheering (g), cross-country running (b,g), dance (g), football (b), gymnastics (g), ice hockey (b,g), indoor track & field (g), martial arts (b,g), nordic skiing (b,g), soccer (b,g), swimming and diving (g), tennis (b,g), volleyball (g); intramural: dressage (g), equestrian sports (g), freestyle skiing (b,g), horseback riding (g), lacrosse (b,g), snowboarding (b,g); coed interscholastic: backpacking, skiing (cross-country), skiing (downhill), track and field; coed intramural: climbing, soccer, wall climbing. 1 PE instructor.
Computers Computer network features include Internet access, wireless campus network, Internet filtering or blocking technology. Campus intranet and student e-mail accounts are available to students. Students grades are available online.
Contact Tammie VanHolland, Director of Admissions. 307-734-3710. Fax: 307-733-3340. E-mail: tammie.vanholland@journeysschool.org. Web site: www.tetonscience.org/index.cfm?id=journeys_home

THE JUDGE ROTENBERG EDUCATIONAL CENTER

Canton, Massachusetts
See Special Needs Schools section.

JUNIPERO SERRA HIGH SCHOOL

14830 South Van Ness Avenue
Gardena, California 90249

Head of School: Mr. Michael Wagner, JD

General Information Coeducational day college-preparatory, arts, and religious studies school, affiliated with Roman Catholic Church. Grades 9–12. Founded: 1950. Setting: urban. 24-acre campus. 10 buildings on campus. Approved or accredited by California Association of Independent Schools, National Catholic Education Association, Western Association of Schools and Colleges, Western Catholic Education Association, and California Department of Education. Member of Secondary School Admission Test Board. Endowment: $200,000. Total enrollment: 686. Upper school average class size: 26. Upper school faculty-student ratio: 1:25. There are 180 required school days per year for Upper School students. Upper School students typically attend 5 days per week. The average school day consists of 5 hours and 45 minutes.
Upper School Student Profile Grade 9: 210 students (146 boys, 64 girls); Grade 10: 191 students (120 boys, 71 girls); Grade 11: 133 students (76 boys, 57 girls); Grade 12: 152 students (87 boys, 65 girls). 45% of students are Roman Catholic.
Faculty School total: 36. In upper school: 22 men, 14 women; 25 have advanced degrees.
Subjects Offered Acting, advanced math, advanced studio art-AP, algebra, American history-AP, American literature, anatomy, biology, biology-AP, calculus-AP, chemistry, choir, computer science, drama, economics, English, English literature, English literature-AP, fine arts, geometry, government, journalism, mathematics, music, photography, physical education, physics, physiology, pre-calculus, religion, science, social studies, Spanish, Spanish-AP, theater, theology, U.S. history, world history, writing.
Graduation Requirements Arts and fine arts (art, music, dance, drama), computer science, English, foreign language, mathematics, physical education (includes health), religion (includes Bible studies and theology), science, social studies (includes history), completion of an SAT or ACT test preperation program, completion of 100 service hours, school does not accept D and F grades as passing. Community service is required.
Special Academic Programs Advanced Placement exam preparation; honors section; study at local college for college credit; academic accommodation for the gifted; remedial reading and/or remedial writing; remedial math.
College Admission Counseling 147 students graduated in 2011; all went to college, including California State University; El Camino College; Loyola Marymount University; University of California, Los Angeles. Mean SAT critical reading: 464, mean SAT math: 452, mean SAT writing: 455, mean composite ACT: 21. 10% scored over 600 on SAT critical reading, 10% scored over 600 on SAT math, 10% scored over 600 on SAT writing, 7% scored over 26 on composite ACT.
Student Life Upper grades have uniform requirement, student council, honor system. Discipline rests primarily with faculty. Attendance at religious services is required.
Tuition and Aid Day student tuition: $6400. Tuition installment plan (FACTS Tuition Payment Plan). Tuition reduction for siblings, merit scholarship grants, need-based scholarship grants available. In 2011–12, 60% of upper-school students received aid; total upper-school merit-scholarship money awarded: $35,000. Total amount of financial aid awarded in 2011–12: $500,000.
Admissions Traditional secondary-level entrance grade is 9. For fall 2011, 400 students applied for upper-level admission, 300 were accepted, 210 enrolled. High School Placement Test required. Deadline for receipt of application materials: none. Application fee required: $75. On-campus interview required.
Athletics Interscholastic: baseball (boys), basketball (b,g), cheering (g), cross-country running (b,g), football (b), golf (b,g), soccer (b,g), softball (g), tennis (b,g), track and field (b,g), volleyball (b,g), winter soccer (b,g), wrestling (b); coed interscholastic: swimming and diving, track and field; coed intramural: basketball, volleyball. 2 PE instructors, 23 coaches, 2 athletic trainers.
Computers Computers are regularly used in art, English, foreign language, history, mathematics, music, science classes. Computer network features include on-campus library services, Internet access, Internet filtering or blocking technology. Computer

access in designated common areas is available to students. Students grades are available online. The school has a published electronic and media policy.

Contact Mr. John Posatko, Admissions Director. 310-324-6675 Ext. 1015. Fax: 310-352-4953. E-mail: jposatko@la-serrahs.org. Web site: www.serrahighschool.com

JUNIPERO SERRA HIGH SCHOOL

451 West 20th Avenue
San Mateo, California 94403-1385

Head of School: Lars Lund

General Information Boys' day college-preparatory, arts, business, religious studies, and technology school, affiliated with Roman Catholic Church. Grades 9–12. Founded: 1944. Setting: suburban. Nearest major city is San Francisco. 13-acre campus. 9 buildings on campus. Approved or accredited by Western Association of Schools and Colleges. Endowment: $2.3 million. Total enrollment: 900. Upper school average class size: 26. Upper school faculty-student ratio: 1:27. There are 180 required school days per year for Upper School students. Upper School students typically attend 5 days per week. The average school day consists of 6 hours and 45 minutes.

Upper School Student Profile Grade 9: 240 students (240 boys); Grade 10: 228 students (228 boys); Grade 11: 201 students (201 boys); Grade 12: 218 students (218 boys). 70% of students are Roman Catholic.

Faculty School total: 74. In upper school: 58 men, 16 women; 35 have advanced degrees.

Subjects Offered Algebra, American history, American history-AP, American literature, architectural drawing, architecture, art, art history-AP, astronomy, band, biology, biology-AP, business, calculus, calculus-AP, chemistry, college admission preparation, college counseling, college planning, community service, comparative government and politics-AP, computer programming, computer science, creative writing, drama, driver education, earth science, economics, electronics, English, English literature, English literature and composition-AP, English literature-AP, ethics, European history, fine arts, French, French language-AP, geography, geology, geometry, German, government and politics-AP, government/civics, grammar, graphic design, health, history, instrumental music, journalism, keyboarding, library skills, literature and composition-AP, Mandarin, mathematics, music, photography, physical education, physics, religion, science, social sciences, social studies, Spanish, Spanish language-AP, speech, statistics, student government, theater, trigonometry, U.S. government and politics-AP, U.S. history-AP, world history, writing.

Graduation Requirements Arts and fine arts (art, music, dance, drama), computer science, English, foreign language, literature, mathematics, physical education (includes health), political systems, religion (includes Bible studies and theology), science, social sciences, social studies (includes history), 80 hours of community service. Community service is required.

Special Academic Programs Advanced Placement exam preparation; honors section; study at local college for college credit.

College Admission Counseling 225 students graduated in 2012; 223 went to college, including College of San Mateo; San Francisco State University; San Jose State University; Santa Clara University; Sonoma State University; University of California, Berkeley. Other: 1 entered military service, 1 entered a postgraduate year.

Student Life Upper grades have specified standards of dress, student council, honor system. Discipline rests primarily with faculty. Attendance at religious services is required.

Summer Programs Remediation, enrichment, advancement, sports, art/fine arts, computer instruction programs offered; session focuses on enrichment and remediation; held on campus; accepts boys and girls; open to students from other schools. 460 students usually enrolled. 2013 schedule: June 17 to July 19. Application deadline: June 14.

Tuition and Aid Day student tuition: $17,120. Tuition installment plan (monthly payment plans, semester payment plan, annual payment plan, direct debit plan). Merit scholarship grants, need-based scholarship grants available. In 2012–13, 35% of upper-school students received aid; total upper-school merit-scholarship money awarded: $55,000. Total amount of financial aid awarded in 2012–13: $2,100,000.

Admissions Traditional secondary-level entrance grade is 9. For fall 2012, 450 students applied for upper-level admission, 320 were accepted, 240 enrolled. High School Placement Test required. Deadline for receipt of application materials: January 10. Application fee required: $75. On-campus interview required.

Athletics Interscholastic: baseball, basketball, crew, cross-country running, diving, football, golf, lacrosse, rowing, soccer, swimming and diving, tennis, track and field, volleyball, water polo, wrestling; intramural: basketball, bicycling, bowling, fishing, fitness, mountain biking, physical training, rock climbing, soccer, softball, strength & conditioning, surfing, touch football, weight lifting. 2 PE instructors, 48 coaches, 1 athletic trainer.

Computers Computers are regularly used in all academic classes. Computer network features include on-campus library services, Internet access, wireless campus network, Internet filtering or blocking technology. Campus intranet and student e-mail accounts are available to students. Students grades are available online. The school has a published electronic and media policy.

Contact Randy Vogel, Director of Admissions. 650-345-8242. Fax: 650-573-6638. E-mail: rvogel@serrahs.com. Web site: www.serrahs.com

KALAMAZOO CHRISTIAN HIGH SCHOOL

2121 Stadium Drive
Kalamazoo, Michigan 49008-1692

Head of School: Mr. Bartel James Huizenga

General Information Coeducational day college-preparatory, general academic, arts, business, vocational, religious studies, bilingual studies, and technology school, affiliated with Christian Reformed Church, Reformed Church in America. Grades 9–12. Founded: 1877. Setting: urban. 3-acre campus. 1 building on campus. Approved or accredited by Christian Schools International, North Central Association of Colleges and Schools, and Michigan Department of Education. Endowment: $1 million. Total enrollment: 810. Upper school average class size: 22. Upper school faculty-student ratio: 1:12. There are 172 required school days per year for Upper School students. Upper School students typically attend 5 days per week. The average school day consists of 6 hours and 45 minutes.

Upper School Student Profile 46% of students are members of Christian Reformed Church, Reformed Church in America.

Faculty School total: 20. In upper school: 14 men, 6 women; 10 have advanced degrees.

Graduation Requirements 50 hours of community service.

Special Academic Programs Advanced Placement exam preparation; honors section; study at local college for college credit.

College Admission Counseling 64 students graduated in 2012; 62 went to college, including Calvin College; Grand Valley State University; Hope College; University of Michigan; Western Michigan University. Other: 2 entered military service. Median composite ACT: 24.

Student Life Upper grades have specified standards of dress, student council, honor system. Discipline rests primarily with faculty. Attendance at religious services is required.

Tuition and Aid Day student tuition: $8070. Tuition installment plan (FACTS Tuition Payment Plan, monthly payment plans, individually arranged payment plans). Tuition reduction for siblings, need-based scholarship grants available. In 2012–13, 50% of upper-school students received aid.

Admissions Traditional secondary-level entrance grade is 9. Deadline for receipt of application materials: none. Application fee required: $100. Interview required.

Athletics Interscholastic: baseball (boys), basketball (b,g), bowling (b,g), cheering (g), cross-country running (b,g), football (b), golf (b), hockey (b), physical fitness (b,g), soccer (b,g), softball (g), strength & conditioning (b,g), tennis (b,g), track and field (b,g), volleyball (g), weight lifting (b,g), weight training (b,g). 2 PE instructors, 32 coaches, 1 athletic trainer.

Computers Computers are regularly used in accounting, business, business applications, business skills, data processing, graphic arts, graphic design, keyboarding, lab/keyboard classes. Computer network features include on-campus library services, online commercial services, Internet access.

Contact Mr. Bartel James Huizenga, Principal. 269-381-2250 Ext. 220. Fax: 269-381-0319. E-mail: bhuizenga@kcsa.org. Web site: www.kcsa.org

THE KARAFIN SCHOOL

Mount Kisco, New York
See Special Needs Schools section.

KAUAI CHRISTIAN ACADEMY

PO Box 1121
4000 Kilauea Road
Kilauea, Hawaii 96754

Head of School: Adm. Daniel A. Moore

General Information Coeducational day college-preparatory, general academic, arts, religious studies, bilingual studies, and technology school, affiliated with Protestant-Evangelical faith, Christian faith. Grades PS–12. Founded: 1973. Setting: rural. Nearest major city is Lihue. 10-acre campus. 3 buildings on campus. Approved or accredited by American Association of Christian Schools and Hawaii Department of Education. Total enrollment: 79. Upper school average class size: 10. Upper school faculty-student ratio: 1:8. There are 171 required school days per year for Upper School students. Upper School students typically attend 5 days per week. The average school day consists of 6 hours and 30 minutes.

Upper School Student Profile Grade 7: 11 students (3 boys, 8 girls); Grade 8: 8 students (6 boys, 2 girls); Grade 9: 4 students (4 girls); Grade 11: 5 students (2 boys, 3 girls); Grade 12: 2 students (2 boys). 75% of students are Protestant-Evangelical faith, Christian faith.

Faculty School total: 9. In upper school: 5 men, 4 women; 3 have advanced degrees.

Subjects Offered Advanced math, agriculture, algebra, American government, American history, ancient history, art, arts, athletics, Basic programming, Bible, Bible as literature, Bible studies, biology, botany, calculus, chemistry, Christian and Hebrew scripture, economics, economics-AP, electives, English, English literature, English literature and composition-AP, family living, geography, geometry, government, history, Latin, music, physical science, pre-algebra, speech, world geography, world history.

Graduation Requirements Arts and fine arts (art, music, dance, drama), computer science, English, Latin, mathematics, science, social studies (includes history), speech, one year of Bible for each year enrolled.

Special Academic Programs Accelerated programs; independent study; remedial reading and/or remedial writing; remedial math.

College Admission Counseling 3 students graduated in 2011; 2 went to college, including Columbia International University; Montana State University. Other: 1 went to work. Median SAT critical reading: 570, median SAT math: 530, median SAT writing: 550, median combined SAT: 1705, median composite ACT: 24. 50% scored over 600 on SAT critical reading, 50% scored over 600 on SAT writing.

Student Life Upper grades have specified standards of dress, honor system. Discipline rests primarily with faculty.

Tuition and Aid Day student tuition: $5875. Tuition installment plan (monthly payment plans, 10-month payment plan). Tuition reduction for siblings, need-based scholarship grants, paying campus jobs available. In 2011–12, 40% of upper-school students received aid. Total amount of financial aid awarded in 2011–12: $40,000.

Admissions Traditional secondary-level entrance grade is 7. For fall 2011, 12 students applied for upper-level admission, 12 were accepted, 12 enrolled. OLSAT, Stanford Achievement Test or Stanford Achievement Test, Otis-Lennon School Ability Test required. Deadline for receipt of application materials: none. Application fee required: $55. Interview recommended.

Computers Computers are regularly used in computer applications, typing classes. Computer network features include Internet access, wireless campus network, Internet filtering or blocking technology. Campus intranet and computer access in designated common areas are available to students.

Contact Adm. Daniel A. Moore, Principal. 808-828-0047. Fax: 808-828-1850. E-mail: dmoore@kcaschool.net. Web site: www.kcaschool.net

KEITH COUNTRY DAY SCHOOL

1 Jacoby Place
Rockford, Illinois 61107

Head of School: Mr. Alan W. Gibby

General Information Coeducational day college-preparatory, arts, and technology school. Grades PK–12. Founded: 1916. Setting: suburban. Nearest major city is Chicago. 15-acre campus. 1 building on campus. Approved or accredited by Independent Schools Association of the Central States and Illinois Department of Education. Member of National Association of Independent Schools. Endowment: $985,000. Total enrollment: 290. Upper school average class size: 16. Upper school faculty-student ratio: 1:6. There are 176 required school days per year for Upper School students. Upper School students typically attend 5 days per week. The average school day consists of 7 hours and 15 minutes.

Upper School Student Profile Grade 9: 14 students (9 boys, 5 girls); Grade 10: 26 students (12 boys, 14 girls); Grade 11: 28 students (17 boys, 11 girls); Grade 12: 19 students (8 boys, 11 girls).

Faculty School total: 44. In upper school: 10 men, 17 women; 24 have advanced degrees.

Subjects Offered Advanced math, Advanced Placement courses, algebra, American history, American literature, Ancient Greek, art, arts, Bible as literature, biology, biology-AP, calculus, ceramics, chemistry, chemistry-AP, college counseling, community service, computer science, design, drama, drawing, economics, English, English literature, English-AP, environmental science, European history, fine arts, French, geography, geometry, government/civics, health, history, Latin, mathematics, music, painting, photography, physical education, physics, pre-calculus, research skills, science, social studies, speech, study skills, theater, trigonometry, world history, world literature.

Graduation Requirements Arts and fine arts (art, music, dance, drama), college counseling, computer science, English, foreign language, mathematics, physical education (includes health), research skills, science, senior project, social studies (includes history), speech, 90 hours of community service.

Special Academic Programs Advanced Placement exam preparation; honors section; study at local college for college credit; study abroad; academic accommodation for the gifted, the musically talented, and the artistically talented; remedial reading and/or remedial writing; programs in general development for dyslexic students.

College Admission Counseling 32 students graduated in 2011; 31 went to college, including Knox College; Purdue University; Saint Louis University; University of Chicago; University of Illinois at Urbana–Champaign; Yale University. Other: 1 went to work. Median SAT critical reading: 621, median SAT math: 634, median SAT writing: 589, median combined SAT: 1844, median composite ACT: 26. 60% scored over 600 on SAT critical reading, 60% scored over 600 on SAT math, 70% scored over 600 on SAT writing, 70% scored over 1800 on combined SAT, 73% scored over 26 on composite ACT.

Student Life Upper grades have specified standards of dress, student council, honor system. Discipline rests equally with students and faculty.

Tuition and Aid Day student tuition: $14,200. Tuition installment plan (monthly payment plans, school's own payment plan). Tuition reduction for siblings, merit scholarship grants, need-based scholarship grants available. In 2011–12, 51% of upper-school students received aid; total upper-school merit-scholarship money awarded: $107,900. Total amount of financial aid awarded in 2011–12: $342,664.

Admissions Traditional secondary-level entrance grade is 9. For fall 2011, 25 students applied for upper-level admission, 24 were accepted, 9 enrolled. ERB, placement test and school's own exam required. Deadline for receipt of application materials: none. Application fee required: $50. On-campus interview required.

Athletics Interscholastic: basketball (boys, girls), physical fitness (b,g), soccer (b,g), tennis (b,g), volleyball (g); coed interscholastic: cross-country running, golf, table tennis; coed intramural: crew. 2 PE instructors, 6 coaches.

Computers Computers are regularly used in English, foreign language, history, mathematics, science, social studies, Spanish, writing, yearbook classes. Computer network features include on-campus library services, Internet access, wireless campus network, Internet filtering or blocking technology. Student e-mail accounts are available to students. Students grades are available online. The school has a published electronic and media policy.

Contact Marcia Aramovich, Director of Admissions. 815-399-8850 Ext. 144. Fax: 815-399-2470. E-mail: marcia.aramovich@keithschool.net. Web site: www.keithschool.com

KENT DENVER SCHOOL

4000 East Quincy Avenue
Englewood, Colorado 80113

Head of School: Todd Horn

General Information Coeducational day college-preparatory and arts school. Grades 6–12. Founded: 1922. Setting: suburban. Nearest major city is Denver. 220-acre campus. 6 buildings on campus. Approved or accredited by Association of Colorado Independent Schools and Colorado Department of Education. Member of National Association of Independent Schools and Secondary School Admission Test Board. Endowment: $43 million. Total enrollment: 672. Upper school average class size: 15. Upper school faculty-student ratio: 1:7. There are 172 required school days per year for Upper School students. Upper School students typically attend 5 days per week. The average school day consists of 7 hours.

Upper School Student Profile Grade 9: 122 students (61 boys, 61 girls); Grade 10: 119 students (56 boys, 63 girls); Grade 11: 103 students (53 boys, 50 girls); Grade 12: 105 students (55 boys, 50 girls).

Faculty School total: 86. In upper school: 61 have advanced degrees.

Subjects Offered African-American literature, algebra, American history, American history-AP, American literature, ancient history, anthropology, art, art history, art history-AP, Asian studies, biology, calculus, calculus-AP, career education internship, ceramics, chemistry, choir, clayworking, college counseling, community service, computer math, computer programming, computer programming-AP, computer science, creative writing, drama, earth science, economics, English, English literature, English literature and composition-AP, environmental science, European history, European history-AP, fine arts, French, French language-AP, French literature-AP, French-AP, general science, genetics, geography, geology, geometry, government/civics, grammar, guitar, health and wellness, history, history-AP, human development, independent study, jazz band, Latin, Mandarin, mathematics, music, music performance, mythology, photography, physical education, physics, pre-calculus, science, social studies, Spanish, Spanish language-AP, Spanish literature-AP, statistics, studio art-AP, theater, Web site design, world history, world literature, writing.

Graduation Requirements Arts and fine arts (art, music, dance, drama), English, foreign language, history, internship, mathematics, participation in sports, science. Community service is required.

Special Academic Programs 15 Advanced Placement exams for which test preparation is offered; honors section; independent study; programs in general development for dyslexic students.

College Admission Counseling 109 students graduated in 2012; all went to college, including Bowdoin College; Miami University; Southern Methodist University; Stanford University; The Colorado College; University of Colorado Boulder. Mean SAT critical reading: 628, mean SAT math: 639, mean SAT writing: 633, mean composite ACT: 28.

Student Life Upper grades have specified standards of dress, student council. Discipline rests equally with students and faculty.

Summer Programs Enrichment, sports, art/fine arts, computer instruction programs offered; session focuses on skill-building, arts, enrichment, athletics; held on campus; accepts boys and girls; open to students from other schools. 1,200 students usually enrolled. 2013 schedule: June 10 to July 26. Application deadline: none.

Tuition and Aid Day student tuition: $21,960. Tuition installment plan (Insured Tuition Payment Plan, Key Tuition Payment Plan, monthly payment plans). Need-based scholarship grants available. In 2012–13, 22% of upper-school students received aid. Total amount of financial aid awarded in 2012–13: $2,000,000.

Admissions Traditional secondary-level entrance grade is 9. For fall 2012, 177 students applied for upper-level admission, 80 were accepted, 55 enrolled. ISEE or SSAT required. Deadline for receipt of application materials: January 31. Application fee required: $60. Interview required.

Athletics Interscholastic: baseball (boys), basketball (b,g), cross-country running (b,g), diving (g), field hockey (g), football (b), golf (b,g), hockey (b), ice hockey (b), lacrosse (b,g), soccer (b,g), swimming and diving (g), tennis (b,g), track and field (b,g), volleyball (g); coed interscholastic: independent competitive sports, outdoor education, yoga; coed intramural: aerobics/Nautilus, bicycling, fitness, mountain biking, outdoor adventure, outdoor education, outdoor skills, physical fitness, physical training, strength & conditioning, weight lifting. 3 PE instructors, 17 coaches, 1 athletic trainer.

Computers Computers are regularly used in art, English, foreign language, history, mathematics, science classes. Computer network features include on-campus library services, online commercial services, Internet access, wireless campus network, Internet filtering or blocking technology. Student e-mail accounts and computer access in designated common areas are available to students. Students grades are available online. The school has a published electronic and media policy.

Contact Susan Green, Admission Office Manager. 303-770-7660 Ext. 237. Fax: 303-770-1398. E-mail: sgreen@kentdenver.org. Web site: www.kentdenver.org

KENT PLACE SCHOOL

42 Norwood Avenue

Summit, New Jersey 07902-0308

Head of School: Mrs. Susan C. Bosland

General Information Coeducational day (boys' only in lower grades) college-preparatory school. Boys grades N–PK, girls grades N–12. Founded: 1894. Setting: suburban. Nearest major city is New York, NY. 25-acre campus. 6 buildings on campus. Approved or accredited by Middle States Association of Colleges and Schools and New Jersey Association of Independent Schools. Member of National Association of Independent Schools and Secondary School Admission Test Board. Endowment: $15 million. Total enrollment: 636. Upper school average class size: 16. Upper school faculty-student ratio: 1:7. There are 167 required school days per year for Upper School students. Upper School students typically attend 5 days per week. The average school day consists of 6 hours and 55 minutes.

Upper School Student Profile Grade 9: 69 students (69 girls); Grade 10: 78 students (78 girls); Grade 11: 67 students (67 girls); Grade 12: 63 students (63 girls).

Faculty School total: 119. In upper school: 7 men, 36 women; 35 have advanced degrees.

Subjects Offered Advanced Placement courses, algebra, American history, American history-AP, American literature, anatomy and physiology, art, art history-AP, biology, biology-AP, calculus, calculus-AP, ceramics, chemistry, chemistry-AP, computer literacy, computer programming-AP, computer science, creative writing, dance, drama, driver education, economics, English, English language-AP, English literature, English literature-AP, environmental science, environmental science-AP, European history, expository writing, fine arts, French, French language-AP, French literature-AP, geometry, government/civics, grammar, health, history, independent study, Latin, Latin-AP, macroeconomics-AP, mathematics, modern European history-AP, music, music theory-AP, photography, physical education, physics, science, social studies, Spanish, Spanish language-AP, Spanish literature-AP, statistics, statistics-AP, theater, trigonometry, world history.

Graduation Requirements Arts and fine arts (art, music, dance, drama), English, foreign language, history, mathematics, physical education (includes health), science.

Special Academic Programs 22 Advanced Placement exams for which test preparation is offered; independent study.

College Admission Counseling 62 students graduated in 2011; all went to college, including Boston College; Colgate University; Cornell University; Princeton University; University of Pennsylvania; Yale University.

Student Life Upper grades have specified standards of dress, student council, honor system. Discipline rests equally with students and faculty.

Tuition and Aid Day student tuition: $32,788. Tuition installment plan (Insured Tuition Payment Plan, Key Tuition Payment Plan, monthly payment plans). Need-based scholarship grants available. In 2011–12, 20% of upper-school students received aid. Total amount of financial aid awarded in 2011–12: $1,299,061.

Admissions Traditional secondary-level entrance grade is 9. ISEE or SSAT required. Deadline for receipt of application materials: January 6. Application fee required: $70. On-campus interview required.

Athletics Interscholastic: basketball, cross-country running, field hockey, indoor track, lacrosse, soccer, softball, swimming and diving, tennis, track and field, volleyball, winter (indoor) track; intramural: dance, fencing, modern dance, physical fitness, squash. 4 PE instructors, 19 coaches, 1 athletic trainer.

Computers Computers are regularly used in all classes. Computer network features include on-campus library services, online commercial services, Internet access, wireless campus network, Internet filtering or blocking technology. Campus intranet, student e-mail accounts, and computer access in designated common areas are available to students. The school has a published electronic and media policy.

Contact Mrs. Julia Wall, Director of Admission and Financial Aid. 908-273-0900 Ext. 254. Fax: 908-273-9390. E-mail: admission@kentplace.org. Web site: www.kentplace.org

KENT SCHOOL

PO Box 2006

Kent, Connecticut 06757

Head of School: Rev. Richardson W. Schell

General Information Coeducational boarding and day college-preparatory, arts, religious studies, technology, and pre-engineering school, affiliated with Episcopal Church. Grades 9–PG. Founded: 1906. Setting: small town. Nearest major city is Hartford. Students are housed in single-sex dormitories. 1,200-acre campus. 17 buildings on campus. Approved or accredited by Association of Independent Schools in New England, Connecticut Association of Independent Schools, National Association of Episcopal Schools, New England Association of Schools and Colleges, New York State Association of Independent Schools, The Association of Boarding Schools, and Connecticut Department of Education. Member of National Association of Independent Schools and Secondary School Admission Test Board. Endowment: $73.5 million. Total enrollment: 565. Upper school average class size: 12. Upper school faculty-student ratio: 1:7.

Upper School Student Profile Grade 9: 77 students (40 boys, 37 girls); Grade 10: 155 students (84 boys, 71 girls); Grade 11: 167 students (79 boys, 88 girls); Grade 12: 157 students (72 boys, 85 girls); Postgraduate: 15 students (1 boy, 14 girls). 90% of students are boarding students. 24% are state residents. 35 states are represented in upper school student body. 28% are international students. International students from Canada, China, Germany, Hong Kong, Republic of Korea, and Thailand; 40 other countries represented in student body.

Faculty School total: 73. In upper school: 43 men, 30 women; 55 have advanced degrees; 66 reside on campus.

Subjects Offered Advanced studio art-AP, African-American history, algebra, American history, American history-AP, American literature, architecture, art, art history-AP, Asian history, astronomy, Bible studies, biology, biology-AP, biotechnology, calculus, calculus-AP, ceramics, chemistry, chemistry-AP, Chinese, classical Greek literature, classical studies, composition-AP, computer math, computer programming, computer science, computer science-AP, digital imaging, drama, ecology, economics, English, English literature, English literature-AP, environmental science-AP, environmental studies, European history, European history-AP, expository writing, fine arts, French, French language-AP, French literature-AP, genetics, geology, geometry, German, German-AP, government and politics-AP, Greek, history, Latin, Latin American history, Latin-AP, law and the legal system, mathematics, meteorology, Middle Eastern history, modern European history-AP, music, music theory-AP, photography, physical education, physics, physics-AP, probability and statistics, psychology-AP, religion, science, sculpture, social studies, Spanish, Spanish language-AP, Spanish literature-AP, statistics-AP, theater, theology, trigonometry, U.S. government and politics-AP, world geography, world history, world literature.

Graduation Requirements Arts and fine arts (art, music, dance, drama), English, foreign language, history, mathematics, music, religion (includes Bible studies and theology), science, U.S. history.

Special Academic Programs 26 Advanced Placement exams for which test preparation is offered; honors section; independent study; academic accommodation for the gifted, the musically talented, and the artistically talented; ESL.

College Admission Counseling 171 students graduated in 2012; all went to college, including Boston University; Carnegie Mellon University; Colgate University; Cornell University; Princeton University; St. Lawrence University.

Student Life Upper grades have specified standards of dress, student council. Discipline rests equally with students and faculty. Attendance at religious services is required.

Tuition and Aid Day student tuition: $39,000; 7-day tuition and room/board: $49,500. Tuition installment plan (Key Tuition Payment Plan, monthly payment plans, individually arranged payment plans). Merit scholarship grants, need-based scholarship grants, need-based loans available. In 2012–13, 43% of upper-school students received aid. Total amount of financial aid awarded in 2012–13: $8,200,000.

Admissions Traditional secondary-level entrance grade is 9. For fall 2012, 1,200 students applied for upper-level admission, 450 were accepted, 190 enrolled. PSAT or SAT for applicants to grade 11 and 12, SSAT or TOEFL required. Deadline for receipt of application materials: January 15. Application fee required: $65. Interview required.

Athletics Interscholastic: baseball (boys), basketball (b,g), crew (b,g), cross-country running (b,g), diving (b,g), field hockey (g), football (b), golf (b,g), hockey (b,g), ice hockey (b,g), lacrosse (b,g), rowing (b,g), soccer (b,g), softball (g), squash (b,g), swimming and diving (b,g), tennis (b,g); intramural: basketball (b), crew (b,g), rowing (b,g); coed interscholastic: crew, dressage, equestrian sports, golf, horseback riding; coed intramural: aerobics/dance, aerobics/Nautilus, alpine skiing, ballet, bicycling, combined training, dance, dressage, equestrian sports, figure skating, fitness, hockey, horseback riding, ice skating, life saving, modern dance, mountain biking, physical fitness, physical training, ropes courses, sailing, skiing (downhill), snowboarding, soccer, squash, strength & conditioning, swimming and diving, tennis, ultimate Frisbee, weight training, yoga. 2 athletic trainers.

Computers Computers are regularly used in all academic, journalism, newspaper, yearbook classes. Computer network features include on-campus library services, online commercial services, Internet access, wireless campus network, students have online storage for schoolwork, Adobe Creative Suite, Autodesk, Mathcad, and Microsoft Office Software for all students. Campus intranet, student e-mail accounts, and computer access in designated common areas are available to students. The school has a published electronic and media policy.

Contact Ms. Kathryn F. Sullivan, Director of Admissions. 860-927-6111. Fax: 860-927-6109. E-mail: admissions@kent-school.edu. Web site: www.kent-school.edu

KENTS HILL SCHOOL

PO Box 257
1614 Main Street, Route 17
Kents Hill, Maine 04349-0257

Head of School: Mr. Jeremy LaCasse

General Information Coeducational boarding and day college-preparatory, arts, technology, environmental studies, and ESL school, affiliated with Methodist Church. Grades 9–PG. Founded: 1824. Setting: rural. Nearest major city is Portland. Students are housed in single-sex dormitories. 400-acre campus. 24 buildings on campus. Approved or accredited by Association of Independent Schools in New England, Independent Schools of Northern New England, New England Association of Schools and Colleges, The Association of Boarding Schools, and Maine Department of Education. Member of National Association of Independent Schools and Secondary School Admission Test Board. Endowment: $4.9 million. Total enrollment: 250. Upper school average class size: 12. Upper school faculty-student ratio: 1:6. Upper School students typically attend 5 days per week. The average school day consists of 7 hours.

Upper School Student Profile Grade 9: 37 students (22 boys, 15 girls); Grade 10: 55 students (33 boys, 22 girls); Grade 11: 74 students (44 boys, 30 girls); Grade 12: 73 students (43 boys, 30 girls); Postgraduate: 10 students (8 boys, 2 girls). 75% of students are boarding students. 33% are state residents. 22 states are represented in upper school student body. 23% are international students. International students from Canada, China, Germany, Mexico, Republic of Korea, and Spain; 10 other countries represented in student body. 3% of students are Methodist.

Faculty School total: 46. In upper school: 26 men, 20 women; 22 have advanced degrees; 40 reside on campus.

Subjects Offered Acting, advanced math, Advanced Placement courses, advanced studio art-AP, African history, African-American literature, algebra, American history, American literature, art, art history, astronomy, biology, biotechnology, calculus, calculus-AP, ceramics, chemistry, college counseling, computer graphics, computer science-AP, computer-aided design, concert choir, creative writing, dance, drama, Eastern religion and philosophy, ecology, economics, English, English literature, environmental science, environmental science-AP, environmental studies, ESL, ethics, ethics and responsibility, European history, filmmaking, fine arts, French, geology, geometry, government/civics, health, history, Holocaust, jazz ensemble, journalism, mathematics, music, photography, physics, psychology, religion, science, Shakespeare, Spanish, theater, U.S. history-AP, Western religions, woodworking, world history, writing.

Graduation Requirements English, environmental studies, foreign language, health, mathematics, science, social studies (includes history), visual and performing arts.

Special Academic Programs 11 Advanced Placement exams for which test preparation is offered; honors section; independent study; term-away projects; study abroad; academic accommodation for the gifted and the artistically talented; programs in general development for dyslexic students; special instructional classes for students with learning differences (through the Learning Skills Center); ESL (24 students enrolled).

College Admission Counseling 76 students graduated in 2012; 69 went to college. Other: 1 entered military service, 5 entered a postgraduate year, 1 had other specific plans.

Student Life Upper grades have specified standards of dress, student council, honor system. Discipline rests equally with students and faculty.

Tuition and Aid Day student tuition: $26,300; 7-day tuition and room/board: $48,300. Tuition installment plan (Insured Tuition Payment Plan, FACTS Tuition Payment Plan, monthly payment plans, individually arranged payment plans, 2-payment plan). Need-based scholarship grants available. In 2012–13, 41% of upper-school students received aid. Total amount of financial aid awarded in 2012–13: $2,200,000.

Admissions Traditional secondary-level entrance grade is 9. Deadline for receipt of application materials: February 1. Application fee required: $50. Interview required.

Athletics Interscholastic: baseball (boys), basketball (b,g), field hockey (g), football (b), ice hockey (b,g), lacrosse (b,g), soccer (b,g), softball (g), tennis (b,g); coed interscholastic: aerobics/dance, alpine skiing, bicycling, cross-country running, fencing, golf, horseback riding, independent competitive sports, mountain biking, skiing (downhill), snowboarding; coed intramural: alpine skiing, backpacking, canoeing/kayaking, dance, equestrian sports, fencing, figure skating, fitness, freestyle skiing, hiking/backpacking, horseback riding, ice skating, kayaking, mountain biking, nordic skiing, outdoor activities, outdoor recreation, physical training, skiing (cross-country), skiing (downhill), snowboarding, snowshoeing, strength & conditioning, tennis. 4 coaches, 1 athletic trainer.

Computers Computers are regularly used in all academic, college planning, desktop publishing, graphic design, media production, newspaper, photojournalism, publications, SAT preparation, video film production, Web site design, yearbook classes. Computer network features include on-campus library services, Internet access, wireless campus network, Internet filtering or blocking technology. Student e-mail accounts and computer access in designated common areas are available to students. Students grades are available online. The school has a published electronic and media policy.

Contact Mrs. Amy Smucker, Director of Admissions. 207-685-4914 Ext. 152. Fax: 207-685-9529. E-mail: asmucker@kentshill.org. Web site: www.kentshill.org

KENTUCKY COUNTRY DAY SCHOOL

4100 Springdale Road
Louisville, Kentucky 40241

Head of School: Mr. Bradley E. Lyman

General Information Coeducational day college-preparatory, arts, technology, honors program, independent study, and advanced programs for academically exceptional students school. Grades JK–12. Founded: 1972. Setting: suburban. 85-acre campus. 3 buildings on campus. Approved or accredited by Independent Schools Association of the Central States. Member of National Association of Independent Schools. Endowment: $10.3 million. Total enrollment: 942. Upper school average class size: 16. Upper school faculty-student ratio: 1:7. There are 170 required school days per year for Upper School students. Upper School students typically attend 5 days per week. The average school day consists of 7 hours and 5 minutes.

Upper School Student Profile Grade 9: 78 students (34 boys, 44 girls); Grade 10: 63 students (30 boys, 33 girls); Grade 11: 66 students (30 boys, 36 girls); Grade 12: 80 students (38 boys, 42 girls).

Faculty School total: 125. In upper school: 22 men, 18 women; 32 have advanced degrees.

Subjects Offered Algebra, American history, American literature, art, biology, calculus, ceramics, chemistry, collage and assemblage, communications, computer math, computer programming, computer science, drama, economics, English, English literature, European history, fine arts, French, geology, geometry, government/civics, history, humanities, instrumental music, Latin, law, mathematics, multimedia, music, physical education, physics, play production, psychology, psychology-AP, science, sculpture, senior internship, senior project, social sciences, social studies, Spanish, Spanish language-AP, speech, stagecraft, statistics, studio art-AP, technical theater, theater, trigonometry, U.S. government and politics-AP, U.S. history-AP.

Graduation Requirements Arts and fine arts (art, music, dance, drama), communications, English, foreign language, mathematics, physical education (includes health), science, social studies (includes history).

Special Academic Programs 20 Advanced Placement exams for which test preparation is offered; honors section; independent study; term-away projects; study abroad; academic accommodation for the gifted, the musically talented, and the artistically talented.

College Admission Counseling 74 students graduated in 2012; all went to college, including Emory University; Indiana University Bloomington; Miami University; University of Kentucky; University of Louisville; University of Michigan. Median SAT critical reading: 570, median SAT math: 600, median SAT writing: 580, median combined SAT: 1750, median composite ACT: 26. 35% scored over 600 on SAT critical reading, 50% scored over 600 on SAT math, 35% scored over 600 on SAT writing, 40% scored over 1800 on combined SAT, 47% scored over 26 on composite ACT.

Student Life Upper grades have specified standards of dress, student council, honor system. Discipline rests equally with students and faculty.

Summer Programs Remediation, enrichment, advancement, sports, art/fine arts, rigorous outdoor training, computer instruction programs offered; session focuses on enrichment; held on campus; accepts boys and girls; open to students from other schools. 200 students usually enrolled. 2013 schedule: June 7 to August 20. Application deadline: none.

Tuition and Aid Day student tuition: $17,800. Tuition installment plan (FACTS Tuition Payment Plan). Merit scholarship grants, need-based scholarship grants available. In 2012–13, 24% of upper-school students received aid; total upper-school merit-scholarship money awarded: $63,610. Total amount of financial aid awarded in 2012–13: $857,180.

Admissions Traditional secondary-level entrance grade is 9. For fall 2012, 40 students applied for upper-level admission, 30 were accepted, 21 enrolled. ERB Reading and Math required. Deadline for receipt of application materials: none. Application fee required: $50. On-campus interview required.

Athletics Interscholastic: baseball (boys), basketball (b,g), cross-country running (b,g), diving (b,g), field hockey (g), football (b), golf (b,g), lacrosse (b,g), soccer (b,g), softball (g), swimming and diving (b,g), tennis (b,g), track and field (b,g), volleyball (g), winter (indoor) track (b,g); coed interscholastic: weight training; coed intramural: bowling, project adventure, ropes courses, weight lifting. 7 PE instructors, 86 coaches, 1 athletic trainer.

Computers Computers are regularly used in all classes. Computer network features include on-campus library services, online commercial services, Internet access, wireless campus network, Internet filtering or blocking technology. Campus intranet and student e-mail accounts are available to students. Students grades are available online. The school has a published electronic and media policy.

Contact Mr. Jeff Holbrook, Director of Admissions. 502-814-4375. Fax: 502-814-4381. E-mail: admissions@kcd.org. Web site: www.kcd.org

KERR-VANCE ACADEMY

700 Vance Academy Road
Henderson, North Carolina 27537

Head of School: Mr. Paul Villatico

General Information Coeducational day college-preparatory school. Grades PK–12. Founded: 1968. Setting: rural. Nearest major city is Raleigh. 25-acre campus. 8 buildings on campus. Approved or accredited by Southern Association of Colleges and Schools and North Carolina Department of Education. Endowment: $40,000. Total enrollment: 472. Upper school average class size: 16. Upper school faculty-student ratio: 1:10. There are 180 required school days per year for Upper School students. Upper School students typically attend 5 days per week. The average school day consists of 6 hours.

Upper School Student Profile Grade 9: 32 students (20 boys, 12 girls); Grade 10: 40 students (16 boys, 24 girls); Grade 11: 30 students (17 boys, 13 girls); Grade 12: 45 students (25 boys, 20 girls).

Faculty School total: 41. In upper school: 5 men, 13 women; 12 have advanced degrees.

Subjects Offered Advanced Placement courses, algebra, American history, American literature, art, art history, biology, calculus, chemistry, computer programming, computer science, creative writing, driver education, earth science, economics, English, English literature, environmental science, French, geography, geometry, government/civics, grammar, Latin, mathematics, music, physical education, physics, psychology, SAT/ACT preparation, science, social sciences, social studies, sociology, Spanish, speech, trigonometry, world history, world literature, writing.

Graduation Requirements Computer science, English, English composition, English literature, foreign language, mathematics, physical education (includes health), science, social sciences, social studies (includes history), writing. Community service is required.

Special Academic Programs International Baccalaureate program; Advanced Placement exam preparation; honors section.

College Admission Counseling 34 students graduated in 2011; all went to college, including East Carolina University; Meredith College; North Carolina State University; The University of North Carolina at Chapel Hill; The University of North Carolina at Greensboro; The University of North Carolina Wilmington. Mean SAT critical reading: 508, mean SAT math: 517, mean composite ACT: 25. 16% scored over 600 on SAT critical reading, 21% scored over 600 on SAT math, 33% scored over 26 on composite ACT.

Student Life Upper grades have specified standards of dress, student council. Discipline rests primarily with faculty.

Tuition and Aid Day student tuition: $8100. Tuition installment plan (monthly payment plans). Tuition reduction for siblings, need-based scholarship grants available. In 2011–12, 5% of upper-school students received aid. Total amount of financial aid awarded in 2011–12: $15,000.

Admissions Traditional secondary-level entrance grade is 9. Admissions testing or writing sample required. Deadline for receipt of application materials: none. Application fee required: $100. On-campus interview required.

Athletics Interscholastic: baseball (boys), basketball (b,g), cheering (g), cross-country running (b,g), golf (b), lacrosse (b), soccer (b,g), softball (g), tennis (b,g), track and field (b,g), volleyball (g), weight training (b,g), wrestling (b); intramural: soccer (b,g), weight lifting (b); coed intramural: swimming and diving, volleyball. 3 PE instructors, 7 coaches, 1 athletic trainer.

Computers Computers are regularly used in art, English, history, library, literary magazine, newspaper, programming, reading, research skills, SAT preparation, science, technology, writing, yearbook classes. Computer network features include on-campus library services, online commercial services, Internet access.

Contact Mrs. Rebecca W. Irvin, Admissions Coordinator. 252-492-0018. Fax: 252-438-4652. E-mail: rirvin@kerrvance.com. Web site: www.kerrvance.com

KESWICK CHRISTIAN SCHOOL

10101 54th Avenue North
St. Petersburg, Florida 33708

Head of School: Supt. Nick Stratis

General Information Coeducational day college-preparatory, arts, business, and religious studies school, affiliated with Bible Fellowship Church. Grades 1–12. Founded: 1953. Setting: rural. Nearest major city is Seminole. 10-acre campus. 3 buildings on campus. Approved or accredited by Florida Department of Education. Upper school average class size: 25. Upper school faculty-student ratio: 1:15. Upper School students typically attend 5 days per week. The average school day consists of 7 hours and 15 minutes.

Upper School Student Profile 50% of students are Bible Fellowship Church.

Faculty School total: 37. In upper school: 6 men, 15 women; 15 have advanced degrees.

Special Academic Programs International Baccalaureate program; Advanced Placement exam preparation; honors section; independent study.

College Admission Counseling 35 students graduated in 2012; 15 went to college. Other: 15 went to work, 1 entered military service, 2 entered a postgraduate year.

Student Life Upper grades have uniform requirement, student council, honor system. Discipline rests primarily with faculty. Attendance at religious services is required.

Tuition and Aid Day student tuition: $6700–$9900. Tuition installment plan (monthly payment plans, individually arranged payment plans). Tuition reduction for siblings, need-based scholarship grants available. In 2012–13, 50% of upper-school students received aid. Total amount of financial aid awarded in 2012–13: $25,000.

Admissions Traditional secondary-level entrance grade is 9. For fall 2012, 85 students applied for upper-level admission, 83 were accepted, 83 enrolled. Deadline for receipt of application materials: none. Application fee required: $225. Interview required.

Athletics Interscholastic: baseball (boys), basketball (b,g), cheering (g), cross-country running (b,g), flag football (b), football (b), golf (b), physical fitness (b), physical training (b), power lifting (b), soccer (b), volleyball (g), weight lifting (b), weight training (b), winter (indoor) track (b,g), winter soccer (b); coed interscholastic: cross-country running, running, swimming and diving, track and field, triathlon, winter (indoor) track. 4 PE instructors, 5 coaches, 1 athletic trainer.

Computers Computer network features include on-campus library services, wireless campus network, Internet filtering or blocking technology. Campus intranet and computer access in designated common areas are available to students. Students grades are available online.

Contact Sue Williams, Admissions Director. 727-393-9100 Ext. 416. Fax: 727-397-5378. E-mail: swilliams@keswickchristian.org. Web site: keswickchristian.org/

THE KEW-FOREST SCHOOL

119-17 Union Turnpike
Forest Hills, New York 11375

Head of School: Mr. Mark P. Fish

General Information Coeducational day college-preparatory and arts school. Grades N–12. Founded: 1918. Setting: urban. Nearest major city is New York. 2-acre campus. 1 building on campus. Approved or accredited by Middle States Association of Colleges and Schools, New York Department of Education, New York State Association of Independent Schools, and New York Department of Education. Member of National Association of Independent Schools and Secondary School Admission Test Board. Total enrollment: 243. Upper school average class size: 13. Upper school faculty-student ratio: 1:8. There are 181 required school days per year for Upper School students. Upper School students typically attend 5 days per week. The average school day consists of 6 hours and 35 minutes.

Upper School Student Profile Grade 9: 22 students (11 boys, 11 girls); Grade 10: 24 students (12 boys, 12 girls); Grade 11: 26 students (13 boys, 13 girls); Grade 12: 26 students (13 boys, 13 girls).

Faculty School total: 34. In upper school: 14 men, 7 women; 18 have advanced degrees.

Subjects Offered Algebra, American history, ancient history, art, biology, biology-AP, calculus, calculus-AP, chemistry, English, English composition, English language and composition-AP, English literature, French, French-AP, geometry, health, history, honors geometry, Latin, Latin-AP, marine biology, modern European history, philosophy, physical education, physics, physics-AP, pre-calculus, Spanish, Spanish-AP, trigonometry, U.S. government and politics.

Graduation Requirements Art, English, history, history of the Catholic Church, mathematics, modern languages, music appreciation, physical education (includes health), science, community service.

Special Academic Programs Advanced Placement exam preparation; honors section; independent study; academic accommodation for the gifted; ESL (20 students enrolled).

College Admission Counseling 32 students graduated in 2012; all went to college, including New York University; Vassar College. Median SAT critical reading: 520, median SAT math: 575, median SAT writing: 580. 25% scored over 600 on SAT critical reading, 40% scored over 600 on SAT math.

Student Life Upper grades have uniform requirement, student council, honor system. Discipline rests primarily with faculty.

Summer Programs Remediation, enrichment, advancement programs offered; session focuses on academic instruction; held on campus; accepts boys and girls; open to students from other schools. 50 students usually enrolled. 2013 schedule: July 1 to August 5.

Tuition and Aid Day student tuition: $30,500. Tuition installment plan (FACTS Tuition Payment Plan, Tuition Management Systems Plan). Need-based scholarship grants available. In 2012–13, 25% of upper-school students received aid. Total amount of financial aid awarded in 2012–13: $983,000.

Admissions Traditional secondary-level entrance grade is 9. ISEE or SSAT required. Deadline for receipt of application materials: none. Application fee required: $75. On-campus interview required.

Athletics Interscholastic: basketball (boys, girls), cross-country running (b,g), rowing (g), soccer (b,g), tennis (b,g), track and field (b,g), volleyball (g); intramural: basketball (b,g), soccer (b,g), tennis (b,g); coed interscholastic: archery, fencing, golf, sailing; coed intramural: badminton, cross-country running, fitness, physical fitness, rock climbing, running, strength & conditioning, volleyball. 2 PE instructors, 5 coaches.

Computers Computers are regularly used in all academic classes. Computer network features include on-campus library services, Internet access, wireless campus network, Internet filtering or blocking technology. Students grades are available online.

Contact Mr. Henry C. Horne, Director of Admission and Enrollment Management. 718-268-4667 Ext. 125. Fax: 718-268-9121. E-mail: hhorne@kewforest.org. Web site: www.kewforest.org

KEY SCHOOL

Fort Worth, Texas

See Special Needs Schools section.

KIMBALL UNION ACADEMY

PO Box 188
Main Street
Meriden, New Hampshire 03770

Head of School: Mr. Michael J. Schafer

General Information Coeducational boarding and day college-preparatory, arts, and environmental science school. Grades 9–PG. Founded: 1813. Setting: small town. Nearest major city is Boston, MA. Students are housed in single-sex dormitories. 1,300-acre campus. 35 buildings on campus. Approved or accredited by Independent Schools of Northern New England, New England Association of Schools and Colleges, The Association of Boarding Schools, The College Board, and New Hampshire Department of Education. Member of National Association of Independent Schools and Secondary School Admission Test Board. Endowment: $11 million. Total enrollment: 314. Upper school average class size: 11. Upper school faculty-student ratio: 1:6. There are 159 required school days per year for Upper School students. Upper School students typically attend 6 days per week. The average school day consists of 5 hours and 8 minutes.

Upper School Student Profile Grade 9: 56 students (32 boys, 24 girls); Grade 10: 77 students (41 boys, 36 girls); Grade 11: 91 students (61 boys, 30 girls); Grade 12: 83 students (43 boys, 40 girls); Postgraduate: 7 students (7 boys). 66% of students are boarding students. 34% are state residents. 22 states are represented in upper school student body. 25% are international students. International students from Canada, China, Mexico, Republic of Korea, Spain, and Turkey; 15 other countries represented in student body.

Faculty School total: 48. In upper school: 32 men, 14 women; 26 have advanced degrees; 32 reside on campus.

Subjects Offered 3-dimensional design, acting, Advanced Placement courses, algebra, American history, American literature, anatomy, anthropology, architecture, art, art history, art history-AP, biology, biology-AP, calculus, calculus-AP, ceramics, chemistry, chemistry-AP, composition-AP, computer programming, creative writing, dance, digital photography, drama, driver education, English, English language and composition-AP, English literature, English literature and composition-AP, English-AP, environmental science, environmental science-AP, environmental studies, European history, fine arts, French, French language-AP, French literature-AP, geology, geometry, government/civics, grammar, health, history, history-AP, honors English, honors geometry, human geography - AP, independent study, international relations, jazz band, jazz ensemble, language-AP, Latin, Latin-AP, Mandarin, mathematical modeling, mathematics, modern European history-AP, modern world history, music, music history, music theory, music theory-AP, peer counseling, photo shop, photography, physics, physics-AP, physiology, playwriting, pottery, probability and statistics, programming, psychology, public speaking, science, social studies, Spanish, Spanish-AP, stagecraft, statistics-AP, student publications, studio art, studio art-AP, theater, theater arts, theater design and production, trigonometry, U.S. government, U.S. history, U.S. history-AP, video film production, visual arts, woodworking, world history, world literature, writing.

Graduation Requirements Art, English, foreign language, history, mathematics, science.

Special Academic Programs 19 Advanced Placement exams for which test preparation is offered; honors section; independent study; term-away projects; study abroad.

College Admission Counseling 86 students graduated in 2012; 80 went to college, including Brandeis University; Colby College; Syracuse University; The George Washington University; Trinity College; University of New Hampshire. Other: 1 entered a postgraduate year, 5 had other specific plans. Median SAT math: 570.

Student Life Upper grades have specified standards of dress, student council, honor system. Discipline rests equally with students and faculty.

Summer Programs Enrichment, ESL, sports, art/fine arts programs offered; session focuses on environmental leadership (EE Just Institute) and ALPS (Accelerated Language Program) with Dartmouth College; held both on and off campus; held at Costa Rica; accepts boys and girls; open to students from other schools. 200 students usually enrolled. 2013 schedule: July 2 to July 30. Application deadline: April 15.

Tuition and Aid Day student tuition: $29,925; 7-day tuition and room/board: $47,830. Tuition installment plan (Insured Tuition Payment Plan, Academic Management Services Plan, Key Tuition Payment Plan, monthly payment plans). Need-based scholarship grants available. In 2012–13, 47% of upper-school students received aid. Total amount of financial aid awarded in 2012–13: $3,369,027.

Admissions Traditional secondary-level entrance grade is 9. For fall 2012, 415 students applied for upper-level admission, 317 were accepted, 117 enrolled. ACT, PSAT or SAT, SLEP, SSAT or TOEFL required. Deadline for receipt of application materials: February 1. Application fee required: $50. Interview required.

Athletics Interscholastic: alpine skiing (boys, girls), baseball (b), basketball (b,g), cross-country running (b,g), equestrian sports (b,g), field hockey (g), freestyle skiing (b,g), golf (b,g), hockey (b,g), horseback riding (b,g), ice hockey (b,g), lacrosse (b,g), nordic skiing (b,g), rugby (b), running (b,g), skiing (cross-country) (b,g), skiing (downhill) (b,g), snowboarding (b,g), soccer (b,g), softball (g), swimming and diving (b,g), tennis (b,g); coed interscholastic: bicycling, mountain biking; coed intramural: alpine skiing, backpacking, canoeing/kayaking, dance, equestrian sports, fitness, freestyle skiing, hiking/backpacking, modern dance, outdoor activities, physical fitness, rock climbing, squash, strength & conditioning, surfing, weight lifting, yoga. 1 coach, 2 athletic trainers.

Computers Computers are regularly used in architecture, literary magazine, theater arts, woodworking classes. Computer network features include on-campus library services, Internet access, wireless campus network, Internet filtering or blocking technology, computer music studio/audio recording. Campus intranet, student e-mail accounts, and computer access in designated common areas are available to students. Students grades are available online. The school has a published electronic and media policy.

Contact Mr. Rich Ryerson, Director of Admissions. 603-469-2100. Fax: 603-469-2041. E-mail: admissions@kua.org. Web site: www.kua.org

KING LOW HEYWOOD THOMAS

1450 Newfield Avenue
Stamford, Connecticut 06905

Head of School: Thomas B. Main

General Information Coeducational day college-preparatory and global studies, language distinctions, independent study school. Grades PK–12. Founded: 1865. Setting: suburban. Nearest major city is New York, NY. 40-acre campus. 3 buildings on campus. Approved or accredited by Connecticut Association of Independent Schools and New England Association of Schools and Colleges. Member of National Association of Independent Schools. Endowment: $18.8 million. Total enrollment: 684. Upper school average class size: 13. Upper school faculty-student ratio: 1:8. Upper School students typically attend 5 days per week. The average school day consists of 7 hours.

Upper School Student Profile Grade 9: 84 students (46 boys, 38 girls); Grade 10: 77 students (41 boys, 36 girls); Grade 11: 80 students (45 boys, 35 girls); Grade 12: 83 students (42 boys, 41 girls).

Faculty School total: 105. In upper school: 24 men, 27 women; 40 have advanced degrees.

Subjects Offered Acting, advanced chemistry, advanced computer applications, advanced math, Advanced Placement courses, algebra, American history, ancient history, ancient world history, ancient/medieval philosophy, anthropology, archaeology, art, biology, calculus, calculus-AP, chemistry, chemistry-AP, Chinese, choral music, college counseling, college planning, computer multimedia, computer programming, digital photography, economics, economics-AP, English, English language and composition-AP, English literature, English literature-AP, environmental studies, ethics, European history, European history-AP, fine arts, forensics, French, French language-AP, general science, geometry, global studies, government, history, Holocaust, honors algebra, honors geometry, honors U.S. history, honors world history, independent study, life skills, literature and composition-AP, macroeconomics-AP, mathematics, microeconomics-AP, model United Nations, modern European history-AP, modern languages, music theory-AP, musical productions, musical theater, oceanography, performing arts, philosophy, physics, physics-AP, play production, pre-calculus, psychology, SAT preparation, SAT/ACT preparation, social studies, Spanish, Spanish language-AP, Spanish literature, Spanish literature-AP, statistics, statistics-AP, student government, student publications, studio art, theater arts, trigonometry, U.S. history-AP, U.S. literature, world history, world religions.

Graduation Requirements Arts and fine arts (art, music, dance, drama), English, ethics, foreign language, history, life skills, mathematics, science, sports, participation in one theater performance before graduation.

Special Academic Programs 17 Advanced Placement exams for which test preparation is offered; honors section; independent study; academic accommodation for the gifted, the musically talented, and the artistically talented.

College Admission Counseling 63 students graduated in 2012; 61 went to college, including Bucknell University; Roger Williams University; Southern Methodist University; The Johns Hopkins University; University of Virginia; Wake Forest University. Other: 1 entered military service, 1 entered a postgraduate year. Median SAT critical reading: 590, median SAT math: 600, median SAT writing: 620, median combined SAT: 1795, median composite ACT: 26. 47% scored over 600 on SAT critical reading, 51% scored over 600 on SAT math, 60% scored over 600 on SAT writing, 49% scored over 1800 on combined SAT, 50% scored over 26 on composite ACT.

Student Life Upper grades have specified standards of dress, student council, honor system. Discipline rests primarily with faculty.

Summer Programs Remediation, enrichment, advancement, sports, art/fine arts programs offered; session focuses on academics (grades 6-12), enrichment (elementary school), and sports (grades 4-8) enrichment; held on campus; accepts boys and girls;

open to students from other schools. 200 students usually enrolled. 2013 schedule: June 17 to August 2. Application deadline: June 1.

Tuition and Aid Day student tuition: $35,120. Tuition installment plan (Key Tuition Payment Plan). Need-based scholarship grants available. In 2012–13, 13% of upper-school students received aid. Total amount of financial aid awarded in 2012–13: $1,152,645.

Admissions Traditional secondary-level entrance grade is 9. For fall 2012, 193 students applied for upper-level admission, 67 were accepted, 35 enrolled. ISEE, school's own test or SSAT required. Deadline for receipt of application materials: January 1. Application fee required: $75. On-campus interview required.

Athletics Interscholastic: baseball (boys), basketball (b,g), cross-country running (b,g), field hockey (g), football (b), golf (b,g), ice hockey (b), independent competitive sports (b,g), lacrosse (b,g), soccer (b,g), softball (g), squash (b,g), tennis (b,g), volleyball (g); intramural: dance (g), physical training (b,g); coed interscholastic: independent competitive sports, squash; coed intramural: aerobics/dance, dance, fitness, physical training, strength & conditioning, weight lifting, weight training. 27 coaches, 2 athletic trainers.

Computers Computers are regularly used in college planning, economics, English, ethics, foreign language, French, history, mathematics, science, technology, writing, yearbook classes. Computer network features include on-campus library services, online commercial services, Internet access, wireless campus network, Internet filtering or blocking technology. Campus intranet, student e-mail accounts, and computer access in designated common areas are available to students. The school has a published electronic and media policy.

Contact Carrie Salvatore, Director of Admission and Financial Aid. 203-322-3496 Ext. 352. Fax: 203-505-6288. E-mail: csalvatore@klht.org. Web site: www.klht.org

THE KING'S ACADEMY

202 Smothers Road
Seymour, Tennessee 37865

Head of School: Mr. Walter Grubb

General Information Coeducational boarding and day and distance learning college-preparatory and religious studies school, affiliated with Southern Baptist Convention. Boarding grades 7–12, day grades K4–12. Distance learning grades 9–12. Founded: 1880. Setting: suburban. Nearest major city is Knoxville. Students are housed in single-sex dormitories. 67-acre campus. 8 buildings on campus. Approved or accredited by Southern Association of Colleges and Schools and Tennessee Department of Education. Endowment: $3.1 million. Total enrollment: 471. Upper school average class size: 14. Upper school faculty-student ratio: 1:14. There are 180 required school days per year for Upper School students. Upper School students typically attend 5 days per week. The average school day consists of 7 hours.

Upper School Student Profile Grade 9: 45 students (25 boys, 20 girls); Grade 10: 40 students (21 boys, 19 girls); Grade 11: 47 students (27 boys, 20 girls); Grade 12: 37 students (23 boys, 14 girls). 24% of students are boarding students. 77% are state residents. 5 states are represented in upper school student body. 19% are international students. International students from China, Japan, Luxembourg, Nigeria, Rwanda, and Thailand; 4 other countries represented in student body. 80% of students are Southern Baptist Convention.

Faculty School total: 47. In upper school: 8 men, 13 women; 9 have advanced degrees; 9 reside on campus.

Subjects Offered Advanced Placement courses, algebra, American history, anatomy, art, Bible studies, biology, calculus, chemistry, Chinese, choir, drama, economics, English, English-AP, ESL, fine arts, geometry, government/civics, grammar, health, health and wellness, history, keyboarding, mathematics, music, orchestra, physical education, physics, physiology, religion, science, social studies, Spanish, world history.

Graduation Requirements Arts and fine arts (art, music, dance, drama), computer science, English, foreign language, mathematics, religion (includes Bible studies and theology), science, social studies (includes history), wellness.

Special Academic Programs Advanced Placement exam preparation; honors section; independent study; study at local college for college credit; ESL (18 students enrolled).

College Admission Counseling 37 students graduated in 2012; 34 went to college, including Boston College; Carson-Newman College; Georgia Institute of Technology; Penn State University Park; Purdue University; The University of Tennessee. Other: 3 went to work.

Student Life Upper grades have uniform requirement, student council. Discipline rests primarily with faculty. Attendance at religious services is required.

Tuition and Aid Day student tuition: $5500–$6600; 5-day tuition and room/board: $15,970–$20,680; 7-day tuition and room/board: $22,680–$27,390. Tuition installment plan (FACTS Tuition Payment Plan, monthly payment plans, individually arranged payment plans). Tuition reduction for siblings, need-based scholarship grants available. In 2012–13, 14% of upper-school students received aid. Total amount of financial aid awarded in 2012–13: $89,610.

Admissions Traditional secondary-level entrance grade is 9. For fall 2012, 34 students applied for upper-level admission, 33 were accepted, 22 enrolled. OLSAT, Stanford Achievement Test or TOEFL required. Deadline for receipt of application materials: none. Application fee required: $50. Interview recommended.

Athletics Interscholastic: baseball (boys), basketball (b,g), cheering (g), football (b), golf (b,g), soccer (b,g), tennis (b,g), volleyball (g), weight lifting (b,g), weight training (b,g); intramural: basketball (b,g), billiards (b,g), table tennis (b,g), tennis (b,g), volleyball (g), weight lifting (b,g), weight training (b,g); coed interscholastic: backpacking, bowling, cross-country running, rappelling, rock climbing, strength & conditioning, track and field; coed intramural: aerobics/Nautilus, canoeing/kayaking, cross-country running, fitness, outdoor education, physical fitness, physical training, rappelling, rock climbing, strength & conditioning, volleyball. 17 coaches, 1 athletic trainer.

Computers Computers are regularly used in business applications, computer applications, keyboarding, yearbook classes. Computer network features include Internet access. Students grades are available online.

Contact Mrs. Janice Mink, Director of Admissions. 865-573-8321. Fax: 865-573-8323. E-mail: jmink@thekingsacademy.net. Web site: www.thekingsacademy.net

KINGS CHRISTIAN SCHOOL

900 East D Street
Lemoore, California 93245

Head of School: Mr. Steven W. Reynolds

General Information Coeducational day college-preparatory, general academic, arts, business, religious studies, and technology school, affiliated with Protestant-Evangelical faith. Grades PK–12. Founded: 1979. Setting: small town. Nearest major city is Fresno. 17-acre campus. 12 buildings on campus. Approved or accredited by Association of Christian Schools International and Western Association of Schools and Colleges. Total enrollment: 294. Upper school average class size: 20. Upper school faculty-student ratio: 1:11. There are 180 required school days per year for Upper School students. Upper School students typically attend 5 days per week. The average school day consists of 6 hours and 45 minutes.

Upper School Student Profile Grade 9: 25 students (7 boys, 18 girls); Grade 10: 19 students (10 boys, 9 girls); Grade 11: 24 students (15 boys, 9 girls); Grade 12: 18 students (13 boys, 5 girls). 70% of students are Protestant-Evangelical faith.

Faculty School total: 26. In upper school: 4 men, 10 women; 3 have advanced degrees.

Subjects Offered Accounting, advanced math, algebra, American government, art, auto mechanics, Bible studies, biology, business, business mathematics, calculus-AP, career education, cheerleading, chemistry, choir, chorus, Christian doctrine, Christian scripture, community service, computer applications, computer literacy, drama, drawing, driver education, economics, English, English composition, English literature-AP, ensembles, finance, fine arts, geography, geometry, health, home economics, HTML design, keyboarding, library skills, life skills, literature, mathematics, music, music theory, novels, painting, personal money management, physical education, physical science, physics, pre-algebra, religion, SAT preparation, science, Shakespeare, social sciences, social studies, Spanish, speech, U.S. history, weight training, word processing, yearbook.

Graduation Requirements Arts and fine arts (art, music, dance, drama), Bible studies, English, foreign language, mathematics, physical education (includes health), portfolio writing, science, social sciences, successfully pass Bible every year of attendance, proof of at least 9th grade proficiency (SAT Test).

Special Academic Programs 2 Advanced Placement exams for which test preparation is offered; honors section; accelerated programs; independent study; remedial reading and/or remedial writing; remedial math.

College Admission Counseling 25 students graduated in 2012; 21 went to college, including Azusa Pacific University; California State University, Fresno; Vanguard University of Southern California; West Hills Community College. Other: 4 went to work. Median SAT critical reading: 580, median SAT math: 500, median SAT writing: 504, median combined SAT: 1584. 20% scored over 600 on SAT critical reading, 30% scored over 600 on SAT math, 30% scored over 600 on SAT writing, 30% scored over 1800 on combined SAT.

Student Life Upper grades have specified standards of dress, student council. Discipline rests primarily with faculty.

Tuition and Aid Day student tuition: $6067. Tuition installment plan (monthly payment plans). Tuition reduction for siblings, need-based scholarship grants, paying campus jobs available. In 2012–13, 21% of upper-school students received aid. Total amount of financial aid awarded in 2012–13: $275,000.

Admissions Traditional secondary-level entrance grade is 9. For fall 2012, 9 students applied for upper-level admission, 8 were accepted, 7 enrolled. PSAT or Terra Nova-CTB required. Deadline for receipt of application materials: none. Application fee required: $150.

Athletics Interscholastic: baseball (boys), basketball (b,g), football (b), softball (g), track and field (b,g), volleyball (g); intramural: physical fitness (b,g), physical training (b,g), power lifting (b), strength & conditioning (b,g), track and field (b,g), weight training (b,g); coed interscholastic: cheering, cross-country running, track and field; coed intramural: badminton, fitness, Frisbee, physical fitness, strength & conditioning, table tennis, track and field, volleyball. 5 PE instructors, 9 coaches, 2 athletic trainers.

Computers Computers are regularly used in Bible studies, college planning, English, introduction to technology, journalism, library skills, programming, SAT preparation, technical drawing, yearbook classes. Computer network features include on-campus library services, Internet access, wireless campus network, Internet filtering or blocking technology.

Contact Leslie Reynolds, Registrar. 559-924-8301 Ext. 107. Fax: 559-924-0607. E-mail: lreynolds@kcsnet.com. Web site: www.kcsnet.com

KING'S-EDGEHILL SCHOOL

254 College Road
Windsor, Nova Scotia B0N 2T0, Canada

Head of School: Mr. Joseph Seagram

General Information Coeducational boarding and day college-preparatory school. Grades 6–12. Founded: 1788. Setting: small town. Nearest major city is Halifax, Canada. Students are housed in single-sex dormitories. 65-acre campus. 17 buildings on campus. Approved or accredited by California Association of Independent Schools and Nova Scotia Department of Education. Language of instruction: English. Total enrollment: 290. Upper school average class size: 15. Upper school faculty-student ratio: 1:10.

Upper School Student Profile Grade 10: 60 students (28 boys, 32 girls); Grade 11: 70 students (37 boys, 33 girls); Grade 12: 70 students (38 boys, 32 girls). 68% of students are boarding students. 55% are province residents. 13 provinces are represented in upper school student body. 30% are international students. International students from Germany, Hong Kong, Mexico, Republic of Korea, and Taiwan; 13 other countries represented in student body.

Faculty School total: 46. In upper school: 19 men, 23 women; 15 have advanced degrees; 22 reside on campus.

Subjects Offered Art, biology, calculus, chemistry, current events, drama, economics, English, French, geography, geology, history, mathematics, music, physics, political science, religion, science, social sciences, social studies, theater, theory of knowledge, world history.

Graduation Requirements English, foreign language, mathematics, science, social sciences, social studies (includes history).

Special Academic Programs International Baccalaureate program; honors section; term-away projects; study abroad; academic accommodation for the gifted; ESL (22 students enrolled).

College Admission Counseling 70 students graduated in 2011; all went to college, including Dalhousie University; McGill University; Queen's University at Kingston; The University of British Columbia; The University of Western Ontario; University of Toronto.

Student Life Upper grades have uniform requirement, student council, honor system. Discipline rests primarily with faculty. Attendance at religious services is required.

Tuition and Aid Day student tuition: CAN$15,050; 7-day tuition and room/board: CAN$35,750. Tuition installment plan (monthly payment plans, individually arranged payment plans). Bursaries, merit scholarship grants available. In 2011–12, 35% of upper-school students received aid. Total amount of financial aid awarded in 2011–12: CAN$900,000.

Admissions Traditional secondary-level entrance grade is 10. OLSAT and English Exam required. Deadline for receipt of application materials: none. Application fee required: CAN$100. Interview required.

Athletics Interscholastic: alpine skiing (boys, girls), aquatics (b,g), badminton (b,g), baseball (b,g), basketball (b,g), biathlon (b,g), bicycling (b,g), cross-country running (b,g), equestrian sports (b,g), fitness (b,g), Frisbee (b,g), golf (b,g), ice hockey (b,g), outdoor recreation (b,g), outdoor skills (b,g), physical fitness (b,g), rugby (b,g), skiing (cross-country) (b,g), skiing (downhill) (b,g), snowboarding (b,g), soccer (b,g), softball (b,g), table tennis (b,g), tennis (b,g), track and field (b,g), ultimate Frisbee (b,g), volleyball (b,g), weight lifting (b,g), wrestling (b,g); intramural: basketball (b,g), bicycling (b,g), cross-country running (b,g), golf (b,g), rugby (b,g), skiing (cross-country) (b,g), skiing (downhill) (b,g), snowboarding (b,g), soccer (b,g), softball (b,g), table tennis (b,g), tennis (b,g), track and field (b,g), weight lifting (b,g), yoga (b,g); coed interscholastic: alpine skiing, aquatics, bicycling, equestrian sports, fitness, Frisbee, outdoor recreation, outdoor skills, physical fitness, table tennis; coed intramural: bowling, curling, field hockey, table tennis, yoga. 2 PE instructors, 30 coaches.

Computers Computers are regularly used in computer applications, English, foreign language, mathematics, music, science classes. Computer network features include on-campus library services, online commercial services, Internet access, Internet filtering or blocking technology. Campus intranet, student e-mail accounts, and computer access in designated common areas are available to students.

Contact Mr. Chris B. Strickey, Director of Admission. 902-798-2278. Fax: 902-798-2105. E-mail: strickey@kes.ns.ca. Web site: www.kes.ns.ca

KING'S HIGH SCHOOL

19303 Fremont Avenue North
Seattle, Washington 98133

Head of School: Bob Ruhlman

General Information Coeducational day college-preparatory, arts, business, religious studies, and technology school, affiliated with Christian faith. Grades PK–12. Founded: 1950. Setting: suburban. 55-acre campus. 6 buildings on campus. Approved or accredited by Association of Christian Schools International, Northwest Accreditation Commission, and Washington Department of Education. Total enrollment: 1,130. Upper school average class size: 25. Upper school faculty-student ratio: 1:15. There are 171 required school days per year for Upper School students. Upper School students typically attend 5 days per week. The average school day consists of 5 hours and 47 minutes.

Upper School Student Profile Grade 9: 127 students (58 boys, 69 girls); Grade 10: 113 students (61 boys, 52 girls); Grade 11: 120 students (62 boys, 58 girls); Grade 12: 111 students (52 boys, 59 girls). 80% of students are Christian faith.

Faculty School total: 89. In upper school: 11 men, 22 women; 20 have advanced degrees.

Subjects Offered Advanced Placement courses, algebra, American history, American literature, anatomy, anatomy and physiology, art, Bible, biology, business, calculus, calculus-AP, ceramics, chemistry, chemistry-AP, choir, choral music, computer science, culinary arts, drama, earth science, English, English literature, English-AP, environmental science, European history, European history-AP, expository writing, fine arts, geography, geometry, health, history, history-AP, honors algebra, honors English, honors geometry, honors U.S. history, journalism, leadership, mathematics, music, orchestra, photography, physical education, physics, pre-calculus, psychology, religion, SAT preparation, science, social studies, Spanish, speech, theater, trigonometry, U.S. history, U.S. history-AP, video film production, vocal ensemble, vocal jazz, world history, writing.

Graduation Requirements Arts and fine arts (art, music, dance, drama), career and technology systems, computer science, English, foreign language, health education, mathematics, physical education (includes health), religion (includes Bible studies and theology), science, social studies (includes history), speech, senior thesis, senior project, senior retreat.

Special Academic Programs Advanced Placement exam preparation; honors section.

College Admission Counseling 102 students graduated in 2011; 100 went to college, including Central Washington University; Seattle Pacific University; University of Washington. Other: 2 went to work. Mean SAT critical reading: 546, mean SAT math: 587, mean SAT writing: 538, mean combined SAT: 1671, mean composite ACT: 24.

Student Life Upper grades have specified standards of dress, student council, honor system. Discipline rests primarily with faculty. Attendance at religious services is required.

Tuition and Aid Day student tuition: $10,660. Tuition installment plan (monthly payment plans). Tuition reduction for siblings, need-based scholarship grants, paying campus jobs available. In 2011–12, 16% of upper-school students received aid. Total amount of financial aid awarded in 2011–12: $572,000.

Admissions Traditional secondary-level entrance grade is 9. For fall 2011, 59 students applied for upper-level admission, 54 were accepted, 50 enrolled. Gates MacGinite Placement Test or TOEFL required. Deadline for receipt of application materials: none. Application fee required: $50. On-campus interview required.

Athletics Interscholastic: basketball (boys, girls), cross-country running (b,g), football (b), golf (b,g), soccer (b,g), track and field (b,g), volleyball (g); coed interscholastic: cheering, physical fitness, physical training, power lifting, strength & conditioning, weight training. 3 PE instructors, 26 coaches, 1 athletic trainer.

Computers Computers are regularly used in English, introduction to technology, journalism, keyboarding, media production, photography, science, study skills, technology, video film production, Web site design, yearbook classes. Computer network features include on-campus library services, online commercial services, Internet access, Internet filtering or blocking technology. Students grades are available online. The school has a published electronic and media policy.

Contact Leslie Young, Secondary Admissions Coordinator. 206-289-7783. Fax: 206-546-7214. E-mail: lyoung@crista.net. Web site: www.kingsschools.org

KING'S RIDGE CHRISTIAN SCHOOL

2765 Bethany Bend
Alpharetta, Georgia 30004

Head of School: Mr. C. David Rhodes III

General Information Coeducational day college-preparatory school, affiliated with Christian faith. Grades K–12. Founded: 2001. Setting: suburban. Nearest major city is Atlanta. 70-acre campus. 3 buildings on campus. Approved or accredited by Georgia Accrediting Commission, Georgia Independent School Association, Southern Association of Colleges and Schools, and Southern Association of Independent Schools. Member of National Association of Independent Schools and Secondary School Admission Test Board. Total enrollment: 713. Upper school average class size: 12. Upper school faculty-student ratio: 1:8. There are 180 required school days per year for Upper School students. Upper School students typically attend 5 days per week. The average school day consists of 6 hours and 45 minutes.

Faculty School total: 120. In upper school: 12 men, 12 women; 14 have advanced degrees.

Subjects Offered Advanced Placement courses, algebra, American government, American history, art, astronomy, biology, calculus-AP, chemistry, Christian doctrine, Christian education, Christian ethics, civics, communication skills, computer programming, drama performance, drawing, English composition, English literature, European history, finance, French, geometry, honors algebra, honors English, honors geometry, honors U.S. history, Life of Christ, music composition, physical fitness, physics, public speaking, SAT preparation, Spanish, speech, statistics, studio art, video film production, yearbook.

Graduation Requirements 50 hours of community service between grades 9-12.

Special Academic Programs Advanced Placement exam preparation; honors section.

College Admission Counseling 16 students graduated in 2011; all went to college, including Auburn University; Georgia College & State University; Georgia Institute of Technology; Samford University; University of Georgia; University of Richmond.

Student Life Upper grades have uniform requirement, student council, honor system. Discipline rests primarily with faculty. Attendance at religious services is required.

Tuition and Aid Day student tuition: $14,643. Tuition installment plan (Insured Tuition Payment Plan, FACTS Tuition Payment Plan). Tuition reduction for siblings, need-based scholarship grants available. In 2011–12, 30% of upper-school students received aid.

Admissions SSAT, ERB, PSAT, SAT, PLAN or ACT required. Deadline for receipt of application materials: none. Application fee required: $75. Interview required.

Athletics Interscholastic: baseball (boys), basketball (b,g), cheering (g), football (b), lacrosse (b), soccer (b,g), softball (g), strength & conditioning (b), swimming and diving (b,g), tennis (b,g), volleyball (g); coed interscholastic: cross-country running, equestrian sports, golf, horseback riding, track and field; coed intramural: weight training. 3 PE instructors, 3 coaches.

Computers Computers are regularly used in all academic classes. Computer network features include online commercial services, Internet access, wireless campus network, Internet filtering or blocking technology, online collaboration of classroom activities. Campus intranet, student e-mail accounts, and computer access in designated common areas are available to students. Students grades are available online. The school has a published electronic and media policy.

Contact Lisa K. McGuire, Director of Admission/Marketing. 770-754-5738 Ext. 118. Fax: 770-754-5544. E-mail: lmcguire@kingsridgecs.org. Web site: www.kingsridgecs.org/

KINGSWAY COLLEGE

1200 Leland Road
Oshawa, Ontario L1K 2H4, Canada

Head of School: Mr. Scott Bowes

General Information Coeducational boarding and day college-preparatory, general academic, arts, business, religious studies, bilingual studies, and technology school, affiliated with Seventh-day Adventists. Grades 9–12. Founded: 1903. Setting: small town. Nearest major city is Toronto, Canada. Students are housed in single-sex by floor dormitories. 100-acre campus. 9 buildings on campus. Approved or accredited by Ontario Ministry of Education and Ontario Department of Education. Language of instruction: English. Endowment: CAN$1.6 million. Total enrollment: 189. Upper school average class size: 25. Upper school faculty-student ratio: 1:13. There are 180 required school days per year for Upper School students. Upper School students typically attend 5 days per week. The average school day consists of 5 hours and 50 minutes.

Upper School Student Profile Grade 9: 45 students (27 boys, 18 girls); Grade 10: 34 students (12 boys, 22 girls); Grade 11: 55 students (32 boys, 23 girls); Grade 12: 55 students (20 boys, 35 girls). 45% of students are boarding students. 85% are province residents. 9 provinces are represented in upper school student body. 4% are international students. International students from Cayman Islands, Democratic People's Republic of Korea, Japan, Serbia and Montenegro, United Kingdom, and United States; 2 other countries represented in student body. 90% of students are Seventh-day Adventists.

Faculty School total: 16. In upper school: 9 men, 6 women; 2 have advanced degrees; 8 reside on campus.

Subjects Offered Accounting, advanced chemistry, advanced computer applications, advanced math, algebra, American history, anthropology, band, biology, business studies, calculus, Canadian geography, Canadian history, Canadian law, career education, ceramics, chemistry, choir, civics, computer applications, computer information systems, computer programming, computer studies, concert band, English, English literature, ESL, French, healthful living, information processing, intro to computers, music, music performance, physical education, physics, psychology, religious education, science, sociology, study skills, U.S. history, visual arts, work-study, world civilizations, world religions.

Graduation Requirements Art, Canadian geography, Canadian history, careers, civics, English, French, mathematics, physical education (includes health), science, all students must take one religion course per year.

Special Academic Programs ESL (3 students enrolled).

College Admission Counseling 52 students graduated in 2012; 37 went to college, including Andrews University; McGill University; Southern Adventist University; University of Michigan; University of Toronto; Walla Walla University.

Student Life Upper grades have specified standards of dress, student council. Discipline rests primarily with faculty.

Tuition and Aid Day student tuition: CAN$11,275; 7-day tuition and room/board: CAN$18,300. Guaranteed tuition plan. Tuition installment plan (monthly payment plans, individually arranged payment plans). Tuition reduction for siblings, merit scholarship grants, need-based scholarship grants, paying campus jobs available. In 2012–13, 45% of upper-school students received aid; total upper-school merit-scholarship money awarded: CAN$24,000. Total amount of financial aid awarded in 2012–13: CAN$200,000.

Admissions Traditional secondary-level entrance grade is 9. For fall 2012, 192 students applied for upper-level admission, 190 were accepted, 189 enrolled. Deadline for receipt of application materials: none. No application fee required. Interview recommended.

Athletics Interscholastic: basketball (boys, girls); intramural: basketball (b,g), flag football (b,g), floor hockey (b,g), ice hockey (b), indoor hockey (b,g), racquetball (b,g), soccer (b,g), softball (b,g), volleyball (b,g); coed intramural: backpacking, badminton, canoeing/kayaking, gymnastics, hiking/backpacking, roller skating, skiing (downhill), snowboarding, volleyball. 1 PE instructor, 2 coaches.

Computers Computers are regularly used in accounting, business, career education, computer applications, data processing, English, ESL, history, programming, science, social sciences classes. Computer network features include Internet access, wireless campus network, Internet filtering or blocking technology. Student e-mail accounts and computer access in designated common areas are available to students. Students grades are available online. The school has a published electronic and media policy.

Contact Ms. Ashley Arriola, Communications Assistant. 905-433-1144 Ext. 211. Fax: 905-433-1156. E-mail: admissions@kingswaycollege.on.ca. Web site: www.kingswaycollege.on.ca

KINGSWOOD-OXFORD SCHOOL

170 Kingswood Road
West Hartford, Connecticut 06119-1430

Head of School: Mr. Dennis Bisgaard

General Information Coeducational day college-preparatory school. Grades 6–12. Founded: 1909. Setting: suburban. Nearest major city is Hartford. 30-acre campus. 11 buildings on campus. Approved or accredited by New England Association of Schools and Colleges and Connecticut Department of Education. Member of National Association of Independent Schools and Secondary School Admission Test Board. Endowment: $25.7 million. Total enrollment: 499. Upper school average class size: 13. Upper school faculty-student ratio: 1:8. There are 160 required school days per year for Upper School students. Upper School students typically attend 5 days per week. The average school day consists of 7 hours.

Upper School Student Profile Grade 9: 93 students (41 boys, 52 girls); Grade 10: 81 students (35 boys, 46 girls); Grade 11: 96 students (48 boys, 48 girls); Grade 12: 75 students (42 boys, 33 girls).

Faculty School total: 53. In upper school: 27 men, 26 women; 33 have advanced degrees.

Subjects Offered Algebra, American history, American literature, art, art history-AP, band, biology, biology-AP, calculus, calculus-AP, chemistry, chemistry-AP, Chinese, Chinese studies, chorus, composition-AP, computer science, computer science-AP, concert band, concert choir, creative writing, digital music, digital photography, dramatic arts, drawing, economics, economics-AP, English, English language-AP, English literature, English literature-AP, environmental science, fine arts, forensics, French, French language-AP, geography, geometry, government/civics, jazz band, jazz ensemble, journalism, Latin, Latin-AP, marine biology, mathematics, media, music, orchestra, photography, physics, physics-AP, political science, public speaking, social studies, Spanish, Spanish language-AP, Spanish-AP, statistics, statistics-AP, theater, U.S. history-AP, visual arts, world history, world literature, writing.

Graduation Requirements Computer science, English, foreign language, mathematics, performing arts, science, social studies (includes history), technology, visual arts, participation on athletic teams, senior thesis in English, 30 hours of community service. Community service is required.

Special Academic Programs 17 Advanced Placement exams for which test preparation is offered; honors section; independent study; term-away projects; study at local college for college credit; study abroad.

College Admission Counseling 101 students graduated in 2012; all went to college, including Boston University; Bucknell University; Gettysburg College; Lehigh University; Union College; University of Connecticut. Median SAT critical reading: 615, median SAT math: 595, median SAT writing: 610, median combined SAT: 1820, median composite ACT: 27.

Student Life Upper grades have specified standards of dress, student council, honor system. Discipline rests equally with students and faculty.

Tuition and Aid Day student tuition: $33,675. Tuition installment plan (Academic Management Services Plan). Merit scholarship grants, need-based scholarship grants available. In 2012–13, 35% of upper-school students received aid; total upper-school merit-scholarship money awarded: $276,500. Total amount of financial aid awarded in 2012–13: $2,300,000.

Admissions Traditional secondary-level entrance grade is 9. For fall 2012, 217 students applied for upper-level admission, 125 were accepted, 64 enrolled. SSAT required. Deadline for receipt of application materials: February 1. Application fee required: $55. On-campus interview required.

Athletics Interscholastic: alpine skiing (boys, girls), baseball (b), basketball (b,g), cross-country running (b,g), diving (b,g), field hockey (g), football (b), ice hockey (b,g), lacrosse (b,g), soccer (b,g), softball (g), squash (b,g), strength & conditioning (b,g),

swimming and diving (b,g), tennis (b,g), track and field (b,g), volleyball (g); intramural: basketball (b,g), ice hockey (b), soccer (b,g), yoga (g); coed interscholastic: golf, skiing (downhill); coed intramural: strength & conditioning. 9 coaches, 2 athletic trainers.
Computers Computers are regularly used in English, foreign language, history, mathematics, music technology, photography, science classes. Computer resources include on-campus library services, Internet access, wireless campus network. Student e-mail accounts and computer access in designated common areas are available to students. Students grades are available online. The school has a published electronic and media policy.
Contact Mr. James E. O?Donnell, Director of Enrollment Management. 860-727-5000. Fax: 860-236-3651. E-mail: odonnell.j@k-o.org. Web site: www.kingswoodoxford.org

THE LAB SCHOOL OF WASHINGTON

Washington, District of Columbia
See Special Needs Schools section.

LA CHEIM SCHOOL

Antioch, California
See Special Needs Schools section.

LADYWOOD HIGH SCHOOL

14680 Newburgh Road
Livonia, Michigan 48154

Head of School: Mrs. Joan L Fitzgerald

General Information Girls' day college-preparatory, arts, business, and religious studies school, affiliated with Roman Catholic Church. Grades 9–12. Founded: 1950. Setting: suburban. Nearest major city is Detroit. 17-acre campus. 1 building on campus. Approved or accredited by National Catholic Education Association, North Central Association of Colleges and Schools, and Michigan Department of Education. Total enrollment: 316. Upper school average class size: 24. Upper school faculty-student ratio: 1:12. There are 179 required school days per year for Upper School students. Upper School students typically attend 5 days per week. The average school day consists of 5 hours and 30 minutes.
Upper School Student Profile Grade 9: 64 students (64 girls); Grade 10: 70 students (70 girls); Grade 11: 79 students (79 girls); Grade 12: 103 students (103 girls). 88% of students are Roman Catholic.
Faculty School total: 34. In upper school: 6 men, 24 women; 14 have advanced degrees.
Subjects Offered Accounting, advanced chemistry, algebra, American government, American history, American history-AP, American literature, anatomy and physiology, art, Asian history, Bible studies, biology, biology-AP, calculus, calculus-AP, career and personal planning, career exploration, career planning, Catholic belief and practice, ceramics, child development, choir, Christian and Hebrew scripture, college writing, composition, computer education, computer science, culinary arts, discrete mathematics, drama performance, drawing and design, economics, English, English composition, English literature and composition-AP, environmental science, environmental science-AP, film appreciation, food science, forensics, French, French language-AP, French-AP, geometry, global issues, graphic arts, health, history of the Catholic Church, independent living, Italian, keyboarding, language and composition, language arts, leadership and service, library assistant, life management skills, oil painting, orchestra, parent/child development, physical education, physics, poetry, prayer/spirituality, pre-calculus, probability and statistics, psychology, religion, scripture, sewing, short story, sociology, Spanish, Spanish language-AP, Spanish-AP, speech, studio art-AP, theater, theater arts, visual and performing arts, water color painting, world studies, writing, yearbook.
Graduation Requirements Algebra, American government, American history, American literature, arts and fine arts (art, music, dance, drama), athletic training, biology, British literature, Catholic belief and practice, chemistry, computer science, economics, English composition, foreign language, geometry, global studies, health education, keyboarding, literature, mathematics, physical education (includes health), religion (includes Bible studies and theology), science, social sciences, speech communications, world literature, service requirement for each grade level.
Special Academic Programs Advanced Placement exam preparation; study at local college for college credit.
College Admission Counseling 86 students graduated in 2011; all went to college, including Grand Valley State University; Michigan State University; University of Michigan–Dearborn; Wayne State University. Median composite ACT: 24. Mean SAT critical reading: 556, mean SAT math: 527, mean SAT writing: 543, mean combined SAT: 1626. 26% scored over 26 on composite ACT.
Student Life Upper grades have uniform requirement, student council, honor system. Discipline rests primarily with faculty. Attendance at religious services is required.
Tuition and Aid Day student tuition: $7650. Tuition installment plan (The Tuition Plan, monthly payment plans, individually arranged payment plans). Tuition reduction for siblings, merit scholarship grants, need-based scholarship grants available. In 2011–12, 14% of upper-school students received aid. Total amount of financial aid awarded in 2011–12: $135,000.
Admissions Traditional secondary-level entrance grade is 9. Catholic High School Entrance Examination required. Deadline for receipt of application materials: none. Application fee required: $300. Interview recommended.
Athletics Interscholastic: basketball, bowling, cheering, cross-country running, equestrian sports, field hockey, figure skating, flag football, golf, ice hockey, lacrosse, pom squad, skiing (downhill), snowboarding, soccer, softball, swimming and diving, tennis, track and field, volleyball; intramural: flag football. 1 PE instructor, 51 coaches, 1 athletic trainer.
Computers Computers are regularly used in accounting, computer applications, data processing, graphic design, keyboarding, Web site design, word processing, yearbook classes. Computer network features include on-campus library services, Internet access, Internet filtering or blocking technology. Campus intranet is available to students. Students grades are available online. The school has a published electronic and media policy.
Contact Mrs. Caryn Epps, Guidance Counselors. 734-591-5492 Ext. 227. Fax: 734-591-4214. E-mail: cepps@ladywood.org. Web site: www.ladywood.org

LA JOLLA COUNTRY DAY SCHOOL

9490 Genesee Avenue
La Jolla, California 92037

Head of School: Mr. Christopher Schuck

General Information Coeducational day college-preparatory, arts, and technology school. Grades N–12. Founded: 1926. Setting: suburban. Nearest major city is San Diego. 24-acre campus. 8 buildings on campus. Approved or accredited by California Association of Independent Schools, Western Association of Schools and Colleges, and California Department of Education. Member of National Association of Independent Schools and Secondary School Admission Test Board. Endowment: $2.4 million. Total enrollment: 1,170. Upper school average class size: 16. Upper school faculty-student ratio: 1:16. There are 171 required school days per year for Upper School students. Upper School students typically attend 5 days per week. The average school day consists of 7 hours.
Upper School Student Profile Grade 9: 111 students (54 boys, 57 girls); Grade 10: 134 students (69 boys, 65 girls); Grade 11: 124 students (63 boys, 61 girls); Grade 12: 123 students (67 boys, 56 girls).
Faculty School total: 103. In upper school: 26 men, 24 women; 32 have advanced degrees.
Subjects Offered Advanced studio art-AP, algebra, Arabic, art, art history-AP, art-AP, ASB Leadership, astronomy, athletic training, band, baseball, basketball, biology, biology-AP, calculus, calculus-AP, ceramics, chemistry, chemistry-AP, choir, choral music, chorus, college counseling, community service, computer graphics, conceptual physics, concert band, creative writing, dance, dance performance, digital photography, drama, economics, economics-AP, English, English language-AP, English literature, English literature and composition-AP, English-AP, environmental science, European history, European history-AP, experiential education, Farsi, film studies, French, French language-AP, French literature-AP, French-AP, freshman seminar, geometry, golf, government, government and politics-AP, government-AP, history of drama, history-AP, honors algebra, honors geometry, independent study, instrumental music, journalism, linear algebra, madrigals, Mandarin, marine biology, modern European history-AP, music appreciation, music theory-AP, music-AP, neuroscience, performing arts, photography, physical education, physics, physics-AP, portfolio art, pre-calculus, programming, psychology, psychology-AP, Spanish, Spanish language-AP, Spanish literature-AP, Spanish-AP, speech, statistics-AP, strings, studio art, studio art-AP, technical theater, theater, theater arts, theater history, theater production, theory of knowledge, U.S. history-AP, world cultures, writing.
Graduation Requirements Arts and fine arts (art, music, dance, drama), English, foreign language, mathematics, performing arts, physical education (includes health), science, senior project, social sciences, speech, 40 hours of community service.
Special Academic Programs Advanced Placement exam preparation; honors section; study abroad.
College Admission Counseling 111 students graduated in 2012; 107 went to college, including New York University; University of California, Berkeley; University of California, Santa Barbara; University of Chicago; University of Southern California; Washington University in St. Louis. Other: 1 went to work, 1 entered military service, 2 had other specific plans. Mean SAT critical reading: 600, mean SAT math: 600, mean SAT writing: 622. 43% scored over 600 on SAT critical reading, 53% scored over 600 on SAT math.
Student Life Upper grades have specified standards of dress, student council. Discipline rests equally with students and faculty.
Summer Programs Remediation, enrichment, advancement, sports, art/fine arts, computer instruction programs offered; session focuses on academics, summer camp, sports camps; held on campus; accepts boys and girls; open to students from other schools. 300 students usually enrolled. 2013 schedule: June 22 to July 31. Application deadline: none.
Tuition and Aid Day student tuition: $27,591. Tuition installment plan (FACTS Tuition Payment Plan, monthly payment plans). Need-based scholarship grants

available. In 2012–13, 27% of upper-school students received aid. Total amount of financial aid awarded in 2012–13: $2,475,780.

Admissions Traditional secondary-level entrance grade is 9. ERB (grade level), ISEE, TerraNova or writing sample required. Deadline for receipt of application materials: February 1. Application fee required: $125. On-campus interview required.

Athletics Interscholastic: aquatics (boys, girls), baseball (b), basketball (b,g), cheering (g), cross-country running (b,g), dance (b,g), fencing (b,g), football (b), golf (b,g), independent competitive sports (b,g), lacrosse (b,g), roller hockey (b), soccer (b,g), softball (g), swimming and diving (b,g), tennis (b,g), track and field (b,g), volleyball (b,g), water polo (b,g); coed interscholastic: physical fitness, physical training, strength & conditioning, surfing, ultimate Frisbee, weight lifting, weight training; coed intramural: dance team, outdoor education, snowboarding. 7 PE instructors, 7 coaches, 1 athletic trainer.

Computers Computers are regularly used in art, English, French, history, mathematics, science, Spanish, technology classes. Computer network features include on-campus library services, online commercial services, Internet access, wireless campus network, Internet filtering or blocking technology, email connection from home. Student e-mail accounts are available to students. The school has a published electronic and media policy.

Contact Mr. Vincent Travaglione, Director of Admission. 858-453-3440 Ext. 117. Fax: 858-453-8210. E-mail: vtravaglione@ljcds.org. Web site: www.ljcds.org

LAKEFIELD COLLEGE SCHOOL

4391 County Road #29
Lakefield, Ontario K0L 2H0, Canada

Head of School: Mr. Struan Robertson

General Information Coeducational boarding and day and distance learning college-preparatory, arts, and athletics, music, outdoor education school, affiliated with Church of England (Anglican). Boarding grades 9–12, day grades 8–12. Distance learning grades 9–12. Founded: 1879. Setting: small town. Nearest major city is Toronto, Canada. Students are housed in single-sex dormitories. 315-acre campus. 25 buildings on campus. Approved or accredited by Canadian Association of Independent Schools, Canadian Educational Standards Institute, The Association of Boarding Schools, and Ontario Department of Education. Affiliate member of National Association of Independent Schools; member of Secondary School Admission Test Board. Language of instruction: English. Endowment: CAN$21 million. Total enrollment: 365. Upper school average class size: 17. Upper school faculty-student ratio: 1:7. There are 185 required school days per year for Upper School students. Upper School students typically attend 6 days per week. The average school day consists of 5 hours.

Upper School Student Profile Grade 9: 48 students (20 boys, 28 girls); Grade 10: 93 students (49 boys, 44 girls); Grade 11: 108 students (60 boys, 48 girls); Grade 12: 102 students (53 boys, 49 girls). 66% of students are boarding students. 60% are province residents. 18 provinces are represented in upper school student body. 36% are international students. International students from Barbados, Bermuda, China, Germany, Mexico, and United States; 23 other countries represented in student body.

Faculty School total: 53. In upper school: 27 men, 22 women; 9 have advanced degrees; 25 reside on campus.

Subjects Offered Algebra, art, art history, biology, calculus, chemistry, computer science, creative writing, drama, earth science, economics, English, English literature, environmental science, fine arts, French, geography, geometry, government/civics, health, history, kinesiology, mathematics, music, outdoor education, physical education, physics, science, social studies, sociology, Spanish, theater, trigonometry, vocal music, world history, world literature.

Graduation Requirements English, foreign language, mathematics, physical education (includes health), science, social studies (includes history).

Special Academic Programs 8 Advanced Placement exams for which test preparation is offered; term-away projects; study abroad.

College Admission Counseling 94 students graduated in 2012; 88 went to college, including Dalhousie University; McGill University; Queen's University at Kingston; The University of Western Ontario; University of Guelph; University of Toronto. Other: 6 had other specific plans.

Student Life Upper grades have uniform requirement, student council, honor system. Discipline rests equally with students and faculty.

Summer Programs Enrichment programs offered; session focuses on online courses; held off campus; held at via distance learning; accepts boys and girls; open to students from other schools. 100 students usually enrolled. 2013 schedule: June 22 to August 30.

Tuition and Aid Day student tuition: CAN$28,330; 7-day tuition and room/board: CAN$49,385. Tuition installment plan (Insured Tuition Payment Plan, monthly payment plans, individually arranged payment plans, 3-payment plans or custom payment plans if req'd). Bursaries, merit scholarship grants, need-based scholarship grants available. In 2012–13, 30% of upper-school students received aid; total upper-school merit-scholarship money awarded: CAN$22,500. Total amount of financial aid awarded in 2012–13: CAN$1,648,600.

Admissions Traditional secondary-level entrance grade is 9. For fall 2012, 232 students applied for upper-level admission, 171 were accepted, 121 enrolled. Otis-Lennon School Ability Test, SSAT or TOEFL or SLEP required. Deadline for receipt of application materials: none. Application fee required: CAN$100. Interview required.

Athletics Interscholastic: alpine skiing (boys, girls), baseball (b), basketball (g), crew (g), cross-country running (b,g), field hockey (g), hockey (b,g), ice hockey (b,g), nordic skiing (b,g), outdoor education (b,g), ropes courses (b,g), rowing (b,g), rugby (b,g), skiing (cross-country) (b,g), skiing (downhill) (b,g), snowboarding (b,g), soccer (b,g), softball (b), tennis (b,g), track and field (b,g), volleyball (g); intramural: aerobics/dance (g), basketball (b,g), cross-country running (b,g), skiing (cross-country) (b,g), tennis (b,g); coed interscholastic: alpine skiing, cross-country running, equestrian sports, Frisbee, hockey, horseback riding, ice hockey, nordic skiing, outdoor education, sailboarding, sailing, skiing (cross-country), skiing (downhill), snowboarding, tennis, track and field, ultimate Frisbee, wall climbing, windsurfing; coed intramural: aerobics/Nautilus, baseball, basketball, bicycling, canoeing/kayaking, climbing, cross-country running, dance, equestrian sports, fitness, ice hockey, kayaking, sailboarding, sailing, skiing (cross-country), skiing (downhill), softball, tennis, weight training, windsurfing, yoga.

Computers Computers are regularly used in all classes. Computer network features include on-campus library services, online commercial services, Internet access, wireless campus network, Internet filtering or blocking technology. Campus intranet, student e-mail accounts, and computer access in designated common areas are available to students. Students grades are available online. The school has a published electronic and media policy.

Contact Mrs. Barbara M. Rutherford, Assistant Director of Admissions. 705-652-3324 Ext. 345. Fax: 705-652-6320. E-mail: admissions@lcs.on.ca. Web site: www.lcs.on.ca

LAKEHILL PREPARATORY SCHOOL

2720 Hillside Drive
Dallas, Texas 75214

Head of School: Roger L. Perry

General Information Coeducational day college-preparatory, arts, bilingual studies, and technology school. Grades K–12. Founded: 1971. Setting: urban. 23-acre campus. 4 buildings on campus. Approved or accredited by Independent Schools Association of the Southwest, Texas Private School Accreditation Commission, The College Board, and Texas Department of Education. Member of National Association of Independent Schools. Endowment: $250,000. Total enrollment: 400. Upper school average class size: 15. Upper school faculty-student ratio: 1:10. There are 175 required school days per year for Upper School students. Upper School students typically attend 5 days per week. The average school day consists of 7 hours and 30 minutes.

Upper School Student Profile Grade 9: 26 students (14 boys, 12 girls); Grade 10: 36 students (18 boys, 18 girls); Grade 11: 25 students (12 boys, 13 girls); Grade 12: 23 students (13 boys, 10 girls).

Faculty School total: 44. In upper school: 10 men, 13 women; 17 have advanced degrees.

Subjects Offered Advanced Placement courses, advanced studio art-AP, algebra, American history, American history-AP, American literature, art, art history, biology, calculus, calculus-AP, chemistry, college counseling, computer math, computer programming, computer programming-AP, computer science, digital photography, drama, earth science, economics, English, English language and composition-AP, English literature, environmental science-AP, European history, French, French language-AP, geography, geometry, government/civics, grammar, health, history, journalism, Latin, mathematics, music, music theater, physical education, physics, psychology, public speaking, publications, science, senior career experience, Shakespeare, social sciences, social studies, Spanish, Spanish language-AP, Spanish literature-AP, speech, statistics, theater, trigonometry, Western civilization, world history, world literature, writing.

Graduation Requirements Arts and fine arts (art, music, dance, drama), computer science, electives, English, foreign language, mathematics, science, social studies (includes history), senior internship program.

Special Academic Programs 14 Advanced Placement exams for which test preparation is offered; honors section; independent study; study abroad.

College Admission Counseling 23 students graduated in 2012; all went to college, including Carnegie Mellon University; Colorado State University; Duke University; Spelman College; Texas A&M University; The University of Texas at Austin. Median SAT critical reading: 576, median SAT math: 585, median SAT writing: 575, median combined SAT: 1736, median composite ACT: 25.

Student Life Upper grades have specified standards of dress, student council, honor system. Discipline rests primarily with faculty.

Summer Programs Enrichment, sports, art/fine arts, computer instruction programs offered; session focuses on enrichment; held on campus; accepts boys and girls; open to students from other schools. 200 students usually enrolled. 2013 schedule: June 10 to August 9. Application deadline: May 15.

Tuition and Aid Day student tuition: $17,525. Tuition installment plan (monthly payment plans). Tuition reduction for siblings, need-based scholarship grants available. In 2012–13, 18% of upper-school students received aid.

Admissions Traditional secondary-level entrance grade is 9. ERB CTP IV, ISEE or Stanford Achievement Test required. Deadline for receipt of application materials: January 18. Application fee required: $150. On-campus interview recommended.

Athletics Interscholastic: baseball (boys), basketball (b,g), cheering (g), cross-country running (b,g), football (b), golf (b,g), paddling (b,g), rock climbing (b,g), running (b,g), softball (g), tennis (b,g), track and field (b,g), volleyball (g), weight training (b,g); coed interscholastic: tennis; coed intramural: bowling. 3 PE instructors, 12 coaches, 1 athletic trainer.

Computers Computers are regularly used in college planning, creative writing, English, graphic design, journalism, mathematics, science, speech, Web site design, word processing, writing, yearbook classes. Computer network features include on-campus library services, online commercial services, Internet access, wireless campus network, Internet filtering or blocking technology. Student e-mail accounts and computer access in designated common areas are available to students. Students grades are available online. The school has a published electronic and media policy.

Contact Holly Walker, Director of Admission. 214-826-2931. Fax: 214-826-4623. E-mail: hwalker@lakehillprep.org. Web site: www.lakehillprep.org

LAKESIDE SCHOOL

14050 First Avenue NE

Seattle, Washington 98125-3099

Head of School: Mr. Bernard Noe

General Information Coeducational day college-preparatory, arts, and technology school. Grades 5–12. Founded: 1919. Setting: urban. 34-acre campus. 19 buildings on campus. Approved or accredited by Northwest Accreditation Commission, Pacific Northwest Association of Independent Schools, and Washington Department of Education. Member of National Association of Independent Schools. Endowment: $188.6 million. Total enrollment: 797. Upper school average class size: 16. Upper school faculty-student ratio: 1:9. There are 164 required school days per year for Upper School students. Upper School students typically attend 5 days per week. The average school day consists of 6 hours and 50 minutes.

Upper School Student Profile Grade 9: 135 students (65 boys, 70 girls); Grade 10: 128 students (65 boys, 63 girls); Grade 11: 143 students (72 boys, 71 girls); Grade 12: 132 students (67 boys, 65 girls).

Faculty School total: 92. In upper school: 33 men, 24 women; 44 have advanced degrees.

Subjects Offered Algebra, American history, American literature, art, biology, calculus, ceramics, chemistry, community service, computer programming, computer science, creative writing, drama, driver education, economics, English, English literature, environmental science, European history, expository writing, fine arts, French, geometry, government/civics, health, history, journalism, Latin, mathematics, music, outdoor education, philosophy, photography, physical education, physics, pre-calculus, science, social studies, Spanish, theater, trigonometry, world history, world literature, writing.

Graduation Requirements Arts, English, foreign language, history, mathematics, outdoor education, physical education (includes health), science. Community service is required.

Special Academic Programs Honors section; independent study; term-away projects; study abroad.

College Admission Counseling 127 students graduated in 2011; 125 went to college, including Columbia University; Stanford University; University of Southern California; University of Washington; Washington University in St. Louis; Whitman College. Other: 2 had other specific plans. Median SAT critical reading: 705, median SAT math: 720, median SAT writing: 690, median combined SAT: 2095, median composite ACT: 31.

Student Life Upper grades have student council, honor system. Discipline rests equally with students and faculty.

Tuition and Aid Day student tuition: $26,200. Tuition installment plan (monthly payment plans). Need-based scholarship grants available. In 2011–12, 28% of upper-school students received aid. Total amount of financial aid awarded in 2011–12: $2,995,770.

Admissions Traditional secondary-level entrance grade is 9. For fall 2011, 362 students applied for upper-level admission, 71 were accepted, 57 enrolled. ISEE, PSAT or SAT for applicants to grade 11 and 12 or SSAT required. Deadline for receipt of application materials: January 26. Application fee required: $25. Interview required.

Athletics Interscholastic: baseball (boys), basketball (b,g), crew (b,g), cross-country running (b,g), diving (b,g), football (b), golf (b,g), lacrosse (b,g), soccer (b,g), softball (g), swimming and diving (b,g), tennis (b,g), track and field (b,g), volleyball (g); coed interscholastic: ultimate Frisbee, wrestling; coed intramural: outdoor education, skiing (cross-country), squash. 5 PE instructors, 71 coaches, 1 athletic trainer.

Computers Computers are regularly used in all academic classes. Computer network features include on-campus library services, online commercial services, Internet access, wireless campus network, Internet filtering or blocking technology, class schedule search, online course registration, online directory. Campus intranet, student e-mail accounts, and computer access in designated common areas are available to students. The school has a published electronic and media policy.

Contact Ms. Margaret Hardy, Admissions Associate. 206-368-3605. Fax: 206-440-2777. E-mail: admissions@lakesideschool.org. Web site: www.lakesideschool.org

LANCASTER COUNTRY DAY SCHOOL

725 Hamilton Road

Lancaster, Pennsylvania 17603

Head of School: Mr. Steven D. Lisk

General Information Coeducational day college-preparatory and arts school. Grades PS–12. Founded: 1943. Setting: suburban. Nearest major city is Philadelphia. 26-acre campus. 1 building on campus. Approved or accredited by Pennsylvania Association of Independent Schools and Pennsylvania Department of Education. Member of National Association of Independent Schools. Endowment: $12.5 million. Total enrollment: 599. Upper school average class size: 12. Upper school faculty-student ratio: 1:8. Upper School students typically attend 5 days per week. The average school day consists of 7 hours.

Upper School Student Profile Grade 9: 51 students (27 boys, 24 girls); Grade 10: 55 students (26 boys, 29 girls); Grade 11: 48 students (21 boys, 27 girls); Grade 12: 50 students (15 boys, 35 girls).

Faculty School total: 78. In upper school: 13 men, 16 women.

Subjects Offered Algebra, Asian studies, athletic training, Basic programming, bioethics, DNA and culture, biology, biology-AP, calculus, calculus-AP, ceramics, chamber groups, chemistry, chemistry-AP, China/Japan history, chorus, computer art, computer graphics, computer programming, computer programming-AP, computer science, computer science-AP, conceptual physics, contemporary history, contemporary issues, contemporary issues in science, creative writing, critical thinking, critical writing, dance, desktop publishing, digital imaging, drama, drawing, driver education, economics, economics and history, English literature, English-AP, ensembles, environmental science, environmental science-AP, European civilization, European history, European literature, fine arts, French, French-AP, geometry, guitar, honors geometry, instrumental music, journalism, Latin, math applications, mathematics, model United Nations, music, music history, painting, photography, physical education, physics, pre-calculus, printmaking, programming, psychology, research seminar, senior project, service learning/internship, Spanish, Spanish-AP, sports medicine, statistics, statistics-AP, theater, trigonometry, U.S. history, U.S. history-AP, U.S. literature, United Nations and international issues, weight training, women in world history, world affairs, world civilizations, world history, world literature, writing, yearbook.

Graduation Requirements Algebra, arts, biology, chemistry, computer science, English, foreign language, geometry, history, Latin, mathematics, physical education (includes health), science, trigonometry.

Special Academic Programs 12 Advanced Placement exams for which test preparation is offered; accelerated programs; independent study; study at local college for college credit; academic accommodation for the gifted, the musically talented, and the artistically talented; ESL.

College Admission Counseling 46 students graduated in 2012; 44 went to college, including Boston College; Franklin & Marshall College; Rochester Institute of Technology; University of Pittsburgh; Washington University in St. Louis. Other: 2 had other specific plans. Median SAT critical reading: 635, median SAT math: 630, median SAT writing: 610, median combined SAT: 1930. 64% scored over 600 on SAT critical reading, 64% scored over 600 on SAT math, 57% scored over 600 on SAT writing, 66% scored over 1800 on combined SAT.

Student Life Upper grades have specified standards of dress, student council, honor system. Discipline rests equally with students and faculty.

Tuition and Aid Day student tuition: $21,200. Tuition installment plan (monthly payment plans, 2-installment plan). Merit scholarship grants, need-based scholarship grants available. In 2012–13, 30% of upper-school students received aid; total upper-school merit-scholarship money awarded: $313,578. Total amount of financial aid awarded in 2012–13: $723,572.

Admissions Traditional secondary-level entrance grade is 9. For fall 2012, 102 students applied for upper-level admission, 45 were accepted, 36 enrolled. ERB CTP III required. Deadline for receipt of application materials: none. Application fee required: $75. Interview required.

Athletics Interscholastic: baseball (boys), basketball (b,g), cross-country running (b,g), dance (b,g), field hockey (g), football (b), lacrosse (b,g), modern dance (b,g), soccer (b,g), softball (g), squash (b,g), swimming and diving (b,g), tennis (b,g), volleyball (b,g), weight training (b,g), wrestling (b,g); coed interscholastic: boxing, golf, track and field, ultimate Frisbee. 3 PE instructors, 5 coaches, 1 athletic trainer.

Computers Computers are regularly used in desktop publishing, ESL, English, graphic arts, history, information technology, journalism, literary magazine, newspaper, programming, psychology, research skills, science, technology, Web site design, word processing, writing, yearbook classes. Computer network features include on-campus library services, online commercial services, Internet access, wireless campus network, Internet filtering or blocking technology, technology-rich environment with SmartBoards in every classroom, I-Pads for all students in grade 9. Student e-mail accounts and computer access in designated common areas are available to students. Students grades are available online. The school has a published electronic and media policy.

Contact Jamie Beth Jamie Beth Schindler Schindler, Assistant Director of Admission. 717-392-2916 Ext. 228. Fax: 717-392-0425. E-mail: schindlerj@lancastercountryday.org. Web site: www.lancastercountryday.org

LANCASTER MENNONITE HIGH SCHOOL

2176 Lincoln Highway East
Lancaster, Pennsylvania 17602

Head of School: Mr. Elvin Kennel

General Information Coeducational boarding and day college-preparatory, general academic, arts, vocational, religious studies, bilingual studies, and agriculture school, affiliated with Mennonite Church. Boarding grades 9–12, day grades 6–12. Founded: 1942. Setting: suburban. Nearest major city is Philadelphia. Students are housed in coed dormitories and single-sex by wings. 100-acre campus. 9 buildings on campus. Approved or accredited by Mennonite Education Agency, Mennonite Schools Council, Middle States Association of Colleges and Schools, and Pennsylvania Department of Education. Endowment: $12 million. Upper school average class size: 18. Upper school faculty-student ratio: 1:15. There are 182 required school days per year for Upper School students. Upper School students typically attend 5 days per week. The average school day consists of 6 hours and 30 minutes.

Upper School Student Profile Grade 9: 118 students (60 boys, 58 girls); Grade 10: 179 students (99 boys, 80 girls); Grade 11: 173 students (85 boys, 88 girls); Grade 12: 170 students (97 boys, 73 girls). 8% of students are boarding students. 89% are state residents. 4 states are represented in upper school student body. 11% are international students. International students from China, Ethiopia, Ethiopia, Hong Kong, Republic of Korea, and Taiwan; 4 other countries represented in student body. 30% of students are Mennonite.

Faculty School total: 77. In upper school: 38 men, 37 women; 50 have advanced degrees; 4 reside on campus.

Subjects Offered 1 1/2 elective credits, 3-dimensional art, 3-dimensional design, accounting, advanced biology, advanced chemistry, advanced math, Advanced Placement courses, agriculture, American government, American history, American history-AP, art appreciation, athletics, band, baseball, basketball, bell choir, Bible, Bible as literature, Bible studies, biology, biology-AP, bowling, business, business mathematics, calculus, calculus-AP, career experience, career exploration, career/college preparation, chemistry, chemistry-AP, Chinese, choir, chorus, Christian doctrine, Christian education, Christian scripture, Christian studies, church history, communications, community service, comparative government and politics, comparative government and politics-AP, concert band, concert choir, creative writing, culinary arts, drama, drawing, driver education, ecology, electives, English, English composition, English language and composition-AP, entrepreneurship, environmental science, ESL, European history, family and consumer science, family living, family studies, fashion, foods, foreign language, French, German, guitar, health education, history, human development, instrumental music, jazz band, language arts, Life of Christ, literary magazine, literature-AP, music, music appreciation, music composition, music performance, music theory, music-AP, musical productions, newspaper, orchestra, painting, parent/child development, participation in sports, performing arts, photography, physical education, physics, physics-AP, psychology, psychology-AP, public speaking, science, senior project, small engine repair, sociology, softball, Spanish, Spanish language-AP, statistics, statistics-AP, strings, student government, student publications, tennis, track and field, U.S. history, U.S. history-AP, U.S. literature, visual and performing arts, visual arts, voice, volleyball, weight training, welding, wind ensemble, wind instruments, woodworking, world history, world history-AP, writing.

Graduation Requirements A certain amount of credits are needed in various academic areas.

Special Academic Programs Advanced Placement exam preparation; honors section; independent study; study at local college for college credit; academic accommodation for the musically talented; remedial reading and/or remedial writing; remedial math; special instructional classes for deaf students, blind students; ESL (40 students enrolled).

College Admission Counseling 147 students graduated in 2012; 96 went to college, including Eastern Mennonite University; Goshen College; Grove City College; Hesston College; Messiah College; Penn State University Park. Other: 26 went to work, 18 had other specific plans. Mean SAT critical reading: 552, mean SAT math: 545, mean SAT writing: 528, mean combined SAT: 1625.

Student Life Upper grades have specified standards of dress, student council. Discipline rests primarily with faculty. Attendance at religious services is required.

Summer Programs Enrichment, sports, art/fine arts programs offered; held on campus; accepts boys and girls; open to students from other schools. 200 students usually enrolled. 2013 schedule: June to August. Application deadline: none.

Tuition and Aid Day student tuition: $7284; 5-day tuition and room/board: $11,312; 7-day tuition and room/board: $14,348. Tuition installment plan (monthly payment plans). Tuition reduction for siblings, merit scholarship grants, need-based scholarship grants, paying campus jobs available. In 2012–13, 40% of upper-school students received aid; total upper-school merit-scholarship money awarded: $20,000. Total amount of financial aid awarded in 2012–13: $2,000,000.

Admissions Traditional secondary-level entrance grade is 9. For fall 2012, 398 students applied for upper-level admission, 390 were accepted, 370 enrolled. Deadline for receipt of application materials: none. Application fee required: $100. Interview recommended.

Athletics Interscholastic: ball hockey (girls), baseball (b), basketball (b,g), cross-country running (b,g), field hockey (g), golf (b), lacrosse (b), soccer (b,g), softball (g), tennis (b,g), track and field (b,g); coed interscholastic: baseball. 4 PE instructors, 20 coaches, 1 athletic trainer.

Computers Computers are regularly used in all academic classes. Computer network features include on-campus library services, Internet access, Internet filtering or blocking technology. Campus intranet and student e-mail accounts are available to students. Students grades are available online. The school has a published electronic and media policy.

Contact Christy L. Horst, Administrative Assistant for Admissions. 717-299-0436 Ext. 312. Fax: 717-299-0823. E-mail: horstcl@lancastermennonite.org. Web site: www.lancastermennonite.org

LANDMARK CHRISTIAN ACADEMY

6502 Johnsontown Road
Louisville, Kentucky 40272

Head of School: Mr. Monte L. Ashworth

General Information Coeducational day college-preparatory and religious studies school, affiliated with Baptist Church. Grades K4–12. Founded: 1978. Setting: suburban. 5-acre campus. 1 building on campus. Approved or accredited by American Association of Christian Schools. Total enrollment: 130. Upper school average class size: 10. Upper school faculty-student ratio: 1:11. There are 177 required school days per year for Upper School students. Upper School students typically attend 5 days per week. The average school day consists of 6 hours and 50 minutes.

Upper School Student Profile Grade 9: 12 students (9 boys, 3 girls); Grade 10: 1 student (1 boy); Grade 11: 5 students (4 boys, 1 girl); Grade 12: 10 students (6 boys, 4 girls). 80% of students are Baptist.

Faculty School total: 13. In upper school: 3 men, 3 women; 2 have advanced degrees.

Subjects Offered Advanced math, algebra, American history, American literature, analytic geometry, ancient history, ancient world history, Bible, biology, business mathematics, chemistry, choir, computer technologies, consumer economics, consumer mathematics, economics, English composition, English literature, general science, geography, geometry, grammar, health, history, home economics, keyboarding, modern history, physical education, physics, pre-algebra, pre-calculus, speech, trigonometry, world geography, world history.

Graduation Requirements Bible, computers, English, foreign language, history, mathematics, science, social sciences.

College Admission Counseling 5 students graduated in 2012; 3 went to college, including Clearwater Christian College; Jefferson Community and Technical College. Other: 2 went to work. Median composite ACT: 23.

Student Life Upper grades have uniform requirement. Discipline rests primarily with faculty.

Tuition and Aid Day student tuition: $3250. Tuition installment plan (FACTS Tuition Payment Plan). Tuition reduction for siblings available.

Admissions Traditional secondary-level entrance grade is 9. For fall 2012, 3 students applied for upper-level admission, 3 were accepted, 3 enrolled. Math and English placement tests required. Deadline for receipt of application materials: none. Application fee required: $275. On-campus interview required.

Athletics Interscholastic: basketball (boys), soccer (b), track and field (b,g), volleyball (g). 1 PE instructor, 3 coaches.

Computers Computers are regularly used in computer applications, keyboarding, Spanish classes. The school has a published electronic and media policy.

Contact Miss Gloria G. Ortegon, School Secretary. 502-933-3000. Fax: 502-933-5179. E-mail: LCAinfo@libcky.com. Web site: LCAky.com

LANDMARK CHRISTIAN SCHOOL

50 South East Broad Street
Fairburn, Georgia 30213

Head of School: Mr. Bill Parsons

General Information Coeducational day college-preparatory, arts, and religious studies school, affiliated with Christian faith, Protestant faith. Grades K4–12. Founded: 1989. Setting: suburban. Nearest major city is Atlanta. 62-acre campus. 4 buildings on campus. Approved or accredited by Southern Association of Colleges and Schools and Georgia Department of Education. Total enrollment: 842. Upper school average class size: 16. Upper school faculty-student ratio: 1:8. There are 179 required school days per year for Upper School students. Upper School students typically attend 5 days per week. The average school day consists of 7 hours and 15 minutes.

Upper School Student Profile Grade 9: 66 students (35 boys, 31 girls); Grade 10: 69 students (31 boys, 38 girls); Grade 11: 59 students (29 boys, 30 girls); Grade 12: 52 students (29 boys, 23 girls). 100% of students are Christian faith, Protestant.

Faculty School total: 79. In upper school: 13 men, 24 women; 17 have advanced degrees.

Subjects Offered Advanced biology, advanced chemistry, advanced math, Advanced Placement courses, advanced studio art-AP, algebra, American government, American literature-AP, anatomy and physiology, art, art-AP, athletics, band, baseball, basketball, Bible, Bible studies, biology, biology-AP, calculus, calculus-AP, chamber groups, cheerleading, chemistry, chemistry-AP, choral music, chorus, Christian studies, communications, composition, computer graphics, computer literacy, computer skills, computer studies, computer technologies, computers, concert band, concert choir, drama, drama performance, economics, electives, English, English language and composition-AP, English literature, English literature-AP, English-AP, fine arts, foreign language, forensics, geography, geometry, golf, government/civics-AP, health, history, history-AP, honors algebra, honors English, honors geometry, honors U.S. history, honors world history, human anatomy, human biology, instrumental music, jazz band, keyboarding, leadership education training, linear algebra, marine biology, music, music appreciation, music theater, physics, physics-AP, physiology, pre-algebra, pre-calculus, public speaking, SAT preparation, SAT/ACT preparation, social studies, Spanish, Spanish language-AP, Spanish-AP, speech, sports medicine, statistics-AP, swimming, tennis, theater arts, U.S. history, U.S. history-AP, vocal ensemble, volleyball, weight training, World-Wide-Web publishing, writing, yearbook.

Special Academic Programs 9 Advanced Placement exams for which test preparation is offered; honors section; academic accommodation for the gifted; remedial reading and/or remedial writing; remedial math; programs in English, mathematics, general development for dyslexic students.

College Admission Counseling 51 students graduated in 2012; all went to college, including Auburn University; Georgia State University; Mississippi State University; The University of Alabama; University of Georgia. Median SAT critical reading: 544, median SAT math: 550, median SAT writing: 535, median combined SAT: 1628, median composite ACT: 24. 25% scored over 600 on SAT critical reading, 28% scored over 600 on SAT math, 25% scored over 600 on SAT writing, 28% scored over 1800 on combined SAT, 41% scored over 26 on composite ACT.

Student Life Upper grades have uniform requirement, student council, honor system. Discipline rests equally with students and faculty. Attendance at religious services is required.

Summer Programs Computer instruction programs offered; held on campus; accepts boys and girls; not open to students from other schools. 20 students usually enrolled.

Tuition and Aid Day student tuition: $13,500. Tuition installment plan (monthly payment plans). Need-based scholarship grants available. In 2012–13, 20% of upper-school students received aid. Total amount of financial aid awarded in 2012–13: $235,650.

Admissions Traditional secondary-level entrance grade is 9. For fall 2012, 39 students applied for upper-level admission, 35 were accepted, 30 enrolled. Deadline for receipt of application materials: none. Application fee required: $100. On-campus interview required.

Athletics Interscholastic: baseball (boys), basketball (b,g), cheering (g), cross-country running (b,g), football (b), golf (b,g), physical training (b,g), soccer (b,g), softball (g), strength & conditioning (b,g), swimming and diving (b,g), tennis (b,g), track and field (b,g), volleyball (g), wrestling (b). 5 PE instructors, 49 coaches, 2 athletic trainers.

Computers Computers are regularly used in all academic classes. Computer network features include on-campus library services, Internet access, Internet filtering or blocking technology, class assignments available online. Computer access in designated common areas is available to students. Students grades are available online.

Contact Mrs. Renee Chastain, Assistant to the Director of Admissions. 770-692-6753. Fax: 770-969-6551. E-mail: admissions@landmark-cs.org. Web site: www.landmarkchristianschool.org

LANDMARK SCHOOL

Prides Crossing, Massachusetts

See Special Needs Schools section.

LANDON SCHOOL

6101 Wilson Lane
Bethesda, Maryland 20817

Head of School: Mr. David M. Armstrong

General Information Boys' day college-preparatory, arts, and music school. Grades 3–12. Founded: 1929. Setting: suburban. Nearest major city is Washington, DC. 75-acre campus. 13 buildings on campus. Approved or accredited by Association of Independent Maryland Schools, Middle States Association of Colleges and Schools, and Maryland Department of Education. Member of National Association of Independent Schools. Endowment: $10.2 million. Total enrollment: 680. Upper school average class size: 15. Upper school faculty-student ratio: 1:6. There are 170 required school days per year for Upper School students. Upper School students typically attend 5 days per week. The average school day consists of 7 hours and 10 minutes.

Upper School Student Profile Grade 9: 90 students (90 boys); Grade 10: 89 students (89 boys); Grade 11: 79 students (79 boys); Grade 12: 78 students (78 boys).

Faculty School total: 108. In upper school: 52 men, 12 women; 40 have advanced degrees.

Subjects Offered Acting, algebra, American Civil War, American foreign policy, American history, American literature, American studies, architecture, art, art history-AP, biology, biology-AP, calculus, calculus-AP, ceramics, chemistry, chemistry-AP, Chinese, Chinese history, classics, computer science, computer science-AP, conceptual physics, constitutional law, creative writing, digital art, drama, drawing, earth science, economics-AP, engineering, English, English literature, environmental science-AP, environmental studies, ethics, European history, expository writing, fine arts, foreign policy, forensics, French, French language-AP, French literature-AP, French studies, freshman foundations, geography, geology, geometry, government/civics, grammar, handbells, health, history, humanities, international relations, jazz band, journalism, justice seminar, Latin, mathematics, meteorology, Middle Eastern history, music, music history, music theory, music theory-AP, oceanography, painting, performing arts, photography, photojournalism, physical education, physics, physics-AP, pre-calculus, science, sculpture, senior project, Shakespeare, social studies, Spanish, Spanish language-AP, Spanish literature, statistics-AP, strings, technological applications, theater, trigonometry, typing, U.S. history, U.S. history-AP, world history, world literature, writing.

Graduation Requirements American Civil War, American government, arts and fine arts (art, music, dance, drama), biology, chemistry, English, ethics, foreign language, government, humanities, mathematics, music, physical education (includes health), pre-calculus, science, social studies (includes history), senior project, 2 year arts requirement, community service requirement in 13-14.

Special Academic Programs Advanced Placement exam preparation; honors section; independent study; term-away projects; study abroad.

College Admission Counseling 77 students graduated in 2012; 76 went to college, including Bucknell University; Davidson College; Trinity College; University of Colorado Boulder; University of Maryland, College Park; University of Virginia. Other: 1 had other specific plans. Mean SAT critical reading: 632, mean SAT math: 648, mean SAT writing: 629, mean combined SAT: 1909, mean composite ACT: 28.

Student Life Upper grades have specified standards of dress, student council, honor system. Discipline rests equally with students and faculty.

Summer Programs Remediation, enrichment, advancement, sports, art/fine arts programs offered; session focuses on enrichment, music, studio arts for Middle and Upper grades; advancement, remediation, and travel for Upper; held both on and off campus; held at locations in France, China and Spain; accepts boys and girls; open to students from other schools. 200 students usually enrolled. 2013 schedule: June 10 to August 2. Application deadline: none.

Tuition and Aid Day student tuition: $32,000. Tuition installment plan (FACTS Tuition Payment Plan, monthly payment plans, individually arranged payment plans, Annual payment and semi-annual payment). Need-based scholarship grants, 50% tuition remission for faculty children available. In 2012–13, 24% of upper-school students received aid. Total amount of financial aid awarded in 2012–13: $1,436,765.

Admissions Traditional secondary-level entrance grade is 9. ISEE or SSAT required. Deadline for receipt of application materials: January 15. Application fee required: $75. On-campus interview required.

Athletics Interscholastic: baseball, basketball, cross-country running, diving, fencing, football, golf, ice hockey, lacrosse, riflery, rugby, soccer, squash, strength & conditioning, swimming and diving, tennis, track and field, ultimate Frisbee, water polo, winter (indoor) track, wrestling; intramural: basketball, Frisbee, physical fitness, softball, strength & conditioning, tennis, ultimate Frisbee, weight lifting. 13 coaches, 1 athletic trainer.

Computers Computers are regularly used in architecture, art, computer applications, photojournalism classes. Computer network features include on-campus library services, online commercial services, Internet access, wireless campus network, Internet filtering or blocking technology, password-accessed Web portals. Campus intranet, student e-mail accounts, and computer access in designated common areas are available to students. Students grades are available online. The school has a published electronic and media policy.

Contact Mr. George C. Mulligan, Director of Admissions. 301-320-1067. Fax: 301-320-1133. E-mail: george_mulligan@landon.net. Web site: www.landon.net

LANSDALE CATHOLIC HIGH SCHOOL

700 Lansdale Avenue
Lansdale, Pennsylvania 19446-2995

Head of School: Mrs. Rita McGovern

General Information Coeducational day and distance learning college-preparatory, general academic, and religious studies school, affiliated with Roman Catholic Church. Grades 9–12. Distance learning grades 9–12. Founded: 1949. Setting: suburban. Nearest major city is Philadelphia. 1 building on campus. Approved or accredited by Middle States Association of Colleges and Schools, National Catholic Education Association, and Pennsylvania Department of Education. Total enrollment: 763. Upper school average class size: 30. There are 190 required school days per year for Upper School students. Upper School students typically attend 5 days per week. The average school day consists of 6 hours and 45 minutes.

Upper School Student Profile Grade 9: 177 students (85 boys, 92 girls); Grade 10: 193 students (98 boys, 95 girls); Grade 11: 213 students (121 boys, 92 girls); Grade 12: 180 students (101 boys, 79 girls). 99% of students are Roman Catholic.

Faculty School total: 37. In upper school: 17 men, 20 women; 18 have advanced degrees.

Subjects Offered Algebra, American government, American history, American history-AP, American literature, art, art history-AP, art-AP, band, biology-AP, business law, calculus, calculus-AP, career education, career planning, career/college preparation, Catholic belief and practice, chemistry, Chinese, choir, chorus, church history, college counseling, college placement, college planning, composition-AP, computer education, computer programming, drama, English language and composition-AP,

English literature and composition-AP, English literature-AP, English/composition-AP, environmental science, European history, European history-AP, French, government-AP, health education, Italian, Latin, mathematics-AP, physical fitness, physical science, physics, pre-calculus, SAT/ACT preparation, Spanish, statistics, statistics-AP, student government, studio art, studio art-AP, The 20th Century, trigonometry, U.S. government and politics, U.S. government and politics-AP, U.S. history, U.S. history-AP, United States government-AP, Western civilization.

Graduation Requirements 30 hour service requirement by the middle of junior year.

Special Academic Programs 17 Advanced Placement exams for which test preparation is offered; honors section; study at local college for college credit.

College Admission Counseling 179 students graduated in 2012; 177 went to college, including Montgomery County Community College; Penn State University Park; Shippensburg University of Pennsylvania; Temple University; West Chester University of Pennsylvania. Other: 1 went to work, 1 entered military service.

Student Life Upper grades have uniform requirement, student council, honor system. Discipline rests primarily with faculty. Attendance at religious services is required.

Summer Programs Remediation, enrichment, advancement, sports, art/fine arts programs offered; held on campus; accepts boys and girls; open to students from other schools. 2013 schedule: June to August.

Tuition and Aid Tuition installment plan (monthly payment plans, individually arranged payment plans). Tuition reduction for siblings, merit scholarship grants, need-based scholarship grants, TAP Program available. In 2012–13, 20% of upper-school students received aid.

Admissions Traditional secondary-level entrance grade is 9. Deadline for receipt of application materials: none. Application fee required. Interview recommended.

Athletics Interscholastic: baseball (boys), basketball (b,g), cheering (g), cross-country running (b,g), dance squad (b,g), field hockey (g), football (b), golf (b,g), ice hockey (b,g), lacrosse (b,g), rugby (b,g), soccer (b,g), softball (g), swimming and diving (b,g), tennis (b,g), track and field (b,g), volleyball (g), weight lifting (b), winter (indoor) track (b,g); intramural: flag football (b), ice hockey (b,g); coed interscholastic: bowling, diving, indoor track, indoor track & field; coed intramural: yoga. 1 PE instructor, 1 athletic trainer.

Computers Computers are regularly used in all classes. Computer network features include on-campus library services, online commercial services, Internet access, wireless campus network, Internet filtering or blocking technology. Computer access in designated common areas is available to students. Students grades are available online. The school has a published electronic and media policy.

Contact Mr. James Casey, President. 215-362-6160 Ext. 133. Fax: 215-362-5746. E-mail: jcasey@lansdalecatholic.com. Web site: www.lansdalecatholic.com

LA SALLE HIGH SCHOOL

3880 East Sierra Madre Boulevard
Pasadena, California 91107-1996

Head of School: Br. Christopher Brady, FSC

General Information Coeducational day college-preparatory, arts, and religious studies school, affiliated with Roman Catholic Church. Grades 9–12. Founded: 1956. Setting: suburban. Nearest major city is Los Angeles. 10-acre campus. 3 buildings on campus. Approved or accredited by California Association of Independent Schools, Christian Brothers Association, Western Association of Schools and Colleges, Western Catholic Education Association, and California Department of Education. Total enrollment: 710. Upper school average class size: 26. Upper school faculty-student ratio: 1:11. There are 180 required school days per year for Upper School students. Upper School students typically attend 5 days per week. The average school day consists of 6 hours and 15 minutes.

Upper School Student Profile Grade 9: 171 students (107 boys, 64 girls); Grade 10: 181 students (95 boys, 86 girls); Grade 11: 179 students (90 boys, 89 girls); Grade 12: 179 students (93 boys, 86 girls). 66% of students are Roman Catholic.

Faculty School total: 69. In upper school: 43 men, 26 women; 44 have advanced degrees.

Subjects Offered 20th century history, acting, Advanced Placement courses, advanced studio art-AP, algebra, American Civil War, American government, American literature-AP, ancient world history, art, art-AP, ASB Leadership, band, biology-AP, business law, calculus, calculus-AP, campus ministry, Catholic belief and practice, chemistry-AP, chorus, Christian and Hebrew scripture, church history, civics, classical civilization, community service, comparative religion, composition, composition-AP, computer applications, computer education, computer graphics, computer literacy, computer programming, concert choir, constitutional history of U.S., creative writing, dance, dance performance, digital photography, drama, dramatic arts, drawing, ecology, environmental systems, economics, economics-AP, education, electives, English, English composition, English language-AP, English literature, English literature and composition-AP, English-AP, fiction, film, fine arts, foreign language, French, general math, general science, geometry, government, government/civics, government/civics-AP, health and safety, health education, Hispanic literature, history, history-AP, honors algebra, honors English, honors U.S. history, honors world history, integrated mathematics, introduction to theater, jazz, jazz band, jazz dance, jazz ensemble, journalism, keyboarding, lab science, lab/keyboard, law and the legal system, leadership, leadership and service, mathematics, mathematics-AP, microbiology, modern European history-AP, musical productions, newspaper, photo shop, photography, physics, physics-AP, play production, pottery, pre-calculus, religion, religion and culture, religious studies, Roman civilization, science, social justice, Spanish, Spanish-AP, student government, studio art, studio art-AP, study skills, tap dance, technical theater, television, theater, theater arts, theater design and production, theater production, trigonometry, U.S. government, U.S. government and politics-AP, U.S. history, U.S. history-AP, U.S. literature, video communication, visual and performing arts, visual arts, wind instruments, world history, writing, yearbook.

Graduation Requirements Algebra, American literature, arts and fine arts (art, music, dance, drama), biology, campus ministry, chemistry, Christian and Hebrew scripture, Christian doctrine, church history, civics, computer literacy, economics, English, English composition, English literature, foreign language, geometry, integrated mathematics, physical education (includes health), physics, religious studies, U.S. history.

Special Academic Programs 15 Advanced Placement exams for which test preparation is offered; honors section.

College Admission Counseling 195 students graduated in 2012; all went to college, including Cornell University; Loyola Marymount University; Northern Arizona University; University of California, Berkeley; University of California, Santa Cruz; University of Southern California. Median SAT critical reading: 580, median SAT math: 590, median SAT writing: 590, median combined SAT: 1780, median composite ACT: 24. 42% scored over 600 on SAT critical reading, 47% scored over 600 on SAT math, 48% scored over 600 on SAT writing, 44% scored over 1800 on combined SAT, 38% scored over 26 on composite ACT.

Student Life Upper grades have uniform requirement, student council, honor system. Discipline rests primarily with faculty. Attendance at religious services is required.

Summer Programs Remediation, enrichment, advancement, sports, art/fine arts, computer instruction programs offered; session focuses on academics and sports camps; held both on and off campus; held at some students do classes online and some students do classes at local Junior Colleges; accepts boys and girls; open to students from other schools. 575 students usually enrolled. 2013 schedule: June 24 to July 18. Application deadline: June 10.

Tuition and Aid Day student tuition: $13,920. Tuition installment plan (monthly payment plans, biannual). Merit scholarship grants, need-based scholarship grants available. In 2012–13, 40% of upper-school students received aid; total upper-school merit-scholarship money awarded: $80,000. Total amount of financial aid awarded in 2012–13: $1,450,000.

Admissions Traditional secondary-level entrance grade is 9. For fall 2012, 599 students applied for upper-level admission, 310 were accepted, 110 enrolled. STS required. Deadline for receipt of application materials: January 13. Application fee required: $80. Interview required.

Athletics Interscholastic: baseball (boys), basketball (b,g), cross-country running (b,g), dance team (g), equestrian sports (g), football (b), golf (b,g), soccer (b,g), softball (g), swimming and diving (b,g), tennis (b,g), track and field (b,g), volleyball (b,g), water polo (b,g); intramural: basketball (b,g), dance team (g), flag football (b); coed interscholastic: cheering, physical fitness, weight training; coed intramural: fitness, Frisbee, physical fitness, weight training. 2 PE instructors, 50 coaches, 2 athletic trainers.

Computers Computers are regularly used in all academic, computer applications, video film production classes. Computer resources include on-campus library services, online commercial services, Internet access. Students grades are available online. The school has a published electronic and media policy.

Contact Ms. Teresa Ring, Admissions Secretary. 626-351-8951. Fax: 626-696-4411. E-mail: tring@lasallehs.org. Web site: www.lasallehs.org

LA SCUOLA D'ITALIA GUGLIELMO MARCONI

12 East 96th Street
New York, New York 10128

Head of School: Prof. Anna Fiore

General Information Coeducational boarding and day and distance learning college-preparatory and bilingual studies school. Distance learning grade X. Founded: 1977. Setting: urban. Nearest major city is Manhattan. 1 building on campus. Approved or accredited by New York Department of Education. Languages of instruction: English, French, and Italian. Total enrollment: 261. Upper school average class size: 10. There are 212 required school days per year for Upper School students. Upper School students typically attend 5 days per week.

Upper School Student Profile Grade 9: 12 students (5 boys, 7 girls); Grade 10: 13 students (7 boys, 6 girls); Grade 11: 11 students (4 boys, 7 girls); Grade 12: 8 students (3 boys, 5 girls).

Faculty School total: 48. In upper school: 6 men, 9 women; 15 have advanced degrees.

Special Academic Programs International Baccalaureate program; Advanced Placement exam preparation; honors section; study at local college for college credit; domestic exchange program; study abroad; remedial reading and/or remedial writing; remedial math; ESL (26 students enrolled).

College Admission Counseling 9 students graduated in 2012; all went to college.

Student Life Upper grades have uniform requirement, honor system. Discipline rests equally with students and faculty.

Admissions Traditional secondary-level entrance grade is 9. For fall 2012, 17 students applied for upper-level admission, 17 were accepted, 16 enrolled. Application fee required: $100. Interview required.

Athletics Coed Interscholastic: artistic gym, basketball, fencing, soccer. 2 PE instructors, 2 coaches, 2 athletic trainers.

Computers Computer network features include on-campus library services, Internet access, Internet filtering or blocking technology. Computer access in designated common areas is available to students. The school has a published electronic and media policy.

Contact Mrs. Pia Pedicini, Deputy Head of School/Director of Admissions. 212-369-3290. Fax: 212-369-1164. E-mail: secretary@lascuoladitalia.org. Web site: www.lascuoladitalia.org

THE LATIN SCHOOL OF CHICAGO

59 West North Boulevard
Chicago, Illinois 60610-1492

Head of School: Randall Dunn

General Information Coeducational day college-preparatory school. Grades JK–12. Founded: 1888. Setting: urban. 1-acre campus. 1 building on campus. Approved or accredited by Independent Schools Association of the Central States and Illinois Department of Education. Member of National Association of Independent Schools and Secondary School Admission Test Board. Endowment: $23.6 million. Total enrollment: 1,110. Upper school average class size: 15. Upper school faculty-student ratio: 1:8. There are 165 required school days per year for Upper School students. Upper School students typically attend 5 days per week. The average school day consists of 6 hours and 30 minutes.

Upper School Student Profile Grade 9: 106 students (49 boys, 57 girls); Grade 10: 111 students (52 boys, 59 girls); Grade 11: 107 students (47 boys, 60 girls); Grade 12: 111 students (54 boys, 57 girls).

Faculty School total: 150. In upper school: 40 men, 37 women; 59 have advanced degrees.

Subjects Offered Advanced Placement courses, advanced studio art-AP, African studies, African-American literature, algebra, American history, American history-AP, American literature, anatomy, animal behavior, art, art history, Asian studies, astronomy, biochemistry, biology, biology-AP, calculus, calculus-AP, chemistry, chemistry-AP, chorus, community service, composition, computer graphics, computer programming, computer science, creative writing, dance, drama, ecology, electives, electronics, English, English literature, environmental science, environmental science-AP, ethics, European civilization, European history, fine arts, French, French language-AP, French literature-AP, geography, geometry, history, history of ideas, honors U.S. history, human relations, human sexuality, humanities, independent study, instrumental music, Latin, Latin American history, Latin American literature, Latin-AP, literature by women, Mandarin, mathematical modeling, mathematics, mathematics-AP, Middle East, Middle Eastern history, music theory, photography, physical education, physics, physics-AP, physiology, poetry, probability and statistics, psychology, religion, science, social studies, Spanish, Spanish language-AP, Spanish literature, Spanish literature-AP, speech, stage design, statistics, studio art-AP, theater, trigonometry, women's literature, world history, world literature, writing.

Graduation Requirements Arts and fine arts (art, music, dance, drama), English, ethics, foreign language, human relations, human sexuality, mathematics, performing arts, physical education (includes health), science, social studies (includes history), technology, one-week non-credit course each year, service learning requirement. Community service is required.

Special Academic Programs Advanced Placement exam preparation; honors section; independent study; study abroad; academic accommodation for the gifted; remedial reading and/or remedial writing; remedial math; programs in general development for dyslexic students.

College Admission Counseling 111 students graduated in 2012; 109 went to college, including Miami University; Northwestern University; Tufts University; University of Chicago; University of Wisconsin–Madison; Yale University. Other: 2 had other specific plans.

Student Life Upper grades have specified standards of dress, student council, honor system. Discipline rests equally with students and faculty.

Summer Programs Remediation, enrichment, advancement, sports, art/fine arts, rigorous outdoor training, computer instruction programs offered; session focuses on enrichment, remediation, sports, travel, and adventure; held both on and off campus; held at lakefront, city parks, wilderness experiences in the United States and abroad; accepts boys and girls; open to students from other schools. 180 students usually enrolled. 2013 schedule: June 10 to August 2. Application deadline: none.

Tuition and Aid Day student tuition: $27,985. Tuition installment plan (Insured Tuition Payment Plan, Key Tuition Payment Plan, FACTS Tuition Payment Plan, monthly payment plans, individually arranged payment plans). Need-based scholarship grants, need-based loans, middle-income loans, Key Education Achiever Loans available. In 2012–13, 20% of upper-school students received aid. Total amount of financial aid awarded in 2012–13: $1,999,129.

Admissions Traditional secondary-level entrance grade is 9. For fall 2012, 222 students applied for upper-level admission, 105 were accepted, 50 enrolled. ISEE required. Deadline for receipt of application materials: December 15. Application fee required: $80. On-campus interview required.

Athletics Interscholastic: aquatics (boys, girls), badminton (g), baseball (b), basketball (b,g), cross-country running (b,g), field hockey (g), golf (b,g), ice hockey (b,g), soccer (b,g), softball (g), swimming and diving (b,g), tennis (b,g), track and field (b,g), volleyball (b,g), water polo (b,g); intramural: life saving (b,g); coed intramural: dance, kayaking, outdoor activities, outdoor adventure, outdoor education, outdoor recreation, physical fitness, physical training, skiing (downhill). 6 PE instructors, 12 coaches, 2 athletic trainers.

Computers Computers are regularly used in art, English, foreign language, mathematics, science classes. Computer network features include on-campus library services, online commercial services, Internet access, wireless campus network. Campus intranet, student e-mail accounts, and computer access in designated common areas are available to students. The school has a published electronic and media policy.

Contact Frankie Brown, Director of Admissions and Financial Aid. 312-582-6060. Fax: 312-582-6061. E-mail: fbrown@latinschool.org. Web site: www.latinschool.org

LAURALTON HALL

200 High Street
Milford, Connecticut 06460

Head of School: Dr. Antoinette Iadarola

General Information Girls' day college-preparatory, arts, religious studies, and technology school, affiliated with Roman Catholic Church. Grades 9–12. Founded: 1905. Setting: suburban. Nearest major city is New Haven. 30-acre campus. 5 buildings on campus. Approved or accredited by Connecticut Association of Independent Schools, Mercy Secondary Education Association, New England Association of Schools and Colleges, and Connecticut Department of Education. Total enrollment: 465. Upper school faculty-student ratio: 1:12. There are 165 required school days per year for Upper School students. Upper School students typically attend 5 days per week. The average school day consists of 6 hours and 15 minutes.

Upper School Student Profile Grade 9: 123 students (123 girls); Grade 10: 115 students (115 girls); Grade 11: 120 students (120 girls); Grade 12: 107 students (107 girls). 76% of students are Roman Catholic.

Faculty School total: 41. In upper school: 3 men, 38 women; 29 have advanced degrees.

Subjects Offered Algebra, American history, American literature, anatomy, art, biology, business, calculus, chemistry, computer math, computer programming, English, English literature, environmental science, European history, fine arts, French, geometry, government/civics, health, history, journalism, Latin, mathematics, music, physical education, physics, physiology, religion, science, social studies, Spanish, trigonometry, world history, writing.

Graduation Requirements Arts and fine arts (art, music, dance, drama), English, foreign language, mathematics, physical education (includes health), religion (includes Bible studies and theology), science, social studies (includes history). Community service is required.

Special Academic Programs Honors section; study at local college for college credit.

College Admission Counseling 108 students graduated in 2012; all went to college, including Boston College; College of the Holy Cross; Fairfield University; Loyola University Maryland; Quinnipiac University; University of Connecticut. Mean SAT critical reading: 544, mean SAT math: 570, mean SAT writing: 563.

Student Life Upper grades have uniform requirement, student council, honor system. Discipline rests primarily with faculty. Attendance at religious services is required.

Tuition and Aid Day student tuition: $16,175. Tuition installment plan (FACTS Tuition Payment Plan, 1- and 2-payment plans). Tuition reduction for siblings, merit scholarship grants, need-based scholarship grants available. In 2012–13, 24% of upper-school students received aid; total upper-school merit-scholarship money awarded: $125,000. Total amount of financial aid awarded in 2012–13: $450,000.

Admissions Traditional secondary-level entrance grade is 9. For fall 2012, 323 students applied for upper-level admission, 247 were accepted, 123 enrolled. High School Placement Test required. Deadline for receipt of application materials: none. Application fee required: $60.

Athletics Interscholastic: basketball, cheering, cross-country running, diving, field hockey, golf, gymnastics, ice hockey, indoor track, lacrosse, running, skiing (downhill), soccer, softball, swimming and diving, tennis, track and field, volleyball; intramural: basketball. 1 PE instructor, 27 coaches, 1 athletic trainer.

Computers Computers are regularly used in mathematics classes. Computer network features include on-campus library services, online commercial services, Internet access, wireless campus network, Internet filtering or blocking technology. Campus intranet, student e-mail accounts, and computer access in designated common areas are available to students. The school has a published electronic and media policy.

Contact Mrs. Kathleen O. Shine, Director of Enrollment Management. 203-878-3333. Fax: 203-876-9760. E-mail: kshine@lauraltonhall.org. Web site: www.lauraltonhall.org

See Display on next page and Close-Up on page 590

THE LAUREATE ACADEMY

Winnipeg, Manitoba, Canada
See Special Needs Schools section.

LAUREL SPRINGS SCHOOL

302 West El Paseo Road
Ojai, California 93023

Head of School: Marilyn Mosley

General Information Distance learning only college-preparatory, arts, vocational, technology, and distance learning school. Distance learning grades K–12. Founded: 1991. Setting: small town. Nearest major city is Los Angeles. 1 building on campus. Approved or accredited by Western Association of Schools and Colleges and California Department of Education. Total enrollment: 1,529. Upper school average class size: 1. Upper school faculty-student ratio: 1:1. The average school day consists of 6 hours.

Upper School Student Profile Grade 9: 178 students (87 boys, 91 girls); Grade 10: 249 students (118 boys, 131 girls); Grade 11: 260 students (124 boys, 136 girls); Grade 12: 189 students (91 boys, 98 girls).

Faculty School total: 86. In upper school: 13 men, 51 women; 46 have advanced degrees.

Subjects Offered Algebra, American literature, art appreciation, art history, biology, biology-AP, British literature, British literature (honors), calculus, calculus-AP, career/college preparation, cartooning/animation, chemistry, chemistry-AP, college admission preparation, college counseling, driver education, earth science, economics, electives, English composition, English language and composition-AP, English literature and composition-AP, environmental education, environmental studies, French, French-AP, geometry, German, health, history of music, honors algebra, honors English, honors geometry, honors U.S. history, honors world history, Latin, macroeconomics-AP, Mandarin, microeconomics-AP, music history, mythology, photo shop, physical education, physics, physics-AP, pre-calculus, psychology, psychology-AP, SAT/ACT preparation, Shakespeare, sociology, Spanish, Spanish language-AP, statistics-AP, trigonometry, U.S. government, U.S. government and politics-AP, U.S. history, U.S. history-AP, world cultures, world history, world literature.

Graduation Requirements Arts and fine arts (art, music, dance, drama), electives, English, foreign language, mathematics, physical education (includes health), science, social studies (includes history).

Special Academic Programs Advanced Placement exam preparation; honors section; accelerated programs; independent study; term-away projects; academic accommodation for the gifted, the musically talented, and the artistically talented; remedial reading and/or remedial writing; remedial math; programs in English, mathematics, general development for dyslexic students; special instructional classes for students needing customized learning options.

College Admission Counseling 102 students graduated in 2012; 94 went to college, including Middle Tennessee State University; New York University; Purdue University; University of California, Los Angeles; University of California, Santa Barbara; University of Southern California. Other: 8 had other specific plans. Mean SAT critical reading: 562, mean SAT math: 519, mean SAT writing: 547, mean composite ACT: 23.

Student Life Upper grades have student council, honor system. Discipline rests equally with students and faculty.

Summer Programs Enrichment, advancement, art/fine arts, computer instruction programs offered; session focuses on accelerated classes; held off campus; held at individual homes of enrolled students; accepts boys and girls; open to students from other schools. Application deadline: none.

Tuition and Aid Tuition installment plan (monthly payment plans, individually arranged payment plans). Tuition reduction for siblings, need-based scholarship grants available.

Admissions Traditional secondary-level entrance grade is 9. For fall 2012, 1,529 students applied for upper-level admission, 1,529 were accepted, 1,529 enrolled. Deadline for receipt of application materials: none. Application fee required: $250.

Computers Computers are regularly used in art, economics, English, foreign language, geography, health, history, independent study, information technology, language development, life skills, mathematics, psychology, SAT preparation, science, social studies, writing classes. Computer network features include on-campus library services, Internet access, 100 online courses. Students grades are available online.

Contact Admissions. 800-377-5890 Ext. 5502. Fax: 805-646-0186. Web site: www.laurelsprings.com

LAUSANNE COLLEGIATE SCHOOL

1381 West Massey Road
Memphis, Tennessee 38120

Head of School: Mr. Stuart McCathie

General Information Coeducational day college-preparatory, arts, bilingual studies, technology, AP courses, honors curriculum, and sports education, electives school. Grades PK–12. Founded: 1926. Setting: suburban. 28-acre campus. 5 buildings on campus. Approved or accredited by National Independent Private Schools Association, Southern Association of Colleges and Schools, Southern Association of Independent Schools, and Tennessee Department of Education. Member of National Association of Independent Schools. Endowment: $700,000. Total enrollment: 809.

Upper school average class size: 15. Upper school faculty-student ratio: 1:9. There are 175 required school days per year for Upper School students. Upper School students typically attend 5 days per week. The average school day consists of 6 hours and 30 minutes.

Upper School Student Profile Grade 9: 77 students (35 boys, 42 girls); Grade 10: 90 students (43 boys, 47 girls); Grade 11: 82 students (41 boys, 41 girls); Grade 12: 70 students (34 boys, 36 girls).

Faculty School total: 95. In upper school: 17 men, 17 women; 20 have advanced degrees.

Subjects Offered Acting, advanced math, algebra, American government, ancient world history, art, art-AP, biology, biology-AP, calculus, chemistry, choir, college admission preparation, comparative government and politics-AP, creative writing, economics, English, English-AP, French, French-AP, geometry, health and wellness, honors algebra, honors English, honors geometry, humanities, instrumental music, international studies, journalism, Latin, modern world history, photography, physical education, physical science, physics, physics-AP, play production, pre-calculus, public policy, short story, Spanish, Spanish-AP, statistics, U.S. history, U.S. history-AP, writing workshop.

Graduation Requirements Arts and fine arts (art, music, dance, drama), English, foreign language, mathematics, physical education (includes health), science, social studies (includes history).

Special Academic Programs International Baccalaureate program; 12 Advanced Placement exams for which test preparation is offered; honors section; independent study; academic accommodation for the gifted, the musically talented, and the artistically talented; ESL (35 students enrolled).

College Admission Counseling 79 students graduated in 2011; all went to college, including Dartmouth College; Northwestern University; Rhodes College; The University of Tennessee; University of Colorado Boulder; Wake Forest University. Mean SAT critical reading: 583, mean SAT math: 595, mean SAT writing: 578, mean combined SAT: 1756, mean composite ACT: 26.

Student Life Upper grades have specified standards of dress, student council, honor system. Discipline rests primarily with faculty.

Tuition and Aid Day student tuition: $16,400. Tuition installment plan (monthly payment plans, Tuition Refund Plan (TRP)). Need-based scholarship grants, tuition remission for children of faculty available. In 2011–12, 18% of upper-school students received aid. Total amount of financial aid awarded in 2011–12: $494,108.

Admissions Traditional secondary-level entrance grade is 9. For fall 2011, 68 students applied for upper-level admission, 60 were accepted, 50 enrolled. ISEE required. Deadline for receipt of application materials: none. Application fee required: $75. Interview required.

Athletics Interscholastic: basketball (boys, girls), cheering (g), cross-country running (b,g), dance squad (g), dance team (g), golf (b,g), gymnastics (b,g), lacrosse (b,g), pom squad (g), soccer (b,g), softball (g), swimming and diving (b,g), tennis (b,g), track and field (b,g), volleyball (g); intramural: ballet (g), basketball (b,g), bowling (b,g), dance team (g), flag football (b,g), Frisbee (b,g), gymnastics (b,g), lacrosse (b,g), outdoor activities (b,g), physical fitness (b,g), soccer (b,g), strength & conditioning (b,g), tennis (b,g), track and field (b,g), ultimate Frisbee (b,g), volleyball (b,g), weight lifting (b,g); coed interscholastic: swimming and diving; coed intramural: basketball, bowling, flag football, Frisbee, lacrosse, martial arts, outdoor activities, physical fitness, soccer, strength & conditioning, tennis, track and field, ultimate Frisbee, volleyball, weight lifting, yoga. 30 coaches, 2 athletic trainers.

Computers Computers are regularly used in all academic, technology classes. Computer network features include on-campus library services, online commercial services, Internet access, wireless campus network, Internet filtering or blocking technology, homework assignments available online. Student e-mail accounts are available to students. Students grades are available online. The school has a published electronic and media policy.

Contact Mrs. Marcie Malin, Admission Coordinator. 901-474-1030. Fax: 901-474-1010. E-mail: mmalin@lausanneschool.com. Web site: www.lausanneschool.com

LAWRENCE ACADEMY

Powderhouse Road
Groton, Massachusetts 01450

Head of School: Mr. Greg Foster

General Information Coeducational boarding and day college-preparatory, interdisciplinary ninth grade curriculum, and student-centered learning school. Grades 9–12. Founded: 1793. Setting: small town. Nearest major city is Boston. Students are housed in single-sex dormitories. 115-acre campus. 31 buildings on campus. Approved or accredited by Association of Independent Schools in New England, New England Association of Schools and Colleges, The Association of Boarding Schools, and Massachusetts Department of Education. Member of National Association of Independent Schools and Secondary School Admission Test Board. Endowment: $18 million. Total enrollment: 399. Upper school average class size: 12. Upper school faculty-student ratio: 1:5. Upper School students typically attend 5 days per week. The average school day consists of 6 hours and 20 minutes.

Upper School Student Profile Grade 9: 79 students (40 boys, 39 girls); Grade 10: 111 students (61 boys, 50 girls); Grade 11: 108 students (59 boys, 49 girls); Grade 12: 101 students (51 boys, 50 girls). 50% of students are boarding students. 60% are state residents. 21 states are represented in upper school student body. 13% are international students. International students from China, Germany, Kazakhstan, Republic of Korea, Russian Federation, and Spain; 15 other countries represented in student body.

Faculty School total: 83. In upper school: 44 men, 39 women; 50 have advanced degrees; 39 reside on campus.

Subjects Offered Advanced Placement courses, African-American literature, algebra, American history, anatomy, art, astronomy, biology, botany, calculus, calculus-AP, ceramics, chemistry, composition, creative writing, criminal justice, dance, drawing, ecology, electives, electronics, English, English literature, entomology, environmental science-AP, ESL, European history, fine arts, finite math, fractal geometry, French, government/civics, history, independent study, John F. Kennedy, Latin, Latin American literature, limnology, marine science, mathematics, microbiology, music, music composition, music technology, music theory, music-AP, ornithology, painting, photography, physics, playwriting, pre-calculus, psychology, scene study, science, sculpture, Shakespeare, social psychology, Spanish, studio art, theater, tropical biology, U.S. government and politics-AP, writing.

Graduation Requirements Arts and fine arts (art, music, dance, drama), English, foreign language, history, mathematics, science, Winterim participation.

Special Academic Programs Advanced Placement exam preparation; honors section; independent study; term-away projects; study abroad; academic accommodation for the musically talented and the artistically talented; special instructional classes for deaf students, blind students; ESL (20 students enrolled).

College Admission Counseling 91 students graduated in 2011; all went to college, including Boston College; Boston University; Colby College; Skidmore College; University of New Hampshire; University of Vermont. Median SAT critical reading: 560, median SAT math: 580, median SAT writing: 570. 34% scored over 600 on SAT critical reading, 46% scored over 600 on SAT math, 40% scored over 600 on SAT writing, 37% scored over 1800 on combined SAT.

Student Life Upper grades have specified standards of dress, student council, honor system. Discipline rests primarily with faculty.

Tuition and Aid Day student tuition: $38,770; 7-day tuition and room/board: $50,375. Tuition installment plan (Key Tuition Payment Plan, monthly payment plans). Need-based scholarship grants, need-based loans, prepGATE loans available. In 2011–12, 29% of upper-school students received aid. Total amount of financial aid awarded in 2011–12: $3,450,000.

Admissions Traditional secondary-level entrance grade is 9. For fall 2011, 682 students applied for upper-level admission, 252 were accepted, 141 enrolled. PSAT or SAT, SSAT or TOEFL required. Deadline for receipt of application materials: February 1. Application fee required: $50. Interview required.

Athletics Interscholastic: baseball (boys), basketball (b,g), cross-country running (b,g), field hockey (g), football (b), golf (b,g), ice hockey (b,g), lacrosse (b,g), soccer (b,g), softball (g), tennis (b,g), track and field (b,g), volleyball (g), wrestling (b); intramural: tennis (b,g); coed interscholastic: alpine skiing, independent competitive sports, mountain biking, skiing (downhill); coed intramural: dance, fitness, independent competitive sports, modern dance, outdoors, physical fitness, physical training, rappelling, skiing (downhill), snowboarding, strength & conditioning, volleyball, weight training, yoga. 5 coaches, 2 athletic trainers.

Computers Computers are regularly used in college planning, computer applications, ESL, library, media production, music, photography, SAT preparation, video film production, yearbook classes. Computer network features include on-campus library services, online commercial services, Internet access, wireless campus network, Internet filtering or blocking technology. Campus intranet, student e-mail accounts, and computer access in designated common areas are available to students. Students grades are available online. The school has a published electronic and media policy.

Contact Tony Hawgood, Director of Admissions. 978-448-6535. Fax: 978-448-1519. E-mail: admiss@lacademy.edu. Web site: www.lacademy.edu

LAWRENCE SCHOOL

Sagamore Hills, Ohio
See Special Needs Schools section.

THE LAWRENCEVILLE SCHOOL

PO Box 6008
2500 Main Street
Lawrenceville, New Jersey 08648

Head of School: Elizabeth A. Duffy

General Information Coeducational boarding and day college-preparatory, arts, religious studies, and technology school. Grades 9–PG. Founded: 1810. Setting: small town. Nearest major city is Philadelphia, PA. Students are housed in single-sex dormitories. 700-acre campus. 39 buildings on campus. Approved or accredited by Middle States Association of Colleges and Schools, New Jersey Association of Independent Schools, The Association of Boarding Schools, and New Jersey Department of Education. Member of National Association of Independent Schools and Secondary School Admission Test Board. Total enrollment: 819. Upper school average class size: 12. Upper school faculty-student ratio: 1:8. Upper School students typically attend 6 days per week. The average school day consists of 7 hours.

Upper School Student Profile 68% of students are boarding students. 45% are state residents. 32 states are represented in upper school student body. 15% are international students. International students from Canada, China, Hong Kong, Japan, Republic of Korea, and Saudi Arabia; 26 other countries represented in student body.

Faculty School total: 145. In upper school: 77 men, 68 women; all have advanced degrees.

Subjects Offered Acting, advanced chemistry, advanced computer applications, advanced studio art-AP, African-American literature, algebra, American Civil War, American foreign policy, American government, American history, American history-AP, American literature, American studies, architecture, art, art history, art history-AP, art-AP, arts, Asian history, astronomy, Basic programming, Bible, Bible studies, bioethics, bioethics, DNA and culture, biology, biology-AP, British literature, Buddhism, calculus, calculus-AP, Central and Eastern European history, ceramics, chamber groups, chemistry, chemistry-AP, China/Japan history, Chinese, Chinese studies, choir, chorus, Christian studies, Civil War, civil war history, classical Greek literature, classical language, comparative government and politics, conceptual physics, constitutional history of U.S., contemporary women writers, critical writing, dance, data analysis, design, digital applications, digital art, drama, dramatic arts, drawing, drawing and design, driver education, Eastern religion and philosophy, economics, electronic music, English, English literature, English literature-AP, English/composition-AP, environmental science, environmental studies, ethics, European history, European history-AP, European literature, evolution, field ecology, film and new technologies, film appreciation, filmmaking, foreign language, foreign policy, French, French language-AP, French literature-AP, French studies, French-AP, geometry, global science, Greek, health and wellness, Hebrew scripture, Hindi, historical foundations for arts, history of China and Japan, Holocaust, human biology, humanities, independent study, instruments, interdisciplinary studies, introduction to literature, introduction to theater, Irish literature, Irish studies, Islamic studies, Japanese, Japanese history, jazz, Jewish studies, John F. Kennedy, journalism, Latin, linear algebra, literature, medieval history, medieval literature, Middle East, Middle Eastern history, nature study, orchestra, organic chemistry, painting, participation in sports, personal development, philosophy, photography, physics, physics-AP, physiology, poetry, pre-algebra, pre-calculus, printmaking, probability and statistics, research seminar, robotics, science, set design, Shakespeare, short story, Southern literature, Spanish, Spanish language-AP, Spanish literature, studio art, the Presidency, the Sixties, theater, theater arts, U.S. constitutional history, U.S. government, U.S. government and politics, U.S. history, visual arts, water color painting, women in world history, world religions, world religions, writing.

Graduation Requirements Arts and fine arts (art, music, dance, drama), English, foreign language, interdisciplinary studies, mathematics, religion (includes Bible studies and theology), science, social sciences, social studies (includes history). Community service is required.

Special Academic Programs Honors section; independent study; term-away projects; study abroad.

College Admission Counseling 232 students graduated in 2012; 230 went to college, including Columbia College; New York University; Princeton University; University of Pennsylvania; Yale University. Other: 1 went to work, 1 entered a postgraduate year. Median SAT critical reading: 676, median SAT math: 697, median SAT writing: 687.

Student Life Upper grades have specified standards of dress, student council, honor system. Discipline rests equally with students and faculty.

Tuition and Aid Day student tuition: $38,050; 7-day tuition and room/board: $46,475. Tuition installment plan (one, two, and nine month installment plans are available). Need-based scholarship grants available. In 2012–13, 29% of upper-school students received aid. Total amount of financial aid awarded in 2012–13: $1,010,000.

Admissions Traditional secondary-level entrance grade is 9. For fall 2012, 1,929 students applied for upper-level admission, 244 enrolled. ISEE, PSAT and SAT for applicants to grade 11 and 12, SSAT or TOEFL or SLEP required. Deadline for receipt of application materials: January 31. Application fee required: $50. Interview required.

Athletics Interscholastic: baseball (boys), basketball (b,g), crew (b,g), cross-country running (b,g), fencing (b,g), field hockey (g), football (b), golf (b,g), hockey (b,g), ice hockey (b,g), indoor track (b,g), indoor track & field (b,g), lacrosse (b,g), rowing (b,g), soccer (b,g), softball (g), squash (b,g), swimming and diving (b,g), tennis (b,g), track and field (b,g), volleyball (b,g), water polo (b,g), winter (indoor) track (b,g); intramural: basketball (b,g), Frisbee (g), handball (b,g), team handball (b,g), ultimate Frisbee (g), weight lifting (b,g), weight training (b,g); coed interscholastic: wrestling; coed intramural: backpacking, bicycling, broomball, canoeing/kayaking, climbing, cricket, dance, fitness, hiking/backpacking, ice skating, kayaking, modern dance, Nautilus, outdoor activities, physical fitness, physical training, rock climbing, ropes courses, squash, strength & conditioning, wall climbing, yoga. 72 coaches, 4 athletic trainers.

Computers Computers are regularly used in art, English, mathematics, music, science, technology classes. Computer network features include on-campus library services, online commercial services, Internet access, wireless campus network, Internet filtering or blocking technology. Campus intranet, student e-mail accounts, and computer access in designated common areas are available to students. Students grades are available online. The school has a published electronic and media policy.

Contact Sally Fitzpatrick, Interim Dean of Admission. 800-735-2030. Fax: 609-895-2217. E-mail: sfitzpatrick@lawrenceville.org. Web site: www.lawrenceville.org

See Display below and Close-Up on page 592.

LEE ACADEMY

26 Winn Road
Lee, Maine 04455

Head of School: Mr. Bruce Lindberg

General Information Coeducational boarding and day college-preparatory, arts, and vocational school. Boarding grades 9–PG, day grades 9–12. Founded: 1845. Setting: rural. Nearest major city is Bangor. Students are housed in single-sex dormitories. 400-acre campus. 15 buildings on campus. Approved or accredited by Independent Schools of Northern New England, New England Association of Schools and Colleges, and Maine Department of Education. Total enrollment: 268. Upper school average class size: 12. Upper school faculty-student ratio: 1:12. There are 175 required school days per year for Upper School students. Upper School students typically attend 5 days per week. The average school day consists of 7 hours and 30 minutes.

Upper School Student Profile Grade 9: 40 students (19 boys, 21 girls); Grade 10: 65 students (35 boys, 30 girls); Grade 11: 72 students (41 boys, 31 girls); Grade 12: 83 students (59 boys, 24 girls); Postgraduate: 8 students (8 boys). 43% of students are boarding students. 57% are state residents. 5 states are represented in upper school student body. 41% are international students. International students from Brazil, China, Democratic People's Republic of Korea, Mali, Senegal, and Turkey; 11 other countries represented in student body.

Faculty School total: 28. In upper school: 15 men, 13 women; 9 have advanced degrees; 11 reside on campus.

Subjects Offered ACT preparation, advanced biology, advanced chemistry, advanced math, Advanced Placement courses, advanced studio art-AP, algebra, American government, American history-AP, anatomy and physiology, art, art-AP, athletics, audio visual/media, band, biology-AP, calculus, calculus-AP, chemistry, chemistry-AP, choir, choral music, chorus, civil rights, comparative government and politics-AP, composition, composition-AP, costumes and make-up, creative drama, developmental math, digital photography, drama, English, English as a foreign language, English language and composition-AP, English language-AP, English literature and composition-AP, English literature-AP, English-AP, English/composition-AP, environmental science-AP, ESL, ESL, foreign language, French, general math, geometry, government and politics-AP, government/civics, guitar, health, health and wellness, history, history-AP, honors English, honors geometry, honors U.S. history, industrial technology, integrated mathematics, introduction to theater, learning lab, literature and composition-AP, literature-AP, media arts, music, music appreciation, music performance, music theater, musical productions, musical theater, performing arts, photography, physical education, physical fitness, physics, physics-AP, piano, pre-college orientation, psychology-AP, SAT preparation, SAT/ACT preparation, Spanish, stage and body movement, stage design, stagecraft, statistics-AP, studio art-AP, theater, theater arts, theater design and production, theater production, TOEFL preparation, U.S. government and politics, U.S. government and politics-AP, U.S. history, U.S. history-AP, vocational skills, wellness, wind ensemble, wind instruments, world cultures, world history, yearbook.

Graduation Requirements Algebra, American history, arts, biology, civics, computer skills, English, foreign language, health and wellness, mathematics, physical education (includes health), science.

Special Academic Programs Advanced Placement exam preparation; honors section; independent study; study abroad; ESL (48 students enrolled).

College Admission Counseling 70 students graduated in 2012; they went to Arizona State University; Saint Joseph's College of Maine; St. Bonaventure University; University of Maine; University of Nevada, Las Vegas. Median SAT critical reading: 560, median SAT math: 622, median SAT writing: 570, median composite ACT: 26.

Student Life Upper grades have specified standards of dress, student council. Discipline rests primarily with faculty.

Summer Programs ESL programs offered; session focuses on ESL; held on campus; accepts boys and girls; open to students from other schools. 60 students usually enrolled. 2013 schedule: July to August. Application deadline: June.

Tuition and Aid Day student tuition: $9000; 7-day tuition and room/board: $32,900. Tuition installment plan (monthly payment plans, individually arranged payment plans). Need-based scholarship grants available.

Admissions Traditional secondary-level entrance grade is 9. TOEFL or SLEP or writing sample required. Deadline for receipt of application materials: none. No application fee required. Interview recommended.

Athletics Interscholastic: baseball (boys), basketball (b,g), cross-country running (b,g), nordic skiing (b,g), soccer (b,g), softball (g), tennis (b,g), track and field (b,g), wrestling (b); intramural: backpacking (b,g); coed interscholastic: alpine skiing, cheering, golf, running, skiing (downhill); coed intramural: aerobics, aerobics/dance, aerobics/Nautilus, archery, badminton, bicycling, billiards, bowling, canoeing/kayaking, climbing, cooperative games, cross-country running, fishing, fitness, fitness walking, freestyle skiing, Frisbee, golf, hiking/backpacking, horseback riding, in-line skating, indoor soccer, jogging, kayaking, kickball, mountain biking, Nautilus, outdoor activities, outdoor recreation, paint ball, physical fitness, physical training, rafting, running, skiing (downhill), snowboarding, ultimate Frisbee, walking, weight lifting, weight training. 1 PE instructor, 11 coaches, 1 athletic trainer.

Computers Computers are regularly used in architecture, drafting, English, ESL, independent study, library, literary magazine, SAT preparation, yearbook classes. Computer resources include on-campus library services, Internet access, wireless campus network, Internet filtering or blocking technology. Campus intranet, student e-mail accounts, and computer access in designated common areas are available to students. Students grades are available online. The school has a published electronic and media policy.

Contact Mrs. Deborah Jacobs, Director of Admission. 207-738-2252 Ext. 115. Fax: 207-738-3257. E-mail: admissions@leeacademy.org. Web site: www.leeacademy.org

LEE ACADEMY

415 Lee Drive
Clarksdale, Mississippi 38614

Head of School: Ricky Weiss

General Information college-preparatory, arts, and business school. Founded: 1970. Setting: small town. Nearest major city is Memphis, TN. 4 buildings on campus. Approved or accredited by Mississippi Private School Association, Southern Association of Colleges and Schools, and Mississippi Department of Education. Total enrollment: 357. Upper school average class size: 22. Upper school faculty-student ratio: 1:20. There are 185 required school days per year for Upper School students. Upper School students typically attend 5 days per week. The average school day consists of 6 hours and 30 minutes.

Upper School Student Profile Grade 6: 24 students (14 boys, 10 girls); Grade 7: 43 students (27 boys, 16 girls); Grade 8: 45 students (28 boys, 17 girls); Grade 9: 44 students (21 boys, 23 girls); Grade 10: 33 students (12 boys, 21 girls); Grade 11: 50 students (27 boys, 23 girls); Grade 12: 48 students (22 boys, 26 girls).

Faculty School total: 45. In upper school: 4 men, 15 women; 8 have advanced degrees.

Subjects Offered ACT preparation, American government, American history, ancient world history, art, athletics, baseball, basketball, Bible, biology, bookkeeping, business, business law, calculus, cheerleading, chemistry, choral music, computer applications, earth and space science, earth science, English, English composition, English literature, foreign language, geography, geometry, guidance, health, Spanish, speech, U.S. history, writing workshop, yearbook.

Graduation Requirements Math methods.

College Admission Counseling 43 students graduated in 2011; all went to college, including Mississippi State University; University of Mississippi.

Student Life Upper grades have uniform requirement, student council. Discipline rests primarily with faculty.

Tuition and Aid Day student tuition: $5000. Tuition installment plan (monthly payment plans). Tuition reduction for siblings, need-based scholarship grants available. In 2011–12, 15% of upper-school students received aid. Total amount of financial aid awarded in 2011–12: $35,000.

Admissions Traditional secondary-level entrance grade is 9. For fall 2011, 177 students applied for upper-level admission, 177 were accepted, 177 enrolled. Deadline for receipt of application materials: February 28. No application fee required.

Athletics Interscholastic: baseball (boys), basketball (b), cheering (g), football (b); coed interscholastic: cross-country running, golf, soccer. 1 PE instructor.

Computers Computer resources include on-campus library services. Computer access in designated common areas is available to students. Students grades are available online.

Contact Ricky Weiss, Headmaster. 662-627-7891. Fax: 662-627-7896. E-mail: leeoffice@acbleone.net. Web site:

LEHIGH VALLEY CHRISTIAN HIGH SCHOOL

330 Howertown Road, Suite 101
Catasauqua, Pennsylvania 18032

Head of School: Mr. Robert J. Brennan Jr.

General Information Coeducational day college-preparatory, general academic, arts, business, religious studies, and technology school, affiliated with Protestant-Evangelical faith. Grades 9–12. Founded: 1988. Setting: urban. Nearest major city is Allentown. 2-acre campus. 1 building on campus. Approved or accredited by Association of Christian Schools International, Middle States Association of Colleges and Schools, and Pennsylvania Department of Education. Total enrollment: 125. Upper school average class size: 20. Upper school faculty-student ratio: 1:7. There are 180 required school days per year for Upper School students. Upper School students typically attend 5 days per week. The average school day consists of 6 hours and 45 minutes.

Upper School Student Profile Grade 9: 22 students (10 boys, 12 girls); Grade 10: 42 students (23 boys, 19 girls); Grade 11: 32 students (12 boys, 20 girls); Grade 12: 29 students (9 boys, 20 girls). 90% of students are Protestant-Evangelical faith.

Faculty School total: 17. In upper school: 7 men, 10 women; 9 have advanced degrees.

Subjects Offered Accounting, Advanced Placement courses, algebra, American history, ancient world history, art, Bible, biology, biology-AP, calculus-AP, chemistry, chemistry-AP, chorus, computer applications, economics, English, English language and composition-AP, English literature and composition-AP, geometry, government, health, history, keyboarding, neuroscience, physical education, physical science, physics, physics-AP, pre-algebra, pre-calculus, Spanish, state history, U.S. history, Western civilization, yearbook.

Graduation Requirements Algebra, American history, American literature, art, Bible, Bible studies, biology, British literature, chemistry, choir, civics, computer applications, English, foreign language, geometry, mathematics, physical education (includes health), physical science, science, social sciences, Western civilization, general lifestyle not harmful to the testimony of the school as a Christian institution, minimum one year of full-time enrollment in LVCH or another Christian high school.

Special Academic Programs Advanced Placement exam preparation; honors section; accelerated programs; independent study; study at local college for college credit; academic accommodation for the gifted; programs in English, mathematics, general development for dyslexic students; special instructional classes for students needing learning support; ESL (6 students enrolled).

College Admission Counseling 41 students graduated in 2012; 40 went to college, including Cairn University; Eastern University; Lehigh University; Liberty University; Moravian College; Penn State University Park. Other: 1 went to work. Mean SAT critical reading: 531, mean SAT math: 539, mean SAT writing: 521, mean combined SAT: 1591.

Student Life Upper grades have uniform requirement, student council. Discipline rests primarily with faculty.

Summer Programs Remediation, advancement programs offered; session focuses on make-up courses; held both on and off campus; held at students' homes (for independent credit); accepts boys and girls; not open to students from other schools. 5 students usually enrolled. 2013 schedule: June 18 to August 11.

Tuition and Aid Day student tuition: $8880. Tuition installment plan (FACTS Tuition Payment Plan, individually arranged payment plans). Tuition reduction for siblings, need-based scholarship grants available. In 2012–13, 35% of upper-school students received aid. Total amount of financial aid awarded in 2012–13: $125,790.

Admissions Traditional secondary-level entrance grade is 9. For fall 2012, 41 students applied for upper-level admission, 41 were accepted, 37 enrolled. Achievement tests, Gates MacGinite Reading Tests or Wide Range Achievement Test required. Deadline for receipt of application materials: none. Application fee required: $200. On-campus interview required.

Athletics Interscholastic: baseball (boys), basketball (b,g), cheering (g), soccer (b,g), volleyball (g); coed interscholastic: cross-country running, track and field; coed intramural: fitness walking. 1 PE instructor, 10 coaches.

Computers Computers are regularly used in graphic arts, keyboarding, library, multimedia, science, technology, writing, yearbook classes. Computer network features include on-campus library services, Internet access, Internet filtering or blocking technology. Students grades are available online. The school has a published electronic and media policy.

Contact Dr. Alan H. Russell, Director of Admissions. 610-403-1000 Ext. 42. Fax: 610-403-1004. E-mail: a.russell@lvchs.org. Web site: www.lvchs.org

LEHMAN HIGH SCHOOL

2400 Saint Mary Avenue
Sidney, Ohio 45365

Head of School: Mr. David Michael Barhorst

General Information Coeducational day and distance learning college-preparatory, arts, business, and religious studies school, affiliated with Roman Catholic Church. Grades 9–12. Distance learning grades 10–12. Founded: 1970. Setting: small town. Nearest major city is Dayton. 50-acre campus. 1 building on campus. Approved or accredited by North Central Association of Colleges and Schools, Ohio Catholic Schools Accreditation Association (OCSAA), and Ohio Department of Education. Endowment: $600,000. Total enrollment: 205. Upper school average class size: 15. Upper school faculty-student ratio: 1:15. There are 178 required school days per year for Upper School students. Upper School students typically attend 5 days per week. The average school day consists of 7 hours.

Upper School Student Profile Grade 9: 46 students (23 boys, 23 girls); Grade 10: 48 students (32 boys, 16 girls); Grade 11: 67 students (33 boys, 34 girls); Grade 12: 44 students (23 boys, 21 girls). 93% of students are Roman Catholic.

Faculty School total: 19. In upper school: 8 men, 11 women; 14 have advanced degrees.

Subjects Offered Accounting, algebra, American government, American literature, anatomy and physiology, art, art history, biology, biology-AP, British literature, British literature (honors), business, calculus, calculus-AP, ceramics, chemistry, chemistry-AP, choir, computer applications, concert band, drafting, earth science, English, English literature and composition-AP, environmental science, geography, geometry, government, health education, history of the Catholic Church, integrated science, intro to computers, Latin, moral theology, newspaper, painting, peace and justice, physical education, physics, pre-algebra, pre-calculus, psychology, sociology, Spanish, studio art, U.S. history, vocal music, weight fitness, world history, yearbook.

Graduation Requirements Biology, business, computer applications, electives, English composition, English literature, health education, mathematics, physical education (includes health), physical science, religion (includes Bible studies and theology), U.S. government, U.S. history, must attend a senior retreat.

Special Academic Programs Advanced Placement exam preparation; honors section; independent study; study at local college for college credit.

College Admission Counseling 47 students graduated in 2012; all went to college, including Miami University; Ohio University; The Ohio State University; University of Cincinnati; University of Dayton. Mean composite ACT: 24. 37% scored over 26 on composite ACT.

Student Life Upper grades have uniform requirement, student council, honor system. Discipline rests primarily with faculty. Attendance at religious services is required.

Tuition and Aid Day student tuition: $7150. Tuition installment plan (FACTS Tuition Payment Plan). Tuition reduction for siblings, need-based scholarship grants available. In 2012–13, 44% of upper-school students received aid. Total amount of financial aid awarded in 2012–13: $353,850.

Admissions Traditional secondary-level entrance grade is 9. For fall 2012, 5 students applied for upper-level admission, 5 were accepted, 5 enrolled. Achievement tests or any standardized test required. Deadline for receipt of application materials: none. Application fee required: $100. Interview recommended.

Athletics Interscholastic: baseball (boys), basketball (b,g), cheering (g), cross-country running (b,g), football (b), golf (b), soccer (b,g), softball (g), swimming and diving (b,g), tennis (b,g), track and field (b,g), volleyball (g), wrestling (b); intramural: strength & conditioning (b,g); coed intramural: indoor track. 1 PE instructor, 35 coaches, 1 athletic trainer.

Computers Computers are regularly used in accounting, computer applications, drafting, newspaper, science, yearbook classes. Computer resources include on-campus library services, Internet access, wireless campus network, Internet filtering or blocking technology. Students grades are available online. The school has a published electronic and media policy.

Contact Mrs. Denise Stauffer, Principal. 937-498-1161 Ext. 115. Fax: 937-492-9877. E-mail: d.stauffer@lehmancatholic.com. Web site: www.lehmancatholic.com/

LE LYCEE FRANCAIS DE LOS ANGELES

3261 Overland Avenue
Los Angeles, California 90034-3589

Head of School: Mrs. Clara-Lisa Kabbaz

General Information Coeducational day college-preparatory, general academic, arts, and bilingual studies school. Grades PS–12. Founded: 1964. Setting: suburban. Nearest major city is West Los Angeles. 12-acre campus. 1 building on campus. Approved or accredited by French Ministry of Education and Western Association of Schools and Colleges. Member of European Council of International Schools. Languages of instruction: English and French. Endowment: $400,000. Total enrollment: 729. Upper school average class size: 17. Upper school faculty-student ratio: 1:15. There are 170 required school days per year for Upper School students. Upper School students typically attend 5 days per week. The average school day consists of 7 hours and 45 minutes.

Upper School Student Profile Grade 9: 39 students (17 boys, 22 girls); Grade 10: 36 students (18 boys, 18 girls); Grade 11: 48 students (18 boys, 30 girls); Grade 12: 25 students (7 boys, 18 girls).

Faculty School total: 85. In upper school: 16 men, 26 women; 31 have advanced degrees.

Subjects Offered 20th century history, 3-dimensional art, Advanced Placement courses, algebra, American history, American literature, anatomy, Ancient Greek, art, arts, ballet, biology, calculus, calculus-AP, ceramics, chemistry, choir, computer programming, computer science, creative writing, dance, drama, earth science, economics, English, English language and composition-AP, English literature, environmental science, ESL, European history, expository writing, fencing, fine arts, French, French as a second language, French language-AP, French studies, gardening, geography, geology, geometry, German, government/civics, grammar, history, Latin, mathematics, microeconomics-AP, music, philosophy, photography, physical education, physics, pre-calculus, SAT preparation, science, social sciences, social studies, Spanish, sports, statistics, theater, theater arts, trigonometry, typing, U.S. history, volleyball, world history, world literature, writing, yoga.

Graduation Requirements Arts and fine arts (art, music, dance, drama), English, foreign language, mathematics, physical education (includes health), science, social sciences, social studies (includes history).

Special Academic Programs International Baccalaureate program; Advanced Placement exam preparation; honors section; remedial reading and/or remedial writing; remedial math; ESL (25 students enrolled).

College Admission Counseling 36 students graduated in 2011; all went to college, including Loyola Marymount University; New York University; University of California, Berkeley; University of California, Los Angeles; University of California, Santa Cruz; University of Southern California. Median SAT critical reading: 600, median SAT math: 590, median SAT writing: 600, median combined SAT: 1790, median composite ACT: 25.

Student Life Upper grades have uniform requirement, student council, honor system. Discipline rests primarily with faculty.

Tuition and Aid Day student tuition: $12,880–$20,350. Bursaries, merit scholarship grants, need-based scholarship grants available. In 2011–12, 12% of upper-school students received aid. Total amount of financial aid awarded in 2011–12: $63,000.

Admissions Traditional secondary-level entrance grade is 9. For fall 2011, 205 students applied for upper-level admission, 155 were accepted, 155 enrolled. School's own exam required. Deadline for receipt of application materials: February 28. Application fee required: $1000. Interview required.

Athletics Interscholastic: basketball (boys, girls), cheering (g), volleyball (b,g); intramural: ballet (g), baseball (g), fencing (b,g), outdoor activities (b,g), outdoor recreation (b,g), physical fitness (b,g); coed interscholastic: soccer; coed intramural: archery, martial arts. 6 PE instructors, 5 coaches, 4 athletic trainers.

Computers Computers are regularly used in English, foreign language, mathematics, science classes. Computer resources include on-campus library services, Internet access, wireless campus network, Internet filtering or blocking technology, Internet Café. Computer access in designated common areas is available to students. The school has a published electronic and media policy.

Contact Mme. Sophie Darmon, Admissions. 310-836-3464 Ext. 315. Fax: 310-558-8069. E-mail: admissions@lyceela.org. Web site: www.LyceeLA.org

LEXINGTON CATHOLIC HIGH SCHOOL

2250 Clays Mill Road
Lexington, Kentucky 40503-1797

Head of School: Dr. Steven Angelucci

General Information Coeducational day college-preparatory and religious studies school, affiliated with Roman Catholic Church. Grades 9–12. Founded: 1823. Setting: urban. 7-acre campus. 3 buildings on campus. Approved or accredited by National Catholic Education Association, Southern Association of Colleges and Schools, and Kentucky Department of Education. Endowment: $600,000. Total enrollment: 802. Upper school average class size: 21. Upper school faculty-student ratio: 1:14. There are 177 required school days per year for Upper School students. Upper School students typically attend 5 days per week. The average school day consists of 7 hours and 15 minutes.

Upper School Student Profile Grade 9: 213 students (97 boys, 116 girls); Grade 10: 207 students (102 boys, 105 girls); Grade 11: 189 students (100 boys, 89 girls); Grade 12: 193 students (103 boys, 90 girls). 81% of students are Roman Catholic.

Faculty School total: 64. In upper school: 32 men, 31 women; 47 have advanced degrees.

Subjects Offered Accounting, advanced chemistry, Advanced Placement courses, advanced studio art-AP, algebra, American government, American history, American history-AP, American literature, anatomy and physiology, art, astronomy, band, Bible as literature, biology, biology-AP, British literature, British literature (honors), calculus, calculus-AP, Catholic belief and practice, ceramics, chemistry, chemistry-AP, choral music, Christian and Hebrew scripture, church history, comparative religion, computer applications, computer programming, creative writing, drama, economics, English-AP, ethics, film, French, French-AP, geography, geology, geometry, government and politics-AP, health, history of the Catholic Church, honors English, honors geometry, honors U.S. history, honors world history, humanities, introduction to literature, Latin, Latin-AP, physical education, physics, psychology, religious studies, sociology, Spanish, Spanish language-AP, U.S. government, U.S. government and politics-AP, U.S. history, U.S. history-AP, world history, world literature.

Graduation Requirements American history, American literature, arts and fine arts (art, music, dance, drama), biology, British literature, Catholic belief and practice, chemistry, Christian and Hebrew scripture, church history, comparative religion, computer applications, English, foreign language, mathematics, physical education (includes health), religion (includes Bible studies and theology), science, U.S. government, U.S. government and politics, U.S. history, world history.

Special Academic Programs 18 Advanced Placement exams for which test preparation is offered; honors section.

College Admission Counseling 203 students graduated in 2012; 198 went to college, including University of Kentucky. Other: 3 went to work, 2 entered military service. Mean SAT critical reading: 577, mean SAT math: 568, mean SAT writing: 558, mean composite ACT: 25. 29% scored over 26 on composite ACT.

Student Life Upper grades have uniform requirement, student council, honor system. Discipline rests primarily with faculty. Attendance at religious services is required.

Tuition and Aid Day student tuition: $8080. Tuition installment plan (monthly payment plans, individually arranged payment plans). Merit scholarship grants, need-based scholarship grants available. In 2012–13, 10% of upper-school students received aid; total upper-school merit-scholarship money awarded: $5000. Total amount of financial aid awarded in 2012–13: $447,000.

Admissions Traditional secondary-level entrance grade is 9. For fall 2012, 240 students applied for upper-level admission, 240 were accepted, 213 enrolled. Scholastic Testing Service High School Placement Test required. Deadline for receipt of application materials: none. Application fee required: $275.

Athletics Interscholastic: baseball (boys), basketball (b,g), cheering (g), cross-country running (b,g), dance team (g), diving (b,g), football (b), golf (b,g), soccer (b,g), softball (g), swimming and diving (b,g), tennis (b,g), track and field (b,g), volleyball (g); intramural: badminton (b,g), basketball (b,g), flag football (g), lacrosse (b), physical training (b,g); coed interscholastic: bowling, ultimate Frisbee; coed intramural: hiking/backpacking, outdoor activities. 2 PE instructors, 2 athletic trainers.

Computers Computers are regularly used in all academic classes. Computer network features include on-campus library services, Internet access, wireless campus network. Computer access in designated common areas is available to students. Students grades are available online. The school has a published electronic and media policy.

Contact Ms. MIndy Towles, Admissions Director. 859-277-7183 Ext. 231. Fax: 859-276-5086. E-mail: mtowles@lexingtoncatholic.com. Web site: www.lexingtoncatholic.com

LIBERTY CHRISTIAN SCHOOL

7661 Warner Avenue
Huntington Beach, California 92647

Head of School: Mrs. Teri Yates

General Information Coeducational day college-preparatory and religious studies school, affiliated with Protestant faith, Baptist Church. Grades K–12. Founded: 1970. Setting: suburban. Nearest major city is Los Angeles. 5-acre campus. 3 buildings on campus. Approved or accredited by Accrediting Commission for Schools, Western Association of Schools and Colleges, and California Department of Education. Total enrollment: 204. Upper school average class size: 20. Upper school faculty-student ratio: 1:6. There are 180 required school days per year for Upper School students. Upper School students typically attend 5 days per week. The average school day consists of 6 hours and 30 minutes.

Upper School Student Profile Grade 9: 31 students (19 boys, 12 girls); Grade 10: 23 students (11 boys, 12 girls); Grade 11: 19 students (11 boys, 8 girls); Grade 12: 20 students (11 boys, 9 girls). 90% of students are Protestant, Baptist.

Faculty School total: 25. In upper school: 8 men, 6 women; 3 have advanced degrees.

Subjects Offered American literature, U.S. government.

Graduation Requirements World cultures.

Special Academic Programs Advanced Placement exam preparation; honors section; independent study.

College Admission Counseling 29 students graduated in 2011; 25 went to college, including California State University, Long Beach; Golden West College; Orange Coast College; Point Loma Nazarene University. Other: 3 went to work, 1 entered military service.

Student Life Upper grades have specified standards of dress, student council, honor system. Discipline rests primarily with faculty.

Tuition and Aid Day student tuition: $8800. Tuition installment plan (SMART Tuition Payment Plan, monthly payment plans). Need-based scholarship grants available. In 2011–12, 60% of upper-school students received aid. Total amount of financial aid awarded in 2011–12: $300,000.

Admissions Traditional secondary-level entrance grade is 9. For fall 2011, 19 students applied for upper-level admission, 19 were accepted, 19 enrolled. Deadline for receipt of application materials: none. Application fee required: $400. On-campus interview required.

Athletics Interscholastic: baseball (boys), basketball (b,g), flag football (b), football (b), power lifting (b), softball (g), volleyball (g); intramural: flag football (g), power lifting (b). 1 PE instructor, 4 coaches.

Computers Computers are regularly used in media classes. Computer network features include on-campus library services, Internet access, wireless campus network. Computer access in designated common areas is available to students. Students grades are available online.

Contact Mrs. Julene Nye, Registrar. 714-842-5992 Ext. 2260. Fax: 714-848-7484. E-mail: jnye@libertychristian.org. Web site: www.libertychristian.org

LIGHTHOUSE CHRISTIAN SCHOOL

4290-50th Street
Sylvan Lake, Alberta T4S 0H3, Canada

Head of School: Dion Krause

General Information Coeducational day college-preparatory, general academic, arts, and religious studies school. Grades PK–12. Setting: small town. Nearest major city is Red Deer, Canada. Approved or accredited by Association of Christian Schools International and Alberta Department of Education. Language of instruction: English. Total enrollment: 84. Upper school faculty-student ratio: 1:15.

Upper School Student Profile Grade 10: 7 students (3 boys, 4 girls); Grade 11: 2 students (1 boy, 1 girl); Grade 12: 4 students (1 boy, 3 girls).

Faculty School total: 11. In upper school: 2 men, 9 women; 8 have advanced degrees.

Student Life Upper grades have specified standards of dress, honor system.

Tuition and Aid Tuition installment plan (individually arranged payment plans).

Admissions Traditional secondary-level entrance grade is 10. For fall 2011, 2 students applied for upper-level admission, 2 were accepted, 2 enrolled. Deadline for receipt of application materials: none. Application fee required. Interview required.

Athletics 1 PE instructor.

Contact Dion Krause, Principal. 403-887-2166. Fax: 403-887-5729. E-mail: lightca@telusplanet.net. Web site:

LINCOLN ACADEMY

81 Academy Hill
Newcastle, Maine 04553

Head of School: Mr. John B. Pinkerton

General Information Coeducational day college-preparatory, general academic, arts, business, vocational, technology, advanced placement, and world languages school. Grades 9–12. Founded: 1801. Setting: small town. Nearest major city is Portland. 85-acre campus. 4 buildings on campus. Approved or accredited by New England Association of Schools and Colleges and Maine Department of Education. Endowment: $5.5 million. Total enrollment: 500. Upper school average class size: 18. Upper school faculty-student ratio: 1:13. There are 176 required school days per year for Upper School students. Upper School students typically attend 5 days per week. The average school day consists of 6 hours and 40 minutes.

Faculty School total: 43.

Subjects Offered 20th century history, 20th century world history, 3-dimensional art, 3-dimensional design, accounting, acting, advanced biology, advanced chemistry, advanced math, Advanced Placement courses, advanced studio art-AP, algebra, American history, American history-AP, American literature, American literature-AP, architectural drawing, art and culture, art-AP, athletics, audio visual/media, auto mechanics, band, basic language skills, biology, biology-AP, bookkeeping, business, business skills, calculus, calculus-AP, career/college preparation, chemistry, chemistry-AP, chorus, computer skills, conceptual physics, concert band, concert choir, desktop publishing, developmental language skills, developmental math, drafting, drama, English composition, English language-AP, English literature-AP, English-AP, English/composition-AP, environmental science-AP, filmmaking, foreign language, French, French-AP, general math, geography, geometry, healthful living, history, history of rock and roll, honors algebra, honors English, honors geometry, honors U.S. history, honors world history, industrial arts, instrumental music, integrated physics, Italian, Japanese, jazz band, language arts, language development, marine science, mechanical drawing, music theory, music theory-AP, musical productions, performing arts, physical education, play production, play/screen writing, poetry, portfolio art, pre-algebra, pre-calculus, psychology, Russian, sculpture, social studies, Spanish, Spanish language-AP, studio art, technical drawing, technical education, U.S. history, U.S. history-AP, U.S. literature, visual and performing arts, work-study, world history, yearbook.

Graduation Requirements English, job shadow experiences, community service.

Special Academic Programs 12 Advanced Placement exams for which test preparation is offered; honors section; independent study.

College Admission Counseling 113 students graduated in 2012.

Student Life Upper grades have specified standards of dress, student council. Discipline rests primarily with faculty.

Tuition and Aid Day student tuition: $10,046.

Admissions Traditional secondary-level entrance grade is 9. CTBS or ERB required. Deadline for receipt of application materials: none. No application fee required. Interview recommended.

Athletics Interscholastic: baseball (boys), basketball (b,g), cheering (g), cross-country running (b,g), field hockey (g), golf (b), lacrosse (b,g), soccer (b,g), softball (g), swimming and diving (b,g), tennis (b,g), track and field (b,g), wrestling (g); coed interscholastic: indoor track, Special Olympics; coed intramural: dance team, outdoor activities.

Computers Computers are regularly used in all classes. Computer network features include on-campus library services, online commercial services, Internet access, wireless campus network. Campus intranet, student e-mail accounts, and computer access in designated common areas are available to students. Students grades are available online. The school has a published electronic and media policy.

Contact Sherry Stearns, Director of Admissions. 207-563-3596. Fax: 207-563-3599. E-mail: stearns@lincolnacademy.org. Web site: www.lincolnacademy.org

LINCOLN SCHOOL

301 Butler Avenue
Providence, Rhode Island 02906-5556

Head of School: Julia Russell Eells

General Information Coeducational day (boys' only in lower grades) college-preparatory, arts, and technology school, affiliated with Society of Friends. Boys grades N–PK, girls grades N–12. Founded: 1884. Setting: urban. 46-acre campus. 5 buildings on campus. Approved or accredited by Association of Independent Schools in New England, Friends Council on Education, New England Association of Schools and Colleges, and Rhode Island Department of Education. Member of National Association of Independent Schools and Secondary School Admission Test Board. Endowment: $7 million. Total enrollment: 337. Upper school average class size: 13. Upper school faculty-student ratio: 1:4. Upper School students typically attend 5 days per week. The average school day consists of 7 hours and 13 minutes.

Upper School Student Profile Grade 9: 43 students (43 girls); Grade 10: 42 students (42 girls); Grade 11: 39 students (39 girls); Grade 12: 33 students (33 girls). 1% of students are members of Society of Friends.

Faculty School total: 75. In upper school: 11 men, 35 women; 24 have advanced degrees.

Subjects Offered Algebra, American history, American literature, anatomy, Arabic, art, biology, biology-AP, calculus, calculus-AP, ceramics, chemistry, chemistry-AP, college awareness, community service, computer science, creative writing, dance, English, English literature, environmental science, ethics, European history, European history-AP, French, French-AP, geometry, health, history, Latin, music, photography, physical education, physics, pre-calculus, Spanish, Spanish language-AP, statistics-AP, theater, trigonometry, U.S. history-AP, visual literacy, women's studies, world history, world literature.

Graduation Requirements Arts and fine arts (art, music, dance, drama), college planning, computer science, English, ethics, foreign language, mathematics, physical education (includes health), science, social studies (includes history), senior service trip. Community service is required.

Special Academic Programs Advanced Placement exam preparation; honors section; independent study; term-away projects; study at local college for college credit; study abroad; programs in general development for dyslexic students.

College Admission Counseling 48 students graduated in 2012; all went to college, including Boston University; Brown University; Hobart and William Smith Colleges; Worcester Polytechnic Institute. Median SAT critical reading: 590, median SAT math: 570, median SAT writing: 609.

Student Life Upper grades have uniform requirement, student council, honor system. Discipline rests equally with students and faculty.

Tuition and Aid Day student tuition: $28,650. Tuition installment plan (FACTS Tuition Payment Plan, Tuition Management Systems Plan). Merit scholarship grants, need-based scholarship grants available. In 2012–13, 40% of upper-school students received aid; total upper-school merit-scholarship money awarded: $15,000. Total amount of financial aid awarded in 2012–13: $2,000,000.

Admissions Traditional secondary-level entrance grade is 9. For fall 2012, 82 students applied for upper-level admission, 59 were accepted, 24 enrolled. ISEE or SSAT required. Deadline for receipt of application materials: February 15. Application fee required: $50. Interview required.

Athletics Interscholastic: basketball, crew, cross-country running, field hockey, lacrosse, soccer, squash, swimming and diving, tennis. 3 PE instructors, 17 coaches, 1 athletic trainer.

Computers Computers are regularly used in English, history, science classes. Computer network features include on-campus library services, Internet access, wireless campus network, Internet filtering or blocking technology. Student e-mail accounts and computer access in designated common areas are available to students. The school has a published electronic and media policy.

Contact Mrs. Diane Mota, Admission Office Administrative Assistant. 401-331-9696 Ext. 3157. Fax: 401-751-6670. E-mail: dmota@lincolnschool.org. Web site: www.lincolnschool.org

LINDEN CHRISTIAN SCHOOL

877 Wilkes Avenue
Winnipeg, Manitoba R3P 1B8, Canada

Head of School: Mr. Robert Charach

General Information Coeducational day college-preparatory, arts, religious studies, and technology school, affiliated with Baptist Church. Grades 9–12. Founded: 1987. Setting: suburban. 1 building on campus. Approved or accredited by Association of Christian Schools International and Manitoba Department of Education. Language of instruction: English. Total enrollment: 876. Upper school average class size: 25. Upper school faculty-student ratio: 1:13.

Upper School Student Profile Grade 9: 77 students (32 boys, 45 girls); Grade 10: 67 students (33 boys, 34 girls); Grade 11: 50 students (19 boys, 31 girls); Grade 12: 69 students (33 boys, 36 girls).

Faculty School total: 61. In upper school: 14 men, 9 women.

Subjects Offered Choir, choral music, computer applications, computer information systems, computer science, computer studies, computer technologies, concert band, drama, dramatic arts, independent study, jazz band, jazz ensemble, leadership, leadership and service, music theater, religious studies, vocal jazz, voice ensemble.

Graduation Requirements Bible studies, English, mathematics, physical education (includes health), science, social studies (includes history).

Special Academic Programs Honors section; independent study.

College Admission Counseling 65 students graduated in 2012; 1 went to college, including Providence College; The University of Winnipeg; University of Manitoba; University of Toronto. Other: 53 entered a postgraduate year.

Student Life Upper grades have specified standards of dress, student council, honor system. Discipline rests primarily with faculty. Attendance at religious services is required.

Tuition and Aid Day student tuition: CAN$2940. Tuition installment plan (monthly payment plans). Tuition reduction for siblings, bursaries available. In 2012–13, 8% of upper-school students received aid.

Admissions Traditional secondary-level entrance grade is 9. PSAT required. Application fee required: CAN$25. Interview required.

Athletics Interscholastic: aerobics (boys, girls), badminton (b,g), baseball (b,g), basketball (b,g), bowling (b,g), broomball (b,g), climbing (b,g), cooperative games (b,g), cross-country running (b,g), curling (b,g), fitness (b,g), flag football (b,g), floor hockey (b,g), football (b,g), golf (b,g), ice hockey (b), life saving (b,g), physical fitness (b,g), soccer (b,g), track and field (b,g), volleyball (b,g); intramural: badminton (b,g), basketball (b,g), cross-country running (b,g), soccer (b,g), volleyball (b,g); coed interscholastic: aerobics, baseball, basketball, bowling, broomball, climbing, cooperative games, cross-country running, curling, fitness, football, golf, life saving, physical fitness, soccer, track and field, volleyball; coed intramural: basketball. 4 PE instructors.

Computers Computers are regularly used in all academic, art, Bible studies, career education, career exploration, Christian doctrine, college planning, creative writing, current events, data processing, desktop publishing, digital applications, drafting, drawing and design, ESL, geography, graphic arts, graphic design, health, history, independent study, information technology, lab/keyboard, learning cognition, library, library skills, life skills, literacy, mathematics, media, music, newspaper, photography, psychology, reading, religion, religious studies, research skills, science, social sciences, social studies, speech, study skills, technology, Web site design, word processing, writing, writing, yearbook classes. Computer network features include on-campus library services, Internet access, wireless campus network, Internet filtering or blocking technology. Student e-mail accounts are available to students. Students grades are available online. The school has a published electronic and media policy.

Contact Mrs. Colleen Job, Registrar. 204-989-6739. Fax: 204-487-7068. E-mail: colleenj@lindenchristian.org. Web site: www.lindenchristian.org/

LINFIELD CHRISTIAN SCHOOL

31950 Pauba Road
Temecula, California 92592

Head of School: Karen Raftery

General Information Coeducational day college-preparatory, arts, religious studies, and technology school, affiliated with Christian faith. Grades K–12. Founded: 1936. Setting: suburban. Nearest major city is San Diego. 105-acre campus. 6 buildings on campus. Approved or accredited by Association of Christian Schools International, Western Association of Schools and Colleges, and California Department of Education. Total enrollment: 758. Upper school average class size: 20. Upper school faculty-student ratio: 1:15. There are 169 required school days per year for Upper School students. Upper School students typically attend 5 days per week. The average school day consists of 6 hours and 55 minutes.

Upper School Student Profile Grade 6: 58 students (28 boys, 30 girls); Grade 7: 65 students (27 boys, 38 girls); Grade 8: 71 students (40 boys, 31 girls); Grade 9: 70 students (43 boys, 27 girls); Grade 10: 84 students (49 boys, 35 girls); Grade 11: 77 students (40 boys, 37 girls); Grade 12: 88 students (37 boys, 51 girls). 70% of students are Christian faith.

Faculty School total: 54. In upper school: 9 men, 17 women; 8 have advanced degrees.

Subjects Offered Advanced math, algebra, American sign language, anatomy and physiology, art, ASB Leadership, athletics, band, Bible, biology, calculus-AP, career/college preparation, chemistry, chemistry-AP, choir, computers, economics, English, English-AP, European history-AP, film, filmmaking, French, freshman foundations, general science, geometry, government, government-AP, health, physical education, physics, pre-calculus, public policy, senior seminar, service learning/internship, Spanish, Spanish-AP, speech and debate, sports medicine, theater, U.S. history, U.S. history-AP, world history, world religions, yearbook.

Graduation Requirements Arts and fine arts (art, music, dance, drama), computer science, economics, English, foreign language, freshman foundations, government, mathematics, physical education (includes health), religion (includes Bible studies and theology), science, senior seminar, social sciences, social studies (includes history), speech and debate. Community service is required.

Special Academic Programs 12 Advanced Placement exams for which test preparation is offered; honors section.

College Admission Counseling 73 students graduated in 2012; 70 went to college, including Azusa Pacific University; California State University, San Marcos; University of California, Riverside; University of California, San Diego. Other: 3 went to work. Mean SAT critical reading: 524, mean SAT math: 573, mean SAT writing: 529, mean combined SAT: 1626.

Student Life Upper grades have uniform requirement, student council, honor system. Discipline rests primarily with faculty. Attendance at religious services is required.

Summer Programs Sports, art/fine arts programs offered; held on campus; accepts boys and girls; open to students from other schools.

Tuition and Aid Day student tuition: $9360. Tuition installment plan (monthly payment plans). Merit scholarship grants, need-based scholarship grants available. In 2012–13, 30% of upper-school students received aid.

Admissions Traditional secondary-level entrance grade is 9. TerraNova and USC/UC Math Diagnostic Test required. Deadline for receipt of application materials: none. Application fee required: $75. On-campus interview required.

Athletics Interscholastic: baseball (boys), basketball (b,g), cheering (g), cross-country running (b,g), equestrian sports (g), football (b), soccer (b,g), softball (g), tennis (b,g), track and field (b,g), volleyball (g); intramural: volleyball (g); coed interscholastic: golf; coed intramural: cross-country running. 3 PE instructors, 16 coaches, 1 athletic trainer.

Computers Computers are regularly used in computer applications, keyboarding, science, senior seminar, yearbook classes. Computer network features include on-campus library services, Internet access, wireless campus network, Internet filtering or blocking technology. Campus intranet and computer access in designated common areas are available to students. Students grades are available online. The school has a published electronic and media policy.

Contact Mrs. Becky Swanson, Assistant Director of Admissions. 951-676-8111 Ext. 1402. Fax: 951-695-1291. E-mail: bswanson@linfield.com. Web site: www.linfield.com

THE LINSLY SCHOOL

60 Knox Lane
Wheeling, West Virginia 26003-6489

Head of School: Mr. Chad Barnett

General Information Coeducational boarding and day college-preparatory, arts, technology, and science, mathematics, humanities, foreign language school. Boarding grades 7–12, day grades 5–12. Founded: 1814. Setting: suburban. Nearest major city is Pittsburgh, PA. Students are housed in single-sex dormitories. 60-acre campus. 19 buildings on campus. Approved or accredited by Independent Schools Association of the Central States, North Central Association of Colleges and Schools, The Association of Boarding Schools, and West Virginia Department of Education. Member of National Association of Independent Schools. Endowment: $16 million. Total enrollment: 450. Upper school average class size: 15. Upper school faculty-student ratio: 1:9. There are 165 required school days per year for Upper School students. Upper School students typically attend 5 days per week. The average school day consists of 6 hours and 30 minutes.

Upper School Student Profile Grade 9: 80 students (49 boys, 31 girls); Grade 10: 71 students (36 boys, 35 girls); Grade 11: 69 students (38 boys, 31 girls); Grade 12: 76 students (44 boys, 32 girls). 32% of students are boarding students. 50% are state residents. 20 states are represented in upper school student body. 9% are international students. International students from Bahamas, Mexico, Republic of Korea, Saudi Arabia, South Africa, and Thailand; 15 other countries represented in student body.

Faculty School total: 51. In upper school: 23 men, 12 women; 26 have advanced degrees; 22 reside on campus.

Subjects Offered Algebra, American history, American literature, art, art history, biology, biology-AP, calculus-AP, character education, chemistry, chemistry-AP, Chinese, chorus, college counseling, communications, computer programming, computer science, concert band, contemporary issues, creative writing, drama, earth science, economics, English, English language-AP, English literature, English literature-AP, environmental science, expository writing, fine arts, French, geometry, German, government/civics, health, history, human geography - AP, humanities, Latin, mathematics, model United Nations, multimedia design, music, newspaper, physical education, physics, physics-AP, psychology, psychology-AP, science, social studies, Spanish, speech, statistics, technology/design, theater, U.S. history-AP, world history, writing, yearbook, zoology.

Graduation Requirements Arts and fine arts (art, music, dance, drama), computer science, English, foreign language, mathematics, physical education (includes health), science, social studies (includes history), Senior Research Essay.

Special Academic Programs 12 Advanced Placement exams for which test preparation is offered; academic accommodation for the gifted.

College Admission Counseling 60 students graduated in 2011; all went to college, including Duquesne University; Marshall University; New York University; Ohio University; West Virginia University. Mean SAT critical reading: 580, mean SAT math: 580, mean SAT writing: 570, mean combined SAT: 1730, mean composite ACT: 26.

Student Life Upper grades have uniform requirement, student council, honor system. Discipline rests primarily with faculty.

Tuition and Aid Day student tuition: $14,280; 5-day tuition and room/board: $29,320; 7-day tuition and room/board: $29,320. Tuition installment plan (Academic Management Services Plan). Need-based scholarship grants available. In 2011–12, 40% of upper-school students received aid. Total amount of financial aid awarded in 2011–12: $900,000.

Admissions Traditional secondary-level entrance grade is 9. Otis-Lennon, Stanford Achievement Test or SSAT required. Deadline for receipt of application materials: January 31. No application fee required. Interview required.

Athletics Interscholastic: baseball (boys), basketball (b,g), cheering (g), cross-country running (b,g), diving (b,g), football (b), golf (b,g), ice hockey (b,g), lacrosse (b), soccer (b,g), softball (g), wrestling (b); intramural: flag football (b,g), floor hockey (b), football (b), hiking/backpacking (b,g), indoor soccer (b,g), indoor track (b,g), indoor track & field (b,g), life saving (b,g), mountain biking (b,g), outdoor activities (b,g), physical fitness (b,g), power lifting (b), rappelling (b,g), rock climbing (b,g), roller blading (b,g), ropes courses (b,g), running (b,g), street hockey (b); coed intramural: backpacking, badminton, bowling, canoeing/kayaking, climbing, combined training, cooperative games, cross-country running, fitness, Frisbee, ice skating, in-line skating, jogging, kayaking, kickball, life saving, mountain biking, Nautilus, physical fitness, physical training, rafting, rock climbing, ropes courses, running, scuba diving, soccer, softball. 4 PE instructors, 4 coaches, 1 athletic trainer.

Computers Computers are regularly used in economics, English, foreign language, humanities, journalism, mathematics, music, psychology, science classes. Computer network features include on-campus library services, online commercial services, Internet access, wireless campus network, Internet filtering or blocking technology.

Student e-mail accounts are available to students. The school has a published electronic and media policy.

Contact Mr. Craig Tredenick, Director of Admissions. 304-233-1436. Fax: 304-234-4614. E-mail: admit@linsly.org. Web site: www.linsly.org

See Display below and Close-Up on page 594.

LITTLE KESWICK SCHOOL

Keswick, Virginia

See Special Needs Schools section.

LODI ACADEMY

1230 South Central Avenue
Lodi, California 95242

Head of School: Mr. Harley Peterson

General Information Coeducational day college-preparatory, general academic, arts, and religious studies school, affiliated with Seventh-day Adventist Church. Boys grade 9, girls grade 12. Founded: 1908. Setting: small town. Nearest major city is Sacramento. 30-acre campus. 9 buildings on campus. Approved or accredited by Western Association of Schools and Colleges and California Department of Education. Endowment: $1.1 million. Total enrollment: 95. Upper school average class size: 24. Upper school faculty-student ratio: 1:13. There are 180 required school days per year for Upper School students. Upper School students typically attend 5 days per week. The average school day consists of 6 hours and 40 minutes.

Upper School Student Profile Grade 9: 18 students (11 boys, 7 girls); Grade 10: 25 students (10 boys, 15 girls); Grade 11: 26 students (12 boys, 14 girls); Grade 12: 26 students (16 boys, 10 girls). 82% of students are Seventh-day Adventists.

Faculty School total: 14. In upper school: 8 men, 6 women; 8 have advanced degrees.

Subjects Offered Accounting, algebra, American history, American literature, art, auto mechanics, band, Bible, biology, chemistry, choir, chorus, computer applications, economics, English, English literature, general math, geography, geometry, government, health, life skills, music appreciation, physical education, physical science, physics, piano, pre-algebra, pre-calculus, Spanish, student publications, U.S. history, U.S. history-AP, work experience, world history, yearbook.

Graduation Requirements Algebra, American history, American literature, applied arts, arts and fine arts (art, music, dance, drama), Bible, biology, chemistry, computer applications, economics, English, English literature, geography, geometry, keyboarding, life skills, physical education (includes health), physical science, Spanish, U.S. government, U.S. history, work experience, world history, 100 hours of community service, 100 hours of paid work experience. Community service is required.

Special Academic Programs 2 Advanced Placement exams for which test preparation is offered.

College Admission Counseling 28 students graduated in 2012; they went to La Sierra University; Pacific Union College; Walla Walla University.

Student Life Upper grades have specified standards of dress, student council. Discipline rests equally with students and faculty. Attendance at religious services is required.

Tuition and Aid Day student tuition: $6350–$7850. Tuition installment plan (monthly payment plans, individually arranged payment plans). Tuition reduction for siblings, merit scholarship grants, need-based scholarship grants, paying campus jobs, low Income tuition available. In 2012–13, 40% of upper-school students received aid; total upper-school merit-scholarship money awarded: $7000. Total amount of financial aid awarded in 2012–13: $33,000.

Admissions Traditional secondary-level entrance grade is 9. Achievement tests or Iowa Tests of Basic Skills required. Deadline for receipt of application materials: none. Application fee required: $300. Interview required.

Athletics Interscholastic: basketball (boys, girls), flag football (b,g), soccer (b,g), volleyball (g); intramural: basketball (b,g), flag football (b,g), volleyball (g); coed interscholastic: golf, softball. 1 PE instructor.

Computers Computers are regularly used in accounting, Bible studies, computer applications, English, mathematics classes. Computer network features include Internet access, wireless campus network, Internet filtering or blocking technology. Student e-mail accounts and computer access in designated common areas are available to students. Students grades are available online. The school has a published electronic and media policy.

Contact Mrs. Dorene Hackett, Registrar. 209-369-2781 Ext. 102. Fax: 209-747-6689. E-mail: dorene@lodiacademy.net. Web site: www.lodiacademy.net

LONG ISLAND LUTHERAN MIDDLE AND HIGH SCHOOL

131 Brookville Road
Brookville, New York 11545-3399

Head of School: Dr. David Hahn

General Information Coeducational day college-preparatory, arts, business, and religious studies school, affiliated with Lutheran Church. Grades 6–12. Founded: 1960. Setting: suburban. Nearest major city is New York. 32-acre campus. 6 buildings on campus. Approved or accredited by Evangelical Lutheran Church in America, Middle States Association of Colleges and Schools, US Department of State, and New York

Department of Education. Member of National Association of Independent Schools. Endowment: $6 million. Total enrollment: 595. Upper school average class size: 18. Upper school faculty-student ratio: 1:9. There are 161 required school days per year for Upper School students. Upper School students typically attend 5 days per week. The average school day consists of 6 hours and 30 minutes.

Upper School Student Profile Grade 9: 97 students (50 boys, 47 girls); Grade 10: 92 students (45 boys, 47 girls); Grade 11: 103 students (62 boys, 41 girls); Grade 12: 110 students (61 boys, 49 girls). 30% of students are Lutheran.

Faculty School total: 58. In upper school: 21 men, 29 women; 47 have advanced degrees.

Subjects Offered Accounting, algebra, American history, American literature, anatomy, art, band, biology, biology-AP, business, business communications, business skills, calculus, calculus-AP, ceramics, choir, college planning, communication skills, computer programming, computer science, computer science-AP, creative writing, dance, decision making skills, driver education, earth science, economics-AP, English, English language-AP, English literature, English literature-AP, environmental science, ethics, European history, European history-AP, fine arts, French, French language-AP, freshman foundations, geography, geometry, government/civics, grammar, graphic arts, health, history, international relations, journalism, Mandarin, marketing, mathematics, multimedia, music, photography, physical education, physics, physics-AP, physiology, psychology, religion, social studies, Spanish, Spanish language-AP, theater, trigonometry, U.S. government and politics-AP, U.S. history-AP, video film production, word processing, world history, writing.

Graduation Requirements Arts and fine arts (art, music, dance, drama), business skills (includes word processing), computer science, English, foreign language, international relations, mathematics, physical education (includes health), religion (includes Bible studies and theology), science, social studies (includes history).

Special Academic Programs 14 Advanced Placement exams for which test preparation is offered; honors section; term-away projects; study at local college for college credit; ESL (10 students enrolled).

College Admission Counseling 101 students graduated in 2012; all went to college, including Binghamton University, State University of New York; Fordham University; Hofstra University; New York University; Penn State University Park; Temple University. Mean SAT critical reading: 572, mean SAT math: 564, mean SAT writing: 595, mean combined SAT: 1731, mean composite ACT: 24. 25% scored over 26 on composite ACT.

Student Life Upper grades have uniform requirement, student council, honor system. Discipline rests primarily with faculty. Attendance at religious services is required.

Summer Programs Sports, art/fine arts, computer instruction programs offered; session focuses on sports, recreation, and education; held both on and off campus; held at local satellite facilities; accepts boys and girls; open to students from other schools. 5,000 students usually enrolled. 2013 schedule: June 24 to August 16. Application deadline: January.

Tuition and Aid Day student tuition: $10,050–$11,990. Tuition installment plan (monthly payment plans, school's own payment plan). Tuition reduction for siblings, merit scholarship grants, need-based scholarship grants available. In 2012–13, 30% of upper-school students received aid; total upper-school merit-scholarship money awarded: $10,000. Total amount of financial aid awarded in 2012–13: $325,000.

Admissions Traditional secondary-level entrance grade is 9. For fall 2012, 144 students applied for upper-level admission, 82 were accepted, 55 enrolled. Cognitive Abilities Test, Math Placement Exam and writing sample required. Deadline for receipt of application materials: none. Application fee required: $100. On-campus interview required.

Athletics Interscholastic: baseball (boys, girls), basketball (b), cheering (g), dance team (g), football (b), lacrosse (b,g), roller hockey (b), soccer (b,g), softball (g), tennis (b,g), volleyball (g), wrestling (b); intramural: dance team (g), flag football (b), horseback riding (b,g); coed interscholastic: cross-country running, golf, running, track and field, winter (indoor) track; coed intramural: bowling, equestrian sports, physical training, skiing (downhill). 3 PE instructors, 30 coaches.

Computers Computers are regularly used in accounting, art, business, business skills, college planning, design, English, graphic design, history, journalism, library skills, mathematics, science classes. Computer network features include on-campus library services, Internet access, wireless campus network, Internet filtering or blocking technology. Student e-mail accounts and computer access in designated common areas are available to students. Students grades are available online. The school has a published electronic and media policy.

Contact Barbara Ward, Director of Admissions. 516-626-1700 Ext. 546. Fax: 516-622-7459. E-mail: barbara.ward@luhi.org. Web site: www.luhi.org

THE LOOMIS CHAFFEE SCHOOL

4 Batchelder Road
Windsor, Connecticut 06095

Head of School: Dr. Sheila Culbert

General Information Coeducational boarding and day college-preparatory and arts school. Grades 9–PG. Founded: 1914. Setting: rural. Nearest major city is Hartford. Students are housed in single-sex dormitories. 300-acre campus. 65 buildings on campus. Approved or accredited by New England Association of Schools and Colleges, The Association of Boarding Schools, and Connecticut Department of Education. Member of National Association of Independent Schools and Secondary School Admission Test Board. Endowment: $200 million. Total enrollment: 682. Upper school average class size: 12. Upper school faculty-student ratio: 1:5. There are 172 required school days per year for Upper School students. Upper School students typically attend 6 days per week. The average school day consists of 8 hours.

Upper School Student Profile Grade 9: 129 students (61 boys, 68 girls); Grade 10: 164 students (86 boys, 78 girls); Grade 11: 168 students (90 boys, 78 girls); Grade 12: 195 students (100 boys, 95 girls); Postgraduate: 26 students (22 boys, 4 girls). 60% of students are boarding students. 50% are state residents. 28 states are represented in upper school student body. 17% are international students. International students from Bermuda, Canada, China, Republic of Korea, Thailand, and Viet Nam; 29 other countries represented in student body.

Faculty School total: 160. In upper school: 75 men, 85 women; 110 have advanced degrees; 70 reside on campus.

Subjects Offered Algebra, American history, American literature, anatomy, art, art history, astronomy, biology, calculus, ceramics, chemistry, creative writing, dance, drama, ecology, economics, English, English literature, environmental science, ethics, European history, expository writing, fine arts, French, geometry, history, history of ideas, history of science, Latin, logic, Mandarin, mathematics, music, philosophy, photography, physical education, physics, physiology, religion, science, Spanish, statistics, theater, video film production, world history, world literature, writing.

Graduation Requirements Arts and fine arts (art, music, dance, drama), English, foreign language, history, mathematics, philosophy, physical education (includes health), science.

Special Academic Programs 19 Advanced Placement exams for which test preparation is offered; honors section; independent study; term-away projects; study at local college for college credit; study abroad.

College Admission Counseling 187 students graduated in 2011; 184 went to college, including Colgate University; Georgetown University; Hamilton College; Syracuse University; The George Washington University; Trinity College. Other: 2 had other specific plans. Mean SAT critical reading: 647, mean SAT math: 659, mean SAT writing: 649, mean combined SAT: 1306, mean composite ACT: 28.

Student Life Upper grades have specified standards of dress, student council. Discipline rests equally with students and faculty.

Tuition and Aid Day student tuition: $35,850; 7-day tuition and room/board: $47,100. Tuition installment plan (Insured Tuition Payment Plan, Key Tuition Payment Plan, monthly payment plans). Need-based scholarship grants, need-based loans available. In 2011–12, 34% of upper-school students received aid. Total amount of financial aid awarded in 2011–12: $7,700,000.

Admissions Traditional secondary-level entrance grade is 9. For fall 2011, 1,680 students applied for upper-level admission, 461 were accepted, 218 enrolled. ISEE, PSAT, SAT, SSAT or TOEFL required. Deadline for receipt of application materials: January 15. Application fee required: $75. Interview required.

Athletics Interscholastic: baseball (boys), basketball (b,g), cross-country running (b,g), field hockey (g), football (b), golf (b,g), ice hockey (b,g), lacrosse (b,g), soccer (b,g), softball (g), squash (b,g), swimming and diving (b,g), tennis (b,g), track and field (b,g), volleyball (g), water polo (b,g), wrestling (b); intramural: ice hockey (b,g), soccer (b,g), volleyball (b,g); coed interscholastic: alpine skiing, diving, skiing (downhill); coed intramural: aerobics, aerobics/dance, aerobics/Nautilus, backpacking, ballet, basketball, bicycling, canoeing/kayaking, climbing, dance, fencing, fitness, Frisbee, hiking/backpacking, jogging, kayaking, life saving, modern dance, mountain biking, Nautilus, outdoor activities, outdoor adventure, physical fitness, physical training, ropes courses, running, scuba diving, soccer, softball, squash, strength & conditioning, swimming and diving, tennis, ultimate Frisbee, weight training, yoga. 5 PE instructors, 2 athletic trainers.

Computers Computers are regularly used in all academic classes. Computer network features include on-campus library services, online commercial services, Internet access, wireless campus network. Campus intranet, student e-mail accounts, and computer access in designated common areas are available to students. Students grades are available online. The school has a published electronic and media policy.

Contact Mr. Erby Mitchell, Assistant Head of School for Enrollment. 860-687-6400. Fax: 860-298-8756. E-mail: erby_mitchell@loomis.org. Web site: www.loomis.org

LORETTO ACADEMY

1300 Hardaway Street
El Paso, Texas 79903

Head of School: Sr. Mary E. (Buffy) Boesen, SL

General Information Coeducational day (boys' only in lower grades) college-preparatory, arts, religious studies, and technology school, affiliated with Roman Catholic Church. Boys grades PK–5, girls grades PK–12. Founded: 1923. Setting: urban. 17-acre campus. 3 buildings on campus. Approved or accredited by Southern Association of Colleges and Schools and Texas Catholic Conference. Endowment: $4.1 million. Total enrollment: 636. Upper school average class size: 20. Upper school faculty-student ratio: 1:20. There are 180 required school days per year for Upper School students. Upper School students typically attend 5 days per week. The average school day consists of 7 hours.

Upper School Student Profile Grade 9: 98 students (98 girls); Grade 10: 89 students (89 girls); Grade 11: 92 students (92 girls); Grade 12: 86 students (86 girls). 90% of students are Roman Catholic.
Faculty School total: 52. In upper school: 7 men, 25 women; 15 have advanced degrees.
Subjects Offered Acting, advanced math, Advanced Placement courses, algebra, American government, American history, anatomy and physiology, art, art appreciation, art-AP, arts, arts and crafts, Bible, biology, business mathematics, calculus, calculus-AP, chemistry, choir, choral music, Christian and Hebrew scripture, college writing, computer applications, computer programming, computer science, English, environmental science, fine arts, French, geology, geometry, government, government-AP, health, honors algebra, honors English, honors geometry, Internet, journalism, keyboarding, life issues, literature, literature-AP, mathematics, modern dance, moral theology, music appreciation, photo shop, physical education, physics, religion, science, social studies, Spanish, Spanish language-AP, Spanish-AP, speech, speech and debate, student government, study skills, technical writing, theater production, world geography, world history, world religions, yearbook, zoology.
Graduation Requirements Algebra, American government, arts and fine arts (art, music, dance, drama), Bible studies, biology, Catholic belief and practice, chemistry, Christian and Hebrew scripture, Christian ethics, Christian studies, church history, computer programming, computer science, digital photography, economics, English, English composition, English literature, environmental science, foreign language, geography, government, health, human anatomy, journalism, lab/keyboard, life issues, mathematics, moral reasoning, physical education (includes health), physical science, physics, psychology, religion (includes Bible studies and theology), science, scripture, social justice, social studies (includes history), sociology, speech communications, technology, theology, world geography, service learning .5 credit, 4 credits of religion.
Special Academic Programs Advanced Placement exam preparation.
College Admission Counseling 76 students graduated in 2012; all went to college, including New Mexico State University; St. Edward's University; St. Mary's University; The University of Texas at El Paso; The University of Texas at San Antonio. Mean SAT critical reading: 508, mean SAT math: 481, mean SAT writing: 521. 14% scored over 600 on SAT critical reading, 8% scored over 600 on SAT math, 25% scored over 600 on SAT writing, 9% scored over 1800 on combined SAT, 5% scored over 26 on composite ACT.
Student Life Upper grades have uniform requirement, student council, honor system. Discipline rests primarily with faculty.
Summer Programs Remediation programs offered; session focuses on remediation; held on campus; accepts girls; not open to students from other schools. 25 students usually enrolled. 2013 schedule: June 1 to July 2.
Tuition and Aid Day student tuition: $6700. Tuition installment plan (FACTS Tuition Payment Plan). Tuition reduction for siblings, need-based scholarship grants, paying campus jobs, need-based financial aid available. In 2012–13, 29% of upper-school students received aid. Total amount of financial aid awarded in 2012–13: $240,000.
Admissions Traditional secondary-level entrance grade is 9. For fall 2012, 72 students applied for upper-level admission, 60 were accepted, 55 enrolled. Educational Development Series or High School Placement Test required. Deadline for receipt of application materials: none. Application fee required: $10. On-campus interview required.
Athletics Interscholastic: aquatics, basketball, cross-country running, dance squad, dance team, golf, modern dance, soccer, softball, swimming and diving, tennis, track and field, volleyball. 2 PE instructors, 17 coaches.
Computers Computers are regularly used in all academic classes. Computer network features include on-campus library services, Internet access, Internet filtering or blocking technology. Computer access in designated common areas is available to students. Students grades are available online. The school has a published electronic and media policy.
Contact Mrs. Lily Miranda, Director of Admissions. 915-566-8400 Ext. 1109. Fax: 915-566-0636. E-mail: lmiranda@loretto.org. Web site: www.loretto.org

LOS ANGELES LUTHERAN HIGH SCHOOL

Now Concordia Jr/Sr High
13570 Eldridge Avenue
Sylmar, California 91342

Head of School: Mr. Edward R. Amey

General Information Coeducational day and distance learning college-preparatory, arts, and religious studies school, affiliated with Lutheran Church–Missouri Synod, Lutheran Church. Grades K–12. Distance learning grades 10–12. Founded: 1953. Setting: suburban. Nearest major city is Los Angeles. 4-acre campus. 3 buildings on campus. Approved or accredited by National Lutheran School Accreditation, Western Association of Schools and Colleges, and California Department of Education. Endowment: $450,000. Total enrollment: 397. Upper school average class size: 22. Upper school faculty-student ratio: 1:10. There are 180 required school days per year for Upper School students. Upper School students typically attend 5 days per week. The average school day consists of 6 hours and 30 minutes.
Upper School Student Profile Grade 9: 20 students (9 boys, 11 girls); Grade 10: 29 students (13 boys, 16 girls); Grade 11: 48 students (29 boys, 19 girls); Grade 12: 49 students (24 boys, 25 girls). 30% of students are Lutheran Church–Missouri Synod, Lutheran.
Faculty School total: 22. In upper school: 11 men, 11 women; 7 have advanced degrees.
Subjects Offered 3-dimensional art, Advanced Placement courses, algebra, American literature, American sign language, anatomy and physiology, ancient history, band, bell choir, Bible, Bible studies, biology, biology-AP, British literature (honors), business applications, business law, business mathematics, calculus, career/college preparation, chemistry, choir, choral music, Christian doctrine, Christian scripture, classical music, composition, concert band, drawing, economics, English literature, English-AP, ESL, ethics, family studies, film appreciation, geography, geometry, German, government, jazz, jazz band, journalism, Life of Christ, math analysis, music theory, painting, physics, psychology, Spanish, U.S. history, world history, yearbook.
Graduation Requirements Advanced math, algebra, American government, American history, American literature, analytic geometry, ancient world history, biology, British literature, career education, chemistry, Christian doctrine, Christian testament, comparative religion, composition, economics, English composition, English literature, geometry, government, keyboarding, physical education (includes health), religious education, Spanish, U.S. government, U.S. history, world history.
Special Academic Programs 6 Advanced Placement exams for which test preparation is offered; honors section; study at local college for college credit; academic accommodation for the gifted, the musically talented, and the artistically talented; ESL (25 students enrolled).
College Admission Counseling 39 students graduated in 2012; 36 went to college, including California College of the Arts; California State University, Northridge; Concordia University. Other: 3 entered military service.
Student Life Upper grades have uniform requirement, student council. Discipline rests primarily with faculty. Attendance at religious services is required.
Summer Programs Remediation, enrichment, ESL, sports programs offered; session focuses on mathematics and English; held on campus; accepts boys and girls; open to students from other schools. 25 students usually enrolled. 2013 schedule: July 7 to July 31. Application deadline: June 15.
Tuition and Aid Day student tuition: $7200. Tuition installment plan (SMART Tuition Payment Plan, monthly payment plans). Merit scholarship grants, need-based scholarship grants available. In 2012–13, 30% of upper-school students received aid; total upper-school merit-scholarship money awarded: $16,000. Total amount of financial aid awarded in 2012–13: $100,000.
Admissions Traditional secondary-level entrance grade is 9. For fall 2012, 43 students applied for upper-level admission, 40 were accepted, 37 enrolled. Achievement/Aptitude/Writing or placement test required. Deadline for receipt of application materials: none. Application fee required: $300. Interview required.
Athletics Interscholastic: baseball (boys), basketball (b,g), cheering (g), drill team (g), flag football (b), football (b), soccer (b), volleyball (b,g); intramural: aerobics (b,g), fitness (b,g), jogging (b,g), physical fitness (b,g), physical training (b,g), strength & conditioning (b), tennis (b,g), track and field (b,g), ultimate Frisbee (b,g), walking (b,g), weight training (b,g); coed interscholastic: flag football, soccer; coed intramural: golf. 4 PE instructors, 8 coaches.
Computers Computers are regularly used in business, business applications, college planning, computer applications, desktop publishing, digital applications, keyboarding, lab/keyboard, media production, religion, science, yearbook classes. Computer network features include on-campus library services, online commercial services, Internet access, Internet filtering or blocking technology. Students grades are available online. The school has a published electronic and media policy.
Contact Ms. Barbara Winslow, Admissions Counselor. 818-362-5861. Fax: 818-367-0043. E-mail: barbara.winslow@concordiaschoolsla.org. Web site: www.concordiahigh.org

LOUISVILLE COLLEGIATE SCHOOL

2427 Glenmary Avenue
Louisville, Kentucky 40204

Head of School: Junius Scott Prince

General Information Coeducational day college-preparatory, arts, and technology school. Grades JK–12. Founded: 1915. Setting: urban. 24-acre campus. 2 buildings on campus. Approved or accredited by Independent Schools Association of the Central States. Member of National Association of Independent Schools and Secondary School Admission Test Board. Endowment: $5.7 million. Total enrollment: 720. Upper school average class size: 15. Upper school faculty-student ratio: 1:8.
Faculty School total: 80. In upper school: 12 men, 10 women; 20 have advanced degrees.
Subjects Offered Algebra, American history, American literature, ancient history, art, art history, biology, calculus, chemistry, Chinese, chorus, community service, composition, computer science, creative writing, discrete mathematics, drama, economics, English, English literature, ensembles, environmental science, European history, fine arts, French, geometry, German, history, mathematics, media, music, music history, physical education, physics, physiology, pre-calculus, science, social studies, Spanish, statistics, studio art, theater, trigonometry, world history, world literature, writing.
Graduation Requirements Arts and fine arts (art, music, dance, drama), English, foreign language, mathematics, physical education (includes health), science,

social studies (includes history), senior symposium in leadership and service, individual and class service projects, senior speech.

Special Academic Programs Advanced Placement exam preparation; honors section; independent study; term-away projects; study abroad.

College Admission Counseling 53 students graduated in 2012; all went to college, including Centre College; Miami University; Northwestern University; University of Louisville; Vanderbilt University; Wake Forest University. Median SAT critical reading: 605, median SAT math: 613, median SAT writing: 625, median composite ACT: 27.

Student Life Upper grades have uniform requirement, student council, honor system. Discipline rests equally with students and faculty.

Summer Programs Enrichment, advancement, sports, art/fine arts, computer instruction programs offered; session focuses on educational enrichment and sports; held both on and off campus; held at Champion's Trace athletic fields; accepts boys and girls; open to students from other schools. 350 students usually enrolled. 2013 schedule: June 1 to July 31. Application deadline: none.

Tuition and Aid Day student tuition: $20,600. Tuition installment plan (The Tuition Plan, monthly payment plans, individually arranged payment plans). Merit scholarship grants, need-based scholarship grants available. In 2012–13, 40% of upper-school students received aid.

Admissions Traditional secondary-level entrance grade is 9. School's own exam and SSAT required. Deadline for receipt of application materials: none. Application fee required: $50. Interview required.

Athletics Interscholastic: basketball (boys, girls), crew (g), cross-country running (b,g), field hockey (g), golf (b,g), indoor track (b,g), lacrosse (b,g), rowing (b,g), soccer (b,g), softball (g), strength & conditioning (b,g), swimming and diving (b,g), tennis (b,g), track and field (b,g), winter (indoor) track (b,g); intramural: basketball (b,g), soccer (b,g), tennis (b,g); coed interscholastic: soccer, strength & conditioning; coed intramural: soccer. 4 PE instructors, 60 coaches, 1 athletic trainer.

Computers Computers are regularly used in art, English, foreign language, history, mathematics, science classes. Computer network features include on-campus library services, online commercial services, Internet access, wireless campus network, Internet filtering or blocking technology. Student e-mail accounts and computer access in designated common areas are available to students. Students grades are available online. The school has a published electronic and media policy.

Contact Lynne Age, Admission Office Administrative Assistant. 502-479-0378. Fax: 502-454-0549. E-mail: lynne_age@loucol.com. Web site: www.loucol.com

LOUISVILLE HIGH SCHOOL

22300 Mulholland Drive
Woodland Hills, California 91364

Head of School: Mrs. Kathleen Vercillo

General Information Girls' day college-preparatory, arts, religious studies, and technology school, affiliated with Roman Catholic Church. Grades 9–12. Founded: 1960. Setting: suburban. Nearest major city is Tarzana. 17-acre campus. 7 buildings on campus. Approved or accredited by National Catholic Education Association, Western Association of Schools and Colleges, Western Catholic Education Association, and California Department of Education. Total enrollment: 428. Upper school average class size: 25. Upper school faculty-student ratio: 1:25. There are 180 required school days per year for Upper School students. Upper School students typically attend 5 days per week. The average school day consists of 6 hours.

Upper School Student Profile Grade 9: 98 students (98 girls); Grade 10: 103 students (103 girls); Grade 11: 115 students (115 girls); Grade 12: 112 students (112 girls). 78% of students are Roman Catholic.

Faculty School total: 38. In upper school: 7 men, 31 women; 26 have advanced degrees.

Subjects Offered Advanced Placement courses, advanced studio art-AP, algebra, American history, American literature, anatomy, art, Bible studies, biology, calculus, calculus-AP, campus ministry, ceramics, chemistry, computer science, creative writing, dance, drama, earth science, economics, English, English literature, European history, fine arts, French, geography, geometry, government/civics, grammar, history, journalism, law, mathematics, music, photography, physical education, physics, physiology, psychology, religion, science, social sciences, social studies, Spanish, speech, theater, trigonometry, video film production, Web site design, world history, world literature.

Graduation Requirements Arts and fine arts (art, music, dance, drama), biology, chemistry, computer science, economics, English, foreign language, mathematics, performing arts, physical education (includes health), religion (includes Bible studies and theology), science, social sciences, social studies (includes history), U.S. government, U.S. history, visual arts, world history. Community service is required.

Special Academic Programs Advanced Placement exam preparation.

College Admission Counseling 79 students graduated in 2012; all went to college, including California State University, Northridge; Loyola Marymount University; Texas Christian University; University of California, Los Angeles; University of San Francisco; University of Southern California.

Student Life Upper grades have uniform requirement, student council, honor system. Discipline rests equally with students and faculty. Attendance at religious services is required.

Summer Programs Sports programs offered; session focuses on skill development; held both on and off campus; held at Los Angeles Pierce Community College and Balboa Park; accepts girls; open to students from other schools. 200 students usually enrolled. 2013 schedule: June 15 to July 26. Application deadline: May 24.

Tuition and Aid Day student tuition: $13,250. Tuition installment plan (FACTS Tuition Payment Plan). Merit scholarship grants, need-based scholarship grants available. In 2012–13, 45% of upper-school students received aid; total upper-school merit-scholarship money awarded: $92,000. Total amount of financial aid awarded in 2012–13: $640,000.

Admissions Traditional secondary-level entrance grade is 9. For fall 2012, 171 students applied for upper-level admission, 155 were accepted, 98 enrolled. High School Placement Test required. Deadline for receipt of application materials: February 1. Application fee required: $100. On-campus interview required.

Athletics Interscholastic: basketball, cross-country running, equestrian sports, field hockey, golf, lacrosse, soccer, softball, swimming and diving, tennis, track and field, volleyball, water polo; intramural: fitness walking, tennis, yoga. 2 PE instructors, 25 coaches, 1 athletic trainer.

Computers Computers are regularly used in all academic, college planning, computer applications, creative writing, economics, English, foreign language, French, graphic design, health, journalism, library, literary magazine, mathematics, media, media production, photography, religion, religious studies, science, social studies, Spanish, speech, technology, yearbook classes. Computer network features include on-campus library services, online commercial services, Internet access, wireless campus network, Internet filtering or blocking technology. Student e-mail accounts are available to students. Students grades are available online. The school has a published electronic and media policy.

Contact Mrs. Linda Klarin, Admissions Coordinator. 818-346-8812 Ext. 1000. Fax: 818-346-9483. E-mail: lklarin@louisvillehs.org. Web site: www.louisvillehs.org

THE LOVETT SCHOOL

4075 Paces Ferry Road NW
Atlanta, Georgia 30327

Head of School: William S. Peebles

General Information Coeducational day college-preparatory school. Grades K–12. Founded: 1926. Setting: suburban. 100-acre campus. 8 buildings on campus. Approved or accredited by Southern Association of Colleges and Schools, Southern Association of Independent Schools, and Georgia Department of Education. Member of National Association of Independent Schools and Secondary School Admission Test Board. Endowment: $70.7 million. Total enrollment: 1,610. Upper school average class size: 15. Upper school faculty-student ratio: 1:8. There are 180 required school days per year for Upper School students. Upper School students typically attend 5 days per week. The average school day consists of 6 hours.

Upper School Student Profile Grade 9: 165 students (79 boys, 86 girls); Grade 10: 149 students (73 boys, 76 girls); Grade 11: 143 students (66 boys, 77 girls); Grade 12: 146 students (70 boys, 76 girls).

Faculty School total: 154. In upper school: 39 men, 36 women; 48 have advanced degrees.

Subjects Offered Advanced chemistry, advanced computer applications, advanced math, Advanced Placement courses, African American history, African history, African literature, African-American literature, algebra, American government, American history, American history-AP, American legal systems, American literature, ancient history, ancient world history, architecture, art, art history, Asian history, Asian studies, band, biology, botany, calculus, calculus-AP, career and personal planning, career/college preparation, ceramics, character education, chemistry, chorus, computer art, computer education, computer graphics, computer programming, computer science, creative writing, dance, debate, drama, driver education, earth science, ecology, economics, electronic music, English, English literature, English-AP, environmental science, ethics, European history, fiction, film history, fine arts, French, French language-AP, French literature-AP, French studies, French-AP, gender issues, genetics, geometry, German, history, human development, jazz dance, journalism, Latin, Latin-AP, leadership, marine biology, mathematics, medieval history, music theory, music theory-AP, newspaper, orchestra, painting, philosophy, photography, physical education, physics, portfolio art, pre-calculus, public speaking, religion, robotics, science, sculpture, social studies, Spanish, Spanish language-AP, Spanish literature-AP, speech, statistics, technical theater, theater, theater arts, trigonometry, U.S. government and politics-AP, video, Western civilization, Western philosophy, world cultures, world history, world literature, world religions, writing workshop, yearbook, zoology.

Graduation Requirements Algebra, American studies, arts and fine arts (art, music, dance, drama), biology, English, foreign language, geometry, history, mathematics, physical education (includes health), religion (includes Bible studies and theology), science, Western civilization.

Special Academic Programs Advanced Placement exam preparation; honors section; independent study; term-away projects; study abroad; academic accommodation for the gifted, the musically talented, and the artistically talented.

College Admission Counseling 149 students graduated in 2012; all went to college, including Miami University; Texas Christian University; The University of Alabama; The University of North Carolina at Chapel Hill; University of Georgia; Wake Forest University.

Student Life Upper grades have uniform requirement, student council, honor system. Discipline rests primarily with faculty. Attendance at religious services is required.

Summer Programs Remediation, enrichment, advancement programs offered; session focuses on academic course work; held on campus; accepts boys and girls; open to students from other schools. 130 students usually enrolled. 2013 schedule: June 3 to July 26. Application deadline: July 24.

Tuition and Aid Day student tuition: $19,210–$22,740. Tuition installment plan (The Tuition Plan, Key Tuition Payment Plan, monthly payment plans, individually arranged payment plans, 1/2 paid in July and 1/2 paid in November). Need-based scholarship grants, local bank loans available. In 2012–13, 15% of upper-school students received aid. Total amount of financial aid awarded in 2012–13: $1,237,420.

Admissions Traditional secondary-level entrance grade is 9. SSAT required. Deadline for receipt of application materials: February 1. Application fee required: $75. On-campus interview required.

Athletics Interscholastic: artistic gym (girls), baseball (b), basketball (b,g), cheering (g), cross-country running (b,g), dance (g), diving (b,g), football (b), golf (b,g), gymnastics (g), lacrosse (b,g), modern dance (g), soccer (b,g), softball (g), swimming and diving (b,g), tennis (b,g), track and field (b,g), volleyball (g), wrestling (b); intramural: aerobics/dance (g), dance (g), in-line hockey (b), modern dance (g), roller hockey (b); coed intramural: backpacking, bicycling, bowling, canoeing/kayaking, climbing, fitness, flag football, Frisbee, hiking/backpacking, kayaking, mountain biking, outdoor activities, physical fitness, physical training, rappelling, rock climbing, ropes courses, strength & conditioning, ultimate Frisbee, wall climbing, weight lifting, weight training, yoga. 3 PE instructors, 26 coaches, 2 athletic trainers.

Computers Computers are regularly used in all academic classes. Computer network features include on-campus library services, online commercial services, Internet access, wireless campus network, Internet filtering or blocking technology, central file storage. Student e-mail accounts and computer access in designated common areas are available to students. Students grades are available online.

Contact Ms. Debbie Lange, Director of Admission. 404-262-3032. Fax: 404-479-8463. E-mail: dlange@lovett.org. Web site: www.lovett.org

LOYOLA-BLAKEFIELD

PO Box 6819
Baltimore, Maryland 21285-6819

Head of School: Mr. Anthony I. Day

General Information Boys' day college-preparatory, arts, and religious studies school, affiliated with Roman Catholic Church. Grades 6–12. Founded: 1852. Setting: suburban. 60-acre campus. 6 buildings on campus. Approved or accredited by Association of Independent Maryland Schools and Jesuit Secondary Education Association. Endowment: $19.7 million. Total enrollment: 988. Upper school average class size: 18. Upper school faculty-student ratio: 1:10. There are 175 required school days per year for Upper School students. Upper School students typically attend 5 days per week. The average school day consists of 7 hours.

Upper School Student Profile Grade 9: 197 students (197 boys); Grade 10: 187 students (187 boys); Grade 11: 182 students (182 boys); Grade 12: 183 students (183 boys). 78% of students are Roman Catholic.

Faculty School total: 98. In upper school: 55 men, 19 women; 54 have advanced degrees.

Subjects Offered Accounting, algebra, American government, American literature, American literature-AP, architecture, art, art history, band, biology, biology-AP, biotechnology, British literature, British literature (honors), calculus, calculus-AP, chemistry, chemistry-AP, chorus, civil war history, composition, composition-AP, computer graphics, computer science, concert band, drawing, driver education, engineering, English, English language-AP, English literature-AP, European history-AP, film studies, fine arts, forensics, French, French language-AP, German, German-AP, government and politics-AP, Greek, history, history of music, honors algebra, honors English, honors geometry, honors U.S. history, honors world history, instrumental music, Italian, jazz ensemble, Latin, Latin-AP, marine science, mathematics, music history, oil painting, painting, photography, physical education, physics, physics-AP, poetry, pre-calculus, psychology, public speaking, religion, science, Spanish, Spanish language-AP, statistics-AP, U.S. government and politics-AP, U.S. history, U.S. history-AP.

Graduation Requirements Arts and fine arts (art, music, dance, drama), computer science, English, foreign language, mathematics, physical education (includes health), religion (includes Bible studies and theology), science, social studies (includes history), 40 hours of Christian service.

Special Academic Programs 19 Advanced Placement exams for which test preparation is offered; honors section; academic accommodation for the gifted, the musically talented, and the artistically talented; programs in English, mathematics, general development for dyslexic students.

College Admission Counseling 183 students graduated in 2012; all went to college, including Loyola University Maryland; Mount St. Mary's University; University of Maryland, College Park; University of South Carolina; Virginia Polytechnic Institute and State University. Median SAT critical reading: 580, median SAT math: 610, median SAT writing: 590, median combined SAT: 1790, median composite ACT: 26. 48% scored over 600 on SAT critical reading, 60% scored over 600 on SAT math, 47% scored over 600 on SAT writing, 49% scored over 1800 on combined SAT, 24% scored over 26 on composite ACT.

Student Life Upper grades have specified standards of dress, student council, honor system. Discipline rests primarily with faculty. Attendance at religious services is required.

Summer Programs Remediation, enrichment, advancement, sports, art/fine arts, computer instruction programs offered; held on campus; accepts boys and girls; open to students from other schools. 600 students usually enrolled. 2013 schedule: June 10 to August 2. Application deadline: none.

Tuition and Aid Day student tuition: $16,935. Tuition installment plan (Tuition Management Systems). Merit scholarship grants, need-based scholarship grants available. In 2012–13, 40% of upper-school students received aid; total upper-school merit-scholarship money awarded: $574,545. Total amount of financial aid awarded in 2012–13: $2,464,636.

Admissions Traditional secondary-level entrance grade is 9. For fall 2012, 290 students applied for upper-level admission, 250 were accepted, 116 enrolled. High School Placement Test or ISEE required. Deadline for receipt of application materials: December 15. No application fee required. On-campus interview required.

Athletics Interscholastic: baseball, basketball, cross-country running, diving, football, golf, ice hockey, indoor track & field, lacrosse, rugby, soccer, squash, swimming and diving, tennis, track and field, volleyball, water polo, winter (indoor) track, wrestling; intramural: basketball, flag football, indoor soccer, lacrosse, martial arts, rock climbing, tennis, ultimate Frisbee. 4 PE instructors, 30 coaches, 1 athletic trainer.

Computers Computers are regularly used in all classes. Computer network features include on-campus library services, online commercial services, Internet access, wireless campus network, Internet filtering or blocking technology. Campus intranet, student e-mail accounts, and computer access in designated common areas are available to students. Students grades are available online. The school has a published electronic and media policy.

Contact Ms. Paddy M. London, Admissions Assistant. 443-841-3680. Fax: 443-841-3105. E-mail: plondon@loyolablakefield.org. Web site: www.loyolablakefield.org

LOYOLA SCHOOL

980 Park Avenue
New York, New York 10028-0020

Head of School: Mr. James F.X. Lyness

General Information Coeducational day college-preparatory school, affiliated with Roman Catholic Church (Jesuit order). Grades 9–12. Founded: 1900. Setting: urban. 2 buildings on campus. Approved or accredited by Jesuit Secondary Education Association, Middle States Association of Colleges and Schools, National Catholic Education Association, New York State Association of Independent Schools, and New York State Board of Regents. Member of National Association of Independent Schools. Total enrollment: 202. Upper school average class size: 17. Upper school faculty-student ratio: 1:9. There are 180 required school days per year for Upper School students. Upper School students typically attend 5 days per week. The average school day consists of 6 hours and 20 minutes.

Upper School Student Profile Grade 9: 49 students (25 boys, 24 girls); Grade 10: 45 students (20 boys, 25 girls); Grade 11: 53 students (25 boys, 28 girls); Grade 12: 55 students (24 boys, 31 girls). 85% of students are Roman Catholic Church (Jesuit order).

Faculty School total: 30. In upper school: 16 men, 14 women; 28 have advanced degrees.

Subjects Offered Advanced Placement courses, algebra, American government, American history, American literature, art, art history, biology, calculus, chemistry, chorus, college counseling, community service, comparative religion, computer programming, computer science, creative writing, death and loss, discrete mathematics, drama, economics, English, English literature, ethics, European history, expository writing, film, film history, fine arts, French, geometry, grammar, health, history, instrumental music, Italian, journalism, language-AP, Latin, mathematics, music history, philosophy, photography, physical education, physics, political science, pre-calculus, religion, science, social studies, Spanish, speech, statistics-AP, student government, student publications, theater, theology, trigonometry, world history, writing.

Graduation Requirements Art history, computer literacy, English, foreign language, guidance, mathematics, music history, physical education (includes health), science, social studies (includes history), speech, theology, Christian service program hours each year.

Special Academic Programs 9 Advanced Placement exams for which test preparation is offered; study at local college for college credit.

College Admission Counseling 55 students graduated in 2012; all went to college, including Cornell University; Fordham University; Georgetown University; New York University; Vanderbilt University. Median SAT critical reading: 620, median SAT math: 600, median SAT writing: 630.

Student Life Upper grades have specified standards of dress, student council, honor system. Discipline rests primarily with faculty. Attendance at religious services is required.

Tuition and Aid Day student tuition: $36,500. Tuition installment plan (Academic Management Services Plan). Merit scholarship grants, need-based scholarship grants available. In 2012–13, 33% of upper-school students received aid; total upper-school merit-scholarship money awarded: $200,000. Total amount of financial aid awarded in 2012–13: $1,194,000.

Admissions Traditional secondary-level entrance grade is 9. High School Placement Test (closed version) from Scholastic Testing Service, ISEE or SSAT required. Deadline for receipt of application materials: November 19. Application fee required: $80. On-campus interview recommended.

Athletics Interscholastic: baseball (boys), basketball (b,g), cross-country running (b,g), soccer (b), softball (g), track and field (b,g), volleyball (g); intramural: basketball (b,g), dance (g); coed interscholastic: golf, physical fitness, soccer; coed intramural: Frisbee, hiking/backpacking, outdoor activities, outdoor adventure, paddle tennis, physical fitness, physical training, track and field. 1 PE instructor, 9 coaches.

Computers Computers are regularly used in all academic classes. Computer network features include on-campus library services, online commercial services, Internet access, wireless campus network, Internet filtering or blocking technology. Campus intranet, student e-mail accounts, and computer access in designated common areas are available to students. The school has a published electronic and media policy.

Contact Mr. Gabriel Rotman, Associate Director of Admissions. 646-346-8131. Fax: 646-346-8175. E-mail: grotman@loyola-nyc.org. Web site: www.loyola-nyc.org

LUTHERAN HIGH SCHOOL NORTH

5401 Lucas Hunt Road
St. Louis, Missouri 63121

Head of School: Mr. Timothy Brackman

General Information Coeducational day college-preparatory, arts, business, religious studies, bilingual studies, and technology school, affiliated with Lutheran Church. Grades 9–12. Founded: 1946. Setting: urban. 47-acre campus. 1 building on campus. Approved or accredited by Lutheran School Accreditation Commission, National Lutheran School Accreditation, North Central Association of Colleges and Schools, and Missouri Department of Education. Endowment: $5.8 million. Total enrollment: 311. Upper school average class size: 20. Upper school faculty-student ratio: 1:10. There are 178 required school days per year for Upper School students. Upper School students typically attend 5 days per week. The average school day consists of 6 hours and 20 minutes.

Upper School Student Profile Grade 9: 88 students (50 boys, 38 girls); Grade 10: 81 students (36 boys, 45 girls); Grade 11: 67 students (35 boys, 32 girls); Grade 12: 75 students (36 boys, 39 girls). 47% of students are Lutheran.

Faculty School total: 30. In upper school: 17 men, 13 women; 26 have advanced degrees.

Subjects Offered Accounting, advanced chemistry, Advanced Placement courses, algebra, American history, American history-AP, American literature, anatomy, art, Bible studies, biology, business, business law, business skills, calculus, calculus-AP, ceramics, chemistry, child development, choir, Christian doctrine, Christian education, Christian ethics, Christian scripture, Christian studies, Christianity, church history, computer applications, computer multimedia, computer science, concert band, concert choir, data analysis, design, drawing, drawing and design, economics, English, English composition, English literature, English literature-AP, entrepreneurship, European history, family and consumer science, fashion, fine arts, finite math, food and nutrition, foods, French, geography, geometry, government, government/civics, health education, history, human anatomy, keyboarding, literature-AP, Mandarin, marketing, mathematics, media studies, multimedia design, music, organic chemistry, painting, physical education, physics, physiology, practical arts, pre-calculus, printmaking, probability and statistics, psychology, religion, research, science, social studies, society and culture, Spanish, speech, statistics, student publications, theology, U.S. government, U.S. history-AP, world geography, world history, world literature, world religions, writing.

Graduation Requirements American history, arts and fine arts (art, music, dance, drama), English, mathematics, physical education (includes health), practical arts, religion (includes Bible studies and theology), science, social studies (includes history), Saved to Serve (community service hours).

Special Academic Programs Advanced Placement exam preparation; honors section; independent study; study at local college for college credit.

College Admission Counseling 79 students graduated in 2012; 78 went to college, including Concordia University Chicago; Southeast Missouri State University; Truman State University; University of Central Missouri; University of Missouri. Other: 1 entered military service. 50% scored over 26 on composite ACT.

Student Life Upper grades have uniform requirement, student council, honor system. Discipline rests primarily with faculty. Attendance at religious services is required.

Summer Programs Enrichment, sports programs offered; session focuses on fundamentals and enrichment; held on campus; accepts boys and girls; not open to students from other schools. 150 students usually enrolled. 2013 schedule: June 1 to July 31.

Tuition and Aid Day student tuition: $9875–$11,075. Tuition installment plan (FACTS Tuition Payment Plan, monthly payment plans, individually arranged payment plans, semester payment plan, full-year payment plan with discount). Tuition reduction for siblings, merit scholarship grants, need-based scholarship grants available. In 2012–13, 66% of upper-school students received aid; total upper-school merit-scholarship money awarded: $22,000. Total amount of financial aid awarded in 2012–13: $750,000.

Admissions Traditional secondary-level entrance grade is 9. For fall 2012, 97 students applied for upper-level admission, 93 were accepted, 86 enrolled. ACT-Explore required. Deadline for receipt of application materials: none. Application fee required: $250. Interview recommended.

Athletics Interscholastic: baseball (boys), basketball (b,g), cheering (g), cross-country running (b,g), dance squad (g), football (b), golf (b), pom squad (g), soccer (b,g), softball (g), tennis (b,g), track and field (b,g), volleyball (g). 2 PE instructors.

Computers Computers are regularly used in art, business education, English, history, mathematics, science, social studies, yearbook classes. Computer network features include on-campus library services, Internet access, wireless campus network, Internet filtering or blocking technology, Internet college work program. Campus intranet and computer access in designated common areas are available to students. Students grades are available online. The school has a published electronic and media policy.

Contact Karen Kersten, Records Clerk. 314-389-3100 Ext. 406. Fax: 314-389-3103. E-mail: kkersten@lhsn.org. Web site: www.lhsn.org

LUTHERAN HIGH SCHOOL NORTHWEST

1000 Bagley Avenue
Rochester Hills, Michigan 48309

Head of School: Mr. Paul Looker

General Information Coeducational day college-preparatory and religious studies school, affiliated with Lutheran Church–Missouri Synod. Grades 9–12. Founded: 1978. Setting: suburban. Nearest major city is Detroit. 30-acre campus. 1 building on campus. Approved or accredited by National Lutheran School Accreditation, North Central Association of Colleges and Schools, and Michigan Department of Education. Endowment: $1 million. Total enrollment: 300. Upper school average class size: 25. Upper school faculty-student ratio: 1:15. There are 185 required school days per year for Upper School students. Upper School students typically attend 5 days per week. The average school day consists of 7 hours and 20 minutes.

Upper School Student Profile Grade 9: 69 students (33 boys, 36 girls); Grade 10: 72 students (32 boys, 40 girls); Grade 11: 81 students (48 boys, 33 girls); Grade 12: 78 students (43 boys, 35 girls). 75% of students are Lutheran Church–Missouri Synod.

Faculty School total: 20. In upper school: 12 men, 8 women; 15 have advanced degrees.

Subjects Offered Accounting, advanced chemistry, algebra, American history, American history-AP, art, audio visual/media, band, Basic programming, biology, biology-AP, bookkeeping, business, business mathematics, calculus, chemistry, chorus, computer science, drawing, drawing and design, Eastern world civilizations, economics, English, English-AP, geography, geometry, German, government/civics, graphic arts, law, mathematics, music, painting, physical education, physical science, physics-AP, psychology, Spanish, statistics-AP, theology, trigonometry, U.S. government and politics-AP, world history.

Graduation Requirements Arts and fine arts (art, music, dance, drama), English, mathematics, physical education (includes health), religion (includes Bible studies and theology), science, social sciences, social studies (includes history). Community service is required.

Special Academic Programs 7 Advanced Placement exams for which test preparation is offered; honors section; independent study; study at local college for college credit.

College Admission Counseling 67 students graduated in 2012; 65 went to college, including Central Michigan University; Concordia University Chicago; Concordia University Wisconsin; Michigan State University; Oakland University; Western Michigan University. Other: 2 went to work. Median composite ACT: 24. 35% scored over 26 on composite ACT.

Student Life Upper grades have specified standards of dress, student council. Discipline rests primarily with faculty. Attendance at religious services is required.

Tuition and Aid Day student tuition: $7550. Tuition installment plan (monthly payment plans). Merit scholarship grants, need-based scholarship grants available. In 2012–13, 2% of upper-school students received aid; total upper-school merit-scholarship money awarded: $20,000. Total amount of financial aid awarded in 2012–13: $20,000.

Admissions Traditional secondary-level entrance grade is 9. High School Placement Test required. Deadline for receipt of application materials: none. Application fee required: $350. On-campus interview required.

Athletics Interscholastic: baseball (boys), basketball (b,g), cheering (g), cross-country running (b,g), dance team (g), football (b), golf (b,g), hockey (b), soccer (b,g), softball (g), track and field (b,g), volleyball (g), wrestling (b); intramural: indoor soccer (b,g); coed intramural: badminton, fitness, physical fitness, physical training, tennis, weight training.

Computers Computers are regularly used in journalism, keyboarding, mathematics, media, research skills, word processing, yearbook classes. Computer network features include Internet access, wireless campus network, Internet filtering or blocking technology. Students grades are available online. The school has a published electronic and media policy.

Contact Mr. Paul Looker, Principal. 248-852-6677. Fax: 248-852-2667. E-mail: plooker@lhsa.com. Web site: www.lhnw.lhsa.com

LUTHERAN HIGH SCHOOL OF HAWAII

1404 University Avenue
Honolulu, Hawaii 96822-2494

Head of School: Daryl S. Utsumi

General Information Coeducational day college-preparatory school, affiliated with Lutheran Church–Missouri Synod. Grades 9–12. Founded: 1988. Setting: urban. 1-acre campus. 3 buildings on campus. Approved or accredited by Lutheran School Accreditation Commission, The Hawaii Council of Private Schools, Western Association of Schools and Colleges, and Hawaii Department of Education. Member of Secondary School Admission Test Board. Endowment: $43,000. Total enrollment: 68. Upper school average class size: 12. Upper school faculty-student ratio: 1:7. There are 170 required school days per year for Upper School students. Upper School students typically attend 5 days per week. The average school day consists of 7 hours and 15 minutes.

Upper School Student Profile Grade 9: 12 students (6 boys, 6 girls); Grade 10: 10 students (3 boys, 7 girls); Grade 11: 23 students (12 boys, 11 girls); Grade 12: 23 students (13 boys, 10 girls). 10% of students are Lutheran Church–Missouri Synod.

Faculty School total: 15. In upper school: 7 men, 8 women; 6 have advanced degrees.

Subjects Offered 20th century history, 3-dimensional art, advanced math, Advanced Placement courses, algebra, American government, American history, American literature, analytic geometry, art, art-AP, Bible studies, biology, British literature, calculus, calculus-AP, chemistry, choir, computer applications, computer programming, computer science, concert band, consumer economics, drama, earth science, economics, English, English literature, European history, expository writing, fine arts, food and nutrition, geometry, government/civics, grammar, health, history, home economics, Japanese, journalism, keyboarding, life skills, marine biology, mathematics, music, oceanography, photography, physical education, physics, psychology, religion, science, social sciences, social studies, Spanish, speech, theater, trigonometry, world history, world literature.

Graduation Requirements Arts and fine arts (art, music, dance, drama), computer science, English, health, mathematics, physical education (includes health), religion (includes Bible studies and theology), science, social studies (includes history).

Special Academic Programs Advanced Placement exam preparation; honors section; study at local college for college credit; academic accommodation for the musically talented and the artistically talented.

College Admission Counseling 30 students graduated in 2012; 29 went to college, including Kapiolani Community College; University of Hawaii at Manoa. Other: 1 went to work. Median composite ACT: 23. Mean SAT critical reading: 525, mean SAT math: 530, mean SAT writing: 525. 10% scored over 600 on SAT critical reading, 15% scored over 600 on SAT math.

Student Life Upper grades have uniform requirement, student council, honor system. Discipline rests primarily with faculty. Attendance at religious services is required.

Summer Programs Remediation, enrichment, advancement, sports, art/fine arts, computer instruction programs offered; held on campus; accepts boys and girls; open to students from other schools. 25 students usually enrolled. 2013 schedule: June 12 to July 20.

Tuition and Aid Day student tuition: $10,490–$10,990. Tuition installment plan (Insured Tuition Payment Plan). Tuition reduction for siblings, merit scholarship grants, need-based scholarship grants available. In 2012–13, 25% of upper-school students received aid; total upper-school merit-scholarship money awarded: $50,000. Total amount of financial aid awarded in 2012–13: $500,000.

Admissions Traditional secondary-level entrance grade is 9. For fall 2012, 45 students applied for upper-level admission, 39 were accepted, 19 enrolled. SSAT required. Deadline for receipt of application materials: none. Application fee required: $30. Interview recommended.

Athletics Interscholastic: baseball (boys), basketball (b,g), bowling (b,g), canoeing/kayaking (b,g), cross-country running (b,g), diving (b,g), golf (b,g), judo (b,g), kayaking (b,g), paddling (b,g), soccer (b,g), softball (g), swimming and diving (b,g), tennis (b,g), track and field (b,g), volleyball (b,g), water polo (b,g), wrestling (b,g); coed interscholastic: cheering, football, gymnastics, sailing, strength & conditioning. 1 PE instructor, 5 coaches, 1 athletic trainer.

Computers Computers are regularly used in art, business applications, desktop publishing, English, history, journalism, library, mathematics, newspaper, photography, photojournalism, science, yearbook classes. Computer network features include on-campus library services, Internet access, Internet filtering or blocking technology. Students grades are available online. The school has a published electronic and media policy.

Contact Lea Dominici, Admissions Officer. 808-949-5302. Fax: 808-947-3701. E-mail: office@lhshawaii.org. Web site: lhshawaii.org

LUTHERAN HIGH SCHOOL OF INDIANAPOLIS

5555 South Arlington Avenue
Indianapolis, Indiana 46237-2366

Head of School: Mr. Michael Brandt

General Information Coeducational day college-preparatory, general academic, and religious studies school, affiliated with Lutheran Church–Missouri Synod. Grades 9–12. Founded: 1976. Setting: suburban. 14-acre campus. 1 building on campus. Approved or accredited by National Lutheran School Accreditation, North Central Association of Colleges and Schools, and Indiana Department of Education. Endowment: $600,000. Total enrollment: 216. Upper school average class size: 18. Upper school faculty-student ratio: 1:15. There are 180 required school days per year for Upper School students. Upper School students typically attend 5 days per week. The average school day consists of 7 hours and 15 minutes.

Upper School Student Profile Grade 9: 47 students (21 boys, 26 girls); Grade 10: 63 students (32 boys, 31 girls); Grade 11: 55 students (28 boys, 27 girls); Grade 12: 51 students (27 boys, 24 girls). 64% of students are Lutheran Church–Missouri Synod.

Faculty School total: 17. In upper school: 12 men, 5 women; 15 have advanced degrees.

Subjects Offered 3-dimensional art, Advanced Placement courses, advanced studio art-AP, algebra, American government, American history, American history-AP, American literature-AP, American sign language, anatomy, anatomy and physiology, art, art-AP, band, biology, biology-AP, calculus, calculus-AP, career experience, ceramics, chemistry, chemistry-AP, choir, chorus, Christian ethics, Christian scripture, Christian testament, computer information systems, computer programming, concert band, current events, desktop publishing, discrete mathematics, earth science, economics, English, English composition, English literature and composition-AP, English literature-AP, ethics, etymology, geography, geometry, German, health and wellness, honors algebra, humanities, integrated physics, math review, music theory, music theory-AP, New Testament, physical education, physical fitness, piano, pre-calculus, psychology, reading/study skills, sociology, Spanish, Spanish-AP, speech, statistics, studio art, U.S. government, U.S. history-AP, world history, world religions.

Graduation Requirements Arts and fine arts (art, music, dance, drama), biology, chemistry, Christian doctrine, Christian ethics, computer applications, economics, foreign language, geography, health and wellness, integrated physics, literature and composition-AP, New Testament, physical education (includes health), U.S. government, U.S. history, world religions.

Special Academic Programs 6 Advanced Placement exams for which test preparation is offered; honors section; independent study; study at local college for college credit; remedial reading and/or remedial writing; remedial math.

College Admission Counseling 74 students graduated in 2012; 72 went to college, including Ball State University; Indiana University Bloomington; Purdue University; Taylor University; University of Indianapolis. Other: 2 went to work. Mean SAT critical reading: 515, mean SAT math: 550, mean SAT writing: 502, mean combined SAT: 1567, mean composite ACT: 23.

Student Life Upper grades have uniform requirement, student council. Discipline rests primarily with faculty. Attendance at religious services is required.

Tuition and Aid Day student tuition: $9150. Tuition installment plan (monthly payment plans, In Full, by semester, or through 10 month payment plan). Tuition reduction for siblings, need-based scholarship grants, paying campus jobs, Simply Giving (Thrivent), church worker grants available. In 2012–13, 81% of upper-school students received aid. Total amount of financial aid awarded in 2012–13: $160,000.

Admissions Traditional secondary-level entrance grade is 9. For fall 2012, 64 students applied for upper-level admission, 61 were accepted, 61 enrolled. Math Placement Exam or SCAT required. Deadline for receipt of application materials: none. Application fee required: $200. On-campus interview required.

Athletics Interscholastic: baseball (boys), basketball (b,g), cross-country running (b,g), football (b), golf (b,g), soccer (b,g), softball (g), strength & conditioning (b,g), tennis (b,g), track and field (b,g), volleyball (b,g), weight lifting (b,g), weight training (b,g); intramural: basketball (b,g); coed interscholastic: cheering, physical fitness, weight training; coed intramural: bowling, fishing, football. 2 PE instructors, 22 coaches.

Computers Computers are regularly used in all academic classes. Computer network features include online commercial services, Internet access, wireless campus network, Internet filtering or blocking technology. Computer access in designated common areas is available to students. Students grades are available online. The school has a published electronic and media policy.

Contact Mrs. Christie Hampton, Director of Admissions. 317-787-5474 Ext. 218. Fax: 317-787-2794. E-mail: admissions@lhsi.org. Web site: www.lhsi.org

LUTHERAN HIGH SCHOOL OF SAN DIEGO

810 Buena Vista Way
Chula Vista, California 91910-6853

Head of School: Mr. Scott Dufresne

General Information Coeducational day and distance learning college-preparatory, arts, religious studies, and technology school, affiliated with Lutheran Church. Grades 9–12. Distance learning grades 9–12. Founded: 1975. Setting: urban. Nearest major city is San Diego. 9-acre campus. 6 buildings on campus. Approved or accredited by National Lutheran School Accreditation, Western Association of Schools and Colleges, and California Department of Education. Total enrollment: 88. Upper school average class size: 12. Upper school faculty-student ratio: 1:12. There are 180 required school days per year for Upper School students. Upper School students typically attend 5 days per week. The average school day consists of 6 hours and 30 minutes.

Upper School Student Profile Grade 9: 16 students (11 boys, 5 girls); Grade 10: 28 students (16 boys, 12 girls); Grade 11: 22 students (12 boys, 10 girls); Grade 12: 22 students (16 boys, 6 girls). 50% of students are Lutheran.

Faculty School total: 9. In upper school: 5 men, 4 women; 6 have advanced degrees.

Subjects Offered Accounting, acting, Advanced Placement courses, algebra, American government, American history, American literature, American literature-AP, analytic geometry, anatomy and physiology, applied arts, applied music, art, art appreciation, art history-AP, ASB Leadership, athletics, band, baseball, basketball, bell choir, Bible, biology, biology-AP, British literature, British literature-AP, calculus-AP, campus ministry, chemistry, choir, choral music, Christian education, Christian ethics, comparative religion, computer literacy, creative writing, drama, driver education, economics, English, English language and composition-AP, English language-AP, English literature and composition-AP, English literature-AP, English-AP, English/composition-AP, European history-AP, French, geometry, government, health education, history, music appreciation, physical education, physics, pre-calculus, softball, Spanish, Spanish language-AP, speech, student government, U.S. government and politics, yearbook.

Special Academic Programs Advanced Placement exam preparation.

College Admission Counseling 18 students graduated in 2012; 17 went to college, including Concordia University; Point Loma Nazarene University; San Diego State University; University of California, Irvine; University of California, Riverside. Other: 1 went to work. Mean SAT critical reading: 537, mean SAT math: 518, mean SAT writing: 540, mean combined SAT: 1595.

Student Life Upper grades have specified standards of dress, student council, honor system. Discipline rests primarily with faculty. Attendance at religious services is required.

Tuition and Aid Day student tuition: $8495. Tuition installment plan (monthly payment plans, individually arranged payment plans, Simply Giving—Thrivent Financial for Lutherans, Tuition Solution). Tuition reduction for siblings, merit scholarship grants, need-based scholarship grants available. In 2012–13, 31% of upper-school students received aid; total upper-school merit-scholarship money awarded: $8000. Total amount of financial aid awarded in 2012–13: $60,000.

Admissions Traditional secondary-level entrance grade is 9. Admissions testing required. Application fee required: $250. On-campus interview required.

Athletics Interscholastic: baseball (boys), basketball (b,g), cross-country running (b,g), football (b), softball (g), volleyball (b,g). 1 PE instructor, 10 coaches.

Computers Computer network features include on-campus library services, Internet access. Students grades are available online.

Contact Debbie Heien, Office Manager. 619-262-4444 Ext. 120. Fax: 619-872-0974. E-mail: debbie.heien@lhssd.org. Web site: www.lutheranhighsandiego.org

LUTHER COLLEGE HIGH SCHOOL

1500 Royal Street
Regina, Saskatchewan S4T 5A5, Canada

Head of School: Dr. Mark Anderson

General Information Coeducational boarding and day college-preparatory, general academic, arts, International Baccalaureate, and ESL school, affiliated with Lutheran Church. Grades 9–12. Founded: 1913. Setting: urban. Nearest major city is Winnipeg, MB, Canada. Students are housed in single-sex dormitories. 27-acre campus. 5 buildings on campus. Approved or accredited by Saskatchewan Department of Education. Language of instruction: English. Endowment: CAN$600,000. Total enrollment: 416. Upper school average class size: 22. Upper school faculty-student ratio: 1:16. There are 190 required school days per year for Upper School students. Upper School students typically attend 5 days per week. The average school day consists of 7 hours.

Upper School Student Profile 14% of students are boarding students. 86% are province residents. 2 provinces are represented in upper school student body. 14% are international students. International students from China, Germany, Hong Kong, Republic of Korea, Taiwan, and Thailand; 6 other countries represented in student body. 22% of students are Lutheran.

Faculty School total: 36. In upper school: 19 men, 17 women; 5 have advanced degrees; 1 resides on campus.

Subjects Offered Band, biology, calculus, chemistry, choir, Christian ethics, computer science, drama, English, ESL, French, German, handbells, history, information processing, International Baccalaureate courses, Latin, mathematics, music, orchestra, physical fitness, physics, psychology, science, video film production.

Graduation Requirements Christian ethics, English, mathematics, science, social studies (includes history).

Special Academic Programs International Baccalaureate program; independent study; study at local college for college credit; study abroad; academic accommodation for the gifted; ESL (15 students enrolled).

College Admission Counseling 91 students graduated in 2012; 75 went to college, including McGill University; University of Alberta; University of Calgary; University of Regina; University of Saskatchewan. Other: 16 went to work. 40% scored over 600 on SAT critical reading, 40% scored over 600 on SAT math, 40% scored over 600 on SAT writing, 20% scored over 1800 on combined SAT.

Student Life Upper grades have specified standards of dress, student council. Discipline rests primarily with faculty. Attendance at religious services is required.

Summer Programs ESL programs offered; session focuses on ESL and cultural experience; held off campus; held at Luther College, University of Regina and Regina, Saskatchewan; accepts boys and girls; open to students from other schools. 7 students usually enrolled. 2013 schedule: July 28 to August 28.

Tuition and Aid Day student tuition: CAN$5030–CAN$12,600; 7-day tuition and room/board: CAN$13,550–CAN$21,200. Tuition installment plan (monthly payment plans, individually arranged payment plans). Tuition reduction for siblings, bursaries, merit scholarship grants, need-based scholarship grants available. In 2012–13, 20% of upper-school students received aid; total upper-school merit-scholarship money awarded: CAN$30,000. Total amount of financial aid awarded in 2012–13: CAN$165,000.

Admissions Traditional secondary-level entrance grade is 9. For fall 2012, 184 students applied for upper-level admission, 174 were accepted, 164 enrolled. English entrance exam required. Deadline for receipt of application materials: none. Application fee required: CAN$300.

Athletics Interscholastic: badminton (boys, girls), baseball (b), basketball (b,g), bicycling (b,g), cheering (g), cross-country running (b,g), curling (b,g), football (b), golf (b,g), hockey (b,g), pom squad (g), rugby (b,g), soccer (b,g), softball (g), volleyball (g); intramural: basketball (b,g), floor hockey (b,g), soccer (b,g), volleyball (g); coed interscholastic: badminton, curling, pom squad, track and field; coed intramural: aerobics/dance, basketball, curling, floor hockey, football, outdoor education, table tennis, ultimate Frisbee. 2 PE instructors, 28 coaches, 2 athletic trainers.

Computers Computers are regularly used in art classes. Computer network features include Internet access, wireless campus network, Internet filtering or blocking technology. Student e-mail accounts and computer access in designated common areas are available to students. Students grades are available online.

Contact Ms. Alanna Kalyniuk, Registrar. 306-791-9154. Fax: 306-359-6962. E-mail: lutherhs@luthercollege.edu. Web site: www.luthercollege.edu

LUTHER NORTH COLLEGE PREP

5700 West Berteau Avenue
Chicago, Illinois 60634

Head of School: Mrs. Joy Mullaney

General Information Coeducational day and distance learning college-preparatory, general academic, arts, business, religious studies, and technology school, affiliated with Lutheran Church–Missouri Synod, Evangelical Lutheran Church in America; primarily serves students with learning disabilities and individuals with Attention Deficit Disorder. Grades 9–12. Distance learning grades 10–12. Founded: 1909. Setting: urban. 10-acre campus. 1 building on campus. Approved or accredited by Evangelical Lutheran Church in America, National Lutheran School Accreditation, North Central Association of Colleges and Schools, and Illinois Department of Education. Endowment: $200,000. Total enrollment: 180. Upper school average class size: 16. Upper school faculty-student ratio: 1:16. There are 179 required school days per year for Upper School students. Upper School students typically attend 5 days per week. The average school day consists of 7 hours.

Upper School Student Profile Grade 9: 45 students (25 boys, 20 girls); Grade 10: 40 students (20 boys, 20 girls); Grade 11: 54 students (29 boys, 25 girls); Grade 12: 41 students (21 boys, 20 girls). 47% of students are Lutheran Church–Missouri Synod, Evangelical Lutheran Church in America.

Faculty School total: 17. In upper school: 7 men, 10 women; 14 have advanced degrees.

Subjects Offered 20th century history, 3-dimensional art, accounting, ACT preparation, advanced computer applications, algebra, American legal systems, anatomy, art, astronomy, band, biology, business, calculus, ceramics, chemistry, chorus, composition, computer science, crafts, drawing, economics, English, English-AP, fine arts, geography, geometry, German, government-AP, government/civics, health, keyboarding, law, mathematics, music, painting, photography, physical education, physics, physiology, psychology, public speaking, reading, science, sewing, social sciences, social studies, Spanish, study skills, theology, trigonometry, U.S. history, word processing.

Graduation Requirements Arts and fine arts (art, music, dance, drama), English, foreign language, mathematics, physical education (includes health), religion (includes Bible studies and theology), science, social sciences, social studies (includes history), word processing, summative portfolio demonstration of faculty selected, extra and co-curricular participation annually.

Special Academic Programs Advanced Placement exam preparation; honors section; accelerated programs; independent study; study at local college for college credit; academic accommodation for the gifted, the musically talented, and the artistically talented; remedial reading and/or remedial writing; remedial math; programs in general development for dyslexic students; special instructional classes for students with learning differences.

College Admission Counseling 54 students graduated in 2012; 48 went to college, including Concordia University; DePaul University; Northeastern Illinois University; University of Illinois at Chicago; University of Illinois at Urbana–Champaign; Valparaiso University. Other: 2 went to work, 2 entered military service, 2 had other specific plans. Median composite ACT: 23. 20% scored over 26 on composite ACT.

Student Life Upper grades have specified standards of dress, student council, honor system. Discipline rests primarily with faculty. Attendance at religious services is required.

Summer Programs Remediation, enrichment, advancement, sports, computer instruction programs offered; session focuses on academics and enrichment for credit; held on campus; accepts boys and girls; open to students from other schools. 300 students usually enrolled. 2013 schedule: June 21 to July 29. Application deadline: June 20.

Tuition and Aid Day student tuition: $9400. Tuition installment plan (Insured Tuition Payment Plan, Academic Management Services Plan, SMART Tuition Payment Plan, monthly payment plans, individually arranged payment plans). Tuition reduction for siblings, merit scholarship grants, need-based scholarship grants, paying campus jobs available. In 2012–13, 70% of upper-school students received aid; total upper-school merit-scholarship money awarded: $30,000.

Admissions Traditional secondary-level entrance grade is 9. For fall 2012, 75 students applied for upper-level admission, 64 were accepted, 62 enrolled. Admissions testing and Stanford Achievement Test, Otis-Lennon School Ability Test required. Deadline for receipt of application materials: none. Application fee required: $175. On-campus interview recommended.

Athletics Interscholastic: baseball (boys), basketball (b,g), cross-country running (b,g), football (b), indoor track & field (b,g), softball (g), track and field (b,g), volleyball (g); coed interscholastic: indoor track; coed intramural: bowling. 2 PE instructors, 10 coaches, 1 athletic trainer.

Computers Computers are regularly used in all academic classes. Computer network features include on-campus library services, online commercial services, Internet access, wireless campus network, Internet filtering or blocking technology, workshops for students and parents in technology. Student e-mail accounts and computer access in designated common areas are available to students. Students grades are available online. The school has a published electronic and media policy.

Contact Mr. Wayne Wenzel, Assistant Principal. 773-286-3600. Fax: 773-286-0304. E-mail: wwenzel@luthernorth.org. Web site: luthernorthcollegeprep.org/

LYCEE INTERNATIONAL DE LOS ANGELES

1105 W Riverside Drive
Burbank, California 91506

Head of School: Mr. Stephane Plancke

General Information Coeducational day and distance learning college-preparatory, arts, bilingual studies, technology, and Math & Sciences school. Grades PS–12. Distance learning grades 11–12. Founded: 1978. Setting: urban. Nearest major city is Los Angeles. 5-acre campus. 1 building on campus. Approved or accredited by French Ministry of Education, International Baccalaureate Organization, Western Association of Schools and Colleges, and California Department of Education. Languages of instruction: English, French, and Spanish. Total enrollment: 934. Upper school average class size: 13. Upper school faculty-student ratio: 1:4. There are 175 required school days per year for Upper School students. Upper School students typically attend 5 days per week. The average school day consists of 7 hours and 38 minutes.

Upper School Student Profile Grade 9: 29 students (12 boys, 17 girls); Grade 10: 28 students (9 boys, 19 girls); Grade 11: 28 students (14 boys, 14 girls); Grade 12: 18 students (10 boys, 8 girls).

Faculty School total: 90. In upper school: 16 men, 15 women; 22 have advanced degrees.

Subjects Offered 20th century world history, advanced biology, advanced chemistry, advanced math, advanced studio art-AP, algebra, analysis and differential calculus, analytic geometry, art, biology, calculus, chemistry, civics, computer applications, economics, English, ESL, European history, film, fine arts, French, geography, geometry, health, history, honors English, industrial arts, integrated arts, integrated mathematics, integrated science, International Baccalaureate courses, lab science, Mandarin, mathematics, music, philosophy, physical education, physical science, physics, psychology, SAT preparation, science, science and technology, social studies, Spanish, technology/design, U.S. government, U.S. history, visual and performing arts, yearbook.

Graduation Requirements Algebra, arts and fine arts (art, music, dance, drama), biology, civics, computer science, English, French, geography, health, integrated mathematics, integrated science, mathematics, music, physical education (includes health), science, social studies (includes history), Spanish, U.S. government, U.S. history, 150 hours of CAS (creativity, action, service).

Special Academic Programs International Baccalaureate program; honors section; independent study; term-away projects; study abroad; ESL (3 students enrolled).

College Admission Counseling 20 students graduated in 2012; 16 went to college, including Bard College, Concordia University, Montreal; McGill University, University of California, Berkeley; University of California, Los Angeles; University of Pennsylvania. Other: 3 went to work, 1 entered military service. Median SAT critical reading: 528, median SAT math: 550, median SAT writing: 512, median combined SAT: 1590, median composite ACT: 26. Mean SAT critical reading: 584, mean SAT math: 594, mean SAT writing: 565, median combined SAT: 1743, mean composite ACT: 29.

Student Life Upper grades have specified standards of dress, student council, honor system. Discipline rests equally with students and faculty.

Tuition and Aid Day student tuition: $14,000–$16,000. Tuition installment plan (SMART Tuition Payment Plan). Tuition reduction for siblings, need-based scholarship grants available. In 2012–13, 21% of upper-school students received aid. Total amount of financial aid awarded in 2012–13: $159,844.

Admissions Traditional secondary-level entrance grade is 11. For fall 2012, 13 students applied for upper-level admission, 13 were accepted, 13 enrolled. Admissions testing, math and English placement tests and writing sample required. Deadline for receipt of application materials: none. Application fee required: $100. Interview required.

Athletics Interscholastic: basketball (boys, girls), volleyball (g); intramural: basketball (b,g), cross-country running (b,g), skiing (downhill) (b,g), snowboarding (b,g), soccer (b), table tennis (b,g), volleyball (b,g); coed intramural: basketball, dance. 1 PE instructor, 3 coaches.

Computers Computers are regularly used in art, computer applications, English, French, science, technology classes. Computer network features include on-campus library services, Internet access, wireless campus network, Internet filtering or blocking technology, homework assignments available online, Smart Boards. Campus intranet, student e-mail accounts, and computer access in designated common areas are available to students. Students grades are available online. The school has a published electronic and media policy.

Contact Mme. Juliette Lange, Admissions Coordinator. 323-665-4526. Fax: 323-665-2607. E-mail: juliette.lange@lilaschool.com. Web site: www.lilaschool.com

LYMAN WARD MILITARY ACADEMY

PO Box 550 P
174 Ward Circle
Camp Hill, Alabama 36850-0550

Head of School: Col. Albert W. Jenrette

General Information Boys' boarding and distance learning college-preparatory and military school, affiliated with Christian faith; primarily serves underachievers. Grades 6–12. Distance learning grades 11–12. Founded: 1898. Setting: small town. Nearest major city is Birmingham. Students are housed in single-sex dormitories. 300-acre campus. 23 buildings on campus. Approved or accredited by Southern Association of Colleges and Schools and Alabama Department of Education. Member of National Association of Independent Schools. Total enrollment: 115. Upper school average class size: 15. Upper school faculty-student ratio: 1:15. There are 180 required school days per year for Upper School students. Upper School students typically attend 5 days per week. The average school day consists of 7 hours.

Upper School Student Profile Grade 9: 20 students (20 boys); Grade 10: 20 students (20 boys); Grade 11: 20 students (20 boys); Grade 12: 25 students (25 boys). 100% of students are boarding students. 50% are state residents. 15 states are represented in upper school student body. 1% are international students. International students from Colombia, Germany, Guatemala, and Mexico; 4 other countries represented in student body. 85% of students are Christian faith.

Faculty School total: 14. In upper school: 8 men, 4 women; 6 have advanced degrees; 2 reside on campus.

Subjects Offered Advanced Placement courses, algebra, band, biology, chemistry, computers, economics, English, geometry, government, health, JROTC, physical science, physiology, pre-algebra, pre-calculus, reading, Spanish, trigonometry, U.S. history, world history.

Special Academic Programs Advanced Placement exam preparation; honors section; remedial reading and/or remedial writing; remedial math.

College Admission Counseling 26 students graduated in 2011; 15 went to college, including Auburn University; Clemson University; Florida State University; North Georgia College & State University; The Citadel, The Military College of South Carolina; The University of Alabama. Other: 5 went to work, 6 entered military service. 5% scored over 600 on SAT critical reading, 5% scored over 600 on SAT math, 5% scored over 26 on composite ACT.

Student Life Upper grades have uniform requirement, student council, honor system. Discipline rests primarily with faculty. Attendance at religious services is required.

Tuition and Aid 7-day tuition and room/board: $16,000. Tuition installment plan (monthly payment plans). Tuition reduction for siblings, merit scholarship grants, need-based scholarship grants available. In 2011–12, 10% of upper-school students received aid. Total amount of financial aid awarded in 2011–12: $50,000.

Admissions Traditional secondary-level entrance grade is 9. Star-9 required. Deadline for receipt of application materials: none. Application fee required: $250. Interview recommended.

Athletics Interscholastic: baseball, basketball, drill team, football, JROTC drill, marksmanship, riflery, soccer; intramural: aquatics, archery, basketball, billiards, canoeing/kayaking, cross-country running, drill team, fishing, fitness, flag football, football, Frisbee, hiking/backpacking, JROTC drill, life saving, marksmanship, outdoor activities, physical fitness, physical training, project adventure, rafting, rappelling, riflery, ropes courses, running, soccer, softball, strength & conditioning, swimming and diving, table tennis, tennis, ultimate Frisbee, volleyball. 2 PE instructors, 3 coaches, 1 athletic trainer.

Computers Computer resources include on-campus library services, Internet access, Internet filtering or blocking technology. Student e-mail accounts are available to students. The school has a published electronic and media policy.

Contact Maj. Joe C. Watson, Assistant to the President/Admissions. 256-896-4127. Fax: 256-896-4661. E-mail: info@lwma.org. Web site: www.lwma.org

LYNDON INSTITUTE

PO Box 127
College Road
Lyndon Center, Vermont 05850-0127

Head of School: Richard D. Hilton

General Information Coeducational boarding and day college-preparatory, general academic, arts, business, technology, and ESL school. Boarding grades 8–12, day grades 9–12. Founded: 1867. Setting: small town. Nearest major city is Burlington. Students are housed in single-sex dormitories. 150-acre campus. 27 buildings on campus. Approved or accredited by Independent Schools of Northern New England, New England Association of Schools and Colleges, The Association of Boarding Schools, and Vermont Department of Education. Endowment: $8 million. Upper school average class size: 16. Upper school faculty-student ratio: 1:10. There are 178 required school days per year for Upper School students. Upper School students typically attend 5 days per week. The average school day consists of 6 hours.

Upper School Student Profile Grade 9: 145 students (62 boys, 83 girls); Grade 10: 158 students (84 boys, 74 girls); Grade 11: 143 students (78 boys, 65 girls); Grade 12: 180 students (91 boys, 89 girls). 14% of students are boarding students. 91% are state residents. 2 states are represented in upper school student body. 9% are international students. International students from Afghanistan, China, Japan, Republic of Korea, Spain, and Taiwan; 1 other country represented in student body.

Faculty School total: 68. In upper school: 36 men, 32 women; 20 have advanced degrees; 3 reside on campus.

Subjects Offered 3-dimensional art, accounting, advanced chemistry, advanced math, algebra, American literature, ancient world history, animal science, art, auto mechanics, band, Basic programming, biology, bookmaking, business, business education, business mathematics, business technology, calculus, chemistry, chemistry-AP, chorus, college counseling, computer applications, computer graphics, computer information systems, computer science, computer skills, computer technologies, computer-aided design, concert band, consumer economics, creative writing, desktop publishing, drafting, drawing, driver education, economics, English, English language and composition-AP, English literature, entrepreneurship, environmental science, European history, family and consumer science, fashion, fine arts, French, general math, geography, geometry, graphic design, health, history, honors algebra, honors English, honors U.S. history, honors world history, industrial arts, information processing, information technology, instrumental music, jazz ensemble, keyboarding, Latin, literary magazine, mathematics, metalworking, music, music theory, philosophy, photography, physical education, physics, printmaking, science, social studies, Spanish, street law, studio art, studio art-AP, theater, theater arts, trigonometry, U.S. history, woodworking, word processing, world cultures, world history, writing.

Graduation Requirements Arts and fine arts (art, music, dance, drama), electives, English, health education, mathematics, physical education (includes health), science, social studies (includes history), U.S. history.

Special Academic Programs Advanced Placement exam preparation; honors section; independent study; study at local college for college credit; remedial reading and/or remedial writing; remedial math; ESL (50 students enrolled).

College Admission Counseling 148 students graduated in 2012; 117 went to college, including Purdue University; Saint Michael's College; University of Illinois at Urbana–Champaign; University of Vermont. Other: 19 went to work, 7 entered military service, 1 entered a postgraduate year, 4 had other specific plans.

Student Life Upper grades have specified standards of dress, student council. Discipline rests primarily with faculty.

Tuition and Aid Day student tuition: $14,004; 5-day tuition and room/board: $31,930; 7-day tuition and room/board: $44,700. Tuition installment plan (monthly payment plans, individually arranged payment plans). Need-based scholarship grants, prepGATE loans available. In 2012–13, 2% of upper-school students received aid.

Admissions Traditional secondary-level entrance grade is 9. International English Language Test, SSAT, ERB, PSAT, SAT, PLAN or ACT or TOEFL or SLEP required. Deadline for receipt of application materials: March 31. Application fee required: $50. Interview recommended.

Athletics Interscholastic: alpine skiing (boys, girls), baseball (b), basketball (b,g), cross-country running (b,g), field hockey (g), golf (b,g), ice hockey (b), nordic skiing (b,g), running (b,g), skiing (cross-country) (b,g), skiing (downhill) (b,g), soccer (b,g), softball (g), track and field (b,g), ultimate Frisbee (b,g); intramural: ballet (g), dance (b,g), volleyball (b,g); coed interscholastic: cheering, football, ice hockey, outdoor activities; coed intramural: aerobics/dance, bicycling, bowling, dance, dance team, equestrian sports, fitness walking, indoor soccer, indoor track, marksmanship, martial arts, modern dance, mountain biking, riflery, weight lifting. 2 PE instructors, 26 coaches, 2 athletic trainers.

Computers Computers are regularly used in architecture, business, business applications, business education, business skills, desktop publishing, drafting, engineering, graphic design, information technology, keyboarding, literary magazine, publishing, SAT preparation, science, technical drawing, technology, word processing, yearbook classes. Computer resources include on-campus library services, Internet access, Internet filtering or blocking technology, Big Chalk eLibrary, Vermont Online Library, NewsBank. Student e-mail accounts and computer access in designated common areas are available to students. The school has a published electronic and media policy.

Contact Mary B. Thomas, Assistant Head for Admissions. 802-626-5232. Fax: 802-626-6138. E-mail: mary.thomas@lyndoninstitute.org. Web site: www.LyndonInstitute.org

See Display on next page and Close-Up on page 596.

MACLACHLAN COLLEGE

337 Trafalgar Road
Oakville, Ontario L6J 3H3, Canada

Head of School: Mr. Michael Piening

General Information Coeducational day college-preparatory, arts, business, and technology school. Grades PK–12. Founded: 1978. Setting: suburban. Nearest major city is Toronto, Canada. 2-acre campus. 1 building on campus. Approved or accredited by Canadian Association of Independent Schools, Canadian Educational Standards Institute, Conference of Independent Schools of Ontario, Ontario Ministry of Education, and Ontario Department of Education. Language of instruction: English. Total enrollment: 344. Upper school average class size: 18. Upper school faculty-student ratio: 1:10. Upper School students typically attend 5 days per week. The average school day consists of 6 hours and 45 minutes.

Upper School Student Profile Grade 9: 28 students (17 boys, 11 girls); Grade 10: 36 students (21 boys, 15 girls); Grade 11: 37 students (21 boys, 16 girls); Grade 12: 32 students (23 boys, 9 girls).

Faculty School total: 30. In upper school: 2 men, 12 women; 7 have advanced degrees.

Subjects Offered 20th century history, accounting, algebra, band, business, business law, business mathematics, calculus, Canadian geography, Canadian history, Canadian law, Canadian literature, career education, chemistry, civics, computer multimedia, computer programming, computer science, drama, economics, English, environmental science, ESL, finite math, French, geography, geometry, health, history, law, marketing, mathematics, multimedia, physical education, physics, science, society challenge and change, TOEFL preparation, visual arts.

Graduation Requirements Arts, careers, civics, English, French, geography, history, mathematics, physical education (includes health), science, pass the grade 10 Ontario Literacy test, 40 hours of community service.

Special Academic Programs Advanced Placement exam preparation; accelerated programs; independent study; ESL (30 students enrolled).

College Admission Counseling 36 students graduated in 2011; they went to Carleton University; Ryerson University; The University of Western Ontario; University of Toronto; University of Waterloo; York University. Other: 36 entered a postgraduate year.

Student Life Upper grades have uniform requirement, student council, honor system. Discipline rests primarily with faculty.

Tuition and Aid Day student tuition: CAN$18,350. Tuition installment plan (monthly payment plans). Tuition reduction for siblings, bursaries available. In 2011–12, 1% of upper-school students received aid. Total amount of financial aid awarded in 2011–12: CAN$9000.

Admissions Traditional secondary-level entrance grade is 11. Deadline for receipt of application materials: none. Application fee required: CAN$250. Interview required.

Athletics Interscholastic: aerobics (boys), wrestling (b); intramural: ball hockey (b), baseball (b,g), basketball (b,g), flag football (b,g), floor hockey (b,g), soccer (b,g), softball (b,g), touch football (b,g), ultimate Frisbee (b,g), volleyball (b,g), wilderness survival (b,g); coed interscholastic: aerobics, archery, backpacking, badminton, ball hockey, baseball, basketball, bowling, canoeing/kayaking, cooperative games, cricket, cross-country running, curling, field hockey, fitness, fitness walking, flag football, flagball, floor hockey, football, golf, gymnastics, hiking/backpacking, ice skating, lacrosse, outdoor activities, outdoor adventure, outdoor education, physical fitness, racquetball, running, soccer, softball, touch football, ultimate Frisbee, volleyball, wilderness survival; coed intramural: football, hiking/backpacking, independent competitive sports. 2 PE instructors.

Computers Computers are regularly used in accounting, art, basic skills, business, business applications, business education, business studies, career education, career exploration, career technology, commercial art, computer applications, creative writing, data processing, design, desktop publishing, digital applications, economics, English, ESL, French, geography, graphic arts, health, history, humanities, information technology, library, mathematics, media arts, multimedia, music, programming, reading, research skills, science, theology, Web site design, wilderness education, writing, writing, yearbook classes. Computer network features include on-campus library services, Internet access, wireless campus network, Internet filtering or blocking technology. Campus intranet, student e-mail accounts, and computer access in designated common areas are available to students. The school has a published electronic and media policy.

Contact Ms. Nancy Norcross, Director of Admissions. 905-844-0372 Ext. 235. Fax: 905-844-9369. E-mail: nnorcross@maclachlan.ca. Web site: www.maclachlan.ca

MADISON ACADEMY

325 Slaughter Road
Madison, Alabama 35758

Head of School: Dr. Robert F. Burton

General Information Coeducational day college-preparatory and religious studies school, affiliated with Church of Christ. Grades PS–12. Founded: 1955. Setting: suburban. Nearest major city is Huntsville. 160-acre campus. 5 buildings on campus. Approved or accredited by Southern Association of Colleges and Schools. Endowment: $1.5 million. Total enrollment: 900. Upper school average class size: 20. Upper school faculty-student ratio: 1:15. There are 180 required school days per year for Upper School students. Upper School students typically attend 5 days per week. The average school day consists of 6 hours.

Upper School Student Profile 35% of students are members of Church of Christ.

Faculty School total: 75. In upper school: 14 men, 20 women; 14 have advanced degrees.

Subjects Offered Accounting, advanced math, Alabama history and geography, algebra, American literature, anatomy, art, art history, arts, band, Bible studies, biology, calculus, calculus-AP, chemistry, choral music, chorus, Christian education, Christian ethics, Christian scripture, Christian studies, church history, community service, computer science, concert choir, consumer mathematics, creative writing, drama, earth science, economics, English, English literature, English/composition-AP, environmental science, European history, expository writing, French, general math, geography, geology, geometry, government/civics, health, human anatomy, journalism, keyboarding, music, photography, physical education, physical science, physics, physics-AP, physiology, pre-algebra, religion, Spanish, speech, studio art, trigonometry, U.S. government, U.S. government and politics, U.S. history, world geography, world history, world literature.

Graduation Requirements English, foreign language, mathematics, religion (includes Bible studies and theology), science, social sciences.

Special Academic Programs Honors section; accelerated programs; study at local college for college credit.

College Admission Counseling 70 students graduated in 2012; all went to college, including Abilene Christian University; Auburn University; Freed-Hardeman University; Lipscomb University; The University of Alabama. Mean composite ACT: 23.

Student Life Upper grades have uniform requirement, student council, honor system. Discipline rests primarily with faculty. Attendance at religious services is required.

Tuition and Aid Day student tuition: $7250. Tuition installment plan (monthly payment plans). Tuition reduction for siblings, need-based scholarship grants available. In 2012–13, 10% of upper-school students received aid. Total amount of financial aid awarded in 2012–13: $100,000.

Admissions Traditional secondary-level entrance grade is 9. For fall 2012, 100 students applied for upper-level admission, 50 were accepted, 41 enrolled. Stanford Achievement Test required. Deadline for receipt of application materials: none. Application fee required: $200. On-campus interview required.

Athletics Interscholastic: baseball (boys), basketball (b,g), cheering (g), football (b), golf (b,g), softball (g), swimming and diving (b,g), tennis (b,g), volleyball (g). 3 PE instructors, 36 coaches, 1 athletic trainer.

Computers Computers are regularly used in art, foreign language, science classes. Computer network features include on-campus library services, Internet access, wireless campus network, Internet filtering or blocking technology. Student e-mail accounts are available to students. The school has a published electronic and media policy.

Contact Dr. Michael Weimer, High School Principal. 256-971-1624. Fax: 256-971-1436. E-mail: mweimer@macademy.org. Web site: www.macademy.org

MADISON-RIDGELAND ACADEMY

7601 Old Canton Road
Madison, Mississippi 39110

Head of School: Tommy Thompson

General Information Coeducational day college-preparatory school, affiliated with Christian faith. Grades 1–12. Founded: 1969. Setting: suburban. Nearest major city is Jackson. 25-acre campus. 6 buildings on campus. Approved or accredited by Mississippi Private School Association, Southern Association of Colleges and Schools, Southern Association of Independent Schools, and Mississippi Department of Education. Endowment: $1 million. Total enrollment: 906. Upper school average class size: 18. Upper school faculty-student ratio: 1:13. There are 180 required school days per year for Upper School students. Upper School students typically attend 5 days per week. The average school day consists of 7 hours and 15 minutes.

Upper School Student Profile Grade 9: 72 students (40 boys, 32 girls); Grade 10: 68 students (43 boys, 25 girls); Grade 11: 59 students (32 boys, 27 girls); Grade 12: 55 students (36 boys, 19 girls). 99% of students are Christian faith.

Faculty School total: 64. In upper school: 10 men, 48 women; 20 have advanced degrees.

Subjects Offered Accounting, algebra, American government, American history, American history-AP, anatomy and physiology, art, Bible, biology, biology-AP, chemistry, chemistry-AP, chorus, civics, communications, computer applications, computer programming, creative writing, debate, drama, driver education, economics, English, European history-AP, forensics, French, French-AP, geography, geometry, global studies, government, graphic arts, health, journalism, keyboarding, music, newspaper, physical fitness, physics, physics-AP, pre-calculus, probability and statistics, psychology, sociology, Spanish, Spanish-AP, speech, trigonometry, U.S. government and politics-AP, Web site design, world history, yearbook.

Graduation Requirements ACT preparation, advanced math, algebra, American government, biology, chemistry, civics, computer applications, economics, electives, English, foreign language, geometry, health, keyboarding, science, social studies (includes history).

Special Academic Programs Advanced Placement exam preparation; honors section; study at local college for college credit; academic accommodation for the gifted.

College Admission Counseling 56 students graduated in 2011; all went to college, including Belhaven University; Millsaps College; Mississippi College; Mississippi State University; University of Mississippi; University of Southern Mississippi. Median SAT critical reading: 705, median SAT math: 620, median composite ACT: 24. 100% scored over 600 on SAT critical reading, 100% scored over 600 on SAT math, 25% scored over 26 on composite ACT.

Student Life Upper grades have uniform requirement, student council, honor system. Discipline rests primarily with faculty. Attendance at religious services is required.

Tuition and Aid Day student tuition: $7680. Tuition installment plan (monthly payment plans, semiannual payment plan). Tuition reduction for siblings, merit scholarship grants, need-based scholarship grants available. In 2011–12, 3% of upper-school students received aid; total upper-school merit-scholarship money awarded: $21,300. Total amount of financial aid awarded in 2011–12: $170,000.

Admissions Traditional secondary-level entrance grade is 9. For fall 2011, 30 students applied for upper-level admission, 23 were accepted, 18 enrolled. Admissions testing, BASIS or Otis-Lennon Ability or Stanford Achievement Test required. Deadline for receipt of application materials: none. Application fee required: $35. On-campus interview required.

Athletics Interscholastic: aquatics (boys, girls), baseball (b), basketball (b,g), cheering (g), cross-country running (b,g), dance team (g), football (b), golf (b), soccer (b,g), softball (g), strength & conditioning (b,g), tennis (b,g), track and field (b,g), volleyball (g); coed interscholastic: aquatics, golf, tennis. 4 PE instructors, 12 coaches, 1 athletic trainer.

Computers Computers are regularly used in accounting, art, business applications, journalism, media, media services, Web site design classes. Computer network features include on-campus library services, Internet access, Internet filtering or blocking technology, Naviance (college guidance). Students grades are available online. The school has a published electronic and media policy.

Contact Mrs. Tammy Synder, Registrar. 601-856-4455. Fax: 601-853-3835. E-mail: tsnyder@mrapats.org. Web site: www.mrapats.com

MAGNIFICAT HIGH SCHOOL

20770 Hilliard Boulevard
Rocky River, Ohio 44116

Head of School: Sr. Carol Anne Smith, HM

General Information Girls' day college-preparatory school, affiliated with Roman Catholic Church. Grades 9–12. Founded: 1955. Setting: suburban. Nearest major city is Cleveland. 20-acre campus. 1 building on campus. Approved or accredited by North Central Association of Colleges and Schools, Ohio Catholic Schools Accreditation Association (OCSAA), and Ohio Department of Education. Total enrollment: 800. Upper school average class size: 22. Upper school faculty-student ratio: 1:12. The average school day consists of 5 hours and 55 minutes.

Upper School Student Profile 93% of students are Roman Catholic.

Faculty School total: 77. In upper school: 4 men, 70 women; 42 have advanced degrees.

Subjects Offered Accounting, algebra, American literature, Arabic, art, art history, art history-AP, arts, band, biology, biology-AP, British literature, business, business technology, calculus-AP, chemistry, chemistry-AP, Chinese, choir, chorus, clayworking, comparative religion, computer applications, computer science-AP, CPR, dance, design, drama, drawing, earth science, economics, economics-AP, electives, English, film and literature, first aid, French, French-AP, geometry, government, health, keyboarding, life issues, mathematics, metalworking, modern languages, music, oral communications, orchestra, painting, photography, physical education, physics, pre-calculus, probability and statistics, programming, psychology, science, social studies, sociology, Spanish, Spanish-AP, statistics, statistics-AP, theology, trigonometry, U.S. history, U.S. history-AP, Web site design, world history, world history-AP, world literature, writing.

Graduation Requirements Art appreciation, electives, English, health education, keyboarding, mathematics, modern languages, physical education (includes health), science, social studies (includes history), theology, word processing, service requirements and senior Genesis Project.

Special Academic Programs 12 Advanced Placement exams for which test preparation is offered; honors section.

College Admission Counseling 205 students graduated in 2011; all went to college, including John Carroll University; Miami University; Ohio University; The Ohio State University; University of Cincinnati; University of Dayton. Mean SAT critical reading: 554, mean SAT math: 544, mean SAT writing: 557, mean composite ACT: 25.

Student Life Upper grades have uniform requirement, student council. Attendance at religious services is required.

Tuition and Aid Day student tuition: $10,900. Tuition installment plan (SMART Tuition Payment Plan). Merit scholarship grants, need-based scholarship grants available. In 2011–12, 46% of upper-school students received aid; total upper-school merit-scholarship money awarded: $82,500. Total amount of financial aid awarded in 2011–12: $900,000.

Admissions Traditional secondary-level entrance grade is 9. High School Placement Test (closed version) from Scholastic Testing Service required. Deadline for receipt of application materials: January 28. No application fee required.

Athletics Interscholastic: basketball, cross-country running, dance team, diving, field hockey, golf, gymnastics, lacrosse, soccer, softball, swimming and diving, tennis, track and field, volleyball. 3 PE instructors, 53 coaches, 1 athletic trainer.

Computers Computers are regularly used in all academic classes. Computer network features include on-campus library services, Internet access. Computer access in designated common areas is available to students. Students grades are available online. The school has a published electronic and media policy.

Contact Ms. Heather Schwager, Director of Admissions. 440-331-1572 Ext. 248. Fax: 440-331-7257. E-mail: hschwager@magnificaths.org. Web site: www.magnificaths.org

MAHARISHI SCHOOL OF THE AGE OF ENLIGHTENMENT

804 Dr. Robert Keith Wallace Drive
Fairfield, Iowa 52556-2200

Head of School: Dr. Richard Beall

General Information Coeducational boarding and day college-preparatory, arts, Science of Creative Intelligence: the study of Natural Law, and Transcendental Meditation: Research in Consciousness school. Boarding grades 9–12, day grades PS–12. Founded: 1972. Setting: small town. Nearest major city is Iowa City. Students are housed in boarding students live with host families. 10-acre campus. 5 buildings on campus. Approved or accredited by Independent Schools Association of the Central States and Iowa Department of Education. Member of National Association of Independent Schools. Total enrollment: 213. Upper school average class size: 15. Upper school faculty-student ratio: 1:12. There are 186 required school days per year for Upper School students. Upper School students typically attend 5 days per week. The average school day consists of 9 hours.

Upper School Student Profile Grade 9: 12 students (7 boys, 5 girls); Grade 10: 28 students (17 boys, 11 girls); Grade 11: 32 students (21 boys, 11 girls); Grade 12: 19 students (12 boys, 7 girls). 13% of students are boarding students. 80% are state residents. 6 states are represented in upper school student body. 10% are international students. International students from China, Germany, Mexico, Nepal, Netherlands, and South Africa; 20 other countries represented in student body.

Faculty School total: 54. In upper school: 11 men, 17 women; 12 have advanced degrees.

Subjects Offered Algebra, American government, American history, American literature, art, art history, basketball, British literature, business mathematics, chemistry, computer science, desktop publishing, digital photography, drama performance, driver education, economics, electives, environmental education, ESL, general math, integrated mathematics, photography, physical education, physiology, pre-calculus, Sanskrit, science project, senior thesis, Spanish, track and field, Vedic science, vocal music, volleyball, world history, world literature, writing, yoga.

Graduation Requirements Art history, computer science, economics, electives, English, foreign language, mathematics, physical education (includes health), science, senior thesis, social studies (includes history), writing, Science of Creative Intelligence course.

Special Academic Programs Honors section; academic accommodation for the gifted, the musically talented, and the artistically talented; remedial reading and/or remedial writing; remedial math; ESL (18 students enrolled).

College Admission Counseling 15 students graduated in 2012; 14 went to college, including Cornell College; Grinnell College; Maharishi University of Management; New York University; The University of Iowa; University of California, San Diego. Other: 1 had other specific plans. Median SAT critical reading: 573, median SAT math: 605, median SAT writing: 589, median combined SAT: 1767, median composite ACT: 26. 58% scored over 600 on SAT critical reading, 42% scored over 600 on SAT math, 58% scored over 600 on SAT writing, 50% scored over 1800 on combined SAT, 43% scored over 26 on composite ACT.

Student Life Upper grades have uniform requirement, student council. Discipline rests primarily with faculty.

Summer Programs Enrichment, ESL, sports, art/fine arts programs offered; session focuses on interscholastic sports, arts; held both on and off campus; held at neighboring schools and universities; accepts boys and girls; not open to students from other schools. 40 students usually enrolled. 2013 schedule: June 15 to August 15. Application deadline: June 12.

Tuition and Aid Day student tuition: $13,900. Tuition installment plan (two semester payments). Tuition reduction for siblings, need-based scholarship grants available. In 2012–13, 85% of upper-school students received aid.
Admissions Traditional secondary-level entrance grade is 9. For fall 2012, 14 students applied for upper-level admission, 14 were accepted, 14 enrolled. International English Language Test or TOEFL or SLEP required. Deadline for receipt of application materials: none. No application fee required. Interview required.
Athletics Interscholastic: basketball (boys, girls), cheering (g), dance team (g), golf (b), indoor track & field (b,g), soccer (b), tennis (b,g), track and field (b,g), volleyball (g), winter (indoor) track (b,g); intramural: archery (b), badminton (b,g), ballet (g), baseball (b), basketball (b,g), canoeing/kayaking (b,g), dance (g), equestrian sports (g), fitness (b,g), fitness walking (g), handball (b,g), hiking/backpacking (b,g), jogging (b,g), life saving (b,g), modern dance (g), outdoor activities (b,g), outdoor recreation (b,g), physical fitness (b,g), physical training (b,g), running (b,g), strength & conditioning (b,g), table tennis (b,g), tennis (b,g), volleyball (g), wall climbing (b,g), winter (indoor) track (b,g), yoga (b,g). 3 PE instructors, 11 coaches.
Computers Computers are regularly used in business education, creative writing, desktop publishing, economics, English, ESL, geography, graphic design, history, independent study, library, library science, library skills, literacy, mathematics, multimedia, photography, programming, publications, science, senior seminar, social sciences, social studies, stock market, typing, video film production, writing classes. Computer network features include Internet access, Internet filtering or blocking technology, file and portfolio management. Campus intranet and computer access in designated common areas are available to students. Students grades are available online. The school has a published electronic and media policy.
Contact Ms. Jane Deans, Director of Admissions. 641-472-9400 Ext. 5538. Fax: 641-472-1211. E-mail: jdeans@msae.edu. Web site: www.maharishischooliowa.org

MAINE CENTRAL INSTITUTE

295 Main Street
Pittsfield, Maine 04967

Head of School: Christopher Hopkins

General Information Coeducational boarding and day college-preparatory, general academic, arts, vocational, bilingual studies, technology, humanities, and mathematics, the sciences school. Grades 9–PG. Founded: 1866. Setting: small town. Nearest major city is Portland. Students are housed in single-sex dormitories and honors dorm is coed. 23-acre campus. Approved or accredited by Independent Schools of Northern New England, New England Association of Schools and Colleges, The Association of Boarding Schools, and Maine Department of Education. Member of National Association of Independent Schools and Secondary School Admission Test Board. Total enrollment: 455. Upper school average class size: 16. Upper school faculty-student ratio: 1:14. There are 175 required school days per year for Upper School students. Upper School students typically attend 5 days per week. The average school day consists of 7 hours and 15 minutes.
Upper School Student Profile Grade 9: 94 students (48 boys, 46 girls); Grade 10: 103 students (61 boys, 42 girls); Grade 11: 123 students (61 boys, 62 girls); Grade 12: 133 students (75 boys, 58 girls). 71% are state residents. 11 states are represented in upper school student body. 85% are international students.
Faculty School total: 41. In upper school: 20 men, 21 women; 14 have advanced degrees; 25 reside on campus.
Subjects Offered Algebra, American history, American literature, anatomy, art, art-AP, Asian studies, astronomy, audio visual/media, ballet, biology, botany, calculus, calculus-AP, career exploration, chemistry, chemistry-AP, child development, civil rights, computer science, concert band, concert choir, contemporary issues, creative writing, drafting, drama, earth science, ecology, economics, electronic publishing, English, English literature, environmental science, ESL, ethics, fine arts, French, geology, geometry, government/civics, health, history, humanities, integrated science, jazz band, jazz dance, jazz ensemble, Latin, life management skills, literature-AP, mathematics, meteorology, music, music appreciation, music composition, music theory, personal finance, philosophy, photography, physical education, physics, physics-AP, piano, psychology, reading/study skills, SAT preparation, science, social sciences, social studies, sociology, Spanish, statistics, theater, trigonometry, video film production, Web site design, world history.
Graduation Requirements Arts and fine arts (art, music, dance, drama), computer skills, English, mathematics, physical education (includes health), science, senior project, social studies (includes history), Manson essay.
Special Academic Programs Advanced Placement exam preparation; honors section; accelerated programs; independent study; study at local college for college credit; study abroad; academic accommodation for the musically talented; remedial reading and/or remedial writing; remedial math; programs in English, mathematics, general development for dyslexic students; ESL (70 students enrolled).
College Admission Counseling 115 students graduated in 2012; 90 went to college, including Husson University; Maine Maritime Academy; University of Maine; University of Maine at Farmington; University of Southern Maine. Other: 15 went to work, 3 entered military service, 6 had other specific plans. Median SAT critical reading: 428, median SAT math: 444, median SAT writing: 442, median combined SAT: 1314.
Student Life Upper grades have specified standards of dress, student council, honor system. Discipline rests primarily with faculty.
Summer Programs ESL, art/fine arts programs offered; session focuses on basic ESL, summer ballet; held on campus; accepts boys and girls; open to students from other schools. 35 students usually enrolled. 2013 schedule: July to August. Application deadline: none.
Tuition and Aid Day student tuition: $10,000; 7-day tuition and room/board: $39,900. Tuition installment plan (Key Tuition Payment Plan, SMART Tuition Payment Plan, school's own payment plan). Merit scholarship grants, need-based scholarship grants available. In 2012–13, 18% of upper-school students received aid; total upper-school merit-scholarship money awarded: $24,430. Total amount of financial aid awarded in 2012–13: $350,000.
Admissions Traditional secondary-level entrance grade is 9. For fall 2012, 385 students applied for upper-level admission, 352 were accepted, 140 enrolled. Deadline for receipt of application materials: none. Application fee required: $50. Interview recommended.
Athletics Interscholastic: baseball (boys), basketball (b,g), field hockey (g), football (b), riflery (b,g); intramural: football (b); coed interscholastic: aerobics/dance, alpine skiing, ballet, cheering, cross-country running, dance, fencing, golf, modern dance, physical training; coed intramural: alpine skiing, backpacking, basketball, billiards, canoeing/kayaking, climbing, cooperative games, fencing, fishing, flagball, floor hockey, handball, outdoor activities, rafting. 1 PE instructor, 30 coaches, 1 athletic trainer.
Computers Computer network features include on-campus library services, Internet access, wireless campus network, Internet filtering or blocking technology. Student e-mail accounts are available to students. Students grades are available online.
Contact Mr. Clint M. Williams, Director of Admission. 207-487-2282 Ext. 128. Fax: 207-487-3512. E-mail: cwilliams@mci-school.org. Web site: www.mci-school.org

See Display on next page and Close-Up on page 598.

MALDEN CATHOLIC HIGH SCHOOL

99 Crystal Street
Malden, Massachusetts 02148

Head of School: Mr. Edward Tyrrell

General Information Boys' day college-preparatory, arts, business, religious studies, bilingual studies, and technology school, affiliated with Roman Catholic Church; primarily serves students with learning disabilities and individuals with Attention Deficit Disorder. Grades 9–12. Founded: 1932. Setting: urban. Nearest major city is Boston. 15-acre campus. 1 building on campus. Approved or accredited by New England Association of Schools and Colleges and Massachusetts Department of Education. Endowment: $2 million. Total enrollment: 700. Upper school average class size: 23. Upper school faculty-student ratio: 1:13. The average school day consists of 6 hours.
Upper School Student Profile Grade 9: 214 students (214 boys); Grade 10: 154 students (154 boys); Grade 11: 162 students (162 boys); Grade 12: 157 students (157 boys). 85% of students are Roman Catholic.
Faculty School total: 52. In upper school: 40 men, 12 women; 43 have advanced degrees.
Subjects Offered 20th century history, 3-dimensional art, accounting, advanced chemistry, advanced math, Advanced Placement courses, algebra, American government, American history-AP, American literature, ancient world history, art, art appreciation, art history, Asian history, athletics, basic language skills, Bible studies, biology, British literature, British literature (honors), British literature-AP, business, calculus-AP, campus ministry, Chinese history, Christian and Hebrew scripture, Christian testament, college admission preparation, community service, computer programming, computer skills, desktop publishing, English language and composition-AP, English-AP, European history, European history-AP, fine arts, foreign language, French, French language-AP, genetics, geometry, global studies, government, health and safety, honors algebra, honors English, honors geometry, honors U.S. history, honors world history, independent study, integrated science, language arts, leadership and service, library studies, marine biology, marine science, math analysis, modern European history, music appreciation, physical education, psychology, religion, SAT preparation, Spanish, Spanish language-AP, studio art, the Sixties, U.S. history, U.S. history-AP, world history, world history-AP.
Graduation Requirements Algebra, American literature, arts and fine arts (art, music, dance, drama), biology, British literature, Catholic belief and practice, chemistry, computer skills, foreign language, geometry, global studies, mathematics, physical education (includes health), religion (includes Bible studies and theology), science, social studies (includes history), Christian service.
Special Academic Programs 12 Advanced Placement exams for which test preparation is offered; honors section; independent study.
College Admission Counseling 175 students graduated in 2011; 170 went to college, including Assumption College; Boston College; Boston University; Merrimack College; Northeastern University; Salem State University. Other: 3 went to work, 2 entered military service.
Student Life Upper grades have specified standards of dress, student council, honor system. Discipline rests primarily with faculty. Attendance at religious services is required.

Tuition and Aid Day student tuition: $11,900. Tuition installment plan (FACTS Tuition Payment Plan, monthly payment plans). Merit scholarship grants, need-based scholarship grants, paying campus jobs available. In 2011–12, 40% of upper-school students received aid; total upper-school merit-scholarship money awarded: $300,000. Total amount of financial aid awarded in 2011–12: $300,000.

Admissions Traditional secondary-level entrance grade is 9. For fall 2011, 400 students applied for upper-level admission, 300 were accepted, 170 enrolled. Archdiocese of Boston High School entrance exam provided by STS required. Deadline for receipt of application materials: December 15. No application fee required. Interview recommended.

Athletics Interscholastic: baseball, basketball, cross-country running, football, golf, hockey, ice hockey, indoor track, indoor track & field, lacrosse, soccer, swimming and diving, tennis, track and field, winter (indoor) track, wrestling; intramural: alpine skiing, badminton, ball hockey, basketball, fitness, flag football, floor hockey, Frisbee, jogging, lacrosse, life saving, nordic skiing, physical fitness, physical training, rugby, skiing (downhill), snowboarding, strength & conditioning, table tennis, weight lifting, weight training. 2 PE instructors, 15 coaches, 1 athletic trainer.

Computers Computers are regularly used in all academic, basic skills, business applications, business studies, design, desktop publishing, graphic arts, graphic design, graphics, information technology, journalism, library, library skills, multimedia, news writing, photography, photojournalism, religion, study skills, technology, theology, Web site design, word processing classes. Computer network features include on-campus library services, online commercial services, Internet access, wireless campus network, Internet filtering or blocking technology. Students grades are available online. The school has a published electronic and media policy.

Contact Mr. Matthew O'Neil, Associate Director of Admissions. 781-475-5308. Fax: 781-397-0573. E-mail: oneilm@maldencatholic.org. Web site: www.maldencatholic.org

MALVERN PREPARATORY SCHOOL

418 South Warren Avenue
Malvern, Pennsylvania 19355-2707

Head of School: Mr. Christian M. Talbot

General Information Boys' day college-preparatory school, affiliated with Roman Catholic Church. Grades 6–12. Founded: 1842. Setting: suburban. Nearest major city is Philadelphia. 104-acre campus. 18 buildings on campus. Approved or accredited by Middle States Association of Colleges and Schools, Pennsylvania Association of Independent Schools, and Pennsylvania Department of Education. Member of National Association of Independent Schools. Endowment: $5.2 million. Total enrollment: 595. Upper school average class size: 18. Upper school faculty-student ratio: 1:9. There are 180 required school days per year for Upper School students. Upper School students typically attend 5 days per week. The average school day consists of 7 hours.

Upper School Student Profile Grade 9: 112 students (112 boys); Grade 10: 110 students (110 boys); Grade 11: 109 students (109 boys); Grade 12: 103 students (103 boys). 85% of students are Roman Catholic.

Faculty School total: 74. In upper school: 54 men, 20 women; 49 have advanced degrees.

Subjects Offered Algebra, American history, American literature, art, Bible studies, biology, business, calculus, ceramics, chemistry, computer math, computer programming, computer science, concert band, creative writing, data analysis, drama, earth science, ecology, economics, English, English literature, environmental science, ethics, European history, expository writing, fine arts, French, geography, geometry, government/civics, grammar, health, history, jazz band, journalism, logic, mathematics, music, music performance, music theory, philosophy, photography, physical education, physics, printmaking, religion, science, sculpture, social sciences, social studies, sociology, Spanish, speech, sports medicine, studio art, theater, theology, trigonometry, world history, world literature, writing.

Graduation Requirements Arts and fine arts (art, music, dance, drama), computer science, English, foreign language, mathematics, physical education (includes health), religion (includes Bible studies and theology), science, senior career experience, social sciences, social studies (includes history). Community service is required.

Special Academic Programs Advanced Placement exam preparation; honors section; independent study.

College Admission Counseling 104 students graduated in 2012; all went to college, including Georgetown University; Penn State University Park; Saint Joseph's University; University of Pennsylvania; Villanova University.

Student Life Upper grades have specified standards of dress, student council. Discipline rests primarily with faculty.

Summer Programs Remediation, enrichment, advancement, sports, art/fine arts, computer instruction programs offered; session focuses on academics; held on campus; accepts boys and girls; open to students from other schools. 2013 schedule: June 21 to July 30. Application deadline: none.

Tuition and Aid Day student tuition: $24,450. Tuition installment plan (Insured Tuition Payment Plan, individually arranged payment plans, Bryn Mawr Trust Loan Program). Merit scholarship grants, need-based scholarship grants available. In 2012–13, 30% of upper-school students received aid; total upper-school merit-scholarship money awarded: $210,600. Total amount of financial aid awarded in 2012–13: $855,650.

Admissions Traditional secondary-level entrance grade is 9. Deadline for receipt of application materials: none. Application fee required: $25. On-campus interview required.
Athletics Interscholastic: aquatics, baseball, basketball, crew, cross-country running, diving, football, golf, ice hockey, lacrosse, soccer, squash, swimming and diving, tennis, track and field, water polo, winter (indoor) track. 4 PE instructors, 23 coaches, 1 athletic trainer.
Computers Computers are regularly used in all academic classes. Computer network features include on-campus library services, online commercial services, Internet access, Discovering Authors, Access PA Power Library, Electric Library, InfoTrac, SIRS Knowledge Source.
Contact William R. Gibson, Dean of Admissions. 484-595-1181. Fax: 484-595-1104. E-mail: wgibson@malvernprep.org. Web site: www.malvernprep.org

MANHATTAN CHRISTIAN HIGH SCHOOL

8000 Churchill Road
Manhattan, Montana 59741

Head of School: Mr. Patrick J. De Jong

General Information Coeducational day and distance learning college-preparatory, general academic, arts, business, religious studies, and technology school, affiliated with Christian Reformed Church, Christian faith; primarily serves students with learning disabilities, individuals with Attention Deficit Disorder, individuals with emotional and behavioral problems, and dyslexic students. Grades PK–12. Distance learning grades 9–12. Founded: 1907. Setting: rural. Nearest major city is Bozeman. 20-acre campus. 1 building on campus. Approved or accredited by Christian Schools International, Office for Standards in Education (OFSTED), The College Board, home study, and Montana Department of Education. Endowment: $5.5 million. Total enrollment: 290. Upper school average class size: 15. Upper school faculty-student ratio: 1:8. There are 175 required school days per year for Upper School students. Upper School students typically attend 5 days per week. The average school day consists of 6 hours and 19 minutes.
Upper School Student Profile Grade 9: 11 students (5 boys, 6 girls); Grade 10: 21 students (15 boys, 6 girls); Grade 11: 19 students (9 boys, 10 girls); Grade 12: 36 students (21 boys, 15 girls). 50% of students are members of Christian Reformed Church, Christian faith.
Faculty School total: 17. In upper school: 4 men, 4 women; 3 have advanced degrees.
Subjects Offered Art, Bible studies, business, community service, English, general science, internship, mathematics, music, physical education, senior project, social studies, Spanish.
Graduation Requirements Arts and fine arts (art, music, dance, drama), business skills (includes word processing), English, mathematics, physical education (includes health), religion (includes Bible studies and theology), science, senior project, social studies (includes history), speech. Community service is required.
Special Academic Programs Advanced Placement exam preparation; honors section; independent study; term-away projects; study at local college for college credit; remedial reading and/or remedial writing; remedial math; programs in English, mathematics, general development for dyslexic students.
College Admission Counseling 17 students graduated in 2012; they went to Azusa Pacific University; Dordt College; Montana State University; The University of Montana Western. Mean composite ACT: 23.
Student Life Upper grades have specified standards of dress, student council, honor system. Discipline rests primarily with faculty. Attendance at religious services is required.
Tuition and Aid Day student tuition: $7200. Guaranteed tuition plan. Tuition installment plan (monthly payment plans, individually arranged payment plans). Tuition reduction for siblings, need-based scholarship grants available. In 2012–13, 80% of upper-school students received aid. Total amount of financial aid awarded in 2012–13: $35,000.
Admissions Traditional secondary-level entrance grade is 9. For fall 2012, 9 students applied for upper-level admission, 8 were accepted, 8 enrolled. Academic Profile Tests or any standardized test required. Deadline for receipt of application materials: none. Application fee required: $35. Interview required.
Athletics Interscholastic: baseball (boys), basketball (b,g), cheering (b,g), cross-country running (b,g), football (b), golf (b,g), track and field (b,g), volleyball (g). 1 PE instructor, 6 coaches, 2 athletic trainers.
Computers Computers are regularly used in business, English, science, senior seminar, social studies classes. Computer network features include on-campus library services, online commercial services, Internet access, Internet filtering or blocking technology. Student e-mail accounts are available to students. Students grades are available online. The school has a published electronic and media policy.
Contact Mrs. Gloria Veltkamp, Admissions Director. 406-282-7261. Fax: 406-282-7701. E-mail: gveltkamp@manhattanchristian.org. Web site: www.manhattanchristian.org

MAPLEBROOK SCHOOL

Amenia, New York
See Special Needs Schools section.

MARANATHA HIGH SCHOOL

169 South Saint John Avenue
Pasadena, California 91105

Head of School: Mrs. Michelle Purghart

General Information Coeducational day college-preparatory, religious studies, and liberal arts school, affiliated with Christian faith. Grades 9–12. Founded: 1965. Setting: urban. Nearest major city is Los Angeles. 11-acre campus. 3 buildings on campus. Approved or accredited by Association of Christian Schools International, Western Association of Schools and Colleges, and California Department of Education. Endowment: $250,000. Total enrollment: 655. Upper school average class size: 22. Upper school faculty-student ratio: 1:13. There are 170 required school days per year for Upper School students. Upper School students typically attend 5 days per week. The average school day consists of 7 hours and 5 minutes.
Faculty School total: 47. In upper school: 25 men, 22 women; 26 have advanced degrees.
Subjects Offered Advanced math, algebra, American history, American history-AP, American literature, American sign language, anatomy and physiology, art, ASB Leadership, Bible, biology, biology-AP, calculus, calculus-AP, chemistry, chemistry-AP, choir, composition, conceptual physics, concert choir, creative writing, drama performance, drawing, economics, English, English language-AP, English literature, English literature-AP, foreign language, French, freshman foundations, geometry, government and politics-AP, government-AP, graphic design, honors algebra, honors English, honors U.S. history, jazz dance, Latin, learning lab, macroeconomics-AP, math analysis, modern world history, music theory, music theory-AP, musical theater, New Testament, orchestra, performing arts, photography, physical education, physical science, physics, physics-AP, psychology, psychology-AP, sociology, Spanish, Spanish language-AP, Spanish-AP, speech and debate, sports medicine, statistics-AP, studio art-AP, swimming, theater, theater arts, theology, theology and the arts, U.S. government, U.S. history-AP, weight training, world geography, world history, yearbook.
Graduation Requirements English, foreign language, history, life science, mathematics, performing arts, physical education (includes health), physical science, theology, visual arts, Theology must be taken every year student attends school. Community service is required.
Special Academic Programs Advanced Placement exam preparation; honors section; study at local college for college credit; academic accommodation for the artistically talented; remedial reading and/or remedial writing; remedial math; special instructional classes for students with learning difficulties and Attention Deficit Disorder.
College Admission Counseling 158 students graduated in 2012; they went to Azusa Pacific University.
Student Life Upper grades have uniform requirement, student council, honor system. Discipline rests primarily with faculty. Attendance at religious services is required.
Summer Programs Remediation, enrichment, advancement, sports, art/fine arts programs offered; session focuses on science and math; held on campus; accepts boys and girls; open to students from other schools. 140 students usually enrolled. 2013 schedule: June 17 to July 26. Application deadline: February 3.
Tuition and Aid Day student tuition: $16,750. Tuition installment plan (SMART Tuition Payment Plan, monthly payment plans). Merit scholarship grants, need-based scholarship grants available. In 2012–13, 25% of upper-school students received aid.
Admissions Traditional secondary-level entrance grade is 9. ISEE required. Deadline for receipt of application materials: none. Application fee required: $75. On-campus interview required.
Athletics Interscholastic: baseball (boys), basketball (b,g), cheering (g), cross-country running (b,g), diving (b,g), football (b), soccer (b,g), softball (g), swimming and diving (b,g), tennis (b,g), track and field (b,g), volleyball (b,g); coed interscholastic: dance team, equestrian sports, golf; coed intramural: climbing, hiking/backpacking, kayaking, mountain biking, outdoor adventure, outdoor skills, wall climbing. 2 PE instructors, 27 coaches, 1 athletic trainer.
Computers Computers are regularly used in college planning, freshman foundations, graphic design, library, photography, research skills, yearbook classes. Computer network features include on-campus library services, online commercial services, Internet access, wireless campus network, Internet filtering or blocking technology, eLibrary. Computer access in designated common areas is available to students. Students grades are available online.
Contact Mrs. Debbie Middlebrook, Admissions Administrative Assistant. 626-817-4021. Fax: 626-817-4040. E-mail: d_middlebrook@mhs-hs.org. Web site: www.maranatha-hs.org

MARET SCHOOL

3000 Cathedral Avenue NW
Washington, District of Columbia 20008

Head of School: Marjo Talbott

General Information Coeducational day college-preparatory, arts, and technology school. Grades K–12. Founded: 1911. Setting: urban. 7-acre campus. 6 buildings on campus. Approved or accredited by Association of Independent Maryland Schools, Association of Independent Schools of Greater Washington, Middle States Association of Colleges and Schools, and District of Columbia Department of Education. Member of National Association of Independent Schools and Secondary School Admission Test Board. Endowment: $19 million. Total enrollment: 635. Upper school average class size: 18. Upper school faculty-student ratio: 1:7. The average school day consists of 7 hours.

Upper School Student Profile Grade 9: 80 students (38 boys, 42 girls); Grade 10: 80 students (41 boys, 39 girls); Grade 11: 83 students (48 boys, 35 girls); Grade 12: 67 students (35 boys, 32 girls).

Faculty School total: 104. In upper school: 37 men, 67 women; 78 have advanced degrees.

Subjects Offered Acting, advanced computer applications, advanced studio art-AP, African-American literature, algebra, American history, American literature, anatomy, art, astronomy, biology, calculus-AP, ceramics, chemistry, civil rights, classical civilization, classical Greek literature, classical language, classics, computer graphics, computer math, computer programming, computer science, creative writing, drama, earth science, ecology, English, English literature, European history, film history, fine arts, French, gender issues, geometry, government/civics, history, humanities, Latin, marine biology, mathematics, music, photography, physical education, physics, physiology, psychology, science, Spanish, statistics, technology, trigonometry, world history, world literature, writing.

Graduation Requirements Arts and fine arts (art, music, dance, drama), English, foreign language, history, mathematics, music, performing arts, physical education (includes health), science, 15 hours of community service in grades 9 and 10, additional 15 hours in grades 11 and 12.

Special Academic Programs 16 Advanced Placement exams for which test preparation is offered; honors section; independent study; study at local college for college credit; study abroad; academic accommodation for the gifted, the musically talented, and the artistically talented.

College Admission Counseling 69 students graduated in 2011; 67 went to college, including Harvard University; Northwestern University; Pomona College; Tufts University; Washington University in St. Louis. Other: 2 entered a postgraduate year.

Student Life Upper grades have student council. Discipline rests primarily with faculty.

Tuition and Aid Day student tuition: $31,670. Tuition installment plan (Key Tuition Payment Plan). Need-based scholarship grants available. In 2011–12, 24% of upper-school students received aid. Total amount of financial aid awarded in 2011–12: $2,800,000.

Admissions Traditional secondary-level entrance grade is 9. For fall 2011, 262 students applied for upper-level admission, 39 were accepted, 25 enrolled. ISEE, PSAT or SSAT required. Deadline for receipt of application materials: January 6. Application fee required: $65. On-campus interview required.

Athletics Interscholastic: baseball (boys), basketball (b,g), football (b), lacrosse (b,g), soccer (b,g), softball (g), tennis (b,g), volleyball (g), wrestling (b); intramural: ice hockey (b), squash (b,g); coed interscholastic: aerobics, cross-country running, diving, flag football, golf, independent competitive sports, martial arts, swimming and diving, track and field, ultimate Frisbee; coed intramural: indoor soccer, ultimate Frisbee, weight lifting, weight training, yoga. 6 PE instructors, 25 coaches, 1 athletic trainer.

Computers Computers are regularly used in graphic design, graphics, programming, publications, Web site design classes. Computer network features include on-campus library services, online commercial services, Internet access, wireless campus network, Internet filtering or blocking technology. Campus intranet and student e-mail accounts are available to students. Students grades are available online. The school has a published electronic and media policy.

Contact Annie M. Farquhar, Director of Admission and Financial Aid. 202-939-8814. Fax: 202-939-8845. E-mail: admissions@maret.org. Web site: www.maret.org

MARIAN CENTRAL CATHOLIC HIGH SCHOOL

1001 McHenry Avenue
Woodstock, Illinois 60098

Head of School: Mr. Charles D. Rakers

General Information Coeducational day college-preparatory, arts, business, religious studies, bilingual studies, and technology school, affiliated with Roman Catholic Church. Grades 9–12. Founded: 1959. Setting: suburban. 42-acre campus. 1 building on campus. Approved or accredited by National Catholic Education Association, North Central Association of Colleges and Schools, and Illinois Department of Education. Endowment: $1.1 million. Total enrollment: 691. Upper school average class size: 24. Upper school faculty-student ratio: 1:18. There are 177 required school days per year for Upper School students. Upper School students typically attend 5 days per week. The average school day consists of 6 hours and 25 minutes.

Upper School Student Profile Grade 9: 178 students (107 boys, 71 girls); Grade 10: 188 students (103 boys, 85 girls); Grade 11: 165 students (82 boys, 83 girls); Grade 12: 160 students (85 boys, 75 girls). 89.5% of students are Roman Catholic.

Faculty School total: 47. In upper school: 24 men, 23 women; 37 have advanced degrees.

Subjects Offered Accounting, advanced biology, advanced chemistry, advanced math, Advanced Placement courses, algebra, American government, art, band, biology, business law, calculus, calculus-AP, chemistry, chemistry-AP, chorus, comparative government and politics-AP, composition, computer applications, consumer economics, desktop publishing, engineering, English, English composition, English literature-AP, first aid, French, general science, geography, geometry, global issues, government, health, honors algebra, honors English, honors geometry, honors U.S. history, integrated science, marketing, photo shop, physical education, physical fitness, physical science, physics, pre-calculus, psychology, psychology-AP, publications, religious studies, Spanish, speech, statistics-AP, theater, U.S. history, U.S. history-AP, Web site design, world history, world history-AP.

Graduation Requirements Art, biology, consumer economics, electives, English, first aid, foreign language, government, mathematics, music, physical education (includes health), religious studies, science, U.S. history.

Special Academic Programs 8 Advanced Placement exams for which test preparation is offered; honors section; remedial reading and/or remedial writing; remedial math.

College Admission Counseling 169 students graduated in 2012; 168 went to college, including Iowa State University of Science and Technology; Loyola University Chicago; Saint Louis University; The University of Iowa; University of Dayton; University of Illinois at Urbana–Champaign. Other: 1 entered military service. Mean composite ACT: 25. 35% scored over 26 on composite ACT.

Student Life Upper grades have uniform requirement, student council. Discipline rests primarily with faculty. Attendance at religious services is required.

Summer Programs Enrichment, sports programs offered; session focuses on sports camps, study skills, Model UN, Scholastic Bowl, Kids in Chemistry, art; held on campus; accepts boys and girls; open to students from other schools. 2013 schedule: June to August.

Tuition and Aid Day student tuition: $5745–$7700. Tuition installment plan (monthly payment plans, quarterly payment plan, semester payment plans, yearly payment plans). Tuition reduction for siblings, need-based scholarship grants, paying campus jobs available. In 2012–13, 22% of upper-school students received aid. Total amount of financial aid awarded in 2012–13: $296,300.

Admissions Traditional secondary-level entrance grade is 9. High School Placement Test (closed version) from Scholastic Testing Service required. Deadline for receipt of application materials: none. No application fee required.

Athletics Interscholastic: baseball (boys), basketball (b,g), cheering (g), cross-country running (b,g), dance team (g), football (b), golf (b,g), soccer (b,g), softball (g), tennis (b,g), track and field (b,g), volleyball (g), wrestling (b); coed interscholastic: fencing, fishing; coed intramural: floor hockey. 3 PE instructors, 52 coaches, 1 athletic trainer.

Computers Computers are regularly used in computer applications, desktop publishing, photography, publications, Web site design classes. Computer resources include on-campus library services, online commercial services, Internet access, Internet filtering or blocking technology. Students grades are available online. The school has a published electronic and media policy.

Contact Mrs. Barbara Villont, Director of Curriculum and Technology. 815-338-4220 Ext. 105. Fax: 815-338-4253. E-mail: bvillont@marian.com. Web site: www.marian.com

MARIAN HIGH SCHOOL

1311 South Logan Street
Mishawaka, Indiana 46544

Head of School: Carl Loesch

General Information Coeducational day college-preparatory, arts, business, vocational, religious studies, bilingual studies, and technology school, affiliated with Roman Catholic Church. Grades 9–12. Founded: 1965. Setting: suburban. 135-acre campus. 1 building on campus. Approved or accredited by North Central Association of Colleges and Schools, The College Board, and Indiana Department of Education. Total enrollment: 719. Upper school average class size: 27. Upper school faculty-student ratio: 1:24. There are 180 required school days per year for Upper School students. Upper School students typically attend 5 days per week. The average school day consists of 6 hours and 30 minutes.

Upper School Student Profile Grade 9: 199 students (89 boys, 110 girls); Grade 10: 182 students (102 boys, 80 girls); Grade 11: 172 students (86 boys, 86 girls); Grade 12: 166 students (82 boys, 84 girls). 83% of students are Roman Catholic.

Faculty School total: 48. In upper school: 18 men, 30 women; 22 have advanced degrees.

Subjects Offered 20th century history, 20th century physics, 20th century world history, 3-dimensional art, 3-dimensional design, accounting, acting, advanced chemistry, advanced computer applications, advanced math, algebra, alternative physical education, American government, American literature, analysis and differential calculus, analytic geometry, anatomy, ancient world history, art, art history, arts and crafts, arts appreciation, business law, calculus, Catholic belief and practice, chemistry, drama, drawing, drawing and design, economics, English composition, English literature-AP, environmental science, environmental studies, environmental systems, family and consumer science, family living, fashion, fine arts, food and nutrition, foods, French, French language-AP, general business, general math, geography, geometry, German, government and politics-AP, government-AP, government/civics, guidance, health, histology, honors world history, independent living, integrated science, keyboarding, Latin, Life of Christ, media, media arts, moral theology, music, music appreciation, nutrition, physics, physics-AP, pre-algebra, pre-calculus, psychology, religion, scripture, senior project, sewing, sociology, Spanish, Spanish language-AP, Spanish-AP, study skills, theology, U.S. government and politics-AP, U.S. history, U.S. history-AP, visual arts, vocal music, Western civilization.

Graduation Requirements Algebra, American government, American history, analytic geometry, arts and fine arts (art, music, dance, drama), biology, chemistry, computer information systems, computer skills, economics, English, English composition, English literature, French, keyboarding, languages, mathematics, science, scripture, writing, four years of theology.

Special Academic Programs Advanced Placement exam preparation; study at local college for college credit; remedial reading and/or remedial writing; remedial math.

College Admission Counseling 162 students graduated in 2012; 155 went to college, including Ball State University; DePaul University; Indiana University–Purdue University Fort Wayne; Indiana University Bloomington; Purdue University; University of Notre Dame. Other: 4 went to work, 1 entered military service, 2 had other specific plans. Mean SAT critical reading: 542, mean SAT math: 541, mean SAT writing: 537, mean composite ACT: 23.

Student Life Upper grades have specified standards of dress, student council, honor system. Discipline rests equally with students and faculty. Attendance at religious services is required.

Summer Programs Sports, art/fine arts, computer instruction programs offered; session focuses on enrichment; held on campus; accepts boys and girls; open to students from other schools. 2013 schedule: June 7 to July 2.

Tuition and Aid Day student tuition: $5575–$6575. Tuition installment plan (The Tuition Plan, FACTS Tuition Payment Plan, individually arranged payment plans). Tuition reduction for siblings, need-based loans available. In 2012–13, 45% of upper-school students received aid. Total amount of financial aid awarded in 2012–13: $350,000.

Admissions Traditional secondary-level entrance grade is 9. For fall 2012, 210 students applied for upper-level admission, 210 were accepted, 199 enrolled. High School Placement Test, Math Placement Exam or placement test required. Deadline for receipt of application materials: September 9. Application fee required: $100. Interview required.

Athletics Interscholastic: aerobics/dance (girls), aquatics (b,g), baseball (b), basketball (b,g), cheering (b,g), Cosom hockey (b), cross-country running (b,g), dance team (g), diving (b,g), flag football (g), football (b), golf (b,g), gymnastics (g), hockey (b), ice hockey (b), indoor hockey (b), lacrosse (b,g), power lifting (b,g), rugby (b), soccer (b,g), softball (g), swimming and diving (b,g), tennis (b,g), track and field (b,g), volleyball (g), weight training (b,g), wrestling (b,g); intramural: basketball (b), flag football (g), pom squad (g); coed interscholastic: cheering, wrestling; coed intramural: alpine skiing, bowling. 2 PE instructors, 42 coaches, 1 athletic trainer.

Computers Computers are regularly used in business education, business skills, career education, commercial art, economics, foreign language, graphic arts, history, library, media arts, occupational education, publications, religion, yearbook classes. Computer network features include on-campus library services, online commercial services, Internet access, Internet filtering or blocking technology. Students grades are available online. The school has a published electronic and media policy.

Contact Mark B. Kirzeder, Assistant Principal of Academics. 574-259-5257 Ext. 318. Fax: 574-258-7668. E-mail: mkirzeder@marianhs.org. Web site: www.marianhs.org/

MARINE MILITARY ACADEMY

320 Iwo Jima Boulevard
Harlingen, Texas 78550

Head of School: Col. R Glenn Hill, USMC-Retd.

General Information Boys' boarding college-preparatory, general academic, and military school; primarily serves underachievers. Grades 8–PG. Founded: 1965. Setting: small town. Students are housed in single-sex dormitories. 142-acre campus. 43 buildings on campus. Approved or accredited by Military High School and College Association, Southern Association of Colleges and Schools, Southern Association of Independent Schools, and Texas Department of Education. Endowment: $18 million. Total enrollment: 250. Upper school average class size: 13. Upper school faculty-student ratio: 1:13.

Upper School Student Profile Grade 8: 17 students (17 boys); Grade 9: 42 students (42 boys); Grade 10: 65 students (65 boys); Grade 11: 57 students (57 boys); Grade 12: 67 students (67 boys); Postgraduate: 3 students (3 boys). 100% of students are boarding students. 37% are state residents. 27 states are represented in upper school student body. 30% are international students. International students from China, Germany, Mexico, Panama, Russian Federation, and United Arab Emirates; 5 other countries represented in student body.

Faculty School total: 34. In upper school: 17 men, 17 women; 16 have advanced degrees; 24 reside on campus.

Subjects Offered Aerospace science, algebra, American history, band, biology, calculus, calculus-AP, chemistry, computer programming, computer science, economics, English, environmental science, geography, geometry, government/civics, history, journalism, JROTC, keyboarding, marine science, mathematics, military science, physics, physics-AP, political science, SAT preparation, science, social sciences, social studies, Spanish, Spanish-AP, speech, world history.

Graduation Requirements Business skills (includes word processing), computer science, English, foreign language, mathematics, military science, physical education (includes health), science, social sciences, social studies (includes history).

Special Academic Programs Advanced Placement exam preparation; honors section; study at local college for college credit; academic accommodation for the gifted; remedial reading and/or remedial writing; remedial math; ESL (60 students enrolled).

College Admission Counseling 54 students graduated in 2012; 53 went to college, including Texas A&M University; Texas Tech University; The Citadel, The Military College of South Carolina; United States Military Academy; United States Naval Academy; Virginia Military Institute. Other: 1 entered military service. 11.7% scored over 600 on SAT critical reading, 14% scored over 600 on SAT math.

Student Life Upper grades have uniform requirement, student council, honor system. Discipline rests equally with students and faculty. Attendance at religious services is required.

Summer Programs ESL, sports, rigorous outdoor training programs offered; session focuses on leadership training; held on campus; accepts boys; open to students from other schools. 360 students usually enrolled. 2013 schedule: June 29 to July 27. Application deadline: none.

Tuition and Aid 7-day tuition and room/board: $33,000. Tuition installment plan (FACTS Tuition Payment Plan, monthly payment plans, individually arranged payment plans, Chief Financial Officer authorization required). Tuition reduction for siblings, merit scholarship grants, need-based scholarship grants, (Parent) Active Duty Military Discount, referral reward discount available. In 2012–13, 12% of upper-school students received aid. Total amount of financial aid awarded in 2012–13: $300,000.

Admissions For fall 2012, 195 students applied for upper-level admission, 172 were accepted, 142 enrolled. Deadline for receipt of application materials: none. Application fee required: $100.

Athletics Interscholastic: baseball, basketball, bicycling, boxing, cross-country running, diving, drill team, football, golf, JROTC drill, marksmanship, physical fitness, riflery, running, soccer, swimming and diving, tennis, track and field, winter soccer; intramural: baseball, basketball, boxing, climbing, fitness, flag football, football, judo, kickball, martial arts, outdoor activities, outdoor adventure, paint ball, physical fitness, physical training, power lifting, racquetball, rappelling, rock climbing, running, sailing, scuba diving, soccer, softball, swimming and diving, track and field, volleyball, wall climbing, weight lifting, weight training. 15 coaches, 1 athletic trainer.

Computers Computers are regularly used in English, foreign language, mathematics, science, yearbook classes. Computer network features include on-campus library services, online commercial services, Internet access, Internet filtering or blocking technology. Student e-mail accounts and computer access in designated common areas are available to students. Students grades are available online.

Contact Mrs. Jay Perez, Assistant Admissions Director. 956-423-6006 Ext. 251. Fax: 956-421-9273. E-mail: admissions@mma-tx.org. Web site: www.mma-tx.org

See Display on next page and Close-Up on page 600.

THE MARIN SCHOOL

100 Ebbtide Avenue #300
Sausalito, California 94965

Head of School: Barbara Brown, EdD

General Information Coeducational day college-preparatory, arts, and film, technology, photography school. Grades 9–12. Founded: 1980. Setting: small town. Nearest major city is San Francisco. 2-acre campus. 4 buildings on campus. Approved or accredited by Western Association of Schools and Colleges and California Department of Education. Member of National Association of Independent Schools. Total enrollment: 100. Upper school average class size: 7. Upper school faculty-student ratio: 1:7. There are 174 required school days per year for Upper School students. Upper School students typically attend 5 days per week. The average school day consists of 6 hours.

Faculty School total: 17. In upper school: 12 men, 5 women; 14 have advanced degrees.

Subjects Offered Algebra, American literature, arts, biology, British literature (honors), calculus, chemistry, civics, community service, composition, drama, earth science, ecology, economics, English, environmental science, fine arts, general science, geography, geometry, health, life science, literature, mathematics, physics, pre-calculus, science, social sciences, social studies, Spanish, trigonometry, U.S. history, visual arts, Western civilization, women's literature.

Graduation Requirements Arts and fine arts (art, music, dance, drama), foreign language, mathematics, physical education (includes health), science, social sciences. Community service is required.

Special Academic Programs Honors section.

College Admission Counseling 25 students graduated in 2011; all went to college, including Bard College; Eugene Lang College The New School for Liberal Arts; Goucher College; Lewis & Clark College; Reed College; The Evergreen State College.

Student Life Upper grades have student council, honor system. Discipline rests primarily with faculty.

Tuition and Aid Day student tuition: $34,800. Tuition installment plan (FACTS Tuition Payment Plan). Need-based scholarship grants available. In 2011–12, 40% of upper-school students received aid.

Admissions ERB, SSAT, Star-9 or STS required. Deadline for receipt of application materials: none. No application fee required. On-campus interview required.

Athletics Coed Interscholastic: basketball, dance, indoor soccer, sailing, soccer; coed intramural: baseball, basketball, bicycling, fencing, mountain biking, sailing, soccer.

Computers Computers are regularly used in all classes. Computer network features include on-campus library services, online commercial services, Internet access, wireless campus network, Internet filtering or blocking technology. Campus intranet and student e-mail accounts are available to students. Students grades are available online. The school has a published electronic and media policy.

Contact Ms. Sierra Antonio, Admissions and Development Assistant. 415-339-9336 Ext. 142. E-mail: santonio@themarinschool.org. Web site: www.themarinschool.org

MARION ACADEMY

1820 Prier Drive
Marion, Alabama 36756

Head of School: Mr. G. Travis Vaughn

General Information Coeducational day college-preparatory, general academic, arts, religious studies, bilingual studies, and technology school, affiliated with Christian faith. Grades K–12. Founded: 1987. Setting: small town. Nearest major city is Tuscaloosa. 5-acre campus. 1 building on campus. Approved or accredited by Southern Association of Colleges and Schools and Alabama Department of Education. Total enrollment: 96. Upper school average class size: 8. Upper school faculty-student ratio: 1:8. There are 180 required school days per year for Upper School students. Upper School students typically attend 5 days per week. The average school day consists of 6 hours and 30 minutes.

Upper School Student Profile Grade 7: 7 students (3 boys, 4 girls); Grade 8: 9 students (6 boys, 3 girls); Grade 9: 8 students (6 boys, 2 girls); Grade 10: 8 students (2 boys, 6 girls); Grade 11: 9 students (3 boys, 6 girls); Grade 12: 9 students (4 boys, 5 girls). 98% of students are Christian.

Faculty School total: 19. In upper school: 5 men, 5 women; 2 have advanced degrees.

Subjects Offered 20th century history, 20th century world history, advanced computer applications, advanced math, Alabama history and geography, algebra, American government, anatomy and physiology, art, athletics, basic language skills, Bible studies, biology, cheerleading, college planning, creative writing, drama, earth science, economics, English language and composition-AP, English language-AP, English literature, English literature and composition-AP, foreign language, general math, geography, government, grammar, health education, history, honors algebra, honors English, human anatomy, Internet, language, language and composition, language arts, library, math applications, math methods, math review, mathematics, mathematics-AP, physical education, SAT/ACT preparation, speech, U.S. government, U.S. history.

Student Life Upper grades have specified standards of dress, student council, honor system. Discipline rests primarily with faculty.

Tuition and Aid Guaranteed tuition plan.

Admissions Traditional secondary-level entrance grade is 9. Deadline for receipt of application materials: none. Application fee required. Interview required.

Athletics Interscholastic: baseball (boys), basketball (b,g), cheering (g), cross-country running (b,g), football (b), softball (g), track and field (b,g), volleyball (g); coed interscholastic: track and field. 1 PE instructor, 2 coaches.

Computers Computers are regularly used in career education, library skills classes. Computer network features include Internet access. Student e-mail accounts are available to students.

Contact Mrs. Margaret S. Hallmon, Secretary. 334-683-8204. Fax: 334-683-4938. E-mail: marionacademy@hotmail.com. Web site: www.marionacademy.org

MARIST SCHOOL

3790 Ashford-Dunwoody Road NE
Atlanta, Georgia 30319-1899

Head of School: Rev. Joel M. Konzen, SM

General Information Coeducational day college-preparatory, arts, business, religious studies, and technology school, affiliated with Roman Catholic Church. Grades 7–12. Founded: 1901. Setting: suburban. 77-acre campus. 18 buildings on campus. Approved or accredited by Southern Association of Colleges and Schools, Southern Association of Independent Schools, and Georgia Department of Education. Member of National Association of Independent Schools and Secondary School Admission Test Board. Endowment: $16.2 million. Total enrollment: 1,081. Upper school average class size: 18. Upper school faculty-student ratio: 1:11. There are 174 required school days per year for Upper School students. Upper School students typically attend 5 days per week. The average school day consists of 5 hours and 30 minutes.

Upper School Student Profile Grade 7: 150 students (75 boys, 75 girls); Grade 8: 146 students (77 boys, 69 girls); Grade 9: 195 students (96 boys, 99 girls); Grade 10: 197 students (96 boys, 101 girls); Grade 11: 201 students (107 boys, 94 girls); Grade 12: 192 students (97 boys, 95 girls). 74% of students are Roman Catholic.

Faculty School total: 96. In upper school: 49 men, 47 women; 70 have advanced degrees.

Subjects Offered Algebra, American history, American literature, ancient history, art, art history, biology, business skills, calculus, ceramics, chemistry, community service, computer programming, computer science, creative writing, dance, drama, driver education, economics, English, English literature, European history, fine arts, French, general science, geography, geology, geometry, German, government/civics, health, history, humanities, journalism, Latin, mathematics, music, peace and justice, philosophy, photography, physical education, physics, religion, science, social studies, Spanish, speech, statistics, studio art, theater, theology, world history, world literature, world religions, writing.

Graduation Requirements Arts and fine arts (art, music, dance, drama), business skills (includes word processing), computer science, English, foreign language, mathematics, physical education (includes health), religion (includes Bible studies and theology), science, social studies (includes history), community service requirements in all grades. Community service is required.

Special Academic Programs Advanced Placement exam preparation; honors section; independent study.

College Admission Counseling 203 students graduated in 2012; 202 went to college, including Auburn University; Clemson University; Georgia College & State University; Georgia Institute of Technology; University of Georgia; University of Mississippi. Other: 1 had other specific plans. 61% scored over 600 on SAT critical reading, 68% scored over 600 on SAT math, 59% scored over 600 on SAT writing, 67% scored over 1800 on combined SAT, 71% scored over 26 on composite ACT.

Student Life Upper grades have uniform requirement, student council, honor system. Discipline rests primarily with faculty. Attendance at religious services is required.

Summer Programs Enrichment, sports, art/fine arts programs offered; held on campus; accepts boys and girls; open to students from other schools.

Tuition and Aid Day student tuition: $16,300. Tuition installment plan (individually arranged payment plans, Tuition Management System). Need-based scholarship grants available. In 2012–13, 17% of upper-school students received aid. Total amount of financial aid awarded in 2012–13: $1,800,000.

Admissions Traditional secondary-level entrance grade is 7. SSAT required. Deadline for receipt of application materials: January 25. Application fee required: $75. On-campus interview required.

Athletics Interscholastic: baseball (boys), basketball (b,g), cheering (g), cross-country running (b,g), diving (b,g), football (b), golf (b,g), lacrosse (b,g), soccer (b,g), softball (g), swimming and diving (b,g), tennis (b,g), track and field (b,g), volleyball (g), weight lifting (b,g), wrestling (b); coed interscholastic: drill team; coed intramural: ultimate Frisbee. 6 PE instructors.

Computers Computers are regularly used in accounting, business applications, computer applications, drawing and design, English, foreign language, mathematics, music, science classes. Computer network features include on-campus library services, online commercial services, Internet access, wireless campus network, Internet filtering or blocking technology. Student e-mail accounts and computer access in designated common areas are available to students. Students grades are available online. The school has a published electronic and media policy.

Contact Mr. Jim Byrne, Director of Admissions. 770-936-2214. Fax: 770-457-8402. E-mail: admissions@marist.com. Web site: www.marist.com

MARLBOROUGH SCHOOL

250 South Rossmore Avenue
Los Angeles, California 90004

Head of School: Ms. Barbara E. Wagner

General Information Girls' day college-preparatory school. Grades 7–12. Founded: 1889. Setting: urban. 4-acre campus. 5 buildings on campus. Approved or accredited by Western Association of Schools and Colleges and California Department of Education. Member of National Association of Independent Schools. Endowment: $36.8 million. Total enrollment: 530. Upper school average class size: 12. Upper school faculty-student ratio: 1:8. There are 166 required school days per year for Upper School students. Upper School students typically attend 5 days per week. The average school day consists of 6 hours and 20 minutes.

Upper School Student Profile Grade 10: 92 students (92 girls); Grade 11: 91 students (91 girls); Grade 12: 91 students (91 girls).

Faculty School total: 77. In upper school: 20 men, 39 women; 47 have advanced degrees.

Subjects Offered Algebra, American literature, American studies, architecture, art history-AP, astronomy, athletic training, ballet technique, biology, biology-AP, calculus, calculus-AP, ceramics, chemistry, chemistry-AP, Chinese history, choral music, choreography, community service, computer programming, creative writing, dance, digital art, drawing, earth systems analysis, economics, English, English literature, English literature and composition-AP, environmental science, environmental science-AP, European history, European history-AP, French, French language-AP, gender issues, geometry, global studies, health, Hispanic literature, instrumental music, internship, journalism, Latin, Latin American literature, Latin-AP, linear algebra, Mandarin, metalworking, modern world history, music theory, newspaper, painting, photography, physical education, physics, physics-AP, political thought, psychology, research, robotics, Russian literature, sculpture, self-defense, social sciences, Spanish, Spanish language-AP, statistics, statistics-AP, studio art-AP, theater, trigonometry, U.S. history, U.S. history-AP, video and animation, world history, world history-AP, world literature, yearbook, yoga.

Graduation Requirements Arts and fine arts (art, music, dance, drama), English, foreign language, history, mathematics, science, social sciences.

Special Academic Programs 21 Advanced Placement exams for which test preparation is offered; honors section; independent study.

College Admission Counseling 84 students graduated in 2011; all went to college, including Carleton College; Columbia University; Stanford University; University of Pennsylvania; University of Southern California; Yale University.

Student Life Upper grades have uniform requirement, student council, honor system. Discipline rests equally with students and faculty.

Tuition and Aid Day student tuition: $31,200. Tuition installment plan (FACTS Tuition Payment Plan, monthly payment plans). Need-based scholarship grants available. In 2011–12, 18% of upper-school students received aid.

Admissions ISEE required. Deadline for receipt of application materials: January 5. Application fee required: $150. On-campus interview required.

Athletics Interscholastic: basketball, cross-country running, equestrian sports, golf, independent competitive sports, soccer, softball, swimming and diving, tennis, track and field, volleyball, water polo. 7 PE instructors, 31 coaches, 1 athletic trainer.

Computers Computers are regularly used in all academic classes. Computer network features include on-campus library services, online commercial services, Internet access, wireless campus network, Internet filtering or blocking technology, videoconferencing. Student e-mail accounts are available to students. Students grades are available online. The school has a published electronic and media policy.

Contact Ms. Jeanette Woo Chitjian, Director of Admissions. 323-964-8450. Fax: 323-933-0542. E-mail: jeanette.woochitjian@marlboroughschool.org. Web site: www.marlboroughschool.org

MARMION ACADEMY

1000 Butterfield Road
Aurora, Illinois 60502

Head of School: Dr. James Quaid

General Information Boys' day college-preparatory, business, religious studies, Junior ROTC, and LEAD (Leadership Education and Development) school, affiliated with Roman Catholic Church. Grades 9–12. Founded: 1933. Setting: suburban. Nearest major city is Chicago. 325-acre campus. 5 buildings on campus. Approved or accredited by National Catholic Education Association, North Central Association of Colleges and Schools, and Illinois Department of Education. Member of Secondary School Admission Test Board. Endowment: $9 million. Total enrollment: 523. Upper school average class size: 27. Upper school faculty-student ratio: 1:11. The average school day consists of 7 hours and 25 minutes.

Upper School Student Profile Grade 9: 109 students (109 boys); Grade 10: 132 students (132 boys); Grade 11: 134 students (134 boys); Grade 12: 148 students (148 boys). 88% of students are Roman Catholic.

Faculty School total: 56. In upper school: 40 men, 16 women; 31 have advanced degrees.

Subjects Offered 1 1/2 elective credits, algebra, American history, American literature, anatomy, art, astronomy, band, biology, biology-AP, botany, calculus, calculus-AP, chemistry, chemistry-AP, community service, computer science, computer-aided design, creative writing, driver education, ecology, economics, English, English literature, English-AP, fine arts, French, French language-AP, general science, geometry, government/civics, history, history-AP, Italian, JROTC, Latin, Latin-AP, leadership, leadership education training, mathematics, mathematics-AP, meteorology, music, music theory-AP, philosophy, physical education, physics, physics-AP, physiology, psychology, religion, science, social sciences, social studies, sociology, Spanish, Spanish language-AP, statistics, statistics-AP, theology, trigonometry, Western civilization, zoology.

Graduation Requirements Arts and fine arts (art, music, dance, drama), English, foreign language, JROTC, leadership education training, mathematics, music appreciation, physical education (includes health), religion (includes Bible studies and theology), science, social sciences, social studies (includes history). Community service is required.

Special Academic Programs Advanced Placement exam preparation; honors section; independent study; academic accommodation for the gifted.

College Admission Counseling 120 students graduated in 2012; all went to college, including Marquette University; Purdue University; Saint Louis University; University of Dayton; University of Illinois. Mean composite ACT: 26.

Student Life Upper grades have uniform requirement, student council. Discipline rests primarily with faculty. Attendance at religious services is required.

Tuition and Aid Day student tuition: $10,100. Tuition installment plan (SMART Tuition Payment Plan, Tuition Management Systems). Merit scholarship grants, need-based scholarship grants, paying campus jobs available. In 2012–13, 30% of upper-school students received aid; total upper-school merit-scholarship money awarded: $155,000. Total amount of financial aid awarded in 2012–13: $342,800.

Admissions Traditional secondary-level entrance grade is 9. For fall 2012, 248 students applied for upper-level admission, 205 were accepted, 148 enrolled. High School Placement Test (closed version) from Scholastic Testing Service required. Deadline for receipt of application materials: none. Application fee required: $50. On-campus interview required.

Athletics Interscholastic: baseball, basketball, cross-country running, diving, football, golf, lacrosse, riflery, soccer, swimming and diving, tennis, track and field, wrestling; intramural: baseball, basketball, fencing, floor hockey, football, JROTC drill, outdoor activities, outdoors, soccer, swimming and diving, table tennis, tennis, volleyball, water polo, weight lifting. 2 PE instructors, 6 coaches, 1 athletic trainer.

Computers Computers are regularly used in design, science classes. Computer network features include on-campus library services, Internet access, wireless campus network, Internet filtering or blocking technology. Computer access in designated common areas is available to students. Students grades are available online. The school has a published electronic and media policy.

Contact William J. Dickson Jr., Director of Admissions. 630-897-6936. Fax: 630-897-7086. Web site: www.marmion.org

MARS HILL BIBLE SCHOOL

698 Cox Creek Parkway
Florence, Alabama 35630

Head of School: Mr. Dexter Rutherford

General Information Coeducational day college-preparatory, arts, and religious studies school, affiliated with Church of Christ. Grades K–12. Founded: 1947. Setting: suburban. Nearest major city is Huntsville. 80-acre campus. 7 buildings on campus. Approved or accredited by National Christian School Association and Southern Association of Colleges and Schools. Endowment: $2.7 million. Total enrollment: 540. Upper school average class size: 22. Upper school faculty-student ratio: 1:14. There are 180 required school days per year for Upper School students. Upper School students typically attend 5 days per week. The average school day consists of 7 hours.

Upper School Student Profile Grade 9: 44 students (17 boys, 27 girls); Grade 10: 39 students (17 boys, 22 girls); Grade 11: 50 students (18 boys, 32 girls); Grade 12: 65 students (26 boys, 39 girls). 82% of students are members of Church of Christ.

Faculty School total: 42. In upper school: 11 men, 12 women; 14 have advanced degrees.

Subjects Offered ACT preparation, algebra, American government, American literature, American literature-AP, anatomy and physiology, ancient world history, band, Bible studies, biology, biology-AP, calculus, calculus-AP, chemistry, chorus, computer literacy, computer programming, computer science, concert band, concert choir, debate, drama, drama performance, driver education, ecology, economics, English, English composition, English literature, English literature and composition-AP, English literature-AP, ensembles, forensics, geometry, health, honors English, human anatomy, Internet research, jazz band, Life of Christ, marine biology, musical productions, physical education, physical science, physics, pre-algebra, pre-calculus, psychology, Spanish, speech, speech and debate, student government, student publications, U.S. history, U.S. history-AP, word processing, world geography, world history, yearbook.

Graduation Requirements Algebra, American government, American history, American literature, ancient world history, art, Bible, biology, British literature, chemistry, college writing, computer applications, computer literacy, economics, English composition, foreign language, geometry, health and wellness, introduction to literature, mathematics, physical education (includes health), physical science, science, social studies (includes history), speech communications. Community service is required.

Special Academic Programs 3 Advanced Placement exams for which test preparation is offered; honors section; independent study; study at local college for college credit; special instructional classes for students with learning disabilities, Attention Deficit Disorder, and dyslexia.

College Admission Counseling 64 students graduated in 2012; all went to college, including Auburn University; Freed-Hardeman University; Harding University; The University of Alabama; The University of Alabama at Birmingham; University of North Alabama. Median composite ACT: 25. 43% scored over 26 on composite ACT.

Student Life Upper grades have specified standards of dress, student council. Discipline rests primarily with faculty. Attendance at religious services is required.

Summer Programs Enrichment, sports, art/fine arts programs offered; session focuses on athletics, driver education, forensics, show choir, band; held on campus; accepts boys and girls; open to students from other schools. 180 students usually enrolled. 2013 schedule: June 1 to July 31. Application deadline: June 1.

Tuition and Aid Day student tuition: $6252. Tuition installment plan (FACTS Tuition Payment Plan, monthly payment plans). Tuition reduction for siblings, need-based scholarship grants available. In 2012–13, 20% of upper-school students received aid. Total amount of financial aid awarded in 2012–13: $150,000.

Admissions Traditional secondary-level entrance grade is 9. For fall 2012, 10 students applied for upper-level admission, 10 were accepted, 8 enrolled. Achievement tests, ACT-Explore, PSAT or Stanford Achievement Test required. Deadline for receipt of application materials: none. Application fee required: $100. Interview required.

Athletics Interscholastic: baseball (boys), basketball (b,g), cheering (g), cross-country running (b,g), football (b), golf (b,g), soccer (b,g), softball (g), tennis (b,g), track and field (b,g), volleyball (g); intramural: basketball (b,g). 3 PE instructors, 7 coaches.

Computers Computers are regularly used in all academic, Bible studies, English, history, remedial study skills, yearbook classes. Computer resources include on-campus library services, online commercial services, Internet access, wireless campus network, Internet filtering or blocking technology. Campus intranet and computer access in designated common areas are available to students. Students grades are available online. The school has a published electronic and media policy.

Contact Mrs. Jeannie Garrett, Director of Admissions. 256-767-1203 Ext. 2005. Fax: 256-767-6304. E-mail: jgarrett@mhbs.org. Web site: www.mhbs.org

MARTIN LUTHER HIGH SCHOOL

60-02 Maspeth Avenue
Maspeth, New York 11378

Head of School: Mr. Randy Gast

General Information Coeducational day college-preparatory, arts, business, religious studies, and technology school, affiliated with Lutheran Church. Grades 6–12. Founded: 1960. Setting: urban. Nearest major city is New York. 1-acre campus. 1 building on campus. Approved or accredited by Middle States Association of Colleges and Schools and New York Department of Education. Total enrollment: 212. Upper school average class size: 22. Upper school faculty-student ratio: 1:12.

Upper School Student Profile Grade 9: 34 students (22 boys, 12 girls); Grade 10: 46 students (20 boys, 26 girls); Grade 11: 51 students (26 boys, 25 girls); Grade 12: 39 students (22 boys, 17 girls). 16% of students are Lutheran.

Faculty School total: 21. In upper school: 7 men, 11 women; 11 have advanced degrees.

Subjects Offered Algebra, American history, art, Bible studies, biology, business, business skills, calculus, calculus-AP, chemistry, chemistry-AP, computer programming, computer science, drama, driver education, earth science, economics, English, English literature, English literature-AP, environmental science-AP, ethics, European history, fine arts, French, geography, geometry, German, government/civics, grammar, health, history, journalism, marine biology, mathematics, music, philosophy, photography, physical education, physics, psychology, religion, science, social studies, Spanish, Spanish-AP, speech, theater, theology, trigonometry, U.S. history-AP, world history.

Graduation Requirements 1 1/2 elective credits, arts and fine arts (art, music, dance, drama), computer applications, English, foreign language, health, mathematics, physical education (includes health), religion (includes Bible studies and theology), science, social studies (includes history), service hours.

Special Academic Programs Advanced Placement exam preparation; honors section; independent study; study at local college for college credit; programs in general development for dyslexic students.

College Admission Counseling 53 students graduated in 2012; 51 went to college, including John Jay College of Criminal Justice of the City University of New York; Queens College of the City University of New York; St. Francis College; St. John's University; St. Joseph's College, New York. Other: 1 went to work, 1 entered military service. Mean SAT critical reading: 430, mean SAT math: 464.

Student Life Upper grades have uniform requirement, student council. Discipline rests primarily with faculty. Attendance at religious services is required.

Summer Programs Remediation, computer instruction programs offered; held on campus; accepts boys and girls; open to students from other schools. 70 students usually enrolled. 2013 schedule: July 2 to August 16. Application deadline: none.

Tuition and Aid Day student tuition: $8150. Tuition installment plan (monthly payment plans, Quarterly payment plan, one payment plan). Tuition reduction for siblings, merit scholarship grants, need-based scholarship grants available. In 2012–13, 50% of upper-school students received aid; total upper-school merit-scholarship money awarded: $40,800. Total amount of financial aid awarded in 2012–13: $1,955,670.

Admissions Traditional secondary-level entrance grade is 9. Iowa Test of Educational Development required. Deadline for receipt of application materials: none. Application fee required: $50. On-campus interview required.

Athletics Interscholastic: baseball (boys), basketball (b,g), cross-country running (b,g), fitness (b,g), soccer (b), softball (g), tennis (b,g), track and field (b,g), volleyball (g), wrestling (b,g); intramural: basketball (b,g), cross-country running (b,g), floor hockey (b,g), indoor hockey (b,g), soccer (b,g), weight lifting (b,g), wrestling (b); coed interscholastic: cross-country running, fitness, soccer; coed intramural: archery, badminton, cross-country running, fitness, handball, paddle tennis, racquetball, track and field, volleyball, wrestling. 2 PE instructors, 15 coaches.

Computers Computers are regularly used in business education, career education, Christian doctrine, computer applications, desktop publishing, history, keyboarding, newspaper, SAT preparation, Spanish, Web site design, yearbook classes. Computer resources include on-campus library services, Internet access. Student e-mail accounts are available to students. Students grades are available online.

Contact Ms. Patricia Dee, Admissions Administrator. 718-894-4000 Ext. 122. Fax: 718-894-1469. E-mail: pdee@martinluthernyc.org. Web site: www.martinluthernyc.org

THE MARVELWOOD SCHOOL

476 Skiff Mountain Road
PO Box 3001
Kent, Connecticut 06757-3001

Head of School: Mr. Arthur Goodearl

General Information Coeducational boarding and day college-preparatory, arts, technology, field science, and community service, ESL school. Grades 9–12. Founded: 1957. Setting: rural. Nearest major city is Hartford. Students are housed in single-sex dormitories. 83-acre campus. 10 buildings on campus. Approved or accredited by New England Association of Schools and Colleges and Connecticut Department of Education. Member of National Association of Independent Schools and Secondary School Admission Test Board. Endowment: $1.6 million. Total enrollment: 165. Upper school average class size: 8. Upper school faculty-student ratio: 1:4. Upper School students typically attend 6 days per week. The average school day consists of 6 hours and 40 minutes.

Upper School Student Profile Grade 9: 20 students (12 boys, 8 girls); Grade 10: 40 students (25 boys, 15 girls); Grade 11: 55 students (37 boys, 18 girls); Grade 12: 37 students (21 boys, 16 girls). 94% of students are boarding students. 21% are state residents. 14 states are represented in upper school student body. 33% are international students. International students from China, Jamaica, Mexico, Republic of Korea, Spain, and United Kingdom; 7 other countries represented in student body.

Faculty School total: 48. In upper school: 19 men, 27 women; 24 have advanced degrees; 35 reside on campus.

Subjects Offered Algebra, American history, American literature, anatomy and physiology, art, art history, biology, calculus, ceramics, chemistry, chorus, college writing, community service, creative writing, drama, driver education, English, English literature, ESL, ethology, European history, film, fine arts, French, geography, geometry, history of China and Japan, Korean literature, limnology, mathematics, music, ornithology, photography, physics, pre-algebra, psychology, religion, SAT preparation, science, Shakespeare, social studies, Spanish, studio art, trigonometry, world cultures, world history, world literature.

Graduation Requirements Arts and fine arts (art, music, dance, drama), English, foreign language, mathematics, science, social studies (includes history), senior service project, daily participation in sports, weekly community service program.

Special Academic Programs Advanced Placement exam preparation; honors section; independent study; remedial reading and/or remedial writing; remedial math; programs in general development for dyslexic students; ESL (32 students enrolled).

College Admission Counseling 41 students graduated in 2012; all went to college, including Pace University; Suffolk University; Syracuse University; University of Hartford; Washington College. Median SAT critical reading: 458, median SAT math: 424, median SAT writing: 458.

Student Life Upper grades have specified standards of dress, student council, honor system. Discipline rests equally with students and faculty.

Summer Programs Remediation, enrichment, ESL, art/fine arts, computer instruction programs offered; session focuses on study skills; held on campus; accepts boys and girls; open to students from other schools. 30 students usually enrolled. 2013 schedule: July 5 to July 31. Application deadline: none.

Tuition and Aid Day student tuition: $31,500; 7-day tuition and room/board: $48,200. Tuition installment plan (Insured Tuition Payment Plan, Academic Management Services Plan, SMART Tuition Payment Plan, individually arranged payment plans). Merit scholarship grants, need-based scholarship grants available. In 2012–13, 30% of upper-school students received aid; total upper-school merit-scholarship money awarded: $48,200. Total amount of financial aid awarded in 2012–13: $950,000.

Admissions Traditional secondary-level entrance grade is 9. For fall 2012, 257 students applied for upper-level admission, 168 were accepted, 58 enrolled. Deadline for receipt of application materials: none. Application fee required: $50. Interview required.

Athletics Interscholastic: baseball (boys), basketball (b,g), cross-country running (b,g), lacrosse (b), soccer (b,g), softball (g), tennis (b,g), volleyball (g), wrestling (b); intramural: lacrosse (g); coed interscholastic: alpine skiing, golf, outdoor activities, skiing (downhill); coed intramural: bicycling, canoeing/kayaking, climbing, dance, fishing, fly fishing, Frisbee, hiking/backpacking, horseback riding, kayaking, mountain biking, mountaineering, outdoor activities, physical training, rock climbing, ropes courses, skiing (downhill), snowboarding, strength & conditioning, weight training, wilderness, wildernessways, yoga. 1 coach, 1 athletic trainer.

Computers Computers are regularly used in computer applications, mathematics, newspaper, photography, science, writing classes. Computer network features include on-campus library services, Internet access, wireless campus network, Internet filtering or blocking technology. Campus intranet, student e-mail accounts, and computer access in designated common areas are available to students. The school has a published electronic and media policy.

Contact Mrs. Maureen Smith, Admissions Associate. 860-927-0047 Ext. 1005. Fax: 860-927-0021. E-mail: maureen.smith@marvelwood.org. Web site: www.marvelwood.org

MARYLAWN OF THE ORANGES

445 Scotland Road
South Orange, New Jersey 07079

Head of School: Dr. Christine H. Lopez

General Information Girls' day college-preparatory, arts, business, religious studies, bilingual studies, and technology school, affiliated with Roman Catholic Church. Grades 6–12. Founded: 1935. Setting: suburban. Nearest major city is Newark. 2 buildings on campus. Approved or accredited by Middle States Association of Colleges and Schools and New Jersey Department of Education. Total enrollment: 145. Upper school average class size: 15. Upper school faculty-student ratio: 1:15. There are 183 required school days per year for Upper School students. Upper School students typically attend 5 days per week. The average school day consists of 7 hours and 15 minutes.

Upper School Student Profile Grade 9: 31 students (31 girls); Grade 10: 23 students (23 girls); Grade 11: 20 students (20 girls); Grade 12: 29 students (29 girls). 25% of students are Roman Catholic.

Faculty School total: 20. In upper school: 7 men, 12 women; 8 have advanced degrees.

Subjects Offered Advanced chemistry, advanced math, algebra, American literature, anatomy and physiology, art, art history, athletics, biology, British literature (honors), calculus, campus ministry, career/college preparation, Catholic belief and practice, cheerleading, chemistry, choir, choral music, Christian ethics, Christian scripture, civics, classical studies, community service, constitutional law, dance, dance performance, dramatic arts, English, English-AP, fine arts, French, geometry, global studies, grammar, health education, honors algebra, honors English, honors geometry, honors U.S. history, Internet research, language arts, Latin, mathematics, moral theology, music theory, physical education, physics, pre-calculus, psychology, SAT/ACT preparation, social studies, Spanish, trigonometry, U.S. history, world history, world religions, yearbook.

Graduation Requirements Arts and fine arts (art, music, dance, drama), electives, English, foreign language, health education, mathematics, physical education (includes health), practical arts, religious studies, science, social studies (includes history), 20 hours of community service (sophomore year), 25 hours of community service (junior year), 40 hours of community service (senior year).

Special Academic Programs 1 Advanced Placement exam for which test preparation is offered; honors section; independent study; study at local college for college credit; academic accommodation for the gifted, the musically talented, and the artistically talented; remedial reading and/or remedial writing; remedial math.

College Admission Counseling 41 students graduated in 2012; 37 went to college, including Felician College; Montclair State University; Pace University; Penn State University Park; Rutgers, The State University of New Jersey, New Brunswick; Seton Hall University. Median SAT critical reading: 450, median SAT math: 420, median SAT writing: 450. 10% scored over 600 on SAT critical reading, 2% scored over 600 on SAT math, 10% scored over 600 on SAT writing.

Student Life Upper grades have uniform requirement, student council. Discipline rests primarily with faculty. Attendance at religious services is required.

Summer Programs Remediation, enrichment, advancement, computer instruction programs offered; session focuses on prep and advancement for secondary school courses, make-up for failed classes; held on campus; accepts boys and girls; open to students from other schools. 75 students usually enrolled. 2013 schedule: June 27 to July 26. Application deadline: June 20.

Tuition and Aid Day student tuition: $8300. Tuition installment plan (monthly payment plans, Tuition Management Systems). Tuition reduction for siblings, merit scholarship grants, need-based scholarship grants available. In 2012–13, 45% of upper-school students received aid; total upper-school merit-scholarship money awarded: $20,000. Total amount of financial aid awarded in 2012–13: $111,850.

Admissions Traditional secondary-level entrance grade is 9. For fall 2012, 130 students applied for upper-level admission, 117 were accepted, 46 enrolled. Cooperative Entrance Exam (McGraw-Hill) required. Deadline for receipt of application materials: none. Application fee required: $125. On-campus interview recommended.

Athletics Interscholastic: basketball, cheering, dance, dance team, drill team, softball, track and field, volleyball; intramural: basketball, dance, dance team, fitness, physical fitness, soccer, softball, tennis, track and field, weight training, winter (indoor) track. 2 PE instructors, 6 coaches.

Computers Computers are regularly used in all academic classes. Computer resources include on-campus library services, Internet access, wireless campus network, Internet filtering or blocking technology. Student e-mail accounts and computer access in designated common areas are available to students. Students grades are available online. The school has a published electronic and media policy.

Contact Ms. Christina Morelli, Admissions Officer. 973-762-9222 Ext. 23. Fax: 973-378-7975. E-mail: cmorelli@marylawn.us. Web site: www.marylawn.us

THE MARY LOUIS ACADEMY

176-21 Wexford Terrace
Jamaica Estates, New York 11432-2926

Head of School: Sr. Kathleen M. McKinney, EdD

General Information Girls' day college-preparatory, arts, religious studies, and technology school, affiliated with Roman Catholic Church. Grades 9–12. Founded: 1936. Setting: suburban. Nearest major city is New York. 5-acre campus. 8 buildings on campus. Approved or accredited by Middle States Association of Colleges and Schools, National Catholic Education Association, New York Department of Education, New York State Board of Regents, and New York Department of Education. Endowment: $3 million. Total enrollment: 909. Upper school average class size: 25. Upper school faculty-student ratio: 1:13. There are 180 required school days per year for Upper School students. Upper School students typically attend 5 days per week. The average school day consists of 6 hours and 30 minutes.

Upper School Student Profile Grade 9: 211 students (211 girls); Grade 10: 219 students (219 girls); Grade 11: 252 students (252 girls); Grade 12: 227 students (227 girls). 74.5% of students are Roman Catholic.

Faculty School total: 75. In upper school: 17 men, 58 women; 65 have advanced degrees.

Subjects Offered 3-dimensional art, 3-dimensional design, Advanced Placement courses, advanced studio art-AP, American history, art, astronomy, biology, business skills, calculus, career exploration, chemistry, college admission preparation, college planning, composition, computer science, current events, drawing, driver education, earth science, economics, engineering, English, English literature, European history, family studies, fine arts, first aid, forensics, French, government/civics, health and wellness, health science, history, human development, Italian, Latin, law, leadership, leadership and service, literature, mathematics, microbiology, music, music theory, nutrition, painting, physical education, physics, political science, religion, robotics, SAT preparation, science, sculpture, social studies, Spanish, speech and debate, vocal music, women in society, women's health, world history, world literature.

Graduation Requirements Arts and fine arts (art, music, dance, drama), English, foreign language, mathematics, music, physical education (includes health), religion (includes Bible studies and theology), science, social studies (includes history), technology, service project.

Special Academic Programs Advanced Placement exam preparation; honors section; study at local college for college credit; academic accommodation for the musically talented and the artistically talented; programs in general development for dyslexic students.

College Admission Counseling 235 students graduated in 2012; all went to college, including Adelphi University; Binghamton University, State University of New York; Hunter College of the City University of New York; Queens College of the City University of New York; St. John's University; St. Joseph's College, New York.

Student Life Upper grades have uniform requirement, student council. Discipline rests primarily with faculty. Attendance at religious services is required.

Summer Programs Remediation, enrichment, sports, art/fine arts programs offered; session focuses on Regents Competency Test preparation, Athletic Camps, Junior High student enrichment; held on campus; accepts girls; open to students from other schools. 100 students usually enrolled. 2013 schedule: July 5 to August 15. Application deadline: June 30.

Tuition and Aid Day student tuition: $7600. Tuition installment plan (monthly payment plans, quarterly payment plan, tuition in full (yearly)). Tuition reduction for siblings, merit scholarship grants, need-based scholarship grants available. In 2012–13, 22% of upper-school students received aid; total upper-school merit-scholarship money awarded: $386,200. Total amount of financial aid awarded in 2012–13: $421,200.

Admissions Traditional secondary-level entrance grade is 9. For fall 2012, 992 students applied for upper-level admission, 413 were accepted, 212 enrolled. Catholic High School Entrance Examination required. Deadline for receipt of application materials: February 1. Application fee required: $300. Interview recommended.

Athletics Interscholastic: aerobics, aerobics/dance, archery, badminton, basketball, billiards, bowling, cheering, cross-country running, dance, dance team, golf, gymnastics, indoor track, indoor track & field, lacrosse, running, self defense, soccer, softball, swimming and diving, tennis, track and field, volleyball, winter (indoor) track, yoga; intramural: basketball, billiards, fitness, self defense, soccer, yoga. 4 PE instructors, 32 coaches.

Computers Computers are regularly used in career exploration, college planning, English, foreign language, history, mathematics, music, science classes. Computer network features include on-campus library services, online commercial services, Internet access, wireless campus network, Internet filtering or blocking technology. Campus intranet and student e-mail accounts are available to students. Students grades are available online. The school has a published electronic and media policy.

Contact Sr. Lorraine O'Neill, CSJ, Administrative Secretary. 718-297-2120 Ext. 228. Fax: 718-739-0037. E-mail: loneill@tmla.org. Web site: www.tmla.org

MARYMOUNT HIGH SCHOOL

10643 Sunset Boulevard
Los Angeles, California 90077

Head of School: Ms. Jacqueline Landry

General Information Girls' day college-preparatory, arts, religious studies, and technology school, affiliated with Roman Catholic Church. Grades 9–12. Founded: 1923. Setting: suburban. 6-acre campus. 6 buildings on campus. Approved or accredited by California Association of Independent Schools, Western Association of Schools and Colleges, Western Catholic Education Association, and California Department of Education. Member of National Association of Independent Schools. Endowment: $5.1 million. Total enrollment: 372. Upper school average class size: 15. Upper school faculty-student ratio: 1:7. There are 170 required school days per year for Upper School students. Upper School students typically attend 5 days per week. The average school day consists of 6 hours and 15 minutes.

Upper School Student Profile Grade 9: 103 students (103 girls); Grade 10: 91 students (91 girls); Grade 11: 83 students (83 girls); Grade 12: 95 students (95 girls). 67% of students are Roman Catholic.

Faculty School total: 50. In upper school: 13 men, 37 women; 41 have advanced degrees.

Subjects Offered Acting, advanced studio art-AP, aerobics, African literature, algebra, American history, American legal systems, American literature, anatomy, art, art history, art-AP, biology, biology-AP, British literature, calculus, calculus-AP, ceramics, chemistry, choir, Christian testament, community service, computer literacy, computer science, contemporary issues, dance, death and loss, design, drama, drawing, ecology, economics, English, English literature, environmental science, environmental science-AP, ethics, fencing, film, fine arts, French, French-AP, gender and religion, geography, geometry, government/civics, Hebrew scripture, human development, Japanese literature, jazz ensemble, journalism, language and composition, literary magazine, literature, literature-AP, music, musical productions, painting, peace studies, performing arts, photography, physical education, physics, physiology, pre-calculus, printmaking, psychology, religion, religious studies, robotics, science, self-defense, social justice, social studies, softball, Spanish, Spanish language-AP, Spanish literature-AP, speech, swimming, theology, trigonometry, U.S. government and politics-AP, U.S. history, U.S. history-AP, vocal music, volleyball, women's studies, world religions, writing.

Graduation Requirements Arts and fine arts (art, music, dance, drama), English, foreign language, mathematics, performing arts, physical education (includes health), religion (includes Bible studies and theology), science, social studies (includes history), 100 hours of community service.

Special Academic Programs 18 Advanced Placement exams for which test preparation is offered; honors section; independent study.

College Admission Counseling 90 students graduated in 2012; 87 went to college, including Boston College; Boston University; New York University; Southern Methodist University; University of California, Santa Cruz; University of Southern California. Other: 1 went to work, 2 entered a postgraduate year. Mean SAT critical reading: 621, mean SAT math: 601, mean SAT writing: 665, mean combined SAT: 1887, mean composite ACT: 26.

Student Life Upper grades have uniform requirement, student council, honor system. Discipline rests equally with students and faculty. Attendance at religious services is required.

Summer Programs Remediation, enrichment, advancement, sports, art/fine arts, computer instruction programs offered; session focuses on enrichment, advancement; held on campus; accepts girls; open to students from other schools. 100 students usually enrolled. 2013 schedule: June 24 to July 26. Application deadline: June 1.

Tuition and Aid Day student tuition: $27,650. Tuition installment plan (FACTS Tuition Payment Plan). Merit scholarship grants, need-based scholarship grants available. In 2012–13, 24% of upper-school students received aid; total upper-school merit-scholarship money awarded: $13,000. Total amount of financial aid awarded in 2012–13: $1,205,000.

Admissions Traditional secondary-level entrance grade is 9. For fall 2012, 267 students applied for upper-level admission, 189 were accepted, 109 enrolled. ISEE required. Deadline for receipt of application materials: January 14. Application fee required: $100. On-campus interview required.

Athletics Interscholastic: basketball, cross-country running, equestrian sports, golf, soccer, softball, swimming and diving, tennis, track and field, volleyball, water polo; intramural: aerobics, aerobics/dance, archery, crew, dance, fitness, physical fitness, self defense, strength & conditioning. 1 PE instructor, 29 coaches, 1 athletic trainer.

Computers Computers are regularly used in all academic classes. Computer network features include on-campus library services, online commercial services, Internet access, wireless campus network, Internet filtering or blocking technology, one to one student laptop program, access to UCLA Library, Loyola Marymount University Library, 14 independent high school libraries. Campus intranet, student e-mail accounts, and computer access in designated common areas are available to students. Students grades are available online. The school has a published electronic and media policy.

Contact Ms. Sarah Jallo, Director of Admission. 310-472-1205 Ext. 306. Fax: 310-440-4316. E-mail: sjallo@mhs-la.org. Web site: www.mhs-la.org

MARYMOUNT INTERNATIONAL SCHOOL

Via di Villa Lauchli 180
Rome 00191, Italy

Head of School: Ms. Maria Castelluccio

General Information Coeducational day college-preparatory school, affiliated with Roman Catholic Church. Grades PK–12. Founded: 1946. Setting: suburban. 16-acre campus. 3 buildings on campus. Approved or accredited by New England Association of Schools and Colleges. Member of European Council of International Schools. Language of instruction: English. Total enrollment: 624. Upper school average class size: 18. Upper school faculty-student ratio: 1:15. There are 170 required school days per year for Upper School students. Upper School students typically attend 5 days per week. The average school day consists of 6 hours and 45 minutes.

Upper School Student Profile Grade 9: 51 students (32 boys, 19 girls); Grade 10: 54 students (20 boys, 34 girls); Grade 11: 50 students (22 boys, 28 girls); Grade 12: 57 students (36 boys, 21 girls). 75% of students are Roman Catholic.

Faculty School total: 84. In upper school: 13 men, 34 women; 40 have advanced degrees.

Subjects Offered Algebra, American history, American literature, art, art history, art history-AP, biology, calculus, ceramics, chemistry, computer science, current events, drama, English, English literature, environmental science, ESL, European history, fine arts, French, geography, geometry, health, history, International Baccalaureate courses, international relations, Italian, Latin, mathematics, music, photography, physical education, physics, pre-calculus, psychology, religious education, science, social studies, Spanish, study skills, theater arts, theory of knowledge, trigonometry, world history.

Graduation Requirements Arts and fine arts (art, music, dance, drama), English, foreign language, mathematics, physical education (includes health), religion (includes Bible studies and theology), science, social studies (includes history).

Special Academic Programs International Baccalaureate program; ESL (30 students enrolled).

College Admission Counseling 51 students graduated in 2012; 49 went to college, including Boston University; New York University; Rensselaer Polytechnic Institute; The Johns Hopkins University; University of Southern California; University of Virginia. Other: 2 had other specific plans. Median SAT critical reading: 500, median SAT math: 500, median SAT writing: 520. 15% scored over 600 on SAT critical reading, 15% scored over 600 on SAT math, 15% scored over 600 on SAT writing.

Student Life Upper grades have specified standards of dress, student council, honor system. Discipline rests primarily with faculty. Attendance at religious services is required.

Tuition and Aid Day student tuition: €18,400.

Admissions Traditional secondary-level entrance grade is 9. For fall 2012, 52 students applied for upper-level admission, 38 were accepted, 24 enrolled. English proficiency or writing sample required. Deadline for receipt of application materials: none. Application fee required: €350. On-campus interview recommended.

Athletics Interscholastic: basketball (boys, girls), cheering (g), cross-country running (b,g), soccer (b,g), tennis (b,g), track and field (b,g), volleyball (b,g). 2 PE instructors, 9 coaches.

Computers Computers are regularly used in graphic arts classes. Computer network features include on-campus library services, Internet access, wireless campus network, Internet filtering or blocking technology, one to one laptop program in the middle school. Student e-mail accounts are available to students.

Contact Ms. Deborah Woods, Admissions Director. 39-063629101 Ext. 212. Fax: 39-0636301738. E-mail: admissions@marymountrome.org. Web site: www.marymountrome.org

MARYMOUNT SCHOOL OF NEW YORK

1026 Fifth Avenue
New York, New York 10028

General Information Coeducational day (boys' only in lower grades) college-preparatory, arts, religious studies, and technology school, affiliated with Roman Catholic Church. Boys grades N–PK, girls grades N–12. Founded: 1926. Setting: urban. 3 buildings on campus. Approved or accredited by New York State Association of Independent Schools. Member of National Association of Independent Schools. Endowment: $800,000. Total enrollment: 608. Upper school average class size: 15. Upper school faculty-student ratio: 1:6. The average school day consists of 7 hours and 30 minutes.

See Display below and Close-Up on page 602.

MARY STAR OF THE SEA HIGH SCHOOL

2500 North Taper Avenue
San Pedro, California 90731

Head of School: Ms. Rita Dever

General Information Coeducational day college-preparatory and religious studies school, affiliated with Roman Catholic Church. Grades 9–12. Founded: 1954. Setting: urban. 1-acre campus. 2 buildings on campus. Approved or accredited by Western Association of Schools and Colleges and California Department of Education. Total enrollment: 517. Upper school average class size: 25. Upper school faculty-student ratio: 1:17. There are 180 required school days per year for Upper School students. Upper School students typically attend 5 days per week. The average school day consists of 6 hours and 20 minutes.

Upper School Student Profile Grade 9: 120 students (63 boys, 57 girls); Grade 10: 137 students (76 boys, 61 girls); Grade 11: 132 students (62 boys, 70 girls); Grade 12: 120 students (63 boys, 57 girls). 96% of students are Roman Catholic.

Faculty School total: 31. In upper school: 19 men, 12 women; 27 have advanced degrees.

Subjects Offered Advanced Placement courses, algebra, American government, American literature, American literature-AP, anatomy and physiology, art, art history, biology, British literature, calculus, calculus-AP, chemistry, choir, consumer mathematics, economics, European history-AP, geometry, government, government-AP, health education, honors algebra, honors English, honors geometry, honors U.S. history, honors world history, human anatomy, Latin, marine biology, physics, pre-algebra, psychology, religion, Spanish, U.S. government and politics-AP, U.S. history, U.S. history-AP, Western civilization.

Graduation Requirements American literature, biology, British literature, chemistry, economics, English, foreign language, geography, geometry, government, religion (includes Bible studies and theology), world history, world literature, service hours.

Special Academic Programs Advanced Placement exam preparation; honors section.

College Admission Counseling 128 students graduated in 2011; 127 went to college, including California State University, Dominguez Hills; California State University, Fullerton; California State University, Long Beach; El Camino College; University of California, Irvine; University of California, San Diego. Other: 1 entered military service.

Student Life Upper grades have uniform requirement, student council. Discipline rests primarily with faculty. Attendance at religious services is required.

Tuition and Aid Day student tuition: $7300. Tuition installment plan (SMART Tuition Payment Plan). Tuition reduction for siblings, merit scholarship grants, need-based scholarship grants available. In 2011–12, 15% of upper-school students received aid. Total amount of financial aid awarded in 2011–12: $145,000.

Admissions Traditional secondary-level entrance grade is 9. Deadline for receipt of application materials: January 21. Application fee required: $75. Interview required.

Athletics Interscholastic: baseball (boys), basketball (b,g), cheering (g), cross-country running (b,g), dance squad (g), football (b), soccer (b,g), softball (g), track and field (b,g), volleyball (b,g); coed interscholastic: swimming and diving. 1 PE instructor, 20 coaches.

Computers Computer resources include on-campus library services, Internet access, wireless campus network, Internet filtering or blocking technology. Computer access in designated common areas is available to students. Students grades are available online. The school has a published electronic and media policy.

Contact Mrs. Nancy Phillips, Registrar. 310-547-1130. Fax: 310-547-1827. E-mail: nphillips@marystarhigh.com. Web site:

THE MASTER'S SCHOOL

36 Westledge Road
West Simsbury, Connecticut 06092-9400

Head of School: Jon F. Holley

General Information Coeducational day college-preparatory, arts, religious studies, and technology school, affiliated with Christian faith. Grades PK–12. Founded: 1970. Setting: suburban. Nearest major city is Hartford. 76-acre campus. 10 buildings on campus. Approved or accredited by Association of Christian Schools International, Connecticut Association of Independent Schools, New England Association of Schools and Colleges, and Connecticut Department of Education. Endowment: $34,000. Total enrollment: 330. Upper school average class size: 15. Upper school faculty-student ratio: 1:7.

Upper School Student Profile Grade 9: 34 students (14 boys, 20 girls); Grade 10: 30 students (16 boys, 14 girls); Grade 11: 31 students (19 boys, 12 girls); Grade 12: 31 students (15 boys, 16 girls).

Faculty School total: 40. In upper school: 9 men, 12 women; 8 have advanced degrees.

Subjects Offered Advanced computer applications, advanced studio art-AP, algebra, American history, American literature, applied music, art, art history, Bible studies, biology, biology-AP, British literature, British literature (honors), calculus, calculus-AP, chemistry, chemistry-AP, chorus, civics, community service, computer applications, computer education, computer literacy, computer math, computer programming, computer skills, creative writing, earth science, English, English literature, English literature-AP, English-AP, ethics, expository writing, fine arts, French, geometry, grammar, health education, history, honors algebra, honors English, honors geometry, honors U.S. history, independent study, instrumental music, keyboarding, mathematics, music, music composition, philosophy, photography, physical education, physics, science, senior seminar, social studies, Spanish, theology, trigonometry, Western civilization, world history, world literature, writing workshop, yearbook.

Graduation Requirements Arts and fine arts (art, music, dance, drama), computer education, English, foreign language, mathematics, physical education (includes health), religion (includes Bible studies and theology), science, senior seminar, social studies (includes history).

Special Academic Programs Advanced Placement exam preparation; honors section; independent study; study at local college for college credit; academic accommodation for the gifted, the musically talented, and the artistically talented.

College Admission Counseling 33 students graduated in 2011; 30 went to college, including Boston College; Grove City College; Hofstra University; Houghton College; Messiah College; University of Connecticut. Other: 3 had other specific plans. Mean SAT critical reading: 545, mean SAT math: 543, mean SAT writing: 522.

Student Life Upper grades have specified standards of dress, student council, honor system. Discipline rests primarily with faculty. Attendance at religious services is required.

Tuition and Aid Day student tuition: $16,500. Tuition installment plan (FACTS Tuition Payment Plan, single payment plan). Tuition reduction for siblings, merit scholarship grants, need-based scholarship grants available. In 2011–12, 35% of upper-school students received aid; total upper-school merit-scholarship money awarded: $25,000. Total amount of financial aid awarded in 2011–12: $250,000.

Admissions Traditional secondary-level entrance grade is 9. For fall 2011, 165 students applied for upper-level admission, 85 were accepted, 72 enrolled. SLEP for foreign students and SSAT required. Deadline for receipt of application materials: none. Application fee required: $50. On-campus interview required.

Athletics Interscholastic: baseball (boys), basketball (b,g), lacrosse (b,g), soccer (b,g), softball (g), ultimate Frisbee (b,g), volleyball (g); intramural: ballet (g), dance (b); coed interscholastic: alpine skiing, Frisbee, golf, skiing (downhill); coed intramural: alpine skiing, cooperative games, fitness, nordic skiing, physical fitness, physical training, skiing (downhill), snowboarding, strength & conditioning, weight lifting, weight training. 3 PE instructors, 12 coaches, 1 athletic trainer.

Computers Computers are regularly used in career education, college planning, computer applications, data processing, desktop publishing, graphic design, keyboarding, mathematics, science, typing, Web site design, word processing, yearbook classes. Computer network features include on-campus library services, Internet access, Internet filtering or blocking technology, MS Office Suite, educational software, digital photography and darkroom facility. Students grades are available online. The school has a published electronic and media policy.

Contact Adm. Robin Egan, Director of Admissions. 860-651-9361 Ext. 5001. Fax: 860-651-9363. E-mail: regan@masterschool.org. Web site: www.masterschool.org

THE MASTERS SCHOOL

49 Clinton Avenue
Dobbs Ferry, New York 10522

Head of School: Dr. Maureen Fonseca

General Information Coeducational boarding and day college-preparatory, arts, and technology school. Boarding grades 9–12, day grades 5–12. Founded: 1877. Setting: suburban. Nearest major city is New York. Students are housed in single-sex dormitories. 96-acre campus. 13 buildings on campus. Approved or accredited by Middle States Association of Colleges and Schools, New York State Association of Independent Schools, The Association of Boarding Schools, and New York Department of Education. Member of National Association of Independent Schools and Secondary School Admission Test Board. Endowment: $25.5 million. Total enrollment: 603. Upper school average class size: 14. Upper school faculty-student ratio: 1:8. Upper School students typically attend 5 days per week. The average school day consists of 6 hours.

Upper School Student Profile Grade 9: 90 students (37 boys, 53 girls); Grade 10: 122 students (55 boys, 67 girls); Grade 11: 110 students (48 boys, 62 girls); Grade 12: 116 students (57 boys, 59 girls). 40% of students are boarding students. 70% are state residents. 17 states are represented in upper school student body. 16% are international students. International students from China, Germany, Republic of Korea, Russian Federation, Switzerland, and Taiwan; 16 other countries represented in student body.

Faculty School total: 97. In upper school: 37 men, 50 women; 70 have advanced degrees; 60 reside on campus.

Subjects Offered Acting, algebra, American history, American literature, art history, biology, biology-AP, calculus, calculus-AP, ceramics, chemistry, chemistry-AP, computer math, computer programming, computer science, creative writing, dance, drama, driver education, earth science, electronics, English, English language-AP, English literature, English literature-AP, environmental science, ESL, ethics, European history, European history-AP, expository writing, fine arts, French, French language-AP, French literature-AP, geography, geometry, grammar, health, health and wellness, health education, jazz, jazz band, journalism, Latin, Latin-AP, mathematics, meteorology, music, music theory-AP, performing arts, photography, physical education, physics, physics-AP, pre-calculus, religion, science, senior thesis, social studies, Spanish, Spanish language-AP, Spanish literature-AP, speech, statistics, statistics-AP, studio art, studio art-AP, theater, trigonometry, U.S. history, U.S. history-AP, world history, world literature, world religions, writing, yearbook, yoga.

Graduation Requirements Arts and fine arts (art, music, dance, drama), computer science, English, foreign language, health, mathematics, physical education (includes health), public speaking, science, U.S. history, world history, world religions.

Special Academic Programs 19 Advanced Placement exams for which test preparation is offered; honors section; independent study; term-away projects; study at local college for college credit; study abroad; academic accommodation for the gifted, the musically talented, and the artistically talented; ESL (20 students enrolled).

College Admission Counseling 95 students graduated in 2011; all went to college, including Cornell University; Middlebury College; New York University; The Johns Hopkins University; University of Chicago; Williams College. Mean SAT critical reading: 660, mean SAT math: 630, mean SAT writing: 700, mean combined SAT: 1990. 61% scored over 600 on SAT critical reading, 57% scored over 600 on SAT math, 68% scored over 600 on SAT writing, 58% scored over 1800 on combined SAT.

Student Life Upper grades have specified standards of dress, student council. Discipline rests equally with students and faculty.

Tuition and Aid Day student tuition: $33,830; 7-day tuition and room/board: $47,780. Tuition installment plan (Insured Tuition Payment Plan, Key Tuition Payment Plan, monthly payment plans, individually arranged payment plans). Need-based scholarship grants available. In 2011–12, 25% of upper-school students received aid. Total amount of financial aid awarded in 2011–12: $4,000,000.

Admissions Traditional secondary-level entrance grade is 9. For fall 2011, 520 students applied for upper-level admission, 243 were accepted, 156 enrolled. ISEE, SSAT or TOEFL required. Deadline for receipt of application materials: February 1. Application fee required: $50. Interview required.

Athletics Interscholastic: baseball (boys), basketball (b,g), cross-country running (b,g), fencing (b,g), field hockey (g), lacrosse (b,g), soccer (b,g), softball (g), tennis (b,g), volleyball (g); coed interscholastic: dance, dance team, golf, indoor track, track and field; coed intramural: aerobics, aerobics/dance, aerobics/Nautilus, combined training, dance squad, dance team, fitness, Frisbee, martial arts, modern dance, outdoor activities, physical fitness, physical training, strength & conditioning, ultimate Frisbee, weight lifting, weight training, yoga. 2 PE instructors, 13 coaches, 1 athletic trainer.

Computers Computers are regularly used in computer applications, English, foreign language, graphic arts, graphic design, history, mathematics, newspaper, photography, programming, publications, science, senior seminar, study skills, video film production, Web site design, writing, yearbook classes. Computer network features include on-campus library services, online commercial services, Internet access, wireless campus network, Internet filtering or blocking technology. Student e-mail accounts and computer access in designated common areas are available to students. The school has a published electronic and media policy.

Contact Office of Admission. 914-479-6420. Fax: 914-693-7295. E-mail: admission@mastersny.org. Web site: www.mastersny.org

MATIGNON HIGH SCHOOL

One Matignon Road
Cambridge, Massachusetts 02140

Head of School: Mr. Thomas F. Galligani

General Information Coeducational day college-preparatory, arts, business, religious studies, and technology school, affiliated with Roman Catholic Church. Grades 9–12. Founded: 1945. Setting: suburban. Nearest major city is Boston. 10-acre campus. 3 buildings on campus. Approved or accredited by Association of Independent Schools in New England, National Catholic Education Association, New England Association of Schools and Colleges, and Massachusetts Department of Education. Endowment: $253,000. Total enrollment: 464. Upper school average class size: 18. Upper school faculty-student ratio: 1:18. Upper School students typically attend 5 days per week. The average school day consists of 7 hours.

Upper School Student Profile Grade 9: 118 students (49 boys, 69 girls); Grade 10: 110 students (47 boys, 63 girls); Grade 11: 120 students (53 boys, 67 girls); Grade 12: 116 students (59 boys, 57 girls). 75% of students are Roman Catholic.

Faculty School total: 37. In upper school: 15 men, 22 women; 23 have advanced degrees.

Subjects Offered 3-dimensional art, 3-dimensional design, accounting, adolescent issues, Advanced Placement courses, algebra, American history, American literature, anatomy and physiology, art, art history, Bible studies, biology, calculus, chemistry, community service, computer science, drawing and design, economics, English, English literature, environmental science, fine arts, French, geometry, government/civics, grammar, health, history, Latin, law, mathematics, physical education, physics, psychology, religion, science, social sciences, social studies, Spanish, theology, trigonometry, world history, writing.

Graduation Requirements 20th century history, accounting, Advanced Placement courses, algebra, American history, anatomy and physiology, arts and fine arts (art, music, dance, drama), chemistry, computer science, English-AP, French, French-AP, geometry, health education, honors algebra, honors English, honors geometry, honors world history, Latin, law, physical education (includes health), psychology, religious studies, SAT preparation, senior internship, Spanish, Spanish-AP, U.S. history, U.S. history-AP, world cultures, world history, Christian service, 45 hours of community service (before junior year).

Special Academic Programs Advanced Placement exam preparation; honors section; independent study; study at local college for college credit; study abroad; ESL (20 students enrolled).

College Admission Counseling 100 students graduated in 2012; 98 went to college, including Boston University; Northeastern University; Saint Anselm College; Suffolk University; University of Massachusetts Amherst; University of Massachusetts Boston. Other: 2 entered military service. Mean SAT critical reading: 500, mean SAT math: 530, mean SAT writing: 503, mean combined SAT: 1533. 21% scored over 600 on SAT critical reading, 23% scored over 600 on SAT math, 14% scored over 600 on SAT writing, 20% scored over 1800 on combined SAT.

Student Life Upper grades have uniform requirement, student council, honor system. Discipline rests primarily with faculty. Attendance at religious services is required.

Summer Programs Remediation, enrichment programs offered; held on campus; accepts boys and girls; open to students from other schools. 80 students usually enrolled. 2013 schedule: June 27 to August 12. Application deadline: none.

Tuition and Aid Day student tuition: $8900. Tuition installment plan (FACTS Tuition Payment Plan, monthly payment plans). Merit scholarship grants, need-based scholarship grants available. In 2012–13, 50% of upper-school students received aid; total upper-school merit-scholarship money awarded: $100,000. Total amount of financial aid awarded in 2012–13: $300,000.

Admissions Traditional secondary-level entrance grade is 9. For fall 2012, 440 students applied for upper-level admission, 390 were accepted, 118 enrolled. Catholic High School Entrance Examination, SSAT or TOEFL or SLEP required. Deadline for receipt of application materials: none. No application fee required. On-campus interview recommended.

Athletics Interscholastic: baseball (boys), basketball (b,g), cheering (g), cross-country running (b,g), football (b), ice hockey (b,g), lacrosse (b,g), soccer (b,g), softball (g), swimming and diving (b,g), tennis (b,g), track and field (b,g), volleyball (g); intramural: aerobics/dance (b,g), dance (b,g), dance squad (b,g), dance team (b,g), figure skating (g), Frisbee (b,g), physical training (b,g), strength & conditioning (b,g), weight lifting (b,g), weight training (b,g); coed interscholastic: golf; coed intramural: table tennis, yoga. 1 PE instructor, 20 coaches, 1 athletic trainer.

Computers Computers are regularly used in all academic classes. Computer network features include on-campus library services, Internet access, wireless campus network, Internet filtering or blocking technology, all academic homework is provided online. Student e-mail accounts and computer access in designated common areas are available to students. Students grades are available online.

Contact Mr. Joseph A. DiSarcina, Principal. 617-876-1212 Ext. 14. Fax: 617-661-3905. E-mail: jdisarcina@matignon-hs.org. Web site: www.matignon-hs.org

MAUI PREPARATORY ACADEMY

5095 Napilihau Street, #109B
PMB #186
Lahaina, Hawaii 96761

Head of School: Mr. George C. Baker

General Information Coeducational boarding and day and distance learning college-preparatory, arts, technology, and Project Based 21st Century Skills school. Grades PK–12. Distance learning grade X. Founded: 2005. Setting: small town. Students are housed in homestay. 20-acre campus. 7 buildings on campus. Approved or accredited by The Hawaii Council of Private Schools, Western Association of Schools and Colleges, and Hawaii Department of Education. Total enrollment: 200. Upper school average class size: 13. Upper school faculty-student ratio: 1:5. There are 178 required school days per year for Upper School students. Upper School students typically attend 5 days per week. The average school day consists of 5 hours and 45 minutes.

Upper School Student Profile Grade 9: 13 students (7 boys, 6 girls); Grade 10: 12 students (5 boys, 7 girls); Grade 11: 15 students (8 boys, 7 girls); Grade 12: 18 students (8 boys, 10 girls). 6% of students are boarding students. 4% are state residents. 2 states are represented in upper school student body. 2% are international students. International students from Canada and Japan.

Faculty School total: 21. In upper school: 8 men, 3 women; 9 have advanced degrees.

Subjects Offered Art, biology, calculus, chemistry, English, environmental science, foreign language, health, history, mathematics, physics, social studies, technology.

Graduation Requirements 1 1/2 elective credits, algebra, all academic, art, athletics, biology, chemistry, college planning, English, foreign language, geometry, science project, 25 hours of community service per year, two varsity teams per year.

Special Academic Programs Advanced Placement exam preparation; independent study; study at local college for college credit.

College Admission Counseling Colleges students went to include Chapman University; University of Miami; University of Oregon; University of San Diego; Utah State University. Mean SAT critical reading: 511, mean SAT math: 541, mean SAT writing: 525.

Student Life Upper grades have uniform requirement, student council, honor system. Discipline rests equally with students and faculty.

Tuition and Aid Day student tuition: $15,910; 7-day tuition and room/board: $27,000. Tuition installment plan (Insured Tuition Payment Plan, FACTS Tuition Payment Plan, monthly payment plans). Tuition reduction for siblings, merit scholarship grants, need-based scholarship grants available. In 2012–13, 40% of upper-school students received aid; total upper-school merit-scholarship money awarded: $123,697. Total amount of financial aid awarded in 2012–13: $465,785.

Admissions Traditional secondary-level entrance grade is 9. For fall 2012, 20 students applied for upper-level admission, 17 were accepted, 15 enrolled. CTP and ERB Mathematics required. Deadline for receipt of application materials: March 30. Application fee required: $100. Interview required.

Athletics Interscholastic: aquatics (boys, girls), canoeing/kayaking (b,g), cross-country running (b,g), golf (b), independent competitive sports (b,g), ocean paddling (b,g), surfing (b,g), swimming and diving (b,g), tennis (b,g), track and field (b,g), volleyball (g); intramural: basketball (b,g), surfing (b,g), windsurfing (b,g); coed interscholastic: ocean paddling; coed intramural: basketball, surfing, windsurfing. 1 PE instructor, 9 coaches.

Computers Computers are regularly used in all classes. Computer network features include on-campus library services, Internet access, wireless campus network. Campus intranet and student e-mail accounts are available to students. Students grades are available online. The school has a published electronic and media policy.

Contact Mrs. Cathi Minami, Admissions Coordinator. 808-665-9966. Fax: 808-665-1075. E-mail: cminami@mauiprep.org. Web site: www.mauiprep.org

MAUR HILL-MOUNT ACADEMY

1000 Green Street
Atchison, Kansas 66002

Head of School: Mr. Phil Baniewicz

General Information Coeducational boarding and day college-preparatory, arts, religious studies, bilingual studies, and English as a Second language school, affiliated with Roman Catholic Church. Grades 9–12. Founded: 1863. Setting: small town. Nearest major city is Kansas City, MO. Students are housed in single-sex dormitories. 90-acre campus. 7 buildings on campus. Approved or accredited by National Catholic Education Association, North Central Association of Colleges and Schools, The Association of Boarding Schools, and Kansas Department of Education. Member of Secondary School Admission Test Board. Total enrollment: 195. Upper school average class size: 17. Upper school faculty-student ratio: 1:9. There are 182 required school days per year for Upper School students. Upper School students typically attend 5 days per week. The average school day consists of 6 hours and 30 minutes.

Upper School Student Profile Grade 9: 43 students (23 boys, 20 girls); Grade 10: 51 students (25 boys, 26 girls); Grade 11: 51 students (27 boys, 24 girls); Grade 12: 50 students (24 boys, 26 girls). 40% of students are boarding students. 50% are state residents. 14 states are represented in upper school student body. 28% are international students. International students from China, Mexico, Republic of Korea, Saudi Arabia, Spain, and Sweden; 9 other countries represented in student body. 65% of students are Roman Catholic.

Faculty School total: 21. In upper school: 13 men, 8 women; 11 have advanced degrees; 3 reside on campus.

Subjects Offered Algebra, American history, American literature, anatomy, art, Bible studies, biology, calculus, chemistry, computer science, drama, economics, English, English literature, ESL, fine arts, geography, geometry, government/civics, grammar, health, history, journalism, mathematics, music, photography, physical education, physics, physiology, psychology, religion, science, social sciences, social studies, sociology, Spanish, speech, theater, theology, trigonometry, typing, world history, world literature, writing.

Graduation Requirements Arts and fine arts (art, music, dance, drama), business skills (includes word processing), computer science, English, foreign language, mathematics, physical education (includes health), religion (includes Bible studies and theology), science, social sciences, social studies (includes history).

Special Academic Programs Advanced Placement exam preparation; honors section; study at local college for college credit; academic accommodation for the gifted; special instructional classes for students with Attention Deficit Disorder; ESL (15 students enrolled).

College Admission Counseling 51 students graduated in 2012; 50 went to college, including Benedictine College; Penn State University Park; Saint Louis University; The University of Kansas; The University of Texas at Austin. Other: 1 entered military service.

Student Life Upper grades have uniform requirement, student council, honor system. Discipline rests primarily with faculty. Attendance at religious services is required.

Summer Programs ESL programs offered; session focuses on activities camp, ESL program; held on campus; accepts boys and girls; open to students from other schools. 17 students usually enrolled. 2013 schedule: July 5 to August 12. Application deadline: June 1.

Tuition and Aid 5-day tuition and room/board: $18,900; 7-day tuition and room/board: $20,500. Tuition installment plan (monthly payment plans, individually arranged payment plans, Sallie Mae). Tuition reduction for siblings, merit scholarship grants, need-based scholarship grants, need-based loans, paying campus jobs available. In 2012–13, 40% of upper-school students received aid. Total amount of financial aid awarded in 2012–13: $291,000.

Admissions Traditional secondary-level entrance grade is 10. For fall 2012, 143 students applied for upper-level admission, 107 were accepted, 73 enrolled. High School Placement Test required. Deadline for receipt of application materials: none. Application fee required: $50. Interview required.

Athletics Interscholastic: aquatics (girls), baseball (b), basketball (b,g), cheering (g), cross-country running (b,g), dance (g), dance squad (g), dance team (g), drill team (g), football (b), swimming and diving (g), tennis (b,g), track and field (b,g), volleyball (g); intramural: boxing (b), field hockey (b), fitness (b), flag football (b), floor hockey (b), football (b), running (b,g), skateboarding (b), skiing (downhill) (b,g), soccer (b,g), swimming and diving (b,g), touch football (b), track and field (b,g), weight lifting (b,g), weight training (b,g); coed interscholastic: bowling, golf, physical fitness, physical training, running, soccer, wrestling; coed intramural: baseball, basketball, Nautilus, physical fitness, physical training, roller blading, table tennis, tennis, volleyball, walking. 1 PE instructor, 10 coaches, 1 athletic trainer.

Computers Computer network features include on-campus library services, Internet access, wireless campus network, Internet filtering or blocking technology. Student e-mail accounts are available to students. Students grades are available online. The school has a published electronic and media policy.

Contact Mr. Deke Nolan, Admissions Director. 913-367-5482 Ext. 210. Fax: 913-367-5096. E-mail: admissions@mh-ma.com. Web site: www.mh-ma.com

MCDONOGH SCHOOL

8600 McDonogh Road
Owings Mills, Maryland 21117-0380

Head of School: Charles W. Britton

General Information Coeducational boarding and day college-preparatory school. Boarding grades 9–12, day grades K–12. Founded: 1873. Setting: suburban. Nearest major city is Baltimore. Students are housed in single-sex dormitories. 800-acre campus. 44 buildings on campus. Approved or accredited by Association of Independent Maryland Schools. Member of National Association of Independent Schools. Endowment: $83 million. Total enrollment: 1,289. Upper school average class size: 15. Upper school faculty-student ratio: 1:9. There are 169 required school days per year for Upper School students. Upper School students typically attend 5 days per week. The average school day consists of 6 hours and 10 minutes.

Upper School Student Profile Grade 9: 149 students (76 boys, 73 girls); Grade 10: 148 students (79 boys, 69 girls); Grade 11: 146 students (77 boys, 69 girls); Grade 12: 145 students (73 boys, 72 girls). 5% of students are boarding students. 98% are state residents. 4 states are represented in upper school student body. 1% are international students.

Faculty School total: 177. In upper school: 35 men, 48 women; 60 have advanced degrees; 35 reside on campus.

Subjects Offered 20th century American writers, acting, Advanced Placement courses, African history, African literature, African-American studies, algebra, American history, American history-AP, American literature, American literature-AP, anatomy, art, art history, art-AP, Asian studies, band, biology, biology-AP, botany, calculus, calculus-AP, ceramics, chemistry, chemistry-AP, Chesapeake Bay studies, classical Greek literature, composition-AP, computer animation, computer graphics, computer music, computer programming, computer science, computer science-AP, concert band, concert choir, creative writing, dance, drama, drawing, ecology, economics, economics-AP, electives, engineering, English, English composition, English literature, English literature and composition-AP, English literature-AP, English-AP, English/composition-AP, environmental science, environmental science-AP, ethics, European history, film, film and literature, fine arts, fitness, foreign language, French, French language-AP, French literature-AP, French-AP, genetics, geology, geometry, German, German-AP, government and politics-AP, government-AP, government/civics, health and wellness, history, history-AP, honors algebra, honors English, honors geometry, honors U.S. history, honors world history, jazz band, jazz dance, journalism, language-AP, languages, Latin, Latin American literature, linguistics, literature and composition-AP, literature by women, marine biology, mathematics, Middle Eastern history, music, music theory, music theory-AP, oceanography, photography, physical education, physical fitness, physics, poetry, pre-calculus, psychology, religion, Russian history, science, senior project, set design, Shakespeare, short story, Spanish, Spanish language-AP, Spanish literature, Spanish literature-AP, Spanish-AP, speech, speech communications, statistics-AP, tap dance, theater, trigonometry, U.S. government and politics-AP, U.S. history, U.S. history-AP, video, visual arts, Web site design, woodworking, world history, world history-AP, world religions, world wide web design, writing workshop, yearbook.

Graduation Requirements Arts and fine arts (art, music, dance, drama), English, foreign language, mathematics, physical education (includes health), science, senior project, social studies (includes history). Community service is required.

Special Academic Programs Advanced Placement exam preparation; honors section; independent study; term-away projects.

College Admission Counseling 145 students graduated in 2012; all went to college, including Davidson College; Harvard University; The George Washington University; The Johns Hopkins University; University of Maryland, College Park; Wake Forest University. Mean SAT critical reading: 615, mean SAT math: 628, mean SAT writing: 606, mean combined SAT: 1850, mean composite ACT: 27.

Student Life Upper grades have uniform requirement, student council, honor system. Discipline rests primarily with faculty.

Summer Programs Enrichment, ESL, sports, art/fine arts, computer instruction programs offered; session focuses on recreation and sports camps; held both on and off campus; held at Gunpowder Falls State Park and Chesapeake Bay; accepts boys and girls; open to students from other schools. 1,700 students usually enrolled. 2013 schedule: June 17 to July 26. Application deadline: May 1.

Tuition and Aid Day student tuition: $25,160; 5-day tuition and room/board: $33,830. Tuition installment plan (Key Tuition Payment Plan, monthly payment plans, individually arranged payment plans). Need-based scholarship grants, need-based

loans, middle-income loans available. In 2012–13, 24% of upper-school students received aid. Total amount of financial aid awarded in 2012–13: $2,415,935.
Admissions Traditional secondary-level entrance grade is 9. For fall 2012, 336 students applied for upper-level admission, 92 were accepted, 70 enrolled. ISEE required. Deadline for receipt of application materials: December 15. Application fee required: $50. On-campus interview required.
Athletics Interscholastic: aquatics (boys, girls), baseball (b), basketball (b,g), cross-country running (b,g), equestrian sports (b,g), field hockey (g), football (b), golf (b,g), indoor track & field (b,g), lacrosse (b,g), soccer (b,g), softball (g), swimming and diving (b,g), tennis (b,g), volleyball (g), water polo (b,g), winter (indoor) track (b,g), wrestling (b); coed interscholastic: cheering, equestrian sports, horseback riding, indoor track & field, squash, track and field; coed intramural: badminton, ballet, dance, fencing, fitness, squash, ultimate Frisbee. 14 PE instructors, 92 coaches, 2 athletic trainers.
Computers Computers are regularly used in all classes. Computer network features include on-campus library services, online commercial services, Internet access, wireless campus network, Internet filtering or blocking technology. Campus intranet, student e-mail accounts, and computer access in designated common areas are available to students. Students grades are available online. The school has a published electronic and media policy.
Contact Tim Fish, Director of Admissions. 410-581-4719. Fax: 410-998-3537. E-mail: tfish@mcdonogh.org. Web site: www.mcdonogh.org

MCGILL-TOOLEN CATHOLIC HIGH SCHOOL

1501 Old Shell Road
Mobile, Alabama 36604-2291

Head of School: Mrs. Michelle T. Haas

General Information Coeducational day college-preparatory, arts, religious studies, and technology school, affiliated with Roman Catholic Church. Grades 9–12. Founded: 1896. Setting: urban. 18-acre campus. 5 buildings on campus. Approved or accredited by Southern Association of Colleges and Schools and Alabama Department of Education. Total enrollment: 1,135. Upper school average class size: 21. Upper school faculty-student ratio: 1:14. There are 180 required school days per year for Upper School students. Upper School students typically attend 5 days per week. The average school day consists of 6 hours and 40 minutes.
Upper School Student Profile Grade 9: 311 students (181 boys, 130 girls); Grade 10: 295 students (164 boys, 131 girls); Grade 11: 263 students (127 boys, 136 girls); Grade 12: 266 students (130 boys, 136 girls). 90.4% of students are Roman Catholic.
Faculty School total: 81. In upper school: 36 men, 42 women; 51 have advanced degrees.
Subjects Offered 3-dimensional art, 3-dimensional design, ACT preparation, advanced biology, advanced chemistry, advanced math, Advanced Placement courses, American government, American history, American history-AP, American literature, analytic geometry, anatomy and physiology, athletic training, band, baseball, basketball, Bible studies, biology, biology-AP, British literature, British literature (honors), calculus, calculus-AP, campus ministry, Catholic belief and practice, ceramics, cheerleading, chemistry, chemistry-AP, choir, choral music, chorus, church history, conceptual physics, concert choir, current events, driver education, economics, English, English composition, English language and composition-AP, English-AP, French, geography, geometry, government, government and politics-AP, graphic design, health, health and wellness, history of the Catholic Church, honors algebra, honors English, honors geometry, honors U.S. history, honors world history, independent study, keyboarding, Latin, marine biology, modern European history-AP, modern world history, multimedia, music appreciation, painting, physical education, physical fitness, physics, physics-AP, pre-algebra, pre-calculus, psychology, reading, reading/study skills, softball, Spanish, Spanish language-AP, speech, studio art, studio art-AP, U.S. government, U.S. government and politics, U.S. government and politics-AP, U.S. history, U.S. history-AP, U.S. literature, video film production, vocal ensemble, volleyball, Web site design, weight fitness, weight training, world geography, world history, world history-AP, world literature, yearbook.
Graduation Requirements Electives, English, keyboarding, mathematics, physical education (includes health), religion (includes Bible studies and theology), science, social studies (includes history).
Special Academic Programs 14 Advanced Placement exams for which test preparation is offered; honors section; remedial reading and/or remedial writing; remedial math.
College Admission Counseling 294 students graduated in 2012; 279 went to college, including Auburn University; Louisiana State University and Agricultural and Mechanical College; Spring Hill College; The University of Alabama; University of South Alabama; University of Southern Mississippi. Other: 9 went to work, 6 entered military service. Median composite ACT: 24. 30% scored over 26 on composite ACT.
Student Life Upper grades have uniform requirement, student council. Discipline rests primarily with faculty. Attendance at religious services is required.
Summer Programs Remediation, enrichment programs offered; session focuses on math/reading/English transition to high school, remediation for religion courses; held on campus; accepts boys and girls; not open to students from other schools. 35 students usually enrolled. 2013 schedule: June 5 to June 27. Application deadline: May 29.
Tuition and Aid Day student tuition: $6500–$7800. Tuition installment plan (monthly payment plans, individually arranged payment plans). Tuition reduction for siblings, need-based scholarship grants available. In 2012–13, 26% of upper-school students received aid. Total amount of financial aid awarded in 2012–13: $958,000.
Admissions ACT-Explore required. Deadline for receipt of application materials: none. Application fee required: $100. On-campus interview recommended.
Athletics Interscholastic: baseball (boys), basketball (b,g), cheering (g), cross-country running (b,g), diving (b,g), football (b), golf (b,g), indoor track (g), soccer (b,g), softball (g), swimming and diving (b,g), tennis (b,g), track and field (b,g), volleyball (g). 4 PE instructors, 3 coaches, 1 athletic trainer.
Computers Computers are regularly used in current events, graphic design, keyboarding, reading, technology, video film production, Web site design, yearbook classes. Computer network features include on-campus library services, Internet access, wireless campus network, Internet filtering or blocking technology. Campus intranet is available to students. Students grades are available online. The school has a published electronic and media policy.
Contact Mr. Paul Knapstein, Director of Enrollment. 251-445-2934. Fax: 251-433-8356. E-mail: knapstp@mcgill-toolen.org. Web site: www.mcgill-toolen.org/

MEADOWRIDGE SCHOOL

12224 240th Street
Maple Ridge, British Columbia V4R 1N1, Canada

Head of School: Mr. Hugh Burke

General Information Coeducational day college-preparatory, arts, and technology school. Grades JK–12. Founded: 1985. Setting: rural. Nearest major city is Vancouver, Canada. 30-acre campus. 1 building on campus. Approved or accredited by Canadian Association of Independent Schools, Canadian Educational Standards Institute, International Baccalaureate Organization, and British Columbia Department of Education. Language of instruction: English. Total enrollment: 540. Upper school average class size: 18. Upper school faculty-student ratio: 1:12. Upper School students typically attend 5 days per week. The average school day consists of 7 hours.
Faculty School total: 50. In upper school: 9 men, 15 women; 6 have advanced degrees.
Subjects Offered Accounting, art, biology, biology-AP, calculus, calculus-AP, career and personal planning, chemistry, comparative civilizations, computer science-AP, computer technologies, drama, English, English literature, English-AP, fencing, filmmaking, forensics, French, geography, history, humanities, marketing, mathematics, photography, physical education, physics, science, Spanish, technology/design, theater, volleyball, weight training.
Graduation Requirements 3 provincially examinable courses, IB Diploma Programme.
Special Academic Programs International Baccalaureate program; study abroad; academic accommodation for the gifted.
College Admission Counseling 31 students graduated in 2012; all went to college, including McGill University; Queen's University at Kingston; Simon Fraser University; The University of British Columbia; University of Toronto; University of Victoria.
Student Life Upper grades have uniform requirement, student council, honor system. Discipline rests equally with students and faculty.
Tuition and Aid Day student tuition: CAN$16,200. Tuition installment plan (Insured Tuition Payment Plan, monthly payment plans). Tuition reduction for siblings, bursaries, merit scholarship grants available. Total upper-school merit-scholarship money awarded for 2012–13: CAN$22,000.
Admissions Traditional secondary-level entrance grade is 8. Admissions testing and writing sample required. Deadline for receipt of application materials: none. Application fee required: CAN$150. On-campus interview required.
Athletics Interscholastic: aerobics/dance (boys, girls), badminton (b,g), basketball (b,g), physical fitness (b,g), rugby (b,g), soccer (b,g), volleyball (b,g); intramural: aerobics/dance (b,g), basketball (b,g); coed interscholastic: aerobics/dance, cross-country running, flag football, outdoor activities, swimming and diving, track and field; coed intramural: aerobics/dance. 2 PE instructors.
Computers Computers are regularly used in information technology, journalism, video film production, yearbook classes. Computer network features include on-campus library services, online commercial services, Internet access, wireless campus network, Internet filtering or blocking technology. Student e-mail accounts and computer access in designated common areas are available to students.
Contact Mr. Daniel Le Page, Director of Admissions. 604-467-4444 Ext. 179. Fax: 604-467-4989. E-mail: daniel.lepage@meadowridge.bc.ca. Web site: www.meadowridge.bc.ca

THE MEADOWS SCHOOL

8601 Scholar Lane
Las Vegas, Nevada 89128-7302

Head of School: Mr. Henry L. Chanin

General Information Coeducational day college-preparatory, arts, technology, and debate, foreign languages school. Grades PK–12. Founded: 1981. Setting: suburban. 42-acre campus. 10 buildings on campus. Approved or accredited by Northwest Accreditation Commission, Pacific Northwest Association of Independent Schools, and Nevada Department of Education. Member of National Association of Independent Schools and Secondary School Admission Test Board. Endowment: $13 million. Total enrollment: 891. Upper school average class size: 12. Upper school faculty-student ratio: 1:11. There are 180 required school days per year for Upper School students. Upper School students typically attend 5 days per week. The average school day consists of 7 hours.

Upper School Student Profile Grade 9: 61 students (26 boys, 35 girls); Grade 10: 65 students (25 boys, 40 girls); Grade 11: 70 students (28 boys, 42 girls); Grade 12: 65 students (31 boys, 34 girls).

Faculty School total: 89. In upper school: 18 men, 20 women; 26 have advanced degrees.

Subjects Offered 20th century American writers, 3-dimensional art, acting, advanced math, Advanced Placement courses, advanced studio art-AP, American literature, anatomy and physiology, anthropology, architecture, art, art history, art history-AP, athletics, band, Basic programming, biology, biology-AP, British literature, British literature (honors), calculus, calculus-AP, ceramics, chemistry, chemistry-AP, choral music, chorus, composition, computer applications, computer graphics, computer literacy, computer programming, computer science, computer science-AP, concert choir, constitutional law, creative writing, dance, digital art, digital photography, drama, drama performance, drawing, drawing and design, economics, engineering, English, English composition, English language and composition-AP, English literature, English literature and composition-AP, European history, European history-AP, film studies, fine arts, finite math, foreign language, forensics, French, French language-AP, genetics, geometry, government-AP, health, honors English, honors geometry, honors U.S. history, honors world history, human anatomy, instrumental music, integrated mathematics, international affairs, international relations, journalism, keyboarding, Latin, Latin-AP, law, literature and composition-AP, macro/microeconomics-AP, money management, music theater, music theory-AP, organic chemistry, painting, photography, physics, physics-AP, policy and value, pre-calculus, psychology-AP, sculpture, Shakespeare, social justice, social sciences, Spanish, Spanish language-AP, Spanish literature, Spanish literature-AP, Spanish-AP, speech, speech and debate, speech and oral interpretations, sports medicine, statistics, statistics-AP, studio art, studio art-AP, technical theater, technology, theater production, trigonometry, U.S. government, U.S. government and politics-AP, U.S. history, U.S. history-AP, yearbook.

Graduation Requirements American literature, ancient world history, arts and fine arts (art, music, dance, drama), biology, English, English composition, English literature, European history, foreign language, geometry, mathematics, physical education (includes health), physics, pre-calculus, science, social studies (includes history), technical skills, U.S. government, U.S. history, seniors have a 24-hour per semester community service requirement, grades 9-11 have a 16-hour per semester community service requirement.

Special Academic Programs 24 Advanced Placement exams for which test preparation is offered; honors section; academic accommodation for the gifted, the musically talented, and the artistically talented.

College Admission Counseling 70 students graduated in 2012; all went to college, including Columbia University; Princeton University; The George Washington University; University of California, Los Angeles; University of Nevada, Las Vegas; University of San Diego. Median SAT critical reading: 680, median SAT math: 680, median SAT writing: 700, median combined SAT: 2060, median composite ACT: 30. 82% scored over 600 on SAT critical reading, 87% scored over 600 on SAT math, 84% scored over 600 on SAT writing, 84% scored over 1800 on combined SAT, 85% scored over 26 on composite ACT.

Student Life Upper grades have uniform requirement, student council, honor system. Discipline rests equally with students and faculty.

Summer Programs Enrichment, sports, art/fine arts programs offered; session focuses on enrichment; held on campus; accepts boys and girls; open to students from other schools. 50 students usually enrolled. 2013 schedule: June 10 to July 5. Application deadline: May 31.

Tuition and Aid Day student tuition: $21,110. Tuition installment plan (Insured Tuition Payment Plan, monthly payment plans, individually arranged payment plans, 2-payment plan, 70% by July 15 and 30% by February 15, 10 monthly payment plan using electronic withdrawal only). Need-based scholarship grants, need-based loans available. In 2012–13, 15% of upper-school students received aid.

Admissions Traditional secondary-level entrance grade is 9. ERB, ISEE, PSAT or SSAT required. Deadline for receipt of application materials: none. Application fee required: $100. On-campus interview required.

Athletics Interscholastic: baseball (boys), basketball (b,g), bowling (b,g), cheering (g), cross-country running (b,g), dance team (g), diving (b,g), football (b), softball (g), tennis (b,g), track and field (b,g), volleyball (g), wrestling (b); coed interscholastic: golf, soccer. 1 PE instructor, 1 athletic trainer.

Computers Computers are regularly used in all academic, college planning, desktop publishing, English, foreign language, graphic design, history, independent study, information technology, introduction to technology, library, mathematics, music, news writing, photography, photojournalism, programming, publications, publishing, science, speech, technology, yearbook classes. Computer network features include on-campus library services, online commercial services, Internet access, wireless campus network, Internet filtering or blocking technology, Neon, SMART boards in all classrooms, three wireless mobile computer labs with notebook computers, course syllabus and homework available online. Computer access in designated common areas is available to students. Students grades are available online. The school has a published electronic and media policy.

Contact 702-254-1610. Fax: 702-254-2452. Web site: www.themeadowsschool.org

MEMORIAL HALL SCHOOL

5400 Mitchelldale, Ste,A-1
Houston, Texas 77092

Head of School: Rev. George C. Aurich

General Information Coeducational day college-preparatory, general academic, and bilingual studies school. Grades 6–12. Founded: 1966. Setting: urban. 1 building on campus. Approved or accredited by Southern Association of Colleges and Schools, Southern Association of Independent Schools, Texas Education Agency, and Texas Department of Education. Total enrollment: 75. Upper school average class size: 14. Upper school faculty-student ratio: 1:14. Upper School students typically attend 4 days per week. The average school day consists of 7 hours and 30 minutes.

Faculty School total: 11. In upper school: 4 men, 7 women; 3 have advanced degrees.

Subjects Offered Algebra, American history, art, biology, business mathematics, business skills, chemistry, computer science, economics, English, ESL, fine arts, geography, geometry, government/civics, health, history, journalism, mathematics, physical education, physics, psychology, science, social sciences, social studies, sociology, Spanish, trigonometry, world history.

Graduation Requirements Arts and crafts, arts and fine arts (art, music, dance, drama), business skills (includes word processing), computer science, English, foreign language, mathematics, physical education (includes health), science, social sciences, social studies (includes history), community service, foreign credit accepted upon completion.

Special Academic Programs Study at local college for college credit; remedial reading and/or remedial writing; remedial math; programs in English, mathematics, general development for dyslexic students; special instructional classes for students with learning disabilities, Attention Deficit Disorder, and dyslexia; ESL (60 students enrolled).

College Admission Counseling 24 students graduated in 2012; 22 went to college, including Baylor University; Sam Houston State University; St. Thomas University; Texas A&M University; The University of Texas at Austin; University of Houston. Other: 2 went to work.

Student Life Upper grades have uniform requirement, student council, honor system. Discipline rests equally with students and faculty.

Summer Programs Remediation, enrichment, advancement, ESL, computer instruction programs offered; session focuses on additional credit enrichment, study skills; held on campus; accepts boys and girls; open to students from other schools. 55 students usually enrolled. 2013 schedule: June 15 to July 30. Application deadline: none.

Tuition and Aid Day student tuition: $12,200. Tuition installment plan (Insured Tuition Payment Plan, monthly payment plans, individually arranged payment plans). Tuition reduction for siblings available. In 2012–13, 5% of upper-school students received aid.

Admissions Traditional secondary-level entrance grade is 9. Stanford Achievement Test required. Deadline for receipt of application materials: none. Application fee required: $300. Interview required.

Athletics Interscholastic: aerobics (boys, girls), aerobics/dance (b,g), bowling (b,g), fitness (b,g), fitness walking (b,g), jump rope (b,g), yoga (b,g); intramural: cheering (g); coed interscholastic: bowling; coed intramural: dance, outdoor activities, physical fitness. 2 PE instructors.

Computers Computers are regularly used in all academic, basic skills, foreign language classes. Campus intranet is available to students.

Contact Ms. Kimberly Smith, Director. 713-688-5566. Fax: 713-956-9751. E-mail: memhallsch@aol.com. Web site: www.memorialhall.org

MEMPHIS CATHOLIC HIGH SCHOOL AND MIDDLE SCHOOL

61 North Mclean Boulevard
Memphis, Tennessee 38104-2644

Head of School: Mr. Nicholas Green

General Information Coeducational day college-preparatory school, affiliated with Roman Catholic Church. Grades 7–12. Founded: 1954. Setting: urban. 4-acre campus. 1 building on campus. Approved or accredited by Southern Association of Colleges and Schools and Tennessee Department of Education. Upper school average class size: 20. Upper school faculty-student ratio: 1:15. There are 180 required school days per year for Upper School students. Upper School students typically attend 5 days per week. The average school day consists of 7 hours and 30 minutes.

Upper School Student Profile 30% of students are Roman Catholic.

Faculty School total: 15. In upper school: 7 men, 8 women; 12 have advanced degrees.

Student Life Upper grades have uniform requirement. Discipline rests equally with students and faculty. Attendance at religious services is required.
Admissions Traditional secondary-level entrance grade is 9. No application fee required.
Contact Mrs. Dell Russell, Admissions and Bookkeeper. 901-276-1221. Fax: 901-725-1447. E-mail: drussell@memphiscatholic.org. Web site: www.memphiscatholic.org

MEMPHIS UNIVERSITY SCHOOL

6191 Park Avenue
Memphis, Tennessee 38119-5399

Head of School: Mr. Ellis L. Haguewood

General Information Boys' day college-preparatory school. Grades 7–12. Founded: 1893. Setting: suburban. 94-acre campus. 8 buildings on campus. Approved or accredited by Southern Association of Colleges and Schools, Southern Association of Independent Schools, and Tennessee Association of Independent Schools. Member of National Association of Independent Schools. Endowment: $21 million. Total enrollment: 660. Upper school average class size: 14. Upper school faculty-student ratio: 1:8. There are 176 required school days per year for Upper School students. Upper School students typically attend 5 days per week. The average school day consists of 7 hours.
Upper School Student Profile Grade 9: 128 students (128 boys); Grade 10: 114 students (114 boys); Grade 11: 129 students (129 boys); Grade 12: 85 students (85 boys).
Faculty School total: 75. In upper school: 47 men, 13 women; 41 have advanced degrees.
Subjects Offered Algebra, American government, American literature, art, art history, art history-AP, arts and crafts, Bible, biology, biology-AP, British literature, calculus, calculus-AP, chemistry, chemistry-AP, choral music, college counseling, college placement, comparative government and politics-AP, comparative religion, composition-AP, computer education, computer programming, computer science, computer science-AP, driver education, earth science, economics, economics and history, English, English composition, English literature, English literature and composition-AP, environmental science, ethics, ethics and responsibility, European history, European history-AP, expository writing, fine arts, foreign language, French, geometry, global studies, government and politics-AP, government/civics, grammar, health, history, humanities, introduction to theater, keyboarding, language and composition, Latin, library skills, literature, mathematics, music, music appreciation, music composition, music theory, physical education, physical science, physics, physics-AP, pre-algebra, pre-calculus, probability and statistics, psychology, religion, research skills, science, social sciences, social studies, Spanish, studio art, study skills, trigonometry, U.S. history, U.S. history-AP, United States government-AP, Western civilization, world history, writing.
Graduation Requirements Arts and fine arts (art, music, dance, drama), English, foreign language, mathematics, physical education (includes health), religion (includes Bible studies and theology), science, social sciences, social studies (includes history).
Special Academic Programs 18 Advanced Placement exams for which test preparation is offered; honors section; study abroad; remedial reading and/or remedial writing; remedial math.
College Admission Counseling 112 students graduated in 2011; all went to college, including Rhodes College; Southern Methodist University; The University of Alabama; The University of Tennessee; University of Mississippi; Vanderbilt University. Median composite ACT: 29. Mean SAT critical reading: 615, mean SAT math: 638, mean SAT writing: 614. 59% scored over 600 on SAT critical reading, 65% scored over 600 on SAT math, 61% scored over 600 on SAT writing, 61% scored over 1800 on combined SAT, 68% scored over 26 on composite ACT.
Student Life Upper grades have specified standards of dress, student council, honor system. Discipline rests primarily with faculty.
Tuition and Aid Day student tuition: $17,500. Tuition installment plan (FACTS Tuition Payment Plan, monthly payment plans, individually arranged payment plans). Need-based scholarship grants available. In 2011–12, 31% of upper-school students received aid. Total amount of financial aid awarded in 2011–12: $1,300,000.
Admissions Traditional secondary-level entrance grade is 9. For fall 2011, 38 students applied for upper-level admission, 35 were accepted, 30 enrolled. ISEE required. Deadline for receipt of application materials: December 10. Application fee required: $50. On-campus interview recommended.
Athletics Interscholastic: baseball, basketball, cross-country running, football, golf, lacrosse, soccer, swimming and diving, tennis, track and field, trap and skeet, weight training, wrestling. 5 PE instructors, 9 coaches, 1 athletic trainer.
Computers Computers are regularly used in all academic, career exploration, college planning, graphic design, library science, newspaper, publications, yearbook classes. Computer network features include on-campus library services, online commercial services, Internet access, wireless campus network, Internet filtering or blocking technology. Campus intranet, student e-mail accounts, and computer access in designated common areas are available to students. Students grades are available online. The school has a published electronic and media policy.
Contact Mrs. Peggy E. Williamson, Director of Admissions. 901-260-1349. Fax: 901-260-1301. E-mail: peggy.williamson@musowls.org. Web site: www.musowls.org

MENAUL SCHOOL

301 Menaul Boulevard NE
Albuquerque, New Mexico 87107

Head of School: Mr. Lindsey R. Gilbert Jr.

General Information Coeducational boarding and day college-preparatory and college prep school, affiliated with Presbyterian Church. Boarding grades 9–12, day grades 6–12. Founded: 1896. Setting: urban. Students are housed in single-sex dormitories. 35-acre campus. 10 buildings on campus. Approved or accredited by Independent Schools Association of the Southwest, North Central Association of Colleges and Schools, The College Board, and New Mexico Department of Education. Endowment: $3.3 million. Total enrollment: 185. Upper school average class size: 12. Upper school faculty-student ratio: 1:9. There are 180 required school days per year for Upper School students. Upper School students typically attend 5 days per week. The average school day consists of 6 hours.
Upper School Student Profile 20% of students are boarding students. 80% are state residents. 3 states are represented in upper school student body. 20% are international students. International students from Belgium, China, Ukraine, and Viet Nam; 4 other countries represented in student body. 20% of students are Presbyterian.
Faculty School total: 25. In upper school: 13 men, 11 women; 16 have advanced degrees; 5 reside on campus.
Subjects Offered ACT preparation, Advanced Placement courses, algebra, American government, American history, American literature, art, arts and crafts, band, Bible studies, biology, calculus-AP, chemistry, clayworking, communications, computer graphics, computer programming, computer science, earth science, economics, English, English literature, English-AP, ethics, fine arts, geography, geometry, government/civics, history, Life of Christ, mathematics, music, Native American arts and crafts, physical education, physics, psychology, religion, science, social sciences, social studies, sociology, Spanish, theology, trigonometry, U.S. government and politics-AP, world history, world literature, writing, yearbook.
Graduation Requirements Arts and fine arts (art, music, dance, drama), communications, computer science, English, foreign language, mathematics, physical education (includes health), religion (includes Bible studies and theology), science, social sciences, social studies (includes history), 100 hours of community service.
Special Academic Programs Advanced Placement exam preparation; honors section; independent study; study at local college for college credit; academic accommodation for the gifted and the artistically talented; ESL (3 students enrolled).
College Admission Counseling 34 students graduated in 2012; all went to college, including New Mexico State University; University of New Mexico. 5% scored over 26 on composite ACT.
Student Life Upper grades have uniform requirement, student council, honor system. Discipline rests primarily with faculty. Attendance at religious services is required.
Summer Programs ESL programs offered; session focuses on ESL and International to U.S. transition; held both on and off campus; held at Albuquerque, various locations in NM and Durango CO; accepts boys and girls; open to students from other schools. 10 students usually enrolled. 2013 schedule: August 1 to August 15. Application deadline: February.
Tuition and Aid Day student tuition: $13,900; 5-day tuition and room/board: $29,000; 7-day tuition and room/board: $33,000. Tuition installment plan (FACTS Tuition Payment Plan). Need-based scholarship grants available. In 2012–13, 50% of upper-school students received aid. Total amount of financial aid awarded in 2012–13: $307,000.
Admissions Traditional secondary-level entrance grade is 9. Admissions testing, ERB, ISEE, SLEP for foreign students or SSAT required. Deadline for receipt of application materials: none. Application fee required: $35. Interview required.
Athletics Interscholastic: basketball (boys, girls), football (b), volleyball (g); intramural: lacrosse (b), soccer (b), touch football (b); coed interscholastic: golf, outdoor education, running, track and field; coed intramural: badminton, dance, modern dance. 2 PE instructors, 6 coaches, 1 athletic trainer.
Computers Computers are regularly used in art, college planning, English, graphics, history, mathematics, psychology, science, yearbook classes. Computer network features include on-campus library services, online commercial services, Internet access, wireless campus network, Internet filtering or blocking technology. Campus intranet and computer access in designated common areas are available to students. Students grades are available online. The school has a published electronic and media policy.
Contact Ericka Paul, Assistant to Admission. 505-341-7250. Fax: 505-344-2517. E-mail: epaul@menaulschool.com. Web site: www.menaulschool.com

MENNONITE COLLEGIATE INSTITUTE

Box 250
Gretna, Manitoba R0G 0V0, Canada

Head of School: Mr. Darryl K. Loewen

General Information Coeducational boarding and day college-preparatory, general academic, arts, business, religious studies, and technology school, affiliated with Mennonite Church, Christian faith; primarily serves students with learning disabilities, individuals with Attention Deficit Disorder, individuals with emotional and behavioral problems, dyslexic students, and physical disabilities. Boarding grades 9–12, day grades 7–12. Founded: 1889. Setting: small town. Nearest major city is Winnipeg,

Canada. Students are housed in single-sex dormitories. 12-acre campus. 5 buildings on campus. Approved or accredited by The College Board and Manitoba Department of Education. Language of instruction: English. Endowment: CAN$500,000. Total enrollment: 130. Upper school average class size: 20. Upper school faculty-student ratio: 1:13. There are 196 required school days per year for Upper School students. Upper School students typically attend 5 days per week. The average school day consists of 7 hours and 10 minutes.

Upper School Student Profile Grade 7: 6 students (2 boys, 4 girls); Grade 8: 4 students (1 boy, 3 girls); Grade 9: 16 students (10 boys, 6 girls); Grade 10: 22 students (14 boys, 8 girls); Grade 11: 45 students (24 boys, 21 girls); Grade 12: 37 students (21 boys, 16 girls). 42% of students are boarding students. 95% are province residents. 3 provinces are represented in upper school student body. 3% are international students. International students from China, Congo, Democratic People's Republic of Korea, Hong Kong, Kenya, and Mexico; 1 other country represented in student body. 70% of students are Mennonite, Christian.

Faculty School total: 12. In upper school: 7 men, 5 women; 2 have advanced degrees; 2 reside on campus.

Subjects Offered Advanced TOEFL/grammar, agriculture, all academic, jazz ensemble, journalism, music.

Graduation Requirements English, geography, history, mathematics, physical education (includes health), compulsory religion courses at each grade level, compulsory religious history courses at one level.

Special Academic Programs 2 Advanced Placement exams for which test preparation is offered; independent study; academic accommodation for the musically talented; remedial reading and/or remedial writing; remedial math; special instructional classes for blind students; ESL (8 students enrolled).

College Admission Counseling 50 students graduated in 2012; 35 went to college, including Cabrillo College; The University of Winnipeg; University of Manitoba. Other: 12 went to work, 3 had other specific plans.

Student Life Upper grades have uniform requirement, student council, honor system. Discipline rests primarily with faculty. Attendance at religious services is required.

Tuition and Aid Day student tuition: CAN$4800; 7-day tuition and room/board: CAN$18,200. Tuition installment plan (monthly payment plans, individually arranged payment plans). Tuition reduction for siblings, bursaries, merit scholarship grants, need-based scholarship grants, middle-income loans available. In 2012–13, 30% of upper-school students received aid; total upper-school merit-scholarship money awarded: CAN$9000. Total amount of financial aid awarded in 2012–13: CAN$40,000.

Admissions Traditional secondary-level entrance grade is 9. For fall 2012, 133 students applied for upper-level admission, 133 were accepted, 130 enrolled. Deadline for receipt of application materials: none. Application fee required: CAN$200. Interview recommended.

Athletics Interscholastic: badminton (boys, girls), baseball (b,g), basketball (b,g), cross-country running (b,g), curling (b,g), golf (b,g), soccer (b,g), track and field (b,g), volleyball (b,g); intramural: floor hockey (b,g), indoor soccer (b,g), paddle tennis (b,g), street hockey (b,g), table tennis (b,g); coed interscholastic: badminton, cross-country running, curling, golf, track and field; coed intramural: floor hockey, indoor soccer, paddle tennis, street hockey, table tennis. 3 PE instructors, 2 athletic trainers.

Computers Computers are regularly used in all academic classes. Computer network features include on-campus library services, Internet access, wireless campus network, Internet filtering or blocking technology. The school has a published electronic and media policy.

Contact Mrs. Tammy Rempel, Admissions Counselor. 204-327-5891. Fax: 204-327-5872. E-mail: admissions@mciblues.net. Web site: www.mciblues.net

MERCHISTON CASTLE SCHOOL

Colinton
Edinburgh EH13 0PU, United Kingdom

Head of School: Mr. Andrew R. Hunter

General Information Boys' boarding and day college-preparatory, arts, business, religious studies, bilingual studies, and technology school, affiliated with Christian faith. Ungraded, ages 8–18. Founded: 1833. Setting: small town. Students are housed in single-sex dormitories. 100-acre campus. 11 buildings on campus. Approved or accredited by Boarding Schools Association (UK) and Independent Schools Council (UK). Language of instruction: English. Upper school average class size: 9. Upper school faculty-student ratio: 1:9. The average school day consists of 9 hours.

Upper School Student Profile 70% of students are boarding students. 18% are international students. International students from China, France, Germany, Hong Kong, Russian Federation, and Spain; 13 other countries represented in student body. 50% of students are Christian faith.

Faculty School total: 64. In upper school: 38 men, 23 women; 37 have advanced degrees; 30 reside on campus.

Subjects Offered Algebra, art, biology, calculus, career education, chemistry, Chinese, computer science, creative writing, design, drama, Dutch, economics, electronics, English, English as a foreign language, English literature, European history, French, geography, geometry, German, government/civics, grammar, history, Italian, Japanese, Latin, Mandarin, mathematics, music, physical education, physics, politics, Portuguese, religion, Russian, science, social studies, Spanish, trigonometry, world history.

Graduation Requirements Any three A-level courses.

Special Academic Programs Independent study; term-away projects; study at local college for college credit; study abroad; academic accommodation for the gifted, the musically talented, and the artistically talented; remedial reading and/or remedial writing; remedial math; programs in English, mathematics, general development for dyslexic students; special instructional classes for deaf students, blind students; ESL (15 students enrolled).

College Admission Counseling 80 students graduated in 2012; 75 went to college. Other: 5 had other specific plans.

Student Life Upper grades have specified standards of dress, student council, honor system. Discipline rests equally with students and faculty.

Summer Programs ESL, sports programs offered; held on campus; accepts boys and girls; open to students from other schools. 40 students usually enrolled.

Tuition and Aid Day student tuition: £12,120–£19,545; 7-day tuition and room/board: £17,070–£26,655. Tuition reduction for siblings, bursaries available. In 2012–13, 20% of upper-school students received aid.

Admissions Traditional secondary-level entrance grade is 8. Traditional secondary-level entrance age is 13. Achievement/Aptitude/Writing, common entrance examinations and school's own exam required. Deadline for receipt of application materials: none. Application fee required: £100. Interview recommended.

Athletics Interscholastic: badminton (boys), ball hockey (b), basketball (b), boxing (b), cricket (b), cross-country running (b), curling (b), fencing (b), Fives (b), football (b), freestyle skiing (b), golf (b), hockey (b), indoor soccer (b), riflery (b), rugby (b), sailing (b), scuba diving (b), skiing (cross-country) (b), skiing (downhill) (b), soccer (b), squash (b), swimming and diving (b), table tennis (b), tennis (b), track and field (b), wall climbing (b); intramural: archery (b), badminton (b), ball hockey (b), basketball (b), bicycling (b), boxing (b), canoeing/kayaking (b), climbing (b), cricket (b), cross-country running (b), curling (b), diving (b), fencing (b), Fives (b), football (b), freestyle skiing (b), golf (b), gymnastics (b), hockey (b), indoor soccer (b), jogging (b), judo (b), life saving (b), marksmanship (b), martial arts (b), mountain biking (b), outdoor activities (b), outdoor education (b), outdoor skills (b), physical fitness (b), riflery (b), rock climbing (b), rugby (b), sailing (b), scuba diving (b), skiing (cross-country) (b), skiing (downhill) (b), soccer (b), squash (b), strength & conditioning (b), swimming and diving (b), table tennis (b), tennis (b), track and field (b), volleyball (b), wall climbing (b). 4 PE instructors, 2 coaches.

Computers Computers are regularly used in all academic, design, music classes. Computer network features include Internet access, wireless campus network, Internet filtering or blocking technology. Campus intranet, student e-mail accounts, and computer access in designated common areas are available to students. The school has a published electronic and media policy.

Contact Mrs. Anne Rickard, Director of Admissions. 44-131-312-2201. Fax: 44-131-441 Ext. 6060. E-mail: admissions@merchiston.co.uk. Web site: www.merchiston.co.uk

MERCY HIGH SCHOOL

1740 Randolph Road
Middletown, Connecticut 06457-5155

Head of School: Sr. Mary McCarthy, RSM

General Information Girls' day college-preparatory, arts, and religious studies school, affiliated with Roman Catholic Church. Grades 9–12. Founded: 1963. Setting: rural. Nearest major city is Hartford. 26-acre campus. 1 building on campus. Approved or accredited by National Catholic Education Association, New England Association of Schools and Colleges, and Connecticut Department of Education. Total enrollment: 651. Upper school average class size: 21. Upper school faculty-student ratio: 1:13. There are 172 required school days per year for Upper School students. Upper School students typically attend 5 days per week. The average school day consists of 6 hours and 30 minutes.

Upper School Student Profile Grade 9: 153 students (153 girls); Grade 10: 165 students (165 girls); Grade 11: 160 students (160 girls); Grade 12: 173 students (173 girls). 85% of students are Roman Catholic.

Faculty School total: 53. In upper school: 9 men, 44 women; 39 have advanced degrees.

Subjects Offered Accounting, advanced math, algebra, American government, American literature, American literature-AP, art, art history, arts and crafts, biology, biology-AP, business, calculus, calculus-AP, Catholic belief and practice, ceramics, chamber groups, chemistry, chemistry-AP, choir, chorus, civics, comparative government and politics, computer applications, concert band, concert choir, creative writing, drama workshop, drawing and design, English, English literature, English-AP, European history, expository writing, French, French language-AP, French literature-AP, French-AP, geometry, government/civics, grammar, health, history, honors algebra, honors English, honors geometry, honors U.S. history, honors world history, humanities, independent study, Italian, journalism, keyboarding, Latin, law, literature-AP, mathematics, modern history, music, musical theater, neuroscience, photography, physical education, physics, physics-AP, physiology, pottery, pre-algebra, pre-calculus, psychology, public speaking, religious studies, science, social studies, Spanish, Spanish language-AP, Spanish-AP, statistics, statistics-AP, theater arts, trigonometry, U.S. history, U.S. history-AP, wind ensemble, word processing, world history, world literature, world religions, writing.

Graduation Requirements Civics, computer applications, English, foreign language, mathematics, physical education (includes health), religion (includes Bible studies and theology), science, social studies (includes history), 100 hours of community service.

Special Academic Programs 12 Advanced Placement exams for which test preparation is offered; honors section; independent study; study at local college for college credit.

College Admission Counseling 170 students graduated in 2011; all went to college, including Central Connecticut State University; Eastern Connecticut State University; Quinnipiac University; Sacred Heart University; Salve Regina University; Southern Connecticut State University. Median SAT critical reading: 525, median SAT math: 510, median SAT writing: 530, median combined SAT: 1555, median composite ACT: 22. 21% scored over 600 on SAT critical reading, 16% scored over 600 on SAT math, 20% scored over 600 on SAT writing, 18% scored over 1800 on combined SAT, 15% scored over 26 on composite ACT.

Student Life Upper grades have uniform requirement, student council. Discipline rests primarily with faculty. Attendance at religious services is required.

Tuition and Aid Day student tuition: $10,350–$10,850. Tuition installment plan (FACTS Tuition Payment Plan, individually arranged payment plans). Tuition reduction for siblings, merit scholarship grants, need-based scholarship grants available.

Admissions Traditional secondary-level entrance grade is 9. For fall 2011, 300 students applied for upper-level admission, 279 were accepted, 174 enrolled. High School Placement Test (closed version) from Scholastic Testing Service required. Deadline for receipt of application materials: none. Application fee required: $50.

Athletics Interscholastic: basketball, cheering, cross-country running, diving, field hockey, golf, indoor track, lacrosse, soccer, softball, swimming and diving, tennis, track and field, volleyball; intramural: basketball, floor hockey, golf, soccer, tennis, volleyball. 1 PE instructor, 30 coaches, 1 athletic trainer.

Computers Computers are regularly used in accounting, all academic, computer applications, desktop publishing, journalism, photography, Web site design, word processing classes. Computer network features include on-campus library services, Internet access, Internet filtering or blocking technology. Campus intranet, student e-mail accounts, and computer access in designated common areas are available to students. Students grades are available online.

Contact Mrs. Diane Santostefano, Director of Admissions. 860-346-6659. Fax: 860-344-9887. E-mail: dsantostefano@mercyhigh.com. Web site: www.mercyhigh.com

MERCY HIGH SCHOOL

1501 South 48th Street
Omaha, Nebraska 68106-2598

Head of School: Ms. Carolyn Jaworski

General Information Girls' day college-preparatory, general academic, arts, business, religious studies, and technology school, affiliated with Roman Catholic Church. Grades 9–12. Founded: 1955. Setting: urban. 2-acre campus. 1 building on campus. Approved or accredited by Mercy Secondary Education Association, National Catholic Education Association, North Central Association of Colleges and Schools, and Nebraska Department of Education. Total enrollment: 360. Upper school average class size: 20. Upper school faculty-student ratio: 1:12. There are 180 required school days per year for Upper School students. Upper School students typically attend 5 days per week. The average school day consists of 7 hours and 15 minutes.

Upper School Student Profile Grade 9: 118 students (118 girls); Grade 10: 89 students (89 girls); Grade 11: 109 students (109 girls); Grade 12: 76 students (76 girls). 90% of students are Roman Catholic.

Faculty School total: 33. In upper school: 6 men, 27 women; 20 have advanced degrees.

Subjects Offered Accounting, algebra, American government, American history, American history-AP, American literature, anatomy and physiology, art, ballet, biology, British literature, British literature-AP, business applications, calculus, calculus-AP, chemistry, chemistry-AP, child development, choir, computer education, consumer mathematics, culinary arts, debate, drama, drawing, ecology, English, French, general math, geometry, health, honors English, honors geometry, journalism, keyboarding, math review, moral theology, painting, participation in sports, peace and justice, physics, physics-AP, play production, pottery, pre-algebra, pre-calculus, psychology, social justice, Spanish, Spanish-AP, speech, speech and debate, sports medicine, stagecraft, statistics, theology, theology and the arts, trigonometry, U.S. government, U.S. history, U.S. history-AP, vocal music, world history, yearbook.

Graduation Requirements Advanced math, algebra, American government, anatomy and physiology, arts and fine arts (art, music, dance, drama), biology, chemistry, computer applications, debate, English, foreign language, geometry, mathematics, physical education (includes health), physics, social studies (includes history), speech, theology, U.S. history, world history, service hours.

Special Academic Programs 5 Advanced Placement exams for which test preparation is offered; honors section; study at local college for college credit; remedial reading and/or remedial writing; remedial math; programs in general development for dyslexic students; special instructional classes for deaf students, blind students, students with LD, ADD, emotional and behavioral problems.

College Admission Counseling 70 students graduated in 2011; 68 went to college, including Creighton University; University of Nebraska–Lincoln; University of Nebraska at Omaha. Other: 2 went to work.

Student Life Upper grades have uniform requirement, student council, honor system. Discipline rests primarily with faculty. Attendance at religious services is required.

Tuition and Aid Day student tuition: $8300. Tuition installment plan (individually arranged payment plans, each family has an individualized tuition based upon their income). Tuition reduction for siblings, merit scholarship grants, need-based scholarship grants, paying campus jobs available. In 2011–12, 85% of upper-school students received aid; total upper-school merit-scholarship money awarded: $100,000. Total amount of financial aid awarded in 2011–12: $1,000,000.

Admissions Traditional secondary-level entrance grade is 9. For fall 2011, 120 students applied for upper-level admission, 120 were accepted, 118 enrolled. STS Examination required. Deadline for receipt of application materials: March 31. Application fee required: $125. Interview required.

Athletics Interscholastic: aerobics, archery, badminton, ballet, basketball, bowling, cheering, cross-country running, dance squad, dance team, diving, fitness walking, golf, independent competitive sports, physical fitness, self defense, soccer, softball, strength & conditioning, swimming and diving, tennis, track and field, volleyball, weight training; intramural: indoor soccer. 2 PE instructors, 15 coaches, 1 athletic trainer.

Computers Computers are regularly used in accounting, business, business applications, business education, business studies, history, journalism, keyboarding, lab/keyboard, library, library skills, mathematics, music, photojournalism, publications, religion, science, yearbook classes. Computer network features include on-campus library services, online commercial services, Internet access, wireless campus network, Internet filtering or blocking technology. Student e-mail accounts and computer access in designated common areas are available to students. Students grades are available online. The school has a published electronic and media policy.

Contact Ms. Anne Zadina, Recruitment Director. 402-553-9424. Fax: 402-553-0394. E-mail: zadinaa@mercyhigh.org. Web site: www.mercyhigh.org

MERCY HIGH SCHOOL COLLEGE PREPARATORY

3250 19th Avenue
San Francisco, California 94132-2000

Head of School: Dr. Dorothy McCrea

General Information Girls' day college-preparatory, arts, and medicine school, affiliated with Roman Catholic Church. Grades 9–12. Founded: 1952. Setting: urban. Nearest major city is Daly City. 6-acre campus. 2 buildings on campus. Approved or accredited by Western Association of Schools and Colleges, Western Catholic Education Association, and California Department of Education. Endowment: $2 million. Total enrollment: 394. Upper school average class size: 25. Upper school faculty-student ratio: 1:14. There are 180 required school days per year for Upper School students. Upper School students typically attend 5 days per week. The average school day consists of 7 hours and 5 minutes.

Upper School Student Profile Grade 9: 83 students (83 girls); Grade 10: 97 students (97 girls); Grade 11: 105 students (105 girls); Grade 12: 109 students (109 girls). 61.9% of students are Roman Catholic.

Faculty School total: 28. In upper school: 3 men, 25 women; 21 have advanced degrees.

Subjects Offered Algebra, American history, American literature, art, biology, business, calculus, ceramics, chemistry, chorus, computer applications, computer programming, creative writing, dance, drama, English, English literature, environmental science, ethnic studies, expository writing, French, geometry, government/civics, keyboarding, mathematics, physical education, physics, physics-AP, religious studies, social justice, social studies, Spanish, speech, statistics, theater, trigonometry, visual and performing arts, world history, world literature.

Graduation Requirements 50 volunteer hours and a senior culminating project, Intersession.

Special Academic Programs Advanced Placement exam preparation; honors section; programs in English, mathematics, general development for dyslexic students; special instructional classes for McAuley Academic Program.

College Admission Counseling 125 students graduated in 2012; all went to college, including Dominican University; San Francisco State University; Skyline College; University of California, Davis; University of California, Irvine; University of San Francisco. Mean SAT critical reading: 477, mean SAT math: 488, mean SAT writing: 507, mean combined SAT: 1472, mean composite ACT: 21. 7% scored over 600 on SAT critical reading, 11% scored over 600 on SAT math, 10.5% scored over 600 on SAT writing, 7% scored over 1800 on combined SAT, 6% scored over 26 on composite ACT.

Student Life Upper grades have uniform requirement, student council, honor system. Discipline rests primarily with faculty. Attendance at religious services is required.

Summer Programs Enrichment, advancement programs offered; session focuses on pre-high program is enrichment only; secondary program is enrichment and remediation; held on campus; accepts boys and girls; open to students from other schools. 350 students usually enrolled. 2013 schedule: June 17 to July 12. Application deadline: June 13.

Tuition and Aid Day student tuition: $15,000. Tuition installment plan (individually arranged payment plans, TADS, 10 months payment (July-April), full pay and semiannual payment (July & December)). Merit scholarship grants, need-based scholarship grants available. In 2012–13, 40% of upper-school students received aid; total upper-school merit-scholarship money awarded: $50,000. Total amount of financial aid awarded in 2012–13: $1,200,000.

Admissions Traditional secondary-level entrance grade is 9. High School Placement Test and TOEFL required. Deadline for receipt of application materials: none. Application fee required: $80. On-campus interview required.

Athletics Interscholastic: basketball, cross-country running, dance, dance squad, self defense, soccer, softball, swimming and diving, tennis, track and field, volleyball. 2 PE instructors, 8 coaches.

Computers Computers are regularly used in all academic classes. Computer network features include on-campus library services, Internet access, wireless campus network, Internet filtering or blocking technology, Hunter Systems. Campus intranet and computer access in designated common areas are available to students. Students grades are available online. The school has a published electronic and media policy.

Contact Michelle Ferrari, Director of Community Outreach and Admissions. 415-584-5929. Fax: 415-334-9726. E-mail: mferrari@mercyhs.org. Web site: www.mercyhs.org

MERCYHURST PREPARATORY SCHOOL

538 East Grandview Boulevard
Erie, Pennsylvania 16504-2697

Head of School: Mrs. Deborah A. Laughlin

General Information Coeducational day college-preparatory, arts, religious studies, and technology school, affiliated with Roman Catholic Church. Grades 9–12. Founded: 1926. Setting: urban. 5-acre campus. 1 building on campus. Approved or accredited by International Baccalaureate Organization, Middle States Association of Colleges and Schools, and Pennsylvania Department of Education. Total enrollment: 624. Upper school average class size: 25. Upper school faculty-student ratio: 1:13. There are 180 required school days per year for Upper School students. Upper School students typically attend 5 days per week. The average school day consists of 6 hours and 15 minutes.

Upper School Student Profile Grade 9: 124 students (38 boys, 86 girls); Grade 10: 175 students (85 boys, 90 girls); Grade 11: 177 students (65 boys, 112 girls); Grade 12: 152 students (50 boys, 102 girls). 81% of students are Roman Catholic.

Faculty School total: 51. In upper school: 19 men, 32 women; 19 have advanced degrees.

Subjects Offered Accounting, algebra, American Civil War, American government, American history, American literature, anatomy, art, art appreciation, art education, art history, astronomy, athletic training, ballet, biology, business skills, calculus, campus ministry, career exploration, ceramics, chemistry, chorus, Christian ethics, civil war history, communications, community service, computer applications, computer programming, computer science, creative arts, dance, digital photography, drama, drama performance, drawing, drawing and design, earth science, English, English literature, environmental science, ethics, European history, expository writing, fine arts, first aid, French, geology, geometry, government/civics, guitar, health, Hebrew scripture, history, Holocaust, humanities, Internet, journalism, keyboarding, leadership, mathematics, multimedia, music, music appreciation, music history, music theory-AP, musical productions, orchestra, painting, photography, physical education, physics, physiology, piano, psychology, public speaking, publications, reading/study skills, religion, SAT preparation, SAT/ACT preparation, science, senior internship, set design, social studies, Spanish, speech, speech and debate, study skills, tap dance, technical theater, technology/design, theater, theater arts, theology, theory of knowledge, trigonometry, typing, U.S. government, U.S. history, visual and performing arts, weight fitness, weightlifting, word processing, world cultures, world history, writing, yearbook.

Graduation Requirements Arts and fine arts (art, music, dance, drama), arts appreciation, business skills (includes word processing), computer science, creative arts, English, foreign language, health and wellness, mathematics, physical education (includes health), public speaking, religion (includes Bible studies and theology), science, social studies (includes history), technological applications, 25 service hours per year.

Special Academic Programs International Baccalaureate program; honors section; independent study; study at local college for college credit; academic accommodation for the gifted, the musically talented, and the artistically talented; remedial reading and/or remedial writing; remedial math; ESL (60 students enrolled).

College Admission Counseling 140 students graduated in 2011; 138 went to college, including Edinboro University of Pennsylvania; Gannon University; Indiana University of Pennsylvania; John Carroll University; Mercyhurst College; Penn State University Park. Other: 1 went to work, 1 entered military service.

Student Life Upper grades have uniform requirement, student council, honor system. Discipline rests primarily with faculty. Attendance at religious services is required.

Tuition and Aid Day student tuition: $7300. Tuition installment plan (FACTS Tuition Payment Plan). Merit scholarship grants, need-based scholarship grants, creative arts scholarships, alumni scholarships, endowment scholarships available. In 2011–12, 51% of upper-school students received aid; total upper-school merit-scholarship money awarded: $89,950. Total amount of financial aid awarded in 2011–12: $578,050.

Admissions Traditional secondary-level entrance grade is 9. For fall 2011, 277 students applied for upper-level admission, 234 were accepted, 121 enrolled. Achievement tests, ACT, High School Placement Test or Iowa Tests of Basic Skills required. Deadline for receipt of application materials: none. Application fee required: $10.

Athletics Interscholastic: ballet (girls), baseball (b), basketball (b,g), bowling (g), cheering (g), crew (b,g), cross-country running (b,g), football (b), golf (b,g), modern dance (g), rowing (b,g), skiing (downhill) (g), soccer (b,g), softball (g), swimming and diving (b,g), tennis (b,g), track and field (b,g), volleyball (g); coed interscholastic: tennis, weight training; coed intramural: weight lifting, weight training. 2 PE instructors, 40 coaches, 1 athletic trainer.

Computers Computers are regularly used in college planning, data processing, design, desktop publishing, English, foreign language, graphic design, history, journalism, mathematics, media, newspaper, photography, photojournalism, programming, publications, publishing, SAT preparation, science, typing, Web site design, word processing, writing, yearbook classes. Computer network features include on-campus library services, online commercial services, Internet access, wireless campus network, Internet filtering or blocking technology. Campus intranet is available to students. Students grades are available online. The school has a published electronic and media policy.

Contact Mrs. Marcia E. DiTullio, Administrative Assistant. 814-824-2323. Fax: 814-824-2116. E-mail: mditullio@mpslakers.com. Web site: www.mpslakers.com

MERION MERCY ACADEMY

511 Montgomery Avenue
Merion Station, Pennsylvania 19066

Head of School: Sr. Barbara Buckley

General Information Girls' day college-preparatory, arts, and religious studies school, affiliated with Roman Catholic Church. Grades 9–12. Founded: 1884. Setting: suburban. Nearest major city is Philadelphia. 35-acre campus. 7 buildings on campus. Approved or accredited by Middle States Association of Colleges and Schools. Endowment: $350,000. Total enrollment: 482. Upper school average class size: 17. Upper school faculty-student ratio: 1:9.

Upper School Student Profile Grade 9: 123 students (123 girls); Grade 10: 116 students (116 girls); Grade 11: 125 students (125 girls); Grade 12: 118 students (118 girls). 90% of students are Roman Catholic.

Faculty School total: 53. In upper school: 6 men, 47 women; 41 have advanced degrees.

Subjects Offered Algebra, American history, American literature, art, art history, biology, business, calculus, chemistry, computer programming, creative writing, drama, economics, English, English literature, environmental science, European history, fine arts, French, geometry, government/civics, grammar, health, history, journalism, Latin, mathematics, music, music history, physical education, physics, physiology, psychology, religion, science, social studies, Spanish, speech, theater, theology, trigonometry, women's studies, world history, world literature, writing.

Graduation Requirements Arts and fine arts (art, music, dance, drama), English, foreign language, mathematics, physical education (includes health), religion (includes Bible studies and theology), science, social studies (includes history).

Special Academic Programs Advanced Placement exam preparation; honors section; study at local college for college credit; academic accommodation for the gifted, the musically talented, and the artistically talented; remedial reading and/or remedial writing; remedial math.

College Admission Counseling 116 students graduated in 2011; all went to college, including Boston College; Georgetown University; Penn State University Park; Saint Joseph's University; The University of Scranton; Villanova University. Mean SAT critical reading: 601, mean SAT math: 573, mean SAT writing: 620.

Student Life Upper grades have uniform requirement, student council, honor system. Discipline rests primarily with faculty. Attendance at religious services is required.

Tuition and Aid Day student tuition: $14,900. Tuition installment plan (The Tuition Plan, monthly payment plans, 2 equal payments plan). Tuition reduction for siblings, merit scholarship grants, need-based scholarship grants, middle-income loans, alumnae, Mercy, and music scholarships available. In 2011–12, 36% of upper-school students received aid; total upper-school merit-scholarship money awarded: $452,150. Total amount of financial aid awarded in 2011–12: $857,600.

Admissions Traditional secondary-level entrance grade is 9. For fall 2011, 300 students applied for upper-level admission, 180 were accepted, 123 enrolled. High School Placement Test required. Deadline for receipt of application materials: November 15. Application fee required: $30. On-campus interview required.

Athletics Interscholastic: basketball, cheering, crew, cross-country running, field hockey, golf, lacrosse, soccer, softball, swimming and diving, tennis, track and field, volleyball, winter (indoor) track; intramural: basketball, dance, tennis. 2 PE instructors, 19 coaches, 1 athletic trainer.

Computers Computers are regularly used in all academic classes. Computer network features include on-campus library services, online commercial services, Internet access, wireless campus network, Internet filtering or blocking technology. Student e-mail accounts and computer access in designated common areas are available to students.

Contact Eileen Killeen, Director of Admissions. 610-664-6655 Ext. 116. Fax: 610-664-6322. E-mail: ekilleen@merion-mercy.com. Web site: www.merion-mercy.com

MESA GRANDE SEVENTH-DAY ACADEMY

975 Fremont Street
Calimesa, California 92320

Head of School: Alfred J. Riddle

General Information Coeducational day college-preparatory, arts, religious studies, and technology school, affiliated with Seventh-day Adventists, Christian faith. Grades K–12. Founded: 1928. Setting: rural. Nearest major city is San Bernardino. 14-acre campus. 3 buildings on campus. Approved or accredited by Western Association of Schools and Colleges and California Department of Education. Endowment: $650,000. Total enrollment: 265. Upper school average class size: 30. Upper school faculty-student ratio: 1:10. There are 180 required school days per year for Upper School students. Upper School students typically attend 5 days per week. The average school day consists of 8 hours.

Upper School Student Profile Grade 9: 31 students (17 boys, 14 girls); Grade 10: 31 students (17 boys, 14 girls); Grade 11: 32 students (16 boys, 16 girls); Grade 12: 29 students (17 boys, 12 girls). 90% of students are Seventh-day Adventists, Christian.

Faculty School total: 23. In upper school: 6 men, 8 women; 8 have advanced degrees.

Subjects Offered Algebra, American literature, arts, ASB Leadership, auto mechanics, bell choir, biology, British literature, career education, chemistry, choral music, community service, composition, computer applications, computer-aided design, computers, concert choir, desktop publishing, drama, economics, economics and history, English, English composition, family living, fine arts, geometry, government/civics, graphic arts, handbells, health, instrumental music, keyboarding, lab science, marine biology, mathematics, music composition, music theory, physical education, physical science, physics, pre-calculus, relationships, religion, religious education, science, social sciences, social studies, Spanish, U.S. government, U.S. history, video film production, world history, world literature, yearbook.

Graduation Requirements Algebra, American government, applied skills, arts and fine arts (art, music, dance, drama), biology, British literature, career education, chemistry, computer education, computer technologies, economics, English, English composition, family living, industrial technology, keyboarding, mathematics, modern languages, physical education (includes health), physical fitness, physical science, physics, religious studies, science, social studies (includes history), Spanish, technical skills, work experience, community service.

College Admission Counseling 20 students graduated in 2012; 18 went to college, including La Sierra University; Pacific Union College; Southern Adventist University; University of California, Irvine; University of California, Los Angeles; Walla Walla University. Other: 2 went to work.

Student Life Upper grades have uniform requirement, student council, honor system. Discipline rests primarily with faculty. Attendance at religious services is required.

Summer Programs Sports programs offered; held both on and off campus; held at Drayson Center, Loma Linda, CA; accepts boys and girls; open to students from other schools. 50 students usually enrolled. 2013 schedule: June 8 to August 3. Application deadline: May 5.

Tuition and Aid Day student tuition: $8000. Tuition installment plan (monthly payment plans, individually arranged payment plans). Need-based scholarship grants, need-based loans, middle-income loans available. In 2012–13, 25% of upper-school students received aid. Total amount of financial aid awarded in 2012–13: $35,000.

Admissions Traditional secondary-level entrance grade is 9. For fall 2012, 30 students applied for upper-level admission, 28 were accepted, 28 enrolled. Any standardized test, ITBS-TAP or Math Placement Exam required. Deadline for receipt of application materials: none. Application fee required: $50. On-campus interview required.

Athletics Interscholastic: baseball (boys), basketball (b,g), flag football (b,g), softball (g), volleyball (b,g); coed interscholastic: cross-country running, golf, physical fitness, weight lifting. 2 PE instructors, 12 coaches, 2 athletic trainers.

Computers Computers are regularly used in art, design, graphic design, library skills, science, technical drawing, technology, typing, video film production, writing, yearbook classes. Computer network features include on-campus library services, online commercial services, Internet access, wireless campus network, Internet filtering or blocking technology. Student e-mail accounts and computer access in designated common areas are available to students. Students grades are available online. The school has a published electronic and media policy.

Contact Lois M. Myhre, Admissions Office. 909-795-1112 Ext. 257. Fax: 909-795-1653. E-mail: lois.myhre@mgak-12.org. Web site: www.mesagrandeacademy.org

MIDDLESEX SCHOOL

1400 Lowell Road
Concord, Massachusetts 01742

Head of School: Kathleen C. Giles

General Information Coeducational boarding and day college-preparatory and arts school. Grades 9–12. Founded: 1901. Setting: suburban. Nearest major city is Boston. Students are housed in single-sex dormitories. 350-acre campus. 31 buildings on campus. Approved or accredited by New England Association of Schools and Colleges. Member of National Association of Independent Schools and Secondary School Admission Test Board. Endowment: $160 million. Total enrollment: 375. Upper school average class size: 12. Upper school faculty-student ratio: 1:6. There are 178 required school days per year for Upper School students. Upper School students typically attend 6 days per week. The average school day consists of 7 hours and 7 minutes.

Upper School Student Profile Grade 9: 78 students (37 boys, 41 girls); Grade 10: 98 students (53 boys, 45 girls); Grade 11: 97 students (52 boys, 45 girls); Grade 12: 102 students (44 boys, 58 girls). 67% of students are boarding students. 56% are state residents. 29 states are represented in upper school student body. 12% are international students. International students from Canada, China, Jamaica, Philippines, Republic of Korea, and United Kingdom; 12 other countries represented in student body.

Faculty School total: 63. In upper school: 35 men, 28 women; 44 have advanced degrees; 52 reside on campus.

Subjects Offered Acting, advanced biology, advanced chemistry, advanced computer applications, Advanced Placement courses, advanced studio art-AP, African American history, African history, African-American history, algebra, American literature, analytic geometry, art, art history, art history-AP, art-AP, Asian literature, astronomy, biology, biology-AP, British literature, calculus, calculus-AP, ceramics, chemistry, chemistry-AP, Chinese, classical Greek literature, computer programming, computer programming-AP, computer science, computer science-AP, creative writing, discrete mathematics, DNA, drama, economics, economics-AP, English, English literature, English literature and composition-AP, environmental science, environmental science-AP, ethics, European history, European history-AP, finite math, forensics, French, French language-AP, French literature-AP, geometry, Greek, history, history of jazz, Holocaust studies, independent study, jazz band, Latin, Latin American history, marine studies, mathematics, media, Middle East, Middle Eastern history, model United Nations, music, music theory, music theory-AP, philosophy, photography, physics, physics-AP, political science, religion, Shakespeare, Spanish, Spanish language-AP, Spanish literature-AP, statistics, statistics-AP, studio art-AP, theater, trigonometry, U.S. government and politics-AP, U.S. history, U.S. history-AP, video film production, Vietnam history, Vietnam War, vocal ensemble, women in world history, woodworking, world history, writing, writing workshop.

Graduation Requirements Algebra, analytic geometry, arts, English, English literature and composition-AP, European history, foreign language, geometry, science, trigonometry, U.S. history, completion of a wooden plaque.

Special Academic Programs 22 Advanced Placement exams for which test preparation is offered; honors section; independent study; academic accommodation for the gifted.

College Admission Counseling 104 students graduated in 2012; 102 went to college, including Boston College; Columbia University; Harvard University; Occidental College; University of Virginia; Williams College. Median SAT critical reading: 690, median SAT math: 700, median SAT writing: 690, median combined SAT: 2080, median composite ACT: 29. 90% scored over 600 on SAT critical reading, 96% scored over 600 on SAT math, 90% scored over 600 on SAT writing, 93% scored over 1800 on combined SAT, 88% scored over 26 on composite ACT.

Student Life Upper grades have specified standards of dress, student council, honor system. Discipline rests equally with students and faculty.

Tuition and Aid Day student tuition: $40,260; 7-day tuition and room/board: $50,320. Guaranteed tuition plan. Tuition installment plan (Insured Tuition Payment Plan, monthly payment plans, semiannual payment plan). Need-based scholarship grants, need-based loans available. In 2012–13, 30% of upper-school students received aid. Total amount of financial aid awarded in 2012–13: $4,100,000.

Admissions Traditional secondary-level entrance grade is 9. For fall 2012, 1,044 students applied for upper-level admission, 107 enrolled. ISEE, SSAT or TOEFL required. Deadline for receipt of application materials: January 15. Application fee required: $50. Interview recommended.

Athletics Interscholastic: alpine skiing (boys, girls), baseball (b), basketball (b,g), crew (b,g), cross-country running (b,g), field hockey (g), football (b), ice hockey (b,g), lacrosse (b,g), skiing (downhill) (b,g), soccer (b,g), softball (g), squash (b,g), tennis (b,g), wrestling (b); coed interscholastic: golf, track and field; coed intramural: dance, fitness, physical training, squash, strength & conditioning, yoga. 1 PE instructor, 18 coaches, 2 athletic trainers.

Computers Computers are regularly used in all classes. Computer network features include on-campus library services, online commercial services, Internet access, wireless campus network, Internet filtering or blocking technology. Campus intranet, student e-mail accounts, and computer access in designated common areas are available to students. Students grades are available online. The school has a published electronic and media policy.

Contact Douglas C. Price, Director of Admissions. 978-371-6524. Fax: 978-402-1400. E-mail: admissions@mxschool.edu. Web site: www.mxschool.edu

MIDDLE TENNESSEE CHRISTIAN SCHOOL

100 East MTCS Road
Murfreesboro, Tennessee 37129

Head of School: Mr. Charles Swift

General Information Coeducational day college-preparatory, arts, religious studies, and technology school, affiliated with Church of Christ. Grades PK–12. Founded: 1962. Setting: suburban. Nearest major city is Nashville. 37-acre campus. 3 buildings on campus. Approved or accredited by National Christian School Association, Southern Association of Colleges and Schools, Tennessee Association of Independent Schools, and Tennessee Department of Education. Member of National

Association of Independent Schools. Total enrollment: 665. Upper school average class size: 18. Upper school faculty-student ratio: 1:18. There are 175 required school days per year for Upper School students. Upper School students typically attend 5 days per week. The average school day consists of 7 hours.

Upper School Student Profile Grade 9: 47 students (29 boys, 18 girls); Grade 10: 47 students (26 boys, 21 girls); Grade 11: 45 students (24 boys, 21 girls); Grade 12: 50 students (28 boys, 22 girls). 52% of students are members of Church of Christ.

Faculty School total: 50. In upper school: 12 men, 14 women; 22 have advanced degrees.

Subjects Offered ACT preparation, advanced math, algebra, American history, American history-AP, American literature, anatomy, art, band, Bible, biology, biology-AP, calculus, chemistry, chorus, computer applications, computer technologies, creative writing, drama, driver education, economics, electives, English, European history, European history-AP, French, geometry, integrated mathematics, keyboarding, physics, pre-algebra, pre-calculus, Spanish, speech, U.S. government, U.S. history, wellness, yearbook.

Graduation Requirements Algebra, arts, Bible, biology, chemistry, computer applications, economics, electives, English, French, geometry, keyboarding, physical science, pre-algebra, Spanish, speech, U.S. government, U.S. history, wellness, world history.

Special Academic Programs Advanced Placement exam preparation.

College Admission Counseling 55 students graduated in 2012; 52 went to college, including Freed-Hardeman University; Harding University; Lipscomb University; Middle Tennessee State University; Tennessee Technological University; The University of Tennessee at Chattanooga. Other: 1 went to work, 2 entered military service. Median composite ACT: 24. 31% scored over 26 on composite ACT.

Student Life Upper grades have specified standards of dress, student council, honor system. Discipline rests primarily with faculty. Attendance at religious services is required.

Tuition and Aid Day student tuition: $7200. Tuition installment plan (monthly payment plans, individually arranged payment plans). Tuition reduction for siblings, need-based scholarship grants available.

Admissions Traditional secondary-level entrance grade is 9. For fall 2012, 39 students applied for upper-level admission, 36 were accepted, 30 enrolled. Achievement tests required. Deadline for receipt of application materials: none. Application fee required: $25. Interview required.

Athletics Interscholastic: baseball (boys), basketball (b,g), bowling (b,g), cheering (g), cross-country running (b,g), football (b), golf (b), skeet shooting (b,g), soccer (b,g), softball (g), tennis (b,g), trap and skeet (b,g), volleyball (g). 2 PE instructors.

Computers Computers are regularly used in engineering, keyboarding, science, writing, yearbook classes. Computer network features include on-campus library services, Internet access, wireless campus network, Internet filtering or blocking technology. Student e-mail accounts and computer access in designated common areas are available to students. Students grades are available online. The school has a published electronic and media policy.

Contact Mrs. Cindy Siler, Director of Admissions and Public Relations. 615-893-0601. Fax: 615-895-8815. E-mail: cindysiler@mtcscougars.org. Web site: www.mtcscougars.org

MIDLAND SCHOOL

PO Box 8
5100 Figueroa Mountain Road
Los Olivos, California 93441

Head of School: Will Graham

General Information Coeducational boarding college-preparatory and environmental studies school. Grades 9–12. Founded: 1932. Setting: rural. Nearest major city is Santa Barbara. Students are housed in single-sex cabins. 2,860-acre campus. Approved or accredited by California Association of Independent Schools, The Association of Boarding Schools, The College Board, US Department of State, and Western Association of Schools and Colleges. Member of National Association of Independent Schools and Secondary School Admission Test Board. Endowment: $14 million. Total enrollment: 80. Upper school average class size: 10. Upper school faculty-student ratio: 1:5. Upper School students typically attend 6 days per week. The average school day consists of 6 hours and 45 minutes.

Upper School Student Profile Grade 9: 16 students (8 boys, 8 girls); Grade 10: 24 students (12 boys, 12 girls); Grade 11: 15 students (8 boys, 7 girls); Grade 12: 25 students (15 boys, 10 girls). 100% of students are boarding students. 70% are state residents. 10 states are represented in upper school student body. 12% are international students. International students from China, Hong Kong, Hungary, Mexico, and Republic of Korea; 5 other countries represented in student body.

Faculty School total: 23. In upper school: 14 men, 9 women; 9 have advanced degrees; 20 reside on campus.

Subjects Offered 3-dimensional art, adolescent issues, advanced chemistry, advanced math, agroecology, algebra, American history, American literature, American studies, anthropology, backpacking, basketball, biology, ceramics, character education, chemistry, Chinese history, clayworking, community service, composition, creative writing, drama, economics, environmental education, environmental studies, equestrian sports, film and literature, foreign language, gardening, geology, geometry, health education, human sexuality, hydrology, integrated science, land and ranch management, leadership, literature by women, metalworking, music, painting, physics, pre-calculus, senior project, senior seminar, senior thesis, sex education, Spanish, Spanish literature, statistics, U.S. history, utopia, volleyball, wilderness education, wilderness experience, world studies.

Graduation Requirements Arts and fine arts (art, music, dance, drama), English, foreign language, history, mathematics, science, senior thesis, independent senior thesis.

Special Academic Programs 7 Advanced Placement exams for which test preparation is offered; honors section; independent study.

College Admission Counseling 22 students graduated in 2012; all went to college, including College of the Atlantic; Cornell University; Hendrix College; Middlebury College; University of California, Davis; University of California, Santa Cruz.

Student Life Upper grades have student council, honor system. Discipline rests equally with students and faculty.

Tuition and Aid 7-day tuition and room/board: $40,500. Tuition installment plan (monthly payment plans, Your Tuition Solution, Tuition Management Systems). Need-based scholarship grants available. In 2012–13, 53% of upper-school students received aid. Total amount of financial aid awarded in 2012–13: $1,000,000.

Admissions Traditional secondary-level entrance grade is 9. For fall 2012, 75 students applied for upper-level admission, 40 were accepted, 29 enrolled. ISEE, SSAT or TOEFL required. Deadline for receipt of application materials: February 15. Application fee required: $50. Interview required.

Athletics Interscholastic: basketball (boys), cross-country running (b,g), lacrosse (b,g), soccer (b,g), volleyball (g); intramural: table tennis (b,g); coed intramural: backpacking, dance, equestrian sports, hiking/backpacking, horseback riding, mountain biking, outdoor adventure, outdoor education, outdoor skills, surfing, touch football, ultimate Frisbee, yoga.

Computers Computer network features include on-campus library services, Internet access, Internet filtering or blocking technology. Student e-mail accounts are available to students. The school has a published electronic and media policy.

Contact Amy E. Graham, Director of Admissions and Financial Aid. 805-688-5114 Ext. 114. Fax: 805-686-2470. E-mail: admissions@midland-school.org. Web site: www.midland-school.org

MID-PACIFIC INSTITUTE

2445 Kaala Street
Honolulu, Hawaii 96822-2299

Head of School: Mr. Joe C. Rice

General Information Coeducational day college-preparatory, arts, bilingual studies, technology, and International Baccalaureate school, affiliated with United Church of Christ. Grades K–12. Founded: 1908. Setting: urban. 38-acre campus. 33 buildings on campus. Approved or accredited by International Baccalaureate Organization and Western Association of Schools and Colleges. Member of National Association of Independent Schools and Secondary School Admission Test Board. Total enrollment: 1,550. Upper school average class size: 20. Upper school faculty-student ratio: 1:20. Upper School students typically attend 5 days per week. The average school day consists of 6 hours and 15 minutes.

Faculty School total: 171. In upper school: 20 have advanced degrees.

Subjects Offered Algebra, American history, American literature, art, art history, astronomy, ballet, band, biology, business skills, calculus, career education, ceramics, chemistry, computer programming, computer science, creative writing, dance, debate, drama, drawing, economics, English, English literature, ESL, film, fine arts, first aid, French, general science, geography, geometry, Hawaiian history, health, history, instrumental music, Japanese, Latin, law, mathematics, oceanography, oral communications, painting, philosophy, photography, physical education, physics, printmaking, psychology, religion, science, sculpture, social sciences, social studies, Spanish, speech, swimming, swimming competency, technological applications, technology, theater, video, weight training, world history, world literature, writing.

Graduation Requirements Arts and fine arts (art, music, dance, drama), business skills (includes word processing), career education, computer science, English, foreign language, mathematics, oral communications, physical education (includes health), religion (includes Bible studies and theology), science, social sciences, social studies (includes history), speech, swimming competency.

Special Academic Programs International Baccalaureate program; Advanced Placement exam preparation; honors section; study at local college for college credit; academic accommodation for the gifted and the artistically talented; ESL (41 students enrolled).

College Admission Counseling 200 students graduated in 2012; all went to college, including Oregon State University; Seattle University; University of Hawaii at Manoa; University of Oregon; University of Southern California.

Student Life Upper grades have specified standards of dress, student council, honor system. Discipline rests primarily with faculty. Attendance at religious services is required.

Summer Programs Enrichment, advancement, ESL, art/fine arts, computer instruction programs offered; session focuses on physical fitness and skills; held on campus; accepts boys and girls; open to students from other schools. 1,200 students usually enrolled. 2013 schedule: June 5 to July 26. Application deadline: April 5.

Tuition and Aid Day student tuition: $18,300. Tuition installment plan (FACTS Tuition Payment Plan, monthly payment plans, semiannual payment plan). Merit scholarship grants, need-based scholarship grants, paying campus jobs, tuition reduction for children of employees available. In 2012–13, 17% of upper-school students received aid. Total amount of financial aid awarded in 2012–13: $2,900,000.

Admissions Traditional secondary-level entrance grade is 9. For fall 2012, 700 students applied for upper-level admission, 220 were accepted, 150 enrolled. SAT, SSAT and TOEFL required. Deadline for receipt of application materials: December 1. Application fee required: $100. Interview required.

Athletics Interscholastic: aquatics (boys, girls), baseball (b), basketball (b,g), bowling (b,g), canoeing/kayaking (b,g), cheering (g), cross-country running (b,g), football (b), golf (b,g), gymnastics (g), independent competitive sports (b,g), kayaking (b,g), ocean paddling (b,g), physical fitness (b,g), physical training (b,g), riflery (b,g), soccer (b,g), softball (g), strength & conditioning (b,g), surfing (b,g), swimming and diving (b,g), tennis (b,g), track and field (b,g), volleyball (b,g), water polo (b,g), wrestling (b,g); intramural: badminton (b,g), weight lifting (b,g), weight training (b,g); coed interscholastic: fitness, modern dance; coed intramural: badminton. 7 PE instructors, 40 coaches, 3 athletic trainers.

Computers Computers are regularly used in English, foreign language, mathematics, media arts, science classes. Computer network features include on-campus library services, online commercial services, Internet access, wireless campus network, Internet filtering or blocking technology. Campus intranet, student e-mail accounts, and computer access in designated common areas are available to students. Students grades are available online. The school has a published electronic and media policy.

Contact Ms. Heidi Bow, Admissions Assistant. 808-973-5005. Fax: 808-973-5099. E-mail: admissions@midpac.edu. Web site: www.midpac.edu

MILLBROOK SCHOOL

131 Millbrook School Road
Millbrook, New York 12545

Head of School: Mr. Drew Casertano

General Information Coeducational boarding and day college-preparatory, arts, environmental stewardship, and community service school. Grades 9–12. Founded: 1931. Setting: rural. Nearest major city is New York. Students are housed in single-sex dormitories. 800-acre campus. 40 buildings on campus. Approved or accredited by The Association of Boarding Schools and New York Department of Education. Member of National Association of Independent Schools and Secondary School Admission Test Board. Endowment: $24 million. Total enrollment: 272. Upper school average class size: 14. Upper school faculty-student ratio: 1:5. There are 179 required school days per year for Upper School students. Upper School students typically attend 6 days per week. The average school day consists of 7 hours.

Upper School Student Profile Grade 9: 40 students (18 boys, 22 girls); Grade 10: 77 students (43 boys, 34 girls); Grade 11: 75 students (38 boys, 37 girls); Grade 12: 75 students (45 boys, 30 girls); Postgraduate: 5 students (3 boys, 2 girls). 80% of students are boarding students. 40% are state residents. 22 states are represented in upper school student body. 15% are international students. International students from Canada, China, Ghana, Republic of Korea, Venezuela, and Viet Nam; 6 other countries represented in student body.

Faculty School total: 55. In upper school: 25 men, 30 women; 30 have advanced degrees; 45 reside on campus.

Subjects Offered Acting, advanced biology, advanced chemistry, advanced math, Advanced Placement courses, advanced studio art-AP, aesthetics, algebra, American history, American literature, ancient history, ancient world history, animal behavior, animal science, anthropology, art, art history, astronomy, biology, calculus, calculus-AP, ceramics, chemistry, choral music, constitutional law, creative writing, dance, dance performance, digital photography, drama, drama performance, drawing, ecology, English, English language-AP, English literature, English-AP, environmental science, European history, fine arts, forensics, French, French language-AP, French-AP, geometry, global studies, history, honors English, honors geometry, human biology, human development, independent study, instrumental music, jazz band, jazz ensemble, journalism, Mandarin, mathematics, medieval history, Middle Eastern history, music, music appreciation, music history, painting, philosophy, photography, physics, pre-calculus, psychology, science, senior project, social sciences, social studies, Spanish, Spanish-AP, studio art, study skills, theater, trigonometry, world history.

Graduation Requirements Biology, English, foreign language, history, mathematics, science, visual and performing arts, Culminating Experience for Seniors.

Special Academic Programs 8 Advanced Placement exams for which test preparation is offered; honors section; independent study; term-away projects; study abroad.

College Admission Counseling 65 students graduated in 2011; 60 went to college, including Barnard College; Cornell University; Dickinson College; Hamilton College; Kenyon College; Wake Forest University. Other: 2 entered a postgraduate year, 3 had other specific plans. Mean SAT critical reading: 576, mean SAT math: 578, mean SAT writing: 586, mean combined SAT: 1740, mean composite ACT: 23.

Student Life Upper grades have specified standards of dress, student council, honor system. Discipline rests equally with students and faculty.

Tuition and Aid Day student tuition: $34,500; 7-day tuition and room/board: $46,950. Tuition installment plan (individually arranged payment plans, Tuition Management Services). Need-based scholarship grants, need-based loans available. In 2011–12, 27% of upper-school students received aid. Total amount of financial aid awarded in 2011–12: $2,148,000.

Admissions Traditional secondary-level entrance grade is 9. For fall 2011, 545 students applied for upper-level admission, 270 were accepted, 96 enrolled. ISEE, PSAT or SAT for applicants to grade 11 and 12, SSAT, TOEFL or writing sample required. Deadline for receipt of application materials: January 15. Application fee required: $50. Interview required.

Athletics Interscholastic: baseball (boys), basketball (b,g), cross-country running (b,g), field hockey (g), ice hockey (b,g), lacrosse (b,g), soccer (b,g), softball (g), squash (b,g), tennis (b,g); coed interscholastic: golf; coed intramural: aerobics/dance, aerobics/Nautilus, alpine skiing, badminton, bicycling, dance, equestrian sports, fitness, hiking/backpacking, horseback riding, modern dance, outdoor education, physical training, running, skiing (downhill), snowboarding, strength & conditioning, weight training, yoga. 1 coach, 1 athletic trainer.

Computers Computers are regularly used in foreign language, history, journalism, mathematics, photography, science, study skills, video film production, yearbook classes. Computer network features include on-campus library services, online commercial services, Internet access, wireless campus network, Internet filtering or blocking technology. Campus intranet, student e-mail accounts, and computer access in designated common areas are available to students. Students grades are available online. The school has a published electronic and media policy.

Contact Mrs. Wendy Greenfield, Admission Office Assistant. 845-677-8261 Ext. 138. Fax: 845-677-1265. E-mail: admissions@millbrook.org. Web site: www.millbrook.org

MILLER SCHOOL OF ALBEMARLE

1000 Samuel Miller Loop
Charlottesville, Virginia 22903-9328

Head of School: Mr. Patrick France

General Information Coeducational boarding and day college-preparatory and arts school. Grades 8–12. Founded: 1878. Setting: small town. Students are housed in single-sex dormitories. 1,600-acre campus. 6 buildings on campus. Approved or accredited by Missouri Independent School Association, The Association of Boarding Schools, Virginia Association of Independent Schools, and Virginia Department of Education. Member of National Association of Independent Schools and Secondary School Admission Test Board. Endowment: $15.4 million. Total enrollment: 173. Upper school average class size: 8. Upper school faculty-student ratio: 1:6. There are 180 required school days per year for Upper School students. Upper School students typically attend 5 days per week. The average school day consists of 5 hours and 10 minutes.

Upper School Student Profile Grade 8: 20 students (15 boys, 5 girls); Grade 9: 27 students (18 boys, 9 girls); Grade 10: 40 students (25 boys, 15 girls); Grade 11: 42 students (24 boys, 18 girls); Grade 12: 44 students (27 boys, 17 girls). 56% of students are boarding students. 60% are state residents. 13 states are represented in upper school student body. 24% are international students. International students from Brazil, China, Germany, Republic of Korea, Spain, and Viet Nam; 6 other countries represented in student body.

Faculty School total: 29. In upper school: 18 men, 11 women; 24 have advanced degrees; 23 reside on campus.

Subjects Offered Algebra, American government, American literature, ancient history, art, arts, baseball, basketball, biology, calculus, calculus-AP, carpentry, chemistry, civics, CPR, creative writing, drama performance, driver education, earth science, economics, economics and history, electives, English, English composition, English language and composition-AP, English language-AP, English literature, English literature and composition-AP, English literature-AP, English-AP, English/composition-AP, environmental science, environmental science-AP, environmental studies, environmental systems, ESL, European history, European history-AP, fine arts, fitness, foreign language, French, French language-AP, French literature-AP, French studies, French-AP, geography, geometry, government, government and politics-AP, government-AP, government/civics, history-AP, independent study, instrumental music, Latin, macroeconomics-AP, mathematics-AP, modern European history, modern European history-AP, music, music performance, musical productions, musical theater, participation in sports, photography, physical education, physical fitness, physical science, physics, poetry, pre-algebra, pre-calculus, reading/study skills, Spanish, Spanish language-AP, Spanish literature-AP, Spanish-AP, sports conditioning, statistics, student government, studio art, studio art-AP, study skills, tennis, trigonometry, U.S. government, U.S. government and politics-AP, U.S. history, U.S. history-AP, visual arts, volleyball, wood processing, woodworking, wrestling, yearbook.

Graduation Requirements Arts and fine arts (art, music, dance, drama), English, foreign language, mathematics, physical education (includes health), science, social studies (includes history). Community service is required.

Special Academic Programs 15 Advanced Placement exams for which test preparation is offered; honors section; accelerated programs; independent study; academic accommodation for the gifted, the musically talented, and the artistically talented; ESL (9 students enrolled).

College Admission Counseling 39 students graduated in 2012; 38 went to college, including James Madison University; Penn State University Park; The College of William and Mary; University of Virginia; Virginia Polytechnic Institute and State University; Washington and Lee University. Other: 1 went to work. Mean SAT critical reading: 510, mean SAT math: 559, mean SAT writing: 516. 40% scored over 600 on SAT critical reading, 40% scored over 600 on SAT math, 40% scored over 600 on SAT writing.

Student Life Upper grades have specified standards of dress, student council, honor system. Discipline rests equally with students and faculty.

Tuition and Aid Day student tuition: $19,000; 5-day tuition and room/board: $36,500; 7-day tuition and room/board: $39,400. Tuition installment plan (Insured Tuition Payment Plan, FACTS Tuition Payment Plan, individually arranged payment plans). Tuition reduction for siblings, need-based scholarship grants available. In 2012–13, 40% of upper-school students received aid. Total amount of financial aid awarded in 2012–13: $1,200,000.

Admissions Traditional secondary-level entrance grade is 9. For fall 2012, 210 students applied for upper-level admission, 102 were accepted, 60 enrolled. PSAT or SAT, SSAT, Stanford Achievement Test or TOEFL or SLEP required. Deadline for receipt of application materials: February 15. Application fee required: $50. Interview required.

Athletics Interscholastic: badminton (boys, girls), baseball (b), basketball (b,g), bicycling (b,g), cross-country running (b,g), lacrosse (b), mountain biking (b,g), outdoor activities (b,g), skiing (downhill) (b,g), snowboarding (b,g), soccer (b,g), tennis (b,g), volleyball (g), wrestling (b); intramural: bicycling (b,g); coed interscholastic: bicycling, equestrian sports, Frisbee, golf, horseback riding, mountain biking; coed intramural: aerobics/dance, basketball, bicycling, canoeing/kayaking, cross-country running, fishing, fitness, fitness walking, flag football, Frisbee, hiking/backpacking, indoor soccer, jogging, mountain biking, outdoor activities, paint ball, physical fitness, physical training, power lifting, running, skateboarding, soccer, softball, street hockey, strength & conditioning, swimming and diving, table tennis, tennis, touch football, ultimate Frisbee, volleyball, walking, weight lifting, weight training. 5 coaches, 1 athletic trainer.

Computers Computers are regularly used in English, foreign language, history, mathematics, science classes. Computer network features include on-campus library services, online commercial services, Internet access, wireless campus network, Internet filtering or blocking technology. Campus intranet and student e-mail accounts are available to students. Students grades are available online. The school has a published electronic and media policy.

Contact Ms. Dee Gregory, Assistant Director of Admissions. 434-823-4805 Ext. 248. Fax: 434-205-5007. E-mail: dgregory@millerschool.org. Web site: www.millerschool.org

MILL SPRINGS ACADEMY

Alpharetta, Georgia

See Special Needs Schools section.

MILTON ACADEMY

170 Centre Street
Milton, Massachusetts 02186

Head of School: Todd Bland

General Information Coeducational boarding and day college-preparatory school. Boarding grades 9–12, day grades K–12. Founded: 1798. Setting: suburban. Nearest major city is Boston. Students are housed in single-sex dormitories. 125-acre campus. 25 buildings on campus. Approved or accredited by Association of Independent Schools in New England, New England Association of Schools and Colleges, The Association of Boarding Schools, and Massachusetts Department of Education. Member of National Association of Independent Schools and Secondary School Admission Test Board. Endowment: $167 million. Total enrollment: 980. Upper school average class size: 14. Upper school faculty-student ratio: 1:5. There are 162 required school days per year for Upper School students. Upper School students typically attend 5 days per week. The average school day consists of 7 hours.

Upper School Student Profile 50% of students are boarding students. 64% are state residents. 26 states are represented in upper school student body. 13% are international students. International students from Hong Kong, Jamaica, Japan, Malaysia, Republic of Korea, and Taiwan; 18 other countries represented in student body.

Faculty School total: 180. In upper school: 62 men, 65 women; 99 have advanced degrees; 102 reside on campus.

Subjects Offered Algebra, American history, American literature, anatomy, architecture, art, art history, astronomy, biology, calculus, ceramics, chemistry, Chinese, computer math, computer programming, computer science, creative writing, current events, dance, drama, earth science, economics, English, English literature, ethics, European history, expository writing, fine arts, French, geography, geometry, government/civics, grammar, Greek, health, history, Latin, mathematics, music, philosophy, photography, physical education, physics, physiology, psychology, religion, science, social studies, sociology, Spanish, speech, statistics, theater, trigonometry, world history, world literature, writing.

Graduation Requirements Arts and fine arts (art, music, dance, drama), current events, English, foreign language, leadership, mathematics, physical education (includes health), public speaking, science, social studies (includes history).

Special Academic Programs Advanced Placement exam preparation; honors section; independent study; term-away projects; study abroad; academic accommodation for the gifted, the musically talented, and the artistically talented.

College Admission Counseling 164 students graduated in 2011; all went to college, including Boston College; Brown University; Columbia University; Georgetown University; Harvard University; Tufts University. Mean SAT critical reading: 680, mean SAT math: 692, mean SAT writing: 693.

Student Life Upper grades have student council, honor system. Discipline rests equally with students and faculty.

Tuition and Aid Day student tuition: $37,530; 7-day tuition and room/board: $45,720. Tuition installment plan (The Tuition Management Systems (TMS)). Need-based scholarship grants available. In 2011–12, 32% of upper-school students received aid. Total amount of financial aid awarded in 2011–12: $7,169,420.

Admissions Traditional secondary-level entrance grade is 9. For fall 2011, 1,100 students applied for upper-level admission, 275 were accepted, 165 enrolled. ISEE, PSAT, SAT, SSAT or TOEFL required. Deadline for receipt of application materials: January 15. Application fee required: $50. Interview required.

Athletics Interscholastic: baseball (boys), basketball (b,g), cross-country running (b,g), field hockey (g), football (b), ice hockey (b,g), lacrosse (b,g), soccer (b,g), softball (g), squash (b,g), tennis (b,g), track and field (b,g), volleyball (g); intramural: basketball (b,g), soccer (b,g), strength & conditioning (b,g); coed interscholastic: alpine skiing, diving, golf, sailing, skiing (downhill), swimming and diving, wrestling; coed intramural: climbing, outdoor activities, outdoor education, project adventure, rock climbing, skiing (downhill), squash, tennis, ultimate Frisbee, yoga. 6 PE instructors, 107 coaches, 3 athletic trainers.

Computers Computers are regularly used in mathematics, science classes. Computer network features include on-campus library services, online commercial services, Internet access, wireless campus network, Internet filtering or blocking technology. Student e-mail accounts and computer access in designated common areas are available to students.

Contact Mrs. Patricia Finn, Admission Assistant. 617-898-2227. Fax: 617-898-1701. E-mail: admissions@milton.edu. Web site: www.milton.edu

See Display on next page and Close-Up on page 604.

MISS EDGAR'S AND MISS CRAMP'S SCHOOL

525 Mount Pleasant Avenue
Montreal, Quebec H3Y 3H6, Canada

Head of School: Ms. Katherine Nikidis

General Information Girls' day college-preparatory, arts, bilingual studies, and technology school. Grades K–11. Founded: 1909. Setting: urban. 4-acre campus. 1 building on campus. Approved or accredited by Canadian Association of Independent Schools, Quebec Association of Independent Schools, and Quebec Department of Education. Affiliate member of National Association of Independent Schools; member of Secondary School Admission Test Board. Languages of instruction: English and French. Total enrollment: 335. Upper school average class size: 19. Upper school faculty-student ratio: 1:9. There are 180 required school days per year for Upper School students. Upper School students typically attend 5 days per week. The average school day consists of 5 hours.

Upper School Student Profile Grade 9: 39 students (39 girls); Grade 10: 40 students (40 girls); Grade 11: 36 students (36 girls).

Faculty School total: 40. In upper school: 3 men, 15 women; 8 have advanced degrees.

Subjects Offered Art, art history, biology, calculus, career exploration, chemistry, computer science, creative writing, drama, ecology, economics, English, environmental science, European history, French, geography, history, mathematics, media, music, physical education, physics, science, social studies, Spanish, theater, women's studies, world history.

Graduation Requirements English, foreign language, mathematics, science, social studies (includes history).

Special Academic Programs 2 Advanced Placement exams for which test preparation is offered; honors section.

College Admission Counseling 41 students graduated in 2012; all went to college, including John Abbott College; Lower Canada College; Marianopolis College.

Student Life Upper grades have uniform requirement, student council, honor system. Discipline rests primarily with faculty.

Tuition and Aid Day student tuition: CAN$15,835. Tuition installment plan (individually arranged payment plans). Bursaries, merit scholarship grants available. In 2012–13, 18% of upper-school students received aid; total upper-school merit-scholarship money awarded: CAN$80,000. Total amount of financial aid awarded in 2012–13: CAN$105,000.

Admissions Traditional secondary-level entrance grade is 9. For fall 2012, 22 students applied for upper-level admission, 15 were accepted, 8 enrolled. CCAT, SSAT or writing sample required. Deadline for receipt of application materials: none. Application fee required: CAN$50. On-campus interview required.

Athletics Interscholastic: badminton, basketball, cross-country running, golf, hockey, ice hockey, running, soccer, swimming and diving, tennis, touch football, track and field, volleyball; intramural: badminton, baseball, basketball, crew, cross-country running, curling, dance, field hockey, gymnastics, ice hockey, outdoor adventure, outdoor education, outdoor skills, physical fitness, rugby, running, skiing (cross-country), soccer, softball, touch football, track and field, volleyball. 3 PE instructors, 11 coaches.

Computers Computers are regularly used in art, English, French, history, newspaper, writing, yearbook classes. Computer network features include on-campus library services, Internet access, wireless campus network, Internet filtering or blocking technology. Campus intranet, student e-mail accounts, and computer access in designated common areas are available to students. The school has a published electronic and media policy.

Contact Ms. Carla Bolsius, Admissions Coordinator. 514-935-6357 Ext. 254. Fax: 514-935-1099. E-mail: bolsiusc@ecs.qc.ca. Web site: www.ecs.qc.ca

MISS HALL'S SCHOOL

492 Holmes Road
Pittsfield, Massachusetts 01201

Head of School: Ms. Jeannie Norris

General Information Girls' boarding and day college-preparatory, arts, technology, community service, and leadership development school. Grades 9–12. Founded: 1898. Setting: suburban. Nearest major city is Albany, NY. Students are housed in single-sex dormitories. 80-acre campus. 9 buildings on campus. Approved or accredited by Association of Independent Schools in New England, New England Association of Schools and Colleges, The Association of Boarding Schools, and Massachusetts Department of Education. Member of National Association of Independent Schools and Secondary School Admission Test Board. Endowment: $16 million. Total enrollment: 180. Upper school average class size: 10. Upper school faculty-student ratio: 1:5.

Upper School Student Profile Grade 9: 50 students (50 girls); Grade 10: 50 students (50 girls); Grade 11: 40 students (40 girls); Grade 12: 40 students (40 girls). 75% of students are boarding students. 34% are state residents. 20 states are represented in upper school student body. 30% are international students. International students from China, Germany, Republic of Korea, Taiwan, and Viet Nam; 14 other countries represented in student body.

Faculty School total: 36. In upper school: 8 men, 28 women; 26 have advanced degrees; 16 reside on campus.

Subjects Offered Advanced Placement courses, algebra, American government, American history, American literature, anatomy, art, art history, biology, business skills, calculus, ceramics, chamber groups, chemistry, college counseling, community service, computer science, CPR, dance, drama, drawing, driver education, ecology, economics, English, English literature, English-AP, environmental science, ESL, ethics, ethics and responsibility, European history, European history-AP, expressive arts, fine arts, forensics, French, geometry, government/civics, health, history, Latin, mathematics, music, music history, painting, photography, physics, physiology, political science, psychology, science, social studies, Spanish, theater, trigonometry, world cultures, world history.

Graduation Requirements Arts and fine arts (art, music, dance, drama), English, foreign language, history, mathematics, physical education (includes health), science. Community service is required.

Special Academic Programs Advanced Placement exam preparation; honors section; independent study; academic accommodation for the gifted, the musically talented, and the artistically talented; special instructional classes for students with mild learning disabilities and Attention Deficit Disorder; ESL (20 students enrolled).

College Admission Counseling 44 students graduated in 2011; all went to college, including New York University; St. Lawrence University; University of Illinois at Urbana–Champaign; University of Vermont.

Student Life Upper grades have specified standards of dress, student council, honor system. Discipline rests equally with students and faculty.

Tuition and Aid Day student tuition: $29,015; 7-day tuition and room/board: $46,970. Tuition installment plan (Insured Tuition Payment Plan, Academic Management Services Plan, Key Tuition Payment Plan, monthly payment plans, individually arranged payment plans). Merit scholarship grants, need-based scholarship grants available. In 2011–12, 48% of upper-school students received aid; total upper-school merit-scholarship money awarded: $275,000. Total amount of financial aid awarded in 2011–12: $2,500,000.

Admissions Traditional secondary-level entrance grade is 9. For fall 2011, 250 students applied for upper-level admission, 122 were accepted, 70 enrolled. PSAT, SAT, SSAT or TOEFL required. Deadline for receipt of application materials: February 15. Application fee required: $50. Interview required.

Athletics Interscholastic: alpine skiing, basketball, cross-country running, field hockey, lacrosse, skiing (downhill), soccer, softball, tennis, volleyball; intramural: aerobics, aerobics/dance, alpine skiing, dance, equestrian sports, fitness, jogging, modern dance, outdoor activities, outdoor education, outdoor skills, physical fitness, rock climbing, ropes courses, running, skiing (cross-country), skiing (downhill), snowboarding, tennis, walking, wall climbing, wilderness, yoga. 3 coaches, 1 athletic trainer.

Computers Computers are regularly used in computer applications, English, foreign language, history, music, newspaper, photography, science, yearbook classes. Computer network features include on-campus library services, online commercial services, Internet access, wireless campus network. Student e-mail accounts and computer access

in designated common areas are available to students. The school has a published electronic and media policy.
Contact Ms. Julie Bradley, Director of Admission. 413-499-1300. Fax: 413-448-2994. E-mail: info@misshalls.org. Web site: www.misshalls.org

MISSOURI MILITARY ACADEMY

204 Grand Avenue
Mexico, Missouri 65265

Head of School: Mr. Charles "Tony" A. McGeorge

General Information Boys' boarding and day college-preparatory, technology, ESL, military science, and military school, affiliated with Christian faith. Boarding grades 6–PG, day grades 6–12. Founded: 1889. Setting: small town. Nearest major city is St. Louis. Students are housed in single-sex dormitories. 288-acre campus. 19 buildings on campus. Approved or accredited by Independent Schools Association of the Central States and The Association of Boarding Schools. Member of National Association of Independent Schools and Secondary School Admission Test Board. Endowment: $39 million. Total enrollment: 232. Upper school average class size: 10. Upper school faculty-student ratio: 1:11. There are 175 required school days per year for Upper School students. Upper School students typically attend 5 days per week. The average school day consists of 5 hours and 50 minutes.
Upper School Student Profile Grade 9: 55 students (55 boys); Grade 10: 52 students (52 boys); Grade 11: 53 students (53 boys); Grade 12: 50 students (50 boys). 99% of students are boarding students. 20% are state residents. 30 states are represented in upper school student body. 40% are international students. International students from China, Mexico, Mongolia, Republic of Korea, Russian Federation, and Taiwan; 10 other countries represented in student body.
Faculty School total: 47. In upper school: 27 men, 7 women; 27 have advanced degrees; 5 reside on campus.
Subjects Offered Algebra, American literature, art, biology, broadcasting, business, business skills, calculus, chemistry, computer science, drama, economics, English, ESL, fine arts, French, geography, geometry, government/civics, history, honors algebra, honors English, honors U.S. history, humanities, instrumental music, Internet, jazz band, journalism, JROTC or LEAD (Leadership Education and Development), keyboarding, languages, Latin American studies, leadership, literary magazine, marching band, mathematics, military science, music, newspaper, physical education, physical science, physics, physics-AP, psychology, science, social studies, sociology, Spanish, speech, statistics, student government, student publications, swimming, theater, track and field, typing, U.S. government, U.S. history, vocal ensemble, vocal music, world history, wrestling, writing, yearbook.
Graduation Requirements Arts and fine arts (art, music, dance, drama), business skills (includes word processing), computer science, English, foreign language, JROTC, mathematics, physical education (includes health), science, social studies (includes history), 20 hours of community service per school year.
Special Academic Programs 9 Advanced Placement exams for which test preparation is offered; honors section; independent study; study at local college for college credit; academic accommodation for the gifted, the musically talented, and the artistically talented; remedial reading and/or remedial writing; remedial math; special instructional classes for students with Attention Deficit Disorder; ESL (33 students enrolled).
College Admission Counseling 52 students graduated in 2012; all went to college, including Saint Louis University; Texas A&M University; The University of Arizona; The University of Texas at Austin; University of Miami; University of Missouri. Median SAT critical reading: 467, median SAT math: 547, median combined SAT: 1016, median composite ACT: 21.
Student Life Upper grades have uniform requirement, student council, honor system. Discipline rests equally with students and faculty. Attendance at religious services is required.
Summer Programs Remediation, enrichment, ESL, sports, rigorous outdoor training programs offered; session focuses on academics and leadership; held both on and off campus; held at water park in Jefferson City, MO and Courtois River for float/canoe trips; accepts boys and girls; open to students from other schools. 70 students usually enrolled. 2013 schedule: June 24 to July 21. Application deadline: June 15.
Tuition and Aid Day student tuition: $8750; 7-day tuition and room/board: $29,900. Guaranteed tuition plan. Tuition installment plan (individually arranged payment plans, school's own payment plan). Tuition reduction for siblings, merit scholarship grants, need-based scholarship grants, need-based loans available. In 2012–13, 30% of upper-school students received aid; total upper-school merit-scholarship money awarded: $25,000. Total amount of financial aid awarded in 2012–13: $875,000.
Admissions Traditional secondary-level entrance grade is 9. For fall 2012, 250 students applied for upper-level admission, 147 were accepted, 135 enrolled. SSAT or TOEFL or SLEP required. Deadline for receipt of application materials: none. Application fee required: $25. Interview required.
Athletics Interscholastic: aquatics, baseball, basketball, cross-country running, drill team, football, golf, JROTC drill, marksmanship, outdoor activities, riflery, soccer, swimming and diving, tennis, track and field, weight training, wrestling; intramural: aquatics, basketball, canoeing/kayaking, equestrian sports, fishing, fitness, fitness walking, flag football, horseback riding, indoor track, marksmanship, martial arts, outdoor activities, outdoor recreation, outdoor skills, paint ball, physical fitness, physical training, rappelling, riflery, roller blading, ropes courses, running, soccer, softball, strength & conditioning, swimming and diving, table tennis, tennis, touch football, track and field, volleyball, weight lifting, weight training, winter (indoor) track, wrestling. 12 coaches, 1 athletic trainer.
Computers Computers are regularly used in business, English, history, journalism, library, mathematics, newspaper, science, yearbook classes. Computer network features include on-campus library services, online commercial services, Internet access, wireless campus network, Internet filtering or blocking technology. Campus intranet, student e-mail accounts, and computer access in designated common areas are available to students. Students grades are available online. The school has a published electronic and media policy.
Contact Ms. Sandy Riutcel, Admissions Office Coordinator. 573-581-1776 Ext. 321. Fax: 573-581-0081. E-mail: sandy.riutcel@missourimilitaryacademy.com. Web site: www.MissouriMilitaryAcademy.org

MISS PORTER'S SCHOOL

60 Main Street
Farmington, Connecticut 06032

Head of School: Dr. Katherine G. Windsor

General Information Girls' boarding and day college-preparatory and arts school. Grades 9–12. Founded: 1843. Setting: suburban. Nearest major city is Hartford. Students are housed in single-sex dormitories. 50-acre campus. 56 buildings on campus. Approved or accredited by New England Association of Schools and Colleges and Connecticut Department of Education. Member of National Association of Independent Schools and Secondary School Admission Test Board. Endowment: $93 million. Upper school average class size: 10. Upper school faculty-student ratio: 1:7.
Upper School Student Profile Grade 9: 61 students (61 girls); Grade 10: 91 students (91 girls); Grade 11: 77 students (77 girls); Grade 12: 78 students (78 girls). 64% of students are boarding students. 54% are state residents. 23 states are represented in upper school student body. 13% are international students. International students from China and Republic of Korea; 28 other countries represented in student body.
Faculty School total: 56. In upper school: 19 men, 37 women; 32 have advanced degrees; all reside on campus.
Subjects Offered Acting, advanced chemistry, advanced computer applications, advanced math, Advanced Placement courses, advanced studio art-AP, African history, algebra, American history, American literature, anatomy and physiology, aquatics, area studies, art history, art history-AP, arts, astronomy, athletics, ballet, biology, biology-AP, British literature, calculus, calculus-AP, career/college preparation, ceramics, chemistry, chemistry-AP, Chinese, Chinese history, classical language, college counseling, college planning, community service, computer applications, computer graphics, computer programming, computer science, creative writing, dance, dance performance, desktop publishing, drama, drama performance, economics, economics and history, engineering, English, English literature, environmental science, environmental science-AP, ethical decision making, ethics, European history, European history-AP, experiential education, expository writing, fitness, foreign language, forensics, French, French language-AP, French literature-AP, geometry, global issues, golf, graphic design, health and wellness, history, honors geometry, human rights, international relations, intro to computers, Japanese history, jazz, jewelry making, languages, Latin, Latin American literature, Latin-AP, leadership, mathematics, Middle Eastern history, model United Nations, modern dance, modern European history-AP, multicultural literature, music, music history, music performance, music theory, participation in sports, performing arts, personal finance, photography, physics, physics-AP, pre-calculus, printmaking, psychology, public speaking, science, Shakespeare, social studies, Spanish, Spanish language-AP, Spanish literature-AP, sports, squash, statistics, statistics-AP, student government, studio art, studio art-AP, swimming, swimming test, tennis, textiles, theater, trigonometry, U.S. history, U.S. history-AP, video film production, visual arts, vocal music, Web site design, Western civilization, writing, yoga.
Graduation Requirements Arts and fine arts (art, music, dance, drama), athletics, computer science, English, experiential education, foreign language, leadership, mathematics, science, social studies (includes history). Community service is required.
Special Academic Programs 26 Advanced Placement exams for which test preparation is offered; honors section; independent study; term-away projects; study abroad; ESL.
College Admission Counseling 91 students graduated in 2012; 87 went to college, including Cornell University; Gettysburg College; Hobart and William Smith Colleges; Northeastern University; University of Pennsylvania; Yale University. Mean SAT critical reading: 644, mean SAT math: 631, mean SAT writing: 645, mean combined SAT: 1920.
Student Life Upper grades have specified standards of dress, student council, honor system. Discipline rests equally with students and faculty.
Summer Programs Enrichment, advancement, art/fine arts programs offered; session focuses on Model UN, leadership; held on campus; accepts girls; open to students from other schools. 60 students usually enrolled. 2013 schedule: July 7 to July 20. Application deadline: none.
Tuition and Aid Day student tuition: $38,510; 7-day tuition and room/board: $48,515. Tuition installment plan (monthly payment plans, individually arranged payment plans). Merit scholarship grants, need-based scholarship grants available. In 2012–13, 38% of upper-school students received aid. Total amount of financial aid awarded in 2012–13: $3,100,000.

Admissions Traditional secondary-level entrance grade is 9. For fall 2012, 400 students applied for upper-level admission, 185 were accepted, 92 enrolled. ISEE, PSAT and SAT for applicants to grade 11 and 12, SSAT or TOEFL required. Deadline for receipt of application materials: January 15. Application fee required: $50. Interview required.

Athletics Interscholastic: alpine skiing, badminton, basketball, crew, cross-country running, dance, diving, equestrian sports, field hockey, golf, horseback riding, independent competitive sports, lacrosse, skiing (downhill), soccer, softball, squash, swimming and diving, tennis, track and field, ultimate Frisbee, volleyball; intramural: aerobics, aerobics/Nautilus, ballet, climbing, dance, equestrian sports, fencing, fitness, fitness walking, golf, horseback riding, jogging, life saving, martial arts, modern dance, physical fitness, self defense, skiing (downhill), snowboarding, squash, strength & conditioning, swimming and diving, tennis, walking, wall climbing, yoga.

Computers Computers are regularly used in computer applications, desktop publishing, graphic design, graphics, introduction to technology, publications, Web site design classes. Computer network features include on-campus library services, online commercial services, Internet access, wireless campus network, Internet filtering or blocking technology. Campus intranet, student e-mail accounts, and computer access in designated common areas are available to students. Students grades are available online. The school has a published electronic and media policy.

Contact Liz Schmitt, Director of Admission. 860-409-3530. Fax: 860-409-3531. E-mail: liz_schmitt@missporters.org. Web site: www.porters.org

MMI PREPARATORY SCHOOL

154 Centre Street
Freeland, Pennsylvania 18224

Head of School: Mr. Thomas G. Hood

General Information Coeducational day college-preparatory, arts, and technology school. Grades 6–12. Founded: 1879. Setting: small town. Nearest major city is Hazleton. 20-acre campus. 1 building on campus. Approved or accredited by Middle States Association of Colleges and Schools and Pennsylvania Department of Education. Member of National Association of Independent Schools. Endowment: $17 million. Total enrollment: 257. Upper school average class size: 16. Upper school faculty-student ratio: 1:11. There are 168 required school days per year for Upper School students. Upper School students typically attend 5 days per week. The average school day consists of 6 hours and 30 minutes.

Upper School Student Profile Grade 9: 36 students (22 boys, 14 girls); Grade 10: 45 students (25 boys, 20 girls); Grade 11: 36 students (18 boys, 18 girls); Grade 12: 44 students (19 boys, 25 girls).

Faculty School total: 27. In upper school: 11 men, 16 women; 20 have advanced degrees.

Subjects Offered Algebra, American history, American literature, anatomy, anthropology, art, art-AP, biology, biology-AP, calculus, chemistry, chemistry-AP, Chinese, computer programming, computer programming-AP, computer science, consumer education, creative writing, earth science, economics, English, English language and composition-AP, English literature, English literature and composition-AP, environmental science, European history, European history-AP, expository writing, fine arts, geography, geometry, German, government/civics, grammar, health, history, keyboarding, Latin, mathematics, music, physical education, physics, physics-AP, physiology, psychology, science, social studies, Spanish, speech, statistics, trigonometry, world history, world literature.

Graduation Requirements Analysis and differential calculus, arts and fine arts (art, music, dance, drama), college counseling, computer science, consumer education, economics, English, foreign language, mathematics, physical education (includes health), science, social studies (includes history), speech, independent research project presentation every spring, public speaking assembly project every year.

Special Academic Programs 10 Advanced Placement exams for which test preparation is offered; honors section; independent study; study at local college for college credit; academic accommodation for the gifted; special instructional classes for blind students.

College Admission Counseling 37 students graduated in 2012; all went to college, including Lehigh University; Penn State University Park; Saint Joseph's University; The University of Scranton; University of Notre Dame; University of Pennsylvania. Mean SAT critical reading: 568, mean SAT math: 577, mean SAT writing: 574, mean combined SAT: 1719.

Student Life Upper grades have uniform requirement, student council, honor system. Discipline rests primarily with faculty.

Summer Programs Remediation, enrichment, advancement, computer instruction programs offered; session focuses on academics; held on campus; accepts boys and girls; open to students from other schools. 25 students usually enrolled. 2013 schedule: June 6 to July 8. Application deadline: May 15.

Tuition and Aid Day student tuition: $13,100. Tuition installment plan (monthly payment plans). Merit scholarship grants, need-based scholarship grants, paying campus jobs available. In 2012–13, 55% of upper-school students received aid; total upper-school merit-scholarship money awarded: $63,750. Total amount of financial aid awarded in 2012–13: $881,500.

Admissions Traditional secondary-level entrance grade is 9. For fall 2012, 36 students applied for upper-level admission, 30 were accepted, 17 enrolled. Cognitive Abilities Test and Iowa Tests of Basic Skills required. Deadline for receipt of application materials: none. Application fee required: $25. On-campus interview required.

Athletics Interscholastic: baseball (boys), basketball (b,g), cross-country running (b,g), soccer (b,g), softball (g), tennis (b,g), volleyball (g); intramural: bowling (b,g); coed interscholastic: golf; coed intramural: skiing (downhill), snowboarding. 2 PE instructors.

Computers Computers are regularly used in all classes. Computer network features include on-campus library services, Internet access, wireless campus network, Internet filtering or blocking technology. Computer access in designated common areas is available to students. Students grades are available online. The school has a published electronic and media policy.

Contact Aprilaurie Whitley, Director of Admissions and Financial Aid. 570-636-1108 Ext. 136. Fax: 570-636-0742. E-mail: awhitley@mmiprep.org. Web site: www.mmiprep.org

MODESTO CHRISTIAN SCHOOL

5901 Sisk Road
Modesto, California 95356

Head of School: Rev. Lance Lowell

General Information Coeducational day college-preparatory, arts, and religious studies school, affiliated with Assembly of God Church; primarily serves students with learning disabilities, individuals with Attention Deficit Disorder, and dyslexic students. Grades K–12. Founded: 1962. Setting: suburban. Nearest major city is Sacramento. 55-acre campus. 6 buildings on campus. Approved or accredited by Association of Christian Schools International, Western Association of Schools and Colleges, and California Department of Education. Total enrollment: 580. Upper school average class size: 20. Upper school faculty-student ratio: 1:11. There are 177 required school days per year for Upper School students. The average school day consists of 6 hours and 45 minutes.

Upper School Student Profile Grade 9: 65 students (41 boys, 24 girls); Grade 10: 66 students (41 boys, 25 girls); Grade 11: 71 students (37 boys, 34 girls); Grade 12: 78 students (43 boys, 35 girls). 10% of students are members of Assembly of God Church.

Faculty School total: 26. In upper school: 10 men, 16 women; 4 have advanced degrees.

Subjects Offered Advanced biology, algebra, American literature, American sign language, anatomy and physiology, arts, band, biology, biology-AP, calculus-AP, career education, chemistry, church history, consumer education, digital photography, drama, economics, English, English literature, environmental science, fine arts, French language-AP, general math, geometry, grammar, health, history, honors English, keyboarding, mathematics, physical education, physics, political science, pre-algebra, pre-calculus, religion, science, social sciences, social studies, Spanish, Spanish language-AP, speech, studio art-AP, study skills, U.S. government, U.S. history, U.S. history-AP, word processing, world history.

Graduation Requirements Arts and fine arts (art, music, dance, drama), computers, English, foreign language, health, mathematics, physical education (includes health), religion (includes Bible studies and theology), science, social studies (includes history), speech.

Special Academic Programs 7 Advanced Placement exams for which test preparation is offered; honors section; remedial reading and/or remedial writing; remedial math; programs in English, mathematics, general development for dyslexic students.

College Admission Counseling 68 students graduated in 2012; 66 went to college, including Azusa Pacific University; California Polytechnic State University, San Luis Obispo; California State University, Stanislaus; Modesto Junior College. Other: 1 went to work, 1 entered military service. Median SAT critical reading: 524, median SAT math: 513, median SAT writing: 505, median combined SAT: 1037, median composite ACT: 24. 10% scored over 600 on SAT critical reading, 10% scored over 600 on SAT math, 6% scored over 600 on SAT writing, 14% scored over 1800 on combined SAT, 18% scored over 26 on composite ACT.

Student Life Upper grades have specified standards of dress, student council. Discipline rests primarily with faculty. Attendance at religious services is required.

Summer Programs Remediation, advancement programs offered; held on campus; accepts boys and girls; not open to students from other schools. 2013 schedule: June 2 to July 8. Application deadline: May 25.

Tuition and Aid Day student tuition: $7295. Tuition installment plan (monthly payment plans, individually arranged payment plans). Tuition reduction for siblings available. In 2012–13, 5% of upper-school students received aid.

Admissions Traditional secondary-level entrance grade is 9. Admissions testing or Stanford Achievement Test required. Deadline for receipt of application materials: none. Application fee required: $200. On-campus interview required.

Athletics Interscholastic: baseball (boys), basketball (b,g), football (b), golf (b,g), soccer (b,g), softball (g), strength & conditioning (b,g), volleyball (g), wrestling (b); coed interscholastic: fitness, tennis, track and field, weight lifting. 2 PE instructors, 20 coaches.

Computers Computers are regularly used in career education, college planning, typing, yearbook classes. Computer resources include on-campus library services, Internet filtering or blocking technology. Students grades are available online. The school has a published electronic and media policy.

Contact Mrs. Rachel Iversen, Admissions Office. 209-343-2340. Fax: 209-545-9930. E-mail: rachel.iversen@modestochristian.org. Web site: www.modestochristian.org

MONSIGNOR DONOVAN HIGH SCHOOL

711 Hooper Avenue
Toms River, New Jersey 08753

Head of School: Edward Gere

General Information Coeducational day college-preparatory school, affiliated with Roman Catholic Church. Grades 9–12. Founded: 1962. Setting: suburban. 1 building on campus. Approved or accredited by Middle States Association of Colleges and Schools, National Catholic Education Association, and New Jersey Department of Education. Total enrollment: 726. Upper school average class size: 30. Upper school faculty-student ratio: 1:15.

Upper School Student Profile Grade 9: 161 students (77 boys, 84 girls); Grade 10: 182 students (79 boys, 103 girls); Grade 11: 181 students (88 boys, 93 girls); Grade 12: 202 students (95 boys, 107 girls). 85% of students are Roman Catholic.

Faculty School total: 61. In upper school: 28 men, 33 women.

Special Academic Programs Advanced Placement exam preparation; honors section; independent study; study at local college for college credit; academic accommodation for the gifted, the musically talented, and the artistically talented; remedial reading and/or remedial writing; remedial math.

College Admission Counseling 210 students graduated in 2012; 208 went to college. Other: 1 entered military service.

Student Life Upper grades have uniform requirement, student council, honor system. Discipline rests equally with students and faculty. Attendance at religious services is required.

Tuition and Aid Day student tuition: $10,875. Tuition installment plan (SMART Tuition Payment Plan, monthly payment plans). Merit scholarship grants, need-based scholarship grants, paying campus jobs available. In 2012–13, 20% of upper-school students received aid. Total amount of financial aid awarded in 2012–13: $400,000.

Admissions Traditional secondary-level entrance grade is 9. High School Placement Test (closed version) from Scholastic Testing Service or Scholastic Testing Service High School Placement Test required. Deadline for receipt of application materials: October 31. Application fee required: $50. On-campus interview recommended.

Athletics Interscholastic: baseball (boys), cheering (g), football (b), golf (b), ice hockey (b), lacrosse (g), softball (g), wrestling (b); coed interscholastic: basketball, bowling, cross-country running, dance, hiking/backpacking, sailing, skiing (cross-country), snowboarding, soccer, strength & conditioning, surfing, swimming and diving, tennis, weight lifting, weight training. 5 PE instructors, 22 coaches, 1 athletic trainer.

Computers Computers are regularly used in all academic classes. Computer network features include on-campus library services, Internet access, wireless campus network, Internet filtering or blocking technology. Student e-mail accounts are available to students. Students grades are available online.

Contact Mrs. Cynthia Saporito, Registrar. 732-349-8801 Ext. 2426. Fax: 732-505-8014. E-mail: csaporito@mondonhs.com. Web site: www.mondonhs.com

MONTCLAIR KIMBERLEY ACADEMY

201 Valley Road
Montclair, New Jersey 07042

Head of School: Mr. Thomas W. Nammack

General Information Coeducational day college-preparatory, arts, and technology school. Grades PK–12. Founded: 1887. Setting: suburban. Nearest major city is New York, NY. 28-acre campus. 1 building on campus. Approved or accredited by Middle States Association of Colleges and Schools and National Lutheran School Accreditation. Member of National Association of Independent Schools and Secondary School Admission Test Board. Endowment: $12 million. Total enrollment: 1,031. Upper school average class size: 12. Upper school faculty-student ratio: 1:6. Upper School students typically attend 5 days per week. The average school day consists of 6 hours and 30 minutes.

Faculty School total: 73. In upper school: 40 men, 33 women; 64 have advanced degrees.

Subjects Offered Acting, advanced chemistry, advanced math, algebra, American history, American literature, architecture, art, astronomy, biology, biology-AP, British literature, calculus, calculus-AP, chemistry, chemistry-AP, Chinese, chorus, communications, concert band, creative writing, dance, digital photography, drama, driver education, ecology, economics, economics-AP, English, English literature, environmental science, ethics, European history, expository writing, fine arts, French, French language-AP, French literature-AP, geometry, government/civics, health, history, Latin, mathematics, music, photography, physical education, physics, physics-AP, post-calculus, Spanish, Spanish language-AP, Spanish literature-AP, statistics-AP, theater, trigonometry, world history, world literature, world wide web design, writing.

Graduation Requirements Art, arts and fine arts (art, music, dance, drama), English, foreign language, history, mathematics, music, physical education (includes health), science, swimming, citizenship. Community service is required.

Special Academic Programs Advanced Placement exam preparation; honors section; independent study; term-away projects; study abroad; academic accommodation for the gifted.

College Admission Counseling 105 students graduated in 2012; 104 went to college, including Georgetown University; Lafayette College; New York University; Penn State University Park; Princeton University; The George Washington University. Other: 1 entered a postgraduate year. Mean SAT critical reading: 630, mean SAT math: 647. 60% scored over 600 on SAT critical reading, 65% scored over 600 on SAT math.

Student Life Upper grades have specified standards of dress, student council, honor system. Discipline rests equally with students and faculty.

Summer Programs Enrichment, advancement, sports, art/fine arts, computer instruction programs offered; held on campus; accepts boys and girls; open to students from other schools. 250 students usually enrolled. 2013 schedule: June 27 to August 5. Application deadline: none.

Tuition and Aid Day student tuition: $32,000. Tuition installment plan (Insured Tuition Payment Plan, monthly payment plans, individually arranged payment plans). Need-based scholarship grants available. In 2012–13, 15% of upper-school students received aid. Total amount of financial aid awarded in 2012–13: $1,281,308.

Admissions Traditional secondary-level entrance grade is 9. ISEE or SSAT required. Deadline for receipt of application materials: January 31. Application fee required: $50. On-campus interview required.

Athletics Interscholastic: baseball (boys), basketball (b,g), cheering (g), cross-country running (b,g), dance (b,g), dance team (b,g), fencing (b,g), field hockey (g), football (b), ice hockey (b), lacrosse (b,g), outdoor activities (b,g), physical fitness (b,g), soccer (b,g), softball (g), swimming and diving (b,g), tennis (b,g), track and field (b,g), volleyball (g), winter (indoor) track (b,g); coed interscholastic: golf. 5 PE instructors, 9 coaches, 2 athletic trainers.

Computers Computers are regularly used in all classes. Computer network features include on-campus library services, online commercial services, Internet access, wireless campus network, Internet filtering or blocking technology, 1:1 laptop school, community Intranet. Campus intranet and student e-mail accounts are available to students. The school has a published electronic and media policy.

Contact Sarah Rowland, Director of Admissions and Financial Aid. 973-509-7930. Fax: 973-509-4526. E-mail: srowland@mka.org. Web site: www.mka.org

MONTGOMERY BELL ACADEMY

4001 Harding Road
Nashville, Tennessee 37205

Head of School: Bradford Gioia

General Information Boys' day college-preparatory and arts school. Grades 7–12. Founded: 1867. Setting: urban. 43-acre campus. 9 buildings on campus. Approved or accredited by Southern Association of Colleges and Schools, Southern Association of Independent Schools, and Tennessee Association of Independent Schools. Member of National Association of Independent Schools and Secondary School Admission Test Board. Endowment: $55.8 million. Total enrollment: 715. Upper school average class size: 12. Upper school faculty-student ratio: 1:8. There are 180 required school days per year for Upper School students. Upper School students typically attend 5 days per week. The average school day consists of 7 hours and 20 minutes.

Upper School Student Profile Grade 9: 123 students (123 boys); Grade 10: 117 students (117 boys); Grade 11: 127 students (127 boys); Grade 12: 119 students (119 boys).

Faculty School total: 96. In upper school: 63 men, 16 women; 62 have advanced degrees.

Subjects Offered Advanced Placement courses, algebra, American history, American history-AP, American literature, American literature-AP, art, art history, art history-AP, biology, biology-AP, calculus, calculus-AP, chemistry, chemistry-AP, Chinese, computer programming, computer science, computer science-AP, drama, earth science, economics, English, English literature, environmental science-AP, European history, European history-AP, fine arts, French, French language-AP, French literature-AP, French-AP, geography, geology, geometry, German, German-AP, government/civics, grammar, Greek, history, Latin, Latin-AP, mathematics, music, music history, music theory, music theory-AP, physical education, physics, physics-AP, science, social studies, Spanish, Spanish-AP, speech, statistics, statistics-AP, theater, trigonometry, U.S. government and politics-AP, U.S. history-AP, world history, world history-AP, writing.

Graduation Requirements Arts and fine arts (art, music, dance, drama), English, foreign language, mathematics, physical education (includes health), science, social studies (includes history).

Special Academic Programs Advanced Placement exam preparation; honors section; term-away projects; study abroad.

College Admission Counseling Colleges students went to include Samford University; Sewanee: The University of the South; The University of Tennessee; Tulane University; University of Mississippi; University of Virginia. Other: 1 entered military service. Mean SAT critical reading: 634, mean SAT math: 648, mean SAT writing: 629, mean combined SAT: 1908, mean composite ACT: 29.

Student Life Upper grades have specified standards of dress, student council, honor system. Discipline rests primarily with faculty.

Summer Programs Remediation, enrichment, sports, art/fine arts, rigorous outdoor training, computer instruction programs offered; session focuses on academics and athletics; held both on and off campus; held at Long Mountain, TN; accepts boys and girls; open to students from other schools. 2,400 students usually enrolled. 2013 schedule: June 1 to July 31.

Tuition and Aid Day student tuition: $21,250. Tuition installment plan (monthly payment plans, Dewar Tuition Refund Plan). Need-based scholarship grants available. In 2012–13, 22% of upper-school students received aid. Total amount of financial aid awarded in 2012–13: $1,750,000.

Admissions Traditional secondary-level entrance grade is 9. For fall 2012, 75 students applied for upper-level admission, 39 were accepted, 28 enrolled. ISEE required. Deadline for receipt of application materials: February 1. Application fee required: $50. Interview required.

Athletics Interscholastic: baseball, basketball, bowling, crew, cross-country running, diving, football, Frisbee, golf, hockey, ice hockey, lacrosse, riflery, rock climbing, rowing, soccer, swimming and diving, tennis, track and field, ultimate Frisbee, wrestling; intramural: backpacking, baseball, basketball, cheering, climbing, crew, cricket, fencing, flag football, fly fishing, football, Frisbee, hiking/backpacking, independent competitive sports, outdoor activities, paddle tennis, running, soccer, strength & conditioning, table tennis, track and field, weight training, wilderness, yoga. 2 PE instructors, 4 coaches, 2 athletic trainers.

Computers Computers are regularly used in all academic classes. Computer network features include on-campus library services, online commercial services, Internet access, wireless campus network, Internet filtering or blocking technology. Student e-mail accounts are available to students. Students grades are available online.

Contact Mr. Greg Ferrell, Director, Admission and Financial Aid. 615-369-5311 Ext. 251. Fax: 615-297-0271. E-mail: greg.ferrell@montgomerybell.edu. Web site: www.montgomerybell.com

MOORESTOWN FRIENDS SCHOOL

110 East Main Street
Moorestown, New Jersey 08057

Head of School: Mr. Laurence Van Meter

General Information Coeducational day college-preparatory, arts, religious studies, and technology school, affiliated with Society of Friends. Grades PS–12. Founded: 1785. Setting: suburban. Nearest major city is Philadelphia, PA. 48-acre campus. 9 buildings on campus. Approved or accredited by Middle States Association of Colleges and Schools and New Jersey Department of Education. Member of National Association of Independent Schools. Endowment: $7.9 million. Total enrollment: 715. Upper school average class size: 18. Upper school faculty-student ratio: 1:9. There are 170 required school days per year for Upper School students. Upper School students typically attend 5 days per week.

Upper School Student Profile Grade 9: 77 students (33 boys, 44 girls); Grade 10: 76 students (39 boys, 37 girls); Grade 11: 71 students (37 boys, 34 girls); Grade 12: 70 students (28 boys, 42 girls). 3% of students are members of Society of Friends.

Faculty School total: 98. In upper school: 24 men, 33 women; 42 have advanced degrees.

Subjects Offered Algebra, American history, American literature, art, art history, biology, calculus, ceramics, chemistry, Chinese, community service, computer programming, computer science, creative writing, drama, driver education, earth science, economics, English, English literature, environmental science, ethics, European history, expository writing, fine arts, French, geometry, government/civics, grammar, health, history, mathematics, music, philosophy, photography, physical education, physics, psychology, religion, science, social studies, Spanish, theater, trigonometry, world history, writing.

Graduation Requirements Arts and fine arts (art, music, dance, drama), English, foreign language, mathematics, physical education (includes health), science, senior project, social studies (includes history). Community service is required.

Special Academic Programs Advanced Placement exam preparation; honors section; independent study; term-away projects; study abroad.

College Admission Counseling 72 students graduated in 2012; all went to college, including Drexel University; Northeastern University; Penn State University Park; Rutgers, The State University of New Jersey, New Brunswick; University of Pennsylvania; Ursinus College. Mean SAT critical reading: 616, mean SAT math: 611, mean SAT writing: 639, mean combined SAT: 1866.

Student Life Upper grades have specified standards of dress, student council, honor system. Discipline rests primarily with faculty. Attendance at religious services is required.

Tuition and Aid Day student tuition: $24,600. Tuition installment plan (Academic Management Services Plan, Tuition Refund Plan). Need-based scholarship grants, need-based loans, tuition reduction for children of faculty and staff available. In 2012–13, 37% of upper-school students received aid. Total amount of financial aid awarded in 2012–13: $1,717,400.

Admissions Traditional secondary-level entrance grade is 9. For fall 2012, 90 students applied for upper-level admission, 34 were accepted, 32 enrolled. ERB CTP required. Deadline for receipt of application materials: none. Application fee required: $45. On-campus interview required.

Athletics Interscholastic: baseball (boys), basketball (b,g), crew (b,g), cross-country running (b,g), fencing (b,g), field hockey (g), independent competitive sports (b,g), lacrosse (b,g), physical training (b,g), soccer (b,g), swimming and diving (b,g), tennis (b,g); intramural: floor hockey (b), roller hockey (b), street hockey (b), weight training (b,g); coed interscholastic: golf. 6 PE instructors, 23 coaches, 1 athletic trainer.

Computers Computers are regularly used in English, foreign language, mathematics, music, science classes. Computer network features include on-campus library services, Internet access, wireless campus network, Internet filtering or blocking technology, campus portal. Campus intranet, student e-mail accounts, and computer access in designated common areas are available to students. Students grades are available online.

Contact Karin B. Miller, Director of Admission and Financial Aid. 856-235-2900 Ext. 227. Fax: 856-235-6684. E-mail: kmiller@mfriends.org. Web site: www.mfriends.org

MOOSEHEART HIGH SCHOOL

255 James J. Davis Drive
Mooseheart, Illinois 60539

Head of School: Mr. Gary Lee Urwiler

General Information Coeducational boarding and day college-preparatory, general academic, arts, business, vocational, religious studies, bilingual studies, technology, nursing, and cosmetology school, affiliated with Protestant faith, Roman Catholic Church; primarily serves underachievers and students in dysfunctional family situations. Grades K–12. Founded: 1913. Setting: small town. Nearest major city is Aurora. Students are housed in family homes. 1,000-acre campus. 40 buildings on campus. Approved or accredited by North Central Association of Colleges and Schools and Illinois Department of Education. Total enrollment: 210. Upper school average class size: 13. Upper school faculty-student ratio: 1:6. There are 176 required school days per year for Upper School students. Upper School students typically attend 5 days per week. The average school day consists of 6 hours and 45 minutes.

Upper School Student Profile Grade 9: 28 students (19 boys, 9 girls); Grade 10: 32 students (24 boys, 8 girls); Grade 11: 41 students (27 boys, 14 girls); Grade 12: 19 students (10 boys, 9 girls). 95% of students are Protestant, Roman Catholic.

Faculty School total: 45. In upper school: 9 men, 11 women; 5 have advanced degrees.

Special Academic Programs Independent study; remedial reading and/or remedial writing; remedial math.

College Admission Counseling 26 students graduated in 2011.

Student Life Upper grades have specified standards of dress, student council, honor system. Discipline rests primarily with faculty. Attendance at religious services is required.

Admissions Traditional secondary-level entrance grade is 9. Mathematics proficiency exam required. Deadline for receipt of application materials: March. No application fee required. Interview recommended.

Athletics Interscholastic: basketball (boys, girls), drill team (b,g), football (b), JROTC drill (b,g), track and field (b,g), volleyball (g), wrestling (b); intramural: aerobics (b), aerobics/dance (g). 2 PE instructors, 10 coaches.

Computers Computers are regularly used in word processing classes. Computer resources include on-campus library services, Internet access, wireless campus network, Internet filtering or blocking technology. Campus intranet and computer access in designated common areas are available to students. The school has a published electronic and media policy.

Contact Kyle Rife, Director of Admission. 630-906-3631 Ext. 3631. Fax: 630-906-3634 Ext. 3634. E-mail: krife@mooseheart.org. Web site:

MORAVIAN ACADEMY

4313 Green Pond Road
Bethlehem, Pennsylvania 18020

Head of School: George N. King Jr.

General Information Coeducational day college-preparatory school, affiliated with Moravian Church. Grades PK–12. Founded: 1742. Setting: rural. Nearest major city is Philadelphia. 120-acre campus. 8 buildings on campus. Approved or accredited by Middle States Association of Colleges and Schools, Pennsylvania Association of Independent Schools, and Pennsylvania Department of Education. Member of National Association of Independent Schools and Secondary School Admission Test Board. Endowment: $15.3 million. Total enrollment: 775. Upper school average class size: 15. Upper school faculty-student ratio: 1:7. There are 173 required school days per year for Upper School students. Upper School students typically attend 5 days per week. The average school day consists of 7 hours and 15 minutes.

Upper School Student Profile Grade 9: 82 students (45 boys, 37 girls); Grade 10: 67 students (33 boys, 34 girls); Grade 11: 76 students (35 boys, 41 girls); Grade 12: 75 students (35 boys, 40 girls).

Faculty School total: 100. In upper school: 21 men, 22 women; 41 have advanced degrees.

Subjects Offered Acting, advanced biology, advanced chemistry, Advanced Placement courses, algebra, American history, American history-AP, American literature, anatomy, ancient history, ancient world history, art, bell choir, biology, biology-AP, botany, calculus, calculus-AP, ceramics, chemistry, chemistry-AP, Chinese, Chinese history, community service, drama, drawing, driver education, ecology, economics, English, English language-AP, English literature, English literature-AP, environmental science, environmental science-AP, ethics, European history, European history-AP, film, fine arts, French, French language-AP, geometry, government, health, history, honors geometry, Latin American history, mathematics, Middle East, music, painting, photography, physical education, physics, playwriting, poetry, probability and statistics, religion, science, short story, Spanish, Spanish language-AP, statistics, statistics-AP, theater, trigonometry, U.S. history-AP, woodworking, world history, world literature, zoology.

Graduation Requirements Arts and fine arts (art, music, dance, drama), English, foreign language, mathematics, physical education (includes health), religion (includes Bible studies and theology), science, social studies (includes history), service project.

Special Academic Programs 12 Advanced Placement exams for which test preparation is offered; honors section; independent study; study at local college for college credit.

College Admission Counseling 62 students graduated in 2012; 59 went to college, including Georgetown University; Lafayette College; Lehigh University; Penn State University Park; The George Washington University; University of Chicago. Other: 3 had other specific plans. Median SAT critical reading: 655, median SAT math: 630, median SAT writing: 645. 73% scored over 600 on SAT critical reading, 71% scored over 600 on SAT math, 74% scored over 600 on SAT writing.

Student Life Upper grades have specified standards of dress, student council. Discipline rests equally with students and faculty. Attendance at religious services is required.

Summer Programs Enrichment, sports, art/fine arts programs offered; session focuses on enrichment; held on campus; accepts boys and girls; open to students from other schools. 2013 schedule: June 10 to August 9.

Tuition and Aid Day student tuition: $23,550. Tuition installment plan (monthly payment plans). Need-based scholarship grants available. In 2012–13, 29% of upper-school students received aid. Total amount of financial aid awarded in 2012–13: $1,124,920.

Admissions Traditional secondary-level entrance grade is 9. For fall 2012, 67 students applied for upper-level admission, 47 were accepted, 34 enrolled. ERB and Otis-Lennon School Ability Test required. Deadline for receipt of application materials: none. Application fee required: $65. On-campus interview required.

Athletics Interscholastic: baseball (boys), basketball (b,g), field hockey (g), football (b), lacrosse (b,g), soccer (b,g), softball (g), tennis (b,g), track and field (b,g), volleyball (g), wrestling (b); coed interscholastic: cross-country running, golf, swimming and diving. 3 PE instructors, 15 coaches, 1 athletic trainer.

Computers Computers are regularly used in all academic, art, English, foreign language, history, mathematics, music, science classes. Computer resources include on-campus library services, Internet access, wireless campus network. Computer access in designated common areas is available to students. The school has a published electronic and media policy.

Contact Daniel Axford, Director of Upper School Admissions. 610-691-1600. Fax: 610-691-3354. E-mail: daxford@moravianacademy.org. Web site: www.moravianacademy.org

See Display below and Close-Up on page 606.

MOREAU CATHOLIC HIGH SCHOOL

27170 Mission Boulevard
Hayward, California 94544

Head of School: Mr. Terry Lee

General Information Coeducational day college-preparatory, arts, business, religious studies, technology, and STEM school, affiliated with Roman Catholic Church. Grades 9–12. Founded: 1965. Setting: suburban. Nearest major city is San Francisco. 14-acre campus. 6 buildings on campus. Approved or accredited by National Catholic Education Association, Western Association of Schools and Colleges, Western Catholic Education Association, and California Department of Education. Total enrollment: 896. Upper school average class size: 24. Upper school faculty-student ratio: 1:18. There are 186 required school days per year for Upper School students. Upper School students typically attend 5 days per week. The average school day consists of 6 hours and 35 minutes.

Upper School Student Profile Grade 9: 256 students (138 boys, 118 girls); Grade 10: 242 students (107 boys, 135 girls); Grade 11: 196 students (105 boys, 91 girls); Grade 12: 202 students (103 boys, 99 girls). 72% of students are Roman Catholic.

Faculty School total: 69. In upper school: 30 men, 23 women; 27 have advanced degrees.

Subjects Offered Advanced Placement courses, aerobics, algebra, American Civil War, American history, American legal systems, American literature, anatomy, art, art history, ASB Leadership, astronomy, athletics, Bible as literature, biology, biology-AP, business, business law, business skills, calculus, calculus-AP, campus ministry, ceramics, cheerleading, chemistry, choral music, Christian ethics, Christian scripture, Christianity, church history, community service, computer education, computer math, computer programming, computer science, concert band, creative writing, drafting, drama, drama performance, driver education, earth science, economics, electronics, engineering, English, English literature, English/composition-AP, ethics, ethics and responsibility, European history, expository writing, fine arts, French, French-AP, geometry, government-AP, government/civics, grammar, health, health education, history, history of the Catholic Church, home economics, honors algebra, honors English, honors geometry, honors U.S. history, honors world history, human biology, instrumental music, jazz band, jazz ensemble, journalism, marching band, mathematics, mechanical drawing, media studies, moral and social development, moral theology, music, music appreciation, newspaper, physical education, physics, physics-AP, physiology, psychology, religion, science, sculpture, social sciences, social studies, Spanish, Spanish language-AP, speech, sports medicine, sports science, student government, student publications, symphonic band, the Sixties, theater, theology, trigonometry, typing, U.S. government, U.S. government and politics-AP, U.S. history, U.S. history-AP, weight training, world history, world literature, writing, yearbook.

Graduation Requirements Arts and fine arts (art, music, dance, drama), computer science, English, foreign language, mathematics, physical education (includes health), religion (includes Bible studies and theology), science, social sciences, social studies (includes history). Community service is required.

Special Academic Programs Advanced Placement exam preparation; honors section; special instructional classes for Saints and Scholars program for students with documented learning disabilities who require accommodations.

College Admission Counseling 229 students graduated in 2012; all went to college, including California State University; Saint Mary's College of California; Santa Clara University; Stanford University; University of California, Berkeley; University of San Francisco. Mean SAT critical reading: 527, mean SAT math: 546, mean SAT writing: 533, mean composite ACT: 24.

Student Life Upper grades have specified standards of dress, student council, honor system. Discipline rests primarily with faculty. Attendance at religious services is required.

Summer Programs Remediation, enrichment, sports programs offered; session focuses on enrichment and remediation; held on campus; accepts boys and girls; open to students from other schools. 2013 schedule: June 17 to July 19. Application deadline: June 7.

Tuition and Aid Day student tuition: $15,096. Tuition installment plan (FACTS Tuition Payment Plan, monthly payment plans). Merit scholarship grants, need-based scholarship grants available. In 2012–13, 37% of upper-school students received aid. Total amount of financial aid awarded in 2012–13: $1,500,000.

Admissions Traditional secondary-level entrance grade is 9. Scholastic Testing Service High School Placement Test required. Deadline for receipt of application materials: January 4. Application fee required: $90. On-campus interview required.

Athletics Interscholastic: aquatics (boys, girls), badminton (b,g), baseball (b), basketball (b,g), cheering (g), cross-country running (b,g), dance squad (g), football (b), golf (b,g), soccer (b,g), softball (g), swimming and diving (b,g), tennis (b,g), track and field (b,g), volleyball (b,g), water polo (b,g); intramural: lacrosse (g); coed interscholastic: aerobics/dance, modern dance; coed intramural: equestrian sports, skiing (downhill), strength & conditioning. 5 PE instructors, 50 coaches, 1 athletic trainer.

Computers Computers are regularly used in career exploration, college planning, English, foreign language, history, journalism, keyboarding, mathematics, newspaper, religious studies, science, Spanish, technology, theology, writing, yearbook classes. Computer network features include on-campus library services, online commercial services, Internet access, wireless campus network, PowerSchool grade program, 1:1 student laptop program (every student at Moreau has a laptop), laptop included in tuition. Campus intranet, student e-mail accounts, and computer access in designated common areas are available to students. Students grades are available online. The school has a published electronic and media policy.

Contact Patricia Bevilacqua, Admissions Assistant. 510-881-4320. Fax: 510-582-8405. E-mail: admissions@moreaucatholic.org. Web site: www.moreaucatholic.org

MORRISTOWN-BEARD SCHOOL

70 Whippany Road
Morristown, New Jersey 07960

Head of School: Mr. Peter Caldwell

General Information Coeducational day college-preparatory and arts school. Grades 6–12. Founded: 1891. Setting: suburban. Nearest major city is New York, NY. 22-acre campus. 11 buildings on campus. Approved or accredited by Middle States Association of Colleges and Schools, New Jersey Association of Independent Schools, and New Jersey Department of Education. Member of National Association of Independent Schools and Secondary School Admission Test Board. Endowment: $11 million. Total enrollment: 557. Upper school average class size: 12. Upper school faculty-student ratio: 1:7. There are 160 required school days per year for Upper School students. Upper School students typically attend 5 days per week. The average school day consists of 7 hours.

Upper School Student Profile Grade 9: 108 students (62 boys, 46 girls); Grade 10: 102 students (60 boys, 42 girls); Grade 11: 96 students (53 boys, 43 girls); Grade 12: 95 students (46 boys, 49 girls).

Faculty School total: 94. In upper school: 33 men, 37 women; 40 have advanced degrees.

Subjects Offered 20th century history, acting, advanced chemistry, advanced math, Advanced Placement courses, advanced studio art-AP, algebra, American history, American legal systems, American studies, anatomy and physiology, ancient world history, architecture, art, art history, astronomy, biology, biology-AP, calculus, calculus-AP, ceramics, chemistry, chemistry-AP, choir, chorus, community service, computer programming, computer science, computer skills, computer studies, constitutional law, creative writing, dance, digital art, drama, drawing, earth science, ecology, engineering, English, English-AP, fine arts, French, geometry, health, instrumental music, journalism, Latin, Middle Eastern history, mythology, nature writers, painting, photography, physical education, physical science, physics, physics-AP, public speaking, rite of passage, Spanish, Spanish-AP, speech, statistics, statistics-AP, studio art-AP, theater, trigonometry, U.S. history-AP, world history.

Graduation Requirements Arts and fine arts (art, music, dance, drama), English, foreign language, mathematics, physical education (includes health), science, service learning/internship, social studies (includes history). Community service is required.

Special Academic Programs 13 Advanced Placement exams for which test preparation is offered; honors section; independent study; term-away projects; study abroad.

College Admission Counseling 98 students graduated in 2012; 95 went to college, including American University; Boston College; Colgate University; New York University; University of Vermont; Wesleyan University. Other: 2 entered a postgraduate year, 1 had other specific plans. Mean SAT critical reading: 589, mean SAT math: 605, mean SAT writing: 613, mean composite ACT: 26.

Student Life Upper grades have specified standards of dress, student council, honor system. Discipline rests equally with students and faculty.

Summer Programs Enrichment, advancement, sports, art/fine arts, computer instruction programs offered; session focuses on traditional day camp; held on campus; accepts boys and girls; open to students from other schools. 700 students usually enrolled. 2013 schedule: June 24 to August 2.

Tuition and Aid Day student tuition: $33,285. Tuition installment plan (Tuition Management Systems). Merit scholarship grants, need-based scholarship grants available. In 2012–13, 14% of upper-school students received aid; total upper-school merit-scholarship money awarded: $85,500. Total amount of financial aid awarded in 2012–13: $2,000,000.

Admissions Traditional secondary-level entrance grade is 9. For fall 2012, 377 students applied for upper-level admission, 225 were accepted, 127 enrolled. ISEE or SSAT required. Deadline for receipt of application materials: February 4. Application fee required: $60. On-campus interview required.

Athletics Interscholastic: baseball (boys), basketball (b,g), field hockey (g), football (b), ice hockey (b,g), lacrosse (b,g), skiing (downhill) (b,g), soccer (b,g), softball (g), swimming and diving (b,g), tennis (b,g), track and field (b,g), volleyball (g); coed interscholastic: alpine skiing, cross-country running, dance, golf, swimming and diving, track and field, yoga; coed intramural: dance, fitness, physical fitness, strength & conditioning. 4 PE instructors, 6 coaches, 1 athletic trainer.

Computers Computers are regularly used in architecture, art, English, foreign language, history, mathematics, music, science classes. Computer network features include on-campus library services, online commercial services, Internet access, wireless campus network, Internet filtering or blocking technology, Jstor, Jerseycat. Student e-mail accounts are available to students. Students grades are available online. The school has a published electronic and media policy.

Contact Mrs. Barbara Luperi, Admission Assistant. 973-539-3032. Fax: 973-539-1590. E-mail: bluperi@mbs.net. Web site: www.mbs.net

MOTHER MCAULEY HIGH SCHOOL

3737 West 99th Street
Chicago, Illinois 60655-3133

Head of School: Mrs. Claudia Woodruff

General Information Girls' day college-preparatory, arts, religious studies, and technology school, affiliated with Roman Catholic Church. Grades 9–12. Founded: 1846. Setting: urban. 21-acre campus. 2 buildings on campus. Approved or accredited by Mercy Secondary Education Association, National Catholic Education Association, North Central Association of Colleges and Schools, The College Board, and Illinois Department of Education. Endowment: $2 million. Total enrollment: 1,215. Upper school average class size: 25. Upper school faculty-student ratio: 1:17. There are 180 required school days per year for Upper School students. Upper School students typically attend 5 days per week. The average school day consists of 6 hours and 30 minutes.

Upper School Student Profile Grade 9: 308 students (308 girls); Grade 10: 291 students (291 girls); Grade 11: 284 students (284 girls); Grade 12: 332 students (332 girls). 87% of students are Roman Catholic.

Faculty School total: 92. In upper school: 12 men, 80 women; 56 have advanced degrees.

Subjects Offered Anatomy and physiology, art history, art history-AP, calculus-AP, ceramics, chemistry-AP, English, English literature, English literature and composition-AP, European history-AP, first aid, French, French-AP, general science, geography, geometry, geometry with art applications, global issues, graphic design, history of the Catholic Church, honors algebra, honors English, honors geometry, honors U.S. history, honors world history, introduction to theater, journalism, Latin, Latin-AP, Life of Christ, marching band, media literacy, music appreciation, newspaper, orchestra, painting, photography, physical education, physics, play production, scripture, Spanish, Spanish-AP, speech, studio art, studio art-AP, theater, theology, U.S. history, U.S. history-AP, U.S. literature, Web site design, wind ensemble, world history, world history-AP, yearbook.

Graduation Requirements Art history, English, lab science, language, mathematics, music, physical education (includes health), social sciences, speech, technology, theology.

Special Academic Programs Advanced Placement exam preparation; honors section; study at local college for college credit.

College Admission Counseling 343 students graduated in 2012; all went to college, including Eastern Illinois University; Illinois State University; Loyola University Chicago; University of Illinois at Chicago; University of Illinois at Urbana–Champaign. Mean composite ACT: 23.

Student Life Upper grades have uniform requirement, student council. Discipline rests primarily with faculty. Attendance at religious services is required.

Summer Programs Remediation, enrichment, advancement, sports, art/fine arts, computer instruction programs offered; session focuses on academics; held on campus; accepts girls; open to students from other schools. 200 students usually enrolled. 2013 schedule: June 11 to July 27. Application deadline: June 8.

Tuition and Aid Day student tuition: $9300. Tuition installment plan (monthly payment plans, individually arranged payment plans). Tuition reduction for siblings, merit scholarship grants, need-based scholarship grants, paying campus jobs available. In 2012–13, 40% of upper-school students received aid; total upper-school merit-scholarship money awarded: $30,000. Total amount of financial aid awarded in 2012–13: $1,000,000.

Admissions Traditional secondary-level entrance grade is 9. For fall 2012, 383 students applied for upper-level admission, 360 were accepted, 308 enrolled. High School Placement Test required. Deadline for receipt of application materials: August 1. Application fee required: $175.

Athletics Interscholastic: basketball, bowling, cross-country running, diving, golf, independent competitive sports, lacrosse, sailing, soccer, softball, swimming and diving, tennis, track and field, volleyball, water polo; intramural: aerobics, basketball, bowling, flag football, Frisbee, softball, touch football, ultimate Frisbee, volleyball. 2 PE instructors, 20 coaches, 1 athletic trainer.

Computers Computers are regularly used in accounting, art, basic skills, business education, drafting, drawing and design, English, foreign language, French, graphics, journalism, Latin, mathematics, music, newspaper, photography, science, social sciences, Spanish, theater, Web site design, writing, yearbook classes. Computer network features include on-campus library services, Internet access, wireless campus network, Internet filtering or blocking technology. Student e-mail accounts and computer access in designated common areas are available to students. Students grades are available online. The school has a published electronic and media policy.

Contact Mrs. Kathryn Klyczek, Director of Admissions and Financial Aid. 773-881-6534. Fax: 773-881-6515. E-mail: kklyczek@mothermcauley.org. Web site: www.mothermcauley.org

MOUNT CARMEL SCHOOL

PO Box 500006
Saipan, Northern Mariana Islands 96950

Head of School: Mr. Galvin S. Deleon Guerrero

General Information Coeducational day college-preparatory, general academic, religious studies, and technology school, affiliated with Roman Catholic Church. Grades 1–12. Founded: 1952. Setting: rural. Nearest major city is Hagatna, Guam. 5-acre campus. 1 building on campus. Approved or accredited by Western Association of Schools and Colleges and Northern Mariana Islands Department of Education. Total enrollment: 378. Upper school average class size: 25. Upper school faculty-student ratio: 1:20. There are 180 required school days per year for Upper School students. Upper School students typically attend 5 days per week. The average school day consists of 6 hours and 5 minutes.

Upper School Student Profile Grade 9: 41 students (19 boys, 22 girls); Grade 10: 28 students (16 boys, 12 girls); Grade 11: 40 students (19 boys, 21 girls); Grade 12: 37 students (21 boys, 16 girls). 95% of students are Roman Catholic.

Faculty School total: 20. In upper school: 3 men, 6 women; 4 have advanced degrees.

Subjects Offered Advanced math, algebra, American government, American history, American history-AP, art, biology, British literature, calculus, calculus-AP, campus ministry, Catholic belief and practice, chemistry, Christian doctrine, Christian scripture, civics, composition, computer applications, computer science, drama, English, English literature, English literature-AP, foreign language, gardening, geometry, history of the Catholic Church, HTML design, independent study, Japanese, literature, media production, moral theology, physical education, physics, pre-calculus, Spanish, state history, theology, trigonometry, world history, world literature, world religions, yearbook.

Graduation Requirements Algebra, American history, art, biology, British literature, Catholic belief and practice, chemistry, Christian ethics, Christian scripture, church history, civics, composition, computer applications, English, English literature, foreign language, geometry, physical education (includes health), physics, theology, U.S. literature, world history.

Special Academic Programs 4 Advanced Placement exams for which test preparation is offered; independent study.

College Admission Counseling 45 students graduated in 2012; 25 went to college, including Northern Marianas College. Other: 3 went to work, 2 entered military service.

Student Life Upper grades have uniform requirement, student council, honor system. Discipline rests primarily with faculty. Attendance at religious services is required.

Summer Programs Remediation, enrichment, advancement, ESL, art/fine arts programs offered; session focuses on remediation/make-up courses; held on campus; accepts boys and girls; open to students from other schools. 20 students usually enrolled. 2013 schedule: July 1 to July 31. Application deadline: June 1.

Tuition and Aid Day student tuition: $3530. Tuition installment plan (monthly payment plans). Tuition reduction for siblings, merit scholarship grants, need-based scholarship grants available. In 2012–13, 25% of upper-school students received aid; total upper-school merit-scholarship money awarded: $1000. Total amount of financial aid awarded in 2012–13: $30,000.

Admissions Traditional secondary-level entrance grade is 9. For fall 2012, 79 students applied for upper-level admission, 79 were accepted, 78 enrolled. Deadline for receipt of application materials: none. Application fee required: $50.

Athletics Interscholastic: aquatics (boys, girls), basketball (b,g), canoeing/kayaking (b,g), flag football (b), ocean paddling (b,g), softball (g), track and field (b,g), volleyball (b,g); intramural: badminton (b,g), basketball (b,g), flag football (b,g), floor hockey (b,g), soccer (b,g), volleyball (b,g); coed interscholastic: aquatics, ocean paddling, volleyball; coed intramural: badminton, soccer, volleyball. 1 PE instructor.

Computers Computers are regularly used in all academic, computer applications classes. Computer network features include on-campus library services, online commercial services, Internet access, wireless campus network, Internet filtering or blocking technology. Campus intranet is available to students. Students grades are available online. The school has a published electronic and media policy.

Contact Mr. Galvin S. Deleon Guerrero, President. 670-234-6184. Fax: 670-235-4751. E-mail: president.mcs@pticom.com. Web site: www.mtcarmel-edu.net

MT. DE SALES ACADEMY

851 Orange Street
Macon, Georgia 31201

Head of School: Mr. David Held

General Information Coeducational day college-preparatory, arts, religious studies, and technology school, affiliated with Roman Catholic Church; primarily serves individuals with Attention Deficit Disorder. Grades 6–12. Founded: 1876. Setting: urban. 10 buildings on campus. Approved or accredited by Georgia Independent School Association, Mercy Secondary Education Association, National Catholic Education Association, Southern Association of Colleges and Schools, Southern Association of Independent Schools, and Georgia Department of Education. Member of National Association of Independent Schools. Endowment: $400,000. Total enrollment: 662. Upper school average class size: 17. Upper school faculty-student ratio: 1:9. There are 180 required school days per year for Upper School students. Upper School students typically attend 5 days per week. The average school day consists of 7 hours.

Upper School Student Profile Grade 6: 57 students (36 boys, 21 girls); Grade 7: 92 students (35 boys, 57 girls); Grade 8: 92 students (49 boys, 43 girls); Grade 9: 103 students (49 boys, 54 girls); Grade 10: 95 students (47 boys, 48 girls); Grade 11: 110 students (46 boys, 64 girls); Grade 12: 113 students (51 boys, 62 girls). 45% of students are Roman Catholic.

Faculty School total: 71. In upper school: 30 men, 19 women; 47 have advanced degrees.

Subjects Offered 20th century world history, advanced biology, advanced chemistry, advanced computer applications, advanced math, Advanced Placement courses, advanced studio art-AP, African American studies, algebra, American Civil War, American government, American history, American history-AP, American literature, American literature-AP, anatomy and physiology, art history-AP, astronomy, athletic training, band, biology, biology-AP, British literature, calculus, calculus-AP, chemistry, chemistry-AP, choral music, chorus, Christian education, Christian scripture, computer applications, computer multimedia, computer programming-AP, drawing and design, economics, English, English language and composition-AP, English literature and composition-AP, European history-AP, forensics, French, government, government and politics-AP, health, Holocaust studies, honors algebra, honors English, honors geometry, New Testament, physical education, physics-AP, portfolio art, pre-calculus, programming, psychology, psychology-AP, Spanish-AP, speech, statistics, statistics-AP, studio art, U.S. government, U.S. government and politics-AP, U.S. history, U.S. history-AP, visual arts, World War II, yearbook.

Graduation Requirements 1 1/2 elective credits, algebra, American government, American history, arts and fine arts (art, music, dance, drama), biology, chemistry, computer applications, economics, English, foreign language, government, health education, physical education (includes health), physics, religion (includes Bible studies and theology), theology, U.S. history, world history.

Special Academic Programs Honors section; study at local college for college credit.

College Admission Counseling 105 students graduated in 2012; all went to college, including Georgia Institute of Technology; Georgia Southern University; Macon State College; University of Georgia. Mean SAT critical reading: 710, mean SAT math: 700, mean SAT writing: 720, mean combined SAT: 2130.

Student Life Upper grades have specified standards of dress, student council, honor system. Discipline rests primarily with faculty. Attendance at religious services is required.

Tuition and Aid Tuition installment plan (FACTS Tuition Payment Plan). Merit scholarship grants, need-based scholarship grants available. In 2012–13, 30% of upper-school students received aid; total upper-school merit-scholarship money awarded: $122,000. Total amount of financial aid awarded in 2012–13: $813,771.

Admissions Traditional secondary-level entrance grade is 9. For fall 2012, 89 students applied for upper-level admission, 65 were accepted, 39 enrolled. Naglieri Nonverbal School Ability Test required. Deadline for receipt of application materials: none. Application fee required: $50.

Athletics Interscholastic: baseball (boys), basketball (b,g), cheering (g), cross-country running (b,g), fitness (b,g), football (b), physical fitness (b,g), physical training (b,g), soccer (b,g), softball (g), strength & conditioning (b,g), swimming and diving (b,g), tennis (b,g), track and field (b,g), weight training (b,g); coed interscholastic: golf. 1 athletic trainer.

Computers Computers are regularly used in all classes. Computer network features include on-campus library services, Internet access, wireless campus network. Campus intranet and student e-mail accounts are available to students. Students grades are available online. The school has a published electronic and media policy.

Contact Mrs. Linda Cardwell, Director of Admissions. 478-751-3244. Fax: 478-751-3241. E-mail: lcardwell@mountdesales.net. Web site: www.mountdesales.net

MOUNT MERCY ACADEMY

88 Red Jacket Parkway
Buffalo, New York 14220

Head of School: Mrs. Margaret Staszak

General Information Girls' day college-preparatory, arts, and religious studies school, affiliated with Roman Catholic Church. Grades 9–12. Founded: 1904. Setting: urban. 2 buildings on campus. Approved or accredited by Middle States Association of Colleges and Schools and New York Department of Education. Total enrollment: 244. Upper school average class size: 20. Upper school faculty-student ratio: 1:20. There are 180 required school days per year for Upper School students. Upper School students typically attend 5 days per week. The average school day consists of 6 hours and 45 minutes.

Upper School Student Profile Grade 9: 67 students (67 girls); Grade 10: 53 students (53 girls); Grade 11: 74 students (74 girls); Grade 12: 50 students (50 girls). 97% of students are Roman Catholic.

Faculty School total: 32. In upper school: 6 men, 26 women.

Special Academic Programs Advanced Placement exam preparation; honors section; independent study.

College Admission Counseling 72 students graduated in 2012; all went to college.

Student Life Upper grades have uniform requirement, student council, honor system. Discipline rests equally with students and faculty. Attendance at religious services is required.

Summer Programs Enrichment programs offered; session focuses on Regents review; held on campus; accepts boys and girls; open to students from other schools. 2013 schedule: July to August.

Tuition and Aid Day student tuition: $7800. Tuition installment plan (FACTS Tuition Payment Plan). Tuition reduction for siblings, merit scholarship grants, need-based scholarship grants, paying campus jobs available.

Admissions Traditional secondary-level entrance grade is 9. Admissions testing or High School Placement Test (closed version) from Scholastic Testing Service required. Deadline for receipt of application materials: none. Application fee required: $20. On-campus interview required.

Athletics Interscholastic: aquatics, basketball, bowling, cross-country running, golf, lacrosse, skiing (downhill), soccer, softball, swimming and diving, tennis, volleyball. 1 PE instructor, 13 coaches.

Computers Computers are regularly used in art, business, desktop publishing, keyboarding, study skills, yearbook classes. Computer network features include on-campus library services, Internet access, wireless campus network, Internet filtering or blocking technology. Campus intranet, student e-mail accounts, and computer access in designated common areas are available to students. Students grades are available online. The school has a published electronic and media policy.

Contact Mrs. Jeanne Burvid, Director of Admissions. 716-825-8796 Ext. 511. Fax: 716-825-0976. E-mail: jburvid@mtmercy.org. Web site: www.mtmercy.org

MOUNT MICHAEL BENEDICTINE SCHOOL

22520 Mount Michael Road
Elkhorn, Nebraska 68022-3400

Head of School: Dr. David Peters

General Information Boys' boarding and day college-preparatory, arts, religious studies, and technology school, affiliated with Roman Catholic Church. Grades 9–12. Founded: 1970. Setting: suburban. Nearest major city is Omaha. Students are housed in single-sex dormitories and private homes. 440-acre campus. 1 building on campus. Approved or accredited by National Catholic Education Association, North Central Association of Colleges and Schools, The College Board, and Nebraska Department of Education. Endowment: $3.2 million. Total enrollment: 221. Upper school average class size: 15. Upper school faculty-student ratio: 1:10. There are 180 required school days per year for Upper School students. Upper School students typically attend 5 days per week. The average school day consists of 6 hours and 27 minutes.

Upper School Student Profile Grade 9: 65 students (65 boys); Grade 10: 59 students (59 boys); Grade 11: 59 students (59 boys); Grade 12: 38 students (38 boys). 62% of students are boarding students. 83% are state residents. 7 states are represented in upper school student body. 14% are international students. International students from China, Germany, Mexico, Republic of Korea, Rwanda, and Viet Nam. 84% of students are Roman Catholic.

Faculty School total: 29. In upper school: 21 men, 8 women; 20 have advanced degrees; 7 reside on campus.

Subjects Offered Accounting, Advanced Placement courses, algebra, American history, American history-AP, American literature, architectural drawing, art, band, Basic programming, basketball, bioethics, DNA and culture, biology, biology-AP, business, business skills, calculus-AP, ceramics, chemistry, chemistry-AP, chorus, Christian doctrine, Christian ethics, Christian scripture, Christianity, community service, computer programming, computer science, critical writing, drafting, drama, economics, English, English language-AP, English literature, English literature and composition-AP, European history, European history-AP, French, French language-AP, geography, geometry, government/civics, health education, Hebrew scripture, history of the Catholic Church, journalism, keyboarding, Latin, math applications, mathematics, music, physical education, physics, physics-AP, psychology-AP, reading, robotics, science, social sciences, social studies, Spanish, speech, theater, theology, trigonometry, weight training, Western civilization, world religions, wrestling, writing, yearbook.

Graduation Requirements Advanced math, algebra, American government, American history, anatomy and physiology, biology, biology-AP, career/college preparation, chemistry, Christian studies, computer science, economics, economics and history, English, foreign language, geometry, government, mathematics, physical education (includes health), physics, pre-calculus, social studies (includes history), speech, Western civilization, world cultures, world religions, service hours requirement. Community service is required.

Special Academic Programs 11 Advanced Placement exams for which test preparation is offered; honors section; independent study; study at local college for college credit.

College Admission Counseling 57 students graduated in 2012; 53 went to college, including Benedictine College; Creighton University; Iowa State University of Science and Technology; Saint John's University; University of Nebraska–Lincoln; University of Wisconsin–Madison. Other: 4 entered military service. Median SAT critical reading: 630, median SAT math: 700, median SAT writing: 660, median combined SAT: 2000, median composite ACT: 28. 80% scored over 600 on SAT critical reading, 80% scored over 600 on SAT math, 100% scored over 600 on SAT writing, 80% scored over 1800 on combined SAT, 67% scored over 26 on composite ACT.

Student Life Upper grades have specified standards of dress, student council, honor system. Discipline rests primarily with faculty. Attendance at religious services is required.

Tuition and Aid Day student tuition: $10,755–$11,075; 5-day tuition and room/board: $15,950–$16,270; 7-day tuition and room/board: $21,795–$22,115. Tuition installment plan (FACTS Tuition Payment Plan). Tuition reduction for siblings, bursaries, merit scholarship grants, need-based loans, paying campus jobs available. In 2012–13, 53% of upper-school students received aid; total upper-school merit-scholarship money awarded: $18,570. Total amount of financial aid awarded in 2012–13: $556,449.

Admissions Traditional secondary-level entrance grade is 9. For fall 2012, 102 students applied for upper-level admission, 77 were accepted, 65 enrolled. California Achievement Test, Explore, High School Placement Test, Iowa Tests of Basic Skills, Stanford Achievement Test or TOEFL required. Deadline for receipt of application materials: July 1. Application fee required: $25. Interview required.

Athletics Interscholastic: baseball, basketball, bowling, cheering, cross-country running, diving, football, golf, soccer, swimming and diving, tennis, trap and skeet, wrestling; intramural: ball hockey, basketball, flag football, floor hockey, physical fitness, physical training, soccer, strength & conditioning, ultimate Frisbee, weight lifting, weight training. 1 PE instructor, 22 coaches, 2 athletic trainers.

Computers Computers are regularly used in architecture, career education, career exploration, career technology, college planning, drafting, economics, French, geography, history, journalism, keyboarding, library, mathematics, newspaper, science, Spanish, stock market, Web site design, yearbook classes. Computer network features include on-campus library services, online commercial services, Internet access, wireless campus network, Internet filtering or blocking technology. Campus intranet, student e-mail accounts, and computer access in designated common areas are available to students. Students grades are available online. The school has a published electronic and media policy.

Contact Mr. Eric Crawford, Director of Admissions. 402-253-0946. Fax: 402-289-4539. E-mail: ecrawford@mountmichael.org. Web site: www.mountmichaelhs.com

MOUNT SAINT CHARLES ACADEMY

800 Logee Street
Woonsocket, Rhode Island 02895-5599

Head of School: Mr. Herve E. Richer Jr.

General Information Coeducational day college-preparatory, arts, and religious studies school, affiliated with Roman Catholic Church. Grades 7–12. Founded: 1924. Setting: suburban. Nearest major city is Providence. 22-acre campus. 2 buildings on campus. Approved or accredited by New England Association of Schools and Colleges and Rhode Island Department of Education. Total enrollment: 774. Upper school average class size: 25. Upper school faculty-student ratio: 1:18. There are 180 required school days per year for Upper School students. The average school day consists of 6 hours and 15 minutes.

Upper School Student Profile Grade 7: 55 students (25 boys, 30 girls); Grade 8: 88 students (41 boys, 47 girls); Grade 9: 120 students (56 boys, 64 girls); Grade 10: 159 students (80 boys, 79 girls); Grade 11: 185 students (78 boys, 107 girls); Grade 12: 167 students (70 boys, 97 girls). 85% of students are Roman Catholic.

Faculty School total: 64. In upper school: 30 men, 34 women; 30 have advanced degrees.

Subjects Offered Advanced computer applications, algebra, American literature, architecture, art, art-AP, band, biology, biology-AP, British literature, calculus, calculus-AP, chemistry, chorus, computer science, creative writing, dance, drama, economics, English, English language and composition-AP, English literature, English literature and composition-AP, English literature-AP, environmental science, environmental science-AP, European history, European history-AP, fine arts, forensics, French, geography, geometry, government, government and politics-AP, government/civics, handbells, health education, history, history of the Catholic Church, honors U.S. history, honors world history, jazz band, mathematics, mathematics-AP, modern European history, music, music theory-AP, physical education, physics, physiology, psychology, psychology-AP, religion, science, social studies, Spanish, theater, trigonometry, U.S. history, U.S. history-AP, world history, world literature, writing, yearbook.

Graduation Requirements Arts and fine arts (art, music, dance, drama), computer science, English, foreign language, mathematics, physical education (includes health), religion (includes Bible studies and theology), science, social studies (includes history).

Special Academic Programs 14 Advanced Placement exams for which test preparation is offered; honors section.

College Admission Counseling 196 students graduated in 2012; 192 went to college. Other: 1 went to work, 2 entered military service, 1 entered a postgraduate year.

Student Life Upper grades have uniform requirement, student council. Discipline rests primarily with faculty. Attendance at religious services is required.

Summer Programs Sports, art/fine arts programs offered; session focuses on fine arts, soccer, hockey, basketball; held on campus; accepts boys and girls; open to students from other schools. 220 students usually enrolled. 2013 schedule: July. Application deadline: none.

Tuition and Aid Day student tuition: $11,500. Tuition installment plan (FACTS Tuition Payment Plan, full payment discount plan). Need-based scholarship grants available. In 2012–13, 38% of upper-school students received aid. Total amount of financial aid awarded in 2012–13: $700,000.

Admissions Traditional secondary-level entrance grade is 7. For fall 2012, 275 students applied for upper-level admission, 225 were accepted, 150 enrolled. Diocesan Entrance Exam, ISEE, SAS, STS-HSPT, SSAT or STS required. Deadline for receipt of application materials: none. Application fee required: $25.

Athletics Interscholastic: baseball (boys), basketball (b,g), cross-country running (b,g), gymnastics (g), ice hockey (b,g), indoor track (b,g), lacrosse (b,g), sailing (b,g), soccer (b,g), softball (g), swimming and diving (b,g), tennis (b,g), track and field (b,g), volleyball (b,g), winter (indoor) track (b,g); intramural: aerobics/dance (g), basketball (b,g), dance (g); coed interscholastic: cheering, golf; coed intramural: billiards, bowling, dance team, flag football, indoor soccer, lacrosse, physical training, soccer, strength & conditioning, touch football. 4 PE instructors, 15 coaches, 1 athletic trainer.

Computers Computers are regularly used in accounting, architecture, art, computer applications, desktop publishing, graphic design, science, yearbook classes. Computer network features include on-campus library services, online commercial services, Internet access, Internet filtering or blocking technology, college/financial aid searches. Campus intranet, student e-mail accounts, and computer access in designated common areas are available to students. Students grades are available online. The school has a published electronic and media policy.

Contact Joseph J. O'Neill Jr., Registrar/Director of Admissions. 401-769-0310 Ext. 137. Fax: 401-762-2327. E-mail: admissions@mountsaintcharles.org. Web site: www.mountsaintcharles.org

MT. SAINT DOMINIC ACADEMY

3 Ryerson Avenue
Caldwell, New Jersey 07006

Head of School: Sr. Frances Sullivan, OP

General Information Girls' day college-preparatory, arts, religious studies, and technology school, affiliated with Roman Catholic Church. Grades 9–12. Founded: 1892. Setting: suburban. Nearest major city is Newark. 70-acre campus. 3 buildings on campus. Approved or accredited by Middle States Association of Colleges and Schools, New Jersey Association of Independent Schools, and New Jersey Department of Education. Endowment: $1.5 million. Total enrollment: 315. Upper school average class size: 12. Upper school faculty-student ratio: 1:12. There are 180 required school days per year for Upper School students. Upper School students typically attend 5 days per week. The average school day consists of 6 hours.

Upper School Student Profile Grade 9: 98 students (98 girls); Grade 10: 65 students (65 girls); Grade 11: 86 students (86 girls); Grade 12: 66 students (66 girls). 88% of students are Roman Catholic.

Faculty School total: 39. In upper school: 5 men, 34 women; 16 have advanced degrees.

Subjects Offered Advanced math, advanced studio art-AP, algebra, American history-AP, American literature, American literature-AP, anatomy and physiology, art, Bible studies, biology, biology-AP, British literature, British literature (honors), calculus, calculus-AP, Catholic belief and practice, chemistry, choir, college counseling, college placement, college planning, communication skills, composition, composition-AP, computer applications, computer science, computer skills, computer technologies, concert choir, contemporary history, creative arts, creative writing, dance, debate, desktop publishing, digital photography, drama, drama workshop, drawing and design, driver education, ecology, environmental systems, English, English language and composition-AP, English literature, English literature and composition-AP, environmental science, forensics, French, geometry, health, history, Holocaust studies, literature, mathematics, music, photography, physical education, physics, pre-calculus, psychology, public speaking, religion, SAT preparation, science, Spanish, studio art-AP, U.S. history, U.S. history-AP, U.S. literature, word processing, world history, world literature, world wide web design.

Graduation Requirements 4 years of community service.

Special Academic Programs Advanced Placement exam preparation; honors section; independent study; academic accommodation for the gifted, the musically talented, and the artistically talented.

College Admission Counseling 99 students graduated in 2012; 96 went to college, including Loyola University Maryland; Montclair State University; Ramapo College of New Jersey; Rutgers, The State University of New Jersey, New Brunswick; Seton Hall University. Median SAT critical reading: 557, median SAT math: 541, median SAT writing: 573. 19% scored over 600 on SAT critical reading, 21% scored over 600 on SAT math, 18% scored over 600 on SAT writing.

Student Life Upper grades have uniform requirement, student council, honor system. Discipline rests primarily with faculty. Attendance at religious services is required.

Summer Programs Enrichment, advancement, sports programs offered; session focuses on mathematics advancement, English and math enrichment; held on campus; accepts girls; open to students from other schools. 15 students usually enrolled. 2013 schedule: June to July. Application deadline: May.

Tuition and Aid Day student tuition: $14,150. Tuition installment plan (individually arranged payment plans, one payment in full, or otherwise monthly, quarterly, or semi-annually). Tuition reduction for siblings, merit scholarship grants, need-based scholarship grants available. In 2012–13, 16% of upper-school students received aid; total upper-school merit-scholarship money awarded: $95,000. Total amount of financial aid awarded in 2012–13: $192,000.

Admissions Traditional secondary-level entrance grade is 9. For fall 2012, 215 students applied for upper-level admission, 211 were accepted, 99 enrolled. Cooperative Entrance Exam (McGraw-Hill) required. Deadline for receipt of application materials: December 15. Application fee required: $40.

Athletics Interscholastic: aerobics/dance, aquatics, basketball, cross-country running, field hockey, indoor track, indoor track & field, lacrosse, soccer, softball, swimming and diving, tennis, track and field, volleyball; intramural: ballet, cheering, dance, dance squad, dance team, field hockey, modern dance. 1 PE instructor, 20 coaches, 1 athletic trainer.

Computers Computers are regularly used in English, foreign language, history, mathematics, music, science classes. Computer network features include on-campus library services, online commercial services, Internet access, wireless campus network, Internet filtering or blocking technology. Student e-mail accounts are available to students. Students grades are available online. The school has a published electronic and media policy.

Contact Pauline Condon, Director of Admission. 973-226-0660 Ext. 1114. Fax: 973-226-2135. E-mail: pcondon@msdacademy.org. Web site: www.msdacademy.org

MOUNT SAINT JOSEPH ACADEMY

120 West Wissahickon Avenue
Flourtown, Pennsylvania 19031

Head of School: Sr. Kathleen Brabson, SSJ

General Information Girls' day college-preparatory school, affiliated with Roman Catholic Church. Grades 9–12. Founded: 1858. Setting: suburban. Nearest major city is Philadelphia. 78-acre campus. 1 building on campus. Approved or accredited by Middle States Association of Colleges and Schools, National Catholic Education Association, Pennsylvania Association of Independent Schools, and Pennsylvania Department of Education. Member of National Association of Independent Schools. Endowment: $4 million. Total enrollment: 550. Upper school average class size: 19. Upper school faculty-student ratio: 1:10. There are 180 required school days per year for Upper School students. Upper School students typically attend 5 days per week. The average school day consists of 6 hours and 45 minutes.

Upper School Student Profile Grade 9: 139 students (139 girls); Grade 10: 137 students (137 girls); Grade 11: 133 students (133 girls); Grade 12: 141 students (141 girls). 95% of students are Roman Catholic.

Faculty School total: 61. In upper school: 14 men, 47 women; 41 have advanced degrees.

Subjects Offered Accounting, algebra, American history, American history-AP, American literature, American studies, art, art history, astronomy, biochemistry, biology, calculus, calculus-AP, chemistry, chorus, communications, computer science, design, desktop publishing, drama, drawing, economics, English, English literature, English literature-AP, ethics, European history, film, fine arts, French, French-AP, geography, geometry, government/civics, health, history, human sexuality, instrumental music, journalism, keyboarding, Latin, literature, mathematics, music, music-AP, painting, physical education, physics, physics-AP, physiology, pre-calculus, psychology, religion, science, social studies, Spanish, Spanish-AP, speech, technology, theater, theology, trigonometry, word processing, world history, world literature, writing.

Graduation Requirements Arts and fine arts (art, music, dance, drama), computer science, English, foreign language, mathematics, physical education (includes health), religion (includes Bible studies and theology), science, social studies (includes history).

Special Academic Programs 13 Advanced Placement exams for which test preparation is offered; honors section; independent study; study at local college for college credit; academic accommodation for the gifted, the musically talented, and the artistically talented.

College Admission Counseling 142 students graduated in 2012; all went to college, including Drexel University; Fordham University; Penn State University Park; Temple University; University of Pennsylvania; University of Pittsburgh. Mean SAT critical reading: 632, mean SAT math: 610, mean SAT writing: 655, mean combined SAT: 1897. 60% scored over 600 on SAT critical reading, 57% scored over 600 on SAT math, 68% scored over 600 on SAT writing, 60% scored over 1800 on combined SAT.

Student Life Upper grades have uniform requirement, student council, honor system. Discipline rests primarily with faculty. Attendance at religious services is required.

Tuition and Aid Day student tuition: $13,800. Tuition installment plan (Higher Education Service, Inc., semester payment plan). Tuition reduction for siblings, merit scholarship grants, need-based scholarship grants available. In 2012–13, 20% of upper-school students received aid; total upper-school merit-scholarship money awarded: $398,900. Total amount of financial aid awarded in 2012–13: $699,113.

Admissions Traditional secondary-level entrance grade is 9. For fall 2012, 285 students applied for upper-level admission, 138 enrolled. High School Placement Test, SAS, STS-HSPT or school's own test required. Deadline for receipt of application materials: October 29. Application fee required: $75.

Athletics Interscholastic: basketball, crew, cross-country running, diving, field hockey, golf, indoor track, lacrosse, soccer, softball, swimming and diving, tennis, track and field, volleyball. 2 PE instructors, 24 coaches, 1 athletic trainer.

Computers Computers are regularly used in art, business studies, career exploration, college planning, commercial art, computer applications, desktop publishing, English, foreign language, graphic design, history, mathematics, music, science, theater arts, writing, writing, yearbook classes. Computer network features include on-campus library services, online commercial services, Internet access, wireless campus network, Internet filtering or blocking technology, video conferencing, SmartBoards. Campus intranet, student e-mail accounts, and computer access in designated common areas are available to students. Students grades are available online. The school has a published electronic and media policy.

Contact Ms. Carol Finney, Director of Admissions. 215-233-9133. Fax: 215-233-5887. E-mail: cfinney@msjacad.org. Web site: www.msjacad.org

MOUNT VERNON PRESBYTERIAN SCHOOL

471 Mt. Vernon Highway NE
Atlanta, Georgia 30328

Head of School: Dr. J. Brett Jacobsen

General Information college-preparatory school, affiliated with Presbyterian Church. Founded: 1972. Setting: suburban. Approved or accredited by Georgia Department of Education. Member of National Association of Independent Schools and Secondary School Admission Test Board.

Student Life Upper grades have uniform requirement, student council, honor system.

Admissions SSAT required. Deadline for receipt of application materials: February 15. Application fee required: $100. Interview required.

Contact Mrs. Kirsten Beard, Director of Admissions. 404-252-3448. Fax: 404-252-7154. E-mail: kbeard@mountvernonschool.org. Web site: www.mountvernonschool.org/

MPS ETOBICOKE

30 Barrhead Crescent
Toronto, Ontario M9W 3Z7, Canada

Head of School: Mrs. Gabrielle Bush

General Information Coeducational day college-preparatory, arts, business, and technology school. Grades JK–12. Founded: 1977. Setting: urban. 1 building on campus. Approved or accredited by Ontario Ministry of Education and Ontario Department of Education. Language of instruction: English. Total enrollment: 255. Upper school average class size: 18. Upper school faculty-student ratio: 1:18. There are 192 required school days per year for Upper School students. Upper School students typically attend 5 days per week. The average school day consists of 6 hours and 30 minutes.

Upper School Student Profile Grade 9: 30 students (18 boys, 12 girls); Grade 10: 27 students (16 boys, 11 girls); Grade 11: 29 students (17 boys, 12 girls); Grade 12: 32 students (23 boys, 9 girls).

Faculty School total: 35. In upper school: 8 men, 8 women; 2 have advanced degrees.

Subjects Offered Accounting, anthropology, biology, Canadian geography, Canadian history, Canadian law, chemistry, civics, communications, data processing, discrete mathematics, dramatic arts, English, film, French, functions, geometry, healthful living, information technology, learning strategies, mathematics, organizational studies, personal finance, philosophy, physics, psychology, reading, science, society challenge and change, sociology, visual arts, world history, writing.

Graduation Requirements English, Ontario Ministry of Education requirements.

Special Academic Programs ESL (15 students enrolled).

College Admission Counseling 47 students graduated in 2012; all went to college, including McMaster University; Ryerson University; University of Guelph; University of Ottawa; University of Toronto; York University.

Student Life Upper grades have uniform requirement, student council, honor system. Discipline rests primarily with faculty.

Summer Programs Remediation, enrichment, advancement, ESL, sports, art/fine arts, computer instruction programs offered; session focuses on academics; held on campus; accepts boys and girls; open to students from other schools. 100 students usually enrolled. 2013 schedule: July 2 to July 26. Application deadline: June 25.

Tuition and Aid Day student tuition: CAN$13,800. Tuition installment plan (individually arranged payment plans, MPS Payment Plan). Tuition reduction for siblings available.

Admissions Traditional secondary-level entrance grade is 9. For fall 2012, 30 students applied for upper-level admission, 30 were accepted, 30 enrolled. Admissions testing required. Deadline for receipt of application materials: October 31. No application fee required. Interview required.

Athletics Interscholastic: baseball (boys, girls), basketball (b,g), flag football (b,g), football (b), indoor track & field (b,g), running (b,g), soccer (b,g), swimming and diving (b,g), track and field (b,g), volleyball (b,g); intramural: basketball (b,g), flag football (b,g), floor hockey (b,g), Frisbee (b,g), indoor hockey (b,g), physical fitness (b,g), rhythmic gymnastics (b,g), running (b,g), soccer (b,g), swimming and diving (b,g), touch football (b,g), track and field (b,g), ultimate Frisbee (b,g), volleyball (b,g), winter (indoor) track (b,g), winter soccer (b,g); coed interscholastic: aquatics, bowling, cross-country running, field hockey, flag football; coed intramural: badminton, baseball, basketball, bowling, cooperative games, cross-country running, flag football, table tennis, tennis. 2 PE instructors.

Computers Computers are regularly used in art, business education, computer applications, graphic arts, media arts, photography classes. Computer resources include Internet access, Internet filtering or blocking technology. The school has a published electronic and media policy.

Contact Mrs. Gabrielle Bush, Director. 416-745-1328. Fax: 416-745-4168. E-mail: gbushmps@rogers.com. Web site: www.mpsetobicoke.com

MU HIGH SCHOOL

28 Heinkel
Columbia, Missouri 65211

Head of School: Dr. Kristi D. Smalley

General Information Coeducational day college-preparatory, general academic, and distance learning school. Grades 9–12. Founded: 1999. Setting: small town. Nearest major city is St. Louis. Approved or accredited by Missouri Independent School Association and North Central Association of Colleges and Schools.

Subjects Offered 1 1/2 elective credits, 20th century American writers, 20th century physics, 20th century world history, 3-dimensional art, accounting, adolescent issues, advanced math, Advanced Placement courses, African-American literature, algebra, American history, ancient world history, art, art appreciation, astronomy, basic language skills, Basic programming, biology, business applications, business mathematics, business skills, business studies, career exploration, career planning, career/college preparation, careers, character education, chemistry, child development, civics, college planning, communication arts, comparative politics, comparative religion, computer applications, computer literacy, computer programming, conservation, consumer education, consumer mathematics, contemporary history, contemporary issues, creative writing, decision making skills, economics, English, English literature and composition-AP, entrepreneurship, environmental science, European literature, family and consumer science, family living, family studies, female experience in America, fiction, film and literature, fitness, food and nutrition, French, general science, geography, geology, geometry, German, government, grammar, health and wellness, history, independent study, integrated mathematics, interpersonal skills, Japanese, keyboarding, language, language arts, Latin, law and the legal system, literature, literature by women, math applications, mathematics, media studies, medieval history, modern history, modern world history, music appreciation, mythology, newspaper, North American literature, novels, parent/child development, personal and social education, personal development, personal fitness, personal money management, photography, poetry, political science, pre-algebra, pre-calculus, psychology, reading/study skills, religious studies, science fiction, Shakespeare, short story, skills for success, social studies, sociology, Spanish, state history, statistics, study skills, trigonometry, U.S. constitutional history, U.S. government and politics, U.S. literature, women's literature, world geography, world religions, writing.

Graduation Requirements Missouri Department of Elementary and Secondary Education requirements.

Special Academic Programs Advanced Placement exam preparation; accelerated programs; independent study; study at local college for college credit; academic accommodation for the gifted; remedial reading and/or remedial writing.

College Admission Counseling 69 students graduated in 2012.

Summer Programs Remediation, enrichment, advancement programs offered; session focuses on online/distance education courses; held off campus; held at students can access coursework from anywhere that has Internet access; accepts boys and girls; open to students from other schools.

Admissions Deadline for receipt of application materials: none. Application fee required: $25.

Athletics 1 PE instructor.

Computers Computers are regularly used in accounting, art, business, business applications, business education, business skills, business studies, career education, career exploration, classics, college planning, computer applications, creative writing, current events, digital applications, economics, English, foreign language, French, French as a second language, geography, health, historical foundations for arts, history, humanities, independent study, information technology, journalism, keyboarding, language development, Latin, life skills, mathematics, media, music, news writing, occupational education, photography, programming, psychology, reading, religious studies, research skills, science, social sciences, social studies, Spanish, study skills, theater, theater arts, typing, writing, writing classes. Computer resources include on-campus library services, INET Library, Britannica Online School Edition, course access. Computer access in designated common areas is available to students. Students grades are available online. The school has a published electronic and media policy.

Contact Alicia Bixby, Counselor. 573-882-7208. Fax: 573-884-9665. E-mail: bixbya@missouri.edu. Web site: muhigh.missouri.edu/

MUNICH INTERNATIONAL SCHOOL

Schloss Buchhof
Starnberg D-82319, Germany

Head of School: Simon Taylor

General Information Coeducational day college-preparatory, arts, business, bilingual studies, and technology school. Grades PK–12. Founded: 1966. Setting: rural. Nearest major city is Munich, Germany. 26-acre campus. 5 buildings on campus. Approved or accredited by Council of International Schools, International Baccalaureate Organization, and New England Association of Schools and Colleges. Affiliate member of National Association of Independent Schools; member of Secondary School Admission Test Board and European Council of International Schools. Language of instruction: English. Total enrollment: 1,206. Upper school average class size: 21. Upper school faculty-student ratio: 1:6. There are 185 required school days per year for Upper School students. Upper School students typically attend 5 days per week. The average school day consists of 6 hours and 55 minutes.

Upper School Student Profile Grade 9: 115 students (55 boys, 60 girls); Grade 10: 106 students (52 boys, 54 girls); Grade 11: 106 students (59 boys, 47 girls); Grade 12: 97 students (45 boys, 52 girls).

Faculty School total: 162. In upper school: 26 men, 46 women; 34 have advanced degrees.

Subjects Offered Adolescent issues, algebra, art, biology, business, calculus, chemistry, computer science, computer-aided design, design, drama, Dutch, economics, English, English literature, ESL, European history, film studies, fine arts, French, geography, geometry, German, grammar, health, health education, history, home economics, Indonesian, information technology, instrumental music, integrated mathematics, International Baccalaureate courses, Japanese, journalism, lab/keyboard, library skills, math methods, mathematics, model United Nations, music, personal and social education, physical education, physics, SAT preparation, science, senior thesis, social sciences, social studies, Spanish, speech and debate, student government, Swedish, technology/design, theater, theory of knowledge, trigonometry, world history, world literature, writing, yearbook.

Graduation Requirements Arts and fine arts (art, music, dance, drama), English, foreign language, mathematics, philosophy, physical education (includes health), science, social sciences, social studies (includes history), theory of knowledge, extended essay, community service. Community service is required.

Special Academic Programs International Baccalaureate program; academic accommodation for the gifted; remedial math; ESL (12 students enrolled).

College Admission Counseling 94 students graduated in 2012; 68 went to college, including California Institute of Technology; Case Western Reserve University; New York University; Rensselaer Polytechnic Institute; Simon Fraser University; The University of British Columbia. Other: 1 went to work, 25 had other specific plans. Median SAT critical reading: 580, median SAT math: 610, median SAT writing: 620, median combined SAT: 1770, median composite ACT: 27. 34% scored over 600 on SAT critical reading, 60% scored over 600 on SAT math, 37% scored over 600 on SAT writing, 43% scored over 1800 on combined SAT, 69% scored over 26 on composite ACT.

Student Life Upper grades have specified standards of dress, student council, honor system. Discipline rests primarily with faculty.

Summer Programs Sports, rigorous outdoor training programs offered; held both on and off campus; held at Lake Garda (Italy); accepts boys and girls; open to students from other schools. 2013 schedule: July 1 to July 15. Application deadline: May 31.

Tuition and Aid Day student tuition: €17,850. Tuition installment plan (monthly payment plans, individually arranged payment plans, Tuition Fee Reduction Programme). Tuition reduction for siblings, need-based tuition remission for current students, need-based tution reduction available. In 2012–13, 1% of upper-school students received aid. Total amount of financial aid awarded in 2012–13: €27,250.

Admissions Traditional secondary-level entrance grade is 9. For fall 2012, 85 students applied for upper-level admission, 67 were accepted, 48 enrolled. English for Non-native Speakers, Math Placement Exam or Secondary Level English Proficiency required. Deadline for receipt of application materials: none. Application fee required: €100. On-campus interview recommended.

Athletics Interscholastic: alpine skiing (boys, girls), basketball (b,g), cross-country running (b,g), freestyle skiing (b,g), golf (b,g), rugby (b), skiing (downhill) (b,g), soccer (b,g), softball (g), swimming and diving (b,g), tennis (b,g), track and field (b,g), volleyball (b,g); intramural: badminton (b,g), ballet (b,g), basketball (b,g), canoeing/kayaking (b,g), climbing (b,g), cross-country running (b,g), dance (b,g), gymnastics (b,g), outdoor skills (b,g), soccer (b,g), strength & conditioning (b,g), swimming and diving (b,g), table tennis (b,g), tennis (b,g), track and field (b,g), volleyball (b,g), wall climbing (b,g); coed interscholastic: alpine skiing, cross-country running, golf, skiing (downhill), swimming and diving, tennis, track and field; coed intramural: ballet, canoeing/kayaking, climbing, dance, gymnastics, outdoor skills, swimming and diving, wall climbing. 5 PE instructors, 10 coaches.

Computers Computers are regularly used in all academic, current events, library skills, newspaper, research skills, yearbook classes. Computer network features include on-campus library services, Internet access, wireless campus network, Internet filtering or blocking technology. Campus intranet and student e-mail accounts are available to students. Students grades are available online. The school has a published electronic and media policy.

Contact Ms. Manuela Black, Director of Admissions. 49-8151-366 Ext. 120. Fax: 49-8151-366 Ext. 129. E-mail: admissions@mis-munich.de. Web site: www.mis-munich.de

See Display on next page and Close-Up on page 608.

NATIVITY B.V.M. HIGH SCHOOL

One Lawtons Hill
Pottsville, Pennsylvania 17901

Head of School: Mrs. Lynn Sabol

General Information college-preparatory and general academic school, affiliated with Roman Catholic Church. Founded: 1955. Setting: small town. 1 building on campus. Approved or accredited by Middle States Association of Colleges and Schools and Pennsylvania Department of Education. Total enrollment: 189. Upper school average class size: 200. Upper school faculty-student ratio: 1:10. There are 180 required school days per year for Upper School students. Upper School students typically attend 5 days per week. The average school day consists of 6 hours and 20 minutes.

Upper School Student Profile Grade 9: 39 students (21 boys, 18 girls); Grade 10: 48 students (22 boys, 26 girls); Grade 11: 41 students (21 boys, 20 girls); Grade 12: 61 students (35 boys, 26 girls). 75% of students are Roman Catholic.

Faculty School total: 21. In upper school: 13 men, 7 women; 6 have advanced degrees.

Special Academic Programs 3 Advanced Placement exams for which test preparation is offered; honors section; independent study; study at local college for college credit; academic accommodation for the gifted.

College Admission Counseling 43 students graduated in 2011; 40 went to college. Other: 2 went to work, 1 had other specific plans.

Student Life Upper grades have uniform requirement, student council, honor system. Discipline rests primarily with faculty. Attendance at religious services is required.

Tuition and Aid Day student tuition: $4750. Tuition installment plan (monthly payment plans, individually arranged payment plans). Tuition reduction for siblings, merit scholarship grants, need-based scholarship grants available. In 2011–12, 65% of upper-school students received aid. Total amount of financial aid awarded in 2011–12: $155,000.

Admissions Traditional secondary-level entrance grade is 9. For fall 2011, 55 students applied for upper-level admission, 55 were accepted, 53 enrolled. Deadline for receipt of application materials: none. Application fee required: $50. Interview recommended.

Athletics Interscholastic: baseball (boys, girls), basketball (b,g), cheering (g), cross-country running (b,g), football (b), golf (b,g), soccer (b,g), softball (g), strength & conditioning (b,g), track and field (b,g), volleyball (g), weight lifting (b). 1 PE instructor, 40 coaches, 1 athletic trainer.

Computers The school has a published electronic and media policy.

Contact Mr. Robert Beruck, Guidance Counselor. 570-622-8110. Fax: 570-622-0454. E-mail: rberuck@nativitybvm.net. Web site:

NAZARETH ACADEMY

1209 West Ogden Avenue
LaGrange Park, Illinois 60526

Head of School: Mrs. Deborah A. Tracy

General Information Coeducational day college-preparatory school, affiliated with Roman Catholic Church. Grades 9–12. Founded: 1900. Setting: suburban. Nearest major city is Chicago. 15-acre campus. 2 buildings on campus. Approved or accredited by North Central Association of Colleges and Schools, The College Board, and Illinois Department of Education. Total enrollment: 802. Upper school average class size: 24. Upper school faculty-student ratio: 1:18. There are 180 required school days per year for Upper School students. Upper School students typically attend 5 days per week. The average school day consists of 7 hours.

Upper School Student Profile Grade 9: 209 students (115 boys, 94 girls); Grade 10: 163 students (90 boys, 73 girls); Grade 11: 219 students (109 boys, 110 girls); Grade 12: 211 students (98 boys, 113 girls). 85% of students are Roman Catholic.

Faculty School total: 49. In upper school: 19 men, 30 women; 40 have advanced degrees.

Subjects Offered 3-dimensional design, acting, algebra, American government, American literature, art, biology, biology-AP, calculus-AP, chemistry, chemistry-AP, computer programming, computer science-AP, concert band, concert choir, creative writing, drawing and design, economics, English, English language and composition-AP, English literature and composition-AP, environmental science, French, geometry, health, Italian, journalism, music theory, photography, physical education, physics, physics-AP, pre-calculus, psychology, religion, scripture, Spanish, speech, studio art, theater, trigonometry, U.S. history, U.S. history-AP, Western civilization, wind ensemble, world history, world literature, world religions.

Graduation Requirements Advanced math, algebra, American literature, arts and fine arts (art, music, dance, drama), biology, chemistry, church history, English, foreign language, geometry, physical education (includes health), physics, religion (includes Bible studies and theology), scripture, U.S. history, Western civilization, world literature, world religions, world studies, service hours, off-campus retreat for juniors.

Special Academic Programs 12 Advanced Placement exams for which test preparation is offered; honors section.

College Admission Counseling 201 students graduated in 2012; all went to college, including Loyola University Chicago; Marquette University; Northwestern University; University of Illinois at Chicago; University of Illinois at Urbana–Champaign; University of Notre Dame. Median composite ACT: 25. 34% scored over 26 on composite ACT.

Student Life Upper grades have uniform requirement, student council, honor system. Discipline rests primarily with faculty. Attendance at religious services is required.

Summer Programs Enrichment, sports, art/fine arts programs offered; session focuses on athletic camps; held on campus; accepts boys and girls; open to students from other schools.

Tuition and Aid Day student tuition: $10,800. Tuition installment plan (monthly payment plans). Tuition reduction for siblings, merit scholarship grants, need-based scholarship grants available. In 2012–13, 22% of upper-school students received aid; total upper-school merit-scholarship money awarded: $40,000. Total amount of financial aid awarded in 2012–13: $300,000.

Admissions Traditional secondary-level entrance grade is 9. For fall 2012, 350 students applied for upper-level admission, 222 enrolled. High School Placement Test required. Deadline for receipt of application materials: June 30. No application fee required.

Athletics Interscholastic: baseball (boys), basketball (b,g), cheering (g), cross-country running (b,g), football (b), golf (b,g), lacrosse (b,g), pom squad (g), soccer (b,g), softball (g), tennis (b,g), track and field (b,g), volleyball (b,g), wrestling (b); intramural: weight training (b,g); coed interscholastic: hockey. 1 PE instructor, 1 coach, 1 athletic trainer.

Computers Computers are regularly used in English, foreign language, history, mathematics, science classes. Computer network features include on-campus library services, Internet access, wireless campus network, Internet filtering or blocking technology. Students grades are available online. The school has a published electronic and media policy.

Contact Mr. John Bonk, Recruitment Director. 708-387-8538. Fax: 708-354-0109. E-mail: jbonk@nazarethacademy.com. Web site: www.nazarethacademy.com

NEBRASKA CHRISTIAN SCHOOLS

1847 Inskip Avenue
Central City, Nebraska 68826

Head of School: Mr. Josh Cumpston

General Information Coeducational boarding and day college-preparatory school, affiliated with Protestant-Evangelical faith. Boarding grades 7–12, day grades K–12. Founded: 1959. Setting: rural. Nearest major city is Lincoln. Students are housed in single-sex dormitories. 27-acre campus. 7 buildings on campus. Approved or accredited by Association of Christian Schools International and Nebraska Department of Education. Endowment: $35,000. Total enrollment: 196. Upper school average class size: 20. Upper school faculty-student ratio: 1:10. There are 155 required school days per year for Upper School students. Upper School students typically attend 4 days per week. The average school day consists of 8 hours.

Upper School Student Profile Grade 9: 23 students (10 boys, 13 girls); Grade 10: 35 students (19 boys, 16 girls); Grade 11: 30 students (17 boys, 13 girls); Grade 12: 36 students (17 boys, 19 girls). 34% of students are boarding students. 74% are state residents. 1 state is represented in upper school student body. 26% are international students. International students from China, Hong Kong, Republic of Korea, Taiwan, Thailand, and Viet Nam. 90% of students are Protestant-Evangelical faith.

Faculty School total: 18. In upper school: 13 men, 5 women; 5 have advanced degrees; 5 reside on campus.

Subjects Offered Accounting, advanced math, algebra, American government, American history, American literature, anatomy and physiology, ancient world history, art, band, Bible, biology, business, business law, chemistry, choir, Christian doctrine, Christian ethics, Christian studies, composition, computer applications, computer programming, concert band, consumer mathematics, creation science, desktop publishing, economics, English, English composition, ESL, family living, fitness, general math, geography, geometry, health and safety, history, keyboarding, lab science, language arts, Life of Christ, life science, literature, mathematics, music, music theory, physical education, physical fitness, physical science, physics, pre-calculus, SAT/ACT preparation, science, science project, social studies, Spanish, speech, trigonometry, vocal ensemble, vocal music, Web site design, word processing, world geography, world history, writing, yearbook.

Graduation Requirements Algebra, American government, American history, American literature, art, Bible, biology, Christian doctrine, economics, English, family living, geometry, history, keyboarding, Life of Christ, physical education (includes health), physical science, world history.

Special Academic Programs Independent study; study at local college for college credit; ESL (16 students enrolled).

College Admission Counseling 26 students graduated in 2012; 25 went to college, including Arizona State University; Hillsdale College; University of Nebraska–Lincoln; University of Nebraska at Kearney; University of Nebraska at Omaha; University of Wisconsin–Madison. Other: 1 went to work. Median composite ACT: 24. 35% scored over 26 on composite ACT.

Student Life Upper grades have specified standards of dress, student council, honor system. Discipline rests primarily with faculty. Attendance at religious services is required.

Tuition and Aid Day student tuition: $5000; 5-day tuition and room/board: $8000; 7-day tuition and room/board: $25,950. Guaranteed tuition plan. Tuition installment plan (FACTS Tuition Payment Plan, individually arranged payment plans). Tuition reduction for siblings, merit scholarship grants, need-based scholarship grants available. In 2012–13, 38% of upper-school students received aid; total upper-school merit-scholarship money awarded: $8500. Total amount of financial aid awarded in 2012–13: $133,000.

Admissions Traditional secondary-level entrance grade is 9. For fall 2012, 24 students applied for upper-level admission, 19 were accepted, 19 enrolled. SLEP for foreign students or TOEFL or SLEP required. Deadline for receipt of application materials: none. Application fee required: $300. Interview recommended.

Athletics Interscholastic: basketball (boys, girls), cross-country running (b,g), football (b), track and field (b,g), volleyball (g), wrestling (b). 2 PE instructors, 7 coaches.

Computers Computers are regularly used in business applications, desktop publishing, programming, Web site design, yearbook classes. Computer network features include Internet access, wireless campus network, Internet filtering or blocking technology. Students grades are available online.

Contact Mr. Larry Hoff, Director, International Programs. 308-946-3836. Fax: 308-946-3837. E-mail: lhoff@nebraskachristian.org. Web site: www.nebraskachristian.org

NERINX HALL

530 East Lockwood Avenue
Webster Groves, Missouri 63119

Head of School: Sr. Barbara Roche, SL

General Information Girls' day college-preparatory and arts school, affiliated with Roman Catholic Church. Grades 9–12. Founded: 1924. Setting: suburban. Nearest major city is St. Louis. 12-acre campus. 4 buildings on campus. Approved or accredited by National Catholic Education Association, North Central Association of Colleges and Schools, and Missouri Department of Education. Endowment: $4.6 million. Total enrollment: 628. Upper school average class size: 20. Upper school faculty-student ratio: 1:12. There are 176 required school days per year for Upper School students. Upper School students typically attend 5 days per week. The average school day consists of 6 hours and 25 minutes.

Upper School Student Profile Grade 9: 158 students (158 girls); Grade 10: 151 students (151 girls); Grade 11: 164 students (164 girls); Grade 12: 155 students (155 girls). 89% of students are Roman Catholic.

Faculty School total: 54. In upper school: 14 men, 40 women; 43 have advanced degrees.

Subjects Offered Acting, advanced math, American government, American history, American literature, anatomy, anthropology, art, astronomy, athletics, biology, business, calculus, ceramics, chemistry, computer applications, computer graphics, conceptual physics, creative writing, death and loss, desktop publishing, drawing and design, Eastern world civilizations, economics, English composition, English literature, film appreciation, French, geology, German, graphics, health, history, Holocaust, honors algebra, honors English, honors geometry, honors U.S. history, instrumental music, jazz band, keyboarding, lab science, Latin, media, Middle East, model United Nations, multimedia, orchestra, painting, performing arts, personal finance, physics, pre-calculus, psychology, public speaking, religious education, Spanish, theology, Web site design, Western civilization.

Graduation Requirements Algebra, arts and fine arts (art, music, dance, drama), biology, chemistry, computer applications, foreign language, geometry, physical education (includes health), physical fitness, physics, public speaking, theology, U.S. government and politics, U.S. history, U.S. literature, world history, writing. Community service is required.

Special Academic Programs 9 Advanced Placement exams for which test preparation is offered; honors section; study at local college for college credit.

College Admission Counseling 155 students graduated in 2012; 154 went to college, including Rockhurst University; Saint Louis University; University of Arkansas; University of Dayton; University of Missouri. Other: 1 had other specific plans. Mean composite ACT: 27.

Student Life Upper grades have uniform requirement, student council, honor system. Discipline rests primarily with faculty. Attendance at religious services is required.

Summer Programs Advancement programs offered; session focuses on advancement; held on campus; accepts girls; not open to students from other schools. 175 students usually enrolled.

Tuition and Aid Day student tuition: $11,300. Tuition installment plan (individually arranged payment plans). Tuition reduction for siblings, need-based scholarship grants, paying campus jobs available. In 2012–13, 28% of upper-school students received aid. Total amount of financial aid awarded in 2012–13: $670,640.

Admissions Traditional secondary-level entrance grade is 9. For fall 2012, 179 students applied for upper-level admission, 173 were accepted, 161 enrolled. Any standardized test or CTBS (or similar from their school) required. Deadline for receipt of application materials: November 21. Application fee required: $10. On-campus interview required.

Athletics Interscholastic: basketball, cross-country running, diving, field hockey, golf, lacrosse, racquetball, soccer, softball, swimming and diving, tennis, track and field, volleyball. 3 PE instructors, 25 coaches.

Computers Computers are regularly used in graphics, humanities, mathematics, science, speech, writing, writing classes. Computer network features include on-campus library services, Internet access, wireless campus network, Internet filtering or blocking technology. Student e-mail accounts are available to students. Students grades are available online. The school has a published electronic and media policy.

Contact Mrs. Mary Ann Gentry, Admissions. 314-968-1505 Ext. 151. Fax: 314-968-0604. E-mail: mgentry@nerinxhs.org. Web site: www.nerinxhs.org

NEUCHATEL JUNIOR COLLEGE

Cret-Taconnet 4
Neuch?l 2002, Switzerland

Head of School: Mr. Bill Boyer

General Information Coeducational boarding college-preparatory, arts, business, bilingual studies, and international development school. Grade 12. Founded: 1956. Setting: urban. Nearest major city is Berne, Switzerland. Students are housed in homes of host families. 1-acre campus. 3 buildings on campus. Approved or accredited by Canadian Association of Independent Schools, Canadian Educational Standards Institute, and state department of education. Languages of instruction: English and French. Endowment: CAN$440,000. Total enrollment: 56. Upper school average class size: 15. Upper school faculty-student ratio: 1:10. Upper School students typically attend 5 days per week. The average school day consists of 5 hours and 15 minutes.

Upper School Student Profile Grade 12: 41 students (15 boys, 26 girls); Postgraduate: 15 students (6 boys, 9 girls). 100% of students are boarding students. 4% are international students. International students from Canada, France, Germany, Japan, United Kingdom, and United States; 1 other country represented in student body.

Faculty School total: 9. In upper school: 3 men, 6 women; 6 have advanced degrees; 1 resides on campus.

Subjects Offered 20th century world history, advanced chemistry, advanced math, Advanced Placement courses, advanced studio art-AP, algebra, analysis and differential calculus, ancient world history, applied arts, art, art history, art history-AP, athletics, biology, biology-AP, British history, calculus, calculus-AP, Canadian history, Canadian law, Canadian literature, chemistry, chemistry-AP, classical civilization, comparative government and politics-AP, comparative politics, debate, dramatic arts, earth science, economics, economics-AP, English, English language and composition-AP, English literature-AP, environmental science, European history, European history-AP, finite math, French as a second language, French language-AP, French literature-AP, German-AP, government and politics-AP, human geography - AP, law, personal and social education, physics, physics-AP, public speaking, studio art-AP, United Nations and international issues, world history-AP, world issues.

Graduation Requirements Minimum of 6 senior year university prep level courses.

Special Academic Programs 8 Advanced Placement exams for which test preparation is offered; study abroad.

College Admission Counseling 83 students graduated in 2011; 81 went to college, including Dalhousie University; Harvard University; McGill University; Queen's University at Kingston; The University of Western Ontario; University of Toronto. Other: 2 had other specific plans.

Student Life Upper grades have specified standards of dress, student council, honor system. Discipline rests primarily with faculty.

Tuition and Aid 7-day tuition and room/board: 47,000 Swiss francs. Bursaries available. In 2011–12, 11% of upper-school students received aid. Total amount of financial aid awarded in 2011–12: 90,000 Swiss francs.

Admissions Traditional secondary-level entrance grade is 12. For fall 2011, 72 students applied for upper-level admission, 56 were accepted, 56 enrolled. Deadline for receipt of application materials: January 16. Application fee required: CAN$175. Interview recommended.

Athletics Interscholastic: field hockey (boys, girls), rugby (b,g), soccer (b,g); intramural: hockey (b,g), ice hockey (b,g), indoor hockey (b,g), rugby (b,g), soccer (b,g); coed interscholastic: alpine skiing, aquatics, snowboarding, swimming and diving; coed intramural: alpine skiing, aquatics, basketball, bicycling, cross-country running, curling, floor hockey, jogging, sailing, snowboarding, volleyball.

Computers Computer network features include on-campus library services, Internet access, wireless campus network. Student e-mail accounts are available to students. The school has a published electronic and media policy.

Contact Ms. Anne Hamilton, Admission Officer. 416-368-8169 Ext. 222. Fax: 416-368-0956. E-mail: admissions@neuchatel.org. Web site: www.njc.ch

NEWARK ACADEMY

91 South Orange Avenue
Livingston, New Jersey 07039-4989

Head of School: M. Donald M. Austin

General Information Coeducational day college-preparatory, arts, technology, and International Baccalaureate school. Grades 6–12. Founded: 1774. Setting: suburban. Nearest major city is Morristown. 68-acre campus. 1 building on campus. Approved or accredited by Middle States Association of Colleges and Schools, New Jersey Association of Independent Schools, and New Jersey Department of Education. Member of National Association of Independent Schools and Secondary School Admission Test Board. Endowment: $20.1 million. Total enrollment: 580. Upper school average class size: 13. Upper school faculty-student ratio: 1:12. There are 165 required school days per year for Upper School students. Upper School students typically attend 5 days per week. The average school day consists of 6 hours.

Upper School Student Profile Grade 9: 108 students (56 boys, 52 girls); Grade 10: 98 students (50 boys, 48 girls); Grade 11: 99 students (46 boys, 53 girls); Grade 12: 104 students (53 boys, 51 girls).

Faculty School total: 84. In upper school: 35 men, 39 women; 73 have advanced degrees.

Subjects Offered Accounting, acting, advanced biology, advanced chemistry, advanced computer applications, advanced math, Advanced Placement courses, advanced studio art-AP, algebra, American history, American literature, anatomy, art, art history, arts, biology, botany, calculus, ceramics, chemistry, chorus, community service, computer programming, computer science, creative writing, drama, driver education, ecology, economics, English, English literature, European history, film studies, filmmaking, finance, fine arts, French, geometry, government/civics, grammar, health, history, history-AP, Holocaust studies, honors algebra, honors geometry, humanities, International Baccalaureate courses, jazz band, leadership, Mandarin, mathematics, mechanical drawing, model United Nations, modern dance, money management, music, musical theater, newspaper, oil painting, participation in sports, peer counseling, philosophy, physical education, physical science, physics, play production, playwriting and directing, poetry, political science, pottery, pre-algebra, pre-calculus, probability and statistics, SAT/ACT preparation, science, Spanish, theater, theory of knowledge, trigonometry, world history, world literature, writing.

Graduation Requirements Arts and fine arts (art, music, dance, drama), computer science, English, foreign language, mathematics, physical education (includes health), science, social studies (includes history), 40-hour senior service project, community service.

Special Academic Programs International Baccalaureate program; 4 Advanced Placement exams for which test preparation is offered; honors section; accelerated programs; independent study; term-away projects; study abroad; academic accommodation for the gifted, the musically talented, and the artistically talented.

College Admission Counseling 93 students graduated in 2012; all went to college, including Cornell University; Georgetown University; Harvard University; New York University; The George Washington University; University of Pennsylvania. Median SAT critical reading: 688, median SAT math: 689, median SAT writing: 706, median combined SAT: 2083, median composite ACT: 30.

Student Life Upper grades have specified standards of dress, student council, honor system. Discipline rests primarily with faculty.

Summer Programs Remediation, enrichment, advancement, sports, art/fine arts, computer instruction programs offered; session focuses on enrichment and advancement; held on campus; accepts boys and girls; open to students from other schools. 850 students usually enrolled. 2013 schedule: June 27 to August 5. Application deadline: May 1.

Tuition and Aid Day student tuition: $30,215. Tuition installment plan (Insured Tuition Payment Plan, Key Tuition Payment Plan, monthly payment plans). Need-based scholarship grants available. In 2012–13, 18% of upper-school students received aid. Total amount of financial aid awarded in 2012–13: $2,109,625.

Admissions Traditional secondary-level entrance grade is 9. For fall 2012, 538 students applied for upper-level admission, 97 were accepted, 44 enrolled. ISEE or SSAT required. Deadline for receipt of application materials: December 10. Application fee required: $75. On-campus interview required.

Athletics Interscholastic: baseball (boys), basketball (b,g), cross-country running (b,g), fencing (b,g), field hockey (g), football (b), golf (b,g), lacrosse (b,g), running (b,g), skiing (downhill) (b,g), soccer (b,g), softball (g), swimming and diving (b,g), tennis (b,g), track and field (b,g), volleyball (g), wrestling (b); intramural: aerobics/dance (b,g), aerobics/Nautilus (b,g), baseball (b), basketball (b,g), bicycling (b,g), cross-country running (b,g), dance (b,g), dance team (b,g), field hockey (g), fitness (b,g), football (b), golf (b,g), hockey (b), ice hockey (b), lacrosse (b,g), modern dance (b,g), soccer (b,g), softball (g), swimming and diving (b,g), tennis (b,g), track and field (b,g), volleyball (g), weight lifting (b,g), wrestling (b), yoga (b,g); coed intramural: aerobics/dance, aerobics/Nautilus, bicycling, cricket, dance, dance team, fitness, modern dance, mountain biking, skiing (downhill), table tennis, ultimate Frisbee, weight lifting, yoga. 5 PE instructors, 10 coaches, 1 athletic trainer.

Computers Computers are regularly used in all academic classes. Computer network features include on-campus library services, online commercial services, Internet access, wireless campus network, Internet filtering or blocking technology. Campus intranet and student e-mail accounts are available to students. Students grades are available online. The school has a published electronic and media policy.

Contact Ms. Imaani F. Sanders, Admission Office Manager. 973-992-7000 Ext. 323. Fax: 973-488-0040. E-mail: Isanders@newarka.edu. Web site: www.newarka.edu

NEW COVENANT ACADEMY

3304 South Cox Road
Springfield, Missouri 65807

Head of School: Mr. Matt Searson

General Information Coeducational day college-preparatory, arts, business, religious studies, technology, and science, math, foreign language, language arts school, affiliated with Christian faith. Grades JK–12. Founded: 1979. Setting: suburban. 22-acre campus. 1 building on campus. Approved or accredited by Association of Christian Schools International and North Central Association of Colleges and Schools. Total enrollment: 371. Upper school faculty-student ratio: 1:10. There are 167 required school days per year for Upper School students. Upper School students typically attend 5 days per week. The average school day consists of 7 hours and 30 minutes.

Upper School Student Profile 99% of students are Christian.

Faculty School total: 30. In upper school: 6 men, 9 women.

Subjects Offered Advanced math, algebra, American government, American history, American literature, anatomy and physiology, ancient world history, art, athletics, Bible, biology, British literature, business, calculus, chemistry, Christianity, comparative government and politics, computer processing, computer technologies, computers, concert choir, economics, English, English composition, geology, geometry, health, history, independent study, Life of Christ, literature, mathematics, music appreciation, New Testament, oceanography, physical education, physics, pre-algebra, robotics, science, scripture, Spanish, trigonometry, world history, yearbook.

Special Academic Programs Independent study; study at local college for college credit.

College Admission Counseling 22 students graduated in 2012.

Student Life Upper grades have specified standards of dress, student council, honor system. Discipline rests primarily with faculty. Attendance at religious services is required.
Tuition and Aid Guaranteed tuition plan. Tuition installment plan (monthly payment plans, individually arranged payment plans). Need-based scholarship grants available.
Admissions Otis-Lennon School Ability Test, SLEP for foreign students or Stanford Achievement Test required. Deadline for receipt of application materials: none. Application fee required: $50. Interview required.
Athletics Interscholastic: basketball (boys, girls), cheering (g), golf (b), soccer (b,g), track and field (b,g), volleyball (g); intramural: basketball (b,g), soccer (b,g); coed interscholastic: golf. 1 PE instructor, 11 coaches.
Computers Computers are regularly used in computer applications, journalism, technology, word processing, yearbook classes. Computer network features include Internet access, Internet filtering or blocking technology. Student e-mail accounts and computer access in designated common areas are available to students. Students grades are available online.
Contact Mrs. Delana Reynolds, Admissions Officer. 417-887-9848 Ext. 6. Fax: 417-887-2419. E-mail: dreynolds@newcovenant.net. Web site: www.newcovenant.net

NEW TRIBES MISSION ACADEMY

PO Box 707
Durham, Ontario N0G 1R0, Canada

Head of School: Helmut Penner

General Information Coeducational day college-preparatory school, affiliated with Baptist Bible Fellowship, Brethren Church. Boys grades K–11, girls grades K–9. Founded: 1992. Setting: small town. 1-acre campus. 1 building on campus. Approved or accredited by Association of Christian Schools International. Language of instruction: English. Total enrollment: 21. Upper school average class size: 5. Upper school faculty-student ratio: 1:3. There are 172 required school days per year for Upper School students. Upper School students typically attend 5 days per week. The average school day consists of 6 hours.
Upper School Student Profile Grade 9: 2 students (1 boy, 1 girl); Grade 10: 1 student (1 boy); Grade 11: 1 student (1 boy). 80% of students are Baptist Bible Fellowship, Brethren.
Faculty School total: 8. In upper school: 3 men, 3 women.
Subjects Offered Algebra, Bible studies, biology, computer applications, English language and composition-AP, French, history, literature, physical education.
Graduation Requirements Advanced math, algebra, Bible studies, biology, Canadian geography, Canadian history, chemistry, computer skills, consumer mathematics, English, English language and composition-AP, English literature and composition-AP, French, history, mathematics, physical education (includes health), physics, science.
Student Life Upper grades have specified standards of dress. Discipline rests equally with students and faculty.
Tuition and Aid Day student tuition: CAN$1200. Tuition installment plan (monthly payment plans).
Admissions For fall 2011, 1 student applied for upper-level admission, 1 was accepted, 1 enrolled. CAT or SAT required. Deadline for receipt of application materials: August 29. No application fee required. Interview recommended.
Athletics Coed Intramural: archery, badminton, ball hockey, basketball, flag football, floor hockey, Frisbee, indoor soccer, soccer, softball, table tennis, tennis, track and field, volleyball. 1 PE instructor.
Computers Computer access in designated common areas is available to students.
Contact Helmut Penner, Principal. 519-369-2622. Fax: 519-369-5828. E-mail: academy@canada.ntm.org. Web site:

NIAGARA CHRISTIAN COMMUNITY OF SCHOOLS

2619 Niagara Boulevard
Fort Erie, Ontario L2A 5M4, Canada

Head of School: Mr. Mark Thiessen

General Information Coeducational boarding and day college-preparatory, general academic, arts, business, vocational, religious studies, bilingual studies, and technology school, affiliated with Brethren in Christ Church. Boarding grades 9–12, day grades 6–12. Founded: 1932. Setting: rural. Nearest major city is Niagara Falls, Canada. Students are housed in single-sex dormitories. 121-acre campus. 11 buildings on campus. Approved or accredited by Ontario Department of Education. Language of instruction: English. Total enrollment: 166. Upper school average class size: 17. Upper school faculty-student ratio: 1:16. There are 170 required school days per year for Upper School students. Upper School students typically attend 5 days per week. The average school day consists of 7 hours.
Upper School Student Profile Grade 9: 19 students (9 boys, 10 girls); Grade 10: 40 students (13 boys, 27 girls); Grade 11: 57 students (29 boys, 28 girls); Grade 12: 43 students (23 boys, 20 girls). 85% of students are boarding students. 15% are province residents. 2 provinces are represented in upper school student body. 85% are international students. International students from Cayman Islands, Hong Kong, Japan, Mexico, Republic of Korea, and Taiwan; 3 other countries represented in student body. 15% of students are Brethren in Christ Church.
Faculty School total: 19. In upper school: 9 men, 10 women; 2 have advanced degrees.
Subjects Offered Accounting, advanced chemistry, advanced computer applications, advanced math, Advanced Placement courses, advanced TOEFL/grammar, algebra, analysis and differential calculus, analysis of data, analytic geometry, anatomy, anthropology, art, art history, athletics, Bible, biology, biology-AP, business, business applications, business education, business mathematics, business technology, calculus, calculus-AP, Canadian geography, Canadian history, Canadian literature, career education, chemistry, choir, civics, computer applications, computer programming, concert choir, CPR, data processing, discrete mathematics, dramatic arts, early childhood, economics, English, English literature, ESL, exercise science, family studies, French as a second language, general math, geography, geometry, guidance, health education, history, information technology, instrumental music, integrated science, international affairs, Italian, leadership education training, Life of Christ, mathematics, media studies, modern world history, music, parenting, physical education, physics, politics, pre-calculus, science, Spanish, TOEFL preparation, world history, world history-AP, world issues, world religions, writing, writing.
Special Academic Programs International Baccalaureate program; independent study; special instructional classes for students with learning disabilities; ESL (85 students enrolled).
College Admission Counseling 78 students graduated in 2012; 75 went to college, including Brock University; McMaster University; The University of Western Ontario; University of Toronto; University of Waterloo; Wilfrid Laurier University. Other: 3 went to work.
Student Life Upper grades have uniform requirement, student council, honor system. Discipline rests primarily with faculty. Attendance at religious services is required.
Summer Programs ESL programs offered; session focuses on ESL; held on campus; accepts boys and girls; not open to students from other schools. 70 students usually enrolled. 2013 schedule: July 9 to August 27. Application deadline: none.
Tuition and Aid Day student tuition: CAN$9050; 5-day tuition and room/board: CAN$29,895; 7-day tuition and room/board: CAN$38,840. Tuition installment plan (monthly payment plans, individually arranged payment plans, quarterly payment plan). Tuition reduction for siblings, bursaries, merit scholarship grants, need-based scholarship grants, paying campus jobs available. In 2012–13, 10% of upper-school students received aid; total upper-school merit-scholarship money awarded: CAN$50,000. Total amount of financial aid awarded in 2012–13: CAN$400,000.
Admissions Traditional secondary-level entrance grade is 9. For fall 2012, 50 students applied for upper-level admission, 46 were accepted, 45 enrolled. Admissions testing and English proficiency required. Deadline for receipt of application materials: none. Application fee required: CAN$100. Interview required.
Athletics Interscholastic: badminton (boys, girls), basketball (b,g), cross-country running (b,g), golf (b), hockey (b,g), ice hockey (b,g), soccer (b,g), track and field (b,g); intramural: basketball (b,g), indoor soccer (b,g); coed interscholastic: badminton; coed intramural: aerobics, alpine skiing, aquatics, badminton, ball hockey, baseball, bowling, canoeing/kayaking, cross-country running, fitness, fitness walking, floor hockey, golf, ice skating, skiing (downhill), soccer. 1 PE instructor, 1 coach.
Computers Computers are regularly used in accounting, all academic, business, data processing, economics, ESL, mathematics, science, yearbook classes. Computer network features include on-campus library services, Internet access, wireless campus network, Internet filtering or blocking technology. Computer access in designated common areas is available to students. Students grades are available online. The school has a published electronic and media policy.
Contact Mr. Tom Auld, Dean of Students. 905-871-6980 Ext. 2280. Fax: 905-871-9260. E-mail: tomauld@niagaracc.com. Web site: www.niagaracc.com

NICHOLS SCHOOL

1250 Amherst Street
Buffalo, New York 14216

Head of School: Richard C. Bryan Jr.

General Information Coeducational day college-preparatory, arts, and technology school. Grades 5–12. Founded: 1892. Setting: urban. 30-acre campus. 8 buildings on campus. Approved or accredited by New York Department of Education and New York Department of Education. Member of National Association of Independent Schools. Endowment: $25 million. Total enrollment: 582. Upper school average class size: 14. Upper school faculty-student ratio: 1:8. Upper School students typically attend 5 days per week. The average school day consists of 7 hours.
Upper School Student Profile Grade 9: 92 students (53 boys, 39 girls); Grade 10: 112 students (62 boys, 50 girls); Grade 11: 101 students (48 boys, 53 girls); Grade 12: 84 students (37 boys, 47 girls).
Faculty School total: 77. In upper school: 26 men, 22 women; 36 have advanced degrees.
Subjects Offered Algebra, American history, American literature, anatomy, art, art history, biology, calculus, chemistry, Chinese, community service, computer graphics, computer math, computer programming, computer science, creative writing, dance, drama, driver education, earth science, economics, English, English literature, environ-

mental science, European history, expository writing, fine arts, French, geology, geometry, government/civics, history, Latin, mathematics, music, photography, physical education, physics, science, social studies, Spanish, speech, theater, trigonometry, world history, world literature.

Graduation Requirements Arts and fine arts (art, music, dance, drama), English, foreign language, mathematics, physical education (includes health), science, social studies (includes history).

Special Academic Programs Advanced Placement exam preparation; honors section; independent study; study abroad.

College Admission Counseling 103 students graduated in 2011; 101 went to college, including Boston College; Canisius College; Hobart and William Smith Colleges; Niagara University; The George Washington University; University at Buffalo, the State University of New York. Other: 1 entered a postgraduate year, 1 had other specific plans. Median SAT critical reading: 550, median SAT math: 580, median SAT writing: 560. 46% scored over 600 on SAT critical reading, 56% scored over 600 on SAT math, 42% scored over 600 on SAT writing.

Student Life Upper grades have specified standards of dress, student council, honor system. Discipline rests equally with students and faculty.

Tuition and Aid Day student tuition: $17,700–$19,400. Tuition installment plan (Insured Tuition Payment Plan, monthly payment plans). Need-based scholarship grants available. In 2011–12, 30% of upper-school students received aid. Total amount of financial aid awarded in 2011–12: $1,720,000.

Admissions Traditional secondary-level entrance grade is 9. For fall 2011, 238 students applied for upper-level admission, 220 were accepted, 136 enrolled. Otis-Lennon and 2 sections of ERB required. Deadline for receipt of application materials: none. Application fee required: $50. On-campus interview required.

Athletics Interscholastic: baseball (boys), basketball (b,g), crew (b,g), cross-country running (b,g), field hockey (g), football (b), golf (b,g), hockey (b,g), ice hockey (b,g), lacrosse (b,g), soccer (b,g), softball (g), squash (b,g), tennis (b,g), volleyball (g), wrestling (b); coed interscholastic: aerobics, aerobics/dance, dance, modern dance; coed intramural: aerobics/dance. 21 coaches, 1 athletic trainer.

Computers Computers are regularly used in art, library skills, newspaper, photography, science, technology, yearbook classes. Computer network features include on-campus library services, online commercial services, Internet access. Student e-mail accounts are available to students. The school has a published electronic and media policy.

Contact Mrs. Heather Newton, Director of Admissions. 716-332-6325. Fax: 716-875-6474. E-mail: hnewton@nicholsschool.org. Web site: www.nicholsschool.org

NOBLE ACADEMY

Greensboro, North Carolina

See Special Needs Schools section.

NOBLE AND GREENOUGH SCHOOL

10 Campus Drive
Dedham, Massachusetts 02026-4099

Head of School: Mr. Robert P. Henderson Jr.

General Information Coeducational boarding and day college-preparatory school. Boarding grades 9–12, day grades 7–12. Founded: 1866. Setting: suburban. Nearest major city is Boston. Students are housed in single-sex dormitories. 187-acre campus. 12 buildings on campus. Approved or accredited by Association of Independent Schools in New England, New England Association of Schools and Colleges, The College Board, and Massachusetts Department of Education. Member of National Association of Independent Schools and Secondary School Admission Test Board. Endowment: $101 million. Total enrollment: 594. Upper school average class size: 14. Upper school faculty-student ratio: 1:7. There are 162 required school days per year for Upper School students. Upper School students typically attend 5 days per week. The average school day consists of 7 hours and 5 minutes.

Upper School Student Profile Grade 9: 111 students (52 boys, 59 girls); Grade 10: 121 students (58 boys, 63 girls); Grade 11: 124 students (68 boys, 56 girls); Grade 12: 119 students (57 boys, 62 girls). 8% of students are boarding students. 99% are state residents. 2 states are represented in upper school student body.

Faculty School total: 125. In upper school: 65 men, 60 women; 34 reside on campus.

Subjects Offered 20th century history, Advanced Placement courses, African-American literature, algebra, American history, American literature, anatomy, ancient history, art, art history, astronomy, biology, calculus, ceramics, chemistry, community service, computer programming, computer science, concert band, creative writing, drama, drawing, earth science, ecology, economics, English, English literature, environmental science, ethics, European history, expository writing, fine arts, French, genetics, geography, geometry, government/civics, grammar, health, history, independent study, Japanese, journalism, Latin, Latin American history, marine biology, mathematics, music, painting, philosophy, photography, physics, physiology, printmaking, psychology, Roman civilization, science, senior internship, senior project, social studies, Spanish, speech, statistics, theater, trigonometry, Vietnam, world history, world literature, writing.

Graduation Requirements Arts and fine arts (art, music, dance, drama), computer science, English, foreign language, mathematics, performing arts, physical education (includes health), science, social studies (includes history), 80 hours of community service must be completed.

Special Academic Programs Advanced Placement exam preparation; honors section; independent study; term-away projects; study abroad; academic accommodation for the gifted, the musically talented, and the artistically talented.

College Admission Counseling 107 students graduated in 2012; all went to college, including Boston College; Dartmouth College; Harvard University; Middlebury College; Trinity College. 72% scored over 600 on SAT critical reading, 75% scored over 600 on SAT math, 80% scored over 600 on SAT writing.

Student Life Upper grades have specified standards of dress, student council, honor system. Discipline rests equally with students and faculty.

Tuition and Aid Day student tuition: $39,150; 5-day tuition and room/board: $44,600. Tuition installment plan (Tuition Management Systems). Need-based scholarship grants, need-based loans available. In 2012–13, 28% of upper-school students received aid. Total amount of financial aid awarded in 2012–13: $3,433,400.

Admissions Traditional secondary-level entrance grade is 9. For fall 2012, 578 students applied for upper-level admission, 140 were accepted, 66 enrolled. ISEE or SSAT required. Deadline for receipt of application materials: January 15. Application fee required: $50. On-campus interview required.

Athletics Interscholastic: baseball (boys), basketball (b,g), crew (b,g), cross-country running (b,g), field hockey (g), football (b); coed intramural: aerobics/dance, dance. 12 coaches, 2 athletic trainers.

Computers Computers are regularly used in English, foreign language, history, journalism, Latin, mathematics, music, science classes. Computer network features include on-campus library services, online commercial services, Internet access, Internet filtering or blocking technology, NoblesNet (first class email and bulletin board with electronic conferencing capability), wireless iBooks. Campus intranet, student e-mail accounts, and computer access in designated common areas are available to students. The school has a published electronic and media policy.

Contact Ms. Jennifer Hines, Dean of Enrollment Management. 781-320-7100. Fax: 781-320-1329. E-mail: admission@nobles.edu. Web site: www.nobles.edu

THE NORA SCHOOL

955 Sligo Avenue
Silver Spring, Maryland 20910

Head of School: David E. Mullen

General Information Coeducational day college-preparatory, arts, and technology school. Grades 9–12. Founded: 1964. Setting: urban. Nearest major city is Washington, DC. 1-acre campus. 1 building on campus. Approved or accredited by Association of Independent Schools of Greater Washington, Middle States Association of Colleges and Schools, and Maryland Department of Education. Member of National Association of Independent Schools. Endowment: $250,000. Total enrollment: 60. Upper school average class size: 8. Upper school faculty-student ratio: 1:5. There are 175 required school days per year for Upper School students. Upper School students typically attend 5 days per week. The average school day consists of 5 hours and 35 minutes.

Upper School Student Profile Grade 9: 12 students (9 boys, 3 girls); Grade 10: 9 students (6 boys, 3 girls); Grade 11: 18 students (11 boys, 7 girls); Grade 12: 19 students (9 boys, 10 girls).

Faculty School total: 10. In upper school: 8 men, 2 women; all have advanced degrees.

Subjects Offered African-American literature, algebra, American literature, American studies, art, art history, astronomy, biology, British literature, calculus, ceramics, chemistry, college writing, community service, computer graphics, conceptual physics, conflict resolution, crafts, creative writing, economics, English composition, environmental science, expository writing, film and literature, forensics, geography, geometry, German, graphic design, illustration, integrated science, peace studies, peer counseling, photo shop, photography, physical education, physics, political science, pre-algebra, pre-calculus, psychology, sculpture, Shakespeare, social justice, Spanish, statistics, street law, studio art, trigonometry, U.S. history, wilderness education, women's literature, world history, world religions, writing.

Graduation Requirements Arts and fine arts (art, music, dance, drama), English, foreign language, lab science, mathematics, personal fitness, science, social studies (includes history), sports, U.S. history, wilderness education, writing, graduation portfolio. Community service is required.

Special Academic Programs Independent study; term-away projects; study at local college for college credit; academic accommodation for the gifted and the artistically talented; remedial reading and/or remedial writing; remedial math; programs in English, mathematics, general development for dyslexic students; special instructional classes for students with Attention Deficit Disorder and learning disabilities, students who have been unsuccessful in a traditional learning environment.

College Admission Counseling 19 students graduated in 2012; all went to college, including Bard College; Dickinson College; Goucher College; Guilford College; Loyola University Maryland; Mount Holyoke College.

Student Life Upper grades have student council. Discipline rests primarily with faculty.

Tuition and Aid Day student tuition: $24,550. Tuition installment plan (monthly payment plans). Need-based scholarship grants, Black Student Fund, Latino Student

Fund, Washington Scholarship Fund available. In 2012–13, 24% of upper-school students received aid. Total amount of financial aid awarded in 2012–13: $167,000.
Admissions Traditional secondary-level entrance grade is 9. For fall 2012, 41 students applied for upper-level admission, 29 were accepted, 19 enrolled. Writing sample required. Deadline for receipt of application materials: none. Application fee required: $75. On-campus interview required.
Athletics Interscholastic: basketball (boys, girls); intramural: cheering (g); coed interscholastic: soccer, softball; coed intramural: alpine skiing, backpacking, bicycling, bowling, canoeing/kayaking, climbing, cooperative games, dance, Frisbee, hiking/backpacking, ice skating, kayaking, outdoor activities, outdoor adventure, rafting, rock climbing, ropes courses, running, skiing (downhill), table tennis, tennis, volleyball, wilderness. 2 coaches.
Computers Computers are regularly used in art, college planning, creative writing, design, drawing and design, English, graphic arts, graphic design, independent study, literary magazine, mathematics, photography, SAT preparation, writing, writing, yearbook classes. Computer network features include on-campus library services, online commercial services, Internet access, wireless campus network, Internet filtering or blocking technology. Students grades are available online. The school has a published electronic and media policy.
Contact Marcia D. Miller, Director of Admissions. 301-495-6672. Fax: 301-495-7829. E-mail: marcia@nora-school.org. Web site: www.nora-school.org

NORFOLK ACADEMY

1585 Wesleyan Drive
Norfolk, Virginia 23502

Head of School: Mr. Dennis G. Manning

General Information Coeducational day college-preparatory school. Grades 1–12. Founded: 1728. Setting: suburban. 70-acre campus. 14 buildings on campus. Approved or accredited by Southern Association of Colleges and Schools, Southern Association of Independent Schools, The College Board, Virginia Association of Independent Schools, and Virginia Department of Education. Member of National Association of Independent Schools and Secondary School Admission Test Board. Endowment: $37 million. Total enrollment: 1,248. Upper school average class size: 15. Upper school faculty-student ratio: 1:10. There are 175 required school days per year for Upper School students. Upper School students typically attend 5 days per week. The average school day consists of 7 hours.
Upper School Student Profile Grade 10: 122 students (66 boys, 56 girls); Grade 11: 135 students (63 boys, 72 girls); Grade 12: 122 students (67 boys, 55 girls).
Faculty School total: 124. In upper school: 39 men, 13 women; 32 have advanced degrees.
Subjects Offered Algebra, American history, American literature, art, art history, band, biology, calculus, chemistry, chorus, computer math, computer programming, computer science, dance, driver education, economics, English, English literature, environmental science, European history, film studies, fine arts, French, geography, geometry, German, government/civics, health, history, instrumental music, Italian, Latin, mathematics, music, music history, music theory, physical education, physics, science, social studies, Spanish, speech, statistics, studio art, theater arts, world history.
Graduation Requirements Arts and fine arts (art, music, dance, drama), English, foreign language, mathematics, physical education (includes health), science, social studies (includes history), 8-minute senior speech, seminar program. Community service is required.
Special Academic Programs Advanced Placement exam preparation; independent study; study abroad; academic accommodation for the gifted, the musically talented, and the artistically talented.
College Admission Counseling 117 students graduated in 2012; all went to college, including Hampden-Sydney College; James Madison University; The College of William and Mary; University of Virginia; Virginia Polytechnic Institute and State University. Mean SAT critical reading: 628, mean SAT math: 648, mean SAT writing: 622.
Student Life Upper grades have specified standards of dress, student council, honor system. Discipline rests equally with students and faculty.
Summer Programs Enrichment, advancement, sports, art/fine arts programs offered; session focuses on academics, arts, athletics, day camp for children; held both on and off campus; held at surfing camp located at beach and Business internships; accepts boys and girls; open to students from other schools. 500 students usually enrolled. 2013 schedule: June 17 to July 26.
Tuition and Aid Day student tuition: $21,000. Tuition installment plan (Key Tuition Payment Plan, monthly payment plans). Need-based scholarship grants available. In 2012–13, 20% of upper-school students received aid.
Admissions Traditional secondary-level entrance grade is 10. For fall 2012, 30 students applied for upper-level admission, 9 were accepted, 8 enrolled. ERB Achievement Test, ERB CTP IV, Otis-Lennon School Ability Test and writing sample required. Deadline for receipt of application materials: January 26. Application fee required: $50. On-campus interview required.
Athletics Interscholastic: baseball (boys), basketball (b,g), cheering (g), crew (b,g), cross-country running (b,g), dance (b,g), diving (b,g), field hockey (g), football (b), golf (b,g), indoor track (b,g), lacrosse (b,g), sailing (b,g), soccer (b,g), softball (g), swimming and diving (b,g), tennis (b,g), track and field (b,g), volleyball (g), winter (indoor) track (b,g), wrestling (b); intramural: dance (g), dance team (g). 2 PE instructors, 3 athletic trainers.
Computers Computers are regularly used in all academic classes. Computer network features include on-campus library services, Internet access, wireless campus network, Internet filtering or blocking technology, online library resources, video production, curriculum-based software, desktop publishing, campus-wide media distribution system. Campus intranet, student e-mail accounts, and computer access in designated common areas are available to students. The school has a published electronic and media policy.
Contact Mr. James H. Lasley Jr., Director of Admissions. 757-455-5582 Ext. 5337. Fax: 757-455-3199. E-mail: jlasley@norfolkacademy.org. Web site: www.norfolkacademy.org

NORTH CATHOLIC HIGH SCHOOL

1400 Troy Hill Road
Pittsburgh, Pennsylvania 15212

Head of School: Mr. Michael Pendred II

General Information Coeducational day college-preparatory school, affiliated with Roman Catholic Church. Grades 9–12. Founded: 1939. Setting: urban. 2 buildings on campus. Approved or accredited by Middle States Association of Colleges and Schools and Pennsylvania Department of Education. Total enrollment: 250. Upper school average class size: 20. There are 180 required school days per year for Upper School students. Upper School students typically attend 5 days per week. The average school day consists of 6 hours and 30 minutes.
Upper School Student Profile 95% of students are Roman Catholic.
Faculty School total: 20. In upper school: 10 men, 7 women.
Special Academic Programs Advanced Placement exam preparation; honors section; independent study; study at local college for college credit; academic accommodation for the gifted; remedial reading and/or remedial writing.
College Admission Counseling 60 students graduated in 2011; 59 went to college. Other: 1 entered military service.
Student Life Upper grades have uniform requirement, student council, honor system. Discipline rests primarily with faculty. Attendance at religious services is required.
Tuition and Aid Day student tuition: $8635. Tuition installment plan (SMART Tuition Payment Plan). Need-based scholarship grants available. In 2011–12, 80% of upper-school students received aid.
Admissions Iowa Tests of Basic Skills required. Deadline for receipt of application materials: none. Application fee required: $35.
Athletics Interscholastic: baseball (boys), basketball (b,g), cheering (g), football (b), softball (g), strength & conditioning (b,g), volleyball (g), weight lifting (b), weight training (b); coed interscholastic: crew, golf, soccer. 2 PE instructors, 9 coaches, 1 athletic trainer.
Computers Computer network features include Internet access, wireless campus network, Internet filtering or blocking technology. Computer access in designated common areas is available to students. Students grades are available online.
Contact Ms. Maura A. DeRiggi, Director of Admissions. 412-321-4823 Ext. 127. Fax: 412-321-0599. E-mail: deriggim@north-catholic.org. Web site: www.north-catholic.org

NORTH CENTRAL TEXAS ACADEMY

3846 North Highway 144
Granbury, Texas 76048

Head of School: Mrs. Jennifer Smith

General Information Coeducational boarding and day and distance learning college-preparatory, arts, and agriculture/FFA school, affiliated with Christian faith. Grades K–12. Distance learning grade X. Founded: 1975. Setting: rural. Nearest major city is Dallas. Students are housed in single-sex residences. 500-acre campus. 1 building on campus. Approved or accredited by Association of Christian Schools International, Southern Association of Colleges and Schools, and The Association of Boarding Schools. Member of National Association of Independent Schools. Total enrollment: 170. Upper school average class size: 8. Upper school faculty-student ratio: 1:7. There are 170 required school days per year for Upper School students. Upper School students typically attend 5 days per week. The average school day consists of 6 hours and 30 minutes.
Upper School Student Profile 70% of students are boarding students. 70% are state residents. 8 states are represented in upper school student body. 10% are international students. International students from China, Hong Kong, Nigeria, Russian Federation, Taiwan, and Viet Nam; 3 other countries represented in student body. 65% of students are Christian.
Faculty School total: 28. In upper school: 4 men, 24 women; 8 have advanced degrees; 10 reside on campus.
Subjects Offered 1 1/2 elective credits, advanced math, Advanced Placement courses, agriculture, algebra, all academic, American history, American literature, animal husbandry, animal science, applied music, art, athletics, basketball, Bible, biology, calculus, cheerleading, chemistry, choir, classical music, computer education,

computer literacy, computer skills, concert choir, desktop publishing, drawing, driver education, economics, economics-AP, electives, English, English literature, English-AP, fine arts, gardening, general math, general science, geometry, golf, government, government-AP, guitar, health, history, horticulture, instruments, journalism, language arts, library, life science, mathematics, mathematics-AP, music, music appreciation, music performance, music theory, newspaper, physical education, physics, pottery, pre-algebra, pre-calculus, science, scripture, social studies, Spanish, speech, sports, tennis, track and field, trigonometry, U.S. government, U.S. history, vocal ensemble, volleyball, weight training, woodworking, world history, yearbook.

Special Academic Programs Honors section; independent study; study at local college for college credit; academic accommodation for the gifted, the musically talented, and the artistically talented; ESL (14 students enrolled).

College Admission Counseling 15 students graduated in 2012; 14 went to college, including Southwestern University; Texas A&M University; Texas Christian University; Texas State University–San Marcos; Texas Wesleyan University; United States Air Force Academy. Other: 1 entered military service.

Student Life Upper grades have uniform requirement, student council, honor system. Discipline rests primarily with faculty. Attendance at religious services is required.

Summer Programs Remediation, enrichment, ESL, sports, art/fine arts programs offered; session focuses on enrichment; held on campus; accepts boys and girls; not open to students from other schools. 160 students usually enrolled. 2013 schedule: June 4 to July 13.

Tuition and Aid Day student tuition: $3000–$8400; 7-day tuition and room/board: $12,000–$36,000. Tuition installment plan (monthly payment plans, individually arranged payment plans). Tuition reduction for siblings, need-based scholarship grants available. In 2012–13, 90% of upper-school students received aid.

Admissions Traditional secondary-level entrance grade is 10. Achievement tests, English for Non-native Speakers, Stanford Achievement Test or writing sample required. Deadline for receipt of application materials: none. Application fee required: $60. Interview required.

Athletics Interscholastic: baseball (boys), basketball (b,g), cheering (g), cross-country running (b,g), football (b), golf (b,g), horseback riding (b,g), outdoor education (b,g), physical fitness (b,g), running (b,g), soccer (g), softball (g), strength & conditioning (b,g), tennis (b,g), track and field (b,g), volleyball (g), weight training (b,g). 2 PE instructors, 4 coaches.

Computers Computers are regularly used in computer applications, creative writing, desktop publishing, English, journalism, library, newspaper, yearbook classes. Computer resources include on-campus library services, Internet access, wireless campus network, Internet filtering or blocking technology. Computer access in designated common areas is available to students. Students grades are available online.

Contact Mr. Todd L. Shipman, President/Chief Financial Officer. 254-897-4822. Fax: 254-897-7650. E-mail: todd@happyhillfarm.org. Web site: www.NorthCentralTexasAcademy.org

NORTH COBB CHRISTIAN SCHOOL

4500 Lakeview Drive
Kennesaw, Georgia 30144

Head of School: Mr. Todd Clingman

General Information Coeducational day college-preparatory, arts, business, and religious studies school, affiliated with Christian faith. Grades PK–12. Founded: 1983. Setting: suburban. Nearest major city is Atlanta. 25-acre campus. 3 buildings on campus. Approved or accredited by Association of Christian Schools International, Georgia Accrediting Commission, and Southern Association of Colleges and Schools. Endowment: $102,225. Total enrollment: 841. Upper school average class size: 13. Upper school faculty-student ratio: 1:10. There are 180 required school days per year for Upper School students. Upper School students typically attend 5 days per week. The average school day consists of 7 hours.

Upper School Student Profile Grade 9: 64 students (38 boys, 26 girls); Grade 10: 55 students (31 boys, 24 girls); Grade 11: 72 students (33 boys, 39 girls); Grade 12: 54 students (28 boys, 26 girls). 95% of students are Christian.

Faculty School total: 75. In upper school: 11 men, 17 women; 10 have advanced degrees.

Subjects Offered Acting, Advanced Placement courses, algebra, American literature, analysis, analysis and differential calculus, anatomy and physiology, band, Bible, Bible studies, biology, British literature, British literature (honors), British literature-AP, calculus, calculus-AP, chemistry, choral music, composition, computer graphics, computer programming, computer skills, computer technology certification, computers, concert band, concert choir, dance, desktop publishing, drama, ecology, economics, economics-AP, electives, English, English literature-AP, English-AP, English/composition-AP, fine arts, French, French-AP, geometry, government, graphic arts, health, honors algebra, honors geometry, honors U.S. history, HTML design, instrumental music, journalism, keyboarding, leadership, life management skills, literature, marching band, math analysis, physical education, physical science, physics, psychology, Spanish, Spanish-AP, statistics, student government, theater, trigonometry, U.S. government, U.S. government and politics-AP, U.S. history, U.S. history-AP, U.S. literature, weight training, word processing, world governments, world history, world history-AP, world literature, world wide web design.

Graduation Requirements Arts and fine arts (art, music, dance, drama), Bible, computers, electives, English, foreign language, mathematics, physical education (includes health), science, social studies (includes history), community service, leadership practicum. Community service is required.

Special Academic Programs Advanced Placement exam preparation; honors section; study at local college for college credit; academic accommodation for the musically talented and the artistically talented.

College Admission Counseling 70 students graduated in 2011; all went to college, including Covenant College; Georgia College & State University; Georgia State University; Kennesaw State University; University of Georgia; Young Harris College. Median SAT critical reading: 570, median SAT math: 550, median SAT writing: 530, median combined SAT: 1570, median composite ACT: 24. 39% scored over 600 on SAT critical reading, 43% scored over 600 on SAT math, 22% scored over 600 on SAT writing, 35% scored over 1800 on combined SAT, 60% scored over 26 on composite ACT.

Student Life Upper grades have specified standards of dress, student council. Discipline rests primarily with faculty. Attendance at religious services is required.

Tuition and Aid Day student tuition: $10,995–$11,545. Tuition installment plan (FACTS Tuition Payment Plan). Tuition reduction for siblings, need-based scholarship grants available. In 2011–12, 30% of upper-school students received aid. Total amount of financial aid awarded in 2011–12: $270,000.

Admissions Traditional secondary-level entrance grade is 9. For fall 2011, 36 students applied for upper-level admission, 25 were accepted, 21 enrolled. Otis-Lennon, Stanford Achievement Test required. Deadline for receipt of application materials: none. Application fee required: $100. Interview required.

Athletics Interscholastic: aerobics (boys, girls), aerobics/dance (g), ballet (g), baseball (b), basketball (b,g), cheering (g), cross-country running (b,g), dance (g), equestrian sports (b,g), football (b), physical fitness (b,g), soccer (b,g), softball (g), swimming and diving (b,g), tennis (b,g), track and field (b,g), volleyball (g); coed interscholastic: aquatics, archery, golf, strength & conditioning, weight training. 6 PE instructors, 6 coaches, 2 athletic trainers.

Computers Computers are regularly used in art, basic skills, desktop publishing, drawing and design, graphic arts, graphic design, keyboarding, library skills, media production, video film production, word processing, yearbook classes. Computer network features include on-campus library services, Internet access, wireless campus network. Computer access in designated common areas is available to students. Students grades are available online. The school has a published electronic and media policy.

Contact Mrs. Joan Carver, Admissions Assistant. 770-975-0252 Ext. 501. Fax: 770-874-9978. E-mail: jcarver@ncchristian.org. Web site: www.ncchristian.org

NORTH COUNTRY SCHOOL

Lake Placid, New York
See Junior Boarding Schools section.

NORTH SHORE COUNTRY DAY SCHOOL

310 Green Bay Road
Winnetka, Illinois 60093-4094

Head of School: Mr. Tom Doar III

General Information Coeducational day college-preparatory, arts, technology, and global service learning school. Grades PK–12. Founded: 1919. Setting: suburban. Nearest major city is Chicago. 16-acre campus. 6 buildings on campus. Approved or accredited by Illinois Department of Education. Member of National Association of Independent Schools and Secondary School Admission Test Board. Endowment: $20 million. Total enrollment: 510. Upper school average class size: 14. Upper school faculty-student ratio: 1:8. Upper School students typically attend 5 days per week. The average school day consists of 6 hours and 30 minutes.

Upper School Student Profile Grade 9: 51 students (23 boys, 28 girls); Grade 10: 51 students (28 boys, 23 girls); Grade 11: 51 students (27 boys, 24 girls); Grade 12: 47 students (24 boys, 23 girls).

Faculty School total: 80. In upper school: 27 men, 35 women; 42 have advanced degrees.

Subjects Offered Algebra, American history, American literature, anatomy, anatomy and physiology, art, art history, Asian studies, biology, biology-AP, calculus, calculus-AP, ceramics, chemistry, chemistry-AP, computer math, computer programming, computer science, creative writing, drama, earth science, ecology, economics, English, English literature, English-AP, European history, expository writing, fine arts, French, French-AP, geography, geometry, government/civics, grammar, industrial arts, journalism, Mandarin, mathematics, music, photography, physical education, physics, physics-AP, science, social studies, Spanish, Spanish-AP, speech, statistics, statistics-AP, technology, theater, trigonometry, U.S. history-AP, world history, world literature, writing.

Graduation Requirements Arts and fine arts (art, music, dance, drama), English, foreign language, mathematics, physical education (includes health), physical fitness, science, service learning/internship, social studies (includes history), technology, one stage performance in four years, completion of senior service project in May, completion of one-week community service project in four years.

Special Academic Programs Advanced Placement exam preparation; independent study; term-away projects; study at local college for college credit; study abroad.
College Admission Counseling 43 students graduated in 2012; all went to college, including University of Illinois at Urbana–Champaign.
Student Life Upper grades have specified standards of dress, student council, honor system. Discipline rests primarily with faculty.
Summer Programs Enrichment, sports, art/fine arts, rigorous outdoor training, computer instruction programs offered; session focuses on academic and artistic enrichment, outdoor expedition, soccer, basketball, field hockey; held both on and off campus; held at lakefront and local preserves and camp sites; accepts boys and girls; open to students from other schools. 750 students usually enrolled. 2013 schedule: June 18 to August 9. Application deadline: none.
Tuition and Aid Day student tuition: $24,800–$25,800. Tuition installment plan (Insured Tuition Payment Plan, Key Tuition Payment Plan, monthly payment plans, individually arranged payment plans, trimester payment plan). Merit scholarship grants, need-based scholarship grants, need-based loans, middle-income loans available. In 2012–13, 15% of upper-school students received aid. Total amount of financial aid awarded in 2012–13: $1,000,000.
Admissions Traditional secondary-level entrance grade is 9. ERB and writing sample required. Deadline for receipt of application materials: February 1. Application fee required: $75. On-campus interview required.
Athletics Interscholastic: baseball (boys), basketball (b,g), cross-country running (b,g), field hockey (g), football (b), golf (b,g), indoor track & field (b,g), soccer (b,g), tennis (b,g), track and field (b,g), volleyball (g); intramural: physical training (b,g), weight lifting (b,g); coed intramural: dance, sailing. 4 PE instructors, 24 coaches, 1 athletic trainer.
Computers Computers are regularly used in all academic classes. Computer network features include on-campus library services, online commercial services, Internet access, wireless campus network, Internet filtering or blocking technology. Campus intranet and student e-mail accounts are available to students. The school has a published electronic and media policy.
Contact Ms. Julie Schmidt, Admissions Liaison. 847-881-8800. Fax: 847-446-0675. E-mail: jschmidt@nscds.org. Web site: www.nscds.org

NORTH TORONTO CHRISTIAN SCHOOL

255 Yorkland Boulevard
Toronto, Ontario M2J 1S3, Canada

Head of School: Mr. Michael Broomer

General Information Coeducational day college-preparatory school, affiliated with Protestant-Evangelical faith. Grades JK–12. Founded: 1981. Setting: urban. 6-acre campus. 1 building on campus. Approved or accredited by Association of Christian Schools International and Ontario Department of Education. Language of instruction: English. Total enrollment: 488. Upper school average class size: 25. Upper school faculty-student ratio: 1:15. There are 184 required school days per year for Upper School students. Upper School students typically attend 5 days per week. The average school day consists of 6 hours.
Faculty School total: 31. In upper school: 12 men, 11 women; 8 have advanced degrees.
Subjects Offered Accounting, biology, business, calculus, Canadian geography, Canadian law, career exploration, chemistry, civics, computer applications, discrete mathematics, English, French, functions, geography, geometry, healthful living, information technology, instrumental music, marketing, physics, visual arts, world history, world issues, world religions.
Graduation Requirements 40 hours of community service, Successful completion of the Ontario Secondary School Literacy Test.
Special Academic Programs Independent study; ESL (18 students enrolled).
College Admission Counseling 56 students graduated in 2012; 54 went to college, including Brock University; McMaster University; Queen's University at Kingston; The University of Western Ontario; University of Toronto; York University. Other: 2 had other specific plans.
Student Life Upper grades have uniform requirement. Discipline rests primarily with faculty. Attendance at religious services is required.
Tuition and Aid Day student tuition: CAN$7296. Tuition installment plan (monthly payment plans, individually arranged payment plans). Tuition reduction for siblings, bursaries available.
Admissions Traditional secondary-level entrance grade is 9. Deadline for receipt of application materials: none. Application fee required: CAN$150. On-campus interview required.
Athletics Interscholastic: rugby (girls); coed interscholastic: aquatics, badminton, ball hockey, basketball, cross-country running, golf, soccer, softball, squash, swimming and diving, table tennis, tennis, track and field, volleyball, wrestling; coed intramural: alpine skiing, canoeing/kayaking, diving, fitness, floor hockey, judo, kayaking, outdoor education, outdoor skills, street hockey, water polo. 6 PE instructors.
Computers Computers are regularly used in business applications, information technology, introduction to technology, keyboarding, mathematics, programming, science, typing, word processing classes. Computer network features include Internet access, wireless campus network. The school has a published electronic and media policy.
Contact Mr. Gordon Cooke, Administrator. 416-491-7667. Fax: 416-491-3806. E-mail: gcooke@ntcs.on.ca. Web site: www.ntcs.on.ca

NORTHWEST ACADEMY

1130 Southwest Main Street
Portland, Oregon 97205

Head of School: Mary Vinton Folberg

General Information Coeducational day college-preparatory, arts, and bilingual studies school. Grades 6–12. Founded: 1996. Setting: urban. 4 buildings on campus. Approved or accredited by Northwest Accreditation Commission, Pacific Northwest Association of Independent Schools, and Oregon Department of Education. Member of National Association of Independent Schools. Total enrollment: 163. Upper school average class size: 16. Upper school faculty-student ratio: 1:4. Upper School students typically attend 5 days per week. The average school day consists of 7 hours and 30 minutes.
Upper School Student Profile Grade 9: 20 students (8 boys, 12 girls); Grade 10: 18 students (6 boys, 12 girls); Grade 11: 17 students (6 boys, 11 girls); Grade 12: 13 students (5 boys, 8 girls).
Faculty School total: 31. In upper school: 14 men, 13 women; 10 have advanced degrees.
Subjects Offered 20th century history, acting, algebra, anatomy and physiology, animation, art history, ballet, biology, calculus, career/college preparation, chemistry, comparative government and politics, comparative politics, comparative religion, computer animation, computer literacy, computer music, creative writing, critical thinking, dance performance, desktop publishing, digital art, drama workshop, drawing, earth and space science, ecology, environmental systems, English literature, European civilization, film studies, French, geometry, history of music, human anatomy, humanities, illustration, independent study, internship, introduction to digital multitrack recording techniques, jazz band, jazz dance, jazz ensemble, journalism, keyboarding, media arts, medieval/Renaissance history, multimedia design, music composition, music history, music performance, musical theater, painting, photo shop, physics, play/screen writing, political systems, pre-calculus, printmaking, senior thesis, Shakespeare, social sciences, Spanish, student publications, tap dance, theater, trigonometry, U.S. government and politics, U.S. history, video film production, visual arts, vocal ensemble, vocal jazz, world cultures, world history, world wide web design, writing, yoga.
Graduation Requirements 4 years of English/humanities, senior thesis seminar, 3 years of both math and science, 2 years of foreign language, 7 units of credit of arts electives, community service, computer literacy, physical education.
Special Academic Programs Accelerated programs; independent study; study at local college for college credit; academic accommodation for the gifted, the musically talented, and the artistically talented.
College Admission Counseling 14 students graduated in 2012; 11 went to college, including Pitzer College. Other: 1 went to work, 2 had other specific plans.
Student Life Upper grades have student council, honor system. Discipline rests primarily with faculty.
Tuition and Aid Day student tuition: $18,500. Tuition installment plan (FACTS Tuition Payment Plan). Need-based scholarship grants available. In 2012–13, 22% of upper-school students received aid.
Admissions Traditional secondary-level entrance grade is 9. For fall 2012, 18 students applied for upper-level admission, 12 were accepted, 11 enrolled. Admissions testing, placement test and writing sample required. Deadline for receipt of application materials: February 1. Application fee required: $100. Interview required.
Athletics Coed Intramural: aerobics/dance, artistic gym, ballet, basketball, cooperative games, dance, modern dance, tai chi, yoga.
Computers Computers are regularly used in all academic, yearbook classes. Computer network features include Internet access, wireless campus network, film and audio editing, sound design, animation, Flash. Campus intranet and computer access in designated common areas are available to students. The school has a published electronic and media policy.
Contact Lainie Keslin Ettinger, Director of Admissions. 503-223-3367 Ext. 104. Fax: 503-402-1043. E-mail: lettinger@nwacademy.org. Web site: www.nwacademy.org

NORTHWEST CATHOLIC HIGH SCHOOL

29 Wampanoag Drive
West Hartford, Connecticut 06117

Head of School: Mrs. Margaret Williamson

General Information Coeducational day college-preparatory school, affiliated with Roman Catholic Church. Grades 9–12. Founded: 1961. Setting: suburban. Nearest major city is Hartford. 1 building on campus. Approved or accredited by New England Association of Schools and Colleges and Connecticut Department of Education. Total enrollment: 603. Upper school average class size: 18. Upper school faculty-student ratio: 1:12. There are 180 required school days per year for Upper School students. Upper School students typically attend 5 days per week. The average school day consists of 6 hours and 18 minutes.

Upper School Student Profile Grade 9: 151 students (76 boys, 75 girls); Grade 10: 147 students (79 boys, 68 girls); Grade 11: 136 students (60 boys, 76 girls); Grade 12: 169 students (85 boys, 84 girls). 80% of students are Roman Catholic.

Faculty School total: 53. In upper school: 23 men, 30 women; 41 have advanced degrees.

Subjects Offered Biology-AP, calculus-AP, chemistry-AP, computer science-AP, English language and composition-AP, English literature and composition-AP, French language-AP, Latin-AP, music theory-AP, physics-AP, Spanish-AP, statistics-AP, studio art-AP, U.S. government and politics-AP, U.S. history-AP.

Graduation Requirements Arts and fine arts (art, music, dance, drama), English, foreign language, health education, mathematics, physical education (includes health), religion (includes Bible studies and theology), science, social studies (includes history), 25 hours of community service.

Special Academic Programs 15 Advanced Placement exams for which test preparation is offered; honors section; study at local college for college credit.

College Admission Counseling 163 students graduated in 2012; 162 went to college, including Assumption College; Boston University; Northeastern University; Providence College; The University of Scranton; University of Connecticut. Other: 1 had other specific plans. Mean SAT critical reading: 525, mean SAT math: 549, mean SAT writing: 532.

Student Life Upper grades have uniform requirement, student council, honor system. Discipline rests primarily with faculty. Attendance at religious services is required.

Summer Programs Sports programs offered; session focuses on grades 3-8; held both on and off campus; held at Northwest Catholic High facilities and St.Thomas Seminary fields; accepts boys and girls; open to students from other schools. 100 students usually enrolled. 2013 schedule: June to August. Application deadline: May 31.

Tuition and Aid Day student tuition: $13,200. Tuition installment plan (monthly payment plans). Tuition reduction for siblings, merit scholarship grants, need-based scholarship grants available. Total amount of financial aid awarded in 2012–13: $1,300,000.

Admissions Traditional secondary-level entrance grade is 9. High School Placement Test required. Deadline for receipt of application materials: March 1. Application fee required: $25.

Athletics Interscholastic: baseball (boys), basketball (b,g), cheering (g), cross-country running (b,g), field hockey (g), golf (b,g), ice hockey (b), indoor track & field (b,g), lacrosse (b,g), soccer (b,g), softball (g), tennis (b,g), track and field (b,g), volleyball (g), winter (indoor) track (b,g); intramural: basketball (b,g); coed interscholastic: diving, football, swimming and diving; coed intramural: canoeing/kayaking, dance team, flag football, indoor soccer, outdoor adventure, rappelling, rock climbing, scuba diving, skiing (downhill), snowboarding, strength & conditioning, ultimate Frisbee, weight training, whiffle ball. 1 PE instructor, 1 athletic trainer.

Computers Computers are regularly used in all academic classes. Computer network features include on-campus library services, Internet access, wireless campus network, Internet filtering or blocking technology. Student e-mail accounts and computer access in designated common areas are available to students. Students grades are available online. The school has a published electronic and media policy.

Contact Mrs. Nancy Scully Bannon, Director of Admissions. 860-236-4221 Ext. 124. Fax: 860-570-0080. E-mail: nbannon@nwcath.org. Web site: www.northwestcatholic.org

THE NORTHWEST SCHOOL

1415 Summit Avenue
Seattle, Washington 98122

Head of School: Mike McGill

General Information Coeducational boarding and day college-preparatory, arts, and ESL school. Boarding grades 9–12, day grades 6–12. Founded: 1978. Setting: urban. Students are housed in coed dormitories. 1-acre campus. 4 buildings on campus. Approved or accredited by Northwest Accreditation Commission, Pacific Northwest Association of Independent Schools, and Washington Department of Education. Member of National Association of Independent Schools. Endowment: $1.6 million. Total enrollment: 478. Upper school average class size: 16. Upper school faculty-student ratio: 1:9. There are 168 required school days per year for Upper School students. Upper School students typically attend 5 days per week. The average school day consists of 7 hours and 20 minutes.

Upper School Student Profile Grade 9: 77 students (38 boys, 39 girls); Grade 10: 101 students (54 boys, 47 girls); Grade 11: 80 students (41 boys, 39 girls); Grade 12: 81 students (43 boys, 38 girls). 14% of students are boarding students. 80% are state residents. 2 states are represented in upper school student body. 20% are international students. International students from China, Japan, Republic of Korea, Taiwan, Thailand, and Viet Nam; 2 other countries represented in student body.

Faculty School total: 75. In upper school: 23 men, 36 women; 40 have advanced degrees.

Subjects Offered Advanced chemistry, algebra, astronomy, biology, calculus, ceramics, chemistry, Chinese, chorus, computer skills, contemporary problems, dance, drama, drawing, earth science, English, ESL, evolution, fiber arts, film, fine arts, French, geometry, health, history, humanities, illustration, improvisation, jazz dance, jazz ensemble, journalism, life science, literature, math analysis, mathematics, mentorship program, musical theater, orchestra, outdoor education, painting, performing arts, philosophy, photography, physical education, physical science, physics, play production, pre-algebra, pre-calculus, printmaking, Spanish, statistics, strings, textiles, theater, trigonometry, U.S. government and politics, U.S. history, visual arts, Washington State and Northwest History, water color painting, wilderness education, world history, writing.

Graduation Requirements English, foreign language, history, humanities, mathematics, physical education (includes health), science, senior project, social studies (includes history), visual and performing arts, participation in environmental maintenance program.

Special Academic Programs ESL (50 students enrolled).

College Admission Counseling 87 students graduated in 2012; 86 went to college, including Brown University; Haverford College; Rhode Island School of Design; The University of British Columbia; University of California, Los Angeles; University of Washington. Other: 1 had other specific plans.

Student Life Upper grades have honor system. Discipline rests primarily with faculty.

Summer Programs Enrichment, ESL, sports, art/fine arts, computer instruction programs offered; session focuses on global connections with international students; held on campus; accepts boys and girls; open to students from other schools. 350 students usually enrolled. 2013 schedule: July 8 to August 16. Application deadline: June 17.

Tuition and Aid Day student tuition: $29,930; 7-day tuition and room/board: $43,655. Tuition installment plan (school's own payment plan). Need-based scholarship grants available. In 2012–13, 16% of upper-school students received aid. Total amount of financial aid awarded in 2012–13: $1,142,451.

Admissions Traditional secondary-level entrance grade is 9. For fall 2012, 252 students applied for upper-level admission, 159 were accepted, 64 enrolled. ISEE, SSAT or TOEFL required. Deadline for receipt of application materials: January 12. Application fee required: $70. Interview required.

Athletics Interscholastic: basketball (boys, girls), cross-country running (b,g), soccer (b,g), track and field (b,g), ultimate Frisbee (b,g), volleyball (g); coed intramural: fitness, hiking/backpacking, outdoor education, physical fitness, rock climbing, ropes courses, skiing (cross-country), skiing (downhill). 2 PE instructors, 30 coaches.

Computers Computers are regularly used in art, English, ESL, foreign language, graphic design, health, history, humanities, journalism, library, mathematics, music, science, social studies, theater, video film production, writing, yearbook classes. Computer network features include on-campus library services, Internet access, wireless campus network, ProQuest, ABC-Cleo, JSTOR, eLibrary, CultureGrams, World Conflicts and Online Encyclopedias. Computer access in designated common areas is available to students. Students grades are available online. The school has a published electronic and media policy.

Contact Douglas Leek, Director of Admissions and Enrollment Management. 206-682-7309. Fax: 206-467-7353. E-mail: douglas.leek@northwestschool.org. Web site: www.northwestschool.org

NORTHWEST YESHIVA HIGH SCHOOL

5017 90th Avenue Southeast
Mercer Island, Washington 98040

Head of School: Rabbi Bernie Fox

General Information Coeducational day college-preparatory and religious studies school, affiliated with Jewish faith. Grades 9–12. Founded: 1974. Setting: suburban. Nearest major city is Seattle. 2-acre campus. 3 buildings on campus. Approved or accredited by Northwest Accreditation Commission and Washington Department of Education. Languages of instruction: English and Hebrew. Endowment: $1.2 million. Total enrollment: 87. Upper school average class size: 12. Upper school faculty-student ratio: 1:4. There are 180 required school days per year for Upper School students. Upper School students typically attend 5 days per week. The average school day consists of 7 hours.

Upper School Student Profile Grade 9: 23 students (13 boys, 10 girls); Grade 10: 20 students (11 boys, 9 girls); Grade 11: 21 students (12 boys, 9 girls); Grade 12: 23 students (12 boys, 11 girls). 100% of students are Jewish.

Faculty School total: 24. In upper school: 15 men, 9 women; 12 have advanced degrees.

Subjects Offered 20th century history, algebra, American legal systems, art, art history, biology, calculus, chemistry, college admission preparation, college counseling, drama, economics, English, film appreciation, fine arts, geometry, Hebrew, Hebrew scripture, integrated mathematics, Jewish history, Judaic studies, lab science, language arts, modern Western civilization, newspaper, philosophy, physical education, physics, prayer/spirituality, pre-algebra, pre-calculus, psychology, Rabbinic literature, religious studies, Spanish, Talmud, U.S. government, U.S. history, U.S. literature, Western civilization, world history, writing, yearbook.

Graduation Requirements Advanced math, arts and fine arts (art, music, dance, drama), biology, conceptual physics, Hebrew, integrated mathematics, Judaic studies, language arts, physics, Spanish, Talmud, U.S. government, U.S. history, world history. Community service is required.

Special Academic Programs Independent study; academic accommodation for the gifted; remedial reading and/or remedial writing; remedial math; special instructional classes for deaf students; ESL (1 student enrolled).

College Admission Counseling 16 students graduated in 2011; 10 went to college, including Brandeis University; University of Washington; Yeshiva University. Other: 6 had other specific plans. Median SAT critical reading: 620, median SAT math: 620, median SAT writing: 630, median combined SAT: 1870. 53% scored over 600 on SAT critical reading, 67% scored over 600 on SAT math, 60% scored over 600 on SAT writing, 53% scored over 1800 on combined SAT.

Student Life Upper grades have specified standards of dress, student council, honor system. Discipline rests primarily with faculty. Attendance at religious services is required.

Tuition and Aid Day student tuition: $14,175. Tuition installment plan (monthly payment plans, individually arranged payment plans). Need-based scholarship grants available. In 2011–12, 50% of upper-school students received aid. Total amount of financial aid awarded in 2011–12: $465,591.

Admissions Traditional secondary-level entrance grade is 9. Deadline for receipt of application materials: none. Application fee required: $250. Interview required.

Athletics Interscholastic: basketball (boys, girls), cross-country running (b,g), golf (b,g), volleyball (g); coed interscholastic: cross-country running, softball. 5 PE instructors, 5 coaches.

Computers Computer network features include Internet access. Student e-mail accounts are available to students.

Contact Mr. Ian Weiner, Director of Student Services. 206-232-5272. Fax: 206-232-2711. E-mail: iw@nyhs.net. Web site: www.nyhs.net

NORTHWOOD SCHOOL

PO Box 1070
92 Northwood Road
Lake Placid, New York 12946

Head of School: Edward M. Good

General Information Coeducational boarding and day college-preparatory and arts school. Grades 9–PG. Founded: 1905. Setting: small town. Nearest major city is Albany. Students are housed in single-sex dormitories. 80-acre campus. 8 buildings on campus. Approved or accredited by New York State Association of Independent Schools and The Association of Boarding Schools. Member of National Association of Independent Schools and Secondary School Admission Test Board. Endowment: $8 million. Total enrollment: 182. Upper school average class size: 9. Upper school faculty-student ratio: 1:6. There are 180 required school days per year for Upper School students. Upper School students typically attend 5 days per week. The average school day consists of 7 hours.

Upper School Student Profile Grade 9: 17 students (8 boys, 9 girls); Grade 10: 48 students (30 boys, 18 girls); Grade 11: 58 students (38 boys, 20 girls); Grade 12: 59 students (38 boys, 21 girls). 79% of students are boarding students. 39% are state residents. 19 states are represented in upper school student body. 36% are international students. International students from Canada, China, Finland, Mexico, Republic of Korea, and Spain; 6 other countries represented in student body.

Faculty School total: 33. In upper school: 22 men, 8 women; 15 have advanced degrees; 17 reside on campus.

Subjects Offered Algebra, American history, American literature, art, biology, calculus, ceramics, chemistry, computer science, drama, earth science, English, English literature, ensembles, environmental science, expository writing, fiber arts, French, geography, geology, geometry, government/civics, great issues, health, history, journalism, mathematics, music, photography, physical education, physics, psychology, SAT preparation, science, social studies, sociology, Spanish, theater, trigonometry, world history.

Graduation Requirements Arts and fine arts (art, music, dance, drama), English, foreign language, mathematics, physical education (includes health), science, social studies (includes history).

Special Academic Programs 5 Advanced Placement exams for which test preparation is offered; honors section; independent study; remedial reading and/or remedial writing; ESL (25 students enrolled).

College Admission Counseling 69 students graduated in 2012; 60 went to college, including Clarkson University; New York University; Penn State University Park; Skidmore College; St. Lawrence University; Syracuse University. Other: 3 entered a postgraduate year, 6 had other specific plans. Median SAT critical reading: 520, median SAT math: 500, median SAT writing: 510.

Student Life Upper grades have specified standards of dress, student council, honor system. Discipline rests primarily with faculty.

Summer Programs Sports programs offered; session focuses on sports camps; held both on and off campus; held at Lake Placid; accepts boys and girls; open to students from other schools. 150 students usually enrolled. 2013 schedule: July to August.

Tuition and Aid Day student tuition: $25,450; 7-day tuition and room/board: $44,425. Tuition installment plan (The Tuition Plan). Need-based scholarship grants available. In 2012–13, 56% of upper-school students received aid.

Admissions Traditional secondary-level entrance grade is 11. For fall 2012, 255 students applied for upper-level admission, 163 were accepted, 99 enrolled. Any standardized test or TOEFL or SLEP required. Deadline for receipt of application materials: none. Application fee required: $50. Interview required.

Athletics Interscholastic: crew (boys, girls), hockey (b,g), ice hockey (b,g), ice skating (b,g), lacrosse (b,g), nordic skiing (b,g), ski jumping (b,g), skiing (downhill) (b,g), soccer (b,g), telemark skiing (b,g), tennis (b,g); intramural: hockey (b,g), ice hockey (b,g), ice skating (b,g), skiing (downhill) (b,g), snowboarding (b,g); coed interscholastic: alpine skiing, figure skating, fitness, freestyle skiing, golf, nordic skiing, skiing (cross-country), snowboarding, telemark skiing; coed intramural: alpine skiing, backpacking, bicycling, canoeing/kayaking, climbing, combined training, cross-country running, figure skating, fishing, fitness, fly fishing, freestyle skiing, golf, hiking/backpacking, jogging, kayaking, luge, mountain biking, mountaineering, nordic skiing, outdoor adventure, physical training, rafting, rappelling, rock climbing, ropes courses, rowing, running, skiing (cross-country), skiing (downhill), snowboarding, street hockey, strength & conditioning, tennis, walking, wall climbing, weight training, wilderness, wilderness survival, wildernessways, winter walking. 1 coach, 1 athletic trainer.

Computers Computers are regularly used in English, foreign language, history, mathematics, science classes. Computer network features include on-campus library services, online commercial services, Internet access, wireless campus network, Internet filtering or blocking technology. Students grades are available online. The school has a published electronic and media policy.

Contact Elenor Mandigo, Admissions Assistant. 518-523-3382 Ext. 204. Fax: 518-523-3405. E-mail: younge@northwoodschool.com. Web site: www.northwoodschool.com

NORTH YARMOUTH ACADEMY

148 Main Street
Yarmouth, Maine 04096

Head of School: Brad Choyt

General Information Coeducational day college-preparatory, arts, and technology school. Grades 5–12. Founded: 1814. Setting: suburban. Nearest major city is Portland. 25-acre campus. 14 buildings on campus. Approved or accredited by Association of Independent Schools in New England, Independent Schools of Northern New England, New England Association of Schools and Colleges, and Maine Department of Education. Member of National Association of Independent Schools and Secondary School Admission Test Board. Endowment: $3 million. Total enrollment: 280. Upper school average class size: 15. Upper school faculty-student ratio: 1:8. There are 277 required school days per year for Upper School students. Upper School students typically attend 5 days per week. The average school day consists of 5 hours and 45 minutes.

Upper School Student Profile Grade 9: 50 students (25 boys, 25 girls); Grade 10: 55 students (31 boys, 24 girls); Grade 11: 47 students (22 boys, 25 girls); Grade 12: 48 students (26 boys, 22 girls).

Faculty School total: 42. In upper school: 16 men, 26 women; 26 have advanced degrees.

Subjects Offered Algebra, American government, American history, American history-AP, ancient world history, art, art history-AP, art-AP, biology-AP, calculus-AP, chemistry, chorus, classical language, college counseling, composition-AP, computer graphics, contemporary issues, drama, drawing and design, earth science, English, English composition, English literature, English literature and composition-AP, English-AP, environmental science-AP, European history, European history-AP, experiential education, fine arts, French, French-AP, genetics, geometry, history, instrumental music, jazz, language-AP, Latin, Latin-AP, mathematics, model United Nations, modern European history, modern European history-AP, music, music theory-AP, music-AP, painting, photography, physical education, physical science, physics, physics-AP, pottery, pre-algebra, pre-calculus, psychology, science, senior project, social issues, social studies, society challenge and change, Spanish, Spanish-AP, statistics, statistics-AP, student publications, studio art, studio art-AP, technology, theater, trigonometry, U.S. government and politics-AP, U.S. history, U.S. history-AP, visual and performing arts, vocal music, world history.

Graduation Requirements Arts and fine arts (art, music, dance, drama), English, foreign language, history, mathematics, science, senior project, speech, two-week volunteer senior service project, senior speech, participation in athletics or performing arts program each season (3).

Special Academic Programs Advanced Placement exam preparation; honors section; study abroad; ESL (6 students enrolled).

College Admission Counseling 52 students graduated in 2012; 50 went to college, including Case Western Reserve University; Colby College; Kalamazoo College; Mount Holyoke College; Tufts University. Other: 2 had other specific plans. Median SAT critical reading: 600, median SAT math: 600. 50% scored over 600 on SAT critical reading, 50% scored over 600 on SAT math.

Student Life Upper grades have specified standards of dress, student council, honor system. Discipline rests equally with students and faculty.

Summer Programs Remediation, enrichment, advancement, sports, art/fine arts programs offered; session focuses on academic enrichment; held on campus; accepts boys and girls; open to students from other schools. 2013 schedule: June 25 to August 15. Application deadline: none.

Tuition and Aid Day student tuition: $25,400; 7-day tuition and room/board: $39,500. Tuition installment plan (Insured Tuition Payment Plan, monthly payment plans). Need-based scholarship grants available. In 2012–13, 45% of upper-school students received aid. Total amount of financial aid awarded in 2012–13: $904,000.

Admissions Traditional secondary-level entrance grade is 9. For fall 2012, 57 students applied for upper-level admission, 45 were accepted, 29 enrolled. School placement exam, SSAT or writing sample required. Deadline for receipt of application materials: February 1. Application fee required: $45. On-campus interview required.

Athletics Interscholastic: baseball (boys), basketball (b,g), crew (b,g), cross-country running (b,g), fencing (b), field hockey (g), golf (b,g), ice hockey (b,g), indoor track (b,g), indoor track & field (b,g), lacrosse (b,g), nordic skiing (b,g), sailing (b,g), skiing (cross-country) (b,g), soccer (b,g), softball (g), swimming and diving (b,g), tennis (b,g), track and field (b,g). 1 PE instructor, 17 coaches, 1 athletic trainer.

Computers Computers are regularly used in English, foreign language, graphic design, history, mathematics, science, technology classes. Computer network features include on-campus library services, Internet access. Campus intranet, student e-mail accounts, and computer access in designated common areas are available to students. The school has a published electronic and media policy.

Contact Laurie D. Hyndman, Director of Admission and Financial Aid. 207-846-2376 Ext. 407. Fax: 207-846-2382. E-mail: admission@nya.org. Web site: www.nya.org

THE NORWICH FREE ACADEMY

305 Broadway
Norwich, Connecticut 06360

Head of School: Mr. David J. Klein

General Information Coeducational day college-preparatory, general academic, arts, business, vocational, bilingual studies, and technology school. Grades 9–12. Founded: 1856. Setting: suburban. 15-acre campus. 11 buildings on campus. Approved or accredited by New England Association of Schools and Colleges and Connecticut Department of Education. Member of National Association of Independent Schools. Total enrollment: 2,265. Upper school average class size: 24. Upper school faculty-student ratio: 1:22. There are 181 required school days per year for Upper School students. Upper School students typically attend 5 days per week. The average school day consists of 7 hours.

Faculty School total: 171. In upper school: 66 men, 105 women.

Subjects Offered 3-dimensional art, 3-dimensional design, accounting, advanced biology, advanced chemistry, advanced computer applications, advanced math, Advanced Placement courses, advanced studio art-AP, algebra, American history, American history-AP, American literature, anatomy and physiology, Arabic, architectural drawing, art, art history-AP, audio visual/media, band, biology, biology-AP, biotechnology, British literature, British literature-AP, business technology, calculus-AP, chemistry, chemistry-AP, Chinese, choir, chorus, civics, composition-AP, computer science-AP, dance, digital photography, discrete mathematics, drafting, drama, drawing, drawing and design, early childhood, economics, economics-AP, English language and composition-AP, English literature and composition-AP, environmental science-AP, European history-AP, exercise science, family and consumer science, finance, foods, forensics, French, French language-AP, geometry, Greek, health, jazz band, jazz dance, journalism, kinesiology, Latin, Latin-AP, marching band, marine biology, marketing, mathematical modeling, metalworking, music theory-AP, oceanography, personal finance, photo shop, photography, physical education, physics, physics-AP, piano, political science, politics, pre-calculus, printmaking, psychology, psychology-AP, public speaking, Spanish language-AP, speech communications, sports science, television, U.S. history, U.S. history-AP, visual arts, vocal ensemble, woodworking, zoology.

Special Academic Programs 20 Advanced Placement exams for which test preparation is offered; honors section; study at local college for college credit; remedial reading and/or remedial writing; remedial math; special instructional classes for students with learning disabilities, Attention Deficit Disorder, emotional and behavioral problems, and dyslexia; ESL (90 students enrolled).

College Admission Counseling 569 students graduated in 2012; 444 went to college. Other: 30 went to work, 10 entered military service, 33 entered a postgraduate year, 16 had other specific plans. Mean SAT critical reading: 513, mean SAT math: 512, mean SAT writing: 508, mean composite ACT: 24.

Student Life Upper grades have specified standards of dress, student council, honor system. Discipline rests primarily with faculty.

Summer Programs Remediation, enrichment, ESL, sports programs offered; held on campus; accepts boys and girls; not open to students from other schools. 250 students usually enrolled. 2013 schedule: July 1 to July 29. Application deadline: June 1.

Tuition and Aid Day student tuition: $11,720.

Admissions Traditional secondary-level entrance grade is 9. Deadline for receipt of application materials: none. No application fee required. Interview required.

Athletics Interscholastic: baseball (boys), basketball (b,g), cheering (b,g), cross-country running (b,g), fencing (b,g), field hockey (g), football (b), golf (b,g), gymnastics (g), hockey (b), ice hockey (b), indoor track (b,g), indoor track & field (b,g), lacrosse (b,g), running (b,g), soccer (b,g), softball (g), Special Olympics (b,g), swimming and diving (b,g), tennis (b,g), track and field (b,g), volleyball (b,g), winter (indoor) track (b,g), wrestling (b); intramural: skiing (downhill) (b,g), snowboarding (b); coed interscholastic: drill team; coed intramural: dance, dance team, physical fitness, physical training, power lifting, skateboarding, snowboarding, strength & conditioning, weight lifting, weight training. 4 PE instructors, 25 coaches, 5 athletic trainers.

Computers Computer network features include on-campus library services, Internet access, wireless campus network, Internet filtering or blocking technology. Student e-mail accounts are available to students. The school has a published electronic and media policy.

Contact Mr. John Iovino, Director of Student Affairs. 860-425-5510. Fax: 860-889-7124. E-mail: iovinoj@nfaschool.org. Web site: www.nfaschool.org

NOTRE DAME ACADEMY

2851 Overland Avenue
Los Angeles, California 90064

Head of School: Mrs. Joan Gumaer Tyhurst

General Information Girls' day college-preparatory, arts, religious studies, technology, and athletics school, affiliated with Roman Catholic Church. Grades 9–12. Founded: 1949. Setting: urban. 1 building on campus. Approved or accredited by Western Association of Schools and Colleges, Western Catholic Education Association, and California Department of Education. Upper school average class size: 23. Upper school faculty-student ratio: 1:13.

Upper School Student Profile 86% of students are Roman Catholic.

Faculty School total: 31. In upper school: 7 men, 24 women.

Subjects Offered Advanced studio art-AP, algebra, American history, art, art history-AP, athletic training, biology, biology-AP, calculus, calculus-AP, campus ministry, chemistry, chemistry-AP, choir, Christian and Hebrew scripture, community service, computer science, dance, design, digital photography, drama, drama performance, economics, English, English language and composition-AP, English literature and composition-AP, European history-AP, French, French-AP, geometry, government and politics-AP, government/civics, health, history, honors geometry, Japanese, law, leadership, photography, physical education, physics, pre-calculus, psychology, psychology-AP, religion, Spanish, Spanish language-AP, speech and oral interpretations, statistics, trigonometry, U.S. government and politics-AP, U.S. history-AP, world civilizations, world history-AP.

Graduation Requirements Arts and fine arts (art, music, dance, drama), computer science, English, foreign language, mathematics, physical education (includes health), religion (includes Bible studies and theology), science, social studies (includes history), speech. Community service is required.

Special Academic Programs 15 Advanced Placement exams for which test preparation is offered; honors section.

College Admission Counseling 99 students graduated in 2012; all went to college, including California State Polytechnic University, Pomona; Cornell University; Loyola Marymount University; University of California, Irvine; University of California, Los Angeles; University of Southern California. Mean SAT critical reading: 571, mean SAT math: 545, mean SAT writing: 598, mean combined SAT: 1714.

Student Life Upper grades have uniform requirement, student council, honor system. Discipline rests primarily with faculty. Attendance at religious services is required.

Summer Programs Remediation, enrichment, advancement, sports, art/fine arts, computer instruction programs offered; session focuses on academic advancement, required prerequisites, enrichment; held both on and off campus; held at various athletic facilities; accepts boys and girls; open to students from other schools. 300 students usually enrolled. 2013 schedule: June 10 to July 12. Application deadline: May.

Tuition and Aid Day student tuition: $11,550. Tuition installment plan (FACTS Tuition Payment Plan, monthly payment plans, quarterly and semester payment plans). Merit scholarship grants, need-based scholarship grants, paying campus jobs available. In 2012–13, 30% of upper-school students received aid.

Admissions Traditional secondary-level entrance grade is 9. For fall 2012, 230 students applied for upper-level admission, 102 enrolled. High School Placement Test (closed version) from Scholastic Testing Service required. Deadline for receipt of application materials: January 6. Application fee required: $75. On-campus interview required.

Athletics Interscholastic: basketball, cross-country running, dance, equestrian sports, soccer, softball, swimming and diving, tennis, track and field, volleyball. 1 PE instructor, 19 coaches, 1 athletic trainer.

Computers Computers are regularly used in all academic, computer applications, design, journalism, photography, yearbook classes. Computer network features include on-campus library services, online commercial services, Internet access, wireless campus network, Internet filtering or blocking technology. Student e-mail accounts and computer access in designated common areas are available to students. Students grades are available online. The school has a published electronic and media policy.

Contact Ms. Brigid Williams, Director of Admissions. 310-839-5289 Ext. 218. Fax: 310-839-7957. E-mail: bwilliams@ndala.com. Web site: www.ndala.com

NOTRE DAME COLLEGE PREP

7655 West Dempster Street
Niles, Illinois 60714-2098

Head of School: Mr. Daniel Tully

General Information Boys' day college-preparatory, arts, business, religious studies, and technology school, affiliated with Roman Catholic Church. Grades 9–12. Founded: 1955. Setting: suburban. Nearest major city is Chicago. 28-acre campus. 1 building on campus. Approved or accredited by National Catholic Education Association, North Central Association of Colleges and Schools, and Illinois Department of Education. Endowment: $1.2 million. Total enrollment: 793. Upper school average class size: 17. Upper school faculty-student ratio: 1:17. There are 174 required school days per year for Upper School students. Upper School students typically attend 5 days per week. The average school day consists of 6 hours and 50 minutes.

Upper School Student Profile Grade 9: 227 students (227 boys); Grade 10: 197 students (197 boys); Grade 11: 193 students (193 boys); Grade 12: 176 students (176 boys). 87% of students are Roman Catholic.

Faculty School total: 58. In upper school: 33 men, 25 women; 39 have advanced degrees.

Subjects Offered 3-dimensional art, accounting, advanced biology, advanced chemistry, advanced math, algebra, American literature, art, art history, art history-AP, band, Bible as literature, Bible studies, bioethics, biology, biology-AP, British literature, British literature (honors), calculus, calculus-AP, Catholic belief and practice, chemistry, chemistry-AP, choir, comedy, computer literacy, computer programming, concert band, contemporary history, creative writing, debate, drama, dramatic arts, economics, English, English-AP, environmental science, ESL, ethics, European history-AP, film appreciation, fine arts, geography, geometry, government-AP, health, history, honors algebra, honors English, honors geometry, Italian, jazz, jazz band, journalism, Latin, Latin-AP, leadership, mathematics, music, music appreciation, music theory, philosophy, physical education, physics, physics-AP, pre-calculus, psychology, reading/study skills, religion, social studies, sociology, Spanish, Spanish-AP, speech, statistics, studio art-AP, theology, trigonometry, U.S. history, U.S. history-AP, Web site design, weight training, weightlifting, Western civilization, world literature, world religions.

Graduation Requirements Algebra, American literature, arts and fine arts (art, music, dance, drama), biology, British literature, computer literacy, constitutional law, English, foreign language, geometry, health, mathematics, physical education (includes health), religion (includes Bible studies and theology), science, social studies (includes history), U.S. history, Western civilization, world literature, four years of religious retreats and community services.

Special Academic Programs 12 Advanced Placement exams for which test preparation is offered; honors section; study at local college for college credit; academic accommodation for the gifted; remedial reading and/or remedial writing; remedial math; special instructional classes for remedial religion, science and social studies; ESL (9 students enrolled).

College Admission Counseling 218 students graduated in 2012; 211 went to college, including DePaul University; Illinois State University; Loyola University Chicago; Northern Illinois University; University of Illinois at Chicago; University of Illinois at Urbana–Champaign. Other: 2 went to work, 3 entered military service, 1 entered a postgraduate year, 1 had other specific plans. Mean composite ACT: 24. 38% scored over 26 on composite ACT.

Student Life Upper grades have specified standards of dress, student council, honor system. Discipline rests primarily with faculty. Attendance at religious services is required.

Summer Programs Remediation, sports, art/fine arts, computer instruction programs offered; session focuses on remediation/make up; held on campus; accepts boys and girls; open to students from other schools. 200 students usually enrolled. 2013 schedule: May 28 to July 26.

Tuition and Aid Day student tuition: $9700. Tuition installment plan (FACTS Tuition Payment Plan, monthly payment plans). Tuition reduction for siblings, merit scholarship grants, need-based scholarship grants, paying campus jobs available. In 2012–13, 36% of upper-school students received aid; total upper-school merit-scholarship money awarded: $94,000. Total amount of financial aid awarded in 2012–13: $3,600,000.

Admissions Traditional secondary-level entrance grade is 9. For fall 2012, 247 students applied for upper-level admission, 241 were accepted, 227 enrolled. High School Placement Test or TOEFL or SLEP required. Deadline for receipt of application materials: June 1. Application fee required: $25. Interview recommended.

Athletics Interscholastic: baseball, basketball, bowling, cross-country running, diving, football, golf, ice hockey, lacrosse, soccer, swimming and diving, tennis, track and field, volleyball, wrestling; intramural: baseball, basketball, boxing, combined training, flag football, floor hockey, football, lacrosse, outdoor adventure, paddle tennis, physical fitness, softball, table tennis, ultimate Frisbee, volleyball, weight lifting, weight training, wrestling. 4 PE instructors, 25 coaches, 1 athletic trainer.

Computers Computers are regularly used in accounting, art, computer applications, English, ESL, geography, health, history, science, Web site design classes. Computer network features include on-campus library services, Internet access, Internet filtering or blocking technology, college search and scholarships. Computer access in designated common areas is available to students. Students grades are available online. The school has a published electronic and media policy.

Contact Mr. Shay Boyle, Director of Enrollment. 847-779-8616. Fax: 847-965-2975. E-mail: sboyle@nddons.org. Web site: www.nddons.org

NOTRE DAME HIGH SCHOOL

596 South Second Street
San Jose, California 95112

Head of School: Mrs. Mary Elizabeth Riley

General Information Girls' day college-preparatory, arts, religious studies, and technology school, affiliated with Roman Catholic Church. Grades 9–12. Founded: 1851. Setting: urban. 2-acre campus. 4 buildings on campus. Approved or accredited by Western Association of Schools and Colleges, Western Catholic Education Association, and California Department of Education. Endowment: $900,000. Total enrollment: 626. Upper school average class size: 24. Upper school faculty-student ratio: 1:11. There are 202 required school days per year for Upper School students. Upper School students typically attend 5 days per week. The average school day consists of 6 hours and 55 minutes.

Upper School Student Profile Grade 9: 162 students (162 girls); Grade 10: 165 students (165 girls); Grade 11: 142 students (142 girls); Grade 12: 157 students (157 girls). 63% of students are Roman Catholic.

Faculty School total: 43. In upper school: 7 men, 36 women; 34 have advanced degrees.

Subjects Offered Advanced biology, advanced chemistry, Advanced Placement courses, algebra, art, ASB Leadership, athletics, Basic programming, biology, biology-AP, calculus, calculus-AP, campus ministry, ceramics, chemistry, Christian and Hebrew scripture, computer programming, computer science, creative writing, dance, decision making skills, digital photography, drama, drama performance, economics, English, English language and composition-AP, English literature, English literature and composition-AP, environmental science-AP, film and literature, fine arts, French, French language-AP, French literature-AP, geography, geometry, global studies, government/civics, healthful living, honors algebra, honors English, honors geometry, honors U.S. history, honors world history, journalism, library research, library skills, mathematics, modern world history, moral and social development, musical theater, painting, peer counseling, peer ministry, philosophy, photography, physical education, physical fitness, physics, post-calculus, pre-calculus, psychology, psychology-AP, public speaking, religion, research skills, robotics, science, service learning/internship, social justice, social psychology, social studies, Spanish, Spanish language-AP, Spanish literature-AP, speech and debate, statistics, study skills, theater, trigonometry, U.S. government, U.S. government and politics-AP, U.S. history, U.S. history-AP, video film production, Web site design, women in society, world history, world history-AP, world religions, yearbook.

Graduation Requirements Arts and fine arts (art, music, dance, drama), computer science, English, foreign language, mathematics, physical education (includes health), religion (includes Bible studies and theology), science, social studies (includes history), community service learning program.

Special Academic Programs 10 Advanced Placement exams for which test preparation is offered; honors section; independent study; study at local college for college credit.

College Admission Counseling 142 students graduated in 2012; all went to college, including California Polytechnic State University, San Luis Obispo; Santa Clara University; Seattle University; Sonoma State University; University of San Francisco; University of Southern California. Median SAT critical reading: 588, median SAT math: 574, median SAT writing: 599. 43% scored over 600 on SAT critical reading, 45% scored over 600 on SAT math, 50% scored over 600 on SAT writing.

Student Life Upper grades have uniform requirement, student council, honor system. Discipline rests primarily with faculty. Attendance at religious services is required.

Summer Programs Enrichment, advancement programs offered; session focuses on enrichment; held on campus; accepts boys and girls; open to students from other schools. 125 students usually enrolled. 2013 schedule: June to July.

Tuition and Aid Day student tuition: $15,368. Tuition installment plan (FACTS Tuition Payment Plan, monthly payment plans, annual payment plan, 2-payment plan). Merit scholarship grants, need-based scholarship grants, individual sponsored grants available. In 2012–13, 24% of upper-school students received aid; total upper-school merit-scholarship money awarded: $7800. Total amount of financial aid awarded in 2012–13: $767,000.

Admissions Traditional secondary-level entrance grade is 9. For fall 2012, 388 students applied for upper-level admission, 273 were accepted, 162 enrolled. High School Placement Test required. Deadline for receipt of application materials: January 23. Application fee required: $65.

Athletics Interscholastic: aquatics, basketball, cross-country running, golf, lacrosse, soccer, softball, swimming and diving, tennis, track and field, volleyball; intramural: badminton, basketball, volleyball. 2 PE instructors, 25 coaches, 2 athletic trainers.

Computers Computers are regularly used in all academic, English, foreign language, history, mathematics, science classes. Computer network features include on-campus library services, online commercial services, Internet access, wireless campus network, Internet filtering or blocking technology. Student e-mail accounts are available to students. Students grades are available online. The school has a published electronic and media policy.

Contact Ms. Susana Garcia, Director of Enrollment Management. 408-294-1113 Ext. 2159. Fax: 408-293-9779. E-mail: sgarcia@ndsj.org. Web site: ndsj.org

NOTRE DAME HIGH SCHOOL

601 Lawrence Road
Lawrenceville, New Jersey 08648

Heads of School: Mr. Barry Edward Breen and Ms. Mary Liz Ivins

General Information Coeducational day college-preparatory school, affiliated with Roman Catholic Church. Grades 9–12. Founded: 1957. Setting: suburban. Nearest major city is Trenton. 100-acre campus. 1 building on campus. Approved or accredited by Middle States Association of Colleges and Schools, National Catholic Education Association, and New Jersey Department of Education. Total enrollment: 1,299. Upper school average class size: 23. Upper school faculty-student ratio: 1:13. There are 180 required school days per year for Upper School students. Upper School students typically attend 5 days per week. The average school day consists of 6 hours and 30 minutes.

Upper School Student Profile Grade 9: 347 students (171 boys, 176 girls); Grade 10: 333 students (168 boys, 165 girls); Grade 11: 312 students (157 boys, 155 girls); Grade 12: 307 students (161 boys, 146 girls). 82% of students are Roman Catholic.

Faculty School total: 96. In upper school: 36 men, 60 women; 42 have advanced degrees.

Subjects Offered 20th century history, 3-dimensional art, 3-dimensional design, accounting, acting, advanced chemistry, advanced computer applications, advanced math, Advanced Placement courses, algebra, American government, American history, American history-AP, American literature, ancient world history, applied music, art, art and culture, art-AP, athletics, Basic programming, Bible studies, biology, biology-AP, British literature, business, business applications, business studies, calculus, calculus-AP, campus ministry, Catholic belief and practice, ceramics, chemistry, chemistry-AP, choir, chorus, Christian doctrine, community service, comparative religion, computer applications, computer science, concert band, concert choir, constitutional law, contemporary issues, creative writing, dance, dance performance, discrete mathematics, drama, driver education, ecology, environmental systems, economics, economics-AP, English, English composition, English language and composition-AP, English literature and composition-AP, English literature-AP, environmental science-AP, etymology, European history-AP, film appreciation, film studies, filmmaking, first aid, French, French-AP, geometry, German, German literature, government-AP, health education, honors algebra, honors English, honors world history, independent study, Italian, Japanese, jazz band, journalism, kinesiology, language-AP, Latin, law, leadership and service, leadership education training, literature and composition-AP, literature-AP, macro/microeconomics-AP, madrigals, math review, media literacy, newspaper, orchestra, painting, peer counseling, peer ministry, personal finance, philosophy, photography, physical education, physics, physics-AP, piano, portfolio art, pottery, pre-algebra, pre-calculus, probability and statistics, psychology, psychology-AP, public speaking, reading/study skills, religion, religion and culture, robotics, Russian, SAT preparation, scripture, senior internship, senior project, service learning/internship, sociology, Spanish, Spanish literature, Spanish-AP, speech and debate, sports medicine, statistics-AP, studio art-AP, U.S. government, U.S. government and politics-AP, U.S. literature, women spirituality and faith, world history, world literature, writing.

Graduation Requirements Biology, English, foreign language, integrated technology fundamentals, lab science, mathematics, physical education (includes health), religion (includes Bible studies and theology), U.S. history, world history, service-learning. Community service is required.

Special Academic Programs 15 Advanced Placement exams for which test preparation is offered; honors section; independent study; study at local college for college credit; remedial reading and/or remedial writing; remedial math.

College Admission Counseling 285 students graduated in 2012; 282 went to college, including Loyola University Maryland; Rutgers, The State University of New Jersey, New Brunswick; Saint Joseph's University; Seton Hall University; The College of New Jersey; University of Delaware. Other: 1 went to work, 2 entered military service. Mean SAT critical reading: 554, mean SAT math: 557, mean SAT writing: 555, mean combined SAT: 1666. 30% scored over 600 on SAT critical reading, 34% scored over 600 on SAT math, 28% scored over 600 on SAT writing, 26% scored over 1800 on combined SAT.

Student Life Upper grades have uniform requirement, student council, honor system. Discipline rests primarily with faculty. Attendance at religious services is required.

Summer Programs Remediation, enrichment, advancement, sports, art/fine arts programs offered; session focuses on sports, arts, academic and writing camps; held on campus; accepts boys and girls; open to students from other schools. 775 students usually enrolled. 2013 schedule: June 19 to August 16. Application deadline: June 19.

Tuition and Aid Day student tuition: $10,920. Tuition installment plan (Tuition Management Systems Plan). Tuition reduction for siblings, need-based scholarship grants available. In 2012–13, 10% of upper-school students received aid. Total amount of financial aid awarded in 2012–13: $375,000.

Admissions Traditional secondary-level entrance grade is 9. For fall 2012, 550 students applied for upper-level admission, 425 were accepted, 347 enrolled. Scholastic Testing Service High School Placement Test required. Deadline for receipt of application materials: November 30. Application fee required: $50. On-campus interview required.

Athletics Interscholastic: baseball (boys), basketball (b,g), cheering (g), cross-country running (b,g), dance (g), field hockey (g), football (b), golf (b,g), ice hockey (b), indoor track (b,g), lacrosse (b,g), soccer (b,g), softball (g), swimming and diving (b,g), tennis (b,g), track and field (b,g), winter (indoor) track (b,g), wrestling (b); intramural: touch football (g), volleyball (b,g); coed interscholastic: cheering, dance, diving, fitness, strength & conditioning; coed intramural: Frisbee, outdoor activities, outdoor recreation, physical fitness, ultimate Frisbee, volleyball, weight lifting, weight training. 9 PE instructors, 65 coaches, 1 athletic trainer.

Computers Computers are regularly used in all academic classes. Computer network features include on-campus library services, online commercial services, Internet access, wireless campus network, Internet filtering or blocking technology. Campus intranet and computer access in designated common areas are available to students. Students grades are available online. The school has a published electronic and media policy.

Contact Ms. Peggy Miller, Director of Enrollment Management. 609-882-7900 Ext. 139. Fax: 609-882-6599. E-mail: miller@ndnj.org. Web site: www.ndnj.org

NOTRE DAME HIGH SCHOOL

2701 Vermont Avenue
Chattanooga, Tennessee 37404

Head of School: Mr. Perry L. Storey

General Information Coeducational day college-preparatory, arts, religious studies, technology, and Microsoft IT Academy Certification school, affiliated with Roman Catholic Church. Grades 9–12. Founded: 1876. Setting: urban. 22-acre campus. 3 buildings on campus. Approved or accredited by Southern Association of Colleges and Schools and Tennessee Department of Education. Endowment: $750,000. Total enrollment: 407. Upper school average class size: 18. Upper school faculty-student ratio: 1:10. There are 180 required school days per year for Upper School students. Upper School students typically attend 5 days per week. The average school day consists of 5 hours and 50 minutes.

Upper School Student Profile Grade 9: 115 students (57 boys, 58 girls); Grade 10: 82 students (42 boys, 40 girls); Grade 11: 107 students (49 boys, 58 girls); Grade 12: 103 students (54 boys, 49 girls). 77% of students are Roman Catholic.

Faculty School total: 40. In upper school: 16 men, 24 women; 27 have advanced degrees.

Subjects Offered 3-dimensional art, ACT preparation, Advanced Placement courses, algebra, American history-AP, American literature, anatomy, anatomy and physiology, art-AP, band, biology, biology-AP, British literature, calculus, Catholic belief and practice, chemistry, choir, civics, conceptual physics, creative dance, criminal justice, drama, economics, electives, English composition, English literature, English-AP, environmental science-AP, European history-AP, foreign language, French, geometry, German, government, government/civics, health and wellness, history-AP, honors algebra, honors English, honors geometry, honors U.S. history, honors world history, Latin, physics, religion, Spanish, U.S. government and politics-AP, weight training, wellness, world geography, world history, world history-AP, writing, yoga.

Special Academic Programs Advanced Placement exam preparation; honors section; independent study; study at local college for college credit.

College Admission Counseling 126 students graduated in 2012; 125 went to college, including Auburn University; Middle Tennessee State University; The University of Tennessee; The University of Tennessee at Chattanooga; University of Georgia. Other: 1 had other specific plans.

Student Life Upper grades have uniform requirement, student council, honor system. Discipline rests primarily with faculty. Attendance at religious services is required.

Summer Programs Enrichment, sports, art/fine arts programs offered; session focuses on enrichment; held both on and off campus; held at various sites in Chattanooga; accepts boys and girls; open to students from other schools. 250 students usually enrolled. 2013 schedule: June 3 to July 26. Application deadline: April 1.

Tuition and Aid Day student tuition: $9150–$11,754. Tuition installment plan (Insured Tuition Payment Plan, FACTS Tuition Payment Plan, monthly payment plans, individually arranged payment plans). Tuition reduction for siblings, need-based scholarship grants available. In 2012–13, 30% of upper-school students received aid. Total amount of financial aid awarded in 2012–13: $378,271.

Admissions Traditional secondary-level entrance grade is 9. ACT-Explore required. Deadline for receipt of application materials: none. Application fee required: $100. On-campus interview required.

Athletics Interscholastic: aerobics/dance (girls), baseball (b), basketball (b,g), bowling (b,g), cross-country running (b,g), dance (g), dance squad (g), dance team (g), diving (b,g), football (b), golf (b,g), modern dance (g), physical training (b,g), running (b,g), soccer (b,g), softball (g), swimming and diving (b,g), tennis (b,g), track and field (b,g), volleyball (g), weight training (b,g), wrestling (b); intramural: aerobics/dance (g), cheering (g), indoor soccer (b), indoor track (b,g), lacrosse (b,g); coed interscholastic: cheering, yoga; coed intramural: backpacking, canoeing/kayaking, climbing, crew, hiking/backpacking, kayaking, mountaineering, outdoors, rafting, rappelling, rock climbing, rowing, skiing (downhill), snowboarding, wall climbing. 4 PE instructors, 30 coaches, 2 athletic trainers.

Computers Computers are regularly used in information technology classes. Computer network features include on-campus library services, Internet access, wireless campus network, Internet filtering or blocking technology, language software labs, Microsoft IT Academy Training. Student e-mail accounts and computer access in designated common areas are available to students. Students grades are available online. The school has a published electronic and media policy.

Contact Ms. Jenny Rittgers, Admissions Director. 423-624-4618 Ext. 1004. Fax: 423-624-4621. E-mail: admissions@myndhs.com. Web site: www.myndhs.com

NOTRE DAME JUNIOR/SENIOR HIGH SCHOOL

60 Spangenburg Avenue
East Stroudsburg, Pennsylvania 18301-2799

Head of School: Mr. Jeffrey Neill Lyons

General Information Coeducational day college-preparatory, arts, and religious studies school, affiliated with Roman Catholic Church. Grades 7–12. Founded: 1967. Setting: suburban. 40-acre campus. 4 buildings on campus. Approved or accredited by Middle States Association of Colleges and Schools, National Catholic Education Association, and Pennsylvania Department of Education. Total enrollment: 233. Upper school average class size: 25. Upper school faculty-student ratio: 1:15. There are 180 required school days per year for Upper School students. Upper School students typically attend 5 days per week. The average school day consists of 6 hours and 30 minutes.

Upper School Student Profile Grade 7: 27 students (9 boys, 18 girls); Grade 8: 19 students (6 boys, 13 girls); Grade 9: 62 students (32 boys, 30 girls); Grade 10: 35 students (18 boys, 17 girls); Grade 11: 43 students (20 boys, 23 girls); Grade 12: 46 students (21 boys, 25 girls). 88% of students are Roman Catholic.

Faculty School total: 25. In upper school: 9 men, 16 women; 12 have advanced degrees.

Graduation Requirements Lab/keyboard, mathematics, moral theology, physical education (includes health), physical science, religion (includes Bible studies and theology), senior project, U.S. history, U.S. literature, word processing, world cultures, world religions.

Special Academic Programs Advanced Placement exam preparation; honors section; study at local college for college credit.

College Admission Counseling 58 students graduated in 2012; 56 went to college, including Marywood University; Mount St. Mary's University; Penn State University Park; Saint Joseph's University; Temple University; The University of Scranton. Other: 2 went to work. Median SAT critical reading: 500, median SAT math: 460, median SAT writing: 500, median combined SAT: 1460. 10% scored over 600 on SAT critical reading, 15% scored over 600 on SAT math, 10% scored over 600 on SAT writing, 25% scored over 1800 on combined SAT.

Student Life Upper grades have uniform requirement, student council. Discipline rests primarily with faculty. Attendance at religious services is required.

Tuition and Aid Tuition installment plan (FACTS Tuition Payment Plan). Tuition reduction for siblings, need-based scholarship grants available. In 2012–13, 30% of upper-school students received aid.

Admissions Traditional secondary-level entrance grade is 7. Achievement tests or TerraNova required. Deadline for receipt of application materials: May 1. No application fee required. Interview required.

Athletics Interscholastic: baseball (boys), basketball (b,g), cheering (g), field hockey (g), soccer (b,g), softball (g), swimming and diving (b,g), tennis (b,g), winter soccer (b,g); coed interscholastic: golf, soccer; coed intramural: cross-country running, indoor soccer, jogging, strength & conditioning. 2 PE instructors, 15 coaches, 1 athletic trainer.

Computers Computer network features include on-campus library services, Internet access, Internet filtering or blocking technology. The school has a published electronic and media policy.

Contact Mr. Jeffrey Neill Lyons, Principal. 570-421-0466. Fax: 570-476-0629. E-mail: principal@ndhigh.org. Web site: www.ndhigh.org

OAK GROVE SCHOOL

220 West Lomita Avenue
Ojai, California 93023

Head of School: Meredy Benson Rice

General Information Coeducational boarding and day college-preparatory and arts school. Boarding grades 9–12, day grades PK–12. Founded: 1975. Setting: small town. Nearest major city is Los Angeles. Students are housed in coed dormitories. 150-acre campus. 6 buildings on campus. Approved or accredited by California Association of Independent Schools, The Association of Boarding Schools, Western Association of Schools and Colleges, and California Department of Education. Member of National Association of Independent Schools and Secondary School Admission Test Board. Endowment: $120,000. Total enrollment: 209. Upper school average class size: 15. Upper school faculty-student ratio: 1:7. There are 170 required school days per year for Upper School students. Upper School students typically attend 5 days per week. The average school day consists of 8 hours and 30 minutes.

Upper School Student Profile 35% of students are boarding students. 83% are state residents. 2 states are represented in upper school student body. 23% are international students. International students from Brazil, China, India, Japan, Republic of Korea, and Viet Nam.

Faculty School total: 35. In upper school: 6 men, 5 women; 5 have advanced degrees; 2 reside on campus.

Subjects Offered Algebra, American history, American literature, anatomy, art, art history, biology, calculus, ceramics, chemistry, communications, community service, comparative religion, computer science, drama, earth science, economics, English, English literature, ethics, film and new technologies, fine arts, gardening, geography, geometry, global studies, history, horticulture, human development, inquiry into relationship, mathematics, music, permaculture, photography, physical education, physics, relationships, religion and culture, science, social studies, Spanish, studio art, theater, world cultures, world history, world literature.

Graduation Requirements Algebra, American history, arts and fine arts (art, music, dance, drama), backpacking, biology, chemistry, college admission preparation, comparative religion, economics and history, English, ethics and responsibility, foreign language, geometry, mathematics, science, social studies (includes history), Spanish, world religions, participation in camping and travel programs and sports, one year of visual and performing arts. Community service is required.

Special Academic Programs 3 Advanced Placement exams for which test preparation is offered; honors section; ESL (4 students enrolled).

College Admission Counseling 12 students graduated in 2012; 11 went to college, including California Institute of the Arts; New York University; Pace University; The Colorado College; University of California, Berkeley. Other: 1 had other specific plans. Mean SAT critical reading: 627, mean SAT math: 580, mean SAT writing: 617. 57% scored over 600 on SAT critical reading, 28% scored over 600 on SAT math, 42% scored over 600 on SAT writing.

Student Life Upper grades have student council, honor system. Discipline rests equally with students and faculty.

Summer Programs ESL programs offered; held on campus; accepts boys and girls; open to students from other schools. 15 students usually enrolled. 2013 schedule: July to August. Application deadline: June.

Tuition and Aid Day student tuition: $16,000; 7-day tuition and room/board: $36,200. Tuition installment plan (FACTS Tuition Payment Plan, annual and semi-annual payment plans). Need-based scholarship grants, African-American scholarships available. In 2012–13, 40% of upper-school students received aid. Total amount of financial aid awarded in 2012–13: $60,000.

Admissions Traditional secondary-level entrance grade is 9. For fall 2012, 31 students applied for upper-level admission, 22 were accepted, 8 enrolled. SSAT or TOEFL or SLEP required. Deadline for receipt of application materials: none. Application fee required: $50. Interview required.

Athletics Interscholastic: soccer (boys, girls), volleyball (b,g); intramural: equestrian sports (g), soccer (b,g), volleyball (b,g); coed intramural: backpacking, fitness, hiking/backpacking, outdoor activities, outdoor education, outdoor skills, physical fitness, ropes courses, skiing (downhill), table tennis, tennis, wilderness. 1 PE instructor, 3 coaches.

Computers Computers are regularly used in art, ESL, graphic arts, history, independent study, library, mathematics, multimedia, photography, SAT preparation, science, technology, typing, writing, yearbook classes. Computer network features include on-campus library services, online commercial services, Internet access, wireless campus network, Internet filtering or blocking technology. Computer access in designated common areas is available to students.

Contact Joy Maguire-Parsons, Director of Admissions. 805-646-8236 Ext. 109. Fax: 805-646-6509. E-mail: enroll@oakgroveschool.com. Web site: www.oakgroveschool.com

OAK HILL ACADEMY

2635 Oak Hill Road
Mouth of Wilson, Virginia 24363

Head of School: Dr. Michael D. Groves

General Information Coeducational boarding and day college-preparatory, general academic, dual-credit courses, and honors classes school, affiliated with Baptist Church. Grades 8–12. Founded: 1878. Setting: rural. Nearest major city is Charlotte, NC. Students are housed in single-sex dormitories. 300-acre campus. 22 buildings on campus. Approved or accredited by Southern Association of Colleges and Schools, Southern Association of Independent Schools, The Association of Boarding Schools, and Virginia Department of Education. Member of Secondary School Admission Test Board. Endowment: $1.9 million. Total enrollment: 122. Upper school average class size: 10. Upper school faculty-student ratio: 1:10. There are 180 required school days per year for Upper School students. Upper School students typically attend 6 days per week. The average school day consists of 7 hours.

Upper School Student Profile Grade 8: 3 students (2 boys, 1 girl); Grade 9: 16 students (9 boys, 7 girls); Grade 10: 19 students (13 boys, 6 girls); Grade 11: 38 students (23 boys, 15 girls); Grade 12: 46 students (25 boys, 21 girls). 98% of students are boarding students. 17% are state residents. 24 states are represented in upper school student body. 22% are international students. International students from Bahamas,

Canada, China, France, Republic of Korea, and Senegal; 7 other countries represented in student body. 18% of students are Baptist.

Faculty School total: 20. In upper school: 8 men, 10 women; 14 have advanced degrees; 11 reside on campus.

Subjects Offered Advanced math, algebra, anatomy and physiology, art, art history, Bible as literature, biology, business, business mathematics, calculus, chemistry, choir, computer programming, creative writing, desktop publishing, digital photography, earth science, English, environmental science, equine science, fine arts, geometry, health, honors algebra, honors English, honors geometry, honors U.S. history, honors world history, instrumental music, intro to computers, keyboarding, mathematics, Microsoft, modern world history, physical education, physics, psychology, reading/study skills, religion, science, social sciences, social studies, Spanish, study skills, trigonometry, U.S. government, U.S. history, world geography, world history, world religions, world studies, yearbook.

Graduation Requirements Arts and fine arts (art, music, dance, drama), computer science, English, foreign language, mathematics, physical education (includes health), religion (includes Bible studies and theology), science, social sciences, social studies (includes history).

Special Academic Programs Honors section; study at local college for college credit; remedial reading and/or remedial writing; special instructional classes for students with Attention Deficit Disorder; ESL (18 students enrolled).

College Admission Counseling 50 students graduated in 2011; 46 went to college, including George Mason University; Indiana University Bloomington; The University of Arizona; The University of Iowa; University of Illinois at Urbana–Champaign; University of Kentucky. Other: 1 entered military service, 3 had other specific plans. Median SAT critical reading: 480, median SAT math: 470. 10% scored over 600 on SAT critical reading, 5% scored over 600 on SAT math, 5% scored over 26 on composite ACT.

Student Life Upper grades have uniform requirement, student council, honor system. Discipline rests primarily with faculty. Attendance at religious services is required.

Tuition and Aid Day student tuition: $9000; 7-day tuition and room/board: $28,700. Tuition installment plan (monthly payment plans, individually arranged payment plans, 12-month interest-free payment plan for those students accepted by June 1). Tuition reduction for siblings, need-based scholarship grants available. In 2011–12, 30% of upper-school students received aid. Total amount of financial aid awarded in 2011–12: $370,000.

Admissions Traditional secondary-level entrance grade is 11. For fall 2011, 69 students applied for upper-level admission, 54 were accepted, 41 enrolled. TOEFL or SLEP required. Deadline for receipt of application materials: none. Application fee required: $50. On-campus interview recommended.

Athletics Interscholastic: baseball (boys), basketball (b,g), cheering (g), tennis (b,g), volleyball (g); intramural: baseball (b), basketball (b,g), billiards (b,g), bowling (b,g), canoeing/kayaking (b,g), equestrian sports (b,g), fishing (b), golf (b,g), hiking/backpacking (b,g), horseback riding (b,g), jogging (b,g), Nautilus (b,g), outdoor recreation (b,g), running (b,g), softball (g), strength & conditioning (b,g), table tennis (b,g), tennis (b,g), walking (g), weight lifting (b,g); coed interscholastic: cross-country running, soccer, track and field; coed intramural: aquatics, fitness walking, flag football, paint ball, skiing (downhill), snowboarding, soccer, swimming and diving, ultimate Frisbee, volleyball, yoga. 1 PE instructor, 1 coach, 1 athletic trainer.

Computers Computers are regularly used in all academic, business education, creative writing, desktop publishing, English, ESL, mathematics, science, yearbook classes. Computer resources include on-campus library services, Internet access, wireless campus network, Internet filtering or blocking technology. Student e-mail accounts are available to students. Students grades are available online. The school has a published electronic and media policy.

Contact Mr. Michael Rodgers, Director of Admissions. 276-579-2619. Fax: 276-579-4722. E-mail: mrodgers@oak-hill.net. Web site: www.oak-hill.net

OAK HILL SCHOOL

86397 Eldon Schafer Drive
Eugene, Oregon 97405-9647

Head of School: Bob Sarkisian

General Information Coeducational day college-preparatory, arts, and technology school. Grades K–12. Founded: 1994. Setting: small town. 72-acre campus. 2 buildings on campus. Approved or accredited by Northwest Accreditation Commission, Pacific Northwest Association of Independent Schools, and Oregon Department of Education. Member of National Association of Independent Schools. Total enrollment: 151. Upper school average class size: 10. Upper school faculty-student ratio: 1:10. There are 175 required school days per year for Upper School students. Upper School students typically attend 5 days per week. The average school day consists of 7 hours.

Faculty School total: 26. In upper school: 5 men, 9 women; 9 have advanced degrees.

Subjects Offered Acting, advanced math, algebra, American literature, analytic geometry, anatomy, art, arts, band, calculus-AP, ceramics, chemistry, comparative government and politics, composition, computer education, drama performance, drawing and design, economics, English composition, English literature, English literature-AP, fitness, French, geometry, health education, history, independent study, Latin, outdoor education, physical education, pre-calculus, probability and statistics, Spanish, Spanish language-AP, Spanish literature-AP, speech communications, theater arts, U.S. government and politics, U.S. history, world history, writing.

Graduation Requirements American government, American history, arts, computer skills, economics, English, English composition, foreign language, French, lab science, mathematics, physical education (includes health), science, Spanish, world history, 70 community service hours.

Special Academic Programs Advanced Placement exam preparation; honors section; academic accommodation for the gifted.

College Admission Counseling 6 students graduated in 2011; all went to college, including Savannah College of Art and Design; Southern Oregon University; University of California, San Diego; University of Oregon; Willamette University. Median SAT critical reading: 560, median SAT math: 610. 27% scored over 600 on SAT critical reading, 27% scored over 600 on SAT math.

Student Life Upper grades have specified standards of dress, student council, honor system. Discipline rests equally with students and faculty.

Tuition and Aid Day student tuition: $15,000. Tuition installment plan (monthly payment plans). Merit scholarship grants, need-based scholarship grants available. In 2011–12, 50% of upper-school students received aid.

Admissions Traditional secondary-level entrance grade is 9. Comprehensive educational evaluation required. Deadline for receipt of application materials: February 15. Application fee required: $100. Interview required.

Athletics Interscholastic: basketball (boys); intramural: basketball (g), volleyball (g); coed interscholastic: cross-country running, indoor track & field, running, track and field; coed intramural: golf, outdoor education, physical training, strength & conditioning. 1 PE instructor, 1 coach.

Computers Computers are regularly used in desktop publishing, graphic arts, graphic design, information technology, introduction to technology, multimedia, publications, technology, Web site design, writing classes. Computer network features include Internet access, wireless campus network, Internet filtering or blocking technology, online homework calendars for each upper school class. Campus intranet, student e-mail accounts, and computer access in designated common areas are available to students. The school has a published electronic and media policy.

Contact Lauren Moody, Admissions Director. 541-744-0954. Fax: 541-741-6968. E-mail: admission@oakhillschool.com. Web site: oakhillschool.net

THE OAKLAND SCHOOL

362 McKee Place
Pittsburgh, Pennsylvania 15213

Head of School: Mr. Jack C. King

General Information Coeducational day college-preparatory and arts school. Grades 8–12. Founded: 1982. Setting: urban. 1 building on campus. Approved or accredited by Pennsylvania Department of Education. Candidate for accreditation by Middle States Association of Colleges and Schools. Total enrollment: 40. Upper school average class size: 6. Upper school faculty-student ratio: 1:6. There are 180 required school days per year for Upper School students. Upper School students typically attend 5 days per week. The average school day consists of 5 hours and 30 minutes.

Upper School Student Profile Grade 8: 2 students (1 boy, 1 girl); Grade 9: 7 students (3 boys, 4 girls); Grade 10: 10 students (5 boys, 5 girls); Grade 11: 10 students (5 boys, 5 girls); Grade 12: 11 students (6 boys, 5 girls).

Faculty School total: 10. In upper school: 3 men, 7 women; 5 have advanced degrees.

Subjects Offered Advanced math, algebra, American history, American literature, art, art history, biology, business skills, calculus, chemistry, computer math, computer science, creative writing, drama, earth science, ecology, economics, English, English literature, environmental science, ESL, expository writing, fine arts, French, geography, geometry, German, government/civics, history, mathematics, physical education, physics, pre-calculus, psychology, SAT/ACT preparation, science, social studies, Spanish, speech, trigonometry, world history, world literature, writing.

Graduation Requirements Arts and fine arts (art, music, dance, drama), computer literacy, English, mathematics, physical education (includes health), science, social studies (includes history), community service.

Special Academic Programs Honors section; accelerated programs; independent study; study at local college for college credit; academic accommodation for the gifted and the artistically talented; remedial reading and/or remedial writing; remedial math; ESL (2 students enrolled).

College Admission Counseling 11 students graduated in 2012; 10 went to college, including Drexel University; Ohio University; Penn State University Park; Rochester Institute of Technology; University of Pittsburgh. Other: 1 had other specific plans. Mean SAT critical reading: 530, mean SAT math: 512, mean SAT writing: 550.

Student Life Upper grades have student council. Discipline rests primarily with faculty.

Tuition and Aid Day student tuition: $9700. Tuition installment plan (monthly payment plans, individually arranged payment plans, quarterly payment plan, semi-annual payment plan). Tuition reduction for siblings, merit scholarship grants, need-based scholarship grants available. In 2012–13, 25% of upper-school students received aid. Total amount of financial aid awarded in 2012–13: $30,000.

Admissions Traditional secondary-level entrance grade is 10. For fall 2012, 26 students applied for upper-level admission, 20 were accepted, 14 enrolled. WRAT

required. Deadline for receipt of application materials: none. Application fee required: $100. On-campus interview required.
Athletics Intramural: aerobics/dance (girls), dance (g); coed intramural: baseball, basketball, bicycling, billiards, bowling, cooperative games, cross-country running, fitness, fitness walking, flag football, Frisbee, golf, hiking/backpacking, ice skating, jogging, jump rope, kickball, martial arts, racquetball, running, skateboarding, skiing (cross-country), skiing (downhill), snowboarding, softball, swimming and diving, tai chi, tennis, volleyball, walking. 1 PE instructor.
Computers Computers are regularly used in all academic classes. Computer network features include Internet access, wireless campus network. Student e-mail accounts and computer access in designated common areas are available to students. Students grades are available online.
Contact Admissions Desk. 412-621-7878. Fax: 412-621-7881. E-mail: oschool@stargate.net. Web site: www.theoaklandschool.org

OAKLAND SCHOOL

Keswick, Virginia
See Special Needs Schools section.

OAK RIDGE MILITARY ACADEMY

2317 Oak Ridge Road
PO Box 498
Oak Ridge, North Carolina 27310

Head of School: Mr. David Johnson

General Information Coeducational boarding and day college-preparatory, leadership, and military school. Grades 7–12. Founded: 1852. Setting: small town. Nearest major city is Greensboro. Students are housed in single-sex dormitories. 101-acre campus. 22 buildings on campus. Approved or accredited by Southern Association of Colleges and Schools, Southern Association of Independent Schools, and North Carolina Department of Education. Member of National Association of Independent Schools. Total enrollment: 65. Upper school average class size: 8. Upper school faculty-student ratio: 1:11. Upper School students typically attend 5 days per week. The average school day consists of 7 hours.
Upper School Student Profile 84% of students are boarding students. 49% are state residents. 16 states are represented in upper school student body. 14% are international students. International students from Bermuda, China, Honduras, Mexico, Philippines, and Republic of Korea; 4 other countries represented in student body.
Faculty School total: 25. In upper school: 12 men, 13 women; 8 have advanced degrees; 9 reside on campus.
Subjects Offered Algebra, American history, American literature, biology, calculus, chemistry, college writing, computer math, computer science, creative writing, driver education, earth science, English, English literature, environmental science, ESL, French, geometry, German, government/civics, grammar, health, JROTC, JROTC or LEAD (Leadership Education and Development), mathematics, military science, music, physical education, physics, SAT preparation, science, social studies, Spanish, trigonometry, world history, writing.
Graduation Requirements Computer science, English, foreign language, mathematics, physical education (includes health), ROTC, SAT preparation, science, social studies (includes history), writing, complete three college applications, 20 hours of community service.
Special Academic Programs Honors section; accelerated programs; study at local college for college credit; academic accommodation for the gifted; special instructional classes for students with Attention Deficit Disorder and Attention Deficit Hyperactivity Disorder; ESL (6 students enrolled).
College Admission Counseling 28 students graduated in 2011; 27 went to college, including Appalachian State University; East Carolina University; North Carolina State University; The Citadel, The Military College of South Carolina; The University of North Carolina at Chapel Hill; The University of North Carolina at Charlotte. Other: 1 entered military service.
Student Life Upper grades have uniform requirement, student council, honor system. Discipline rests equally with students and faculty. Attendance at religious services is required.
Tuition and Aid Day student tuition: $12,815; 5-day tuition and room/board: $22,195; 7-day tuition and room/board: $25,095. Tuition installment plan (Key Tuition Payment Plan, SMART Tuition Payment Plan, monthly payment plans). Tuition reduction for siblings, merit scholarship grants, USS Education Loan Program available. In 2011–12, 24% of upper-school students received aid.
Admissions Traditional secondary-level entrance grade is 10. Deadline for receipt of application materials: none. Application fee required: $200. Interview recommended.
Athletics Interscholastic: baseball (boys), basketball (b,g), football (b), golf (b), soccer (b,g), swimming and diving (b,g), tennis (b), track and field (b,g), volleyball (g), wrestling (b); intramural: basketball (b,g), flag football (b), outdoor adventure (b,g), paint ball (b,g), rappelling (b,g), scuba diving (b,g), skydiving (b,g), strength & conditioning (b,g), weight lifting (b,g); coed interscholastic: cross-country running, drill team, JROTC drill, marksmanship, riflery, swimming and diving, track and field; coed intramural: outdoor adventure, paint ball, pistol, rappelling, scuba diving, skydiving, softball, strength & conditioning, weight lifting. 1 PE instructor, 10 coaches, 1 athletic trainer.
Computers Computers are regularly used in English, mathematics, science classes. Computer resources include on-campus library services, Internet access.
Contact Mr. Bob Lipke, Director of Admissions. 336-643-4131 Ext. 196. Fax: 336-643-1797. E-mail: blipke@ormila.com. Web site: www.oakridgemilitary.com

THE OAKRIDGE SCHOOL

5900 West Pioneer Parkway
Arlington, Texas 76013-2899

Head of School: Mr. Jonathan Kellam

General Information Coeducational day college-preparatory, arts, and technology school. Grades PS–12. Founded: 1979. Setting: suburban. 90-acre campus. 12 buildings on campus. Approved or accredited by Independent Schools Association of the Southwest and Texas Department of Education. Member of National Association of Independent Schools. Endowment: $672,406. Total enrollment: 858. Upper school average class size: 16. Upper school faculty-student ratio: 1:11. There are 171 required school days per year for Upper School students. Upper School students typically attend 5 days per week. The average school day consists of 7 hours.
Upper School Student Profile Grade 9: 82 students (41 boys, 41 girls); Grade 10: 75 students (38 boys, 37 girls); Grade 11: 83 students (36 boys, 47 girls); Grade 12: 74 students (42 boys, 32 girls).
Faculty School total: 82. In upper school: 12 men, 14 women; 26 have advanced degrees.
Subjects Offered 3-dimensional art, acting, Advanced Placement courses, advanced studio art-AP, algebra, American history, American history-AP, American literature, anatomy, ancient world history, anthropology, archaeology, art, art history-AP, athletics, biology, British literature, calculus, calculus-AP, chemistry, chemistry-AP, Chinese, choir, choral music, college admission preparation, college counseling, college writing, community service, comparative religion, composition-AP, computer art, computer graphics, computer literacy, computer multimedia, computer science-AP, concert choir, creative writing, current events, desktop publishing, digital applications, digital art, digital imaging, digital photography, discrete mathematics, drama, drama performance, drama workshop, dramatic arts, drawing, drawing and design, economics, economics and history, English, English language and composition-AP, English literature and composition-AP, environmental science-AP, European civilization, European history-AP, expository writing, film and literature, fine arts, fractal geometry, French, French language-AP, French-AP, geometry, golf, government, government and politics-AP, government-AP, government/civics, graphic arts, graphic design, graphics, honors algebra, honors English, honors geometry, honors world history, human biology, independent study, language and composition, language arts, literature and composition-AP, modern European history-AP, modern world history, music theory, music theory-AP, musical productions, physics, physics-AP, play production, poetry, portfolio art, portfolio writing, pre-algebra, pre-calculus, probability and statistics, programming, public service, public speaking, reading/study skills, SAT preparation, SAT/ACT preparation, Spanish, Spanish-AP, strings, theater, track and field, U.S. government, U.S. government and politics, U.S. government and politics-AP, U.S. history, U.S. history-AP, United States government-AP, video, video communication, video film production, visual and performing arts, voice, voice ensemble, Web site design, weightlifting, world history.
Graduation Requirements Arts and fine arts (art, music, dance, drama), English, foreign language, mathematics, physical education (includes health), science, social studies (includes history), participation in six seasons of athletics, 60 hours of community service. Community service is required.
Special Academic Programs 21 Advanced Placement exams for which test preparation is offered; honors section; independent study; study at local college for college credit; study abroad; academic accommodation for the gifted, the musically talented, and the artistically talented.
College Admission Counseling 78 students graduated in 2012; all went to college, including Austin College; Oklahoma State University; Texas A&M University; Texas Christian University; The University of Texas at Austin; University of Arkansas. Mean SAT critical reading: 600, mean SAT math: 619, mean SAT writing: 595, mean combined SAT: 1814, mean composite ACT: 27.
Student Life Upper grades have uniform requirement, student council, honor system. Discipline rests primarily with faculty.
Summer Programs Remediation, enrichment, advancement, sports, art/fine arts, rigorous outdoor training, computer instruction programs offered; session focuses on enrichment; held both on and off campus; held at museums and recreational facilities; accepts boys and girls; open to students from other schools. 317 students usually enrolled. 2013 schedule: June 10 to July 19. Application deadline: none.
Tuition and Aid Day student tuition: $18,300. Tuition installment plan (FACTS Tuition Payment Plan, early discount option). Need-based scholarship grants available. In 2012–13, 22% of upper-school students received aid. Total amount of financial aid awarded in 2012–13: $523,375.
Admissions Traditional secondary-level entrance grade is 9. For fall 2012, 49 students applied for upper-level admission, 38 were accepted, 31 enrolled. ERB Reading and Math, ISEE or Otis-Lennon School Ability Test required. Deadline for receipt of application materials: March 1. Application fee required: $75. Interview required.

Athletics Interscholastic: baseball (boys), basketball (b,g), cheering (g), cross-country running (b,g), field hockey (g), football (b), golf (b,g), physical fitness (b,g), physical training (b,g), power lifting (b), soccer (b,g), softball (g), strength & conditioning (b,g), swimming and diving (b,g), tennis (b,g), track and field (b,g), volleyball (g), weight lifting (b), wrestling (b); intramural: fitness (b,g), physical fitness (b,g), physical training (b,g), strength & conditioning (b,g), weight lifting (b), weight training (b); coed intramural: outdoor activities, outdoor education. 7 PE instructors, 10 coaches, 2 athletic trainers.

Computers Computers are regularly used in art, English, foreign language, history, mathematics, programming, science, stock market, technology, video film production, Web site design, writing, yearbook classes. Computer network features include on-campus library services, online commercial services, Internet access, wireless campus network, Internet filtering or blocking technology. Campus intranet, student e-mail accounts, and computer access in designated common areas are available to students. Students grades are available online. The school has a published electronic and media policy.

Contact Dr. Jerry A. Davis Jr., Director of Admissions. 817-451-4994 Ext. 2708. Fax: 817-457-6681. E-mail: jadavis@theoakridgeschool.org. Web site: www.theoakridgeschool.org

OAKWOOD FRIENDS SCHOOL

22 Spackenkill Road
Poughkeepsie, New York 12603

Head of School: Peter F. Baily

General Information Coeducational boarding and day college-preparatory and arts school, affiliated with Society of Friends. Boarding grades 9–12, day grades 6–12. Founded: 1796. Setting: suburban. Nearest major city is New York. Students are housed in single-sex dormitories. 63-acre campus. 22 buildings on campus. Approved or accredited by Friends Council on Education, New York State Association of Independent Schools, New York State Board of Regents, The Association of Boarding Schools, and New York Department of Education. Member of National Association of Independent Schools and Secondary School Admission Test Board. Endowment: $3 million. Total enrollment: 125. Upper school average class size: 11. Upper school faculty-student ratio: 1:4. There are 167 required school days per year for Upper School students. Upper School students typically attend 5 days per week. The average school day consists of 5 hours.

Upper School Student Profile Grade 9: 23 students (15 boys, 8 girls); Grade 10: 24 students (9 boys, 15 girls); Grade 11: 32 students (17 boys, 15 girls); Grade 12: 26 students (17 boys, 9 girls). 50% of students are boarding students. 74% are state residents. 8 states are represented in upper school student body. 33% are international students. International students from Canada, China, Ghana, Republic of Korea, Rwanda, and Spain; 2 other countries represented in student body. 1% of students are members of Society of Friends.

Faculty School total: 33. In upper school: 15 men, 14 women; 23 have advanced degrees; 24 reside on campus.

Subjects Offered Acting, algebra, American history, American literature, American sign language, anthropology, art, art history, biology, calculus, ceramics, chemistry, community service, computer applications, conceptual physics, critical thinking, directing, drama, drawing, ecology, English, English literature, ensembles, environmental science, ESL, European history, existentialism, expository writing, fashion, fine arts, French, geometry, health, history, interdisciplinary studies, introduction to theater, mathematics, media arts, music, music theater, painting, photography, physical education, physics, playwriting and directing, pre-calculus, psychology, public speaking, Quakerism and ethics, robotics, science, sculpture, social studies, Spanish, statistics-AP, theater, world history, writing.

Graduation Requirements Advanced math, algebra, American history, arts and fine arts (art, music, dance, drama), biology, chemistry, computer literacy, conceptual physics, English, foreign language, geometry, health, interdisciplinary studies, physical education (includes health), Quakerism and ethics, U.S. history, world history, senior orientation trip in September, senior evaluation trip in June, community service. Community service is required.

Special Academic Programs 8 Advanced Placement exams for which test preparation is offered; independent study; special instructional classes for students with mild learning differences; ESL (44 students enrolled).

College Admission Counseling 35 students graduated in 2012; all went to college, including American University; Goucher College; Hobart and William Smith Colleges; Rensselaer Polytechnic Institute; Skidmore College; The George Washington University. Median SAT critical reading: 530, median SAT math: 500, median SAT writing: 530. 15% scored over 600 on SAT critical reading, 38% scored over 600 on SAT math, 27% scored over 600 on SAT writing.

Student Life Upper grades have specified standards of dress, student council, honor system. Discipline rests equally with students and faculty. Attendance at religious services is required.

Tuition and Aid Day student tuition: $24,220; 5-day tuition and room/board: $36,598; 7-day tuition and room/board: $41,980. Tuition installment plan (FACTS Tuition Payment Plan, monthly payment plans). Tuition reduction for siblings, need-based scholarship grants available. In 2012–13, 39% of upper-school students received aid. Total amount of financial aid awarded in 2012–13: $808,000.

Admissions Traditional secondary-level entrance grade is 9. For fall 2012, 110 students applied for upper-level admission, 75 were accepted, 40 enrolled. TOEFL or writing sample required. Deadline for receipt of application materials: none. Application fee required: $40. Interview required.

Athletics Interscholastic: baseball (boys), basketball (b,g), cross-country running (b,g), Frisbee (b,g), independent competitive sports (b,g), running (b,g), soccer (b,g), softball (g), tennis (b,g), volleyball (g); coed interscholastic: swimming and diving, ultimate Frisbee; coed intramural: badminton, basketball, bowling, cooperative games, cross-country running, dance team, fitness, fitness walking, indoor soccer, jogging, kickball, martial arts, outdoor activities, physical training, ropes courses, running, strength & conditioning, table tennis, tai chi, ultimate Frisbee, volleyball, walking, weight lifting, whiffle ball, yoga.

Computers Computers are regularly used in computer applications, English, foreign language, history, science, writing classes. Computer network features include on-campus library services, online commercial services, Internet access, wireless campus network, Internet filtering or blocking technology. Computer access in designated common areas is available to students. Students grades are available online. The school has a published electronic and media policy.

Contact Barbara Lonczak, Director of Admissions. 845-462-4200 Ext. 215. Fax: 845-462-4251. E-mail: blonczak@oakwoodfriends.org. Web site: www.oakwoodfriends.org

OJAI VALLEY SCHOOL

723 El Paseo Road
Ojai, California 93023

Head of School: Mr. Michael J. Hall-Mounsey

General Information Coeducational boarding and day college-preparatory, arts, and technology school; primarily serves students with learning disabilities, individuals with Attention Deficit Disorder, and dyslexic students. Boarding grades 3–12, day grades PK–12. Founded: 1911. Setting: rural. Nearest major city is Los Angeles. Students are housed in single-sex dormitories. 200-acre campus. 13 buildings on campus. Approved or accredited by California Association of Independent Schools, The Association of Boarding Schools, Western Association of Schools and Colleges, and California Department of Education. Member of National Association of Independent Schools and Secondary School Admission Test Board. Endowment: $1 million. Total enrollment: 288. Upper school average class size: 12. Upper school faculty-student ratio: 1:6.

Upper School Student Profile Grade 9: 24 students (15 boys, 9 girls); Grade 10: 31 students (12 boys, 19 girls); Grade 11: 24 students (14 boys, 10 girls); Grade 12: 30 students (19 boys, 11 girls). 72% of students are boarding students. 46% are state residents. 7 states are represented in upper school student body. 44% are international students. International students from China, Japan, Mexico, Republic of Korea, Taiwan, and Thailand; 3 other countries represented in student body.

Faculty School total: 54. In upper school: 11 men, 12 women; 10 have advanced degrees; 10 reside on campus.

Subjects Offered 20th century history, algebra, American history, American literature, art, art history, biology, biology-AP, calculus-AP, chemistry, chemistry-AP, community service, computer science, conceptual physics, creative writing, drama, ecology, economics, English, English literature, English-AP, environmental science, equestrian sports, ESL, fine arts, geography, geometry, government/civics, grammar, history, honors English, humanities, independent study, mathematics, music, music theory-AP, photography, physical education, physics, psychology, science, social studies, Spanish, Spanish-AP, speech, statistics, studio art, studio art-AP, theater, trigonometry, wilderness education, world history, writing.

Graduation Requirements Arts and fine arts (art, music, dance, drama), economics, English, foreign language, government, mathematics, science, social studies (includes history).

Special Academic Programs 11 Advanced Placement exams for which test preparation is offered; honors section; accelerated programs; independent study; study abroad; academic accommodation for the gifted and the artistically talented; remedial reading and/or remedial writing; remedial math; ESL (12 students enrolled).

College Admission Counseling 23 students graduated in 2012; all went to college, including Boston University; New York University; The Johns Hopkins University; University of California, Riverside; University of California, Santa Barbara. Median SAT critical reading: 540, median SAT math: 625, median SAT writing: 585, median combined SAT: 1750. 25% scored over 600 on SAT math.

Student Life Upper grades have specified standards of dress, student council, honor system. Discipline rests equally with students and faculty.

Summer Programs Remediation, enrichment, advancement, ESL, art/fine arts, computer instruction programs offered; session focuses on academic and course credit; held on campus; accepts boys and girls; open to students from other schools. 300 students usually enrolled. 2013 schedule: June 24 to August 2. Application deadline: none.

Tuition and Aid Day student tuition: $19,500; 7-day tuition and room/board: $47,950. Tuition installment plan (individually arranged payment plans). Need-based scholarship grants, need-based loans available. In 2012–13, 15% of upper-school students received aid. Total amount of financial aid awarded in 2012–13: $347,360.

Admissions Traditional secondary-level entrance grade is 9. For fall 2012, 150 students applied for upper-level admission, 65 were accepted, 32 enrolled. Any standardized test, SSAT or TOEFL required. Deadline for receipt of application materials: none. Application fee required: $50. Interview required.

Athletics Interscholastic: baseball (boys), basketball (b,g), cross-country running (b,g), dressage (b,g), football (b), lacrosse (b,g), soccer (b,g), volleyball (b,g); coed interscholastic: equestrian sports, golf, track and field; coed intramural: backpacking, basketball, bicycling, climbing, cross-country running, equestrian sports, fencing, fitness, fitness walking, golf, hiking/backpacking, horseback riding, kayaking, martial arts, mountain biking, outdoor education, physical fitness, rappelling, rock climbing, ropes courses, surfing, swimming and diving, weight training, yoga. 2 PE instructors, 2 coaches, 2 athletic trainers.

Computers Computers are regularly used in economics, English, ESL, geography, history, humanities, journalism, mathematics, music, photography, SAT preparation, science, social sciences, yearbook classes. Computer resources include on-campus library services, online commercial services, Internet access, wireless campus network, Internet filtering or blocking technology. The school has a published electronic and media policy.

Contact Ms. Tracy Wilson, Director of Admission. 805-646-1423. Fax: 805-646-0362. E-mail: admission@ovs.org. Web site: www.ovs.org

OLDENBURG ACADEMY

1 Twister Circle
Oldenburg, Indiana 47036

Head of School: Sr. Therese Gillman, OSF

General Information Coeducational day college-preparatory, arts, and religious studies school, affiliated with Roman Catholic Church. Grades 9–12. Founded: 1852. Setting: small town. Nearest major city is Cincinnati, OH. 23-acre campus. 3 buildings on campus. Approved or accredited by North Central Association of Colleges and Schools and Indiana Department of Education. Total enrollment: 202. Upper school average class size: 15. Upper school faculty-student ratio: 1:12. There are 180 required school days per year for Upper School students. The average school day consists of 7 hours.

Upper School Student Profile Grade 9: 48 students (20 boys, 28 girls); Grade 10: 53 students (21 boys, 32 girls); Grade 11: 32 students (10 boys, 22 girls); Grade 12: 69 students (32 boys, 37 girls). 80% of students are Roman Catholic.

Faculty School total: 17. In upper school: 7 men, 10 women; 11 have advanced degrees.

Graduation Requirements 40 hours of community service.

Special Academic Programs Advanced Placement exam preparation; honors section.

College Admission Counseling Colleges students went to include Butler University; Indiana University Bloomington; Purdue University.

Student Life Upper grades have uniform requirement, student council, honor system. Discipline rests primarily with faculty. Attendance at religious services is required.

Tuition and Aid Day student tuition: $7200. Tuition installment plan (FACTS Tuition Payment Plan). Tuition reduction for siblings, merit scholarship grants, need-based scholarship grants available. In 2012–13, 35% of upper-school students received aid. Total amount of financial aid awarded in 2012–13: $65,000.

Admissions Traditional secondary-level entrance grade is 9. High School Placement Test (closed version) from Scholastic Testing Service required. Deadline for receipt of application materials: none. Application fee required: $350. Interview recommended.

Athletics Interscholastic: baseball (boys), basketball (b,g), cheering (g), cross-country running (b,g), dance (b,g), dance team (g), physical fitness (b,g), soccer (b,g), softball (g), swimming and diving (b,g), tennis (b,g), track and field (b,g), volleyball (g), wrestling (b). 1 PE instructor, 9 coaches, 1 athletic trainer.

Computers Computers are regularly used in all academic classes. Computer network features include on-campus library services, Internet access, wireless campus network, Internet filtering or blocking technology, one to one student iPad program. Campus intranet, student e-mail accounts, and computer access in designated common areas are available to students. Students grades are available online. The school has a published electronic and media policy.

Contact Mrs. Bettina Rose, Principal. 812-934-4440 Ext. 223. Fax: 812-934-4838. E-mail: brose@oldenburgacademy.org. Web site:

THE OLIVERIAN SCHOOL

Haverhill, New Hampshire
See Special Needs Schools section.

THE O'NEAL SCHOOL

3300 Airport Road
PO Box 290
Southern Pines, North Carolina 28388-0290

Head of School: Mr. Alan Barr

General Information Coeducational day college-preparatory school. Grades PK–12. Founded: 1971. Setting: small town. Nearest major city is Raleigh. 40-acre campus. 3 buildings on campus. Approved or accredited by North Carolina Association of Independent Schools, Southern Association of Colleges and Schools, Southern Association of Independent Schools, and North Carolina Department of Education. Member of National Association of Independent Schools. Endowment: $1.4 million. Total enrollment: 435. Upper school average class size: 15. Upper school faculty-student ratio: 1:12. There are 175 required school days per year for Upper School students. Upper School students typically attend 5 days per week. The average school day consists of 7 hours.

Upper School Student Profile Grade 9: 45 students (19 boys, 26 girls); Grade 10: 44 students (19 boys, 25 girls); Grade 11: 40 students (19 boys, 21 girls); Grade 12: 39 students (18 boys, 21 girls).

Faculty School total: 54. In upper school: 8 men, 8 women; 8 have advanced degrees.

Subjects Offered Algebra, American history, American literature, art, art history, art history-AP, biology, biology-AP, calculus-AP, chemistry, community service, computer science, creative writing, drama, economics, English, English language-AP, English literature, English literature-AP, environmental science, environmental science-AP, European history, European history-AP, expository writing, film, fine arts, French, geometry, government-AP, Latin, mathematics, music, philosophy, photography, physical education, physics-AP, political science, pottery, pre-calculus, science, social studies, Spanish, statistics-AP, U.S. history-AP, world history, world literature, yearbook.

Graduation Requirements Arts and fine arts (art, music, dance, drama), English, foreign language, mathematics, physical education (includes health), science, social studies (includes history), 36 hours of community service.

Special Academic Programs 13 Advanced Placement exams for which test preparation is offered; independent study; study at local college for college credit.

College Admission Counseling 34 students graduated in 2012; 33 went to college, including Appalachian State University; East Carolina University; North Carolina State University; The University of North Carolina at Chapel Hill; The University of North Carolina at Charlotte; The University of North Carolina Wilmington. Other: 1 entered military service. Median SAT critical reading: 540, median SAT math: 530, median SAT writing: 510, median combined SAT: 1580. 29% scored over 600 on SAT critical reading, 30% scored over 600 on SAT math, 19% scored over 600 on SAT writing, 19% scored over 1800 on combined SAT.

Student Life Upper grades have specified standards of dress, student council, honor system. Discipline rests primarily with faculty.

Tuition and Aid Day student tuition: $15,500. Tuition installment plan (Insured Tuition Payment Plan, monthly payment plans, individually arranged payment plans). Merit scholarship grants, need-based scholarship grants available. In 2012–13, 32% of upper-school students received aid; total upper-school merit-scholarship money awarded: $62,000. Total amount of financial aid awarded in 2012–13: $471,500.

Admissions Traditional secondary-level entrance grade is 9. For fall 2012, 33 students applied for upper-level admission, 29 were accepted, 23 enrolled. Admissions testing, essay, OLSAT, Stanford Achievement Test, PSAT and SAT for applicants to grade 11 and 12, WRAT or writing sample required. Deadline for receipt of application materials: none. Application fee required: $100. On-campus interview required.

Athletics Interscholastic: baseball (boys), basketball (b,g), cheering (g), cross-country running (b,g), soccer (b,g), swimming and diving (b,g), tennis (b,g), track and field (b,g), volleyball (g); coed interscholastic: golf. 2 PE instructors, 2 coaches.

Computers Computers are regularly used in all academic classes. Computer network features include on-campus library services, Internet access, wireless campus network, Internet filtering or blocking technology, EBSCO, World Book Online. Student e-mail accounts and computer access in designated common areas are available to students. The school has a published electronic and media policy.

Contact Mrs. Alice Droppers, Director of Admissions and Financial Aid. 910-692-6920 Ext. 103. Fax: 910-692-6930. E-mail: adroppers@onealschool.org. Web site: www.onealschool.org

ONEIDA BAPTIST INSTITUTE

11 Mulberry Street
Oneida, Kentucky 40972

Head of School: Dr. Paul Davidson

General Information Coeducational boarding and day college-preparatory, general academic, arts, vocational, religious studies, bilingual studies, and agriculture school, affiliated with Southern Baptist Convention. Grades 6–12. Founded: 1899. Setting: rural. Nearest major city is Lexington. Students are housed in single-sex dormitories. 200-acre campus. 15 buildings on campus. Approved or accredited by The Kentucky Non-Public School Commission, The National Non-Public School Commission, and Kentucky Department of Education. Endowment: $15 million. Total enrollment: 275. Upper school average class size: 11. Upper school faculty-student ratio: 1:11. There are 174 required school days per year for Upper School students. Upper School students typically attend 5 days per week. The average school day consists of 6 hours.

Upper School Student Profile Grade 9: 56 students (35 boys, 21 girls); Grade 10: 43 students (20 boys, 23 girls); Grade 11: 57 students (32 boys, 25 girls); Grade 12: 54 students (33 boys, 21 girls). 85% of students are boarding students. 30% are state residents. 22 states are represented in upper school student body. 35% are international students. International students from China, Ethiopia, Liberia, Nigeria, Republic of

Korea, and Thailand; 14 other countries represented in student body. 25% of students are Southern Baptist Convention.

Faculty School total: 42. In upper school: 16 men, 15 women; 10 have advanced degrees; all reside on campus.

Subjects Offered Agriculture, algebra, art, band, Bible, biology, biology-AP, calculus-AP, chemistry, child development, choir, commercial art, computers, cultural geography, drama, earth and space science, English, English-AP, ESL, geography, geometry, government, government-AP, guitar, health, language arts, life skills, literature, mathematics, physical education, physical science, piano, pre-calculus, social sciences, Spanish, stagecraft, U.S. history, U.S. history-AP, weight training, world history.

Graduation Requirements Arts and fine arts (art, music, dance, drama), Bible, computer literacy, English, foreign language, mathematics, physical education (includes health), science, social studies (includes history), field placement.

Special Academic Programs 6 Advanced Placement exams for which test preparation is offered; independent study; remedial reading and/or remedial writing; remedial math; ESL (37 students enrolled).

College Admission Counseling 48 students graduated in 2012; 45 went to college, including Berea College; California State University, Long Beach; Eastern Kentucky University; Lindsey Wilson College; University of Kentucky; University of the Cumberlands. Other: 2 went to work, 1 entered military service.

Student Life Upper grades have specified standards of dress. Discipline rests primarily with faculty. Attendance at religious services is required.

Summer Programs Remediation, enrichment, advancement programs offered; session focuses on remediation and make-up courses; held on campus; accepts boys and girls; open to students from other schools. 125 students usually enrolled. 2013 schedule: June 10 to July 20. Application deadline: none.

Tuition and Aid 7-day tuition and room/board: $5250–$11,000. Tuition installment plan (monthly payment plans). Need-based scholarship grants available. In 2012–13, 100% of upper-school students received aid.

Admissions Traditional secondary-level entrance grade is 9. Deadline for receipt of application materials: none. Application fee required: $35. On-campus interview required.

Athletics Interscholastic: baseball (boys), basketball (b,g), cheering (g), cross-country running (b,g), softball (g), swimming and diving (b,g), tennis (b,g), track and field (b,g), volleyball (g); coed interscholastic: soccer. 2 PE instructors.

Computers Computers are regularly used in commercial art classes. Computer resources include Internet access, Internet filtering or blocking technology. The school has a published electronic and media policy.

Contact Admissions. 606-847-4111 Ext. 233. Fax: 606-847-4496. E-mail: admissions@oneidaschool.org. Web site: www.oneidaschool.org

OREGON EPISCOPAL SCHOOL

6300 Southwest Nicol Road
Portland, Oregon 97223-7566

Head of School: Mrs. Mo Copeland

General Information Coeducational boarding and day college-preparatory, arts, religious studies, technology, and science school, affiliated with Episcopal Church. Boarding grades 9–12, day grades PK–12. Founded: 1869. Setting: suburban. Students are housed in single-sex dormitories. 59-acre campus. 9 buildings on campus. Approved or accredited by National Association of Episcopal Schools, Northwest Accreditation Commission, Pacific Northwest Association of Independent Schools, and Oregon Department of Education. Member of National Association of Independent Schools and Secondary School Admission Test Board. Endowment: $20.9 million. Total enrollment: 851. Upper school average class size: 15. Upper school faculty-student ratio: 1:7. There are 175 required school days per year for Upper School students. Upper School students typically attend 5 days per week. The average school day consists of 7 hours.

Upper School Student Profile Grade 9: 86 students (49 boys, 37 girls); Grade 10: 79 students (39 boys, 40 girls); Grade 11: 79 students (43 boys, 36 girls); Grade 12: 67 students (29 boys, 38 girls). 18% of students are boarding students. 81% are state residents. 4 states are represented in upper school student body. 15% are international students. International students from Canada, China, Hong Kong, Republic of Korea, Taiwan, and Thailand. 10% of students are members of Episcopal Church.

Faculty School total: 121. In upper school: 19 men, 28 women; 36 have advanced degrees; 12 reside on campus.

Subjects Offered Advanced chemistry, advanced math, Advanced Placement courses, algebra, American history, American literature, American studies, anatomy, anatomy and physiology, Arabic studies, art, Asian history, astronomy, athletic training, Basic programming, biology, Buddhism, calculus, calculus-AP, ceramics, chemistry, Chinese, chorus, Christian studies, Christianity, college counseling, college planning, college writing, community service, computer graphics, computer science, computer science-AP, constitutional law, creative writing, dance, debate, discrete mathematics, drama, drawing, driver education, East Asian history, ecology, electronics, engineering, English, English literature, environmental science, ESL, ESL, European history, fencing, film, film and literature, filmmaking, fine arts, finite math, foreign language, foreign policy, French, French language-AP, French-AP, freshman seminar, functions, gardening, geology, geometry, graphic arts, graphic design, graphics, health, health and wellness, history, history of China and Japan, history of ideas, history of rock and roll, history-AP, human anatomy, human relations, human sexuality, humanities, independent study, international affairs, international relations, jazz band, jazz dance, jazz ensemble, journalism, literature, marine biology, marine ecology, mathematics, mathematics-AP, microbiology, model United Nations, modern Chinese history, music, music history, music technology, musical productions, musical theater, newspaper, painting, personal finance, personal fitness, philosophy, photography, photojournalism, physical education, physical fitness, physics, playwriting and directing, poetry, pre-algebra, pre-calculus, psychology, psychology-AP, religion, religion and culture, research, science, science project, science research, service learning/internship, sex education, sexuality, Shakespeare, social studies, Spanish, Spanish language-AP, Spanish literature, Spanish-AP, speech, stagecraft, statistics, statistics-AP, tennis, theater, theater design and production, theology, track and field, trigonometry, U.S. history, U.S. history-AP, urban studies, video and animation, video film production, visual arts, vocal ensemble, vocal music, weight training, weightlifting, wellness, wilderness education, wilderness experience, world history, world literature, world religions, world religions, world wide web design, yearbook, yoga, zoology.

Graduation Requirements Arts and fine arts (art, music, dance, drama), electives, English, foreign language, health education, humanities, mathematics, philosophy, physical education (includes health), religion (includes Bible studies and theology), science, service learning/internship, U.S. history, Winterim, College Decisions (for juniors).

Special Academic Programs Advanced Placement exam preparation; honors section; independent study; term-away projects; study abroad; academic accommodation for the gifted; ESL (9 students enrolled).

College Admission Counseling 74 students graduated in 2012; all went to college, including Boston University; Santa Clara University; Stanford University; University of Oregon; University of Southern California; University of Washington. Median SAT critical reading: 680, median SAT math: 680, median SAT writing: 680, median combined SAT: 1990, median composite ACT: 30. 70% scored over 600 on SAT critical reading, 78% scored over 600 on SAT math, 73% scored over 600 on SAT writing, 81% scored over 1800 on combined SAT, 74% scored over 26 on composite ACT.

Student Life Upper grades have specified standards of dress, student council. Discipline rests equally with students and faculty. Attendance at religious services is required.

Summer Programs Remediation, enrichment, advancement, sports, art/fine arts, computer instruction programs offered; session focuses on a variety of academic, sports, and artistic enrichment programs; held both on and off campus; held at local/regional trips are offered through summer programs for experiential education and science and research: marine ecology trip on Oregon Coast, backpacking on Mt. Hood, etc.; accepts boys and girls; open to students from other schools. 2,000 students usually enrolled. 2013 schedule: June 18 to August 24.

Tuition and Aid Day student tuition: $25,340; 7-day tuition and room/board: $48,410. Tuition installment plan (Insured Tuition Payment Plan, monthly payment plans). Need-based scholarship grants available. In 2012–13, 18% of upper-school students received aid. Total amount of financial aid awarded in 2012–13: $663,000.

Admissions Traditional secondary-level entrance grade is 9. For fall 2012, 136 students applied for upper-level admission, 75 were accepted, 49 enrolled. SSAT or TOEFL required. Deadline for receipt of application materials: February 1. Application fee required: $75. Interview required.

Athletics Interscholastic: alpine skiing (boys, girls), basketball (b,g), cross-country running (b,g), fencing (b,g), golf (b,g), lacrosse (b,g), skiing (downhill) (b,g), soccer (b,g), tennis (b,g), track and field (b,g), volleyball (g); intramural: backpacking (b,g), dance (b,g), hiking/backpacking (b,g), outdoor activities (b,g), snowboarding (b,g), yoga (b,g); coed intramural: outdoor education, physical fitness, physical training, rock climbing, ropes courses. 2 PE instructors, 33 coaches, 1 athletic trainer.

Computers Computers are regularly used in art, English, foreign language, history, humanities, independent study, mathematics, music, philosophy, religion, science, social sciences, technology classes. Computer network features include on-campus library services, online commercial services, Internet access, wireless campus network, Internet filtering or blocking technology. Campus intranet, student e-mail accounts, and computer access in designated common areas are available to students. Students grades are available online. The school has a published electronic and media policy.

Contact Ms. Marcy Morris, Admissions Associate. 503-768-3115. Fax: 503-768-3140. E-mail: admit@oes.edu. Web site: www.oes.edu

ORINDA ACADEMY

19 Altarinda Road
Orinda, California 94563-2602

Head of School: Ron Graydon

General Information Coeducational day college-preparatory, general academic, and arts school. Grades 6–12. Founded: 1982. Setting: suburban. Nearest major city is Walnut Creek. 1-acre campus. 2 buildings on campus. Approved or accredited by East Bay Independent Schools Association, The College Board, and Western Association of Schools and Colleges. Total enrollment: 90. Upper school average class size: 10. Upper school faculty-student ratio: 1:9. There are 175 required school days per year for Upper School students. Upper School students typically attend 5 days per week. The average school day consists of 6 hours and 30 minutes.

Upper School Student Profile Grade 9: 15 students (7 boys, 8 girls); Grade 10: 21 students (15 boys, 6 girls); Grade 11: 23 students (11 boys, 12 girls); Grade 12: 17 students (11 boys, 6 girls).

Faculty School total: 17. In upper school: 7 men, 9 women; 9 have advanced degrees.

Subjects Offered Algebra, American history, American literature, art, basketball, biology, calculus, chemistry, community service, computer graphics, computer multimedia, computer music, contemporary issues, creative writing, dance, drama, earth science, economics, English, English literature, English literature and composition-AP, ensembles, environmental science, ESL, European history, film history, fine arts, French, geography, geometry, government/civics, health, history, history of music, introduction to theater, journalism, mathematics, music, music performance, musical productions, performing arts, physical education, physics, science, social studies, Spanish, Spanish language-AP, theater, trigonometry, visual arts, yearbook.

Graduation Requirements Algebra, biology, civics, composition, economics, English, foreign language, geometry, physical education (includes health), science, trigonometry, U.S. history, visual and performing arts. Community service is required.

Special Academic Programs 2 Advanced Placement exams for which test preparation is offered; honors section; accelerated programs; academic accommodation for the gifted; ESL (2 students enrolled).

College Admission Counseling 15 students graduated in 2012; 13 went to college, including DePaul University; Smith College; The Evergreen State College; University of California, Berkeley; University of Oregon; Willamette University. Other: 1 went to work, 1 had other specific plans. Mean SAT critical reading: 548, mean SAT math: 493, mean SAT writing: 541, mean combined SAT: 1582. 33% scored over 600 on SAT critical reading, 7% scored over 600 on SAT writing, 7% scored over 1800 on combined SAT.

Student Life Upper grades have specified standards of dress, student council, honor system. Discipline rests primarily with faculty.

Summer Programs Remediation, enrichment, advancement programs offered; session focuses on academics; held on campus; accepts boys and girls; open to students from other schools. 50 students usually enrolled. 2013 schedule: June 17 to August 2. Application deadline: none.

Tuition and Aid Day student tuition: $30,475. Tuition installment plan (FACTS Tuition Payment Plan). Tuition reduction for siblings, need-based scholarship grants available. In 2012–13, 25% of upper-school students received aid. Total amount of financial aid awarded in 2012–13: $400,000.

Admissions Traditional secondary-level entrance grade is 9. For fall 2012, 60 students applied for upper-level admission, 36 were accepted, 23 enrolled. ISEE or SSAT required. Deadline for receipt of application materials: January 18. Application fee required: $75. On-campus interview required.

Athletics Interscholastic: baseball (boys), basketball (b,g); coed interscholastic: soccer; coed intramural: soccer, softball. 1 PE instructor, 1 coach.

Computers Computers are regularly used in English, social sciences, writing, yearbook classes. Computer network features include Internet access, Internet filtering or blocking technology. Student e-mail accounts and computer access in designated common areas are available to students. The school has a published electronic and media policy.

Contact Laurel Evans, Director of Admissions. 925-254-7553 Ext. 305. Fax: 925-254-4768. E-mail: laurel@orindaacademy.org. Web site: www.orindaacademy.org

OUR LADY ACADEMY

222 South Beach Boulevard
Bay St. Louis, Mississippi 38520-4320

Head of School: Mrs. Tiffany Lindmark

General Information Girls' day and distance learning college-preparatory and religious studies school, affiliated with Roman Catholic Church. Grades 7–12. Distance learning grades 10–12. Founded: 1971. Setting: small town. Nearest major city is New Orleans, LA. 3-acre campus. 4 buildings on campus. Approved or accredited by Mercy Secondary Education Association, National Catholic Education Association, and Southern Association of Colleges and Schools. Endowment: $2 million. Total enrollment: 220. Upper school average class size: 22. Upper school faculty-student ratio: 1:13. There are 150 required school days per year for Upper School students. Upper School students typically attend 5 days per week. The average school day consists of 7 hours.

Upper School Student Profile Grade 9: 40 students (40 girls); Grade 10: 35 students (35 girls); Grade 11: 50 students (50 girls); Grade 12: 25 students (25 girls). 85% of students are Roman Catholic.

Faculty School total: 20. In upper school: 1 man, 19 women; 8 have advanced degrees.

Subjects Offered Advanced biology, advanced math, aquatics, band, Catholic belief and practice, choral music, Christian ethics, Christian studies, English composition, English literature, European history-AP, fine arts, integrated science, Latin, learning strategies, minority studies, moral reasoning, mythology, oral communications, physics, physiology, scripture, theater, theater arts, U.S. government, world religions.

Graduation Requirements Art, computers, English, foreign language, mathematics, physical education (includes health), religious studies, science, social sciences.

Special Academic Programs 10 Advanced Placement exams for which test preparation is offered; honors section; independent study; programs in English, general development for dyslexic students; ESL (3 students enrolled).

College Admission Counseling 45 students graduated in 2011; 37 went to college, including Louisiana State University and Agricultural and Mechanical College; Mississippi State University; University of Mississippi; University of South Alabama; University of Southern Mississippi. Median composite ACT: 25. 33% scored over 26 on composite ACT.

Student Life Upper grades have uniform requirement, student council, honor system. Discipline rests primarily with faculty. Attendance at religious services is required.

Tuition and Aid Day student tuition: $5200. Tuition installment plan (The Tuition Plan, monthly payment plans, individually arranged payment plans). Need-based scholarship grants available. In 2011–12, 8% of upper-school students received aid. Total amount of financial aid awarded in 2011–12: $40,000.

Admissions Traditional secondary-level entrance grade is 9. For fall 2011, 47 students applied for upper-level admission, 40 were accepted, 40 enrolled. CTBS, Stanford Achievement Test, any other standardized test, Metropolitan Achievement Short Form and Stanford Achievement Test required. Deadline for receipt of application materials: none. No application fee required. On-campus interview required.

Athletics Interscholastic: basketball, cheering, cross-country running, dance squad, drill team, sailing, soccer, softball, track and field, volleyball; coed interscholastic: swimming and diving, tennis. 1 PE instructor, 8 coaches, 1 athletic trainer.

Computers Computers are regularly used in accounting, business, college planning, creative writing, desktop publishing, English, foreign language, keyboarding, library science, newspaper, typing, Web site design, word processing, writing, yearbook classes. Computer network features include Internet access, wireless campus network, Internet filtering or blocking technology. Campus intranet and computer access in designated common areas are available to students. Students grades are available online. The school has a published electronic and media policy.

Contact Mrs. Tiffany Lindmark, Principal. 228-467-7048 Ext. 12. Fax: 228-467-1666. E-mail: tiffany.lindmark@ourladyacademy.com. Web site: www.ourladyacademy.com

OUR LADY OF MERCY ACADEMY

1001 Main Road
Newfield, New Jersey 08344

Head of School: Sr. Grace Marie Scandale

General Information Girls' day college-preparatory, arts, religious studies, bilingual studies, and technology school, affiliated with Roman Catholic Church. Grades 9–12. Founded: 1962. Setting: rural. Nearest major city is Vineland. 58-acre campus. 2 buildings on campus. Approved or accredited by British Accreditation Council, Middle States Association of Colleges and Schools, and National Catholic Education Association. Endowment: $250,000. Total enrollment: 150. Upper school average class size: 20. Upper school faculty-student ratio: 1:11. There are 180 required school days per year for Upper School students. Upper School students typically attend 5 days per week. The average school day consists of 6 hours and 30 minutes.

Upper School Student Profile Grade 9: 39 students (39 girls); Grade 10: 33 students (33 girls); Grade 11: 44 students (44 girls); Grade 12: 34 students (34 girls); Postgraduate: 150 students (150 girls). 90% of students are Roman Catholic.

Faculty School total: 22. In upper school: 22 women; 10 have advanced degrees.

Subjects Offered Algebra, American history, American literature, art, biology, botany, British literature (honors), career and personal planning, Catholic belief and practice, chemistry, choral music, chorus, Christian ethics, Christian scripture, Christian testament, Christianity, college counseling, computer technologies, CPR, current events, death and loss, driver education, economics, electronic publishing, English literature, first aid, food and nutrition, French, graphic design, honors algebra, honors geometry, Middle Eastern history, physics, pre-calculus, probability and statistics, psychology, publications, religion, social justice, sociology, technology, Western civilization.

Graduation Requirements Algebra, biology, chemistry, English, geometry, physical education (includes health), religion (includes Bible studies and theology), religious studies, technology, U.S. history, Western civilization.

Special Academic Programs Honors section; study at local college for college credit.

College Admission Counseling 35 students graduated in 2012; all went to college, including La Salle University; Rutgers, The State University of New Jersey, New Brunswick; Saint Joseph's University; Seton Hall University; The University of Scranton; University of Pennsylvania.

Student Life Upper grades have uniform requirement, student council, honor system. Discipline rests primarily with faculty. Attendance at religious services is required.

Tuition and Aid Day student tuition: $10,044. Tuition installment plan (SMART Tuition Payment Plan, monthly payment plans, individually arranged payment plans). Tuition reduction for siblings, merit scholarship grants, need-based scholarship grants, paying campus jobs available. In 2012–13, 15% of upper-school students received aid; total upper-school merit-scholarship money awarded: $34,500. Total amount of financial aid awarded in 2012–13: $35,000.

Admissions Traditional secondary-level entrance grade is 9. For fall 2012, 59 students applied for upper-level admission, 50 were accepted, 40 enrolled. High School

Placement Test (closed version) from Scholastic Testing Service required. Deadline for receipt of application materials: none. Application fee required: $200.

Athletics Interscholastic: basketball, cheering, crew, lacrosse, soccer, softball, strength & conditioning, swimming and diving, tennis, track and field, volleyball; intramural: badminton, basketball, flag football, golf, gymnastics, physical fitness, soccer, softball, synchronized swimming, volleyball. 2 PE instructors, 12 coaches.

Computers Computers are regularly used in all academic, career exploration, college planning, creative writing, graphic design, graphics, library, library skills, photography, publications, research skills, technology, typing, Web site design, word processing, yearbook classes. Computer network features include on-campus library services, Internet access, wireless campus network, Internet filtering or blocking technology. Computer access in designated common areas is available to students. Students grades are available online. The school has a published electronic and media policy.

Contact Sr. Grace Marie Scandale, Principal. 856-697-2008. Fax: 856-697-2887. E-mail: srgrace@olmanj.org. Web site: www.olmanj.org

OUR LADY OF MERCY HIGH SCHOOL

1437 Blossom Road
Rochester, New York 14610

Head of School: Mr. Terence Quinn

General Information Girls' day college-preparatory, arts, business, religious studies, and technology school, affiliated with Roman Catholic Church. Grades 7–12. Founded: 1928. Setting: suburban. 1 building on campus. Approved or accredited by Mercy Secondary Education Association, Middle States Association of Colleges and Schools, National Catholic Education Association, and New York State Board of Regents. Total enrollment: 691. Upper school average class size: 22. Upper school faculty-student ratio: 1:11. There are 177 required school days per year for Upper School students. Upper School students typically attend 5 days per week. The average school day consists of 6 hours and 35 minutes.

Upper School Student Profile Grade 9: 120 students (120 girls); Grade 10: 144 students (144 girls); Grade 11: 147 students (147 girls); Grade 12: 143 students (143 girls). 78% of students are Roman Catholic.

Faculty School total: 61. In upper school: 14 men, 47 women.

Subjects Offered Accounting, algebra, American history, American history-AP, American literature, art, biology, biology-AP, business, calculus-AP, ceramics, chemistry, chemistry-AP, creative writing, drama, earth science, economics, English, English literature, English literature-AP, entrepreneurship, European history-AP, finance, French, French-AP, geometry, government/civics, health, Latin, Latin-AP, mathematics, music, orchestra, photography, physical education, physics, physics-AP, prayer/spirituality, pre-calculus, psychology, psychology-AP, science, scripture, social justice, Spanish, Spanish-AP, speech, studio art, theater, theater arts, theology, world history, world history-AP, world literature, writing.

Graduation Requirements Arts and fine arts (art, music, dance, drama), English, foreign language, mathematics, physical education (includes health), science, social studies (includes history), theology.

Special Academic Programs 12 Advanced Placement exams for which test preparation is offered; honors section; study at local college for college credit; ESL.

College Admission Counseling 125 students graduated in 2011; all went to college, including Nazareth College of Rochester; Rochester Institute of Technology; University of Rochester. Mean SAT critical reading: 564, mean SAT math: 555, mean SAT writing: 600. 39% scored over 26 on composite ACT.

Student Life Upper grades have specified standards of dress, student council, honor system. Discipline rests primarily with faculty. Attendance at religious services is required.

Tuition and Aid Day student tuition: $8100. Tuition installment plan (monthly payment plans, individually arranged payment plans, 2-payment plan). Merit scholarship grants, need-based scholarship grants available. In 2011–12, 20% of upper-school students received aid; total upper-school merit-scholarship money awarded: $1,200,000. Total amount of financial aid awarded in 2011–12: $1,200,000.

Admissions Traditional secondary-level entrance grade is 9. For fall 2011, 103 students applied for upper-level admission, 88 were accepted, 55 enrolled. Educational Development Series, High School Placement Test (closed version) from Scholastic Testing Service or Scholastic Testing Service High School Placement Test required. Deadline for receipt of application materials: none. Application fee required: $200. On-campus interview recommended.

Athletics Interscholastic: basketball, bowling, cheering, crew, cross-country running, diving, golf, indoor track, lacrosse, sailing, skiing (downhill), soccer, softball, swimming and diving, tennis, track and field, volleyball. 3 PE instructors, 12 coaches, 1 athletic trainer.

Computers Computers are regularly used in accounting, all academic, business, business education, career exploration, college planning, English, keyboarding, library skills, literary magazine, mathematics, newspaper, photography, publications, research skills, science, technology, yearbook classes. Computer resources include on-campus library services, Internet access. The school has a published electronic and media policy.

Contact Mary Elizabeth McCahill, Director of Admissions. 585-288-7120 Ext. 310. Fax: 585-288-7966. E-mail: mmccahill@mercyhs.com. Web site: www.mercyhs.com

OUT-OF-DOOR-ACADEMY

5950 Deer Drive
Sarasota, Florida 34240

Head of School: Mr. David Mahler

General Information Coeducational day college-preparatory school. Grades PK–12. Founded: 1924. Setting: suburban. Nearest major city is Tampa. 85-acre campus. 9 buildings on campus. Approved or accredited by Florida Council of Independent Schools. Member of National Association of Independent Schools. Endowment: $7.5 million. Total enrollment: 615. Upper school average class size: 16. Upper school faculty-student ratio: 1:13. There are 172 required school days per year for Upper School students. Upper School students typically attend 5 days per week. The average school day consists of 7 hours.

Upper School Student Profile Grade 9: 64 students (27 boys, 37 girls); Grade 10: 57 students (28 boys, 29 girls); Grade 11: 53 students (21 boys, 32 girls); Grade 12: 56 students (32 boys, 24 girls).

Faculty School total: 75. In upper school: 13 men, 19 women; 18 have advanced degrees.

Subjects Offered Advanced Placement courses, advanced studio art-AP, algebra, American history-AP, art history, biology, biology-AP, British literature, calculus, calculus-AP, chemistry, chemistry-AP, college counseling, computers, drama, drama performance, dramatic arts, English, English composition, English language and composition-AP, English literature, English literature and composition-AP, English-AP, European history-AP, expository writing, French, French language-AP, geometry, graphic design, health and wellness, history-AP, honors algebra, honors geometry, Latin, Latin-AP, literature, literature and composition-AP, music, newspaper, photography, portfolio art, Spanish, Spanish language-AP, studio art, studio art-AP, U.S. government, U.S. history, U.S. history-AP, women's studies, world cultures, world literature, world studies, yearbook, zoology.

Graduation Requirements Arts and fine arts (art, music, dance, drama), electives, English, foreign language, health, history, mathematics, performing arts, personal fitness, science. Community service is required.

Special Academic Programs 21 Advanced Placement exams for which test preparation is offered; honors section; independent study.

College Admission Counseling 53 students graduated in 2011; all went to college, including Colgate University; New York University; Syracuse University; Trinity College; Vanderbilt University. Mean SAT critical reading: 622, mean SAT math: 618, mean SAT writing: 613, mean combined SAT: 1854. 59% scored over 600 on SAT critical reading, 59% scored over 600 on SAT math, 61% scored over 600 on SAT writing, 61% scored over 1800 on combined SAT.

Student Life Upper grades have specified standards of dress, student council, honor system. Discipline rests equally with students and faculty.

Tuition and Aid Day student tuition: $18,460. Tuition installment plan (FACTS Tuition Payment Plan). Need-based scholarship grants, faculty/staff tuition remission available. In 2011–12, 28% of upper-school students received aid. Total amount of financial aid awarded in 2011–12: $650,465.

Admissions Traditional secondary-level entrance grade is 9. For fall 2011, 67 students applied for upper-level admission, 41 were accepted, 35 enrolled. ERB or SSAT required. Deadline for receipt of application materials: March 2. Application fee required: $100. Interview required.

Athletics Interscholastic: baseball (boys), basketball (b,g), cheering (g), cross-country running (b,g), football (b), golf (b,g), independent competitive sports (b,g), lacrosse (b,g), soccer (b,g), softball (g), swimming and diving (b,g), tennis (b,g), track and field (b,g), volleyball (g); intramural: fitness (b,g); coed interscholastic: sailing; coed intramural: physical fitness, physical training, strength & conditioning, weight training. 3 PE instructors, 21 coaches, 1 athletic trainer.

Computers Computers are regularly used in computer applications, English, foreign language, French, graphic design, history, Latin, mathematics, newspaper, science, senior seminar, social studies, Spanish, yearbook classes. Computer network features include on-campus library services, online commercial services, Internet access, wireless campus network, Internet filtering or blocking technology, digital video production. Campus intranet and computer access in designated common areas are available to students. Students grades are available online. The school has a published electronic and media policy.

Contact Mr. Jamie Carver, Director of Middle and Upper School Admissions. 941-554-5954. Fax: 941-907-1251. E-mail: jcarver@oda.edu. Web site: www.oda.edu

THE OVERLAKE SCHOOL

20301 Northeast 108th Street
Redmond, Washington 98053

Head of School: Matthew P. Horvat

General Information Coeducational day college-preparatory and arts school. Grades 5–12. Founded: 1967. Setting: rural. Nearest major city is Seattle. 75-acre campus. 22 buildings on campus. Approved or accredited by Northwest Accreditation Commission, Pacific Northwest Association of Independent Schools, The College Board, and Washington Department of Education. Member of National Association of Independent Schools. Endowment: $15 million. Total enrollment: 521. Upper school average class size: 14. Upper school faculty-student ratio: 1:9. There are 173 required school days per year for Upper School students. Upper School students typically attend 5 days per week. The average school day consists of 6 hours.

Upper School Student Profile Grade 9: 80 students (39 boys, 41 girls); Grade 10: 76 students (39 boys, 37 girls); Grade 11: 73 students (36 boys, 37 girls); Grade 12: 68 students (36 boys, 32 girls).

Faculty School total: 65. In upper school: 19 men, 25 women; 34 have advanced degrees.

Subjects Offered 3-dimensional art, 3-dimensional design, acting, advanced chemistry, Advanced Placement courses, aerobics, African studies, algebra, American history, American literature, art, art history-AP, arts, athletic training, athletics, backpacking, band, Basic programming, bioethics, biology-AP, calculus, calculus-AP, career/college preparation, ceramics, chamber groups, chemistry, chemistry-AP, Chinese, choir, chorus, college admission preparation, community service, comparative religion, computer graphics, computer programming, computer science, computer science-AP, concert band, concert choir, constitutional history of U.S., constitutional law, creative arts, dance, drama, drama performance, drawing, English, English literature, English literature and composition-AP, English literature-AP, environmental science, European literature, fine arts, fitness, foreign language, forensics, French, French language-AP, French-AP, geometry, global issues, graphic design, health, Holocaust and other genocides, Holocaust studies, honors algebra, honors U.S. history, industrial arts, instrumental music, integrated science, Japanese, jazz, jazz band, jazz ensemble, lab science, Latin, Latin American literature, Latin-AP, life skills, literature, mathematics, metalworking, Middle East, modern history, music, music theater, musical productions, orchestra, outdoor education, painting, participation in sports, performing arts, personal fitness, photography, physical education, physics-AP, pre-calculus, programming, psychology, science, senior project, Spanish, Spanish language-AP, Spanish literature-AP, Spanish-AP, sports conditioning, sports medicine, stage design, stagecraft, statistics-AP, studio art, theater, theater arts, traditional camping, U.S. history, video film production, vocal music, woodworking, world history, world literature, yearbook.

Graduation Requirements Arts and fine arts (art, music, dance, drama), English, foreign language, history, lab science, mathematics, outdoor education, physical education (includes health), senior project, annual Project Week, 3 co-curricular activities. Community service is required.

Special Academic Programs 14 Advanced Placement exams for which test preparation is offered; honors section; independent study; term-away projects; study abroad; academic accommodation for the gifted, the musically talented, and the artistically talented.

College Admission Counseling 68 students graduated in 2012; 66 went to college, including Brown University; Chapman University; Santa Clara University; Stanford University; Tufts University; University of Washington. Other: 1 entered a postgraduate year, 1 had other specific plans. Median SAT critical reading: 640, median SAT math: 650, median SAT writing: 630, median combined SAT: 1930, median composite ACT: 29. 79% scored over 600 on SAT critical reading, 85% scored over 600 on SAT math, 67% scored over 600 on SAT writing, 74% scored over 1800 on combined SAT, 100% scored over 26 on composite ACT.

Student Life Upper grades have student council. Discipline rests equally with students and faculty.

Summer Programs Sports programs offered; session focuses on skill-building sports camps; held both on and off campus; held at sports programs are on campus; outdoor program trips are in the mountains, etc.; accepts boys and girls; not open to students from other schools. 75 students usually enrolled. 2013 schedule: August 1 to August 15. Application deadline: June 30.

Tuition and Aid Day student tuition: $26,856. Tuition installment plan (monthly payment plans). Need-based scholarship grants, 50% tuition remission for faculty and staff, Malone Scholarship, Gibson Scholarship available. In 2012–13, 18% of upper-school students received aid. Total amount of financial aid awarded in 2012–13: $675,904.

Admissions Traditional secondary-level entrance grade is 9. For fall 2012, 72 students applied for upper-level admission, 31 were accepted, 21 enrolled. ISEE or SSAT required. Deadline for receipt of application materials: January 15. Application fee required: $50. Interview required.

Athletics Interscholastic: baseball (boys), basketball (b,g), cross-country running (b,g), golf (b,g), lacrosse (b,g), soccer (b,g), tennis (b,g), ultimate Frisbee (b,g), volleyball (g); intramural: basketball (b,g), physical fitness (b,g), strength & conditioning (b,g), weight lifting (b,g), weight training (b,g); coed interscholastic: squash, tennis; coed intramural: backpacking, basketball, bicycling, canoeing/kayaking, climbing, dance, fitness, hiking/backpacking, kayaking, mountain biking, mountaineering, outdoor activities, outdoor education, outdoor skills, physical fitness, physical training, rafting, rappelling, rock climbing, ropes courses, skiing (downhill), snowshoeing, table tennis, wall climbing, wilderness, yoga. 4 PE instructors, 45 coaches, 2 athletic trainers.

Computers Computers are regularly used in all classes. Computer network features include on-campus library services, online commercial services, Internet access, wireless campus network. Campus intranet and computer access in designated common areas are available to students. Students grades are available online. The school has a published electronic and media policy.

Contact Lori Maughan, Director of Admission and Financial Aid. 425-868-1000. Fax: 425-868-5771. E-mail: lmaughan@overlake.org. Web site: www.overlake.org

THE OXFORD ACADEMY

1393 Boston Post Road
Westbrook, Connecticut 06498-0685

Head of School: Philip B. Cocchiola

General Information Boys' boarding college-preparatory, general academic, arts, bilingual studies, and ESL school. Grades 9–PG. Founded: 1906. Setting: small town. Nearest major city is New Haven. Students are housed in single-sex dormitories. 13-acre campus. 8 buildings on campus. Approved or accredited by Connecticut Association of Independent Schools, New England Association of Schools and Colleges, The Association of Boarding Schools, and Connecticut Department of Education. Member of National Association of Independent Schools and Secondary School Admission Test Board. Endowment: $250,000. Total enrollment: 38. Upper school average class size: 1. Upper school faculty-student ratio: 1:1.

Upper School Student Profile Grade 9: 4 students (4 boys); Grade 10: 5 students (5 boys); Grade 11: 10 students (10 boys); Grade 12: 17 students (17 boys). 100% of students are boarding students. 35% are state residents. 8 states are represented in upper school student body. 33% are international students. International students from Bahamas, Bermuda, France, Mexico, Republic of Korea, and Saudi Arabia.

Faculty School total: 22. In upper school: 15 men, 7 women; 10 have advanced degrees; 12 reside on campus.

Subjects Offered Algebra, American history, American literature, anatomy, astronomy, biology, botany, calculus, chemistry, creative writing, earth science, ecology, economics, English, English literature, environmental science, ESL, European history, expository writing, French, geography, geology, geometry, German, government/civics, grammar, history, Latin, marine biology, mathematics, oceanography, paleontology, philosophy, physical education, physics, physiology, psychology, science, social studies, sociology, Spanish, study skills, trigonometry, world history, world literature, writing, zoology.

Graduation Requirements English, foreign language, mathematics, science, social studies (includes history). Community service is required.

Special Academic Programs Advanced Placement exam preparation; honors section; accelerated programs; independent study; academic accommodation for the gifted; remedial reading and/or remedial writing; remedial math; special instructional classes for students with mild ADD and learning differences; ESL (6 students enrolled).

College Admission Counseling 17 students graduated in 2012; all went to college, including Bucknell University; Georgia Southern University; Lynn University; Rhode Island School of Design; Suffolk University; Wheaton College. 20% scored over 600 on SAT critical reading, 20% scored over 600 on SAT math, 20% scored over 600 on SAT writing.

Student Life Upper grades have specified standards of dress, student council, honor system. Discipline rests equally with students and faculty.

Summer Programs Remediation, enrichment, advancement, ESL programs offered; session focuses on acceleration of academics, study skills; held on campus; accepts boys; open to students from other schools. 25 students usually enrolled. 2013 schedule: June 17 to July 19. Application deadline: none.

Tuition and Aid 7-day tuition and room/board: $54,900. Tuition installment plan (monthly payment plans, individually arranged payment plans). Tuition reduction for siblings, need-based scholarship grants available. In 2012–13, 1% of upper-school students received aid.

Admissions For fall 2012, 22 students applied for upper-level admission, 19 were accepted, 13 enrolled. SLEP for foreign students, Stanford Achievement Test, Otis-Lennon School Ability Test, TOEFL, WISC or WAIS or Woodcock-Johnson required. Deadline for receipt of application materials: none. Application fee required: $65. Interview recommended.

Athletics Interscholastic: basketball, soccer, tennis; intramural: basketball, flag football, Frisbee, golf, hiking/backpacking, paint ball, physical fitness, power lifting, roller blading, running, sailing, skateboarding, strength & conditioning, table tennis, tennis, ultimate Frisbee, walking, weight lifting, weight training. 6 coaches.

Computers Computers are regularly used in mathematics classes. Computer network features include Internet access. Student e-mail accounts are available to students. The school has a published electronic and media policy.

Contact Mrs. Patricia Davis, Director of Admissions. 860-399-6247 Ext. 100. Fax: 860-399-6805. E-mail: admissions@oxfordacademy.net. Web site: www.oxfordacademy.net

PACIFIC ACADEMY

679 Encinitas Boulevard
Suite 205
Encinitas, California 92024

Head of School: Dr. Erika Sanchez

General Information Coeducational day college-preparatory and arts school; primarily serves students with learning disabilities, individuals with Attention Deficit Disorder, and dyslexic students. Grades 7–12. Founded: 1997. Setting: small town. Nearest major city is San Diego. 1 building on campus. Approved or accredited by Western Association of Schools and Colleges and California Department of Education. Languages of instruction: English and Spanish. Total enrollment: 21. Upper school average class size: 6. Upper school faculty-student ratio: 1:5.

Faculty School total: 5. In upper school: 3 men, 2 women; 4 have advanced degrees.
Subjects Offered Algebra, American government, American literature, American studies, art history, biology, business mathematics, chemistry, computer applications, earth science, economics, English, ethnic studies, general math, geography, geometry, history, language arts, life science, literature, physical science, physics, pre-algebra, pre-calculus, Spanish, U.S. history, world history, world literature.
Graduation Requirements Arts and fine arts (art, music, dance, drama), computer studies, English, foreign language, mathematics, physical education (includes health), practical arts, science, social studies (includes history), community service hours in 11th and 12th grade.
Special Academic Programs Advanced Placement exam preparation; honors section; accelerated programs; academic accommodation for the gifted.
College Admission Counseling 5 students graduated in 2012.
Student Life Upper grades have honor system. Discipline rests primarily with faculty.
Summer Programs Remediation, enrichment, advancement programs offered; session focuses on academics; held on campus; accepts boys and girls; open to students from other schools. 38 students usually enrolled. 2013 schedule: June 23 to August 1. Application deadline: June 15.
Tuition and Aid Day student tuition: $13,600–$15,000. Tuition installment plan (monthly payment plans). Tuition reduction for siblings available. In 2012–13, 5% of upper-school students received aid.
Admissions Traditional secondary-level entrance grade is 10. California Achievement Test required. Deadline for receipt of application materials: none. Application fee required: $50. On-campus interview required.
Athletics 1 PE instructor.
Computers Computers are regularly used in all academic, yearbook classes. Computer network features include online commercial services, Internet access, wireless campus network.
Contact Ms. Annie Chang, Director of Admissions. 760-634-1188. Fax: 760-436-5718. E-mail: achang@pacificacademy.org. Web site: www.pacificacademy.org

PACIFIC CREST COMMUNITY SCHOOL

116 Northeast 29th Street
Portland, Oregon 97232

Head of School: Becky Lukens

General Information Coeducational day college-preparatory and arts school. Grades 6–12. Founded: 1993. Setting: urban. 1 building on campus. Approved or accredited by Northwest Accreditation Commission and Oregon Department of Education. Total enrollment: 85. Upper school average class size: 10. Upper school faculty-student ratio: 1:9. There are 180 required school days per year for Upper School students. Upper School students typically attend 5 days per week. The average school day consists of 6 hours.
Faculty School total: 12. In upper school: 5 men, 7 women; 11 have advanced degrees.
Graduation Requirements Senior seminar/dissertation.
Special Academic Programs Independent study; study at local college for college credit; academic accommodation for the gifted.
College Admission Counseling 16 students graduated in 2012; 13 went to college. Other: 3 had other specific plans.
Student Life Discipline rests equally with students and faculty.
Tuition and Aid Day student tuition: $11,500. Tuition installment plan (monthly payment plans). Need-based scholarship grants available. In 2012–13, 15% of upper-school students received aid. Total amount of financial aid awarded in 2012–13: $50,000.
Admissions Traditional secondary-level entrance grade is 9. For fall 2012, 22 students applied for upper-level admission, 19 were accepted, 19 enrolled. Deadline for receipt of application materials: none. Application fee required: $100. Interview required.
Athletics Coed Intramural: artistic gym, basketball, bicycling, bowling, canoeing/kayaking, hiking/backpacking, outdoor adventure, outdoor education, outdoor skills, rock climbing, running, skiing (cross-country). 2 PE instructors.
Computers Computer network features include Internet access, wireless campus network. Student e-mail accounts are available to students.
Contact Jenny Osborne, Co-Director. 503-234-2826. Fax: 503-234-3186. E-mail: Jenny@pcrest.org. Web site: www.pcrest.org

PACIFIC HILLS SCHOOL

8628 Holloway Drive
West Hollywood, California 90069

Head of School: Dr. Peter Temes

General Information Coeducational day college-preparatory school. Grades 6–12. Founded: 1983. Setting: urban. Nearest major city is Beverly Hills. 2-acre campus. 2 buildings on campus. Approved or accredited by Western Association of Schools and Colleges and California Department of Education. Member of National Association of Independent Schools. Total enrollment: 207. Upper school average class size: 15. Upper school faculty-student ratio: 1:10. There are 175 required school days per year for Upper School students. Upper School students typically attend 5 days per week. The average school day consists of 6 hours and 35 minutes.
Upper School Student Profile Grade 9: 23 students (13 boys, 10 girls); Grade 10: 41 students (22 boys, 19 girls); Grade 11: 35 students (23 boys, 12 girls); Grade 12: 51 students (33 boys, 18 girls).
Faculty School total: 27. In upper school: 16 men, 11 women; 9 have advanced degrees.
Subjects Offered Advanced Placement courses, aerobics, algebra, American history, American literature, anatomy, art, biology, calculus-AP, cheerleading, chemistry, computers, economics, English, English literature, film, French, geometry, government, human development, music, newspaper, photography, physical education, physics, pre-calculus, Spanish, speech, theater arts, yearbook.
Graduation Requirements Arts and fine arts (art, music, dance, drama), English, foreign language, mathematics, outdoor education, physical education (includes health), science, social sciences, social studies (includes history). Community service is required.
Special Academic Programs 9 Advanced Placement exams for which test preparation is offered; honors section.
College Admission Counseling 32 students graduated in 2011; all went to college, including California State University, Northridge; Loyola Marymount University; University of California, Irvine; University of California, Los Angeles; University of California, San Diego; University of Southern California. Mean SAT critical reading: 525, mean SAT math: 510, mean SAT writing: 532. 17% scored over 600 on SAT critical reading, 15% scored over 600 on SAT math, 15% scored over 600 on SAT writing.
Student Life Upper grades have specified standards of dress, student council, honor system. Discipline rests primarily with faculty.
Tuition and Aid Day student tuition: $20,950. Tuition installment plan (Insured Tuition Payment Plan, monthly payment plans, individually arranged payment plans). Tuition reduction for siblings, need-based scholarship grants, need-based loans available. In 2011–12, 52% of upper-school students received aid.
Admissions Traditional secondary-level entrance grade is 9. For fall 2011, 118 students applied for upper-level admission, 61 were accepted, 54 enrolled. CTBS (or similar from their school), ERB or ISEE required. Deadline for receipt of application materials: none. Application fee required: $100. On-campus interview required.
Athletics Interscholastic: baseball (boys), basketball (b,g), cheering (g), flag football (b), softball (g), volleyball (b,g); coed interscholastic: cross-country running, dance team, outdoor education, soccer, track and field. 3 PE instructors, 7 coaches.
Computers Computers are regularly used in graphic design, journalism, yearbook classes. Computer network features include Internet access, wireless campus network, Internet filtering or blocking technology. Computer access in designated common areas is available to students. Students grades are available online. The school has a published electronic and media policy.
Contact Ms. Lynne Bradshaw, Admissions Assistant. 310-276-3068 Ext. 112. Fax: 310-657-3831. E-mail: lbradshaw@phschool.org. Web site: www.phschool.org

PADUA FRANCISCAN HIGH SCHOOL

6740 State Road
Parma, Ohio 44134-4598

Head of School: Mr. David Stec

General Information Coeducational day college-preparatory, arts, business, religious studies, and technology school, affiliated with Roman Catholic Church. Grades 9–12. Founded: 1961. Setting: suburban. Nearest major city is Cleveland. 40-acre campus. 1 building on campus. Approved or accredited by North Central Association of Colleges and Schools, Ohio Catholic Schools Accreditation Association (OCSAA), and Ohio Department of Education. Endowment: $1.5 million. Total enrollment: 805. Upper school average class size: 25. Upper school faculty-student ratio: 1:19. There are 179 required school days per year for Upper School students. Upper School students typically attend 5 days per week. The average school day consists of 6 hours and 30 minutes.
Upper School Student Profile Grade 9: 180 students (87 boys, 93 girls); Grade 10: 230 students (130 boys, 100 girls); Grade 11: 186 students (99 boys, 87 girls); Grade 12: 208 students (108 boys, 100 girls). 90% of students are Roman Catholic.
Faculty School total: 55. In upper school: 24 men, 31 women; 30 have advanced degrees.
Subjects Offered Accounting, algebra, American government, art appreciation, biology-AP, business, calculus-AP, chemistry, child development, Christian ethics, church history, computers, concert band, concert choir, consumer economics, current events, design, drawing, earth science, economics, English, English language-AP, ensembles, fitness, food and nutrition, French, French-AP, geography, geometry, German, German-AP, honors algebra, honors English, honors geometry, honors U.S. history, integrated science, interior design, Italian, Latin, Latin-AP, marching band, marketing, math analysis, music appreciation, music theory, orchestra, painting, photography, physics, pre-calculus, programming, psychology, social issues, social justice, sociology, Spanish, Spanish-AP, stagecraft, symphonic band, theater, trigonometry, U.S. history, U.S. history-AP, world cultures, world history.

Graduation Requirements Arts and fine arts (art, music, dance, drama), computer science, English, foreign language, lab science, mathematics, physical education (includes health), social studies (includes history), theology, four years of service projects.

Special Academic Programs Advanced Placement exam preparation; honors section; accelerated programs; study at local college for college credit; study abroad; remedial reading and/or remedial writing; remedial math; programs in English, mathematics for dyslexic students; special instructional classes for students with learning disabilities.

College Admission Counseling 202 students graduated in 2012; 198 went to college, including Bowling Green State University; Kent State University; Miami University; The University of Akron; The University of Toledo; University of Dayton. Other: 2 went to work, 2 entered military service. Median SAT critical reading: 537, median SAT math: 530, median composite ACT: 23.

Student Life Upper grades have specified standards of dress, student council, honor system. Discipline rests primarily with faculty. Attendance at religious services is required.

Summer Programs Enrichment, sports, art/fine arts, computer instruction programs offered; session focuses on introducing students to school, programs, coaches, and other students; PE for credit; held on campus; accepts boys and girls; open to students from other schools. 175 students usually enrolled. 2013 schedule: June 17 to June 21. Application deadline: May 17.

Tuition and Aid Day student tuition: $9350. Tuition installment plan (monthly payment plans, individually arranged payment plans). Tuition reduction for siblings, merit scholarship grants, need-based scholarship grants, paying campus jobs available. In 2012–13, 45% of upper-school students received aid; total upper-school merit-scholarship money awarded: $343,750. Total amount of financial aid awarded in 2012–13: $373,825.

Admissions Traditional secondary-level entrance grade is 9. For fall 2012, 218 students applied for upper-level admission, 212 were accepted, 180 enrolled. High School Placement Test or STS required. Deadline for receipt of application materials: January 31. Application fee required: $50.

Athletics Interscholastic: aquatics (boys, girls), baseball (b), basketball (b,g), cheering (g), combined training (b,g), cross-country running (b,g), dance team (g), diving (b,g), football (b), golf (b,g), ice hockey (b), lacrosse (b), physical fitness (b,g), soccer (b,g), softball (g), strength & conditioning (b,g), swimming and diving (b,g), tennis (g), track and field (b,g), volleyball (g), wrestling (b); intramural: basketball (b), flag football (b), football (b), freestyle skiing (b,g), golf (g), gymnastics (g), power lifting (b), touch football (b), weight lifting (b), weight training (b,g), winter soccer (b), yoga (b); coed interscholastic: figure skating, fitness; coed intramural: alpine skiing, backpacking, canoeing/kayaking, fishing, hiking/backpacking, skiing (downhill), snowboarding, wilderness, wilderness survival, wildernessways. 3 PE instructors, 30 coaches, 5 athletic trainers.

Computers Computers are regularly used in all academic classes. Computer network features include on-campus library services, online commercial services, Internet access, wireless campus network. Computer access in designated common areas is available to students. Students grades are available online. The school has a published electronic and media policy.

Contact Mrs. Nancy Hodas, Admissions Coordinator. 440-845-2444 Ext. 112. Fax: 440-845-5710. E-mail: nhodas@paduafranciscan.com. Web site: www.paduafranciscan.com

THE PAIDEIA SCHOOL

1509 Ponce de Leon Avenue
Atlanta, Georgia 30307

Head of School: Paul F. Bianchi

General Information Coeducational day college-preparatory, arts, and technology school. Grades PK–12. Founded: 1971. Setting: urban. 28-acre campus. 13 buildings on campus. Approved or accredited by Georgia Independent School Association, Southern Association of Colleges and Schools, Southern Association of Independent Schools, and Georgia Department of Education. Endowment: $10.8 million. Total enrollment: 975. Upper school average class size: 12. Upper school faculty-student ratio: 1:9. There are 179 required school days per year for Upper School students. Upper School students typically attend 5 days per week. The average school day consists of 6 hours and 45 minutes.

Upper School Student Profile Grade 9: 102 students (55 boys, 47 girls); Grade 10: 108 students (53 boys, 55 girls); Grade 11: 107 students (48 boys, 59 girls); Grade 12: 98 students (51 boys, 47 girls).

Faculty School total: 135. In upper school: 33 men, 33 women; 55 have advanced degrees.

Subjects Offered African-American history, algebra, American culture, American government, American history, American literature, anatomy, archaeology, art, art history, Asian history, Asian studies, auto mechanics, bioethics, biology, biology-AP, calculus, ceramics, chemistry, chemistry-AP, chorus, community service, comparative religion, computer programming, creative writing, drama, drawing, ecology, environmental systems, economics, English, English literature, environmental science, ethics, European history-AP, expository writing, fine arts, forensics, French, French studies, geography, geology, geometry, government/civics, health, history, humanities, jazz, journalism, literature, mathematics, medieval history, organic chemistry, photography, physical education, physics, physics-AP, physiology, poetry, pre-calculus, psychology, psychology-AP, Shakespeare, social studies, sociology, Spanish, Spanish literature, speech, statistics, statistics-AP, theater, trigonometry, U.S. history, Web site design, weight training, women's health, women's studies, world history, world literature, writing.

Graduation Requirements Arts and fine arts (art, music, dance, drama), English, foreign language, mathematics, physical education (includes health), science, social studies (includes history). Community service is required.

Special Academic Programs 11 Advanced Placement exams for which test preparation is offered; honors section; independent study.

College Admission Counseling 95 students graduated in 2011; 94 went to college, including Eckerd College; Elon University; Emory University; University of Georgia. Other: 1 entered a postgraduate year.

Student Life Upper grades have student council, honor system. Discipline rests equally with students and faculty.

Tuition and Aid Day student tuition: $19,563. Tuition installment plan (bank-arranged tuition loan program). Need-based tuition assistance available. In 2011–12, 18% of upper-school students received aid. Total amount of financial aid awarded in 2011–12: $1,156,509.

Admissions Traditional secondary-level entrance grade is 9. Deadline for receipt of application materials: February 1. Application fee required: $75. On-campus interview required.

Athletics Interscholastic: baseball (boys), basketball (b,g), cross-country running (b,g), diving (b,g), soccer (b,g), softball (g), swimming and diving (b,g), tennis (b,g), track and field (b,g), ultimate Frisbee (b,g), volleyball (g); coed interscholastic: golf, ultimate Frisbee; coed intramural: aerobics, basketball, bicycling, bowling, fitness, flag football, hiking/backpacking, lacrosse, outdoor education, soccer, softball, tai chi, ultimate Frisbee, yoga. 2 PE instructors, 1 athletic trainer.

Computers Computers are regularly used in art, English, foreign language, graphic arts, history, journalism, mathematics, music, science classes. Computer network features include on-campus library services, Internet access, wireless campus network, Internet filtering or blocking technology, technology assistant program, computer borrowing program for students, technology courses. Campus intranet, student e-mail accounts, and computer access in designated common areas are available to students. The school has a published electronic and media policy.

Contact Admissions Office. 404-270-2312. Fax: 404-270-2312. E-mail: admissions@paideiaschool.org. Web site: www.paideiaschool.org

PALMA SCHOOL

919 Iverson Street
Salinas, California 93901

Head of School: Br. Patrick D. Dunne, CFC

General Information Boys' day college-preparatory and religious studies school, affiliated with Roman Catholic Church. Grades 7–12. Founded: 1951. Setting: suburban. Nearest major city is San Jose. 25-acre campus. 16 buildings on campus. Approved or accredited by Western Association of Schools and Colleges, Western Catholic Education Association, and California Department of Education. Endowment: $200,000. Total enrollment: 534. Upper school average class size: 25. Upper school faculty-student ratio: 1:15. Upper School students typically attend 5 days per week.

Upper School Student Profile Grade 9: 116 students (116 boys); Grade 10: 102 students (102 boys); Grade 11: 107 students (107 boys); Grade 12: 77 students (77 boys). 69% of students are Roman Catholic.

Faculty School total: 31. In upper school: 26 men, 5 women; 19 have advanced degrees.

Subjects Offered Algebra, American history, American literature, anatomy, art, art history, band, biology, business, calculus, calculus-AP, chemistry, Chinese, Christian and Hebrew scripture, church history, civics, community service, computer applications, computer art, computer math, computer multimedia, computer programming, computer programming-AP, computer science, computer-aided design, creative writing, debate, digital art, driver education, earth science, economics, English, English language and composition-AP, English literature, English literature-AP, ethics, European history, European history-AP, expository writing, film, film studies, fine arts, French, geography, geometry, government/civics, grammar, health, health education, history, honors algebra, honors geometry, Japanese, jazz ensemble, journalism, Latin, mathematics, music, participation in sports, physical education, physical science, physics, pre-calculus, psychology, religion, Russian, Russian literature, science, social studies, Spanish, Spanish language-AP, speech, statistics-AP, student government, theology, trigonometry, typing, U.S. government and politics-AP, U.S. history-AP, video film production, world history, world literature, world religions, writing.

Graduation Requirements Advanced biology, arts and fine arts (art, music, dance, drama), English, foreign language, mathematics, physical education (includes health), religion (includes Bible studies and theology), science, social studies (includes history), religious retreat (8th, 9th, 10th grades), 60 hours of community service, must take the ACT College Entrance Exam.

Special Academic Programs Advanced Placement exam preparation; honors section; study at local college for college credit.

College Admission Counseling 115 students graduated in 2012; 111 went to college, including California Polytechnic State University, San Luis Obispo; California State University, Fresno; California State University, Monterey Bay; Saint Mary's College of California; Santa Clara University; University of California, Davis. Other: 2 went to work, 2 entered military service.

Student Life Upper grades have specified standards of dress, student council, honor system. Discipline rests primarily with faculty. Attendance at religious services is required.

Summer Programs Remediation, enrichment, advancement programs offered; session focuses on remediation and advancement; held on campus; accepts boys and girls; open to students from other schools. 150 students usually enrolled. 2013 schedule: June 15 to July 25. Application deadline: March 1.

Tuition and Aid Day student tuition: $9900. Tuition installment plan (Insured Tuition Payment Plan, monthly payment plans, 2-payment plan). Merit scholarship grants, need-based scholarship grants available. In 2012–13, 15% of upper-school students received aid. Total amount of financial aid awarded in 2012–13: $229,000.

Admissions Traditional secondary-level entrance grade is 9. For fall 2012, 65 students applied for upper-level admission, 45 were accepted, 40 enrolled. ETS high school placement exam and ETS HSPT (closed) required. Deadline for receipt of application materials: none. Application fee required: $75. On-campus interview required.

Athletics Interscholastic: baseball, basketball, cross-country running, diving, football, golf, soccer, swimming and diving, track and field, volleyball, water polo, wrestling; intramural: basketball, indoor soccer. 4 PE instructors, 15 coaches, 1 athletic trainer.

Computers Computers are regularly used in art, economics, English, foreign language, history, mathematics, multimedia, music, newspaper, photography, science, social sciences, video film production, writing, yearbook classes. Computer network features include on-campus library services, online commercial services, Internet access, wireless campus network, Internet filtering or blocking technology. Computer access in designated common areas is available to students. Students grades are available online. The school has a published electronic and media policy.

Contact Mr. Chris Dalman, Director of Admissions. 831-422-6391. Fax: 831-422-5065. E-mail: dalman@palmahs.org. Web site: www.palmahs.org

PALMER TRINITY SCHOOL

7900 Southwest 176th Street
Palmetto Bay, Florida 33157

Head of School: Sean Murphy

General Information Coeducational day college-preparatory, arts, religious studies, technology, and ESL school, affiliated with Episcopal Church. Grades 6–12. Founded: 1972. Setting: suburban. Nearest major city is Miami. 55-acre campus. 10 buildings on campus. Approved or accredited by Florida Council of Independent Schools, National Association of Episcopal Schools, Southern Association of Colleges and Schools, Southern Association of Independent Schools, and Florida Department of Education. Member of National Association of Independent Schools and Secondary School Admission Test Board. Endowment: $5 million. Total enrollment: 660. Upper school average class size: 13. Upper school faculty-student ratio: 1:50. There are 175 required school days per year for Upper School students. Upper School students typically attend 5 days per week. The average school day consists of 6 hours.

Upper School Student Profile Grade 9: 100 students (48 boys, 52 girls); Grade 10: 93 students (45 boys, 48 girls); Grade 11: 105 students (42 boys, 63 girls); Grade 12: 83 students (40 boys, 43 girls). 10% of students are members of Episcopal Church.

Faculty School total: 89. In upper school: 22 men, 33 women; 55 have advanced degrees.

Subjects Offered Algebra, American government, American studies, art, art-AP, Basic programming, biology, biology-AP, British literature, calculus, calculus-AP, ceramics, chemistry, chemistry-AP, choir, computer science, concert band, creative writing, dance, drama, earth science, ecology, economics, English, English language and composition-AP, English literature, English literature and composition-AP, environmental studies, ESL, European history, European history-AP, film, fine arts, forensics, French, French language-AP, geometry, global studies, guitar, health and wellness, history, honors algebra, honors English, honors geometry, honors U.S. history, honors world history, journalism, keyboarding, literature, macroeconomics-AP, marine biology, mathematics, model United Nations, multimedia, music, newspaper, physical education, physical science, physics, physics-AP, pre-algebra, pre-calculus, psychology, religion, religion and culture, science, sculpture, Spanish, Spanish language-AP, Spanish literature-AP, theater, U.S. history, U.S. history-AP, United States government-AP, world history, world literature, yearbook.

Graduation Requirements 1 1/2 elective credits, arts and fine arts (art, music, dance, drama), computer programming, English, foreign language, history, humanities, mathematics, physical education (includes health), religious studies, science, minimum 20 hours of community service per year.

Special Academic Programs 21 Advanced Placement exams for which test preparation is offered; honors section; accelerated programs; independent study; term-away projects; study at local college for college credit; study abroad; academic accommodation for the gifted, the musically talented, and the artistically talented; ESL (27 students enrolled).

College Admission Counseling 85 students graduated in 2012; all went to college, including Boston College; Florida State University; Texas Christian University; The George Washington University; University of Florida; University of Miami. Mean SAT critical reading: 616, mean SAT math: 618, mean SAT writing: 628, mean combined SAT: 1872, mean composite ACT: 27.

Student Life Upper grades have uniform requirement, student council, honor system. Discipline rests equally with students and faculty.

Summer Programs Remediation, enrichment, advancement, ESL, sports, art/fine arts, rigorous outdoor training, computer instruction programs offered; session focuses on academics; held on campus; accepts boys and girls; open to students from other schools. 100 students usually enrolled. 2013 schedule: June 17 to July 26. Application deadline: May 1.

Tuition and Aid Day student tuition: $26,000. Tuition installment plan (Insured Tuition Payment Plan, monthly payment plans). Need-based scholarship grants available. In 2012–13, 17% of upper-school students received aid. Total amount of financial aid awarded in 2012–13: $940,300.

Admissions Traditional secondary-level entrance grade is 9. For fall 2012, 119 students applied for upper-level admission, 64 were accepted, 39 enrolled. ACT, ISEE, PSAT and SAT for applicants to grade 11 and 12, SLEP for foreign students or SSAT required. Deadline for receipt of application materials: February 1. Application fee required: $115. On-campus interview required.

Athletics Interscholastic: baseball (boys), basketball (b,g), cheering (g), cross-country running (b,g), dance (g), football (b), golf (b,g), lacrosse (b,g), soccer (b,g), softball (g), strength & conditioning (b), tennis (b,g), track and field (b,g), volleyball (g), wrestling (b); intramural: basketball (b,g), dance team (g), floor hockey (b), hockey (b), in-line hockey (b), in-line skating (b), rugby (b), volleyball (g), weight training (b,g); coed intramural: climbing, ice hockey, outdoor education, physical training, rock climbing, strength & conditioning, weight training. 3 PE instructors, 20 coaches, 1 athletic trainer.

Computers Computers are regularly used in all academic, art, college planning, design, desktop publishing, graphic arts, library skills classes. Computer network features include on-campus library services, online commercial services, Internet access, wireless campus network, Internet filtering or blocking technology, laptop program in all academic areas. Student e-mail accounts are available to students. Students grades are available online. The school has a published electronic and media policy.

Contact Danny Reynolds, Director of Admission, College Counseling, and Financial Aid. 305-969-4204. Fax: 305-251-0607. E-mail: dreynolds@palmertrinity.org. Web site: www.palmertrinity.org

PALO ALTO PREPARATORY SCHOOL

2462 Wyandotte Street
Mountain View, California 94043

Head of School: Christopher Morley Keck

General Information Coeducational day and distance learning college-preparatory school. Grades 8–12. Distance learning grades 9–12. Founded: 1986. Setting: suburban. Nearest major city is Palo Alto. 1 building on campus. Approved or accredited by Western Association of Schools and Colleges and California Department of Education. Total enrollment: 65. Upper school average class size: 8. Upper school faculty-student ratio: 1:6. There are 180 required school days per year for Upper School students. Upper School students typically attend 5 days per week. The average school day consists of 6 hours.

Upper School Student Profile Grade 8: 2 students (2 boys); Grade 9: 16 students (11 boys, 5 girls); Grade 10: 15 students (9 boys, 6 girls); Grade 11: 19 students (11 boys, 8 girls); Grade 12: 19 students (12 boys, 7 girls).

Faculty School total: 11. In upper school: 7 men, 4 women; 5 have advanced degrees.

Subjects Offered 3-dimensional design.

Graduation Requirements Senior Project.

Special Academic Programs 3 Advanced Placement exams for which test preparation is offered; accelerated programs; independent study.

College Admission Counseling 17 students graduated in 2012; 16 went to college, including California State University, Dominguez Hills. Other: 1 had other specific plans.

Student Life Upper grades have specified standards of dress, student council, honor system. Discipline rests primarily with faculty.

Summer Programs Remediation, rigorous outdoor training programs offered; session focuses on outdoor excursions and classes for makeup or to get ahead; held on campus; accepts boys and girls; open to students from other schools. 40 students usually enrolled. 2013 schedule: July 1 to August 9. Application deadline: May 15.

Tuition and Aid Tuition installment plan (SMART Tuition Payment Plan). Need-based scholarship grants available.

Admissions Traditional secondary-level entrance grade is 8. Deadline for receipt of application materials: none. No application fee required. On-campus interview required.

Computers Computer network features include Internet access, wireless campus network, Internet filtering or blocking technology. Campus intranet and student e-mail accounts are available to students. Students grades are available online. The school has a published electronic and media policy.

Contact Lisa Ohearn-Keck, Dean of Students. 650-493-7071 Ext. 102. Fax: 650-493-7073. E-mail: lisa@paloaltoprep.com. Web site: www.paloaltoprep.com

PARADISE ADVENTIST ACADEMY

5699 Academy Drive
PO Box 2169
Paradise, California 95969

Head of School: Mr. Lance Taggart

General Information Coeducational day college-preparatory school, affiliated with Seventh-day Adventists. Grades K–12. Founded: 1908. Setting: small town. Nearest major city is Sacramento. 12-acre campus. 6 buildings on campus. Approved or accredited by Western Association of Schools and Colleges and California Department of Education. Endowment: $200,000. Total enrollment: 196. Upper school average class size: 20. Upper school faculty-student ratio: 1:8. There are 180 required school days per year for Upper School students. Upper School students typically attend 5 days per week. The average school day consists of 8 hours and 5 minutes.

Upper School Student Profile Grade 9: 15 students (11 boys, 4 girls); Grade 10: 26 students (11 boys, 15 girls); Grade 11: 14 students (8 boys, 6 girls); Grade 12: 26 students (15 boys, 11 girls). 80% of students are Seventh-day Adventists.

Faculty School total: 20. In upper school: 7 men, 3 women; 6 have advanced degrees.

Subjects Offered Advanced biology, advanced computer applications, advanced math, algebra, American government, American history, auto mechanics, band, basketball, Bible, biology, career education, carpentry, chemistry, choir, computer applications, computers, drama, earth science, English, geometry, health, keyboarding, military history, physical education, physical science, physics, pre-algebra, pre-calculus, Spanish, speech, U.S. government, U.S. history, volleyball, weightlifting, woodworking, world history, yearbook.

Graduation Requirements Advanced computer applications, algebra, American government, American history, arts and fine arts (art, music, dance, drama), Bible, biology, career and personal planning, career education, chemistry, computer literacy, electives, English, keyboarding, languages, life skills, physical education (includes health), physics, Spanish, world history, 100 hours of community service, 20 credits of fine arts, 100 hours of work experience.

Special Academic Programs Accelerated programs; independent study.

College Admission Counseling 21 students graduated in 2012; all went to college, including Azusa Pacific University; Concordia University; Pacific Union College; Pepperdine University; Southern Adventist University; Walla Walla University. Median SAT critical reading: 620, median SAT math: 530, median SAT writing: 530, median combined SAT: 1750, median composite ACT: 27. 54% scored over 600 on SAT critical reading, 38% scored over 600 on SAT math, 38% scored over 600 on SAT writing, 31% scored over 1800 on combined SAT, 80% scored over 26 on composite ACT.

Student Life Upper grades have specified standards of dress, student council. Discipline rests primarily with faculty. Attendance at religious services is required.

Summer Programs Sports programs offered; session focuses on basketball; held on campus; accepts boys and girls; open to students from other schools. 20 students usually enrolled. 2013 schedule: June 17 to June 21. Application deadline: June 17.

Tuition and Aid Day student tuition: $8450. Tuition installment plan (monthly payment plans, individually arranged payment plans, By year-$50 off, 10 or 12 month plan, Automatic Bank withdrawal). Tuition reduction for siblings, merit scholarship grants, need-based scholarship grants, paying campus jobs available. In 2012–13, 25% of upper-school students received aid; total upper-school merit-scholarship money awarded: $800. Total amount of financial aid awarded in 2012–13: $50,000.

Admissions Traditional secondary-level entrance grade is 9. For fall 2012, 9 students applied for upper-level admission, 9 were accepted, 9 enrolled. Any standardized test required. Deadline for receipt of application materials: August 17. Application fee required: $50. Interview required.

Athletics Interscholastic: basketball (boys, girls), cheering (g), football (b,g), soccer (b), volleyball (g). 1 PE instructor, 2 coaches.

Computers Computers are regularly used in all academic classes. Computer network features include on-campus library services, Internet access, wireless campus network, Internet filtering or blocking technology. Campus intranet, student e-mail accounts, and computer access in designated common areas are available to students. Students grades are available online. The school has a published electronic and media policy.

Contact Mrs. Brenda Muth, Registrar. 530-877-6540 Ext. 3010. Fax: 530-877-0870. E-mail: bmuth@mypaa.net. Web site: www.mypaa.net

PARISH EPISCOPAL SCHOOL

4101 Sigma Road
Dallas, Texas 75244

Head of School: Mr. Dave Monaco

General Information Coeducational day college-preparatory school, affiliated with Episcopal Church. Grades PK–12. Founded: 1972. Setting: suburban. 50-acre campus. 1 building on campus. Approved or accredited by Independent Schools Association of the Southwest, Southwest Association of Episcopal Schools, and Texas Department of Education. Member of National Association of Independent Schools. Endowment: $10 million. Total enrollment: 1,100. Upper school average class size: 18.

Upper School Student Profile 25% of students are members of Episcopal Church.

Special Academic Programs Honors section.

Student Life Upper grades have uniform requirement, student council, honor system. Discipline rests primarily with faculty. Attendance at religious services is required.

Summer Programs Enrichment, advancement, sports, art/fine arts, computer instruction programs offered; held on campus; accepts boys and girls; open to students from other schools. 2013 schedule: June 1 to August 3. Application deadline: none.

Tuition and Aid Day student tuition: $22,000. Guaranteed tuition plan. Tuition installment plan (Insured Tuition Payment Plan, FACTS Tuition Payment Plan). Need-based scholarship grants available.

Admissions Deadline for receipt of application materials: January 18. Application fee required: $150. Interview required.

Athletics Interscholastic: baseball (boys), basketball (b,g), cheering (g), dance (b,g), dance squad (b,g), drill team (g), field hockey (g), football (b), golf (b,g), lacrosse (b,g), soccer (b,g), softball (g), strength & conditioning (b,g), swimming and diving (b,g), track and field (b,g), volleyball (g), weight training (b,g), winter soccer (b,g); intramural: aerobics/dance (g), dance (g); coed interscholastic: cross-country running, golf, tennis; coed intramural: physical fitness, strength & conditioning, weight training.

Computers Computer resources include on-campus library services, Internet access, Internet filtering or blocking technology. Campus intranet, student e-mail accounts, and computer access in designated common areas are available to students. Students grades are available online. The school has a published electronic and media policy.

Contact Ms. Gina Wallace, Admission Coordinator. 972-239-8011. Fax: 972-991-1237. E-mail: gwallace@parishepiscopal.org. Web site: www.parishepiscopal.org

THE PARK SCHOOL OF BALTIMORE

2425 Old Court Road
Baltimore, Maryland 21208

Head of School: Mr. Daniel Paradis

General Information Coeducational day college-preparatory school. Grades PK–12. Founded: 1912. Setting: suburban. 100-acre campus. 4 buildings on campus. Approved or accredited by Association of Independent Maryland Schools and Maryland Department of Education. Member of National Association of Independent Schools. Endowment: $26.9 million. Total enrollment: 850. Upper school average class size: 15. Upper school faculty-student ratio: 1:7. There are 170 required school days per year for Upper School students. Upper School students typically attend 5 days per week. The average school day consists of 7 hours.

Faculty School total: 120. In upper school: 36 have advanced degrees.

Subjects Offered 20th century world history, 3-dimensional art, acting, advanced chemistry, advanced math, anatomy, animal behavior, architectural drawing, art history, astronomy, audio visual/media, biochemistry, biology, British literature, calculus, ceramics, chemistry, Chinese, Chinese history, Chinese literature, choir, choral music, computer animation, computer programming, debate, design, digital art, digital music, digital photography, discrete mathematics, drama workshop, drawing, economics, English, English composition, English literature, entomology, environmental science, equality and freedom, etymology, European history, film studies, filmmaking, French, French studies, functions, genetics, Greek drama, health education, human sexuality, illustration, independent study, Irish studies, Islamic studies, jazz ensemble, jewelry making, keyboarding, Latin American studies, madrigals, mathematics, Middle East, modern languages, modern politics, multicultural studies, music composition, music performance, musical theater, organic chemistry, painting, photography, physical education, physics, playwriting and directing, poetry, publications, sculpture, senior project, set design, Shakespeare, social justice, Spanish, Spanish literature, statistics, studio art, theater, theater arts, U.S. history, visual and performing arts, vocal ensemble, Web site design, women in literature, woodworking, world religions, World-Wide-Web publishing, writing workshop.

Graduation Requirements Arts and fine arts (art, music, dance, drama), English, history, mathematics, modern languages, physical education (includes health), science.

Special Academic Programs Advanced Placement exam preparation; independent study; term-away projects; study abroad; academic accommodation for the gifted, the musically talented, and the artistically talented.

College Admission Counseling 82 students graduated in 2012; 81 went to college, including Emory University; New York University; Tulane University; University of Maryland, College Park; Yale University. Other: 1 had other specific plans. 78% scored over 600 on SAT critical reading, 75% scored over 600 on SAT math, 75% scored over 600 on SAT writing, 75% scored over 1800 on combined SAT, 79% scored over 26 on composite ACT.

Student Life Upper grades have student council. Discipline rests equally with students and faculty.

Tuition and Aid Day student tuition: $25,420. Tuition installment plan (The Tuition Plan, Insured Tuition Payment Plan, FACTS Tuition Payment Plan, monthly payment plans). Need-based scholarship grants available. In 2012–13, 31% of upper-school students received aid. Total amount of financial aid awarded in 2012–13: $1,279,390.

Admissions Traditional secondary-level entrance grade is 9. For fall 2012, 90 students applied for upper-level admission, 55 were accepted, 29 enrolled. Deadline for receipt of application materials: January 1. Application fee required: $50. Interview required.

Athletics Interscholastic: baseball (boys), basketball (b,g), cross-country running (b,g), field hockey (g), indoor soccer (g), lacrosse (b,g), soccer (b,g), softball (g), squash (b,g), tennis (b,g), winter soccer (g); coed intramural: climbing, Frisbee, strength & conditioning, ultimate Frisbee, wall climbing, yoga. 3 PE instructors, 30 coaches, 1 athletic trainer.
Computers Computers are regularly used in art, computer applications, creative writing, desktop publishing, English, foreign language, French, graphic design, history, journalism, library skills, mathematics, media production, music, music technology, news writing, newspaper, photojournalism, programming, publications, science, Spanish, theater, theater arts, video film production, woodworking, writing, writing, yearbook classes. Computer network features include on-campus library services, online commercial services, Internet access, wireless campus network, Internet filtering or blocking technology, access to course materials and assignments through faculty Web pages and wikis, discounted software purchase plan. Campus intranet, student e-mail accounts, and computer access in designated common areas are available to students. Students grades are available online. The school has a published electronic and media policy.
Contact Rachel Hockett, Administrative Assistant. 410-339-4130. Fax: 410-339-4127. E-mail: admission@parkschool.net. Web site: www.parkschool.net

THE PARK SCHOOL OF BUFFALO

4625 Harlem Road
Snyder, New York 14226

Head of School: Christopher J. Lauricella

General Information Coeducational day college-preparatory and arts school. Grades PK–12. Founded: 1912. Setting: suburban. Nearest major city is Buffalo. 34-acre campus. 15 buildings on campus. Approved or accredited by National Independent Private Schools Association, New York Department of Education, New York State Association of Independent Schools, and New York Department of Education. Member of National Association of Independent Schools. Endowment: $1.3 million. Total enrollment: 250. Upper school average class size: 14. Upper school faculty-student ratio: 1:8. There are 167 required school days per year for Upper School students. Upper School students typically attend 5 days per week. The average school day consists of 7 hours.
Upper School Student Profile Grade 9: 26 students (12 boys, 14 girls); Grade 10: 28 students (15 boys, 13 girls); Grade 11: 30 students (23 boys, 7 girls); Grade 12: 26 students (10 boys, 16 girls).
Faculty School total: 39. In upper school: 13 men, 12 women; 20 have advanced degrees.
Subjects Offered Advanced studio art-AP, algebra, American history, American history-AP, American literature, American literature-AP, art, band, biology, biology-AP, calculus, calculus-AP, ceramics, chemistry, chorus, college admission preparation, college counseling, community service, computer applications, computer programming, critical thinking, drama, drawing, economics, English, environmental science, fine arts, forensics, French, French language-AP, freshman seminar, geometry, government/civics, health, junior and senior seminars, marine biology, media, media production, metalworking, music, orchestra, organic chemistry, photography, physical education, physics, senior project, senior seminar, senior thesis, sophomore skills, Spanish, Spanish-AP, studio art-AP, trigonometry, U.S. government and politics-AP, woodworking, world history, yearbook.
Graduation Requirements Arts and fine arts (art, music, dance, drama), computer science, English, foreign language, mathematics, physical education (includes health), science, senior project, senior thesis, social sciences, social studies (includes history). Community service is required.
Special Academic Programs Advanced Placement exam preparation; honors section; accelerated programs; independent study; study at local college for college credit; study abroad; academic accommodation for the gifted; ESL (23 students enrolled).
College Admission Counseling 27 students graduated in 2012; 26 went to college, including Bard College; Goucher College; Temple University; The Johns Hopkins University; University at Buffalo, the State University of New York; Wesleyan University. Other: 1 went to work. Median SAT critical reading: 611, median SAT math: 567, median SAT writing: 591, median combined SAT: 1752, median composite ACT: 24. 50% scored over 600 on SAT critical reading, 43% scored over 600 on SAT math, 52% scored over 600 on SAT writing, 35% scored over 1800 on combined SAT, 55% scored over 26 on composite ACT.
Student Life Upper grades have specified standards of dress, student council, honor system. Discipline rests equally with students and faculty.
Summer Programs Remediation, enrichment, advancement, ESL, sports, art/fine arts programs offered; session focuses on recreational day camp, basketball camps, soccer camp, ESL, summer scholars; held on campus; accepts boys and girls; open to students from other schools. 585 students usually enrolled. 2013 schedule: July 6 to August 14. Application deadline: January 16.
Tuition and Aid Day student tuition: $18,475–$19,600. Tuition installment plan (Insured Tuition Payment Plan, FACTS Tuition Payment Plan). Tuition reduction for siblings, merit scholarship grants, need-based scholarship grants available. In 2012–13, 59% of upper-school students received aid; total upper-school merit-scholarship money awarded: $58,238. Total amount of financial aid awarded in 2012–13: $567,832.
Admissions Traditional secondary-level entrance grade is 9. For fall 2012, 50 students applied for upper-level admission, 37 were accepted, 28 enrolled. ERB Reading and Math, Otis-Lennon School Ability Test or TOEFL required. Deadline for receipt of application materials: none. Application fee required: $50. Interview required.
Athletics Interscholastic: basketball (boys, girls), bowling (b,g), golf (b), lacrosse (b), soccer (b,g), tennis (b,g); coed interscholastic: soccer; coed intramural: bicycling, cooperative games, cross-country running, fitness, flag football, floor hockey, Frisbee, hiking/backpacking, indoor soccer, outdoor activities, outdoor adventure, outdoor education, outdoor recreation, outdoor skills, outdoors, physical fitness, running, skiing (downhill), snowboarding, snowshoeing, soccer, strength & conditioning, weight lifting, weight training, winter walking, yoga. 2 PE instructors, 14 coaches.
Computers Computers are regularly used in creative writing, current events, data processing, English, graphic arts, independent study, mathematics, media, media arts, media services, newspaper, photography, science, word processing, yearbook classes. Computer network features include on-campus library services, online commercial services, Internet access, wireless campus network, Internet filtering or blocking technology. Campus intranet, student e-mail accounts, and computer access in designated common areas are available to students. Students grades are available online. The school has a published electronic and media policy.
Contact Marnie Cerrato, Director of Enrollment Management. 716-839-1242 Ext. 107. Fax: 716-408-9511. E-mail: mcerrato@theparkschool.org. Web site: www.theparkschool.org

PARKVIEW ADVENTIST ACADEMY

5505 College Avenue
Lacombe, Alberta T4L 2E7, Canada

Head of School: Ms. Angie Bishop

General Information Coeducational boarding and day college-preparatory, general academic, arts, vocational, religious studies, and technology school, affiliated with Seventh-day Adventist Church. Grades 10–12. Founded: 1907. Setting: small town. Nearest major city is Edmonton, Canada. Students are housed in single-sex by floor dormitories. Approved or accredited by National Council for Private School Accreditation and Alberta Department of Education. Language of instruction: English. Upper school average class size: 20. Upper school faculty-student ratio: 1:10. There are 188 required school days per year for Upper School students. Upper School students typically attend 5 days per week. The average school day consists of 5 hours and 50 minutes.
Upper School Student Profile Grade 10: 30 students (15 boys, 15 girls); Grade 11: 32 students (17 boys, 15 girls); Grade 12: 45 students (24 boys, 21 girls). 40% of students are boarding students. 70% are province residents. 4 provinces are represented in upper school student body. 1% are international students. International students from Rwanda; 3 other countries represented in student body. 80% of students are Seventh-day Adventists.
Faculty School total: 9. In upper school: 3 men, 6 women; 2 have advanced degrees; 1 resides on campus.
Subjects Offered Advanced math, art, arts, band, biology, career and technology systems, chemistry, choir, choral music, English, fine arts, foods, French, home economics, industrial arts, instrumental music, language arts, mathematics, mechanics, metalworking, music, photography, physical education, physics, religion, religious studies, science, social sciences, social studies, welding, woodworking.
Graduation Requirements Computer processing, keyboarding, physical education (includes health), word processing.
Special Academic Programs ESL.
College Admission Counseling 36 went to college. Other: 3 went to work.
Student Life Upper grades have specified standards of dress, student council, honor system. Discipline rests primarily with faculty. Attendance at religious services is required.
Tuition and Aid Day student tuition: CAN$5657; 7-day tuition and room/board: CAN$11,724. Tuition installment plan (monthly payment plans, individually arranged payment plans). Tuition reduction for siblings, merit scholarship grants available.
Admissions Traditional secondary-level entrance grade is 10. Deadline for receipt of application materials: none. Application fee required: CAN$20. Interview required.
Athletics Interscholastic: aquatics (boys), basketball (b,g), hockey (b), soccer (b), volleyball (b,g); intramural: basketball (b,g), football (b), softball (g); coed interscholastic: baseball, basketball, soccer; coed intramural: baseball, basketball. 1 PE instructor, 3 coaches.
Computers Computer network features include on-campus library services, Internet access, wireless campus network, Internet filtering or blocking technology. Student e-mail accounts are available to students. Students grades are available online. The school has a published electronic and media policy.
Contact Mr. Rodney Jamieson, Vice Principal. 403-782-3381 Ext. 4111. Fax: 866-931-2652. E-mail: rjamieso@paa.ca. Web site: www.paa.ca/

THE PATHWAY SCHOOL

Norristown, Pennsylvania
See Special Needs Schools section.

PATTEN ACADEMY OF CHRISTIAN EDUCATION

2433 Coolidge Avenue
Oakland, California 94601

Head of School: Dr. Sharon Anderson

General Information Coeducational day college-preparatory, arts, religious studies, and bilingual studies school, affiliated with Christian faith. Grades K–12. Founded: 1944. Setting: urban. Nearest major city is San Francisco. 3 buildings on campus. Approved or accredited by Western Association of Schools and Colleges and California Department of Education. Total enrollment: 117. Upper school average class size: 11. Upper school faculty-student ratio: 1:6. There are 185 required school days per year for Upper School students. Upper School students typically attend 5 days per week. The average school day consists of 6 hours and 45 minutes.

Upper School Student Profile Grade 9: 12 students (7 boys, 5 girls); Grade 10: 11 students (6 boys, 5 girls); Grade 11: 12 students (6 boys, 6 girls); Grade 12: 9 students (4 boys, 5 girls). 11% of students are Christian faith.

Faculty School total: 14. In upper school: 5 men, 2 women; 6 have advanced degrees.

Subjects Offered Algebra, American literature, art, arts, band, Bible studies, biology, chemistry, choir, community service, computer science, economics, English, English literature, fine arts, geometry, health, instrumental music, introduction to literature, language arts, life skills, mathematics, music, physical education, physical science, physics, piano, pre-calculus, religion, science, social studies, Spanish, strings, U.S. government, U.S. history, vocal music, world geography, world history, world literature, writing.

Graduation Requirements Arts and fine arts (art, music, dance, drama), environmental science, foreign language, mathematics, science, social studies (includes history). Community service is required.

College Admission Counseling 12 students graduated in 2012; 11 went to college, including California State University, East Bay; Morehouse College; Patten University; Saint Mary's College of California; University of California, Berkeley. Other: 1 went to work.

Student Life Upper grades have uniform requirement, student council, honor system. Discipline rests primarily with faculty. Attendance at religious services is required.

Tuition and Aid Day student tuition: $5999. Tuition installment plan (monthly payment plans). Tuition reduction for siblings, need-based scholarship grants available. In 2012–13, 27% of upper-school students received aid. Total amount of financial aid awarded in 2012–13: $23,797.

Admissions Traditional secondary-level entrance grade is 9. For fall 2012, 10 students applied for upper-level admission, 9 were accepted, 9 enrolled. Deadline for receipt of application materials: none. Application fee required: $50. On-campus interview required.

Athletics Interscholastic: basketball (boys, girls), volleyball (b,g). 1 PE instructor.

Computers Computer network features include Internet access.

Contact Mrs. Sharon Moncher, Coordinator. 510-533-3121. Fax: 510-535-9381. Web site: www.pattenacademy.org

PEDDIE SCHOOL

201 South Main Street
Hightstown, New Jersey 08520

Head of School: John F. Green

General Information Coeducational boarding and day college-preparatory, arts, and technology school. Grades 9–PG. Founded: 1864. Setting: small town. Nearest major city is Princeton. Students are housed in single-sex dormitories. 230-acre campus. 53 buildings on campus. Approved or accredited by Middle States Association of Colleges and Schools, The Association of Boarding Schools, and New Jersey Department of Education. Member of National Association of Independent Schools and Secondary School Admission Test Board. Endowment: $278 million. Total enrollment: 550. Upper school average class size: 12. Upper school faculty-student ratio: 1:6. Upper School students typically attend 6 days per week. The average school day consists of 7 hours.

Upper School Student Profile Grade 9: 114 students (61 boys, 53 girls); Grade 10: 133 students (71 boys, 62 girls); Grade 11: 144 students (73 boys, 71 girls); Grade 12: 141 students (70 boys, 71 girls); Postgraduate: 16 students (13 boys, 3 girls). 63% of students are boarding students. 24 states are represented in upper school student body. 13% are international students. International students from China, Hong Kong, Japan, Republic of Korea, Thailand, and United Kingdom; 34 other countries represented in student body.

Faculty School total: 84. In upper school: 48 men, 36 women; 58 have advanced degrees; 72 reside on campus.

Subjects Offered Acting, African studies, algebra, American history, American literature, American studies, anatomy, architecture, art, art history, art history-AP, Asian studies, astronomy, Bible studies, biology, biology-AP, calculus, calculus-AP, chemistry, Chinese, comedy, comparative religion, computer programming, computer science, creative writing, debate, digital imaging, DNA, DNA science lab, drama, earth science, ecology, economics, English, English literature, environmental science, environmental science-AP, European history, European history-AP, expository writing, film history, fine arts, forensics, French, French language-AP, French literature-AP, geometry, global issues, global science, government/civics, health, history, information technology, Latin, Latin-AP, mathematics, Middle East, music, music theory-AP, neuroscience, philosophy, photography, physical education, physics, physics-AP, psychology, psychology-AP, robotics, science, Shakespeare, social studies, Spanish, Spanish language-AP, Spanish literature-AP, speech, statistics, statistics-AP, studio art-AP, theater, trigonometry, U.S. history, U.S. history-AP, video film production, world history, world literature, World War I, World War II, writing.

Graduation Requirements Arts and fine arts (art, music, dance, drama), computer science, English, foreign language, history, mathematics, physical education (includes health), science. Community service is required.

Special Academic Programs Advanced Placement exam preparation; honors section; independent study; term-away projects; study abroad.

College Admission Counseling 140 students graduated in 2012; all went to college, including Carnegie Mellon University; Cornell University; Princeton University; The George Washington University; The Johns Hopkins University; University of Pennsylvania.

Student Life Upper grades have specified standards of dress, student council. Discipline rests primarily with faculty.

Summer Programs Enrichment, advancement, sports, art/fine arts programs offered; session focuses on enrichment; held on campus; accepts boys and girls; open to students from other schools. 175 students usually enrolled. 2013 schedule: June 21 to August 2. Application deadline: none.

Tuition and Aid Day student tuition: $39,000; 7-day tuition and room/board: $47,500. Tuition installment plan (Academic Management Services Plan, monthly payment plans, individually arranged payment plans). Merit scholarship grants, need-based scholarship grants, need-based loans available. In 2012–13, 40% of upper-school students received aid; total upper-school merit-scholarship money awarded: $70,000. Total amount of financial aid awarded in 2012–13: $5,000,000.

Admissions Traditional secondary-level entrance grade is 9. For fall 2012, 1,561 students applied for upper-level admission, 310 were accepted, 171 enrolled. ISEE or SSAT required. Deadline for receipt of application materials: January 15. Application fee required: $50. Interview required.

Athletics Interscholastic: baseball (boys), basketball (b,g), crew (b,g), cross-country running (b,g), diving (b,g), field hockey (g), fitness (b,g), football (b), golf (b,g), indoor track & field (b,g), lacrosse (b,g), soccer (b,g), softball (g), strength & conditioning (b,g), swimming and diving (b,g), tennis (b,g), track and field (b,g), winter (indoor) track (b,g), wrestling (b), yoga (b,g); intramural: weight lifting (b,g), weight training (b,g); coed intramural: bicycling, bowling, dance, physical fitness, physical training, softball. 9 coaches, 3 athletic trainers.

Computers Computers are regularly used in English, foreign language, history, mathematics, science classes. Computer network features include on-campus library services, online commercial services, Internet access, wireless campus network, Internet filtering or blocking technology, NewsBank, Britannica, GaleNet, Electric Library. Student e-mail accounts are available to students. Students grades are available online. The school has a published electronic and media policy.

Contact Raymond H. Cabot, Director of Admission. 609-944-7501. Fax: 609-944-7901. E-mail: admission@peddie.org. Web site: www.peddie.org

THE PENNINGTON SCHOOL

112 West Delaware Avenue
Pennington, New Jersey 08534-1601

Head of School: Mrs. Stephanie (Penny) G. Townsend

General Information Coeducational boarding and day college-preparatory and arts school, affiliated with Methodist Church. Boarding grades 8–12, day grades 6–12. Founded: 1838. Setting: small town. Nearest major city is Philadelphia, PA. Students are housed in single-sex by floor dormitories and single-sex dormitories. 54-acre campus. 17 buildings on campus. Approved or accredited by Middle States Association of Colleges and Schools, National Independent Private Schools Association, New Jersey Association of Independent Schools, The Association of Boarding Schools, The College Board, University Senate of United Methodist Church, and New Jersey Department of Education. Member of National Association of Independent Schools and Secondary School Admission Test Board. Endowment: $25 million. Total enrollment: 485. Upper school average class size: 13. Upper school faculty-student ratio: 1:8. There are 180 required school days per year for Upper School students. Upper School students typically attend 5 days per week. The average school day consists of 7 hours.

Upper School Student Profile Grade 9: 89 students (44 boys, 45 girls); Grade 10: 104 students (58 boys, 46 girls); Grade 11: 95 students (56 boys, 39 girls); Grade 12: 100 students (57 boys, 43 girls). 25% of students are boarding students. 66% are state residents. 7 states are represented in upper school student body. 13% are international students. International students from China, Germany, Republic of Korea, South Africa, Taiwan, and Thailand; 10 other countries represented in student body. 5% of students are Methodist.

Faculty School total: 87. In upper school: 31 men, 38 women; 55 have advanced degrees; 49 reside on campus.

Subjects Offered Advanced studio art-AP, advanced TOEFL/grammar, African-American history, algebra, American history, American literature, anatomy, anatomy and physiology, art, bioethics, DNA and culture, biology, British literature-AP, calculus-AP, cheerleading, chemistry, chemistry-AP, Chinese, chorus, computer applications, computer skills, drama, economics, English, English literature, English literature-AP, English-AP, environmental science, ESL, fine arts, forensics, French, French language-AP, genetics, geometry, German, government and politics-AP, Greek, Greek culture, health, history-AP, honors algebra, honors English, honors geometry, honors U.S. history, jazz ensemble, Latin, macroeconomics-AP, music, music history, music theory, organic chemistry, photography, physics, physics-AP, pottery, pre-calculus, psychology, public speaking, religion, robotics, senior internship, Spanish, Spanish literature, Spanish-AP, stage design, stagecraft, technical theater, U.S. government and politics-AP, Web site design, weight training, world history, world history-AP.

Graduation Requirements Algebra, American history, arts and fine arts (art, music, dance, drama), athletics, biology, chemistry, computer education, English, foreign language, geometry, health education, public speaking, religion (includes Bible studies and theology), religion and culture, world history.

Special Academic Programs 18 Advanced Placement exams for which test preparation is offered; honors section; independent study; term-away projects; study at local college for college credit; study abroad; academic accommodation for the gifted; programs in English for dyslexic students; ESL (41 students enrolled).

College Admission Counseling 99 students graduated in 2012; all went to college, including Carnegie Mellon University; Georgetown University; Muhlenberg College; New York University; Penn State University Park; Quinnipiac University. Mean SAT critical reading: 526, mean SAT math: 548, mean SAT writing: 537, mean combined SAT: 1611, mean composite ACT: 24.

Student Life Upper grades have specified standards of dress, student council, honor system. Discipline rests equally with students and faculty. Attendance at religious services is required.

Tuition and Aid Day student tuition: $30,950; 7-day tuition and room/board: $46,100. Tuition installment plan (Key Tuition Payment Plan). Merit scholarship grants, need-based scholarship grants available. In 2012–13, 28% of upper-school students received aid; total upper-school merit-scholarship money awarded: $201,600. Total amount of financial aid awarded in 2012–13: $2,500,000.

Admissions Traditional secondary-level entrance grade is 9. For fall 2012, 501 students applied for upper-level admission, 154 were accepted, 130 enrolled. SSAT or TOEFL required. Deadline for receipt of application materials: February 1. Application fee required: $50. Interview required.

Athletics Interscholastic: baseball (boys), basketball (b,g), cheering (g), field hockey (g), football (b), ice hockey (b), lacrosse (b,g), soccer (b,g), softball (g), tennis (b,g); intramural: aquatics (b,g), bowling (b,g); coed interscholastic: cross-country running, golf, indoor track, judo, swimming and diving, track and field, water polo, weight training, winter (indoor) track; coed intramural: dance team, fitness, physical training, strength & conditioning, weight training. 3 coaches, 2 athletic trainers.

Computers Computers are regularly used in art, college planning, computer applications, creative writing, desktop publishing, graphic design, library, literary magazine, mathematics, music, newspaper, research skills, science, video film production, yearbook classes. Computer network features include on-campus library services, online commercial services, Internet access, wireless campus network, Internet filtering or blocking technology. Campus intranet, student e-mail accounts, and computer access in designated common areas are available to students. Students grades are available online. The school has a published electronic and media policy.

Contact Ms. Grace Megaffin, Admission Office Fellow. 609-737-6128. Fax: 609-730-1405. E-mail: gmegaffin@pennington.org. Web site: www.pennington.org

See Display below and Close-Up on page 610.

PENSACOLA CATHOLIC HIGH SCHOOL

3043 West Scott Street
Pensacola, Florida 32505

Head of School: Sr. Kierstin Martin

General Information Coeducational day college-preparatory and technology school, affiliated with Roman Catholic Church. Grades 9–12. Founded: 1941. Setting: urban. 25-acre campus. 5 buildings on campus. Approved or accredited by Southern Association of Colleges and Schools. Total enrollment: 595. Upper school average class size: 25. Upper school faculty-student ratio: 1:18. The average school day consists of 7 hours.

Upper School Student Profile Grade 9: 147 students (87 boys, 60 girls); Grade 10: 161 students (94 boys, 67 girls); Grade 11: 154 students (87 boys, 67 girls); Grade 12: 133 students (71 boys, 62 girls). 70% of students are Roman Catholic.

Faculty School total: 50. In upper school: 15 men, 35 women; 15 have advanced degrees.

Subjects Offered Advanced math, Advanced Placement courses, algebra, American government, American history, American history-AP, American literature, analysis and differential calculus, analytic geometry, anatomy and physiology, art, art appreciation, arts and crafts, athletics, band, baseball, basketball, Bible, Bible studies, biology, botany, British literature, broadcast journalism, business law, calculus, calculus-AP, campus ministry, Catholic belief and practice, chemistry, Christian ethics, Christian scripture, Christian studies, Christian testament, church history, civics, college counseling, comparative religion, composition, composition-AP, computer applications, computer graphics, consumer mathematics, CPR, creative arts, criminal justice, desktop publishing, digital photography, drawing, earth science, economics, electives, English, English composition, English language and composition-AP, English literature, English literature and composition-AP, environmental science, fabric arts, film appreciation, film history, filmmaking, foreign language, French, general science, genetics, geography, geometry, government, government-AP, grammar, graphic arts, guidance, health education, history, history of the Catholic Church, honors algebra, honors English, honors geometry, honors U.S. history, honors world history, human sexuality, journalism, keyboarding, lab science, library, library assistant, Life of Christ, literature and composition-AP, marine biology, music appreciation, music history, physical education, physical science, physics, pottery, pre-algebra, pre-calculus, probability and statistics, reading, religion, sex education, social studies, Spanish, student government, student publications, telecommunications and the Internet, television, the Web, trigonometry, U.S. government, U.S. government and politics-AP, U.S. history, U.S. literature, vocal music, weight training, Western civilization, world geography, world history, world religions.

Special Academic Programs Advanced Placement exam preparation; honors section; independent study; study at local college for college credit; academic accommodation for the gifted; remedial reading and/or remedial writing; remedial math; programs in English, mathematics, general development for dyslexic students; special instructional classes for deaf students, blind students.

College Admission Counseling 120 students graduated in 2012; 117 went to college, including Florida State University; Mississippi State University; Pensacola State College; The University of Alabama; University of Florida. Other: 2 entered military service, 1 had other specific plans. Mean SAT critical reading: 541, mean SAT math: 535, mean SAT writing: 548, mean combined SAT: 1624, mean composite ACT: 23.

Student Life Upper grades have specified standards of dress, student council. Discipline rests primarily with faculty. Attendance at religious services is required.

Summer Programs Remediation, enrichment programs offered; session focuses on religion courses, enrichment, and study skills; held on campus; accepts boys and girls; not open to students from other schools. 25 students usually enrolled.

Tuition and Aid Tuition installment plan (individually arranged payment plans). Tuition reduction for siblings, need-based scholarship grants available.

Admissions Traditional secondary-level entrance grade is 9. ETS high school placement exam required. Deadline for receipt of application materials: none. Application fee required: $125. On-campus interview required.

Athletics Interscholastic: baseball (boys), basketball (b,g), cheering (b,g), golf (b,g), physical training (b), soccer (b,g), softball (g), swimming and diving (b,g), wrestling (b).

Computers Computers are regularly used in Bible studies, computer applications, creative writing, desktop publishing, foreign language, French, geography, graphic design, history, independent study, keyboarding, mathematics, publications, reading, religion, science, social studies, Spanish, stock market, study skills, video film production, Web site design, word processing, yearbook classes. Computer network features include on-campus library services, online commercial services, Internet access, wireless campus network, Internet filtering or blocking technology. Student e-mail accounts and computer access in designated common areas are available to students. Students grades are available online. The school has a published electronic and media policy.

Contact Mary Kyte, Senior Guidance Counselor. 850-436-6400 Ext. 120. Fax: 850-436-6405. E-mail: mkyte@pensacolachs.org. Web site: www.pensacolachs.org

PEOPLES CHRISTIAN ACADEMY

245 Renfrew Drive
Markham, Ontario L3R 6G3, Canada

Head of School: Mr. Reg Andrews

General Information Coeducational day college-preparatory and religious studies school, affiliated with Christian faith. Grades JK–12. Founded: 1971. Setting: urban. Nearest major city is Toronto, Canada. 5-acre campus. 1 building on campus. Approved or accredited by Association of Christian Schools International, Christian Schools International, Ontario Ministry of Education, and Ontario Department of Education. Language of instruction: English. Endowment: CAN$15,000. Total enrollment: 339. Upper school average class size: 20. Upper school faculty-student ratio: 1:10. There are 176 required school days per year for Upper School students. Upper School students typically attend 5 days per week. The average school day consists of 7 hours.

Upper School Student Profile Grade 9: 22 students (13 boys, 9 girls); Grade 10: 29 students (12 boys, 17 girls); Grade 11: 27 students (16 boys, 11 girls); Grade 12: 32 students (15 boys, 17 girls). 85% of students are Christian.

Faculty School total: 36. In upper school: 9 men, 13 women; 4 have advanced degrees.

Subjects Offered Accounting, Bible, biology, calculus, Canadian geography, Canadian history, Canadian law, careers, chemistry, civics, discrete mathematics, dramatic arts, economics, English, exercise science, family studies, French, functions, geography, geometry, health education, healthful living, ideas, information technology, instrumental music, journalism, keyboarding, literature, mathematics, media arts, organizational studies, philosophy, physical education, physics, psychology, science, sociology, visual arts, vocal music, world history, world religions, writing.

Graduation Requirements Arts, Canadian geography, Canadian history, careers, civics, English, French as a second language, mathematics, physical education (includes health), science, must complete Bible course curriculum for all grades.

College Admission Counseling 42 students graduated in 2012; 40 went to college, including McMaster University; The University of Western Ontario; University of Guelph; University of Toronto; Wilfrid Laurier University; York University. Other: 2 had other specific plans.

Student Life Upper grades have uniform requirement, student council, honor system. Discipline rests primarily with faculty. Attendance at religious services is required.

Tuition and Aid Day student tuition: CAN$9630. Tuition installment plan (monthly payment plans). Tuition reduction for siblings, bursaries, need-based scholarship grants, alumni scholarships, prepayment tuition reduction available. In 2012–13, 2% of upper-school students received aid. Total amount of financial aid awarded in 2012–13: CAN$30,000.

Admissions Traditional secondary-level entrance grade is 9. For fall 2012, 15 students applied for upper-level admission, 10 were accepted, 10 enrolled. CTBS (or similar from their school) required. Deadline for receipt of application materials: none. Application fee required: CAN$150. Interview required.

Athletics Interscholastic: badminton (boys, girls), baseball (b,g), basketball (b,g), cross-country running (b,g), Frisbee (b,g), running (b,g), track and field (b,g), volleyball (b,g); intramural: badminton (b,g), basketball (b,g), cross-country running (b,g), floor hockey (b,g), running (b,g); coed interscholastic: badminton, baseball, basketball, cross-country running, Frisbee, running, swimming and diving, track and field; coed intramural: badminton, basketball, cross-country running, floor hockey, running, volleyball. 2 PE instructors.

Computers Computers are regularly used in business studies, drawing and design, graphics, information technology, introduction to technology, journalism, mathematics, yearbook classes. Computer network features include Internet access, Internet filtering or blocking technology. The school has a published electronic and media policy.

Contact School Office. 416-733-2010 Ext. 204. Fax: 416-733-2011. E-mail: admissions@pca.ca. Web site: www.pca.ca

PHILADELPHIA-MONTGOMERY CHRISTIAN ACADEMY

35 Hillcrest Avenue
Erdenheim, Pennsylvania 19038

Head of School: Mr. Donald B. Beebe

General Information Coeducational day college-preparatory, arts, and religious studies school, affiliated with Christian faith. Grades PK–12. Founded: 1943. Setting: suburban. Nearest major city is Philadelphia. 1-acre campus. 1 building on campus. Approved or accredited by Christian Schools International and Middle States Association of Colleges and Schools. Endowment: $150,205. Total enrollment: 304. Upper school average class size: 18. Upper school faculty-student ratio: 1:10. There are 178 required school days per year for Upper School students. Upper School students typically attend 5 days per week. The average school day consists of 6 hours and 50 minutes.

Upper School Student Profile Grade 9: 35 students (17 boys, 18 girls); Grade 10: 32 students (15 boys, 17 girls); Grade 11: 38 students (19 boys, 19 girls); Grade 12: 19 students (11 boys, 8 girls). 99% of students are Christian.

Faculty School total: 33. In upper school: 11 men, 8 women; 10 have advanced degrees.

Subjects Offered Algebra, American history, American literature, art, art history, biology, calculus, ceramics, chemistry, creative writing, drama, English, English literature, ethics, European history, fine arts, geography, geometry, German, government/civics, grammar, health, history, mathematics, music, physical education, physics, religion, science, social studies, sociology, Spanish, theater, trigonometry, typing, world history, writing.

Graduation Requirements Arts and fine arts (art, music, dance, drama), Bible, English, mathematics, physical education (includes health), science, social studies (includes history).

Special Academic Programs 4 Advanced Placement exams for which test preparation is offered; honors section; academic accommodation for the gifted, the musically talented, and the artistically talented.

College Admission Counseling 37 students graduated in 2012; 35 went to college, including Holy Family University; Liberty University; Penn State University Park; Temple University; West Chester University of Pennsylvania. Other: 2 went to work. Mean SAT critical reading: 268, mean SAT math: 551, mean SAT writing: 557, mean combined SAT: 1676.

Student Life Upper grades have uniform requirement, student council. Discipline rests primarily with faculty. Attendance at religious services is required.

Tuition and Aid Day student tuition: $12,153. Tuition installment plan (FACTS Tuition Payment Plan). Tuition reduction for siblings, need-based scholarship grants available. In 2012–13, 50% of upper-school students received aid. Total amount of financial aid awarded in 2012–13: $500,000.

Admissions Traditional secondary-level entrance grade is 9. For fall 2012, 26 students applied for upper-level admission, 21 were accepted, 17 enrolled. Iowa Tests of Basic Skills required. Deadline for receipt of application materials: none. Application fee required: $100. On-campus interview required.

Athletics Interscholastic: baseball (boys), basketball (b,g), soccer (b,g), softball (g), tennis (g), track and field (b,g), wrestling (b); coed interscholastic: cross-country running. 2 PE instructors, 6 coaches.

Computers Computers are regularly used in art, English, mathematics, yearbook classes. Computer resources include on-campus library services, Internet access, Internet filtering or blocking technology, online college search. Students grades are available online. The school has a published electronic and media policy.

Contact Phil VanVeldhuizen, Admissions and Marketing Manager. 215-233-0782 Ext. 408. Fax: 215-233-0829. E-mail: admissions@phil-mont.com. Web site: www.phil-mont.com

PHILLIPS ACADEMY (ANDOVER)

180 Main Street
Andover, Massachusetts 01810-4161

Head of School: John G. Palfrey Jr.

General Information Coeducational boarding and day college-preparatory school. Grades 9–PG. Founded: 1778. Setting: suburban. Nearest major city is Boston. Students are housed in single-sex dormitories and 9th graders housed separately from other students. 500-acre campus. 160 buildings on campus. Approved or accredited by New England Association of Schools and Colleges and The Association of Boarding Schools. Member of National Association of Independent Schools and Secondary School Admission Test Board. Endowment: $785 million. Total enrollment: 1,143. Upper school average class size: 13. Upper school faculty-student ratio: 1:5. There are 157 required school days per year for Upper School students. Upper School students typically attend 5 days per week. The average school day consists of 8 hours.

Upper School Student Profile Grade 9: 214 students (106 boys, 108 girls); Grade 10: 293 students (151 boys, 142 girls); Grade 11: 308 students (160 boys, 148 girls); Grade 12: 328 students (166 boys, 162 girls); Postgraduate: 28 students (20 boys, 8 girls). 75% of students are boarding students. 41% are state residents. 47 states are represented in upper school student body. 8% are international students. International students from Canada, China, Hong Kong, Republic of Korea, Thailand, and United Kingdom; 35 other countries represented in student body.

Faculty School total: 219. In upper school: 105 men, 114 women; 171 have advanced degrees; 190 reside on campus.

Subjects Offered Algebra, American history, American literature, ancient history, animal behavior, animation, Arabic studies, architecture, art, art history, astronomy, band, Bible studies, biology, calculus, ceramics, chamber groups, chemistry, Chinese, chorus, computer graphics, computer programming, computer science, creative writing, dance, drama, drawing, driver education, ecology, economics, English, English literature, environmental science, ethics, European history, expository writing, film, fine arts, French, geology, geometry, German, government/civics, grammar, Greek, health, history, international relations, Japanese, jazz, Latin, Latin American studies, life issues, literature, mathematics, Middle Eastern history, music, mythology, oceanography, painting, philosophy, photography, physical education, physics, physiology, printmaking, psychology, religion, Russian, Russian studies, science, sculpture, social sciences, social studies, sociology, Spanish, speech, swimming, theater, trigonometry, video, world history, writing.

Graduation Requirements Arts and fine arts (art, music, dance, drama), English, foreign language, history, life issues, mathematics, philosophy, physical education (includes health), religion (includes Bible studies and theology), science, social sciences, swimming test.

Special Academic Programs Advanced Placement exam preparation; honors section; independent study; term-away projects; study abroad; academic accommodation for the gifted, the musically talented, and the artistically talented; programs in English, mathematics, general development for dyslexic students; special instructional classes for deaf students, blind students.

College Admission Counseling 313 students graduated in 2012; 306 went to college, including Columbia University; Cornell University; Stanford University; University of Pennsylvania; Wesleyan University; Yale University. Other: 7 had other specific plans. Mean SAT critical reading: 678, mean SAT math: 684, mean SAT writing: 675.

Student Life Upper grades have student council, honor system. Discipline rests primarily with faculty.

Summer Programs Remediation, enrichment, advancement, ESL, art/fine arts, computer instruction programs offered; session focuses on academics; held both on and off campus; held at Colorado; accepts boys and girls; open to students from other schools. 550 students usually enrolled. 2013 schedule: June 24 to August 1. Application deadline: none.

Tuition and Aid Day student tuition: $34,500; 7-day tuition and room/board: $44,500. Tuition installment plan (individually arranged payment plans, The Andover Plan). Need-based scholarship grants, middle-income loans, Andover is a true need-blind school that admits students without regard to a family's financial situation available. In 2012–13, 46% of upper-school students received aid. Total amount of financial aid awarded in 2012–13: $18,157,000.

Admissions For fall 2012, 3,154 students applied for upper-level admission, 444 were accepted, 371 enrolled. ISEE or SSAT required. Deadline for receipt of application materials: February 1. Application fee required: $40. Interview required.

Athletics Interscholastic: baseball (boys), basketball (b,g), bicycling (b,g), crew (b,g), cross-country running (b,g), diving (b,g), field hockey (g), football (b), golf (b,g), ice hockey (b,g), indoor track & field (b,g), lacrosse (b,g), nordic skiing (b,g), skiing (cross-country) (b,g), soccer (b,g), softball (g), squash (b,g), swimming and diving (b,g), tennis (b,g), track and field (b,g), volleyball (b,g), water polo (b,g), winter (indoor) track (b,g), wrestling (b); intramural: aerobics/dance (b,g), backpacking (b,g), basketball (b,g), crew (b,g), martial arts (b,g), physical fitness (b,g), physical training (b,g); coed interscholastic: bicycling, Frisbee, golf, ultimate Frisbee, wrestling; coed intramural: badminton, ballet, canoeing/kayaking, cheering, cross-country running, dance, fencing, fitness, fitness walking, hiking/backpacking, martial arts, modern dance, outdoor adventure, outdoor education, physical fitness, physical training, rappelling, rock climbing, ropes courses, soccer, softball, strength & conditioning, tennis, wall climbing. 7 PE instructors, 25 coaches, 3 athletic trainers.

Computers Computers are regularly used in animation, architecture, art, classics, computer applications, digital applications, English, foreign language, history, mathematics, music, photography, psychology, religious studies, science, theater, video film production classes. Computer network features include on-campus library services, online commercial services, Internet access, wireless campus network. Campus intranet and student e-mail accounts are available to students. The school has a published electronic and media policy.

Contact Jim Ventre, Interim Dean of Admission and Director of Financial Aid. 978-749-4050. Fax: 978-749-4068. E-mail: admissions@andover.edu. Web site: www.andover.edu

PHILLIPS EXETER ACADEMY

20 Main Street
Exeter, New Hampshire 03833-2460

Head of School: Mr. Thomas E. Hassan

General Information Coeducational boarding and day college-preparatory school. Grades 9–PG. Founded: 1781. Setting: small town. Nearest major city is Boston, MA. Students are housed in single-sex dormitories. 670-acre campus. 130 buildings on campus. Approved or accredited by Association of Independent Schools in New England, New England Association of Schools and Colleges, and The Association of Boarding Schools. Member of National Association of Independent Schools and Secondary School Admission Test Board. Endowment: $969.1 million. Upper school average class size: 12. Upper school faculty-student ratio: 1:5.

Upper School Student Profile 80% of students are boarding students. 45 states are represented in upper school student body. 10% are international students.

Faculty School total: 209. In upper school: 103 men, 106 women.

Subjects Offered Algebra, American history, American literature, anatomy, anthropology, Arabic, archaeology, architecture, art, art history, astronomy, biology, botany, calculus, ceramics, chemistry, Chinese, classics, computer programming, computer science, creative writing, dance, discrete mathematics, drama, driver education, ecology, economics, electronics, English, English literature, environmental science, ethics, European history, evolution, existentialism, expository writing, film, fine arts, French, genetics, geology, geometry, German, Greek, health, history, Italian, Japanese, Latin, linear algebra, logic, marine biology, mathematics, music, music composition, ornithology, philosophy, photography, physical education, physics, physiology, psychology, religion, Russian, science, sculpture, Spanish, statistics, theater, trigonometry, world literature, writing, Zen Buddhism.

Graduation Requirements American history, art, biology, computer science, English, foreign language, mathematics, physical education (includes health), physical science, religion (includes Bible studies and theology), science.

Special Academic Programs Advanced Placement exam preparation; honors section; independent study; term-away projects; study abroad; academic accommodation for the gifted, the musically talented, and the artistically talented.

College Admission Counseling Colleges students went to include Harvard University; New York University; Stanford University; The George Washington University; The Johns Hopkins University; University of Pennsylvania.

Student Life Upper grades have specified standards of dress, student council, honor system. Discipline rests primarily with faculty.

Tuition and Aid Day student tuition: $32,470; 7-day tuition and room/board: $41,800. Tuition installment plan (Academic Management Services Plan, Tuition Management Systems Plan). Need-based scholarship grants available. In 2011–12, 47% of upper-school students received aid. Total amount of financial aid awarded in 2011–12: $15,635,367.

Admissions Traditional secondary-level entrance grade is 9. PSAT or SAT, SSAT or TOEFL required. Deadline for receipt of application materials: January 15. Application fee required: $50. Interview required.

Athletics Interscholastic: baseball (boys), basketball (b,g), crew (b,g), cross-country running (b,g), field hockey (g), football (b), golf (b,g), ice hockey (b,g), lacrosse (b,g), soccer (b,g), softball (g), squash (b,g), swimming and diving (b,g), tennis (b,g), track and field (b,g), volleyball (g), water polo (b,g), wrestling (b); coed interscholastic: bicycling, winter (indoor) track.

Computers Computers are regularly used in computer applications, foreign language, mathematics, science classes. Computer network features include on-campus library services, Internet access, Internet filtering or blocking technology. Campus intranet and student e-mail accounts are available to students.

Contact Mr. Michael Gary, Director of Admissions. 603-777-3437. Fax: 603-777-4399. E-mail: admit@exeter.edu. Web site: www.exeter.edu

See Summer Program Close-Up on page 712.

PHOENIX CHRISTIAN UNIFIED SCHOOLS

1751 West Indian School Road
Phoenix, Arizona 85015

Head of School: Dr. Phil Adams

General Information Coeducational day college-preparatory, general academic, religious studies, and AP/Honors school, affiliated with Christian faith. Grades PS–12. Founded: 1949. Setting: suburban. 12-acre campus. 10 buildings on campus. Approved or accredited by Association of Christian Schools International, North Central Association of Colleges and Schools, and Arizona Department of Education. Total enrollment: 380. Upper school average class size: 20. Upper school faculty-student ratio: 1:20. There are 180 required school days per year for Upper School students. Upper School students typically attend 5 days per week. The average school day consists of 6 hours and 40 minutes.

Upper School Student Profile Grade 6: 15 students (7 boys, 8 girls); Grade 7: 26 students (11 boys, 15 girls); Grade 8: 24 students (14 boys, 10 girls); Grade 9: 52 students (28 boys, 24 girls); Grade 10: 48 students (27 boys, 21 girls); Grade 11: 68 students (38 boys, 30 girls); Grade 12: 45 students (26 boys, 19 girls).

Faculty School total: 23. In upper school: 12 men, 9 women; 17 have advanced degrees.

Subjects Offered Advanced computer applications, algebra, American literature, American literature-AP, anatomy, art, arts, band, Bible, biology, biology-AP, calculus, calculus-AP, career and personal planning, chemistry, choir, choral music, computer applications, computers, creative writing, culinary arts, drama, drama performance, drawing, economics, English, English literature, English literature-AP, English-AP, geometry, government, government-AP, home economics, instrumental music, integrated science, internship, intro to computers, language-AP, library, literature, literature-AP, marching band, photography, physical education, physics, pre-algebra, pre-calculus, psychology, religious education, sociology, Spanish, Spanish language-AP, statistics, student government, study skills, U.S. government, U.S. history, U.S. history-AP, Web site design, world history, yearbook.

Graduation Requirements Advanced math, Advanced Placement courses, algebra, American literature, arts and fine arts (art, music, dance, drama), biology, British literature, chemistry, computer education, economics, English, English composition, English literature, foreign language, geometry, government, integrated science, pre-calculus, religious studies, study skills, U.S. history, world history, world literature.

Special Academic Programs Advanced Placement exam preparation; honors section; independent study; study at local college for college credit; ESL (11 students enrolled).

College Admission Counseling 58 students graduated in 2012; 49 went to college, including Arizona Christian University; Arizona State University; Grand Canyon University; Northern Arizona University; The University of Arizona. Other: 1 entered military service, 4 entered a postgraduate year, 1 had other specific plans. Mean SAT critical reading: 544, mean SAT math: 544, mean SAT writing: 532, mean composite ACT: 23.

Student Life Upper grades have uniform requirement, student council. Discipline rests primarily with faculty.

Summer Programs Sports programs offered; session focuses on skill building; social; held on campus; accepts boys and girls; not open to students from other schools. 25 students usually enrolled. 2013 schedule: June 1 to July 31. Application deadline: May 15.

Tuition and Aid Day student tuition: $8100. Tuition installment plan (FACTS Tuition Payment Plan, monthly payment plans, individually arranged payment plans). Tuition reduction for siblings, need-based scholarship grants available.

Admissions Traditional secondary-level entrance grade is 9. Achievement tests or any standardized test required. Deadline for receipt of application materials: none. Application fee required: $200. Interview required.

Athletics Interscholastic: baseball (boys), basketball (b,g), cheering (g), drill team (g), football (b), softball (g), volleyball (g), wrestling (b); coed interscholastic: cross-country running, diving, golf, soccer, swimming and diving, tennis, track and field, weight lifting, weight training. 1 PE instructor, 4 coaches, 1 athletic trainer.

Computers Computers are regularly used in career exploration, college planning, computer applications, keyboarding, library, media services, Web site design, yearbook classes. Computer resources include on-campus library services, Internet access, wireless campus network, Internet filtering or blocking technology. Campus intranet and computer access in designated common areas are available to students. Students grades are available online. The school has a published electronic and media policy.

Contact Mrs. Gretchen Janes, Admissions & Development Rep. 602-265-4707 Ext. 270. Fax: 602-277-7170. E-mail: gjanes@phoenixchristian.org. Web site: www.phoenixchristian.org

PHOENIX COUNTRY DAY SCHOOL

3901 East Stanford Drive
Paradise Valley, Arizona 85253

Head of School: Mr. Andrew Rodin

General Information Coeducational day college-preparatory, arts, performing and studio arts, extensive athletics, and community service, global citizenship, and travel school. Grades PK–12. Founded: 1961. Setting: suburban. Nearest major city is Phoenix. 40-acre campus. 8 buildings on campus. Approved or accredited by Independent Schools Association of the Southwest and National Independent Private Schools Association. Member of National Association of Independent Schools. Endowment: $15 million. Total enrollment: 724. Upper school average class size: 15. Upper school faculty-student ratio: 1:8. There are 173 required school days per year for Upper School students. Upper School students typically attend 5 days per week. The average school day consists of 5 hours.

Upper School Student Profile Grade 9: 70 students (33 boys, 37 girls); Grade 10: 64 students (29 boys, 35 girls); Grade 11: 57 students (20 boys, 37 girls); Grade 12: 62 students (25 boys, 37 girls).

Faculty School total: 90. In upper school: 17 men, 13 women; 23 have advanced degrees.

Subjects Offered Acting, advanced biology, advanced chemistry, advanced math, Advanced Placement courses, African-American literature, algebra, American government, American history, American history-AP, American literature, anatomy, anatomy and physiology, anthropology, art, art history, art history-AP, astronomy, band, baseball, basketball, biology, biology-AP, British literature, calculus, calculus-AP, ceramics, chemistry, chemistry-AP, Chinese, Chinese studies, choir, chorus, computer programming, computer science, creative writing, digital photography, directing, discrete mathematics, drawing, ecology, English, English composition, English literature, environmental science, environmental science-AP, ethics, European history, evolution, fine arts, French, French-AP, geography, geology, geometry, government/civics, history, Holocaust studies, jazz band, journalism, Latin, Latin American literature, Latin-AP, literature, Mandarin, marine biology, mathematics, music, oceanography, orchestra, painting, photography, physical education, physics, physics-AP, physiology, pre-calculus, probability and statistics, psychology, scene study, science, Shakespeare, social sciences, social studies, Spanish, Spanish-AP, speech, statistics, statistics-AP, theater, theater arts, trigonometry, world history, world literature, world religions.

Graduation Requirements Advanced biology, American history, American literature, ancient world history, arts and fine arts (art, music, dance, drama), biology, chemistry, English, foreign language, mathematics, physical education (includes health), physics, science, U.S. history, Western civilization, world history, 40 hours of community service.

Special Academic Programs 15 Advanced Placement exams for which test preparation is offered; honors section; independent study; study abroad.

College Admission Counseling 58 students graduated in 2012; all went to college, including Arizona State University; Harvard University; Massachusetts Institute of Technology; New York University; Southern Methodist University; University of Southern California. Median SAT critical reading: 670, median SAT math: 680, median SAT writing: 690, median combined SAT: 2010, median composite ACT: 29. 77% scored over 600 on SAT critical reading, 86% scored over 600 on SAT math, 86% scored over 600 on SAT writing, 86% scored over 1800 on combined SAT, 78% scored over 26 on composite ACT.

Student Life Upper grades have specified standards of dress, student council, honor system. Discipline rests primarily with faculty.

Summer Programs Enrichment, advancement, sports, art/fine arts, computer instruction programs offered; session focuses on academics/sports camp/arts program; held on campus; accepts boys and girls; open to students from other schools. 500 students usually enrolled. 2013 schedule: June 4 to July 13. Application deadline: none.

Tuition and Aid Day student tuition: $22,100. Tuition installment plan (Insured Tuition Payment Plan, monthly payment plans, individually arranged payment plans, 10 months, quarterly, semiannual, and yearly payment plans). Need-based scholarship grants available. In 2012–13, 21% of upper-school students received aid. Total amount of financial aid awarded in 2012–13: $1,016,600.

Admissions Traditional secondary-level entrance grade is 9. For fall 2012, 82 students applied for upper-level admission, 45 were accepted, 31 enrolled. Achievement/Aptitude/Writing, ERB CTP IV, Math Placement Exam, Otis-Lennon IQ and writing sample required. Deadline for receipt of application materials: March 1. Application fee required: $100. Interview required.

Athletics Interscholastic: baseball (boys), basketball (b,g), cheering (g), diving (b,g), flag football (b), golf (b,g), lacrosse (b,g), soccer (b,g), softball (g), winter soccer (g); intramural: archery (b,g), badminton (b,g), basketball (b,g), lacrosse (b,g), outdoor education (b,g), outdoor recreation (b,g), physical fitness (b,g), softball (g), strength & conditioning (b,g), yoga (b,g); coed interscholastic: cheering, diving, swimming and diving, tennis, volleyball; coed intramural: basketball, cross-country running, flag football, golf, hiking/backpacking, running, soccer, swimming and diving, tennis, volleyball, weight lifting, winter soccer. 5 PE instructors, 23 coaches, 1 athletic trainer.

Computers Computers are regularly used in art, college planning, creative writing, data processing, desktop publishing, economics, engineering, English, foreign language, French, history, humanities, independent study, information technology, keyboarding, library, library skills, literary magazine, mathematics, news writing, newspaper, photography, programming, publications, research skills, science, social sciences, social studies, Spanish, stock market, Web site design, writing, yearbook classes. Computer network features include on-campus library services, online commercial services, Internet access, wireless campus network, Internet filtering or blocking technology. Campus intranet, student e-mail accounts, and computer access in designated common areas are available to students. Students grades are available online. The school has a published electronic and media policy.

Contact Sandy Orrick, Admissions Assistant. 602-955-8200 Ext. 2255. Fax: 602-381-4554. E-mail: sandy.orrick@pcds.org. Web site: www.pcds.org

PICKENS ACADEMY

225 Ray Bass Road
Carrollton, Alabama 35447

Head of School: Mr. Brach White

General Information Coeducational day college-preparatory, general academic, and technology school. Grades K4–12. Founded: 1970. Setting: rural. Nearest major city is Tuscaloosa. 3 buildings on campus. Approved or accredited by Distance Education and Training Council, Southern Association of Colleges and Schools, and Alabama Department of Education. Total enrollment: 265. Upper school average class size: 25. Upper school faculty-student ratio: 1:20. There are 180 required school days per year for Upper School students. Upper School students typically attend 5 days per week. The average school day consists of 7 hours.

Upper School Student Profile Grade 7: 25 students (11 boys, 14 girls); Grade 8: 28 students (11 boys, 17 girls); Grade 9: 15 students (7 boys, 8 girls); Grade 10: 26 students (13 boys, 13 girls); Grade 11: 19 students (7 boys, 12 girls); Grade 12: 34 students (15 boys, 19 girls).

Faculty School total: 21. In upper school: 5 men, 16 women; 8 have advanced degrees.

Subjects Offered 20th century history, 20th century world history, advanced chemistry, advanced computer applications, advanced math, Alabama history and geography, algebra, American democracy, American government, American history, American literature, anatomy and physiology, ancient history, ancient world history, applied music, art, band, baseball, basketball, biology, British literature, business mathematics, calculus, career/college preparation, cheerleading, chemistry, civics, college admission preparation, composition, computer literacy, consumer economics, CPR, creative writing, desktop publishing, economics, English composition, English literature, environmental science, family and consumer science, French, geography, government, grammar, health education, history, keyboarding, land management, leadership education training, library assistant, Microsoft, music, music appreciation, physical education, physical science, physics, research skills, science, student government, trigonometry, U.S. government and politics, Web site design, weight training, weightlifting.

Graduation Requirements 20th century world history, advanced math, American government, American history, anatomy and physiology, calculus, economics, English, English composition, English literature, physics, research skills, trigonometry.

Special Academic Programs Study at local college for college credit.

College Admission Counseling 24 students graduated in 2012; 17 went to college, including Auburn University; Mississippi State University; The University of Alabama. Other: 1 went to work, 1 entered military service. Median composite ACT: 21. 8% scored over 26 on composite ACT.

Student Life Upper grades have specified standards of dress, student council. Discipline rests primarily with faculty.

Summer Programs Sports programs offered; session focuses on conditioning; held on campus; accepts boys and girls; not open to students from other schools. 2013 schedule: June 1 to July 30. Application deadline: May 15.

Tuition and Aid Day student tuition: $3000. Guaranteed tuition plan. Tuition installment plan (Insured Tuition Payment Plan, monthly payment plans).

Admissions Traditional secondary-level entrance grade is 9. PSAT or Stanford Achievement Test, Otis-Lennon School Ability Test required. Deadline for receipt of application materials: none. No application fee required. On-campus interview required.

Athletics Interscholastic: baseball (boys), basketball (b,g), cheering (g), cross-country running (b,g), danceline (g), football (b), golf (b,g), softball (g), volleyball (g), weight lifting (b,g); coed interscholastic: tennis, track and field. 1 PE instructor, 2 coaches.

Computers Computers are regularly used in all academic classes. Computer network features include on-campus library services, Internet access, Internet filtering or blocking technology. Student e-mail accounts are available to students. Students grades are available online. The school has a published electronic and media policy.

Contact Admissions. 205-367-8144. Fax: 205-367-8145. Web site: www.pickensacademy.com

PICKERING COLLEGE

16945 Bayview Avenue
Newmarket, Ontario L3Y 4X2, Canada

Head of School: Mr. Peter C. Sturrup

General Information Coeducational boarding and day college-preparatory, arts, technology, film studies and radio station, and leadership school. Boarding grades 7–12, day grades JK–12. Founded: 1842. Setting: suburban. Nearest major city is Toronto, Canada. Students are housed in single-sex dormitories. 42-acre campus. 6 buildings on campus. Approved or accredited by Canadian Association of Independent Schools, Canadian Educational Standards Institute, National Independent Private Schools Association, Ontario Ministry of Education, The Association of Boarding Schools, and Ontario Department of Education. Affiliate member of National Association of Independent Schools; member of Secondary School Admission Test Board. Language of instruction: English. Total enrollment: 373. Upper school average class size: 18. Upper school faculty-student ratio: 1:9. There are 164 required school days per year for Upper School students. Upper School students typically attend 5 days per week. The average school day consists of 8 hours.

Upper School Student Profile Grade 9: 42 students (26 boys, 16 girls); Grade 10: 54 students (32 boys, 22 girls); Grade 11: 57 students (31 boys, 26 girls); Grade 12: 65 students (32 boys, 33 girls). 35% of students are boarding students. 60% are province residents. 40% are international students. International students from Barbados, China, Germany, Japan, Mexico, and Russian Federation; 18 other countries represented in student body.

Faculty School total: 42. In upper school: 17 men, 12 women; 7 have advanced degrees; 15 reside on campus.

Subjects Offered Algebra, art, art history, biology, business, business skills, business studies, calculus, Canadian geography, Canadian history, careers, chemistry, community service, computer applications, computer multimedia, computer programming, computer science, concert band, creative writing, drama, dramatic arts, economics, English, English composition, English literature, entrepreneurship, environmental science, ESL, experiential education, family studies, filmmaking, fine arts, finite math, French, geography, geometry, government/civics, guitar, health, health education, history, instrumental music, jazz band, law, leadership, literature, mathematics, media studies, music, physical education, physics, politics, science, social sciences, social studies, theater, video film production, visual arts, vocal music, world history.

Graduation Requirements English, 60 hours of community service completed over 4 years before graduation.

Special Academic Programs Independent study; ESL (25 students enrolled).

College Admission Counseling 69 students graduated in 2012; 67 went to college, including Dalhousie University; McGill University; Queen's University at Kingston; The University of Western Ontario; University of Toronto; University of Waterloo. Other: 1 entered military service, 1 had other specific plans.

Student Life Upper grades have uniform requirement, student council, honor system. Discipline rests equally with students and faculty.

Summer Programs ESL programs offered; session focuses on ESL summer camp; held on campus; accepts boys and girls; open to students from other schools. 70 students usually enrolled. 2013 schedule: June 23 to August 16. Application deadline: May.

Tuition and Aid Day student tuition: CAN$19,130–CAN$23,000; 7-day tuition and room/board: CAN$47,700–CAN$49,930. Tuition installment plan (Insured Tuition Payment Plan, monthly payment plans). Tuition reduction for siblings, bursaries, merit scholarship grants, need-based scholarship grants available. In 2012–13, 4% of upper-school students received aid; total upper-school merit-scholarship money awarded: CAN$13,000. Total amount of financial aid awarded in 2012–13: CAN$100,000.

Admissions Traditional secondary-level entrance grade is 9. For fall 2012, 109 students applied for upper-level admission, 52 enrolled. CAT, International English Language Test, SLEP for foreign students, SSAT or TOEFL required. Deadline for receipt of application materials: none. Application fee required: CAN$200. Interview required.

Athletics Interscholastic: badminton (boys, girls), basketball (b,g), cross-country running (b,g), figure skating (b,g), hockey (b), horseback riding (b,g), ice hockey (b), ice skating (b,g), rugby (b,g), skiing (downhill) (b,g), snowboarding (b,g), soccer (b,g), softball (b,g), swimming and diving (b,g), tennis (b,g), track and field (b,g), volleyball (b,g); intramural: badminton (b,g), ball hockey (b,g), combined training (b,g), figure skating (b,g), floor hockey (b,g), hockey (b,g), horseback riding (b,g), ice skating (b,g), outdoor activities (b,g), outdoor adventure (b,g), outdoor recreation (b,g), paddle tennis (b,g), physical training (b,g), running (b,g), skiing (downhill) (b,g), soccer (b,g), strength & conditioning (b,g), swimming and diving (b,g), tennis (b,g), track and field (b,g), volleyball (b,g); coed interscholastic: alpine skiing, aquatics, badminton, cross-country running, equestrian sports, figure skating, hockey, horseback riding, ice hockey, ice skating, mountain biking, skiing (downhill), snowboarding, soccer, swimming and diving, tennis, track and field; coed intramural: aerobics/dance, badminton, ball hockey, basketball, bowling, broomball, canoeing/kayaking, cooperative games, cross-country running, dance squad, equestrian sports, figure skating, fitness, floor hockey, Frisbee, golf, hockey, horseback riding, ice skating, indoor soccer, mountain biking, nordic skiing, outdoor adventure, outdoor education, paint ball, rock climbing, skiing (downhill), soccer, strength & conditioning, swimming and diving, table tennis, tennis, touch football, track and field, volleyball, wilderness survival, yoga. 3 PE instructors, 2 coaches, 1 athletic trainer.

Computers Computers are regularly used in all classes. Computer network features include on-campus library services, Internet access, wireless campus network, Internet filtering or blocking technology. Student e-mail accounts are available to students. Students grades are available online. The school has a published electronic and media policy.

Contact Mrs. Susan Hundert, Admission Associate, Day and North American Boarding. 905-895-1700 Ext. 259. Fax: 905-895-1306. E-mail: admission@pickeringcollege.on.ca. Web site: www.pickeringcollege.on.ca

PIC RIVER PRIVATE HIGH SCHOOL

21 Rabbit Drive
PO Box 216
Heron Bay, Ontario P0T 1R0, Canada

Head of School: Mrs. Lisa Michano-Courchene

General Information Coeducational day college-preparatory school, affiliated with Roman Catholic Church. Grades K–12. Founded: 1993. Setting: small town. Nearest major city is Thunder Bay, Canada. 2-acre campus. 1 building on campus. Approved or accredited by Ontario Department of Education. Language of instruction: English. Upper school average class size: 22. Upper school faculty-student ratio: 1:10. There are 194 required school days per year for Upper School students. Upper School students typically attend 5 days per week. The average school day consists of 3 hours.

Upper School Student Profile 100% of students are Roman Catholic.

Faculty School total: 1. In upper school: 1 man.

Student Life Discipline rests primarily with faculty.

Admissions No application fee required.

Computers Computer network features include on-campus library services, Internet access, Internet filtering or blocking technology. Campus intranet and student e-mail accounts are available to students.

Contact Mr. Douglas L. Vollett, Teacher. 807-229-3726. Fax: 807-229-1944. E-mail: dvollett@picriver.com. Web site:

PIEDMONT ACADEMY

PO Box 231
126 Highway 212 West
Monticello, Georgia 31064

Head of School: Mr. Tony Tanner

General Information Coeducational day college-preparatory, arts, business, vocational, religious studies, bilingual studies, technology, and joint enrollment with Georgia Military College school, affiliated with Protestant faith. Grades 1–12. Founded: 1970. Setting: rural. Nearest major city is Atlanta. 22-acre campus. 8 buildings on campus. Approved or accredited by Georgia Accrediting Commission and Georgia Independent School Association. Total enrollment: 270. Upper school average class size: 15. Upper school faculty-student ratio: 1:13. There are 180 required school days per year for Upper School students. Upper School students typically attend 5 days per week. The average school day consists of 7 hours.

Upper School Student Profile Grade 9: 23 students (12 boys, 11 girls); Grade 10: 28 students (20 boys, 8 girls); Grade 11: 28 students (14 boys, 14 girls); Grade 12: 26 students (9 boys, 17 girls). 98% of students are Protestant.

Faculty School total: 31. In upper school: 6 men, 15 women; 15 have advanced degrees.

Subjects Offered Advanced chemistry, advanced computer applications, advanced math, algebra, American government, American history, American history-AP, anatomy and physiology, band, biology, business law, calculus, calculus-AP, chemistry, chemistry-AP, civics, computer science, computer science-AP, computers, concert band, concert choir, consumer economics, consumer law, economics, English, English-AP, geometry, government and politics-AP, government-AP, government/civics, grammar, health education, honors algebra, honors English, honors geometry, Internet, intro to computers, keyboarding, language arts, leadership and service, literature, mathematics, performing arts, personal finance, physical fitness, physical science, physics, pre-calculus, science, sociology, Spanish, student government, wind instruments, world history, yearbook.

Graduation Requirements Algebra, American government, American literature, biology, calculus, chemistry, civics, English composition, English literature, geometry, government, grammar, history, keyboarding, mathematics, physical education (includes health), physical science, science, Spanish.

Special Academic Programs Study at local college for college credit.

College Admission Counseling 19 students graduated in 2012; 18 went to college, including Georgia Perimeter College; North Georgia College & State University; University of Georgia. Other: 1 entered military service.

Student Life Upper grades have uniform requirement, student council, honor system. Discipline rests primarily with faculty.

Tuition and Aid Day student tuition: $4480–$6360. Guaranteed tuition plan. Tuition installment plan (monthly payment plans, individually arranged payment plans, APOGEE School Choice Scholarship). Tuition reduction for siblings, need-based scholarship grants available. In 2012–13, 10% of upper-school students received aid. Total amount of financial aid awarded in 2012–13: $25,000.

Admissions For fall 2012, 46 students applied for upper-level admission, 43 were accepted, 40 enrolled. OLSAT, Stanford Achievement Test or WAIS, WICS required. Deadline for receipt of application materials: none. Application fee required: $75. Interview required.

Athletics Interscholastic: baseball (boys), basketball (b,g), cheering (b,g), fitness (b,g), flag football (b,g), football (b), golf (b,g), power lifting (b,g); coed interscholastic: cross-country running; coed intramural: cross-country running, flag football. 6 PE instructors, 10 coaches.

Computers Computers are regularly used in all academic classes. Computer network features include on-campus library services, online commercial services, Internet access, wireless campus network, Internet filtering or blocking technology. Campus intranet is available to students. Students grades are available online. The school has a published electronic and media policy.

Contact Judy M. Nelson, Director of Admissions/Public and Alumni Relations. 706-468-8818 Ext. 19. Fax: 706-468-2409. E-mail: judy_nelson@piedmontacademy.com. Web site: www.piedmontacademy.com

PINECREST ACADEMY

955 Peachtree Parkway
Cumming, Georgia 30041

Head of School: Fr. Robert Presutti, LC, PhD

General Information Coeducational day college-preparatory, arts, religious studies, and technology school, affiliated with Roman Catholic Church. Grades PK–12. Founded: 1993. Setting: suburban. Nearest major city is Atlanta. 70-acre campus. 4 buildings on campus. Approved or accredited by Georgia Independent School Association, National Catholic Education Association, Southern Association of Colleges and Schools, The College Board, and Georgia Department of Education. Member of Secondary School Admission Test Board. Total enrollment: 752. Upper school average class size: 18. Upper school faculty-student ratio: 1:10. There are 180 required school days per year for Upper School students. Upper School students typically attend 5 days per week. The average school day consists of 7 hours and 30 minutes.

Upper School Student Profile Grade 9: 69 students (34 boys, 35 girls); Grade 10: 55 students (26 boys, 29 girls); Grade 11: 52 students (26 boys, 26 girls); Grade 12: 51 students (25 boys, 26 girls). 85% of students are Roman Catholic.

Faculty School total: 73. In upper school: 19 men, 25 women; 31 have advanced degrees.

Subjects Offered Advanced chemistry, advanced math, Advanced Placement courses, advanced studio art-AP, anatomy and physiology, art-AP, band, biology, biology-AP, British literature, British literature-AP, calculus, calculus-AP, chemistry, chemistry-AP, chorus, Christian ethics, church history, classical language, concert band, economics, English composition, English language and composition-AP, English literature, English literature and composition-AP, European history-AP, geometry, government and politics-AP, health education, honors algebra, honors English, honors world history, journalism, literature and composition-AP, macroeconomics-AP, microeconomics-AP, music theory, painting, physical education, physics, pre-algebra, precalculus, psychology, Spanish language-AP, Spanish literature-AP, statistics, statistics-AP, studio art, studio art-AP, symphonic band, technology, theology, trigonometry, U.S. government and politics, U.S. government and politics-AP, U.S. history, U.S. history-AP, yearbook.

Special Academic Programs 22 Advanced Placement exams for which test preparation is offered; honors section.

College Admission Counseling 54 students graduated in 2012; all went to college, including Emory University; Georgia Institute of Technology; University of Georgia.

Student Life Upper grades have uniform requirement, student council, honor system. Discipline rests primarily with faculty. Attendance at religious services is required.

Tuition and Aid Day student tuition: $13,300. Tuition installment plan (monthly payment plans). Tuition reduction for siblings, need-based scholarship grants available.

Admissions Traditional secondary-level entrance grade is 9. For fall 2012, 154 students applied for upper-level admission, 124 were accepted, 95 enrolled. Admissions testing, Individual IQ, Achievement and behavior rating scale, PSAT or SAT for applicants to grade 11 and 12, psychoeducational evaluation, school's own exam, SSAT or TOEFL required. Deadline for receipt of application materials: none. Application fee required: $150. Interview required.

Athletics Interscholastic: baseball (boys), basketball (b,g), cheering (g), cross-country running (b,g), football (b), golf (b), soccer (b,g), swimming and diving (b,g), tennis (b,g), track and field (b,g), volleyball (g), weight training (b,g); intramural: baseball (b), basketball (b,g), cheering (g), cross-country running (b,g), football (b), soccer (b,g), swimming and diving (b,g), tennis (b,g), track and field (b,g), volleyball (g). 3 PE instructors, 13 coaches.

Computers Computers are regularly used in all classes. Computer network features include on-campus library services, online commercial services, Internet access, wireless campus network, Internet filtering or blocking technology, homework is available online. Campus intranet and computer access in designated common areas are available to students. Students grades are available online. The school has a published electronic and media policy.

Contact Ms. Melissa McWaters, Admissions Assistant. 770-888-4477 Ext. 245. Fax: 770-888-0404. E-mail: mmcwaters@pinecrestacademy.org. Web site: www.pinecrestacademy.org/

PINE CREST SCHOOL

1501 Northeast 62nd Street
Fort Lauderdale, Florida 33334-5116

Head of School: Dr. Dana Markham

General Information Coeducational day college-preparatory school. Grades PK–12. Founded: 1934. Setting: urban. 49-acre campus. 22 buildings on campus. Approved or accredited by Florida Council of Independent Schools, Southern Association of Colleges and Schools, and Southern Association of Independent Schools. Member of National Association of Independent Schools and Secondary School Admission Test Board. Endowment: $36.2 million. Total enrollment: 1,755. Upper school average class size: 17. Upper school faculty-student ratio: 1:14. The average school day consists of 6 hours and 30 minutes.

Upper School Student Profile Grade 9: 214 students (98 boys, 116 girls); Grade 10: 200 students (107 boys, 93 girls); Grade 11: 185 students (97 boys, 88 girls); Grade 12: 207 students (101 boys, 106 girls).

Faculty School total: 219. In upper school: 42 men, 59 women; 61 have advanced degrees.

Subjects Offered Algebra, American history, art, art history, ballet, band, biology, calculus, ceramics, chemistry, Chinese, chorus, comparative government and politics-AP, computer graphics, computer programming, computer science, dance, drama, economics, English, environmental science, ethics, European history, fine arts, forensics, French, geometry, German, government/civics, history, mathematics, music, orchestra, photography, physical education, physics, psychology, Spanish, speech, statistics.

Graduation Requirements Arts and fine arts (art, music, dance, drama), English, ethics, foreign language, humanities, mathematics, physical education (includes health), science, social studies (includes history), speech.

Special Academic Programs Advanced Placement exam preparation; honors section; ESL (12 students enrolled).

College Admission Counseling 206 students graduated in 2012; 205 went to college, including Cornell University; The George Washington University; The Johns Hopkins University; University of Florida; University of Miami; University of Pennsylvania. Other: 1 entered a postgraduate year. Median SAT critical reading: 640, median SAT math: 650, median SAT writing: 650, median combined SAT: 1950, median composite ACT: 29. 70% scored over 600 on SAT critical reading, 77% scored over 600 on SAT math, 69% scored over 600 on SAT writing, 76% scored over 1800 on combined SAT, 80% scored over 26 on composite ACT.

Student Life Upper grades have uniform requirement, student council, honor system. Discipline rests primarily with faculty.

Summer Programs Enrichment, advancement, sports programs offered; session focuses on competitive swimming, dance, summer school (grades 9-12); held on campus; accepts boys and girls; open to students from other schools. 300 students usually enrolled. 2013 schedule: June to July. Application deadline: none.

Tuition and Aid Day student tuition: $24,440. Tuition installment plan (The Tuition Refund Plan). Need-based scholarship grants available. In 2012–13, 18% of upper-school students received aid. Total amount of financial aid awarded in 2012–13: $1,888,380.

Admissions Traditional secondary-level entrance grade is 9. For fall 2012, 187 students applied for upper-level admission, 114 were accepted, 76 enrolled. SSAT required. Deadline for receipt of application materials: none. Application fee required: $100. Interview required.

Athletics Interscholastic: aquatics (boys, girls), baseball (b), basketball (b,g), crew (b,g), cross-country running (b,g), diving (b,g), football (b), golf (b,g), lacrosse (b,g), physical fitness (b,g), soccer (b,g), softball (g), strength & conditioning (b,g), swimming and diving (b,g), tennis (b,g), track and field (b,g), volleyball (b,g), weight lifting (b,g); intramural: aquatics (b,g), swimming and diving (b,g); coed interscholastic: ballet, cheering; coed intramural: ballet, physical training, strength & conditioning. 8 PE instructors, 1 athletic trainer.

Computers Computer network features include on-campus library services, online commercial services, Internet access, wireless campus network, Internet filtering or blocking technology, laptop program (grades 6-12), SmartBoards in classrooms. Campus intranet and student e-mail accounts are available to students. Students grades are available online. The school has a published electronic and media policy.

Contact Mrs. Elena Del Alamo, Director of Admission and Financial Aid. 954-492-4103. Fax: 954-492-4188. E-mail: pcadmit@pinecrest.edu. Web site: www.pinecrest.edu

PINEHURST SCHOOL

St. Catharines, Ontario, Canada
See Special Needs Schools section.

THE PINE SCHOOL

12350 SE Federal Highway
Hobe Sound, Florida 33455

Head of School: Mr. Stephen M. Mandell

General Information college-preparatory school. Founded: 1969. Setting: small town. Nearest major city is West Palm Beach. Approved or accredited by Florida Department of Education. Member of National Association of Independent Schools. Upper school average class size: 9. Upper school faculty-student ratio: 1:9. Upper School students typically attend 5 days per week.

Special Academic Programs Advanced Placement exam preparation; honors section; study abroad.

Student Life Upper grades have uniform requirement, student council, honor system. Discipline rests primarily with faculty.

Tuition and Aid Financial aid available to upper-school students. In 2011–12, 29% of upper-school students received aid. Total amount of financial aid awarded in 2011–12: $1,000,000.

Admissions Deadline for receipt of application materials: none. Application fee required: $60. Interview required.

Computers Computer network features include on-campus library services, Internet access, wireless campus network, Internet filtering or blocking technology. Student e-mail accounts and computer access in designated common areas are available to students. Students grades are available online. The school has a published electronic and media policy.

Contact 772-675-7005. Web site: www.thepineschool.org

PINEWOOD - THE INTERNATIONAL SCHOOL OF THESSALONIKI, GREECE

PO Box 60606
Thermi
Thessaloniki 57001, Greece

Head of School: Dr. Roxanne Giampapa

General Information Coeducational boarding and day college-preparatory, arts, and bilingual studies school. Boarding grades 7–12, day grades PK–12. Founded: 1950. Setting: suburban. Students are housed in coed dormitories. 4-acre campus. 2 buildings on campus. Approved or accredited by International Baccalaureate Organization, Middle States Association of Colleges and Schools, The College Board, US Department of State, and state department of education. Member of European Council of International Schools. Language of instruction: English. Total enrollment: 205. Upper school average class size: 10. Upper school faculty-student ratio: 1:5. There are 174 required school days per year for Upper School students. The average school day consists of 6 hours and 30 minutes.

Upper School Student Profile Grade 9: 15 students (9 boys, 6 girls); Grade 10: 10 students (5 boys, 5 girls); Grade 11: 25 students (12 boys, 13 girls); Grade 12: 25 students (14 boys, 11 girls). 10% of students are boarding students. 80% are international students. International students from Bulgaria, China, Italy, Spain, and United States; 20 other countries represented in student body.

Faculty School total: 35. In upper school: 7 men, 14 women; 14 have advanced degrees.

Subjects Offered Algebra, art, biology, chemistry, computer applications, computer science, computers, economics, electives, English, English literature, ESL, European history, French, general science, geography, geometry, Greek, Greek culture, history, honors English, honors U.S. history, library, literature, math methods, mathematics, modern European history, music, physical education, physical science, physics, pre-algebra, psychology, science, social sciences, social studies, U.S. history, world cultures, world geography, world history, world literature, yearbook.

Graduation Requirements Electives, English, European history, foreign language, mathematics, physical education (includes health), science, social studies (includes history), world history.

Special Academic Programs International Baccalaureate program; honors section; accelerated programs; independent study; study at local college for college credit; ESL (30 students enrolled).

College Admission Counseling 8 students graduated in 2012; 7 went to college, including Bard College. Other: 1 had other specific plans.

Student Life Upper grades have specified standards of dress, student council, honor system. Discipline rests primarily with faculty.

Tuition and Aid Day student tuition: €10,812; 7-day tuition and room/board: €22,500. Tuition installment plan (monthly payment plans, individually arranged payment plans, 3-payment plan). Merit scholarship grants, need-based scholarship grants available. In 2012–13, 5% of upper-school students received aid.

Admissions Traditional secondary-level entrance grade is 10. English entrance exam or English language required. Deadline for receipt of application materials: none. No application fee required. Interview required.

Athletics Interscholastic: aerobics/dance (girls), basketball (b,g), dance (g), fitness (b,g), football (b), soccer (b,g), volleyball (b,g); intramural: basketball (b,g), cheering (g), flag football (b,g), floor hockey (b,g), football (b), soccer (b,g), table tennis (b,g), tennis (b,g), volleyball (b,g); coed interscholastic: gymnastics, indoor soccer, juggling; coed intramural: baseball, gymnastics, juggling, softball, table tennis. 2 PE instructors, 3 coaches, 2 athletic trainers.

Computers Computers are regularly used in English, science, word processing, yearbook classes. Computer network features include on-campus library services, Internet access, wireless campus network. Student e-mail accounts are available to students. Students grades are available online. The school has a published electronic and media policy.

Contact Mrs. Youli Andrianopoulou, Executive Assistant to the Director/Head of Admissions. 30-2310-301221 Ext. 13. Fax: 30-2310-323196. E-mail: admissions@pinewood.gr. Web site: www.pinewood.gr

THE PINGREE SCHOOL

537 Highland Street

South Hamilton, Massachusetts 01982

Head of School: Dr. Timothy M. Johnson

General Information Coeducational day college-preparatory school. Grades 9–12. Founded: 1961. Setting: suburban. Nearest major city is Boston. 100-acre campus. 2 buildings on campus. Approved or accredited by Association of Independent Schools in New England, National Independent Private Schools Association, and New England Association of Schools and Colleges. Member of National Association of Independent Schools and Secondary School Admission Test Board. Endowment: $11 million. Total enrollment: 334. Upper school average class size: 15. Upper school faculty-student ratio: 1:7. There are 162 required school days per year for Upper School students. Upper School students typically attend 5 days per week. The average school day consists of 8 hours.

Upper School Student Profile Grade 9: 85 students (42 boys, 43 girls); Grade 10: 81 students (39 boys, 42 girls); Grade 11: 83 students (33 boys, 50 girls); Grade 12: 85 students (34 boys, 51 girls).

Faculty School total: 58. In upper school: 23 men, 35 women; 45 have advanced degrees.

Subjects Offered Algebra, American history, American literature, American studies, art, art history, astronomy, biology, calculus, ceramics, chemistry, computer programming, computer science, creative writing, dance, drama, driver education, earth science, ecology, economics, engineering, English, English literature, European history, fine arts, French, geometry, history, Latin, mathematics, music, oceanography, philosophy, photography, physics, psychology, Russian literature, science, social studies, Spanish, theater, trigonometry, writing.

Graduation Requirements Arts and fine arts (art, music, dance, drama), English, foreign language, mathematics, science, social studies (includes history), 50 hours of community service, senior projects.

Special Academic Programs Advanced Placement exam preparation; honors section; independent study; term-away projects.

College Admission Counseling 79 students graduated in 2012; 78 went to college, including Elon University; Providence College; Skidmore College; The George Washington University; Trinity College; University of Vermont. Other: 1 went to work. Median SAT critical reading: 590, median SAT math: 610, median SAT writing: 620, median combined SAT: 1850, median composite ACT: 26. 49% scored over 600 on SAT critical reading, 59% scored over 600 on SAT math, 65% scored over 600 on SAT writing, 56% scored over 1800 on combined SAT, 50% scored over 26 on composite ACT.

Student Life Upper grades have specified standards of dress, student council, honor system. Discipline rests equally with students and faculty.

Tuition and Aid Day student tuition: $36,100. Tuition installment plan (Academic Management Services Plan). Merit scholarship grants, need-based scholarship grants, need-based loans available. In 2012–13, 30% of upper-school students received aid; total upper-school merit-scholarship money awarded: $144,000. Total amount of financial aid awarded in 2012–13: $2,500,000.

Admissions Traditional secondary-level entrance grade is 9. For fall 2012, 400 students applied for upper-level admission, 200 were accepted, 100 enrolled. ISEE or SSAT required. Deadline for receipt of application materials: January 15. Application fee required: $50. On-campus interview required.

Athletics Interscholastic: baseball (boys), basketball (b,g), cross-country running (b,g), field hockey (g), football (b), golf (b,g), ice hockey (b,g), lacrosse (b,g), running (b,g), soccer (b,g), softball (g), swimming and diving (b,g), tennis (b,g), volleyball (g); coed interscholastic: Frisbee, sailing, ultimate Frisbee; coed intramural: dance, fitness, golf, hiking/backpacking, modern dance, mountaineering, outdoor adventure, outdoor education, outdoor skills, physical fitness, physical training, skiing (downhill), strength & conditioning, weight lifting, weight training, wilderness. 24 coaches, 2 athletic trainers.

Computers Computers are regularly used in college planning, computer applications, desktop publishing, digital applications, drawing and design, English, foreign language, graphic arts, graphic design, independent study, information technology, mathematics, programming, publications, science, technology, Web site design, word processing, writing, yearbook classes. Computer network features include on-campus library services, online commercial services, Internet access, Internet filtering or blocking technology. Student e-mail accounts are available to students. Students grades are available online.

Contact Mrs. Jody MacWhinnie, Admission Office Coordinator. 978-468-4415 Ext. 262. Fax: 978-468-3758. E-mail: jmacwhinnie@pingree.org. Web site: www.pingree.org

THE PINGRY SCHOOL

Martinsville Road

PO Box 366

Martinsville, New Jersey 08836

Head of School: Mr. Nathaniel Conard

General Information Coeducational day college-preparatory and arts school. Grades K–12. Founded: 1861. Setting: suburban. Nearest major city is New York, NY. 240-acre campus. 1 building on campus. Approved or accredited by Middle States Association of Colleges and Schools and New Jersey Department of Education. Member of National Association of Independent Schools. Endowment: $60 million. Total enrollment: 1,077. Upper school average class size: 14. Upper school faculty-student ratio: 1:8. There are 168 required school days per year for Upper School students. Upper School students typically attend 5 days per week. The average school day consists of 6 hours and 15 minutes.

Upper School Student Profile Grade 9: 138 students (65 boys, 73 girls); Grade 10: 146 students (75 boys, 71 girls); Grade 11: 134 students (71 boys, 63 girls); Grade 12: 132 students (70 boys, 62 girls).

Faculty School total: 120. In upper school: 47 men, 37 women; 61 have advanced degrees.

Subjects Offered Algebra, American literature, analysis, analysis and differential calculus, anatomy, architecture, art, art history-AP, biology, biology-AP, brass choir, calculus, chemistry, chemistry-AP, Chinese, clayworking, comparative cultures, computer science-AP, creative writing, drafting, drama, driver education, English, ethics, European literature, filmmaking, French, French-AP, geometry, German, German-AP, Greek drama, health, jazz band, jewelry making, Latin, literature by women, macro/microeconomics-AP, macroeconomics-AP, modern European history, music theory, mythology, orchestra, painting, peer counseling, photography, physics, physics-AP, physiology, psychology, psychology-AP, sculpture, Shakespeare, Spanish, Spanish-AP, studio art-AP, trigonometry, U.S. government and politics-AP, U.S. history-AP, wind ensemble, world literature, yearbook.

Graduation Requirements Arts and fine arts (art, music, dance, drama), English, foreign language, mathematics, physical education (includes health), science, social studies (includes history). Community service is required.

Special Academic Programs 20 Advanced Placement exams for which test preparation is offered; honors section; independent study; term-away projects; study abroad; academic accommodation for the gifted.

College Admission Counseling 131 students graduated in 2012; 126 went to college, including Boston College; Cornell University; Georgetown University; Hamilton College; Princeton University; University of Pennsylvania. Other: 2 entered a postgraduate year, 3 had other specific plans. Mean SAT critical reading: 686, mean SAT math: 693, mean SAT writing: 698, mean composite ACT: 30.

Student Life Upper grades have specified standards of dress, student council, honor system. Discipline rests equally with students and faculty.

Summer Programs Enrichment, sports programs offered; session focuses on enrichment, writing, and study skills; held on campus; accepts boys and girls; open to students from other schools. 30 students usually enrolled. 2013 schedule: June 27 to August 5.

Tuition and Aid Day student tuition: $25,670–$30,225. Tuition installment plan (monthly payment plans, individually arranged payment plans, My Tuition Solutions). Need-based scholarship grants available. In 2012–13, 15% of upper-school students received aid. Total amount of financial aid awarded in 2012–13: $199,259.

Admissions Traditional secondary-level entrance grade is 9. For fall 2012, 288 students applied for upper-level admission, 131 were accepted, 102 enrolled. ERB, ISEE, SSAT or Wechsler Intelligence Scale for Children required. Deadline for receipt of application materials: December 17. Application fee required: $75. On-campus interview required.

Athletics Interscholastic: alpine skiing (boys, girls), baseball (b), basketball (b,g), cross-country running (b,g), fencing (b,g), field hockey (g), football (b), golf (b,g), ice hockey (b,g), indoor track & field (b,g), lacrosse (b,g), skiing (downhill) (b,g), soccer (b,g), softball (g), squash (b,g), swimming and diving (b,g), tennis (b,g), track and field (b,g), wrestling (b); intramural: fitness (b,g), yoga (b,g); coed interscholastic: dance, physical fitness, physical training, water polo. 3 PE instructors, 15 coaches, 1 athletic trainer.

Computers Computers are regularly used in all academic classes. Computer network features include on-campus library services, online commercial services, Internet access, wireless campus network, Internet filtering or blocking technology. Campus intranet, student e-mail accounts, and computer access in designated common areas are available to students. The school has a published electronic and media policy.

Contact Mrs. Samantha Schifano, Admission Coordinator and Counselor. 908-647-5555 Ext. 1228. Fax: 908-647-4395. E-mail: sschifano@pingry.org. Web site: www.pingry.org

PIONEER VALLEY CHRISTIAN SCHOOL

965 Plumtree Road
Springfield, Massachusetts 01119

Head of School: Mr. Timothy L. Duff

General Information Coeducational day college-preparatory, religious studies, bilingual studies, and technology school, affiliated with Protestant faith, Evangelical faith. Grades PS–12. Founded: 1972. Setting: suburban. 25-acre campus. 1 building on campus. Approved or accredited by Association of Christian Schools International, New England Association of Schools and Colleges, and Massachusetts Department of Education. Total enrollment: 265. Upper school average class size: 20. Upper school faculty-student ratio: 1:5. There are 181 required school days per year for Upper School students. Upper School students typically attend 5 days per week. The average school day consists of 6 hours and 40 minutes.

Upper School Student Profile Grade 9: 24 students (15 boys, 9 girls); Grade 10: 20 students (12 boys, 8 girls); Grade 11: 11 students (5 boys, 6 girls); Grade 12: 22 students (11 boys, 11 girls). 95% of students are Protestant, members of Evangelical faith.

Faculty School total: 31. In upper school: 6 men, 10 women; 9 have advanced degrees.

Subjects Offered Advanced math, algebra, American literature, American literature-AP, anatomy, art, athletics, baseball, basketball, bell choir, Bible studies, biology, British literature, British literature-AP, calculus-AP, chemistry, choir, choral music, Christian education, drama, economics, English, English-AP, French, geometry, government, history, instrumental music, music, physical education, physical science, physics, pre-algebra, sociology, softball, Spanish, speech, sports, technology, tennis, U.S. history, volleyball, weight training, Western civilization, world history, yearbook.

Graduation Requirements Algebra, American literature, arts and fine arts (art, music, dance, drama), Bible, biology, British literature, economics, English, foreign language, government, physical education (includes health), physical science, sociology, speech, U.S. history, Christian/community service hours.

Special Academic Programs Advanced Placement exam preparation; honors section; remedial reading and/or remedial writing; remedial math; programs in English, mathematics, general development for dyslexic students; special instructional classes for students with learning disabilities, Attention Deficit Disorder, and dyslexia.

College Admission Counseling 32 students graduated in 2012; all went to college, including Anderson University; Berklee College of Music; Holyoke Community College; Western New England University. Median SAT critical reading: 485, median SAT math: 480, median SAT writing: 480, median composite ACT: 19.

Student Life Upper grades have uniform requirement, honor system. Discipline rests primarily with faculty. Attendance at religious services is required.

Tuition and Aid Day student tuition: $10,300. Tuition installment plan (monthly payment plans, Electronic Funds Transfer, weekly, biweekly, monthly). Need-based scholarship grants, need-based financial aid and scholarship available. In 2012–13, 38% of upper-school students received aid. Total amount of financial aid awarded in 2012–13: $80,300.

Admissions Traditional secondary-level entrance grade is 9. For fall 2012, 10 students applied for upper-level admission, 10 were accepted, 10 enrolled. Admissions testing required. Deadline for receipt of application materials: none. Application fee required: $80. Interview required.

Athletics Interscholastic: baseball (boys), basketball (b,g), softball (g), tennis (b,g), volleyball (g); intramural: soccer (b,g); coed interscholastic: soccer, weight training; coed intramural: combined training, physical training, soccer, strength & conditioning. 2 PE instructors, 16 coaches.

Computers Computers are regularly used in all academic classes. Computer network features include Internet access, Internet filtering or blocking technology, homework assignments available online.

Contact Mr. Pat Sterlacci, Director of Admissions. 413-782-8031. Fax: 413-782-8033. E-mail: psterlacci@pvcs.org. Web site: www.pvcs.org

POPE JOHN XXIII REGIONAL HIGH SCHOOL

28 Andover Road
Sparta, New Jersey 07871

Head of School: Mrs. Gloria Shope

General Information Coeducational day college-preparatory, arts, business, religious studies, and technology school, affiliated with Roman Catholic Church. Grades 8–12. Founded: 1956. Setting: suburban. Nearest major city is New York, NY. 15-acre campus. 1 building on campus. Approved or accredited by Department of Defense Dependents Schools and New Jersey Department of Education. Total enrollment: 972. Upper school average class size: 20. Upper school faculty-student ratio: 1:13. There are 180 required school days per year for Upper School students. Upper School students typically attend 5 days per week. The average school day consists of 5 hours and 42 minutes.

Upper School Student Profile Grade 8: 127 students (62 boys, 65 girls); Grade 9: 196 students (87 boys, 109 girls); Grade 10: 217 students (119 boys, 98 girls); Grade 11: 208 students (97 boys, 111 girls); Grade 12: 224 students (118 boys, 106 girls). 80% of students are Roman Catholic.

Faculty School total: 78. In upper school: 36 men, 42 women; 35 have advanced degrees.

Subjects Offered Advanced chemistry, advanced computer applications, advanced math, Advanced Placement courses, algebra, American literature, American studies, anatomy and physiology, art, biology, biology-AP, British literature, business, business law, calculus, calculus-AP, chemistry, chemistry-AP, choral music, computer literacy, computer science, computer science-AP, conceptual physics, concert choir, earth science, economics, English, English language-AP, English literature, English literature and composition-AP, environmental science, environmental science-AP, European history-AP, fine arts, French, French-AP, geometry, German, global issues, government and politics-AP, graphic arts, health and safety, history-AP, honors algebra, honors English, honors geometry, honors U.S. history, honors world history, Italian, Japanese, jazz band, journalism, lab science, Latin, macroeconomics-AP, microeconomics-AP, modern politics, music theory, physical education, physics, physics-AP, pre-calculus, psychology, public speaking, reading/study skills, robotics, Spanish, Spanish language-AP, statistics, statistics-AP, theater arts, theology, U.S. government, U.S. government and politics-AP, U.S. history, U.S. history-AP, world cultures, world history-AP, writing, zoology.

Graduation Requirements Arts and fine arts (art, music, dance, drama), English, foreign language, health and safety, mathematics, science, social studies (includes history), theology, 60 hours of community service (15 hours per year).

Special Academic Programs Advanced Placement exam preparation; honors section; ESL (19 students enrolled).

College Admission Counseling 252 students graduated in 2012; 251 went to college, including High Point University; Manhattan College; Seton Hall University; Susquehanna University; The Catholic University of America; The College of New Jersey. Other: 1 had other specific plans. Mean SAT critical reading: 540, mean SAT math: 560, mean SAT writing: 540, mean combined SAT: 1640.

Student Life Upper grades have uniform requirement, student council. Discipline rests primarily with faculty. Attendance at religious services is required.

Summer Programs Remediation, enrichment, sports programs offered; session focuses on sports; held on campus; accepts boys and girls; open to students from other schools. 200 students usually enrolled.

Tuition and Aid Day student tuition: $14,000. Guaranteed tuition plan. Tuition installment plan (SMART Tuition Payment Plan). Need-based scholarship grants available.

Admissions Traditional secondary-level entrance grade is 9. CTB/McGraw-Hill/Macmillan Co-op Test, Math Placement Exam, placement test and writing sample required. Deadline for receipt of application materials: none. No application fee required. Interview required.

Athletics Interscholastic: baseball (boys), basketball (b,g), cheering (g), cross-country running (b,g), field hockey (g), football (b), ice hockey (b), indoor track & field (b,g), lacrosse (b,g), running (b,g), skiing (downhill) (b,g), softball (g), swimming and diving (b,g), tennis (b,g), track and field (b,g), volleyball (b,g), winter (indoor) track (b,g), wrestling (b); coed interscholastic: golf.

Computers Computers are regularly used in graphic arts, programming classes. Computer network features include Internet access, Internet filtering or blocking technology, Naviance Succeed. Computer access in designated common areas is available to students. The school has a published electronic and media policy.

Contact Mrs. Anne Kaiser, Administrative Assistant for Admissions. 973-729-6125 Ext. 255. Fax: 973-729-4536. E-mail: annekaiser@popejohn.org. Web site: www.popejohn.org

PORTER-GAUD SCHOOL

300 Albemarle Road
Charleston, South Carolina 29407

Head of School: Mr. David DuBose Egleston Jr.

General Information Coeducational day college-preparatory, arts, religious studies, and technology school, affiliated with Christian faith, Episcopal Church. Grades 1–12. Founded: 1867. Setting: suburban. 80-acre campus. 7 buildings on campus. Approved or accredited by National Association of Episcopal Schools, South Carolina Independent School Association, Southern Association of Colleges and Schools, Southern Association of Independent Schools, and South Carolina Department of Education. Member of National Association of Independent Schools and Secondary School Admission Test Board. Endowment: $12 million. Total enrollment: 889. Upper school average class size: 12. Upper school faculty-student ratio: 1:12. There are 175 required school days per year for Upper School students. Upper School students typically attend 5 days per week. The average school day consists of 7 hours and 15 minutes.

Upper School Student Profile Grade 9: 86 students (58 boys, 28 girls); Grade 10: 83 students (48 boys, 35 girls); Grade 11: 93 students (60 boys, 33 girls); Grade 12: 80 students (50 boys, 30 girls); Postgraduate: 342 students (216 boys, 126 girls). 80% of students are Christian, members of Episcopal Church.

Faculty School total: 94. In upper school: 15 men, 25 women; 30 have advanced degrees.

Subjects Offered Advanced Placement courses, algebra, American history, American literature, art, art history, art-AP, biology, calculus, calculus-AP, chemistry, computer programming, computer science, drama, economics, English, English literature, ethics, European history, expository writing, fine arts, French, geometry, government/civics, health, Latin, Latin-AP, music, music appreciation, music theory-AP, physical education, physics, pre-calculus, Spanish, Spanish language-AP, world history, world literature.

Graduation Requirements Algebra, American literature, art education, arts and fine arts (art, music, dance, drama), biology, chemistry, computer science, English, English composition, English literature, European history, foreign language, geometry, health, physical education (includes health), physics, pre-calculus, religion (includes Bible studies and theology), trigonometry, U.S. history, world history.

Special Academic Programs 19 Advanced Placement exams for which test preparation is offered; honors section; independent study.

College Admission Counseling 85 students graduated in 2012; all went to college, including Clemson University; Georgetown University; Sewanee: The University of the South; University of South Carolina; University of Southern California; Vanderbilt University. Mean SAT critical reading: 629, mean SAT math: 624, mean SAT writing: 640, mean combined SAT: 1893, mean composite ACT: 28.

Student Life Upper grades have uniform requirement, student council, honor system. Discipline rests equally with students and faculty. Attendance at religious services is required.

Summer Programs Remediation, enrichment programs offered; session focuses on remedial; held on campus; open to students from other schools. 15 students usually enrolled. 2013 schedule: June to August. Application deadline: June.

Tuition and Aid Day student tuition: $18,610. Tuition installment plan (monthly payment plans, individually arranged payment plans, 60/40 payment plan). Need-based scholarship grants available. In 2012–13, 20% of upper-school students received aid. Total amount of financial aid awarded in 2012–13: $467,620.

Admissions Traditional secondary-level entrance grade is 9. For fall 2012, 60 students applied for upper-level admission, 53 were accepted, 29 enrolled. ISEE or SSAT required. Deadline for receipt of application materials: January 30. Application fee required: $75. Interview required.

Athletics Interscholastic: baseball (boys), basketball (b,g), cheering (g), fencing (b), football (b), hockey (b), ice hockey (b), lacrosse (b), physical training (b,g), soccer (b,g), softball (b,g), squash (b), strength & conditioning (b,g), swimming and diving (b,g), tennis (b,g), track and field (b,g), volleyball (g), weight lifting (b,g), weight training (b,g), wrestling (b); intramural: basketball (b,g), Frisbee (b,g), lacrosse (b); coed interscholastic: cross-country running, golf, Nautilus, sailing; coed intramural: Frisbee, ultimate Frisbee. 4 PE instructors, 26 coaches, 1 athletic trainer.

Computers Computers are regularly used in all classes. Computer network features include on-campus library services, Internet access, wireless campus network, Internet filtering or blocking technology, 4 year Computer Science degree with college credit earned. Campus intranet, student e-mail accounts, and computer access in designated common areas are available to students. Students grades are available online. The school has a published electronic and media policy.

Contact Mrs. Eleanor W. Hurtes, Director of Admissions. 843-402-4775. Fax: 843-556-7404. E-mail: eleanor.hurtes@portergaud.edu. Web site: www.portergaud.edu

PORTSMOUTH ABBEY SCHOOL

285 Cory's Lane
Portsmouth, Rhode Island 02871

Head of School: Dr. James De Vecchi

General Information Coeducational boarding and day college-preparatory, arts, religious studies, and music, classics, humanities school, affiliated with Roman Catholic Church. Grades 9–12. Founded: 1926. Setting: small town. Nearest major city is Providence. Students are housed in single-sex dormitories. 550-acre campus. 36 buildings on campus. Approved or accredited by Association of Independent Schools in New England, National Independent Private Schools Association, New England Association of Schools and Colleges, and The Association of Boarding Schools. Member of National Association of Independent Schools and Secondary School Admission Test Board. Endowment: $30 million. Total enrollment: 357. Upper school average class size: 13. Upper school faculty-student ratio: 1:7. There are 180 required school days per year for Upper School students. Upper School students typically attend 6 days per week. The average school day consists of 7 hours.

Upper School Student Profile Grade 9: 77 students (42 boys, 35 girls); Grade 10: 111 students (64 boys, 47 girls); Grade 11: 76 students (42 boys, 34 girls); Grade 12: 93 students (44 boys, 49 girls). 70% of students are boarding students. 35% are state residents. 22 states are represented in upper school student body. 19% are international students. International students from China, Dominican Republic, Guatemala, Republic of Korea, Spain, and Trinidad and Tobago; 10 other countries represented in student body. 60% of students are Roman Catholic.

Faculty School total: 52. In upper school: 35 men, 17 women; 41 have advanced degrees; 34 reside on campus.

Subjects Offered Algebra, American literature, art, art history, art history-AP, art-AP, biology, biology-AP, calculus, calculus-AP, chemistry, chemistry-AP, Chinese, Christian doctrine, Christian ethics, computer programming-AP, computer science, computer science-AP, creative writing, drama, drama workshop, economics, English, English language and composition-AP, English literature, English literature and composition-AP, fine arts, French, French language-AP, French literature-AP, geometry, government/civics, Greek, health, history, history-AP, humanities, international relations, Latin, Latin-AP, Mandarin, marine biology, mathematics, mathematics-AP, modern European history-AP, music, music composition, music theory, music theory-AP, philosophy, photography, physics, physics-AP, physiology, political science, religion, science, social sciences, Spanish, Spanish language-AP, Spanish literature-AP, statistics-AP, studio art-AP, theater, theology, trigonometry, U.S. history, U.S. history-AP, world history, writing workshop.

Graduation Requirements Arts and fine arts (art, music, dance, drama), English, foreign language, history, Latin, mathematics, religion (includes Bible studies and theology), science, humanities.

Special Academic Programs 19 Advanced Placement exams for which test preparation is offered; honors section; independent study; academic accommodation for the gifted.

College Admission Counseling 105 students graduated in 2012; all went to college, including Boston College; Brown University; Georgetown University; New York University; Northeastern University; The George Washington University.

Student Life Upper grades have specified standards of dress, student council, honor system. Discipline rests primarily with faculty. Attendance at religious services is required.

Summer Programs Enrichment, advancement, ESL, sports, art/fine arts programs offered; session focuses on Academic; held on campus; accepts boys and girls; open to students from other schools. 90 students usually enrolled. 2013 schedule: June 30 to July 27. Application deadline: none.

Tuition and Aid Day student tuition: $33,025; 7-day tuition and room/board: $48,850. Tuition installment plan (monthly payment plans, individually arranged payment plans, Tuition Management Systems Plan). Merit scholarship grants, need-based scholarship grants available. In 2012–13, 37% of upper-school students received aid; total upper-school merit-scholarship money awarded: $300,000. Total amount of financial aid awarded in 2012–13: $3,600,000.

Admissions Traditional secondary-level entrance grade is 9. For fall 2012, 512 students applied for upper-level admission, 246 were accepted, 117 enrolled. PSAT or SAT for applicants to grade 11 and 12, SSAT and TOEFL required. Deadline for receipt of application materials: January 31. Application fee required: $50. Interview required.

Athletics Interscholastic: baseball (boys), basketball (b,g), cross-country running (b,g), field hockey (g), football (b), golf (b,g), ice hockey (b,g), lacrosse (b,g), soccer (b,g), softball (g), squash (b,g), swimming and diving (b,g), tennis (b,g), track and field (b,g), wrestling (g); coed interscholastic: cross-country running, sailing, swimming and diving, track and field; coed intramural: ballet, dance, equestrian sports, fitness, horseback riding, modern dance, strength & conditioning, weight training. 1 athletic trainer.

Computers Computer network features include on-campus library services, Internet access, wireless campus network. Campus intranet and student e-mail accounts are available to students. Students grades are available online.

Contact Mrs. Ann Motta, Admissions Coordinator. 401-643-1248. Fax: 401-643-1355. E-mail: admissions@portsmouthabbey.org. Web site: www.portsmouthabbey.org

PORTSMOUTH CHRISTIAN ACADEMY

20 Seaborne Drive
Dover, New Hampshire 03820

Head of School: Mr. Dennis Runey

General Information Coeducational day college-preparatory, arts, religious studies, technology, science/mathematics, and communication school, affiliated with Christian faith. Grades K–12. Founded: 1979. Setting: rural. Nearest major city is Portsmouth. 50-acre campus. 3 buildings on campus. Approved or accredited by Association of Christian Schools International, New England Association of Schools and Colleges, and New Hampshire Department of Education. Total enrollment: 617. Upper school average class size: 17. Upper school faculty-student ratio: 1:13. There are 172 required school days per year for Upper School students. Upper School students typically attend 5 days per week. The average school day consists of 7 hours and 5 minutes.

Upper School Student Profile Grade 9: 46 students (21 boys, 25 girls); Grade 10: 51 students (25 boys, 26 girls); Grade 11: 36 students (21 boys, 15 girls); Grade 12: 48 students (15 boys, 33 girls). 70% of students are Christian faith.

Faculty School total: 71. In upper school: 11 men, 13 women; 14 have advanced degrees.

Subjects Offered 20th century American writers, 20th century history, 3-dimensional art, 3-dimensional design, ACT preparation, advanced chemistry, advanced computer applications, advanced math, Advanced Placement courses, advanced studio art-AP, African drumming, algebra, alternative physical education, American history, American literature, American literature-AP, analysis and differential calculus, anatomy and physiology, applied music, art, art appreciation, art education, art history, art history-AP, arts appreciation, astronomy, athletic training, athletics, band, baseball, basketball, Bible, Bible studies, biochemistry, biology, British literature, British literature (honors), calculus, calculus-AP, chemistry, chemistry-AP, choir, choral music, chorus, Christian doctrine, Christian education, Christian ethics, Christian scripture, Christian studies, Christian testament, Christianity, church history, civics, college admission preparation, college awareness, college counseling, college placement, college planning, college writing, comparative religion, composition, composition-AP, computer applications, computer education, computer graphics, computer processing, computer resources, computer skills, computer-aided design, contemporary issues, current history, debate, digital art, digital photography, drama, drama performance, drama workshop, drawing, drawing and design, driver education, economics, economics and history, English, English as a foreign language, English composition, English language and composition-AP, English literature and composition-AP, English literature-AP, English-AP, environmental science, European history, film and literature, foreign language, French, French language-AP, French studies, geometry, government, government/civics, guitar, health, health and wellness, honors algebra, honors English, honors geometry, honors world history, human anatomy, instrumental music, integrated physics, jazz band, lab science, law studies, learning lab, literature, literature and composition-AP, literature-AP, logic, rhetoric, and debate, marine science, math review, mathematics, microbiology, modern European history, modern history, music, music appreciation, musical productions, musical theater, New Testament, novels, performing arts, photography, physics, physics-AP, physiology, political economy, pre-calculus, religion and culture, rhetoric, SAT preparation, SAT/ACT preparation, Shakespeare, Spanish, Spanish language-AP, Spanish-AP, student government, symphonic band, theater arts, theology, U.S. history, U.S. history-AP, U.S. literature, world history, World War II, writing, writing workshop, yearbook.

Graduation Requirements 20th century history, algebra, arts and fine arts (art, music, dance, drama), biology, chemistry, comparative cultures, composition, computer skills, foreign language, geometry, physical education (includes health), physical science, U.S. history, writing, one Bible course for each year of Upper School attendance, service hours.

Special Academic Programs Advanced Placement exam preparation; honors section; accelerated programs; independent study; study at local college for college credit; academic accommodation for the gifted and the musically talented; special instructional classes for students with Attention Deficit Disorder and dyslexia; ESL (22 students enrolled).

College Admission Counseling 34 students graduated in 2012; 33 went to college, including Pepperdine University; Rochester Institute of Technology; Seattle Pacific University; Texas A&M University; University of Massachusetts Amherst; University of New Hampshire. Other: 1 had other specific plans. Mean SAT critical reading: 562, mean SAT math: 536, mean SAT writing: 551.

Student Life Upper grades have specified standards of dress, student council, honor system. Discipline rests primarily with faculty.

Summer Programs Remediation, enrichment, sports programs offered; session focuses on soccer, basketball, and volleyball; held on campus; accepts boys and girls; open to students from other schools. 40 students usually enrolled. 2013 schedule: July 1 to August 25. Application deadline: June 1.

Tuition and Aid Day student tuition: $10,115. Tuition installment plan (FACTS Tuition Payment Plan). Tuition reduction for siblings, merit scholarship grants, need-based scholarship grants available. In 2012–13, 26% of upper-school students received aid; total upper-school merit-scholarship money awarded: $8000. Total amount of financial aid awarded in 2012–13: $180,000.

Admissions Traditional secondary-level entrance grade is 9. Achievement tests, PSAT or SAT, PSAT or SAT for applicants to grade 11 and 12, PSAT, SAT, or ACT for applicants to grade 11 and 12, SAT, standardized test scores, Stanford Achievement Test, Test of Achievement and Proficiency, TOEFL, TOEFL or SLEP or writing sample required. Deadline for receipt of application materials: none. Application fee required: $100. Interview required.

Athletics Interscholastic: baseball (boys), basketball (b,g), cross-country running (b,g), indoor track & field (b,g), soccer (b,g), softball (g), tennis (b,g), track and field (b,g), volleyball (g), winter (indoor) track (b,g); intramural: golf (b,g), skiing (cross-country) (b,g), skiing (downhill) (b,g), snowboarding (b,g), tennis (b,g); coed interscholastic: alpine skiing, cross-country running, fitness, indoor track & field, winter (indoor) track; coed intramural: skiing (cross-country), skiing (downhill), snowboarding, tennis. 1 PE instructor, 14 coaches.

Computers Computers are regularly used in art, Bible studies, career education, Christian doctrine, classics, college planning, desktop publishing, economics, English, foreign language, graphic design, history, humanities, independent study, library, library skills, mathematics, media arts, photography, religion, religious studies, SAT preparation, science, social studies, writing, yearbook classes. Computer network features include on-campus library services, online commercial services, Internet access, Internet filtering or blocking technology. Computer access in designated common areas is available to students. Students grades are available online. The school has a published electronic and media policy.

Contact Mrs. Diane Sipp, Director of Admissions. 603-742-3617 Ext. 116. Fax: 603-750-0490. E-mail: dsipp@pcaschool.org. Web site: www.pcaschool.org

THE POTOMAC SCHOOL

1301 Potomac School Road
McLean, Virginia 22101

Head of School: Geoffrey Jones

General Information Coeducational day college-preparatory and liberal arts, arts, athletics, and character education school. Grades K–12. Founded: 1904. Setting: suburban. Nearest major city is Washington, DC. 90-acre campus. Approved or accredited by Association of Independent Schools of Greater Washington and Virginia Association of Independent Schools. Member of National Association of Independent Schools and Secondary School Admission Test Board. Endowment: $28 million. Total enrollment: 1,007. Upper school average class size: 14. Upper school faculty-student ratio: 1:6.

Upper School Student Profile Grade 9: 109 students (54 boys, 55 girls); Grade 10: 93 students (48 boys, 45 girls); Grade 11: 102 students (54 boys, 48 girls); Grade 12: 106 students (52 boys, 54 girls).

Faculty School total: 150. In upper school: 27 men, 34 women; 45 have advanced degrees.

Subjects Offered 20th century American writers, 20th century history, 20th century world history, 3-dimensional art, 3-dimensional design, acting, advanced computer applications, advanced math, Advanced Placement courses, advanced studio art-AP, African history, African-American literature, African-American studies, algebra, American foreign policy, American literature, ancient history, art, art history, Asian studies, band, bell choir, Bible as literature, bioethics, biology, British literature, calculus, calculus-AP, cell biology, ceramics, chamber groups, character education, chemistry, chemistry-AP, Chinese history, choral music, civil war history, community service, comparative religion, computer programming, computer programming-AP, computer science, conceptual physics, concert band, creative writing, debate, directing, drama, drama performance, drawing and design, economics and history, engineering, English, English literature, environmental science, European history, expository writing, film and literature, fine arts, French, French language-AP, French literature-AP, functions, geometry, global studies, government/civics, handbells, Harlem Renaissance, historical research, history of jazz, history of music, independent study, jazz band, Latin, Latin American history, Latin-AP, leadership, literary magazine, madrigals, mathematics, medieval history, Middle Eastern history, model United Nations, modern European history, music, music composition, music theory-AP, newspaper, painting, performing arts, photography, physical education, physics, physics-AP, portfolio art, pre-calculus, robotics, science, science and technology, sculpture, senior project, Shakespeare, short story, Spanish, Spanish language-AP, Spanish literature-AP, stagecraft, statistics-AP, strings, student government, studio art-AP, theater arts, trigonometry, U.S. government and politics, U.S. history-AP, vocal music, World War II, yearbook.

Graduation Requirements Arts and fine arts (art, music, dance, drama), English, ethics, foreign language, history, mathematics, physical education (includes health), science, senior project, month-long senior project.

Special Academic Programs Advanced Placement exam preparation; honors section; independent study.

College Admission Counseling 98 students graduated in 2011; 96 went to college, including Columbia University; Cornell University; Georgetown University; Southern Methodist University; University of Virginia; Villanova University. Median SAT critical reading: 690, median SAT math: 700.

Student Life Upper grades have specified standards of dress, student council, honor system. Discipline rests equally with students and faculty.

Tuition and Aid Day student tuition: $28,915. Tuition installment plan (Insured Tuition Payment Plan, monthly payment plans). Need-based scholarship grants available. In 2011–12, 15% of upper-school students received aid. Total amount of financial aid awarded in 2011–12: $1,293,670.

Admissions Traditional secondary-level entrance grade is 9. ISEE or SSAT required. Deadline for receipt of application materials: January 10. Application fee required: $65. On-campus interview required.

Athletics Interscholastic: baseball (boys), basketball (b,g), cross-country running (b,g), field hockey (g), football (b), lacrosse (b,g), soccer (b,g), softball (g), squash (b,g), tennis (b,g), track and field (b,g), wrestling (b); intramural: weight lifting (b,g); coed interscholastic: golf, ice hockey, swimming and diving, winter (indoor) track; coed intramural: canoeing/kayaking, fitness, hiking/backpacking, ice hockey, outdoor education, physical fitness, physical training, sailing, strength & conditioning, weight training. 5 PE instructors, 33 coaches, 2 athletic trainers.

Computers Computers are regularly used in all academic, computer applications, drawing and design, independent study, literary magazine, newspaper, photography, programming, yearbook classes. Computer network features include on-campus library services, online commercial services, Internet access, wireless campus network, Internet filtering or blocking technology, ebooks. Campus intranet and student e-mail accounts are available to students. The school has a published electronic and media policy.

Contact Leslie Vorndran, Admission Services Coordinator. 703-749-6313. Fax: 703-356-1764. Web site: www.potomacschool.org

POWERS CATHOLIC HIGH SCHOOL

G-2040 West Carpenter Road
Flint, Michigan 48505-1028

Head of School: Mr. Thomas Furnas

General Information Coeducational day college-preparatory, arts, business, religious studies, and technology school, affiliated with Roman Catholic Church. Grades 9–12. Founded: 1970. Setting: urban. 67-acre campus. 1 building on campus. Approved or accredited by National Catholic Education Association, North Central Association of Colleges and Schools, and Michigan Department of Education. Endowment: $3 million. Total enrollment: 511. Upper school average class size: 25. Upper school faculty-student ratio: 1:18. There are 188 required school days per year for Upper School students. Upper School students typically attend 5 days per week. The average school day consists of 6 hours and 40 minutes.

Upper School Student Profile Grade 9: 122 students (66 boys, 56 girls); Grade 10: 148 students (69 boys, 79 girls); Grade 11: 118 students (59 boys, 59 girls); Grade 12: 123 students (76 boys, 47 girls). 75% of students are Roman Catholic.
Faculty School total: 29. In upper school: 12 men, 17 women; 20 have advanced degrees.
Subjects Offered Art, art-AP, biology, biology-AP, calculus-AP, ceramics, chemistry, choir, computer skills, concert band, drafting, economics, English, English literature and composition-AP, European history-AP, French, geometry, government, government-AP, health, honors algebra, honors English, honors geometry, integrated science, interdisciplinary studies, macroeconomics-AP, marching band, math analysis, math applications, mechanical drawing, physics, pre-algebra, pre-calculus, psychology, psychology-AP, public speaking, religion, social justice, Spanish, state history, studio art-AP, theology, trigonometry, U.S. history, wind ensemble, world geography, world history, world religions, yearbook.
Graduation Requirements American history, English, government, health, mathematics, science, theology, world history, 40 hours of community service.
Special Academic Programs 7 Advanced Placement exams for which test preparation is offered; honors section; remedial reading and/or remedial writing; remedial math.
College Admission Counseling 147 students graduated in 2012; 144 went to college, including Central Michigan University; Grand Valley State University; Michigan State University; Saginaw Valley State University; University of Michigan; University of Michigan–Dearborn. Other: 1 went to work, 2 entered military service. Mean composite ACT: 22.
Student Life Upper grades have uniform requirement, student council. Discipline rests primarily with faculty. Attendance at religious services is required.
Tuition and Aid Day student tuition: $8200. Tuition installment plan (SMART Tuition Payment Plan). Tuition reduction for siblings, need-based scholarship grants available. In 2012–13, 33% of upper-school students received aid. Total amount of financial aid awarded in 2012–13: $450,300.
Admissions Traditional secondary-level entrance grade is 9. ACT-Explore required. Deadline for receipt of application materials: none. Application fee required: $100. Interview required.
Athletics Interscholastic: alpine skiing (boys, girls), baseball (b), basketball (b,g), bowling (b,g), cross-country running (b,g), dance squad (g), dance team (g), diving (b,g), football (b), golf (b,g), ice hockey (b), lacrosse (b,g), skiing (downhill) (b,g), soccer (b,g), softball (g), swimming and diving (b,g), tennis (b,g), track and field (b,g), volleyball (g), wrestling (b); coed interscholastic: cheering, equestrian sports, indoor track, power lifting, skeet shooting, strength & conditioning, weight lifting; coed intramural: ultimate Frisbee, weight training. 1 PE instructor.
Computers Computers are regularly used in accounting, business applications, drafting, graphic design, keyboarding, yearbook classes. Computer resources include on-campus library services, Internet access, wireless campus network, Internet filtering or blocking technology. Computer access in designated common areas is available to students. Students grades are available online. The school has a published electronic and media policy.
Contact Ms. Sally Bartos, Assistant Principal for Instruction. 810-591-4741. Fax: 810-591-0383. E-mail: sbartos@powerscatholic.org. Web site: www.powerscatholic.org/

THE PRAIRIE SCHOOL

4050 Lighthouse Drive
Racine, Wisconsin 53402

Head of School: Mr. Wm. Mark H. Murphy

General Information Coeducational day college-preparatory, arts, and technology school. Grades PK–12. Founded: 1965. Setting: small town. Nearest major city is Milwaukee. 33-acre campus. 2 buildings on campus. Approved or accredited by Independent Schools Association of the Central States and Wisconsin Department of Education. Member of National Association of Independent Schools. Endowment: $38 million. Total enrollment: 687. Upper school average class size: 17. Upper school faculty-student ratio: 1:17. There are 175 required school days per year for Upper School students. Upper School students typically attend 5 days per week. The average school day consists of 7 hours.
Upper School Student Profile Grade 9: 67 students (34 boys, 33 girls); Grade 10: 60 students (24 boys, 36 girls); Grade 11: 63 students (34 boys, 29 girls); Grade 12: 75 students (38 boys, 37 girls).
Faculty School total: 75. In upper school: 19 men, 15 women; 18 have advanced degrees.
Subjects Offered Algebra, American history, American history-AP, American literature, anatomy and physiology, art, athletic training, biology, biology-AP, calculus, calculus-AP, ceramics, chemistry, chemistry-AP, Chinese, choir, community service, computer science, CPR, creative writing, dance, digital imaging, drama, drawing and design, earth and space science, ecology, economics, English, English literature, English-AP, environmental science, environmental science-AP, European history, European history-AP, film studies, fine arts, French, French language-AP, geometry, glassblowing, government/civics, health, history, international relations, jazz ensemble, mathematics, multicultural literature, music, music theory-AP, orchestra, philosophy, photography, physical education, physics, physics-AP, pre-calculus, probability and statistics, public speaking, science, social studies, Spanish, Spanish language-AP, speech, statistics, statistics-AP, study skills, theater, trigonometry, Western literature, world geography, world history, world literature, writing.
Graduation Requirements Arts and fine arts (art, music, dance, drama), English, foreign language, mathematics, physical education (includes health), science, social studies (includes history), study skills, spring Interim program (including on-campus seminars, community service, off-campus internships), 100-hour service requirement.
Special Academic Programs 14 Advanced Placement exams for which test preparation is offered; honors section; independent study; term-away projects; academic accommodation for the gifted, the musically talented, and the artistically talented; remedial reading and/or remedial writing; special instructional classes for blind students; ESL (2 students enrolled).
College Admission Counseling 72 students graduated in 2011; all went to college, including Marquette University; The University of Tampa; University of Denver; University of Minnesota, Twin Cities Campus; University of Wisconsin–Madison; University of Wisconsin–Milwaukee. Median SAT math: 595, median SAT writing: 590, median combined SAT: 1185, median composite ACT: 27.
Student Life Upper grades have specified standards of dress, student council, honor system. Discipline rests primarily with faculty.
Tuition and Aid Day student tuition: $14,040. Tuition installment plan (FACTS Tuition Payment Plan). Tuition reduction for siblings, merit scholarship grants, need-based scholarship grants available. In 2011–12, 43% of upper-school students received aid; total upper-school merit-scholarship money awarded: $98,000. Total amount of financial aid awarded in 2011–12: $120,000.
Admissions Traditional secondary-level entrance grade is 9. For fall 2011, 35 students applied for upper-level admission, 26 were accepted, 16 enrolled. Admissions testing, school's own exam or TerraNova required. Deadline for receipt of application materials: none. Application fee required: $50. On-campus interview required.
Athletics Interscholastic: baseball (boys), basketball (b,g), soccer (b,g), tennis (b,g), volleyball (g); coed interscholastic: cross-country running, golf, modern dance, outdoor activities, track and field. 7 PE instructors, 13 coaches, 1 athletic trainer.
Computers Computers are regularly used in all academic classes. Computer network features include on-campus library services, Internet access, wireless campus network, Internet filtering or blocking technology. Campus intranet, student e-mail accounts, and computer access in designated common areas are available to students. Students grades are available online. The school has a published electronic and media policy.
Contact Ms. Molly Lofquist Johnson, Director of Admissions. 262-260-4393. Fax: 262-260-3790. E-mail: mlofquist@prairieschool.com. Web site: www.prairieschool.com

PRESBYTERIAN PAN AMERICAN SCHOOL

PO Box 1578
223 North FM Road 772
Kingsville, Texas 78364-1578

Head of School: Dr. Doug Dalglish

General Information Coeducational boarding and day and distance learning college-preparatory school, affiliated with Presbyterian Church (U.S.A.). Grades 9–12. Distance learning grades 9–12. Founded: 1912. Setting: rural. Nearest major city is Corpus Christi. Students are housed in single-sex dormitories. 670-acre campus. 22 buildings on campus. Approved or accredited by Southern Association of Colleges and Schools, Texas Private School Accreditation Commission, and Texas Department of Education. Endowment: $5.3 million. Total enrollment: 163. Upper school average class size: 20. Upper school faculty-student ratio: 1:10. There are 180 required school days per year for Upper School students. Upper School students typically attend 5 days per week. The average school day consists of 8 hours.
Upper School Student Profile Grade 9: 44 students (16 boys, 28 girls); Grade 10: 33 students (17 boys, 16 girls); Grade 11: 34 students (15 boys, 19 girls); Grade 12: 52 students (25 boys, 27 girls). 100% of students are boarding students. 6% are state residents. 2 states are represented in upper school student body. 94% are international students. International students from China, Colombia, Democratic People's Republic of Korea, Mexico, and Rwanda. 40% of students are Presbyterian Church (U.S.A.).
Faculty School total: 17. In upper school: 5 men, 11 women; 5 have advanced degrees; 3 reside on campus.
Subjects Offered Algebra, American history, American literature, animal science, art, arts, Bible studies, biology, calculus, career exploration, chemistry, choir, communications, computer science, debate, economics, English, English literature, ESL, geography, geometry, government/civics, health, horticulture, journalism, literary genres, mathematical modeling, physical education, physics, pre-calculus, religion, Spanish, theater arts, U.S. history, world history, world literature, yearbook.
Graduation Requirements Arts and fine arts (art, music, dance, drama), career exploration, economics, English, foreign language, mathematics, religion (includes Bible studies and theology), science, social sciences, social studies (includes history), TOEFL score of 550, or SAT Reading of 550.
Special Academic Programs Study at local college for college credit; ESL (59 students enrolled).

College Admission Counseling 45 students graduated in 2012; all went to college, including Abilene Christian University; Schreiner University; Texas A&M University; The University of Texas at Austin; The University of Texas at San Antonio; University of Houston. Median SAT critical reading: 410, median SAT math: 450, median SAT writing: 420. 4% scored over 600 on SAT critical reading, 5% scored over 600 on SAT math.

Student Life Upper grades have uniform requirement, student council, honor system. Discipline rests primarily with faculty. Attendance at religious services is required.

Tuition and Aid Day student tuition: $8500; 7-day tuition and room/board: $15,000. Guaranteed tuition plan. Tuition installment plan (monthly payment plans, individually arranged payment plans, quarterly payment plan, semester payment plan). Tuition reduction for siblings, merit scholarship grants, need-based scholarship grants, need-based financial aid, discounts tied to enrollment referred by current student families available. In 2012–13, 89% of upper-school students received aid. Total amount of financial aid awarded in 2012–13: $1,196,250.

Admissions Traditional secondary-level entrance grade is 9. For fall 2012, 106 students applied for upper-level admission, 83 were accepted, 57 enrolled. Secondary Level English Proficiency and TOEFL required. Deadline for receipt of application materials: none. Application fee required: $75. Interview recommended.

Athletics Interscholastic: baseball (boys), basketball (b,g), cheering (b,g), cross-country running (b,g), soccer (b,g), track and field (b,g), volleyball (g); intramural: billiards (b), jogging (b,g), life saving (b,g), paddle tennis (b,g), physical fitness (b,g), strength & conditioning (b,g), table tennis (b,g), tennis (b,g), volleyball (b), walking (b,g), winter walking (b,g); coed intramural: aquatics, fitness walking, jogging, life saving, paddle tennis, strength & conditioning, table tennis, volleyball, walking, winter walking. 2 PE instructors, 5 coaches, 1 athletic trainer.

Computers Computers are regularly used in all academic, English, ESL, mathematics, publications, yearbook classes. Computer resources include on-campus library services, Internet access, Internet filtering or blocking technology. Campus intranet, student e-mail accounts, and computer access in designated common areas are available to students. Students grades are available online. The school has a published electronic and media policy.

Contact Joe L. Garcia, Director of Admission/Registrar. 361-592-4307. Fax: 361-592-6126. E-mail: jlgarcia@ppas.org. Web site: www.ppas.org

See Display below and Close-Up on page 612.

PRESTONWOOD CHRISTIAN ACADEMY

6801 West Park Boulevard
Plano, Texas 75093

Head of School: Dr. Larry Taylor

General Information Coeducational day and distance learning college-preparatory and Bible courses school, affiliated with Southern Baptist Convention. Grades PK–12. Distance learning grades 6–12. Founded: 1997. Setting: suburban. Nearest major city is Dallas. 44-acre campus. 2 buildings on campus. Approved or accredited by Southern Association of Colleges and Schools and Texas Department of Education. Total enrollment: 1,472. Upper school average class size: 18. Upper school faculty-student ratio: 1:11. There are 172 required school days per year for Upper School students. Upper School students typically attend 5 days per week. The average school day consists of 7 hours and 35 minutes.

Upper School Student Profile Grade 9: 130 students (75 boys, 55 girls); Grade 10: 125 students (55 boys, 70 girls); Grade 11: 122 students (60 boys, 62 girls); Grade 12: 114 students (63 boys, 51 girls). 66% of students are Southern Baptist Convention.

Faculty School total: 115. In upper school: 17 men, 23 women; 20 have advanced degrees.

Subjects Offered 20th century history, 20th century physics, advanced chemistry, advanced math, Advanced Placement courses, algebra, American history-AP, American literature, anatomy and physiology, art, art-AP, band, Bible, biology, biology-AP, British literature, calculus-AP, ceramics, chemistry, choir, Christian doctrine, computer applications, conceptual physics, debate, drama, drawing, economics, ethics, fine arts, fitness, geometry, government, government-AP, health, honors algebra, honors English, honors geometry, honors U.S. history, honors world history, internship, language-AP, leadership education training, learning lab, literature-AP, logic, multimedia, multimedia design, newspaper, painting, performing arts, personal fitness, philosophy, photo shop, physical fitness, physics, physics-AP, pre-calculus, printmaking, sculpture, service learning/internship, Spanish, Spanish-AP, speech, statistics, strings, student government, studio art, U.S. government and politics-AP, U.S. history, Web site design, Western literature, world history, world religions, yearbook.

Graduation Requirements 1 1/2 elective credits, algebra, arts and fine arts (art, music, dance, drama), Bible, biology, British literature, chemistry, Christian doctrine, computer applications, economics, English, English literature, ethics, foreign language, geometry, government, mathematics, philosophy, physical education (includes health), physics, speech, U.S. history, Western literature, world history, mission trip.

Special Academic Programs Advanced Placement exam preparation; honors section; academic accommodation for the gifted.

College Admission Counseling 124 students graduated in 2012; all went to college, including Baylor University; Oklahoma State University; Southern Methodist University; Texas A&M University; The University of Texas at Austin; University of

Oklahoma. Median SAT critical reading: 560, median SAT math: 550, median SAT writing: 550, median combined SAT: 1540, median composite ACT: 24. 37% scored over 600 on SAT critical reading, 35% scored over 600 on SAT math, 31% scored over 600 on SAT writing, 47% scored over 1800 on combined SAT, 38% scored over 26 on composite ACT.

Student Life Upper grades have uniform requirement, student council, honor system. Discipline rests primarily with faculty.

Summer Programs Remediation, enrichment, advancement, sports, art/fine arts, rigorous outdoor training, computer instruction programs offered; held on campus; accepts boys and girls; open to students from other schools. 800 students usually enrolled. 2013 schedule: June 1 to August 5. Application deadline: May 1.

Tuition and Aid Day student tuition: $16,297–$16,779. Tuition installment plan (FACTS Tuition Payment Plan, monthly payment plans, individually arranged payment plans). Tuition reduction for siblings, need-based scholarship grants available. In 2012–13, 21% of upper-school students received aid. Total amount of financial aid awarded in 2012–13: $734,381.

Admissions Traditional secondary-level entrance grade is 9. For fall 2012, 109 students applied for upper-level admission, 65 were accepted, 54 enrolled. ISEE or Stanford Achievement Test required. Deadline for receipt of application materials: none. Application fee required: $100. Interview required.

Athletics Interscholastic: baseball (boys), basketball (b,g), cheering (g), cross-country running (b,g), drill team (g), football (b), golf (b,g), soccer (b,g), softball (g), swimming and diving (b,g), tennis (b,g), track and field (b,g), volleyball (g). 42 coaches.

Computers Computers are regularly used in all academic, technology classes. Computer network features include on-campus library services, Internet access, wireless campus network, Internet filtering or blocking technology. Student e-mail accounts are available to students. Students grades are available online. The school has a published electronic and media policy.

Contact Mrs. Marsha Backof, Admissions Assistant. 972-930-4010. Fax: 972-930-4008. E-mail: mbackof@prestonwoodchristian.org. Web site: www.prestonwoodchristian.org

PROCTOR ACADEMY

PO Box 500
204 Main Street
Andover, New Hampshire 03216

Head of School: Mr. Michael Henriques

General Information Coeducational boarding and day college-preparatory, arts, technology, environmental studies, and experiential learning programs school. Grades 9–12. Founded: 1848. Setting: small town. Nearest major city is Concord. Students are housed in single-sex dormitories. 3,000-acre campus. 45 buildings on campus. Approved or accredited by Association for Experiential Education, Association of Independent Schools in New England, Independent Schools of Northern New England, New England Association of Schools and Colleges, The Association of Boarding Schools, and New Hampshire Department of Education. Member of National Association of Independent Schools and Secondary School Admission Test Board. Endowment: $25 million. Total enrollment: 360. Upper school average class size: 12. Upper school faculty-student ratio: 1:5. There are 170 required school days per year for Upper School students. Upper School students typically attend 6 days per week. The average school day consists of 5 hours and 35 minutes.

Upper School Student Profile Grade 9: 65 students (37 boys, 28 girls); Grade 10: 92 students (49 boys, 43 girls); Grade 11: 93 students (59 boys, 34 girls); Grade 12: 108 students (58 boys, 50 girls); Postgraduate: 4 students (4 boys). 77% of students are boarding students. 31% are state residents. 30 states are represented in upper school student body. 9% are international students. International students from China, Hong Kong, Mexico, Republic of Korea, Spain, and Viet Nam; 9 other countries represented in student body.

Faculty School total: 85. In upper school: 39 men, 46 women; 66 have advanced degrees; 35 reside on campus.

Subjects Offered Algebra, American history, American literature, art, art history, biology, boat building, calculus, ceramics, chemistry, computer math, computer programming, creative writing, drama, economics, English, English literature, environmental science, European history, fine arts, finite math, forestry, French, genetics, geometry, health, history, industrial arts, mathematics, Middle Eastern history, music, music history, music technology, Native American history, performing arts, photography, physical education, physics, piano, play/screen writing, poetry, political thought, probability and statistics, psychology, public speaking, publications, robotics, science, senior project, social sciences, Spanish, sports medicine, studio art, study skills, the Web, theater, theater history, U.S. government and politics-AP, U.S. history-AP, Vietnam history, voice, voice ensemble, wilderness experience, woodworking, world literature, writing, writing workshop.

Graduation Requirements Arts and fine arts (art, music, dance, drama), English, foreign language, mathematics, science, social sciences.

Special Academic Programs 14 Advanced Placement exams for which test preparation is offered; honors section; independent study; term-away projects; study at local college for college credit; study abroad; academic accommodation for the gifted; programs in general development for dyslexic students; ESL (5 students enrolled).

College Admission Counseling 98 students graduated in 2012; 90 went to college, including St. Lawrence University; University of New Hampshire; University of Vermont. Other: 8 had other specific plans. Mean SAT critical reading: 555, mean SAT math: 560, mean SAT writing: 545, mean combined SAT: 1660, mean composite ACT: 23. 20% scored over 600 on SAT critical reading, 24% scored over 600 on SAT math, 22% scored over 600 on SAT writing, 24% scored over 26 on composite ACT.

Student Life Upper grades have student council, honor system. Discipline rests equally with students and faculty.

Tuition and Aid Day student tuition: $26,200; 7-day tuition and room/board: $48,950. Tuition installment plan (Academic Management Services Plan, monthly payment plans). Need-based scholarship grants available. In 2012–13, 28% of upper-school students received aid. Total amount of financial aid awarded in 2012–13: $3,200,000.

Admissions Traditional secondary-level entrance grade is 9. For fall 2012, 566 students applied for upper-level admission, 221 were accepted, 131 enrolled. ISEE, PSAT or SAT for applicants to grade 11 and 12, SSAT, TOEFL or SLEP, WISC/Woodcock-Johnson or writing sample required. Deadline for receipt of application materials: February 1. Application fee required: $50. Interview required.

Athletics Interscholastic: alpine skiing (boys, girls), baseball (b), basketball (b,g), bicycling (b,g), canoeing/kayaking (b,g), cross-country running (b,g), field hockey (g), football (b), hockey (b,g), ice hockey (b,g), lacrosse (b,g), nordic skiing (b,g), skiing (downhill) (b,g), snowboarding (b,g), soccer (b,g), softball (g), tennis (b,g); intramural: alpine skiing (b,g), snowboarding (b,g); coed interscholastic: dance, freestyle skiing, golf, horseback riding, kayaking, ski jumping, skiing (cross-country); coed intramural: aerobics/dance, aerobics/Nautilus, backpacking, ballet, broomball, canoeing/kayaking, climbing, combined training, dance, equestrian sports, fencing, fitness, Frisbee, hiking/backpacking, horseback riding, kayaking, martial arts, modern dance, mountain biking, mountaineering, outdoor activities, outdoor adventure, outdoor education, outdoor recreation, outdoor skills, outdoors, paint ball, rock climbing, running, skiing (downhill), snowshoeing, strength & conditioning, ultimate Frisbee, wall climbing, weight lifting, weight training, wilderness, yoga. 5 coaches, 3 athletic trainers.

Computers Computers are regularly used in all academic classes. Computer network features include on-campus library services, online commercial services, Internet access, wireless campus network, Internet filtering or blocking technology. Campus intranet and student e-mail accounts are available to students. Students grades are available online. The school has a published electronic and media policy.

Contact Charlie Durell, Admissions Coordinator. 603-735-6312. Fax: 603-735-6284. E-mail: charlie_durell@proctornet.com. Web site: www.proctoracademy.org

PROFESSIONAL CHILDREN'S SCHOOL

132 West 60th Street
New York, New York 10023

Head of School: Dr. James Dawson

General Information Coeducational day college-preparatory school. Grades 6–12. Founded: 1914. Setting: urban. 1 building on campus. Approved or accredited by New York State Association of Independent Schools. Member of National Association of Independent Schools. Endowment: $2.7 million. Total enrollment: 193. Upper school average class size: 10. Upper school faculty-student ratio: 1:8. There are 163 required school days per year for Upper School students. Upper School students typically attend 5 days per week. The average school day consists of 7 hours.

Upper School Student Profile Grade 9: 19 students (8 boys, 11 girls); Grade 10: 36 students (12 boys, 24 girls); Grade 11: 50 students (18 boys, 32 girls); Grade 12: 56 students (19 boys, 37 girls).

Faculty School total: 30. In upper school: 11 men, 19 women; 27 have advanced degrees.

Subjects Offered Advanced math, algebra, American government, American history, biology, calculus, chemistry, chorus, computer education, constitutional history of U.S., constitutional law, creative writing, drama, English, English literature, environmental science, ESL, foreign language, French, general math, geometry, health education, introduction to literature, keyboarding, library research, library skills, physical education, physics, pre-algebra, pre-calculus, Spanish, studio art, U.S. government, U.S. history.

Graduation Requirements Art, English, foreign language, health, history, mathematics, science.

Special Academic Programs ESL (26 students enrolled).

College Admission Counseling 53 students graduated in 2012; 46 went to college, including Columbia University; Eugene Lang College The New School for Liberal Arts; Fordham University; New York University; Princeton University. Other: 4 went to work, 3 had other specific plans.

Student Life Upper grades have student council, honor system. Discipline rests primarily with faculty.

Tuition and Aid Day student tuition: $33,700. Tuition installment plan (Tuition Management Systems). Need-based scholarship grants available. In 2012–13, 29% of upper-school students received aid. Total amount of financial aid awarded in 2012–13: $805,000.

Admissions Traditional secondary-level entrance grade is 9. For fall 2012, 113 students applied for upper-level admission, 80 were accepted, 63 enrolled. ERB, ISEE, SSAT or Stanford Achievement Test required. Deadline for receipt of application materials: none. Application fee required: $75. On-campus interview recommended.
Athletics 1 PE instructor.
Computers Computers are regularly used in all academic classes. Computer network features include on-campus library services, Internet access, wireless campus network, Internet filtering or blocking technology. Student e-mail accounts and computer access in designated common areas are available to students. The school has a published electronic and media policy.
Contact Ms. Sherrie A. Hinkle, Director of Admissions. 212-582-3116 Ext. 112. Fax: 212-307-6542. E-mail: info@pcs-nyc.org. Web site: www.pcs-nyc.org

THE PROUT SCHOOL

4640 Tower Hill Road
Wakefield, Rhode Island 02879

Head of School: Mr. David Carradini

General Information Coeducational day college-preparatory, arts, religious studies, and technology school, affiliated with Roman Catholic Church. Grades 9–12. Founded: 1966. Setting: small town. Nearest major city is Providence. 25-acre campus. 1 building on campus. Approved or accredited by International Baccalaureate Organization, New England Association of Schools and Colleges, Rhode Island State Certified Resource Progam, and Rhode Island Department of Education. Total enrollment: 640. Upper school average class size: 23. Upper school faculty-student ratio: 1:18. There are 182 required school days per year for Upper School students. Upper School students typically attend 5 days per week. The average school day consists of 6 hours and 30 minutes.
Upper School Student Profile 75% of students are Roman Catholic.
Faculty School total: 53. In upper school: 25 men, 28 women; 40 have advanced degrees.
Subjects Offered Acting, American literature, anatomy and physiology, art education, art history, athletic training, ballet, ballet technique, band, biology, calculus, chemistry, Chinese, choir, chorus, Christian doctrine, Christian education, Christian ethics, Christian scripture, Christian studies, Christianity, church history, clayworking, college planning, college writing, community service, comparative religion, computer applications, computer art, computer education, computer graphics, computer multimedia, computer programming, computer science, computer skills, computer studies, contemporary history, contemporary issues, costumes and make-up, CPR, creative dance, creative drama, creative thinking, critical studies in film, critical writing, dance performance, drama performance, drama workshop, dramatic arts, drawing, drawing and design, earth science, economics, economics and history, English, English composition, English literature, environmental science, environmental studies, first aid, fitness, food and nutrition, foreign language, French, general science, government, graphic arts, graphic design, health, health and wellness, history, history of the Catholic Church, honors English, honors U.S. history, honors world history, human anatomy, instruments, introduction to theater, Italian, jazz band, keyboarding, lab science, language, language and composition, law and the legal system, life science, marine science, mathematics, modern history, music performance, music theater, musical theater, musical theater dance, oceanography, personal fitness, physical fitness, physics, play production, portfolio art, pre-calculus, public service, religion, religion and culture, religious education, religious studies, scene study, science, science research, scripture, set design, Spanish, sports nutrition, stage and body movement, stage design, theater, theater arts, theater design and production, theater history, visual and performing arts, yearbook.
Graduation Requirements Computers, English, foreign language, health education, history, lab science, mathematics, oceanography, physical education (includes health), religion (includes Bible studies and theology), science.
Special Academic Programs International Baccalaureate program; Advanced Placement exam preparation; honors section.
College Admission Counseling 158 students graduated in 2012; 152 went to college, including Johnson & Wales University; Providence College; Salve Regina University; University of New Hampshire; University of Rhode Island. Other: 1 went to work, 2 entered military service, 3 entered a postgraduate year.
Student Life Upper grades have uniform requirement, student council, honor system. Discipline rests primarily with faculty. Attendance at religious services is required.
Tuition and Aid Day student tuition: $10,750. Tuition installment plan (FACTS Tuition Payment Plan). Tuition reduction for siblings, need-based scholarship grants available. In 2012–13, 28% of upper-school students received aid. Total amount of financial aid awarded in 2012–13: $225,000.
Admissions Traditional secondary-level entrance grade is 9. For fall 2012, 310 students applied for upper-level admission, 228 were accepted, 167 enrolled. Admissions testing and essay required. Deadline for receipt of application materials: December 22. Application fee required: $25.
Athletics Interscholastic: baseball (boys), basketball (b,g), cheering (g), cross-country running (b,g), gymnastics (g), lacrosse (b,g), soccer (b,g), softball (g), swimming and diving (b,g), tennis (b,g), track and field (b,g), volleyball (g); intramural: dance (g), outdoor recreation (b,g); coed interscholastic: aquatics, golf, ice hockey; coed intramural: aerobics, aerobics/dance, ballet, bicycling, fitness, outdoor recreation, sailing, strength & conditioning, table tennis, weight lifting, weight training. 3 PE instructors, 14 coaches.
Computers Computers are regularly used in all academic classes. Computer resources include on-campus library services, Internet access, Internet filtering or blocking technology. Computer access in designated common areas is available to students. The school has a published electronic and media policy.
Contact Ms. Kristen Need, Director of Admissions. 401-789-9262 Ext. 515. Fax: 401-782-2262. E-mail: kneed@theproutschool.org. Web site: www.theproutschool.org

PROVIDENCE CATHOLIC SCHOOL, THE COLLEGE PREPARATORY SCHOOL FOR GIRLS GRADES 6-12

1215 North St. Mary's
San Antonio, Texas 78215-1787

Head of School: Ms. Alicia Garcia

General Information Girls' day college-preparatory, arts, and religious studies school, affiliated with Roman Catholic Church. Grades 6–12. Founded: 1951. Setting: urban. 3-acre campus. 4 buildings on campus. Approved or accredited by Southern Association of Colleges and Schools, Southern Association of Independent Schools, Texas Catholic Conference, and Texas Education Agency. Total enrollment: 346. Upper school average class size: 22. Upper school faculty-student ratio: 1:11. There are 186 required school days per year for Upper School students. Upper School students typically attend 5 days per week. The average school day consists of 7 hours.
Upper School Student Profile Grade 9: 49 students (49 girls); Grade 10: 50 students (50 girls); Grade 11: 57 students (57 girls); Grade 12: 50 students (50 girls). 80% of students are Roman Catholic.
Faculty School total: 34. In upper school: 5 men, 26 women; 28 have advanced degrees.
Subjects Offered Acting, advanced biology, advanced chemistry, advanced math, Advanced Placement courses, aerobics, algebra, American history, American history-AP, American literature, American literature-AP, anatomy, ancient world history, art, athletics, audio visual/media, band, biology, biology-AP, British literature, British literature-AP, broadcast journalism, broadcasting, calculus-AP, career education internship, Catholic belief and practice, cheerleading, chemistry, choir, choral music, church history, composition-AP, computer information systems, concert band, concert choir, conflict resolution, creative writing, dance, dance performance, desktop publishing, drama, drama performance, drama workshop, economics, English, English language and composition-AP, English language-AP, English literature, English literature and composition-AP, English literature-AP, English-AP, film, fitness, foreign language, French, geography, government, government and politics-AP, history, history-AP, human anatomy, jazz band, journalism, JROTC, JROTC or LEAD (Leadership Education and Development), Latin, law, leadership, literature and composition-AP, music theory, newspaper, peer ministry, personal fitness, photography, photojournalism, physical education, physical fitness, physical science, physics, play production, psychology, social justice, sociology, softball, Spanish, Spanish language-AP, Spanish-AP, speech, sports, statistics-AP, student government, student publications, swimming, swimming competency, tennis, Texas history, the Web, theater, theater arts, theater design and production, theater production, theology, track and field, U.S. government and politics, U.S. government and politics-AP, U.S. history, U.S. history-AP, volleyball, Web site design, world geography, world history, yearbook.
Graduation Requirements All academic, 100 hours of community service completed by grade 12, senior retreat participation.
Special Academic Programs International Baccalaureate program; 13 Advanced Placement exams for which test preparation is offered; honors section; independent study; study at local college for college credit.
College Admission Counseling 42 students graduated in 2011; all went to college, including St. Mary's University; Texas A&M University; The University of Texas at Austin; The University of Texas at San Antonio; University of the Incarnate Word.
Student Life Upper grades have uniform requirement, student council, honor system. Discipline rests primarily with faculty. Attendance at religious services is required.
Tuition and Aid Day student tuition: $7035. Tuition installment plan (monthly payment plans, Middle School Tuition $4,202). Tuition reduction for siblings, merit scholarship grants, need-based scholarship grants available. In 2011–12, 20% of upper-school students received aid; total upper-school merit-scholarship money awarded: $55,500. Total amount of financial aid awarded in 2011–12: $200,000.
Admissions Traditional secondary-level entrance grade is 9. High School Placement Test or QUIC required. Deadline for receipt of application materials: none. No application fee required. On-campus interview recommended.
Athletics Interscholastic: aerobics, aerobics/dance, basketball, bowling, cheering, cross-country running, dance, dance team, drill team, JROTC drill, physical fitness, physical training, running, soccer, softball, tennis, track and field, volleyball, weight training, winter soccer; coed interscholastic: aquatics. 2 PE instructors, 7 coaches, 1 athletic trainer.
Computers Computers are regularly used in desktop publishing, journalism, newspaper, Web site design, yearbook classes. Computer network features include on-campus library services, online commercial services, Internet access, Internet filtering or blocking technology, online classrooms. Campus intranet and student e-mail

accounts are available to students. Students grades are available online. The school has a published electronic and media policy.

Contact Mrs. Nora Walsh, Enrollment Director. 210-224-6651 Ext. 210. Fax: 210-224-6214. E-mail: nwalsh@providencehs.net. Web site: www.providencehs.net

PROVIDENCE CHRISTIAN SCHOOL

P.O. Box 240
Monarch, Alberta T0L 1M0, Canada

Head of School: Mr. Chris Heikoop

General Information Coeducational day college-preparatory, general academic, and religious studies school, affiliated with Calvinist faith, Reformed Church. Grades K–12. Founded: 1994. Setting: rural. Nearest major city is Lethbridge, Canada. 5-acre campus. 1 building on campus. Approved or accredited by Alberta Department of Education. Language of instruction: English. Total enrollment: 120. Upper school average class size: 12. Upper school faculty-student ratio: 1:11. There are 180 required school days per year for Upper School students. Upper School students typically attend 4 days per week. The average school day consists of 6 hours and 25 minutes.

Upper School Student Profile Grade 10: 7 students (2 boys, 5 girls); Grade 11: 6 students (2 boys, 4 girls); Grade 12: 8 students (4 boys, 4 girls). 90% of students are Calvinist, Reformed.

Faculty School total: 10. In upper school: 3 men, 2 women.

Subjects Offered Accounting, advanced biology, advanced math, Bible, Bible studies, bookkeeping, business applications, business education, business law, business studies, career and personal planning, career and technology systems, Christian doctrine, Christian scripture, church history, civil rights, computer technologies, critical thinking, English, ESL, finance, first aid, French, general science, health education, human sexuality, information processing, information technology, integrated mathematics, integrated physics, integrated science, keyboarding, language arts, library, life skills, mathematics, music, music appreciation, participation in sports, personal finance, physics, reading, religious education, science project, sewing, sex education, social studies, sports, Web site design.

Graduation Requirements Alberta Ministry of Education requirements.

Special Academic Programs International Baccalaureate program; ESL (6 students enrolled).

College Admission Counseling 6 students graduated in 2011; 1 went to college. Other: 3 went to work, 2 entered a postgraduate year.

Student Life Upper grades have specified standards of dress, student council, honor system. Discipline rests primarily with faculty. Attendance at religious services is required.

Tuition and Aid Day student tuition: CAN$5100. Tuition installment plan (The Tuition Plan). Tuition reduction for siblings available.

Admissions Traditional secondary-level entrance grade is 10. For fall 2011, 21 students applied for upper-level admission, 21 were accepted, 21 enrolled. Deadline for receipt of application materials: September 30. No application fee required. Interview required.

Athletics 2 PE instructors.

Computers Computers are regularly used in all classes. Computer network features include Internet access, wireless campus network, Internet filtering or blocking technology. The school has a published electronic and media policy.

Contact Mr. Chris Heikoop, Principal. 403-381-4418. Fax: 403-381-4428. E-mail: principal@pcsmonarch.com. Web site: www.pcsmonarch.com/

PROVIDENCE COUNTRY DAY SCHOOL

660 Waterman Avenue
East Providence, Rhode Island 02914-1724

Head of School: Mr. Vince Watchorn

General Information Coeducational day college-preparatory and arts school. Grades 6–12. Founded: 1923. Setting: suburban. Nearest major city is Providence. 18-acre campus. 6 buildings on campus. Approved or accredited by Association of Independent Schools in New England, New England Association of Schools and Colleges, The College Board, and Rhode Island Department of Education. Member of National Association of Independent Schools and Secondary School Admission Test Board. Endowment: $1.5 million. Total enrollment: 201. Upper school average class size: 12. Upper school faculty-student ratio: 1:7. The average school day consists of 6 hours and 50 minutes.

Upper School Student Profile Grade 9: 34 students (21 boys, 13 girls); Grade 10: 42 students (26 boys, 16 girls); Grade 11: 41 students (24 boys, 17 girls); Grade 12: 48 students (32 boys, 16 girls).

Faculty School total: 34. In upper school: 15 men, 17 women; 19 have advanced degrees.

Subjects Offered Advanced Placement courses, algebra, American government, American history, American history-AP, American literature, ancient history, art, art history-AP, Asian studies, Bible as literature, bioethics, biology, biology-AP, British literature, calculus, calculus-AP, ceramics, chemistry, choir, computer graphics, conceptual physics, creative writing, drama, earth science, electives, English, English literature, English literature-AP, environmental science, European civilization, European history, European history-AP, expository writing, fine arts, foreign language, forensics, French, geography, geometry, government/civics, graphic design, health, history, independent study, jazz ensemble, journalism, Latin, mathematics, media production, modern European history, music, performing arts, photography, physical education, physics, pottery, pre-algebra, pre-calculus, public speaking, science, senior internship, social studies, Spanish, Spanish language-AP, studio art, theater, trigonometry, U.S. government and politics-AP, visual arts, world history, writing.

Graduation Requirements Arts and fine arts (art, music, dance, drama), English, foreign language, history, mathematics, physical education (includes health), science, senior independent project, community service hours.

Special Academic Programs 9 Advanced Placement exams for which test preparation is offered; honors section; independent study; term-away projects; academic accommodation for the gifted, the musically talented, and the artistically talented.

College Admission Counseling 49 students graduated in 2012; all went to college, including Boston College; Emerson College; The George Washington University; Trinity College; University of Rhode Island; Worcester Polytechnic Institute. Mean SAT critical reading: 568, mean SAT math: 580, mean SAT writing: 572, mean combined SAT: 1721, mean composite ACT: 23.

Student Life Upper grades have specified standards of dress, student council, honor system. Discipline rests primarily with faculty.

Summer Programs Sports, art/fine arts programs offered; held on campus; accepts boys and girls; not open to students from other schools.

Tuition and Aid Day student tuition: $29,400–$29,900. Tuition installment plan (SMART Tuition Payment Plan, monthly payment plans). Need-based scholarship grants available. In 2012–13, 41% of upper-school students received aid. Total amount of financial aid awarded in 2012–13: $1,500,000.

Admissions Traditional secondary-level entrance grade is 9. For fall 2012, 127 students applied for upper-level admission, 116 were accepted, 47 enrolled. ISEE or SSAT required. Deadline for receipt of application materials: February 1. Application fee required: $55. On-campus interview required.

Athletics Interscholastic: baseball (boys), basketball (b,g), cross-country running (b,g), football (b), golf (b,g), ice hockey (b), indoor track & field (b,g), lacrosse (b,g), sailing (b,g), soccer (b,g), swimming and diving (b,g), tennis (b,g), track and field (b,g), winter (indoor) track (b,g), wrestling (b); coed interscholastic: physical fitness, yoga; coed intramural: strength & conditioning, weight training. 2 PE instructors, 8 coaches, 1 athletic trainer.

Computers Computers are regularly used in art, English, foreign language, history, mathematics, music, science classes. Computer network features include on-campus library services, online commercial services, Internet access, Internet filtering or blocking technology. Campus intranet, student e-mail accounts, and computer access in designated common areas are available to students. The school has a published electronic and media policy.

Contact Ms. Ashley E. Randlett, Director of Admissions and Financial Aid. 401-438-5170 Ext. 102. Fax: 401-435-4514. E-mail: randlett@providencecountryday.org. Web site: www.providencecountryday.org

PROVIDENCE DAY SCHOOL

5800 Sardis Road
Charlotte, North Carolina 28270

Head of School: Dr. Glyn Cowlishaw

General Information Coeducational day college-preparatory and global studies diploma program school. Grades PK–12. Founded: 1971. Setting: suburban. 44-acre campus. 18 buildings on campus. Approved or accredited by Southern Association of Colleges and Schools, Southern Association of Independent Schools, and North Carolina Department of Education. Member of National Association of Independent Schools. Endowment: $4 million. Total enrollment: 1,501. Upper school average class size: 18. Upper school faculty-student ratio: 1:12. There are 177 required school days per year for Upper School students. Upper School students typically attend 5 days per week. The average school day consists of 7 hours and 10 minutes.

Upper School Student Profile Grade 9: 148 students (76 boys, 72 girls); Grade 10: 129 students (68 boys, 61 girls); Grade 11: 120 students (55 boys, 65 girls); Grade 12: 137 students (81 boys, 56 girls).

Faculty School total: 148. In upper school: 46 men, 34 women; 56 have advanced degrees.

Subjects Offered 3-dimensional design, accounting, African-American history, algebra, American history, American literature, art, art history-AP, Asian history, band, biology, biology-AP, calculus-AP, chemistry, chemistry-AP, chorus, Civil War, composition, computer graphics, computer programming, computer science, computer science-AP, drama, economics, English, English literature, English-AP, environmental science, environmental science-AP, fine arts, French, French-AP, geometry, German, German-AP, government-AP, government/civics, health, history, history-AP, instrumental music, international relations, journalism, Judaic studies, keyboarding, Latin, Latin-AP, literature, Mandarin, mathematics, music-AP, photography, physical education, physical science, physics, physics-AP, political science, pre-calculus, psychology, science, set design, social studies, Spanish, Spanish-AP, sports medicine, statistics-AP, theater, word processing, world history, writing, yearbook.

Graduation Requirements Arts and fine arts (art, music, dance, drama), computer science, English, foreign language, mathematics, physical education (includes health), science, social studies (includes history), Global Studies Diploma.

Special Academic Programs 24 Advanced Placement exams for which test preparation is offered; honors section; accelerated programs; domestic exchange program; study abroad; academic accommodation for the gifted, the musically talented, and the artistically talented.

College Admission Counseling 118 students graduated in 2011; all went to college, including Appalachian State University; Duke University; North Carolina State University; The University of North Carolina at Chapel Hill; University of Virginia; Wake Forest University. Median SAT critical reading: 650, median SAT math: 660, median SAT writing: 650, median combined SAT: 1960, median composite ACT: 28. 73% scored over 600 on SAT critical reading, 80% scored over 600 on SAT math, 71% scored over 600 on SAT writing, 73% scored over 1800 on combined SAT.

Student Life Upper grades have specified standards of dress, student council, honor system. Discipline rests equally with students and faculty.

Tuition and Aid Day student tuition: $20,730. Tuition installment plan (Academic Management Services Plan, monthly payment plans). Need-based scholarship grants available. In 2011–12, 14% of upper-school students received aid. Total amount of financial aid awarded in 2011–12: $1,056,585.

Admissions Traditional secondary-level entrance grade is 9. For fall 2011, 113 students applied for upper-level admission, 65 were accepted, 39 enrolled. Cognitive Abilities Test, ERB CTP IV, ISEE, SSAT, ERB, PSAT, SAT, PLAN or ACT or Woodcock-Johnson Educational Evaluation, WISC III required. Deadline for receipt of application materials: January 15. Application fee required: $90. On-campus interview required.

Athletics Interscholastic: aerobics/dance (girls), baseball (b), basketball (b,g), cheering (g), cross-country running (b,g), dance squad (g), field hockey (g), football (b), golf (b,g), lacrosse (b,g), soccer (b,g), softball (g), swimming and diving (b,g), tennis (b,g), track and field (b,g), volleyball (g), wrestling (b); intramural: indoor hockey (b,g), indoor soccer (b,g), Newcombe ball (b,g), physical fitness (b,g), pillo polo (b,g), soccer (b,g), softball (b,g), strength & conditioning (b,g), volleyball (b,g); coed intramural: indoor hockey, indoor soccer, Newcombe ball, physical fitness, pillo polo, soccer, softball, strength & conditioning, tennis, volleyball. 4 PE instructors, 36 coaches, 2 athletic trainers.

Computers Computers are regularly used in English, mathematics, science, technology, word processing classes. Computer network features include on-campus library services, online commercial services, Internet access, wireless campus network, Internet filtering or blocking technology, wireless iBook lab available for individual student check-out, ipads. Student e-mail accounts and computer access in designated common areas are available to students. Students grades are available online. The school has a published electronic and media policy.

Contact Mrs. Carissa Goddard, Admissions Assistant. 704-887-7040. Fax: 704-887-7520 Ext. 7041. E-mail: carissa.goddard@providenceday.org. Web site: www.providenceday.org

PROVIDENCE HIGH SCHOOL

511 South Buena Vista Street
Burbank, California 91505-4865

Head of School: Mr. Joe Sciuto

General Information Coeducational day college-preparatory, arts, religious studies, and technology school, affiliated with Roman Catholic Church. Grades 9–12. Founded: 1955. Setting: urban. Nearest major city is Los Angeles. 4-acre campus. 7 buildings on campus. Approved or accredited by California Association of Independent Schools, National Catholic Education Association, The College Board, Western Association of Schools and Colleges, Western Catholic Education Association, and California Department of Education. Endowment: $1.6 million. Total enrollment: 417. Upper school average class size: 21. Upper school faculty-student ratio: 1:9. There are 183 required school days per year for Upper School students. Upper School students typically attend 5 days per week. The average school day consists of 6 hours.

Upper School Student Profile Grade 9: 122 students (58 boys, 64 girls); Grade 10: 129 students (56 boys, 73 girls); Grade 11: 79 students (38 boys, 41 girls); Grade 12: 87 students (46 boys, 41 girls). 71% of students are Roman Catholic.

Faculty School total: 44. In upper school: 18 men, 26 women; 27 have advanced degrees.

Subjects Offered 3-dimensional art, accounting, advanced computer applications, Advanced Placement courses, advanced studio art-AP, algebra, American history, American history-AP, American literature, American literature-AP, Basic programming, Bible studies, biology, biology-AP, calculus, calculus-AP, Catholic belief and practice, ceramics, chemistry, choral music, chorus, community service, computer animation, computer art, computer programming, computer science, digital photography, drama, economics, economics-AP, English, English literature, English literature and composition-AP, environmental science, ethics, film, fine arts, French, geometry, graphic arts, history, instruments, journalism, language-AP, Latin, law, Mandarin, mathematics, media studies, music, photography, physical education, physics, physics-AP, pre-calculus, psychology, psychology-AP, religion, robotics, science, social studies, Spanish, Spanish-AP, theater, trigonometry, U.S. government, U.S. government and politics-AP, U.S. history-AP, United States government-AP, video, video and animation, video film production, visual and performing arts, volleyball, world cultures, world history, world religions, world religions, writing, yearbook, yoga.

Graduation Requirements Advanced math, American government, American history, American literature, art, biology, British literature, chemistry, comparative religion, computer science, economics, electives, English, ethics, foreign language, mathematics, physical education (includes health), religion (includes Bible studies and theology), science, social studies (includes history), world history, world literature, completion of Christian Service hours.

Special Academic Programs 11 Advanced Placement exams for which test preparation is offered; honors section; academic accommodation for the musically talented and the artistically talented.

College Admission Counseling 98 students graduated in 2012; 95 went to college, including California State University, Los Angeles; California State University, Northridge; Loyola Marymount University; Pasadena City College; Santa Monica College; University of California, Los Angeles. Other: 3 had other specific plans. Median SAT critical reading: 530, median SAT math: 525, median SAT writing: 537, median composite ACT: 23.

Student Life Upper grades have uniform requirement, student council. Discipline rests equally with students and faculty. Attendance at religious services is required.

Summer Programs Remediation, enrichment, advancement, sports, art/fine arts, computer instruction programs offered; session focuses on enrichment, remediation, and extracurricular activities; held on campus; accepts boys and girls; open to students from other schools. 250 students usually enrolled. 2013 schedule: June 17 to July 12. Application deadline: June 3.

Tuition and Aid Day student tuition: $13,255. Tuition installment plan (The Tuition Plan, 1-payment plan: payment in full due July 1st, 2-payment plan-60% due July 1st, 40% due January 1st, 10-payment plan: monthly beginning July 1, ending April 1). Tuition reduction for siblings, merit scholarship grants, need-based scholarship grants, PSJMC Employee Discount available. In 2012–13, 46% of upper-school students received aid; total upper-school merit-scholarship money awarded: $129,000. Total amount of financial aid awarded in 2012–13: $382,000.

Admissions Traditional secondary-level entrance grade is 9. For fall 2012, 289 students applied for upper-level admission, 266 were accepted, 137 enrolled. Admissions testing or Catholic High School Entrance Examination required. Deadline for receipt of application materials: January 11. Application fee required: $65. On-campus interview recommended.

Athletics Interscholastic: baseball (boys), basketball (b,g), combined training (b), cross-country running (b,g), fitness (b,g), golf (b), physical fitness (b,g), soccer (b,g), softball (g), strength & conditioning (b,g), volleyball (b,g), weight training (b); coed interscholastic: cheering, cross-country running, dance team, track and field, yoga; coed intramural: kickball, volleyball. 2 PE instructors, 23 coaches.

Computers Computers are regularly used in accounting, animation, computer applications, desktop publishing, digital applications, information technology, journalism, library, literary magazine, media, media production, newspaper, photography, programming, publications, video film production, Web site design, word processing, writing, yearbook classes. Computer network features include on-campus library services, online commercial services, Internet access, wireless campus network, Microsoft Office Suite XP Professional, extranet portal. Student e-mail accounts are available to students. Students grades are available online. The school has a published electronic and media policy.

Contact Mrs. Judy Umeck, Director of Admissions. 818-846-8141 Ext. 501. Fax: 818-843-8421. E-mail: judy.umeck@providencehigh.org. Web site: www.providencehigh.org

PUNAHOU SCHOOL

1601 Punahou Street
Honolulu, Hawaii 96822

Head of School: Dr. James K. Scott

General Information Coeducational day and distance learning college-preparatory, arts, bilingual studies, and technology school. Grades K–12. Distance learning grades 9–12. Founded: 1841. Setting: urban. 76-acre campus. 21 buildings on campus. Approved or accredited by Western Association of Schools and Colleges. Member of National Association of Independent Schools and Secondary School Admission Test Board. Endowment: $186.8 million. Total enrollment: 3,743. Upper school average class size: 21. Upper school faculty-student ratio: 1:11. There are 170 required school days per year for Upper School students. Upper School students typically attend 5 days per week. The average school day consists of 7 hours.

Upper School Student Profile Grade 9: 443 students (217 boys, 226 girls); Grade 10: 419 students (205 boys, 214 girls); Grade 11: 429 students (205 boys, 224 girls); Grade 12: 422 students (202 boys, 220 girls).

Faculty School total: 330. In upper school: 70 men, 95 women; 116 have advanced degrees.

Subjects Offered Acting, Advanced Placement courses, algebra, American literature, American studies, anatomy and physiology, anthropology, Asian history, astronomy, ballet, Bible as literature, bioethics, biology, biology-AP, British literature, calculus, calculus-AP, career/college preparation, ceramics, character education, chemistry, chemistry-AP, child development, choir, choral music, chorus, clayworking, college admission preparation, college counseling, college planning, college writing, community garden, composition, computer science, computer science-AP, concert band, contemporary issues, CPR, creative writing, dance, digital art, drama performance, drawing, driver education, economics, English, English composition, environmental science, environmental science-AP, European history, European history-AP, film and literature, French, French language-AP, geometry, glassblowing, government and politics-AP, guitar, Hawaiian history, Hawaiian language, humanities, independent study, Japanese, jewelry making, journalism, JROTC or LEAD (Leadership Education and Development), law, Mandarin, marching band, marine biology, mechanical drawing, medieval history, money management, music theory, musical theater, oceanography, painting, peer counseling, photography, physical education, physics, physics-AP, pre-calculus, psychology, psychology-AP, religion, robotics, sculpture, Shakespeare, social studies, Spanish, Spanish-AP, statistics-AP, studio art, studio art-AP, symphonic band, technical theater, theater design and production, U.S. government and politics-AP, U.S. history, U.S. history-AP, video, video film production, Western literature, wind ensemble, world civilizations, world literature, writing, yoga.

Graduation Requirements Electives, English, foreign language, mathematics, physical education (includes health), science, social studies (includes history), visual and performing arts, seniors are required to take a CapSeeds course that combines economics and community service, one course with the Spiritual, Ethical, Community Responsibility (SECR) designation.

Special Academic Programs 17 Advanced Placement exams for which test preparation is offered; honors section; independent study; study abroad.

College Admission Counseling 426 students graduated in 2012; 420 went to college, including Creighton University; Santa Clara University; Seattle University; University of Hawaii at Manoa; University of Southern California; University of Washington. Other: 1 went to work, 5 had other specific plans. Median SAT critical reading: 610, median SAT math: 660, median SAT writing: 620, median combined SAT: 1890. 51% scored over 600 on SAT critical reading, 75% scored over 600 on SAT math, 57% scored over 600 on SAT writing, 63% scored over 1800 on combined SAT.

Student Life Upper grades have specified standards of dress, student council, honor system. Discipline rests primarily with faculty. Attendance at religious services is required.

Summer Programs Enrichment, advancement, sports, art/fine arts programs offered; session focuses on enrichment and graduation credit; held both on and off campus; held at Japan, Costa Rica, China; accepts boys and girls; not open to students from other schools. 3,915 students usually enrolled. 2013 schedule: June 10 to July 19. Application deadline: April 26.

Tuition and Aid Day student tuition: $19,200. Tuition installment plan (Insured Tuition Payment Plan, monthly payment plans, semester payment plan; annual payment plan). Merit scholarship grants, need-based scholarship grants available. In 2012–13, 15% of upper-school students received aid; total upper-school merit-scholarship money awarded: $235,400. Total amount of financial aid awarded in 2012–13: $2,386,690.

Admissions Traditional secondary-level entrance grade is 9. For fall 2012, 394 students applied for upper-level admission, 129 were accepted, 94 enrolled. SAT or SSAT required. Deadline for receipt of application materials: October 1. Application fee required: $125. Interview required.

Athletics Interscholastic: baseball (boys), basketball (b,g), bowling (b,g), canoeing/kayaking (b,g), cheering (g), cross-country running (b,g), football (b), golf (b,g), judo (b,g), kayaking (b,g), paddling (b,g), riflery (b,g), sailing (b,g), soccer (b,g), softball (g), swimming and diving (b,g), tennis (b,g), track and field (b,g), volleyball (b,g), water polo (b,g), wrestling (b,g); coed interscholastic: canoeing/kayaking, paddling. 4 PE instructors, 266 coaches, 4 athletic trainers.

Computers Computers are regularly used in all academic classes. Computer network features include on-campus library services, online commercial services, Internet access, wireless campus network, Internet filtering or blocking technology. Campus intranet, student e-mail accounts, and computer access in designated common areas are available to students. The school has a published electronic and media policy.

Contact Mrs. Betsy S. Hata, Director of Admission and Financial Aid. 808-944-5714. Fax: 808-943-3602. E-mail: admission@punahou.edu. Web site: www.punahou.edu

QUEEN MARGARET'S SCHOOL

660 Brownsey Avenue

Duncan, British Columbia V9L 1C2, Canada

Head of School: Mrs. Wilma Jamieson

General Information Girls' boarding and coeducational day college-preparatory, arts, technology, equestrian studies, and STEM school, affiliated with Anglican Church of Canada. Boarding girls grades 6–12, day boys grades PS–8, day girls grades PS–12. Founded: 1921. Setting: small town. Nearest major city is Victoria, Canada. Students are housed in single-sex dormitories. 27-acre campus. 8 buildings on campus. Approved or accredited by Canadian Association of Independent Schools, Canadian Educational Standards Institute, The Association of Boarding Schools, and British Columbia Department of Education. Affiliate member of National Association of Independent Schools; member of Secondary School Admission Test Board and Canadian Association of Independent Schools. Language of instruction: English. Endowment: CAN$500,000. Total enrollment: 316. Upper school average class size: 16. Upper school faculty-student ratio: 1:8. There are 168 required school days per year for Upper School students. Upper School students typically attend 5 days per week. The average school day consists of 7 hours.

Upper School Student Profile Grade 8: 24 students (5 boys, 19 girls); Grade 9: 27 students (27 girls); Grade 10: 36 students (36 girls); Grade 11: 35 students (35 girls); Grade 12: 29 students (29 girls). 66% of students are boarding students. 47% are province residents. 7 provinces are represented in upper school student body. 45% are international students. International students from China, Germany, Hong Kong, Japan, Mexico, and United States; 20 other countries represented in student body.

Faculty School total: 45. In upper school: 5 men, 18 women; 9 have advanced degrees; 4 reside on campus.

Subjects Offered Advanced math, advanced studio art-AP, algebra, all academic, animal science, applied skills, art, biology, business education, business skills, calculus, calculus-AP, Canadian history, career and personal planning, career exploration, chemistry, chorus, college planning, computer science, creative writing, drama, English, English literature, equestrian sports, equine management, equine science, equitation, ESL, fine arts, French, geography, geometry, grammar, health, history, home economics, instrumental music, international relations, international studies, Japanese, journalism, leadership and service, mathematics, photography, physical education, physics, science, social studies, society, politics and law, speech, sports, sports psychology, theater, TOEFL preparation, trigonometry, visual arts, world history, writing.

Graduation Requirements Arts and fine arts (art, music, dance, drama), career and personal planning, computer science, English, foreign language, mathematics, physical education (includes health), science, social studies (includes history). Community service is required.

Special Academic Programs Advanced Placement exam preparation; independent study; study at local college for college credit; academic accommodation for the gifted, the musically talented, and the artistically talented; ESL (40 students enrolled).

College Admission Counseling 33 students graduated in 2012; 31 went to college, including Acadia University; Carleton University; Pratt Institute; Queen's University at Kingston; University of Victoria; University of Waterloo. Other: 2 went to work.

Student Life Upper grades have uniform requirement, student council, honor system. Discipline rests primarily with faculty. Attendance at religious services is required.

Summer Programs Enrichment, ESL, sports programs offered; session focuses on ESL group camps, equestrian riding, and pre-vet camp; held on campus; accepts boys and girls; open to students from other schools. 25 students usually enrolled. 2013 schedule: July 6 to August 29. Application deadline: May 15.

Tuition and Aid Day student tuition: CAN$8500–CAN$12,750; 7-day tuition and room/board: CAN$33,790–CAN$49,790. Tuition installment plan (Insured Tuition Payment Plan, monthly payment plans, individually arranged payment plans). Tuition reduction for siblings, bursaries, merit scholarship grants, need-based scholarship grants, tuition reduction for children of staff available. In 2012–13, 30% of upper-school students received aid; total upper-school merit-scholarship money awarded: CAN$50,000. Total amount of financial aid awarded in 2012–13: CAN$150,000.

Admissions Traditional secondary-level entrance grade is 8. Otis-Lennon School Ability Test, SLEP or Stanford Achievement Test required. Deadline for receipt of application materials: none. Applieation fee required: CAN$200. Interview required.

Athletics Interscholastic: aquatics (girls), badminton (g), basketball (g), canoeing/kayaking (g), cross-country running (b,g), dressage (g), equestrian sports (b,g), field hockey (g), golf (g), horseback riding (g), soccer (g), tennis (g), track and field (b,g), volleyball (g), wrestling (g); intramural: aerobics (g), aerobics/dance (g), ballet (g), flag football (g), golf (b,g), modern dance (g), rafting (g), rappelling (g), rugby (b), sailing (g), scuba diving (g), sea rescue (g), snowshoeing (g), surfing (g), ultimate Frisbee (g), volleyball (g), yoga (g); coed intramural: alpine skiing, aquatics, archery, backpacking, ball hockey, baseball, basketball, bowling, canoeing/kayaking, climbing, cooperative games, cross-country running, dance, dressage, equestrian sports, field hockey, figure skating, fitness, floor hockey, freestyle skiing, Frisbee, gymnastics, hiking/backpacking, hockey, horseback riding, ice skating, indoor hockey, indoor soccer, jogging, kayaking, ocean paddling, outdoor activities, outdoor adventure, outdoor education, outdoor recreation, outdoor skills, outdoors, paddling, physical fitness, physical training, running, skiing (downhill), snowboarding, soccer, softball, street hockey, swimming and diving, tennis. 2 PE instructors, 2 coaches, 2 athletic trainers.

Computers Computers are regularly used in all academic, career education, career exploration, college planning, creative writing, English, ESL, French, information technology, introduction to technology, journalism, mathematics, media arts, media production, science, social sciences, technology classes. Computer network features include on-campus library services, Internet access, wireless campus network, Internet filtering or blocking technology. Campus intranet and student e-mail accounts are available to students. The school has a published electronic and media policy.

Contact Admissions Coordinator. 250-746-4185. Fax: 250-746-4187. E-mail: admissions@qms.bc.ca. Web site: www.qms.bc.ca

QUINTE CHRISTIAN HIGH SCHOOL

138 Wallbridge-Loyalist Road
RR 2
Belleville, Ontario K8N 4Z2, Canada

Head of School: Mr. Johan Cooke

General Information Coeducational day college-preparatory, general academic, arts, business, vocational, religious studies, bilingual studies, and technology school, affiliated with Christian faith, Protestant faith. Grades 9–12. Founded: 1977. Setting: suburban. Nearest major city is Toronto, Canada. 25-acre campus. 1 building on campus. Approved or accredited by Christian Schools International, Ontario Ministry of Education, and Ontario Department of Education. Language of instruction: English. Total enrollment: 161. Upper school average class size: 15. Upper school faculty-student ratio: 1:15. There are 176 required school days per year for Upper School students. Upper School students typically attend 5 days per week. The average school day consists of 6 hours and 10 minutes.

Upper School Student Profile Grade 9: 36 students (22 boys, 14 girls); Grade 10: 35 students (16 boys, 19 girls); Grade 11: 37 students (13 boys, 24 girls); Grade 12: 45 students (25 boys, 20 girls). 90% of students are Christian, Protestant.

Faculty School total: 16. In upper school: 9 men, 7 women; 2 have advanced degrees.

Subjects Offered Accounting, art, Bible, biology, calculus, careers, chemistry, Christian education, civics, computers, drama, English, English literature, ESL, French, geography, history, law, leadership education training, mathematics, mathematics-AP, media, music, peer counseling, physical education, physics, religious education, science, shop, society challenge and change, technical education, transportation technology, world issues, world religions.

Graduation Requirements Accounting, applied arts, careers, Christian education, civics, computers, English, French, geography, mathematics, physical education (includes health), religious education, science, social studies (includes history), world religions, Ontario Christian School diploma requirements.

Special Academic Programs Special instructional classes for students with learning disabilities.

College Admission Counseling 39 students graduated in 2012; 20 went to college, including Calvin College; Dordt College; Queen's University at Kingston; Redeemer University College; University of Guelph; University of Waterloo. 100% scored over 26 on composite ACT.

Student Life Upper grades have specified standards of dress, student council, honor system. Discipline rests primarily with faculty. Attendance at religious services is required.

Tuition and Aid Day student tuition: CAN$12,200. Tuition installment plan (monthly payment plans, individually arranged payment plans). Tuition reduction for siblings, need-based scholarship grants available. In 2012–13, 18% of upper-school students received aid.

Admissions Traditional secondary-level entrance grade is 9. Deadline for receipt of application materials: March 31. Application fee required: CAN$250. Interview required.

Athletics Interscholastic: badminton (boys, girls), basketball (b,g), cross-country running (b,g), track and field (b,g), volleyball (b,g); coed interscholastic: badminton; coed intramural: badminton, basketball, fitness walking, indoor soccer, physical training, volleyball. 3 PE instructors.

Computers Computers are regularly used in all classes. Computer network features include on-campus library services, Internet access, wireless campus network, Internet filtering or blocking technology. Campus intranet, student e-mail accounts, and computer access in designated common areas are available to students. The school has a published electronic and media policy.

Contact Mrs. Hermien Hogewoning, Administrative Assistant. 613-968-7870. Fax: 613-968-7970. E-mail: admin@qchs.ca. Web site: www.qchs.ca

RABBI ALEXANDER S. GROSS HEBREW ACADEMY

2425 Pine Tree Drive
Miami Beach, Florida 33140

Head of School: Dr. Roni Raab

General Information Coeducational day college-preparatory, general academic, religious studies, and technology school, affiliated with Jewish faith. Grades N–12. Founded: 1948. Setting: urban. 4-acre campus. 1 building on campus. Approved or accredited by Massachusetts Office of Child Care Services, Southern Association of Colleges and Schools, and Florida Department of Education. Member of Secondary School Admission Test Board. Languages of instruction: English and Hebrew. Endowment: $650,000. Total enrollment: 468. Upper school average class size: 18. Upper school faculty-student ratio: 1:4.

Upper School Student Profile Grade 9: 45 students (20 boys, 25 girls); Grade 10: 38 students (20 boys, 18 girls); Grade 11: 32 students (15 boys, 17 girls); Grade 12: 40 students (20 boys, 20 girls). 100% of students are Jewish.

Faculty School total: 70. In upper school: 21 men, 18 women; 23 have advanced degrees.

Subjects Offered Algebra, audio visual/media, Bible studies, biology, biology-AP, calculus, calculus-AP, chemistry, chemistry-AP, computers, economics, English, English-AP, environmental science, geometry, Jewish studies, life science, physical education, physics, political science, pre-calculus, SAT preparation, social studies, Spanish, Talmud, technology.

Graduation Requirements Arts and fine arts (art, music, dance, drama), business skills (includes word processing), computer science, English, foreign language, mathematics, physical education (includes health), religion (includes Bible studies and theology), science, social sciences, social studies (includes history). Community service is required.

Special Academic Programs 7 Advanced Placement exams for which test preparation is offered; honors section; independent study; study at local college for college credit; academic accommodation for the gifted; ESL (3 students enrolled).

College Admission Counseling 57 students graduated in 2011; 56 went to college, including Florida International University; Florida State University; University of Florida; University of Maryland, College Park; Yeshiva University. Other: 1 went to work. Mean SAT critical reading: 544, mean SAT math: 542, mean SAT writing: 521, mean combined SAT: 1607, mean composite ACT: 23.

Student Life Upper grades have specified standards of dress, student council, honor system. Discipline rests primarily with faculty. Attendance at religious services is required.

Tuition and Aid Day student tuition: $14,000. Tuition installment plan (monthly payment plans, individually arranged payment plans). Tuition reduction for siblings, need-based scholarship grants available. In 2011–12, 46% of upper-school students received aid. Total amount of financial aid awarded in 2011–12: $300,000.

Admissions Traditional secondary-level entrance grade is 9. For fall 2011, 40 students applied for upper-level admission, 33 were accepted, 30 enrolled. SSAT required. Deadline for receipt of application materials: none. No application fee required. On-campus interview required.

Athletics Interscholastic: basketball (boys, girls), soccer (b), tennis (b,g), volleyball (g); intramural: basketball (b,g), soccer (b), tennis (b,g), volleyball (g). 2 PE instructors, 3 coaches.

Computers Computers are regularly used in English, mathematics, religion, science classes. Computer network features include Internet access. Student e-mail accounts are available to students.

Contact Mrs. Dara Lieber, Assistant Principal. 305-532-6421 Ext. 217. Fax: 305-604-0011. E-mail: dlieber@rasg.org. Web site: www.rasg.org

RAMONA CONVENT SECONDARY SCHOOL

1701 West Ramona Road
Alhambra, California 91803-3080

Head of School: Ms. Tina Bonacci

General Information Girls' day college-preparatory, arts, business, religious studies, bilingual studies, and technology school, affiliated with Roman Catholic Church. Grades 7–12. Founded: 1889. Setting: suburban. Nearest major city is Los Angeles. 19-acre campus. 10 buildings on campus. Approved or accredited by Western Association of Schools and Colleges, Western Catholic Education Association, and California Department of Education. Endowment: $2 million. Total enrollment: 272. Upper school average class size: 22. Upper school faculty-student ratio: 1:9. There are 180 required school days per year for Upper School students. Upper School students typically attend 5 days per week. The average school day consists of 6 hours and 30 minutes.

Upper School Student Profile Grade 9: 60 students (60 girls); Grade 10: 53 students (53 girls); Grade 11: 69 students (69 girls); Grade 12: 76 students (76 girls). 88% of students are Roman Catholic.

Faculty School total: 30. In upper school: 6 men, 24 women; all have advanced degrees.

Subjects Offered Advanced Placement courses, advanced studio art-AP, algebra, American history, American literature, art history, Bible studies, biology, biology-AP, calculus, calculus-AP, ceramics, chemistry, chemistry-AP, computer programming, computer science, dance, drama, economics, English, English literature, environmental science, European history, European history-AP, fine arts, French, French-AP, geography, geometry, government/civics, grammar, graphic arts, health, history, honors English, honors geometry, mathematics, music, photography, physical education, physics, pre-calculus, religion, science, social sciences, social studies, Spanish, Spanish language-AP, Spanish literature-AP, speech, theater, theology, trigonometry, U.S. government and politics-AP, visual arts, word processing, world history, world literature.

Graduation Requirements Arts and fine arts (art, music, dance, drama), business skills (includes word processing), computer science, English, foreign language, mathematics, physical education (includes health), religion (includes Bible studies and theology), science, social studies (includes history), speech, passing grade in the Ramona Arithmetic Proficiency Test.

Special Academic Programs Advanced Placement exam preparation; honors section; independent study; study abroad; academic accommodation for the gifted, the musically talented, and the artistically talented.

College Admission Counseling 89 students graduated in 2012; all went to college, including California State University, Los Angeles; Loyola Marymount University; Mount St. Mary's College; Pitzer College; University of California, Irvine; University of California, Los Angeles. Mean SAT critical reading: 532, mean SAT math: 511, mean SAT writing: 536.

Student Life Upper grades have uniform requirement, student council, honor system. Discipline rests primarily with faculty. Attendance at religious services is required.
Summer Programs Remediation, enrichment, advancement, sports, art/fine arts, computer instruction programs offered; session focuses on academics; held on campus; accepts boys and girls; open to students from other schools. 200 students usually enrolled. 2013 schedule: July 1 to July 26. Application deadline: June 1.
Tuition and Aid Day student tuition: $12,000. Tuition installment plan (monthly payment plans, quarterly and semester payment plans). Merit scholarship grants, need-based scholarship grants, paying campus jobs available. In 2012–13, 33% of upper-school students received aid; total upper-school merit-scholarship money awarded: $18,000. Total amount of financial aid awarded in 2012–13: $350,000.
Admissions Traditional secondary-level entrance grade is 9. For fall 2012, 190 students applied for upper-level admission, 150 were accepted, 78 enrolled. High School Placement Test required. Deadline for receipt of application materials: January 24. Application fee required: $75. On-campus interview required.
Athletics Interscholastic: basketball, cross-country running, soccer, softball, swimming and diving, tennis, track and field, volleyball. 1 PE instructor, 9 coaches.
Computers Computers are regularly used in all academic classes. Computer network features include on-campus library services, Internet access, wireless campus network, Internet filtering or blocking technology. Student e-mail accounts and computer access in designated common areas are available to students. Students grades are available online. The school has a published electronic and media policy.
Contact Mrs. Veronica Fernandez, Associate Director of Enrollment and Public Relations. 626-282-4151 Ext. 168. Fax: 626-281-0797. E-mail: vfernandez@ramonaconvent.org. Web site: www.ramonaconvent.org

RANDOLPH-MACON ACADEMY

200 Academy Drive
Front Royal, Virginia 22630

Head of School: Maj. Gen. Henry M. Hobgood

General Information Coeducational boarding and day college-preparatory, religious studies, technology, Air Force Junior ROTC, ESL, and military school, affiliated with Methodist Church. Grades 6–PG. Founded: 1892. Setting: small town. Nearest major city is Washington, DC. Students are housed in single-sex dormitories. 135-acre campus. 9 buildings on campus. Approved or accredited by Southern Association of Colleges and Schools, The Association of Boarding Schools, University Senate of United Methodist Church, Virginia Association of Independent Schools, and Virginia Department of Education. Member of National Association of Independent Schools. Endowment: $5 million. Total enrollment: 367. Upper school average class size: 13. Upper school faculty-student ratio: 1:9. There are 180 required school days per year for Upper School students. Upper School students typically attend 5 days per week. The average school day consists of 7 hours.
Upper School Student Profile Grade 9: 57 students (37 boys, 20 girls); Grade 10: 57 students (39 boys, 18 girls); Grade 11: 81 students (55 boys, 26 girls); Grade 12: 78 students (55 boys, 23 girls); Postgraduate: 2 students (1 boy, 1 girl). 80% of students are boarding students. 48% are state residents. 20 states are represented in upper school student body. 23% are international students. International students from Angola, China, Democratic People's Republic of Korea, Nigeria, Portugal, and Viet Nam; 9 other countries represented in student body. 12% of students are Methodist.
Faculty School total: 39. In upper school: 23 men, 9 women; 19 have advanced degrees; 16 reside on campus.
Subjects Offered Advanced math, aerospace science, algebra, American government, American history, American history-AP, American literature, American literature-AP, anatomy, anatomy and physiology, art, art history, art history-AP, Asian history, aviation, band, Bible studies, biology, biology-AP, British literature, calculus, calculus-AP, career education, chemistry, chorus, college counseling, comparative religion, composition-AP, computer applications, computer literacy, conceptual physics, concert band, concert choir, critical thinking, desktop publishing, discrete mathematics, drama, English, English composition, English literature, English literature and composition-AP, English-AP, epic literature, ESL, European history-AP, flight instruction, geometry, German, German-AP, government/civics, handbells, history, honors algebra, honors English, honors geometry, honors U.S. history, independent study, journalism, JROTC, keyboarding, life management skills, mathematics, music, music appreciation, New Testament, personal finance, personal fitness, photography, physical education, physics, physics-AP, physiology, pre-algebra, pre-calculus, psychology, religion, SAT preparation, science, senior seminar, Shakespeare, social studies, Spanish, Spanish literature-AP, speech and debate, statistics-AP, studio art, theater arts, trigonometry, U.S. government, U.S. history, world history, yearbook.
Graduation Requirements Aerospace science, arts and fine arts (art, music, dance, drama), computer science, English, foreign language, mathematics, physical education (includes health), religion (includes Bible studies and theology), science, social studies (includes history), Air Force Junior ROTC for each year student is enrolled.
Special Academic Programs Advanced Placement exam preparation; honors section; independent study; study at local college for college credit; study abroad; academic accommodation for the gifted; ESL (18 students enrolled).
College Admission Counseling 81 students graduated in 2012; all went to college, including James Madison University; Norwich University; Penn State University Park; United States Air Force Academy; University of California, Berkeley; Virginia Commonwealth University. Median SAT critical reading: 522, median SAT math: 560, median SAT writing: 511, median combined SAT: 1590, median composite ACT: 22.
Student Life Upper grades have uniform requirement, student council, honor system. Discipline rests equally with students and faculty. Attendance at religious services is required.
Summer Programs Remediation, enrichment, advancement, ESL, art/fine arts, computer instruction programs offered; session focuses on remediation, new courses, ESL, flight, college counseling; held on campus; accepts boys and girls; open to students from other schools. 180 students usually enrolled. 2013 schedule: June 30 to July 26. Application deadline: June 21.
Tuition and Aid Day student tuition: $16,091; 7-day tuition and room/board: $32,211. Tuition installment plan (monthly payment plans, 2-payment plan). Tuition reduction for siblings, merit scholarship grants, need-based scholarship grants, paying campus jobs, Methodist Church scholarships available. In 2012–13, 20% of upper-school students received aid; total upper-school merit-scholarship money awarded: $72,000. Total amount of financial aid awarded in 2012–13: $436,000.
Admissions Traditional secondary-level entrance grade is 9. For fall 2012, 132 students applied for upper-level admission, 128 were accepted, 94 enrolled. Any standardized test or SSAT required. Deadline for receipt of application materials: none. Application fee required: $75. Interview required.
Athletics Interscholastic: baseball (boys), basketball (b,g), cross-country running (b,g), football (b), lacrosse (b), soccer (b,g), softball (g), swimming and diving (b,g), tennis (b,g), track and field (b,g), volleyball (b,g), wrestling (b); intramural: basketball (b,g), horseback riding (g), independent competitive sports (b,g), soccer (b,g), softball (g), strength & conditioning (b,g), swimming and diving (b,g), tennis (b,g), track and field (b,g), volleyball (b,g); coed interscholastic: cheering, drill team, golf, JROTC drill; coed intramural: golf, horseback riding, indoor soccer, jogging, JROTC drill, outdoor activities, outdoor recreation, physical fitness, soccer, strength & conditioning, swimming and diving, table tennis, volleyball, weight lifting, weight training. 2 PE instructors, 1 athletic trainer.
Computers Computers are regularly used in aerospace science, aviation, English, ESL, foreign language, independent study, mathematics, science, yearbook classes. Computer network features include on-campus library services, online commercial services, Internet access, Internet filtering or blocking technology. Campus intranet and student e-mail accounts are available to students. Students grades are available online. The school has a published electronic and media policy.
Contact Mrs. Paula Brady, Admission Coordinator. 540-636-5484. Fax: 540-636-5419. E-mail: pbrady@rma.edu. Web site: www.rma.edu

RANDOLPH SCHOOL

1005 Drake Avenue SE
Huntsville, Alabama 35802

Head of School: Dr. Byron C. Hulsey

General Information Coeducational day college-preparatory and arts school. Grades K–12. Founded: 1959. Setting: suburban. 67-acre campus. 3 buildings on campus. Approved or accredited by Southern Association of Colleges and Schools, Southern Association of Independent Schools, and The College Board. Member of National Association of Independent Schools. Endowment: $11 million. Total enrollment: 1,001. Upper school average class size: 13. Upper school faculty-student ratio: 1:10. The average school day consists of 7 hours.
Faculty School total: 106. In upper school: 16 men, 25 women; 21 have advanced degrees.
Subjects Offered 3-dimensional art, acting, algebra, American history, American history-AP, American literature, anatomy, art, art-AP, band, biology, biology-AP, calculus, calculus-AP, ceramics, chemistry, chemistry-AP, comparative government and politics-AP, computer math, concert choir, creative writing, drama, drama workshop, economics, English, English literature, English-AP, environmental science, European history, European history-AP, film appreciation, filmmaking, fine arts, French, French-AP, geometry, history, journalism, Latin, marine biology, mathematics, music, music theory-AP, physical education, physics, physics-AP, physiology, psychology, science, social studies, Southern literature, Spanish, Spanish-AP, speech, stage design, stagecraft, student publications, studio art-AP, theater, trigonometry, U.S. government and politics-AP, U.S. history-AP, world history, world history-AP, world literature, writing, yearbook.
Graduation Requirements Algebra, arts and fine arts (art, music, dance, drama), biology, chemistry, English, foreign language, geometry, health, literature, mathematics, science, social studies (includes history), U.S. history, world history.
Special Academic Programs 12 Advanced Placement exams for which test preparation is offered; honors section; independent study; study at local college for college credit.
College Admission Counseling 80 students graduated in 2012; all went to college, including Auburn University; Birmingham-Southern College; Sewanee: The University of the South; The University of Alabama; The University of Alabama at Birmingham; Vanderbilt University. Mean SAT critical reading: 632, mean SAT math: 637, mean SAT writing: 634, mean combined SAT: 1903, mean composite ACT: 28. 53% scored over 600 on SAT critical reading, 57% scored over 600 on SAT math, 55%

scored over 600 on SAT writing, 55% scored over 1800 on combined SAT, 66% scored over 26 on composite ACT.

Student Life Upper grades have specified standards of dress, student council, honor system. Discipline rests primarily with faculty.

Summer Programs Enrichment, sports programs offered; session focuses on sports, arts, academics; held on campus; accepts boys and girls; open to students from other schools. 140 students usually enrolled. 2013 schedule: June 1 to July 31. Application deadline: April 30.

Tuition and Aid Day student tuition: $12,460–$16,615. Tuition installment plan (Insured Tuition Payment Plan, 2- and 10-month payment plans). Need-based scholarship grants, middle-income loans available. In 2012–13, 9% of upper-school students received aid. Total amount of financial aid awarded in 2012–13: $258,240.

Admissions Traditional secondary-level entrance grade is 9. For fall 2012, 42 students applied for upper-level admission, 27 were accepted, 22 enrolled. ISEE or writing sample required. Deadline for receipt of application materials: none. Application fee required: $75. On-campus interview required.

Athletics Interscholastic: baseball (boys), basketball (b,g), cheering (g), cross-country running (b,g), diving (b,g), football (b), golf (b,g), indoor track & field (b,g), physical fitness (b,g), physical training (b,g), soccer (b,g), softball (g), swimming and diving (b,g), tennis (b,g), track and field (b,g), volleyball (g), winter (indoor) track (b,g); coed interscholastic: diving. 2 PE instructors, 19 coaches, 2 athletic trainers.

Computers Computers are regularly used in all academic classes. Computer network features include on-campus library services, online commercial services, Internet access, wireless campus network, Internet filtering or blocking technology, laptops. Campus intranet, student e-mail accounts, and computer access in designated common areas are available to students. Students grades are available online. The school has a published electronic and media policy.

Contact Glynn Below, Director of Admissions. 256-799-6104. Fax: 256-881-1784. E-mail: gbelow@randolphschool.net. Web site: www.randolphschool.net

RANNEY SCHOOL

235 Hope Road
Tinton Falls, New Jersey 07724

Head of School: Dr. Lawrence S. Sykoff

General Information Coeducational day college-preparatory school. Grades N–12. Founded: 1960. Setting: suburban. Nearest major city is New York, NY. 60-acre campus. 3 buildings on campus. Approved or accredited by Middle States Association of Colleges and Schools and New Jersey Department of Education. Member of National Association of Independent Schools and Secondary School Admission Test Board. Total enrollment: 821. Upper school average class size: 15. Upper school faculty-student ratio: 1:9. The average school day consists of 7 hours.

Upper School Student Profile Grade 9: 80 students (30 boys, 50 girls); Grade 10: 82 students (29 boys, 53 girls); Grade 11: 59 students (30 boys, 29 girls); Grade 12: 50 students (24 boys, 26 girls).

Faculty School total: 94.

Subjects Offered ACT preparation, Advanced Placement courses, algebra, American history, American literature, anatomy and physiology, art, art history, art history-AP, astronomy, biology, biology-AP, British literature (honors), calculus, calculus-AP, ceramics, chemistry, chemistry-AP, computer programming, computer science, computer science-AP, ecology, environmental systems, economics, economics-AP, English, English language-AP, English literature, English literature-AP, environmental science, environmental science-AP, ethics, European history, European history-AP, fine arts, French, French-AP, geometry, government, government and politics-AP, grammar, health, history, honors English, honors geometry, journalism, macro/microeconomics-AP, macroeconomics-AP, Mandarin, marine biology, mathematics, music, music history, music theory-AP, music-AP, physical education, physics, SAT preparation, science, senior internship, senior thesis, Spanish, Spanish language-AP, strings, studio art, studio art-AP, theater arts, world history, world history-AP, world literature, writing.

Graduation Requirements Arts and fine arts (art, music, dance, drama), English, foreign language, history, mathematics, physical education (includes health), science.

Special Academic Programs 19 Advanced Placement exams for which test preparation is offered; honors section.

College Admission Counseling 56 students graduated in 2012; all went to college, including Franklin & Marshall College; New York University; The George Washington University; University of Notre Dame; University of Pennsylvania. Mean SAT critical reading: 626, mean SAT math: 621, mean SAT writing: 638, mean combined SAT: 1884.

Student Life Upper grades have specified standards of dress, student council, honor system. Discipline rests equally with students and faculty.

Summer Programs Enrichment, sports, art/fine arts, computer instruction programs offered; session focuses on academic, enrichment, and Gifted and Talented; held on campus; accepts boys and girls; open to students from other schools. 200 students usually enrolled. 2013 schedule: July 1 to August 23. Application deadline: March 30.

Tuition and Aid Day student tuition: $21,650–$25,500. Tuition installment plan (Tuiton Management Systems (TMS)). Need-based scholarship grants, reduced tuition for children of employees available. In 2012–13, 6% of upper-school students received aid. Total amount of financial aid awarded in 2012–13: $267,000.

Admissions Traditional secondary-level entrance grade is 9. For fall 2012, 65 students applied for upper-level admission, 51 were accepted, 42 enrolled. ERB required. Deadline for receipt of application materials: none. Application fee required: $75. On-campus interview required.

Athletics Interscholastic: baseball (boys), basketball (b,g), cheering (g), field hockey (g), lacrosse (b,g), soccer (b,g), softball (g), tennis (b,g); coed interscholastic: aquatics, crew, cross-country running, golf, swimming and diving, track and field; coed intramural: aquatics, climbing, crew, dance team, fencing, fishing, fitness, ropes courses, running, squash, strength & conditioning, weight training. 6 PE instructors, 18 coaches, 1 athletic trainer.

Computers Computers are regularly used in all academic classes. Computer network features include on-campus library services, Internet access, wireless campus network, Internet filtering or blocking technology, 1:1 laptop program in grades 6-12. Campus intranet, student e-mail accounts, and computer access in designated common areas are available to students. Students grades are available online. The school has a published electronic and media policy.

Contact Joseph M. Tweed, Director of Admissions and Financial Aid. 732-542-4777 Ext. 1107. Fax: 732-460-1078. E-mail: jtweed@ranneyschool.org. Web site: www.ranneyschool.org

See Display on next page and Close-Up on page 614.

RANSOM EVERGLADES SCHOOL

3575 Main Highway
Miami, Florida 33133

Head of School: Mrs. Ellen Y. Moceri

General Information Coeducational day college-preparatory school. Grades 6–12. Founded: 1903. Setting: urban. 11-acre campus. 19 buildings on campus. Approved or accredited by Southern Association of Colleges and Schools, Southern Association of Independent Schools, and Florida Department of Education. Member of National Association of Independent Schools and Secondary School Admission Test Board. Endowment: $23.5 million. Total enrollment: 1,075. Upper school average class size: 14. Upper school faculty-student ratio: 1:10. There are 175 required school days per year for Upper School students. Upper School students typically attend 5 days per week. The average school day consists of 7 hours and 30 minutes.

Upper School Student Profile Grade 9: 152 students (76 boys, 76 girls); Grade 10: 155 students (74 boys, 81 girls); Grade 11: 155 students (79 boys, 76 girls); Grade 12: 151 students (82 boys, 69 girls).

Faculty School total: 97. In upper school: 31 men, 26 women; 46 have advanced degrees.

Subjects Offered Advanced Placement courses, algebra, American history, American history-AP, American literature, anatomy and physiology, art, art history, art history-AP, Asian studies, astronomy, band, biology, calculus, calculus-AP, ceramics, chemistry, chemistry-AP, Chinese, choir, chorus, college counseling, comparative government and politics-AP, computer math, computer programming, computer science, computer science-AP, computer-aided design, concert band, creative writing, dance, dance performance, debate, digital photography, drama, earth science, ecology, economics, economics-AP, engineering, English, English literature, English literature and composition-AP, English-AP, environmental science, environmental science-AP, environmental studies, ethical decision making, ethics, ethics and responsibility, European history, European history-AP, experiential education, fine arts, French, French language-AP, French-AP, geography, geology, geometry, government and politics-AP, government/civics, grammar, graphic design, guitar, health, health and wellness, history, history-AP, human anatomy, interdisciplinary studies, jazz ensemble, journalism, macro/microeconomics-AP, macroeconomics-AP, Mandarin, marine biology, mathematics, mathematics-AP, music, music theory, music theory-AP, music-AP, mythology, philosophy, photography, physical education, physics, physics-AP, probability and statistics, psychology, psychology-AP, robotics, science, sculpture, social studies, sociology, Spanish, Spanish language-AP, Spanish literature-AP, speech, speech and debate, statistics, statistics-AP, theater, theory of knowledge, trigonometry, U.S. government and politics-AP, U.S. history, U.S. history-AP, world history, world history-AP, world literature, writing, yearbook.

Graduation Requirements Arts and fine arts (art, music, dance, drama), computer science, English, foreign language, mathematics, physical education (includes health), science, social studies (includes history).

Special Academic Programs 21 Advanced Placement exams for which test preparation is offered; honors section.

College Admission Counseling 141 students graduated in 2012; all went to college, including Harvard University; New York University; The George Washington University; University of Miami; University of Pennsylvania; Vanderbilt University. Median SAT critical reading: 650, median SAT math: 670, median SAT writing: 670, median combined SAT: 1970, median composite ACT: 30.

Student Life Upper grades have specified standards of dress, student council, honor system. Discipline rests primarily with faculty.

Summer Programs Enrichment, advancement, computer instruction programs offered; session focuses on enrichment to reinforce basic skills and advancement for credit; held on campus; accepts boys and girls; open to students from other schools. 130

students usually enrolled. 2013 schedule: June 10 to July 19. Application deadline: June 7.

Tuition and Aid Day student tuition: $28,040. Tuition installment plan (monthly payment plans, 60%/40% payment plan). Need-based scholarship grants available. In 2012–13, 16% of upper-school students received aid. Total amount of financial aid awarded in 2012–13: $2,224,990.

Admissions Traditional secondary-level entrance grade is 9. For fall 2012, 126 students applied for upper-level admission, 14 were accepted, 9 enrolled. SSAT required. Deadline for receipt of application materials: December 1. Application fee required: $100. On-campus interview required.

Athletics Interscholastic: baseball (boys), basketball (b,g), canoeing/kayaking (b,g), cheering (g), crew (b,g), cross-country running (b,g), dance (g), dance team (g), football (b), golf (b,g), kayaking (b,g), lacrosse (b), physical training (b,g), sailing (b,g), soccer (b,g), softball (g), swimming and diving (b,g), tennis (b,g), track and field (b,g), volleyball (b,g), water polo (b,g), wrestling (b); coed interscholastic: crew, kayaking, sailing. 4 PE instructors, 80 coaches, 2 athletic trainers.

Computers Computers are regularly used in all classes. Computer network features include on-campus library services, online commercial services, Internet access, wireless campus network, Internet filtering or blocking technology. Student e-mail accounts and computer access in designated common areas are available to students. Students grades are available online. The school has a published electronic and media policy.

Contact Amy Sayfie, Director of Admission. 305-250-6875. Fax: 305-854-1846. E-mail: asayfie@ransomeverglades.org. Web site: www.ransomeverglades.org

RAVENSCROFT SCHOOL

7409 Falls of the Neuse Road
Raleigh, North Carolina 27615

Head of School: Mrs. Doreen C. Kelly

General Information Coeducational day college-preparatory, arts, and technology school. Grades PK–12. Founded: 1862. Setting: suburban. 127-acre campus. 13 buildings on campus. Approved or accredited by Southern Association of Colleges and Schools, Southern Association of Independent Schools, and North Carolina Department of Education. Member of National Association of Independent Schools. Endowment: $15 million. Total enrollment: 1,210. Upper school average class size: 13. Upper school faculty-student ratio: 1:8. There are 179 required school days per year for Upper School students. Upper School students typically attend 5 days per week. The average school day consists of 7 hours and 10 minutes.

Faculty School total: 156. In upper school: 25 men, 30 women; 42 have advanced degrees.

Subjects Offered Advanced Placement courses, algebra, American history, American literature, anatomy, art, art history, astronomy, biology, biotechnology, calculus, chemistry, computer programming, computer science, discrete mathematics, drama, economics, engineering, English, English literature, environmental science, environmental science-AP, European history, expository writing, fine arts, French, geometry, government/civics, Greek, health, history, journalism, Latin, mathematics, music, photography, physical education, physics, psychology, science, social sciences, social studies, Spanish, speech, sports medicine, stagecraft, statistics-AP, theater, world history, writing.

Graduation Requirements Arts and fine arts (art, music, dance, drama), composition, English, foreign language, mathematics, physical education (includes health), science, social sciences, social studies (includes history). Community service is required.

Special Academic Programs 24 Advanced Placement exams for which test preparation is offered; honors section; independent study; term-away projects; study at local college for college credit; study abroad; academic accommodation for the gifted, the musically talented, and the artistically talented.

College Admission Counseling 115 students graduated in 2012; 114 went to college, including Appalachian State University; Davidson College; East Carolina University; North Carolina State University; The University of North Carolina at Chapel Hill; Virginia Polytechnic Institute and State University. Other: 1 entered a postgraduate year. Median SAT critical reading: 640, median SAT math: 660, median SAT writing: 640, median combined SAT: 1950, median composite ACT: 27. 61% scored over 600 on SAT critical reading, 71% scored over 600 on SAT math, 62% scored over 600 on SAT writing, 68% scored over 1800 on combined SAT, 55% scored over 26 on composite ACT.

Student Life Upper grades have specified standards of dress, student council, honor system. Discipline rests equally with students and faculty.

Summer Programs Enrichment, advancement, sports, art/fine arts, computer instruction programs offered; session focuses on enrichment; held on campus; accepts boys and girls; open to students from other schools. 2,000 students usually enrolled. 2013 schedule: June 17 to August 9. Application deadline: none.

Tuition and Aid Day student tuition: $19,550. Tuition installment plan (individually arranged payment plans). Merit scholarship grants, need-based scholarship grants, need-based loans available. In 2012–13, 7% of upper-school students received aid.

Admissions Traditional secondary-level entrance grade is 9. ERB and SSAT required. Deadline for receipt of application materials: none. Application fee required: $70. On-campus interview required.

Athletics Interscholastic: baseball (boys), basketball (b,g), cheering (g), cross-country running (b,g), dance squad (g), field hockey (g), fitness (b,g), football (b), golf (b,g), lacrosse (b,g), physical training (b,g), soccer (b,g), softball (g), strength & conditioning (b,g), swimming and diving (b,g), tennis (b,g), track and field (b,g), volleyball (g), weight training (b,g), wrestling (b); intramural: baseball (b), basketball (b,g), cheering (g), dance team (g), football (b,g), lacrosse (b), soccer (b,g), softball (g), strength & conditioning (b,g), swimming and diving (b,g), tennis (b,g), track and field (b,g), volleyball (g), wrestling (b); coed interscholastic: life saving. 10 PE instructors, 68 coaches, 2 athletic trainers.
Computers Computers are regularly used in economics, English, foreign language, history, mathematics, science, social studies, writing classes. Computer network features include on-campus library services, online commercial services, Internet access, wireless campus network, Internet filtering or blocking technology. Campus intranet, student e-mail accounts, and computer access in designated common areas are available to students. Students grades are available online. The school has a published electronic and media policy.
Contact Mrs. Pamela J. Jamison, Director of Admissions. 919-847-0900 Ext. 2226. Fax: 919-846-2371. E-mail: admissions@ravenscroft.org. Web site: www.ravenscroft.org

REALMS OF INQUIRY

120 W. Vine Street
Murray, Utah 84107

Head of School: Mr. Jochen Schmidt

General Information Coeducational day college-preparatory, general academic, arts, bilingual studies, and outdoor education school; primarily serves underachievers and gifted students. Grades 6–12. Founded: 1972. Setting: urban. Nearest major city is Salt Lake City. 1-acre campus. 1 building on campus. Approved or accredited by Northwest Accreditation Commission and Utah Department of Education. Total enrollment: 22. Upper school average class size: 7. Upper school faculty-student ratio: 1:7. There are 180 required school days per year for Upper School students. Upper School students typically attend 5 days per week. The average school day consists of 6 hours and 15 minutes.
Upper School Student Profile Grade 9: 4 students (4 boys); Grade 10: 3 students (1 boy, 2 girls); Grade 11: 4 students (2 boys, 2 girls); Grade 12: 1 student (1 boy).
Faculty School total: 5. In upper school: 3 men, 1 woman; 1 has an advanced degree.
Subjects Offered Algebra, art, band, biology, calculus, chemistry, computer literacy, drama, earth science, English, French, geometry, history, life skills, outdoor education, photography, physical education, physics, pre-calculus, Spanish, writing.
Graduation Requirements Arts and fine arts (art, music, dance, drama), computer science, English, foreign language, mathematics, outdoor education, physical education (includes health), science, social sciences, social studies (includes history), 30 volunteer service hours per year.
Special Academic Programs Accelerated programs; independent study; study at local college for college credit; study abroad; academic accommodation for the gifted, the musically talented, and the artistically talented; programs in English, mathematics, general development for dyslexic students.
College Admission Counseling 5 students graduated in 2012; 4 went to college, including Beloit College; University of Utah; Westminster College. Other: 1 had other specific plans. Median SAT critical reading: 690, median SAT math: 640, median SAT writing: 670, median combined SAT: 2000, median composite ACT: 28. 100% scored over 600 on SAT critical reading, 100% scored over 600 on SAT math, 100% scored over 600 on SAT writing, 100% scored over 1800 on combined SAT, 100% scored over 26 on composite ACT.
Student Life Upper grades have student council, honor system. Discipline rests equally with students and faculty.
Summer Programs Rigorous outdoor training programs offered; session focuses on climbing, rafting, wilderness skills; held both on and off campus; held at various locations; accepts boys and girls; open to students from other schools. 10 students usually enrolled.
Tuition and Aid Day student tuition: $12,900. Tuition installment plan (monthly payment plans, individually arranged payment plans). Tuition reduction for siblings, need-based scholarship grants available. In 2012–13, 30% of upper-school students received aid. Total amount of financial aid awarded in 2012–13: $40,000.
Admissions Traditional secondary-level entrance grade is 9. Admissions testing, WISC-III and Woodcock-Johnson, WISC/Woodcock-Johnson or Woodcock-Johnson required. Deadline for receipt of application materials: none. Application fee required: $25. Interview required.
Athletics Coed Interscholastic: backpacking, bicycling, canoeing/kayaking, climbing, combined training, cooperative games, cross-country running, dance, fencing, fishing, fitness, flag football, Frisbee, gymnastics, hiking/backpacking, independent competitive sports, jogging, kayaking, life saving, martial arts, modern dance, mountain biking, mountaineering, nordic skiing, outdoor activities, outdoor adventure, outdoor education, outdoor recreation, outdoor skills, outdoors, paddling, physical fitness, physical training, project adventure, rafting, rappelling, rock climbing, running, skateboarding, ski jumping, skiing (cross-country), skiing (downhill), snowboarding, snowshoeing, soccer, strength & conditioning, swimming and diving, table tennis, telemark skiing, touch football, ultimate Frisbee, unicycling, volleyball, walking, wall climbing, weight lifting, weight training, wilderness, wilderness survival, wildernessways, winter walking, yoga.
Computers Computers are regularly used in all academic, career exploration, college planning, commercial art, computer applications, creative writing, current events, design, desktop publishing, digital applications, drafting, drawing and design, engineering, English, foreign language, graphic design, graphics, history, independent study, mathematics, media, media arts, media production, media services, music, photography, photojournalism, publishing, research skills, SAT preparation, science, social sciences, social studies classes. Computer network features include on-campus library services, Internet access, wireless campus network. Computer access in designated common areas is available to students. Students grades are available online. The school has a published electronic and media policy.
Contact Front Desk. 801-467-5911. Fax: 801-467-5932. E-mail: frontdesk@realmsofinquiry.org. Web site: www.realmsofinquiry.org

THE RECTORY SCHOOL

Pomfret, Connecticut
See Junior Boarding Schools section.

REDWOOD CHRISTIAN SCHOOLS

4200 James Avenue
Castro Valley, California 94546

Head of School: Mr. Bruce D. Johnson

General Information Coeducational day college-preparatory and religious studies school, affiliated with Christian faith. Grades K–12. Founded: 1970. Setting: urban. Nearest major city is Oakland. 10-acre campus. 11 buildings on campus. Approved or accredited by Association of Christian Schools International, Western Association of Schools and Colleges, and California Department of Education. Total enrollment: 648. Upper school average class size: 18. Upper school faculty-student ratio: 1:10. There are 175 required school days per year for Upper School students. Upper School students typically attend 5 days per week. The average school day consists of 6 hours and 50 minutes.
Upper School Student Profile Grade 9: 66 students (38 boys, 28 girls); Grade 10: 67 students (38 boys, 29 girls); Grade 11: 60 students (30 boys, 30 girls); Grade 12: 67 students (41 boys, 26 girls). 50% of students are Christian.
Faculty School total: 27. In upper school: 16 men, 11 women; 9 have advanced degrees.
Subjects Offered Advanced math, Advanced Placement courses, algebra, art, athletics, band, baseball, basketball, Bible studies, biology, chemistry, choir, computer literacy, concert band, drama, economics, English, European history-AP, fitness, geometry, honors English, keyboarding, macro/microeconomics-AP, physical education, physical science, physics, softball, Spanish, speech, track and field, trigonometry, U.S. government, U.S. history, vocal music, woodworking, world history, world history-AP, yearbook.
Graduation Requirements Arts and fine arts (art, music, dance, drama), Bible, computer literacy, electives, English, foreign language, mathematics, physical education (includes health), science, speech, world history.
Special Academic Programs Advanced Placement exam preparation; honors section; study at local college for college credit; remedial reading and/or remedial writing; remedial math; programs in English, mathematics, general development for dyslexic students; ESL (30 students enrolled).
College Admission Counseling 56 students graduated in 2012; 54 went to college, including Azusa Pacific University; California State University, East Bay; Seattle Pacific University; Simpson University; University of California, Davis; University of California, Irvine. Other: 2 went to work. Mean SAT critical reading: 610, mean SAT math: 627, mean SAT writing: 603, mean combined SAT: 1840. 50% scored over 600 on SAT critical reading, 52% scored over 600 on SAT math, 55% scored over 600 on SAT writing, 52% scored over 1800 on combined SAT.
Student Life Upper grades have specified standards of dress, student council, honor system. Discipline rests primarily with faculty.
Tuition and Aid Day student tuition: $10,362–$15,543. Tuition installment plan (monthly payment plans, individually arranged payment plans). Tuition reduction for siblings, merit scholarship grants, need-based scholarship grants, paying campus jobs available. In 2012–13, 65% of upper-school students received aid; total upper-school merit-scholarship money awarded: $356,524. Total amount of financial aid awarded in 2012–13: $356,524.
Admissions Traditional secondary-level entrance grade is 9. For fall 2012, 76 students applied for upper-level admission, 74 were accepted, 58 enrolled. Stanford Achievement Test required. Deadline for receipt of application materials: none. Application fee required: $125. On-campus interview required.
Athletics Interscholastic: baseball (boys), basketball (b,g), cross-country running (b,g), soccer (b,g), softball (g), tennis (b,g), track and field (b,g), volleyball (b,g). 2 PE instructors, 1 coach.
Computers Computers are regularly used in computer applications, keyboarding, yearbook classes. Computer network features include on-campus library services, Internet access. Campus intranet is available to students. Students grades are available online. The school has a published electronic and media policy.

Contact Mrs. Deborah Wright, Administrative Assistant. 510-889-7526. Fax: 510-881-0127. E-mail: deborahwright@rcs.edu. Web site: www.rcs.edu

REGIS HIGH SCHOOL

55 East 84th Street
New York, New York 10028-0884

Head of School: Dr. Gary J. Tocchet

General Information Boys' day college-preparatory school, affiliated with Roman Catholic Church. Grades 9–12. Founded: 1914. Setting: urban. 3-acre campus. 1 building on campus. Approved or accredited by Jesuit Secondary Education Association, Middle States Association of Colleges and Schools, and New York Department of Education. Total enrollment: 530. Upper school average class size: 15. Upper school faculty-student ratio: 1:15. There are 180 required school days per year for Upper School students. Upper School students typically attend 5 days per week. The average school day consists of 6 hours and 50 minutes.

Upper School Student Profile Grade 9: 136 students (136 boys); Grade 10: 132 students (132 boys); Grade 11: 131 students (131 boys); Grade 12: 131 students (131 boys). 100% of students are Roman Catholic.

Faculty School total: 66. In upper school: 40 men, 22 women; 52 have advanced degrees.

Subjects Offered Algebra, American history, American literature, art, art history, band, biology, calculus, chemistry, Chinese, computer programming, computer science, creative writing, drama, driver education, economics, English, English literature, ethics, European history, expository writing, film, French, geometry, German, health, history, Latin, mathematics, music, physical education, physics, psychology, social studies, Spanish, speech, statistics, theater, theology, trigonometry, writing.

Graduation Requirements Art, computer literacy, English, foreign language, history, mathematics, music, physical education (includes health), science, theology, Christian service program.

Special Academic Programs 14 Advanced Placement exams for which test preparation is offered; independent study; study abroad.

College Admission Counseling 135 students graduated in 2012; all went to college, including Boston College; College of the Holy Cross; Columbia University; Fordham University; Georgetown University; Villanova University. Mean SAT critical reading: 713, mean SAT math: 713, mean SAT writing: 719, mean combined SAT: 2145.

Student Life Upper grades have specified standards of dress, student council. Discipline rests primarily with faculty. Attendance at religious services is required.

Tuition and Aid Tuition-free school available.

Admissions Traditional secondary-level entrance grade is 9. For fall 2012, 771 students applied for upper-level admission, 144 were accepted, 136 enrolled. Admissions testing required. Deadline for receipt of application materials: October 19. Application fee required: $50. On-campus interview required.

Athletics Interscholastic: baseball, basketball, cross-country running, fencing, floor hockey, indoor track & field, volleyball; intramural: baseball, basketball, cross-country running, floor hockey, indoor soccer. 2 PE instructors, 10 coaches.

Computers Computers are regularly used in all academic classes. Computer network features include on-campus library services, Internet access, wireless campus network, Internet filtering or blocking technology. Campus intranet, student e-mail accounts, and computer access in designated common areas are available to students.

Contact Mr. Eric P. DiMichele, Director of Admissions. 212-288-1100 Ext. 2057. Fax: 212-794-1221. E-mail: edimiche@regis.org. Web site: www.regis.org

REGIS JESUIT HIGH SCHOOL, GIRLS DIVISION

6300 South Lewiston Way
Aurora, Colorado 80016

Head of School: Ms. Gretchen M. Kessler

General Information Coeducational day college-preparatory, arts, and religious studies school, affiliated with Roman Catholic Church (Jesuit order). Grades 9–12. Founded: 2003. Setting: suburban. 64-acre campus. 2 buildings on campus. Approved or accredited by American Association of Christian Schools and Colorado Department of Education. Total enrollment: 1,700. Upper school average class size: 20. Upper school faculty-student ratio: 1:8. Upper School students typically attend 5 days per week. The average school day consists of 6 hours and 45 minutes.

Upper School Student Profile Grade 9: 460 students (270 boys, 190 girls); Grade 10: 420 students (240 boys, 180 girls); Grade 11: 420 students (240 boys, 180 girls); Grade 12: 400 students (225 boys, 175 girls). 65% of students are Roman Catholic Church (Jesuit order).

Faculty School total: 175. In upper school: 24 men, 57 women.

Special Academic Programs International Baccalaureate program; Advanced Placement exam preparation; academic accommodation for the gifted, the musically talented, and the artistically talented; remedial reading and/or remedial writing; remedial math; special instructional classes for deaf students, blind students.

College Admission Counseling Colleges students went to include Adams State University.

Student Life Upper grades have specified standards of dress, student council, honor system. Discipline rests primarily with faculty. Attendance at religious services is required.

Summer Programs Remediation, enrichment, advancement, sports, art/fine arts, computer instruction programs offered; held on campus; accepts boys and girls; not open to students from other schools. 50 students usually enrolled.

Tuition and Aid Financial aid available to upper-school students. In 2012–13, 35% of upper-school students received aid.

Admissions Traditional secondary-level entrance grade is 9. For fall 2012, 900 students applied for upper-level admission, 500 were accepted, 460 enrolled. Deadline for receipt of application materials: December 12. Application fee required.

Athletics Interscholastic: aerobics/dance (girls), aquatics (b,g), baseball (b,g), basketball (b,g), cheering (g), cross-country running (b,g), dance (g), dance team (g), field hockey (g), fitness (b,g), football (b), golf (b,g), ice hockey (b), modern dance (g), physical fitness (b,g), power lifting (b), rhythmic gymnastics (g), rugby (b), running (b,g), soccer (b,g), swimming and diving (b,g), tennis (b,g), track and field (b,g), volleyball (b,g), wrestling (b); intramural: basketball (b,g), flag football (b), football (b), golf (b,g), soccer (b,g), whiffle ball (b). 10 PE instructors, 30 coaches, 3 athletic trainers.

Computers Computer network features include on-campus library services, Internet access, wireless campus network, Internet filtering or blocking technology. Campus intranet, student e-mail accounts, and computer access in designated common areas are available to students. Students grades are available online. The school has a published electronic and media policy.

Contact Ms. Patricia Long, Director of Admissions. 303-269-8164. Fax: 303-221-4776. E-mail: plong@regisjesuit.com. Web site: www.regisjesuit.com

REITZ MEMORIAL HIGH SCHOOL

1500 Lincoln Avenue
Evansville, Indiana 47714

Head of School: Cynthia Schneider

General Information Coeducational day college-preparatory, arts, business, religious studies, and technology school, affiliated with Roman Catholic Church. Grades 9–12. Founded: 1925. Setting: urban. Nearest major city is Indianapolis. 2 buildings on campus. Approved or accredited by National Catholic Education Association, North Central Association of Colleges and Schools, The College Board, and Indiana Department of Education. Total enrollment: 781. Upper school average class size: 25. Upper school faculty-student ratio: 1:14. There are 180 required school days per year for Upper School students. Upper School students typically attend 5 days per week. The average school day consists of 7 hours and 15 minutes.

Upper School Student Profile Grade 9: 176 students (92 boys, 84 girls); Grade 10: 211 students (107 boys, 104 girls); Grade 11: 204 students (110 boys, 94 girls); Grade 12: 190 students (93 boys, 97 girls). 85% of students are Roman Catholic.

Faculty School total: 52. In upper school: 17 men, 35 women; 37 have advanced degrees.

Subjects Offered 20th century American writers, 20th century history, 3-dimensional art, accounting, advanced biology, advanced chemistry, advanced computer applications, Advanced Placement courses, algebra, American government, American history, American literature, anatomy, anatomy and physiology, anthropology, applied music, art, art appreciation, art history, band, Basic programming, biology, biology-AP, botany, British literature, business, business communications, business law, business skills, calculus, calculus-AP, Catholic belief and practice, ceramics, chemistry, chemistry-AP, choir, choral music, chorus, church history, commercial art, composition, computer applications, computer programming, computer skills, concert band, concert choir, consumer economics, current events, digital photography, dramatic arts, drawing, drawing and design, driver education, earth and space science, earth science, ecology, environmental systems, English, English composition, English literature and composition-AP, English-AP, entomology, environmental science, environmental studies, etymology, fitness, foreign language, forensics, French, French language-AP, French-AP, geometry, German, government, grammar, guitar, health and wellness, history of the Catholic Church, honors algebra, honors English, honors geometry, honors U.S. history, honors world history, instrumental music, integrated physics, jewelry making, journalism, keyboarding, law, law and the legal system, library assistant, Life of Christ, literary genres, literature, marching band, media arts, moral theology, music appreciation, music composition, music history, New Testament, newspaper, oil painting, orchestra, painting, peace and justice, personal finance, photography, physical education, physics, physics-AP, physiology, piano, play production, portfolio art, prayer/spirituality, precalculus, printmaking, psychology, publications, SAT/ACT preparation, social justice, sociology, Spanish, Spanish language-AP, Spanish-AP, sports conditioning, state history, studio art, theater, theater arts, theater design and production, theology, trigonometry, U.S. history, Web site design, weight fitness, weight training, world history, world history-AP, yearbook.

Graduation Requirements Service hours.

Special Academic Programs 8 Advanced Placement exams for which test preparation is offered; honors section; study at local college for college credit.

College Admission Counseling 184 students graduated in 2011; 171 went to college, including Indiana University Bloomington; Purdue University; University of Evansville; University of Kentucky; University of Mississippi; Western Kentucky University. Other: 3 went to work, 3 entered military service, 7 entered a postgraduate year. Mean SAT critical reading: 522, mean SAT math: 540, mean SAT writing: 526, mean combined SAT: 1588, mean composite ACT: 24.

Student Life Upper grades have uniform requirement, student council. Discipline rests primarily with faculty. Attendance at religious services is required.

Tuition and Aid Day student tuition: $4500–$7050. Tuition installment plan (monthly payment plans, ETFCU Loans). Tuition reduction for siblings, need-based scholarship grants, need-based loans available. In 2011–12, 12% of upper-school students received aid. Total amount of financial aid awarded in 2011–12: $264,840.

Admissions Traditional secondary-level entrance grade is 9. For fall 2011, 781 students applied for upper-level admission, 781 were accepted, 781 enrolled. ACT-Explore required. Deadline for receipt of application materials: none. Application fee required: $180.

Athletics Interscholastic: baseball (boys), basketball (b,g), cheering (g), dance squad (g), dance team (g), diving (b,g), drill team (g), football (b), golf (b,g), soccer (b,g), softball (g), swimming and diving (b,g), tennis (b,g), track and field (b,g), volleyball (g), weight training (b), wrestling (b); intramural: bowling (b,g), lacrosse (b,g), paint ball (b); coed interscholastic: cross-country running; coed intramural: ice hockey, table tennis. 4 PE instructors, 1 athletic trainer.

Computers Computers are regularly used in all classes. Computer network features include on-campus library services, Internet access, wireless campus network, Internet filtering or blocking technology. Campus intranet and computer access in designated common areas are available to students. Students grades are available online. The school has a published electronic and media policy.

Contact Mrs. Lisa Popham, Assistant Principal. 812-476-4973 Ext. 205. Fax: 812-474-2942. E-mail: lisapopham@reitzmemorial.org. Web site: www.reitzmemorial.org

REJOICE CHRISTIAN SCHOOLS

12200 East 86th Street North
Owasso, Oklahoma 74055

Head of School: Dr. Craig D. Shaw

General Information Coeducational day college-preparatory school, affiliated with Free Will Baptist Church. Grades P3–12. Founded: 1992. Setting: suburban. Nearest major city is Tulsa. 1 building on campus. Approved or accredited by Association of Christian Schools International and Oklahoma Department of Education. Total enrollment: 713. Upper school average class size: 12. Upper school faculty-student ratio: 1:12.

Upper School Student Profile Grade 6: 36 students (14 boys, 22 girls); Grade 7: 40 students (17 boys, 23 girls); Grade 8: 37 students (20 boys, 17 girls); Grade 9: 35 students (14 boys, 21 girls); Grade 10: 17 students (8 boys, 9 girls); Grade 11: 17 students (10 boys, 7 girls); Grade 12: 15 students (9 boys, 6 girls). 30% of students are Free Will Baptist Church.

Faculty School total: 22. In upper school: 5 men, 17 women; 8 have advanced degrees.

Subjects Offered Advanced biology, advanced chemistry, Advanced Placement courses, algebra, American democracy, American government, American history, American history-AP, anatomy, anatomy and physiology, art, art appreciation, art education, art history, athletic training, athletics, band, basketball, Bible, Bible studies, biology, biology-AP, business, business education, calculus, calculus-AP, cheerleading, chemistry, chemistry-AP, choir, chorus, Christian education, civics, computer skills, electives, English, English language-AP, English literature and composition-AP, English literature-AP, English-AP, English/composition-AP, fitness, general business, general math, geography, geometry, golf, government, government and politics-AP, government-AP, government/civics, government/civics-AP, history, honors algebra, honors English, honors geometry, honors U.S. history, honors world history, journalism, language, language arts, library, mathematics, mathematics-AP, media, music, novels, physical education, physical fitness, physical science, pre-algebra, pre-calculus, Spanish, Spanish language-AP, speech, speech and debate, sports, sports conditioning, state history, technology, track and field, trigonometry, U.S. government, U.S. government and politics-AP, U.S. history, U.S. history-AP, weight training, world history, world history-AP, yearbook.

Special Academic Programs Honors section; study at local college for college credit.

Student Life Upper grades have student council, honor system. Discipline rests primarily with faculty.

Tuition and Aid Tuition installment plan (SMART Tuition Payment Plan, monthly payment plans). Need-based scholarship grants available.

Admissions Gates MacGinite Reading Tests, Gates MacGinite Reading/Key Math or Stanford Achievement Test required. Deadline for receipt of application materials: none. Application fee required: $160. Interview required.

Athletics Interscholastic: basketball (boys, girls), cheering (g), cross-country running (b,g), fitness (b,g), flag football (b,g), football (b), golf (b,g), jogging (b,g), outdoor activities (b,g), outdoor recreation (b,g), physical fitness (b,g), physical training (b,g), ropes courses (b,g), running (b,g), strength & conditioning (b,g), track and field (b,g), volleyball (g), weight lifting (b), weight training (b,g). 2 PE instructors, 15 coaches, 2 athletic trainers.

Computers Computers are regularly used in English, journalism, library, media, newspaper, yearbook classes. Computer network features include on-campus library services, Internet access, wireless campus network, Internet filtering or blocking technology. Campus intranet is available to students. Students grades are available online. The school has a published electronic and media policy.

Contact Mrs. Julie Long, High School Registrar. 918-516-0050. Fax: 918-516-0299. E-mail: jlong@rejoiceschool.com. Web site: www.rejoiceschool.com

RIDLEY COLLEGE

2 Ridley Road
St. Catharines, Ontario L2R7C3, Canada

Head of School: Mr. Edward Kidd

General Information Coeducational boarding and day college-preparatory, arts, business, and technology school, affiliated with Church of England (Anglican). Boarding grades 5–PG, day grades JK–PG. Founded: 1889. Setting: suburban. Nearest major city is Buffalo, NY. Students are housed in single-sex dormitories. 100-acre campus. 13 buildings on campus. Approved or accredited by Canadian Association of Independent Schools, Canadian Educational Standards Institute, Conference of Independent Schools of Ontario, Headmasters' Conference, International Baccalaureate Organization, National Independent Private Schools Association, Ontario Ministry of Education, The Association of Boarding Schools, and Ontario Department of Education. Affiliate member of National Association of Independent Schools; member of Secondary School Admission Test Board. Language of instruction: English. Endowment: CAN$23 million. Total enrollment: 630. Upper school average class size: 17. Upper school faculty-student ratio: 1:7. There are 232 required school days per year for Upper School students. Upper School students typically attend 6 days per week. The average school day consists of 6 hours.

Upper School Student Profile Grade 9: 53 students (34 boys, 19 girls); Grade 10: 113 students (69 boys, 44 girls); Grade 11: 132 students (75 boys, 57 girls); Grade 12: 145 students (82 boys, 63 girls); Postgraduate: 3 students (1 boy, 2 girls). 64% of students are boarding students. 63% are province residents. 25 provinces are represented in upper school student body. 32% are international students. International students from China, Germany, Hong Kong, Mexico, United States, and Venezuela; 30 other countries represented in student body. 20% of students are members of Church of England (Anglican).

Faculty School total: 77. In upper school: 37 men, 40 women; 26 have advanced degrees; 40 reside on campus.

Subjects Offered Accounting, Advanced Placement courses, algebra, American history, anthropology, art, art history, biology, business mathematics, business skills, calculus, Canadian history, Canadian law, chemistry, computer programming, computer science, creative writing, drafting, drama, dramatic arts, driver education, economics, English, English literature, ESL, finance, fine arts, French, geography, German, International Baccalaureate courses, kinesiology, Latin, Mandarin, mathematics, music, physical education, physics, science, social sciences, social studies, Spanish, sports science, theater, world history, world religions, writing.

Graduation Requirements Arts and fine arts (art, music, dance, drama), business skills (includes word processing), English, foreign language, mathematics, physical education (includes health), science, social sciences, social studies (includes history).

Special Academic Programs International Baccalaureate program; 12 Advanced Placement exams for which test preparation is offered; honors section; independent study; study abroad; academic accommodation for the musically talented and the artistically talented; ESL (20 students enrolled).

College Admission Counseling 126 students graduated in 2012; 116 went to college, including Brock University; Queen's University at Kingston; The University of Western Ontario; University of Guelph; University of Toronto; University of Waterloo. Other: 4 entered a postgraduate year, 6 had other specific plans.

Student Life Upper grades have uniform requirement, student council, honor system. Discipline rests primarily with faculty. Attendance at religious services is required.

Tuition and Aid Day student tuition: CAN$27,912; 5-day tuition and room/board: CAN$36,768; 7-day tuition and room/board: CAN$49,332. Tuition installment plan (monthly payment plans, individually arranged payment plans). Bursaries, merit scholarship grants, need-based scholarship grants, need-based loans available. In 2012–13, 38% of upper-school students received aid; total upper-school merit-scholarship money awarded: CAN$300,000. Total amount of financial aid awarded in 2012–13: CAN$3,000,000.

Admissions Traditional secondary-level entrance grade is 9. For fall 2012, 407 students applied for upper-level admission, 307 were accepted, 190 enrolled. Deadline for receipt of application materials: none. Application fee required: CAN$150. Interview required.

Athletics Interscholastic: aerobics/dance (girls), artistic gym (g), baseball (b,g), basketball (b,g), crew (b,g), cross-country running (b,g), dance (g), dance squad (g), dance team (g), field hockey (g), fitness walking (g), gymnastics (g), hockey (b,g), ice hockey (b,g), rowing (b,g), rugby (b,g), running (b,g), soccer (b,g), softball (b,g), squash (b,g), swimming and diving (b,g), tennis (b,g), track and field (b,g), volleyball (g); intramural: aerobics (g), aerobics/dance (g), ball hockey (b), ballet (g), Cosom hockey (g), hockey (b,g), ice hockey (b,g), running (b,g); coed interscholastic: golf, tennis; coed intramural: alpine skiing, aquatics, backpacking, badminton, baseball, basketball, bicycling, bowling, canoeing/kayaking, climbing, cooperative games, curling, drill team, equestrian sports, fencing, fitness, Frisbee, golf, hiking/backpacking, horseback riding, ice skating, jogging, life saving, martial arts, modern dance, outdoor activities, outdoor education, outdoor recreation, outdoor skills, physical fitness, physical training, power lifting, racquetball, rock climbing, ropes courses, sailing, scuba diving, self defense, skiing (cross-country), skiing (downhill), snowboarding, snowshoeing, soccer, softball, squash, strength & conditioning, swimming and diving, table tennis, tennis, track and field, triathlon, ultimate Frisbee, volleyball, walking, wall climbing, weight lifting, weight training, wilderness survival, yoga. 8 coaches, 3 athletic trainers.

Computers Computers are regularly used in all academic classes. Computer network features include on-campus library services, online commercial services, Internet access, wireless campus network, Internet filtering or blocking technology. Student e-mail accounts and computer access in designated common areas are available to students. Students grades are available online. The school has a published electronic and media policy.

Contact Mrs. Stephanie Park, Admissions Administrative Assistant. 905-684-1889 Ext. 2207. Fax: 905-684-8875. E-mail: admissions@ridleycollege.com. Web site: www.ridleycollege.com

See Display below and Close-Up on page 616.

RIPON CHRISTIAN SCHOOLS

435 North Maple Avenue
Ripon, California 95366

Head of School: Mrs. Mary Ann Sybesma

General Information Coeducational day college-preparatory, arts, business, vocational, religious studies, and technology school, affiliated with Calvinist faith; primarily serves students with learning disabilities. Grades K–12. Founded: 1946. Setting: small town. Nearest major city is San Francisco. 34-acre campus. 5 buildings on campus. Approved or accredited by Association of Christian Schools International, Christian Schools International, Western Association of Schools and Colleges, and California Department of Education. Endowment: $2.5 million. Total enrollment: 659. Upper school average class size: 22. Upper school faculty-student ratio: 1:18. There are 175 required school days per year for Upper School students. Upper School students typically attend 5 days per week. The average school day consists of 6 hours and 40 minutes.

Upper School Student Profile 50% of students are Calvinist.

Faculty School total: 47. In upper school: 10 men, 11 women; 10 have advanced degrees.

Subjects Offered 20th century American writers, accounting, advanced computer applications, algebra, American history, anatomy and physiology, animal science, art, band, Bible studies, biology, business, business mathematics, calculus, calculus-AP, ceramics, chemistry, choir, computer applications, computer education, computer science, computer-aided design, drafting, English, English language and composition-AP, English literature and composition-AP, environmental education, environmental science, ethics, family living, fine arts, geography, geometry, government/civics, grammar, health, history, keyboarding, leadership, life skills, mathematics, music, physical education, physics, psychology, science, social sciences, social studies, Spanish, Spanish-AP, U.S. history-AP, weightlifting, welding, woodworking, world history, yearbook.

Graduation Requirements Computer science, English, mathematics, physical education (includes health), religion (includes Bible studies and theology), science, social sciences, social studies (includes history), 10 service hours per semester are required of all students.

Special Academic Programs 4 Advanced Placement exams for which test preparation is offered; independent study; academic accommodation for the musically talented and the artistically talented; remedial math.

College Admission Counseling 55 students graduated in 2011; 52 went to college, including Azusa Pacific University; California Polytechnic State University, San Luis Obispo; California State University, Stanislaus; Dordt College; Modesto Junior College; Trinity Christian College. Other: 1 went to work, 2 entered military service.

Student Life Upper grades have specified standards of dress, student council. Discipline rests primarily with faculty. Attendance at religious services is required.

Tuition and Aid Day student tuition: $8150. Tuition installment plan (FACTS Tuition Payment Plan, individually arranged payment plans, 1-payment plan, biannual payment plan, quarterly payment plan). Tuition reduction for siblings, need-based scholarship grants, need-based financial assistance, TRIP program available. In 2011–12, 10% of upper-school students received aid. Total amount of financial aid awarded in 2011–12: $20,000.

Admissions Traditional secondary-level entrance grade is 9. For fall 2011, 16 students applied for upper-level admission, 14 were accepted, 14 enrolled. Kaufman Test of Educational Achievement or Woodcock-Johnson required. Deadline for receipt of application materials: none. No application fee required. On-campus interview required.

Athletics Interscholastic: baseball (boys), basketball (b,g), football (b), golf (b,g), physical fitness (b,g), physical training (b,g), soccer (b,g), softball (g), tennis (b,g), volleyball (g), weight training (b,g); intramural: indoor soccer (b); coed interscholastic: tennis; coed intramural: tennis. 2 PE instructors, 15 coaches.

Computers Computers are regularly used in business skills classes. Computer network features include on-campus library services, Internet access, wireless campus network, Internet filtering or blocking technology. Students grades are available online. The school has a published electronic and media policy.

Contact Mrs. Mary Ann Sybesma, Principal. 209-599-2155. Fax: 209-599-2170. E-mail: msybesma@rcschools.com. Web site: www.rcschools.com

RIVERDALE COUNTRY SCHOOL

5250 Fieldston Road
Bronx, New York 10471-2999

Head of School: Dominic A.A. Randolph

General Information Coeducational day college-preparatory school. Grades PK–12. Founded: 1907. Setting: suburban. Nearest major city is New York. 27-acre campus. 9 buildings on campus. Approved or accredited by New York Department of Education. Member of National Association of Independent Schools and Secondary School Admission Test Board. Endowment: $47.1 million. Upper school average class size: 16. Upper school faculty-student ratio: 1:8. Upper School students typically attend 5 days per week.

Faculty School total: 185.

Subjects Offered Algebra, American literature, anatomy, art, art history, biology, calculus, ceramics, chemistry, community service, computer math, computer programming, computer science, creative writing, drama, driver education, earth science, ecology, economics, English, English literature, environmental science, European history, expository writing, fine arts, French, geology, geometry, government/civics, grammar, health, history, history of science, introduction to liberal studies, Japanese, journalism, Latin, Mandarin, marine biology, mathematics, music, oceanography, philosophy, photography, physical education, physics, psychology, science, social studies, Spanish, speech, statistics, theater, theory of knowledge, trigonometry, world history, writing.

Graduation Requirements American studies, arts and fine arts (art, music, dance, drama), computer science, English, foreign language, mathematics, physical education (includes health), science, social studies (includes history), integrated liberal studies. Community service is required.

Special Academic Programs Honors section; independent study; term-away projects; study abroad; academic accommodation for the gifted, the musically talented, and the artistically talented.

College Admission Counseling 121 students graduated in 2012; all went to college, including Cornell University; Dartmouth College; Duke University; Harvard University; Stanford University; Yale University.

Student Life Upper grades have student council, honor system. Discipline rests equally with students and faculty.

Summer Programs Enrichment programs offered; session focuses on science research; held on campus; accepts boys and girls; not open to students from other schools.

Tuition and Aid Day student tuition: $42,000. Tuition installment plan (monthly payment plans). Need-based scholarship grants available. In 2012–13, 20% of upper-school students received aid.

Admissions Traditional secondary-level entrance grade is 9. ISEE or SSAT required. Deadline for receipt of application materials: November 15. Application fee required: $60. On-campus interview required.

Athletics Interscholastic: baseball (boys), basketball (b,g), field hockey (g), football (b), gymnastics (g), lacrosse (b,g), soccer (b,g), softball (g), tennis (b,g), volleyball (g), wrestling (b); intramural: baseball (b), basketball (b,g), field hockey (g), football (b), gymnastics (g), lacrosse (b,g), soccer (b,g), softball (g), tennis (b,g), volleyball (g), wrestling (b); coed interscholastic: cross-country running, fencing, golf, squash, swimming and diving, track and field, ultimate Frisbee; coed intramural: cross-country running, dance, fencing, fitness, physical fitness, squash, swimming and diving, tennis, track and field, ultimate Frisbee, yoga. 7 PE instructors, 31 coaches, 1 athletic trainer.

Computers Computers are regularly used in art, English, foreign language, history, mathematics, music, science classes. Computer network features include on-campus library services, online commercial services, Internet access, wireless campus network, Internet filtering or blocking technology, off-campus email, off-campus library services. Student e-mail accounts and computer access in designated common areas are available to students. The school has a published electronic and media policy.

Contact Jenna Rogers King, Director of Middle and Upper School Admission. 718-519-2715. Fax: 718-519-2793. E-mail: jrking@riverdale.edu. Web site: www.riverdale.edu

RIVERMONT COLLEGIATE

1821 Sunset Drive
Bettendorf, Iowa 52722

Head of School: Mr. Richard E. St. Laurent

General Information Coeducational day college-preparatory, arts, and technology school. Grades PS–12. Founded: 1884. Setting: suburban. Nearest major city is Davenport. 16-acre campus. 4 buildings on campus. Approved or accredited by Independent Schools Association of the Central States and Iowa Department of Education. Member of National Association of Independent Schools and Secondary School Admission Test Board. Total enrollment: 192. Upper school average class size: 9. Upper school faculty-student ratio: 1:2. Upper School students typically attend 5 days per week.

Faculty School total: 31. In upper school: 4 men, 14 women; 6 have advanced degrees.

Subjects Offered Acting, advanced chemistry, advanced math, Advanced Placement courses, algebra, animation, art, arts, band, basketball, biology, biology-AP, calculus, calculus-AP, character education, cheerleading, chemistry, chemistry-AP, Chinese, choir, choral music, chorus, college counseling, college writing, computer animation, computer graphics, computer multimedia, computer programming, computer science, concert band, concert choir, creative drama, creative writing, desktop publishing, digital photography, drama, drama performance, drama workshop, dramatic arts, drawing, drawing and design, earth science, economics, English, English language and composition-AP, English literature, English literature and composition-AP, English-AP, environmental science-AP, fine arts, foreign language, French, French language-AP, French literature-AP, French-AP, geography, geometry, global science, government/civics, guidance, health, health education, Hispanic literature, history, history-AP, honors algebra, honors English, HTML design, human biology, humanities, independent study, instrumental music, Latin, Latin American literature, life science, literature and composition-AP, macro/microeconomics-AP, mathematics, media, media arts, microeconomics, Middle East, model United Nations, multimedia, multimedia design, music, music theater, musical productions, musical theater, oral communications, performing arts, photography, physical education, physical fitness, physics, physics-AP, play production, pre-algebra, pre-calculus, probability and statistics, psychology, psychology-AP, public speaking, science, science project, science research, senior career experience, senior internship, senior project, service learning/internship, social studies, Spanish, Spanish language-AP, Spanish literature, Spanish literature-AP, Spanish-AP, speech, speech and debate, stage design, statistics-AP, studio art, symphonic band, theater, theater arts, theater design and production, theater production, U.S. government, U.S. government and politics, U.S. government and politics-AP, U.S. history, U.S. history-AP, United States government-AP, visual and performing arts, visual arts, vocal ensemble, voice, Web site design, wilderness education, wilderness experience, wind ensemble, wind instruments, world history, world history-AP, writing, yearbook.

Graduation Requirements Senior Project/Internship, Junior Service Project.

Special Academic Programs Advanced Placement exam preparation; honors section; independent study; study at local college for college credit; academic accommodation for the gifted, the musically talented, and the artistically talented.

College Admission Counseling 11 students graduated in 2011; they went to Cairn University; Case Western Reserve University; Pratt Institute; The University of Iowa; University of Illinois at Urbana–Champaign; University of Miami.

Student Life Upper grades have specified standards of dress, student council, honor system. Discipline rests primarily with faculty.

Tuition and Aid Tuition installment plan (Insured Tuition Payment Plan, monthly payment plans, individually arranged payment plans). Tuition reduction for siblings, merit scholarship grants, need-based scholarship grants available.

Admissions Otis-Lennon Ability or Stanford Achievement Test, Otis-Lennon School Ability Test, Otis-Lennon School Ability Test, ERB CPT III, Otis-Lennon School Ability Test/writing sample, Otis-Lennon, Stanford Achievement Test, Wide Range Achievement Test or WRAT required. Deadline for receipt of application materials: none. Application fee required: $50. Interview required.

Athletics Interscholastic: basketball (boys, girls), cheering (g), cross-country running (b,g), running (b,g), track and field (b,g), volleyball (g); intramural: basketball (b,g), cheering (g), cross-country running (b,g), running (b,g), track and field (b,g), volleyball (g). 1 PE instructor, 4 coaches.

Computers Computer network features include on-campus library services, online commercial services, Internet access, wireless campus network, Internet filtering or blocking technology. Campus intranet and student e-mail accounts are available to students. Students grades are available online. The school has a published electronic and media policy.

Contact Mrs. Brittany A. Marietta, Director of Admission/Marketing Coordinator. 563-359-1366 Ext. 302. Fax: 563-359-7576. E-mail: marietta@rvmt.org. Web site: www.rvmt.org

RIVER OAKS BAPTIST SCHOOL

2300 Willowick
Houston, Texas 77027

Head of School: Mrs. Leanne Reynolds

General Information Coeducational day college-preparatory and Character education school, affiliated with Christian faith. Grades PK–8. Founded: 1955. Setting: urban. Approved or accredited by Accreditation Commission of the Texas Association of Baptist Schools, Independent Schools Association of the Southwest, and Texas Department of Education. Member of National Association of Independent Schools. Endowment: $30 million. Total enrollment: 732. There are 187 required school days per year for Upper School students.

Upper School Student Profile Grade 6: 80 students (40 boys, 40 girls); Grade 7: 80 students (40 boys, 40 girls); Grade 8: 80 students (40 boys, 40 girls). 95% of students are Christian.

Faculty School total: 91.

Student Life Upper grades have uniform requirement, honor system. Discipline rests primarily with faculty. Attendance at religious services is required.

Tuition and Aid Tuition installment plan (Insured Tuition Payment Plan, monthly payment plans). Need-based scholarship grants available.

Admissions Individual IQ, ISEE and OLSAT, Stanford Achievement Test required. Deadline for receipt of application materials: none. Application fee required: $100. On-campus interview required.

Computers Computer network features include on-campus library services, wireless campus network, Internet filtering or blocking technology. Campus intranet and student e-mail accounts are available to students. Students grades are available online. The school has a published electronic and media policy.

Contact Mrs. Kristin Poe, Director of Admission. 713-623-6938. Fax: 713-623-0650. E-mail: kpoe@robs.org. Web site: www.robs.org

RIVERSIDE MILITARY ACADEMY

2001 Riverside Drive
Gainesville, Georgia 30501

Head of School: Dr. James H. Benson, Col., USMC-Retd.

General Information Boys' boarding and day college-preparatory, arts, technology, JROTC (grades 9-12), and military school, affiliated with Christian faith. Grades 7–12. Founded: 1907. Setting: suburban. Nearest major city is Atlanta. Students are housed in single-sex dormitories. 206-acre campus. 9 buildings on campus. Approved or accredited by Southern Association of Colleges and Schools, Southern Association of Independent Schools, and Georgia Department of Education. Member of National Association of Independent Schools. Endowment: $52 million. Total enrollment: 423. Upper school average class size: 14. Upper school faculty-student ratio: 1:14. There are 180 required school days per year for Upper School students. Upper School students typically attend 5 days per week. The average school day consists of 5 hours and 45 minutes.

Upper School Student Profile Grade 9: 74 students (74 boys); Grade 10: 69 students (69 boys); Grade 11: 97 students (97 boys); Grade 12: 98 students (98 boys). 95% of students are boarding students. 56% are state residents. 30 states are represented in upper school student body. 29% are international students. International students from China, Colombia, Dominican Republic, Kazakhstan, Mexico, and Republic of Korea; 16 other countries represented in student body. 80% of students are Christian faith.

Faculty School total: 45. In upper school: 35 men, 10 women; 30 have advanced degrees; 20 reside on campus.

Subjects Offered Algebra, American literature, art, art appreciation, band, biology, biology-AP, calculus, calculus-AP, ceramics, chemistry, chemistry-AP, chorus, computer applications, computer education, computer programming, computer science, computer skills, computer studies, computer technologies, desktop publishing, drama, drawing, earth science, economics, English, English composition, English literature, English/composition-AP, ESL, ethics, European history, fine arts, geography, geometry, German, government/civics, grammar, health, history-AP, honors English, honors geometry, honors U.S. history, honors world history, JROTC, keyboarding, Latin, leadership, mathematics, military science, modern world history, music, music technology, music theory, painting, physical education, physics, physics-AP, pre-algebra, pre-calculus, science, social studies, Spanish, statistics, swimming, theater, U.S. government, U.S. government and politics-AP, U.S. history, U.S. history-AP, U.S. literature, visual arts, weight training, world geography, world history, world history-AP, world literature, yearbook.

Graduation Requirements Arts and fine arts (art, music, dance, drama), computer science, electives, English, foreign language, JROTC, lab science, mathematics, military science, physical education (includes health), science, social studies (includes history).

Special Academic Programs 8 Advanced Placement exams for which test preparation is offered; honors section; independent study; special instructional classes for Attention Deficit Hyperactivity Disorder, Attention Deficit Disorder; ESL (24 students enrolled).

College Admission Counseling 83 students graduated in 2012; 64 went to college, including The Citadel, The Military College of South Carolina; The University of Alabama; University of California, Los Angeles; University of Florida; University of Georgia. Other: 2 went to work, 3 entered military service. Median SAT critical reading: 484, median SAT math: 511, median SAT writing: 462, median combined SAT: 1458, median composite ACT: 20.

Student Life Upper grades have uniform requirement, student council, honor system. Discipline rests equally with students and faculty. Attendance at religious services is required.

Summer Programs Remediation, enrichment, advancement, ESL, sports, art/fine arts, rigorous outdoor training, computer instruction programs offered; session focuses on academics; held on campus; accepts boys; open to students from other schools. 130 students usually enrolled. 2013 schedule: July 8 to August 2. Application deadline: none.

Tuition and Aid Day student tuition: $17,150; 7-day tuition and room/board: $28,600. Tuition installment plan (Key Tuition Payment Plan, FACTS Tuition Payment Plan, monthly payment plans). Need-based scholarship grants available. In 2012–13, 10% of upper-school students received aid.

Admissions Traditional secondary-level entrance grade is 10. Any standardized test required. Deadline for receipt of application materials: none. Application fee required: $100. Interview required.

Athletics Interscholastic: aquatics, baseball, basketball, crew, cross-country running, drill team, football, golf, JROTC drill, lacrosse, marksmanship, outdoor adventure, outdoor skills, paint ball, riflery, ropes courses, soccer, strength & conditioning, swimming and diving, tennis, track and field, weight lifting, weight training, wrestling; intramural: aquatics, backpacking, baseball, basketball, billiards, canoeing/kayaking, cheering, climbing, combined training, crew, cross-country running, fencing, fishing, fitness, flag football, football, hiking/backpacking, indoor soccer, indoor track, indoor track & field, jogging, JROTC drill, kayaking, marksmanship, mountaineering, outdoor activities, paddle tennis, physical fitness, physical training, rafting, rappelling, riflery, rock climbing, ropes courses, running, skateboarding, soccer, softball, swimming and diving, table tennis, tennis, volleyball, wall climbing, water polo, water volleyball, weight lifting, wilderness. 5 PE instructors, 20 coaches, 1 athletic trainer.

Computers Computers are regularly used in college planning, desktop publishing, English, ESL, foreign language, library, mathematics, multimedia, music, SAT preparation, science, Spanish, technology, theater, yearbook classes. Computer network features include on-campus library services, Internet access, wireless campus network, Internet filtering or blocking technology. Campus intranet, student e-mail accounts, and computer access in designated common areas are available to students. Students grades are available online. The school has a published electronic and media policy.

Contact Admissions Office. 800-462-2338. Fax: 678-291-3364. E-mail: apply@riversidemilitary.com. Web site: www.riversidemilitary.com

THE RIVERS SCHOOL

333 Winter Street
Weston, Massachusetts 02493-1040

Head of School: Thomas P. Olverson

General Information Coeducational day college-preparatory and arts school. Grades 6–12. Founded: 1915. Setting: suburban. Nearest major city is Boston. 53-acre campus. 8 buildings on campus. Approved or accredited by Association of Independent Schools in New England and New England Association of Schools and Colleges. Member of National Association of Independent Schools and Secondary School Admission Test Board. Endowment: $18.5 million. Total enrollment: 479. Upper school average class size: 12. Upper school faculty-student ratio: 1:6. Upper School students typically attend 5 days per week. The average school day consists of 7 hours and 15 minutes.

Upper School Student Profile Grade 9: 93 students (43 boys, 50 girls); Grade 10: 90 students (50 boys, 40 girls); Grade 11: 93 students (56 boys, 37 girls); Grade 12: 83 students (42 boys, 41 girls).

Faculty School total: 86. In upper school: 43 men, 43 women; 54 have advanced degrees.

Subjects Offered Advanced Placement courses, algebra, American history, American literature, art, art history, art history-AP, astronomy, biochemistry, biology, biology-AP, calculus, calculus-AP, ceramics, chamber groups, chemistry, chemistry-AP, chorus, civil rights, Civil War, computer graphics, computer science, computer science-AP, creative writing, drama, earth science, economics-AP, English, English language and composition-AP, English literature, English literature and composition-AP, environmental science-AP, European history, expository writing, film studies, filmmaking, fine arts, French, French-AP, geography, geometry, history, Holocaust, jazz band, journalism, kinesiology, Latin, Latin-AP, Mandarin, mathematics, modern European history-AP, music, photography, physics, physics-AP, playwriting, science, Spanish, Spanish-AP, statistics-AP, the Presidency, theater, theater arts, trigonometry, U.S. history-AP, world history, world literature.

Graduation Requirements Algebra, athletics, English, foreign language, geometry, history, mathematics, modern European history, science, U.S. history, visual and performing arts, participation in athletics. Community service is required.

Special Academic Programs Advanced Placement exam preparation; honors section; independent study; study at local college for college credit.

College Admission Counseling 84 students graduated in 2012; all went to college, including Babson College; Brown University; Bucknell University; Colby College; Colgate University; Lehigh University. Median SAT critical reading: 650, median SAT math: 690, median SAT writing: 680, median combined SAT: 2000. 82% scored over 600 on SAT critical reading, 75% scored over 600 on SAT math, 76% scored over 600 on SAT writing, 82% scored over 1800 on combined SAT.

Student Life Upper grades have specified standards of dress, student council, honor system. Discipline rests primarily with faculty.

Tuition and Aid Day student tuition: $38,600. Tuition installment plan (Academic Management Services Plan, Key Tuition Payment Plan, monthly payment plans). Need-based scholarship grants available. In 2012–13, 30% of upper-school students received aid. Total amount of financial aid awarded in 2012–13: $3,065,050.

Admissions Traditional secondary-level entrance grade is 9. ISEE or SSAT required. Deadline for receipt of application materials: February 1. Application fee required: $40. On-campus interview required.

Athletics Interscholastic: alpine skiing (boys, girls), baseball (b), basketball (b,g), cross-country running (b,g), field hockey (g), football (b), ice hockey (b,g), lacrosse (b,g), skiing (downhill) (b,g), soccer (b,g), softball (g), strength & conditioning (b,g), tennis (b,g); intramural: basketball (b,g), tennis (g); coed interscholastic: fitness, physical training, track and field, weight lifting, weight training; coed intramural: strength & conditioning. 4 coaches, 2 athletic trainers.

Computers Computers are regularly used in art, English, foreign language, history, humanities, language development, mathematics, newspaper, publications, science, writing, yearbook classes. Computer network features include on-campus library services, online commercial services, Internet access, wireless campus network, Internet filtering or blocking technology, language lab. Campus intranet, student e-mail accounts, and computer access in designated common areas are available to students. Students grades are available online. The school has a published electronic and media policy.

Contact Gillian Lloyd, Director of Admissions. 781-235-9300. Fax: 781-239-3614. E-mail: g.lloyd@rivers.org. Web site: www.rivers.org

ROBERT LAND ACADEMY

Wellandport, Ontario, Canada

See Special Needs Schools section.

ROBERT LOUIS STEVENSON SCHOOL

New York, New York

See Special Needs Schools section.

ROCK POINT SCHOOL

1 Rock Point Road
Burlington, Vermont 05408

Head of School: C.J. Spirito

General Information Coeducational boarding and day college-preparatory and arts school, affiliated with Episcopal Church. Grades 9–12. Founded: 1928. Setting: small town. Students are housed in single-sex by floor dormitories. 130-acre campus. 3 buildings on campus. Approved or accredited by Association of Independent Schools in New England, Independent Schools of Northern New England, National Association of Episcopal Schools, New England Association of Schools and Colleges, The Association of Boarding Schools, and Vermont Department of Education. Member of National Association of Independent Schools. Endowment: $2.5 million. Total enrollment: 29. Upper school average class size: 10. Upper school faculty-student ratio: 1:5. There are 167 required school days per year for Upper School students. Upper School students typically attend 5 days per week. The average school day consists of 6 hours and 45 minutes.

Upper School Student Profile Grade 9: 4 students (2 boys, 2 girls); Grade 10: 6 students (4 boys, 2 girls); Grade 11: 7 students (4 boys, 3 girls); Grade 12: 12 students (6 boys, 6 girls). 80% of students are boarding students. 15% are state residents. 9 states are represented in upper school student body. 7% are international students. International students from India and United Kingdom. 12% of students are members of Episcopal Church.

Faculty School total: 9. In upper school: 2 men, 6 women; 3 have advanced degrees.

Subjects Offered Algebra, American history, American literature, ancient history, animation, art, art history, biology, calculus, chemistry, community service, creative thinking, critical thinking, drawing, earth science, English, geometry, health, historical foundations for arts, history, mathematics, painting, photography, physical education, poetry, portfolio art, pre-calculus, science, stained glass, Western civilization, world history, world literature.

Graduation Requirements Art, art history, English, history, mathematics, physical education (includes health), science. Community service is required.

Special Academic Programs Independent study; term-away projects; study at local college for college credit; special instructional classes for students who need structure and personal attention; ESL.

College Admission Counseling 8 students graduated in 2011; 7 went to college, including Roger Williams University. Other: 1 went to work. Median SAT critical reading: 540, median SAT math: 490, median SAT writing: 490, median combined SAT: 1500. 29% scored over 600 on SAT critical reading, 14% scored over 600 on SAT math, 14% scored over 600 on SAT writing, 29% scored over 1800 on combined SAT.

Student Life Upper grades have specified standards of dress. Discipline rests primarily with faculty.

Tuition and Aid Day student tuition: $26,500; 7-day tuition and room/board: $51,000. Tuition installment plan (individually arranged payment plans, deposit and two installment plan (September 1 and December 1);, other specially created plans with a family.). Need-based scholarship grants available. In 2011–12, 31% of upper-school students received aid. Total amount of financial aid awarded in 2011–12: $150,000.

Admissions Traditional secondary-level entrance grade is 10. For fall 2011, 20 students applied for upper-level admission, 17 were accepted, 15 enrolled. Essay or writing sample required. Deadline for receipt of application materials: none. Application fee required. On-campus interview required.

Athletics Coed Interscholastic: basketball; coed intramural: alpine skiing, backpacking, ball hockey, basketball, bicycling, billiards, broomball, climbing, cooperative games, fitness, fitness walking, Frisbee, hiking/backpacking, jogging, kickball, martial arts, outdoor activities, outdoor adventure, outdoor recreation, physical fitness, physical training, rock climbing, ropes courses, running, skateboarding, skiing (downhill), snowboarding, soccer, softball, touch football, ultimate Frisbee, walking, weight lifting, winter walking, yoga. 7 PE instructors.

Computers Computers are regularly used in all academic, animation, art, college planning, creative writing, media, music, photography, video film production, word processing classes. Computer network features include Internet access, Internet filtering or blocking technology. Student e-mail accounts are available to students.

Contact Hillary Kramer, Director of Admissions. 802-863-1104 Ext. 12. Fax: 802-863-6628. E-mail: hkramer@rockpoint.org. Web site: www.rockpoint.org

ROCKWAY MENNONITE COLLEGIATE

110 Doon Road
Kitchener, Ontario N2G 3C8, Canada

Head of School: Mr. Dennis Wikerd

General Information Coeducational boarding and day college-preparatory, arts, religious studies, and technology school, affiliated with Mennonite Church USA. Grades 7–12. Founded: 1945. Setting: suburban. Nearest major city is Toronto, Canada. Students are housed in host family homes. 14-acre campus. 7 buildings on campus. Approved or accredited by Mennonite Schools Council and Ontario Department of Education. Language of instruction: English. Endowment: CAN$450,000. Total enrollment: 285. Upper school average class size: 19. Upper school faculty-student ratio: 1:10. There are 194 required school days per year for Upper School students. Upper School students typically attend 5 days per week. The average school day consists of 5 hours and 55 minutes.

Upper School Student Profile 1% of students are boarding students. 85% are province residents. 1 province is represented in upper school student body. 15% are international students. International students from China, Democratic People's Republic of Korea, Germany, Hong Kong, Japan, and Taiwan; 2 other countries represented in student body. 38% of students are Mennonite Church USA.

Faculty School total: 45. In upper school: 20 men, 20 women; 8 have advanced degrees.

Subjects Offered Algebra, auto mechanics, Bible, biology, calculus, Canadian history, career education, chemistry, choral music, civics, computer science, computer studies, construction, dramatic arts, English, entrepreneurship, ESL, family studies, finite math, food and nutrition, French, functions, geography, geometry, German, guidance, health, healthful living, history, information technology, instrumental music, integrated technology fundamentals, Mandarin, mathematics, music, orchestra, parenting, personal finance, philosophy, physical education, physics, religious studies, science, strings, technology/design, transportation technology, visual arts, vocal music, wind instruments, world history, world religions.

Graduation Requirements Ontario Ministry of Education requirements, 2 credits in a language other than English, religious studies courses through grade 10.

Special Academic Programs Independent study; academic accommodation for the gifted; ESL (34 students enrolled).

College Admission Counseling 68 students graduated in 2012; 58 went to college, including Carleton University; The University of Western Ontario; University of Guelph; University of Toronto; University of Waterloo; Wilfrid Laurier University. Other: 8 went to work, 2 had other specific plans.

Student Life Upper grades have specified standards of dress, student council. Discipline rests primarily with faculty. Attendance at religious services is required.

Tuition and Aid Day student tuition: CAN$12,360; 7-day tuition and room/board: CAN$20,860. Tuition installment plan (monthly payment plans, individually arranged payment plans). Tuition reduction for siblings, bursaries, need-based scholarship grants, paying campus jobs available. In 2012–13, 25% of upper-school students received aid. Total amount of financial aid awarded in 2012–13: CAN$170,000.

Admissions Traditional secondary-level entrance grade is 9. For fall 2012, 60 students applied for upper-level admission, 56 were accepted, 55 enrolled. Deadline for receipt of application materials: none. Application fee required: CAN$100.

Athletics Interscholastic: badminton (boys, girls), baseball (b,g), basketball (b,g), cross-country running (b,g), soccer (b), softball (b,g), track and field (b,g), volleyball (b,g), wrestling (b,g); intramural: ball hockey (b,g), baseball (b,g), basketball (b,g), cooperative games (b,g), dance (b,g), field hockey (b,g), flag football (b,g), flagball (b,g), floor hockey (b,g), football (b,g), indoor soccer (b,g), nordic skiing (b,g), outdoor education (b,g), physical training (b,g), power lifting (b,g), rock climbing (b,g), rugby (b,g), skiing (downhill) (b,g), soccer (b,g), strength & conditioning (b,g), volleyball (b,g); coed interscholastic: soccer; coed intramural: baseball, canoeing/kayaking, cooperative games, outdoor education, roller skating, skiing (downhill), street hockey, table tennis, track and field. 4 PE instructors.

Computers Computers are regularly used in Bible studies, business, career technology, college planning, construction, drafting, English, geography, library, mathematics, religious studies, science, typing, Web site design classes. Computer resources include on-campus library services, Internet access, Internet filtering or blocking technology.

Contact Mr. Tom Bileski, Director of Community Relations. 519-342-0007 Ext. 3029. Fax: 519-743-5935. E-mail: admin@rockway.ca. Web site: www.rockway.ca

THE ROEPER SCHOOL

41190 Woodward Avenue
Bloomfield Hills, Michigan 48304

Head of School: Philip Deely

General Information Coeducational day college-preparatory school. Grades PK–12. Founded: 1941. Setting: urban. Nearest major city is Birmingham. 1-acre campus. 1 building on campus. Approved or accredited by Independent Schools Association of the Central States. Member of National Association of Independent Schools. Endowment: $6 million. Total enrollment: 551. Upper school average class size: 14. Upper school faculty-student ratio: 1:6. There are 165 required school days per year for Upper School students. Upper School students typically attend 5 days per week. The average school day consists of 7 hours and 10 minutes.

Upper School Student Profile Grade 9: 44 students (29 boys, 15 girls); Grade 10: 52 students (24 boys, 28 girls); Grade 11: 47 students (29 boys, 18 girls); Grade 12: 48 students (23 boys, 25 girls).

Faculty School total: 90. In upper school: 14 men, 24 women; 21 have advanced degrees.

Subjects Offered Algebra, American history, American literature, art, art history, biology, calculus, chemistry, computer programming, creative writing, dance, drama, English, English literature, European history, fine arts, French, geometry, government/civics, health, history, journalism, Latin, mathematics, music, philosophy, photography, physical education, physics, science, social studies, Spanish, speech, statistics, theater, trigonometry, world history, world literature, writing.

Graduation Requirements Arts and fine arts (art, music, dance, drama), computer science, English, foreign language, government, health, mathematics, science, social studies (includes history).

Special Academic Programs 13 Advanced Placement exams for which test preparation is offered; independent study; academic accommodation for the gifted, the musically talented, and the artistically talented; programs in English, mathematics, general development for dyslexic students.

College Admission Counseling 49 students graduated in 2011; all went to college, including Kalamazoo College; Northwestern University; University of Chicago; University of Michigan; Western Michigan University.

Student Life Upper grades have student council, honor system. Discipline rests primarily with faculty.

Tuition and Aid Day student tuition: $22,250. Tuition installment plan (FACTS Tuition Payment Plan, individually arranged payment plans). Need-based scholarship grants available. In 2011–12, 31% of upper-school students received aid. Total amount of financial aid awarded in 2011–12: $384,375.

Admissions Traditional secondary-level entrance grade is 9. For fall 2011, 31 students applied for upper-level admission, 29 were accepted, 16 enrolled. Individual IQ required. Deadline for receipt of application materials: none. Application fee required: $75. On-campus interview required.

Athletics Interscholastic: baseball (boys), basketball (b,g), cross-country running (b,g), golf (b,g), physical training (b,g), soccer (b,g), strength & conditioning (b,g), track and field (b,g), volleyball (g), weight lifting (b,g); intramural: indoor soccer (b,g); coed intramural: physical training, strength & conditioning, weight lifting. 4 PE instructors, 30 coaches.

Computers Computers are regularly used in English, journalism, library, mathematics, publishing, science, yearbook classes. Computer network features include on-campus library services, online commercial services, Internet access. Student e-mail accounts and computer access in designated common areas are available to students. Students grades are available online.

Contact Lori Zinser, Director of Admissions. 248-203-7302. Fax: 248-203-7310. E-mail: lori.zinser@roeper.org. Web site: www.roeper.org

ROLAND PARK COUNTRY SCHOOL

5204 Roland Avenue
Baltimore, Maryland 21210

Head of School: Mrs. Jean Waller Brune

General Information Girls' day and distance learning college-preparatory and arts school. Grades K–12. Distance learning grades 9–12. Founded: 1901. Setting: suburban. 21-acre campus. 1 building on campus. Member of National Association of Independent Schools and Secondary School Admission Test Board. Endowment: $49 million. Total enrollment: 650. Upper school average class size: 14. Upper school faculty-student ratio: 1:7. There are 176 required school days per year for Upper School students. Upper School students typically attend 5 days per week. The average school day consists of 7 hours and 45 minutes.

Upper School Student Profile Grade 9: 74 students (74 girls); Grade 10: 71 students (71 girls); Grade 11: 80 students (80 girls); Grade 12: 62 students (62 girls).

Faculty School total: 100. In upper school: 8 men, 42 women; 38 have advanced degrees.

Subjects Offered 3-dimensional art, advanced biology, advanced chemistry, advanced math, Advanced Placement courses, advanced studio art-AP, algebra, American history-AP, American literature, American literature-AP, anatomy, ancient world history, Arabic, archaeology, art, art history, art history-AP, astronomy, biology, biology-AP, calculus, calculus-AP, ceramics, chemistry, chemistry-AP, Chesapeake Bay studies, Chinese, community service, computer programming, computer science, creative writing, dance, drama, ecology, economics, engineering, English, English language-AP, English literature, English literature-AP, English-AP, environmental science, environmental studies, European civilization, European history, European history-AP, French, French language-AP, French literature-AP, geometry, German, government/civics, Greek, health, integrated mathematics, Latin, music, philosophy, photography, physical education, physics, physiology, religion, Russian, science, social studies, Spanish, speech, statistics, theater, trigonometry, world history.

Graduation Requirements Adolescent issues, arts and fine arts (art, music, dance, drama), biology, chemistry, English, foreign language, history, mathematics, physical education (includes health), physics, public speaking, science. Community service is required.

Special Academic Programs Advanced Placement exam preparation; honors section; independent study; term-away projects; study abroad.

College Admission Counseling 62 students graduated in 2012; all went to college, including Bucknell University; Clemson University; The Johns Hopkins University; University of Maryland, College Park; University of Virginia. Mean SAT critical reading: 606, mean SAT math: 623, mean SAT writing: 640, mean combined SAT: 1869, mean composite ACT: 26.

Student Life Upper grades have uniform requirement, student council, honor system. Discipline rests equally with students and faculty.

Summer Programs Remediation, enrichment, advancement, sports, art/fine arts programs offered; session focuses on summer camp, arts, some academics; held both on and off campus; held at off-site pool and venues for outdoor education programs and various sites around Baltimore for art projects; accepts boys and girls; open to students from other schools. 600 students usually enrolled. 2013 schedule: June 17 to August 23. Application deadline: none.

Tuition and Aid Day student tuition: $24,035. Tuition installment plan (FACTS Tuition Payment Plan, individually arranged payment plans). Need-based scholarship grants, paying campus jobs available. In 2012–13, 29% of upper-school students received aid. Total amount of financial aid awarded in 2012–13: $1,208,315.

Admissions Traditional secondary-level entrance grade is 9. For fall 2012, 117 students applied for upper-level admission, 86 were accepted, 38 enrolled. ERB CTP IV or ISEE required. Deadline for receipt of application materials: December 17. Application fee required: $60. Interview required.

Athletics Interscholastic: badminton, basketball, crew, cross-country running, field hockey, golf, independent competitive sports, indoor soccer, indoor track, lacrosse, soccer, softball, squash, swimming and diving, tennis, volleyball, winter (indoor) track, winter soccer; intramural: dance, fitness, modern dance, outdoor education, physical fitness, rock climbing, strength & conditioning. 7 PE instructors, 1 athletic trainer.

Computers Computers are regularly used in all classes. Computer network features include on-campus library services, online commercial services, Internet access, wireless campus network, Internet filtering or blocking technology, online database. Campus intranet, student e-mail accounts, and computer access in designated common areas are available to students. Students grades are available online. The school has a published electronic and media policy.

Contact Peggy Wolf, Director of Admissions. 410-323-5500. Fax: 410-323-2164. E-mail: admissions@rpcs.org. Web site: www.rpcs.org

ROLLING HILLS PREPARATORY SCHOOL

One Rolling Hills Prep Way
San Pedro, California 90732

Head of School: Peter McCormack

General Information Coeducational day college-preparatory, arts, and technology school. Grades 6–12. Founded: 1981. Setting: suburban. Nearest major city is Los Angeles. 21-acre campus. 20 buildings on campus. Approved or accredited by California Association of Independent Schools, Western Association of Schools and Colleges, and California Department of Education. Member of National Association of Independent Schools. Endowment: $100,000. Total enrollment: 225. Upper school average class size: 16. Upper school faculty-student ratio: 1:9. There are 180 required school days per year for Upper School students. Upper School students typically attend 5 days per week. The average school day consists of 6 hours.

Upper School Student Profile Grade 9: 30 students (15 boys, 15 girls); Grade 10: 32 students (16 boys, 16 girls); Grade 11: 31 students (16 boys, 15 girls); Grade 12: 37 students (21 boys, 16 girls).

Faculty School total: 36. In upper school: 7 men, 21 women; 13 have advanced degrees.

Subjects Offered Algebra, American history, American literature, American sign language, anatomy, art, biology, calculus, ceramics, chemistry, Chinese, computer science, creative writing, drama, economics, English, English literature, European history, fine arts, French, geography, geometry, government/civics, history, mathematics, music, photography, physical education, physics, pre-calculus, robotics, science, social studies, Spanish, speech, statistics, theater, trigonometry, world history.

Graduation Requirements Arts and fine arts (art, music, dance, drama), English, foreign language, mathematics, outdoor education, physical education (includes health), science, social studies (includes history), two-week senior internship, senior speech.

Special Academic Programs 10 Advanced Placement exams for which test preparation is offered; honors section; independent study; academic accommodation for the gifted; programs in general development for dyslexic students; ESL (16 students enrolled).

College Admission Counseling 45 students graduated in 2012; 43 went to college, including Berklee College of Music; Carnegie Mellon University; Lewis & Clark College; University of California, Berkeley; University of California, Los Angeles; University of Southern California. Other: 2 had other specific plans. Mean SAT critical reading: 580, mean SAT math: 560, mean SAT writing: 610. 45% scored over 600 on SAT critical reading, 40% scored over 600 on SAT math, 45% scored over 600 on SAT writing.

Student Life Upper grades have specified standards of dress, student council, honor system. Discipline rests primarily with faculty.

Summer Programs Enrichment, art/fine arts programs offered; session focuses on algebra and photography; held on campus; accepts boys and girls; open to students from other schools. 30 students usually enrolled. 2013 schedule: June 26 to August 28. Application deadline: June 1.

Tuition and Aid Day student tuition: $24,650. Tuition installment plan (Insured Tuition Payment Plan, Key Tuition Payment Plan, monthly payment plans). Merit scholarship grants, need-based scholarship grants available. In 2012–13, 35% of upper-school students received aid. Total amount of financial aid awarded in 2012–13: $560,000.

Admissions Traditional secondary-level entrance grade is 9. For fall 2012, 22 students applied for upper-level admission, 15 were accepted, 10 enrolled. ISEE or SLEP for foreign students required. Deadline for receipt of application materials: none. Application fee required: $150. Interview required.

Athletics Interscholastic: baseball (boys), basketball (b,g), cheering (g), football (b), soccer (b,g), softball (g), track and field (g), volleyball (b,g); intramural: cheering (g), dance (g); coed interscholastic: cross-country running, golf, roller hockey, running, track and field; coed intramural: backpacking, climbing, fitness, hiking/backpacking, outdoor education, physical fitness, rock climbing, ropes courses. 4 PE instructors, 10 coaches, 1 athletic trainer.

Computers Computers are regularly used in English, foreign language, history, mathematics, photography, science classes. Computer network features include on-campus library services, Internet access, wireless campus network. The school has a published electronic and media policy.

Contact Bryonna Fisco, Director of Admission. 310-791-1101 Ext. 148. Fax: 310-373-4931. E-mail: bfisco@rollinghillsprep.org. Web site: www.rollinghillsprep.org

ROSSEAU LAKE COLLEGE

1967 Bright Street
Rosseau, Ontario P0C 1J0, Canada

Head of School: Mr. Lance Postma

General Information Coeducational boarding and day college-preparatory, arts, business, and technology school. Grades 7–12. Founded: 1967. Setting: rural. Nearest major city is Toronto, Canada. Students are housed in single-sex dormitories. 53-acre campus. 13 buildings on campus. Approved or accredited by Canadian Association of Independent Schools, Canadian Educational Standards Institute, The Association of Boarding Schools, and Ontario Department of Education. Languages of instruction: English and French. Endowment: CAN$100,000. Total enrollment: 81. Upper school average class size: 12. Upper school faculty-student ratio: 1:6. There are 176 required school days per year for Upper School students. Upper School students typically attend 5 days per week. The average school day consists of 5 hours and 30 minutes.

Upper School Student Profile Grade 9: 14 students (5 boys, 9 girls); Grade 10: 18 students (10 boys, 8 girls); Grade 11: 14 students (12 boys, 2 girls); Grade 12: 18 students (12 boys, 6 girls). 45% of students are boarding students. 80% are province residents. 2 provinces are represented in upper school student body. 20% are international students. International students from China, Democratic People's Republic of Korea, Japan, Mexico, Nigeria, and Spain; 4 other countries represented in student body.

Faculty School total: 19. In upper school: 8 men, 11 women; 5 have advanced degrees; 11 reside on campus.

Subjects Offered Accounting, algebra, art, art history, biology, business, calculus, Canadian law, career and personal planning, chemistry, civics, computer programming, computer science, data analysis, economics, English, entrepreneurship, ESL, European history, experiential education, fine arts, French, geography, geometry, health, history, information technology, marketing, mathematics, music, outdoor education, physical education, physics, political science, science, social sciences, trigonometry, visual arts, world governments, writing.

Graduation Requirements Arts and fine arts (art, music, dance, drama), business skills (includes word processing), career planning, civics, computer science, English, foreign language, mathematics, physical education (includes health), science, social studies (includes history).

Special Academic Programs Accelerated programs; independent study; term-away projects; study abroad; academic accommodation for the gifted; remedial reading and/or remedial writing; remedial math; ESL (18 students enrolled).

College Admission Counseling 16 students graduated in 2011; all went to college, including McMaster University; Queen's University at Kingston; The University of Western Ontario; University of Guelph; University of Toronto; York University.

Student Life Upper grades have uniform requirement, student council, honor system. Discipline rests primarily with faculty.

Tuition and Aid Day student tuition: CAN$17,700; 7-day tuition and room/board: CAN$40,500. Tuition installment plan (monthly payment plans, individually arranged payment plans). Merit scholarship grants, need-based scholarship grants available. In 2011–12, 10% of upper-school students received aid; total upper-school merit-scholarship money awarded: CAN$40,000. Total amount of financial aid awarded in 2011–12: CAN$160,000.

Admissions Traditional secondary-level entrance grade is 9. Admissions testing and English Composition Test for ESL students required. Deadline for receipt of application materials: none. Application fee required: CAN$150. Interview required.

Athletics Interscholastic: baseball (boys), basketball (b,g), cross-country running (b,g), field hockey (g), hockey (b), ice hockey (b), mountain biking (b,g), nordic skiing (b,g), rugby (b), running (b,g), skiing (cross-country) (b,g), snowboarding (b,g), soccer (b,g), softball (b), swimming and diving (b,g), tennis (b,g), track and field (b,g), volleyball (b,g); intramural: alpine skiing (b,g), baseball (b), basketball (b,g), cross-country running (b,g), field hockey (g), hockey (b,g), ice hockey (b,g), rugby (b), running (b,g), skiing (cross-country) (b,g), snowboarding (b,g); coed interscholastic: bicycling, canoeing/kayaking, climbing, golf, kayaking, mountain biking, nordic skiing, running, skiing (cross-country), skiing (downhill), snowboarding, softball, track and field; coed intramural: aerobics, aerobics/dance, aquatics, backpacking, ball hockey, baseball, basketball, bicycling, bowling, broomball, canoeing/kayaking, climbing, combined training, cooperative games, Cosom hockey, cross-country running, equestrian sports, fishing, fitness, fitness walking, flag football, floor hockey, fly fishing, freestyle skiing, Frisbee, golf, hiking/backpacking, horseback riding, ice skating, indoor hockey, indoor soccer, jogging, kayaking, life saving, mountain biking, mountaineering, nordic skiing, outdoor activities, paddle tennis, paddling, physical fitness, physical training, rappelling, rock climbing, ropes courses, sailboarding, sailing, scuba diving, skateboarding, skiing (cross-country), skiing (downhill), snowboarding, snowshoeing, soccer, softball, squash, street hockey, strength & conditioning, swimming and diving, table tennis, tennis, track and field, triathlon, ultimate Frisbee, volleyball, walking, wall climbing, water skiing, weight lifting, weight training, wilderness, wilderness survival, wildernessways, windsurfing, winter walking, yoga. 2 PE instructors, 2 coaches.

Computers Computers are regularly used in geography, graphic arts, information technology classes. Computer network features include on-campus library services, Internet access, wireless campus network, Internet filtering or blocking technology. Campus intranet, student e-mail accounts, and computer access in designated common areas are available to students. The school has a published electronic and media policy.

Contact Ms. Lynda Marshall, Director of Admissions. 705-732-4351 Ext. 12. Fax: 705-732-6319. E-mail: lynda.marshall@rlc.on.ca. Web site: www.rosseaulakecollege.com

ROSS SCHOOL

18 Goodfriend Drive
East Hampton, New York 11937

Head of School: Dr. Gregg Maloberti

General Information Coeducational boarding and day college-preparatory, globally-focused, integrated curriculum, and ESOL curriculum school. Boarding grades 7–12, day grades N–12. Founded: 1991. Setting: small town. Nearest major city is New York City. Students are housed in single-sex dormitories. 100-acre campus. 7 buildings on campus. Approved or accredited by Middle States Association of Colleges and Schools and New York Department of Education. Member of National Association of Independent Schools and Secondary School Admission Test Board. Upper school average class size: 15. Upper school faculty-student ratio: 1:7. There are 175 required school days per year for Upper School students. Upper School students typically attend 5 days per week. The average school day consists of 7 hours and 25 minutes.

Upper School Student Profile 35% of students are boarding students. 6 states are represented in upper school student body. International students from Brazil, China, Germany, Republic of Korea, and Taiwan; 29 other countries represented in student body.

Faculty School total: 85. In upper school: 27 reside on campus.

Subjects Offered Advanced biology, advanced chemistry, advanced math, art history, athletics, Chinese, college counseling, computer multimedia, English literature, ESL, French, health and wellness, independent study, jazz band, media studies, model United Nations, music, philosophy, physics, SAT preparation, science and technology, senior internship, senior project, Spanish, theater arts, United Nations and international issues, visual arts, world history.

Graduation Requirements 30 hours of community service.

Special Academic Programs 9 Advanced Placement exams for which test preparation is offered; honors section; independent study; term-away projects; ESL (40 students enrolled).

College Admission Counseling 51 students graduated in 2012; all went to college, including American University; Bard College; Boston University; Princeton University; The Johns Hopkins University; Wesleyan University.

Student Life Upper grades have uniform requirement, student council, honor system. Discipline rests primarily with faculty.

Summer Programs ESL, sports, art/fine arts programs offered; session focuses on sports and fine arts; held on campus; accepts boys and girls; open to students from other schools. 2013 schedule: June 25 to August 17. Application deadline: none.
Tuition and Aid Day student tuition: $34,350; 5-day tuition and room/board: $50,650. Tuition installment plan (monthly payment plans). Tuition reduction for siblings, need-based scholarship grants available. In 2012–13, 45% of upper-school students received aid.
Admissions Traditional secondary-level entrance grade is 9. Any standardized test required. Deadline for receipt of application materials: January 31. Application fee required: $50. Interview required.
Athletics Interscholastic: baseball (boys), basketball (b,g), cross-country running (b,g), lacrosse (b,g), soccer (b,g), softball (g), tennis (b,g), track and field (b,g), volleyball (b,g); intramural: archery (b,g); coed interscholastic: cheering, golf, sailing; coed intramural: dance, fitness, kayaking, modern dance, mountain biking, sailing, surfing, tai chi, yoga. 14 coaches.
Computers Computers are regularly used in all classes. Computer network features include on-campus library services, online commercial services, Internet access, wireless campus network, Internet filtering or blocking technology. Campus intranet and student e-mail accounts are available to students. Students grades are available online. The school has a published electronic and media policy.
Contact Ms. Kristin Eberstadt, Assistant Director of Admissions. 631-907-5205. Fax: 631-907-5563. E-mail: keberstadt@ross.org. Web site: www.ross.org

ROTHESAY NETHERWOOD SCHOOL

40 College Hill Road
Rothesay, New Brunswick E2E 5H1, Canada

Head of School: Mr. Paul G. Kitchen

General Information Coeducational boarding and day college-preparatory, arts, and technology school, affiliated with Anglican Church of Canada. Grades 6–12. Founded: 1877. Setting: small town. Nearest major city is Saint John, Canada. Students are housed in single-sex dormitories. 260-acre campus. 26 buildings on campus. Approved or accredited by Canadian Association of Independent Schools, Conference of Independent Schools of Ontario, International Baccalaureate Organization, The Association of Boarding Schools, and New Brunswick Department of Education. Affiliate member of National Association of Independent Schools. Languages of instruction: English and French. Endowment: CAN$3.5 million. Total enrollment: 265. Upper school average class size: 16. Upper school faculty-student ratio: 1:8. There are 176 required school days per year for Upper School students. Upper School students typically attend 5 days per week. The average school day consists of 7 hours and 45 minutes.
Upper School Student Profile Grade 9: 41 students (21 boys, 20 girls); Grade 10: 52 students (28 boys, 24 girls); Grade 11: 47 students (20 boys, 27 girls); Grade 12: 64 students (39 boys, 25 girls). 58% of students are boarding students. 66% are province residents. 9 provinces are represented in upper school student body. 17% are international students. International students from Bermuda, China, Dominica, Germany, Mexico, and Republic of Korea; 8 other countries represented in student body. 30% of students are members of Anglican Church of Canada.
Faculty School total: 42. In upper school: 15 men, 15 women; 6 have advanced degrees; 35 reside on campus.
Subjects Offered 3-dimensional design, advanced chemistry, art, art history, biology, Canadian history, chemistry, computer programming, computer science, CPR, digital art, drama, driver education, English, English literature, ESL, European history, fine arts, French, geography, geometry, health, history, information technology, International Baccalaureate courses, leadership, math applications, mathematics, music, outdoor education, physical education, physics, science, social studies, Spanish, theater arts, world history, writing.
Graduation Requirements Arts and fine arts (art, music, dance, drama), computer science, English, foreign language, mathematics, physical education (includes health), science, social sciences, social studies (includes history), IB Theory of Knowledge, IB designation CAS hours (creativity, action, service), Extended Essay, Outward Bound adventure.
Special Academic Programs International Baccalaureate program; honors section; independent study; term-away projects; study at local college for college credit; academic accommodation for the gifted, the musically talented, and the artistically talented; ESL (10 students enrolled).
College Admission Counseling 59 students graduated in 2012; all went to college, including Acadia University; Dalhousie University; Mount Allison University; Queen's University at Kingston; St. Francis Xavier University; University of Toronto.
Student Life Upper grades have uniform requirement, student council, honor system. Discipline rests primarily with faculty. Attendance at religious services is required.
Tuition and Aid Day student tuition: CAN$19,850; 7-day tuition and room/board: CAN$32,840. Tuition installment plan (monthly payment plans, individually arranged payment plans). Tuition reduction for siblings, bursaries, merit scholarship grants, need-based scholarship grants available. In 2012–13, 32% of upper-school students received aid.
Admissions Traditional secondary-level entrance grade is 9. For fall 2012, 91 students applied for upper-level admission, 82 were accepted, 63 enrolled. Deadline for receipt of application materials: none. Application fee required: CAN$100. Interview required.
Athletics Interscholastic: basketball (boys, girls), crew (b,g), cross-country running (b,g), field hockey (g), ice hockey (b,g), rowing (b,g), rugby (b,g), running (b,g), soccer (b,g), squash (b,g), tennis (b,g), track and field (b,g), volleyball (b,g); intramural: crew (b,g), cross-country running (b,g), golf (b,g), ice hockey (b,g), indoor soccer (b), squash (b,g), tennis (b,g), track and field (b,g), yoga (g); coed interscholastic: badminton, crew, cross-country running, ice hockey, rowing, tennis, track and field; coed intramural: aerobics, aerobics/dance, backpacking, badminton, bicycling, billiards, broomball, canoeing/kayaking, climbing, cooperative games, crew, cross-country running, fitness, fitness walking, floor hockey, golf, hiking/backpacking, ice hockey, ice skating, indoor soccer, jogging, kayaking, outdoor activities, outdoor education, physical fitness, physical training, rock climbing, running, skiing (cross-country), skiing (downhill), snowboarding, snowshoeing, squash, street hockey, strength & conditioning, tennis, track and field, ultimate Frisbee, volleyball, walking, wall climbing, weight training. 3 PE instructors.
Computers Computers are regularly used in all classes. Computer network features include on-campus library services, Internet access, wireless campus network, Internet filtering or blocking technology, Web site for each academic course, informative, interactive online community for parents, teachers, and students. Campus intranet and student e-mail accounts are available to students. Students grades are available online. The school has a published electronic and media policy.
Contact Mrs. Elizabeth Kitchen, Associate Director of Admission. 506-848-0866. Fax: 506-848-0851. E-mail: Elizabeth.Kitchen@rns.cc. Web site: www.rns.cc

ROWLAND HALL

843 South Lincoln Street
Salt Lake City, Utah 84102

Head of School: Mr. Alan C. Sparrow

General Information Coeducational day college-preparatory school. Grades PK–12. Founded: 1867. Setting: urban. 4-acre campus. 1 building on campus. Approved or accredited by National Association of Episcopal Schools, Northwest Accreditation Commission, Pacific Northwest Association of Independent Schools, The College Board, and Utah Department of Education. Member of National Association of Independent Schools. Endowment: $7.2 million. Total enrollment: 980. Upper school average class size: 16. Upper school faculty-student ratio: 1:8. There are 170 required school days per year for Upper School students. Upper School students typically attend 5 days per week. The average school day consists of 6 hours.
Upper School Student Profile Grade 9: 85 students (34 boys, 51 girls); Grade 10: 63 students (24 boys, 39 girls); Grade 11: 75 students (41 boys, 34 girls); Grade 12: 87 students (43 boys, 44 girls).
Faculty School total: 40. In upper school: 21 men, 19 women; 30 have advanced degrees.
Subjects Offered Adolescent issues, algebra, biology, biology-AP, calculus, calculus-AP, ceramics, chemistry, chemistry-AP, Chinese, chorus, computer graphics, creative writing, dance, debate, drama, English, English language and composition-AP, English literature and composition-AP, environmental science, ethics, European history-AP, French, French language-AP, French literature-AP, geometry, graphic arts, graphic design, history, human development, jazz band, Latin, Latin-AP, math applications, modern European history-AP, music theory, newspaper, orchestra, photography, physical education, physics, physics-AP, political science, pre-calculus, psychology-AP, Spanish, Spanish-AP, statistics-AP, studio art, studio art-AP, theater, trigonometry, U.S. history, U.S. history-AP, Web site design, weight training, Western civilization, world cultures, world religions, yearbook.
Graduation Requirements American history, arts and fine arts (art, music, dance, drama), biology, chemistry, English, ethics, foreign language, health education, mathematics, physical education (includes health), physics, science, social studies (includes history), world religions.
Special Academic Programs 17 Advanced Placement exams for which test preparation is offered; honors section; independent study.
College Admission Counseling 66 students graduated in 2012; all went to college, including Babson College; University of Puget Sound; University of Southern California; University of Utah; Wesleyan University; Westminster College. Median SAT critical reading: 620, median SAT math: 640, median SAT writing: 620, median combined SAT: 1870, median composite ACT: 29. 53% scored over 600 on SAT critical reading, 63% scored over 600 on SAT math, 53% scored over 600 on SAT writing, 58% scored over 1800 on combined SAT, 65% scored over 26 on composite ACT.
Student Life Upper grades have specified standards of dress, student council, honor system. Discipline rests equally with students and faculty.
Summer Programs Enrichment, advancement, sports, art/fine arts, computer instruction programs offered; session focuses on advancement and elective courses; held on campus; accepts boys and girls; open to students from other schools. 40 students usually enrolled. 2013 schedule: June 17 to August 9. Application deadline: none.
Tuition and Aid Day student tuition: $17,505. Tuition installment plan (monthly payment plans, individually arranged payment plans, 2-installment plan). Merit scholarship grants, need-based scholarship grants, Ethnic/Racial Diversity scholarship grants, Malone Family Foundation Academically Talented/Need-Based Scholarships available. In 2012–13, 23% of upper-school students received aid; total upper-school

merit-scholarship money awarded: $53,500. Total amount of financial aid awarded in 2012–13: $591,190.

Admissions Traditional secondary-level entrance grade is 9. For fall 2012, 55 students applied for upper-level admission, 33 were accepted, 24 enrolled. ACT-Explore, ERB CTP IV, ISEE, PSAT, TOEFL or writing sample required. Deadline for receipt of application materials: March 1. Application fee required: $50. Interview recommended.

Athletics Interscholastic: alpine skiing (boys, girls), baseball (b), basketball (b,g), golf (b,g), skiing (downhill) (b,g), soccer (b,g), softball (g), swimming and diving (b,g), tennis (b,g), volleyball (g); intramural: skiing (downhill) (b,g); coed interscholastic: alpine skiing, cross-country running, dance, modern dance, skiing (downhill), track and field; coed intramural: climbing, deck hockey, hiking/backpacking, mountain biking, outdoor activities, outdoor education, physical fitness, physical training, rock climbing, ropes courses, skiing (cross-country), skiing (downhill), snowboarding, strength & conditioning, swimming and diving, telemark skiing, weight training, yoga. 6 PE instructors, 22 coaches, 1 athletic trainer.

Computers Computers are regularly used in desktop publishing, graphic design, yearbook classes. Computer network features include on-campus library services, Internet access, wireless campus network, Internet filtering or blocking technology, all students have their own laptop computer. Campus intranet, student e-mail accounts, and computer access in designated common areas are available to students. Students grades are available online. The school has a published electronic and media policy.

Contact Kathryn B. Gundersen, Director of Admission. 801-924-2950. Fax: 801-363-5521. E-mail: kathygundersen@rowlandhall.org. Web site: www.rowlandhall.org

THE ROXBURY LATIN SCHOOL

101 St. Theresa Avenue
West Roxbury, Massachusetts 02132

Head of School: Mr. Kerry Paul Brennan

General Information Boys' day college-preparatory school. Grades 7–12. Founded: 1645. Setting: urban. Nearest major city is Boston. 117-acre campus. 10 buildings on campus. Approved or accredited by Association of Independent Schools in New England, Headmasters' Conference, and New England Association of Schools and Colleges. Member of National Association of Independent Schools and Secondary School Admission Test Board. Endowment: $105 million. Total enrollment: 297. Upper school average class size: 13. Upper school faculty-student ratio: 1:7. There are 176 required school days per year for Upper School students. Upper School students typically attend 5 days per week. The average school day consists of 6 hours and 30 minutes.

Upper School Student Profile Grade 7: 42 students (42 boys); Grade 8: 43 students (43 boys); Grade 9: 52 students (52 boys); Grade 10: 56 students (56 boys); Grade 11: 53 students (53 boys); Grade 12: 51 students (51 boys).

Faculty School total: 41. In upper school: 36 men, 5 women; 29 have advanced degrees.

Subjects Offered Advanced biology, advanced chemistry, advanced math, algebra, American Civil War, American government, American history, American literature, American studies, analysis, analytic geometry, Ancient Greek, ancient history, ancient world history, applied arts, art, art history, arts, biology, calculus, calculus-AP, chemistry, classical Greek literature, classical language, college counseling, college placement, computer science, computer science-AP, creative writing, design, drama, earth science, English, English literature, environmental science, European history, expository writing, fine arts, French, French language-AP, geometry, global studies, government/civics, grammar, history, Indian studies, Latin, Latin-AP, life science, macro/microeconomics-AP, mathematics, Middle East, model United Nations, music, music theory-AP, personal development, photography, physical education, physical science, physics, pre-algebra, science, senior project, Spanish, Spanish language-AP, statistics-AP, studio art, theater, trigonometry, U.S. government and politics-AP, U.S. history, visual arts, water color painting, Western civilization, world history, writing.

Graduation Requirements Arts, English, foreign language, history, Latin, mathematics, science, U.S. history, Western civilization, independent senior project.

Special Academic Programs Advanced Placement exam preparation; honors section; independent study; academic accommodation for the gifted, the musically talented, and the artistically talented.

College Admission Counseling 51 students graduated in 2012; all went to college, including Columbia University; Dartmouth College; Georgetown University; Harvard University; Princeton University; Stanford University. Median SAT critical reading: 740, median SAT math: 740, median SAT writing: 750, median combined SAT: 2240. 96% scored over 600 on SAT critical reading, 98% scored over 600 on SAT math, 98% scored over 600 on SAT writing, 98% scored over 1800 on combined SAT.

Student Life Upper grades have specified standards of dress, student council, honor system. Discipline rests equally with students and faculty.

Summer Programs Enrichment, sports, computer instruction programs offered; held on campus; accepts boys and girls; open to students from other schools.

Tuition and Aid Day student tuition: $24,300. Tuition installment plan (Insured Tuition Payment Plan, Key Tuition Payment Plan, 2-payment plan). Need-based scholarship grants available. In 2012–13, 35% of upper-school students received aid. Total amount of financial aid awarded in 2012–13: $1,805,675.

Admissions Traditional secondary-level entrance grade is 7. For fall 2012, 482 students applied for upper-level admission, 65 were accepted, 54 enrolled. ISEE or SSAT required. Deadline for receipt of application materials: January 4. No application fee required. On-campus interview required.

Athletics Interscholastic: baseball, basketball, cross-country running, football, ice hockey, lacrosse, soccer, tennis, track and field, wrestling. 7 coaches, 1 athletic trainer.

Computers Computers are regularly used in all academic, desktop publishing, literary magazine, newspaper, yearbook classes. Computer network features include on-campus library services, online commercial services, Internet access, wireless campus network, Internet filtering or blocking technology. Campus intranet, student e-mail accounts, and computer access in designated common areas are available to students. The school has a published electronic and media policy.

Contact Ms. Lindsay Schuyler, Assistant Director of Admission. 617-325-4920. Fax: 617-325-3585. E-mail: admission@roxburylatin.org. Web site: www.roxburylatin.org

ROYAL CANADIAN COLLEGE

8610 Ash Street
Vancouver, British Columbia V6P 3M2, Canada

Head of School: Mr. Howard H. Jiang

General Information Coeducational day college-preparatory and general academic school. Grades 8–12. Founded: 1989. Setting: suburban. 1-acre campus. 2 buildings on campus. Approved or accredited by British Columbia Department of Education. Language of instruction: English. Total enrollment: 88. Upper school average class size: 20. Upper school faculty-student ratio: 1:15. There are 197 required school days per year for Upper School students. Upper School students typically attend 5 days per week. The average school day consists of 5 hours and 30 minutes.

Upper School Student Profile Grade 10: 8 students (6 boys, 2 girls); Grade 11: 31 students (20 boys, 11 girls); Grade 12: 49 students (32 boys, 17 girls).

Faculty School total: 7. In upper school: 5 men, 2 women; 1 has an advanced degree.

Subjects Offered Accounting, applied skills, biology, calculus, Canadian history, career planning, chemistry, communications, computer science, computer science-AP, drama, economics, English, ESL, fine arts, general science, geography, history, information technology, Mandarin, mathematics, physical education, physics, pre-calculus, social justice, social sciences, world history, writing.

Graduation Requirements Applied skills, arts and fine arts (art, music, dance, drama), career and personal planning, language arts, mathematics, science, social studies (includes history).

Special Academic Programs ESL (10 students enrolled).

College Admission Counseling 26 students graduated in 2012; 25 went to college, including McGill University; Simon Fraser University; The University of British Columbia; University of Toronto; University of Victoria. Other: 1 had other specific plans.

Student Life Upper grades have student council, honor system. Discipline rests primarily with faculty.

Summer Programs ESL programs offered; session focuses on learning survival English conversational skills, and Canadian cultural experience; held on campus; accepts boys and girls; open to students from other schools. 30 students usually enrolled. 2013 schedule: July 1 to August 23. Application deadline: May 31.

Tuition and Aid Day student tuition: CAN$13,500. Merit scholarship grants available. In 2012–13, 4% of upper-school students received aid; total upper-school merit-scholarship money awarded: CAN$10,000. Total amount of financial aid awarded in 2012–13: CAN$18,000.

Admissions Traditional secondary-level entrance grade is 11. For fall 2012, 30 students applied for upper-level admission, 27 were accepted, 27 enrolled. English language required. Deadline for receipt of application materials: none. Application fee required: CAN$200. Interview recommended.

Athletics Intramural: badminton (boys, girls), baseball (b,g), basketball (b,g), soccer (b,g), ultimate Frisbee (b,g); coed intramural: badminton, baseball, soccer, ultimate Frisbee. 1 PE instructor.

Computers Computers are regularly used in accounting, career exploration, English, information technology, programming, science, social studies classes. Computer network features include Internet access, wireless campus network, Internet filtering or blocking technology. Computer access in designated common areas is available to students.

Contact Ms. Alice Syn, Admissions Manager. 604-738-2221. Fax: 604-738-2282. E-mail: alice.syn@royalcanadiancollege.com. Web site: www.royalcanadiancollege.com

ROYCEMORE SCHOOL

1200 Davis Street
Evanston, Illinois 60201

Head of School: Mr. Joseph A. Becker

General Information Coeducational day college-preparatory and arts school. Grades PK–12. Founded: 1915. Setting: suburban. Nearest major city is Chicago. 2.4-acre campus. 1 building on campus. Approved or accredited by Independent Schools Association of the Central States and Illinois Department of Education. Member of National Association of Independent Schools. Endowment: $11,000. Total enrollment: 292. Upper school average class size: 9. Upper school faculty-student ratio: 1:5. There are 172 required school days per year for Upper School students. Upper School students typically attend 5 days per week. The average school day consists of 7 hours.

Upper School Student Profile Grade 9: 21 students (9 boys, 12 girls); Grade 10: 27 students (14 boys, 13 girls); Grade 11: 20 students (12 boys, 8 girls); Grade 12: 28 students (13 boys, 15 girls).

Faculty School total: 40. In upper school: 5 men, 15 women; 14 have advanced degrees.

Subjects Offered African-American literature, algebra, American literature, art, biology, biology-AP, calculus-AP, chemistry, choir, comedy, composition, drawing, English language and composition-AP, English literature, environmental science, European history-AP, French, French-AP, geometry, government/civics, human development, independent study, international relations, introduction to theater, literature-AP, microeconomics, modern European history, music composition, music history, music theory, music theory-AP, mythology, painting, physical education, physics, physics-AP, pottery, public speaking, sculpture, society, politics and law, sociology, Spanish, Spanish-AP, studio art-AP, trigonometry, U.S. history, U.S. history-AP, world history, world literature, world religions, yearbook.

Graduation Requirements Arts and fine arts (art, music, dance, drama), English, foreign language, mathematics, physical education (includes health), science, social studies (includes history), participation in a 3-week January short-term project each year.

Special Academic Programs 10 Advanced Placement exams for which test preparation is offered; accelerated programs; independent study; study at local college for college credit.

College Admission Counseling 32 students graduated in 2012; all went to college, including DePaul University; Indiana University Bloomington; Knox College; University of Illinois at Urbana–Champaign; University of Wisconsin–Madison. Median SAT critical reading: 630, median SAT math: 630, median SAT writing: 560, median combined SAT: 1760, median composite ACT: 26. 55% scored over 600 on SAT critical reading, 55% scored over 600 on SAT math, 38% scored over 600 on SAT writing, 52% scored over 1800 on combined SAT, 48% scored over 26 on composite ACT.

Student Life Upper grades have specified standards of dress, student council, honor system. Discipline rests primarily with faculty.

Tuition and Aid Day student tuition: $24,425. Tuition installment plan (individually arranged payment plans, semi-annual payment plan, 9-month payment plan). Merit scholarship grants, need-based scholarship grants, discounts for children of Northwestern University and NorthShore University HealthSystem employees available. In 2012–13, 47% of upper-school students received aid; total upper-school merit-scholarship money awarded: $66,150. Total amount of financial aid awarded in 2012–13: $699,821.

Admissions Traditional secondary-level entrance grade is 9. Any standardized test or writing sample required. Deadline for receipt of application materials: none. Application fee required: $75. Interview required.

Athletics Interscholastic: basketball (boys, girls), volleyball (g); intramural: softball (b), strength & conditioning (b), volleyball (b); coed interscholastic: soccer; coed intramural: gymnastics, table tennis. 3 PE instructors, 2 coaches.

Computers Computers are regularly used in all academic classes. Computer network features include on-campus library services, Internet access, wireless campus network. The school has a published electronic and media policy.

Contact Ms. Amanda Avery, Director of Admissions. 847-866-6055. Fax: 847-866-6545. E-mail: aavery@roycemoreschool.org. Web site: www.roycemoreschool.org

RUMSEY HALL SCHOOL

Washington Depot, Connecticut

See Junior Boarding Schools section.

RUNDLE COLLEGE

4411 Manitoba Road SE
Calgary, Alberta T2G 4B9, Canada

Head of School: Mr. David Hauk

General Information Coeducational day college-preparatory, arts, business, bilingual studies, and technology school. Grades PK–12. Founded: 1985. Setting: suburban. 20-acre campus. 1 building on campus. Approved or accredited by Canadian Association of Independent Schools and Alberta Department of Education. Member of Secondary School Admission Test Board. Language of instruction: English. Total enrollment: 811. Upper school average class size: 14. Upper school faculty-student ratio: 1:14. There are 187 required school days per year for Upper School students. Upper School students typically attend 5 days per week. The average school day consists of 6 hours.

Upper School Student Profile Grade 10: 84 students (37 boys, 47 girls); Grade 11: 94 students (46 boys, 48 girls); Grade 12: 78 students (41 boys, 37 girls).

Faculty School total: 45. In upper school: 14 men, 31 women; 15 have advanced degrees.

Subjects Offered Accounting, art, band, biology, calculus, chemistry, computer science, drama, English, French, general science, mathematics, physical education, physics, science, social studies, Spanish, theater.

Graduation Requirements Career and personal planning, English, mathematics, physical education (includes health), science, social sciences.

Special Academic Programs Honors section; study abroad.

College Admission Counseling 81 students graduated in 2012; 79 went to college, including Queen's University at Kingston; St. Francis Xavier University; The University of British Columbia; University of Alberta; University of Calgary; University of Victoria. Other: 1 went to work, 1 had other specific plans.

Student Life Upper grades have uniform requirement, student council, honor system. Discipline rests primarily with faculty.

Tuition and Aid Day student tuition: CAN$12,000. Tuition installment plan (monthly payment plans). Bursaries, merit scholarship grants available. In 2012–13, 1% of upper-school students received aid; total upper-school merit-scholarship money awarded: CAN$24,000. Total amount of financial aid awarded in 2012–13: CAN$90,000.

Admissions Traditional secondary-level entrance grade is 10. For fall 2012, 50 students applied for upper-level admission, 25 were accepted, 20 enrolled. Achievement tests and SSAT or WISC III required. Deadline for receipt of application materials: none. Application fee required: CAN$100. On-campus interview required.

Athletics Interscholastic: badminton (boys, girls), basketball (b,g), cross-country running (b,g), curling (b,g), dance squad (b,g), flag football (b,g), floor hockey (b,g), football (b), golf (b,g), rugby (b,g), soccer (b,g), track and field (b,g), volleyball (b,g), wrestling (b,g); intramural: aerobics (g), badminton (b,g), dance (g), football (b); coed interscholastic: badminton, softball; coed intramural: badminton, baseball, basketball, cross-country running, flag football, football, lacrosse, outdoor recreation, skiing (downhill), soccer, table tennis, track and field, volleyball, weight lifting, wrestling. 4 PE instructors.

Computers Computers are regularly used in technology classes. Computer network features include Internet access, wireless campus network, Web page hosting, multimedia productions, streaming video student news. Student e-mail accounts and computer access in designated common areas are available to students. Students grades are available online. The school has a published electronic and media policy.

Contact Ms. Nicola Spencer, Director of Admissions. 403-291-3866 Ext. 106. Fax: 403-291-5458. E-mail: spencer@rundle.ab.ca. Web site: www.rundle.ab.ca

RYE COUNTRY DAY SCHOOL

Cedar Street
Rye, New York 10580-2034

Head of School: Mr. Scott A. Nelson

General Information Coeducational day college-preparatory, arts, and technology school. Grades PK–12. Founded: 1869. Setting: suburban. Nearest major city is New York. 30-acre campus. 8 buildings on campus. Approved or accredited by New York Department of Education. Member of National Association of Independent Schools and Secondary School Admission Test Board. Endowment: $29 million. Total enrollment: 886. Upper school average class size: 13. Upper school faculty-student ratio: 1:7. There are 165 required school days per year for Upper School students. Upper School students typically attend 5 days per week. The average school day consists of 6 hours and 50 minutes.

Upper School Student Profile Grade 9: 102 students (44 boys, 58 girls); Grade 10: 106 students (60 boys, 46 girls); Grade 11: 87 students (43 boys, 44 girls); Grade 12: 98 students (46 boys, 52 girls).

Faculty School total: 125. In upper school: 21 men, 28 women; 49 have advanced degrees.

Subjects Offered 20th century history, algebra, American history, American history-AP, American literature, American literature-AP, art, art history, art history-AP, art-AP, astronomy, biology, biology-AP, calculus, calculus-AP, ceramics, chemistry, chemistry-AP, chorus, classics, computer music, computer programming, computer science-AP, computer-aided design, CPR, creative writing, dance, drama, driver education, economics, English, English literature, English literature-AP, English-AP, environmental science, environmental science-AP, European history, European history-AP, expository writing, fencing, fine arts, forensics, French, French-AP, geometry, government, government and politics-AP, government-AP, Greek, health, history, honors English, honors geometry, independent study, instrumental music, interdisciplinary studies, jazz band, Latin, Latin-AP, Mandarin, mathematics, mechanical drawing, modern European history-AP, music, music theory-AP, oceanography, philosophy, photography, physical education, physics, physics-AP, psychology, psychology-AP, science, social studies, Spanish, Spanish-AP, speech, squash, statistics-AP, studio art-AP, The 20th Century, the Sixties, theater, theater arts, trigonometry, U.S. government and politics-AP, U.S. history, U.S. history-AP, U.S. literature, weight training, wind ensemble, world civilizations, writing.

Graduation Requirements Arts and fine arts (art, music, dance, drama), English, foreign language, life management skills, mathematics, physical education (includes health), science, social studies (includes history).

Special Academic Programs 26 Advanced Placement exams for which test preparation is offered; honors section; independent study; academic accommodation for the gifted; special instructional classes for deaf students.

College Admission Counseling 97 students graduated in 2011; all went to college, including Boston University; Lehigh University; Syracuse University; University of Michigan; University of Pennsylvania. Mean SAT critical reading: 667, mean SAT math: 674, mean SAT writing: 695, mean combined SAT: 2039, mean composite ACT: 30.

Student Life Upper grades have student council. Discipline rests primarily with faculty.

Tuition and Aid Day student tuition: $32,800. Tuition installment plan (monthly payment plans, individually arranged payment plans). Need-based scholarship grants available. In 2011–12, 19% of upper-school students received aid. Total amount of financial aid awarded in 2011–12: $2,300,000.

Admissions Traditional secondary-level entrance grade is 9. For fall 2011, 226 students applied for upper-level admission, 52 were accepted, 35 enrolled. ISEE or SSAT required. Deadline for receipt of application materials: December 15. Application fee required: $75. On-campus interview required.

Athletics Interscholastic: baseball (boys), basketball (b,g), cross-country running (b,g), fencing (b,g), field hockey (g), football (b), golf (b,g), ice hockey (b,g), lacrosse (b,g), sailing (b,g), soccer (b,g), softball (g), squash (b,g), tennis (b,g), track and field (b,g), wrestling (b); intramural: basketball (b), fitness (b,g), physical fitness (b,g), physical training (b,g), squash (b,g), strength & conditioning (b,g), tennis (b,g), ultimate Frisbee (b), weight training (b,g), wrestling (b); coed intramural: aerobics, aerobics/dance, ballet, cross-country running, dance, dance squad, fitness, ice skating, jogging, modern dance, running, squash, yoga. 4 PE instructors, 19 coaches, 2 athletic trainers.

Computers Computers are regularly used in art, classics, English, foreign language, history, mathematics, music, photography, publishing, science, technology, yearbook classes. Computer network features include on-campus library services, online commercial services, Internet access, wireless campus network, Internet filtering or blocking technology. Campus intranet and student e-mail accounts are available to students. Students grades are available online. The school has a published electronic and media policy.

Contact Mr. Matthew J.M. Suzuki, Director of Admissions. 914-925-4513. Fax: 914-921-2147. E-mail: matt_suzuki@ryecountryday.org. Web site: www.ryecountryday.org

See Display on this page and Close-Up on page 618.

SACRAMENTO ADVENTIST ACADEMY

5601 Winding Way
Carmichael, California 95608-1298

Head of School: John Soule

General Information Coeducational day college-preparatory, general academic, arts, business, vocational, religious studies, bilingual studies, and technology school, affiliated with Seventh-day Adventist Church. Grades K–12. Founded: 1957. Setting: suburban. Nearest major city is Sacramento. 36-acre campus. 5 buildings on campus. Approved or accredited by Board of Regents, General Conference of Seventh-day Adventists, National Council for Private School Accreditation, Western Association of Schools and Colleges, and California Department of Education. Total enrollment: 222. Upper school average class size: 29. Upper school faculty-student ratio: 1:12. There are 180 required school days per year for Upper School students. Upper School students typically attend 5 days per week. The average school day consists of 7 hours and 15 minutes.

Upper School Student Profile 96% of students are Seventh-day Adventists.

Faculty School total: 25. In upper school: 8 men, 4 women; 4 have advanced degrees.

Subjects Offered Accounting, advanced math, Advanced Placement courses, algebra, art, band, Bible, biology, biology-AP, business technology, calculus-AP, chemistry, choir, computer applications, computer education, conceptual physics, concert band, consumer mathematics, driver education, economics, English, English composition, English language and composition-AP, geometry, graphic design, handbells, health, health education, keyboarding, life skills, microcomputer technology applications, photography, physical education, physics, public speaking, religion, softball, Spanish, Spanish-AP, speech, technical skills, U.S. government, U.S. history, word processing, world history, world history-AP, World War I.

Graduation Requirements Arts and fine arts (art, music, dance, drama), biology, computer applications, economics, English, keyboarding, life skills, mathematics, physical education (includes health), religion (includes Bible studies and theology), science, U.S. government, U.S. history, 100 hours of documented work experience, 25 hours of documented community service per year of attendance.

Special Academic Programs 2 Advanced Placement exams for which test preparation is offered; honors section; accelerated programs; study at local college for college credit; remedial math.

College Admission Counseling 27 students graduated in 2012; 24 went to college, including American River College; La Sierra University; Pacific Union College; Sierra College; Walla Walla University. Other: 2 went to work, 1 entered military service. Mean SAT critical reading: 559, mean SAT math: 566, mean composite ACT: 23. 22% scored over 600 on SAT critical reading, 44% scored over 600 on SAT math, 45% scored over 26 on composite ACT.

Student Life Upper grades have specified standards of dress, student council. Discipline rests primarily with faculty.

Tuition and Aid Day student tuition: $5470–$9740. Tuition installment plan (monthly payment plans, individually arranged payment plans). Tuition reduction for siblings, paying campus jobs, academy day scholarships available. In 2012–13, 5% of upper-school students received aid. Total amount of financial aid awarded in 2012–13: $10,000.

Admissions Traditional secondary-level entrance grade is 9. Deadline for receipt of application materials: none. Application fee required: $25. Interview required.

Athletics Interscholastic: baseball (girls), basketball (b,g), flag football (b,g), golf (b), softball (b,g), volleyball (g). 1 PE instructor, 1 coach.

Computers Computers are regularly used in accounting, business applications, English, history, keyboarding, religion, word processing classes. Computer network features include on-campus library services, online commercial services, Internet access.

Contact Mrs. Sheri Miller, Registrar/Guidance Counselor. 916-481-2300 Ext. 102. Fax: 916-481-7426. E-mail: smiller@sacaa.org. Web site: www.sacaa.org

SACRAMENTO COUNTRY DAY SCHOOL

2636 Latham Drive
Sacramento, California 95864-7198

Head of School: Stephen T. Repsher

General Information Coeducational day college-preparatory, arts, and technology school. Grades PK–12. Founded: 1964. Setting: suburban. 12-acre campus. 8 buildings on campus. Approved or accredited by California Association of Independent Schools and Western Association of Schools and Colleges. Member of National Association of Independent Schools. Endowment: $2 million. Total enrollment: 469. Upper school average class size: 12. Upper school faculty-student ratio: 1:9. There are 175 required school days per year for Upper School students. Upper School students typically attend 5 days per week. The average school day consists of 6 hours and 25 minutes.

Upper School Student Profile Grade 9: 35 students (15 boys, 20 girls); Grade 10: 33 students (16 boys, 17 girls); Grade 11: 27 students (13 boys, 14 girls); Grade 12: 40 students (21 boys, 19 girls).

Faculty School total: 65. In upper school: 18 men, 10 women; 19 have advanced degrees.

Subjects Offered Acting, algebra, American history, American literature, ancient history, ancient/medieval philosophy, art, art history, art history-AP, art-AP, band, biology, biology-AP, British literature, calculus, calculus-AP, ceramics, chamber groups, chemistry, chemistry-AP, community service, computer skills, computer technologies, concert band, creative writing, digital imaging, digital music, drama, drama performance, drawing, earth science, economics, English, English literature, European history, fine arts, French, French-AP, geography, geometry, government/civics, grammar, history, international relations, jazz band, journalism, language and composition, Latin, Latin-AP, mathematics, microeconomics, newspaper, nutrition, orchestra, physical education, physics, physics-AP, physiology, pre-calculus, public speaking, science, social studies, Spanish, Spanish-AP, speech, studio art, studio art-AP, technology/design, theater, trigonometry, U.S. history, U.S. history-AP, world history, world literature, writing.

Graduation Requirements Arts and fine arts (art, music, dance, drama), computer science, electives, English, foreign language, history, interdisciplinary studies, mathematics, physical education (includes health), science, 40-hour senior project. Community service is required.

Special Academic Programs Advanced Placement exam preparation; independent study; study at local college for college credit; ESL (6 students enrolled).

College Admission Counseling 34 students graduated in 2012; all went to college, including Cornell University; University of California, Los Angeles; University of California, San Diego; University of California, Santa Barbara; University of Southern California; Williams College. Median SAT critical reading: 628, median SAT math: 643, median SAT writing: 643, median combined SAT: 1914.

Student Life Upper grades have specified standards of dress, student council, honor system. Discipline rests primarily with faculty.

Tuition and Aid Day student tuition: $16,970–$20,960. Tuition installment plan (Insured Tuition Payment Plan, monthly payment plans, individually arranged payment plans). Need-based scholarship grants available. In 2012–13, 26% of upper-school students received aid. Total amount of financial aid awarded in 2012–13: $501,860.

Admissions Traditional secondary-level entrance grade is 9. For fall 2012, 35 students applied for upper-level admission, 20 were accepted, 17 enrolled. ERB, Otis-Lennon Mental Ability Test and writing sample required. Deadline for receipt of application materials: none. Application fee required: $25. Interview required.

Athletics Interscholastic: baseball (boys), basketball (b,g), flag football (b), lacrosse (b), soccer (b,g), softball (g), swimming and diving (b,g), track and field (b,g), volleyball (b,g); coed interscholastic: cross-country running, golf, skiing (downhill), snowboarding, tennis, wrestling. 3 PE instructors, 14 coaches.

Computers Computers are regularly used in all academic classes. Computer network features include on-campus library services, online commercial services, Internet access, Internet filtering or blocking technology. Campus intranet and student e-mail accounts are available to students. The school has a published electronic and media policy.

Contact Lonna Bloedau, Director of Admission. 916-481-8811. Fax: 916-481-6016. E-mail: lbloedau@saccds.org. Web site: www.saccds.org

SACRED HEART/GRIFFIN HIGH SCHOOL

1200 West Washington
Springfield, Illinois 62702-4794

Head of School: Sr. Margaret Joanne Grueter, OP

General Information Coeducational day college-preparatory school, affiliated with Roman Catholic Church. Grades 9–12. Founded: 1895. Setting: urban. 13-acre campus. 2 buildings on campus. Approved or accredited by National Catholic Education Association, North Central Association of Colleges and Schools, and Illinois Department of Education. Endowment: $8.7 million. Total enrollment: 781. Upper school average class size: 24. Upper school faculty-student ratio: 1:24. There are 176 required school days per year for Upper School students. Upper School students typically attend 5 days per week. The average school day consists of 7 hours.

Upper School Student Profile Grade 9: 207 students (91 boys, 116 girls); Grade 10: 192 students (101 boys, 91 girls); Grade 11: 217 students (122 boys, 95 girls); Grade 12: 165 students (84 boys, 81 girls). 88% of students are Roman Catholic.

Faculty School total: 52. In upper school: 24 men, 28 women; 26 have advanced degrees.

Subjects Offered Advanced biology.

Graduation Requirements 80 hours of service to community or approved organizations.

Special Academic Programs 9 Advanced Placement exams for which test preparation is offered; honors section; academic accommodation for the gifted, the musically talented, and the artistically talented.

College Admission Counseling 191 students graduated in 2012; 187 went to college. Other: 2 entered military service, 2 had other specific plans. Median composite ACT: 24.

Student Life Upper grades have uniform requirement, student council, honor system. Discipline rests primarily with faculty. Attendance at religious services is required.

Summer Programs Enrichment, advancement, sports programs offered; session focuses on physical education and health; held on campus; accepts boys and girls; open to students from other schools. 300 students usually enrolled. 2013 schedule: May 28 to June 28. Application deadline: April 15.

Tuition and Aid Day student tuition: $7275. Tuition installment plan (FACTS Tuition Payment Plan, individually arranged payment plans). Tuition reduction for siblings, merit scholarship grants, need-based scholarship grants available. In 2012–13, 30% of upper-school students received aid; total upper-school merit-scholarship money awarded: $12,900. Total amount of financial aid awarded in 2012–13: $443,093.

Admissions Traditional secondary-level entrance grade is 9. For fall 2012, 207 students applied for upper-level admission, 207 were accepted, 207 enrolled. Explore required. Deadline for receipt of application materials: none. Application fee required: $225. Interview recommended.

Athletics Interscholastic: aquatics (boys, girls), baseball (b), basketball (b,g), cheering (g), cross-country running (b,g), diving (b,g), football (b), golf (b,g), hockey (b), pom squad (g), soccer (b,g), softball (g), tennis (b,g), track and field (b,g), volleyball (g). 1 PE instructor, 3 coaches, 1 athletic trainer.

Computers Computers are regularly used in all academic classes. Computer network features include on-campus library services, Internet access, wireless campus network, Internet filtering or blocking technology. Students grades are available online. The school has a published electronic and media policy.

Contact Erica Cusumano, Marketing/Alumni Coordinator. 217-787-9732. Fax: 217-726-9791. E-mail: Cusumano@shg.org. Web site: www.shg.org

SACRED HEART SCHOOL OF HALIFAX

5820 Spring Garden Road
Halifax, Nova Scotia B3H 1X8, Canada

Head of School: Sr. Anne Wachter

General Information Coeducational day college-preparatory and religious studies school, affiliated with Roman Catholic Church. Grades K–12. Founded: 1849. Setting: urban. 1 building on campus. Approved or accredited by Canadian Association of Independent Schools and Nova Scotia Department of Education. Language of instruction: English. Total enrollment: 461. Upper school average class size: 18. Upper school faculty-student ratio: 1:15. There are 175 required school days per year for Upper School students. Upper School students typically attend 5 days per week. The average school day consists of 7 hours.

Upper School Student Profile Grade 7: 51 students (8 boys, 43 girls); Grade 8: 61 students (22 boys, 39 girls); Grade 9: 64 students (23 boys, 41 girls); Grade 10: 32 students (11 boys, 21 girls); Grade 11: 39 students (8 boys, 31 girls); Grade 12: 39 students (13 boys, 26 girls). 60% of students are Roman Catholic.

Faculty School total: 65. In upper school: 7 men, 28 women; 22 have advanced degrees.

Subjects Offered 20th century history, 20th century world history, algebra, art, Bible studies, biology, calculus, Canadian history, chemistry, creative writing, earth science, economics, English, English literature, environmental science, European history, expository writing, French, geography, geometry, government/civics, grammar, health, history, mathematics, music, physical education, physics, religion, science, social studies, sociology, Spanish, theater, trigonometry, world history, writing.

Graduation Requirements Arts and fine arts (art, music, dance, drama), English, foreign language, history, mathematics, physical education (includes health), religion (includes Bible studies and theology), science. Community service is required.

Special Academic Programs 8 Advanced Placement exams for which test preparation is offered; honors section; domestic exchange program (with Network of Sacred Heart Schools); study abroad; ESL (19 students enrolled).

College Admission Counseling 35 students graduated in 2012; 32 went to college, including Acadia University; Carleton University; Dalhousie University; Mount Allison University; Saint Mary's University; St. Francis Xavier University. Other: 2 went to work, 1 had other specific plans.

Student Life Upper grades have uniform requirement, student council, honor system. Discipline rests primarily with faculty. Attendance at religious services is required.

Summer Programs Remediation, enrichment programs offered; session focuses on French remediation, debate; held on campus; accepts boys and girls; open to students from other schools. 50 students usually enrolled. Application deadline: none.

Tuition and Aid Day student tuition: CAN$12,977. Tuition installment plan (monthly payment plans, individually arranged payment plans). Tuition reduction for siblings, bursaries, merit scholarship grants, need-based scholarship grants available. In 2012–13, 12% of upper-school students received aid; total upper-school merit-scholarship money awarded: CAN$106,000. Total amount of financial aid awarded in 2012–13: CAN$138,000.

Admissions Traditional secondary-level entrance grade is 7. Otis-Lennon School Ability Test and school's own test required. Deadline for receipt of application materials: none. Application fee required: CAN$100. On-campus interview required.

Athletics Interscholastic: aquatics (girls), badminton (b,g), basketball (b,g), cross-country running (b,g), field hockey (g), ice hockey (b), soccer (b,g), swimming and diving (b,g), tennis (g), volleyball (g); intramural: alpine skiing (b,g), badminton (b,g), basketball (b,g), cross-country running (b,g), curling (g), fitness walking (g), jogging (b,g), running (b,g), skiing (downhill) (b,g), soccer (b,g), swimming and diving (b), tennis (g), track and field (g), volleyball (g). 3 PE instructors.

Computers Computer network features include on-campus library services, Internet access, wireless campus network, Internet filtering or blocking technology. Campus intranet and student e-mail accounts are available to students. The school has a published electronic and media policy.

Contact Ms. Pauline Scott, Principal, Sacred Heart High School. 902-422-4459 Ext. 209. Fax: 902-423-7691. E-mail: pscott@shsh.ca. Web site: www.sacredheartschool.ns.ca

SADDLEBACK VALLEY CHRISTIAN SCHOOL

26333 Oso Road
San Juan Capistrano, California 92675

Head of School: Mr. Edward Carney

General Information Coeducational day college-preparatory, general academic, arts, religious studies, and technology school, affiliated with Christian faith. Grades PK–12. Founded: 1997. Setting: suburban. Nearest major city is Irvine/Anaheim. 69-acre campus. 6 buildings on campus. Approved or accredited by Association of Christian Schools International, Western Association of Schools and Colleges, and California Department of Education. Total enrollment: 911. Upper school average class size: 24. Upper school faculty-student ratio: 1:15. There are 180 required school days per year for Upper School students. Upper School students typically attend 5 days per week. The average school day consists of 6 hours and 35 minutes.

Upper School Student Profile Grade 9: 89 students (49 boys, 40 girls); Grade 10: 108 students (49 boys, 59 girls); Grade 11: 103 students (55 boys, 48 girls); Grade 12: 76 students (36 boys, 40 girls). 75% of students are Christian faith.

Faculty School total: 75. In upper school: 12 men, 22 women; 10 have advanced degrees.

Subjects Offered 1 1/2 elective credits, algebra, American history, American history-AP, American literature, American sign language, anatomy and physiology, applied arts, art, art history-AP, ASB Leadership, athletic training, Bible, Bible as literature, biology, biology-AP, British literature, business mathematics, calculus-AP, chemistry, computers, concert choir, debate, drama, English language and composition-AP, English literature and composition-AP, environmental science, ESL, geography, geometry, government and politics-AP, history, honors English, music, musical theater, oceanography, psychology-AP, public speaking, religious studies, science, senior project, Spanish, Spanish language-AP, speech and debate, sports, statistics-AP, studio art-AP, trigonometry, U.S. government and politics, U.S. government and politics-AP, U.S. history, U.S. history-AP, visual and performing arts, world history, world literature, world religions, yearbook.

Graduation Requirements Algebra, American history, American literature, anatomy and physiology, art, Bible, biology, British literature, earth science, English, English literature, foreign language, geometry, history, life science, physical education (includes health), physical science, science, senior project, Spanish, speech, trigonometry, U.S. history, visual arts, world history, Senior Project required for seniors to graduate.

Special Academic Programs 11 Advanced Placement exams for which test preparation is offered; honors section; independent study; study at local college for college credit; study abroad; remedial reading and/or remedial writing; remedial math; programs in English, mathematics, general development for dyslexic students; special instructional classes for students with learning disabilities; ESL (24 students enrolled).

College Admission Counseling 64 students graduated in 2012; 50 went to college, including Biola University; California Polytechnic State University, San Luis Obispo; Point Loma Nazarene University; University of California, Los Angeles; University of California, San Diego. Other: 10 went to work, 4 had other specific plans. Median SAT critical reading: 540, median SAT math: 540, median SAT writing: 540, median combined SAT: 1620, median composite ACT: 22. 32% scored over 600 on SAT critical reading, 21% scored over 600 on SAT math, 32% scored over 600 on SAT writing, 26% scored over 1800 on combined SAT, 27% scored over 26 on composite ACT.

Student Life Upper grades have uniform requirement, student council, honor system. Discipline rests primarily with faculty. Attendance at religious services is required.

Summer Programs Remediation programs offered; session focuses on make-up of school work; held on campus; accepts boys and girls; not open to students from other schools. 10 students usually enrolled. 2013 schedule: June 20 to July 31. Application deadline: June 5.

Tuition and Aid Day student tuition: $8600. Tuition installment plan (monthly payment plans). Tuition reduction for siblings, need-based scholarship grants available. In 2012–13, 25% of upper-school students received aid. Total amount of financial aid awarded in 2012–13: $175,000.

Admissions Traditional secondary-level entrance grade is 9. For fall 2012, 70 students applied for upper-level admission, 65 were accepted, 60 enrolled. Placement test required. Deadline for receipt of application materials: none. Application fee required: $200. Interview required.

Athletics Interscholastic: baseball (boys), basketball (b,g), cheering (g), cross-country running (b,g), football (b), golf (b,g), soccer (b,g), softball (g), swimming and diving (b,g), tennis (g), track and field (b,g), volleyball (b,g); intramural: equestrian sports (g); coed interscholastic: dance team. 5 PE instructors, 15 coaches, 4 athletic trainers.

Computers Computers are regularly used in computer applications classes. Computer network features include Internet access, Internet filtering or blocking technology. Student e-mail accounts are available to students. Students grades are available online. The school has a published electronic and media policy.

Contact Mrs. Denise Karlsen, Registrar. 949-443-4050 Ext. 1201. Fax: 949-443-3941. E-mail: denisek@svcschools.org. Web site: www.svcschools.org

SADDLEBROOK PREPARATORY SCHOOL

5700 Saddlebrook Way
Wesley Chapel, Florida 33543

Head of School: Mr. Larry W. Robison

General Information Coeducational boarding and day college-preparatory school. Boarding grades 6–12, day grades 3–12. Founded: 1993. Setting: suburban. Nearest major city is Tampa. Students are housed in single-sex dormitories. 50-acre campus. 8 buildings on campus. Approved or accredited by Florida Council of Independent Schools, Southern Association of Colleges and Schools, and Florida Department of Education. Upper school average class size: 8. Upper school faculty-student ratio: 1:8. There are 175 required school days per year for Upper School students. Upper School students typically attend 5 days per week. The average school day consists of 7 hours and 15 minutes.

Upper School Student Profile Grade 9: 13 students (10 boys, 3 girls); Grade 10: 16 students (10 boys, 6 girls); Grade 11: 22 students (17 boys, 5 girls); Grade 12: 17 students (10 boys, 7 girls); Postgraduate: 2 students (2 boys). 60% of students are boarding students. 14% are state residents. 16 states are represented in upper school student body. 69% are international students. International students from Brazil, China, Germany, India, Mexico, and Switzerland; 17 other countries represented in student body.

Faculty School total: 11. In upper school: 3 men, 6 women; 6 have advanced degrees; 1 resides on campus.

Subjects Offered Algebra, American government, American history, anatomy and physiology, biology, calculus, chemistry, economics, English, geometry, physical science, physics, pre-algebra, pre-calculus, SAT preparation, Spanish, world geography, world history.

Graduation Requirements Algebra, American government, American history, biology, chemistry, economics, English, geometry, mathematics, physical education (includes health), physical science, science, social studies (includes history), world history.

Special Academic Programs Honors section; ESL (18 students enrolled).

College Admission Counseling 28 students graduated in 2012; 21 went to college, including College of Charleston; Georgia Institute of Technology; Hofstra University; New York University; Pepperdine University; University of San Francisco. Other: 7 had other specific plans.

Student Life Upper grades have uniform requirement, student council, honor system. Discipline rests primarily with faculty.

Summer Programs Remediation, enrichment, advancement, ESL, sports, art/fine arts programs offered; session focuses on academics; held on campus; accepts boys and girls; open to students from other schools. 8 students usually enrolled. 2013 schedule: June 5 to July 31. Application deadline: May 25.

Tuition and Aid Day student tuition: $16,885; 7-day tuition and room/board: $32,885. Tuition installment plan (individually arranged payment plans). Tuition reduction for siblings available.

Admissions Traditional secondary-level entrance grade is 12. For fall 2012, 60 students applied for upper-level admission, 51 were accepted, 46 enrolled. Deadline for receipt of application materials: none. Application fee required: $50. Interview recommended.

Athletics Interscholastic: golf (boys). 28 coaches, 3 athletic trainers.

Computers Computers are regularly used in English, foreign language, history, mathematics, science classes. Computer network features include on-campus library services, online commercial services, Internet access, wireless campus network, Internet filtering or blocking technology, RenWeb. Student e-mail accounts and computer access in designated common areas are available to students. Students grades are available online. The school has a published electronic and media policy.

Contact Ms. Donna Claggett, Administrative Manager. 813-907-4525. Fax: 813-991-4713. E-mail: dclaggett@saddlebrookresort.com. Web site: www.saddlebrookprep.com

SAGE HILL SCHOOL

20402 Newport Coast Drive
Newport Coast, California 92657-0300

Head of School: Mr. Gordon McNeill

General Information Coeducational day college-preparatory and arts school. Grades 9–12. Founded: 2000. Setting: suburban. Nearest major city is Newport Beach. 30-acre campus. 6 buildings on campus. Approved or accredited by Western Association of Schools and Colleges and California Department of Education. Member of National Association of Independent Schools. Endowment: $10 million. Total enrollment: 466. Upper school average class size: 15. Upper school faculty-student ratio: 1:10. There are 170 required school days per year for Upper School students. Upper School students typically attend 5 days per week. The average school day consists of 6 hours and 20 minutes.

Upper School Student Profile Grade 9: 122 students (62 boys, 60 girls); Grade 10: 117 students (57 boys, 60 girls); Grade 11: 109 students (52 boys, 57 girls); Grade 12: 118 students (49 boys, 69 girls).

Faculty School total: 46. In upper school: 22 men, 24 women; 24 have advanced degrees.

Subjects Offered Advanced chemistry, advanced math, Advanced Placement courses, algebra, American history, American history-AP, art, art history-AP, athletics, biology, biology-AP, British literature, calculus, calculus-AP, ceramics, chemistry, chemistry-AP, Chinese, choral music, computer science-AP, dance, dance performance, digital art, economics-AP, English, English literature and composition-AP, English-AP, environmental science-AP, film history, French, French language-AP, geometry, honors algebra, honors English, honors geometry, instrumental music, Latin, marine science, modern dance, music, physical science, physics-AP, pre-calculus, psychology, Spanish, Spanish-AP, statistics-AP, studio art-AP, theater, theater design and production, U.S. history, U.S. history-AP, United States government-AP, wind ensemble.

Graduation Requirements Arts, English, history, languages, mathematics, physical education (includes health), science.

Special Academic Programs 19 Advanced Placement exams for which test preparation is offered; honors section; independent study; academic accommodation for the gifted, the musically talented, and the artistically talented.

College Admission Counseling 97 students graduated in 2012; all went to college, including Chapman University; New York University; Southern Methodist University; Stanford University; University of San Francisco; University of Southern California. Mean combined SAT: 1920.

Student Life Upper grades have specified standards of dress, student council, honor system. Discipline rests equally with students and faculty.

Summer Programs Remediation, enrichment, advancement, sports, art/fine arts programs offered; session focuses on academics; held on campus; accepts boys and girls; open to students from other schools. 280 students usually enrolled. 2013 schedule: June to July.

Tuition and Aid Day student tuition: $30,400. Tuition installment plan (SMART Tuition Payment Plan, monthly payment plans). Need-based scholarship grants available. In 2012–13, 14% of upper-school students received aid. Total amount of financial aid awarded in 2012–13: $1,857,570.

Admissions Traditional secondary-level entrance grade is 9. For fall 2012, 272 students applied for upper-level admission, 206 were accepted, 130 enrolled. ISEE required. Deadline for receipt of application materials: February 15. Application fee required: $100. On-campus interview required.

Athletics Interscholastic: baseball (boys), basketball (b,g), cross-country running (b,g), diving (b,g), football (b), golf (b,g), lacrosse (b,g), soccer (b,g), swimming and diving (b,g), tennis (b,g), track and field (b,g), volleyball (b,g), water polo (b). 3 PE instructors, 44 coaches, 1 athletic trainer.

Computers Computers are regularly used in computer applications, digital applications, video film production classes. Computer network features include on-campus library services, online commercial services, Internet access, wireless campus network, Internet filtering or blocking technology. Student e-mail accounts and computer access in designated common areas are available to students. Students grades are available online. The school has a published electronic and media policy.

Contact Ms. Elaine Mijalis-Kahn, Director of Admission and Financial Aid. 949-219-1337. Fax: 949-219-1399. E-mail: mijaliskahne@sagehillschool.org. Web site: www.sagehillschool.org

SAGE RIDGE SCHOOL

2515 Crossbow Court
Reno, Nevada 89511

General Information Coeducational day college-preparatory, arts, and technology school. Grades 5–12. Founded: 1997. Setting: suburban. 44-acre campus. 2 buildings on campus. Approved or accredited by Pacific Northwest Association of Independent Schools and Nevada Department of Education. Member of National Association of Independent Schools. Total enrollment: 215. Upper school average class size: 14. Upper school faculty-student ratio: 1:6. There are 180 required school days per year for Upper School students. Upper School students typically attend 5 days per week. The average school day consists of 7 hours and 10 minutes.

Upper School Student Profile Grade 9: 31 students (18 boys, 13 girls); Grade 10: 18 students (9 boys, 9 girls); Grade 11: 20 students (11 boys, 9 girls); Grade 12: 16 students (6 boys, 10 girls).

Faculty School total: 32. In upper school: 8 men, 8 women; 9 have advanced degrees.

Subjects Offered Advanced chemistry, algebra, American history-AP, American literature, American literature-AP, analytic geometry, anatomy and physiology, ancient world history, art history, biology, biology-AP, British literature, British literature-AP, calculus, calculus-AP, ceramics, chemistry, choir, classical language, college counseling, conceptual physics, creative writing, debate, drama performance, electives, English language and composition-AP, English language-AP, English literature and composition-AP, English literature-AP, European history, European literature, foreign language, geometry, honors algebra, honors English, lab science, language-AP, Latin, Latin-AP, medieval history, modern European history, music history, music performance, music theory, outdoor education, philosophy, physical education, physical fitness, physics, playwriting and directing, poetry, pre-algebra, pre-calculus, probability and statistics, public speaking, senior internship, senior seminar, senior thesis, Spanish, Spanish language-AP, Spanish literature, Spanish literature-AP, Spanish-AP, statistics, studio art, studio art-AP, theater, theater arts, theater history, theory of knowledge, trigonometry, U.S. government and politics-AP, U.S. history, U.S. history-AP, Western literature, world history.

Graduation Requirements 20th century world history, algebra, American history, American literature, analytic geometry, ancient world history, art history, biology, British literature, chemistry, conceptual physics, English composition, European history, foreign language, history of music, modern European history, music, outdoor education, participation in sports, pre-calculus, public speaking, science, senior internship, senior thesis, speech, theater history, trigonometry, U.S. history, 15 hours of community service per year, senior thesis and senior internship, two mini-semester seminars per year.

Special Academic Programs 16 Advanced Placement exams for which test preparation is offered; honors section; independent study.

College Admission Counseling 20 students graduated in 2012; all went to college, including Dartmouth College; Duke University; Pepperdine University. Mean SAT critical reading: 612, mean SAT math: 660, mean SAT writing: 636, mean combined SAT: 1907, mean composite ACT: 27.

Student Life Upper grades have uniform requirement, student council, honor system. Discipline rests equally with students and faculty.

Summer Programs Enrichment, art/fine arts programs offered; session focuses on enrichment for middle school students; held on campus; accepts boys and girls; open to students from other schools. 150 students usually enrolled. 2013 schedule: July 12 to July 30.

Tuition and Aid Day student tuition: $18,300. Tuition installment plan (Insured Tuition Payment Plan). Need-based scholarship grants available. In 2012–13, 13% of upper-school students received aid. Total amount of financial aid awarded in 2012–13: $179,225.

Admissions Traditional secondary-level entrance grade is 9. ERB required. Deadline for receipt of application materials: none. Application fee required: $50. Interview required.

Athletics Interscholastic: alpine skiing (boys, girls), basketball (b,g), cross-country running (b,g), golf (b), skiing (downhill) (b,g), track and field (b,g), volleyball (g), wrestling (b,g); intramural: alpine skiing (b,g), basketball (b,g), cross-country running (b,g), golf (b,g), skiing (downhill) (b,g), swimming and diving (b,g), track and field (b,g), volleyball (g); coed intramural: bicycling, Frisbee, lacrosse, outdoor education, ropes courses, soccer. 2 PE instructors, 13 coaches.

Computers Computers are regularly used in art, classics, college planning, current events, English, foreign language, history, humanities, independent study, Latin, literary magazine, mathematics, newspaper, publications, SAT preparation, science, senior seminar, social sciences, social studies, Spanish, speech, word processing, writing, yearbook classes. Computer network features include on-campus library services, online commercial services, Internet access, wireless campus network, Internet filtering or blocking technology. Student e-mail accounts are available to students. Students grades are available online. The school has a published electronic and media policy.

Contact Mrs. Laurice Antoun-Becker, Director of Admission. 775-852-6222 Ext. 509. Fax: 775-852-6228. E-mail: LBecker@sageridge.org. Web site: www.sageridge.org

ST. AGNES ACADEMY

9000 Bellaire Boulevard
Houston, Texas 77036

Head of School: Sr. Jane Meyer

General Information Girls' day college-preparatory, arts, business, religious studies, and technology school, affiliated with Roman Catholic Church. Grades 9–12. Founded: 1906. Setting: urban. 33-acre campus. 3 buildings on campus. Approved or accredited by Southern Association of Colleges and Schools, Texas Catholic Conference, and Texas Department of Education. Endowment: $6 million. Total enrollment: 890. Upper school average class size: 22. Upper school faculty-student ratio: 1:15. There are 180 required school days per year for Upper School students. Upper School students typically attend 5 days per week. The average school day consists of 6 hours and 50 minutes.

Upper School Student Profile Grade 9: 239 students (239 girls); Grade 10: 238 students (238 girls); Grade 11: 210 students (210 girls); Grade 12: 203 students (203 girls). 78% of students are Roman Catholic.

Faculty School total: 80. In upper school: 18 men, 62 women; 51 have advanced degrees.

Subjects Offered Accounting, acting, algebra, American history, American literature, art, art history, biology, business law, business skills, calculus, chemistry, community service, computer programming, computer science, creative writing, dance, digital photography, drama, economics, English, English literature, European history, fine arts, French, geology, geometry, government/civics, health, history, integrated physics, journalism, keyboarding, Latin, marine biology, mathematics, music, philosophy, photography, physical education, physics, physiology, psychology, religion, science, social sciences, social studies, Spanish, speech, theater, theology, trigonometry, video film production, world history, world literature.

Graduation Requirements Advanced Placement courses, arts and fine arts (art, music, dance, drama), computer science, electives, English, foreign language, mathematics, physical education (includes health), religion (includes Bible studies and theology), science, social sciences, social studies (includes history), speech, 100 hours of community service.

Special Academic Programs Advanced Placement exam preparation; honors section; independent study.

College Admission Counseling 207 students graduated in 2012; all went to college, including Louisiana State University and Agricultural and Mechanical College; St. Edward's University; Texas A&M University; The University of Texas at Austin; The University of Texas at San Antonio. Mean SAT critical reading: 620, mean SAT math: 620, mean composite ACT: 26. 56% scored over 600 on SAT critical reading, 58% scored over 600 on SAT math, 50% scored over 26 on composite ACT.

Student Life Upper grades have uniform requirement, student council, honor system. Discipline rests primarily with faculty. Attendance at religious services is required.

Summer Programs Remediation, art/fine arts, computer instruction programs offered; session focuses on remediation and elective credit; held on campus; accepts girls; not open to students from other schools. 100 students usually enrolled. 2013 schedule: June to June.

Tuition and Aid Day student tuition: $14,400. Tuition installment plan (plans arranged through local bank). Merit scholarship grants, need-based scholarship grants available. In 2012–13, 30% of upper-school students received aid; total upper-school merit-scholarship money awarded: $24,000. Total amount of financial aid awarded in 2012–13: $800,000.

Admissions Traditional secondary-level entrance grade is 9. For fall 2012, 558 students applied for upper-level admission, 311 were accepted, 239 enrolled. High School Placement Test or ISEE required. Deadline for receipt of application materials: January 15. Application fee required: $75.

Athletics Interscholastic: aquatics, basketball, cheering, cross-country running, dance team, diving, field hockey, golf, lacrosse, soccer, softball, swimming and diving, tennis, track and field, volleyball, water polo, winter soccer; intramural: badminton, floor hockey, volleyball. 4 PE instructors, 6 coaches, 1 athletic trainer.

Computers Computers are regularly used in all classes. Computer network features include on-campus library services, online commercial services, Internet access, wireless campus network, Internet filtering or blocking technology. Campus intranet and student e-mail accounts are available to students. Students grades are available online. The school has a published electronic and media policy.

Contact Maddy Echols, Admissions Coordinator. 713-219-5400. Fax: 713-219-5499. E-mail: maddy.echols@st-agnes.org. Web site: www.st-agnes.org

SAINT AGNES BOYS HIGH SCHOOL

555 West End Avenue
New York, New York 10024

Head of School: Robert J. Conte

General Information Boys' day college-preparatory and religious studies school, affiliated with Roman Catholic Church. Grades 9–12. Founded: 1892. Setting: urban. 1 building on campus. Approved or accredited by Middle States Association of Colleges and Schools, New York State Board of Regents, New York State University, and New York Department of Education. Language of instruction: Spanish. Upper school average class size: 25. Upper school faculty-student ratio: 1:16. There are 180 required school days per year for Upper School students. Upper School students typically attend 5 days per week. The average school day consists of 6 hours and 6 minutes.

Upper School Student Profile Grade 9: 70 students (70 boys); Grade 10: 60 students (60 boys); Grade 11: 70 students (70 boys); Grade 12: 55 students (55 boys). 85% of students are Roman Catholic.

Faculty School total: 25. In upper school: 18 men, 7 women; 20 have advanced degrees.

Special Academic Programs 3 Advanced Placement exams for which test preparation is offered; honors section.

College Admission Counseling 71 students graduated in 2011; all went to college, including Binghamton University, State University of New York; Hunter College of the City University of New York; Manhattan College; St. John's University. Mean SAT critical reading: 450, mean SAT math: 450.

Student Life Upper grades have specified standards of dress. Discipline rests primarily with faculty. Attendance at religious services is required.

Tuition and Aid Day student tuition: $5350. Tuition installment plan (monthly payment plans). Need-based scholarship grants available. In 2011–12, 60% of upper-school students received aid.

Admissions Traditional secondary-level entrance grade is 9. For fall 2011, 390 students applied for upper-level admission, 280 were accepted, 70 enrolled. Cooperative Entrance Exam (McGraw-Hill) required. Deadline for receipt of application materials: none. No application fee required. Interview recommended.

Athletics Interscholastic: baseball, basketball, bowling, cross-country running, soccer; intramural: basketball, floor hockey, table tennis, volleyball. 1 PE instructor, 5 coaches.

Computers Computer network features include on-campus library services, Internet access. The school has a published electronic and media policy.

Contact Principal. 212-873-9100. Fax: 212-873-9292. Web site: www.staghs.org

ST. ALBANS SCHOOL

Mount Saint Alban
Washington, District of Columbia 20016

Head of School: Mr. Vance Wilson

General Information Boys' boarding and day college-preparatory school, affiliated with Episcopal Church. Boarding grades 9–12, day grades 4–12. Founded: 1909. Setting: urban. Students are housed in single-sex dormitories. 54-acre campus. 7 buildings on campus. Approved or accredited by Association of Independent Maryland Schools, Association of Independent Schools of Greater Washington, The Association of Boarding Schools, and District of Columbia Department of Education. Member of National Association of Independent Schools and Secondary School Admission Test Board. Endowment: $51.3 million. Total enrollment: 586. Upper school average class size: 13. Upper school faculty-student ratio: 1:7. There are 170 required school days per year for Upper School students. Upper School students typically attend 5 days per week.

Upper School Student Profile Grade 9: 85 students (85 boys); Grade 10: 79 students (79 boys); Grade 11: 79 students (79 boys); Grade 12: 79 students (79 boys). 9% of students are boarding students. 47% are state residents. 5 states are represented in upper school student body. 2% are international students. International students from Bulgaria, China, and United Kingdom. 20% of students are members of Episcopal Church.

Faculty School total: 80. In upper school: 49 men, 21 women; 45 have advanced degrees; 4 reside on campus.

Subjects Offered Advanced Placement courses, algebra, American history, American literature, Ancient Greek, art, art history, art history-AP, Bible studies, biology, biotechnology, calculus, ceramics, chemistry, Chinese, community service, computer math, computer programming, computer science, creative writing, dance, directing, drama, earth science, economics, engineering, English, English literature, ethics, European history, expository writing, filmmaking, fine arts, French, geography, geology, geometry, government/civics, Greek, history, Japanese, Latin, marine biology, mathematics, music, photography, physical education, physics, religion, science, sculpture, social studies, Spanish, speech, stagecraft, theater, zoology.

Graduation Requirements American history, ancient history, arts and fine arts (art, music, dance, drama), English, ethics, foreign language, mathematics, physical education (includes health), science, participation in athletic program. Community service is required.

Special Academic Programs Advanced Placement exam preparation; honors section; independent study; term-away projects; study abroad.

College Admission Counseling 76 students graduated in 2012; all went to college, including Dartmouth College; Georgetown University; Harvard University; University of Pennsylvania; Wake Forest University; Yale University.
Student Life Upper grades have specified standards of dress, student council, honor system. Discipline rests equally with students and faculty. Attendance at religious services is required.
Summer Programs Remediation, enrichment, advancement, ESL, sports, art/fine arts, rigorous outdoor training, computer instruction programs offered; session focuses on academics, day camp, and sports camps; held on campus; accepts boys and girls; open to students from other schools. 1,500 students usually enrolled. 2013 schedule: June 10 to August 23. Application deadline: none.
Tuition and Aid Day student tuition: $36,973; 7-day tuition and room/board: $52,301. Tuition installment plan (Insured Tuition Payment Plan, monthly payment plans, individually arranged payment plans). Need-based scholarship grants, need-based loans available. In 2012–13, 28% of upper-school students received aid. Total amount of financial aid awarded in 2012–13: $2,482,572.
Admissions Traditional secondary-level entrance grade is 9. For fall 2012, 138 students applied for upper-level admission, 61 were accepted, 35 enrolled. ISEE or SSAT required. Deadline for receipt of application materials: January 4. Application fee required: $80. Interview required.
Athletics Interscholastic: aquatics, baseball, basketball, canoeing/kayaking, climbing, crew, cross-country running, diving, football, golf, ice hockey, independent competitive sports, indoor soccer, indoor track, indoor track & field, kayaking, lacrosse, rappelling, rock climbing, soccer, swimming and diving, tennis, track and field, wall climbing, weight training, winter (indoor) track, winter soccer, wrestling; intramural: aquatics, basketball, combined training, dance, fitness, indoor soccer, outdoor activities, physical training, tennis, track and field, yoga. 5 coaches, 2 athletic trainers.
Computers Computers are regularly used in all academic, mathematics, programming, science classes. Computer network features include on-campus library services, online commercial services, Internet access, wireless campus network. Campus intranet and student e-mail accounts are available to students. The school has a published electronic and media policy.
Contact Mrs. Melissa Larocque, Admissions and Financial Aid Coordinator. 202-537-6440. Fax: 202-537-2225. E-mail: mlarocque@cathedral.org. Web site: www.stalbansschool.org/

SAINT ALBERT JUNIOR-SENIOR HIGH SCHOOL

400 Gleason Avenue
Council Bluffs, Iowa 51503

Head of School: Mr. David M. Schweitzer

General Information college-preparatory school, affiliated with Roman Catholic Church. Founded: 1963. Setting: urban. 5-acre campus. 1 building on campus. Approved or accredited by North Central Association of Colleges and Schools and Iowa Department of Education. Endowment: $1 million. Total enrollment: 752. Upper school average class size: 20. Upper school faculty-student ratio: 1:11. There are 190 required school days per year for Upper School students. Upper School students typically attend 5 days per week. The average school day consists of 7 hours.
Upper School Student Profile Grade 6: 50 students (30 boys, 20 girls); Grade 7: 70 students (34 boys, 36 girls); Grade 8: 48 students (17 boys, 31 girls); Grade 9: 55 students (24 boys, 31 girls); Grade 10: 56 students (34 boys, 22 girls); Grade 11: 62 students (42 boys, 20 girls); Grade 12: 43 students (24 boys, 19 girls). 90% of students are Roman Catholic.
Faculty School total: 32. In upper school: 13 men, 19 women; 21 have advanced degrees.
Graduation Requirements World religions.
Special Academic Programs 9 Advanced Placement exams for which test preparation is offered; study at local college for college credit; academic accommodation for the gifted; remedial reading and/or remedial writing; remedial math; special instructional classes for deaf students.
College Admission Counseling 46 students graduated in 2012; all went to college, including Iowa State University of Science and Technology; Northwest Missouri State University; University of Nebraska–Lincoln; University of Nebraska at Omaha; University of Northern Iowa. Median composite ACT: 22. 21.7% scored over 26 on composite ACT.
Student Life Upper grades have uniform requirement, student council. Discipline rests primarily with faculty. Attendance at religious services is required.
Tuition and Aid Day student tuition: $7200. Tuition installment plan (monthly payment plans, individually arranged payment plans). Tuition reduction for siblings, merit scholarship grants, need-based scholarship grants, paying campus jobs available. In 2012–13, 30% of upper-school students received aid; total upper-school merit-scholarship money awarded: $15,000. Total amount of financial aid awarded in 2012–13: $380,000.
Admissions Traditional secondary-level entrance grade is 9. For fall 2012, 15 students applied for upper-level admission, 15 were accepted, 15 enrolled. Deadline for receipt of application materials: none. No application fee required. Interview recommended.
Athletics Interscholastic: baseball (boys), basketball (b,g), bowling (b,g), cheering (g), cross-country running (b,g), dance (g), dance squad (g), dance team (g), football (b), golf (b,g), soccer (b,g), softball (g), swimming and diving (b,g), tennis (b,g), track and field (b,g), wrestling (b). 2 PE instructors, 53 coaches, 1 athletic trainer.
Computers Computer network features include Internet access, wireless campus network. Campus intranet and student e-mail accounts are available to students. Students grades are available online. The school has a published electronic and media policy.
Contact Ms. Abby Jares, Admissions Coordinator. 712-328-2316. Fax: 712-328-0228. E-mail: jaresa@saintalbertschools.org. Web site: www.saintalbertschools.org/

ST. ANDREW'S COLLEGE

15800 Yonge Street
Aurora, Ontario L4G 3H7, Canada

Head of School: Mr. Kevin R. McHenry

General Information Boys' boarding and day college-preparatory, arts, business, and technology school. Grades 5–12. Founded: 1899. Setting: small town. Nearest major city is Toronto, Canada. Students are housed in single-sex dormitories. 110-acre campus. 24 buildings on campus. Approved or accredited by Canadian Association of Independent Schools, Canadian Educational Standards Institute, Conference of Independent Schools of Ontario, Ontario Ministry of Education, The Association of Boarding Schools, and Ontario Department of Education. Affiliate member of National Association of Independent Schools; member of Secondary School Admission Test Board. Language of instruction: English. Endowment: CAN$23.3 million. Total enrollment: 614. Upper school average class size: 17. Upper school faculty-student ratio: 1:9. There are 158 required school days per year for Upper School students. Upper School students typically attend 5 days per week. The average school day consists of 5 hours and 20 minutes.
Upper School Student Profile Grade 9: 97 students (97 boys); Grade 10: 111 students (111 boys); Grade 11: 103 students (103 boys); Grade 12: 135 students (135 boys). 50% of students are boarding students. 73% are province residents. 6 provinces are represented in upper school student body. 27% are international students. International students from China, Hong Kong, Jamaica, Mexico, Republic of Korea, and Taiwan; 26 other countries represented in student body.
Faculty School total: 72. In upper school: 43 men, 9 women; 17 have advanced degrees; 23 reside on campus.
Subjects Offered Accounting, Advanced Placement courses, algebra, American history, art, biology, business, calculus, chemistry, communications, community service, computer science, creative writing, drama, economics, English, English literature, environmental science, fine arts, French, geography, geometry, health, history, mathematics, music, physical education, physics, physiology, science, social sciences, social studies, sociology, Spanish, statistics, world history, world religions.
Graduation Requirements Arts, arts and fine arts (art, music, dance, drama), business, careers, civics, computer science, dance, drama, English, foreign language, French, geography, health education, history, mathematics, physical education (includes health), science, science and technology, social sciences. Community service is required.
Special Academic Programs 10 Advanced Placement exams for which test preparation is offered; honors section; accelerated programs; independent study; term-away projects; study abroad; ESL (38 students enrolled).
College Admission Counseling 113 students graduated in 2012; all went to college, including Queen's University at Kingston; The University of British Columbia; The University of Western Ontario; University of Guelph; University of Toronto; Wilfrid Laurier University.
Student Life Upper grades have uniform requirement, student council, honor system. Discipline rests equally with students and faculty. Attendance at religious services is required.
Summer Programs ESL, sports, art/fine arts programs offered; session focuses on Scottish music (piping and drumming), sports/arts camps, leadership camps, academics; held on campus; accepts boys and girls; open to students from other schools. 1,200 students usually enrolled. 2013 schedule: June 20 to August 16. Application deadline: none.
Tuition and Aid Day student tuition: CAN$29,115; 5-day tuition and room/board: CAN$46,850; 7-day tuition and room/board: CAN$46,850. Tuition installment plan (monthly payment plans, one-time payment, three installments plan, Plastiq). Bursaries, merit scholarship grants, need-based scholarship grants available. In 2012–13, 26% of upper-school students received aid; total upper-school merit-scholarship money awarded: CAN$354,000. Total amount of financial aid awarded in 2012–13: CAN$1,897,830.
Admissions Traditional secondary-level entrance grade is 9. For fall 2012, 166 students applied for upper-level admission, 118 were accepted, 96 enrolled. CAT, SSAT or TOEFL or SLEP required. Deadline for receipt of application materials: none. Application fee required: CAN$150. Interview required.
Athletics Interscholastic: alpine skiing, aquatics, badminton, baseball, basketball, biathlon, cricket, cross-country running, curling, fencing, football, golf, ice hockey, indoor track, indoor track & field, lacrosse, marksmanship, nordic skiing, rugby, running, skiing (cross-country), skiing (downhill), soccer, softball, squash, swimming and diving, table tennis, tennis, track and field, triathlon, volleyball, winter (indoor) track; intramural: aquatics, archery, backpacking, badminton, ball hockey, baseball, basketball, canoeing/kayaking, climbing, cooperative games, cross-country running,

curling, fencing, fitness, flag football, floor hockey, football, Frisbee, golf, hiking/backpacking, ice hockey, ice skating, jogging, lacrosse, marksmanship, mountain biking, nordic skiing, outdoor activities, outdoor education, outdoor skills, physical fitness, rock climbing, ropes courses, running, scuba diving, self defense, skiing (cross-country), skiing (downhill), snowboarding, soccer, softball, squash, strength & conditioning, swimming and diving, table tennis, tennis, touch football, track and field, triathlon, ultimate Frisbee, volleyball, wall climbing, water polo, weight training, wilderness survival. 7 athletic trainers.

Computers Computers are regularly used in all academic classes. Computer network features include on-campus library services, online commercial services, Internet access, wireless campus network, Internet filtering or blocking technology. The school has a published electronic and media policy.

Contact Mrs. Natascia Stewart, Admission Associate. 905-727-3178 Ext. 303. Fax: 905-727-9032. E-mail: admission@sac.on.ca. Web site: www.sac.on.ca

ST. ANDREW'S EPISCOPAL SCHOOL

8804 Postoak Road
Potomac, Maryland 20854

Head of School: Mr. Robert Kosasky

General Information Coeducational day college-preparatory school, affiliated with Episcopal Church. Grades PS–12. Founded: 1978. Setting: suburban. Nearest major city is Washington, DC. 19-acre campus. 5 buildings on campus. Approved or accredited by Association of Independent Maryland Schools, Association of Independent Schools of Greater Washington, Middle States Association of Colleges and Schools, and National Association of Episcopal Schools. Member of National Association of Independent Schools and Secondary School Admission Test Board. Endowment: $6 million. Total enrollment: 506. Upper school average class size: 13. Upper school faculty-student ratio: 1:6. There are 172 required school days per year for Upper School students. Upper School students typically attend 5 days per week. The average school day consists of 6 hours and 40 minutes.

Upper School Student Profile Grade 9: 53 students (36 boys, 17 girls); Grade 10: 64 students (26 boys, 38 girls); Grade 11: 59 students (35 boys, 24 girls); Grade 12: 72 students (43 boys, 29 girls). 20% of students are members of Episcopal Church.

Faculty School total: 82. In upper school: 23 men, 28 women; 37 have advanced degrees.

Subjects Offered 20th century history, 3-dimensional art, 3-dimensional design, acting, Advanced Placement courses, advanced studio art-AP, algebra, American history, American literature, art, art history, art history-AP, art-AP, athletics, band, Bible, biology, biology-AP, British literature, calculus, calculus-AP, ceramics, chemistry, chorus, civics, college counseling, composition-AP, computer animation, computer art, computer graphics, computer science, creative writing, dance, digital photography, drama, dramatic arts, earth science, English, English literature, English literature and composition-AP, English-AP, ethics, European history, fine arts, French, French language-AP, French literature-AP, geography, geometry, global studies, government/civics, guitar, health, history, instrumental music, jazz band, journalism, Latin, Latin American studies, Latin-AP, mathematics, modern European history, music, musical theater, newspaper, orchestra, organic biochemistry, painting, photography, physical education, physical science, physics, physics-AP, pre-algebra, pre-calculus, public speaking, religion, robotics, science, service learning/internship, Spanish, Spanish language-AP, Spanish literature-AP, Spanish-AP, sports, stage design, statistics, student publications, studio art, studio art-AP, theater, theater design and production, theology, trigonometry, U.S. history, U.S. history-AP, video, visual and performing arts, vocal music, world cultures, world history, world religions, writing, yearbook.

Graduation Requirements English, foreign language, history, mathematics, performing arts, physical education (includes health), religion (includes Bible studies and theology), science, senior thesis, visual arts. Community service is required.

Special Academic Programs Advanced Placement exam preparation; independent study; special instructional classes for deaf students; ESL (4 students enrolled).

College Admission Counseling 68 students graduated in 2012; all went to college, including American University; Duke University; Franklin & Marshall College; University of Delaware; University of Maryland, College Park; Wake Forest University.

Student Life Upper grades have specified standards of dress, student council, honor system. Discipline rests primarily with faculty. Attendance at religious services is required.

Summer Programs Enrichment, advancement, sports, art/fine arts programs offered; session focuses on advancement and enrichment; held on campus; accepts boys and girls; open to students from other schools. 400 students usually enrolled. 2013 schedule: June 17 to August 2. Application deadline: none.

Tuition and Aid Day student tuition: $34,835. Tuition installment plan (FACTS Tuition Payment Plan, monthly payment plans). Need-based scholarship grants, Achiever Loans (Key Education Resources) available. In 2012–13, 22% of upper-school students received aid. Total amount of financial aid awarded in 2012–13: $2,193,800.

Admissions Traditional secondary-level entrance grade is 9. Comprehensive educational evaluation, ISEE or SSAT required. Deadline for receipt of application materials: January 15. Application fee required: $50. On-campus interview required.

Athletics Interscholastic: baseball (boys), basketball (b,g), cross-country running (b,g), lacrosse (b,g), soccer (b,g), softball (g), tennis (b,g), volleyball (g); coed interscholastic: equestrian sports, golf, track and field, wrestling; coed intramural: dance, fitness, physical fitness, weight training. 12 coaches, 1 athletic trainer.

Computers Computers are regularly used in English, foreign language, graphic arts, history, journalism, mathematics, music, science classes. Computer network features include on-campus library services, online commercial services, Internet access, wireless campus network, Internet filtering or blocking technology. Campus intranet and student e-mail accounts are available to students. Students grades are available online. The school has a published electronic and media policy.

Contact Mrs. Aileen Moodie, Associate Director of Admission and Admission Office Coordinator. 301-983-5200 Ext. 236. Fax: 301-983-4620. E-mail: admission@saes.org. Web site: www.saes.org

ST. ANDREW'S PRIORY SCHOOL

224 Queen Emma Square
Honolulu, Hawaii 96813

Head of School: Ms. Sandra J. Theunick

General Information Girls' day college-preparatory, arts, and technology school, affiliated with Episcopal Church. Grades K–12. Founded: 1867. Setting: urban. 3-acre campus. 7 buildings on campus. Approved or accredited by National Association of Episcopal Schools, The College Board, The Hawaii Council of Private Schools, Western Association of Schools and Colleges, and Hawaii Department of Education. Member of National Association of Independent Schools and Secondary School Admission Test Board. Endowment: $3.2 million. Total enrollment: 401. Upper school average class size: 12. Upper school faculty-student ratio: 1:8. There are 175 required school days per year for Upper School students. Upper School students typically attend 5 days per week. The average school day consists of 7 hours and 15 minutes.

Upper School Student Profile Grade 9: 26 students (26 girls); Grade 10: 32 students (32 girls); Grade 11: 40 students (40 girls); Grade 12: 25 students (25 girls). 15% of students are members of Episcopal Church.

Faculty School total: 55. In upper school: 13 men, 25 women; 27 have advanced degrees.

Subjects Offered Algebra, American government, American history, American literature, ancient history, applied arts, applied music, art, art history, Asian studies, Bible studies, biology, biology-AP, British literature, British literature-AP, calculus, calculus-AP, ceramics, chemistry, chemistry-AP, choir, college counseling, college placement, community service, competitive science projects, computer art, computer education, computer graphics, computer literacy, computer multimedia, computer programming, computer science, computer technology certification, creative writing, drama, economics, economics and history, English, English literature, English literature-AP, ESL, European history, expository writing, fine arts, French, geography, geometry, government/civics, grammar, guidance, handbells, Hawaiian history, Hawaiian language, health, history, honors U.S. history, humanities, Japanese, journalism, Latin, leadership, life skills, mathematics, mechanical drawing, medieval history, microbiology, modern world history, music, Pacific Island studies, photography, physical education, physics, physics-AP, physiology, Polynesian dance, pre-algebra, pre-calculus, psychology, religion, science, science research, social sciences, social studies, sociology, Spanish, Spanish-AP, speech, speech communications, theater, theology, trigonometry, U.S. history-AP, United States government-AP, video and animation, visual and performing arts, wind ensemble, women's studies, world civilizations, world history, world literature, world wide web design, writing workshop, yearbook.

Graduation Requirements Advanced Placement courses, arts and fine arts (art, music, dance, drama), computer science, English, foreign language, Hawaiian history, mathematics, physical education (includes health), religion (includes Bible studies and theology), science, science research, social sciences, social studies (includes history), speech, technological applications. Community service is required.

Special Academic Programs 8 Advanced Placement exams for which test preparation is offered; honors section; independent study; study at local college for college credit; academic accommodation for the musically talented and the artistically talented; ESL (10 students enrolled).

College Admission Counseling 41 students graduated in 2011; all went to college, including American University; Barnard College; The George Washington University; University of California, Berkeley; University of Hawaii at Manoa; Vassar College.

Student Life Upper grades have uniform requirement, student council, honor system. Discipline rests primarily with faculty. Attendance at religious services is required.

Tuition and Aid Day student tuition: $15,000. Tuition installment plan (SMART Tuition Payment Plan, monthly payment plans, individually arranged payment plans). Tuition reduction for siblings, merit scholarship grants, need-based scholarship grants, middle-income loans available. In 2011–12, 32% of upper-school students received aid; total upper-school merit-scholarship money awarded: $139,500. Total amount of financial aid awarded in 2011–12: $491,650.

Admissions Traditional secondary-level entrance grade is 9. PSAT or SAT for applicants to grade 11 and 12 or SSAT required. Deadline for receipt of application materials: none. Application fee required: $50. On-campus interview required.

Athletics Interscholastic: basketball, bowling, canoeing/kayaking, cheering, cross-country running, dance team, diving, drill team, golf, gymnastics, martial arts, ocean paddling, sailing, soccer, softball, swimming and diving, tennis, track and field, volleyball, water polo, wrestling; intramural: aerobics/dance, badminton, dance squad, drill team, fitness, flag football, jogging, outdoor activities, outdoor adventure, physical fitness, ropes courses, self defense, strength & conditioning, tai chi, weight training, windsurfing. 4 PE instructors, 18 coaches.

Computers Computers are regularly used in animation, art, college planning, English, ESL, foreign language, graphic design, history, humanities, independent study, library, literary magazine, mathematics, media arts, music, newspaper, photojournalism, psychology, religion, science, speech, technology, writing, yearbook classes. Computer network features include on-campus library services, online commercial services, Internet access, wireless campus network, Internet filtering or blocking technology. Campus intranet and student e-mail accounts are available to students. Students grades are available online. The school has a published electronic and media policy.

Contact Ms. Sue Ann Wargo, Director of Admissions. 808-532-2418. Fax: 808-531-8426. E-mail: sawargo@priory.net. Web site: www.priory.net

ST. ANDREW'S REGIONAL HIGH SCHOOL

880 Mckenzie Avenue
Victoria, British Columbia V8X 3G5, Canada

Head of School: Mr. Andrew Keleher

General Information Coeducational day college-preparatory, general academic, and religious studies school, affiliated with Roman Catholic Church. Grades 8–12. Founded: 1983. Setting: urban. 2-acre campus. 1 building on campus. Approved or accredited by British Columbia Department of Education. Language of instruction: English. Upper school average class size: 24. Upper school faculty-student ratio: 1:14. There are 178 required school days per year for Upper School students. Upper School students typically attend 5 days per week. The average school day consists of 5 hours.

Upper School Student Profile 65% of students are Roman Catholic.

Faculty School total: 34. In upper school: 16 men, 15 women; 11 have advanced degrees.

Subjects Offered Religious education, yoga.

Graduation Requirements Religious studies.

Special Academic Programs Honors section.

College Admission Counseling 103 students graduated in 2011. Other: 10 went to work, 90 entered a postgraduate year, 3 had other specific plans.

Student Life Upper grades have uniform requirement, student council, honor system. Discipline rests primarily with faculty. Attendance at religious services is required.

Tuition and Aid Tuition reduction for siblings, bursaries available.

Admissions Deadline for receipt of application materials: February 28. Application fee required: CAN$50. Interview required.

Athletics Interscholastic: badminton (boys, girls), basketball (b,g), bicycling (b,g), cross-country running (b,g); intramural: basketball (b,g); coed interscholastic: aquatics; coed intramural: dance team, floor hockey, indoor soccer.

Computers Computers are regularly used in business education, career education, computer applications, digital applications, photography classes. Computer resources include on-campus library services, Internet access, Internet filtering or blocking technology. The school has a published electronic and media policy.

Contact Diane Chimich, Vice Principal. 250-479-1414. Fax: 250-479-5356. E-mail: dchimich@cisdv.bc.ca. Web site: www.standrewshigh.ca/

ST. ANDREW'S SCHOOL

350 Noxontown Road
Middletown, Delaware 19709

Head of School: Daniel T. Roach

General Information Coeducational boarding college-preparatory, arts, and religious studies school, affiliated with Episcopal Church. Grades 9–12. Founded: 1929. Setting: small town. Nearest major city is Wilmington. Students are housed in single-sex dormitories. 2,200-acre campus. 16 buildings on campus. Approved or accredited by Middle States Association of Colleges and Schools, National Association of Episcopal Schools, The Association of Boarding Schools, The College Board, and Delaware Department of Education. Member of National Association of Independent Schools and Secondary School Admission Test Board. Endowment: $170 million. Total enrollment: 297. Upper school average class size: 11. Upper school faculty-student ratio: 1:5.

Upper School Student Profile Grade 9: 65 students (33 boys, 32 girls); Grade 10: 72 students (38 boys, 34 girls); Grade 11: 77 students (42 boys, 35 girls); Grade 12: 83 students (43 boys, 40 girls). 100% of students are boarding students. 12% are state residents. 26 states are represented in upper school student body. 14% are international students. International students from Bermuda, China, India, Italy, Republic of Korea, and Viet Nam; 8 other countries represented in student body. 30% of students are members of Episcopal Church.

Faculty School total: 60. In upper school: 35 men, 25 women; 52 have advanced degrees.

Subjects Offered 20th century world history, acting, advanced chemistry, advanced math, algebra, American history, American literature, art, art history, art history-AP, Asian history, biology, calculus, calculus-AP, ceramics, chemistry, Chinese, choir, choral music, college counseling, comparative religion, computer literacy, computer programming, concert choir, creative writing, digital music, drama, drawing, driver education, East Asian history, English, English literature, English literature-AP, environmental science, ethics, European history, European history-AP, film, film studies, fine arts, French, French literature-AP, geometry, Greek, history, honors geometry, improvisation, Islamic history, Latin, Latin-AP, mathematics, Middle Eastern history, modern European history, music, music theory, organic chemistry, painting, philosophy, photography, physics, physics-AP, poetry, pottery, psychology, religion, religious studies, science, science research, Spanish, Spanish literature-AP, speech, statistics-AP, theater, trigonometry, U.S. history, Western religions.

Graduation Requirements Arts and fine arts (art, music, dance, drama), English, foreign language, history, mathematics, religion (includes Bible studies and theology), science.

Special Academic Programs Honors section; independent study; academic accommodation for the gifted, the musically talented, and the artistically talented.

College Admission Counseling 68 students graduated in 2011; all went to college, including Davidson College; University of Delaware; University of Virginia; Vassar College; Williams College. Mean SAT critical reading: 629, mean SAT math: 651, mean SAT writing: 625.

Student Life Upper grades have specified standards of dress, student council, honor system. Discipline rests equally with students and faculty. Attendance at religious services is required.

Tuition and Aid 7-day tuition and room/board: $47,000. Tuition installment plan (Key Tuition Payment Plan, monthly payment plans). Need-based scholarship grants available. In 2011–12, 46% of upper-school students received aid. Total amount of financial aid awarded in 2011–12: $4,950,000.

Admissions Traditional secondary-level entrance grade is 9. For fall 2011, 450 students applied for upper-level admission, 125 were accepted, 77 enrolled. ISEE, SSAT or TOEFL required. Deadline for receipt of application materials: January 15. Application fee required: $50. On-campus interview required.

Athletics Interscholastic: aquatics (boys, girls), baseball (b), basketball (b,g), crew (b,g), cross-country running (b,g), field hockey (g), football (b), lacrosse (b,g), rowing (b,g), soccer (b,g), squash (b,g), swimming and diving (b,g), tennis (b,g), volleyball (g), wrestling (b); coed intramural: aerobics, aerobics/dance, canoeing/kayaking, dance, fencing, fishing, fitness, Frisbee, indoor soccer, kayaking, outdoors, paddle tennis, physical training, rowing, sailboarding, sailing, weight lifting, weight training, windsurfing, yoga. 1 athletic trainer.

Computers Computers are regularly used in English, foreign language, history, mathematics, science classes. Computer network features include on-campus library services, online commercial services, Internet access, Internet filtering or blocking technology. Campus intranet, student e-mail accounts, and computer access in designated common areas are available to students. The school has a published electronic and media policy.

Contact Louisa H. Zendt, Director of Admission. 302-285-4230. Fax: 302-378-7120. E-mail: lzendt@standrews-de.org. Web site: www.standrews-de.org

ST. ANDREW'S SCHOOL

63 Federal Road
Barrington, Rhode Island 02806

Head of School: Mr. John D. Martin

General Information Coeducational boarding and day college-preparatory and arts school. Boarding grades 9–12, day grades 3–12. Founded: 1893. Setting: suburban. Nearest major city is Providence. Students are housed in single-sex dormitories. 100-acre campus. 33 buildings on campus. Approved or accredited by Massachusetts Department of Education, National Association of Episcopal Schools, New England Association of Schools and Colleges, Rhode Island State Certified Resource Progam, The Association of Boarding Schools, and Rhode Island Department of Education. Member of National Association of Independent Schools and Secondary School Admission Test Board. Endowment: $15.2 million. Total enrollment: 215. Upper school average class size: 12. Upper school faculty-student ratio: 1:5. There are 150 required school days per year for Upper School students. Upper School students typically attend 5 days per week. The average school day consists of 8 hours.

Upper School Student Profile Grade 9: 35 students (19 boys, 16 girls); Grade 10: 47 students (30 boys, 17 girls); Grade 11: 51 students (33 boys, 18 girls); Grade 12: 45 students (30 boys, 15 girls); Postgraduate: 3 students (3 boys). 38% of students are boarding students. 54% are state residents. 11 states are represented in upper school student body. 25% are international students. International students from China, India, Kenya, Republic of Korea, Taiwan, and Turkey; 2 other countries represented in student body.

Faculty School total: 44. In upper school: 16 men, 28 women; 31 have advanced degrees; 22 reside on campus.

Subjects Offered Advanced biology, Advanced Placement courses, algebra, American history, ancient history, art, astronomy, biology, calculus, calculus-AP, ceramics, chemistry, chorus, college counseling, computer applications, creative writing, digital applications, digital photography, drawing, English, environmental science, ESL, European history, French, geometry, honors world history, human anatomy, humanities, jewelry making, lab science, music history, music theory, music theory-AP, oceanography, oral communications, physical education, physics, physics-

AP, pre-calculus, printmaking, probability and statistics, remedial study skills, SAT preparation, Spanish, statistics-AP, studio art, study skills, technical theater, theater, TOEFL preparation, trigonometry, water color painting, yearbook.

Graduation Requirements Arts and fine arts (art, music, dance, drama), English, mathematics, physical education (includes health), science, social studies (includes history), community service.

Special Academic Programs Advanced Placement exam preparation; honors section; independent study; remedial reading and/or remedial writing; programs in English for dyslexic students; special instructional classes for students with mild language-based learning disabilities, students with attention/organizational issues (ADHD); ESL (28 students enrolled).

College Admission Counseling 40 students graduated in 2012; 38 went to college, including Brown University; Dartmouth College; Lehigh University; Skidmore College; University of California, Davis; University of Rochester. Other: 1 went to work, 1 entered military service. Median SAT critical reading: 480, median SAT math: 540, median SAT writing: 490, median combined SAT: 1510. 6% scored over 600 on SAT critical reading, 47% scored over 600 on SAT math, 13% scored over 600 on SAT writing, 13% scored over 1800 on combined SAT.

Student Life Upper grades have specified standards of dress, student council. Discipline rests primarily with faculty.

Summer Programs Remediation, enrichment, advancement, ESL, sports, art/fine arts, rigorous outdoor training, computer instruction programs offered; session focuses on skills development; held on campus; accepts boys and girls; open to students from other schools. 1,200 students usually enrolled. 2013 schedule: June 25 to August 16. Application deadline: June 15.

Tuition and Aid Day student tuition: $31,400; 7-day tuition and room/board: $47,000. Tuition installment plan (Key Tuition Payment Plan). Need-based scholarship grants, need-based loans available. In 2012–13, 53% of upper-school students received aid. Total amount of financial aid awarded in 2012–13: $2,125,550.

Admissions Traditional secondary-level entrance grade is 9. For fall 2012, 261 students applied for upper-level admission, 110 were accepted, 56 enrolled. Any standardized test required. Deadline for receipt of application materials: January 15. Application fee required: $50. Interview required.

Athletics Interscholastic: basketball (boys, girls), cross-country running (b,g), golf (b), lacrosse (b,g), soccer (b,g), tennis (b,g); coed interscholastic: soccer; coed intramural: badminton, ball hockey, basketball, bicycling, billiards, bocce, cooperative games, croquet, dance, fitness, fitness walking, flag football, floor hockey, Frisbee, horseshoes, jogging, physical fitness, project adventure, ropes courses, running, soccer, strength & conditioning, tennis, touch football, ultimate Frisbee, walking, weight lifting, weight training, yoga. 1 PE instructor, 20 coaches, 1 athletic trainer.

Computers Computers are regularly used in all academic, computer applications, library skills, multimedia, photography, SAT preparation, yearbook classes. Computer network features include on-campus library services, Internet access, wireless campus network, Internet filtering or blocking technology, NetClassroom is available for parents and students. Campus intranet, student e-mail accounts, and computer access in designated common areas are available to students. Students grades are available online. The school has a published electronic and media policy.

Contact Mary Bishop, Administrative Assistant to Admissions. 401-246-1230 Ext. 3025. Fax: 401-246-0510. E-mail: mbishop@standrews-ri.org. Web site: www.standrews-ri.org

See Display below and Close-Up on page 620.

ST. ANDREW'S–SEWANEE SCHOOL

290 Quintard Road
Sewanee, Tennessee 37375-3000

Head of School: Rev. John T. Thomas

General Information Coeducational boarding and day college-preparatory, arts, and science school, affiliated with Episcopal Church. Boarding grades 9–12, day grades 6–12. Founded: 1868. Setting: small town. Nearest major city is Chattanooga. Students are housed in single-sex dormitories. 550-acre campus. 19 buildings on campus. Approved or accredited by National Association of Episcopal Schools, Southern Association of Colleges and Schools, Southern Association of Independent Schools, The Association of Boarding Schools, and Tennessee Department of Education. Member of National Association of Independent Schools and Secondary School Admission Test Board. Endowment: $11 million. Total enrollment: 248. Upper school average class size: 13. Upper school faculty-student ratio: 1:4. There are 168 required school days per year for Upper School students. Upper School students typically attend 5 days per week. The average school day consists of 4 hours and 30 minutes.

Upper School Student Profile Grade 9: 38 students (17 boys, 21 girls); Grade 10: 44 students (31 boys, 13 girls); Grade 11: 59 students (16 boys, 43 girls); Grade 12: 45 students (27 boys, 18 girls). 44% of students are boarding students. 72% are state residents. 14 states are represented in upper school student body. 16% are international students. International students from China, Costa Rica, Denmark, Germany, Republic of Korea, and Taiwan; 10 other countries represented in student body. 33% of students are members of Episcopal Church.

Faculty School total: 39. In upper school: 13 men, 23 women; 24 have advanced degrees; 26 reside on campus.

Subjects Offered 20th century history, acting, adolescent issues, advanced biology, advanced chemistry, advanced TOEFL/grammar, aerobics, African history, African-American literature, algebra, American history, American literature, American studies, art, Asian history, band, biology, British literature, British literature (honors), calculus, chamber groups, chemistry, Chinese, choir, college counseling, community service, comparative religion, creative writing, drama, dramatic arts, ecology, English, English literature, environmental systems, ESL, European literature, filmmaking, fine arts, general science, geometry, history, humanities, Latin, Latin American literature, leadership, literature, mathematics, minority studies, music, philosophy, physical education, physics, poetry, pottery, pre-algebra, psychology, religion, religious studies, science, social studies, Southern literature, Spanish, statistics, theater, trigonometry, world history, yearbook.

Graduation Requirements Arts and fine arts (art, music, dance, drama), English, foreign language, mathematics, physical education (includes health), religion (includes Bible studies and theology), science, social studies (includes history), senior lecture series, creedal statement. Community service is required.

Special Academic Programs Advanced Placement exam preparation; independent study; term-away projects; study at local college for college credit; study abroad; academic accommodation for the gifted, the musically talented, and the artistically talented; remedial reading and/or remedial writing; remedial math; ESL (16 students enrolled).

College Admission Counseling 46 students graduated in 2012; 42 went to college, including Northeastern University; Sewanee: The University of the South. Other: 4 went to work.

Student Life Upper grades have specified standards of dress, student council, honor system. Discipline rests equally with students and faculty. Attendance at religious services is required.

Summer Programs Sports, art/fine arts programs offered; session focuses on sports, outdoor adventure, art; held both on and off campus; held at surrounding natural areas; accepts boys and girls; open to students from other schools. 140 students usually enrolled. 2013 schedule: May 20 to July 22. Application deadline: none.

Tuition and Aid Day student tuition: $16,500; 7-day tuition and room/board: $40,000. Tuition installment plan (monthly payment plans). Merit scholarship grants, need-based scholarship grants available. In 2012–13, 48% of upper-school students received aid; total upper-school merit-scholarship money awarded: $148,000. Total amount of financial aid awarded in 2012–13: $1,365,590.

Admissions Traditional secondary-level entrance grade is 9. For fall 2012, 118 students applied for upper-level admission, 68 were accepted, 48 enrolled. SLEP, TOEFL or writing sample required. Deadline for receipt of application materials: none. Application fee required: $50. Interview required.

Athletics Interscholastic: baseball (boys), basketball (b,g), cross-country running (b,g), football (b), soccer (b,g), softball (g), swimming and diving (b,g), tennis (b,g), track and field (b,g), volleyball (g), wrestling (b,g); intramural: ballet (g); coed interscholastic: bicycling, cross-country running, golf, mountain biking, ultimate Frisbee; coed intramural: aerobics, aerobics/dance, backpacking, bicycling, billiards, canoeing/kayaking, climbing, combined training, dance, dance team, fishing, fitness, fly fishing, hiking/backpacking, independent competitive sports, kayaking, modern dance, mountain biking, mountaineering, outdoor activities, outdoor adventure, outdoor education, outdoor recreation, outdoor skills, outdoors, paint ball, physical fitness, physical training, rafting, rappelling, rock climbing, ropes courses, running, soccer, strength & conditioning, table tennis, tennis, touch football, triathlon, walking, wall climbing, weight training, wilderness, wilderness survival, yoga. 8 coaches.

Computers Computers are regularly used in all academic, art, college planning, creative writing, design, desktop publishing, digital applications, English, foreign language, graphic arts, graphic design, history, humanities, introduction to technology, Latin, literary magazine, mathematics, religion, SAT preparation, science, Spanish, yearbook classes. Computer network features include on-campus library services, online commercial services, Internet access, wireless campus network, Internet filtering or blocking technology, access to University of the South technology facilities. Student e-mail accounts and computer access in designated common areas are available to students. Students grades are available online.

Contact Ms. Anne Chenoweth, Director of Admission and Financial Aid. 931-598-5651 Ext. 2117. Fax: 931-914-1222. E-mail: admission@sasweb.org. Web site: www.sasweb.org

ST. ANNE'S–BELFIELD SCHOOL

2132 Ivy Road
Charlottesville, Virginia 22903

Head of School: Mr. David S. Lourie

General Information Coeducational boarding and day college-preparatory, arts, religious studies, and ESL school, affiliated with Christian faith. Boarding grades 9–12, day grades PK–12. Founded: 1910. Setting: small town. Nearest major city is Washington, DC. Students are housed in coed dormitories. 49-acre campus. 6 buildings on campus. Approved or accredited by The Association of Boarding Schools and Virginia Association of Independent Schools. Member of National Association of Independent Schools and Secondary School Admission Test Board. Endowment: $25 million. Total enrollment: 869. Upper school average class size: 12. Upper school faculty-student ratio: 1:8. There are 180 required school days per year for Upper School students. Upper School students typically attend 5 days per week. The average school day consists of 7 hours and 30 minutes.

Upper School Student Profile Grade 9: 94 students (49 boys, 45 girls); Grade 10: 86 students (42 boys, 44 girls); Grade 11: 78 students (34 boys, 44 girls); Grade 12: 88 students (49 boys, 39 girls). 18% of students are boarding students. 87% are state residents. 7 states are represented in upper school student body. 9% are international students. International students from Azerbaijan, China, Ethiopia, Republic of Korea, Saint Kitts and Nevis, and South Africa; 22 other countries represented in student body.

Faculty School total: 111. In upper school: 16 men, 25 women; 35 have advanced degrees; 7 reside on campus.

Subjects Offered 1968, algebra, art, biology, biology-AP, calculus-AP, ceramics, chemistry, chemistry-AP, choir, conceptual physics, drama, economics, English, environmental science-AP, ESL, French, French language-AP, geometry, honors algebra, honors geometry, humanities, Latin, Latin-AP, modern European history-AP, modern world history, music theory, music theory-AP, orchestra, photography, physics, physics-AP, pre-calculus, religion, sculpture, Spanish, Spanish language-AP, statistics, statistics-AP, theology, trigonometry, U.S. history, U.S. history-AP, video, world history, writing workshop.

Graduation Requirements Art, English, foreign language, history, mathematics, physical education (includes health), religion (includes Bible studies and theology), science. Community service is required.

Special Academic Programs 14 Advanced Placement exams for which test preparation is offered; honors section; independent study; study at local college for college credit; ESL (12 students enrolled).

College Admission Counseling Colleges students went to include James Madison University; Lynchburg College; The College of William and Mary; University of Mary Washington; University of Virginia; Virginia Commonwealth University. Other: 1 had other specific plans. Median SAT critical reading: 630, median SAT math: 620. Mean SAT writing: 622. 59% scored over 600 on SAT critical reading, 57% scored over 600 on SAT math, 68% scored over 600 on SAT writing, 72% scored over 1800 on combined SAT.

Student Life Upper grades have uniform requirement, student council, honor system. Discipline rests primarily with faculty. Attendance at religious services is required.

Summer Programs Remediation, enrichment, ESL, sports programs offered; session focuses on academic enrichment and remediation through 8th grade, ESL Summer Program; held on campus; accepts boys and girls; open to students from other schools. 350 students usually enrolled. 2013 schedule: June 15 to July 31. Application deadline: none.

Tuition and Aid Day student tuition: $22,000; 5-day tuition and room/board: $36,200; 7-day tuition and room/board: $46,000. Tuition installment plan (Insured Tuition Payment Plan, FACTS Tuition Payment Plan, monthly payment plans). Need-based scholarship grants, need-based financial aid available. In 2012–13, 38% of upper-school students received aid. Total amount of financial aid awarded in 2012–13: $4,500,000.

Admissions Traditional secondary-level entrance grade is 9. For fall 2012, 104 students applied for upper-level admission, 60 were accepted, 45 enrolled. ERB verbal, ERB math, SSAT, TOEFL or writing sample required. Deadline for receipt of application materials: February 15. Application fee required: $30. Interview required.

Athletics Interscholastic: baseball (boys), basketball (b,g), cross-country running (b,g), field hockey (g), football (b), golf (b,g), lacrosse (b,g), soccer (b,g), softball (g), squash (b,g), swimming and diving (b,g), tennis (b,g), track and field (b,g), volleyball (g), wrestling (b); coed interscholastic: cross-country running, golf, squash, swimming and diving, track and field; coed intramural: aerobics, aerobics/dance, alpine skiing, dance, fitness, physical fitness, yoga. 6 PE instructors, 8 coaches, 2 athletic trainers.

Computers Computers are regularly used in all academic classes. Computer network features include on-campus library services, online commercial services, Internet access, wireless campus network. Student e-mail accounts and computer access in designated common areas are available to students. Students grades are available online. The school has a published electronic and media policy.

Contact Mrs. Kai'li Millner, Assistant Director of Admission for Grades 5-12. 434-296-5106. Fax: 434-979-1486. E-mail: kmillner@stab.org. Web site: www.stab.org

ST. ANTHONY CATHOLIC HIGH SCHOOL

3200 McCullough Avenue
San Antonio, Texas 78212-3099

Head of School: Mr. Rene Escobedo

General Information Coeducational boarding and day and distance learning college-preparatory, arts, religious studies, technology, AP Dual Credit, and college course credit school, affiliated with Roman Catholic Church. Grades 9–12. Distance learning grades 9–12. Founded: 1903. Setting: urban. Students are housed in single-sex by floor dormitories. 14-acre campus. 5 buildings on campus. Approved or accredited by National Catholic Education Association, Southern Association of Colleges and Schools, Texas Catholic Conference, The College Board, and Texas Department of Education. Total enrollment: 391. Upper school average class size: 19. Upper school faculty-student ratio: 1:12. There are 180 required school days per year for Upper School students. Upper School students typically attend 5 days per week. The average school day consists of 7 hours.

Upper School Student Profile Grade 9: 96 students (59 boys, 37 girls); Grade 10: 93 students (50 boys, 43 girls); Grade 11: 108 students (65 boys, 43 girls); Grade 12: 94 students (55 boys, 39 girls). 4% of students are boarding students. 89% are state residents. 1 state is represented in upper school student body. 11% are international students. International students from China, Japan, Mexico, Republic of Korea, Spain, and

Viet Nam; 1 other country represented in student body. 85% of students are Roman Catholic.

Faculty School total: 35. In upper school: 19 men, 16 women; 19 have advanced degrees.

Subjects Offered Advanced biology, advanced chemistry, advanced math, Advanced Placement courses, algebra, anatomy and physiology, art, athletics, band, Bible studies, biology, calculus, Catholic belief and practice, chemistry, choir, computer graphics, computer literacy, dance, drama, economics, English, English language and composition-AP, English literature, English literature and composition-AP, environmental science, ESL, film appreciation, geology, geometry, government, graphic arts, graphic design, health, history, history of the Catholic Church, honors algebra, Japanese, jazz band, keyboarding, Latin, mathematical modeling, media literacy, moral theology, photography, photojournalism, physical education, physics, pre-calculus, psychology, sexuality, sociology, Spanish, Spanish-AP, speech, theater, theater arts, theology, trigonometry, U.S. government, U.S. history, U.S. history-AP, world history, world history-AP, world religions, writing, yearbook.

Graduation Requirements Arts and fine arts (art, music, dance, drama), computer applications, economics, English, foreign language, government, health, mathematics, physical education (includes health), religion (includes Bible studies and theology), science, speech, U.S. history, world history.

Special Academic Programs Advanced Placement exam preparation; honors section; independent study; study at local college for college credit; study abroad; academic accommodation for the gifted; ESL (34 students enrolled).

College Admission Counseling 109 students graduated in 2012; all went to college, including San Antonio College; St. Mary's University; Texas A&M University; The University of Texas at San Antonio; University of the Incarnate Word. 8.3% scored over 600 on SAT critical reading, 15.6% scored over 600 on SAT math, 5.5% scored over 600 on SAT writing, 5.5% scored over 1800 on combined SAT, 4.6% scored over 26 on composite ACT.

Student Life Upper grades have uniform requirement, student council, honor system. Discipline rests primarily with faculty. Attendance at religious services is required.

Summer Programs Remediation, enrichment, advancement, sports, art/fine arts, computer instruction programs offered; session focuses on enrichment/advancement; held both on and off campus; held at Incarnate Word High School; accepts boys and girls; open to students from other schools. 200 students usually enrolled. 2013 schedule: June 1 to June 29. Application deadline: May 30.

Tuition and Aid Day student tuition: $8575; 7-day tuition and room/board: $19,000. Tuition installment plan (monthly payment plans). Tuition reduction for siblings, merit scholarship grants, need-based scholarship grants available. In 2012–13, 37% of upper-school students received aid; total upper-school merit-scholarship money awarded: $50,000. Total amount of financial aid awarded in 2012–13: $175,000.

Admissions Traditional secondary-level entrance grade is 9. For fall 2012, 422 students applied for upper-level admission, 402 were accepted, 391 enrolled. High School Placement Test required. Deadline for receipt of application materials: none. No application fee required. Interview required.

Athletics Interscholastic: baseball (boys), basketball (b,g), cross-country running (b,g), dance team (g), football (b), lacrosse (b), soccer (b,g), softball (g), swimming and diving (b,g), tennis (b,g), track and field (b,g), volleyball (g); coed interscholastic: cheering, golf. 2 PE instructors, 32 coaches, 1 athletic trainer.

Computers Computers are regularly used in all academic classes. Computer network features include on-campus library services, Internet access, wireless campus network, Internet filtering or blocking technology. Student e-mail accounts are available to students. Students grades are available online. The school has a published electronic and media policy.

Contact Mr. Alejandro Calderon, Director of Enrollment. 210-832-5632. Fax: 210-832-5633. E-mail: sachs@uiwtx.edu. Web site: www.sachs.org

SAINT ANTHONY HIGH SCHOOL

620 Olive Avenue
Long Beach, California 90802

Head of School: Mr. Mike Schabert

General Information Coeducational day college-preparatory, arts, business, religious studies, technology, Marine Science Academy, and Theatre Arts Program school, affiliated with Roman Catholic Church. Grades 9–12. Founded: 1920. Setting: urban. 15-acre campus. 5 buildings on campus. Approved or accredited by National Catholic Education Association, Western Association of Schools and Colleges, Western Catholic Education Association, and California Department of Education. Total enrollment: 480. Upper school average class size: 25. Upper school faculty-student ratio: 1:19. There are 180 required school days per year for Upper School students. Upper School students typically attend 5 days per week. The average school day consists of 7 hours and 15 minutes.

Upper School Student Profile 80% of students are Roman Catholic.

Faculty School total: 25. In upper school: 13 men, 12 women; 23 have advanced degrees.

Subjects Offered ACT preparation, acting, Advanced Placement courses, algebra, American history, American history-AP, American literature-AP, anatomy, anatomy and physiology, art, ASB Leadership, athletics, band, Bible studies, biology, biology-AP, British literature, calculus, calculus-AP, campus ministry, career and personal planning, career/college preparation, Catholic belief and practice, ceramics, cheerleading, chemistry, chemistry-AP, choir, Christian doctrine, Christian ethics, Christian scripture, Christian studies, Christian testament, Christianity, church history, civics, college admission preparation, college awareness, college counseling, college planning, college writing, comparative religion, computer resources, computer technologies, constitutional history of U.S., drama, economics, economics-AP, English, English language and composition-AP, English language-AP, English literature, English literature and composition-AP, English literature-AP, English-AP, environmental science, environmental science-AP, ethics, fine arts, geometry, government, government-AP, government/civics, health, health education, history, honors English, honors geometry, honors U.S. history, honors world history, integrated technology fundamentals, jazz band, leadership, leadership and service, Life of Christ, literature and composition-AP, macroeconomics-AP, marching band, marine biology, marine science, mathematics, mathematics-AP, music, music appreciation, musical productions, New Testament, peace and justice, physical education, physics, physics-AP, play production, prayer/spirituality, pre-algebra, pre-calculus, religion, religious education, religious studies, SAT/ACT preparation, science, social justice, social sciences, social studies, Spanish, Spanish language-AP, Spanish-AP, student government, theater, U.S. government, U.S. government and politics, U.S. government and politics-AP, U.S. history, U.S. history-AP, world history, world history-AP, world religions, yearbook.

Graduation Requirements Arts and fine arts (art, music, dance, drama), English, foreign language, mathematics, physical education (includes health), religion (includes Bible studies and theology), science, social sciences, social studies (includes history), Christian service hours. Community service is required.

Special Academic Programs Advanced Placement exam preparation; honors section; academic accommodation for the gifted and the artistically talented; remedial reading and/or remedial writing; remedial math.

College Admission Counseling 59 students graduated in 2012; 58 went to college, including California State University, Dominguez Hills; California State University, Long Beach; Loyola Marymount University; University of California, Irvine; University of California, Los Angeles; University of California, San Diego. Other: 1 entered military service. Mean SAT critical reading: 471, mean SAT math: 445, mean SAT writing: 451, mean combined SAT: 1367. 7% scored over 600 on SAT critical reading, 5% scored over 600 on SAT math, 4% scored over 600 on SAT writing, 4% scored over 1800 on combined SAT.

Student Life Upper grades have uniform requirement, student council, honor system. Discipline rests primarily with faculty. Attendance at religious services is required.

Summer Programs Remediation, enrichment, sports programs offered; session focuses on remediation/make-up; held both on and off campus; held at Clark Field; accepts boys and girls; open to students from other schools.

Tuition and Aid Day student tuition: $6400. Tuition installment plan (SMART Tuition Payment Plan, monthly payment plans, individually arranged payment plans). Tuition reduction for siblings, merit scholarship grants, need-based scholarship grants, Catholic Education Foundation (CEF) assistance available. In 2012–13, 55% of upper-school students received aid.

Admissions Traditional secondary-level entrance grade is 9. For fall 2012, 250 students applied for upper-level admission, 130 enrolled. High School Placement Test required. Deadline for receipt of application materials: none. Application fee required: $50. On-campus interview required.

Athletics Interscholastic: baseball (boys), basketball (b,g), cheering (g), cross-country running (b,g), dance squad (g), diving (b,g), football (b), independent competitive sports (b,g), running (b,g), soccer (b,g), softball (g), strength & conditioning (b,g), track and field (b,g), volleyball (b,g), weight training (b,g); coed interscholastic: aquatics, cheering; coed intramural: fitness, golf, physical fitness, roller blading, roller hockey, running, tennis. 31 coaches, 1 athletic trainer.

Computers Computers are regularly used in aerospace science, all academic, aviation, basic skills, Bible studies, business, career education, Christian doctrine, college planning, creative writing, current events, design, drawing and design, economics, English, foreign language, graphic arts, graphic design, graphics, historical foundations for arts, history, journalism, keyboarding, library, mathematics, media, media arts, media production, media services, mentorship program, multimedia, news writing, newspaper, photojournalism, publications, publishing, religion, religious studies, remedial study skills, research skills, SAT preparation, science, technology, theater arts, word processing, writing, writing, yearbook classes. Computer network features include online commercial services, Internet access, wireless campus network, Internet filtering or blocking technology, fiber optic, multimedia laboratory, iPad for every student. Campus intranet, student e-mail accounts, and computer access in designated common areas are available to students. Students grades are available online. The school has a published electronic and media policy.

Contact Ms. Lori Tribble, Registrar. 562-435-4496 Ext. 1200. Fax: 562-437-3055. E-mail: lori.tribble@longbeachsaints.org. Web site: www.longbeachsaints.org

SAINT ANTHONY HIGH SCHOOL

304 East Roadway Avenue
Effingham, Illinois 62401

Head of School: Mr. Greg Fearday

General Information Coeducational day college-preparatory, arts, business, religious studies, bilingual studies, and technology school, affiliated with Roman Catholic

Church. Grades 9–12. Setting: small town. Nearest major city is St. Louis, MO. 1 building on campus. Approved or accredited by Illinois Department of Education. Total enrollment: 190. Upper school average class size: 20. Upper school faculty-student ratio: 1:10. There are 176 required school days per year for Upper School students. Upper School students typically attend 5 days per week. The average school day consists of 5 hours and 42 minutes.

Upper School Student Profile Grade 9: 41 students (16 boys, 25 girls); Grade 10: 49 students (27 boys, 22 girls); Grade 11: 39 students (23 boys, 16 girls); Grade 12: 52 students (23 boys, 29 girls). 97% of students are Roman Catholic.

Faculty School total: 21. In upper school: 6 men, 15 women; 8 have advanced degrees.

Subjects Offered Accounting, advanced math, algebra, American government, anatomy, art appreciation, band, biology, British literature, calculus-AP, career exploration, Catholic belief and practice, ceramics, chemistry, chorus, communications, composition, computer applications, conceptual physics, concert band, consumer education, criminal justice, current events, drawing, earth science, English literature, English-AP, environmental science, finite math, forensics, general math, geography, geometry, health, microbiology, music appreciation, physical education, physical science, physics, pre-algebra, psychology, publications, Spanish, statistics-AP, U.S. history, world history, world wide web design.

Graduation Requirements American government, arts and fine arts (art, music, dance, drama), computer science, consumer education, English, mathematics, physical education (includes health), religion (includes Bible studies and theology), science, social sciences, speech, U.S. history, world history.

Special Academic Programs International Baccalaureate program; 3 Advanced Placement exams for which test preparation is offered; independent study; study at local college for college credit; remedial math; special instructional classes for deaf students.

College Admission Counseling 52 students graduated in 2012; 51 went to college, including Eastern Illinois University; Southern Illinois University Edwardsville; University of Illinois at Urbana–Champaign. Other: 1 entered military service. Median composite ACT: 24.

Student Life Upper grades have specified standards of dress, student council. Discipline rests primarily with faculty. Attendance at religious services is required.

Tuition and Aid Tuition installment plan (monthly payment plans). Need-based scholarship grants available.

Admissions Traditional secondary-level entrance grade is 9. Deadline for receipt of application materials: none. No application fee required.

Athletics Interscholastic: baseball (boys), basketball (b,g), bowling (b,g), cheering (g), dance team (g), golf (b,g), soccer (b,g), softball (g), tennis (b,g), track and field (b,g), volleyball (g), wrestling (b); coed interscholastic: cross-country running. 2 PE instructors, 19 coaches.

Computers Computers are regularly used in drafting, publications, yearbook classes. Computer network features include on-campus library services, Internet access, Internet filtering or blocking technology. Student e-mail accounts are available to students. Students grades are available online. The school has a published electronic and media policy.

Contact Mr. Greg Fearday, Principal. 217-342-6969. Fax: 217-342-6997. E-mail: gfearday@stanthony.com. Web site: www.stanthony.com

ST. ANTHONY'S JUNIOR-SENIOR HIGH SCHOOL

1618 Lower Main Street
Wailuku, Hawaii 96793

Head of School: Mrs. Patricia Rickard

General Information Coeducational day college-preparatory, general academic, arts, religious studies, technology, and college courses offered for dual credit school, affiliated with Roman Catholic Church. Grades 7–12. Founded: 1848. Setting: small town. 15-acre campus. 13 buildings on campus. Approved or accredited by National Catholic Education Association, Western Association of Schools and Colleges, and Hawaii Department of Education. Member of National Association of Independent Schools. Endowment: $216,177. Total enrollment: 155. Upper school average class size: 22. Upper school faculty-student ratio: 1:10. There are 180 required school days per year for Upper School students. Upper School students typically attend 5 days per week. The average school day consists of 6 hours and 45 minutes.

Upper School Student Profile Grade 9: 34 students (14 boys, 20 girls); Grade 10: 18 students (10 boys, 8 girls); Grade 11: 32 students (18 boys, 14 girls); Grade 12: 22 students (10 boys, 12 girls). 65% of students are Roman Catholic.

Faculty School total: 20. In upper school: 8 men, 12 women; 10 have advanced degrees.

Subjects Offered Advanced math, American government, American history, American literature, anatomy and physiology, applied arts, art, athletic training, athletics, baseball, basic skills, basketball, Bible, Bible as literature, Bible studies, biology, bowling, British literature, business, calculus-AP, campus ministry, chemistry, college counseling, college planning, computer education, computer graphics, computer literacy, computer skills, computer technologies, computer technology certification, computer tools, computers, drawing, drawing and design, electives, English, English language and composition-AP, English literature, English literature and composition-AP, environmental science, environmental science-AP, foreign language, health, keyboarding, mathematics, music, physical education, pre-algebra, pre-calculus, religion, religious studies, SAT preparation, SAT/ACT preparation, science, social studies, sports medicine, standard curriculum, technology, U.S. history-AP, world geography, writing, writing, yearbook.

Graduation Requirements Art, English, languages, mathematics, physical education (includes health), religion (includes Bible studies and theology), science, social studies (includes history), technology.

Special Academic Programs 6 Advanced Placement exams for which test preparation is offered; honors section; study at local college for college credit.

College Admission Counseling 24 students graduated in 2012; all went to college, including University of Hawaii at Manoa; University of Notre Dame; University of Portland; Western Washington University. Median SAT critical reading: 518, median SAT math: 526, median SAT writing: 495, median combined SAT: 1539, median composite ACT: 22. 33% scored over 600 on SAT critical reading, 33% scored over 600 on SAT math, 33% scored over 600 on SAT writing, 33% scored over 1800 on combined SAT.

Student Life Upper grades have uniform requirement, student council. Discipline rests primarily with faculty. Attendance at religious services is required.

Summer Programs Remediation, enrichment programs offered; session focuses on remediation; held on campus; accepts boys and girls; open to students from other schools. 100 students usually enrolled. 2013 schedule: June 10 to July 12. Application deadline: June 1.

Tuition and Aid Day student tuition: $7500–$10,300. Tuition installment plan (FACTS Tuition Payment Plan). Tuition reduction for siblings, merit scholarship grants, need-based scholarship grants, alumni discount, new student referral discount available. In 2012–13, 50% of upper-school students received aid; total upper-school merit-scholarship money awarded: $4000. Total amount of financial aid awarded in 2012–13: $207,000.

Admissions Traditional secondary-level entrance grade is 9. For fall 2012, 27 students applied for upper-level admission, 27 were accepted, 20 enrolled. Achievement tests, Educational Development Series or standardized test scores required. Deadline for receipt of application materials: none. Application fee required: $300. Interview required.

Athletics Interscholastic: aquatics (boys, girls), baseball (b), basketball (b), bowling (b,g), canoeing/kayaking (b,g), cross-country running (b,g), drill team (b,g), football (b), golf (b,g), judo (b,g), ocean paddling (b,g), paddling (b,g), racquetball (b,g), riflery (b,g), running (b,g), soccer (b,g), softball (g), strength & conditioning (b,g), surfing (b,g), swimming and diving (b,g), tennis (b,g), track and field (b,g), volleyball (g), weight lifting (b,g), weight training (b,g), wrestling (b,g); intramural: basketball (b,g), flag football (b,g); coed interscholastic: cheering, flag football, paddling, racquetball; coed intramural: flag football. 2 PE instructors, 36 coaches, 1 athletic trainer.

Computers Computers are regularly used in college planning, computer applications, digital applications, graphic design, independent study, photography, technology, Web site design, yearbook classes. Computer network features include on-campus library services, Internet access, Internet filtering or blocking technology. Student e-mail accounts and computer access in designated common areas are available to students. Students grades are available online. The school has a published electronic and media policy.

Contact Mrs. Cindy Martin, Guidance/College Counselor. 808-244-4190 Ext. 224. Fax: 808-242-8081. E-mail: cmartin@sasmaui.org. Web site: www.sasmaui.org

ST. AUGUSTINE HIGH SCHOOL

3266 Nutmeg Street
San Diego, California 92104-5199

Head of School: James Walter Horne

General Information Boys' day college-preparatory and religious studies school, affiliated with Roman Catholic Church; primarily serves students with learning disabilities, individuals with Attention Deficit Disorder, dyslexic students, and We have limited accomodations based on the IEP results.. Grades 9–12. Founded: 1922. Setting: urban. 6-acre campus. 10 buildings on campus. Approved or accredited by National Catholic Education Association, Western Association of Schools and Colleges, and Western Catholic Education Association. Endowment: $1 million. Total enrollment: 700. Upper school average class size: 28. Upper school faculty-student ratio: 1:28. There are 180 required school days per year for Upper School students. Upper School students typically attend 5 days per week. The average school day consists of 5 hours and 50 minutes.

Upper School Student Profile Grade 9: 190 students (190 boys); Grade 10: 180 students (180 boys); Grade 11: 170 students (170 boys); Grade 12: 160 students (160 boys). 95% of students are Roman Catholic.

Faculty School total: 50. In upper school: 38 men, 12 women; 40 have advanced degrees.

Subjects Offered Algebra, American history, American literature, anatomy, art, art history, arts, Bible studies, biology, calculus, chemistry, computer science, driver education, economics, economics-AP, English, English literature, English-AP, ethics, fine arts, French, geometry, government/civics, grammar, health, history, Latin, Latin-AP, mathematics, music, philosophy, physical education, physics, physiology, psychology, religion, science, social studies, Spanish, speech, theology, trigonometry, world history, world literature, writing.

Graduation Requirements Arts and fine arts (art, music, dance, drama), English, foreign language, mathematics, physical education (includes health), religion (includes Bible studies and theology), science, social studies (includes history), speech, 100 hours of Christian service over four years.

Special Academic Programs Advanced Placement exam preparation; honors section; study abroad; academic accommodation for the gifted; remedial reading and/or remedial writing; remedial math; programs in English, mathematics, general development for dyslexic students; special instructional classes for blind students.

College Admission Counseling 169 students graduated in 2012; all went to college, including Gonzaga University; San Diego State University; University of California, Los Angeles; University of California, San Diego; University of Notre Dame; University of San Diego. 45% scored over 600 on SAT critical reading, 45% scored over 600 on SAT math, 45% scored over 600 on SAT writing, 55% scored over 26 on composite ACT.

Student Life Upper grades have specified standards of dress, student council, honor system. Discipline rests primarily with faculty. Attendance at religious services is required.

Summer Programs Remediation, enrichment, advancement, sports, rigorous outdoor training programs offered; session focuses on preparing students for fall semester; held on campus; accepts boys and girls; open to students from other schools. 150 students usually enrolled. 2013 schedule: June 20 to July 29. Application deadline: none.

Tuition and Aid Day student tuition: $14,000. Tuition installment plan (SMART Tuition Payment Plan, monthly payment plans, quarterly and annual payment plans). Merit scholarship grants, need-based scholarship grants, paying campus jobs available. In 2012–13, 40% of upper-school students received aid.

Admissions Traditional secondary-level entrance grade is 9. For fall 2012, 340 students applied for upper-level admission, 220 were accepted, 190 enrolled. ACT-Explore required. Deadline for receipt of application materials: January 26. Application fee required: $50. Interview required.

Athletics Interscholastic: baseball, basketball, cross-country running, diving, football, golf, in-line hockey, lacrosse, rugby, running, soccer, surfing, swimming and diving, tennis, track and field, volleyball, winter soccer, wrestling; intramural: basketball, bicycling, crew, fishing, fitness, flag football, Frisbee, kickball, mountain biking, ocean paddling, outdoor activities, outdoor adventure, outdoor education, outdoor recreation, physical fitness, physical training, racquetball, scuba diving, speedball, street hockey, strength & conditioning, table tennis, ultimate Frisbee, volleyball, weight lifting, weight training, yoga. 5 PE instructors, 26 coaches, 1 athletic trainer.

Computers Computers are regularly used in foreign language, mathematics, science, Web site design, writing classes. Computer resources include on-campus library services, online commercial services, Internet access, wireless campus network, Internet filtering or blocking technology, online databases, remote access. Campus intranet, student e-mail accounts, and computer access in designated common areas are available to students. Students grades are available online. The school has a published electronic and media policy.

Contact Jeannie Oliwa, Registrar. 619-282-2184 Ext. 5512. Fax: 619-282-1203. E-mail: joliwa@sahs.org. Web site: www.sahs.org

SAINT AUGUSTINE PREPARATORY SCHOOL

611 Cedar Avenue
PO Box 279
Richland, New Jersey 08350

Head of School: Rev. Donald F. Reilly, OSA

General Information Boys' day college-preparatory and religious studies school, affiliated with Roman Catholic Church. Grades 9–12. Founded: 1959. Setting: rural. Nearest major city is Vineland. 120-acre campus. 4 buildings on campus. Approved or accredited by Middle States Association of Colleges and Schools, National Catholic Education Association, New Jersey Association of Independent Schools, and New Jersey Department of Education. Endowment: $250,000. Total enrollment: 682. Upper school average class size: 17. Upper school faculty-student ratio: 1:12. There are 180 required school days per year for Upper School students. Upper School students typically attend 5 days per week. The average school day consists of 6 hours and 8 minutes.

Upper School Student Profile Grade 9: 191 students (191 boys); Grade 10: 184 students (184 boys); Grade 11: 159 students (159 boys); Grade 12: 173 students (173 boys). 78% of students are Roman Catholic.

Faculty School total: 62. In upper school: 48 men, 14 women; 23 have advanced degrees.

Subjects Offered 20th century history, accounting, advanced chemistry, Advanced Placement courses, advanced studio art-AP, algebra, American Civil War, American history-AP, American literature, anatomy and physiology, ancient world history, Arabic, Arabic studies, art, band, Bible, biology, biology-AP, British literature, British literature (honors), calculus, calculus-AP, Catholic belief and practice, chemistry, chemistry-AP, choir, Christian and Hebrew scripture, Christian doctrine, Christian ethics, church history, classical language, college counseling, college planning, community service, comparative religion, computer applications, computer programming, computer science, computer science-AP, computer-aided design, concert choir, culinary arts, current events, drama, drama performance, driver education, engineering, English, English composition, English literature, English literature-AP, environmental education, ethics and responsibility, European history, European history-AP, finance, French, geometry, German, grammar, guitar, history, history-AP, Holocaust, Holocaust and other genocides, honors algebra, honors English, honors geometry, honors U.S. history, independent study, jazz band, jazz ensemble, lab science, language-AP, Latin, marine biology, mathematics-AP, model United Nations, moral theology, music theory, music theory-AP, peer ministry, philosophy, photojournalism, physical education, physics, physics-AP, political science, pre-calculus, psychology, psychology-AP, public speaking, religion, religious studies, SAT preparation, scripture, service learning/internship, social skills, sociology, Spanish, Spanish language-AP, Spanish literature-AP, Spanish-AP, studio art, theater, travel, U.S. history-AP, vocal music, Web site design, world cultures, world religions, writing.

Graduation Requirements Electives, English, foreign language, lab science, mathematics, religion (includes Bible studies and theology), science, service learning/internship, U.S. history, world cultures, social service project (approximately 100 hours), retreat experiences, third semester experiences (travel); hands-on learning.

Special Academic Programs 18 Advanced Placement exams for which test preparation is offered; honors section; independent study; study at local college for college credit; study abroad; programs in general development for dyslexic students.

College Admission Counseling 144 students graduated in 2012; 140 went to college, including Drexel University; La Salle University; Rutgers, The State University of New Jersey, Newark; Saint Joseph's University; Temple University; Villanova University. Other: 1 entered military service, 3 had other specific plans. Mean SAT critical reading: 547, mean SAT math: 567, mean SAT writing: 537, mean combined SAT: 1651, mean composite ACT: 23. 24% scored over 600 on SAT critical reading, 42% scored over 600 on SAT math, 22% scored over 600 on SAT writing, 27% scored over 1800 on combined SAT.

Student Life Upper grades have uniform requirement, student council, honor system. Discipline rests primarily with faculty. Attendance at religious services is required.

Summer Programs Enrichment, advancement, sports, art/fine arts, rigorous outdoor training programs offered; session focuses on academic enrichment, community relations, sports camps; held both on and off campus; held at crew camp on nearby lake; accepts boys and girls; open to students from other schools. 656 students usually enrolled. 2013 schedule: July 8 to August 9. Application deadline: June 15.

Tuition and Aid Day student tuition: $15,300. Tuition installment plan (FACTS Tuition Payment Plan, individually arranged payment plans, credit card payment; discount for pre-payment). Merit scholarship grants, need-based scholarship grants available. In 2012–13, 31% of upper-school students received aid; total upper-school merit-scholarship money awarded: $206,500. Total amount of financial aid awarded in 2012–13: $1,010,000.

Admissions Traditional secondary-level entrance grade is 9. For fall 2012, 350 students applied for upper-level admission, 240 were accepted, 191 enrolled. School's own exam required. Deadline for receipt of application materials: January 31. Application fee required: $75. On-campus interview recommended.

Athletics Interscholastic: baseball, basketball, bowling, crew, cross-country running, fencing, football, golf, ice hockey, indoor track, lacrosse, rowing, rugby, sailing, soccer, swimming and diving, tennis, track and field, volleyball, winter (indoor) track, wrestling; intramural: basketball, ultimate Frisbee, weight training. 2 PE instructors, 11 coaches, 1 athletic trainer.

Computers Computers are regularly used in all academic, art, career education, design, photojournalism, SAT preparation classes. Computer network features include on-campus library services, online commercial services, Internet access, wireless campus network, Internet filtering or blocking technology, syllabus, current grades, and assignments available online for all courses. Student e-mail accounts and computer access in designated common areas are available to students. Students grades are available online. The school has a published electronic and media policy.

Contact Mr. Stephen Cappuccio, Dean of Enrollment Management. 856-697-2600 Ext. 112. Fax: 856-697-8389. E-mail: mr.cappuccio@hermits.com. Web site: www.hermits.com

SAINT BASIL ACADEMY

711 Fox Chase Road
Jenkintown, Pennsylvania 19046

Head of School: Sr. Carla Hern?ez

General Information Girls' day college-preparatory, arts, business, religious studies, bilingual studies, and technology school, affiliated with Roman Catholic Church. Grades 9–12. Founded: 1931. Setting: suburban. Nearest major city is Philadelphia. 28-acre campus. 1 building on campus. Approved or accredited by Middle States Association of Colleges and Schools and Pennsylvania Department of Education. Endowment: $350,000. Total enrollment: 324. Upper school average class size: 18. Upper school faculty-student ratio: 1:10. There are 180 required school days per year for Upper School students. Upper School students typically attend 5 days per week. The average school day consists of 6 hours and 30 minutes.

Upper School Student Profile Grade 9: 71 students (71 girls); Grade 10: 83 students (83 girls); Grade 11: 79 students (79 girls); Grade 12: 91 students (91 girls). 96% of students are Roman Catholic.

Faculty School total: 36. In upper school: 9 men, 25 women; 22 have advanced degrees.

Subjects Offered Accounting, advanced biology, algebra, American history, American history-AP, American literature, anatomy, art, band, biology, British literature, business, calculus-AP, chemistry, Christian and Hebrew scripture, computer applications, concert choir, creative writing, desktop publishing, digital applications, economics, English, English language-AP, English literature, English literature-AP, ensembles, environmental science, European history, fine arts, French, French literature-AP, geometry, German, government/civics, guitar, health, Hebrew scripture, history, honors algebra, honors English, honors geometry, Italian, journalism, keyboarding, Latin, mathematics, music, physical education, physics, pre-calculus, probability and statistics, psychology, religion, religious studies, SAT preparation, science, Shakespeare, social studies, sociology, Spanish, Spanish literature-AP, Spanish-AP, statistics, trigonometry, U.S. government and politics-AP, U.S. history, U.S. history-AP, Ukrainian, world cultures, world history.

Graduation Requirements Arts and fine arts (art, music, dance, drama), English, foreign language, keyboarding, mathematics, physical education (includes health), religion (includes Bible studies and theology), science, social studies (includes history). Community service is required.

Special Academic Programs Advanced Placement exam preparation; honors section; study at local college for college credit.

College Admission Counseling 102 students graduated in 2011; all went to college, including Drexel University; La Salle University; Penn State University Park; Saint Joseph's University; Temple University; West Chester University of Pennsylvania. Mean SAT critical reading: 576, mean SAT math: 550, mean SAT writing: 600, mean combined SAT: 1726, mean composite ACT: 24.

Student Life Upper grades have uniform requirement, student council, honor system. Discipline rests primarily with faculty. Attendance at religious services is required.

Tuition and Aid Tuition installment plan (monthly payment plans, 2-installments (pay 1/2 tuition July 15, 1/2 tuition November 15), first installment (due July 15 (3 months), 7 installments (pay Oct. 15-April 15)). Tuition reduction for siblings, merit scholarship grants, need-based scholarship grants, Ellis Grant for children of single parents living in Philadelphia, BLOCS scholarships and foundations available. In 2011–12, 20% of upper-school students received aid; total upper-school merit-scholarship money awarded: $193,925. Total amount of financial aid awarded in 2011–12: $268,175.

Admissions Traditional secondary-level entrance grade is 9. For fall 2011, 162 students applied for upper-level admission, 71 enrolled. High School Placement Test required. Deadline for receipt of application materials: October 24. Application fee required: $40.

Athletics Interscholastic: basketball, cheering, cross-country running, field hockey, indoor track, lacrosse, soccer, softball, tennis, track and field, volleyball, winter (indoor) track. 1 PE instructor, 25 coaches.

Computers Computers are regularly used in accounting, computer applications, creative writing, desktop publishing, digital applications, economics, journalism, keyboarding, science classes. Computer network features include Internet access, wireless campus network, Internet filtering or blocking technology, student accessible server storage space, on-campus and Web-based library services (catalog and book request). Student e-mail accounts are available to students. The school has a published electronic and media policy.

Contact Mrs. Maureen Walsh, Director of Admissions. 215-885-6952. Fax: 215-885-0395. E-mail: mwalsh@stbasilacademy.org. Web site: www.stbasilacademy.org

ST. BENEDICT AT AUBURNDALE

8250 Varnavas Drive
Cordova, Tennessee 38016

Head of School: Mr. George D. Valadie

General Information Coeducational day college-preparatory, arts, business, religious studies, bilingual studies, and technology school, affiliated with Roman Catholic Church. Grades 9–12. Founded: 1966. Setting: suburban. Nearest major city is Memphis. 40-acre campus. 1 building on campus. Approved or accredited by National Catholic Education Association, Southern Association of Colleges and Schools, and Tennessee Department of Education. Endowment: $100,000. Total enrollment: 982. Upper school average class size: 26. Upper school faculty-student ratio: 1:16. There are 186 required school days per year for Upper School students. Upper School students typically attend 5 days per week. The average school day consists of 7 hours and 15 minutes.

Upper School Student Profile Grade 9: 254 students (110 boys, 144 girls); Grade 10: 255 students (125 boys, 130 girls); Grade 11: 245 students (110 boys, 135 girls); Grade 12: 228 students (102 boys, 126 girls). 85% of students are Roman Catholic.

Faculty School total: 65. In upper school: 15 men, 50 women; 40 have advanced degrees.

Subjects Offered Accounting, algebra, American government, American history, American history-AP, American literature-AP, anatomy and physiology, applied music, art, art appreciation, art education, art history, art-AP, astronomy, band, biology, calculus, calculus-AP, Catholic belief and practice, chemistry, choir, choral music, choreography, chorus, church history, cinematography, clayworking, comparative religion, composition-AP, computer graphics, computer multimedia, computers, creative writing, dance, digital art, digital photography, drama, drama performance, drawing, driver education, ecology, economics, economics-AP, English, English language-AP, English literature-AP, English-AP, English/composition-AP, etymology, European history, film, filmmaking, fine arts, first aid, fitness, forensics, French, French-AP, general business, geometry, German, government, government-AP, graphic arts, graphic design, health and wellness, health education, history, history of the Catholic Church, history-AP, honors algebra, honors English, honors geometry, honors U.S. history, human anatomy, human biology, instrumental music, internship, jazz band, jazz dance, journalism, keyboarding, lab/keyboard, Latin, literature-AP, macroeconomics-AP, marketing, modern history, music appreciation, music history, music theory, newspaper, performing arts, personal finance, photography, physical education, physical science, physics, play production, pre-algebra, pre-calculus, psychology, religion, set design, sociology, Spanish, Spanish-AP, speech, sports conditioning, stage design, statistics-AP, student publications, U.S. government and politics-AP, U.S. history-AP, world geography, world history, yearbook.

Graduation Requirements Arts and fine arts (art, music, dance, drama), economics, English, foreign language, government, mathematics, physical education (includes health), religion (includes Bible studies and theology), science, social studies (includes history), technology, theology.

Special Academic Programs 10 Advanced Placement exams for which test preparation is offered; study at local college for college credit; academic accommodation for the gifted, the musically talented, and the artistically talented; remedial reading and/or remedial writing; remedial math; programs in English, mathematics, general development for dyslexic students; special instructional classes for students with diagnosed learning disabilities and Attention Deficit Disorder.

College Admission Counseling 232 students graduated in 2012; all went to college, including Christian Brothers University; Middle Tennessee State University; Mississippi State University; The University of Alabama; The University of Tennessee; University of Memphis. Mean SAT critical reading: 570, mean SAT math: 560, mean composite ACT: 24. 38% scored over 600 on SAT critical reading, 37% scored over 600 on SAT math, 30% scored over 26 on composite ACT.

Student Life Upper grades have uniform requirement, student council, honor system. Discipline rests primarily with faculty. Attendance at religious services is required.

Summer Programs Remediation, enrichment programs offered; session focuses on enrichment for math and language; held on campus; accepts boys and girls; not open to students from other schools. 30 students usually enrolled. 2013 schedule: July 5 to July 29. Application deadline: none.

Tuition and Aid Day student tuition: $8000. Tuition installment plan (FACTS Tuition Payment Plan, monthly payment plans, individually arranged payment plans). Merit scholarship grants, need-based scholarship grants available. In 2012–13, 4% of upper-school students received aid; total upper-school merit-scholarship money awarded: $30,000. Total amount of financial aid awarded in 2012–13: $35,000.

Admissions Traditional secondary-level entrance grade is 9. For fall 2012, 287 students applied for upper-level admission, 280 were accepted, 273 enrolled. High School Placement Test required. Deadline for receipt of application materials: none. Application fee required: $75. Interview required.

Athletics Interscholastic: baseball (boys), basketball (b,g), bowling (b,g), cheering (g), cross-country running (b,g), dance (g), dance squad (g), dance team (g), football (b), Frisbee (b,g), golf (b,g), lacrosse (b,g), pom squad (g), soccer (b,g), softball (g), strength & conditioning (b), swimming and diving (b,g), tennis (b,g), track and field (b,g), volleyball (g), weight lifting (b), weight training (b), wrestling (b); coed interscholastic: water polo; coed intramural: Frisbee. 4 PE instructors, 17 coaches, 1 athletic trainer.

Computers Computers are regularly used in all academic, art, business, commercial art, current events, dance, design, desktop publishing, economics, French, graphic arts, graphic design, health, history, journalism, lab/keyboard, Latin, mathematics, music, newspaper, photography, psychology, publications, religion, science, social sciences, social studies, Spanish, speech, study skills, technology, theater, theater arts, theology, Web site design, writing, yearbook classes. Computer network features include on-campus library services, Internet access, wireless campus network, Internet filtering or blocking technology. Students grades are available online. The school has a published electronic and media policy.

Contact Mrs. Ann O'Leary, Director of Admissions. 901-260-2875. Fax: 901-260-2850. E-mail: olearya@sbaeagles.org. Web site: www.sbaeagles.org

ST. BENEDICT'S PREPARATORY SCHOOL

520 Dr. Martin Luther King, Jr. Boulevard
Newark, New Jersey 07102-1314

Head of School: Rev. Edwin D. Leahy, OSB

General Information Boys' day college-preparatory school, affiliated with Roman Catholic Church. Grades 7–12. Founded: 1868. Setting: urban. 12-acre campus. 15 buildings on campus. Approved or accredited by Middle States Association of Colleges and Schools, New Jersey Association of Independent Schools, and New Jersey Department of Education. Endowment: $28 million. Total enrollment: 562. Upper school average class size: 20. Upper school faculty-student ratio: 1:11. Upper School students typically attend 5 days per week. The average school day consists of 6 hours.

Upper School Student Profile Grade 9: 132 students (132 boys); Grade 10: 118 students (118 boys); Grade 11: 116 students (116 boys); Grade 12: 109 students (109 boys). 40% of students are Roman Catholic.

Faculty School total: 55. In upper school: 44 men, 8 women; 40 have advanced degrees.

Subjects Offered Algebra, American history, American literature, architecture, art, astronomy, Bible studies, biology, Black history, calculus, chemistry, computer science, creative writing, drama, economics, English, English literature, ESL, European history, French, geometry, health, Hispanic literature, history, Latin, mathematics, mechanical drawing, music, physical education, physics, religion, social studies, sociology, Spanish, theater, trigonometry, world history.

Graduation Requirements English, foreign language, mathematics, physical education (includes health), religion (includes Bible studies and theology), science, social studies (includes history), spring projects, summer phase courses.

Special Academic Programs Term-away projects; domestic exchange program (with The Network Program Schools); remedial reading and/or remedial writing; remedial math; ESL (20 students enrolled).

College Admission Counseling 119 students graduated in 2011; 115 went to college, including Boston College; College of the Holy Cross; Rutgers, The State University of New Jersey, Newark; Saint John's University; Saint Peter's University; University of Notre Dame. Other: 2 went to work, 2 entered military service. Mean SAT critical reading: 468, mean SAT math: 492, mean SAT writing: 476, mean combined SAT: 1436.

Student Life Upper grades have uniform requirement, student council, honor system. Discipline rests equally with students and faculty. Attendance at religious services is required.

Tuition and Aid Day student tuition: $8500. Tuition installment plan (FACTS Tuition Payment Plan). Need-based scholarship grants available. In 2011–12, 75% of upper-school students received aid. Total amount of financial aid awarded in 2011–12: $1,908,723.

Admissions For fall 2011, 365 students applied for upper-level admission, 281 were accepted, 175 enrolled. Deadline for receipt of application materials: December 31. No application fee required. On-campus interview required.

Athletics Interscholastic: baseball, basketball, cross-country running, fencing, golf, indoor track & field, soccer, swimming and diving, tennis, track and field, water polo, winter (indoor) track, wrestling; intramural: basketball, flag football, floor hockey, hiking/backpacking, life saving, outdoor adventure, outdoor skills, physical training, soccer, swimming and diving, weight lifting. 2 PE instructors, 20 coaches.

Computers Computers are regularly used in English, information technology, journalism, science classes. Computer network features include on-campus library services, online commercial services, Internet access, wireless campus network, Internet filtering or blocking technology. Student e-mail accounts are available to students. The school has a published electronic and media policy.

Contact Ms. Doris Lamourt, Admissions Administrative Assistant. 973-792-5744. Fax: 973-792-5706. E-mail: DLamourt@sbp.org. Web site: www.sbp.org

ST. BERNARD HIGH SCHOOL

1593 Norwich-New London Turnpike
Uncasville, Connecticut 06382

Head of School: Mr. Thomas J. Doherty III

General Information Coeducational day college-preparatory school, affiliated with Roman Catholic Church. Grades 6–12. Founded: 1956. Setting: suburban. Nearest major city is Hartford. 113-acre campus. 2 buildings on campus. Approved or accredited by New England Association of Schools and Colleges and Connecticut Department of Education. Member of National Association of Independent Schools. Endowment: $1 million. Total enrollment: 369. Upper school average class size: 20. Upper school faculty-student ratio: 1:12. There are 177 required school days per year for Upper School students. Upper School students typically attend 5 days per week. The average school day consists of 6 hours.

Upper School Student Profile Grade 9: 57 students (30 boys, 27 girls); Grade 10: 72 students (26 boys, 46 girls); Grade 11: 60 students (34 boys, 26 girls); Grade 12: 72 students (36 boys, 36 girls). 60% of students are Roman Catholic.

Faculty School total: 33. In upper school: 19 men, 12 women; 26 have advanced degrees.

Subjects Offered 3-dimensional art, accounting, acting, algebra, anatomy and physiology, athletic training, biology, biology-AP, calculus, calculus-AP, chemistry, chemistry-AP, Christian doctrine, Christian ethics, Christian scripture, church history, conceptual physics, concert band, concert choir, creative writing, design, drawing and design, economics, English, English literature and composition-AP, environmental science, European history-AP, fine arts, forensics, French, French-AP, geometry, global issues, health, honors algebra, honors English, honors geometry, honors U.S. history, honors world history, integrated science, intro to computers, modern world history, moral theology, music, music theory, music theory-AP, Native American studies, nutrition, organic chemistry, painting, peace and justice, peer counseling, peer ministry, performing arts, personal finance, personal fitness, philosophy, photography, physical education, physics, pottery, pre-algebra, pre-calculus, printmaking, psychology-AP, public speaking, religious studies, scripture, sociology, Spanish, Spanish-AP, sports conditioning, sports nutrition, statistics, street law, strings, studio art, technology, theater arts, U.S. history, U.S. history-AP, world history.

Graduation Requirements Art, biology, chemistry, English, health education, history, intro to computers, mathematics, physical education (includes health), theology, U.S. history, world history, all students are required to complete 100 hours of community service prior to high school graduation.

Special Academic Programs Honors section; study at local college for college credit.

College Admission Counseling 74 students graduated in 2012; 72 went to college, including Keene State College; Providence College; Roger Williams University; Saint Michael's College; University of Connecticut; Worcester Polytechnic Institute. Other: 2 entered military service. Mean SAT critical reading: 546, mean SAT math: 518, mean SAT writing: 533.

Student Life Upper grades have uniform requirement, student council, honor system. Discipline rests primarily with faculty. Attendance at religious services is required.

Summer Programs Art/fine arts, computer instruction programs offered; held on campus; accepts boys and girls; not open to students from other schools. 2013 schedule: June to August.

Tuition and Aid Day student tuition: $11,400. Tuition installment plan (SMART Tuition Payment Plan, FACTS Tuition Payment Plan, monthly payment plans, individually arranged payment plans). Tuition reduction for siblings, merit scholarship grants, need-based scholarship grants available. In 2012–13, 32% of upper-school students received aid; total upper-school merit-scholarship money awarded: $166,050. Total amount of financial aid awarded in 2012–13: $354,257.

Admissions Traditional secondary-level entrance grade is 9. For fall 2012, 136 students applied for upper-level admission, 120 were accepted, 110 enrolled. High School Placement Test (closed version) from Scholastic Testing Service and Scholastic Testing Service required. Deadline for receipt of application materials: January 15. No application fee required. On-campus interview recommended.

Athletics Interscholastic: baseball (boys), basketball (b,g), cheering (g), cross-country running (b,g), diving (b,g), fencing (b,g), football (b), golf (b,g), ice hockey (b), indoor track & field (b,g), lacrosse (b,g), physical fitness (b,g), soccer (b,g), softball (g), swimming and diving (b,g), tennis (b,g), track and field (b,g), wrestling (b,g); coed interscholastic: cheering, cross-country running, fencing, golf, physical fitness, soccer, swimming and diving, wrestling; coed intramural: skiing (cross-country), skiing (downhill), snowboarding, strength & conditioning, volleyball, weight training. 2 PE instructors, 50 coaches, 1 athletic trainer.

Computers Computers are regularly used in computer applications, design classes. Computer resources include on-campus library services, Internet access, wireless campus network, Internet filtering or blocking technology. Campus intranet, student e-mail accounts, and computer access in designated common areas are available to students. Students grades are available online. The school has a published electronic and media policy.

Contact Mrs. Cathy Brown, Director of Admissions (gr. 6-8) and International Programs. 860-848-1271 Ext. 108. Fax: 860-848-1274. E-mail: Admissions@Saint-Bernard.com. Web site: www.saint-bernard.com

ST. BERNARD'S CATHOLIC SCHOOL

222 Dollison Street
Eureka, California 95501

Head of School: Mr. David Sharp

General Information Coeducational boarding and day college-preparatory and religious studies school, affiliated with Roman Catholic Church. Boarding grades 9–12, day grades PK–12. Founded: 1912. Setting: small town. Nearest major city is San Francisco. 5-acre campus. 4 buildings on campus. Approved or accredited by National Catholic Education Association, Western Association of Schools and Colleges, Western Catholic Education Association, and California Department of Education. Endowment: $63,000. Total enrollment: 300. Upper school average class size: 20. Upper school faculty-student ratio: 1:12. There are 162 required school days per year for Upper School students. Upper School students typically attend 5 days per week. The average school day consists of 6 hours.

Upper School Student Profile 25% of students are boarding students. 75% are state residents. 25% are international students. International students from China, Republic of Korea, and Viet Nam. 35% of students are Roman Catholic.

Faculty School total: 20. In upper school: 9 men, 11 women; 5 have advanced degrees.

Subjects Offered Arts, community service, English, fine arts, mathematics, physical education, religion, science, social studies.

Graduation Requirements Arts and fine arts (art, music, dance, drama), English, foreign language, mathematics, physical education (includes health), science, social studies (includes history), theology, follow the University of California requirements (250 units). Community service is required.

Special Academic Programs Advanced Placement exam preparation; honors section; remedial reading and/or remedial writing; remedial math; special instructional classes for students with learning disabilities.

College Admission Counseling 44 students graduated in 2012; 43 went to college, including College of the Redwoods; Humboldt State University; Pacific University; Sonoma State University; University of California, San Diego; University of San Francisco. Other: 1 entered military service.

Student Life Upper grades have specified standards of dress, student council. Discipline rests equally with students and faculty. Attendance at religious services is required.

Summer Programs Remediation programs offered; session focuses on make-up work; held on campus; accepts boys and girls; open to students from other schools. 10 students usually enrolled. 2013 schedule: June 16 to July 23. Application deadline: June 6.

Tuition and Aid Day student tuition: $6300. Tuition installment plan (monthly payment plans, individually arranged payment plans, 3% reduction if paid in full by July 10). Tuition reduction for siblings, merit scholarship grants, need-based scholarship grants, paying campus jobs available. In 2012–13, 47% of upper-school students received aid; total upper-school merit-scholarship money awarded: $2500. Total amount of financial aid awarded in 2012–13: $55,000.

Admissions Traditional secondary-level entrance grade is 9. Admissions testing required. Deadline for receipt of application materials: none. Application fee required: $40. Interview required.

Athletics Interscholastic: baseball (boys), basketball (b,g), football (b), golf (b,g), soccer (b,g), softball (g), tennis (b,g), volleyball (g), wrestling (b); intramural: cheering (g); coed interscholastic: track and field. 1 PE instructor, 15 coaches, 1 athletic trainer.

Computers Computers are regularly used in graphic design, journalism, yearbook classes. Computer network features include on-campus library services, Internet access, wireless campus network, Internet filtering or blocking technology. Students grades are available online. The school has a published electronic and media policy.

Contact Mrs. Shirley Sobol, Domestic Admissions. 707-443-2735 Ext. 115. Fax: 707-443-4723. E-mail: sobol@saintbernards.us. Web site: www.saintbernards.us/

ST. BRENDAN HIGH SCHOOL

2950 Southwest 87th Avenue
Miami, Florida 33165-3295

Head of School: Mr. Jose Rodelgo-Bueno

General Information Coeducational day college-preparatory, general academic, arts, business, religious studies, bilingual studies, and technology school, affiliated with Roman Catholic Church. Grades 9–12. Founded: 1975. Setting: urban. 34-acre campus. 3 buildings on campus. Approved or accredited by Southern Association of Colleges and Schools and Florida Department of Education. Total enrollment: 1,118. Upper school average class size: 28. Upper school faculty-student ratio: 1:15. There are 180 required school days per year for Upper School students. Upper School students typically attend 5 days per week. The average school day consists of 7 hours and 45 minutes.

Upper School Student Profile 98% of students are Roman Catholic.

Faculty School total: 76. In upper school: 22 men, 54 women; 34 have advanced degrees.

Graduation Requirements Algebra, students must complete 100 community service hours in their four years of high school.

Special Academic Programs 10 Advanced Placement exams for which test preparation is offered; honors section; study at local college for college credit; academic accommodation for the gifted; remedial reading and/or remedial writing; remedial math.

College Admission Counseling 315 students graduated in 2012; 310 went to college, including Florida International University; Florida State University; Miami Dade College; University of Central Florida; University of Florida; University of Miami. Other: 5 had other specific plans. Median SAT critical reading: 480, median SAT math: 460, median SAT writing: 470, median combined SAT: 1410, median composite ACT: 20. 10% scored over 26 on composite ACT.

Student Life Upper grades have uniform requirement, student council, honor system. Discipline rests primarily with faculty. Attendance at religious services is required.

Summer Programs Remediation, enrichment, advancement, computer instruction programs offered; held on campus; accepts boys and girls; open to students from other schools. 270 students usually enrolled.

Tuition and Aid Tuition installment plan (FACTS Tuition Payment Plan, monthly payment plans). Need-based scholarship grants, paying campus jobs available. In 2012–13, 23% of upper-school students received aid. Total amount of financial aid awarded in 2012–13: $266,000.

Admissions Traditional secondary-level entrance grade is 9. Catholic High School Entrance Examination or placement test required. Deadline for receipt of application materials: January 22. Application fee required: $50.

Athletics Interscholastic: baseball (boys), basketball (b,g), cheering (g), cross-country running (b,g), dance team (g), soccer (b,g), softball (g), swimming and diving (b,g), tennis (b,g), track and field (b,g), volleyball (b,g). 2 PE instructors, 17 coaches, 1 athletic trainer.

Computers Computers are regularly used in business, computer applications, graphic design, mathematics, media arts, media production, newspaper, programming, reading, remedial study skills, research skills, science, speech, Web site design, word processing, yearbook classes. Computer network features include on-campus library services, Internet access, wireless campus network, Internet filtering or blocking technology, 1:1 iPad program. Computer access in designated common areas is available to students. Students grades are available online. The school has a published electronic and media policy.

Contact Melissa Ferrer, Director of Admissions. 305-223-5181 Ext. 578. Fax: 305-220-7434. E-mail: mferrer@stbhs.org. Web site: www.stbhs.org

ST. CATHERINE'S ACADEMY

Anaheim, California

See Junior Boarding Schools section.

ST. CHRISTOPHER'S SCHOOL

711 St. Christopher's Road
Richmond, Virginia 23226

Head of School: Mr. Charles M. Stillwell

General Information Boys' day college-preparatory school, affiliated with Episcopal Church. Grades JK–12. Founded: 1911. Setting: suburban. 46-acre campus. 9 buildings on campus. Approved or accredited by National Association of Episcopal Schools and Virginia Association of Independent Schools. Member of National Association of Independent Schools and Secondary School Admission Test Board. Endowment: $61.6 million. Total enrollment: 956. Upper school average class size: 15. Upper school faculty-student ratio: 1:6. Upper School students typically attend 5 days per week. The average school day consists of 7 hours and 30 minutes.

Upper School Student Profile Grade 9: 86 students (86 boys); Grade 10: 65 students (65 boys); Grade 11: 67 students (67 boys); Grade 12: 75 students (75 boys). 45% of students are members of Episcopal Church.

Faculty School total: 157. In upper school: 32 men, 17 women; 32 have advanced degrees.

Subjects Offered Algebra, American history, American literature, ancient history, architecture, art, art history, astronomy, Bible studies, biology, calculus, ceramics, chemistry, Chinese, community service, computer math, computer programming, computer science, creative thinking, creative writing, dance, drama, driver education, ecology, economics, English, English literature, environmental science, ethics, European history, expository writing, fine arts, French, geography, geology, geometry, government/civics, grammar, Greek, health, history, industrial arts, journalism, Latin, mathematics, music, philosophy, photography, physics, public speaking, religion, science, social studies, Spanish, speech, statistics, theater, theology, trigonometry, typing, woodworking, writing.

Graduation Requirements 1 1/2 elective credits, algebra, American history, American literature, ancient history, arts and fine arts (art, music, dance, drama), biology, British literature, chemistry, church history, computer science, English, English literature, European history, foreign language, geometry, physical education (includes health), physics, public speaking, religion (includes Bible studies and theology), speech, U.S. history. Community service is required.

Special Academic Programs 20 Advanced Placement exams for which test preparation is offered; honors section; independent study; academic accommodation for the gifted, the musically talented, and the artistically talented.

College Admission Counseling 73 students graduated in 2011; all went to college, including Hampden-Sydney College; Sewanee: The University of the South; The College of William and Mary; University of Virginia; Virginia Polytechnic Institute and State University; Washington and Lee University.

Student Life Upper grades have specified standards of dress, student council, honor system. Discipline rests equally with students and faculty. Attendance at religious services is required.

Tuition and Aid Day student tuition: $21,835. Tuition installment plan (Academic Management Services Plan, monthly payment plans, individually arranged payment plans, Tuition Refund Plan). Merit scholarship grants, need-based scholarship grants available. In 2011–12, 27% of upper-school students received aid; total upper-school merit-scholarship money awarded: $3000. Total amount of financial aid awarded in 2011–12: $783,200.

Admissions Traditional secondary-level entrance grade is 9. For fall 2011, 56 students applied for upper-level admission, 36 were accepted, 19 enrolled. SSAT and writing sample required. Deadline for receipt of application materials: none. Application fee required: $50. On-campus interview required.

Athletics Interscholastic: baseball, basketball, cross-country running, diving, football, golf, indoor soccer, indoor track & field, lacrosse, sailing, soccer, squash, strength & conditioning, swimming and diving, tennis, track and field, weight lifting, weight training, winter (indoor) track, wrestling; coed interscholastic: canoeing/kayaking, climbing, dance, martial arts, outdoor adventure, rappelling. 5 coaches, 2 athletic trainers.

Computers Computers are regularly used in computer applications, desktop publishing, digital applications, English, foreign language, health, history, journalism, literary magazine, mathematics, music, photography, publications, science classes. Computer network features include on-campus library services, online commercial services, Internet access, wireless campus network, Internet filtering or blocking technology. Student e-mail accounts and computer access in designated common areas are available to students. Students grades are available online. The school has a published electronic and media policy.

Contact Cary C. Mauck, Director of Admission. 804-282-3185 Ext. 2388. Fax: 804-673-6632. E-mail: mauckc@stcva.org. Web site: www.stchristophers.com

SAINT CLEMENT ACADEMY

88 Main St
Ottawa, Ontario K1S 1C2, Canada

Head of School: Mrs. Beryl Devine

General Information Coeducational day college-preparatory school, affiliated with Roman Catholic Church. Grades 7–12. Founded: 1996. Setting: urban. Approved or accredited by Ontario Department of Education. Language of instruction: English. Total enrollment: 20. Upper school average class size: 9. Upper school faculty-student ratio: 1:3. There are 181 required school days per year for Upper School students. Upper School students typically attend 5 days per week. The average school day consists of 6 hours.

Upper School Student Profile Grade 9: 4 students (2 boys, 2 girls); Grade 10: 2 students (1 boy, 1 girl); Grade 11: 5 students (2 boys, 3 girls); Grade 12: 2 students (1 boy, 1 girl). 100% of students are Roman Catholic.

Faculty School total: 15. In upper school: 7 men, 4 women; 9 have advanced degrees.

Subjects Offered Advanced math, algebra, arts and crafts, calculus, Canadian geography, Canadian history, Catholic belief and practice, chemistry, choir, church history, English literature and composition-AP, French, French as a second language, geometry, Greek, history, Latin, mathematics, music history, music theory, physical education, science, world history.

Graduation Requirements Biology, calculus, chemistry, church history, English, French, French as a second language, Greek, Latin, mathematics, music history, music theory, physics, religion (includes Bible studies and theology).

Special Academic Programs Honors section; ESL.

College Admission Counseling 4 students graduated in 2011; all went to college.

Student Life Upper grades have uniform requirement, honor system. Discipline rests primarily with faculty. Attendance at religious services is required.

Tuition and Aid Day student tuition: CAN$3700. Tuition installment plan (full payment in advance, 5-month payment plan). Tuition reduction for siblings available.

Admissions Traditional secondary-level entrance grade is 9. Canadian Standardized Test required. Deadline for receipt of application materials: April 1. No application fee required. On-campus interview required.

Athletics Coed Intramural: fitness, Frisbee, independent competitive sports, paddle tennis, physical training, running, soccer, tennis, touch football, track and field, volleyball. 2 PE instructors.

Computers Computer resources include Internet access, word processing, encyclopedia.

Contact Mrs. Beryl Devine, Headmistress. 613-236-7231. Fax: 613-236-9159. E-mail: st.clementacademy@bellnet.ca. Web site:

ST. CLEMENT'S SCHOOL

21 St. Clements Avenue
Toronto, Ontario M4R 1G8, Canada

Head of School: Ms. Martha Perry

General Information Girls' day college-preparatory, arts, business, and technology school, affiliated with Anglican Church of Canada. Grades 1–12. Founded: 1901. Setting: urban. 1-acre campus. 1 building on campus. Approved or accredited by Canadian Association of Independent Schools, Canadian Educational Standards Institute, Conference of Independent Schools of Ontario, and Ontario Department of Education. Affiliate member of National Association of Independent Schools; member of Secondary School Admission Test Board. Language of instruction: English. Total enrollment: 473. Upper school average class size: 16. Upper school faculty-student ratio: 1:7. Upper School students typically attend 5 days per week.

Upper School Student Profile Grade 10: 60 students (60 girls); Grade 11: 60 students (60 girls); Grade 12: 60 students (60 girls).

Faculty School total: 62. In upper school: 7 men, 43 women; 20 have advanced degrees.

Subjects Offered Accounting, Advanced Placement courses, algebra, Ancient Greek, ancient world history, art, art history-AP, art-AP, band, biology, biology-AP, business, business studies, calculus, calculus-AP, Canadian geography, Canadian history, Canadian law, Canadian literature, career and personal planning, career education, character education, chemistry, chemistry-AP, civics, classics, college admission preparation, communication arts, computer science, creative writing, dance, data processing, design, drama, economics, economics-AP, English, English language-AP, English literature, English literature and composition-AP, environmental science, environmental science-AP, European history, European history-AP, exercise science, film studies, fine arts, finite math, French, French-AP, geography, geometry, grammar, graphic design, guidance, health, history, history-AP, human geography - AP, instrumental music, interdisciplinary studies, jazz ensemble, keyboarding, kinesiology, language and composition, language arts, Latin, Latin-AP, law, leadership and service, library, macro/microeconomics-AP, Mandarin, mathematics, modern Western civilization, music, music theory-AP, musical theater, philosophy, photography, physical education, physics, physics-AP, physiology, religion, science, social sciences, social studies, Spanish, Spanish-AP, statistics-AP, studio art-AP, theater, trigonometry, U.S. history-AP, Western civilization, world history, world issues, writing workshop.

Graduation Requirements Arts, business skills (includes word processing), career/college preparation, civics, computer science, English, foreign language, geography, mathematics, physical education (includes health), science, social studies (includes history).

Special Academic Programs 20 Advanced Placement exams for which test preparation is offered; independent study; academic accommodation for the gifted.

College Admission Counseling 57 students graduated in 2011; all went to college, including Dalhousie University; McGill University; Queen's University at Kingston; The University of British Columbia; The University of Western Ontario; University of Toronto.

Student Life Upper grades have uniform requirement, student council, honor system. Discipline rests equally with students and faculty. Attendance at religious services is required.

Tuition and Aid Day student tuition: CAN$24,150. Tuition installment plan (monthly payment plans, individually arranged payment plans). Bursaries, merit scholarship grants, need-based scholarship grants available. In 2011–12, 8% of upper-school students received aid.

Admissions SSAT required. Deadline for receipt of application materials: December 16. Application fee required: CAN$150. Interview required.

Athletics Interscholastic: alpine skiing, badminton, basketball, cross-country running, dance, dance team, equestrian sports, field hockey, hockey, ice hockey, nordic skiing, running, skiing (downhill), soccer, softball, swimming and diving, tennis, track and field, volleyball; intramural: aerobics, aerobics/dance, backpacking, badminton, basketball, bocce, canoeing/kayaking, cooperative games, cross-country running, dance, dance team, field hockey, fitness, floor hockey, hiking/backpacking, indoor soccer, jogging, life saving, outdoor education, paddle tennis, running, soccer, softball, swimming and diving, table tennis, tennis, track and field, ultimate Frisbee, volleyball, wilderness survival, yoga. 5 PE instructors, 12 coaches.

Computers Computers are regularly used in all academic classes. Computer network features include on-campus library services, online commercial services, Internet access, wireless campus network, Internet filtering or blocking technology. Campus intranet, student e-mail accounts, and computer access in designated common areas are available to students. The school has a published electronic and media policy.

Contact Mrs. Jennifer Gray, Director of Admissions. 416-483-4414 Ext. 2227. Fax: 416-483-8242. E-mail: jgray@scs.on.ca. Web site: www.scs.on.ca

ST. CROIX COUNTRY DAY SCHOOL

RR #1, Box 6199
Kingshill, Virgin Islands 00850-9807

Head of School: Mr. William D. Sinfield

General Information Coeducational day college-preparatory and technology school. Grades N–12. Founded: 1964. Setting: rural. Nearest major city is Christiansted, U.S. Virgin Islands. 25-acre campus. 6 buildings on campus. Approved or accredited by Middle States Association of Colleges and Schools and Virgin Islands Department of Education. Member of National Association of Independent Schools. Endowment: $574,000. Total enrollment: 413. Upper school average class size: 14. Upper school faculty-student ratio: 1:12. Upper School students typically attend 5 days per week. The average school day consists of 7 hours.

Upper School Student Profile Grade 9: 22 students (15 boys, 7 girls); Grade 10: 32 students (13 boys, 19 girls); Grade 11: 23 students (14 boys, 9 girls); Grade 12: 32 students (19 boys, 13 girls).

Faculty School total: 51. In upper school: 6 men, 17 women; 11 have advanced degrees.

Subjects Offered Algebra, American history, American literature, art, art history, arts, band, biology, calculus, ceramics, chemistry, chorus, community service, computer programming, computer science, creative writing, current events, dance, drama, earth science, ecology, economics, electronics, English, English literature, film, fine arts, French, geometry, government/civics, health, history, journalism, keyboarding, marine biology, mathematics, music, Native American studies, photography, physical education, physical science, physics, pre-calculus, psychology, public speaking, science, social studies, sociology, Spanish, statistics, swimming, theater, trigonometry, world history.

Graduation Requirements Arts and fine arts (art, music, dance, drama), computer science, English, foreign language, mathematics, physical education (includes health), science, social studies (includes history), swimming, typing. Community service is required.

Special Academic Programs Advanced Placement exam preparation.

College Admission Counseling 44 students graduated in 2012; all went to college, including Michigan Technological University; University of Pennsylvania; University of Pittsburgh; Vassar College. Median SAT critical reading: 520, median SAT math: 540, median composite ACT: 22. 35% scored over 600 on SAT critical reading, 25% scored over 600 on SAT math, 19% scored over 26 on composite ACT.

Student Life Upper grades have specified standards of dress, student council, honor system. Discipline rests primarily with faculty.

Tuition and Aid Day student tuition: $14,000. Tuition installment plan (monthly payment plans, individually arranged payment plans, semiannual and annual payment plans). Merit scholarship grants, need-based scholarship grants available. In 2012–13,

33% of upper-school students received aid; total upper-school merit-scholarship money awarded: $42,500. Total amount of financial aid awarded in 2012–13: $265,550.

Admissions Traditional secondary-level entrance grade is 9. For fall 2012, 25 students applied for upper-level admission, 10 were accepted, 10 enrolled. Essay and Test of Achievement and Proficiency required. Deadline for receipt of application materials: none. Application fee required: $150. On-campus interview required.

Athletics Interscholastic: baseball (boys), basketball (b,g), football (b), softball (g), tennis (b,g), volleyball (b,g); intramural: volleyball (b,g); coed interscholastic: aerobics, aquatics, basketball, cross-country running, sailing, soccer; coed intramural: basketball, soccer, ultimate Frisbee. 3 PE instructors, 4 coaches.

Computers Computers are regularly used in mathematics, music, science, yearbook classes. Computer network features include on-campus library services, online commercial services, Internet access. The school has a published electronic and media policy.

Contact Mrs. Alma V. Castro-Nieves, Registrar. 340-778-1974 Ext. 2108. Fax: 340-779-3331. E-mail: anieves@stxcountryday.com. Web site: www.stxcountryday.com

ST. CROIX SCHOOLS

1200 Oakdale Avenue
West St. Paul, Minnesota 55118

Head of School: Dr. Gene Pfeifer

General Information Coeducational boarding and day college-preparatory, general academic, arts, business, vocational, religious studies, bilingual studies, technology, and ESL school, affiliated with Wisconsin Evangelical Lutheran Synod, Christian faith. Grades 6–12. Founded: 1958. Setting: suburban. Nearest major city is St. Paul. Students are housed in single-sex dormitories. 30-acre campus. 3 buildings on campus. Approved or accredited by Minnesota Department of Education. Endowment: $1.6 million. Total enrollment: 500. Upper school average class size: 21. Upper school faculty-student ratio: 1:15. There are 176 required school days per year for Upper School students. Upper School students typically attend 5 days per week. The average school day consists of 5 hours and 30 minutes.

Upper School Student Profile Grade 9: 110 students (52 boys, 58 girls); Grade 10: 110 students (57 boys, 53 girls); Grade 11: 110 students (56 boys, 54 girls); Grade 12: 110 students (53 boys, 57 girls). 30% of students are boarding students. 74% are state residents. 7 states are represented in upper school student body. 22% are international students. International students from China, Japan, Republic of Korea, Taiwan, Thailand, and Viet Nam; 11 other countries represented in student body. 67% of students are Wisconsin Evangelical Lutheran Synod, Christian.

Faculty School total: 35. In upper school: 24 men, 11 women; 21 have advanced degrees; 4 reside on campus.

Subjects Offered Accounting, advanced biology, advanced chemistry, advanced math, Advanced Placement courses, algebra, American history, American literature, applied skills, art, band, Bible studies, biology, biology-AP, business skills, calculus, chemistry, choir, chorus, computer programming, computer science, drama, economics, engineering, English, English literature, environmental science, general science, geography, geology, geometry, German, home economics, keyboarding, Latin, literature, Mandarin, mathematics, music, physical education, physics, pre-algebra, reading, religion, science, social sciences, social studies, Spanish, speech, trigonometry, world history, writing.

Graduation Requirements Algebra, arts and fine arts (art, music, dance, drama), biology, chemistry, English, English composition, English literature, foreign language, geometry, government, grammar, literature, physical education (includes health), physics, religion (includes Bible studies and theology), science, social studies (includes history), speech, world geography.

Special Academic Programs 12 Advanced Placement exams for which test preparation is offered; honors section; independent study; academic accommodation for the gifted, the musically talented, and the artistically talented; remedial reading and/or remedial writing; remedial math; programs in English for dyslexic students; special instructional classes for students with learning disabilities; ESL (30 students enrolled).

College Admission Counseling 115 students graduated in 2012; 111 went to college, including Bethany Lutheran College; Cornell College; Martin Luther College; Minnesota State University Mankato; University of Minnesota, Twin Cities Campus; University of Wisconsin–Madison. Other: 1 went to work, 3 entered military service. Mean composite ACT: 25.

Student Life Upper grades have specified standards of dress, student council, honor system. Discipline rests equally with students and faculty.

Summer Programs ESL, sports programs offered; session focuses on ESL and activities, and a variety of sports camps; held on campus; accepts boys and girls; open to students from other schools. 80 students usually enrolled. 2013 schedule: July 15 to August 2. Application deadline: May 15.

Tuition and Aid 7-day tuition and room/board: $26,800. Tuition installment plan (SMART Tuition Payment Plan). Merit scholarship grants, need-based scholarship grants available. In 2012–13, 40% of upper-school students received aid; total upper-school merit-scholarship money awarded: $25,000. Total amount of financial aid awarded in 2012–13: $600,000.

Admissions Traditional secondary-level entrance grade is 9. For fall 2012, 163 students applied for upper-level admission, 124 were accepted, 100 enrolled. Secondary Level English Proficiency or writing sample required. Deadline for receipt of application materials: none. Application fee required: $100. Interview recommended.

Athletics Interscholastic: baseball (boys), basketball (b,g), bowling (b,g), cheering (g), cross-country running (b,g), dance team (g), football (b), golf (b,g), hockey (b,g), ice hockey (b,g), soccer (b,g), softball (g), swimming and diving (b,g), tennis (b,g), track and field (b,g), volleyball (g), wrestling (b); intramural: badminton (b,g), basketball (b,g); coed intramural: alpine skiing, ball hockey, basketball, bowling, cheering, cross-country running, dance team, flag football, floor hockey, Frisbee, jogging, juggling, kickball, physical fitness, physical training, power lifting, skiing (downhill), snowboarding, softball, strength & conditioning, swimming and diving, table tennis, tennis, touch football, track and field, ultimate Frisbee, volleyball, weight lifting, weight training, whiffle ball. 3 PE instructors, 3 coaches, 2 athletic trainers.

Computers Computers are regularly used in accounting, computer applications, desktop publishing, economics, graphic design, keyboarding, media production, writing, yearbook classes. Computer network features include on-campus library services, online commercial services, Internet access, wireless campus network, Internet filtering or blocking technology. Computer access in designated common areas is available to students. Students grades are available online. The school has a published electronic and media policy.

Contact Dr. Jeff Lemke, Admissions Director. 651-455-1521. Fax: 651-451-3968. E-mail: international@stcroixlutheran.org. Web site: www.stcroixlutheran.org

SAINT DOMINIC ACADEMY

Bishop Joseph OSB Boulevard
121 Gracelawn Road
Auburn, Maine 04210

Head of School: Mr. Donald Fournier

General Information Coeducational day and distance learning college-preparatory, arts, business, and religious studies school, affiliated with Roman Catholic Church. Grades 9–12. Distance learning grades 11–12. Founded: 1941. Setting: suburban. 70-acre campus. 1 building on campus. Approved or accredited by Maine Department of Education. Total enrollment: 571. Upper school average class size: 17. Upper school faculty-student ratio: 1:12. There are 175 required school days per year for Upper School students. Upper School students typically attend 5 days per week. The average school day consists of 6 hours and 15 minutes.

Upper School Student Profile Grade 9: 43 students (23 boys, 20 girls); Grade 10: 57 students (28 boys, 29 girls); Grade 11: 48 students (23 boys, 25 girls); Grade 12: 54 students (29 boys, 25 girls). 70% of students are Roman Catholic.

Faculty School total: 25. In upper school: 10 men, 15 women.

Special Academic Programs International Baccalaureate program; Advanced Placement exam preparation; honors section; independent study.

College Admission Counseling 73 students graduated in 2012; 67 went to college. Other: 2 went to work, 1 entered military service, 1 entered a postgraduate year, 2 had other specific plans. Median SAT critical reading: 542, median SAT math: 534, median SAT writing: 524, median combined SAT: 1600.

Student Life Upper grades have specified standards of dress, student council, honor system. Discipline rests primarily with faculty. Attendance at religious services is required.

Summer Programs Enrichment, sports, art/fine arts programs offered; session focuses on recreation/theater/math and science; held both on and off campus; held at various venues; accepts boys and girls; open to students from other schools.

Tuition and Aid Day student tuition: $10,975. Tuition installment plan (FACTS Tuition Payment Plan). Merit scholarship grants, need-based scholarship grants available. In 2012–13, 33% of upper-school students received aid.

Admissions Traditional secondary-level entrance grade is 9. Scholastic Testing Service High School Placement Test required. Deadline for receipt of application materials: none. Application fee required: $50. On-campus interview required.

Athletics Interscholastic: baseball (boys), basketball (b,g), field hockey (g), hockey (b,g), indoor hockey (b,g), indoor track & field (b,g), soccer (b,g), softball (b,g), swimming and diving (b); coed interscholastic: alpine skiing, aquatics, cheering, cross-country running, dance team, golf. 1 PE instructor, 30 coaches.

Computers Computer network features include on-campus library services, online commercial services, Internet access, wireless campus network, Internet filtering or blocking technology. Campus intranet, student e-mail accounts, and computer access in designated common areas are available to students. Students grades are available online. The school has a published electronic and media policy.

Contact Mr. James Boulet, Director of Admissions. 207-782-6911 Ext. 2110. Fax: 207-795-6439. E-mail: james.boulet@portlanddiocese.org. Web site: www.st-dominic.net

SAINT EDWARD'S SCHOOL

1895 Saint Edward's Drive
Vero Beach, Florida 32963

Head of School: Mr. Michael J. Mersky

General Information Coeducational day college-preparatory, technology, and Advanced Placement school, affiliated with Episcopal Church. Grades PK–12. Founded: 1965. Setting: suburban. Nearest major city is West Palm Beach. 33-acre campus. 12 buildings on campus. Approved or accredited by Florida Council of Independent Schools, National Association of Episcopal Schools, Southern Association of Colleges and Schools, and The College Board. Member of National Association of Independent Schools and Secondary School Admission Test Board. Endowment: $4 million. Total enrollment: 500. Upper school average class size: 12. Upper school faculty-student ratio: 1:7. There are 175 required school days per year for Upper School students. Upper School students typically attend 5 days per week. The average school day consists of 5 hours and 45 minutes.

Upper School Student Profile Grade 9: 57 students (32 boys, 25 girls); Grade 10: 51 students (23 boys, 28 girls); Grade 11: 46 students (22 boys, 24 girls); Grade 12: 70 students (32 boys, 38 girls).

Faculty School total: 62. In upper school: 12 men, 16 women; 20 have advanced degrees.

Subjects Offered Advanced Placement courses, algebra, American history, American literature, anatomy and physiology, art, band, biology, biology-AP, calculus, calculus-AP, chemistry, chemistry-AP, Chinese, choir, choral music, chorus, Christian ethics, computer science-AP, concert band, concert choir, contemporary issues, contemporary studies, drama, economics, economics-AP, English, English as a foreign language, English language and composition-AP, English literature and composition-AP, ethics, fine arts, geometry, global studies, government, government-AP, graphic design, health and wellness, honors algebra, honors English, honors geometry, human geography - AP, instrumental music, Internet research, Mandarin, marine biology, mathematics, model United Nations, modern European history-AP, music, music theory-AP, performing arts, physical education, physical fitness, physics, physics-AP, pre-calculus, psychology, religion, science, senior internship, senior project, social sciences, social studies, sociology, Spanish, Spanish language-AP, statistics-AP, theater arts, U.S. government and politics-AP, U.S. history-AP, world history, world history-AP.

Graduation Requirements Arts and fine arts (art, music, dance, drama), English, foreign language, mathematics, physical education (includes health), religion (includes Bible studies and theology), science, social sciences, social studies (includes history), 25 hours of community service each year of high school.

Special Academic Programs Advanced Placement exam preparation; honors section; independent study; study at local college for college credit; study abroad; academic accommodation for the gifted, the musically talented, and the artistically talented; ESL (10 students enrolled).

College Admission Counseling 62 students graduated in 2011; all went to college, including Florida State University; New York University; The University of Alabama at Birmingham; University of Colorado Boulder; University of Florida; University of Miami. Mean SAT critical reading: 599, mean SAT math: 611, mean SAT writing: 596, mean combined SAT: 1807, mean composite ACT: 26. 53% scored over 600 on SAT critical reading, 58% scored over 600 on SAT math, 53% scored over 600 on SAT writing, 58% scored over 1800 on combined SAT, 57% scored over 26 on composite ACT.

Student Life Upper grades have specified standards of dress, student council, honor system. Discipline rests primarily with faculty. Attendance at religious services is required.

Tuition and Aid Day student tuition: $5800–$23,900. Tuition installment plan (FACTS Tuition Payment Plan, 1-, 2-, and 10-payment plans). Need-based scholarship grants available. In 2011–12, 32% of upper-school students received aid. Total amount of financial aid awarded in 2011–12: $889,050.

Admissions Traditional secondary-level entrance grade is 9. For fall 2011, 52 students applied for upper-level admission, 37 were accepted, 22 enrolled. ACT, PSAT, SAT or SSAT required. Deadline for receipt of application materials: February 15. Application fee required: $50. Interview recommended.

Athletics Interscholastic: baseball (boys), basketball (b,g), cheering (g), crew (b,g), cross-country running (b,g), football (b), golf (b,g), independent competitive sports (b,g), lacrosse (b,g), soccer (b,g), swimming and diving (b,g), tennis (b,g), volleyball (g), weight lifting (b,g); intramural: baseball (b), basketball (b,g), cheering (g), cross-country running (b,g), flagball (b), football (b), golf (b,g), lacrosse (b,g), physical fitness (b,g), sailing (b,g), soccer (b,g), tennis (b,g), volleyball (g); coed interscholastic: aquatics, swimming and diving; coed intramural: aquatics, outdoor education, physical fitness, soccer, softball. 4 PE instructors, 14 coaches, 1 athletic trainer.

Computers Computers are regularly used in all academic classes. Computer network features include on-campus library services, online commercial services, Internet access, wireless campus network, Internet filtering or blocking technology, issuance of tablet technology to all students in grades 6-12, electronic submission of homework, class assignments and homework available online. Campus intranet and student e-mail accounts are available to students. Students grades are available online. The school has a published electronic and media policy.

Contact Ms. Peggy Anderson, Director of Admission. 772-492-2364. Fax: 772-231-2427. E-mail: panderson@steds.org. Web site: www.steds.org

SAINT ELIZABETH HIGH SCHOOL

1530 34th Avenue
Oakland, California 94601

Head of School: Mr. Martin Procaccio

General Information Coeducational day college-preparatory, arts, and religious studies school, affiliated with Roman Catholic Church. Grades 9–12. Founded: 1921. Setting: urban. Nearest major city is Berkeley. 2-acre campus. 1 building on campus. Approved or accredited by National Catholic Education Association, Western Association of Schools and Colleges, and California Department of Education. Endowment: $100,000. Total enrollment: 142. Upper school average class size: 16. Upper school faculty-student ratio: 1:15. There are 180 required school days per year for Upper School students. Upper School students typically attend 5 days per week. The average school day consists of 6 hours and 48 minutes.

Upper School Student Profile Grade 9: 35 students (20 boys, 15 girls); Grade 10: 34 students (21 boys, 13 girls); Grade 11: 39 students (22 boys, 17 girls); Grade 12: 34 students (21 boys, 13 girls). 80% of students are Roman Catholic.

Faculty School total: 17. In upper school: 6 men, 10 women; 9 have advanced degrees.

Subjects Offered Advanced math, algebra, American literature, American literature-AP, anatomy and physiology, art and culture, biology, business mathematics, calculus-AP, Catholic belief and practice, chemistry, Christian and Hebrew scripture, Christian testament, civics, composition, computer applications, computer graphics, computer literacy, creative writing, drawing and design, economics, economics and history, English, English literature and composition-AP, geometry, journalism, learning strategies, moral and social development, physical education, physical science, physics, pre-algebra, pre-calculus, psychology, social justice, Spanish, Spanish language-AP, Spanish literature-AP, speech, speech communications, trigonometry, U.S. history, world cultures, world geography, world history, world religions.

Graduation Requirements Arts and fine arts (art, music, dance, drama), electives, English, foreign language, mathematics, physical education (includes health), religious studies, science, social sciences, 100 hours of community service.

Special Academic Programs 3 Advanced Placement exams for which test preparation is offered; honors section; remedial reading and/or remedial writing; remedial math; programs in English, mathematics for dyslexic students; special instructional classes for students with learning disabilities, Attention Deficit Disorder, dyslexia, and emotional and behavioral problems.

College Admission Counseling 42 students graduated in 2012; all went to college, including California State University, East Bay; San Francisco State University; San Jose State University; University of California, Berkeley; University of California, Davis.

Student Life Upper grades have specified standards of dress, honor system. Discipline rests primarily with faculty. Attendance at religious services is required.

Summer Programs Remediation programs offered; session focuses on academics; held on campus; accepts boys and girls; not open to students from other schools. 25 students usually enrolled. 2013 schedule: June 17 to July 16. Application deadline: June 1.

Tuition and Aid Day student tuition: $10,700. Tuition reduction for siblings, merit scholarship grants, need-based scholarship grants available. In 2012–13, 90% of upper-school students received aid; total upper-school merit-scholarship money awarded: $56,000. Total amount of financial aid awarded in 2012–13: $980,000.

Admissions Traditional secondary-level entrance grade is 9. For fall 2012, 77 students applied for upper-level admission, 63 were accepted, 41 enrolled. High School Placement Test required. Deadline for receipt of application materials: none. Application fee required: $75. Interview required.

Athletics Interscholastic: baseball (boys), basketball (b,g), football (b), soccer (b,g), softball (g), track and field (b,g), volleyball (b,g). 1 PE instructor, 5 coaches.

Computers Computer network features include on-campus library services, Internet access, wireless campus network, Internet filtering or blocking technology. Students grades are available online. The school has a published electronic and media policy.

Contact Lisseth Aguilar, Secretary. 510-532-8947. Fax: 510-532-9754. E-mail: laguilar@stliz-hs.org. Web site: www.stliz-hs.org

ST. FRANCIS DE SALES HIGH SCHOOL

2323 West Bancroft Street
Toledo, Ohio 43607

Head of School: Mr. Eric J. Smola

General Information Boys' day college-preparatory, religious studies, AP courses, and community service school, affiliated with Roman Catholic Church. Grades 9–12. Founded: 1955. Setting: urban. Nearest major city is Cleveland. 25-acre campus. 1 building on campus. Approved or accredited by Ohio Catholic Schools Accreditation Association (OCSAA) and Ohio Department of Education. Endowment: $7.1 million. Total enrollment: 612. Upper school average class size: 24. Upper school faculty-student ratio: 1:14. There are 180 required school days per year for Upper School students. Upper School students typically attend 5 days per week. The average school day consists of 6 hours and 30 minutes.

Upper School Student Profile Grade 9: 148 students (148 boys); Grade 10: 174 students (174 boys); Grade 11: 164 students (164 boys); Grade 12: 126 students (126 boys). 71% of students are Roman Catholic.

Faculty School total: 58. In upper school: 44 men, 14 women; 37 have advanced degrees.
Subjects Offered Advanced Placement courses, advanced studio art-AP, algebra, American history, American history-AP, American literature, American literature-AP, anatomy, animation, art, biology, biology-AP, British literature, calculus, calculus-AP, ceramics, chemistry, chemistry-AP, Chinese, chorus, church history, community service, computer science, computer-aided design, creative writing, criminal justice, drawing, economics, English literature, English-AP, environmental science, expository writing, French, French-AP, geometry, government/civics, grammar, graphic design, health, journalism, Latin, Latin-AP, macroeconomics-AP, math analysis, mathematics, microeconomics-AP, military history, music, mythology, New Testament, physical education, physical science, physics, physics-AP, pre-calculus, psychology, psychology-AP, public speaking, science, social justice, social studies, sociology, Spanish, Spanish-AP, statistics, theology, trigonometry, U.S. government, U.S. government and politics-AP, U.S. history-AP, Web site design, world geography, world history, yearbook.
Graduation Requirements Art, computer science, English, foreign language, mathematics, physical education (includes health), religion (includes Bible studies and theology), science, social studies (includes history), participation in religious retreats four of 4 years. Community service is required.
Special Academic Programs Advanced Placement exam preparation; honors section; study at local college for college credit; ESL (9 students enrolled).
College Admission Counseling 150 students graduated in 2012; 149 went to college, including Bowling Green State University; Eastern Michigan University; The Ohio State University; The University of Toledo; University of Cincinnati; University of Dayton. Other: 1 entered military service. Mean SAT critical reading: 544, mean SAT math: 550, mean SAT writing: 517, mean composite ACT: 24.
Student Life Upper grades have specified standards of dress, student council. Discipline rests primarily with faculty. Attendance at religious services is required.
Summer Programs Enrichment programs offered; session focuses on mathematics, English, reading; held on campus; accepts boys; not open to students from other schools. 100 students usually enrolled. 2013 schedule: June 12 to July 2. Application deadline: June 1.
Tuition and Aid Day student tuition: $9800. Tuition installment plan (monthly payment plans, quarterly payment plan). Tuition reduction for siblings, merit scholarship grants, need-based scholarship grants, paying campus jobs available. In 2012–13, 66% of upper-school students received aid; total upper-school merit-scholarship money awarded: $45,000. Total amount of financial aid awarded in 2012–13: $1,600,000.
Admissions Traditional secondary-level entrance grade is 9. For fall 2012, 197 students applied for upper-level admission, 178 were accepted, 149 enrolled. STS required. Deadline for receipt of application materials: none. No application fee required. On-campus interview required.
Athletics Interscholastic: baseball, basketball, bowling, crew, cross-country running, diving, football, golf, ice hockey, lacrosse, soccer, swimming and diving, tennis, track and field, water polo, winter (indoor) track, wrestling; intramural: basketball, football. 4 PE instructors, 49 coaches, 2 athletic trainers.
Computers Computers are regularly used in animation, art, desktop publishing, English, mathematics, science, Web site design classes. Computer network features include Internet access, Internet filtering or blocking technology. Student e-mail accounts and computer access in designated common areas are available to students. Students grades are available online. The school has a published electronic and media policy.
Contact Mrs. Jacqueline VanDemark, Administrative Assistant. 419-531-1618. Fax: 419-531-9740. E-mail: jvandemark@sfstoledo.org. Web site: www.sfstoledo.org

SAINT FRANCIS HIGH SCHOOL

200 Foothill Boulevard
La Canada Flintridge, California 91011

Head of School: Mr. Thomas G. Moran

General Information Boys' day college-preparatory and religious studies school, affiliated with Roman Catholic Church. Grades 9–12. Founded: 1946. Setting: suburban. Nearest major city is Los Angeles. 19-acre campus. 5 buildings on campus. Approved or accredited by Western Association of Schools and Colleges and Western Catholic Education Association. Total enrollment: 671. Upper school average class size: 28. Upper school faculty-student ratio: 1:15. There are 182 required school days per year for Upper School students. Upper School students typically attend 5 days per week. The average school day consists of 6 hours.
Upper School Student Profile Grade 9: 196 students (196 boys); Grade 10: 168 students (168 boys); Grade 11: 166 students (166 boys); Grade 12: 141 students (141 boys). 70% of students are Roman Catholic.
Faculty School total: 48. In upper school: 38 men, 10 women; 20 have advanced degrees.
Subjects Offered Advanced Placement courses, English, fine arts, foreign language, health, history, mathematics, physical education, religion, science, social sciences, technology.
Graduation Requirements Arts and fine arts (art, music, dance, drama), English, foreign language, mathematics, physical education (includes health), religion (includes Bible studies and theology), science, social sciences, technology, Christian service hours, retreat each year of attendance. Community service is required.
Special Academic Programs Advanced Placement exam preparation; honors section.
College Admission Counseling 165 students graduated in 2012; all went to college, including California State University, Northridge; Loyola Marymount University; Texas Christian University. Mean SAT critical reading: 561, mean SAT math: 557, mean SAT writing: 538, mean composite ACT: 23.
Student Life Upper grades have specified standards of dress, student council. Discipline rests primarily with faculty. Attendance at religious services is required.
Summer Programs Remediation, enrichment, sports programs offered; session focuses on remediation and enrichment; held on campus; accepts boys and girls; open to students from other schools. 400 students usually enrolled. 2013 schedule: June 24 to July 26. Application deadline: June 17.
Tuition and Aid Day student tuition: $12,500. Tuition installment plan (FACTS Tuition Payment Plan, monthly payment plans). Merit scholarship grants, need-based scholarship grants available. In 2012–13, 20% of upper-school students received aid; total upper-school merit-scholarship money awarded: $35,000. Total amount of financial aid awarded in 2012–13: $500,000.
Admissions Traditional secondary-level entrance grade is 9. For fall 2012, 420 students applied for upper-level admission, 220 were accepted, 196 enrolled. High School Placement Test required. Deadline for receipt of application materials: January 26. Application fee required: $75. On-campus interview required.
Athletics Interscholastic: baseball, basketball, cross-country running, football, golf, lacrosse, soccer, tennis, track and field, volleyball. 3 PE instructors, 14 coaches, 1 athletic trainer.
Computers Computers are regularly used in all academic, yearbook classes. Computer network features include on-campus library services, Internet access, wireless campus network, Internet filtering or blocking technology. Students grades are available online. The school has a published electronic and media policy.
Contact Mrs. Stephanie Martinez, Registrar. 818-790-0325 Ext. 502. Fax: 818-790-5542. E-mail: martinezs@sfhs.net. Web site: www.sfhs.net

ST. FRANCIS HIGH SCHOOL

233 West Broadway
Louisville, Kentucky 40202

Head of School: Ms. Alexandra Schreiber Thurstone

General Information Coeducational day college-preparatory and arts school. Grades 9–12. Founded: 1976. Setting: urban. 2-acre campus. 1 building on campus. Approved or accredited by Independent Schools Association of the Central States and Kentucky Department of Education. Member of National Association of Independent Schools. Endowment: $1 million. Total enrollment: 136. Upper school average class size: 11. Upper school faculty-student ratio: 1:7. There are 174 required school days per year for Upper School students. Upper School students typically attend 5 days per week. The average school day consists of 7 hours.
Upper School Student Profile Grade 9: 24 students (12 boys, 12 girls); Grade 10: 33 students (12 boys, 21 girls); Grade 11: 43 students (25 boys, 18 girls); Grade 12: 32 students (18 boys, 14 girls).
Faculty School total: 20. In upper school: 12 men, 8 women; 15 have advanced degrees.
Subjects Offered African studies, algebra, American history, ancient history, ancient world history, art, biology, biology-AP, business, calculus, calculus-AP, chemistry, chemistry-AP, Chinese, Chinese history, civil rights, community service, creative writing, drama, drawing, English, English literature, English literature-AP, environmental science, environmental science-AP, European history, European history-AP, film studies, filmmaking, fine arts, finite math, French, French language-AP, French literature-AP, French-AP, gender and religion, gender issues, geometry, health, history-AP, journalism, law, medieval history, modern civilization, photography, physical education, physics, physics-AP, playwriting, pre-calculus, senior project, Spanish, Spanish language-AP, Spanish literature-AP, Spanish-AP, statistics, statistics-AP, The 20th Century, U.S. history-AP, video film production, world history, writing, zoology.
Graduation Requirements Arts and fine arts (art, music, dance, drama), English, foreign language, history, mathematics, physical education (includes health), science, senior project (year-long research project on a topic of student's choice). Community service is required.
Special Academic Programs Advanced Placement exam preparation; independent study; study abroad; academic accommodation for the gifted and the artistically talented.
College Admission Counseling 34 students graduated in 2012; 33 went to college. Other: 1 entered military service.
Student Life Upper grades have student council. Discipline rests equally with students and faculty.
Summer Programs Remediation, enrichment, advancement, sports programs offered; session focuses on enrichment; held on campus; accepts boys and girls; open to students from other schools. 40 students usually enrolled. 2013 schedule: June 1 to August 13. Application deadline: April 1.
Tuition and Aid Day student tuition: $18,950. Tuition installment plan (Insured Tuition Payment Plan, FACTS Tuition Payment Plan, monthly payment plans). Merit scholarship grants, need-based scholarship grants, tuition remission for children of faculty and staff available. In 2012–13, 46% of upper-school students received aid; total

upper-school merit-scholarship money awarded: $44,710. Total amount of financial aid awarded in 2012–13: $615,000.

Admissions Traditional secondary-level entrance grade is 9. For fall 2012, 47 students applied for upper-level admission, 42 were accepted, 39 enrolled. Deadline for receipt of application materials: January 15. Application fee required: $50. On-campus interview required.

Athletics Interscholastic: basketball (boys, girls), bicycling (b,g), bowling (g), field hockey (g), fitness (b,g), lacrosse (b), running (b,g), tennis (b,g), track and field (b,g), volleyball (g); intramural: indoor hockey (g), indoor soccer (b); coed interscholastic: indoor track & field, soccer; coed intramural: dance team, fitness, physical fitness, physical training, power lifting, racquetball, rowing, ultimate Frisbee, wall climbing, wallyball, weight lifting, weight training, yoga. 1 PE instructor, 12 coaches.

Computers Computers are regularly used in English, French, history, mathematics, science, Spanish classes. Computer network features include Internet access, wireless campus network, word processing, publishing, and Web page programs. Student e-mail accounts and computer access in designated common areas are available to students. The school has a published electronic and media policy.

Contact Ms. Annie Murphy, Director of Admissions. 502-736-1009. Fax: 502-736-1049. E-mail: murphy@stfrancisschool.org. Web site: www.stfrancisschool.org

SAINT FRANCIS SCHOOL

2707 Pamoa Road
Honolulu, Hawaii 96822

Head of School: Sr. Joan of Arc Souza

General Information Coeducational day college-preparatory, arts, religious studies, bilingual studies, technology, and ESL school, affiliated with Roman Catholic Church. Boys grades K–11, girls grades K–12. Founded: 1924. Setting: suburban. 11-acre campus. 9 buildings on campus. Approved or accredited by Western Association of Schools and Colleges, Western Catholic Education Association, and Hawaii Department of Education. Member of National Association of Independent Schools. Total enrollment: 445. Upper school average class size: 20. Upper school faculty-student ratio: 1:20. There are 180 required school days per year for Upper School students. Upper School students typically attend 5 days per week. The average school day consists of 6 hours and 30 minutes.

Upper School Student Profile Grade 9: 75 students (47 boys, 28 girls); Grade 10: 71 students (43 boys, 28 girls); Grade 11: 79 students (59 boys, 20 girls); Grade 12: 41 students (41 girls). 60% of students are Roman Catholic.

Faculty School total: 46. In upper school: 13 men, 33 women; 21 have advanced degrees.

Subjects Offered Algebra, American history, American literature, American sign language, ancient history, art, band, Bible studies, biology, biology-AP, calculus-AP, Catholic belief and practice, ceramics, chemistry, choir, chorus, cinematography, college admission preparation, college counseling, college planning, computer literacy, computer technologies, creative writing, earth science, English, English language and composition-AP, English literature, English literature and composition-AP, environmental science, ESL, fine arts, geography, geometry, government-AP, government/civics, grammar, health, history, humanities, Japanese, journalism, keyboarding, mathematics, medieval/Renaissance history, music, newspaper, NJROTC, oral communications, physical education, physical science, physics, pre-algebra, pre-calculus, psychology, religion, SAT preparation, science, social studies, Spanish, Spanish language-AP, speech, theater, TOEFL preparation, trigonometry, U.S. history-AP, world history, world literature, world religions, writing, yearbook.

Graduation Requirements Algebra, American history, American literature, arts and fine arts (art, music, dance, drama), biology, chemistry, computer applications, computer skills, English, foreign language, humanities, keyboarding, mathematics, physical education (includes health), religion (includes Bible studies and theology), science, social studies (includes history), U.S. history, 100 hours of community service. Community service is required.

Special Academic Programs 7 Advanced Placement exams for which test preparation is offered; honors section; independent study; study at local college for college credit; ESL (15 students enrolled).

College Admission Counseling 56 students graduated in 2011; 53 went to college, including Chaminade University of Honolulu; Hawai`i Pacific University; Seattle University; Southern Oregon University; University of Hawaii at Manoa; University of Oregon. Other: 3 went to work.

Student Life Upper grades have uniform requirement, student council, honor system. Discipline rests primarily with faculty. Attendance at religious services is required.

Tuition and Aid Day student tuition: $8600. Tuition installment plan (FACTS Tuition Payment Plan, monthly payment plans, individually arranged payment plans, semi-annual payment plan). Tuition reduction for siblings, merit scholarship grants, need-based scholarship grants, alumni scholarships, Support A Student Scholarships, Alverna Scholarships available. In 2011–12, 38% of upper-school students received aid; total upper-school merit-scholarship money awarded: $173,000. Total amount of financial aid awarded in 2011–12: $317,000.

Admissions Traditional secondary-level entrance grade is 9. For fall 2011, 291 students applied for upper-level admission, 227 were accepted, 137 enrolled. School placement exam or SSAT required. Deadline for receipt of application materials: none. Application fee required: $40. Interview required.

Athletics Interscholastic: baseball (boys), basketball (b,g), bowling (g), canoeing/kayaking (b,g), cheering (b,g), football (b), ocean paddling (g), paddling (g), riflery (b,g), running (g), soccer (g), softball (g), swimming and diving (b,g), tennis (b,g), track and field (b,g), volleyball (g), water polo (g), wrestling (b,g); coed interscholastic: cross-country running, golf, JROTC drill, weight training. 2 PE instructors, 36 coaches, 1 athletic trainer.

Computers Computers are regularly used in art, English, foreign language, mathematics, music, newspaper, religion, science, social studies, yearbook classes. Computer network features include on-campus library services, Internet access, wireless campus network, Internet filtering or blocking technology. Computer access in designated common areas is available to students. Students grades are available online. The school has a published electronic and media policy.

Contact Karen Curry, Director of Admissions. 808-988-4111 Ext. 712. Fax: 808-988-5497. E-mail: kcurry@stfrancis-oahu.org. Web site: www.stfrancis-oahu.org

ST. GEORGE'S INDEPENDENT SCHOOL

1880 Wolf River Road
Collierville, Tennessee 38017

Head of School: Mr. William W. Taylor

General Information Coeducational day college-preparatory school, affiliated with Christian faith. Grades PK–12. Founded: 1959. Setting: suburban. Nearest major city is Memphis. 250-acre campus. 5 buildings on campus. Approved or accredited by Southern Association of Colleges and Schools and Southern Association of Independent Schools. Member of National Association of Independent Schools. Endowment: $3.4 million. Total enrollment: 1,195. Upper school average class size: 19. Upper school faculty-student ratio: 1:7. There are 175 required school days per year for Upper School students. Upper School students typically attend 5 days per week. The average school day consists of 7 hours and 18 minutes.

Upper School Student Profile Grade 9: 108 students (55 boys, 53 girls); Grade 10: 99 students (54 boys, 45 girls); Grade 11: 87 students (46 boys, 41 girls); Grade 12: 95 students (50 boys, 45 girls).

Faculty School total: 148. In upper school: 28 men, 27 women; 34 have advanced degrees.

Subjects Offered Algebra, American literature, astronomy, band, biology, biology-AP, calculus, calculus-AP, chemistry, chemistry-AP, chorus, computer programming, drawing, English, English language and composition-AP, English literature and composition-AP, environmental science, ethics, European history-AP, European literature, film, French, French language-AP, geometry, global studies, government/civics, honors algebra, honors geometry, human anatomy, independent study, journalism, Latin, Latin-AP, painting, philosophy, photography, physics, physics-AP, pottery, pre-calculus, printmaking, psychology, religion, short story, social justice, Southern literature, Spanish, Spanish language-AP, statistics-AP, theater, trigonometry, U.S. history, U.S. history-AP, visual arts, wellness, world history, world history-AP.

Graduation Requirements Art, electives, English, history, independent study, language, mathematics, religion (includes Bible studies and theology), science, wellness, senior independent study, senior Global Challenge.

Special Academic Programs Advanced Placement exam preparation; honors section; independent study.

College Admission Counseling 103 students graduated in 2012; all went to college, including Baylor University; Mississippi State University; The University of Alabama; The University of Tennessee; University of Memphis; University of Mississippi. Mean SAT critical reading: 626, mean SAT math: 594, mean SAT writing: 606, mean combined SAT: 1826, mean composite ACT: 27.

Student Life Upper grades have specified standards of dress, student council, honor system. Discipline rests equally with students and faculty. Attendance at religious services is required.

Summer Programs Remediation, enrichment, advancement, sports, art/fine arts, computer instruction programs offered; session focuses on enrichment; held on campus; accepts boys and girls; open to students from other schools. 2013 schedule: June to August. Application deadline: June.

Tuition and Aid Day student tuition: $16,590. Tuition installment plan (individually arranged payment plans, One payment per year, two payments per year, and four payments per year.). Need-based scholarship grants available. In 2012–13, 14% of upper-school students received aid. Total amount of financial aid awarded in 2012–13: $389,652.

Admissions Traditional secondary-level entrance grade is 9. For fall 2012, 46 students applied for upper-level admission, 28 were accepted, 23 enrolled. Admissions testing or ISEE required. Deadline for receipt of application materials: none. Application fee required: $50. Interview required.

Athletics Interscholastic: baseball (boys), basketball (b,g), cheering (g), cross-country running (b,g), football (b), golf (b,g), lacrosse (b,g), pom squad (g), soccer (b,g), softball (g), tennis (b,g), track and field (b,g), volleyball (g), wrestling (b); coed interscholastic: swimming and diving; coed intramural: equestrian sports. 5 PE instructors, 24 coaches, 2 athletic trainers.

Computers Computers are regularly used in all classes. Computer network features include on-campus library services, Internet access, wireless campus network, Internet filtering or blocking technology. Campus intranet, student e-mail accounts, and computer access in designated common areas are available to students. Students grades are available online. The school has a published electronic and media policy.

Contact Mrs. Jennifer Taylor, Director of Admission. 901-457-2000. Fax: 901-457-2111. E-mail: jtaylor@sgis.org. Web site: www.sgis.org

ST. GEORGE'S SCHOOL

372 Purgatory Road
Middletown, Rhode Island 02842-5984

Head of School: Eric F. Peterson

General Information Coeducational boarding and day college-preparatory, arts, religious studies, technology, and marine sciences school, affiliated with Episcopal Church. Grades 9–12. Founded: 1896. Setting: suburban. Nearest major city is Providence. Students are housed in single-sex dormitories. 150-acre campus. 47 buildings on campus. Approved or accredited by Association of Independent Schools in New England, National Association of Episcopal Schools, New England Association of Schools and Colleges, The Association of Boarding Schools, and Rhode Island Department of Education. Member of National Association of Independent Schools and Secondary School Admission Test Board. Endowment: $110 million. Total enrollment: 365. Upper school average class size: 11. Upper school faculty-student ratio: 1:6. Upper School students typically attend 6 days per week. The average school day consists of 6 hours and 50 minutes.

Upper School Student Profile Grade 9: 70 students (39 boys, 31 girls); Grade 10: 98 students (47 boys, 51 girls); Grade 11: 101 students (50 boys, 51 girls); Grade 12: 96 students (50 boys, 46 girls). 82% of students are boarding students. 21% are state residents. 31 states are represented in upper school student body. 15% are international students. International students from Canada, China, Germany, and Republic of Korea; 16 other countries represented in student body.

Faculty School total: 69. In upper school: 32 men, 37 women; 55 have advanced degrees; 56 reside on campus.

Subjects Offered 3-dimensional art, 3-dimensional design, acting, advanced biology, advanced chemistry, advanced computer applications, advanced math, Advanced Placement courses, advanced studio art-AP, African American history, African American studies, algebra, American history, American history-AP, American literature, American literature-AP, American studies, analytic geometry, architectural drawing, architecture, art, art history, art-AP, Asian studies, Bible, Bible as literature, Bible studies, biology, biology-AP, calculus, calculus-AP, ceramics, chemistry, chemistry-AP, Chinese, computer graphics, computer math, computer programming, computer science, computer science-AP, creative writing, dance, DNA, drama, dramatic arts, drawing, ecology, economics, economics-AP, English, English language and composition-AP, English literature, English literature-AP, environmental science, environmental science-AP, ethics, European history, European history-AP, expository writing, fine arts, French, French language-AP, geometry, global studies, government/civics, grammar, health, history, journalism, Latin, Latin-AP, law, logic, macro/microeconomics-AP, Mandarin, marine biology, mathematics, microbiology, music, music theory-AP, navigation, oceanography, philosophy, photography, physics, physics-AP, psychology, public speaking, religion, robotics, science, sculpture, social studies, Spanish, Spanish language-AP, Spanish literature-AP, statistics, studio art-AP, theater, theology, trigonometry, U.S. government and politics-AP, veterinary science, world history, world history-AP, world literature, writing.

Graduation Requirements Arts and fine arts (art, music, dance, drama), computer science, English, foreign language, mathematics, physical education (includes health), religion (includes Bible studies and theology), science, social studies (includes history).

Special Academic Programs Advanced Placement exam preparation; honors section; independent study; term-away projects; study abroad; academic accommodation for the gifted, the musically talented, and the artistically talented.

College Admission Counseling 89 students graduated in 2012; all went to college, including Babson College; Boston College; Georgetown University; Middlebury College; The George Washington University; Wake Forest University. Mean SAT critical reading: 626, mean SAT math: 651, mean SAT writing: 628, mean combined SAT: 1905.

Student Life Upper grades have specified standards of dress, student council, honor system. Discipline rests primarily with faculty. Attendance at religious services is required.

Tuition and Aid Day student tuition: $34,150; 7-day tuition and room/board: $49,750. Tuition installment plan (Insured Tuition Payment Plan, Academic Management Services Plan, Key Tuition Payment Plan, monthly payment plans, individually arranged payment plans). Need-based scholarship grants, need-based loans, middle-income loans available. In 2012–13, 30% of upper-school students received aid.

Admissions Traditional secondary-level entrance grade is 9. For fall 2012, 690 students applied for upper-level admission, 188 were accepted, 103 enrolled. ISEE, PSAT, SSAT or TOEFL required. Deadline for receipt of application materials: February 1. Application fee required: $50. Interview required.

Athletics Interscholastic: baseball (boys), basketball (b,g), cross-country running (b,g), field hockey (g), football (b), hockey (b,g), ice hockey (b,g), lacrosse (b,g), sailing (b,g), soccer (b,g), softball (g), squash (b,g), swimming and diving (b,g), tennis (b,g), track and field (b,g); coed interscholastic: dance, sailing; coed intramural: aerobics/dance, dance, modern dance, mountain biking, Nautilus, soccer, softball, squash, strength & conditioning. 3 coaches, 3 athletic trainers.

Computers Computers are regularly used in art, English, foreign language, history, mathematics, music, religion, science, theater classes. Computer network features include on-campus library services, online commercial services, Internet access, wireless campus network, Internet filtering or blocking technology, scanners, digital cameras, and access to printers. Campus intranet, student e-mail accounts, and computer access in designated common areas are available to students. Students grades are available online. The school has a published electronic and media policy.

Contact Ryan P. Mulhern, Director of Admission. 401-842-6600. Fax: 401-842-6696. E-mail: admission@stgeorges.edu. Web site: www.stgeorges.edu

ST. GEORGE'S SCHOOL

4175 West 29th Avenue
Vancouver, British Columbia V6S 1V1, Canada

Head of School: Dr. Tom Matthews

General Information Boys' boarding and day college-preparatory, arts, bilingual studies, and technology school. Boarding grades 7–12, day grades 1–12. Founded: 1930. Setting: suburban. Students are housed in single-sex dormitories. 27-acre campus. 2 buildings on campus. Approved or accredited by Canadian Association of Independent Schools, The Association of Boarding Schools, and British Columbia Department of Education. Affiliate member of National Association of Independent Schools; member of Secondary School Admission Test Board. Language of instruction: English. Total enrollment: 1,157. Upper school average class size: 19. Upper school faculty-student ratio: 1:10. The average school day consists of 6 hours.

Upper School Student Profile Grade 8: 144 students (144 boys); Grade 9: 149 students (149 boys); Grade 10: 157 students (157 boys); Grade 11: 156 students (156 boys); Grade 12: 155 students (155 boys). 18% of students are boarding students. 91% are province residents. 9 provinces are represented in upper school student body. 9% are international students. International students from Germany, Hong Kong, Mexico, Republic of Korea, Taiwan, and United States; 4 other countries represented in student body.

Faculty School total: 130. In upper school: 63 men, 23 women; 35 have advanced degrees; 9 reside on campus.

Subjects Offered Advanced chemistry, advanced computer applications, advanced math, algebra, analysis and differential calculus, applied arts, applied music, applied skills, architecture, art, art history, art history-AP, biology, biology-AP, business, business skills, calculus, calculus-AP, Canadian geography, Canadian history, Canadian literature, career and personal planning, ceramics, chemistry, chemistry-AP, comparative government and politics-AP, computer graphics, computer programming, computer programming-AP, computer science, computer science-AP, creative writing, critical thinking, debate, drama, drama performance, dramatic arts, earth science, economics, economics-AP, English, English literature, English literature-AP, environmental science, European history, expository writing, film, fine arts, French, French-AP, geography, geology, geometry, German, German-AP, government/civics, grammar, history, industrial arts, introduction to theater, Japanese, journalism, Latin, Latin-AP, law, library, Mandarin, mathematics, mathematics-AP, music, music-AP, performing arts, photography, physical education, physical fitness, physics, physics-AP, psychology, psychology-AP, science, social studies, society, politics and law, Spanish, Spanish-AP, speech and debate, studio art, studio art-AP, technical theater, theater, trigonometry, typing, U.S. history-AP, United States government-AP, Western civilization, world history, world literature, writing.

Graduation Requirements Arts and fine arts (art, music, dance, drama), business skills (includes word processing), English, foreign language, mathematics, physical education (includes health), science, social studies (includes history).

Special Academic Programs Advanced Placement exam preparation; honors section; remedial reading and/or remedial writing.

College Admission Counseling 155 students graduated in 2012; 152 went to college, including McGill University; Queen's University at Kingston; The University of British Columbia; The University of Western Ontario; University of Toronto; University of Victoria.

Student Life Upper grades have uniform requirement, student council, honor system. Discipline rests primarily with faculty.

Summer Programs Advancement, ESL, sports, art/fine arts, computer instruction programs offered; session focuses on recreation and enrichment; held both on and off campus; held at other schools in area (outdoor education); accepts boys and girls; open to students from other schools. 1,000 students usually enrolled. 2013 schedule: July 2 to August 15. Application deadline: none.

Tuition and Aid Day student tuition: CAN$15,355–CAN$46,000; 7-day tuition and room/board: CAN$37,470–CAN$46,000. Tuition installment plan (monthly payment plans, individually arranged payment plans, term payment plan, one-time payment plan). Tuition reduction for siblings, bursaries, merit scholarship grants, need-based scholarship grants available. In 2012–13, 12% of upper-school students received aid; total upper-school merit-scholarship money awarded: CAN$75,000. Total amount of financial aid awarded in 2012–13: CAN$800,000.

Admissions Traditional secondary-level entrance grade is 8. For fall 2012, 250 students applied for upper-level admission, 90 were accepted, 50 enrolled. School's own exam and SSAT required. Deadline for receipt of application materials: February 10. Application fee required: CAN$200. Interview required.

Athletics Interscholastic: badminton, basketball, cricket, cross-country running, field hockey, golf, ice hockey, rowing, rugby, soccer, swimming and diving, tennis, track and field, triathlon, volleyball, water polo; intramural: badminton, ball hockey, basketball, bicycling, canoeing/kayaking, cross-country running, flag football, floor hockey, ice hockey, martial arts, outdoor education, outdoor recreation, physical fitness, rugby, running, sailing, skiing (downhill), soccer, softball, squash, swimming and diving, table tennis, tennis, track and field, ultimate Frisbee, volleyball, water polo, weight lifting. 4 PE instructors, 8 coaches.

Computers Computers are regularly used in desktop publishing, history, information technology, mathematics, media, publications, science, technology classes. Computer network features include on-campus library services, online commercial services, Internet access. The school has a published electronic and media policy.

Contact Mr. Gordon C. Allan, Director of Admissions. 604-221-3881. Fax: 604-224-5820. E-mail: gallan@stgeorges.bc.ca. Web site: www.stgeorges.bc.ca

ST. GEORGE'S SCHOOL OF MONTREAL

3100 The Boulevard
Montreal, Quebec H3Y 1R9, Canada

Head of School: Mr. James A. Officer

General Information Coeducational day college-preparatory, arts, bilingual studies, technology, Sports études, and Performing Arts études school. Grades K–11. Founded: 1930. Setting: urban. 2-acre campus. 1 building on campus. Approved or accredited by Canadian Association of Independent Schools, Quebec Association of Independent Schools, and Quebec Department of Education. Affiliate member of National Association of Independent Schools. Languages of instruction: English and French. Total enrollment: 426. Upper school average class size: 19. Upper school faculty-student ratio: 1:15. There are 181 required school days per year for Upper School students. Upper School students typically attend 5 days per week. The average school day consists of 6 hours and 45 minutes.

Upper School Student Profile Grade 7: 50 students (25 boys, 25 girls); Grade 8: 45 students (28 boys, 17 girls); Grade 9: 47 students (36 boys, 11 girls); Grade 10: 58 students (31 boys, 27 girls); Grade 11: 36 students (17 boys, 19 girls).

Faculty School total: 33. In upper school: 12 men, 21 women; 16 have advanced degrees.

Subjects Offered Advanced math, advanced studio art-AP, algebra, ancient history, art, art appreciation, art history, biology, calculus, calculus-AP, Canadian history, chemistry, college counseling, communication skills, community service, competitive science projects, computer animation, computer art, computer multimedia, concert band, concert choir, contemporary issues, creative thinking, creative writing, critical thinking, dance, debate, desktop publishing, digital art, drama, drama performance, earth science, English, English literature and composition-AP, English-AP, environmental education, environmental science, ESL, ethics, experimental science, expository writing, filmmaking, fine arts, fitness, food and nutrition, French as a second language, French studies, French-AP, general math, general science, geography, government/civics, health education, independent study, instrumental music, integrated science, interdisciplinary studies, Internet research, jazz band, jazz ensemble, leadership, leadership education training, library research, marine biology, mathematics, media arts, media literacy, mentorship program, model United Nations, music, music appreciation, musical productions, musical theater dance, oral communications, outdoor education, performing arts, photography, physical education, physical fitness, physics, play production, play/screen writing, portfolio art, pre-calculus, psychology, psychology-AP, research skills, robotics, science and technology, science project, set design, sex education, social studies, Spanish, sports science, student publications, studio art-AP, swimming, tennis, track and field, writing, yoga.

Graduation Requirements Art, economics, electives, English, ethics, French as a second language, mathematics, physical education (includes health), science, social studies (includes history), community service learning.

Special Academic Programs 7 Advanced Placement exams for which test preparation is offered; honors section; independent study; academic accommodation for the gifted, the musically talented, and the artistically talented; remedial reading and/or remedial writing; remedial math; ESL (7 students enrolled).

College Admission Counseling 58 students graduated in 2012; all went to college.

Student Life Upper grades have specified standards of dress, student council. Discipline rests primarily with faculty.

Tuition and Aid Guaranteed tuition plan. Tuition installment plan (4 Payments (1, 2 or 4 Payments)). Tuition reduction for siblings, need-based scholarship grants available.

Admissions Traditional secondary-level entrance grade is 7. For fall 2012, 132 students applied for upper-level admission, 70 were accepted, 49 enrolled. Academic Profile Tests or placement test required. Deadline for receipt of application materials: January 25. Application fee required: CAN$50. Interview required.

Athletics Interscholastic: badminton (boys, girls), basketball (b,g), cross-country running (b,g), flag football (g), football (b), golf (b,g), rugby (b), running (b,g), soccer (b,g), swimming and diving (b,g), tennis (b,g), track and field (b,g); intramural: badminton (b,g); coed interscholastic: aquatics, independent competitive sports, indoor soccer, jogging; coed intramural: aerobics, alpine skiing, aquatics, ball hockey, baseball, basketball, bicycling, canoeing/kayaking, Circus, climbing, cooperative games, Cosom hockey, cross-country running, curling, dance, fencing, fitness, fitness walking, floor hockey, ice hockey, indoor soccer, jogging, lacrosse, life saving, martial arts, outdoor recreation, physical fitness, scuba diving, self defense, skiing (cross-country), soccer, squash, track and field, volleyball, wall climbing, yoga. 3 PE instructors, 5 coaches.

Computers Computers are regularly used in all classes. Computer network features include on-campus library services, Internet access, wireless campus network, Internet filtering or blocking technology. Campus intranet and student e-mail accounts are available to students. The school has a published electronic and media policy.

Contact Ms. Kathay Carson, Director of Admissions. 514-904-0542. Fax: 514-933-3621. E-mail: kathay.carson@stgeorges.qc.ca. Web site: www.stgeorges.qc.ca

ST. GREGORY COLLEGE PREPARATORY SCHOOL

3231 North Craycroft Road
Tucson, Arizona 85712

Head of School: Mr. A. Richard Belding

General Information Coeducational day college-preparatory and arts school. Grades 6–12. Founded: 1980. Setting: suburban. 40-acre campus. 9 buildings on campus. Approved or accredited by Independent Schools Association of the Southwest, The College Board, and Arizona Department of Education. Member of National Association of Independent Schools and Secondary School Admission Test Board. Total enrollment: 299. Upper school average class size: 16. Upper school faculty-student ratio: 1:9. Upper School students typically attend 5 days per week. The average school day consists of 7 hours and 30 minutes.

Upper School Student Profile Grade 9: 41 students (19 boys, 22 girls); Grade 10: 42 students (21 boys, 21 girls); Grade 11: 54 students (31 boys, 23 girls); Grade 12: 52 students (27 boys, 25 girls).

Faculty School total: 34. In upper school: 11 men, 12 women; 17 have advanced degrees.

Subjects Offered Advanced studio art-AP, algebra, American history, American literature, anatomy and physiology, ancient world history, art, art history, band, biology, biology-AP, calculus, ceramics, chemistry, chemistry-AP, choir, chorus, college counseling, college placement, community service, comparative government and politics-AP, computer programming, creative writing, drama, earth science, ecology, economics, English, English literature, English-AP, ethics, European history, European history-AP, expository writing, fine arts, finite math, French, French language-AP, French-AP, geography, geology, geometry, government and politics-AP, government/civics, government/civics-AP, grammar, history, history of drama, history of music, humanities, independent study, jazz band, journalism, Latin, Latin-AP, literature, marine biology, mathematics, music, music theory, music theory-AP, newspaper, photography, physical education, physical science, physics, pre-calculus, religion, SAT preparation, science, social studies, Spanish, Spanish language-AP, Spanish-AP, speech, stage design, stagecraft, studio art-AP, theater, trigonometry, U.S. government and politics-AP, U.S. history-AP, world history, writing.

Graduation Requirements Arts and fine arts (art, music, dance, drama), English, foreign language, history, humanities, mathematics, science, senior internships. Community service is required.

Special Academic Programs Advanced Placement exam preparation; honors section; accelerated programs; independent study; term-away projects; study at local college for college credit; academic accommodation for the gifted, the musically talented, and the artistically talented.

College Admission Counseling 29 students graduated in 2012; 28 went to college, including Brown University; Princeton University; Smith College; Stanford University; The University of Arizona. Other: 1 went to work. Mean SAT critical reading: 573, mean SAT math: 590, mean composite ACT: 26.

Student Life Upper grades have specified standards of dress, student council, honor system. Discipline rests primarily with faculty.

Tuition and Aid Day student tuition: $14,950–$15,950. Tuition installment plan (monthly payment plans; 2- and 10-payment plans). Need-based scholarship grants available. In 2012–13, 42% of upper-school students received aid. Total amount of financial aid awarded in 2012–13: $1,200,000.

Admissions Traditional secondary-level entrance grade is 9. ERB CTP IV and writing sample required. Deadline for receipt of application materials: February. Application fee required: $45. Interview recommended.

Athletics Interscholastic: baseball (boys), basketball (b,g), golf (b,g), soccer (b,g), softball (g), swimming and diving (b,g), tennis (b,g), volleyball (b,g); intramural: touch football (b); coed interscholastic: cross-country running, hiking/backpacking, outdoor education, ropes courses, strength & conditioning; coed intramural: basketball, cooperative games, cross-country running, dance, flag football, football, hiking/backpacking, outdoor education, outdoor recreation, outdoor skills, physical training, ropes courses, strength & conditioning, volleyball, weight training, yoga. 3 PE instructors, 12 coaches, 1 athletic trainer.

Computers Computers are regularly used in English, foreign language, history, journalism, mathematics, newspaper, photography, science classes. Computer network features include on-campus library services, online commercial services, Internet access, wireless campus network, Internet filtering or blocking technology. Campus intranet, student e-mail accounts, and computer access in designated common areas are available to students. Students grades are available online. The school has a published electronic and media policy.

Contact Director of Admissions. 520-327-6395 Ext. 209. Fax: 520-327-8276. E-mail: admissions@stgregoryschool.org. Web site: www.stgregoryschool.org

SAINT JOAN ANTIDA HIGH SCHOOL

1341 North Cass Street
Milwaukee, Wisconsin 53202

Head of School: Mr. Paul Gessner

General Information Girls' day college-preparatory, arts, business, religious studies, technology, and engineering school, affiliated with Roman Catholic Church. Grades 9–12. Founded: 1954. Setting: urban. 2 buildings on campus. Approved or accredited by North Central Association of Colleges and Schools and Wisconsin Department of Education. Total enrollment: 250. Upper school average class size: 25. Upper school faculty-student ratio: 1:14. Upper School students typically attend 5 days per week.

Upper School Student Profile Grade 9: 83 students (83 girls); Grade 10: 66 students (66 girls); Grade 11: 46 students (46 girls); Grade 12: 52 students (52 girls). 50% of students are Roman Catholic.

Faculty School total: 25. In upper school: 7 men, 18 women; 9 have advanced degrees.

Subjects Offered 3-dimensional art, advanced chemistry, advanced math, Advanced Placement courses, algebra, American history-AP, American literature, American literature-AP, anatomy, art, bell choir, biology, biotechnology, British literature, business, calculus, campus ministry, career planning, career/college preparation, Catholic belief and practice, ceramics, chemistry, chemistry-AP, choir, Christian and Hebrew scripture, church history, clayworking, college admission preparation, college counseling, composition, composition-AP, concert choir, keyboarding, leadership and service.

Graduation Requirements Advanced Placement courses, algebra, American history, chemistry, Christian studies, church history, composition, electives, English composition, English literature, history, history of the Americas, history of the Catholic Church, physics, religion (includes Bible studies and theology), science, speech.

Special Academic Programs Advanced Placement exam preparation; honors section; study at local college for college credit; remedial reading and/or remedial writing; remedial math.

College Admission Counseling 52 students graduated in 2012; 50 went to college, including University of Wisconsin–Milwaukee. Other: 2 went to work.

Student Life Upper grades have uniform requirement, student council, honor system. Discipline rests primarily with faculty. Attendance at religious services is required.

Tuition and Aid Day student tuition: $6500. Tuition installment plan (SMART Tuition Payment Plan). Merit scholarship grants, need-based scholarship grants available. In 2012–13, 98% of upper-school students received aid.

Admissions Traditional secondary-level entrance grade is 9. For fall 2012, 150 students applied for upper-level admission, 120 were accepted, 118 enrolled. Explore required. Deadline for receipt of application materials: December 31. No application fee required. On-campus interview recommended.

Athletics Interscholastic: basketball, cheering, cross-country running, drill team, soccer, tennis, volleyball. 1 PE instructor.

Computers Computers are regularly used in business, engineering, keyboarding classes. Computer network features include on-campus library services, Internet access, wireless campus network, Internet filtering or blocking technology. The school has a published electronic and media policy.

Contact Ms. Marcela O. Garcia, Director of Admissions. 414-274-4709. Fax: 414-272-3135. E-mail: mgarcia@saintjoanantida.org. Web site: www.saintjoanantida.org/

ST. JOHN'S PREPARATORY SCHOOL

72 Spring Street
Danvers, Massachusetts 01923

Head of School: Dr. Edward P. Hardiman

General Information Boys' day college-preparatory, arts, religious studies, and technology school, affiliated with Roman Catholic Church. Grades 9–12. Founded: 1907. Setting: suburban. Nearest major city is Boston. 175-acre campus. 9 buildings on campus. Approved or accredited by National Catholic Education Association and New England Association of Schools and Colleges. Member of National Association of Independent Schools. Endowment: $1.2 million. Total enrollment: 1,200. Upper school average class size: 18. Upper school faculty-student ratio: 1:12. There are 161 required school days per year for Upper School students. Upper School students typically attend 5 days per week. The average school day consists of 6 hours and 9 minutes.

Upper School Student Profile Grade 9: 300 students (300 boys); Grade 10: 300 students (300 boys); Grade 11: 300 students (300 boys); Grade 12: 300 students (300 boys). 70% of students are Roman Catholic.

Faculty School total: 102. In upper school: 66 men, 36 women; 83 have advanced degrees.

Subjects Offered Accounting, acting, algebra, American history, American history-AP, American literature, anatomy and physiology, art, biology, biology-AP, business, calculus, calculus-AP, ceramics, chemistry, chemistry-AP, Chinese, chorus, computer programming, computer science, computer science-AP, desktop publishing, drama, driver education, economics, economics-AP, English, English literature, English-AP, environmental science, environmental studies, ethics, European history, European history-AP, geometry, German, German-AP, government/civics, Latin, Latin-AP, mathematics, music, neuroscience, physical education, physics, physics-AP, religion, robotics, science, sculpture, social studies, society, politics and law, Spanish, Spanish-AP, statistics, statistics-AP, studio art, technology, trigonometry, U.S. government and politics-AP, U.S. history-AP, video, world history, world religions.

Graduation Requirements Arts and fine arts (art, music, dance, drama), English, foreign language, mathematics, physical education (includes health), religion (includes Bible studies and theology), science, social studies (includes history).

Special Academic Programs Advanced Placement exam preparation; honors section; independent study; study abroad; academic accommodation for the gifted, the musically talented, and the artistically talented.

College Admission Counseling 276 students graduated in 2012; all went to college, including Boston College; College of the Holy Cross; Fairfield University; Northeastern University; University of Massachusetts Amherst; University of Vermont. Mean SAT critical reading: 589, mean SAT math: 608, mean SAT writing: 591.

Student Life Upper grades have specified standards of dress, student council. Discipline rests primarily with faculty. Attendance at religious services is required.

Summer Programs Enrichment, advancement, sports, art/fine arts, computer instruction programs offered; session focuses on academic enrichment, study skills, arts, and fitness; held on campus; accepts boys and girls; open to students from other schools.

Tuition and Aid Day student tuition: $19,250. Tuition installment plan (monthly payment plans). Merit scholarship grants, need-based scholarship grants available. In 2012–13, 31% of upper-school students received aid. Total amount of financial aid awarded in 2012–13: $2,900,000.

Admissions Traditional secondary-level entrance grade is 9. SSAT or STS, Diocese Test required. Deadline for receipt of application materials: December 15. No application fee required.

Athletics Interscholastic: alpine skiing, baseball, basketball, cross-country running, fencing, football, Frisbee, golf, hockey, ice hockey, indoor track, lacrosse, rugby, sailing, skiing (downhill), soccer, swimming and diving, tennis, track and field, ultimate Frisbee, volleyball, water polo, winter (indoor) track, wrestling; intramural: baseball, basketball, bicycling, bocce, bowling, boxing, climbing, combined training, cooperative games, crew, flag football, floor hockey, Frisbee, golf, ice hockey, martial arts, mountain biking, Nautilus, physical fitness, rowing, sailing, skiing (downhill), snowboarding, strength & conditioning, surfing, table tennis, tennis, touch football, ultimate Frisbee, volleyball, weight lifting, weight training, whiffle ball. 2 PE instructors, 57 coaches, 2 athletic trainers.

Computers Computers are regularly used in all academic, career exploration, college planning, research skills classes. Computer network features include on-campus library services, Internet access, wireless campus network, Internet filtering or blocking technology, student access to 300 computer workstations. Student e-mail accounts are available to students. Students grades are available online. The school has a published electronic and media policy.

Contact Ms. Maureen Ward, Admissions Assistant. 978-624-1301. Fax: 978-624-1315. E-mail: mward@stjohnsprep.org. Web site: www.stjohnsprep.org

SAINT JOHN'S PREPARATORY SCHOOL

Box 4000
2280 Watertower Road
Collegeville, Minnesota 56321

Head of School: Fr. Timothy Backous, OSB

General Information Coeducational boarding and day college-preparatory, arts, religious studies, bilingual studies, and theatre school, affiliated with Roman Catholic Church. Boarding grades 9–PG, day grades 6–PG. Founded: 1857. Setting: rural. Nearest major city is St. Cloud. Students are housed in single-sex dormitories. 2,700-acre campus. 23 buildings on campus. Approved or accredited by Independent Schools Association of the Central States, Midwest Association of Boarding Schools, The Association of Boarding Schools, and Minnesota Department of Education. Member of National Association of Independent Schools. Endowment: $9 million. Total enrollment: 315. Upper school average class size: 16. Upper school faculty-student ratio: 1:10. There are 172 required school days per year for Upper School students. Upper School students typically attend 5 days per week. The average school day consists of 5 hours and 35 minutes.

Upper School Student Profile Grade 9: 45 students (25 boys, 20 girls); Grade 10: 74 students (47 boys, 27 girls); Grade 11: 56 students (23 boys, 33 girls); Grade 12: 55 students (31 boys, 24 girls); Postgraduate: 3 students (2 boys, 1 girl). 37% of students are boarding students. 63% are state residents. 4 states are represented in upper school student body. 25% are international students. International students from Austria, Chile, China, Mexico, Republic of Korea, and Taiwan; 18 other countries represented in student body. 50% of students are Roman Catholic.

Faculty School total: 34. In upper school: 18 men, 16 women; 24 have advanced degrees; 2 reside on campus.

Subjects Offered 3-dimensional design, advanced chemistry, Advanced Placement courses, algebra, American history, American literature, art, art history, band, Bible studies, biology, biology-AP, British literature, calculus, ceramics, chemistry, Chinese, choir, civics, conceptual physics, creative writing, current events, drawing, earth science, economics, English, English literature, English-AP, environmental science-AP, ESL, European history, fine arts, geometry, German, government/civics, health, history, International Baccalaureate courses, mathematics, music, orchestra, photography, physical education, physics, pre-calculus, religion, science, social studies, Spanish, speech, statistics, theology, trigonometry, world history, world literature, writing.

Graduation Requirements American literature, British literature, English, theology and the arts, world literature.

Special Academic Programs International Baccalaureate program; Advanced Placement exam preparation; honors section; independent study; term-away projects; study at local college for college credit; study abroad; ESL (23 students enrolled).

College Admission Counseling 52 students graduated in 2012; all went to college, including Carleton College; College of Saint Benedict; St. John's University; University of Minnesota, Twin Cities Campus; University of Portland. Mean SAT critical reading: 713, mean SAT math: 685, mean SAT writing: 672, mean combined SAT: 2070, mean composite ACT: 27.

Student Life Upper grades have specified standards of dress, student council, honor system. Discipline rests primarily with faculty. Attendance at religious services is required.

Summer Programs Enrichment, advancement, art/fine arts programs offered; session focuses on fun camp experiences; held on campus; accepts boys and girls; open to students from other schools. 1,000 students usually enrolled. 2013 schedule: June 14 to August 6. Application deadline: June 1.

Tuition and Aid Day student tuition: $14,659; 5-day tuition and room/board: $28,949; 7-day tuition and room/board: $32,354. Tuition installment plan (monthly payment plans, individually arranged payment plans, semester payment plan). Merit scholarship grants, need-based scholarship grants, paying campus jobs available. In 2012–13, 46% of upper-school students received aid; total upper-school merit-scholarship money awarded: $30,000. Total amount of financial aid awarded in 2012–13: $700,000.

Admissions Traditional secondary-level entrance grade is 9. For fall 2012, 122 students applied for upper-level admission, 72 were accepted, 56 enrolled. SLEP required. Deadline for receipt of application materials: none. Application fee required: $25. Interview required.

Athletics Interscholastic: alpine skiing (boys, girls), aquatics (g), baseball (b), basketball (b,g), cross-country running (b,g), diving (g), football (b), gymnastics (g), ice hockey (b,g), indoor track & field (b,g), nordic skiing (b,g), soccer (b,g), softball (g), swimming and diving (g), tennis (b,g), track and field (b,g); intramural: aerobics (g), aerobics/dance (g), dance (g), figure skating (g), golf (b,g), ice skating (g); coed intramural: bicycling, canoeing/kayaking, cross-country running, fitness, fitness walking, flag football, floor hockey, Frisbee, indoor soccer, mountain biking, nordic skiing, physical fitness, physical training, racquetball, rock climbing, roller blading, skiing (cross-country), skiing (downhill), soccer, strength & conditioning, swimming and diving, ultimate Frisbee, volleyball, walking, wall climbing, wallyball, weight lifting, weight training, winter (indoor) track, winter soccer, winter walking, yoga. 1 PE instructor, 21 coaches.

Computers Computers are regularly used in all academic, English, science classes. Computer network features include on-campus library services, Internet access, Internet filtering or blocking technology. Student e-mail accounts and computer access in designated common areas are available to students. Students grades are available online. The school has a published electronic and media policy.

Contact Jennine Klosterman, Director of Admissions. 320-363-3321. Fax: 320-363-3322. E-mail: jklosterman@sjprep.net. Web site: www.sjprep.net

ST. JOHN'S-RAVENSCOURT SCHOOL

400 South Drive
Winnipeg, Manitoba R3T 3K5, Canada

Head of School: Dr. Stephen Johnson

General Information Coeducational boarding and day college-preparatory school. Boarding grades 8–12, day grades K–12. Founded: 1820. Setting: suburban. Students are housed in single-sex dormitories. 23-acre campus. 6 buildings on campus. Approved or accredited by Canadian Association of Independent Schools, Canadian Educational Standards Institute, The Association of Boarding Schools, and Manitoba Department of Education. Language of instruction: English. Endowment: CAN$8.3 million. Total enrollment: 822. Upper school average class size: 20. Upper school faculty-student ratio: 1:9. There are 172 required school days per year for Upper School students.

Upper School Student Profile Grade 9: 96 students (49 boys, 47 girls); Grade 10: 88 students (53 boys, 35 girls); Grade 11: 100 students (60 boys, 40 girls); Grade 12: 89 students (47 boys, 42 girls). 4% of students are boarding students. 96% are province residents. 5 provinces are represented in upper school student body. 2% are international students. International students from China, Democratic People's Republic of Korea, Germany, Hong Kong, Taiwan, and United States; 2 other countries represented in student body.

Faculty School total: 78. In upper school: 25 men, 23 women; 13 have advanced degrees; 4 reside on campus.

Subjects Offered Advanced Placement courses, algebra, American history, animation, art, biology, biology-AP, calculus, calculus-AP, Canadian geography, Canadian history, chemistry, chemistry-AP, computer science, debate, drama, driver education, economics, English, English literature, European history, European history-AP, French, French-AP, geography, geometry, history, information technology, law, linear algebra, mathematics, music, physical education, physics, physics-AP, pre-calculus, psychology, psychology-AP, science, social studies, Spanish, theater, visual arts, Web site design, world issues.

Graduation Requirements Canadian geography, Canadian history, computer science, English, French, geography, history, mathematics, physical education (includes health), pre-calculus, science, social sciences.

Special Academic Programs Advanced Placement exam preparation; honors section; independent study; study at local college for college credit; ESL (27 students enrolled).

College Admission Counseling 99 students graduated in 2012; 98 went to college, including McGill University; Queen's University at Kingston; The University of British Columbia; The University of Western Ontario; University of Manitoba; University of Toronto.

Student Life Upper grades have uniform requirement, student council, honor system. Discipline rests equally with students and faculty.

Tuition and Aid Day student tuition: CAN$18,650; 7-day tuition and room/board: CAN$34,790–CAN$45,400. Tuition installment plan (monthly payment plans, individually arranged payment plans). Bursaries, merit scholarship grants available. In 2012–13, 21% of upper-school students received aid; total upper-school merit-scholarship money awarded: CAN$95,000. Total amount of financial aid awarded in 2012–13: CAN$262,250.

Admissions Traditional secondary-level entrance grade is 9. For fall 2012, 72 students applied for upper-level admission, 47 were accepted, 39 enrolled. Otis-Lennon School Ability Test, school's own exam or TOEFL or SLEP required. Deadline for receipt of application materials: none. Application fee required: CAN$125. Interview recommended.

Athletics Interscholastic: aerobics (boys, girls), badminton (b,g), basketball (b,g), cross-country running (b,g), Frisbee (b,g), golf (b), hockey (b,g), ice hockey (b,g), indoor track (b,g), indoor track & field (b,g), lacrosse (b,g); intramural: badminton (b,g), basketball (b,g), cross-country running (b,g), dance (b,g), hockey (b,g); coed interscholastic: badminton, Frisbee, physical fitness; coed intramural: badminton, flag football, floor hockey. 6 PE instructors.

Computers Computers are regularly used in business skills, career exploration, college planning, creative writing, English, history, library skills, newspaper, science, social studies, yearbook classes. Computer network features include on-campus library services, Internet access, wireless campus network, Internet filtering or blocking technology, EBSCO. Campus intranet and student e-mail accounts are available to students. The school has a published electronic and media policy.

Contact Mr. Paul Prieur, Director of Admissions and Marketing. 204-477-2400. Fax: 204-477-2429. E-mail: admissions@sjr.mb.ca. Web site: www.sjr.mb.ca

ST. JOSEPH ACADEMY

155 State Road 207
St. Augustine, Florida 32084

Head of School: Mr. Michael H. Heubeck

General Information Coeducational day college-preparatory, arts, religious studies, and technology school, affiliated with Roman Catholic Church. Grades 9–12. Founded: 1866. Setting: suburban. 33-acre campus. 13 buildings on campus. Approved or accredited by Southern Association of Colleges and Schools and Florida Department of Education. Total enrollment: 260. Upper school average class size: 14. Upper school faculty-student ratio: 1:11. There are 184 required school days per year for Upper School students. Upper School students typically attend 5 days per week. The average school day consists of 5 hours and 6 minutes.

Upper School Student Profile Grade 9: 58 students (26 boys, 32 girls); Grade 10: 74 students (36 boys, 38 girls); Grade 11: 72 students (32 boys, 40 girls); Grade 12: 56 students (27 boys, 29 girls). 84% of students are Roman Catholic.

Faculty School total: 24. In upper school: 12 men, 12 women; 10 have advanced degrees.

Subjects Offered Advanced computer applications, advanced math, Advanced Placement courses, advanced studio art-AP, algebra, American government, American history, American sign language, anatomy and physiology, ancient world history, applied arts, art, art history, Bible studies, biology, calculus-AP, career education, career exploration, career planning, Catholic belief and practice, chemistry, Christianity, church history, clayworking, college counseling, college placement, college planning, community service, computer applications, computer education, computer skills, costumes and make-up, creative drama, drama, drama performance, drama workshop, drawing, English, English composition, English language-AP, environmental science, government, history of the Catholic Church, honors algebra, honors English, honors geometry, honors U.S. history, honors world history, integrated mathematics, Internet

research, life management skills, marine biology, Microsoft, moral theology, peer ministry, personal fitness, physical education, physics, play production, playwriting and directing, portfolio art, pottery, pre-algebra, pre-calculus, psychology, religious education, senior career experience, Shakespeare, Spanish, Spanish language-AP, Spanish literature-AP, theology, U.S. history, weight training.

Graduation Requirements Advanced Placement courses, career/college preparation, Catholic belief and practice, college writing, computer literacy, dramatic arts, economics, English, environmental science, foreign language, government, mathematics, physical education (includes health), religion (includes Bible studies and theology), social studies (includes history), theology.

Special Academic Programs Advanced Placement exam preparation; study at local college for college credit; academic accommodation for the gifted and the artistically talented; special instructional classes for students with Attention Deficit Disorder.

College Admission Counseling 74 students graduated in 2011; all went to college, including Florida Atlantic University; University of Central Florida; University of Florida; University of North Florida.

Student Life Upper grades have uniform requirement, student council, honor system. Discipline rests primarily with faculty. Attendance at religious services is required.

Tuition and Aid Day student tuition: $7665–$9780. Tuition installment plan (FACTS Tuition Payment Plan). Need-based scholarship grants available. In 2011–12, 42% of upper-school students received aid. Total amount of financial aid awarded in 2011–12: $119,467.

Admissions Traditional secondary-level entrance grade is 9. For fall 2011, 63 students applied for upper-level admission, 58 were accepted, 58 enrolled. ACT-Explore, Iowa Tests of Basic Skills, Iowa Tests of Basic Skills-Grades 7-8, Archdiocese HSEPT-Grade 9, PSAT or SAT required. Deadline for receipt of application materials: none. Application fee required: $580. Interview required.

Athletics Interscholastic: baseball (boys), basketball (b,g), cheering (g), cross-country running (b,g), flag football (g), football (b), golf (b,g), physical fitness (b,g), physical training (b,g), soccer (b,g), softball (g), swimming and diving (b,g), tennis (b,g), track and field (b,g), volleyball (g), weight training (b), winter soccer (b,g), wrestling (b). 1 PE instructor, 3 coaches, 2 athletic trainers.

Computers Computers are regularly used in all academic classes. Computer network features include on-campus library services, Internet access, Internet filtering or blocking technology. Students grades are available online. The school has a published electronic and media policy.

Contact Mr. Patrick M. Keane, Director of Admissions. 904-824-0431 Ext. 305. Fax: 904-824-4412. E-mail: admissions@sjaweb.org. Web site: www.sjaweb.org

SAINT JOSEPH ACADEMY HIGH SCHOOL

3470 Rocky River Drive
Cleveland, Ohio 44111

Head of School: Dr. Jim Cantwell

General Information Girls' day college-preparatory, technology, pre-engineering, and Mandarin school, affiliated with Roman Catholic Church. Grades 9–12. Founded: 1890. Setting: urban. 44-acre campus. 2 buildings on campus. Approved or accredited by North Central Association of Colleges and Schools, Ohio Catholic Schools Accreditation Association (OCSAA), and Ohio Department of Education. Endowment: $3.5 million. Upper school average class size: 23. Upper school faculty-student ratio: 1:12. The average school day consists of 7 hours.

Upper School Student Profile Grade 9: 180 students (180 girls); Grade 10: 175 students (175 girls); Grade 11: 148 students (148 girls); Grade 12: 162 students (162 girls). 90% of students are Roman Catholic.

Faculty School total: 63. In upper school: 15 men, 48 women; 38 have advanced degrees.

Subjects Offered ACT preparation, advanced biology, advanced chemistry, Advanced Placement courses, advanced studio art-AP, algebra, art, biology-AP, calculus, calculus-AP, chemistry-AP, Chinese, creative writing, English language-AP, European history-AP, film studies, filmmaking, French-AP, geometry, government and politics-AP, graphic design, Greek, honors U.S. history, honors world history, Latin, Latin-AP, model United Nations, physics-AP, psychology-AP, Spanish, Spanish-AP, speech and debate, statistics-AP, studio art-AP, U.S. history-AP, world history-AP.

Graduation Requirements 4 credits of Theology, 4 credits of Mathematics.

Special Academic Programs 13 Advanced Placement exams for which test preparation is offered; honors section; independent study; study abroad.

College Admission Counseling 163 students graduated in 2012; 161 went to college, including Cleveland State University; John Carroll University; Kent State University; Miami University; Ohio University; University of Dayton. Other: 2 went to work. Mean SAT critical reading: 557, mean SAT math: 531, mean SAT writing: 554, mean combined SAT: 1642, mean composite ACT: 24.

Student Life Upper grades have uniform requirement, student council, honor system. Discipline rests primarily with faculty. Attendance at religious services is required.

Tuition and Aid Day student tuition: $10,600. Tuition installment plan (monthly payment plans). Tuition reduction for siblings, merit scholarship grants, need-based scholarship grants, need-based loans, paying campus jobs available. In 2012–13, 65% of upper-school students received aid; total upper-school merit-scholarship money awarded: $130,000. Total amount of financial aid awarded in 2012–13: $900,000.

Admissions Traditional secondary-level entrance grade is 9. For fall 2012, 245 students applied for upper-level admission, 195 were accepted, 181 enrolled. ACT-Explore required. Deadline for receipt of application materials: none. No application fee required. Interview required.

Athletics Interscholastic: basketball, cheering, crew, cross-country running, diving, golf, rugby, soccer, softball, swimming and diving, tennis, track and field, volleyball; intramural: alpine skiing, dance team, physical fitness, strength & conditioning. 2 PE instructors, 14 coaches, 1 athletic trainer.

Computers Computer network features include on-campus library services, Internet access, wireless campus network, Internet filtering or blocking technology. Student e-mail accounts and computer access in designated common areas are available to students. Students grades are available online. The school has a published electronic and media policy.

Contact Ms. Diane Marie Kanney, Director of Admissions. 216-251-4868 Ext. 220. Fax: 216-251-5809. E-mail: admissions@sja1890.org. Web site: www.sja1890.org

ST. JOSEPH HIGH SCHOOL

2320 Huntington Turnpike
Trumbull, Connecticut 06611

Head of School: Pres. William J. Fitzgerald, PhD

General Information Coeducational day college-preparatory, arts, business, religious studies, and technology school, affiliated with Roman Catholic Church; primarily serves students with learning disabilities and individuals with Attention Deficit Disorder. Grades 9–12. Founded: 1962. Setting: suburban. Nearest major city is Bridgeport. 25-acre campus. 2 buildings on campus. Approved or accredited by New England Association of Schools and Colleges and Connecticut Department of Education. Total enrollment: 830. Upper school average class size: 24. Upper school faculty-student ratio: 1:20. Upper School students typically attend 5 days per week. The average school day consists of 6 hours.

Upper School Student Profile Grade 9: 222 students; Grade 10: 212 students; Grade 11: 205 students; Grade 12: 209 students. 85% of students are Roman Catholic.

Faculty School total: 64. In upper school: 25 men, 39 women; 50 have advanced degrees.

Subjects Offered Accounting, Advanced Placement courses, algebra, American history, American literature, art, art history, band, biology, business skills, calculus, chemistry, chorus, community service, computer applications, current events, design, drawing, earth science, ecology, economics, English, English literature, European history, finance, fine arts, French, geography, geometry, government/civics, health, history, international relations, Italian, journalism, law, mathematics, music, painting, philosophy, physical education, physics, poetry, pre-calculus, psychology, religion, science, sculpture, Shakespeare, social studies, sociology, Spanish, statistics, study skills, theology, trigonometry, word processing.

Graduation Requirements Arts and fine arts (art, music, dance, drama), English, foreign language, mathematics, physical education (includes health), religion (includes Bible studies and theology), science, social studies (includes history). Community service is required.

Special Academic Programs 7 Advanced Placement exams for which test preparation is offered; honors section; study at local college for college credit; academic accommodation for the gifted; special instructional classes for students with learning disabilities and Attention Deficit Disorder.

College Admission Counseling 182 students graduated in 2012; 175 went to college, including Boston College; Boston University; Fairfield University; Providence College; Southern Connecticut State University; University of Connecticut. Other: 1 entered military service, 1 entered a postgraduate year. Mean SAT critical reading: 535, mean SAT math: 516, mean SAT writing: 540, mean combined SAT: 1597, mean composite ACT: 21.

Student Life Upper grades have uniform requirement, student council. Discipline rests primarily with faculty. Attendance at religious services is required.

Summer Programs Sports programs offered; session focuses on soccer and basketball; held on campus. 2013 schedule: July 1 to August 30.

Tuition and Aid Day student tuition: $9775. Tuition installment plan (monthly payment plans, one lump sum payment with discount by June 1 or two payments by semester, payment plan through People's Bank). Tuition reduction for siblings, merit scholarship grants, need-based scholarship grants available. In 2012–13, 34% of upper-school students received aid; total upper-school merit-scholarship money awarded: $148,000. Total amount of financial aid awarded in 2012–13: $235,000.

Admissions Admissions testing, High School Placement Test and STS - Educational Development Series required. Deadline for receipt of application materials: December 1. Application fee required: $50.

Athletics Interscholastic: baseball (boys), basketball (b,g), cheering (g), cross-country running (b,g), diving (g), football (b), hockey (b,g), ice hockey (b), indoor track & field (b,g), lacrosse (b,g), softball (g), swimming and diving (g), tennis (b,g), track and field (b,g), volleyball (b,g); coed interscholastic: bowling, golf. 2 PE instructors, 65 coaches, 2 athletic trainers.

Computers Computer network features include on-campus library services, online commercial services, Internet access, wireless campus network, Internet filtering or blocking technology. Campus intranet and student e-mail accounts are available to students. Students grades are available online. The school has a published electronic and media policy.

Contact Peggy Kuhar Marino '71, Director of Admission. 203-378-9378 Ext. 308. Fax: 203-378-7306. E-mail: pmarino@sjcadets.org. Web site: www.sjcadets.org

SAINT JOSEPH HIGH SCHOOL

10900 West Cermak Road
Westchester, Illinois 60154-4299

Head of School: Mr. Ronald Hoover

General Information Coeducational day college-preparatory, arts, business, vocational, religious studies, bilingual studies, and technology school, affiliated with Roman Catholic Church. Grades 9–12. Founded: 1960. Setting: suburban. Nearest major city is Chicago. 21-acre campus. 2 buildings on campus. Approved or accredited by Christian Brothers Association, North Central Association of Colleges and Schools, and Illinois Department of Education. Total enrollment: 524. Upper school average class size: 27. Upper school faculty-student ratio: 1:16. There are 176 required school days per year for Upper School students. Upper School students typically attend 5 days per week. The average school day consists of 6 hours and 30 minutes.

Upper School Student Profile Grade 9: 114 students (73 boys, 41 girls); Grade 10: 140 students (76 boys, 64 girls); Grade 11: 125 students (67 boys, 58 girls); Grade 12: 145 students (85 boys, 60 girls). 39% of students are Roman Catholic.

Faculty School total: 34. In upper school: 20 men, 14 women; 15 have advanced degrees.

Subjects Offered Accounting, ACT preparation, acting, algebra, American history, anatomy and physiology, art, band, biology, business law, calculus, calculus-AP, chemistry, Christian ethics, computer applications, computer graphics, computer programming, computer-aided design, concert band, creative writing, current events, digital photography, economics, English, English-AP, film studies, fine arts, geography, geometry, graphic arts, health, human biology, Italian, jazz band, journalism, Mandarin, marching band, moral and social development, music appreciation, peace and justice, peer ministry, photography, physical education, physics, pre-algebra, pre-calculus, reading, reading/study skills, sociology, Spanish, Spanish-AP, speech, sports conditioning, studio art, theater production, U.S. history, video and animation, video film production, Web site design, world cultures, world religions.

Graduation Requirements Arts and fine arts (art, music, dance, drama), economics, English, foreign language, health, mathematics, physical education (includes health), religion (includes Bible studies and theology), science, social studies (includes history), each student must complete 40 community service hours.

Special Academic Programs 5 Advanced Placement exams for which test preparation is offered; honors section; independent study; study at local college for college credit; remedial reading and/or remedial writing; remedial math; special instructional classes for deaf students, blind students.

College Admission Counseling 146 students graduated in 2012; 141 went to college, including DePaul University; Illinois State University; Loyola University Chicago; Northern Illinois University; University of Illinois at Urbana–Champaign; Western Illinois University. Other: 1 went to work, 4 entered military service. Median composite ACT: 20. 14% scored over 26 on composite ACT.

Student Life Upper grades have uniform requirement, student council, honor system. Discipline rests primarily with faculty. Attendance at religious services is required.

Summer Programs Remediation, sports programs offered; session focuses on remediation/make-up; held on campus; accepts boys and girls; open to students from other schools. 200 students usually enrolled. 2013 schedule: June 17 to July 29. Application deadline: June 3.

Tuition and Aid Day student tuition: $9100. Tuition installment plan (monthly payment plans, individually arranged payment plans, based on parents income special arrangements are made with income tax return). Tuition reduction for siblings, merit scholarship grants, need-based scholarship grants, paying campus jobs available. In 2012–13, 65% of upper-school students received aid; total upper-school merit-scholarship money awarded: $80,000. Total amount of financial aid awarded in 2012–13: $800,000.

Admissions Traditional secondary-level entrance grade is 9. For fall 2012, 250 students applied for upper-level admission, 250 were accepted, 114 enrolled. High School Placement Test (closed version) from Scholastic Testing Service required. Deadline for receipt of application materials: none. Application fee required: $300. On-campus interview required.

Athletics Interscholastic: aerobics/dance (girls), baseball (b), basketball (b,g), bowling (b,g), cheering (g), cross-country running (b,g), dance team (g), football (b), golf (b,g), hockey (g), indoor soccer (b,g), indoor track (b,g), soccer (b,g), softball (g), strength & conditioning (b,g), tennis (b,g), track and field (b,g), volleyball (b,g), wrestling (b). 4 PE instructors, 30 coaches, 1 athletic trainer.

Computers Computers are regularly used in business applications, current events, economics, English, graphic arts, graphic design, health, history, journalism, mathematics, music, newspaper, photography, reading, religion, science, social studies, Spanish, speech, technology, theater arts, video film production, writing, yearbook classes. Computer network features include Internet access, wireless campus network, Internet filtering or blocking technology, all students have a laptop computer with wireless access to the Internet, anywhere on campus. Campus intranet and student e-mail accounts are available to students. Students grades are available online. The school has a published electronic and media policy.

Contact Mrs. Tricia McGleam, Admissions Director. 708-562-4433 Ext. 117. Fax: 708-562-4459. E-mail: tmcgleam@stjoeshs.org. Web site: www.stjoeshs.org/se3bin/clientschool.cgi?schoolname=school8

SAINT JOSEPH HIGH SCHOOL

328 Vine Street
Hammonton, New Jersey 08037

Head of School: Mrs. Lynn Domenico

General Information Coeducational day college-preparatory, arts, religious studies, technology, and global studies/distance learning school, affiliated with Roman Catholic Church. Grades 9–12. Founded: 1939. Setting: small town. Nearest major city is Philadelphia, PA. 7-acre campus. 2 buildings on campus. Approved or accredited by Middle States Association of Colleges and Schools and New Jersey Department of Education. Total enrollment: 380. Upper school average class size: 25. Upper school faculty-student ratio: 1:17. There are 180 required school days per year for Upper School students. Upper School students typically attend 5 days per week. The average school day consists of 5 hours and 30 minutes.

Upper School Student Profile Grade 9: 96 students (57 boys, 39 girls); Grade 10: 92 students (39 boys, 53 girls); Grade 11: 100 students (51 boys, 49 girls); Grade 12: 98 students (52 boys, 46 girls). 90% of students are Roman Catholic.

Faculty School total: 33. In upper school: 12 men, 15 women; 12 have advanced degrees.

Subjects Offered Advanced Placement courses, algebra, American history, American history-AP, American literature-AP, anatomy and physiology, biology, biology-AP, British literature, British literature (honors), business law, business technology, calculus, calculus-AP, chemistry, chemistry-AP, choral music, Christian doctrine, Christian scripture, church history, community service, composition-AP, computer applications, creative writing, desktop publishing, earth science, economics, English, English composition, English language and composition-AP, English literature and composition-AP, environmental science, European history, finite math, foreign language, forensics, French, geometry, global studies, health, health education, history, honors algebra, honors English, honors geometry, honors U.S. history, honors world history, lab science, Latin, music, physical education, physical science, physics, pre-calculus, psychology, religion, religious education, SAT preparation, Spanish, statistics, theater arts, U.S. history, U.S. history-AP, world cultures, world history.

Graduation Requirements 20th century history, algebra, American history, American literature, biology, British literature, chemistry, church history, computer education, driver education, English, English literature, European history, geometry, health, history of the Catholic Church, lab science, languages, mathematics, religious education, science, social studies (includes history), theology, U.S. history, world cultures. Community service is required.

Special Academic Programs Academic accommodation for the gifted; remedial reading and/or remedial writing; programs in English, mathematics, general development for dyslexic students.

College Admission Counseling 98 students graduated in 2011; 96 went to college, including Penn State University Park; Widener University. Other: 1 went to work, 1 entered military service. Median SAT critical reading: 500, median SAT math: 490, median SAT writing: 450, median combined SAT: 1440. 4% scored over 600 on SAT critical reading, 11% scored over 600 on SAT math, 3% scored over 600 on SAT writing, 1% scored over 1800 on combined SAT.

Student Life Upper grades have uniform requirement, student council, honor system. Discipline rests primarily with faculty. Attendance at religious services is required.

Tuition and Aid Day student tuition: $7650. Tuition installment plan (SMART Tuition Payment Plan). Tuition reduction for siblings, merit scholarship grants, need-based scholarship grants available. In 2011–12, 20% of upper-school students received aid; total upper-school merit-scholarship money awarded: $10,000. Total amount of financial aid awarded in 2011–12: $50,000.

Admissions Traditional secondary-level entrance grade is 9. For fall 2011, 400 students applied for upper-level admission, 304 were accepted, 96 enrolled. Admissions testing, CAT, Catholic High School Entrance Examination, CTBS, Stanford Achievement Test, any other standardized test, Iowa Tests of Basic Skills, Stanford Achievement Test, STS Examination or Terra Nova-CTB required. Deadline for receipt of application materials: none. Application fee required: $200. Interview recommended.

Athletics Interscholastic: baseball (boys, girls), basketball (b,g), bowling (b,g), cheering (b,g), cross-country running (b,g), dance (g), field hockey (g), football (b), golf (b,g), gymnastics (g), ice hockey (b), ice skating (g), indoor track (b,g), indoor track & field (b,g), lacrosse (b,g), physical training (b,g), power lifting (b,g), soccer (b,g), softball (g), swimming and diving (g), track and field (b,g), volleyball (g), weight lifting (b,g), weight training (b,g), winter (indoor) track (b,g), wrestling (b); coed interscholastic: bowling; coed intramural: bowling, snowboarding, weight training. 3 PE instructors, 43 coaches, 1 athletic trainer.

Computers Computers are regularly used in business applications, desktop publishing classes. Computer network features include on-campus library services, Internet access, wireless campus network, Internet filtering or blocking technology. Campus intranet and student e-mail accounts are available to students. Students grades are available online. The school has a published electronic and media policy.

Contact Mr. Renee DeFinis, Administrative Assistant to the Principal. 609-561-8700. Fax: 609-561-8701. E-mail: rdefinis@stjoek12.org. Web site: www.stjoek12.org

SAINT JOSEPH HIGH SCHOOL

145 Plainfield Avenue
Metuchen, New Jersey 08840

Head of School: Mr. John A. Anderson '70

General Information Boys' day college-preparatory, arts, religious studies, and technology school, affiliated with Roman Catholic Church. Grades 9–12. Founded: 1961. Setting: suburban. Nearest major city is New York, NY. 68-acre campus. 8 buildings on campus. Approved or accredited by Middle States Association of Colleges and Schools, National Catholic Education Association, and New Jersey Department of Education. Endowment: $2 million. Total enrollment: 760. Upper school average class size: 24. Upper school faculty-student ratio: 1:16. There are 170 required school days per year for Upper School students. Upper School students typically attend 5 days per week. The average school day consists of 6 hours and 12 minutes.

Upper School Student Profile Grade 9: 181 students (181 boys); Grade 10: 200 students (200 boys); Grade 11: 210 students (210 boys); Grade 12: 170 students (170 boys). 75% of students are Roman Catholic.

Faculty School total: 68. In upper school: 44 men, 24 women; 44 have advanced degrees.

Subjects Offered Accounting, acting, Advanced Placement courses, algebra, American Civil War, American government, American history, American literature, art, arts, astronomy, biology, biology-AP, calculus, calculus-AP, campus ministry, career education, Catholic belief and practice, chemistry, chemistry-AP, Christian ethics, Christian scripture, Christian studies, Christianity, church history, computer animation, computer applications, computer programming, computer science, computer science-AP, desktop publishing, discrete mathematics, driver education, English, English literature, English-AP, European history, European history-AP, French, French as a second language, French-AP, geometry, German, German literature, guitar, health, history, lab science, Latin, mathematics, mathematics-AP, meteorology, music, personal finance, photo shop, photography, physical education, physics, physics-AP, pre-calculus, public speaking, religion, social studies, Spanish, Spanish-AP, technical drawing, theology, U.S. government and politics-AP, U.S. history-AP, Web site design, world history, world literature, writing.

Graduation Requirements Arts and fine arts (art, music, dance, drama), career education, computer science, English, foreign language, lab science, mathematics, physical education (includes health), religion (includes Bible studies and theology), science, social studies (includes history). Community service is required.

Special Academic Programs 33 Advanced Placement exams for which test preparation is offered; honors section; independent study; study at local college for college credit; academic accommodation for the gifted.

College Admission Counseling 184 students graduated in 2012; all went to college, including Penn State University Park; Rutgers, The State University of New Jersey, Rutgers College; Saint Joseph's University; Seton Hall University; The College of New Jersey; University of Notre Dame. Mean SAT critical reading: 551, mean SAT math: 587, mean SAT writing: 551.

Student Life Upper grades have specified standards of dress, student council, honor system. Discipline rests primarily with faculty. Attendance at religious services is required.

Summer Programs Remediation, enrichment, advancement, sports, computer instruction programs offered; session focuses on remediation and enrichment; held on campus; accepts boys and girls; open to students from other schools. 205 students usually enrolled. 2013 schedule: June to July. Application deadline: June.

Tuition and Aid Tuition installment plan (FACTS Tuition Payment Plan, monthly payment plans, individually arranged payment plans). Merit scholarship grants, need-based scholarship grants available. In 2012–13, 10% of upper-school students received aid; total upper-school merit-scholarship money awarded: $150,000. Total amount of financial aid awarded in 2012–13: $250,000.

Admissions Traditional secondary-level entrance grade is 9. For fall 2012, 400 students applied for upper-level admission, 280 were accepted, 225 enrolled. High School Placement Test required. Deadline for receipt of application materials: none. No application fee required. On-campus interview recommended.

Athletics Interscholastic: baseball, basketball, bowling, cross-country running, football, golf, ice hockey, indoor track & field, lacrosse, soccer, swimming and diving, tennis, track and field, volleyball, winter (indoor) track; intramural: crew, flag football, Frisbee, skiing (downhill), snowboarding, strength & conditioning, ultimate Frisbee, volleyball, weight lifting, weight training. 3 PE instructors, 41 coaches, 1 athletic trainer.

Computers Computers are regularly used in animation, computer applications, desktop publishing, desktop publishing, ESL, drawing and design, graphic design, graphics, journalism, lab/keyboard, mathematics, news writing, newspaper, photography, publications, publishing, science, technical drawing, technology, Web site design, word processing, yearbook classes. Computer network features include on-campus library services, online commercial services, Internet access, Internet filtering or blocking technology. Students grades are available online. The school has a published electronic and media policy.

Contact Mr. Marc Moreau, Director of Admissions. 732-549-7600 Ext. 221. Fax: 732-549-0282. E-mail: admissions@stjoes.org. Web site: www.stjoes.org

SAINT JOSEPH JUNIOR-SENIOR HIGH SCHOOL

1000 Ululani Street
Hilo, Hawaii 96720

Head of School: Ms. Victoria Torcolini

General Information Coeducational day college-preparatory, arts, religious studies, and technology school, affiliated with Roman Catholic Church. Grades 7–12. Founded: 1948. Setting: urban. 14-acre campus. 3 buildings on campus. Approved or accredited by The Hawaii Council of Private Schools, Western Association of Schools and Colleges, Western Catholic Education Association, and Hawaii Department of Education. Member of National Association of Independent Schools. Total enrollment: 193. Upper school average class size: 18. Upper school faculty-student ratio: 1:12. There are 176 required school days per year for Upper School students. Upper School students typically attend 5 days per week. The average school day consists of 5 hours and 25 minutes.

Upper School Student Profile 55% of students are Roman Catholic.

Faculty School total: 32. In upper school: 8 men, 8 women; 6 have advanced degrees.

Subjects Offered Advanced Placement courses, algebra, American history, American literature, art, astronomy, biology, British literature, British literature-AP, calculus, calculus-AP, chemistry, composition-AP, computer science, concert band, creative writing, criminal justice, cultural geography, drama, earth science, English, English literature, European history, European history-AP, expository writing, fine arts, geometry, government and politics-AP, government/civics, Hawaiian history, history, Japanese, JROTC, life skills, marine biology, marine science, mathematics, music, physical education, physics, physiology, psychology, religion, science, senior project, social studies, sociology, Spanish, speech, theology, trigonometry, typing, world history, world literature, yearbook.

Graduation Requirements Arts and fine arts (art, music, dance, drama), English, foreign language, mathematics, physical education (includes health), religion (includes Bible studies and theology), science, social studies (includes history).

Special Academic Programs Advanced Placement exam preparation; honors section; independent study; study at local college for college credit; academic accommodation for the gifted; remedial math; ESL (6 students enrolled).

College Admission Counseling 28 students graduated in 2011; 27 went to college, including Chaminade University of Honolulu; The George Washington University; University of Alaska Anchorage; University of California, Davis; University of Hawaii at Hilo; University of Hawaii at Manoa. Other: 1 had other specific plans. Median SAT critical reading: 510, median SAT math: 489, median composite ACT: 21.

Student Life Upper grades have uniform requirement, student council, honor system. Discipline rests primarily with faculty. Attendance at religious services is required.

Tuition and Aid Day student tuition: $8000. Tuition installment plan (FACTS Tuition Payment Plan, individually arranged payment plans). Tuition reduction for siblings, need-based scholarship grants, paying campus jobs available. In 2011–12, 45% of upper-school students received aid. Total amount of financial aid awarded in 2011–12: $225,000.

Admissions For fall 2011, 43 students applied for upper-level admission, 36 were accepted. 3-R Achievement Test and English proficiency required. Deadline for receipt of application materials: none. Application fee required: $25. Interview required.

Athletics Interscholastic: aquatics (girls), basketball (b,g), bowling (b,g), cheering (g), cross-country running (b,g), golf (g), paddling (b,g), riflery (b,g), running (b), soccer (b,g), swimming and diving (b,g), tennis (b,g), track and field (b), volleyball (b,g); coed interscholastic: paddling. 1 PE instructor.

Computers Computers are regularly used in college planning, creative writing, data processing, desktop publishing, ESL, English, ESL, foreign language, geography, graphic arts, graphic design, graphics, health, history, keyboarding, lab/keyboard, library, life skills, mathematics, newspaper, publications, science, technology, typing, word processing, writing, writing, yearbook classes. Computer network features include on-campus library services, Internet access, wireless campus network, Internet filtering or blocking technology, State of Hawaii's College and Career Information Delivery System. Student e-mail accounts are available to students. Students grades are available online.

Contact Mrs. Rachel Dawson, Registrar. 808-935-4936 Ext. 226. Fax: 808-969-9019. Web site: www.sjhshilo.org

ST. JOSEPH'S ACADEMY

3015 Broussard Street
Baton Rouge, Louisiana 70808

Head of School: Mrs. Linda Fryoux Harvison

General Information Girls' day college-preparatory, arts, religious studies, and technology school, affiliated with Roman Catholic Church. Grades 9–12. Founded: 1868. Setting: urban. 14-acre campus. 8 buildings on campus. Approved or accredited by National Catholic Education Association, Southern Association of Colleges and Schools, Southern Association of Independent Schools, and Louisiana Department of

Education. Endowment: $3.6 million. Total enrollment: 1,022. Upper school average class size: 24. Upper school faculty-student ratio: 1:15. There are 179 required school days per year for Upper School students. Upper School students typically attend 5 days per week. The average school day consists of 7 hours and 20 minutes.

Upper School Student Profile Grade 9: 268 students (268 girls); Grade 10: 252 students (252 girls); Grade 11: 252 students (252 girls); Grade 12: 250 students (250 girls). 96% of students are Roman Catholic.

Faculty School total: 69. In upper school: 9 men, 60 women; 37 have advanced degrees.

Subjects Offered Accounting, acting, advanced biology, advanced chemistry, advanced computer applications, advanced math, Advanced Placement courses, algebra, American history, American history-AP, American literature, American literature-AP, analysis, analysis and differential calculus, art, art appreciation, band, Basic programming, biology, biology-AP, business law, calculus-AP, campus ministry, Catholic belief and practice, chemistry, child development, choir, choral music, chorus, Christian and Hebrew scripture, church history, civics, civics/free enterprise, computer applications, computer information systems, computer multimedia, computer programming, computer technologies, computer technology certification, CPR, critical studies in film, dance, desktop publishing, drama, drama performance, economics, English, English literature-AP, English-AP, environmental science, European history-AP, family and consumer science, film and literature, fine arts, foreign language, French, French as a second language, geometry, grammar, health, health and safety, health education, Hebrew scripture, honors algebra, honors English, honors geometry, human sexuality, independent study, information technology, Latin, marching band, media arts, media production, music, novels, physical education, physical fitness, physics, poetry, pre-calculus, public speaking, religion, research, Shakespeare, social justice, Spanish, speech, speech communications, technology, the Web, transition mathematics, U.S. history, U.S. history-AP, U.S. literature, visual arts, vocal ensemble, vocal music, Web authoring, Web site design, world history-AP.

Graduation Requirements Advanced math, algebra, American history, arts and fine arts (art, music, dance, drama), biology, chemistry, civics, computer applications, English, foreign language, geometry, physical education (includes health), physical science, physics, religion (includes Bible studies and theology), world history, service hours.

Special Academic Programs Advanced Placement exam preparation; honors section; independent study; study at local college for college credit.

College Admission Counseling 216 students graduated in 2012; all went to college, including Auburn University; Louisiana State University and Agricultural and Mechanical College; Louisiana Tech University; Loyola University New Orleans; The University of Alabama; University of Louisiana at Lafayette. 72% scored over 26 on composite ACT.

Student Life Upper grades have uniform requirement, student council, honor system. Discipline rests primarily with faculty. Attendance at religious services is required.

Summer Programs Computer instruction programs offered; session focuses on computer orientation for incoming 9th grade students; held on campus; accepts girls; not open to students from other schools. 254 students usually enrolled. 2013 schedule: June 3 to June 14. Application deadline: March 15.

Tuition and Aid Day student tuition: $9420. Tuition installment plan (monthly debit plan). Need-based scholarship grants available. In 2012–13, 6% of upper-school students received aid. Total amount of financial aid awarded in 2012–13: $375,000.

Admissions Traditional secondary-level entrance grade is 9. For fall 2012, 310 students applied for upper-level admission, 272 were accepted, 268 enrolled. ACT-Explore required. Deadline for receipt of application materials: November 16. Application fee required: $45. On-campus interview required.

Athletics Interscholastic: ballet, basketball, bowling, cheering, cross-country running, dance squad, golf, gymnastics, indoor track, modern dance, physical fitness, physical training, rodeo, running, soccer, softball, strength & conditioning, swimming and diving, tennis, track and field, triathlon, volleyball, weight training, winter (indoor) track, winter soccer; coed intramural: volleyball. 6 PE instructors, 9 coaches, 1 athletic trainer.

Computers Computers are regularly used in all classes. Computer network features include on-campus library services, online commercial services, Internet access, wireless campus network, Internet filtering or blocking technology, administrative software/grading/scheduling. Student e-mail accounts are available to students. Students grades are available online. The school has a published electronic and media policy.

Contact Mrs. Sheri Gillio, Assistant Principal. 225-388-2243. Fax: 225-344-5714. E-mail: gillios@sjabr.org. Web site: www.sjabr.org

ST. JOSEPH'S CATHOLIC SCHOOL

100 St. Joseph's Drive
Greenville, South Carolina 29607

Head of School: Mr. Keith F. Kiser

General Information Coeducational day college-preparatory school, affiliated with Roman Catholic Church. Grades 6–12. Founded: 1993. Setting: suburban. 36-acre campus. 3 buildings on campus. Approved or accredited by South Carolina Independent School Association and South Carolina Department of Education. Total enrollment: 644. Upper school average class size: 19. Upper school faculty-student ratio: 1:13. There are 175 required school days per year for Upper School students. Upper School students typically attend 5 days per week. The average school day consists of 7 hours and 10 minutes.

Upper School Student Profile Grade 9: 111 students (57 boys, 54 girls); Grade 10: 105 students (56 boys, 49 girls); Grade 11: 102 students (51 boys, 51 girls); Grade 12: 77 students (37 boys, 40 girls). 73% of students are Roman Catholic.

Faculty School total: 56. In upper school: 17 men, 22 women; 19 have advanced degrees.

Subjects Offered Algebra, American history, American literature, art, arts appreciation, bell choir, biology, biology-AP, calculus-AP, chemistry, chemistry-AP, chorus, Christian doctrine, Christian ethics, church history, composition, computer applications, computer graphics, dance, drama workshop, drawing, economics, economics-AP, English literature and composition-AP, English-AP, ensembles, European history, European history-AP, European literature, exercise science, film studies, fine arts, forensics, French, geometry, government, government-AP, honors algebra, honors English, honors geometry, human movement and its application to health, Latin, literature, medieval/Renaissance history, moral theology, newspaper, personal money management, physical education, physics, physics-AP, pre-calculus, science fiction, Shakespeare, Spanish, Spanish-AP, speech, statistics-AP, strings, theater arts, theater production, U.S. history, U.S. history-AP, yearbook.

Graduation Requirements 65 hours of community service.

Special Academic Programs Advanced Placement exam preparation; honors section.

College Admission Counseling 71 students graduated in 2012; 70 went to college, including Anderson University; Clemson University; College of Charleston; Furman University; University of Notre Dame; University of South Carolina. Other: 1 entered military service. Median SAT critical reading: 623, median SAT math: 620, median SAT writing: 612, median combined SAT: 1854, median composite ACT: 27.

Student Life Upper grades have uniform requirement, student council, honor system. Discipline rests primarily with faculty. Attendance at religious services is required.

Summer Programs Sports, art/fine arts programs offered; held on campus; accepts boys and girls; open to students from other schools. 2013 schedule: June to August.

Tuition and Aid Day student tuition: $9795. Tuition installment plan (monthly payment plans, yearly payment plan, semiannual payment plan). Tuition reduction for siblings, merit scholarship grants, need-based scholarship grants, tuition reduction for staff available. In 2012–13, 31% of upper-school students received aid; total upper-school merit-scholarship money awarded: $36,633. Total amount of financial aid awarded in 2012–13: $446,439.

Admissions Traditional secondary-level entrance grade is 9. For fall 2012, 72 students applied for upper-level admission, 63 were accepted, 48 enrolled. High School Placement Test (closed version) from Scholastic Testing Service required. Deadline for receipt of application materials: none. Application fee required: $125. On-campus interview required.

Athletics Interscholastic: baseball (boys), basketball (b,g), cheering (g), cross-country running (b,g), football (b), golf (b), soccer (b,g), softball (g), swimming and diving (b,g), tennis (b,g), track and field (b,g), volleyball (g), wrestling (b); intramural: basketball (b,g), flag football (b), Frisbee (b,g), soccer (b,g), volleyball (g); coed interscholastic: golf; coed intramural: dance, weight training.

Computers Computers are regularly used in computer applications, graphic design, keyboarding, programming, yearbook classes. Computer network features include Internet access.

Contact Mrs. Barbara L. McGrath, Director of Admissions. 864-234-9009 Ext. 104. Fax: 864-234-5516. E-mail: bmcgrath@sjcatholicschool.org. Web site: www.sjcatholicschool.org

ST. JOSEPH'S PREPARATORY SCHOOL

1733 Girard Avenue
Philadelphia, Pennsylvania 19130

Head of School: Rev. George W. Bur, SJ

General Information Boys' day college-preparatory, arts, and religious studies school, affiliated with Roman Catholic Church. Grades 9–12. Founded: 1851. Setting: urban. 7-acre campus. 3 buildings on campus. Approved or accredited by Jesuit Secondary Education Association, Middle States Association of Colleges and Schools, National Catholic Education Association, and Pennsylvania Department of Education. Member of National Association of Independent Schools. Endowment: $9 million. Total enrollment: 993. Upper school average class size: 22. Upper school faculty-student ratio: 1:16. There are 156 required school days per year for Upper School students. Upper School students typically attend 5 days per week. The average school day consists of 6 hours.

Upper School Student Profile Grade 9: 257 students (257 boys); Grade 10: 262 students (262 boys); Grade 11: 243 students (243 boys); Grade 12: 231 students (231 boys). 95% of students are Roman Catholic.

Faculty School total: 75. In upper school: 60 men, 15 women; 65 have advanced degrees.

Subjects Offered Algebra, American history, American literature, anatomy, archaeology, art, biology, business, calculus, chemistry, classics, computer math, computer programming, computer science, earth science, economics, English, English literature, environmental science, ethics, European history, fine arts, French, geometry, German, government/civics, Greek, history, Latin, Mandarin, marine biology, mathematics, photography, physical education, physics, physiology, religion, science, social sciences, social studies, Spanish, speech, trigonometry, world history, world literature.

Graduation Requirements Arts and fine arts (art, music, dance, drama), classics, computer science, English, foreign language, mathematics, physical education (includes health), religion (includes Bible studies and theology), science, social sciences, social studies (includes history), Christian service hours in junior and senior year.

Special Academic Programs International Baccalaureate program; 15 Advanced Placement exams for which test preparation is offered; honors section; independent study; study at local college for college credit; study abroad; academic accommodation for the gifted, the musically talented, and the artistically talented.

College Admission Counseling 230 students graduated in 2012; all went to college, including Fordham University; Penn State University Park; Saint Joseph's University; Temple University; University of Pennsylvania; University of Pittsburgh. Mean SAT critical reading: 621, mean SAT math: 619, mean SAT writing: 609, mean combined SAT: 1849. 55% scored over 600 on SAT critical reading, 55% scored over 600 on SAT math, 55% scored over 600 on SAT writing, 55% scored over 1800 on combined SAT.

Student Life Upper grades have specified standards of dress, student council. Discipline rests primarily with faculty. Attendance at religious services is required.

Summer Programs Remediation, enrichment, sports, art/fine arts, computer instruction programs offered; session focuses on pre-8th grade enrichment; held on campus; accepts boys and girls; open to students from other schools. 500 students usually enrolled. 2013 schedule: June 26 to July 26. Application deadline: none.

Tuition and Aid Day student tuition: $19,200. Tuition installment plan (monthly payment plans). Tuition reduction for siblings, merit scholarship grants, need-based scholarship grants, need-based loans, middle-income loans, paying campus jobs available. In 2012–13, 36% of upper-school students received aid; total upper-school merit-scholarship money awarded: $500,000. Total amount of financial aid awarded in 2012–13: $2,000,000.

Admissions Traditional secondary-level entrance grade is 9. For fall 2012, 645 students applied for upper-level admission, 310 were accepted, 258 enrolled. 3-R Achievement Test, High School Placement Test or High School Placement Test (closed version) from Scholastic Testing Service required. Deadline for receipt of application materials: November 16. Application fee required: $50. On-campus interview recommended.

Athletics Interscholastic: baseball, basketball, bowling, crew, cross-country running, diving, football, Frisbee, golf, ice hockey, indoor track & field, lacrosse, rowing, rugby, running, soccer, squash, swimming and diving, tennis, track and field, ultimate Frisbee, winter (indoor) track, wrestling; intramural: basketball, flag football, handball, martial arts, paint ball, physical fitness, table tennis, team handball, volleyball, water polo. 35 coaches, 1 athletic trainer.

Computers Computers are regularly used in English, mathematics, science classes. Computer network features include on-campus library services, online commercial services, Internet access, wireless campus network, Internet filtering or blocking technology. Student e-mail accounts and computer access in designated common areas are available to students. Students grades are available online. The school has a published electronic and media policy.

Contact Jason M. Zazyczny, Director of Admission. 215-978-1958. Fax: 215-978-1920. E-mail: jzazyczny@sjprep.org. Web site: www.sjprep.org

ST. JUDE'S SCHOOL

888 Trillium Drive
Kitchener, Ontario N2R 1K4, Canada

Head of School: Mr. Frederick T. Gore

General Information Coeducational day college-preparatory, arts, and bright learning disabled school; primarily serves underachievers, students with learning disabilities, individuals with Attention Deficit Disorder, and dyslexic students. Grades 1–12. Founded: 1982. Setting: small town. Nearest major city is Toronto, Canada. 10-acre campus. 1 building on campus. Approved or accredited by Ontario Ministry of Education and Ontario Department of Education. Language of instruction: English. Total enrollment: 30. Upper school average class size: 6. Upper school faculty-student ratio: 1:6. There are 200 required school days per year for Upper School students. Upper School students typically attend 5 days per week. The average school day consists of 7 hours.

Upper School Student Profile Grade 10: 2 students (2 boys); Grade 11: 1 student (1 boy).

Faculty School total: 6. In upper school: 3 men, 3 women; 3 have advanced degrees.

Subjects Offered 20th century history, 20th century physics, 20th century world history, accounting, acting, adolescent issues, advanced chemistry, advanced math, algebra, analytic geometry, ancient history, ancient world history, ancient/medieval philosophy, anthropology, applied arts, art, art appreciation, art education, art history, basic skills, biology, bookkeeping, business education, business law, business mathematics, business studies, calculus, Canadian history, Canadian law, Canadian literature, career and personal planning, career education, chemistry, civics, college counseling, communication skills, computer literacy, computer science, computer skills, computer studies, discrete mathematics, dramatic arts, drawing and design, earth and space science, ecology, ecology, environmental systems, economics, economics and history, English, English literature, environmental studies, ESL, family studies, fencing, finite math, general science, geography, health, health education, history, honors algebra, honors English, honors geometry, independent study, intro to computers, keyboarding, law, law studies, marketing, media studies, modern Western civilization, modern world history, philosophy, physical education, physical fitness, remedial study skills, remedial/makeup course work, science, science and technology, society, politics and law, sociology, Spanish, study skills, visual arts, Western philosophy, world issues.

Graduation Requirements Ontario requirements.

Special Academic Programs Remedial reading and/or remedial writing; remedial math; programs in English, mathematics, general development for dyslexic students; special instructional classes for students with learning disabilities, Attention Deficit Disorder, and dyslexia; ESL (2 students enrolled).

College Admission Counseling 5 students graduated in 2012; all went to college, including University of Waterloo; Wilfrid Laurier University.

Student Life Upper grades have uniform requirement, student council, honor system. Discipline rests primarily with faculty.

Summer Programs Session focuses on English and math; held on campus; accepts boys and girls; open to students from other schools. 15 students usually enrolled. 2013 schedule: July 1 to July 30. Application deadline: June 1.

Tuition and Aid Day student tuition: CAN$16,900. Tuition installment plan (monthly payment plans, individually arranged payment plans).

Admissions For fall 2012, 5 students applied for upper-level admission, 5 were accepted, 5 enrolled. Academic Profile Tests, achievement tests, Woodcock Reading Mastery Key Math and Woodcock-Johnson Educational Evaluation, WISC III required. Deadline for receipt of application materials: none. No application fee required. Interview required.

Athletics Interscholastic: synchronized swimming (girls); coed interscholastic: basketball, bowling, cross-country running, fencing, golf; coed intramural: badminton, ball hockey, baseball, basketball, bowling, cross-country running, curling, fencing, fitness, floor hockey, golf, martial arts. 2 PE instructors.

Computers Computers are regularly used in all classes. Computer network features include Internet access, Internet filtering or blocking technology.

Contact Frederick T. Gore, Director of Education. 519-888-0807. Fax: 519-888-0316. E-mail: director@stjudes.com. Web site: www.stjudes.com

SAINT LAWRENCE ACADEMY

2000 Lawrence Court
Santa Clara, California 95051

Head of School: Mrs. Christie Filios

General Information Coeducational day college-preparatory, arts, business, religious studies, and technology school, affiliated with Roman Catholic Church. Grades 9–12. Founded: 1975. Setting: urban. Nearest major city is San Jose. 9-acre campus. 3 buildings on campus. Approved or accredited by National Catholic Education Association, Western Association of Schools and Colleges, and California Department of Education. Total enrollment: 250. Upper school average class size: 21. Upper school faculty-student ratio: 1:15. There are 169 required school days per year for Upper School students. Upper School students typically attend 5 days per week. The average school day consists of 6 hours and 35 minutes.

Upper School Student Profile 65% of students are Roman Catholic.

Faculty School total: 27. In upper school: 12 men, 15 women; 17 have advanced degrees.

Subjects Offered Accounting, algebra, American history, American history-AP, American literature, American sign language, art, Bible studies, biology, career exploration, chemistry, computer programming, computer science, consumer economics, drama, earth science, economics, English, English literature, ethics, geometry, government/civics, health, keyboarding, mathematics, music, physical education, physical science, physics, religion, science, social studies, Spanish, Spanish-AP, technology, theater, trigonometry, word processing, world history, world literature, yearbook.

Graduation Requirements Arts and fine arts (art, music, dance, drama), computer science, English, foreign language, mathematics, physical education (includes health), religion (includes Bible studies and theology), science, social sciences. Community service is required.

Special Academic Programs Study at local college for college credit; remedial reading and/or remedial writing; remedial math; programs in English, mathematics, general development for dyslexic students; special instructional classes for students with learning disabilities, Attention Deficit Disorder, and dyslexia.

College Admission Counseling 55 students graduated in 2012; 54 went to college, including De Anza College; San Francisco State University; San Jose State University; Santa Clara University; University of California, Irvine; West Valley College. Other: 1 went to work. Mean SAT critical reading: 526, mean SAT math: 545. 13% scored over 600 on SAT critical reading, 20% scored over 600 on SAT math.

Student Life Upper grades have uniform requirement, student council, honor system. Discipline rests primarily with faculty. Attendance at religious services is required.

Tuition and Aid Day student tuition: $14,500. Tuition installment plan (monthly payment plans). Tuition reduction for siblings, merit scholarship grants, need-based scholarship grants, diocesan scholarship for Catholic students available.

Admissions Traditional secondary-level entrance grade is 9. Catholic High School Entrance Examination required. Deadline for receipt of application materials: January 31. Application fee required: $65. Interview required.

Athletics Interscholastic: baseball (boys), basketball (b,g), cross-country running (b,g), golf (b), roller hockey (b), soccer (b), tennis (b,g), track and field (b,g), volleyball (g); coed interscholastic: golf, roller hockey, soccer, track and field. 3 coaches, 1 athletic trainer.

Computers Computers are regularly used in all academic, science classes. Computer network features include Internet access, wireless campus network, Internet filtering or blocking technology. Campus intranet and student e-mail accounts are available to students. Students grades are available online. The school has a published electronic and media policy.

Contact Mrs. Mary Dixon, Admissions Director. 408-296-6391. Fax: 408-296-3794. E-mail: mdixon@saintlawrence.org. Web site: saintlawrenceacademy.com

ST. LAWRENCE SEMINARY HIGH SCHOOL

301 Church Street
Mount Calvary, Wisconsin 53057

Head of School: Fr. John Holly, OFMCAP

General Information Boys' boarding college-preparatory and religious studies school, affiliated with Roman Catholic Church. Grades 9–12. Founded: 1860. Setting: rural. Nearest major city is Milwaukee. Students are housed in single-sex dormitories. 150-acre campus. 11 buildings on campus. Approved or accredited by National Catholic Education Association, North Central Association of Colleges and Schools, and Wisconsin Department of Education. Total enrollment: 191. Upper school average class size: 17. Upper school faculty-student ratio: 1:9. There are 167 required school days per year for Upper School students. Upper School students typically attend 5 days per week. The average school day consists of 7 hours and 25 minutes.

Upper School Student Profile Grade 9: 46 students (46 boys); Grade 10: 65 students (65 boys); Grade 11: 43 students (43 boys); Grade 12: 37 students (37 boys). 100% of students are boarding students. 30% are state residents. 18 states are represented in upper school student body. 12% are international students. International students from Ghana, India, Philippines, Republic of Korea, Saudi Arabia, and Viet Nam; 4 other countries represented in student body. 100% of students are Roman Catholic.

Faculty School total: 25. In upper school: 19 men, 6 women; 12 have advanced degrees; 6 reside on campus.

Subjects Offered Accounting, algebra, American history, American literature, art, biology, business, business law, calculus, chemistry, classical studies, computer science, English, English literature, fine arts, geometry, German, government/civics, health, health and wellness, humanities, industrial arts, lab/keyboard, Latin, literary genres, mathematics, mechanical drawing, music, physical education, physics, psychology, religion, science, socioeconomic problems, Spanish, theology, trigonometry, world history, world literature.

Graduation Requirements Arts and fine arts (art, music, dance, drama), business skills (includes word processing), computer science, English, foreign language, health education, humanities, mathematics, physical education (includes health), religion (includes Bible studies and theology), science, social studies (includes history), study skills, ministry hours.

Special Academic Programs Study at local college for college credit.

College Admission Counseling 44 students graduated in 2012; all went to college, including Marquette University; Saint Xavier University; University of Chicago; University of Dallas; University of Minnesota, Duluth; University of Wisconsin–Madison. Median SAT critical reading: 550, median SAT math: 600, median SAT writing: 540, median combined SAT: 1630, median composite ACT: 23. 10% scored over 600 on SAT critical reading, 50% scored over 600 on SAT math, 20% scored over 600 on SAT writing, 30% scored over 1800 on combined SAT, 23% scored over 26 on composite ACT.

Student Life Upper grades have specified standards of dress, student council, honor system. Discipline rests primarily with faculty. Attendance at religious services is required.

Tuition and Aid 7-day tuition and room/board: $10,300. Tuition installment plan (SMART Tuition Payment Plan, monthly payment plans, individually arranged payment plans). Need-based scholarship grants available. In 2012–13, 73% of upper-school students received aid. Total amount of financial aid awarded in 2012–13: $778,110.

Admissions Traditional secondary-level entrance grade is 9. For fall 2012, 67 students applied for upper-level admission, 65 were accepted, 61 enrolled. 3-R Achievement Test and any standardized test required. Deadline for receipt of application materials: none. Application fee required: $300. Interview recommended.

Athletics Interscholastic: baseball, basketball, cross-country running, soccer, tennis, track and field, wrestling; intramural: basketball, bicycling, billiards, bowling, floor hockey, Frisbee, handball, kickball, outdoor activities, outdoor recreation, physical fitness, physical training, racquetball, skiing (downhill), softball, table tennis, tennis, volleyball, wallyball, weight lifting, winter soccer. 3 PE instructors, 8 coaches, 1 athletic trainer.

Computers Computers are regularly used in accounting, business education, classics, creative writing, drafting, economics, English, keyboarding, mathematics, psychology, science, typing, writing, yearbook classes. Computer network features include on-campus library services, Internet access, Internet filtering or blocking technology. Campus intranet, student e-mail accounts, and computer access in designated common areas are available to students. The school has a published electronic and media policy.

Contact Mrs. Deann Sippel, Administrative Assistant to Admissions. 920-753-7570. Fax: 920-753-7507. E-mail: dsippel@stlawrence.edu. Web site: www.stlawrence.edu

SAINT LUCY'S PRIORY HIGH SCHOOL

655 West Sierra Madre Avenue
Glendora, California 91741-1997

Head of School: Sr. Monica Collins, OSB

General Information Girls' day college-preparatory, arts, religious studies, and technology school, affiliated with Roman Catholic Church. Grades 9–12. Founded: 1962. Setting: suburban. Nearest major city is Pasadena. 14-acre campus. 4 buildings on campus. Approved or accredited by Western Association of Schools and Colleges and California Department of Education. Endowment: $2 million. Total enrollment: 647. Upper school average class size: 17. Upper school faculty-student ratio: 1:17. There are 182 required school days per year for Upper School students. Upper School students typically attend 5 days per week. The average school day consists of 6 hours and 45 minutes.

Upper School Student Profile Grade 9: 166 students (166 girls); Grade 10: 151 students (151 girls); Grade 11: 152 students (152 girls); Grade 12: 178 students (178 girls). 80% of students are Roman Catholic.

Faculty School total: 41. In upper school: 9 men, 32 women; 15 have advanced degrees.

Subjects Offered Adolescent issues, advanced math, algebra, art, art appreciation, ASB Leadership, athletics, Bible studies, biology, biology-AP, calculus, calculus-AP, calligraphy, chemistry, child development, Christian ethics, Christian scripture, church history, commercial art, computer art, creative dance, creative writing, dance, drama, drawing, early childhood, economics, English, English language and composition-AP, English literature, English literature-AP, ethics, European history-AP, film studies, French, geometry, health, health education, Hebrew scripture, journalism, kinesiology, library assistant, literary magazine, mechanical drawing, media arts, meditation, modern European history-AP, moral and social development, moral theology, musical productions, painting, physical education, physical science, physics, physiology, psychology, religion, sculpture, sewing, Spanish, Spanish-AP, studio art, theater production, trigonometry, U.S. government, U.S. government and politics-AP, U.S. history, U.S. history-AP, voice, world history, yearbook.

Graduation Requirements Arts and fine arts (art, music, dance, drama), English, foreign language, mathematics, physical education (includes health), religion (includes Bible studies and theology), science, social sciences, social studies (includes history).

Special Academic Programs Advanced Placement exam preparation; honors section.

College Admission Counseling 171 students graduated in 2012; all went to college, including Azusa Pacific University; California State Polytechnic University, Pomona; Loyola Marymount University; Mount St. Mary's College; University of California, Irvine; University of California, Riverside. Mean SAT critical reading: 540, mean SAT math: 521, mean SAT writing: 548, mean composite ACT: 23. 40% scored over 600 on SAT critical reading, 20% scored over 600 on SAT math, 35% scored over 600 on SAT writing, 46% scored over 26 on composite ACT.

Student Life Upper grades have uniform requirement, student council. Discipline rests equally with students and faculty. Attendance at religious services is required.

Summer Programs Remediation programs offered; session focuses on remediation; held on campus; accepts girls; not open to students from other schools. 80 students usually enrolled. 2013 schedule: June 20 to July 15. Application deadline: June 1.

Tuition and Aid Day student tuition: $7800. Tuition installment plan (SMART Tuition Payment Plan, monthly payment plans, individually arranged payment plans, quarterly payment plan). Tuition reduction for siblings, merit scholarship grants, need-based scholarship grants available. In 2012–13, 5% of upper-school students received aid; total upper-school merit-scholarship money awarded: $3500. Total amount of financial aid awarded in 2012–13: $90,000.

Admissions Traditional secondary-level entrance grade is 9. STS required. Deadline for receipt of application materials: January 21. Application fee required: $75. On-campus interview required.

Athletics Interscholastic: basketball, cheering, cross-country running, drill team, soccer, softball, swimming and diving, tennis, track and field, volleyball, water polo; intramural: badminton, basketball, cheering, dance, dance squad, dance team, jogging, physical fitness, soccer, softball, yoga. 2 PE instructors, 36 coaches, 1 athletic trainer.

Computers Computers are regularly used in art, drawing and design, English, graphic arts, history, journalism, library science, literary magazine, mathematics, media production, music, psychology, science, yearbook classes. Computer resources include Internet access, wireless campus network, Internet filtering or blocking technology. Campus intranet and computer access in designated common areas are available to students. Students grades are available online.

Contact Mrs. Irma Esparza, Secretary. 626-335-3322. Fax: 626-335-4373. Web site: www.stlucys.com

ST. MARK'S HIGH SCHOOL

2501 Pike Creek Road
Wilmington, Delaware 19808

Head of School: Mark J. Freund

General Information Coeducational day college-preparatory, arts, business, religious studies, and technology school, affiliated with Roman Catholic Church. Grades 9–12. Founded: 1969. Setting: suburban. Nearest major city is Philadelphia, PA. 60-acre campus. 1 building on campus. Approved or accredited by Middle States Association of Colleges and Schools, National Catholic Education Association, and Delaware Department of Education. Member of National Association of Independent Schools. Endowment: $3 million. Total enrollment: 1,100. Upper school average class size: 24. Upper school faculty-student ratio: 1:11. There are 180 required school days per year for Upper School students. Upper School students typically attend 5 days per week. The average school day consists of 6 hours and 25 minutes.

Upper School Student Profile Grade 9: 245 students (125 boys, 120 girls); Grade 10: 260 students (135 boys, 125 girls); Grade 11: 300 students (160 boys, 140 girls); Grade 12: 295 students (140 boys, 155 girls). 80% of students are Roman Catholic.

Faculty School total: 105. In upper school: 47 men, 58 women; 60 have advanced degrees.

Subjects Offered Advanced Placement courses, art, business, computer science, drama, driver education, English, family and consumer science, fine arts, French, general science, German, history, Italian, mathematics, media, music, physical education, reading, religion, science, social studies, Spanish, theater.

Graduation Requirements Arts and fine arts (art, music, dance, drama), English, health education, mathematics, physical education (includes health), religion (includes Bible studies and theology), science, social studies (includes history).

Special Academic Programs 22 Advanced Placement exams for which test preparation is offered; honors section; study at local college for college credit; study abroad; academic accommodation for the gifted; remedial reading and/or remedial writing; remedial math; programs in general development for dyslexic students; special instructional classes for deaf students, blind students, students with learning challenges.

College Admission Counseling 341 students graduated in 2011; 334 went to college, including Neumann University; Penn State University Park; Towson University; University of Delaware; University of Maryland, College Park; West Chester University of Pennsylvania. Other: 6 went to work, 1 entered military service. Median SAT critical reading: 530, median SAT math: 520, median SAT writing: 520, median combined SAT: 1600, median composite ACT: 23. 28% scored over 600 on SAT critical reading, 25% scored over 600 on SAT math, 21% scored over 600 on SAT writing, 22% scored over 1800 on combined SAT, 29% scored over 26 on composite ACT.

Student Life Upper grades have uniform requirement, student council. Discipline rests primarily with faculty. Attendance at religious services is required.

Tuition and Aid Day student tuition: $9900. Tuition installment plan (monthly payment plans). Merit scholarship grants, need-based scholarship grants, full academic scholarships for gifted students available. In 2011–12, 25% of upper-school students received aid; total upper-school merit-scholarship money awarded: $50,000. Total amount of financial aid awarded in 2011–12: $1,000,000.

Admissions Traditional secondary-level entrance grade is 9. For fall 2011, 380 students applied for upper-level admission, 375 were accepted, 275 enrolled. High School Placement Test or STS required. Deadline for receipt of application materials: none. Application fee required: $100.

Athletics Interscholastic: baseball (boys), basketball (b,g), cheering (g), crew (b,g), cross-country running (b,g), dance team (g), field hockey (g), football (b), ice hockey (b), indoor track & field (b,g), lacrosse (b,g), soccer (b,g), softball (g), swimming and diving (b,g), tennis (b,g), track and field (b,g), volleyball (b,g), wrestling (b); coed interscholastic: golf; coed intramural: bowling, Frisbee, ultimate Frisbee. 4 PE instructors, 6 coaches, 1 athletic trainer.

Computers Computers are regularly used in all classes. Computer network features include on-campus library services, online commercial services, Internet access, wireless campus network, Internet filtering or blocking technology, PowerSchool system for parents to monitor child's progress. Campus intranet is available to students. Students grades are available online. The school has a published electronic and media policy.

Contact Mrs. Clarice G. Kwasnieski, Director of Admissions. 302-757-8723. Fax: 302-738-5132. E-mail: ckwasnieski@stmarkshs.net. Web site: www.stmarkshs.net

ST. MARK'S SCHOOL OF TEXAS

10600 Preston Road
Dallas, Texas 75230-4000

Head of School: Mr. Arnold E. Holtberg

General Information Boys' day college-preparatory, arts, technology, and advanced placement school. Grades 1–12. Founded: 1906. Setting: urban. 40-acre campus. 13 buildings on campus. Approved or accredited by Independent Schools Association of the Southwest. Member of National Association of Independent Schools and Secondary School Admission Test Board. Endowment: $104.9 million. Total enrollment: 851. Upper school average class size: 14. Upper school faculty-student ratio: 1:8. There are 172 required school days per year for Upper School students. Upper School students typically attend 5 days per week. The average school day consists of 7 hours and 55 minutes.

Upper School Student Profile Grade 9: 94 students (94 boys); Grade 10: 91 students (91 boys); Grade 11: 89 students (89 boys); Grade 12: 93 students (93 boys).

Faculty School total: 102. In upper school: 39 men, 19 women; 48 have advanced degrees.

Subjects Offered 3-dimensional art, acting, algebra, American history-AP, ancient world history, art, art history, astronomy, Basic programming, biology, biology-AP, calculus, calculus-AP, ceramics, chemistry, chemistry-AP, Chinese, choir, civil rights, community service, computer programming, computer science, computer science-AP, conceptual physics, concert band, creative drama, creative writing, debate, digital art, digital photography, directing, DNA, DNA science lab, drama, drama workshop, economics, economics-AP, English, English literature and composition-AP, English literature-AP, environmental science-AP, European history, European history-AP, film studies, fine arts, gender issues, geology, geometry, history, honors English, honors geometry, humanities, independent study, Japanese, journalism, Latin, Latin-AP, macroeconomics-AP, marine ecology, mathematics, microeconomics-AP, modern European history-AP, modern world history, music, oceanography, photography, physical education, physics, physics-AP, piano, science, science fiction, sculpture, senior project, short story, Spanish, Spanish language-AP, Spanish literature-AP, statistics-AP, strings, theater, trigonometry, U.S. history, video film production, Web site design, woodworking, world history, world religions.

Graduation Requirements Arts and fine arts (art, music, dance, drama), English, foreign language, mathematics, physical education (includes health), science, social studies (includes history), senior exhibition. Community service is required.

Special Academic Programs Advanced Placement exam preparation; honors section; independent study; term-away projects; study abroad; academic accommodation for the gifted.

College Admission Counseling 90 students graduated in 2012; 89 went to college, including Princeton University; Rice University; Texas A&M University; The University of Texas at Austin; Vanderbilt University; Washington University in St. Louis. Other: 1 entered a postgraduate year. Mean SAT critical reading: 679, mean SAT math: 714, mean SAT writing: 679, mean combined SAT: 2072, mean composite ACT: 31.

Student Life Upper grades have uniform requirement, student council, honor system. Discipline rests primarily with faculty. Attendance at religious services is required.

Summer Programs Session focuses on day camp; held on campus; accepts boys and girls; open to students from other schools. 700 students usually enrolled. 2013 schedule: June 10 to July 19. Application deadline: none.

Tuition and Aid Day student tuition: $24,404–$26,004. Tuition installment plan (Insured Tuition Payment Plan, individually arranged payment plans, financial aid student monthly payment plan). Need-based scholarship grants, tuition remission for sons of faculty and staff, need-based middle-income financial aid available. In 2012–13, 18% of upper-school students received aid. Total amount of financial aid awarded in 2012–13: $1,064,791.

Admissions Traditional secondary-level entrance grade is 9. For fall 2012, 123 students applied for upper-level admission, 20 were accepted, 12 enrolled. ISEE required. Deadline for receipt of application materials: January 11. Application fee required: $125. Interview required.

Athletics Interscholastic: backpacking, baseball, basketball, cheering, climbing, crew, cross-country running, diving, fencing, football, golf, hiking/backpacking, hockey, ice hockey, lacrosse, outdoor education, outdoor skills, physical fitness, physical training, soccer, strength & conditioning, swimming and diving, tennis, track and field, volleyball, wall climbing, water polo, weight training, wilderness, winter soccer, wrestling; intramural: basketball, bicycling, cooperative games, cross-country running, fitness, flag football, floor hockey, jump rope, kickball, lacrosse, physical fitness, physical training, soccer, softball, swimming and diving, table tennis, team handball, tennis, track and field, volleyball, water polo, weight training, winter soccer, wrestling. 8 PE instructors, 9 coaches, 2 athletic trainers.

Computers Computers are regularly used in English, foreign language, humanities, mathematics, science classes. Computer network features include on-campus library services, online commercial services, Internet access, wireless campus network, Internet filtering or blocking technology. Student e-mail accounts are available to students. The school has a published electronic and media policy.

Contact Mr. David P. Baker, Director of Admission and Financial Aid. 214-346-8700. Fax: 214-346-8701. E-mail: admission@smtexas.org. Web site: www.smtexas.org

See Display on next page and Close-Up on page 622.

ST. MARTIN'S EPISCOPAL SCHOOL

225 Green Acres Road
Metairie, Louisiana 70003

Head of School: Merry Sorrells

General Information Coeducational day college-preparatory school, affiliated with Episcopal Church. Grades PK–12. Founded: 1947. Setting: suburban. Nearest major city is New Orleans. 18-acre campus. 13 buildings on campus. Approved or accredited by Independent Schools Association of the Southwest, National Association of Episcopal Schools, Southern Association of Colleges and Schools, Southwest Association of Episcopal Schools, The College Board, and Louisiana Department of Education. Member of National Association of Independent Schools. Endowment: $7.2 million. Total enrollment: 526. Upper school average class size: 17. Upper school faculty-student ratio: 1:8. There are 179 required school days per year for Upper School students. Upper School students typically attend 5 days per week. The average school day consists of 6 hours.

Upper School Student Profile Grade 9: 59 students (34 boys, 25 girls); Grade 10: 58 students (32 boys, 26 girls); Grade 11: 61 students (32 boys, 29 girls); Grade 12: 57 students (33 boys, 24 girls). 9.5% of students are members of Episcopal Church.

Faculty School total: 65. In upper school: 16 men, 17 women; 19 have advanced degrees.

Subjects Offered Advanced chemistry, advanced math, Advanced Placement courses, advanced studio art-AP, algebra, American history, American history-AP, American literature, American literature-AP, art, art history, band, baseball, basketball, bell choir, Bible studies, biology, biology-AP, calculus, calculus-AP, career education internship, career/college preparation, ceramics, cheerleading, chemistry, chemistry-AP, Chinese studies, chorus, civics, college counseling, community garden, community service, computer literacy, creative writing, digital photography, drama, earth science, economics, economics and history, English, English language and composition-AP, English literature, English literature and composition-AP, English literature-AP, environmental science, ethics, European history-AP, film studies, fine arts, French, French-AP, geography, geology, geometry, grammar, history-AP, honors algebra, honors English, honors geometry, humanities, internship, journalism, lab science, Latin, Latin-AP, leadership and service, life management skills, life skills, literary magazine, Mandarin, mathematics, model United Nations, music, music appreciation, music-AP, musical productions, newspaper, philosophy, physical education, physics, pre-algebra, publications, religion, SAT preparation, science, scripture, senior internship, social studies, softball, Spanish, Spanish-AP, speech, statistics-AP, student government, studio art, studio art-AP, swimming, tennis, theater, theater design and production, theology, track and field, trigonometry, U.S. history-AP, volleyball, world history, world literature, world religions, writing.

Graduation Requirements Arts and fine arts (art, music, dance, drama), electives, English, foreign language, life skills, mathematics, physical education (includes health), religion (includes Bible studies and theology), science, senior internship, social studies (includes history), senior intern program, 50 hours of community service.

Special Academic Programs 12 Advanced Placement exams for which test preparation is offered; honors section; independent study.

College Admission Counseling 54 students graduated in 2012; all went to college, including Auburn University; Louisiana State University and Agricultural and Mechanical College; Loyola University New Orleans; Rhodes College; Texas Christian University; Tulane University. Median SAT critical reading: 590, median SAT math: 600, median SAT writing: 560, median combined SAT: 1750, median composite ACT: 26. 36% scored over 600 on SAT critical reading, 51% scored over 600 on SAT math, 30% scored over 600 on SAT writing, 30% scored over 1800 on combined SAT, 40% scored over 26 on composite ACT.

Student Life Upper grades have specified standards of dress, student council, honor system. Discipline rests primarily with faculty. Attendance at religious services is required.

Summer Programs Remediation, enrichment, advancement, sports, art/fine arts, computer instruction programs offered; session focuses on academics, athletics, creative arts, and enrichment; held on campus; accepts boys and girls; open to students from other schools. 485 students usually enrolled. 2013 schedule: June 1 to August 7. Application deadline: May 15.

Tuition and Aid Day student tuition: $18,250. Tuition installment plan (local bank-arranged plan). Merit scholarship grants, need-based scholarship grants available. In 2012–13, 36% of upper-school students received aid; total upper-school merit-scholarship money awarded: $238,125. Total amount of financial aid awarded in 2012–13: $761,225.

Admissions Traditional secondary-level entrance grade is 9. For fall 2012, 55 students applied for upper-level admission, 46 were accepted, 31 enrolled. Admissions testing, CTP, ISEE, math and English placement tests, WISC III or other aptitude measures; standardized achievement test or writing sample required. Deadline for receipt of application materials: none. Application fee required: $50. On-campus interview required.

Athletics Interscholastic: baseball (boys), basketball (b,g), cross-country running (b,g), flag football (b), football (b), golf (b,g), soccer (b,g), softball (g), swimming and diving (b,g), tennis (b,g), track and field (b,g), volleyball (g); intramural: basketball (b,g), cheering (b,g), cross-country running (b,g), dance squad (g), golf (b,g), outdoor adventure (b), ropes courses (b,g), soccer (b,g), swimming and diving (b,g), tennis (b,g), track and field (b,g), volleyball (g); coed intramural: project adventure. 5 PE instructors, 5 coaches, 1 athletic trainer.

Computers Computers are regularly used in all academic classes. Computer network features include on-campus library services, online commercial services, Internet access, wireless campus network, Internet filtering or blocking technology, VPN for teachers, staff, and students. Campus intranet, student e-mail accounts, and computer access in designated common areas are available to students. Students grades are available online. The school has a published electronic and media policy.

Contact Mrs. Mary White, Assistant Director of Admission. 504-736-9918. Fax: 504-736-8802. E-mail: mary.white@stmsaints.com. Web site: www.stmsaints.com

SAINT MARY'S COLLEGE HIGH SCHOOL

1294 Albina Avenue
Peralta Park
Berkeley, California 94706

Head of School: Dr. Peter Imperial

General Information Coeducational day college-preparatory school, affiliated with Roman Catholic Church. Grades 9–12. Founded: 1863. Setting: urban. Nearest major city is Oakland. 13-acre campus. 9 buildings on campus. Approved or accredited by National Catholic Education Association, Western Association of Schools and Colleges, and Western Catholic Education Association. Endowment: $4.2 million. Total enrollment: 625. Upper school average class size: 28. Upper school faculty-student ratio: 1:16. There are 180 required school days per year for Upper School students. Upper School students typically attend 5 days per week. The average school day consists of 6 hours and 50 minutes.

Upper School Student Profile Grade 9: 160 students (79 boys, 81 girls); Grade 10: 165 students (86 boys, 79 girls); Grade 11: 146 students (65 boys, 81 girls); Grade 12: 148 students (73 boys, 75 girls). 51% of students are Roman Catholic.

Faculty School total: 44. In upper school: 26 men, 16 women; 26 have advanced degrees.

Subjects Offered Algebra, American history, American literature, art, band, biology, biology-AP, calculus-AP, chemistry, chorus, conceptual physics, concert band, dance, diversity studies, economics, English, English language and composition-AP, English literature, English literature and composition-AP, finite math, forensics, French, French language-AP, geometry, government-AP, government/civics, graphic design, health education, jazz band, math analysis, mathematics, philosophy, photography, physical education, physics, physics-AP, psychology, religion, scripture, Spanish, Spanish language-AP, sports medicine, studio art-AP, theater, trigonometry, U.S. government and politics-AP, U.S. history-AP, world history, world history-AP, world religions, world religions, yearbook.

Graduation Requirements Electives, English, foreign language, health and wellness, lab science, mathematics, physical education (includes health), religious studies, U.S. history, visual and performing arts, world history, service learning, enrichment week mini-course (once a year).

Special Academic Programs 13 Advanced Placement exams for which test preparation is offered; honors section.

College Admission Counseling 146 students graduated in 2011; 142 went to college, including California State University, Monterey Bay; California State University, Sacramento; Saint Mary's College of California; San Francisco State University; University of California, Berkeley; University of California, Santa Cruz. Other: 4 had other specific plans.

Student Life Upper grades have specified standards of dress, student council, honor system. Discipline rests primarily with faculty. Attendance at religious services is required.

Tuition and Aid Day student tuition: $17,500. Tuition installment plan (monthly payment plans). Merit scholarship grants, need-based scholarship grants available. In 2011–12, 42% of upper-school students received aid; total upper-school merit-scholarship money awarded: $10,000. Total amount of financial aid awarded in 2011–12: $2,220,840.

Admissions Traditional secondary-level entrance grade is 9. For fall 2011, 413 students applied for upper-level admission, 327 were accepted, 167 enrolled. High School Placement Test and writing sample required. Deadline for receipt of application materials: January 5. Application fee required: $85. Interview required.

Athletics Interscholastic: baseball (boys), basketball (b,g), cross-country running (b,g), football (b), golf (b,g), lacrosse (b), soccer (b,g), softball (g), tennis (b,g), track and field (b,g), volleyball (b,g); coed interscholastic: cheering, diving, swimming and diving; coed intramural: basketball. 1 PE instructor, 45 coaches, 1 athletic trainer.

Computers Computers are regularly used in all academic, art, college planning, graphic arts, yearbook classes. Computer network features include on-campus library services, online commercial services, Internet access, wireless campus network, Internet filtering or blocking technology. Student e-mail accounts are available to students. Students grades are available online. The school has a published electronic and media policy.

Contact Lawrence Puck, Director of Admissions. 510-559-6235. Fax: 510-559-6277. E-mail: lpuck@stmchs.org. Web site: www.saintmaryschs.org

ST. MARY'S EPISCOPAL SCHOOL

60 Perkins Extended
Memphis, Tennessee 38117-3199

Head of School: Mr. Albert L. Throckmorton

General Information Girls' day college-preparatory, arts, religious studies, technology, and global issues school, affiliated with Episcopal Church. Grades PK–12. Founded: 1847. Setting: urban. 25-acre campus. 8 buildings on campus. Approved or accredited by National Association of Episcopal Schools, Southern Association of Colleges and Schools, Southern Association of Independent Schools, Tennessee Association of Independent Schools, The College Board, and Tennessee Department of Education. Member of National Association of Independent Schools. Endowment: $17.2 million. Total enrollment: 846. Upper school average class size: 13. Upper school faculty-student ratio: 1:13. There are 175 required school days per year for Upper School students. Upper School students typically attend 5 days per week. The average school day consists of 6 hours and 40 minutes.

Upper School Student Profile Grade 9: 67 students (67 girls); Grade 10: 54 students (54 girls); Grade 11: 58 students (58 girls); Grade 12: 64 students (64 girls). 15% of students are members of Episcopal Church.

Faculty School total: 114. In upper school: 10 men, 27 women; 27 have advanced degrees.

Subjects Offered Algebra, anatomy and physiology, art history, art history-AP, biology, biology-AP, calculus, calculus-AP, chamber groups, chemistry, chemistry-AP, choir, comparative religion, economics, English, English language and composition-AP, English literature and composition-AP, ethics, French, French-AP, geography, geometry, global issues, guitar, health, humanities, instrumental music, Latin, Latin-AP, Mandarin, microbiology, music theory-AP, performing arts, physical education, physics, physics-AP, pre-calculus, psychology, religion, robotics, Spanish, Spanish-AP, speech, studio art, studio art-AP, technology, theater, U.S. government, U.S. history, U.S. history-AP, wind ensemble, world history, world history-AP.

Graduation Requirements 1 1/2 elective credits, algebra, arts and fine arts (art, music, dance, drama), biology, calculus, chemistry, computer skills, economics, English, English language-AP, English literature-AP, foreign language, geometry, physical education (includes health), physics, pre-calculus, religion (includes Bible studies and theology), social studies (includes history), U.S. history, world history.

Special Academic Programs 16 Advanced Placement exams for which test preparation is offered; honors section; independent study; academic accommodation for the gifted, the musically talented, and the artistically talented.

College Admission Counseling 60 students graduated in 2012; all went to college, including Rhodes College; Samford University; Texas Christian University; The University of Texas at Austin; University of Arkansas; University of Mississippi. Median SAT critical reading: 680, median SAT math: 670, median SAT writing: 710, median combined SAT: 1990, median composite ACT: 29. 61% scored over 600 on SAT critical reading, 54% scored over 600 on SAT math, 69% scored over 600 on SAT writing, 63% scored over 1800 on combined SAT, 83% scored over 26 on composite ACT.

Student Life Upper grades have specified standards of dress, student council, honor system. Discipline rests equally with students and faculty. Attendance at religious services is required.

Summer Programs Enrichment, sports, art/fine arts programs offered; session focuses on summer enrichment; held both on and off campus; held at predominantly held on the school campus. Swimming component at a neighborhood pool; accepts boys and girls; open to students from other schools. 450 students usually enrolled. 2013 schedule: May 29 to August 10. Application deadline: none.

Tuition and Aid Day student tuition: $17,500. Tuition installment plan (monthly payment plans, credit card payment). Need-based scholarship grants, discounts for children of faculty, staff, and clergy available. In 2012–13, 18% of upper-school students received aid. Total amount of financial aid awarded in 2012–13: $318,200.

Admissions Traditional secondary-level entrance grade is 9. For fall 2012, 28 students applied for upper-level admission, 24 were accepted, 18 enrolled. ISEE and writing sample required. Deadline for receipt of application materials: none. Application fee required: $75. On-campus interview required.

Athletics Interscholastic: basketball, bowling, cross-country running, dance team, golf, lacrosse, soccer, softball, swimming and diving, tennis, track and field, volleyball. 1 PE instructor, 7 coaches, 1 athletic trainer.

Computers Computers are regularly used in all academic, career exploration, college planning, creative writing, library, literary magazine, music, newspaper, research skills, SAT preparation, speech, theater arts, yearbook classes. Computer network features include on-campus library services, Internet access, wireless campus network, Internet filtering or blocking technology, online database services for research available at school and at home. Campus intranet, student e-mail accounts, and computer access in designated common areas are available to students. Students grades are available online. The school has a published electronic and media policy.

Contact Ms. Nicole Hernandez, Director of Admission and Financial Aid. 901-537-1405. Fax: 901-685-1098. E-mail: nhernandez@stmarysschool.org. Web site: www.stmarysschool.org

SAINT MARY'S HALL

9401 Starcrest Drive
San Antonio, Texas 78217

Head of School: Mr. Bob Windham

General Information Coeducational day college-preparatory and arts school. Grades PK–12. Founded: 1879. Setting: suburban. 60-acre campus. 15 buildings on campus. Approved or accredited by Independent Schools Association of the Southwest. Member of National Association of Independent Schools and Secondary School Admission Test Board. Endowment: $31.7 million. Total enrollment: 991. Upper school average class size: 15. Upper school faculty-student ratio: 1:6. There are 173 required school days per year for Upper School students. Upper School students typically attend 5 days per week. The average school day consists of 7 hours and 15 minutes.

Upper School Student Profile Grade 9: 102 students (53 boys, 49 girls); Grade 10: 91 students (49 boys, 42 girls); Grade 11: 103 students (45 boys, 58 girls); Grade 12: 94 students (46 boys, 48 girls).

Faculty School total: 102. In upper school: 29 men, 20 women; 37 have advanced degrees.

Subjects Offered 3-dimensional art, Advanced Placement courses, algebra, American history-AP, American literature, anatomy and physiology, art, art history, art history-AP, art-AP, athletic training, ballet, baseball, basketball, biology, biology-AP, British literature, calculus, calculus-AP, cell biology, ceramics, chemistry, chemistry-AP, choir, college counseling, composition, computer science, computer science-AP, concert choir, creative writing, dance, digital photography, directing, drama, drawing, drawing and design, economics, economics-AP, English language and composition-AP, English literature and composition-AP, environmental science-AP, European history, European history-AP, fitness, French, French language-AP, genetics, geology, geometry, golf, government/civics, great books, guitar, health, human geography - AP, jazz band, Latin, Latin-AP, literary magazine, marine biology, model United Nations, music theory, painting, photography, physical education, physics, physics-AP, piano, pre-calculus, religious studies, science research, sculpture, set design, softball, Spanish, Spanish language-AP, Spanish literature-AP, speech, statistics-AP, swimming, technical theater, tennis, track and field, U.S. history, voice, volleyball, Web site design, world geography, world history, world literature, world religions, yearbook, zoology.

Graduation Requirements Arts and fine arts (art, music, dance, drama), athletics, electives, English, foreign language, mathematics, physical education (includes health), science, social studies (includes history), 40 hours of community service.

Special Academic Programs 25 Advanced Placement exams for which test preparation is offered; honors section; independent study; study abroad.

College Admission Counseling 79 students graduated in 2012; all went to college, including Harvard University; Southern Methodist University; The University of Texas at Austin; Trinity University; University of Southern California; Vanderbilt University. Median SAT critical reading: 610, median SAT math: 623, median SAT writing: 615.

Student Life Upper grades have uniform requirement, student council, honor system. Discipline rests primarily with faculty. Attendance at religious services is required.

Summer Programs Enrichment, sports, art/fine arts, computer instruction programs offered; held on campus; accepts boys and girls; open to students from other schools. 837 students usually enrolled. 2013 schedule: June 1 to August 5. Application deadline: May 13.

Tuition and Aid Day student tuition: $20,435. Tuition installment plan (monthly payment plans, individually arranged payment plans, full-year payment plan, 2-payment plan, monthly payment plan). Merit scholarship grants, need-based scholarship grants available. In 2012–13, 22% of upper-school students received aid; total upper-school merit-scholarship money awarded: $538,960. Total amount of financial aid awarded in 2012–13: $621,990.

Admissions Traditional secondary-level entrance grade is 9. For fall 2012, 133 students applied for upper-level admission, 79 were accepted, 47 enrolled. ISEE required. Deadline for receipt of application materials: November 14. Application fee required: $50. Interview required.

Athletics Interscholastic: ballet (boys, girls), baseball (b), basketball (b,g), cheering (g), dance (b,g), field hockey (g), fitness (b,g), football (b), golf (b,g), independent competitive sports (b,g), lacrosse (b), soccer (b,g), softball (g), volleyball (b,g); coed interscholastic: cross-country running, physical fitness, physical training, strength & conditioning, tennis, track and field, weight training. 14 coaches, 2 athletic trainers.

Computers Computers are regularly used in media arts classes. Computer network features include on-campus library services, Internet access, wireless campus network, Internet filtering or blocking technology, SmartBoards. Student e-mail accounts are available to students. Students grades are available online. The school has a published electronic and media policy.

Contact Mrs. Julie Hellmund, Director of Admission. 210-483-9234. Fax: 210-655-5211. E-mail: jhellmund@smhall.org. Web site: www.smhall.org

SAINT MARY'S HIGH SCHOOL

2525 North Third Street
Phoenix, Arizona 85004

Head of School: Mrs. Suzanne M. Fessler

General Information Coeducational day college-preparatory, general academic, arts, and religious studies school, affiliated with Roman Catholic Church. Grades 9–12. Founded: 1917. Setting: urban. 6-acre campus. 5 buildings on campus. Approved or accredited by North Central Association of Colleges and Schools, Western Catholic Education Association, and Arizona Department of Education. Endowment: $1 million. Total enrollment: 504. Upper school average class size: 25. Upper school faculty-student ratio: 1:15. There are 180 required school days per year for Upper School students. Upper School students typically attend 5 days per week. The average school day consists of 6 hours and 45 minutes.

Upper School Student Profile Grade 9: 144 students (68 boys, 76 girls); Grade 10: 128 students (67 boys, 61 girls); Grade 11: 109 students (43 boys, 66 girls); Grade 12: 123 students (58 boys, 65 girls). 80% of students are Roman Catholic.

Faculty School total: 33. In upper school: 13 men, 20 women; 20 have advanced degrees.

Subjects Offered Advanced Placement courses, algebra, American government, American history, American history-AP, American literature, art, band, biology, British literature, British literature (honors), calculus-AP, Catholic belief and practice, chemistry, chorus, Christian and Hebrew scripture, composition, computer graphics, conceptual physics, dance, drama, economics, electives, English, English composition, English language and composition-AP, English literature, English literature and composition-AP, fine arts, foreign language, French, geometry, health, history, history of the Catholic Church, honors algebra, honors English, honors geometry, honors U.S. history, intro to computers, journalism, Life of Christ, personal finance, physical education, physical science, physics, prayer/spirituality, pre-algebra, pre-calculus, religious education, remedial study skills, social studies, Spanish, Spanish language-AP, standard curriculum, state government, state history, theology, trigonometry, U.S. government and politics-AP, world geography, world history, world religions, yearbook.

Graduation Requirements Advanced math, algebra, American government, American history, American literature, anatomy and physiology, arts and fine arts (art, music, dance, drama), biology, British literature, Catholic belief and practice, chemistry, Christian and Hebrew scripture, composition, economics, electives, English, foreign language, geometry, health education, history of the Catholic Church, language and composition, physical education (includes health), physics, pre-calculus, theology, trigonometry, world history, world literature, 90 hours of Christian community service, 4 credtis of Catholic Theology courses.

Special Academic Programs 6 Advanced Placement exams for which test preparation is offered; honors section; study at local college for college credit; remedial reading and/or remedial writing; remedial math.

College Admission Counseling 116 students graduated in 2012; 111 went to college, including Arizona State University; Grand Canyon University; Northern Arizona University; The University of Arizona. Other: 3 went to work, 2 entered military service. Mean SAT critical reading: 463, mean SAT math: 474, mean SAT writing: 455, mean composite ACT: 21. 5% scored over 600 on SAT critical reading, 6% scored over 600 on SAT math, 5% scored over 600 on SAT writing, 12% scored over 26 on composite ACT.

Student Life Upper grades have uniform requirement, student council. Discipline rests primarily with faculty. Attendance at religious services is required.

Summer Programs Remediation, enrichment, advancement, sports, art/fine arts programs offered; session focuses on high school preparation for incoming freshmen; held on campus; accepts boys and girls; open to students from other schools. 200 students usually enrolled. 2013 schedule: June 4 to July 12. Application deadline: May 10.

Tuition and Aid Day student tuition: $9108–$11,748. Tuition installment plan (monthly payment plans, individually arranged payment plans, quarterly and semester payment plans). Need-based scholarship grants, paying campus jobs available. In 2012–13, 80% of upper-school students received aid. Total amount of financial aid awarded in 2012–13: $2,200,000.

Admissions Traditional secondary-level entrance grade is 9. For fall 2012, 160 students applied for upper-level admission, 155 were accepted, 144 enrolled. High School Placement Test required. Deadline for receipt of application materials: none. Application fee required: $300. On-campus interview required.

Athletics Interscholastic: baseball (boys), basketball (b,g), cheering (g), football (b), golf (b,g), physical fitness (b,g), soccer (b,g), softball (g), strength & conditioning (b,g), tennis (b,g), volleyball (b,g), weight training (b,g), winter soccer (b,g); intramural: dance (g); coed interscholastic: cross-country running, physical fitness, strength & conditioning, swimming and diving, track and field, weight training; coed intramural: bowling. 3 PE instructors, 20 coaches, 1 athletic trainer.

Computers Computers are regularly used in computer applications, graphics, Web site design, yearbook classes. Computer resources include on-campus library services, Internet access, Internet filtering or blocking technology. Students grades are available online. The school has a published electronic and media policy.

Contact Mr. Jonathon Ciani, Director of Admissions. 602-251-2515. Fax: 602-251-2595. E-mail: jciani@smknights.org. Web site: www.smknights.org

SAINT MARY'S HIGH SCHOOL

113 Duke of Gloucester Street
Annapolis, Maryland 21401

Head of School: Mr. Richard Bayhan

General Information Coeducational day college-preparatory, arts, religious studies, bilingual studies, and technology school, affiliated with Roman Catholic Church. Grades 9–12. Founded: 1946. Setting: small town. 5-acre campus. 3 buildings on campus. Approved or accredited by Southern Association of Independent Schools and Maryland Department of Education. Total enrollment: 485. Upper school average class size: 22. Upper school faculty-student ratio: 1:15. Upper School students typically attend 5 days per week. The average school day consists of 6 hours and 25 minutes.

Upper School Student Profile 80% of students are Roman Catholic.

Faculty School total: 32. In upper school: 17 men, 15 women.

Subjects Offered Accounting, algebra, American government, American literature, art, art history, art history-AP, biology, biology-AP, British literature, calculus-AP, Catholic belief and practice, chemistry, chemistry-AP, Christian scripture, Christianity, cinematography, computer applications, creative writing, current events, drama, economics, environmental science, European history-AP, fiction, forensics, French, geography, geometry, health, integrated mathematics, interdisciplinary studies, Irish literature, Latin, literature and composition-AP, math analysis, mathematics, mechanical drawing, microbiology, musical theater, peace and justice, physical education, physical science, physics, physics-AP, pre-calculus, psychology, public speaking, relationships, religion, religion and culture, senior project, Shakespeare, social justice, sociology, Spanish, sports conditioning, studio art, trigonometry, U.S. government and politics-AP, U.S. history, U.S. history-AP, weight training, world arts, world history, world literature, writing, zoology.

Graduation Requirements Arts and fine arts (art, music, dance, drama), computers, English, foreign language, mathematics, physical education (includes health), religion (includes Bible studies and theology), science, social studies (includes history).

Special Academic Programs Advanced Placement exam preparation; honors section; study at local college for college credit; study abroad; academic accommodation for the gifted.

College Admission Counseling 122 students graduated in 2012; all went to college, including United States Naval Academy; University of Maryland, College Park; Washington College.

Student Life Upper grades have uniform requirement, student council, honor system. Discipline rests primarily with faculty. Attendance at religious services is required.

Tuition and Aid Day student tuition: $13,660. Tuition installment plan (monthly payment plans). Merit scholarship grants, need-based scholarship grants available. In 2012–13, 25% of upper-school students received aid; total upper-school merit-scholarship money awarded: $30,000. Total amount of financial aid awarded in 2012–13: $250,000.

Admissions Traditional secondary-level entrance grade is 9. For fall 2012, 285 students applied for upper-level admission, 138 enrolled. High School Placement Test required. Deadline for receipt of application materials: January 4. Application fee required: $75.

Athletics Interscholastic: baseball (boys), basketball (b,g), cross-country running (b,g), dance team (g), field hockey (g), football (b), golf (b,g), lacrosse (b,g), soccer (b,g), swimming and diving (b,g), tennis (b,g), track and field (b,g), volleyball (g), wrestling (b); intramural: crew (g); coed interscholastic: weight training; coed intramural: dance team, fishing, Frisbee, sailing, yoga. 2 PE instructors, 56 coaches, 1 athletic trainer.

Computers Computers are regularly used in all classes. Computer network features include on-campus library services, online commercial services, Internet access, wireless campus network. The school has a published electronic and media policy.

Contact Mrs. Chrissie Chomo, Director of Admissions. 410-990-4236. Fax: 410-269-7843. E-mail: cchomo@stmarysannapolis.org. Web site: www.stmarysannapolis.org

ST. MARY'S PREPARATORY SCHOOL

3535 Indian Trail
Orchard Lake, Michigan 48324

Head of School: James Glowacki

General Information Boys' boarding and day college-preparatory school, affiliated with Roman Catholic Church. Grades 9–12. Founded: 1885. Setting: suburban. Nearest major city is Detroit. Students are housed in single-sex dormitories. 80-acre campus. 12 buildings on campus. Approved or accredited by Michigan Association of Non-Public Schools and Michigan Department of Education. Total enrollment: 480. Upper school average class size: 18. Upper school faculty-student ratio: 1:10. There are 185 required school days per year for Upper School students. Upper School students typically attend 5 days per week. The average school day consists of 7 hours.

Upper School Student Profile Grade 9: 147 students (147 boys); Grade 10: 130 students (130 boys); Grade 11: 122 students (122 boys); Grade 12: 94 students (94 boys). 15% of students are boarding students. 80% are state residents. 5 states are represented in upper school student body. 15% are international students. International students from Brazil, China, Poland, Republic of Korea, Russian Federation, and Taiwan. 80% of students are Roman Catholic.

Faculty School total: 58. In upper school: 43 men, 15 women; 16 have advanced degrees; 6 reside on campus.

Subjects Offered Algebra, American history, American literature, art, band, Bible studies, biology, business, business skills, calculus, chemistry, Chinese, computer programming, computer science, creative writing, drafting, driver education, earth science, ecology, economics, English, English literature, expository writing, fine arts, French, geometry, government/civics, grammar, health, history, journalism, law, mathematics, music technology, mythology, physical education, physics, Polish, psychology, religion, robotics, science, social sciences, social studies, Spanish, speech, theology, trigonometry, world history, writing.

Graduation Requirements Arts and fine arts (art, music, dance, drama), business skills (includes word processing), computer science, English, foreign language, mathematics, physical education (includes health), religion (includes Bible studies and theology), science, social sciences, social studies (includes history).

Special Academic Programs Advanced Placement exam preparation; honors section; study at local college for college credit; academic accommodation for the musically talented and the artistically talented; programs in general development for dyslexic students; special instructional classes for students with learning disabilities, Attention Deficit Disorder, and dyslexia; ESL (60 students enrolled).

College Admission Counseling 125 students graduated in 2012; 119 went to college, including Michigan State University; Oakland University; University of Detroit Mercy; University of Michigan; Wayne State University; Western Michigan University. Other: 1 entered a postgraduate year, 5 had other specific plans. Median SAT critical reading: 503, median SAT math: 600, median SAT writing: 510, median combined SAT: 1613, median composite ACT: 25. 5% scored over 600 on SAT critical reading, 15% scored over 600 on SAT math, 40% scored over 26 on composite ACT.

Student Life Upper grades have specified standards of dress, student council, honor system. Discipline rests primarily with faculty. Attendance at religious services is required.

Summer Programs Sports programs offered; session focuses on football, basketball, and lacrosse; held on campus; accepts boys and girls; open to students from other schools. 400 students usually enrolled. 2013 schedule: June to August. Application deadline: June.

Tuition and Aid Day student tuition: $9800; 5-day tuition and room/board: $20,000; 7-day tuition and room/board: $22,000. Tuition installment plan (FACTS Tuition Payment Plan, individually arranged payment plans). Tuition reduction for siblings, merit scholarship grants, need-based scholarship grants available. In 2012–13, 80% of upper-school students received aid.

Admissions Traditional secondary-level entrance grade is 9. For fall 2012, 300 students applied for upper-level admission, 200 were accepted, 150 enrolled. STS and TOEFL required. Deadline for receipt of application materials: none. Application fee required: $35. Interview recommended.

Athletics Interscholastic: alpine skiing, baseball, basketball, crew, cross-country running, football, freestyle skiing, golf, hockey, ice hockey, indoor track, indoor track & field, jogging, lacrosse, rowing, skiing (downhill), soccer, track and field, wrestling; intramural: aerobics/Nautilus, aquatics, basketball, bicycling, billiards, bowling, broomball, fitness, Frisbee, golf, hockey, ice hockey, ice skating, indoor hockey, indoor soccer, indoor track, jogging, lacrosse, mountain biking, Nautilus, physical fitness, physical training, rowing, running, skeet shooting, skiing (downhill), snowboarding, soccer, strength & conditioning, swimming and diving, table tennis, tennis, weight lifting, weight training, whiffle ball. 2 PE instructors, 25 coaches, 3 athletic trainers.

Computers Computers are regularly used in desktop publishing, drafting, engineering, yearbook classes. Computer network features include on-campus library services, Internet access, Internet filtering or blocking technology. Campus intranet and student e-mail accounts are available to students. Students grades are available online.

Contact Candace Knight, Dean of Admissions. 248-683-0514. Fax: 248-683-1740. E-mail: cknight@stmarysprep.com. Web site: www.stmarysprep.com/

SAINT MARY'S SCHOOL

900 Hillsborough Street
Raleigh, North Carolina 27603-1689

Head of School: Dr. Monica M. Gillespie

General Information Girls' boarding and day college-preparatory, arts, religious studies, bilingual studies, and technology school, affiliated with Episcopal Church. Grades 9–12. Founded: 1842. Setting: urban. Students are housed in single-sex dormitories. 23-acre campus. 26 buildings on campus. Approved or accredited by National Association of Episcopal Schools, North Carolina Association of Independent Schools, Southern Association of Colleges and Schools, Southern Association of Independent Schools, and The Association of Boarding Schools. Member of National Association of Independent Schools and Secondary School Admission Test Board. Total enrollment: 237. Upper school average class size: 12. Upper school faculty-student ratio: 1:8. Upper School students typically attend 5 days per week. The average school day consists of 7 hours.

Upper School Student Profile Grade 9: 49 students (49 girls); Grade 10: 67 students (67 girls); Grade 11: 63 students (63 girls); Grade 12: 58 students (58 girls). 48% of students are boarding students. 78% are state residents. 12 states are represented in upper school student body. 11% are international students. International students from China, Republic of Korea, Russian Federation, Spain, United Kingdom, and Viet Nam; 1 other country represented in student body. 20% of students are members of Episcopal Church.

Faculty School total: 40. In upper school: 10 men, 30 women; 30 have advanced degrees; 36 reside on campus.

Subjects Offered 3-dimensional art, acting, advanced chemistry, advanced math, Advanced Placement courses, algebra, American government, American history, American history-AP, American literature, anatomy, art, astronomy, athletics, ballet, biology, biology-AP, calculus, calculus-AP, ceramics, chemistry, chemistry-AP, choir, choral music, computer science, dance, drama, drama performance, drawing, drawing and design, earth science, ecology, English, English literature, English literature-AP, European history, French, French language-AP, geometry, government, government-AP, government/civics, honors English, honors geometry, honors U.S. history, honors world history, Latin, Latin-AP, mathematics, philosophy, physical education, physics, physics-AP, piano, psychology-AP, religion, senior project, Spanish, Spanish language-AP, speech, U.S. government and politics-AP, U.S. history, U.S. history-AP, Western civilization, world literature, yearbook, yoga.

Graduation Requirements Algebra, arts and fine arts (art, music, dance, drama), biology, electives, English, foreign language, geometry, government, physical education (includes health), physical science, religion (includes Bible studies and theology), social sciences, U.S. history, Western civilization.

Special Academic Programs Advanced Placement exam preparation; honors section; independent study; study at local college for college credit; study abroad; academic accommodation for the gifted, the musically talented, and the artistically talented.

College Admission Counseling 71 students graduated in 2012; all went to college, including Clemson University; Elon University; North Carolina State University; The University of North Carolina at Chapel Hill; University of Georgia; University of South Carolina.

Student Life Upper grades have specified standards of dress, student council, honor system. Discipline rests equally with students and faculty. Attendance at religious services is required.

Summer Programs Enrichment, sports, art/fine arts, computer instruction programs offered; held on campus; accepts boys and girls; open to students from other schools.

Tuition and Aid Day student tuition: $19,100; 7-day tuition and room/board: $40,800. Tuition installment plan (FACTS Tuition Payment Plan, monthly payment plans). Merit scholarship grants, need-based scholarship grants available.

Admissions Traditional secondary-level entrance grade is 9. For fall 2012, 183 students applied for upper-level admission, 127 were accepted, 81 enrolled. SSAT and TOEFL required. Deadline for receipt of application materials: none. Application fee required: $100. Interview required.

Athletics Interscholastic: basketball, cross-country running, field hockey, golf, lacrosse, soccer, softball, swimming and diving, tennis, track and field, volleyball; intramural: ballet, dance, dance team, modern dance. 2 PE instructors, 32 coaches, 1 athletic trainer.

Computers Computers are regularly used in dance, English, foreign language, history, introduction to technology, mathematics, newspaper, publications, science, senior seminar, writing, yearbook classes. Computer network features include on-campus library services, online commercial services, Internet access, wireless campus network, Internet filtering or blocking technology. Student e-mail accounts are available to students. Students grades are available online. The school has a published electronic and media policy.

Contact Mrs. Elizabeth Lynnes, Manager of Admission Systems and Data. 919-424-4003. Fax: 919-424-4122. E-mail: admission@sms.edu. Web site: www.sms.edu

ST. MARY'S SCHOOL

816 Black Oak Drive
Medford, Oregon 97504-8504

Head of School: Mr. Frank Phillips

General Information Coeducational boarding and day college-preparatory, arts, religious studies, and ESL school, affiliated with Roman Catholic Church. Boarding grades 9–12, day grades 6–12. Founded: 1865. Setting: small town. Nearest major city is Eugene. Students are housed in single-sex dormitories. 23-acre campus. 9 buildings on campus. Approved or accredited by National Catholic Education Association, Northwest Accreditation Commission, Pacific Northwest Association of Independent Schools, and Oregon Department of Education. Member of National Association of Independent Schools. Total enrollment: 468. Upper school average class size: 18. Upper school faculty-student ratio: 1:11. There are 180 required school days per year for Upper School students. Upper School students typically attend 5 days per week. The average school day consists of 7 hours and 15 minutes.

Upper School Student Profile Grade 9: 85 students (47 boys, 38 girls); Grade 10: 88 students (34 boys, 54 girls); Grade 11: 80 students (42 boys, 38 girls); Grade 12: 79 students (45 boys, 34 girls). 15% of students are boarding students. 85% are state residents. 2 states are represented in upper school student body. 15% are international students. International students from China, Mexico, Republic of Korea, and Rwanda; 4 other countries represented in student body. 35% of students are Roman Catholic.

Faculty School total: 48. In upper school: 22 men, 26 women; 21 have advanced degrees; 2 reside on campus.

Subjects Offered Adolescent issues, Advanced Placement courses, algebra, American history, American history-AP, American literature, ancient history, art, art history-AP, biology, biology-AP, calculus-AP, chamber groups, chemistry, chemistry-AP, chorus, community service, computer programming-AP, computer science, creative writing, drama, earth science, economics-AP, English, English-AP, environmental science-AP, ESL, ethics, European history, European history-AP, expository writing, fine arts, general science, geometry, German, government/civics, government/civics-AP, grammar, health, history, human geography - AP, instrumental music, jazz band, Latin, Latin-AP, mathematics, music theory-AP, physical education, physics, physics-AP, religion, science, social sciences, social studies, Spanish, Spanish-AP, speech, studio art-AP, theater, trigonometry, world history, world literature, writing.

Graduation Requirements Arts and fine arts (art, music, dance, drama), electives, English, foreign language, mathematics, physical education (includes health), religion (includes Bible studies and theology), science, social sciences, social studies (includes history), 100 hours of community service (25 each year in Upper School).

Special Academic Programs 20 Advanced Placement exams for which test preparation is offered; independent study; study at local college for college credit; academic accommodation for the gifted, the musically talented, and the artistically talented; ESL (35 students enrolled).

College Admission Counseling 77 students graduated in 2012; 76 went to college, including Oregon State University; Portland State University; Santa Clara University; University of Oregon; University of Portland; University of San Diego. Other: 1 went to work. Mean SAT critical reading: 608, mean SAT math: 582, mean SAT writing: 608, mean combined SAT: 1798, mean composite ACT: 24.

Student Life Upper grades have specified standards of dress, student council, honor system. Discipline rests equally with students and faculty. Attendance at religious services is required.

Summer Programs Enrichment, advancement, sports programs offered; session focuses on enrichment and SAT prep; held on campus; accepts boys and girls; open to students from other schools. 75 students usually enrolled. 2013 schedule: July 1 to August 27. Application deadline: none.

Tuition and Aid Day student tuition: $12,600. Tuition installment plan (monthly payment plans, annual payment plans). Need-based scholarship grants available. In 2012–13, 47% of upper-school students received aid. Total amount of financial aid awarded in 2012–13: $650,000.

Admissions Traditional secondary-level entrance grade is 9. For fall 2012, 178 students applied for upper-level admission, 158 were accepted. Deadline for receipt of application materials: February 15. Application fee required: $50. Interview required.

Athletics Interscholastic: baseball (boys), basketball (b,g), combined training (b,g), cross-country running (b,g), football (b), golf (b,g), independent competitive sports (b,g), soccer (b,g), softball (g), tennis (b,g), track and field (b,g), volleyball (g); intramural: alpine skiing (b,g), canoeing/kayaking (b,g), equestrian sports (b,g), flag football (g), hiking/backpacking (b,g); coed interscholastic: martial arts; coed intramural: backpacking, fitness, floor hockey, outdoor adventure, skiing (cross-country), strength & conditioning, tennis, weight lifting. 2 PE instructors.

Computers Computers are regularly used in English, history, mathematics, science, speech classes. Computer network features include on-campus library services, online commercial services, Internet access, wireless campus network, Internet filtering or blocking technology, access to homework, daily bulletins, and teachers via email, Wifi. Campus intranet and computer access in designated common areas are available to students. Students grades are available online. The school has a published electronic and media policy.

Contact Ms. Rebecca Naumes, Director of Admissions. 541-773-7877. Fax: 541-772-8973. E-mail: admissions@smschool.us. Web site: www.smschool.us

SAINT MAUR INTERNATIONAL SCHOOL

83 Yamate-cho, Naka-ku
Yokohama 231-8654, Japan

Head of School: Jeanette K. Thomas

General Information Coeducational day college-preparatory, general academic, arts, religious studies, technology, and science school, affiliated with Roman Catholic Church. Grades PK–12. Founded: 1872. Setting: urban. 1-hectare campus. 7 buildings on campus. Approved or accredited by Council of International Schools, East Asia Regional Council of Schools, International Baccalaureate Organization, Ministry of Education, Japan, and New England Association of Schools and Colleges. Language of instruction: English. Total enrollment: 406. Upper school average class size: 15. Upper school faculty-student ratio: 1:4. There are 175 required school days per year for Upper School students. Upper School students typically attend 5 days per week. The average school day consists of 5 hours and 30 minutes.

Upper School Student Profile Grade 9: 36 students (15 boys, 21 girls); Grade 10: 33 students (16 boys, 17 girls); Grade 11: 19 students (10 boys, 9 girls); Grade 12: 26 students (12 boys, 14 girls). 25% of students are Roman Catholic.

Faculty School total: 59. In upper school: 14 men, 12 women; 12 have advanced degrees.

Subjects Offered 20th century history, art, Asian studies, biology, calculus-AP, chemistry, computer science, drama, drama performance, economics, economics-AP, English, fine arts, French, geography, information technology, Japanese, Japanese history, mathematics, music, music performance, physical education, physics, psychology, religious education, religious studies, robotics, science, social studies, Spanish, theory of knowledge, TOEFL preparation, visual arts, world history.

Graduation Requirements Arts and fine arts (art, music, dance, drama), English, foreign language, mathematics, physical education (includes health), religion (includes Bible studies and theology), science, social studies (includes history), graduation requirements for IB diploma differ.

Special Academic Programs International Baccalaureate program; 10 Advanced Placement exams for which test preparation is offered; independent study; academic accommodation for the gifted, the musically talented, and the artistically talented; ESL (49 students enrolled).

College Admission Counseling 25 students graduated in 2012; all went to college, including Brown University; Keio University, Japan; London School of Economics; University of British Columbia; University of London; Waseda University, Japan. Median combined SAT: 1760. Mean SAT critical reading: 524, mean SAT math: 653, mean SAT writing: 569. 40% scored over 1800 on combined SAT.

Student Life Upper grades have uniform requirement, student council. Discipline rests primarily with faculty. Attendance at religious services is required.

Summer Programs Enrichment, advancement, ESL, sports, art/fine arts, computer instruction programs offered; session focuses on TOEFL and SAT preparation; held both on and off campus; held at various off-campus locations; accepts boys and girls; open to students from other schools. 60 students usually enrolled. 2013 schedule: June 17 to July 5. Application deadline: May 15.

Tuition and Aid Day student tuition: ¥2,107,000.

Admissions For fall 2012, 19 students applied for upper-level admission, 12 were accepted, 11 enrolled. School's own test required. Deadline for receipt of application materials: none. Application fee required: ¥20,000. On-campus interview required.

Athletics Interscholastic: baseball (boys), basketball (b,g), cross-country running (b,g), soccer (b,g), volleyball (g); intramural: soccer (b); coed interscholastic: table tennis. 2 PE instructors.

Computers Computers are regularly used in computer applications, economics, English, foreign language, French, geography, independent study, information technology, mathematics, media, music, SAT preparation, science, social studies, Spanish, technology classes. Computer network features include on-campus library services, Internet access, wireless campus network, Internet filtering or blocking technology. Campus intranet and computer access in designated common areas are available to students. Students grades are available online. The school has a published electronic and media policy.

Contact Jeanette K. Thomas, School Head. 81-(0) 45-641-5751. Fax: 81-(0) 45-641-6688. E-mail: jthomas@stmaur.ac.jp. Web site: www.stmaur.ac.jp

ST. MICHAEL'S COLLEGE SCHOOL

1515 Bathurst Street
Toronto, Ontario M5P 3H4, Canada

Head of School: Mr. Terrance Sheridan

General Information Boys' day college-preparatory and religious studies school, affiliated with Roman Catholic Church. Grades 7–12. Founded: 1852. Setting: urban. 10-acre campus. 2 buildings on campus. Approved or accredited by Ontario Ministry of Education and Ontario Department of Education. Member of Secondary School Admission Test Board. Language of instruction: English. Total enrollment: 1,078. Upper school average class size: 24. Upper school faculty-student ratio: 1:16. There are 184 required school days per year for Upper School students. Upper School students typically attend 5 days per week. The average school day consists of 6 hours and 10 minutes.

Upper School Student Profile Grade 9: 228 students (228 boys); Grade 10: 215 students (215 boys); Grade 11: 218 students (218 boys); Grade 12: 221 students (221 boys). 90% of students are Roman Catholic.

Faculty School total: 73. In upper school: 59 men, 13 women; 20 have advanced degrees.

Subjects Offered Advanced Placement courses, all academic, American history, anatomy and physiology, ancient history, art, biology, calculus, calculus-AP, Canadian geography, Canadian history, Canadian law, Canadian literature, career and personal planning, career education, chemistry, civics, computer multimedia, economics, English, English composition, English literature, finite math, French, functions, geography, history, history-AP, Italian, Latin, leadership, mathematics, media arts, modern Western civilization, outdoor education, physical education, religion, science, Spanish, theology, world religions.

Graduation Requirements 20 hours of community service, 20 hours of Christian service must be completed over the 4 years of high school.

Special Academic Programs Advanced Placement exam preparation.

College Admission Counseling 217 students graduated in 2012; all went to college, including Queen's University at Kingston; Ryerson University; The University of Western Ontario; University of Guelph; University of Toronto; York University.

Student Life Upper grades have uniform requirement, student council, honor system. Discipline rests primarily with faculty. Attendance at religious services is required.

Tuition and Aid Day student tuition: CAN$16,200. Tuition installment plan (monthly payment plans, individually arranged payment plans, all up front-$300 discount, three monthly installments (March, June, August)-$100 discount). Bursaries, merit scholarship grants, need-based scholarship grants available. In 2012–13, 15% of upper-school students received aid; total upper-school merit-scholarship money awarded: CAN$105,000. Total amount of financial aid awarded in 2012–13: CAN$1,800,000.

Admissions Traditional secondary-level entrance grade is 9. For fall 2012, 306 students applied for upper-level admission, 219 were accepted, 149 enrolled. SSAT required. Deadline for receipt of application materials: none. Application fee required: CAN$100.

Athletics Interscholastic: alpine skiing, aquatics, archery, badminton, baseball, basketball, cross-country running, football, golf, ice hockey, indoor track & field, lacrosse, mountain biking, nordic skiing, rugby, skiing (cross-country), skiing (downhill), snowboarding, soccer, softball, swimming and diving, tennis, track and field, volleyball; intramural: archery, badminton, ball hockey, basketball, fishing, fitness, flag football, ice hockey, indoor soccer, outdoor education, power lifting, soccer, tennis, touch football.

Computers Computers are regularly used in all academic, media arts classes. Computer network features include on-campus library services, Internet access, wireless campus network, Internet filtering or blocking technology. Student e-mail accounts are available to students. The school has a published electronic and media policy.

Contact Ms. Marilyn Furgiuele, Admissions Assistant. 416-653-3180 Ext. 438. Fax: 416-653-7704. E-mail: furgiuele@smcsmail.com. Web site: www.stmichaelscollegeschool.com

ST. MICHAEL'S PREPARATORY SCHOOL OF THE NORBERTINE FATHERS

19292 El Toro Road
Silverado, California 92676-9710

Head of School: Rev. Victor J. Szczurek, OPRAEM

General Information Boys' boarding college-preparatory and religious studies school, affiliated with Roman Catholic Church. Grades 9–12. Founded: 1961. Setting: suburban. Nearest major city is Los Angeles. Students are housed in single-sex dormitories. 35-acre campus. 4 buildings on campus. Approved or accredited by National Catholic Education Association, Western Association of Schools and Colleges, and California Department of Education. Total enrollment: 66. Upper school average class size: 12. Upper school faculty-student ratio: 1:3. Upper School students typically attend 5 days per week. The average school day consists of 7 hours.

Upper School Student Profile 100% of students are boarding students. 90% are state residents. 4 states are represented in upper school student body. 4% are international students. International students from China, Hong Kong, Spain, and Viet Nam; 1 other country represented in student body. 95% of students are Roman Catholic.

Faculty School total: 20. In upper school: 18 men, 2 women; 18 have advanced degrees; 13 reside on campus.

Subjects Offered Algebra, American history, American history-AP, American literature, ancient history, art history, Bible studies, biology, calculus-AP, chemistry, chorus, economics, economics-AP, English, English literature, ethics, fine arts, geography, geometry, government-AP, government/civics, Greek, health, history, Latin, Latin-AP, mathematics, philosophy, physical education, physical science, physics, pre-calculus, religion, science, social studies, Spanish, Spanish-AP, theology, trigonometry, world literature.

Graduation Requirements Arts and fine arts (art, music, dance, drama), English, foreign language, mathematics, physical education (includes health), religion (includes Bible studies and theology), science, social studies (includes history), Senior Matura.

Special Academic Programs Advanced Placement exam preparation; honors section; independent study; ESL (1 student enrolled).

College Admission Counseling 11 students graduated in 2012; all went to college, including California State Polytechnic University, Pomona; California State University, Fullerton; California State University, Long Beach; Thomas Aquinas College; University of California, Davis; University of Notre Dame. Mean SAT critical reading: 514, mean SAT math: 530.

Student Life Upper grades have uniform requirement, student council, honor system. Discipline rests equally with students and faculty. Attendance at religious services is required.

Tuition and Aid 5-day tuition and room/board: $17,900. Tuition installment plan (FACTS Tuition Payment Plan, monthly payment plans, individually arranged payment plans). Need-based scholarship grants available. Total amount of financial aid awarded in 2012–13: $350,000.

Admissions Traditional secondary-level entrance grade is 9. High School Placement Test required. Deadline for receipt of application materials: June 30. Application fee required: $100. Interview required.

Athletics Interscholastic: baseball, basketball, cross-country running, football, soccer; intramural: field hockey, outdoor activities, swimming and diving, table tennis, volleyball, weight lifting. 1 PE instructor, 2 coaches.

Computers Computers are regularly used in English, mathematics, science classes. Computer resources include on-campus library services, Internet access, Internet filtering or blocking technology. Computer access in designated common areas is available to students. Students grades are available online.

Contact Mrs. Pamela M. Christian, School Secretary. 949-858-0222 Ext. 237. Fax: 949-858-7365. E-mail: admissions@stmichaelsprep.org. Web site: www.stmichaelsprep.org

ST. PATRICK CATHOLIC HIGH SCHOOL

18300 St. Patrick Road
Biloxi, Mississippi 39532

Head of School: Mr. Bobby Trosclair

General Information Coeducational day college-preparatory and religious studies school, affiliated with Roman Catholic Church. Grades 7–12. Founded: 2007. Setting: suburban. 32-acre campus. 7 buildings on campus. Approved or accredited by Southern Association of Colleges and Schools and Mississippi Department of Education. Endowment: $400,000. Total enrollment: 474. Upper school average class size: 20. Upper school faculty-student ratio: 1:14. There are 180 required school days per year for Upper School students. Upper School students typically attend 5 days per week. The average school day consists of 6 hours and 45 minutes.

Upper School Student Profile Grade 7: 75 students (38 boys, 37 girls); Grade 8: 102 students (52 boys, 50 girls); Grade 9: 82 students (45 boys, 37 girls); Grade 10: 72 students (37 boys, 35 girls); Grade 11: 73 students (37 boys, 36 girls); Grade 12: 70 students (35 boys, 35 girls). 80% of students are Roman Catholic.
Faculty In upper school: 15 men, 20 women; 18 have advanced degrees.
Subjects Offered Accounting, advanced chemistry, advanced computer applications, advanced math, Advanced Placement courses, algebra, American government, American history, American literature, analytic geometry, anatomy and physiology, art, athletics, band, baseball, Basic programming, basketball, biology, British literature, business applications, business law, calculus, calculus-AP, campus ministry, Catholic belief and practice, cheerleading, chemistry, chemistry-AP, choral music, Christian and Hebrew scripture, church history, civics, college counseling, college placement, college planning, composition-AP, computer applications, creative writing, desktop publishing, drama, driver education, earth science, economics, English, English literature and composition-AP, environmental science, French, geometry, global studies, health, introduction to theater, journalism, keyboarding, law, Life of Christ, marching band, marine biology, marine science, oral communications, physical education, physical science, pre-algebra, pre-calculus, probability and statistics, psychology, softball, Spanish, track and field, trigonometry, U.S. government, U.S. history, U.S. history-AP, volleyball, Web site design, weight fitness, weight training, weightlifting, wood processing, world geography, world history, yearbook.
Graduation Requirements Algebra, American history, American literature, art, biology, British literature, cell biology, chemistry, computer applications, English literature, foreign language, physical education (includes health), state history, U.S. government, U.S. history, world geography, world history, world literature.
Special Academic Programs Advanced Placement exam preparation; study at local college for college credit; remedial reading and/or remedial writing.
College Admission Counseling 72 students graduated in 2011; 71 went to college, including Louisiana State University and Agricultural and Mechanical College; Millsaps College; Mississippi State University; University of Mississippi; University of South Alabama; University of Southern Mississippi. Other: 1 went to work. Mean SAT critical reading: 576, mean SAT math: 619, mean SAT writing: 640, mean composite ACT: 24. 38% scored over 600 on SAT critical reading, 75% scored over 600 on SAT math, 63% scored over 600 on SAT writing, 41% scored over 26 on composite ACT.
Student Life Upper grades have uniform requirement, student council, honor system. Discipline rests primarily with faculty. Attendance at religious services is required.
Tuition and Aid Day student tuition: $5900. Tuition installment plan (monthly payments through local bank). Tuition reduction for siblings, need-based scholarship grants available. In 2011–12, 4% of upper-school students received aid. Total amount of financial aid awarded in 2011–12: $176,590.
Admissions Traditional secondary-level entrance grade is 7. For fall 2011, 402 students applied for upper-level admission, 400 were accepted, 396 enrolled. Deadline for receipt of application materials: none. No application fee required. Interview required.
Athletics Interscholastic: baseball (boys), basketball (b,g), cheering (g), cross-country running (b,g), dance team (g), football (b), golf (b,g), power lifting (b,g), soccer (b,g), softball (g), swimming and diving (b,g), tennis (b,g), track and field (b,g), volleyball (g), weight lifting (b,g), weight training (b,g); intramural: bicycling (b,g); coed interscholastic: sailing; coed intramural: sailing. 3 PE instructors, 18 coaches, 1 athletic trainer.
Computers Computers are regularly used in accounting, business applications, business education, computer applications, desktop publishing, mathematics, newspaper, Web site design, word processing, yearbook classes. Computer network features include on-campus library services, Internet access, Internet filtering or blocking technology. Campus intranet and computer access in designated common areas are available to students. Students grades are available online.
Contact Renee McDaniel, Vice Principal. 228-702-0500. Fax: 228-702-0511. E-mail: rmcdaniel@stpatrickhighschool.net. Web site: www.stpatrickhighschool.net

SAINT PATRICK HIGH SCHOOL

5900 West Belmont Avenue
Chicago, Illinois 60634

Head of School: Br. Konrad Diebold

General Information Boys' day college-preparatory, arts, and religious studies school, affiliated with Roman Catholic Church. Grades 9–12. Founded: 1861. Setting: urban. 1 building on campus. Approved or accredited by Christian Brothers Association, National Catholic Education Association, North Central Association of Colleges and Schools, and Illinois Department of Education. Endowment: $6.8 million. Total enrollment: 710. Upper school average class size: 22. Upper school faculty-student ratio: 1:17. There are 178 required school days per year for Upper School students. Upper School students typically attend 5 days per week. The average school day consists of 6 hours and 40 minutes.
Upper School Student Profile Grade 9: 154 students (154 boys); Grade 10: 204 students (204 boys); Grade 11: 183 students (183 boys); Grade 12: 169 students (169 boys). 75% of students are Roman Catholic.
Faculty School total: 59. In upper school: 43 men, 16 women; 39 have advanced degrees.
Subjects Offered Accounting, algebra, American history, American literature, anatomy, art, art history, biology, broadcasting, business, business skills, calculus, chemistry, Chinese, chorus, computer graphics, computer science, creative writing, drama, driver education, ecology, economics, English, English literature, ESL, ethics, European history, fine arts, French, geography, geometry, government/civics, grammar, health, history, journalism, keyboarding, mathematics, music, physical education, physics, psychology, religion, science, social sciences, social studies, sociology, Spanish, speech, theater, trigonometry, word processing, world history, writing.
Graduation Requirements Arts and fine arts (art, music, dance, drama), business skills (includes word processing), computer science, English, mathematics, physical education (includes health), religion (includes Bible studies and theology), science, service learning/internship, social sciences, social studies (includes history), participation in a retreat program. Community service is required.
Special Academic Programs Advanced Placement exam preparation; honors section; study at local college for college credit; remedial reading and/or remedial writing; remedial math.
College Admission Counseling 195 students graduated in 2012; 183 went to college, including DePaul University; Lewis University; Northeastern Illinois University; Northern Illinois University; University of Illinois at Chicago; University of Illinois at Urbana–Champaign. Other: 2 went to work, 3 entered military service, 7 had other specific plans. Mean composite ACT: 21. 28% scored over 26 on composite ACT.
Student Life Upper grades have specified standards of dress, student council, honor system. Discipline rests primarily with faculty. Attendance at religious services is required.
Summer Programs Remediation, enrichment, sports, art/fine arts, computer instruction programs offered; session focuses on remediation; held on campus; accepts boys and girls; open to students from other schools. 225 students usually enrolled. 2013 schedule: June 17 to August 10. Application deadline: June 13.
Tuition and Aid Day student tuition: $9400. Tuition installment plan (monthly payment plans, quarterly payment plan). Merit scholarship grants, need-based scholarship grants, legacy (sons and grandsons of alumni) available. In 2012–13, 50% of upper-school students received aid. Total amount of financial aid awarded in 2012–13: $1,025,000.
Admissions Traditional secondary-level entrance grade is 9. For fall 2012, 212 students applied for upper-level admission, 210 were accepted, 154 enrolled. ACT-Explore or any standardized test required. Deadline for receipt of application materials: none. No application fee required. On-campus interview required.
Athletics Interscholastic: baseball, basketball, bowling, cross-country running, diving, fishing, football, golf, hockey, soccer, swimming and diving, tennis, track and field, volleyball, water polo, wrestling; intramural: basketball, football, volleyball. 4 PE instructors, 19 coaches, 1 athletic trainer.
Computers Computers are regularly used in business, English, foreign language, geography, graphic arts, graphic design, graphics, history, information technology, introduction to technology, library skills, mathematics, media arts, media production, media services, newspaper, photojournalism, religion, remedial study skills, research skills, science, typing, word processing, yearbook classes. Computer network features include on-campus library services, online commercial services, Internet access, wireless campus network, Internet filtering or blocking technology. Student e-mail accounts are available to students. Students grades are available online. The school has a published electronic and media policy.
Contact Christopher Perez, Director of Curriculum. 773-282-8844 Ext. 228. Fax: 773-282-2361. E-mail: cperez@stpatrick.org. Web site: www.stpatrick.org

SAINT PATRICK - SAINT VINCENT HIGH SCHOOL

1500 Benicia Road
Vallejo, California 94591

Head of School: Ms. Mary Ellen Ryan

General Information Coeducational day college-preparatory, arts, business, religious studies, and technology school, affiliated with Roman Catholic Church. Grades 9–12. Founded: 1870. Setting: suburban. 31-acre campus. 8 buildings on campus. Approved or accredited by Western Association of Schools and Colleges, Western Catholic Education Association, and California Department of Education. Total enrollment: 502. Upper school average class size: 30. Upper school faculty-student ratio: 1:30. There are 180 required school days per year for Upper School students. Upper School students typically attend 5 days per week. The average school day consists of 6 hours and 15 minutes.
Upper School Student Profile Grade 9: 117 students (46 boys, 71 girls); Grade 10: 129 students (63 boys, 66 girls); Grade 11: 119 students (72 boys, 47 girls); Grade 12: 137 students (64 boys, 73 girls). 80% of students are Roman Catholic.
Faculty School total: 43. In upper school: 19 men, 21 women; 24 have advanced degrees.
Subjects Offered Algebra, art, biology, calculus-AP, campus ministry, Catholic belief and practice, chemistry, chemistry-AP, choir, civics, college counseling, college planning, computer multimedia, computer science-AP, concert bell choir, concert choir, economics, English, English-AP, environmental science, environmental studies, ethnic studies, film appreciation, French, French language-AP, geometry, health, history-AP, honors English, human biology, keyboarding, leadership, organic chemistry, physical education, physics, psychology, religion, science, Spanish, Spanish language-AP, statistics, statistics-AP, studio art-AP, theater arts, U.S. history, vocal jazz, world history, world history-AP.

Graduation Requirements English, foreign language, mathematics, physical education (includes health), religion (includes Bible studies and theology), science, social studies (includes history), Christian service.

Special Academic Programs 8 Advanced Placement exams for which test preparation is offered; honors section; academic accommodation for the gifted; remedial math.

College Admission Counseling 140 students graduated in 2012; 137 went to college, including California State University, Sacramento; San Jose State University; Sonoma State University; University of California, Davis; University of California, Los Angeles; University of California, San Diego. Other: 3 entered military service.

Student Life Upper grades have specified standards of dress, student council, honor system. Discipline rests primarily with faculty. Attendance at religious services is required.

Summer Programs Remediation, enrichment, sports, art/fine arts programs offered; session focuses on enrichment; held on campus; accepts boys and girls; open to students from other schools. 350 students usually enrolled. 2013 schedule: June 17 to July 19. Application deadline: June 3.

Tuition and Aid Day student tuition: $11,650. Tuition installment plan (FACTS Tuition Payment Plan). Tuition reduction for siblings, need-based scholarship grants available. In 2012–13, 30% of upper-school students received aid. Total amount of financial aid awarded in 2012–13: $680,000.

Admissions Traditional secondary-level entrance grade is 9. For fall 2012, 179 students applied for upper-level admission, 165 were accepted, 131 enrolled. High School Placement Test required. Deadline for receipt of application materials: none. Application fee required: $50. Interview required.

Athletics Interscholastic: baseball (boys), basketball (b,g), cross-country running (b,g), golf (b,g), soccer (b,g), softball (g), swimming and diving (b,g), tennis (b,g), track and field (b,g), volleyball (b,g), water polo (b,g), wrestling (b,g); coed interscholastic: cheering, football, yoga. 3 PE instructors, 67 coaches, 1 athletic trainer.

Computers Computers are regularly used in business applications, business education, business studies, career education, career exploration, college planning, computer applications, desktop publishing, drawing and design, economics, English, foreign language, graphic arts, graphic design, history, library, library skills, mathematics, psychology, religious studies, science, social studies, Spanish, theater arts, theology, Web site design, word processing, yearbook classes. Computer network features include on-campus library services, Internet access, wireless campus network, Internet filtering or blocking technology. Student e-mail accounts are available to students. Students grades are available online. The school has a published electronic and media policy.

Contact Mrs. Sheila Williams, Director of Admissions. 707-644-4425 Ext. 448. Fax: 707-644-4770. E-mail: s.williams@spsv.org. Web site: spsv.org

ST. PATRICK'S REGIONAL SECONDARY

115 East 11th Avenue
Vancouver, British Columbia V5T 2C1, Canada

Head of School: Mr. John V. Bevacqua

General Information Coeducational day college-preparatory, general academic, arts, business, religious studies, and technology school, affiliated with Roman Catholic Church. Grades 8–12. Founded: 1923. Setting: urban. 2 buildings on campus. Approved or accredited by British Columbia Department of Education. Language of instruction: English. Total enrollment: 500. Upper school average class size: 25. The average school day consists of 6 hours.

Upper School Student Profile Grade 8: 99 students (38 boys, 61 girls); Grade 9: 101 students (35 boys, 66 girls); Grade 10: 104 students (33 boys, 71 girls); Grade 11: 101 students (36 boys, 65 girls); Grade 12: 101 students (38 boys, 63 girls). 97% of students are Roman Catholic.

Faculty School total: 35. In upper school: 15 men, 15 women; 8 have advanced degrees.

Special Academic Programs Advanced Placement exam preparation; ESL (15 students enrolled).

College Admission Counseling 100 students graduated in 2012; all went to college, including University of Alaska Fairbanks.

Student Life Upper grades have uniform requirement. Attendance at religious services is required.

Tuition and Aid Tuition installment plan (monthly payment plans).

Admissions Application fee required: CAN$100. Interview required.

Athletics Interscholastic: basketball (boys, girls), soccer (b,g), track and field (b,g), volleyball (g), wrestling (b,g); coed intramural: badminton. 5 PE instructors, 5 coaches.

Contact Mr. John V. Bevacqua, Principal. 604-874-6422. Fax: 604-874-5176. E-mail: administration@stpats.bc.ca. Web site: www.stpats.bc.ca

ST. PAUL ACADEMY AND SUMMIT SCHOOL

1712 Randolph Avenue
St. Paul, Minnesota 55105

Head of School: Bryn S. Roberts

General Information Coeducational day college-preparatory school. Grades K–12. Founded: 1900. Setting: urban. 32-acre campus. 4 buildings on campus. Approved or accredited by Independent Schools Association of the Central States and Minnesota Department of Education. Member of National Association of Independent Schools. Endowment: $31 million. Total enrollment: 884. Upper school average class size: 14. Upper school faculty-student ratio: 1:7. Upper School students typically attend 5 days per week.

Upper School Student Profile Grade 9: 98 students (43 boys, 55 girls); Grade 10: 91 students (43 boys, 48 girls); Grade 11: 95 students (45 boys, 50 girls); Grade 12: 89 students (43 boys, 46 girls).

Faculty School total: 108. In upper school: 15 men, 25 women; 32 have advanced degrees.

Subjects Offered Algebra, American literature, art, biology, calculus, ceramics, chemistry, Chinese, creative writing, current events, debate, drama, earth science, economics, English, English literature, European history, expository writing, fine arts, French, geometry, German, journalism, law and the legal system, marine biology, mathematics, multicultural studies, music, music theory, newspaper, photography, physical education, physics, psychology, science, senior project, Shakespeare, social psychology, social studies, sociology, space and physical sciences, Spanish, trigonometry, world history, world literature, world religions, yearbook.

Graduation Requirements Arts and fine arts (art, music, dance, drama), English, foreign language, mathematics, physical education (includes health), science, social studies (includes history), month-long senior project, senior speech.

Special Academic Programs Honors section; independent study; term-away projects; study abroad.

College Admission Counseling 77 students graduated in 2012; all went to college, including Boston University; Carleton College; Colgate University; St. Olaf College; University of Minnesota, Twin Cities Campus; University of Wisconsin–Madison. Mean SAT critical reading: 617, mean SAT math: 624, mean SAT writing: 628, mean combined SAT: 1900, mean composite ACT: 29.

Student Life Upper grades have specified standards of dress, student council. Discipline rests equally with students and faculty.

Summer Programs Enrichment programs offered; held on campus; accepts boys and girls; open to students from other schools.

Tuition and Aid Day student tuition: $23,310–$25,560. Tuition installment plan (Insured Tuition Payment Plan, monthly payment plans). Need-based scholarship grants available. In 2012–13, 29% of upper-school students received aid. Total amount of financial aid awarded in 2012–13: $1,797,260.

Admissions Traditional secondary-level entrance grade is 9. For fall 2012, 83 students applied for upper-level admission, 46 were accepted, 29 enrolled. SSAT, ERB, PSAT, SAT, PLAN or ACT or writing sample required. Deadline for receipt of application materials: February 1. Application fee required: $75. Interview required.

Athletics Interscholastic: alpine skiing (boys, girls), baseball (b), basketball (b,g), cross-country running (b,g), dance (g), dance team (g), diving (b,g), fencing (b,g), football (b), golf (b,g), ice hockey (b,g), skiing (cross-country) (b,g), skiing (downhill) (b,g), soccer (b,g), softball (g), swimming and diving (b,g), tennis (b,g); intramural: outdoor adventure (b,g); coed interscholastic: lacrosse, strength & conditioning, track and field; coed intramural: hiking/backpacking, physical fitness, snowboarding, table tennis. 1 PE instructor, 85 coaches, 1 athletic trainer.

Computers Computers are regularly used in all academic classes. Computer network features include on-campus library services, online commercial services, Internet access, wireless campus network, Internet filtering or blocking technology, laptop program (beginning in grade 7). Student e-mail accounts and computer access in designated common areas are available to students. The school has a published electronic and media policy.

Contact Mrs. Heather Cameron Ploen, Director of Admission and Financial Aid. 651-698-2451. Fax: 651-698-6787. E-mail: hploen@spa.edu. Web site: www.spa.edu

ST. PAUL'S EPISCOPAL SCHOOL

161 Dogwood Lane
Mobile, Alabama 36608

Head of School: Mr. F. Martin Lester Jr.

General Information Coeducational day college-preparatory, arts, technology, and honors, Advanced Placement school, affiliated with Episcopal Church. Grades PK–12. Founded: 1947. Setting: suburban. 32-acre campus. 10 buildings on campus. Approved or accredited by National Association of Episcopal Schools, Southern Association of Colleges and Schools, Southern Association of Independent Schools, and Alabama Department of Education. Member of National Association of Independent Schools and Secondary School Admission Test Board. Endowment: $1.6 million. Total enrollment: 1,222. Upper school average class size: 20. Upper school faculty-student ratio: 1:12. There are 177 required school days per year for Upper School students. Upper School students typically attend 5 days per week. The average school day consists of 6 hours and 10 minutes.

Upper School Student Profile Grade 9: 102 students (56 boys, 46 girls); Grade 10: 98 students (52 boys, 46 girls); Grade 11: 89 students (40 boys, 49 girls); Grade 12: 92 students (48 boys, 44 girls).

Faculty School total: 143. In upper school: 21 men, 35 women; 48 have advanced degrees.

Subjects Offered Advanced biology, advanced chemistry, advanced math, Advanced Placement courses, advanced studio art-AP, algebra, American history, American literature, anatomy and physiology, art, arts, band, biology, biology-AP, calculus, calculus-AP, chemistry, chemistry-AP, choir, choral music, civics, composition, computer science, concert choir, digital photography, drama, driver education, economics, economics-AP, English, English literature, English-AP, environmental science, environmental science-AP, European history, European history-AP, fine arts, foreign language, French, French-AP, geometry, government-AP, government/civics, grammar, history, history-AP, honors algebra, honors English, honors geometry, human anatomy, instrumental music, journalism, Latin, marching band, marine biology, mathematics, music, oil painting, painting, photography, physical education, physics, physics-AP, pre-algebra, pre-calculus, public service, Spanish, speech, theater, theater arts, trigonometry, U.S. history-AP, weight training, world history, yearbook.

Graduation Requirements Arts and fine arts (art, music, dance, drama), electives, English, foreign language, history, mathematics, science, 4 years of English, mathematics, social studies, and science, 2 year minimum foreign language, 60 hours of community service. Community service is required.

Special Academic Programs Advanced Placement exam preparation; honors section; study at local college for college credit; remedial reading and/or remedial writing; remedial math; special instructional classes for students with diagnosed learning disabilities.

College Admission Counseling 130 students graduated in 2012; all went to college, including Auburn University; Birmingham-Southern College; The University of Alabama; University of Mississippi; University of South Alabama; Vanderbilt University.

Student Life Upper grades have uniform requirement, student council, honor system. Discipline rests primarily with faculty. Attendance at religious services is required.

Summer Programs Remediation, enrichment, advancement, sports, art/fine arts, computer instruction programs offered; session focuses on enrichment; held both on and off campus; held at trip abroad; accepts boys and girls; open to students from other schools. 2013 schedule: June 1 to August 1. Application deadline: none.

Tuition and Aid Tuition installment plan (Insured Tuition Payment Plan, monthly payment plans, individually arranged payment plans, semiannual payment plan). Need-based scholarship grants available.

Admissions Traditional secondary-level entrance grade is 9. ERB CTP IV or Otis-Lennon and 2 sections of ERB required. Deadline for receipt of application materials: none. Application fee required. Interview required.

Athletics Interscholastic: baseball (boys), basketball (b,g), cheering (g), cross-country running (b,g), diving (b,g), football (b), golf (b,g), indoor track & field (b,g), soccer (b,g), softball (g), strength & conditioning (b,g), swimming and diving (b,g), tennis (b,g), track and field (b,g), volleyball (g), weight training (b), winter (indoor) track (b,g); intramural: basketball (b,g), soccer (b,g), volleyball (g), weight training (b); coed interscholastic: fencing. 6 PE instructors, 13 coaches, 4 athletic trainers.

Computers Computers are regularly used in economics, English, foreign language, history, independent study, journalism, keyboarding, mathematics, newspaper, publications, science, Spanish, writing, yearbook classes. Computer network features include on-campus library services, online commercial services, Internet access, wireless campus network, Internet filtering or blocking technology. Campus intranet, student e-mail accounts, and computer access in designated common areas are available to students. Students grades are available online. The school has a published electronic and media policy.

Contact Ms. Julie L. Taylor, Admissions Director. 251-461-2129. Fax: 251-342-1844. E-mail: jtaylor@stpaulsmobile.net. Web site: www.stpaulsmobile.net

ST. PAUL'S HIGH SCHOOL

2200 Grant Avenue
Winnipeg, Manitoba R3P 0P8, Canada

Head of School: Fr. Alan Fogarty, SJ

General Information Boys' day college-preparatory, arts, religious studies, and technology school, affiliated with Roman Catholic Church. Grades 9–12. Founded: 1926. Setting: suburban. 18-acre campus. 5 buildings on campus. Approved or accredited by Jesuit Secondary Education Association and Manitoba Department of Education. Language of instruction: English. Endowment: CAN$7.5 million. Total enrollment: 596. Upper school average class size: 26. Upper school faculty-student ratio: 1:14. There are 196 required school days per year for Upper School students. Upper School students typically attend 5 days per week. The average school day consists of 5 hours and 50 minutes.

Upper School Student Profile Grade 9: 156 students (156 boys); Grade 10: 156 students (156 boys); Grade 11: 146 students (146 boys); Grade 12: 138 students (138 boys). 67% of students are Roman Catholic.

Faculty School total: 44. In upper school: 35 men, 9 women; 16 have advanced degrees.

Subjects Offered Algebra, American history, art, biology, calculus, chemistry, classics, computer science, current events, economics, English, ethics, French, geography, geometry, history, law, mathematics, media, multimedia, multimedia design, music, physical education, physics, political science, psychology, religion, science, social studies, speech, theology, world wide web design.

Graduation Requirements English, mathematics, physical education (includes health), religion (includes Bible studies and theology), science, social studies (includes history), completion of Christian service program.

Special Academic Programs Advanced Placement exam preparation; honors section; remedial math.

College Admission Counseling 151 students graduated in 2012; 145 went to college, including McGill University; Queen's University at Kingston; The University of British Columbia; The University of Winnipeg; University of Manitoba; University of Toronto. Other: 4 went to work, 2 had other specific plans.

Student Life Upper grades have specified standards of dress, student council, honor system. Discipline rests primarily with faculty. Attendance at religious services is required.

Summer Programs Sports programs offered; session focuses on sport skills and relationship building; held on campus; accepts boys; open to students from other schools. 80 students usually enrolled. 2013 schedule: August 20 to September 2.

Tuition and Aid Day student tuition: CAN$7490. Tuition installment plan (Insured Tuition Payment Plan, monthly payment plans, individually arranged payment plans). Bursaries, need-based loans available. In 2012–13, 18% of upper-school students received aid. Total amount of financial aid awarded in 2012–13: CAN$320,000.

Admissions Traditional secondary-level entrance grade is 9. For fall 2012, 310 students applied for upper-level admission, 170 were accepted, 165 enrolled. Achievement tests and STS required. Deadline for receipt of application materials: February 3. Application fee required: CAN$100. On-campus interview required.

Athletics Interscholastic: badminton, basketball, cross-country running, curling, football, golf, ice hockey, indoor track, indoor track & field, rugby, soccer, track and field, volleyball, wrestling; intramural: badminton, basketball, curling, flag football, golf, physical fitness, physical training, skiing (downhill), strength & conditioning, table tennis, volleyball, weight training. 4 PE instructors, 1 athletic trainer.

Computers Computers are regularly used in French, French as a second language, geography, mathematics, multimedia, religious studies, science, Web site design classes. Computer network features include on-campus library services, online commercial services, Internet access, Internet filtering or blocking technology. Campus intranet, student e-mail accounts, and computer access in designated common areas are available to students. Students grades are available online. The school has a published electronic and media policy.

Contact Mr. Tom Lussier, Principal. 204-831-2300. Fax: 204-831-2340. E-mail: tlussier@stpauls.mb.ca. Web site: www.stpauls.mb.ca

ST. PETER'S PREPARATORY SCHOOL

144 Grand Street
Jersey City, New Jersey 07302

Head of School: Rev. Robert E. Reiser, SJ

General Information Boys' day college-preparatory, arts, technology, and music school, affiliated with Roman Catholic Church. Grades 9–12. Founded: 1872. Setting: urban. Nearest major city is New York, NY. 7-acre campus. 8 buildings on campus. Approved or accredited by Jesuit Secondary Education Association, Middle States Association of Colleges and Schools, and New Jersey Department of Education. Endowment: $18 million. Total enrollment: 966. Upper school average class size: 22. Upper school faculty-student ratio: 1:12. There are 170 required school days per year for Upper School students. Upper School students typically attend 5 days per week. The average school day consists of 6 hours.

Upper School Student Profile Grade 9: 280 students (280 boys); Grade 10: 249 students (249 boys); Grade 11: 209 students (209 boys); Grade 12: 228 students (228 boys). 80% of students are Roman Catholic.

Faculty School total: 80. In upper school: 51 men, 27 women; 46 have advanced degrees.

Subjects Offered Advanced Placement courses, algebra, American history, American history-AP, American legal systems, American literature, Ancient Greek, art, art history, biology, biology-AP, calculus, calculus-AP, ceramics, chemistry, chemistry-AP, choral music, Christian ethics, community service, computer programming, computer science, concert band, creative writing, drawing, English, English language-AP, English literature, English literature-AP, European history, French, geometry, German, government and politics-AP, health, history, human anatomy, Italian, jazz band, Latin, Latin-AP, mathematics, music, music theory, physical education, physics, religion, sculpture, social justice, Spanish, Spanish language-AP, Spanish literature-AP, statistics-AP, studio art, theology, trigonometry, Web site design, world civilizations, world history, world literature, writing.

Graduation Requirements Algebra, American history, American literature, ancient world history, art, Basic programming, biology, British literature, chemistry, computer education, English, geometry, Latin, modern languages, music, physical education (includes health), physics, religion (includes Bible studies and theology), U.S. history, world civilizations, 20 hours of community service in freshman and sophomore years, 60 hours in the third (junior) year.

Special Academic Programs International Baccalaureate program; 13 Advanced Placement exams for which test preparation is offered; honors section; study at local college for college credit; study abroad.

College Admission Counseling 189 students graduated in 2011; 186 went to college, including Boston College; Georgetown University; Rutgers, The State University of New Jersey, Rutgers College; Saint Joseph's University; Saint Peter's University; The College of New Jersey. Other: 2 went to work, 1 entered military service. Median SAT critical reading: 570, median SAT math: 590. Mean SAT writing: 570, mean combined SAT: 1715. 44% scored over 600 on SAT critical reading, 48% scored over 600 on SAT math, 50% scored over 600 on SAT writing, 50% scored over 1800 on combined SAT.

Student Life Upper grades have specified standards of dress, student council, honor system. Discipline rests primarily with faculty.

Tuition and Aid Day student tuition: $11,500. Tuition installment plan (SMART Tuition Payment Plan, monthly payment plans). Merit scholarship grants, need-based scholarship grants, paying campus jobs available. In 2011–12, 46% of upper-school students received aid; total upper-school merit-scholarship money awarded: $1,000,000. Total amount of financial aid awarded in 2011–12: $1,000,000.

Admissions Traditional secondary-level entrance grade is 9. For fall 2011, 904 students applied for upper-level admission, 455 were accepted, 280 enrolled. Cooperative Entrance Exam (McGraw-Hill) or SSAT required. Deadline for receipt of application materials: November 15. No application fee required.

Athletics Interscholastic: baseball, basketball, bowling, crew, cross-country running, diving, fencing, football, golf, ice hockey, indoor track, indoor track & field, lacrosse, rugby, soccer, swimming and diving, tennis, track and field, volleyball, water polo, winter (indoor) track, wrestling; intramural: basketball, flag football, Frisbee, handball, indoor soccer, outdoor recreation, team handball, touch football, ultimate Frisbee, weight lifting, whiffle ball. 4 PE instructors, 23 coaches, 1 athletic trainer.

Computers Computers are regularly used in all academic classes. Computer network features include on-campus library services, online commercial services, Internet access, wireless campus network, Internet filtering or blocking technology. Campus intranet and student e-mail accounts are available to students. Students grades are available online. The school has a published electronic and media policy.

Contact Mr. John T. Irvine, Director of Admissions. 201-547-6389. Fax: 201-547-2341. E-mail: Irvinej@spprep.org. Web site: www.spprep.org

ST. PIUS X CATHOLIC HIGH SCHOOL

2674 Johnson Road NE
Atlanta, Georgia 30345

Head of School: Mr. Steve Spellman

General Information Coeducational day college-preparatory school, affiliated with Roman Catholic Church. Grades 9–12. Founded: 1958. Setting: suburban. 33-acre campus. 8 buildings on campus. Approved or accredited by National Catholic Education Association, Southern Association of Colleges and Schools, Southern Association of Independent Schools, The College Board, and Georgia Department of Education. Member of Secondary School Admission Test Board. Total enrollment: 1,100. Upper school average class size: 21. Upper school faculty-student ratio: 1:12. There are 180 required school days per year for Upper School students. The average school day consists of 7 hours.

Upper School Student Profile Grade 9: 295 students (148 boys, 147 girls); Grade 10: 285 students (140 boys, 145 girls); Grade 11: 260 students (130 boys, 130 girls); Grade 12: 260 students (130 boys, 130 girls). 82% of students are Roman Catholic.

Faculty School total: 97. In upper school: 49 men, 45 women; 67 have advanced degrees.

Subjects Offered Accounting, algebra, American history, American literature, anatomy, art, band, biology, business, business law, calculus, ceramics, chemistry, chorus, computer programming, computer science, creative writing, current events, dance, drama, driver education, economics, English, English literature, European history, expository writing, French, geography, geometry, German, government/civics, health, history, instrumental music, journalism, Latin, mathematics, music, physical education, physical science, physics, physiology, psychology, religion, science, social studies, sociology, Spanish, speech, statistics, theater, trigonometry, word processing, world history, world literature.

Graduation Requirements American history, computer science, English, foreign language, mathematics, physical education (includes health), religion (includes Bible studies and theology), science, social studies (includes history), Works of Mercy.

Special Academic Programs 20 Advanced Placement exams for which test preparation is offered; honors section; special instructional classes for students with learning disabilities and Attention Deficit Disorder.

College Admission Counseling 260 students graduated in 2012; 259 went to college, including Emory University; Georgia Institute of Technology; Georgia Southern University; Georgia State University; University of Georgia; University of Notre Dame. Other: 1 entered military service. 60% scored over 600 on SAT critical reading, 60% scored over 600 on SAT math, 50% scored over 26 on composite ACT.

Student Life Upper grades have uniform requirement, student council, honor system. Discipline rests equally with students and faculty. Attendance at religious services is required.

Summer Programs Enrichment, sports, art/fine arts programs offered; held on campus; accepts boys and girls; open to students from other schools. 500 students usually enrolled. 2013 schedule: June 3 to July 30.

Tuition and Aid Day student tuition: $11,400. Tuition installment plan (FACTS Tuition Payment Plan, monthly payment plans). Tuition reduction for siblings, need-based scholarship grants available. In 2012–13, 18% of upper-school students received aid. Total amount of financial aid awarded in 2012–13: $400,000.

Admissions Traditional secondary-level entrance grade is 9. For fall 2012, 525 students applied for upper-level admission, 325 were accepted, 290 enrolled. SSAT required. Deadline for receipt of application materials: February 1. Application fee required: $100.

Athletics Interscholastic: baseball (boys), basketball (b,g), cheering (b,g), cross-country running (b,g), dance (b), dance squad (g), dance team (g), diving (b,g), drill team (g), football (b), golf (b,g), lacrosse (b,g), soccer (b,g), softball (g), strength & conditioning (b,g), swimming and diving (b,g), tennis (b,g), track and field (b,g), volleyball (g), water polo (b,g), weight training (b,g), wrestling (b); coed interscholastic: sailing, water polo. 4 PE instructors, 35 coaches, 1 athletic trainer.

Computers Computers are regularly used in all academic classes. Computer network features include on-campus library services, online commercial services, Internet access, wireless campus network, Internet filtering or blocking technology. Campus intranet, student e-mail accounts, and computer access in designated common areas are available to students. Students grades are available online. The school has a published electronic and media policy.

Contact Terry Sides, Coordinator of Admissions. 404-636-0323 Ext. 291. Fax: 404-636-2118. E-mail: tsides@spx.org. Web site: www.spx.org

ST. PIUS X HIGH SCHOOL

811 West Donovan Street
Houston, Texas 77091-5699

Head of School: Sr. Donna M. Pollard, OP

General Information Coeducational day college-preparatory, arts, business, religious studies, and technology school, affiliated with Roman Catholic Church. Grades 9–12. Founded: 1956. Setting: urban. 26-acre campus. 1 building on campus. Approved or accredited by Southern Association of Colleges and Schools, Texas Catholic Conference, Texas Education Agency, The College Board, and Texas Department of Education. Endowment: $3.5 million. Total enrollment: 649. Upper school average class size: 20. Upper school faculty-student ratio: 1:12. There are 180 required school days per year for Upper School students. Upper School students typically attend 5 days per week. The average school day consists of 7 hours.

Upper School Student Profile Grade 9: 159 students (93 boys, 66 girls); Grade 10: 168 students (93 boys, 75 girls); Grade 11: 167 students (85 boys, 82 girls); Grade 12: 155 students (82 boys, 73 girls). 71% of students are Roman Catholic.

Faculty School total: 57. In upper school: 21 men, 36 women; 41 have advanced degrees.

Subjects Offered Advanced chemistry, advanced computer applications, advanced math, Advanced Placement courses, advanced studio art-AP, algebra, American history-AP, American literature, American literature-AP, art, band, biology, biology-AP, business law, calculus, calculus-AP, campus ministry, Catholic belief and practice, chemistry, choir, chorus, Christian ethics, church history, college counseling, communications, community service, computer applications, computer multimedia, computer programming, computer science-AP, cultural geography, dance, death and loss, desktop publishing, earth and space science, economics, English language-AP, English literature-AP, environmental science, film history, fine arts, foreign language, French, geography, geometry, graphic design, health, health education, history of the Catholic Church, honors geometry, honors world history, introduction to theater, jewelry making, language arts, Latin, Latin-AP, library assistant, marching band, modern world history, moral and social development, moral theology, musical productions, painting, personal finance, philosophy, photography, physical education, physics, psychology, reading/study skills, SAT/ACT preparation, Shakespeare, social justice, sociology, Spanish, Spanish language-AP, Spanish-AP, speech, speech communications, stagecraft, student government, student publications, technical theater, theology, U.S. government, U.S. government and politics-AP, U.S. history, U.S. history-AP, Web site design, world history, world religions, yearbook.

Graduation Requirements Advanced math, algebra, American government, American history, ancient world history, art, biology, chemistry, communications, economics, electives, English, geometry, government, health, integrated physics, physical education (includes health), physics, theology, 2 years of foreign language or reading development, Christian Service Learning (100 hours of community service), 4 years of theology.

Special Academic Programs 10 Advanced Placement exams for which test preparation is offered; honors section; study at local college for college credit; remedial reading and/or remedial writing; remedial math; programs in English, mathematics, general development for dyslexic students.

College Admission Counseling 170 students graduated in 2012; 99 went to college, including Stephen F. Austin State University; Texas A&M University; Texas State University–San Marcos; Texas Tech University; The University of Texas at San Antonio; University of Houston. Mean SAT critical reading: 517, mean SAT math: 505, mean SAT writing: 492, mean combined SAT: 1517, mean composite ACT: 23. 12%

scored over 600 on SAT critical reading, 12% scored over 600 on SAT math, 13% scored over 600 on SAT writing, 11% scored over 1800 on combined SAT, 19% scored over 26 on composite ACT.

Student Life Upper grades have uniform requirement, student council, honor system. Discipline rests primarily with faculty. Attendance at religious services is required.

Summer Programs Enrichment, sports, art/fine arts, computer instruction programs offered; held on campus; accepts boys and girls; not open to students from other schools. 100 students usually enrolled. 2013 schedule: June 6 to July 30. Application deadline: May 1.

Tuition and Aid Day student tuition: $11,700. Tuition installment plan (monthly payment plans, individually arranged payment plans). Tuition reduction for siblings, merit scholarship grants, need-based scholarship grants available. In 2012–13, 26% of upper-school students received aid; total upper-school merit-scholarship money awarded: $53,500. Total amount of financial aid awarded in 2012–13: $711,000.

Admissions Traditional secondary-level entrance grade is 9. For fall 2012, 375 students applied for upper-level admission, 275 were accepted, 199 enrolled. Catholic High School Entrance Examination required. Deadline for receipt of application materials: January 15. Application fee required: $50. Interview required.

Athletics Interscholastic: baseball (boys), basketball (b,g), cheering (g), cross-country running (b,g), dance squad (g), dance team (b,g), drill team (g), football (b), golf (b,g), rugby (b,g), soccer (b,g), softball (g), swimming and diving (b,g), tennis (b,g), track and field (b,g), volleyball (g), wrestling (b). 1 PE instructor, 1 athletic trainer.

Computers Computers are regularly used in art, career exploration, career technology, desktop publishing, drawing and design, graphic design, journalism, mathematics, multimedia, news writing, newspaper, publications, technology, video film production, yearbook classes. Computer network features include on-campus library services, Internet access, wireless campus network, Internet filtering or blocking technology, faculty Web pages for courses. Student e-mail accounts and computer access in designated common areas are available to students. Students grades are available online. The school has a published electronic and media policy.

Contact Ms. Susie Kramer, Admissions Director. 713-579-7507. Fax: 713-692-5725. E-mail: kramers@stpiusx.org. Web site: www.stpiusx.org

ST. SEBASTIAN'S SCHOOL

1191 Greendale Avenue
Needham, Massachusetts 02492

Head of School: Mr. William L. Burke III

General Information Boys' day college-preparatory school, affiliated with Roman Catholic Church. Grades 7–12. Founded: 1941. Setting: suburban. Nearest major city is Boston. 25-acre campus. 5 buildings on campus. Approved or accredited by New England Association of Schools and Colleges and Massachusetts Department of Education. Member of National Association of Independent Schools and Secondary School Admission Test Board. Endowment: $10.4 million. Total enrollment: 360. Upper school average class size: 11. Upper school faculty-student ratio: 1:7.

Upper School Student Profile Grade 9: 66 students (66 boys); Grade 10: 62 students (62 boys); Grade 11: 63 students (63 boys); Grade 12: 66 students (66 boys). 80% of students are Roman Catholic.

Faculty School total: 61. In upper school: 48 men, 13 women; 35 have advanced degrees.

Subjects Offered Algebra, American history, American literature, art, art history, biology, calculus, chemistry, computer science, drama, economics, English, English literature, ethics, European history, fine arts, geography, geometry, government/civics, Greek, history, Latin, mathematics, music, philosophy, photography, physical education, physics, religion, science, social studies, Spanish, speech, theater, trigonometry, world history, world literature, writing.

Graduation Requirements Arts and fine arts (art, music, dance, drama), English, foreign language, mathematics, physical education (includes health), religion (includes Bible studies and theology), science, social studies (includes history), senior service, chapel speaking program.

Special Academic Programs Advanced Placement exam preparation; honors section; independent study; academic accommodation for the gifted, the musically talented, and the artistically talented.

College Admission Counseling 55 students graduated in 2011; 54 went to college, including College of the Holy Cross; Hobart and William Smith Colleges; Loyola University Maryland; Stonehill College; University of Richmond; Villanova University. Median SAT critical reading: 640, median SAT math: 640.

Student Life Upper grades have specified standards of dress, student council, honor system. Discipline rests primarily with faculty. Attendance at religious services is required.

Tuition and Aid Day student tuition: $31,550. Tuition installment plan (Academic Management Services Plan, Key Tuition Payment Plan). Need-based scholarship grants, need-based loans available. In 2011–12, 26% of upper-school students received aid. Total amount of financial aid awarded in 2011–12: $1,750,000.

Admissions Traditional secondary-level entrance grade is 9. For fall 2011, 100 students applied for upper-level admission, 34 were accepted, 17 enrolled. ISEE or SSAT required. Deadline for receipt of application materials: January 15. Application fee required: $40. On-campus interview required.

Athletics Interscholastic: baseball, basketball, cross-country running, football, golf, ice hockey, lacrosse, sailing, skiing (downhill), soccer, squash, swimming and diving, tennis; intramural: strength & conditioning, ultimate Frisbee, weight lifting, whiffle ball, wrestling. 1 athletic trainer.

Computers Computers are regularly used in English, foreign language, mathematics, science, social studies, writing classes. Computer network features include on-campus library services, Internet access, wireless campus network, Internet filtering or blocking technology. Campus intranet is available to students. The school has a published electronic and media policy.

Contact Mrs. Helen Maxwell, Assistant to Dean of Admissions. 781-449-5200 Ext. 125. Fax: 781-449-5630. E-mail: admissions@stsebs.org. Web site: www.saintsebastiansschool.org

SAINTS PETER AND PAUL HIGH SCHOOL

900 High Street
Easton, Maryland 21601

Head of School: Mr. James Edward Nemeth

General Information Coeducational day college-preparatory school, affiliated with Roman Catholic Church. Grades 9–12. Founded: 1958. Setting: small town. Nearest major city is Baltimore. 4-acre campus. 4 buildings on campus. Approved or accredited by Middle States Association of Colleges and Schools, National Catholic Education Association, and Maryland Department of Education. Endowment: $125,000. Total enrollment: 214. Upper school average class size: 16. Upper school faculty-student ratio: 1:9. There are 183 required school days per year for Upper School students. Upper School students typically attend 5 days per week. The average school day consists of 6 hours and 30 minutes.

Upper School Student Profile Grade 9: 62 students (37 boys, 25 girls); Grade 10: 51 students (29 boys, 22 girls); Grade 11: 49 students (23 boys, 26 girls); Grade 12: 52 students (17 boys, 35 girls). 68% of students are Roman Catholic.

Faculty School total: 22. In upper school: 11 men, 10 women; 15 have advanced degrees.

Subjects Offered Advanced computer applications, algebra, American government, American literature, anatomy and physiology, art and culture, biology, biology-AP, British literature, British literature (honors), calculus, calculus-AP, campus ministry, Catholic belief and practice, chemistry, chemistry-AP, Christian and Hebrew scripture, Christian ethics, Christianity, church history, computer multimedia, computer programming, computer science, conceptual physics, creative writing, drama, earth science, economics, English language and composition-AP, English literature and composition-AP, environmental science, geography, geometry, health and wellness, Hebrew scripture, honors algebra, honors English, honors geometry, honors U.S. history, honors world history, Microsoft, moral theology, music theory, philosophy, physical education, physics, pre-calculus, probability and statistics, Spanish, speech, studio art-AP, theology, U.S. government and politics-AP, U.S. history, U.S. history-AP, Web site design, world history, yearbook.

Graduation Requirements Algebra, American literature, arts and fine arts (art, music, dance, drama), biology, British literature, Catholic belief and practice, chemistry, Christian and Hebrew scripture, Christianity, computer applications, computer science, English, foreign language, geometry, history of the Catholic Church, mathematics, moral theology, physical education (includes health), physics, pre-algebra, social justice, U.S. government, U.S. history, world history.

Special Academic Programs 7 Advanced Placement exams for which test preparation is offered; honors section; independent study.

College Admission Counseling 46 students graduated in 2011; all went to college, including Loyola University Maryland; Salisbury University; University of Maryland, College Park; Washington College. Median SAT critical reading: 530, median SAT math: 520, median SAT writing: 520. 18% scored over 600 on SAT critical reading, 18% scored over 600 on SAT math, 30% scored over 600 on SAT writing.

Student Life Upper grades have uniform requirement. Discipline rests primarily with faculty. Attendance at religious services is required.

Tuition and Aid Day student tuition: $10,600. Tuition installment plan (FACTS Tuition Payment Plan). Tuition reduction for siblings, need-based scholarship grants, parish subsidies available. In 2011–12, 3% of upper-school students received aid. Total amount of financial aid awarded in 2011–12: $6500.

Admissions Traditional secondary-level entrance grade is 9. For fall 2011, 68 students applied for upper-level admission, 62 were accepted, 62 enrolled. Diocesan Entrance Exam required. Deadline for receipt of application materials: none. Application fee required: $50. On-campus interview required.

Athletics Interscholastic: baseball (boys), basketball (b,g), cross-country running (b,g), field hockey (g), golf (b), ice hockey (b), lacrosse (b,g), soccer (b,g), softball (g), swimming and diving (b,g), tennis (b,g). 1 PE instructor, 23 coaches.

Computers Computers are regularly used in all academic classes. Computer network features include on-campus library services, Internet access, wireless campus network, Internet filtering or blocking technology. Students grades are available online. The school has a published electronic and media policy.

Contact Mrs. Carolyn Smith Hayman, Administrative Assistant. 410-822-2275 Ext. 150. Fax: 410-822-1767. E-mail: chayman@ssppeaston.org. Web site: www.ssppeaston.org

ST. STANISLAUS COLLEGE

304 South Beach Boulevard
Bay St. Louis, Mississippi 39520

Head of School: Br. Bernard Couvillion, SC

General Information Boys' boarding and day college-preparatory, business, religious studies, technology, and ESL school, affiliated with Roman Catholic Church. Grades 7–PG. Founded: 1854. Setting: small town. Nearest major city is New Orleans, LA. Students are housed in single-sex dormitories. 30-acre campus. 8 buildings on campus. Approved or accredited by National Catholic Education Association, Southern Association of Colleges and Schools, Southern Association of Independent Schools, and Mississippi Department of Education. Member of National Association of Independent Schools. Endowment: $5 million. Total enrollment: 352. Upper school average class size: 22. Upper school faculty-student ratio: 1:12. There are 180 required school days per year for Upper School students. Upper School students typically attend 5 days per week. The average school day consists of 6 hours and 23 minutes.

Upper School Student Profile Grade 9: 65 students (65 boys); Grade 10: 64 students (64 boys); Grade 11: 66 students (66 boys); Grade 12: 55 students (55 boys). 25% of students are boarding students. 1% are state residents. 6 states are represented in upper school student body. 8% are international students. International students from Angola, China, Mexico, Republic of Korea, Taiwan, and Thailand. 70% of students are Roman Catholic.

Faculty School total: 34. In upper school: 28 men, 6 women; 21 have advanced degrees; 8 reside on campus.

Subjects Offered Accounting, ACT preparation, advanced biology, advanced chemistry, advanced computer applications, advanced math, Advanced Placement courses, algebra, American history, American history-AP, American literature, anatomy, art, astronomy, biology, biology-AP, business, business education, business law, calculus, calculus-AP, campus ministry, ceramics, chemistry, chemistry-AP, computer programming, computer science, computer science-AP, creative writing, desktop publishing, drama, economics, economics and history, English, English language and composition-AP, English literature, English literature and composition-AP, environmental science, ESL, finance, French, French as a second language, genetics, geography, geology, geometry, government, government/civics, grammar, guidance, health, health education, history, journalism, law, marine biology, marine science, mathematics, music, music performance, physical education, physics, physics-AP, pre-calculus, psychology, psychology-AP, religion, science, scuba diving, short story, social sciences, social studies, sociology, Spanish, speech, swimming, symphonic band, theater, theater arts, theology, track and field, trigonometry, typing, U.S. history-AP, world history, world literature.

Graduation Requirements Arts and fine arts (art, music, dance, drama), computer science, English, foreign language, mathematics, physical education (includes health), religion (includes Bible studies and theology), science, social sciences, social studies (includes history), service hours are required.

Special Academic Programs 8 Advanced Placement exams for which test preparation is offered; honors section; remedial reading and/or remedial writing; remedial math; programs in English, general development for dyslexic students; ESL (10 students enrolled).

College Admission Counseling 64 students graduated in 2012; all went to college, including Louisiana State University and Agricultural and Mechanical College; Mississippi State University; University of Mississippi; University of New Orleans; University of South Alabama; University of Southern Mississippi. Median SAT critical reading: 520, median SAT math: 620, median SAT writing: 570, median composite ACT: 21. 40% scored over 600 on SAT critical reading, 50% scored over 600 on SAT math, 35% scored over 600 on SAT writing, 22% scored over 1800 on combined SAT, 17% scored over 26 on composite ACT.

Student Life Upper grades have uniform requirement, student council. Discipline rests primarily with faculty. Attendance at religious services is required.

Summer Programs ESL programs offered; session focuses on outdoor summer camp and ESL, cultural summer camp; held both on and off campus; held at Mississippi, Louisiana, and Florida; accepts boys; open to students from other schools. 180 students usually enrolled. 2013 schedule: June 15 to July 13. Application deadline: none.

Tuition and Aid Day student tuition: $5600; 7-day tuition and room/board: $21,650. Tuition installment plan (monthly payment plans, individually arranged payment plans). Need-based scholarship grants, need-based loans, paying campus jobs available.

Admissions Traditional secondary-level entrance grade is 9. For fall 2012, 100 students applied for upper-level admission, 90 were accepted, 80 enrolled. Deadline for receipt of application materials: none. Application fee required: $100. On-campus interview recommended.

Athletics Interscholastic: baseball, basketball, cross-country running, football, golf, power lifting, soccer, track and field; intramural: baseball, basketball, billiards, cheering, fishing, flag football, floor hockey, football, hiking/backpacking, jogging, outdoor activities, outdoor adventure, outdoor education, outdoor recreation, outdoor skills, outdoors, physical fitness, physical training, power lifting, scuba diving, swimming and diving, table tennis, tennis, touch football, volleyball, water polo, water skiing, weight lifting, weight training; coed interscholastic: sailing, swimming and diving, tennis. 5 PE instructors, 16 coaches, 1 athletic trainer.

Computers Computers are regularly used in accounting, English, mathematics, religion, SAT preparation, science, Spanish classes. Computer network features include on-campus library services, online commercial services, Internet access, wireless campus network, Internet filtering or blocking technology. Campus intranet and computer access in designated common areas are available to students. Students grades are available online.

Contact Mr. John Thibodeaux, Director of Admissions. 228-467-9057 Ext. 226. Fax: 228-466-2972. E-mail: admissions@ststan.com. Web site: www.ststan.com

ST. STEPHEN'S & ST. AGNES SCHOOL

1000 St. Stephen's Road
Alexandria, Virginia 22304

Head of School: Mrs. Joan G. Ogilvy Holden

General Information Coeducational day college-preparatory, arts, religious studies, and technology school, affiliated with Episcopal Church. Grades JK–12. Founded: 1924. Setting: suburban. Nearest major city is Washington, DC. 35-acre campus. 5 buildings on campus. Approved or accredited by Association of Independent Schools of Greater Washington, National Association of Episcopal Schools, and Virginia Association of Independent Schools. Member of National Association of Independent Schools and Secondary School Admission Test Board. Endowment: $20.3 million. Total enrollment: 1,143. Upper school average class size: 14. Upper school faculty-student ratio: 1:9. There are 170 required school days per year for Upper School students. Upper School students typically attend 5 days per week. The average school day consists of 7 hours and 10 minutes.

Upper School Student Profile Grade 9: 113 students (54 boys, 59 girls); Grade 10: 108 students (51 boys, 57 girls); Grade 11: 120 students (70 boys, 50 girls); Grade 12: 112 students (52 boys, 60 girls). 22% of students are members of Episcopal Church.

Faculty School total: 133. In upper school: 26 men, 26 women; 38 have advanced degrees.

Subjects Offered 1 1/2 elective credits, Advanced Placement courses, algebra, American history, American literature, art, art history, art history-AP, bioethics, biology, biology-AP, calculus, calculus-AP, ceramics, chemistry, chemistry-AP, Christian education, Christian ethics, Christian scripture, Christian testament, comparative government and politics-AP, concert choir, directing, drama, drawing, economics, English, English-AP, ensembles, environmental science-AP, ethics, European history, European history-AP, forensics, French, French language-AP, geometry, government/civics-AP, history, honors English, honors geometry, honors U.S. history, honors world history, instrumental music, jazz ensemble, Latin, Latin-AP, macro/microeconomics-AP, Mandarin, mathematics, medieval history, medieval/Renaissance history, microeconomics-AP, music, music theory-AP, newspaper, painting, physical education, physics, physics-AP, playwriting and directing, pre-calculus, psychology-AP, religion, sculpture, senior project, Spanish, Spanish language-AP, Spanish literature-AP, sports, sports medicine, statistics-AP, studio art, studio art-AP, technical theater, theater, theater arts, trigonometry, U.S. history-AP, world history, writing, yearbook, yoga.

Graduation Requirements Arts and fine arts (art, music, dance, drama), English, family studies, foreign language, history, mathematics, physical education (includes health), religion (includes Bible studies and theology), science, technological applications, senior year independent off-campus project, 40 hours of community service.

Special Academic Programs 22 Advanced Placement exams for which test preparation is offered; honors section; independent study; term-away projects; study abroad; academic accommodation for the gifted, the musically talented, and the artistically talented.

College Admission Counseling 96 students graduated in 2012; all went to college, including Dartmouth College; New York University; Stanford University; The College of William and Mary; The University of North Carolina at Chapel Hill; University of Virginia. Mean SAT critical reading: 612, mean SAT math: 624, mean SAT writing: 621, mean combined SAT: 1857.

Student Life Upper grades have specified standards of dress, student council, honor system. Discipline rests equally with students and faculty. Attendance at religious services is required.

Summer Programs Enrichment, advancement, sports, art/fine arts, computer instruction programs offered; session focuses on enrichment; held both on and off campus; held at Chesapeake Bay, DC, VA and MD area, Auxiliary camps held on our campus—Johns Hopkins University, Center for Talented Youth, and ASM Summer Tennis Camp, Terrence Austin's Football Camp, USA Chess Camp and Animation Creation; accepts boys and girls; open to students from other schools. 1,750 students usually enrolled. 2013 schedule: June 17 to August 16. Application deadline: April 5.

Tuition and Aid Day student tuition: $30,765. Tuition installment plan (FACTS Tuition Payment Plan). Need-based scholarship grants available. In 2012–13, 26% of upper-school students received aid. Total amount of financial aid awarded in 2012–13: $2,198,325.

Admissions Traditional secondary-level entrance grade is 9. ISEE or SSAT required. Deadline for receipt of application materials: January 15. Application fee required: $70. Interview required.

Athletics Interscholastic: baseball (boys), basketball (b,g), field hockey (g), football (b), ice hockey (b), lacrosse (b,g), soccer (b,g), softball (g), swimming and diving (b,g), tennis (b,g), track and field (b,g), volleyball (g), winter soccer (g), wrestling (b); intramural: dance team (g), independent competitive sports (b,g); coed interscholastic: cross-country running, diving, golf, winter (indoor) track; coed intramural: basketball, fitness, independent competitive sports, jogging, physical fitness, physical training, strength & conditioning, weight lifting, weight training, yoga. 6 PE instructors, 14 coaches, 2 athletic trainers.

Computers Computers are regularly used in all academic classes. Computer network features include on-campus library services, online commercial services, Internet access, wireless campus network, Internet filtering or blocking technology, computer labs for foreign language, math, technology, library, newspaper, physics, and chemistry, homework assignments posted online, mobile wireless laptop cart (180 laptops), iPads, computers available in study hall and library. Campus intranet, student e-mail accounts, and computer access in designated common areas are available to students. Students grades are available online. The school has a published electronic and media policy.

Contact Mr. Jon Kunz, Director of Admission, Grades 6-12. 703-212-2706. Fax: 703-212-2788. E-mail: jkunz@sssas.org. Web site: www.sssas.org

SAINT STEPHEN'S EPISCOPAL SCHOOL

315 41st Street West
Bradenton, Florida 34209

Head of School: Janet S. Pullen

General Information Coeducational day college-preparatory, arts, religious studies, and marine science school, affiliated with Episcopal Church. Grades PK–12. Founded: 1970. Setting: small town. Nearest major city is Tampa. 35-acre campus. 3 buildings on campus. Approved or accredited by Florida Council of Independent Schools, National Association of Episcopal Schools, Southern Association of Colleges and Schools, and Southern Association of Independent Schools. Member of National Association of Independent Schools. Endowment: $1.2 million. Total enrollment: 654. Upper school average class size: 11. Upper school faculty-student ratio: 1:11. There are 177 required school days per year for Upper School students. Upper School students typically attend 5 days per week. The average school day consists of 7 hours.

Upper School Student Profile Grade 9: 62 students (32 boys, 30 girls); Grade 10: 54 students (26 boys, 28 girls); Grade 11: 73 students (38 boys, 35 girls); Grade 12: 70 students (34 boys, 36 girls); Postgraduate: 2 students (2 boys). 15% of students are members of Episcopal Church.

Faculty School total: 90. In upper school: 13 men, 18 women; 21 have advanced degrees.

Subjects Offered 3-dimensional art, Advanced Placement courses, advanced studio art-AP, algebra, American government, American history, American history-AP, American literature, art, art history, art history-AP, art-AP, astronomy, band, biology, biology-AP, British literature, broadcast journalism, calculus, calculus-AP, ceramics, chemistry, chemistry-AP, choir, chorus, community service, comparative religion, composition, composition-AP, computer programming, computer programming-AP, computer science, computer science-AP, conceptual physics, debate, digital art, digital photography, discrete mathematics, drama, economics, English, English language and composition-AP, English language-AP, English literature, English literature and composition-AP, English literature-AP, English-AP, environmental science-AP, European history, European history-AP, French, French language-AP, geometry, graphic design, humanities, international relations, journalism, Latin, Latin-AP, marine biology, marine science, music, newspaper, organic chemistry, painting, photography, physical education, physics, physics-AP, portfolio art, pre-calculus, probability and statistics, psychology, public speaking, science research, Spanish, Spanish language-AP, speech and debate, studio art, studio art-AP, trigonometry, U.S. history, U.S. history-AP, weight training, Western civilization, world history, world history-AP.

Graduation Requirements Arts and fine arts (art, music, dance, drama), electives, English, foreign language, mathematics, physical education (includes health), science, social studies (includes history), senior speech. Community service is required.

Special Academic Programs 17 Advanced Placement exams for which test preparation is offered; honors section.

College Admission Counseling 52 students graduated in 2012; all went to college, including Florida State University; University of Central Florida; University of Florida; University of Miami; University of South Florida. Mean SAT critical reading: 570, mean SAT math: 614, mean SAT writing: 579, mean composite ACT: 25. 39% scored over 600 on SAT critical reading, 56% scored over 600 on SAT math, 36% scored over 600 on SAT writing, 38% scored over 26 on composite ACT.

Student Life Upper grades have specified standards of dress, student council, honor system. Discipline rests primarily with faculty. Attendance at religious services is required.

Summer Programs Enrichment, advancement, sports, art/fine arts, computer instruction programs offered; session focuses on academic enrichment and sports; held on campus; accepts boys and girls; open to students from other schools. 500 students usually enrolled. 2013 schedule: June 13 to August 12. Application deadline: June 1.

Tuition and Aid Day student tuition: $18,550. Tuition installment plan (monthly payment plans). Need-based scholarship grants available. In 2012–13, 6% of upper-school students received aid. Total amount of financial aid awarded in 2012–13: $9250.

Admissions Traditional secondary-level entrance grade is 9. For fall 2012, 37 students applied for upper-level admission, 34 were accepted, 34 enrolled. School's own exam required. Deadline for receipt of application materials: none. Application fee required: $100. Interview recommended.

Athletics Interscholastic: aerobics/dance (girls), aquatics (b,g), baseball (b), basketball (b,g), cheering (g), cross-country running (b,g), dance (g), dance team (g), diving (b,g), football (b), golf (b,g), independent competitive sports (b,g), lacrosse (b), soccer (b,g), softball (g), swimming and diving (b,g), tennis (b,g), track and field (b,g), volleyball (g), winter soccer (b,g), wrestling (b); intramural: aerobics/dance (g), ballet (g), basketball (b,g), cheering (g), cross-country running (b,g), dance (g), fitness (b,g), horseback riding (b,g), jogging (b,g), lacrosse (b,g), physical fitness (b,g), physical training (b,g), running (b,g), sailing (b,g), soccer (b,g), softball (b,g), strength & conditioning (b,g), tennis (b,g), track and field (b,g), volleyball (b,g), weight training (b,g), wrestling (b); coed intramural: kayaking, yoga. 8 PE instructors, 14 coaches, 1 athletic trainer.

Computers Computers are regularly used in art, computer applications, foreign language, journalism, library, mathematics, media, science, social sciences, word processing, writing, yearbook classes. Computer network features include on-campus library services, online commercial services, Internet access, wireless campus network, Internet filtering or blocking technology, Microsoft Office. Computer access in designated common areas is available to students. Students grades are available online. The school has a published electronic and media policy.

Contact Linda G. Lutz, Director of Admissions. 941-746-2121 Ext. 1568. Fax: 941-345-1237. E-mail: llutz@saintstephens.org. Web site: www.saintstephens.org

ST. STEPHEN'S EPISCOPAL SCHOOL

6500 St. Stephen's Drive
Austin, Texas 78746

Head of School: Mr. Robert Kirkpatrick

General Information Coeducational boarding and day college-preparatory and theater school, affiliated with Episcopal Church. Boarding grades 8–12, day grades 6–12. Founded: 1950. Setting: suburban. Students are housed in single-sex dormitories. 370-acre campus. 45 buildings on campus. Approved or accredited by Independent Schools Association of the Southwest, National Association of Episcopal Schools, The Association of Boarding Schools, and Texas Department of Education. Member of National Association of Independent Schools and Secondary School Admission Test Board. Endowment: $320,000. Total enrollment: 669. Upper school average class size: 17. Upper school faculty-student ratio: 1:8. There are 165 required school days per year for Upper School students. Upper School students typically attend 5 days per week. The average school day consists of 7 hours and 35 minutes.

Upper School Student Profile Grade 9: 120 students (62 boys, 58 girls); Grade 10: 124 students (65 boys, 59 girls); Grade 11: 113 students (56 boys, 57 girls); Grade 12: 107 students (53 boys, 54 girls). 35% of students are boarding students. 80% are state residents. 9 states are represented in upper school student body. 20% are international students. International students from Bahamas, China, Mexico, Republic of Korea, Saudi Arabia, and Taiwan; 10 other countries represented in student body. 18% of students are members of Episcopal Church.

Faculty School total: 98. In upper school: 31 men, 26 women; 45 have advanced degrees; 36 reside on campus.

Subjects Offered 3-dimensional design, acting, algebra, American history, American history-AP, anthropology, art, art history, astrophysics, ballet, band, biology, calculus, ceramics, chamber groups, chemistry, Chinese, choreography, classics, computer applications, computer math, computer science, computer studies, creative writing, directing, drama, English, English literature, environmental science, European history, fine arts, French, geology, geometry, government/civics, graphic design, history, jazz band, Latin, mathematics, music, musical theater, photography, physical education, physics, physics-AP, play/screen writing, pre-calculus, psychology, public policy issues and action, public speaking, religion, science, social studies, Spanish, theater arts, theology, video, world history, world literature.

Graduation Requirements Arts and fine arts (art, music, dance, drama), electives, English, foreign language, mathematics, physical education (includes health), religion (includes Bible studies and theology), science, social studies (includes history), community service requirement in middle and upper schools.

Special Academic Programs Advanced Placement exam preparation; honors section; independent study; study abroad; ESL (23 students enrolled).

College Admission Counseling 122 students graduated in 2012; all went to college, including Reed College; Santa Clara University; The Colorado College; The Johns Hopkins University; The University of Texas at Austin; University of California, Berkeley. Mean SAT critical reading: 620, mean SAT math: 666, mean SAT writing: 637, mean combined SAT: 1923.

Student Life Upper grades have specified standards of dress, student council. Discipline rests equally with students and faculty. Attendance at religious services is required.

Summer Programs Sports, art/fine arts programs offered; session focuses on soccer, tennis, travel abroad, foreign language/culture, fine arts, community service; held both on and off campus; held at locations in Europe, El Salvador, Nicaragua, Costa Rica, American wilderness areas; accepts boys and girls; open to students from other schools. 120 students usually enrolled. 2013 schedule: June 1 to July 31. Application deadline: none.

Tuition and Aid Day student tuition: $22,630; 7-day tuition and room/board: $45,500. Tuition installment plan (individually arranged payment plans). Merit scholarship grants, need-based scholarship grants available. In 2012–13, 15% of upper-school students received aid; total upper-school merit-scholarship money awarded: $30,000. Total amount of financial aid awarded in 2012–13: $2,800,000.

Admissions Traditional secondary-level entrance grade is 9. For fall 2012, 299 students applied for upper-level admission, 137 were accepted, 78 enrolled. ISEE or SSAT required. Deadline for receipt of application materials: February 1. Application fee required: $75. Interview required.

Athletics Interscholastic: baseball (boys), basketball (b,g), cheering (b,g), crew (b,g), cross-country running (b,g), field hockey (g), football (b), golf (b,g), lacrosse (b,g), running (b,g), soccer (b,g), softball (g), swimming and diving (b,g), tennis (b,g), track and field (b,g), volleyball (g), winter soccer (b,g); intramural: bicycling (b,g), climbing (b,g), combined training (b,g), dance (b,g), fitness (b,g), hiking/backpacking (b,g), independent competitive sports (b,g), indoor hockey (b,g), modern dance (b,g), mountain biking (b,g), mountaineering (b,g), outdoor adventure (b,g), outdoor education (b,g), physical fitness (b,g), physical training (b,g), rappelling (b,g), rock climbing (b,g), ropes courses (b,g), strength & conditioning (b,g), surfing (b,g), wall climbing (b,g), weight training (b,g). 2 PE instructors, 9 coaches, 3 athletic trainers.

Computers Computer network features include on-campus library services, online commercial services, Internet access, wireless campus network, Internet filtering or blocking technology, online schedules, syllabi, homework, examples, and links to information sources. Campus intranet, student e-mail accounts, and computer access in designated common areas are available to students. Students grades are available online.

Contact Lawrence Sampleton, Director of Admission. 512-327-1213 Ext. 210. Fax: 512-327-6771. E-mail: admission@sstx.org. Web site: www.sstx.org

ST. STEPHEN'S SCHOOL, ROME

Via Aventina 3
Rome 00153, Italy

Head of School: Ms. Lesley Jane Murphy

General Information Coeducational boarding and day college-preparatory, arts, and bilingual studies school. Grades 9–PG. Founded: 1964. Setting: urban. Students are housed in single-sex by floor dormitories. 2-acre campus. 2 buildings on campus. Approved or accredited by International Baccalaureate Organization, New England Association of Schools and Colleges, and US Department of State. Affiliate member of National Association of Independent Schools; member of European Council of International Schools. Language of instruction: English. Endowment: $3 million. Total enrollment: 259. Upper school average class size: 13. Upper school faculty-student ratio: 1:7. There are 175 required school days per year for Upper School students. Upper School students typically attend 5 days per week. The average school day consists of 7 hours.

Upper School Student Profile Grade 9: 49 students (24 boys, 25 girls); Grade 10: 67 students (28 boys, 39 girls); Grade 11: 80 students (38 boys, 42 girls); Grade 12: 63 students (29 boys, 34 girls). 13% of students are boarding students. 62% are international students. International students from Brazil, China, Germany, Sri Lanka, United Kingdom, and United States; 26 other countries represented in student body.

Faculty School total: 44. In upper school: 9 men, 35 women; 36 have advanced degrees; 7 reside on campus.

Subjects Offered 20th century history, algebra, American literature, art, art history, biology, calculus, chemistry, chorus, classical studies, creative writing, dance, drama, economics, English, English literature, environmental systems, European history, French, geometry, health, Islamic studies, Italian, Latin, music theory, photography, physical education, physics, pre-calculus, Roman civilization, sculpture, Spanish, theory of knowledge, trigonometry, U.S. history, world literature.

Graduation Requirements Arts and fine arts (art, music, dance, drama), English, foreign language, mathematics, physical education (includes health), science, social studies (includes history), senior essay, computer proficiency examination, service.

Special Academic Programs International Baccalaureate program; 6 Advanced Placement exams for which test preparation is offered; domestic exchange program (with Buckingham Browne & Nichols School, Choate Rosemary Hall); ESL (9 students enrolled).

College Admission Counseling 67 students graduated in 2012; 61 went to college, including Barnard College; Boston University; Bryn Mawr College; Georgia Institute of Technology; New York University; Yale University. Other: 6 had other specific plans. Mean SAT critical reading: 609, mean SAT math: 613, mean SAT writing: 614, mean combined SAT: 1836.

Student Life Upper grades have student council. Discipline rests equally with students and faculty.

Summer Programs Enrichment, art/fine arts programs offered; session focuses on liberal arts/pre-college; held both on and off campus; held at off-campus sites include museum visits and visits to various historical sites within the city; accepts boys and girls; open to students from other schools. 50 students usually enrolled. 2013 schedule: July 2 to August 5. Application deadline: June 19.

Tuition and Aid Day student tuition: €22,340–€22,840; 7-day tuition and room/board: €33,590–€34,090. Tuition installment plan (individually arranged payment plans). Tuition reduction for siblings, merit scholarship grants, need-based scholarship grants available. In 2012–13, 23% of upper-school students received aid; total upper-school merit-scholarship money awarded: €30,000. Total amount of financial aid awarded in 2012–13: €405,150.

Admissions Traditional secondary-level entrance grade is 9. For fall 2012, 178 students applied for upper-level admission, 117 were accepted, 88 enrolled. School's own exam required. Deadline for receipt of application materials: February 8. Application fee required: €150. Interview required.

Athletics Interscholastic: soccer (boys, girls), volleyball (b,g); intramural: basketball (b,g), soccer (b,g), tennis (b,g), volleyball (b,g); coed intramural: dance, physical training, track and field. 1 PE instructor, 6 coaches.

Computers Computers are regularly used in English, foreign language, mathematics, photography, science, social studies classes. Computer network features include on-campus library services, Internet access, wireless campus network, Internet filtering or blocking technology. Campus intranet and computer access in designated common areas are available to students. Students grades are available online. The school has a published electronic and media policy.

Contact Ms. Alex Perniciaro, Admissions Coordinator. 39-06-575-0605. Fax: 39-06-574-1941. E-mail: admissions@ststephens-rome.com. Web site: www.sssrome.it

SAINT TERESA'S ACADEMY

5600 Main Street
Kansas City, Missouri 64113

Head of School: Mrs. Nan Tiehen Bone

General Information Girls' day college-preparatory school, affiliated with Roman Catholic Church. Grades 9–12. Founded: 1866. Setting: urban. 20-acre campus. 4 buildings on campus. Approved or accredited by National Catholic Education Association, North Central Association of Colleges and Schools, and Missouri Department of Education. Endowment: $150,000. Total enrollment: 580. Upper school average class size: 21. Upper school faculty-student ratio: 1:12. There are 174 required school days per year for Upper School students. Upper School students typically attend 5 days per week. The average school day consists of 6 hours and 40 minutes.

Upper School Student Profile Grade 9: 162 students (162 girls); Grade 10: 145 students (145 girls); Grade 11: 138 students (138 girls); Grade 12: 135 students (135 girls). 87% of students are Roman Catholic.

Faculty School total: 48. In upper school: 8 men, 40 women; 33 have advanced degrees.

Subjects Offered Advanced chemistry, advanced math, algebra, American government, American history, American history-AP, American literature, American literature-AP, analysis, anatomy and physiology, art, athletics, basketball, biology, biology-AP, botany, British literature, calculus, career/college preparation, chamber groups, chemistry, chemistry-AP, choir, chorus, computer graphics, computer programming, current events, dance, directing, drama, drawing, ecology, English, English language and composition-AP, English language-AP, English literature, European history-AP, fiber arts, fitness, foreign language, forensics, French, French language-AP, French-AP, freshman seminar, geometry, golf, graphic design, health, independent study, journalism, keyboarding, language arts, Latin, Latin History, music-AP, newspaper, painting, physical education, physics, piano, playwriting, portfolio art, pre-calculus, probability and statistics, psychology, psychology-AP, Shakespeare, social issues, social studies, sociology, softball, Spanish, Spanish language-AP, Spanish literature-AP, Spanish-AP, speech, speech and debate, speech communications, sports conditioning, sports performance development, stagecraft, swimming, technical theater, tennis, theater, theology and the arts, track and field, trigonometry, U.S. government, U.S. government and politics, U.S. government and politics-AP, U.S. history, U.S. history-AP, volleyball, Western civilization, women in literature, women spirituality and faith, world geography, world religions, world religions, writing, writing, yearbook.

Graduation Requirements Arts and fine arts (art, music, dance, drama), computer science, electives, English, foreign language, mathematics, physical education (includes health), science, social studies (includes history), theology. Community service is required.

Special Academic Programs 10 Advanced Placement exams for which test preparation is offered; honors section; study at local college for college credit.

College Admission Counseling 130 students graduated in 2012; 129 went to college, including Kansas State University; Saint Louis University; The University of Kansas; University of Arkansas; University of Missouri. Other: 1 had other specific plans. Mean SAT critical reading: 600, mean SAT math: 580, mean SAT writing: 610, mean combined SAT: 1780, mean composite ACT: 26.

Student Life Upper grades have uniform requirement, student council. Discipline rests primarily with faculty. Attendance at religious services is required.

Summer Programs Sports, art/fine arts, computer instruction programs offered; session focuses on fine arts, sports and remedial summer school programs; held on campus; accepts girls; open to students from other schools. 145 students usually enrolled. 2013 schedule: June 3 to July 15. Application deadline: May 1.

Tuition and Aid Day student tuition: $10,150. Tuition installment plan (SMART Tuition Payment Plan). Tuition reduction for siblings, merit scholarship grants, need-based scholarship grants available. In 2012–13, 25% of upper-school students received aid; total upper-school merit-scholarship money awarded: $125,000. Total amount of financial aid awarded in 2012–13: $130,000.

Admissions Traditional secondary-level entrance grade is 9. For fall 2012, 181 students applied for upper-level admission, 175 were accepted, 162 enrolled. Placement test required. Deadline for receipt of application materials: February 28. No application fee required.

Athletics Interscholastic: aerobics/dance, basketball, cross-country running, diving, drill team, golf, lacrosse, soccer, softball, swimming and diving, tennis, track and field, volleyball; intramural: aerobics/dance, badminton, fitness, fitness walking, jogging, physical fitness, physical training, running, strength & conditioning, table tennis, volleyball, walking, weight lifting, weight training. 1 PE instructor, 25 coaches, 1 athletic trainer.

Computers Computers are regularly used in business education, creative writing, graphics, journalism, library, newspaper, photography, research skills, science, writing, yearbook classes. Computer network features include on-campus library services, Internet access, wireless campus network, Internet filtering or blocking technology. Campus intranet is available to students. Students grades are available online. The school has a published electronic and media policy.

Contact Mrs. Roseann Hudnall, Admissions Director. 816-501-0011 Ext. 135. Fax: 816-523-0232. E-mail: rhudnall@stteresasacademy.org. Web site: www.stteresasacademy.org

SAINT THOMAS ACADEMY

949 Mendota Heights Road
Mendota Heights, Minnesota 55120

Head of School: Thomas B. Mich, PhD

General Information Boys' day college-preparatory and military school, affiliated with Roman Catholic Church. Grades 7–12. Founded: 1885. Setting: suburban. Nearest major city is St. Paul. 72-acre campus. 4 buildings on campus. Approved or accredited by Independent Schools Association of the Central States. Member of National Association of Independent Schools. Endowment: $16.3 million. Total enrollment: 671. Upper school average class size: 18. Upper school faculty-student ratio: 1:10. There are 172 required school days per year for Upper School students. Upper School students typically attend 5 days per week. The average school day consists of 6 hours and 40 minutes.

Upper School Student Profile Grade 9: 126 students (126 boys); Grade 10: 148 students (148 boys); Grade 11: 129 students (129 boys); Grade 12: 143 students (143 boys). 80% of students are Roman Catholic.

Faculty School total: 59. In upper school: 37 men, 17 women; 48 have advanced degrees.

Subjects Offered Advanced biology, advanced computer applications, advanced math, Advanced Placement courses, algebra, American democracy, American government, American history, American history-AP, American literature, American literature-AP, American studies, art, art and culture, art appreciation, art history, band, biology, biology-AP, calculus, campus ministry, chemistry, Chinese, computer science, creative writing, earth science, economics, English, English literature, environmental studies, fine arts, French, geometry, government/civics, health, history, JROTC, Latin, mathematics, military science, music, physical education, physics, psychology, religion, science, social studies, Spanish, trigonometry, world history, world literature, writing.

Graduation Requirements Arts and fine arts (art, music, dance, drama), biology, chemistry, English, foreign language, health education, JROTC or LEAD (Leadership Education and Development), mathematics, physical education (includes health), science, social studies (includes history), theology, U.S. history, world history, 100 hours of community service in 12th grade.

Special Academic Programs 11 Advanced Placement exams for which test preparation is offered; honors section; independent study; study at local college for college credit.

College Admission Counseling 120 students graduated in 2012; 118 went to college, including Boston College; Iowa State University of Science and Technology; University of Minnesota, Twin Cities Campus; University of Notre Dame; University of St. Thomas; University of Wisconsin–Madison. Other: 2 had other specific plans. Mean SAT critical reading: 611, mean SAT math: 626, mean SAT writing: 586, mean composite ACT: 26.

Student Life Upper grades have uniform requirement, student council, honor system. Discipline rests primarily with faculty. Attendance at religious services is required.

Summer Programs Enrichment programs offered; session focuses on study and organizational strategies, time management, test preparation and orientation, writing skills; held on campus; accepts boys and girls; not open to students from other schools. 150 students usually enrolled. 2013 schedule: July 9 to August 9. Application deadline: May 25.

Tuition and Aid Day student tuition: $17,950. Tuition installment plan (SMART Tuition Payment Plan, monthly payment plans, individually arranged payment plans, quarterly payment plan). Merit scholarship grants, need-based scholarship grants available. In 2012–13, 40% of upper-school students received aid; total upper-school merit-scholarship money awarded: $115,000. Total amount of financial aid awarded in 2012–13: $2,500,000.

Admissions Traditional secondary-level entrance grade is 9. For fall 2012, 125 students applied for upper-level admission, 112 were accepted, 82 enrolled. Cognitive Abilities Test required. Deadline for receipt of application materials: none. No application fee required. On-campus interview recommended.

Athletics Interscholastic: alpine skiing, baseball, basketball, cross-country running, drill team, fitness, football, golf, hockey, ice hockey, JROTC drill, lacrosse, marksmanship, nordic skiing, outdoor skills, physical fitness, riflery, skiing (cross-country), skiing (downhill), soccer, swimming and diving, tennis, track and field, wrestling; intramural: basketball, bowling, football, hockey, physical training, strength & conditioning, table tennis, weight lifting, weight training. 3 PE instructors, 1 athletic trainer.

Computers Computers are regularly used in all academic, art, foreign language, music classes. Computer network features include on-campus library services, online commercial services, Internet access, wireless campus network, Internet filtering or blocking technology. Student e-mail accounts are available to students. Students grades are available online. The school has a published electronic and media policy.

Contact Peggy Mansur, Admissions Assistant. 651-683-1515. Fax: 651-683-1576. E-mail: pmansur@cadets.com. Web site: www.cadets.com

ST. THOMAS AQUINAS HIGH SCHOOL

2801 Southwest 12th Street
Fort Lauderdale, Florida 33312-2999

Head of School: Mrs. Tina Jones

General Information Coeducational day college-preparatory, arts, religious studies, technology, Campus Ministry, and college preparatory school, affiliated with Roman Catholic Church. Grades 9–12. Founded: 1936. Setting: suburban. 24-acre campus. 23 buildings on campus. Approved or accredited by National Catholic Education Association, Southern Association of Colleges and Schools, and Florida Department of Education. Total enrollment: 2,239. Upper school average class size: 25. Upper school faculty-student ratio: 1:18. There are 180 required school days per year for Upper School students. Upper School students typically attend 5 days per week. The average school day consists of 6 hours and 30 minutes.

Upper School Student Profile Grade 9: 575 students (276 boys, 299 girls); Grade 10: 558 students (284 boys, 274 girls); Grade 11: 546 students (280 boys, 266 girls); Grade 12: 560 students (273 boys, 287 girls). 96% of students are Roman Catholic.

Faculty School total: 123. In upper school: 65 men, 55 women; 71 have advanced degrees.

Subjects Offered 20th century history, 20th century world history, 3-dimensional art, acting, advanced chemistry, advanced computer applications, advanced math, Advanced Placement courses, advanced studio art-AP, algebra, American government, American history, American history-AP, American literature, anatomy and physiology, art, art appreciation, art history-AP, athletics, biology, biology-AP, British literature, British literature (honors), British literature-AP, broadcast journalism, calculus, calculus-AP, chemistry, chemistry-AP, Chinese, choir, choral music, chorus, Christianity, church history, comparative government and politics-AP, comparative political systems-AP, composition-AP, computer art, computer graphics, computer programming-AP, computer science-AP, debate, desktop publishing, digital art, digital imaging, directing, drama, drama performance, drawing, economics-AP, electives, English, English language and composition-AP, English literature, English literature and composition-AP, English literature-AP, English-AP, English/composition-AP, environmental science, environmental science-AP, European history, European history-AP, film and literature, film and new technologies, fitness, food science, forensics, French, French language-AP, French literature-AP, French-AP, general science, geometry, government, government and politics-AP, government-AP, government/civics-AP, grammar, graphic arts, graphic design, health, health and safety, health and wellness, health education, health enhancement, health science, healthful living, Hispanic literature, history, history of drama, history-AP, Holocaust, honors algebra, honors English, honors geometry, honors U.S. history, honors world history, human anatomy, human geography - AP, jazz, jazz band, journalism, keyboarding, lab science, language, language and composition, language arts, language-AP, Latin, Latin-AP, leadership, leadership and service, leadership education training, Life of Christ, literature, literature and composition-AP, literature-AP, macro/microeconomics-AP, macroeconomics-AP, marine biology, marine studies, mathematics-AP, media, microeconomics, microeconomics-AP, model United Nations, modern European history, modern European history-AP, news writing, newspaper, nutrition, oral expression, orchestra, peace and justice, peace education, peace studies, performing arts, photography, photojournalism, physical education, physical fitness, physics, physics-AP, play production, playwriting and directing, poetry, political systems, pottery, pre-algebra, pre-calculus, probability and statistics, psychology, psychology-AP, public speaking, reading, SAT preparation, SAT/ACT preparation, Spanish, Spanish language-AP, Spanish literature, Spanish literature-AP, Spanish-AP, speech, speech and debate, speech and oral interpretations, speech communications, sports team management, stage design, stagecraft, statistics, statistics-AP, student government, student publications, studio art, technical theater, television, trigonometry, U.S. government and politics-AP, U.S. history, U.S. history-AP, United States government-AP, world history, world history-AP.

Graduation Requirements Arts and fine arts (art, music, dance, drama), computer science, electives, English, foreign language, health, mathematics, personal fitness, science, social sciences, theology.

Special Academic Programs Advanced Placement exam preparation; honors section; remedial reading and/or remedial writing; remedial math.

College Admission Counseling 525 students graduated in 2012; 219 went to college, including Florida Atlantic University; Florida State University; University of Central Florida; University of Florida; University of Miami; University of North Florida. Other: 6 had other specific plans. Mean SAT critical reading: 573, mean SAT math: 572, mean SAT writing: 582, mean combined SAT: 1727, mean composite ACT: 24.

Student Life Upper grades have uniform requirement, student council, honor system. Discipline rests primarily with faculty. Attendance at religious services is required.

Summer Programs Remediation, enrichment, advancement, art/fine arts, computer instruction programs offered; session focuses on enrichment; held on campus; accepts boys and girls; open to students from other schools. 1,000 students usually enrolled. 2013 schedule: June 10 to June 26. Application deadline: June 10.

Tuition and Aid Day student tuition: $9600. Tuition installment plan (monthly payment plans, TADS). Need-based scholarship grants available.

Admissions Traditional secondary-level entrance grade is 9. For fall 2012, 800 students applied for upper-level admission, 590 were accepted, 575 enrolled. High School Placement Test required. Deadline for receipt of application materials: March 15. Application fee required: $50. Interview required.

Athletics Interscholastic: baseball (boys), basketball (b,g), bowling (b,g), cheering (g), cross-country running (b,g), dance (b,g), dance squad (g), diving (b,g), drill team (g), football (b), golf (b,g), lacrosse (b,g), physical fitness (b,g), running (b,g), sailing (b,g), soccer (b,g), softball (g), swimming and diving (b,g), tennis (b,g), track and field (b,g), volleyball (b,g), water polo (b,g), wrestling (b); intramural: dance team (g), danceline (g), drill team (g); coed interscholastic: ballet, bowling, hockey, ice hockey, indoor hockey, physical training; coed intramural: physical training, running. 2 PE instructors, 39 coaches, 1 athletic trainer.

Computers Computers are regularly used in all academic, data processing, desktop publishing, graphic arts, graphic design, graphics, journalism, keyboarding, lab/keyboard, media, media arts, media production, media services, news writing, newspaper, programming, publications, publishing, technology, video film production, Web site design, word processing classes. Computer network features include on-campus library services, online commercial services, Internet access, wireless campus network, Internet filtering or blocking technology. Campus intranet, student e-mail accounts, and computer access in designated common areas are available to students. Students grades are available online. The school has a published electronic and media policy.

Contact Admissions Office. 954-581-2127 Ext. 8623. Fax: 954-327-2193. E-mail: mary.facella@aquinas-sta.org. Web site: www.aquinas-sta.org

SAINT THOMAS AQUINAS HIGH SCHOOL

11411 Pflumm Road
Overland Park, Kansas 66215-4816

Head of School: Dr. William P. Ford

General Information Coeducational day college-preparatory, religious studies, and technology school, affiliated with Roman Catholic Church. Grades 9–12. Founded: 1988. Setting: suburban. Nearest major city is Kansas City, MO. 44-acre campus. 2 buildings on campus. Approved or accredited by National Catholic Education Association, North Central Association of Colleges and Schools, and Kansas Department of Education. Total enrollment: 937. Upper school average class size: 24. Upper school faculty-student ratio: 1:15. There are 180 required school days per year for Upper School students. Upper School students typically attend 5 days per week. The average school day consists of 7 hours.

Upper School Student Profile Grade 9: 224 students (106 boys, 118 girls); Grade 10: 243 students (120 boys, 123 girls); Grade 11: 225 students (111 boys, 114 girls); Grade 12: 245 students (111 boys, 134 girls). 97% of students are Roman Catholic.

Faculty School total: 66. In upper school: 30 men, 36 women; 64 have advanced degrees.

Graduation Requirements Arts and fine arts (art, music, dance, drama), computer technologies, electives, English, Latin, mathematics, modern languages, physical education (includes health), science, social studies (includes history), speech, theology, service (one fourth credit each of 4 years).

Special Academic Programs Advanced Placement exam preparation; honors section; study at local college for college credit; academic accommodation for the gifted; remedial reading and/or remedial writing; remedial math.

College Admission Counseling 261 students graduated in 2012; 254 went to college, including Benedictine College; Johnson County Community College; Kansas State University; Saint Louis University; The University of Kansas; University of Notre Dame. Other: 1 entered military service. Mean SAT critical reading: 619, mean SAT math: 638, mean SAT writing: 603, mean composite ACT: 25.

Student Life Upper grades have uniform requirement, student council. Discipline rests primarily with faculty. Attendance at religious services is required.

Summer Programs Remediation, advancement, sports, computer instruction programs offered; session focuses on sports camps and selected academic coursework; held on campus; accepts boys and girls; open to students from other schools.

Tuition and Aid Day student tuition: $7800–$8800. Tuition installment plan (SMART Tuition Payment Plan). Need-based scholarship grants available.

Admissions Traditional secondary-level entrance grade is 9. ACT-Explore required. Deadline for receipt of application materials: none. Application fee required: $175. Interview required.

Athletics Interscholastic: baseball (boys), basketball (b,g), bowling (b,g), cross-country running (b,g), dance team (g), diving (b,g), football (b), golf (b,g), soccer (b,g), softball (g), swimming and diving (b,g), tennis (b,g), track and field (b,g), volleyball (g), wrestling (b); intramural: field hockey (g), lacrosse (b); coed interscholastic: cheering; coed intramural: table tennis, ultimate Frisbee. 3 PE instructors, 1 athletic trainer.

Computers Computers are regularly used in all academic, computer applications, desktop publishing, programming, video film production, Web site design classes. Computer network features include on-campus library services, Internet access, wireless campus network, computer labs and laptop carts. Student e-mail accounts are available to students. Students grades are available online. The school has a published electronic and media policy.

Contact Mrs. Diane Pyle, Director of Admissions. 913-319-2423. Fax: 913-345-2319. E-mail: dpyle@stasaints.net. Web site: www.stasaints.net

ST. THOMAS AQUINAS HIGH SCHOOL

197 Dover Point Road
Dover, New Hampshire 03820

Head of School: Mr. Kevin Collins

General Information Coeducational day college-preparatory and religious studies school, affiliated with Roman Catholic Church. Grades 9–12. Founded: 1960. Setting: small town. Nearest major city is Boston, MA. 11-acre campus. 2 buildings on campus. Approved or accredited by New England Association of Schools and Colleges and New Hampshire Department of Education. Total enrollment: 630. Upper school average class size: 18. Upper school faculty-student ratio: 1:14. There are 186 required school days per year for Upper School students. Upper School students typically attend 5 days per week. The average school day consists of 6 hours and 25 minutes.

Faculty School total: 51. In upper school: 27 men, 24 women; 25 have advanced degrees.

Subjects Offered Algebra, anatomy and physiology, biology, biology-AP, calculus, calculus-AP, chemistry, chorus, Christian ethics, civics, concert band, contemporary studies, drawing, economics, English, environmental science-AP, finite math, French, geography, geometry, honors algebra, honors English, honors geometry, humanities, international relations, introduction to technology, Latin, marine biology, math applications, media arts, music appreciation, music theory, painting, physics, prayer/spirituality, pre-calculus, psychology, science, scripture, sculpture, social justice, sociology, Spanish, statistics-AP, studio art, theology, trigonometry, U.S. government and politics-AP, U.S. history, U.S. history-AP, wellness, Western civilization, world religions.

Graduation Requirements Arts and fine arts (art, music, dance, drama), Christian ethics, electives, English, foreign language, freshman seminar, mathematics, prayer/spirituality, science, scripture, social justice, social studies (includes history), theology, world religions, 40 hour community service requirement.

Special Academic Programs Advanced Placement exam preparation; honors section; independent study.

College Admission Counseling 165 students graduated in 2012; 151 went to college, including Keene State College; Providence College; Rochester Institute of Technology; Roger Williams University; University of New Hampshire; University of Southern Maine. Other: 3 entered military service, 6 entered a postgraduate year, 5 had other specific plans. Mean SAT critical reading: 554, mean SAT math: 562, mean SAT writing: 552, mean composite ACT: 24.

Student Life Upper grades have specified standards of dress, student council. Discipline rests primarily with faculty. Attendance at religious services is required.

Summer Programs Enrichment, advancement programs offered; held on campus; accepts boys and girls; not open to students from other schools.

Tuition and Aid Day student tuition: $10,700. Tuition installment plan (annual, semiannual, and 10-month payment plans). Need-based scholarship grants available. In 2012–13, 25% of upper-school students received aid.

Admissions Traditional secondary-level entrance grade is 9. Scholastic Testing Service High School Placement Test required. Deadline for receipt of application materials: December 20. Application fee required: $40.

Athletics Interscholastic: baseball (boys), basketball (b,g), cross-country running (b,g), field hockey (g), football (b), golf (b,g), ice hockey (b,g), lacrosse (b,g), skiing (downhill) (b,g), soccer (b,g), softball (g), swimming and diving (b,g), tennis (b,g), track and field (b,g), volleyball (g), winter (indoor) track (b,g), wrestling (b); intramural: dance team (g). 51 coaches, 1 athletic trainer.

Computers Computers are regularly used in introduction to technology, media arts classes. Computer network features include on-campus library services, Internet access, wireless campus network. Student e-mail accounts and computer access in designated common areas are available to students. Students grades are available online.

Contact Mr. Scott Rafferty, Director of Admissions. 603-742-3206. Fax: 603-749-7822. E-mail: srafferty@stalux.org. Web site: www.stalux.org

ST. THOMAS CHOIR SCHOOL

New York, New York

See Junior Boarding Schools section.

ST. THOMAS HIGH SCHOOL

4500 Memorial Drive

Houston, Texas 77007-7332

Head of School: Rev. Patrick Fulton, CSB

General Information Boys' day college-preparatory and religious studies school, affiliated with Roman Catholic Church. Grades 9–12. Founded: 1900. Setting: urban. 37-acre campus. 6 buildings on campus. Approved or accredited by Southern Association of Colleges and Schools, Texas Catholic Conference, Texas Education Agency, and Texas Department of Education. Member of National Association of Independent Schools. Endowment: $12 million. Total enrollment: 752. Upper school average class size: 18. Upper school faculty-student ratio: 1:14. There are 185 required school days per year for Upper School students. Upper School students typically attend 5 days per week. The average school day consists of 7 hours and 20 minutes.

Upper School Student Profile Grade 9: 230 students (230 boys); Grade 10: 175 students (175 boys); Grade 11: 179 students (179 boys); Grade 12: 173 students (173 boys). 72% of students are Roman Catholic.

Faculty School total: 54. In upper school: 33 men, 21 women; 28 have advanced degrees.

Subjects Offered Algebra, American government, American history, American history-AP, American literature, anatomy and physiology, ancient history, art, arts, Basic programming, Bible studies, bioethics, biology, biology-AP, British literature, calculus, calculus-AP, ceramics, chemistry, chemistry-AP, civics/free enterprise, classical civilization, college counseling, comparative government and politics-AP, computer applications, computer information systems, computer programming, computer studies, creative writing, critical thinking, critical writing, decision making skills, desktop publishing, digital photography, drama, drawing, ecology, environmental systems, economics, economics-AP, English, English language-AP, English literature, English literature-AP, environmental education, environmental science, ethics, European history, fine arts, forensics, French, geography, geology, geometry, government and politics-AP, government/civics, grammar, guidance, health, health education, history of the Catholic Church, Holocaust studies, instrumental music, jazz band, journalism, Latin, marine biology, mathematics, military history, oceanography, oral communications, orchestra, painting, photography, physical education, physics, physics-AP, pre-calculus, programming, public speaking, publications, religion, social studies, Spanish, Spanish language-AP, speech, student government, student publications, theater, theology, trigonometry, U.S. government and politics-AP, world history, world literature.

Graduation Requirements Arts and fine arts (art, music, dance, drama), computer applications, English, foreign language, mathematics, physical education (includes health), religion (includes Bible studies and theology), science, social studies (includes history).

Special Academic Programs 10 Advanced Placement exams for which test preparation is offered; honors section.

College Admission Counseling 171 students graduated in 2012; all went to college, including Louisiana State University and Agricultural and Mechanical College; Texas A&M University; Texas Tech University; The University of Texas at Austin; The University of Texas at San Antonio; University of Houston. Mean composite ACT: 26.

Student Life Upper grades have specified standards of dress, student council, honor system. Discipline rests primarily with faculty. Attendance at religious services is required.

Summer Programs Remediation programs offered; held on campus; accepts boys; not open to students from other schools. 20 students usually enrolled. 2013 schedule: June 5 to June 26.

Tuition and Aid Day student tuition: $13,250. Tuition installment plan (monthly payment plans). Merit scholarship grants, need-based scholarship grants, middle-income loans available. In 2012–13, 34% of upper-school students received aid; total upper-school merit-scholarship money awarded: $200,000. Total amount of financial aid awarded in 2012–13: $1,300,000.

Admissions Traditional secondary-level entrance grade is 9. For fall 2012, 587 students applied for upper-level admission, 315 were accepted, 232 enrolled. High School Placement Test required. Deadline for receipt of application materials: January 15. Application fee required: $75.

Athletics Interscholastic: baseball, basketball, cross-country running, football, golf, lacrosse, rugby, soccer, swimming and diving, tennis, track and field, wrestling; intramural: basketball, bowling, flag football, Frisbee, roller hockey, table tennis, weight lifting. 2 PE instructors, 2 coaches, 1 athletic trainer.

Computers Computers are regularly used in data processing, desktop publishing, multimedia, newspaper, photography, programming, publications, Web site design, word processing classes. Computer network features include on-campus library services, Internet access, wireless campus network, Internet filtering or blocking technology. Campus intranet, student e-mail accounts, and computer access in designated common areas are available to students. Students grades are available online. The school has a published electronic and media policy.

Contact Ms. Christine Westman, Assistant Principal. 713-864-6348. Fax: 713-864-5750. E-mail: chris.westman@sths.org. Web site: www.sths.org

ST. TIMOTHY'S SCHOOL

8400 Greenspring Avenue

Stevenson, Maryland 21153

Head of School: Randy S. Stevens

General Information Girls' boarding and day college-preparatory, arts, and IB (International Baccalaureate diploma program) school, affiliated with Episcopal Church. Grades 9–12. Founded: 1882. Setting: suburban. Nearest major city is Baltimore. Students are housed in single-sex dormitories. 145-acre campus. 23 buildings on campus. Approved or accredited by Association of Independent Maryland Schools, International Baccalaureate Organization, Middle States Association of Colleges and Schools, National Association of Episcopal Schools, The Association of Boarding Schools, and Maryland Department of Education. Member of National Association of Independent Schools and Secondary School Admission Test Board. Endowment: $10 million. Total enrollment: 157. Upper school average class size: 10. Upper school faculty-student ratio: 1:6. Upper School students typically attend 5 days per week. The average school day consists of 6 hours.

Upper School Student Profile Grade 9: 40 students (40 girls); Grade 10: 44 students (44 girls); Grade 11: 33 students (33 girls); Grade 12: 40 students (40 girls). 70% of students are boarding students. 37% are state residents. 14 states are represented in upper school student body. 33% are international students. International students from Afghanistan, China, Germany, Jamaica, Mexico, and Republic of Korea; 10 other countries represented in student body.

Faculty School total: 39. In upper school: 9 men, 30 women; 21 have advanced degrees; 19 reside on campus.

Subjects Offered Algebra, American literature, art, art history, bell choir, biology, British literature, calculus, chemistry, Chinese, choir, college counseling, comparative politics, creative writing, dance, drama, drama performance, drama workshop, English, English composition, English literature, ESL, ethics, European history, fine arts, foreign language, French, geometry, history, integrated mathematics, International Baccalaureate courses, Latin, Mandarin, mathematics, modern dance, music, photography, physics, piano, religion, SAT preparation, science, Spanish, U.S. history, world history, world literature, writing.

Graduation Requirements Arts and fine arts (art, music, dance, drama), English, foreign language, history, mathematics, physical education (includes health), religion (includes Bible studies and theology), science, Theory of Knowledge course, extended essay, Community, Action, and Service (CAS). Community service is required.

Special Academic Programs International Baccalaureate program; independent study; ESL (15 students enrolled).

College Admission Counseling 35 students graduated in 2012; all went to college, including Brown University; Pratt Institute; University of Maryland, College Park; University of Southern California; University of Virginia; Wake Forest University.

Student Life Upper grades have uniform requirement, student council, honor system. Discipline rests equally with students and faculty. Attendance at religious services is required.

Summer Programs Enrichment, ESL programs offered; session focuses on global immersion/intensive language and college prep; held on campus; accepts boys and girls; open to students from other schools.

Tuition and Aid Day student tuition: $27,200; 5-day tuition and room/board: $46,800; 7-day tuition and room/board: $46,800. Tuition installment plan (FACTS Tuition Payment Plan). Merit scholarship grants, need-based scholarship grants, need-based loans available. In 2012–13, 45% of upper-school students received aid; total upper-school merit-scholarship money awarded: $100,000. Total amount of financial aid awarded in 2012–13: $2,500,000.

Admissions Traditional secondary-level entrance grade is 9. For fall 2012, 233 students applied for upper-level admission, 117 were accepted, 61 enrolled. ISEE, SLEP for foreign students, SSAT or TOEFL required. Deadline for receipt of application materials: February 1. Application fee required: $50. Interview required.

Athletics Interscholastic: badminton, basketball, dressage, equestrian sports, field hockey, golf, horseback riding, ice hockey, indoor soccer, lacrosse, soccer, softball, squash, tennis, volleyball; intramural: ballet, dance, dance squad, equestrian sports, horseback riding, modern dance, outdoor adventure, weight training, yoga. 3 coaches, 1 athletic trainer.

Computers Computers are regularly used in art, college planning, English, mathematics, publications, SAT preparation, science, yearbook classes. Computer network features include on-campus library services, online commercial services, Internet access, wireless campus network, Internet filtering or blocking technology. Student e-mail accounts are available to students. The school has a published electronic and media policy.

Contact Anne Mickle, Director of Admissions. 410-486-7401. Fax: 410-486-1167. E-mail: amickle@stt.org. Web site: www.stt.org

SAINT URSULA ACADEMY

4025 Indian Road
Toledo, Ohio 43606

Head of School: Mrs. Mary Werner

General Information Girls' day college-preparatory, arts, business, religious studies, bilingual studies, technology, and College Preparatory school, affiliated with Roman Catholic Church. Grades 6–12. Founded: 1854. Setting: suburban. 16-acre campus. 1 building on campus. Approved or accredited by North Central Association of Colleges and Schools, Ohio Catholic Schools Accreditation Association (OCSAA), and Ohio Department of Education. Total enrollment: 549. Upper school average class size: 16. Upper school faculty-student ratio: 1:16. There are 180 required school days per year for Upper School students. Upper School students typically attend 5 days per week. The average school day consists of 7 hours and 20 minutes.

Upper School Student Profile Grade 9: 151 students (151 girls); Grade 10: 121 students (121 girls); Grade 11: 115 students (115 girls); Grade 12: 135 students (135 girls). 75% of students are Roman Catholic.

Faculty School total: 51. In upper school: 8 men, 43 women; 32 have advanced degrees.

Subjects Offered 3-dimensional art, accounting, Advanced Placement courses, advanced studio art-AP, algebra, American government, American history, American history-AP, American literature, anatomy, anatomy and physiology, art, art-AP, ballet, biology, British literature, British literature-AP, business law, calculus-AP, career exploration, Catholic belief and practice, ceramics, chemistry, chemistry-AP, choral music, choreography, chorus, church history, comparative government and politics-AP, comparative religion, composition-AP, computer applications, computer graphics, concert choir, dance, digital photography, drama, drawing, economics, electives, engineering, English language and composition-AP, English literature and composition-AP, fashion, female experience in America, film history, foreign language, French language-AP, geometry, government, government and politics-AP, graphic arts, health, history of the Catholic Church, honors algebra, honors English, honors geometry, honors world history, human geography - AP, instrumental music, Latin, Latin-AP, literature, literature and composition-AP, Mandarin, marketing, mathematics-AP, microeconomics, music, music theory-AP, New Testament, orchestra, painting, personal finance, photography, physical education, physics, physiology, pre-calculus, printmaking, probability and statistics, psychology, psychology-AP, religion and culture, religious education, sculpture, single survival, social psychology, Spanish, Spanish language-AP, speech, statistics, statistics-AP, student publications, studio art-AP, symphonic band, theology, trigonometry, U.S. government and politics, U.S. government and politics-AP, U.S. history, U.S. history-AP, U.S. literature, United States government-AP, vocal music, women's health, women's studies, yearbook.

Graduation Requirements Arts and fine arts (art, music, dance, drama), computers, English, foreign language, mathematics, physical education (includes health), science, social studies (includes history), theology, community service, Career Exploration Experience.

Special Academic Programs 15 Advanced Placement exams for which test preparation is offered; honors section; study at local college for college credit.

College Admission Counseling 125 students graduated in 2012; 123 went to college, including Miami University; The Ohio State University; The University of Toledo; University of Dayton; University of Michigan. Other: 1 went to work, 1 entered military service. Mean SAT critical reading: 570, mean SAT math: 554, mean SAT writing: 577, mean composite ACT: 25. 40% scored over 600 on SAT critical reading, 25% scored over 600 on SAT math, 58% scored over 600 on SAT writing, 37% scored over 26 on composite ACT.

Student Life Upper grades have uniform requirement, student council, honor system. Discipline rests primarily with faculty. Attendance at religious services is required.

Summer Programs Enrichment, advancement, sports, art/fine arts, computer instruction programs offered; session focuses on athletics and academics; held both on and off campus; held at golf course; accepts girls; open to students from other schools. 300 students usually enrolled. 2013 schedule: June 6 to July 29. Application deadline: June 1.

Tuition and Aid Tuition installment plan (SMART Tuition Payment Plan). Tuition reduction for siblings, merit scholarship grants, need-based scholarship grants, paying campus jobs available. In 2012–13, 68% of upper-school students received aid. Total amount of financial aid awarded in 2012–13: $1,299,000.

Admissions Traditional secondary-level entrance grade is 9. For fall 2012, 160 students applied for upper-level admission, 151 were accepted, 121 enrolled. High School Placement Test or placement test required. Deadline for receipt of application materials: December. Application fee required.

Athletics Interscholastic: aerobics/dance, ballet, basketball, bowling, broomball, cheering, crew, cross-country running, dance team, diving, equestrian sports, fencing, golf, gymnastics, horseback riding, independent competitive sports, lacrosse, modern dance, physical fitness, physical training, rowing, soccer, softball, swimming and diving, tennis, track and field, volleyball, water polo, weight training; intramural: badminton, cooperative games, volleyball. 1 PE instructor, 32 coaches, 1 athletic trainer.

Computers Computers are regularly used in accounting, computer applications, graphic arts, newspaper, Web site design, yearbook classes. Computer network features include on-campus library services, Internet access, wireless campus network, Internet filtering or blocking technology. Campus intranet, student e-mail accounts, and computer access in designated common areas are available to students. Students grades are available online. The school has a published electronic and media policy.

Contact Mrs. Nichole Flores, Principal. 419-329-2279. Fax: 419-531-4575. E-mail: nflores@toledosua.org. Web site: www.toledosua.org

SAINT VIATOR HIGH SCHOOL

1213 East Oakton Street
Arlington Heights, Illinois 60004

Head of School: Rev. Robert M. Egan, CSV

General Information Coeducational day college-preparatory, arts, religious studies, bilingual studies, and technology school, affiliated with Roman Catholic Church. Grades 9–12. Founded: 1961. Setting: suburban. Nearest major city is Chicago. 1 building on campus. Approved or accredited by North Central Association of Colleges and Schools and Illinois Department of Education. Upper school average class size: 25. Upper school faculty-student ratio: 1:18. There are 190 required school days per year for Upper School students. Upper School students typically attend 5 days per week. The average school day consists of 6 hours and 35 minutes.

Faculty School total: 67. In upper school: 25 men, 42 women; 50 have advanced degrees.

Graduation Requirements 25 hours of Christian Service each year (100 total hours).

College Admission Counseling 237 students graduated in 2012; all went to college, including DePaul University; Indiana University Bloomington; Loyola University Chicago; The University of Iowa; University of Dayton; University of Illinois at Urbana–Champaign. Mean composite ACT: 26.

Student Life Upper grades have specified standards of dress, student council, honor system. Discipline rests primarily with faculty. Attendance at religious services is required.

Summer Programs Enrichment, advancement, sports, art/fine arts, computer instruction programs offered; held on campus; accepts boys and girls; not open to students from other schools. 2013 schedule: June 10 to July 26.

Tuition and Aid Day student tuition: $11,400. Tuition installment plan (monthly payment plans). Need-based scholarship grants available. In 2012–13, 27% of upper-school students received aid. Total amount of financial aid awarded in 2012–13: $1,200,000.

Admissions Traditional secondary-level entrance grade is 9. ETS high school placement exam required. Application fee required: $400.

Athletics Interscholastic: baseball (boys), basketball (b,g), cheering (g), cross-country running (b,g), football (b), golf (b,g), ice hockey (b), lacrosse (b,g), pom squad (g), soccer (b,g), softball (g), swimming and diving (b,g), tennis (b,g), track and field (b,g), volleyball (b,g), water polo (b,g), wrestling (b); coed intramural: outdoor adventure. 3 PE instructors, 101 coaches, 2 athletic trainers.

Computers Computer network features include Internet access, wireless campus network, Internet filtering or blocking technology, faculty Web pages. Students grades are available online. The school has a published electronic and media policy.

Contact Mrs. Eileen Manno, Principal. 847-392-4050 Ext. 229. Fax: 847-392-4101. E-mail: emanno@saintviator.com. Web site: www.saintviator.com

ST. XAVIER CATHOLIC SCHOOL

200 North Washington
Junction City, Kansas 66441

General Information college-preparatory and general academic school. Approved or accredited by Kansas Department of Education. Upper school average class size: 12.

Student Life Attendance at religious services is required.

Admissions Application fee required. On-campus interview required.

Athletics Interscholastic: basketball (boys, girls), cross-country running (b), volleyball (g); coed interscholastic: cheering, track and field.

Contact 785-238-2841. Fax: 785-238-5021. Web site: www.saintxrams.org

SALEM ACADEMY

500 Salem Avenue
Winston-Salem, North Carolina 27101-0578

Head of School: Mr. Karl Sjolund

General Information Girls' boarding and day college-preparatory and arts school, affiliated with Moravian Church; primarily serves students with learning disabilities, individuals with Attention Deficit Disorder, and dyslexic students. Grades 9–12. Founded: 1772. Setting: urban. Students are housed in single-sex dormitories. 60-acre campus. 4 buildings on campus. Approved or accredited by Southern Association of Colleges and Schools, The Association of Boarding Schools, and North Carolina Department of Education. Member of National Association of Independent Schools and Secondary School Admission Test Board. Endowment: $7 million. Total enrollment: 160. Upper school average class size: 10. Upper school faculty-student ratio: 1:7. There are 172 required school days per year for Upper School students. Upper School students typically attend 5 days per week. The average school day consists of 7 hours and 30 minutes.

Upper School Student Profile Grade 9: 31 students (31 girls); Grade 10: 47 students (47 girls); Grade 11: 41 students (41 girls); Grade 12: 41 students (41 girls). 60% of students are boarding students. 30% are state residents. 11 states are represented in upper school student body. 33% are international students. International students from China, Germany, and Republic of Korea; 3 other countries represented in student body. 4% of students are Moravian.

Faculty School total: 24. In upper school: 2 men, 22 women; 13 have advanced degrees; 3 reside on campus.

Subjects Offered Algebra, American history, art, biology, calculus, chemistry, dance, drama, economics, English, European history, fine arts, French, geometry, government/civics, Latin, mathematics, music, physical education, physics, pre-calculus, psychology, religion, science, social sciences, social studies, Spanish, theater, trigonometry, world history.

Graduation Requirements Arts and fine arts (art, music, dance, drama), English, foreign language, mathematics, physical education (includes health), religion (includes Bible studies and theology), science, social sciences, social studies (includes history), completion of January term.

Special Academic Programs 8 Advanced Placement exams for which test preparation is offered; honors section; term-away projects; study at local college for college credit; study abroad; programs in general development for dyslexic students; ESL (8 students enrolled).

College Admission Counseling 40 students graduated in 2012; all went to college, including New York University; Penn State University Park; The University of North Carolina at Chapel Hill; The University of North Carolina at Greensboro. Mean SAT critical reading: 575, mean SAT math: 631, mean SAT writing: 598, mean combined SAT: 1876.

Student Life Upper grades have specified standards of dress, student council, honor system. Discipline rests equally with students and faculty.

Tuition and Aid Day student tuition: $19,940; 7-day tuition and room/board: $40,490. Tuition installment plan (Key Tuition Payment Plan, monthly payment plans). Merit scholarship grants, need-based scholarship grants available. In 2012–13, 45% of upper-school students received aid; total upper-school merit-scholarship money awarded: $123,100. Total amount of financial aid awarded in 2012–13: $1,033,794.

Admissions Traditional secondary-level entrance grade is 9. For fall 2012, 160 students applied for upper-level admission, 85 were accepted, 65 enrolled. ACT, PSAT, SAT, SSAT or TOEFL required. Deadline for receipt of application materials: none. Application fee required: $50. Interview required.

Athletics Interscholastic: basketball, cross-country running, fencing, field hockey, golf, soccer, softball, swimming and diving, tennis, track and field, volleyball; intramural: aerobics/dance, archery, badminton, dance, fitness, flag football, floor hockey, golf, horseback riding, indoor hockey, indoor soccer, self defense. 2 PE instructors, 15 coaches, 1 athletic trainer.

Computers Computers are regularly used in all academic classes. Computer network features include on-campus library services, online commercial services, Internet access, wireless campus network. Student e-mail accounts and computer access in designated common areas are available to students. Students grades are available online.

Contact C. Lucia Higgins, Director of Admissions. 336-721-2643. Fax: 336-917-5340. E-mail: academy@salem.edu. Web site: www.salemacademy.com

SALEM ACADEMY

942 Lancaster Drive NE
Salem, Oregon 97301

Head of School: Tina deVries

General Information Coeducational day college-preparatory, general academic, arts, vocational, religious studies, bilingual studies, and technology school, affiliated with Protestant Church. Grades K–12. Founded: 1945. Setting: suburban. 34-acre campus. 6 buildings on campus. Approved or accredited by Association of Christian Schools International, Northwest Accreditation Commission, and Oregon Department of Education. Total enrollment: 594. Upper school average class size: 20. Upper school faculty-student ratio: 1:9. Upper School students typically attend 5 days per week. The average school day consists of 7 hours and 15 minutes.

Upper School Student Profile 90% of students are Protestant.

Faculty School total: 48. In upper school: 16 men, 15 women; 4 have advanced degrees.

Subjects Offered Advanced chemistry, Advanced Placement courses, algebra, American history, American literature, anatomy and physiology, art, athletics, auto mechanics, baseball, Bible, Bible studies, biology, business, calculus, ceramics, cheerleading, chemistry, choir, college counseling, college writing, computer programming, computer science, drama, drama performance, economics, English, English literature, English literature and composition-AP, English literature-AP, ESL, foods, geography, geometry, government/civics, grammar, health, history, history-AP, home economics, honors English, industrial arts, Japanese, jazz ensemble, mathematics, music, physical education, physical science, physics, psychology, religion, SAT preparation, science, shop, social sciences, social studies, softball, Spanish, speech, track and field, typing, U.S. history-AP, vocal music, volleyball, weight training, woodworking, world history, world literature, writing.

Graduation Requirements English, foreign language, mathematics, physical education (includes health), religion (includes Bible studies and theology), science, social sciences, social studies (includes history), one credit in biblical studies for each year attended, 40 hours of community service (high school).

Special Academic Programs 7 Advanced Placement exams for which test preparation is offered; honors section; independent study; study at local college for college credit; academic accommodation for the musically talented and the artistically talented; ESL (23 students enrolled).

College Admission Counseling 62 students graduated in 2012; 56 went to college, including Chemeketa Community College; Corban University; George Fox University; Oregon State University; University of Oregon; Washington State University. Other: 4 went to work, 2 entered military service. Mean SAT critical reading: 551, mean SAT math: 595, mean SAT writing: 535, mean combined SAT: 1681.

Student Life Upper grades have specified standards of dress, student council, honor system. Discipline rests primarily with faculty.

Tuition and Aid Tuition installment plan (monthly payment plans). Tuition reduction for siblings, need-based scholarship grants available. In 2012–13, 25% of upper-school students received aid.

Admissions Traditional secondary-level entrance grade is 9. Math Placement Exam, Reading for Understanding, school's own exam and writing sample required. Deadline for receipt of application materials: none. Application fee required: $50. On-campus interview required.

Athletics Interscholastic: baseball (boys), basketball (b,g), cheering (g), cross-country running (b,g), football (b), golf (b,g), softball (g), track and field (b,g), volleyball (g); coed interscholastic: equestrian sports, swimming and diving; coed intramural: racquetball. 2 PE instructors, 36 coaches.

Computers Computers are regularly used in computer applications, design, digital applications, media, media production, multimedia, music technology, photography, photojournalism, video film production, yearbook classes. Computer network features include on-campus library services, Internet access, wireless campus network, Internet filtering or blocking technology. Students grades are available online. The school has a published electronic and media policy.

Contact Mr. Shannon deVries, Dean of Students. 503-378-1211. Fax: 503-375-3265. E-mail: sdevries@salemacademy.org. Web site: www.salemacademy.org

SALESIAN HIGH SCHOOL

2851 Salesian Avenue
Richmond, California 94804

Head of School: Mr. Timothy J. Chambers

General Information Coeducational day college-preparatory, arts, religious studies, and technology school, affiliated with Roman Catholic Church. Grades 9–12. Founded: 1960. Setting: urban. Nearest major city is San Francisco. 21-acre campus. 3 buildings on campus. Approved or accredited by National Catholic Education Association, Western Association of Schools and Colleges, Western Catholic Education Association, and California Department of Education. Endowment: $200,000. Total enrollment: 473. Upper school average class size: 18. Upper school faculty-student ratio: 1:18. There are 177 required school days per year for Upper School students. Upper School students typically attend 5 days per week. The average school day consists of 6 hours and 50 minutes.

Upper School Student Profile Grade 9: 107 students (55 boys, 52 girls); Grade 10: 130 students (68 boys, 62 girls); Grade 11: 106 students (57 boys, 49 girls); Grade 12: 130 students (58 boys, 72 girls). 65% of students are Roman Catholic.

Faculty School total: 36. In upper school: 17 men, 15 women; 25 have advanced degrees.

Subjects Offered Advanced math, advanced studio art-AP, algebra, American history-AP, American literature, American literature-AP, anatomy, ancient world history, art, art history, art history-AP, biology, calculus, calculus-AP, Catholic belief and practice, Christian scripture, Christianity, classical language, computer literacy, drama, dramatic arts, economics, English, English composition, English language and composition-AP, English literature, English literature-AP, English-AP, environmental science, French, French language-AP, French-AP, geometry, government, government/civics, health and wellness, history of the Catholic Church, history-AP, honors U.S. history, mathematics, mathematics-AP, performing arts, physical education, physics, pre-algebra, pre-calculus, psychology, religion, SAT preparation, science, Spanish, Spanish language-AP, Spanish-AP, U.S. government, U.S. history, visual and performing arts, world history, world religions.

Graduation Requirements Arts and fine arts (art, music, dance, drama), English, foreign language, mathematics, physical education (includes health), religion (includes Bible studies and theology), science, social sciences, theology, Christian service projects.

Special Academic Programs 11 Advanced Placement exams for which test preparation is offered; honors section; remedial reading and/or remedial writing; remedial math.

College Admission Counseling 144 students graduated in 2012; 142 went to college, including San Francisco State University; University of California, Berkeley; University of California, Davis; University of California, Santa Cruz. Other: 2 entered military service.

Student Life Upper grades have uniform requirement, student council. Discipline rests primarily with faculty. Attendance at religious services is required.
Summer Programs Remediation, enrichment, advancement, sports, art/fine arts, computer instruction programs offered; session focuses on enrichment, remediation and recruitment of 6, 7, and 8th grade students; held on campus; accepts boys and girls; open to students from other schools. 280 students usually enrolled. 2013 schedule: June 24 to July 26. Application deadline: June 21.
Tuition and Aid Day student tuition: $13,250. Tuition installment plan (SMART Tuition Payment Plan). Merit scholarship grants, need-based scholarship grants available. In 2012–13, 45% of upper-school students received aid; total upper-school merit-scholarship money awarded: $50,000. Total amount of financial aid awarded in 2012–13: $1,400,000.
Admissions Traditional secondary-level entrance grade is 9. For fall 2012, 270 students applied for upper-level admission, 150 were accepted, 107 enrolled. High School Placement Test and High School Placement Test (closed version) from Scholastic Testing Service required. Deadline for receipt of application materials: none. Application fee required: $850. On-campus interview required.
Athletics Interscholastic: baseball (boys), basketball (b,g), cheering (g), cross-country running (b,g), football (b), physical training (b), soccer (b,g), softball (g), swimming and diving (b,g), volleyball (b,g), weight training (b), winter soccer (b,g); intramural: basketball (b,g), floor hockey (b,g), football (b), weight training (b); coed interscholastic: cross-country running, golf, track and field. 1 PE instructor, 25 coaches.
Computers Computers are regularly used in all academic, computer applications, history, library, stock market, yearbook classes. Computer network features include on-campus library services, Internet access, wireless campus network, Internet filtering or blocking technology. Student e-mail accounts and computer access in designated common areas are available to students. Students grades are available online. The school has a published electronic and media policy.
Contact Mrs. Connie Decuir, Director of Admissions. 510-234-4433 Ext. 1128. Fax: 510-236-4636. E-mail: cdecuir@salesian.com. Web site: www.salesian.com

SALESIANUM SCHOOL

1801 North Broom Street
Wilmington, Delaware 19802-3891

Head of School: Rev. J. Christian Beretta, OSFS

General Information Boys' day college-preparatory school, affiliated with Roman Catholic Church. Grades 9–12. Founded: 1903. Setting: suburban. 22-acre campus. 1 building on campus. Approved or accredited by Middle States Association of Colleges and Schools and Delaware Department of Education. Total enrollment: 970. Upper school average class size: 20. Upper school faculty-student ratio: 1:12.
Upper School Student Profile Grade 9: 258 students (258 boys); Grade 10: 245 students (245 boys); Grade 11: 235 students (235 boys); Grade 12: 232 students (232 boys). 87% of students are Roman Catholic.
Faculty School total: 92. In upper school: 67 men, 25 women; 53 have advanced degrees.
Subjects Offered Algebra, American history, American history-AP, American literature, anatomy, architecture, art, art-AP, band, biology, biology-AP, business, business law, calculus, calculus-AP, career/college preparation, chemistry, chemistry-AP, chorus, community service, computer applications, computer programming, computer science, computer science-AP, drafting, driver education, ecology, economics, English, English literature, English-AP, ensembles, environmental science-AP, European history-AP, fine arts, foreign policy, French, French-AP, geometry, German-AP, government/civics, health, journalism, Latin, law, literature, marketing, mathematics, physical education, physics, physics-AP, pre-calculus, psychology, psychology-AP, religion, science, social sciences, social studies, Spanish, Spanish-AP, statistics, statistics-AP, television, trigonometry, U.S. government and politics-AP, video, Western literature, world affairs, world history, world literature.
Graduation Requirements Arts and fine arts (art, music, dance, drama), college planning, computer science, driver education, electives, English, foreign language, mathematics, physical education (includes health), religion (includes Bible studies and theology), science, social sciences, social studies (includes history). Community service is required.
Special Academic Programs Advanced Placement exam preparation; honors section; independent study; study at local college for college credit; domestic exchange program (with Ursuline Academy, Padua Academy); academic accommodation for the gifted; remedial reading and/or remedial writing; remedial math.
College Admission Counseling 261 students graduated in 2012; 258 went to college, including Penn State University Park; Saint Joseph's University; University of Delaware; Villanova University; Virginia Polytechnic Institute and State University. Other: 2 went to work, 1 entered military service. Mean SAT critical reading: 574, mean SAT math: 589, mean SAT writing: 558, mean combined SAT: 1721. 32% scored over 600 on SAT critical reading, 41% scored over 600 on SAT math, 27% scored over 600 on SAT writing.
Student Life Upper grades have specified standards of dress, student council. Discipline rests primarily with faculty. Attendance at religious services is required.
Summer Programs Enrichment, computer instruction programs offered; session focuses on freshman transition and technology; held on campus; accepts boys; not open to students from other schools.
Tuition and Aid Day student tuition: $12,600. Tuition installment plan (Insured Tuition Payment Plan, monthly payment plans, semester payment plan, annual payment plan, monthly payment plan). Merit scholarship grants, need-based scholarship grants, paying campus jobs available. In 2012–13, 23% of upper-school students received aid; total upper-school merit-scholarship money awarded: $315,000. Total amount of financial aid awarded in 2012–13: $650,000.
Admissions Traditional secondary-level entrance grade is 9. Scholastic Testing Service High School Placement Test required. Deadline for receipt of application materials: November 30. Application fee required: $65.
Athletics Interscholastic: baseball, basketball, cross-country running, diving, football, golf, ice hockey, lacrosse, soccer, swimming and diving, tennis, track and field, volleyball, wrestling; intramural: basketball, bowling, flag football, Frisbee, lacrosse, roller hockey, rowing, skateboarding, tennis, ultimate Frisbee, weight lifting. 4 PE instructors, 58 coaches, 1 athletic trainer.
Computers Computers are regularly used in architecture, college planning, drafting, English, foreign language, mathematics, science, social studies, yearbook classes. Computer network features include on-campus library services, online commercial services, Internet access, wireless campus network, Internet filtering or blocking technology. Campus intranet and computer access in designated common areas are available to students. Students grades are available online.
Contact Mrs. Barbara Palena, Administrative Assistant to the Admissions Office. 302-654-2495 Ext. 148. Fax: 302-654-7767. E-mail: bpalena@salesianum.org. Web site: www.salesianum.org

SALPOINTE CATHOLIC HIGH SCHOOL

1545 East Copper Street
Tucson, Arizona 85719-3199

Head of School: Mrs. Kay Sullivan

General Information Coeducational day college-preparatory and Humanities school, affiliated with Roman Catholic Church. Grades 9–12. Founded: 1950. Setting: urban. 40-acre campus. 10 buildings on campus. Approved or accredited by North Central Association of Colleges and Schools, Western Catholic Education Association, and Arizona Department of Education. Endowment: $2.7 million. Total enrollment: 1,094. Upper school average class size: 24. Upper school faculty-student ratio: 1:15. There are 180 required school days per year for Upper School students. Upper School students typically attend 5 days per week. The average school day consists of 6 hours and 50 minutes.
Upper School Student Profile Grade 9: 274 students (138 boys, 136 girls); Grade 10: 266 students (143 boys, 123 girls); Grade 11: 268 students (141 boys, 127 girls); Grade 12: 286 students (155 boys, 131 girls). 77% of students are Roman Catholic.
Faculty School total: 80. In upper school: 29 men, 44 women; 62 have advanced degrees.
Subjects Offered 3-dimensional art, 3-dimensional design, accounting, acting, advanced biology, advanced chemistry, advanced math, Advanced Placement courses, advanced studio art-AP, aerobics, algebra, American culture, American government, American history, American history-AP, American literature, American literature-AP, American studies, analysis and differential calculus, animation, art, art appreciation, art history, art history-AP, art-AP, arts, athletic training, athletics, band, Bible studies, biology, biology-AP, bookkeeping, British literature, British literature (honors), business, calculus, calculus-AP, career and personal planning, career and technology systems, career planning, career technology, career/college preparation, Catholic belief and practice, ceramics, chemistry, chemistry-AP, choir, choral music, classics, comparative religion, composition, computer animation, computer art, computer programming, computer science, computer skills, computer-aided design, computers, concert band, concert choir, constitutional history of U.S., consumer economics, creative writing, dance, desktop publishing, digital art, digital photography, discrete mathematics, drama, drama performance, drawing and design, earth science, economics, electives, electronic publishing, engineering, English, English literature, English literature and composition-AP, English literature-AP, environmental science, environmental science-AP, European history, film and literature, finance, fitness, French, French language-AP, French literature-AP, French-AP, general business, general math, geography, geometry, government, government and politics-AP, government/civics, history, Holocaust, honors algebra, honors English, honors geometry, honors U.S. history, humanities, instrumental music, jazz, jazz band, jazz ensemble, journalism, language arts, Latin, Latin-AP, law, leadership, leadership and service, learning lab, Life of Christ, literary magazine, macroeconomics-AP, marching band, marketing, music history, music theory, newspaper, non-Western literature, orchestra, painting, performing arts, personal fitness, philosophy, photo shop, photography, photojournalism, physical fitness, physics, physics-AP, play production, politics, pottery, pre-algebra, pre-calculus, probability and statistics, programming, psychology, rhetoric, SAT/ACT preparation, scripture, sculpture, Shakespeare, social justice, softball, space and physical sciences, Spanish, Spanish language-AP, Spanish literature, Spanish literature-AP, Spanish-AP, sports conditioning, sports medicine, statistics, statistics-AP, student government, student publications, studio art, studio art-AP, symphonic band, theater, theology, trigonometry, U.S. government and politics, U.S. history-AP, United States government-AP, visual and performing arts, visual arts, vocal music, voice ensemble, water color painting, weight

fitness, weight training, weightlifting, world history, world history-AP, world literature, world religions, world studies, writing, writing workshop, yearbook.

Graduation Requirements Arts and fine arts (art, music, dance, drama), career and technology systems, English, exercise science, mathematics, modern languages, science, social studies (includes history), theology.

Special Academic Programs 18 Advanced Placement exams for which test preparation is offered; honors section; study at local college for college credit; remedial reading and/or remedial writing; remedial math; programs in English, mathematics, general development for dyslexic students.

College Admission Counseling 266 students graduated in 2012; 264 went to college, including Arizona State University; Northern Arizona University; Pima Community College; The University of Arizona; University of Colorado Boulder; University of San Diego. Other: 1 went to work, 1 entered military service. Median SAT critical reading: 530, median SAT math: 520, median SAT writing: 530, median combined SAT: 1570, median composite ACT: 24. 36% scored over 600 on SAT critical reading, 30% scored over 600 on SAT math, 30% scored over 600 on SAT writing, 29% scored over 1800 on combined SAT, 28% scored over 26 on composite ACT.

Student Life Upper grades have specified standards of dress, student council, honor system. Discipline rests primarily with faculty. Attendance at religious services is required.

Summer Programs Remediation, enrichment, advancement, sports, computer instruction programs offered; session focuses on advancement, remediation, sports camps; held on campus; accepts boys and girls; open to students from other schools. 1,100 students usually enrolled. 2013 schedule: May 28 to July 2. Application deadline: May 25.

Tuition and Aid Day student tuition: $7750–$8200. Tuition installment plan (monthly payment plans, individually arranged payment plans). Merit scholarship grants, need-based scholarship grants, USS Education Loan Program available. In 2012–13, 39% of upper-school students received aid; total upper-school merit-scholarship money awarded: $32,500. Total amount of financial aid awarded in 2012–13: $1,350,000.

Admissions Traditional secondary-level entrance grade is 9. For fall 2012, 409 students applied for upper-level admission, 380 were accepted, 305 enrolled. High School Placement Test required. Deadline for receipt of application materials: none. Application fee required: $60. On-campus interview required.

Athletics Interscholastic: aerobics/dance (girls), baseball (b), basketball (b,g), cheering (g), cross-country running (b,g), dance team (g), diving (b,g), football (b), golf (b,g), lacrosse (b), soccer (b,g), softball (g), strength & conditioning (b,g), swimming and diving (b,g), tennis (b,g), track and field (b,g), volleyball (b,g), weight lifting (b,g), wrestling (b); intramural: aerobics (g), basketball (b,g), bicycling (b,g), dance (g), fitness (b,g), flag football (b,g), floor hockey (b,g), ice hockey (b), independent competitive sports (b,g), indoor soccer (b,g), jogging (b,g), lacrosse (b), physical fitness (b,g), physical training (b,g), running (b,g), soccer (b,g), strength & conditioning (b,g), volleyball (b,g), weight lifting (b,g), weight training (b,g), whiffle ball (b,g), yoga (b,g); coed interscholastic: strength & conditioning; coed intramural: basketball, bowling, fitness, flag football, floor hockey, Frisbee, independent competitive sports, indoor soccer, jogging, outdoor adventure, physical fitness, physical training, running, soccer, strength & conditioning, ultimate Frisbee, volleyball, weight lifting, weight training, whiffle ball, yoga. 3 PE instructors, 110 coaches, 2 athletic trainers.

Computers Computers are regularly used in all academic classes. Computer network features include on-campus library services, Internet access, wireless campus network, Internet filtering or blocking technology. Campus intranet, student e-mail accounts, and computer access in designated common areas are available to students. Students grades are available online. The school has a published electronic and media policy.

Contact Mrs. Meg Gossmann, Admissions Coordinator. 520-547-4460. Fax: 520-327-8477. E-mail: mgossmann@salpointe.org. Web site: www.salpointe.org

SALTUS GRAMMAR SCHOOL

PO Box HM 2224
Hamilton HM JX, Bermuda

Head of School: Mr. E.G. (Ted) Staunton

General Information Coeducational day college-preparatory, general academic, arts, business, and technology school, affiliated with Church of England (Anglican). Grades K–12. Founded: 1888. Setting: suburban. 6 buildings on campus. Approved or accredited by Canadian Association of Independent Schools. Affiliate member of National Association of Independent Schools. Language of instruction: English. Endowment: 5 million Bermuda dollars. Total enrollment: 961. Upper school average class size: 17. Upper school faculty-student ratio: 1:13. There are 195 required school days per year for Upper School students. Upper School students typically attend 5 days per week. The average school day consists of 5 hours and 30 minutes.

Upper School Student Profile Grade 9: 53 students (30 boys, 23 girls); Grade 10: 47 students (24 boys, 23 girls); Grade 11: 51 students (28 boys, 23 girls); Grade 12: 47 students (25 boys, 22 girls).

Faculty School total: 95. In upper school: 18 men, 18 women; 20 have advanced degrees.

Subjects Offered Advanced Placement courses, American history, art, art history, biology, business, chemistry, computer programming, computer science, design, drama, earth science, economics, electronics, English, English literature, environmental science, European history, French, geography, health, history, mathematics, music, photography, physical education, physics, psychology, social studies, sociology, Spanish, speech, statistics, theater, trigonometry, world history.

Graduation Requirements English, mathematics. Community service is required.

Special Academic Programs 17 Advanced Placement exams for which test preparation is offered.

College Admission Counseling 69 students graduated in 2011; 68 went to college, including Acadia University; Dalhousie University; McGill University; Queen's University at Kingston; The University of Western Ontario; University of Guelph. Other: 1 went to work.

Student Life Upper grades have uniform requirement, student council, honor system. Discipline rests primarily with faculty.

Tuition and Aid Day student tuition: 17,980 Bermuda dollars–18,900 Bermuda dollars. Tuition installment plan (monthly payment plans, One Payment Plan, Two payment plan). Bursaries, merit scholarship grants, need-based scholarship grants available. In 2011–12, 16% of upper-school students received aid; total upper-school merit-scholarship money awarded: 268,302 Bermuda dollars. Total amount of financial aid awarded in 2011–12: 359,400 Bermuda dollars.

Admissions Traditional secondary-level entrance grade is 11. Admissions testing, grade equivalent tests, school placement exam or writing sample required. Deadline for receipt of application materials: none. Application fee required: 50 Bermuda dollars. On-campus interview required.

Athletics Interscholastic: badminton (boys, girls), basketball (b,g), cricket (b), cross-country running (b,g), field hockey (g), netball (g), rugby (b), running (b,g), soccer (b,g), softball (b,g), swimming and diving (b,g), track and field (b,g), volleyball (b,g); intramural: badminton (b,g), basketball (b,g), cricket (b), cross-country running (b,g), field hockey (b,g), gymnastics (b,g), indoor soccer (b), lacrosse (b,g), netball (g), physical fitness (b,g), physical training (b,g), rowing (b,g), rugby (b), running (b,g), sailing (b,g), scuba diving (b,g), soccer (b,g), softball (b,g), squash (b,g), strength & conditioning (b,g), swimming and diving (b,g), table tennis (b,g), tennis (b,g), touch football (b,g), track and field (b,g), volleyball (b,g), wall climbing (b,g), weight training (b,g); coed interscholastic: badminton, basketball, field hockey, running, swimming and diving, water polo; coed intramural: badminton, field hockey, gymnastics, running, scuba diving, swimming and diving, table tennis, water polo. 5 PE instructors.

Computers Computers are regularly used in all classes. Computer network features include on-campus library services, Internet access, wireless campus network, Internet filtering or blocking technology. Campus intranet and student e-mail accounts are available to students. The school has a published electronic and media policy.

Contact Mr. Malcolm J. Durrant, Deputy Headmaster. 441-292-6177. Fax: 441-295-4977. E-mail: mdurrant@saltus.bm. Web site: www.saltus.bm

SANDIA PREPARATORY SCHOOL

532 Osuna Road NE
Albuquerque, New Mexico 87113

Head of School: B. Stephen Albert

General Information Coeducational day college-preparatory and arts school. Grades 6–12. Founded: 1966. Setting: suburban. 27-acre campus. 13 buildings on campus. Approved or accredited by Independent Schools Association of the Southwest and New Mexico Department of Education. Member of National Association of Independent Schools. Endowment: $4 million. Total enrollment: 625. Upper school average class size: 17. Upper school faculty-student ratio: 1:10. There are 180 required school days per year for Upper School students. The average school day consists of 7 hours and 30 minutes.

Upper School Student Profile Grade 9: 92 students (44 boys, 48 girls); Grade 10: 90 students (38 boys, 52 girls); Grade 11: 86 students (42 boys, 44 girls); Grade 12: 101 students (58 boys, 43 girls).

Faculty School total: 74. In upper school: 40 men, 33 women; 47 have advanced degrees.

Subjects Offered 20th century American writers, 3-dimensional art, adolescent issues, advanced biology, advanced chemistry, advanced computer applications, advanced math, algebra, American history, American literature, American politics in film, anatomy and physiology, ancient world history, art, astronomy, band, biology, calculus, ceramics, chemistry, chorus, computer programming, computer science, creative writing, drawing, earth science, ecology, environmental systems, economics, English, English literature, environmental science, film, film history, filmmaking, fine arts, foreign language, French, French as a second language, geology, geometry, global issues, grammar, guitar, healthful living, history, jazz band, journalism, language arts, library skills, life science, mathematics, media communications, modern world history, music, newspaper, orchestra, outdoor education, painting, performing arts, personal development, philosophy, photography, physical education, physics, pottery, pre-algebra, pre-calculus, science, Shakespearean histories, social studies, Spanish, state history, statistics, technical theater, technology, theater, trigonometry, women in world history, world history, world literature, World War I, World War II, yearbook.

Graduation Requirements Arts and fine arts (art, music, dance, drama), electives, English, foreign language, mathematics, physical education (includes health), science, social studies (includes history), completion of a one-month volunteer Senior

Experience in a professional, academic, or volunteer area of interest during May of senior year.

Special Academic Programs Independent study; study at local college for college credit; study abroad; academic accommodation for the gifted.

College Admission Counseling 91 students graduated in 2012; all went to college, including Carnegie Mellon University; Duke University; Knox College; Lake Forest Academy; Trinity University; University of New Mexico. Median SAT critical reading: 660, median SAT math: 610, median composite ACT: 27. 65% scored over 600 on SAT critical reading, 59% scored over 600 on SAT math, 60% scored over 26 on composite ACT.

Student Life Upper grades have specified standards of dress, student council. Discipline rests primarily with faculty.

Summer Programs Enrichment, sports, art/fine arts, computer instruction programs offered; session focuses on summer enrichment; held on campus; accepts boys and girls; open to students from other schools. 350 students usually enrolled. 2013 schedule: June 1 to July 18. Application deadline: May 1.

Tuition and Aid Day student tuition: $18,400. Tuition installment plan (FACTS Tuition Payment Plan, monthly payment plans). Need-based scholarship grants available. In 2012–13, 20% of upper-school students received aid. Total amount of financial aid awarded in 2012–13: $950,000.

Admissions Traditional secondary-level entrance grade is 9. For fall 2012, 315 students applied for upper-level admission, 277 were accepted, 122 enrolled. Deadline for receipt of application materials: February 6. Application fee required: $55. On-campus interview required.

Athletics Interscholastic: baseball (boys), basketball (b,g), cross-country running (b,g), dance squad (g), golf (b,g), soccer (b,g), softball (g), swimming and diving (b,g), table tennis (b), tennis (b,g), track and field (b,g), volleyball (g); intramural: basketball (b,g), self defense (g); coed interscholastic: archery, dance, kickball; coed intramural: backpacking, bocce, canoeing/kayaking, climbing, Frisbee, hiking/backpacking, kayaking, lacrosse, modern dance, nordic skiing, ocean paddling, outdoor adventure, outdoor education, outdoor skills, rock climbing, yoga. 5 PE instructors, 40 coaches, 1 athletic trainer.

Computers Computers are regularly used in art, college planning, graphic arts, history, information technology, journalism, library skills, literacy, mathematics, multimedia, newspaper, photography, publications, science, study skills, technology, typing, word processing, yearbook classes. Computer network features include on-campus library services, online commercial services, Internet access, Internet filtering or blocking technology, individual student accounts, productivity software. Student e-mail accounts are available to students. Students grades are available online. The school has a published electronic and media policy.

Contact Ester Tomelloso, Director of Admissions. 505-338-3000. Fax: 505-338-3099. E-mail: etomelloso@sandiaprep.org. Web site: www.sandiaprep.org

SAN DOMENICO SCHOOL

1500 Butterfield Road
San Anselmo, California 94960

Head of School: Dr. David Behrs

General Information Girls' boarding and coeducational day college-preparatory, arts, religious studies, music, and theater arts, dance school, affiliated with Roman Catholic Church. Boarding girls grades 9–12, day boys grades PK–8, day girls grades PK–12. Founded: 1850. Setting: suburban. Nearest major city is San Francisco. Students are housed in single-sex dormitories. 515-acre campus. 4 buildings on campus. Approved or accredited by California Association of Independent Schools, Western Association of Schools and Colleges, and Western Catholic Education Association. Member of National Association of Independent Schools. Endowment: $8.5 million. Total enrollment: 598. Upper school average class size: 12. Upper school faculty-student ratio: 1:5. There are 180 required school days per year for Upper School students. Upper School students typically attend 5 days per week. The average school day consists of 7 hours.

Upper School Student Profile Grade 9: 44 students (44 girls); Grade 10: 49 students (49 girls); Grade 11: 32 students (32 girls). 59% of students are boarding students. 58% are state residents. 2 states are represented in upper school student body. 42% are international students. International students from China, Hong Kong, Mexico, Republic of Korea, Taiwan, and Viet Nam. 25% of students are Roman Catholic.

Faculty School total: 35. In upper school: 7 men, 28 women; 17 have advanced degrees; 7 reside on campus.

Subjects Offered Acting, algebra, American history, American literature, art, art history, biology, biology-AP, calculus, calculus-AP, ceramics, chemistry, chemistry-AP, community service, drama, English, English language and composition-AP, English literature, English literature-AP, environmental science, environmental science-AP, ESL, ethics, European history, expository writing, fine arts, geometry, government/civics, grammar, history, Mandarin, mathematics, modern world history, music, music composition, music theater, music theory, music theory-AP, musical productions, musicianship, photography, physical education, physics, physics-AP, psychology-AP, religion, science, social studies, sociology, Spanish, Spanish language-AP, statistics-AP, studio art-AP, theater, theology, trigonometry, U.S. history-AP, world history, world literature.

Graduation Requirements Arts and fine arts (art, music, dance, drama), English, foreign language, health, mathematics, physical education (includes health), religion (includes Bible studies and theology), science, social studies (includes history). Community service is required.

Special Academic Programs Advanced Placement exam preparation; honors section; independent study; academic accommodation for the musically talented; ESL (37 students enrolled).

College Admission Counseling 30 students graduated in 2012; all went to college, including New York University; University of Southern California. Mean SAT critical reading: 584, mean SAT math: 606, mean SAT writing: 592, mean combined SAT: 1782, mean composite ACT: 29.

Student Life Upper grades have specified standards of dress, student council, honor system. Discipline rests primarily with faculty. Attendance at religious services is required.

Tuition and Aid Day student tuition: $33,650; 5-day tuition and room/board: $49,000; 7-day tuition and room/board: $49,000. Tuition installment plan (Insured Tuition Payment Plan, monthly payment plans). Need-based scholarship grants available. In 2012–13, 47% of upper-school students received aid. Total amount of financial aid awarded in 2012–13: $1,000,000.

Admissions Traditional secondary-level entrance grade is 9. For fall 2012, 184 students applied for upper-level admission, 112 were accepted, 63 enrolled. High School Placement Test, ISEE or SSAT required. Deadline for receipt of application materials: January 17. Application fee required: $100. Interview required.

Athletics Interscholastic: badminton, basketball, cross-country running, equestrian sports, horseback riding, soccer, swimming and diving, tennis, volleyball; intramural: dance, golf, modern dance. 1 PE instructor, 5 coaches.

Computers Computers are regularly used in English, mathematics, science, social studies, yearbook classes. Computer network features include on-campus library services, online commercial services, Internet access, wireless campus network, Internet filtering or blocking technology. Student e-mail accounts are available to students. Students grades are available online. The school has a published electronic and media policy.

Contact Mr. Sean Kenney, Executive Director, Admissions and Financial Aid. 415-258-1905. Fax: 415-258-1906. E-mail: admissions@sandomenico.org. Web site: www.sandomenico.org/

SANDY SPRING FRIENDS SCHOOL

16923 Norwood Road
Sandy Spring, Maryland 20860

Head of School: Thomas R. Gibian

General Information Coeducational boarding and day college-preparatory, arts, and ESL school, affiliated with Society of Friends. Boarding grades 9–12, day grades PK–12. Founded: 1961. Setting: suburban. Nearest major city is Washington, DC. Students are housed in single-sex by floor dormitories. 140-acre campus. 15 buildings on campus. Approved or accredited by Association of Independent Maryland Schools, Association of Independent Schools of Greater Washington, Friends Council on Education, The Association of Boarding Schools, and Maryland Department of Education. Member of National Association of Independent Schools and Secondary School Admission Test Board. Endowment: $1.1 million. Total enrollment: 572. Upper school average class size: 14. Upper school faculty-student ratio: 1:8. There are 171 required school days per year for Upper School students. Upper School students typically attend 5 days per week. The average school day consists of 7 hours and 30 minutes.

Upper School Student Profile Grade 9: 57 students (19 boys, 38 girls); Grade 10: 59 students (30 boys, 29 girls); Grade 11: 75 students (33 boys, 42 girls); Grade 12: 72 students (47 boys, 25 girls). 11% of students are boarding students. 82% are state residents. 7 states are represented in upper school student body. 8% are international students. International students from China, Ethiopia, Republic of Korea, Taiwan, Thailand, and Viet Nam; 2 other countries represented in student body. 11% of students are members of Society of Friends.

Faculty School total: 74. In upper school: 17 men, 16 women; 21 have advanced degrees; 17 reside on campus.

Subjects Offered Algebra, American history, American literature, art, biology, British literature-AP, calculus, calculus-AP, ceramics, chemistry, chemistry-AP, choral music, creative writing, cultural geography, dance, dance performance, desktop publishing, drama, drawing, English, English as a foreign language, English literature and composition-AP, English literature-AP, environmental science-AP, ESL, ESL, French, French language-AP, geology, geometry, grammar, history, mathematics, music, music theory-AP, Native American history, painting, photography, physical education, physics, poetry, Quakerism and ethics, Russian literature, science, Spanish, Spanish language-AP, statistics-AP, trigonometry, U.S. history-AP, weaving, Western civilization, world literature.

Graduation Requirements Art, English, foreign language, history, mathematics, physical education (includes health), religion (includes Bible studies and theology), science. Community service is required.

Special Academic Programs 15 Advanced Placement exams for which test preparation is offered; honors section; independent study; academic accommodation for the gifted, the musically talented, and the artistically talented; ESL (25 students enrolled).

College Admission Counseling 76 students graduated in 2011; all went to college, including Bowdoin College; Connecticut College; Dickinson College; Haverford College; The College of Wooster; University of Maryland, College Park. Median SAT critical reading: 620, median SAT math: 610, median SAT writing: 620, median combined SAT: 1850, median composite ACT: 27.

Student Life Upper grades have specified standards of dress, student council, honor system. Discipline rests equally with students and faculty. Attendance at religious services is required.

Tuition and Aid Day student tuition: $27,500; 5-day tuition and room/board: $40,500; 7-day tuition and room/board: $50,700. Tuition installment plan (FACTS Tuition Payment Plan). Need-based scholarship grants available. In 2011–12, 31% of upper-school students received aid. Total amount of financial aid awarded in 2011–12: $3,035,000.

Admissions Traditional secondary-level entrance grade is 9. For fall 2011, 198 students applied for upper-level admission, 106 were accepted, 57 enrolled. SSAT or TOEFL or SLEP required. Deadline for receipt of application materials: January 15. Application fee required: $75. Interview required.

Athletics Interscholastic: baseball (boys), basketball (b,g), cross-country running (b,g), lacrosse (b,g), soccer (b,g), softball (g), tennis (b,g), volleyball (g); coed interscholastic: cooperative games, modern dance, running, track and field; coed intramural: dance, fitness, flag football, Frisbee, hiking/backpacking, jogging, outdoor activities, outdoor adventure, outdoor education, outdoor recreation, outdoor skills, outdoors, physical fitness, physical training, rappelling, rock climbing, ropes courses, running, skiing (downhill), strength & conditioning, table tennis, track and field, ultimate Frisbee, walking, wall climbing, weight lifting, weight training, wilderness, wilderness survival, wrestling, yoga. 5 PE instructors, 3 coaches, 1 athletic trainer.

Computers Computers are regularly used in all academic classes. Computer network features include on-campus library services, Internet access, wireless campus network. Student e-mail accounts and computer access in designated common areas are available to students. Students grades are available online.

Contact Yasmin McGinnis, Director of Enrollment Management. 301-774-7455 Ext. 182. Fax: 301-924-1115. E-mail: yasmin.mcginnis@ssfs.org. Web site: www.ssfs.org

See Display below and Close-Up on page 624.

SANFORD SCHOOL

6900 Lancaster Pike
PO Box 888
Hockessin, Delaware 19707-0888

Head of School: Mark J. Anderson

General Information Coeducational day college-preparatory school. Grades PK–12. Founded: 1930. Setting: suburban. Nearest major city is Wilmington. 100-acre campus. 6 buildings on campus. Approved or accredited by Middle States Association of Colleges and Schools and Delaware Department of Education. Member of National Association of Independent Schools and Secondary School Admission Test Board. Endowment: $7 million. Total enrollment: 599. Upper school average class size: 14. Upper school faculty-student ratio: 1:8. There are 169 required school days per year for Upper School students. Upper School students typically attend 5 days per week. The average school day consists of 5 hours and 15 minutes.

Upper School Student Profile Grade 9: 65 students (28 boys, 37 girls); Grade 10: 52 students (22 boys, 30 girls); Grade 11: 61 students (30 boys, 31 girls); Grade 12: 61 students (28 boys, 33 girls).

Faculty School total: 82. In upper school: 11 men, 19 women; 20 have advanced degrees.

Subjects Offered Algebra, American literature, anatomy and physiology, art, biology, biology-AP, calculus-AP, ceramics, chemistry, chemistry-AP, choir, Civil War, collage and assemblage, computer art, computer graphics, computer science-AP, concert band, drawing, driver education, ecology, ecology, environmental systems, economics, engineering, English, English language-AP, English literature, English literature-AP, environmental science-AP, fine arts, French, French-AP, functions, geometry, German, German-AP, graphic design, health, history, jazz band, Latin, Latin-AP, mathematics, music, music appreciation, painting, photography, physics, physics-AP, pre-calculus, printmaking, psychology, social studies, Spanish, Spanish-AP, statistics, statistics-AP, studio art-AP, technology, trigonometry, U.S. history, U.S. history-AP, video film production, visual arts, vocal ensemble, voice, world civilizations, world history, world history-AP, world literature, writing, yearbook.

Graduation Requirements Arts and fine arts (art, music, dance, drama), athletics, computer science, electives, English, foreign language, health, lab science, mathematics, music, social sciences, 2-week senior project/internship in May.

Special Academic Programs Advanced Placement exam preparation; honors section; independent study.

College Admission Counseling 54 students graduated in 2011; all went to college, including College of the Holy Cross; High Point University; Syracuse University; Towson University; University of Delaware; Washington College.

Student Life Upper grades have specified standards of dress, student council, honor system. Discipline rests equally with students and faculty.

Tuition and Aid Day student tuition: $20,350–$22,000. Tuition installment plan (Tuition Management System (TMS)). Need-based scholarship grants available. In 2011–12, 44% of upper-school students received aid. Total amount of financial aid awarded in 2011–12: $1,375,825.

Admissions Traditional secondary-level entrance grade is 9. For fall 2011, 73 students applied for upper-level admission, 62 were accepted, 36 enrolled. ERB CTP IV, ISEE or SSAT required. Deadline for receipt of application materials: January 6. Application fee required: $40. On-campus interview required.

Athletics Interscholastic: baseball (boys), basketball (b,g), cross-country running (b,g), field hockey (g), lacrosse (b,g), soccer (b,g), swimming and diving (b,g), tennis (b,g), volleyball (g), wrestling (b); coed interscholastic: golf, indoor track; coed intramural: physical fitness. 27 coaches, 1 athletic trainer.

Computers Computers are regularly used in art, computer applications, English, foreign language, history, mathematics, newspaper, science, yearbook classes. Computer network features include on-campus library services, online commercial services, Internet access, Internet filtering or blocking technology. Campus intranet and student e-mail accounts are available to students. Students grades are available online. The school has a published electronic and media policy.

Contact Ceil Baum, Admission Administrative Assistant. 302-239-5263 Ext. 265. Fax: 302-239-1912. E-mail: admission@sanfordschool.org. Web site: www.sanfordschool.org

SAN MARCOS BAPTIST ACADEMY

2801 Ranch Road Twelve
San Marcos, Texas 78666-9406

Head of School: Dr. John H. Garrison

General Information Coeducational boarding and day college-preparatory, arts, business, religious studies, technology, learning skills, and ESL school, affiliated with Baptist General Conference. Grades 7–12. Founded: 1907. Setting: small town. Nearest major city is Austin. Students are housed in single-sex dormitories. 220-acre campus. 9 buildings on campus. Approved or accredited by Accreditation Commission of the Texas Association of Baptist Schools, Southern Association of Colleges and Schools, Texas Education Agency, and Texas Department of Education. Member of National Association of Independent Schools. Endowment: $5.8 million. Total enrollment: 287. Upper school average class size: 12. Upper school faculty-student ratio: 1:7. There are 180 required school days per year for Upper School students. Upper School students typically attend 5 days per week. The average school day consists of 7 hours and 40 minutes.

Upper School Student Profile Grade 9: 48 students (31 boys, 17 girls); Grade 10: 55 students (31 boys, 24 girls); Grade 11: 71 students (46 boys, 25 girls); Grade 12: 66 students (46 boys, 20 girls). 65% of students are boarding students. 58% are state residents. 6 states are represented in upper school student body. 38% are international students. International students from China, Mexico, Nigeria, Republic of Korea, Saudi Arabia, and Viet Nam; 6 other countries represented in student body. 12% of students are Baptist General Conference.

Faculty School total: 41. In upper school: 19 men, 22 women; 22 have advanced degrees; 5 reside on campus.

Subjects Offered Advanced math, Advanced Placement courses, algebra, American government, American history, American literature, analysis and differential calculus, analytic geometry, anatomy and physiology, ancient world history, applied arts, applied music, art, athletic training, athletics, band, baseball, Basic programming, basketball, Bible, Bible studies, biology, biology-AP, British literature, British literature (honors), British literature-AP, business applications, calculus, calculus-AP, career/college preparation, character education, cheerleading, chemistry, choir, Christian scripture, Christian testament, Christianity, civics, civics/free enterprise, clayworking, college admission preparation, college counseling, college planning, communication skills, community service, comparative religion, computer applications, computer information systems, computer programming, computer science, computers, concert band, concert choir, contemporary art, critical thinking, desktop publishing, digital photography, drama, drama performance, drama workshop, dramatic arts, drawing, driver education, earth and space science, earth science, economics, economics and history, English, English as a foreign language, English composition, English literature, English literature and composition-AP, English literature-AP, English-AP, ESL, family and consumer science, fine arts, foreign language, French, geography, geometry, golf, government/civics, grammar, guidance, health, health education, history, history of the Americas, honors algebra, honors geometry, honors U.S. history, honors world history, HTML design, human anatomy, human biology, instrumental music, instruments, intro to computers, introduction to theater, jazz band, journalism, JROTC, JROTC or LEAD (Leadership Education and Development), keyboarding, language and composition, language arts, leadership, leadership and service, leadership education training, learning strategies, library, library skills, library studies, Life of Christ, life skills, literature, literature and composition-AP, literature-AP, logic, mathematical modeling, mathematics, mathematics-AP, military science, music, music appreciation, music performance, music theory, musical productions, musical theater, musicianship, New Testament, news writing, newspaper, novels, painting, participation in sports, personal and social education, personal fitness, personal growth, photography, photojournalism, physical education, physical fitness, physical science, physics, piano, play production, pottery, prayer/spirituality, pre-calculus, psychology, public speaking, reading, reading/study skills, religion, religious education, remedial study skills, research skills, SAT preparation, SAT/ACT preparation, science, social skills, social studies, society and culture, sociology, softball, Spanish, speech, speech and debate, speech communications, sports, sports conditioning, sports performance development, sports team management, state government, state history, stock market, student government, student publications, study skills, swimming, tennis, Texas history, theater, theater arts, theater production, theology, TOEFL preparation, track and field, U.S. government, U.S. government and politics, U.S. history, U.S. literature, visual arts, vocal ensemble, vocal jazz, vocal music, voice, voice and diction, voice ensemble, volleyball, Web site design, weight training, weightlifting, Western civilization, world civilizations, world cultures, world geography, world history, world issues, world literature, world religions, world religions, world studies, world wide web design, yearbook.

Graduation Requirements Arts and fine arts (art, music, dance, drama), computer science, economics, electives, English, foreign language, JROTC or LEAD (Leadership Education and Development), mathematics, physical education (includes health), religion (includes Bible studies and theology), science, social studies (includes history), speech.

Special Academic Programs 6 Advanced Placement exams for which test preparation is offered; honors section; accelerated programs; independent study; study at local college for college credit; academic accommodation for the gifted, the musically talented, and the artistically talented; remedial reading and/or remedial writing; remedial math; programs in English, mathematics, general development for dyslexic students; special instructional classes for deaf students, students with Section 504 learning disabilities, Attention Deficit Disorder, and dyslexia; ESL (27 students enrolled).

College Admission Counseling 71 students graduated in 2012; 70 went to college, including Indiana University Bloomington; Michigan State University; Texas State University–San Marcos; Texas Tech University; The University of Texas at Austin; United States Military Academy. Other: 1 entered military service. Median combined SAT: 450, median composite ACT: 19. Mean SAT critical reading: 459, mean SAT math: 525, mean SAT writing: 460. 16.4% scored over 600 on SAT critical reading, 32.8% scored over 600 on SAT math, 14.9% scored over 600 on SAT writing, 14.9% scored over 1800 on combined SAT, 7% scored over 26 on composite ACT.

Student Life Upper grades have uniform requirement, student council, honor system. Discipline rests primarily with faculty. Attendance at religious services is required.

Tuition and Aid Day student tuition: $8518; 7-day tuition and room/board: $28,790. Guaranteed tuition plan. Tuition installment plan (monthly payment plans, individually arranged payment plans). Need-based scholarship grants available. In 2012–13, 39% of upper-school students received aid. Total amount of financial aid awarded in 2012–13: $483,546.

Admissions Traditional secondary-level entrance grade is 9. For fall 2012, 104 students applied for upper-level admission, 85 were accepted, 50 enrolled. Deadline for receipt of application materials: none. Application fee required: $100. Interview required.

Athletics Interscholastic: baseball (boys), basketball (b,g), cross-country running (b,g), football (b), golf (b,g), JROTC drill (b,g), power lifting (b,g), softball (g), swimming and diving (b,g), tennis (b,g), track and field (b,g), volleyball (g), weight lifting (b,g); coed interscholastic: equestrian sports, flag football, marksmanship, soccer, winter soccer; coed intramural: cheering, Frisbee, horseback riding, ropes courses, table tennis, weight lifting, weight training. 3 PE instructors, 20 coaches, 1 athletic trainer.

Computers Computers are regularly used in all classes. Computer network features include on-campus library services, online commercial services, Internet access, wireless campus network, Internet filtering or blocking technology, 1:1 computer device program for 9th and 10th grade students. Student e-mail accounts and computer access in designated common areas are available to students. Students grades are available online. The school has a published electronic and media policy.

Contact Mr. Jeffrey D. Baergen, Director of Admissions. 800-428-5120. Fax: 512-753-8031. E-mail: admissions@smba.org. Web site: www.smabears.org

SANTA CATALINA SCHOOL

1500 Mark Thomas Drive
Monterey, California 93940-5291

Head of School: Sr. Claire Barone

General Information Girls' boarding and day college-preparatory and liberal arts school, affiliated with Roman Catholic Church. Grades 9–12. Founded: 1950. Setting: small town. Nearest major city is San Francisco. Students are housed in single-sex dormitories. 36-acre campus. 21 buildings on campus. Approved or accredited by California Association of Independent Schools, National Christian School Association, The Association of Boarding Schools, The College Board, Western Association of Schools and Colleges, and California Department of Education. Member of National Association of Independent Schools and Secondary School Admission Test Board. Endowment: $24 million. Total enrollment: 258. Upper school average class size: 13. Upper school faculty-student ratio: 1:8. There are 168 required school days per year for Upper School students. Upper School students typically attend 5 days per week. The average school day consists of 5 hours and 25 minutes.

Upper School Student Profile Grade 9: 62 students (62 girls); Grade 10: 57 students (57 girls); Grade 11: 80 students (80 girls); Grade 12: 59 students (59 girls). 47%

of students are boarding students. 78% are state residents. 12 states are represented in upper school student body. 16% are international students. International students from Canada, China, Democratic People's Republic of Korea, Germany, Mexico, and Turkey; 4 other countries represented in student body. 45% of students are Roman Catholic.

Faculty School total: 34. In upper school: 16 men, 16 women; 27 have advanced degrees; 19 reside on campus.

Subjects Offered Algebra, American literature, art, art history-AP, ballet, biology, biology-AP, calculus, calculus-AP, ceramics, chemistry, chemistry-AP, Chinese, choir, college counseling, conceptual physics, dance, digital art, drama, drama performance, English, English language-AP, English literature, English literature-AP, ensembles, environmental science-AP, European history, fine arts, French, French language-AP, geometry, health, honors algebra, honors English, honors geometry, jazz dance, Latin, Latin-AP, Mandarin, marine science, media arts, music, music performance, peace and justice, philosophy, photography, physical education, physics, physics-AP, pre-calculus, Spanish, Spanish language-AP, Spanish literature-AP, studio art, studio art-AP, theater, theology, trigonometry, U.S. history, U.S. history-AP, women spirituality and faith, world history, world history-AP, world issues, world literature, world religions.

Graduation Requirements Arts, English, foreign language, history, lab science, mathematics, physical education (includes health), religious studies.

Special Academic Programs 16 Advanced Placement exams for which test preparation is offered; honors section; academic accommodation for the gifted, the musically talented, and the artistically talented.

College Admission Counseling 46 students graduated in 2012; all went to college, including Boston University; Georgetown University; Santa Clara University; Southern Methodist University; University of Oregon; University of San Francisco. Mean SAT critical reading: 595, mean SAT math: 600, mean SAT writing: 598.

Student Life Upper grades have uniform requirement, student council. Discipline rests equally with students and faculty. Attendance at religious services is required.

Summer Programs Enrichment, sports, art/fine arts programs offered; session focuses on recreation and enrichment fun; held on campus; accepts girls; open to students from other schools. 215 students usually enrolled. 2013 schedule: June 23 to July 27. Application deadline: none.

Tuition and Aid Day student tuition: $29,900; 7-day tuition and room/board: $46,000. Tuition installment plan (monthly payment plans, Tuition Management Systems). Merit scholarship grants, need-based scholarship grants available. In 2012–13, 42% of upper-school students received aid. Total amount of financial aid awarded in 2012–13: $2,094,575.

Admissions Traditional secondary-level entrance grade is 9. For fall 2012, 235 students applied for upper-level admission, 131 were accepted, 78 enrolled. ISEE, SSAT or TOEFL required. Deadline for receipt of application materials: February 1. Application fee required: $75. Interview required.

Athletics Interscholastic: basketball, cross-country running, diving, equestrian sports, field hockey, golf, lacrosse, soccer, softball, swimming and diving, tennis, track and field, volleyball, water polo; intramural: ballet, canoeing/kayaking, dance, fencing, fitness, horseback riding, kayaking, modern dance, outdoor activities, physical fitness, rafting, rock climbing, self defense, strength & conditioning, surfing, weight training, yoga. 2 PE instructors, 26 coaches.

Computers Computers are regularly used in English, foreign language, mathematics, media arts, science, yearbook classes. Computer network features include on-campus library services, Internet access, wireless campus network, Internet filtering or blocking technology, iPad initiative for freshman class. Campus intranet, student e-mail accounts, and computer access in designated common areas are available to students. The school has a published electronic and media policy.

Contact Mrs. Jamie Buffington Browne '85, Director of Admission. 831-655-9356. Fax: 831-655-7535. E-mail: jamie.brown@santacatalina.org. Web site: www.santacatalina.org

SANTA FE PREPARATORY SCHOOL

1101 Camino de la Cruz Blanca
Santa Fe, New Mexico 87505

Head of School: Mr. James W. Leonard

General Information Coeducational day college-preparatory, arts, and community service school. Grades 7–12. Founded: 1961. Setting: suburban. 13-acre campus. 4 buildings on campus. Approved or accredited by Independent Schools Association of the Southwest and New Mexico Department of Education. Member of National Association of Independent Schools. Endowment: $4.3 million. Total enrollment: 303. Upper school average class size: 13. Upper school faculty-student ratio: 1:16. There are 171 required school days per year for Upper School students. Upper School students typically attend 5 days per week. The average school day consists of 6 hours and 23 minutes.

Upper School Student Profile Grade 9: 49 students (30 boys, 19 girls); Grade 10: 74 students (31 boys, 43 girls); Grade 11: 39 students (24 boys, 15 girls); Grade 12: 42 students (16 boys, 26 girls).

Faculty School total: 48. In upper school: 19 men, 20 women; 27 have advanced degrees.

Subjects Offered Acting, advanced chemistry, advanced computer applications, advanced math, algebra, American Civil War, American culture, American democracy, American government, American history, American history-AP, American literature, analytic geometry, art, art appreciation, art history, art history-AP, arts, athletics, basketball, biology, calculus, calculus-AP, ceramics, chemistry, chemistry-AP, chorus, clayworking, college counseling, community service, computer applications, computer graphics, computer literacy, computer programming, computer science, conceptual physics, creative writing, drama, drama performance, dramatic arts, driver education, earth science, English, English literature, European history, fine arts, French, geography, geometry, health, history, humanities, journalism, keyboarding, Latin, mathematics, music, photography, physical education, physics, psychology, science, social studies, Spanish, theater, trigonometry, world history, world literature, writing.

Graduation Requirements Arts and fine arts (art, music, dance, drama), computer science, English, foreign language, history, humanities, mathematics, music appreciation, physical education (includes health), science, social studies (includes history), senior seminar program. Community service is required.

Special Academic Programs 5 Advanced Placement exams for which test preparation is offered; honors section; independent study; study at local college for college credit; study abroad.

College Admission Counseling 52 students graduated in 2012; all went to college, including Middlebury College; University of Denver; University of New Mexico; University of Redlands; Whitman College; Williams College. Median SAT critical reading: 620, median SAT math: 610, median SAT writing: 600, median combined SAT: 1850, median composite ACT: 28. 61% scored over 600 on SAT critical reading, 61% scored over 600 on SAT math, 54% scored over 600 on SAT writing, 61% scored over 1800 on combined SAT, 58% scored over 26 on composite ACT.

Student Life Upper grades have specified standards of dress, student council. Discipline rests equally with students and faculty.

Tuition and Aid Day student tuition: $18,906. Tuition installment plan (individually arranged payment plans, Tuition Management Systems Plan). Need-based scholarship grants, tuition remission for faculty available. In 2012–13, 30% of upper-school students received aid.

Admissions Traditional secondary-level entrance grade is 9. For fall 2012, 22 students applied for upper-level admission, 22 were accepted, 22 enrolled. Mathematics proficiency exam required. Deadline for receipt of application materials: none. Application fee required: $55. On-campus interview required.

Athletics Interscholastic: baseball (boys), basketball (b,g), cross-country running (b,g), diving (b,g), lacrosse (b,g), soccer (b,g), softball (g), swimming and diving (b,g), tennis (b,g), track and field (b,g), volleyball (g); intramural: basketball (b,g), cross-country running (b,g), football (b,g), soccer (b,g), tennis (b,g), track and field (b,g), volleyball (g); coed interscholastic: aerobics/dance, dance team; coed intramural: basketball, bowling, skiing (downhill), swimming and diving. 1 PE instructor, 16 coaches, 1 athletic trainer.

Computers Computers are regularly used in current events, English, French, freshman foundations, geography, graphic arts, history, humanities, journalism, library, literary magazine, mathematics, newspaper, photography, photojournalism, science, social sciences, writing, yearbook classes. Computer network features include on-campus library services, Internet access, wireless campus network, Internet filtering or blocking technology. Campus intranet, student e-mail accounts, and computer access in designated common areas are available to students. The school has a published electronic and media policy.

Contact Michael Multari, Director of Admissions. 505-982-1829 Ext. 1212. Fax: 505-982-2897. E-mail: mmultari@sfprep.org. Web site: www.santafeprep.org

SAYRE SCHOOL

194 North Limestone Street
Lexington, Kentucky 40507

Head of School: Mr. Clayton G. Chambliss

General Information Coeducational day college-preparatory, arts, and technology school. Grades PK–12. Founded: 1854. Setting: urban. 60-acre campus. 10 buildings on campus. Approved or accredited by Independent Schools Association of the Central States and Kentucky Department of Education. Member of National Association of Independent Schools and Secondary School Admission Test Board. Endowment: $64 million. Total enrollment: 549. Upper school average class size: 14. Upper school faculty-student ratio: 1:9. There are 179 required school days per year for Upper School students. Upper School students typically attend 5 days per week. The average school day consists of 6 hours and 15 minutes.

Upper School Student Profile Grade 9: 56 students (29 boys, 27 girls); Grade 10: 52 students (28 boys, 24 girls); Grade 11: 57 students (26 boys, 31 girls); Grade 12: 49 students (26 boys, 23 girls).

Faculty School total: 32. In upper school: 12 men, 16 women; 22 have advanced degrees.

Subjects Offered Algebra, American history, American literature, art, art history, biology, calculus, chemistry, community service, computer science, creative writing, drama, earth science, English, English literature, fine arts, French, geometry, government/civics, health, history, journalism, mathematics, music, photography, physical education, physics, public speaking, science, social studies, Spanish, speech, statistics, theater, U.S. constitutional history, world history, writing.

Graduation Requirements Arts and fine arts (art, music, dance, drama), computer science, creative writing, English, foreign language, mathematics, physical education (includes health), public speaking, science, social studies (includes history), senior project internship, senior seminars. Community service is required.

Special Academic Programs 13 Advanced Placement exams for which test preparation is offered; honors section; independent study; term-away projects; study at local college for college credit; academic accommodation for the gifted and the artistically talented.

College Admission Counseling 65 students graduated in 2011; all went to college, including Centre College; Miami University; University of Georgia; University of Kentucky; Vanderbilt University. Median SAT critical reading: 570, median SAT math: 580, median SAT writing: 580, median combined SAT: 1760, median composite ACT: 25. 38% scored over 600 on SAT critical reading, 42% scored over 600 on SAT math, 44% scored over 600 on SAT writing, 41% scored over 1800 on combined SAT, 41% scored over 26 on composite ACT.

Student Life Upper grades have specified standards of dress, student council, honor system. Discipline rests equally with students and faculty.

Tuition and Aid Day student tuition: $18,020–$19,520. Tuition installment plan (Insured Tuition Payment Plan, monthly payment plans, individually arranged payment plans). Merit scholarship grants, need-based scholarship grants available. In 2011–12, 21% of upper-school students received aid. Total amount of financial aid awarded in 2011–12: $6,000,000.

Admissions Traditional secondary-level entrance grade is 9. For fall 2011, 36 students applied for upper-level admission, 27 were accepted, 25 enrolled. Admissions testing, Math Placement Exam, PSAT and SAT for applicants to grade 11 and 12, school's own exam or writing sample required. Deadline for receipt of application materials: none. Application fee required: $75. On-campus interview required.

Athletics Interscholastic: baseball (boys), basketball (b,g), cheering (g), diving (b,g), golf (b,g), lacrosse (b), physical fitness (b), physical training (b,g), soccer (b,g), softball (g), swimming and diving (b,g), tennis (b,g); coed interscholastic: cross-country running. 5 PE instructors, 10 coaches, 1 athletic trainer.

Computers Computers are regularly used in English, foreign language, history, mathematics, music, science classes. Computer network features include on-campus library services, online commercial services, Internet access, wireless campus network, Internet filtering or blocking technology. Student e-mail accounts are available to students. Students grades are available online. The school has a published electronic and media policy.

Contact Mr. John W. Hackworth, Director of Admission. 859-254-1361 Ext. 207. Fax: 859-254-5627. E-mail: jwhackworth@sayreschool.org. Web site: www.sayreschool.org

SBEC (SOUTHERN BAPTIST EDUCATIONAL CENTER)

7400 Getwell Road
Southaven, Mississippi 38672

Head of School: Mr. David H. Manley

General Information Coeducational day college-preparatory, arts, religious studies, and technology school, affiliated with Christian faith, Baptist Church. Grades PK–12. Founded: 1972. Setting: suburban. Nearest major city is Memphis, TN. 61-acre campus. 2 buildings on campus. Approved or accredited by Southern Association of Independent Schools. Total enrollment: 1,077. Upper school average class size: 21. Upper school faculty-student ratio: 1:13. There are 177 required school days per year for Upper School students. Upper School students typically attend 5 days per week. The average school day consists of 7 hours and 5 minutes.

Upper School Student Profile Grade 7: 79 students (41 boys, 38 girls); Grade 8: 69 students (39 boys, 30 girls); Grade 9: 84 students (42 boys, 42 girls); Grade 10: 74 students (35 boys, 39 girls); Grade 11: 81 students (38 boys, 43 girls); Grade 12: 87 students (40 boys, 47 girls). 90% of students are Christian, Baptist.

Faculty School total: 99. In upper school: 11 men, 30 women; 16 have advanced degrees.

Subjects Offered Advanced math, algebra, American government, American history, anatomy and physiology, art, arts, band, Bible, Bible studies, biology, calculus-AP, chemistry, computer programming, computer science, drafting, drama, driver education, economics, English, English-AP, French, geometry, home economics, journalism, keyboarding, Latin, physical education, physics, pre-algebra, psychology, sociology, Spanish, U.S. government and politics-AP, vocal music, world history, yearbook.

Graduation Requirements 20th century world history, advanced math, algebra, American history, anatomy and physiology, Bible, chemistry, Christian studies, computer programming, economics, English, French, geometry, independent living, Latin, physical education (includes health), physics, psychology, Spanish, U.S. government and politics-AP, world history, world history-AP.

Special Academic Programs Advanced Placement exam preparation; honors section; academic accommodation for the gifted; remedial reading and/or remedial writing; remedial math; programs in English, mathematics, general development for dyslexic students.

College Admission Counseling 85 students graduated in 2012; 83 went to college, including Mississippi College; Mississippi State University; Samford University; University of Memphis; University of Mississippi. Other: 1 went to work, 1 had other specific plans. Mean composite ACT: 31. 35% scored over 26 on composite ACT.

Student Life Upper grades have specified standards of dress, student council. Discipline rests primarily with faculty. Attendance at religious services is required.

Summer Programs Sports programs offered; session focuses on driver's education; held both on and off campus; held at Classroom portion done on campus. Driving portion and done on the highways and towns in north Mississippi; accepts boys and girls; open to students from other schools. 15 students usually enrolled. 2013 schedule: May 30 to June 30. Application deadline: April 1.

Tuition and Aid Day student tuition: $4756–$5300. Tuition installment plan (monthly payment arrangements with local bank). Tuition reduction for siblings, need-based scholarship grants available. In 2012–13, 13% of upper-school students received aid. Total amount of financial aid awarded in 2012–13: $67,675.

Admissions Traditional secondary-level entrance grade is 8. For fall 2012, 40 students applied for upper-level admission, 38 were accepted, 36 enrolled. Admissions testing required. Deadline for receipt of application materials: none. Application fee required: $225. On-campus interview required.

Athletics Interscholastic: baseball (boys), basketball (b,g), cheering (g), cross-country running (b,g), drill team (g), football (b), golf (b,g), soccer (b,g), softball (g), strength & conditioning (b,g), swimming and diving (b,g), tennis (b,g), track and field (b,g), volleyball (g); intramural: soccer (b,g); coed intramural: soccer. 2 PE instructors, 1 coach, 1 athletic trainer.

Computers Computers are regularly used in all classes. Computer network features include on-campus library services, Internet access, wireless campus network. Students grades are available online.

Contact Mrs. Sheila Sheron, Director of Admission. 662-349-5127. Fax: 662-349-4962. E-mail: ssheron@sbectrojans.com. Web site:

SCHOLAR'S HALL PREPARATORY SCHOOL

888 Trillium Drive
Kitchener, Ontario N2R 1K4, Canada

Head of School: Mr. Frederick T. Gore

General Information Coeducational day college-preparatory, general academic, arts, and business school. Grades JK–12. Founded: 1997. Setting: small town. Nearest major city is Toronto, Canada. 10-acre campus. 1 building on campus. Approved or accredited by Ontario Department of Education. Language of instruction: English. Total enrollment: 105. Upper school average class size: 10. Upper school faculty-student ratio: 1:10. There are 200 required school days per year for Upper School students. Upper School students typically attend 5 days per week. The average school day consists of 7 hours.

Upper School Student Profile Grade 6: 10 students (5 boys, 5 girls); Grade 7: 10 students (5 boys, 5 girls); Grade 8: 10 students (5 boys, 5 girls); Grade 9: 10 students (5 boys, 5 girls); Grade 10: 10 students (5 boys, 5 girls); Grade 11: 10 students (5 boys, 5 girls); Grade 12: 10 students (5 boys, 5 girls).

Faculty School total: 10. In upper school: 5 men, 5 women; 5 have advanced degrees.

Special Academic Programs ESL (20 students enrolled).

College Admission Counseling 10 students graduated in 2012; 2 went to college, including The University of Western Ontario; University of Waterloo; Wilfrid Laurier University. Other: 8 entered a postgraduate year.

Student Life Upper grades have uniform requirement, student council, honor system. Discipline rests primarily with faculty.

Summer Programs Remediation, advancement, ESL programs offered; session focuses on academics; held on campus; accepts boys and girls; open to students from other schools. 100 students usually enrolled. 2013 schedule: July 1 to August 30. Application deadline: May 30.

Tuition and Aid Day student tuition: CAN$10,900. Guaranteed tuition plan. Tuition installment plan (The Tuition Plan, monthly payment plans, individually arranged payment plans). Tuition reduction for siblings, bursaries available. In 2012–13, 10% of upper-school students received aid. Total amount of financial aid awarded in 2012–13: CAN$20,000.

Admissions Traditional secondary-level entrance grade is 9. For fall 2012, 20 students applied for upper-level admission, 15 were accepted, 15 enrolled. Woodcock-Johnson Educational Evaluation, WISC III required. Deadline for receipt of application materials: June 1. No application fee required. Interview required.

Athletics Coed Interscholastic: badminton, ball hockey, baseball, basketball, cross-country running, fencing, fitness, fitness walking, flag football, floor hockey, Frisbee, golf, independent competitive sports, martial arts, outdoor activities, outdoor education, physical fitness, self defense, soccer, softball, table tennis, volleyball; coed intramural: badminton, ball hockey, baseball, basketball, bowling, cross-country running, fencing, fitness, fitness walking, flag football, floor hockey, Frisbee, golf, martial arts, outdoor activities, outdoor education, physical fitness, self defense, soccer, softball, table tennis, volleyball. 2 PE instructors.

Computers Computers are regularly used in all classes. Computer network features include Internet access, wireless campus network, Internet filtering or blocking technology. Campus intranet is available to students. The school has a published electronic and media policy.

Contact 519-888-6620. Fax: 519-884-0316. Web site: www.scholarshall.com

SCICORE ACADEMY

120 Main Street
Hightstown, New Jersey 08520

Head of School: Arthur T. Poulos, PhD

General Information Coeducational day college-preparatory school. Grades K–12. Founded: 2002. Setting: small town. Nearest major city is Trenton. 5-acre campus. 1 building on campus. Approved or accredited by Middle States Association of Colleges and Schools. Total enrollment: 95. Upper school average class size: 13. Upper school faculty-student ratio: 1:7. There are 170 required school days per year for Upper School students. Upper School students typically attend 5 days per week. The average school day consists of 6 hours and 30 minutes.

Faculty School total: 16. In upper school: 9 men, 5 women; 6 have advanced degrees.

Subjects Offered 3-dimensional design, advanced biology, advanced chemistry, advanced math, algebra, American government, American history, American literature, anatomy and physiology, art, Basic programming, biology, biology-AP, biotechnology, British literature, calculus, chemistry, chemistry-AP, Chinese, choir, drafting, drama, electronics, English composition, French, history of science, Italian, Japanese, lab science, logic, rhetoric, and debate, microcomputer technology applications, moral reasoning, music appreciation, optics, physics, pre-calculus, programming, public speaking, SAT preparation, science project, senior project, Spanish, speech and debate, U.S. history, Western civilization, world literature.

Graduation Requirements Advanced math, algebra, American government, American history, American literature, biology, British literature, chemistry, civics, computer programming, English composition, foreign language, geometry, lab science, logic, rhetoric, and debate, physical education (includes health), physics, programming, SAT preparation, science project, U.S. history, Western civilization, world literature.

Special Academic Programs 3 Advanced Placement exams for which test preparation is offered; honors section; independent study; academic accommodation for the gifted and the artistically talented; ESL (4 students enrolled).

College Admission Counseling 5 students graduated in 2011; all went to college, including Bryn Mawr College; Drexel University; New Jersey Institute of Technology; University of Chicago; University of Connecticut.

Student Life Upper grades have specified standards of dress, honor system. Discipline rests primarily with faculty.

Tuition and Aid Day student tuition: $9120. Tuition installment plan (monthly payment plans). Tuition reduction for siblings available.

Admissions Traditional secondary-level entrance grade is 9. Admissions testing required. Deadline for receipt of application materials: none. No application fee required. Interview required.

Athletics Interscholastic: basketball (boys); intramural: aerobics/dance (g); coed interscholastic: cross-country running, golf, soccer; coed intramural: cross-country running, equestrian sports, fencing, horseback riding. 2 PE instructors, 1 coach.

Computers Computers are regularly used in English, foreign language, French, programming, science, Spanish, yearbook classes. Computer resources include Internet access, wireless campus network. Computer access in designated common areas is available to students. The school has a published electronic and media policy.

Contact Mrs. Danette N. Poulos, Vice Principal. 609-448-8950. Fax: 609-448-8952. E-mail: atpoulos@scicore.org. Web site: www.scicore.org/

SCOTTSDALE CHRISTIAN ACADEMY

14400 North Tatum Boulevard
Phoenix, Arizona 85032

Head of School: Mr. Peter Laugen

General Information Coeducational day college-preparatory and religious studies school, affiliated with Christian faith. Grades PK–12. Founded: 1968. Setting: suburban. 11-acre campus. 6 buildings on campus. Approved or accredited by Association of Christian Schools International and North Central Association of Colleges and Schools. Total enrollment: 821. Upper school average class size: 22. Upper school faculty-student ratio: 1:13. There are 180 required school days per year for Upper School students. Upper School students typically attend 5 days per week. The average school day consists of 7 hours.

Upper School Student Profile 99% of students are Christian.

Faculty School total: 61. In upper school: 14 men, 8 women.

Subjects Offered Advanced Placement courses, algebra, American history, American history-AP, American literature, anatomy, art, Bible studies, biology, calculus, chemistry, creative writing, drama, economics, English, English-AP, fine arts, French, geography, geometry, government/civics, graphic design, guitar, history, honors geometry, honors U.S. history, mathematics, music, physical education, physical science, physics, physics-AP, religion, science, social studies, Spanish, speech, trigonometry, world history.

Graduation Requirements American government, American history, ancient world history, arts and fine arts (art, music, dance, drama), Bible, biology, chemistry, Christian ethics, economics, English, foreign language, government, mathematics, physical education (includes health), religion (includes Bible studies and theology), science, social sciences, social studies (includes history), speech, U.S. history, world history.

Special Academic Programs Advanced Placement exam preparation; honors section; independent study; study at local college for college credit.

College Admission Counseling 69 students graduated in 2012; 67 went to college, including Arizona Christian University; Arizona State University; Baylor University; Grand Canyon University; Paradise Valley Community College; The University of Arizona.

Student Life Upper grades have specified standards of dress, student council. Discipline rests primarily with faculty. Attendance at religious services is required.

Summer Programs Sports, art/fine arts programs offered; session focuses on camps; held on campus; accepts boys and girls; open to students from other schools. 300 students usually enrolled. 2013 schedule: June to June.

Tuition and Aid Day student tuition: $10,000. Tuition installment plan (Academic Management Services Plan). Need-based scholarship grants available.

Admissions Traditional secondary-level entrance grade is 9. Deadline for receipt of application materials: none. Application fee required: $100. On-campus interview required.

Athletics Interscholastic: baseball (boys), basketball (b,g), cheering (g), cross-country running (b,g), football (b), golf (b,g), soccer (b,g), softball (g), swimming and diving (b,g), tennis (b,g), track and field (b,g), volleyball (g), winter soccer (b); intramural: weight lifting (b); coed intramural: martial arts. 3 PE instructors, 50 coaches, 1 athletic trainer.

Computers Computers are regularly used in computer applications, graphic design, Latin, photography, video film production, yearbook classes. Computer network features include on-campus library services, Internet access, wireless campus network, Internet filtering or blocking technology, EXPAN. Student e-mail accounts are available to students. Students grades are available online. The school has a published electronic and media policy.

Contact Joan Rockwell, Admissions. 602-992-5100 Ext. 1095. Fax: 602-992-0575. E-mail: jrockwell@scottsdalechristian.org. Web site: www.scottsdalechristian.org

SCOTUS CENTRAL CATHOLIC HIGH SCHOOL

1554 18th Avenue
Columbus, Nebraska 68601-5132

Head of School: Mr. Wayne Morfeld

General Information Coeducational day college-preparatory, arts, business, religious studies, and technology school, affiliated with Roman Catholic Church. Grades 7–12. Founded: 1884. Setting: small town. Nearest major city is Omaha. 1-acre campus. 1 building on campus. Approved or accredited by National Catholic Education Association, North Central Association of Colleges and Schools, and Nebraska Department of Education. Endowment: $7.2 million. Total enrollment: 396. Upper school average class size: 20. Upper school faculty-student ratio: 1:14. There are 174 required school days per year for Upper School students. Upper School students typically attend 5 days per week. The average school day consists of 6 hours and 40 minutes.

Upper School Student Profile Grade 9: 67 students (38 boys, 29 girls); Grade 10: 60 students (29 boys, 31 girls); Grade 11: 63 students (29 boys, 34 girls); Grade 12: 68 students (26 boys, 42 girls). 96% of students are Roman Catholic.

Faculty School total: 28. In upper school: 10 men, 18 women; 9 have advanced degrees.

Subjects Offered Accounting, advanced math, Advanced Placement courses, algebra, American history, art, astronomy, band, Bible studies, biology, bookkeeping, calculus, calculus-AP, campus ministry, career and personal planning, career exploration, career/college preparation, Catholic belief and practice, character education, chemistry, child development, choir, choral music, chorus, community service, computer applications, computer multimedia, computer technologies, concert band, concert choir, consumer economics, consumer mathematics, contemporary problems, CPR, current events, digital applications, drama, earth science, economics, English, fabric arts, family and consumer science, fitness, food and nutrition, geography, government, guidance, health and safety, history, human development, instrumental music, jazz band, jazz ensemble, journalism, keyboarding, life management skills, life skills, marching band, modern world history, personal fitness, physical education, physical science, physics, physiology, psychology, reading/study skills, sociology, Spanish, speech, speech and debate, student publications, textiles, theater, U.S. history, vocal ensemble, weight training, world history, yearbook.

Graduation Requirements Algebra, American government, American history, biology, chemistry, computer applications, electives, English, geometry, mathematics, modern history, physical education (includes health), religion (includes Bible studies and theology), Spanish, speech, U.S. history, world history, 80 hours of Living the Faith community/church/school service.

Special Academic Programs Advanced Placement exam preparation; study at local college for college credit.

College Admission Counseling 65 students graduated in 2012; all went to college, including Creighton University; The University of South Dakota; University of Nebraska–Lincoln; University of Nebraska at Kearney; University of Nebraska at Omaha; University of Notre Dame. Median composite ACT: 22. 21% scored over 26 on composite ACT.

Student Life Upper grades have uniform requirement, student council. Discipline rests equally with students and faculty. Attendance at religious services is required.

Tuition and Aid Day student tuition: $2400–$2500. Tuition installment plan (monthly payment plans). Need-based scholarship grants, paying campus jobs available. In 2012–13, 26% of upper-school students received aid. Total amount of financial aid awarded in 2012–13: $109,250.
Admissions Traditional secondary-level entrance grade is 9. Deadline for receipt of application materials: none. No application fee required.
Athletics Interscholastic: baseball (boys), basketball (b,g), cheering (g), cross-country running (b,g), football (b), golf (b,g), soccer (b,g), softball (g), swimming and diving (b,g), tennis (b,g), track and field (b,g), volleyball (g), wrestling (b). 3 PE instructors, 15 coaches, 2 athletic trainers.
Computers Computers are regularly used in business, computer applications, journalism, keyboarding, newspaper, publications, technology, Web site design, word processing, yearbook classes. Computer network features include on-campus library services, Internet access, wireless campus network, Internet filtering or blocking technology. Campus intranet, student e-mail accounts, and computer access in designated common areas are available to students. Students grades are available online. The school has a published electronic and media policy.
Contact Mrs. Pamela K. Weir, 7-12 Guidance Counselor. 402-564-7165. Fax: 402-564-6004. E-mail: pweir@esu7.org. Web site: www.scotuscc.org

SEABURY HALL

480 Olinda Road
Makawao, Hawaii 96768-9399

Head of School: Mr. Joseph J. Schmidt

General Information Coeducational day college-preparatory, arts, and technology school, affiliated with Episcopal Church. Grades 6–12. Founded: 1964. Setting: rural. Nearest major city is Kahului. 73-acre campus. 8 buildings on campus. Approved or accredited by Western Association of Schools and Colleges. Member of National Association of Independent Schools and Secondary School Admission Test Board. Endowment: $27 million. Total enrollment: 443. Upper school average class size: 16. Upper school faculty-student ratio: 1:11. There are 175 required school days per year for Upper School students. Upper School students typically attend 5 days per week. The average school day consists of 7 hours and 30 minutes.
Upper School Student Profile Grade 9: 82 students (32 boys, 50 girls); Grade 10: 82 students (29 boys, 53 girls); Grade 11: 70 students (28 boys, 42 girls); Grade 12: 77 students (34 boys, 43 girls). 5% of students are members of Episcopal Church.
Faculty School total: 56. In upper school: 23 men, 15 women; 23 have advanced degrees.
Subjects Offered Acting, algebra, American history, American history-AP, American literature, American literature-AP, art, band, biology, biology-AP, calculus-AP, ceramics, chemistry, chorus, college counseling, college placement, college planning, community service, comparative religion, computer programming, dance, drawing, economics, engineering, English, English literature, ethics, European history-AP, expository writing, fine arts, geometry, global studies, government, Hawaiian history, Hawaiian language, history, Japanese, keyboarding, mathematics, mythology, painting, philosophy, physical education, physical science, physics, physics-AP, political science, pre-algebra, pre-calculus, religion, SAT preparation, science, set design, social studies, Spanish, Spanish-AP, speech, studio art-AP, yearbook.
Graduation Requirements Arts and fine arts (art, music, dance, drama), English, foreign language, mathematics, physical education (includes health), religion (includes Bible studies and theology), science, social studies (includes history), speech. Community service is required.
Special Academic Programs 13 Advanced Placement exams for which test preparation is offered; honors section; independent study; academic accommodation for the gifted.
College Admission Counseling 72 students graduated in 2012; 71 went to college, including California Polytechnic State University, San Luis Obispo; Chapman University; Colorado State University; University of Colorado Boulder; University of Hawaii at Manoa; University of San Francisco. Other: 1 entered military service. Mean SAT critical reading: 550, mean SAT math: 570, mean SAT writing: 565, mean combined SAT: 1685, mean composite ACT: 25.
Student Life Upper grades have specified standards of dress, student council, honor system. Discipline rests primarily with faculty.
Summer Programs Enrichment, sports, art/fine arts programs offered; session focuses on enrichment; held on campus; accepts boys and girls; open to students from other schools. 170 students usually enrolled. 2013 schedule: June 10 to July 5. Application deadline: June 10.
Tuition and Aid Day student tuition: $17,330. Tuition installment plan (FACTS Tuition Payment Plan). Need-based scholarship grants available. In 2012–13, 36% of upper-school students received aid. Total amount of financial aid awarded in 2012–13: $956,860.
Admissions Traditional secondary-level entrance grade is 9. For fall 2012, 173 students applied for upper-level admission, 136 were accepted, 102 enrolled. ERB CTP III, ISEE or SSAT required. Deadline for receipt of application materials: February 16. Application fee required: $65. Interview required.
Athletics Interscholastic: basketball (boys, girls), cross-country running (b,g), dance (g), golf (b,g), paddling (b,g), physical fitness (b,g), soccer (b,g), swimming and diving (b,g), tennis (b,g), track and field (b,g), volleyball (b,g); intramural: basketball (b,g), dance (g), fitness (b,g), strength & conditioning (b,g); coed interscholastic: baseball, dance, paddling, physical fitness; coed intramural: ballet, baseball, cross-country running, dance, fitness, track and field, volleyball. 4 PE instructors, 12 coaches, 1 athletic trainer.
Computers Computers are regularly used in art, economics, English, foreign language, geography, history, journalism, mathematics, newspaper, science, speech, yearbook classes. Computer network features include on-campus library services, online commercial services, Internet access, wireless campus network, Internet filtering or blocking technology. Campus intranet, student e-mail accounts, and computer access in designated common areas are available to students. Students grades are available online. The school has a published electronic and media policy.
Contact Elaine V. Nelson, Director of Admissions. 808-572-0807. Fax: 808-572-2042. E-mail: enelson@seaburyhall.org. Web site: www.seaburyhall.org

SEATTLE ACADEMY OF ARTS AND SCIENCES

1201 East Union Street
Seattle, Washington 98122

Head of School: Joe Puggelli

General Information Coeducational day college-preparatory, arts, and technology school. Grades 6–12. Founded: 1983. Setting: urban. 3-acre campus. 5 buildings on campus. Approved or accredited by Northwest Accreditation Commission, Pacific Northwest Association of Independent Schools, and Washington Department of Education. Member of National Association of Independent Schools. Endowment: $10.9 million. Total enrollment: 686. Upper school average class size: 18. Upper school faculty-student ratio: 1:9. There are 174 required school days per year for Upper School students. Upper School students typically attend 5 days per week. The average school day consists of 6 hours and 45 minutes.
Upper School Student Profile Grade 9: 126 students (66 boys, 60 girls); Grade 10: 106 students (52 boys, 54 girls); Grade 11: 106 students (53 boys, 53 girls); Grade 12: 103 students (50 boys, 53 girls).
Faculty School total: 104. In upper school: 46 men, 58 women; 72 have advanced degrees.
Subjects Offered Acting, advanced chemistry, algebra, American history, American literature, Asian studies, biology, biotechnology, calculus, chemistry, choir, civics, community service, dance, debate, drawing, economics, English, environmental systems, French, geometry, health, history, humanities, independent study, instrumental music, lab science, literature, Mandarin, marine science, math analysis, musical productions, painting, physical education, physics, printmaking, robotics, sculpture, Spanish, speech, stagecraft, statistics, visual arts, vocal music, world literature, yearbook.
Graduation Requirements Arts and fine arts (art, music, dance, drama), English, foreign language, history, mathematics, physical education (includes health), science, social studies (includes history). Community service is required.
Special Academic Programs Honors section; independent study; term-away projects; study abroad; academic accommodation for the gifted, the musically talented, and the artistically talented; remedial reading and/or remedial writing; remedial math; programs in English, mathematics, general development for dyslexic students.
College Admission Counseling 86 students graduated in 2012; 85 went to college, including Lewis & Clark College; New York University; Occidental College; Santa Clara University; University of Colorado Boulder; University of Washington. Other: 1 had other specific plans. Mean SAT critical reading: 622, mean SAT math: 580, mean SAT writing: 610, mean combined SAT: 1812, mean composite ACT: 26. 65% scored over 600 on SAT critical reading, 45% scored over 600 on SAT math, 56% scored over 600 on SAT writing, 52% scored over 1800 on combined SAT, 59% scored over 26 on composite ACT.
Student Life Upper grades have student council, honor system. Discipline rests equally with students and faculty.
Summer Programs Enrichment, sports, art/fine arts programs offered; held both on and off campus; held at outdoor trips to various national and international locations; accepts boys and girls; open to students from other schools. 100 students usually enrolled. 2013 schedule: June 24 to August 9.
Tuition and Aid Day student tuition: $27,156. Tuition installment plan (Academic Management Services Plan, monthly payment plans). Need-based scholarship grants available. In 2012–13, 20% of upper-school students received aid.
Admissions Traditional secondary-level entrance grade is 9. ISEE required. Deadline for receipt of application materials: January 15. Application fee required: $100. Interview required.
Athletics Interscholastic: basketball (boys, girls), cross-country running (b,g), golf (b,g), soccer (b,g), tennis (b,g), track and field (b,g), ultimate Frisbee (b,g), volleyball (g); coed interscholastic: dance, dance squad, dance team, Frisbee; coed intramural: bowling, in-line skating, outdoor activities, paint ball, roller blading, roller skating, skateboarding, skiing (cross-country), skiing (downhill), snowboarding, squash. 5 PE instructors, 30 coaches, 2 athletic trainers.
Computers Computers are regularly used in all academic, computer applications, English, foreign language, graphic design, history, mathematics, newspaper, science, speech, study skills, theater arts, video film production, Web site design, yearbook classes. Computer network features include on-campus library services, online commercial services, Internet access, wireless campus network, Internet filtering or

blocking technology. Student e-mail accounts are available to students. Students grades are available online. The school has a published electronic and media policy.

Contact Jim Rupp, Admission Director. 206-324-7227. Fax: 206-323-6618. E-mail: jrupp@seattleacademy.org. Web site: www.seattleacademy.org

SEATTLE CHRISTIAN SCHOOLS

18301 Military Road South
Seattle, Washington 98188

Head of School: Ms. Gloria Hunter

General Information Coeducational day college-preparatory, general academic, and religious studies school, affiliated with Christian faith. Grades K–12. Founded: 1946. Setting: suburban. 13-acre campus. 1 building on campus. Approved or accredited by Association of Christian Schools International, Northwest Accreditation Commission, and Washington Department of Education. Endowment: $987,200. Total enrollment: 538. Upper school average class size: 17. Upper school faculty-student ratio: 1:10. There are 180 required school days per year for Upper School students. Upper School students typically attend 5 days per week. The average school day consists of 7 hours.

Upper School Student Profile Grade 9: 59 students (29 boys, 30 girls); Grade 10: 45 students (24 boys, 21 girls); Grade 11: 51 students (25 boys, 26 girls); Grade 12: 58 students (31 boys, 27 girls). 100% of students are Christian faith.

Faculty School total: 21. In upper school: 11 men, 10 women; 16 have advanced degrees.

Subjects Offered Algebra, American literature, anatomy and physiology, art, band, Bible, biology, business mathematics, calculus, calculus-AP, chemistry, Christian education, Christian studies, civics, desktop publishing, English-AP, ensembles, geometry, Greek, health, language arts, Latin, Life of Christ, math analysis, multimedia, music, Pacific Northwest seminar, physical education, physics, physics-AP, psychology, Spanish, theater arts, U.S. history, U.S. history-AP, weight training, world history, world literature, yearbook.

Graduation Requirements Algebra, arts and fine arts (art, music, dance, drama), Bible, biology, chemistry, civics, foreign language, geometry, language arts, Life of Christ, mathematics, occupational education, Pacific Northwest seminar, physical education (includes health), physics, science, U.S. history, world history, UTT-Understanding the Times, Acts and Paul and Life of Christ, Bible Survey.

Special Academic Programs 4 Advanced Placement exams for which test preparation is offered; honors section; study at local college for college credit; remedial reading and/or remedial writing; programs in English for dyslexic students.

College Admission Counseling 50 students graduated in 2011; all went to college, including Bellevue College; Biola University; Green River Community College; Highline Community College; Seattle Pacific University; South Seattle Community College. Median SAT critical reading: 540, median SAT math: 510, median SAT writing: 530, median combined SAT: 1580, median composite ACT: 24. 17% scored over 600 on SAT critical reading, 23% scored over 600 on SAT math, 27% scored over 600 on SAT writing, 22% scored over 1800 on combined SAT, 48% scored over 26 on composite ACT.

Student Life Upper grades have specified standards of dress, student council, honor system. Discipline rests primarily with faculty. Attendance at religious services is required.

Tuition and Aid Day student tuition: $9180. Tuition installment plan (FACTS Tuition Payment Plan, monthly payment plans). Tuition reduction for siblings, need-based scholarship grants available. In 2011–12, 47% of upper-school students received aid. Total amount of financial aid awarded in 2011–12: $110,098.

Admissions Traditional secondary-level entrance grade is 9. For fall 2011, 16 students applied for upper-level admission, 14 were accepted, 13 enrolled. Stanford Achievement Test or WRAT required. Deadline for receipt of application materials: none. Application fee required: $75. On-campus interview required.

Athletics Interscholastic: baseball (boys), basketball (b,g), cheering (g), cross-country running (b,g), golf (b,g), soccer (b,g), softball (g), track and field (b,g), volleyball (g); coed interscholastic: cross-country running, track and field; coed intramural: archery, badminton, baseball, basketball, field hockey, fitness, floor hockey, juggling, lacrosse, softball, strength & conditioning, touch football, weight training. 1 PE instructor.

Computers Computers are regularly used in art, library, mathematics, multimedia, reading, science, social studies, Web site design, yearbook classes. Computer network features include on-campus library services, Internet access, Internet filtering or blocking technology, accelerated reading and math program. Computer access in designated common areas is available to students. Students grades are available online. The school has a published electronic and media policy.

Contact Fran Hubeek, Admissions Coordinator. 206-246-8241 Ext. 1301. Fax: 206-246-9066. E-mail: admissions@seattlechristian.org. Web site: www.seattlechristian.org

SEISEN INTERNATIONAL SCHOOL

12-15 Yoga 1-chome, Setagaya-ku
Tokyo 158-0097, Japan

Head of School: Sr. Margaret Scott

General Information Coeducational day (boys' only in lower grades) college-preparatory school, affiliated with Roman Catholic Church. Boys grade K, girls grades K–12. Founded: 1962. Setting: urban. 1-hectare campus. 3 buildings on campus. Approved or accredited by Council of International Schools, Department of Defense Dependents Schools, International Baccalaureate Organization, Ministry of Education, Japan, National Catholic Education Association, and New England Association of Schools and Colleges. Member of Secondary School Admission Test Board. Language of instruction: English. Total enrollment: 613. Upper school average class size: 19. Upper school faculty-student ratio: 1:7. There are 176 required school days per year for Upper School students. Upper School students typically attend 5 days per week. The average school day consists of 6 hours.

Upper School Student Profile Grade 9: 61 students (61 girls); Grade 10: 42 students (42 girls); Grade 11: 36 students (36 girls); Grade 12: 32 students (32 girls). 20% of students are Roman Catholic.

Faculty School total: 84. In upper school: 12 men, 37 women; 29 have advanced degrees.

Subjects Offered 3-dimensional art, advanced math, art, bell choir, biology, business, career planning, chemistry, choir, college planning, computer graphics, computers, Danish, drama, English, environmental studies, ESL, French, geography, geometry, health education, history, honors algebra, honors geometry, information technology, International Baccalaureate courses, Japanese, journalism, Korean, library, math methods, mathematics, model United Nations, music, music composition, music performance, painting, performing arts, personal and social education, physical education, physics, pottery, psychology, religion, science, social sciences, social studies, Spanish, speech, theory of knowledge, trigonometry, visual arts, world history, yearbook.

Graduation Requirements Electives, English, foreign language, mathematics, physical education (includes health), religion (includes Bible studies and theology), science, social studies (includes history).

Special Academic Programs International Baccalaureate program; honors section; independent study; remedial reading and/or remedial writing; remedial math; ESL (11 students enrolled).

College Admission Counseling 40 students graduated in 2012; all went to college, including Nagoya University, Japan; Oberlin College; Sophia University, Japan; University of British Columbia, Canada; University of Sussex, UK; and Waseda University, Japan. Median SAT critical reading: 520, median SAT math: 590, median SAT writing: 550, median combined SAT: 1670. 13% scored over 600 on SAT critical reading, 48% scored over 600 on SAT math, 26% scored over 600 on SAT writing, 26% scored over 1800 on combined SAT.

Student Life Upper grades have uniform requirement, student council, honor system. Discipline rests primarily with faculty.

Summer Programs Remediation, ESL programs offered; session focuses on high school remedial work only; held on campus; accepts girls; not open to students from other schools. 8 students usually enrolled. 2013 schedule: June 10 to June 28. Application deadline: May 1.

Tuition and Aid Day student tuition: ¥1,940,000. Tuition installment plan (monthly payment plans, individually arranged payment plans). Tuition reduction for siblings, need-based scholarship grants available. In 2012–13, 2% of upper-school students received aid. Total amount of financial aid awarded in 2012–13: ¥1,990,000.

Admissions Traditional secondary-level entrance grade is 9. For fall 2012, 24 students applied for upper-level admission, 19 were accepted, 18 enrolled. Admissions testing, mathematics proficiency exam, Reading for Understanding or writing sample required. Deadline for receipt of application materials: none. Application fee required: ¥20,000. On-campus interview required.

Athletics Interscholastic: basketball, cross-country running, running, soccer, swimming and diving, tennis, track and field, volleyball; intramural: badminton, outdoor activities, running, soccer, table tennis, tennis, winter soccer. 2 PE instructors.

Computers Computers are regularly used in art, business studies, career education, college planning, English, foreign language, graphic design, history, information technology, journalism, mathematics, music, psychology, science, study skills, writing, yearbook classes. Computer network features include on-campus library services, online commercial services, Internet access, wireless campus network, Internet filtering or blocking technology. Campus intranet and computer access in designated common areas are available to students.

Contact Sr. Margaret Scott, School Head. 81-3-3704-2661. Fax: 81-3-3701-1033. E-mail: sisinfo@seisen.com. Web site: www.seisen.com

SETON CATHOLIC CENTRAL HIGH SCHOOL

70 Seminary Avenue
Binghamton, New York 13905

Head of School: Mr. Richard Bucci

General Information Coeducational day college-preparatory, arts, business, vocational, religious studies, technology, and cybersecurity school, affiliated with

Roman Catholic Church. Grades 7–12. Founded: 1963. Setting: suburban. Nearest major city is Syracuse. 4-acre campus. 1 building on campus. Approved or accredited by Middle States Association of Colleges and Schools, National Catholic Education Association, New York State Board of Regents, The College Board, and New York Department of Education. Total enrollment: 380. Upper school average class size: 23. Upper school faculty-student ratio: 1:23. There are 200 required school days per year for Upper School students. Upper School students typically attend 5 days per week. The average school day consists of 6 hours and 45 minutes.

Upper School Student Profile 90% of students are Roman Catholic.

Faculty School total: 43. In upper school: 16 men, 19 women; 27 have advanced degrees.

Subjects Offered 3-dimensional design, accounting, advanced computer applications, Advanced Placement courses, advertising design, algebra, alternative physical education, American government, American history-AP, American legal systems, American literature, American literature-AP, ancient world history, applied music, architectural drawing, art-AP, band, Bible, biology, biology-AP, business, business law, business mathematics, calculus, calculus-AP, chemistry, chemistry-AP, chorus, Christian scripture, church history, comparative religion, computer applications, computer programming, computer programming-AP, creative drama, criminal justice, dramatic arts, economics, English, English language and composition-AP, English literature and composition-AP, entrepreneurship, environmental science, ethical decision making, ethics and responsibility, European history-AP, food and nutrition, foreign language, forensics, French, government/civics, guitar, health, honors English, honors geometry, instrumental music, integrated mathematics, keyboarding, Latin, Latin-AP, law and the legal system, literature and composition-AP, math applications, mathematics-AP, music theater, music theory, performing arts, photography, physical education, physics, physics-AP, pre-algebra, religion, social psychology, Spanish, Spanish-AP, studio art-AP, theater arts, theology, U.S. history, U.S. history-AP, wood processing, work-study, world history-AP, world religions.

Graduation Requirements Arts and fine arts (art, music, dance, drama), English, foreign language, mathematics, physical education (includes health), science, social studies (includes history), theology.

Special Academic Programs 18 Advanced Placement exams for which test preparation is offered; honors section; study at local college for college credit; academic accommodation for the gifted and the artistically talented; remedial reading and/or remedial writing; remedial math.

College Admission Counseling 82 students graduated in 2011; all went to college, including Binghamton University, State University of New York; Le Moyne College; Marywood University; The University of Scranton; Villanova University. Mean SAT critical reading: 561, mean SAT math: 587, mean SAT writing: 561.

Student Life Upper grades have specified standards of dress, student council, honor system. Discipline rests primarily with faculty.

Tuition and Aid Tuition installment plan (monthly payment plans). Tuition reduction for siblings, merit scholarship grants, need-based scholarship grants available. In 2011–12, 40% of upper-school students received aid. Total amount of financial aid awarded in 2011–12: $200,000.

Admissions Traditional secondary-level entrance grade is 7. Deadline for receipt of application materials: none. Application fee required: $100. Interview required.

Athletics Interscholastic: baseball (boys), basketball (b,g), cross-country running (b,g), field hockey (g), football (b), ice hockey (b), indoor track & field (b,g), lacrosse (b,g), soccer (b,g), softball (g), swimming and diving (b,g), tennis (b,g), track and field (b,g), winter (indoor) track (b,g); intramural: snowboarding (b,g), strength & conditioning (b,g), weight training (b,g); coed interscholastic: cheering, golf; coed intramural: alpine skiing. 2 PE instructors, 25 coaches, 1 athletic trainer.

Computers Computers are regularly used in business applications, computer applications, desktop publishing, economics, English, foreign language, history, keyboarding, Latin, mathematics, science, social studies, Spanish, technology, yearbook classes. Computer network features include on-campus library services, online commercial services, Internet access, wireless campus network, Internet filtering or blocking technology. Computer access in designated common areas is available to students. The school has a published electronic and media policy.

Contact Guidance Office. 607-723-5307. Fax: 607-723-4811. E-mail: secathb@syrdiocese.org. Web site: www.setoncchs.com

SETON CATHOLIC HIGH SCHOOL

1150 North Dobson Road
Chandler, Arizona 85224

Head of School: Patricia L. Collins

General Information Coeducational day college-preparatory, arts, religious studies, technology, and dual enrollment with Seton Hill Univ. in specific classes school, affiliated with Roman Catholic Church. Grades 9–12. Founded: 1954. Setting: suburban. Nearest major city is Phoenix. 30-acre campus. 11 buildings on campus. Approved or accredited by North Central Association of Colleges and Schools, Western Catholic Education Association, and Arizona Department of Education. Endowment: $342,000. Total enrollment: 553. Upper school average class size: 22. Upper school faculty-student ratio: 1:13. There are 182 required school days per year for Upper School students. Upper School students typically attend 5 days per week. The average school day consists of 5 hours and 30 minutes.

Upper School Student Profile Grade 9: 145 students (69 boys, 76 girls); Grade 10: 158 students (82 boys, 76 girls); Grade 11: 113 students (60 boys, 53 girls); Grade 12: 110 students (54 boys, 56 girls). 95% of students are Roman Catholic.

Faculty School total: 42. In upper school: 19 men, 23 women; 29 have advanced degrees.

Subjects Offered Aerobics, algebra, American government, American history, anatomy, art, athletic training, Basic programming, biology, biology-AP, calculus, chemistry, chemistry-AP, choir, Christian and Hebrew scripture, Christian scripture, church history, computer applications, dance, drama, drawing, economics, English, English-AP, European history-AP, fitness, foreign language, French, geometry, government, guitar, health, honors English, honors geometry, honors U.S. history, keyboarding, Latin, Latin-AP, personal fitness, photography, physics, pre-calculus, psychology, reading/study skills, religion, scripture, social justice, Spanish, Spanish-AP, study skills, television, theology, U.S. government, U.S. history, video film production, weight training, world history, world religions, yearbook.

Graduation Requirements Arts and fine arts (art, music, dance, drama), computer applications, computer literacy, English, foreign language, mathematics, physical education (includes health), religion (includes Bible studies and theology), science, social studies (includes history), study skills.

Special Academic Programs 11 Advanced Placement exams for which test preparation is offered; honors section.

College Admission Counseling 123 students graduated in 2011; 122 went to college, including Arizona State University; Northern Arizona University; The University of Arizona. Other: 1 had other specific plans. Mean SAT critical reading: 565, mean SAT math: 572, mean SAT writing: 543, mean composite ACT: 24. 26% scored over 600 on SAT critical reading, 31% scored over 600 on SAT math, 20% scored over 600 on SAT writing.

Student Life Upper grades have uniform requirement, student council, honor system. Discipline rests primarily with faculty. Attendance at religious services is required.

Tuition and Aid Day student tuition: $11,880. Tuition installment plan (FACTS Tuition Payment Plan, monthly payment plans). Merit scholarship grants, need-based scholarship grants, Catholic Tuition Organization of Diocese of Phoenix available. In 2011–12, 34% of upper-school students received aid; total upper-school merit-scholarship money awarded: $44,000. Total amount of financial aid awarded in 2011–12: $705,000.

Admissions Traditional secondary-level entrance grade is 9. For fall 2011, 249 students applied for upper-level admission, 185 were accepted, 164 enrolled. Catholic High School Entrance Examination or Scholastic Testing Service High School Placement Test required. Deadline for receipt of application materials: January 31. Application fee required: $75. Interview required.

Athletics Interscholastic: baseball (boys), basketball (b,g), cheering (g), cross-country running (b,g), dance squad (g), danceline (g), diving (b,g), football (b), golf (b,g), soccer (b,g), swimming and diving (b,g), tennis (b,g), track and field (b,g), volleyball (b,g), wrestling (b); coed interscholastic: aerobics/dance, dance, dance team, football, physical fitness, strength & conditioning, weight training. 2 PE instructors, 1 athletic trainer.

Computers Computers are regularly used in all academic, religious studies, yearbook classes. Computer network features include on-campus library services, Internet access, wireless campus network, Internet filtering or blocking technology, Turnitin®. Campus intranet and student e-mail accounts are available to students. Students grades are available online. The school has a published electronic and media policy.

Contact Mr. Chris Moore, Director of Admissions. 480-963-1900 Ext. 2008. Fax: 480-963-1974. E-mail: cmoore@setonchs.org. Web site: www.setoncatholic.org

THE SEVEN HILLS SCHOOL

5400 Red Bank Road
Cincinnati, Ohio 45227

Head of School: Mr. Christopher P. Garten

General Information Coeducational day college-preparatory, arts, and technology school. Grades PK–12. Founded: 1974. Setting: suburban. 35-acre campus. 16 buildings on campus. Approved or accredited by Ohio Department of Education. Member of National Association of Independent Schools and Secondary School Admission Test Board. Endowment: $19.2 million. Total enrollment: 1,011. Upper school average class size: 15. Upper school faculty-student ratio: 1:9. There are 178 required school days per year for Upper School students. Upper School students typically attend 5 days per week. The average school day consists of 7 hours and 5 minutes.

Upper School Student Profile Grade 9: 79 students (37 boys, 42 girls); Grade 10: 81 students (46 boys, 35 girls); Grade 11: 62 students (31 boys, 31 girls); Grade 12: 83 students (38 boys, 45 girls).

Faculty School total: 128. In upper school: 20 men, 25 women; 40 have advanced degrees.

Subjects Offered Acting, advanced computer applications, Advanced Placement courses, algebra, American history, American literature, ancient history, art, art history, biology, British literature, calculus, ceramics, chemistry, computer programming, computer science, economics, English, European history, fine arts, French, geometry, journalism, Latin, linear algebra, Mandarin, medieval/Renaissance history, modern political theory, music, physical education, physics, pre-calculus, psychology, Spanish, speech, theater, world history, world literature, writing.

Graduation Requirements Algebra, arts and fine arts (art, music, dance, drama), biology, chemistry, computer science, English, foreign language, geometry, performing arts, physical education (includes health), physics, U.S. history, U.S. literature, completion of a personal challenge project, successfully pass writing competency exam, 30 hours of community service.

Special Academic Programs 16 Advanced Placement exams for which test preparation is offered; honors section; independent study; term-away projects; study abroad; academic accommodation for the gifted.

College Admission Counseling 61 students graduated in 2012; all went to college, including Duke University; Massachusetts Institute of Technology; Miami University; Northwestern University; Tufts University; Washington University in St. Louis. Median SAT critical reading: 661, median SAT math: 663, median SAT writing: 666, median composite ACT: 29. 74% scored over 600 on SAT critical reading, 87% scored over 600 on SAT math, 84% scored over 600 on SAT writing.

Student Life Upper grades have specified standards of dress, student council. Discipline rests primarily with faculty.

Summer Programs Enrichment programs offered; session focuses on SAT review, sports clinics, and acting workshop; held on campus; accepts boys and girls; open to students from other schools. 400 students usually enrolled. 2013 schedule: June 14 to August 10. Application deadline: none.

Tuition and Aid Day student tuition: $20,459–$20,988. Tuition installment plan (monthly payment plans, individually arranged payment plans). Merit scholarship grants, need-based scholarship grants available. In 2012–13, 17% of upper-school students received aid; total upper-school merit-scholarship money awarded: $157,900. Total amount of financial aid awarded in 2012–13: $530,000.

Admissions Traditional secondary-level entrance grade is 9. For fall 2012, 72 students applied for upper-level admission, 54 were accepted, 38 enrolled. ISEE required. Deadline for receipt of application materials: December 2. Application fee required: $50. On-campus interview required.

Athletics Interscholastic: baseball (boys), basketball (b,g), cheering (g), cross-country running (b,g), golf (b), gymnastics (g), lacrosse (b,g), soccer (b,g), softball (g), swimming and diving (b,g), tennis (b,g), volleyball (g); coed interscholastic: track and field. 3 PE instructors, 9 coaches.

Computers Computers are regularly used in foreign language, mathematics, science classes. Computer network features include on-campus library services, online commercial services, Internet access, wireless campus network, Internet filtering or blocking technology. Computer access in designated common areas is available to students. Students grades are available online.

Contact Mrs. Janet S. Hill, Director of Admission and Financial Aid. 513-728-2405. Fax: 513-728-2409. E-mail: janet.hill@7hills.org. Web site: www.7hills.org

SEVERN SCHOOL

201 Water Street
Severna Park, Maryland 21146

Head of School: Douglas H. Lagarde

General Information Coeducational day college-preparatory, arts, and technology school. Grades 6–12. Founded: 1914. Setting: suburban. Nearest major city is Annapolis. 19-acre campus. 8 buildings on campus. Approved or accredited by Association of Independent Maryland Schools, Middle States Association of Colleges and Schools, and Maryland Department of Education. Member of National Association of Independent Schools and Secondary School Admission Test Board. Endowment: $6 million. Total enrollment: 582. Upper school average class size: 15. Upper school faculty-student ratio: 1:8. There are 175 required school days per year for Upper School students. Upper School students typically attend 5 days per week. The average school day consists of 6 hours and 35 minutes.

Upper School Student Profile Grade 9: 99 students (43 boys, 56 girls); Grade 10: 105 students (47 boys, 58 girls); Grade 11: 94 students (51 boys, 43 girls); Grade 12: 89 students (48 boys, 41 girls).

Faculty School total: 81. In upper school: 27 men, 30 women; 38 have advanced degrees.

Subjects Offered Algebra, American history, American literature, art, biology, calculus, ceramics, chemistry, community service, computer programming, computer science, CPR, creative writing, dance, desktop publishing, digital art, digital imaging, digital photography, discrete mathematics, drama, drama performance, dramatic arts, drawing, drawing and design, earth science, ecology, economics, economics-AP, English, English literature, environmental science, environmental systems, European civilization, European history, European history-AP, expository writing, fine arts, forensics, French, French language-AP, French literature-AP, geometry, government/civics, grammar, graphic arts, health, history, journalism, Latin, marine biology, mathematics, multimedia, music, photography, physical education, physics, psychology, science, social studies, Spanish, speech, theater, trigonometry, world history, world literature, writing.

Graduation Requirements Arts and fine arts (art, music, dance, drama), computer science, CPR, English, foreign language, mathematics, physical education (includes health), science, social studies (includes history). Community service is required.

Special Academic Programs Advanced Placement exam preparation; honors section; independent study; study abroad; academic accommodation for the gifted, the musically talented, and the artistically talented.

College Admission Counseling 100 students graduated in 2012; all went to college, including Boston University; Elon University; The George Washington University; The Johns Hopkins University; The University of Alabama; University of Maryland, College Park. Median SAT critical reading: 600, median SAT math: 630, median SAT writing: 620, median combined SAT: 1860, median composite ACT: 26. 47% scored over 600 on SAT critical reading, 56% scored over 600 on SAT math, 55% scored over 600 on SAT writing, 58% scored over 1800 on combined SAT, 47% scored over 26 on composite ACT.

Student Life Upper grades have uniform requirement, student council, honor system. Discipline rests primarily with faculty.

Summer Programs Remediation, enrichment, advancement, sports, art/fine arts, computer instruction programs offered; session focuses on advanced math, day camp, and sports camps; held both on and off campus; held at SPY swimming pool; accepts boys and girls; open to students from other schools. 250 students usually enrolled. 2013 schedule: June 23 to August 1.

Tuition and Aid Day student tuition: $22,150. Tuition installment plan (Academic Management Services Plan). Need-based scholarship grants available. In 2012–13, 24% of upper-school students received aid. Total amount of financial aid awarded in 2012–13: $1,115,305.

Admissions Traditional secondary-level entrance grade is 9. For fall 2012, 105 students applied for upper-level admission, 55 were accepted, 44 enrolled. ISEE required. Deadline for receipt of application materials: January 20. Application fee required: $55. On-campus interview required.

Athletics Interscholastic: baseball (boys), basketball (b,g), combined training (b,g), dance team (g), field hockey (g), football (b), lacrosse (b,g), soccer (b,g), tennis (b,g), wrestling (b); coed interscholastic: cross-country running, dance, diving, fitness, golf, outdoor education, physical fitness, sailing, strength & conditioning, swimming and diving, track and field, weight training; coed intramural: aerobics/dance, ice hockey, outdoor adventure, paint ball, table tennis. 4 PE instructors, 56 coaches, 2 athletic trainers.

Computers Computers are regularly used in all academic classes. Computer network features include on-campus library services, online commercial services, Internet access, Internet filtering or blocking technology. Campus intranet, student e-mail accounts, and computer access in designated common areas are available to students. Students grades are available online. The school has a published electronic and media policy.

Contact Ellen Murray, Associate Director of Admissions. 410-647-7701 Ext. 2266. Fax: 410-544-9451. E-mail: e.murray@severnschool.com. Web site: www.severnschool.com

SEWICKLEY ACADEMY

315 Academy Avenue
Sewickley, Pennsylvania 15143

Head of School: Mr. Kolia J. O'Connor

General Information Coeducational day college-preparatory, arts, and technology school. Grades PK–12. Founded: 1838. Setting: suburban. Nearest major city is Pittsburgh. 30-acre campus. 10 buildings on campus. Approved or accredited by National Independent Private Schools Association and Pennsylvania Department of Education. Member of National Association of Independent Schools and Secondary School Admission Test Board. Endowment: $27.8 million. Total enrollment: 702. Upper school average class size: 15. Upper school faculty-student ratio: 1:7. There are 167 required school days per year for Upper School students. Upper School students typically attend 5 days per week. The average school day consists of 7 hours.

Upper School Student Profile Grade 9: 75 students (38 boys, 37 girls); Grade 10: 81 students (36 boys, 45 girls); Grade 11: 63 students (25 boys, 38 girls); Grade 12: 75 students (39 boys, 36 girls).

Faculty School total: 106. In upper school: 28 men, 28 women; 32 have advanced degrees.

Subjects Offered Advanced chemistry, advanced studio art-AP, African studies, algebra, American history, American history-AP, American literature, American literature-AP, art, art-AP, astronomy, band, biology, biology-AP, calculus, calculus-AP, ceramics, chemistry, chemistry-AP, choral music, chorus, clayworking, computer applications, computer art, computer programming, computer science, computer science-AP, concert band, concert choir, contemporary issues, creative writing, dance, dance performance, digital art, drama, drama performance, drama workshop, drawing, driver education, economics, English, English literature, environmental science, ethics, European history, European history-AP, expository writing, fine arts, French, French language-AP, French literature-AP, geometry, German, German-AP, government/civics, health, health education, history, Italian, keyboarding, Mandarin, music, musical theater, performing arts, photography, physical education, physics, physics-AP, pre-calculus, psychology, psychology-AP, senior project, Spanish, Spanish literature, Spanish-AP, speech and debate, statistics, statistics-AP, studio art, theater, trigonometry, U.S. history-AP, U.S. literature, Vietnam War, world history, world literature, writing.

Graduation Requirements Arts and fine arts (art, music, dance, drama), English, foreign language, health education, mathematics, physical education (includes health), science, social studies (includes history), U.S. history, world cultures, world studies. Community service is required.

Special Academic Programs Advanced Placement exam preparation; honors section; independent study; term-away projects; study at local college for college credit; study abroad.

College Admission Counseling 75 students graduated in 2011; all went to college, including Boston University; Bucknell University; Colgate University; Dartmouth College; Emory University; Princeton University.

Student Life Upper grades have specified standards of dress, student council, honor system. Discipline rests equally with students and faculty.

Tuition and Aid Day student tuition: $22,025. Tuition installment plan (monthly payment plans). Need-based scholarship grants available. In 2011–12, 20% of upper-school students received aid. Total amount of financial aid awarded in 2011–12: $600,000.

Admissions Traditional secondary-level entrance grade is 9. For fall 2011, 66 students applied for upper-level admission, 43 were accepted, 26 enrolled. ISEE or SSAT required. Deadline for receipt of application materials: February 8. Application fee required: $50. Interview required.

Athletics Interscholastic: baseball (boys), basketball (b,g), cross-country running (b,g), golf (b,g), ice hockey (b), lacrosse (b,g), physical fitness (b,g), soccer (b,g), softball (g), tennis (b,g); coed interscholastic: bowling, diving, field hockey, physical fitness, swimming and diving, track and field. 5 PE instructors, 5 coaches, 1 athletic trainer.

Computers Computers are regularly used in all academic classes. Computer network features include on-campus library services, online commercial services, Internet access, wireless campus network, Internet filtering or blocking technology. Campus intranet, student e-mail accounts, and computer access in designated common areas are available to students. The school has a published electronic and media policy.

Contact Ms. Wendy Berns, Admission Assistant. 412-741-2235. Fax: 412-741-1411. E-mail: wberns@sewickley.org. Web site: www.sewickley.org

SHADY SIDE ACADEMY

423 Fox Chapel Road
Pittsburgh, Pennsylvania 15238

Head of School: Mr. Thomas Cangiano

General Information Coeducational boarding and day college-preparatory school. Boarding grades 9–12, day grades PK–12. Founded: 1883. Setting: suburban. Students are housed in single-sex dormitories. 130-acre campus. 26 buildings on campus. Approved or accredited by Middle States Association of Colleges and Schools, Pennsylvania Association of Independent Schools, The Association of Boarding Schools, and Pennsylvania Department of Education. Member of National Association of Independent Schools. Endowment: $46.2 million. Total enrollment: 931. Upper school average class size: 13. Upper school faculty-student ratio: 1:8. There are 172 required school days per year for Upper School students. Upper School students typically attend 5 days per week.

Upper School Student Profile Grade 9: 126 students (71 boys, 55 girls); Grade 10: 116 students (61 boys, 55 girls); Grade 11: 130 students (64 boys, 66 girls); Grade 12: 117 students (68 boys, 49 girls). 11% of students are boarding students. 97% are state residents. 8 states are represented in upper school student body.

Faculty School total: 117. In upper school: 28 men, 29 women; 36 have advanced degrees; 19 reside on campus.

Subjects Offered 3-dimensional art, advanced biology, advanced chemistry, advanced computer applications, advanced math, Advanced Placement courses, algebra, American history, American literature, architectural drawing, architecture, art, art history, band, biology, calculus, calculus-AP, ceramics, chemistry, Chinese, Chinese history, choir, college counseling, computer graphics, computer math, computer programming, computer science, computer science-AP, concert band, creative writing, drama, economics, English, English literature, environmental science, ethics, European history, expository writing, film and literature, fine arts, fractal geometry, French, French-AP, gender issues, geography, geometry, German, German-AP, health, history, introduction to theater, jazz ensemble, Latin, linear algebra, logic, mathematics, music, music technology, musical theater, philosophy, photography, physical education, physics, pre-calculus, probability and statistics, religion and culture, science, senior project, social studies, Spanish, Spanish-AP, speech, statistics, studio art, technical theater, theater arts, trigonometry, world history, world literature, writing.

Graduation Requirements Art, athletics, computer science, English, foreign language, history, mathematics, physical education (includes health), science, participation in five seasons of athletics.

Special Academic Programs 6 Advanced Placement exams for which test preparation is offered; honors section; accelerated programs; independent study; term-away projects; study at local college for college credit; study abroad; academic accommodation for the gifted, the musically talented, and the artistically talented.

College Admission Counseling 128 students graduated in 2012; 125 went to college, including Carnegie Mellon University; Northwestern University; Penn State University Park; University of Pennsylvania; University of Pittsburgh; Villanova University. Other: 1 entered military service, 2 had other specific plans. Median SAT critical reading: 620, median SAT math: 640, median SAT writing: 640, median combined SAT: 1890, median composite ACT: 26. 56% scored over 600 on SAT critical reading, 73% scored over 600 on SAT math, 63% scored over 600 on SAT writing, 60% scored over 1800 on combined SAT, 56% scored over 26 on composite ACT.

Student Life Upper grades have specified standards of dress, student council. Discipline rests primarily with faculty.

Summer Programs Remediation, enrichment, advancement, sports, art/fine arts, computer instruction programs offered; session focuses on academic and non-academic enrichment; held on campus; accepts boys and girls; open to students from other schools. 1,150 students usually enrolled. 2013 schedule: June 10 to August 16. Application deadline: none.

Tuition and Aid Day student tuition: $27,000; 5-day tuition and room/board: $37,900. Tuition installment plan (monthly payment plans, Tuition Refund Plan available through Dewar's). Tuition reduction for siblings, merit scholarship grants, need-based scholarship grants, merit-based scholarships are for boarding students, FAME awards (Fund for the Advancement of Minorities Through Education), partial tuition remission for children of full-time employees available. In 2012–13, 23% of upper-school students received aid; total upper-school merit-scholarship money awarded: $50,000. Total amount of financial aid awarded in 2012–13: $2,030,930.

Admissions Traditional secondary-level entrance grade is 9. For fall 2012, 131 students applied for upper-level admission, 102 were accepted, 64 enrolled. ISEE, SSAT or TOEFL required. Deadline for receipt of application materials: February 4. Application fee required: $50. On-campus interview required.

Athletics Interscholastic: baseball (boys), basketball (b,g), crew (g), cross-country running (b,g), field hockey (g), football (b), golf (b,g), ice hockey (b,g), lacrosse (b,g), soccer (b,g), softball (g), squash (b,g), swimming and diving (b,g), tennis (b,g), track and field (b,g), wrestling (b); intramural: cheering (g), volleyball (g); coed interscholastic: ultimate Frisbee; coed intramural: aerobics/dance, backpacking, badminton, bowling, cricket, ultimate Frisbee, weight lifting. 1 PE instructor, 47 coaches, 2 athletic trainers.

Computers Computers are regularly used in all classes. Computer network features include on-campus library services, online commercial services, Internet access, wireless campus network, Internet filtering or blocking technology, report cards are available online four times a year. Student e-mail accounts and computer access in designated common areas are available to students. The school has a published electronic and media policy.

Contact Ms. Katherine H. Mihm, Director of Enrollment Management and Marketing. 412-968-3179. Fax: 412-968-3213. E-mail: kmihm@shadysideacademy.org. Web site: www.shadysideacademy.org

SHATTUCK-ST. MARY'S SCHOOL

1000 Shumway Avenue
PO Box 218
Faribault, Minnesota 55021

Head of School: Kathy Layendecker

General Information Coeducational boarding and day college-preparatory, arts, and BioScience, STEM Education school, affiliated with Episcopal Church. Grades 6–PG. Founded: 1858. Setting: small town. Nearest major city is Minneapolis/St. Paul. Students are housed in single-sex dormitories. 250-acre campus. 10 buildings on campus. Approved or accredited by Independent Schools Association of the Central States, Midwest Association of Boarding Schools, National Association of Episcopal Schools, The Association of Boarding Schools, and Minnesota Department of Education. Member of National Association of Independent Schools and Secondary School Admission Test Board. Total enrollment: 438. Upper school average class size: 11. Upper school faculty-student ratio: 1:9. There are 167 required school days per year for Upper School students. The average school day consists of 7 hours.

Upper School Student Profile Grade 9: 63 students (41 boys, 22 girls); Grade 10: 102 students (69 boys, 33 girls); Grade 11: 124 students (74 boys, 50 girls); Grade 12: 105 students (60 boys, 45 girls); Postgraduate: 4 students (1 boy, 3 girls). 75% of students are boarding students. 25% are state residents. 44 states are represented in upper school student body. 32% are international students. International students from Canada, China, Japan, Republic of Korea, Sweden, and Taiwan; 31 other countries represented in student body.

Faculty School total: 80. In upper school: 25 men, 30 women; 42 have advanced degrees; 60 reside on campus.

Subjects Offered 20th century world history, Advanced Placement courses, advanced studio art-AP, advanced TOEFL/grammar, algebra, American Civil War, American history, American history-AP, American literature, American sign language, anatomy and physiology, art, art history, astronomy, ballet, band, Bible studies, bioethics, biology, British literature, calculus, calculus-AP, ceramics, chamber groups, chemistry, chemistry-AP, choir, choral music, community service, composition, dance, digital photography, drama, drawing, economics, English, English language and composition-AP, English literature, English literature and composition-AP, environmental science-AP, ESL, ethics, European civilization, European history, European history-AP, expository writing, field ecology, film studies, fine arts, French, French language-AP, geography, geometry, government/civics, grammar, Greek, high adventure outdoor program, history, human anatomy, Latin, Latin American history, Mandarin, mathematics, microbiology, Middle Eastern history, music, Native American history, oil painting, orchestra, painting, physics, physics-AP, piano, pottery, pre-algebra, pre-calculus, psychology, psychology-AP, public speaking, religion, robotics, Roman civilization, science, social studies, South African history, Spanish, Spanish-AP, speech, statistics, statistics-AP, theater, trigonometry, U.S. history-AP, world geography, world history, world history-AP, writing.

Graduation Requirements Arts and fine arts (art, music, dance, drama), English, foreign language, mathematics, religion (includes Bible studies and theology), science, social studies (includes history), 20 hours of community service per year.

Special Academic Programs 14 Advanced Placement exams for which test preparation is offered; honors section; independent study; academic accommodation for the gifted and the musically talented; remedial reading and/or remedial writing; remedial math; programs in English, mathematics, general development for dyslexic students; ESL (85 students enrolled).

College Admission Counseling 104 students graduated in 2012; 100 went to college, including Butler University; Cornell University; University of Illinois at Urbana–Champaign; University of Minnesota, Twin Cities Campus; University of Rochester; University of Wisconsin–Madison. Other: 2 entered a postgraduate year, 2 had other specific plans.

Student Life Upper grades have specified standards of dress, student council. Discipline rests primarily with faculty. Attendance at religious services is required.

Summer Programs ESL, sports, art/fine arts programs offered; session focuses on challenging, diversified instruction in the arts and athletics; ESL summer program; held on campus; accepts boys and girls; open to students from other schools.

Tuition and Aid Day student tuition: $26,950; 7-day tuition and room/board: $40,450. Tuition installment plan (Insured Tuition Payment Plan, monthly payment plans). Merit scholarship grants, need-based scholarship grants, performing arts scholarship, Headmasters scholarship available. In 2012–13, 44% of upper-school students received aid. Total amount of financial aid awarded in 2012–13: $3,900,000.

Admissions Traditional secondary-level entrance grade is 9. For fall 2012, 1,012 students applied for upper-level admission, 312 were accepted, 184 enrolled. SLEP, SSAT or TOEFL required. Deadline for receipt of application materials: none. Application fee required: $75. Interview required.

Athletics Interscholastic: baseball (boys), basketball (b,g), fencing (b,g), golf (b,g), ice hockey (b,g), indoor hockey (b,g), indoor soccer (b,g), lacrosse (b,g), soccer (b,g), tennis (b,g), track and field (b,g), volleyball (g); intramural: drill team (b,g), weight training (b,g); coed interscholastic: figure skating, soccer; coed intramural: aerobics/dance, badminton, basketball, dance, dance team, Frisbee, ice skating, jogging, martial arts, outdoor activities, outdoor recreation, ropes courses, strength & conditioning, table tennis, ultimate Frisbee. 29 coaches, 3 athletic trainers.

Computers Computers are regularly used in animation, college planning, creative writing, English, ESL, foreign language, history, independent study, mathematics, photography, SAT preparation, science, senior seminar, speech, writing, writing, yearbook classes. Computer network features include on-campus library services, Internet access, wireless campus network, Internet filtering or blocking technology. Campus intranet, student e-mail accounts, and computer access in designated common areas are available to students. Students grades are available online. The school has a published electronic and media policy.

Contact Mr. Jesse W. Fortney, Director of Admissions. 800-421-2724. Fax: 507-333-1661. E-mail: admissions@s-sm.org. Web site: www.s-sm.org

SHAWE MEMORIAL JUNIOR/SENIOR HIGH SCHOOL

201 West State Street
Madison, Indiana 47250-2899

Head of School: Mr. Philip J. Kahn

General Information Coeducational day college-preparatory and religious studies school, affiliated with Roman Catholic Church. Grades 7–12. Founded: 1954. Setting: small town. 30-acre campus. 1 building on campus. Approved or accredited by North Central Association of Colleges and Schools and Indiana Department of Education. Total enrollment: 342. Upper school average class size: 11. Upper school faculty-student ratio: 1:9. There are 180 required school days per year for Upper School students. Upper School students typically attend 5 days per week. The average school day consists of 8 hours and 15 minutes.

Upper School Student Profile Grade 9: 25 students (12 boys, 13 girls); Grade 10: 23 students (11 boys, 12 girls); Grade 11: 41 students (22 boys, 19 girls); Grade 12: 19 students (11 boys, 8 girls). 70% of students are Roman Catholic.

Faculty School total: 22. In upper school: 4 men, 17 women; 10 have advanced degrees.

Special Academic Programs International Baccalaureate program; Advanced Placement exam preparation; honors section; independent study; study at local college for college credit; academic accommodation for the gifted; remedial reading and/or remedial writing; special instructional classes for deaf students, some special needs students can be accommodated on an individual basis.

College Admission Counseling 27 students graduated in 2011; all went to college, including Ball State University; Indiana University Bloomington; Purdue University; University of Kentucky. Mean SAT critical reading: 539, mean SAT math: 506, mean SAT writing: 504, mean combined SAT: 1549.

Student Life Upper grades have specified standards of dress, student council. Discipline rests primarily with faculty. Attendance at religious services is required.

Tuition and Aid Day student tuition: $5915. Tuition installment plan (The Tuition Plan, FACTS Tuition Payment Plan, individually arranged payment plans, multiple options). Tuition reduction for siblings, need-based scholarship grants available. In 2011–12, 35% of upper-school students received aid. Total amount of financial aid awarded in 2011–12: $161,537.

Admissions Traditional secondary-level entrance grade is 9. For fall 2011, 23 students applied for upper-level admission, 19 were accepted, 19 enrolled. Deadline for receipt of application materials: none. Application fee required: $150. Interview required.

Athletics Interscholastic: archery (boys), baseball (b), basketball (b,g), cheering (g), cross-country running (b,g), fencing (b), golf (b,g), soccer (b,g), softball (g), tennis (b,g), track and field (b,g), volleyball (g). 2 PE instructors, 10 coaches, 1 athletic trainer.

Computers Computer network features include on-campus library services, Internet access, wireless campus network, Internet filtering or blocking technology. Campus intranet is available to students. Students grades are available online.

Contact Mr. Philip J. Kahn, President. 812-273-5835 Ext. 245. Fax: 812-273-8975. E-mail: poppresident@popeace.org. Web site:

SHAWNIGAN LAKE SCHOOL

1975 Renfrew Road
Postal Bag 2000
Shawnigan Lake, British Columbia V0R 2W1, Canada

Head of School: Mr. David Robertson

General Information Coeducational boarding and day college-preparatory, fine arts, athletics, leadership, citizenship, and entrepreneurship, and language studies school. Grades 8–12. Founded: 1916. Setting: rural. Nearest major city is Victoria, Canada. Students are housed in single-sex dormitories. 300-acre campus. 50 buildings on campus. Approved or accredited by British Columbia Independent Schools Association, Canadian Association of Independent Schools, The Association of Boarding Schools, Western Boarding Schools Association, and British Columbia Department of Education. Affiliate member of National Association of Independent Schools. Languages of instruction: English and French. Endowment: CAN$8 million. Total enrollment: 453. Upper school average class size: 15. Upper school faculty-student ratio: 1:8. Upper School students typically attend 6 days per week.

Upper School Student Profile Grade 8: 46 students (30 boys, 16 girls); Grade 9: 55 students (34 boys, 21 girls); Grade 10: 105 students (56 boys, 49 girls); Grade 11: 122 students (66 boys, 56 girls); Grade 12: 125 students (67 boys, 58 girls). 91% of students are boarding students. 65% are province residents. 17 provinces are represented in upper school student body. 22% are international students. International students from China, Democratic People's Republic of Korea, Germany, Hong Kong, Mexico, and United States; 19 other countries represented in student body.

Faculty School total: 59. In upper school: 39 men, 20 women; 22 have advanced degrees; 45 reside on campus.

Subjects Offered Advanced Placement courses, advanced studio art-AP, algebra, art, art history, art history-AP, biology, biology-AP, business skills, calculus, calculus-AP, career and personal planning, chemistry, chemistry-AP, computer science, computer science-AP, creative writing, earth science, economics, English, English language and composition-AP, English literature, English literature and composition-AP, English-AP, environmental science, European history-AP, expository writing, fine arts, French, French language-AP, French literature-AP, French-AP, geography, geometry, German, health, history, human geography - AP, industrial arts, mathematics, media studies, music, physical education, physics, physics-AP, religion, science, social studies, Spanish, sports science, study skills, trigonometry, U.S. history-AP, writing.

Graduation Requirements Acting, arts and fine arts (art, music, dance, drama), athletics, band, biology, career and personal planning, chemistry, drama, English, foreign language, geography, mathematics, music, physical education (includes health), physics, science, social studies (includes history), graduation requirements are mandated by the BC Provincial Government and include English 12 plus 4 additional grade 12 courses, and 30 hours of work experience, refer to the curriculum courses to see the subject offerings.

Special Academic Programs Advanced Placement exam preparation; honors section; academic accommodation for the gifted; remedial reading and/or remedial writing; remedial math; special instructional classes for students with learning disabilities; ESL (10 students enrolled).

College Admission Counseling 97 students graduated in 2012; 94 went to college, including McGill University; Queen's University at Kingston; The University of British Columbia; The University of Western Ontario; University of Alberta; University of Victoria. Other: 1 went to work, 1 entered military service, 1 had other specific plans.

Student Life Upper grades have uniform requirement, student council, honor system. Discipline rests equally with students and faculty. Attendance at religious services is required.

Summer Programs Sports programs offered; session focuses on rugby; held on campus; accepts boys and girls; open to students from other schools. 2013 schedule: July 1 to July 6. Application deadline: June 1.

Tuition and Aid Day student tuition: CAN$20,410; 7-day tuition and room/board: CAN$40,000–CAN$53,000. Tuition installment plan (Insured Tuition Payment Plan, individually arranged payment plans). Tuition reduction for siblings, bursaries, merit scholarship grants available. In 2012–13, 25% of upper-school students received aid; total upper-school merit-scholarship money awarded: CAN$200,000. Total amount of financial aid awarded in 2012–13: CAN$800,000.

Admissions Traditional secondary-level entrance grade is 8. For fall 2012, 341 students applied for upper-level admission, 167 were accepted, 153 enrolled. English entrance exam and Math Placement Exam required. Deadline for receipt of application materials: none. Application fee required: CAN$200. Interview required.

Athletics Interscholastic: basketball (boys, girls), crew (b,g), cross-country running (b,g), field hockey (g), golf (b,g), hockey (b), ice hockey (b), rowing (b,g), rugby (b,g), soccer (b,g), squash (b,g), tennis (b,g), volleyball (g); intramural: alpine skiing (b,g), ballet (g), basketball (b,g), crew (b,g), field hockey (g), golf (b,g), rowing (b,g), rugby (b,g), soccer (b,g), squash (b,g), strength & conditioning (b,g), tennis (b,g), volleyball (g), weight training (b,g), winter soccer (g); coed interscholastic: hockey, ice hockey, track and field; coed intramural: aerobics, aerobics/dance, alpine skiing, aquatics, backpacking, badminton, canoeing/kayaking, climbing, cross-country running, dance, fitness, golf, hiking/backpacking, jogging, kayaking, modern dance, nordic skiing, ocean paddling, outdoor activities, outdoor adventure, outdoor education, outdoor recreation, outdoor skills, outdoors, physical fitness, riflery, running, swimming and diving, track and field, wilderness survival, yoga. 4 PE instructors, 20 coaches, 2 athletic trainers.

Computers Computers are regularly used in animation, art, business, computer applications, creative writing, design, drawing and design, English, foreign language, graphic arts, history, library, mathematics, photography, research skills, science, social studies, video film production, yearbook classes. Computer network features include on-campus library services, online commercial services, Internet access, wireless campus network, Internet filtering or blocking technology. Campus intranet and student e-mail accounts are available to students. Students grades are available online. The school has a published electronic and media policy.

Contact Ms. Margot Allen, Associate Director of Admission. 250-743-6207. Fax: 250-743-6280. E-mail: admissions@shawnigan.ca. Web site: www.shawnigan.ca

SHELTON SCHOOL AND EVALUATION CENTER

Dallas, Texas

See Special Needs Schools section.

THE SHIPLEY SCHOOL

814 Yarrow Street
Bryn Mawr, Pennsylvania 19010-3525

Head of School: Dr. Steven S. Piltch

General Information Coeducational day college-preparatory school. Grades PK–12. Founded: 1894. Setting: suburban. Nearest major city is Philadelphia. 36-acre campus. 4 buildings on campus. Approved or accredited by Middle States Association of Colleges and Schools and Pennsylvania Association of Independent Schools. Member of National Association of Independent Schools and Secondary School Admission Test Board. Endowment: $31.1 million. Total enrollment: 834. Upper school average class size: 12. Upper school faculty-student ratio: 1:7. There are 167 required school days per year for Upper School students. Upper School students typically attend 5 days per week. The average school day consists of 7 hours and 30 minutes.

Upper School Student Profile Grade 9: 83 students (39 boys, 44 girls); Grade 10: 100 students (51 boys, 49 girls); Grade 11: 76 students (41 boys, 35 girls); Grade 12: 83 students (41 boys, 42 girls).

Faculty School total: 130. In upper school: 28 men, 45 women; 32 have advanced degrees.

Subjects Offered Advanced studio art-AP, algebra, American history, American literature, ancient world history, art, art history, athletic training, athletics, band, bioethics, biology, calculus, chamber groups, chemistry, chorus, classical language, college admission preparation, college counseling, conceptual physics, concert bell choir, CPR, drama, drama performance, dramatic arts, ecology, environmental systems, economics, economics and history, English, English literature, European history, film studies, fine arts, forensics, French, geometry, global issues, global studies, grammar, health, health and wellness, health education, Homeric Greek, honors English, honors geometry, honors U.S. history, honors world history, independent study, introduction to theater, jazz band, Latin, leadership, library skills, Mandarin, mathematics, medieval history, Middle East, model United Nations, music, music theory, musical productions, orchestra, performing arts, philosophy, photography, physical education, physical fitness, physics, pre-calculus, research skills, science, senior project, senior seminar, service learning/internship, Shakespeare, Spanish, speech and debate, statistics, student publications, studio art-AP, theater, theater arts, urban studies, wind ensemble, world history, world literature.

Graduation Requirements English, foreign language, interdisciplinary studies, mathematics, performing arts, physical education (includes health), research skills, science, senior project, senior seminar, social studies (includes history), studio art, 40 hours of community service/service learning.

Special Academic Programs 1 Advanced Placement exam for which test preparation is offered; honors section; accelerated programs; independent study; term-away projects; study abroad; academic accommodation for the gifted.

College Admission Counseling 87 students graduated in 2012; 86 went to college, including Brown University; Drexel University; Penn State University Park; Syracuse University; The George Washington University; University of Pennsylvania. Other: 1 entered a postgraduate year. Mean SAT critical reading: 626, mean SAT math: 631, mean SAT writing: 646, mean combined SAT: 1903, mean composite ACT: 29.

Student Life Upper grades have specified standards of dress, student council, honor system. Discipline rests equally with students and faculty.

Summer Programs Sports programs offered; session focuses on sports; held on campus; accepts boys and girls; open to students from other schools. 29 students usually enrolled. 2013 schedule: June 20 to July 29.

Tuition and Aid Day student tuition: $31,375. Tuition installment plan (monthly payment plans). Need-based scholarship grants available. In 2012–13, 26% of upper-school students received aid. Total amount of financial aid awarded in 2012–13: $2,453,825.

Admissions Traditional secondary-level entrance grade is 9. For fall 2012, 321 students applied for upper-level admission, 216 were accepted, 128 enrolled. ISEE, SSAT or Wechsler Intelligence Scale for Children required. Deadline for receipt of application materials: January 11. Application fee required: $50. On-campus interview required.

Athletics Interscholastic: baseball (boys), basketball (b,g), crew (b,g), cross-country running (b,g), field hockey (g), independent competitive sports (b,g), lacrosse (b,g), rowing (b,g), soccer (b,g), softball (g), squash (b,g), tennis (b,g), volleyball (g), weight training (b,g); intramural: aerobics (b,g), aerobics/Nautilus (b,g), dance (g), modern dance (g), Nautilus (b,g); coed interscholastic: diving, golf, independent competitive sports, swimming and diving, weight training; coed intramural: aerobics, aerobics/Nautilus, fitness, Nautilus, physical fitness, yoga. 11 PE instructors, 51 coaches, 2 athletic trainers.

Computers Computers are regularly used in all classes. Computer network features include on-campus library services, online commercial services, Internet access, wireless campus network, Internet filtering or blocking technology, all progress, midterm, and final reports are online, 3D printer. Campus intranet, student e-mail accounts, and computer access in designated common areas are available to students. Students grades are available online. The school has a published electronic and media policy.

Contact Mrs. Zoe Marshall, Assistant to the Director of Admissions. 610-525-4300 Ext. 4118. Fax: 610-525-5082. E-mail: zmarshall@shipleyschool.org. Web site: www.shipleyschool.org

SHOORE CENTRE FOR LEARNING

Toronto, Ontario, Canada

See Special Needs Schools section.

SHORELINE CHRISTIAN

2400 Northeast 147th Street
Shoreline, Washington 98155

Head of School: Mr. Timothy E. Visser

General Information Coeducational day college-preparatory and general academic school, affiliated with Christian faith. Grades PS–12. Founded: 1952. Setting: suburban. Nearest major city is Seattle. 7-acre campus. 2 buildings on campus. Approved or accredited by Christian Schools International, Northwest Accreditation Commission, and Washington Department of Education. Total enrollment: 212. Upper school average class size: 20. Upper school faculty-student ratio: 1:7. There are 180 required school days per year for Upper School students. Upper School students typically attend 5 days per week. The average school day consists of 6 hours and 30 minutes.

Upper School Student Profile Grade 7: 8 students (5 boys, 3 girls); Grade 8: 13 students (6 boys, 7 girls); Grade 9: 17 students (9 boys, 8 girls); Grade 10: 16 students (9 boys, 7 girls); Grade 11: 18 students (12 boys, 6 girls); Grade 12: 25 students (13 boys, 12 girls). 100% of students are Christian faith.

Faculty School total: 23. In upper school: 6 men, 7 women; 5 have advanced degrees.

Subjects Offered 20th century history, advanced computer applications, advanced math, Advanced Placement courses, algebra, American history, American literature, art, band, Bible, biology, British literature, calculus, chemistry, choir, Christian doctrine, college writing, composition, computer applications, consumer education, creative writing, current events, current history, drama, drawing, English, geometry, global studies, government, health, human anatomy, jazz band, keyboarding, life science, life skills, literature, media, music appreciation, physical education, physical science, physics, pre-calculus, psychology, sculpture, sociology, Spanish, speech, study skills, Washington State and Northwest History, weight training, Western civilization, world literature, world religions, yearbook.

Graduation Requirements American government, American literature, Bible, British literature, college writing, composition, electives, English, foreign language, global issues, keyboarding, life skills, mathematics, occupational education, physical education (includes health), science, social sciences, speech, U.S. history, Washington State and Northwest History, Western civilization, world literature.

Special Academic Programs Honors section; independent study; study at local college for college credit; remedial reading and/or remedial writing.

College Admission Counseling 14 students graduated in 2012; all went to college, including Calvin College; University of Washington; Washington State University.

Student Life Upper grades have specified standards of dress, student council. Discipline rests primarily with faculty. Attendance at religious services is required.

Tuition and Aid Day student tuition: $10,600–$11,100. Tuition installment plan (monthly payment plans, individually arranged payment plans, prepaid cash tuition discount, quarterly or semi-annual payment plans). Tuition reduction for siblings, need-based scholarship grants, discount for qualifying Pastor families available. In 2012–13, 29% of upper-school students received aid. Total amount of financial aid awarded in 2012–13: $340,000.

Admissions Traditional secondary-level entrance grade is 9. Deadline for receipt of application materials: none. Application fee required: $100. Interview required.

Athletics Interscholastic: baseball (boys), basketball (b,g), soccer (b), volleyball (g); coed interscholastic: golf, soccer, track and field. 1 PE instructor.

Computers Computers are regularly used in all academic, art, library, media, music, occupational education, research skills, yearbook classes. Computer network features include on-campus library services, Internet access, wireless campus network, Internet filtering or blocking technology. Computer access in designated common areas is available to students. Students grades are available online. The school has a published electronic and media policy.

Contact Mrs. Laurie Dykstra, Director of Development. 206-364-7777 Ext. 308. Fax: 206-364-0349. E-mail: ldykstra@shorelinechristian.org. Web site: www.shorelinechristian.org

SIGNET CHRISTIAN SCHOOL

95 Jonesville Crescent
North York, Ontario M4A 1H2, Canada

Head of School: Mr. Trent Mansell

General Information Coeducational day college-preparatory and business school, affiliated with Christian faith. Grades JK–12. Founded: 1975. Setting: urban. Nearest major city is Toronto, Canada. 1-acre campus. 1 building on campus. Approved or accredited by Association of Christian Schools International and Ontario Department of Education. Language of instruction: English. Total enrollment: 40. Upper school average class size: 6. Upper school faculty-student ratio: 1:5. There are 178 required school days per year for Upper School students. Upper School students typically attend 5 days per week. The average school day consists of 6 hours and 30 minutes.

Upper School Student Profile Grade 9: 2 students (1 boy, 1 girl); Grade 10: 5 students (3 boys, 2 girls); Grade 11: 10 students (8 boys, 2 girls); Grade 12: 5 students (4 boys, 1 girl). 80% of students are Christian.

Faculty School total: 11. In upper school: 2 men, 3 women; 1 has an advanced degree.

Subjects Offered Biology, business studies, calculus, Canadian geography, Canadian history, career education, chemistry, civics, English, ESL, French as a second language, math analysis, math applications, physics, science, visual arts.

Graduation Requirements English, Ontario Ministry of Education requirements.

Special Academic Programs Independent study; ESL (9 students enrolled).

Student Life Upper grades have uniform requirement, student council. Discipline rests primarily with faculty. Attendance at religious services is required.

Tuition and Aid Day student tuition: CAN$6120. Tuition installment plan (individually arranged payment plans). Tuition reduction for siblings available. In 2012–13, 20% of upper-school students received aid.

Admissions Traditional secondary-level entrance grade is 9. For fall 2012, 13 students applied for upper-level admission, 13 were accepted, 9 enrolled. SLEP required. Deadline for receipt of application materials: none. No application fee required.

Athletics Coed Intramural: basketball, bowling, cross-country running, ice skating, skiing (downhill), snowboarding, soccer, table tennis, track and field.

Computers Computers are regularly used in English, mathematics, technology classes. Computer network features include Internet access.

Contact Admissions. 416-750-7515. Fax: 416-750-7720. E-mail: scs@titan.tcn.net. Web site: www.signetschool.ca

SMITH SCHOOL

New York, New York
See Special Needs Schools section.

SOLOMON COLLEGE

Suite 228, 10621 100th Avenue
Edmonton, Alberta T5J 0B3, Canada

Head of School: Ms. Ping Ping Lee

General Information Coeducational day and distance learning college-preparatory, general academic, vocational, bilingual studies, and ESL school. Grades 10–12. Distance learning grades 10–12. Founded: 1994. Setting: urban. 1 building on campus. Approved or accredited by Association of Independent Schools and Colleges of Alberta and Alberta Department of Education. Language of instruction: English. Total enrollment: 25. Upper school average class size: 10. Upper school faculty-student ratio: 1:10. There are 225 required school days per year for Upper School students. Upper School students typically attend 5 days per week. The average school day consists of 4 hours and 30 minutes.

Upper School Student Profile Grade 11: 3 students (3 boys); Grade 12: 10 students (5 boys, 5 girls).

Faculty School total: 5. In upper school: 2 men, 3 women; 2 have advanced degrees.

Subjects Offered Biology, calculus, career and personal planning, chemistry, Chinese, computer information systems, computer skills, computer technologies, English literature, ESL, keyboarding, mathematics, physics, social studies.

Special Academic Programs ESL (80 students enrolled).

College Admission Counseling 10 students graduated in 2012; 8 went to college, including University of Alberta; University of Calgary; University of Lethbridge.

Student Life Discipline rests equally with students and faculty.

Tuition and Aid Day student tuition: CAN$5800.

Admissions Traditional secondary-level entrance grade is 10. For fall 2012, 13 students applied for upper-level admission, 13 were accepted, 13 enrolled. Placement test required. Deadline for receipt of application materials: August 31. Application fee required: CAN$200.

Computers Computer network features include Internet access, wireless campus network, Internet filtering or blocking technology. Campus intranet is available to students.

Contact Mr. Sunny Ip, Registrar. 780-431-1516. Fax: 780-431-1644. E-mail: sunnyi@solomoncollege.ca. Web site: www.solomoncollege.ca/index_home.htm

SONOMA ACADEMY

2500 Farmers Lane
Santa Rosa, California 95404

Head of School: Janet Durgin

General Information Coeducational day college-preparatory and Environmental Leadership & Global Citizenship concentrations school. Grades 9–12. Founded: 1999. Nearest major city is San Francisco. 34-acre campus. 3 buildings on campus. Approved or accredited by California Association of Independent Schools, Western Association of Schools and Colleges, and California Department of Education. Member of National Association of Independent Schools. Total enrollment: 246. Upper school average class size: 15. Upper school faculty-student ratio: 1:12. Upper School students typically attend 5 days per week. The average school day consists of 6 hours and 30 minutes.

Upper School Student Profile Grade 9: 62 students (31 boys, 31 girls); Grade 10: 68 students (35 boys, 33 girls); Grade 11: 68 students (28 boys, 40 girls); Grade 12: 48 students (27 boys, 21 girls); Grade 13: 246 students (120 boys, 126 girls).

Faculty School total: 24. In upper school: 11 men, 13 women; 19 have advanced degrees.

Subjects Offered Algebra, anatomy and physiology, art history, arts, British literature, calculus, calculus-AP, chemistry, chemistry-AP, choir, comparative religion, computer programming, creative writing, digital photography, economics, engineering, English language and composition-AP, English literature and composition-AP, environmental studies, expository writing, French, genetics, geometry, literature, Mandarin, music history, Native American studies, oceanography, oral expression, philosophy, physics, physics-AP, Shakespeare, Spanish, Spanish language-AP, studio art, theater.

Special Academic Programs 6 Advanced Placement exams for which test preparation is offered; honors section; independent study; study abroad.

College Admission Counseling 56 students graduated in 2012; all went to college, including Arizona State University; Carnegie Mellon University; Reed College; Saint Mary's College of California; University of San Diego. Mean SAT critical reading: 624, mean SAT math: 618, mean SAT writing: 631, mean combined SAT: 1873.

Student Life Upper grades have student council. Discipline rests equally with students and faculty.

Tuition and Aid Day student tuition: $34,900. Tuition installment plan (Insured Tuition Payment Plan, monthly payment plans). Need-based scholarship grants, STEM Scholarships available. In 2012–13, 56% of upper-school students received aid. Total amount of financial aid awarded in 2012–13: $2,600,000.

Admissions Traditional secondary-level entrance grade is 9. SSAT required. Deadline for receipt of application materials: January 2. Application fee required: $85. Interview required.

Athletics Interscholastic: baseball (boys), basketball (b,g), cross-country running (b,g), lacrosse (b,g), soccer (b,g), track and field (b,g), volleyball (g); coed intramural: aerobics/dance, combined training, dance, fencing, fitness, flag football, kickball, martial arts, outdoor education, physical fitness, physical training, power lifting, softball, strength & conditioning, tai chi, ultimate Frisbee, weight training, whiffle ball, yoga. 9 coaches.

Computers Computers are regularly used in all classes. Computer network features include on-campus library services, online commercial services, Internet access, wireless campus network, Internet filtering or blocking technology, one to one laptop program, digital technology center, broadcast studio. Campus intranet and student e-mail accounts are available to students. Students grades are available online. The school has a published electronic and media policy.

Contact Sandy Stack, Director of Enrollment and Marketing. 707-545-1770. Fax: 707-636-2474. E-mail: sandy.stack@sonomaacademy.org. Web site: www.sonomaacademy.org/

SOUNDVIEW PREPARATORY SCHOOL

370 Underhill Avenue
Yorktown Heights, New York 10598

Head of School: W. Glyn Hearn

General Information Coeducational day college-preparatory, arts, and technology school. Grades 6–PG. Founded: 1989. Setting: suburban. Nearest major city is New York. 13.8-acre campus. 7 buildings on campus. Approved or accredited by New York State Association of Independent Schools and New York Department of Education. Member of National Association of Independent Schools. Total enrollment: 70. Upper school average class size: 7. Upper school faculty-student ratio: 1:4. There are 164 required school days per year for Upper School students. Upper School students typically attend 5 days per week. The average school day consists of 6 hours and 47 minutes.

Upper School Student Profile Grade 9: 13 students (7 boys, 6 girls); Grade 10: 9 students (3 boys, 6 girls); Grade 11: 18 students (9 boys, 9 girls); Grade 12: 18 students (8 boys, 10 girls).

Faculty School total: 18. In upper school: 4 men, 13 women; 13 have advanced degrees.

Subjects Offered Advanced Placement courses, algebra, American history, American literature, art, art-AP, astronomy, biology, calculus, chemistry, computer science, contemporary issues in science, creative writing, drama, earth science, English, English literature, European history-AP, French, geometry, health, Italian, Latin, mathematics, music, physical education, physics, science, social studies, Spanish, study skills, U.S. history-AP, world history.

Graduation Requirements Art, electives, English, foreign language, health, history, mathematics, physical education (includes health), science.

Special Academic Programs 6 Advanced Placement exams for which test preparation is offered; honors section; accelerated programs; independent study; academic accommodation for the gifted and the artistically talented; special instructional classes for students needing wheelchair accessibility.

College Admission Counseling 18 students graduated in 2012; all went to college, including High Point University; Ithaca College; Muhlenberg College; Oberlin College; State University of New York at New Paltz; The Ohio State University. Mean SAT critical reading: 600, mean SAT math: 590, mean SAT writing: 540, mean composite ACT: 25.

Student Life Discipline rests primarily with faculty.

Tuition and Aid Day student tuition: $33,300–$34,500. Need-based scholarship grants available. In 2012–13, 20% of upper-school students received aid. Total amount of financial aid awarded in 2012–13: $420,000.

Admissions Traditional secondary-level entrance grade is 9. For fall 2012, 27 students applied for upper-level admission, 14 were accepted, 12 enrolled. ERB (CTP-Verbal, Quantitative) or ERB Mathematics required. Deadline for receipt of application materials: none. Application fee required: $50. On-campus interview required.

Athletics Interscholastic: basketball (girls); coed interscholastic: basketball, soccer, tennis, ultimate Frisbee; coed intramural: cheering, sailing, skiing (downhill), volleyball. 1 PE instructor, 1 coach.

Computers Computers are regularly used in all academic classes. Computer network features include Internet access, wireless campus network, Internet filtering or blocking technology. Campus intranet and student e-mail accounts are available to students. The school has a published electronic and media policy.

Contact Mary E. Ivanyi, Assistant Head. 914-962-2780. Fax: 914-302-2769. E-mail: mivanyi@soundviewprep.org. Web site: www.soundviewprep.org

See Display below and Close-Up on page 626.

SOUTHFIELD CHRISTIAN HIGH SCHOOL

28650 Lahser Road
Southfield, Michigan 48034-2099

Head of School: Mrs. Margie Baldwin

General Information Coeducational day and distance learning college-preparatory, arts, religious studies, and technology school, affiliated with Christian faith, Evangelical faith. Grades PK–12. Distance learning grades 9–12. Founded: 1970. Setting: suburban. Nearest major city is Detroit. 28-acre campus. 1 building on campus. Approved or accredited by Association of Christian Schools International, Independent Schools Association of the Central States, North Central Association of Colleges and Schools, and Michigan Department of Education. Endowment: $1.5 million. Total enrollment: 567. Upper school average class size: 22. Upper school faculty-student ratio: 1:20. There are 176 required school days per year for Upper School students. Upper School students typically attend 5 days per week. The average school day consists of 6 hours and 30 minutes.

Upper School Student Profile Grade 9: 50 students (26 boys, 24 girls); Grade 10: 48 students (27 boys, 21 girls); Grade 11: 58 students (22 boys, 36 girls); Grade 12:

41 students (15 boys, 26 girls). 100% of students are Christian faith, members of Evangelical faith.
Faculty School total: 28. In upper school: 14 men, 14 women; 12 have advanced degrees.
Subjects Offered Accounting, Advanced Placement courses, algebra, American government, American history, American history-AP, American literature, American literature-AP, ancient world history, art, band, Bible, biology, biology-AP, British literature, calculus-AP, chemistry, chemistry-AP, choir, chorus, communication arts, composition-AP, computer applications, computer programming, conceptual physics, creative writing, drawing and design, economics, English language-AP, English literature and composition-AP, film and literature, French, geography, geometry, government, graphic design, health, instrumental music, Life of Christ, literature and composition-AP, Middle Eastern history, New Testament, organic chemistry, photography, physical education, physics-AP, pre-calculus, probability and statistics, Russian history, senior project, Spanish, speech and debate, U.S. history, vocal music, Web site design, world studies, yearbook.
Special Academic Programs Advanced Placement exam preparation; honors section; independent study.
College Admission Counseling 53 students graduated in 2012; all went to college, including Grand Valley State University; Hope College; Michigan State University; Oakland University; University of Michigan; Wheaton College. Median SAT critical reading: 460, median SAT math: 430, median SAT writing: 480, median composite ACT: 23. 21% scored over 26 on composite ACT.
Student Life Upper grades have uniform requirement, student council. Discipline rests primarily with faculty. Attendance at religious services is required.
Summer Programs Rigorous outdoor training programs offered; session focuses on physical education; held on campus; accepts boys and girls; not open to students from other schools. 10 students usually enrolled. 2013 schedule: June 10 to June 28. Application deadline: May 1.
Tuition and Aid Day student tuition: $8630. Tuition installment plan (FACTS Tuition Payment Plan). Tuition reduction for siblings, need-based scholarship grants available. In 2012–13, 10% of upper-school students received aid.
Admissions Traditional secondary-level entrance grade is 9. For fall 2012, 70 students applied for upper-level admission, 50 were accepted, 39 enrolled. Any standardized test required. Deadline for receipt of application materials: none. No application fee required. On-campus interview required.
Athletics Interscholastic: baseball (boys), basketball (b,g), cheering (g), cross-country running (b,g), football (b), soccer (b,g), softball (g), track and field (b,g), volleyball (g); coed interscholastic: golf; coed intramural: skiing (downhill), weight lifting. 1 PE instructor, 1 athletic trainer.
Computers Computers are regularly used in art, commercial art, computer applications, creative writing, drawing and design, graphic arts, graphic design, independent study, media production, programming, publishing, Web site design, writing, yearbook classes. Computer network features include on-campus library services, Internet access, wireless campus network, Internet filtering or blocking technology. Student e-mail accounts are available to students. Students grades are available online. The school has a published electronic and media policy.
Contact Mrs. Sue Hoffenbacher, High School Principal. 248-357-3660 Ext. 278. Fax: 248-357-5271. E-mail: shoffenbacher@southfieldchristian.org. Web site: www.southfieldchristian.org

SOUTHFIELD SCHOOL

10 Newton Street
Brookline, Massachusetts 02445

Head of School: Mr. Todd A. Vincent

General Information Girls' day college-preparatory and arts school. Grades PK–12. Founded: 1992. Setting: suburban. Nearest major city is Boston. 36-acre campus. 4 buildings on campus. Approved or accredited by Association of Independent Schools in New England and Massachusetts Department of Education. Candidate for accreditation by New England Association of Schools and Colleges. Endowment: $8 million. Total enrollment: 319. Upper school average class size: 14. Upper school faculty-student ratio: 1:7. There are 172 required school days per year for Upper School students. Upper School students typically attend 5 days per week. The average school day consists of 6 hours and 45 minutes.
Upper School Student Profile Grade 9: 25 students (25 girls); Grade 10: 25 students (25 girls); Grade 11: 13 students (13 girls); Grade 12: 19 students (19 girls).
Faculty School total: 110. In upper school: 26 men, 23 women; 31 have advanced degrees.
Subjects Offered Advanced studio art-AP, algebra, American government, American history, American history-AP, American literature, anatomy and physiology, Ancient Greek, ancient world history, art, art history, astronomy, biology, biology-AP, British history, British literature, British literature (honors), calculus-AP, chemistry, chemistry-AP, Chinese history, choir, college counseling, community service, computer music, constitutional history of U.S., digital imaging, digital photography, drama performance, drama workshop, earth and space science, English, English language-AP, English literature-AP, environmental science, equality and freedom, ethics, European history, European history-AP, French, French-AP, geometry, grammar, health and wellness, honors algebra, honors English, honors geometry, human anatomy, jazz ensemble, Latin, Latin-AP, marine biology, music technology, music theory-AP, painting, physics, physics-AP, physiology, pre-calculus, probability and statistics, public speaking, SAT preparation, senior project, shop, space and physical sciences, Spanish, Spanish language-AP, statistics-AP, studio art, studio art-AP, The 20th Century, U.S. history, U.S. history-AP, world history, world history-AP.
Graduation Requirements All academic.
Special Academic Programs 13 Advanced Placement exams for which test preparation is offered; honors section; independent study.
College Admission Counseling 15 students graduated in 2012; all went to college, including Columbia University; Dartmouth College; Harvard University; Massachusetts Institute of Technology; The George Washington University; Trinity College.
Student Life Upper grades have specified standards of dress, student council, honor system. Discipline rests equally with students and faculty. Attendance at religious services is required.
Tuition and Aid Day student tuition: $39,995. Tuition installment plan (monthly payment plans). Need-based scholarship grants available. In 2012–13, 29% of upper-school students received aid. Total amount of financial aid awarded in 2012–13: $3,000,000.
Admissions Traditional secondary-level entrance grade is 9. For fall 2012, 39 students applied for upper-level admission, 29 were accepted, 9 enrolled. ISEE, PSAT and SAT for applicants to grade 11 and 12, SSAT or TOEFL required. Deadline for receipt of application materials: February 1. Application fee required: $50. Interview required.
Athletics Interscholastic: basketball, crew, cross-country running, curling, field hockey, ice hockey, independent competitive sports, lacrosse, physical fitness, rowing, soccer, softball, squash, tennis, weight training; intramural: dance, hiking/backpacking, life saving. 4 coaches, 2 athletic trainers.
Computers Computers are regularly used in all classes. Computer network features include on-campus library services, online commercial services, Internet access, wireless campus network, Internet filtering or blocking technology, one to one device program. Campus intranet and student e-mail accounts are available to students. The school has a published electronic and media policy.
Contact Mrs. Jennifer DaPonte, Admissions Office Manager. 617-454-2721. Fax: 617-928-7691. E-mail: admissions@southfield.org. Web site: www.southfield.org

SOUTHLAND ACADEMY, INC.

PO Box 1127
Americus, Georgia 31709

Head of School: Mr. William E. Stubbs

General Information Coeducational day college-preparatory school. Grades PK–12. Setting: small town. 4 buildings on campus. Approved or accredited by Southern Association of Colleges and Schools and Georgia Department of Education. Member of National Association of Independent Schools. Total enrollment: 565. Upper school average class size: 18. There are 180 required school days per year for Upper School students. Upper School students typically attend 5 days per week. The average school day consists of 5 hours.
Upper School Student Profile Grade 9: 50 students (29 boys, 21 girls); Grade 10: 47 students (24 boys, 23 girls); Grade 11: 38 students (18 boys, 20 girls); Grade 12: 44 students (26 boys, 18 girls).
College Admission Counseling 40 students graduated in 2011; all went to college.
Student Life Upper grades have specified standards of dress, student council, honor system.
Admissions No application fee required. Interview required.
Athletics Interscholastic: baseball (boys), basketball (b,g), cheering (g), cross-country running (b,g), dance squad (g), football (b), golf (b), soccer (g), softball (g), swimming and diving (b,g), tennis (b,g), track and field (b,g), wrestling (b). 4 PE instructors, 8 coaches.
Contact 912-924-4406. Fax: 912-924-2996. Web site:

SOUTHWEST CHRISTIAN SCHOOL, INC.

7001 Benbrook Lake Drive
Fort Worth, Texas 76132

Head of School: Dr. Penny Armstrong

General Information Coeducational day college-preparatory, arts, religious studies, and technology school, affiliated with Christian faith. Grades PK–12. Founded: 1969. Setting: suburban. 39-acre campus. 3 buildings on campus. Approved or accredited by Southern Association of Colleges and Schools and Texas Department of Education. Member of National Association of Independent Schools. Total enrollment: 861. Upper school average class size: 16. Upper school faculty-student ratio: 1:11. There are 176 required school days per year for Upper School students. Upper School students typically attend 5 days per week. The average school day consists of 7 hours.
Upper School Student Profile Grade 7: 76 students (35 boys, 41 girls); Grade 8: 67 students (28 boys, 39 girls); Grade 9: 65 students (21 boys, 44 girls); Grade 10: 85 students (39 boys, 46 girls); Grade 11: 79 students (43 boys, 36 girls); Grade 12: 68 students (33 boys, 35 girls).

Faculty School total: 130. In upper school: 13 men, 35 women; 34 have advanced degrees.
Subjects Offered 1 1/2 elective credits, advanced math, algebra, American government, American literature, American literature-AP, anatomy and physiology, art, Bible studies, biology, biology-AP, British literature, British literature-AP, calculus, calculus-AP, chemistry, chemistry-AP, choir, drama, English, English literature-AP, English-AP, foreign language, French, geometry, government, history, honors algebra, honors English, honors geometry, honors U.S. history, honors world history, journalism, keyboarding, lab science, leadership, literature and composition-AP, physics, physics-AP, pre-algebra, pre-calculus, psychology, SAT preparation, Spanish, speech, technology, U.S. history, U.S. history-AP, Web site design.
Graduation Requirements 4 years of Bible courses.
Special Academic Programs Advanced Placement exam preparation; honors section; accelerated programs; study at local college for college credit; study abroad; academic accommodation for the gifted.
College Admission Counseling 77 students graduated in 2012; 74 went to college. Other: 3 entered military service.
Student Life Upper grades have uniform requirement, student council, honor system. Discipline rests primarily with faculty. Attendance at religious services is required.
Summer Programs Enrichment, sports, art/fine arts, computer instruction programs offered; session focuses on enrichment, athletics; held on campus; accepts boys and girls; open to students from other schools. 2013 schedule: June to June. Application deadline: June.
Tuition and Aid Day student tuition: $10,275–$13,700. Tuition installment plan (FACTS Tuition Payment Plan). Need-based scholarship grants available. In 2012–13, 20% of upper-school students received aid. Total amount of financial aid awarded in 2012–13: $455,000.
Admissions Traditional secondary-level entrance grade is 9. For fall 2012, 106 students applied for upper-level admission, 99 were accepted, 62 enrolled. Stanford 9 required. Deadline for receipt of application materials: none. No application fee required. Interview required.
Athletics Interscholastic: aerobics/dance (girls), baseball (b), basketball (b,g), cheering (g), cross-country running (b,g), dance team (g), equestrian sports (b,g), football (b), golf (b,g), soccer (b,g), softball (g), track and field (b,g), volleyball (g), wrestling (b); intramural: physical training (b,g); coed interscholastic: aquatics, equestrian sports, paint ball, rodeo; coed intramural: aquatics, fitness, strength & conditioning, weight training. 2 PE instructors, 12 coaches, 1 athletic trainer.
Computers Computers are regularly used in all academic classes. Computer network features include on-campus library services, online commercial services, Internet access, wireless campus network, Internet filtering or blocking technology, computer carts for classroom use. Student e-mail accounts and computer access in designated common areas are available to students. Students grades are available online. The school has a published electronic and media policy.
Contact Mr. Travis Crow, Dean of Student Services. 817-294-9596 Ext. 207. Fax: 817-294-9603. E-mail: tcrow@southwestchristian.org. Web site: www.southwestchristian.org

SOUTHWESTERN ACADEMY

Beaver Creek Ranch Campus
Rimrock, Arizona 86335

Head of School: Mr. Kenneth R. Veronda

General Information Coeducational boarding and day college-preparatory, general academic, and arts school. Grades 9–PG. Founded: 1963. Setting: rural. Nearest major city is Sedona. Students are housed in single-sex dormitories. 185-acre campus. 24 buildings on campus. Approved or accredited by Arizona Association of Independent Schools, The Association of Boarding Schools, and Arizona Department of Education. Member of Secondary School Admission Test Board. Endowment: $10 million. Total enrollment: 27. Upper school average class size: 6. Upper school faculty-student ratio: 1:4. There are 184 required school days per year for Upper School students. Upper School students typically attend 5 days per week. The average school day consists of 8 hours.
Upper School Student Profile Grade 9: 3 students (3 boys); Grade 10: 7 students (5 boys, 2 girls); Grade 11: 12 students (5 boys, 7 girls); Grade 12: 5 students (3 boys, 2 girls). 100% of students are boarding students. 3% are state residents. 3 states are represented in upper school student body. 60% are international students. International students from China, Indonesia, and Serbia and Montenegro.
Faculty School total: 12. In upper school: 5 men, 7 women; 4 have advanced degrees; 7 reside on campus.
Subjects Offered Advanced math, Advanced Placement courses, algebra, American history, American literature, American literature-AP, art, art appreciation, art history, astronomy, biology, biology-AP, British literature, calculus, chemistry, earth science, ecology, economics, English, English composition, environmental education, environmental science, environmental studies, ESL, fashion, fine arts, general math, geometry, health, integrated science, Latin, math review, mathematics, music, music appreciation, outdoor education, physics, pre-algebra, Spanish, studio art, U.S. government, world cultures, yearbook.
Graduation Requirements Algebra, American government, American history, American literature, British literature, computer literacy, economics, electives, English, foreign language, geometry, lab science, mathematics, physical education (includes health), visual and performing arts, world cultures. Community service is required.
Special Academic Programs 4 Advanced Placement exams for which test preparation is offered; honors section; accelerated programs; independent study; term-away projects; study at local college for college credit; ESL (6 students enrolled).
College Admission Counseling 8 students graduated in 2012; all went to college, including Arizona State University; Drexel University; The University of Arizona; University of Nevada, Las Vegas. Median SAT critical reading: 550, median SAT math: 700, median SAT writing: 550, median combined SAT: 1800.
Student Life Upper grades have specified standards of dress, student council, honor system. Discipline rests primarily with faculty.
Summer Programs Remediation, enrichment, advancement, ESL, art/fine arts, rigorous outdoor training programs offered; session focuses on academics and outdoor/environmental education; held on campus; accepts boys and girls; open to students from other schools. 30 students usually enrolled. 2013 schedule: June 17 to August 16. Application deadline: none.
Tuition and Aid Day student tuition: $16,550; 7-day tuition and room/board: $33,750. Tuition installment plan (monthly payment plans, individually arranged payment plans). Need-based scholarship grants available. In 2012–13, 40% of upper-school students received aid. Total amount of financial aid awarded in 2012–13: $445,000.
Admissions Traditional secondary-level entrance grade is 9. For fall 2012, 49 students applied for upper-level admission, 28 were accepted, 17 enrolled. English language, English proficiency, ESL, High School Placement Test, International English Language Test, international math and English tests, SLEP, SLEP for foreign students, TOEFL or writing sample required. Deadline for receipt of application materials: none. Application fee required: $100. Interview recommended.
Athletics Interscholastic: basketball (boys, girls), volleyball (g); coed interscholastic: golf, soccer; coed intramural: alpine skiing, aquatics, archery, backpacking, badminton, ballet, baseball, basketball, bicycling, billiards, canoeing/kayaking, climbing, croquet, cross-country running, equestrian sports, fishing, fitness, fitness walking, flag football, Frisbee, golf, hiking/backpacking, horseback riding, horseshoes, ice skating, mountain biking, outdoor activities, outdoor adventure, outdoor education, outdoor recreation, outdoor skills, outdoors, paint ball, physical fitness, rafting, rock climbing, ropes courses, running, skiing (cross-country), skiing (downhill), snowboarding, soccer, softball, swimming and diving, table tennis, tennis, touch football, track and field, volleyball, walking, weight lifting, weight training, wilderness. 1 PE instructor, 2 coaches.
Computers Computers are regularly used in all academic, animation, architecture, art, basic skills, career education, career exploration, classics, college planning, commercial art, computer applications, creative writing, current events, data processing, design, digital applications, drafting, drawing and design, economics, English, ESL, ethics, foreign language, geography, graphic arts, graphic design, graphics, health, historical foundations for arts, history, humanities, independent study, information technology, journalism, keyboarding, lab/keyboard, language development, learning cognition, library, life skills, literacy, literary magazine, mathematics, media, media arts, media production, media services, mentorship program, multimedia, music, music technology, news writing, newspaper, occupational education, philosophy, photography, photojournalism, programming, psychology, publications, publishing, reading, research skills, SAT preparation, science, senior seminar, social sciences, social studies, Spanish, speech, stock market, study skills, technical drawing, technology, theater, theater arts, typing, video film production, vocational-technical courses, Web site design, wilderness education, word processing, writing, writing, yearbook classes. Computer network features include on-campus library services, Internet access, wireless campus network, Internet filtering or blocking technology. Student e-mail accounts and computer access in designated common areas are available to students.
Contact Mr. Joseph M. Blake, Director of Admissions and Outreach. 626-799-5010 Ext. 203. Fax: 626-799-0407. E-mail: jblake@southwesternacademy.edu. Web site: www.southwesternacademy.edu

See Display on next page, Close-Up on page 628, and Summer Program Close-Up on page 714.

SOUTHWESTERN ACADEMY

2800 Monterey Road
San Marino, California 91108

Head of School: Mr. Kenneth R. Veronda

General Information Coeducational boarding and day college-preparatory, general academic, arts, and ESL school. Grades 6–PG. Founded: 1924. Setting: suburban. Nearest major city is Pasadena. Students are housed in single-sex dormitories. 8-acre campus. 9 buildings on campus. Approved or accredited by The Association of Boarding Schools, Western Association of Schools and Colleges, and California Department of Education. Member of Secondary School Admission Test Board. Endowment: $15 million. Upper school average class size: 12. Upper school faculty-student ratio: 1:6. There are 184 required school days per year for Upper School students. Upper School students typically attend 5 days per week. The average school day consists of 8 hours.
Upper School Student Profile Grade 9: 18 students (14 boys, 4 girls); Grade 10: 35 students (21 boys, 14 girls); Grade 11: 29 students (15 boys, 14 girls); Grade 12: 36 students (24 boys, 12 girls); Postgraduate: 2 students (2 girls). 75% of students are

boarding students. 29% are state residents. 7 states are represented in upper school student body. 55% are international students. International students from China, Germany, Indonesia, Japan, Taiwan, and Viet Nam; 19 other countries represented in student body.

Faculty School total: 29. In upper school: 12 men, 11 women; 15 have advanced degrees; 10 reside on campus.

Subjects Offered Algebra, American history, American literature, animation, art, art history, audio visual/media, biology, calculus, calculus-AP, chemistry, college counseling, creative writing, drama, earth science, economics, English, English literature, ESL, European history, expository writing, fashion, fine arts, geography, geology, geometry, government/civics, grammar, health, history, journalism, mathematics, music, photography, physical education, physics, psychology, science, social sciences, social studies, Spanish, speech, world cultures, world history, world literature, writing.

Graduation Requirements Algebra, American government, American history, American literature, biology, British literature, computer literacy, economics, electives, English, foreign language, geometry, lab science, mathematics, physical education (includes health), visual and performing arts, world cultures, 100 hours of community service. Community service is required.

Special Academic Programs Advanced Placement exam preparation; honors section; independent study; study at local college for college credit; academic accommodation for the musically talented and the artistically talented; ESL (39 students enrolled).

College Admission Counseling 34 students graduated in 2012; all went to college, including Drexel University; Marymount College, Palos Verdes, California; Pepperdine University; Syracuse University; University of California, Los Angeles; University of California, San Diego.

Student Life Upper grades have specified standards of dress, student council, honor system. Discipline rests primarily with faculty.

Summer Programs Remediation, enrichment, advancement, ESL, art/fine arts, computer instruction programs offered; session focuses on academics; held on campus; accepts boys and girls; open to students from other schools. 60 students usually enrolled. 2013 schedule: June 14 to September 17. Application deadline: none.

Tuition and Aid Day student tuition: $16,550; 7-day tuition and room/board: $33,750. Tuition installment plan (monthly payment plans, individually arranged payment plans). Need-based scholarship grants available. In 2012–13, 20% of upper-school students received aid. Total amount of financial aid awarded in 2012–13: $450,000.

Admissions Traditional secondary-level entrance grade is 9. For fall 2012, 193 students applied for upper-level admission, 68 were accepted, 41 enrolled. TOEFL or SLEP or writing sample required. Deadline for receipt of application materials: none. Application fee required: $100. Interview recommended.

Athletics Interscholastic: baseball (boys), basketball (b,g), track and field (b,g), volleyball (b,g); intramural: baseball (b), basketball (b,g), track and field (b,g), volleyball (b,g); coed interscholastic: baseball, bowling, climbing, cross-country running, fishing, fitness, fitness walking, flag football, horseback riding, soccer, tennis; coed intramural: archery, backpacking, baseball, bicycling, bowling, climbing, cross-country running, fishing, fitness, fitness walking, golf, hiking/backpacking, horseback riding, jogging, mountain biking, outdoor activities, outdoor adventure, outdoor education, outdoor recreation, outdoor skills, outdoors, paddle tennis, physical fitness, physical training, skiing (downhill), snowboarding, soccer, table tennis, tennis, weight training. 2 PE instructors, 4 coaches, 1 athletic trainer.

Computers Computers are regularly used in all academic, animation, art, career exploration, classics, college planning, computer applications, creative writing, current events, design, desktop publishing, digital applications, economics, English, ESL, foreign language, geography, graphic arts, graphic design, graphics, historical foundations for arts, history, humanities, independent study, journalism, language development, library, life skills, literary magazine, mathematics, media, media arts, media production, media services, mentorship program, multimedia, music, music technology, news writing, photography, photojournalism, publications, publishing, reading, SAT preparation, science, senior seminar, social sciences, social studies, Spanish, speech, study skills, technology, theater, theater arts, typing, video film production, word processing, writing, writing, yearbook classes. Computer network features include on-campus library services, online commercial services, Internet access, wireless campus network, Internet filtering or blocking technology. Student e-mail accounts and computer access in designated common areas are available to students. The school has a published electronic and media policy.

Contact Mr. Joseph M. Blake, Director of Admissions and Outreach. 626-799-5010 Ext. 1203. Fax: 626-799-0407. E-mail: jblake@southwesternacademy.edu. Web site: www.SouthwesternAcademy.edu

See Display on next page, Close-Up on page 630, and Summer Program Close-Up on page 716.

SPARTANBURG DAY SCHOOL

1701 Skylyn Drive
Spartanburg, South Carolina 29307

Head of School: Mrs. Rachel S. Deems

General Information Coeducational day college-preparatory and arts school. Grades PK–12. Founded: 1957. Setting: suburban. Nearest major city is Greenville. 52-acre campus. 10 buildings on campus. Approved or accredited by Southern Association of Colleges and Schools and Southern Association of Independent Schools. Member of National Association of Independent Schools. Endowment: $4.1 million. Total enrollment: 449. Upper school average class size: 12. Upper school faculty-student ratio: 1:9. There are 175 required school days per year for Upper School students. Upper School students typically attend 5 days per week. The average school day consists of 8 hours and 45 minutes.

Upper School Student Profile Grade 9: 40 students (18 boys, 22 girls); Grade 10: 35 students (16 boys, 19 girls); Grade 11: 36 students (16 boys, 20 girls); Grade 12: 34 students (20 boys, 14 girls).

Faculty School total: 55. In upper school: 8 men, 14 women; 19 have advanced degrees.

Subjects Offered Advanced chemistry, advanced math, Advanced Placement courses, algebra, American government, American history, American history-AP, American literature, applied music, art, art history-AP, arts appreciation, band, biology, biology-AP, calculus, calculus-AP, career/college preparation, character education, chemistry, chemistry-AP, chorus, college counseling, college placement, college writing, community service, computer education, concert band, creative drama, creative writing, critical thinking, critical writing, cultural arts, debate, drama performance, drawing, drawing and design, earth science, English, English composition, English literature, English literature-AP, European history, fine arts, French, French language-AP, geometry, government/civics, history, jazz band, keyboarding, Latin, Latin-AP, mathematics, modern European history-AP, music, music theory, philosophy, physics, physics-AP, science, Spanish, Spanish language-AP, speech, statistics, statistics-AP, studio art-AP, trigonometry, U.S. government and politics-AP, world history.

Graduation Requirements Algebra, arts and fine arts (art, music, dance, drama), biology, chemistry, English, foreign language, geometry, history, physics, Ancient or European history, one additional lab science, participation in one sport per year.

Special Academic Programs 19 Advanced Placement exams for which test preparation is offered; honors section; study at local college for college credit; academic accommodation for the gifted and the artistically talented; programs in English, mathematics, general development for dyslexic students; ESL (3 students enrolled).

College Admission Counseling 27 students graduated in 2012; all went to college, including College of Charleston; University of Virginia; Washington and Lee University; Wofford College. Mean SAT critical reading: 595, mean SAT math: 602, mean SAT writing: 584.

Student Life Upper grades have specified standards of dress, student council, honor system. Discipline rests primarily with faculty.

Summer Programs Enrichment, sports, art/fine arts, computer instruction programs offered; session focuses on enrichment; held on campus; accepts boys and girls; open to students from other schools. 10 students usually enrolled. 2013 schedule: June 4 to August 4. Application deadline: May 1.

Tuition and Aid Day student tuition: $14,425. Tuition installment plan (monthly payment plans, tuition insurance). Merit scholarship grants, need-based scholarship grants, tuition reduction for children of faculty and staff, tuition reduction for children of benefit-receiving employees of Wofford College, Converse College, UCSUpstate available. In 2012–13, 24% of upper-school students received aid.

Admissions Traditional secondary-level entrance grade is 9. ERB, Kaufman Test of Educational Achievement, Metropolitan Test, ITBS, Otis-Lennon School Ability Test, Stanford Achievement Test or writing sample required. Deadline for receipt of application materials: none. Application fee required: $50. On-campus interview recommended.

Athletics Interscholastic: baseball (boys), basketball (b,g), cheering (g), soccer (b,g), swimming and diving (b,g), tennis (b,g), volleyball (g); coed interscholastic: aquatics, cooperative games, cross-country running, fitness, golf, martial arts, physical fitness, physical training, track and field, weight training. 4 PE instructors, 8 coaches, 1 athletic trainer.

Computers Computers are regularly used in art, English, French, history, Latin, mathematics, philosophy, science, Spanish classes. Computer network features include on-campus library services, Internet access, wireless campus network, Internet filtering or blocking technology, multimedia presentation stations. Student e-mail accounts are available to students. The school has a published electronic and media policy.

Contact Mr. Shawn Wilson, Director of Admissions. 864-582-7539 Ext. 2906. Fax: 864-582-7530. E-mail: shawn.wilson@sdsgriffin.org. Web site: www.spartanburgdayschool.org

THE SPENCE SCHOOL

22 East 91st Street
New York, New York 10128-0657

Head of School: Ellanor N. (Bodie) Brizendine

General Information Girls' day college-preparatory and arts school. Grades K–12. Founded: 1892. Setting: urban. 1 building on campus. Approved or accredited by New York State Association of Independent Schools. Member of National Association of Independent Schools and Secondary School Admission Test Board. Total enrollment: 720. Upper school average class size: 14. Upper school faculty-student ratio: 1:7. There are 163 required school days per year for Upper School students. Upper School students typically attend 5 days per week. The average school day consists of 7 hours.

Upper School Student Profile Grade 9: 61 students (61 girls); Grade 10: 59 students (59 girls); Grade 11: 57 students (57 girls); Grade 12: 60 students (60 girls).

Faculty School total: 127. In upper school: 25 men, 41 women; 52 have advanced degrees.

Subjects Offered 20th century history, 20th century world history, acting, advanced chemistry, advanced math, aerobics, African history, African literature, African-

American literature, algebra, American culture, American history, American literature, art, art history, art-AP, Asian history, Asian literature, astronomy, bioethics, biology, calculus, ceramics, chemistry, Chinese, Chinese history, Chinese literature, civil rights, composition, computer programming, computer science, CPR, critical writing, dance, design, digital imaging, digital photography, drama, drama performance, dramatic arts, drawing, earth science, economics, English, environmental science, equality and freedom, European history, exercise science, fiber arts, film studies, first aid, fitness, French, geometry, health, health and wellness, history, Indian studies, Japanese history, Japanese literature, Latin, Latin American history, Latin American literature, Latin American studies, linear algebra, literature, mathematics, media literacy, Middle East, multimedia, music, music composition, non-Western literature, novels, painting, performing arts, photo shop, photography, physical education, physics, poetry, pre-algebra, psychology, robotics, science, science research, sculpture, self-defense, Shakespeare, Spanish, Spanish literature, speech, statistics, technology, theater production, U.S. history, video film production, visual and performing arts, women's studies, world history, world religions, world studies, yoga.

Graduation Requirements Advanced math, algebra, American literature, art, biology, chemistry, computer science, dance, English, European history, foreign language, geometry, global studies, health, history, languages, music, non-Western societies, performing arts, physical education (includes health), physics, science, Shakespeare, speech, technology, U.S. history, visual and performing arts, visual arts, world religions, world studies.

Special Academic Programs 1 Advanced Placement exam for which test preparation is offered; independent study; term-away projects; study abroad.

College Admission Counseling 48 students graduated in 2012; all went to college, including Brown University; Dartmouth College; Duke University; Harvard University; University of Pennsylvania; Yale University. Median SAT critical reading: 720, median SAT math: 700, median SAT writing: 720, median combined SAT: 2140, median composite ACT: 30. 98% scored over 600 on SAT critical reading, 98% scored over 600 on SAT math, 100% scored over 600 on SAT writing, 100% scored over 1800 on combined SAT, 100% scored over 26 on composite ACT.

Student Life Upper grades have uniform requirement, student council. Discipline rests primarily with faculty.

Tuition and Aid Day student tuition: $39,200. Tuition installment plan (Academic Management Services Plan). Need-based scholarship grants, prepGATE loans, Academic Management Services private loans available. In 2012–13, 27% of upper-school students received aid. Total amount of financial aid awarded in 2012–13: $2,014,982.

Admissions Traditional secondary-level entrance grade is 9. For fall 2012, 127 students applied for upper-level admission, 11 enrolled. ISEE, school's own test and SSAT required. Deadline for receipt of application materials: December 1. Application fee required: $65. On-campus interview required.

Athletics Interscholastic: badminton, basketball, cross-country running, field hockey, lacrosse, soccer, softball, squash, swimming and diving, tennis, track and field, volleyball; intramural: fencing. 8 PE instructors, 29 coaches, 2 athletic trainers.

Computers Computers are regularly used in art, computer applications, creative writing, design, economics, foreign language, history, independent study, journalism, mathematics, science, technology classes. Computer network features include on-campus library services, online commercial services, Internet access, wireless campus network, iPads for every 9th grader to keep throughout Upper School, all classrooms equipped with SMART Boards. Campus intranet, student e-mail accounts, and computer access in designated common areas are available to students. The school has a published electronic and media policy.

Contact Susan Parker, Director of Admissions. 212-710-8140. Fax: 212-289-6025. E-mail: sparker@spenceschool.org. Web site: www.spenceschool.org

SPRING CREEK ACADEMY

6000 Custer Road
Building 5
Plano, Texas 75023

General Information Coeducational boarding and day and distance learning college-preparatory school. Grades K–12. Distance learning grade X. Founded: 1997. Setting: suburban. Nearest major city is Dallas. 3 buildings on campus. Approved or accredited by Southern Association of Colleges and Schools, Texas Education Agency, Texas Private School Accreditation Commission, and Texas Department of Education. Upper school average class size: 6. Upper school faculty-student ratio: 1:6. There are 180 required school days per year for Upper School students. Upper School students typically attend 5 days per week. The average school day consists of 2 hours and 30 minutes.

Faculty School total: 22. In upper school: 4 men, 18 women; 12 have advanced degrees.

Special Academic Programs Advanced Placement exam preparation; honors section.

College Admission Counseling 14 students graduated in 2012; all went to college.

Student Life Upper grades have specified standards of dress, student council, honor system. Discipline rests primarily with faculty.

Summer Programs Remediation, enrichment, advancement, art/fine arts programs offered; held on campus; accepts boys and girls; open to students from other schools. 2013 schedule: June to July. Application deadline: May.

Admissions Iowa Tests of Basic Skills required. Deadline for receipt of application materials: none. Application fee required: $300. On-campus interview required.

Computers Computer network features include Internet access, wireless campus network, Internet filtering or blocking technology. Computer access in designated common areas is available to students. Students grades are available online. The school has a published electronic and media policy.

Contact 972-517-6730. Fax: 972-517-8750. Web site: springcreekacademy.com/

SPRINGSIDE CHESTNUT HILL ACADEMY

500 West Willow Grove Avenue
Philadelphia, Pennsylvania 19118

Head of School: Dr. Priscilla Sands

General Information Coeducational day college-preparatory, arts, technology, science, and math school. Grades PK–12. Founded: 1861. Setting: suburban. 65-acre campus. 4 buildings on campus. Approved or accredited by Pennsylvania Association of Independent Schools and Pennsylvania Department of Education. Member of National Association of Independent Schools and Secondary School Admission Test Board. Endowment: $36 million. Total enrollment: 1,129. Upper school average class size: 16. Upper school faculty-student ratio: 1:6. There are 174 required school days per year for Upper School students. Upper School students typically attend 5 days per week. The average school day consists of 7 hours and 30 minutes.

Upper School Student Profile Grade 9: 107 students (53 boys, 54 girls); Grade 10: 112 students (55 boys, 57 girls); Grade 11: 101 students (48 boys, 53 girls); Grade 12: 128 students (59 boys, 69 girls).

Faculty School total: 137. In upper school: 27 men, 34 women; 40 have advanced degrees.

Subjects Offered Advanced math, Advanced Placement courses, African studies, algebra, American history, art, art history, biology, biology-AP, calculus, calculus-AP, ceramics, chamber groups, chemistry, Chinese, choral music, college counseling, community service, comparative government and politics-AP, computer animation, computer programming, computer science, dance, dance performance, drama, drawing and design, East Asian history, English, English literature, English-AP, environmental science, European history, European history-AP, fine arts, forensics, French, French language-AP, geometry, handbells, health, history-AP, independent study, jazz ensemble, Latin, mathematics, music, oceanography, orchestra, peer counseling, photography, physical education, physics, physics-AP, physiology, printmaking, robotics, science, senior project, social studies, Spanish, Spanish-AP, statistics, statistics-AP, theater, trigonometry, U.S. government and politics-AP, U.S. history, weight reduction, woodworking, world history, world history-AP, writing, writing workshop, yearbook.

Graduation Requirements English, foreign language, health, history, mathematics, music, physical education (includes health), science, senior project, sports, Senior speech. Community service is required.

Special Academic Programs 9 Advanced Placement exams for which test preparation is offered; honors section; independent study.

College Admission Counseling 106 students graduated in 2011; all went to college, including Franklin & Marshall College; Lehigh University; The George Washington University; Trinity College; University of Pennsylvania; Yale University. Mean SAT critical reading: 612, mean SAT math: 611, mean SAT writing: 624, mean composite ACT: 25.

Student Life Upper grades have uniform requirement, student council, honor system. Discipline rests equally with students and faculty.

Tuition and Aid Day student tuition: $27,400. Tuition installment plan (monthly payment plans, Higher Education Service, Inc). Merit scholarship grants, need-based scholarship grants available. In 2011–12, 38% of upper-school students received aid. Total amount of financial aid awarded in 2011–12: $3,146,250.

Admissions Traditional secondary-level entrance grade is 9. For fall 2011, 177 students applied for upper-level admission, 88 were accepted, 46 enrolled. ACT-Explore or SSAT required. Deadline for receipt of application materials: January 15. Application fee required: $50. On-campus interview required.

Athletics Interscholastic: basketball (boys, girls), crew (b,g), cross-country running (b,g), field hockey (g), golf (b,g), ice hockey (b), independent competitive sports (g), lacrosse (b,g), rowing (b,g), soccer (b,g), softball (g), squash (b,g), swimming and diving (b,g), tennis (b,g), track and field (b,g), volleyball (g), winter (indoor) track (b,g), wrestling (b); intramural: aerobics (g), aerobics/dance (g), badminton (g), basketball (g), dance (g), fitness (g), golf (g), outdoor activities (g), physical fitness (g), physical training (g), power lifting (g), ropes courses (g), soccer (g), softball (g), volleyball (g), weight training (g), yoga (g). 9 PE instructors, 53 coaches, 2 athletic trainers.

Computers Computers are regularly used in all classes. Computer network features include on-campus library services, online commercial services, Internet access, wireless campus network, Internet filtering or blocking technology. Student e-mail accounts and computer access in designated common areas are available to students. Students grades are available online. The school has a published electronic and media policy.

Contact Ms. Murielle Telemaque, Admissions Office Manager. 215-247-7007. Fax: 215-247-7308. E-mail: mtelemaque@sch.org. Web site: www.sch.org

SQUAW VALLEY ACADEMY

235 Squaw Valley Road
Olympic Valley, California 96146

Head of School: Mr. Donald Rees

General Information Coeducational boarding and day college-preparatory and arts school. Grades 9–12. Founded: 1978. Setting: rural. Nearest major city is Reno, NV. Students are housed in single-sex by floor dormitories and single-sex dormitories. 3-acre campus. 4 buildings on campus. Approved or accredited by Western Association of Schools and Colleges and California Department of Education. Total enrollment: 100. Upper school average class size: 8. Upper school faculty-student ratio: 1:8. Upper School students typically attend 5 days per week. The average school day consists of 8 hours.

Upper School Student Profile 100% of students are boarding students. 75% are international students. International students from Armenia, China, Germany, Republic of Korea, Russian Federation, and Saudi Arabia; 8 other countries represented in student body.

Faculty School total: 12. In upper school: 9 men, 3 women; 6 have advanced degrees; 4 reside on campus.

Subjects Offered Addiction, advanced biology, advanced chemistry, advanced math, Advanced Placement courses, advanced TOEFL/grammar, algebra, American democracy, American government, American history, American history-AP, American literature, American literature-AP, anatomy, applied arts, applied music, art, art education, art history, backpacking, band, biology, biology-AP, calculus, calculus-AP, ceramics, chemistry, civics, college admission preparation, college counseling, college placement, college planning, college writing, computer science, computers, creative writing, drama, English, English literature, environmental science, expository writing, fine arts, French, geography, geometry, government/civics, grammar, health, history, history-AP, instruments, Internet, Internet research, jazz, language-AP, linear algebra, literature-AP, martial arts, mathematics, mathematics-AP, music, music appreciation, music history, music performance, music theory, novels, outdoor education, photography, physical education, physics, physics-AP, pre-calculus, psychology, publications, research and reference, SAT preparation, SAT/ACT preparation, science, social sciences, social studies, Spanish, Spanish-AP, student government, student publications, studio art, surfing, swimming, TOEFL preparation, travel, trigonometry, typing, video, visual and performing arts, weight fitness, world history, world history-AP, writing, yearbook, yoga.

Graduation Requirements Arts and fine arts (art, music, dance, drama), college admission preparation, English, foreign language, mathematics, physical education (includes health), science, social sciences, participation in skiing and snowboarding, seniors must gain acceptance into a minimum of one (1) college or university.

Special Academic Programs 9 Advanced Placement exams for which test preparation is offered; honors section; accelerated programs; independent study; study at local college for college credit; academic accommodation for the gifted, the musically talented, and the artistically talented; programs in English, mathematics for dyslexic students; special instructional classes for students with ADD and dyslexia; ESL (15 students enrolled).

College Admission Counseling 17 students graduated in 2011; all went to college, including Michigan State University; Penn State University Park; The Johns Hopkins University; University of California, Davis; University of Colorado Boulder; University of Oregon. Median SAT critical reading: 410, median SAT math: 550, median SAT writing: 445, median combined SAT: 1405. 20% scored over 600 on SAT critical reading, 40% scored over 600 on SAT math, 20% scored over 600 on SAT writing, 20% scored over 1800 on combined SAT.

Student Life Upper grades have uniform requirement, student council, honor system. Discipline rests primarily with faculty.

Tuition and Aid Day student tuition: $17,010; 7-day tuition and room/board: $44,298. Tuition installment plan (individually arranged payment plans). Tuition reduction for siblings, need-based scholarship grants available. In 2011–12, 10% of upper-school students received aid.

Admissions Traditional secondary-level entrance grade is 10. For fall 2011, 120 students applied for upper-level admission, 110 were accepted, 100 enrolled. Math Placement Exam and writing sample required. Deadline for receipt of application materials: none. Application fee required: $100. Interview required.

Athletics Interscholastic: alpine skiing (boys, girls), freestyle skiing (b,g), golf (b,g), skiing (downhill) (b,g), snowboarding (b,g); intramural: aerobics (b,g), aerobics/Nautilus (b,g), alpine skiing (b,g), aquatics (b,g), backpacking (b,g), badminton (b,g), basketball (b,g), bicycling (b,g), billiards (b,g), blading (b,g), bowling (b,g), canoeing/kayaking (b,g), climbing (b,g), combined training (b,g), croquet (b,g), cross-country running (b,g), field hockey (b,g), fishing (b,g), fitness (b,g), fitness walking (b,g), flag football (b,g), fly fishing (b,g), freestyle skiing (b,g), Frisbee (b,g), golf (b,g), hiking/backpacking (b,g), horseback riding (b,g), ice skating (b,g), jogging (b,g), kayaking (b,g), mountain biking (b,g), mountaineering (b,g), nordic skiing (b,g), outdoor activities (b,g), outdoor adventure (b,g), outdoor education (b,g), outdoor recreation (b,g), outdoor skills (b,g), outdoors (b,g), paddling (b,g), paint ball (b,g), physical fitness (b,g), physical training (b,g), rafting (b,g), rock climbing (b,g), ropes courses (b,g), running (b,g), self defense (b,g), skateboarding (b,g), skiing (cross-country) (b,g), skiing (downhill) (b,g), snowboarding (b,g), snowshoeing (b,g), strength & conditioning (b,g), swimming and diving (b,g), table tennis (b,g), telemark skiing (b,g), tennis (b,g), ultimate Frisbee (b,g), volleyball (b,g), walking (b,g), wall climbing (b,g), weight lifting (b,g), weight training (b,g), yoga (b,g); coed interscholastic: alpine skiing, freestyle skiing, golf, skiing (downhill), snowboarding, soccer; coed intramural: aerobics, aerobics/Nautilus, alpine skiing, aquatics, backpacking, badminton, baseball, basketball, bicycling, billiards, blading, bowling, canoeing/kayaking, climbing, combined training, croquet, cross-country running, field hockey, fishing, fitness, fitness walking, flag football, fly fishing, freestyle skiing, Frisbee, golf, hiking/backpacking, horseback riding, ice skating, jogging, kayaking, mountain biking, mountaineering, nordic skiing, outdoor activities, outdoor adventure, outdoor education, outdoor recreation, outdoor skills, outdoors, paddling, paint ball, physical fitness, physical training, rafting, rock climbing, ropes courses, running, self defense, skateboarding, skiing (cross-country), skiing (downhill), snowboarding, snowshoeing, soccer, softball, strength & conditioning, swimming and diving, table tennis, telemark skiing, tennis, ultimate Frisbee, volleyball, walking, wall climbing, weight lifting, weight training, yoga.

Computers Computers are regularly used in all academic classes. Computer network features include on-campus library services, online commercial services, Internet access, wireless campus network, Internet filtering or blocking technology. Computer access in designated common areas is available to students.

Contact Adrienne Forbes, M.Ed., Admissions Director. 530-583-9393 Ext. 105. Fax: 530-581-1111. E-mail: enroll@sva.org. Web site: www.sva.org

STEPHEN T. BADIN HIGH SCHOOL

571 New London Road
Hamilton, Ohio 45013

Head of School: Mr. Brian Pendergest

General Information Coeducational day college-preparatory, general academic, arts, business, vocational, religious studies, and technology school, affiliated with Roman Catholic Church. Grades 9–12. Founded: 1966. Setting: urban. Nearest major city is Cincinnati. 22-acre campus. 2 buildings on campus. Approved or accredited by National Catholic Education Association, North Central Association of Colleges and Schools, Ohio Catholic Schools Accreditation Association (OCSAA), and Ohio Department of Education. Endowment: $120,000. Total enrollment: 509. Upper school average class size: 24. Upper school faculty-student ratio: 1:19. There are 182 required school days per year for Upper School students. Upper School students typically attend 5 days per week. The average school day consists of 6 hours and 55 minutes.

Upper School Student Profile Grade 9: 158 students (83 boys, 75 girls); Grade 10: 126 students (68 boys, 58 girls); Grade 11: 125 students (65 boys, 60 girls); Grade 12: 100 students (60 boys, 40 girls). 90% of students are Roman Catholic.

Faculty School total: 35. In upper school: 19 men, 15 women; 23 have advanced degrees.

Subjects Offered Accounting, algebra, American history, American literature, art, band, biology, British literature, calculus, calculus-AP, chemistry, chorus, computer programming, computer resources, consumer economics, consumer mathematics, economics, English, English literature, English-AP, French, geometry, government-AP, government/civics, history, integrated science, intro to computers, journalism, Latin, marketing, mathematics, music, music theory, physical education, physical science, physics, physiology, pre-calculus, publications, religion, science, social studies, Spanish, Web site design, Western literature, world history.

Graduation Requirements Computer science, English, mathematics, physical education (includes health), religion (includes Bible studies and theology), science, social studies (includes history), 15 hours of community service per year for seniors.

Special Academic Programs 8 Advanced Placement exams for which test preparation is offered; honors section; study at local college for college credit; study abroad; remedial reading and/or remedial writing; remedial math.

College Admission Counseling 124 students graduated in 2012; 120 went to college, including College of Mount St. Joseph; Miami University; Ohio University; The Ohio State University; University of Cincinnati; Xavier University. Other: 2 went to work, 2 entered military service. Median SAT critical reading: 526, median SAT math: 521, median SAT writing: 529, median combined SAT: 1574, median composite ACT: 23. 21% scored over 600 on SAT critical reading, 11% scored over 600 on SAT math, 16% scored over 600 on SAT writing, 20% scored over 1800 on combined SAT, 25% scored over 26 on composite ACT.

Student Life Upper grades have uniform requirement, student council. Discipline rests primarily with faculty. Attendance at religious services is required.

Tuition and Aid Day student tuition: $7800. Tuition installment plan (monthly payment plans, individually arranged payment plans, quarterly payment plan). Merit scholarship grants, need-based scholarship grants, paying campus jobs available. In 2012–13, 36% of upper-school students received aid; total upper-school merit-scholarship money awarded: $23,000. Total amount of financial aid awarded in 2012–13: $300,000.

Admissions Traditional secondary-level entrance grade is 9. Deadline for receipt of application materials: none. No application fee required. On-campus interview recommended.

Athletics Interscholastic: aquatics (boys, girls), baseball (b), basketball (b,g), bowling (b,g), cheering (g), diving (b,g), football (b), golf (b,g), gymnastics (g), hockey (b), ice hockey (b), rowing (b), soccer (b,g), softball (g), swimming and diving (b,g), tennis (g), volleyball (b,g); coed interscholastic: fishing. 2 PE instructors, 35 coaches, 1 athletic trainer.

Computers Computers are regularly used in mathematics, music, science, Web site design classes. Computer network features include on-campus library services, Internet access, wireless campus network, Internet filtering or blocking technology, scanners, travelling laptops, digital cameras. Campus intranet, student e-mail accounts, and computer access in designated common areas are available to students. Students grades are available online. The school has a published electronic and media policy.

Contact Mrs. Angie Gray, Director of Recruitment. 513-863-3993 Ext. 145. Fax: 513-785-2844. E-mail: agray@mail.badinhs.org. Web site: www.badinhs.org/index.asp

STEVENSON SCHOOL

3152 Forest Lake Road
Pebble Beach, California 93953

Head of School: Mr. Joseph E. Wandke

General Information Coeducational boarding and day college-preparatory, arts, and technology school. Boarding grades 9–12, day grades K–12. Founded: 1952. Setting: suburban. Nearest major city is San Francisco. Students are housed in single-sex by floor dormitories. 70-acre campus. 22 buildings on campus. Approved or accredited by Western Association of Schools and Colleges and California Department of Education. Member of National Association of Independent Schools and Secondary School Admission Test Board. Endowment: $21 million. Total enrollment: 747. Upper school average class size: 14. Upper school faculty-student ratio: 1:10. Upper School students typically attend 5 days per week. The average school day consists of 6 hours.

Upper School Student Profile Grade 9: 109 students (61 boys, 48 girls); Grade 10: 139 students (74 boys, 65 girls); Grade 11: 143 students (68 boys, 75 girls); Grade 12: 129 students (62 boys, 67 girls). 56% of students are boarding students. 70% are state residents. 20 states are represented in upper school student body. 20% are international students. International students from China, Hong Kong, Republic of Korea, Singapore, Taiwan, and Viet Nam; 14 other countries represented in student body.

Faculty School total: 65. In upper school: 37 men, 17 women; 36 have advanced degrees; 28 reside on campus.

Subjects Offered 3-dimensional art, advanced chemistry, Advanced Placement courses, algebra, American history, American literature, American literature-AP, architecture, art, art history, art-AP, biology, biology-AP, broadcasting, calculus, calculus-AP, ceramics, chemistry, chemistry-AP, Chinese, computer programming, computer science, concert band, creative writing, dance, dance performance, drama, drama performance, drama workshop, dramatic arts, drawing, drawing and design, driver education, economics, economics-AP, English, English literature, English-AP, environmental science, environmental science-AP, ethics, European civilization, European history, expository writing, fine arts, French, French-AP, geometry, German-AP, government/civics, grammar, history of ideas, history-AP, honors algebra, honors English, honors geometry, honors U.S. history, Japanese, jazz, jazz band, jazz ensemble, jazz theory, journalism, Latin, Latin-AP, macroeconomics-AP, marine biology, mathematics, mathematics-AP, microbiology, music, musical productions, musical theater, ornithology, photography, physical education, physics, physics-AP, portfolio art, pre-calculus, psychology, science, social studies, Spanish, Spanish-AP, speech, stage design, stagecraft, studio art-AP, tap dance, theater, trigonometry, U.S. history-AP, visual and performing arts, visual arts, vocal ensemble, wilderness education, wilderness experience, wind ensemble, world cultures, world history, world literature, world studies, writing, yearbook.

Graduation Requirements Arts and fine arts (art, music, dance, drama), English, foreign language, mathematics, physical education (includes health), science, social studies (includes history).

Special Academic Programs 22 Advanced Placement exams for which test preparation is offered; honors section; independent study; term-away projects; study abroad.

College Admission Counseling 133 students graduated in 2012; all went to college, including Boston University; New York University; University of California, Davis; University of California, Los Angeles; University of Oregon; University of Pennsylvania. Mean SAT critical reading: 615, mean SAT math: 668, mean SAT writing: 652, mean combined SAT: 1935, mean composite ACT: 25. 52% scored over 600 on SAT critical reading, 60% scored over 600 on SAT math, 52% scored over 600 on SAT writing, 58% scored over 1800 on combined SAT, 50% scored over 26 on composite ACT.

Student Life Upper grades have specified standards of dress, student council, honor system. Discipline rests equally with students and faculty.

Summer Programs Enrichment programs offered; held on campus; accepts boys and girls; open to students from other schools. 140 students usually enrolled. 2013 schedule: June 23 to July 26. Application deadline: none.

Tuition and Aid Day student tuition: $31,600; 7-day tuition and room/board: $51,900. Tuition installment plan (Insured Tuition Payment Plan). Need-based scholarship grants available. In 2012–13, 22% of upper-school students received aid. Total amount of financial aid awarded in 2012–13: $3,100,000.

Admissions Traditional secondary-level entrance grade is 9. For fall 2012, 499 students applied for upper-level admission, 264 were accepted, 162 enrolled. SSAT required. Deadline for receipt of application materials: February 1. Application fee required: $75. Interview required.

Athletics Interscholastic: baseball (boys), basketball (b,g), cross-country running (b,g), diving (b,g), field hockey (g), football (b), golf (b,g), lacrosse (b,g), sailing (b,g), soccer (b,g), softball (g), swimming and diving (b,g), tennis (b,g), track and field (b,g), volleyball (g), water polo (b,g); intramural: dance (b,g), golf (b,g), horseback riding (b,g), kayaking (b,g), modern dance (b,g), mountaineering (b,g), outdoor education (b,g), outdoors (b,g), power lifting (b,g), rock climbing (b,g), strength & conditioning (b,g), table tennis (b,g), weight lifting (b,g), wilderness (b,g), yoga (b,g); coed interscholastic: sailing; coed intramural: basketball, bicycling, climbing, dance, equestrian sports, fencing, horseback riding, kayaking, modern dance, mountaineering, outdoor education, outdoors, rock climbing, sailing, softball, strength & conditioning, table tennis, weight lifting, wilderness, yoga. 22 coaches.

Computers Computers are regularly used in all classes. Computer network features include on-campus library services, online commercial services, Internet access, wireless campus network, Internet filtering or blocking technology. Campus intranet and student e-mail accounts are available to students. Students grades are available online. The school has a published electronic and media policy.

Contact Mr. Thomas W. Sheppard, Director of Enrollment Management. 831-625-8309. Fax: 831-625-5208. E-mail: info@stevensonschool.org. Web site: www.stevensonschool.org

STONELEIGH–BURNHAM SCHOOL

574 Bernardston Road
Greenfield, Massachusetts 01301

Head of School: Sally Mixsell

General Information Girls' boarding and day college-preparatory and arts school. Grades 7–PG. Founded: 1869. Setting: small town. Nearest major city is Boston. Students are housed in single-sex dormitories. 100-acre campus. 7 buildings on campus. Approved or accredited by Association of Independent Schools in New England, International Baccalaureate Organization, New England Association of Schools and Colleges, The Association of Boarding Schools, and Massachusetts Department of Education. Member of National Association of Independent Schools. Endowment: $2.8 million. Total enrollment: 127. Upper school average class size: 10. Upper school faculty-student ratio: 1:6. Upper School students typically attend 5 days per week. The average school day consists of 7 hours and 30 minutes.

Upper School Student Profile Grade 9: 18 students (18 girls); Grade 10: 24 students (24 girls); Grade 11: 27 students (27 girls); Grade 12: 23 students (23 girls). 71% of students are boarding students. 35% are state residents. 12 states are represented in upper school student body. 38% are international students. International students from China, Japan, Mexico, Republic of Korea, and Taiwan.

Faculty School total: 33. In upper school: 7 men, 16 women; 14 have advanced degrees; 13 reside on campus.

Subjects Offered Acting, Advanced Placement courses, algebra, American history, art, band, biology, biology-AP, calculus, calculus-AP, ceramics, chemistry, Chinese, conceptual physics, dance, desktop publishing, drama, drawing, ecology, English, English-AP, environmental science-AP, equine science, ESL, ethical decision making, European history, European history-AP, fine arts, French, French-AP, geometry, graphic arts, history, International Baccalaureate courses, mathematics, music, music theory, photography, physics, poetry, psychology, public speaking, science, senior seminar, social studies, Spanish, Spanish-AP, sports medicine, theater, U.S. history-AP, values and decisions, water color painting, weaving, yearbook.

Graduation Requirements Art, arts and fine arts (art, music, dance, drama), English, foreign language, history, mathematics, physical education (includes health), science, U.S. history.

Special Academic Programs International Baccalaureate program; Advanced Placement exam preparation; honors section; independent study; ESL (9 students enrolled).

College Admission Counseling Colleges students went to include Brown University; Georgetown University; Mount Holyoke College; Smith College; The George Washington University; Tufts University.

Student Life Upper grades have specified standards of dress, student council, honor system. Discipline rests equally with students and faculty.

Tuition and Aid Day student tuition: $28,890; 7-day tuition and room/board: $48,443. Tuition installment plan (monthly payment plans). Merit scholarship grants, need-based scholarship grants available. In 2011–12, 22% of upper-school students received aid; total upper-school merit-scholarship money awarded: $20,000. Total amount of financial aid awarded in 2011–12: $904,000.

Admissions Traditional secondary-level entrance grade is 9. For fall 2011, 107 students applied for upper-level admission, 44 were accepted, 15 enrolled. ISEE, SAT, SSAT or TOEFL or SLEP required. Deadline for receipt of application materials: February 15. Application fee required: $50. Interview required.

Athletics Interscholastic: aerobics/dance, ballet, basketball, cross-country running, dance, dressage, equestrian sports, horseback riding, lacrosse, modern dance, soccer, softball, tennis, volleyball; intramural: alpine skiing, cross-country running, fitness, golf, horseback riding, ice skating, skiing (downhill), snowboarding, strength & conditioning, tennis. 1 athletic trainer.

Computers Computers are regularly used in all classes. Computer network features include on-campus library services, Internet access, wireless campus network, Internet filtering or blocking technology. Campus intranet, student e-mail accounts, and computer access in designated common areas are available to students. The school has a published electronic and media policy.

Contact Laura Lavallee, Associate Director of Admissions. 413-774-2711 Ext. 257. Fax: 413-772-2602. E-mail: admissions@sbschool.org. Web site: www.sbschool.org

THE STORM KING SCHOOL

314 Mountain Road
Cornwall-on-Hudson, New York 12520-1899

Head of School: Mr. Paul Domingue

General Information Coeducational boarding and day college-preparatory and arts school. Grades 8–12. Founded: 1867. Setting: small town. Nearest major city is New York. Students are housed in single-sex dormitories. 55-acre campus. 24 buildings on campus. Approved or accredited by Middle States Association of Colleges and Schools, New York State Association of Independent Schools, The Association of Boarding Schools, and New York Department of Education. Member of National Association of Independent Schools and Secondary School Admission Test Board. Endowment: $1 million. Total enrollment: 127. Upper school average class size: 12. Upper school faculty-student ratio: 1:6. There are 166 required school days per year for Upper School students. Upper School students typically attend 5 days per week. The average school day consists of 8 hours.

Upper School Student Profile Grade 8: 7 students (5 boys, 2 girls); Grade 9: 21 students (10 boys, 11 girls); Grade 10: 28 students (19 boys, 9 girls); Grade 11: 41 students (23 boys, 18 girls); Grade 12: 30 students (16 boys, 14 girls). 85% of students are boarding students. 32% are state residents. 3 states are represented in upper school student body. 60% are international students. International students from China, Italy, Republic of Korea, Russian Federation, Taiwan, and Viet Nam; 10 other countries represented in student body.

Faculty School total: 36. In upper school: 21 men, 15 women; 23 have advanced degrees; 16 reside on campus.

Subjects Offered Acting, Advanced Placement courses, advanced studio art-AP, advanced TOEFL/grammar, algebra, American history, American literature, American sign language, art, art history-AP, art-AP, astronomy, athletics, biology, biology-AP, calculus, calculus-AP, chemistry, Chinese, choir, choral music, college counseling, college planning, community service, computer graphics, computer programming-AP, computer science-AP, creative writing, dance, dance performance, digital art, drama, drawing, earth science, economics, economics-AP, English, English literature, English literature-AP, English-AP, environmental science, ESL, ESL, fine arts, foreign language, geometry, government/civics, guitar, health, health education, high adventure outdoor program, history, humanities, literacy, literature, macro/microeconomics-AP, macroeconomics-AP, Mandarin, mathematics, music, music composition, musical productions, outdoor education, painting, performing arts, photography, physical education, physics, physics-AP, piano, pre-calculus, psychology, psychology-AP, SAT preparation, science, Spanish, stage design, stagecraft, statistics-AP, student government, studio art-AP, theater, theater design and production, U.S. history, world history, world literature, writing, yearbook.

Graduation Requirements English, foreign language, Internet, mathematics, performing arts, public speaking, science, social studies (includes history), visual arts, at least two community service, outdoor adventure, and cultural experiences per year. Community service is required.

Special Academic Programs 10 Advanced Placement exams for which test preparation is offered; honors section; academic accommodation for the gifted, the musically talented, and the artistically talented; remedial reading and/or remedial writing; programs in English, mathematics, general development for dyslexic students; ESL (50 students enrolled).

College Admission Counseling 42 students graduated in 2012; all went to college, including Drexel University; Pace University; Penn State University Park; Rensselaer Polytechnic Institute; University of Connecticut; University of Rochester. Median SAT critical reading: 530, median SAT math: 620, median SAT writing: 500, median combined SAT: 1580, median composite ACT: 19. 15% scored over 600 on SAT critical reading, 57% scored over 600 on SAT math, 15% scored over 600 on SAT writing, 18% scored over 1800 on combined SAT, 22% scored over 26 on composite ACT.

Student Life Upper grades have specified standards of dress, student council, honor system. Discipline rests primarily with faculty.

Tuition and Aid Day student tuition: $22,700; 7-day tuition and room/board: $42,500. Tuition installment plan (individually arranged payment plans). Tuition reduction for siblings, merit scholarship grants, need-based scholarship grants available. In 2012–13, 26% of upper-school students received aid; total upper-school merit-scholarship money awarded: $32,500. Total amount of financial aid awarded in 2012–13: $405,575.

Admissions Traditional secondary-level entrance grade is 9. For fall 2012, 153 students applied for upper-level admission, 123 were accepted, 47 enrolled. Admissions testing, SSAT or TOEFL or SLEP required. Deadline for receipt of application materials: none. Application fee required: $85. Interview required.

Athletics Interscholastic: basketball (boys, girls), lacrosse (b,g), soccer (b,g), softball (g), volleyball (g), wrestling (b); coed interscholastic: crew, cross-country running, fencing, golf, jogging, rowing, running, skiing (downhill), snowboarding, tennis; coed intramural: aerobics/dance, alpine skiing, backpacking, ballet, bicycling, bocce, bowling, canoeing/kayaking, climbing, dance, fitness, fitness walking, freestyle skiing, golf, hiking/backpacking, ice skating, jogging, kayaking, modern dance, mountain biking, mountaineering, Nautilus, outdoor activities, outdoor adventure, outdoor education, outdoor recreation, outdoor skills, outdoors, paddle tennis, paddling, physical fitness, physical training, power lifting, rafting, rappelling, rock climbing, ropes courses, skiing (cross-country), skiing (downhill), snowboarding, snowshoeing, strength & conditioning, table tennis, tennis, touch football, track and field, walking, wall climbing, weight lifting, weight training, wilderness, winter walking, yoga. 3 coaches, 1 athletic trainer.

Computers Computers are regularly used in all academic, art, college planning, computer applications, drawing and design, economics, English, ESL, foreign language, graphic design, history, mathematics, music technology, photography, psychology, video film production, yearbook classes. Computer network features include on-campus library services, online commercial services, Internet access, wireless campus network, Internet filtering or blocking technology, parent/student/teacher communication portal. Campus intranet, student e-mail accounts, and computer access in designated common areas are available to students. Students grades are available online. The school has a published electronic and media policy.

Contact Mrs. Joanna Evans, Director of Admissions. 845-534-9860 Ext. 242. Fax: 845-534-4128. E-mail: admissions@sks.org. Web site: www.sks.org

See Display on next page and Close-Up on page 632.

STRAKE JESUIT COLLEGE PREPARATORY

8900 Bellaire Boulevard
Houston, Texas 77036

Head of School: Fr. Dan Lahart, SJ

General Information Boys' day college-preparatory school, affiliated with Roman Catholic Church (Jesuit order). Grades 9–12. Founded: 1960. Setting: suburban. 44-acre campus. 21 buildings on campus. Approved or accredited by Jesuit Secondary Education Association, Southern Association of Colleges and Schools, Texas Catholic Conference, Texas Education Agency, and Texas Department of Education. Endowment: $8 million. Total enrollment: 904. Upper school average class size: 25. Upper school faculty-student ratio: 1:11. There are 180 required school days per year for Upper School students. Upper School students typically attend 5 days per week. The average school day consists of 7 hours.

Upper School Student Profile Grade 9: 249 students (249 boys); Grade 10: 220 students (220 boys); Grade 11: 229 students (229 boys); Grade 12: 206 students (206 boys). 74% of students are Roman Catholic Church (Jesuit order).

Faculty School total: 80. In upper school: 59 men, 21 women; 26 have advanced degrees.

Subjects Offered Accounting, algebra, American history, American literature, art, art history, band, biology, broadcasting, calculus, chemistry, chorus, community service, computer science, debate, drama, drawing, economics, English, English literature, French, geography, geometry, government/civics, health, journalism, Latin, mathematics, music, music theory, oceanography, orchestra, painting, physical education, physical science, physics, physiology, pre-calculus, reading, religion, science, social studies, Spanish, speech, television, theater, theology, trigonometry, video, word processing, world history, world literature.

Graduation Requirements Arts and fine arts (art, music, dance, drama), business skills (includes word processing), computer science, English, foreign language, geography, health, mathematics, physical education (includes health), religion (includes Bible studies and theology), science, social studies (includes history), speech. Community service is required.

Special Academic Programs Advanced Placement exam preparation; honors section; study at local college for college credit.

College Admission Counseling 208 students graduated in 2011; 206 went to college, including Louisiana State University in Shreveport; Rice University; Texas A&M University; The University of Texas at Austin; The University of Texas at San Antonio; University of Notre Dame. Other: 2 had other specific plans. Median SAT critical reading: 630, median SAT math: 650, median SAT writing: 640, median combined SAT: 1910, median composite ACT: 28. 74% scored over 26 on composite ACT.

Student Life Upper grades have specified standards of dress, student council, honor system. Discipline rests primarily with faculty. Attendance at religious services is required.

Tuition and Aid Day student tuition: $15,150. Tuition installment plan (monthly payment plans). Need-based scholarship grants available. In 2011–12, 14% of upper-school students received aid. Total amount of financial aid awarded in 2011–12: $1,350,000.

Admissions Traditional secondary-level entrance grade is 9. For fall 2011, 554 students applied for upper-level admission, 357 were accepted, 249 enrolled. High School Placement Test (closed version) from Scholastic Testing Service required. Deadline for receipt of application materials: January 15. Application fee required: $50.

Athletics Interscholastic: baseball, basketball, cross-country running, football, golf, lacrosse, rugby, soccer, swimming and diving, tennis, track and field, water polo, wrestling. 4 PE instructors, 33 coaches, 2 athletic trainers.

Computers Computer network features include on-campus library services, online commercial services, Internet access. Student e-mail accounts are available to students. Students grades are available online. The school has a published electronic and media policy.

Contact Mrs. Patti McNeil, Assistant to the Director of Admissions. 713-490-8113. Fax: 713-272-4300. E-mail: pledesma@strakejesuit.org. Web site: www.strakejesuit.org

STRATFORD ACADEMY

6010 Peake Road
Macon, Georgia 31220-3903

Head of School: Dr. Robert E. Veto

General Information Coeducational day college-preparatory, arts, and technology school. Grades 1–12. Founded: 1960. Setting: suburban. Nearest major city is Atlanta. 70-acre campus. 4 buildings on campus. Approved or accredited by Georgia Independent School Association, Southern Association of Colleges and Schools, Southern Association of Independent Schools, and Georgia Department of Education. Member of National Association of Independent Schools. Endowment: $1 million. Total enrollment: 962. Upper school average class size: 17. Upper school faculty-student ratio: 1:13. There are 180 required school days per year for Upper School students. Upper School students typically attend 5 days per week. The average school day consists of 6 hours.

Faculty School total: 89. In upper school: 24 men, 23 women; 25 have advanced degrees.

Subjects Offered Advanced Placement courses, algebra, American history, American literature, anatomy, art, art history, art-AP, athletics, baseball, basketball, biology, biology-AP, calculus, calculus-AP, chemistry, chemistry-AP, community service, comparative government and politics-AP, computer programming, computer science, creative writing, drama, drama performance, driver education, earth science, economics, English, English literature, English literature-AP, English-AP, European history, European history-AP, expository writing, French, French-AP, geography, geometry, government/civics, grammar, history, history-AP, humanities, journalism, keyboarding, Latin, Latin-AP, madrigals, mathematics, mathematics-AP, music, physical education, physical science, physics, pre-calculus, science, social sciences, social studies, sociology, Spanish, Spanish-AP, speech, speech and debate, theater, trigonometry, U.S. government and politics-AP, water color painting, world history, world literature, writing.

Graduation Requirements English, foreign language, math applications, mathematics, science, senior seminar, social sciences, social studies (includes history), community service. Community service is required.

Special Academic Programs Advanced Placement exam preparation; independent study; special instructional classes for students with learning disabilities, Attention Deficit Disorder, and dyslexia.

College Admission Counseling 73 students graduated in 2012; all went to college, including Auburn University; Davidson College; Georgia Institute of Technology; Georgia Southern University; Harvard University; University of Georgia.

Student Life Upper grades have uniform requirement, student council, honor system. Discipline rests primarily with faculty.

Summer Programs Enrichment, sports, art/fine arts programs offered; held on campus; accepts boys and girls; open to students from other schools. 250 students usually enrolled.

Tuition and Aid Day student tuition: $12,995. Tuition installment plan (Insured Tuition Payment Plan, monthly payment plans, individually arranged payment plans). Merit scholarship grants, need-based scholarship grants available. Total upper-school merit-scholarship money awarded for 2012–13: $12,995.

Admissions Traditional secondary-level entrance grade is 9. ERB required. Deadline for receipt of application materials: none. Application fee required: $50. On-campus interview required.

Athletics Interscholastic: aerobics (girls), aquatics (b,g), baseball (b), basketball (b,g), cheering (g), cross-country running (b,g), dance team (g), drill team (g), fitness (b,g), football (b), horseback riding (b,g), physical training (b,g), soccer (b,g), softball (g), tennis (b,g), track and field (b,g), volleyball (g), wrestling (b), yoga (g); coed interscholastic: badminton, golf. 9 PE instructors, 6 coaches, 2 athletic trainers.

Computers Computers are regularly used in art, creative writing, English, French, graphics, information technology, Spanish classes. Computer network features include on-campus library services, Internet access, wireless campus network. Computer access in designated common areas is available to students. The school has a published electronic and media policy.

Contact Mrs. Lori Palmer, Associate Director of Admissions. 478-477-8073 Ext. 298. Fax: 478-477-0299. E-mail: lori.palmer@stratford.org. Web site: www.stratford.org

STRATHCONA-TWEEDSMUIR SCHOOL

RR 2
Okotoks, Alberta T1S 1A2, Canada

Head of School: Mr. William Jones

General Information Coeducational day college-preparatory, arts, and technology school. Grades 1–12. Founded: 1905. Setting: rural. Nearest major city is Calgary, Canada. 200-acre campus. 1 building on campus. Approved or accredited by Canadian Association of Independent Schools, Canadian Educational Standards Institute, International Baccalaureate Organization, and Alberta Department of Education. Affiliate member of National Association of Independent Schools; member of Secondary School Admission Test Board. Language of instruction: English. Endowment: CAN$5 million. Total enrollment: 667. Upper school average class size:

20. Upper school faculty-student ratio: 1:9. There are 174 required school days per year for Upper School students. Upper School students typically attend 5 days per week. The average school day consists of 6 hours and 40 minutes.

Upper School Student Profile Grade 6: 44 students (27 boys, 17 girls); Grade 7: 65 students (26 boys, 39 girls); Grade 8: 68 students (33 boys, 35 girls); Grade 9: 74 students (44 boys, 30 girls); Grade 10: 85 students (46 boys, 39 girls); Grade 11: 79 students (44 boys, 35 girls); Grade 12: 79 students (41 boys, 38 girls).

Faculty School total: 80. In upper school: 24 men, 27 women; 15 have advanced degrees.

Subjects Offered Art, band, biology, calculus, chemistry, computer science, drama, English, fine arts, French, Latin, mathematics, music, outdoor education, physical education, physics, science, social sciences, social studies, Spanish, theater.

Graduation Requirements Arts and fine arts (art, music, dance, drama), business skills (includes word processing), English, foreign language, mathematics, physical education (includes health), science, social sciences, social studies (includes history).

Special Academic Programs International Baccalaureate program; term-away projects.

College Admission Counseling 75 students graduated in 2012; all went to college, including Acadia University; Queen's University at Kingston; The University of British Columbia; The University of Western Ontario; University of Calgary; University of Victoria.

Student Life Upper grades have uniform requirement, student council, honor system. Discipline rests primarily with faculty.

Tuition and Aid Day student tuition: CAN$15,760–CAN$18,090. Tuition installment plan (monthly payment plans). Bursaries, merit scholarship grants, need-based scholarship grants available. In 2012–13, 10% of upper-school students received aid; total upper-school merit-scholarship money awarded: CAN$100,000. Total amount of financial aid awarded in 2012–13: CAN$137,913.

Admissions Traditional secondary-level entrance grade is 10. CTBS, OLSAT, Differential Aptitude Test, Henmon-Nelson or SSAT required. Deadline for receipt of application materials: none. Application fee required: CAN$100. Interview required.

Athletics Interscholastic: badminton (boys, girls), basketball (b,g), canoeing/kayaking (b,g), cross-country running (b,g), fencing (b,g), field hockey (g), golf (b,g), hiking/backpacking (b,g), jump rope (b,g), nordic skiing (b,g), outdoor activities (b,g), outdoor education (b,g), rugby (b), soccer (g), telemark skiing (b,g), track and field (b,g), triathlon (b,g), volleyball (b,g), wall climbing (b,g); coed interscholastic: alpine skiing, backpacking, badminton, bicycling, canoeing/kayaking, climbing, cross-country running, hiking/backpacking, jump rope, mountain biking, mountaineering, nordic skiing, outdoor activities, outdoor education; coed intramural: basketball, volleyball. 10 PE instructors, 38 coaches, 2 athletic trainers.

Computers Computers are regularly used in all classes. Computer network features include on-campus library services, online commercial services, Internet access, wireless campus network, Internet filtering or blocking technology. Campus intranet and student e-mail accounts are available to students. Students grades are available online. The school has a published electronic and media policy.

Contact Ms. Lydia J Hawkins, Director of Enrollment. 403-938-8303. Fax: 403-938-4492. E-mail: hawkinl@sts.ab.ca. Web site: www.sts.ab.ca

STRATTON MOUNTAIN SCHOOL

World Cup Circle
Stratton Mountain, Vermont 05155

Head of School: Christopher G. Kaltsas

General Information Coeducational boarding and day college-preparatory, arts, bilingual studies, and technology school. Grades 7–PG. Founded: 1972. Setting: rural. Nearest major city is Albany, NY. Students are housed in single-sex by floor dormitories. 12-acre campus. 7 buildings on campus. Approved or accredited by New England Association of Schools and Colleges and Vermont Department of Education. Member of National Association of Independent Schools. Endowment: $2.4 million. Total enrollment: 124. Upper school average class size: 10. Upper school faculty-student ratio: 1:6. There are 170 required school days per year for Upper School students. Upper School students typically attend 5 days per week. The average school day consists of 5 hours.

Upper School Student Profile Grade 9: 23 students (11 boys, 12 girls); Grade 10: 26 students (17 boys, 9 girls); Grade 11: 18 students (9 boys, 9 girls); Grade 12: 24 students (11 boys, 13 girls); Postgraduate: 10 students (5 boys, 5 girls). 54% of students are boarding students. 46% are state residents. 22 states are represented in upper school student body. 5% are international students. International students from Australia, Italy, Japan, New Zealand, and Switzerland.

Faculty School total: 21. In upper school: 7 men, 10 women; 8 have advanced degrees; 8 reside on campus.

Subjects Offered Algebra, American history, American literature, art, biology, calculus, chemistry, computer science, English, English literature, environmental science, French, geography, geometry, grammar, health, history, journalism, mathematics, nutrition, physical education, physics, science, social studies, Spanish, world history.

Graduation Requirements Arts and fine arts (art, music, dance, drama), computer education, English, foreign language, health education, mathematics, science, social studies (includes history), superior competence in winter sports (skiing/snowboarding). Community service is required.

Special Academic Programs Independent study; ESL (3 students enrolled).

College Admission Counseling 21 students graduated in 2012; 14 went to college, including Dartmouth College; Middlebury College; St. Lawrence University; University of Colorado Boulder; University of New Hampshire; University of Vermont. Other: 7 entered a postgraduate year. Mean SAT critical reading: 580, mean SAT math: 570, mean SAT writing: 600, mean combined SAT: 1750. 32% scored over 600 on SAT critical reading, 21% scored over 600 on SAT math, 47% scored over 600 on SAT writing, 42% scored over 1800 on combined SAT.

Student Life Upper grades have specified standards of dress, student council, honor system. Discipline rests primarily with faculty.

Tuition and Aid Day student tuition: $32,500; 7-day tuition and room/board: $44,500. Tuition installment plan (choice of one or two tuition installments plus advance deposit). Need-based scholarship grants, need-based loans available. In 2012–13, 48% of upper-school students received aid. Total amount of financial aid awarded in 2012–13: $800,000.

Admissions Traditional secondary-level entrance grade is 9. For fall 2012, 50 students applied for upper-level admission, 30 were accepted, 22 enrolled. Mathematics proficiency exam required. Deadline for receipt of application materials: March 15. Application fee required: $100. On-campus interview required.

Athletics Interscholastic: alpine skiing (boys, girls), bicycling (b,g), cross-country running (b,g), freestyle skiing (b,g), golf (b,g), lacrosse (b,g), mountain biking (b,g), nordic skiing (b,g), skiing (cross-country) (b,g), skiing (downhill) (b,g), snowboarding (b,g), soccer (b,g), tennis (b,g); intramural: strength & conditioning (b,g), tennis (b,g), yoga (b,g); coed intramural: skateboarding, tennis, yoga. 24 coaches, 1 athletic trainer.

Computers Computers are regularly used in computer applications, graphic design, mathematics, media production, research skills, science, Web site design, yearbook classes. Computer network features include on-campus library services, online commercial services, Internet access, Internet filtering or blocking technology. Student e-mail accounts are available to students. The school has a published electronic and media policy.

Contact Mrs. Kate Nolan Joyce, Director of Admissions. 802-856-1124. Fax: 802-297-0020. E-mail: knolan@gosms.org. Web site: www.gosms.org

STUART HALL

235 West Frederick Street
PO Box 210
Staunton, Virginia 24401

Head of School: Mr. Mark H. Eastham

General Information Girls' boarding and coeducational day college-preparatory and arts school, affiliated with Episcopal Church. Boarding girls grades 8–12, day boys grades PK–12, day girls grades PK–12. Founded: 1844. Setting: small town. Nearest major city is Richmond. Students are housed in single-sex dormitories. 8-acre campus. 6 buildings on campus. Approved or accredited by National Association of Episcopal Schools, Virginia Association of Independent Schools, and Virginia Department of Education. Member of National Association of Independent Schools and Secondary School Admission Test Board. Endowment: $1 million. Total enrollment: 300. Upper school average class size: 10. Upper school faculty-student ratio: 1:12. There are 172 required school days per year for Upper School students. Upper School students typically attend 5 days per week. The average school day consists of 6 hours and 20 minutes.

Upper School Student Profile Grade 9: 22 students (7 boys, 15 girls); Grade 10: 32 students (4 boys, 28 girls); Grade 11: 36 students (4 boys, 32 girls); Grade 12: 34 students (6 boys, 28 girls). 48% of students are boarding students. 82% are state residents. 3 states are represented in upper school student body. 17% are international students. International students from China, Republic of Korea, and Rwanda; 3 other countries represented in student body. 25% of students are members of Episcopal Church.

Faculty School total: 40. In upper school: 12 men, 12 women; 16 have advanced degrees; 4 reside on campus.

Subjects Offered Algebra, American literature, ancient world history, applied arts, applied music, art appreciation, art history, biology, biology-AP, British literature, calculus-AP, career education, career/college preparation, ceramics, chamber groups, chemistry, chemistry-AP, choir, choral music, chorus, civics, college counseling, composition, creative writing, drama, drama performance, dramatic arts, English, English composition, English language and composition-AP, English literature-AP, English-AP, environmental science, environmental science-AP, ESL, fine arts, French, French language-AP, geometry, grammar, guitar, health education, history of drama, history of music, history-AP, honors algebra, honors English, honors geometry, honors world history, instrumental music, lab science, language and composition, learning lab, mathematics, modern world history, music, music composition, music history, music performance, music theater, music theory, philosophy, photography, physical education, physical fitness, physics, piano, playwriting and directing, portfolio art, pre-algebra, pre-calculus, probability and statistics, religion, SAT preparation, science, social studies, Spanish, Spanish language-AP, Spanish-AP, stage and body movement, stage design, strings, student government, student publications, study skills, theater, theater arts, theater history, theater production, trigonometry, U.S. government, U.S. government and politics-AP, U.S. history, U.S. history-AP, visual and performing arts, visual arts, vocal ensemble, vocal music, voice, voice ensemble, world geography, world history, world history-AP, world literature, yearbook.

Graduation Requirements Arts and fine arts (art, music, dance, drama), English, foreign language, mathematics, philosophy, physical education (includes health), religion (includes Bible studies and theology), SAT preparation, science, social studies (includes history).

Special Academic Programs Advanced Placement exam preparation; honors section; study at local college for college credit; academic accommodation for the gifted, the musically talented, and the artistically talented; ESL (30 students enrolled).

College Admission Counseling 31 students graduated in 2012; 26 went to college, including Brandeis University; New England Conservatory of Music; Roanoke College; University of Virginia; Virginia Military Institute; Virginia Polytechnic Institute and State University. Mean SAT critical reading: 577, mean SAT math: 567, mean SAT writing: 561.

Student Life Upper grades have specified standards of dress, student council, honor system. Discipline rests equally with students and faculty.

Tuition and Aid Day student tuition: $13,400; 5-day tuition and room/board: $28,000; 7-day tuition and room/board: $41,500. Tuition installment plan (Insured Tuition Payment Plan, monthly payment plans, individually arranged payment plans). Need-based scholarship grants available. In 2012–13, 33% of upper-school students received aid. Total amount of financial aid awarded in 2012–13: $850,000.

Admissions Traditional secondary-level entrance grade is 10. For fall 2012, 10 students applied for upper-level admission, 6 were accepted, 6 enrolled. TOEFL or SLEP required. Deadline for receipt of application materials: February 1. Application fee required: $45. Interview required.

Athletics Interscholastic: basketball (boys, girls), cheering (g), golf (b,g), horseback riding (b,g), jogging (b,g), lacrosse (b,g), soccer (b,g), track and field (b,g), volleyball (g); intramural: cheering (g), skiing (downhill) (b,g), snowboarding (b,g); coed interscholastic: cross-country running, lacrosse, running, soccer; coed intramural: golf. 1 PE instructor, 1 coach.

Computers Computers are regularly used in all classes. Computer network features include on-campus library services, Internet access, wireless campus network, Internet filtering or blocking technology. Student e-mail accounts and computer access in designated common areas are available to students. The school has a published electronic and media policy.

Contact Mrs. Mia Kivlighan, Director, Day Enrollment. 888-306-8926. Fax: 540-886-2275. E-mail: mkivlighan@stuart-hall.org. Web site: www.stuart-hall.org

THE SUDBURY VALLEY SCHOOL

2 Winch Street
Framingham, Massachusetts 01701

Head of School: Samuel McGuire

General Information Coeducational day college-preparatory and general academic school. Grades PS–12. Founded: 1968. Setting: suburban. Nearest major city is Boston. 10-acre campus. 2 buildings on campus. Approved or accredited by Massachusetts Department of Education. Total enrollment: 160. Upper school faculty-student ratio: 1:16. There are 180 required school days per year for Upper School students. Upper School students typically attend 5 days per week. The average school day consists of 6 hours.

Faculty School total: 10. In upper school: 4 men, 6 women; 3 have advanced degrees.

Subjects Offered Algebra, American history, American literature, anatomy, anthropology, archaeology, art, art history, Bible studies, biology, botany, business, calculus, ceramics, chemistry, computer programming, computer science, creative writing, dance, drama, economics, English, English literature, ethics, European history, expository writing, French, geography, geometry, German, government/civics, grammar, Hebrew, history, history of ideas, history of science, home economics, Latin, mathematics, music, philosophy, photography, physical education, physics, physiology, psychology, religion, social studies, Spanish, speech, theater, trigonometry, typing, world history, world literature, writing.

Graduation Requirements Students must justify the proposition that they have developed the problem solving skill, the adaptability, and the abilities needed to function, independently in the world.

Special Academic Programs Independent study.

College Admission Counseling 20 students graduated in 2012; 15 went to college. Other: 5 went to work.

Student Life Upper grades have student council, honor system. Discipline rests equally with students and faculty.

Tuition and Aid Day student tuition: $7800. Tuition reduction for siblings available.

Admissions Deadline for receipt of application materials: none. Application fee required: $50. On-campus interview required.

Computers Computer network features include on-campus library services, Internet access. Student e-mail accounts are available to students. The school has a published electronic and media policy.

Contact Hanna Greenberg, Admissions Clerk. 508-877-3030. Fax: 508-788-0674. E-mail: office@sudval.org. Web site: www.sudval.org

SUFFIELD ACADEMY

185 North Main Street
Suffield, Connecticut 06078

Head of School: Mr. Charles Cahn III

General Information Coeducational boarding and day college-preparatory, arts, technology, and leadership school. Grades 9–PG. Founded: 1833. Setting: small town. Nearest major city is Hartford. Students are housed in single-sex dormitories. 340-acre campus. 49 buildings on campus. Approved or accredited by Connecticut Association of Independent Schools, New England Association of Schools and Colleges, and The Association of Boarding Schools. Member of National Association of Independent Schools and Secondary School Admission Test Board. Endowment: $31 million. Total enrollment: 412. Upper school average class size: 10. Upper school faculty-student ratio: 1:5. There are 180 required school days per year for Upper School students. Upper School students typically attend 6 days per week. The average school day consists of 5 hours and 35 minutes.

Upper School Student Profile Grade 9: 82 students (43 boys, 39 girls); Grade 10: 106 students (58 boys, 48 girls); Grade 11: 101 students (56 boys, 45 girls); Grade 12: 108 students (51 boys, 57 girls); Postgraduate: 15 students (14 boys, 1 girl). 66% of students are boarding students. 36% are state residents. 17 states are represented in upper school student body. 23% are international students. International students from China, Jamaica, Norway, Republic of Korea, Thailand, and United Kingdom; 20 other countries represented in student body.

Faculty School total: 81. In upper school: 45 men, 36 women; 54 have advanced degrees; 65 reside on campus.

Subjects Offered Acting, Advanced Placement courses, algebra, American history, American literature, anatomy and physiology, archaeology, art, art history, biology, biology-AP, calculus, calculus-AP, ceramics, chemistry, chemistry-AP, Chinese, computer math, computer programming, computer science, constitutional law, dance, drama, economics, economics-AP, English, English literature, English-AP, environmental science, ESL, ethics, European history, expository writing, fine arts, French, French-AP, geometry, government-AP, government/civics, grammar, health, history, jazz band, leadership, mathematics, mechanical drawing, music, music theory, news writing, philosophy, photography, physical education, physics, physics-AP, probability and statistics, religion, science, senior seminar, short story, social studies, sociology, Spanish, Spanish-AP, statistics, statistics-AP, technology, theater, theater arts, trigonometry, U.S. history, U.S. history-AP, visual and performing arts, visual arts, voice ensemble, wilderness education, wind ensemble, wind instruments, woodworking, world history, writing.

Graduation Requirements Arts and fine arts (art, music, dance, drama), English, foreign language, leadership, mathematics, physical education (includes health), religion (includes Bible studies and theology), science, social studies (includes history), technology portfolio.

Special Academic Programs 17 Advanced Placement exams for which test preparation is offered; honors section; independent study; academic accommodation for the gifted, the musically talented, and the artistically talented; ESL (12 students enrolled).

College Admission Counseling 131 students graduated in 2011; 130 went to college, including Bentley University; Boston College; Georgetown University; Gettysburg College; Southern Methodist University; Trinity College. Other: 1 entered a postgraduate year. Mean SAT critical reading: 553, mean SAT math: 577, mean SAT writing: 554, mean combined SAT: 1684, mean composite ACT: 24. 27% scored over 600 on SAT critical reading, 43% scored over 600 on SAT math, 30% scored over 600 on SAT writing, 33% scored over 1800 on combined SAT, 52% scored over 26 on composite ACT.

Student Life Upper grades have specified standards of dress, student council, honor system. Discipline rests primarily with faculty.

Tuition and Aid Day student tuition: $32,900; 7-day tuition and room/board: $46,500. Tuition installment plan (monthly payment plans). Need-based scholarship grants, tuition remission for children of faculty and staff who meet years of service requirement available. In 2011–12, 33% of upper-school students received aid. Total amount of financial aid awarded in 2011–12: $3,500,000.

Admissions Traditional secondary-level entrance grade is 9. For fall 2011, 934 students applied for upper-level admission, 287 were accepted, 145 enrolled. PSAT or SAT, SSAT or TOEFL required. Deadline for receipt of application materials: January 15. Application fee required: $50. Interview required.

Athletics Interscholastic: aquatics (boys, girls), baseball (b), basketball (b,g), cross-country running (b,g), field hockey (g), football (b), lacrosse (b,g), soccer (b,g), softball (g), squash (b,g), swimming and diving (b,g), tennis (b,g), track and field (b,g), volleyball (g), water polo (b,g); coed interscholastic: alpine skiing, backpacking, canoeing/kayaking, climbing, dance, diving, fitness, golf, outdoors, riflery, rock climbing, ropes courses, skiing (downhill), snowboarding, wrestling; coed intramural: rock climbing, ropes courses, weight lifting. 3 coaches, 2 athletic trainers.

Computers Computers are regularly used in architecture, art, English, foreign language, history, mathematics, science classes. Computer network features include on-campus library services, online commercial services, Internet access, wireless campus network. Student e-mail accounts are available to students. The school has a published electronic and media policy.

Contact Terry Breault, Director of Admissions and Financial Aid. 860-386-4440. Fax: 860-668-2966. E-mail: saadmit@suffieldacademy.org. Web site: www.suffieldacademy.org

SUMMERFIELD WALDORF SCHOOL

655 Willowside Road
Santa Rosa, California 95401

Head of School: Ms. Renate Lundberg

General Information Coeducational day college-preparatory, arts, and Waldorf Curriculum school. Grades K–12. Founded: 1974. Setting: rural. 38-acre campus. 8 buildings on campus. Approved or accredited by Association of Waldorf Schools of North America, Western Association of Schools and Colleges, and California Department of Education. Total enrollment: 385. Upper school average class size: 28. Upper school faculty-student ratio: 1:7. Upper School students typically attend 5 days per week. The average school day consists of 7 hours.

Upper School Student Profile Grade 9: 25 students (11 boys, 14 girls); Grade 10: 25 students (13 boys, 12 girls); Grade 11: 23 students (7 boys, 16 girls); Grade 12: 26 students (13 boys, 13 girls).

Faculty School total: 23. In upper school: 11 men, 12 women; all have advanced degrees.

Subjects Offered Advanced chemistry, arts, history, humanities, literature, mathematics, music, science.

Graduation Requirements All , Senior Thesis Project.

Special Academic Programs Honors section; study abroad.

College Admission Counseling 26 students graduated in 2012; 23 went to college, including Bennington College; Cornell University; Oberlin College; Sonoma State University; University of California, Davis; University of Redlands. Other: 1 went to work, 2 had other specific plans.

Student Life Upper grades have specified standards of dress, student council. Discipline rests primarily with faculty.

Tuition and Aid Day student tuition: $16,750. Tuition installment plan (FACTS Tuition Payment Plan, monthly payment plans). Tuition reduction for siblings, need-based scholarship grants available. In 2012–13, 40% of upper-school students received aid.

Admissions Traditional secondary-level entrance grade is 9. For fall 2012, 36 students applied for upper-level admission, 30 were accepted, 30 enrolled. Deadline for receipt of application materials: January 17. Application fee required: $75. On-campus interview required.

Athletics Interscholastic: baseball (boys), basketball (b,g), soccer (b,g); intramural: volleyball (b,g); coed interscholastic: tennis. 5 PE instructors, 5 coaches.

Computers The school has a published electronic and media policy.

Contact Ms. Sallie Miller, Admissions Director. 707-575-7194 Ext. 102. Fax: 707-575-3217. E-mail: sallie@summerfieldwaldof.org. Web site: www.summerfieldwaldorf.org

THE SUMMIT COUNTRY DAY SCHOOL

2161 Grandin Road
Cincinnati, Ohio 45208-3300

Head of School: Mr. Rich Wilson

General Information Coeducational day college-preparatory school, affiliated with Roman Catholic Church. Grades PK–12. Founded: 1890. Setting: suburban. 24-acre campus. 2 buildings on campus. Approved or accredited by Independent Schools Association of the Central States, Ohio Association of Independent Schools, The College Board, and Ohio Department of Education. Member of National Association of Independent Schools. Endowment: $20 million. Total enrollment: 1,071. Upper school average class size: 16. Upper school faculty-student ratio: 1:9. There are 187 required school days per year for Upper School students. Upper School students typically attend 5 days per week. The average school day consists of 6 hours and 30 minutes.

Upper School Student Profile Grade 9: 88 students (34 boys, 54 girls); Grade 10: 99 students (50 boys, 49 girls); Grade 11: 98 students (46 boys, 52 girls); Grade 12: 97 students (46 boys, 51 girls). 60% of students are Roman Catholic.

Faculty School total: 136. In upper school: 14 men, 23 women; 31 have advanced degrees.

Subjects Offered Advanced Placement courses, algebra, American history, American history-AP, American literature, anatomy and physiology, archaeology, art, biology, biology-AP, business law, calculus, calculus-AP, ceramics, chemistry, chemistry-AP, chorus, college admission preparation, college placement, community service, computer applications, computer science, computer science-AP, concert choir, critical studies in film, drama, economics, English, English literature, English-AP, environmental science, European history, European history-AP, fine arts, French, French-AP, geometry, government-AP, government/civics, grammar, graphic design, health, history, history of science, history-AP, Holocaust studies, language-AP, Latin, Latin-AP, leadership, leadership and service, leadership education training, literary magazine, mathematics, music, music theory-AP, music-AP, philosophy, physical education, physics, physics-AP, pre-calculus, psychology, psychology-AP, public speaking, religion, religious studies, science, senior career experience, service learning/internship, social studies, Spanish, Spanish language-AP, Spanish-AP, speech, speech communications, statistics-AP, student government, studio art, studio art-AP, study skills, theater, trigonometry, U.S. government and politics-AP, world history, world history-AP, world literature, world religions, writing.

Graduation Requirements Arts and fine arts (art, music, dance, drama), computer applications, computer science, English, foreign language, mathematics, physical education (includes health), religion (includes Bible studies and theology), science, social sciences, social studies (includes history), speech communications, junior year leadership course (one semester), junior year speech course, 40 hours of Christian service, senior search (2-week field experience in career of interest area).

Special Academic Programs 19 Advanced Placement exams for which test preparation is offered; honors section; independent study; study abroad; academic accommodation for the gifted.

College Admission Counseling 97 students graduated in 2012; all went to college, including Denison University; Indiana University Bloomington; Miami University; The George Washington University; University of Cincinnati; University of Notre Dame. Median SAT critical reading: 631, median SAT math: 609, median composite ACT: 28.

Student Life Upper grades have uniform requirement, student council, honor system. Discipline rests equally with students and faculty. Attendance at religious services is required.

Summer Programs Enrichment, advancement, sports, art/fine arts, computer instruction programs offered; session focuses on enrichment, academic advancement; held both on and off campus; held at 16-acre athletic sports complex; accepts boys and girls; open to students from other schools. 2013 schedule: June 7 to August 15. Application deadline: none.

Tuition and Aid Day student tuition: $18,700–$19,300. Tuition installment plan (monthly payment plans, individually arranged payment plans). Merit scholarship grants, need-based scholarship grants available. In 2012–13, 50% of upper-school students received aid.

Admissions Traditional secondary-level entrance grade is 9. For fall 2012, 80 students applied for upper-level admission, 72 were accepted, 47 enrolled. High School Placement Test or ISEE required. Deadline for receipt of application materials: December 14. Application fee required: $50. On-campus interview recommended.

Athletics Interscholastic: baseball (boys, girls), basketball (b,g), bowling (b,g), cheering (g), cross-country running (b,g), diving (b,g), field hockey (g), football (b), golf (b,g), lacrosse (b), soccer (b,g), softball (g), swimming and diving (b,g), tennis (b,g), track and field (b,g), volleyball (g), wrestling (b); intramural: dance team (g); coed interscholastic: weight lifting. 52 coaches, 1 athletic trainer.

Computers Computers are regularly used in all classes. Computer network features include on-campus library services, online commercial services, Internet access, wireless campus network, Internet filtering or blocking technology, mobile laptop computer lab, Basmati Grades, Blackboard, Sketchpad, 8 full-text databases including Big Chalk, World Book, Children's Lit, SIRS, Biography Resource Center, Wilson Web, INFOhio, JSTOR. Campus intranet, student e-mail accounts, and computer access in designated common areas are available to students. Students grades are available online. The school has a published electronic and media policy.

Contact Mrs. Kelley Schiess, Director of Admission. 513-871-4700 Ext. 207. Fax: 513-533-5350. E-mail: schiess_k@summitcds.org. Web site: www.summitcds.org

SUNSHINE BIBLE ACADEMY

400 Sunshine Drive
Miller, South Dakota 57362-6821

Head of School: Jason Watson

General Information Coeducational boarding and day college-preparatory, general academic, arts, business, vocational, religious studies, bilingual studies, and technology school, affiliated with Christian faith. Boarding grades 8–12, day grades K–12. Founded: 1951. Setting: rural. Nearest major city is Pierre. Students are housed in single-sex dormitories. 160-acre campus. 20 buildings on campus. Approved or accredited by Association of Christian Schools International and South Dakota Department of Education. Total enrollment: 86. Upper school average class size: 20. Upper school faculty-student ratio: 1:9. There are 180 required school days per year for Upper School students. Upper School students typically attend 5 days per week. The average school day consists of 6 hours and 40 minutes.

Upper School Student Profile Grade 9: 11 students (5 boys, 6 girls); Grade 10: 15 students (10 boys, 5 girls); Grade 11: 17 students (8 boys, 9 girls); Grade 12: 22 students (14 boys, 8 girls). 91% of students are boarding students. 72% are state residents. 7 states are represented in upper school student body. 15% are international students. International students from Ethiopia, Japan, and Republic of Korea. 100% of students are Christian faith.

Faculty School total: 16. In upper school: 8 men, 6 women; 4 have advanced degrees; 13 reside on campus.

Subjects Offered Accounting, advanced math, algebra, American history, American literature, band, bell choir, Bible, Bible studies, biology, chemistry, choir, Christian doctrine, Christian ethics, computer science, creative writing, drama, drama performance, economics, English, English literature, ethics, fine arts, geography, geometry, government/civics, grammar, health, history, HTML design, journalism,

mathematics, music, music appreciation, music composition, music history, music performance, newspaper, physical education, physics, science, social sciences, social studies, Spanish, speech, speech and oral interpretations, trigonometry, typing, U.S. government, U.S. history, vocal music, world geography, world history, writing, yearbook.

Graduation Requirements Arts and fine arts (art, music, dance, drama), Bible, computer science, English, mathematics, science, social sciences, social studies (includes history).

Special Academic Programs Independent study; study at local college for college credit; academic accommodation for the musically talented; remedial math.

College Admission Counseling 20 students graduated in 2012; 18 went to college, including Dordt College; South Dakota State University. Other: 1 went to work, 1 entered military service. Median composite ACT: 23. 8% scored over 26 on composite ACT.

Student Life Upper grades have specified standards of dress, student council, honor system. Discipline rests primarily with faculty. Attendance at religious services is required.

Tuition and Aid Day student tuition: $5565; 5-day tuition and room/board: $7950; 7-day tuition and room/board: $7950. Tuition installment plan (monthly payment plans). Tuition reduction for siblings, need-based scholarship grants available. In 2012–13, 20% of upper-school students received aid. Total amount of financial aid awarded in 2012–13: $38,520.

Admissions Traditional secondary-level entrance grade is 9. For fall 2012, 13 students applied for upper-level admission, 13 were accepted, 13 enrolled. Deadline for receipt of application materials: none. Application fee required: $50. On-campus interview required.

Athletics Interscholastic: basketball (boys, girls), cheering (g), cross-country running (b,g), football (b), track and field (b,g), volleyball (g), wrestling (b); intramural: physical fitness (b,g), physical training (b,g), strength & conditioning (b,g), weight lifting (b,g), weight training (b,g). 1 PE instructor, 6 coaches.

Computers Computers are regularly used in art, journalism, newspaper, publications, publishing, research skills, speech, typing, Web site design, writing, yearbook classes. Computer resources include on-campus library services, Internet access, wireless campus network, Internet filtering or blocking technology. Student e-mail accounts are available to students.

Contact Andrew Boersma, Dean of Students. 605-853-3071. Fax: 605-853-3072. Web site: www.sunshinebible.org

TABOR ACADEMY

66 Spring Street
Marion, Massachusetts 02738

Head of School: Mr. Jay S. Stroud

General Information Coeducational boarding and day college-preparatory and arts school. Grades 9–12. Founded: 1876. Setting: suburban. Nearest major city is Boston. Students are housed in single-sex dormitories. 85-acre campus. 42 buildings on campus. Approved or accredited by Association of Independent Schools in New England, New England Association of Schools and Colleges, and The Association of Boarding Schools. Member of National Association of Independent Schools and Secondary School Admission Test Board. Endowment: $36.5 million. Total enrollment: 519. Upper school average class size: 12. Upper school faculty-student ratio: 1:6. There are 157 required school days per year for Upper School students. Upper School students typically attend 5 days per week. The average school day consists of 7 hours.

Upper School Student Profile Grade 9: 92 students (47 boys, 45 girls); Grade 10: 141 students (78 boys, 63 girls); Grade 11: 129 students (74 boys, 55 girls); Grade 12: 157 students (92 boys, 65 girls). 69% of students are boarding students. 58% are state residents. 20 states are represented in upper school student body. 18% are international students. International students from China, Germany, Japan, Republic of Korea, Taiwan, and Viet Nam; 13 other countries represented in student body.

Faculty School total: 90. In upper school: 52 men, 38 women; 55 have advanced degrees; 59 reside on campus.

Subjects Offered Algebra, American history, American literature, ancient history, architecture, art, art history, astronomy, biology, calculus, celestial navigation, ceramics, chemistry, creative writing, drama, ecology, economics, English, English literature, European history, fine arts, French, freshman foundations, geology, geometry, German, Greek, health, history, Latin, maritime history, mathematics, meteorology, microbiology, music, navigation, oceanography, photography, physics, physiology, science, social sciences, social studies, Spanish, speech, statistics, theater, trigonometry, world history, world literature.

Graduation Requirements Algebra, arts and fine arts (art, music, dance, drama), biology, English, foreign language, geometry, mathematics, science, social sciences, social studies (includes history).

Special Academic Programs Advanced Placement exam preparation; honors section; independent study; term-away projects; academic accommodation for the gifted, the musically talented, and the artistically talented; ESL (12 students enrolled).

College Admission Counseling 132 students graduated in 2011; 127 went to college, including Boston College; Boston University; Hobart and William Smith Colleges; The George Washington University; University of Colorado Boulder; University of Vermont. Other: 1 entered a postgraduate year, 4 had other specific plans. Mean SAT critical reading: 592, mean SAT math: 619, mean SAT writing: 592, mean combined SAT: 1812.

Student Life Upper grades have specified standards of dress, student council, honor system. Discipline rests primarily with faculty.

Tuition and Aid Day student tuition: $34,000; 7-day tuition and room/board: $47,500. Tuition installment plan (Academic Management Services Plan, Key Tuition Payment Plan, monthly payment plans, Tuition Management Systems Plan). Need-based scholarship grants available. In 2011–12, 30% of upper-school students received aid. Total amount of financial aid awarded in 2011–12: $3,650,000.

Admissions Traditional secondary-level entrance grade is 9. For fall 2011, 806 students applied for upper-level admission, 415 were accepted, 160 enrolled. ISEE, PSAT or SSAT required. Deadline for receipt of application materials: January 31. Application fee required: $50. Interview required.

Athletics Interscholastic: baseball (boys), basketball (b,g), crew (b,g), cross-country running (b,g), field hockey (g), football (b), ice hockey (b,g), lacrosse (b,g), sailing (b,g), soccer (b,g), softball (g), squash (b,g), tennis (b,g), track and field (b,g), wrestling (b); intramural: crew (b,g), ice hockey (g), squash (b,g), tennis (b,g); coed interscholastic: dance, dance team, golf; coed intramural: aerobics, canoeing/kayaking, combined training, dance, fitness, Frisbee, kayaking, physical training, sailing, strength & conditioning, weight training. 2 athletic trainers.

Computers Computers are regularly used in English, foreign language, history, literary magazine, mathematics, newspaper, photography, publications, science, yearbook classes. Computer network features include on-campus library services, online commercial services, Internet access, wireless campus network, Internet filtering or blocking technology, digital media labs. Campus intranet, student e-mail accounts, and computer access in designated common areas are available to students. The school has a published electronic and media policy.

Contact Leslie Geil, Admissions Assistant. 508-291-8300. Fax: 508-291-8301. E-mail: admissions@taboracademy.org. Web site: www.taboracademy.org

THE TAFT SCHOOL

110 Woodbury Road
Watertown, Connecticut 06795

Head of School: Mr. William R. MacMullen

General Information Coeducational boarding and day college-preparatory, arts, and humanities school. Grades 9–PG. Founded: 1890. Setting: small town. Nearest major city is Waterbury. Students are housed in single-sex dormitories. 224-acre campus. 20 buildings on campus. Approved or accredited by Connecticut Association of Independent Schools, New England Association of Schools and Colleges, The Association of Boarding Schools, The College Board, and Connecticut Department of Education. Member of National Association of Independent Schools and Secondary School Admission Test Board. Endowment: $191.8 million. Total enrollment: 586. Upper school average class size: 12. Upper school faculty-student ratio: 1:5. Upper School students typically attend 6 days per week. The average school day consists of 7 hours.

Upper School Student Profile Grade 9: 107 students (54 boys, 53 girls); Grade 10: 151 students (70 boys, 81 girls); Grade 11: 162 students (80 boys, 82 girls); Grade 12: 151 students (81 boys, 70 girls); Postgraduate: 15 students (12 boys, 3 girls). 80% of students are boarding students. 36% are state residents. 37 states are represented in upper school student body. 15% are international students. International students from Canada, China, Hong Kong, Republic of Korea, Spain, and Taiwan; 21 other countries represented in student body.

Faculty School total: 124. In upper school: 66 men, 58 women; 92 have advanced degrees; 118 reside on campus.

Subjects Offered Acting, adolescent issues, advanced biology, advanced chemistry, advanced computer applications, advanced math, Advanced Placement courses, advanced studio art-AP, African-American literature, algebra, American history, American history-AP, American literature, anatomy, anatomy and physiology, animal behavior, architectural drawing, architecture, art, art history, art history-AP, astronomy, biology, biology-AP, calculus, calculus-AP, ceramics, chamber groups, character education, chemistry, chemistry-AP, Chinese, computer math, computer programming, computer science, computer science-AP, concert choir, creative writing, dance, design, digital imaging, drama, drawing, ecology, economics, economics-AP, English, English literature, English literature-AP, environmental science, environmental science-AP, ethics, European history, European history-AP, expository writing, film studies, fine arts, forensics, French, French language-AP, geography, geology, geometry, government-AP, government/civics, grammar, Greek, history, history of rock and roll, history of science, honors algebra, honors English, honors geometry, human rights, humanities, Islamic studies, Japanese, jazz band, Latin, Mandarin, marine biology, mathematics, music, music theory-AP, philosophy, photography, physical education, physics, physics-AP, physiology, pre-calculus, psychology, religion, science, senior project, senior thesis, service learning/internship, sex education, South African history, Spanish, Spanish literature-AP, Spanish-AP, speech, statistics, statistics-AP, studio art-AP, theater, theology, trigonometry, U.S. government and politics-AP, U.S. history-AP, video film production, world history, world literature, writing, zoology.

Graduation Requirements American history, arts and fine arts (art, music, dance, drama), English, foreign language, mathematics, science, social studies (includes history), three semesters of arts.

Special Academic Programs 27 Advanced Placement exams for which test preparation is offered; honors section; independent study; term-away projects; study abroad; academic accommodation for the gifted, the musically talented, and the artistically talented.

College Admission Counseling 169 students graduated in 2012; 167 went to college, including Amherst College; Cornell University; The George Washington University; Trinity College; Tufts University. Other: 2 entered a postgraduate year. Mean SAT critical reading: 630, mean SAT math: 650, mean SAT writing: 648, mean combined SAT: 1928. 75% scored over 600 on SAT critical reading, 75% scored over 600 on SAT math, 76% scored over 600 on SAT writing, 78% scored over 1800 on combined SAT.

Student Life Upper grades have specified standards of dress, student council, honor system. Discipline rests equally with students and faculty.

Summer Programs Enrichment, ESL, sports, art/fine arts programs offered; session focuses on academic enrichment; held on campus; accepts boys and girls; open to students from other schools. 150 students usually enrolled. 2013 schedule: June 25 to July 30. Application deadline: none.

Tuition and Aid Day student tuition: $35,775; 7-day tuition and room/board: $48,360. Tuition installment plan (Key Tuition Payment Plan). Need-based scholarship grants, need-based loans available. In 2012–13, 37% of upper-school students received aid. Total amount of financial aid awarded in 2012–13: $7,045,000.

Admissions Traditional secondary-level entrance grade is 9. For fall 2012, 1,656 students applied for upper-level admission, 375 were accepted, 197 enrolled. SSAT required. Deadline for receipt of application materials: January 15. Application fee required: $50. Interview required.

Athletics Interscholastic: alpine skiing (boys, girls), baseball (b), basketball (b,g), crew (b,g), cross-country running (b,g), field hockey (g), football (b), golf (b,g), hockey (b,g), ice hockey (b,g), lacrosse (b,g), rowing (b,g), soccer (b,g), softball (g), squash (b,g), tennis (b,g), track and field (b,g), ultimate Frisbee (b,g), volleyball (g), wrestling (b); coed interscholastic: dressage, equestrian sports, horseback riding; coed intramural: aerobics, aerobics/dance, ballet, basketball, climbing, cross-country running, dance, dressage, equestrian sports, figure skating, fitness, fitness walking, Frisbee, hockey, horseback riding, ice hockey, ice skating, jogging, martial arts, modern dance, outdoor activities, physical fitness, rock climbing, rowing, running, soccer, squash, strength & conditioning, tennis, track and field, ultimate Frisbee, walking, wall climbing, weight lifting, weight training, yoga. 1 coach, 3 athletic trainers.

Computers Computers are regularly used in art, English, foreign language, geography, history, mathematics, music, science classes. Computer network features include on-campus library services, online commercial services, Internet access, wireless campus network, Internet filtering or blocking technology. Campus intranet, student e-mail accounts, and computer access in designated common areas are available to students. The school has a published electronic and media policy.

Contact Mr. Peter A. Frew, Director of Admissions. 860-945-7700. Fax: 860-945-7808. E-mail: admissions@taftschool.org. Web site: www.taftschool.org

TAIPEI AMERICAN SCHOOL

800 Chung Shan North Road, Section 6
Taipei 11152, Taiwan

Head of School: Dr. Sharon Hennessy

General Information Coeducational day college-preparatory, arts, technology, and fine and performing arts, STEM, robotics school. Grades PK–12. Founded: 1949. Setting: urban. 15-acre campus. 5 buildings on campus. Approved or accredited by International Baccalaureate Organization, US Department of State, and Western Association of Schools and Colleges. Affiliate member of National Association of Independent Schools; member of European Council of International Schools. Language of instruction: English. Endowment: 499 million Taiwan dollars. Total enrollment: 2,235. Upper school average class size: 17. Upper school faculty-student ratio: 1:9. There are 180 required school days per year for Upper School students. Upper School students typically attend 5 days per week. The average school day consists of 6 hours and 40 minutes.

Upper School Student Profile Grade 9: 215 students (120 boys, 95 girls); Grade 10: 225 students (107 boys, 118 girls); Grade 11: 216 students (97 boys, 119 girls); Grade 12: 228 students (116 boys, 112 girls).

Faculty School total: 249. In upper school: 53 men, 50 women; 85 have advanced degrees.

Subjects Offered Advanced math, Advanced Placement courses, advanced studio art-AP, algebra, American literature, art history, Asian studies, biology, business, calculus, ceramics, chemistry, chemistry-AP, Chinese, choir, computer science, computer science-AP, contemporary history, current history, dance, debate, digital photography, drawing, earth science, English, English language-AP, English literature-AP, environmental science-AP, European history-AP, expository writing, fitness, forensics, French, French-AP, geography, geometry, health, International Baccalaureate courses, Japanese, jazz ensemble, journalism, Latin, linear algebra, macro/microeconomics-AP, macroeconomics-AP, Mandarin, microeconomics-AP, music theory-AP, orchestra, physical education, physics, physics-AP, pre-algebra, pre-calculus, psychology, research seminar, rhetoric, robotics, Spanish, Spanish-AP, speech and debate, statistics-AP, theater, theory of knowledge, trigonometry, U.S. history, U.S. history-AP, video film production, visual arts, wind ensemble, world cultures, world history, world literature, yearbook.

Graduation Requirements English, mathematics, modern languages, performing arts, physical education (includes health), public speaking, science, social studies (includes history).

Special Academic Programs International Baccalaureate program; 26 Advanced Placement exams for which test preparation is offered; honors section; ESL.

College Admission Counseling 217 students graduated in 2012; 214 went to college, including New York University; University of California, Berkeley; University of California, Los Angeles; University of California, San Diego; University of Pennsylvania; University of Southern California. Other: 2 entered military service, 1 had other specific plans. Mean SAT critical reading: 614, mean SAT math: 684, mean SAT writing: 631, mean combined SAT: 1929.

Student Life Upper grades have specified standards of dress, student council, honor system. Discipline rests primarily with faculty.

Summer Programs Remediation, enrichment, advancement, computer instruction programs offered; session focuses on internships, advancement, and make-up courses; honors math and science, robotics, writing, public speaking; held on campus; accepts boys and girls; open to students from other schools. 400 students usually enrolled. 2013 schedule: June 10 to July 5. Application deadline: May 31.

Tuition and Aid Day student tuition: 563,855 Taiwan dollars. Tuition installment plan (individually arranged payment plans).

Admissions Traditional secondary-level entrance grade is 9. For fall 2012, 117 students applied for upper-level admission, 68 were accepted, 54 enrolled. California Achievement Test, English for Non-native Speakers, ERB CTP IV, Iowa Tests of Basic Skills, ISEE, latest standardized score from previous school, PSAT, SAT, SSAT or Stanford Achievement Test required. Deadline for receipt of application materials: none. Application fee required: 10,000 Taiwan dollars.

Athletics Interscholastic: badminton (boys, girls), basketball (b,g), cross-country running (b,g), dance (b,g), golf (b,g), rugby (b,g), soccer (b,g), softball (b,g), swimming and diving (b,g), tennis (b,g), track and field (b,g), volleyball (b,g); intramural: swimming and diving (b,g). 6 PE instructors, 1 athletic trainer.

Computers Computers are regularly used in all academic classes. Computer network features include on-campus library services, online commercial services, Internet access, wireless campus network, Internet filtering or blocking technology. Campus intranet, student e-mail accounts, and computer access in designated common areas are available to students. Students grades are available online. The school has a published electronic and media policy.

Contact Dr. Winnie Tang, Admissions Officer. 886-2-2873-9900 Ext. 328. Fax: 886-2-2873-1641. E-mail: admissions@tas.edu.tw. Web site: www.tas.edu.tw

TAKOMA ACADEMY

8120 Carroll Avenue
Takoma Park, Maryland 20912-7397

Head of School: Mr. David Daniels

General Information Coeducational day college-preparatory and religious studies school, affiliated with Seventh-day Adventist Church. Grades 9–12. Founded: 1904. Setting: urban. 10-acre campus. 1 building on campus. Approved or accredited by Middle States Association of Colleges and Schools and Maryland Department of Education. Endowment: $400,000. Total enrollment: 230. Upper school average class size: 20. Upper school faculty-student ratio: 1:12. There are 180 required school days per year for Upper School students. Upper School students typically attend 5 days per week. The average school day consists of 5 hours and 20 minutes.

Upper School Student Profile Grade 9: 55 students (23 boys, 32 girls); Grade 10: 59 students (35 boys, 24 girls); Grade 11: 47 students (32 boys, 15 girls); Grade 12: 68 students (25 boys, 43 girls). 80% of students are Seventh-day Adventists.

Faculty School total: 20. In upper school: 9 men, 11 women; 8 have advanced degrees.

Subjects Offered Accounting, Advanced Placement courses, algebra, American government, American history, anatomy and physiology, art, art and culture, auto mechanics, band, Bible, biology, calculus-AP, career and personal planning, chemistry, choir, computer applications, computer skills, conceptual physics, drama performance, earth science, English, English-AP, geography, geometry, handbells, health education, honors algebra, honors English, honors geometry, honors U.S. history, honors world history, personal finance, physical education, physics, pre-calculus, Spanish, U.S. government and politics, U.S. government and politics-AP, world history.

Special Academic Programs Advanced Placement exam preparation; honors section; study at local college for college credit; remedial reading and/or remedial writing.

College Admission Counseling 70 students graduated in 2011.

Student Life Upper grades have uniform requirement, student council, honor system. Discipline rests primarily with faculty. Attendance at religious services is required.

Tuition and Aid Tuition installment plan (FACTS Tuition Payment Plan). Tuition reduction for siblings, merit scholarship grants, need-based scholarship grants, paying campus jobs available.

Admissions Traditional secondary-level entrance grade is 9. Application fee required: $75. On-campus interview recommended.

Athletics Interscholastic: basketball (boys, girls), cross-country running (b,g), flag football (b); intramural: basketball (b,g). 1 PE instructor.

Computers Computer resources include on-campus library services, Internet access, wireless campus network, Internet filtering or blocking technology. Campus intranet and student e-mail accounts are available to students. Students grades are available online.

Contact Mrs. Leah Daniels, Assistant Registrar. 301-434-4700. Fax: 301-434-4814. E-mail: ldaniels@ta.edu. Web site: www.ta.edu

TANDEM FRIENDS SCHOOL

279 Tandem Lane
Charlottesville, Virginia 22902

Head of School: Andy Jones-Wilkins

General Information Coeducational day college-preparatory and arts school, affiliated with Society of Friends. Grades 5–12. Founded: 1970. Setting: small town. Nearest major city is Richmond. 23-acre campus. 7 buildings on campus. Approved or accredited by Friends Council on Education and Virginia Association of Independent Schools. Member of National Association of Independent Schools. Endowment: $3.3 million. Total enrollment: 207. Upper school average class size: 12. Upper school faculty-student ratio: 1:6. There are 180 required school days per year for Upper School students. Upper School students typically attend 5 days per week. The average school day consists of 7 hours.

Upper School Student Profile Grade 9: 30 students (13 boys, 17 girls); Grade 10: 21 students (12 boys, 9 girls); Grade 11: 27 students (9 boys, 18 girls); Grade 12: 31 students (13 boys, 18 girls). 3% of students are members of Society of Friends.

Faculty School total: 36. In upper school: 7 men, 10 women; 10 have advanced degrees.

Subjects Offered Algebra, American literature, anatomy, art, bioethics, biology, biology-AP, calculus, calculus-AP, ceramics, chemistry, chemistry-AP, college counseling, computer applications, creative writing, cultural geography, discrete mathematics, drama, economics, economics and history, English, English-AP, environmental science-AP, expository writing, fine arts, French, French-AP, geometry, health and wellness, jazz ensemble, Latin, Latin-AP, marine biology, media studies, modern world history, music, musical productions, performing arts, photo shop, photography, physics, Quakerism and ethics, senior project, Spanish, Spanish-AP, statistics, statistics-AP, student government, student publications, studio art, theater, trigonometry, U.S. government, U.S. history, U.S. history-AP, weaving, world history, world literature, writing, yearbook.

Graduation Requirements Arts and fine arts (art, music, dance, drama), computer science, English, foreign language, government/civics, history, mathematics, science, senior year independent experiential learning project. Community service is required.

Special Academic Programs Advanced Placement exam preparation; independent study; academic accommodation for the gifted; remedial reading and/or remedial writing; remedial math.

College Admission Counseling 36 students graduated in 2012; 32 went to college, including Bates College; James Madison University; The College of William and Mary; The University of North Carolina at Asheville; University of Virginia; Virginia Polytechnic Institute and State University. Other: 4 had other specific plans. Median SAT critical reading: 642, median SAT math: 599, median SAT writing: 620, median combined SAT: 1241, median composite ACT: 26.

Student Life Upper grades have student council, honor system. Discipline rests equally with students and faculty. Attendance at religious services is required.

Summer Programs Art/fine arts programs offered; session focuses on arts, grades K-8; held on campus; accepts boys and girls; open to students from other schools. 125 students usually enrolled. 2013 schedule: June 17 to July 26. Application deadline: May.

Tuition and Aid Day student tuition: $17,900. Tuition installment plan (Insured Tuition Payment Plan, monthly payment plans, individually arranged payment plans). Need-based scholarship grants, tuition remission for children of full-time faculty available. In 2012–13, 34% of upper-school students received aid. Total amount of financial aid awarded in 2012–13: $379,110.

Admissions Traditional secondary-level entrance grade is 9. For fall 2012, 76 students applied for upper-level admission, 71 were accepted, 59 enrolled. Woodcock-Johnson required. Deadline for receipt of application materials: none. Application fee required: $50. Interview required.

Athletics Interscholastic: basketball (boys, girls), field hockey (g), lacrosse (b,g), soccer (b,g), tennis (b,g), volleyball (g); coed interscholastic: cross-country running, fencing, golf, mountain biking, track and field; coed intramural: fencing. 2 PE instructors, 24 coaches.

Computers Computers are regularly used in all academic classes. Computer network features include on-campus library services, online commercial services, Internet access, wireless campus network, Internet filtering or blocking technology, virtual classroom, iPad program for grades 5, 6, and 9. Student e-mail accounts and computer access in designated common areas are available to students. Students grades are available online. The school has a published electronic and media policy.

Contact Louise DeCamp Cole, Director of Admissions. 434-951-9314. Fax: 434-296-1886. E-mail: lcole@tandemfs.org. Web site: www.tandemfs.org

TAPPLY BINET COLLEGE

245 Garner Road West
Ancaster, Ontario L9G 3K9, Canada

Head of School: Ms. Sue Davidson

General Information Coeducational day college-preparatory and general academic school. Grades 7–12. Founded: 1997. Setting: small town. Nearest major city is Hamilton, Canada. 1-acre campus. 1 building on campus. Approved or accredited by Ontario Ministry of Education and Ontario Department of Education. Language of instruction: English. Total enrollment: 17. Upper school average class size: 6. Upper school faculty-student ratio: 1:3.

Upper School Student Profile Grade 9: 2 students (1 boy, 1 girl); Grade 10: 3 students (2 boys, 1 girl); Grade 11: 2 students (1 boy, 1 girl); Grade 12: 10 students (7 boys, 3 girls).

Faculty School total: 6. In upper school: 1 man, 3 women; 3 have advanced degrees.

College Admission Counseling 4 students graduated in 2012; they went to Brock University; Trent University; Wilfrid Laurier University.

Student Life Upper grades have uniform requirement, student council, honor system. Discipline rests primarily with faculty.

Summer Programs Enrichment programs offered; session focuses on academics; held on campus; accepts boys and girls; open to students from other schools. 6 students usually enrolled. 2013 schedule: July 1 to August 31.

Admissions Battery of testing done through outside agency required. Deadline for receipt of application materials: none. No application fee required.

Athletics Coed Interscholastic: aerobics/Nautilus. 1 PE instructor.

Contact Ms. Sue Davidson, Principal. 905-648-2737. Fax: 905-648-8762. E-mail: tapplybinetcollege@cogeco.net. Web site: www.tapplybinetcollege.com

TASIS THE AMERICAN SCHOOL IN ENGLAND

Coldharbour Lane
Thorpe, Surrey TW20 8TE, United Kingdom

Head of School: Mr. Michael McBrien

General Information Coeducational boarding and day college-preparatory and arts school. Boarding grades 9–13, day grades N–13. Founded: 1976. Setting: rural. Nearest major city is London, United Kingdom. Students are housed in single-sex dormitories. 46-acre campus. 26 buildings on campus. Approved or accredited by Council of International Schools, International Baccalaureate Organization, New England Association of Schools and Colleges, Office for Standards in Education (OFSTED), The Association of Boarding Schools, and state department of education. Affiliate member of National Association of Independent Schools; member of Secondary School Admission Test Board and European Council of International Schools. Language of instruction: English. Total enrollment: 750. Upper school average class size: 15. Upper school faculty-student ratio: 1:8. There are 171 required school days per year for Upper School students. Upper School students typically attend 5 days per week. The average school day consists of 6 hours.

Upper School Student Profile Grade 9: 70 students (38 boys, 32 girls); Grade 10: 85 students (47 boys, 38 girls); Grade 11: 115 students (60 boys, 55 girls); Grade 12: 120 students (60 boys, 60 girls). 46% of students are boarding students. 39% are international students. International students from China, Russian Federation, Saudi Arabia, Spain, Taiwan, and United States; 36 other countries represented in student body.

Faculty School total: 112. In upper school: 24 men, 27 women; 38 have advanced degrees; 23 reside on campus.

Subjects Offered 20th century history, acting, algebra, American history, American history-AP, American literature, ancient history, art, art history, art history-AP, biology, biology-AP, calculus-AP, ceramics, chemistry, chemistry-AP, choir, computer graphics, computer science-AP, debate, drawing, economics, economics-AP, English, English language and composition-AP, English literature, English literature and composition-AP, ensembles, environmental science, environmental science-AP, ESL, European history, European history-AP, French, French-AP, geometry, German, government and politics-AP, health and wellness, humanities, international affairs, international relations, Internet, journalism, keyboarding, Latin, Latin-AP, mathematics, music, music technology, music theory, music theory-AP, painting, photography, physical education, physical science, physics, physics-AP, pre-calculus, printmaking, psychology, public speaking, Russian, sculpture, senior humanities, Shakespeare, Spanish, Spanish-AP, statistics-AP, theater arts, theory of knowledge, visual arts, Web site design, Western civilization, word processing, world history, yearbook.

Graduation Requirements Arts and fine arts (art, music, dance, drama), computer science, English, foreign language, history, lab science, mathematics, physical education (includes health), senior humanities, sports. Community service is required.

Special Academic Programs International Baccalaureate program; 21 Advanced Placement exams for which test preparation is offered; independent study; academic accommodation for the gifted; remedial reading and/or remedial writing; ESL (76 students enrolled).

College Admission Counseling 107 students graduated in 2011; 106 went to college, including McGill University; Texas A&M University; University of Richmond; University of South Carolina; University of Southern California. Other: 1 had other specific plans.

Student Life Upper grades have uniform requirement, student council. Discipline rests primarily with faculty.

Tuition and Aid Day student tuition: £19,210; 7-day tuition and room/board: £32,130. Tuition installment plan (monthly payment plans, individually arranged payment plans). Need-based scholarship grants available.

Admissions TOEFL or SLEP required. Deadline for receipt of application materials: none. Application fee required: £125. Interview recommended.

Athletics Interscholastic: baseball (boys), basketball (b,g), cross-country running (b,g), rugby (b), soccer (b,g), softball (g), tennis (b,g), volleyball (b,g); intramural: aerobics (g), aerobics/dance (g), badminton (b,g), ballet (g), cricket (b,g), dance (g), dance team (g), field hockey (b,g), fitness (b,g), floor hockey (b,g), gymnastics (b,g), handball (b,g), indoor soccer (b,g), jump rope (b,g), lacrosse (b,g), modern dance (b,g), outdoor activities (b,g), outdoor adventure (b,g), physical fitness (b,g), physical training (b,g), rhythmic gymnastics (b,g), rugby (b), running (b,g), scooter football (b,g), soccer (b,g), softball (b,g), strength & conditioning (b,g), team handball (b,g), weight training (b,g), winter soccer (b,g); coed interscholastic: cheering, golf; coed intramural: basketball, bicycling, golf, gymnastics, handball, horseback riding, indoor soccer, lacrosse, martial arts, outdoor activities, outdoor adventure, squash, strength & conditioning, swimming and diving, table tennis, team handball, tennis, track and field, volleyball, weight training, winter soccer. 5 PE instructors, 10 coaches, 1 athletic trainer.

Computers Computers are regularly used in all academic classes. Computer network features include on-campus library services, online commercial services, Internet access, wireless campus network, Internet filtering or blocking technology. Campus intranet, student e-mail accounts, and computer access in designated common areas are available to students. The school has a published electronic and media policy.

Contact Ms. Karen House, Director of Admissions. 44-1932-582316. Fax: 44-1932-564644. E-mail: ukadmissions@tasisengland.org. Web site: www.tasis.com/England/

See Display below, Close-Up on page 634, and Summer Program Close-Up on page 718.

TASIS, THE AMERICAN SCHOOL IN SWITZERLAND

Via Collina d'Oro
Montagnola-Lugano CH-6926, Switzerland

Head of School: Mr. Michael Ulku-Steiner

General Information Coeducational boarding and day college-preparatory, arts, and sports school. Boarding grades 7–PG, day grades 1–PG. Founded: 1956. Setting: small town. Nearest major city is Lugano, Switzerland. Students are housed in single-sex dormitories. 9-acre campus. 19 buildings on campus. Approved or accredited by New England Association of Schools and Colleges and Swiss Federation of Private Schools. Affiliate member of National Association of Independent Schools; member of Secondary School Admission Test Board. Language of instruction: English. Total enrollment: 642. Upper school average class size: 14. Upper school faculty-student ratio: 1:5. Upper School students typically attend 5 days per week.

Upper School Student Profile Grade 9: 61 students (30 boys, 31 girls); Grade 10: 82 students (41 boys, 41 girls); Grade 11: 114 students (57 boys, 57 girls); Grade 12: 78 students (32 boys, 46 girls); Postgraduate: 4 students (4 girls). 80% of students are boarding students. 82% are international students. International students from Brazil, Germany, Italy, and United States; 4 other countries represented in student body.

Faculty In upper school: 30 men, 39 women; 39 have advanced degrees; 32 reside on campus.

Subjects Offered Advanced Placement courses, algebra, American history, American literature, ancient history, art, art history, art history-AP, biology, biology-AP, calculus, calculus-AP, ceramics, chemistry, chemistry-AP, digital photography, drama, economics, economics-AP, English, English language and composition-AP, English literature, English literature and composition-AP, environmental science, ESL, European history, European history-AP, fine arts, French, French language-AP, geography, geometry, German-AP, graphic design, health, history, international relations, Italian, mathematics, medieval/Renaissance history, music, photography, physical education, physics, science, social studies, Spanish, Spanish language-AP, theater, theory of knowledge, U.S. government, U.S. history-AP, world cultures, world history, world literature.

Graduation Requirements Arts, English, European history, foreign language, mathematics, science, senior humanities, sports, U.S. history. Community service is required.

Special Academic Programs International Baccalaureate program; Advanced Placement exam preparation; honors section; ESL (235 students enrolled).

College Admission Counseling 72 students graduated in 2011; 70 went to college, including Pace University; The American University of Paris; The George Washington University. Other: 2 entered a postgraduate year. Median SAT critical reading: 570, median SAT math: 570. 30% scored over 600 on SAT critical reading, 22% scored over 600 on SAT math.

Student Life Upper grades have specified standards of dress, student council, honor system. Discipline rests equally with students and faculty.

Tuition and Aid Day student tuition: 43,140 Swiss francs; 7-day tuition and room/board: 69,000 Swiss francs. Tuition installment plan (individually arranged payment plans). Need-based scholarship grants available. In 2011–12, 15% of upper-school students received aid.

Admissions Traditional secondary-level entrance grade is 11. TOEFL or SLEP required. Deadline for receipt of application materials: none. Application fee required: 300 Swiss francs. Interview recommended.

Athletics Interscholastic: basketball (boys, girls), golf (b), rugby (b), soccer (b,g), swimming and diving (b,g), tennis (b,g), track and field (b,g), volleyball (b,g); intramural: basketball (b,g), rugby (b); coed interscholastic: softball, swimming and diving, track and field; coed intramural: aerobics, aerobics/dance, aerobics/Nautilus, basketball, climbing, combined training, cross-country running, dance, fitness, flag football, floor hockey, golf, horseback riding, indoor soccer, jogging, lacrosse, martial arts, modern dance, physical fitness, physical training, rock climbing, running, sailing, soccer, softball, squash, strength & conditioning, swimming and diving, tennis, ultimate Frisbee, volleyball, weight lifting, weight training. 2 PE instructors.

Computers Computers are regularly used in art, English, ESL, foreign language, history, photography, science classes. Computer network features include on-campus library services, Internet access, wireless campus network, Internet filtering or blocking technology. Student e-mail accounts are available to students. Students grades are available online. The school has a published electronic and media policy.

Contact William E. Eichner, Director of Admissions. 41-91-960-5151. Fax: 41-91-993-2979. E-mail: admissions@tasis.ch. Web site: www.tasis.com

See Display below, Close-Up on page 636, and Summer Program Close-Up on page 720.

TELLURIDE MOUNTAIN SCHOOL

200 San Miguel River Drive
Telluride, Colorado 81435

Head of School: Mr. Joseph Stefani

General Information Coeducational day college-preparatory, arts, technology, and music, visual and dramatic arts school. Grades PK–12. Founded: 1999. Setting: small town. Nearest major city is Denver. 1 building on campus. Approved or accredited by Colorado Department of Education. Member of National Association of Independent Schools. Total enrollment: 100. Upper school average class size: 6. Upper school faculty-student ratio: 1:10. There are 165 required school days per year for Upper School students. Upper School students typically attend 5 days per week. The average school day consists of 6 hours and 30 minutes.

Upper School Student Profile Grade 9: 10 students (7 boys, 3 girls); Grade 10: 4 students (2 boys, 2 girls); Grade 12: 4 students (1 boy, 3 girls).

Faculty School total: 16. In upper school: 3 men, 3 women; 3 have advanced degrees.

Subjects Offered Algebra, alternative physical education, American Civil War, American history, American literature, ancient world history, applied music, art, backpacking, biology, calculus, character education, chemistry, civil rights, college admission preparation, college counseling, college planning, community service, computer education, computer literacy, computer multimedia, computer music, CPR, creative writing, critical thinking, critical writing, digital music, drama, dramatic arts, English composition, English literature, environmental education, European history, film studies, geography, geology, geometry, grammar, guitar, history, history of rock and roll, instrumental music, Internet research, keyboarding, Latin American literature, leadership, leadership and service, music, music performance, music technology, outdoor education, painting, portfolio writing, pre-algebra, pre-calculus, public speaking, reading/study skills, Spanish, Spanish literature, studio art, trigonometry, video film production, visual arts, white-water trips, wilderness education, world history.

Graduation Requirements Algebra, biology, chemistry, college admission preparation, college counseling, dramatic arts, English, English composition, English literature, geometry, grammar, history, music, physics, pre-calculus, Spanish, trigonometry, U.S. history, visual arts, wilderness education, world history.

Special Academic Programs Independent study; study abroad.

College Admission Counseling 4 students graduated in 2012; all went to college, including Bowdoin College; Fort Lewis College; Macalester College; University of Colorado Boulder.

Student Life Upper grades have specified standards of dress. Discipline rests primarily with faculty.

Tuition and Aid Day student tuition: $22,050. Tuition installment plan (monthly payment plans, individually arranged payment plans). Merit scholarship grants, need-based scholarship grants available. In 2012–13, 39% of upper-school students received aid. Total amount of financial aid awarded in 2012–13: $117,000.

Admissions Traditional secondary-level entrance grade is 9. For fall 2012, 2 students applied for upper-level admission, 2 were accepted, 2 enrolled. Deadline for receipt of application materials: none. Application fee required: $50. Interview required.

Athletics Interscholastic: alpine skiing (boys, girls), freestyle skiing (b,g), skiing (cross-country) (b,g), skiing (downhill) (b,g), snowboarding (b,g); coed interscholastic: backpacking, canoeing/kayaking, climbing, cooperative games, hiking/backpacking, ice skating, kayaking, mountaineering, nordic skiing, outdoor activities, outdoor adventure, outdoor education, outdoor recreation, outdoor skills, outdoors, rafting, rappelling, rock climbing, wilderness, wilderness survival, yoga; coed intramural: alpine skiing, lacrosse, rock climbing, snowshoeing, street hockey, telemark skiing, wilderness. 1 PE instructor, 5 coaches.

Computers Computers are regularly used in all classes. Computer network features include Internet access, wireless campus network. Campus intranet, student e-mail accounts, and computer access in designated common areas are available to students. The school has a published electronic and media policy.

Contact Mrs. Jamie Intemann, Program Coordinator. 970-728-1969. Fax: 970-369-4412. E-mail: jintemann@telluridemtnschool.org. Web site: www.telluridemtnschool.org/

TEMPLE GRANDIN SCHOOL

Boulder, Colorado

See Special Needs Schools section.

THE TENNEY SCHOOL

2055 South Gessner
Houston, Texas 77063

Head of School: Mr. Michael E. Tenney

General Information Coeducational day college-preparatory and general academic school; primarily serves students with learning disabilities and individuals with Attention Deficit Disorder. Grades 6–12. Founded: 1973. Setting: suburban. 1-acre campus. 1 building on campus. Approved or accredited by Southern Association of Colleges and Schools and Texas Department of Education. Total enrollment: 55. Upper school average class size: 1. Upper school faculty-student ratio: 1:2. There are 170 required school days per year for Upper School students. Upper School students typically attend 5 days per week. The average school day consists of 5 hours and 30 minutes.

Upper School Student Profile Grade 6: 4 students (1 boy, 3 girls); Grade 7: 3 students (1 boy, 2 girls); Grade 8: 6 students (2 boys, 4 girls); Grade 9: 12 students (7 boys, 5 girls); Grade 10: 9 students (6 boys, 3 girls); Grade 11: 6 students (4 boys, 2 girls); Grade 12: 15 students (11 boys, 4 girls).

Faculty School total: 25. In upper school: 2 men, 22 women; 13 have advanced degrees.

Subjects Offered Accounting, algebra, American history, American literature, biology, British literature, business law, calculus, chemistry, computer programming, computer studies, creative writing, economics, English, fine arts, geometry, government, health, independent study, journalism, keyboarding, mathematics, microcomputer technology applications, physical education, physical science, physics, precalculus, psychology, science, social studies, sociology, Spanish, studio art, study skills, world geography, world history, world literature, yearbook.

Graduation Requirements American government, American history.

Special Academic Programs Advanced Placement exam preparation; honors section; academic accommodation for the gifted, the musically talented, and the artistically talented; remedial reading and/or remedial writing; remedial math; special instructional classes for deaf students; ESL (10 students enrolled).

College Admission Counseling 10 students graduated in 2012; all went to college, including Houston Baptist University; St. Thomas University; Texas A&M University; The University of Texas at Austin; University of Houston.

Student Life Upper grades have specified standards of dress. Discipline rests primarily with faculty.

Summer Programs Remediation, enrichment, advancement programs offered; session focuses on academic course work; held on campus; accepts boys and girls; open to students from other schools. 45 students usually enrolled. 2013 schedule: June 6 to June 28. Application deadline: June 1.

Tuition and Aid Day student tuition: $23,000.

Admissions Traditional secondary-level entrance grade is 9. For fall 2012, 40 students applied for upper-level admission, 26 were accepted, 24 enrolled. Naglieri Nonverbal School Ability Test or Scholastic Achievement Test required. Deadline for receipt of application materials: none. No application fee required. On-campus interview required.

Athletics 1 PE instructor.

Computers Computers are regularly used in computer applications, creative writing, desktop publishing, English, foreign language, journalism, keyboarding, speech, word processing, yearbook classes. Computer network features include on-campus library services, Internet access, wireless campus network, Internet filtering or blocking technology. Campus intranet and computer access in designated common areas are available to students. Students grades are available online.

Contact Mr. Michael E. Tenney, Director. 713-783-6990. Fax: 713-783-0786. E-mail: mtenney@tenneyschool.com. Web site: www.tenneyschool.com

TEURLINGS CATHOLIC HIGH SCHOOL

139 Teurlings Drive
Lafayette, Louisiana 70501-3832

Head of School: Mr. Michael Harrison Boyer

General Information Coeducational day and distance learning college-preparatory and religious studies school, affiliated with Roman Catholic Church. Grades 9–12. Distance learning grades 10–12. Founded: 1955. Setting: urban. Nearest major city is Baton Rouge. 25-acre campus. 13 buildings on campus. Approved or accredited by National Catholic Education Association, Southern Association of Colleges and Schools, and Louisiana Department of Education. Endowment: $140,000. Total enrollment: 658. Upper school average class size: 21. Upper school faculty-student ratio: 1:21. There are 179 required school days per year for Upper School students. Upper School students typically attend 5 days per week. The average school day consists of 6 hours and 50 minutes.

Upper School Student Profile Grade 9: 161 students (78 boys, 83 girls); Grade 10: 179 students (91 boys, 88 girls); Grade 11: 165 students (86 boys, 79 girls); Grade 12: 153 students (69 boys, 84 girls). 94% of students are Roman Catholic.

Faculty School total: 44. In upper school: 16 men, 25 women; 13 have advanced degrees.

Subjects Offered 20th century history, accounting, acting, advanced chemistry, advanced computer applications, advanced math, algebra, American history, American literature, anatomy and physiology, art, biology, business applications, business law, calculus, campus ministry, chemistry, choral music, civics/free enterprise, computer science, drama, earth science, English, entrepreneurship, environmental science, fine arts, food and nutrition, French, geography, geometry, health, honors algebra, honors English, honors geometry, honors U.S. history, honors world history, interpersonal skills, keyboarding, Latin, music, newspaper, physical education, physical science, physics, psychology, public speaking, publications, Spanish, speech, sports medicine, theology, Web site design, world history.

Graduation Requirements Advanced math, algebra, American history, American literature, biology, chemistry, civics, civics/free enterprise, electives, English, geometry, literature, physical education (includes health), physical science, theology, world geography, world history.

Special Academic Programs Honors section; study at local college for college credit.

College Admission Counseling 166 students graduated in 2011; 158 went to college, including Centenary College of Louisiana; Louisiana State University and Agricultural and Mechanical College; Louisiana State University at Eunice; Northwestern State University of Louisiana; Spring Hill College; University of Louisiana at Lafayette. Other: 2 went to work, 3 entered military service, 3 had other specific plans. Median composite ACT: 21. 12% scored over 26 on composite ACT.

Student Life Upper grades have uniform requirement, student council. Discipline rests equally with students and faculty. Attendance at religious services is required.

Tuition and Aid Day student tuition: $5400. Tuition installment plan (monthly payment plans). Need-based scholarship grants, paying campus jobs available. In 2011–12, 20% of upper-school students received aid. Total amount of financial aid awarded in 2011–12: $84,000.

Admissions Traditional secondary-level entrance grade is 9. For fall 2011, 202 students applied for upper-level admission, 181 were accepted, 151 enrolled. ACT, ACT-Explore, Explore or Stanford Achievement Test required. Deadline for receipt of application materials: January 27. No application fee required.

Athletics Interscholastic: baseball (boys), basketball (b,g), bowling (b,g), cheering (b,g), cross-country running (b,g), dance team (g), football (b), golf (b,g), gymnastics (b), indoor track & field (b,g), soccer (b,g), softball (g), strength & conditioning (b,g), swimming and diving (b,g), tennis (b,g), track and field (b,g), volleyball (g), winter (indoor) track (b,g), wrestling (b); intramural: cheering (g); coed interscholastic: riflery, skeet shooting, trap and skeet. 3 coaches.

Computers Computer network features include on-campus library services, Internet access, wireless campus network, Internet filtering or blocking technology. Student e-mail accounts and computer access in designated common areas are available to students. Students grades are available online. The school has a published electronic and media policy.

Contact Mrs. Kathy Dodson, Administrative Secretary. 337-235-5711 Ext. 101. Fax: 337-234-8057. E-mail: kdodson@tchs.net. Web site: www.tchs.net

THE THACHER SCHOOL

5025 Thacher Road
Ojai, California 93023

Head of School: Mr. Michael K. Mulligan

General Information Coeducational boarding and day college-preparatory, arts, and technology school. Grades 9–12. Founded: 1889. Setting: small town. Nearest major city is Santa Barbara. Students are housed in single-sex dormitories. 450-acre campus. 89 buildings on campus. Approved or accredited by California Association of Independent Schools, The Association of Boarding Schools, Western Association of Schools and Colleges, and California Department of Education. Member of National Association of Independent Schools and Secondary School Admission Test Board. Endowment: $111.4 million. Total enrollment: 246. Upper school average class size: 11. Upper school faculty-student ratio: 1:6. Upper School students typically attend 5 days per week. The average school day consists of 7 hours.

Upper School Student Profile Grade 9: 58 students (29 boys, 29 girls); Grade 10: 63 students (33 boys, 30 girls); Grade 11: 56 students (28 boys, 28 girls); Grade 12: 69 students (34 boys, 35 girls). 90% of students are boarding students. 53% are state residents. 26 states are represented in upper school student body. 11% are international students. International students from Australia, Canada, Hong Kong, Japan, Saudi Arabia, and Taiwan; 11 other countries represented in student body.

Faculty School total: 45. In upper school: 23 men, 21 women; 31 have advanced degrees; 42 reside on campus.
Subjects Offered 3-dimensional art, ACT preparation, acting, advanced chemistry, advanced math, Advanced Placement courses, advanced studio art-AP, algebra, American history, American history-AP, American literature, art, art history, art history-AP, astronomy, biology, biology-AP, calculus, calculus-AP, ceramics, chemistry, chemistry-AP, Chinese, computer math, computer science, computer science-AP, conceptual physics, creative writing, dance, drama, ecology, economics, economics and history, electronic music, English, English literature, English literature-AP, English/composition-AP, environmental science, environmental science-AP, European history, European history-AP, film, fine arts, French, French language-AP, French literature-AP, geography, geometry, health, history, journalism, Latin, logic, marine biology, mathematics, music, music theory-AP, philosophy, photography, physical education, physics, physics-AP, psychology, religion, science, social studies, Spanish, Spanish language-AP, Spanish literature-AP, statistics, studio art-AP, theater, trigonometry, U.S. history-AP, world history, world literature, writing.
Graduation Requirements Arts and fine arts (art, music, dance, drama), English, foreign language, mathematics, physical education (includes health), science, social studies (includes history), senior exhibition program (students choose an academic topic of interest and study it for one year, culminating in a school-wide presentation).
Special Academic Programs 17 Advanced Placement exams for which test preparation is offered; honors section; independent study; study abroad; academic accommodation for the gifted, the musically talented, and the artistically talented.
College Admission Counseling 61 students graduated in 2012; all went to college, including Brown University; Columbia College; Dartmouth College; Middlebury College; Stanford University. Mean SAT critical reading: 660, mean SAT math: 650, mean SAT writing: 660, mean combined SAT: 1970.
Student Life Upper grades have specified standards of dress, student council, honor system. Discipline rests equally with students and faculty.
Tuition and Aid Day student tuition: $31,750; 7-day tuition and room/board: $47,950. Tuition installment plan (monthly payment plans). Need-based scholarship grants available. In 2012–13, 27% of upper-school students received aid. Total amount of financial aid awarded in 2012–13: $2,181,350.
Admissions Traditional secondary-level entrance grade is 9. For fall 2012, 643 students applied for upper-level admission, 82 were accepted, 67 enrolled. ACT-Explore, ISEE, PSAT or SSAT required. Deadline for receipt of application materials: January 15. Application fee required: $75. Interview required.
Athletics Interscholastic: baseball (boys), basketball (b,g), cross-country running (b,g), dance (b,g), football (b), lacrosse (b,g), soccer (b,g), tennis (b,g), track and field (b,g), volleyball (g); intramural: backpacking (b,g), ballet (b,g), bicycling (b,g), canoeing/kayaking (b,g), climbing (b,g), dance (b,g), horseback riding (b,g), outdoor activities (b,g), weight training (b,g), wilderness (b,g), wilderness survival (b,g), yoga (b,g); coed interscholastic: dance, equestrian sports; coed intramural: backpacking, ballet, bicycling, bowling, canoeing/kayaking, climbing, dance, equestrian sports, fencing, golf, handball, hiking/backpacking, horseback riding, modern dance, outdoor activities, pistol, polo, Polocrosse, riflery, rock climbing, rodeo, skiing (downhill), surfing, trap and skeet, ultimate Frisbee, wall climbing, weight lifting, yoga. 18 coaches, 1 athletic trainer.
Computers Computers are regularly used in English, foreign language, history, mathematics, science classes. Computer network features include on-campus library services, online commercial services, Internet access, wireless campus network, Internet filtering or blocking technology. Campus intranet and student e-mail accounts are available to students. Students grades are available online. The school has a published electronic and media policy.
Contact Mr. William P. McMahon, Director of Admission. 805-640-3210. Fax: 805-640-9377. E-mail: admission@thacher.org. Web site: www.thacher.org

THETFORD ACADEMY

PO Box 190
Thetford, Vermont 05074

Head of School: Torrelee Fisher-Sass

General Information Coeducational day college-preparatory, arts, and vocational school. Grades 7–12. Founded: 1819. Setting: rural. Nearest major city is Montpelier. 240-acre campus. 4 buildings on campus. Approved or accredited by Association of Independent Schools in New England, Commission on Independent Schools, New England Association of Schools and Colleges, and Vermont Department of Education. Endowment: $2 million. Total enrollment: 300. Upper school average class size: 15. Upper school faculty-student ratio: 1:7. There are 176 required school days per year for Upper School students. Upper School students typically attend 5 days per week. The average school day consists of 6 hours and 30 minutes.
Upper School Student Profile Grade 9: 49 students (23 boys, 26 girls); Grade 10: 67 students (32 boys, 35 girls); Grade 11: 63 students (30 boys, 33 girls); Grade 12: 59 students (28 boys, 31 girls).
Faculty School total: 34. In upper school: 16 men, 18 women; 17 have advanced degrees.
Subjects Offered Acting, advanced math, algebra, anatomy, art, art history, biology, British history, calculus, ceramics, chemistry, community service, computer science, current events, drama, driver education, English, forestry, French, geometry, government, health, history, horticulture, industrial arts, Latin, mathematics, music, painting, physical education, physics, physiology, study skills, U.S. history, voice, world cultures, world history.
Special Academic Programs Independent study; term-away projects; study at local college for college credit; ESL (4 students enrolled).
College Admission Counseling 53 went to college, including Plymouth State University. Other: 6 went to work, 2 entered military service, 44 entered a postgraduate year, 1 had other specific plans.
Student Life Upper grades have specified standards of dress, student council, honor system. Discipline rests primarily with faculty.
Tuition and Aid Day student tuition: $17,890.
Admissions Traditional secondary-level entrance grade is 9. For fall 2011, 22 students applied for upper-level admission, 21 were accepted, 20 enrolled. Canada Quick Individual Educational Test required. Deadline for receipt of application materials: none. No application fee required. Interview recommended.
Athletics Interscholastic: alpine skiing (boys, girls), baseball (b), basketball (b,g), cross-country running (b,g), skiing (downhill) (b,g), soccer (b,g), softball (g), track and field (b,g); coed interscholastic: cross-country running; coed intramural: archery, nordic skiing, skiing (cross-country). 2 PE instructors, 7 coaches, 1 athletic trainer.
Computers Computers are regularly used in all classes. Computer network features include on-campus library services, Internet access, wireless campus network, Internet filtering or blocking technology. Campus intranet, student e-mail accounts, and computer access in designated common areas are available to students. The school has a published electronic and media policy.
Contact Marceny Bourne, Director of Counseling. 802-785-4805 Ext. 212. Fax: 802-785-4085. E-mail: marceny.bourne@thet.net. Web site: www.thetfordacademy.org

THINK GLOBAL SCHOOL

One Embarcadero Center
Suite 500
San Francisco, California 94111

Head of School: Mr. Alun Cooper

General Information Coeducational boarding college-preparatory and IB curriculum school. Grades 9–12. Founded: 2009. Setting: Traveling global high school.. Students are housed in coed facilities in host city. Approved or accredited by International Baccalaureate Organization and Western Association of Schools and Colleges. Endowment: $10 million. Total enrollment: 36. Upper school average class size: 12. Upper school faculty-student ratio: 1:3. There are 193 required school days per year for Upper School students. Upper School students typically attend 5 days per week. The average school day consists of 6 hours and 45 minutes.
Upper School Student Profile Grade 9: 6 students (2 boys, 4 girls); Grade 10: 12 students (5 boys, 7 girls); Grade 11: 18 students (8 boys, 10 girls). 100% of students are boarding students. 9 states are represented in upper school student body. 75% are international students. International students from Bhutan, Singapore, Sweden, Thailand, and United Kingdom; 14 other countries represented in student body.
Faculty School total: 14. In upper school: 7 men, 7 women; 10 have advanced degrees; 13 reside on campus.
Subjects Offered All academic.
Special Academic Programs International Baccalaureate program; study abroad.
Student Life Upper grades have specified standards of dress, student council, honor system. Discipline rests equally with students and faculty.
Tuition and Aid 7-day tuition and room/board: $79,000. Tuition installment plan (monthly payment plans, individually arranged payment plans). Need-based scholarship grants available.
Admissions Traditional secondary-level entrance grade is 9. For fall 2012, 135 students applied for upper-level admission, 14 were accepted, 13 enrolled. Admissions testing or English proficiency required. Deadline for receipt of application materials: none. No application fee required. Interview required.
Computers Computers are regularly used in all classes. Computer network features include Internet access, wireless campus network, Internet filtering or blocking technology, all students are provided with laptops, iPads, and phones. Campus intranet and student e-mail accounts are available to students. Students grades are available online. The school has a published electronic and media policy.
Contact Mrs. Lily Just, Director of Admissions. 202-580-8405. E-mail: ljust@thinkglobalschool.org. Web site: www.thinkglobalschool.org

See Display on next page and Close-Up on page 638.

THOMAS JEFFERSON SCHOOL

4100 South Lindbergh Boulevard
St. Louis, Missouri 63127

Head of School: Dr. Elizabeth L. Holekamp

General Information Coeducational boarding and day college-preparatory and classical liberal-arts education school. Grades 7–PG. Founded: 1946. Setting: suburban. Students are housed in single-sex dormitories. 20-acre campus. 12 buildings on campus.

Approved or accredited by Independent Schools Association of the Central States, Midwest Association of Boarding Schools, and The Association of Boarding Schools. Member of National Association of Independent Schools and Secondary School Admission Test Board. Endowment: $1.5 million. Total enrollment: 91. Upper school average class size: 14. Upper school faculty-student ratio: 1:6. There are 130 required school days per year for Upper School students. Upper School students typically attend 5 days per week. The average school day consists of 8 hours and 30 minutes.

Upper School Student Profile Grade 9: 16 students (10 boys, 6 girls); Grade 10: 17 students (10 boys, 7 girls); Grade 11: 17 students (11 boys, 6 girls); Grade 12: 18 students (10 boys, 8 girls). 57% of students are boarding students. 43% are state residents. 10 states are represented in upper school student body. 30% are international students. International students from Canada, China, Japan, Poland, Republic of Korea, and Taiwan; 3 other countries represented in student body.

Faculty School total: 19. In upper school: 5 men, 8 women; 10 have advanced degrees; 5 reside on campus.

Subjects Offered Advanced Placement courses, algebra, American history-AP, ancient history, ancient world history, art, art history, biology, biology-AP, calculus, calculus-AP, ceramics, chemistry, chemistry-AP, dance, earth science, English, English language-AP, English literature-AP, ESL, fine arts, French, geography, geometry, government and politics-AP, government/civics, Greek, history, Homeric Greek, Italian, Latin, life science, mathematics, music, physical science, physics, physics-AP, science, social studies, trigonometry, U.S. history-AP, world history, world history-AP.

Graduation Requirements Arts and fine arts (art, music, dance, drama), English, foreign language, mathematics, science, social studies (includes history). Community service is required.

Special Academic Programs 10 Advanced Placement exams for which test preparation is offered; honors section; academic accommodation for the gifted; ESL (10 students enrolled).

College Admission Counseling 14 students graduated in 2012; all went to college, including Cornell University; Haverford College; Mount Holyoke College; Stanford University; University of Chicago; University of Illinois at Urbana–Champaign. Median SAT critical reading: 700, median SAT math: 660, median SAT writing: 690, median combined SAT: 2050.

Student Life Upper grades have specified standards of dress, student council, honor system. Discipline rests equally with students and faculty.

Tuition and Aid Day student tuition: $22,750; 5-day tuition and room/board: $37,750; 7-day tuition and room/board: $39,500. Tuition installment plan (monthly payment plans, individually arranged payment plans, Sallie Mae TuitionPay). Merit scholarship grants, need-based scholarship grants, paying campus jobs available. In 2012–13, 35% of upper-school students received aid; total upper-school merit-scholarship money awarded: $10,000. Total amount of financial aid awarded in 2012–13: $640,000.

Admissions Traditional secondary-level entrance grade is 9. For fall 2012, 47 students applied for upper-level admission, 14 were accepted, 11 enrolled. SSAT or TOEFL required. Deadline for receipt of application materials: February 15. Application fee required: $40. Interview required.

Athletics Interscholastic: basketball (boys, girls), soccer (b,g), volleyball (b,g); intramural: basketball (b,g), soccer (b,g), volleyball (b,g); coed interscholastic: soccer; coed intramural: dance, fitness, physical fitness, tennis, weight training, yoga.

Computers Computers are regularly used in foreign language, mathematics, science, yearbook classes. Computer network features include online commercial services, Internet access, wireless campus network, Internet filtering or blocking technology. Campus intranet, student e-mail accounts, and computer access in designated common areas are available to students. The school has a published electronic and media policy.

Contact Mrs. Barbara Fraser, Director of Admissions. 314-843-4151 Ext. 2341. Fax: 314-843-3527. E-mail: admissions@tjs.org. Web site: www.tjs.org

See Display on next page and Close-Up on page 640.

TIDEWATER ACADEMY

217 Church Street
Post Office Box 1000
Wakefield, Virginia 23888

Head of School: Mr. Rodney L. Taylor

General Information Coeducational day college-preparatory, arts, and technology school. Grades PK–12. Founded: 1964. Setting: rural. Nearest major city is Richmond. 10-acre campus. 4 buildings on campus. Approved or accredited by Virginia Association of Independent Schools. Total enrollment: 153. Upper school average class size: 15. Upper school faculty-student ratio: 1:15. There are 180 required school days per year for Upper School students. Upper School students typically attend 5 days per week. The average school day consists of 6 hours and 50 minutes.

Upper School Student Profile Grade 8: 14 students (6 boys, 8 girls); Grade 9: 11 students (8 boys, 3 girls); Grade 10: 14 students (6 boys, 8 girls); Grade 11: 12 students (4 boys, 8 girls); Grade 12: 11 students (7 boys, 4 girls).

Faculty School total: 25. In upper school: 4 men, 9 women; 2 have advanced degrees.

Subjects Offered Algebra, American history, American literature, art, arts, biology, calculus, chemistry, computer applications, creative writing, driver education, earth science, English, English literature, English-AP, fine arts, geography, geometry, government/civics, grammar, health, history, journalism, life skills, mathematics, music, physical education, science, social sciences, social studies, Spanish, world history, world literature, writing.

Graduation Requirements Arts and fine arts (art, music, dance, drama), business skills (includes word processing), computer science, English, foreign language, mathematics, physical education (includes health), science, social sciences, social studies (includes history).

Special Academic Programs 6 Advanced Placement exams for which test preparation is offered; honors section; independent study.

College Admission Counseling 23 students graduated in 2012; 18 went to college, including James Madison University; Lynchburg College; Radford University; Randolph-Macon College. Other: 4 went to work, 1 entered military service. Median SAT critical reading: 516, median SAT math: 501. 5% scored over 600 on SAT critical reading.

Student Life Upper grades have specified standards of dress, student council, honor system. Discipline rests primarily with faculty.

Tuition and Aid Day student tuition: $6575. Tuition installment plan (FACTS Tuition Payment Plan, monthly payment plans, individually arranged payment plans). Need-based scholarship grants available. In 2012–13, 40% of upper-school students received aid. Total amount of financial aid awarded in 2012–13: $125,000.

Admissions Traditional secondary-level entrance grade is 10. For fall 2012, 9 students applied for upper-level admission, 6 were accepted, 6 enrolled. Any standardized test required. Deadline for receipt of application materials: none. Application fee required: $25. On-campus interview required.

Athletics Interscholastic: baseball (boys), basketball (b,g), cheering (g), football (b), softball (g), tennis (b,g), volleyball (g). 2 PE instructors, 2 coaches.

Computers Computers are regularly used in yearbook classes. Computer network features include on-campus library services, Internet access, wireless campus network. Campus intranet is available to students.

Contact Robyn Croft, Admissions Counselor. 757-899-5401. Fax: 757-899-2521. E-mail: r_croft@tidewateracademy-pvt-va.us. Web site: www.tawarriors.org

TILTON SCHOOL

30 School Street
Tilton, New Hampshire 03276

Head of School: Peter Saliba

General Information Coeducational boarding and day college-preparatory school; primarily serves students with learning disabilities, individuals with Attention Deficit Disorder, and dyslexic students. Grades 9–PG. Founded: 1845. Setting: small town. Nearest major city is Concord. Students are housed in single-sex by floor dormitories and single-sex dormitories. 150-acre campus. 30 buildings on campus. Approved or accredited by Association of Independent Schools in New England, Independent Schools of Northern New England, New England Association of Schools and Colleges, The Association of Boarding Schools, and New Hampshire Department of Education. Member of National Association of Independent Schools and Secondary School Admission Test Board. Endowment: $14.6 million. Total enrollment: 241. Upper school average class size: 12. Upper school faculty-student ratio: 1:6. There are 187 required school days per year for Upper School students. Upper School students typically attend 6 days per week. The average school day consists of 7 hours.

Upper School Student Profile Grade 9: 25 students (15 boys, 10 girls); Grade 10: 50 students (35 boys, 15 girls); Grade 11: 68 students (45 boys, 23 girls); Grade 12: 79 students (49 boys, 30 girls); Postgraduate: 19 students (16 boys, 3 girls). 75% of students are boarding students. 35% are state residents. 22 states are represented in upper school student body. 20% are international students. International students from Bermuda, Canada, China, Republic of Korea, Spain, and Taiwan; 7 other countries represented in student body.

Faculty School total: 43. In upper school: 29 men, 14 women; 18 have advanced degrees; 40 reside on campus.

Subjects Offered Advanced chemistry, advanced math, advanced studio art-AP, algebra, American history, American literature, anatomy and physiology, art, band, biology, biology-AP, calculus, calculus-AP, chemistry, chemistry-AP, chorus, clay-working, college counseling, computer graphics, criminal justice, debate, drama, drawing, ecology, economics, English, English language and composition-AP, English literature-AP, ESL, European history-AP, forensics, French, French-AP, functions, geology, geometry, honors algebra, honors English, honors geometry, independent study, integrated mathematics, integrated science, leadership, marine ecology, music, music appreciation, music theory, musical productions, newspaper, painting, photography, physics, physics-AP, politics, pre-calculus, psychology-AP, SAT preparation, sociology, Spanish, Spanish-AP, statistics, studio art, studio art-AP, theater, trigonometry, wilderness education, world cultures, world literature, world religions, yearbook.

Graduation Requirements American history, arts and fine arts (art, music, dance, drama), English, foreign language, history, lab science, mathematics, science, annual participation in Plus/5 (including activities in art and culture, athletics, community service, leadership, and outdoor experience).

Special Academic Programs 11 Advanced Placement exams for which test preparation is offered; honors section; independent study; ESL (22 students enrolled).

College Admission Counseling 75 students graduated in 2012; they went to Dartmouth College; James Madison University; Norwich University; Rensselaer Polytechnic Institute; Roger Williams University; University of New Hampshire. Mean SAT critical reading: 521, mean SAT math: 546, mean SAT writing: 530, mean combined SAT: 1597.

Student Life Upper grades have specified standards of dress, student council, honor system. Discipline rests primarily with faculty.

Tuition and Aid Day student tuition: $27,400; 7-day tuition and room/board: $47,600. Tuition installment plan (FACTS Tuition Payment Plan, individually arranged payment plans). Merit scholarship grants, need-based scholarship grants, need-based loans available. In 2012–13, 41% of upper-school students received aid; total upper-school merit-scholarship money awarded: $422,250. Total amount of financial aid awarded in 2012–13: $2,237,570.

Admissions Traditional secondary-level entrance grade is 9. For fall 2012, 449 students applied for upper-level admission, 289 were accepted, 87 enrolled. ACT, PSAT, PSAT or SAT for applicants to grade 11 and 12, SAT, SLEP, SSAT, SSAT, ERB, PSAT, SAT, PLAN or ACT, TOEFL, TOEFL or SLEP, WAIS, WICS or writing sample required. Deadline for receipt of application materials: February 1. Application fee required: $50. Interview required.

Athletics Interscholastic: baseball (boys), basketball (b,g), field hockey (g), football (b), ice hockey (b,g), lacrosse (b,g), soccer (b,g), softball (g), tennis (b,g); coed interscholastic: alpine skiing, cross-country running, golf, mountain biking, skiing (downhill), snowboarding, weight lifting, weight training, wrestling; coed intramural: canoeing/kayaking, hiking/backpacking, outdoor activities, outdoor education, outdoor skills, rock climbing, squash, strength & conditioning, wall climbing, weight training, wilderness survival. 1 athletic trainer.

Computers Computers are regularly used in English, foreign language, graphic arts, history, mathematics, newspaper, science, yearbook classes. Computer network features include on-campus library services, online commercial services, Internet access, wireless campus network, Internet filtering or blocking technology, USB ports, Smart Media Readers. Campus intranet, student e-mail accounts, and computer access in designated common areas are available to students. Students grades are available online. The school has a published electronic and media policy.

Contact Sharon Trudel, Admissions Assistant. 603-286-1733. Fax: 603-286-1705. E-mail: admissions@tiltonschool.org. Web site: www.tiltonschool.org

TIMOTHY CHRISTIAN HIGH SCHOOL

1061 South Prospect Avenue
Elmhurst, Illinois 60126

Head of School: Mr. Bradford Mitchell

General Information Coeducational day college-preparatory, general academic, arts, business, vocational, religious studies, and technology school, affiliated with Christian faith. Grades K–12. Founded: 1911. Setting: suburban. Nearest major city is Chicago. 26-acre campus. 1 building on campus. Approved or accredited by Christian Schools International, North Central Association of Colleges and Schools, and Illinois Department of Education. Total enrollment: 1,052. Upper school average class size: 13. Upper school faculty-student ratio: 1:13. There are 176 required school days per year for Upper School students. Upper School students typically attend 5 days per week. The average school day consists of 6 hours and 45 minutes.

Upper School Student Profile Grade 9: 103 students (48 boys, 55 girls); Grade 10: 81 students (48 boys, 33 girls); Grade 11: 95 students (39 boys, 56 girls); Grade 12: 101 students (53 boys, 48 girls). 99% of students are Christian.

Faculty School total: 30. In upper school: 19 men, 11 women; 24 have advanced degrees.

Subjects Offered Advanced math, algebra, American literature, anatomy and physiology, art, band, Bible, biology, British literature, business studies, calculus-AP, ceramics, chemistry, child development, choir, Christian doctrine, Christian ethics, church history, communication skills, community service, computer applications, computer art, computer graphics, computer-aided design, concert choir, desktop publishing, drafting, drawing and design, economics, electives, English, English literature-AP, expository writing, food and nutrition, geometry, health, home economics, honors algebra, honors geometry, human anatomy, independent living, industrial arts, industrial technology, instrumental music, interior design, jazz ensemble, music, music appreciation, music theory, New Testament, oral communications, orchestra, parent/child development, photography, physical education, physics, physics-AP, pre-calculus, psychology, sewing, Spanish, trigonometry, U.S. government, U.S. history, U.S. history-AP, United States government-AP, Western civilization, world cultures, world literature.

Graduation Requirements Computer processing, English, mathematics, music, physical education (includes health), religious studies, science, social studies (includes history), senior service retreat at end of 12th grade, service requirement in grades 9-11 (10 hours per year).

Special Academic Programs 6 Advanced Placement exams for which test preparation is offered; honors section; remedial reading and/or remedial writing.

College Admission Counseling 99 students graduated in 2012; 97 went to college, including Calvin College; Dordt College; Hope College; Marquette University; Trinity Christian College. Other: 1 went to work, 1 had other specific plans.

Student Life Upper grades have specified standards of dress, student council, honor system. Discipline rests primarily with faculty. Attendance at religious services is required.

Summer Programs Sports, art/fine arts programs offered; session focuses on athletics; held on campus; accepts boys and girls; open to students from other schools. 136 students usually enrolled.

Tuition and Aid Day student tuition: $8710–$17,250. Tuition installment plan (FACTS Tuition Payment Plan, FACTS is required unless paying the total tuition at once). Need-based scholarship grants, some need-based financial assistance available through school foundation available. In 2012–13, 13% of upper-school students received aid.

Admissions Traditional secondary-level entrance grade is 9. Scholastic Testing Service, Scholastic Testing Service High School Placement Test or school's own exam required. Deadline for receipt of application materials: none. Application fee required: $50. On-campus interview required.

Athletics Interscholastic: baseball (boys), basketball (b,g), cross-country running (b,g), pom squad (g), soccer (b,g), softball (g), tennis (b,g), track and field (b,g), volleyball (g); intramural: basketball (b), flag football (b); coed interscholastic: cheering, golf; coed intramural: volleyball. 2 PE instructors, 1 athletic trainer.

Computers Computers are regularly used in art, computer applications, English, graphic design, industrial technology, keyboarding, science, writing classes. Computer network features include on-campus library services, Internet access, wireless campus network, Internet filtering or blocking technology. Student e-mail accounts are available to students. Students grades are available online. The school has a published electronic and media policy.

Contact Mr. Rudi Gesch, Marketing Director. 630-782-4043. Fax: 630-833-9238. E-mail: gesch@timothychristian.com. Web site: www.timothychristian.com

TMI - THE EPISCOPAL SCHOOL OF TEXAS

20955 West Tejas Trail
San Antonio, Texas 78257

Head of School: Dr. John W. Cooper

General Information Coeducational boarding and day college-preparatory, arts, and religious studies school, affiliated with Episcopal Church, Christian faith. Boarding grades 9–12, day grades 6–12. Founded: 1893. Setting: suburban. Students are housed in single-sex dormitories. 80-acre campus. 17 buildings on campus. Approved or accredited by Independent Schools Association of the Southwest, National Association of Episcopal Schools, Southwest Association of Episcopal Schools, The Association of Boarding Schools, and Texas Department of Education. Total enrollment: 435. Upper school average class size: 16. Upper school faculty-student ratio: 1:10. There are 168 required school days per year for Upper School students. Upper School students typically attend 5 days per week. The average school day consists of 6 hours and 10 minutes.

Upper School Student Profile 17% of students are boarding students. 96% are state residents. 5 states are represented in upper school student body. 3% are international students. International students from China, Mexico, Panama, Republic of Korea, and Viet Nam; 2 other countries represented in student body. 83% of students are members of Episcopal Church, Christian.

Faculty School total: 60. In upper school: 27 men, 13 women; 25 have advanced degrees; 13 reside on campus.

Subjects Offered 20th century history, acting, Advanced Placement courses, advanced studio art-AP, algebra, American Civil War, American history, American literature, anatomy and physiology, astronomy, athletics, biology, British literature, calculus, ceramics, chemistry, choir, computer programming, conceptual physics, earth science, economics, English, English literature, environmental science, fine arts, geometry, government, Greek, history, JROTC, Latin, meteorology, military history, philosophy, photography, physics, playwriting, religion, Spanish, statistics, studio art, theater arts, theater design and production, world history, writing.

Graduation Requirements Arts and fine arts (art, music, dance, drama), electives, English, foreign language, history, mathematics, philosophy, physical education (includes health), religion (includes Bible studies and theology), science, students must pass the Assessment of Basic English Skills, senior chapel talk, community service requirement.

Special Academic Programs Advanced Placement exam preparation; honors section; independent study.

College Admission Counseling 63 students graduated in 2012; all went to college, including Baylor University; Harvard University; Rice University; Southern Methodist University; Texas A&M University; Texas Christian University. Median SAT critical reading: 600, median SAT math: 590, median SAT writing: 610, median combined SAT: 1800.

Student Life Upper grades have uniform requirement, student council, honor system. Discipline rests equally with students and faculty. Attendance at religious services is required.

Summer Programs Enrichment, advancement, sports programs offered; session focuses on academics and enrichment; held on campus; accepts boys and girls; open to students from other schools. 30 students usually enrolled. 2013 schedule: June 8 to July 17. Application deadline: May 28.

Tuition and Aid Day student tuition: $17,995; 5-day tuition and room/board: $32,495; 7-day tuition and room/board: $36,740. Tuition installment plan (Academic Management Services Plan, FACTS Tuition Payment Plan, monthly payment plans). Merit scholarship grants, need-based scholarship grants, tuition remission for children of faculty available. In 2012–13, 25% of upper-school students received aid; total upper-school merit-scholarship money awarded: $55,000. Total amount of financial aid awarded in 2012–13: $555,500.

Admissions Traditional secondary-level entrance grade is 9. For fall 2012, 75 students applied for upper-level admission, 71 were accepted, 60 enrolled. ISEE required. Deadline for receipt of application materials: January 15. Application fee required: $75. Interview required.

Athletics Interscholastic: baseball (boys), basketball (b,g), cheering (g), cross-country running (b,g), diving (b,g), fitness (b,g), football (b), golf (b,g), lacrosse (b,g), soccer (b,g), softball (g), strength & conditioning (b,g), swimming and diving (b,g), tennis (b,g), track and field (b,g), volleyball (g), weight training (b,g); coed interscholastic: JROTC drill, marksmanship, physical training, riflery, strength & conditioning. 10 coaches, 1 athletic trainer.

Computers Computers are regularly used in journalism, language development, literary magazine, newspaper, programming, science, yearbook classes. Computer network features include on-campus library services, online commercial services, Internet access, Internet filtering or blocking technology. Campus intranet, student e-mail accounts, and computer access in designated common areas are available to students. Students grades are available online. The school has a published electronic and media policy.

Contact Mr. Aaron Hawkins, Associate Director. 210-564-6152. Fax: 210-698-0715. E-mail: a.hawkins@tmi-sa.org. Web site: www.tmi-sa.org

TORONTO DISTRICT CHRISTIAN HIGH SCHOOL

377 Woodbridge Avenue
Woodbridge, Ontario L4L 2V7, Canada

Head of School: Mr. William Groot

General Information Coeducational day college-preparatory, general academic, arts, business, religious studies, bilingual studies, and technology school, affiliated with Christian faith, Christian faith. Grades 9–12. Founded: 1963. Setting: urban. Nearest major city is Toronto, Canada. 12-acre campus. 1 building on campus. Approved or accredited by Association of Christian Schools International, Christian Schools International, Ontario Ministry of Education, and Ontario Department of Education. Language of instruction: English. Endowment: CAN$100,000. Total enrollment: 430. Upper school average class size: 22. Upper school faculty-student ratio: 1:14. The average school day consists of 5 hours and 20 minutes.

Upper School Student Profile Grade 9: 94 students (46 boys, 48 girls); Grade 10: 100 students (51 boys, 49 girls); Grade 11: 121 students (57 boys, 64 girls); Grade 12: 122 students (59 boys, 63 girls). 99% of students are Christian faith, Christian.

Faculty School total: 33. In upper school: 21 men, 12 women; 8 have advanced degrees.

Subjects Offered 20th century history, advanced math, ancient history, art, athletic training, Bible, biology, bookkeeping, business applications, business education, business mathematics, business technology, cabinet making, calculus, Canadian geography, Canadian history, career and personal planning, chemistry, choir, civics, computer applications, computer multimedia, computer programming, concert band, creative writing, discrete mathematics, dramatic arts, economics, English, English literature, environmental studies, ESL, family living, family studies, French, geography, global issues, guitar, health, history, industrial arts, keyboarding, law, media studies, modern Western civilization, music, philosophy, physical education, physics, remedial study skills, science, social justice, theater arts, video film production, visual arts, Western civilization, world issues, world religions.

Graduation Requirements Ontario Ministry of Education requirements.

Special Academic Programs Honors section; term-away projects; study abroad; remedial reading and/or remedial writing; remedial math; programs in English, mathematics, general development for dyslexic students; ESL (21 students enrolled).

College Admission Counseling 109 students graduated in 2011; 87 went to college, including McMaster University; Redeemer University College; University of Guelph; University of Toronto; University of Waterloo; York University. Other: 10 went to work, 12 had other specific plans.

Student Life Upper grades have specified standards of dress, student council, honor system. Discipline rests equally with students and faculty.

Tuition and Aid Day student tuition: CAN$9250–CAN$12,020. Tuition installment plan (monthly payment plans, individually arranged payment plans). Tuition reduction for siblings, need-based scholarship grants available.

Admissions Traditional secondary-level entrance grade is 9. Deadline for receipt of application materials: none. Application fee required: CAN$400. On-campus interview required.

Athletics Interscholastic: badminton (boys, girls), basketball (b,g), hockey (b), soccer (b,g), volleyball (b,g), water badminton (b); intramural: badminton (b,g), water badminton (b); coed interscholastic: badminton, cross-country running, track and field, ultimate Frisbee; coed intramural: badminton, ice hockey. 5 PE instructors, 5 coaches.

Computers Computers are regularly used in accounting, all academic, business applications, programming, technology, video film production, yearbook classes. Computer network features include on-campus library services, Internet access, wireless campus network, Internet filtering or blocking technology. Campus intranet, student e-mail accounts, and computer access in designated common areas are available to students. Students grades are available online. The school has a published electronic and media policy.

Contact Mr. Tim Bentum, Vice Principal, Students and Admissions. 905-851-1772 Ext. 202. Fax: 905-851-9992. E-mail: bentum@tdchristian.ca. Web site: www.tdchristian.ca

TOWER HILL SCHOOL

2813 West 17th Street
Wilmington, Delaware 19806

Head of School: Dr. Christopher D. Wheeler

General Information Coeducational day college-preparatory, arts, and technology school. Grades PS–12. Founded: 1919. Setting: suburban. Nearest major city is Philadelphia, PA. 45-acre campus. 4 buildings on campus. Approved or accredited by Middle States Association of Colleges and Schools and Delaware Department of Education. Member of National Association of Independent Schools and Secondary School Admission Test Board. Endowment: $28 million. Total enrollment: 748. Upper school average class size: 14. Upper school faculty-student ratio: 1:6. There are 162 required school days per year for Upper School students. Upper School students typically attend 5 days per week. The average school day consists of 7 hours.

Upper School Student Profile Grade 9: 66 students (38 boys, 28 girls); Grade 10: 67 students (33 boys, 34 girls); Grade 11: 56 students (34 boys, 22 girls); Grade 12: 55 students (28 boys, 27 girls).

Faculty School total: 111. In upper school: 23 men, 21 women; 34 have advanced degrees.

Subjects Offered Acting, advanced biology, advanced chemistry, advanced computer applications, advanced math, advanced studio art-AP, algebra, American literature, art, art history, band, biology, British literature, calculus, calculus-AP, chemistry, China/Japan history, chorus, civil rights, classical Greek literature, community service, computer science, creative writing, current events, DNA, drama, drawing, driver education, engineering, English, English literature, European history, film, fine arts, French, geometry, health and wellness, historical research, history, human anatomy, jazz band, Latin, Latin American literature, mathematics, music, music theory, organic chemistry, painting, photography, physical science, physics, poetry, politics, pre-calculus, psychology, science, Shakespeare, Spanish, Spanish literature, strings, theater, theater design and production, U.S. constitutional history, U.S. history, U.S. history-AP, Vietnam War, woodworking, world history, writing, writing.

Graduation Requirements Arts and fine arts (art, music, dance, drama), athletics, English, foreign language, mathematics, science, social studies (includes history). Community service is required.

Special Academic Programs Advanced Placement exam preparation; honors section; independent study; academic accommodation for the gifted, the musically talented, and the artistically talented.

College Admission Counseling 52 students graduated in 2012; all went to college, including American University; Cornell University; Emory University; New York University; University of Delaware; University of Virginia. Mean SAT critical reading: 614, mean SAT math: 638, mean SAT writing: 611, mean composite ACT: 27. 42% scored over 600 on SAT critical reading, 53% scored over 600 on SAT math, 43% scored over 600 on SAT writing, 59% scored over 26 on composite ACT.

Student Life Upper grades have specified standards of dress, student council, honor system. Discipline rests equally with students and faculty.

Summer Programs Enrichment, sports programs offered; session focuses on sports camps and science enrichments; held on campus; accepts boys and girls; open to students from other schools. 60 students usually enrolled. 2013 schedule: June 17 to August 10. Application deadline: May 1.

Tuition and Aid Day student tuition: $25,110–$25,675. Tuition installment plan (The Tuition Plan, monthly payment plans, individually arranged payment plans, 60/40). Merit scholarship grants, need-based scholarship grants available. In 2012–13, 20% of upper-school students received aid; total upper-school merit-scholarship money awarded: $80,000. Total amount of financial aid awarded in 2012–13: $1,022,687.

Admissions Traditional secondary-level entrance grade is 9. For fall 2012, 72 students applied for upper-level admission, 37 were accepted, 18 enrolled. ISEE, PSAT or SAT for applicants to grade 11 and 12, SSAT or writing sample required. Deadline for receipt of application materials: January 2. Application fee required: $40. On-campus interview required.

Athletics Interscholastic: baseball (boys), basketball (b,g), cross-country running (b,g), field hockey (g), football (b), indoor track (b,g), lacrosse (b,g), soccer (b,g), swimming and diving (b,g), tennis (b,g), track and field (b,g), volleyball (g), winter (indoor) track (b,g), wrestling (b); intramural: fitness (g), self defense (g), yoga (g); coed interscholastic: golf; coed intramural: aerobics/Nautilus, strength & conditioning, weight lifting. 10 coaches, 2 athletic trainers.

Computers Computers are regularly used in all academic classes. Computer network features include on-campus library services, Internet access, wireless campus network, Internet filtering or blocking technology. Student e-mail accounts and computer access in designated common areas are available to students. Students grades are available online. The school has a published electronic and media policy.

Contact Mr. William R. Ushler, Associate Director of Admission. 302-657-8350. Fax: 302-657-8377. E-mail: wushler@towerhill.org. Web site: www.towerhill.org

TRAFALGAR CASTLE SCHOOL

401 Reynolds Street

Whitby, Ontario L1N 3W9, Canada

Head of School: Mr. Adam de Pencier

General Information Girls' boarding and day college-preparatory, arts, business, bilingual studies, and technology school. Boarding grades 7–12, day grades 5–12. Founded: 1874. Setting: small town. Nearest major city is Toronto, Canada. Students are housed in single-sex dormitories. 28-acre campus. 2 buildings on campus. Approved or accredited by Canadian Association of Independent Schools, Canadian Educational Standards Institute, Conference of Independent Schools of Ontario, Ontario Ministry of Education, The Association of Boarding Schools, and Ontario Department of Education. Language of instruction: English. Endowment: CAN$153,000. Total enrollment: 181. Upper school average class size: 15. Upper school faculty-student ratio: 1:9. There are 170 required school days per year for Upper School students. Upper School students typically attend 5 days per week. The average school day consists of 7 hours and 30 minutes.

Upper School Student Profile Grade 9: 28 students (28 girls); Grade 10: 32 students (32 girls); Grade 11: 39 students (39 girls); Grade 12: 24 students (24 girls). 38% of students are boarding students. 75% are province residents. 2 provinces are represented in upper school student body. 25% are international students. International students from Bahamas, Barbados, China, Democratic People's Republic of Korea, Mexico, and Republic of Korea; 1 other country represented in student body.

Faculty School total: 27. In upper school: 7 men, 20 women; 9 have advanced degrees; 5 reside on campus.

Subjects Offered Algebra, art, art history, biology, business skills, calculus, chemistry, computer math, computer science, creative writing, drama, earth science, economics, English, English literature, environmental science, ESL, European history, fine arts, French, geography, geometry, grammar, Latin, law, mathematics, music, photography, physical education, physics, science, social studies, world history, world literature, writing.

Graduation Requirements Arts and fine arts (art, music, dance, drama), business skills (includes word processing), computer science, English, foreign language, mathematics, physical education (includes health), science, social studies (includes history).

Special Academic Programs Advanced Placement exam preparation; honors section; independent study; term-away projects; domestic exchange program; special instructional classes for students with slight learning disabilities; ESL (20 students enrolled).

College Admission Counseling 34 students graduated in 2011; all went to college, including McGill University; Queen's University at Kingston; The University of Western Ontario; University of Toronto; University of Waterloo; Wilfrid Laurier University.

Student Life Upper grades have uniform requirement, student council. Discipline rests primarily with faculty.

Tuition and Aid Day student tuition: CAN$18,700–CAN$21,700; 5-day tuition and room/board: CAN$36,000–CAN$37,600; 7-day tuition and room/board: CAN$39,000–CAN$44,900. Tuition installment plan (monthly payment plans, individually arranged payment plans, early payment discounts). Tuition reduction for siblings, bursaries, merit scholarship grants, need-based scholarship grants available. In 2011–12, 3% of upper-school students received aid; total upper-school merit-scholarship money awarded: CAN$16,000. Total amount of financial aid awarded in 2011–12: CAN$43,000.

Admissions Traditional secondary-level entrance grade is 9. For fall 2011, 75 students applied for upper-level admission, 70 were accepted, 64 enrolled. Cognitive Abilities Test required. Deadline for receipt of application materials: none. Application fee required: CAN$2500. Interview required.

Athletics Interscholastic: badminton, baseball, basketball, cross-country running, field hockey, gymnastics, ice hockey, independent competitive sports, soccer, softball, swimming and diving, synchronized swimming, tennis, track and field, volleyball; intramural: badminton, baseball, basketball, cross-country running, dance team, field hockey, fitness, fitness walking, gymnastics, ice hockey, outdoor activities, outdoor adventure, outdoor education, physical fitness, ropes courses, rowing, running, skiing (cross-country), skiing (downhill), snowboarding, soccer, softball, swimming and diving, synchronized swimming, tennis, track and field, volleyball, yoga. 3 PE instructors.

Computers Computers are regularly used in all academic classes. Computer network features include on-campus library services, Internet access, wireless campus network, Internet filtering or blocking technology. Campus intranet and student e-mail accounts are available to students. Students grades are available online. The school has a published electronic and media policy.

Contact Irene Talent, Admissions Officer. 905-668-3358 Ext. 227. Fax: 905-668-4136. E-mail: talenti@castle-ed.com. Web site: www.castle-ed.com

TRI-CITY CHRISTIAN ACADEMY

2211 W Germann Road

Chandler, Arizona 85286

Head of School: Pastor Thad E. Todd

General Information Coeducational day college-preparatory, religious studies, and music school, affiliated with Baptist Church. Grades K4–12. Founded: 1971. Setting: suburban. Nearest major city is Phoenix. 9-acre campus. 1 building on campus. Approved or accredited by Association of Christian Schools International and North Central Association of Colleges and Schools. Total enrollment: 304. Upper school average class size: 23. Upper school faculty-student ratio: 1:16. There are 169 required school days per year for Upper School students. Upper School students typically attend 5 days per week. The average school day consists of 7 hours and 5 minutes.

Upper School Student Profile Grade 9: 30 students (13 boys, 17 girls); Grade 10: 17 students (10 boys, 7 girls); Grade 11: 23 students (12 boys, 11 girls); Grade 12: 22 students (11 boys, 11 girls). 40% of students are Baptist.

Faculty School total: 19. In upper school: 6 men, 4 women; 2 have advanced degrees.

Subjects Offered 20th century history, 20th century world history, algebra, American government, American history, American literature, applied music, athletic training, athletics, band, basic language skills, basketball, bell choir, Bible, Bible studies, biology, brass choir, business mathematics, calculus, career and personal planning, career/college preparation, cheerleading, chemistry, choir, choral music, chorus, Christian doctrine, Christian education, Christian ethics, Christian scripture, civics, computer applications, computer studies, computers, concert choir, debate, drama, drama performance, dramatic arts, English, English composition, English literature, ESL, foreign language, geometry, government, journalism, keyboarding, library skills, public speaking, Spanish, strings, U.S. history, voice and diction, volleyball, wind instruments, world history, yearbook.

Special Academic Programs Independent study; study at local college for college credit; ESL (10 students enrolled).

College Admission Counseling 15 students graduated in 2012; 13 went to college, including Arizona State University; Bob Jones University; Northern Arizona University. Other: 2 went to work.

Student Life Upper grades have uniform requirement, student council, honor system. Discipline rests primarily with faculty.

Tuition and Aid Day student tuition: $5125. Tuition installment plan (monthly payment plans). Tuition reduction for siblings, tuition tax scholarships available. In 2012–13, 30% of upper-school students received aid. Total amount of financial aid awarded in 2012–13: $25,000.

Admissions Traditional secondary-level entrance grade is 9. For fall 2012, 13 students applied for upper-level admission, 13 were accepted, 12 enrolled. Deadline for receipt of application materials: none. Application fee required: $225. On-campus interview required.

Athletics Interscholastic: basketball (boys), golf (b), soccer (b,g), volleyball (g); coed interscholastic: soccer. 2 PE instructors.

Computers Computers are regularly used in ESL, foreign language, journalism classes. Computer resources include Internet access. Students grades are available online.

Contact 480-245-7902. Fax: 480-245-7908. Web site: www.tcawarriors.org

TRI-CITY CHRISTIAN SCHOOLS

1737 West Vista Way

Vista, California 92083

Head of School: Mr. Clark Gilbert

General Information Coeducational day college-preparatory, general academic, arts, vocational, religious studies, bilingual studies, and technology school, affiliated with Christian faith. Grades PK–12. Founded: 1971. Setting: suburban. Nearest major city is San Diego. 4-acre campus. 4 buildings on campus. Approved or accredited by Association of Christian Schools International and Western Association of Schools and Colleges. Endowment: $100,000. Total enrollment: 571. Upper school average class size: 22. Upper school faculty-student ratio: 1:12. There are 180 required school days per year for Upper School students. Upper School students typically attend 5 days per week. The average school day consists of 7 hours and 25 minutes.

Upper School Student Profile Grade 9: 47 students (24 boys, 23 girls); Grade 10: 52 students (23 boys, 29 girls); Grade 11: 50 students (22 boys, 28 girls); Grade 12: 71 students (28 boys, 43 girls). 25% of students are Christian faith.

Faculty School total: 25. In upper school: 9 men, 16 women; 12 have advanced degrees.

Subjects Offered Algebra, American literature, American sign language, art, Bible studies, biology, biology-AP, British literature (honors), business mathematics, calculus, calculus-AP, chemistry, civics, computer science, drama, economics, English, English language-AP, English literature, English literature-AP, environmental science, European history, geometry, government/civics, guitar, health education, history, honors English, honors U.S. history, honors world history, journalism, library studies, mathematics, philosophy, physical education, physical science, physiology, religion, science, social studies, Spanish, speech, trigonometry, U.S. history, U.S. history-AP, world history, world literature.

Graduation Requirements Arts and fine arts (art, music, dance, drama), computer studies, English, foreign language, mathematics, physical education (includes health), religion (includes Bible studies and theology), science, social studies (includes history), speech, student portfolio. Community service is required.

Special Academic Programs International Baccalaureate program; Advanced Placement exam preparation; honors section; independent study.

College Admission Counseling 77 students graduated in 2012; all went to college, including Azusa Pacific University; California State University, San Marcos; MiraCosta College; Palomar College; Point Loma Nazarene University; Vanguard University of Southern California. Mean SAT critical reading: 546, mean SAT math: 532, mean SAT writing: 544.

Student Life Upper grades have uniform requirement, student council. Discipline rests primarily with faculty. Attendance at religious services is required.

Summer Programs Remediation, advancement, sports programs offered; session focuses on development; held both on and off campus; held at other area schools; accepts boys and girls; open to students from other schools. 60 students usually enrolled. 2013 schedule: June 1 to August 1.

Tuition and Aid Day student tuition: $7100–$9100. Tuition installment plan (monthly payment plans, individually arranged payment plans). Tuition reduction for siblings, need-based scholarship grants, paying campus jobs, church affiliation grants available. In 2012–13, 5% of upper-school students received aid. Total amount of financial aid awarded in 2012–13: $50,000.

Admissions Traditional secondary-level entrance grade is 9. Any standardized test, English entrance exam and Math Placement Exam required. Deadline for receipt of application materials: none. Application fee required: $425. On-campus interview required.

Athletics Interscholastic: aerobics/dance (girls), baseball (b), basketball (b,g), cheering (g), cross-country running (b,g), flag football (b), football (b), golf (b), soccer (b,g), softball (g), tennis (b,g), touch football (b), track and field (b,g), volleyball (b,g), weight training (b,g); intramural: dance (g), physical fitness (b,g); coed interscholastic: equestrian sports, golf, horseback riding, lacrosse, martial arts, snowboarding. 2 PE instructors, 20 coaches, 1 athletic trainer.

Computers Computers are regularly used in animation, business applications, career exploration, computer applications, media production, news writing, science, video film production classes. Computer network features include on-campus library services, Internet access, Internet filtering or blocking technology. Campus intranet and student e-mail accounts are available to students. Students grades are available online. The school has a published electronic and media policy.

Contact Mrs. Terri Montano, Registrar. 760-806-8247 Ext. 200. Fax: 760-906-9002. E-mail: Terri.Montano@tccs.org. Web site: www.tccs.org

TRINITY CHRISTIAN ACADEMY

10 Windy City Road
Jackson, Tennessee 38305

Head of School: Mr. Jon Holley

General Information Coeducational day college-preparatory school. Grades PS–12. Founded: 1986. Setting: small town. Nearest major city is Memphis. 30-acre campus. 1 building on campus. Approved or accredited by Association of Christian Schools International, Southern Association of Colleges and Schools, and Tennessee Department of Education. Total enrollment: 751. Upper school average class size: 22. Upper school faculty-student ratio: 1:10. There are 176 required school days per year for Upper School students. Upper School students typically attend 5 days per week. The average school day consists of 5 hours and 20 minutes.

Upper School Student Profile Grade 9: 64 students (30 boys, 34 girls); Grade 10: 56 students (34 boys, 22 girls); Grade 11: 60 students (24 boys, 36 girls); Grade 12: 61 students (31 boys, 30 girls).

Faculty School total: 60. In upper school: 10 men, 11 women; 19 have advanced degrees.

Subjects Offered Algebra, art, Bible studies, biology, biology-AP, British literature, British literature (honors), calculus-AP, chemistry, choir, computers, drama, economics, English, etymology, fine arts, forensics, geography, geometry, government, photography, physical fitness, physical science, physics, physics-AP, pre-calculus, U.S. history, U.S. history-AP, wellness, world history, yearbook.

Graduation Requirements Arts and fine arts (art, music, dance, drama), Bible, computers, English, foreign language, history, mathematics, science, wellness, 80 hours of community service and participation in the Footprints program.

Special Academic Programs Honors section; study at local college for college credit.

College Admission Counseling 57 students graduated in 2012; 56 went to college, including Jackson State Community College; The University of Tennessee; The University of Tennessee at Chattanooga; The University of Tennessee at Martin; Union University. Other: 1 went to work. Median composite ACT: 23.

Student Life Upper grades have uniform requirement, student council, honor system. Discipline rests primarily with faculty. Attendance at religious services is required.

Tuition and Aid Day student tuition: $7780. Tuition installment plan (FACTS Tuition Payment Plan, monthly payment plans). Need-based scholarship grants available.

Admissions Traditional secondary-level entrance grade is 9. For fall 2012, 48 students applied for upper-level admission, 48 were accepted, 48 enrolled. SAT required. Deadline for receipt of application materials: none. Application fee required: $200. On-campus interview required.

Athletics Interscholastic: baseball (girls), basketball (b,g), cheering (b), cross-country running (b,g), football (g), golf (b,g), in-line hockey (b), soccer (b,g), softball (g), tennis (b,g), track and field (b,g), trap and skeet (b), volleyball (b). 2 PE instructors.

Computers Computers are regularly used in computer applications classes. Computer resources include Internet access, Internet filtering or blocking technology. Students grades are available online.

Contact Mrs. Andrea Moody, Admissions Director. 731-668-8500 Ext. 107. Fax: 731-668-3232. E-mail: amoody@tcalions.com. Web site: www.tcalions.com

TRINITY COLLEGE SCHOOL

55 Deblaquire Street North
Port Hope, Ontario L1A 4K7, Canada

Head of School: Mr. Stuart K.C. Grainger

General Information Coeducational boarding and day college-preparatory and arts school, affiliated with Church of England (Anglican). Boarding grades 9–12, day grades 5–12. Founded: 1865. Setting: small town. Nearest major city is Toronto, Canada. Students are housed in single-sex dormitories. 100-acre campus. 15 buildings on campus. Approved or accredited by Canadian Association of Independent Schools, Canadian Educational Standards Institute, Conference of Independent Schools of Ontario, The Association of Boarding Schools, and Ontario Department of Education. Affiliate member of National Association of Independent Schools; member of Secondary School Admission Test Board. Language of instruction: English. Endowment: CAN$24 million. Total enrollment: 545. Upper school average class size: 16. Upper school faculty-student ratio: 1:8. There are 165 required school days per year for Upper School students. Upper School students typically attend 5 days per week. The average school day consists of 6 hours.

Upper School Student Profile 60% of students are boarding students. 61% are province residents. 8 provinces are represented in upper school student body. 33% are international students. International students from Bahamas, Bermuda, China, Germany, Mexico, and Republic of Korea; 23 other countries represented in student body. 30% of students are members of Church of England (Anglican).

Faculty School total: 86. In upper school: 37 men, 29 women; 17 have advanced degrees; 11 reside on campus.

Subjects Offered Algebra, art, art history-AP, astronomy, biology, biology-AP, calculus, calculus-AP, Canadian geography, Canadian history, career education, career/college preparation, chemistry, chemistry-AP, civics, classical civilization, classics, community service, computer programming, computer science, creative writing, dramatic arts, earth science, economics, English, English literature, English-AP, environmental science, environmental studies, ESL, European history, fine arts, finite math, French, French-AP, general science, geography, geometry, German, guidance, health, history, independent study, Latin, law, mathematics, modern Western civilization, music, philosophy, physical education, physics, physics-AP, political science, science, social sciences, social studies, Spanish.

Graduation Requirements Arts and fine arts (art, music, dance, drama), Canadian geography, Canadian history, civics, English, French, guidance, mathematics, physical education (includes health), science, social sciences, technology, minimum 40 hours of community service.

Special Academic Programs Advanced Placement exam preparation; independent study; term-away projects; study abroad; ESL (15 students enrolled).

College Admission Counseling 119 students graduated in 2012; 1 went to college, including Dalhousie University; McGill University; Queen's University at Kingston; The University of Western Ontario; University of Guelph; University of Toronto. Other: 5 had other specific plans. 25.5% scored over 600 on SAT critical reading, 30% scored over 600 on SAT math, 23% scored over 600 on SAT writing, 30% scored over 1800 on combined SAT.

Student Life Upper grades have uniform requirement, student council, honor system. Discipline rests primarily with faculty. Attendance at religious services is required.

Summer Programs Advancement, art/fine arts, computer instruction programs offered; session focuses on advancement through cultural enrichment; held off campus; held at England; accepts boys and girls; open to students from other schools. 30 students usually enrolled. 2013 schedule: July 3 to July 25. Application deadline: April 12.

Tuition and Aid Day student tuition: CAN$21,100–CAN$29,250; 7-day tuition and room/board: CAN$48,250–CAN$48,750. Tuition installment plan (monthly payment plans, quarterly payment plan). Bursaries, need-based scholarship grants available. In 2012–13, 26% of upper-school students received aid. Total amount of financial aid awarded in 2012–13: CAN$1,000,000.

Admissions Traditional secondary-level entrance grade is 9. For fall 2012, 198 students applied for upper-level admission, 198 were accepted, 134 enrolled. Otis-Lennon Ability or Stanford Achievement Test, SSAT, ERB, PSAT, SAT, PLAN or ACT or TOEFL required. Deadline for receipt of application materials: none. Application fee required: CAN$150. Interview required.

Athletics Interscholastic: baseball (boys), basketball (b,g), cricket (b), field hockey (g), football (b), ice hockey (b,g), rugby (b,g), soccer (b,g), softball (g), squash (b,g), tennis (b,g), volleyball (b,g); coed interscholastic: badminton, cross-country running, dressage, equestrian sports, golf, nordic skiing, outdoor education, rowing, skiing (cross-country), swimming and diving, track and field; coed intramural: aerobics, aerobics/dance, alpine skiing, badminton, basketball, bicycling, cricket, cross-country running, dance, equestrian sports, fitness, golf, horseback riding, ice hockey, jogging, mountain biking, paddling, skiing (downhill), snowboarding, soccer, softball, squash, strength & conditioning, swimming and diving, table tennis, tennis, water polo, weight lifting, weight training, yoga. 4 PE instructors, 5 coaches, 2 athletic trainers.

Computers Computers are regularly used in career education, college planning, English, ESL, foreign language, French, geography, history, humanities, independent study, information technology, mathematics, music, science, technology classes. Computer network features include on-campus library services, Internet access, wireless campus network. Student e-mail accounts are available to students. The school has a published electronic and media policy.

Contact Ms. Kathryn A. LaBranche, Director of Admissions. 905-885-3209. Fax: 905-885-7444. E-mail: admissions@tcs.on.ca. Web site: www.tcs.on.ca

TRINITY HIGH SCHOOL

4011 Shelbyville Road
Louisville, Kentucky 40207-9427

Head of School: Robert J. Mullen, EdD

General Information Boys' day college-preparatory, arts, business, religious studies, and technology school, affiliated with Roman Catholic Church. Grades 9–12. Founded: 1953. Setting: suburban. 110-acre campus. 11 buildings on campus. Approved or accredited by National Catholic Education Association, Southern Association of Colleges and Schools, Southern Association of Independent Schools, and Kentucky Department of Education. Member of National Association of Independent Schools. Endowment: $10 million. Total enrollment: 1,320. Upper school average class size: 20. Upper school faculty-student ratio: 1:12. There are 175 required school days per year for Upper School students. Upper School students typically attend 5 days per week. The average school day consists of 7 hours.

Upper School Student Profile Grade 9: 349 students (349 boys); Grade 10: 324 students (324 boys); Grade 11: 318 students (318 boys); Grade 12: 329 students (329 boys). 84% of students are Roman Catholic.

Faculty School total: 120. In upper school: 88 men, 30 women; 110 have advanced degrees.

Subjects Offered 20th century history, 3-dimensional art, accounting, acting, adolescent issues, advanced chemistry, advanced computer applications, advanced math, Advanced Placement courses, advanced studio art-AP, algebra, American Civil War, American democracy, American foreign policy, American government, American history, American history-AP, American literature, American literature-AP, analysis and differential calculus, analysis of data, anatomy and physiology, ancient history, ancient world history, applied arts, applied music, art, art and culture, art appreciation, art education, art history, art-AP, arts, arts appreciation, athletic training, athletics, band, banking, Basic programming, Bible as literature, biology, biology-AP, broadcasting, business, business education, business law, business mathematics, business studies, business technology, calculus, calculus-AP, campus ministry, career exploration, career planning, career/college preparation, cell biology, character education, cheerleading, chemistry, chemistry-AP, choir, choral music, chorus, Christian doctrine, Christian ethics, Christian scripture, church history, cinematography, civics, Civil War, classical civilization, classical Greek literature, classical music, college admission preparation, college awareness, college counseling, college placement, college planning, communication arts, communication skills, community service, comparative cultures, comparative government and politics, composition-AP, computer animation, computer applications, computer art, computer education, computer graphics, computer information systems, computer literacy, computer math, computer multimedia, computer music, computer processing, computer programming, computer science, computer skills, computer studies, computer technologies, computer technology certification, computer tools, computers, concert band, concert choir, conflict resolution, constitutional law, contemporary art, CPR, creative writing, critical studies in film, critical thinking, critical writing, data analysis, data processing, death and loss, decision making skills, developmental math, digital photography, DNA research, drama, drama performance, drawing, drawing and design, earth and space science, earth science, ecology, economics, economics and history, economics-AP, English, English language and composition-AP, English literature, English-AP, environmental studies, European civilization, European history, evolution, family living, fencing, film, film studies, finite math, first aid, forensics, French, general science, geography, geometry, German, health, health science, Hebrew scripture, Holocaust studies, HTML design, humanities, independent study, information technology, instrumental music, integrated mathematics, interdisciplinary studies, Internet, jazz band, journalism, keyboarding, language arts, leadership and service, literature, literature-AP, martial arts, mathematics, modern civilization, moral and social development, multimedia design, music performance, musical theater, New Testament, news writing, newspaper, oil painting, painting, peace and justice, philosophy, photography, photojournalism, physical education, physical fitness, physical science, physics, physics-AP, post-calculus, pottery, pre-algebra, precalculus, probability and statistics, programming, psychology, public speaking, religion, religious studies, Roman civilization, Romantic period literature, Russian history, SAT/ACT preparation, science, sculpture, senior seminar, social justice, social psychology, social sciences, social studies, sociology, software design, space and physical sciences, Spanish, Spanish literature, Spanish-AP, speech and debate, sports medicine, sports nutrition, stage design, stained glass, statistics, student government, student publications, technology, trigonometry, U.S. government and politics-AP, U.S. history-AP, video film production, Web site design, weight training, Western civilization, work-study, world civilizations, world history, world history-AP, yearbook.

Graduation Requirements Communication arts, English, foreign language, humanities, lab science, mathematics, physical education (includes health), religion (includes Bible studies and theology), science, social studies (includes history), several elective offerings, Must have taken the ACT. Community service is required.

Special Academic Programs Advanced Placement exam preparation; honors section; independent study; study at local college for college credit; study abroad; academic accommodation for the gifted, the musically talented, and the artistically talented; remedial reading and/or remedial writing; remedial math; programs in English, mathematics, general development for dyslexic students; special instructional classes for deaf students, blind students.

College Admission Counseling 307 students graduated in 2012; 304 went to college, including Bellarmine University; Eastern Kentucky University; Indiana University Bloomington; University of Dayton; University of Kentucky; University of Louisville. Other: 3 entered military service. Mean combined SAT: 1854, mean composite ACT: 23.

Student Life Upper grades have specified standards of dress, student council, honor system. Discipline rests primarily with faculty. Attendance at religious services is required.

Summer Programs Remediation, enrichment, advancement, sports, art/fine arts, computer instruction programs offered; session focuses on academic advancement and enrichment/sports camps; held on campus; accepts boys; not open to students from other schools. 1,000 students usually enrolled. 2013 schedule: June 1 to August 3. Application deadline: May 15.

Tuition and Aid Day student tuition: $11,325. Guaranteed tuition plan. Tuition installment plan (monthly payment plans, individually arranged payment plans, Tuition Management Systems). Merit scholarship grants, need-based scholarship grants, paying campus jobs available. In 2012–13, 40% of upper-school students received aid; total upper-school merit-scholarship money awarded: $120,000. Total amount of financial aid awarded in 2012–13: $2,200,000.

Admissions Traditional secondary-level entrance grade is 9. High School Placement Test required. Deadline for receipt of application materials: none. Application fee required: $75. Interview required.

Athletics Interscholastic: archery, baseball, basketball, bicycling, bowling, cheering, crew, cross-country running, diving, football, golf, hockey, ice hockey, lacrosse, power lifting, rugby, soccer, swimming and diving, tennis, track and field, volleyball, weight lifting, wrestling; intramural: alpine skiing, basketball, bocce, climbing, cricket, fencing, fishing, flag football, freestyle skiing, Frisbee, golf, hiking/backpacking, indoor soccer, kickball, life saving, martial arts, mountain biking, paddle tennis, rock climbing, skiing (downhill), snowboarding, soccer, softball, strength & conditioning, table tennis, ultimate Frisbee, volleyball, water polo, weight lifting, weight training; coed intramural: bowling. 5 PE instructors, 30 coaches, 3 athletic trainers.

Computers Computers are regularly used in all classes. Computer network features include on-campus library services, online commercial services, Internet access, wireless campus network, Internet filtering or blocking technology. Campus intranet, student e-mail accounts, and computer access in designated common areas are available to students. Students grades are available online. The school has a published electronic and media policy.

Contact Mr. Joseph M. Porter Jr., Vice President for Advancement. 502-736-2119. Fax: 502-899-2052. E-mail: porter@thsrock.net. Web site: www.trinityrocks.com

TRINITY HIGH SCHOOL

581 Bridge Street
Manchester, New Hampshire 03104

Head of School: Mr. Denis Mailloux

General Information Coeducational day college-preparatory, arts, religious studies, and technology school, affiliated with Roman Catholic Church. Grades 9–12. Founded: 1886. Setting: urban. Nearest major city is Boston, MA. 5-acre campus. 2 buildings on campus. Approved or accredited by National Catholic Education Association, New England Association of Schools and Colleges, and New Hampshire Department of Education. Total enrollment: 447. Upper school average class size: 15. Upper school faculty-student ratio: 1:12. There are 180 required school days per year for Upper School students. Upper School students typically attend 5 days per week. The average school day consists of 6 hours and 30 minutes.

Upper School Student Profile Grade 9: 120 students (76 boys, 44 girls); Grade 10: 107 students (58 boys, 49 girls); Grade 11: 119 students (62 boys, 57 girls); Grade 12: 101 students (50 boys, 51 girls). 80% of students are Roman Catholic.

Faculty School total: 37. In upper school: 19 men, 18 women; 19 have advanced degrees.

Subjects Offered 3-dimensional art, advanced biology, advanced math, Advanced Placement courses, algebra, American government, American history, American history-AP, American literature, analysis, anatomy and physiology, art, Bible studies, biology, calculus, calculus-AP, chemistry, computer science, driver education, English, English literature, English-AP, ethics, French, geometry, grammar, health, history, human development, journalism, Latin, mathematics, physical education, physics, psychology, psychology-AP, religion, science, social studies, sociology, Spanish, theology, trigonometry, U.S. history-AP, world history, world literature.

Special Academic Programs 5 Advanced Placement exams for which test preparation is offered; honors section; study at local college for college credit.

College Admission Counseling 90 students graduated in 2012; 88 went to college, including Saint Anselm College; Stonehill College; University of New Hampshire. Other: 1 entered military service, 1 entered a postgraduate year.

Student Life Upper grades have specified standards of dress, student council, honor system. Discipline rests primarily with faculty. Attendance at religious services is required.

Tuition and Aid Day student tuition: $8940. Tuition installment plan (FACTS Tuition Payment Plan). Need-based scholarship grants available. In 2012–13, 10% of upper-school students received aid.

Admissions Traditional secondary-level entrance grade is 9. STS required. Deadline for receipt of application materials: none. Application fee required: $50. Interview recommended.

Athletics Interscholastic: baseball (boys), basketball (b,g), cheering (g), cross-country running (b,g), football (b), gymnastics (g), hockey (b), ice hockey (b), indoor track & field (b,g), lacrosse (b), skiing (cross-country) (b,g), skiing (downhill) (b,g), soccer (b,g), softball (g), swimming and diving (b,g), tennis (b,g), volleyball (g), winter (indoor) track (b,g), wrestling (b); coed interscholastic: alpine skiing, golf, track and field; coed intramural: gymnastics. 1 PE instructor, 25 coaches, 1 athletic trainer.

Computers Computers are regularly used in English, journalism, science, social sciences, yearbook classes. Computer network features include Internet access, wireless campus network. Campus intranet and student e-mail accounts are available to students. Students grades are available online.

Contact Mr. Patrick Smith, Dean of Students and Director of Admissions. 603-668-2910 Ext. 18. Fax: 603-668-2913. E-mail: psmith@trinity-hs.org. Web site: www.trinity-hs.org

TRINITY HIGH SCHOOL

12425 Granger Road
Garfield Heights, Ohio 44125

Head of School: Mrs. Linda Bacho

General Information Coeducational day college-preparatory, arts, business, religious studies, technology, technical, and medical school, affiliated with Roman Catholic Church. Grades 9–12. Founded: 1926. Setting: suburban. Nearest major city is Cleveland. 26-acre campus. 3 buildings on campus. Approved or accredited by National Catholic Education Association, North Central Association of Colleges and Schools, Ohio Catholic Schools Accreditation Association (OCSAA), and Ohio Department of Education. Total enrollment: 352. Upper school average class size: 17. Upper school faculty-student ratio: 1:10. There are 199 required school days per year for Upper School students. Upper School students typically attend 5 days per week. The average school day consists of 7 hours.

Upper School Student Profile Grade 9: 106 students (42 boys, 64 girls); Grade 10: 70 students (23 boys, 47 girls); Grade 11: 87 students (46 boys, 41 girls); Grade 12: 89 students (39 boys, 50 girls). 89% of students are Roman Catholic.

Faculty School total: 35. In upper school: 14 men, 21 women; 16 have advanced degrees.

Subjects Offered 3-dimensional art, accounting, advanced biology, advanced chemistry, advanced computer applications, advanced math, Advanced Placement courses, advanced studio art-AP, algebra, American government, American history, American history-AP, American literature, analysis and differential calculus, anatomy and physiology, animation, art, athletics, automated accounting, band, Bible, Bible studies, biology, bookkeeping, British literature, British literature (honors), business applications, business skills, business technology, calculus-AP, campus ministry, career and personal planning, career education, career education internship, career experience, career exploration, career planning, career/college preparation, Catholic belief and practice, ceramics, chemistry, choir, Christian and Hebrew scripture, Christian doctrine, Christian ethics, Christian scripture, Christian testament, church history, college admission preparation, college awareness, college counseling, college placement, college planning, college writing, communication skills, community service, comparative religion, competitive science projects, computer animation, computer applications, computer art, computer education, computer graphics, computer information systems, computer multimedia, computer technologies, computer technology certification, computer-aided design, concert band, concert choir, consumer economics, creative writing, critical thinking, critical writing, culinary arts, digital applications, drama performance, drawing and design, earth science, economics and history, electives, English, English literature and composition-AP, environmental science, ethics, European history, food and nutrition, foods, foreign language, four units of summer reading, geometry, global studies, government-AP, graphic arts, graphic design, graphics, guidance, health education, honors algebra, honors English, honors geometry, human anatomy, human biology, instrumental music, integrated mathematics, Internet research, internship, lab science, library, life issues, Life of Christ, marching band, marine biology, Microsoft, moral theology, musical theater, neuroscience, oral communications, participation in sports, peace and justice, peer ministry, personal finance, photo shop, physical education, physics, play production, portfolio art, prayer/spirituality, pre-algebra, pre-calculus, psychology, public speaking, SAT/ACT preparation, speech, sports, studio art-AP, study skills, symphonic band, theology, U.S. government and politics-AP, video, video and animation, vocal ensemble, Web site design, wind ensemble, word processing, world history, yearbook.

Graduation Requirements Arts and fine arts (art, music, dance, drama), electives, English, government, human relations, mathematics, physical education (includes health), science, social studies (includes history), theology, Western civilization, service hours, internship.

Special Academic Programs Advanced Placement exam preparation; honors section; independent study; academic accommodation for the gifted and the artistically talented; remedial math; programs in English, mathematics, general development for dyslexic students.

College Admission Counseling 78 students graduated in 2012; 74 went to college, including John Carroll University; Kent State University; Miami University; Ohio University; The Ohio State University; University of Dayton. Other: 2 went to work, 1 entered military service, 1 had other specific plans. Median SAT critical reading: 485, median SAT math: 450, median SAT writing: 450, median combined SAT: 1385, median composite ACT: 21. 27% scored over 600 on SAT critical reading, 18% scored over 600 on SAT math, 18% scored over 600 on SAT writing, 10% scored over 1800 on combined SAT, 11% scored over 26 on composite ACT.

Student Life Upper grades have uniform requirement, student council. Discipline rests primarily with faculty. Attendance at religious services is required.

Summer Programs Enrichment, advancement, sports, art/fine arts programs offered; session focuses on recruitment; held both on and off campus; held at other schools; accepts boys and girls; open to students from other schools. 125 students usually enrolled. 2013 schedule: June to August. Application deadline: May.

Tuition and Aid Day student tuition: $9900. Guaranteed tuition plan. Tuition installment plan (individually arranged payment plans, private bank loans). Tuition reduction for siblings, need-based scholarship grants, middle-income loans, private bank loans available. In 2012–13, 25% of upper-school students received aid. Total amount of financial aid awarded in 2012–13: $138,000.

Admissions Traditional secondary-level entrance grade is 9. For fall 2012, 112 students applied for upper-level admission, 110 were accepted, 106 enrolled. Scholastic Testing Service High School Placement Test required. Deadline for receipt of application materials: none. Application fee required: $20. On-campus interview required.

Athletics Interscholastic: baseball (boys), basketball (b,g), cheering (g), cross-country running (b,g), danceline (g), football (b), soccer (b,g), softball (g), track and field (b,g), volleyball (g), wrestling (b); intramural: danceline (g); coed interscholastic: golf, indoor track & field; coed intramural: skiing (downhill), snowboarding. 1 PE instructor, 34 coaches, 1 athletic trainer.

Computers Computers are regularly used in all academic classes. Computer network features include on-campus library services, online commercial services, Internet access, wireless campus network, Internet filtering or blocking technology, Citrix, network printing, personal storage on network, weekly email grade reports, electronic newsletters, remote access, school Web site, online homework tracking system. Computer access in designated common areas is available to students. Students grades are available online. The school has a published electronic and media policy.

Contact Sr. Dian Majsterek, Administrative Assistant, Admissions and Marketing. 216-581-1061. Fax: 216-581-9348. E-mail: SisterDian@ths.org. Web site: www.ths.org

TRINITY-PAWLING SCHOOL

700 Route 22
Pawling, New York 12564

Head of School: Mr. Archibald A. Smith III

General Information Boys' boarding and day college-preparatory, arts, religious studies, technology, and ESL school, affiliated with Episcopal Church. Boarding grades 9–PG, day grades 7–PG. Founded: 1907. Setting: small town. Nearest major city is New York. Students are housed in single-sex dormitories. 140-acre campus. 27 buildings on campus. Approved or accredited by New York State Association of Independent Schools, New York State Board of Regents, and The Association of Boarding Schools. Member of National Association of Independent Schools and Secondary School Admission Test Board. Endowment: $35 million. Total enrollment: 293. Upper school average class size: 12. Upper school faculty-student ratio: 1:8. There are 186 required school days per year for Upper School students. Upper School students typically attend 6 days per week. The average school day consists of 6 hours and 30 minutes.

Upper School Student Profile Grade 9: 33 students (33 boys); Grade 10: 68 students (68 boys); Grade 11: 78 students (78 boys); Grade 12: 72 students (72 boys); Postgraduate: 20 students (20 boys). 80% of students are boarding students. 20% are state residents. 19 states are represented in upper school student body. 25% are international students. International students from Brazil, Canada, China, Republic of Korea, Saudi Arabia, and Viet Nam; 14 other countries represented in student body. 20% of students are members of Episcopal Church.

Faculty School total: 53. In upper school: 36 men, 15 women; 40 have advanced degrees; 50 reside on campus.

Subjects Offered Advanced Placement courses, advanced studio art-AP, algebra, American government, American history, American legal systems, American literature, American studies, anatomy, anatomy and physiology, architectural drawing, art, art history, art history-AP, Asian history, Asian studies, astronomy, Bible, biology, biology-

AP, calculus, calculus-AP, ceramics, chemistry, chemistry-AP, choir, chorus, Christian ethics, civil rights, composition-AP, computer applications, computer information systems, computer math, computer music, computer programming, computer science, computer science-AP, computer technologies, constitutional history of U.S., data analysis, drafting, drama, drama performance, earth science, East Asian history, ecology, economics, economics-AP, English, English language-AP, English literature, English literature-AP, English-AP, English/composition-AP, environmental science, environmental science-AP, environmental studies, ESL, ethics, European history, European history-AP, fine arts, French, French language-AP, French studies, geology, geometry, government, government and politics-AP, government/civics, grammar, health science, history, honors algebra, honors English, honors geometry, honors U.S. history, honors world history, human anatomy, keyboarding, Latin, Latin American literature, Latin-AP, law and the legal system, literature, literature and composition-AP, Mandarin, mathematics, mechanical drawing, model United Nations, music, philosophy, photography, physical education, physics, physics-AP, physiology, political science, pre-calculus, probability and statistics, psychology, public speaking, reading/study skills, religion, religious education, religious studies, SAT preparation, science, Shakespeare, social justice, social sciences, social studies, Spanish, Spanish language-AP, Spanish literature-AP, statistics-AP, studio art, studio art-AP, study skills, theater, theology, trigonometry, U.S. government and politics, U.S. history, U.S. history-AP, Vietnam War, word processing, world history, writing, yearbook.

Graduation Requirements Arts and fine arts (art, music, dance, drama), English, foreign language, mathematics, physical education (includes health), religion (includes Bible studies and theology), science, social studies (includes history).

Special Academic Programs 17 Advanced Placement exams for which test preparation is offered; honors section; remedial reading and/or remedial writing; programs in English for dyslexic students; ESL (25 students enrolled).

College Admission Counseling 86 students graduated in 2012; all went to college, including Boston University; Hobart and William Smith Colleges; Syracuse University; The Johns Hopkins University; The University of Arizona; University of New Hampshire. Mean SAT critical reading: 580, mean SAT math: 570.

Student Life Upper grades have specified standards of dress, student council, honor system. Discipline rests equally with students and faculty. Attendance at religious services is required.

Tuition and Aid Day student tuition: $35,000; 7-day tuition and room/board: $49,250. Tuition installment plan (Academic Management Services Plan, individually arranged payment plans, payment plans arranged directly with the school business office). Need-based scholarship grants, need-based loans available. In 2012–13, 35% of upper-school students received aid. Total amount of financial aid awarded in 2012–13: $3,200,000.

Admissions Traditional secondary-level entrance grade is 9. For fall 2012, 352 students applied for upper-level admission, 242 were accepted, 112 enrolled. PSAT or SAT, SSAT, TOEFL, Wechsler Intelligence Scale for Children III or WISC-R required. Deadline for receipt of application materials: February 1. Application fee required: $50. On-campus interview required.

Athletics Interscholastic: alpine skiing, baseball, basketball, cross-country running, football, golf, hockey, ice hockey, lacrosse, ropes courses, skiing (downhill), soccer, squash, strength & conditioning, tennis, track and field, weight lifting, weight training, wrestling; intramural: alpine skiing, basketball, bicycling, climbing, fishing, fitness, floor hockey, fly fishing, Frisbee, golf, hiking/backpacking, ice skating, mountain biking, outdoor education, outdoor recreation, physical training, polo, rock climbing, running, skiing (downhill), snowboarding, soccer, softball, squash, strength & conditioning, tennis, trap and skeet, ultimate Frisbee, wall climbing, weight lifting. 30 coaches, 2 athletic trainers.

Computers Computers are regularly used in English, history, mathematics, remedial study skills, science classes. Computer network features include on-campus library services, online commercial services, Internet access, wireless campus network, Internet filtering or blocking technology. Campus intranet, student e-mail accounts, and computer access in designated common areas are available to students. Students grades are available online.

Contact Mrs. Denise Palmer, Admission Office Manager. 845-855-4825. Fax: 845-855-4827. E-mail: denisepalmer@trinitypawling.org. Web site: www.trinitypawling.org

See Display below and Close-Up on page 642.

TRINITY PREPARATORY SCHOOL

5700 Trinity Prep Lane
Winter Park, Florida 32792

Head of School: Craig S. Maughan

General Information Coeducational day college-preparatory, arts, technology, and Stanford Online video conferencing courses school, affiliated with Episcopal Church. Grades 6–12. Founded: 1966. Setting: suburban. Nearest major city is Orlando. 100-acre campus. 12 buildings on campus. Approved or accredited by Florida Council of Independent Schools and Florida Department of Education. Member of National Association of Independent Schools and Secondary School Admission Test Board. Endowment: $9.2 million. Total enrollment: 860. Upper school average class size: 17. Upper school faculty-student ratio: 1:9. There are 175 required school days per year for Upper School students. Upper School students typically attend 5 days per week. The average school day consists of 5 hours and 45 minutes.

Upper School Student Profile Grade 9: 130 students (72 boys, 58 girls); Grade 10: 133 students (69 boys, 64 girls); Grade 11: 128 students (62 boys, 66 girls); Grade 12: 121 students (71 boys, 50 girls). 7% of students are members of Episcopal Church.

Faculty School total: 78. In upper school: 25 men, 35 women; 40 have advanced degrees.

Subjects Offered 20th century American writers, 20th century world history, 3-dimensional art, advanced math, Advanced Placement courses, advanced studio art-AP, algebra, American history, American literature, anatomy, animal science, art, athletic training, audio visual/media, band, Basic programming, Bible, biology, biology-AP, calculus, calculus-AP, character education, chemistry, chemistry-AP, chorus, civics, Civil War, comparative religion, computer graphics, computer multimedia, computer processing, computer programming, computer programming-AP, concert band, concert choir, creative writing, critical studies in film, digital photography, drama, drawing, economics, economics-AP, English, English language and composition-AP, English literature, English literature and composition-AP, environmental science, environmental science-AP, ethics, European history, European history-AP, filmmaking, fine arts, forensics, French, French language-AP, French literature-AP, geography, geometry, government and politics-AP, health, honors algebra, honors English, honors geometry, journalism, Latin, Latin-AP, life management skills, mathematics, music, music theory-AP, newspaper, painting, physical education, physics, physics-AP, portfolio art, pottery, pre-algebra, pre-calculus, probability and statistics, psychology, psychology-AP, science, sculpture, social studies, Spanish, Spanish language-AP, Spanish literature-AP, speech, strings, studio art-AP, theater, trigonometry, U.S. government and politics-AP, U.S. history-AP, weight training, world history, world wide web design, writing, yearbook.

Graduation Requirements Arts and fine arts (art, music, dance, drama), computer science, electives, English, foreign language, life management skills, mathematics, physical education (includes health), science, social sciences, 1/2 additional social studies credit.

Special Academic Programs 25 Advanced Placement exams for which test preparation is offered; honors section; independent study; study at local college for college credit; academic accommodation for the gifted, the musically talented, and the artistically talented.

College Admission Counseling 113 students graduated in 2012; all went to college, including Emory University; Florida State University; University of Central Florida; University of Florida; University of Virginia. Mean SAT critical reading: 647, mean SAT math: 662, mean SAT writing: 637, mean combined SAT: 1956, mean composite ACT: 28. 74% scored over 600 on SAT critical reading, 79% scored over 600 on SAT math, 76% scored over 600 on SAT writing, 79% scored over 1800 on combined SAT, 80% scored over 26 on composite ACT.

Student Life Upper grades have specified standards of dress, student council, honor system. Discipline rests primarily with faculty. Attendance at religious services is required.

Summer Programs Remediation, enrichment, advancement, sports, art/fine arts, computer instruction programs offered; session focuses on enrichment; held on campus; accepts boys and girls; open to students from other schools. 300 students usually enrolled. 2013 schedule: June 14 to August 8. Application deadline: none.

Tuition and Aid Day student tuition: $17,500. Tuition installment plan (Insured Tuition Payment Plan, monthly payment plans, semiannual and annual payment plans). Need-based scholarship grants available. In 2012–13, 25% of upper-school students received aid. Total amount of financial aid awarded in 2012–13: $1,828,500.

Admissions Traditional secondary-level entrance grade is 9. For fall 2012, 52 students applied for upper-level admission, 23 were accepted, 20 enrolled. CTP, ISEE, PSAT, SAT or SSAT required. Deadline for receipt of application materials: February 8. Application fee required: $75. Interview required.

Athletics Interscholastic: baseball (boys), basketball (b,g), bowling (b,g), cheering (g), cross-country running (b,g), diving (b,g), fitness (b,g), football (b), golf (b,g), lacrosse (b,g), physical fitness (b,g), soccer (b,g), softball (g), strength & conditioning (b,g), swimming and diving (b,g), tennis (b,g), track and field (b,g), volleyball (g), weight lifting (b,g), weight training (b,g); intramural: ropes courses (b,g), strength & conditioning (b,g). 5 PE instructors, 48 coaches, 1 athletic trainer.

Computers Computers are regularly used in all classes. Computer network features include on-campus library services, online commercial services, Internet access, wireless campus network, Internet filtering or blocking technology. Student e-mail accounts and computer access in designated common areas are available to students. Students grades are available online. The school has a published electronic and media policy.

Contact Sherryn M. Hay, Director of Admission. 321-282-2523. Fax: 407-671-6935. E-mail: hays@trinityprep.org. Web site: www.trinityprep.org

TRINITY SCHOOL OF TEXAS

215 Teague Street
Longview, Texas 75601

Head of School: Mr. Richard L. Beard

General Information Coeducational day and distance learning college-preparatory, arts, religious studies, and technology school, affiliated with Episcopal Church. Grades PK–12. Distance learning grades 10–12. Founded: 1957. Setting: small town. Nearest major city is Dallas. 14-acre campus. 4 buildings on campus. Approved or accredited by National Association of Episcopal Schools, Southern Association of Colleges and Schools, Southwest Association of Episcopal Schools, and Texas Department of Education. Endowment: $315,000. Total enrollment: 300. Upper school average class size: 12: Upper school faculty-student ratio: 1:8. There are 174 required school days per year for Upper School students. Upper School students typically attend 5 days per week. The average school day consists of 6 hours and 20 minutes.

Upper School Student Profile Grade 9: 15 students (9 boys, 6 girls); Grade 10: 15 students (6 boys, 9 girls); Grade 11: 11 students (7 boys, 4 girls); Grade 12: 12 students (4 boys, 8 girls). 11% of students are members of Episcopal Church.

Faculty School total: 38. In upper school: 3 men, 13 women; 3 have advanced degrees.

Subjects Offered Advanced studio art-AP, algebra, American history, art, astronomy, athletics, biology, biology-AP, calculus, calculus-AP, Central and Eastern European history, character education, chemistry, chemistry-AP, choir, choral music, college admission preparation, college writing, community service, computer applications, computer literacy, conflict resolution, creative writing, desktop publishing, digital photography, drama performance, earth science, economics, English-AP, environmental science, environmental studies, European history-AP, geography, geometry, government, government/civics, grammar, health, junior and senior seminars, keyboarding, language and composition, language arts, leadership and service, library, life science, literature and composition-AP, mathematics, modern European history, modern Western civilization, modern world history, music, music performance, mythology, newspaper, participation in sports, personal finance, photography, photojournalism, physical education, physical fitness, physical science, physics, pre-algebra, pre-calculus, probability and statistics, psychology, psychology-AP, religious studies, research seminar, research skills, SAT preparation, SAT/ACT preparation, sociology, Spanish, Spanish language-AP, sports, statistics, strings, student publications, studio art, Texas history, U.S. government, U.S. history, world geography, world history, world religions, yearbook.

Graduation Requirements Arts and fine arts (art, music, dance, drama), computers, English, government/civics, languages, mathematics, physical education (includes health), science, social sciences, speech, theology.

Special Academic Programs Advanced Placement exam preparation; accelerated programs; independent study; term-away projects; study at local college for college credit; study abroad; academic accommodation for the gifted, the musically talented, and the artistically talented; programs in English, mathematics for dyslexic students.

College Admission Counseling 16 students graduated in 2011; all went to college, including LeTourneau University; Morehouse College; Northeastern University; Texas A&M University; The University of Texas at Arlington; The University of Texas at Austin. Median SAT critical reading: 530, median SAT math: 620, median SAT writing: 535, median combined SAT: 1690, median composite ACT: 23. 18% scored over 600 on SAT critical reading, 23% scored over 600 on SAT math, 13% scored over 600 on SAT writing, 42% scored over 26 on composite ACT.

Student Life Upper grades have specified standards of dress, student council, honor system. Discipline rests primarily with faculty. Attendance at religious services is required.

Tuition and Aid Day student tuition: $7139–$7897. Tuition installment plan (FACTS Tuition Payment Plan, monthly payment plans, individually arranged payment plans, semester payment plan). Merit scholarship grants, need-based scholarship grants available. In 2011–12, 12% of upper-school students received aid; total upper-school merit-scholarship money awarded: $74,497. Total amount of financial aid awarded in 2011–12: $99,875.

Admissions Traditional secondary-level entrance grade is 9. For fall 2011, 12 students applied for upper-level admission, 12 were accepted, 12 enrolled. Otis-Lennon, Stanford Achievement Test, PSAT or SAT for applicants to grade 11 and 12, Woodcock-Johnson Revised Achievement Test and writing sample required. Deadline for receipt of application materials: none. Application fee required: $850. On-campus interview required.

Athletics Interscholastic: baseball (boys), basketball (b,g), cheering (g), football (b), golf (b,g), physical fitness (b), power lifting (b), tennis (b,g), track and field (b,g), volleyball (g); intramural: football (b), physical fitness (b,g), tennis (b,g), volleyball (g); coed interscholastic: soccer; coed intramural: soccer, track and field, weight training. 2 PE instructors, 4 coaches.

Computers Computers are regularly used in college planning, computer applications, creative writing, English, geography, history, journalism, keyboarding, library, mathematics, newspaper, photography, photojournalism, psychology, publications, publishing, research skills, SAT preparation, science, senior seminar, Spanish, technology, writing, yearbook classes. Computer network features include on-campus library services, online commercial services, Internet access, Internet filtering or blocking technology. The school has a published electronic and media policy.

Contact Mrs. Jill Galvez, Director of Admission. 903-753-0612 Ext. 236. Fax: 903-753-4812. E-mail: jgalvez@trinityschooloftexas.com. Web site: www.trinityschooloftexas.com

TRINITY VALLEY SCHOOL

7500 Dutch Branch Road
Fort Worth, Texas 76132

Head of School: Dr. Gary Krahn

General Information Coeducational day college-preparatory school. Grades K–12. Founded: 1959. Setting: urban. 75-acre campus. 7 buildings on campus. Approved or accredited by Independent Schools Association of the Southwest and Texas Department of Education. Member of National Association of Independent Schools. Endowment: $28.7 million. Total enrollment: 957. Upper school average class size: 16. Upper school faculty-student ratio: 1:8. There are 176 required school days per year for Upper School students. Upper School students typically attend 5 days per week. The average school day consists of 5 hours and 30 minutes.

Upper School Student Profile Grade 9: 85 students (42 boys, 43 girls); Grade 10: 86 students (40 boys, 46 girls); Grade 11: 74 students (31 boys, 43 girls); Grade 12: 91 students (45 boys, 46 girls).

Faculty School total: 110. In upper school: 18 men, 23 women; 36 have advanced degrees.

Subjects Offered Algebra, American culture, American history, American history-AP, ancient history, ancient world history, art, Asian history, biology, biology-AP, British history, calculus, calculus-AP, ceramics, chemistry, chemistry-AP, Chinese, choir, computer graphics, computer science, computer science-AP, constitutional law, creative writing, debate, digital imaging, economics, economics-AP, English, English language-AP, English literature-AP, environmental science, French, French-AP, geometry, government/civics, humanities, Latin, Latin-AP, leadership, modern European history, photography, physical education, physics, physics-AP, psychology-AP, Spanish, Spanish-AP, statistics, statistics-AP, technical theater, theater arts, U.S. government, U.S. government and politics-AP, video film production, writing workshop, yearbook.

Graduation Requirements Algebra, American government, American history, arts and fine arts (art, music, dance, drama), biology, chemistry, economics, English, foreign language, geometry, physical education (includes health), physics, pre-calculus, Western civilization, students must complete 60 hours of community service in the U.S.. Community service is required.

Special Academic Programs 22 Advanced Placement exams for which test preparation is offered; honors section; academic accommodation for the gifted, the musically talented, and the artistically talented.

College Admission Counseling 88 students graduated in 2011; all went to college, including Southern Methodist University; Texas A&M University; Texas Christian University; The University of Alabama; The University of Texas at Austin; University of Oklahoma.

Student Life Upper grades have uniform requirement, student council, honor system. Discipline rests equally with students and faculty.

Tuition and Aid Day student tuition: $17,560. Tuition installment plan (monthly payment plans). Need-based scholarship grants available. In 2011–12, 14% of upper-school students received aid. Total amount of financial aid awarded in 2011–12: $511,265.

Admissions Traditional secondary-level entrance grade is 9. For fall 2011, 46 students applied for upper-level admission, 29 were accepted, 15 enrolled. ISEE required. Deadline for receipt of application materials: March 2. Application fee required: $75. Interview required.

Athletics Interscholastic: baseball (boys), basketball (b,g), cross-country running (b,g), field hockey (g), football (b), golf (b,g), soccer (b,g), softball (g), tennis (b,g), track and field (b,g), volleyball (b,g). 5 PE instructors, 6 coaches, 2 athletic trainers.

Computers Computers are regularly used in all academic classes. Computer network features include on-campus library services, online commercial services, Internet access, wireless campus network, Internet filtering or blocking technology. Campus intranet, student e-mail accounts, and computer access in designated common areas are available to students. Students grades are available online. The school has a published electronic and media policy.

Contact Judith Kinser, Director of Admissions and Financial Aid. 817-321-0116. Fax: 817-321-0105. E-mail: kinserj@trinityvalleyschool.org. Web site: www.trinityvalleyschool.org

TURNING WINDS ACADEMIC INSTITUTE

Bonners Ferry, Idaho
See Special Needs Schools section.

TUSCALOOSA ACADEMY

420 Rice Valley Road North
Tuscaloosa, Alabama 35406

Head of School: Dr. Jeffrey Mitchell

General Information Coeducational day college-preparatory, arts, bilingual studies, technology, and ESL school. Grades PK–12. Founded: 1967. Setting: suburban. Nearest major city is Birmingham. 35-acre campus. 2 buildings on campus. Approved or accredited by Southern Association of Colleges and Schools and Southern Association of Independent Schools. Member of National Association of Independent Schools. Total enrollment: 418. Upper school average class size: 15. Upper school faculty-student ratio: 1:15. There are 177 required school days per year for Upper School students. Upper School students typically attend 5 days per week. The average school day consists of 6 hours and 55 minutes.

Upper School Student Profile Grade 9: 28 students (17 boys, 11 girls); Grade 10: 32 students (18 boys, 14 girls); Grade 11: 35 students (17 boys, 18 girls); Grade 12: 24 students (12 boys, 12 girls).

Faculty School total: 56. In upper school: 10 men, 12 women; 11 have advanced degrees.

Subjects Offered ACT preparation, advanced math, Advanced Placement courses, algebra, American government, American history, American history-AP, American literature, American literature-AP, anatomy, art, art history, art-AP, baseball, basketball, biology, biology-AP, calculus, calculus-AP, cheerleading, chemistry, chemistry-AP, choir, choral music, chorus, college counseling, computer programming, computer science, computer studies, creative writing, drama, earth science, economics, English, English literature, English-AP, English/composition-AP, European history, expository writing, fine arts, French, French language-AP, French-AP, geography, geometry, German, golf, government-AP, government/civics, grammar, health, history, history-AP, journalism, Latin, Latin-AP, literature-AP, mathematics, mathematics-AP, music, physical education, pre-calculus, psychology, psychology-AP, SAT preparation, SAT/ACT preparation, science, senior thesis, social studies, sociology, softball, Spanish, Spanish language-AP, Spanish-AP, speech, sports conditioning, studio art, studio art-AP, theater, track and field, trigonometry, U.S. history-AP, world history, world literature, yearbook.

Graduation Requirements Algebra, American government, American history, arts and fine arts (art, music, dance, drama), biology, chemistry, computer science, electives, English, foreign language, geometry, literature, mathematics, modern European history, physical education (includes health), physical science, pre-calculus, science, social studies (includes history), speech, U.S. history, 80 community service hours.

Special Academic Programs Advanced Placement exam preparation; honors section; independent study; study at local college for college credit; study abroad; academic accommodation for the gifted; ESL (81 students enrolled).

College Admission Counseling 31 students graduated in 2011; all went to college, including Auburn University; Birmingham-Southern College; Shelton State Community College; The University of Alabama; University of Mississippi.

Student Life Upper grades have specified standards of dress, student council, honor system. Discipline rests primarily with faculty.

Tuition and Aid Day student tuition: $7334–$8792. Guaranteed tuition plan. Tuition installment plan (Insured Tuition Payment Plan, monthly payment plans, semester payment plan, annual payment plan). Tuition reduction for siblings, merit scholarship grants, need-based scholarship grants available. In 2011–12, 20% of upper-school students received aid; total upper-school merit-scholarship money awarded: $27,000. Total amount of financial aid awarded in 2011–12: $160,000.

Admissions Traditional secondary-level entrance grade is 9. For fall 2011, 25 students applied for upper-level admission, 23 were accepted, 18 enrolled. Any standardized test, Star-9 and writing sample required. Deadline for receipt of application materials: none. Application fee required: $75. Interview required.

Athletics Interscholastic: baseball (boys), basketball (b,g), cheering (g), cross-country running (b,g), dance team (g), football (b), golf (b,g), softball (g), strength & conditioning (b), tennis (b,g), track and field (b,g), volleyball (g), weight training (b); coed interscholastic: soccer. 2 coaches, 6 athletic trainers.

Computers Computers are regularly used in journalism, keyboarding, yearbook classes. Computer network features include on-campus library services, online commercial services, Internet access, wireless campus network, Internet filtering or blocking technology, laptop program. Campus intranet, student e-mail accounts, and computer access in designated common areas are available to students. Students grades are available online. The school has a published electronic and media policy.

Contact Anne D. Huffaker, Director of Admission. 205-758-4462 Ext. 202. Fax: 205-758-4418. E-mail: ahuffaker@tuscaloosaacademy.org. Web site: www.tuscaloosaacademy.org or www.WhyTa.org

TYLER STREET CHRISTIAN ACADEMY

915 West 9th Street
Dallas, Texas 75208

Head of School: Dr. Karen J. Egger

General Information Coeducational day college-preparatory, general academic, arts, religious studies, and technology school, affiliated with Christian faith. Grades P3–12. Founded: 1972. Setting: urban. 5-acre campus. 2 buildings on campus. Approved or accredited by Association of Christian Schools International, Southern Association of Colleges and Schools, Texas Private School Accreditation Commission, and Texas Department of Education. Endowment: $120,000. Total enrollment: 198. Upper school average class size: 10. Upper school faculty-student ratio: 1:13. There are 176 required school days per year for Upper School students. Upper School students typically attend 5 days per week. The average school day consists of 7 hours and 40 minutes.

Upper School Student Profile Grade 9: 32 students (14 boys, 18 girls); Grade 10: 12 students (8 boys, 4 girls); Grade 11: 10 students (4 boys, 6 girls); Grade 12: 12 students (7 boys, 5 girls). 75% of students are Christian faith.

Faculty School total: 31. In upper school: 6 men, 8 women; 5 have advanced degrees.
Subjects Offered Advanced Placement courses, algebra, American government, American history, art, art appreciation, art history, arts and crafts, athletic training, ballet, band, bell choir, Bible studies, biology, British literature, British literature (honors), calculus, calculus-AP, cheerleading, chemistry, choir, choral music, Christian education, college admission preparation, college counseling, college planning, community service, composition, computer applications, computer literacy, computer skills, computer technologies, computer-aided design, concert band, concert bell choir, CPR, critical writing, economics, English literature, family living, freshman seminar, geography, geometry, government, grammar, guidance, health, history, Holocaust studies, honors algebra, honors English, honors geometry, human anatomy, human biology, integrated physics, keyboarding, lab science, lab/keyboard, leadership, leadership and service, literature, mathematics-AP, musical productions, physical education, physical science, physics, physiology, pre-calculus, religion, robotics, science, social studies, Spanish, speech communications, student government, track and field, U.S. government, U.S. history, U.S. literature, volleyball, weight training, world geography, world history, world literature, yearbook.
Graduation Requirements Algebra, American government, arts and fine arts (art, music, dance, drama), Bible, biology, calculus, chemistry, computer science, economics, English, geometry, physical education (includes health), physical science, physics, Spanish, speech communications, U.S. history, world geography, world history.
Special Academic Programs International Baccalaureate program; 1 Advanced Placement exam for which test preparation is offered; honors section; independent study; study at local college for college credit.
College Admission Counseling 12 students graduated in 2012; all went to college, including Baylor University; Rice University; Texas A&M University; Texas Tech University; The University of Texas at Arlington; University of North Texas. Mean SAT critical reading: 564, mean SAT math: 506, mean composite ACT: 25. 43% scored over 600 on SAT critical reading, 15% scored over 600 on SAT math, 28% scored over 600 on SAT writing, 15% scored over 1800 on combined SAT, 9% scored over 26 on composite ACT.
Student Life Upper grades have uniform requirement, student council, honor system. Discipline rests primarily with faculty. Attendance at religious services is required.
Summer Programs Session focuses on summer camp PK-6th grade; held on campus; accepts boys and girls; open to students from other schools. 25 students usually enrolled. 2013 schedule: June 4 to August 7. Application deadline: April 27.
Tuition and Aid Day student tuition: $6450. Tuition installment plan (FACTS Tuition Payment Plan). Merit scholarship grants, need-based scholarship grants available. In 2012–13, 55% of upper-school students received aid; total upper-school merit-scholarship money awarded: $2500. Total amount of financial aid awarded in 2012–13: $157,000.
Admissions Traditional secondary-level entrance grade is 9. For fall 2012, 51 students applied for upper-level admission, 49 were accepted, 34 enrolled. Admissions testing, English entrance exam, mathematics proficiency exam and writing sample required. Deadline for receipt of application materials: none. Application fee required: $50. On-campus interview required.
Athletics Interscholastic: ballet (boys, girls), basketball (b,g), cheering (g), dance squad (b,g), football (b), independent competitive sports (b,g), life saving (b,g), martial arts (b,g), modern dance (g), physical training (b,g), strength & conditioning (b,g), track and field (b,g), volleyball (g), weight lifting (b,g), weight training (b,g); coed interscholastic: cooperative games, life saving, physical training. 1 PE instructor, 4 coaches, 1 athletic trainer.
Computers Computers are regularly used in business applications, career exploration, computer applications, data processing, desktop publishing, graphic arts, information technology, introduction to technology, keyboarding, lab/keyboard, library, library skills, literacy, photojournalism, reading, technology, word processing, yearbook classes. Computer network features include on-campus library services, Internet access, Internet filtering or blocking technology, on-campus library services for Accelerated Reader Program. Computer access in designated common areas is available to students. Students grades are available online. The school has a published electronic and media policy.
Contact Mrs. Perla Gonzalez, Registrar. 214-941-9717 Ext. 200. Fax: 214-941-0324. E-mail: perlagonzalez@tsca.org. Web site: www.tsca.org

UNITED MENNONITE EDUCATIONAL INSTITUTE

614 Mersea Road 6, RR 5
Leamington, Ontario N8H 3V8, Canada

Head of School: Mrs. Sonya A. Bedal

General Information Coeducational day college-preparatory, arts, and religious studies school, affiliated with Mennonite Church USA. Grades 9–12. Founded: 1945. Setting: rural. Nearest major city is Windsor, Canada. 12-acre campus. 3 buildings on campus. Approved or accredited by Ontario Department of Education. Language of instruction: English. Total enrollment: 50. Upper school average class size: 18. Upper school faculty-student ratio: 1:15.
Upper School Student Profile Grade 9: 9 students (4 boys, 5 girls); Grade 10: 11 students (4 boys, 7 girls); Grade 11: 11 students (6 boys, 5 girls); Grade 12: 21 students (6 boys, 15 girls). 65% of students are Mennonite Church USA.
Faculty School total: 9. In upper school: 3 men, 6 women; 1 has an advanced degree.
Subjects Offered 20th century physics, advanced chemistry, advanced math, algebra, American history, ancient world history, art, Bible, biology, business studies, career exploration, chemistry, choir, choral music, Christian ethics, church history, civics, communication arts, computer applications, computer studies, computer technologies, English, environmental geography, family studies, film and new technologies, foreign language, French as a second language, German, instrumental music, introduction to theater, mathematics, orchestra, parenting, religious studies, society challenge and change, theater arts.
Graduation Requirements Arts, Canadian geography, Canadian history, careers, civics, English, French, mathematics, physical education (includes health), science.
College Admission Counseling 11 students graduated in 2011; 10 went to college. Other: 1 went to work.
Student Life Upper grades have specified standards of dress, student council. Discipline rests equally with students and faculty. Attendance at religious services is required.
Tuition and Aid Day student tuition: CAN$6300. Tuition installment plan (monthly payment plans). Tuition reduction for siblings, bursaries, need-based scholarship grants, need-based loans available. In 2011–12, 5% of upper-school students received aid. Total amount of financial aid awarded in 2011–12: CAN$4000.
Admissions Traditional secondary-level entrance grade is 9. Deadline for receipt of application materials: none. No application fee required.
Athletics Interscholastic: badminton (boys, girls), baseball (b,g), basketball (b,g), cross-country running (b,g), floor hockey (b,g), golf (b), softball (g), volleyball (b,g); intramural: badminton (b,g), baseball (b,g), basketball (b,g), bicycling (b), football (b), indoor soccer (b,g), volleyball (b,g); coed intramural: skiing (downhill), ultimate Frisbee. 1 PE instructor.
Computers Computers are regularly used in all classes. Computer network features include on-campus library services, Internet access, Internet filtering or blocking technology.
Contact Mrs. Sonya A. Bedal, Principal. 519-326 7448. Fax: 519-326 0278. E-mail: umeiadm@gmail.com. Web site: www.umei.on.ca

UNITED NATIONS INTERNATIONAL SCHOOL

24-50 Franklin Roosevelt Drive
New York, New York 10010-4046

Head of School: Mr. George Dymond

General Information Coeducational day college-preparatory, arts, technology, English as Second Language and Eight Mother Tongue programs, and International Baccalaureate, Eight 3rd Language Programs school. Grades K–12. Founded: 1947. Setting: urban. 3-acre campus. 1 building on campus. Approved or accredited by International Baccalaureate Organization, New York State Association of Independent Schools, New York State Board of Regents, and New York Department of Education. Member of National Association of Independent Schools. Endowment: $13.3 million. Total enrollment: 1,542. Upper school average class size: 20. Upper school faculty-student ratio: 1:3. There are 172 required school days per year for Upper School students. Upper School students typically attend 5 days per week. The average school day consists of 6 hours and 40 minutes.
Upper School Student Profile Grade 9: 110 students (57 boys, 53 girls); Grade 10: 114 students (58 boys, 56 girls); Grade 11: 117 students (57 boys, 60 girls); Grade 12: 117 students (51 boys, 66 girls).
Faculty School total: 221. In upper school: 64 men, 82 women; 44 have advanced degrees.
Subjects Offered 3-dimensional art, algebra, American history, American literature, American studies, anthropology, Arabic, art, biology, calculus, chemistry, Chinese, community service, computer applications, computer science, creative writing, drama, economics, English, English literature, ESL, European history, expository writing, film, film studies, fine arts, French, geometry, German, history, humanities, Italian, Japanese, journalism, languages, library, mathematics, media production, modern languages, music, philosophy, photography, physical education, physics, psychology, Russian, science, social sciences, social studies, Spanish, theater arts, theory of knowledge, United Nations and international issues, video, video and animation, video communication, video film production, world history, world literature, writing.
Graduation Requirements Art, electives, English, health and wellness, humanities, independent study, mathematics, modern languages, music, physical education (includes health), science, International Baccalaureate, Theory of Knowledge, extended essay, Creative Aesthetic Service, individual project. Community service is required.
Special Academic Programs International Baccalaureate program; independent study; academic accommodation for the gifted, the musically talented, and the artistically talented; ESL (185 students enrolled).
College Admission Counseling 126 students graduated in 2011; 121 went to college, including Barnard College; Boston College; Cornell University; Northeastern University; Syracuse University; University of Chicago. Other: 1 entered military service, 4 had other specific plans. Median SAT critical reading: 600, median SAT math: 600, median SAT writing: 610, median combined SAT: 1810, median composite ACT: 26. 56% scored over 600 on SAT critical reading, 57% scored over 600 on SAT math, 66% scored over 600 on SAT writing, 58% scored over 1800 on combined SAT, 64% scored over 26 on composite ACT.

Student Life Upper grades have student council. Discipline rests primarily with faculty.

Tuition and Aid Day student tuition: $24,900–$25,450. Tuition installment plan (Tuition Management System (formerly Key Tuition Plan)). Bursaries available. In 2011–12, 7% of upper-school students received aid. Total amount of financial aid awarded in 2011–12: $286,290.

Admissions Traditional secondary-level entrance grade is 9. For fall 2011, 75 students applied for upper-level admission, 46 were accepted, 36 enrolled. ISEE, PSAT and SAT for applicants to grade 11 and 12 or SSAT required. Deadline for receipt of application materials: November 15. Application fee required: $75. On-campus interview required.

Athletics Interscholastic: baseball (boys), basketball (b,g), indoor track (b,g), indoor track & field (b,g), soccer (b,g), softball (g), track and field (b,g), volleyball (b,g); intramural: volleyball (b,g); coed interscholastic: swimming and diving; coed intramural: aerobics, aerobics/dance, aerobics/Nautilus, aquatics, badminton, ball hockey, basketball, canoeing/kayaking, climbing, cooperative games, dance, field hockey, fitness, flag football, floor hockey, gymnastics, handball, hiking/backpacking, independent competitive sports, indoor hockey, indoor soccer, indoor track, indoor track & field, jogging, jump rope, life saving, martial arts, modern dance, outdoor activities, physical fitness, physical training, rock climbing, ropes courses, rounders, running, soccer, softball, strength & conditioning, swimming and diving, table tennis, team handball, tennis, touch football, track and field, volleyball, wall climbing, weight training. 10 PE instructors, 26 coaches.

Computers Computers are regularly used in all academic, animation, art, basic skills, career education, career exploration, career technology, classics, college planning, computer applications, creative writing, current events, data processing, desktop publishing, desktop publishing, ESL, digital applications, drawing and design, economics, English, ESL, foreign language, French, French as a second language, graphic arts, graphic design, graphics, health, history, humanities, independent study, information technology, introduction to technology, journalism, keyboarding, lab/keyboard, learning cognition, library, library science, library skills, life skills, literacy, literary magazine, mathematics, media, media arts, media production, media services, multimedia, music, music technology, news writing, newspaper, philosophy, photography, photojournalism, programming, publications, publishing, research skills, science, social sciences, social studies, Spanish, study skills, technology, theater, theater arts, video film production, Web site design, writing, yearbook classes. Computer network features include on-campus library services, online commercial services, Internet access, wireless campus network, Internet filtering or blocking technology, media lab, TV studio, Web portal, film production, digital video streaming, digital video editing. Campus intranet, student e-mail accounts, and computer access in designated common areas are available to students. Students grades are available online.

Contact Admissions Office. 212-584-3071. Fax: 212-685-5023. E-mail: admissions@unis.org. Web site: www.unis.org

THE UNITED WORLD COLLEGE - USA

PO Box 248
State Road 65
Montezuma, New Mexico 87731

Head of School: Lisa A. H. Darling

General Information Coeducational boarding college-preparatory, arts, bilingual studies, wilderness, search and rescue, conflict resolution, and service, science, humanities school. Grades 11–12. Founded: 1982. Setting: small town. Nearest major city is Santa Fe. Students are housed in single-sex dormitories. 320-acre campus. 20 buildings on campus. Approved or accredited by Independent Schools Association of the Southwest, International Baccalaureate Organization, and New Mexico Department of Education. Member of National Association of Independent Schools. Languages of instruction: English, French, and Spanish. Endowment: $91 million. Upper school average class size: 9. Upper school faculty-student ratio: 1:9. There are 245 required school days per year for Upper School students. Upper School students typically attend 5 days per week. The average school day consists of 6 hours and 30 minutes.

Upper School Student Profile Grade 11: 106 students (52 boys, 54 girls); Grade 12: 106 students (54 boys, 52 girls). 100% of students are boarding students. 5% are state residents. 37 states are represented in upper school student body. 82% are international students. International students from Canada, China, Germany, Mexico, Spain, and Venezuela; 81 other countries represented in student body.

Faculty School total: 28. In upper school: 14 men, 12 women; 20 have advanced degrees; 17 reside on campus.

Subjects Offered Anthropology, art, biology, calculus, chemistry, community service, conflict resolution, economics, English, English literature, environmental geography, environmental science, environmental studies, environmental systems, ESL, fine arts, French, German, history, information technology, International Baccalaureate courses, mathematics, music, physics, science, social sciences, social studies, Spanish, theater arts, theory of knowledge, world history, world literature, world religions.

Graduation Requirements American history, arts and fine arts (art, music, dance, drama), biology, calculus, chemistry, comparative religion, economics, English literature, environmental geography, environmental systems, European history, foreign language, French, French as a second language, geography, German, German literature, global issues, global studies, history of the Americas, International Baccalaureate courses, literature, math methods, mathematics, music, music theory, organic chemistry, peace studies, physics, post-calculus, pre-algebra, pre-calculus, research, science, senior thesis, social justice, social sciences, Spanish, Spanish literature, statistics, studio art, theater, theater arts, theory of knowledge, visual arts, wilderness education, wilderness experience, world religions, extended essay, independent research, theory of knowledge. Community service is required.

Special Academic Programs International Baccalaureate program; honors section; independent study; academic accommodation for the musically talented and the artistically talented; ESL (43 students enrolled).

College Admission Counseling 100 students graduated in 2011; 94 went to college, including Brown University; Dartmouth College; Earlham College; Harvard University; Princeton University; Trinity College. Other: 3 entered military service, 3 entered a postgraduate year. 25% scored over 600 on SAT critical reading, 75% scored over 600 on SAT math, 95% scored over 26 on composite ACT.

Student Life Upper grades have student council, honor system. Discipline rests equally with students and faculty.

Tuition and Aid 7-day tuition and room/board: $18,000. Guaranteed tuition plan. Tuition installment plan (all accepted U.S. students are awarded full merit scholarships, need-based aid available to all other students). Merit scholarship grants, need-based scholarship grants, full tuition merit scholarships awarded to all admitted U.S. citizens available. In 2011–12, 85% of upper-school students received aid; total upper-school merit-scholarship money awarded: $2,800,000. Total amount of financial aid awarded in 2011–12: $2,800,000.

Admissions Traditional secondary-level entrance grade is 11. For fall 2011, 440 students applied for upper-level admission, 52 were accepted, 52 enrolled. ACT, PSAT or SAT or PSAT, SAT, or ACT for applicants to grade 11 and 12 required. Deadline for receipt of application materials: January 10. No application fee required. Interview required.

Athletics Coed Intramural: aerobics, aerobics/dance, aerobics/Nautilus, alpine skiing, aquatics, backpacking, badminton, ballet, baseball, basketball, bicycling, billiards, canoeing/kayaking, climbing, combined training, cooperative games, cricket, cross-country running, dance, fitness, Frisbee, hiking/backpacking, jogging, modern dance, mountaineering, nordic skiing, outdoor activities, physical training, racquetball, ropes courses, running, sailing, skiing (cross-country), skiing (downhill), snowboarding, snowshoeing, soccer, softball, squash, strength & conditioning, swimming and diving, table tennis, tennis, volleyball, walking, weight lifting, weight training, wilderness, wilderness survival, yoga. 1 PE instructor, 12 athletic trainers.

Computers Computers are regularly used in art, English, ESL, foreign language, mathematics, music, science classes. Computer network features include on-campus library services, Internet access, wireless campus network, Internet filtering or blocking technology. Campus intranet, student e-mail accounts, and computer access in designated common areas are available to students. Students grades are available online.

Contact Mr. Tim Smith, Director of Admissions. 505-454-4201. Fax: 505-454-4294. E-mail: tim.smith@uwc-usa.org. Web site: www.uwc-usa.org

UNIVERSITY LIGGETT SCHOOL

1045 Cook Road
Grosse Pointe Woods, Michigan 48236

Head of School: Dr. Joseph P. Healey

General Information Coeducational day college-preparatory, arts, and technology school. Grades PK–12. Founded: 1878. Setting: suburban. Nearest major city is Detroit. 50-acre campus. 4 buildings on campus. Approved or accredited by Independent Schools Association of the Central States. Member of National Association of Independent Schools. Endowment: $38 million. Total enrollment: 616. Upper school average class size: 14. Upper school faculty-student ratio: 1:8. There are 170 required school days per year for Upper School students. The average school day consists of 7 hours.

Upper School Student Profile Grade 9: 73 students (36 boys, 37 girls); Grade 10: 75 students (36 boys, 39 girls); Grade 11: 65 students (34 boys, 31 girls); Grade 12: 68 students (34 boys, 34 girls).

Faculty School total: 94. In upper school: 23 men, 16 women; 27 have advanced degrees.

Subjects Offered Advanced Placement courses, algebra, American history, American literature, art, art history, biology, calculus, ceramics, chemistry, creative writing, drama, engineering, English, English literature, environmental science-AP, European history, fine arts, French, geology, geometry, government/civics, Greek, health and wellness, history of jazz, instrumental music, Latin, mathematics, media arts, modern languages, photography, physical education, physical fitness, physics, physiology, psychology, SAT preparation, science, social studies, Spanish, technology, theater, Vietnam, world history.

Graduation Requirements Algebra, arts and fine arts (art, music, dance, drama), biology, chemistry, computer science, English, foreign language, geometry, government, mathematics, physical education (includes health), science, U.S. history, world history, Advanced Research Project. Community service is required.

Special Academic Programs Honors section; independent study; term-away projects; study abroad; academic accommodation for the gifted, the musically talented, and the artistically talented; special instructional classes for deaf students.

College Admission Counseling 77 students graduated in 2012; all went to college, including Boston College; Kalamazoo College; Michigan State University; University of Michigan; Western Michigan University; Williams College. Mean SAT critical reading: 610, mean SAT math: 590, mean SAT writing: 590, mean composite ACT: 27. 54% scored over 600 on SAT critical reading, 43% scored over 600 on SAT math, 54% scored over 600 on SAT writing.
Student Life Upper grades have specified standards of dress, student council, honor system. Discipline rests primarily with faculty.
Summer Programs Remediation, enrichment, sports programs offered; session focuses on SAT preparation; held on campus; accepts boys and girls; open to students from other schools. 400 students usually enrolled. 2013 schedule: June 22 to August 12. Application deadline: none.
Tuition and Aid Day student tuition: $17,880–$22,480. Tuition installment plan (Insured Tuition Payment Plan, monthly payment plans, individually arranged payment plans, 2- and 4-payment plans). Tuition reduction for siblings, merit scholarship grants, need-based scholarship grants, scholarships for children of alumni available. In 2012–13, 35% of upper-school students received aid; total upper-school merit-scholarship money awarded: $250,000. Total amount of financial aid awarded in 2012–13: $2,600,000.
Admissions Traditional secondary-level entrance grade is 9. For fall 2012, 285 students applied for upper-level admission, 72 were accepted, 44 enrolled. ERB CTP III or SSAT required. Deadline for receipt of application materials: none. Application fee required: $50. Interview required.
Athletics Interscholastic: baseball (boys), basketball (b,g), field hockey (g), football (b), golf (b), ice hockey (b,g), lacrosse (b,g), soccer (b,g), softball (g), tennis (b,g), volleyball (g); coed interscholastic: physical training, swimming and diving; coed intramural: aerobics/dance, ultimate Frisbee, weight lifting. 4 PE instructors, 15 coaches, 1 athletic trainer.
Computers Computers are regularly used in all academic classes. Computer network features include on-campus library services, online commercial services, Internet access, wireless campus network, Internet filtering or blocking technology. Campus intranet, student e-mail accounts, and computer access in designated common areas are available to students. Students grades are available online. The school has a published electronic and media policy.
Contact Mr. Kevin Breen, Director of Enrollment. 313-884-4444 Ext. 405. Fax: 313-884-1775. E-mail: kbreen@uls.org. Web site: www.uls.org

UNIVERSITY OF CHICAGO LABORATORY SCHOOLS

1362 East 59th Street
Chicago, Illinois 60637

Head of School: Dr. David W. Magill

General Information Coeducational day college-preparatory school. Grades N–12. Founded: 1896. Setting: urban. 11-acre campus. 3 buildings on campus. Approved or accredited by Independent Schools Association of the Central States, North Central Association of Colleges and Schools, and Illinois Department of Education. Member of National Association of Independent Schools. Endowment: $17.7 million. Total enrollment: 1,825. Upper school average class size: 16. Upper school faculty-student ratio: 1:10. There are 170 required school days per year for Upper School students. Upper School students typically attend 5 days per week. The average school day consists of 7 hours and 5 minutes.
Upper School Student Profile Grade 9: 134 students (67 boys, 67 girls); Grade 10: 122 students (60 boys, 62 girls); Grade 11: 109 students (57 boys, 52 girls); Grade 12: 131 students (51 boys, 80 girls).
Faculty School total: 221. In upper school: 29 men, 41 women; 52 have advanced degrees.
Subjects Offered Acting, advanced biology, advanced chemistry, African-American history, algebra, American history, art, art history, biology, calculus, calculus-AP, chemistry, Chinese, community service, computer science, computer science-AP, CPR, creative writing, discrete mathematics, drama, drawing, driver education, English, English literature, European history, expository writing, fine arts, French, French-AP, geometry, German, German-AP, government/civics, history, Holocaust, jazz band, journalism, Latin, Mandarin, mathematics, modern European history, music, music theory-AP, newspaper, orchestra, painting, photography, photojournalism, physical education, physics, play production, post-calculus, science, sculpture, social studies, Spanish, Spanish language-AP, Spanish-AP, statistics, statistics-AP, studio art, theater, trigonometry, U.S. history, Web site design, Western civilization, world history, writing, yearbook.
Graduation Requirements Arts and fine arts (art, music, dance, drama), computer science, English, foreign language, mathematics, music, physical education (includes health), science, social studies (includes history). Community service is required.
Special Academic Programs 8 Advanced Placement exams for which test preparation is offered; accelerated programs; independent study; study at local college for college credit.
College Admission Counseling 117 students graduated in 2012; 116 went to college, including Beloit College; Dartmouth College; Tufts University; University of Chicago; University of Illinois at Urbana–Champaign; University of Southern California. Other: 1 had other specific plans. Median SAT critical reading: 693, median SAT math: 696, median SAT writing: 690, median combined SAT: 2080, median composite ACT: 30. 84% scored over 600 on SAT critical reading, 86% scored over 600 on SAT math, 74% scored over 600 on SAT writing, 81% scored over 1800 on combined SAT, 59% scored over 26 on composite ACT.
Student Life Upper grades have student council. Discipline rests primarily with faculty.
Summer Programs Enrichment, advancement, sports programs offered; session focuses on advancement of placement in courses; held on campus; accepts boys and girls; open to students from other schools. 125 students usually enrolled. 2013 schedule: June 24 to August 2. Application deadline: May 15.
Tuition and Aid Day student tuition: $26,520. Tuition installment plan (monthly payment plans, quarterly payment plan). Need-based scholarship grants available. In 2012–13, 17% of upper-school students received aid. Total amount of financial aid awarded in 2012–13: $1,139,925.
Admissions Traditional secondary-level entrance grade is 9. For fall 2012, 157 students applied for upper-level admission, 52 were accepted, 26 enrolled. ISEE required. Deadline for receipt of application materials: November 30. Application fee required: $80. On-campus interview required.
Athletics Interscholastic: baseball (boys), basketball (b,g), cross-country running (b,g), indoor track & field (b,g), soccer (b,g), swimming and diving (b,g), tennis (b,g), track and field (b,g), volleyball (g), winter (indoor) track (b,g); intramural: dance squad (g), weight training (b,g); coed interscholastic: cross-country running, fencing, golf; coed intramural: life saving. 12 PE instructors, 31 coaches, 1 athletic trainer.
Computers Computers are regularly used in mathematics, music, newspaper, science, yearbook classes. Computer network features include on-campus library services, Internet access, wireless campus network. Student e-mail accounts and computer access in designated common areas are available to students. Students' grades are available online. The school has a published electronic and media policy.
Contact Irene Reed, Executive Director of Admissions and Financial Aid. 773-702-9451. Fax: 773-702-7455. E-mail: ireed@ucls.uchicago.edu. Web site: www.ucls.uchicago.edu/

See Close-Up on page 644.

UNIVERSITY OF DETROIT JESUIT HIGH SCHOOL AND ACADEMY

8400 South Cambridge Avenue
Detroit, Michigan 48221

Head of School: Mr. Anthony Trudel

General Information Boys' day college-preparatory, arts, religious studies, and technology school, affiliated with Roman Catholic Church (Jesuit order). Grades 7–12. Founded: 1877. Setting: urban. 12-acre campus. 1 building on campus. Approved or accredited by Jesuit Secondary Education Association, Michigan Association of Non-Public Schools, North Central Association of Colleges and Schools, and Michigan Department of Education. Endowment: $15 million. Total enrollment: 873. Upper school average class size: 22. Upper school faculty-student ratio: 1:14. There are 183 required school days per year for Upper School students. Upper School students typically attend 5 days per week. The average school day consists of 6 hours and 45 minutes.
Upper School Student Profile Grade 9: 212 students (212 boys); Grade 10: 190 students (190 boys); Grade 11: 190 students (190 boys); Grade 12: 160 students (160 boys). 72% of students are Roman Catholic Church (Jesuit order).
Faculty School total: 61. In upper school: 41 men, 20 women; 40 have advanced degrees.
Subjects Offered Acting, African-American history, algebra, American history, American history-AP, American literature, anatomy, art, Bible studies, biochemistry, biology, biology-AP, calculus, calculus-AP, ceramics, chemistry, chemistry-AP, Chinese, Christian and Hebrew scripture, Christian doctrine, Christian education, Christian ethics, Christian studies, Christian testament, church history, comparative religion, computer applications, computer programming, computer-aided design, drawing, earth science, economics, English, English literature, English literature-AP, English-AP, environmental science, ethics, European history, expository writing, French, geography, geometry, government-AP, government/civics, history, history of the Catholic Church, history-AP, Latin, Latin-AP, Mandarin, mathematics, music, physical education, physical science, physics, physics-AP, psychology, public speaking, religion, science, social studies, sociology, Spanish, Spanish-AP, speech, theology, trigonometry, U.S. government and politics-AP, U.S. history, U.S. history-AP, world history, world literature, writing.
Graduation Requirements Arts and fine arts (art, music, dance, drama), business skills (includes word processing), English, foreign language, mathematics, physical education (includes health), public speaking, religion (includes Bible studies and theology), science, social studies (includes history), senior community service program.
Special Academic Programs 14 Advanced Placement exams for which test preparation is offered; honors section; independent study; study at local college for college credit.
College Admission Counseling 156 students graduated in 2012; 155 went to college, including Michigan State University; University of Dayton; University of

Michigan; University of Michigan–Dearborn; University of Notre Dame; Wayne State University. Other: 1 had other specific plans. Mean SAT critical reading: 593, mean SAT math: 603, mean SAT writing: 611.

Student Life Upper grades have specified standards of dress, student council, honor system. Discipline rests primarily with faculty. Attendance at religious services is required.

Summer Programs Art/fine arts, computer instruction programs offered; session focuses on computer applications and art; held on campus; accepts boys; not open to students from other schools. 50 students usually enrolled. 2013 schedule: June 20 to July 22.

Tuition and Aid Day student tuition: $10,980. Tuition installment plan (FACTS Tuition Payment Plan). Merit scholarship grants, need-based scholarship grants available. In 2012–13, 34% of upper-school students received aid; total upper-school merit-scholarship money awarded: $250,000. Total amount of financial aid awarded in 2012–13: $1,610,000.

Admissions Traditional secondary-level entrance grade is 9. For fall 2012, 500 students applied for upper-level admission, 360 were accepted, 212 enrolled. Scholastic Testing Service High School Placement Test or STS - Educational Development Series required. Deadline for receipt of application materials: none. No application fee required. On-campus interview recommended.

Athletics Interscholastic: baseball, basketball, bowling, cross-country running, diving, football, golf, ice hockey, lacrosse, skiing (downhill), soccer, swimming and diving, tennis, track and field, wrestling; intramural: basketball, bowling, flag football, football, Frisbee, soccer, ultimate Frisbee. 2 PE instructors, 15 coaches, 2 athletic trainers.

Computers Computers are regularly used in all academic, art, history, mathematics, science, speech classes. Computer network features include on-campus library services, online commercial services, Internet access, wireless campus network, Internet filtering or blocking technology. Student e-mail accounts are available to students. Students grades are available online. The school has a published electronic and media policy.

Contact Mr. Atif Lodhi, Director of Admissions. 313-862-5400 Ext. 2380. Fax: 313-862-3299. E-mail: atif.lodhi@uofdjesuit.org. Web site: www.uofdjesuit.org/

UNIVERSITY PREP

8000 25th Avenue NE
Seattle, Washington 98115

Head of School: Erica L. Hamlin

General Information Coeducational day college-preparatory, arts, bilingual studies, technology, and global education school; primarily serves students with learning disabilities, individuals with Attention Deficit Disorder, and dyslexic students. Grades 6–12. Founded: 1976. Setting: urban. 6-acre campus. 5 buildings on campus. Approved or accredited by Northwest Accreditation Commission, Pacific Northwest Association of Independent Schools, and Washington Department of Education. Member of National Association of Independent Schools. Endowment: $6 million. Total enrollment: 511. Upper school average class size: 17. Upper school faculty-student ratio: 1:9. There are 169 required school days per year for Upper School students. Upper School students typically attend 5 days per week. The average school day consists of 6 hours and 50 minutes.

Upper School Student Profile Grade 9: 80 students (40 boys, 40 girls); Grade 10: 77 students (41 boys, 36 girls); Grade 11: 78 students (40 boys, 38 girls); Grade 12: 67 students (32 boys, 35 girls).

Faculty School total: 59. In upper school: 20 men, 23 women; 30 have advanced degrees.

Subjects Offered 3-dimensional art, advanced chemistry, advanced math, African-American studies, algebra, American government, American history, American literature, applied arts, applied music, art, art and culture, art history, Asian literature, Asian studies, astronomy, athletics, audio visual/media, band, biology, British literature, calculus, career and personal planning, career planning, career/college preparation, chemistry, Chinese, Chinese studies, choir, chorus, civil rights, classical civilization, college counseling, college placement, college planning, community service, comparative government and politics, comparative religion, composition, computer art, computer literacy, computer science, conceptual physics, creative dance, creative drama, creative writing, critical thinking, critical writing, dance, decision making skills, democracy in America, design, digital art, digital photography, diversity studies, drafting, drama, drama performance, dramatic arts, drawing, ecology, economics, electives, English, English composition, English literature, ensembles, environmental education, environmental science, environmental studies, ethnic studies, European history, expository writing, film studies, fine arts, fitness, foreign language, French, freshman seminar, geography, geometry, global studies, golf, government, government/civics, graphic design, health, history, history of religion, independent study, information technology, introduction to technology, Japanese, Japanese history, Japanese studies, jazz ensemble, journalism, languages, Latin American studies, library, life skills, literary magazine, mathematics, media, medieval/Renaissance history, minority studies, multicultural studies, music, music performance, music theory, orchestra, Pacific Northwest seminar, painting, performing arts, personal fitness, philosophy, photography, physical education, physical fitness, physics, play production, play/screen writing, poetry, political science, politics, psychology, public policy, publishing, research, Russian studies, science, senior thesis, social justice, Spanish, stagecraft, statistics, student publications, theater, theater arts, theater design and production, trigonometry, vocal ensemble, weight training, weightlifting, wilderness education, wilderness experience, women in society, world literature, yearbook.

Graduation Requirements American history, arts and fine arts (art, music, dance, drama), biology, chemistry, English, foreign language, life skills, mathematics, Pacific Northwest seminar, physical education (includes health), physics, science, senior thesis, social studies (includes history). Community service is required.

Special Academic Programs Independent study; term-away projects; domestic exchange program; study abroad; programs in English, mathematics, general development for dyslexic students; special instructional classes for college-bound students with high intellectual potential who have diagnosed specific learning disability.

College Admission Counseling 68 students graduated in 2012; all went to college, including Chapman University; Dartmouth College; Occidental College; Santa Clara University; University of Pennsylvania; University of Washington. Median SAT critical reading: 620, median SAT math: 610, median SAT writing: 620, median combined SAT: 1855, median composite ACT: 28. 60% scored over 600 on SAT critical reading, 52% scored over 600 on SAT math, 60% scored over 600 on SAT writing, 57% scored over 1800 on combined SAT, 64% scored over 26 on composite ACT.

Student Life Upper grades have student council, honor system. Discipline rests equally with students and faculty.

Tuition and Aid Day student tuition: $28,080. Tuition installment plan (Insured Tuition Payment Plan, Key Tuition Payment Plan, monthly payment plans, individually arranged payment plans, Dewar Tuition Refund Plan). Need-based scholarship grants available. In 2012–13, 21% of upper-school students received aid. Total amount of financial aid awarded in 2012–13: $1,392,423.

Admissions Traditional secondary-level entrance grade is 9. For fall 2012, 206 students applied for upper-level admission, 43 were accepted, 23 enrolled. ISEE required. Deadline for receipt of application materials: January 15. Application fee required: $75. On-campus interview required.

Athletics Interscholastic: baseball (boys), basketball (b,g), cross-country running (b,g), flag football (b), Frisbee (b,g), soccer (b,g), softball (g), tennis (b,g), track and field (b,g), volleyball (g); intramural: golf (b,g), ultimate Frisbee (b,g); coed interscholastic: ultimate Frisbee; coed intramural: aerobics, aerobics/dance, backpacking, climbing, dance, fitness, hiking/backpacking, modern dance, outdoor activities, outdoor adventure, outdoor education, outdoor skills, outdoors, rock climbing, skiing (downhill), snowboarding, strength & conditioning, ultimate Frisbee, wall climbing, weight training, wilderness, yoga. 5 PE instructors, 65 coaches, 1 athletic trainer.

Computers Computers are regularly used in all academic, art, creative writing, English, foreign language, geography, history, information technology, journalism, library, mathematics, media, music, photography, publications, publishing, research skills, science, technology, writing, writing, yearbook classes. Computer network features include on-campus library services, online commercial services, Internet access, wireless campus network, Internet filtering or blocking technology, RYOD - Required your on device. Campus intranet, student e-mail accounts, and computer access in designated common areas are available to students. Students grades are available online. The school has a published electronic and media policy.

Contact Melaine Taylor, Associate Director of Admission. 206-523-6407. Fax: 206-525-5320. E-mail: admissionoffice@universityprep.org. Web site: www.universityprep.org

UNIVERSITY SCHOOL OF JACKSON

232/240 McClellan Road
Jackson, Tennessee 38305

Head of School: Clay Lilienstern

General Information Coeducational day college-preparatory, arts, and technology school. Grades PK–12. Founded: 1970. Setting: suburban. 140-acre campus. 3 buildings on campus. Approved or accredited by Southern Association of Colleges and Schools and Tennessee Department of Education. Member of National Association of Independent Schools. Endowment: $85,000. Total enrollment: 1,196. Upper school average class size: 20. Upper school faculty-student ratio: 1:13. There are 180 required school days per year for Upper School students. Upper School students typically attend 5 days per week. The average school day consists of 7 hours and 10 minutes.

Upper School Student Profile Grade 9: 94 students (51 boys, 43 girls); Grade 10: 79 students (37 boys, 42 girls); Grade 11: 66 students (34 boys, 32 girls); Grade 12: 88 students (49 boys, 39 girls).

Faculty School total: 96. In upper school: 15 men, 18 women; 30 have advanced degrees.

Subjects Offered 3-dimensional art, 3-dimensional design, accounting, acting, advanced biology, advanced chemistry, advanced math, Advanced Placement courses, advanced studio art-AP, algebra, American history, American literature, anatomy, anatomy and physiology, art, band, biology, biology-AP, broadcast journalism, calculus, calculus-AP, character education, chemistry, chemistry-AP, chorus, computer applications, computer programming, computer science, creative writing, current events, dramatic arts, ecology, economics, economics and history, English, English language-AP, English literature and composition-AP, English literature-AP, environmental science, environmental science-AP, European history, fine arts, French, geography, geology, geometry, government, government/civics, honors algebra, honors English, honors geometry, humanities, keyboarding, macroeconomics-AP, mathematics, music theory, music theory-AP, music-AP, performing arts, photography, physical education, physical science, physics, pre-calculus, psychology, science, social studies, Spanish, Spanish language-AP, studio art-AP, trigonometry, U.S. history, U.S. history-AP, vocal ensemble, world history, world religions, yearbook.

Graduation Requirements Arts and fine arts (art, music, dance, drama), computer science, English, foreign language, mathematics, science, social studies (includes history), 50 hours of community service.

Special Academic Programs 11 Advanced Placement exams for which test preparation is offered; honors section; academic accommodation for the gifted, the musically talented, and the artistically talented; ESL (10 students enrolled).

College Admission Counseling 103 students graduated in 2012; all went to college, including Mississippi State University; Rhodes College; Tennessee Technological University; The University of Tennessee; Union University; University of Arkansas. Median SAT critical reading: 546, median SAT math: 563, median SAT writing: 546, median combined SAT: 1656, median composite ACT: 27. 20% scored over 600 on SAT critical reading, 20% scored over 600 on SAT math, 20% scored over 600 on SAT writing, 20% scored over 1800 on combined SAT, 45% scored over 26 on composite ACT.

Student Life Upper grades have uniform requirement, student council, honor system. Discipline rests equally with students and faculty.

Summer Programs Remediation, enrichment, sports, art/fine arts, computer instruction programs offered; session focuses on enrichment and remediation; held on campus; accepts boys and girls; open to students from other schools. 500 students usually enrolled. 2013 schedule: June 1 to July 31. Application deadline: none.

Tuition and Aid Day student tuition: $6140–$8125. Tuition installment plan (monthly payment plans, quarterly payment plan). Tuition reduction for siblings, need-based scholarship grants, need-based financial aid available. In 2012–13, 3% of upper-school students received aid. Total amount of financial aid awarded in 2012–13: $130,000.

Admissions Traditional secondary-level entrance grade is 9. For fall 2012, 37 students applied for upper-level admission, 32 were accepted, 27 enrolled. Math Placement Exam, Otis-Lennon School Ability Test, SCAT and writing sample required. Deadline for receipt of application materials: none. Application fee required: $50. On-campus interview required.

Athletics Interscholastic: baseball (boys), basketball (b,g), cheering (g), cross-country running (b,g), football (b), golf (b,g), physical fitness (b,g), soccer (b,g), softball (g), tennis (b,g), track and field (b,g), volleyball (g), weight lifting (b,g), weight training (b,g); intramural: bowling (b,g), in-line hockey (b); coed intramural: bowling. 2 coaches.

Computers Computers are regularly used in art, English, foreign language, history, journalism, keyboarding, music, science, technology, theater arts, word processing, writing, yearbook classes. Computer network features include on-campus library services, online commercial services, Internet access, wireless campus network, Internet filtering or blocking technology. Campus intranet and computer access in designated common areas are available to students. Students grades are available online. The school has a published electronic and media policy.

Contact Kay Shearin, Director of Admissions. 731-660-1692. Fax: 731-668-6910. E-mail: kshearin@usjbruins.org. Web site: www.usjbruins.org

UNIVERSITY SCHOOL OF MILWAUKEE

2100 West Fairy Chasm Road
Milwaukee, Wisconsin 53217

Head of School: Laura J. Fuller

General Information Coeducational day college-preparatory, arts, and technology school. Grades PK–12. Founded: 1851. Setting: suburban. 131-acre campus. 2 buildings on campus. Approved or accredited by Independent Schools Association of the Central States and Wisconsin Department of Education. Member of National Association of Independent Schools and Secondary School Admission Test Board. Endowment: $47 million. Total enrollment: 1,082. Upper school average class size: 15. Upper school faculty-student ratio: 1:9. There are 178 required school days per year for Upper School students. Upper School students typically attend 5 days per week. The average school day consists of 6 hours and 45 minutes.

Upper School Student Profile Grade 9: 100 students (59 boys, 41 girls); Grade 10: 89 students (43 boys, 46 girls); Grade 11: 99 students (50 boys, 49 girls); Grade 12: 76 students (37 boys, 39 girls).

Faculty School total: 121. In upper school: 24 men, 30 women; 35 have advanced degrees.

Subjects Offered Algebra, American history, American literature, art, art history, band, biology, calculus, chemistry, computer programming, computer science, concert choir, discrete mathematics, drama, drawing, economics, English, English literature, European history, expository writing, French, geometry, health, Latin, mathematics, music, orchestra, painting, photography, physical education, physics, printmaking, psychology, SAT/ACT preparation, sculpture, Spanish, statistics, theater, U.S. history, world history, world literature.

Graduation Requirements Arts and fine arts (art, music, dance, drama), English, foreign language, history, mathematics, physical education (includes health), science, 40 hours of community service.

Special Academic Programs Advanced Placement exam preparation; honors section; independent study; study at local college for college credit.

College Admission Counseling 93 students graduated in 2012; all went to college, including Elon University; High Point University; Marquette University; Miami University; Saint Louis University; University of Wisconsin–Madison. Mean SAT critical reading: 653, mean SAT math: 638, mean SAT writing: 642, mean combined SAT: 1934, mean composite ACT: 29. 71% scored over 600 on SAT critical reading, 71% scored over 600 on SAT math, 68% scored over 600 on SAT writing, 71% scored over 1800 on combined SAT, 80% scored over 26 on composite ACT.

Student Life Upper grades have specified standards of dress, student council, honor system. Discipline rests equally with students and faculty.

Summer Programs Enrichment, sports, art/fine arts, computer instruction programs offered; session focuses on reading, writing, math, science, sports, visual arts, music, drama, and computer enrichment/instruction; held on campus; accepts boys and girls; open to students from other schools. 1,400 students usually enrolled. 2013 schedule: June 10 to August 16. Application deadline: none.

Tuition and Aid Day student tuition: $21,200. Tuition installment plan (SMART Tuition Payment Plan). Merit scholarship grants, need-based scholarship grants available. In 2012–13, 22% of upper-school students received aid; total upper-school merit-scholarship money awarded: $247,835. Total amount of financial aid awarded in 2012–13: $1,000,450.

Admissions Traditional secondary-level entrance grade is 9. For fall 2012, 86 students applied for upper-level admission, 58 were accepted, 48 enrolled. ERB Achievement Test required. Deadline for receipt of application materials: January 3. Application fee required: $50. Interview required.

Athletics Interscholastic: baseball (boys), basketball (b,g), cross-country running (b,g), dance team (g), diving (b,g), field hockey (g), football (b), golf (b), ice hockey (b,g), lacrosse (b), skiing (downhill) (b,g), soccer (b,g), swimming and diving (b,g), tennis (b,g), track and field (b,g), volleyball (g). 2 PE instructors, 46 coaches, 2 athletic trainers.

Computers Computers are regularly used in college planning, creative writing, English, foreign language, history, journalism, mathematics, science, yearbook classes. Computer network features include on-campus library services, online commercial services, Internet access, wireless campus network, Internet filtering or blocking technology. Student e-mail accounts are available to students. Students grades are available online. The school has a published electronic and media policy.

Contact Kathleen Friedman, Director of Admissions. 414-540-3321. Fax: 414-352-8076. E-mail: kfriedman@usmk12.org. Web site: www.usmk12.org

UNIVERSITY SCHOOL OF NOVA SOUTHEASTERN UNIVERSITY

3375 SW 75 Avenue
Lower School Building
Fort Lauderdale, Florida 33314

Head of School: Dr. Jerome S. Chermak

General Information Coeducational day college-preparatory, arts, and technology school. Grades PK–12. Founded: 1970. Setting: suburban. 300-acre campus. 4 buildings on campus. Approved or accredited by Association of Independent Schools of Florida, Southern Association of Colleges and Schools, and Florida Department of Education. Member of National Association of Independent Schools. Endowment: $750,000. Total enrollment: 1,885. Upper school average class size: 20. Upper school faculty-student ratio: 1:11. There are 180 required school days per year for Upper School students. Upper School students typically attend 5 days per week. The average school day consists of 6 hours.

Upper School Student Profile Grade 9: 167 students (84 boys, 83 girls); Grade 10: 188 students (100 boys, 88 girls); Grade 11: 180 students (99 boys, 81 girls); Grade 12: 179 students (89 boys, 90 girls).

Faculty School total: 181. In upper school: 26 men, 35 women; 43 have advanced degrees.

Subjects Offered 1 1/2 elective credits, Advanced Placement courses, advanced studio art-AP, algebra, American government, American history, American literature, anatomy, art, band, biology, calculus, ceramics, chemistry, chorus, community service, computer programming, computer science, concert choir, creative writing, debate, directing, drawing and design, economics, English, English literature, environmental science, expository writing, fine arts, forensics, French, geometry, grammar, guitar, Internet, journalism, keyboarding, Latin, media production, music, music appreciation, music theory, orchestra, performing arts, personal fitness, physical education, physics, portfolio art, pre-calculus, psychology, public speaking, Spanish, speech, theater, trigonometry, video film production, world geography, world history, world literature, writing.

Graduation Requirements Art, computer science, electives, English, expository writing, foreign language, health education, journalism, mathematics, music, personal fitness, physical education (includes health), public speaking, science, social studies (includes history), speech and debate. Community service is required.

Special Academic Programs Advanced Placement exam preparation; honors section; accelerated programs; independent study; term-away projects; study at local college for college credit; academic accommodation for the gifted, the musically talented, and the artistically talented; remedial reading and/or remedial writing; ESL (3 students enrolled).

College Admission Counseling 166 students graduated in 2012; all went to college, including Boston University; Florida State University; University of Central Florida; University of Florida; University of Miami; University of Pennsylvania.

Student Life Upper grades have uniform requirement, student council. Discipline rests primarily with faculty.

Summer Programs Remediation, enrichment, advancement, sports, art/fine arts programs offered; session focuses on sports, arts, and academics; held on campus; accepts boys and girls; open to students from other schools. 400 students usually enrolled. 2013 schedule: June 4 to August 11. Application deadline: none.

Tuition and Aid Day student tuition: $20,500. Tuition installment plan (Key Tuition Payment Plan). Tuition reduction for siblings, need-based scholarship grants available. In 2012–13, 15% of upper-school students received aid. Total amount of financial aid awarded in 2012–13: $1,500,000.

Admissions Traditional secondary-level entrance grade is 9. For fall 2012, 175 students applied for upper-level admission, 116 were accepted, 75 enrolled. SSAT required. Deadline for receipt of application materials: none. Application fee required: $100. Interview required.

Athletics Interscholastic: baseball (boys), basketball (b,g), cheering (g), crew (b,g), cross-country running (b,g), dance team (g), diving (b,g), football (b), golf (b,g), ice hockey (b), lacrosse (b,g), soccer (b,g), softball (g), swimming and diving (b,g), tennis (b,g), track and field (b,g), volleyball (b,g), wrestling (b); coed interscholastic: cross-country running, dance. 3 PE instructors, 43 coaches, 1 athletic trainer.

Computers Computers are regularly used in all classes. Computer network features include on-campus library services, online commercial services, Internet access, wireless campus network, Internet filtering or blocking technology. Student e-mail accounts and computer access in designated common areas are available to students. Students grades are available online. The school has a published electronic and media policy.

Contact Ms. Allison Musso, Coordinator of Admissions. 954-262-4405. Fax: 954-262-3691. E-mail: amusso@nova.edu. Web site: www.uschool.nova.edu

UPPER CANADA COLLEGE

200 Lonsdale Road
Toronto, Ontario M4V 1W6, Canada

Head of School: Dr. Jim Power

General Information Boys' boarding and day college-preparatory, bilingual studies, and technology school. Boarding grades 8–12, day grades K–12. Founded: 1829. Setting: urban. 16-hectare campus. 3 buildings on campus. Approved or accredited by Canadian Association of Independent Schools, Conference of Independent Schools of Ontario, International Baccalaureate Organization, The Association of Boarding Schools, and Ontario Department of Education. Affiliate member of National Association of Independent Schools. Language of instruction: English. Total enrollment: 1,154. Upper school average class size: 20. Upper school faculty-student ratio: 1:8. There are 210 required school days per year for Upper School students. Upper School students typically attend 5 days per week. The average school day consists of 6 hours.

Upper School Student Profile 8% of students are boarding students. 90% are province residents. 9 provinces are represented in upper school student body. 10% are international students. International students from China, Colombia, Germany, Hong Kong, Russian Federation, and United States; 25 other countries represented in student body.

Faculty School total: 138. In upper school: 57 men, 28 women; 17 reside on campus.

Subjects Offered Algebra, American history, art, athletics, biology, calculus, career and personal planning, chemistry, Chinese, civics, community service, computer multimedia, computer programming, computer science, creative writing, digital art, drama, economics, English, English literature, environmental science, European history, expository writing, film, fine arts, French, geography, geometry, German, health, history, Latin, mathematics, music, physical education, physics, science, social sciences, social studies, Spanish, theater, theater arts, theory of knowledge, trigonometry, visual arts, world history, writing.

Graduation Requirements English, foreign language, mathematics, science, social sciences. Community service is required.

Special Academic Programs International Baccalaureate program; honors section.

College Admission Counseling 160 students graduated in 2012; they went to Cornell University; McGill University; Queen's University at Kingston; The University of Western Ontario; University of Toronto; University of Waterloo. Other: 7 had other specific plans.

Student Life Upper grades have specified standards of dress, student council. Discipline rests equally with students and faculty.

Summer Programs Remediation, advancement, art/fine arts, computer instruction programs offered; session focuses on enrichment and credit courses; held on campus; accepts boys and girls; open to students from other schools. 300 students usually enrolled. 2013 schedule: June 15 to August 30. Application deadline: none.

Tuition and Aid Day student tuition: CAN$30,000; 5-day tuition and room/board: CAN$53,000. Tuition installment plan (The Tuition Plan, monthly payment plans, term payment plan, full-payment discount plan). Bursaries, merit scholarship grants, need-based financial assistance available. In 2012–13, 11% of upper-school students received aid.

Admissions ACT, SAT or SSAT required. Deadline for receipt of application materials: none. Application fee required: CAN$200. Interview required.

Athletics Interscholastic: aquatics, badminton, baseball, basketball, crew, cricket, cross-country running, dance, football, golf, hockey, ice hockey, lacrosse, rowing, rugby, running, soccer, softball, squash, swimming and diving, tennis, track and field, volleyball; intramural: ball hockey, basketball, bicycling, canoeing/kayaking, climbing, combined training, cooperative games, fencing, floor hockey, Frisbee, hiking/backpacking, hockey, ice hockey, in-line hockey, indoor hockey, indoor soccer, kayaking, martial arts, mountain biking, outdoor activities, outdoor adventure, outdoor education, physical training, power lifting, rock climbing, ropes courses, self defense, soccer, softball, strength & conditioning, tai chi, ultimate Frisbee, volleyball, wall climbing, weight training, wilderness.

Computers Computer network features include on-campus library services, online commercial services, wireless campus network. Student e-mail accounts and computer access in designated common areas are available to students. The school has a published electronic and media policy.

Contact Tricia Rankin, Associate Director of Admission. 416-488-1125 Ext. 2221. Fax: 416-484-8618. E-mail: trankin@ucc.on.ca. Web site: www.ucc.on.ca

THE URSULINE ACADEMY OF DALLAS

4900 Walnut Hill Lane
Dallas, Texas 75229

Head of School: Ms. Elizabeth Bourgeois

General Information Girls' day college-preparatory, arts, religious studies, and technology school, affiliated with Roman Catholic Church. Grades 9–12. Founded: 1874. Setting: urban. 26-acre campus. 5 buildings on campus. Approved or accredited by Independent Schools Association of the Southwest, National Catholic Education Association, Texas Catholic Conference, The College Board, and Texas Department of Education. Total enrollment: 800. Upper school average class size: 18. Upper school faculty-student ratio: 1:10.

Upper School Student Profile Grade 9: 200 students (200 girls); Grade 10: 200 students (200 girls); Grade 11: 200 students (200 girls); Grade 12: 200 students (200 girls). 85% of students are Roman Catholic.

Faculty School total: 91. In upper school: 15 men, 76 women; 68 have advanced degrees.

Subjects Offered 20th century history, Advanced Placement courses, algebra, anatomy, anatomy and physiology, Arabic, band, biology, bookbinding, calculus, ceramics, chemistry, choir, Christian and Hebrew scripture, community service, comparative government and politics, comparative religion, computer programming, computer science, concert choir, creative writing, current events, dance, design, digital imaging, digital photography, discrete mathematics, drama, drawing, economics, English literature, environmental science, ethics, European history, fitness, French, geography, geology, geometry, government, government/civics, graphic design, health and wellness, journalism, Latin, Latin American literature, Mandarin, newspaper, oceanography, orchestra, painting, peer ministry, photography, physical education, physics, pre-calculus, printmaking, psychology, social justice, Spanish, speech, statistics, theater, theology, U.S. history, U.S. literature, Web authoring, Western civilization, world history, world literature, yearbook.

Graduation Requirements Arts and fine arts (art, music, dance, drama), computer science, English, foreign language, mathematics, physical education (includes health), religion (includes Bible studies and theology), science, social studies (includes history), speech. Community service is required.

Special Academic Programs Advanced Placement exam preparation; honors section; independent study.

College Admission Counseling 191 students graduated in 2012; all went to college, including Louisiana State University and Agricultural and Mechanical College; Southern Methodist University; Texas A&M University; Texas Christian University; The University of Texas at Austin; University of Oklahoma. Mean SAT critical reading: 614, mean SAT math: 608, mean SAT writing: 619, mean combined SAT: 1841, mean composite ACT: 28.

Student Life Upper grades have uniform requirement, student council, honor system. Discipline rests equally with students and faculty. Attendance at religious services is required.

Summer Programs Remediation, advancement, art/fine arts, computer instruction programs offered; session focuses on remediation and advancement; held on campus; accepts girls; not open to students from other schools. 200 students usually enrolled. 2013 schedule: June 10 to June 28. Application deadline: January 11.

Tuition and Aid Day student tuition: $16,660. Tuition installment plan (individually arranged payment plans, annual, semi-annual, and monthly (by bank draft) payment plans). Merit scholarship grants, need-based scholarship grants available. In 2012–13, 23% of upper-school students received aid. Total amount of financial aid awarded in 2012–13: $851,300.

Admissions Traditional secondary-level entrance grade is 9. For fall 2012, 411 students applied for upper-level admission, 215 enrolled. ISEE required. Deadline for receipt of application materials: January 11. Application fee required: $60. Interview required.

Athletics Interscholastic: basketball, cheering, crew, cross-country running, diving, drill team, golf, lacrosse, soccer, softball, swimming and diving, tennis, track and field, volleyball; intramural: crew, drill team. 3 PE instructors, 15 coaches, 1 athletic trainer.

Computers Computers are regularly used in all classes. Computer network features include on-campus library services, online commercial services, Internet access, wireless campus network. Campus intranet and student e-mail accounts are available to students. Students grades are available online.

Contact Ms. Emily Howse, Admissions Assistant. 469-232-1804. Fax: 469-232-1836. E-mail: ehowse@ursulinedallas.org. Web site: www.ursulinedallas.org

VAIL MOUNTAIN SCHOOL

3000 Booth Falls Road
Vail, Colorado 81657

Head of School: Mr. Peter M. Abuisi

General Information Coeducational day college-preparatory school. Grades K–12. Founded: 1962. Setting: small town. Nearest major city is Denver. 10-acre campus. 2 buildings on campus. Approved or accredited by Association of Colorado Independent Schools, National Independent Private Schools Association, and Colorado Department of Education. Member of National Association of Independent Schools. Endowment: $1.5 million. Total enrollment: 349. Upper school average class size: 15. Upper school faculty-student ratio: 1:8. There are 175 required school days per year for Upper School students. Upper School students typically attend 5 days per week. The average school day consists of 7 hours.

Upper School Student Profile Grade 9: 36 students (16 boys, 20 girls); Grade 10: 25 students (12 boys, 13 girls); Grade 11: 24 students (15 boys, 9 girls); Grade 12: 21 students (9 boys, 12 girls).

Faculty School total: 37. In upper school: 10 have advanced degrees.

Subjects Offered Advanced Placement courses, algebra, American history, American literature, art, arts, biology, calculus, chemistry, computer math, computer science, creative writing, drama, earth science, English, English literature, environmental science, ethics, European history, expository writing, fine arts, geography, geometry, government/civics, grammar, history, Latin, Latin American literature, mathematics, photography, physical education, physics, poetry, psychology, science, Shakespeare, social sciences, social studies, Spanish, theater, trigonometry, world history, writing.

Graduation Requirements Arts and fine arts (art, music, dance, drama), English, foreign language, mathematics, physical education (includes health), psychology, science, social sciences, social studies (includes history), Spanish, acceptance into a four-year college or university.

Special Academic Programs 8 Advanced Placement exams for which test preparation is offered; ESL (6 students enrolled).

College Admission Counseling 22 students graduated in 2011; all went to college, including Cornell University; University of Colorado Boulder; University of Southern California; Washington University in St. Louis.

Student Life Upper grades have specified standards of dress, honor system. Discipline rests primarily with faculty.

Tuition and Aid Day student tuition: $18,500. Tuition installment plan (monthly payment plans, individually arranged payment plans). Need-based scholarship grants, need-based loans available. In 2011–12, 33% of upper-school students received aid. Total amount of financial aid awarded in 2011–12: $390,000.

Admissions Traditional secondary-level entrance grade is 9. For fall 2011, 18 students applied for upper-level admission, 10 were accepted, 7 enrolled. Any standardized test required. Deadline for receipt of application materials: January 28. Application fee required: $50. Interview required.

Athletics Interscholastic: alpine skiing (boys, girls), freestyle skiing (b,g), golf (b,g), nordic skiing (b,g), skiing (cross-country) (b,g), skiing (downhill) (b,g), soccer (b,g), tennis (g); intramural: backpacking (b,g), basketball (b,g), dance team (g), ice hockey (b), independent competitive sports (b,g), indoor soccer (b,g), jogging (b,g), outdoor activities (b,g), outdoor adventure (b,g), outdoor education (b,g), physical fitness (b,g), physical training (b,g), rock climbing (b,g), skiing (cross-country) (b,g), skiing (downhill) (b,g), strength & conditioning (b,g), telemark skiing (b,g), volleyball (g), weight lifting (b,g); coed interscholastic: freestyle skiing, nordic skiing, snowboarding; coed intramural: backpacking, basketball, canoeing/kayaking, climbing, fishing, fitness, Fives, fly fishing, Frisbee, hiking/backpacking, indoor soccer, jogging, jump rope, kayaking, mountain biking, mountaineering, outdoor activities, outdoor adventure, outdoor education, physical fitness, physical training, rafting, rock climbing, ropes courses, running, snowboarding, snowshoeing, strength & conditioning, telemark skiing, touch football, ultimate Frisbee, weight lifting, wilderness survival, yoga. 1 PE instructor, 15 coaches, 1 athletic trainer.

Computers Computers are regularly used in all academic, art, basic skills, college planning, computer applications, creative writing, desktop publishing, English, ethics, foreign language, graphic arts, history, humanities, independent study, introduction to technology, keyboarding, library, library skills, music technology, photography, reading, research skills, senior seminar, social sciences, social studies, Spanish, study skills, technology, Web site design, word processing, writing, writing, yearbook classes. Computer network features include on-campus library services, online commercial services, Internet access, wireless campus network, Internet filtering or blocking technology. Campus intranet and student e-mail accounts are available to students. Students grades are available online. The school has a published electronic and media policy.

Contact Mr. Jeremy Thelen, Director of Admission. 970-477-7164. Fax: 970-476-3860. E-mail: admissions@vms.edu. Web site: www.vms.edu

VALLE CATHOLIC HIGH SCHOOL

40 North Fourth Street
Ste. Genevieve, Missouri 63670

Head of School: Dr. Mark Gilligan

General Information Coeducational day college-preparatory, arts, business, vocational, religious studies, and technology school, affiliated with Roman Catholic Church. Grades 9–12. Founded: 1837. Setting: small town. Nearest major city is St. Louis. 3-acre campus. 4 buildings on campus. Approved or accredited by North Central Association of Colleges and Schools and Missouri Department of Education. Endowment: $2 million. Total enrollment: 134. Upper school average class size: 15. Upper school faculty-student ratio: 1:9. There are 171 required school days per year for Upper School students. Upper School students typically attend 5 days per week. The average school day consists of 6 hours.

Upper School Student Profile Grade 9: 30 students (19 boys, 11 girls); Grade 10: 40 students (19 boys, 21 girls); Grade 11: 40 students (16 boys, 24 girls); Grade 12: 23 students (10 boys, 13 girls). 98% of students are Roman Catholic.

Faculty School total: 13. In upper school: 5 men, 8 women; 6 have advanced degrees.

Subjects Offered 20th century American writers, accounting, advanced chemistry, advanced computer applications, advanced math, algebra, American democracy, American history, American literature, analysis and differential calculus, anatomy and physiology, architectural drawing, art, art history, arts, band, biology, British literature, business, business applications, business communications, business law, business mathematics, business skills, business studies, calculus, calculus-AP, Catholic belief and practice, chemistry-AP, Christian and Hebrew scripture, Christian scripture, church history, civics, civics/free enterprise, classics, communications, comparative religion, composition, computer applications, computer multimedia, computer science, computer skills, concert band, consumer economics, consumer education, consumer law, consumer mathematics, drafting, drama, drama performance, dramatic arts, drawing, earth science, ecology, environmental systems, economics, economics and history, English, entrepreneurship, environmental science, environmental systems, foreign language, freshman seminar, geography, geometry, history of the Catholic Church, honors algebra, honors English, honors U.S. history, human anatomy, journalism, keyboarding, marching band, math analysis, mathematics, media communications, moral theology, novels, orchestra, painting, peace and justice, physical education, physics, practical arts, psychology, religion, science, social studies, sociology, Spanish, technical drawing, U.S. government, values and decisions, visual arts, Western civilization, yearbook.

Graduation Requirements Advanced math, algebra, American history, American literature, biology, Catholic belief and practice, chemistry, Christian and Hebrew scripture, civics, English, English composition, ethical decision making, foreign language, geometry, government/civics, history of the Catholic Church, mathematics, physical education (includes health), practical arts, religion (includes Bible studies and theology), science, senior composition, social justice, social studies (includes history), Spanish, 80 hours of community service.

Special Academic Programs 1 Advanced Placement exam for which test preparation is offered; honors section; study at local college for college credit; academic accommodation for the gifted and the artistically talented; remedial reading and/or remedial writing; remedial math.

College Admission Counseling 33 students graduated in 2012; 32 went to college, including Missouri State University; Saint Louis University; Southeast Missouri State University; Truman State University; University of Missouri. Other: 1 went to work. Mean SAT critical reading: 720, mean SAT math: 780, mean composite ACT: 24. 100% scored over 600 on SAT critical reading, 100% scored over 600 on SAT math, 26% scored over 26 on composite ACT.

Student Life Upper grades have uniform requirement, student council, honor system. Discipline rests primarily with faculty. Attendance at religious services is required.

Summer Programs Remediation, enrichment, advancement programs offered; session focuses on advancement and remediation/make-up; held on campus; accepts boys and girls; not open to students from other schools. 2 students usually enrolled. 2013 schedule: June 3 to July 31.

Tuition and Aid Day student tuition: $3800. Tuition installment plan (The Tuition Plan, monthly payment plans, individually arranged payment plans, tuition assistance through the St. Louis Archdiocese and Scholarships available through the School). Tuition reduction for siblings, merit scholarship grants, need-based scholarship grants, tuition relief funds available from St. Louis Archdiocese available. In 2012–13, 20% of upper-school students received aid; total upper-school merit-scholarship money awarded: $10,000. Total amount of financial aid awarded in 2012–13: $165,000.

Admissions Traditional secondary-level entrance grade is 9. For fall 2012, 33 students applied for upper-level admission, 33 were accepted, 30 enrolled. Any standardized test, school placement exam and writing sample required. Deadline for receipt of application materials: none. Application fee required: $25. Interview recommended.

Athletics Interscholastic: baseball (boys), basketball (b,g), dance team (g), drill team (g), football (b), track and field (b,g), volleyball (g), weight training (b); coed interscholastic: cheering, cross-country running, golf, physical training, strength & conditioning, weight lifting. 1 PE instructor.

Computers Computers are regularly used in accounting, business, career exploration, classics, college planning, economics, English, foreign language, geography, history, humanities, journalism, mathematics, psychology, religion, science, Spanish, writing, yearbook classes. Computer network features include Internet access, Internet filtering or blocking technology. Student e-mail accounts and computer access in designated common areas are available to students. The school has a published electronic and media policy.

Contact Mrs. Dawn C. Basler, Registrar. 573-883-7496 Ext. 242. Fax: 573-883-9142. E-mail: baslerd@valleschools.org. Web site: www.valleschools.org

VALLEY CHRISTIAN HIGH SCHOOL

7500 Inspiration Drive
Dublin, California 94568

Head of School: Mr. Larry Lopez

General Information Coeducational day college-preparatory, arts, and religious studies school, affiliated with Assemblies of God. Grades 6–12. Founded: 1981. Setting: suburban. Nearest major city is Pleasanton. 49-acre campus. 3 buildings on campus. Approved or accredited by Association of Christian Schools International, Western Association of Schools and Colleges, and California Department of Education. Total enrollment: 471. Upper school average class size: 22. Upper school faculty-student ratio: 1:13. Upper School students typically attend 5 days per week. The average school day consists of 5 hours and 36 minutes.

Upper School Student Profile 10% of students are Assemblies of God.

Faculty School total: 39. In upper school: 11 men, 27 women; 7 have advanced degrees.

Subjects Offered Acting, advanced math, Advanced Placement courses, advanced studio art-AP, algebra, American government, American history, American history-AP, American literature, American sign language, anatomy and physiology, art, arts, ASB Leadership, athletics, baseball, basketball, Bible, Bible studies, biology, British literature, business mathematics, calculus, calculus-AP, campus ministry, career and personal planning, career education, career exploration, career planning, career/college preparation, careers, ceramics, character education, cheerleading, chemistry, choir, choral music, Christian doctrine, Christian ethics, Christian scripture, Christian studies, Christian testament, church history, college admission preparation, college awareness, college counseling, college planning, competitive science projects, composition, computer graphics, computer literacy, computer resources, conceptual physics, constitutional history of U.S., creation science, creative writing, critical thinking, critical writing, debate, decision making skills, digital photography, directing, drama, drama performance, drama workshop, earth science, economics, electives, English, English language and composition-AP, English literature, English literature and composition-AP, English literature-AP, English-AP, English/composition-AP, epic literature, ESL, ethical decision making, ethics, European literature, expository writing, expressive arts, fiction, fine arts, fitness, foreign language, geography, geometry, German, German-AP, golf, government, grammar, graphic design, great books, Harlem Renaissance, health, health and wellness, health education, history, history of religion, history-AP, Holocaust, honors algebra, honors English, honors geometry, human anatomy, humanities, ideas, illustration, improvisation, journalism, keyboarding, lab science, language arts, language structure, language-AP, languages, leadership, leadership and service, library, Life of Christ, life science, literary genres, literature, literature and composition-AP, literature-AP, macro/microeconomics-AP, marine biology, math analysis, math applications, mathematics, mathematics-AP, mechanics of writing, medieval literature, methods of research, modern history, modern languages, moral theology, music, music appreciation, music theory, newspaper, novels, oral communications, oral expression, painting, participation in sports, performing arts, physical education, physical fitness, physics, physics-AP, play production, poetry, pre-algebra, pre-calculus, pre-college orientation, psychology, public speaking, reading, reading/study skills, regional literature, religion, religious education, religious studies, remedial study skills, research and reference, research skills, Russian literature, science fiction, science project, scripture, Shakespeare, Shakespearean histories, short story, softball, Spanish, Spanish language-AP, Spanish-AP, speech, sports, sports conditioning, statistics-AP, student government, studio art, studio art-AP, study skills, swimming, tennis, theater, theater arts, theater design and production, U.S. government, U.S. government and politics, U.S. history, U.S. history-AP, U.S. literature, values and decisions, visual and performing arts, volleyball, weight training, world geography, world history, world history-AP, world literature, world religions, world wide web design, yearbook.

Graduation Requirements Art, Christian doctrine, Christian ethics, Christian scripture, composition, economics, foreign language, geography, grammar, health, history, keyboarding, literature, mathematics, moral reasoning, religious studies, science, U.S. government, World War II.

Special Academic Programs Honors section; independent study; academic accommodation for the gifted; programs in English, general development for dyslexic students.

College Admission Counseling 71 students graduated in 2011; 69 went to college, including Arizona State University; Azusa Pacific University; University of California, Davis; University of California, Irvine; University of California, San Diego. Other: 2 had other specific plans. Median SAT critical reading: 574, median SAT math: 570, median SAT writing: 561, median composite ACT: 24.

Student Life Upper grades have specified standards of dress, student council, honor system. Discipline rests primarily with faculty. Attendance at religious services is required.

Tuition and Aid Day student tuition: $11,550. Tuition installment plan (FACTS Tuition Payment Plan). Tuition reduction for siblings, need-based scholarship grants available. In 2011–12, 10% of upper-school students received aid. Total amount of financial aid awarded in 2011–12: $30,000.

Admissions Traditional secondary-level entrance grade is 9. For fall 2011, 50 students applied for upper-level admission, 47 were accepted, 41 enrolled. SSAT, TOEFL or SLEP or writing sample required. Deadline for receipt of application materials: none. Application fee required: $375. On-campus interview required.

Athletics Interscholastic: baseball (boys), basketball (b,g), cheering (g), cross-country running (b,g), flag football (b), football (b), golf (b), soccer (b,g), softball (g), tennis (b,g), track and field (b,g), volleyball (b,g), weight training (b,g), wrestling (b). 4 PE instructors, 20 coaches, 3 athletic trainers.

Computers Computers are regularly used in business skills, graphic design, journalism, keyboarding, lab/keyboard, media arts, publications, Web site design, yearbook classes. Computer network features include on-campus library services, online commercial services, Internet access, wireless campus network. Campus intranet is available to students. Students grades are available online. The school has a published electronic and media policy.

Contact Mrs. Lori Umidon, Admissions Administrative Assistant. 925-560-6256. Fax: 925-828-5658. E-mail: lumidon@dublinvcc.org. Web site: www.valleychristianschools.org

VALLEY CHRISTIAN HIGH SCHOOL

100 Skyway Drive
San Jose, California 95111

Head of School: Dr. Clifford Daugherty

General Information Coeducational day and distance learning college-preparatory, arts, religious studies, technology, Conservatory of the Arts, and Applied Math, Science and Engineering Institute school, affiliated with Christian faith. Grades K–12. Distance learning grades 8–12. Founded: 1960. Setting: suburban. 53-acre campus. 6 buildings on campus. Approved or accredited by Association of Christian Schools International, Western Association of Schools and Colleges, and California Department of Education. Total enrollment: 2,400. Upper school average class size: 28. Upper school faculty-student ratio: 1:17. There are 174 required school days per year for Upper School students. Upper School students typically attend 5 days per week. The average school day consists of 6 hours and 45 minutes.

Upper School Student Profile Grade 9: 344 students (172 boys, 172 girls); Grade 10: 332 students (170 boys, 162 girls); Grade 11: 329 students (173 boys, 156 girls); Grade 12: 313 students (168 boys, 145 girls). 85% of students are Christian.

Faculty School total: 142. In upper school: 37 men, 49 women; 24 have advanced degrees.

Subjects Offered 20th century American writers, acting, advanced chemistry, advanced computer applications, advanced math, Advanced Placement courses, advanced studio art-AP, algebra, American history, American literature, American sign language, anatomy and physiology, ancient world history, applied music, art, audio visual/media, Basic programming, Bible, Bible studies, biology, biology-AP, British literature-AP, broadcasting, calculus-AP, career and personal planning, cheerleading, chemistry, chemistry-AP, Chinese, choir, choral music, choreography, Christian doctrine, Christian ethics, Christian scripture, Christian studies, college admission preparation, college counseling, college planning, comparative political systems-AP, composition-AP, computer art, computer literacy, computer music, computer science-AP, concert choir, consumer mathematics, critical studies in film, dance, dance performance, digital art, drama, drama performance, dramatic arts, electronics, engineering, English, English language and composition-AP, English literature-AP, environmental science-AP, European history-AP, filmmaking, finite math, foreign language, French, French studies, geometry, global studies, government, grammar, health education, health science, history, history of music, honors English, honors U.S. history, honors world history, HTML design, instrumental music, introduction to theater, Japanese, Japanese as Second Language, jazz band, jazz dance, jazz ensemble, journalism, keyboarding, Latin, leadership, leadership and service, literature and composition-AP, macro/microeconomics-AP, Mandarin, marching band, mathematics, mathematics-AP, Microsoft, music theater, music theory-AP, musical productions, musical theater, photo shop, photojournalism, physical science, physics, physics-AP, play/screen writing, pre-algebra, pre-calculus, radio broadcasting, SAT preparation, sign language, Spanish, Spanish-AP, stage design, statistics, statistics-AP, student government, studio art-AP, symphonic band, tap dance, technical theater, telecommunications, theater arts, theater production, trigonometry, typing, U.S. government, U.S. government and politics-AP, U.S. history, U.S. history-AP, video film production, vocal ensemble, weight training, wind ensemble, world history, yearbook.

Graduation Requirements Arts and fine arts (art, music, dance, drama), biology, Christian and Hebrew scripture, Christian doctrine, Christian studies, computers, economics, economics and history, English, English composition, English literature, foreign language, global studies, mathematics, physical education (includes health), physical science, science, technology, U.S. government, U.S. history, world geography, world history.

Special Academic Programs 22 Advanced Placement exams for which test preparation is offered; honors section; programs in English, mathematics, general development for dyslexic students.

College Admission Counseling 325 students graduated in 2012; 324 went to college, including Azusa Pacific University; California Polytechnic State University, San Luis Obispo; California State University, Chico; San Jose State University; University of California, Berkeley; University of California, Davis. Other: 1 entered military service. Median SAT critical reading: 540, median SAT math: 530, median SAT writing: 590, median combined SAT: 1660. 35% scored over 600 on SAT critical reading, 38% scored over 600 on SAT math, 32% scored over 600 on SAT writing, 31% scored over 1800 on combined SAT.

Student Life Upper grades have specified standards of dress, student council, honor system. Discipline rests primarily with faculty.

Summer Programs Remediation, enrichment, advancement, sports, art/fine arts, computer instruction programs offered; session focuses on advancement, remediation, and enrichment; held on campus; accepts boys and girls; open to students from other schools. 400 students usually enrolled. 2013 schedule: June 21 to July 30. Application deadline: none.

Tuition and Aid Day student tuition: $15,200. Tuition installment plan (FACTS Tuition Payment Plan). Tuition reduction for siblings, need-based scholarship grants available. In 2012–13, 20% of upper-school students received aid. Total amount of financial aid awarded in 2012–13: $1,300,000.

Admissions Traditional secondary-level entrance grade is 9. For fall 2012, 405 students applied for upper-level admission, 315 were accepted, 246 enrolled. Admissions testing, essay, Iowa Subtests, mathematics proficiency exam, school's own test or TOEFL or SLEP required. Deadline for receipt of application materials: none. Application fee required: $70. Interview required.

Athletics Interscholastic: aquatics (boys, girls), baseball (b), basketball (b,g), cheering (b,g), cross-country running (b,g), dance squad (b,g), dance team (b), diving (b,g), football (b), golf (b,g), ice hockey (b,g), soccer (b,g), softball (g), swimming and diving (b,g), tennis (b,g), track and field (b,g), volleyball (b,g), water polo (b,g), weight training (b,g), wrestling (b); intramural: weight training (b,g). 3 PE instructors, 23 coaches, 2 athletic trainers.

Computers Computers are regularly used in Bible studies, computer applications, digital applications, engineering, foreign language, graphic arts, graphic design, journalism, keyboarding, lab/keyboard, library, mathematics, media arts, music, music technology, news writing, newspaper, photography, photojournalism, research skills, science, technology, typing, video film production, Web site design, word processing, writing, yearbook classes. Computer network features include on-campus library services, Internet access, wireless campus network, Internet filtering or blocking technology, ten online classes, through two online learning labs. Campus intranet, student e-mail accounts, and computer access in designated common areas are available to students. Students grades are available online. The school has a published electronic and media policy.

Contact Alana James, High School Admissions Coordinator. 408-513-2512. Fax: 408-513-2517. E-mail: ajames@vcs.net. Web site: www.vcs.net

VALLEY FORGE MILITARY ACADEMY & COLLEGE

1001 Eagle Road
Wayne, Pennsylvania 19087-3695

Head of School: Col. James J. Doyle, USMC-Retd.

General Information Boys' boarding and day college-preparatory, arts, business, religious studies, bilingual studies, technology, music, and military school. Boarding grades 7–PG, day grades 7–12. Founded: 1928. Setting: suburban. Nearest major city is Philadelphia. Students are housed in single-sex dormitories. 100-acre campus. 83 buildings on campus. Approved or accredited by Middle States Association of Colleges and Schools, The Association of Boarding Schools, and Pennsylvania Department of Education. Member of National Association of Independent Schools and Secondary School Admission Test Board. Endowment: $12 million. Total enrollment: 248. Upper school average class size: 12. Upper school faculty-student ratio: 1:11. There are 175 required school days per year for Upper School students. Upper School students typically attend 5 days per week. The average school day consists of 5 hours and 50 minutes.

Upper School Student Profile Grade 9: 34 students (34 boys); Grade 10: 37 students (37 boys); Grade 11: 74 students (74 boys); Grade 12: 59 students (59 boys); Postgraduate: 23 students (23 boys). 100% of students are boarding students. 30% are state residents. 35 states are represented in upper school student body. 15% are international students. International students from China, Egypt, Mexico, Republic of Korea, Russian Federation, and Saudi Arabia; 29 other countries represented in student body.

Faculty School total: 30. In upper school: 16 men, 12 women; 18 have advanced degrees; 14 reside on campus.

Subjects Offered ACT preparation, algebra, American government, American history-AP, anatomy and physiology, ancient world history, applied music, art, biology, calculus, chemistry, Chinese, computer programming, creative writing, driver education, earth science, English, English literature and composition-AP, ESL, ESL, European history, French, French studies, geometry, government/civics, health, health education, honors geometry, honors U.S. history, instrumental music, Latin, mathematics, modern world history, music, music theory, physical education, physics, physics-AP, pre-algebra, Russian, social sciences, sociology, Spanish, speech, statistics-AP, TOEFL preparation, U.S. government, U.S. history, U.S. history-AP, world history, world religions, world religions.

Special Academic Programs Advanced Placement exam preparation; honors section; independent study; study at local college for college credit; study abroad; academic accommodation for the musically talented and the artistically talented; remedial reading and/or remedial writing; remedial math; ESL (24 students enrolled).

College Admission Counseling 73 students graduated in 2012; 65 went to college, including Drexel University; George Mason University; Penn State University Park; United States Military Academy; United States Naval Academy; University of Chicago. Other: 3 went to work, 1 entered a postgraduate year, 4 had other specific plans. Median SAT critical reading: 500, median SAT math: 530, median SAT writing: 450, median combined SAT: 1440. 28% scored over 600 on SAT critical reading, 38% scored over 600 on SAT math, 16% scored over 600 on SAT writing, 16% scored over 1800 on combined SAT.

Student Life Upper grades have uniform requirement, student council, honor system. Discipline rests equally with students and faculty. Attendance at religious services is required.

Tuition and Aid Day student tuition: $21,250; 5-day tuition and room/board: $34,000; 7-day tuition and room/board: $32,500. Tuition installment plan (monthly payment plans, individually arranged payment plans, HES). Tuition reduction for siblings, merit scholarship grants, need-based scholarship grants available. In 2012–13, 73% of upper-school students received aid; total upper-school merit-scholarship money awarded: $2,230,907. Total amount of financial aid awarded in 2012–13: $2,230,907.

Admissions Traditional secondary-level entrance grade is 11. For fall 2012, 339 students applied for upper-level admission, 204 were accepted, 105 enrolled. TOEFL or SLEP required. Deadline for receipt of application materials: none. Application fee required: $100. Interview required.

Athletics Interscholastic: baseball, basketball, climbing, cross-country running, dressage, drill team, equestrian sports, fitness, football, golf, horseback riding, indoor track, judo, lacrosse, marksmanship, outdoor activities, outdoor recreation, physical fitness, physical training, soccer, swimming and diving, weight lifting, weight training, wrestling; intramural: boxing, fencing, hockey, indoor hockey, indoor soccer, life saving, martial arts, paint ball, physical training, rugby, scuba diving, soccer, street hockey, ultimate Frisbee. 3 PE instructors, 12 coaches, 2 athletic trainers.

Computers Computers are regularly used in all classes. Computer network features include on-campus library services, Internet access, wireless campus network, Internet filtering or blocking technology, Blackboard. Campus intranet, student e-mail accounts, and computer access in designated common areas are available to students. Students grades are available online. The school has a published electronic and media policy.

Contact Col. John Ford, Academy Headmaster and Interim Director of Enrollment. 610-989-1490. Fax: 610-340-2194. E-mail: admissions@vfmac.edu. Web site: www.vfmac.edu

VALLEY LUTHERAN HIGH SCHOOL

5199 North 7th Avenue
Phoenix, Arizona 85013-2043

Head of School: Mr. Robert Koehne

General Information Coeducational day college-preparatory, arts, religious studies, and technology school, affiliated with Lutheran Church–Missouri Synod. Grades 9–12. Founded: 1981. Setting: urban. 10-acre campus. 4 buildings on campus. Approved or accredited by National Lutheran School Accreditation, North Central Association of Colleges and Schools, and Arizona Department of Education. Total enrollment: 184. Upper school average class size: 15. Upper school faculty-student ratio: 1:10. There are 180 required school days per year for Upper School students. Upper School students typically attend 5 days per week. The average school day consists of 6 hours and 45 minutes.

Upper School Student Profile Grade 9: 37 students (20 boys, 17 girls); Grade 10: 45 students (23 boys, 22 girls); Grade 11: 60 students (38 boys, 22 girls); Grade 12: 42 students (23 boys, 19 girls). 56% of students are Lutheran Church–Missouri Synod.

Faculty School total: 18. In upper school: 10 men, 8 women; 7 have advanced degrees.

Subjects Offered Advanced Placement courses, advanced studio art-AP, algebra, American government, American history, American history-AP, American literature, American politics in film, anatomy and physiology, art, athletics, band, Bible, biology, British literature, British literature (honors), calculus, calculus-AP, career and personal planning, chemistry, choir, choral music, chorus, Christian doctrine, Christian education, Christian ethics, computer skills, concert band, consumer mathematics, creative writing, current history, economics, English, English literature and composition-AP, environmental science, film history, foreign language, freshman seminar, geography, government, government-AP, honors algebra, honors geometry, human biology, intro to computers, music, music appreciation, New Testament, oral communications, physical education, physical fitness, physics, portfolio art, pre-algebra, pre-calculus, psychology, religion, SAT preparation, SAT/ACT preparation, Spanish, speech, speech communications, trigonometry, U.S. government, U.S. history-AP, United States government-AP, weightlifting, world geography, world history, world literature, World-Wide-Web publishing, yearbook.

Special Academic Programs 4 Advanced Placement exams for which test preparation is offered; honors section; term-away projects; academic accommodation for the gifted; remedial math; special instructional classes for deaf students.

College Admission Counseling 63 students graduated in 2012; 50 went to college, including Arizona State University; Azusa Pacific University; Concordia University; Grand Canyon University; Northern Arizona University; The University of Arizona. Other: 3 went to work, 8 entered military service, 1 entered a postgraduate year, 1 had other specific plans. Median SAT critical reading: 550, median SAT math: 560, median SAT writing: 500, median combined SAT: 1610, median composite ACT: 24.

Student Life Upper grades have specified standards of dress, student council, honor system. Discipline rests primarily with faculty. Attendance at religious services is required.

Tuition and Aid Day student tuition: $8500. Tuition installment plan (monthly payment plans, individually arranged payment plans, Vanco Services online payments). Merit scholarship grants, need-based scholarship grants, association grants, Christian worker discounts available. In 2012–13, 30% of upper-school students received aid. Total amount of financial aid awarded in 2012–13: $166,770.

Admissions Traditional secondary-level entrance grade is 9. For fall 2012, 68 students applied for upper-level admission, 68 were accepted, 64 enrolled. High School Placement Test and school's own test required. Deadline for receipt of application materials: none. Application fee required: $50. On-campus interview required.

Athletics Interscholastic: baseball (boys), basketball (b,g), cheering (g), cross-country running (b,g), football (b), pom squad (g), soccer (b,g), softball (g), track and field (b,g), volleyball (g), wrestling (b); coed interscholastic: golf, running, strength & conditioning, tennis, weight training. 13 coaches.

Computers Computers are regularly used in computer applications, desktop publishing, photography, Web site design, word processing, yearbook classes. Computer network features include Internet access, Internet filtering or blocking technology. Students grades are available online. The school has a published electronic and media policy.

Contact Mr. Robert Koehne, Principal. 602-230-1600 Ext. 120. Fax: 602-230-1602. E-mail: rkoehne@vlhs.org. Web site: www.vlhs.org/

THE VALLEY SCHOOL

5255 S. Linden Rd.
Swartz Creek, Michigan 48473

Head of School: Kaye C. Panchula

General Information Coeducational day college-preparatory and arts school. Grades PK–12. Founded: 1970. Setting: urban. Nearest major city is Flint. 5-acre campus. 1 building on campus. Candidate for accreditation by Independent Schools Association of the Central States. Total enrollment: 62. Upper school average class size: 17. Upper school faculty-student ratio: 1:8. There are 180 required school days per year for Upper School students. Upper School students typically attend 5 days per week. The average school day consists of 5 hours and 30 minutes.

Upper School Student Profile Grade 9: 7 students (4 boys, 3 girls); Grade 10: 1 student (1 girl); Grade 11: 4 students (4 boys); Grade 12: 5 students (3 boys, 2 girls).

Faculty School total: 13. In upper school: 4 men, 3 women; 4 have advanced degrees.

Subjects Offered Algebra, American history, American literature, anatomy, art, art history, biology, chemistry, current events, earth science, English, English literature, European history, expository writing, fine arts, geometry, government/civics, grammar, history, mathematics, music, physical education, physics, probability and statistics, SAT/ACT preparation, science, social sciences, Spanish, trigonometry, world cultures, world history, world literature, writing.

Graduation Requirements Arts and fine arts (art, music, dance, drama), English, foreign language, mathematics, physical education (includes health), science, social sciences, social studies (includes history), senior project off campus.

Special Academic Programs Independent study; term-away projects; study at local college for college credit; academic accommodation for the gifted and the artistically talented.

College Admission Counseling 5 students graduated in 2012; all went to college, including Baylor University; Eastern Michigan University; Kalamazoo College; University of Chicago; University of Michigan. Median composite ACT: 26.

Student Life Upper grades have student council. Discipline rests equally with students and faculty.

Tuition and Aid Day student tuition: $9399. Tuition installment plan (FACTS Tuition Payment Plan). Tuition reduction for siblings, merit scholarship grants, need-based scholarship grants available. In 2012–13, 83% of upper-school students received aid; total upper-school merit-scholarship money awarded: $28,199. Total amount of financial aid awarded in 2012–13: $51,376.

Admissions Traditional secondary-level entrance grade is 9. For fall 2012, 10 students applied for upper-level admission, 10 were accepted, 10 enrolled. School's own exam required. Deadline for receipt of application materials: none. No application fee required. On-campus interview required.

Athletics Interscholastic: baseball (boys), basketball (b,g), golf (b), outdoor skills (b,g), outdoors (b,g), physical fitness (b,g), soccer (b,g), tennis (g), volleyball (g). 1 PE instructor, 3 coaches.

Computers Computers are regularly used in art, English, mathematics, science, social sciences, stock market, study skills, writing classes. Computer resources include Internet access, wireless campus network. Computer access in designated common areas is available to students.

Contact Ms. Minka Owens, Director of Admissions. 810-767-4004. Fax: 810-655-0853. E-mail: email@valleyschool.org. Web site: www.valleyschool.org

VALLEY VIEW SCHOOL

North Brookfield, Massachusetts
See Special Needs Schools section.

VENTA PREPARATORY SCHOOL

2013 Old Carp Road
Ottawa, Ontario K0A 1L0, Canada

Head of School: Ms. Marilyn Mansfield

General Information Coeducational boarding and day college-preparatory, arts, and music school. Grades 1–10. Founded: 1981. Setting: small town. Students are housed in single-sex by floor dormitories. 50-acre campus. 8 buildings on campus. Approved or accredited by Ontario Department of Education. Language of instruction: English. Total enrollment: 82. Upper school average class size: 12. Upper school faculty-student ratio: 1:6. There are 175 required school days per year for Upper School students. Upper School students typically attend 5 days per week. The average school day consists of 8 hours and 30 minutes.

Upper School Student Profile Grade 8: 7 students (5 boys, 2 girls); Grade 9: 8 students (3 boys, 5 girls); Grade 10: 8 students (7 boys, 1 girl). 40% of students are boarding students. 90% are province residents. 2 provinces are represented in upper school student body. International students from Bermuda, China, Hong Kong, Mexico, and United States.

Faculty School total: 18. In upper school: 7 men, 11 women; 4 have advanced degrees; 6 reside on campus.

Special Academic Programs Independent study; academic accommodation for the gifted; remedial reading and/or remedial writing; remedial math; programs in English, mathematics, general development for dyslexic students.

Student Life Upper grades have uniform requirement, honor system. Discipline rests primarily with faculty.

Tuition and Aid Day student tuition: CAN$17,070–CAN$18,585; 5-day tuition and room/board: CAN$30,965–CAN$33,895; 7-day tuition and room/board: CAN$34,465–CAN$37,395. Tuition installment plan (monthly payment plans, individually arranged payment plans). Tuition reduction for siblings, merit scholarship grants available.

Admissions Traditional secondary-level entrance grade is 9. Psychoeducational evaluation required. Deadline for receipt of application materials: none. Application fee required: CAN$75. On-campus interview required.

Athletics Coed Interscholastic: basketball, rugby, soccer; coed intramural: ball hockey, baseball, basketball, canoeing/kayaking, fitness, football, ice hockey, jogging, outdoor recreation, running, soccer, track and field, ultimate Frisbee. 4 PE instructors.

Computers Computers are regularly used in current events, geography, keyboarding, mathematics, research skills, science, Web site design classes. Computer network features include Internet access, wireless campus network, Internet filtering or blocking technology. The school has a published electronic and media policy.

Contact Ms. Tanya Kaye, Manager, Marketing and Admissions. 613-839-2175 Ext. 240. Fax: 613-839-1956. E-mail: info@ventaprep.com. Web site: www.ventapreparatoryschool.com

VIANNEY HIGH SCHOOL

1311 South Kirkwood Road
St. Louis, Missouri 63122

Head of School: Dr. Timothy Dilg

General Information Boys' day college-preparatory, arts, business, religious studies, and technology school, affiliated with Roman Catholic Church. Grades 9–12. Founded: 1960. Setting: suburban. 37-acre campus. 6 buildings on campus. Approved or accredited by National Catholic Education Association, North Central Association of Colleges and Schools, and The College Board. Total enrollment: 640. Upper school average class size: 22. Upper school faculty-student ratio: 1:13. There are 165 required school days per year for Upper School students. Upper School students typically attend 5 days per week. The average school day consists of 6 hours and 5 minutes.

Upper School Student Profile Grade 9: 163 students (163 boys); Grade 10: 165 students (165 boys); Grade 11: 172 students (172 boys); Grade 12: 140 students (140 boys). 98% of students are Roman Catholic.

Faculty School total: 50. In upper school: 40 men, 8 women; 37 have advanced degrees.

Subjects Offered Accounting, advanced chemistry, Advanced Placement courses, algebra, American government, American history, American literature, analysis, analytic geometry, architectural drawing, art, art education, art history, arts appreciation, athletic training, band, British literature (honors), business law, business mathematics, calculus, calculus-AP, Catholic belief and practice, chemistry, Christian and Hebrew scripture, Christian ethics, Christian studies, college writing, communication skills, composition, computer applications, computer programming, computer skills, constitutional history of U.S., consumer education, current events, drama, economics, English composition, English literature, European history, expository writing, foreign language, fractal geometry, French, geometry, German, German literature, government, health and wellness, honors algebra, honors English, honors geometry, honors U.S. history, journalism, keyboarding, leadership, mythology, probability and statistics, publications, research skills, scripture, sex education, Shakespeare, Spanish, Spanish literature, sports conditioning, stage design, stagecraft, technical drawing, technology, technology/design, the Web, theater arts, theater design and production, theater history, trigonometry, U.S. government, U.S. history, U.S. literature, Web site design, weight training, world civilizations, world history, writing.

Graduation Requirements American history, American literature, arts and fine arts (art, music, dance, drama), biology, English, English composition, food science, foods, foreign language, government/civics, grammar, history, keyboarding, mathematics, physical education (includes health), physical fitness, religious studies, science, social issues, 100 hours of community service, forensic science.

Special Academic Programs 5 Advanced Placement exams for which test preparation is offered; honors section; study at local college for college credit; special instructional classes for students with learning disabilities, Attention Deficit Disorder, dyslexia, emotional and behavioral problems.

College Admission Counseling 147 students graduated in 2012; 146 went to college, including Missouri State University; Saint Louis University; Southeast Missouri State University; St. Louis Community College at Meramec; University of Missouri. Other: 1 entered military service. Median composite ACT: 24. 25% scored over 26 on composite ACT.

Student Life Upper grades have specified standards of dress, student council, honor system. Discipline rests primarily with faculty. Attendance at religious services is required.

Summer Programs Sports programs offered; session focuses on reinforcing athletic skills; held on campus; accepts boys and girls; open to students from other schools. 1,100 students usually enrolled. 2013 schedule: June 8 to July 27. Application deadline: May 28.

Tuition and Aid Day student tuition: $12,000. Tuition installment plan (The Tuition Plan, FACTS Tuition Payment Plan, monthly payment plans, individually arranged payment plans). Tuition reduction for siblings, merit scholarship grants, need-based scholarship grants, paying campus jobs available. In 2012–13, 27% of upper-school students received aid; total upper-school merit-scholarship money awarded: $135,127. Total amount of financial aid awarded in 2012–13: $316,127.

Admissions Traditional secondary-level entrance grade is 9. For fall 2012, 172 students applied for upper-level admission, 167 were accepted, 163 enrolled. Explore required. Deadline for receipt of application materials: none. No application fee required. On-campus interview required.

Athletics Interscholastic: aquatics, baseball, basketball, cross-country running, diving, football, golf, ice hockey, lacrosse, racquetball, roller hockey, soccer, swimming and diving, tennis, track and field, volleyball, wrestling; intramural: bowling, flag football, paint ball, Special Olympics, touch football. 3 PE instructors, 40 coaches, 1 athletic trainer.

Computers Computers are regularly used in all academic, architecture, computer applications, creative writing, drafting, journalism, yearbook classes. Computer network features include on-campus library services, online commercial services, Internet access, wireless campus network, Internet filtering or blocking technology. Campus intranet, student e-mail accounts, and computer access in designated common areas are available to students. Students grades are available online. The school has a published electronic and media policy.

Contact Mr. Tom Mulvihill, Director of Admissions. 314-965-4853 Ext. 142. Fax: 314-965-1950. E-mail: tmulvihill@vianney.com. Web site: www.vianney.com

VICKSBURG CATHOLIC SCHOOL

1900 Grove Street
Vicksburg, Mississippi 39183

Head of School: Mrs. Michele Connelly

General Information Coeducational day college-preparatory and religious studies school, affiliated with Roman Catholic Church. Grades PK–12. Founded: 1860. Setting: urban. Nearest major city is Jackson. 8-acre campus. 2 buildings on campus. Approved or accredited by National Catholic Education Association, Southern Association of Colleges and Schools, and Mississippi Department of Education. Endowment: $350,000. Total enrollment: 569. Upper school average class size: 16. Upper school faculty-student ratio: 1:10. There are 180 required school days per year for Upper School students. Upper School students typically attend 5 days per week. The average school day consists of 5 hours and 50 minutes.

Upper School Student Profile Grade 7: 42 students (20 boys, 22 girls); Grade 8: 49 students (28 boys, 21 girls); Grade 9: 39 students (24 boys, 15 girls); Grade 10: 48 students (23 boys, 25 girls); Grade 11: 38 students (22 boys, 16 girls); Grade 12: 37 students (19 boys, 18 girls). 50% of students are Roman Catholic.

Faculty School total: 50. In upper school: 9 men, 14 women; 5 have advanced degrees.

Subjects Offered Accounting, ACT preparation, algebra, American government, American history, anatomy, anatomy and physiology, art, band, biology, biology-AP, calculus-AP, chemistry, chemistry-AP, choir, computer applications, desktop publishing, drama, earth science, economics, English, English language and composition-AP, environmental science, foreign language, geography, geology, geometry, government and politics-AP, health, honors algebra, honors English, honors geometry, humanities, keyboarding, learning lab, music, personal finance, physical education, physics, physics-AP, pre-algebra, pre-calculus, psychology, public speaking, sociology, Spanish, state history, theology, trigonometry, U.S. government, U.S. history, world history, yearbook.

Graduation Requirements Algebra, American government, American history, biology, computer skills, economics, English, geography, geometry, government, health, history, lab science, law, physical education (includes health), Spanish, theology, U.S. government, U.S. history, world history, Mississippi state requirements.

Special Academic Programs 6 Advanced Placement exams for which test preparation is offered; honors section; special instructional classes for students with learning disabilities, Attention Deficit Disorder, dyslexia, emotional and behavioral problems.

College Admission Counseling 38 students graduated in 2012; all went to college, including Delta State University; Hinds Community College; Louisiana State University and Agricultural and Mechanical College; Mississippi State University; University of Mississippi; University of Southern Mississippi. Median composite ACT: 20. 18% scored over 26 on composite ACT.

Student Life Upper grades have uniform requirement, student council, honor system. Discipline rests primarily with faculty. Attendance at religious services is required.

Tuition and Aid Day student tuition: $6100. Tuition installment plan (FACTS Tuition Payment Plan). Tuition reduction for siblings, need-based scholarship grants available. In 2012–13, 14% of upper-school students received aid. Total amount of financial aid awarded in 2012–13: $75,000.

Admissions Traditional secondary-level entrance grade is 7. For fall 2012, 23 students applied for upper-level admission, 19 were accepted, 17 enrolled. Admissions testing required. Deadline for receipt of application materials: none. Application fee required: $75. Interview required.

Athletics Interscholastic: baseball (boys), basketball (b,g), cheering (g), cross-country running (b,g), dance squad (g), football (b), golf (b,g), power lifting (b), soccer (b,g), softball (g), swimming and diving (b,g), tennis (b,g), track and field (b,g); coed interscholastic: swimming and diving, tennis. 2 PE instructors, 4 coaches.

Computers Computers are regularly used in accounting, computer applications, desktop publishing, keyboarding classes. Computer network features include on-campus library services, online commercial services, Internet access, Internet filtering or blocking technology. Students grades are available online. The school has a published electronic and media policy.

Contact Mrs. Patricia Rabalais, Registrar. 601-636-2256 Ext. 16. Fax: 601-631-0430. E-mail: patricia.rabalais@vicksburgcatholic.org. Web site: www.vicksburgcatholic.org

VILLA ANGELA-ST. JOSEPH HIGH SCHOOL

18491 Lakeshore Boulevard
Cleveland, Ohio 44119-1212

Head of School: Mr. Dave Csank

General Information Coeducational day college-preparatory, general academic, arts, business, religious studies, and technology school, affiliated with Roman Catholic Church. Grades 9–12. Founded: 1990. Setting: urban. 5-acre campus. 2 buildings on campus. Approved or accredited by North Central Association of Colleges and Schools and Ohio Department of Education. Endowment: $3 million. Total enrollment: 310. Upper school average class size: 20. Upper school faculty-student ratio: 1:15. Upper School students typically attend 5 days per week. The average school day consists of 7 hours and 8 minutes.

Upper School Student Profile 50% of students are Roman Catholic.

Faculty School total: 50. In upper school: 28 men, 19 women; 27 have advanced degrees.

Subjects Offered 20th century American writers, 20th century history, 20th century physics, 20th century world history, 3-dimensional art, 3-dimensional design, accounting, ACT preparation, advanced chemistry, advanced computer applications, advanced math, Advanced Placement courses, African American history, African-American history, algebra, alternative physical education, American Civil War, American culture, American democracy, American government, American history, American history-AP, American literature, analysis, analytic geometry, anatomy, anatomy and physiology, applied skills, architectural drawing, art, art and culture, art appreciation, art education, art history, arts, arts and crafts, arts appreciation, audio visual/media, auto mechanics, band, basic skills, Bible, Bible studies, biology, biology-AP, British literature, British literature (honors), business, business skills, business studies, calculus, calculus-AP, campus ministry, career and personal planning, career education, career education internship, career experience, career exploration, career planning, career/college preparation, carpentry, cartooning/animation, Catholic belief and practice, chemistry, chemistry-AP, child development, choir, choral music, chorus,

Christian doctrine, Christian education, Christian ethics, Christian scripture, Christian studies, Christian testament, Christianity, church history, civics, Civil War, civil war history, college admission preparation, college placement, community service, composition, computer education, computer information systems, computer literacy, computer multimedia, computer programming, computer resources, computer science, computer skills, computer studies, computer technologies, computer technology certification, computer tools, computer-aided design, computers, conceptual physics, concert band, creative arts, creative writing, critical thinking, critical writing, culinary arts, current events, current history, debate, design, desktop publishing, diversity studies, drawing, drawing and design, early childhood, engineering, English, English composition, English language and composition-AP, English language-AP, English literature, English literature and composition-AP, English literature-AP, English-AP, English/composition-AP, environmental education, environmental geography, environmental science, environmental studies, epic literature, ethnic literature, ethnic studies, European civilization, European history, expressive arts, family and consumer science, family living, family studies, fiction, fine arts, food and nutrition, foods, foreign language, French, freshman foundations, functions, gender and religion, general, general business, general math, general science, geography, geometry, global issues, global science, government, government-AP, government/civics, health, health education, health science, history, history of religion, history of the Catholic Church, history-AP, honors algebra, honors English, honors geometry, honors U.S. history, honors world history, human development, human relations, human sexuality, independent living, industrial arts, industrial technology, instrumental music, instruments, interactive media, Internet, Internet research, intro to computers, introduction to literature, introduction to technology, keyboarding, lab science, lab/keyboard, language and composition, language arts, languages, Latin, life management skills, life science, life skills, literary genres, literary magazine, literature, literature and composition-AP, literature-AP, logarithms, logic, rhetoric, and debate, math analysis, math applications, math methods, math review, mathematical modeling, mathematics, mathematics-AP, mechanics of writing, Microsoft, minority studies, modern civilization, modern European history, modern history, modern politics, modern Western civilization, modern world history, moral and social development, multicultural studies, multimedia design, music, music performance, music theater, musical productions, musical theater, newspaper, nutrition, painting, parent/child development, peer ministry, performing arts, personal and social education, physical education, physical science, physics, physics-AP, prayer/spirituality, pre-algebra, pre-calculus, programming, publications, reading, reading/study skills, relationships, religion, religion and culture, religious education, religious studies, research skills, Romantic period literature, SAT preparation, SAT/ACT preparation, science, science and technology, scripture, sculpture, sewing, sex education, shop, skills for success, social education, social issues, social justice, social sciences, social studies, society, politics and law, space and physical sciences, Spanish, Spanish literature, speech and debate, student government, student publications, studio art, study skills, technology, technology/design, the Web, theology, theology and the arts, trigonometry, typing, U.S. government, U.S. government and politics, U.S. government and politics-AP, U.S. history, U.S. literature, U.S. Presidents, United Nations and international issues, United States government-AP, Vietnam, Vietnam history, Vietnam War, visual and performing arts, visual arts, vocal ensemble, vocal music, vocational skills, vocational-technical courses, Web authoring, Web site design, Western civilization, Western literature, wood lab, woodworking, word processing, world civilizations, world cultures, world geography, world governments, world history, world issues, world literature, world religions, world religions, world studies, World War I, World War II, world wide web design, writing, writing, writing workshop, yearbook.

Graduation Requirements Students are required to complete a total of 50 hours of service work to be eligible for graduation.

Special Academic Programs Advanced Placement exam preparation; honors section; study at local college for college credit; remedial reading and/or remedial writing; remedial math.

College Admission Counseling 82 students graduated in 2012; all went to college, including Bowling Green State University; John Carroll University; Kent State University; Ohio University; The Ohio State University; University of Dayton.

Student Life Upper grades have uniform requirement, student council. Discipline rests primarily with faculty. Attendance at religious services is required.

Summer Programs Remediation, sports, art/fine arts programs offered; session focuses on athletic and summer camps; held on campus; accepts boys and girls; open to students from other schools. 70 students usually enrolled. 2013 schedule: June to August. Application deadline: June.

Tuition and Aid Day student tuition: $7950. Tuition installment plan (monthly payment plans). Merit scholarship grants, need-based scholarship grants available. In 2012–13, 85% of upper-school students received aid.

Admissions Traditional secondary-level entrance grade is 9. No application fee required. On-campus interview required.

Athletics Interscholastic: baseball (boys), basketball (b,g), cheering (g), cross-country running (b,g), dance team (g), football (b), golf (b,g), hockey (b), ice hockey (b), indoor track (b,g), indoor track & field (b,g), soccer (b,g), softball (g), track and field (b,g), volleyball (g), wrestling (g); intramural: basketball (b,g), flag football (g); coed interscholastic: bowling; coed intramural: flag football, Frisbee, touch football, ultimate Frisbee, volleyball. 1 PE instructor, 60 coaches, 2 athletic trainers.

Computers Computers are regularly used in architecture, business, career education, career exploration, college planning, creative writing, data processing, design, desktop publishing, drafting, drawing and design, English, industrial technology, information technology, introduction to technology, keyboarding, lab/keyboard, literary magazine, newspaper, publications, publishing, research skills, science, technical drawing, technology, typing, vocational-technical courses, Web site design, word processing, writing, writing, yearbook classes. Computer network features include on-campus library services, Internet access, wireless campus network, Internet filtering or blocking technology, Schoology (online learning information system). Student e-mail accounts are available to students. Students grades are available online. The school has a published electronic and media policy.

Contact Mrs. Terri Richards, Director of Admissions. 216-481-8414 Ext. 254. Fax: 216-486-1035. E-mail: trichards@vasj.com. Web site: www.vasj.com

VILLA DUCHESNE AND OAK HILL SCHOOL

801 South Spoede Road
St. Louis, Missouri 63131

Head of School: Sr. Lucie Nordmann, RSCJ

General Information Coeducational day college-preparatory, arts, religious studies, and technology school, affiliated with Roman Catholic Church. Boys grades JK–6, girls grades JK–12. Founded: 1929. Setting: suburban. 60-acre campus. 2 buildings on campus. Approved or accredited by Independent Schools Association of the Central States, National Catholic Education Association, Network of Sacred Heart Schools, North Central Association of Colleges and Schools, and Missouri Department of Education. Member of National Association of Independent Schools. Total enrollment: 640. Upper school average class size: 15. Upper school faculty-student ratio: 1:9. There are 180 required school days per year for Upper School students. Upper School students typically attend 5 days per week. The average school day consists of 7 hours.

Upper School Student Profile 88% of students are Roman Catholic.

Faculty School total: 89. In upper school: 13 men, 44 women; 40 have advanced degrees.

Subjects Offered American government, American literature, American literature-AP, anatomy and physiology, art, biology, biology-AP, British literature, calculus, calculus-AP, campus ministry, ceramics, chemistry, chorus, civics, computers, creative writing, discrete mathematics, drawing, economics, English, European history, European history-AP, Far Eastern history, French, geography, geometry, health, integrated physics, math analysis, Middle East, music, newspaper, painting, personal development, physical education, physics, pre-algebra, pre-calculus, printmaking, psychology, public speaking, religion, scripture, sculpture, social justice, Spanish, studio art, studio art-AP, theater arts, U.S. history, U.S. history-AP, Western civilization, women's studies, world literature, yearbook.

Graduation Requirements All academic, students must perform community service to graduate.

Special Academic Programs International Baccalaureate program; 11 Advanced Placement exams for which test preparation is offered; honors section; independent study; term-away projects; study at local college for college credit; domestic exchange program (with Network of Sacred Heart Schools); study abroad; remedial reading and/or remedial writing; remedial math.

College Admission Counseling 97 students graduated in 2012; all went to college, including Marquette University; Saint Louis University; Texas Christian University; University of Missouri. Mean combined SAT: 1827, mean composite ACT: 28.

Student Life Upper grades have uniform requirement, student council, honor system. Discipline rests primarily with faculty. Attendance at religious services is required.

Summer Programs Enrichment, advancement, sports, art/fine arts, computer instruction programs offered; session focuses on enrichment and college preparation; held on campus; accepts boys and girls; open to students from other schools. 150 students usually enrolled. 2013 schedule: June 10 to June 28. Application deadline: May 30.

Tuition and Aid Day student tuition: $17,980. Tuition installment plan (monthly payment plans, individually arranged payment plans, 8-month plan, trimester plan, or full-payment plan). Tuition reduction for siblings, need-based scholarship grants available. In 2012–13, 31% of upper-school students received aid. Total amount of financial aid awarded in 2012–13: $1,148,249.

Admissions Traditional secondary-level entrance grade is 9. SSAT required. Deadline for receipt of application materials: November 21. Application fee required: $40. On-campus interview required.

Athletics Interscholastic: basketball (girls), cross-country running (g), diving (g), field hockey (g), golf (g), lacrosse (g), racquetball (g), soccer (g), softball (g), swimming and diving (g), tennis (g), track and field (g), volleyball (g). 7 PE instructors, 34 coaches, 1 athletic trainer.

Computers Computers are regularly used in all academic classes. Computer network features include on-campus library services, online commercial services, Internet access, wireless campus network, Internet filtering or blocking technology, students in grades 7 to 12 have personal HP tablet PCs. Campus intranet, student e-mail accounts, and computer access in designated common areas are available to students. Students grades are available online. The school has a published electronic and media policy.

Contact Mrs. Elaine Brooks, Admissions Assistant. 314-810-3566. Fax: 314-432-0199. E-mail: ebrooks@vdoh.org. Web site: www.vdoh.org

VILLA JOSEPH MARIE HIGH SCHOOL

1180 Holland Road
Holland, Pennsylvania 18966

Head of School: Mrs. Mary T. Michel

General Information Girls' day college-preparatory, arts, religious studies, and drama school, affiliated with Roman Catholic Church. Grades 9–12. Founded: 1932. Setting: suburban. Nearest major city is Philadelphia. 55-acre campus. 3 buildings on campus. Approved or accredited by Middle States Association of Colleges and Schools and Pennsylvania Department of Education. Total enrollment: 367. Upper school average class size: 15. Upper school faculty-student ratio: 1:10. There are 167 required school days per year for Upper School students. Upper School students typically attend 5 days per week. The average school day consists of 6 hours and 45 minutes.

Upper School Student Profile Grade 9: 109 students (109 girls); Grade 10: 87 students (87 girls); Grade 11: 87 students (87 girls); Grade 12: 84 students (84 girls). 98% of students are Roman Catholic.

Faculty School total: 36. In upper school: 6 men, 30 women; 27 have advanced degrees.

Subjects Offered Algebra, American government, American history, American history-AP, anatomy and physiology, ancient history, art, art appreciation, biology, biology-AP, business mathematics, calculus-AP, chemistry, chemistry-AP, chorus, conceptual physics, dance, drama, earth science, English, English literature-AP, environmental science, environmental science-AP, European history-AP, film and literature, forensics, French, geometry, health, Italian, Latin, music, physical education, physics, physics-AP, pre-calculus, psychology, psychology-AP, sociology, Spanish, speech, studio art, theology, trigonometry, world history, writing.

Graduation Requirements Arts and fine arts (art, music, dance, drama), English, foreign language, mathematics, physical education (includes health), religion (includes Bible studies and theology), science, social sciences, social studies (includes history), service hours requirement.

Special Academic Programs 13 Advanced Placement exams for which test preparation is offered; honors section; independent study; study at local college for college credit; academic accommodation for the gifted, the musically talented, and the artistically talented.

College Admission Counseling 88 students graduated in 2012; all went to college, including Drexel University; Penn State University Park; Saint Joseph's University; The University of Scranton; University of Delaware; Ursinus College. Mean SAT critical reading: 580, mean SAT math: 555, mean SAT writing: 603.

Student Life Upper grades have uniform requirement, student council, honor system. Discipline rests primarily with faculty. Attendance at religious services is required.

Summer Programs Enrichment, advancement, sports programs offered; session focuses on enrichment; held on campus; accepts girls; open to students from other schools. 45 students usually enrolled. 2013 schedule: July to July.

Tuition and Aid Day student tuition: $11,650. Tuition installment plan (monthly payment plans). Tuition reduction for siblings, merit scholarship grants, need-based scholarship grants available. In 2012–13, 6% of upper-school students received aid; total upper-school merit-scholarship money awarded: $160,000.

Admissions Traditional secondary-level entrance grade is 9. For fall 2012, 200 students applied for upper-level admission, 130 were accepted, 109 enrolled. High School Placement Test required. Deadline for receipt of application materials: November 16. Application fee required: $65. On-campus interview required.

Athletics Interscholastic: basketball, cheering, cross-country running, field hockey, golf, indoor track, lacrosse, soccer, softball, swimming and diving, tennis, track and field, volleyball, winter (indoor) track. 1 PE instructor, 9 coaches, 1 athletic trainer.

Computers Computers are regularly used in art, college planning, creative writing, English, foreign language, health, history, library, literary magazine, mathematics, religion, science, yearbook classes. Computer network features include on-campus library services, online commercial services, Internet access, wireless campus network, Internet filtering or blocking technology. Computer access in designated common areas is available to students. Students grades are available online. The school has a published electronic and media policy.

Contact Mrs. Laura Lasky, Director of Admissions. 215-357-8810 Ext. 193. Fax: 215-357-9410. E-mail: llasky@vjmhs.org. Web site: www.vjmhs.org

VILLA MARIA ACADEMY

2403 West Eighth Street
Erie, Pennsylvania 16505-4492

Head of School: Fr. Scott Jabo

General Information Girls' day college-preparatory school, affiliated with Roman Catholic Church. Grades 9–12. Founded: 1892. Setting: suburban. 4 buildings on campus. Approved or accredited by Middle States Association of Colleges and Schools and National Catholic Education Association. Total enrollment: 323. Upper school average class size: 14. Upper school faculty-student ratio: 1:10. There are 180 required school days per year for Upper School students. Upper School students typically attend 5 days per week. The average school day consists of 5 hours and 36 minutes.

Upper School Student Profile Grade 9: 82 students (82 girls); Grade 10: 97 students (97 girls); Grade 11: 71 students (71 girls); Grade 12: 73 students (73 girls). 85% of students are Roman Catholic.

Faculty School total: 33. In upper school: 10 men, 23 women; 15 have advanced degrees.

Subjects Offered 3-dimensional art, advanced math, Advanced Placement courses, algebra, art, art appreciation, art-AP, arts, athletics, audio visual/media, biology, biology-AP, calculus, calculus-AP, ceramics, chemistry, chemistry-AP, choir, chorus, community service, computer applications, computer science, computer skills, computer technologies, creative writing, dance, drawing, driver education, English, English-AP, environmental science, ESL, family and consumer science, film history, fine arts, foods, foreign language, forensics, French, geometry, government, graphic arts, health, honors algebra, honors English, honors geometry, honors U.S. history, honors world history, integrated science, journalism, keyboarding, Latin, mathematics, music history, newspaper, photography, physical education, physical fitness, physics, physiology, piano, practical arts, probability and statistics, psychology, religious education, SAT preparation, SAT/ACT preparation, science, senior project, social studies, Spanish, speech, student government, technology, textiles, theater, theology, trigonometry, U.S. history, U.S. history-AP, Web site design, word processing, world history, yearbook.

Graduation Requirements Arts and fine arts (art, music, dance, drama), English, foreign language, health, mathematics, physical education (includes health), religion (includes Bible studies and theology), science, social studies (includes history), speech, technology. Community service is required.

Special Academic Programs 6 Advanced Placement exams for which test preparation is offered; honors section; study at local college for college credit; ESL (14 students enrolled).

College Admission Counseling 57 students graduated in 2012; 55 went to college, including Gannon University; Indiana University of Pennsylvania; John Carroll University; Mercyhurst College; Seton Hill University. Other: 2 went to work.

Student Life Upper grades have uniform requirement, student council, honor system. Discipline rests primarily with faculty.

Summer Programs Remediation programs offered; session focuses on remediation; held on campus; accepts girls; not open to students from other schools. 12 students usually enrolled.

Tuition and Aid Day student tuition: $7345–$7670. Tuition installment plan (FACTS Tuition Payment Plan). Tuition reduction for siblings, merit scholarship grants, need-based scholarship grants available. In 2012–13, 85% of upper-school students received aid; total upper-school merit-scholarship money awarded: $85,433. Total amount of financial aid awarded in 2012–13: $428,004.

Admissions Traditional secondary-level entrance grade is 9. For fall 2012, 171 students applied for upper-level admission, 155 were accepted, 86 enrolled. Placement test required. Deadline for receipt of application materials: none. No application fee required.

Athletics Interscholastic: basketball, bowling, cheering, cross-country running, golf, lacrosse, soccer, softball, swimming and diving, tennis, track and field, volleyball, water polo; intramural: bowling. 2 PE instructors, 30 coaches, 1 athletic trainer.

Computers Computers are regularly used in all academic classes. Computer network features include on-campus library services, online commercial services, Internet access, wireless campus network, Internet filtering or blocking technology. Campus intranet, student e-mail accounts, and computer access in designated common areas are available to students. Students grades are available online. The school has a published electronic and media policy.

Contact Ms. Amy Oldach, Admissions Coordinator. 814-838-2061 Ext. 3239. Fax: 814-836-0881. E-mail: Amy.Oldach@prep-villa.com. Web site: www.prep-villa.com

VILLA MARIA ACADEMY

370 Old Lincoln Highway
Malvern, Pennsylvania 19355

Head of School: Sr. Marita Carmel McCarthy, IHM

General Information Girls' day college-preparatory, arts, religious studies, and technology school, affiliated with Roman Catholic Church. Grades 9–12. Founded: 1872. Setting: suburban. Nearest major city is Philadelphia. 28-acre campus. 4 buildings on campus. Approved or accredited by Middle States Association of Colleges and Schools, The College Board, and Pennsylvania Department of Education. Total enrollment: 425. Upper school average class size: 15. Upper school faculty-student ratio: 1:9. There are 172 required school days per year for Upper School students. Upper School students typically attend 5 days per week. The average school day consists of 6 hours and 30 minutes.

Upper School Student Profile Grade 9: 102 students (102 girls); Grade 10: 104 students (104 girls); Grade 11: 106 students (106 girls); Grade 12: 113 students (113 girls). 95% of students are Roman Catholic.

Faculty School total: 51. In upper school: 9 men, 41 women; 40 have advanced degrees.

Subjects Offered Accounting, advanced chemistry, advanced math, algebra, American government, American literature, analysis, art, Bible, biology, biology-AP, British literature, British literature (honors), calculus, calculus-AP, Catholic belief and practice, chemistry, chemistry-AP, choral music, church history, college counseling, computer applications, computer literacy, discrete mathematics, drama, driver education, English, English composition, English language-AP, English literature, English literature-AP, environmental science, European history, European history-AP, first aid, French, French-AP, geography, geometry, government-AP, grammar, guidance, health education, history of the Catholic Church, honors algebra, honors English, honors geometry, honors U.S. history, honors world history, information design technology, keyboarding, Latin, library skills, literary magazine, modern European history, modern European history-AP, music performance, music theory, music-AP, orchestra, physical education, physics, physics-AP, piano, psychology-AP, religious studies, social studies, Spanish, Spanish language-AP, statistics, statistics-AP, studio art, studio art-AP, trigonometry, U.S. history, U.S. history-AP, vocal ensemble, voice, Western civilization, world issues.

Graduation Requirements Catholic belief and practice, college admission preparation, computer applications, English, foreign language, mathematics, physical education (includes health), science, social studies (includes history), theology.

College Admission Counseling 111 students graduated in 2011; 109 went to college, including Drexel University; Penn State University Park; Saint Joseph's University; University of Delaware; University of Pittsburgh; Villanova University. Other: 1 went to work, 1 entered military service. 38% scored over 600 on SAT critical reading, 39% scored over 600 on SAT math, 49% scored over 600 on SAT writing, 47% scored over 1800 on combined SAT, 42% scored over 26 on composite ACT.

Student Life Upper grades have uniform requirement, student council, honor system. Discipline rests equally with students and faculty. Attendance at religious services is required.

Tuition and Aid Day student tuition: $14,100. Tuition installment plan (monthly payment plans). Tuition reduction for siblings, merit scholarship grants, need-based scholarship grants available. In 2011–12, 28% of upper-school students received aid; total upper-school merit-scholarship money awarded: $248,600. Total amount of financial aid awarded in 2011–12: $506,986.

Admissions Traditional secondary-level entrance grade is 9. For fall 2011, 226 students applied for upper-level admission, 185 were accepted, 102 enrolled. High School Placement Test required. Deadline for receipt of application materials: December 8. Application fee required: $50. On-campus interview recommended.

Athletics Interscholastic: basketball, cross-country running, dance team, field hockey, golf, indoor track, indoor track & field, lacrosse, soccer, softball, swimming and diving, tennis, track and field, volleyball, winter (indoor) track. 2 PE instructors, 12 coaches, 1 athletic trainer.

Computers Computers are regularly used in accounting, art, Bible studies, Christian doctrine, college planning, economics, English, French, geography, health, history, humanities, Latin, library skills, mathematics, music, psychology, publications, religious studies, science, social studies, Spanish, theology, writing, yearbook classes. Computer network features include on-campus library services, online commercial services, Internet access, wireless campus network, Internet filtering or blocking technology. Campus intranet, student e-mail accounts, and computer access in designated common areas are available to students. Students grades are available online. The school has a published electronic and media policy.

Contact Mrs. Mary Kay D. Napoli, Director of Admissions. 610-644-2551 Ext. 1020. Fax: 610-644-2866. E-mail: mknapoli@vmahs.org. Web site: www.vmahs.org

VILLA VICTORIA ACADEMY

376 West Upper Ferry Road
Ewing, New Jersey 08628

Head of School: Sr. Lillian Harrington, MPF

General Information Girls' day college-preparatory, arts, religious studies, and technology school, affiliated with Roman Catholic Church. Grades PK–12. Founded: 1933. Setting: suburban. Nearest major city is Trenton. 44-acre campus. 7 buildings on campus. Approved or accredited by Middle States Association of Colleges and Schools, National Catholic Education Association, and New Jersey Department of Education. Member of National Association of Independent Schools and Secondary School Admission Test Board. Total enrollment: 202. Upper school average class size: 12. Upper school faculty-student ratio: 1:6. There are 180 required school days per year for Upper School students. Upper School students typically attend 5 days per week. The average school day consists of 6 hours and 20 minutes.

Upper School Student Profile Grade 9: 16 students (16 girls); Grade 10: 16 students (16 girls); Grade 11: 17 students (17 girls); Grade 12: 18 students (18 girls). 65% of students are Roman Catholic.

Faculty School total: 31. In upper school: 5 men, 15 women; 13 have advanced degrees.

Subjects Offered Algebra, American literature, art, art history, art-AP, arts, arts appreciation, athletics, Bible studies, biology, calculus, calculus-AP, campus ministry, career and personal planning, career exploration, career planning, career/college preparation, Catholic belief and practice, ceramics, character education, chemistry, chemistry-AP, Chinese studies, choir, choral music, chorus, Christian education, Christian ethics, Christianity, church history, clayworking, college admission preparation, college awareness, college counseling, college placement, college planning, college writing, communication skills, community service, computer science, concert band, concert choir, creative thinking, creative writing, critical thinking, critical writing, cultural arts, current events, drama, drawing, drawing and design, earth science, English, English composition, English language and composition-AP, English literature, English literature-AP, English-AP, ethics and responsibility, European history, fiction, fine arts, French, French language-AP, French studies, French-AP, gender and religion, general business, general math, general science, geography, geometry, global issues, government, government and politics-AP, government-AP, government/civics, government/civics-AP, grammar, health, health and safety, health and wellness, health education, history, history of music, history of religion, history of the Americas, history of the Catholic Church, history-AP, honors algebra, honors English, honors geometry, honors U.S. history, honors world history, humanities, independent study, interdisciplinary studies, Internet, Internet research, interpersonal skills, language and composition, Latin, leadership, leadership and service, library research, library skills, life management skills, Life of Christ, linguistics, literary magazine, literature, literature-AP, math analysis, math applications, math methods, math review, mathematics, mathematics-AP, mechanics of writing, modern history, modern languages, modern world history, money management, moral and social development, moral reasoning, moral theology, multimedia, music, music appreciation, music history, music performance, music theater, music theory, musical productions, musical theater, musical theater dance, oil painting, painting, participation in sports, peer ministry, performing arts, personal development, personal finance, personal fitness, personal money management, photography, physical education, physics, physics-AP, play production, poetry, portfolio art, pottery, prayer/spirituality, pre-algebra, pre-calculus, public service, public speaking, qualitative analysis, reading/study skills, religion, religion and culture, religious education, research, research skills, rhetoric, SAT preparation, SAT/ACT preparation, science, science and technology, sculpture, senior humanities, senior project, senior seminar, set design, Shakespeare, skills for success, social skills, social studies, society and culture, Spanish, Spanish language-AP, Spanish-AP, sports, sports conditioning, stage design, stagecraft, strategies for success, student government, student publications, theater, theater design and production, trigonometry, U.S. history, United States government-AP, values and decisions, visual and performing arts, visual arts, vocal ensemble, world civilizations, world cultures, world history, world issues, world literature, world religions, writing.

Graduation Requirements American literature, art history, arts and fine arts (art, music, dance, drama), biology, British literature, chemistry, computer science, English, foreign language, mathematics, physical education (includes health), physics, religion (includes Bible studies and theology), SAT/ACT preparation, science, social studies (includes history), world cultures, world literature, interdisciplinary humanities. Community service is required.

Special Academic Programs Advanced Placement exam preparation; honors section; independent study; academic accommodation for the gifted, the musically talented, and the artistically talented.

College Admission Counseling 17 students graduated in 2012; all went to college, including Boston University; Fordham University; New York University; The George Washington University; University of Pennsylvania; Villanova University. Median combined SAT: 1814.

Student Life Upper grades have uniform requirement, student council, honor system. Discipline rests primarily with faculty. Attendance at religious services is required.

Summer Programs Enrichment, art/fine arts programs offered; session focuses on art and theater, enrichment; held on campus; accepts boys and girls; open to students from other schools. 25 students usually enrolled. 2013 schedule: June to July.

Tuition and Aid Day student tuition: $11,850. Tuition installment plan (FACTS Tuition Payment Plan, individually arranged payment plans, 2-payment plan). Tuition reduction for siblings, merit scholarship grants, need-based scholarship grants available. In 2012–13, 30% of upper-school students received aid; total upper-school merit-scholarship money awarded: $50,000.

Admissions Traditional secondary-level entrance grade is 9. School placement exam or SSAT required. Deadline for receipt of application materials: December 13. Application fee required: $50. On-campus interview required.

Athletics Interscholastic: basketball, cross-country running, soccer, softball, tennis, track and field; intramural: dance, outdoor activities, outdoor education, walking. 1 PE instructor, 4 coaches.

Computers Computers are regularly used in art, English, foreign language, history, mathematics, music, SAT preparation, science, theater classes. Computer network features include on-campus library services, Internet access, wireless campus network, Internet filtering or blocking technology, each student in 9-11 grade have their own NetBook for use in school and home. Computer access in designated common areas is available to students. Students grades are available online. The school has a published electronic and media policy.

Contact Ms. Lori Hoffman, Director of Admissions. 609-882-1700 Ext. 19. Fax: 609-882-8421. E-mail: lhoffman@villavictoria.org. Web site: www.villavictoria.org

VILLA WALSH ACADEMY

455 Western Avenue
Morristown, New Jersey 07960

Head of School: Sr. Patricia Pompa

General Information Girls' day college-preparatory, arts, religious studies, and technology school, affiliated with Roman Catholic Church. Grades 7–12. Founded: 1967. Setting: suburban. Nearest major city is New York, NY. 130-acre campus. 3 buildings on campus. Approved or accredited by Middle States Association of Colleges and Schools, National Catholic Education Association, and New Jersey Department of

Education. Endowment: $5 million. Total enrollment: 260. Upper school average class size: 12. Upper school faculty-student ratio: 1:8. There are 176 required school days per year for Upper School students. Upper School students typically attend 5 days per week. The average school day consists of 6 hours and 30 minutes.

Upper School Student Profile Grade 9: 58 students (58 girls); Grade 10: 59 students (59 girls); Grade 11: 56 students (56 girls); Grade 12: 57 students (57 girls). 90% of students are Roman Catholic.

Faculty School total: 35. In upper school: 3 men, 32 women; 20 have advanced degrees.

Subjects Offered Advanced Placement courses, algebra, American history, American literature, anatomy and physiology, art, Bible as literature, biology, biology-AP, British literature, British literature (honors), calculus, calculus-AP, career/college preparation, chemistry, chemistry-AP, choral music, chorus, church history, college admission preparation, computer applications, computer graphics, computer literacy, computer processing, computer programming, computer science, computer skills, CPR, creative writing, desktop publishing, driver education, economics, economics and history, English, English language and composition-AP, English literature, ethics, European civilization, European history-AP, family living, finite math, first aid, French, French language-AP, French-AP, geometry, health education, honors English, honors geometry, honors U.S. history, Italian, keyboarding, life science, mathematics, modern European history, moral theology, philosophy, physical education, physics, physics-AP, pre-algebra, pre-calculus, psychology, psychology-AP, religion, Spanish, Spanish-AP, statistics-AP, studio art, theology, U.S. government and politics, U.S. history, U.S. history-AP, voice ensemble, Web site design, world history, world literature.

Graduation Requirements Arts and fine arts (art, music, dance, drama), English, foreign language, mathematics, physical education (includes health), science, social studies (includes history), theology.

Special Academic Programs 12 Advanced Placement exams for which test preparation is offered; honors section; independent study; academic accommodation for the gifted, the musically talented, and the artistically talented.

College Admission Counseling 54 students graduated in 2012; all went to college, including Boston College; Boston University; College of the Holy Cross; Cornell University; University of Pennsylvania; Villanova University. Mean SAT critical reading: 660, mean SAT math: 660, mean SAT writing: 700, mean combined SAT: 2020.

Student Life Upper grades have uniform requirement, student council, honor system. Discipline rests primarily with faculty. Attendance at religious services is required.

Tuition and Aid Day student tuition: $17,000. Tuition installment plan (Insured Tuition Payment Plan, Key Tuition Payment Plan, individually arranged payment plans). Merit scholarship grants, need-based scholarship grants available. In 2012–13, 12% of upper-school students received aid; total upper-school merit-scholarship money awarded: $10,000. Total amount of financial aid awarded in 2012–13: $140,000.

Admissions Traditional secondary-level entrance grade is 9. For fall 2012, 150 students applied for upper-level admission, 70 were accepted, 60 enrolled. Math, reading, and mental ability tests and writing sample required. Deadline for receipt of application materials: none. Application fee required: $50. On-campus interview required.

Athletics Interscholastic: basketball, cross-country running, indoor track, lacrosse, soccer, softball, swimming and diving, tennis, track and field, volleyball, winter (indoor) track. 1 PE instructor, 32 coaches, 1 athletic trainer.

Computers Computers are regularly used in college planning, desktop publishing, independent study, keyboarding, library science, mathematics, newspaper, programming, SAT preparation, science, technology, Web site design, word processing, yearbook classes. Computer network features include on-campus library services, Internet access, wireless campus network, Internet filtering or blocking technology. Campus intranet is available to students. The school has a published electronic and media policy.

Contact Sr. Doris Lavinthal, Director. 973-538-3680 Ext. 175. Fax: 973-538-6733. E-mail: lavinthald@aol.com. Web site: www.villawalsh.org

VISITATION ACADEMY OF ST. LOUIS COUNTY

3020 North Ballas Road
St. Louis, Missouri 63131

Head of School: Mrs. Rosalie Henry

General Information Coeducational day (boys' only in lower grades) college-preparatory, arts, and technology school, affiliated with Roman Catholic Church. Boys grade PK, girls grades PK–12. Founded: 1833. Setting: suburban. 30-acre campus. 1 building on campus. Approved or accredited by Independent Schools Association of the Central States, National Catholic Education Association, North Central Association of Colleges and Schools, and Missouri Department of Education. Member of National Association of Independent Schools. Endowment: $7 million. Total enrollment: 633. Upper school average class size: 18. Upper school faculty-student ratio: 1:9. There are 176 required school days per year for Upper School students. Upper School students typically attend 5 days per week. The average school day consists of 7 hours.

Upper School Student Profile Grade 7: 54 students (54 girls); Grade 8: 77 students (77 girls); Grade 9: 96 students (96 girls); Grade 10: 96 students (96 girls); Grade 11: 64 students (64 girls); Grade 12: 71 students (71 girls). 85% of students are Roman Catholic.

Faculty School total: 52. In upper school: 8 men, 44 women; 31 have advanced degrees.

Subjects Offered Adolescent issues, advanced biology, advanced chemistry, advanced math, Advanced Placement courses, algebra, American history, American history-AP, American literature, American literature-AP, anatomy, anatomy and physiology, art, art appreciation, art history, bell choir, Bible studies, biology, biology-AP, calculus, calculus-AP, ceramics, character education, chemistry, chemistry-AP, choral music, chorus, Christian studies, Christian testament, church history, civics, classical language, computer art, computer math, computer programming, computer science, concert choir, creative writing, drama, earth science, economics, economics and history, English, English literature, English literature-AP, environmental science, European history, European history-AP, expository writing, fine arts, French, French-AP, genetics, geography, geometry, government/civics, grammar, health, history, independent study, journalism, keyboarding, Latin, mathematics, music, New Testament, photo shop, photography, physical education, physical science, physics, pre-calculus, psychology, science, social studies, Spanish, speech, statistics-AP, theater, theology, trigonometry, U.S. history-AP, world geography, world literature.

Graduation Requirements Arts and fine arts (art, music, dance, drama), computers, electives, English, foreign language, mathematics, physical education (includes health), science, social studies (includes history), theology, 120 hours of community service.

Special Academic Programs 12 Advanced Placement exams for which test preparation is offered; honors section; independent study; study at local college for college credit; special instructional classes for mild learning differences.

College Admission Counseling 88 students graduated in 2011; all went to college, including Auburn University; Indiana University Bloomington; Saint Louis University; Spring Hill College; University of Missouri; Washington University in St. Louis. Median SAT critical reading: 605, median SAT math: 620, median SAT writing: 610, median combined SAT: 1840, median composite ACT: 29.

Student Life Upper grades have uniform requirement, student council. Discipline rests primarily with faculty. Attendance at religious services is required.

Tuition and Aid Day student tuition: $15,775. Tuition installment plan (FACTS Tuition Payment Plan). Need-based scholarship grants available. In 2011–12, 10% of upper-school students received aid.

Admissions Traditional secondary-level entrance grade is 7. For fall 2011, 92 students applied for upper-level admission, 90 were accepted, 71 enrolled. SSAT required. Deadline for receipt of application materials: January 20. Application fee required: $75. On-campus interview required.

Athletics Interscholastic: basketball, cheering, cross-country running, dance, diving, field hockey, golf, lacrosse, racquetball, soccer, softball, swimming and diving, tennis, track and field, volleyball; intramural: cheering, dance. 4 PE instructors, 17 coaches, 1 athletic trainer.

Computers Computers are regularly used in art, English, foreign language, history, mathematics, science, theology classes. Computer network features include on-campus library services, Internet access, wireless campus network, Internet filtering or blocking technology. Campus intranet and student e-mail accounts are available to students. Students grades are available online. The school has a published electronic and media policy.

Contact Mrs. Ashley Giljum, Director of Admission. 314-625-9102. Fax: 314-432-7210. E-mail: agiljum@visitationacademy.org. Web site: www.visitationacademy.org

WAKEFIELD SCHOOL

4439 Old Tavern Road
PO Box 107
The Plains, Virginia 20198

Head of School: Mr. Peter A. Quinn

General Information Coeducational day college-preparatory and arts school; primarily serves students with learning disabilities. Grades PS–12. Founded: 1972. Setting: rural. Nearest major city is Washington, DC. 65-acre campus. 6 buildings on campus. Approved or accredited by Virginia Association of Independent Schools and Virginia Department of Education. Member of National Association of Independent Schools. Total enrollment: 397. Upper school average class size: 16. Upper school faculty-student ratio: 1:16. There are 180 required school days per year for Upper School students. Upper School students typically attend 5 days per week. The average school day consists of 7 hours.

Upper School Student Profile Grade 9: 49 students (22 boys, 27 girls); Grade 10: 43 students (19 boys, 24 girls); Grade 11: 28 students (14 boys, 14 girls); Grade 12: 32 students (11 boys, 21 girls).

Faculty School total: 83. In upper school: 15 men, 13 women; 13 have advanced degrees.

Subjects Offered Acting, Advanced Placement courses, algebra, American government, American history-AP, American literature, art, art history, bell choir, biology, biology-AP, British history, British literature, calculus, calculus-AP, chemistry, chemistry-AP, chorus, classical language, composition, computer applications, computer programming, conservation, drama, dramatic arts, earth science, Eastern world civilizations, ecology, English language and composition-AP, English literature and composition-AP, environmental science, environmental science-AP, European history-AP, French, French language-AP, geometry, geopolitics, government and politics-AP, government/civics, Latin, Latin-AP, model United Nations, music, music composition, music history, music theory, music theory-AP, physical fitness, physics, physics-AP, political science, psychology, publications, Spanish, Spanish language-AP, statistics, statistics-AP, studio art, studio art-AP, U.S. history, world civilizations.

Graduation Requirements Advanced math, algebra, American history, American literature, arts, biology, British literature, chemistry, composition, computer literacy, English, foreign language, geometry, government/civics, grammar, language, literature, physical education (includes health), pre-calculus, world civilizations, 2 interdisciplinary compositions, 2 thesis and portfolio projects, including senior thesis.

Special Academic Programs 11 Advanced Placement exams for which test preparation is offered; honors section; independent study; programs in general development for dyslexic students.

College Admission Counseling 40 students graduated in 2012; all went to college, including American University; Old Dominion University; University of Virginia; Wake Forest University. Mean SAT critical reading: 622, mean SAT math: 597, mean SAT writing: 601, mean combined SAT: 1820.

Student Life Upper grades have uniform requirement, student council, honor system. Discipline rests equally with students and faculty.

Summer Programs Remediation, enrichment, advancement, sports, art/fine arts, computer instruction programs offered; session focuses on academics, athletics, fine arts, fun; held both on and off campus; held at various locations; accepts boys and girls; open to students from other schools. 200 students usually enrolled. 2013 schedule: June 17 to July 26.

Tuition and Aid Day student tuition: $3040–$22,700. Tuition installment plan (FACTS Tuition Payment Plan, monthly payment plans, The Tuition Refund Plan). Need-based scholarship grants available. In 2012–13, 25% of upper-school students received aid. Total amount of financial aid awarded in 2012–13: $1,000,000.

Admissions Traditional secondary-level entrance grade is 9. Admissions testing or SSAT required. Deadline for receipt of application materials: none. Application fee required: $60. Interview required.

Athletics Interscholastic: basketball (boys, girls), field hockey (g), lacrosse (b,g), soccer (b,g), squash (b), strength & conditioning (b,g), tennis (b,g), volleyball (g); intramural: field hockey (g), fitness (b,g), lacrosse (b,g), outdoor activities (b,g), soccer (b,g), squash (b), strength & conditioning (b,g), tennis (b,g), volleyball (g), weight training (b,g); coed interscholastic: aquatics, cross-country running, fitness, golf, physical fitness, squash, swimming and diving; coed intramural: aquatics, cross-country running, squash, swimming and diving. 4 PE instructors, 3 coaches, 1 athletic trainer.

Computers Computers are regularly used in all academic, publications, yearbook classes. Computer network features include on-campus library services, online commercial services, Internet access, wireless campus network, Internet filtering or blocking technology, new Science and Technology building opened in January 2007, student center login/password protected portal for students on new Web site. Campus intranet, student e-mail accounts, and computer access in designated common areas are available to students. Students grades are available online. The school has a published electronic and media policy.

Contact Office of Admissions. 540-253-7600. Fax: 540-253-5492. E-mail: admissions@wakefieldschool.org. Web site: www.wakefieldschool.org

WALDORF HIGH SCHOOL OF MASSACHUSETTS BAY

160 Lexington Street
Belmont, Massachusetts 02478

Head of School: Mara D. White

General Information Coeducational day college-preparatory and arts school. Grades 9–12. Founded: 1996. Setting: suburban. Nearest major city is Boston. 1 building on campus. Approved or accredited by Association of Independent Schools in New England, Association of Waldorf Schools of North America, New England Association of Schools and Colleges, and Massachusetts Department of Education. Total enrollment: 57. Upper school average class size: 14. Upper school faculty-student ratio: 1:7. There are 165 required school days per year for Upper School students. Upper School students typically attend 5 days per week. The average school day consists of 6 hours and 30 minutes.

Upper School Student Profile Grade 9: 17 students (5 boys, 12 girls); Grade 10: 13 students (5 boys, 8 girls); Grade 11: 11 students (3 boys, 8 girls); Grade 12: 16 students (7 boys, 9 girls).

Faculty School total: 12. In upper school: 4 men, 4 women; 3 have advanced degrees.

Subjects Offered Algebra, American history, American literature, American studies, analysis and differential calculus, anatomy and physiology, ancient history, ancient world history, art, art history, astronomy, athletics, Bible as literature, biology, bookbinding, botany, calculus, chamber groups, chemistry, chorus, classical Greek literature, college admission preparation, college counseling, college placement, community service, computer applications, computer programming, creative writing, current events, digital art, drama, drama performance, earth science, electives, English, English literature, epic literature, European history, expository writing, fine arts, fitness, geography, geometry, global studies, grammar, health education, jazz ensemble, mathematics, medieval/Renaissance history, model United Nations, modern history, music, Native American history, painting, photography, physical education, physics, play production, poetry, projective geometry, Russian literature, SAT preparation, senior internship, senior seminar, Spanish, theory of knowledge, trigonometry, U.S. government, woodworking, world history, world literature, writing, yearbook, zoology.

Graduation Requirements Algebra, arts and fine arts (art, music, dance, drama), chemistry, English, English literature, foreign language, geometry, global studies, mathematics, music, performing arts, physical education (includes health), physics, practical arts, science, social studies (includes history). Community service is required.

Special Academic Programs Honors section; independent study; term-away projects; study abroad.

College Admission Counseling 13 students graduated in 2012; 8 went to college, including Boston University; Connecticut College; Oberlin College; University of California, Santa Barbara; Wheaton College. Other: 5 went to work.

Student Life Upper grades have specified standards of dress, student council. Discipline rests primarily with faculty.

Tuition and Aid Day student tuition: $25,200. Tuition installment plan (monthly payment plans, individually arranged payment plans). Tuition reduction for siblings, merit scholarship grants, need-based scholarship grants available. In 2012–13, 40% of upper-school students received aid; total upper-school merit-scholarship money awarded: $4000. Total amount of financial aid awarded in 2012–13: $357,455.

Admissions Traditional secondary-level entrance grade is 9. For fall 2012, 33 students applied for upper-level admission, 30 were accepted, 24 enrolled. Essay, grade equivalent tests or math and English placement tests required. Deadline for receipt of application materials: none. Application fee required: $50. Interview required.

Athletics Interscholastic: basketball (boys, girls), soccer (b,g); coed intramural: running, ultimate Frisbee. 2 coaches.

Computers Computers are regularly used in college planning, creative writing, current events, independent study, mathematics, photography, research skills, SAT preparation, Spanish, yearbook classes. Computer network features include Internet access, Internet filtering or blocking technology. Computer access in designated common areas is available to students. The school has a published electronic and media policy.

Contact Susan Morris, Enrollment Coordinator. 617-489-6600 Ext. 11. Fax: 617-489-6619. E-mail: s.morris@waldorfhighschool.org. Web site: www.waldorfhighschool.org

THE WALDORF SCHOOL OF GARDEN CITY

225 Cambridge Avenue
Garden City, New York 11530

Head of School: Ms. Sabine Kully

General Information Coeducational day college-preparatory, arts, and liberal arts school. Grades N–12. Founded: 1947. Setting: suburban. Nearest major city is New York. 10-acre campus. 1 building on campus. Approved or accredited by Association of Waldorf Schools of North America, Middle States Association of Colleges and Schools, New York State Association of Independent Schools, and New York Department of Education. Member of National Association of Independent Schools and Secondary School Admission Test Board. Total enrollment: 350. Upper school average class size: 25. Upper school faculty-student ratio: 1:5. There are 170 required school days per year for Upper School students. Upper School students typically attend 5 days per week. The average school day consists of 7 hours and 10 minutes.

Upper School Student Profile Grade 6: 21 students (11 boys, 10 girls); Grade 7: 23 students (7 boys, 16 girls); Grade 8: 23 students (10 boys, 13 girls); Grade 9: 29 students (14 boys, 15 girls); Grade 10: 25 students (13 boys, 12 girls); Grade 11: 24 students (11 boys, 13 girls); Grade 12: 27 students (14 boys, 13 girls).

Faculty School total: 50. In upper school: 9 men, 12 women; 14 have advanced degrees.

Subjects Offered Algebra, American history, American literature, anatomy, art, art history, biology, botany, calculus, cartography, chemistry, computer science, creative writing, dance, drama, earth science, economics, English, English literature, European history, expository writing, fine arts, French, geography, geology, geometry, German, government/civics, grammar, health, history, mathematics, model United Nations, music, physical education, physics, physiology, science, sculpture, social studies, speech, trigonometry, woodworking, world history, world literature, writing, zoology.

Graduation Requirements Applied arts, arts and fine arts (art, music, dance, drama), English, French, German, history of architecture, history of drama, history of music, history of science, literature, medieval history, medieval/Renaissance history, music, organic chemistry, physical education (includes health), science, social studies (includes history).

Special Academic Programs 3 Advanced Placement exams for which test preparation is offered; independent study; study abroad; academic accommodation for the musically talented and the artistically talented.

College Admission Counseling Colleges students went to include American University; Boston College; Dartmouth College; Fordham University; Rochester Institute of Technology; Wellesley College. 35% scored over 600 on SAT critical reading, 40% scored over 600 on SAT math, 14% scored over 600 on SAT writing, 45% scored over 26 on composite ACT.

Student Life Upper grades have specified standards of dress, student council, honor system. Discipline rests equally with students and faculty.

Summer Programs Enrichment programs offered; session focuses on music, drama, field trips, tennis, painting, crafts, puppetry, swimming, athletics; held both on and off campus; held at Camp Glen Brook (programs in summer and winter); accepts boys and girls; open to students from other schools. 80 students usually enrolled. 2013 schedule: June 25 to August 3. Application deadline: none.

Tuition and Aid Day student tuition: $19,000. Tuition installment plan (FACTS Tuition Payment Plan). Merit scholarship grants, need-based scholarship grants available. In 2012–13, 35% of upper-school students received aid; total upper-school merit-scholarship money awarded: $30,000. Total amount of financial aid awarded in 2012–13: $180,000.

Admissions SSAT required. Deadline for receipt of application materials: none. Application fee required: $50. On-campus interview required.

Athletics Interscholastic: baseball (boys, girls), basketball (b,g), cross-country running (b,g), independent competitive sports (b,g), physical fitness (b,g), soccer (b,g), softball (g), volleyball (g); intramural: artistic gym (b,g), cooperative games (b,g), dance (b,g), fitness (b,g), volleyball (b,g); coed interscholastic: baseball, outdoor education, ropes courses, soccer; coed intramural: artistic gym, dance, fitness, volleyball. 2 PE instructors, 6 coaches.

Computers Computers are regularly used in research skills, science, yearbook classes. Computer network features include Internet access, wireless campus network, Internet filtering or blocking technology. Computer access in designated common areas is available to students. The school has a published electronic and media policy.

Contact Mrs. Carol Proctor, Admissions Assistant. 516-742-3434 Ext. 129. Fax: 516-742-3457. E-mail: proctorc@waldorfgarden.org. Web site: www.waldorfgarden.org

THE WALDORF SCHOOL OF SARATOGA SPRINGS

122 Regent Street
Saratoga Springs, New York 12866

Head of School: Ms. Katherine Scharff

General Information Coeducational day college-preparatory, general academic, and arts school. Grades PK–12. Founded: 1981. Setting: suburban. 5-acre campus. 1 building on campus. Approved or accredited by Association of Waldorf Schools of North America, New York State Association of Independent Schools, and New York Department of Education. Total enrollment: 252. Upper school average class size: 13. Upper school faculty-student ratio: 1:3. There are 170 required school days per year for Upper School students. Upper School students typically attend 5 days per week. The average school day consists of 7 hours and 20 minutes.

Upper School Student Profile Grade 9: 9 students (2 boys, 7 girls); Grade 10: 14 students (9 boys, 5 girls); Grade 11: 15 students (8 boys, 7 girls); Grade 12: 9 students (5 boys, 4 girls).

Faculty School total: 24. In upper school: 6 men, 9 women; 7 have advanced degrees.

Graduation Requirements Art, chemistry, earth science, English, eurythmy, foreign language, history, life science, mathematics, music, physical education (includes health), physics, juniors must complete an internship program, seniors must complete a senior project.

Special Academic Programs Study abroad.

College Admission Counseling 13 students graduated in 2012; 11 went to college, including Drexel University; Eugene Lang College The New School for Liberal Arts; Massachusetts Institute of Technology; Rhode Island School of Design; University at Albany, State University of New York; Wesleyan University. Other: 2 had other specific plans.

Student Life Upper grades have specified standards of dress, honor system. Discipline rests primarily with faculty.

Tuition and Aid Day student tuition: $12,800. Tuition installment plan (monthly payment plans). Tuition reduction for siblings, need-based scholarship grants available. In 2012–13, 30% of upper-school students received aid.

Admissions Traditional secondary-level entrance grade is 9. Non-standardized placement tests required. Deadline for receipt of application materials: none. No application fee required. Interview required.

Athletics Interscholastic: cross-country running (boys, girls), rowing (b,g); coed intramural: archery, climbing, fencing, hiking/backpacking, ice skating, outdoor activities, outdoor adventure, outdoor recreation, outdoor skills. 2 PE instructors.

Computers The school has a published electronic and media policy.

Contact Ms. Debra Nicastro, Admissions Coordinator. 518-587-2224. Fax: 518-581-1466. E-mail: admissions@waldorfsaratoga.org. Web site: www.waldorfsaratoga.org/

THE WALKER SCHOOL

700 Cobb Parkway North
Marietta, Georgia 30062

Head of School: Jack Hall

General Information Coeducational day college-preparatory, arts, bilingual studies, and technology school. Grades PK–12. Founded: 1957. Setting: suburban. Nearest major city is Atlanta. 32-acre campus. 7 buildings on campus. Approved or accredited by Southern Association of Colleges and Schools and Southern Association of Independent Schools. Member of National Association of Independent Schools and Secondary School Admission Test Board. Endowment: $1.8 million. Total enrollment: 1,049. Upper school average class size: 15. Upper school faculty-student ratio: 1:15. There are 178 required school days per year for Upper School students. Upper School students typically attend 5 days per week. The average school day consists of 7 hours.

Upper School Student Profile Grade 9: 96 students (46 boys, 50 girls); Grade 10: 86 students (43 boys, 43 girls); Grade 11: 103 students (55 boys, 48 girls); Grade 12: 94 students (52 boys, 42 girls).

Faculty School total: 130. In upper school: 28 men, 17 women; 42 have advanced degrees.

Subjects Offered Acting, algebra, American history, American literature, analysis, anatomy, ancient world history, art, art-AP, band, biology, biology-AP, calculus, calculus-AP, chemistry, chemistry-AP, chorus, comparative government and politics-AP, computer science, computer science-AP, dance, drama, economics, economics-AP, English, English composition, English language and composition-AP, English literature, English literature and composition-AP, English-AP, European history, expository writing, fine arts, fitness, French, French language-AP, French literature-AP, genetics, geometry, German, German-AP, government and politics-AP, government-AP, government/civics, grammar, history, history-AP, honors English, honors geometry, Latin, Latin-AP, law, linear algebra, literature and composition-AP, macro/microeconomics-AP, mathematics, modern world history, multimedia design, music, music theory-AP, musical theater, newspaper, oceanography, orchestra, personal finance, philosophy, physical education, physics, physics-AP, play production, post-calculus, psychology, public speaking, science, science research, social studies, Spanish, Spanish-AP, stagecraft, statistics, statistics-AP, trigonometry, U.S. history-AP, Web site design, world history, world history-AP, world literature, writing.

Graduation Requirements Advanced Placement courses, American government, arts and fine arts (art, music, dance, drama), computer science, English, English composition, English literature, foreign language, mathematics, physical education (includes health), science, social studies (includes history).

Special Academic Programs 25 Advanced Placement exams for which test preparation is offered; honors section; independent study; study abroad; academic accommodation for the gifted, the musically talented, and the artistically talented.

College Admission Counseling 80 students graduated in 2011; all went to college, including Auburn University; Elon University; Georgia College & State University; Georgia Institute of Technology; Georgia Southern University; University of Georgia. 49% scored over 600 on SAT critical reading, 53% scored over 600 on SAT math, 43% scored over 600 on SAT writing, 43% scored over 1800 on combined SAT, 41% scored over 26 on composite ACT.

Student Life Upper grades have specified standards of dress, student council, honor system. Discipline rests equally with students and faculty.

Tuition and Aid Day student tuition: $17,950. Tuition installment plan (school's own payment plan (1, 3, or 7 payments)). Need-based scholarship grants available. In 2011–12, 17% of upper-school students received aid. Total amount of financial aid awarded in 2011–12: $480,600.

Admissions Traditional secondary-level entrance grade is 9. For fall 2011, 93 students applied for upper-level admission, 73 were accepted, 49 enrolled. Otis-Lennon School Ability Test, SSAT or WISC III or Stanford Achievement Test required. Deadline for receipt of application materials: February 20. Application fee required: $75. On-campus interview required.

Athletics Interscholastic: aquatics (boys, girls), baseball (b), basketball (b,g), cheering (g), cross-country running (b,g), football (b), golf (b,g), physical training (b,g), soccer (b,g), softball (g), swimming and diving (b,g), tennis (b,g), track and field (b,g), volleyball (g), wrestling (b); intramural: aerobics (g), cross-country running (g), strength & conditioning (b,g), weight training (b,g); coed interscholastic: cross-country running, diving, golf, swimming and diving; coed intramural: fishing, fly fishing, rugby. 3 PE instructors, 3 coaches, 2 athletic trainers.

Computers Computers are regularly used in art, drawing and design, English, foreign language, history, information technology, introduction to technology, literary magazine, mathematics, news writing, newspaper, science, writing classes. Computer network features include on-campus library services, online commercial services, Internet access, wireless campus network, Internet filtering or blocking technology. Student e-mail accounts are available to students. Students grades are available online. The school has a published electronic and media policy.

Contact Patricia H. Mozley, Director of Admission. 678-581-6921. Fax: 770-514-8122. E-mail: patty.mozley@thewalkerschool.org. Web site: www.thewalkerschool.org

WALNUT HILL SCHOOL FOR THE ARTS

12 Highland Street
Natick, Massachusetts 01760-2199

Head of School: Mr. Antonio Viva

General Information Coeducational boarding and day college-preparatory and arts school. Grades 9–PG. Founded: 1893. Setting: suburban. Nearest major city is Boston. Students are housed in single-sex dormitories. 30-acre campus. 19 buildings on campus. Approved or accredited by New England Association of Schools and Colleges and Massachusetts Department of Education. Member of National Association of Independent Schools and Secondary School Admission Test Board. Endowment: $12 million. Total enrollment: 298. Upper school average class size: 14. Upper school faculty-student ratio: 1:6.

Upper School Student Profile Grade 9: 43 students (15 boys, 28 girls); Grade 10: 71 students (19 boys, 52 girls); Grade 11: 86 students (27 boys, 59 girls); Grade 12:

98 students (36 boys, 62 girls). 80% of students are boarding students. 31% are state residents. 32 states are represented in upper school student body. 32% are international students. International students from Canada, China, Republic of Korea, Taiwan, Thailand, and United Kingdom; 6 other countries represented in student body.

Faculty School total: 51. In upper school: 24 men, 27 women; 47 have advanced degrees; 20 reside on campus.

Subjects Offered 20th century world history, 3-dimensional art, acting, advanced chemistry, advanced math, algebra, American history, American literature, art history, arts, ballet, ballet technique, biology, calculus, ceramics, chemistry, choral music, choreography, chorus, classical music, college counseling, community service, creative writing, dance, directing, drama, drawing, English, English literature, environmental science, ESL, fine arts, French, geometry, health, history, history of dance, jazz dance, mathematics, modern dance, music history, music theory, musical theater, musical theater dance, opera, orchestra, painting, photography, physics, piano, poetry, pre-calculus, research seminar, science, sculpture, set design, Shakespeare, social studies, Spanish, stage design, technical theater, theater, theater design and production, theater production, U.S. history, visual and performing arts, visual arts, vocal music, voice, voice ensemble, world history, writing.

Graduation Requirements Arts, English, foreign language, mathematics, science, social studies (includes history), U.S. history, completion of arts portfolio, body of writing, or participation in performing arts ensembles and/or solo recital.

Special Academic Programs Advanced Placement exam preparation; honors section; independent study; academic accommodation for the gifted, the musically talented, and the artistically talented; ESL (35 students enrolled).

College Admission Counseling 96 students graduated in 2012; 90 went to college, including New England Conservatory of Music; New York University; Peabody Conservatory of The Johns Hopkins University; Pratt Institute; School of the Art Institute of Chicago; The Juilliard School. Other: 6 had other specific plans. Median SAT critical reading: 590, median SAT math: 580, median SAT writing: 580, median composite ACT: 26.

Student Life Upper grades have student council. Discipline rests equally with students and faculty.

Summer Programs Art/fine arts programs offered; session focuses on theater, ballet, writing, and opera; held both on and off campus; held at Italy (opera); accepts boys and girls; open to students from other schools. 300 students usually enrolled. 2013 schedule: June to August. Application deadline: none.

Tuition and Aid Day student tuition: $35,000; 7-day tuition and room/board: $45,900. Tuition installment plan (Insured Tuition Payment Plan, Academic Management Services Plan, monthly payment plans). Need-based scholarship grants available. In 2012–13, 50% of upper-school students received aid. Total amount of financial aid awarded in 2012–13: $2,900,000.

Admissions Traditional secondary-level entrance grade is 10. For fall 2012, 407 students applied for upper-level admission, 178 were accepted, 119 enrolled. Any standardized test, audition, TOEFL or SLEP or writing sample required. Deadline for receipt of application materials: February 1. Application fee required: $65. Interview recommended.

Athletics Intramural: self defense (girls); coed intramural: aerobics, aerobics/dance, ballet, dance, fitness, modern dance, outdoor activities, physical fitness, physical training, self defense, yoga. 3 athletic trainers.

Computers Computer network features include on-campus library services, Internet access, wireless campus network, Internet filtering or blocking technology. Campus intranet, student e-mail accounts, and computer access in designated common areas are available to students. The school has a published electronic and media policy.

Contact Mike Bucco Sr., Acting Director of Admission. 508-650-5020. Fax: 508-655-3726. E-mail: admissions@walnuthillarts.org. Web site: why.walnuthillarts.org/

WALSINGHAM ACADEMY

1100 Jamestown Road
PO Box 8702
Williamsburg, Virginia 23187-8702

Head of School: Sr. Mary Jeanne Oesterle, RSM

General Information Coeducational day college-preparatory, arts, religious studies, and technology school, affiliated with Roman Catholic Church. Grades PK–12. Founded: 1947. Setting: small town. Nearest major city is Richmond. 30-acre campus. 2 buildings on campus. Approved or accredited by National Catholic Education Association and Southern Association of Colleges and Schools. Endowment: $3 million. Total enrollment: 533. Upper school average class size: 16. Upper school faculty-student ratio: 1:7. There are 182 required school days per year for Upper School students. Upper School students typically attend 5 days per week. The average school day consists of 6 hours and 30 minutes.

Upper School Student Profile Grade 8: 47 students (21 boys, 26 girls); Grade 9: 41 students (23 boys, 18 girls); Grade 10: 35 students (18 boys, 17 girls); Grade 11: 53 students (32 boys, 21 girls); Grade 12: 43 students (19 boys, 24 girls). 47% of students are Roman Catholic.

Faculty School total: 30. In upper school: 9 men, 21 women; 25 have advanced degrees.

Subjects Offered 3-dimensional art, advanced math, Advanced Placement courses, advanced studio art-AP, algebra, American history, American history-AP, American literature, American literature-AP, ancient world history, art, band, Bible, Bible studies, biology, biology-AP, British literature-AP, calculus, calculus-AP, Catholic belief and practice, chemistry, chemistry-AP, choral music, Christian ethics, Christian scripture, church history, driver education, earth science, economics, English, English language and composition-AP, English literature, English literature and composition-AP, English literature-AP, environmental science, environmental science-AP, fine arts, French, French-AP, geography, geometry, government/civics, health, history, honors English, independent study, Latin, Latin-AP, marine science, mathematics, medieval/Renaissance history, modern world history, music, music theory-AP, newspaper, physical education, physics, physics-AP, pre-calculus, psychology, public speaking, religion, science, social justice, social studies, Spanish, Spanish-AP, statistics, statistics-AP, studio art-AP, theology, trigonometry, U.S. government and politics-AP, U.S. history-AP, world history, yearbook.

Graduation Requirements Arts and fine arts (art, music, dance, drama), English, foreign language, mathematics, physical education (includes health), religion (includes Bible studies and theology), science, social studies (includes history), 20 hours of community service each year.

Special Academic Programs 16 Advanced Placement exams for which test preparation is offered; honors section; independent study.

College Admission Counseling 62 students graduated in 2012; all went to college, including James Madison University; The Catholic University of America; University of Georgia; University of Virginia; Virginia Polytechnic Institute and State University; Wake Forest University. Mean SAT critical reading: 570, mean SAT math: 589, mean SAT writing: 574.

Student Life Upper grades have uniform requirement, student council, honor system. Discipline rests primarily with faculty. Attendance at religious services is required.

Tuition and Aid Day student tuition: $12,534. Tuition installment plan (FACTS Tuition Payment Plan). Tuition reduction for siblings, need-based scholarship grants available. Total amount of financial aid awarded in 2012–13: $190,000.

Admissions Traditional secondary-level entrance grade is 8. For fall 2012, 21 students applied for upper-level admission, 20 were accepted, 20 enrolled. Kulhmann-Anderson Level G (for grades 7-9) or Level H (for grades 10-12), TerraNova or TOEFL or SLEP required. Deadline for receipt of application materials: none. Application fee required: $100. On-campus interview required.

Athletics Interscholastic: baseball (boys), basketball (b,g), cross-country running (b,g), field hockey (g), golf (b,g), lacrosse (b,g), soccer (b,g), swimming and diving (b,g), tennis (b,g), track and field (b,g), volleyball (g); coed interscholastic: sailing. 2 PE instructors, 32 coaches, 1 athletic trainer.

Computers Computers are regularly used in all classes. Computer network features include on-campus library services, Internet access, wireless campus network, Internet filtering or blocking technology. Students grades are available online. The school has a published electronic and media policy.

Contact Mrs. Anita Magliola, Director of Admissions. 757-229-6026. E-mail: amagliola@walsingham.org. Web site: www.walsingham.org

WARING SCHOOL

35 Standley Street
Beverly, Massachusetts 01915

Head of School: Mr. Peter L. Smick

General Information Coeducational day college-preparatory school. Grades 6–12. Founded: 1972. Setting: suburban. Nearest major city is Boston. 32-acre campus. 6 buildings on campus. Approved or accredited by Association of Independent Schools in New England and New England Association of Schools and Colleges. Endowment: $4 million. Total enrollment: 152. Upper school average class size: 14. Upper school faculty-student ratio: 1:8. There are 170 required school days per year for Upper School students. Upper School students typically attend 5 days per week. The average school day consists of 9 hours.

Upper School Student Profile Grade 9: 31 students (14 boys, 17 girls); Grade 10: 27 students (12 boys, 15 girls); Grade 11: 26 students (15 boys, 11 girls); Grade 12: 21 students (7 boys, 14 girls).

Faculty School total: 45. In upper school: 14 men, 16 women; 17 have advanced degrees.

Subjects Offered Adolescent issues, advanced biology, advanced math, Advanced Placement courses, African studies, algebra, American studies, athletics, biology, calculus, calculus-AP, chemistry, chorus, college counseling, drama, drawing, earth science, European history, European literature, fine arts, French, French language-AP, functions, geometry, graphic design, great books, music appreciation, music performance, music theory, photography, physics, statistics, theater, theater arts, trigonometry, writing, yearbook.

Graduation Requirements Advanced math, algebra, arts and fine arts (art, music, dance, drama), biology, chemistry, drawing, English, foreign language, French, geometry, history, literature, mathematics, music, physical education (includes health), physics, science, social sciences, writing, musical performance.

Special Academic Programs 2 Advanced Placement exams for which test preparation is offered; honors section; independent study; term-away projects; study abroad;

academic accommodation for the gifted, the musically talented, and the artistically talented.

College Admission Counseling 24 students graduated in 2011; 23 went to college, including Brown University; Colby College; Ithaca College; Kenyon College; Skidmore College; University of Chicago. Median SAT critical reading: 690, median SAT math: 630, median SAT writing: 690, median combined SAT: 2010. 90% scored over 600 on SAT critical reading, 60% scored over 600 on SAT math, 80% scored over 600 on SAT writing, 82% scored over 1800 on combined SAT.

Student Life Upper grades have student council, honor system. Discipline rests primarily with faculty.

Tuition and Aid Day student tuition: $25,171. Tuition installment plan (Insured Tuition Payment Plan, monthly payment plans, TMS). Need-based scholarship grants available. In 2011–12, 36% of upper-school students received aid. Total amount of financial aid awarded in 2011–12: $588,000.

Admissions Traditional secondary-level entrance grade is 9. For fall 2011, 91 students applied for upper-level admission, 40 were accepted, 31 enrolled. Deadline for receipt of application materials: January 20. Application fee required: $50. On-campus interview required.

Athletics Interscholastic: basketball (boys, girls), lacrosse (b,g), soccer (b,g); coed interscholastic: cross-country running; coed intramural: basketball, dance, fitness, lacrosse, mountain biking, running, soccer, yoga. 15 coaches, 1 athletic trainer.

Computers Computers are regularly used in all academic, literary magazine, mathematics, music, publications, science, writing, yearbook classes. Computer network features include on-campus library services, Internet access, wireless campus network, Internet filtering or blocking technology. Campus intranet and computer access in designated common areas are available to students. The school has a published electronic and media policy.

Contact Ms. Dorothy Wang, Assistant Head of School and Director of Admissions. 978-927-8793 Ext. 226. Fax: 978-921-2107. E-mail: dwang@waringschool.org. Web site: www.waringschool.org

WASATCH ACADEMY

120 South 100 West
Mt. Pleasant, Utah 84647

Head of School: Mr. Joseph Loftin

General Information Coeducational boarding and day college-preparatory, arts, bilingual studies, technology, and debate school. Grades 8–PG. Founded: 1875. Setting: small town. Nearest major city is Provo. Students are housed in single-sex dormitories. 30-acre campus. 23 buildings on campus. Approved or accredited by Northwest Accreditation Commission, Pacific Northwest Association of Independent Schools, The Association of Boarding Schools, and Utah Department of Education. Member of National Association of Independent Schools. Endowment: $2 million. Total enrollment: 304. Upper school average class size: 12. Upper school faculty-student ratio: 1:10.

Upper School Student Profile Grade 9: 27 students (16 boys, 11 girls); Grade 10: 73 students (43 boys, 30 girls); Grade 11: 96 students (59 boys, 37 girls); Grade 12: 93 students (62 boys, 31 girls); Postgraduate: 1 student (1 boy). 78% of students are boarding students. 26% are state residents. 25 states are represented in upper school student body. 53% are international students. International students from China, France, Mali, Republic of Korea, Taiwan, and Viet Nam; 26 other countries represented in student body.

Faculty School total: 53. In upper school: 25 men, 26 women; 19 have advanced degrees; 48 reside on campus.

Subjects Offered Acting, Advanced Placement courses, advanced studio art-AP, advanced TOEFL/grammar, algebra, anatomy, ballet, biology, biology-AP, calculus-AP, ceramics, chemistry, chemistry-AP, choir, college counseling, college placement, comedy, community garden, community service, dance, design, drama, drawing, drawing and design, driver education, earth science, electronic music, English, English-AP, equine science, ESL, European history-AP, fencing, film, filmmaking, fine arts, forensics, French, geography, geology, global issues, golf, guitar, honors algebra, honors English, honors U.S. history, jewelry making, Latin, learning strategies, math applications, music, music theory, outdoor education, painting, performing arts, philosophy, photography, physical education, physical science, physics, piano, play production, pottery, pre-calculus, reading, SAT/ACT preparation, Spanish, Spanish-AP, speech and debate, stained glass, statistics-AP, study skills, theater, TOEFL preparation, U.S. history, U.S. history-AP, weightlifting, Western civilization, woodworking, world religions, yoga.

Graduation Requirements Arts and fine arts (art, music, dance, drama), computer literacy, English, foreign language, mathematics, physical education (includes health), science, social sciences, social studies (includes history), U.S. history, outdoor, cultural, community service, and recreational requirements.

Special Academic Programs Advanced Placement exam preparation; honors section; accelerated programs; independent study; study at local college for college credit; programs in English, mathematics, general development for dyslexic students; ESL (29 students enrolled).

College Admission Counseling 87 students graduated in 2012; 86 went to college, including Cornell University; Northeastern Illinois University; Savannah College of Art and Design; Syracuse University; University of Pennsylvania; University of Utah. Other: 1 had other specific plans. Median SAT critical reading: 500, median SAT math: 480, median composite ACT: 22. Mean SAT writing: 564, mean combined SAT: 1892. 13% scored over 600 on SAT critical reading, 9% scored over 600 on SAT math, 27% scored over 26 on composite ACT.

Student Life Upper grades have specified standards of dress, student council, honor system. Discipline rests primarily with faculty.

Summer Programs Remediation, enrichment, advancement, ESL programs offered; held on campus; accepts boys and girls; open to students from other schools. 40 students usually enrolled. 2013 schedule: June 23 to August 3. Application deadline: none.

Tuition and Aid Day student tuition: $24,500; 5-day tuition and room/board: $41,700; 7-day tuition and room/board: $44,700. Tuition installment plan (Key Tuition Payment Plan, monthly payment plans, individually arranged payment plans). Merit scholarship grants, need-based scholarship grants, need-based loans available. In 2012–13, 38% of upper-school students received aid; total upper-school merit-scholarship money awarded: $126,000. Total amount of financial aid awarded in 2012–13: $2,650,000.

Admissions Traditional secondary-level entrance grade is 9. For fall 2012, 188 students applied for upper-level admission, 153 were accepted, 111 enrolled. ACT, ISEE, SSAT or Stanford Achievement Test required. Deadline for receipt of application materials: none. Application fee required: $75. Interview required.

Athletics Interscholastic: alpine skiing (boys, girls), baseball (b), basketball (b,g), climbing (b,g), cross-country running (b,g), dance (b,g), dressage (b,g), equestrian sports (b,g), fencing (b,g), golf (b,g), horseback riding (b,g), outdoor activities (b,g), outdoor education (b,g), paint ball (b,g), physical training (b,g), rodeo (b,g), running (b,g), skiing (cross-country) (b,g), skiing (downhill) (b,g), snowboarding (b,g), snowshoeing (b,g), soccer (b,g), tennis (b,g), track and field (b,g), volleyball (g), weight training (b,g); intramural: dance (g), skiing (downhill) (b,g), soccer (b,g), table tennis (b,g); coed interscholastic: aerobics/dance, archery, backpacking, ballet, bicycling, canoeing/kayaking, cheering, climbing, combined training, cross-country running, dance, dressage, equestrian sports, fencing, fishing, fly fishing, golf, hiking/backpacking, horseback riding, kayaking, life saving, martial arts, modern dance, mountain biking, nordic skiing, outdoor activities, paint ball, physical training, rock climbing, rodeo, running, ski jumping, skiing (cross-country), skiing (downhill), snowboarding, snowshoeing, swimming and diving, table tennis, telemark skiing, tennis, track and field, weight training, yoga; coed intramural: aerobics/dance, aquatics, archery, backpacking, badminton, ballet, bicycling, billiards, blading, bowling, canoeing/kayaking, climbing, combined training, cooperative games, dance team, equestrian sports, fishing, fitness, flag football, fly fishing, freestyle skiing, Frisbee, golf, hiking/backpacking, horseback riding, horseshoes, jogging, lacrosse, life saving, modern dance, mountain biking, nordic skiing, outdoor activities, paint ball, physical training, power lifting, rafting, rappelling, rock climbing, running, skateboarding, skiing (downhill), snowshoeing, swimming and diving, table tennis, telemark skiing, ultimate Frisbee, volleyball, weight lifting, weight training, yoga. 2 coaches, 1 athletic trainer.

Computers Computers are regularly used in all academic classes. Computer network features include on-campus library services, online commercial services, Internet access, wireless campus network, Internet filtering or blocking technology. Campus intranet and student e-mail accounts are available to students. Students grades are available online.

Contact Mrs. Carol Reeve, Director of Admissions. 435-462-1415. Fax: 435-462-1450. E-mail: carol.reeve@wasatchacademy.org. Web site: www.wasatchacademy.org

WASHINGTON INTERNATIONAL SCHOOL

3100 Macomb Street NW
Washington, District of Columbia 20008

Head of School: Clayton W. Lewis

General Information Coeducational day college-preparatory, bilingual studies, and International Baccalaureate school. Grades PK–12. Founded: 1966. Setting: urban. 6-acre campus. 8 buildings on campus. Approved or accredited by Association of Independent Schools of Greater Washington, International Baccalaureate Organization, Middle States Association of Colleges and Schools, and District of Columbia Department of Education. Member of National Association of Independent Schools, Secondary School Admission Test Board, and European Council of International Schools. Languages of instruction: English, French, and Spanish. Endowment: $3.8 million. Total enrollment: 901. Upper school average class size: 12. Upper school faculty-student ratio: 1:8. There are 175 required school days per year for Upper School students. Upper School students typically attend 5 days per week. The average school day consists of 5 hours and 25 minutes.

Upper School Student Profile Grade 9: 66 students (35 boys, 31 girls); Grade 10: 64 students (25 boys, 39 girls); Grade 11: 72 students (36 boys, 36 girls); Grade 12: 61 students (31 boys, 30 girls).

Faculty School total: 105. In upper school: 12 men, 23 women; 21 have advanced degrees.

Subjects Offered Advanced chemistry, advanced math, art, arts, biology, calculus, chemistry, chorus, community service, comparative government and politics, contemporary history, drama, Dutch, economics, English, English literature, environmental science, ESL, fine arts, French, geography, history, information technology, integrated mathematics, International Baccalaureate courses, Italian, Japanese, literature seminar, music, musical productions, physical education, physics, science, social sciences, Spanish, theater, theory of knowledge, world history.

Graduation Requirements Algebra, arts, arts and fine arts (art, music, dance, drama), biology, calculus, chemistry, economics, English, environmental science, foreign language, geography, geometry, physical education (includes health), physics, trigonometry, world history, world literature, IB program. Community service is required.

Special Academic Programs International Baccalaureate program; ESL (10 students enrolled).

College Admission Counseling 59 students graduated in 2012; all went to college, including American University; Columbia University; McGill University; Northwestern University; Stanford University; University of Virginia. Mean SAT critical reading: 632, mean SAT math: 630, mean SAT writing: 628.

Student Life Upper grades have specified standards of dress, student council, honor system. Discipline rests primarily with faculty.

Summer Programs Enrichment, ESL programs offered; held on campus; accepts boys and girls; open to students from other schools. 40 students usually enrolled. 2013 schedule: June 23 to August 1. Application deadline: April 30.

Tuition and Aid Day student tuition: $32,250. Tuition installment plan (monthly payment plans, 2-payment plan). Need-based scholarship grants available. In 2012–13, 14% of upper-school students received aid.

Admissions Traditional secondary-level entrance grade is 9. School's own exam required. Deadline for receipt of application materials: January 10. Application fee required: $50. On-campus interview required.

Athletics Interscholastic: baseball (boys), basketball (b,g), soccer (b,g), softball (g), tennis (b,g), track and field (b,g), volleyball (g); coed interscholastic: cross-country running, golf; coed intramural: swimming and diving. 3 PE instructors, 1 athletic trainer.

Computers Computers are regularly used in all classes. Computer network features include on-campus library services, online commercial services, Internet access, wireless campus network, Internet filtering or blocking technology. Campus intranet and student e-mail accounts are available to students. The school has a published electronic and media policy.

Contact Ms. Mary Hastings Moore, Associate Director of Admissions. 202-243-1815. Fax: 202-243-1807. E-mail: moore@wis.edu. Web site: www.wis.edu

WASHINGTON WALDORF SCHOOL

4800 Sangamore Road
Bethesda, Maryland 20816

Head of School: Mrs. Natalie Adams

General Information Coeducational day college-preparatory and arts school. Grades PS–12. Founded: 1969. Setting: suburban. Nearest major city is Washington, DC. 6-acre campus. 1 building on campus. Approved or accredited by Association of Independent Schools of Greater Washington, Association of Waldorf Schools of North America, Middle States Association of Colleges and Schools, and Maryland Department of Education. Member of National Association of Independent Schools. Total enrollment: 236. Upper school average class size: 18. Upper school faculty-student ratio: 1:7. There are 175 required school days per year for Upper School students. Upper School students typically attend 5 days per week. The average school day consists of 7 hours.

Upper School Student Profile Grade 9: 9 students (5 boys, 4 girls); Grade 10: 10 students (3 boys, 7 girls); Grade 11: 11 students (2 boys, 9 girls); Grade 12: 17 students (6 boys, 11 girls).

Faculty School total: 38. In upper school: 8 men, 8 women; 9 have advanced degrees.

Subjects Offered 3-dimensional art, African-American history, algebra, American Civil War, American literature, anatomy and physiology, ancient world history, art, art and culture, art history, biochemistry, biology, bookbinding, botany, British literature, calculus, calculus-AP, chamber groups, chemistry, choir, chorus, civil rights, classical civilization, crafts, critical thinking, critical writing, drama performance, ecology, epic literature, eurythmy, fine arts, general math, general science, geology, geometry, German, grammar, history of architecture, history of music, human anatomy, human development, lab science, medieval literature, metalworking, modern history, modern world history, mythology, oil painting, optics, physical education, pre-calculus, printmaking, research skills, sculpture, Shakespeare, Spanish, stone carving, trigonometry, U.S. constitutional history, weaving, Western literature, writing, zoology.

Graduation Requirements Arts and fine arts (art, music, dance, drama), comparative religion, constitutional history of U.S., crafts, English, eurythmy, foreign language, history of drama, history of music, mathematics, physical education (includes health), science, social studies (includes history).

Special Academic Programs 1 Advanced Placement exam for which test preparation is offered; study abroad; academic accommodation for the musically talented and the artistically talented.

College Admission Counseling 15 students graduated in 2011; all went to college, including Bard College; Bowdoin College; Clemson University; Rochester Institute of Technology; Sarah Lawrence College; The University of North Carolina at Chapel Hill. Median SAT critical reading: 648, median SAT math: 578, median SAT writing: 652.

Student Life Upper grades have specified standards of dress, student council. Discipline rests primarily with faculty.

Tuition and Aid Day student tuition: $22,300. Tuition installment plan (FACTS Tuition Payment Plan, monthly payment plans, individually arranged payment plans, self-insured tuition insurance). Tuition reduction for siblings, need-based scholarship grants, need-based assistance grants, tuition remission for children of faculty, one full scholarship for an inner-city student available. In 2011–12, 25% of upper-school students received aid. Total amount of financial aid awarded in 2011–12: $38,000.

Admissions Traditional secondary-level entrance grade is 9. For fall 2011, 9 students applied for upper-level admission, 7 were accepted, 5 enrolled. Math and English placement tests required. Deadline for receipt of application materials: none. Application fee required: $60. On-campus interview required.

Athletics Interscholastic: baseball (boys), basketball (b,g), cross-country running (b,g), soccer (b,g), softball (g); coed intramural: golf, outdoor education, table tennis, volleyball, yoga. 1 PE instructor, 3 coaches.

Computers Computers are regularly used in graphic design, technology classes. Computer resources include Internet access.

Contact Ms. Lezlie Lawson, Admissions/Enrollment Director. 301-229-6107 Ext. 154. Fax: 301-229-9379. E-mail: llawson@washingtonwaldorf.org. Web site: www.washingtonwaldorf.org

THE WATERFORD SCHOOL

1480 East 9400 South
Sandy, Utah 84093

Head of School: Mrs. Nancy M. Heuston

General Information Coeducational day college-preparatory, arts, technology, and visual arts, music, photography, dance, and theater school. Grades PK–12. Founded: 1981. Setting: suburban. Nearest major city is Salt Lake City. 40-acre campus. 10 buildings on campus. Approved or accredited by Northwest Accreditation Commission, Pacific Northwest Association of Independent Schools, and Utah Department of Education. Member of National Association of Independent Schools. Endowment: $2 million. Total enrollment: 875. Upper school average class size: 16. Upper school faculty-student ratio: 1:5. There are 169 required school days per year for Upper School students. Upper School students typically attend 5 days per week. The average school day consists of 6 hours.

Upper School Student Profile Grade 9: 77 students (45 boys, 32 girls); Grade 10: 65 students (33 boys, 32 girls); Grade 11: 60 students (24 boys, 36 girls); Grade 12: 56 students (27 boys, 29 girls).

Faculty School total: 110. In upper school: 37 men, 31 women; 54 have advanced degrees.

Subjects Offered 20th century history, 3-dimensional design, acting, advanced math, Advanced Placement courses, aerobics, algebra, American history, American history-AP, American literature, art, Asian history, basketball, biology, biology-AP, British literature, calculus, calculus-AP, ceramics, chemistry, chemistry-AP, chorus, computer applications, computer art, computer graphics, computer programming, computer science, computer science-AP, creative writing, debate, drama, drama performance, drama workshop, drawing, ecology, economics, English-AP, European history, European history-AP, French, French-AP, geology, geometry, German, German-AP, Japanese, jazz ensemble, Latin, Latin American literature, music history, music performance, music theater, outdoor education, painting, philosophy, photography, physical education, physics, physics-AP, pre-calculus, probability and statistics, psychology, sculpture, Spanish, Spanish-AP, statistics-AP, strings, studio art-AP, trigonometry, voice ensemble, volleyball, weight training, wind ensemble, world literature, writing workshop, yearbook, zoology.

Graduation Requirements 20th century world history, algebra, American history, American literature, biology, British literature, calculus, chemistry, computer science, English, European history, foreign language, geometry, music performance, physics, pre-calculus, trigonometry, visual arts, world history, writing workshop, six terms of physical education or participation on athletic teams.

Special Academic Programs 15 Advanced Placement exams for which test preparation is offered; honors section; independent study; term-away projects; academic accommodation for the gifted, the musically talented, and the artistically talented.

College Admission Counseling 55 students graduated in 2012; all went to college. Mean SAT critical reading: 618, mean SAT math: 633, mean SAT writing: 616, mean combined SAT: 1867, mean composite ACT: 26.

Student Life Upper grades have uniform requirement, student council, honor system. Discipline rests equally with students and faculty.

Summer Programs Enrichment, advancement, sports, art/fine arts, rigorous outdoor training programs offered; session focuses on enrichment and advancement; held both on and off campus; held at various locations in Utah and abroad; accepts boys and girls; not open to students from other schools. 100 students usually enrolled. 2013 schedule: June 10 to August 15. Application deadline: March 15.

Tuition and Aid Day student tuition: $19,200. Guaranteed tuition plan. Tuition installment plan (Insured Tuition Payment Plan, monthly payment plans). Tuition reduction for siblings, need-based scholarship grants available. In 2012–13, 21% of upper-school students received aid. Total amount of financial aid awarded in 2012–13: $140,162.

Admissions Traditional secondary-level entrance grade is 9. For fall 2012, 56 students applied for upper-level admission, 32 were accepted, 27 enrolled. ERB CTP IV required. Deadline for receipt of application materials: none. Application fee required: $35. On-campus interview required.

Athletics Interscholastic: basketball (boys, girls), crew (b,g), cross-country running (b,g), golf (b,g), lacrosse (b,g), soccer (b,g), tennis (b,g), volleyball (g); coed interscholastic: alpine skiing, aquatics, ballet, dance, Frisbee, racquetball, skiing (downhill); coed intramural: aerobics, backpacking, climbing, crew, nordic skiing, outdoor education, outdoor recreation, rock climbing, weight training. 6 PE instructors, 15 coaches.

Computers Computers are regularly used in animation, college planning, graphic design, library, literary magazine, newspaper, photography, publications, yearbook classes. Computer network features include on-campus library services, online commercial services, Internet access, wireless campus network, Internet filtering or blocking technology. Campus intranet, student e-mail accounts, and computer access in designated common areas are available to students. Students grades are available online. The school has a published electronic and media policy.

Contact Mr. Todd Winters, Director of Admissions. 801-816-2213. Fax: 801-572-1787. E-mail: toddwinters@waterfordschool.org. Web site: www.waterfordschool.org

WATKINSON SCHOOL

180 Bloomfield Avenue
Hartford, Connecticut 06105

Head of School: Mr. John W. Bracker

General Information Coeducational day college-preparatory, arts, technology, and athletics, global studies school. Grades 6–PG. Founded: 1881. Setting: suburban. 40-acre campus. 5 buildings on campus. Approved or accredited by Association of Independent Schools in New England, New England Association of Schools and Colleges, and Connecticut Department of Education. Member of National Association of Independent Schools and Secondary School Admission Test Board. Endowment: $4 million. Total enrollment: 240. Upper school average class size: 12. Upper school faculty-student ratio: 1:6. There are 165 required school days per year for Upper School students. Upper School students typically attend 5 days per week. The average school day consists of 7 hours and 30 minutes.

Upper School Student Profile Grade 9: 42 students (22 boys, 20 girls); Grade 10: 48 students (28 boys, 20 girls); Grade 11: 43 students (23 boys, 20 girls); Grade 12: 31 students (14 boys, 17 girls); Postgraduate: 1 student (1 girl).

Faculty School total: 49. In upper school: 12 men, 27 women; 25 have advanced degrees.

Subjects Offered African history, algebra, American history, American literature, American sign language, anatomy, ancient world history, art, Asian history, biology, calculus, ceramics, chemistry, creative writing, dance, drama, drawing, earth science, English, English literature, environmental science, European history, expository writing, fine arts, forensics, French, geography, geometry, health, history, internship, mathematics, modern European history, painting, photography, physics, pottery, science, social studies, Spanish, theater, U.S. history, world history, world literature, writing.

Graduation Requirements Arts and fine arts (art, music, dance, drama), English, foreign language, health and wellness, mathematics, science, social studies (includes history), technology.

Special Academic Programs Independent study; study at local college for college credit; academic accommodation for the gifted, the musically talented, and the artistically talented; programs in English, mathematics, general development for dyslexic students; special instructional classes for deaf students.

College Admission Counseling 45 students graduated in 2012; 44 went to college, including Eastern Connecticut State University; Fairfield University; Sacred Heart University; Smith College; University of Hartford. Other: 1 had other specific plans. Median SAT critical reading: 550, median SAT math: 520, median SAT writing: 530, median combined SAT: 1590, median composite ACT: 26. 34% scored over 600 on SAT critical reading, 24% scored over 600 on SAT math, 27% scored over 600 on SAT writing, 29% scored over 1800 on combined SAT, 35% scored over 26 on composite ACT.

Student Life Upper grades have specified standards of dress, student council. Discipline rests equally with students and faculty.

Summer Programs Remediation, enrichment programs offered; session focuses on academics; held on campus; accepts boys and girls; open to students from other schools. 28 students usually enrolled. 2013 schedule: June 24 to August 2. Application deadline: none.

Tuition and Aid Day student tuition: $34,125. Tuition installment plan (Insured Tuition Payment Plan, Sallie Mae). Need-based scholarship grants available. In 2012–13, 41% of upper-school students received aid. Total amount of financial aid awarded in 2012–13: $1,510,932.

Admissions Traditional secondary-level entrance grade is 9. For fall 2012, 91 students applied for upper-level admission, 54 were accepted, 35 enrolled. ISEE or SSAT required. Deadline for receipt of application materials: February 1. Application fee required: $50. On-campus interview required.

Athletics Interscholastic: baseball (boys), basketball (b,g), crew (b,g), cross-country running (b,g), lacrosse (b,g), soccer (b,g), softball (g), tennis (b,g), volleyball (g); coed interscholastic: crew, cross-country running, tennis, ultimate Frisbee; coed intramural: alpine skiing, ballet, Circus, climbing, combined training, dance, fencing, fitness, juggling, martial arts, outdoor activities, outdoor adventure, physical fitness, physical training, skiing (downhill), snowboarding, street hockey, strength & conditioning, tennis, ultimate Frisbee, volleyball, weight lifting, yoga. 4 coaches.

Computers Computers are regularly used in computer applications, desktop publishing classes. Computer network features include on-campus library services, online commercial services, Internet access, wireless campus network, Internet filtering or blocking technology. Campus intranet, student e-mail accounts, and computer access in designated common areas are available to students. The school has a published electronic and media policy.

Contact Mrs. Cathy Batson, Admissions Office Assistant. 860-236-5618 Ext. 136. Fax: 860-233-8295. E-mail: cathy_batson@watkinson.org. Web site: www.watkinson.org

WAYNFLETE SCHOOL

360 Spring Street
Portland, Maine 04102

Head of School: Dr. Mark Segar

General Information Coeducational day college-preparatory school. Grades PK–12. Founded: 1898. Setting: urban. Nearest major city is Boston, MA. 37-acre campus. 10 buildings on campus. Approved or accredited by Association of Independent Schools in New England, Independent Schools of Northern New England, New England Association of Schools and Colleges, The College Board, and Maine Department of Education. Member of National Association of Independent Schools. Endowment: $18.7 million. Total enrollment: 567. Upper school average class size: 14. Upper school faculty-student ratio: 1:12. There are 172 required school days per year for Upper School students. Upper School students typically attend 5 days per week. The average school day consists of 7 hours and 15 minutes.

Upper School Student Profile Grade 9: 60 students (28 boys, 32 girls); Grade 10: 72 students (33 boys, 39 girls); Grade 11: 65 students (28 boys, 37 girls); Grade 12: 62 students (28 boys, 34 girls).

Faculty School total: 75. In upper school: 18 men, 24 women; 29 have advanced degrees.

Subjects Offered 20th century American writers, 20th century history, advanced biology, algebra, American history, American literature, ancient/medieval philosophy, art appreciation, art history, bioethics, biology, calculus, ceramics, chemistry, composition, computer science, constitutional history of U.S., creative writing, drama, drama workshop, English, English composition, English literature, environmental science, equality and freedom, European history, expository writing, film and literature, fine arts, French, geometry, government/civics, grammar, health, jazz ensemble, Latin, Mandarin, marine biology, modern European history, music, physical education, physics, pre-calculus, printmaking, psychology, senior project, Spanish, studio art, theater, trigonometry, U.S. constitutional history, Vietnam, world history, world literature, writing.

Graduation Requirements Arts, biology, English, foreign language, geometry, history, mathematics, performing arts, science, sports, U.S. history, Seniors may design a month-long Senior Project, which allows them to pursue academic interests, potential careers, fine arts, or community service. Community service is required.

Special Academic Programs Independent study; term-away projects; study abroad.

College Admission Counseling 58 students graduated in 2012; 56 went to college, including Bates College; Boston College; Colby College; Middlebury College; The George Washington University; University of Vermont. Other: 1 went to work, 1 had other specific plans. Median SAT critical reading: 630, median SAT math: 610, median SAT writing: 630, median combined SAT: 1870. 57% scored over 600 on SAT critical reading, 60% scored over 600 on SAT math, 60% scored over 600 on SAT writing, 59% scored over 1800 on combined SAT.

Student Life Upper grades have student council. Discipline rests primarily with faculty.

Summer Programs Enrichment, sports, art/fine arts programs offered; session focuses on sports, gymnastics, martial arts, robotics, fine/performing arts, digital media, sustainable ocean studies; held both on and off campus; held at Fore River Fields, Portland, ME and Pensobscot Bay, Darling Marine Center, Mt. Desert Island; accepts boys and girls; open to students from other schools. 750 students usually enrolled. 2013 schedule: June 10 to July 26. Application deadline: July 1.

Tuition and Aid Day student tuition: $25,275. Tuition installment plan (Insured Tuition Payment Plan, monthly payment plans). Need-based scholarship grants available. In 2012–13, 40% of upper-school students received aid. Total amount of financial aid awarded in 2012–13: $1,553,768.

Admissions Traditional secondary-level entrance grade is 9. For fall 2012, 76 students applied for upper-level admission, 33 were accepted, 26 enrolled. Writing sample required. Deadline for receipt of application materials: February 10. Application fee required: $40. Interview required.

Athletics Interscholastic: baseball (boys), basketball (b,g), cross-country running (b,g), field hockey (g), golf (b,g), lacrosse (b,g), skiing (cross-country) (b,g), soccer (b,g), tennis (b,g); intramural: backpacking (b,g); coed interscholastic: crew, nordic skiing, rowing, sailing, swimming and diving, track and field; coed intramural: dance, fitness walking, modern dance, physical fitness, sailing, swimming and diving, tennis, weight lifting, weight training, yoga. 4 PE instructors, 20 coaches, 1 athletic trainer.

Computers Computers are regularly used in all academic classes. Computer network features include on-campus library services, online commercial services, Internet access, wireless campus network, Internet filtering or blocking technology, Google doc accounts; academic data bases, including JSTOR, MARVEL, Infotrac, Noodle Tools, and URSUS. Student e-mail accounts and computer access in designated common areas are available to students. The school has a published electronic and media policy.

Contact Admission Office. 207-774-5721 Ext. 1224. Fax: 207-772-4782. E-mail: admissionoffice@waynflete.org. Web site: www.waynflete.org

THE WEBB SCHOOL

319 Webb Road East
PO Box 488
Bell Buckle, Tennessee 37020

Head of School: Mr. Ray Broadhead

General Information Coeducational boarding and day college-preparatory, arts, technology, wilderness leadership, and ethics school. Boarding grades 7–12, day grades 6–12. Founded: 1870. Setting: rural. Nearest major city is Nashville. Students are housed in single-sex dormitories. 145-acre campus. 17 buildings on campus. Approved or accredited by Southern Association of Colleges and Schools, Southern Association of Independent Schools, The Association of Boarding Schools, and Tennessee Department of Education. Member of National Association of Independent Schools and Secondary School Admission Test Board. Endowment: $22 million. Total enrollment: 304. Upper school average class size: 12. Upper school faculty-student ratio: 1:7. There are 175 required school days per year for Upper School students. Upper School students typically attend 5 days per week. The average school day consists of 6 hours and 30 minutes.

Upper School Student Profile Grade 9: 43 students (23 boys, 20 girls); Grade 10: 66 students (37 boys, 29 girls); Grade 11: 63 students (30 boys, 33 girls); Grade 12: 56 students (21 boys, 35 girls). 33% of students are boarding students. 85% are state residents. 11 states are represented in upper school student body. 15% are international students. International students from Bahamas, China, Jamaica, Republic of Korea, Taiwan, and Viet Nam; 6 other countries represented in student body.

Faculty School total: 46. In upper school: 18 men, 28 women; 31 have advanced degrees; 17 reside on campus.

Subjects Offered Advanced Placement courses, algebra, American Civil War, American government, American history, American literature, American literature-AP, anatomy, art, art appreciation, art education, art history, arts appreciation, biology, biology-AP, calculus, calculus-AP, ceramics, chemistry, chemistry-AP, choir, chorus, computer programming, computer science, creative writing, drama, driver education, earth science, ecology, economics, economics-AP, English, English literature, English literature-AP, English-AP, ESL, ESL, ethical decision making, ethics, European history, European history-AP, fine arts, French, geography, geometry, German, government/civics, grammar, health, history, history of rock and roll, history-AP, honors algebra, honors English, honors geometry, honors U.S. history, journalism, Latin, macroeconomics-AP, mathematics, microeconomics-AP, modern European history-AP, music, music appreciation, music history, music performance, music theory, outdoor education, physical education, physics, physics-AP, physiology, piano, poetry, pre-algebra, pre-calculus, psychology, religion, Russian history, science, Shakespeare, social sciences, social studies, Spanish, speech, speech communications, statistics, statistics-AP, technology, theater, theater arts, trigonometry, U.S. history, U.S. history-AP, Western civilization, wilderness education, world geography, world history, world literature.

Graduation Requirements American government, American history, arts and fine arts (art, music, dance, drama), computer science, economics, English, ethics, foreign language, mathematics, physical education (includes health), science, senior thesis, social sciences, social studies (includes history), speech, Public Exhibition Program—declamation, oration, performance piece, original creative work.

Special Academic Programs 13 Advanced Placement exams for which test preparation is offered; honors section; independent study; study abroad; academic accommodation for the gifted; programs in English, mathematics, general development for dyslexic students; special instructional classes for deaf students, blind students; ESL (21 students enrolled).

College Admission Counseling 48 students graduated in 2011; 47 went to college, including Belmont University; Clemson University; Sewanee: The University of the South; The University of Tennessee; The University of Tennessee at Chattanooga; Vanderbilt University. Other: 1 entered military service. Mean SAT critical reading: 626, mean SAT math: 623, mean SAT writing: 600, mean combined SAT: 1849, mean composite ACT: 26.

Student Life Upper grades have uniform requirement, student council, honor system. Discipline rests equally with students and faculty.

Tuition and Aid Day student tuition: $16,500; 5-day tuition and room/board: $29,950; 7-day tuition and room/board: $38,500. Tuition installment plan (FACTS Tuition Payment Plan, monthly payment plans, individually arranged payment plans). Merit scholarship grants, need-based scholarship grants available. In 2011–12, 40% of upper-school students received aid; total upper-school merit-scholarship money awarded: $154,000. Total amount of financial aid awarded in 2011–12: $1,200,000.

Admissions Traditional secondary-level entrance grade is 9. For fall 2011, 82 students applied for upper-level admission, 54 were accepted, 33 enrolled. ISEE, SSAT or TOEFL required. Deadline for receipt of application materials: February 15. Application fee required: $50. Interview required.

Athletics Interscholastic: baseball (boys), basketball (b,g), cross-country running (b,g), football (b), golf (b,g), lacrosse (b,g), soccer (b,g); intramural: aerobics (g), aerobics/Nautilus (b,g), volleyball (g); coed interscholastic: marksmanship, running, trap and skeet; coed intramural: aerobics/Nautilus, aquatics, backpacking, badminton, ballet, bowling, canoeing/kayaking, climbing, combined training, fishing, fitness, fitness walking, fly fishing, Frisbee, hiking/backpacking, horseback riding, kayaking, outdoor activities, physical fitness, physical training, rock climbing, ropes courses, skeet shooting, table tennis, ultimate Frisbee, wall climbing, weight lifting, weight training, wilderness survival, yoga. 1 PE instructor, 17 coaches, 1 athletic trainer.

Computers Computers are regularly used in computer applications, English, foreign language, history, mathematics, science, writing classes. Computer network features include on-campus library services, online commercial services, Internet access, wireless campus network, Internet filtering or blocking technology. Campus intranet, student e-mail accounts, and computer access in designated common areas are available to students. Students grades are available online. The school has a published electronic and media policy.

Contact Mrs. Julie Harris, Director of Admissions. 931-389-6003. Fax: 931-389-6657. E-mail: admissions@webbschool.com. Web site: www.thewebbschool.com

WEBB SCHOOL OF KNOXVILLE

9800 Webb School Drive
Knoxville, Tennessee 37923-3399

Head of School: Mr. Scott L. Hutchinson

General Information Coeducational day college-preparatory, arts, religious studies, and technology school. Grades K–12. Founded: 1955. Setting: urban. Nearest major city is Chattanooga. 114-acre campus. 8 buildings on campus. Approved or accredited by Southern Association of Colleges and Schools, Southern Association of Independent Schools, and Tennessee Department of Education. Member of National Association of Independent Schools and Secondary School Admission Test Board. Endowment: $28.8 million. Total enrollment: 1,023. Upper school average class size: 16. Upper school faculty-student ratio: 1:10. There are 175 required school days per year for Upper School students. Upper School students typically attend 5 days per week. The average school day consists of 8 hours and 5 minutes.

Upper School Student Profile Grade 9: 106 students (54 boys, 52 girls); Grade 10: 130 students (71 boys, 59 girls); Grade 11: 113 students (59 boys, 54 girls); Grade 12: 106 students (47 boys, 59 girls).

Faculty School total: 94. In upper school: 20 men, 24 women; 40 have advanced degrees.

Subjects Offered 3-dimensional design, algebra, American sign language, anatomy and physiology, art history-AP, biology, biology-AP, calculus, calculus-AP, ceramics, chamber groups, chemistry, chemistry-AP, computer science-AP, concert choir, creative writing, digital imaging, drama, dramatic arts, drawing, economics, economics-AP, engineering, English, English language and composition-AP, English literature and composition-AP, English-AP, environmental science-AP, forensics, French, French-AP, freshman foundations, geometry, government and politics-AP, honors algebra, honors English, honors geometry, honors world history, independent study, journalism, Latin, Latin-AP, Mandarin, math applications, modern European history-AP, modern history, modern world history, music theory-AP, painting, photography, physics, physics-AP, pre-calculus, probability and statistics, psychology-AP, robotics, Spanish, Spanish-AP, speech communications, stage design, statistics-AP, strings, studio art-AP, U.S. government and politics, U.S. government and politics-AP, U.S. history, U.S. history-AP, video film production, wind ensemble, world history, world history-AP, world religions, yearbook.

Graduation Requirements Algebra, American history, arts and fine arts (art, music, dance, drama), biology, chemistry, English, foreign language, freshman foundations, geometry, mathematics, physical education (includes health), public service, science, world history, world religions, public speaking (two chapel talks), 25 hours of community service per year.

Special Academic Programs 22 Advanced Placement exams for which test preparation is offered; honors section; independent study; study abroad; remedial reading and/or remedial writing; remedial math.

College Admission Counseling 118 students graduated in 2012; all went to college, including Auburn University; Belmont University; Duke University; The University of Tennessee; University of Mississippi; Vanderbilt University. Mean SAT critical reading: 620, mean SAT math: 610, mean SAT writing: 610, mean composite ACT: 28. 64% scored over 600 on SAT critical reading, 60% scored over 600 on SAT math, 62% scored over 600 on SAT writing, 72% scored over 26 on composite ACT.

Student Life Upper grades have uniform requirement, student council, honor system. Discipline rests equally with students and faculty.

Summer Programs Remediation, enrichment, advancement, sports, art/fine arts programs offered; session focuses on academic and sports-oriented fun; held on campus; accepts boys and girls; open to students from other schools. 2013 schedule: June 3 to August 2. Application deadline: June 3.

Tuition and Aid Day student tuition: $16,640. Tuition installment plan (monthly payment plans, individually arranged payment plans, Tuition Payments can also be paid in two installments-last calendar day in July and November). Need-based scholarship

grants available. In 2012–13, 16% of upper-school students received aid. Total amount of financial aid awarded in 2012–13: $720,250.
Admissions Traditional secondary-level entrance grade is 9. For fall 2012, 42 students applied for upper-level admission, 30 were accepted, 22 enrolled. ISEE required. Deadline for receipt of application materials: January 20. Application fee required: $75. On-campus interview required.
Athletics Interscholastic: baseball (boys), basketball (b,g), bowling (b,g), cheering (g), climbing (b,g), cross-country running (b,g), dance squad (g), field hockey (g), football (b), golf (b,g), lacrosse (b), soccer (b,g), softball (g), swimming and diving (b,g), tennis (b,g), track and field (b,g), volleyball (g), wrestling (b); coed interscholastic: sailing. 18 coaches, 1 athletic trainer.
Computers Computers are regularly used in all classes. Computer network features include on-campus library services, Internet access, wireless campus network, Internet filtering or blocking technology, all students in grades 3-12 own/lease iPads for school. Student e-mail accounts are available to students. Students grades are available online. The school has a published electronic and media policy.
Contact Mrs. Christy Widener, Admissions Administrative Assistant. 865-291-3830. Fax: 865-291-1532. E-mail: christy_widener@webbschool.org. Web site: www.webbschool.org

THE WEBB SCHOOLS

1175 West Baseline Road
Claremont, California 91711

Head of School: Mr. Taylor Stockdale

General Information Coeducational boarding and day college-preparatory school. Grades 9–12. Founded: 1922. Setting: suburban. Nearest major city is Pasadena. Students are housed in single-sex dormitories. 70-acre campus. 57 buildings on campus. Approved or accredited by California Association of Independent Schools, The Association of Boarding Schools, Western Association of Schools and Colleges, and California Department of Education. Member of National Association of Independent Schools and Secondary School Admission Test Board. Endowment: $33.6 million. Total enrollment: 410. Upper school average class size: 15. Upper school faculty-student ratio: 1:8.
Upper School Student Profile Grade 9: 93 students (50 boys, 43 girls); Grade 10: 108 students (51 boys, 57 girls); Grade 11: 113 students (57 boys, 56 girls); Grade 12: 96 students (51 boys, 45 girls). 65% of students are boarding students. 66% are state residents. 18 states are represented in upper school student body. 23% are international students. International students from China, Democratic People's Republic of Korea, Germany, Hong Kong, Russian Federation, and Saudi Arabia; 13 other countries represented in student body.
Faculty School total: 56. In upper school: 31 men, 25 women; 44 have advanced degrees; 45 reside on campus.
Subjects Offered Advanced Placement courses, algebra, American history, American history-AP, American literature, art, astronomy, biology, biology-AP, calculus, calculus-AP, chamber groups, chemistry, chemistry-AP, chorus, composition-AP, computer math, discrete mathematics, drama, economics, English, English language and composition-AP, English literature, English literature and composition-AP, environmental science, environmental science-AP, European history, European history-AP, fine arts, French, French language-AP, French literature-AP, freshman foundations, geometry, government/civics, health and wellness, history, integrated mathematics, literature, modern European history-AP, modern world history, museum science, orchestra, paleontology, performing arts, physical education, physics, physics-AP, precalculus, psychology, SAT preparation, Spanish, Spanish language-AP, Spanish literature-AP, statistics-AP, theater, trigonometry, U.S. history-AP, world history, world history-AP, writing.
Graduation Requirements Arts and fine arts (art, music, dance, drama), English, foreign language, health, history, mathematics, physical education (includes health), science.
Special Academic Programs 15 Advanced Placement exams for which test preparation is offered; honors section; study at local college for college credit; academic accommodation for the gifted.
College Admission Counseling 111 students graduated in 2012; all went to college, including Boston College; Cornell University; New York University; University of California, Berkeley; University of Southern California; Wellesley College. Mean combined SAT: 1990.
Student Life Upper grades have specified standards of dress, student council, honor system. Discipline rests equally with students and faculty.
Summer Programs Enrichment, advancement, sports, art/fine arts, computer instruction programs offered; session focuses on academic enrichment; held on campus; accepts boys and girls; open to students from other schools. 300 students usually enrolled. 2013 schedule: June to July. Application deadline: none.
Tuition and Aid Day student tuition: $35,395; 7-day tuition and room/board: $49,775. Tuition installment plan (Insured Tuition Payment Plan, monthly payment plans). Merit scholarship grants available. In 2012–13, 33% of upper-school students received aid; total upper-school merit-scholarship money awarded: $3,400,000. Total amount of financial aid awarded in 2012–13: $3,400,000.
Admissions Traditional secondary-level entrance grade is 9. For fall 2012, 443 students applied for upper-level admission, 183 were accepted, 130 enrolled. ISEE or SSAT required. Deadline for receipt of application materials: January 15. Application fee required: $75. On-campus interview required.
Athletics Interscholastic: baseball (boys), basketball (b,g), cross-country running (b,g), diving (b,g), football (b), golf (b,g), independent competitive sports (b,g), soccer (b,g), softball (g), swimming and diving (b,g), tennis (b,g), track and field (b,g), volleyball (b,g), water polo (b,g), winter soccer (g), wrestling (b); intramural: weight lifting (b); coed interscholastic: badminton; coed intramural: backpacking, bicycling, climbing, dance, fitness, fitness walking, Frisbee, hiking/backpacking, indoor soccer, kayaking, mountain biking, outdoor activities, physical fitness, rock climbing, running, snowboarding, strength & conditioning, surfing, triathlon, ultimate Frisbee, yoga. 12 coaches, 1 athletic trainer.
Computers Computers are regularly used in English, foreign language, health, history, journalism, mathematics, science classes. Computer network features include on-campus library services, Internet access, wireless campus network, Internet filtering or blocking technology. Campus intranet and student e-mail accounts are available to students. Students grades are available online. The school has a published electronic and media policy.
Contact Mr. Leo G. Marshall, Director of Admission and Financial Aid. 909-482-5214. Fax: 909-445-8269. E-mail: admission@webb.org. Web site: www.webb.org/admission

WELLSPRING FOUNDATION

Bethlehem, Connecticut
See Special Needs Schools section.

WELLSPRINGS FRIENDS SCHOOL

3590 West 18th Avenue
Eugene, Oregon 97402

Head of School: Dennis Hoerner

General Information Coeducational day college-preparatory and general academic school, affiliated with Society of Friends; primarily serves underachievers. Grades 9–12. Founded: 1994. Setting: small town. Nearest major city is Portland. 4-acre campus. 2 buildings on campus. Approved or accredited by Northwest Accreditation Commission and Oregon Department of Education. Endowment: $8,000. Total enrollment: 60. Upper school average class size: 10. Upper school faculty-student ratio: 1:8. The average school day consists of 6 hours.
Upper School Student Profile Grade 9: 7 students (7 girls); Grade 10: 12 students (5 boys, 7 girls); Grade 11: 24 students (13 boys, 11 girls); Grade 12: 18 students (7 boys, 11 girls); Grade 13: 1 student (1 girl).
Faculty School total: 10. In upper school: 5 men, 5 women; 4 have advanced degrees.
Subjects Offered 20th century world history, advanced math, algebra, creative writing, English, film, finance, fine arts, geometry, German, government, human sexuality, life science, personal finance, physical education, physical science, poetry, pre-algebra, reading, Spanish, U.S. history.
Graduation Requirements English, foreign language, mathematics, science, social studies (includes history). Community service is required.
Special Academic Programs Independent study; remedial reading and/or remedial writing; remedial math.
College Admission Counseling 21 students graduated in 2012; 8 went to college, including Lane Community College; University of Oregon. Other: 6 went to work, 2 entered military service, 5 had other specific plans.
Student Life Upper grades have student council. Discipline rests equally with students and faculty.
Tuition and Aid Day student tuition: $6000. Tuition installment plan (monthly payment plans, individually arranged payment plans). Need-based scholarship grants available.
Admissions Traditional secondary-level entrance grade is 9. For fall 2012, 15 students applied for upper-level admission, 15 were accepted, 14 enrolled. Deadline for receipt of application materials: none. No application fee required. Interview required.
Athletics Coed Intramural: basketball, bocce, football, Frisbee, hiking/backpacking, physical fitness, skateboarding, table tennis, yoga. 1 PE instructor.
Computers Computers are regularly used in career education, career exploration, music, writing, yearbook classes. Computer network features include Internet access, wireless campus network.
Contact Office Manager. 541-686-1223. Fax: 541-687-1493. E-mail: info@wellspringsfriends.org. Web site: www.wellspringsfriends.org

WESLEYAN ACADEMY

PO Box 1489
Guaynabo, Puerto Rico 00970-1489

Head of School: Rev. Fernando Vazquez

General Information Coeducational day college-preparatory school, affiliated with Wesleyan Church. Grades PK–12. Founded: 1955. Setting: urban. Nearest major city is San Juan. 6-acre campus. 1 building on campus. Approved or accredited by Association of Christian Schools International, Middle States Association of Colleges and Schools, and Puerto Rico Department of Education. Total enrollment: 927. Upper school average class size: 25. Upper school faculty-student ratio: 1:23. There are 180 required school days per year for Upper School students. Upper School students typically attend 6 days per week. The average school day consists of 6 hours and 15 minutes.

Upper School Student Profile Grade 9: 53 students (28 boys, 25 girls); Grade 10: 53 students (27 boys, 26 girls); Grade 11: 51 students (27 boys, 24 girls); Grade 12: 40 students (21 boys, 19 girls). 50% of students are members of Wesleyan Church.

Faculty School total: 72. In upper school: 7 men, 14 women; 5 have advanced degrees.

Subjects Offered Accounting, algebra, American history, anatomy and physiology, art, Bible, biology, calculus, career and personal planning, choir, college planning, computer skills, critical writing, dance, drama, English, French, general math, general science, geography, geometry, global studies, golf, guidance, guitar, handbells, health, history, Internet, intro to computers, keyboarding, lab science, library, mathematics, music, music appreciation, personal development, piano, poetry, pre-algebra, pre-calculus, pre-college orientation, Puerto Rican history, science, social sciences, Spanish, swimming, trigonometry, U.S. government, volleyball, world affairs, world history, yearbook.

Graduation Requirements American government, American history, Bible, computer science, electives, English, foreign language, health, history, lab science, mathematics, physical education (includes health), science, service learning/internship, social sciences, social studies (includes history), Spanish, 84 accumulative hours of community service during high school years.

Special Academic Programs Advanced Placement exam preparation; honors section; independent study.

College Admission Counseling 47 students graduated in 2012; 46 went to college, including Embry-Riddle Aeronautical University–Daytona; Georgia Institute of Technology; Penn State University Park; Purdue University; The Johns Hopkins University; University of Florida. Other: 1 had other specific plans. Mean SAT critical reading: 537, mean SAT math: 500, mean SAT writing: 531, mean combined SAT: 1037. 24% scored over 600 on SAT critical reading, 14% scored over 600 on SAT math, 48% scored over 600 on SAT writing, 14% scored over 1800 on combined SAT.

Student Life Upper grades have uniform requirement, student council, honor system. Discipline rests primarily with faculty.

Summer Programs Remediation, enrichment, advancement programs offered; session focuses on remediation and enrichment classes; held on campus; accepts boys and girls; open to students from other schools. 100 students usually enrolled. 2013 schedule: June 4 to June 29. Application deadline: May 31.

Tuition and Aid Day student tuition: $6700. Guaranteed tuition plan. Tuition installment plan (monthly payment plans, full-payment discount plan, semester payment plan). Need-based scholarship grants, need-based financial aid available. In 2012–13, 2% of upper-school students received aid. Total amount of financial aid awarded in 2012–13: $1000.

Admissions Traditional secondary-level entrance grade is 9. For fall 2012, 165 students applied for upper-level admission, 150 were accepted, 143 enrolled. Academic Profile Tests, admissions testing, mathematics proficiency exam and Metropolitan Achievement Test required. Deadline for receipt of application materials: none. Application fee required: $100. On-campus interview required.

Athletics Interscholastic: basketball (boys, girls), golf (b,g), indoor soccer (b,g), soccer (b,g), swimming and diving (b,g), tennis (b,g), track and field (b,g), volleyball (b,g); intramural: basketball (b,g), indoor soccer (b,g), soccer (b,g), track and field (b,g), volleyball (b,g); coed interscholastic: tennis. 3 PE instructors, 3 coaches.

Computers Computers are regularly used in all academic classes. Computer network features include on-campus library services, Internet access, wireless campus network, Internet filtering or blocking technology. Computer access in designated common areas is available to students. The school has a published electronic and media policy.

Contact Mrs. Mae Ling Cardona, Admissions Clerk. 787-720-8959 Ext. 235. Fax: 787-790-0730. E-mail: mcardona@wesleyanacademy.org. Web site: www.wesleyanacademy.org

WESTBURY CHRISTIAN SCHOOL

10420 Hillcroft
Houston, Texas 77096

Head of School: Mr. Greg J. Glenn

General Information Coeducational day college-preparatory, arts, business, and religious studies school, affiliated with Church of Christ. Grades PK–12. Founded: 1975. Setting: urban. 13-acre campus. 1 building on campus. Approved or accredited by National Christian School Association, Southern Association of Colleges and Schools, Texas Private School Accreditation Commission, The College Board, and Texas Department of Education. Endowment: $300,000. Total enrollment: 579. Upper school average class size: 22. Upper school faculty-student ratio: 1:10. There are 180 required school days per year for Upper School students. Upper School students typically attend 5 days per week. The average school day consists of 7 hours and 45 minutes.

Upper School Student Profile Grade 9: 74 students (46 boys, 28 girls); Grade 10: 72 students (48 boys, 24 girls); Grade 11: 62 students (36 boys, 26 girls); Grade 12: 59 students (27 boys, 32 girls). 18% of students are members of Church of Christ.

Faculty School total: 62. In upper school: 20 men, 21 women; 13 have advanced degrees.

Subjects Offered Accounting, algebra, anatomy and physiology, art, athletics, band, basketball, Bible, biology, biology-AP, business, calculus-AP, cheerleading, chemistry, chemistry-AP, community service, computer applications, drama, economics, English, English language and composition-AP, English literature and composition-AP, entrepreneurship, geography, geometry, government, government-AP, health, human geography - AP, macro/microeconomics-AP, marketing, photography, physical education, physical science, physics, pre-calculus, psychology-AP, Spanish, speech, statistics-AP, studio art-AP, U.S. history, U.S. history-AP, vocal music, weight training, world history, world history-AP, yearbook.

Graduation Requirements Arts and fine arts (art, music, dance, drama), Bible, electives, English, foreign language, geometry, mathematics, physical education (includes health), science, social studies (includes history), speech, continuous participation in student activities programs, community service each semester.

Special Academic Programs 15 Advanced Placement exams for which test preparation is offered; independent study.

College Admission Counseling 53 students graduated in 2012; 51 went to college, including Harding University; Houston Baptist University; Texas A&M University; Texas Tech University; The University of Texas at Austin; University of Houston. Other: 1 went to work, 1 entered a postgraduate year. Mean SAT critical reading: 482, mean SAT math: 552, mean SAT writing: 489, mean combined SAT: 1523, mean composite ACT: 23. 15% scored over 600 on SAT critical reading, 24% scored over 600 on SAT math, 9% scored over 600 on SAT writing, 11% scored over 1800 on combined SAT, 28% scored over 26 on composite ACT.

Student Life Upper grades have uniform requirement, student council, honor system. Discipline rests primarily with faculty.

Summer Programs Sports programs offered; session focuses on week-long basketball, football, and volleyball instruction camps; held both on and off campus; held at Wildcat athletic complex, 10402 Fondren, Houston; accepts boys and girls; open to students from other schools. 200 students usually enrolled. 2013 schedule: June 3 to July 26. Application deadline: none.

Tuition and Aid Day student tuition: $11,840. Tuition installment plan (FACTS Tuition Payment Plan). Tuition reduction for siblings, merit scholarship grants, need-based scholarship grants available. In 2012–13, 23% of upper-school students received aid; total upper-school merit-scholarship money awarded: $20,000. Total amount of financial aid awarded in 2012–13: $325,000.

Admissions Traditional secondary-level entrance grade is 9. For fall 2012, 140 students applied for upper-level admission, 100 were accepted, 86 enrolled. ISEE, Otis-Lennon School Ability Test or SLEP for foreign students required. Deadline for receipt of application materials: none. Application fee required: $75. Interview required.

Athletics Interscholastic: baseball (boys), basketball (b,g), cheering (g), cross-country running (b,g), football (b), golf (b,g), soccer (b,g), softball (g), strength & conditioning (b,g), swimming and diving (b,g), tennis (b,g), track and field (b,g), volleyball (g). 1 PE instructor, 7 coaches, 1 athletic trainer.

Computers Computers are regularly used in all academic classes. Computer network features include on-campus library services, online commercial services, Internet access, wireless campus network, Internet filtering or blocking technology. Campus intranet and student e-mail accounts are available to students. Students grades are available online. The school has a published electronic and media policy.

Contact Mrs. Phylis Frye, Director of Admissions. 713-551-8100 Ext. 1018. Fax: 713-551-8117. E-mail: admissions@westburychristian.org. Web site: www.westburychristian.org

WEST CATHOLIC HIGH SCHOOL

1801 Bristol Avenue NW
Grand Rapids, Michigan 49504

Head of School: Mrs. Cynthia Kneibel

General Information Coeducational day college-preparatory and religious studies school, affiliated with Roman Catholic Church. Grades 9–12. Founded: 1962. Setting: urban. 20-acre campus. 1 building on campus. Approved or accredited by National Catholic Education Association, North Central Association of Colleges and Schools, and Michigan Department of Education. Endowment: $1 million. Total enrollment: 437. Upper school average class size: 30. Upper school faculty-student ratio: 1:30. There are 181 required school days per year for Upper School students. Upper School students typically attend 5 days per week. The average school day consists of 6 hours.

Upper School Student Profile Grade 9: 87 students (43 boys, 44 girls); Grade 10: 117 students (60 boys, 57 girls); Grade 11: 112 students (69 boys, 43 girls); Grade 12: 121 students (60 boys, 61 girls). 95% of students are Roman Catholic.

Faculty School total: 26. In upper school: 13 men, 13 women; 20 have advanced degrees.

Subjects Offered 20th century world history, acting, advanced chemistry, advanced computer applications, advanced math, American government, American literature, anatomy, art, band, Basic programming, biology, biology-AP, calculus, calculus-AP, career planning, chemistry, choir, Christian doctrine, composition, composition-AP, computer applications, computer programming, concert band, desktop publishing, drama, drawing, earth science, economics, economics-AP, English, English language and composition-AP, English literature, English literature and composition-AP, English literature-AP, environmental science, family living, French, general math, geometry, government, government and politics-AP, government-AP, government/civics, history, history of the Catholic Church, honors algebra, honors English, honors geometry, honors world history, human anatomy, intro to computers, jazz band, journalism, marching band, physics, pre-algebra, pre-calculus, psychology, sexuality, social justice, sociology, Spanish, U.S. government and politics-AP, U.S. history, Web site design, world history, yearbook.

Graduation Requirements Economics, electives, English composition, foreign language, government, health, mathematics, religion (includes Bible studies and theology), science, social studies (includes history), U.S. history, visual arts.

Special Academic Programs Advanced Placement exam preparation; honors section; independent study; remedial reading and/or remedial writing.

College Admission Counseling 121 students graduated in 2012; 117 went to college, including Central Michigan University; Grand Valley State University; Loyola University Chicago; Saint Mary's College; University of Dayton. Other: 1 went to work, 3 entered military service. 45% scored over 600 on SAT critical reading, 67% scored over 600 on SAT math, 45% scored over 600 on SAT writing, 45% scored over 1800 on combined SAT, 31% scored over 26 on composite ACT.

Student Life Upper grades have uniform requirement, student council, honor system. Discipline rests primarily with faculty. Attendance at religious services is required.

Summer Programs Remediation, sports programs offered; session focuses on sports enrichment; held on campus; accepts boys and girls; not open to students from other schools. 150 students usually enrolled. 2013 schedule: June 10 to July 31. Application deadline: June 1.

Tuition and Aid Day student tuition: $8170. Tuition installment plan (FACTS Tuition Payment Plan, individually arranged payment plans). Need-based scholarship grants available. In 2012–13, 25% of upper-school students received aid.

Admissions Traditional secondary-level entrance grade is 9. For fall 2012, 10 students applied for upper-level admission, 10 were accepted, 10 enrolled. Essay, High School Placement Test and Math Placement Exam required. Deadline for receipt of application materials: February 1. Application fee required: $150.

Athletics Interscholastic: baseball (boys), basketball (b,g), bowling (b,g), cheering (g), cross-country running (b,g), diving (b,g), football (b), golf (b,g), gymnastics (g), hockey (b), ice hockey (b), pom squad (g), skiing (downhill) (b,g), soccer (b,g), softball (g), swimming and diving (b,g), tennis (b,g), track and field (b,g), volleyball (g), weight lifting (b), weight training (b), wrestling (b); intramural: basketball (b,g). 1 PE instructor, 66 coaches, 2 athletic trainers.

Computers Computers are regularly used in all academic classes. Computer network features include Internet access, wireless campus network, Internet filtering or blocking technology. Student e-mail accounts and computer access in designated common areas are available to students. Students grades are available online. The school has a published electronic and media policy.

Contact Mrs. Lauri Ford, Guidance Secretary. 616-233-5909. Fax: 616-453-4320. E-mail: lauriford@grcss.org. Web site: www.grwestcatholic.org

WESTCHESTER COUNTRY DAY SCHOOL

2045 North Old Greensboro Road
High Point, North Carolina 27265

Head of School: Mr. Cobb Atkinson

General Information Coeducational day and distance learning college-preparatory, arts, bilingual studies, and technology school. Grades PK–12. Distance learning grades 6–12. Founded: 1967. Setting: rural. 53-acre campus. 6 buildings on campus. Approved or accredited by North Carolina Association of Independent Schools, Southern Association of Colleges and Schools, Southern Association of Independent Schools, and North Carolina Department of Education. Member of National Association of Independent Schools. Endowment: $2.5 million. Total enrollment: 384. Upper school average class size: 16. Upper school faculty-student ratio: 1:6. There are 176 required school days per year for Upper School students. Upper School students typically attend 5 days per week. The average school day consists of 5 hours and 40 minutes.

Upper School Student Profile Grade 9: 35 students (22 boys, 13 girls); Grade 10: 25 students (14 boys, 11 girls); Grade 11: 39 students (26 boys, 13 girls); Grade 12: 43 students (18 boys, 25 girls).

Faculty School total: 73. In upper school: 9 men, 16 women; 25 have advanced degrees.

Subjects Offered Advanced chemistry, Advanced Placement courses, advanced studio art-AP, algebra, American history, American literature, American literature-AP, art, art history-AP, art-AP, athletics, biology, biology-AP, British literature, calculus, calculus-AP, chamber groups, character education, chemistry, chemistry-AP, choral music, chorus, college admission preparation, college counseling, college placement, college planning, college writing, computer science, creative writing, dance, debate, earth science, economics, English, English language-AP, English literature, English literature-AP, environmental science, European history, European history-AP, exercise science, film and literature, fine arts, French, geography, geometry, global studies, government/civics, grammar, health, health education, history, Mandarin, mathematics, music, physical education, physics, probability and statistics, science, social studies, Spanish, Spanish language-AP, statistics-AP, theater, U.S. history-AP, voice ensemble, Web site design, world history, world literature, writing.

Graduation Requirements Arts and fine arts (art, music, dance, drama), civics, English, foreign language, mathematics, physical education (includes health), science, social studies (includes history), community service project, senior speech.

Special Academic Programs 12 Advanced Placement exams for which test preparation is offered; honors section; independent study.

College Admission Counseling 30 students graduated in 2012; all went to college, including Appalachian State University; High Point University; North Carolina State University; Roanoke College; The University of North Carolina at Chapel Hill. Median SAT critical reading: 560, median SAT math: 570, median SAT writing: 550, median combined SAT: 1110.

Student Life Upper grades have specified standards of dress, student council, honor system. Discipline rests primarily with faculty.

Summer Programs Enrichment, sports, art/fine arts, computer instruction programs offered; session focuses on academics, sports, hobby-related; held on campus; accepts boys and girls; open to students from other schools. 200 students usually enrolled. 2013 schedule: May 31 to August 12. Application deadline: none.

Tuition and Aid Day student tuition: $6000–$14,760. Guaranteed tuition plan. Tuition installment plan (FACTS Tuition Payment Plan, monthly payment plans). Tuition reduction for siblings, need-based scholarship grants available. In 2012–13, 13% of upper-school students received aid. Total amount of financial aid awarded in 2012–13: $524,945.

Admissions Traditional secondary-level entrance grade is 9. Brigance Test of Basic Skills, ERB CTP IV, grade equivalent tests, Metropolitan Achievement Test, Wide Range Achievement Test or Woodcock-Johnson Revised Achievement Test required. Deadline for receipt of application materials: none. Application fee required: $75. Interview recommended.

Athletics Interscholastic: baseball (boys), basketball (b,g), cheering (g), dance (g), dance team (g), soccer (b,g), softball (g), tennis (b,g), volleyball (g); coed interscholastic: aquatics, cross-country running, golf, physical fitness, swimming and diving, track and field. 2 PE instructors, 12 coaches.

Computers Computers are regularly used in English, foreign language, history, library science, mathematics, science, Web site design, yearbook classes. Computer network features include on-campus library services, Internet access, wireless campus network, Internet filtering or blocking technology. Campus intranet, student e-mail accounts, and computer access in designated common areas are available to students. Students grades are available online. The school has a published electronic and media policy.

Contact Mrs. Kerie Beth Scott, Director of Admissions. 336-822-4005. Fax: 336-869-6685. E-mail: keriebeth.scott@westchestercds.org. Web site: www.westchestercds.org

WESTERN MENNONITE SCHOOL

9045 Wallace Road NW
Salem, Oregon 97304-9716

Head of School: Darrel Camp

General Information Coeducational boarding and day college-preparatory, general academic, and religious studies school, affiliated with Mennonite Church USA. Boarding grades 9–12, day grades 6–12. Founded: 1945. Setting: rural. Students are housed in single-sex dormitories. 45-acre campus. 10 buildings on campus. Approved or accredited by Mennonite Education Agency, Mennonite Schools Council, Northwest Accreditation Commission, and Oregon Department of Education. Endowment: $1 million. Total enrollment: 230. Upper school average class size: 16. Upper school faculty-student ratio: 1:14. There are 173 required school days per year for Upper School students. Upper School students typically attend 5 days per week. The average school day consists of 5 hours and 25 minutes.

Upper School Student Profile Grade 9: 35 students (17 boys, 18 girls); Grade 10: 35 students (18 boys, 17 girls); Grade 11: 33 students (16 boys, 17 girls); Grade 12: 51 students (26 boys, 25 girls). 12% of students are boarding students. 85% are state residents. 3 states are represented in upper school student body. 12% are international students. International students from China, Germany, Hong Kong, Japan, Republic of Korea, and Taiwan; 7 other countries represented in student body. 18% of students are Mennonite Church USA.

Faculty School total: 26. In upper school: 12 men, 14 women; 8 have advanced degrees; 10 reside on campus.

Subjects Offered Accounting, advanced math, algebra, anatomy and physiology, art, Bible studies, biology, calculus, career and personal planning, career education, chemistry, choral music, Christian education, Christian scripture, church history, computer applications, computer programming, drawing and design, economics, English, English composition, English literature, general math, geography, geometry, government, health education, human anatomy, instrumental music, intro to computers, keyboarding, mathematics, music, music performance, novels, physical education, physical fitness, physical science, physics, pre-algebra, pre-calculus, psychology, religious education, religious studies, research, science, Spanish, U.S. government, U.S. history, U.S. literature, woodworking, yearbook.

Graduation Requirements Algebra, applied arts, Bible studies, biology, career education, chemistry, choir, economics, English, English literature, geometry, global studies, music, physical education (includes health), Spanish, U.S. government, U.S. history, U.S. literature, world geography, Mini-Term—one week of co-curricular activity at end of academic year (sophomore through senior year).

Special Academic Programs Independent study; term-away projects; study at local college for college credit.

College Admission Counseling 42 students graduated in 2011; 38 went to college, including Chemeketa Community College; Corban University; Eastern Mennonite University; Oregon State University; Seattle Pacific University; Western Oregon University. Median SAT math: 520, median composite ACT: 27. 11% scored over 600 on SAT math, 50% scored over 26 on composite ACT.

Student Life Upper grades have specified standards of dress, student council, honor system. Discipline rests primarily with faculty. Attendance at religious services is required.

Tuition and Aid Day student tuition: $7700; 5-day tuition and room/board: $11,748; 7-day tuition and room/board: $13,431. Tuition installment plan (monthly payment plans, individually arranged payment plans). Tuition reduction for siblings, merit scholarship grants, need-based scholarship grants, paying campus jobs available. In 2011–12, 41% of upper-school students received aid.

Admissions Traditional secondary-level entrance grade is 9. Deadline for receipt of application materials: none. Application fee required: $50. Interview recommended.

Athletics Interscholastic: baseball (boys, girls), basketball (b,g), cross-country running (b), soccer (b,g), volleyball (g); coed intramural: softball. 5 PE instructors, 8 coaches.

Computers Computers are regularly used in independent study, introduction to technology, keyboarding, yearbook classes. Computer network features include on-campus library services, online commercial services, Internet access, wireless campus network, Internet filtering or blocking technology. Campus intranet, student e-mail accounts, and computer access in designated common areas are available to students. Students grades are available online. The school has a published electronic and media policy.

Contact Mr. Rich Martin, Admissions Coordinator. 503-363-2000 Ext. 121. Fax: 503-370-9455. E-mail: rmartin@westernmennoniteschool.org. Web site: www.westernmennoniteschool.org

WESTGATE MENNONITE COLLEGIATE

86 West Gate
Winnipeg, Manitoba R3C 2E1, Canada

Head of School: Mr. Bob Hummelt

General Information Coeducational day college-preparatory, general academic, arts, religious studies, technology, and music, German, and French school, affiliated with Mennonite Church USA. Grades 7–12. Founded: 1958. Setting: urban. 3-acre campus. 1 building on campus. Approved or accredited by Canadian Association of Independent Schools and Manitoba Department of Education. Language of instruction: English. Total enrollment: 340. Upper school average class size: 25. Upper school faculty-student ratio: 1:15. Upper School students typically attend 5 days per week. The average school day consists of 6 hours and 30 minutes.

Upper School Student Profile Grade 10: 71 students (36 boys, 35 girls); Grade 11: 48 students (24 boys, 24 girls); Grade 12: 64 students (39 boys, 25 girls). 55% of students are Mennonite Church USA.

Faculty School total: 27. In upper school: 15 men, 11 women; 5 have advanced degrees.

Special Academic Programs Advanced Placement exam preparation; independent study; term-away projects.

College Admission Counseling 51 students graduated in 2011; they went to The University of Winnipeg; University of Manitoba.

Student Life Upper grades have specified standards of dress, student council. Discipline rests primarily with faculty. Attendance at religious services is required.

Tuition and Aid Day student tuition: CAN$4800. Tuition installment plan (monthly payment plans, individually arranged payment plans). Tuition reduction for siblings, bursaries, merit scholarship grants, need-based scholarship grants available. In 2011–12, 10% of upper-school students received aid; total upper-school merit-scholarship money awarded: CAN$5000. Total amount of financial aid awarded in 2011–12: CAN$36,000.

Admissions Traditional secondary-level entrance grade is 10. Deadline for receipt of application materials: March 10. Application fee required: CAN$50. Interview required.

Athletics Interscholastic: badminton (boys, girls), baseball (b,g), basketball (b,g), bowling (b,g), cheering (b,g), cross-country running (b,g), curling (b,g), floor hockey (b,g), golf (b), gymnastics (b,g), outdoor education (b,g), outdoor skills (b,g), rock climbing (b,g), running (b,g), soccer (b,g), strength & conditioning (b,g), volleyball (b,g); intramural: aerobics/dance (b,g), backpacking (b,g), badminton (b,g), basketball (b,g), bicycling (b,g), broomball (b,g), canoeing/kayaking (b,g), cross-country running (b,g), curling (b,g), field hockey (b,g), floor hockey (b,g), football (b,g), gymnastics (b,g), hiking/backpacking (b,g), ice hockey (b,g), ice skating (b,g), outdoor education (b,g), paddle tennis (b,g), racquetball (b,g), rock climbing (b,g), running (b,g), soccer (b,g), strength & conditioning (b,g), swimming and diving (b,g), volleyball (b,g), wall climbing (b,g); coed interscholastic: badminton, baseball, basketball, bowling, cheering, cross-country running, curling, floor hockey, gymnastics, outdoor education, outdoor skills, rock climbing, running, soccer, strength & conditioning, ultimate Frisbee, volleyball; coed intramural: aerobics/dance, backpacking, badminton, basketball, bicycling, broomball, canoeing/kayaking, cross-country running, curling, field hockey, floor hockey, football, gymnastics, hiking/backpacking, ice hockey, ice skating, outdoor education, paddle tennis, racquetball, rock climbing, running, soccer, strength & conditioning, swimming and diving, volleyball, wall climbing. 3 PE instructors, 7 coaches.

Computers Computer network features include on-campus library services, online commercial services, Internet access. The school has a published electronic and media policy.

Contact Mr. Bob Hummelt, Principal. 204-775-7111 Ext. 202. Fax: 204-786-1651. E-mail: westgate@westgatemennonite.ca. Web site: www.westgatemennonite.ca

WEST ISLAND COLLEGE

7410 Blackfoot Trail SE
Calgary, Alberta T2H IM5, Canada

Head of School: Ms. Carol Grant-Watt

General Information Coeducational day college-preparatory, arts, business, bilingual studies, technology, and advanced placement school. Grades 7–12. Founded: 1982. Setting: urban. 18-acre campus. 2 buildings on campus. Approved or accredited by Canadian Association of Independent Schools and Alberta Department of Education. Languages of instruction: English, French, and Spanish. Total enrollment: 451. Upper school average class size: 18. Upper school faculty-student ratio: 1:17. There are 182 required school days per year for Upper School students. Upper School students typically attend 5 days per week. The average school day consists of 6 hours and 13 minutes.

Upper School Student Profile Grade 10: 75 students (36 boys, 39 girls); Grade 11: 95 students (45 boys, 50 girls); Grade 12: 68 students (33 boys, 35 girls).

Faculty School total: 45. In upper school: 20 men, 21 women; 15 have advanced degrees.

Subjects Offered Advanced Placement courses, anthropology, art, arts, biology, business, chemistry, choral music, communications, debate, drama, English, European history, experiential education, French, French studies, health, information processing, information technology, leadership, literature, mathematics, modern languages, music, outdoor education, philosophy, physical education, physics, political thought, politics, psychology, public speaking, science, social sciences, social studies, sociology, Spanish, standard curriculum, study skills, world geography, world history, world religions.

Graduation Requirements Alberta Education requirements.

Special Academic Programs 10 Advanced Placement exams for which test preparation is offered; honors section; independent study; study abroad; academic accommodation for the gifted.

College Admission Counseling 71 students graduated in 2012; 69 went to college, including McGill University; Queen's University at Kingston; The University of British Columbia; University of Alberta; University of Calgary; University of Victoria. Other: 2 had other specific plans.

Student Life Upper grades have uniform requirement, student council, honor system. Discipline rests equally with students and faculty.

Summer Programs Enrichment, advancement, sports, computer instruction programs offered; session focuses on study skills and academic preparedness; held both on and off campus; held at various public parks in the city; accepts boys and girls; not open to students from other schools. 50 students usually enrolled. 2013 schedule: August 19 to August 23. Application deadline: May 30.

Tuition and Aid Day student tuition: CAN$12,800. Tuition installment plan (monthly payment plans).

Admissions Traditional secondary-level entrance grade is 10. For fall 2012, 24 students applied for upper-level admission, 23 were accepted, 19 enrolled. 3-R Achievement Test, CCAT, CTBS, OLSAT, Gates MacGinite Reading Tests and Otis-Lennon IQ Test required. Deadline for receipt of application materials: none. Application fee required: CAN$100. Interview required.

Athletics Interscholastic: basketball (boys, girls), field hockey (g), rugby (b), track and field (b,g), volleyball (b,g); intramural: aquatics (b,g), basketball (b,g), floor hockey (b,g), track and field (b,g), volleyball (b,g); coed interscholastic: badminton, climbing, cross-country running, soccer; coed intramural: alpine skiing, backpacking, badminton, bicycling, bowling, canoeing/kayaking, climbing, cross-country running, curling, dance, fitness, golf, hiking/backpacking, kayaking, mountaineering, nordic skiing, outdoor activities, outdoor education, physical fitness, physical training, rock climbing, sailing, skiing (cross-country), skiing (downhill), snowboarding, soccer, wilderness survival, wildernessways. 4 PE instructors, 10 coaches, 2 athletic trainers.

Computers Computers are regularly used in business, career education, career exploration, career technology, economics, English, French, independent study, mathematics, media arts, media production, multimedia, science, social studies, technology, word processing classes. Computer network features include on-campus library services, online commercial services, Internet access, wireless campus network, Internet filtering or blocking technology. Campus intranet, student e-mail accounts, and computer access in designated common areas are available to students. Students grades are available online. The school has a published electronic and media policy.

Contact Ms. Nicole Bernard, Director of Admissions. 403-444-0023. Fax: 403-444-2820. E-mail: admissions@westislandcollege.ab.ca. Web site: www.westislandcollege.ab.ca

WESTMARK SCHOOL

Encino, California

See Special Needs Schools section.

WESTMINSTER CHRISTIAN ACADEMY

237 Johns Road
Huntsville, Alabama 35806

Head of School: Mr. Craig L. Bouvier

General Information Coeducational day college-preparatory, general academic, arts, religious studies, and technology school, affiliated with Presbyterian Church in America. Grades K–12. Founded: 1964. Setting: suburban. Nearest major city is Birmingham. 42-acre campus. 5 buildings on campus. Approved or accredited by Christian Schools International, Southern Association of Colleges and Schools, and Alabama Department of Education. Member of Secondary School Admission Test Board. Endowment: $243,000. Total enrollment: 733. Upper school average class size: 17. Upper school faculty-student ratio: 1:13. There are 180 required school days per year for Upper School students. Upper School students typically attend 5 days per week. The average school day consists of 7 hours and 10 minutes.

Upper School Student Profile Grade 9: 73 students (34 boys, 39 girls); Grade 10: 70 students (41 boys, 29 girls); Grade 11: 70 students (42 boys, 28 girls); Grade 12: 44 students (19 boys, 25 girls). 15% of students are Presbyterian Church in America.

Faculty School total: 62. In upper school: 16 men, 21 women; 9 have advanced degrees.

Subjects Offered Advanced computer applications, algebra, American history, American history-AP, art, band, Bible studies, biology, botany, business mathematics, business skills, calculus, calculus-AP, chemistry, choir, civics, computer programming, computer programming-AP, concert choir, consumer mathematics, CPR, drama, drama performance, economics-AP, English, English-AP, ensembles, environmental science, first aid, fitness, French, geography, geometry, government, government-AP, health education, home economics, interior design, journalism, keyboarding, Latin, modern dance, painting, photography, physical education, physical science, physics, physiology, pre-calculus, psychology, Spanish, Web site design, world history, yearbook.

Graduation Requirements Arts and fine arts (art, music, dance, drama), computer applications, electives, English, foreign language, mathematics, physical education (includes health), religion (includes Bible studies and theology), science, social studies (includes history).

Special Academic Programs Advanced Placement exam preparation; honors section; independent study; study at local college for college credit.

College Admission Counseling 57 students graduated in 2011; 55 went to college, including Auburn University; The University of Alabama; The University of Alabama in Huntsville. Other: 1 went to work, 1 entered military service. 35% scored over 600 on SAT critical reading, 50% scored over 600 on SAT math, 65% scored over 26 on composite ACT.

Student Life Upper grades have specified standards of dress, student council. Discipline rests primarily with faculty. Attendance at religious services is required.

Tuition and Aid Day student tuition: $7484. Guaranteed tuition plan. Tuition installment plan (monthly payment plans, Semi-Annual Payments, Annual Payments). Tuition reduction for siblings, need-based scholarship grants, reduced tuition for children of faculty available. In 2011–12, 4% of upper-school students received aid. Total amount of financial aid awarded in 2011–12: $35,149.

Admissions Traditional secondary-level entrance grade is 9. For fall 2011, 57 students applied for upper-level admission, 33 were accepted, 30 enrolled. Any standardized test, school's own test or writing sample required. Deadline for receipt of application materials: none. Application fee required: $75. Interview required.

Athletics Interscholastic: baseball (boys), basketball (b,g), cheering (g), cross-country running (b,g), drill team (g), football (b), golf (b,g), physical training (b,g), soccer (b,g), softball (g), swimming and diving (b,g), track and field (b,g), volleyball (g), weight training (b,g), wrestling (b); intramural: physical fitness (b,g), physical training (b,g), strength & conditioning (b,g), weight training (b,g); coed interscholastic: cheering; coed intramural: weight training. 2 PE instructors, 6 coaches, 1 athletic trainer.

Computers Computers are regularly used in all academic classes. Computer network features include on-campus library services, Internet access, wireless campus network, Internet filtering or blocking technology. Student e-mail accounts and computer access in designated common areas are available to students. Students grades are available online. The school has a published electronic and media policy.

Contact Mrs. Leslie Parker, Admissions Director. 256-705-8229. Fax: 256-705-8001. E-mail: leslie.parker@wca-hsv.org. Web site: www.wca-hsv.org

WESTMINSTER CHRISTIAN ACADEMY

186 Westminster Drive
Opelousas, Louisiana 70570

Head of School: Mrs. Merida Brooks

General Information Coeducational day college-preparatory, arts, religious studies, bilingual studies, and technology school, affiliated with Protestant-Evangelical faith, Christian faith. Grades PK–12. Founded: 1978. Setting: rural. Nearest major city is Lafayette. 30-acre campus. 6 buildings on campus. Approved or accredited by Association of Christian Schools International and Louisiana Department of Education. Endowment: $200,000. Total enrollment: 1,123. Upper school average class size: 23. Upper school faculty-student ratio: 1:13. There are 175 required school days per year for Upper School students. Upper School students typically attend 5 days per week. The average school day consists of 7 hours.

Upper School Student Profile Grade 9: 74 students (42 boys, 32 girls); Grade 10: 70 students (34 boys, 36 girls); Grade 11: 51 students (28 boys, 23 girls); Grade 12: 50 students (27 boys, 23 girls). 95% of students are Protestant-Evangelical faith, Christian faith.

Faculty School total: 66. In upper school: 13 men, 12 women; 5 have advanced degrees.

Subjects Offered Advanced math, algebra, American history, art, biology, calculus, calculus-AP, ceramics, chemistry, chemistry-AP, civics, concert choir, creative writing, drama, economics, English, English-AP, fine arts, French, geometry, guitar, history-AP, Latin, music, physics, religion, Spanish, world history, yearbook.

Graduation Requirements Arts and fine arts (art, music, dance, drama), computer literacy, English, foreign language, mathematics, physical education (includes health), religion (includes Bible studies and theology), science, social studies (includes history).

Special Academic Programs 6 Advanced Placement exams for which test preparation is offered; honors section; accelerated programs; special instructional classes for students with mild learning disabilities and Attention Deficit Disorder.

College Admission Counseling 52 students graduated in 2012; 50 went to college, including Baylor University; Louisiana State University and Agricultural and Mechanical College; Louisiana Tech University; Loyola University New Orleans; University of Louisiana at Lafayette. Other: 2 went to work. Mean SAT math: 581, mean SAT writing: 680, mean composite ACT: 26.

Student Life Upper grades have uniform requirement, student council. Discipline rests primarily with faculty. Attendance at religious services is required.

Summer Programs Sports programs offered; session focuses on training for football; held on campus; accepts boys; not open to students from other schools. 85 students usually enrolled. 2013 schedule: July 31.

Tuition and Aid Day student tuition: $5935. Tuition installment plan (monthly payment plans, individually arranged payment plans, annual and biannual payment plans). Need-based scholarship grants, pastor discounts available. In 2012–13, 10% of upper-school students received aid. Total amount of financial aid awarded in 2012–13: $70,000.

Admissions Traditional secondary-level entrance grade is 9. For fall 2012, 26 students applied for upper-level admission, 23 were accepted, 21 enrolled. School's own exam and Stanford Achievement Test required. Deadline for receipt of application materials: none. Application fee required: $150. On-campus interview required.

Athletics Interscholastic: baseball (boys), basketball (b,g), cheering (g), cross-country running (b,g), football (b), soccer (b,g), softball (g), swimming and diving (b,g), track and field (b,g), volleyball (g); coed interscholastic: golf, hiking/backpacking, soccer, wilderness survival. 2 PE instructors, 2 coaches, 1 athletic trainer.

Computers Computers are regularly used in all classes. Computer network features include on-campus library services, Internet access, wireless campus network, Internet filtering or blocking technology. Student e-mail accounts are available to students. Students grades are available online. The school has a published electronic and media policy.

Contact Mrs. Michelle Nezat, Director of Institutional Advancement. 337-948-4623 Ext. 123. Fax: 337-948-4090. E-mail: mnezat@wcala.org. Web site: www.wcala.org

WESTMINSTER SCHOOL

995 Hopmeadow Street
Simsbury, Connecticut 06070

Head of School: Mr. William V.N. Philip

General Information Coeducational boarding and day college-preparatory, arts, and technology school. Grades 9–PG. Founded: 1888. Setting: suburban. Nearest major city is Hartford. Students are housed in single-sex dormitories. 230-acre campus. 38 buildings on campus. Approved or accredited by Connecticut Association of Independent Schools, New England Association of Schools and Colleges, The Association of Boarding Schools, and Connecticut Department of Education. Member of National Association of Independent Schools and Secondary School Admission Test Board. Endowment: $77 million. Total enrollment: 390. Upper school average class size: 12. Upper school faculty-student ratio: 1:6. There are 185 required school days per year for Upper School students. Upper School students typically attend 6 days per week. The average school day consists of 6 hours and 30 minutes.

Upper School Student Profile Grade 9: 84 students (44 boys, 40 girls); Grade 10: 101 students (54 boys, 47 girls); Grade 11: 103 students (55 boys, 48 girls); Grade 12: 92 students (51 boys, 41 girls); Postgraduate: 13 students (13 boys). 67% of students are boarding students. 49% are state residents. 26 states are represented in upper school student body. 13% are international students. International students from Bermuda, Canada, China, Hong Kong, Republic of Korea, and Taiwan; 14 other countries represented in student body.

Faculty School total: 62. In upper school: 35 men, 27 women; 52 have advanced degrees; 51 reside on campus.

Subjects Offered Acting, advanced chemistry, advanced computer applications, advanced math, Advanced Placement courses, advanced studio art-AP, African American history, algebra, American history, American history-AP, American literature, American literature-AP, anatomy and physiology, Ancient Greek, architecture, art, art history, art history-AP, art-AP, Asian history, astronomy, athletics, band, biology, biology-AP, calculus, calculus-AP, character education, chemistry, chemistry-AP, Chinese, choir, choral music, comparative government and politics-AP, computer programming, computer science-AP, creative writing, dance, discrete mathematics, drama, drama workshop, drawing, drawing and design, driver education, ecology, economics, economics-AP, English, English literature, English-AP, English/composition-AP, environmental science-AP, ethics, ethics and responsibility, European history, European history-AP, female experience in America, fine arts, French, French language-AP, French literature-AP, geology, geometry, graphic design, health, history, honors algebra, honors English, honors geometry, illustration, Latin, Latin-AP, literature and composition-AP, macro/microeconomics-AP, mathematics, mathematics-AP, mechanical drawing, modern European history-AP, music, music appreciation, music composition, music theory-AP, musical theater, Native American history, painting, philosophy, photography, physics, physics-AP, pre-calculus, probability and statistics, psychology-AP, SAT preparation, SAT/ACT preparation, science, set design, social studies, Spanish, Spanish language-AP, Spanish literature, Spanish literature-AP, stagecraft, statistics, statistics-AP, studio art-AP, theater, trigonometry, U.S. history-AP, world history, writing.

Graduation Requirements Arts, English, foreign language, history, mathematics, science.

Special Academic Programs 23 Advanced Placement exams for which test preparation is offered; honors section; independent study; term-away projects; study abroad.

College Admission Counseling 113 students graduated in 2012; all went to college, including Boston College; Duke University; Middlebury College; Trinity College; University of Richmond. Median SAT critical reading: 617, median SAT math: 619, median SAT writing: 626, median combined SAT: 1862.

Student Life Upper grades have specified standards of dress, student council. Discipline rests primarily with faculty.

Summer Programs Enrichment, sports programs offered; session focuses on soccer, science; held on campus; accepts boys and girls; open to students from other schools. 350 students usually enrolled. 2013 schedule: July 9 to August 3.

Tuition and Aid Day student tuition: $36,800; 7-day tuition and room/board: $49,500. Tuition installment plan (Academic Management Services Plan). Need-based scholarship grants available. In 2012–13, 31% of upper-school students received aid. Total amount of financial aid awarded in 2012–13: $4,020,700.

Admissions Traditional secondary-level entrance grade is 9. For fall 2012, 1,175 students applied for upper-level admission, 279 were accepted, 137 enrolled. PSAT and SAT for applicants to grade 11 and 12, SSAT or TOEFL required. Deadline for receipt of application materials: January 15. Application fee required: $75. On-campus interview required.

Athletics Interscholastic: baseball (boys), basketball (b,g), cross-country running (b,g), diving (b,g), field hockey (g), football (b), golf (b,g), hockey (b,g), ice hockey (b,g), lacrosse (b,g), soccer (b,g), softball (g), squash (b,g), swimming and diving (b,g), tennis (b,g), track and field (b,g); intramural: strength & conditioning (b,g); coed interscholastic: dance, martial arts, modern dance; coed intramural: aerobics/dance, ballet, bowling, canoeing/kayaking, dance, fly fishing, freestyle skiing, ice skating, modern dance, mountain biking, outdoor activities, rugby, skiing (cross-country), skiing (downhill), table tennis, unicycling. 2 athletic trainers.

Computers Computers are regularly used in English, foreign language, history, mathematics, science classes. Computer network features include on-campus library services, online commercial services, Internet access, wireless campus network, Internet filtering or blocking technology. Campus intranet, student e-mail accounts, and computer access in designated common areas are available to students. The school has a published electronic and media policy.

Contact Mrs. Rhonda Smith, Admissions Assistant. 860-408-3060. Fax: 860-408-3042. E-mail: admit@westminster-school.org. Web site: www.westminster-school.org

WESTOVER SCHOOL

1237 Whittemore Road
Middlebury, Connecticut 06762

Head of School: Mrs. Ann S. Pollina

General Information Girls' boarding and day college-preparatory, arts, technology, and mathematics and science school. Grades 9–12. Founded: 1909. Setting: small town. Nearest major city is New York, NY. Students are housed in single-sex dormitories. 145-acre campus. 11 buildings on campus. Approved or accredited by Association of Independent Schools in New England, New England Association of Schools and Colleges, The Association of Boarding Schools, and Connecticut Department of Education. Member of National Association of Independent Schools and Secondary School Admission Test Board. Endowment: $48 million. Total enrollment: 209. Upper school average class size: 12. Upper school faculty-student ratio: 1:12. There are 183 required school days per year for Upper School students. Upper School students typically attend 6 days per week. The average school day consists of 6 hours.

Upper School Student Profile Grade 9: 44 students (44 girls); Grade 10: 59 students (59 girls); Grade 11: 46 students (46 girls); Grade 12: 60 students (60 girls). 62% of students are boarding students. 53% are state residents. 16 states are represented in upper school student body. 19% are international students. International students from China, Japan, Netherlands, Republic of Korea, Russian Federation, and Turkey; 11 other countries represented in student body.

Faculty School total: 37. In upper school: 13 men, 24 women; 29 have advanced degrees; 20 reside on campus.

Subjects Offered Advanced chemistry, Advanced Placement courses, African-American studies, algebra, American history, American history-AP, American literature, art, art history, art-AP, astronomy, ballet technique, bell choir, biology, biology-AP, calculus, calculus-AP, ceramics, chemistry, clayworking, community service, computer literacy, computer science, computer science-AP, creative writing, dance, drama, drawing, English, English language and composition-AP, English literature, environmental science, ESL, etymology, European history, European history-AP, filmmaking, fine arts, French, French-AP, geography, geometry, grammar, health and wellness, journalism, Latin, mathematics, model United Nations, music, music theory-AP, musical productions, painting, performing arts, photo shop, photography, physics, physics-AP, poetry, politics, portfolio art, pre-calculus, religion, robotics, science, sculpture, Shakespeare, short story, social studies, Spanish, Spanish-AP, speech, studio art-AP, theater, trigonometry, wilderness education, women's studies, world history, writing.

Graduation Requirements Art, athletics, English, foreign language, general science, mathematics, science, summer reading. Community service is required.

Special Academic Programs 15 Advanced Placement exams for which test preparation is offered; honors section; independent study; term-away projects; study abroad; academic accommodation for the gifted, the musically talented, and the artistically talented; special instructional classes for deaf students; ESL (5 students enrolled).

College Admission Counseling 48 students graduated in 2012; all went to college, including Barnard College; Bates College; Brown University; Columbia University; University of California, Santa Cruz; University of Notre Dame. Median composite ACT: 27. Mean SAT critical reading: 597, mean SAT math: 594, mean SAT writing: 621. 61% scored over 600 on SAT critical reading, 59% scored over 600 on SAT math, 64% scored over 600 on SAT writing, 54% scored over 1800 on combined SAT, 56% scored over 26 on composite ACT.

Student Life Upper grades have specified standards of dress, student council, honor system. Discipline rests equally with students and faculty.

Tuition and Aid Day student tuition: $33,950; 7-day tuition and room/board: $47,250. Tuition installment plan (The Tuition Plan, Insured Tuition Payment Plan, FACTS Tuition Payment Plan, monthly payment plans). Need-based scholarship grants, need-based loans, middle-income loans available. In 2012–13, 50% of upper-school students received aid.

Admissions Traditional secondary-level entrance grade is 9. For fall 2012, 226 students applied for upper-level admission, 113 were accepted, 56 enrolled. ISEE, SSAT or TOEFL required. Deadline for receipt of application materials: January 14. Application fee required: $50. On-campus interview required.

Athletics Interscholastic: basketball, cross-country running, field hockey, golf, independent competitive sports, lacrosse, outdoor activities, soccer, softball, squash, swimming and diving, tennis, volleyball; intramural: aerobics, aerobics/dance, alpine skiing, backpacking, ballet, canoeing/kayaking, climbing, dance, fitness, fitness walking, Frisbee, hiking/backpacking, jogging, kayaking, modern dance, outdoor activities, outdoor education, outdoor skills, outdoors, paddle tennis, physical fitness, physical training, rappelling, rock climbing, running, self defense, skiing (downhill), snowboarding, strength & conditioning, tennis, ultimate Frisbee, walking, wall climbing, weight lifting, weight training, wilderness, yoga. 2 PE instructors, 10 coaches, 1 athletic trainer.

Computers Computers are regularly used in all academic classes. Computer network features include on-campus library services, online commercial services, Internet access, wireless campus network, Internet filtering or blocking technology. Campus intranet, student e-mail accounts, and computer access in designated common areas are available to students. Students grades are available online. The school has a published electronic and media policy.

Contact Mrs. Laura Volovski, Director of Admission. 203-577-4521. Fax: 203-577-4588. E-mail: admission@westoverschool.org. Web site: www.westoverschool.org

WESTRIDGE SCHOOL

324 Madeline Drive
Pasadena, California 91105-3399

Head of School: Ms. Elizabeth J. McGregor

General Information Girls' day college-preparatory, arts, and technology school. Grades 4–12. Founded: 1913. Setting: suburban. Nearest major city is Los Angeles. 9-

acre campus. 11 buildings on campus. Approved or accredited by California Association of Independent Schools, National Independent Private Schools Association, The College Board, Western Association of Schools and Colleges, and California Department of Education. Member of National Association of Independent Schools. Endowment: $14.6 million. Total enrollment: 480. Upper school average class size: 12. Upper school faculty-student ratio: 1:6. Upper School students typically attend 5 days per week. The average school day consists of 6 hours and 30 minutes.

Upper School Student Profile Grade 9: 52 students (52 girls); Grade 10: 64 students (64 girls); Grade 11: 73 students (73 girls); Grade 12: 67 students (67 girls).

Faculty School total: 68. In upper school: 12 men, 24 women; 27 have advanced degrees.

Subjects Offered Acting, Advanced Placement courses, algebra, American history, American literature, art, art history, biology, calculus, cell biology, ceramics, chemistry, Chinese, chorus, classical language, college counseling, computer applications, computer graphics, computer science, creative writing, dance, directing, drama, earth science, English, English literature, environmental science, European history, fine arts, French, geometry, government/civics, history, Latin, life science, Mandarin, mathematics, modern languages, music, orchestra, photography, physical education, physical science, physics, physiology, pre-calculus, science, Spanish, Spanish literature, statistics, studio art, theater, trigonometry, video, visual and performing arts, visual arts, world history, world literature.

Graduation Requirements Art, college counseling, cultural arts, English, foreign language, history, mathematics, music, physical education (includes health), science, senior project, statistics. Community service is required.

Special Academic Programs Advanced Placement exam preparation; honors section; independent study.

College Admission Counseling 71 students graduated in 2012; all went to college, including Georgetown University; New York University; The Johns Hopkins University; University of California, Los Angeles; University of Chicago; University of Southern California. Median SAT critical reading: 610-720, median SAT math: 580-690, median SAT writing: 640-760, median combined SAT: 1180-2150, median composite ACT: 26-31. Mean SAT critical reading: 670, mean SAT math: 645, mean SAT writing: 694, median combined SAT: 2010, mean composite ACT: 28.

Student Life Upper grades have uniform requirement, student council. Discipline rests primarily with faculty.

Tuition and Aid Day student tuition: $30,600. Tuition installment plan (monthly payment plans, full payment, two payment plan, 10-month tuition payment). Need-based scholarship grants available. In 2012–13, 33% of upper-school students received aid. Total amount of financial aid awarded in 2012–13: $1,523,099.

Admissions Traditional secondary-level entrance grade is 9. For fall 2012, 62 students applied for upper-level admission, 43 were accepted, 9 enrolled. ISEE or writing sample required. Deadline for receipt of application materials: January 25. Application fee required: $85. On-campus interview required.

Athletics Interscholastic: aerobics/dance, basketball, cross-country running, dance, diving, fencing, golf, lacrosse, martial arts, modern dance, physical fitness, soccer, softball, swimming and diving, tennis, track and field, volleyball, water polo, yoga. 28 coaches, 2 athletic trainers.

Computers Computers are regularly used in art, English, foreign language, history, library skills, mathematics, science, yearbook classes. Computer network features include on-campus library services, online commercial services, Internet access, wireless campus network, Internet filtering or blocking technology, course Web sites, remote access to email and files, school Internet portal/Web site. Student e-mail accounts are available to students. The school has a published electronic and media policy.

Contact Ms. Helen V. Hopper, Director of Admissions. 626-799-1153 Ext. 213. Fax: 626-799-7068. E-mail: hhopper@westridge.org. Web site: www.westridge.org

WEST SOUND ACADEMY

16571 Creative Drive NE
Poulsbo, Washington 98370

Head of School: Barrie Hillman

General Information Coeducational boarding and day college-preparatory, arts, and International Baccalaureate school. Boarding grades 9–12, day grades 6–12. Founded: 1998. Setting: rural. Nearest major city is Seattle. Students are housed in coed dormitories. 20-acre campus. 4 buildings on campus. Approved or accredited by International Baccalaureate Organization, Northwest Accreditation Commission, Pacific Northwest Association of Independent Schools, and Washington Department of Education. Total enrollment: 92. Upper school average class size: 11. Upper school faculty-student ratio: 1:7. There are 178 required school days per year for Upper School students. Upper School students typically attend 5 days per week. The average school day consists of 6 hours and 15 minutes.

Upper School Student Profile Grade 9: 19 students (14 boys, 5 girls); Grade 10: 19 students (11 boys, 8 girls); Grade 11: 18 students (9 boys, 9 girls); Grade 12: 10 students (4 boys, 6 girls). 17% of students are boarding students. 62% are state residents. 2 states are represented in upper school student body. 35% are international students. International students from China, Germany, Ghana, Mexico, Republic of Korea, and Turkey; 2 other countries represented in student body.

Faculty School total: 19. In upper school: 6 men, 8 women; 9 have advanced degrees.

Subjects Offered Advanced biology, advanced chemistry, advanced math, advanced TOEFL/grammar, algebra, American history, American literature, analytic geometry, ancient world history, art, art history, biology, calculus, chemistry, college counseling, college planning, community service, contemporary issues, creative writing, dance, drama, drawing, earth science, electives, English, ESL, film studies, fitness, four units of summer reading, French, geometry, global issues, guitar, history, International Baccalaureate courses, linear algebra, literary magazine, logarithms, marine biology, music, music performance, non-Western literature, non-Western societies, outdoor education, painting, photography, physics, poetry, portfolio art, portfolio writing, SAT preparation, senior thesis, Spanish, sports, studio art, technology, theory of knowledge, U.S. history, visual arts, Washington State and Northwest History, Western civilization, Western literature, wilderness experience, world cultures, world history, world literature, yearbook.

Graduation Requirements Biology, chemistry, English, foreign language, history, International Baccalaureate courses, mathematics, senior thesis, service learning/internship, theory of knowledge, visual arts, West Sound Academy has a 4-1-4 academic calendar; students are required to complete a Jan-Term, courses are 3-week-long short courses of intense study in a variety of subjects outside the usual curriculum, fall and spring trips to varied locations teach leadership, environmental ethics, and technical skills.

Special Academic Programs International Baccalaureate program; independent study; term-away projects; academic accommodation for the gifted, the musically talented, and the artistically talented; ESL (17 students enrolled).

College Admission Counseling 8 students graduated in 2012; 7 went to college, including Drexel University; Edmonds Community College; Hampshire College; Randolph-Macon College; University of Wisconsin–Madison; Western Washington University. Other: 1 entered a postgraduate year. Median SAT critical reading: 500, median SAT math: 510, median SAT writing: 495, median combined SAT: 1460. 14% scored over 600 on SAT critical reading, 14% scored over 600 on SAT math, 29% scored over 600 on SAT writing, 29% scored over 1800 on combined SAT.

Student Life Upper grades have specified standards of dress, honor system. Discipline rests primarily with faculty.

Summer Programs ESL programs offered; session focuses on ESL coursework with arts workshops, marine science classes, and guided excursions to local visitor attractions; held both on and off campus; held at International students stay in Murphy International House, West Sound Academy's off-campus dormitory, program includes both on-campus classes and off-campus field trips to various places of interest, and Seattle, Mount Rainier, Olympic National Park, Mt. St. Helens; accepts boys and girls; open to students from other schools. 15 students usually enrolled. 2013 schedule: July 8 to August 9. Application deadline: March 1.

Tuition and Aid Day student tuition: $15,805; 7-day tuition and room/board: $38,500. Tuition installment plan (Insured Tuition Payment Plan). Merit scholarship grants, need-based scholarship grants available. In 2012–13, 50% of upper-school students received aid; total upper-school merit-scholarship money awarded: $110,225. Total amount of financial aid awarded in 2012–13: $254,180.

Admissions Traditional secondary-level entrance grade is 9. For fall 2012, 30 students applied for upper-level admission, 29 were accepted, 26 enrolled. TOEFL or SLEP required. Deadline for receipt of application materials: none. Application fee required: $60. Interview required.

Athletics Interscholastic: basketball (boys), lacrosse (g), sailing (b), swimming and diving (b), volleyball (g); coed intramural: hiking/backpacking, kayaking, outdoor education, rafting, rock climbing.

Computers Computers are regularly used in all classes. Computer network features include on-campus library services, Internet access, wireless campus network. Student e-mail accounts are available to students. The school has a published electronic and media policy.

Contact Lisa Gsellman, Director of Admissions. 360-598-5954. Fax: 360-598-5494. E-mail: lgsellman@westsoundacademy.org. Web site: www.westsoundacademy.org/

WESTTOWN SCHOOL

975 Westtown Road
West Chester, Pennsylvania 19382-5700

Head of School: John W. Baird

General Information Coeducational boarding and day college-preparatory, arts, and religious studies school, affiliated with Society of Friends. Boarding grades 9–12, day grades PK–10. Founded: 1799. Setting: suburban. Nearest major city is Philadelphia. Students are housed in single-sex by floor dormitories and single-sex dormitories. 600-acre campus. 38 buildings on campus. Approved or accredited by Friends Council on Education, Middle States Association of Colleges and Schools, Pennsylvania Association of Independent Schools, and Pennsylvania Department of Education. Member of National Association of Independent Schools and Secondary School Admission Test Board. Endowment: $70 million. Total enrollment: 642. Upper school average class size: 15. Upper school faculty-student ratio: 1:8. Upper School students typically attend 5 days per week. The average school day consists of 9 hours and 20 minutes.

Upper School Student Profile Grade 9: 85 students (40 boys, 45 girls); Grade 10: 80 students (46 boys, 34 girls); Grade 11: 122 students (55 boys, 67 girls); Grade 12: 83 students (32 boys, 51 girls). 77% of students are boarding students. 59% are state residents. 20 states are represented in upper school student body. 10% are international students. International students from Austria, China, Colombia, Germany, Republic of Korea, and Viet Nam; 14 other countries represented in student body. 15% of students are members of Society of Friends.

Faculty School total: 112. In upper school: 32 men, 34 women; 52 have advanced degrees; 58 reside on campus.

Subjects Offered 3-dimensional art, ACT preparation, advanced biology, advanced chemistry, advanced math, algebra, American culture, American foreign policy, American history, American literature, Ancient Greek, ancient history, art, Asian history, astronomy, astrophysics, ballet, band, baseball, basketball, Bible, Bible studies, biology, botany, British literature, calculus, Chinese, choir, choral music, chorus, Christian and Hebrew scripture, classical language, classical studies, comparative religion, computer applications, concert band, concert choir, crafts, creative dance, creative writing, dance, dance performance, drama, drama performance, drama workshop, drawing, drawing and design, earth science, Eastern religion and philosophy, ecology, ecology, environmental systems, electives, English, English as a foreign language, English composition, English literature, environmental science, environmental studies, ESL, European history, film and literature, folk art, foreign language, foreign policy, fractal geometry, French, functions, geometry, German, graphic design, Greek, Holocaust and other genocides, honors algebra, honors geometry, honors U.S. history, honors world history, Japanese, jazz, jazz band, jazz dance, jazz ensemble, lab science, language, Latin, Latin American history, leadership, library research, linear algebra, literature, literature seminar, Mandarin, mathematics, model United Nations, modern dance, music, music composition, music performance, music theater, musical theater, mythology, nature writers, non-Western literature, peace and justice, physics, piano, play production, playwriting and directing, pre-algebra, pre-calculus, Quakerism and ethics, religion, robotics, SAT preparation, science, senior project, senior seminar, Shakespeare, Spanish, Spanish literature, stage design, statistics, student government, student publications, studio art, swimming, tennis, theater, theater design and production, theater history, theater production, trigonometry, U.S. history, U.S. literature, visual and performing arts, visual arts, vocal ensemble, vocal music, water color painting, weight fitness, Western civilization, Western literature, Western religions, woodworking, world history, world literature, world religions, wrestling, writing, writing workshop, yearbook.

Graduation Requirements Arts and fine arts (art, music, dance, drama), English, foreign language, mathematics, physical education (includes health), religion (includes Bible studies and theology), religious studies, science, service learning/ internship, social sciences.

Special Academic Programs Advanced Placement exam preparation; honors section; independent study; study abroad; academic accommodation for the gifted, the musically talented, and the artistically talented; remedial math; ESL (18 students enrolled).

College Admission Counseling 109 students graduated in 2012; 108 went to college, including American University; Dickinson College; Drexel University; Gettysburg College; The George Washington University; University of Richmond. Other: 1 had other specific plans.

Student Life Upper grades have specified standards of dress, student council. Discipline rests equally with students and faculty. Attendance at religious services is required.

Tuition and Aid Day student tuition: $29,120; 7-day tuition and room/board: $46,400. Tuition installment plan (Key Tuition Payment Plan, monthly payment plans). Merit scholarship grants, need-based scholarship grants available. In 2012–13, 41% of upper-school students received aid; total upper-school merit-scholarship money awarded: $32,800. Total amount of financial aid awarded in 2012–13: $4,848,091.

Admissions Traditional secondary-level entrance grade is 9. For fall 2012, 355 students applied for upper-level admission, 173 were accepted, 83 enrolled. SSAT or TOEFL required. Deadline for receipt of application materials: none. Application fee required: $50. Interview required.

Athletics Interscholastic: baseball (boys), basketball (b,g), cross-country running (b,g), field hockey (g), independent competitive sports (b,g), lacrosse (b,g), soccer (b,g), softball (g), swimming and diving (b,g), tennis (b,g), track and field (b,g), volleyball (g); coed interscholastic: dance, dance team, golf, independent competitive sports, indoor track, indoor track & field; coed intramural: aquatics, ballet, basketball, canoeing/kayaking, combined training, dance, fitness, hiking/backpacking, indoor soccer, life saving, modern dance, outdoor activities, outdoor education, outdoor recreation, physical fitness, physical training, ropes courses, running, strength & conditioning, weight training, yoga. 18 coaches, 2 athletic trainers.

Computers Computers are regularly used in all academic, art, career exploration, college planning, current events, desktop publishing, digital applications, introduction to technology, library, library skills, literary magazine, publications, research skills, theater classes. Computer network features include on-campus library services, online commercial services, Internet access, wireless campus network, Internet filtering or blocking technology. Campus intranet, student e-mail accounts, and computer access in designated common areas are available to students. Students grades are available online. The school has a published electronic and media policy.

Contact Nathan Bohn, Director of Admission. 610-399-7900. Fax: 610-399-7909. E-mail: admissions@westtown.edu. Web site: www.westtown.edu

WHEATON ACADEMY

900 Prince Crossing Road
West Chicago, Illinois 60185

Head of School: Dr. Gene Frost

General Information Coeducational day college-preparatory and religious studies school, affiliated with Christian faith. Grades 9–12. Founded: 1853. Setting: suburban. Nearest major city is Chicago. 43-acre campus. 8 buildings on campus. Approved or accredited by Association of Christian Schools International, North Central Association of Colleges and Schools, and Illinois Department of Education. Total enrollment: 640. Upper school average class size: 20. Upper school faculty-student ratio: 1:15. There are 175 required school days per year for Upper School students. Upper School students typically attend 5 days per week. The average school day consists of 6 hours and 30 minutes.

Upper School Student Profile Grade 9: 152 students (74 boys, 78 girls); Grade 10: 154 students (73 boys, 81 girls); Grade 11: 166 students (82 boys, 84 girls); Grade 12: 165 students (81 boys, 84 girls). 98% of students are Christian faith.

Faculty School total: 48. In upper school: 28 men, 20 women; 31 have advanced degrees.

Subjects Offered ACT preparation, algebra, art, arts and crafts, band, Bible, Bible studies, biology, biology-AP, British literature, business, business applications, calculus, calculus-AP, ceramics, chemistry, chemistry-AP, child development, choir, Christian doctrine, Christian education, classics, comparative government and politics-AP, computer art, computer education, computer graphics, computer multimedia, computer processing, computer programming-AP, computer science, concert choir, consumer economics, creative writing, debate, desktop publishing, drama, drama workshop, drawing, driver education, earth science, economics, English, English language and composition-AP, English literature, English literature and composition-AP, environmental science, environmental science-AP, European history, European history-AP, family living, fiber arts, fine arts, foods, French, French language-AP, freshman seminar, geology, geometry, government/civics, graphic design, Greek, health, health and wellness, history, honors English, honors geometry, honors U.S. history, industrial arts, internship, journalism, keyboarding, leadership, literature, mathematics, multimedia design, music, music theory-AP, novels, orchestra, personal growth, physical education, physics, physics-AP, portfolio art, pre-algebra, psychology, publications, science, social sciences, social studies, sociology, Spanish, Spanish language-AP, speech, statistics, statistics-AP, student publications, theater, theology, trigonometry, U.S. government, U.S. government and politics-AP, U.S. history, U.S. history-AP, U.S. literature, world history, world history-AP, world literature, writing.

Graduation Requirements Arts and fine arts (art, music, dance, drama), English, mathematics, physical education (includes health), religion (includes Bible studies and theology), science, social sciences, social studies (includes history), Winterim (3-week period during January allowing students to take two classes beyond the typical curriculum).

Special Academic Programs 16 Advanced Placement exams for which test preparation is offered; honors section; independent study; term-away projects; study at local college for college credit; academic accommodation for the gifted, the musically talented, and the artistically talented; remedial reading and/or remedial writing; remedial math; special instructional classes for students with learning disabilities; ESL (40 students enrolled).

College Admission Counseling 140 students graduated in 2012; 134 went to college, including Baylor University; Calvin College; Hope College; Taylor University; University of Illinois at Urbana–Champaign; Wheaton College. Other: 2 went to work, 4 had other specific plans. Median composite ACT: 25. 45% scored over 26 on composite ACT.

Student Life Upper grades have specified standards of dress, honor system. Discipline rests primarily with faculty. Attendance at religious services is required.

Summer Programs Enrichment, advancement, sports, art/fine arts, computer instruction programs offered; held on campus; accepts boys and girls; open to students from other schools. 75 students usually enrolled. 2013 schedule: June 10 to June 28.

Tuition and Aid Day student tuition: $13,500. Tuition installment plan (monthly payment plans, semester payment plan). Tuition reduction for siblings, merit scholarship grants, need-based scholarship grants, paying campus jobs available. In 2012–13, 30% of upper-school students received aid; total upper-school merit-scholarship money awarded: $15,000. Total amount of financial aid awarded in 2012–13: $500,000.

Admissions Traditional secondary-level entrance grade is 9. ACT-Explore or placement test required. Deadline for receipt of application materials: none. Application fee required: $50. On-campus interview required.

Athletics Interscholastic: baseball (boys), basketball (b,g), cheering (g), cross-country running (b,g), dance team (g), football (b), golf (b,g), ice hockey (b), pom squad (g), soccer (b,g), softball (g), tennis (b,g), track and field (b,g), volleyball (b,g); intramural: aerobics (g), flagball (g), ice hockey (b), wilderness survival (b); coed interscholastic: modern dance, physical training, running; coed intramural: climbing, floor hockey, hiking/backpacking, outdoor education, outdoor skills, power lifting, project adventure, rock climbing, skiing (cross-country), strength & conditioning, wall climbing, weight lifting, weight training. 2 PE instructors, 6 coaches, 1 athletic trainer.

Computers Computers are regularly used in Bible studies, graphic design, independent study, mathematics, multimedia, writing, yearbook classes. Computer network features include on-campus library services, online commercial services, Internet access, wireless campus network, Internet filtering or blocking technology. Student e-mail accounts are available to students. Students grades are available online. The school has a published electronic and media policy.

Contact Mr. Ryan Hall, Admissions Counselor. 630-562-7500 Ext. 7501. Fax: 630-231-0842. E-mail: rhall@wheatonacademy.org. Web site: www.wheatonacademy.org

THE WHEELER SCHOOL

216 Hope Street
Providence, Rhode Island 02906

Head of School: Mr. Dan Miller, PhD

General Information Coeducational day college-preparatory, arts, Community Action Program (service-based learning), and AERIE Program (individual academic enrichment grades 9-12) school. Grades N–12. Founded: 1889. Setting: urban. 5-acre campus. 8 buildings on campus. Approved or accredited by Association of Independent Schools in New England, New England Association of Schools and Colleges, and Rhode Island Department of Education. Member of National Association of Independent Schools. Endowment: $21.3 million. Total enrollment: 839. Upper school average class size: 15. Upper school faculty-student ratio: 1:8. There are 165 required school days per year for Upper School students. Upper School students typically attend 5 days per week. The average school day consists of 6 hours and 25 minutes.

Upper School Student Profile Grade 9: 100 students (54 boys, 46 girls); Grade 10: 82 students (41 boys, 41 girls); Grade 11: 80 students (39 boys, 41 girls); Grade 12: 81 students (39 boys, 42 girls).

Faculty School total: 115. In upper school: 15 men, 25 women; 29 have advanced degrees.

Subjects Offered 20th century American writers, 20th century world history, acting, Advanced Placement courses, advanced studio art-AP, algebra, American history, anatomy, art, art history, biology, biology-AP, biotechnology, Black history, broadcasting, business skills, calculus, calculus-AP, ceramics, chemistry, Chinese, Chinese studies, choral music, civil rights, computer programming, computer science, contemporary issues, dance, drama, drawing, economics, engineering, English, English literature, English-AP, environmental science, environmental science-AP, European history, film studies, fine arts, forensics, French, geometry, guitar, Japanese, jazz ensemble, kinesiology, Latin, Latin American history, Latin American studies, mathematics, Middle Eastern history, music, nutrition, photography, physical education, physics, physiology, pre-calculus, printmaking, psychology, research, science, sculpture, social studies, Spanish, statistics, theater, trigonometry, Web site design, Western civilization.

Graduation Requirements Arts and fine arts (art, music, dance, drama), English, foreign language, history, mathematics, performing arts, physical education (includes health), science, community service, Unity and Diversity curriculum.

Special Academic Programs 18 Advanced Placement exams for which test preparation is offered; honors section; independent study; term-away projects; study at local college for college credit; study abroad; academic accommodation for the gifted; programs in general development for dyslexic students.

College Admission Counseling 72 students graduated in 2012; 71 went to college, including Dickinson College; Harvard University; Northwestern University; The George Washington University; Wheaton College. Other: 1 entered a postgraduate year. Mean SAT critical reading: 640, mean SAT math: 650, mean SAT writing: 650, mean combined SAT: 1290, mean composite ACT: 28.

Student Life Upper grades have specified standards of dress, student council. Discipline rests equally with students and faculty.

Summer Programs Enrichment, sports, art/fine arts programs offered; session focuses on Jazz Camp, Basketball Camp, Kayaking/Voyager Camps, Sports Academy; held on campus; accepts boys and girls; open to students from other schools. 175 students usually enrolled. 2013 schedule: June 18 to August 10. Application deadline: none.

Tuition and Aid Day student tuition: $26,640–$28,960. Tuition installment plan (Key Tuition Payment Plan, monthly payment plans). Need-based scholarship grants available. In 2012–13, 25% of upper-school students received aid. Total amount of financial aid awarded in 2012–13: $1,360,353.

Admissions Traditional secondary-level entrance grade is 9. For fall 2012, 188 students applied for upper-level admission, 89 were accepted, 37 enrolled. ISEE or SSAT required. Deadline for receipt of application materials: January 31. Application fee required: $60. On-campus interview required.

Athletics Interscholastic: baseball (boys), basketball (b,g), cross-country running (b,g), field hockey (g), football (b), ice hockey (b,g), lacrosse (b,g), soccer (b,g), softball (g), swimming and diving (b,g), tennis (b,g), track and field (b,g), winter (indoor) track (b,g); coed interscholastic: golf, squash. 6 PE instructors, 30 coaches, 1 athletic trainer.

Computers Computers are regularly used in all classes. Computer network features include on-campus library services, online commercial services, Internet access, wireless campus network. Campus intranet and student e-mail accounts are available to students. The school has a published electronic and media policy.

Contact Jeanette Epstein, Director of Admission. 401-421-8100. Fax: 401-751-7674. E-mail: jeanetteepstein@wheelerschool.org. Web site: www.wheelerschool.org

WHITEFIELD ACADEMY

1 Whitefield Drive SE
Mableton, Georgia 30126

Head of School: Dr. John H. Lindsell

General Information Coeducational day college-preparatory, arts, religious studies, technology, and life and career planning school, affiliated with Christian faith. Grades PK–12. Founded: 1996. Setting: suburban. Nearest major city is Atlanta. 75-acre campus. 5 buildings on campus. Approved or accredited by Southern Association of Colleges and Schools and Southern Association of Independent Schools. Member of Secondary School Admission Test Board. Total enrollment: 649. Upper school average class size: 18. Upper school faculty-student ratio: 1:18. The average school day consists of 6 hours and 45 minutes.

Upper School Student Profile Grade 9: 48 students (27 boys, 21 girls); Grade 10: 58 students (30 boys, 28 girls); Grade 11: 48 students (24 boys, 24 girls); Grade 12: 62 students (32 boys, 30 girls). 100% of students are Christian faith.

Faculty School total: 122. In upper school: 12 men, 11 women; 13 have advanced degrees.

Graduation Requirements Algebra, American history, American literature, arts and fine arts (art, music, dance, drama), biology, British literature, chemistry, Christian studies, English, foreign language, geometry, health education, modern European history, physical fitness, physics, pre-calculus, public speaking, Western civilization, Life and Career Planning program; Community Service Hour Requirements. Community service is required.

Special Academic Programs Advanced Placement exam preparation; honors section; independent study; special instructional classes for deaf students, blind students.

College Admission Counseling 68 students graduated in 2012; all went to college, including Auburn University; Furman University; Georgia Institute of Technology; The University of Alabama; University of Georgia.

Student Life Upper grades have uniform requirement, student council, honor system. Discipline rests primarily with faculty. Attendance at religious services is required.

Summer Programs Remediation, enrichment, sports, art/fine arts programs offered; session focuses on skills improvement; held on campus; accepts boys and girls; open to students from other schools. 150 students usually enrolled. 2013 schedule: June to July.

Tuition and Aid Day student tuition: $19,410. Tuition installment plan (FACTS Tuition Payment Plan). Need-based financial assistance (through SSS application), AchieverLoans, and PrepGATE loans available. In 2012–13, 18% of upper-school students received aid. Total amount of financial aid awarded in 2012–13: $800,000.

Admissions Traditional secondary-level entrance grade is 9. SSAT required. Deadline for receipt of application materials: February 15. Application fee required: $65. Interview required.

Athletics Interscholastic: baseball (boys), basketball (b,g), cheering (g), cross-country running (b,g), diving (b,g), football (b), golf (b,g), lacrosse (b), physical fitness (b,g), physical training (b,g), soccer (b,g), softball (g), strength & conditioning (b,g), swimming and diving (b,g), tennis (b,g), track and field (b,g), volleyball (g), weight lifting (b,g), weight training (b,g), wrestling (b); coed interscholastic: cross-country running, diving, golf, physical fitness, physical training, strength & conditioning, swimming and diving, tennis, track and field, weight lifting, weight training. 2 PE instructors, 5 coaches, 2 athletic trainers.

Computers Computer network features include on-campus library services, online commercial services, Internet access, wireless campus network, Internet filtering or blocking technology. Students grades are available online. The school has a published electronic and media policy.

Contact Mrs. Linda J. Simpson, Admission Director. 678-305-3027. Fax: 678-305-3010. E-mail: lsimpson@whitefieldacademy.com. Web site: www.whitefieldacademy.com

WHITEFIELD ACADEMY

7711 Fegenbush Lane
Louisville, Kentucky 40228

Head of School: Mr. Chip Evans

General Information Coeducational day college-preparatory, arts, religious studies, and technology school, affiliated with Baptist Church. Grades PS–12. Founded: 1976. Setting: suburban. 30-acre campus. 2 buildings on campus. Approved or accredited by Association of Christian Schools International, CITA (Commission on International and Trans-Regional Accreditation), Council of Accreditation and School Improvement, Southern Association of Colleges and Schools, and Kentucky Department of Education. Total enrollment: 731. Upper school average class size: 20. Upper school faculty-student ratio: 1:20. There are 178 required school days per year for Upper School students. Upper School students typically attend 5 days per week. The average school day consists of 6 hours and 25 minutes.

Upper School Student Profile Grade 9: 50 students (30 boys, 20 girls); Grade 10: 52 students (23 boys, 29 girls); Grade 11: 55 students (25 boys, 30 girls); Grade 12: 43 students (20 boys, 23 girls). 45% of students are Baptist.

Faculty School total: 55. In upper school: 11 men, 11 women; 9 have advanced degrees.

Subjects Offered Adolescent issues, advanced math, algebra, anatomy, art, arts, band, Bible studies, biology, calculus, calculus-AP, chemistry, choir, choral music, chorus, Christian education, Christian studies, college placement, college planning, college writing, communication skills, composition, computer applications, computer education, computers, current events, drama, drama performance, economics, English, English composition, English literature, English literature-AP, foreign language, geometry, history, honors English, library, mathematics, music, political science, pre-calculus, reading, SAT/ACT preparation, science, science project, sex education, social sciences, Spanish, speech and debate, student government, student publications, U.S. history, U.S. history-AP.

Graduation Requirements Arts and fine arts (art, music, dance, drama), Bible, electives, English, foreign language, health, mathematics, physical education (includes health), science, social studies (includes history).

Special Academic Programs 6 Advanced Placement exams for which test preparation is offered; honors section; independent study; academic accommodation for the gifted.

College Admission Counseling 42 students graduated in 2012; 41 went to college, including Bellarmine University; Eastern Kentucky University; Jefferson Community and Technical College; University of Kentucky; University of Louisville; Western Kentucky University. Other: 1 had other specific plans. Median composite ACT: 26. 46% scored over 26 on composite ACT.

Student Life Upper grades have uniform requirement, student council, honor system. Discipline rests primarily with faculty. Attendance at religious services is required.

Summer Programs Enrichment, sports programs offered; held on campus; accepts boys and girls; open to students from other schools. 60 students usually enrolled.

Tuition and Aid Day student tuition: $6300. Tuition installment plan (FACTS Tuition Payment Plan, annual payment in full plan). Tuition reduction for siblings, need-based scholarship grants available. In 2012–13, 13% of upper-school students received aid. Total amount of financial aid awarded in 2012–13: $42,175.

Admissions Traditional secondary-level entrance grade is 9. For fall 2012, 16 students applied for upper-level admission, 16 were accepted, 16 enrolled. Stanford Achievement Test required. Deadline for receipt of application materials: none. Application fee required: $350. On-campus interview required.

Athletics Interscholastic: aquatics (boys, girls), baseball (b), basketball (b,g), cheering (b,g), cross-country running (b,g), golf (b,g), soccer (b,g), softball (g), swimming and diving (b,g), tennis (b,g), track and field (b,g), volleyball (g); intramural: aerobics (g), fitness (b,g), outdoor activities (b,g), physical fitness (b,g), volleyball (g), weight lifting (b,g). 3 PE instructors.

Computers Computers are regularly used in all academic, college planning, library, newspaper, SAT preparation, theater arts, yearbook classes. Computer network features include on-campus library services, Internet access, wireless campus network, Internet filtering or blocking technology. Computer access in designated common areas is available to students. Students grades are available online. The school has a published electronic and media policy.

Contact Mrs. Diane Fow, Director of Admissions. 502-231-6261. Fax: 502-239-3144. E-mail: dfow@whitefield.org. Web site: www.whitefield.org/

THE WHITE MOUNTAIN SCHOOL

371 West Farm Road
Bethlehem, New Hampshire 03574

General Information Coeducational boarding and day college-preparatory, arts, and sustainability studies school, affiliated with Episcopal Church. Grades 9–PG. Founded: 1886. Setting: rural. Nearest major city is Concord. Students are housed in single-sex dormitories. 250-acre campus. 13 buildings on campus. Approved or accredited by Association for Experiential Education, National Association of Episcopal Schools, New England Association of Schools and Colleges, The Association of Boarding Schools, and New Hampshire Department of Education. Member of National Association of Independent Schools and Secondary School Admission Test Board. Endowment: $1.5 million. Total enrollment: 99. Upper school average class size: 9. Upper school faculty-student ratio: 1:5. Upper School students typically attend 5 days per week. The average school day consists of 5 hours and 45 minutes.

See Display below and Close-Up on page 646.

THE WILLIAMS SCHOOL

182 Mohegan Avenue
New London, Connecticut 06320-4110

Head of School: Mr. Mark Fader

General Information Coeducational day college-preparatory and arts school. Grades 7–12. Founded: 1891. Setting: urban. 25-acre campus. 2 buildings on campus. Approved or accredited by Connecticut Association of Independent Schools, New England Association of Schools and Colleges, and Connecticut Department of Education. Member of National Association of Independent Schools and Secondary School Admission Test Board. Endowment: $4 million. Total enrollment: 238. Upper school average class size: 13. Upper school faculty-student ratio: 1:9. There are 165 required school days per year for Upper School students. Upper School students typically attend 5 days per week. The average school day consists of 6 hours and 48 minutes.

Upper School Student Profile Grade 9: 43 students (16 boys, 27 girls); Grade 10: 40 students (21 boys, 19 girls); Grade 11: 50 students (24 boys, 26 girls); Grade 12: 54 students (23 boys, 31 girls).

Faculty School total: 36. In upper school: 18 men, 18 women; 26 have advanced degrees.
Subjects Offered Algebra, American history, art, band, biology, biology-AP, calculus, calculus-AP, chemistry, chemistry-AP, chorus, dance, digital art, drama, economics, English, English literature, English-AP, environmental science, European history, expository writing, fine arts, French, French-AP, geography, geometry, Greek, history, jazz, Latin-AP, mathematics, modern European history, music, music composition, music history, music theory, music theory-AP, physical education, physics, physics-AP, pre-calculus, science, social studies, Spanish, Spanish-AP, theater, trigonometry, world history, world literature.
Graduation Requirements Arts and fine arts (art, music, dance, drama), classical language, English, foreign language, mathematics, physical education (includes health), science, senior project, social studies (includes history), at least one year of Latin, four years of math in Upper School or through precalculus.
Special Academic Programs 10 Advanced Placement exams for which test preparation is offered; honors section; independent study; study at local college for college credit; study abroad; academic accommodation for the gifted, the musically talented, and the artistically talented.
College Admission Counseling 67 students graduated in 2012; all went to college, including Boston University; Connecticut College; Goucher College; New York University; Tufts University; University of Connecticut. Mean SAT critical reading: 614, mean SAT math: 584, mean SAT writing: 590, mean combined SAT: 1788, mean composite ACT: 26. 67% scored over 600 on SAT critical reading, 45% scored over 600 on SAT math, 46% scored over 600 on SAT writing.
Student Life Upper grades have specified standards of dress, student council. Discipline rests primarily with faculty.
Summer Programs Advancement, sports programs offered; session focuses on lacrosse, basketball, and mathematics; held on campus; accepts boys and girls; open to students from other schools. 160 students usually enrolled. 2013 schedule: June 21 to August 20. Application deadline: June 15.
Tuition and Aid Day student tuition: $26,600. Tuition installment plan (Insured Tuition Payment Plan, FACTS Tuition Payment Plan, monthly payment plans, individually arranged payment plans). Need-based scholarship grants available. In 2012–13, 40% of upper-school students received aid. Total amount of financial aid awarded in 2012–13: $1,270,680.
Admissions Traditional secondary-level entrance grade is 9. For fall 2012, 68 students applied for upper-level admission, 61 were accepted, 30 enrolled. SSAT required. Deadline for receipt of application materials: February 1. Application fee required: $50. On-campus interview required.
Athletics Interscholastic: baseball (boys), basketball (b,g), field hockey (g), lacrosse (b,g), soccer (b,g), tennis (b,g); intramural: dance (b,g), dance team (b,g), fencing (b,g), fitness (b,g), yoga (b); coed interscholastic: cross-country running, sailing, squash, swimming and diving; coed intramural: dance, dance team, fencing, fitness, golf, modern dance, weight training. 2 PE instructors, 19 coaches, 1 athletic trainer.
Computers Computers are regularly used in creative writing, English, French, graphic design, history, Latin, mathematics, music, photography, SAT preparation, science, social studies, Spanish, study skills, theater, writing, yearbook classes. Computer network features include on-campus library services, online commercial services, Internet access, wireless campus network, Internet filtering or blocking technology. Campus intranet, student e-mail accounts, and computer access in designated common areas are available to students. The school has a published electronic and media policy.
Contact Cristan Harris, Director of Admission. 860-439-2789. Fax: 860-439-2796. E-mail: charris@williamsschool.org. Web site: www.williamsschool.org

THE WILLISTON NORTHAMPTON SCHOOL

19 Payson Avenue
Easthampton, Massachusetts 01027

Head of School: Mr. Robert W. Hill III

General Information Coeducational boarding and day college-preparatory school. Boarding grades 9–PG, day grades 7–12. Founded: 1841. Setting: small town. Nearest major city is Northampton. Students are housed in single-sex dormitories. 125-acre campus. 57 buildings on campus. Approved or accredited by Association of Independent Schools in New England, New England Association of Schools and Colleges, and The Association of Boarding Schools. Member of National Association of Independent Schools and Secondary School Admission Test Board. Endowment: $40 million. Total enrollment: 534. Upper school average class size: 13. Upper school faculty-student ratio: 1:6. There are 160 required school days per year for Upper School students. Upper School students typically attend 5 days per week. The average school day consists of 8 hours and 30 minutes.
Upper School Student Profile Grade 9: 76 students (35 boys, 41 girls); Grade 10: 123 students (62 boys, 61 girls); Grade 11: 138 students (79 boys, 59 girls); Grade 12: 107 students (58 boys, 49 girls); Postgraduate: 10 students (9 boys, 1 girl). 64% of students are boarding students. 40% are state residents. 22 states are represented in upper school student body. 18% are international students. International students from Bermuda, Canada, China, Hong Kong, Republic of Korea, and Taiwan; 24 other countries represented in student body.
Faculty School total: 70. In upper school: 35 men, 35 women; 49 have advanced degrees; 59 reside on campus.
Subjects Offered African-American history, algebra, American history, American literature, anatomy and physiology, animal behavior, art, art history, astronomy, biology, biology-AP, calculus, calculus-AP, chemistry, chemistry-AP, China/Japan history, Chinese, choral music, choreography, Christian and Hebrew scripture, comparative government and politics-AP, comparative politics, computer math, computer programming, computer science, computer science-AP, constitutional law, creative writing, dance, discrete mathematics, drama, economics, economics and history, economics-AP, English, English language-AP, English literature, English literature-AP, environmental science, ESL, ethics, European history, expository writing, fine arts, French, French language-AP, French literature-AP, French-AP, genetics, geometry, global studies, government/civics, health, history, history of jazz, honors algebra, honors English, honors geometry, Islamic studies, Latin, Latin American history, Latin-AP, mathematics, music, music theory, organic biochemistry, organic chemistry, philosophy, photography, photojournalism, physics, physics-AP, play production, playwriting, poetry, psychology, psychology-AP, religion, religion and culture, Russian history, science, sculpture, social studies, Spanish, Spanish language-AP, Spanish literature-AP, statistics-AP, theater, theology, trigonometry, U.S. history-AP, world history, world literature, writing workshop.
Graduation Requirements Arts and fine arts (art, music, dance, drama), English, foreign language, history, mathematics, science, participation in Afternoon Program.
Special Academic Programs 18 Advanced Placement exams for which test preparation is offered; honors section; independent study; term-away projects; study abroad; academic accommodation for the gifted, the musically talented, and the artistically talented; special instructional classes for deaf students; ESL (12 students enrolled).
College Admission Counseling 125 students graduated in 2012; 121 went to college, including Bates College; Berklee College of Music; Colby College; Connecticut College; Hobart and William Smith Colleges; New York University. Other: 1 entered a postgraduate year, 3 had other specific plans. Mean SAT critical reading: 574, mean SAT math: 609, mean SAT writing: 591, mean combined SAT: 1773, mean composite ACT: 25.
Student Life Upper grades have specified standards of dress, student council, honor system. Discipline rests equally with students and faculty.
Summer Programs Sports, art/fine arts programs offered; session focuses on sports camps and summer theater; held on campus; accepts boys and girls; open to students from other schools. 2013 schedule: June 19 to August 19.
Tuition and Aid Day student tuition: $33,800; 7-day tuition and room/board: $49,400. Tuition installment plan (Insured Tuition Payment Plan, monthly payment plans, individually arranged payment plans, Tuition Management Systems). Merit scholarship grants, need-based scholarship grants available. In 2012–13, 42% of upper-school students received aid; total upper-school merit-scholarship money awarded: $84,000. Total amount of financial aid awarded in 2012–13: $5,767,000.
Admissions Traditional secondary-level entrance grade is 9. For fall 2012, 807 students applied for upper-level admission, 338 were accepted, 119 enrolled. ACT, ISEE, PSAT or SAT for applicants to grade 11 and 12, SSAT or TOEFL required. Deadline for receipt of application materials: January 15. Application fee required: $50. Interview required.
Athletics Interscholastic: alpine skiing (boys, girls), baseball (b), basketball (b,g), crew (b,g), cross-country running (b,g), field hockey (g), football (b), golf (b,g), ice hockey (b,g), lacrosse (b,g), soccer (b,g), softball (g), squash (b,g), strength & conditioning (b,g), swimming and diving (b,g), tennis (b,g), track and field (b,g), volleyball (g), water polo (b,g), wrestling (b); intramural: self defense (g); coed interscholastic: dance, diving, ultimate Frisbee; coed intramural: aerobics, aerobics/dance, dance, dance team, equestrian sports, fitness, Frisbee, horseback riding, judo, martial arts, modern dance, mountain biking, snowboarding, weight lifting, weight training, yoga. 1 PE instructor, 5 coaches, 2 athletic trainers.
Computers Computers are regularly used in college planning, geography, graphic design, history, library, mathematics, newspaper, photography, photojournalism, programming, science, yearbook classes. Computer network features include on-campus library services, online commercial services, Internet access, wireless campus network, Internet filtering or blocking technology. Campus intranet, student e-mail accounts, and computer access in designated common areas are available to students. Students grades are available online. The school has a published electronic and media policy.
Contact Mr. Derek Cunha, Associate Director of Admission. 413-529-3432. Fax: 413-527-9494. E-mail: dcunha@williston.com. Web site: www.williston.com

See Display on next page and Close-Up on page 648.

THE WILLOWS ACADEMY

1015 Rose Avenue
Des Plaines, Illinois 60016

Head of School: Mrs. Jeanne Petros

General Information Girls' day college-preparatory, arts, religious studies, technology, and College Preparatory school, affiliated with Roman Catholic Church. Grades 6–12. Founded: 1974. Setting: suburban. Nearest major city is Chicago. 4-acre campus. 1 building on campus. Approved or accredited by Illinois Department of Education. Total enrollment: 230. Upper school average class size: 18. Upper school faculty-student ratio: 1:10. Upper School students typically attend 5 days per week. The average school day consists of 6 hours and 30 minutes.

Upper School Student Profile Grade 6: 23 students (23 girls); Grade 7: 29 students (29 girls); Grade 8: 25 students (25 girls); Grade 9: 42 students (42 girls); Grade 10: 37 students (37 girls); Grade 11: 30 students (30 girls); Grade 12: 42 students (42 girls). 85% of students are Roman Catholic.

Faculty School total: 35. In upper school: 27 women; 15 have advanced degrees.

Subjects Offered Algebra, American history, American literature, art, biology, calculus, chemistry, choir, choral music, computer graphics, computer programming, computer science, economics, English, English literature, ethics, European history, fine arts, four units of summer reading, French, geography, geometry, government/civics, grammar, health, history, instrumental music, Latin, mathematics, music, music history, music theory, musical productions, philosophy, physical education, physics, pre-calculus, science, social studies, Spanish, statistics, theology, visual arts, vocal music, world history, world literature, writing.

Graduation Requirements Arts and fine arts (art, music, dance, drama), English, foreign language, four units of summer reading, mathematics, physical education (includes health), religion (includes Bible studies and theology), science, social studies (includes history), 40 hours of service work per year.

Special Academic Programs Advanced Placement exam preparation; honors section.

College Admission Counseling 35 students graduated in 2012; all went to college, including Marquette University; Northwestern University; Purdue University; University of Dallas; University of Illinois at Urbana–Champaign; University of Notre Dame. Mean SAT critical reading: 695, mean SAT math: 658, mean SAT writing: 672, mean composite ACT: 26.

Student Life Upper grades have uniform requirement, student council, honor system. Discipline rests primarily with faculty.

Summer Programs Enrichment, sports programs offered; session focuses on athletic camps and enrichment; held on campus; accepts girls; open to students from other schools. 30 students usually enrolled. 2013 schedule: June 1 to July 31. Application deadline: none.

Tuition and Aid Day student tuition: $14,000. Tuition installment plan (Insured Tuition Payment Plan, monthly payment plans, quarterly, semiannual, and annual payment plans). Tuition reduction for siblings, need-based scholarship grants available. In 2012–13, 30% of upper-school students received aid.

Admissions Traditional secondary-level entrance grade is 9. For fall 2012, 80 students applied for upper-level admission, 80 were accepted, 66 enrolled. Any standardized test, ISEE or school's own exam required. Deadline for receipt of application materials: none. Application fee required: $50. On-campus interview required.

Athletics Interscholastic: basketball, cross-country running, dance team, soccer, softball, swimming and diving, volleyball; intramural: strength & conditioning. 1 PE instructor, 8 coaches.

Computers Computers are regularly used in graphic design, history, mathematics, music, music technology, science classes. Computer network features include Internet access, Internet filtering or blocking technology. Computer access in designated common areas is available to students. Students grades are available online.

Contact Stephanie Sheffield, Director of Admissions. 847-824-6900. Fax: 847-824-7089. E-mail: sheffield@willowsacademy.org. Web site: www.willowsacademy.org

WILLOW WOOD SCHOOL

55 Scarsdale Road
Don Mills, Ontario M3B 2R3, Canada

Head of School: Ms. Joy Kurtz

General Information Coeducational day college-preparatory, general academic, arts, technology, and sports school; primarily serves students with learning disabilities and individuals with Attention Deficit Disorder. Grades 1–12. Founded: 1980. Setting: suburban. Nearest major city is Toronto, Canada. 3-acre campus. 1 building on campus. Approved or accredited by Ontario Ministry of Education and Ontario Department of Education. Languages of instruction: English, French, and Spanish. Total enrollment: 190. Upper school average class size: 16. Upper school faculty-student ratio: 1:7. There are 185 required school days per year for Upper School students. Upper School students typically attend 5 days per week. The average school day consists of 7 hours and 15 minutes.

Upper School Student Profile Grade 9: 27 students (24 boys, 3 girls); Grade 10: 25 students (17 boys, 8 girls); Grade 11: 35 students (27 boys, 8 girls); Grade 12: 35 students (23 boys, 12 girls).

Faculty School total: 35. In upper school: 9 men, 7 women; 4 have advanced degrees.

Subjects Offered 20th century world history, accounting, advanced chemistry, advanced math, algebra, ancient world history, applied arts, art, art history, biology, business applications, business mathematics, calculus, Canadian geography, Canadian history, Canadian law, Canadian literature, career and personal planning, careers, chemistry, civics, computer applications, computer graphics, computer information systems, computer literacy, computer multimedia, computer science, creative writing, data processing, dramatic arts, economics, English, English composition, English literature, environmental science, ESL, family studies, film studies, finite math, French as a second language, geography, geometry, global issues, guidance, health education, history, independent study, keyboarding, learning strategies, mathematics, media studies, medieval history, modern Western civilization, philosophy, photography, physical education, physics, politics, psychology, reading/study skills, remedial/makeup course work, research skills, science and technology, skills for success, social skills, society challenge and change, society, politics and law, Spanish, study skills, The 20th Century, visual arts, world history, world religions, yearbook.

Graduation Requirements Arts, business, Canadian geography, Canadian history, career education, civics, computer technologies, electives, English, French, history, mathematics, physical education (includes health), science, social sciences, Provincial Literacy Test requirement, community service hours.

Special Academic Programs Accelerated programs; independent study; study abroad; academic accommodation for the gifted and the artistically talented; remedial reading and/or remedial writing; remedial math; programs in English, mathematics, general development for dyslexic students; special instructional classes for students with learning disabilities and Attention Deficit Disorder; ESL (12 students enrolled).

College Admission Counseling 22 students graduated in 2011; all went to college, including Brock University; Queen's University at Kingston; Trent University; University of Guelph; University of Toronto; York University.

Student Life Upper grades have uniform requirement, student council, honor system. Discipline rests primarily with faculty.

Tuition and Aid Day student tuition: CAN$17,100. Tuition installment plan (individually arranged payment plans, 10% due upon acceptance; balance divided into three equal payments due June 1, October 1, December 1). Tuition reduction for siblings available. In 2011–12, 5% of upper-school students received aid. Total amount of financial aid awarded in 2011–12: CAN$60,000.

Admissions Traditional secondary-level entrance grade is 9. For fall 2011, 25 students applied for upper-level admission, 15 were accepted, 15 enrolled. Achievement/Aptitude/Writing, CTBS, Stanford Achievement Test, any other standardized test, grade equivalent tests, non-standardized placement tests, school's own test, Wechsler Individual Achievement Test or writing sample required. Deadline for receipt of application materials: none. No application fee required. On-campus interview required.

Athletics Interscholastic: badminton (boys, girls), ball hockey (b,g), basketball (b,g), cooperative games (b,g), croquet (b,g), flag football (b,g), floor hockey (b,g), hockey (b), track and field (b,g), volleyball (b,g); intramural: ball hockey (b,g), basketball (b,g), cooperative games (b,g), flag football (b,g), floor hockey (b,g), indoor hockey (b,g), track and field (b,g); coed interscholastic: badminton, ball hockey, baseball, bowling, cross-country running, curling, fitness walking, Frisbee, golf, hockey, ice hockey, indoor soccer, jogging, outdoor education, outdoor recreation, physical fitness, physical training, running, soccer, softball, table tennis, ultimate Frisbee, walking; coed intramural: aerobics, badminton, ball hockey, baseball, bowling, curling, fitness, fitness walking, hockey, ice hockey, indoor soccer, jogging, outdoor education, outdoor recreation, physical fitness, physical training, running, soccer, softball, strength & conditioning, table tennis, ultimate Frisbee, volleyball, walking. 2 PE instructors, 1 athletic trainer.

Computers Computers are regularly used in accounting, business applications, career exploration, college planning, creative writing, data processing, English, ESL, geography, graphic arts, independent study, learning cognition, publishing, remedial study skills, typing, Web site design, writing, yearbook classes. Computer network features include on-campus library services, online commercial services, Internet access, wireless campus network, Internet filtering or blocking technology. Computer access in designated common areas is available to students. Students grades are available online. The school has a published electronic and media policy.

Contact Ms. Joy Kurtz, Director. 416-444-7644. Fax: 416-444-1801. E-mail: joykurtz@willowwoodschool.ca. Web site: www.willowwoodschool.ca

WILMINGTON CHRISTIAN SCHOOL

825 Loveville Road
Hockessin, Delaware 19707

Head of School: Mr. William F. Stevens Jr.

General Information Coeducational day college-preparatory, arts, religious studies, and technology school, affiliated with Protestant faith. Grades PK–12. Founded: 1946. Setting: suburban. Nearest major city is Wilmington. 15-acre campus. 1 building on campus. Approved or accredited by Association of Christian Schools International, Middle States Association of Colleges and Schools, and Delaware Department of Education. Endowment: $400,000. Total enrollment: 517. Upper school average class size: 25. Upper school faculty-student ratio: 1:15. There are 177 required school days per year for Upper School students. Upper School students typically attend 5 days per week. The average school day consists of 6 hours and 40 minutes.

Upper School Student Profile Grade 9: 54 students (33 boys, 21 girls); Grade 10: 64 students (30 boys, 34 girls); Grade 11: 57 students (25 boys, 32 girls); Grade 12: 56 students (22 boys, 34 girls). 90% of students are Protestant.

Faculty School total: 52. In upper school: 7 men, 17 women; 9 have advanced degrees.

Subjects Offered Accounting, advanced math, algebra, American history, American history-AP, American minority experience, anatomy and physiology, art, band, biology, calculus, calculus-AP, chemistry, chorus, Christian doctrine, Christian ethics, church history, civics, computer applications, consumer mathematics, creative writing, democracy in America, driver education, ecology, economics, English, geometry, German, health, honors algebra, honors English, honors geometry, information processing, journalism, lab science, library assistant, marine biology, modern history, music theory, novels, physical education, physical science, physics, pre-calculus, Spanish, speech, study skills, trigonometry, world civilizations, world religions, yearbook.

Graduation Requirements Bible studies, English, foreign language, health education, mathematics, physical education (includes health), science, social studies (includes history), 40 hours of community service.

Special Academic Programs Advanced Placement exam preparation; honors section; study at local college for college credit; remedial reading and/or remedial writing; remedial math; ESL (9 students enrolled).

College Admission Counseling 52 students graduated in 2012; all went to college, including Drexel University; Eastern University; Gordon College; Liberty University; Messiah College; University of Delaware.

Student Life Upper grades have uniform requirement, student council, honor system. Discipline rests primarily with faculty. Attendance at religious services is required.

Summer Programs Remediation, advancement programs offered; session focuses on to attract more students to the school; held on campus; accepts boys and girls; open to students from other schools. 12 students usually enrolled. 2013 schedule: June 15 to August 5.

Tuition and Aid Day student tuition: $11,870. Tuition installment plan (STEP Plan (monthly deduction from a checking account)). Tuition reduction for siblings, need-based scholarship grants available. In 2012–13, 47% of upper-school students received aid. Total amount of financial aid awarded in 2012–13: $292,720.

Admissions Traditional secondary-level entrance grade is 9. For fall 2012, 37 students applied for upper-level admission, 34 were accepted, 26 enrolled. Stanford Achievement Test required. Deadline for receipt of application materials: August 1. Application fee required: $125. On-campus interview required.

Athletics Interscholastic: baseball (boys), basketball (b,g), cheering (g), field hockey (g), lacrosse (b), soccer (b,g), softball (g), volleyball (g), wrestling (b); coed interscholastic: cross-country running, golf, running. 2 PE instructors, 16 coaches, 1 athletic trainer.

Computers Computers are regularly used in accounting, business education, data processing, information technology, newspaper, yearbook classes. Computer network features include on-campus library services, Internet access. The school has a published electronic and media policy.

Contact Mrs. Carol Allston-Stiles, Admissions/Assistant to the Head of School. 302-239-2121 Ext. 3205. Fax: 302-239-2778. E-mail: admissions@WilmingtonChristian.org. Web site: www.wilmingtonchristian.org

WILSON HALL

520 Wilson Hall Road
Sumter, South Carolina 29150

Head of School: Mr. Frederick B. Moulton Sr.

General Information Coeducational day college-preparatory, arts, and technology school. Grades PS–12. Founded: 1966. Setting: small town. Nearest major city is Columbia. 17-acre campus. 6 buildings on campus. Approved or accredited by Southern Association of Colleges and Schools, Southern Association of Independent Schools, and South Carolina Department of Education. Endowment: $280,000. Total enrollment: 825. Upper school average class size: 18. Upper school faculty-student ratio: 1:13. There are 180 required school days per year for Upper School students. Upper School students typically attend 5 days per week. The average school day consists of 6 hours and 20 minutes.

Upper School Student Profile Grade 9: 68 students (32 boys, 36 girls); Grade 10: 58 students (27 boys, 31 girls); Grade 11: 59 students (36 boys, 23 girls); Grade 12: 68 students (33 boys, 35 girls).

Faculty School total: 84. In upper school: 15 men, 28 women; 22 have advanced degrees.

Subjects Offered 3-dimensional design, algebra, anatomy, biology-AP, calculus-AP, chemistry-AP, computer applications, computer programming, computer programming-AP, drawing, economics, English, English language-AP, English literature-AP, environmental science, European history-AP, French, French language-AP, government, government-AP, journalism, Latin, Latin-AP, Middle Eastern history, multimedia, music theory-AP, philosophy, physical education, physical science, physics-AP, pottery, sculpture, Spanish, Spanish language-AP, studio art-AP, trigonometry, U.S. history-AP, world history.

Graduation Requirements Arts and fine arts (art, music, dance, drama), computer science, English, foreign language, mathematics, physical education (includes health), science, social studies (includes history), acceptance into four-year college or university, 20 hours community service.

Special Academic Programs Advanced Placement exam preparation; honors section.

College Admission Counseling 53 students graduated in 2012; all went to college, including Clemson University; College of Charleston; Duke University; Furman University; The Citadel, The Military College of South Carolina; University of South Carolina. Mean SAT critical reading: 568, mean SAT math: 588, mean SAT writing: 554, mean combined SAT: 1711, mean composite ACT: 24.

Student Life Upper grades have specified standards of dress, honor system. Discipline rests primarily with faculty.

Summer Programs Enrichment, sports, art/fine arts, computer instruction programs offered; session focuses on enrichment; held on campus; accepts boys and girls; not open to students from other schools. 100 students usually enrolled. 2013 schedule: June 1 to July 15. Application deadline: May 20.
Tuition and Aid Day student tuition: $5175–$5995. Tuition installment plan (monthly payment plans). Need-based scholarship grants available. In 2012–13, 6% of upper-school students received aid. Total amount of financial aid awarded in 2012–13: $135,000.
Admissions Traditional secondary-level entrance grade is 9. For fall 2012, 140 students applied for upper-level admission, 101 were accepted, 101 enrolled. ACT, CTBS, OLSAT, Iowa Tests of Basic Skills, PSAT and SAT for applicants to grade 11 and 12, school's own test or Stanford Achievement Test, Otis-Lennon School Ability Test required. Deadline for receipt of application materials: none. Application fee required: $150. Interview recommended.
Athletics Interscholastic: baseball (boys), basketball (b,g), bowling (b,g), cheering (g), cross-country running (b,g), equestrian sports (g), fishing (b), football (b), golf (b,g), marksmanship (b), Nautilus (b,g), riflery (b), running (b,g), skeet shooting (b), softball (g), strength & conditioning (b,g), swimming and diving (b,g), tennis (b,g), track and field (b,g), trap and skeet (b), volleyball (g), wrestling (b); intramural: table tennis (b), weight lifting (b,g), weight training (b,g); coed interscholastic: climbing, outdoor adventure, outdoor education, paint ball, riflery, skeet shooting, soccer; coed intramural: archery, outdoor adventure, rafting, rock climbing, ropes courses, table tennis. 5 PE instructors, 12 coaches.
Computers Computers are regularly used in computer applications, English, journalism, literary magazine, technology, yearbook classes. Computer network features include on-campus library services, online commercial services, Internet access, wireless campus network, Internet filtering or blocking technology. Students grades are available online. The school has a published electronic and media policy.
Contact Mr. Sean Hoskins, Director of Admissions and Public Relations. 803-469-3475 Ext. 107. Fax: 803-469-3477. E-mail: sean_hoskins@hotmail.com. Web site: www.wilsonhall.org

WINCHESTER THURSTON SCHOOL

555 Morewood Avenue
Pittsburgh, Pennsylvania 15213-2899

Head of School: Mr. Gary J. Niels

General Information Coeducational day college-preparatory and arts school. Grades PK–12. Founded: 1887. Setting: urban. 5-acre campus. 2 buildings on campus. Approved or accredited by Middle States Association of Colleges and Schools, Pennsylvania Association of Independent Schools, The College Board, and Pennsylvania Department of Education. Member of National Association of Independent Schools. Endowment: $9 million. Total enrollment: 643. Upper school average class size: 15. Upper school faculty-student ratio: 1:8. There are 175 required school days per year for Upper School students. Upper School students typically attend 5 days per week. The average school day consists of 6 hours and 50 minutes.
Upper School Student Profile Grade 9: 61 students (32 boys, 29 girls); Grade 10: 65 students (40 boys, 25 girls); Grade 11: 62 students (26 boys, 36 girls); Grade 12: 56 students (34 boys, 22 girls).
Faculty School total: 91. In upper school: 16 men, 16 women; 16 have advanced degrees.
Subjects Offered Algebra, American history, American history-AP, American literature, animal behavior, art, art history, biology, biology-AP, calculus, calculus-AP, ceramics, chemistry, Chinese, choir, chorus, classics, composition-AP, computer programming, computer science, computer science-AP, creative writing, dance, drama, drawing, economics, economics-AP, English, English literature, English literature-AP, English-AP, European history, European history-AP, expository writing, filmmaking, French, French-AP, geometry, government/civics, health, history, journalism, Latin, Latin-AP, mathematics, music, music theory, philosophy, photography, physical education, physics, physics-AP, psychology, SAT preparation, science, social studies, Spanish, Spanish-AP, speech, statistics-AP, visual arts, world history, world literature, writing, yearbook.
Graduation Requirements Arts and fine arts (art, music, dance, drama), computer science, English, foreign language, mathematics, physical education (includes health), science, social studies (includes history), speech, City As Our Campus coursework, a unique program which connects our students with various educational opportunities within the city of Pittsburgh, (examples of these opportunities include internships, research programs, and service learning options).
Special Academic Programs Advanced Placement exam preparation; independent study; term-away projects; study at local college for college credit; study abroad; academic accommodation for the gifted, the musically talented, and the artistically talented; ESL (2 students enrolled).
College Admission Counseling 63 students graduated in 2011; 62 went to college, including Boston University; Carnegie Mellon University; Haverford College; Haverford College; Lehigh University; University of Pittsburgh. Other: 1 had other specific plans. Mean SAT math: 611, mean SAT writing: 640, mean combined SAT: 1884, mean composite ACT: 26. 49% scored over 600 on SAT critical reading, 42% scored over 600 on SAT math, 46% scored over 600 on SAT writing, 66% scored over 1800 on combined SAT, 67% scored over 26 on composite ACT.
Student Life Upper grades have specified standards of dress, student council. Discipline rests equally with students and faculty.
Tuition and Aid Day student tuition: $22,600–$24,600. Tuition installment plan (monthly payment plans). Need-based scholarship grants available. In 2011–12, 31% of upper-school students received aid. Total amount of financial aid awarded in 2011–12: $1,249,000.
Admissions Traditional secondary-level entrance grade is 9. For fall 2011, 98 students applied for upper-level admission, 63 were accepted, 40 enrolled. ISEE or TOEFL or SLEP required. Deadline for receipt of application materials: December 15. Application fee required: $50. Interview required.
Athletics Interscholastic: basketball (boys, girls), drill team (g), field hockey (g), lacrosse (b,g), rowing (b,g), running (b,g), tennis (b,g); intramural: squash (b); coed interscholastic: crew, cross-country running, fencing, golf, soccer, squash, track and field; coed intramural: basketball, dance, Frisbee, independent competitive sports, outdoor activities, physical fitness, physical training, soccer, strength & conditioning, ultimate Frisbee, weight training, winter soccer, yoga. 4 PE instructors, 24 coaches, 1 athletic trainer.
Computers Computers are regularly used in art, college planning, computer applications, creative writing, English, foreign language, history, library, mathematics, music, photography, science, senior seminar, social studies, writing, writing, yearbook classes. Computer network features include on-campus library services, online commercial services, Internet access, wireless campus network, Internet filtering or blocking technology. Campus intranet, student e-mail accounts, and computer access in designated common areas are available to students. Students grades are available online. The school has a published electronic and media policy.
Contact Mr. Scot Lorenzi, Associate Director of Admission. 412-578-3738. Fax: 412-578-7504. E-mail: lorenzis@winchesterthurston.org. Web site: www.winchesterthurston.org

WINDELLS ACADEMY

PO Box 6
Brightwood, Oregon 97011

Head of School: Mike Hanley

General Information Coeducational boarding college-preparatory, general academic, and skateboarding, freestyle skiing, and snowboarding school. Grades 9–12. Founded: 2009. Setting: rural. Nearest major city is Portland. Students are housed in single-sex dormitories. 53-acre campus. 16 buildings on campus. Approved or accredited by Northwest Accreditation Commission and Oregon Department of Education. Upper school average class size: 25. Upper school faculty-student ratio: 1:7. There are 208 required school days per year for Upper School students. Upper School students typically attend 7 days per week. The average school day consists of 4 hours.
Upper School Student Profile Grade 9: 2 students (2 boys); Grade 10: 7 students (7 boys); Grade 11: 4 students (4 boys); Grade 12: 12 students (9 boys, 3 girls). 100% of students are boarding students. 4% are state residents. 17 states are represented in upper school student body. 32% are international students. International students from Australia, Canada, Chile, France, Switzerland, and Thailand.
Faculty School total: 6. In upper school: 1 man, 2 women; 3 have advanced degrees.
Subjects Offered Accounting, ACT preparation, advanced biology, advanced chemistry, advanced math, Advanced Placement courses, algebra, American government, American history, American legal systems, American literature, art history, arts appreciation, biology, biology-AP, business law, business skills, calculus, calculus-AP, career planning, chemistry, chemistry-AP, Chinese, civics, computer literacy, computer science, computer science-AP, consumer mathematics, contemporary issues, creative writing, digital imaging, digital photography, driver education, earth and space science, earth science, economics, economics and history, economics-AP, English, English as a foreign language, English language-AP, English literature, English literature-AP, English-AP, environmental science, environmental science-AP, European history, European history-AP, fine arts, French, French language-AP, French studies, French-AP, geography, geometry, German, German-AP, grammar, health, health and wellness, integrated mathematics, Japanese, journalism, Latin, life science, life skills, Mandarin, marketing, personal finance, physical education, physical fitness, physical science, physics, physics-AP, pre-algebra, pre-calculus, programming, psychology, psychology-AP, skills for success, sociology, Spanish, statistics, statistics-AP, trigonometry, U.S. government, U.S. government and politics, U.S. government and politics-AP, U.S. history, U.S. history-AP, video, video film production, world history, world history-AP, world literature.
Graduation Requirements Our students receive a diploma through the Keystone online school.
College Admission Counseling 5 students graduated in 2012; 2 went to college, including University of Utah. Other: 1 went to work, 2 had other specific plans.
Student Life Discipline rests primarily with faculty.
Summer Programs Sports, rigorous outdoor training programs offered; session focuses on school and training; held both on and off campus; accepts boys and girls; open to students from other schools. 12 students usually enrolled. 2013 schedule: June 3 to August 9.
Tuition and Aid 7-day tuition and room/board: $35,000–$40,000. Guaranteed tuition plan. Tuition installment plan (monthly payment plans, individually arranged payment plans). Merit scholarship grants, need-based scholarship grants, academic

scholarships, athletic scholarships, and partial media scholarships available. In 2012–13, 20% of upper-school students received aid.

Admissions Traditional secondary-level entrance grade is 10. For fall 2012, 27 students applied for upper-level admission, 25 were accepted, 25 enrolled. Deadline for receipt of application materials: none. No application fee required. On-campus interview required.

Athletics Intramural: skateboarding (boys, girls), ski jumping (b,g), snowboarding (b,g); coed intramural: skateboarding, ski jumping, snowboarding. 4 coaches.

Computers Computers are regularly used in all classes. Computer resources include Internet access, wireless campus network. Computer access in designated common areas is available to students. Students grades are available online.

Contact Ally Ryoppy, Academy Director. 503-622-8751. Fax: 503-622-4582. E-mail: ally@windellsacademy.com. Web site: windellsacademy.com/

WINDERMERE PREPARATORY SCHOOL

6189 Winter Garden-Vineland Road
Windermere, Florida 34786

Head of School: Mrs. Donna Montague-Russell

General Information Boys' boarding and coeducational day college-preparatory, arts, and technology school. Boarding boys grades 9–12, day boys grades PK–12, day girls grades PK–12. Founded: 2000. Setting: small town. Nearest major city is Orlando. Students are housed in single-sex dormitories. 48-acre campus. 3 buildings on campus. Approved or accredited by Association of Independent Schools of Florida, International Baccalaureate Organization, National Independent Private Schools Association, Southern Association of Colleges and Schools, Southern Association of Independent Schools, and Florida Department of Education. Total enrollment: 1,043. Upper school average class size: 18. Upper school faculty-student ratio: 1:11. There are 180 required school days per year for Upper School students. Upper School students typically attend 5 days per week. The average school day consists of 7 hours and 15 minutes.

Upper School Student Profile Grade 9: 60 students (30 boys, 30 girls); Grade 10: 97 students (46 boys, 51 girls); Grade 11: 96 students (48 boys, 48 girls); Grade 12: 64 students (31 boys, 33 girls). 9% of students are boarding students. 91% are state residents. 9% are international students. International students from Austria, Canada, China, Germany, Switzerland, and Turkey; 8 other countries represented in student body.

Faculty School total: 103. In upper school: 20 men, 20 women; 30 have advanced degrees; 3 reside on campus.

Subjects Offered 20th century history, 3-dimensional art, acting, Advanced Placement courses, algebra, American government, American history, American literature, art, biology, biology-AP, business, calculus, calculus-AP, ceramics, chemistry, chemistry-AP, choir, chorus, composition-AP, creative writing, dance, dance performance, drama, drama performance, economics, economics-AP, electives, engineering, English, English composition, English language and composition-AP, English literature, English literature and composition-AP, environmental science, ethics, film, forensics, French, geometry, graphic design, honors algebra, honors English, honors U.S. history, honors world history, Latin, music, music theory, personal fitness, physical education, physics, physics-AP, pre-calculus, psychology, psychology-AP, Spanish, speech and debate, theory of knowledge, world history, world history-AP, world literature, yearbook.

Graduation Requirements Arts and fine arts (art, music, dance, drama), electives, English, foreign language, history, mathematics, performing arts, physical fitness, science, 6 additional elective credits. Community service is required.

Special Academic Programs International Baccalaureate program; 11 Advanced Placement exams for which test preparation is offered; honors section; independent study; academic accommodation for the musically talented and the artistically talented.

College Admission Counseling 54 students graduated in 2011; all went to college, including Boston College; Elon University; Rollins College; University of Central Florida; University of Florida; University of North Florida. Median SAT critical reading: 578, median SAT math: 592, median SAT writing: 563.

Student Life Upper grades have uniform requirement, student council, honor system. Discipline rests primarily with faculty.

Tuition and Aid Day student tuition: $14,025; 7-day tuition and room/board: $38,950. Tuition installment plan (monthly payment plans). Need-based scholarship grants available. In 2011–12, 9% of upper-school students received aid. Total amount of financial aid awarded in 2011–12: $126,672.

Admissions Traditional secondary-level entrance grade is 9. For fall 2011, 100 students applied for upper-level admission, 75 were accepted, 70 enrolled. Achievement tests or SSAT, ERB, PSAT, SAT, PLAN or ACT required. Deadline for receipt of application materials: none. Application fee required: $100. Interview recommended.

Athletics Interscholastic: ballet (girls), baseball (b), basketball (b,g), cheering (g), dance (g), dance team (g), golf (b,g), lacrosse (b), modern dance (g), physical fitness (b,g), physical training (b,g), soccer (b,g), softball (g), strength & conditioning (g), swimming and diving (b), tennis (b,g), track and field (b,g), volleyball (g), weight training (g); coed interscholastic: crew, cross-country running, equestrian sports, track and field; coed intramural: flag football, golf. 8 PE instructors, 25 coaches, 2 athletic trainers.

Computers Computers are regularly used in all academic classes. Computer network features include on-campus library services, Internet access, wireless campus network, Internet filtering or blocking technology. Student e-mail accounts are available to students. Students grades are available online. The school has a published electronic and media policy.

Contact Mrs. Carol Riggs, Director of Admissions. 407-905-7737. Fax: 407-905-7710. E-mail: carol.riggs@windermereprep.com. Web site: www.windermereprep.com

THE WINDSOR SCHOOL

37-02 Main St. / 4th Floor
Flushing, New York 11354

Head of School: Mr. James Seery

General Information Coeducational day college-preparatory and arts school. Grades 6–PG. Founded: 1968. Setting: urban. Nearest major city is New York. 1 building on campus. Approved or accredited by Middle States Association of Colleges and Schools, New York Department of Education, New York State Association of Independent Schools, New York State Board of Regents, The College Board, and US Department of State. Total enrollment: 152. Upper school average class size: 12. Upper school faculty-student ratio: 1:14. There are 185 required school days per year for Upper School students. Upper School students typically attend 5 days per week. The average school day consists of 6 hours.

Upper School Student Profile Grade 9: 12 students (4 boys, 8 girls); Grade 10: 30 students (22 boys, 8 girls); Grade 11: 38 students (21 boys, 17 girls); Grade 12: 68 students (34 boys, 34 girls).

Faculty School total: 14. In upper school: 5 men, 9 women; all have advanced degrees.

Subjects Offered Advanced Placement courses, algebra, American history, American literature, art, basic skills, biology, business, business applications, calculus, ceramics, chemistry, computer programming, computer science, computer skills, computer studies, creative writing, driver education, economics, English, English literature, environmental science, ESL, European history, fine arts, French, geometry, government/civics, grammar, health, marketing, mathematics, music, physical education, physics, pre-calculus, psychology, science, social sciences, social studies, Spanish, trigonometry, world affairs, world history.

Graduation Requirements Arts and fine arts (art, music, dance, drama), English, foreign language, mathematics, physical education (includes health), science, social sciences, social studies (includes history).

Special Academic Programs Advanced Placement exam preparation; honors section; accelerated programs; independent study; academic accommodation for the gifted, the musically talented, and the artistically talented; remedial reading and/or remedial writing; remedial math; ESL (19 students enrolled).

College Admission Counseling 68 students graduated in 2012; all went to college, including Binghamton University, State University of New York; Penn State University Park; Queens College of the City University of New York; St. John's University. Median SAT critical reading: 440, median SAT math: 550, median SAT writing: 460. 10% scored over 600 on SAT critical reading, 35% scored over 600 on SAT math, 10% scored over 600 on SAT writing.

Student Life Upper grades have specified standards of dress. Discipline rests primarily with faculty.

Summer Programs Remediation, enrichment, advancement, ESL, art/fine arts, computer instruction programs offered; session focuses on advancement, enrichment, remediation; held on campus; accepts boys and girls; open to students from other schools. 600 students usually enrolled. 2013 schedule: July 1 to August 18. Application deadline: June 30.

Tuition and Aid Day student tuition: $21,600. Tuition installment plan (individually arranged payment plans). Financial aid available to upper-school students. In 2012–13, 10% of upper-school students received aid. Total amount of financial aid awarded in 2012–13: $30,000.

Admissions Traditional secondary-level entrance grade is 9. For fall 2012, 80 students applied for upper-level admission, 76 were accepted, 73 enrolled. School's own exam required. Deadline for receipt of application materials: none. No application fee required. On-campus interview required.

Athletics Interscholastic: basketball (boys, girls), soccer (b,g), softball (b,g); intramural: aerobics (b,g), basketball (b,g), cooperative games (b,g), fitness (b,g), jump rope (g), physical fitness (b,g), soccer (b,g), softball (b,g), tennis (b,g), volleyball (b,g); coed interscholastic: basketball, soccer, softball; coed intramural: basketball, fitness, jump rope, physical fitness, soccer, softball, table tennis, tennis, volleyball. 2 PE instructors, 2 coaches.

Computers Computers are regularly used in art, business applications, mathematics, research skills, typing, yearbook classes. Computer resources include Internet access.

Contact Ms. Emily Yu, Director of Admissions. 718-359-8300. Fax: 718-359-1876. E-mail: admin@thewindsorschool.com. Web site: www.windsorschool.com

WINDWARD SCHOOL

11350 Palms Boulevard
Los Angeles, California 90066

Head of School: Tom Gilder

General Information Coeducational day college-preparatory school. Grades 7–12. Founded: 1971. Setting: urban. 9-acre campus. 11 buildings on campus. Approved or accredited by California Association of Independent Schools and Western Association of Schools and Colleges. Member of National Association of Independent Schools. Total enrollment: 541. Upper school average class size: 16. Upper school faculty-student ratio: 1:7. There are 165 required school days per year for Upper School students. Upper School students typically attend 5 days per week. The average school day consists of 7 hours.

Upper School Student Profile Grade 9: 80 students (38 boys, 42 girls); Grade 10: 94 students (46 boys, 48 girls); Grade 11: 91 students (48 boys, 43 girls); Grade 12: 89 students (43 boys, 46 girls).

Faculty School total: 65. In upper school: 32 men, 27 women; 37 have advanced degrees.

Subjects Offered 3-dimensional art, acting, advanced biology, advanced chemistry, Advanced Placement courses, algebra, American history, American literature, art, art history, ballet, biology, calculus, ceramics, chemistry, Chinese, chorus, computer science, creative writing, dance, drama, English, English literature, environmental science, European history, fine arts, French, geometry, government/civics, health, history, journalism, Latin, marine biology, mathematics, music, performing arts, photography, photojournalism, physical education, physiology, robotics, science, senior internship, social studies, Spanish, theater, trigonometry, world history.

Graduation Requirements Arts and fine arts (art, music, dance, drama), English, foreign language, mathematics, physical education (includes health), science, social studies (includes history).

Special Academic Programs 16 Advanced Placement exams for which test preparation is offered; honors section; independent study; study at local college for college credit.

College Admission Counseling 89 students graduated in 2011; all went to college, including Dartmouth College; Northwestern University; Tufts University; University of California, Berkeley; Williams College; Yale University. Mean SAT critical reading: 650, mean SAT math: 645, mean SAT writing: 671, mean combined SAT: 1966.

Student Life Upper grades have specified standards of dress, student council, honor system. Discipline rests primarily with faculty.

Tuition and Aid Day student tuition: $33,505. Tuition installment plan (Key Tuition Payment Plan, monthly payment plans). Need-based scholarship grants, need-based loans available. In 2011–12, 17% of upper-school students received aid. Total amount of financial aid awarded in 2011–12: $1,367,106.

Admissions Traditional secondary-level entrance grade is 9. For fall 2011, 149 students applied for upper-level admission, 30 were accepted, 23 enrolled. ISEE required. Deadline for receipt of application materials: December 14. Application fee required: $100. On-campus interview required.

Athletics Interscholastic: baseball (boys), basketball (b,g), football (b); coed interscholastic: cross-country running, flag football. 5 PE instructors, 15 coaches, 2 athletic trainers.

Computers Computers are regularly used in art, English, history, mathematics, science classes. Computer network features include on-campus library services, online commercial services, Internet access, wireless campus network, Internet filtering or blocking technology. Student e-mail accounts are available to students. The school has a published electronic and media policy.

Contact Sharon Pearline, Director of Admissions. 310-391-7127. Fax: 310-397-5655. Web site: www.windwardschool.org

See Display on next page and Close-Up on page 650.

THE WINSOR SCHOOL

103 Pilgrim Road
Boston, Massachusetts 02215

Head of School: Mrs. Rachel Friis Stettler

General Information Girls' day college-preparatory school. Grades 5–12. Founded: 1886. Setting: urban. 8-acre campus. 2 buildings on campus. Approved or accredited by Association of Independent Schools in New England, New England Association of Schools and Colleges, and Massachusetts Department of Education. Member of National Association of Independent Schools. Endowment: $62.5 million. Total enrollment: 434. Upper school average class size: 13. Upper school faculty-student ratio: 1:5. There are 163 required school days per year for Upper School students. Upper School students typically attend 5 days per week. The average school day consists of 6 hours and 30 minutes.

Upper School Student Profile Grade 9: 65 students (65 girls); Grade 10: 66 students (66 girls); Grade 11: 59 students (59 girls); Grade 12: 51 students (51 girls).

Faculty School total: 72. In upper school: 11 men, 38 women; 39 have advanced degrees.

Subjects Offered Acting, advanced studio art-AP, African history, African literature, algebra, architecture, art, art history, astronomy, biology, biology-AP, British literature (honors), calculus, calculus-AP, ceramics, chemistry, chemistry-AP, Chinese, computer programming, contemporary history, creative writing, digital art, drama, engineering, English, environmental science-AP, expository writing, fine arts, French, French-AP, geometry, health, Islamic history, Latin, Latin-AP, literature, macroeconomics-AP, marine biology, Middle Eastern history, music, photography, physical education, physics, physics-AP, pre-calculus, sculpture, senior project, Spanish, Spanish-AP, statistics, statistics-AP, theater, U.S. history, U.S. literature, Web site design.

Graduation Requirements Algebra, art, biology, chemistry, English, foreign language, geometry, health and wellness, health education, non-Western literature, non-Western societies, physical education (includes health), physics, pre-calculus, senior project, U.S. history, world history, 1 semester quantitative course senior year.

Special Academic Programs 11 Advanced Placement exams for which test preparation is offered; honors section; term-away projects.

College Admission Counseling 54 students graduated in 2011; all went to college, including Boston College; Dartmouth College; Harvard University; The Johns Hopkins University; Vanderbilt University; Yale University. Median SAT critical reading: 710, median SAT math: 700, median SAT writing: 750, median combined SAT: 2160, median composite ACT: 30. 93% scored over 600 on SAT critical reading, 93% scored over 600 on SAT math, 98% scored over 600 on SAT writing, 96% scored over 1800 on combined SAT.

Student Life Upper grades have specified standards of dress, student council, honor system. Discipline rests primarily with faculty.

Tuition and Aid Day student tuition: $35,500. Tuition installment plan (Tuition Management Systems). Need-based scholarship grants available. In 2011–12, 24% of upper-school students received aid. Total amount of financial aid awarded in 2011–12: $1,735,291.

Admissions Traditional secondary-level entrance grade is 9. For fall 2011, 104 students applied for upper-level admission, 19 were accepted, 12 enrolled. ISEE or SSAT required. Deadline for receipt of application materials: December 17. Application fee required: $45. On-campus interview required.

Athletics Interscholastic: basketball, crew, cross-country running, field hockey, ice hockey, lacrosse, sailing, soccer, softball, squash, swimming and diving, tennis, track and field. 4 PE instructors, 4 coaches, 1 athletic trainer.

Computers Computers are regularly used in photography, programming, Web site design classes. Computer network features include on-campus library services, Internet access, wireless campus network, Internet filtering or blocking technology. Campus intranet and student e-mail accounts are available to students. The school has a published electronic and media policy.

Contact Mrs. Pamela Parks McLaurin, Director of Admission. 617-735-9503. Fax: 617-912-1381. Web site: www.winsor.edu/

WINSTON PREPARATORY SCHOOL

New York, New York
See Special Needs Schools section.

THE WINSTON SCHOOL SAN ANTONIO

San Antonio, Texas
See Special Needs Schools section.

THE WOODHALL SCHOOL

PO Box 550
58 Harrison Lane
Bethlehem, Connecticut 06751

Head of School: Matthew C. Woodhall

General Information Boys' boarding and day college-preparatory, arts, and ESL school; primarily serves students with above-average intellectual ability who have had difficulties in traditional school environments. Grades 9–PG. Founded: 1983. Setting: rural. Nearest major city is Waterbury. Students are housed in single-sex dormitories. 38-acre campus. 5 buildings on campus. Approved or accredited by Association of Independent Schools in New England, New England Association of Schools and Colleges, and Connecticut Department of Education. Member of National Association of Independent Schools. Endowment: $120,000. Total enrollment: 39. Upper school average class size: 4. Upper school faculty-student ratio: 1:4. There are 184 required school days per year for Upper School students. Upper School students typically attend 6 days per week.

Upper School Student Profile Grade 9: 5 students (5 boys); Grade 10: 10 students (10 boys); Grade 11: 12 students (12 boys); Grade 12: 12 students (12 boys). 100% of students are boarding students. 15% are state residents. 22 states are represented in upper school student body. 1% are international students. International students from Canada.

Faculty School total: 16. In upper school: 13 men, 3 women; 11 have advanced degrees; 11 reside on campus.
Subjects Offered Algebra, American history, anatomy, art, biology, calculus, chemistry, comparative government and politics, drama, English, environmental science, geometry, Greek, language and composition, Latin, physics, pre-calculus, Spanish, world civilizations.
Graduation Requirements Arts and fine arts (art, music, dance, drama), communication skills, English, foreign language, mathematics, physical education (includes health), science, social studies (includes history).
Special Academic Programs Advanced Placement exam preparation; independent study; special instructional classes for students with Attention Deficit Disorder and non-verbal learning disabilities; ESL.
College Admission Counseling 13 students graduated in 2012; 11 went to college, including Guilford College; Keene State College; Lynchburg College; Northeastern University; University of the Ozarks; University of Vermont. Other: 2 had other specific plans. Median SAT critical reading: 652, median SAT math: 500, median SAT writing: 569, median combined SAT: 574.
Student Life Upper grades have specified standards of dress, student council, honor system. Discipline rests primarily with faculty.
Tuition and Aid Day student tuition: $45,810; 7-day tuition and room/board: $59,500. Tuition installment plan (individually arranged payment plans).
Admissions Traditional secondary-level entrance grade is 10. Deadline for receipt of application materials: none. Application fee required: $100. On-campus interview required.
Athletics Interscholastic: basketball, cross-country running, lacrosse, soccer, wrestling; intramural: alpine skiing, basketball, bicycling, bowling, canoeing/kayaking, cross-country running, fishing, fitness, fitness walking, Frisbee, hiking/backpacking, ice skating, jogging, lacrosse, mountain biking, outdoor activities, outdoor education, outdoor recreation, physical fitness, physical training, rafting, running, skiing (cross-country), skiing (downhill), snowboarding, soccer, street hockey, strength & conditioning, table tennis, volleyball, walking, wall climbing, weight lifting, winter walking, wrestling.
Computers Computers are regularly used in art, English, foreign language, history, mathematics, science, social sciences classes. Computer resources include Internet access. The school has a published electronic and media policy.
Contact Matthew C. Woodhall, Head of School. 203-266-7788. Fax: 203-266-5896. E-mail: mwoodhall@woodhallschool.org. Web site: www.woodhallschool.org

WOODLYNDE SCHOOL

445 Upper Gulph Road
Strafford, Pennsylvania 19087

Head of School: Christopher M. Fulco, EdD

General Information Coeducational day college-preparatory, arts, and technology school; primarily serves individuals with Attention Deficit Disorder, dyslexic students, and language-based learning disabilities. Grades K–12. Founded: 1976. Setting: suburban. Nearest major city is Philadelphia. 8-acre campus. 2 buildings on campus. Approved or accredited by Pennsylvania Association of Independent Schools and Pennsylvania Department of Education. Member of National Association of Independent Schools. Endowment: $559,699. Total enrollment: 262. Upper school average class size: 10. Upper school faculty-student ratio: 1:5. There are 168 required school days per year for Upper School students. Upper School students typically attend 5 days per week. The average school day consists of 6 hours and 55 minutes.
Upper School Student Profile Grade 9: 22 students (12 boys, 10 girls); Grade 10: 22 students (12 boys, 10 girls); Grade 11: 26 students (14 boys, 12 girls); Grade 12: 28 students (20 boys, 8 girls).
Faculty School total: 62. In upper school: 11 men, 10 women; 7 have advanced degrees.
Subjects Offered Algebra, American history, American literature, art, art-AP, arts, biology, chemistry, creative writing, earth science, English, English literature, English-AP, European history, fine arts, French, geometry, government/civics, health, history, journalism, mathematics, music, photography, physical education, physics, political science, psychology, science, social studies, Spanish, studio art, world history, world literature, writing.
Graduation Requirements Arts and fine arts (art, music, dance, drama), English, foreign language, mathematics, physical education (includes health), science, social studies (includes history), community service, senior project, senior speech.
Special Academic Programs Honors section; remedial reading and/or remedial writing.
College Admission Counseling 27 students graduated in 2012; 26 went to college, including West Chester University of Pennsylvania; Widener University. Other: 1 went to work.
Student Life Upper grades have specified standards of dress, student council. Discipline rests primarily with faculty.
Summer Programs Remediation, enrichment, advancement, sports, art/fine arts programs offered; session focuses on mathematics and reading enrichment; held on campus; accepts boys and girls; open to students from other schools. 75 students usually enrolled. 2013 schedule: June 20 to July 22. Application deadline: May 30.

Tuition and Aid Day student tuition: $29,150. Tuition installment plan (FACTS Tuition Payment Plan). Need-based scholarship grants available. In 2012–13, 35% of upper-school students received aid. Total amount of financial aid awarded in 2012–13: $525,475.

Admissions Traditional secondary-level entrance grade is 9. For fall 2012, 19 students applied for upper-level admission, 10 were accepted, 6 enrolled. Individual IQ required. Deadline for receipt of application materials: none. Application fee required: $100. On-campus interview required.

Athletics Interscholastic: basketball (boys, girls), lacrosse (b,g), soccer (b,g), softball (g), tennis (b,g), volleyball (g); intramural: aerobics/dance (b,g); coed interscholastic: cross-country running. 4 PE instructors, 10 coaches, 1 athletic trainer.

Computers Computers are regularly used in all academic, art, creative writing, drawing and design, English, foreign language, French, graphic arts, graphic design, history, music, newspaper, publications, social studies, Spanish, study skills, technology, word processing, writing, yearbook classes. Computer network features include on-campus library services, Internet access, wireless campus network, Internet filtering or blocking technology. Campus intranet and student e-mail accounts are available to students. The school has a published electronic and media policy.

Contact Dorinda Shank, Director of Admissions. 610-687-9660 Ext. 624. Fax: 610-687-4752. E-mail: shankd@woodlynde.org. Web site: www.woodlynde.org

WOODWARD ACADEMY

1662 Rugby Avenue

College Park, Georgia 30337

Head of School: Mr. Stuart Gulley, PhD

General Information Coeducational day college-preparatory and arts school. Grades PK–12. Founded: 1900. Setting: suburban. Nearest major city is Atlanta. 90-acre campus. 50 buildings on campus. Approved or accredited by Georgia Independent School Association, Southern Association of Colleges and Schools, and Georgia Department of Education. Member of National Association of Independent Schools and Secondary School Admission Test Board. Endowment: $120.7 million. Total enrollment: 2,662. Upper school average class size: 17.

Faculty School total: 384. In upper school: 45 men, 68 women; 85 have advanced degrees.

Subjects Offered 20th century world history, 3-dimensional art, 3-dimensional design, acting, Advanced Placement courses, algebra, American government, American history, American history-AP, anatomy and physiology, art, astronomy, audio visual/media, band, biology, biology-AP, calculus, calculus-AP, ceramics, chemistry, chemistry-AP, choir, choral music, chorus, comparative religion, computer education, computer programming, computer programming-AP, computer science, computer science-AP, concert band, contemporary history, contemporary issues, creative writing, dance, debate, digital music, drama, drama performance, drawing, drawing and design, earth science, ecology, economics, economics and history, economics-AP, English, English language and composition-AP, English literature, English literature and composition-AP, English-AP, environmental science, environmental science-AP, European history, European history-AP, fine arts, French, French language-AP, French-AP, geography, geometry, government and politics-AP, government/civics, grammar, health, history, history-AP, honors English, honors geometry, honors U.S. history, honors world history, independent study, Japanese, jewelry making, journalism, Latin, literature and composition-AP, marching band, marine ecology, mathematics, meteorology, microeconomics-AP, Middle East, modern European history-AP, multicultural literature, music, oceanography, performing arts, personal fitness, photography, physical education, physics, physics-AP, pre-calculus, probability and statistics, science, social studies, Spanish, Spanish language-AP, Spanish-AP, speech communications, statistics, statistics-AP, television, the Sixties, theater, trigonometry, U.S. government and politics, U.S. government and politics-AP, U.S. history, U.S. history-AP, video, voice ensemble, world history, world literature, world religions, yearbook.

Graduation Requirements Arts and fine arts (art, music, dance, drama), computer science, English, foreign language, mathematics, physical education (includes health), religion (includes Bible studies and theology), science, social studies (includes history).

Special Academic Programs 22 Advanced Placement exams for which test preparation is offered; honors section; independent study.

College Admission Counseling 269 students graduated in 2011; all went to college, including Auburn University; Georgia Institute of Technology; Georgia Southern University; The University of Alabama; University of Georgia.

Student Life Upper grades have uniform requirement, student council, honor system. Discipline rests primarily with faculty.

Tuition and Aid Day student tuition: $21,300. Tuition installment plan (SMART Tuition Payment Plan, Your Tuition Solution—Springstone Financial, Sallie Mae). Need-based scholarship grants available. In 2011–12, 10% of upper-school students received aid.

Admissions Traditional secondary-level entrance grade is 9. SSAT required. Deadline for receipt of application materials: March 1. Application fee required: $75. On-campus interview required.

Athletics Interscholastic: baseball (boys), basketball (b,g), cheering (g), cross-country running (b,g), diving (b,g), football (b), golf (b,g), lacrosse (b,g), soccer (b,g), softball (g), swimming and diving (b,g), tennis (b,g), track and field (b,g), volleyball (g); intramural: basketball (b,g), cheering (g), football (b), soccer (b,g), softball (g), swimming and diving (b,g), tennis (b,g), track and field (b,g), volleyball (g); coed interscholastic: Frisbee, power lifting, ultimate Frisbee, weight lifting; coed intramural: fencing, horseback riding. 4 PE instructors, 34 coaches, 1 athletic trainer.

Computers Computers are regularly used in creative writing, English, foreign language, graphic design, journalism, literary magazine, mathematics, media production, newspaper, science, yearbook classes. Computer network features include on-campus library services, online commercial services, Internet access, wireless campus network. Student e-mail accounts are available to students. Students grades are available online.

Contact Russell L. Slider, Vice President/Dean of Admissions. 404-765-4001. Fax: 404-765-4009. E-mail: rusty.slider@woodward.edu. Web site: www.woodward.edu

THE WOODWARD SCHOOL

1102 Hancock Street

Quincy, Massachusetts 02169

Head of School: Carol Andrews, JD

General Information Girls' day college-preparatory, arts, and technology school. Grades 6–12. Founded: 1869. Setting: urban. Nearest major city is Boston. 2-acre campus. 2 buildings on campus. Approved or accredited by Association of Independent Schools in New England, New England Association of Schools and Colleges, and Massachusetts Department of Education. Total enrollment: 125. Upper school average class size: 12. Upper school faculty-student ratio: 1:8. There are 165 required school days per year for Upper School students. Upper School students typically attend 5 days per week. The average school day consists of 6 hours and 35 minutes.

Upper School Student Profile Grade 9: 19 students (19 girls); Grade 10: 20 students (20 girls); Grade 11: 20 students (20 girls); Grade 12: 22 students (22 girls).

Faculty School total: 19. In upper school: 3 men, 16 women; 12 have advanced degrees.

Subjects Offered Advanced computer applications, algebra, American history, American literature, anatomy, art, arts, biology, calculus, calculus-AP, chemistry, chorus, classical studies, classics, community service, computer graphics, computer math, computer science, computer skills, constitutional law, drama, ecology, English, English language and composition-AP, environmental science, filmmaking, fine arts, French, health and wellness, health science, language arts, Latin, Latin-AP, law and the legal system, literature, literature and composition-AP, mathematics, media studies, music, music appreciation, physics, physics-AP, physiology, political science, portfolio art, pre-algebra, psychology, rhetoric, SAT preparation, science, senior project, social sciences, social studies, sociology, Spanish, study skills, theater arts, U.S. government, U.S. history, Web authoring, Web site design, world history, world literature, World War II, writing.

Graduation Requirements Arts and fine arts (art, music, dance, drama), computer science, English, foreign language, mathematics, science, senior project, social studies (includes history). Community service is required.

Special Academic Programs 6 Advanced Placement exams for which test preparation is offered; honors section; independent study; ESL (11 students enrolled).

College Admission Counseling 22 students graduated in 2012; all went to college, including Boston College; Boston University; Northeastern University; University of Massachusetts Amherst; University of Massachusetts Boston.

Student Life Upper grades have specified standards of dress, student council, honor system. Discipline rests primarily with faculty.

Tuition and Aid Day student tuition: $12,775. Tuition installment plan (SMART Tuition Payment Plan, monthly payment plans, individually arranged payment plans). Tuition reduction for siblings, merit scholarship grants, need-based scholarship grants, prepGATE K-12 education loan available. In 2012–13, 47% of upper-school students received aid; total upper-school merit-scholarship money awarded: $27,000. Total amount of financial aid awarded in 2012–13: $185,240.

Admissions Traditional secondary-level entrance grade is 9. For fall 2012, 37 students applied for upper-level admission, 22 were accepted, 15 enrolled. ISEE, school's own exam, SSAT or writing sample required. Deadline for receipt of application materials: December 14. Application fee required: $40. Interview required.

Athletics Interscholastic: basketball, soccer, softball. 2 PE instructors, 6 coaches, 1 athletic trainer.

Computers Computers are regularly used in all classes. Computer network features include on-campus library services, Internet access, wireless campus network, Internet filtering or blocking technology. Computer access in designated common areas is available to students. The school has a published electronic and media policy.

Contact Sarah Jacobs, Director of Admissions. 617-773-5610. Fax: 617-770-1551. E-mail: sjacobs@thewoodwardschool.org. Web site: www.thewoodwardschool.org

WORCESTER PREPARATORY SCHOOL

508 South Main Street
PO Box 1006
Berlin, Maryland 21811

Head of School: Dr. Barry W. Tull

General Information Coeducational day college-preparatory, arts, and technology school. Grades PK–12. Founded: 1970. Setting: small town. Nearest major city is Ocean City. 45-acre campus. 7 buildings on campus. Approved or accredited by Association of Independent Maryland Schools, Middle States Association of Colleges and Schools, and Maryland Department of Education. Member of National Association of Independent Schools. Total enrollment: 532. Upper school average class size: 14. Upper school faculty-student ratio: 1:9. There are 173 required school days per year for Upper School students. Upper School students typically attend 5 days per week. The average school day consists of 6 hours and 30 minutes.

Upper School Student Profile Grade 9: 47 students (25 boys, 22 girls); Grade 10: 53 students (24 boys, 29 girls); Grade 11: 53 students (25 boys, 28 girls); Grade 12: 47 students (27 boys, 20 girls).

Faculty School total: 62. In upper school: 13 men, 21 women; 29 have advanced degrees.

Subjects Offered Advanced Placement courses, algebra, American history, American literature, art, art history, biology, biology-AP, calculus, calculus-AP, chemistry, chemistry-AP, computer programming, computer programming-AP, computer science, creative writing, dance, dance performance, drama, earth science, economics, English, English literature, English literature and composition-AP, English-AP, European history, fine arts, French, geography, geometry, government/civics, Latin, literature and composition-AP, literature-AP, mathematics, military history, music, music theory, physical education, physics, physics-AP, psychology, SAT preparation, science, social sciences, social studies, Spanish, speech, statistics, technological applications, technology/design, theater, typing, U.S. history-AP, vocal music, world history, world history-AP, world literature, writing.

Graduation Requirements Art appreciation, arts and fine arts (art, music, dance, drama), computer science, English, foreign language, mathematics, music appreciation, physical education (includes health), science, social sciences.

Special Academic Programs 8 Advanced Placement exams for which test preparation is offered; honors section; independent study; academic accommodation for the gifted.

College Admission Counseling 57 students graduated in 2012; all went to college, including Furman University; Massachusetts Institute of Technology; The Johns Hopkins University; The University of Alabama; University of Pennsylvania; Vanderbilt University.

Student Life Upper grades have uniform requirement, student council, honor system. Discipline rests primarily with faculty.

Tuition and Aid Day student tuition: $11,950. Tuition installment plan (Key Tuition Payment Plan, monthly payment plans, individually arranged payment plans). Need-based scholarship grants available. In 2012–13, 1% of upper-school students received aid.

Admissions Traditional secondary-level entrance grade is 9. For fall 2012, 16 students applied for upper-level admission, 13 were accepted, 11 enrolled. Achievement/Aptitude/Writing and writing sample required. Deadline for receipt of application materials: none. Application fee required: $50. On-campus interview required.

Athletics Interscholastic: basketball (boys, girls), field hockey (g), lacrosse (b,g), soccer (b,g), tennis (b,g), volleyball (g), weight training (b,g), winter soccer (b,g); intramural: basketball (b,g), dance (b,g), dance squad (b,g), flag football (b,g), soccer (b,g); coed interscholastic: cheering, golf, tennis; coed intramural: dance, dance squad. 3 PE instructors, 3 coaches, 1 athletic trainer.

Computers Computers are regularly used in all classes. Computer network features include on-campus library services, online commercial services, Internet access, wireless campus network, Internet filtering or blocking technology. Campus intranet, student e-mail accounts, and computer access in designated common areas are available to students. The school has a published electronic and media policy.

Contact Tara F. Becker, Director of Admissions. 410-641-3575 Ext. 107. Fax: 410-641-3586. E-mail: tbecker@worcesterprep.org. Web site: www.worcesterprep.org

WYOMING SEMINARY

201 North Sprague Avenue
Kingston, Pennsylvania 18704-3593

Head of School: Dr. Kip P. Nygren

General Information Coeducational boarding and day college-preparatory school, affiliated with United Methodist Church. Grades 9–PG. Founded: 1844. Setting: suburban. Nearest major city is Wilkes-Barre. Students are housed in single-sex dormitories. 22-acre campus. 12 buildings on campus. Approved or accredited by Middle States Association of Colleges and Schools, Pennsylvania Association of Independent Schools, The Association of Boarding Schools, The College Board, University Senate of United Methodist Church, and Pennsylvania Department of Education. Member of National Association of Independent Schools and Secondary School Admission Test Board. Endowment: $50 million. Total enrollment: 756. Upper school average class size: 14. Upper school faculty-student ratio: 1:8. There are 170 required school days per year for Upper School students. Upper School students typically attend 5 days per week. The average school day consists of 7 hours.

Upper School Student Profile Grade 9: 80 students (40 boys, 40 girls); Grade 10: 103 students (47 boys, 56 girls); Grade 11: 121 students (67 boys, 54 girls); Grade 12: 100 students (47 boys, 53 girls); Postgraduate: 15 students (11 boys, 4 girls). 41% of students are boarding students. 66% are state residents. 17 states are represented in upper school student body. 25% are international students. International students from Canada, China, Germany, Republic of Korea, Taiwan, and Viet Nam; 10 other countries represented in student body. 10% of students are United Methodist Church.

Faculty School total: 57. In upper school: 31 men, 26 women; 42 have advanced degrees; 37 reside on campus.

Subjects Offered 20th century world history, 3-dimensional design, algebra, alternative physical education, American Civil War, American history, American literature, analysis and differential calculus, analytic geometry, anatomy and physiology, ancient world history, art, art appreciation, art history, art history-AP, Bible studies, biology, biology-AP, botany, British literature, calculus, calculus-AP, ceramics, chemistry, chemistry-AP, choral music, college admission preparation, college counseling, computer programming, computer science, conceptual physics, creative writing, critical writing, discrete mathematics, drama, drawing and design, ecology, English, English literature, environmental science, environmental science-AP, ESL, European history, European history-AP, expository writing, fine arts, forensics, French, French-AP, geometry, health education, history, history of music, independent study, Judaic studies, Latin, Latin-AP, mathematics, music, music theory, music theory-AP, philosophy, photography, physics, poetry, pre-calculus, printmaking, psychology, psychology-AP, public speaking, religion, Russian, science, science research, Shakespeare, social studies, sociology, Spanish, Spanish-AP, statistics, statistics-AP, studio art-AP, theater, trigonometry, U.S. government and politics-AP, U.S. history-AP, women in literature, world civilizations, world cultures, world history, world literature, world religions, World War II, zoology.

Graduation Requirements Art history, Bible as literature, biology, computer science, English, foreign language, health education, mathematics, music history, physical education (includes health), public speaking, science, social studies (includes history), U.S. history, world civilizations, 40 hours of community service, extracurricular participation.

Special Academic Programs 21 Advanced Placement exams for which test preparation is offered; honors section; independent study; term-away projects; study at local college for college credit; study abroad; ESL (47 students enrolled).

College Admission Counseling 100 students graduated in 2012; 98 went to college, including Boston University; Bucknell University; Drexel University; New York University; Penn State University Park. Other: 1 went to work, 1 entered a postgraduate year. Mean SAT critical reading: 572, mean SAT math: 633, mean SAT writing: 582, mean combined SAT: 1787.

Student Life Upper grades have specified standards of dress, student council, honor system. Discipline rests equally with students and faculty. Attendance at religious services is required.

Summer Programs Enrichment, advancement, ESL, sports, art/fine arts programs offered; session focuses on performing arts and ESL; held on campus; accepts boys and girls; open to students from other schools. 400 students usually enrolled. 2013 schedule: June 23 to August 22. Application deadline: June 1.

Tuition and Aid Day student tuition: $21,850; 7-day tuition and room/board: $43,200. Tuition installment plan (FACTS Tuition Payment Plan, monthly payment plans). Merit scholarship grants, need-based scholarship grants, need-based loans, prepGATE loans available. In 2012–13, 50% of upper-school students received aid; total upper-school merit-scholarship money awarded: $400,000. Total amount of financial aid awarded in 2012–13: $6,000,000.

Admissions Traditional secondary-level entrance grade is 9. For fall 2012, 356 students applied for upper-level admission, 199 were accepted, 106 enrolled. ACT, PSAT or SAT for applicants to grade 11 and 12, SSAT or TOEFL or SLEP required. Deadline for receipt of application materials: none. Application fee required: $75. Interview required.

Athletics Interscholastic: baseball (boys), basketball (b,g), cross-country running (b,g), diving (b,g), field hockey (g), ice hockey (b,g), lacrosse (b,g), soccer (b,g), softball (g), swimming and diving (b,g), tennis (b,g), wrestling (b); coed interscholastic: golf, strength & conditioning; coed intramural: ballet, combined training, dance, fitness, martial arts, modern dance, outdoor activities, outdoor recreation, physical training, wall climbing. 2 PE instructors, 6 coaches, 1 athletic trainer.

Computers Computers are regularly used in art, English, foreign language, history, mathematics, music, science classes. Computer network features include on-campus library services, online commercial services, Internet access, wireless campus network, Internet filtering or blocking technology. Campus intranet, student e-mail accounts, and computer access in designated common areas are available to students. Students grades are available online. The school has a published electronic and media policy.

Contact Mr. Eric Turner, Director of Enrollment Management. 570-270-2160. Fax: 570-270-2191. E-mail: admission@wyomingseminary.org. Web site: www.wyomingseminary.org

XAVERIAN HIGH SCHOOL

7100 Shore Road
Brooklyn, New York 11209

Head of School: Mr. Robert Alesi

General Information Boys' day college-preparatory, arts, business, religious studies, and technology school, affiliated with Roman Catholic Church. Grades 9–12. Founded: 1957. Setting: urban. 1 building on campus. Approved or accredited by Middle States Association of Colleges and Schools, New York Department of Education, New York State Board of Regents, and New York Department of Education. Total enrollment: 1,088. Upper school average class size: 27. Upper school faculty-student ratio: 1:26. There are 180 required school days per year for Upper School students. Upper School students typically attend 5 days per week. The average school day consists of 6 hours.

Special Academic Programs Advanced Placement exam preparation; honors section; study at local college for college credit; academic accommodation for the gifted and the musically talented; remedial reading and/or remedial writing; remedial math; programs in English, mathematics, general development for dyslexic students.

College Admission Counseling 270 students graduated in 2012.

Student Life Upper grades have uniform requirement. Attendance at religious services is required.

Summer Programs Remediation, enrichment, sports programs offered; session focuses on academic enrichment and recreation; held on campus; accepts boys; open to students from other schools. 60 students usually enrolled. 2013 schedule: July 1 to August 1. Application deadline: May 1.

Tuition and Aid Day student tuition: $11,600. Tuition installment plan (SMART Tuition Payment Plan). Merit scholarship grants, need-based scholarship grants, need-based loans available. In 2012–13, 30% of upper-school students received aid.

Admissions For fall 2012, 800 students applied for upper-level admission. New York Archdiocesan Cooperative Entrance Examination required. Deadline for receipt of application materials: December 1. No application fee required.

Athletics Interscholastic: aquatics, baseball, basketball, billiards, bowling, cross-country running, diving, fitness, football, golf, handball, ice hockey, indoor track, indoor track & field, jogging, lacrosse, physical fitness, physical training, power lifting, running, soccer, strength & conditioning, swimming and diving, team handball, tennis, track and field, volleyball, weight lifting, weight training, winter (indoor) track, wrestling; intramural: Frisbee, independent competitive sports, Nautilus, ultimate Frisbee.

Computers Computers are regularly used in all classes. Computer network features include on-campus library services, online commercial services, Internet access, wireless campus network, Internet filtering or blocking technology, students are issued iPad 2s when they enter the school. Campus intranet and student e-mail accounts are available to students. Students grades are available online. The school has a published electronic and media policy.

Contact Deacon Kevin McCormack, Principal. 718-836-7100. Fax: 718-836-7114. E-mail: kmccormack@xaverian.org. Web site: www.xaverian.org

YORK CATHOLIC HIGH SCHOOL

601 East Springettsbury Avenue
York, Pennsylvania 17403

Head of School: Mrs. Adrienne K. Seufert

General Information Coeducational day college-preparatory and general academic school, affiliated with Roman Catholic Church. Grades 7–12. Founded: 1927. Setting: suburban. 19-acre campus. 1 building on campus. Approved or accredited by Middle States Association of Colleges and Schools, National Catholic Education Association, and Pennsylvania Department of Education. Total enrollment: 636. Upper school average class size: 21. Upper school faculty-student ratio: 1:16. There are 180 required school days per year for Upper School students. Upper School students typically attend 5 days per week. The average school day consists of 6 hours and 15 minutes.

Upper School Student Profile Grade 9: 99 students (40 boys, 59 girls); Grade 10: 106 students (49 boys, 57 girls); Grade 11: 136 students (60 boys, 76 girls); Grade 12: 99 students (52 boys, 47 girls). 89% of students are Roman Catholic.

Faculty School total: 46. In upper school: 16 men, 30 women.

Special Academic Programs Advanced Placement exam preparation; honors section; study at local college for college credit.

College Admission Counseling 110 students graduated in 2012; 104 went to college. Other: 6 entered military service. Median SAT critical reading: 547, median SAT math: 533, median SAT writing: 546, median combined SAT: 1626.

Student Life Upper grades have uniform requirement, student council, honor system. Discipline rests primarily with faculty. Attendance at religious services is required.

Tuition and Aid Day student tuition: $4800. Tuition installment plan (SMART Tuition Payment Plan). Tuition reduction for siblings, need-based scholarship grants available. In 2012–13, 28% of upper-school students received aid. Total amount of financial aid awarded in 2012–13: $250,000.

Admissions Traditional secondary-level entrance grade is 9. Deadline for receipt of application materials: none. No application fee required. Interview required.

Athletics Interscholastic: baseball (boys), basketball (b,g), cheering (g), cross-country running (b,g), football (b), golf (b,g), lacrosse (b,g), running (b,g), soccer (b,g), softball (g), tennis (b,g), track and field (b,g), volleyball (g), wrestling (b); intramural: strength & conditioning (b); coed intramural: bowling, ice hockey, skiing (downhill), table tennis.

Computers Computer resources include on-campus library services, Internet access, Internet filtering or blocking technology. Campus intranet is available to students. Students grades are available online. The school has a published electronic and media policy.

Contact Ms. Heather Hoffman, Director of Admissions. 717-846-8871 Ext. 20. Fax: 717-843-4588. E-mail: hhoffman@yorkcatholic.org. Web site: www.yorkcatholic.org

YORK COUNTRY DAY SCHOOL

1071 Regents Glen Boulevard
York, Pennsylvania 17403

Head of School: Nathaniel W. Coffman

General Information Coeducational day college-preparatory, arts, and bilingual studies school. Grades PS–12. Founded: 1953. Setting: suburban. Nearest major city is Baltimore, MD. 15-acre campus. 1 building on campus. Approved or accredited by Middle States Association of Colleges and Schools, Pennsylvania Association of Independent Schools, and Pennsylvania Department of Education. Member of National Association of Independent Schools. Endowment: $1.3 million. Total enrollment: 217. Upper school average class size: 12. Upper school faculty-student ratio: 1:6. There are 170 required school days per year for Upper School students. Upper School students typically attend 5 days per week. The average school day consists of 7 hours and 30 minutes.

Upper School Student Profile Grade 9: 14 students (5 boys, 9 girls); Grade 10: 13 students (9 boys, 4 girls); Grade 11: 18 students (12 boys, 6 girls); Grade 12: 16 students (7 boys, 9 girls).

Faculty School total: 42. In upper school: 10 men, 8 women; 12 have advanced degrees.

Subjects Offered Advanced biology, advanced chemistry, advanced studio art-AP, algebra, American history, American history-AP, American literature, art, art history, biochemistry, biology, calculus, calculus-AP, chemistry, choral music, community service, computer programming, computer science, creative writing, drama, English, English literature, English literature-AP, European history, fine arts, French, French-AP, geography, geometry, government/civics, health, history, Latin, literature, mathematics, music, physical education, physics, psychology, public speaking, science, social studies, Spanish, Spanish language-AP, studio art-AP, theater, world history, world history-AP.

Graduation Requirements Arts and fine arts (art, music, dance, drama), English, foreign language, history, independent study, mathematics, physical education (includes health), public speaking, science, visual arts, independent study (3 semesters) through our Magnet Program, two semester classes. Community service is required.

Special Academic Programs Advanced Placement exam preparation; honors section; independent study; term-away projects; study at local college for college credit; study abroad; academic accommodation for the gifted, the musically talented, and the artistically talented.

College Admission Counseling 14 students graduated in 2011; all went to college, including Gettysburg College; Penn State University Park; University of Pittsburgh; University of Richmond; Ursinus College; York College of Pennsylvania. Median SAT critical reading: 540, median SAT math: 510.

Student Life Upper grades have specified standards of dress, student council, honor system. Discipline rests equally with students and faculty.

Tuition and Aid Day student tuition: $16,850. Tuition installment plan (Insured Tuition Payment Plan, monthly payment plans, semester payment plan). Need-based scholarship grants available. In 2011–12, 39% of upper-school students received aid. Total amount of financial aid awarded in 2011–12: $306,250.

Admissions Traditional secondary-level entrance grade is 9. 3-R Achievement Test, Academic Profile Tests, California Achievement Test, ISEE, Otis-Lennon Ability or Stanford Achievement Test or PSAT and SAT for applicants to grade 11 and 12 required. Deadline for receipt of application materials: none. Application fee required: $35. On-campus interview required.

Athletics Interscholastic: baseball (boys), basketball (b,g), bowling (b,g), cross-country running (b,g), field hockey (g), football (b), golf (b,g), soccer (b,g), softball (g), swimming and diving (b,g), tennis (b,g), volleyball (g), wrestling (b); intramural: basketball (b,g), soccer (b,g); coed intramural: soccer. 2 PE instructors, 6 coaches.

Computers Computers are regularly used in all academic classes. Computer network features include on-campus library services, online commercial services, Internet access, Internet filtering or blocking technology. Student e-mail accounts are available to students.

Contact Ms. Alison C. Greer, Director of Admission and Communication. 717-843-9805. Fax: 717-815-6769. E-mail: agreer@ycds.org. Web site: www.ycds.org

YORK PREPARATORY SCHOOL

40 West 68th Street
New York, New York 10023-6092

Head of School: Ronald P. Stewart

General Information Coeducational day college-preparatory, arts, technology, music (practical and theory), and drama school. Grades 6–12. Founded: 1969. Setting: urban. 1 building on campus. Approved or accredited by Middle States Association of Colleges and Schools, National Independent Private Schools Association, and New York Department of Education. Member of National Association of Independent Schools. Total enrollment: 358. Upper school average class size: 15. Upper school faculty-student ratio: 1:6. There are 158 required school days per year for Upper School students. Upper School students typically attend 5 days per week. The average school day consists of 6 hours and 30 minutes.

Upper School Student Profile Grade 9: 73 students (44 boys, 29 girls); Grade 10: 64 students (35 boys, 29 girls); Grade 11: 61 students (36 boys, 25 girls); Grade 12: 64 students (40 boys, 24 girls).

Faculty School total: 64. In upper school: 24 men, 40 women; 48 have advanced degrees.

Subjects Offered 20th century history, 20th century world history, 3-dimensional art, advanced chemistry, advanced computer applications, Advanced Placement courses, advanced studio art-AP, algebra, American history, American history-AP, American literature, anatomy, animation, anthropology, art, art appreciation, astronomy, biology, calculus, calculus-AP, ceramics, chemistry, chemistry-AP, comparative religion, computer math, computer programming, computer science, computer skills, concert band, creative writing, current events, drama, drama performance, driver education, earth science, economics, English, English literature, English-AP, environmental science, ethics, European history, expository writing, filmmaking, fine arts, French, genetics, geography, geology, geometry, government/civics, grammar, health education, Holocaust studies, law, literary magazine, mathematics, music, music history, philosophy, photography, physical education, physics, physiology, political science, politics, pre-calculus, psychology, reading/study skills, research skills, SAT preparation, science, science project, social studies, Spanish, statistics, theater, trigonometry, typing, world history, world literature, writing, zoology.

Graduation Requirements Arts and fine arts (art, music, dance, drama), English, foreign language, mathematics, physical education (includes health), science, social studies (includes history). Community service is required.

Special Academic Programs Advanced Placement exam preparation; honors section; independent study; study at local college for college credit; academic accommodation for the gifted, the musically talented, and the artistically talented; programs in English, mathematics, general development for dyslexic students; special instructional classes for students with mild learning issues (extra tutoring program).

College Admission Counseling 51 students graduated in 2012; all went to college, including American University; Boston University; Harvard University; Massachusetts Institute of Technology; Syracuse University; The Johns Hopkins University.

Student Life Upper grades have specified standards of dress, student council, honor system. Discipline rests primarily with faculty.

Summer Programs Remediation, advancement programs offered; held on campus; accepts boys and girls; not open to students from other schools. 30 students usually enrolled. 2013 schedule: June 10 to July 31. Application deadline: none.

Tuition and Aid Day student tuition: $40,700–$41,300. Tuition installment plan (Insured Tuition Payment Plan, monthly payment plans, individually arranged payment plans). Tuition reduction for siblings, merit scholarship grants, need-based scholarship grants available. In 2012–13, 20% of upper-school students received aid. Total amount of financial aid awarded in 2012–13: $1,000,000.

Admissions Traditional secondary-level entrance grade is 9. ISEE or SSAT required. Deadline for receipt of application materials: January 15. Application fee required: $50. On-campus interview required.

Athletics Interscholastic: baseball (boys), basketball (b,g), cross-country running (b,g), soccer (b,g), softball (b,g), volleyball (b,g); intramural: cheering (g), volleyball (b,g); coed interscholastic: basketball, cross-country running, golf, tennis, track and field; coed intramural: aerobics, aerobics/Nautilus, aquatics, basketball, bicycling, combined training, cross-country running, dance, fitness, Frisbee, golf, indoor track, physical fitness, physical training, skiing (downhill), soccer, softball, swimming and diving, ultimate Frisbee, weight training, yoga. 6 PE instructors, 6 coaches, 2 athletic trainers.

Computers Computers are regularly used in all academic classes. Computer network features include on-campus library services, online commercial services, Internet access, wireless campus network, Internet filtering or blocking technology. Computer access in designated common areas is available to students. Students grades are available online. The school has a published electronic and media policy.

Contact Ms. Cathy Minaudo, Director of Admissions. 212-362-0400 Ext. 106. Fax: 212-362-7424. E-mail: cminaudo@yorkprep.org. Web site: www.yorkprep.org

See Display on this page and Close-Up on page 652.

YORK SCHOOL

9501 York Road
Monterey, California 93940

Head of School: Chuck Harmon

General Information Coeducational day college-preparatory, arts, bilingual studies, and technology school, affiliated with Episcopal Church. Grades 8–12. Founded: 1959. Setting: suburban. Nearest major city is San Jose. 126-acre campus. 6 buildings on campus. Approved or accredited by California Association of Independent Schools, National Association of Episcopal Schools, Western Association of Schools and Colleges, and California Department of Education. Member of National Association of Independent Schools. Endowment: $5.8 million. Total enrollment: 225. Upper school average class size: 14. Upper school faculty-student ratio: 1:8. Upper School students typically attend 5 days per week. The average school day consists of 7 hours.

Upper School Student Profile Grade 8: 18 students (7 boys, 11 girls); Grade 9: 62 students (34 boys, 28 girls); Grade 10: 56 students (28 boys, 28 girls); Grade 11: 43 students (17 boys, 26 girls); Grade 12: 50 students (27 boys, 23 girls).

Faculty School total: 32. In upper school: 16 men, 16 women; 24 have advanced degrees.

Subjects Offered Advanced studio art-AP, algebra, American history-AP, anatomy, ancient history, art, art history, Asian history, band, biology, biology-AP, calculus, calculus-AP, chemistry, chemistry-AP, choir, community service, computer science, creative writing, digital art, drama, English, English-AP, environmental science, film, fine arts, French, French language-AP, geometry, Greek, jazz, Latin, Latin-AP, marine biology, mathematics, music, music theory-AP, orchestra, painting, philosophy, photography, physical education, physical science, physics, physics-AP, physiology, pre-calculus, psychology-AP, science, social studies, Spanish, Spanish language-AP, statistics, studio art, U.S. history, U.S. history-AP, world history, yearbook.

Graduation Requirements Arts and fine arts (art, music, dance, drama), computer science, English, foreign language, mathematics, physical education (includes health), science, social studies (includes history), ensemble participation. Community service is required.

Special Academic Programs Advanced Placement exam preparation; honors section.

College Admission Counseling 49 students graduated in 2012; 46 went to college, including Boston University; Princeton University; University of California, Santa Barbara; Whittier College. Other: 3 had other specific plans. Mean SAT critical reading: 670, mean SAT math: 657, mean SAT writing: 665, mean combined SAT: 1992, mean composite ACT: 28.

Student Life Upper grades have specified standards of dress, student council, honor system. Discipline rests primarily with faculty.

Tuition and Aid Day student tuition: $27,600. Tuition installment plan (individually arranged payment plans, 2 Payments, 10 Payments). Need-based scholarship grants available. In 2012–13, 46% of upper-school students received aid. Total amount of financial aid awarded in 2012–13: $1,463,100.

Admissions Traditional secondary-level entrance grade is 9. For fall 2012, 133 students applied for upper-level admission. Admissions testing required. Deadline for receipt of application materials: February 1. Application fee required: $75. Interview required.

Athletics Interscholastic: basketball (boys, girls), cross-country running (b,g), diving (b,g), field hockey (g), golf (b,g), soccer (b,g), softball (g), swimming and diving (b,g), tennis (b,g), volleyball (g); coed interscholastic: dance, lacrosse; coed intramural: badminton, basketball, fitness walking, independent competitive sports, jogging, soccer, ultimate Frisbee, volleyball, walking, weight training, yoga. 18 coaches.

Computers Computers are regularly used in computer applications, technology, yearbook classes. Computer network features include on-campus library services, Internet access, wireless campus network. The school has a published electronic and media policy.

Contact Rachel Gaudoin, Admission Associate. 831-372-7338 Ext. 116. Fax: 831-372-8055. E-mail: rachel@york.org. Web site: www.york.org

ZURICH INTERNATIONAL SCHOOL

Steinacherstrasse 140
W?nswil 8820, Switzerland

Head of School: Jeff Paulson

General Information Coeducational day college-preparatory, technology, and International Baccalaureate Diploma and Advanced Placement school. Grades PS–13. Founded: 1963. Setting: suburban. Nearest major city is Zurich, Switzerland. 6-acre campus. 1 building on campus. Approved or accredited by International Baccalaureate Organization, New England Association of Schools and Colleges, and Swiss Federation of Private Schools. Member of European Council of International Schools. Language of instruction: English. Total enrollment: 1,493. Upper school average class size: 16. Upper school faculty-student ratio: 1:7. There are 175 required school days per year for Upper School students. Upper School students typically attend 5 days per week. The average school day consists of 7 hours.

Upper School Student Profile Grade 9: 111 students (61 boys, 50 girls); Grade 10: 110 students (50 boys, 60 girls); Grade 11: 122 students (70 boys, 52 girls); Grade 12: 117 students (49 boys, 68 girls).

Faculty School total: 230. In upper school: 31 men, 35 women; 46 have advanced degrees.

Subjects Offered Acting, Advanced Placement courses, art history, art history-AP, art-AP, biology, biology-AP, calculus, calculus-AP, chemistry-AP, computer programming-AP, concert band, concert choir, digital photography, drama, drama performance, economics, economics-AP, English, English language and composition-AP, English literature, English literature and composition-AP, ESL, European history-AP, fine arts, French, French language-AP, German, German-AP, health, history, history-AP, International Baccalaureate courses, journalism, macro/microeconomics-AP, macroeconomics-AP, mathematics, microeconomics-AP, music, philosophy, photography, physical education, physics-AP, pre-calculus, psychology-AP, public speaking, robotics, science, social studies, Spanish language-AP, statistics-AP, studio art, studio art-AP, theater, U.S. history-AP, visual arts, world history, world history-AP, writing.

Graduation Requirements Arts and fine arts (art, music, dance, drama), English, foreign language, mathematics, physical education (includes health), science, social studies (includes history), completion of a yearly service project. Community service is required.

Special Academic Programs International Baccalaureate program; 22 Advanced Placement exams for which test preparation is offered; honors section; independent study; remedial reading and/or remedial writing; remedial math; ESL (9 students enrolled).

College Admission Counseling 121 students graduated in 2012; 110 went to college, including Northeastern University; Northwestern University; Princeton University; University of California, Los Angeles; University of Chicago; University of Virginia. Other: 2 went to work, 3 entered military service, 6 had other specific plans. Median SAT critical reading: 570, median SAT math: 560, median SAT writing: 570, median combined SAT: 1700. 46% scored over 600 on SAT critical reading, 39% scored over 600 on SAT math, 42% scored over 600 on SAT writing.

Student Life Upper grades have specified standards of dress, student council. Discipline rests primarily with faculty.

Summer Programs Held both on and off campus; held at in and around the greater Zurich area; accepts boys and girls; open to students from other schools. 100 students usually enrolled.

Tuition and Aid Day student tuition: 33,900 Swiss francs. Tuition installment plan (monthly payment plans). Need-based scholarship grants available. In 2012–13, 3% of upper-school students received aid. Total amount of financial aid awarded in 2012–13: 67,700 Swiss francs.

Admissions Traditional secondary-level entrance grade is 9. For fall 2012, 141 students applied for upper-level admission, 58 were accepted, 58 enrolled. English for Non-native Speakers or math and English placement tests required. Deadline for receipt of application materials: none. Application fee required: 500 Swiss francs.

Athletics Interscholastic: basketball (boys, girls), rugby (b), soccer (b,g), softball (g), tennis (b,g), volleyball (b,g); intramural: indoor soccer (b,g); coed interscholastic: alpine skiing, cross-country running, golf, skiing (cross-country), skiing (downhill), swimming and diving, track and field, ultimate Frisbee; coed intramural: aerobics/dance, badminton, basketball, canoeing/kayaking, climbing, dance, fitness, Frisbee, juggling, kayaking, outdoor activities, rock climbing, sailing, swimming and diving, wall climbing, yoga. 5 PE instructors, 15 coaches.

Computers Computers are regularly used in all classes. Computer network features include on-campus library services, online commercial services, Internet access, wireless campus network, one to one Tablet Program, Moodle, VHS, MAC lab, iPad pilot in upper school. Campus intranet, student e-mail accounts, and computer access in designated common areas are available to students. Students grades are available online. The school has a published electronic and media policy.

Contact Dale Braunschweig, Head Admissions. 41-58 750 2531. Fax: 41-58 750 2501. E-mail: dbraunschweig@zis.ch. Web site: www.zis.ch

Traditional Day and Boarding School Close-Ups

AMERICAN HERITAGE SCHOOL

Plantation and Delray Beach, Florida

Type: Coeducational, day, independent, nonsectarian
Grades: PK-3–grade 12
Enrollment: 2,400, Plantation campus; 1,057, Boca/Delray campus
Head of School: William Laurie, President and Founder

THE SCHOOL

American Heritage School's mission is to graduate students who are prepared in mind, body, and spirit to meet the requirements of the colleges of their choice. To this end, the School strives to offer a challenging college preparatory curriculum, opportunities for leadership, and superior programs in the arts and athletics. American Heritage is committed to providing a safe and nurturing environment for learning so that children of average to gifted intelligence may achieve their full potential to be intelligent, creative, and contributing members of society. Students receive a well-rounded education that provides opportunities for leadership and character building and extensive opportunities for growth in the arts, athletics, and new technology.

ACADEMIC PROGRAM

The curriculum for the preprimary child is developmental and age appropriate at each level. Daily language, speech, and auditory development activities help children to listen, understand, speak, and learn effectively. The program seeks to maximize the academic potential of each child, while fostering a positive self-image and providing the skills necessary for the next level of education.

The Lower School is committed to developing a student's basic skills, helping the student master content areas, and maintaining the student's enthusiasm for learning. Students learn the fundamentals of reading, process writing, mathematics, and English through a logical progressive sequence, and they learn social studies, handwriting, spelling, science, and health, with an emphasis on the development of good study skills. In math and reading, students are grouped according to ability. Enrichment classes in computer education, art, media center, music, Spanish, Chinese, physical education, and investigative science lab are offered. Field trips, special projects and events, and assemblies supplement the work introduced in class.

Math, reading, grammar, literature, social studies, and science are the core subjects of the junior high curriculum, where critical-thinking skills become increasingly important. Writing skills are emphasized, helping students become literate and articulate thinkers and writers. Enrichment courses are an important part of the junior high curriculum, with courses rotated on a nine-week basis. Honors classes are available in all core subject areas.

At the high school level, emphasis is placed on college preparation and on higher-level thinking skills. Students are challenged by required research and speech and writing assignments in all subject areas. An extensive variety of classes in all areas of the fine arts is available. A selection of electives—from marine biology to Advanced Placement Chinese to stagecraft—rounds out the students' schedules, allowing them to explore other interests and talents. In addition to traditional lecture and discussion, teachers supplement the text curriculum with activities, projects, and field trips that make subjects more relevant and meaningful to the students.

Honors and Advanced Placement (AP) courses are available to qualified students. Students may gain college credit as a benefit of the successful completion of AP courses, which include American government, American history, biology, calculus, chemistry, economics, English language, English literature, environmental studies, European history, French, music theory, physics, psychology, Spanish, and world history.

American Heritage School offers unique premedical, prelaw, and pre-engineering programs to qualified high school students. The programs challenge those ninth- through twelfth-grade students who have an interest in these fields of study and encourage students to consider these areas as potential career choices. The many course offerings are most often taught by working professionals in each area. In addition to course work for both programs, there are required internships that match students with professionals in their area of study.

In 2012, the school had 30 National Merit Scholarship Finalists and was the top-ranked private school at the National Mu Alpha Theta (mathematics honor society) annual conference.

Through the international program, in addition to an international student's regular academic classes, one to two hours of English language instruction is provided daily. Living with an American family produces more opportunity for language development and practice.

FACULTY AND ADVISERS

The students at American Heritage are served by 211 teachers, counselors, and administrators at the Plantation location, and 122 teachers, counselors, and administrators at the Delray campus. Sixty-two percent hold master's or doctoral degrees. Teachers actively seek out both school-year and summer workshops to attend, and they return with creative ideas for their teaching. Faculty turnover is minimal. The faculty is also committed to the Heritage philosophy of developing good character and self-esteem as well as the reinforcement of traditional values in students. Teachers maintain close communication with parents regarding their child's progress, with frequent written progress reports, phone calls, and scheduled conference days. The school provides a Web-based service, Edline, on which students and parents can access information ranging from general school, club, and sports topics to specific content for individual classes. Classes are small, with a 17:1 student-teacher ratio.

COLLEGE ADMISSION COUNSELING

At American Heritage, the goal is to send seniors to colleges that match their goals and expectations for college life. There are 10 full-time guidance counselors in the high school, including a Director of College Placement and a Scholarship Specialist.

The college placement process begins in seventh grade with academic advising about curriculum and course selection and continues through high school with college-preparation advising. The counselors keep abreast of current admissions trends through attendance at national and local conferences and frequent contact with college admissions representatives.

The preparation for college intensifies as students in grades 9 through 12 follow a program designed to help them score well on the SATs. The program includes SAT prep mini-exercises in their English and math classes. In tenth grade and above, students may take an intensive daily SAT prep class taught on campus during the regular school day.

At this level, academic counseling gives consideration to graduation requirements and course selection, study skills and time management, leadership and club involvement, and referral to mentoring or professional tutoring, if needed. College advising is offered in the classroom on topics such as standardized test taking, the college application process, resume and essay writing, and searching for colleges and majors. The School reviews all college applications sent, writes letters of recommendation, finds scholarships for students, prepares students for college interviews, invites college admission representatives to campus, hosts a college fair, and proctors AP exams.

Virtually all graduates continue their educations and are admitted to the nation's finest colleges and universities. In recent years, graduates have been admitted to such schools as Boston College, Colgate, Columbia, Cornell, Duke, Harvard, Georgetown, MIT, NYU, Pepperdine, Princeton, Rutgers, Tufts, Wake Forest, West Point, Yale, and the Universities of Connecticut, Maryland, Pennsylvania, and Southern California.

STUDENT BODY AND CONDUCT

In the Lower School, the PK-3 classes enroll about 16 students; PK-4, 17; Kindergarten, 18; grades 1 and 2, 21; grades 3 and 4, 22; and grades 5 and 6, 23. In preschool through grade six, each class has a teacher and a full-time assistant. Grades 7 through 12 in the Upper School average 17 students.

The Plantation campus has 2,400 students, with 733 in the Lower School and 1,667 in the Upper School. The Boca/Delray student population totals 1,057 with 241 students in the Lower School and 816 in the Upper School. The School's day population is culturally diverse, with students representing forty-three countries from around the world.

ACADEMIC FACILITIES

The Plantation campus includes a fully equipped science lab, ten state-of-the-art computer rooms, and a $25-million Center for the Arts that houses a state-of-the-art 800-seat theater, a black-box theater, spacious art studios, a graphic design lab, choral and band rooms, and individual practice rooms. There are two new library/media centers, one that services the Lower School and another that meets all the technological requirements of students in the Upper School. Heritage has an excellent physical education center that includes an Olympic-sized swimming and diving facility, a gymnasium, six tennis courts, a track, four modern locker rooms, a weight-training room, and acres of well-maintained athletic fields.

The American Heritage Boca/Delray campus provides seven state-of-the-art iMac computer labs, fully equipped science labs, art studios, a college guidance computer lab, a library/media center and research lab, a new $20 million center for the arts, an Olympic-sized swimming pool with eight racing lanes, a 2,600-square-foot teaching pool, a 25,000-square-foot gymnasium/auditorium, six lighted tennis courts, a football and soccer field, fully equipped weight training room, locker rooms, two well-equipped playgrounds, acres of well-maintained baseball and softball fields, practice fields for soccer and football, and beautifully landscaped grounds and courtyards.

ATHLETICS

The athletic program is an important part of the sense of community that has developed at Heritage. Parents, teachers, administrators, and students develop a special kind of camaraderie while cheering on the Patriot teams. Awards evenings are held for athletes and parents at the conclusion of each season. Heritage offers a complete competitive sports program. A "no-cut" policy allows every student who wants to participate an opportunity to play on the Patriot team of his or her choice. Coaches provide high-quality instruction in all sports. Sportsmanship, teamwork, recognition of effort, and thorough training and preparation are the goals toward which the School works every day. Each year, a number of student-athletes receive financial help for their college education based on their athletic ability and their performance. More importantly, however, for those who do not have the ability—or maybe the desire—to participate at the collegiate level, athletic opportunities offer a very enjoyable and memorable experience, with accomplishments and relationships that last a lifetime. American Heritage competes as a member of the Florida High School Activities Association, and the athletics programs are consistently ranked in the top ten in the state of Florida.

EXTRACURRICULAR OPPORTUNITIES

The extensive activities offered at Heritage serve several purposes. Primarily, they assist in the growth and development of students, but they also provide opportunities for leadership and excellence, which are increasingly required for college admission. Among the activities and clubs offered to high school students are the National Honor Society; Student Council; Spanish/French Honor Society; Premed, Prelaw, and Pre-engineering Clubs; the Modern Language Club; Mu Alpha Theta (math club); SADD; the computer club; yearbook; the student newspaper; thespians; marching band; orchestra; jazz band; and chorus. Lower School students can take after-school classes in art, dance, instrumental music, karate, cooking, computers, and other areas of interest. Students may also participate in Student Council, Junior Thespians, or advanced math competitions.

American Heritage School provides an outstanding fine arts program to students in PK-3 through grade 12. The Center for the Arts is a beautiful, specially designed facility that enhances the arts program. Students participating in art, music, and drama programs have won awards at local, state, and national levels of competition in recent years. This recognition includes the Florida State Thespians Critics Choice awards, Florida Vocal Association (superior ratings for choir, solo, and ensemble), Florida Orchestra Association (superior ratings for solo and ensemble/guitar and strings), American Choral Directors Award, and National Scholastic Art Competition (gold and silver medals).

Many students participate in enrichment and leadership programs offered in Broward County, including the National Conference for Community and Justice, Leadership Broward, Boys and Girls Clubs, Silver Knights, and the Institute for Math and Computer Science. Nationally, students have participated in Hugh O'Brian Youth Foundation, Freedoms Foundation, Presidential Classroom, and Global Young Leaders Conference. In addition, American Heritage School is home to two nonprofit organizations: Mosaic Theatre, an organization committed to promoting the dramatic arts, where students are able to work alongside professional actors, and the Center for the Arts Scholarship Foundation, a fund-raising organization that awards scholarships to talented students in the arts.

SUMMER PROGRAMS

American Heritage has provided summer fun for young campers since 1981. Summer camp provides activities that help build confidence and self-esteem. Campers enjoy the challenges and rewards of teamwork as they work and play. Through the numerous activities that are offered, campers continue to develop the socialization skills begun in school. Campers enjoy good relationships with the high school and college counselors, who serve as role models for them. American Heritage Day Camp sessions are available for students 13 years old and under.

For students who have failed a credit course in high school or have been required by their current school to attend summer school in order to pass to the next grade level, summer school is a necessity. However, many others can benefit from American Heritage's summer academic program, including preschoolers who need readiness skills to succeed in kindergarten or first grade; elementary and junior high students who need practice and development of basic skills in math, reading, and language arts; any students who perform one or two years below grade level; students for whom English is a second language; high school students who want to advance themselves academically by earning extra credits during the summer; and high school students who will soon take the SAT or ACT tests for college admission. More information can be obtained by contacting the American Heritage School.

COSTS AND FINANCIAL AID

In 2012–13, tuition and fees total between $18,238 for preschoolers and $22,954 for twelfth-grade students. An international program is available at additional cost for the academic school year—August through May—and includes tuition, housing, three meals a day, books, uniforms, and 2 hours a day of English language.

American Heritage offers financial aid to parents who qualify.

ADMISSIONS INFORMATION

Enrollment at American Heritage School is limited to students who are above average to gifted in intelligence and who are working at or above grade level. Math, reading, vocabulary, and IQ tests are administered and are used to determine if the student has the background and basic skills necessary to be successful. The results of these entrance exams are discussed with the parents at a conference following the testing. I-20 visas are granted to international students who are accepted. Details are available from the Director of Admissions. Students are admitted without regard to race, creed, or national origin.

For acceptance into American Heritage's international program, families must supply complete academic records from the age of 12, translated into English; two teacher letters of recommendation, translated into English; copies of the student's passport; and a completed American Heritage School application form. The American Heritage Admissions Committee reviews the student's records and determines suitable placement. Full tuition for the school year is due upon acceptance. After tuition has been received, the School issues an I-20 form, which must be taken to the U.S. Embassy in the student's country to obtain a student visa.

APPLICATION TIMETABLE

First-semester classes begin in late August. For information regarding specific deadlines, students should contact American Heritage School's Plantation campus.

ADMISSIONS CORRESPONDENCE

Attn: Admissions

American Heritage School
12200 West Broward Boulevard
Plantation, Florida 33325
United States
Phone: 954-472-0022
E-mail: admissions@ahschool.com
Web site: http://www.ahschool.com

American Heritage School Boca/Delray
6200 Linton Boulevard
Delray Beach, Florida 33484
United States
Phone: 561-495-7272
E-mail: admissions.bd@ahschool.com
Web site: http://www.ahschool.com

THE ATHENIAN SCHOOL

Danville, California

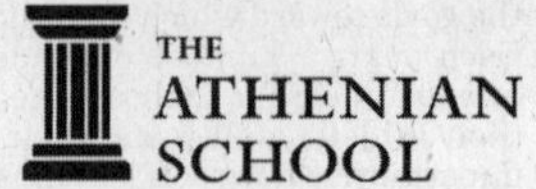

Type: Coeducational day and boarding college-preparatory school
Grades: 6–12: Middle School, 6–8; Upper School, 9–12
Enrollment: School total: 450; Upper School: 306
Head of School: Eric Niles, Head

THE SCHOOL

Founded in 1965 by Dyke Brown, a graduate of Yale Law School and Vice President of the Ford Foundation, Athenian has as its goal the development of each student for a life of purpose and personal fulfillment as a citizen of the world. An Athenian education equips graduates with a deep understanding of themselves, extraordinary skills for achievement, and the compassion to make a positive difference in the world.

With distinctive programs, Athenian goes far beyond preparing students for outstanding colleges by engaging them in their education. Meaningful hands-on classes and programs make learning exciting and motivating. Classes average 15 to 16 students, so teachers know each student and involve them in discussion and activities. Athenian's diverse student body comes from throughout the East Bay and more than ten other countries. The international programs broaden students' perspectives, with opportunities across the globe for exchanges, service projects, interim trips, and conferences. Students build important skills in activities such as an electric car project, a championship robotics team, athletics, and art, music, chorus, and theater. All students participate in community service each year and, in grade 11, complete the Athenian Wilderness Experience. Few schools offer an experience as academically and personally enriching as Athenian's.

Nearly 100 percent of Athenian graduates are admitted to an outstanding array of four-year colleges and universities. Athenian helps students find the colleges that fit them best. Most importantly, Athenian inspires students to become lifelong learners and confident, successful adults.

Athenian's beautiful 75-acre campus of rolling hills is located 32 miles east of San Francisco at the base of Mt. Diablo. Athenian students access the cultural and educational resources of the San Francisco Bay Area via Athenian's shuttles, buses, and nearby BART stations (the Bay Area rapid transit system). Students also enjoy activities on the nearby Pacific Coast and the majestic Sierra mountains.

A nonprofit institution, Athenian is governed by a 25-member Board of Trustees. The School's operating budget was $12.5 million for 2010–11. The endowment is $7 million.

The Athenian School is fully accredited by the Western Association of Schools and Colleges. It is a member of the National Association of Independent Schools, the California Association of Independent Schools, the National Network of Complementary Schools, A Better Chance, Western Boarding Schools, the College Board, the National Association for College Admission Counseling, and the Round Square Conference of International Schools.

ACADEMIC PROGRAM

Athenian's exciting broad curriculum develops analytical thinking and communication skills in all disciplines, offering a wide variety of enriching courses in English, history, math, science, fine arts, foreign language, and physical education. The ninth-grade humanities program studies major world cultures through literature, history, and art courses. The sophomore humanities program focuses on American studies in history and literature. Juniors and seniors choose enriching and varied seminars in history and literature. Athenian's mathematics program features statistics and AP statistics courses in addition to two yearlong AP calculus courses. Science features first-year and second-year courses in physics, chemistry, and biology in addition to environmental science, geology, applied science, and the art of science and making. Modern languages offer courses with honors and/or AP options in French, Mandarin Chinese, and Spanish. Fine and performing arts feature courses in drawing, painting, sculpture, pottery, stained glass, photography, dance, musical performance, drama, theater tech, and several arts and society courses. Many honors or Advanced Placement and/or honors options are offered.

The academic year is divided into two semesters. The daily schedule includes six academic periods ranging from 50 to 85 minutes each. Each course meets four times a week.

Courses required for graduation are as follows: English, 4 years; laboratory science, 3 years; mathematics, 3 years; history, 3 years (including freshman humanities, American studies, and three 1-semester elective history seminars in the junior or senior year); 3 years of a foreign language; and 2.5 years of fine arts. Most students exceed these requirements. Students also fulfill graduation requirements in community service each year and must participate in the Athenian Wilderness Experience in grade 11.

Some of the electives offered are studio arts, drama workshops, instrumental ensembles, and additional courses in academic subjects. Required seminars (chosen by students) for English and history may include Shakespeare, science fiction, Russian fiction, Latin American fiction, African American studies, creative writing, or women writers. Science offers inspiring applied science, geology, and environmental science courses and extracurricular programs in building an electric car and robotics. Mathematics courses go beyond two Advanced Placement calculus courses to offer statistics and AP statistics yearlong courses.

Class size varies from 8 to 20, and the average class has 15 students. The overall student-teacher ratio is 10:1. Study for boarding students is supervised by faculty members assigned to dormitories during the evenings.

Athenian offers intermediate and advanced English learning courses to students for whom English is not the first language. ESL students take part in the in the regular curriculum for subjects other than English and history. Field trips help familiarize international students with northern California and U.S. culture.

Opportunities for independent study are provided for selected students by the academic departments. Student exchanges can be arranged either domestically or internationally. The Athenian School is a founding member of a notable consortium of international schools, The Round Square, which offers students academic exchanges, international community service opportunities, and participation in an annual international student conference. Athenian also belongs to the National Network of Complementary Schools, which arranges short-term exchanges of students across the country between member schools that have diverse strengths and resources.

Class field trips in the San Francisco Bay Area are frequent. Students may also participate in off-campus internships oriented toward community service and career exploration. Qualified seniors may take advantage of an accelerated high school program arrangement at the University of California at Berkeley.

A distinctive element of the curriculum is the Athenian Wilderness Experience, required of all students in their junior year. AWE enhances self-confidence, communication skills, and perseverance in addition to fostering an appreciation of the environment.

FACULTY AND ADVISERS

There are 55 full-time and 15 part-time faculty members, 42 of whom hold advanced degrees. Twenty-five faculty members live on-campus with their families.

Eric Niles, Head since 2009, has graduated from the University of Pennsylvania, Wharton School of Economics, and UCLA Law School. Prior to his career in education, he served as counsel to a member of the House of Representatives. Beginning in 1995 he taught and served as Dean of Students at Midland School and then Emma Willard School, where he became Assistant Head in 2005. In 2009 the Athenian Board of Trustees and community selected Mr. Niles as Athenian's Head of School.

The Athenian School maintains an excellent faculty by seeking the most talented people in their respective fields, by encouraging teachers to continue their education, and by providing financial support for professional growth. Enthusiasm for teaching and teaching skills for this age group are qualities also sought in faculty members.

Faculty members perform dormitory supervision, take charge of activities several weekends a year, organize community service activities, and lead adventurous trips and activities during Interim period each spring. Each faculty member also acts as an adviser for 8 to 10 students.

COLLEGE ADMISSION COUNSELING

Two college counselors provide expert advice to students choosing colleges. College counseling starts in the junior year and includes sessions with each student and with parents, as well as preparation for the PSAT and SAT. Trips to campuses throughout the country are available. The Athenian School is visited by numerous college representatives each year.

The following is a representative list of the institutions to which graduates have been admitted: Amherst, Brown, Columbia, Cornell, Dartmouth, Duke, Evergreen State, Georgetown, Johns Hopkins, MIT, NYU, Occidental, Pomona, Princeton, Reed, Stanford, USC, Yale, and the Universities of California (all campuses), Chicago, and Pennsylvania.

STUDENT BODY AND CONDUCT

In 2011–12, there were 74 freshmen (37 boys and 37 girls), 78 sophomores (39 boys and 39 girls), 79 juniors (36 boys and 43 girls), and 75 seniors (37 boys and 38 girls). Of these 306 students, 40 (19 boys and 21 girls) were boarders and 266 (130 boys and 136 girls) were day students.

Eighty-nine percent of the students are from California, and 10 percent are international students from more than ten different countries. Forty-three percent are members of ethnic minority groups.

Living as a community—especially a community as democratic as the one at Athenian—requires cooperation, social responsibility, and a sense of having a real influence on the quality of life and the decision-making process. An informal atmosphere promotes a good rapport between students and faculty members, and faculty members help students behave with respect toward themselves, others, and the school community.

The rules encourage high ethical standards and the ability to live with others harmoniously. The use of tobacco, alcohol, and illegal drugs is prohibited. Cheating and stealing are also major rule violations. Infractions of these rules often result either in referral by the Dean of Students to the Student Discipline Committee or expulsion. Town Meeting is the student government of the School and provides a forum for the discussion of community issues and standards.

ACADEMIC FACILITIES

Academic facilities include classrooms; a science building with four labs; a library holding 16,000 print volumes, forty-three periodical subscriptions, and six electronic subscriptions; a Center for the Arts with gallery, black box theater, drawing and painting, sculpture and pottery, and a dance studio; a new music and multipurpose building, which houses large choral and instrumental rooms, an ensemble room, and two smaller practice rooms; several computer labs; and the improved and renamed Maker's Studio, a significant facility for applied science and robotics.

BOARDING AND GENERAL FACILITIES

There are two dormitories and eleven faculty homes. A number of faculty members reside in apartments or town houses on campus.

Returning students in grades 11 and 12 generally choose single rooms. The Director of the Boarding Program and dormitory parents match the new and younger students with roommates for the double rooms. Ninth graders receive support and guidance from carefully selected seniors through this all-important transition. Supervision of each dorm at the School is the responsibility of a faculty dorm head, assisted by older students who act as proctors.

Students most often arrange to spend the two-week winter and spring vacations with nearby relatives or friends, if they do not travel back to their homes. If needed, the School assists international students in finding suitable homestays during shorter vacation periods. Some trips are also provided during vacations.

The Fuller Commons Building serves as the student recreation and meeting center. The Dyke Brown Main Hall contains the kitchen, dining area, and administrative offices. The Boarding Center provides a gathering place for resident students.

The School nurse visits the dorms each day and advises what action should be taken for any students reported ill. She is available for emergencies as well as drop-in visits during scheduled hours. The School counselor is also available as a resource if needed.

ATHLETICS

Physical education, interscholastic sport, or dance is required of all students.

Athenian teams compete with other schools in the North Bay Conference of the California Interscholastic Federation. The School fields interscholastic teams in thirteen sports—seven for boys and six for girls. These are baseball (for boys), basketball, cross-country, soccer, swimming, tennis, and volleyball. There are also junior varsity teams in basketball, soccer, and girls' volleyball. Athenian's teams have won league championships in a number of sports in recent years.

Noncompetitive activities include rock-climbing, hiking, downhill and cross-country skiing, bicycling, and jazz dance.

Campus facilities include a gym, two tennis courts, a 25-meter pool, a soccer field, a second playing field, and baseball and softball diamonds.

EXTRACURRICULAR OPPORTUNITIES

The School plans occasional trips to museums, plays, the opera, concerts, art exhibits, and lectures in the Bay Area. There are also skiing trips to the Sierra Nevada and excursions to spots on the coast.

On-campus activities include the School newspaper, debate, Interweave, yearbook, and Multicultural Alliance, among many others.

Community service is required of all students. Service projects include cross-country skiing with the visually handicapped, running the scholarship auction, helping at soup kitchens in San Francisco, working with disadvantaged children or the elderly, and working on environmental projects.

DAILY LIFE

A typical day begins with breakfast between 7:30 and 8. Day students arrive in time for classes, which begin at 8:10. A hot lunch prepared at the School is served at noon. Classes end at 2:40 and are followed by sports and performing arts. Dinner is at 6. Clubs, activities, School meetings, and study occupy a portion of each day.

Faculty-supervised evening study hours are from 7:30 to 9:30, when the dormitories are kept quiet. All boarding students are in their dorms by 10:30 p.m., Sunday through Thursday, and by midnight on Friday and Saturday.

WEEKEND LIFE

Weekend activities are arranged by faculty members on duty. They may include hikes on Mt. Diablo, visits to San Francisco and Berkeley, trips to the coast or the Sierra, and an attendance of the Oregon Shakespeare Festival. Boarding students may spend weekends off campus with permission from the Dean of Students and their parents.

Day students are encouraged to participate in all activities available to boarding students and to spend the night on campus from time to time. An outdoor education program is available throughout the year.

COSTS AND FINANCIAL AID

Tuition for 2012–13 is $31,950 for day students and $50,800 for boarding students. Additional expenditures are estimated at $1000. They include such expenses as books, music lessons, field trips, and athletic uniforms. Tuition insurance and a tuition payment plan are available.

Financial aid is based on need; eligibility is determined by the School and Student Service for Financial Aid. For 2011–12, scholarship aid of over $2 million was awarded to 90 students.

ADMISSIONS INFORMATION

Admission is open to all qualified and motivated persons without regard to race, creed, or color. Athenian seeks students who will prosper in an informal, caring environment, want a rigorous academic course of studies, support Athenian's mission, and will contribute to the on-campus community. Admission is selective and based upon the applicant's intellectual ability, academic achievement, character, motivation, creativity, talents, and interests. The School seeks a student body that includes a diversity of geographical, economic, cultural, and ethnic backgrounds.

Each applicant must submit an application, including transcripts and recommendations, have a personal interview, and take an entrance examination, the ISEE, or the SSAT. ESL candidates must take the TOEFL, IELTS, or SLEP.

Priority is given to ninth graders and then to tenth graders. Admission is granted to a smaller number of eleventh graders and occasionally to a twelfth grader.

APPLICATION TIMETABLE

Initial inquiries should be made in the fall of the year preceding anticipated entrance. The School catalog and application forms are available from the Admission Office upon request. Campus visits and interviews may be arranged at any time during the academic year on weekdays between 8:30 and 3. The application deadline is January 15, and notification of admission is given no later than March 19. After this date, applications may still be received and reviewed until all places are filled.

ADMISSIONS CORRESPONDENCE

Christopher Beeson, Director of Admission
The Athenian School
2100 Mt. Diablo Scenic Boulevard
Danville, California 94506
United States
Phone: 925-362-7223
Fax: 925-362-7228
E-mail: admission@athenian.org
Web site: http://www.athenian.org

THE BEEKMAN SCHOOL AND THE TUTORING SCHOOL

New York, New York

Type: Coeducational day college-preparatory and general academic school
Grades: 9–12, postgraduate year
Enrollment: 80
Head of School: George Higgins, Headmaster

THE SCHOOL

The Beekman School/The Tutoring School of New York was founded by George Matthew in 1925. The School was organized to offer a college-preparatory curriculum with the advantage of highly individualized instruction. Since each student has different abilities, learning issues, or goals, teaching is geared to the needs of the individual student. Thus, classes are limited to a maximum of 10 students in The Beekman School and a maximum of 3 students in The Tutoring School.

In addition to having small classes, The Beekman School combines a traditional academic education with a flexible yet structured approach. For instance, some students are eager to complete high school in less than four years for reasons that range from having been retained in a grade earlier in their education to feeling a natural desire to move ahead to college. If there appears (to all concerned) to be a readiness to accomplish this, the School proceeds with a program that will achieve this goal. This is done by adding one or two extra classes to the student's schedule and/or through attendance in the summer session.

In order for students to move effectively at their own pace, the School provides them with the proper level of classes in as many subjects as seems appropriate. Some students require more support to facilitate their learning in the state-mandated academic curriculum. Teachers have several periods free each day to meet with students, and there are supervised study halls each period throughout the day until 5 p.m. In addition, all homework assignments are posted on the School's Web site daily. Upon request, tutors are available through The Tutoring School.

The Tutoring School is a program within The Beekman School. This program specializes in educating students who require private or semiprivate classes. The Tutoring School teaches college-level courses as well as standard courses. Its mission is to provide a supportive environment in which students can realize their academic potential and achieve their educational goals. Generally, incoming students follow The Beekman School's college-preparatory curriculum and receive credit from The Beekman School. However, if necessary, The Tutoring School can follow any school's course syllabus, and course credit is granted by that school upon successful completion of all course work. After-school or home tutoring is available for midterm and final-exam preparation, SAT preparation, or academic support in any subject. In addition, The Tutoring School can arrange at-home schooling, if necessary.

The Beekman School is registered by the Board of Regents of the State of New York and is a member of the College Entrance Examination Board and the Educational Records Bureau.

ACADEMIC PROGRAM

The requirements of the Board of Regents of the State of New York form the core of the college-preparatory curriculum at The Beekman School and The Tutoring School. It is strongly advised, however, that students exceed these requirements, especially in the areas of mathematics, the sciences, and humanities. In addition to the requirements, The Beekman School faculty has developed many interesting and challenging elective courses from which students may choose. Some of these are psychology, bioethics, ecology, computer animation, creative writing, modern politics, filmmaking, darkroom photography, Eastern and Western philosophy, poetry, and art. Students also participate in after-school activities, such as the literary magazine, yearbook projects, and the School's volunteer program. Students can elect to study music, music theory, voice, various musical instruments, or composition at the Turtle Bay Music School, which is a 2-block walk from The Beekman School. If 6 or more students wish to form a particular course, the administration will offer the course at The Beekman School. If 1 to 3 students wish to take a particular course, it will be offered through The Tutoring School. Otherwise, students are encouraged to take specialized elective courses at various institutions throughout the city.

If students take an elective course off campus, they must complete 48 course hours to earn a semester credit and 96 course hours to earn a full-year credit. For the college-bound student, the suggested academic high school program consists of the following courses: 4 years of English, 4 years of history (including a senior-year program that consists of a semester of U.S. government and a semester of economics), 3 years of mathematics (through algebra II/trigonometry), 3 years of science (including 1 year of a lab science), 3 years of a foreign language, 1 year of art or music, several elective courses, and 1 semester of health education and computer science.

The grading system of the School is A to D (passing) and F (failing). Sixty percent is the minimum passing grade. Midway through each quarter, an interim progress report is mailed home to any student who is earning below 70 percent in any course. Weekly updates by phone can be arranged so that parents always know the academic status of their child.

Because of the independent nature and small size of the School community, the scheduling of classes and the number of classes in which a student enrolls are flexible. Students can begin their day with the first, second, or third period. For the same reasons of independence and adaptability, the School also tries to accommodate any reasonable requests of the students for additional courses. Similarly, tutoring for study and organizational skills and remediation courses in English and math are offered through The Tutoring School.

FACULTY AND ADVISERS

There are 14 full-time members of The Beekman School faculty.

The current Headmaster, George Higgins, has been at the School since 1980, first as a teacher, then as Assistant Headmaster, before serving the School as Headmaster.

All faculty members have graduate degrees or are enrolled in a graduate degree program. In addition to teaching, faculty members also act as advisers to small groups of students. Faculty advisers review progress reports with students and hold meetings periodically to listen to student concerns and discuss upcoming events. Parent conferences are held as frequently as they are needed or requested. Twice during the school year, parents are invited to the School to attend open-house evenings, at which time they can discuss their child's progress with the teachers. When necessary, the Headmaster or classroom teacher calls parents to keep them informed of their child's homework and general behavior.

The School's offices are open to the students almost all day, every day. Students feel welcome to visit the Headmaster to talk, complain, laugh, or ask questions.

COLLEGE ADMISSION COUNSELING

Each year, approximately 96 percent of the graduating class attends college. The aim of the School's college guidance program is to find the right college for each graduating senior. Major considerations include how competitive an environment the student wants, what area of study the student is leaning toward, what size of school would be conducive to success, and where the student would like to live (i.e., city, suburb, East Coast, West Coast). In the past five years, graduates of the School have been accepted at the following colleges and universities: Bard, Boston University, Bennington, Cornell, Duke, Vassar, Fordham, Chapman, NYU, Sarah Lawrence, School of Visual Arts, SUNY at Purchase, and the University of Colorado, to name a few. The Beekman School's staff and faculty members make every effort to examine not just where a student will likely be admitted but where that student will learn, grow, and feel successful for the next four years.

The senior class numbers approximately 25 students. Each student is carefully guided through the college application process, as are his or her parents. A Parents' College Evening, hosted by the School's college guidance counselor, is held each fall for the parents of seniors. It is always an informative evening for parents; the guest speaker is an administrator from the admissions office of a nearby university, who is also there to answer questions. The college guidance counselor schedules several individual appointments with all seniors in order to help them navigate the college application process.

STUDENT BODY AND CONDUCT

Each year, The Beekman School begins the fall term with approximately 70 students. Its rolling admissions policy means that the School adds members to the student body until it reaches its maximum enrollment of 80 students. The enrollment is generally evenly divided between boys and girls. All students are from the immediate tristate area of Connecticut, New Jersey, and New York and its suburbs. The success of The Beekman School's philosophy is proven by the distance students gladly travel in order to be in a school where the enrollment and class size are small, the faculty is supportive and caring, and the education is challenging yet can be paced according to the student's abilities and needs.

There is a School code of behavior that has been shaped by the students and teachers of the School. The main tenet of the code is based on the Golden Rule—"Do unto others as you would have others do unto you." The small, intimate environment makes any type of behavior problem untenable; if the code of the School is violated, there is always an appropriate response. There have been no serious discipline or behavior issues at the School; Beekman students respect their school and its philosophy and recognize the need for tolerance, compassion, and respect in this global community.

ACADEMIC FACILITIES

The School is located in an East Side Manhattan town house. There are eight classrooms; a small library; a state-of-the-art laboratory for biology, chemistry, and physics; a Smart Board in every classroom; a computer lab updated with the latest technology; a study hall equipped with computers; a beautifully landscaped garden; and a student lounge where students can eat lunch and socialize. Rapid Internet access is available throughout the School. Each administrator and teacher has an e-mail address, so parents and students can easily communicate with staff members.

ATHLETICS

The Beekman School meets the New York State requirements for physical education by providing a gym program at a nearby athletic facility. Students may participate in the School's program or design their own program; for example, they may wish to attend their neighborhood gym while being supervised by a private trainer, or they may decide to take dance lessons, karate lessons, or other lessons. Students must exercise for 2 hours each week. In the School's program, an instructor is provided, and students begin the year with aerobics and weight training. Activities in the gym program vary throughout the year and include volleyball, basketball, cardiovascular exercise, and instruction in the proper use of the facility's fitness equipment. If a student is seriously involved in an intramural activity outside the School, such as soccer or tennis, he or she may be excused from the School's sports program.

EXTRACURRICULAR OPPORTUNITIES

The School's Manhattan location gives it the opportunity to use New York City and its immediate environs as an extension of the classroom. Groups from the School attend plays, films, operas, and dance performances and visit various museums, exhibitions, historical sites, and other points of interest in and around Manhattan and as far away as Philadelphia.

Any student who wants to work on the yearbook or school literary magazine is welcome to do so, and about one third of the student body participates in one way or another. Additional after-school activities have included a drama club, photography club, and film club. Upperclassmen can also take part in a community volunteer program if the desire and maturity are present.

DAILY LIFE

Students' schedules reflect their individual needs. The school day begins at 8:45 a.m. and continues until 3:50 p.m. When possible, students who have a long commuting distance can be scheduled to begin classes at 9:30 or 10:15. Students with professional programs outside of school can have classes arranged for mornings or afternoons. Supervised study halls are provided throughout the day from 8:45 a.m. to 5 p.m. Lunch periods are scheduled throughout the day on a staggered basis.

SUMMER PROGRAMS

The Beekman School is in session almost year-round. In June, when the academic year is over, the School begins a three-week mini-session of intensive work for students who want or need private tutoring in a specific subject area, who need to make up work in a course for which they received an incomplete, or who exceeded the School's attendance policy (sixteen absences are allowed in a year course, and eight are allowed in a semester course).

Following the mini-session, The Beekman School operates a six-week summer session, which is attended by the School's students and by students from boarding and other private day schools who wish to accelerate in any major academic course, enrich their knowledge of a particular subject, or repeat a course. Each summer class is 2 hours long; there are four classes each day, and the program lasts for twenty-four days. The Beekman School's summer session is approved by the New York State Education Department.

COSTS AND FINANCIAL AID

The annual tuition is $34,500, which is divided into four payments. In addition, an activity fee and an administrative fee ($250 each) are charged. All twelfth-grade students pay a senior fee of $500.

The tuition for the mini-session depends upon the individual's length of study. The tuition for the six-week summer session is $2300 per 2-hour course.

If a student wishes to take a course in The Tutoring School (average student-teacher ratio is 2:1), tuition is $9450 for each yearlong course and $4985 for each semester course. Activity and administration fees are included. Currently, there is no financial aid.

ADMISSIONS INFORMATION

It is a reflection of the School's philosophy that it does not use admissions tests as a means to determine a prospective student's eligibility to attend the School. The Headmaster or Director meets with each prospective student and his or her parents in an intensive interview so that all may better understand each other. Together, they try to assess whether the School would be a good match for the student. Previous school transcripts and records of testing are reviewed but are not solely used to determine a course of study. Prospective students are also welcome to observe for a half or full day so they can gain a clearer understanding of the style of the School. Informal evaluations in math and English may be administered to determine the best course placement for various students.

APPLICATION TIMETABLE

Since there are several different types of secondary schools offering many different programs, it is advisable that interviews take place during the early spring of the year prior to entry. Selecting a school in which to study and socialize is an important process, and students and their families should take the time to look closely at several schools before coming to a final decision. Occasionally, students choose a school that is not a good fit for them. Because Beekman has a rolling admissions policy, even if the traditional day program is filled, students can begin their day in the afternoon and take classes into the late afternoon or early evening. These courses are usually semiprivate and cost more than the regular Beekman tuition. The School believes that a successful secondary education is of vital importance to all young adults; its goal is to make the School available to any student who wishes to actively participate in his or her education.

ADMISSIONS CORRESPONDENCE

George Higgins, Headmaster
The Beekman School
220 East 50th Street
New York, New York 10022
Phone: 212-755-6666
Fax: 212-888-6085
E-mail: georgeh@beekmanschool.org
Web site: http://www.beekmanschool.org

BERKELEY PREPARATORY SCHOOL

Tampa, Florida

Type: Coeducational independent college-preparatory day school
Grades: PK–12: Lower Division, prekindergarten–5; Middle Division, 6–8; Upper Division, 9–12
Enrollment: School total: 1,290; Lower Division: 425; Middle Division: 300; Upper Division: 565
Head of School: Joseph W. Seivold, Headmaster

THE SCHOOL

The Latin words *Disciplina, Diligentia,* and *Integritas* in Berkeley's motto describe the school's mission to nurture students' intellectual, emotional, spiritual and physical development so they can achieve their highest human potential. Episcopal in heritage, Berkeley was founded in 1960 and opened for grades 7–12 the following year. Kindergarten through grade 6 was added in 1967, and prekindergarten began in 1988. Berkeley's purpose is to enable its students to achieve academic excellence in preparation for higher education and to instill in students a strong sense of morality, ethics, and social responsibility.

Berkeley is located on an 80-acre campus in Tampa, Florida, a location that attracts students from Hillsborough, Pinellas, Pasco, Polk, and Hernando Counties and throughout the greater Tampa Bay area. Private bus transportation is available.

Berkeley is incorporated as a nonprofit institution and is governed by a 27-member Board of Trustees that includes alumni, parents of current students, and parents of alumni. The presidents of the Alumni Association and Parents' Club are also members of the Board.

ACADEMIC PROGRAM

The school year runs from the end of August to the first week of June and includes Thanksgiving, Christmas, and spring vacations. The curriculum naturally varies within each division.

In the Lower Division, the program seeks to provide appropriate, challenging learning experiences in a safe environment that reflects the academic, social, moral, and ethical values the school espouses in its philosophy. Curricular emphasis is on core subjects of reading and mathematics. An interdisciplinary approach is used in world language and social studies, and manipulatives are used extensively in the science and mathematics programs. Each student also receives instruction in library skills and integration of technology and learning.

Academic requirements in the Middle Division, where classes average 16 to 20 students, are English, English expression, mathematics, global studies, world language, science, technology, physical education, art, drama, and music. All students in grades 6 and 7 take Latin and their choice of French, Spanish, or Chinese. Continuing grade 8 students have the option of Latin, French, Spanish, or Chinese. Classes meet five days a week on a rotating schedule. Extra help is available from teachers, and grades are sent to parents four times a year.

The Upper Division program, with an average class size of 15 to 20 students, requires students to take four or five credit courses a year, in addition to fine arts and physical education requirements. To graduate, a student must complete 23 credits, including 4 in English, 4 in mathematics, and 3 in history, science, and foreign language. Students must also complete one year of personal fitness/health and an additional year of physical education, two years of fine arts, and two electives. In addition, Berkeley students are required to take a semester of religious studies each year and complete 76 hours of community service. More than twenty Advanced Placement courses are offered.

FACULTY AND ADVISERS

There are more than 150 full-time faculty members and administrators. They hold baccalaureate, more than 85 graduate, and several doctoral degrees. Headmaster Seivold graduated Phi Beta Kappa from the University of North Carolina at Chapel Hill with a degree in history. He holds a master's degree in education administration from St. Mary's University of Minnesota. He came to Berkeley from The Blake School in Minnesota.

In addition to teaching responsibilities, faculty members are involved in Berkeley's cocurricular programs as coaches and student activity advisers. In the Upper Division, 3 teach part-time and serve as academic grade advisers for students in grades 9 and 10, and 3 full-time college counselors assist students in grades 11 and 12 with academic advising and the college process. Berkeley faculty members receive support for professional development opportunities and several faculty members have been recognized as some of the top teachers among their peers nationally.

COLLEGE ADMISSION COUNSELING

Traditionally, Berkeley's entire graduating class goes on to attend college. Although Berkeley does not rank its students, more than 125 colleges visit the School each year to recruit its graduates. The mean SAT scores for the class of 2011–12 were 616 critical reading, 632 writing, and 633 math. Berkeley's college counseling department works to assist students and their families in selecting colleges that best suit their academic, financial, and social needs.

Recent graduates are attending Boston College, Brown, Cornell, Dartmouth, Duke, Emory, Georgetown, Harvard, Northwestern, Notre Dame, NYU, Princeton, Stanford, Vanderbilt, Villanova, Yale, and the Universities of Florida, Miami, Michigan, North Carolina, Pennsylvania, and Virginia. Scholarship offers totaling more than $8.5 million were made to the class of 2012, and 12 percent of the graduates committed to pursuing athletic competition at the collegiate level.

STUDENT BODY AND CONDUCT

In all divisions, Berkeley students are expected to maintain high standards. Mature conduct and use of manners are expected, and an honor code outlines students' responsibilities. In exchange, students are entrusted with certain privileges, such as direct access to the administration and the opportunity to initiate School-sponsored clubs. Students wear uniforms to class.

ACADEMIC FACILITIES

The 80-acre campus is located in Town 'n' Country, a suburb of Tampa. The campus consists of classrooms, a fine arts wing, a science wing, two libraries, technology labs, general convocation rooms, physical education fields, a 19,000-square-foot student center, a prekindergarten wing, and administrative offices for the Lower, Middle, and Upper Divisions.

The fine arts program is enhanced by the Lykes Center for the Arts, a 634-seat performing arts center, which also includes a gallery for visual arts displays, a flex studio for dance and small drama productions, dressing rooms, and an orchestra pit.

ATHLETICS

Varsity sports for boys include baseball, basketball, crew, cross-country, diving, football, golf, lacrosse, soccer, hockey, swimming, tennis, track, and wrestling. Girls compete in basketball, crew, cross-country, diving, golf, lacrosse, soccer, softball, swimming, tennis, track, and volleyball. Berkeley has been recognized as the Florida High School Athletic Association's overall 4A state academic champion for two consecutive years and has several individual and team champions.

Berkeley's athletic facilities include the new 53,000 square-foot Straz Family Field House; two gymnasiums; a junior Olympic swimming pool; a wrestling/gymnastics room; a weight room; a rock-climbing wall; a varsity level soccer field; a tennis complex; a high- and low-ropes course; a baseball and softball complex; a state-of-the-art track, a stadium; and practice fields for football, soccer, and lacrosse.

Seasonal sports award banquets and a homecoming football game are scheduled annually.

EXTRACURRICULAR OPPORTUNITIES

In addition to its broad-based commitment to student organizations and clubs and its community service requirements, Berkeley offers its students a vast array of possibilities beyond the classrooms. Berkeley's Pipe and Drum Corps continues to make a significant impact in the community by performing at several special events, including the Boston St. Patrick's Day Parade and Walt Disney World. Student artwork is accepted each year into the prestigious Scarfone Gallery Art Show, and several students receive gold key awards each year from the Alliance for Young Artists and Writers. An after-school Lower Division chess club attracts close to 50 students from kindergarten through grade 5. Middle and Upper Division students, as well as many faculty members, participate in several international experiences, visiting countries such as England, New Zealand, the Dominican Republic, the Galapagos Islands, Australia, China, France, Italy, Switzerland, and Spain.

DAILY LIFE

Students in prekindergarten through grade 5 attend classes from 8 to 3:10. Middle and Upper Division students also begin at 8 and end at 3:20. Teachers are available to assist students and offer extra help during activity periods, which are scheduled into each class day. Supervised study halls are also scheduled for some students.

SUMMER PROGRAMS

A six-week summer academic program for prekindergarten through grade 12 students is offered.

COSTS AND FINANCIAL AID

The tuition schedule for 2012–13 is as follows: $17,010 for prekindergarten–grade 5, $18,820 for grades 6–8, and $20,110 for grades 9–12. Tuition is payable in eight installments and must be paid in full by January 1. Tuition payments do not cover costs of uniforms, laptops, supplies, transportation, special event admission fees, or other expenses incurred in the ordinary course of student activities at Berkeley.

Berkeley makes all admission decisions without regard to financial status. Families who have reviewed their financial situation and feel that help may be needed in paying tuition should apply for aid. Financial aid awards are available at any grade level to students who demonstrate need. In determining need, the guidelines of the School and Student Service for Financial Aid (SSS) are used. Each award is individualized based upon the financial assessment of each applicant. It is important to note that Berkeley may not be able to accommodate all financial aid applications in a given year.

Berkeley is also fortunate to have a number of scholarships available to students. In addition to demonstrated financial need, specific criteria such as academic achievement and leadership potential are also components of a separate scholarship application process. Receiving a scholarship is a great honor; therefore, the process is both competitive and selective. A selection committee will review the completed applications and announce the scholarship recipients in early March.

ADMISSIONS INFORMATION

In considering applicants, Berkeley evaluates a student's talent, academic skills, personal interests, motivation to learn, and desire to attend. Special consideration is given to qualified applicants who are children of faculty members or alumni or who have siblings currently attending Berkeley.

Lower Division candidates visit age-appropriate classrooms and are evaluated through grade level assessments. Middle and Upper Division candidates are required to take the Secondary School Admissions Test (SSAT) and generally register for a November, December, or January test date. In addition to the SSAT, all applicants schedule an appointment with the Admissions Office for Otis-Lennon testing and a writing sample. Entering juniors and seniors may submit PSAT, SAT, PLAN, or ACT scores in place of sitting for the SSAT.

The admission process is selective and is based on information gathered from the application form, interviews, the candidate's record, admission tests, and teacher recommendations.

Berkeley admits students of any race, color, sex, religion, and national or ethnic origin and does not discriminate on the basis of any category protected by law in the administration of its educational policies; admission policies; and scholarship, financial aid, athletic, and other school-administered programs.

APPLICATION TIMETABLE

Applications should be submitted by the fall one year prior to the student's entrance into Berkeley. The Lower and Upper Division Admissions Committees begin evaluation of applicants in mid-February and decisions are made in March. The Middle Division Admissions Committee begins evaluation of completed files in mid-January with notification on a rolling basis from the end of January until vacancies are filled. All applications after the initial selection process are considered on a space-available basis.

Berkeley welcomes inquiries from families throughout the year. However, because of the competitive nature of the admission process, families are encouraged to visit the campus as early as possible to become familiar with the School, its programs, and its admission procedure.

ADMISSIONS CORRESPONDENCE

Janie McIlvaine
Director of Admissions
Berkeley Preparatory School
4811 Kelly Road
Tampa, Florida 33615
United States
Phone: 813-885-1673
Fax: 813-886-6933
E-mail: mcilvjan@berkeleyprep.org
Web site: www.berkeleyprep.org/admissions

BERKSHIRE SCHOOL

Sheffield, Massachusetts

Type: Coeducational boarding and day college-preparatory school
Grades: 9–12 (Forms III–VI), postgraduate year
Enrollment: 386
Head of School: Michael J. Maher

THE SCHOOL

"At Berkshire, we want every student to craft an educational master plan which makes a difference to this community and to the world; to discover and develop a passion; to respect the natural environment; and to recognize the interdependence of the world. No student is anonymous here, and we value all opinions, backgrounds and nationalities as each add to the richness of the community and to the experience of the Berkshire education."

~Michael J. Maher, Head of School

Berkshire School is a coed, college preparatory boarding and day school that prepares 386 ninth through twelfth graders and postgraduates for a global future. Pioneering programs—such as Advanced Math/Science Research, Advanced Humanities Research, and Sustainability and Resource Management—coexist with advanced sections and AP offerings in all disciplines. With a range of artistic and athletic offerings; a new, state-of-the-art math and science center; a 117,000-square-foot athletic facility; an 8-acre solar field providing 48 percent of the School's energy needs; and national recognition for its efforts in environmental conservation, Berkshire School is an extraordinary setting in which students are encouraged to embrace the school motto: *Pro Vita Non Pro Schola Discimus,* "Learning—not just for school, but for life."

In 1907, Mr. and Mrs. Seaver B. Buck, graduates of Harvard and Smith respectively, rented the building of Glenny Farm at the foot of Mt. Everett and founded Berkshire School. For thirty-five years, the Bucks devoted themselves to educating young men to the values of academic excellence, physical vigor, and high personal standards. In 1969, this commitment to excellence was extended to include girls.

Situated at the base of Mt. Everett, the second-highest mountain in Massachusetts, Berkshire's campus spans 400 acres. It is a 75-minute drive to both Albany International Airport and Hartford's Bradley International Airport, and just over 2 hours from Boston and New York City.

Berkshire School is incorporated as a not-for-profit institution, governed by a 29-member self-perpetuating Board of Trustees. The School has a $91-million endowment. Annual operating expenses exceed $23 million. Annual Giving in 2011–12 exceeded $2.6 million. The Berkshire Chapter of the Cum Laude Society was established in 1942.

Berkshire School is accredited by the New England Association of Schools and Colleges and holds memberships in the Independent School Association of Massachusetts, the National Association of Independent Schools, the College Entrance Examination Board, the National Association for College Admission Counseling, the Secondary School Admission Test Board, and the Association of Boarding Schools.

ACADEMIC PROGRAM

Berkshire's academic program is firmly rooted in a college-preparatory curriculum that features advanced and AP courses across all disciplines. In addition, unique opportunities to excel in math/science research, student-directed independent study, and electives in science, history, and fine arts allow students to pursue advanced study at Berkshire. As creative and agile problem solvers, strong critical thinkers, persuasive communicators, and active global citizens, Berkshire's students are equipped with the skills required to excel in the twenty-first century. The School's balance between academic rigor and possibility allows students to flourish as independent learners, community members, and professionals.

Believing that the best preparation for college is the acquisition of knowledge from a variety of disciplines, Berkshire requires the following credits: 4 years of English; 3 years each of mathematics, a foreign language, and history; 2 years of science; and 1 year of the visual or performing arts. All departments provide for accelerated sections, and students are placed at a level commensurate with their skills and talent. Many students take one or more of the sixteen Advanced Placement courses offered.

Most students carry five courses. The average number of students in a class is 12, and the student-teacher ratio is 5:1. The academic year is divided into two semesters, each culminating with an assessment period. Students receive grades, teacher comments, and adviser letters twice each semester. Berkshire uses a traditional letter-grading system of A–F (D is passing).

In 2007, Berkshire introduced its Advanced Math/Science Research course in which students use the strong foundation of knowledge acquired in the regular Berkshire curriculum as a springboard for beyond-the-curriculum projects in areas of cutting-edge research and other fields. Students intern with a professional scientist to conduct research in facilities located in the nearby Hartford, Connecticut and Albany, New York areas. Students work closely with their mentor in the field of their choice for 4 to 8 hours a week. The course culminates with a critical review paper and a research paper, both in scientific format.

FACULTY AND ADVISERS

The Berkshire teaching faculty numbers 67, and 89 including nonteaching. Forty-two teachers hold a master's degree and 6 hold doctorates. Faculty members contribute to both the academic and personal development of each student. The small size of the Berkshire community permits faculty members to become involved in students' lives outside, as well as inside, the classroom. Each student is paired with a faculty adviser who provides guidance, monitors academic progress, and serves as a liaison with the student's family. Berkshire also retains the services of 4 pediatricians, a nurse practitioner, 4 registered nurses, and 2 certified athletic trainers.

Michael J. Maher was named Berkshire's fifteenth head of school in the spring of 2004. He holds a bachelor's degree in political science from the University of Vermont and a master's degree in liberal studies from Wesleyan University. Mr. Maher is in his ninth year at Berkshire. He and his wife, Jean, an associate director of admission and a member of the Foreign Language Department, have 3 children including one Berkshire alumnus and a current student.

COLLEGE ADMISSION COUNSELING

College counseling at Berkshire is the responsibility of 5 professionals who assist students and their parents in the search for an appropriate college or university. The formal process begins in the Fifth Form, with individual conferences with the college counselors, and the opportunity to meet with some of the approximately 100 college admissions representatives who visit the campus. In February, Fifth Formers and their parents attend a two-day seminar on the college admission process. Admission strategies are discussed and specific institutions are identified for each student's consideration. During the summer, students are encouraged to visit colleges and write the first draft of their college application essay. The application process is generally completed by winter vacation in the Sixth Form year.

Members of the classes of 2009–2012 enrolled at a variety of four-year colleges or universities, including Bard, Bates, Berkeley, Boston College, Boston University, Bowdoin, Brown, Bucknell, Caltech, Carnegie Mellon, Colby, Colgate, Columbia, Cornell, Dartmouth, Denison, Dickinson, Emory, Hamilton, Harvard, Johns Hopkins, Kenyon, Lehigh, Middlebury, MIT, NYU, Northeastern, Northwestern, SMU, St. Lawrence, Syracuse, Union, USC, Villanova, Whitman, Williams, Yale, and the Universities of Connecticut, Maine, Massachusetts, Michigan, New Hampshire, Pennsylvania, Vermont, and Wisconsin.

STUDENT BODY AND CONDUCT

In the 2012–13 academic year, there are 354 boarders and 32 day students; with 2 students studying abroad in the first semester. The student body is drawn from twenty-seven states and twenty-seven countries.

Students contribute directly to the life of the school community through involvement in the Student Government, the Prefect Program, dormitory life, and various clubs and activities. Participation gives students a positive growth experience in keeping with the School's motto, *Pro Vita Non Pro Schola Discimus,* "Learning—not just for school, but for life." The rules at Berkshire are simple and straightforward and are consistent with the values and ideals of the School. They are designed to help students live orderly lives within an environment of mutual trust and respect.

ACADEMIC FACILITIES

Berkshire Hall, the primary academic facility built in 1930 and the centerpiece of the campus, reopened in the fall of 2008 after a full renovation. It now features larger classrooms with state-of-the-art technology, new administrative offices, a two-story atrium, and a Great Room for student study and special functions. A new music center opened in the fall of 2010, featuring two specially designed classrooms to meet the needs of the instrumental, choral, and chamber music programs. The center has five practice rooms, plenty of spacious storage cabinets for instruments, a recording studio, and storage and office space for the music program. A new dance studio also opened in the fall of 2010 as part of the existing gymnasium. Godman Dormitory is home to several darkrooms and a digital art and electronic music studio, and deWindt Dormitory houses a visual arts studio. In 2009, the School opened its Center for Writing and Critical Thinking, which is home to a nightly writing tutoring program. The center also hosts faculty forums and guest speakers.

In the fall of 2011, Allen Theater reopened after a complete renovation. The Allen renovation also included new academic spaces for the Kenefick Center for Learning, new classrooms for the theater and film department and the SAT tutoring program, and a new studio for WBSL, the School's own radio station.

In October 2012, Berkshire inaugurated the state-of-the-art Bellas/Dixon Math and Science Center. This new, 48,000-square-foot building provides students and teachers with facilities that will allow them to pursue academic excellence and innovation at the highest level while adhering to the School's commitment to sustainability.

The Geier Library contains approximately 43,000 volumes in open stacks, an extensive reference collection in both print and electronic format, numerous periodicals, and a fine audiovisual collection. The library has wireless Internet access, as well as twenty computers with Internet access and an online card catalog for student use. ProQuest Direct, the Expanded Academic Index ASAP, the *New York Times* full text (1994 to present), and the current ninety days' full text of 150 Northeastern newspapers, including the *Wall Street Journal* online, keep the library fully up-to-date on breaking information. In addition, in 2011 the Library acquired access to JSTOR, an online database of more than 1,000 academic journals, containing literally millions of peer-reviewed articles, images, reviews, and primary sources.

At the Dixon Observatory, computer-synchronized telescopes make it possible to view and photograph objects in the solar system and beyond. Given the combination of equipment, software, and location, Berkshire's observatory is among the best in New England.

BOARDING AND GENERAL FACILITIES

Berkshire has ten residential houses, including two girls' dormitories that were completed in the fall of 2002. Three faculty families generally reside in each house along with a prefect—Sixth Formers whose primary responsibility is to assist dorm parents with daily routines, such as study hall and room inspection. Dorm rooms all have Internet access and private phone lines. There is a common room in each house, where students may relax or study. Benson Commons, the school center, features a dining hall, a post office, the School bookstore, the Music Center, the Student Life office, and recreational spaces. In 2011 an 8-acre solar field was built on campus and it now provides up to 48 percent of the School's electricity needs.

ATHLETICS

Berkshire enjoys a proud tradition of athletic excellence. The School provides competition in twenty-seven interscholastic sports, including baseball, basketball, crew, cross-country running, field hockey, football, golf, ice hockey, lacrosse, mountain biking, skiing, soccer, softball, squash, tennis, track and field, and volleyball. Students may also participate in the Ritt Kellogg Mountain Program, a program that utilizes Berkshire's natural environment and its proximity to the Appalachian Trail to present athletic challenges, teach leadership, and foster environmental responsibility.

In January 2009, the 117,000-square-foot Jackman L. Stewart Athletic Center opened. The facility offers two ice rinks (one Olympic-size), fourteen locker rooms, seating for 800 spectators, a 34-machine fitness center and athletic training rooms. It can also be used for indoor tennis and can accommodate all-school functions. A second athletic center features full-size courts for basketball and volleyball, four international squash courts, a climbing wall, and a dance studio. Other facilities include the new Thomas H. Young Field for baseball, softball fields, an all-weather track, a lighted football field, and two synthetic-turf fields. A twelve-court tennis facility was completed in the fall of 2010.

EXTRACURRICULAR OPPORTUNITIES

Berkshire offers students a variety of opportunities to express their talents and passions. Students publish a newspaper, a yearbook, and a literary magazine that features student writing, art, and photography. The Ritt Kellogg Mountain Program offers backcountry skills, boatbuilding, fly fishing, hiking, kayaking, rock climbing, and winter mountaineering.

There are a number of active clubs, including the Drama Club, the International Club, the Investment Club, the Maple Syrup Program, the Philanthropy Society, and a Student Activities Committee.

Berkshire's student-run FM radio station, WBSL, operates with a power of 250 watts and is capable of reaching 10,000 listeners. Berkshire is one of the few secondary schools to hold membership in the Intercollegiate Broadcasting System and the only one affiliated with both the Associated Press wire service and its radio service.

Berkshire students pursue the arts in the classroom and in extracurricular activities. The theater program offers two plays in the fall and spring as well as a winter musical. There are three choral groups: Ursa Major, an all-school chorus; Ursa Minor, a girls' a cappella group; and Greensleeves, an all male chorus. There are two music groups: a jazz band and a chamber music ensemble. Students can also take private voice and instrumental lessons. Each season the Berkshire community looks forward to various performances, such as dance and music recitals, a jazz café, and poetry readings. Visual arts include painting, drawing, sculpture, digital art, photography, and ceramics. Students display their work in galleries in the Student Center and in Berkshire Hall.

DAILY LIFE

The first of the six class periods in a school day begins at 8 a.m., and the final class concludes at 2:45 p.m., except on Wednesday and Saturday, when the last class ends by 11:35 a.m. Berkshire follows a rotating schedule in which classes meet at different times each day.

Athletics, outdoor experiences, and art activities occupy the afternoon. Clubs often meet after dinner, before the 2-hour supervised study period that begins at 8 p.m.

WEEKEND LIFE

Weekend activities are planned by a Director of Student Activities and include first-run movies, dances with live bands, and other dances hosted by DJs. There are trips to local amusement parks and theaters as well as shopping trips to Hartford and Albany. In addition, students and faculty members journey to New York and Boston to visit museums, attend theater and music productions, or take in professional sports events.

COSTS AND FINANCIAL AID

For the 2012–13 academic year, tuition is $49,900 for boarding students and $39,900 for day students. For most students, $100 a month is sufficient personal spending money. Ten percent of the tuition is paid upon enrollment, 50 percent is payable on July 1, and 40 percent is payable on November 30. Various tuition payment plans are available.

Financial aid is awarded on the basis of need to about 30 percent of the student body. The total financial aid spent in 2012–13 was $5.0 million. The School and Student Service (SSS) Parents Financial Statement and a 1040 form are required.

ADMISSIONS INFORMATION

Berkshire adheres to the principle that in diversity there is strength and therefore, actively seeks students from a broad range of geographic, ethnic, religious, and socioeconomic backgrounds. Admission is most common in the Third and Fourth Forms, and the School enrolls a small number of postgraduates each year.

In order to assess the student's academic record, potential, character, and contributions to his or her school, Berkshire requires a personal interview, a transcript, test scores, and recommendations from English and mathematics teachers, along with the actual application. Candidates should have their Secondary School Admission Test (SSAT) scores forwarded to Berkshire School (school code 1612).

APPLICATION TIMETABLE

Interested families are encouraged to visit the campus in the fall or winter preceding the September in which admission is desired. Visits are arranged according to the academic schedule, Monday through Friday, from 8 a.m. to 2 p.m. and Saturday from 8 to 10:45 a.m. January 15 is the deadline for submitting applications; late applications are accepted as long as space is anticipated. Berkshire adheres to the standard notification date of March 10 and the families' reply date of April 10. Depending on availability, late applications are processed on a rolling basis. Applications for admission are available online at the School's Web site: http://www.berkshireschool.org.

ADMISSIONS CORRESPONDENCE

Andrew Bogardus, Director of Admission
Berkshire School
245 North Undermountain Road
Sheffield, Massachusetts 01257
United States
Phone: 413-229-1003
Fax: 413-229-1016
E-mail: admission@berkshireschool.org
Web site: http://www.berkshireschool.org

THE BIRCH WATHEN LENOX SCHOOL

New York, New York

Type: Coeducational, college-preparatory day school
Grades: K–12
Enrollment: 565
Head of School: Frank J. Carnabuci III

THE SCHOOL

The Birch Wathen Lenox School (BWL) is a kindergarten through grade twelve, independent, coeducational, college-preparatory school in New York City. BWL blends over 150 years of strong legacies from two highly esteemed private schools: The Lenox School, founded in 1916, and The Birch Wathen School, founded in 1921, were consolidated in 1991. The School is committed to a structured and traditionally rigorous academic program, while placing an uncommon emphasis on nurturing the individual. Frequent class trips throughout New York City (as well as around the world through the Overseas Study Program) reinforce the academic principles students learn in the classroom. The same diversity that enriches the School socially and culturally also offers young people a clear perspective on the various faiths and beliefs that shape today's world.

The School has an endowment of $7.2 million and is governed by the Board of Trustees. There is an active Alumni Association, with over 3,000 members, overseen by a full-time Alumni Director. Events are hosted throughout the year in New York City as well as several other cities throughout the United States and Europe. The Birch Wathen Lenox School is accredited by NYSAIS, ISAAGNY, NAIS, NACAC, ISAL, and GISAL.

ACADEMIC PROGRAM

BWL promotes a broad and rich study of all academic subjects, including foreign languages, English, history, science, writing, and mathematics, as well as music, art, computer science, and physical education. A focus on study skills and work ethic is always a top priority. BWL fosters traditional academics in a supportive setting, maximized by state-of-the-art facilities and small class sizes. The average class size is 15, and the student faculty ratio is 5:1. Class groupings in the Lower School are arranged according to ability for math and reading.

The typical program for students in grade 9–12 is six courses per year, plus physical education, as well as weekly courses in grammar and composition, art history, health, critical writing, and freshman seminar. The graduation requirements include 4 years of English, 3 years of history, 3 years of math, 3 years of science, 3 years of foreign language, 2 years of fine arts, and 4 years of physical education, as well as electives and mandatory community service. Advanced placement courses are offered in biology, physics, calculus AB, English literature, Spanish language, and U.S. history.

The Lower and Upper School divisions operate on a semester basis, and the Middle School operates on a trimester. Progress reports and parent-teacher conferences occur several times per year.

FACULTY AND ADVISERS

There are approximately 110 full-time faculty members at BWL, and 97 percent have advanced degrees. The staff includes music and art instructors, reading specialists, science and mathematics coordinators, a full-time nurse, a librarian, 3 computer specialists, a college guidance counselor, and 2 school psychologists.

Frank J. Carnabuci III, formerly assistant headmaster of the Dalton School, was appointed headmaster in 1992. He holds a B.A. degree from Drew University and master's degrees from Columbia and Harvard.

COLLEGE ADMISSION COUNSELING

The School's thorough and comprehensive college guidance program begins in the early stages of Upper School with gatherings and special events designed to acquaint students and their families with the college application process. These meetings, both individual and group, along with visits from various college representatives, allow students and parents to benefit from presentations and question-answer sessions. In autumn of their junior year, students take the PSAT and receive their results during a one-on-one appointment with a college counselor. The mean SAT scores are 600 for critical reading, 588 for math, and 616 for writing. One-hundred percent of BWL graduates are admitted to four-year colleges or universities, including Brown, Colgate, Columbia, Cornell, Duke, Harvard, Northwestern, Princeton, Tufts, Yale, and the University of Pennsylvania.

STUDENT BODY AND CONDUCT

The Birch Wathen Lenox School is comprised of approximately 565 students (K–12) from all five boroughs of New York City and the surrounding area. Eighteen percent of the student body comes from a diverse background. BWL is further enriched by its international makeup; about 20 percent of the School's families were either foreign born or have lived overseas.

Ethics are interwoven into daily life at BWL by instilling in every student the values found in the School's motto, "Integrity, loyalty, civility." The peer relations program and mandatory community service both inspire responsible citizenship within the School community and beyond.

ACADEMIC FACILITIES

The entire school is housed in a traditional, spacious building on Manhattan's Upper East Side. Facilities include a gymnasium, library (with 30,000 volumes of books plus various online memberships for student research), auditorium, cafeteria/commons area, music and art studios, three computer labs, multiple science laboratories, and a rooftop play area. A $19-million renovation of the School's facilities was completed in 2006.

ATHLETICS

The School offers 39 competitive teams for Middle and Upper School students, including ice hockey, golf, swimming, tennis, lacrosse, and squash. After-school sports programs and intramurals are available to students in the Lower School. The physical education department ensures that the course of each student's athletic development receives the attention and encouragement it deserves. The focus is on sportsmanship and fair play as much as on athletic excellence. A modern gymnasium, complete with bleacher seating, is complemented by the use of other venues outside of School, allowing BWL students to play sports almost every day. Locations beyond the gymnasium and play roof include Central Park, Randall's Island, Sokol Gymnasium, Basketball City, Asphalt Green, Riverbank State Park, and Lasker Ice Rink, in addition to the many schools where students travel for New York State Independent School Athletic League competitions.

EXTRACURRICULAR OPPORTUNITIES

After-school enrichment classes are offered to students in the Lower School, including arts and crafts, chess, gymnastics, martial arts, and yoga.

Middle and Upper School students have numerous opportunities to participate in extracurricular programs, including drama, chorus, student government, yearbook, school newspaper, photography, Model United Nations, foreign language clubs, and an overseas study program. The School also offers a variety of clubs including Community Service, Election Club, Drug Awareness Club, Earth Club, Business Investment Club, Improv Club, Chess Club, and Music Appreciation Club.

DAILY LIFE

The School operates on a five-day class schedule that runs from 8:15 a.m. until 3 p.m. Each period is approximately 45 minutes in length. Homework is assigned in all grades beginning in kindergarten. There is standardized testing throughout the year in all three divisions.

SUMMER PROGRAM

In addition to a two-week day camp for students in grades K through 6, BWL offers summer courses designed for Middle and Upper School Students. Options include a dynamic SAT/ACT prep program that comes to BWL from AlphaPrep, one of the nation's premier tutoring and college admissions counseling organizations; two Middle School courses, Science In the City, and Bards In the City.

COSTS AND FINANCIAL AID

Tuition for the 2012–13 academic year ranges from $37,923 for kindergarten to $38,950 for Grade Twelve. Additional fees include the lunch program (K–9), activities fees (K–12), and Parents' Association dues (K–12). Sixteen percent of students receive full or partial financial aid grants; annual financial aid awarded is $2.7 million. A tuition payment plan is available as well as alternative methods of financing for families who qualify.

ADMISSIONS INFORMATION

The Birch Wathen Lenox School adheres to the admissions guidelines and notification dates established by the Independent School Admissions Association of Greater New York (ISAAGNY). The School maintains membership with the Education Records Bureau (ERB) and National Association of Independent Schools (NAIS) and is accredited by the New York State Association of Independent Schools (NYSAIS).

APPLICATION TIMETABLE

The School recommends that parents contact the admissions office during the early months of the fall semester in order to apply for enrollment in the following academic year. Applications (and $50 fee) will be received after September 1. Applications are available on the School website at www.bwl.org.

The admissions process includes a parent tour and student interview. There is no formal parent interview. The admissions committee will review academic records (minimum two years), standardized test scores (ERB, ISEE, or SAT), teacher evaluations, and a parent essay as part of the admissions process. There is also an Early Notification Program available to sibling and legacy families.

ADMISSIONS CORRESPONDENCE

Julianne Kaplan, Director of Admissions
Danielle Tormey Lambert, Assistant Director of Admissions
Barbara B. Kaplan, Assistant Director of Admissions
Billie Williams, Admissions Coordinator
The Birch Wathen Lenox School
210 East 77th Street
New York, New York 10075
Phone: 212-861-0404, Ext. 135
Fax: 212-879-3388
E-mail: admissions@bwl.org
Web site: http://www.bwl.org

The Birch Wathen Lenox School does not discriminate in its admission and employment policies and practices on the basis of race, creed, color, sex, or national origin.

BLAIR ACADEMY

Blairstown, New Jersey

Type: Coeducational boarding and day college-preparatory school
Grades: 9–12, postgraduate year
Enrollment: 450
Head of School: T. Chandler Hardwick III

THE SCHOOL

In its 165th year, Blair Academy continues to offer a superior college-preparatory program while holding firmly to its tradition of being a community fully focused on the development of each individual student. In this environment, students learn to advocate for themselves, become service-minded, and develop the leadership skills necessary for success in college and beyond. Students balance their academic responsibilities with extensive opportunities to develop in theater, music, competitive athletics, and numerous extracurricular activities. The balance between high academic and personal expectations, and a willingness to provide individual focus are among Blair's greatest strengths.

Situated on 425 hilltop acres adjacent to Blairstown in one of New Jersey's most scenic counties, Blair is just 10 minutes from the Appalachian Trail and the Delaware Water Gap, only 60 miles from New York City, and 2 hours from Philadelphia.

Blair maintains an enrollment of 450 students on average, large enough to support a broad program of studies, activities, and athletics, yet small enough so that everyone can receive individualized instruction and ample attention. The average class size is 11 students, and the dual-advisory system also makes for close relationships between students and faculty members. Blair maintains a ratio of boarding to day students of 80:20.

A Board of Trustees directs the school, and alumni are well represented on the Board. The school's endowment is currently estimated at approximately $70 million. Blair received $5.7 million in capital gifts for 2011–12 and the Blair Fund raised $2.3 million.

Blair Academy is accredited by the Middle States Association of Colleges and Schools. Its memberships include the Cum Laude Society, New Jersey Association of Independent Schools, National Association of Independent Schools, The Association of Boarding Schools, Council for Advancement and Support of Education, and Secondary School Admission Test Board.

ACADEMIC PROGRAM

With twenty-three Advanced Placement (AP) courses and a wide range of electives such as Roman history, epidemiology, marine biology, ethical philosophy, architecture, robotics and video production, Blair students enhance their potential and awaken new interests with the guidance of committed teachers. The talented and diverse faculty brings enthusiasm, passion, and global perspective to lessons. Caring and committed to each individual student, the faculty members serve as housemasters, advisers, coaches, and friends while laying the necessary foundation for academic success at Blair and beyond.

Blair boasts a notable fine and performing arts program that is integral to its well-rounded curriculum. From introductory-level to advanced, art courses encourage students to think and express themselves creatively through various mediums, including canvas, dance, music, theater, film, graphic design, and ceramics. In the spring of 2009, the Blair wind symphony and string ensemble joined together to form the first-ever Blair Academy Orchestra, a momentous occasion for the music program. With vocal and instrumental performance tours across Eastern Europe, musicians and vocalists at Blair are able to explore international travel while performing at some of Europe's most historic concert venues.

History teacher Quint Clarke, affectionately known as Q, has taken students to such faraway places as Vietnam, Beijing, and many locations in Africa. A trip to Kenya he conducted several years ago as a community service effort was so successful and meaningful that it has now become Q's annual summer trip with students. Other faculty members have also taken students on trips abroad, most recently to Spain, Tunisia, France, and China. Spring break offers an opportunity to travel to countries like Russia, France, and Greece, while Long Winter Weekend allows marine science students to expand upon their classroom studies in the Cayman Islands.

FACULTY AND ADVISERS

For the 2012–13 academic year, Blair employed 80 full-time faculty members and administrators, more than half of whom hold graduate degrees. Ninety-two percent of faculty members and administrators live on campus, many as houseparents in the dormitories. They also serve as coaches, academic monitors, and advisers. Faculty members have high expectations for their students and seek to provide individual focus in addition to the rigorous and challenging academic program. Encouraging students to excel in a particular area is what motivates every faculty member at Blair. Teachers are exceptionally talented, with diverse and outstanding educational backgrounds and a wide range of interests. This allows each student to cultivate positive relationships with many adults in the Blair community. Through a dual advisory system, faculty advisers and academic monitors guide Blair students' personal growth. Blair is further set apart by allowing each student to choose his or her own adviser, which allows students to develop a strong sense of independence, responsibility, and confidence in engaging the world around them.

T. Chandler Hardwick III was appointed the Academy's fifteenth Headmaster in 1989. A graduate of the University of North Carolina (B.A., 1975) and Middlebury College (M.A., 1983), Mr. Hardwick previously taught English and was Senior Dean at the Taft School, as well as the Director of the Taft Summer School.

COLLEGE ADMISSION COUNSELING

College counselors begin working with students and their families in January of their junior year. Each student is required to have at least five private meetings with a college counselor to map out their college search and application process. Counselors communicate regularly with parents to keep them informed and involved. Parents of juniors are invited to spend a day on campus for an informational introduction to the Blair College Counseling Office and process: often, with Deans of Admissions from the country's top universities serving as guest speakers. In addition, Blair hosts on-campus visits from representatives of at least seventy colleges and universities each year.

Blair works with each individual student to craft an academic program that emphasizes areas of strength while fulfilling the expectations of competitive college admissions. Students from recent graduating classes are attending colleges and universities such as Brown, Colgate, Columbia, Cornell, Davidson, Georgetown, Harvard, Middlebury, NYU, Princeton, Stanford, U.S. Military Academy, U.S. Naval Academy, Williams, Yale, and the Universities of Pennsylvania and Virginia.

STUDENT BODY AND CONDUCT

Blair attempts to maintain a geographically, ethnically, and socioeconomically diverse student body. For 2012–13, Blair welcomed students from nineteen states and twenty-six countries, including Austria, Hong Kong, South Africa, Spain, Thailand, United Arab Emirates and Zimbabwe. The composition of the 2012–13 student body was as follows: senior class and postgraduate year, 74 boys, 60 girls; junior class, 76 boys, 54 girls; sophomore class, 55 boys, 40 girls; and freshman class, 44 boys, 43 girls. Of the total enrollment of 450, there were 104 day and 346 boarding students.

ACADEMIC FACILITIES

At the center of the campus are the four major classroom buildings: Clinton Hall, Bogle Hall, Timken Library, and Armstrong-Hipkins Center for the Arts. Bogle Hall, dedicated in 1989, provides laboratories and classrooms for the math and science departments and includes a state-of-the-art computer laboratory and a 150-seat auditorium. Armstrong-Hipkins Center for the Arts was dedicated in 1997 and includes DuBois auditorium, which seats 500 people and is where school meetings are held. Additional arts facilities include a black box theater, outdoor theater, soundproof practice rooms, two dance/yoga studios, various painting/drawing studios, ceramics room, architecture studio, photography darkroom, and digital video laboratory. A renovated Timken Library, which includes classrooms and a computer center, opened in 1998 and houses over 20,000 volumes. The library also subscribes to several excellent databases. These are recognized academic sites with information that has been collected and reviewed specifically for student use.

BOARDING AND GENERAL FACILITIES

In the spring of 2013, Blair is scheduled to break ground on the newest additions to the campus: two dorms overlooking Blair Lake for upperclass boys and girls. Recent additions to campus were completed in 2009 and consisted of several additions to the exterior sports facilities including a new turf field, ten new tennis courts, an improved all-weather track, stadium seating to accompany the turf field, and a tennis house. A new interior athletic space houses seven squash courts, a weight-lifting center, a fitness center, three basketball courts, a six-lane swimming pool, a wrestling room, and ample locker space for students and coaches. The bookstore, canteen, and college counseling suite moved to the activities portion of the new building. Both the athletic facility and student activities center have quickly become an integral part of campus life and complement Blair's existing facilities.

There is also an ongoing initiative to improve the physical campus as part of Blair's Ever Always campaign. These improvements saw changes to central campus, where only pedestrian traffic is allowed now as part of a plan to develop a park-like setting for recreation and study through improvements to the campus infrastructure and landscaping.

Eleven dormitories house boarding students. The housemaster and other dorm faculty members play a unique role in residential life. They help create a community and ensure that students adapt to dorm life and school. They make sure the dorm offers an atmosphere conducive to study but also provides a social liveliness that builds dorm spirit. In addition to having a housemaster and dorm parents in residence, each underclass dormitory unit has prefects who live in the underclass dormitories. Prefects are seniors who are selected by the faculty for their leadership ability and commitment to Blair; they devote their senior year to living with the younger students in order to help them make a smooth transition to Blair, all the while balancing their own college applications, varsity athletics, and demanding course schedules of honors and AP courses.

ATHLETICS

Blair's philosophy is that physical education is beneficial and important; hence all students participate in a program of athletics or supervised recreational sports. Blair fields twenty-eight competitive varsity teams in baseball, basketball, crew, cross-country, field hockey, football, golf, lacrosse, skiing, soccer, softball, squash, swimming, tennis, wrestling, and winter and spring track. Because participation is key to Blair's sports program, most sports field junior varsity and thirds-level competitive teams.

EXTRACURRICULAR OPPORTUNITIES

Blair students are also offered numerous learning opportunities outside of the classroom, ranging from weekly lectures as part of the Society of Skeptics, to travel abroad with faculty and peers. The Society of Skeptics, the longest continuously running high school lecture series in the country (now in its thirty-fifth year), was an outgrowth of the Blair International Society, begun in 1962, and has served as a forum for the discussion and debate of important national and international issues. For more than three decades, under the tutelage of Dr. Martin Miller, the weekly lecture series has featured a wide variety of speakers who are engaging, accomplished in their respective fields, and often controversial.

The Nevett Bartow Series brings to campus some twenty programs each year. The mission of the Bartow Series is to expand the artistic experiences of Blair students by bringing professional performers from far and wide to the Blair stage, including such offerings as Rockapella, Solid Brass, Loudon Wainwright III, the Cincinnati Boys Choir, the David Grisman Quintet, Tom Chapin, Judy Collins, Arlo Guthrie, and visiting lecturers. Day trips are arranged to the theater, concerts, opera, ballet, and museums in New York City.

Among popular campus organizations are the Blair Academy Singers, the Blair Academy Players, the String Orchestra, the Wind Symphony and Jazz Ensemble, the Community Service and Environmental Clubs, Model United Nations, and the Investment Club. The outdoor-skills group takes full advantage of Blair's proximity to the Delaware Water Gap and the Appalachian Trail, while the Ski Club utilizes the Pocono Mountains for daily skiing excursions. Students write for the school newspaper, *The Blair Breeze,* compose the yearbook, and publish a literary magazine each year. Service-oriented organizations, such as the Blue and White Key, encourage students to become engaged and active citizens within the Blair community.

DAILY LIFE

Classes are 55 minutes long and meet four times during a six-day week. Four days per week, classes end at 3:10 p.m. Wednesday and Saturday are shortened days, with afternoons dedicated to athletic competitions and extended theater practices.

Afternoons are devoted to athletics practices and games, play rehearsals, recreational sports, or activities. Family-style dinner, a formal dining room meal, is held two to three days per week for boarding students. Each dormitory, including senior dorms, has monitored evening study hours from 8 to 10 p.m. Students who have earned study privileges (known as honor nights) can be in their rooms, the library, the canteen, computer labs, or receive tutoring from an individual faculty member during these hours. Most importantly, faculty members do not disappear into their apartments at the end of the school day but instead are present around campus as mentors, friends, and houseparents.

WEEKEND LIFE

The campus bustles with activity on the weekends. Every Saturday evening, there is a community-focused event, such as athletic competitions, a dance, movie night, open-mic night, musical performances, and student theater productions. In addition, the Residential Life Office sponsors numerous off-campus trips (New York City, movies, mall trips, hikes, local festivals) as well as other low-key entertainment events (Blair intramural games, volleyball tournaments, scavenger hunts) throughout the weekends. Highlights include International Weekend, the midwinter formal, Super Sunday, and Peddie Week. Closed weekends during examinations and the first two weeks of September require all boarding students to remain on campus. Otherwise, students are allowed to take weekends away from campus according to a scale based on their grade in school.

COSTS AND FINANCIAL AID

Tuition for 2012–13 is $49,500 for boarders and $35,100 for day students. Additional deposits or fees are charged for the use of certain equipment, private music lessons, and extra medical services.

Financial aid is awarded on the basis of demonstrated financial need and proven personal and academic merit in accordance with procedures established by the School and Student Service for Financial Aid. Approximately $5 million in aid was distributed to 33 percent of the student body for the 2012–13 academic year.

ADMISSIONS INFORMATION

Blair is interested in students who seek the satisfaction of personal achievement through an experience that is both broad and challenging. Blair students are determined to make the most of their secondary school years and to prepare for college and beyond by being active participants in an engaging environment. Academic preparation is only part of being ready for college; Blair also emphasizes social responsibility, involvement, and leadership. Students take on such roles as team captains, dormitory prefects, or members of class council, and play an important part in shaping the Blair experience for those around them. They share in school planning and decision-making, and serve with faculty members on committees involving residential life, discipline, academic honor, multiculturalism, health, and student activities. Each student leader has an opportunity to influence the direction of Blair and impact the experiences of his or her classmates—skills that he or she will carry beyond Blair.

Blair enrolls students in grades 9–11 each year and also admits a limited number of high school graduates who wish to pursue a postgraduate year of study.

In addition to a personal interview, several written components complete the formal application. To complement the school transcript and teachers' recommendations, Blair requests results from a standardized test: the SSAT or ISEE for grades 9–10; and the PSAT, SAT, or ACT for eleventh-grade entry and postgraduates. Application forms must be accompanied by a nonrefundable fee of $50 ($125 for international applicants). The application deadline is February 1.

APPLICATION TIMETABLE

The initial inquiry is welcome at any time. An official inquiry can be made by visiting the Academy's Web site at www.blair.edu. The Admission Office is open for interviews and tours by appointment on weekdays and Saturdays. The application deadline is January 15, 2013. Those applicants who complete the admissions process prior to this date are notified of the decision on March 9, 2013.

ADMISSIONS CORRESPONDENCE

Peter G. Curran, Dean of Admissions
Blair Academy
P.O. Box 600
Blairstown, New Jersey 07825-0600
United States
Phone: 908-362-2024
800-462-5247 (toll-free)
Fax: 908-362-7975
E-mail: admissions@blair.edu
Web site: http://www.blair.edu

THE BOLLES SCHOOL

Jacksonville, Florida

Type: Coeducational boarding (7–12) and day (PK–12) college-preparatory school
Grades: PK–12: Lower Schools, PK–5; Middle School, 6–8; Upper School, 9–12
Enrollment: School total: 1,648; Lower Schools, 462; Middle School, 405; Upper School, 781
Head of School: Brian Johnson, President and Head of School

THE SCHOOL

Bolles offers a comprehensive college-preparatory program. Bolles prepares students for the future by offering them an education that challenges and guides them in the belief that all things are possible. Moral development is encouraged by an emphasis on respect for self and others, volunteerism, and personal responsibility.

Bolles has served as the educational inspiration for three generations, with a strong and unshakable commitment to providing the finest preparatory education possible for each student. Located in Jacksonville, Florida, Bolles was founded in 1933 as an all-boys military school on the San Jose Campus. In 1962, the School dropped its military status; in 1971, it began admitting girls.

In 1981, the Lower School Whitehurst Campus for grades K–5 was begun. A separate campus for middle school students in grades 6–8 was achieved in 1991 with the acquisition of Bartram School, an independent girls' school operating since 1934 and now known as the Bolles Middle School Bartram Campus. In 1998, the Bolles Lower School Ponte Vedra Beach Campus opened its doors to serve students in pre-kindergarten through grade 5.

Today, with nearly 1,700 students on four campuses, Bolles is recognized as one of the finest college-preparatory institutions in the nation. All of its students are college-bound. Bolles students consistently place in the top 10 percent of Advanced Placement scores from throughout the country. The School prepares students for the future by providing them with a variety of activities and a myriad of challenges that promote growth and development in four primary areas: academics, arts, activities, and athletics. Students learn to make decisions and budget time by balancing homework, sports, extracurricular, family, and community service responsibilities.

Students from all walks of life, cultures, religions, and races learn together at Bolles, a microcosm of the world that they will inherit. The School's excellent academic and athletic offerings attracted students from twenty countries and eight states to participate in the resident program for the 2011–12 school year. This blend of cultures and interests sets Bolles apart from other independent college-preparatory institutions in the Southeast and fosters a level of mutual respect that is crucial in learning how to meet global challenges.

The School's locations are in suburban neighborhoods. The Upper School San Jose Campus and the Lower School Whitehurst Campus occupy 52 acres on the St. Johns River. Five miles to the northeast, the Middle School Bartram Campus is set on 23 acres. The Bolles Lower School Ponte Vedra Beach Campus is located on 12 acres in Ponte Vedra Beach, east of Jacksonville.

Jacksonville, a major metropolitan area in northeast Florida, is home to the Jaguars National Football League team and many cultural associations, such as the Jacksonville Symphony, the Florida Ballet, several professional theater companies, three major museums, the Jacksonville Zoo, and several professional sports teams. Downtown Jacksonville is located approximately 35 minutes from the Jacksonville Beach area, which includes Ponte Vedra Beach, and about an hour from St. Augustine, the oldest city in the United States.

A not-for-profit institution, Bolles is governed by a self-perpetuating board of 32 trustees. The School also works with a 37-member Board of Visitors and an Alumni Board that represents more than 8,300 living graduates.

The School's operating budget is more than $30 million. The annual giving goal for 2012–13 was $2.08 million, which included more than $900,000 in unrestricted funds. The School's endowment is more than $11.6 million.

The School is accredited by the Southern Association of Colleges and Schools and the Florida Council of Independent Schools and holds membership in the National Association of Independent Schools, the Council for Spiritual and Ethical Education, the Secondary School Admission Test Board, and the Southeastern Association of Boarding Schools.

ACADEMIC PROGRAM

The Middle School curriculum includes English, government, world cultures, world geography, U.S. history, mathematics through algebra, and science, and world languages. Students may select from a varied fine and performing arts program and may choose among band, chorus, drama, dance, graphics, drawing and painting, ceramics and sculpture, and computer elective. Each student has an adviser, and a full-time, on-campus guidance counselor assists with decision-making skills, peer relations, and alcohol- and drug-abuse awareness.

Upper School students must earn 22 credits for graduation, with a college-certifying grade of at least C-. Specific requirements are 4 years of English; 2 of a single foreign language; 3 of social studies, including U.S. and world history; 3 of mathematics through algebra II; 3 of science, including biology and chemistry; 2 of physical education; 1 of fine arts; ½ year of life management skills; and 3½ years of additional electives. The average class size is 15 students.

Among the full-year courses are English, French, Latin, Spanish, Japanese, Chinese, world and U.S. history, algebra, geometry, pre-calculus, physical science, biology, chemistry, marine science, environmental science, band, introduction to dance, intermediate dance, upper-level dance, AP drawing, AP portfolio 2-D, AP portfolio 3-D, advanced acting, portfolio development honors, men's chorus, women's chorus, concert choir, and symphonic band. There are honors sections in English, geometry, algebra, biology, chemistry, physics, neurobiology, languages, and social studies. Courses designed to prepare students for Advanced Placement examinations are available in English, U.S. and European history, American and comparative government, languages (French, Latin, Spanish, and Chinese), calculus, computer science, statistics, biology, chemistry, physics, computer science, statistics, portfolio art, and art history. A postgraduate program is available to students seeking an additional year of academics prior to entering college.

Students choose from such semester electives as composition, Latin American history, Middle Eastern history, art history, humanities, economics, human anatomy, neuroscience, psychology, mythology, foundations of studio art, drawing and painting, ceramics and sculpture, creative writing, acting, directing, production, public speaking, computer or multimedia applications, robotics, statistics, algebra III, and trigonometry.

The school offers an English as a second language curriculum to students in grades 7–12 for those students whose level of proficiency indicates this need.

Opportunities for off-campus projects sponsored directly by the School include the Outdoor Academy and French, Spanish, Japanese, and Chinese exchange programs as well as a study-abroad experience to Spain.

Grades, with narrative reports from faculty advisers, are sent to parents twice each quarter.

FACULTY AND ADVISERS

Brian Johnson was appointed President and Head of School in 2012. Johnson holds a Bachelor of Arts in Public Policy from Stanford and a Master of Education in Administration, Planning, and Social Policy from Harvard. Selected for this position because of his strong background in independent education and innovative approach, Johnson possesses the character, energy, and foresight to provide quality leadership. His concern for the entire Bolles community is evident through his efforts to meet students, faculty, staff, and other constituents on an individual basis.

Bolles has 130 full-time faculty members and 7 part-time faculty members; there are 70 professional staff members who hold master's degrees and 11 who hold doctorates.

Each student in the Middle and Upper Schools is assigned to a faculty member, whose primary responsibility is to serve as an adviser. A minimal class load makes the adviser readily accessible to both students and parents. The School maintains an Office of Student Counseling to assist students in addressing issues that fall outside the traditional categories of academic advising.

COLLEGE ADMISSION COUNSELING

The aim of the college counseling program is to help students and their families to find college options and ultimately to find the most appropriate college choice. At the start of the second semester of the junior year, a daylong meeting is held to begin the more structured aspect of the process, and each student is assigned a college-placement adviser. An evening parent meeting provides additional information. The Williams Guidance Center offers a full range of up-to-date college reference materials, which include catalogs, videotapes, and computer search programs. In addition, approximately 100 college representatives visit the campus each year to meet with students, counselors, and parents.

In each of the past five years, 98 percent of graduates have attended four-year colleges and universities. A small number of students defer admission, and a small percentage attends two-year schools.

The middle 50 percent of scores for the last three graduating classes on the SAT Reasoning Test are 1070–1310 on a 1600 scale. The middle 50 percent of ACT scores are 22–28. Teachers in English and mathematics classes work with students in preparation for college admission testing.

STUDENT BODY AND CONDUCT

The Upper School numbers 781 students, with between 190 and 200 students in each grade. There are 86 boarding students.

There is an Honor Code and a Values Statement, and the Honor Council of Upper School students administers the Code and serves as the judiciary court for infractions against the Code. The Student Council is very active and serves as a proactive body for legislation of student privileges, organizes activities, and offers advice to the Upper School administration.

ACADEMIC FACILITIES

On the Upper School San Jose Campus, Bolles Hall houses classrooms, boys' dormitory rooms, a dining room and kitchen, offices, and three meeting rooms. Other academic buildings are Clifford G. Schultz Hall, with seventeen classrooms; the Michael

Marco Science Center, which houses three science labs; the Joan W. and Martin E. Stein Computer Laboratory; the Hirsig Life Science Center; Ulmer Hall, which includes fifteen classrooms, a language lab, and two science labs; and a marine science classroom along the St. Johns River. In 2012 the traffic flow and parking areas were completely restructured and paved, and iron security gates were added to the entrance.

The Swisher Library houses the Meadow Multimedia Center, with a large-screen television, two satellite dishes, and computer labs. Other facilities include the McGehee Auditorium, which seats more than 600, and the Cindy and Jay Stein Fine Arts Center, which contains the Independent Life Music Building, the Lucy B. Gooding Art Gallery, and the Lynch Theater.

Middle School academic facilities include Murchison-Lane Hall for classrooms and administrative offices, the Art Barn, a marine science classroom along Pottsburg Creek, girls' dormitory rooms, the Pratt Library, and the Betsy Lovett Arts Center, which opened in 2007.

The Lower School Whitehurst Campus houses each grade separately in homelike classrooms set around a natural playground. The Lower School Ponte Vedra Beach Campus is a modern campus that includes an administration/classroom facility as well as the McLauchlan-Evans Building, housing classrooms, and the River Branch Building, which is the location of both the Ullmann Family Art Room and the Loeb-Lovett Family Music Room. In 2012 an area below the main building was completely renovated and is now a cafetorium with a large open space. This building also houses a new campus store.

BOARDING AND GENERAL FACILITIES

All boarding students are housed in rooms that accommodate 2 students. Boys and girls reside on separate campuses. Students are assigned roommates based upon age and interests.

Upper School athletic facilities include Collins Stadium at the Donovan Baseball Field, Hodges Field, the Bent Tennis Complex, the Baker-Gate Petroleum Company Track Facility, and Skinner-Barco Stadium. The Davis Sports Complex includes the Huston Student Center, basketball and volleyball courts, the 25-yard Lobrano and 50-meter Uible swimming pools, the Cassidy Aquatic Fitness Center, and the Garces Diving Facility. The Agnes Cain Gymnasium features a wrestling room and athletic offices. The newly constructed Peyton Boathouse and Rice Family Crew Complex, and the Bent Student Center are proud additions to the San Jose Campus.

Among the Middle School athletic facilities are a football and soccer field, the Conroy Athletic Center, and Meninak Field, which includes Collins Baseball Stadium.

ATHLETICS

Bolles is a member of the Florida High School Athletic Association. Boys' teams compete in baseball, basketball, crew, cross-country, football, golf, lacrosse, soccer, swimming, tennis, track, wrestling, and weightlifting. Girls' teams compete in basketball, cheerleading, crew, cross-country, golf, soccer, softball, swimming, tennis, track, and volleyball. Middle School boys' teams compete in baseball, basketball, crew, football, lacrosse, soccer, swimming, track, and wrestling. Middle School girls' teams compete in basketball, cheerleading, crew, soccer, softball, swimming, track, and volleyball.

EXTRACURRICULAR OPPORTUNITIES

Extracurricular activities offered include Student Government; National Honor Society; language honor societies; Amnesty International; Interact, a service club; a mentor program; three student after-school tutoring programs; Student Advocate Council, which promotes community spirit among the students; an array of other community service opportunities; language clubs; special interest clubs; Community Service Leadership Council; Sophomore Leadership Council; class-sponsored activities; *Turris* (yearbook); *The Bugle* (newspaper); and *Perspective* (literary magazine).

DAILY LIFE

The daily schedule for the Upper School, which lasts from 8 a.m. until 3:45 p.m., includes seven 45-minute periods and "Zero Hour," a 30-minute period reserved for individual conferences and extra help. Boarders have evening study in their rooms, with faculty members available for extra help, and supervised study halls are provided for students needing more structured assistance.

WEEKEND LIFE

Resident students are strongly encouraged to take advantage of the excellent recreational facilities at Bolles. On weekends, the waterfront is open for resident students, weather permitting. In addition, regular off-campus trips are organized, as are, from time to time, special trips.

COSTS AND FINANCIAL AID

Upper School tuition costs for the 2012–13 school year are as follows: tuition, room, and meals for boarding students (grades 7–12) totals $41,450, and tuition for day students (grades 9–12) totals $20,280. Additional fees include $500–$750 for books, $30–$35 per gym uniform set, $375 for driver education, a one-time $500 facilities fee, and $45–$65 for the yearbook. Essential services fees for boarding students include $250 for the School clinic, $100 for emergency escrow, and an allowance of $40 per week ($1440 per school year) for students in grades 7–8, $45 per week ($1620 per school year) for students in grades 9–11, and $50 per week ($1800 per school year) for students in grade 12. Lunches and snacks are available for purchase by day students.

The School awarded over $3 million in financial aid for the 2011–12 academic year.

ADMISSIONS INFORMATION

The School seeks students who demonstrate the ability to meet the requirements of a rigorous college-preparatory curriculum. In addition, special talents and strengths that allow the applicant to achieve distinction within the applicant pool are desired. The ISEE or its equivalent is required of all applicants, as are a personal interview, teacher recommendations, and transcripts. There is a $45 application fee for day students and a $75 application fee for international students.

APPLICATION TIMETABLE

The Admission Office accepts applications beginning in the fall, with an initial deadline of January 10. Applications received after that date are considered on a rolling basis as space becomes available. Upon acceptance, the applicant must respond with a deposit of 10 percent of the total tuition and pay the facilities fee within two weeks.

ADMISSIONS CORRESPONDENCE

The Bolles School
7400 San Jose Boulevard
Jacksonville, Florida 32217
United States
Phone: 904-256-5030
Fax: 904-739-9929
Web site: http://www.Bolles.org

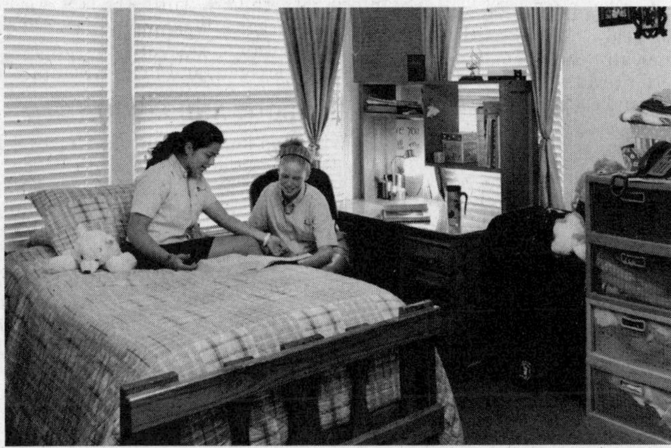

CAMPBELL HALL (EPISCOPAL)

North Hollywood, California

Type: Coeducational day college-preparatory school
Grades: K–12: Lower School, K–6; Middle School, 7–8; Upper School, 9–12
Enrollment: School total: 1,100; Upper School: 544
Head of School: The Reverend Canon Julian Bull, Headmaster

THE SCHOOL

"Campbell Hall is a community of inquiry committed to academic excellence and to the nurturing of decent, loving, and responsible human beings." So says the mission statement for this independent, K–12, coeducational, nonprofit day school.

Campbell Hall is both progressive and traditional, with one of the most innovative schedules in the independent school world and a dynamic, research-based educational program. Affiliated with the Episcopal Church and its 500-year history of academic excellence, Campbell Hall is also one of the most religiously and racially diverse schools in Southern California. Believing both discipline and balance to be crucial in healthy, productive lives, the program provides a vast range of possibilities for intellectual, creative, and athletic pursuits.

Located in the San Fernando Valley, Campbell Hall is a 15-acre campus with lush landscaping and the atmosphere of an oasis in the midst of the city. In addition to classroom spaces, the campus comprises athletic fields, six science labs, playgrounds, four art studios, two gymnasiums, a theater, three dance studios, music practice rooms, nine computer labs, amphitheaters, and other outdoor teaching spaces. The Arts and Education Center, which houses new classrooms, music and art rooms, a video production studio and lab, a recording studio, a photography and digital arts center, and an art gallery, opened in 2012.

Campbell Hall was founded in 1944 by the Reverend Alexander K. Campbell as a school dedicated not only to the finest in academic education but also to the discovery of the values of a religious heritage. Campbell Hall enrolls students in kindergarten through the twelfth grade.

The basic structure and operation of the school and the formulation of educational and other school policies are guided by a 24-member Board of Directors. The board is composed of community leaders, alumni, and parents of Campbell Hall students. The Headmaster has traditionally served as a liaison between the board and the various segments of the school community.

The school's advancement programs include annual and capital campaigns.

Campbell Hall is accredited by the Western Association of Schools and Colleges and the California Association of Independent Schools. The school is also accredited by the Episcopal Diocesan Commission on Schools. It holds memberships in the National Association of Independent Schools, National Association of Episcopal Schools, Episcopal Diocesan Commission on Schools, Educational Records Bureau, National Association of College Admission Counselors, Council for Advancement and Support of Education, College Board, Council for Religion in Independent Schools, and Cum Laude Society.

ACADEMIC PROGRAM

Students at the high school must complete 7½ units in the humanities, including 4 units of the English component, 3 units of the history component, and ½ unit of senior seminar. Other requirements for graduation include 3 units of mathematics, 3 of a world language, 3 of a laboratory science, 2 years of physical education, 1 year of a visual or performing art, ½ year of art history, ½ year of music history, and ½ year of human development. In addition to the graduation requirements, students must complete additional units chosen from electives, such as music theory, creative writing, economics, ethics, physiology, poetry, computer programming, philosophy, psychology, and visual and performing arts. Students must also complete 20 hours of approved community service each year.

A number of special academic options attract qualified students. Twenty-one Advanced Placement courses and eighteen honors courses are offered and include calculus (AB and BC), probability and statistics, English, French, Japanese, Spanish, European history, U.S. history, government/politics, human geography, biology, chemistry, physics, music theory, art history, psychology, economics, and computer science. In addition, qualified seniors may take college-level courses through the Talented High School Student Program of the California State University at Northridge, through local community colleges, through the UCLA High School Scholars' Program, and through approved online course providers.

Classes range in size from 8 or fewer students in advanced courses to 19 in some of the required courses. An online pilot program is available to students who wish to petition for specific courses in which they are particularly interested that are not part of the curriculum.

The school's grading system uses percentages: 100–90 is an A; 89–80 is a B; 79–70 is a C; 69–60 is a D, and no credit is given for a grade of 59 or below. Report cards, which are issued electronically each semester and trimester, include letter grades, as well as evaluations of work habits and cooperation.

At the end of each year, students who earn all A's in all classes are eligible for the Headmaster's List; students who earn a 3.6 academic average qualify for the Honor Roll primarily on the basis of grade point average. Academically outstanding juniors and seniors are eligible for membership in the Cum Laude Society.

FACULTY AND ADVISERS

There are 152 teaching faculty members; 58 hold master's degrees and 5 have doctorates. The school has a strong professional growth and development program, funded in part by the school's charitable giving program. Faculty members are encouraged to attend seminars and conferences in their fields. In addition to giving academic and social guidance to individual students, faculty advisers work closely with class officers to ensure unity and success in various class projects and social activities.

The Reverend Canon Julian Bull was appointed Headmaster in 2003. He is a graduate of Dartmouth (B.A., 1982), Boston College (M.A., 1988), and received his M.Div. from Virginia Theological Seminary in 2007. Mr. Bull was formerly Head of School at Trinity Episcopal in New Orleans, Louisiana.

COLLEGE ADMISSION COUNSELING

The college counseling office provides students with support and guidance to facilitate their postsecondary educational plans. College counselors work with individual students on a personalized basis to find the best option that is consistent with each student's interests, values, abilities, and educational goals. Students are encouraged to seek opportunities that will best allow them to continue their intellectual and personal development.

In October, all sophomores and juniors take the PSAT. Throughout their high school years, students receive extensive college counseling through group workshops and in-depth individual conferences with the college counseling staff members. Throughout the school year, the college counseling office offers a number of programs to help students and parents understand the college admissions process. These programs often include college admission representatives. In recent years, speakers from Brown, California Institute of the Arts, Columbia, Duke, NYU, Northwestern, Pitzer College, Sarah Lawrence, Stanford, UCLA, and USC have participated in these programs. One hundred percent of Campbell Hall graduates are accepted to four-year colleges or universities. They are drawn to a broad range of schools, and in recent years have enrolled at Berklee College of Music, Berkeley, Brown, Carnegie Mellon, Claremont McKenna, Columbia, Cornell, Duke, Emory, Georgetown, Grinnell College, Julliard, Middlebury, NYU, Northwestern, Pomona, Rhode Island School of Design, Rice, Scripps, UCLA, USC, Spelman, Stanford, Swarthmore, Tufts, the U.S. Air Force Academy, Vassar, Washington (St. Louis), Wesleyan, Whitman, Yale, and the Universities of Chicago, Michigan, and Pennsylvania.

STUDENT BODY AND CONDUCT

Of the 544 boys and girls in the Upper School (grades 9–12), 158 are in the ninth grade, 122 in the tenth, 133 in the eleventh, and 131 in the twelfth. Most students live in the suburban areas of Los Angeles.

Because Campbell Hall is concerned with the formation of character traits and values that reflect a sense of responsibility as well as a concern for the needs of others, misconduct is subject to disciplinary action. Violation of school rules and regulations may result in suspension or expulsion.

ACADEMIC FACILITIES

Campus academic facilities include classroom complexes, seven science labs, four computer labs, the Fine Arts Building, the Arts and Education Center, and a theater. A 22,000-square-foot library and academic center serves as the hub for the school's state-of-the-art technological resources which include campus-wide high-speed wireless Internet access and hundreds of laptops, tablets, and desktops deployed throughout the campus. Carefully researched iPad pilot programs and online education and digital media projects ensure that the school continues to teach for the twenty-first century; its philosophy blends technological sophistication with a strong sense of community and opportunity in this world center for the arts, sciences, and communications. All faculty members have school-supplied iPads and laptops and significant professional development resources available to them. The school library subscribes to a number of online databases.

The new 111,000-square-foot Arts and Education Center includes 3 two-story connected buildings, a multilevel subterranean parking garage, twenty-four state-of-the-art classrooms, an art gallery, a television studio, a video production lab, a photography lab and darkroom, a recording studio, a faculty resource center, outdoor learning spaces, terraces, and gardens, with extensive use of multimedia throughout. Designed by Gensler, an architectural firm renowned for its expertise in education design and innovative sustainability practices, the project is LEED certified.

ATHLETICS

There are two basic components to the athletics program. First, physical education courses provide basic and advanced instruction for sports that are in season; and second, Campbell Hall is a member of the California Interscholastic Federation (Gold Coast Athletic Association) and field teams in baseball, basketball, cheerleading, cross-country, 11-man tackle football, equestrian, golf, soccer, softball, tennis, track and field, and volleyball.

The school has two well-equipped gymnasiums, a baseball diamond, an artificial turf football and soccer field, a softball field, and five outdoor basketball/volleyball courts.

EXTRACURRICULAR OPPORTUNITIES

An active student government with elected officers represents each division of the student body. Among the student-planned events are dances; homecoming; the Winter Formal; and the Halloween, Christmas, and Valentine's Day celebrations. The year's social schedule culminates in a spring prom, planned by the student activities committee to honor the senior class.

There are also many curricular field trips and about sixty special interest groups, such as the Speech and Debate Team, Highlanders, the Cultural Awareness Club, the Spirit Club, Thespians, the Creative Writing Club, Amnesty International, Junior Statesmen of America, GSA, the Community Service Committee, and the High School Academic Honor Board.

DAILY LIFE

Monday through Thursday, there are four 75-minute blocks that meet between 8:50 a.m. and 3:40 p.m. Four days per week, 40 minutes are devoted to chapel (every Monday and Thursday), advisee group meetings, or clubs. On Wednesdays, the secondary school begins at 9:30 a.m. to allow for student/faculty conferences. There is a daily 45-minute lunch break. Interspersed among the academic courses are electives that provide enrichment in the fine arts (painting, drawing, ceramics, sculpture, and photography), the performing arts (chorus, instrumental music, drama, stagecraft, and dance), sports (physical education and team sports), robotics, computer programming, etc. Yearbook, newspaper, and journalism are also available as curricular classes.

SUMMER PROGRAMS

The school offers a full complement of summer programs for students in kindergarten through grade 12, including academic courses, a creative arts academy, and sports camps. Additional information may be obtained by contacting the Summer Programs Director.

COSTS AND FINANCIAL AID

Tuition for 2012–13, including fees, is $25,590 to $31,710. Tuition payments may be made annually, biannually or in ten monthly installments. Students may either bring their own lunches to school or purchase them at the student store or from a school-sponsored caterer at the school at lunchtime. Uniforms are worn Monday through Thursday, with free dress on Fridays. There are four bus routes.

Financial aid is available and is awarded on the basis of family need. Continuing students have priority for renewal. In 2012–13, 24 percent of Middle and Upper School students received financial aid.

ADMISSIONS INFORMATION

The school seeks students who are able to benefit from a rigorous college-preparatory curriculum and who will contribute to extracurricular as well as other community activities. Campbell Hall admits students of any race, color, national or ethnic origin to all the rights, privileges, programs, and activities generally accorded or made available to the students at the school. It does not discriminate on the basis of race, color, national or ethnic origin, or any other legally protected status in administration of its educational policies, admissions policies, scholarship programs and athletic and other school-administered programs. Campbell Hall is a diverse school community. Students of color make up 33 percent of the student body, and a variety of different faiths and family structures are also represented.

An entrance examination is required, as are recommendations from 2 teachers, a transcript from the school in which the applicant is currently enrolled, and an interview.

APPLICATION TIMETABLE

The Admissions Office is open from 8 a.m. to 4 p.m., Monday through Friday, to answer inquiries and to arrange interviews and campus visits. Applicants for the 2013–14 school year should file an application, accompanied by a $125 fee, by January 18, 2013. Most applications are submitted by December of the year preceding the desired entrance. Applicants take the Independent School Entrance Examination.

The school makes most decisions concerning new admissions by March. Parents are expected to reply to an offer of acceptance within two weeks and to pay a deposit, which is credited toward the first semester's tuition.

ADMISSIONS CORRESPONDENCE

Alice Fleming, Director of Admissions
George White, Associate Director
Campbell Hall
4533 Laurel Canyon Boulevard
P.O. Box 4036
North Hollywood, California 91617-9985
United States
Phone: 818-980-7280
Web site: http://www.campbellhall.org

CANTERBURY SCHOOL

Ft. Myers, Florida

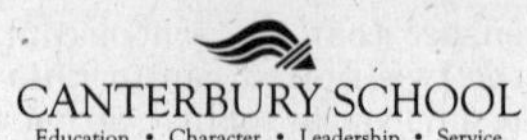

Type: Coeducational, day, college-preparatory
Grades: Prekindergarten–12: Lower School, Pre-K–3; Intermediate School, 4–6; Middle School, 7–8; Upper School, 9–12
Enrollment: 615; Upper School, 203
Head of School: Anthony J. Paulus

THE SCHOOL

Founded in 1964, the Canterbury School sits on 32 acres located on College Parkway between U.S. 41 and McGregor Boulevard. The School is dedicated to academic excellence within a caring and supportive community, preparing students of ability, promise, and diverse backgrounds for selective colleges. Canterbury's motto, "Education, character, leadership, service," defines the focus of the School's program and underscores all that its students do in and out of the classroom.

There are four divisions—Lower (grades prekindergarten–3), Intermediate (grades 4–6), Middle (grades 7–8), and Upper (grades 9–12). At all levels, the academic program emphasizes individual growth, skill development, a high caliber of instruction, collaboration, and high standards. Canterbury provides all students with an opportunity to challenge themselves and take risks in an atmosphere of mutual respect and partnership among students, parents, and teachers. Canterbury's integrated, innovative curriculum emphasizes group and individual study of the liberal arts, in addition to experiential learning and community service opportunities.

The Canterbury School is accredited by the Southern Association of Independent Schools (SAIS), Southern Association of Colleges and Schools/Council on Accreditation and School Improvement (SACS/CASI), Florida Council of Independent Schools (FCIS), the College Board, and the Florida Kindergarten Council (FKC).

ACADEMIC PROGRAM

All students pursue a demanding schedule of college-preparatory classes for four years in the Upper School, earning a minimum of 26 credits to graduate. Students play an active role in their course of study, and juniors and seniors may pursue advanced work in areas of significant interest or expertise. Although Honors and Advanced Placement courses, as well as independent studies, give students extra challenges, even the standard-level courses thoroughly prepare students for college work. Offering a rigorous and rewarding liberal arts curriculum, the Upper School program is rich in math, science, modern and classical languages, music, visual arts, social sciences, foreign language, and drama, with a special emphasis on writing, research, and the discourse of ideas. Study strategies, self-discipline, academic responsibility, and fluency in technology are underscored in each content area. Students learn academic honesty, competitive fair play, and good citizenship through a respected honor code. Students master key skills that will serve them well in their college careers as they actively participate in intellectual inquiry, analysis, and evaluation.

Middle School students take one course in each of the major disciplines every year—English, mathematics, science, social studies, and foreign language—and classes in the arts and in physical education/health, as well as other electives.

Canterbury's Intermediate School offers instruction in a math, science, and technology triad, as well as the Writing Across the Curriculum initiative, which links critical thinking and written expression in every curriculum area. Lower School celebrates childhood in an age-appropriate, developmental learning environment for students in prekindergarten through third grade; a balance between hard work and fun creates an environment where children are encouraged to take risks and assume personal responsibility for their learning as they embark upon their learning journey.

FACULTY AND ADVISERS

There are 80 faculty members, 38 of whom teach in the Upper School. Canterbury's talented and dedicated faculty seeks to inspire young minds through a rigorous and rewarding curriculum. Passionate about ideas and mentoring, instructors understand how students learn most effectively. Teaching is more than facts, figures, and formulas—it's a way of life. Canterbury's teachers personalize their approach to meet individual student needs. Small class sizes allow one-on-one time for personal attention, challenging and supporting students as they stretch their minds and their opportunities.

COLLEGE ADMISSION COUNSELING

College preparation is a primary focus of Canterbury's curriculum, so students receive the highly personalized direction and encouragement they need to choose the undergraduate institution with the right fit. An experienced college counselor guides juniors and seniors, as well as their families, through the process—helping them gain a comprehensive understanding of college acceptance practices. The result? An ongoing tradition of a 100 percent college-acceptance rate among Canterbury graduates. Recent graduates have been accepted to such distinguished institutions as Carnegie Mellon, Dartmouth, Georgetown, Harvard, Princeton, and Yale.

STUDENT BODY AND CONDUCT

Six hundred students are enrolled in grades prekindergarten–12. They come from diverse backgrounds, but the majority live in Fort Myers, Cape Coral, Sanibel, and the surrounding area.

ACADEMIC FACILITIES

The Canterbury School Libraries offer instruction, materials, and technology to promote the skills of information literacy and fluency, the love of reading, and the joy of intellectual discovery. By providing resources for both academic and recreational reading needs, the libraries help students develop research competencies for college and facilitate lifelong learning. The libraries also provide space for individual reflection and creation, as well as a forum for the sharing of ideas within the Canterbury community. The Ellenberg Library (grades 6–12) has established several special collections, in addition to the familiar biography, fiction, nonfiction, periodical, reference, and story collections. The Hilliard Library serves students from pre-K through fifth grade and their teachers. The library collection, of both print and nonprint resources, includes books, videotapes, magazines, Internet access, professional resources, and online subscription databases.

The Lower and Intermediate schools have dedicated art and music classrooms, science laboratories, computer labs and classrooms. They share a library. The Middle and Upper schools share a library, a language listening lab, and music and art classrooms, but they have separate science laboratories, computer labs, classrooms, and commons areas. The entire school shares the dining hall, a gymnasium and a sports center, an outdoor marine biology touch tank and classroom, and the Performing Arts Center.

ATHLETICS

At Canterbury, the life of the mind is complemented by a strong athletic program. Canterbury School fields teams in soccer, basketball, baseball, six-man football, volleyball, swimming, tennis, golf, cross-country, track and field, and lacrosse. Students are encouraged to become involved with athletics; around 85 percent of all Middle and Upper School students participate in interscholastic sports. Canterbury School is a member of the Florida High School Athletic Association (FHSAA) and is accredited by the Southern Association of Schools and Colleges (SACS). The Middle School belongs to the Suncoast Middle School League.

EXTRACURRICULAR OPPORTUNITIES

Clubs and organizations play key roles in student life. Students can choose from more than twenty active clubs on campus, including yearbook, newspaper, chess, mock trial, and Model UN, which meet regularly throughout the year. Students can also participate in a variety of local, state, national, and international scholastic competitions.

DAILY LIFE

Students spend their days in class, followed by after-school activities ranging from community service, student government, and athletics to clubs and study groups.

SUMMER PROGRAMS

Summer academic programs are available to students of all ages. Students can brush up their math, writing, or Spanish skills or take SAT-prep courses. Canterbury provides a recommended summer reading list for prekindergarten to fifth grade students so that they can begin, continue, and support the process of developing comprehension and analytical skills. Students in grades 6–12 receive a required summer reading list to support their academic course selection for the following year.

COSTS AND FINANCIAL AID

Upper School students pay $18,550 plus fees per academic year. Tuition is $13,995 for prekindergarten and kindergarten, $16,080 for grades 1–3, $17,350 for grades 4–6, and $17,960 for Middle School. Fees are additional. In 2012–13, Canterbury provided more than $1.46 million in financial assistance to 25 percent of the student body, with awards ranging from 20 percent to 95 percent of tuition.

Tuition payments include both a nonrefundable deposit and the remaining tuition balance. The nonrefundable 20 percent deposit is due upon enrollment and must accompany the student's enrollment contract. On July 1, another 30 percent of tuition is due, and the remaining 50 percent is due October 1. With this plan, tuition refund insurance is optional. Payment plan options are presented in the addendum to the enrollment contract.

ADMISSIONS INFORMATION

As a college-preparatory school with high academic standards, Canterbury seeks students of demonstrated abilities with potential for intellectual growth. Boys and girls entering prekindergarten through grade eleven are invited to apply, beginning the fall prior to the school year they wish to attend. Applications can be submitted online or by mail and must include the $75 application fee.

Applicants are first evaluated by testing, using the ERB, CTP 4 Test, or the SSAT in grades 3–11. Next, candidates' files are forwarded to the Admission Committee, which assesses each application based on the student's past academic achievement, performance on the admission test, a written essay, personal recommendations, and an interview with the division head and director of admission.

APPLICATION TIMETABLE

Open houses are scheduled October through April; attendees must reserve a space by contacting the admission office. Applications are accepted continually.

ADMISSIONS CORRESPONDENCE

Julie Peters, Director of Admissions
Canterbury School
8141 College Parkway
Fort Myers, Florida 33919
United States
Phone: 239-415-8945
Fax: 239-481-8339
E-mail: jpeters@canterburyfortmyers.org
Web site:
http://www.canterburyfortmyers.org/

CHARLOTTE LATIN SCHOOL

Charlotte, North Carolina

Type: Independent, college-preparatory, nonsectarian, coeducational day school
Grades: Transitional kindergarten–Grade 12
Enrollment: 1,402
Head of School: Arch N. McIntosh, Jr., Headmaster

THE SCHOOL

Founded in 1970, Charlotte Latin School (CLS) is located on a 122-acre campus in southeast Charlotte, North Carolina. The school community, which includes students, parents, alumni, and faculty and staff members, embraces a shared mission, core values, and a commitment to academic excellence. Latin is a school that is traditional by design yet innovative in implementation. The School's emphasis is for its students to maintain balance in their lives, which is enhanced by a curriculum built upon a foundation of academic rigor, the arts, and athletics. Students are presented with many growth-promoting opportunities to explore and develop their interests, including a variety of co-curricular options and a TK–12 community service program that fosters a lifelong commitment to service through age-appropriate activities. Students also are encouraged to explore their world and are supported in this endeavor through active international sister schools and study-abroad programs.

Charlotte Latin remains true to its founding parents' original vision as a place where a stimulating learning environment is united with a vibrant family life. Named for America's early Latin schools, in which colonial children pursued classical studies under the careful tutelage of their teachers, Charlotte Latin similarly fosters a close relationship between its faculty and students. With their teachers' guidance, students of all ages study and serve the community that surrounds them and the world that beckons them, in preparation to care for and succeed in the global community they will inherit as adults. Their parents, too, are partners with the School in their education and are frequently seen on campus attending special events, cheering on a Hawks athletic team, sharing lunch with their children in Founders' Hall, or serving on the Board of Trustees, Parents' Council, or one of the many volunteer committees that make Charlotte Latin a special place. Alumni, too, often return to campus to visit former teachers, and in some cases, to visit their own children at Latin. More than 3,400 alumni are members of the active CLS Alumni Association.

Charlotte Latin School is accredited by and is a member of the National, Southern, and North Carolina Associations of Independent Schools. The most recent reaccreditation by SAIS-SACS (the Southern Association of Independent Schools and Southern Association of Colleges and Schools) was in 2011. The School is also accredited by the North Carolina Department of Public Instruction. Latin is the youngest school in the United States to receive a Cum Laude chapter, and it has been named a Blue Ribbon School of Excellence three times by the U.S. Department of Education.

ACADEMIC PROGRAM

Charlotte Latin is organized into three divisions: the Lower School includes transitional kindergarten through fifth grade; the Middle School encompasses the sixth through eighth grades; and the Upper School comprises the ninth through twelfth grades.

The academic program prepares students to succeed in college and beyond by instilling a lifelong love of learning. Charlotte Latin School's curriculum is designed so that each successive grade adds to the students' mastery of skills and continued maturation. Through the leadership of the Division Heads and Curriculum Coordinator, the curriculum is constantly reviewed and refined to ensure that best practices are adopted to create a strong academic foundation.

The class of 2012's SAT scores reflect this academic strength. The middle 50 percent of scores are 580–690 for critical reading, 610–720 for mathematics, and 570–690 for writing. The class's middle 50 percent ACT composite score is 26–31.

While Latin has high expectations for its students, the School provides a nurturing environment and individual support, including a learning resources coordinator and guidance counselor for each division.

FACULTY AND ADVISORS

At Latin's core is a dedicated faculty composed of more than 185 experienced educators. The School's low student-teacher ratios and considerable professional development resources demonstrate that Latin values its teachers and celebrates learning. Active Middle School and Upper School advisory programs foster strong ties between faculty members and students, which enable these adults to serve as positive role models for maturing adolescents.

COLLEGE ADMISSION COUNSELING

As a college preparatory school, Charlotte Latin provides a College Center that guides students and their families through every step of the college admission process. The College Center is staffed by 3 full-time college counselors and a full-time registrar who work actively with both students and their families throughout the Upper School years. The support is individualized and proactive, and is designed to empower the student to take ownership of the process. The success of Latin's approach to college admissions is evidenced annually; 100 percent of the School's graduates are accepted to prestigious colleges and universities across the United States and beyond.

STUDENT BODY AND CONDUCT

The Charlotte Latin community is guided by the CLS Honor Code. A plaque bearing the inscription "Honor above all" is posted in every classroom as a constant reminder of the importance of this creed in the life of Charlotte Latin School. Adherence to the Honor Pledge is a condition of enrollment in the Upper School. Students may participate with administrators and faculty members as representatives of the Upper School Honor Council after demonstrating successive levels of leadership and personally modeling honorable conduct.

ACADEMIC FACILITIES

Latin's campus features distinct areas and buildings for each of the three divisions as well as shared facilities, such as the 17,630-square-foot Media Center and 13,275-square-foot Founders' Hall dining facility. Connected by covered walkways, each area of campus is appropriate for the developmental stage of the students while also enhancing a sense of school unity. The Horne Performing Arts Center, which opened in 2011, provides state-of-the-art instructional and performance spaces for the vocal and instrumental music programs. The theater program benefits from the performing arts center's 740-seat Thies Auditorium and Anne's Black Box Theater.

Wired and wireless computer connectivity is available in every building via a campuswide fiber-optic network and a dedicated 40MB line for high-speed data transmission. Computer labs and mobile laptop labs are utilized by students at all grade levels. Internet access via the academic network is filtered by the School to ensure that students view only appropriate online content.

ATHLETICS

Interscholastic athletics have a long and rich tradition at Charlotte Latin School. Throughout its more than forty-year history, students have proven they can compete on the playing field as well as in the classroom. Along with the many conference and state titles earned over the years, the School has always placed a premium on the values instilled and the life lessons learned from athletic competition.

Latin sponsors more than sixty-five athletic teams in seventeen men's and women's sports, and more than 90 percent of students in grades 7–12 participate in at least one sport.

Athletic facilities include three gymnasiums, an all-weather track surrounding the 1,450-seat Patten Stadium; six tennis courts; seven playing fields; an Olympic-quality natatorium; a cross-country course; and the Beck Student Activities Center, which includes an arena, fitness facility, indoor track, and dedicated wrestling room.

The Charlotte Latin Hawks have won the Wachovia Cup for overall excellence in high school athletics every year from 2005 through 2011. A commitment to athletic excellence is not only reflected in the many championship banners collected over the years but also through Latin's adherence to high standards of personal conduct and good sportsmanship on the part of student athletes, coaches, and fans.

EXTRACURRICULAR OPPORTUNITIES

Charlotte Latin offers a balanced program that provides creative outlets for students' intellectual and physical energies. Beginning in the fourth grade, a broad selection of clubs and organizations is available to encourage students to pursue their interests and explore new opportunities. Leadership development is a key component of participation, with students accepting increasing responsibility for managing organizations such as the Student Council, Service Program, and the Mosaic Club, which fosters inclusiveness and promotes awareness of diversity issues.

SUMMER PROGRAMS

The goal of Charlotte Latin Summer Programs is to provide an environment that promotes a joy for learning, where campers can develop cognitively, socially, emotionally, and physically through growth-promoting experiences. A professional and caring staff sustains a safe, structured, and innovative environment that sparks children's excitement about exploring new possibilities. Camps are primarily designed for boys and girls in Lower School and Middle School. Fees vary depending on the camp(s) selected. For more information, call 704-846-7277.

COSTS AND FINANCIAL AID

Tuition for the 2012–2013 school year is as follows: transitional kindergarten and kindergarten, $15,650; grades 1–5, $18,200; and grades 6–12, $19,650.

Charlotte Latin has need-based financial aid funds available for qualified families. Application for financial aid is made during the admissions application process. Charlotte Latin is a Malone Scholar School, and other scholarships are available to students based upon specific qualifying criteria.

ADMISSIONS INFORMATION

Charlotte Latin School's admission policies were established to fulfill the School's philosophy: to initiate in its students a love of and a respect for learning, to help them develop self-discipline, and to encourage creativity. The School seeks to attract a variety of students who demonstrate motivation and the ability to respond to the total School program. Charlotte Latin welcomes students who indicate a willingness to participate and a desire to do their best. The School believes that students with a breadth of talents and interests will contribute to the creation of a dynamic learning environment. Charlotte Latin School does not discriminate on the basis of sex, race, color, religion, sexual orientation, or national origin in the administration of its educational programs, admissions policies, financial aid policies, employment practices, or other School-administered programs.

APPLICATION TIMETABLE

Additional information about Charlotte Latin School's admissions process and key dates is available online at www.charlottelatin.org/admissions.

ADMISSIONS CORRESPONDENCE

Charlotte Latin School
9502 Providence Road
Charlotte, North Carolina 28277
United States
Phone: 704-846-1100
E-mail: inquiries@charlottelatin.org
Web site: http://www.charlottelatin.org

CONVENT OF THE SACRED HEART

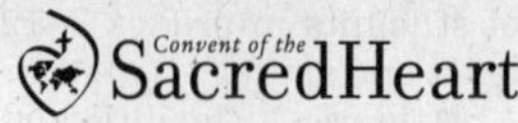

Greenwich, Connecticut

Type: Independent, Catholic day school for girls
Grades: P–12: Lower School, Preschool–4; Middle School, 5–8; Upper School, 9–12
Enrollment: School total: 775; Upper School: 300
Head of School: Pamela Juan Hayes, Head of School

THE SCHOOL

Convent of the Sacred Heart is situated on a beautiful 118-acre wooded campus in Greenwich, Connecticut. Greenwich is a suburban town located about 30 miles from New York City and 40 minutes from New Haven. An independent Catholic school for girls in preschool through grade 12, Sacred Heart was first established in New York City in 1848 and moved to Greenwich in 1945. Convent of the Sacred Heart is one of twenty-two Sacred Heart schools in the United States and part of an international network of schools that includes more than 200 schools in twenty-eight countries around the world.

A Sacred Heart education provides a strong academic foundation appropriate to each student's individual talents and abilities within an environment that fosters the development of her spiritual life and a strong sense of personal values. True to its international heritage, the school welcomes students and faculty members of diverse backgrounds and faiths, so that each student will grow in her understanding of different cultures and peoples. Graduates are prepared to become leaders with broad intellectual and spiritual horizons.

Convent of the Sacred Heart is a nonprofit institution governed by a 22-member Board of Trustees, which is responsible to the Society of the Sacred Heart for the implementation of the society's educational philosophy. Parents, religious, alumnae, and educators serve on the board. Sacred Heart benefits from the active involvement and strong support of its parent and alumnae organizations.

The school is accredited by the New England Association of Schools and Colleges and approved by the Connecticut State Board of Education. It is a member of the National Association of Independent Schools, the Connecticut Association of Independent Schools, the Cum Laude Society, the College Board, the National Association of College Admissions Counselors, the National Coalition of Girls' Schools, and the Network of Sacred Heart Schools in the United States.

ACADEMIC PROGRAM

Sacred Heart is committed to the development of each student's intellectual, physical, spiritual, and emotional well-being. The academic program in the Upper School provides a rigorous educational foundation that enables students to become independent and creative thinkers. Students are active participants in the learning process, expanding their experience through exploration, inquiry, and discovery. Students analyze, critique, evaluate, and make important connections with the concepts they learn.

Sacred Heart's academic program is comprehensive, rigorous, and flexible. Serious study is emphasized, and the development of essential academic skills necessary for success in college and life is encouraged. College-preparatory, honors, and advanced-placement courses are offered throughout the core curriculum, which includes mathematics, science, English, history and social sciences, world languages, theology, and the arts. A student is afforded opportunities for exploration of her own talents and interests through special projects, study abroad, summer programs, and independent study. Emphasizing the connection between the disciplines is critical to learning at Sacred Heart. Faculty collaboration helps students in discovering and understanding the relevance of all subject areas and the importance of their learning in relationship to society and their daily lives.

A student's schedule for the three-term academic year is planned individually. The student plans her course of study with the support of her teachers and her Academic Dean. Course levels are chosen according to academic readiness, ability, and talent in an academic area. Each student typically takes between 6 and 8 credits per school year in a combination of required courses and electives.

Graduation requirements are based on the expectations of highly selective colleges and universities; all of Sacred Heart's graduates choose to attend college. To receive a diploma, students must complete a minimum of 25 credits, although the majority of students complete more than this minimum number. The requirements include 4 credits of English, 4 credits in theology, 3 credits in history, 3 credits in mathematics, 3 credits in a world language, 3 credits in science, and 2 elective credits, at least 1 of which must be in the arts. Students must also complete 2 years of physical education and a 2-year health education requirement.

All academic disciplines employ the computer as a tool for writing, research, analysis, and presentation, including the use of multimedia presentations, spreadsheets and databases for organization and analysis, and desktop publishing. The program also addresses the possibilities and responsibilities associated with the use of technology in today's society. All students in grades 6–12 use laptop computers in the classroom and anywhere else they study or work.

FACULTY AND ADVISERS

High expectations and positive role models are important to the success of girls and young women. A student-faculty ratio of 7:1 and an average class size of approximately 13 students ensure the teachers know every student. Assured of the faculty's support, students are motivated to take risks through which confidence and self-discipline develop. Individual teaching styles are complemented by a common commitment to the goals and criteria of a Sacred Heart education.

Convent of the Sacred Heart has 122 faculty members, with 50 full-time and 5 part-time members teaching in the Upper School. They also serve as academic advisers to small groups of about 10 advisees, and many serve as club moderators and coaches as well. Students meet with their advisers regularly during a special advisory period. Each day begins with an all-school assembly and students and faculty members attend an Upper School chapel service once per cycle.

Teachers regularly participate in workshops, summer study, curriculum development, travel, and research. Approximately 82 percent of the faculty members hold advanced degrees, including 9 who have doctoral degrees. The full-time faculty has an average of fifteen years of teaching experience.

COLLEGE ADMISSION COUNSELING

The College Guidance Department at Sacred Heart believes in the importance of an individualized college process and works hard to find the best match possible for each student. An informational parent meeting in the sophomore year helps to set this tone. The Directors of College Guidance also review PSAT scores, and help their student advisees plan schedules for appropriate SAT Subject Tests.

In junior year, students and parents meet with the Directors of College Guidance to identify goals and discuss expectations about college plans. The college search process is explained at an evening winter program, which features college representatives and the college counselors. Juniors also attend guidance classes that explore issues surrounding the college selection process, including identifying prospective colleges, the campus visit and interview, the college essay, and financial aid and scholarships. Students have access to a variety of college search resources, including guidebooks, Internet search engines, and an internal software program. Students are also encouraged to take advantage of opportunities to meet with the many college representatives who visit Sacred Heart in the fall.

During the senior year, each student and her parents examine the more specific details of the application process: deadlines, the submission of standardized test scores, the college essay, resumes, and financial aid. In the school's 164-year history, Sacred Heart graduates have attended many of the nation's finest colleges and universities. Recent graduates are currently attending schools such as Boston College, Brown, Georgetown, Harvard, Holy Cross, Johns Hopkins, Notre Dame, Stanford, Wellesley, Yale, and the University of Pennsylvania.

STUDENT BODY AND CONDUCT

There are 775 students enrolled in preschool through grade 12, with 300 students enrolled in the Upper School. Students join the high school from more than sixty-seven different communities, coming from public, private, and parochial schools in Connecticut and New York State. The student body includes a diversity of ethnic, socioeconomic, and religious backgrounds that allows for a dynamic community with a wide range of interests, talents, and passions.

School policies and practices foster the acceptance of responsibility, self-discipline, respect for the self and others, and caring for the school and wider community. The student government, student/faculty disciplinary board, and the administration work together to establish and enforce policies and minimal rules that govern the school community.

ACADEMIC FACILITIES

Overlooking Long Island Sound, the campus consists of modern classrooms, science laboratories, an observatory, playgrounds, synthetic-turf fields, a media center, a theater, a chapel, a broadcast journalism studio, a gymnasium, a fitness room, a swimming pool, and a dance studio.

The media center holds a collection of 30,000 books, 1,000 e-books, online databases and encyclopedias, and DVDs and videos in a fully wireless environment.

A 29,000-square-foot science center has state-of-the-art science laboratories for all three divisions, including the Upper School's Science Research Program, in addition to space for the Upper School art studio, special space for drama and music, classrooms, and offices. On campus, there is a free-standing state-of-the-art observatory, which offers students interested in astronomy the opportunity for viewings of the night sky through a computerized, 16-inch telescope with 800x magnification. In addition, outside the observatory there is a pad with ten 8-inch telescopes.

The broadcast journalism studio consists of control, editing, and recording rooms. Students learn how to operate camera, audio, lighting, and editing equipment to tell their stories. This state-of-the-art space provides students with the opportunity to practice media literacy in a meaningful, hands-on fashion.

Students studying art, environmental science, and ecology make frequent use of the school's acres of woods, trails, fields, and a working vegetable garden. The campus is further enlivened by traditions and events unique to Convent of the Sacred Heart.

ATHLETICS

The energy of the Sacred Heart community extends beyond the walls of the school buildings. The indoor competition swimming pool, tennis courts, and the synthetic and grass playing fields outside are showcases for girls accepting challenges, testing limits, and cooperating with teammates. Sacred Heart provides a full schedule of varsity, junior varsity, and thirds sports, including basketball, crew, cross-country, field hockey, golf, lacrosse, soccer, softball, squash, swimming and diving, tennis, and volleyball. The teams are supported with the very best facilities and equipment, including two synthetic-turf fields. Convent of the Sacred Heart is a member of the twelve-school Fairchester League and the New England Preparatory School Athletic Council (NEPSAC). A certified athletic trainer services both the Middle and Upper School student-athletes.

The physical education program is designed to develop skills for a healthy and active life. Opportunities are provided for competition, excellence, and fun in a variety of activities for all students.

EXTRACURRICULAR OPPORTUNITIES

A wide range of clubs, committees, and activities provide opportunities for students to contribute to the school community, pursue their interests, and develop leadership and team skills. Students produce major theatrical productions, govern the student body through extensive collaboration with student-elected representatives, and produce award-winning publications, which include a school newspaper and a literary and art magazine in English and another in a variety of world languages. Sacred Heart students participate in local, regional, and national competitions with their peers from other schools through programs such as forensics/speech and debate, science research, broadcast journalism, and Model United Nations. These programs are designed to promote self-expression, intellectual challenge, and individual leadership opportunities.

Music, dramatic readings, and gallery art shows are an important part of the Upper School experience. Diverse curricular offerings in visual arts, theater, and music provide opportunities for interdisciplinary study, and core academic classes often collaborate on thematic projects with the arts departments.

Recognizing that one's own creative development emerges from exposure to the creativity of others, Sacred Heart emphasizes a balance between performance and appreciation. Guest artists, performers, and lecturers regularly visit the school. Proximity to New York City creates opportunities to investigate unlimited cultural resources, while student exhibitions and performances showcase the talents cultivated in the school's classes and studios.

The Community Service Program is also an integral part of the Upper School experience at Sacred Heart. Using age-appropriate tools, students study a wide range of issues, including racism, poverty, housing, and education. Analysis of social injustices helps the students recognize that they can use their talents to be agents of change in the world. The Community Service Program explores domestic and global issues and includes guest speakers, individual yearly projects, service trips, and retreats. While service is required for Upper School students, most exceed the graduation requirement of 100 hours with extra volunteer work. The Barat Foundation is a student-run philanthropic organization that awards grants to community nonprofits and teaches financial literacy to students.

The Sacred Heart Exchange Program allows students to experience different cultures in the United States and around the world. Upper School students may complete an academic exchange of two to ten weeks at another Sacred Heart school. Convent of the Sacred Heart also welcomes exchange students to its campus. Recently, Sacred Heart students have studied in California, Chicago, Houston, Miami, New Orleans, and Seattle and abroad in England, France, Spain, Taiwan, Australia, Chile, Mexico, and Nova Scotia. Upon graduating, students are given an international Sacred Heart Passport listing the Sacred Heart schools throughout the world where they are always welcome.

DAILY LIFE

The first academic period begins at 8:25 a.m. The school day includes six academic periods with time built in for advisory periods, assembly periods, and activities and club meetings. The day concludes at 3:25 p.m. Sports and a variety of activities occur after school. Students may buy or bring their lunch. A hot lunch is provided for a yearly fee.

SUMMER PROGRAMS

Convent of the Sacred Heart offers a summer enrichment program for its students and siblings in June. In August, the School hosts a study skills development program for incoming Middle School students.

In addition, as part of its mission Sacred Heart hosts an annual Summer Outreach Program for 250 boys and girls in grades 2 through 9 from low-income families. The five-week academic program is augmented with extracurricular activities, including team sports, swimming lessons, and hands-on experience with a vegetable garden.

COSTS AND FINANCIAL AID

An education at Sacred Heart is an investment that provides many important and valuable opportunities. Tuition for 2012–13 was $34,500 for grades 9–12. The Financial Aid Committee is committed to helping families find ways to make an education at Convent of the Sacred Heart affordable. The Financial Aid Committee works with families to determine personalized need-based assistance and financial planning. Applying for financial aid has no bearing on admission to Convent of the Sacred Heart.

ADMISSIONS INFORMATION

Sacred Heart admits students without regard to race, religion, nationality, or ethnic origin. Applicants are considered on the basis of their school records, teacher recommendations, admission test scores, class visit, and personal interview. Entrance exams are administered at the school in November and January and at other local independent schools throughout the fall.

Families are encouraged to attend the All-School Open House in November or Thursday morning Tour Day programs (October, November, December, and January). Sacred Heart also hosts an evening Upper School Open House in October for students interested in grades 9–12. Specific dates for these events will be available on the School's Web site at http://www.cshgreenwich.org. Individual tours and interviews are also available.

APPLICATION TIMETABLE

All application materials and visits must be completed by February 1. Decision letters are mailed by March 1. Applications for financial aid with supporting documentation are due by February 15.

ADMISSIONS CORRESPONDENCE

Catherine Cullinane, Director of Admission and Financial Aid
Convent of the Sacred Heart
1177 King Street
Greenwich, Connecticut 06831
United States
Phone: 203-532-3534
Fax: 203-532-3301
E-mail: admission@cshgreenwich.org
Web site: http://www.cshgreenwich.org

CRANBROOK SCHOOLS

Bloomfield Hills, Michigan

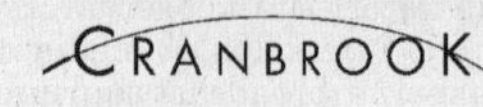

Type: Coeducational day and boarding college-preparatory school

Grades: PK–12: Brookside Lower School, Prekindergarten–5; Cranbrook Kingswood Middle School, 6–8; Cranbrook Kingswood Upper School, 9–12

Enrollment: School total: 1,666; Upper School: 797; Middle School: 351; Lower School: 518

Head of School: Arlyce M. Seibert, Director of Schools

THE SCHOOL

First established in 1922, Cranbrook Schools seek to prepare young men and women from diverse backgrounds to develop intellectually, morally, and physically; to move into higher education with competence and confidence; and to appreciate the arts. The Schools also strive to instill in their students a strong sense of social responsibility and the ability to contribute in an increasingly complex world.

Its founders, George and Ellen Scripps Booth, believed that "a life without beauty is only half lived." Critics have called the 315-acre Cranbrook campus "a masterpiece of American architecture." The buildings, gardens, and fountains were designed by Finnish architect, Eliel Saarinen, and offer students an exquisite environment in which to live and learn.

The Schools are a division of Cranbrook Educational Community, which also includes Cranbrook Institute of Science (a natural history and science museum serving Michigan and the Great Lakes region) and Cranbrook Academy of Art, known worldwide for its prestigious graduate programs in fine arts and architecture as well as its Art Museum. The entire complex has been designated a National Historic Landmark.

Cranbrook offers a comprehensive college-preparatory education that commences with Brookside (PK–5), continues in Cranbrook Kingswood Middle School (6–8, separate programs for boys and girls), and culminates in the opportunity and possibility that is provided by graduation from Cranbrook Kingswood Upper School (day and boarding, 9–12).

Bloomfield Hills is a residential suburb (population 3,985) approximately 25 minutes northwest of Detroit and 5 minutes from Birmingham.

A nonprofit corporation, Cranbrook is directed by a 21-member, self-perpetuating Board of Trustees, which meets four times a year. The corporation has a $209 million endowment.

Cranbrook Kingswood is accredited by the Independent Schools Association of the Central States. It is a member of the National Association of Independent Schools.

ACADEMIC PROGRAM

The school year, from September to early June, is divided into semesters. Classes, which enroll an average of 16 students each, meet five days a week. Eight academic periods are scheduled daily. All boarding students participate in supervised evening study hours from Sunday through Thursday. Grades are sent to parents quarterly, written evaluations are given semiannually, and progress reports for new students are issued in October.

Promotion from one class level to another is contingent upon faculty recommendations and is necessary for graduation. Each student is expected to take five academic classes each semester, along with a class chosen from the fine arts, performing arts, or computer departments. In order to graduate, students must complete the following minimum unit requirements: English, 4; mathematics, 4; foreign language, 2; social science/history, 2½; science, 3; religion/philosophy, 1; and performing or fine arts, 1. (One unit is the equivalent of a full-year course.)

In addition to seventy full-year courses, Cranbrook Kingswood Upper School offers seventy-five semester courses, including Anatomy, Astronomy, Eastern Religious Traditions, Ethics, Genetics, Geology, Law and Literature, Literature and Film, World Mythology, Principles of Macroeconomics, Principles of Psychology, and Russia and Eastern Europe. An extensive fine and performing arts program includes basic design, drawing, painting, sculpture, metalsmithing, ceramics, weaving, photography, dance, concert band, symphony orchestra, madrigals, jazz band, mastersingers, concert choir, acting, and speech.

Advanced Placement (AP) courses are available in English, foreign languages, mathematics, and social sciences. Honors courses and directed-study programs are also offered for qualified students. ESL is offered for international students who demonstrate a strong academic record and a high intermediate level of English proficiency.

The Tennessee Wilderness Expedition (modeled on Outward Bound) is available to tenth graders each March. Seniors can participate in Senior May (off-campus internships) during the spring term.

Students are graded on an A–E scale, although some elective courses are pass/fail. Students must maintain a minimum C-average to avoid academic probation. Classes are generally grouped by ability within grade level. The student-teacher ratio is 8:1.

FACULTY AND ADVISERS

More than 70 percent of the 95 full-time Cranbrook Kingswood Upper School faculty members reside on campus; 52 are men and 43 are women; 87 percent of the Upper School faculty members hold master's degrees or Ph.D.'s in the subject area that they teach. The average tenure of a Cranbrook Schools teacher is more than fourteen years.

In selecting its faculty, Cranbrook Kingswood seeks men and women with educational and intellectual curiosity. Faculty members are encouraged to explore special interests and talents that extend beyond their academic discipline. They are continually involved in professional advancement programs—course work, conferences, and workshops, the cost of which Cranbrook Kingswood largely underwrites. All faculty members are involved in some type of extracurricular activity, and each is an adviser to an average of 8 students, helping them in all aspects of school life from course selection to peer relationships.

Arlyce M. Seibert was appointed Vice President of Cranbrook Educational Community and the Director of Schools in 1996. Mrs. Seibert joined the Upper School in 1970 and has served in many capacities in her forty-two years with the Schools.

COLLEGE ADMISSION COUNSELING

Four full-time counselors help students select colleges, and representatives from more than 135 colleges visit Cranbrook Kingswood each year. The selection process begins in the junior year, involving both students and parents.

Among Cranbrook Kingswood's 2012 graduates, the mean SAT scores were 631critical reading, 666 math, and 646 writing. A total of 189 graduates are attending such colleges and universities as Amherst, Carnegie Mellon, Columbia, Cornell, Dartmouth, Emory, Georgetown, Johns Hopkins, MIT, Middlebury, Northwestern, Princeton, USC, Vanderbilt, Wellesley, Yale, and the Universities of Chicago, Michigan, and Pennsylvania.

STUDENT BODY AND CONDUCT

The 2012–13 Upper School was composed of 156 boarding boys, 246 day boys, 102 boarding girls, and 293 day girls, distributed as follows: 171 in the ninth grade, 216 in tenth, 206 in eleventh, and 204 in twelfth. Twenty-three states and nineteen countries were represented. Forty-five percent of students identified themselves as members of minority groups, and international students made up 11 percent of the student body.

Cranbrook Kingswood's disciplinary system is designed to be educative, not punitive. Honest conduct, regular attendance, punctual completion of assignments, and thoughtful adherence to school policies and rules are the minimum commitments expected of students. A Discipline Committee, consisting of faculty members, the deans, and elected students, assumes responsibility in matters of conduct. Major offenses may result in dismissal.

Students participate in several committees that help to shape life at Cranbrook Schools, such as the Conduct Review Board, the Dormitory Council, the Athletic Committee, the Diversity Committee, the Student Leadership Task Force, and the President's Council.

ACADEMIC FACILITIES

Students have the advantage of full access to two educational campuses. Kingswood's world-famous, Saarinen-designed building is a single continuous unit that includes a library with 23,500 volumes, a gymnasium, and six separate art studios. A new girls' middle school was completed during the 2010–11 school year.

Cranbrook's classrooms are located around a quadrangle in Lindquist Hall (1927) and Hoey Hall (1927). Other facilities that compose the quadrangle complex are a library with more than 21,500 volumes, a dining hall, boys' dormitories, and a student center. A performing arts center and the Gordon Science Center are located adjacent to the quadrangle.

Students take shuttle buses from one campus to another according to their class schedules. Students not only have access to the museums and other resources at the Cranbrook Institute of Science and the Cranbrook Art Museum, a number of classes across all departments utilize the museums during the year.

BOARDING AND GENERAL FACILITIES

Cranbrook Kingswood maintains single-sex boarding facilities. The campus buildings are linked by a fiber-optic network and provide telephone, computer, and video access in each dormitory room, classroom, lab, and faculty and student work area. The campus is equipped with more than ninety SmartBoards. For the last several years, Cranbrook has been one of only twenty-five schools nationwide to be named a SMART Showcase Elite School and was also the 2012 SMART Showcase School of the Year.

The Kingswood dormitory for girls, adjacent to Kingswood Lake, houses 102 girls. Most live in suites that contain two single or double bedrooms with adjoining bath. The dormitory has two lounges with televisions, stereo equipment, and a piano. Two kitchenettes and laundry facilities are available, in addition to a four-lane bowling alley.

At the Cranbrook campus, there are single rooms for 158 boys, who are divided according to their grade. The student activity center has a dance floor, a snack bar, a performance space, recently renovated kitchen, and a small theater for videotape recording and viewing.

Many Cranbrook Kingswood faculty members live in the dormitories with their families. Others live in faculty homes clustered throughout the grounds. Resident Advisers (senior students) live on each floor and act as confidants and helpmates to their fellow boarders.

ATHLETICS

Cranbrook Kingswood Upper School provides the opportunity for participation in eighteen interscholastic sports, including baseball, basketball, cross-country, crew, fencing, field hockey, football, golf, ice hockey, lacrosse, skiing, soccer, softball, swimming, tennis, track, volleyball, and wrestling. Recent state championships include boys' and girls' tennis, girls' golf, girls' swimming, and boys' and girls' hockey. Among the intramural and noncompetitive athletic activities are martial arts, yoga, rock climbing, strength and fitness, and walking for fitness.

Athletics facilities include a football stadium, a track, fifteen outdoor tennis courts, a dance studio, an indoor ice arena, four gymnasiums, and numerous playing fields. The School's award-winning natatorium was designed by a Cranbrook graduate.

EXTRACURRICULAR OPPORTUNITIES

Cranbrook Kingswood offers over fifty student organizations, including Model UN, forensics, ethnic clubs, dramatics, community service, and two award-winning publications, the student-run newspaper and an arts and literary publication. Other clubs meet to discuss topics as varied as politics and racial diversity.

The cultural and educational events on campus include the exhibitions, lectures, films, and concerts offered through the science and art museums, highlighted by regular planetarium and laser shows, a world-class collection of modern American and European paintings, and traveling exhibits. The spacious grounds, wooded areas, lakes and indoor and outdoor theaters provide a serene setting for cross-country skiing, biking, jogging, swimming, and canoeing, as well as the Cranbrook Music Festival, the American Artists Series, the Cranbrook Kingswood Film Program, the Symposium Series, and the Cranbrook Retreat for Writers and Artists.

DAILY LIFE

The school day is divided into eight 45-minute classes between 8 a.m. and 3:20 p.m., including lunch, Monday through Friday. After-school activities such as class meetings, extra-help sessions, and athletics follow. Dinner for boarders begins at 5:30 weekdays, followed by a study period from 8 to 10 p.m.

WEEKEND LIFE

Boarding students have an unusual opportunity to take part in urban and rural activities on the weekends. Although students may go home some weekends with parental permission, there are weekends during the year when all boarding students must stay on the campus for special activities. Shuttle buses drive students to nearby Birmingham for shopping and entertainment, and groups can go to places such as Detroit and Ann Arbor for professional sporting events and cultural activities. There are frequent weekend camping, hiking, rock climbing, and skiing trips during the year. On-campus activities include dances, concerts, exhibits, lectures, sporting events, and recent movies at the student center.

SUMMER PROGRAMS

The Cranbrook Educational Community conducts several summer programs for day and boarding students and the community at large. These include day camps, a theater school, art programs, a soccer clinic, a filmmaking seminar, a compensatory educational program for youngsters from low-income families, a jazz ensemble, and ice hockey, lacrosse, robotics, and tennis camps.

COSTS AND FINANCIAL AID

The 2012–13 fees are $38,900 for boarding students and $28,300 for day students. Other expenses are for books ($500) and a room deposit fee ($200). A tuition-payment plan, health insurance plan, and tuition insurance are offered.

In 2012–13, 32 percent of the Upper School students received some amount of tuition aid, some as much as 50 percent of day or boarding tuition. Aid is based on financial need, following procedures established by the School and Student Service for Financial Aid.

ADMISSIONS INFORMATION

Cranbrook admits day students in preschool through grade 12 and boarding students in grades 9 through 12. The Schools accept students without regard to race, religion, national origin, sex, or handicap. Admission is based on recommendations, past performance, a personal interview, a writing sample, and results of the SSAT or other standardized examinations. Recommended grades for entrance are all A's or A's and B's.

APPLICATION TIMETABLE

An initial inquiry is welcome at any time, although the recommended application completion date is January 31. Campus tours and interviews are arranged on weekdays through the admissions office. Notification of acceptance begins in February. The application fee is $50.

ADMISSIONS CORRESPONDENCE

Drew Miller
Dean of Admission and Financial Aid
Cranbrook Schools
39221 Woodward Avenue
P.O. Box 801
Bloomfield Hills, Michigan 48303-0801
United States
Phone: 248-645-3610
Fax: 248-645-3025
E-mail: admission@cranbrook.edu
Web site: http://www.schools.cranbrook.edu

CUSHING ACADEMY

Ashburnham, Massachusetts

Type: Coeducational boarding and day college-preparatory school
Grades: 9–12, postgraduate year
Enrollment: 454
Head of School: Dr. James Tracy, Ph.D., M.B.A.

THE SCHOOL

Cushing Academy, founded in 1865, opened as a coeducational boarding school with funds provided by Thomas Parkman Cushing. Since its founding, Cushing Academy has prepared boys and girls in grades 9 through 12 and postgraduate to be contributing members of colleges and universities and of the modern world. Students live and learn with students from over thirty countries and thirty states in a quiet, safe, and supportive community. At Cushing Academy, students are prepared for the technological, political, artistic, environmental, scientific, cultural, and ethical issues already present in their lives—the big questions of this new century that frame their academics, athletics, activities, and life on campus. Cushing builds students' global awareness, helps them to fulfill their aspirations, and enables them to learn the skills they will need to succeed throughout their lives.

Cushing's 162-acre campus lies in the small, rural town of Ashburnham in north-central Massachusetts, 55 miles west of Boston and 10 miles south of the New Hampshire border. Proximity to Boston permits extensive use of the city's cultural, entertainment, and commercial resources.

The Academy is governed by a 13-member Board of Trustees, 6 of whom are alumni. The operating budget for 2012–13 was $25.7 million, and the endowment was estimated at $29 million. Total voluntary support received in 2011–12 exceeded $4.1 million.

Cushing is accredited by the New England Association of Schools and Colleges. The Academy is a member of the National Association of Independent Schools, the Association of Independent Schools in New England, the Secondary School Admission Test Board, and the Cum Laude Society.

ACADEMIC PROGRAM

The hub of Cushing's academic program is the Cushing Innovation Lab, founded in 2012, and designed to prepare students to meet the challenges and opportunities of this century. The Innovation Lab facilitates teachers and students working with one another outside the boundaries of traditional academic disciplines to envision and develop student-centered approaches to teaching and learning. The Lab is aimed at addressing the emerging needs, interests, and aspirations of Cushing's diverse community of learners. The Innovation Lab also provides leadership and entrepreneurial opportunities on campus; experiential opportunities off campus; and coordinates the Cushing Scholars, an enrichment program for students selected on the basis of intellectual, athletic, and artistic promise, as well as leadership potential.

The Academy offers more than 150 full-year courses and seminars, including ten laboratory courses and fifteen advanced-level courses. Advanced independent study programs may be arranged through the Dean of Academics.

Typically, Cushing Academy students carry five major courses every trimester, in addition to a required elective in the visual or performing arts. To satisfy Cushing's diploma requirements, students must earn a minimum of 18 credits distributed as follows: English, 4; mathematics, 4; foreign language, 2; history and social science, 2; and science, 2. The remaining requirements may be filled by choosing from numerous electives, including ethics, creative writing, visual and performing arts, ecology, marine biology, economics, comparative religions, global diplomacy, and leadership.

All teachers are available in their classrooms during a daily extra-help period. Informal tutoring may also take place after dinner or during free time.

The Academy offers a structured Academic Support Program staffed by 6 educational specialists who work with students on a variety of strategies to assist them with their studies. Students who enroll in the Academic Support Program, either through the admissions process or who are identified as needing additional support after they arrive at Cushing, take one or more courses with the Academic Support specialists, concurrent with their other classes, for an additional fee. With students from thirty countries, Cushing also has a thriving international community. Students entering Cushing in need of English as a second language enroll in the ESL program for one or more years and then transition into the standard academic offerings.

The academic year is divided into three terms of twelve, ten, and nine weeks in length. Cumulative final exams are given at the end of fall and spring terms in all academic courses. Evaluations are sent home six times each year. Letters warning of academic difficulty are written at the discretion of the Academic Dean.

Cushing uses a letter grading system that follows a 4.0 scale; 1.2 is passing, 3.3–3.6 is honors, and 3.7 and above is high honors. Class placement is determined by demonstrated ability and past performance in each subject area. The average class size is 12 students. The student-teacher ratio is approximately 8:1. On weeknights from 8 to 10 p.m., students work quietly in their rooms or in the library during supervised study hall.

FACULTY AND ADVISERS

In 2012–13, the faculty and administration consisted of 92 full-time teachers and administrators—45 women and 47 men, of whom 52 had master's degrees, and 7 had earned their Ph.D.s. Seventy percent of faculty members live on campus, and all faculty members are involved in the daily life of students beyond the classroom experience. Each teacher is responsible for the academic, social, extracurricular, and dorm life for 5 to 7 student advisees.

The Headmaster, Dr. James Tracy, joined the Cushing community in 2006. He received an M.A. from the University of Massachusetts, a Ph.D. from Stanford University, and an M.B.A. from Boston University.

COLLEGE ADMISSION COUNSELING

Staffed by 5 experienced professionals, the Cushing Academy College Counseling Office is a resource available to all students and parents. The counseling process begins when a student enters the school, at which time a comprehensive College Counseling Guide is presented to each student and his or her parents. Cushing believes in engaging the students at all levels and that the college advising process should focus on each student's particular needs, aspirations, and abilities. The goal is to provide students and parents with information that will help all to feel knowledgeable, confident, and organized as they move through this exciting time.

Group meetings are held regularly for each of the various grade levels on such topics as summer activities, college research, campus visits, athletic recruitment, interviews, financial aid, applications, and standardized tests. Workshops for parents are presented during family weekends in the fall and spring. During the winter and spring trimesters, juniors meet individually with a member of the College Counseling staff to establish a prospective list of colleges. The following fall, a new round of group meetings and individual interviews take place to aid the seniors in completing their applications to universities of responsible choice.

Standardized tests, including the SAT and the ACT, are administered on-site at Cushing throughout the year, beginning with the PSAT in October. Individual tutoring and group test preparation is available for an additional fee.

The College Counseling Office utilizes Naviance, a Web-based counseling tool and database that aids the students and the office in the research process as well as in the organization and management of the application process. In addition, a library of college counseling books, course catalogs, viewbooks, DVDs, and other college materials are available in the College Counseling Office.

Recent college enrollments include Boston College, Boston University, Bowdoin, Brown, Cornell, College of the Holy Cross, Dartmouth, George Washington, Hofstra, Parsons School of Design, Purdue, Syracuse, University of Virginia, Vanderbilt, and Wellesley. Admissions representatives from over eighty colleges and universities visit the Cushing Academy campus each fall to meet with the students and College Counseling staff.

STUDENT BODY AND CONDUCT

The 2012–13 student body consists of 41 boys and 24 girls in the freshman class; 67 boys and 40 girls in the sophomore class; 71 boys and 69 girls in the junior class; 70 boys and 40 girls in the senior class; and 25 boys and 6 girls in the postgraduate class.

Of these 454 students, 372 were boarders. Students were predominantly from Massachusetts (136) and other parts of New England (59), as well as from New Jersey (16), New York (11), Florida (11), and Georgia (7), and Texas (7). Thirty states and Puerto Rico, as well as thirty countries, ranging from Indonesia to Germany, were represented. Of the total enrollment, 8 percent were African American.

Students play an active role in school governance through their participation in the school's thriving student organizations, such as student proctors, class officers, student-faculty senate, and tour guides, and through participation in the school's discipline committee process. Through these and other organizations, students influence decision-making at the school and serve as leaders for the community.

ACADEMIC FACILITIES

At the center of Cushing's campus is the Main Building, which houses classrooms, offices, and Cowell Chapel, where members of the community gather for all-school meetings and performing arts productions. Also in the Main Building is the Fisher-Watkins Library, which was transformed in 2009 to a digital learning center. In addition to its collection of e-readers and online data sources, the library features collaborative instruction space, large-screen monitors for viewing interactive data and news feeds from around the world, quiet study carrels, and a cyber café. The Joseph R. Curry Academic Center houses mathematics, the sciences, and the performing arts. This state-of-the-art facility of more than 56,000 square feet includes instructional laboratories, studios, student project rooms, and seminar space. The

English Building houses seven newly renovated classrooms, many with flex-furniture to facilitate collaborative learning. The Emily Fisher Landau Center for Visual Arts has both studio and gallery space for students to create and display professional-quality work in a variety of media, including fused and stained glass, silver, ceramics, photography, painting, and sculpture. Cushing Academy students have been invited to display their artwork in galleries in Santa Fe, New York, and at Oxford University.

The Cushing Network, a campuswide wireless computer network, may be accessed throughout the school, including all classrooms and dormitory rooms. CushNet and MyCushing, the school's intranet systems, allow students to send e-mail, join bulletin-board discussions for classes, communicate with teachers and friends, follow campus happenings, monitor homework and submit assignments. Parents and guardians of Cushing students may log in to a separate portal where they may access their students' course syllabi, school news items, calendars, and events. SmartBoard technology is available in all classrooms and the Academy is rolling out its newly designed interactive iClass Tables in various departments, and an iPad pilot program is underway.

BOARDING AND GENERAL FACILITIES

The Academy houses more than 350 students in seven dormitories and six student-faculty houses that vary in capacity from 3 to 81 students each. Almost all rooms are doubles, and returning students select rooms through a room-draw system that favors seniority. New students are assigned rooms by the Co-Directors of Admission and the Student Life Office. The ratio of faculty to students in the dormitories is generally 1:12.

Cushing's Dining Commons houses a newly renovated student center on the lower level, which includes a recreational area, snack bar, bookstore, and post office. Formal family-style dinners are served once a month.

ATHLETICS

In the belief that physical fitness and agility enrich both the individual and the community, Cushing's renowned athletic program is designed to involve everyone in physical endeavors. There are boys' interscholastic teams in baseball, basketball, cross-country, football, golf, ice hockey, lacrosse, skiing, soccer, tennis, and track; girls compete in basketball, cross-country, field hockey, ice hockey, lacrosse, skiing, soccer, softball, tennis, track, and volleyball. Organized recreational sports include aerobics, dance, figure skating, horseback riding, skiing, snowboarding, tennis, and weight lifting.

The Heslin Gymnasium contains four locker rooms, the John Biggs Jr. Memorial Fitness Center, a training room, and a basketball/volleyball court. There are also six playing fields and six tennis courts. In addition to year-round ice skating, the Theodore Iorio Ice Arena offers boys' and girls' locker rooms, workout facilities, a multipurpose function room, and a snack bar. Cushing's Athletic Leadership Program further challenges student-athletes who wish to take their drive beyond the playing fields through workshops, guest speakers, and off-campus opportunities.

EXTRACURRICULAR OPPORTUNITIES

In addition to their commitments in the classroom and on the playing fields, Cushing students take advantage of the many opportunities to join or start up clubs and to organize campus events. Always based on student interest, clubs in recent years have included Open Doors, International Club, Environmental Club, Cushing Academy Music Association, Literary Magazine, Mock Trial, Model United Nations, and Book Club. Students are also involved in coordinating campus events.

Cushing's proximity to Boston enables students to have access to the city's resources—museums, sporting events, shopping, theater—and regular trips to take advantage of these opportunities are scheduled throughout the year. Students interested in exploring opportunities in business, the arts, law, or other fields can also pursue opportunities with Boston-area professionals.

DAILY LIFE

The Monday-through-Friday schedule, which begins with classes at 8 a.m., provides time for an extra-help period, activities, and athletics before evening study hall at 8 p.m. Lights-out is at 10:30 p.m. for underclassmen and 11 p.m. for seniors and postgraduates. Classes are 40 minutes long on Mondays and Fridays and 55 minutes long on Tuesdays, Wednesdays, and Thursdays. Courses, activities, and athletics are all centrally scheduled to avoid unnecessary conflicts. On weekdays, the hours from 3 to 5 p.m. are reserved for athletics, arts, and activities; interscholastic competitions occur on Wednesday, Friday (occasionally), and Saturday.

WEEKEND LIFE

On a typical weekend at the Academy, students enjoy many off-campus trips with faculty chaperones. Movies are shown on campus each weekend, while dances and concerts are often scheduled in the evening. Students are permitted to spend a number of weekends off campus, but on any given weekend 70 to 75 percent of the boarding population chooses to remain at school. One weekend each month is designated an on-campus weekend, during which students remain at Cushing to enjoy performances and sporting events, and participate in special activities as a community.

SUMMER PROGRAMS

During the five-week summer session, Cushing offers a unique boarding school experience for girls and boys ages 12–18 from throughout the United States and around the world. The program features Prep for Success for middle school students, regular and advanced college-preparatory courses for high school students, intensive art, and extensive English as a second language instruction. Each program is combined with interesting artistic and athletic electives as well as exciting excursions throughout New England. For further information, students should contact Margaret Lee, Director of Summer Programs at mlee@cushing.org or 978-827-7700.

COSTS AND FINANCIAL AID

Tuition and required fees for 2012–13 are $51,575 for boarding students and $37,500 for day students. There are optional fees for skiing, music lessons, and fine arts materials. A $5158 nonrefundable enrollment deposit ($3750 for day students) is credited toward the balance due; half of the remaining total is due on July 1 and the balance on December 1.

In 2012–13, 26 percent of the student body received $3.2 million in financial aid. Funds are awarded on the basis of need as demonstrated by established criteria of the School and Student Service for Financial Aid. Financial aid is renewed annually, subject to continued need and availability of funds.

ADMISSIONS INFORMATION

Cushing Academy seeks students who are interested in taking an active role in promoting their own academic and social growth. Cushing values strong character, motivation, diversity, and strength in extracurricular activities. Candidates are evaluated based on school performance, SSAT, PSAT, SAT, ACT, TOEFL, or other tests, and a personal interview. If travel is too difficult, international applicants may request a video interview via Skype.

APPLICATION TIMETABLE

Initial inquiries are welcome at any time. Application materials are available online and are provided, along with the school's viewbook, upon request. Interviews and campus tours are scheduled Monday through Friday and some Saturdays.

Completed applications should be submitted, along with the $50 nonrefundable application fee ($100 for international students), by February 1. Applications may be submitted after February 1, and will be acted on after March 10, subject to the availability of spaces in the classes. Decisions are mailed out on March 10 for students submitting applications by the deadline and for others on a rolling basis as space permits.

ADMISSIONS CORRESPONDENCE

Deborah Gustafson, Co-Director of Admission
Adam Payne, Co-Director of Admission
Cushing Academy
39 School Street
P.O. Box 8000
Ashburnham, Massachusetts 01430
United States
Phone: 978-827-7300
Fax: 978-827-6253
E-mail: admissions@cushing.org
Web site: http://www.cushing.org

DEERFIELD ACADEMY

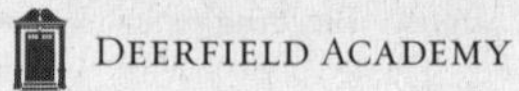

Deerfield, Massachusetts

Type: Coeducational boarding and day college-preparatory school
Grades: 9–12, postgraduate year
Enrollment: 630
Head of School: Dr. Margarita O'Byrne Curtis

THE SCHOOL

Since its founding in 1797, Deerfield Academy has provided a unique and challenging opportunity for young people. Deerfield Academy is a vibrant learning community nurturing high standards of scholarship, citizenship, and personal responsibility. Through a demanding liberal arts curriculum, extensive cocurricular program, and supportive residential environment, Deerfield encourages each student to develop an inquisitive and creative mind, sound body, strong moral character, and commitment to service. The setting of the campus, which is rich in tradition and beauty, inspires reflection, study and play, the cultivation of friendships, and the growth of a defining community spirit.

The school's 280-acre campus is located in the center of Historic Deerfield, a restored Colonial village in western Massachusetts, 90 miles from Boston and 55 miles from Hartford. Only 20 minutes south is the five-college area that includes Amherst, Smith, Mount Holyoke, and Hampshire Colleges and the University of Massachusetts, providing rich cultural and intellectual resources.

A 30-member Board of Trustees is the Academy's governing body. The endowment is valued at approximately $398 million. In 2011–12, operating expenses totaled $50.7 million, capital gifts amounted to $15.8 million, and Annual Giving was $5.79 million, with 41.1 percent of the 9,811 alumni participating.

Deerfield is accredited by the New England Association of Schools and Colleges. It is a member of the National Association of Independent Schools, the Independent School Association of Massachusetts, and the Secondary School Admission Test Board.

ACADEMIC PROGRAM

Deerfield's curriculum is designed to enable its students to assume active and intelligent roles in the world community. Courses and teaching methods are aimed at developing logical and imaginative thinking, systematic approaches to problem solving, clear and correct expression in writing and speech, and the confidence to pursue creatively one's interests and talents. Students take five courses per trimester. Their schedules are planned individually in consultation with advisers and the Academic Dean.

Graduation requirements include English, 4 years; mathematics, 3 years; foreign language, 3 years of a language (Arabic, Chinese, French, Greek, Latin, or Spanish); history, 2 years (including 1 year of U.S. history); laboratory science, 2 years; fine arts, two terms; and philosophy and religious studies, one term. All sophomores take a one-term course in health issues. In addition, all new students take a required course in library skills. Honors and Advanced Placement (AP) courses are offered in nineteen subject areas. Last year, 320 students sat for 709 AP exams. Ninety-one percent of the tests received qualifying scores of 3 or better. Independent study is offered in all departments.

During the spring term, seniors may engage in off-campus alternate-studies projects, ranging from working in a local hospital to serving as an intern for a member of Congress. Juniors may spend half of their year at the Maine Coast Semester, which combines regular classes with studies of environmental issues; at the Mountain School in Vermont; or at a boarding school in South Africa, Botswana, or Kenya. Sophomores and juniors may spend a semester at the Island School on Eleuthera in the Bahamas. The Swiss Semester in Zermatt is a program that gives sophomores an opportunity to study geology, European history, and foreign language at the foot of the Matterhorn. Deerfield participates in the School Year Abroad program in China, France, Italy, Japan, Spain, and Vietnam, which is available for juniors and seniors. Students may also choose from many exchange programs, including programs in Australia, Hong Kong, Jordan, and New Zealand. Summer opportunities are available in China, the Dominican Republic, France, Greece, Italy, Spain, and Uruguay.

The average class size is 12. The overall faculty-student ratio is 1:6. Placement in AP courses, honors sections, and accelerated courses is based upon preparedness, ability, and interest. All students have study hours Sunday through Thursday evenings.

The school year is divided into three 11-week terms. Grades are sent at the end of each term and at midterm. In the fall and spring, the student's academic adviser prepares a formal written report, commenting extensively on the student's academic performance, attitude, work habits, dormitory life, and participation in athletics and cocurricular activities and as a citizen of the school.

Grading is based on a numerical scale of 0 to 100; 60 is passing. The honor roll is made up of students with minimum averages of 90, and the high honor roll recognizes students with averages of 93 and above. Students in academic difficulty are reviewed by the Academic Standing Committee at the end of each term. Teachers are available during evenings, weekends, and free periods to assist students individually. Students can also get help from the Study Skills Coordinator.

FACULTY AND ADVISERS

The high quality of Deerfield's faculty is the school's greatest endowment.

The faculty consists of 124 members (57 women and 67 men); 71 percent hold advanced degrees. Ninety-five percent reside on campus or live in the village of Deerfield. All faculty members act as advisers to students, coach sports, head tables in the dining hall, and serve on various committees. Teachers receive summer grants and time away from the Academy for advanced study, travel, and exchange teaching.

Dr. Margarita O'Byrne Curtis was appointed Head of School in July 2006. She earned her B.A. from Tulane, her B.S. from Mankato State, and a Ph.D. in Romance languages and literature from Harvard.

COLLEGE ADMISSION COUNSELING

College advising is coordinated by 4 college advisers. Beginning in their junior year, all students attend small-group discussions that help them make informed decisions about college. In mid-winter, every junior is assigned to an individual college adviser, who further develops, with parental consultation, a list of prospective colleges. In the fall of the senior year, college advisers assist students in narrowing their college choices and in making the most effective presentation of their strengths. During the fall, representatives of approximately 160 colleges visit the Academy for presentations and interviews.

Normally, sophomores and juniors take the PSAT in October. Juniors take the SAT in January; SAT Subject Tests in December, May, and June; and Advanced Placement (AP) tests in May. Seniors, whenever advisable, take the SAT in the fall and additional AP tests later in the year. The midrange of SAT scores for the class of 2011 was 620–700 critical reading, 620–720 math, and 620–720 writing.

Of the 197 graduates in 2012, 190 are attending college, 7 students deferred admission to college for a year. Colleges attended by 5 or more students are: Princeton (11); Dartmouth and Yale (10 each); Harvard (9); Georgetown (7); Davidson; the Universities of Pennsylvania and Virginia (6 each); and Boston College, Brown, Duke, and Trinity College (5 each).

STUDENT BODY AND CONDUCT

In fall 2012, Deerfield enrolled 633 students: 309 girls and 324 boys. There are 95 boarders and 17 day students in the ninth grade, 125 boarders and 26 day students in the tenth grade, 148 boarders and 18 day students in the eleventh grade, and 188 boarders and 16 day students in the twelfth grade (including 20 postgraduates). Recognizing that diversity enriches the school, the Academy seeks to foster an appreciation of difference. To that end, international students make up 16 percent of the student body, and those from minority groups make up 30 percent. Deerfield students come from thirty-nine states and thirty-three countries.

In all communities, a healthy tension exists between the need for individuality and the need for common values and standards. A community's shared values define the place, giving it a distinct sense of itself. In all facets of school life, Deerfield strives to teach that honesty, tolerance, compassion, and responsibility are essential to the well-being of the individual, the school, and society. Deerfield Academy is a residential community in which students learn to conduct themselves according to high standards of citizenship. Expectations for students are clear, and the response to misbehavior is timely and as supportive as possible of the students involved.

ACADEMIC FACILITIES

Deerfield's campus has eighty-one buildings. The Frank L. Boyden Library has a collection of more than 85,000 books, periodicals, and films. Most of the library's collection is accessible via a fully integrated online catalog. The Koch Center, a new, state-of-the-art 80,000-square-foot center for science, mathematics, and technology, includes a new planetarium; thirty classroom and laboratory spaces, including dedicated spaces for independent research; a 225-seat auditorium; the Star Terrace; and a central atrium.

The Memorial Building contains the main auditorium, Hilson Gallery, Russell Gallery, art studios, a black-box theater, a dance facility, and music recital and practice rooms.

BOARDING AND GENERAL FACILITIES

There are eighteen dormitories. Faculty members live in apartments attached to each dorm corridor and maintain a close, supportive relationship with students. Two senior proctors also live on the freshman and sophomore corridors. Eighty-five percent of the boarding students have single rooms.

The fifteen-bed health center, Dewey House, is staffed full-time by a physician and registered nurses.

ATHLETICS

Participation in sports—at the student's level of ability—is the athletic program's central focus. The Academy fields interscholastic teams in baseball, basketball, crew, cross-country, cycling, diving, field hockey, football, golf, ice hockey, lacrosse, skiing, soccer, softball, squash, swimming, tennis, track, volleyball, water polo, and wrestling. Supervised recreational activities include aerobics, cycling, dance, skiing, squash, strength training, tennis, and an outdoor skills program.

Deerfield's gymnasium complex contains three basketball courts; a wrestling arena; an indoor hockey rink; a new 5,500-square-foot fitness center with state-of-the-art cardiovascular and weight lifting equipment, trainer's room, and locker rooms; the Dewey Squash Center, a 16,000-square-foot facility housing ten international squash courts and tournament seating; and the largest preparatory school natatorium in New England, which includes an indoor, eight-lane, 25-yard pool with a separate diving well. Ninety acres of playing fields include three football fields, twelve soccer/lacrosse fields, three field hockey fields, eighteen tennis courts, a major-league-quality baseball field, a softball field, paddle tennis courts, a new boathouse and crew facility, and a new eight-lane track. Two synthetic turf fields were added in the summer of 2008.

EXTRACURRICULAR OPPORTUNITIES

Deerfield students and faculty members are extraordinarily productive in the performing and visual arts. Musical groups include wind ensemble, chamber music, string orchestra, jazz ensemble, Deerfield Choral Society, madrigal singers, a cappella groups, and the Academy Chorus. Many opportunities exist for acting as well. In addition to the three major theater productions each year, plays and scenes are also performed by advanced acting classes. Students who are interested in dance may explore modern, jazz, and ballet, with the opportunity to perform all three terms.

Cocurricular organizations include Peer Counselors, the Diversity Task Force, Amnesty International, and debate, photography, and political clubs. Outing groups offer opportunities to ski, rock climb, and bike on weekends. Publications include an award-winning campus newspaper, the yearbook, and literary publications.

Students provide service as tutors, dormitory proctors, tour guides, and waiters in the dining hall. Students serve responsibly on various standing and ad hoc administrative committees and play an especially important role on the disciplinary committee. Students are also involved in various community service projects. The Community Service program encourages Deerfield students and faculty members to broaden their perspectives by sharing with and learning from people of different ages, abilities, cultures, and economic backgrounds. Ongoing projects include mentoring at nearby schools, volunteering in shelters and day-care centers, tutoring, organic farming and on-campus recycling, visiting nursing homes, and sponsoring Red Cross blood drives. Some students also serve as Big Brothers or Big Sisters to local youth. In addition, each sophomore also participates in Deerfield Perspectives, an on-campus service program.

DAILY LIFE

Students normally take five courses each term, and each course meets four times per week. The length of a class period ranges from 45 to 70 minutes. Classes begin at 8:30 and end at 3:05, except on Wednesday, when classes end at 12:45 and are followed by interscholastic athletics and cocurricular activities. Classes do not meet on Saturdays. One morning a week, students and faculty members gather together for a school meeting, and students and faculty members attend seven family-style meals per week. All sports and drama activities take place after classes. Clubs and cocurricular groups meet between dinner and study hours or on weekends.

Students study in their dormitory rooms between 7:45 and 9:45 p.m., Sunday through Thursday. They may also study in the library, perform laboratory experiments, or seek help from a faculty member or the student tutoring service. During the school week, the curfew for freshmen and sophomores is 7:45; for juniors and seniors, it is 9:45.

WEEKEND LIFE

In addition to athletic events on Saturday afternoon, there are films, theatrical productions, and musical performances. Social activities, sponsored by the Student Activities Committee and chaperoned by faculty members, include coffeehouses, talent shows, concerts, and dances. Deerfield's rural setting and extensive athletic facilities are ideal for recreational hiking, rock climbing, skiing, swimming, ice skating, and other activities.

The Academy Events Committee plans and sponsors events throughout the school year. The Robert Crow Lecture Series brings to the Academy leaders in politics, government, education, science, and journalism. Students attend concerts and film series. Art exhibitions and numerous dramatic productions provide recognition for promising young artists, photographers, and actors. Students also have access to cultural programs in the five-college area.

Freshmen may take two weekends off campus in the fall term and three each in the winter and spring terms; sophomores may take two weekends in fall, three in winter, and an unlimited number in spring; juniors and seniors in good standing may take unlimited weekends. On weekends, the curfew for freshmen and sophomores is at 10:30 p.m. on Friday and 11 on Saturday. For juniors and seniors, Friday curfew is at 11; Saturday curfew is at 11:30.

COSTS AND FINANCIAL AID

For 2012–13 school year, the cost for boarding students is $47,500; for day students, it is $34,050. Additional fees include $2045 for books, infirmary, and technology. Tuition is payable in two installments, on August 1 and December 1. A $2500 deposit (credited to the August tuition bill) is due within four weeks of the student's acceptance by Deerfield.

Deerfield awards financial aid to 35 percent of its students. Financial aid totaled more than $7 million for the 2012–13 academic year; grants, based on demonstrated need and procedures established by the School and Student Service for Financial Aid, range from $2500 to full tuition.

ADMISSIONS INFORMATION

Deerfield maintains rigorous academic standards and seeks a diverse student body—geographic, socioeconomic, and racial. Selection is based upon academic ability and performance, character and maturity, and promise as a positive community citizen. The Admission Committee closely examines candidates' teacher and school recommendations and personal essays.

The SSAT or ISEE is required of applicants for grades 9 and 10 and should be taken during an applicant's current academic year. The SSAT, ISEE, or PSAT is required for eleventh-grade applicants, and the PSAT, SAT or ACT is required for twelfth-grade and postgraduate candidates. The TOEFL may be taken in place of the aforementioned tests by students for whom English is not their first language.

Deerfield Academy does not discriminate on the basis of race, color, creed, handicap, sexual orientation, or national or ethnic origin in its admission policies or financial aid program.

APPLICATION TIMETABLE

Applicants normally visit the Academy in the year prior to the proposed date of entrance. Campus tours and interviews are conducted from 8:30 to 2:20 on Monday, Tuesday, Thursday, and Friday; from 8:15 to noon on Wednesday; and at 9, 10, and 11 on Saturday. Weekdays are preferable, since there are no Saturday classes. The completed application—including teacher recommendations, the school transcript, and essays—should be submitted no later than the January 15 deadline. Applicants receive notification of the admission decision on March 10. The candidate reply date is April 10. Specific dates can be found on the Academy's Web site at http://deerfield.edu/apply/how-to-apply.

ADMISSIONS CORRESPONDENCE

Patricia L. Gimbel
Dean of Admission and Financial Aid
Deerfield Academy
Deerfield, Massachusetts 01342
United States
Phone: 413-774-1400
E-mail: admission@deerfield.edu
Web site: http://www.deerfield.edu

DELBARTON SCHOOL

Morristown, New Jersey

Type: Boys' day college-preparatory school
Grades: 7–12: Middle School, 7–8; Upper School, 9–12
Enrollment: School total: 554; Upper School: 487
Head of School: Br. Paul Diveny, O.S.B., Headmaster

THE SCHOOL

Delbarton School was established in 1939 by the Benedictine monks of Saint Mary's Abbey as an independent boarding and day school. Now a day school, Delbarton is located on a 200-acre woodland campus 3 miles west of historic Morristown and 30 miles west of New York City. Adjacent to the campus is Jockey Hollow, a national historic park.

Delbarton School seeks to enroll boys of good character who have demonstrated scholastic achievement and the capacity for further growth. The faculty strives to support each boy's efforts toward intellectual development and to reinforce his commitment to help build a community of responsible individuals. The faculty encourages each boy to become an independent seeker of information, not a passive recipient, and to assume responsibility for gaining both knowledge and judgment that will strengthen his contribution to the life of the School and his later contribution to society. While the School offers much, it also seeks boys who are willing to give much and who are eager to understand as well as to be understood.

The School is governed by the 9-member Board of Trustees of the Order of Saint Benedict of New Jersey, located at Saint Mary's Abbey in Morristown. Delbarton's 2011–12 annual operating expenses totaled $20.5 million. It has an endowment of $29 million. This includes annual fund-raising support from 36 percent of the alumni.

Delbarton School is accredited by the Middle States Association of Colleges and Schools and approved by the Department of Education of the State of New Jersey. It is a member of the National Association of Independent Schools, the New Jersey Association of Independent Schools, the Council for Advancement and Support of Education, the National Catholic Educational Association, and the New Jersey State Interscholastic Athletic Association.

ACADEMIC PROGRAM

The academic program in the Upper School is college preparatory. The course of study offers preparation in all major academic subjects and a number of electives. The studies are intended to help a boy shape a thought and a sentence, speak clearly about ideas and effectively about feelings, and suspend judgment until all the facts are known. Course work, on the whole, is intensive and involves about 20 hours of outside preparation each week. The curriculum contains both a core of required subjects that are fundamental to a liberal education and various elective courses that are designed to meet the individual interests of the boys. Instruction is given in all areas that are necessary for gaining admission to liberal arts or technical institutions of higher learning.

The school year is divided into three academic terms. In each term, every boy must take five major courses, physical education, and religious studies. The specific departmental requirements in grades 9 through 12 are English (4 years), mathematics (4 years), foreign language (3 years), science (3 years), history (3 years), religious studies (2 terms in each of 4 years), physical education and health (4 years), fine arts (1 major course, 1 term of art, and 1 term of music), and computer technology (2 terms). For qualified boys in the junior and senior years, all departments offer Advanced Placement courses, and it is also possible in certain instances to pursue work through independent study or to study at neighboring colleges.

The grading system uses 4 to 0 (failing) designations with pluses and minuses. Advisory reports are sent to parents in the middle of each term as well as at the end of the three terms. Parents are also contacted when a student has received an academic warning or is placed on probation. The average class size is 15, and the student-teacher ratio is about 7:1, which fosters close student-faculty relations.

FACULTY AND ADVISERS

In 2012–13 the faculty consisted of 9 Benedictine monks and 72 lay teachers. Sixty-one are full-time members, with 57 holding advanced degrees.

Br. Paul Diveny, O.S.B., became Headmaster in July 2007. Br. Paul received his B.A. from the Catholic University of America in 1975; his diploma in Monastic Studies from the Pontificio Ateneo Sant'Anselmo in Rome, Italy in 1982; and his M.A. in German from Middlebury College in 1987. He has served the School previously as a teacher of Latin, German, ancient history, and religious studies, and as Assistant Headmaster.

The teaching tradition of the School has called upon faculty members to serve as coaches, counselors, or administrators. A genuine interest in the development of people leads the faculty to be involved in many student activities. Every boy is assigned to a guidance counselor, who advises in the selection of courses that meet School and college requirements as well as personal interests. Individual conferences are regularly arranged to discuss academic and personal development. The counselor also contacts the boy's parents when it seems advisable.

COLLEGE ADMISSION COUNSELING

Preparation for college begins when a boy enters Delbarton. The PSAT is given to everyone in the tenth and eleventh grades. Guidance for admission to college is directed by the senior class counselor. This process generally begins in the fall of the junior year, when the junior class counselor meets with each boy to help clarify his goals and interests. Many college admissions officers visit the School annually for conferences. Every effort is made to direct each boy toward an institution that will challenge his abilities and satisfy his interests.

The mean SAT critical reading and math score for the class of 2012 was 1350. More than 25 percent of the young men in the classes of 2009, 2010, 2011, and 2012 have been named National Merit Scholars, Semifinalists, or Commended Students. In addition, 85 percent of the members of the class of 2012 were enrolled in at least one AP course.

All of the graduates of the classes of 2009, 2010, 2011, and 2012 went on to college, with 5 or more attending such schools as Boston College, Columbia, Cornell, Dartmouth, Duke, Georgetown, Harvard, Holy Cross, Johns Hopkins, Middlebury, Notre Dame, Princeton, Villanova, Williams, Yale, and the Universities of Pennsylvania and Virginia.

STUDENT BODY AND CONDUCT

The 2012–13 Upper School student body consisted of 119 ninth graders, 120 tenth graders, 131 eleventh graders, and 117 twelfth graders. The Middle School has 33 seventh and 34 eighth graders. All of the students are from New Jersey, particularly the counties of Morris, Essex, Somerset, Union, Bergen, Hunterdon, Passaic, and Sussex.

Regulations, academic and social, are relatively few. The School eschews the manipulative, the coercive, the negative, or the merely punitive approach to discipline. The basic understanding underlying the School's regulations is that each boy, entering with others in a common educational enterprise, shares responsibility with his fellow students and with faculty members for developing and maintaining standards that contribute to the welfare of the entire School community. Moreover, shared responsibility is essential to the growth of the community; at the same time, much of an individual boy's growth, the increase in his capacity for self-renewal, his sense of belonging, and his sense of identity spring from his eagerness and willingness to contribute to the life of the School. Each class has a moderator, who is available for advice and assistance. The moderator works closely with the boys, assisting them in their progress.

ACADEMIC FACILITIES

The physical facilities include two classroom buildings, a fine arts center, a science pavilion, a greenhouse, the church, and the dining hall. Academic facilities include thirty-four classrooms, six science laboratories, art and music studios, a language laboratory, and a library of more than 20,000 volumes. The five computer laboratories consist of 250 workstations in a networked system. Also, the music department provides twelve personal computers for the advanced study of music and composition.

ATHLETICS

Sports at the School are an integral part of student life. The School holds the traditional belief that much can be learned about cooperation, competition, and character through participating in sports. Almost 80 percent of the boys participate on one or more interscholastic athletics teams. Varsity sports offered in the fall term are football, soccer, and cross-country; in the winter term, basketball, wrestling, track, hockey, squash, bowling, and swimming (in an off-campus pool); and in the spring, baseball, track, lacrosse, tennis, and golf. In most of these sports, there are junior varsity, freshman, and Middle School teams. Some intramural sports are available, depending upon interest, every year.

The facilities consist of two gymnasiums, eight athletics fields, six tennis courts, and an outdoor pool for swimming during warm weather. Students who join the golf team are able to play at nearby golf clubs.

EXTRACURRICULAR OPPORTUNITIES

The School provides opportunities for individual development outside the classroom as well as within. The faculty encourages the boys to express their intellectual, cultural, social, and recreational interests through a variety of activities and events. For example, fine arts at Delbarton are available both within and outside the curriculum. Studio hours accommodate boys after school, and students visit galleries and museums. In the music department, vocal and instrumental instruction is available. Performing ensembles include an orchestra, band, and chorus and smaller vocal and instrumental ensembles. Under the aegis of the Abbey Players, drama productions are staged three times a year, involving boys in a wide variety of experiences.

Other activities include Deaneries (student support groups promoting School unity and spirit), the *Courier* (the School newspaper), the *Archway* (the yearbook), *Schola Cantorum* (a vocal ensemble), the Abbey Orchestra, and the Model UN, Mock Trial, Speech and Debate, Junior Statesmen, Art, History, Chess, Cycling, Stock Exchange, and Future Business Leaders clubs. In addition, faculty moderators of the Ski Club regularly organize and chaperone trips during School vacations.

To expose students to other cultures and to enhance their understanding of the world, faculty members have organized trips to Europe, Africa, and Latin America. The Campus Ministry office is active in sponsoring several outreach programs that lead boys to an awareness of the needs of others and the means to answer calls for help. The outreach programs include community soup kitchens, Big Brothers of America, Adopt-a-Grandparent, Basketball Clinic for exceptional children, and a program in which volunteers travel to Appalachia during break to contribute various services to the poor of that area.

Students' imagination and initiative are also given opportunities for expression through Student Council committees and assemblies. The students are also offered School-sponsored trips to cultural and recreational events at area colleges and in nearby cities.

DAILY LIFE

Classes begin at 8:15 a.m. and end at 2:34 p.m. The average number of classes per day for each student is six. Two classes are an hour long, while the remainder are 40 minutes each. The School operates on a six-day cycle, and each class meets five days per cycle. Physical education classes are held during the school day. After classes, students are involved in athletics and the arts. Clubs and organizations also meet after school, while many meet at night.

COSTS AND FINANCIAL AID

Charges at Delbarton for the 2012–13 academic year are $30,200. These are comprehensive fees that include a daily hot lunch as well as library and athletics fees. The only other major expenses are the bookstore bill and transportation, the cost of which varies. Optional expenses may arise for such items as the yearbook, music lessons, or trips.

Because of the School's endowment and generous alumni and parent support, a financial aid program enables many boys to attend the School. All awards are based on financial need, as determined by the criteria set by the School and Student Service for Financial Aid. No academic or athletics scholarships are awarded. Financial aid is granted to boys in grades 7 through 12. This year, the School was able to grant $1.6 million to students.

ADMISSIONS INFORMATION

Delbarton School selects students whose academic achievement and personal promise indicate that they are likely to become positive members of the community. The object of the admissions procedure is for the School and prospective student to learn as much as possible about each other. Admission is based on the candidate's overall qualifications, without regard to race, color, religion, or national or ethnic origin.

The typical applicant takes one of the three entrance tests administered by the School in October, November, and December. Candidates are considered on the basis of their transcript, recommendations, test results, and personal interview in addition to the formal application. In 2012–13, 378 students were tested for entrance in grades 7 and 9; of these, 149 were accepted. Eighty-nine percent of the students who were accepted for the seventh grade were enrolled; 77 percent of those accepted for the ninth grade were enrolled. Delbarton does not admit postgraduate students or students who are entering the twelfth grade.

APPLICATION TIMETABLE

The School welcomes inquiries at any time during the year. Students who apply are invited to spend a day at Delbarton attending classes with a School host. Interested applicants should arrange this day visit through the Admissions Office. Tours of the campus are generally given in conjunction with interviews, from 9 a.m. to noon on Saturdays in the fall, or by special arrangement. The formal application for admission must be accompanied by a nonrefundable fee of $65. Application fee waivers are available upon request.

It is advisable to initiate the admissions process in the early fall. Acceptance notifications for applicants to grades 7 and 9 are made by the end of January. Applicants to all remaining grades, as well as students placed in a wait pool, are given acceptance notification as late as June. Parents are expected to reply to acceptances two to three weeks after notification. A refundable deposit is also required. Application for financial aid should be made as early as possible; the committee hopes to notify financial aid applicants by the middle of March.

ADMISSIONS CORRESPONDENCE

Dr. David Donovan
Dean of Admissions
Delbarton School
Morristown, New Jersey 07960
United States
Phone: 973-538-3231 Ext. 3019
Fax: 973-538-8836
E-mail: admissions@delbarton.org
Web site: http://www.delbarton.org/admissions

THE DERRYFIELD SCHOOL

Manchester, New Hampshire

Type: Coeducational, college-preparatory day school
Grades: Grades 6–12
Enrollment: Total: 365; Middle School: 116; Upper School: 249
Head of School: Mary Halpin Carter, Ph.D., Interim Head of School

THE SCHOOL

The Derryfield School, an independent, coeducational, college-preparatory day school, was founded by local citizens in 1964 to provide an outstanding secondary education for students who want to live at home.

Derryfield inspires bright, motivated young people to be their best, and provides them with the skills and experiences needed to be valued, dynamic, confident, and purposeful members of any community.

The School is governed by a 20-member Board of Trustees and, in addition to tuition, is supported financially through annual giving and an endowment fund of more than $4.4 million.

Derryfield is accredited by the New England Association of Schools and Colleges and is a member of the National Association of Independent Schools (NAIS), the Association of Independent Schools of New England (AISNE), and the Independent Schools Association of Northern New England (ISANNE).

ACADEMIC PROGRAM

Derryfield's challenging academic program combines a seriousness of purpose with a sense of spirit. A core college-preparatory curriculum is enhanced by more than seventy elective classes and independent learning opportunities.

Students entering Derryfield in the Middle School participate in a curriculum that provides a firm background in skills and basic discipline areas in preparation for Upper School courses. All students in grades 6, 7, and 8 take English, mathematics, science, history, and a foreign language. In addition, all Middle School students participate in drama, music, wellness, physical education, and art.

Students entering the Upper School (grades 9–12) plan their course of study in the context of graduation requirements, college plans, and interests. A total of 18 academic credits is required with the following departmental distribution: 4 credits in English, 2 credits in history, 3 credits in mathematics, 3 credits in a world language, 2-1/3 credits in science, 1 credit in fine arts, and participation in either the alternative sports program or a team sport two seasons per year. Each student carries a minimum of five courses each term. The academic year consists of three terms.

The Independent Senior Project is an option for seniors during the final six weeks of the spring term. The project allows students to explore their interests and to gain practical experience outside of the classroom.

FACULTY AND ADVISERS

The Derryfield faculty consists of 43 members (24 men and 19 women). Master's degrees are held by 22 members and Ph.D.'s are held by 4 members. Twenty-four faculty members have taught at Derryfield for ten or more years, and annual faculty turnover is low. The student-faculty ratio is 8:1.

Faculty members are hired on the basis of a high level of expertise in their academic areas as well as enthusiasm to contribute to the overall success of their students and the School. In addition to their classroom obligations, faculty members advise approximately 8 students, coach Derryfield's athletic and academic teams, advise student activities, and make themselves available to counsel students in other areas of student life.

COLLEGE ADMISSION COUNSELING

A dedicated college counselor begins working with students in February of their junior year. College counseling is an active process that includes group seminars and individual meetings with students and their families. More than 50 college representatives visit Derryfield each year.

The average SAT scores for the class of 2012 were 638 in critical reading, 638 in math, and 643 in the writing section. Sixty-six students graduated in 2012, with 100 percent of the class going to college. A sampling of the colleges and universities currently attended by 2 or more Derryfield graduates includes Bates, Bentley, Boston College, Boston University, Brandeis, Bucknell, Carnegie Mellon, Clemson, Colby, Colgate, Cornell, Emory, Hamilton, Middlebury, Rensselaer, RIT, Syracuse, Trinity, Tufts, and the Universities of Chicago, New Hampshire, St. Andrews (Scotland), and Vermont.

STUDENT BODY AND CONDUCT

Of the 365 students enrolled at The Derryfield School, 116 students attend the Middle School program and 249 students attend the Upper School program. Students come from fifty local communities.

Violations of School rules are handled by the Discipline Committee, which consists of elected students and faculty members who evaluate discipline issues and make recommendations to the Head of School.

ACADEMIC FACILITIES

Derryfield's academic facilities include classroom buildings with five fully equipped science laboratories, a STEM classroom, a technology center with workstations and laptops, a 95-seat multimedia lyceum, a 17,000-volume library with a large subscription database, two art studios, an art gallery, and a 400-seat performing arts center. Outdoor classroom facilities include several miles of cross-country trails, high and low ropes courses, and many acres of woods. A turf field, a full-sized gymnasium, weight-training area, and trainer's room are also valuable learning sites for courses in physical education and health and wellness. In addition, the School opened the new 8,000-square-foot Gateway Building in 2011, which houses administrative offices, the Breakthrough Manchester Program, and two additional teaching spaces.

ATHLETICS

"A sound mind in a healthy body" defined the Greek ideal and is the concept at the core of Derryfield's physical education, health and wellness, and athletics philosophy.

All Middle Schoolers (grades 6–8) take physical education and health and wellness. Seventh and eighth graders also have competitive athletic requirements. Offerings include baseball, basketball, cross-country running, field hockey, lacrosse, Nordic and Alpine skiing, soccer, softball, and tennis.

In the Upper School (grades 9–12), two levels of competitive sports teams (junior varsity and varsity), as well as some alternative physical activities (e.g., yoga, weight training) are offered. Upper School athletics include baseball, basketball, crew, cross-country running, equestrian, field hockey, golf, lacrosse, Nordic and Alpine skiing, soccer, softball, swimming, and tennis. The School also honors areas of physical interest that it does not offer on site; students may request that an independent physical activity be a replacement for one of the two required seasons.

Derryfield is a member of the New Hampshire Interscholastic Athletic Association, participating in Divisions I, III, and IV, according to sport. Derryfield currently has the most athletic offerings of any Division IV school in New Hampshire and has garnered more than twenty-five state championships in the last ten years.

EXTRACURRICULAR OPPORTUNITIES

Derryfield's commitment to the arts is evident. High school students perform two large-scale drama productions each year, while seventh and eighth graders take part in their own musical. Each sixth grade drama class produces its own junior musical. Instrumental ensembles that include classical, jazz, and orchestral instruments are active in both the Middle and Upper School. There are vocal groups in both schools, and Upper School students may audition for a select chorus. All musicians participate in two concerts per year and frequently in talent shows and assemblies. Students are encouraged to audition for the New Hampshire All-State Chorus and Band. Visual art students regularly submit materials to the New Hampshire Student Artist Awards and the Boston Globe Scholastic Art Awards, and help organize displays of their own work in Derryfield's art gallery openings.

In each of the two schools, Middle and Upper, students participate in more than a dozen student-organized clubs. Choices include School Council, Conservation Club, Art Club, Gay/Straight Alliance, Medical Club, Robotics Club, and Chinese Culture Club, among others. Derryfield also offers competitive clubs, including Math Team, Debate Team, Mock Trial, Granite State Challenge, and Model United Nations. Student publications include newspapers, literary magazines, academic journals, and a yearbook.

Field trips, organized through classes or clubs, include regular visits to New York City, Boston, and Manchester museums, theaters, courtrooms, and outdoor areas of interest. Each year, different faculty members lead groups of students on cultural or service-learning outings. Trips for the 2012–13 school year include Ecuador, the Dominican Republic, China, Peru, New York City, and a Habitat for Humanity work project in one of the Mid-Atlantic States. In the summer of 2013, Derryfield will have its first exchange experience with a school in South Africa.

In its dedication to local and global communities, Derryfield's Key Club actively partners with the National Honor Society and more than a dozen organizations, including the New Hampshire Food Bank, the American Cancer Society, New Horizons Soup Kitchen, Boys and Girls Club, and local immigrant relocation programs.

Breakthrough Manchester, a year-round, tuition-free academic program, is also an important part of The Derryfield School. Breakthrough offers motivated students from Manchester's public elementary schools the opportunity to learn from outstanding high school and college students. Several Derryfield faculty members work as mentor teachers, while a large number of Derryfield students teach for Breakthrough.

Traditional Derryfield events and celebrations include Founders' Day, Winter Carnival, Grandparents' Day, Head's Holiday, Country Fair, Moose Revue talent show, and the Prom.

DAILY LIFE

Because Derryfield students come from approximately forty different surrounding towns, the School itself becomes a hub for learning, playing, serving, and socializing.

A full Derryfield School day begins at 7:55 a.m. and ends between 2:45 and 3:20 p.m. Departure times vary, depending on grade, a student's level of involvement in extracurricular activities or desire to obtain extra help from a teacher, use the library, or attend study hall.

Homeroom gatherings occur two mornings per week, and advisories meet three times per week. The Tuesday and Friday class schedules allow time for an activities period, during which clubs meet. A 30-minute all-school assembly takes place each Monday morning. The class schedule is a seven-period, seven-"day," rotating schedule.

SUMMER PROGRAMS

Derryfield offers several summer camps, including tennis and two drama camps.

COSTS AND FINANCIAL AID

Tuition and fees for 2012–13 are $27,730. In addition to the need-based Financial Aid Program and the Merit Scholarship Program, which offer direct grants, the School offers installment payment options.

The Financial Aid Program is designed to make a Derryfield education accessible to qualified students who could not otherwise afford the cost of attending. On average, Derryfield provides financial assistance to 26 percent of the student body, with awards that vary from 5 to 95 percent of tuition. Derryfield awards nearly $1.5 million in financial aid grants annually.

The Merit Scholarship Program is designed to recognize students who demonstrate qualities that will add meaning and vitality to Derryfield's core values or are distinguished by a commitment to purposeful involvement in both the local and global community. Awards of up to $15,000 are made annually.

The Malone Scholars Program was established in 2012 with a $2 million award from the Malone Foundation in recognition of the School's academic program. The Foundation's goal is to improve access to quality education for gifted students who lack the financial resources to develop their talents. Currently, the school has two Malone Scholars, and anticipates that two additional Scholars will be added for the 2013–14 school year.

ADMISSIONS INFORMATION

The Admission Committee considers applications from students entering grades 6 through 12. Although the largest number of students enters in grades 6, 7, 8, and 9, spaces are often available in other grades as well.

Applicants are required to complete an on-campus interview and a written application. The SSAT is required for all applications to grades 6 through 9. Applicants to grade 10, 11, and 12 have the option to submit their PSAT or SAT scores.

APPLICATION TIMETABLE

The priority deadline for applications is February 1. Tours and interviews are offered through the Admission Office. There is a $50 preliminary application fee for applicants.

Notification of acceptance is mailed on March 10, and families are expected to reply by April 10.

ADMISSIONS CORRESPONDENCE

Admission Office
The Derryfield School
2108 River Road
Manchester, New Hampshire 03104-1396
United States
Phone: 603-669-4524
Fax: 603-641-9521
E-mail: admission@derryfield.org
Web site: http://www.derryfield.org

ELGIN ACADEMY

Elgin, Illinois

Type: Independent, coeducational, college-preparatory day school
Grades: PS (age 3) through Grade 12
Enrollment: 430
Head of School: Seth L. Hanford

THE SCHOOL

Elgin Academy is a preschool through grade 12, independent, college-preparatory, coeducational day school committed to developing the full potential of each student. Through a proactive partnership among faculty, parents, and students in a nurturing, dynamic, challenging, and diverse community, Elgin Academy creates an environment where students may acquire the knowledge, skills, and attitudes necessary to become intellectually engaged and confident about their place in the world.

Elgin Academy is dedicated to its challenging liberal arts and college-preparatory curriculum, a belief in equal standards for both genders, the development of high moral character, and a true spirit of community. Admission is selective and focuses on commitment to learning, academic record, entrance examination, and personal interviews.

The 18-acre campus is located 35 miles northwest of Chicago. The school draws families from Elgin, Barrington, St. Charles, Dundee, Algonquin, and approximately thirty-five other communities, thus creating a culturally and economically diverse student body.

Elgin Academy is recognized by the Illinois State Board of Education and is a proud member of the following associations: NAIS (National Association of Independent Schools), ISACS (Independent Schools Association of the Central States), LMAIS (Lake Michigan Association of Independent Schools), ISM (Independent School Management), ICNS (Illinois Coalition of Non-Public Schools), CAPE (Council for American Private Education), IHSA (Illinois High School Association), and the Cum Laude Society (founded in 1906; honors scholastic achievement in secondary schools).

ACADEMIC PROGRAM

Elgin Academy's approach to its Early Childhood curriculum is focused on active learning. The Academy constantly seeks to provide children with opportunities to find learning joyful. Elgin Academy's approach is integrated and holistic, offering developmental opportunities not only in cognitive areas but also in the social, emotional, and physical aspects of the child's growth. The Academy's philosophy includes an enduring respect for developing the individuality, creativity, and self-esteem of each child. Material presented to children is developmentally appropriate at all times. Meaningful learning for young children takes place when the information presented is relevant to the child's experience. A child's initiative comes from a natural curiosity about the world around them. The educational environment is relevant and children are motivated and engaged in the learning process.

While the Lower School (Grades K–4) curriculum provides significant structure and ensures a core background, it also allows each individual the flexibility of a program that is appropriate, challenging, and of particular interest. Students are required to take language arts, mathematics, science, social studies, music, visual arts, a world language, and physical education.

Elgin Academy's Middle School (Grades 5–8) students are required to take mathematics, English, science, social studies, geography, videography, humanities, a world language (French, Spanish, or Latin), the arts (music, visual arts, and performing arts), either study skills or writer's workshop, and physical education. Underlying the core curriculum is an acknowledgment of the importance of character education.

The Upper School (Grades 9–12) curriculum is structured with college preparation in mind. A series of courses provides all students with the depth and breadth expected by the finest colleges. Advanced Placement (AP) courses are offered in the following seven subjects: American history, biology, calculus AB, chemistry, European history, psychology, and studio art. Students may choose to prepare for AP examinations in the following fourteen subjects: calculus BC, comparative government and politics, computer science, English language, English literature, environmental science, French language, French literature, Latin, music theory, physics, Spanish language, Spanish literature, and U.S. government and politics. Honors courses are offered in chemistry and physics. For graduation, students must complete 24½ credit hours. While the program provides significant structure and ensures a core background for all students, it also allows each individual the flexibility needed to build a selection of courses that is appropriate, challenging, and of particular interest.

FACULTY AND ADVISERS

The faculty is recruited nationally, with an average of twenty years of teaching experience. Seventy percent of all faculty members and 88 percent of the Upper School faculty hold advanced degrees. The Academy's PS–12 faculty consists of 56 teachers and administrators. Seventy-five percent of the Upper School faculty members have at least fifteen years of teaching experience and more than 65 percent have at least twenty years of teaching experience. The student-teacher ratio is 7:1.

COLLEGE ADMISSION COUNSELING

Elgin Academy has two college counselors and an administrative assistant, all of whom have many opportunities to get to know students in a variety of different ways. As a result, the process is first and foremost a personal one built upon solid relationships. Nationally, the ratio of high school students to counselors who provide college counseling is approximately 300:1. The comparable figure at the Academy is 151:1.

The college counseling office provides the following services: the availability of a counselor who knows each student at all points in the process; Sophomore College Night, an evening geared to introduce each family to the college process and the components of each student's application; College Night for Juniors, the formal beginning of the process during which families receive the extensive "College Handbook," a complete resource for every aspect of the process and discuss with representatives from local colleges and universities, the college search and application process; and many college visits by representatives from schools all over the country that come to recruit Elgin Academy students.

One hundred percent of Elgin Academy graduates are admitted to four-year colleges, with most students admitted to highly selective colleges and universities (as classified by *U.S. News & World Report*). Approximately 80 percent of the members of the classes of 2009–2011 earned grades of 3 or higher on AP exams. Eighty-two percent of the members of the class of 2013 who took AP Exams as juniors earned a 3 or higher. Forty-one percent of the class of 2012 earned the status of AP Scholar or higher for their performance on these exams.

In recent years, between 10 and 20 percent of the senior class have earned commended status or higher from the National Merit Scholarship Corporation. Two students have been named National Merit Finalists. The amount of merit scholarship dollars earned by students in the classes of 2010, 2011, and 2012 averaged $2.2 million dollars.

The following is a partial list of schools to which Elgin Academy seniors have been accepted in the last five years: Augustana, American, Bates, Boston University, Bradley, Case Western Reserve, Caltech, Colby, Colgate, Columbia, Cornell, Davidson, DePaul, DePauw, Duke, Furman, Georgetown, George Washington, Grinnell, Illinois Wesleyan, Knox, Lawrence, Macalester, Miami (Ohio), Tulane, Vanderbilt, Vassar, Wake Forest, Washington (St. Louis), Wheaton (Massachusetts), Xavier, William and Mary, and the Universities of Chicago, Edinburgh (UK), Illinois, Iowa, Manchester (UK), Rochester, St. Andrews (Scotland), and Wisconsin.

STUDENT BODY AND CONDUCT

Elgin Academy is coed and nonsectarian, with an enrollment of 430 students. The school's population of students has had the honor of representing over twenty states and such countries as Brazil, China, India, Japan, Korea, Pakistan, Vietnam, Portugal, France, and the United Kingdom.

ACADEMIC FACILITIES

The campus contains the following buildings: Old Main (special rooms for select Upper School classes and Elgin Historical Society), Raymond House (Business Office), Penney House (Offices of Admissions & Marketing, Development, and Alumni Relations), Sears Gallery and Theatre, North Hall (Lower School, PS–4), Sears Hall (Middle School, Grades 5–8), Edwards Hall (Upper School, Grades 9–12), the Gymnasium, and the Harold D. Rider Family Media, Science, and Fine Arts Center (Media Center/Library, Kimball Street Theatre, Fine Arts classrooms, and Liautaud-Lyons Upper School Accelerated classes), which earned LEED Gold certification from the U.S. Green Building Council. The Rider Center is now a living laboratory for science and math students interested in technology, materials, and design/construction techniques. The Rider Center is one of the most environmentally friendly school facilities in the nation.

ATHLETICS

An extensive selection of interscholastic sports is offered to Middle and Upper School students in grades 6–12. Sports offered to both girls and boys include basketball, cross-country, golf, soccer, tennis, track, and girls' field hockey. The Academy competes against other schools in the Independent School League, including North Shore Country Day School, Latin School, Lake Forest Academy, The University of Chicago Lab School, and Francis Parker School.

The Athletics facilities include the on-campus Gymnasium, off-campus athletic fields (on Franklin Boulevard), and regular use of The Centre of Elgin (the recreation center of the City of Elgin).

EXTRACURRICULAR OPPORTUNITIES

A long list of options includes Model United Nations, Worldwide Youth in Science and Engineering, musical and theatrical productions, formal and informal dances, Mock Trial, National Honor Society, student government, Athletic Council, Community Service Club, literary magazine, yearbook, Environmental Club, Baking Club, French Club, Art Club, and the Stock Market Club. There are also several courses to choose from in the Academy's Accelerated Program with the Northwestern University's Center for Talent Development.

Community service opportunities include projects with local agencies and an annual service trip to volunteer at orphanages in the Dominican Republic and Nicaragua.

DAILY LIFE

Classes take place Monday–Friday, 8:15 a.m. to 2:45 p.m. Office Hours are Monday–Friday, 8 a.m. to 4:30 p.m. Younger students have frequent field trips, and students in grades 6–12 participate in extended educational trips, including many high-adventure outdoor education experiences. All trips include faculty members and focus on team building. Recent trips have included the Canadian boundary waters; the Apostle Islands; the Appalachian Mountains; Montana's Missouri River; Texas' Big Bend; the Pine Ridge Indian Reservation in South Dakota; Washington, DC; Costa Rica; and Italy.

SUMMER PROGRAMS

The following camps are offered in conjunction with Summer at the Academy enrichment programs and are available to both Elgin Academy and non–Elgin Academy students: Summer Science Academy, Summer Arts Academy, Summer Athletics Academy, and Adventure Camp.

COSTS AND FINANCIAL AID

Tuition for Elgin Academy is estimated to be between $13,990 and $22,780. Need-based financial aid grants can help cover the tuition cost. Nearly 40 percent of students who attend the Academy receive some level of financial aid.

ADMISSIONS INFORMATION

To start the admission process, prospective families should request an information packet by completing the online inquiry form. The Admission Office will then contact students and their families and give further details on applying for admission. For domestic students, the application fee is $50, which is submitted with the completed application. The Academy recommends that families schedule a screening/visit and parent tour. After receiving the student's Teacher Recommendation Forms, report cards, and Entrance Exam scores (Middle and Upper School), the Admission Office will notify parents of the admit/deny status. For international students, the application process includes additional steps (TOEFL or SLEP exam results and online Skype interviews). Questions or requests for additional information should be e-mailed to admissions@elginacademy.org.

APPLICATION TIMETABLE

Elgin Academy utilizes a rolling admission process until the grade is at optimum enrollment. Prospective families should contact the Academy to inquire about particular grades and available space. The Admission Office adheres to the following schedule:

- Begin admission application process: September (one year in advance)
- Deadline to complete admission application process: January 15
- Entrance exam (Grades 6–12): Pre-registration required, early December, register by e-mail
- Apply online for financial aid: between November 1 and January 15
- Deposit deadline: March 1.

ADMISSIONS CORRESPONDENCE

Office of Admissions
Elgin Academy
350 Park Street
Elgin, Illinois
United States
Phone: 847-695-0303
E-mail: admissions@elginacademy.org
Web site: http://www.elginacademy.org

EMMA WILLARD SCHOOL

Troy, New York

Type: Girls' boarding and day college-preparatory school
Grades: 9–12, postgraduate year
Enrollment: 329
Head of School: Trudy E. Hall

THE SCHOOL

In 1814, Emma Hart Willard founded the school that now bears her name, making it the oldest nondenominational school for young women in the United States. Her belief in the intellectual and world-change potential of each young women is the cornerstone of a curriculum that has challenged Emma Willard students for nearly 200 years.

The exceptionally beautiful 137-acre campus has forty-two buildings. Often called the Castle on the Hill, the gothic buildings of Emma Willard are striking. Emma Willard School is located on the edge of the city of Troy, New York, 7 miles from Albany, at the crossroads of the Berkshires, the Adirondacks, and the Catskills.

The 31-member Board of Trustees includes 18 alumnae, 4 parents, and 1 faculty member. Three of the members are ex officio. An operating budget of $18 million is supported in part through a $78.5-million endowment and Annual Giving that exceeds $1.9 million.

Emma Willard School is accredited by the New York State Association of Independent Schools and by the New York State Board of Regents. It is a member of the National Association of Independent Schools, the New York State Association of Independent Schools, the Cum Laude Society, and the National Coalition of Girls Schools.

ACADEMIC PROGRAM

The individualized education at Emma Willard School develops the abilities and qualities of mind that are essential for success, while also taking into account the individual goals and talents of each girl. The rigorous college-preparatory curriculum ensures a strong foundation in all major academic areas in addition to extensive exposure to the arts. Emma Willard celebrates leadership, rewards successes, offers appropriate support, and reminds girls of the limitless possibilities the world presents an educated woman.

Each student's faculty adviser helps her plan her courses in coordination with the Director of College Counseling and the Academic Office. The school year is divided into two semesters, and most students take five academic classes per term. Core requirements for graduation include a minimum of 4 units of English; 3 of history, foreign language, and mathematics; and 2 of laboratory science and visual/ performing arts. All students are required to participate in physical education. The School offers more than 130 courses, including Advanced Placement (AP) preparation in all academic departments. A student who wishes to study subjects beyond the curriculum offerings may arrange individualized tutorials with faculty supervision.

The School's Practicum program offers individualized learning opportunities in various academic, professional, artistic, and athletic fields. Recent Practicum projects have focused on broadcasting, publishing, microbiology, veterinary medicine, law, environmental engineering, photojournalism, biotechnology, advertising, government, and architecture. The curriculum is complemented by the Serving and Shaping Her World Speakers Series, which invites accomplished and renowned experts in various fields to speak at assemblies throughout the school year.

All boarding underclass women are assigned to a supervised study hall each evening during the fall term; students in good academic standing are excused from this study hall at the end of the term. There is a 2-hour evening study period Sunday through Thursday for all boarding students all year. Students may be assigned by their advisers to a supervised evening study hall. The library is open 15 hours a day, seven days a week. At least one professional librarian is on duty 66 hours a week.

Emma Willard students may take courses for credit at nearby universities. In addition, the School is a member of the National Network of Complementary Schools, which offers students an opportunity to pursue special programs on an exchange basis. Service and educational trips abroad, as well as work with Habitat for Humanity, are undertaken by students with faculty chaperones each year; groups have traveled to Austria, Belize, China, Ethiopia, France, Germany, Greece, Ireland, Italy, Mongolia, Russia, and Spain. These trips often focus on nontraditional parts of the world to open students to entirely new ways of life and service to the world.

The grading system uses letter grades with plus and minus notations. A few courses are graded Credit/No Credit. Grades and comments are issued to parents and students at midterm and at the end of each semester.

FACULTY AND ADVISERS

The faculty numbers 48 (43 full-time and 5 part-time); 73 percent are women and 27 percent are men. The student-faculty ratio is 6:1. Most faculty members reside on campus. Thirty-six percent of the faculty members hold a master's or doctoral degree. The faculty members hold degrees from institutions such as Amherst, Boston College, Carnegie Mellon, Colgate, Cornell, Dartmouth, New England Conservatory, Princeton, Rensselaer, Smith, St. Lawrence, Trinity (Dublin), Vassar, Wellesley, Wesleyan, Williams, and Yale.

Trudy E. Hall was appointed Head of School in 1999. She holds a B.S. from St. Lawrence University, an M.Ed. from Harvard University, and an M.A.L.S. from Duke University. Hall is also the president of the board of the National Coalition of Girl's Schools and an international advocate and expert in the education of young women.

In selecting its teachers, Emma Willard looks for adults who are dedicated to enriching the lives of young women in and out of the classroom. Faculty development grants are available to those who wish to pursue advanced degrees or enrich their current areas of study and to those who wish to develop new courses. Sabbaticals and travel funds are available to all faculty members. Most dormitory staff members are dedicated full-time residence personnel and do not teach. All faculty members act as advisers to 3 to 6 students each. Faculty members chaperone weekend activities, sit on School committees, and advise student organizations. Annual faculty turnover is typically less than 10 percent.

COLLEGE ADMISSION COUNSELING

Formal college counseling begins in the junior year. The director of college counseling supervises all college placement testing (the PSAT, the SAT, and Subject Tests), coordinates visits to Emma Willard by college admissions officers, assists students in college planning and college applications, and writes a comprehensive recommendation for each senior, based on the student's academic record and teachers' written evaluations.

In 2012, 100 percent of seniors enrolled in colleges and universities, including: Amherst, Babson, Boston College, Brown, Carnegie Mellon, Columbia College, Cornell, Dartmouth, George Washington, Georgetown, Hamilton, Hampshire College, Ithaca, Johns Hopkins, Mount Holyoke, Northeastern, NYU, Parsons, Rensselaer, Skidmore, Smith, St. Lawrence, Stanford, Syracuse, Trinity (Hartford), Vassar, Wellesley, and Williams. The average SAT scores for the class of 2012 were 626 (critical reading), 624 (math), and 648 (writing).

STUDENT BODY AND CONDUCT

In 2012–13, Emma Willard has 202 boarding and 127 day students, as follows: grade 9, 77; grade 10, 73; grade 11, 90; and grade 12, 86. Students come from twenty-one states and twenty-six countries. Sixty-three are students of color, 89 are international students, and 49 have an alumna or current sister relationship to the school.

The School seeks to enroll girls who are responsible and mature enough not to require rigid structure, but all are expected to abide by the fundamental rules that govern major issues of discipline.

Students do not wear uniforms, but they are expected to meet standards of neatness and cleanliness in dress code during the academic day or in the dormitories. Dress for plays, concerts, and academic ceremonies is more formal.

ACADEMIC FACILITIES

The Emma Willard campus is listed on the National Register of History Places for its historic and beautiful buildings, which have been featured in numerous major motion pictures. The oldest buildings, of Tudor Gothic design, include the Alumnae Chapel and Slocum Hall, which contain classrooms, offices, Kiggins Hall (the main auditorium), a lab theater, and a dance studio. The Hunter Science Center, an addition to Weaver Hall, opened in 1996. Hunter includes computer equipment integrated with fractal laboratories. Completing the main quadrangle is the art, music, and library complex designed by Edward Larabee Barnes and constructed from 1967 to 1971. Other campus buildings house an additional auditorium and dance studio, ten music practice rooms, twenty-one grand pianos, six science laboratories, an audiovisual center, two photography darkrooms, a microcomputer center, and a weaving studio.

The William Moore Dietel Library holds more than 35,000 volumes in addition to a growing collection of e-books, CDs, DVDs, and an impressive variety of periodicals. Students have access to many online databases that augment the journal collection. The school archives contain school records dating back to the early 1800s. Some of the collections include nineteenth-century photographs and student manuscripts, and Emma Willard's papers.

BOARDING AND GENERAL FACILITIES

Students reside in three connected dormitories, Sage, Hypen, and Kellas. Sophomores, juniors, and seniors live together on various halls; ninth grade students live together on the same hall. There are single rooms, doubles, and suites. Professional residential faculty members supervise student life in the dormitories. A team of faculty affiliates, student proctors, and peer educators shares in dormitory responsibilities. Day students are assigned to residence halls to facilitate their integration into the residential program.

In 2004, the School embarked on a $32-million adaptive reuse project of the first and garden levels of the residence halls to create new community spaces. The design included a new state-of-the-art dining hall, student center, student study lounge, e-café, admissions suite, and student services offices. A large percentage of faculty and staff members live on the campus to best support students either within residential halls or in on-campus faculty residences.

ATHLETICS

Emma Willard encourages students to combine lifetime sports with competition. Students can fulfill the physical activities requirement through team sports, individual sports, or dance. Emma Willard teams compete in a league with local public and private schools in basketball, crew, cross-country, field hockey, lacrosse, soccer, softball, swimming, tennis, track, and volleyball. Recreational activities include cross-country skiing, dance, skating, swimming, tennis, volleyball, weight conditioning, yoga, and more. In addition to the Mott Gymnasium, which includes two indoor tennis courts and full facilities for basketball, volleyball, and fitness training, facilities also include six outdoor tennis courts, three large playing fields, and an all-weather 400-meter track. The Helen S. Cheel Aquatics and Fitness Center offers a competition-size swimming pool and state-of-the-art fitness equipment. The athletics staff includes a trained strength and conditioning coach.

EXTRACURRICULAR OPPORTUNITIES

The Speakers Series brings prominent individuals to campus for lectures, classroom interaction, and residencies. Speakers have included Poet Laureate Billy Collins; mathematician and author Edward Burger; ABC news correspondent Lynn Sherr; science writer Margaret Wertheim; Pulitzer Prize–winning authors Nicholas Kristof and Sheryl WuDunn; artist, slam poet, and filmmaker Kip Fulbeck; and award-winning novelist Tobias Wolff. The Emma Willard arts calendar features an impressive array of renowned chamber groups, dance companies, artists, and exhibitions.

The surrounding region offers performances at the historic Troy Music Hall, the Saratoga Performing Arts Center, and Tanglewood; events at the Empire State Performing Arts Center in Albany; ethnic festivals; sports events; theater; and activities at nearby colleges and universities. The School sponsors a world-class chamber music series and all students are required to attend at least two cultural events each term.

Among the many clubs and organizations are the Outing Club, Slavery No More, EMMA Green (environmental group), Quiz Team, Fair Trade, Foreign and American Student Organization, Black and Hispanic Awareness, Phila (charitable service club), and various singing groups. There are also four student publications: *Triangle,* the arts and literary magazine; *The Clock,* the School newspaper; *Gargoyle,* the yearbook; and Emma Now, a student-run news blog. Through Interact, girls may serve the community in volunteer projects. Traditions include the start-of-school Opening Convocation, fall and spring senior dinners, dances with neighboring schools, holiday Eventide, Revels, the surprise holiday Principal's Play Day, May Day, and the Flame Ceremony.

DAILY LIFE

Classes are held Monday through Friday from 8 a.m. to 3:30 p.m. in time blocks of 50-minute and 75-minute periods. On Wednesdays, students and teachers gather to participate in schoolwide academic activities, such as the service program and the Serving and Shaping Her World Speakers Series. A midmorning all-school meeting is held three times a week. Team sports, choir, some dance classes, and drama rehearsals meet after 3:30. Dinner is served from 5:30 to 7 p.m., and quiet study hours are 7:30 to 9:30 p.m. All students must be on their floor by 10:30 and in their rooms by 11 p.m.

WEEKEND LIFE

An extensive weekend activities program is developed and coordinated by the Director of Student Activities. Generally, 75 to 80 percent of the boarders remain on campus during the weekend, and day students are encouraged to participate in weekend activities. The Emma Willard campus is at the crossroads of New England, the Adirondacks, the Catskills, and the Berkshires. This location gives students an exciting array of cultural and recreational venues. Weekend activities include sports events, dances with boys' schools, dinner in the Capital District, movies on and off campus, and trips to Boston, New York, and Montreal. Transportation to area events and places of worship is provided.

COSTS AND FINANCIAL AID

Tuition, room, and board in 2012–13 is $48,480. Day student tuition was $29,690. A SmartCard fee of $600 for boarding students in grades 9–11 ($650 for seniors) and $400 for day students in grades 9–11 ($450 for seniors) covers testing, field trips, and other class-related expenses. Emma Willard requires all students to have a laptop computer.

Families purchase textbooks directly from the School's online vendor. The average cost of books per year is $500. Special-fee courses include private music lessons, ballet, skiing, and horseback riding. A 10 percent deposit is required to confirm enrollment; School fees are billed in July and December, and families may elect to pay 60 percent in August, with the remainder due in January. Families that wish to make monthly tuition payments may do so through the School's ten-month installment plan.

Emma Willard is committed to maintaining the diversity of its student body and allocated more than $4.2 million in financial aid to the student body during 2012–13. Aid is awarded on the basis of academic promise and family financial need, as determined by the parents' financial statement to the School and Student Service for Financial Aid. Applications for financial aid must be submitted by February 1. As long as a student is in good standing and family circumstances warrant continued assistance, grants are renewed from year to year.

ADMISSIONS INFORMATION

Emma Willard seeks students of above-average to superior academic ability who are self-motivated, responsible, interested in learning, and involved in activities outside the classroom. All candidates for admission must submit an application, a personal essay, transcripts, three recommendations, and the results of the SSAT. Students for whom English is not their first language should submit the results of the TOEFL in lieu of the SSAT. An interview is strongly encouraged. Applicants for the postgraduate year should submit SAT scores.

APPLICATION TIMETABLE

Initial inquiries are welcome at any time. Campus visits include tours for parents and daughters, interviews, a class visit, and occasionally a meal. On weekdays, office hours are 8 a.m. to 4 p.m. Appointments may be made at any time of year, but October through April visits are strongly recommended. Open House programs are scheduled in the fall.

The application fee of $50 ($100 for international students) is nonrefundable. The application deadline is February 1. Prospective students and their parents are notified of the Admission Committee's decision in March. Applications received after that time are accepted on a space-available basis.

ADMISSIONS CORRESPONDENCE

Director of Admissions
Emma Willard School
285 Pawling Avenue
Troy, New York 12180
United States
Phone: 518-833-1320
Fax: 518-833-1805
E-mail: admissions@emmawillard.org
Web site: http://www.emmawillard.org

THE EPISCOPAL ACADEMY

Newtown Square, Pennsylvania

Type: Coeducational day college-preparatory school
Grades: Lower School, Prekindergarten–5; Middle School, 6–8; Upper School, 9–12
Enrollment: School total: 1,227; Upper School: 516
Head of School: Mr. L. Hamilton Clark, The Greville Haslam Head of School (through June 30, 2013); Mr. Thomas J. Locke (new head effective July 1, 2013)

THE SCHOOL

The Episcopal Academy is a coeducational day school that has educated the whole child—Mind, Body, and Spirit—for over 225 years. Founded in 1785 by The Right Reverend William White, the first Bishop of Pennsylvania, Episcopal's original purpose was to teach Anglican doctrine and train the clergy. However, Bishop White believed in free education for the poor, and in 1789, the Academy set up free schools for more than 100 children. After moving to a number of sites in Philadelphia, the Academy moved to the suburbs of Merion in 1921. Originally all boys, in 1974, Episcopal became coed and opened a second campus in Devon.

In 2001, Episcopal Academy's Board of Trustees launched an initiative to provide its community with the facilities it needed to do its best work, to experience a greater sense of unity, and to accommodate future plans. This endeavor was to build a new school, uniting two campuses, on 123 acres in Newtown Square, Pennsylvania. In August of 2008, Episcopal opened one of the finest day school campuses in the country. The facilities allow academic, athletic, and arts programs to flourish and Episcopal to stay at the forefront of curricular development and expansion for decades to come. The campus is valued at $189 million.

Hamilton Clark, The Greville Haslam Head of School, has led Episcopal for 10 years. A fundamental value of being an Episcopalian school is religious openness and acceptance, in every way respectful of all faiths, and the recognition that the presence of students, families, and faculty members of varied religions and backgrounds is vital to the vibrancy of the Academy's diverse community. Episcopal students are drawn from wide geographic and demographic backgrounds. There are over 1,200 students currently on the Newtown Square campus.

The Episcopal Academy takes every opportunity to keep alumni integrated in the life of the school, most specifically in counselor and mentor programs. Passing on the rich history and traditions to current students is part of the school's legacy.

Episcopal also has a very active parents association that sponsors events and provides services throughout the community. Through association activities, parents become involved in the day-to-day life of the school and contribute time and effort on behalf of their children and those of others.

The Episcopal Academy is accredited by the Middle States Association of Colleges and Secondary Schools and the Pennsylvania Association of Private Academic Schools. It holds membership in the National Association of Independent Schools, the Pennsylvania Association of Independent Schools, the National Association of Episcopal Schools, the National Association of Principals of Schools for Girls, the Association of Delaware Valley Schools, and the National Association of College Admission Counselors in compliance with the NACAC Statement of Principles of Good Practice.

ACADEMIC PROGRAM

The Episcopal Academy is renowned for its classical education, which combines the humanities and sciences with a focus on social responsibility and an individual approach to each child. The development of each student's Mind, Body, and Spirit begins in pre-kindergarten and continues through senior year.

The Upper School curriculum stresses clear, concise writing; reading; mathematics; the natural sciences; social studies; the arts; and foreign language proficiency. Added emphasis is also placed on preparing students for college and postgraduate study and in teaching students to take personal responsibility for their own education. All graduates go off to a four-year college, and a significant number of seniors are honored each year in the National Merit Scholarship competition.

To graduate, a student must acquire 19 credits (1 credit equals one full-year course). Graduation requirements include 4 credits in English, 3 credits in mathematics, 3 credits in science, 3 credits in history, 2 credits in world languages, 1 credit in religion, 1 credit in the arts distributed among at least two of the arts areas (music, theater, dance, and visual art), and successful participation in after-school athletic programs. Advanced Placement courses are offered in French and Spanish language, Latin (Vergil), calculus (AB and BC), statistics, Computer Science A, biology, chemistry, physics, studio art, art history, music theory, European history, U.S history, U.S. government and politics, and macroeconomics. In addition to AP courses, students may take honors courses in Latin, Greek, Algebra II, geometry, precalculus (AB and BC), Mandarin, Spanish, French, biology, chemistry, physics, and art.

Each student has a faculty adviser who supervises his or her progress and provides counsel in times of difficulty. The adviser and parents are encouraged to remain in close touch on both academic and nonacademic matters. In addition, each grade has a dean who remains with them for all four years.

The Upper School operates on a 12-day rotating schedule. The school year consists of two semesters. The recommended course load for all students is six courses during each semester. Teacher reports are sent out at midpoints of each semester.

Chapel is an important part of the Episcopal community. Upper and Middle School attend every other day, and Lower School students attend twice every 12 days. It is an affirmation of a wide range of faiths, cultures, and traditions and the powerful conservations that enrich individual understanding.

FACULTY AND ADVISERS

Episcopal's faculty (7:1 student-teacher ratio) is committed to each student's educational and individual growth. Close contact with faculty members enhances the quality of learning. In their roles as educators, advisers, and coaches, the Academy's teachers take notice and action—the "teacher-counselor-coach."

New faculty members are hired for their academic credentials, experience, and ability to contribute to school life beyond the classroom. Salaries are competitive, and turnover is low. Of the 176 faculty in the entire school, many hold advanced degrees as well as have served the school for 10 years or more. The school provides continuing education, collaborative summer work, enrichment, travel grants, and a sabbatical program for faculty members to continue study in their field.

COLLEGE PLACEMENT

The college planning process begins in the ninth grade. College guidance counselors meet with parents and begin to guide students through a process of self-evaluation in both individual conferences and class meetings. During their junior year, students build their Episcopal resume and begin the application process. More than 100 schools send admission representatives to Episcopal each year to meet with students. Through this guidance process, students and their families choose the most appropriate college, university, or program.

Episcopal students are consistently accepted by the nation's most selective colleges. Eight or more members of the classes of 2008–2012 have gone to Boston College, Boston University, Bucknell, Colgate, Cornell, Franklin & Marshall, Georgetown, Gettysburg, Harvard, Johns Hopkins, Lehigh, Penn State, Princeton, Syracuse, Trinity, Vanderbilt, Villanova, and Yale, and the Universities of Delaware, Pennsylvania, Pittsburgh, and Richmond.

STUDENT BODY AND CONDUCT

In 2012–13, the Upper School has 516 students: 275 boys and 241 girls. Eighteen percent are members of minority groups. Students come from Philadelphia, its northern and western suburbs as far as Lancaster, and nearby New Jersey. Students from Europe, China, and Australia have enrolled at Episcopal through various exchange programs.

The Student Council (2 faculty members and 24 students) is the elected Upper School student government. They represent a voice for the entire student body and serve in an advisory role for the administration while promoting school spirit, morale, and extracurricular activities.

ACADEMIC FACILITIES

At the Newtown Square campus, there is an individual building for Lower, Middle, and Upper School; an athletic center; a chapel; a campus center; a science center; a community garden, a greenhouse; the Sherrerd Alumni House; a maintenance facility; an outdoor playground and basketball courts; turf fields; grass fields; tennis courts; and a cross-country course as well as parking for 600. There are also two state-of-the-art libraries.

With more than 600 computers on campus, students and faculty and staff members have access to educational technology throughout the school. The entire campus is fully networked. In 2012, Episcopal launched a one-to-one laptop computer program in the fifth grade in order to facilitate collaboration and innovative teaching, and to give students access to a tremendous wealth of learning opportunities.

ATHLETICS

Episcopal has a strong physical education curriculum for pre-kindergarten through fifth grade. Athletics are required for grades 6–12. There are 30 varsity sports, and Episcopal's student-athletes compete at the highest levels. On the field, students learn honor in victory and grace in defeat, as well as how to accomplish a common goal by relying on others. Weight training, fitness, paddleball, bike polo, and dance options are also offered.

EXTRACURRICULAR OPPORTUNITIES

The Community Service Program is entirely voluntary yet enormously successful. Everyone, including faculty and staff, is encouraged to get involved. Approximately 97 percent of all students participate in the program.

In the Arts, students are able to participate in instrumental, vocal, drama, and dance groups during the school year. They can also work on the newspaper, yearbook, and literary arts magazine.

There are a multitude of clubs developed from student and faculty interests, including art, debate, television production, photography, poetry, stock market, cooking, chess, French, Student Council, Vestry, Social Impact, robotics, World Affairs, PRISM, science, and Community Connections, to name a few.

DAILY LIFE

The Upper School academic day begins with homeroom at 8 a.m. There is a 30-minute lunch at midday. Students attend Chapel every other day. Required athletics begin at 3:45 p.m. daily and end at 5 p.m. for those in intramural sports and approximately 6 p.m. for those on interscholastic teams.

SUMMER PROGRAMS

The Episcopal Academy offers a coeducational summer program for students entering grades K–12 that features personal and academic enrichment activities including visual and performing arts, athletics, science, and technology. Students can also take courses for credit to fulfill graduation requirements.

COSTS AND FINANCIAL AID

Episcopal Academy is committed to enrolling a diverse student body from varying economic backgrounds. Financial aid and admission are two separate processes; financial aid requests have no impact on the admission decisions made by the Admission Committees.

Upper School tuition for 2012–13 is $28,970. Additional costs vary by student. All financial aid is based on demonstrated financial need, as determined by the information families provide the Student and School Service (SSS), an independent scholarship processing center. A copy of the most recent 1040 form(s) is also needed, in addition to completing The Episcopal Academy Application for Financial Aid.

ADMISSIONS INFORMATION

Through a review of academic records, testing, and interviews, the family and the school carefully examine whether Episcopal will meet the needs of the student. The process helps establish the candidate's potential to benefit from the academic, physical, spiritual, and social/emotional atmosphere at Episcopal.

APPLICATION TIMETABLE

Application can be made by mail or online. Decisions on admission are made by an Admission Committee, which considers all the information, including the candidate's academic ability, achievements, and other interests. Early application is advised.

ADMISSIONS CORRESPONDENCE

Rachel G. Tilney, Director of Enrollment Management
The Episcopal Academy
1785 Bishop White Drive
Newtown Square, Pennsylvania 19073
United States
Phone: 610-414-1445
Fax: 484-424-1604
E-mail: rtilney@episocpalacademy.org
Web site: http://www.episcopalacademy.org/

GRIER SCHOOL

Tyrone, Pennsylvania

Type: Girls' boarding and day college-preparatory school
Grades: 7–PG: Middle School, 7–8; Upper School: 9–12, postgraduate year
Enrollment: School total: 290
Heads of School: Douglas A. Grier, Director; Andrew Wilson, Headmaster; Gina Borst, Head of School

THE SCHOOL

Grier School was founded in 1853 as the Mountain Female Seminary and was reincorporated in 1857 under the direction of Dr. Lemuel Grier. The School has been successfully operated under the management of four generations of the Grier family. In 1957, the School was reincorporated as a nonprofit foundation administered by an alumnae Board of Trustees. Grier is located on a 300-acre campus in the country, 3 miles from Tyrone, Pennsylvania, and halfway between State College (where Penn State University is located) and Altoona.

The School is committed to a highly supportive philosophy aimed at developing each girl's full potential as an individual. Competitive sports are offered but do not overshadow the many intramural, life-sports, and creative arts opportunities available to each girl. Grier does not seek an elitist or high-pressure label and is proud of its family-like environment. "Friendliness" is the word most often used by visitors to describe the atmosphere.

The current endowment stands at approximately $16 million, supplemented by $500,000 raised through the most recent Annual and Capital Giving program.

Grier School is accredited by the Middle States Association of Colleges and Schools. It has memberships in the National Association of Independent Schools, the Pennsylvania Association of Independent Schools, and the Secondary School Admission Test Board.

ACADEMIC PROGRAM

Grier offers a multi-track academic program. The Elite Scholars Program is well suited for high-achieving students interested in honors and AP courses. AP courses are offered in all subject areas as seventeen class offerings. While all classes are college preparatory in nature, the LEAP! program ensures that all students receive the support they need to empower themselves as learners. Every attempt is made to pace the curriculum to the needs of individual students, and crossover is permitted between the academic tracks according to the abilities of the students.

Learning Skills, a course taught by 3 specialists, is available for students who require additional academic structure and offered as part of LEAP! to provide opportunities for tutoring and the development of strong study habits. This program serves the needs of approximately 50 students at Grier. A comprehensive English as a second language program is offered to international students. Girls who test below 100 on the TOEFL Internet-based test are required to attend an intensive summer session.

Students are encouraged to take at least one elective in the arts each year. The variety of course offerings is designed to provide students with the opportunity to pursue areas of interest and to develop and enhance their individual talents. Strong programs are offered in studio art, ceramics, jewelry making, photography, weaving, costume design, dance, music, and drama. Art faculty members help students assemble portfolios in preparation for higher education.

FACULTY AND ADVISERS

The full-time faculty consists of 42 women and 18 men, more than half of whom have received advanced degrees.

Douglas A. Grier, Director of the School for the past thirty years, is a graduate of Princeton and has an M.A. and a Ph.D. from the University of Michigan. Andrew Wilson and Gina Borst are co-heads of the School. Headmaster Andrew Wilson has a B.A. from Middlebury College and has worked at Grier for twenty-six years. Head of School Gina Borst has a B.S. and an M.Ed. from Penn State University. She has worked at Grier for twenty years.

Many faculty members live on campus, and 22 housemothers supervise the dormitories. Faculty members are available for extra academic help on a daily basis. Faculty members also serve as advisers to students and participate in various clubs and sports activities.

COLLEGE ADMISSION COUNSELING

The School has a full-time college counselor who works with students in their junior and senior years. College counseling begins in the winter term of the junior year with class discussions about colleges, admissions requirements, and application procedures. The college counselor then discusses specific colleges with each student individually and helps the student develop a preliminary list of colleges to investigate and visit over the summer, thus refining the list. In the fall of the senior year, the counselor reviews each student's list again and encourages the student to apply to at least six colleges. Applications are usually sent by Thanksgiving (or before Christmas break at the latest).

Graduates of the class of 2012 were accepted at various colleges and universities, including Boston College, Bryn Mawr, College of William and Mary, Dickinson, Fashion Institute of Technology, Lehigh, Mount Holyoke, Parsons, Purdue, Skidmore, UCLA, and the University of Wisconsin.

STUDENT BODY AND CONDUCT

Students come from twenty-two states and fourteen other countries.

Students are expected to follow the rules as defined in the student handbook. A Discipline Committee composed of students, faculty members, and administrators handles all infractions. Grier believes that good citizenship should be encouraged through incentive, and girls earn merits for good conduct, honors grades, and academic effort.

The student government consists of a Student Council with representatives from each class. The council serves as a forum for student concerns and helps plan the weekend programs.

ACADEMIC FACILITIES

Trustees Building is a modern classroom facility that was completely remodeled in summer 2002. It houses classrooms, two science labs, a supervised study room, and studios for ceramics, batik, and photo printmaking. Adjoining buildings house computer studios, language classrooms, and the Landon Library, which houses 16,000 volumes. The Fine Arts Center, housing extensive facilities for music and art classes, opened in January 2002. The Science Center opened in August 2003. Grier's Performing Arts Center, containing practice and performance space for dance and drama, opened in June 2006. Three new classrooms and four music practice rooms were added to the academic facilities when a new dormitory was completed in September 2012.

BOARDING AND GENERAL FACILITIES

The living quarters consist of seven dormitory areas and five cottages. The dorms and cottages provide a modern private bath for every two rooms. Two girls share a room, and each combination of two rooms and bath is called a suite. All students must leave the campus for Thanksgiving, Christmas, and spring break, though the School does sponsor trips during Thanksgiving and spring break.

Multiple student lounges with TVs and games are available, and a School-operated snack bar is located in a remodeled eighteenth-century log cabin.

The Health Center is located on the campus and is staffed at all times for emergencies or any medical concern that may arise.

ATHLETICS

Students of all ability levels are encouraged to participate in either the interscholastic sports program, which includes riding, dance, basketball, soccer, volleyball, and tennis, or the life-sports program of riding, dance, swimming, tennis, fencing, archery, badminton, yoga, body sculpting, scuba diving, and skiing/snowboarding. Grier has an excellent horseback riding program with 3 full-time instructors and 1 part-time instructor. Four stables accommodate 35 School horses and up to 15 privately owned horses. Two indoor and two outdoor rings are located on the campus within an easy walking distance of the dorm. Grier's Western indoor ring was completed in September of 2012.

The School's gymnasium is well suited for basketball and volleyball. Grier's state-of-the-art fitness center opened in September 2006. Five tennis courts and ample playing fields round out the School's physical education facilities.

EXTRACURRICULAR OPPORTUNITIES

Student groups active on campus include Grier Dance; Grier Equestrians; the Athletic Association; drama, cooking, baking, outing, ecology, modern languages, and Grier Giving Back clubs; and the yearbook and School newspaper. In addition, students participate in "Green and Gold" intramural sports, which often include soccer, volleyball, basketball, softball, and horseback riding.

Creative arts play an important part in School life, and girls can participate in several activities for enjoyment and credit, including drama, photography, art, instrumental music, voice, and dance.

Nearby Penn State University provides many cultural, social, and educational opportunities. A wide variety of field trips are offered each year, ranging from rock concerts to ski weekends to trips to Washington, D.C., Pittsburgh, and New York City. A regular schedule of visiting artists and a movie series complete the social activities.

DAILY LIFE

Classes begin at 8 and run until 2:37, Monday through Friday; sports activities are scheduled during the next 3 hours. A 40-minute period is set aside daily for student-teacher conferences, and an all-School meeting is held daily. Students have a 105-minute supervised study period in the dormitories Sunday through Thursday nights.

WEEKEND LIFE

Because most of Grier's students are boarders, a comprehensive program of weekend activities is planned. Approximately eight dances are planned annually, usually for Saturday evenings. The Outing Club uses the nearby facilities of Raystown Lake for camping and hiking, and canoeing and white-water rafting on the Youghiogheny River are also popular. Tussey Mountain Ski Resort, near Penn State University, is 40 minutes away.

COSTS AND FINANCIAL AID

Tuition, room, and board for the 2012–13 school year was $46,800. Books cost approximately $400 per year. Off-campus entertainment is optional, with additional costs charged based on individual participation. A deposit of $4000 is due with the Enrollment Contract. Parents may elect to pay the entire tuition by July 1 or pay 80 percent in July and the balance in December.

Financial aid is based primarily on need. To apply, parents must submit the Parents' Financial Statement to the School and Student Service for Financial Aid in Princeton, New Jersey. In 2011–12, 35 percent of the student body received a total of $1.5 million in financial aid.

ADMISSIONS INFORMATION

Grier seeks college-bound students of average to above-average ability who possess interest in sports and the arts as well as a desire to work in a challenging yet supportive academic atmosphere. Applicants are accepted in grades 7 through 12 (and occasionally for a postgraduate year) on the basis of previous record, recommendations, and an interview. Grier School admits students of any race, nationality, religion, or ethnic background.

Approximately 50 percent of all applicants are accepted for admission.

APPLICATION TIMETABLE

Grier has rolling admissions, and the Selection Committee meets on a regular basis to consider students whose files are complete. Candidates are asked to file an application and transcript release form with a $50 application fee, submit two teacher's recommendations, and have a personal interview on campus. The Admissions Office is open for interviews and tours during both the academic year and the summer.

ADMISSIONS CORRESPONDENCE

Andrew Wilson, Director of Admissions
Grier School
Tyrone, Pennsylvania 16686
United States
Phone: 814-684-3000
Fax: 814-684-2177
E-mail: admissions@grier.org
Web site: http://www.grier.org

GRIGGS INTERNATIONAL ACADEMY

Berrien Springs, Michigan

Type: Christian distance education school
Grades: Kindergarten–Grade 12
Enrollment: Approximately 1,500
Head of School: La Ronda Forsey, K–12 Principal

THE SCHOOL

For parents seeking academic excellence for their children in a nontraditional educational setting, the distance education programs offered by Griggs International Academy (GIA) could very well be their answer. Griggs is a Christian online high school in America with dual accreditation—both regional (the same as classroom schools) and national (for distance education programs).

Since 1909 Griggs International Academy, together with Griggs University, has enrolled more than a quarter-million students from around the world. In July 2011, Griggs International Academy moved its main operations to Berrien Springs, Michigan. Griggs is now owned and operated by Andrews University, the premier university in the Seventh-day Adventist global education system. Identified by *U.S. News & World Report* to be one of the most culturally and internationally diverse universities in the nation, Andrews University is also listed as one of the top 650 colleges and universities in the country by *Forbes* magazine.

Griggs offers both online and print-based distance education courses, with reasonable tuition and a flexible schedule to fit the needs of the distance-learning student. Studies can be completed at a pace that fits the student's schedule with open enrollment allowing twelve months to finish any course.

In addition to a full diploma program, single courses are available as make-up credits or as supplements to a traditional classroom education. Thanks to Griggs' regional accreditation, most credits can be transferred to Griggs from a student's current school. Credits can also be transferred from GIA to schools in the United States as long as they are approved by the school's registrar.

Most of the school's junior and senior high school courses are available online, and both college prep and general high school curricula are offered. Dual enrollment is possible for academically advanced high school students. The school's teachers and administrative staff are readily available for aid and support as needed by each student and his or her parent.

Full-semester tuition amounts may be paid over several months with no interest charges. Griggs also offers a tuition refund policy for its diploma-seeking students, should they need to withdraw from courses.

Griggs has numerous accreditations and recognitions that reflect the high level of academic excellence in all of its programs and courses:

- Southern Association of Colleges and Schools (SACS) Commissions on Elementary, Middle, and Secondary Schools (regional accreditation)
- Distance Education and Training Council (national accreditation for distance programs)
- Middle States Association of Colleges and Schools (MSA) Commission on Elementary Schools
- Commission on International and Trans-Regional Accreditation (CITA)
- Accrediting Association of Seventh-day Adventist Schools, Colleges, and Universities (AAA)
- Approval as a nonpublic school by the State of Maryland

From its humble beginnings in a one-room school in 1909, Griggs International Academy has grown into a worldwide Christian school that maintains high academic standards with solid accreditations, and teachers who truly care about their students.

ACADEMIC PROGRAM

GIA offers a basic high school diploma and a college-preparatory diploma, with many courses offered both online and in print-based formats. The basic diploma requires 21 Carnegie units, which must include 4 units of English, 3 units of math, 3 units of social studies (one of which must be U.S. history), 2 units of science, and 4 units of Bible study (students may be excused from the Bible requirement if their personal convictions and familial belief systems so dictate). One half-credit is given toward a Griggs diploma for a student who has taken driver's education.

The college-preparatory diploma requires 24 units, including those listed for the basic diploma plus an additional unit in science and 2 units of a second language.

Many parents prefer homeschooling because it gives them more opportunities to interact and build solid relationships with their children. With the support and guidance of GIA, parents can manage what their children learn and when they learn it. Parents can also limit negative influences that children might be exposed to in a local school. Another advantage of homeschooling is that the family is not bound by typical school restrictions; they can travel and engage in experiential learning while still following a basic curriculum.

Each Griggs course comes equipped with the course instructional guide. All learning objectives, instructional sections, reading assignments, supplemental information, self-diagnostic tools, and lessons/submissions are included. The student also receives a full set of supplies, including a textbook and, when needed, additional electronic materials, lab equipment, and reading supplements. Experienced, certified teachers are assigned to each course to provide positive, individual interaction with students.

For most courses, two examinations are required each semester—a midterm and a semester examination. All examinations must be supervised by a school or community official (such as a teacher or registrar). If a student is enrolled in another school while taking GIA courses, the examinations should be taken under the direction of that school's registrar or testing department. Final grades are issued as A, B, C, D, or F. At the high school level, pluses and minuses (e.g., B+ and B–) are also used.

Because GIA's high school program offers year-round registration and self-paced instruction, students may adapt their class schedules to meet learning needs. The instructional materials engender self-discipline and motivation as well as academic excellence.

FACULTY AND ADVISERS

The writers for GIA courses are exceptional professionals in their specialties. The courses are intellectually stimulating and designed to foster the student's academic growth and curiosity. Griggs has dozens of faculty members and nonteaching professionals to provide assistance to students and parents. The majority of Griggs' faculty members have advanced degrees.

Faculty members are chosen on the basis of their expertise in their disciplines and their ability to counsel, advise, and instruct an international, multicultural student body in an online and distance-education environment.

COLLEGE ADMISSION COUNSELING

Graduates of GIA attend colleges and universities throughout the world. High school and college advisers provide guidance counseling and college placement information to all interested students.

STUDENT BODY AND CONDUCT

The GIA student body includes thousands of students across the United States as well as other countries.

Because Griggs is not limited to a traditional school year, enrollment figures may vary from month to month as new students enroll and others finish their programs. Griggs also provides opportunities for supplementing and augmenting programs for students attending traditional secondary schools.

DAILY LIFE

Distance education students can progress at their own speed, and they have the flexibility to plan the study portion of their day in shorter blocks of time than a traditional school. This allows for holistic personal development, providing time for greater physical, social, and spiritual development, and integrating academic learning into daily life activities and service to others. Full-time Griggs students can enjoy sport groups and have extra time to use libraries, museums, and faith-based activities in their communities. On average, full-time students spend 4 to 5 hours a day on their studies.

COSTS AND FINANCIAL AID

GIA offers two options for grades K–8—the Accredited Plan and the Non-Accredited Plan.

The Accredited Plan is approved and includes tuition, textbooks and instructional guides, daily lesson plans, exams, teacher assistance, grading services, record keeping, report cards, and transcript services. In the 2012–13 school year, the costs for core subjects for one full year, including a $25 enrollment fee, are:

- kindergarten, $337
- grade 1, $1086
- grade 2, $1194
- grade 3, $1069
- grade 4, $1036
- grade 5, $1371
- grade 6, $848

The grade 6 curriculum is also available online for $831.

The Non-Accredited Plan (K–8 only) is for those who choose not to use Griggs International Academy's teaching, grading, advising, or record-keeping services. However, this plan does offer instructional guides, activity sheets, tests (no answer keys for tests), and placement advising for the student (if necessary). Prices for the Non-Accredited Plan are substantially lower, and financial aid is not available. For the 2012–13 school year, costs for the core curriculum are:

- kindergarten, $167
- grade 1, $630
- grade 2, $715
- grade 3, $609
- grade 4, $556
- grade 5, $882
- grade 6, $441

The junior high program (grades 7 and 8) allows for more immediate interaction between parent and student. The programs are available online or in print-based formats. The 2012–13 prices for the four core courses, including an $80 enrollment fee, are: grade 7, $1100 and grade 8, $1139. This does not include the cost of shipping and handling. Sales tax is added if shipping to Maryland or Michigan.

The 2012–13 high school tuition is $240 per course per semester, plus the cost of books and supplies, an $80 enrollment fee, and shipping.

Because of its reasonable tuition and fees, Griggs does not offer financial aid. Parents are offered a payment plan that allows tuition to be paid over a period of three months. The school also offers a generous tuition refund policy for students who must withdraw from semesters or courses before they are completed. Please visit the Griggs Web site for details.

Online courses are not available in the Non-Accredited Plan. All prices are subject to change July 1 each year.

ADMISSIONS INFORMATION

Griggs accepts applications for admission at any time. Applications can be completed online at www.griggs.edu. Questions can be e-mailed to enrollgia@andrews.edu.

ADMISSIONS CORRESPONDENCE

Gabriela Melgar, Enrollment Counselor
Griggs International Academy
8903 U.S. Highway 31
Berrien Springs, Michigan 49104
United States
Phone: 269-471-6570
800-782-4769 (toll-free; inquiries only)
E-mail: enrollgia@andrews.edu
Web site: www.griggs.edu

THE HILL SCHOOL

Pottstown, Pennsylvania

Type: Coeducational boarding and day college-preparatory school
Grades: 9–PG (Forms III–VI)
Enrollment: 512
Head of School: Zachary G. Lehman, Headmaster

THE SCHOOL

The Hill School prepares young men and women from across the country and around the world for college, careers, and life. Founded in 1851 by Matthew Meigs, The Hill School is a purposefully small and close learning community—a place where academic excellence is based upon a challenging liberal arts curriculum; a faculty of highly qualified, dedicated teachers; a noteworthy breadth of advanced and honors course offerings; and a structured atmosphere that blends high expectations with meaningful support. Within a family school environment and a rigorous liberal arts curriculum, Hill challenges its students to work hard; think and reason; be fulfilled; serve the common good; and be prepared to lead as citizens of the world, uniquely guided by the motto, "Whatsoever things are true."

The Hill School operates as a not-for-profit institution with a 25-member Board of Trustees. In 1998, the School began admitting young women and became a coeducational institution.

The Hill's 200-acre campus in Pottstown is located 37 miles northwest of Philadelphia and 125 miles from New York City. Because of its Mid-Atlantic location, students at The Hill can take advantage of a balanced climate, including warm autumn weather and a winter season that makes possible such activities as skiing in the nearby Pocono Mountains.

The School's endowment is approximately $130 million. The amount of Annual Giving for 2011–12 was more than $2.5 million, with approximately 20 percent alumni participation.

The Hill School is accredited by the Middle States Association of Colleges and Schools and is a member of the Secondary School Admission Test Board and the National Association of Independent Schools.

ACADEMIC PROGRAM

The Hill School's principal academic goal is to instill in each student the capacity and desire to learn. The School maintains a student-faculty ratio of approximately 7:1 and an average class size of 13 students.

The Hill's graduation requirements include English in every year; mathematics through Algebra II; completion of three levels of one foreign or classical language (or two years in each of two languages); two years of history (one of which must be U.S. History, or U.S. History AP); two years of laboratory science (biology, chemistry, physics, environmental); and a course in the arts as well as one in religion or philosophy. Language offerings include Latin (through Vergil AP and post-AP offerings); four levels of Greek; Spanish (including both language and literature AP courses); French (including language AP and post-AP), and four years of Chinese including Chinese AP. Additional courses offered within the Department of History include World History; Modern European History AP; Islamic, Latin American, and Native American Civilizations; Government AP; Economics and Economics AP; and Psychology and Psychology AP. Department of Mathematics offerings include Algebra I and II, Geometry, Pre-calculus, Functions and Discrete Math, Calculus, Calculus AB AP, Graph Theory, Statistics and Statistics AP, Multivariable Calculus, and advanced topics. Science courses include Biology 1 and 2 AP; Chemistry 1, 1 Honors, and 2 AP; Physics 1 Honors; Physics Mechanics AP, and Physics E&M AP; as well as three levels of Computer Science, including Introductory, AP, and an advanced seminar in iOS development. Environmental Science Honors, Astronomy, Human Physiology, and Kinesiology also are offered. Current Arts courses include Photography, Studio Art, Theatre, Digital Arts, Woodworking, Speech, Chorus, Jazz ensemble, and Orchestra. History of Art and Music is required for all freshmen; Art History AP also is offered. Religion options include World Views and World Religions, Philosophy Seminar, Biblical Criticism, and God and Free Will, which is an honors-level course. Twenty-four Advanced Placement (AP) courses are offered; in 2012, 173 students took 384 AP exams.

Academic reports are sent home at the conclusion of each of the three terms. Comments from instructors, the dorm parent, and the academic adviser are mailed to parents after the fall and spring terms. Students have seven-day-a-week access to the teaching faculty, nearly all of whom live on campus; many faculty members live in the residence halls as dormitory parents. The School library is open every school day as well as weekends.

FACULTY AND ADVISERS

The Hill has 69 teaching faculty members. Seventy percent hold or are working toward advanced degrees. Nearly all reside in dormitories serving as dorm parents or live in homes on campus with their families.

Zachary Gimbel Lehman and his family arrived at The Hill School in July 2012. He is the School's eleventh headmaster. Zack came to the School after serving for six years as the assistant head of school for advancement at Gould Academy, a coeducational ninth through twelfth grade and postgraduate year boarding school in Bethel, Maine. At Gould, Zack also taught filmmaking, was the head coach for the boys' varsity lacrosse team, was an academic student adviser, and worked in the dormitories. From 2000 to 2006, Zack was the founding executive director of MetroLacrosse, a not-for-profit community organization that provides integrated lacrosse and character education programs to youth from underserved urban communities in Greater Boston and today has a national presence. Prior to leading MetroLacrosse, Zack was an attorney at Ropes & Gray and previously clerked for the chief judge of the United States District Court in Boston. A *magna cum laude* graduate of Harvard Law School, Zack also distinguished himself at Dartmouth College, where he earned a B.A. degree in geography, with *cum laude* and *Phi Beta Kappa* distinctions. At Dartmouth, Zack played varsity lacrosse and football; was an Academic All-American in football; and, as a Senior Fellow, produced an animated film that earned a Student Academy Award from the Academy of Motion Picture Arts and Sciences. Prior to Dartmouth, Zack attended Phillips Exeter Academy for four years, where he played three varsity sports, was a prep school All-American in wrestling, and graduated with high honors.

COLLEGE ADMISSION COUNSELING

For more than 160 years, The Hill School has prepared students for outstanding colleges and universities throughout the United States. The College Advising Office, staffed by 5 individuals, is devoted exclusively to helping students select appropriate colleges and universities and to helping them plan and prepare college admission materials.

Each year, more than 100 college and university representatives visit The Hill to present information about their institutions. Interested students are invited to attend these sessions, and Sixth Form students may schedule formal interviews with college representatives. During the Fifth Form year, students participate in a college forum class, which addresses the college application process. Topics covered include decision making, career interest identification, essay writing, interview techniques, methods of quality assessment, and SAT practice tests.

A complete range of standardized tests is administered on campus, including SAT and SAT Subject Tests, ACT, Advanced Placement, and TOEFL; students generally take those exams at regular intervals during the Fifth and Sixth Form years. The middle 50 percent ranges on the SAT for the class of 2012 were 550–670 critical reading, 580–680 math, and 570–690 writing.

Recent graduates are attending such colleges and universities as Amherst, Brown, Bowdoin, Bucknell, Colgate, Cornell, Dickinson, George Washington, Georgetown, Harvard, Princeton, Tufts, the United States Naval Academy, Wellesley, William and Mary, Yale, and the Universities of Pennsylvania, Richmond, St. Andrews (Scotland), and the South.

STUDENT BODY AND CONDUCT

In the Third Form, there are 62 boarding and 38 day students; in the Fourth Form, there are 90 boarding and 50 day students; in the Fifth Form, there are 97 boarding and 40 day students; in the Sixth Form, there are 135 students; and in the PG class, there are 19 students. Students come from twenty-eight states and eighteen other countries. Sixty-nine percent of the students come from Middle Atlantic states, with the rest of the students coming in equal measure from New England, the Southeast, and Midwestern and Western states. Thirty-four percent of Hill's student body is multicultural.

In 1997, the Hill School students and faculty members adopted a student-initiated Honor Code to promote an environment of mutual trust and respect and to uphold the School's principles of trust, honor, and integrity in all intellectual, athletic, and social pursuits. Most disciplinary matters are handled by either the Discipline Committee or Honor Council, depending on the nature of the offense. Both groups consist of students and faculty members who have been chosen by their peers.

ACADEMIC FACILITIES

The Hill School's academic facilities include the Humphrey Family Writing Center; the John P. Ryan Library, which houses two computer labs featuring brand new Apple computers equipped with the latest digital editing software; Harry Elkins Widener Memorial Science Building; the Center For The Arts visual and performing arts center, which includes The Boyer Gallery; and the Academic Center, home of the McIlvain Multimedia Learning Classroom, the George Berman Center for College Advising, and the Students Center and Grille.

BOARDING AND GENERAL FACILITIES

The Hill School's 12 dormitories are divided into residential units that most often house 12–16 students. Faculty members and their families reside in apartments connected to the dorms. Housing has been designed for 2 students per dormitory room. Two selected Sixth Form prefects, who share some supervisory responsibilities with the residential faculty family, live on each dormitory hall. New students are assigned roommates by the Residential Life and Admission Offices; in subsequent years, however, roommate selections are made by each student. There is a formal dining room where students and faculty families enjoy seated family-style and buffet meals.

The Student Health Service is staffed by full-time registered nurses and 2 physicians who are on call around the clock.

ATHLETICS

Athletics are an integral part of The Hill's educational offering. A program of twenty-nine sports enables each student to compete and develop expertise in the sports of their choice.

The athletic facilities at The Hill include a 34,000-square-foot field house and seven squash courts, a gymnasium complex, four basketball courts, a six-lane swimming pool, and a fitness center that includes twenty cardiovascular machines, Body Masters strength training equipment, and free weights. Additional structures include a collegiate-sized indoor ice-hockey arena and a wrestling room. The Hill shares an eighteen-hole golf course and owns eleven tennis courts and 90 acres of playing fields for baseball, cross-country, field hockey, football, lacrosse, and soccer.

EXTRACURRICULAR OPPORTUNITIES

Students at The Hill are involved in many pursuits that take them well beyond the classroom and frequently beyond the campus itself. The students publish a newspaper, a literary magazine, and a yearbook. Students fulfill a community service requirement, and they also initiate a variety of community-wide service projects. For students interested in music, there are several instrumental and vocal groups, including the Hilltones and Hilltrebles (a cappella groups), jazz ensemble, orchestra, chorus, and chamber choir. Other student organizations include the Hill Athletic Association, Student Government Association, Ellis Theatre Guild, and numerous clubs that reflect special interests.

Students also have many opportunities to enjoy trips to cultural events such as performances by the Philadelphia Orchestra or exhibits at the Philadelphia Museum of Art. In addition, numerous on-campus lectures, concerts, plays, and exhibits are scheduled to stimulate and enrich students' cultural life.

DAILY LIFE

Classes are held six days a week, with a midmorning chapel service on Monday and Thursday. A full academic day is divided into eight 40-minute periods, beginning at 8:25 a.m. and ending at 3:30 p.m. Wednesday and Saturday classes meet in the morning only. Athletic practice takes place between 3:45 and 5:45 p.m. Additional help with faculty members can be scheduled during free periods and in the evening. Student organizations typically meet after dinner. Evening study hours are supervised by faculty members and prefects.

Every Hill student gives back to the School by completing specifically assigned jobs within the School community several times each week for approximately 40 minutes each session.

WEEKEND LIFE

The Student Activities Office organizes weekend activities for Hill students. Off-campus activities include trips to movie theaters and malls, sporting events, amusement parks, outdoor activities (skiing, snow tubing, paintball), and excursions to Baltimore, Philadelphia, the Jersey shore, New York City, and Washington, D.C. Special on-campus events include concerts, dances, karaoke night, outdoor movie nights, the International Food Fair, and Spring Fling, where student participate in school-wide volleyball competitions and rock climbing, listen to live bands, and more.

COSTS AND FINANCIAL AID

The annual charge for boarding students in 2012–13 is $49,400. This fee covers instruction, board, room, concerts, lectures, movies, athletic contests, services of the School physician and nurses at daily dispensaries, and athletic equipment on an issue basis. It also includes subscriptions for the newspaper and the literary magazine. There is an optional laundry service for an additional fee.

The day student tuition in 2012–13 is $34,100, which includes lunch for every day except Sunday. All day students are required to board for one year.

Financial aid is awarded to students whose parents are unable to meet the full cost of tuition. Aid is granted without regard to race, color, or ethnic origin. Financial aid grants are based on the guidelines established by the School and Student Service for Financial Aid. Grants are renewed annually; parents must submit the School and Student Service for Financial Aid form each year. About 40 percent of students receive financial aid. Applications for financial aid should be submitted by December 15.

ADMISSIONS INFORMATION

The Hill School seeks to enroll students who show academic promise, intellectual curiosity, and strong character. The School encourages applications from students who demonstrate involvement in the arts, athletics, and community service. The following credentials are required for admission: a formal application; a writing sample; a transcript of grades; results from the SSAT, ISEE, PSAT, SAT, or ACT; a letter of recommendation from the school counselor and English and mathematics teachers; and an interview.

APPLICATION TIMETABLE

During the year preceding the applicant's proposed entrance, a formal application for admission should be filed, accompanied by a nonrefundable application fee of $50 ($100 for international students). January 31 is the deadline for consideration in the first round; late applications are considered on a space-available basis.

Families are encouraged to visit The Hill during the school term to meet members of the faculty and student body. An appointment should be made in advance.

ADMISSIONS CORRESPONDENCE

Thomas Eccleston IV, '87
Assistant Headmaster for Enrollment Management
The Hill School
717 East High Street
Pottstown, Pennsylvania 19464
United States
Phone: 610-326-1000
Fax: 610-705-1753
E-mail: admission@thehill.org
Web site: http://www.thehill.org

THE HOCKADAY SCHOOL

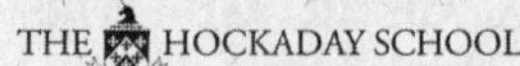

Dallas, Texas

Type: Girls' day college-preparatory (prekindergarten–grade 12) and boarding (grades 8–12) school
Grades: Prekindergarten–12: Lower School, prekindergarten–4; Middle School, 5–8; Upper School, 9–12 (Forms I–IV)
Enrollment: School total: 1,085
Head of School: Kim Wargo, Eugene McDermott Headmistress

THE SCHOOL

The Hockaday School, founded in 1913, provides a nationally recognized college-preparatory education for bright girls of strong potential who will assume positions of responsibility and leadership in a rapidly changing world. Ela Hockaday dedicated herself to giving each girl a foundation for living based on scholarship, character, courtesy, and athletics—the traditional Four Cornerstones that remain the dominant influence in the School's educational philosophy today.

Hockaday's campus encompasses almost 100 acres of open fields and wooded creeks in residential north Dallas. The School's contemporary architectural setting features an academic quadrangle built to provide views of exterior gardens and landscaped terraces. The science center and Clements Lecture Hall opened in 1983, the Ashley Priddy Lower School Building in 1984, the Biggs Dining Room and Whittenburg Dining Terrace in 1985, the Fine Arts Wing in 1987, the Lower School addition in 2001, the Liza Lee Academic Research Center in 2002 (renovated in 2012 to become the media epicenter of the School), the renovated Middle and Upper Schools in 2005, and the renovated Clements Lecture Hall in 2007.

A Board of Trustees is the governing body. The School's endowment is more than $120 million, and the operating income is supplemented by Annual Fund giving of more than $2 million. The Alumnae Association, with more than 7,000 graduates and former students, contributes significantly to the ongoing programs of the School.

The Hockaday School is accredited by the Independent Schools Association of the Southwest. It holds membership in the National Association of Independent Schools, the National Association of Principals of Schools for Girls, the College Board, the National Association for College Admission Counseling, the Educational Records Bureau, the National Coalition of Girls' Schools, the Online School for Girls, and the Secondary School Admission Test Board.

ACADEMIC PROGRAM

Students are exposed to a rigorous academic curriculum that offers core educational subjects as well as unique offerings in technology, the arts, and leadership and personal development. Graduation requirements (in years) include English, 4; mathematics, 3; history, 2.5; foreign language, 2; laboratory science, 3; fine arts, 1.5; physical education and health, 4; and academic electives from any department, 2, plus basic proficiency in computer usage. Hockaday offers 121 courses, including many honors courses. Advanced Placement courses are offered in eighteen subjects, including English, modern European history, U.S. history, AB and BC calculus, statistics, physics, chemistry, biology, studio art, Latin, French, Spanish, computer science, and economics. For some selected courses, Hockaday has a cooperative program with St. Mark's School of Texas, a boys' school in Dallas. Private lessons are available in cello, flute, guitar, piano, violin, and voice.

An English for speakers of other languages (ESOL) program is offered to students at the intermediate and advanced levels. Intensive language training in academic writing, critical reading, listening, and speaking skills is the focus of the program. Students may continue at Hockaday after the first year, following acceptance into the regular academic program. International students with intermediate or advanced English proficiency may study at Hockaday. Along with these special classes, students may study math, science, fine arts, and other courses in the mainstream curriculum. First-year ESOL students travel to the Texas Hill Country and Washington, D.C.

Class sizes average 15 students, with an overall student-teacher ratio of 10:1.

The grading system in grades 7–12 uses A to F designations with pluses and minuses. Reports are sent to parents at the end of each quarter period. High achievement in the Upper School is recognized by inclusion on the Headmistress's List and by initiation into a number of honor societies, including the Cum Laude Society.

Each student receives careful counseling throughout her Hockaday career. Academic counseling begins even in the admissions process and continues under the supervision of the counseling office, which coordinates the faculty adviser system and general counseling program. Each student has an interested, concerned faculty adviser to assist her with academic or personal matters on a daily basis.

FACULTY AND ADVISERS

The Hockaday faculty is represented by accomplished individuals, most of whom have advanced degrees, with 9 holding doctoral degrees.

Hockaday's teachers are chosen for their depth of knowledge in their fields of specialization, personal integrity, and the ability to facilitate the progress of individual students. Many are successful writers, lecturers, artists, musicians, photographers, or composers. Summer study grants are awarded to faculty members to encourage both research and professional development.

Ms. Kim Wargo, Eugene McDermott Headmistress, holds a bachelor's degree in journalism from Louisiana State University, where she graduated summa cum laude with minors in history and English. She earned a master's degree in history from Tulane University.

COLLEGE ADMISSION COUNSELING

The college counselors work directly with Upper School students in their college planning. Each student participates with her parents in conferences with the counselor concerning applications and final selection.

In 2011, SAT scores ranged from 620 to 740 in critical reading, 620 to 740 in math, and 650 to 780 in writing. The class of 2012 had 20 National Merit Finalists, 20 National Merit Semifinalists, 25 National Merit Commended Students, 1 National Achievement Finalist, 1 National Achievement Scholar, 1 National Achievement Outstanding Participants, and 3 National Hispanic Honorable Mention Finalists. Hockaday alumnae include Hesburgh-Yusko Scholars (Notre Dame), Jefferson-Echols Scholars (Virginia), Marshall Scholars, Morehead-Cain Scholars (UNC-CH), a Rhodes Scholar, and Truman Scholars. They have received the Michael C. Rockefeller Memorial Fellowship at Harvard and have been named to the Gates Millennium Scholars Program. Traditionally, 100 percent of Hockaday graduates attend four-year colleges or universities. The 120 members of the class of 2012 were accepted for admission by 175 institutions, including Bowdoin, Carnegie Mellon, Claremont McKenna, Duke, George Washington, Harvard, McGill (Canada), Middlebury, Northwestern, Oxford (England), Princeton, SMU, Stanford, Vanderbilt, Wake Forest, Washington (St. Louis), Yale, and the Universities of Chicago and Texas at Austin, among others.

STUDENT BODY AND CONDUCT

The student body is composed of 1,085 girls (75 of whom board) from eight states and eleven countries besides the United States. Thirty-eight percent of the girls are members of minority groups.

The Upper School Student Council and the Honor Council exert strong, active, and responsible leadership in student affairs. In addition to planning activities, allocating funds, and serving as a forum for student concerns, these councils promote and exemplify the School's written Honor Code.

Students are expected to abide by the guidelines set forth in the Upper School manual. Disciplinary measures rest primarily with the Head of the Upper School and the Headmistress.

ACADEMIC FACILITIES

The campus includes twelve buildings. The Liza Lee Academic Research Center is 52,000-square-feet and hosts two expansive libraries, several computer labs, debate team space, a state-of-the-art newsroom, a versatile hall that doubles as a lecture facility and audiovisual theater, a blue room, and an editing suite. In the academic area are classrooms; laboratories for languages, computers, and reading; and a study center. The campus is fully wireless, and all classrooms are equipped with SmartBoard technology for use in conjunction with students' laptops, required for every girl in grades 6–12. The Fine Arts facilities include a 600-seat auditorium, instrumental and voice studios, practice rooms, a painting studio, ceramics facilities with outdoor kilns, a photography laboratory, printmaking facilities, and an electronic music studio. The Science Center contains a recently renovated lecture hall, study lounges, classrooms, ten major laboratories, a computer lab, and a greenhouse. The Wellness Center includes the 5,000-square-foot Hill Family Fitness Center, an 1,800-square-foot aerobics room with state-of-the-art aerobic and resistance equipment, and athletic training facilities fully equipped for the treatment of sports-related injuries.

BOARDING AND GENERAL FACILITIES

Accommodations for boarding students are comfortable dormitories, updated study areas, and lounges. Girls of similar grades are normally housed on the same hall, each with its own lounge, kitchen, large-screen plasma television, DVR, and laundry room. The dormitories are wireless and all laptops are equipped with Skype. An additional common lounge has also been updated with a large-screen television, kitchen, and fireplace, which overlooks an outdoor swimming pool and tennis courts. Rooms are shared by two students, and each hall contains a small suite for the dorm mom in charge. The dormitories are closed for Thanksgiving, Christmas, and spring vacations.

The School's Health Center is located on the ground floor of the dormitory area, with a registered nurse on duty at all times and the School doctor on call. Campus security is maintained 24 hours a day.

The Wellness Center features an aerobics center, a fitness testing area, a trainer's facility, and the Hill Fitness Center, a 5,000-square-foot facility offering aerobic, resistance, and circuit training equipment.

ATHLETICS

Athletic facilities include two gymnasiums housing basketball courts (convertible to volleyball and indoor tennis courts), a climbing wall, two racquetball courts, a swimming pool, and a dance studio. On the grounds are six athletic fields, a softball complex, an all-weather track, a tennis center with ten courts and seating for 90 people. Interscholastic sports include basketball, crew, cross-country, fencing, field hockey, golf, lacrosse, soccer, softball, swimming and diving, tennis, track, and volleyball.

EXTRACURRICULAR OPPORTUNITIES

The Hockaday educational experience includes far more than just the classroom. There is a vast range of extracurricular opportunities for students to take part in: more than fifty student clubs, community service projects that impact the world beyond the campus, class bonding trips that build lifelong friendships, world-renowned speakers who expand students' perspectives, talent showcases at the Coffeehouse, and more.

To encourage student creativity, the Upper School sponsors a literary and journalistic magazine, a newspaper, and the Hockaday yearbook. These publications are edited by students with the guidance of faculty advisers. The literary magazine, *Vibrato,* won a gold medal with one all-Columbian honor from the Columbia Scholastic Press Association (CSPA). *Vibrato* has won top distinctions in ten of the last eleven years. Hockaday's student newspaper, *The Fourcast,* was awarded a gold medal with three all-Columbian honors, the highest score possible. NSPA rated the magazine first class with two marks of distinction. The yearbook, *Cornerstones,* was featured in a full-page treatment in the 2010 edition of Taylor Publishing's *Yearbook Yearbook.* All three of Hockaday's scholastic press publications were featured in the NSPA's *Best of the High School Press.*

Service to the School and its surrounding community is an important part of a girl's life at Hockaday. Each Upper School student is required to contribute a minimum of 15 volunteer hours per year in service to the wider community.

DAILY LIFE

Upper School classes begin at 8 a.m. and end at 3:45 p.m. Monday through Friday. The daily schedule provides time for academic help sessions and club meetings.

Varsity sports meet after the close of the regular school day. Boarding students have a 2-hour required study time, Sunday through Thursday nights.

WEEKEND LIFE

Off-campus activities each weekend enable resident students to take advantage of the many cultural and recreational resources in the Dallas–Fort Worth area. Faculty members are frequently involved in boarding activities, as are families of the Hockaday Parents' Association, who sponsor girls who are new to Hockaday and include them in family activities. Each resident student is matched with a local Dallas family through the Host Family Program. The host families offer local support for the girls and encourage their participation in social activities outside of school.

SUMMER PROGRAMS

A six-week coed academic summer session is offered for day and boarding students. Students may attend three- or six-week sessions beginning in June and July. Summer boarding is limited to girls ages 12–17. Programs in language immersion, math and science enrichment, computers, sports, SAT preparation, study skills, English, creative writing, and arts/theater are offered. Academic courses focus on enrichment opportunities. English as a second language, an international program lasting three weeks, begins in July. Information on the summer session is available in late spring. Applications are accepted until all spaces are filled, although students are encouraged to apply early to ensure their preferred course selection.

COSTS AND FINANCIAL AID

In 2012–13, tuition for Upper School day students averages $24,000. For resident students, costs are approximately $42,000 for tuition, room, and board. Additional expenses for both day and resident students include, among others, those for books and uniforms. A deposit of $1000 is due with the signed enrollment contract, and the balance of tuition and fees is due by July 1, prior to entrance in August. Partial payment for room and board for resident students is also made at this time. The room and board balance for resident students is payable by December 1 following entrance in August.

The Hockaday Financial Aid Program offers assistance based on financial need. Parents of all applicants for financial aid must provide financial information as required by the Financial Aid Committee. Over $3 million was awarded to students in 2012–13. Details of the programs are available from the Admission Office.

ADMISSIONS INFORMATION

Applicants to Hockaday's Upper School are considered on the basis of their previous academic records, results of aptitude and achievement testing, teacher and head of school evaluations, and, in most cases, a personal interview. There is no discrimination because of race, creed, or nationality. Because the School requires a student to attend the School for at least two years to be eligible for graduation, new students are not normally admitted to the senior class. In order to qualify for admission and have a successful experience at Hockaday, girls need to possess strong potential and a desire to learn.

APPLICATION TIMETABLE

Initial inquiries are welcome at any time, and applications are received continuously. There is a nonrefundable application fee for both day-student and boarding-student applications. Entrance tests are scheduled in December, January, and February and periodically throughout the spring and summer. Campus tours are available at convenient times during the year. Notification of the admission decision is made approximately six weeks after testing. Parents are expected to reply to an offer of admission within two weeks.

ADMISSIONS CORRESPONDENCE

Jen Liggitt, Assistant Head for Enrollment Management
The Hockaday School
11600 Welch Road
Dallas, Texas 75229-2999
United States
Phone: 214-363-6311
Fax: 214-265-1649
E-mail: admissions@mail.hockaday.org
Web site: http://www.hockaday.org

LAURALTON HALL, THE ACADEMY OF OUR LADY OF MERCY

Milford, Connecticut

Type: Girls college-preparatory day school
Grades: 9–12
Enrollment: 460+
Head of School: Antoinette Iadarola, Ph.D., President

THE ACADEMY

Lauralton Hall, the Academy of Our Lady of Mercy, is a Catholic college-preparatory high school, founded in 1905 by the Sisters of Mercy. The first independent Catholic college-prep school for young women in Connecticut, it is over 100 years old—a major milestone for any school and even more significant for a Catholic girls' school. A member of the National Coalition of Girls' Schools, Lauralton Hall is accredited by the New England Association of Schools and Colleges and the Connecticut Department of Education. The Lauralton day-school experience prepares girls to become competent, confident, and compassionate women, giving of themselves—especially to those in need. Students are challenged to succeed academically.

Lauralton Hall is one of a select group of Catholic girls' schools that has remained true to its original mission, which is to foster a community atmosphere enriched by the Mercy tradition and to educate young women to pursue knowledge, recognize truth, and respond to the needs of others. This empowers young women to excel in any endeavor, to find their own voices, and to be bearers of mercy for others. Since Lauralton believes character formation is as essential as academic achievement, the core values of a Mercy education play an integral role in a Lauralton Hall education: compassion and service, educational excellence, concern for women and women's issues, global vision and responsibility, spiritual growth and development, and collaboration.

Centrally located in historic downtown Milford and within walking distance of a train station, Lauralton attracts more than 460 students from over 35 towns. Students come by train, car, or bus, seeking the same rigorous preparation for college as the more than 6,000 alumnae who have passed through Lauralton's halls for over 100 years. The student body is composed of young women from diverse socioeconomic, religious, and ethnic backgrounds.

ACADEMIC PROGRAM

The well-rounded Lauralton Hall curriculum fully prepares students for college study, with demanding honors and advanced placement classes offered in all academic disciplines. As an added dimension, the formation of character is valued as highly as intellectual achievement. In keeping with the tradition of the Sisters of Mercy, students are constantly challenged to think of others and to reach out to those in need. They are expected to become Renaissance women for the twenty-first century—articulate and poised, confident and compassionate, gracious in their strength, at home in their own times, respectful of the past, and fully prepared to embrace the future.

Lauralton strives to develop clear, independent thinkers who appreciate knowledge and the learning process. The school offers a solid and well-balanced college-preparatory curriculum, which emphasizes a mastery of analytical and critical thinking skills, problem solving, and the ability to communicate ideas effectively. Challenging and demanding college-preparatory, honors, and advanced placement courses are offered. Courses are also available through the UConn Early College Experience (ECE), a concurrent enrollment program that allows motivated high school students to take UConn courses at their high schools for both high school and college credit. Every course taken through the UConn ECE is equivalent to the same course at the University of Connecticut. Established in 1955, the UConn ECE is the nation's longest running concurrent enrollment program and is nationally accredited by the National Alliance of Concurrent Enrollment Partnerships (NACEP).

Lauralton Hall offers advanced placement (AP) courses in calculus, chemistry, English language and composition, English literature and composition, environmental science, European history, French, Latin, music theory, physics, Spanish, and United States history. UConn ECE courses are offered in biology, elementary discrete mathematics, English literature and composition, European history, finite mathematics, French, fundamentals of music theory, Spanish IV, and U.S. history.

In order to graduate, a minimum of 25 credits must be earned, which must include six major subject areas (English, world languages, history, mathematics, science, and religion), a fine arts course, physical education, and 75 hours of community service.

FACULTY AND ADVISERS

There are 41 faculty members, 7 administrators, 4 guidance counselors, and 2 library media specialists. About 81 percent of the faculty members hold advanced degrees. The school is privileged to have the presence of 2 sisters on the school campus and 3 sisters active on the Board of Trustees.

COLLEGE ADMISSION COUNSELING

Individual conferences and group sessions are an integral, ongoing part of each student's guidance experience during her four years at Lauralton Hall. The counselors guide students in making appropriate college choices and help students with the application process.

All 108 members of Lauralton's class of 2012 pursued higher education after graduating. Sixty-nine percent of the class of 2012 were honor students. Well over $7 million in merit-based scholarships were awarded to the class of 2012.

In recent years, Lauralton Hall graduates have attended top-tier institutions such as Boston College, Brown, Carnegie Mellon, College of the Holy Cross, Columbia, Dartmouth, Duke, Georgetown, Harvard, Rensselaer Polytechnic Institute, the United States Military Academy, the United States Naval Academy, the University of Pennsylvania, Vanderbilt, and Vassar, to name a few.

STUDENT BODY AND CONDUCT

More than 460 young women from 35 Connecticut towns attend Lauralton Hall. The students are from diverse socioeconomic, religious, and ethnic backgrounds; about 77 percent are Catholic, and 18 percent are members of minority groups. Students are expected to abide by the codes of conduct found in the school's Student/Parent Handbook of Standards and Expectations.

ACADEMIC FACILITIES

The beautiful 30-acre campus surrounds a Victorian Gothic mansion built in 1864. The mansion and its property were purchased by the Sisters of Mercy in 1905 for use as a school. The administrative building, known as Mercy Hall, and the St. Joseph school building were added to provide classrooms, offices, an auditorium, a library/media center, and the school chapel. The school also has a music building, an athletic center, five new state-of-the-art science labs, and recently renovated art rooms.

ATHLETICS

At Lauralton Hall, students have the opportunity to participate in many different interscholastic athletics and are required to take physical education classes. "We've got the spirit!" summarizes what student athletes at Lauralton Hall experience: the joy of competition, pride in school and personal accomplishments, and the ability to win or lose with heads held high. Lauralton Hall athletes are expected to play fair, enjoy honest competition, and demonstrate sportsmanship, dedication, and compassion for one another, opponents, officials, and spectators. The school is a member of the Connecticut Interscholastic Athletic Conference (CIAC) and the South West Conference (SWC). There are fifteen varsity sports: basketball, cheerleading, cross-country, field hockey, golf, gymnastics, ice hockey, lacrosse, skiing, soccer, softball, swimming and diving, tennis, track and field, and volleyball. The campus has its own playing fields and an athletic center, which houses a basketball court as well as a fully equipped fitness center.

EXTRACURRICULAR OPPORTUNITIES

In preparing its young women to become visionary leaders and active members of their communities, Lauralton encourages each student to become involved in at least one extracurricular activity. Clubs, organizations, and activities bring new experiences, new challenges, and new friends. With more than thirty clubs and organizations to choose from, there is something to fit the interest of every young woman. Extracurricular activities include culture trips, student council, national and language honor societies, a fall musical, a spring play, Christmas and spring concerts, art club, youth and government, environmental club, percussion ensemble, Shakespeare club, humanities, classic film, dance club, Key club, debate club, world language clubs, student literary publications, yearbook, and school mixers/dances. New groups and activities are added yearly, based on student interest.

CAMPUS MINISTRY

Lauralton students are sisters in faith. They help the less fortunate and are stewards of the earth. They have retreats, liturgies, and prayer services.

The Office of Campus Ministry annually sponsors special collections to benefit those less fortunate. Lauralton's students generously embrace these initiatives. The four-year service program builds compassion and links the school to the global community through national and international mission trips.

The Lauralton Hall Women of Mercy award was created in 2004 to recognize young women, chosen by their peers, who exemplify the qualities of mercy established by Catherine McAuley: compassion, kindness, honesty, integrity, and care for the least of God's people.

DAILY LIFE

Classes begin at 8 a.m. with homeroom and end at 2:20 p.m., Monday through Friday. Sports and activities are offered after school.

SUMMER PROGRAMS

Lauralton Hall offers summer sports and enrichment programs for girls and boys. A qualified adult staff guides children through a week of learning and fun in a safe environment. Open to students ages 6 and up, these high-quality, educational, fun programs offer participants an opportunity to experience community and engage in diverse activities on the beautiful Lauralton Hall campus at various times and dates from the end of June through August.

Enrichment programs include a variety of offerings in art, sports, science, writing, cooking, and more. Recent sessions have included STEM Gems, video making, baking, all levels of cooking, Art Adventure, Fun Adventures, creative writing, CSI, physics, soccer, basketball, baseball, field hockey, lacrosse, softball, and cheerleading.

COSTS AND FINANCIAL AID

Tuition for 2012–13 is $16,175, plus the cost of books and uniform. There is also a $150 athletics fee per sport per athlete. Financial aid and scholarships are available. About 24 percent of students receive financial aid.

ADMISSIONS INFORMATION

Interested parents and prospective students, including transfer students, may request information by contacting Mrs. Kathleen O. Shine, Director of Enrollment Management at kshine@lauraltonhall.org or 203-878-3333. Information can also be accessed on the school Web site, www.lauraltonhall.org. Prospective students are also welcome to spend a day at the school.

APPLICATION TIMETABLE

Inquiries are welcome anytime. Applications should be submitted online by November 15, but they are accepted later, space permitting. The application fee is $60.

ADMISSIONS CORRESPONDENCE

Admissions Office
Lauralton Hall
200 High Street
Milford, Connecticut 06460
United States
Phone: 203-878-3333
Fax: 203-876-9760
E-mail: admission@lauraltonhall.org
Web site: http://www.lauraltonhall.org

THE LAWRENCEVILLE SCHOOL

Lawrenceville, New Jersey

Type: Coeducational boarding and day college-preparatory school
Grades: 9–PG (Second–Fifth Forms): Lower School, Second Form; Circle/Crescent Level, Third–Fourth Forms; Fifth Form
Enrollment: 819
Head of School: Elizabeth A. Duffy, Head Master

THE SCHOOL

The Lawrenceville School was founded in 1810 by Isaac Van Arsdale Brown as the Maidenhead Academy. Throughout the 1900s, Lawrenceville continued to develop as a leader in academic innovation, including early adoption of Advanced Placement (AP) courses and the introduction of nationally and internationally known guest speakers designed to broaden the intellectual horizons of young Lawrentians. Among the most-lasting changes was the introduction in 1936 of the Harkness method of education, which sought to bring the benefits of the House system to the classroom by providing an intimate environment for intellectual discourse.

Discussion of coeducation began in earnest in the 1970s, and after a lengthy, but thoughtful analysis of what it would mean both pedagogically and practically to the school, the Board elected to accept female students in 1985. The first girls arrived on campus in 1987 and brought a new vitality to the campus community. As the twentieth century drew to a close, the School embraced the ever-increasing diversity of its students in gender, geography, faith, race, and socioeconomic status, focusing on the need for a Lawrentian education to include broad exposure to all facets of the global community and an appreciation for and understanding of multiculturalism.

For more than 200 years, Lawrenceville graduates have gone on to success in their chosen fields, prepared by their education for the changing world around them. As the School enters its third century of educating students, it welcomes new students to join the legacy of Lawrenceville and discover what it means to be a Lawrentian in the twenty-first century.

The Lawrenceville School is located on 700 acres in the historic village of Lawrenceville, New Jersey.

The mission of the School is to inspire and educate promising young people from diverse backgrounds for responsible leadership, personal fulfillment, and enthusiastic participation in the world. Through its unique House system, collaborative Harkness approach to teaching and learning, close mentoring relationships, and extensive co-curricular opportunities, Lawrenceville helps students to develop high standards of character and scholarship; a passion for learning; an appreciation for diversity; a global perspective; and strong commitments to personal, community, and environmental responsibility.

Lawrenceville is accredited by the Middle States Association of Colleges and Schools and is a member of the Secondary School Admission Test Board, the National Association of Independent Schools, the New Jersey Association of Independent Schools, and the Council for Religion in Independent Schools.

ACADEMIC PROGRAM

The School's graduation requirements are designed to ensure students receive a strong foundation in all disciplines during their first two years that can be built upon in the upper forms. The requirements meet NCAA standards and are aligned with standard requirements for college admissions.

The requirements for entering Second Formers are: arts, 3 terms; English, 9 terms; history, 6 terms; humanities–English, 3 terms; humanities–cultural studies, 3 terms; interdisciplinary, 2 terms (at the advanced level); language through unit 9 (foundational level–through unit 6)*; mathematics through advanced algebra or precalculus (foundational level–through math 3)*; religion and philosophy, 2 terms; and science, 9 terms (foundational level–6 terms)*. Students are also required to give at least 40 hours of community service before they graduate. (*Students may opt to finish their course work in one of these disciplines at the foundational level with approval.)

Individual participation is encouraged in small classroom sections that average 12 students. Classes are grouped randomly and are taught around a large oval table called the Harkness table. Evening study periods, held in the Houses, are supervised by the Housemaster, the Assistant Housemaster, or an Associate Housemaster.

Students may also apply for independent study, off-campus projects, or the Lawrenceville international programs. Recent destinations include China, the Dominican Republic, Mexico, Japan, France, Peru, Nicaragua, Ghana, the Galapagos, Great Britain, South Africa, and Tanzania. Other opportunities include language immersion trips, where students reside with host families. Driver's education is also available.

Lawrenceville uses a letter grading system (A–F) in which D– is passing and B+ qualifies for honors.

The school year is divided into three 10-week terms. Full reports are sent home at the end of each term, with interim reports at midterm. The full reports include comments and grades from each of a student's teachers indicating his or her accomplishments, efforts, and attitudes. Less formal progress reports are also written by teachers throughout the term as needed. Students in academic difficulty are placed on academic review, which entails close supervision and additional communication with parents.

FACULTY AND ADVISERS

There are 143 full-time and two part-time faculty members, all of whom hold numerous degrees: bachelor's, 30; master's, 94; Ed.D., 1; M.D., 1; Ph.D., 17; J.D., 1; and professional, 1. Most faculty members reside on the campus, and many serve as residential Housemasters, coaches, and club advisers. All are active in advising and counseling students.

Elizabeth A. Duffy was appointed the twelfth Head Master of the Lawrenceville School in 2003. Ms. Duffy graduated magna cum laude from Princeton University in 1988 with an A.B. in molecular biology. In 1993, she received an M.B.A. from the Graduate School of Business at Stanford University and an A.M. in administration and policy analysis from the School of Education there. She has spent her entire career working with educators at all levels.

COLLEGE ADMISSION COUNSELING

The College Counseling Office supports, informs, and encourages students and their families as they navigate the exciting, complex, and ever-changing process of college admissions. The counselors educate students and families about the nuances of admissions, advise students about college options that best suit their individual needs, and support and encourage students as they complete the application process.

Lawrenceville's college counselors offer students decades of professional experience as college counselors and college admissions officers. The counseling staff provides valuable and timely advice to families as the process unfolds and helps students present their abilities, talents, and experiences to colleges in the most appropriate manner. The 5 counselors carry a small average case load of 45 students, which allows for personal attention and sustained involvement in all aspects of the residential school community. Over the course of their Lawrenceville careers, families and students receive information through form-specific newsletters, classwide meetings, and Parent Weekend programming. They also have access to Naviance, an online college admission management tool. All of these resources help ensure that students and their families are well prepared to embrace the college counseling process when students are officially assigned to individual counselors in the middle of their Fourth Form year.

The class of 2011's median SAT scores were: 676 critical reading, 683 math, and 687 writing. Between 2010 and 2012, the twenty colleges most attended by Lawrenceville students were: Princeton (43), Duke (31), Georgetown (29), NYU (24), Pennsylvania (20), Columbia (18), Brown (18), Dartmouth (16), Trinity (15), Cornell (14), Yale (14), Stanford (14), George Washington (13), Johns Hopkins (13), Virginia (12), Boston College (10), Chicago (9), Harvard (9), Williams (9), and Northwestern (8).

STUDENT BODY AND CONDUCT

For 2012–13, there are 819 students: boarding 561, day 258, boys 419, and girls 400. Students are from thirty-two states and thirty-four countries.

Lawrenceville expects its students to achieve good records and develop self-control, systematic study habits, and a clear sense of responsibility. The School has a high regard for energy, initiative, a positive attitude, and active cooperation. Students accepting this premise have no trouble following the basic regulations.

The student body elects 5 governing officers from among students in the Fifth Form, and each House elects its own Student Council.

ACADEMIC FACILITIES

Lawrenceville's first rate, state-of-the art academic facilities, which include the Kirby Arts Center, Gruss Center of Visual Arts, the F.M. Kirby Science Center, the Juliet Lyell Staunton Clark Music Center, Bunn Library, and the Noyes History Center, offer a unique opportunity for all students. Each building houses an entire academic discipline, so students are immersed within a particular subject from the minute they enter the building until the minute they leave.

Lawrenceville supports excellent teaching with outstanding educational and campus resources. The Bicentennial Campaign, completed in 2010 in honor of the School's 200th anniversary, demonstrated the intense willingness of alumni, parents, and friends to provide the absolute best facilities and support for students and faculty. This most ambitious campaign raised $218.5 million, exceeding the $200 million goal, for student financial aid, faculty support, academic programs, and student life. Among the campaign's successes were the new Al Rashid Health and Wellness Center, a state-of-the-art facility for both treatment and prevention; Carter House, a Fifth girls' residential house (opened fall 2010); and lighted turf fields of the Getz Sports Complex.

BOARDING AND GENERAL FACILITIES

Lawrenceville's most distinguishing feature is its House system. In each of the twenty Houses, the Housemaster maintains close contact with the residents. House athletics teams compete on an intramural level, and House identity is maintained through separate dining rooms in the Irwin Dining Center for the underformers. This distinctive system provides a small social environment in which each student's contribution is important and measurable.

Services in the Edith Memorial Chapel are nondenominational. The Al Rashid Health and Wellness Center offers inpatient and outpatient medical care, including psychological counseling services, and a consulting staff who offer gynecological care, orthopedic/sports medicine, and nutrition. Certified athletic trainers provide rehabilitation services for injuries. The Center's health professionals seek to educate and encourage students to develop the knowledge and skills needed to sustain a lifetime of healthy function.

ATHLETICS

Lawrenceville regards athletics as yet another educational opportunity for students and a valuable complement to the School's rigorous academic expectations. The importance of commitment; satisfaction of teamwork; hard lessons of failure; courage to surmount pain, fatigue, and frustration for a common goal; the virtue of physical conditioning; imperatives of sportsmanship; and the sheer joy of healthy competition are values Lawrenceville's athletic program is uniquely suited to teach. In addition, the School's proud interscholastic tradition and comprehensive intramural program, along with instruction in lifetime sports, ensure that each student experiences the challenge and reward of athletic competition.

The School takes pride in its first-class outdoor sports facilities: two FieldTurf artificial playing surfaces with lights for field hockey, lacrosse, and soccer; and eighteen other multipurpose natural grass athletic fields, including five intramural fields and two softball and two baseball diamonds. There are also twelve tennis courts, a nine-hole golf course, and a quarter-mile all-weather track. The crew program enjoys the use of a bay and other facilities at the Mercer Lake Rowing Association boathouse.

The Edward J. Lavino Field House is one of the finest in any independent school. The main arena has a Mondo surface with three combination basketball-volleyball-tennis courts; a four-lane 200-meter banked indoor track, with an eight-lane straightaway; and long jump, shot put, pole vault, and high jump areas. Along each side of the arena are two gymnasiums, a six-lane competition swimming pool, a wrestling room, a performance center, and an athletic training wellness room. A modern, enclosed ice hockey rink is attached to the Lavino Field House, and there are ten Anderson international squash courts. Nearby, a separate building houses the state-of-the-art, 4,500-square-foot Al Rashid Strength and Conditioning Center that is supervised by 2 certified coaches.

Students must participate in an approved form of athletic activity each term. Rehabilitation of athletic injuries and fitness testing are an important part of the athletic program and are available to students by Lawrenceville's 2 certified athletic trainers.

The School's outdoor, experientially based programs and initiatives educate students in responsible leadership, community membership, and character development and provide interactions in the outdoor environment, enhancing both academic and nonacademic skills development. Lawrentians have traveled the globe through outdoor program courses, scaling glaciers in Patagonia, trekking through the desert in South Africa, and sea kayaking among icebergs in Newfoundland. Athletic credit is given to participants.

Lawrenceville's ropes course offers students the opportunity to accept a challenge and work toward conquering it as a group. The course, created and built by an outdoor experiential education expert, is designed to help students listen to each other, trust each other, and work toward a common goal.

EXTRACURRICULAR OPPORTUNITIES

Lawrenceville provides a numerous opportunities for students to explore outside the classroom. There are more than eighty clubs and organizations specializing in interests such as writing, acting, debate, music, art, history, religion, science, photography, woodworking, and scuba diving.

Through the required Community Service Program, students serve as tutors, elementary school study center supervisors, and group activity counselors. The School sponsors organized educational and cultural trips to New York City and Washington, D.C.

Exhibits occur throughout the year. Several lecture programs bring speakers and artists to the campus. Annual events include Parents' Weekend in the fall, Parents' Winter Gathering, and Alumni Weekend in the spring.

DAILY LIFE

Lawrenceville students have their schedules packed full of classes, study hours, athletic practice, rehearsals, and time for friends, special events, eating, and sleeping. Students learn to manage their time, meet their commitments, and enjoy their friendships.

Classes begin at 8 a.m. on most days, and the dining center opens at 7 a.m. for breakfast. Each class meets four times a week for 55-minute sessions. Science and advanced classes have an additional 55-minute period each week for labs, extended discussions, test practice, writing workshops, etc. There also are three 40-minute periods each week for student-teacher consultations. Students are highly encouraged to take advantage of consultation periods.

The entire School eats lunch at the same time, and each House dines together. This tradition is yet another example of how the House system defines the Lawrenceville experience. On Mondays, students take lunch with their academic advisers. Each advisee group shares a table, and time is spent discussing both individual and group concerns; if needed, students can schedule a private meeting with their adviser.

The entire School assembles once a week for an all-School community meeting. These gatherings feature readings, reflections, and announcements. School meeting agendas include outside speakers, special guests, musical presentations, and opportunities to examine student issues.

Classes end at 3:05 p.m., but then there is more to do—sports or community service. On Wednesdays, classes end at 12:20 p.m., and students have the option of studying, rehearsing, practicing sports, working on publications, or fulfilling their community service requirement. Saturday classes end at 11:30 a.m..

Dinner is served from 5:30 to 7 p.m. All Forms eat in the Irwin Dining Center, except for the Fifth Form, which takes meals in the Abbott Dining Room in the Upper House. After dinner, there is time for clubs, activities, homework, and socializing. Check-in is at 8 p.m. for Lower School, 8:30 p.m. for Crescent and Circle Houses, and 9 p.m. for the Fifth Form, Sunday–Friday. Permission to leave the House after check-in to go to the library, rehearsals, club meetings, or to meet a teacher for consultation is granted after check-in time, but students must check back in with the Housemaster on duty by 10 p.m. (11 p.m. on Saturday).

WEEKEND LIFE

On weekends, at least one House sponsors an all-School social event, which may include carnivals, concerts, formal dinners, and dances. Faculty members are on hand to take trips to local shopping areas and movie theaters. Reach Out to the Arts is a faculty-led club that takes weekly trips to cultural events in New York. Day students are encouraged to attend all-campus activities.

COSTS AND FINANCIAL AID

The annual charges for 2012–13 are $51,025 for boarding students and $42,185 for day students.

Through the generosity of alumni, friends, and foundations, approximately $10.1 million in funds are available to provide financial assistance to qualified students. Currently, 29 percent of the student body receives assistance. Awards are made on the basis of character, ability, past performance, and future promise. Amounts are based solely on need and are determined by procedures established by the School and Student Service for Financial Aid.

ADMISSIONS INFORMATION

All students who enter must be able to meet the academic standards. Lawrenceville also looks for students who possess the potential to become vitally interested members of the student body—students who make individual contributions.

Selection is based on all-around qualifications without regard to race, creed, or national origin. Character, seriousness of purpose, and future promise as well as past performance, the recommendation of a headmaster or principal, and SSAT results are all taken into consideration by the Admission Committee.

For fall 2012, there were 2,063 formal applications for grades 9–12, of which 249 enrolled. Thirty-three percent were from public schools, 43 percent from private schools, 16 percent from international schools, and 8 percent from church-related schools.

Required for admission is the formal application, which includes a written essay, a transcript of the applicant's school record, a letter of recommendation from the head of the current school, three reference letters, SSAT or ISEE and/or TOEFL scores, and an on-campus interview.

APPLICATION TIMETABLE

Campus interviews are conducted during the week from 9 a.m. to 2 p.m. Monday, Tuesday, Thursday, and Friday. Applicants can also interview on Wednesdays from 9 to 10:30 and on Saturdays from 8:30 to 10:30. Interviews are not conducted on Saturdays during the summer months.

The application deadline is January 31 for boarding students and January 14 for day students, at which time all application materials must be submitted and interviews completed. The notification date is March 10, and parents reply by April 10.

ADMISSIONS CORRESPONDENCE

Dean of Admission
The Lawrenceville School
2500 Main Street
P.O. Box 6008
Lawrenceville, New Jersey 08648
United States
Phone: 609-895-2030
800-735-2030 (toll-free outside New Jersey)
Fax: 609-895-2217
E-mail: admissions@lawrenceville.org
Web site: http://www.lawrenceville.org

THE LINSLY SCHOOL

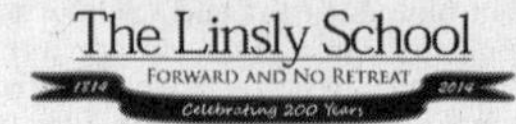

Wheeling, West Virginia

Type: Independent, coeducational, college-preparatory boarding and day school
Grades: 5–12
Enrollment: 440 students; 100 boarding students
Head of School: Chad Barnett

THE SCHOOL

Founded in 1814, the Linsly School is a private, independent day and boarding school for students in grades 5 through 12. Located in Wheeling, West Virginia, the School offers a college-preparatory curriculum that combines the traditional values of hard work, respect, honor, honesty, and self-discipline within a challenging academic program designed to unlock the potential of each student.

The family-like atmosphere at Linsly helps students grow and develop under the guidance of faculty members who know them by name and care about their future. Learning is not limited to the classroom—it happens over lunch, dinner, evening study hall, and at any time—learning at Linsly never ends.

Linsly is a place where lifelong friendships between students and faculty are formed. Students wear uniforms, not to encourage conformity, but to ensure that they are known for their unique ideas and abilities. Linsly is a school where long-forgotten traditional values live on in everyday curriculum.

With 100 percent college placement, Linsly's record as an excellent college-preparatory academy speaks for itself. But the School also teaches that there is more to education than test scores and college acceptance letters. Every day, students learn by living many of life's most important principles: responsibility, commitment, time management, sportsmanship, maturity, and even disappointment. The School's no-quit policy teaches students to finish what they start and to follow through with their commitments.

The education a student earns at Linsly is both deep and lasting because life's lessons continually emerge. The experience fosters lifelong learning to prepare students for college and life.

ACADEMIC PROGRAM

At Linsly, academic excellence has always been developed through a traditional curriculum enhanced with contemporary courses. While some schools claim to go back to basics, Linsly is proud to have never left them.

The academic program is rigorous and challenging to every student. Advanced-level courses are available in both the high school and the middle school curriculum, ensuring that even the most gifted students will be intellectually challenged.

Class grades are computed on a numerical basis. All grades below 70 percent are considered failing. Certain grades are indicated by letter grade (92 and up, A; 83–91, B; 74–82, C; 70–73, D). Report cards are mailed home four times a year at the end of every grading period. Students receive a separate report for each subject. A student having attained an average of 92 percent has earned second honors. A student having received an average of 95 percent has earned first honors. In addition, deficiency reports and/or progress reports are mailed to parents at the midpoint of each grading period. Lower School students receive letter grades in computer and physical education/health twice a year, at the end of each semester. Lower School students receive letter grades in fine arts courses every grading period.

A full program of college preparatory subjects is offered at Linsly. All students must carry a five-course per semester class load (excluding physical education). Full credit courses meet five times weekly for the entire year. However, there are certain half-credit courses which meet three times weekly for a year, or every day for a semester. Twenty credits are required for graduation and must include the following minimums: 4 credits of English, 4 credits of mathematics, 3 credits of social studies, 3 credits of the same foreign language, 3 credits of science (2 laboratory sciences), physical education, 1 Full credit of Fine Arts including Art Appreciation and Music Appreciation, ½ credit of computer science, and the Senior Research Essay.

FACULTY AND ADVISERS

Linsly teachers share a common calling. They are not individuals who see education as an 8-to-3 job. They are not individuals who see themselves as specialists in a very narrow area, uninterested in broadening the education of their students. Linsly teachers are interested in the complete development of their students. They are diverse in their talents, varied in their interests, and committed to a model of education that places the relationship with their students at the heart of the teaching experience.

Many of Linsly's faculty members live on campus, making them readily accessible for extra help and counsel. As advisers, the faculty members build strong and lasting relationships with their students. This strong sense of community is felt in all aspects of school life at Linsly. The School is extremely proud of its accomplished and respected faculty and administrative team.

Linsly's Advisory Program provides guidance from the faculty members in both academic and personal matters and allows a small group of students and a faculty mentor to get to know one another personally outside of the academic environment. Students meet daily for the first 10 minutes of the academic day with other advisees. While this is an ideal time for group discussions, students may call upon their faculty adviser for help or advice whenever needed. The average advisory group consists of 10 students. New students are assigned advisers, and returning students choose their adviser at the end of every year. The adviser becomes the student's close personal contact with the School, and advisers are available to offer assistance in all areas of a student's life.

COLLEGE ADMISSION COUNSELING

Linsly's college counseling office seeks to find the best college or university to match each individual student's needs and interests. The School's director of college counseling conducts a thorough program of testing and interviews with both students and parents throughout each high school student's Linsly career. College counseling begins in the sophomore year when students sit for their first PSAT and SAT tests. Taking these exams early allows students to become familiar with their test-taking abilities and provides instructors with the data necessary to help meet the academic needs of a particular individual or body of students.

A multiyear, comprehensive SAT-preparation program begins in the sophomore year and concludes prior to the student's first senior SAT. In addition to regular administration of the PSAT, SAT, and SAT Subject Tests, each student goes through a thorough interview process including the Strong Interest Inventory to help them discover academic and career interests. This individual attention and concern helps students gain an understanding of their academic and personal priorities when selecting institutions of higher learning.

STUDENT BODY AND CONDUCT

There are approximately 440 students enrolled at the Linsly School during the academic year. Students in grades 5 through 8 are considered members of Linsly's Lower School. The Upper School is comprised of students in grades 9 through 12.

Daily life at Linsly is based on principles of mutual respect and cooperation. Students are encouraged to accept responsibility, express themselves openly, and develop a strong sense of self-awareness and self-confidence. Boys and girls adhere to a dress code designed to distinguish themselves by their accomplishments rather than by their appearance.

ACADEMIC FACILITIES

Linsly's scenic 65-acre campus offers an ideal setting for a safe and vibrant learning community. Tucked behind Wheeling's historic National Road, and bordered by Wheeling Creek, the Linsly campus functions as an extensive classroom. The School's location makes it an attractive educational option for families throughout West Virginia, Pennsylvania, Ohio, and beyond.

With nearly twenty faculty residences situated throughout campus, Linsly's neighborhood feeling provides all students an encouraging and attentive place to grow and learn.

Linsly's Banes Hall serves as the School's primary academic building. The 80,000-square-foot structure houses twenty-seven classrooms, modern science laboratories, upgraded computer centers, a technology-rich library, music room, swimming pool, and cafeteria. The Williams Visual Arts Center provides top-quality studio, classroom, and gallery space, while the Hess Center offers equipment for students interested in woodworking. The Dlesk Conference Center is a unique place for meetings or searching the Linsly history archives housed there.

BOARDING AND GENERAL FACILITIES

Any student living outside the day student area (as defined by the School) must live in a Linsly dormitory. Weiss Hall, Merriman Hall, Yost Hall, and the Dicke Dorm are operated for those students who reside outside the Wheeling area and who have a strong desire to participate in the Linsly education program.

The layout of each of the dormitories is different. Within each dormitory there are faculty members assigned a specific section or wing. The Dormitory Master for that section is responsible for prescribing specific rules and the conduct of the residents. Students are not permitted in other dormitories or in other wings without consent.

The Linsly campus is located approximately 1 hour from the Pittsburgh International Airport. If necessary, the School can help parents arrange transportation to and from the airport for boarding students.

ATHLETICS

At Linsly, athletics are an important part of a well-rounded education; they not only contribute to physical well-being, but they also teach valuable lessons. Through athletics, students learn that hard work, perseverance, sportsmanship, and teamwork count at least as much as winning.

Every Linsly student is encouraged to participate in athletics. Lower School students can play on interscholastic teams, and all participate in a spring intramural sports program. The Upper School athletic program includes more than twenty interscholastic teams, which compete in both the Ohio Valley Athletic Conference (OVAC) and the Interstate Prep School League. Even students who are not athletically inclined can choose an appropriate sport and work with a coach to gain satisfaction of meeting the sport's physical and mental challenges.

EXTRACURRICULAR OPPORTUNITIES

Linsly provides a wide range of extracurricular options considered essential to the overall educational process. The Student Life program gives each student the opportunity to express his or her individuality through participation in activities that meet a variety of needs and interests.

Throughout the year, the School sponsors dances, fun activities, and on-campus events that highlight the talents of the diverse student body. A weekly all-school meeting is held to recognize accomplishments both in and outside of school.

Linsly offers a variety of special interest and community service clubs and organizations to give students the opportunity to participate in areas where they have interests and abilities. Participation helps each student develop a sense of responsibility for their community that is important to the individual and the school. Once a student begins a commitment, they must finish the commitment. The clubs and organizations meet regularly during specified times during the school day or after school. Some of the extracurricular activities offered include animal shelter club, Lower School band, yearbook, newspaper, chorus, Upper and Lower School drama, stage band, forensics, French club, German club, Fellowship of Christian Athletes, Key Club, Shakespeare club, Spanish club, Upper School math club, chess club, Lower School newspaper, classical club, puzzlemaniacs, history club, Model United Nations, environmental club, outdoor adventure club, multicultural club, technology club, Scrabble club, and Students Against Destructive Decisions.

DAILY LIFE

The school day begins at 8 a.m. when students meet in adviser groups for 10 minutes. Fifty-minute academic periods begin at 8:10. At 9:50 there is a half-hour flexible period to allow School clubs and class meetings to take place. The five remaining 50-minute periods are broken up by a half-hour lunch period. The Lower School eats at noon, and the Upper School eats at 12:50.

COSTS AND FINANCIAL AID

Tuition for the 2012–13 academic year is $14,920 for day students and $30,710 for boarding students. The cost of books, uniforms, and supplies is approximately $1000.

The Linsly School seeks to attract and maintain a highly capable and diverse student body. To help meet that commitment the School offers financial aid to qualified students on the basis of the demonstrated financial need of the family and the availability of funds. Families should not be discouraged from applying because of limited financial resources. For the 2012–13 academic year, 44 percent of Linsly students received awards totaling $1.8 million.

The Linsly School now proudly ranks among fifty other independent schools across the United States to have been awarded the prestigious Malone Scholars Grant, a $2 million endowment designed to support the School's scholarship program.

The Linsly School does not offer merit scholarships; the financial aid program is need-based. It is the School's expectation that families receiving financial assistance embrace the value of a Linsly education and make it a priority in their financial planning.

Financial aid decisions are made independent of admission decisions. Once students who have applied for financial aid are accepted in the admission process, they are referred to the Financial Aid Committee, which reviews the family's financial information, calculates their demonstrated need, and determines their financial aid awards.

Questions or concerns about financial aid or the financial aid application process should be directed to Craig Tredenick, Linsly's Director of Admissions and Financial Aid.

ADMISSIONS INFORMATION

Families interested in learning more about Linsly can request information by calling the Admissions Office at 304-233-1436 or e-mailing admit@linsly.org. In addition, families can submit an inquiry form via the Linsly School's Web site at www.linsly.org/admissions.

There are three main steps to Linsly's admissions process. The first is to schedule a visit by contacting the Admissions Office, Monday–Friday, 8 a.m. to 4 p.m. Weekend visits are also available. A campus visit will last approximately 2 hours and will include a tour of campus, an interview with the admissions director, and the completion of the School's admissions test. Interested students may also attend a Campus Visit Day.

The second step is to complete and submit an application and supporting materials (two essays, teacher recommendations, standardized test scores, and a parent survey). Finally, if the applicant family plans to apply for financial aid, they need to notify the admissions office; the application information will be forwarded to them.

Once an application for admission is completed, the admissions committee meets to discuss each applicant. When a decision is made, the admissions office will notify the applicant of the decision.

APPLICATION TIMETABLE

An application for admissions and all supporting documents should be submitted to the admissions office by mid-December (decision by mid-January) or mid-February (decision by mid-March). Specific deadline dates for each year are available on the School's Web site. The deadline for International Student applications is usually the end of January.

ADMISSIONS CORRESPONDENCE

Craig Tredenick
Director of Admissions
Linsly School
60 Knox Lane
Wheeling, West Virginia 26003
United States
Phone: 304-233-1436
E-mail: admit@linsly.org
Web site: http://www.linsly.org/admissions

LYNDON INSTITUTE

Lyndon Center, Vermont

Type: College-preparatory and general academic coeducational day and boarding school
Grades: 9–12
Enrollment: 600 (approximate)
Head of School: Richard D. Hilton, Headmaster

THE SCHOOL

Lyndon Institute is an academic community providing students with excellent preparation for success in school, college, careers, and life.

Lyndon Institute (LI) was founded in 1867 in the tradition of the New England academy. The Institute still shows the effects of the shaping hand of T. N. Vail, founder of AT&T, who served as president of LI in the early 1900s and was responsible for considerable growth in its programs and facilities.

An accomplished faculty that includes published authors, noted artists, college faculty members, and others active in their professional fields provides a challenging, comprehensive educational program in a picturesque Vermont village setting. Lyndon students enjoy personal attention from the faculty members, genuine respect for their individuality and unique talents, a truly inclusive environment, and outstanding preparation for their choices of colleges and careers.

Lyndon Institute consists of three adjacent campuses on 150 acres centered on the village green of historic Lyndon Center, Vermont. It is a safe, supportive community of exceptional beauty.

LI is located 10 miles north of St. Johnsbury on Interstate 91. Boston and Hartford are 3–4 hours away by car. Burlington, Vermont, and Montreal, Quebec are only 2 hours from the campus. Airline service to Burlington; Manchester, New Hampshire; or Boston, Massachusetts, provides easy access. Burke Mountain Ski Area is 7 miles away.

The school's operating budget is $10.1 million; parents, friends, and an active alumni group raise about $250,000 in annual support. The endowment is $8 million.

Lyndon Institute is accredited by the New England Association of Schools and Colleges and approved by the Vermont Department of Education. Memberships include the Independent School Association of Northern New England, the Vermont Independent School Association, the Secondary School Admission Test Board, and The Association of Boarding Schools.

ACADEMIC PROGRAM

Lyndon Institute is a comprehensive secondary school offering college-preparatory and fine arts programs of study as well as graphic arts and graphic engineering courses. Twenty-two credits are required for graduation, with the following distribution: English, 4 credits; social studies, 3 credits; mathematics, 3 credits; science, 3 credits; fine arts, 1 credit; health and physical education, 2½ credits; and electives, 4½ credits.

Other course offerings include French, 4 years; Mandarin Chinese, 1 year; Latin, 4 years; Spanish, 4 years; Russian, 4 years; band and chorus, 4 years; art, 4 years; theater, 1 year; advanced math, 2 years; algebra, 2 years; geometry, 1 year; Calculus, 2 years; biology, 2 years; chemistry, 2 years; physics, 2 years; technology, 14 courses; drafting, 5 courses, including computer-aided design. Honors courses are offered in American literature, English literature, algebra 1 and 2, geometry, world geography, U.S. history, contemporary U.S. history, world civilizations, biology, chemistry, physics, and advanced art. LI offers Advanced Placement courses in English composition, English literature, biology, chemistry, physics B, environmental science, European history, U.S. history, calculus A/B and B/C, studio art in both drawing and design, and music theory.

The fine and performing arts program allows students to take a series of courses within the fine arts concentration, which includes concert band, improvisation, music theory, chorus, select chorus, world music, art, art 4, advanced art, book arts, painting, printmaking, 2-D design, photography, dance, jazz dance, lyrical ballet, and acting.

Classes are grouped on the basis of ability. The student-teacher ratio is 10:1, with an average class size of 18. The grading system ranges from A to F and is calculated on a 4-point scale: A, 4.0; B, 3.0; C, 2.0; D, 1.0; and F, 0.0. The academic year is divided into two semesters consisting of two quarters each. Exchange trips are available during vacation times, and many opportunities for class travel are offered throughout the year.

FACULTY AND ADVISERS

There are 54 full-time and part-time faculty members at Lyndon Institute. Fifty-five percent have earned a master's degree or higher.

Richard D. Hilton was appointed Headmaster in 1999. He holds a B.A. in English from Notre Dame and a master's degree from Villanova.

COLLEGE ADMISSION COUNSELING

College planning is accomplished through individual and small-group counseling beginning in the freshman year. Two full-time counselors work in concert with students and families to develop postsecondary plans. In a student's junior year, counselors from the Student Services Office help with coordinating college applications and essay writing.

Representatives from more than thirty colleges visit Lyndon Institute annually. LI cosponsors the Northeast Kingdom College Night program each spring with representatives from more than 100 colleges and universities in attendance.

Last year, 86 percent of LI graduates pursued postsecondary options. Recent graduates have attended Berkeley, Boston College, Boston University, Brown, Clarkson, Cornell, Dartmouth, Fordham, Georgia Tech, Harvard, Indiana, Michigan State, Northeastern, Parsons, Penn State, Purdue, Rensselaer, Smith, St. Lawrence, Syracuse, and the Universities of Arizona, Connecticut, Illinois, Maine, Massachusetts, Michigan, New Hampshire, Vermont, Washington, and Wisconsin.

STUDENT BODY AND CONDUCT

The total enrollment is approximately 600 students, who come from the surrounding communities in Vermont and New Hampshire and from countries around the globe. The school implemented a boarding program in 2003–04, which included 100 students in grades 9–12 during the 2011–12 school year. Countries represented in the international program in the last five years include Afghanistan, China, the Czech Republic, Germany, Jamaica, Japan, Kazakhstan, Korea, Mexico, Pakistan, Poland, Rwanda, Spain, Sweden, Taiwan, and the Bahamas.

The Code of Conduct is established by the faculty members, the administration, and the Board of Trustees and is based on common courtesy, mutual respect, and socially acceptable behavior.

ACADEMIC FACILITIES

Lyndon Institute comprises three adjacent campuses. The Darling Campus consists of the Main Building, containing ten classrooms, four science labs, a small performing arts space, administrative offices, and a multilevel media center; Pierce Hall, containing seven classrooms, and a 250-seat cafeteria; Alumni Wing, which houses a 550-seat gymnasium and a 650-seat auditorium; and Lewis Field.

The Harris Campus consists of nine main buildings, including the school's health center; two dormitories; Brown building, which houses the language class rooms and a fully networked computer aided design (CAD) lab; and Sanborn Hall, which provides locker rooms, athletic training facilities, and a full-size auxiliary gymnasium.

The Vail Campus comprises fourteen buildings, four of which house technology classrooms, workshops, an art center, and five residence dormitories. The Admissions Office is also located on Vail Campus.

BOARDING AND GENERAL FACILITIES

Seven dorms make up the housing for boarding students at Lyndon Institute, including a new dormitory for 20 students. The dormitories can accommodate 106 students in single (seventy-six) or double rooms (fifteen), as well as 15 resident dorm parents.

ATHLETICS

In the 2011–12 school year, roughly 60 percent of the student body participated in the fall sports program. Lyndon Institute is involved in fifteen interscholastic sports as well as five club sports and students can use the multiple game and practice fields; the Fenton Chester Ice Arena, which is adjacent to the school; and Burke Mountain Ski Area, just 7 miles from campus. The golf team practices at nearby St. Johnsbury Country Club's championship golf course. In the last five years, LI teams have won state championships in baseball, cross-country running, golf, Nordic skiing, softball, and track.

EXTRACURRICULAR OPPORTUNITIES

Student clubs and organizations include Student Council, National Honor Society, Volunteer Club, and USA Skills/Vocational Industrial Clubs of America. Students may join the jazz ensemble; choral and drama groups; French, Latin, and Spanish clubs; the forensics team; and the scholars bowl team. The award-winning art and literature magazine, *Janus* and the yearbook, *Cynosure* offer students writing, editing, and desktop publishing opportunities.

The French and Spanish clubs organize trips abroad in alternating years. Students can take advantage of the cultural events and concerts at LSC, the Catamount Film and Arts Center in St. Johnsbury, and the Hopkins Center at Dartmouth College. The Music, Dance, and Art Departments offer students opportunities to work and perform with guest artists-in-residence. In addition to dances, plays, concerts, and athletics events, Spirit Week and Winter Carnival are two schoolwide events that engage the entire student body. Kingdom Trails offers a network of trails in the region for mountain biking in the summer and fall, and cross-country skiing and snowshoeing in the winter. Numerous field trips throughout Vermont and New England are offered throughout the year.

DAILY LIFE

Classes begin each day at 7:50 a.m. and end at 2:45 p.m. There are eight class periods of 50 minutes each. Faculty members remain in their classrooms until 3 p.m. to assist students. Activities are scheduled at 3 p.m. or later to allow students additional time to meet with faculty members as needed. The library is open from 7:30 a.m. to 4 p.m.

WEEKEND LIFE

Weekends in the Northeast Kingdom are always an adventure. Many interscholastic events take place on Saturday. Trips are scheduled to nearby ski areas and to the urban centers of Burlington, Hanover, and New Hampshire. Catamount Film and Arts Center in St. Johnsbury frequently hosts special events or series in the area, some of which are scheduled at LI and Lyndon State College. Students in good standing and with advance permission have the option to spend the weekend with a host family in the area or to travel home.

SUMMER PROGRAMS

Lyndon Institute sponsors day camps for football, basketball, and soccer in late July and August, and it sponsors camps for dance and theater in July.

COSTS AND FINANCIAL AID

Tuition for boarding students for 2012–13 is $44,700. A deposit of $2000 is due by May 31 to reserve a place. The Institute works with parents to arrange alternative payment schedules when needed.

Financial aid is based on need as determined by the School's Financial Aid Committee.

ADMISSIONS INFORMATION

Acceptance to Lyndon Institute is based on academic performance and potential, school citizenship, and motivation. The SSAT is required for domestic students. The TOEFL or TOEFL Junior is required for international students whose native language is not English.

Lyndon Institute admits students of any race, color, or national or ethnic origin to all the rights, privileges, programs, and activities generally accorded or made available to students at the school. LI does not discriminate on the basis of race, color, or national or ethnic origin in the administration of its educational policies, admission policies, scholarships, and loan programs or athletics and other school-administered programs.

APPLICATION TIMETABLE

Inquiries are welcome at any time. An interview is strongly suggested. Interviews and tours are scheduled between 10 a.m. and 2 p.m., Monday through Friday. Weekend appointments are available by special arrangement. Admissions decisions are made on a rolling basis. Since the boarding program is limited in enrollment, early application (by March 31) is recommended.

ADMISSIONS CORRESPONDENCE

Mary B. Thomas, Assistant Head for Admissions
Donald F. Steen, Assistant Director of Admissions
Lyndon Institute
P.O. Box 127
Lyndon Center, Vermont 05850-0127
United States
Phone: 802-626-5232
Fax: 802-626-6138
E-mail: admissions@lyndon.institute.org
Web site: http://www.lyndoninstitute.org

MAINE CENTRAL INSTITUTE

Pittsfield, Maine

Type: Coeducational traditional boarding and day college-preparatory and comprehensive curriculum
Grades: 9–12, postgraduate year
Enrollment: 452
Head of School: Christopher Hopkins

THE SCHOOL

Founded in 1866 by Free Will Baptists, Maine Central Institute (MCI) retains the inventive spirit and philosophy of its founders but no longer has a formal affiliation with the church. During the school's pioneer years, MCI served as a feeder school to Bates College in nearby Lewiston, Maine. Although adhering to upstanding and traditional educational values, MCI is progressive and broadminded, pledging to provide a comprehensive college-preparatory education to a multicultural student body diverse in talents, abilities, and interests.

MCI regards each student as an individual with individual needs and aspirations. In keeping with its belief in individuality, MCI strives to foster an overall environment of mutual respect, cooperation, and tolerance among all of its members and with the surrounding community. In a safe and caring atmosphere, students are encouraged to develop a moral and social consciousness, self-esteem, and social responsibility and to become globally aware, lifelong learners.

The rural town of Pittsfield (population 4,500) is nestled in between the Atlantic Ocean and the mountains of western Maine. The region of central Maine provides prime opportunities for hiking, skiing, biking, fishing, skating, and snowmobiling. The campus is within walking distance of local eateries, recreational parks, shopping, hiking trials, and a movie theater.

Maine Central Institute is accredited by the New England Association of Schools and Colleges and approved by the State of Maine Department of Education. MCI is also a member of the College Board and the National Association of Independent Schools.

ACADEMIC PROGRAM

MCI offers a rigorous comprehensive curriculum to accommodate various learning styles and academic abilities. MCI fosters the intellectual curiosities of its student body by offering accelerated and advanced placement courses in all core subject areas.

For grades 9–12, 20 credits are required for graduation. Students must successfully complete units in English (4), mathematics (4), social studies (3, including U.S. history), science (4), physical education (1), fine arts (1), computer science (½), and health (½). Students are required to take the equivalent of at least 5 units each semester. MCI also offers a postgraduate academic year with college prep and, more specifically, SAT prep.

MCI's math and science programs exceed national standards and utilize state-of-the-art technology and academic facilities. Students in MCI's well-known humanities program understand the culture of an era through a study of its history, literature, and art. The Institute has an award-winning music program.

The foreign language program includes four levels of French and Spanish. In 2009, MCI added a Chinese Mandarin program to the foreign languages, which is taught by an exchange teacher from China. In addition to the traditional offerings, students may take courses in psychology, music composition, the Internet, sociology, child development, computer-assisted drawing, personal finance, vocational subjects, and philosophy.

MCI offers a structured ESL program for the international student who is planning for a university education. Students receive individual testing before placement at one of three levels of ESL. The extensive ESL program includes American history for international students and carefully structured math classes that focus on the development of math language skills. MCI also offers a four-week summer program for ESL.

FACULTY AND ADVISERS

The 2012–13 faculty consists of 44 full-time members. More than a quarter of the faculty and staff members reside on campus, while the rest live in nearby towns such as Newport, Waterville, and Bangor.

Faculty members are selected on the basis of three main criteria. They must possess a strong subject-matter background, the ability to relate to students, and an educational philosophy consistent with that of the institution and its mission. Faculty members are also expected to become actively involved in coaching, supervising dormitories, advising, counseling, and student affairs.

COLLEGE ADMISSION COUNSELING

A guidance team of 4 professionals is available for students. Counselors are responsible primarily for helping students with postsecondary placement and academic program planning. Approximately 75 college admissions representatives visit MCI's campus annually. Career counseling is also an integral part of the guidance department. Financial aid workshops for seniors, postgraduates, and their parents are offered. Preparation for the SAT and ACT is offered within the math and English curricula.

MCI has a strong history of placing students in postsecondary school. Schools attended by recent graduates include Bates, Boston University, Colby, Cornell, Emerson, Emory, George Mason, Gettysburg, Hofstra, Husson, Maine Maritime Academy, Michigan State, Muhlenberg, Northeastern, Syracuse, Tufts, Worcester Polytechnic, and the Universities of Connecticut, Maine, New England, New Hampshire, and Rhode Island.

STUDENT BODY AND CONDUCT

The 2012–13 enrollment of 452 includes day and boarding students. Students come to MCI from eight states and thirteen countries.

Students at MCI are expected to be good citizens and are held responsible for their behavior. The rules that provide the structure for the school community are written in the student handbook. Disciplinary issues are the responsibility of the administration, the faculty, and the residence hall staff.

ACADEMIC FACILITIES

There are seventeen buildings housed on the 23-acre campus. Visitors are greeted upon entrance with the stoic simplicity of the campus with its brick-front buildings and the historic bell tower of Founder's Hall.

The Math and Science Center is a 23,000-square-foot recent addition to MCI, including fourteen instructional spaces, two computer classrooms, and a botany area. More than 210 computers are available for student use campuswide, many of which have Internet and e-mail access. The 12,000-volume Powell Memorial Library has a computerized card catalogue as well as Internet access. The Pittsfield Public Library is also available for school use.

BOARDING AND GENERAL FACILITIES

Boarding students reside in single-sex residence halls on campus, supervised by resident faculty and staff members. Each residence hall has its own recreation room and laundry facilities. MCI celebrated the opening in fall 2007 of an Honors Dormitory, converted from a home owned by the school to reward the highest-achieving residential students. Construction of the Donna Leavitt Furman Student Center was a second notable addition to the MCI campus in 2007. It is home to the dining hall, student lounge, and garden sitting area, including a performance stage, food court, garden benches, and game room.

Weymouth Hall houses the Student Services Center, consisting of the student union, snack machines, the Wellness Center, and the school bookstore.

MCI offers a unique Host Family Program. Participating students are paired with a family from the community that

makes the student a part of its family for the school year. Students may spend time with their host family on weekends, after school, and during vacations, if so desired.

ATHLETICS

MCI believes that athletics not only provide a wholesome outlet for youthful energies but also help students apply and further develop their skills in various sports. The school strives to furnish opportunities for participation by students of all abilities by offering JV, varsity, and club-level sports. MCI also provides an opportunity for postgraduate basketball, and many alumni have gone on to play in the NCAA Division 1 and 9 and also in the NBA.

There are seventeen sports teams for boys and girls, including baseball, basketball, cheering, field hockey, football, golf, rifle, skiing, soccer, softball, tennis, track, and wrestling.

Wright Gymnasium and Parks Gymnasium are multiple-use athletic facilities, and each contains a weight room and locker facilities. Located on the main campus are a football field, a practice field, a ¼-mile track, two tennis courts, and a rifle range. Manson Park has fields for soccer, field hockey, baseball, and softball as well as three tennis courts. The school has the use of a local golf course and ski areas for competitive teams and recreation.

EXTRACURRICULAR OPPORTUNITIES

MCI students may choose from among more than thirty campus organizations, which represent some of the following interests: drama production; foreign languages and travel to places such as Spain, England, and Russia; chess; hiking; weight lifting; Future Problem Solvers; Key Club, which is the school's community service organization; computer science; and public speaking. Students may participate in Student Council; MCI's strong, award-winning music program includes concert band, concert choir, chamber choir, vocal jazz ensemble, instrumental jazz ensemble, jazz combo, percussion ensemble, and pep band; and the Math Team and the Science Olympiad, which compete locally and statewide.

Bossov Ballet Theatre offers MCI students a unique opportunity to study classical ballet as part of the academic curriculum. Ballet classes are taught by Andrei Bossov, a world-renowned teacher who previously taught at the Vaganova Academy in Saint Petersburg, Russia. The program consists of a preprofessional-level syllabus that prepares students for a professional ballet career.

DAILY LIFE

The school day begins at 7:40 a.m. and ends at 2:36 p.m., with a 42-minute lunch break beginning at 11:30. Classes run from Monday through Friday, with dinner served from 5 to 6:30 p.m.

Sunday through Thursday, there is a mandatory supervised study hall from 7 to 8:30 p.m. for all boarding students.

WEEKEND LIFE

Supervised weekend activities include trips to Canada, Boston, the nearby capital of Augusta, the city of Portland, historic ports, lighthouses and coastal towns along the Atlantic shoreline, and cultural and athletic events both on and off campus. Activities such as whale watching, white-water rafting, and skiing at Sugarloaf Resort are also offered. With parental permission, students are allowed to go home on weekends or visit the home of their host family.

COSTS AND FINANCIAL AID

The 2012–13 tuition, room, and board are $40,850 for boarding students, and tuition is $10,000 for private day students. The cost for ESL support is $2500 for the first class and $1500 for each additional class. The nonrefundable deposit of $3000 is due within two weeks of an offer of admission. A variety of payment plans are available.

Financial aid is awarded on a need basis, determined by information shown on the Parents' Confidential Statement and any additional financial information that is requested.

ADMISSIONS INFORMATION

MCI's Admissions Committee screens all applicants to determine their compatibility with MCI's philosophy that students should assume a mature responsibility for their own education. No entrance tests are required, but an on-campus interview with each student and his or her parents is strongly recommended. School transcripts and results of standardized tests are used to determine academic ability and appropriate academic placement in classes in accordance with the student's individual needs, abilities, and interests.

Maine Central Institute does not discriminate on the basis of race, sex, age, sexual preference, disability, religion, or national or ethnic origin in the administration of its educational and admission policies, financial aid programs, and athletic or other school-administered programs and activities.

APPLICATION TIMETABLE

Inquiries and applications are welcome at any time; however, applying by June 1 is recommended. Visits may be scheduled at any time during the year but are most effective when school is in session. Tours and interviews can be arranged by calling the Admissions Office, which is open Monday through Friday from 8 to 4:30. A nonrefundable application fee of $50 is required.

ADMISSIONS CORRESPONDENCE

Clint M. Williams, Director of Admission
Maine Central Institute
295 Main Street
Pittsfield, Maine 04967
United States
Phone: 207-487-2282
Fax: 207-487-3512
E-mail: cwilliams@mci-school.org
Web site: http://www.mci-school.org

MARINE MILITARY ACADEMY

Harlingen, Texas

Type: All-boys, college-preparatory, military boarding school
Grades: 8–12 with an optional postgraduate year
Enrollment: 230
Head of School: Col R. Glenn Hill, USMC (Ret.)

THE SCHOOL

Marine Military Academy (MMA) is a private, college-preparatory, boarding school for young men in grades 8–12 with an optional postgraduate year. Located in sunny South Texas, MMA is the only private secondary school based on the traditions, values, and ideals of the U.S. Marine Corps. Since 1965, MMA has been home to adolescent sons from all over the world. MMA takes young men and fuels their minds, bodies, and spirits.

MMA's purpose is to inspire positive academic, physical, and moral growth in every cadet. To achieve this, MMA provides a structured, distraction-free setting that allows cadets to focus on their educational and personal development. At the center of this environment are eight principles that govern each cadet's actions: leadership, character, confidence, courage, responsibility, self-discipline, loyalty, and respect.

Throughout this journey, cadets learn to take ownership of their lives and develop the critical tools they need to succeed, not only in college, but in life. MMA's proven education model makes it among the world's top private military schools for adolescent males.

In the early 1960s, Capt William A. Gary, an Arizona rancher and retired U.S. Marine Corps Reservist, wanted to send his son to a school that embraced the ideology of the Marine Corps. He believed that the Marine Corps concepts of leadership, discipline, responsibility, and moral values could be successfully applied to a college-preparatory education. Captain Gary could not find such a school, so in 1963 he and a group of retired Marines set out on a mission to start one.

Captain Gary and his team discovered a former Air Force navigation school in Harlingen, Texas, a city located in the southernmost part of the state. The Marines envisioned the 142-acre campus as an all-boys, military boarding school and began building the educational laboratory that would develop today's young men into tomorrow's leaders.

In September 1965, Marine Military Academy opened its doors to 58 cadets; six would comprise the first graduating class of 1966. Today, MMA is home to hundreds of young men from across the globe and the alma mater to thousands of alumni.

ACADEMIC PROGRAM

To prepare cadets for the rigor of college course work and help them earn college credit, MMA offers and promotes dual-enrollment and Advanced Placement (AP) courses. MMA's academic program is accredited by the Southern Association of Colleges and Schools. One hundred percent of MMA graduates are accepted into colleges or universities.

In addition to its core classes, MMA offers two popular elective classes: aerospace/flight training and marine science/sailing.

When school is out, MMA holds a four-week summer camp for boys who wish to engage in numerous outdoor activities and challenges designed to build their strength, confidence, concentration, and self-discipline. MMA also offers a concurrent ESL Summer Camp for students who wish to learn English.

FACULTY AND ADVISERS

With a student-teacher ratio of 11:1, MMA provides small class sizes so cadets receive more personalized instruction. The daily afternoon tutorial period allows cadets to seek extra assistance from their teachers on subjects they find challenging. The grade point average (GPA) for new cadets increases by an average of 1.71.

COLLEGE ADMISSION COUNSELING

The College Placement Officer at MMA assists all cadets with their college or service academy selection and the application process. The College Placement Officer is located in the College Placement Office, a library that houses hundreds of resources, such as college catalogs, study guides for college admission tests, financial aid and scholarship information, and other print and online data.

MMA's distinguished Marine Corps Junior ROTC program makes it a Naval Honor School. As a Naval Honor School, MMA has the privilege of nominating cadets each year for placement in the U.S. service academies.

STUDENT BODY AND CONDUCT

Approximately 230 cadets attend MMA. As an international boarding school, MMA cadets represent at least twelve different countries. No matter where they hail from, all cadets form a bond of brotherhood and become part of the "Leatherneck" family.

The Marine Military Academy's mission is to develop disciplined, morally strong, college-ready young men who are prepared for responsible leadership. MMA provides sound academic preparation so cadets may enter the university or service academy of their choice. In addition, MMA is globally recognized as a premier private school for adolescent men on course to achieve their post-secondary education and career goals.

MMA is guided by three key values as well: honor, courage, and commitment. Cadets are held to the highest ethical and moral standards. Respect for others is essential. Cadets will face their fears and overcome them. They will do what is right no matter the consequences. Cadets strive for excellence and never give up. Duty to others is fundamental.

ACADEMIC FACILITIES

MMA is located on a 142-acre, gated campus in Harlingen, Texas and offers an impressive array of facilities for academics, athletics, and ceremonies. The Tom T. East Center is home to the mathematics and science departments and the synergistic lab, which allows cadets to explore a wide variety of physical phenomena in a hands-on manner including light, sound, flight, and bridge design. Coleman Hall houses the English department, SAT prep computer lab, and College Placement Office. The social sciences and foreign language departments are located in Belle Blaschke Hall. With over 18,000 books and hundreds of print and online resources, the Harold James Memorial Library reinforces MMA's strong educational program and is the nucleus for academic activities.

The Col Philip J. Yeckel Memorial Auditorium seats 1,070 people and is used for concerts, theater productions, and special events. Throughout the school year, MMA hosts a number of battalion-size parades that are open to the public on its Parade Ground.

MMA is also proud to serve as the home of the Iwo Jima Monument. On February 23, 1945, news photographer Joe Rosenthal captured five Marines and one Navy Corpsman erecting an American flag atop Mount Suribachi. At the time the photo was released, sculptor Dr. Felix W. de Weldon was on duty with the U.S. Navy. After World War II ended, de Weldon felt that the inspiring event should be depicted on a massive scale in our nation's capital. Over a nine-and-a-half-year period, he created a statue that would be cast in bronze and erected in Arlington, Virginia. It would be known as the Iwo Jima Memorial.

In 1981, de Weldon gifted the original working model of the Iwo Jima Memorial to MMA. The statue, which came in numerous parts, arrived at MMA on October 10, 1981. Just six months later, on April 16, 1982, MMA held the dedication ceremony for this distinguished American icon.

There were several important reasons why MMA was selected by de Weldon as the monument's home. The main street of the campus was appropriately named Iwo Jima Boulevard by its founders in 1965. The fairly constant temperature and humidity in Harlingen, Texas, are ideal for the preservation of the plaster figures. The Marine depicted at the base of the flagpole was a South Texas native, Cpl Harlon H. Block of Weslaco, Texas; his gravesite is directly behind the Iwo Jima Monument. In addition, MMA is the only place outside of Washington where proper honors are rendered with battalion-size, dress-blue parades.

Since 1982, the Jima Monument has been an inspiration to MMA cadets and visitors from all over the world. All MMA parades are held in front of this magnificent sculpture and an American flag flies above it 24 hours a day.

ATHLETICS AND EXTRACURRICULAR OPPORTUNITIES

All MMA cadets are required to participate in at least one sport or activity. MMA offers fifteen sports and three activities for cadets to join. The campus boasts four athletic fields, three tennis courts, three gyms, a swimming pool, a marksmanship center, and the 40-acre Leadership Enhancement and Development (LEAD) Complex.

The sports and activities MMA currently offers include band, boxing, baseball, basketball, cross-country, cycling, drill team and color guard, football, golf, jujitsu, rifle team, rock climbing, soccer, swimming, track and field, tennis, weightlifting, and wrestling.

DAILY LIFE

Cadets reside in barracks with a live-in drill instructor. There are approximately 45 cadets in each barrack; two cadets share a room equipped with a bathroom. Each barrack has two community rooms, a computer study room with filtered Internet access and a television room. Cadets eat three times a day in the Mess Hall.

A typical day for the cadets includes the following:

6 a.m.—Reveille
6:10—Physical training
6:40—Breakfast
7:30—Clean up and prepare for school
8:35—Morning colors
8:50—Morning classes
12:10 p.m.—Pass in review/formation and lunch
1:15—Afternoon classes
2:55—Tutoring
3:35—Activities
6—Dinner
7—Study period
9:15—Free time
10—Lights out

Cadets earn liberty on the weekends and may leave the MMA campus for leisure, such as spending a day at the local movie theater or mall. The young men often use their liberty to perform community service. MMA cadets contribute approximately 3,000 hours a year to the local community.

COSTS AND FINANCIAL AID

Tuition and fees for the school year are $33,000, and the uniform fee is $1400. The application fee is $100 and a security deposit of $1800 is required. Payment plan information is available by contacting the Admissions Office at 956-421-9252 or admissions@MMA-TX.org.

Financial assistance is available in the form of scholarships. Scholarships are never full, only partial. Prospective students can contact MMA's chief financial officer at 956-421-9240 for more scholarship information.

ADMISSIONS INFORMATION

Applications for the school year are accepted all year, but students enter at the beginning of the fall or spring semester. Acceptance to MMA is based on a number of factors: prior academic history and curriculum, discipline history, health history, and, very importantly, potential. Because of the nature of the academic setting, the committee looks for young men who have the potential to adapt to MMA's program.

A guided tour is highly recommended as it gives the applicant and his family a sense of daily life at MMA. Ideally located, MMA is just a 5-minute walk from Valley International Airport, the region's largest airport, and a 40-minute drive from South Padre Island. To schedule a tour, contact Admissions at 956-421-9252 or admissions@MMA-TX.org.

Marine Military Academy does not discriminate on the basis of race, religion, color, or national or ethnic origin in the administration of its educational policies, admission policies, scholarship or loan programs, or athletic and other academy-administered programs.

ADMISSIONS CORRESPONDENCE

Marine Military Academy
Admissions Office
320 Iwo Jima Boulevard
Harlingen, Texas 78550
United States
Phone: 956-421-9252
Fax: 956-421-9273
E-mail: admissions@MMA-TX.org
Web site: http://www.MMA-TX.org/Apply

MARYMOUNT SCHOOL OF NEW YORK

New York, New York

Type: Girls' independent college-preparotory Catholic day school
Grades: N–XII: Lower School, Nursery–III; Middle School, IV–VII; Upper School, VIII–XII
Enrollment: School total: 676; Upper School: 256
Head of School: Concepcion R. Alvar ,

THE SCHOOL

Marymount School of New York is an independent Catholic day school that educates girls in a tradition of academic excellence and moral values. The School promotes in each student a respect for her own unique abilities and provides a foundation for exploring and acting on questions of integrity and ethical decision-making. Founded by Mother Marie Joseph Butler in 1926 as part of a worldwide network of schools directed by the Religious of the Sacred Heart of Mary, Marymount remains faithful to its mission "to educate young women who question, risk, and grow; young women who care, serve, and lead; young women prepared to challenge, shape, and change the world." Committed to its Catholic heritage, the School welcomes and values the religious diversity of its student body and seeks to give all students a deeper understanding of the role of the spiritual in life. The School also has an active social service program and integrates social justice and human rights into the curriculum.

Marymount occupies three adjoining landmark Beaux Arts mansions, located on Fifth Avenue's historic Museum Mile, and a fourth mansion on East 82nd Street. The School has recently expanded to include an additional facility with 42,000-square-feet of space on East 97th Street. The Metropolitan Museum of Art and Central Park, both located directly across the street from the School, provide resources that are integral to the School's academic and extracurricular programs. Middle School art classes meet once a week in studios at the Museum. As part of the Class IX humanities curriculum and in advanced Art History courses, Upper School students visit the Museum as often as twice a week. Central Park is used for science and physical education classes as well as extracurricular activities. Other city sites, such as the United Nations, the Tenement Museum, Ellis Island, the New York Zoological Society, the American Museum of Natural History, the Rose Planetarium, the Frick and Guggenheim Museums, and El Museo Del Barrio are also frequent extensions of the classroom for Marymount students.

Since 1969, the School has been independently incorporated under the direction of a 30-member Board of Trustees made up of parents, alumnae, educators, and members of the founding order. The School benefits from a strong Parents' Association; an active Alumnae Association; the involvement of parents, alumnae, and student volunteers; and a successful Annual Giving Program.

Marymount is accredited by the New York State Association of Independent Schools (NYSAIS). The School holds membership in the National Association of Independent Schools (NAIS), NYSAIS, the Independent Schools Admissions Association of Greater New York, the National Catholic Education Association, the National Coalition of Girls' Schools (NCGS), and the Educational Records Bureau.

ACADEMIC PROGRAM

The study of classic disciplines at Marymount is dynamic and innovative. The rigorous college-preparatory curriculum emphasizes critical thinking, collaboration, communication, and creativity. Students are encouraged to question and explore topics in depth, to take intellectual risks, and to work independently and collaboratively to find alternative approaches to problems. With its focus on the education of young women, Marymount allows each student to find her own voice. Students develop the skills necessary to succeed in competitive colleges and in life beyond the classroom: self-confidence, leadership ability, a risk-taking spirit, and joy in learning.

A commitment to the study of science, technology, engineering, and mathematics (STEM) is reflected in Marymount's curriculum, which fully integrates information and communication technologies into all subject areas. Students have access to desktop and laptop computers, iPads, and other mobile computing devices throughout the School. Students in Classes K through V use iPads for individual and collaborative exploration, creation, and communication. Students in Classes VI through XII and staff members each have a school-supplied MacBook, school e-mail, and Google account and use digital media to carry out research, create presentations, publish work, communicate, and demonstrate ideas and concepts. Students learn a wide variety of authoring tools as well as programming languages to create and publish digital media. Using an array of interactive media, students extend discussions and collaborations beyond the classroom. Using online tools and video-conferencing, students collaborate on projects with other Marymount Schools and with students and researchers around the globe.

Marymount's position at the forefront of educational technology relies on more than the investment in laptops, iPads, interactive displays, software, and networks. To maintain its cutting-edge program—which has been recognized for excellence by NAIS, NCGS, and Apple Inc.—the School offers technology seminars every summer and workshops during the school year for the faculty and other NAIS-school faculty members.

High school graduation requirements include satisfactory completion of 4 years of English, 3 years of history, 3 years of math, 3 years of laboratory science, 3 years of a world language, 4 years of religious studies, 4 years of physical education, 1 year of studio art, 1 year of computer science, 6 semesters of health/guidance, and 1 semester of speech. These requirements provide a broad, solid base of knowledge while sharpening problem-solving and research skills and promoting critical and creative thinking.

The School offers honors and Advanced Placement courses as well as electives such as AP art history, economics, classical Greek, music history, history of theater, two AP studio art courses, African studies, Latin American studies, Middle Eastern studies, history of modern China, and programming languages. In senior English, students choose from seminars that cover topics from Shakespeare's history plays to contemporary American drama to the literature of African-American and Asian-American women writers. Most students elect to take a fourth year of math; advanced offerings include AP calculus AB, AP calculus BC, AP statistics, and calculus. Fourth-year science courses include AP biology, AP chemistry, AP physics C, advanced physics, molecular biology, and atmospheric science. Class XII students may elect to take AP psychology or other advanced courses through Marymount's affiliate membership in Online School for Girls. The science program connects with and utilizes the research of numerous institutions, including the New York Academy of Sciences and Princeton University, as well as participating in the STEM Internship Program and the STEM Research Program.

While a leader in science and technological education, Marymount is also committed to the study of humanities. All Class IX students take part in the Integrated Humanities program, an interdisciplinary curriculum that focuses on history, literature, and art history in the study of ancient civilizations. Classes are held at the Metropolitan Museum of Art at least once a week. The program includes a performance-based World Civilizations Festival and collaborative research projects in history and art history. As a culminating project, seniors must submit an interdisciplinary writing portfolio of selected work from their last three years of high school.

The visual arts department offers studio art, AP 2-D design, and AP drawing. The performing arts program includes a school chorus, a chamber choir, courses in music history and the history of theater, dramatic arts classes, and two stage productions annually.

The religious studies program includes comparative religions, Hebrew scriptures, the New Testament, social justice, and ethics. With a focus on moral and ethical decision-making, students analyze systemic social issues and immerse themselves in the community through numerous service projects, as well as the Youth and Philanthropy Initiative. The Catholic-Jewish Initiative provides students with a deeper understanding of the Judeo-Christian tradition and includes Holocaust studies and a trip to the National Holocaust Museum in Washington, D.C.

During the last four weeks of the academic year, each senior participates in an off-campus internship to gain exposure to a career of interest. Students have interned at hospitals, research laboratories, law firms, financial organizations, theaters, schools, nonprofit organizations, and corporations. They also attend a career day, with visiting alumnae as guest speakers. A financial literacy program prepares graduates for the financial challenges of college and life.

As members of a worldwide network of schools, students may opt to spend the second semester of their sophomore year at a Marymount International School in London or Rome. Annual concert and study tours and service trips extend the curriculum. Recent study tours have included the scientists and poets in England and Scotland, mathematics and culture of ancient Greece, the ecology of the Galapagos Islands, the theater and literature of Shakespeare's London and Stratford-upon-Avon, and the music, language, and culture of Italy, France, and Spain. Recent service trips have brought students to work with disabled orphans in Jamaica, rebuild homes in New Orleans, and promote justice for trafficked women in New York City. The Marymount Singers enjoys an annual concert tour every spring and have performed in Italy, France, Austria, the Czech Republic, Ireland, Portugal, and Spain.

Upper School students are formally evaluated four times a year, using an A–F grading system. The evaluation process includes written reports and biannual parent/student/teacher conferences.

The Middle School curriculum welcomes the diverse interests of young adolescents and is structured to channel their energy and natural love of learning. The integrated core curriculum gradually increases in the degree of departmentalization at each grade level, and challenging learning activities and flexible groupings in main subject areas ensure that the students achieve their full potential. In Class IV, students study a trimester of French, Latin, and Spanish; in Class V, students choose to pursue a three-year sequence in one of these languages. The Middle School years culminate in a study tour to France and Spain; the integration of language, mathematics, social studies, science, architecture, religious studies, and art makes the study tour a rich intellectual experience as well as accentuating the relevance of the students' classroom study to the world at large. All students enjoy regular visits to the Metropolitan Museum of Art, including studio art classes.

Twice-weekly speech classes prepare the girls for dramatic presentations reflective of their social studies and literature curriculum: *Revolutionary Voices, Greek Mythology,* and scenes from *The Canterbury Tales* and *A Midsummer Night's Dream.* Uptown Broadway, an extracurricular option offered each semester, allows the students to participate in a full-scale musical production. The Middle School celebrates music and voice at its annual spring concert.

The Lower School provides child-centered, creative learning within a challenging, structured environment. The curriculum focuses on the acquisition of foundational skills, often through an interdisciplinary approach. Programs engage students in the exciting process of learning about themselves, their surroundings, and the larger world. Introductory lessons in Spanish complement the social studies curriculum. A hands-on science program, an emphasis on technology integration, a study of robotics, a popular School chorus, and an extensive after-school program are some highlights of the Lower School.

FACULTY AND ADVISERS

There are 102 full-time and 14 part-time faculty members, allowing for a 6:1 student-teacher ratio. Eighty-three percent of the faculty members hold master's degrees, and 11 percent hold doctoral degrees. In Nursery through Class III, each class has a head teacher and at least one assistant teacher. In the Middle School, students make the transition from having homeroom teachers to having advisers. In Classes IV and V, each class has two homeroom teachers. In Classes V–XII, each student has a homeroom teacher and an adviser, usually one of her teachers, who follows her academic progress and provides guidance and support. Learning resource specialists, school nurses, an athletic trainer, artists-in-residence, a school counselor, and school psychologists work with students throughout the School.

Concepcion R. Alvar was appointed Headmistress in 2004 after serving thirteen years as the Director of Admissions and three years as a head teacher. She also served as the Director and Supervisor of Marymount Summer for sixteen years. Mrs. Alvar holds a B.S. from Maryknoll College (Philippines) and an M.A. from Columbia University, Teachers College.

COLLEGE ADMISSION COUNSELING

Under the guidance of the Director of College Counseling, Marymount's formal college counseling program begins during the junior year. In the second semester, two College Nights are held for students and parents. Individual counseling throughout the semester directs each student to those colleges that best match her achievements and interests. Students participate in weekly guidance classes to learn about general requirements for college admission, the application process, and standardized tests. During the fall of their senior year, students continue the weekly sessions, focusing on essay writing, admissions interviews, and financial aid applications.

Graduates from recent classes are attending the following colleges and universities: Amherst, Barnard, Boston College, Boston University, Bowdoin, Brown, Columbia, Cooper Union, Connecticut, Cornell, Dartmouth, Davidson, Duke, Fairfield, Fordham, George Washington, Georgetown, Harvard, Holy Cross, Kenyon, Middlebury, NYU, Oberlin, Princeton, Skidmore, Smith, Stanford, Trinity, Tufts, Vanderbilt, Villanova, Wake Forest, Wellesley, Wesleyan, Wheaton, Williams, Yale, and the Universities of Notre Dame, Pennsylvania, St. Andrew's (Scotland), and Virginia.

STUDENT BODY AND CONDUCT

Marymount's enrollment is 676 students in Nursery through Class XII, with 256 girls in the Upper School. Most students reside in the five boroughs of New York City; however, Upper School students also commute from Long Island, New Jersey, and Westchester County. Students wear uniforms, except on special days; participate in athletic and extracurricular activities; and attend weekly chapel services, all-school masses, and annual class retreats.

Marymount encourages students to be active participants in their education and in the life of the School community. Students seek out leadership and volunteer opportunities, serving as advocates for one another through peer mentoring, retreat teams, and the Big Sister/Little Sister program. Student government and campus ministry provide social and service opportunities that enable students to broaden their perspectives, develop as leaders, sharpen public-speaking skills, and form lasting friendships. Teachers and administrators encourage each student to respect herself and others and to be responsible members of the community.

ACADEMIC FACILITIES

The Beaux Arts mansions on Fifth Avenue provide rooms for Lower and Upper School classes, and include four science laboratories, two art studios, a math center, a gymnasium, an auditorium, a courtyard play area, a chapel, and a library complex. The East 82nd Street facility is the home of the Middle School. Students in the Middle and Upper Schools also attend classes at the East 97th Street campus. This renovated facility includes a gymnasium, cafeteria, and three floors of classrooms. The fourth floor of 116 East 97th Street features several science classrooms and laboratories as well as a media-production lab, and a "fab lab" where students can design, engineer, and fabricate an array of objects and solutions using 3-D printers, laser cutters, and other fabrication tools. The additional campus also offers classrooms for humanities classes, space for visual and performing arts, and a fitness room. All classrooms feature interactive boards and multimedia displays.

ATHLETICS

The athletic program promotes good health, physical fitness, coordination, skill development, confidence, and a spirit of competition and collaboration through its physical education classes, the electives program for Classes X–XII, and individual and team sports.

Marymount provides a full schedule for varsity and junior varsity sports, as well as Middle School teams at the V/VI and VII/VIII class levels. Participants in Classes V/VI stay two days per week for an after-school sports program; students in Classes VII/VIII commit to three afternoons per week. The junior varsity and varsity teams compete within the Athletic Association of Independent Schools League (AAIS) in badminton, basketball, cross-country, fencing, field hockey, lacrosse, soccer, softball, swimming, tennis, track and field, and volleyball.

In addition to its gymnasiums, Marymount uses the facilities of nearby Catholic schools, the Harlem Armory, Riverbank State Park, and Roberto Clemente State Park. Central Park, Randall's Island, and Van Cortlandt Park are sites for field sports. Tennisport, Riverbank State Park, and Flushing Meadows are competitive sites for the tennis and swim teams. Additional facilities are used throughout New York City.

EXTRACURRICULAR OPPORTUNITIES

A wide range of clubs and activities complement the academic program, promote student initiative, and provide opportunities to contribute to the School community and develop communication, cooperation, and leadership skills. Student-led clubs include Amnesty International, book club, digital photography, science and the environment club, film club, finance club, forensics team, Mathletes, philosophy club, set design/tech crew, student government, and women in the world. Campus Ministry, CAMBIAS (Cultural Awareness Club), Marymount Singers, Marymount Players, Mock Trial, Model UN, and National Honor Society offer additional opportunities for student service, leadership, and performance. Student publications include a yearbook (*Marifia*), a newspaper (*Joritan*), and an award-winning literary/arts journal (*Muse*). A wide range of Friday noontime clubs in the Middle School includes Student Council; Italian, Latin, and French clubs; altar servers; handbells; environmental science; art; drama; handwork; and the literary magazine, *Chez Nous.*

Each year, the Upper School presents two dramatic productions, including a musical; organizes either a Harambee Celebration during Black History Month or a Bias Awareness Day; sponsors an Art Festival; and participates in numerous community service projects, local and national competitions, and conferences with other schools.

The School brings people of stature and high achievement to address students, including Nobel Peace Prize winner Leymah Gbowee, former poet laureate Billy Collins, athlete Tegla Laroupe, author Jhumpa Lahiri, bioethicist Ronald Green, nanotechnologist Dr. Susan Arney, African American painter Philomena Williamson, feminist Gloria Steinem, Sr. Helen Prejean, author of *Dead Man Walking,* and Sheryl WuDunn, coauthor of *Half the Sky.* The Maggie Murray Fund supports a series of writing-related events to enrich the students' literary experiences and has given students the opportunity to attend conversations with such celebrated writers as Toni Morrison and Chinua Achebe.

Students have the opportunity to interact with boys from neighboring schools through dramatic productions, community service projects, walkathons, dances, and other student-run social activities.

DAILY LIFE

Upper School classes are held from 8 a.m. to 3:30 p.m. on Monday, Tuesday, and Thursday. To accommodate electives, extracurricular activities, and team sports, classes end at 2:45 p.m. on Wednesdays and Fridays. Class periods are 45, 60, or 90 minutes in length and typically meet eight out of ten days in a two-week cycle. Designated "community time" during the day allows students to meet with their advisors, teachers, or other students. After classes have ended, most students remain for sports, extracurricular activities, and/or independent study.

COSTS AND FINANCIAL AID

The tuition for the 2012–13 academic year ranges from $22,926 for Nursery to $39,874 for Class XII. In February, parents are required to make a deposit of $5000, which is credited toward the November tuition. The Key Education Resources Payment Plan is available.

Roughly $3 million in financial aid was awarded in 2011–12 to students after establishing need through School and Student Services. Twenty-five percent of Marymount students receive need-based financial aid.

ADMISSIONS INFORMATION

As a college-preparatory school, Marymount aims to enroll young women of academic promise and sound character who seek a challenging educational environment and opportunities for learning outside the classroom. Educational Records Bureau tests, school records, and interviews are used in selecting students.

The School admits students of any race, color, and national or ethnic origin to all the rights, privileges, programs, and activities generally accorded or made available to students at the School and does not discriminate on these bases in the administration of its educational policies, admissions policies, scholarship or loan programs, athletic programs, or other School programs.

APPLICATION TIMETABLE

Interested students are encouraged to contact the Admissions Office as early as possible in the fall for admission the following year. The application deadline is November 30, but may be changed at the discretion of the Director of Admissions. Notification of admissions decisions is sent during February, according to the dates established by the Independent School Admissions Association of Greater New York.

ADMISSIONS CORRESPONDENCE

Lillian Issa
Deputy Head/Director of Admissions
Marymount School of New York
1026 Fifth Avenue
New York, New York 10028
United States
Phone: 212-744-4486
Fax: 212-744-0163 (general)
212-744-0716 (admissions)
E-mail: admissions@marymountnyc.org
Web site: http://marymountnyc.org

MILTON ACADEMY

Milton, Massachusetts

Type: Coeducational boarding and day college-preparatory school
Grades: K–12: (Lower School: K–8; Upper School: 9–12)
Enrollment: School total: 980; Upper School: 675
Head of School: Todd Bland

THE SCHOOL

The Academy received its charter in 1798 under the Massachusetts land-grant policy. It bequeathed to the school a responsibility to "open the way for all the people to a higher order of education than the common schools can supply." Milton's motto, "Dare to be true," not only states a core value, it describes Milton's culture. Milton fosters intellectual inquiry and encourages initiative and the open exchange of ideas. Teaching and learning at Milton are active processes that recognize the intelligence, talents, and potential of each member of the Academy.

For more than 200 years, Milton has developed confident, independent thinkers in an intimate, friendly setting where students and faculty members understand that the life of the mind is the pulse of the school. A gifted and dedicated faculty motivates a diverse student body, providing students with the structure to learn and the support to take risks. The faculty's teaching expertise and passion for scholarship generates extraordinary growth in students who learn to expect the most of themselves. The Milton community connects purposefully with world issues. Students graduate with a clear sense of themselves, their world, and how to contribute.

From Milton Academy's suburban 125-acre campus, 8 miles south of Boston in the town of Milton (population 26,000), students and faculty members access the vast cultural resources of Boston and Cambridge. Minutes from campus is the Blue Hills Reservation, 6,000 wooded acres of hiking trails and ski slopes.

Milton Academy is a nonprofit organization with a self-perpetuating Board of Trustees. Its endowment is $193 million (as of June 1, 2012).

Milton Academy is accredited by the New England Association of Schools and Colleges and holds memberships in the National Association of Independent Schools, the Cum Laude Society, and the Association of Independent Schools in New England.

ACADEMIC PROGRAM

Milton students and faculty members are motivated participants in the world of ideas, concepts, and values. Milton's curriculum provides rigorous preparation for college and includes more than 182 courses in nine academic departments. For students entering Milton in the ninth grade, a minimum of 18 credits are required for graduation. This includes 4 years of English, 2 years of history (including U.S. and modern world history), 2 years of science, 1 year of an arts course, and successful completion of algebra II, geometry, and a level III foreign language course. Noncredit requirements include current events/public speaking, physical education, a ninth-grade arts course (music/drama/visual arts), and a four-year affective education curriculum that includes health, values, social awareness, and senior transitions.

Electives are offered in all academic areas. Examples of electives include computer programming, comparative government, performing literature, Spanish film and social change, advanced architecture, philosophy and literature, choreography, film and video production, psychology, engineering, nuclear physics, issues in environmental science, creative writing, music theory, observational astronomy, and marine biology. Students may petition to take independent study courses, and Advanced Placement courses leading to college credit are offered in most subject areas.

In January, seniors submit a proposal for a five-week spring independent project, on or off campus. Senior projects give students the opportunity to pursue in-depth interests stemming from their work at Milton.

The typical class size is 14 students, and the overall student-teacher ratio is 5:1. Nightly 2-hour study periods in the houses are supervised for boarding students.

Faculty members are available for individual help throughout the day and in the houses at night. Students seeking assistance with assignments or help with specific skills, organization, and/or time management visit the Academic Skills Center, which is staffed throughout the day.

The school year, which is divided into two semesters, runs from early September to early June with an examination period at the end of January. Students typically take five courses per semester. Students earn letter grades from E (failure) through A+, and comments prepared by each student's teachers and adviser are sent to parents three times a year in November, February, and June.

All academic buildings and residential houses are part of a campuswide computer network. MiltONline, the Academy's e-mail and conferencing system, allows students to join conference discussions for many classes and extracurricular activities, communicate with faculty members and friends, and submit assignments. Students have access to the Milton Intranet as well as the Internet.

Class II students (eleventh graders) may apply to spend either the fall or spring semester at the Mountain School Program of Milton Academy (an interdisciplinary academic program set on a working 300-acre farm in Vermont); at CITYterm at the Master's School in Dobbs Ferry, New York; or at the Maine Coast Semester at Chewonki. Through School Year Abroad, Milton provides opportunities in Spain, France, Italy, and China. Milton also offers six- to eight-week exchange programs with schools in Spain, France, and China.

FACULTY AND ADVISERS

The deep commitment of a learned and experienced group of teachers is Milton's greatest treasure. Teaching in Classes IV-I (grades 9–12) are133 full-time faculty members, 78 percent of whom hold advanced degrees (Ph.D. and master's degrees). Eighty-five percent of faculty members live on campus.

In addition to teaching, faculty members also serve as house parents and coaches, as well as advisers to student clubs, organizations, publications, and activities. Each faculty member is an adviser to a group of 6 to 8 students and supports the students' emotional, social, and academic well-being at Milton.

COLLEGE ADMISSION COUNSELING

Four college counselors work one-on-one with students, beginning in their Class II (eleventh grade) year, in a highly personal and effective approach toward the college admissions process.

For the graduating classes of 2010, 2011, and 2012 the top college enrollments were Harvard (29), Boston College (21), Tufts (20), Georgetown (16), NYU (15), Columbia (14), Colby College (14), Amherst College (13), and Brown (13).

STUDENT BODY AND CONDUCT

Of the 675 students in the Upper School, 50 percent are boys and 50 percent are girls; 50 percent are boarding students and 50 percent are day students. Forty percent of Milton's enrolled students are students of color. Ten percent of the Upper School students are international, coming from twenty-four countries across the globe. Thirty-two percent of Milton students receive financial aid, and the average grants account for 75 percent of tuition.

All Upper School students from Classes IV-I (grades 9–12) participate in the Self-Governing Association, led by 2 elected student representatives, 1 senior girl and 1 senior boy. Elected class representatives serve with faculty members on the Discipline Committee, which recommends to the Head of School appropriate responses when infractions of major school rules occur. Rules at Milton Academy foster the cohesion and morale of the community and enhance education by upholding standards of conduct developed by generations of students and faculty members.

ACADEMIC FACILITIES

Among the prominent buildings on the Milton campus are three primarily academic buildings: Warren Hall (English), Wigglesworth Hall (history), and Ware Hall (math and foreign languages); the Kellner Performing Arts Center, with a 350-seat teaching theater, a studio theater, dressing rooms, scene shop, practice rooms, orchestral rehearsal room, dance studio, and speech/debate room; the Athletic and Convocation Center, with a hockey rink, a fitness center, three basketball courts, and an indoor track; the Williams Squash Courts; the Ayer Observatory; and Apthorp Chapel. The Pritzker Science Center, which opened in 2010, integrates classroom areas with laboratory tables and equipment to create an environment that allows students to work collaboratively and move seamlessly between discussion and hands-on lab work. The Art and Media Center is home to numerous visual art studios and public display spaces, including the Nesto Gallery and the Greely auditorium.

Cox Library contains more than 46,000 volumes, more than 150 periodicals with back issues on microfilm, and a newspaper collection dating back to 1704. It also provides CD-ROM sources, Internet access and online search capabilities. Within Cox Library is one of several computer laboratories.

BOARDING AND GENERAL FACILITIES

Milton Academy students live in one of eight single-sex houses ranging in size from 31 to 48 students; four for boys and four for girls. Single rooms house one third of the students, while the other two thirds of the students reside in double rooms. Milton houses include all four classes as well as faculty members' families. Students spend all their Milton years in one house, experiencing a family-at-school context for developing close relationships with valued adults, learning about responsibility to the community, taking leadership roles with peers, and sharing social and cultural traditions. All rooms are networked, and school computers are available for student use in the house common rooms.

The Health and Counseling Center and the Academic Skills Center, as well as house parents in each residential house, class deans, and the office of the school chaplain, are available to meet students' needs.

ATHLETICS

Milton believes that teamwork, sportsmanship, and the pursuit of excellence are important values and that regular vigorous exercise is a foundation of good health. Milton offers a comprehensive athletic program that includes physical education classes and a range of intramural and interscholastic sports geared to the needs and interests of every student.

The school's offerings in interscholastic sports are Alpine skiing, baseball, basketball, cross-country, field hockey, football, golf, ice hockey, lacrosse, sailing, soccer, softball, squash, swimming and diving, tennis, track, volleyball, and wrestling.

Intramural offerings include the outdoor program, Pilates, soccer, squash, strength and conditioning, tennis, Ultimate (Frisbee), and yoga.

Sports facilities include four athletic buildings, an ice hockey rink and fitness center, two indoor climbing walls, twelve playing fields, seventeen tennis courts, seven international squash courts, an all-weather track, a cross-country course, and a ropes course.

EXTRACURRICULAR OPPORTUNITIES

The breadth of extracurricular opportunities means that every student finds a niche—a comfortable place to develop new skills, take on leadership, show commitment, make friends, and have fun. Clubs and organizations include cultural groups such as the Asian Society, Latino Association, Onyx, and Common Ground (an umbrella organization for the various groups); the Arts Board; the Outdoor Club; the Chinese, French, and Spanish clubs; the debate, math, and speech teams; and Students for Gender Equality. There are eleven student publications, among them *The Asian, La Voz, MAGUS/MÁBUS, Mille Tonnes, Milton Measure, Milton Paper,* and the yearbook. Music programs include the chamber singers, the gospel choir, the glee club, the orchestra, improvisational jazz combos, and five a cappella groups. The performing arts are an important part of the extracurricular offerings at Milton. Main stage theater productions, studio theater productions, play readings, and speech and debate team are a few of the available opportunities. Milton stages twelve major theater productions each year, including a Class IV (ninth grade) play, student directed one-act plays, a dance concert, and a biennial musical. Service opportunities include the audiovisual crew, community service, Lorax (environmental group), Orange and Blue Key (admission tour guides and leaders), and the Public Issues Board.

DAILY LIFE

The academic day runs from 8 a.m. to 2:55 p.m., except on Wednesday, when classes end at 1:15 p.m. There are no classes on Saturday or Sunday. Cafeteria-style lunch is served from 11 a.m. to 1:30 p.m., and students eat during a free period within that time. The students' activities period is from 3 to 3:30 p.m. Athletics and extracurricular activities take place from 3:30 to 5:30 p.m. Family-style dinner is at 6 p.m., and the evening study period runs from 7:30 to 9:30 p.m. Lights-out time depends on the grade level of each student.

WEEKEND LIFE

Interscholastic games are held on Wednesday, Friday, and Saturday afternoons. Social activities on Friday and Saturday evenings are planned by the Student Activities Association. Day students join boarders every weekend for events such as dances with live or recorded music, classic and new films, concerts, plays, drama readings, dormitory open houses, and trips to professional sports events, arts events, or local museums.

Prior to leaving campus, students must check their plans with house parents, who must approve their whereabouts and any overnight plans.

SUMMER PROGRAMS

Milton Academy does not run its own summer programs on campus. Professional development opportunities are made available to faculty members, including the Cultural Diversity Institute and the Boarding Staff Conference for teachers from across the country. In addition, Milton hosts many outside programs, including sports camps and academic enrichment programs.

COSTS AND FINANCIAL AID

For the 2012–13 academic year, tuition is $47,520 for boarding students and $39,000 for day students.

Milton seeks to enroll the most qualified applicants regardless of their financial circumstances. To that end, more than $8.3 million in financial aid will be provided to students in the 2013–14 school year. All financial aid at Milton is awarded on the basis of need. In addition to the program of direct grants, the school offers installment payment options and two low-interest loan programs.

ADMISSIONS INFORMATION

Milton Academy seeks students who are able, energetic, intellectually curious, and have strong values and a willingness to grow. Applicants must submit the Secondary School Admission Test (SSAT) scores (students applying for eleventh grade may submit PSAT or SAT scores if applicable). All applicants must also submit a school transcript, teacher recommendations, parental statement, and two essays. An interview, on or off campus, is also required.

APPLICATION TIMETABLE

The deadline for applying is January 15. Notification letters are sent out March 10; the reply date is April 10. There is a $50 application fee for U.S. applicants and a $100 fee for international applicants.

ADMISSIONS CORRESPONDENCE

Paul Rebuck, Dean of Admission
Milton Academy
170 Centre Street
Milton, Massachusetts 02186
United States
Phone: 617-898-2227
Fax: 617-898-1701
E-mail: admissions@milton.edu
Web site: http://www.milton.edu

MORAVIAN ACADEMY

Bethlehem, Pennsylvania

Type: Day college-preparatory school
Grades: PK–12: Lower School, Prekindergarten–5; Middle School, 6–8; Upper School, 9–12
Enrollment: School total: 775 ; Upper School: 300
Head of School: George N. King Jr., Headmaster

THE SCHOOL

Moravian Academy (MA) traces its origin back to 1742 and the Moravians who settled Bethlehem. Guided by the wisdom of John Amos Comenius, Moravian bishop and renowned educator, the Moravian Church established schools in every community in which it settled. Moravian Academy became incorporated in 1971 when Moravian Seminary for Girls and Moravian Preparatory School were merged. The school has two campuses: the Lower–Middle School campus in the historic downtown area of Bethlehem and the Upper School campus on a 120-acre estate 6 miles to the east.

For more than 270 years, Moravian Academy has encouraged sound innovations to meet contemporary challenges while recognizing the permanence of basic human values. The school seeks to promote young people's full development in mind, body, and spirit by fostering a love for learning, respect for others, joy in participation and service, and skill in decision-making. Preparation for college occurs in an atmosphere characterized by an appreciation for the individual.

Moravian Academy is governed by a Board of Trustees. Six members are representatives of the Moravian Church. As of June 30, 2012, the net asset value of the Academy is $36.1 million, of which $15.3 million is endowment. In 2011–12, Annual Giving was $415,888, and operating expenses were $14.9 million.

Moravian Academy is accredited by the Middle States Association of Colleges and Schools and the Pennsylvania Association of Independent Schools. The school is a member of the National Association of Independent Schools, the Association of Delaware Valley Independent Schools, the College Board, the Council for Spiritual and Ethical Education, the School and Student Service for Financial Aid, and the Secondary School Admission Test Board.

Moravian Academy does not discriminate on the basis of race, nationality, sex, sexual orientation, religious affiliation, or ethnic origin in the administration of its educational and admission policies, financial aid awards, and athletic or other school-administered programs. Applicants who are disabled (or applicants' family members who are disabled) and require any type of accommodation during the application process, or at any other time, are encouraged to identify themselves and indicate what type of accommodation is needed.

ACADEMIC PROGRAM

Students are required to carry five major courses per year. Minimum graduation requirements include English, 4 credits; mathematics, 3 credits; lab sciences, 3 credits; global language, 3 credits; social studies, 3 credits; fine arts, 2 credits; and physical education and health. All students must successfully complete a semester course in world religions or ethics. Community service is an integral part of the curriculum. Electives are offered in many areas, such as fine and performing arts, sciences, English, math, history, and global language. Moravian Academy offers Advanced Placement courses, numerous honors courses, and the opportunity to pursue an honors independent study project under the mentorship of a faculty member. The Academy also participates in a high school scholars program that enables a small number of highly qualified students to take college courses at no cost. The overall student-faculty ratio is about 9:1, with classes ranging from 10 to 18 students.

Grades in most courses are A–F; D is a passing grade. However, a C- is required to advance to the next level in math and global languages. Reports are sent to parents on a monthly basis, and parent-conference opportunities are scheduled in the fall semester. Faculty and staff members are available for additional conferences whenever necessary. Examinations are held at the end of each seventeen-week semester in all major subjects. In the senior year, final examinations are given in May to allow seniors time for a two-week Post Term Experience before graduation.

FACULTY AND ADVISERS

The Upper School has 39 full-time and 4 part-time faculty members. Ninety-five percent of the full-time Upper School faculty members have advanced degrees. Several faculty members have degrees in counseling in addition to other subjects, and the entire faculty shares in counseling through the Faculty-Student Adviser Program.

George N. King Jr. was appointed Headmaster in 2007. He previously served as the Head of the Wooster School in Danbury, Connecticut. Mr. King received his B.A. from Murray State University and his M.A. from the New England Conservatory of Music.

COLLEGE ADMISSION COUNSELING

The Director of College Counseling begins group work in college guidance in the tenth grade. Tenth graders take a practice PSAT and repeat it the following year. Sophomore Seminar encourages students to familiarize themselves with the college application process; the focus is on understanding academic options and participation in school and community life. College Night is held annually for juniors and their parents. Junior Seminar meets weekly in small groups for college counseling during the second semester and includes an individual family conference in the spring. They take the PSAT, SAT, and Subject Tests. Some students also elect to take the ACT in their junior or senior year. Senior Seminar meets weekly in small groups during the first semester for additional guidance and seniors are led through the college application process. They take the SAT and Subject Tests again, if necessary. In recent years, approximately 85 to 90 percent of the senior class takes at least one Advanced Placement exam and earns a score of 3 or higher.

Average SAT scores of 2012 graduates were 649 critical reading, 636 math, and 650 writing. Graduates of 2012 are attending Bates, Boston College, Boston University, Bucknell, Columbia, Davidson, Duke, Emory, Georgetown, George Washington, Lafayette, Lehigh, Notre Dame, Penn State, United States Naval Academy, Richmond, Tufts, Vanderbilt, Villanova, Wake Forest, Washington (St. Louis), Wellesley, and the Universities of Chicago, Pennsylvania, and Pittsburgh. Some students participate in travel abroad or gap year programs before attending college.

STUDENT BODY AND CONDUCT

The Upper School has 300 students. The school understands the value of diversity in the educational setting. In all divisions, students and faculty members from a variety of ethnic, cultural, religious, and socioeconomic backgrounds carry on this commitment. Through classroom activities, nondenominational chapel services discussing many faiths, and active engagement with each other, students at Moravian Academy are encouraged to appreciate one another's individuality.

Students enjoy the small classes and the opportunity for participation in sports and other activities. Students are expected to wear clothing that is neat and appropriate for school. Denim is not permitted during the school day, and a school uniform is required for members of performing groups. Students participate actively in a Student Council. Serious matters of discipline come before a faculty-student discipline committee.

ACADEMIC FACILITIES

Snyder House, Walter Hall, Couch Fine Arts Center, and the Heath Science Complex hold the classrooms, studios, and laboratories (chemistry, physics, biology, and computer). In September 2007, the Academy dedicated the new Van S. Merle-Smith Woodworking Studio. All of the library's resources are integrated with the instructional program to intensify and individualize the educational experience. Technology plays an important role in enhancing learning and students get hands-on experience with the latest equipment in classrooms and labs. There are dedicated computer labs, additional computers in the library, portable wireless labs, and a computer in every classroom. SmartBoards are used in all divisions to enhance the learning process. The Couch Fine Arts Center houses the studio arts department. A 350-seat auditorium enhances the music and theater programs. Students can also use the resources and facilities of the seven colleges and universities in the area.

ATHLETICS

A strong athletics program meets the guidelines of the school's philosophy that a person must be nurtured in body, as well as in mind and spirit, and that respect for others and participation are important goals. A large gymnasium, eight athletics fields, and six tennis courts provide the school with facilities for varsity and junior varsity teams in boys' and girls' lacrosse and baseball; girls' field hockey; boys' and girls' basketball, cross-country, soccer, swimming, and tennis; coeducational golf; and a girls' varsity softball team. Students also have the opportunity to participate in girls' volleyball, football, track, and wrestling in co-operative programs with a local school. A gymnasium that includes a weight room complements the physical education facilities in Walter Hall. An outdoor recreational pool is available for special student functions as well as the Academy's summer day camp program for younger children.

All students take part in team sports. In any given athletic season, more than one third of the Upper School student body participates in after-school athletics at the Academy.

EXTRACURRICULAR OPPORTUNITIES

Moravian Academy's activity program provides opportunities for varied interests and talents. Included are service projects, outdoor education, International Club, *Legacy* (yearbook), *The Moravian Star* (newspaper), *Green Ponderer* (literary magazine), Model Congress, Model UN, PJAS, Scholastic Scrimmage, and a variety of activities that change in response to student interests. A fine arts series combines music, art, drama, and dance. In addition, the Academy's outdoor education program offers a variety of off-campus experiences in hiking, rock climbing, and white water rafting/kayaking. The annual Country Fair gives students an opportunity to work with the Parents' Association to create a family fun day for the school and Lehigh Valley community. Rooted in Moravian tradition, a strong appreciation of music has continued. There are several student musical groups, including chorale, MA Chamber Singers, a cappella group, handbell choirs, and instrumental ensembles. Highlights of the year include the Christmas Vespers Service and the spring concert.

DAILY LIFE

A typical school day begins at 8 a.m., and classes run until 3:15 p.m. on Monday, Tuesday, Wednesday, and Friday. On Thursday, classes conclude at 2:45. The average length of class periods is about 40 minutes. Students usually take six classes a day.

A weekly nondenominational chapel service is held on Thursday mornings. On Monday, Tuesday, Wednesday, and Friday, there is a period for class, school, advisory meetings, or activity periods.

COSTS AND FINANCIAL AID

Tuition for 2012–13 is $23,550. There is an additional dining fee for students. An initial deposit of $1000 is required upon acceptance, and the remainder of the fee is to be paid in two installments, unless other arrangements are made. An additional fee for tuition insurance is recommended for all new students.

Financial aid is available. Moravian Academy uses the services of the School and Student Service for Financial Aid by NAIS. Aid is awarded on the basis of demonstrated financial need. Aid is received by approximately 29 percent of Upper School students.

ADMISSIONS INFORMATION

Students are admitted in grades 9–11. Each applicant is carefully considered. Students who demonstrate an ability and willingness to handle a rigorous academic program as well as such qualities as intellectual curiosity, responsibility, creativity, and cooperation, are encouraged to apply. Scores on tests administered by the school are also used in the admission process. In addition, school records, recommendations, and a personal interview are required. Admissions are usually completed by May, but there are sometimes openings available after that time.

APPLICATION TIMETABLE

Inquiries are welcome at any time. The Admission Office makes arrangements for tours and classroom visits during the school week. If necessary, other arrangements for tours can be made. The application fee is $65. Test dates are scheduled on specified Saturday mornings from January through March. Notifications are sent after February 15, and families are asked to respond within two weeks.

ADMISSIONS CORRESPONDENCE

Daniel J. Axford
Director of Admissions, Upper School
Moravian Academy
4313 Green Pond Road
Bethlehem, Pennsylvania 18020
United States
Phone: 610-691-1600
Web site: http://www.moravianacademy.org

MUNICH INTERNATIONAL SCHOOL

Starnberg, Germany

Type: Coeducational day college-preparatory school
Grades: PK–12: Junior School, Early Childhood (ages 4 and 5)–grade 4; Middle School, grades 5–8; Senior School, grades 9–12
Enrollment: School total: 1,202; Junior School: 405, Middle School: 375, Senior School: 422
Head of School: Simon Taylor

THE SCHOOL

Munich International School (MIS) is a nonprofit coeducational primary and secondary day school that serves students from early childhood (ages 4 and 5) through grade 12, with English as the language of instruction. A total of 1,202 students who represent about fifty countries and nationalities attend MIS. Students are accepted without regard to race, creed, nationality, or religion. The 26-acre MIS campus lies in an environmentally protected area of woodlands and farmland near scenic Lake Starnberg, some 20 kilometres (12 miles) south of Munich. School buses serve the cities of Munich and Starnberg and the surrounding region.

Founded in 1966, the School serves the international community in and around Munich, Germany, as well as those from the local community who wish to take advantage of the unique MIS educational experience. As an exemplary English language International Baccalaureate (I.B.) World School, MIS inspires students to be interculturally aware and achieve their potential within a stimulating and caring learning environment. The curriculum follows the frameworks of the I.B. Primary Years Programme (IBPYP) and the I.B. Middle Years Programme (IBMYP), which culminate in the final two years with the International Baccalaureate Diploma (IBDP) or the American high school diploma.

MIS regards the acquisition of knowledge, concepts, and skills as essential. They are seen as part of a broad and significant process of personal development toward independence, understanding, and tolerance. Learning is a lifelong process, and students are encouraged to cultivate a respect for learning and the ability and wisdom to use it well. Furthermore, since the School is an international and multicultural community, it seeks to develop in young people an active and lasting commitment to international cooperation.

All parents whose children attend MIS constitute the membership of the MIS Association, a tax-exempt, nonprofit organisation that elects a Board of Directors from its membership to operate the School in accordance with its Articles of Association.

Munich International School is fully accredited by the Council of International Schools (CIS) and the New England Association of Schools and Colleges (NEASC) and is approved by the German and Bavarian Educational Authorities.

ACADEMIC PROGRAMME

The academic programme throughout the School covers English language and literature, mathematics, humanities (including history, business and management, economics, geography, and social studies), sciences (including biology, chemistry, and physics), foreign languages, computer science, the fine arts, and film studies.

In the belief that students best benefit from the experience of living in Germany if they are able to communicate effectively and take part in local culture, MIS offers German language instruction to all students in early childhood classes through grade 12. Furthermore, comprehensive instruction in English as a second language (ESL) is offered to students who come to MIS with minimal or no English language skills. In the Senior School, however, English language competence is required for admission.

The School programme is designed so that all students have the opportunity to pursue studies in the fine arts (art, music, drama, and film studies) and computing, athletic, and recreational skills.

The Junior School (early childhood–grade 4) follows the curriculum of the IBPYP, which emphasises an inquiry-based approach to learning across all core academic subjects. The children are taught in self-contained classes in a nurturing environment. The early childhood classes prepare the students for successful entry into grade 1.

The Middle School (grades 5–8) provides a caring, stable environment with a balance of challenging academic studies and opportunities for curricular and extracurricular skill development. The curriculum conforms to the frameworks of the IBMYP in grades 5–8. The IBMYP is also part of the curriculum in grades 9 and 10. Studies emphasise the development of skills that involve moral reasoning, aesthetic judgment, and the use of scientific method. The Middle School is committed to providing students with the knowledge, learning strategies, and study skills necessary for the demanding Senior School programme. Food technology and ethics are introduced in grade 6, and French and Spanish are offered as electives from grade 6 onwards. Additional programmes that focus on health, design and technology, social skills, and the importance of the environment are also provided.

The academic programme of the Senior School (grades 9–12) is designed to prepare students for higher education. The guidance counselor especially encourages career planning to make students aware of the education and skills necessary to pursue lifetime goals. The academic programme culminates in grades 11 and 12, with studies leading to a full International Baccalaureate Diploma or an American high school diploma.

FACULTY AND ADVISERS

At MIS, more than 160 teachers from twenty-three nations are part of this broad international experience, coming from such countries as Australia, Canada, France, Germany, Great Britain, Hungary, Ireland, the Netherlands, New Zealand, Sri Lanka, and the United States. The faculty members are fully qualified; many have taught overseas and hold advanced degrees.

COLLEGE ADMISSION COUNSELING

Students have the opportunity to prepare and sit for the American PSAT, SAT, and ACT—tests normally needed for U.S. college entrance. About 90 percent of MIS graduates continue their education at universities and colleges in the world, including Columbia, Duke, the London School of Economics and Political Science, Middlebury, Politecnico Milano (Italy), Sciences Po (France), Tokyo Institute of Technology, Universita Bocconi (Italy), University of Munich, and the University of St. Andrews (Scotland), to cite some recent examples.

STUDENT BODY AND CONDUCT

The strong MIS community of students, teachers, and parents works together. MIS teachers and administrators understand the uncertainties and complexities that accompany a student's transition from one country to another and from one school to another, as well as the normal challenges of growing up. A coordinated support system across the School consists of homeroom teachers, grade coordinators, year coordinators, year advisers, IBPYP/IBMYP/IB coordinators, and guidance counselors.

ACADEMIC FACILITIES

The Junior School is housed in a modern facility, with spacious, light-filled classrooms that radiate from a central multipurpose activity area. There are rooms for computing, German, ESL, learning support, art, and music classes as well as a large, well-equipped library. The Health Office and the School cafeteria, which serves hot meals, are also located in this building.

The Middle School is also located in a modern building. The architectural concept maximizes the use of windows, allowing students to feel close to the natural beauty of the campus. In addition to the spacious classrooms, there are two science laboratories, and a multipurpose auditorium as well as rooms for ESL, academic support, music, and food technology.

The Senior School combines a new building and a traditional Bavarian-style building. Multipurpose classrooms are enhanced by five science laboratories, music and computer rooms, a library, a student lounge, and a performing arts center.

Stately Schloss Buchhof, an original manor house of the area that dates back to 1875, has been renovated to house the Middle and Senior School fine arts departments as well as the administrative offices of the School.

ATHLETICS

Sports activities, which play an important role at MIS, are conducted for all ages after school and during weekends. Soccer, skiing, volleyball, basketball, track and field, tennis, cross-country, and softball are the main sports offered. Tennis courts, several sports fields, and a well-equipped triple gymnasium are available on campus.

The School competes in several ISST tournaments and participates in local leagues and events under the auspices of a School-sponsored sports club. Middle and Senior School teams represent MIS at various international school competitions across Europe.

EXTRACURRICULAR OPPORTUNITIES

In order to take advantage of the experience of living in Germany and Europe, there is a wide range of half- or full-day field trips at all school levels. There are overnight trips for the Middle and Senior School, when teachers and students travel both within Germany and beyond for educational and cultural experiences.

Students may select from a variety of activities in the fine arts, ranging from painting, drawing, and ceramics to handicrafts, drama, and dance. There are several School choirs, bands, and an orchestra. Private instrumental instruction is available. A number of student drama productions are performed throughout the year. Senior and Middle School students participate in the International School Theatre Festival, the Speech and Debate Team, and several international school tournaments. Students in grades 11 and 12 have a weekly period set aside for recreational sports and service activities. They may take part in the Business@School and Model United Nations programmes.

Each year, a group of 8 to 10 students travels to Tanzania to visit project sites funded by donations from the MIS community. The travelling students present their findings at special assemblies held in each division of the School.

An active Parent-Teacher Organisation (PTO) operates as a voluntary support group for the School and fellow parents. The PTO organises a wide range of activities throughout the year, including a Ski Swap, Winterfest, and, in the spring, Frühlingsfest.

DAILY LIFE

The school year begins at the end of August and ends in late June. It is interspersed with short vacations, usually a week at the end of October, two weeks at Christmas, a Ski Week, and two weeks for Spring Break.

The school day starts at 9:10 a.m.; it ends at 3:15 p.m. for Junior School students and at 4 p.m. for Middle and Senior School students. Buses organised by the School and serving most areas in and around Munich provide transportation for nearly 80 percent of the students.

SUMMER PROGRAMMES

A two-week daytime sports programme at the beginning of July includes a week of camping in the Dolomite Mountains in northern Italy.

COSTS AND FINANCIAL AID

In the school year 2011–12, tuition was €12 400 for pre-reception–grade 5, €14 175 for grades 6–8, and €15 550–15 700 for grades 9–12. There is also an entrance fee of €7000 per child upon initial admission and an additional €3000 per child in each of the following two school years.

ADMISSIONS INFORMATION

Applicants are advised that the School does not have the facilities to serve the educational needs of students who have mental, emotional, or physical handicaps or severe learning disabilities. The School does not have boarding facilities.

APPLICATION TIMETABLE

Interested students are required to submit a completed MIS application packet. Following submission of all required documentation, applicants are screened. Based on the School's judgment of the suitability of the educational programme for the prospective student and on space availability, applicants are admitted throughout the year. Earliest acceptance of application material is six months prior to attendance and/or January of that particular year. A nonrefundable application fee is paid in advance of admission decisions being made.

ADMISSIONS CORRESPONDENCE

Admissions Office
Munich International School
Schloss Buchhof
D-82319 Starnberg
Germany
Phone: 49-8151-366-120
Fax: 49-8151-366-129
E-mail: admissions@mis-munich.de
Web site: http://www.mis-munich.de

THE PENNINGTON SCHOOL

Pennington, New Jersey

Type: Coeducational day and boarding college-preparatory school
Grades: 6–12: Middle School, 6–8; Upper School, 9–12
Enrollment: School total: 485; Middle School, 87; Upper School: 397
Head of School: Stephanie G. Townsend, Head of School

THE SCHOOL

The Pennington School is an independent coeducational school for students in grades 6 through 12, with both day and boarding programs. The curriculum is college preparatory, with an emphasis on fostering the development of the whole student through academics, athletics, community service, and the creative and performing arts. There are also specialized programs within the curriculum for international students and for students with learning differences. Founded in 1838, The Pennington School values both tradition and innovation, applying the values gleaned from centuries of learning along with the most up-to-date knowledge, to a rapidly changing world. The School's faculty members focus not only on what they can teach the students but also on what the varied perspectives of the student body can impart to the overall educational experience.

The 54-acre campus is strategically located in a suburban setting just 60 miles from New York City, 40 miles from Philadelphia, and within 8 miles of Princeton. This location makes it convenient for cultural and educational field trips.

The governing body is a 36-member Board of Trustees. Pennington's endowment currently stands at $26 million.

The Pennington School is accredited by the Middle States Association of Colleges and Schools and approved by the New Jersey Association of Independent Schools. It is a member of the National Association of Independent Schools, the New Jersey Association of Independent Schools, and the Secondary School Admission Test Board. The Pennington School is affiliated with the University Senate and the Board of Higher Education and Ministry of the United Methodist Church.

ACADEMIC PROGRAM

The Pennington School's objectives are to offer a challenging and broad academic program that best prepares its students for life as college students.

Middle School students concentrate on five major subject areas: math, English, social studies, science, and foreign language. All students rotate through a series of exploratory courses during the year, including art/drama, music, health, technology, writing workshop, and ethics.

Students in the Upper School usually take six classes per day. The minimum number of credits necessary for graduation is 20. Requirements include the following: English, 4; mathematics, 3; history, 3; science, 3; foreign language, 2; religion, 1; art, 1; health, 1; technology, ½; and public speaking, ¼. Honors and Advanced Placement courses are offered in all disciplines.

The student-teacher ratio is 8:1, and the average class size is 13, with a maximum of 18 students in any one class. A 2-hour evening study period for boarders is supervised. The School library is open a half-hour before the school day begins until the conclusion of study hall on school nights and for limited hours on weekends.

The School uses the semester system, but, with midterm evaluations, there are four marking periods. Parent-teacher or parent-adviser-student conferences are held twice a year. Individual conferences are arranged as required.

Official grades are issued at the conclusion of each semester. The Pennington School uses a letter grading system in which D– (60) is a passing grade but C– (70) is the minimum grade for a course to count toward graduation requirements.

The Pennington School has two unique programs: a Center for Learning, a program designed for bright, academically talented students with language-based learning differences, and an English as a second language (ESL) program.

FACULTY AND ADVISERS

The faculty consists of 100 men and women, about half of whom live on campus. The Seventy percent of the faculty members hold advanced degrees. Faculty members serve as advisers for 6 to 8 students, and oversee each student's life at the school. Trained counselors are also available to all students for specific needs. Teachers also serve as hall parents, providing the basis for yet another kind of close relationship.

Stephanie (Penny) Townsend, appointed Head of School in 2006, earned her bachelor's degree from the University of Connecticut and her master's degree from Middlebury College. Before coming to The Pennington School, she taught Spanish at Northfield Mount Hermon School in Massachusetts and at the Taft School in Connecticut. Most recently, Townsend served as the Dean of Faculty at the Taft School.

COLLEGE ADMISSION COUNSELING

College guidance is the responsibility of trained counselors who coordinate all aspects of the college planning and placement process, including the taking of PSAT, SAT, TOEFL, and Advanced Placement tests. Representatives from almost 200 colleges visit The Pennington School each year to meet with students. Juniors and seniors meet individually with their college counselors and attend college admission panels. Juniors attend special college programs, including two spring on-campus college fairs, and take a college admission seminar.

The School's recent graduates attend such colleges and universities including American, Boston College, Boston University, Brown, Bucknell, Columbia, Emory, Georgetown, Harvey Mudd, Hofstra, Lafayette, Lehigh, NYU, Parsons, Rutgers, Syracuse, Trinity (Hartford), Villanova, Williams, the University of Pennsylvania, and the University of Saint Andrews (Scotland).

STUDENT BODY AND CONDUCT

Of The Pennington School's 485 students, 87 are in the Middle School and 397 are in the Upper School; 383 are day students, and 101 are boarding students. Current students represent seven states and come from a number of countries, including the Bahamas, Bulgaria, China, Korea, Russia, Spain, Taiwan, Uzbekistan, and the West Indies. Twenty percent of the students belong to minority groups.

There is a student government, elected by the student body. Students are expected to follow the rules defined in the *Student/Parent Handbook*. Violations may be dealt with by the Behavior Review Board, which is made up of students and faculty members.

During class hours, Upper School boys must wear collared shirts, slacks, and dress shoes; on certain days, shirts and ties are required. Upper School girls must wear slacks or skirts with collared shirts or blouses. Middle School students wear polo shirts and khakis. Monday night formal dinners and certain programs call for jackets and ties for boys and dresses or skirts and blouses for girls. The dress code permits jeans, T-shirts, and sneakers to be worn by students after class hours, on weekends, and on dress-down days but not during class time.

ACADEMIC FACILITIES

The centers of academic activities are Stainton Hall, a classroom/administration building; the Campus Center, containing art and music studios, a theater, foreign language classrooms, science labs and the Student Center; Meckler Library, which contains the academic book collection, online databases, and the Computer Center; and Old Main, which houses classrooms and five residence halls.

BOARDING AND GENERAL FACILITIES

In addition to Old Main, there are two dormitories containing another five residence halls: Becher Hall, a one-story residence with ten student rooms and two faculty apartments, and Buck Hall, containing four halls with double rooms and private bathrooms. There are eight faculty apartments in this building. The School has an attractive dining facility and a health center, with 2 registered nurses in residence. Boarding facilities close for the Thanksgiving, Christmas, and spring holidays, so all students must leave the campus during those vacation periods. The Pennington School also has numerous athletic facilities, as described below.

ATHLETICS

The Pennington School believes that the lessons learned through athletics involvement are valuable ones. Thus, every student is expected to participate in a team or individual sport that fits his or her own ability level. Although The Pennington School's athletic teams are very successful and frequently win state championships, the emphasis is on participation, collective effort, sportsmanship, and personal growth. All students must participate in at least one sport per year. Boarders must take three terms of activities. When boarding students are not involved in a sport, they must be involved in other extracurricular activities.

The sports available for boys and girls in grades 9 to 12 are basketball, cheerleading, cross-country, golf, lacrosse, soccer, swimming, tennis, track and field, and water polo. In addition, field hockey and softball are available for girls, and baseball, football, and ice hockey are offered for boys.

In addition to a gymnasium/swimming pool complex, The Pennington School has five tennis courts, 30 acres of playing fields, an all-weather-surface track, and a lighted artificial turf field lined for lacrosse, soccer, and football. The School also offers weight training with a facility housing the SOURCE Institute for Human Performance.

EXTRACURRICULAR OPPORTUNITIES

Life at The Pennington School is more than classrooms, laboratories, and the library, essential as these are. Opportunities exist for participation in a wide range of extracurricular activities.

Apart from the athletics program, there are many clubs and organizations that students may join. These include three drama productions a year, the Pennington Singers, Mock Trial, Peer Leadership, National Honor Society, Photography Club, International Club, International Thespian Society, Model United Nations, Pennington Sports News, Youth Service Fellowship, Campus Guides, United People of Many Colors, jazz ensemble, chamber ensemble, Junior Proctors, foreign language clubs, and staffs of the yearbook, newspaper, and literary magazine, which contains creative writing and artistic work of students. All students are encouraged to do community service during the year. Students do volunteer work for hospitals and charitable organizations in Pennington, Princeton, and Trenton and travel globally on service-related trips during School vacations.

A student activities program provides for social events such as dances, ski trips, movies, theater presentations, and visits to area places of interest.

Life at The Pennington School also includes a weekly chapel service. Chapel services are a peaceful time for reflection and thought about life and love, friendship and community, right and wrong—themes that are important in every religion and in every country. The School's students are multidenominational, believing in Christianity, Hinduism, Islam, Judaism, Quakerism, and Buddhism.

DAILY LIFE

The day's activities begin at 8 a.m. and conclude at 2:45 p.m. There is an activities period on Fridays and a bimonthly community meeting on Wednesdays. There are two lunch periods. An extra-help conference period follows the class day. Sports practice takes place from 3:15 to 5:15, and dinner follows at 5:30 for boarding students. A monitored study period for boarders from 7:30 to 9:30 completes the day. Lights are out at 10:30 p.m. on weekdays.

WEEKEND LIFE

Day students and boarders are encouraged to participate in weekend activities coordinated by residential faculty. These include functions on campus as well as trips off campus to attend plays, museums, festivals, and professional sports contests. The library, swimming pool, and gymnasium are open on weekends. Transportation is also provided to shopping centers, where students may shop, eat, or see a movie.

COSTS AND FINANCIAL AID

The 2012–13 charges are $30,950 for day students and $46,100 for boarding students, with additional charges for Center for Learning and ESL classes. Additional costs are a book deposit of $500 or $600, and an activity fee of $150 or $350. There are special fees for private music lessons and tutoring. An allowance of $15 to $25 per week is recommended for spending money for residential students.

When an enrollment contract is signed, a nonrefundable deposit of 10 percent of tuition for day students and boarders is required to hold a space for the student; it is applied toward the year's tuition. The remainder of the tuition may be paid in installments of one half on July 15 and the remaining half on November 1, or tuition may be paid through a ten-month payment plan. Enrollment in school tuition insurance is required.

Financial aid is based on demonstrated need. Parents applying for aid must submit the required paperwork and forms through TADS. Financial aid is granted on an annual basis. Thirty percent of the students received financial aid for the 2012–13 school year.

ADMISSIONS INFORMATION

The Pennington School seeks students who have strong academic ability, as demonstrated on their school transcript and the SSAT, good character, and a record of good citizenship. Approximately 37 percent of the applicants are accepted for admission.

The School does not discriminate on the basis of race, color, religion, gender, or national or ethnic origin in the administration of its admission or educational policies or the financial aid, athletic, or other School-administered programs.

APPLICATION TIMETABLE

Students should begin the application process for The Pennington School early in the fall. The School uses a March 10 notification date, an April 10 reply date, and then rolling admissions as space is available. Students who wish to be considered in March should have all materials and the $50 application fee submitted online and the interview completed by February 1. The Admission Office is open throughout the year for interviews and tours of the campus from 8:15 to 2:00, Monday through Friday, by appointment.

ADMISSIONS CORRESPONDENCE

Stephen D. Milich
Director of Admission and Financial Aid
The Pennington School
Pennington, New Jersey 08534
United States
Phone: 609-737-6128
Fax: 609-730-1405
E-mail: admiss@pennington.org
Web site: http://www.pennington.org

PRESBYTERIAN PAN AMERICAN SCHOOL

Kingsville, Texas

Type: Coeducational college-preparatory boarding school and day school
Grades: 9–12 plus a fifth/bridge year
Enrollment: 170
Head of School: Dr. Robert L. (Doug) Dalglish

THE SCHOOL

Founded in 1911 on land from the world-renowned King Ranch, Presbyterian Pan American School (Pan Am) has distinguished itself over the past century for its commitment to preparing international students, along with racial and ethnic minorities, for a university-level education. Although students come from many countries in addition to the United States, all classroom instruction is in English. English as a second language (ESL) is the foundation of an international student's first year, with faculty and classes assigned on the basis of proficiency testing administered during the first week on campus.

Pan Am seeks applicants who show clear evidence of a lively intelligence—students who are at ease communicating with others, open to experiencing the wider world, and eager to discover and explore the possibilities it holds for them.

Enrollment at Pan Am ranges from 150 to 175, with approximately the same number of boys and girls. In recent years students have come from South Korea, Mexico, China, Japan, Rwanda, Ecuador, Peru, Bolivia, Hong Kong, Taiwan, Guatemala, Colombia, Costa Rica, Spain, Equatorial Guinea, and the United States.

As a mission school of the Presbyterian Church (U.S.A.), Pan Am offers a generous program of financial aid. The majority of students come from Christian families, either Protestant or Roman Catholic; however, the admissions process is blind to both religion and a family's economic situation. Students attend chapel services and take elective courses in Bible. In their upperclass semesters they participate in usually spirited seminars that require critical thinking about selected topics in ethics, economic justice, and human rights, particularly as informed by the teachings and ideals of the Protestant Reformation. However, the School does not attempt to proselytize and indeed prizes and teaches a wholesome respect for the reality and diversity of God's creation.

Pan Am is located on a 670-acre working cattle ranch in Kingsville, Texas, less than an hour's drive from the Corpus Christi International Airport and about an hour and a half north of the U.S. border with Mexico.

The School is accredited by the Southern Association of Colleges and Schools (SACS), is a member of the Texas Association of Non-Public Schools (TANS), and follows graduation requirements set forth by the Texas Education Agency (TEA).

ACADEMIC PROGRAM

Classroom instruction, along with a student's social formation, is designed to equip the student for success in college and eventually in a satisfying career. A student who fully utilizes Pan American School's many resources should be able to achieve a minimum average grade of 85 in college. Each student is coached to attain a score of 550 on the standardized Test of English as a Foreign Language (TOEFL).

In addition to traditional high school subjects, Pan Am offers instruction in speech, journalism, economics, fine arts, computers, horticulture and agriculture, health and hygiene, physical education, and religious studies. Practical experience in robotics is offered when instructors are available. For those students eager for the experience, the School offers a supervised 4-H program in which participants raise their own animal, which will eventually be sold at the annual livestock show and auction. No previous ranch experience is required.

Classes average about 20 students each. The student-faculty ratio is 10:1.

Senior students who score well on a college placement exam have the option of taking college-level classes for dual credit at Coastal Bend College. In a typical year, up to one third of the senior class graduates with college credits in math, English, government, or economics.

Pan Am also offers a fifth "bridge" year for international students who are academically strong but whose command of English might place them at a competitive disadvantage in a U.S. college classroom. The emphasis of the bridge year is strengthening a student's English reading comprehension, speaking, writing, and listening skills.

FACULTY AND ADVISERS

The professional staff includes classroom teachers; resource specialists; specialists in art, music, and physical education; a school principal (or dean); academic and psychological counselors; a computer network engineer; and a library and media specialist. Many are graduates of Texas A&M University–Kingsville and/or are working toward advanced degrees on that campus.

Several staff members, including the president and spiritual life director, live on campus. Parents are invited to visit, phone, or e-mail faculty members. Each student's family receives an online password to access their child's grades, along with comments and observations from teachers and counselors.

COLLEGE ADMISSION COUNSELING

Academic counselors advise each student regarding options for college. Each senior is required to apply to a minimum of three colleges or universities, which may be in the United States, the student's home country, or elsewhere in the world. Many choose to study in Texas before returning home.

Presbyterian Pan American School is proud of its nearly 100 percent college acceptance rate among senior class students. In recent years, Pan Am's graduates have been accepted by such fine institutions as Baylor, Dordt, Schreiner, Technológico de Monterrey, Texas A&M, Trinity (San Antonio), Universidad Autónoma de Nuevo León, Universidad Iberoamericana, Universidad Nacional Autónoma de México, University of Houston, The University of Texas at Austin, and other locations in The University of Texas and Texas A&M University systems.

ACADEMIC FACILITIES

The campus includes four classroom buildings offering science labs, an art studio, choir room, and computer lab and a library with a media center. The campus is served by multiple T-1 high-speed Internet lines and also provides wireless access. Also, at this time, all students have a school e-mail address.

BOARDING AND GENERAL FACILITIES

In addition to the academic facilities, there are a number of other buildings on the 50-acre campus. A kitchen and a dining hall serves three meals daily to the student body and staff. The Morris Chapel is the center of worship and spiritual life. Boys and girls live in their respective dormitory complexes, each with lounge facilities and a resident adult staff of dorm parents and assistants. A gymnasium contains basketball and volleyball courts. In addition there are administrative offices, a teachers' lounge and offices, and a student union building.

ATHLETICS

Presbyterian Pan American School points proudly to a string of Texas state championships in boys' soccer. In addition, the School offers girls' soccer, both boys' and girls' basketball, girls' volleyball, cheerleading, girls' and boys' track, and boys' baseball. There is also an outdoor basketball court, a tennis court, a soccer field and track, and a swimming pool. Student lifeguards are Red Cross–trained and certified. The boys' and girls' dorm complexes include fitness facilities and boys' and girls' centers.

EXTRACURRICULAR OPPORTUNITIES

Pan Am firmly believes that social and personal formation is at least as vital as academic information in preparing young people to take their places in the world. While athletics offer the most obvious extracurricular outlets, the School provides additional activities as well. A professionally led choir affords training and vocal coaching. Choir members have the opportunity to compete at the annual TAAPS All-State Choir competition. The Morris Chapel Choir visits around the state and serves as a powerful outreach for the School. The 4-H Club presents opportunities to participate in raising lambs on the School's extensive ranch. Quilting and photography students are also able to participate and compete through 4-H competitions. Student Council, drama club, yearbook, and National Honor Society further develop leadership and organizational ability. The chapel's praise band offers students the opportunity to perform in an organized musical group. Student-led committees abound, ranging from worship to waste recycling, and there are frequent class fund-raising projects and opportunities to contribute to the student-produced newspaper.

DAILY LIFE

Students clean their rooms each morning in preparation for inspection. Breakfast is at 7:15 a.m. on weekdays and later on weekends. The first class of the day begins at 7:45. The work program, choir, and athletic activities are held after classes dismiss in the afternoon. Computer lab is held on alternate evenings for boys and girls. Free time for informal athletics, board games, jogging, and other recreation is available following dinner. There is a required chapel worship service twice a week and on Sunday, with students working alongside the director of spiritual life to plan and lead the worship. Students typically have several hours of homework to complete before lights-out at 10:30 p.m.

Since the School's founding in 1911, the student work program has been an integral component of the weekday routine. Each student is required to perform 6 hours per week of supervised on-campus work, which may include cleaning the library or public areas of the dorms, assisting in the kitchen, sanitizing tables in the dining hall, maintenance of facilities, collecting trash, gardening, or other routine tasks.

Weekends at Pan Am are as important as weekdays and begin just as the last class ends on Friday. There is no work program on Fridays. Friday evening activities are usually in the Student Union Building (SUB), where there are movies and dances, cards and chess, and pool and ping-pong. Saturdays and Sundays are also times when students may be driven into Kingsville or the malls in Corpus Christi to shop and hang out together. Weekend activities also include occasional barbecues over native mesquite cut from the ranch, outings to NCAA Division II athletic events, or gatherings at the swimming pool in season. Many students enjoy the tree-covered campus as a pleasant place to come together to play the guitar, sing, and be with friends. Students attend mandatory worship services on Sunday mornings. Students who live within driving distance of the campus can sign out of the dorm with parental permission and spend an occasional weekend at home, often inviting friends and roommates to go with them.

COSTS AND FINANCIAL AID

Tuition and fees in 2012–13 were $15,000 for boarding students and $8500 for day students. This includes room, board, tuition, and test fees for PSAT, SAT, and TOEFL.

The School offers a tuition installment plan and is able to accept online payments via credit card. As a mission school of the Presbyterian Church (U.S.A.), Pan Am remains committed to being financially accessible to families with modest financial resources. Most years, about 85 percent of the student body receives some degree of need-based financial aid. Nearly $1,000,000 was awarded for the 2011–12 school year.

ADMISSIONS INFORMATION

Presbyterian Pan American School admits students into grades 9 through 12 and also offers a post–high school year of intensive English language studies for international students who are preparing to apply to a U.S. college. Interested parents and prospective students may find further information online at www.ppas.org. Admission packets are available on the website or by contacting the Office of Admissions. Visits to the campus are recommended. For families living far from the United States, the director of admissions can conduct a webcam interview over the Internet.

Once an international student has been admitted, the School will issue a U.S. Department of Homeland Security Form I-20, which is the application for an F-1 Student Visa. Once the Form I-20 has been received, students must make an appointment with the U.S. Embassy or a consular office in their home country, where they will be interviewed regarding their reasons for wishing to study in the United States and their future plans back home.

APPLICATION TIMETABLE

Inquiries are welcome at any time. The School begins receiving applications in January of each year but cannot make an admissions decision until the applicant's file is complete. Applications should be submitted by June 30 of each year, although they may be accepted later if space is available. The application fee is $75, payable either in cash or online.

ADMISSIONS CORRESPONDENCE

Mr. Joe L. Garcia, Director of Admissions
Presbyterian Pan American School
Post Office Box 1578
223 North FM Road 772
Kingsville, Texas 78364
United States
Phone: 361-592-4307
Fax: 361-592-6126
E-mail: jlgarcia@ppas.org
Web site: www.ppas.org

RANNEY SCHOOL

Tinton Falls, New Jersey

Type: Coeducational college-preparatory day school
Grades: BG (3 years old)–grade 12: Lower School, BG–Grade 5; Middle School, Grades 6–8; Upper School, Grades 9–12
Enrollment: School total: 818
Head of School: Lawrence S. Sykoff, Ed.D.

THE SCHOOL

Ranney School was founded in 1960 by Russell G. Ranney for the purpose of fostering high academic achievement. A former Associate Director of the New York University Reading Institute, Mr. Ranney was a firm believer in the three R's. A 19-member Board of Trustees, plus the Head of School, supervises the School's operation on its campus of more than 60 acres in a residential neighborhood located approximately 45 miles south of New York City.

Ranney School is dedicated to engaging its students in an exemplary, well-rounded education, one that promotes the development of every child's intellectual, personal, creative, and moral promise. By serving a diverse community that values a rigorous, wide-ranging program of study, Ranney students are inspired to reach their full potential. Guided by dedicated and compassionate professionals, the Ranney experience is distinguished by the heartfelt bond between student and teacher—the hallowed principle celebrating the unique nature of every child. In an environment with contemporary learning resources, students learn the value of contributing to their local and global communities through leadership and service. The School's motto, "knowledge, vision, honor," is as much an inspiration as it is a social imperative, one that informs the thinking and actions the School's students. Awakening students' intellectual potential and encouraging them to communicate with confidence in their own unique voice remains fundamental to the Ranney experience. The ultimate success of Ranney students is the result of a simple yet powerful mission-promise, that every child will be known and valued.

The Board of Trustees is the School's governing body. During 2011–12, annual giving totaled $754,000; annual operating expenses average $22 million.

Ranney School alumni number approximately 1,710. An Alumni Council oversees alumni activities.

Ranney School is accredited by the Middle States Association of Colleges and Schools. The School maintains active membership in the National Association of Independent Schools (NAIS), the New Jersey Association of Independent Schools (NJAIS), the Council for Advancement and Support of Education (CASE), the Educational Records Bureau (ERB), and the National Association for College Admission Counseling (NACAC).

ACADEMIC PROGRAM

The Lower School (beginners [age 3] through grade 5) curriculum is designed to stimulate a child's natural love of learning. Goals are set forth in a program consistent with the early stages of child development. The primary goal is to maximize the growth of each individual. The curriculum remains rooted in the development of language arts. Course time is allotted to vocabulary building, spelling, grammar usage, reading, and the development of writing skills. Strong programs in mathematics, science, social studies, instrumental music, and computer education complement these courses. Students are also introduced to studies in the fine arts, music, and world languages. Aquatics and physical education complete the course of study. Teaching strategies include cooperative learning, interdisciplinary arrangements, and individual attention.

The Middle School (grades 6 through 8) curriculum is designed to provide a special community in which students can grow, learn about themselves, develop personal and group values, and prepare for the challenges of higher learning, particularly within the Ranney Upper School. The comprehensive English and mathematics programs initiated in the Lower School continue through the middle years, along with additional concentrations in science, history, and world languages, including Mandarin Chinese. A one-to-one laptop program begins in Middle School, with courses in computer fundamentals, art, music, drama, word processing, physical education, and aquatics. To provide flexibility in instruction, some classes in math, history, and world languages are arranged to cover the curriculum over a two-year period.

The Upper School (grades 9 through 12) graduation requirements include a minimum of 20 academic credits, plus 4 units in health and physical education. All students are expected to take 5 full credits of course work each year. Specific requirements include English (4 credits), world language (3 credits), history (3 credits, 2 of which must be American history), mathematics (3 credits), science (2 credits with lab, including biology and either chemistry or physics), art (1 credit), and physical education (4 credits). In addition to required courses, a number of single-semester and full-year electives are available to sophomores, juniors, and seniors. The Upper School curriculum also offers many honors and college-level Advanced Placement (AP) courses. Nineteen AP units are available to students who are capable of accelerated study. All Upper School students receive a laptop computer in addition to the digital media center on campus.

Ranney utilizes a numeric grading system with a 100-point scale. The school year consists of two semesters and four marking periods, with grades and written evaluations being sent home at the end of the first and third marking periods. Report cards with grades only are sent at the end of each semester. Midterm exams are given in January and final exams in June.

FACULTY AND ADVISERS

There are 92 full-time faculty members, plus 4 part-time instructors. Fifty-one faculty members have master's degrees or higher. Each Middle and Upper School faculty member serves as an adviser to an average of 6 to 8 students. Ranney faculty members are accomplished and recognized professionals whose contributions to the growth and status of their calling often extend outside the School community.

Dr. Lawrence S. Sykoff was appointed Headmaster in June 1993. He holds degrees from the University of San Diego (Ed.D. and M.Ed.) and Baruch College of Business Administration of the City University of New York (B.B.A.).

COLLEGE ADMISSION COUNSELING

The College Guidance Office is one of the distinguishing features of Ranney School. It all starts in ninth grade, where all student schedules pass through the college guidance office for review. Staff members then work closely with students, parents, and advisers throughout the Upper School years to ensure that each student follows an appropriate academic course, with clear and achievable goals. Beginning in tenth grade, students take the PSAT and the PLAN test and are guided by their college counselor to focus on either the ACT or SAT exam.

During the junior year, Ranney's college counselors meet one-on-one with students and parents to discuss all the variables in the college selection process and help focus each student's priorities, goals, and aspirations. Students enter the admission process well-prepared and well-informed, benefiting from individualized counseling designed to ensure success. Ranney's success is evident: 100 percent of graduates go on to attend four-year schools, 80 percent are admitted to their first- or second-choice college, and Ranney students regularly earn more than $2 million in scholarships.

All seniors receive direction from the College Guidance Office in writing college essays, interviewing skills, and preparing their final applications.

The mean SAT scores for 2012 graduates were 620 critical reading, 630 writing, and 620 math.

The senior class of 2012 achieved 100 percent college acceptance at schools such as Bucknell, Dartmouth, George Washington, NYU, Northeastern, and the University of Pennsylvania.

STUDENT BODY AND CONDUCT

The 2012–13 student body consists of 818 students, as follows: 168 boys and 170 girls in the Lower School, 115 boys and 94 girls in the Middle School, and 113 boys and 158 girls in the Upper School.

Ranney's families represent many countries, including China, India, Japan, and Russia. The School sponsors an International Week of Celebration each year in all three divisions.

A Judicial Board handles routine disciplinary issues in the Upper School. The board consists of 2 faculty members and 2 students and is chaired by the Dean of Students. Recommendations are given to the Principal and the Headmaster for review and decision.

ACADEMIC FACILITIES

The Lower School is comprised of three buildings and has its own computer lab, two science labs, and library. Ranney is a completely wireless campus with over fifty laptops and 100 iPads available in the Lower School. In addition, each classroom is equipped with two computers. The Middle School and Upper School are housed in Ranney's modern and high-tech academic complex. The facility offers thirty-three classrooms; state-of-the-art biology, chemistry, physics, and robotics laboratories; a world language laboratory; a college guidance center; a modern library with digital media center;

student assembly areas; 300 computers; and a unique Distance Learning Center. The entire building offers wireless Internet access. In addition, the Middle and Upper Schools have their own dining hall.

ATHLETICS

Ranney School encourages students to participate in sports and views athletics as an important part of the educational program. All students are eligible to participate regardless of ability. Ranney School offers twenty-five varsity-level sport teams, as well as a coed squash club. Ranney School also offers fourteen interscholastic teams on the middle school level, along with four club sports, including winter track, fencing, crew, and golf. Ranney competes against other accredited public and private schools in the area and maintains active membership in the Shore Conference of High Schools, the New Jersey Independent School Athletic Association, and the New Jersey State Interscholastic Athletic Association. Interscholastic competition begins in the sixth grade. The School has two gymnasiums; a newly renovated 25-meter indoor swimming pool; five new tennis courts; a baseball and softball field; and brand-new athletic facilities, including a synthetic turf field and all-weather track. In addition, there is a new fitness center with a certified athletic trainer on duty.

EXTRACURRICULAR OPPORTUNITIES

Ranney Plus is a robust, all-inclusive, after-school program that enriches opportunities for students of all ages at the School. Across the divisions, Ranney Plus plays an important role for students. It provides opportunities for students to explore activities that encompass global perspectives in the areas of performing arts, technology, science, math, and athletics, and also allows them to receive teacher-supported assistance with homework, study skills, or preparation for a specific subject assessment or project. Each division offers an array of selections for students to explore after school, such as clubs, specialized student activities, and athletic teams and interscholastic sports. Ranney Plus also provides complimentary after-care programs for students in the Lower and Middle Schools and late bus transportation for students in all divisions, grades 3–12. More information about Ranney Plus, registration forms, and transportation permission slips are available on the School's Web site.

In addition to Ranney Plus, the Lower School offers a variety of extracurricular and after-school activities for grades kindergarten through 5, including computers, art instruction, creative writing, chorus, band, cooking, swimming, and other sports.

Both the Middle and Upper Schools have a broad selection of student organizations in which to participate. Both schools have a student council, world language clubs, and excellent forensics teams. Students in grades 6 through 9 are eligible to join the Science Olympiad Team, which travels to Rider University for participation in the New Jersey State Science Olympiad.

The Upper School has an active chapter of the National Honor Society, seven academic honor societies, and a Cum Laude Society chapter. Students can also participate in Mock Trial, math, chess, and academic bowl teams. Chorus and drama clubs offer students an opportunity to perform for friends, parents, and peers. Publications include *Horizons* (the School's award-winning yearbook), *The Torch*, *The Beacon* (college guidance magazine), and *RSVP (Ranney School Verse & Prose)*, which showcases the talents of Ranney's young artists and authors.

Throughout the year, the Ranney School Fine Arts Department and Thespian Troupe present art exhibitions, music recitals, and two major drama productions. Traditional events include Spirit Day/Homecoming, International Week, Halloween Parade, Grandparents' Thanksgiving Feast, Parents' Day Tea, and Lower, Middle, and Upper School Carnivals (fund-raisers). Field trips, both interstate and intrastate, offer cultural exposure outside the Ranney campus for students in the middle and upper divisions. International student travel takes place each year, with students immersed in the culture of countries such as England, France, Italy, and Spain.

DAILY LIFE

The typical school day consists of six 45-minute academic periods and one 60-minute period, with a 10-minute break between second and third periods, plus a lunch period. Assemblies are held throughout the year. Each week, grades 6–12 meet with their advisers for approximately 20 minutes during an adviser period. School begins at 8:25 a.m. and ends at 3:25 p.m. The cafeteria serves hot and cold lunches. Bus transportation is available to most students.

SUMMER PROGRAMS

Students can enroll for two through six weeks to take enhancement and/or credit courses in several academic subject areas. Most courses are taught by Ranney School faculty members. In addition, an eight-, six-, or four-week summer day camp program is available for boys and girls ages 3 through 13. Ranney-in-the-Summer is fully accredited by the American Camping Association.

COSTS AND FINANCIAL AID

Tuition for 2012–13 ranges from $10,550 to $25,750. Extras include books (Lower School: $150–$550; Middle School: $400–$650; Upper School: $600–$900) and transportation ($4500–$5000). Parents of students in grades pre-K through 12 are required to purchase a $1000 bond, which is redeemed when the child either graduates or leaves Ranney School.

Ranney School is committed to awarding financial aid to those students who demonstrate a financial need. Families who feel that a need for assistance exists are encouraged to apply. The Financial Aid Committee of the Board of Trustees bases financial aid decisions on the formula provided by the School and Student Service for Financial Aid (SSS) in Princeton, New Jersey. The Financial Aid Committee diligently reviews each application in order to distribute available funds equitably. All applications are held in strict confidence. Each student applying for aid must be in good standing in all aspects of student life. Parents must complete the SSS financial aid form annually and should send it to Princeton as early as possible. Inquiries should be directed to the Associate Head for Admissions and Marketing.

Parents can arrange to pay the tuition over a ten-month period through Tuition Management Services. An enrollment deposit must be paid directly to the School upon registration.

ADMISSIONS INFORMATION

Standardized placement tests are administered on an individual or small-group basis. Transferring students should forward a completed application and appropriate school records to the Admission Office prior to the scheduled date of the placement exam. All candidates must complete an interview with appropriate members of the Admission Committee. Ranney School does not discriminate on the basis of sex, race, religion, ethnic origin, or disabilities in the administration of its education, hiring, and admission policies; financial aid program; and athletic or other School-administered programs.

APPLICATION TIMETABLE

Ranney School does not stipulate a formal application deadline, but it strongly recommends that parents contact the Admission Office during the fall to enroll for the next academic year. There is a $75 application fee.

ADMISSIONS CORRESPONDENCE

Joseph M. Tweed, Director of Admissions and Financial Aid
Ranney School
235 Hope Road
Tinton Falls, New Jersey 07724
United States
Phone: 732-542-4777 Ext. 1107
Fax: 732-460-1078
E-mail: jtweed@ranneyschool.org
Web site: http://www.ranneyschool.org

RIDLEY COLLEGE

St. Catharines, Ontario, Canada

Type: Coeducational, college-preparatory, boarding and day school
Grades: Lower School, JK–8; Upper School, 9–12/PG
Enrollment: School total: 627; Upper School, 444; Lower School, 183
Head of School: J. Edward Kidd, Headmaster

THE SCHOOL

Established in 1889, Ridley College was founded by a group of Anglican clergymen intending to provide boys in Ontario with an education that emphasized strong academic and religious values. Named after Bishop Nicholas Ridley, a sixteenth-century churchman in England martyred during the Protestant Reformation, the School was originally known as Bishop Ridley College. Ridley became coeducational in 1973. Ridley's school life philosophy embraces four essential qualities: academics, athletics, citizenship, and faith.

Ridley College is a university preparatory school that offers junior kindergarten through grade 12 with a postgraduate option. The campus is built on 100 acres of land near Lake Ontario, a few minutes from Niagara Falls. It is conveniently located 45 minutes from the Toronto Airport and Buffalo Airport.

Ridley College is accredited to the Canadian Accredited Independent Schools (CAIS) under the Ridley College Board of Governors. Ridley's endowment is currently $21.9 million. Ridley is a member of the National Association of Boarding Schools (NAIS), Conference of Independent Schools of Ontario (CIS), The Association of Boarding Schools (TABS), Canadian Association of Independent Schools (CAIS) and the Headmasters' and Headmistresses' Conference (HMC).

ACADEMIC PROGRAM

In September 2012, Ridley College began offering the International Baccalaureate Diploma Program alongside the Ontario Secondary School Diploma. Ridley College offers eighteen Advanced Placement courses. The average class size is 14.5 students, and the student-teacher ratio is 8:1. During weeknights there is mandatory study time set aside in the houses for boarding students. Evening study is also open to day students who wish to stay. Students have an opportunity to meet with their teachers after school and in the evening for tutorial sessions. Ridley College offers English language development classes and individual learning skills sessions for students with specific learning needs. Students can participate in an exchange program in their tenth-grade year; Ridley students have travelled to Australia, South Africa, Scotland, and Spain on exchange. The school year is divided into three trimesters, known as the Michaelmas, Lent, and Trinity terms. Progress reports are distributed throughout the term, and a final report is given at the end of each term. Teachers, coaches, housemasters, and academic advisers contribute individual comments to the reports.

FACULTY AND ADVISORS

There are 70 faculty members at Ridley College. Twenty-eight percent of the faculty members have master's degrees. Twenty-two of the faculty members live on campus. Each faculty member at Ridley is an academic advisor to approximately 5 students. Advisers meet with their students on a regular basis and ensure that they are doing well academically, physically, and emotionally. Faculty members also coach sports, coordinate activities and community service, and supervise students in the boarding house several times a month.

Headmaster Edward Kidd was born in the Ottawa Valley and went to Queen's University, where he completed both his Bachelor of Arts and Bachelor of Education degrees. During his time at Queen's he was a captain of the varsity football team and a member of the 1992 Vanier Cup–winning team. Mr. Kidd earned his Master of Science degree from the State University of New York at Buffalo. He began his teaching career in 1994 at North Grenville High School. In 1996 he moved to the Seoul International School in Seoul, South Korea to teach English literature. In 1998 he joined Shanghai American School, also as an English teacher. In 2009, Shanghai American School appointed him principal of the high school. Mr. Kidd has first-hand teaching and leadership experience with both the International Baccalaureate (IB) and Advanced Placement programs. He was a member of the team who planned and introduced the IB philosophy and IB diploma program to Shanghai American School. His leadership training includes principal's qualifications from Queen's, Miami, and Harvard.

COLLEGE ADMISSION COUNSELING

The Ridley College Guidance Department works to assist students with their academic progression through the School and with gaining entry to college or university. The department maintains a current and comprehensive library of career and educational resources and a website of guidance-related links and maintains academic records in compliance with the Ontario Ministry of Education and Training. The department can also provide personal counseling when the need arises and refer students to specialists or agencies if warranted.

Ninety-nine percent of Ridley College students are university-bound. Alumni pursue postsecondary degrees at top Canadian universities, including Dalhousie, McGill, McMaster, Queen's, Toronto, Waterloo, and Western as well as top schools in the United States and Europe including Cambridge, Cornell, Durham, Georgetown, Harvard, Imperial College, London School of Economics, Newcastle, Oxford, Princeton, Spelman, St. Andrew's, Yale, and the Universities of Edinburgh and London.

STUDENT BODY AND CONDUCT

The Upper School is composed of 444 students: 260 boys and 184 girls, 277 boarding students and 182 day students. The Lower School is composed of 183 students: 100 boys and 83 girls, 23 boarding students and 160 day students

There are 199 international students attending Ridley College, representing more than thirty countries, including the Bahamas, Bangladesh, Barbados, Bermuda, the Cayman Islands, China, France, Germany, Hong Kong, Japan, Republic of Korea, Mexico, Nigeria, Russian Federation, Saudi Arabia, Taiwan, the United States, and Venezuela.

Social discipline in the residential setting is based on the demerit system, and accumulations of demerits lead to the imposition of "gatings," during which students are prohibited from leaving the campus and must check-in with the faculty member on duty each half-hour, on the half-hour, when not engaged in classroom work or having meals.

ACADEMIC FACILITIES

The Upper School, or School House, building has a campus co-op store, a computer help desk, a dining hall, and classrooms. The Second Century Building (2CB) houses the science department, art department, and music and drama department. The latter includes several labs and various studio rooms. The Mandeville Theatre, with a capacity of 350 guests, serves as an auditorium for various local public schools and production companies. The Memorial Chapel was built during the 1920s and is dedicated to the memory of Ridley alumni who died in World War I.

The Lower School is located across the campus from the Upper School. The Lower School has a JK/SK class, one class each for grades 1 through 6, and two classes each for grades 7 and 8. The Lower School building also offers a design shop; an art room; a resource centre; and a junior boarding residence for students in grades 5–8.

BOARDING AND GENERAL FACILITIES

Ridley has ten boarding houses. A unique feature of the Ridley boarding experience is the fact that all day students have study and storage space within the houses and opportunities for overnight stays when necessary. The residences are home base for the term. Here belongings are kept, pictures put up, and study time is observed. Recreational areas also exist for students. Much emphasis has been put into the public areas where students relax, visit, and socialize with their friends.

Each house has a housemaster living in a family home adjacent to the house as well as an assistant housemaster. A full-duty team of advisers watches over the welfare and personal and academic progress of every student in their care. This team is the main point of contact for parents. North American students typically return to their families during School holidays, and international students who choose not to return to their home countries (or are unable to due to time constraints) are often billeted with Ridley families or go on school trips.

The Schmon Health Centre is dedicated to the promotion of health and the total well-being of the Ridley community. It is located behind Upper School and the Athletic Therapy Clinic is located in the field house. A registered practical nurse and/or a registered nurse are on duty during regular hours of operation. A nurse is available for emergencies during overnight hours. A physician is also on campus four days a week, and is available by phone 24 hours a day for emergencies. The Athletic Therapy Clinic is open Monday through Saturday in the mid-afternoon. The St. Catharines General Hospital is located about 2 kilometres from the campus, should a student require additional medical evaluation and/or treatment.

ATHLETICS

Sport is an integral part of the fabric of the Ridley community. The College believes that physical fitness and active participation are a crucial part of student life. Ridley annually fields more than forty-five competitive teams. The variety of competitive sport offered at Ridley is unparalleled in the independent system, and the annual competitive success rivals that of any comparable-size high school in the country. Ridley College has four program development sports: basketball, ice hockey, rowing, and soccer. Ridley also fields teams for all ages in field hockey, gymnastics, rugby, squash, swimming, tennis, and volleyball, with Upper School teams in cross-country and track and field. Each program has represented the school at the provincial championships in the last decade. While Ridley students do enjoy winning, the athletic program pushes its athletes toward being triple-impact competitors, with a focus on personal mastery of skill, developing leadership and interpersonal skills, and honouring the game that they play. Ridley College's athletic facilities include two gyms, a new arena and field-house built in 2010, new $12 million ice rink, a swimming pool, five outdoor tennis courts, three indoor squash courts, a dance studio and fitness/strength training centre, Concept 2 rowing ergometer room, and five natural turf playing fields.

EXTRACURRICULAR OPPORTUNITIES

Ridley College offers a wide range of extracurricular activities including computer club, dance club, debate club, drama club, international club, math club, Model UN, peer tutoring, photography club, quiz bowl, radio station, running club, school band, ski club, student government, student publications, tour guides, and yearbook.

One of Ridley's most notable traditions is the Snake Dance, a school spirit-building celebration to inaugurate the fall sports season. Other traditions include an annual cross-country run, intramural competition among residences for the Bradley Shield (girls) and Bermuda Cup (boys) trophies, the Chimes Challenge (a sprinting contest held during the midday chimes of the clock tower), and the annual Prize Day that concludes the school year. Ridley's motto is *Terar dum prosim*—"may I be consumed in service"—and students take this to heart. Ridley students participate in community service on a regular basis and raise money and awareness for their house charities.

DAILY LIFE

Ridley College has a balanced day schedule. From 6:30 to 8 a.m. on Monday, Tuesday, Thursday, Friday and Saturday, students may have practice for one of the four major sports (rowing, ice hockey, basketball, or soccer), music or band practice, fitness class, or community service, depending on their involvement. From 6:15 to 8:15 a.m., breakfast is available in the dining hall. Chapel is held on Monday and Tuesday mornings and Friday afternoons. There is an assembly to share news on Thursday morning. Classes run from 8:45 a.m. to 3:45 p.m. on Monday, Tuesday, Thursday, and Friday. There are two nutrition breaks and a lunch period from 11:30 a.m. to 12:30 p.m. There is also a tutorial period during the day where students can receive academic assistance from their teachers. Sports, community service, and other activities begin at 4 p.m., except on Wednesdays and Saturdays, when they begin at 2:15 and 1 p.m., respectively. On Wednesdays, breakfast begins at 8 a.m., and classes start at 9:30 a.m. and finish at 2:15 p.m. On Saturdays, classes begin at 8:30 and finish at 10 a.m., with community service, sports, or activities taking place until 5:30 p.m. Dinner is served in the dining hall every evening from approximately 5:15 to 7:15 p.m., depending on the day. Evening study is from 7:30 to 9:30 p.m. on weekdays. Sunday is a day to rest and catch up on homework. Sunday afternoons are designated for residential programs or free time.

WEEKEND LIFE

There is a varied and comprehensive weekend program planned for students on campus. All varsity athletes are engaged each weekend in practices or games. The Sport for Life group involves intramural athletics, and also meets for scheduled fitness activities on Saturdays. Most of the fun, supervised weekend activities take place in the afternoon or evening and participation is voluntary. Students are required to sign-in with the faculty member who is on duty in their house on the weekends. Each grade is given a curfew time and places that they are allowed to visit on weekends. There is a movie bus on most weekends that takes students to the local theatre and many students go to restaurants and coffee shops near the campus. Day students are more than welcome to join in activities on campus over the weekend. Junior boarders go on weekend trips with their housemaster and housemates. Past trips have included Canada's Wonderland, go-karting, Sugar Bush, and movies. On long weekend breaks, Duke of Edinburgh trips are offered for those students working towards their Bronze, Silver, or Gold certification. During the November midterm break, a trip to Ottawa and Montreal is offered in order to tour historical Canadian landmarks. In February, a ski trip to Mont Tremblant, Quebec, allows students to experience a true Canadian winter wonderland and to ski at a top-ranked ski resort.

COSTS AND FINANCIAL AID

Tuition is Can$47,900 for seven-day boarding students, Can$35,700 for five-day boarding students, and Can$27,100 for day students. The standard payment plan allows tuition to be paid in four installments; a monthly payment plan is available for families living in Canada or the United States, using preauthorized payments or postdated cheques.

Students in grades 9–12 are required to purchase a laptop equipment bundle (Can$2260 in 2011–12). A technology fee is charged each year for software upgrades and technical support. General expenses include campus store purchases, textbooks, athletic uniforms, dry cleaning and mending, prescriptions, tutoring, theatre tickets, school ski trip, school pictures, courier charges, dances, and September camp. Other estimated fees for Upper School students are Can$3000–$3500 for boarders and Can$2000–$2500 for day students. This amount does not include the laptop bundle, major trips, or some tournament travel for sports teams. Lower School charges are generally less than those noted. Boarding students in grades 5–8 are allocated pocket money each week and parents are billed at the end of each term. Pocket money for boarding students in grades 9–12/PG is not provided.

In the 2011–12 academic year, approximately 206 students received financial assistance. Ridley attempts to meet the needs of all students with academic promise and worthy character through merit-based scholarships, need-based bursaries, and a deferred payment plan. The average merit scholarship was Can$5534 while the average bursary was Can$13,996.

Merit scholarships are available only to new students seeking entrance to Ridley. These scholarships offer awards up to Can$10,000 annually. Merit scholarships are awarded according to the following criteria: past academic achievement; the score from the SSAT; and the potential to contribute to the Ridley community either through the arts, athletics, community service, or leadership. Scholarship awards are renewed annually during a student's Ridley career, conditional upon maintaining academic honours (80 percent and above) and continuing a positive contribution to school life.

Need-based bursaries are offered to assist with a family's financial contribution to Ridley. These bursaries are based on the family's ability to afford a Ridley education and do not need to be repaid. In order to apply for a bursary, families are required to complete the FACS (Financial Aid for Canadian Students) application. This application requests information on family assets, liabilities, income, expenses, and special circumstances.

Deferred payment or loans are also available to families with demonstrated need.

ADMISSIONS INFORMATION

Ridley College admits students who are well rounded. Admissions officers look for students who are involved in a wide range of activities from music to athletics to community service—students who thrive on being engaged and involved. Ridley no longer requires standardized admissions testing as a part of the application process. Applicants interested in applying for a merit-based scholarship are required to write the SSAT (Secondary School Admission Test). Ridley's SSAT number is 6036. Registration and more SSAT information is available at www.ssat.org/ontario. Ridley reserves the right to require results from standardized admissions testing in certain circumstances, particularly from candidates for whom English is a second language.

Applicants to grade 2 and above are asked to submit their most recent school reports as well as transcripts including grades from the previous two years. All accepted students are asked to submit their final year grades as well.

APPLICATION TIMETABLE

While admission to Ridley is on a rolling basis, the Admissions Office encourages families to begin the process during the fall and spring of the preceding academic year.

A campus visit can be scheduled Monday through Friday between 8:15 a.m. and 3:30 p.m. The Admissions Office is also open for visits on select Saturday mornings throughout the academic year. A campus visit or interview can be scheduled by calling the Admissions Office at 905-684-1889 Ext. 2207 or e-mailing admissions@ridleycollege.com.

The Ridley College application can be completed online at https://apply.ridleycollege.com. The application fee for domestic students is Can$100 and Can$150 for international boarding students. Once an application is complete, a prospective student will typically receive an answer from the Admissions Committee in two to three weeks.

ADMISSIONS CORRESPONDENCE

Dr. Andrew T. Weller, Dean of Admissions
Ridley College
2 Ridley Road
St. Catharines, Ontario L2R7C3
Canada
Phone: 905-684-1889 Ext. 2207
866-603-1889 (toll-free in North America only)
E-mail: admissions@ridleycollege.com
Web site: http://www.ridleycollege.com

RYE COUNTRY DAY SCHOOL

Rye, New York

Type: Coeducational day college-preparatory school
Grades: P–12: Lower School, Prekindergarten–4; Middle School, 5–8; Upper School, 9–12
Enrollment: School total: 881; Upper School: 387
Head of School: Scott A. Nelson, Headmaster

THE SCHOOL

Founded in 1869, Rye Country Day School (RCDS) is entering its 143rd year. Reflecting and reaffirming the School's purposes, the RCDS mission statement states, "Rye Country Day School is a coeducational, college-preparatory school dedicated to providing students from Pre-Kindergarten through Grade Twelve with an excellent education using both traditional and innovative approaches. In a nurturing and supportive environment, we offer a challenging program that stimulates individuals to achieve their maximum potential through academic, athletic, creative, and social endeavors. We are actively committed to diversity. We expect and promote moral responsibility, and strive to develop strength of character within a respectful school community. Our goal is to foster a lifelong passion for learning, understanding, and service in an ever-changing world."

Rye Country Day School acts consciously and deliberately in order to create and sustain an inclusive community. According to the School's diversity mission statement, "At Rye Country Day, we believe that diversity is the existence of human variety. As such, each one of us is diverse in multiple ways and in a variety of contexts. We recognize diversity as including, but not limited to, differences in ability/disability, age, ethnicity, family structures, gender, geographic origin, life experiences, physical appearance, race, religion, sexual orientation, and socioeconomic status. As educators, we are committed to creating and sustaining a school community that is diverse and inclusive, one in which all members can participate fully and maximize their potential. We believe that only an inclusive school community can be equitable and just. We are proactive about teaching our students the importance of diversity and inclusion in an increasingly interconnected, multicultural, and ever-changing world. As we prepare our students for leadership in the world beyond Rye Country Day, we are responsible for teaching them how to communicate with and be respectful of others—beginning with those in our school community and extending to those who live beyond our nation's borders. Every global citizen should be able to thrive in a diverse and interconnected society. Our commitment to inclusion enriches our community with diverse ideas and perspectives. Students grow and flourish in this type of environment, where they can safely explore their individual identity while developing and exercising strength of character, healthy self-esteem, and confidence. Through our commitment to diversity and inclusion, we strive to be good role models for the individuals in our care so that their present and future actions and choices may positively impact the world."

The 26-acre campus is located in Rye at the junction of routes I-95 and I-287, one block from the train station. The School's location, 25 miles from Manhattan, provides easy access to both New York City and to a suburban setting with ample playing fields and open spaces. Through frequent field trips, internships, and community service projects, the School takes considerable advantage of the cultural opportunities in the New York metropolitan area.

A nonprofit, nonsectarian institution, Rye Country Day is governed by a 26-member Board of Trustees that includes parents and alumni. The annual operating budget is $27.7 million, and the physical plant assets have a book value in excess of $53.5 million. Annual gifts from parents, alumni, and friends amount to more than $3.4 million. The endowment of the School is valued at more than $31.2 million.

Rye Country Day School is accredited by the Middle States Association of Colleges and Schools and the New York State Association of Independent Schools and is chartered and registered by the New York State Board of Regents. It is a member of the National Association of Independent Schools, the New York State Association of Independent Schools, the Educational Records Bureau, the College Board, and the National Association for College Admission Counseling.

ACADEMIC PROGRAM

Leading to the college-preparatory program of the Upper School, the program in the Middle School (grades 5–8) emphasizes the development of skills and the acquisition of information needed for success at the secondary school level by exposing students to a wide range of opportunities. The academic program is fully departmentalized. Spanish or French is offered to all students in grades 2–5. Starting in grade 6 students may choose Latin or Mandarin Chinese or continue with Spanish or French. The math, foreign language, and writing programs lead directly into the Upper School curriculum. Programs in art, music (vocal and instrumental), computer use, and dramatics are offered in all grades. Students in kindergarten through grade 6 are scheduled for sports for 45 to 75 minutes daily, and a full interscholastic sports program is available to both boys and girls in grades 7 and 8, and in the Upper School.

Sixteen courses are required for Upper School graduation, including 4 years of English, 3 years of mathematics, 3 years of one foreign language, 2 years of science, and 2 years of history. Students entering the School by grade 9 must complete ½ unit in art and music survey, and ½ unit in the arts. Seniors must successfully complete an off-campus Senior Term community service program in June. Students are expected to carry five academic courses per year.

Full-year courses in English include English 9, 10, and 11; major American writers; English and American literature; and creative and expository writing. Required mathematics courses are algebra I, algebra II, trigonometry, and geometry. Regular course work extends through calculus BC, and tutorials are available for more advanced students. Yearlong courses in science are environmental science, biology, chemistry, and physics. Science courses are laboratory based. The computer department offers beginning and advanced programming, software applications courses, desktop publishing, and independent study opportunities.

The modern language department offers five years of Mandarin Chinese, French, and Spanish, and the classics department teaches five years of Latin. History courses include world civilizations, U.S. history, government, and modern European history. Semester electives in the humanities include philosophy, psychology, government, and economics.

In the arts, full-year courses in studio art, art history, and music theory are available. Participation in the Concert Choir and Wind Ensemble earns students full academic credit. Semester courses in drawing, printmaking, sculpture, graphic design, ceramics, and photography are available. The drama department offers electives in technique, history, oral presentation, technical theater, and dance.

Advanced Placement courses leading to the AP examinations are offered in biology, environmental science, chemistry, physics, psychology, economics, statistics, calculus, English, U.S. government, U.S. and modern European history, Mandarin Chinese, French, Spanish, Latin, music theory, photography, studio art, history of art, and computer science. Honors sections are scheduled in tenth- and eleventh-grade English, math, physics, biology, and chemistry, and in foreign languages at all levels. Independent study is available in grades 11 and 12 in all disciplines.

The student-teacher ratio is 8:1, and the average class size in the Upper School is 12. Extra help is provided for students as needed.

The year is divided into two semesters. Examinations are given in March. Grades are scaled from A to F and are given four times a year. Written comments accompany grades at the end of each quarter.

Academic classes travel to New York City and other areas to supplement classroom work. Although not a graduation requirement, all students are involved in community service programs. Semester class projects as well as individual experiences involve work with local charities and schools, YMCA, Midnight Run, United Cerebral Palsy, Big Brother-Big Sister, Doctors Without Borders, AmeriCares, and numerous local organizations.

Students in grades 7–12 are required to have laptop computers. The campus supports wireless Internet connection and provides appropriate filters for student and faculty educational use. A technology department supports and updates the network and assists students with software and hardware issues. Students receiving financial aid awards receive new laptop computers from the school which are replaced every three years.

FACULTY AND ADVISERS

The Upper School faculty consists of 65 full-time teachers—35 men and 30 women, the large majority of whom hold at least one advanced degree. The average length of service is eight years, and annual faculty turnover averages fewer than 6 teachers.

Scott A. Nelson became Headmaster in 1993. He holds a B.A. from Brown University and an M.A. from Fordham University. Prior to his appointment at Rye, he served as Upper School Director both at the Marlborough School in Los Angeles and at the Hackley School in Tarrytown, New York. Mr. Nelson and his family reside on campus.

Nearly all faculty members in the Middle and Upper Schools serve as advisers for 5 to 12 students each. In addition to helping students select courses, faculty advisers monitor the students' progress in all areas of school life and provide ongoing support. The advisers also meet with students' parents at various times throughout the year.

Rye Country Day seeks faculty members who are effective teachers in their field and who, by virtue of their sincere interest in the students' overall well-being, will further the broad goals of the School's philosophy. The School supports the continuing education of its faculty through grants and summer sabbaticals totaling more than $401,000 a year.

COLLEGE ADMISSION COUNSELING

The college selection process is supervised by a full-time Director of College Counseling and 2 Associate Directors, and support is provided by an administrative assistant. Advising is done in groups and on an individual basis, with the staff meeting with both students and their families. More than 100 college representatives visit the campus each year.

The 98 graduates of the class of 2012 enrolled in fifty-three colleges and universities, including Amherst, Barnard, Brown, Colgate, Columbia, Cornell, Dartmouth, Duke, Georgetown, Harvard, Johns Hopkins, McGill, Michigan, Middlebury, Northwestern, Notre Dame, Pomona, Stanford, Tufts, USC, Vanderbilt, Washington (St. Louis), Wesleyan, William and Mary, Williams, Yale, and the Universities of Pennsylvania and Texas.

STUDENT BODY AND CONDUCT

The Upper School enrollment for 2012–13 totaled 387: 195 boys and 192 girls. There were 97 students in grade 9, 105 in grade 10, 100 in grade 11, and 85 in grade 12. Members of minority groups represented 29 percent of the student body in grades 5–12. Students came from roughly forty different school districts in Westchester and Fairfield counties as well as New York City. Students holding citizenship in eighteen countries were enrolled.

While School regulations are few, the School consciously and directly emphasizes a cooperative, responsible, and healthy community life. The Student Council plays a major role in administering School organizations and activities. Minor disciplinary problems are handled by the Division Principal or Grade Level Dean; more serious matters in the Upper School may be brought before the Disciplinary Committee. There is student representation on the Academic Affairs and other major committees.

ACADEMIC FACILITIES

Academic facilities at Rye Country Day School include the Main Building (1927) and Main Building Addition (2002), with separate areas for kindergarten through grade 4, grades 5 and 6, and grades 7 and 8. The Lower and Middle School divisions have separate art, computer, and science facilities.

The Upper School is housed in the Pinkham Building (1964), which was completely renovated in 2010. The new 14,000-square-foot addition includes a 140-seat auditorium, a college counseling center, faculty offices, classrooms, and three science labs.

There are two libraries on campus—the Lower School Library (2002) and the Klingenstein Library (1984), which serves the Middle and Upper School divisions. The Klingenstein Library contains more than 25,000 volumes with fully automated circulation and collection management technology. Resources include significant periodical and reference materials that are available via direct online services and the Internet, CD-ROM, and substantial videotape collection.

The school has invested in technology infrastructure and classroom SmartBoards in all three divisions. Laptop computers, which are required for all students in grades 7 through 12, are used extensively throughout the curriculum. Access to the RCDS network and Internet is via a campuswide wireless network. In total, there are 650 networked computers on campus.

The performing arts programs are housed in the Dunn Performing Arts Center (1990), which includes a 400-seat theater-auditorium and classroom spaces for vocal music, instrumental music, and a dance studio. There also are five music practice rooms which adjunct faculty use for private music lessons.

ATHLETICS

Rye Country Day's athletic program offers seventy-two interscholastic teams for students in grades 7 through 12. Varsity competition includes boys' and girls' teams in soccer, cross-country, basketball, ice hockey, fencing, squash, tennis, golf, track and field, sailing, and lacrosse, as well as football, field hockey, wrestling, baseball, and softball. Approximately 70 percent of the students participate in at least one team sport.

The physical education department offers classes throughout the year in fitness center training, yoga, boot camp, kickboxing, Zumba, tennis, squash, dance, running, and skating.

Athletic facilities include the LaGrange Field House (1972) with its indoor ice rink/tennis courts; a multipurpose gymnasium which serves as the home for the wrestling and fencing programs; the Scott A. Nelson Athletic Center (2000), which houses a two-court gymnasium, four squash courts, four locker rooms, and an athletic training facility; a multipurpose room; and a state-of-the-art fitness center. Between 2007 and 2009, the School installed four artificial turf fields, making it the premier outdoor athletic facility in the area.

EXTRACURRICULAR OPPORTUNITIES

More than fifty extracurricular activities are available. Students can choose vocal music (Concert Choir, Madrigal Singers, and solfeggio classes) and instrumental music (Wind Ensemble, Concert Band, and Jazz Band). Many of these offerings have curricular status. The performance groups give local concerts and occasionally travel to perform at schools and universities here and abroad. In addition, professional instructors offer private instrumental and voice lessons during and after the school day. The drama department presents major productions three times a year. Recent productions have included *The Laramie Project, South Pacific, Dark of the Moon, The Mystery of Edwin Drood, Macbeth, The Pajama Game, The Arabian Nights, Anything Goes, Alice in Wonderland, Urinetown, Museum, Bye Bye Birdie,The Comedy of Errors, The Boys from Syracuse,* and *Working.*

Student publications include a yearbook, newspaper, literary magazine, graphic arts and photography magazines, and a public affairs journal, each of which is composed using student publications desktop publishing facilities. The School's Web site (http://www.ryecountryday.org) is an ever-changing location for student- and staff-provided information on and perspectives of the School. Students participate in Model Congress programs on campus and at other schools and colleges.

The School's new focus on public purpose goes beyond community service by challenging community members to identify, examine, and research social inequities in order to plan a course of action that is responsive, that is partnership-based, and that utilizes rich and varied methods. Using a service-learning approach, the School encourages students to strengthen their skills and realize their potential to empower others and themselves. Rye Country Day is committed to leveraging its human and educational resources to co-create sustainable solutions to real-world problems. The School's public purpose mission statement reads: "Since 1869, Rye Country Day School's motto, 'Not for self, but for service,' has been integral to the culture of the School. The Rye Country Day School philosophy states, 'A superior education embraces the concept that to educate is to do more than to teach.' Through service learning, we will provide transformative educational opportunities that prepare our students to be responsible citizens with an ethic of service and empathy for our shared human experience. We believe that meaningful and mutually beneficial partnerships emanate from a curriculum enhanced by community engagement. Rye Country Day School's sustained commitment to making a positive impact on the community and contributing to the common good defines our public purpose."

DAILY LIFE

Beginning each day at 8:05, the Upper School utilizes a six-day schedule cycle. Most courses meet five of the six days, with one or two longer, 70-minute periods per cycle. The day includes an activity/meeting period and two lunch periods as well as seven class periods. Class periods end at 2:50, and team sport practices and games begin at 3:30. Breakfast and lunch may be purchased in the school dining room; seniors may have lunch off campus. Study halls are required for grade 9.

SUMMER PROGRAMS

The Rye Country Day Summer School enrolls approximately 100 students—rising students to grades 6 to postgraduate—in remedial, enrichment, and advanced-standing courses. Some courses prepare students for the New York State Regents exams that may be taken at the local public schools. The program is six weeks long and runs on a five-period schedule from 8 a.m. to noon, Monday through Friday. Tuition averages $1300 per course. A brochure is available after April 1 from the Director of the Summer School or on the School's Web site.

In addition to the Summer School, Rye conducts a summer program, the ACTION Program, an academic enrichment program at Rye for highly motivated public school students who will be entering grades 7, 8, and 9. The ACTION Program seeks to expand the academic and intellectual horizons of very capable and responsible students from local communities who may not have the resources available to provide such summer programs. The program promotes confidence and strength of character while helping students grow academically and develop as leaders.

The ACTION Program runs for four weeks in July. Its philosophy emphasizes learning for the sake of learning. All students take project-based courses in math, science, history, leadership, Presidential election coverage, creative writing, drama, and yoga/kickboxing. Once a week, the curriculum is reinforced with experiential learning opportunities outside the classroom. Field trips include seeing a Broadway musical, participating in a high ropes adventures program, and sailing aboard a schooner in the Long Island Sound.

COSTS AND FINANCIAL AID

Tuition for grade 9 for 2012–13 is $33,900. Additional charges are made for textbooks, lunches, sports, field trips, and private music lessons, as appropriate.

Tuition aid is available on a need basis. For the 2012–13 academic year, 131 students received a total of more than $3.8 million in aid. All aid applications are processed through the School and Student Service for Financial Aid.

ADMISSIONS INFORMATION

Students are accepted in all grades. In 2012–13, 23 new students enrolled in the ninth grade, and 5 in the tenth grade. Academic readiness is a prerequisite; a diversity of skills and interests, as well as general academic aptitude, is eagerly sought. The School seeks and enrolls students of all backgrounds; a diverse student body is an important part of the School's educational environment.

Required in the admissions process are the results of the Educational Records Bureau's ISEE or the Secondary School Admission Test (SSAT); the student's school record; and school and faculty recommendations. A visit to the campus and an interview are also required.

APPLICATION TIMETABLE

Inquiries are welcome throughout the year. Interviews and tours of the campus begin in late September. To be considered in initial admissions decisions, applicants must fully complete the Application by December 15. All other parts of the Application Folder (transcripts, testing, recommendation forms, interview, etc.) are due by January 15. Candidates whose Application Folders are complete by that date are notified by approximately February 15. Applications received after December 15 are evaluated on a rolling basis. All application materials are available online (www.ryecountryday.org/admissions).

ADMISSIONS CORRESPONDENCE

Matthew J. M. Suzuki, Director of Admissions
Rye Country Day School
Cedar Street
Rye, New York 10580-2034
United States
Phone: 914-925-4513
Fax: 914-921-2147
E-mail: matt_suzuki@ryecountryday.org
Web site: http://www.ryecountryday.org

ST. ANDREW'S SCHOOL

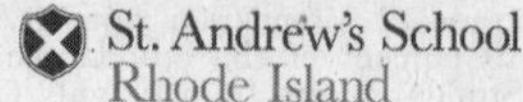

Barrington, Rhode Island

Type: Coeducational, boarding and day college-preparatory school
Grades: 3–PG: Lower School, 3–5; Middle School, 6–8; Upper School and Boarding, 9–Postgraduate (PG)
Enrollment: School total: 215; Upper School: 181
Head of School: John D. Martin

THE SCHOOL

St. Andrew's School is a coeducational boarding and day school for students in grades 3–PG, with the boarding program starting in the ninth grade. The School is located on a 100-acre campus in Barrington (population approximately 16,000), a suburban community 10 miles southeast of Providence on Narragansett Bay. The campus contains open space and woodlands. Its proximity to Providence and Newport, as well as Boston, offers a wide variety of cultural opportunities for students.

St. Andrew's School was founded in 1893 by Rev. William Merrick Chapin as a school for homeless boys. From these simple beginnings through its years as a working farm school to its present role as a coeducational boarding and day college preparatory school, St. Andrew's steadfastly maintains the same sense of purpose and concern for the individual. The curriculum is designed primarily to prepare students for college, with emphasis on helping them to develop stronger academic skills, study habits, and self-esteem.

Every St. Andrew's teacher is trained to teach using a multisensory approach for the different ways students may learn. St. Andrew's students find that when they get to college, they are well prepared to handle the course work because they have a true understanding of how they learn and an awareness of the tools they need to achieve their best.

St. Andrew's School is a nonsectarian, nonprofit corporation. A Board of Trustees governs the School; this 21-member board meets five times a year. The School's physical plant is valued at approximately $45 million. The School's endowment is currently valued at more than $15.2 million.

St. Andrew's is accredited by the New England Association of Schools and Colleges. It is a member of the National Association of Independent Schools, the Association of Independent Schools in New England, the Association of Boarding Schools, and the Independent Schools Association of Rhode Island.

ACADEMIC PROGRAM

St. Andrew's School believes that every student can find success in the classroom. With a 5:1 student-teacher ratio, the average class size at St. Andrew's is 7–10 students with a class maximum of 12. Small classes, along with twice-daily adviser meetings, help to ensure that no student is overlooked. The homelike community, nurturing environment, and hands-on approach to learning and teaching help maintain close student-teacher relationships.

To graduate from the Upper School, a student must complete 26 credits: 24 academic credits and 2 credits in physical education. Students are expected to take course work in English, math, science, social studies, and physical education each year. Preparation in a foreign language is also highly recommended. Students may only have one study hall in their schedule. Seniors must pass the equivalent of five full-credit courses in order to graduate. Specific minimum requirements for Upper School students are 4 credits in English, 3 credits in social studies (including 1 in U.S. history), 3 credits in mathematics, 3 credits in science (including 2 in a lab science), 2 credits in physical education, 1 credit in art, and 10 elective credits. An English as a Second Language (ESL) Program is provided for international students. The School's computer network, which is available to all students, provides Internet access from all classrooms, dorm rooms, and offices.

The School's Learning Services program, for students who have been identified with language-based learning differences or attentional challenges, is taught by learning support teachers. All students enrolled in a program receive instruction and support to enable academic success in the School's college-preparatory course of study. An Individual Education Plan is designed and updated annually with input from the student, family, and each teacher. This plan identifies both the skills and support to be provided throughout the year to guide learning success. Individualized programs are available to support the advancement of reading, writing, speech and language, and study skills (e.g., materials management, test preparation, focus and homework strategies, time management, organization, and planning).

The school year runs on a semester basis. Students are evaluated frequently by their teachers so that each student's progress is monitored closely throughout the year. Each advisee meets twice a day with his or her adviser to discuss issues pertaining to the student's academic progress and his or her involvement in the School community. Advisers communicate with families every three weeks by phone or e-mail.

FACULTY AND ADVISERS

The faculty numbers 44, with 16 men and 28 women. Twenty-one reside with their families on campus and seven of them serve as dorm parents. All full-time faculty members serve as advisers. John D. Martin was appointed Head of School on July 1, 1996, and has an extensive background in independent schools, including teaching and administrative positions at Sewickley Academy, Peddie School, and Tabor Academy. He holds a Master of Divinity degree from Yale University, a Master of Education degree from American International College, and a Bachelor of Arts degree from Tufts University.

COLLEGE ADMISSION COUNSELING

All of St. Andrew's graduates enter four-year colleges, two-year colleges, postgraduate programs, or technical schools upon graduation each year. Goal setting, short- and long-term planning, and informal discussions about careers and postsecondary plans are ongoing between students and advisers from the moment a student enters the Upper School. Formal college counseling begins in the eleventh grade. The college counselor works with students and their parents to assist in determining the best steps for each student. The advisers and other faculty members assist the college counselor in assessing each student's options. PSATs are given in the fall of sophomore year and again at the start of junior year. SATs should be taken during the junior and senior years. College representatives visit the campus throughout the year to meet with interested students.

St. Andrew's graduates have matriculated to colleges and universities such as Boston University, Brandeis, Brown, Dartmouth, Emmanuel, Emory, Fairfield, Indiana, Michigan State, Mount Holyoke, Parsons, Penn State, Pratt, Providence, Ringling College of Art and Design, Rhode Island College, Roger Williams, Sacred Heart, Salve Regina, Seton Hall, Suffolk, Syracuse, Tulane, and the Universities of California, Hawaii, Illinois, Massachusetts, Rhode Island, Vermont, and Washington.

STUDENT BODY AND CONDUCT

The School enrolls both boarding and day students. Approximately one third of the Upper School population boards. Approximately 21 percent of the School's population is enrolled in the Lower and Middle Schools, and less than 40 percent of the School's population participates in the Resource/Focus Programs.

Over the years, St. Andrew's School has attracted boarding students from all corners of the United States and other countries, including Canada, China, France, Germany, Greece, Haiti, India, Israel, Jamaica, Japan, Montenegro, Senegal, South Korea, Taiwan, and Turkey.

Each student is required to read the *Parent and Student Handbook,* which defines expectations for students within the community. Difficulties, if they arise, are handled according to degree; minor issues are handled by teachers and dorm parents, while major offenses are handled by the Director of Student Life in conjunction with a joint student-faculty disciplinary committee. Faculty advisers play a major role in working with students to help them understand the expectations of them as members of the community.

ACADEMIC FACILITIES

Stone Academic Center (1988) houses fifteen classrooms, a renovated resource wing with five classrooms for instruction, a computer lab, academic offices, and a faculty workroom. It is also the site of the library, which features study carrels, meeting rooms, and computer workstations. Hardy Hall (1898) was renovated in 2008 and houses the Middle School (6–8) and Lower School (3–5). The classrooms are designed for interactive learning in groups of 5 to 12 students. The George M. Sage Gymnasium (2001) and the Karl P. Jones Gymnasium (1965) each house a full-size gymnasium and locker room facilities. The Annie Lee Steele Adams Memorial Student Service Center (1997) houses the Health Center, classrooms, and additional office space. The David A. Brown '52 Science Center houses four science labs, two regular classrooms, and the office of the Director of College Counseling. The Norman E. and Dorothy R. McCulloch Center for the Arts (2004) houses a 287-seat theater, two visual art classrooms, a ceramics lab, a music classroom, music practice rooms, a black-box/theater classroom, a computer graphics lab, storage, and theater scene shop.

BOARDING AND GENERAL FACILITIES

Upper School girls live in the newly renovated Margot's House (1969). Upper School boys live in Bill's House (1970), Coleman House (circa 1795), and Perry Hall (1927). Students are assigned to single or double rooms. Each dormitory is supervised by faculty dorm parents, who are aided by the Director of Residential Life and the Director of Student Life. Each dorm has a common room, laundry facilities, access to a kitchen area, and ample storage space. The recently renovated Gardiner Hall (1926) has seating for 175 and the Head Master's Dining Room. McVickar Hall (1913) houses the Admissions office, the Head Master's office, the Development and Communications department, and reception area. Peck Hall (circa 1895) contains the Business office. Clark Hall (1899) houses the Student Center, offering students space for entertainment and relaxation. The second floor provides faculty housing.

Coleman House and the Rectory, the Head Master's house, are late-eighteenth-century buildings that were acquired by the School from two local estates. Both buildings are said to have been stops for travelers on the Underground Railroad. The Rectory has a hidden back staircase and room.

ATHLETICS

Upper School students participate in athletics at the completion of each class day. St. Andrew's fields varsity teams in boys' and girls' basketball, cross-country, golf, lacrosse, soccer, and tennis. Intramural sports programs are also offered and include fitness training, weight training, yoga, biking, lawn games, and Project Adventure Ropes Course. St. Andrew's also offers a state-of-the-art health and fitness center that comprises separate cardio and weight-training facilities.

EXTRACURRICULAR OPPORTUNITIES

The School's proximity to Providence, Newport, and Boston provides a myriad of cultural and recreational activities. Students may take advantage of museums, movies, concerts, plays, rock climbing, skating, bowling, skiing, and professional and collegiate sporting events. Among the on-campus extracurricular activities are theater, photography, debate club, and yearbook. The St. Andrew's Parent Association (SAPA) organizes a wide variety of social activities for students throughout the year, from dances to laser tag to paintball to barbecues.

DAILY LIFE

Boarding students generally rise at about 7 a.m. and are responsible for making their beds, cleaning their rooms, and performing other assorted dorm chores. Breakfast is served at 7:30 and is a favorite gathering time for day and boarding students alike. Students assemble for Morning Meeting at 8 and then meet in their advising groups. Classes begin at 8:30. Adviser meetings are held again at the end of the day. Activities and athletics begin at 3 p.m. and run until approximately 4. Students may leave the campus between athletics and dinner if they are in good standing in the community. Dinner is at 5:30, and evening study hall is from 7:30 to 9:30. All study halls are proctored by faculty members, who are able to provide extra academic assistance if needed. During study hall, the library is open for those students who need to conduct research.

The Student Center is open on weekdays from 11 a.m. to 1 p.m., all day Saturday, and at other times depending on scheduled special activities.

WEEKEND LIFE

Weekend activities are planned by the Director of Student Life and the Coordinator of Weekend Activities, with student and faculty input. Students choose from an array of on- and off-campus activities, including sporting events, concerts, movies, plays, hayrides, open gymnasium, bicycle riding, skiing, attending performances by special guests on campus, dances, skating, festivals and fairs, hiking, and shopping. Visits to nearby cities and other places of interest are also offered. Boarders may leave for the weekend, with parental permission, either to go home or to visit a day student's family. Each weekend, approximately 75 percent of the boarding community remains on campus.

COSTS AND FINANCIAL AID

Tuition for a boarder in 2012–13 is $47,000; for a day student, it is $31,400. Additional costs for the Resource and Focus Programs are $10,100. The yearly book fee is about $650. Parents of a boarding student should plan to set up an account in the on-campus bank for weekly allowance needs. The amount varies from family to family and student to student.

Approximately 53 percent of students received financial aid for the 2012–13 academic year, with more than $2.5 million offered in grants and loans. Financial aid is based solely on need. St. Andrew's School is affiliated with School and Student Services by National Association of Independent Schools (NAIS) in Randolph, Massachusetts for financial aid and works in conjunction with this organization to provide an objective and fair basis for awarding financial aid. All required information is due to the School by February 12. Final awards are determined by the School's Financial Aid Committee.

ADMISSIONS INFORMATION

In order to assess the match between student and school and to plan an appropriate academic program, the School requires a tour, a personal interview, an application with a fee of $50 ($100 for international students), a school transcript covering the last three years, three teacher recommendations, and standardized test scores. For applicants to the Resource Program, an educational evaluation and a psychological evaluation (both within eighteen months of potential enrollment) and a current Individualized Education Plan (if applicable) are required. A student applying to the Focus Program must establish a history of attention difficulties and supply the School with a medical diagnosis from a physician and appropriate testing results. International students must also submit results from an SLEP or TOEFL evaluation.

APPLICATION TIMETABLE

Parents and prospective students are encouraged to contact the Admissions Office for information during the fall semester. Because the School considers a visit to the campus and a personal interview with the candidate to be such a critical part of the admissions process, it asks that all families call for an appointment. It is best to visit the School during the fall if considering enrollment for the following September, although the School welcomes campus visitors throughout the year.

St. Andrew's School does not discriminate on the basis of race, creed, gender, or handicap in the administration of policies, practices, and procedures.

Applications are due by January 28. Students are notified of acceptance by March 11, and the School holds a place for accepted students until April 10. Depending on available space, rolling admission may be offered thereafter. A nonrefundable deposit of $1000 ($5000 for international students) is due when students agree to attend and is credited toward tuition.

ADMISSIONS CORRESPONDENCE

R. Scott Telford
Director of Admissions
St. Andrew's School
63 Federal Road
Barrington, Rhode Island 02806
Phone: 401-246-1230
Fax: 401-246-0510
E-mail: inquiry@standrews-ri.org
Web site: http://www.standrews-ri.org

ST. MARK'S SCHOOL OF TEXAS

Dallas, Texas

Type: Boys' day college-preparatory school
Grades: 1–12: Lower School, 1–4; Middle School, 5–8; Upper School, 9–12
Enrollment: School total: 851; Upper: 367; Middle: 332; Lower: 152
Head of School: Arnold E. Holtberg, Eugene McDermott Headmaster

THE SCHOOL

St. Mark's is the descendant of three former Dallas boys' schools: Terrill School (1906–1944), Texas Country Day School (1933–1950), and Cathedral School (1944–1950). St. Mark's was organized in 1950 on the Preston Road campus of Texas Country Day School (TCD) when the Cathedral School merged with TCD. The campus is located on 43 acres in the residential area of North Dallas.

St. Mark's college-preparatory program is synchronized to the unique learning styles and maturity rates of boys. Free from traditional gender assumptions, boys are encouraged to discover and develop their intellectual, academic, and artistic interests. Challenging studies in the sciences, arts, and humanities form the basis of a St. Mark's education. Teachers work to instill an enthusiasm for learning, encourage independent and critical judgment, and demonstrate the methods for making sound inquiries and for using effective communication. St. Mark's aims to prepare young men for responsible lives of leadership and service.

St. Mark's Lower School (grades 1–4) is housed in a single building and has approximately 25 faculty members. The program offers diverse learning activities, including academic instruction in Spanish language and culture, language arts, mathematics, science, and social studies; regular instruction in the arts (visual arts, music, creative dramatics); and a developmental physical education program that teaches fundamental skills at a level geared to the age and abilities of the child.

St. Mark's School of Texas is accredited by the Independent Schools Association of the Southwest. Its memberships include the National Association of Independent Schools, the Cum Laude Society, the International Boys' School Coalition, and the College Board.

ACADEMIC PROGRAM

The academic program in the Upper School is designed to satisfy the most exacting requirements for admission to colleges and universities across the country, but the program is more broadly defined by the School and the faculty as preparation for personal independence, enlightenment, and maturity.

There are required courses, Advanced Placement courses, and many electives available. Graduation requirements are 4 years of English, 3 years of a foreign language, 3 years of mathematics, 4 years of physical education or athletics, 3 years of social studies, 3 years of a laboratory science, 1 year in fine arts, a senior exhibition, and 15 hours of community service each Upper School year. Each student takes five classes per year, and some students, with the permission of the Head of the Upper School, may take more.

The individual teaching sections average about 15 students. In most classes, the students are randomly grouped; the notable exceptions are in honors and Advanced Placement courses.

The School operates on a trimester system. Grade reports are given three times a year and are made available to the parents with written comments. Interim reports are also written to help ensure adequate reporting to the parents. Parents are encouraged to communicate at any time with their son's adviser. Only final grades in Upper School classes are recorded for transcript purposes.

FACULTY AND ADVISERS

For the academic year 2012–13, the non-administrative faculty consisted of 98 full-time members; 72 hold master's degrees, and 6 have earned doctoral degrees.

The Eugene McDermott Headmaster, Arnold E. Holtberg, graduated cum laude from Princeton University in 1970 with a baccalaureate degree in sociology. He also received a master's degree in pastoral care and counseling in 1976 from the Lutheran Theological Seminary in Philadelphia, Pennsylvania.

The School seeks to employ faculty members who are willing to participate fully in the many areas of school life. The School compensates teachers in the top 10 percent of independent schools nationally and supports fourteen endowed teaching positions.

COLLEGE ADMISSION COUNSELING

The Director of College Counseling and staff members coordinate college planning and counseling. All Upper School students are encouraged to attend the College Previews, held in September, and are welcome to utilize the college office. Several required college conferences are scheduled with students and parents, beginning in the junior year. The SAT mean scores for the class of 2013 were critical reading, 689; math, 715; and writing, 686. The mean ACT scores were 32.

St. Mark's graduates attend major universities throughout the country. Ten or more students in the classes of 2008 through 2012 have enrolled at Dartmouth, Duke, Northwestern, Princeton, Rice, Southern Methodist, Stanford, Texas A&M, Vanderbilt, Yale, and the Universities of Pennsylvania, Southern California, and Texas at Austin.

STUDENT BODY AND CONDUCT

In 2012–13, there were 94 boys in grade 9, 91 in grade 10, 89 in grade 11, and 93 in grade 12. Since St. Mark's is a day school, almost all of the boys come from the Dallas area. Approximately 40 percent of the boys are students of color.

While the rules that govern the School are published by the School, these rules or guidelines provide only a part of the criteria that determine student behavior. Students are also encouraged to take responsibility for their own actions, with the guidance of the faculty and class sponsors. A faculty- and student-led Discipline Council deals with some disciplinary problems.

Each boy has a faculty adviser who is available for personal counseling and advice and is responsible for reporting to the parents and the School on the student's overall performance.

ACADEMIC FACILITIES

Among the campus buildings are Centennial Hall and the Robert K. Hoffman Center, both new facilities for fall 2008; the Green-McDermott Science and Mathematics Center; the Cecil and Ida Green Library; Nearburg Hall; the H. Ben Decherd Center for the Arts; the St. Mark's Chapel; Thomas O. Hicks Family Athletic Center; Mullen Family Fitness Center; the A. Earl Cullum, Jr., Alumni Commons; and the Athletic Center, which includes the Morris G. Spencer Gymnasium and the Ralph B. Rogers Natatorium.

The Cecil and Ida Green Library houses 56,000 volumes and a state-of-the-art computer laboratory for research and Internet access, which includes online subscription databases. Three professional librarians and a technical assistant staff the library. The School has an integrated campuswide technology network that includes video projection systems in more than 90 percent of the classrooms and numerous labs and access to extensive advanced information systems.

ATHLETICS

Every boy at St. Mark's is required to participate daily in some form of athletics. Upper School boys may select either the physical education program or one of the sports teams.

In physical education, the School is concerned with students' neuromuscular and cardiovascular development, as well as their development of an appreciation of physical fitness, through the specialty classes and intramural program.

The School provides many levels of interscholastic team sports to fit the needs of each student. There are sixteen different sports that are available to Middle and Upper School students, including baseball, basketball, crew, cross-country, cheerleading, fencing, football, golf, lacrosse, soccer, swimming, tennis, track and field, volleyball, water polo, and wrestling. For the 2011–12 school year, St. Mark's was awarded its eleventh consecutive Athletic Director's trophy for the best overall boys' athletic program in the Southwest Preparatory Conference.

EXTRACURRICULAR OPPORTUNITIES

Students at St. Mark's are encouraged to do more than excel in their academic subjects. Boys have the opportunity to participate in speech and debate, the Student Council, the mathematics team, the robotics team, the School's yearbook and newspaper, drama activities, the environmental club, the letterman's club, the Cum Laude Society, the Lion and Sword Society, the tutorial program, the astronomy club, the School's literary magazine, and many other activities.

DAILY LIFE

The school day begins at 8 a.m. for all boys and ends at 3:55 p.m. for grades 9–12. Most classes, except science and fine arts, last 45 minutes. Sports and extracurricular activities for grades 9–12 are from 4 to 6 p.m.

COSTS AND FINANCIAL AID

In 2012–13, tuition, including textbooks and supplies, lunches, and fees, is $26,004 for grade 9, $24,404 for grades 10 and 11, and $25,194 for grade 12. At the time of enrollment, a deposit of $1000 is due with the signed enrollment contract, and the balance of the tuition is due by July 1 prior to entrance in August.

Financial aid awards are based on need and require annual qualification. Approximately 15 percent of the students receive financial aid. Parents are expected to furnish all of the financial information, as requested by the financial aid committee. Specific details are available from the Office of Admission.

ADMISSIONS INFORMATION

Applicants receive information about the School upon request or at the School's Web site at http://www.smtexas.org. Parents are asked to file an application, obtain a teacher's recommendation, and send a transcript of the applicant's prior work. Applicants take general aptitude, reading comprehension, vocabulary, and mathematics tests. A writing sample and on-campus interviews are also required. The application fee is $50 for grade 1 and $125 for grades 2–12.

APPLICATION TIMETABLE

Inquiries are welcome at any time. Group tours and individual tours are recommended. Applications should be submitted by December for grade 1 and by November for grades 2 through 4. Applications for grades 5 through 12 are due in January. Testing and interviewing are completed in February, and decision letters are mailed in mid-March.

ADMISSIONS CORRESPONDENCE

David Baker
Director of Admission and Financial Aid
St. Mark's School of Texas
10600 Preston Road
Dallas, Texas 75230-4047
United States
Phone: 214-346-8700
Fax: 214-346-8701
E-mail: admission@smtexas.org
Web site: http://www.smtexas.org

SANDY SPRING FRIENDS SCHOOL

Sandy Spring, Maryland

Type: Coeducational day and five- and seven-day boarding college-preparatory school
Grades: PK –12: Lower School, PK–5; Middle School 6–8; Upper School 9–12
Enrollment: School total: 552; Lower School: 162; Middle School: 121; Upper School: 269
Head of School: Thomas R. Gibian

THE SCHOOL

Sandy Spring Friends School (SSFS) was founded by Brook Moore in 1961 under the care of the Sandy Spring Monthly Meeting of Friends. The School provides a college-preparatory liberal arts curriculum for students of varying ethnic, economic, and religious backgrounds. It is situated on a 140-acre campus that contains woodlands, a pond and stream, walking and biking paths, playing fields, and one of the largest aerial ropes courses in the United States, the Adventure Park of Sandy Spring. Sandy Spring is in Montgomery County and is located approximately 35 minutes from both Washington, D.C., and Baltimore.

As a Quaker school, Sandy Spring Friends School shares the Quaker philosophy for the unique worth of the individual. Intellectual traits along with qualities of sensitivity, inventiveness, persistence, and humor are valued. The School's goal is to help each student develop a sense of personal integrity while growing academically and learning to be a responsible member of the community. The School offers a diverse liberal arts curriculum, with courses ranging from college-preparatory to Advanced Placement courses. Performing and fine arts courses and athletics are an important part of the curriculum.

The 24-member Board of Trustees includes appointments by the Baltimore Yearly Meeting, the Sandy Spring Monthly Meeting, and Sandy Spring Friends School. The 2011–12 budget exceeds $15 million, with a growing endowment program that began in 1989.

The School is accredited by the Association of Independent Maryland Schools and approved by the State of Maryland Department of Education. It is a member of the National Association of Independent Schools, the Association of Independent Maryland Schools, the Association of Independent Schools of Greater Washington, the Association of Boarding Schools, the Friends Council on Education, the Secondary School Admission Test Board, the Education Records Bureau, A Better Chance, the National Association for College Admission Counseling, the Black Student Fund, the Potomac and Chesapeake Association of College Admissions Counselors, and the College Board.

ACADEMIC PROGRAM

The curriculum at Sandy Spring Friends School is intended to prepare students for college as well as for being valuable citizens of the world. It focuses on Quaker values, academic excellence, and personal growth in an environment that values personal responsibility. The school year, from early September to early June, includes Thanksgiving, winter, and spring vacations. A typical daily schedule includes six academic periods, jobs, lunch, an electives period, and sports. The school day is from 8 to 3:20, with sports and activities after school. Boarding students are required to attend dinner at 6 and study hall from 7:30 to 9:30 p.m. The average class size is 14, with a faculty-student ratio of 1:8.

Meeting for Worship is required once a week for Lower, Middle, and Upper School students.

The required academic load for an Upper School student is six courses. To graduate, students must earn 24 credits, including English, 4; foreign language, 3; history, 3 (including United States history); mathematics, 3; science, 3; fine arts, 3; and electives, 3. Additional requirements are participating in a physical activity two times per year, passing a semester course on Quakerism, and community service. Advanced Placement courses are available in English, Spanish, French, history, math, art, and science. The ESL program is open to students in grades 9–12; currently, 61 students are enrolled.

Intersession week in March gives Upper School students an opportunity to participate in off-campus activities that supplement the standard curriculum. Projects have included trips to countries such as Belize, Brazil, France, Greece, Italy, Korea, Senegal, and Turkey after intensive study; community service projects in Georgia, Maryland, New York, North Carolina, Tennessee, Virginia, and Washington, D.C.; intensive arts workshops in modern dance, improvisational theater, spinning and weaving, and other arts; and numerous opportunities for outdoor exploration by foot, bike, and boat.

The Upper School operates on a semester schedule, and the grading systems vary by division according to the developmental needs of the students in the age group. The Lower School works within the framework of parent and teacher conferences with extensive comments; the Middle and Upper Schools use letter grades, with additional comments and parent-teacher conferences.

FACULTY AND ADVISERS

There are 66 full-time and 7 part-time teachers and administrators who teach. Seventeen live on campus, 6 with their families. Twenty-eight faculty members hold advanced degrees.

Tom Gibian, the seventh Head of School, came to Sandy Spring Friends School in July, 2010 after ten years as CEO, managing director, and founding partner of Emerging Capital Partners, the largest fund manager working across the African continent. Prior to returning to the Washington D.C. area, he was Executive Director in the Asia-Pacific region of Goldman Sachs (Asia) Limited from 1992 to 1995, having joined Goldman Sachs in 1987 as vice president. Throughout his career, he has focused on staying true to his Quaker values and using them in the business world. He has served on both the Sandy Spring Friends School and the Sidwell School Boards, and has dedicated his volunteer efforts to the governance of Quaker schools.

Mr. Gibian grew up in Sandy Spring, Maryland, and is a member of Sandy Spring Monthly Meeting. He received a bachelor's degree with honors from the College of Wooster in Ohio, and an M.B.A. in finance from the University of Pennsylvania's Wharton School of Business. As a college senior, his independent study project at College of Wooster was entitled "Dissent and Experimentation in American Schools, 1900–1960." He taught at Wooster High School and received a secondary school teaching certificate. After college he was a community organizer and, later, an administrator in a local anti-poverty agency.

Sandy Spring faculty members share a variety of nonacademic duties, including supervising student activities, proctoring the dorms, and advising students. The School encourages and supports faculty members in the pursuit of educational interests by providing funding and by supporting a professional development committee of the School.

Middle and Upper School students have a strong adviser-advisee relationship that is based on developing a mutual trust and respect. It provides parents with a personal contact when they have questions or concerns about their child's progress.

COLLEGE ADMISSION COUNSELING

Active college planning begins in the junior year with individual meetings with the College Guidance Director to discuss the general admissions process and to identify colleges of interest. Parents and students attend College Night Programs that include information regarding common admission and application for financial aid procedures. Also, many college representatives make personal visits to the School each year. The School's goal is to match the student with the right school.

One hundred percent of the students in the class of 2011 were accepted to college. They are attending institutions such as American, Bowdoin, Boston Conservatory, College of Wooster, Dartmouth, Dickinson, Earlham, Emerson, Georgia Tech, Haverford, Johns Hopkins, Penn State, St. Mary's (Maryland), Tufts, Xavier, and the Universities of Delaware, Maryland, Pittsburgh, Vermont, Virginia, and Washington.

STUDENT BODY AND CONDUCT

In 2012–13, the Upper School enrolled 269 students, 126 boys and 142 girls, as follows: 60 in grade 9, 71 in grade 10, 66 in grade 11, and 71 in grade 12. The boarding program enrolled 60 students from the mid-Atlantic region and eight countries. Nine percent are members of the Religious Society of Friends, and 26 percent are students of color. International students represent 25 percent of the Upper School student body.

The Torch Committee, the student government organization, includes day and boarding students as well as faculty and administration representatives. The committee, operating by consensus, considers student concerns and makes recommendations to faculty committees and to the administration. A student member of Torch is invited to attend faculty and business meetings and meetings of the Board of Trustees.

ACADEMIC FACILITIES

The School's physical plant, which is valued at more than $41 million, includes a science center; a Lower School building and a Middle School building; a dormitory and dining hall; three major classroom buildings and an administration building; a performing arts center with a fine arts wing; an athletic complex; and Yarnall Hall, a $1.75-million resource center that houses a 20,000-volume library, a gymnasium, and an observatory. Computers are integrated into many aspects of the curriculum. Every division of the School is equipped with its own computer lab, and every classroom includes at least one computer and is wired for network and Internet access. The School's library includes computers for online research through the public library system, subscription to online reference tools, and the Internet. A fiber-optic backbone connects the network, and a T1 line connects the Internet and e-mail accounts to students and faculty members. All faculty members and students use Moodle (a course management software).

BOARDING AND GENERAL FACILITIES

All of the boarding students live with their roommates in one 2-story dormitory. Boys and girls each have a separate floor. Community life for boarders includes regular dorm meetings (with decisions reached by consensus), committee-style sponsored activities, family-style dinners with resident staff members, and visits to the homes of day student friends. The dorm staff members (6 adults for 61 boarders in 2010–11) all reside in either apartments or town houses located near the Westview dormitory.

The School nurse assists with the appropriate care for students who may become ill. The School's infirmary is open all day for the entire school year.

ATHLETICS

Sandy Spring Friends School is a member of the Potomac Valley Athletic Conference. The Middle and Upper School teams compete in the following interscholastic sports: baseball, basketball, cross-country, golf, lacrosse, soccer, softball, tennis, track and field, and volleyball. Other activities include weight lifting and outdoor exploration.

The athletic facilities include a complex with a 9,000-square-foot gymnasium, a fully equipped fitness center, and state-of-the-art training and locker room facilities. The 140-acre campus includes four soccer and lacrosse fields, baseball and softball fields, and a 5-kilometer cross-country course. A new 40-foot by 50-foot teaching climbing wall was added in 2011.

EXTRACURRICULAR OPPORTUNITIES

Getting involved is made easy at Sandy Spring Friends by a weekly activities period that allows students to participate in clubs such as Amnesty International (now in its tenth year at SSFS), the Multicultural Club, the International Student Club, the Open Door Club, the ski club (eight weeks of Friday-night skiing plus other trips), the chess club, and the outdoor exploration club. The yearbook and the award-winning literary magazine are also popular activities for students.

The Community Service Program at Sandy Spring Friends School seeks to respond to the needs of others and enrich the School community and the lives of its members. Every student at the School completes 100 community service hours as a requirement for graduation. The service programs are diverse and allow for individual interests to be pursued.

DAILY LIFE

Breakfast for the boarding community begins at 7. Classes begin at 8 and end at 3:20. Advisory and tutorial periods occur once a week, Meeting for Worship occurs once each week, and a "jobs" period is scheduled daily for dorm students. Lunch is served cafeteria-style daily.

Athletics take place between 3:30 and 5:30, and dinner is served family-style at 6. Dorm meetings or activity groups frequently meet before the study hours, which begin nightly at 7:30, Sunday through Thursday.

WEEKEND LIFE

Weekends at the School are relaxed. Activities, which are frequently designed by both students and faculty members, have included adventures such as day trips into Washington, D.C., for a museum visit, a march on the Mall, lunch at Planet Hollywood and a show at the Kennedy Center, or shopping in Georgetown. In addition, the students have visited Baltimore's Inner Harbor, Harper's Ferry, and various hot spots around the School. While boarding students are not required to stay at the School on weekends, all students can choose the weekend activities in which they wish to participate (day students and five-day boarders are charged an appropriate fee for the off-campus activities). One third of the weekends during the school year include on-campus activities such as School dances; student performances in theater, music, and modern dance; art shows; and special concerts and symposiums in the areas of science and the arts.

COSTS AND FINANCIAL AID

In 2012–13, tuition ranges from $20,475 to 23,050 in the Lower School, and is $25,520 in the Middle School, and $28,300 in the Upper School. Boarding tuition was $41,700 for five days and $52,200 for seven days. A hot lunch is provided beginning in the first grade. Additional costs include an incidental account for the School store, student allowances, laboratory fees, and art supplies.

Sandy Spring Friends School offers financial aid on the basis of need. The financial aid decisions for applications submitted by January 15 are made by mid-March for the following year. Thirty-three percent of the students received financial aid for the 2012–13 school year. The average award was $30,000 for boarders and $14,000 for day students in the Upper School.

ADMISSIONS INFORMATION

Sandy Spring Friends School actively seeks a diverse, curious, and enthusiastic community of students. The student body is diverse in race, creed, and economic and social background. The admissions process allows prospective students and their families to become familiar with as many aspects of the School as possible. New students enter at all grade levels as space permits.

APPLICATION TIMETABLE

Inquiries are welcome at any time. The Admissions Office is open from 8 a.m. to 4:30 p.m., Monday through Friday. Application forms are due by January 1. The application process must be completed by February 15 to ensure first-round consideration. Applications received after January 1 are reviewed as space permits.

ADMISSIONS CORRESPONDENCE

Yasmin McGinnis, Director of Enrollment Management
Sandy Spring Friends School
16923 Norwood Road
Sandy Spring, Maryland 20860-1199
United States
Phone: 301-774-7455 Ext. 182
Fax: 301-924-1115
E-mail: admissions@ssfs.org
Web site: http://www.ssfs.org

SOUNDVIEW PREPARATORY SCHOOL

Yorktown Heights, New York

Type: Coeducational day college-preparatory school
Grades: Middle School, 6–8; Upper School, 9–12
Enrollment: Total, 70; Middle School, 12; Upper School, 58
Head of School: W. Glyn Hearn, Headmaster

THE SCHOOL

Soundview Preparatory School, a coeducational, college-preparatory school for grades 6 through 12, was founded in 1989 on the belief that the best environment for students is one where classes are small, teachers know the learning style and interests of each student, and an atmosphere of mutual trust prevails. At Soundview, students and teachers work in close collaboration in classes with an average size of 7 students.

The School's mission is to provide a college-preparatory education in a supportive and noncompetitive environment that requires rigorous application to academics, instills respect for ethical values, and fosters self-confidence by helping each student feel recognized and valued. Soundview empowers students to develop their potential and reach their own goals in a setting that promotes respect for others and a sense of community.

Soundview Prep opened its doors with 13 students in the spring of 1989. In the spring of 1998, having outgrown its original quarters in Pocantico Hills, New York, the School moved to a larger facility in Mount Kisco, New York. On January 14, 2008, Soundview moved to its first permanent home, a 13.8-acre campus in Yorktown Heights, New York. New York City, only an hour away, provides a wealth of cultural opportunities for Soundview students to explore on class trips.

The School is governed by a 7-member Board of Trustees. The current operating budget is $2.085 million. In 2011–12, Soundview raised a gross total amount of $176,112 through the Annual Fund and fund-raising events, and from parents, alumni families, grandparents, friends, foundations, and corporations.

Soundview is chartered by the New York State Board of Regents and is accredited by the New York State Association of Independent Schools. The School is a member of the National Association of Independent Schools, the Education Records Bureau, and the Council for Advancement and Support of Education.

ACADEMIC PROGRAM

Soundview provides a rigorous academic program to ensure that students not only develop the skills and acquire the knowledge needed for college work but also have the opportunity to pursue their own personal goals.

The academic day is carefully structured but informal, with nurture a crucial ingredient. Soundview's student-teacher ratio of 4:1 guarantees that students are monitored closely and receive the support they need. At the same time, the School provides advanced courses for students who wish to go beyond the high school level or take a subject that is not usually offered, allowing students to soar academically and truly develop their potential.

The Middle School curriculum is designed to establish a foundation of knowledge and skills in each academic discipline, strong comprehension and communication skills, good work habits and study skills, confidence in using technology, and creativity in the arts.

The Upper School curriculum provides a traditional college-preparatory education in academics and the arts. In addition to the core subjects—English, history, math, and science—Soundview offers four languages (Latin, French, Spanish, and Italian); studio art; music; and electives such as history of philosophy, drama, computer science, astronomy, journalism, environmental science, and contemporary issues in science.

AP courses are made available according to students' abilities and interests. Recently, AP courses have been offered in calculus, biology, physics, U.S. history, European history, government, and art.

Academic requirements for graduation are 4 years each of English and history, 3 years each of math and science, 3 years of one foreign language or 2 years each of two different languages, 1 year of art or music, and ½ year of health.

Computer technology at Soundview is integrated into the curriculum. Teachers post assignments on the School's Web site, and students upload completed work into teachers' folders. The School is wired for wireless technology and has a well-equipped computer lab.

The School's annual two-week trips abroad (to Argentina, Russia, China, England, Spain and Italy over the last six years) offer students experience with other cultures.

The school year is divided into two semesters, with letter grades sent out at the end of each. Individual conferences with parents, students, faculty members, and the Headmaster are arranged throughout the year.

Students take the Educational Records Bureau (ERB) standardized tests every year for use by the School in monitoring each student's progress.

FACULTY AND ADVISERS

The faculty consists of 17 teachers (13 women and 4 men); the majority hold advanced degrees. Three teachers are part-time; the rest, full-time. Turnover is low, with an average of one replacement or addition per year.

Each teacher serves as adviser to up to 5 students. Most faculty members supervise a club or publication or coach an athletic team.

W. Glyn Hearn has served as Headmaster since the School was founded in 1989. He obtained his B.A. in English at the University of Texas at Austin and his M.A. in American literature at Texas Tech University. He spent twelve years at the Awty International School of Houston, Texas, where he served as Principal of the Lower, Middle, and Upper Schools and Head of the American Section, before becoming Assistant Headmaster and then Headmaster of the American Renaissance School in Westchester County in 1987.

COLLEGE ADMISSION COUNSELING

College placement at Soundview is directed by Carol Gill, president of Carol Gill Associates and one of the nation's leading college counseling experts. The process starts early on, when eighth, ninth, and tenth graders plan and refine a course sequence that is appropriate for a competitive college. In the junior year, students and their parents begin meeting with Ms. Gill to discuss the college application process, develop lists of colleges, and plan college visits. The meetings continue through the senior year to complete applications. Representatives from approximately twenty colleges visit Soundview every year to speak with students.

Because of the School's small size, the faculty and staff members know each student well and are able to assist students in selecting colleges that are the right match for them. The Headmaster writes a personal recommendation for each senior.

College acceptances in recent years include Bard, Barnard, Bates, Brandeis, Brown, Carnegie Mellon, Clark, Columbia, Dickinson, Duke, Emerson, Franklin & Marshall, Gettysburg, Hampshire, Hartwick, High Point, Hobart, Ithaca, Manhattanville, Maryland Institute College of Art, Muhlenberg, Northeastern, NYU, Oberlin, Reed, Rensselaer, Rhode Island School of Design, Roger Williams, Sarah Lawrence, St. John's (Santa Fe), SUNY, Susquehanna, Vassar, Williams, and the Universities of Maine and Vermont.

STUDENT BODY AND CONDUCT

Soundview reflects the diversity—ethnic, religious, and economic—of American society. The 32 boys and 38 girls come from Westchester, Fairfield, and Rockland Counties and New York City. Approximately 13 percent of the student body are members of minority groups.

Respect for ethical values such as kindness, honesty, and respect for others are paramount at Soundview, where individual responsibility and a sense of community are stressed.

The School's disciplinary structure is informal, since it is based on the assumption that students attending the School desire to be there and are therefore willing to adhere to a code of conduct that demonstrates awareness that the community is based upon a shared sense of purpose and commitment. Despite the cordiality of its atmosphere, Soundview has high expectations of personal conduct. The result of this policy is a remarkably cooperative, considerate group of students who value each other and who appreciate their teachers.

Attire appropriate for a school is expected of all students, although there is no formal dress code.

ACADEMIC FACILITIES

Soundview's campus consists of 13.8 rustic acres with a historic main house, numerous outbuildings, a large pond, meadows, and woods, all in the heart of the village of Yorktown Heights, New York. The main house, the former Underhill mansion built by Yorktown's leading family in the nineteenth century, contains classrooms, administrative offices, the computer lab, and meeting rooms. A large barn houses the science lab, art studios, additional classrooms, and a cafeteria-meeting hall, while a third building is home to the Middle School. A fourth building provides another large meeting and performance space, while a small former chapel is used for the music program. Woodland paths and footbridges lead across streams and around the property.

ATHLETICS

Physical education and sports at Soundview offer students the opportunity to develop leadership and teamwork skills as well as to excel in individual sports. Students participate on coed soccer, coed basketball, girls' basketball, and Ultimate Frisbee teams that compete against other independent schools in the Hudson Valley region. Depending upon student interest in a given year, other sports, such as tennis, softball, and baseball are also offered. Any student who wishes to play is accepted, regardless of ability.

The Ski and Snowboard Club offers opportunities for noncompetitive sports. For physical education, students play intramural sports, work out on exercise equipment, and participate in the Outdoors Club, clearing trails and planting gardens on school property.

Soundview's home gym is the Solaris Sports Club in Yorktown Heights, a state-of-the-art multisport center just blocks from the School. The facility includes tennis courts, a large indoor basketball court, and exercise equipment.

EXTRACURRICULAR OPPORTUNITIES

Soundview offers a wide range of clubs and activities, with additional choices added each year by students themselves.

Drama is important at Soundview. Students perform at School functions, attend plays on Broadway, and meet backstage with theater professionals. The School sponsors activities to expose students to other cultures, such as trips to art exhibitions, dance performances, concerts, and plays. The Community Service Club works on such projects as collecting food for local food banks and toys for the children of women incarcerated at a nearby correctional facility.

Other activities students are likely to sign up for include yearbook, literary magazine, student newspaper, the mock trial program, Outdoors Club, Chess Club, Politics Club, Art Club, Music Club and New York! New York (that explores New York's architectural and historical sites on foot).

Major annual functions at Soundview include the Back-to-School Picnic; the Spring Gala, a dinner and fund-raiser for the Soundview community; the Talent Show, which involves every student in the School; Texas Day, a lighthearted event featuring a barbecue, games, and spoofs on the Headmaster's home state; and the Graduation Dinner, an evening for Soundview parents to honor the graduating class.

DAILY LIFE

The school day begins at 8:10 with Morning Meeting, when the entire student body, faculty, and staff assemble to hear announcements about ongoing activities, listen to presentations by clubs, and discuss the day's national and international news. The Head of School encourages students to express their views and helps them to assess events that are unfolding in the world around them.

Classes begin at 8:25 and end at 3:25. There are eight academic periods plus lunch.

SUMMER PROGRAMS

Soundview offers a small summer school on an as-needed basis, with classes that vary each year. A typical offering includes English, writing, math, history, a science, and a language. Students have the opportunity to work one-on-one with a teacher or in small classes to skip ahead in a given subject or fulfill a requirement.

COSTS AND FINANCIAL AID

Tuition and fees for 2012–13 are $36,800 for Middle School and $38,000 for Upper School. Fees include gym, books, art and lab fees, ERB exams, and literary publications.

In 2011–12, the School provided a total of $411,950 in financial aid to approximately 30 percent of the student body.

ADMISSIONS INFORMATION

Soundview operates on a rolling admissions policy, with students accepted throughout the year in all grades except twelfth. Families of prospective students meet with the Admissions Director, after which the student spends a day at the School. The SSAT is not required, but portions of the ERB standardized examination are administered (unless the applicant provides the School with sufficient, current test data).

Students of all backgrounds are welcomed. The academic program is demanding, but the School's small size allows it to work with each individual student in order to develop strategies for success.

APPLICATION TIMETABLE

Soundview accepts applications on a rolling basis throughout the year. The application fee is $50.

ADMISSIONS CORRESPONDENCE

Mary E. Ivanyi
Director of Admissions and Assistant Head
Soundview Preparatory School
370 Underhill Road
Yorktown Heights, New York 10598
United States
Phone: 914-962-2780
E-mail: info@soundviewprep.org
Web site: http://www.soundviewprep.org

SOUTHWESTERN ACADEMY

Beaver Creek Ranch, Arizona

Type: Coeducational boarding and day college-preparatory and general academic school
Grades: 9–12, postgraduate year
Enrollment: 32
Head of School: Kenneth R. Veronda, Headmaster

THE SCHOOL

Southwestern Academy offers achievement-based, departmentalized, and supportively structured classes limited to 9 to 12 students. Small classes allow for individualized attention in a noncompetitive environment. Southwestern was founded by Maurice Veronda in 1924 as a college-preparatory program "for capable students who could do better" in small, supportive classes. While maintaining that commitment, Southwestern Academy includes U.S. and international students with strong academic abilities who are eager to learn and strengthen English-language skills as well as pursue a general scholastic program in a small, supportive school structure. Southwestern Academy is accredited by the Western Association of Schools and Colleges (WASC).

Southwestern Academy offers students the opportunity to study at either of two distinctly different and beautiful campuses. The Arizona campus, which is known as Beaver Creek Ranch, is located deep in a red-rock canyon in northern Arizona. The San Marino, California, campus is situated in a historic orange grove area near Pasadena. Students may attend either campus and, if space permits, may divide the academic year between the two.

The Beaver Creek campus is a 185-acre ranch located 100 miles north of Phoenix, 12 miles from the resort community of Sedona, and 45 miles south of Flagstaff. The San Marino campus occupies 8 acres in a residential suburb 10 miles from downtown Los Angeles and immediately south of Pasadena, home to the renowned Tournament of Roses Parade. Although the program and philosophies are the same at both campuses, each offers a very different learning environment. Students studying at the Beaver Creek Ranch campus enjoy a living and learning environment that takes full advantage of the rich cultural, scenic, and environmentally significant region. Students at the California campus draw on the offerings of the urban setting.

A mix of U.S. and international students from several countries offers a unique blend of cultural, social, and educational opportunities for all. Every effort is made to enroll a well-balanced student body that represents the rich ethnic diversity of U.S. citizens and students from around the world. The student body consists of college-bound students who prefer a small, personalized education; above-average students who have the potential to become excellent academic achievers in the right learning environment; and average students who, with a supportive structure, can achieve academic success.

Southwestern Academy is incorporated as a not-for-profit organization. Operating expenses are approximately $4.5 million per annum and are met by tuition (93 percent) and grants and annual giving (7 percent). The Academy has no indebtedness.

ACADEMIC PROGRAM

High school classes are divided by grade level, and students are assigned based on ability and achievement.

High school graduation requirements are based on University of California requirements and include completion of a minimum of 200 academic credits plus 40 credit hours of physical education. The academic term is mid-September through mid-June, with a summer quarter offered at both campuses. Requirements include 4 years of English, 3 years of mathematics, 2 years of a foreign language, 2 years of laboratory sciences, and 1 year each of U.S. history and world cultures, plus one semester of U.S. government and economics and 2 years of visual/performing arts. Proficiency exams in English, mathematics, and computer literacy, as well as community service hours, are also required for graduation.

A typical semester of course work includes six classes plus physical education. Advanced Placement classes are available in English, history, language, math, and science. Review and remedial classes are made available to students who need additional instruction. International students are offered three levels of classes in English as a second language (ESL), including an introductory class, to prepare them to enter and succeed in other academic areas.

Teachers are available daily during a midafternoon study period to work individually with students and meet with parents. There is no extra charge for this tutoring. Boarding students are required to attend a monitored evening study hall, where additional teacher assistance is available.

Student achievement is recognized with a grading system that ranges from A to F. Progress letters are sent monthly to parents and report cards are sent quarterly. The minimum college-recommending grade upon completion of academic requirements is C.

Students studying at the Beaver Creek Ranch campus attend classes on a block schedule, Monday through Thursday. Each Friday, students participate in educational, project-oriented, and assignment-based field trips. Experiential learning allows students to apply knowledge from the classroom. It also supports an integrated academic element that links core subject areas in a practical, applied manner, promoting understanding and retention of key concepts.

FACULTY AND ADVISERS

Headmaster Kenneth Veronda was born at the San Marino campus that his father founded. Mr. Veronda attended classes at Southwestern, graduated, and completed undergraduate and graduate work in American history and foreign relations at Stanford University. The majority of 30 faculty members, 8 in Arizona and 22 in California, hold advanced degrees in their subject areas. Each teacher serves as a faculty adviser to a few students and meets with them individually throughout the school year. On-campus college and career counselors are also available to meet with and assist students in making post–high school graduation plans.

COLLEGE ADMISSION COUNSELING

The college counselors closely monitor the advisement and placement needs of each student. Beginning in the ninth grade, every effort is made to assist students in researching a variety of colleges and universities that match their interests and academic achievement levels. Students are provided a college planning handbook that offers helpful hints and suggestions regarding college application processes. A variety of college representatives are invited annually to visit each campus and meet with students.

Approximately 35 students graduate each year from Southwestern Academy. Almost all enter a U.S. college or university. Some choose to attend a local two-year community college before transferring to a four-year college or university. In recent years, Southwestern Academy graduates have been accepted to the following schools: American University; Arizona State; Art Center College of Design; Azusa Pacific; Boston College; Boston University; Brown; Butler; California State, Fullerton, Monterey Bay, and Northridge; California State Polytechnic, Pomona; Columbia; Hampton; Howard; Loyola; Marymount; Menlo College; Mills; Occidental; Oregon State; Parsons; Penn State; Pepperdine; Pitzer; Temple; USC, Whittier; Woodbury; Wooster; Xavier; and the Universities of California, Irvine, La Verne, Nevada, New Orleans, the Pacific, San Diego, San Francisco, St. Louis, and Washington (Seattle).

ACADEMIC FACILITIES

At the Beaver Creek Ranch campus, newly renovated classrooms, a learning resource center, and the dormitories blend into the picturesque setting. The campus also includes recreation rooms, a gymnasium, several large activity fields, and an indoor, solar-heated swimming pool.

The San Marino campus includes seven buildings encircling a large multisport athletic field. Lincoln Hall, the main academic building, houses morning assembly and study hall, ten classrooms, science and computer labs, and the library. Pioneer Hall includes several classrooms, a kitchen, dining rooms, and business offices. A separate building is home to large music and art studios and an additional science classroom and lab.

BOARDING AND GENERAL FACILITIES

The Beaver Creek Ranch Campus offers dorm rooms that accommodate 1 to 4 people. Meals are served in the dining room and sometimes in the charming courtyard. Picnics are also popular. A lounge with a huge fireplace is a favorite spot for students to watch movies and DirectTV®.

Seven stone cottages are home to faculty and staff members and sometimes upperclassmen and are set along the trout-filled Beaver Creek. Two fishing ponds, pastures, prehistoric Indian caves, and a favorite swimming hole in the creek are found on campus. Even in this remote, rugged environment, students can e-mail friends and surf the Internet, thanks to the T-1 wireless connectivity.

Four dormitory halls are located on the San Marino campus. Each is designed to accommodate up to 20 boys in double and single rooms. Two off-campus dormitories (located within a mile) house a total of 32 girls. Dorm parents live in apartments adjoining each hall.

ATHLETICS

Gyms and playing fields are available to all students at both campuses, where sports opportunities exist for physical education requirements and recreation. As a member of federated leagues in Arizona and California, Southwestern Academy fields teams at both campuses in all major sports except tackle football. Athletic events are held in late afternoon following the regular school day.

EXTRACURRICULAR OPPORTUNITIES

At the Beaver Creek Ranch campus, students can learn to ride and care for horses or swing on a rope over the creek—and drop in for a swim! The indoor pool is heated for those who prefer warmer water. The campus offers a full program of sports, including golf, and a full range of art classes. Wildlife, including mule deer, bighorn sheep, and javelina, can be seen on hikes. Other recreation opportunities include camping, hiking, mountain biking, fishing, and backpacking.

Southwestern offers a wide range of co-curricular and extracurricular activities and opportunities, including art, drama, music, journalism, student government, and student clubs. Current clubs include chess, Interact, International, the Southwestern Arts Society, Southwestern Environmental Associates, and tennis. Frequent class trips to southern California and northern Arizona places of interest, such as tide pools, museums, archaeological sites, art galleries, and live theater, are great learning experiences for students at both campuses.

DAILY LIFE

Boarding students begin each school day with a breakfast buffet at 7:30. Following breakfast, day and boarding students meet for a required assembly at 8:10, with classes following from 8:30 to 2:45. Required study halls and optional clubs and athletic events are held between 2:50 and 4:30. Dinner is served at 6 and is followed by a monitored study hall lasting until 8. Lights out is at 10:30 for middle school students and 11 for those in high school.

SUMMER PROGRAMS

Summer school sessions are offered at both campuses. Both offer intensive yet enjoyable individualized classes in English and other subjects, plus educational and recreational trips to interesting places in northern Arizona and southern California.

Summer sessions at Beaver Creek Ranch combine review and enrichment courses with experiential learning and high-adventure activities in classwork, camp-type activities, and travel in northern Arizona. ESL is offered at the Beaver Creek campus during the summer.

The summer program in San Marino is an excellent opportunity for domestic students to catch up, if needed, or to move ahead academically in order to take more advanced courses before graduation. For non-English-speaking international students, the summer session can provide an entire semester of the appropriate ESL level necessary to successfully complete a college-preparatory curriculum.

COSTS AND FINANCIAL AID

Tuition for a 2012–13 U.S. boarding student is $33,750. International student tuition was $41,000. The cost for a day student (U.S. citizens) was $16,500. An incidental account containing $2000 for boarding students or $1000 for day students is required of all students to cover expenses such as books, school supplies, physical education uniforms, and discretionary spending money. Payment is due in advance unless other arrangements are made with the business office.

Financial aid is awarded based on financial need. More than $440,000 was awarded in 2012–13.

ADMISSIONS INFORMATION

Southwestern Academy admits students of any race, color, national and ethnic origin, creed, or sex. A completed application packet is required, followed by a personal on-campus interview with students and parents. A daylong visit to classes (and an overnight for prospective boarding students) is strongly encouraged for prospective students already living in the United States. Interviews with prospective international students and parents are scheduled by the international admissions director and do not require a campus visit.

Each campus offers exceptional learning opportunities. Prospective students are encouraged to seriously consider both campuses and apply to the one that seems better suited to them.

Admission materials and other information can be downloaded from the Southwestern Academy Web site. It can also be obtained by contacting the Office of Admissions.

APPLICATION TIMETABLE

Admission offers are made throughout the year, as space permits. Appointments are required for interviews and campus tours at both locations. The admissions office for both campus locations is located in San Marino. Students should write or call the San Marino office for information on either campus.

ADMISSIONS CORRESPONDENCE

Office of Admissions
Southwestern Academy
2800 Monterey Road
San Marino, California 91108
United States
Phone: 626-799-5010 Ext. 203
Fax: 626-799-0407
E-mail: jblake@southwesternacademy.edu
Web site:
http://www.southwesternacademy.edu

SOUTHWESTERN ACADEMY

San Marino, California

Type: Coeducational boarding and day college-preparatory and general academic school
Grades: 6–12, postgraduate year
Enrollment: 140
Head of School: Kenneth R. Veronda, Headmaster

THE SCHOOL

Southwestern Academy offers achievement-based, departmentalized, and supportively structured classes limited to 9 to 12 students. Small classes allow for individualized attention in a noncompetitive environment. Southwestern was founded by Maurice Veronda in 1924 as a college-preparatory program "for capable students who could do better" in small, supportive classes. While maintaining that commitment, Southwestern Academy includes U.S. and international students with strong academic abilities who are eager to learn and strengthen English-language skills as well as pursue a general scholastic program in a small, supportive school structure. Southwestern Academy is accredited by the Western Association of Schools and Colleges (WASC).

Southwestern Academy offers students the opportunity to study at either of two distinctly different and beautiful campuses. The San Marino, California, campus is situated in a historic orange grove area near Pasadena. The Arizona campus, which is known as Beaver Creek Ranch, is located deep in a red-rock canyon in northern Arizona. Students may attend either campus and, if space permits, may divide the academic year between the two.

The San Marino campus occupies 8 acres in a residential suburb 10 miles from downtown Los Angeles and immediately south of Pasadena, home to the renowned Tournament of Roses Parade. The Beaver Creek campus is a 185-acre ranch located 100 miles north of Phoenix, 12 miles from the resort community of Sedona, and 45 miles south of Flagstaff. Although the program and philosophies are the same at both campuses, each offers a very different learning environment. Students at the California campus draw on the offerings of the urban setting. Students studying at the Beaver Creek Ranch campus enjoy a living and learning environment that takes full advantage of the rich cultural, scenic, and environmentally significant region.

A mix of U.S. and international students from several countries offers a unique blend of cultural, social, and educational opportunities for all. Every effort is made to enroll a well-balanced student body that represents the rich ethnic diversity of U.S. citizens and students from around the world. The student body consists of college-bound students who prefer a small, personalized education; above-average students who have the potential to become excellent academic achievers in the right learning environment; and average students who, with a supportive structure, can achieve academic success.

Southwestern Academy is incorporated as a not-for-profit organization. Operating expenses are approximately $4.5 million per annum and are met by tuition (93 percent) and grants and annual giving (7 percent). The Academy has no indebtedness.

ACADEMIC PROGRAM

Middle school students are placed in classes based on individual achievement levels. High school classes are divided by grade level, and students are assigned based on ability and achievement.

High school graduation requirements are based on University of California requirements and include completion of a minimum of 200 academic credits plus 40 credit hours of physical education. The academic term is mid-September through mid-June, with a summer quarter offered at both campuses. Requirements include 4 years of English, 3 years of mathematics, 2 years of a foreign language, 2 years of laboratory sciences, and 1 year each of U.S. history and world cultures, plus one semester of U.S. government and economics and 2 years of visual/performing arts. Proficiency exams in English, mathematics, and computer literacy, as well as community service hours, are also required for graduation.

A typical semester of course work includes six classes plus physical education. Advanced Placement classes are available in English, history, language, math, and science. Review and remedial classes are made available to students who need additional instruction. International students are offered three levels of classes in English as a second language (ESL), including an introductory class, to prepare them to enter and succeed in other academic areas.

Teachers are available daily during a midafternoon study period to work individually with students and meet with parents. There is no extra charge for this tutoring. Boarding students are required to attend a monitored evening study hall, where additional teacher assistance is available.

Student achievement is recognized with a grading system that ranges from A to F. Progress letters are sent monthly to parents and report cards are sent quarterly. The minimum college-recommending grade upon completion of academic requirements is C.

While studying at the Beaver Creek Ranch campus, students attend classes on a block schedule, Monday through Thursday. Each Friday, students participate in educational, project-oriented, and assignment-based field trips. Experiential learning allows students to apply knowledge from the classroom. It also supports an integrated academic element that links core subject areas in a practical, applied manner, promoting understanding and retention of key concepts.

FACULTY AND ADVISERS

Headmaster Kenneth Veronda was born at the San Marino campus that his father founded. Mr. Veronda attended classes at Southwestern, graduated, and completed undergraduate and graduate work in American history and foreign relations at Stanford University. The majority of 31 faculty members, 22 in California and 9 in Arizona, hold advanced degrees in their subject areas. Each teacher serves as a faculty adviser to a few students and meets with them individually throughout the school year. On-campus college and career counselors are also available to meet with and assist students in making post–high school graduation plans.

COLLEGE ADMISSION COUNSELING

The college counselors closely monitor the advisement and placement needs of each student. Beginning in the ninth grade, every effort is made to assist students in researching a variety of colleges and universities that match their interests and academic achievement levels. Students are provided a college planning handbook that offers helpful hints and suggestions regarding college application processes. A variety of college representatives are invited annually to visit each campus and meet with students.

Approximately 35 students graduate each year from Southwestern Academy. Almost all enter a U.S. college or university. Some choose to attend a local two-year community college before transferring to a four-year college or university. In recent years, Southwestern Academy graduates have been accepted to the following schools: American University; Arizona State; Art Center College of Design; Azusa Pacific; Boston College; Boston University; Brown; Butler; California State, Fullerton, Monterey Bay, and Northridge; California State Polytechnic, Pomona; Columbia; Hampton; Howard; Loyola; Marymount; Menlo College; Mills; Occidental; Oregon State; Parsons; Penn State; Pepperdine; Pitzer; Temple; USC, Whittier; Woodbury; Wooster; Xavier; and the Universities of California, La Verne, Nevada, New Orleans, the Pacific, San Diego, San Francisco, St. Louis, and Washington (Seattle).

ACADEMIC FACILITIES

The San Marino campus includes seven buildings encircling a large multisport athletic field. Lincoln Hall, the main academic building, houses morning assembly and study hall, ten classrooms, science and computer labs, and the library. Pioneer Hall includes several classrooms, a kitchen, dining rooms, and business offices. A separate building is home to large music and art studios and an additional science classroom and lab.

Newly renovated classrooms, a learning resource center, and the dormitories blend into the picturesque setting along Beaver Creek.

BOARDING AND GENERAL FACILITIES

Four dormitory halls are located on the San Marino campus. Each is designed to accommodate up to 20 boys in double and single rooms. Two off-campus dormitories (located within a mile) house a total of 32 girls. Dorm parents live in apartments adjoining each hall.

At Beaver Creek, seven stone cottages encircle the main campus area and provide faculty/staff housing. Four recently renovated residence halls accommodate up to 56 students. The Beaver Creek Ranch campus includes recreation rooms, a gymnasium, several large activity fields, and an indoor, solar-heated swimming pool.

ATHLETICS

Gyms and playing fields are available to all students at both campuses, where sports opportunities exist for physical education requirements and recreation. As a member of federated leagues in California and Arizona, Southwestern Academy fields teams at both campuses in all major sports except tackle football. Athletic events are held in late afternoon, following the regular school day.

EXTRACURRICULAR OPPORTUNITIES

Southwestern offers a wide range of cocurricular and extracurricular activities and opportunities, including art, drama, music, journalism, student government, and student clubs. Current clubs include chess, Interact, International, the Southwestern Arts Society, Southwestern Environmental Associates, and tennis. Frequent class trips to southern California and northern Arizona places of interest, such as tide pools, museums, archaeological sites, art galleries, and live theater, are great learning experiences for students at both campuses.

DAILY LIFE

Boarding students begin each school day with a breakfast buffet at 7:30. Following breakfast, day and boarding students meet for a required assembly at 8:10, with classes following from 8:30 to 2:45. Required study halls and optional clubs and athletic events are held between 2:50 and 4:30. Dinner is served at 6 and is followed by a monitored study hall lasting until 8. Lights out is at 10:30 for middle school students and 11 for high school students.

WEEKEND LIFE

Students in good standing may leave the campus, with permission, during any weekend. Many students take advantage of the planned activities that are arranged for them, including theater performances, shopping at the malls and Old Town Pasadena, barbecues, beach parties, and movies. Visits are planned to Disneyland, Magic Mountain, and Big Surf, and the other attractions of the two-state areas are a part of the social program at Southwestern Academy. Day students are welcome to attend all weekend activities if space permits.

SUMMER PROGRAMS

Summer school sessions are offered at both campuses. Both offer intensive yet enjoyable individualized classes in English and other subjects, plus educational and recreational trips to interesting places in southern California and northern Arizona.

The summer program in San Marino is an excellent opportunity for domestic students to catch up, if needed, or to move ahead academically in order to take more advanced courses before graduation. For non-English-speaking international students, the summer session can provide an entire semester of the appropriate ESL level necessary to successfully complete a college-preparatory curriculum.

Summer sessions at Beaver Creek Ranch combine review and enrichment courses with experiential learning and high-adventure activities in classwork, camp-type activities, and travel in northern Arizona. ESL is offered at the Beaver Creek campus during the summer.

COSTS AND FINANCIAL AID

Tuition for the 2012–13 U.S. boarding student is $33,750. International student tuition is $41,000. The cost for a day student (U.S. citizens) is $16,500. An incidental account containing $2000 for boarding students or $1000 for day students is required of all students to cover expenses such as books, school supplies, physical education uniforms, and discretionary spending money. Payment is due in advance unless other arrangements are made with the business office.

Financial aid is awarded based on financial need. More than $440,000 was awarded in the 2012–13 school year.

ADMISSIONS INFORMATION

Southwestern Academy admits students of any race, color, national and ethnic origin, creed, or sex. A completed application packet is required, followed by a personal on-campus interview with students and parents. A daylong visit to classes (and an overnight for prospective boarding students) is strongly encouraged for prospective students already living in the United States. Interviews with prospective international students and parents are scheduled by the international admissions director and do not require a campus visit.

Each campus offers exceptional learning opportunities. Prospective students are encouraged to seriously consider both campuses and apply to the one that seems better suited to them.

Admission materials and other information can be downloaded from the Southwestern Academy Web site. It can also be obtained by contacting the Office of Admissions.

APPLICATION TIMETABLE

Admission offers are made throughout the year, as space permits. Appointments are required for interviews and campus tours at both locations. The admissions office for both campus locations is located in San Marino. Students should write or call the San Marino office for information on either campus.

ADMISSIONS CORRESPONDENCE

Office of Admissions
Southwestern Academy
2800 Monterey Road
San Marino, California 91108
United States
Phone: 626-799-5010 Ext. 203
Fax: 626-799-0407
E-mail: jblake@southwesternacademy.edu
Web site:
http://www.southwesternacademy.edu

requirements and recreation. As a member of federated leagues in California and Arizona, Southwestern Academy fields teams at both campuses in all major sports except tackle football. Athletic events are held in late afternoon, following the regular school day.

EXTRACURRICULAR OPPORTUNITIES

Southwestern offers a wide range of cocurricular and extracurricular activities and opportunities, including art, drama, music, journalism, student government, and student clubs. Current clubs include chess, Interact, International, the Southwestern Arts Society, Southwestern Environmental Associates, and tennis. Frequent class trips to southern California and northern Arizona places of interest, such as tide pools, museums, archaeological sites, art galleries, and live theater, are great learning experiences for students at both campuses.

DAILY LIFE

Boarding students begin each school day with a breakfast buffet at 7:30. Following breakfast, day and boarding students meet for a required assembly at 8:10, with classes following from 8:30 to 2:45. Required study halls and optional clubs and athletic events are held between 2:50 and 4:30. Dinner is served at 6 and is followed by a monitored study hall lasting until 8. Lights out is at 10:30 for middle school students and 11 for high school students.

WEEKEND LIFE

Students in good standing may leave the campus, with permission, during any weekend. Many students take advantage of the planned activities that are arranged for them, including theater performances, shopping at the malls and Old Town Pasadena, barbecues, beach parties, and movies. Visits are planned to Disneyland, Magic Mountain, and Big Surf, and the other attractions of the two-state areas are a part of the social program at Southwestern Academy. Day students are welcome to attend all weekend activities if space permits.

SUMMER PROGRAMS

Summer school sessions are offered at both campuses. Both offer intensive yet enjoyable individualized classes in English and other subjects, plus educational and recreational trips to interesting places in southern California and northern Arizona.

The summer program in San Marino is an excellent opportunity for domestic students to catch up, if needed, or to move ahead academically in order to take more advanced courses before graduation. For non-English-speaking international students, the summer session can provide an entire semester of the appropriate ESL level necessary to successfully complete a college-preparatory curriculum.

Summer sessions at Beaver Creek Ranch combine review and enrichment courses with experiential learning and high-adventure activities in classwork, camp-type activities, and travel in northern Arizona. ESL is offered at the Beaver Creek campus during the summer.

COSTS AND FINANCIAL AID

Tuition for the 2012–13 U.S. boarding student is $33,750. International student tuition is $41,000. The cost for a day student (U.S. citizens) is $16,500. An incidental account containing $2000 for boarding students or $1000 for day students is required of all students to cover expenses such as books, school supplies, physical education uniforms, and discretionary spending money. Payment is due in advance unless other arrangements are made with the business office.

Financial aid is awarded based on financial need. More than $440,000 was awarded in the 2012–13 school year.

ADMISSIONS INFORMATION

Southwestern Academy admits students of any race, color, national and ethnic origin, creed, or sex. A completed application packet is required, followed by a personal on-campus interview with students and parents. A daylong visit to classes (and an overnight for prospective boarding students) is strongly encouraged for prospective students already living in the United States. Interviews with prospective international students and parents are scheduled by the international admissions director and do not require a campus visit.

Each campus offers exceptional learning opportunities. Prospective students are encouraged to seriously consider both campuses and apply to the one that seems better suited to them.

Admission materials and other information can be downloaded from the Southwestern Academy Web site. It can also be obtained by contacting the Office of Admissions.

APPLICATION TIMETABLE

Admission offers are made throughout the year, as space permits. Appointments are required for interviews and campus tours at both locations. The admissions office for both campus locations is located in San Marino. Students should write or call the San Marino office for information on either campus.

ADMISSIONS CORRESPONDENCE

Office of Admissions
Southwestern Academy
2800 Monterey Road
San Marino, California 91108
United States
Phone: 626-799-5010 Ext. 203
Fax: 626-799-0407
E-mail: jblake@southwesternacademy.edu
Web site:
http://www.southwesternacademy.edu

THE STORM KING SCHOOL

Cornwall-on-Hudson, New York

Type: Coeducational boarding and day college-preparatory school
Grades: 8–12
Enrollment: 135
Head of School: Paul C. Domingue

THE SCHOOL

The Storm King School was founded in 1867 as a college-preparatory school by the Reverend Louis P. Ledoux. In 1928, it was chartered by the Board of Regents of the State University of New York as a nonprofit institution governed by a self-perpetuating 18-member Board of Trustees. The School has an endowment of $1 million and an active Annual Giving campaign.

The Storm King School seeks to provide a caring, structured residential life and an academic program that prepares students for college. The School helps students stretch themselves by building upon their strengths while realistically acknowledging and addressing their weaknesses. Storm King believes that art, theater, music, and athletics are components of a good education. Therefore, they are a part of daily life at the School. Central to Storm King's philosophy is the belief that the School is a learning community that creates success from students' potential.

The School is located near the crest of Storm King Mountain on the west bank of the Hudson River. The 55-acre campus offers a serene setting and a magnificent view of a sweeping bend in the river, the Shawangunk Mountains, and the distant Catskills. The 4,000-acre Black Rock Forest, a wilderness preserved by environmentalists, adjoins the campus to the south; West Point Military reservation and Bear Mountain Preserve are nearby, as are the estates of several long-established Hudson Highlands families. New York City, about 50 miles away, is within easy reach via the Palisades Parkway or via the Metro-North Hudson Line.

The Storm King School has a Middle School program for grade 8. The focus of this program is to help students develop and retain a sense of responsibility and individuality. The Middle School curriculum offers the basic core courses as well as technology, athletics, and performing and visual arts. Students are allowed to be creative and self-exploring while fulfilling an educationally intensive program.

The School is accredited by the Middle States Association of Colleges and Schools. It is a member of the Cum Laude Society, the National Honor Society, the New York State Association of Independent Schools, the National Association of Independent Schools, The Associations of Boarding Schools, and the College Board.

ACADEMIC PROGRAM

College and university preparation is a goal of The Storm King School; therefore, the School emphasizes the development of present skills and talents as the best way to prepare for the future. The School seeks to discover and extend what a student has learned and to identify and develop what he or she has not. The curriculum focuses on skill development as well as content knowledge. The English and history programs stress reading and writing skills and include both required and elective courses; offerings range from creative writing to the British novel and from contemporary world history to psychology and economics. Advanced placement courses include English literature, macroeconomics, psychology, and computer science. To graduate, a student must also complete a course in health and in public speaking.

The School believes that all students can improve their mathematical skills and reasoning ability. The flexible curriculum encourages students to remedy any past deficiencies in mathematics and to move forward. Courses range from algebra and geometry to Advanced Placement (AP) calculus and statistics. The science program includes biology, chemistry, physics, environmental science, and other electives. Advanced Placement biology and physics courses are available. The foreign language program ensures that all students become familiar with the language, history, and culture of other countries. The School offers Spanish, Mandarin Chinese, and American Sign Language (ASL).

The fine, performing, and creative arts programs encourage students' creative potential through the exploration of artistic expression. All students are required to take at least one performing arts (theater or music) and one visual arts course. Students who are interested in pursuing the arts at the university level are given advanced, individualized attention in their area of interest to develop their creative repertoire and portfolios. The Department of Fine Arts offers courses in ceramics, graphic design, drawing, painting, photography, sculpture, and AP Studio Art: Drawing, among others. Excellent faculty members encourage and inspire students to create works of art that far exceed students' personal expectations. The Department of Music offers chorus, digital recording and studio production, as well as individual instruction in piano, guitar, and other instruments by special arrangement. Students learn performance techniques and are prepared for public recitals. The Dance Department offers instruction in classical ballet, tap, jazz, hip-hop, and modern dance. Dance students present their work in public recitals. The Department of Theatre Arts offers performance, stagecraft, theater history, theater appreciation, and courses in design and production. Students apply classroom instruction in rehearsals and production work through the two or three Storm King Theatre Ensemble productions, on which the entire division collaborates. Arts education and training at The Storm King School enhance a student's education and development through academic courses in the arts and are supported by opportunities for practical application in every creative area.

The Learning Center (TLC) helps selected students develop the skills and self-confidence that are essential for academic independence. TLC emphasizes the development of strong executive functioning skills. TLC works collaboratively with teachers in order to plan instruction that is directly related to classroom curriculum. The Learning Center focuses on building current strengths while improving academics and organization. Study skills work includes note-taking, outlining, researching, test taking, and time management.

In 2004, The Storm King School established a small program called the Mountain Center, using the same curriculum as the Upper School. This program is designed for bright, college-bound students who have an Individual Education Plan (IEP), or the equivalent, developed to address different learning styles. The program does not accept students who have significant emotional or behavioral problems. The Mountain Center presents core subjects (English, math, science, social studies) in a 5:1 ratio setting. The center uses a variety of methods that are appropriate to the needs of each student to accomplish the desired outcome.

Graduation requirements for all students include 4 years each of English and history, 3–4 years of mathematics, 3–4 years of science (with a total of at least 7 credits in math and science), 2 years or the equivalent of a foreign language, 1 year each in the visual and performing arts, 1 credit public speaking, ½ credit in health, and community service.

Grades are based on a numeric system. These grades are sent to parents four times a year, but for guidance purposes, progress reports are sent out in the middle of each marking period. The academic year is divided into trimesters.

FACULTY AND ADVISERS

Sixty-five percent of the faculty members live on campus—either in the dormitories or in campus housing—and are available for extra help, especially in the evening. All faculty members are active in advising and counseling students and provide a critical link between the family and the School. Of the 30 full-time and 6 part-time faculty members, 24 hold advanced degrees. The School provides funds for continuing education.

Paul Domingue was appointed the sixteenth Head of School in July 2012.

COLLEGE ADMISSION COUNSELING

Guidance is a continuing process that takes place throughout a student's entire stay at Storm King and sometimes even after graduation. College guidance begins in the sophomore year. In group meetings, students and their advisers discuss what lies ahead; individual conferences take place frequently and often include parents. There are many "right" colleges for each student. In recent years, 2 or more graduates have attended the following colleges, among others: Bennington, Boston University, Bucknell, Emerson, George Washington, Hamilton, Iona, Northeastern, NYU, NYU-SVA, Parsons, Pratt, Roger Williams, Skidmore, Smith, several campuses of the State University of New York, Syracuse, Tufts, Virginia Tech, and the Universities of Colorado, Hartford, Illinois at Urbana-Champaign, Massachusetts, Miami, Southern California, and Vermont. In recent years, the senior class has consistently been offered more than $1 million in scholarships.

STUDENT BODY AND CONDUCT

The Storm King School student body represents a wide spectrum of socioeconomic backgrounds from nine states and fifteen other countries.

The student body includes 115 boarding and 20 day students. About 50 new students enroll annually.

A disciplinary committee and the Head of School determine consequences for disciplinary infractions. Major offenses may result in withdrawal. Student and faculty groups are consulted in policy formation. Students are expected to be supportive of School policies and to take an active and positive part in the School's programs and activities.

ACADEMIC FACILITIES

Stillman Hall contains mathematics and science classrooms, laboratories, and department offices. There is a greenhouse located down the hill from Stillman Hall. Dyar Hall provides humanities classrooms. The Ogden Library is a split-level learning center with study desks, language classrooms, and the Computer Center, which is equipped with seventeen computer workstations. The Walter Reade Jr. Theater was dedicated in 1984. The Cobb-Matthiessen Astronomy Observatory was dedicated in 1990. The Allison Vladimir Art Center, a converted barn, is a beautiful facility with a spectacular view of the Black Rock wilderness area. The center was dedicated in 1994.

BOARDING AND GENERAL FACILITIES

There are four dormitories: Highmount, McConnell, Dempsey, and Cottage. Each dormitory has two faculty apartments. Most of the rooms are doubles; there are a few triples for girls and several singles available to student leaders. Orr Commons contains a chorus room, music practice studios, a recording studio, a video recording and production studio, a ceramics room, a darkroom, and modern kitchen and dining room facilities. All equipment and software in the audio and video studios is professional grade. The health center is on the ground floor of Stillman Hall. An admissions/development complex opened in 1992. Also on campus are several faculty residences; the Administration Building; and Spy Rock House, the Head's residence. New faculty residences were completed in December 2003.

ATHLETICS

Athletics at Storm King include recreational and competitive activities as well as an outdoor adventure program (including activities such as hiking, rock climbing, and kayaking).

Each student must participate in a sport in at least two of the three seasons each year. Students may elect to take sports in all three seasons.

The gymnasium provides a basketball court, weight-lifting and fitness equipment, a wrestling room, and a dance studio.

With sixteen teams across eleven sports, the School offers students lots of choices in its athletic program. In the fall, students may select from soccer, volleyball, crew, and cross-country. In winter, choices include basketball, wrestling, fencing, and ski/snowboarding club. Springtime offerings are lacrosse, softball, golf, tennis, and crew. Students are also encouraged to take advantage of opportunities for outdoor adventure such as hiking, rock climbing, and kayaking. For one season each year, a student may select a club instead of a sport.

EXTRACURRICULAR OPPORTUNITIES

The Student Activities Committee oversees many extracurricular activities. Among the student activities are the yearbook, photography, art, the literary magazine, the environmental club, and recycling club. A work program involves students in routine chores on campus. Service learning opportunities are available on and off campus.

DAILY LIFE

Classes are 45 minutes long and meet five times a week. The day begins with breakfast from 7:15 to 7:50, followed by a morning meeting and classes, which end by 4. This is followed by required activities from 4 to 5:30. Thursday dinners are served family style, with formal dress required every four to six weeks. A 2-hour supervised study hall, either in the dorm or in the library, and some free time cap off the evening. The day ends at 10 p.m. Students are quiet and in their rooms by 10:30; lights are out by 11 p.m.

WEEKEND LIFE

The School's location provides various opportunities for social, cultural, and entertainment activities. Students may attend theater performances and concerts in New York City. The activities director and a student committee plan weekend activities, such as movies, dances, intramural athletics, hikes, skiing, horseback riding, visits to museums, and trips to special events and points of interest in the Northeast and as far south as Washington, D.C. There are shopping, movie, community service, cultural, and outdoor adventure trips offered every weekend. The School plans an international trip each year; most recently, students have visited Ireland and Scotland, Italy, and France. Students may go home any weekend after their obligations have been met.

COSTS AND FINANCIAL AID

For 2012–13, costs for Upper School boarding students total $42,500; for Upper School day students, costs totaled $22,700. There are additional fees for English as a second language (ESL), the Learning Center (TLC), and the Mountain Center. Costs for books, insurance, and laundry are additional. Students pay for transportation to and from the School. Families may establish student accounts at the School, from which spending money may be drawn.

Financial assistance totaling about $511,000 is awarded annually according to guidelines determined by the School and Student Service for Financial Aid, to about 28 percent of the student body. Some small merit scholarships, especially in the arts, are also available

ADMISSIONS INFORMATION

The School accepts students in grades 8 through 12 as well as a few academic postgraduates. Selections are made without regard to race or creed and are based upon the applicant's promise of success and past record. An interview at the School is highly desirable. The School also offers prospective students the opportunity to participate in the student-for-a-day program to help them feel more comfortable and to enable them to learn about the School directly from their peers. The Director of Admissions recommends candidates for consideration to the Admissions Committee.

APPLICATION TIMETABLE

Initial inquiries are welcome at any time, and campus interviews can be arranged from 8:30 to 3:30 during the week. A nonrefundable $85 fee ($125 for international applications) must accompany the application. Acceptance notifications are sent beginning in mid-February for fall enrollment, or for students applying after the February 1 priority deadline, as soon as all information is complete and the Admissions Committee makes a decision.

ADMISSIONS CORRESPONDENCE

Joanna Evans
Director of Admissions
The Storm King School
314 Mountain Road
Cornwall-on-Hudson, New York 12520-1899
United States
Phone: 845-534-9860
800-225-9144 (toll-free)
Fax: 845-534-4128
E-mail: admissions@sks.org
Web site: http://www.sks.org

TASIS THE AMERICAN SCHOOL IN ENGLAND

Thorpe, Surrey, England

Type: Coeducational boarding and day college-preparatory school
Grades: Nursery–13: Lower School, Nursery–4; Middle School, 5–8; Upper School, 9–13
Enrollment: Total: 760; Lower School: 160; Middle School: 200; Upper School: 400
Head of School: Mr. Michael McBrien, Headmaster

THE SCHOOL

TASIS The American School in England was founded in 1976 by Mrs. M. Crist Fleming and is a sister school of The American School in Switzerland (TASIS), which she established in 1956. In fulfillment of its mission statement, the School seeks to balance the pursuit of knowledge with the love of wisdom, and promotes the skills of lifelong learning, an appreciation for beauty, and the development of character.

TASIS England offers a challenging and traditional college-preparatory program. While academics are emphasized, a wide variety of sports, extracurricular activities, cultural excursions, and weekend trips ensure a balanced education.

The 46-acre campus is set in the country village of Thorpe in the heart of the beautiful Thames valley, only 18 miles from central London and 6 miles from Heathrow Airport. The School takes full advantage of its location and the opportunities that England and Europe offer as extensions to classroom learning.

The TASIS Schools and Summer Programs are owned and fully controlled by the TASIS Foundation, a Swiss, independent, not-for-profit educational foundation, registered in Delémont, Switzerland. The Board of Directors of each school is responsible for providing its governance structure, determining its policies and strategies, providing trusteeship over its financial position, and appointing and evaluating its headmaster.

TASIS England is an International Baccalaureate (IB) World School, is accredited by the Council of International Schools (CIS) and the New England Association of Schools and Colleges (NEASC), and is a member of the National Association of Independent Schools (NAIS) and The Association of Boarding Schools (TABS).

ACADEMIC PROGRAM

The Upper School comprises grades 9 to 13. The minimum requirements for graduation from the Upper School are 4 years of English, 3 years of history (including U.S. history at the eleventh- or twelfth-grade level), a third-level proficiency in a foreign language, 3 years of mathematics (through algebra II), three laboratory sciences (including a biological and a physical science), and 1 year of fine arts. All seniors are required to take a full-year humanities course. Students who have attended TASIS England for three years or more are expected to complete 19 credits. A normal course load consists of six courses per year. Advanced Placement courses are offered for qualified students and include art history, biology, calculus, chemistry, computer science, economics, English, environmental science, French, government and politics, music theory, physics, Spanish, statistics, and U.S. history.

TASIS also offers the International Baccalaureate (IB) diploma. Students may apply to this program for their final two years at TASIS, and successful IB diploma candidates can earn both the IB diploma and the TASIS England high school diploma. Entry into the IB Program is made in consultation between the School, student, and family and is open to highly motivated students with strong academic, time management, and study skills.

With an average class size of 15, and a teacher-student ratio of 1:8, the School provides an intimate learning environment that challenges a young person to realize his or her full potential. The Advisory Program enhances this aspect of a TASIS education, as the advisers are charged with the social and academic well-being of each advisee.

A student's day is fully structured. Participation in supervised evening study hall for boarding students is a requirement for all but those who have earned the privilege of independent study in their rooms.

The academic year is divided into two semesters, ending in January and June, respectively. Grades and comments are e-mailed home to parents four times a year at mid-semester and end-of-semester breaks, together with a summary report from the adviser. The grading system uses A to F, indicating achievement levels, and 1 to 5 as a measure of a student's attitude, effort, and application to his or her work.

An educational travel program during the October break is mandatory for all boarding students and is included in the tuition. Past trips have included such destinations as Austria, France, Germany, Greece, Hungary, Italy, Poland, Romania, Russia, Spain, and Switzerland. These school trips are also an option for day students.

FACULTY AND ADVISERS

Mr. Michael McBrien was appointed as headmaster of TASIS England in 2010. He holds a master's degree in education and a Bachelor of Arts in counseling, psychology, and communication. He has twenty-four years of experience in education and has worked as an administrator at the University of California, Berkeley, and at Babson College and Frontier Academy, in Colorado. Mr. McBrien was previously Head of Baylor School in Tennessee, an independent, coeducational college preparatory, day, and boarding school.

The faculty represents one of the School's strongest assets. Its members are dedicated professionals with a true sense of vocation. Duties are not limited to teaching but encompass the responsibilities of advisers, sports coaches, dorm parents, community service aides, and trip chaperones. There are 104 full-time faculty members—42 men and 62 women—and 15 part-time teachers. Approximately 60 percent of them have advanced degrees and 21 live on campus. In addition, music specialists visit the School for private instruction by arrangement.

COLLEGE ADMISSION COUNSELING

TASIS England employs 3 full-time college counselors who provide guidance about university choices and assist in managing the details of the search/application process at every stage of an Upper School student's academic career. They meet with students in small groups in the freshman and sophomore years, and individually with students in their junior and senior years to discuss academic programs, careers, and college plans. Support programs include student seminars, essay-writing workshops, U.S. and U.K. case studies, and informational events for parents. The counselors have a welcoming University and College Counseling Center that maintains a reference library of college catalogs, provides access to computer software, and familiarizes students with the range of opportunities available to them.

The counselors coordinate visits to the School by college admissions officers from universities in the United States and around the world, and administer the college admissions testing programs. TASIS England is a test center for the Plan, Explore, ACT, PSAT, and SAT, as well as the Advanced Placement and International Baccalaureate examinations. The range of SAT scores achieved by TASIS students graduating in 2012 (45 percent of whom speak English as an alternate language) were: math 540–690, critical reading 470–630, and writing 510–620.

TASIS graduates are accepted by universities around the world and have recently attended such schools as Boston University, Bowdoin, Cornell, Duke, NYU, Rhode Island School of Design, UCLA, United States Air Force Academy, and the University of Pennsylvania (U.S.); Bath, Bristol, Durham, Imperial College, King's College London, London School of Economics, St. George's Medical School, University College London, and York (U.K.); Trinity College Dublin (Ireland); and McGill, Queen's, and the University of British Columbia (Canada). TASIS believes that students should be encouraged to think deeply about the purposes of higher education, about the intangible benefits of genuine intellectual activity, and about the range of philosophical options offered by educational institutions. The major responsibility for college choices lies with each student, but the School provides as much advice and support as possible.

STUDENT BODY AND CONDUCT

For the 2012–13 academic year, there are 400 students in the Upper School (grades 9–13), including 180 boarding students. Year groups include: 105 seniors, 119 juniors, 108 sophomores, and 68 freshmen. Overall, the ratio of boys to girls in each grade level is close to 1:1. In some cases, boarding students' parents are expatriates undertaking assignments overseas, such as in Saudi Arabia, Africa, Europe, and various parts of the British Isles. The student body is culturally diverse, with about half of the students in the Upper School representing approximately fifty countries other than the United States. In the Lower School (nursery–grade 4), there are 160 children, and the Middle School (grades 5–8) has 200 students.

TASIS England promotes a purposeful environment for learning and growing, including demonstrating respect for one's self and for others. The *Student Handbook* clearly identifies the accepted codes of conduct within the School community. A uniform is required for Upper School students. Lower and Middle School students wear white and navy blue. An infraction of a major school rule is dealt with by the Upper School administration with the Disciplinary Advisory Board. TASIS England reserves the right to dismiss at any time a student who has proved to be an unsatisfactory member of the school community, even though there may have been no infraction of a specific rule.

In the Upper School, the Student Council is made up of representatives from all grade levels and is the vehicle of student government. Prefects, as student leaders, carry special responsibilities in dormitory and general school life.

ACADEMIC FACILITIES

Two large Georgian mansions and purpose-built classrooms are the focal points of the campus. There are computer centers and a library for each school division, with the Upper School library alone holding over 12,000 volumes. Additional facilities include art studios, a darkroom, an art gallery, music rooms, a language laboratory, a 24-hour health center, two multipurpose gymnasiums, a fitness center, two drama/dance studios, and a 350-seat theater. TASIS England is implementing a ten-year master plan to enhance all campus facilities. The most recent development, a state-of-the-art Science Center with three floors of classrooms and well-equipped laboratories, opened in 2011 and augments the School's vibrant science program. Wi-Fi is available throughout the campus.

BOARDING AND GENERAL FACILITIES

Approximately 180 boarding students (grades 9–13) are accommodated in single-sex dormitories supervised by a faculty resident dorm parent, assisted by prefects. Each unit holds 13–16 students, usually in 2- or 3-person rooms, which are located in the top floors of the main buildings as well as in the adjacent cottages, such as Tudor House, Orchard, Shepherd's Cottage, and Vicarage Mews. The Boarding Program is coordinated by two staff members, both of whom are experienced in providing boarding care and serving the needs of young people. All meals are provided, and the campus Health Center has an experienced 24-hour nursing staff, and a school doctor on call. A new student center, opened in 2012, provides an innovative and relaxed café-style space for both boarding and day students to meet friends and relax.

ATHLETICS

An awareness of physical fitness, the discipline of training the body as well as the mind, and the spirit of competition are viewed as important elements in a student's education at TASIS England. All Upper School students participate in the afternoon sports/activities program, which operates on a three-term basis, reflecting seasonal sports. The minimum requirement is participation for two afternoons a week.

Varsity sports include basketball, cross-country, dance, golf, lacrosse, soccer, tennis, and volleyball as well as boys' teams in rugby and baseball and girls' teams in cheering and softball. Recreational sports include badminton, basketball, golf, lacrosse, running, soccer, squash, swimming, tennis, and a conditioning program.

There are four large playing fields on campus, six all-weather tennis courts, two gymnasiums, and a fitness center that offers a complete weight-training circuit and a wide variety of cardiovascular machines. The nearby Egham Sports Center offers fine supplementary facilities.

Besides participating in local sports events, the School competes in International Schools Sports Tournaments (ISSTs) with other international schools throughout Europe and North Africa.

EXTRACURRICULAR OPPORTUNITIES

England's capital city, London, only 18 miles away, provides an unrivaled opportunity for students to enjoy such pleasures as theater, opera, concerts, art galleries, and museums. Through course-related study or School-chaperoned trips, in the evenings and on weekends, students are regularly encouraged to participate in as many enriching and fun educational experiences as possible.

On-campus activities include drama productions; musical groups; choir; the School newspaper; Model UN; the Duke of Edinburgh Award Program; art, debate, and drama clubs; and the yearbook committee, as well as School dances and movies.

A committee of students and teachers coordinates and plans on-campus and off-campus recreational activities, including day trips (sightseeing, for example) and weekends away. Traditionally, the International Festival, Christmas Dinner Dance, Spring Prom, and May Fair are the highlights of the year.

The Community Service Program aims to help each student to develop skills leading to a sense of involvement and greater responsibility for others. The minimum commitment involves approximately 1 hour a week. Students may serve the School community in a variety of ways, e.g., by helping in the library or tutoring younger children. They may serve the local community by visiting homes for the elderly, working with the disabled, participating in conservation projects, and raising funds for local charities. Special summer projects are also available.

DAILY LIFE

Classes commence at 8:20 (9:15 on Wednesdays) and end at 3:15. Each Upper School class meets four times a week, allowing a structured advisory and tutorial period during the day. Sports/activities time is between 3:30 and 5 p.m. each day, except Fridays. An Upper School meeting is regularly scheduled for Wednesdays. No classes are held on Saturday or Sunday.

WEEKEND LIFE

Day students as well as boarders participate freely in organized social events on the weekends. The Activities Coordinator and Student Council members collaborate to develop a wide variety of activities. These can include on-campus activities such as dances and bonfire night as well as trips to the theater and concerts, the ballet, and professional sports events.

Students are encouraged to initiate weekend day trips to destinations in the U.K. such as Stratford-upon-Avon, Salisbury, Cambridge, Oxford, Canterbury, and Bath. Organized excursions are chaperoned by members of the faculty.

SUMMER PROGRAMS

During the summer, six-week credit-based academic courses are offered in such subjects as algebra II and geometry, as well as enrichment courses such as the ShakespeareXperience, Theater in London, SAT Review, English as a Second Language, International Business, Television Broadcasting, Photography in London, and Art. Some 450 students regularly participate from schools in the United States and from international schools all over the world. Qualified teachers and counselors from the United States and around the world make up the summer programs administration and faculty. Weekend travel to a variety of destinations in England, theater trips, and other excursions are included in the program.

In addition to the courses in England, TASIS offers a variety of summer programs in France, Spain, and Switzerland to students from all over the world. From intensive study of painting, photography, and architecture at Les Tapies in the Ardèche to learning Spanish in Salamanca or French at Chateaux d'Oex in Switzerland, TASIS summer courses enrich the talents, skills, and interests of its participants.

COSTS AND FINANCIAL AID

In 2012–13, tuition and fees for day students are £6105–£19,810 per annum. Fees include lunches, loan of textbooks, IT and laboratory fees, most classroom materials, and the cost of most curriculum-related activities and field trips. Optional expenses, including costs for music lessons, are by private arrangement. Boarding fees are £33,760 and include tuition, room, full board, loan of textbooks, most IT and laboratory fees, annual laptop maintenance, some classroom materials, the cost of most curriculum-related activities and field trips, weekly laundry service for bed linen and towels, and travel insurance for school-sponsored trips. Costs for the October Travel Week are also included in the boarding fees. A recommended personal allowance is £50 per week.

There is a one-time-only Development Fund Fee of £750 per student for on-campus building projects and an enrollment deposit of £1000 for day students and £2000 for boarders. The balance of fees becomes payable for each semester by June 1 and November 15.

Students are invited to apply for financial aid, which is granted on the basis of merit, need, and available funds. In 2012–13, 27 students, including 15 in the Upper School, were awarded aid. Early application for financial help is recommended, and students who have been awarded financial aid must reapply for continued assistance each academic year. Each year the School awards approximately £150,000–£200,000 in financial aid.

ADMISSIONS INFORMATION

Applications for admission are considered by the Admissions Committee upon receipt of a completed application form together with the application fee, three teachers' recommendations, and a transcript. Standardized test scores are requested, and a student questionnaire is required. A School visit is recommended unless distance is a prohibiting factor. A decision is reached on the basis of a student's academic and behavioral acceptability to the TASIS England School community. A student's nationality, religion, ethnic background, and gender play no part in the committee's decision, although availability of space in the dormitories (all are grouped by gender) is sometimes a limiting factor.

APPLICATION TIMETABLE

Applications are processed throughout the year. Visitors are welcome on campus at any time of the year other than the period between Christmas and New Year, when the School is closed. An interview by prior arrangement, even on very short notice, is recommended. It is preferable for visitors to choose days when school is in session in order to appreciate the working atmosphere of the community.

While early applications are encouraged, there is no final deadline, since a rolling admissions policy exists. Acceptances are made with the provision that students complete their current year in good standing. There is an application fee of £125.

ADMISSIONS CORRESPONDENCE

Karen House, Director of Admissions
TASIS The American School in England
Coldharbour Lane
Thorpe, Nr Egham
Surrey TW20 8TE
England
Phone: +44-1932-582316
Fax: +44-1932-564644
E-mail: ukadmissions@tasisengland.org
Web site: http://www.tasisengland.org

TASIS Schools and Summer Programs in Europe
112 South Royal Street
Alexandria, Virginia 22314
United States
Phone: 703-299-8150
800-442-6005 (toll-free)
Fax: 703-299-8157
E-mail: usadmissions@tasis.com
Web site: http://www.tasis.com

TASIS THE AMERICAN SCHOOL IN SWITZERLAND

Montagnola-Lugano, Switzerland

Type: Coeducational boarding and day college-preparatory school
Grades: Pre-K–12, PG: Elementary School, pre-K–5; Middle School, 6–8; High School, 9–12, postgraduate year
Enrollment: School total: 650; High School: 450; Middle School: 95; Elementary School: 105
Head of School: Michael Ulku-Steiner, Headmaster

THE SCHOOL

TASIS The American School in Switzerland was founded in 1956 by Mrs. M. Crist Fleming to offer a strong American college-preparatory education in a European setting. TASIS was the first American boarding school established in Europe. Over time, it has become a school for students from more than fifty countries seeking an American independent school experience. The International Baccalaureate (I.B.) Program is also offered within this setting.

The objective of the School is to foster both a vital enthusiasm for learning and habits that are essential to a full realization of each student's moral and intellectual potential. The curriculum gives special emphasis to the achievements of the Western heritage, many elements of which are easily accessible from the School's location. By providing an international dimension to education, the School stresses the need for young people to mature with confidence and competence in an increasingly interrelated world.

The beautiful campus is in the village of Montagnola, overlooking the city and the lake of Lugano, nestled among the southernmost of the Swiss Alps in the Italian-speaking canton of Ticino. Ideally situated in the heart of Europe, the School makes the most of its location by introducing students to European cultures and languages through extensive travel programs.

The TASIS Foundation, a not-for-profit Swiss foundation, owns the School. The TASIS Foundation also has a school near London and offers summer programs in England, Spain, and Italy as well as Switzerland. Alumni provide enthusiastic support for the School's activities and participate in annual reunions and other special events.

TASIS is accredited by the Council of International Schools (CIS) and the New England Association of Schools and Colleges (NEASC) and is a member of the National Association of Independent Schools and the Swiss Group of International Schools.

ACADEMIC PROGRAM

The minimum requirements for graduation from the high school college-preparatory program are 4 years of English, 3 years of history (including European and U.S. history), a third-year proficiency in a modern foreign language, 3 years of mathematics (through algebra II), 3 years of laboratory science (including physical and biological sciences), and 1 year of fine arts, plus senior humanities, sports/physical education, and community service requirements. Students must satisfactorily complete a minimum of 19 credits. Students are required to enroll in a minimum of five full-credit courses per year or the equivalent. A normal course load for students consists of six courses.

TASIS offers an extensive English as an additional language program that focuses on oral and written academic English skills and competence in a high school curriculum leading to the TASIS college-preparatory diploma.

TASIS offers a diverse and challenging curriculum, including the Advanced Placement Program (AP), the International Baccalaureate (I.B.) Diploma Programme, and a wide range of required and elective courses. In 2012, 40 students took sixty-eight AP exams in eleven subject areas; 44 percent of the scores were 4 or above and 13 percent earned the top score of 5. Students may also select I.B. courses and can earn subject-specific certificates or the full diploma.

The average class size is 12; the teacher-student ratio is 1:6. The student's day is fully structured, including time for academics, sports and activities, meals and socializing, and supervised evening study hours. The grading system uses A to F for performance and assigns effort grades of 1 to 5, reflecting students' attitudes and application to their work. The academic year is divided into two semesters and grades and comment reports are e-mailed to parents five times a year.

The postgraduate year presents an additional opportunity to high school graduates who wish to spend an interim year in Europe before going on to college. Each postgraduate student can design a tailor-made course of study with the assistance and approval of the Academic Dean that enables him or her to explore and develop new interests, strengthen academic weaknesses, or concentrate in areas of strength or particular interest. It includes a course-related Academic Travel program.

FACULTY AND ADVISERS

The faculty represents one of the School's strongest assets. Its members are a group of dedicated professionals who are enthusiastic about working with young people. The TASIS faculty includes 108 full-time teaching administrators and faculty members, of whom 57 are women and 51 are men. Seventy-one percent of the faculty members have advanced degrees. Thirty-two faculty members live on campus; the rest live nearby and participate in most campus activities. In addition to teaching, faculty members act as advisers, sports coaches, trip chaperones, and dormitory residents and help to create a warm, family-like atmosphere.

COLLEGE ADMISSION COUNSELING

The School employs 3 full-time college counselors, who meet with students individually and in groups during their junior and senior years. The college counseling office maintains a reference library of university catalogs from around the world so that students can familiarize themselves with the wide variety of opportunities that are open to them. As a counseling resource, the School provides a small computer lab for college research. Many college admissions officers from universities in the U.S. and Europe visit the School and speak to students. TASIS is an official testing center for the PSAT, SAT, SAT Subject Tests, ACT, PLAN, and all AP and I.B. examinations.

Recent graduates attend such institutions as Edinburgh, Reading, and Nottingham Universities in the U.K. and Boston University, Colorado College, George Washington, Middlebury, Notre Dame, Northwestern, Stanford, and Tufts in the United States.

STUDENT BODY AND CONDUCT

Each student is honor bound to abide by the rules, as defined in the TASIS *Student Handbook*. The School employs a variety of counseling, disciplinary, and administrative responses to rules violations, determined on a case-by-case basis. The School administration and Conduct Review Board handle more serious offenses. All responses take into account the seriousness of the offense, the number of previous offenses, any mitigating circumstances, and the student's record as a member of the TASIS community.

Students at TASIS bear a serious responsibility to conduct themselves not only in a way that does credit to them, to their School, and to their country of origin, but also in a way that is consistent with the high standards set by the citizens of the European countries they visit. For this reason, TASIS has established reasonable but definitive standards of behavior, attitude, and appearance for all of its students. The School reserves the right to ask any student to withdraw for failure to maintain these standards.

ACADEMIC FACILITIES

The campus comprises twenty-three buildings, a combination of historical villas restored for school use and new, purpose-built facilities. The seventeenth century Villa De Nobili was the School's original building and houses the dining hall, dormitories, administrative offices, and science laboratories. Hadsall House contains classrooms and dormitories. Villa Monticello contains modern classrooms, a computer center, a computer-based language lab, and dormitories. Next to Villa Monticello is the 22,000-volume M. Crist Fleming Library. Villa Aurora provides new classrooms for the Middle School. Classes are also held in the Belvedere and Villa Del Sole dormitories. The Palestra houses a sports complex with a gymnasium, fitness center, dance studio, locker rooms, student lounge with café, and music rooms. The School recently completed the John E. Palmer Cultural Center, which includes a state-of-the-art theater, and Fiammetta, which houses classrooms. Lanterna is the newest building, which includes classrooms and the health center. The newly renovated Casa Al Focolare houses Elementary School students from prekindergarten to first grade. A second gymnasium and new arts center opened in September 2012. The new Ferit Sahenk ('83) Arts Center houses spaces for art studios, architecture and design, painting and drawing, ceramics and sculpture; and photography.

BOARDING AND GENERAL FACILITIES

The campus includes ten dormitories, each of which houses from 6 to 43 students. Dormitories are located in the Villa De Nobili, Villa Monticello, Hadsall House, Villa Del Sole, Balmelli, Giani, Belvedere, and Lanterna buildings. All dormitories are supervised, and some faculty members live in the dormitories. Rooms accommodate from 2 to 4 students each. Although School facilities are closed during the winter and spring vacations, optional faculty-chaperoned trips are offered for students who are unable to return home.

Two recreation centers and a snack bar serve as focal points for student social activities. Three fully qualified nurses are in residence.

ATHLETICS

Students are required to participate in either a varsity sport three days a week or recreational sports after classes. Sports available include soccer, basketball, fitness training, mountain biking, volleyball, rugby, tennis, track and field, squash, swimming, rock climbing, and aerobics. Horseback riding and tennis are available at an extra cost. On weekends, students often go on hiking and mountain-climbing trips in the Swiss Alps during the fall and spring and go skiing during the winter. During Ski Week in Crans-Montana (High School) or Verbier (Middle School), every student takes lessons in downhill or cross-country skiing or snowboarding. The Fleming Cup ski race and a faculty versus students hockey game are held during the Crans-Montana week.

Varsity sports give students the opportunity to compete against many schools in Switzerland and other countries and to take part in tournaments sponsored by the Swiss Group of International Schools. Varsity sports include soccer, volleyball, basketball, tennis, and track and field. Students also have the opportunity to enroll in the AC Milan soccer program, run by the coaches of the renowned Italian soccer team AC Milan.

Facilities include a playing field, a gym, and an outdoor basketball/volleyball area. The newly constructed Palestra sports complex includes a gymnasium with seating for up to 400 spectators, a dance studio, a fitness center, changing rooms, and a student lounge with a café.

EXTRACURRICULAR OPPORTUNITIES

The School's location in central Europe offers an enviable range of cultural opportunities. Trips to concerts, art galleries, and museums in Lugano, Locarno, and Milan extend education beyond the classroom. All students participate in the Academic Travel program, a four-day, faculty-chaperoned trip in the fall and a seven-day, faculty-chaperoned trip in the spring to such cities as Athens, Barcelona, Florence, Madrid, Munich, Nice, Paris, Prague, Rome, Venice, and Vienna.

On-campus activities include drama productions, choral and instrumental music, Model Congress, Environmental Club, Student Council, yearbook, and the Student Weekend Activities Team (SWAT). The Service Learning program focuses on the TASIS community, the local community, the interschool community, and the global community. Opportunities include peer tutoring, volunteering at a local domestic violence shelter, participating in Model UN, and work with Habitat for Humanity. TASIS also offers an annual summer service trip to Africa. Special annual social events include Family Weekend, dinner dances at the beginning of the academic year and at Christmas, prom, and the spring arts festival, along with a special graduation banquet and ceremony for seniors.

DAILY LIFE

Classes start at 8 a.m. and follow a rotating schedule. Classes meet from 50 to 65 minutes. There are weekly all-School assemblies, and students meet with their advisers every day. Sports and activities take place after school until 5:30 p.m. Meals are served buffet-style except for Wednesday evenings, when students share a formal dinner with their adviser group. Evening study is from 7 until 10.

WEEKEND LIFE

Both day and boarding students are encouraged to participate in organized events on weekends, including mountain-climbing and camping trips to scenic areas in Switzerland, shopping trips to open-air markets in northern Italy, and sightseeing excursions to Zurich, Milan, Venice, or Florence. On-campus events include talent shows, open-mic coffeehouse afternoons, films, and discotheque dances.

On weekends, students have Lugano town privileges if they have no School commitments and are in good academic and social standing. All excursions beyond Lugano are chaperoned by a member of the faculty, except those for seniors and some juniors, who, with parental permission, enjoy the privilege of independent travel in groups of 2 or more.

COSTS AND FINANCIAL AID

The all-inclusive tuition fee for boarding students is CHF 70,380 for the 2012–13 academic year, with an enrollment deposit of CHF 3000. This includes all fees that are necessary for attendance: room, board, tuition, eleven days of academic travel, Ski Week, all textbooks, laundry, activities, and most lab fees. A monthly personal allowance of CHF 250–300 is recommended. Seventy percent of the tuition is due by July 1 and the remainder by November 15.

Students may apply for financial assistance, which is granted on the basis of merit, need, and the student's ability to contribute to the School community.

ADMISSIONS INFORMATION

All applicants are considered on the basis of previous academic records, three teachers' evaluations, a personal statement, and a parental statement. The SSAT is recommended, and the SLEP test is required for students whose native language is not English. TASIS does not discriminate on the basis of race, color, nationality, or ethnic origin in its admissions policies and practices.

Application for entrance is recommended only for those students with sufficient academic interest and motivation to benefit from the program. The School accepts students from prekindergarten to grade 12 and at the postgraduate level.

APPLICATION TIMETABLE

TASIS has a rolling admissions policy and considers applications throughout the year. Applicants are encouraged to make an appointment to visit the campus. Within ten days of receipt of a completed application, the CHF 300 application fee, an official transcript from the previous school, and three teachers' evaluations, the Admissions Committee notifies the parents of its decision.

ADMISSIONS CORRESPONDENCE

Mr. William E. Eichner, Director of Admissions
TASIS The American School in Switzerland
CH-6926 Montagnola-Lugano
Switzerland
Phone: 41-91-960-5151
Fax: 41-91-993-2979
E-mail: admissions@tasis.ch
Web site: http://www.tasis.com

or

The TASIS Schools
112 South Royal Street
Alexandria, Virginia 22314
United States
Phone: 703-299-8150
Fax: 703-299-8157
E-mail: usadmissions@tasis.com

THINK GLOBAL SCHOOL

International – three different countries each year

Type: Coeducational International Baccalaureate (IB) boarding school
Grades: 9–12
Enrollment: 36
Head of School: Mr. Alun Cooper, M.A. Ed.

THE SCHOOL

THINK Global School (TGS), founded in 2009, was the concept of Joann McPike, a philanthropist and parent who saw the need for a school that would teach different ways of seeing the world. The idea of a traveling high school, where the students and faculty live and study in three different countries each year, was born. One unique aspect of TGS is that there is no stationary, brick-and-mortar school facility. Instead, in each city THINK Global partners with a local host school that provides classroom facilities, laboratories, and other learning spaces. The host schools also offer incredible opportunities to foster cultural exchange and mutual learning. TGS has been to Sweden, Australia, China, Ecuador, Thailand, Germany, and Argentina, with plans to visit five additional countries in the next two years.

TGS students spend as much time on classwork and homework as their counterparts at other top international high schools, but they combine a challenging curriculum with a wealth of educational adventures in the host city and its surroundings. The mission of THINK Global School is to provide a challenging academic experience for multinational students in a multicultural learning environment, with a specific focus on engaging with the local culture, and integrating those experiences into the academic curriculum.

The school seeks to prepare the next generation of global citizens for tertiary education and beyond. Classroom instruction is teacher-led but student-driven, with an emphasis on investigative inquiry in real-world settings and deliberative dialogue where every view is discussed with interest and compassion.

TGS is governed by a six-member Board of Directors, which includes the original two founders and representatives with extensive experience in education, finance, and psychology. The Head of School also sits on the Board as a nonvoting member. The operating budget is $5 million per annum.

THINK Global School is authorized as an official IB World School by the International Baccalaureate Organization and is accredited by the U.S.–based Western Association of Schools and Colleges (WASC).

ACADEMIC PROGRAM

Core academic courses provide the backbone of the IB curriculum, and all TGS classes are taught by TGS faculty.

The pre-IB curriculum for ninth and tenth grades includes English (world literature), Global Studies (anthropology, current events, geography, history), Science (biology, chemistry, physics), Math (statistics, geometry, algebra, precalculus), World Languages (Spanish 1, 2, 3 and Mandarin 1, 2, 3), and Visual Arts (photography, film, drawing, painting).

All TGS students in grades 11 and 12 enroll in the International Baccalaureate Diploma Programme (IBDP) and study for IB diplomas. The basic IB diploma requirements include three core courses (Theory of Knowledge; Creativity, Action, Service; Extended Essay) and one course each from IB groups listed below. Diploma candidates must take six group courses in total, three at Standard Level (SL) and three at Higher Level (HL).

- Group 1: Language A1 (world literature)
- Group 2: Second Language B (Spanish SL/HL or Mandarin)
- Group 3: Individuals and Societies (History Route–two SL/HL, Economics HL–online, Information Technology in a Global Society SL/HL–online, Business and Management–online, Psychology–online)
- Group 4: Experimental Sciences (Environmental Systems and Societies)
- Group 5: Mathematics and Computer Science (Math SL/HL)

The average class size is 12, with a student- faculty ratio of 3:1. The school year comprises two semesters plus a January intersession. Each teacher makes formal, cumulative assessments of student work at least twice per semester, using the IB grading scale of 1–7. Faculty communicate regularly with students and parents, sharing grades and narrative assessments of each student's progress.

The integrated technology program facilitates both group collaboration and individual exploration. Teachers post weekly course outlines, requirements, and due dates on the TGS proprietary, online educational platform, THINK Spot. Students access the portal from their iPads, iPhones, and MacBooks (provided by the school), submitting assignments, essays, and exams while interacting with teachers, parents, and other teenagers around the world.

FACULTY AND ADVISERS

Head of School, Mr. Alun Cooper, M.A.Ed., began teaching in England in 1974 and taught in Argentina, Chile, Liberia, Egypt, Bahrain, Vietnam, and Belgium before joining TGS in 2012. He has served as a Boarding House Master, Head of English, Secondary Principal, IB Coordinator, and Head of School.

Faculty members reside with students in each host country. Ten of the 14 faculty members hold advanced degrees, and there is an equal distribution of male and female teachers. The interdisciplinary and experiential curriculum, flexible schedules, and small class sizes at THINK Global School allow teachers to individually tailor the educational process. Faculty members are assigned 3 to 4 advisees and serve as their adviser throughout the school year.

As the school grows, TGS seeks additional faculty with an unusually strong dedication to the craft of teaching, a sense of adventure, and an ability to explore the interconnections between academic disciplines and real-world experiences that leverage the school's global destinations. Applicants must be aware of the exigencies of working in a boarding school, particularly one that travels extensively. Teachers attend continuing education programs in their respective fields annually.

COLLEGE ADMISSION COUNSELING

TGS utilizes the professional skills and experiences of two college counselors from the consulting firm Popacademics. College preparation begins at the end of grade 9 when TGS students discuss future aspirations with their adviser and college counselor. In grade 10, they select their IB courses and complete practice college entrance tests. Counselors guide grade 11 students through the college selection and application processes and will work with grade 12 students to complete application to their university of choice. TGS will graduate its first class in 2014.

STUDENT BODY AND CONDUCT

THINK Global School enrolls students in grades 9–12, with an average of 12 students per grade. Seventy-five percent of students are from outside the United States, representing twenty different countries of citizenship.

Safety and security are top concerns for a school that travels to multiple nations and geographic regions. Students are expected to conduct themselves appropriately, honor the laws and customs of the host country, and follow all school safety guidelines. Students shall behave in accordance with the expectations and rules of TGS (established by the official Handbook and Student Council), both during and after normal school hours. Faculty and staff monitor student whereabouts at all times. TGS's security solutions incorporate the latest technology and trained personnel to ensure an anxiety-free experience for all.

ACADEMIC FACILITIES

In each city visited, THINK Global School partners with a local IB host school. That school provides classroom facilities, laboratories and other learning and recreational spaces for students and staff.

BOARDING AND GENERAL FACILITIES

Students, teachers, and Residential Life staff live, work and eat together as they travel the world. TGS provides student accommodations in each host city, and no two are quite the same. All accommodations meet top international boarding quality, and students benefit from experiencing a variety of living situations within different cultural settings. Students share rooms with classmates of the same gender. The Residential Life team supervises students whenever they are out of class. They also offer support and guidance to students as they travel the globe, learning about the world, themselves, and each other. Because cuisine is an integral part of learning and understanding a culture, the boarding program features local and nutritious fare.

ATHLETICS

TGS students participate in a variety of fitness and/or sport-based activities designed to promote an active, healthy lifestyle. The types of athletic activities students enjoy vary depending on the host country. Physical education activities have included soccer, swimming, tai chi, tennis, scuba diving, and fencing.

EXTRACURRICULAR OPPORTUNITIES

The boundary between "school" and "life" at TGS is much thinner than it would be at a more traditional school. Students have unique opportunities for learning, adventure, and community service in each host city. They might attend an educational workshop with a local expert; take advantage of museums or educational events in the host city, or head out of the city for a scientific or cultural trip.

DAILY LIFE

A typical day at TGS starts with early morning breakfast, then students and teachers head straight to class. Block sessions are held throughout the day, with a lunch break at the host school or surrounding area. In the late afternoon, students have independent study time and physical education. Dinner is followed by free time until the lights-out bed check, conducted by Residential Life staff at 10 p.m.

COSTS AND FINANCIAL AID

The cost for one year (including room, board, international insurance, computer equipment, and all other fees) is $79,000. The endowment allows the school to work with families individually in determining a fair and reasonable contribution toward educational expenses, and assistance is available to accepted students who demonstrate a need for financial support. TGS does not offer academic or athletic merit scholarships.

ADMISSIONS INFORMATION

TGS seeks international students from varied backgrounds with a combination of academic strength and intellectual curiosity, a desire to experience new cultures, and a willingness to engage in a tight-knit school community. The acceptance rate is 12 percent and successful applicants demonstrate the following characteristics: a strong academic record across multiple subject areas; an adventurous spirit, curious mind, and desire for hands-on engagement with global issues; advanced written and oral English skills (English is the language of instruction); self-motivation and a desire to succeed; teamwork skills and a friendly, positive attitude; and supportive parents who are active participants in the innovative school community.

TGS does not unlawfully discriminate on the basis of age, color, creed, disability, national or ethnic origin, race, religion, sex, or sexual orientation.

APPLICATION TIMETABLE

Initial inquiries are welcome up to two years in advance of intended enrollment, and completed applications are due in the winter prior to the upcoming September start date. There is no application fee and no testing is required prior to applying. The application includes questionnaires for students and parents, an essay, a media project of the student's choice, an English class writing sample, three recommendations, and transcripts for the last two school years.

After completing the online application, the remaining admissions process continues for approximately 30 days. First, selected students and their parents will be invited for a Skype admissions interview. Students who advance from the admissions interview stage will be invited to complete a nonverbal reasoning test and an emotional quotient inventory. Students whose native language is not English will also be asked to complete an English proficiency test. When testing is completed, qualifying students will be invited to interview with teachers and the Residential Life Director (also via Skype). Acceptance notifications are made once this process is complete, and continue until classes are full.

ADMISSIONS CORRESPONDENCE

Lily A. Just, Director of Admissions
THINK Global School
E-mail: ljust@thinkglobalschool.org
Web site: http://www.thinkglobalschool.org

THOMAS JEFFERSON SCHOOL

St. Louis, Missouri

Type: Coeducational boarding and day college-preparatory school
Grades: 7–12
Enrollment: 91
Head of School: Elizabeth L. Holekamp, Ph.D.

THE SCHOOL

Thomas Jefferson School was founded in 1946. It has received national attention for its academic excellence and its teacher-trustee system, the two guiding ideas of the founders. It became coeducational in 1971. The campus is a 20-acre estate in Sunset Hills, a suburb 15 miles southwest of downtown St. Louis.

The School's mission is to give its students the strongest possible academic background through a classical education. Within a nurturing community, students develop a responsibility for their own learning and a desire to lift up the world with beauty and intellect. Many of the School's distinctive features, such as the daily schedule, are outgrowths of this mission.

The School is unique in its business organization. A majority of the members of its Board of Trustees must be teachers in the School; moreover, no one may teach full-time for more than five years without becoming a trustee. The Head of School and the other teacher-trustees make up the administration of the School, with the exception of the Directors of Admissions and Development, who are not faculty members. This structure gives teachers a greater stake in the School and a breadth of experience that produces better teaching.

Thomas Jefferson School is a member of the National Association of Independent Schools, the Association of Boarding Schools, the Independent Schools Association of the Central States, Midwest Boarding Schools, the School and Student Service for Financial Aid, and the Educational Records Bureau.

ACADEMIC PROGRAM

Thomas Jefferson offers a challenging approach to learning, with the emphasis on the student's own efforts. Classes are short, and the teachers seldom lecture; instead, all students are called on to answer questions and generate discussion. During afternoon and evening study time, the students have a good deal of freedom in choosing when and where to do their homework, with help readily available from faculty members.

Seventh and eighth graders take English, mathematics, science, social studies, and Latin. In the ninth through twelfth grades, students take 4 years of English; 4 years of mathematics through calculus; 2 years of Ancient Greek (ninth and tenth grades); 2 years of Italian or French (tenth and eleventh); at least 3 years of science, including an AP course; and at least 2 years of history, including AP U.S. History. Electives include additional language, science, and history courses. Advanced Placement exams are a standard part of the courses in the social sciences, calculus, biology, physics, chemistry, advanced languages, and junior and senior English. The faculty members can also help students work toward AP exams in other subject areas.

The English curriculum gives students intensive training in grammar, vocabulary, and writing skills. They also read and discuss a great deal of literature, including recognized classics (Shakespeare, the Bible, and epics), time-tested authors (Austen, Dickens, Dostoyevsky, Fitzgerald, Manzoni, Melville, and Shaw), and more contemporary major authors, such as Amy Tan, Ralph Ellison, and Chaim Potok.

A special feature is the study of classical Greek, which contributes to intellectual development (including concrete benefits such as enhanced vocabulary) and cultural background. This subject, in which the School is a national leader, continues to stir curiosity and ambition. A number of graduates continue to study it in college; others do so independently or later in life.

The average class size is 15, and the overall student-teacher ratio is 7:1. During the day, teachers are accessible to everyone and are ready to help; one teacher is on duty each evening and visits the students' rooms to assist with homework. Younger new students and those having academic difficulty are placed in supervised afternoon or evening study halls.

The grading system uses letter grades of A, B, C, D, and E. An average of B– is Honors; an average of A– is High Honors. To remain in good standing, a student must have no more than one D in any marking period; students in their first year, however, are allowed extra time to adjust. One-hour examinations are given at the end of the first and third quarters (October and April), and 2- to 3-hour examinations are given at midyear and at the end of the year. Following each exam period, a student's adviser sends the parents a letter discussing the student's progress and giving the latest grades and teachers' comments.

The unusually long winter and spring vacations (about one month each) give students an opportunity to unwind, spend time with their families, and do independent work for extra credit.

FACULTY AND ADVISERS

The faculty, including the Head of School, consists of 7 women and 5 men. Faculty members hold twelve baccalaureate degrees, ten master's degrees, one law degree, and four Ph.D.'s.

Dr. Elizabeth Holekamp became the fourth Head of School in the summer of 2011. Dr. Holekamp attended the University of Missouri and holds a Ph.D. from Indiana University.

All faculty members are expected to continue educating themselves by regular reading, both within and outside the subject areas they teach. They meet periodically to report on their reading and to discuss it.

Currently, 5 of the 12 faculty members live on the campus, along with 3 resident assistants and one staff member. Each teacher, whether resident or not, has several duties besides teaching, such as athletics supervision, evening study help, and advising students. Teachers meet with each of their advisees regularly to check the student's grades and to keep in touch with his or her personal development.

COLLEGE ADMISSION COUNSELING

Three experienced faculty members serve as college advisers, guiding the seniors through the process, helping them develop a realistic list of choices, and offering advice on writing personal essays. They also spend many hours following up with colleges by phone and e-mail.

In sixty-six years, the School has had 611 graduates; all have gone to college—most to well-known, selective institutions. Among the colleges and universities attended by Thomas Jefferson graduates in the past nine years are Boston University (6), Brown (2), Caltech (2), Carnegie Mellon (1), Carleton (1), Claremont-McKenna (2), Columbia (2), Cornell (2), Duke (3), Emory (3), Harvard (1), Haverford (5), Johns Hopkins (4), Lake Forest (3), Northwestern (6), Pitzer (2), Pomona (3), Reed (3), Rensselaer (2), Rhodes (5), Smith (2), Stanford (2), Swarthmore (2), Vanderbilt (4), Washington (St. Louis) (10), Wesleyan (3), the University of Chicago (7), the University of Missouri (7), and the University of Pennsylvania (1).

Ten-year medians for the SAT are 700 critical reading, 660 math, and 680 writing.

STUDENT BODY AND CONDUCT

In 2012–13, the School has 91 students (52 boarding, 39 day). Most students come from the region between the Appalachians and the Great Plains. Approximately one third are international students from various countries (ESL instruction is available, although knowledge of English is required for admission). Most grades have girls and boys in about equal numbers.

A Student Council, whose members are elected twice a year, brings student concerns before the faculty and helps maintain a healthy, studious atmosphere. Collectively, the council has one vote in faculty meetings on any decision concerning student life.

Demerits are given for misconduct, lateness, and other routine matters; a student who receives too many demerits in one week has to do chores around the campus on Saturday. Students may appeal any demerits, even those given by the Head of School, before a Student Appeals Court.

ACADEMIC FACILITIES

The Main Building, a former residence, provides a comfortable, homelike setting for classes and meals; it also contains faculty and administrative offices, the library, computer terminals, and an art gallery. Sayers Hall, next to the Main Building, provides science laboratories, classrooms, and a library/computer annex. In 2008, the School opened a new art facility and built an addition onto the gymnasium.

BOARDING AND GENERAL FACILITIES

Boarders live in the Gables—a smaller building from the original estate—and in five modern one-story houses, built in 1960, plus one additional, similar house added in 1994. Each house has four double rooms; each room has an outside entrance, a private bath, large windows, wall-to-wall carpeting, and air conditioning. The houses were designed to provide quiet, privacy, and independence. Normally, 2 or 3 boarding students share a room with 1 or 2 day students. All dorm rooms provide wireless Internet access.

ATHLETICS

Thomas Jefferson School athletics are meant to help students relax, stay in shape, and study better. Outdoor sports include intramural tennis (five courts), varsity soccer, and fitness; indoor sports are volleyball and basketball (both varsity and JV), yoga, and general fitness. Athletics are required on Monday, Tuesday, Thursday, and Friday afternoons. Teams compete with other local schools in basketball, soccer, and volleyball.

EXTRACURRICULAR OPPORTUNITIES

St. Louis has a wealth of resources in art, music, and theater, as well as an excellent zoo, a science museum, and a world-renowned botanical garden. The faculty members keep the students informed about opportunities around town and help provide them with transportation and tickets whenever possible. Teachers often take groups of students on informal weekend field trips. In recent years, groups have gone to the Ozarks for camping, to the Mississippi River to see bald eagles, and to many symphony concerts, ballets, and plays. Students also attend movies, sports events, and concerts.

Volunteer service is a required part of the program, and the School helps students find opportunities for service. All students must plan and complete a required amount of voluntary community service before they graduate. Students are encouraged to pursue their own interests, such as music lessons, and the School helps make arrangements. A piano is available. Over the years, students have initiated and sustained major activities, such as the School yearbook, a student newspaper, mock trial, and the all-school play.

DAILY LIFE

A school day begins with breakfast at 7:45. Eight 35-minute class periods (and lunch) take place between 8:30 and 1:10. In grades 11 and 12, students take four classes and in grades 7 through 10, they take five. Classes meet daily, but AP classes, which have longer assignments, may meet only four days a week. After lunch, a student may have a science lab, a language lab, or other supplementary academic work. Then they have an hour of athletics, perhaps a meeting with their adviser or study help from another teacher, and some independent time in which they are expected to start their homework for the next day. Dinner is at 6:15, and evenings are devoted to study. On Wednesday and Friday afternoons, there are fine-arts classes in such subjects as drawing, photography, ceramics, and art and music appreciation, and students may leave the campus for nearby shopping centers. Day students are on campus from about 8:30 to 5.

WEEKEND LIFE

Weekends are leisure time. As long as students are in good standing academically, they have considerable freedom and may leave the campus for movies, shopping, and the like. A driver is employed on the weekends to provide student transportation. Older students may keep cars on campus at the discretion of the faculty. The sports facilities are available for weekend use. Dances and other events and outings are organized by the Student Council, the Student Activities Committee, and the on-campus staff.

SUMMER PROGRAMS

The School organizes summer trips to Europe for students in grades 10–12, often led by the Head of School or other experienced faculty members. Students in grades 7–9 may participate in a weeklong trip to London in the spring.

COSTS AND FINANCIAL AID

Charges for 2012–13 are $39,500 for full boarding, $37,750 for weekday boarding, and $22,750 for day students. This includes room plus all meals for boarders and all lunches for day students. Approximately $2000 covers books, school supplies, and other expenses related to School activities. Optional off-campus activities such as music lessons (and the necessary transportation) cost extra.

A $2000 deposit, nonrefundable but credited to tuition, is required when a student enrolls. The balance of the tuition is paid through Sallie Mae's TuitionPay program.

Financial aid is available, based on a family's need. Thirty-five percent of the student body currently receives some financial aid; the total amount awarded is more than $630,000. An applicant's family must file a statement with the School and Student Service, and this information is used in judging need. Many middle-income families receive some assistance.

ADMISSIONS INFORMATION

The School looks for signs of native intelligence, liveliness, energy, ambition, and curiosity. Strong grades and test scores are important considerations but not always the deciding ones. A candidate should submit the results of the Secondary School Admission Test (SSAT); international students submit the results of the TOEFL. About 60 percent of those who complete the application process are accepted.

APPLICATION TIMETABLE

Inquiries and applications are welcome at any time, but the School has three rounds of admissions: early decision applicants submit their materials by mid-December and receive an answer in early January; regular decision applicants submit their materials by mid-February and receive an answer in early March; after April, applications for any remaining openings are considered as they are received. As part of the application process, prospective students usually spend a day at the School visiting classes, having lunch, and spending time with the admissions staff to ask questions and have an interview. There is a $40 fee for domestic applications, and a $100 fee for international applications.

ADMISSIONS CORRESPONDENCE

Barbara Fraser, Director of Admissions
Thomas Jefferson School
4100 South Lindbergh Boulevard
St. Louis, Missouri 63127
United States
Phone: 314-843-4151
Fax: 314-843-3527
E-mail: admissions@tjs.org
Web site: http://www.tjs.org

TRINITY–PAWLING SCHOOL

Pawling, New York

Type: Boys' boarding (9–PG) and day (7–PG) college-preparatory school
Grades: 7–12, postgraduate year
Enrollment: 300
Head of School: Archibald A. Smith III, Headmaster

THE SCHOOL

The Pawling School was founded in 1907 by Dr. Frederick Gamage. In 1946, it was renamed Trinity-Pawling School in recognition of its ties with Trinity School of New York City. In 1978, Trinity-Pawling School became a separate educational and corporate entity. Trinity-Pawling's Episcopal background is reflected in daily chapel services and course offerings in religion, ethics, and psychology.

The School is located 68 miles north of New York City along the Connecticut border; regular train service is available from Grand Central Station to Pawling (population 5,000). The campus, set on 140 acres of rolling hills, is just over an hour's drive from New York's major airports. On vacations, the School transports students to and from the airports and train stations.

It is Trinity-Pawling's belief that an appreciation of one's own worth can best be discovered by experiencing the worth of others, by understanding the value of one's relationship with others, and by acquiring a sense of self-confidence that comes through living and working competently at the level of one's own potential. Trinity-Pawling respects and recognizes the differences in individuals and the different processes required to achieve their educational potential.

The School is governed by a self-perpetuating 26-member Board of Trustees. The School raises more than $4 million in annual giving, in part from its more than 5,000 alumni. The School's endowment exceeds $32 million, and its operating budget for 2012–13 is more than $10 million.

Trinity-Pawling is accredited by the New York State Association of Independent Schools and chartered by the New York State Board of Regents. It is a member of the National Association of Independent Schools, the Secondary School Admission Test Board, the New York State Association of Independent Schools (NYSAIS), and the National Association of Episcopal Schools.

ACADEMIC PROGRAM

To graduate from Trinity-Pawling, a student must obtain a minimum of 112 credits in eight disciplines to earn a diploma. A full-year course is worth 6 credits, and a term course (trimester) is worth 2 credits. If a student enters after grade 9, his school record is evaluated and translated into Trinity-Pawling's system.

Students are required to complete 90 credits in the following subjects: 24 credits in English; 18 credits in mathematics; 18 credits in a laboratory science; 18 credits in history; 12 credits in a foreign language (excluding Language Program students); 6 credits in fine, performing, or studio arts (music, art, drafting, or drama); 4 credits in religion or philosophy; and 2 credits in health. Additionally, students must take 22 credits of elective courses. Advanced Placement courses are offered in English, U.S. history, European history, economics, chemistry, physics, biology, environmental science, mathematics, computer science, Latin, French, and Spanish.

Students carry a minimum of five courses per term. Evening study periods, held in student residences, are supervised by dorm masters. Students with academic difficulty have a formally supervised study hall. Teachers are available to give students extra help at any time that is agreeable to both. Reports are posted online for parents three times per term. Trinity-Pawling uses a number grading system (0–100) in which 60 is passing, 80 qualifies for honors, and 85 qualifies for high honors.

In addition to academic grades, the School utilizes a unique effort system to rank students based on overall effort in many aspects of School life, including academics, athletics, clubs, and dormitory life. A student's privileges are then tied to his overall effort ranking. This program is designed to work in conjunction with the School's philosophy of encouraging each student to work toward his own personal potential.

The Language Program, open to a maximum of 40 students, is initiated in the ninth and tenth grades. A modification of the Orton-Gillingham method, it strives to retrain students with developmental dyslexia. First-year students work in pairs with tutors. In addition, they take a skills-oriented language arts course. Phonetics, sequencing ideas, handwriting, memorization, and other language skills are emphasized. The second-year student is placed in an analytical writing class in addition to a skills-level English class. All students in the program also take basic science, mathematics, and history courses. The program's goal is to enable students to complete Trinity-Pawling's regular college-preparatory curriculum. Students in the program are not required to take a foreign language but may elect to do so.

FACULTY AND ADVISERS

There are 60 full-time members of the faculty, all of whom reside on the campus. Members of the teaching faculty hold fifty-eight baccalaureate and thirty-five graduate degrees. All participate in counseling and advising students. The School actively supports advanced study for its teachers during summers and other holidays.

Archibald A. Smith III was appointed Headmaster in 1990, after having served at Trinity-Pawling as a chemistry teacher, Director of College Placement, and Assistant Headmaster at various times since 1975. He is a graduate of St. John's School in Houston, Texas; Trinity College (Hartford) (B.S., 1972); and Wesleyan University (M.S., 1980). His career also includes teaching at the Northwood School in Lake Placid, New York. Mr. Smith is the past president of the New York State Association of Independent Schools and a member of the Accreditation Council of NYSAIS. He is a trustee of Dutchess Day School, a trustee of the International Boys School Coalition, a trustee of the Parents' League of New York, and is a member of the Headmasters Association.

COLLEGE ADMISSION COUNSELING

Trinity-Pawling's Director of College Counseling works closely with other administrators and faculty members to advise and aid students and their families with college placement. Individual meetings and group workshops are held on a regular basis, and more than 100 college representatives visit the campus each fall for presentations and interviews. More than 95 percent of the class of 2012 gained admission to their first- or second-choice college.

All of the 2012 graduates earned college or university acceptances. Among those they attend are Berkeley, Carnegie Mellon, Columbia, Cornell, George Washington, Northwestern, Occidental, Princeton, Purdue, Skidmore, Syracuse, Trinity, USC, U.S. Military Academy at West Point, and U.S. Naval Academy at Annapolis.

STUDENT BODY AND CONDUCT

Boarding students number 240, and day students number 60. Students come from twenty-nine states and thirteen countries. Students from minority groups make up 10 percent of the total enrollment. Students who choose Trinity-Pawling tend to desire a reasonably structured community that is dedicated to individual growth. A strong academic program in harmony with fine athletics and activities programs brings the School together. The School seeks students who want to actively pursue their academic and social development in a caring atmosphere.

Major violations of community rules are handled by a Faculty-Student Disciplinary Committee, which makes recommendations to the Headmaster. Less serious breaches are handled by the Dean of Students and others.

The Student-Faculty Senate is composed of School prefects and elected student and faculty representatives. The senate works to develop self-government, plans School activities, and fosters a bond between the students and the faculty. It consists of six committees, each with a responsibility for specific areas of School life.

ACADEMIC FACILITIES

The Dann Building (1964) and the Science and Technology Center (2002) house classrooms and science and computer labs. The Art Building, completed in 2004, houses the fine arts, theater, and music programs. This building contains a theater that is used for student productions, lectures, and visiting professional performances. The library features an online catalog, more than 28,000 volumes, and available computers. It is located in the historic Cluett Building, which also contains administrative offices and the student center.

BOARDING AND GENERAL FACILITIES

Students reside in single or double rooms in eighteen dormitory units located in eight buildings, including Starr Hall (1984), Starr East (1987), and Cluett (renovated 1995). Each is under the supervision of 1 or more faculty members aided by senior proctors. Students are allowed to choose roommates, and, whenever possible, housing choice is granted. Students are grouped in housing units according to grade level. A student's dorm master is usually his adviser, so a strong personal relationship often develops. Trinity-Pawling stresses the value of close student-faculty relationships.

Students enjoy a School store and snack bar that are open daily. The Scully Dining Hall was completed in 2009. Medical services are provided by the Health Center, staffed by a resident nurse and a doctor who makes daily visits. Several hospitals serve the area. Trinity-Pawling is within walking distance of the village of Pawling.

ATHLETICS

Trinity-Pawling is a member of the New England Private School Athletic Conference and the Founders League, which affords it the opportunity to play schools in New England, such as Avon, Choate, Hotchkiss, Kent, Loomis Chaffee, Salisbury, Taft, and Westminster. Because the School believes that athletics and physical development are key ingredients in a student's growth, all students are required to participate in the program during the school year. Three or four levels of teams are formed in each interscholastic sport, including baseball, basketball, cross-country, football, golf, hockey, lacrosse, soccer, squash, tennis, track and field, and wrestling. Also offered at both the interscholastic and intramural levels are running, skiing, and weight training.

The Carleton Gymnasium contains a 50-foot by 90-foot basketball court with two cross courts for practice. The lower floor and wing contain weight-training rooms, five international squash courts, and locker rooms. There are also six soccer fields, a new football field, baseball fields, an all-weather track, twelve tennis courts, three lacrosse fields, ponds for skating and fishing, the McGraw wrestling pavilion, and the enclosed Tirrell Hockey Rink, which underwent a $1 million renovation in 2007.

EXTRACURRICULAR OPPORTUNITIES

Each student is encouraged to participate in one or more of the twenty-four activities offered on the campus. These activities are often initiated and directed by the students with the guidance of an interested faculty adviser. Among the offerings are the student newspaper, Model United Nations, the Minority Student Union, the yearbook, the choir, the photography club, the dramatic club, the chess club, the computer club, the fishing club, foreign language clubs, jazz groups, and the outing club. Trinity-Pawling encourages student initiative in starting new activities.

The School sponsors regular trips to nearby areas of educational and cultural interest, including museums and theaters in New York City. Annual events include Parents' Weekend, Junior Parents' Weekend, and several alumni functions. The concert series, offering five concerts annually, brings a rich variety of musical talent to the campus during the school year.

Each student participates in the work program that emphasizes the School's policy of self-responsibility and economy of operation. Boys assist with parts of the routine maintenance work throughout the buildings and on the grounds.

DAILY LIFE

At 8 a.m., three mornings a week, a brief community chapel service is held for all students. A more formal Episcopal service is held for the entire school mid-morning on Tuesdays. Classes are scheduled from 8:20 until 2:40 four days a week and until noon on Wednesdays and Saturdays. Wednesday and Saturday afternoons are reserved for interscholastic sports events. Athletic practices take place in the afternoon, while most extracurricular activities are scheduled in the evening. Lunches are generally served cafeteria-style, dinners sit-down family-style. Students are required to study from 8:00 to 9:30 in their rooms, the library, or the study hall, depending upon their academic status.

WEEKEND LIFE

Dances, plays, concerts, trips to New York City, and informal activities are planned for weekends. The Student-Faculty Senate organizes and plans many of the weekend activities. Social activities are also arranged with girls' schools in the area. Weekend leaves from the School are based upon a group rating, which encompasses a student's record in academic effort and achievement, general citizenship, and dormitory life. In general, as the group rating increases, so do the amount and nature of privileges. Students are evaluated twice per term.

COSTS AND FINANCIAL AID

Charges for 2012–13 are $49,250 for boarding students, $35,000 for day students in ninth through twelfth grade, and $24,000 for day students in seventh and eighth grade. Extra expenses total approximately $2000 per year. The Language Program is an additional $5300–$7600 per year, depending on the grade. A tuition payment plan and tuition insurance are available.

Thirty-five percent of the students receive a total of over $3.3 million in financial aid each year. Trinity-Pawling subscribes to the School and Student Service for Financial Aid and grants aid on the basis of need.

ADMISSIONS INFORMATION

Trinity-Pawling seeks the well-rounded student who will both gain from and give to the School. New students are accepted in all grades; a limited number are accepted for the postgraduate year. Selection is based upon all-around qualifications without regard to race, color, creed, or national origin. Candidates must submit a complete transcript plus two or three teachers' recommendations, have a personal interview at the School, and take the SSAT. Candidates for the Language Program are asked to have completed a Wechsler Test (WISC-R). International students are required to sit for the TOEFL test.

In 2011, there were 350 applicants, of whom 250 were accepted and 110 enrolled.

APPLICATION TIMETABLE

Initial inquiries are welcome at any time. Campus tours and interviews (allow 1½–2 hours) can be arranged by appointment, Monday through Friday, 8:30–1:30, and on Saturday, 8:30–11. All candidates must have an interview. The completed forms must be submitted by the February 1 deadline and must be accompanied by a nonrefundable fee of $50 ($100 for international students).

Fall is the usual time for applying, and notification of acceptance begins in early March. Parents are expected to reply to acceptances one month after notification.

ADMISSIONS CORRESPONDENCE

MacGregor Robinson
Assistant Headmaster for External Affairs
Trinity-Pawling School
Pawling, New York 12564
United States
Phone: 845-855-4825
Fax: 845-855-4827
E-mail: denisepalmer@trinitypawling.org
Web site: http://www.trinitypawling.org

THE UNIVERSITY OF CHICAGO LABORATORY SCHOOLS

Chicago, Illinois

Type: Coeducational, day, college-preparatory school
Grades: N–12
Enrollment: Approximately 1,800
Head of School: Dr. David W. Magill

THE SCHOOL

The University of Chicago Laboratory Schools (Lab) is an independent, coeducational day school enrolling approximately 1,800 students from nursery school through twelfth grade. Founded in 1896 by John Dewey, Lab's progressive education is broad and deep, with an emphasis on the arts, humanities, math, and science. Lab is a division of the University of Chicago, and Lab students benefit from access to University professors, classes, and facilities. Lab prepares students to be critical thinkers who are equipped to handle the rigors of a complex and changing world. Each year, Lab graduates matriculate at top four-year colleges throughout the United States and abroad.

Lab is approved or accredited by the Independent Schools Association of the Central States, North Central Association of Colleges and Schools, and the Illinois Department of Education. Lab is a member of the National Association of Independent Schools.

ACADEMIC PROGRAM

The Laboratory Schools do not specialize in a particular academic area. Rather, Lab prepares students to be creative, in-depth thinkers who are lifelong learners, ready to face the challenges of an increasingly complex global society.

All students are required to take math, science, English, history, a world language (French, German, Spanish, Latin, and Mandarin), computer science, physical education, music, community learning, and fine arts. In addition, high school students may enroll in University of Chicago classes, utilize University libraries, and intern with University of Chicago faculty members. Lab graduates enter a variety of fields, including education, law, medicine, and others.

Students at University High (U-High) pursue a comprehensive liberal arts program that emphasizes analytical reading, writing, research, and strong math and science skills. Through discussion, hands-on lab work, research, and other school work, Lab students learn to read closely, form independent ideas, and write analytically. Approximately 90 percent enroll in at least one of the eight Advanced Placement or ten advanced topics courses.

FACULTY AND ADVISERS

Approximately 230 teachers, counselors, librarians, and assistant teachers comprise the faculty at the Laboratory Schools. Most have higher degrees and many have doctoral degrees.

A total of 8 current or former teachers throughout the Laboratory Schools have won the coveted Golden Apple Award for excellence in teaching, awarded by Illinois' Golden Apple Foundation, more than any other school.

COLLEGE ADMISSION COUNSELING

Three full-time college placement counselors provide step-by-step guidance to juniors, seniors, and their parents as they navigate the college admission and selection process. This includes conducting workshops on various college topics and directing families to appropriate information at each stage of the process. In 2007, the *Wall Street Journal* named the Laboratory Schools' college placement office the fourth best in the nation.

STUDENT BODY AND CONDUCT

Lab enrolls approximately 1,800 students from nursery school through twelfth grade, with a largely equal number of boys and girls. Lab students speak more than forty languages at home, and identify themselves as having fifty-nine different nationalities. The Nursery/Kindergarten program enrolls approximately 340 students, the Primary School (grades 1 and 2) enrolls approximately 230 students, the Lower School (grades 3–5) enrolls approximately 350 students, and the Middle School (grades 6–8) enrolls approximately 380 students. Lab's high school, University High (U-High), enrolls approximately 500 students. Lab students live throughout the greater Chicago area, with approximately half coming from the Hyde Park/Kenwood area. Approximately 50 percent of Lab students have parents who are affiliated with the University of Chicago.

ACADEMIC FACILITIES

Lab's campus consists of Blaine Hall (the Lower School), Belfield (the Middle School), and the University High building. Judd Hall contains Lab's administrative offices, as well as some additional classrooms. The lower, middle, and high school libraries together contain more than 100,000 volumes. Lab has art studios, a darkroom, music classrooms and practice rooms, a state-of-the-art language lab, a dance studio, and a theater. Wireless Internet access is available for students and faculty throughout the school.

Athletic facilities are located in Sunny and Kovler Gymnasium, steps away from the main buildings. In addition, Lab students have access to the academic and athletic facilities at the University of Chicago.

In 2013, Lab anticipates opening Earl Shapiro Hall, on the Early Childhood Campus, which will house students from Nursery 3 through second grade.

ATHLETICS

The 2012–13 school year marks the 109th year that the Laboratory Schools have offered students interscholastic athletic competition. During the previous year, 660 students from middle through high school competed in the athletic program on one or more of Lab's forty-four different teams. Over the last four years Lab's varsity teams have won seven sectional and sixteen regional championships in nine different varsity sports. All told, Lab has 57 coaches currently, 24 of whom are faculty members. Lab's no-cut policy ensures that all students may participate in any sport they choose. The Laboratory Schools are part of the Illinois High School Association (IHSA) as a nonboundaried school.

EXTRACURRICULAR OPPORTUNITIES

In the high school, students run more than forty school-sponsored organizations, ranging from religious and ethnic clubs to activities in the arts, culture, academics, philanthropy, and social activism. University High students devote significant time to many different extracurricular activities: joining sports, math, science, debate, or Model UN teams; writing and publishing the School's newspaper or yearbook; serving in student government or community service roles; and participating in theater productions or musical performances. Many of these extracurricular activities begin in the Middle School.

DAILY LIFE

Because Lab begins with children who are 3 years old, and slightly over half continue at Lab until they graduate from U-High in twelfth grade, there are enormous variances in the students' daily schedules and activities.

The nursery and kindergarten classrooms at Lab are busy, with many different activities going on at one time. This is Lab's negotiated curriculum in action: teachers prepare an environment filled with possibilities and encourage choice, initiative, exploration, and collaboration.

Lab's Primary and Lower School curricula (first through fifth grades) are designed to help children master the skills that will serve as the foundation to their intellectual life. Children entering the Middle School years (sixth through eighth grade) begin an intense period of social, emotional, physical, moral, and intellectual growth.

U-Highers are an independent group whose high expectations go hand in hand with a demanding workload and a great deal of personal freedom. Each year, Lab students are better able to think for themselves, challenge assumptions, and, most importantly, take on increasing levels of responsibility for their own education.

SUMMER PROGRAMS

Summer Lab is a six-week program that includes Summer School, Adventure Kids Day Camp, sports camps, Fun in the Sun, and Summer Lab on Stage. Summer Lab Field Study stages domestic and international summer travel. Summer Lab embodies the notion that love of learning never goes on vacation. Approximately 900 students, from ages 3 to 18, participated last summer in the rich and diverse program, mixing Labbies with children from all around the city of Chicago, the United States, and the world.

COSTS AND FINANCIAL AID

Tuition costs for the 2012–13 academic year are as follows: $16,584 for the nursery school half-day program; $23,526 for the nursery and kindergarten full-day program; $23,526 for grades 1–5; $25,326 for grades 6–8; and $26,520 for grades 9–12.

Each year, Lab provides financial assistance to help meet the needs of students and their families. Lab does not have a specific income threshold for financial aid. Rather, the Financial Aid Committee reviews a family's entire financial picture, including income, expenses, and other circumstances. Financial aid awards are not automatically renewed; families are required to reapply for aid each year. Awards are recalculated annually based on the most recent financial data.

ADMISSIONS INFORMATION

Every applicant family receives personal attention, including a meeting with an admissions officer, a tour of the schools, and an opportunity to interact with other students and faculty. Lab believes that each applicant is unique and possesses special qualities that cannot always be captured by test scores and applications alone. Lab learns about its applicants through playgroups, classroom visits, interviews, shadow days, and tours. Applicant families also learn more about Lab's special character through this process.

APPLICATION TIMETABLE

Historically, most students enter Lab at either Nursery 3 (3 years old) or ninth grade and begin the application process in August or September of the year prior to enrollment. Admissions deadlines and details on the application process for all grades are available on Lab's website at www.ucls.uchicago.edu.

ADMISSIONS CORRESPONDENCE

Irene M. Reed, Executive Director
Admissions and Financial Aid
University of Chicago Laboratory Schools
1362 East 59th Street
Chicago, Illinois 60637
United States
Phone: 773-702-9451
Fax: 773-702-1520
E-mail: admissions@ucls.uchicago.edu
Web site: http://www.ucls.uchicago.edu

THE WHITE MOUNTAIN SCHOOL

Bethlehem, New Hampshire

Type: Coeducational boarding and day college-preparatory school
Grades: 9–12, postgraduate year
Enrollment: 110
Head of School: Timothy Breen, Ph.D.

THE SCHOOL

The White Mountain School is an independent boarding and day school dedicated to preparing young people for college studies and life beyond formal academics. Through challenging coursework and innovative instruction, students learn to think critically and creatively; they are encouraged to "own" their education and become responsible, independent young adults. Local and international community service, sustainability studies, performing and fine arts, field courses in the fall and spring, and team and individual sports are integral parts of the School's program.

Founded in 1886 as Saint Mary's School in Concord, New Hampshire, the School moved to Bethlehem in 1935. The move north, adjacent to the spectacular 600,000-acre White Mountain National Forest, was made to offer students an opportunity to live in and among things that were greater than themselves, to help them gain perspective, and to give them a sense of appreciation for the natural environment. The School changed its name to The White Mountain School in 1972.

As an Episcopal school, The White Mountain School honors and celebrates the unique worth of each individual. Students of all faiths are welcome and students are encouraged to pursue their own understanding of spirituality. The School's Episcopal heritage inspires a commitment to community service (local and international), instills a connection to the natural world, and respects each student's individual talents and passions.

Governed by a 16-member Board of Trustees, The White Mountain School is fully accredited by the New England Association of Schools and Colleges (NEASC). It is a member of the National Association of Independent Schools (NAIS), the Independent School Association of Northern New England (ISANNE), the Association of Boarding Schools (TABS), the National Association of Episcopal Schools (NAES) and the Council for Advancement and Support of Education (CASE). The White Mountain School is proud of its recognized outdoor education program which is accredited by the Association of Experiential Education (AEE), and the American Mountain Guides Association (AMGA).

ACADEMIC PROGRAM

The White Mountain School's academic philosophy combines a college-preparatory curriculum involving innovative and engaging classes with the development of practical life skills that fully prepare students for success in college and beyond. AP and honors courses are offered in every discipline. With an average class size of 10 students and a student-faculty ratio of 5:1, teachers are able to create discussion-based classes where every student is engaged. Fifty-eight percent of the faculty members hold advanced degrees.

Independent projects are an integral component of the School's academic program. They allow students to pursue topics that pique their curiosity and develop their passions. Independent projects provide the students with an opportunity to become fully immersed in a specific realm of interest that is important to them.

To graduate, students must earn 19 academic credits, including a minimum of 4 credits in English, 2½ credits in history, 3 credits in mathematics, 3 credits in science, 2 credits in world language, 1 credit in the arts, ½ credit in philosophy and religious studies, and ½ credit in sustainability studies. Year-long courses are worth one credit; semester courses are worth ½ credit. Parents receive grade reports and teacher comments four times per year. Advisers maintain close contact with students and parents to ensure that students receive both the challenge and support they need.

The White Mountain School recognizes that each student learns differently and is committed to challenging and supporting every student. The School's Learning Center provides additional support to students who are capable of pursuing a rigorous college preparatory curriculum and who have a diagnosed learning difference. This program is designed to give each student the tools needed to become an involved learner as well as to understand their own strengths, weaknesses, and distinct learning styles. English as a second language (ESL) is also offered to qualified international students.

Outside the classroom, The White Mountain School offers students special opportunities for academic experiences. Through week-long field courses, which are offered twice a year, students explore the world around them and put theoretical understanding into action. They gain new perspective and appreciation for different cultures, the environment, and their place within the world. Recent courses have included studies of Buddhism; Green Living in an Urban Setting; Winter Weather in the White Mountains; playwriting; the Island Culture and Ecology of Isle Au Haut, Maine; domestic service projects with Habitat for Humanity; international service projects in Nicaragua and the Dominican Republic; and a student exchange program in France.

FACULTY AND ADVISERS

At The White Mountain School, faculty members strive to engage their students wherever they work with them—in the classroom, on the playing field, in extracurricular or weekend activities, and in residential life. Students and teachers are on a first-name basis, living and learning in a community of respect. Nearly all the teachers and administrators live on campus. Students know the faculty members as dorm parents, coaches, and participants in weekend activities and extracurricular clubs, as well as inspirational teachers. Every student has a faculty adviser who serves as the primary contact for parents. Fifty-eight percent of the faculty members hold advanced degrees as well as a variety of additional certifications important for their teaching and coaching responsibilities.

COLLEGE ADMISSION COUNSELING

The college counselor works extensively with students and their parents during their time at The White Mountain School, but particularly during the junior and senior years. The college counseling program is firmly rooted in the principle that discovering good matches between students and postsecondary institutions is the ultimate outcome of the college application process. Ninety-nine percent of White Mountain graduates attend college within the first year after graduation. Recent graduates have attended colleges and universities that include Boston University, Colby, Cornell, Duke, Fordham, Mount Holyoke, NYU, Purdue, Temple, Warren Wilson, and the Universities of Chicago, Connecticut, Michigan, New Hampshire, and Vermont.

STUDENT BODY AND CONDUCT

The White Mountain School enrolls approximately 110 students from around the country and the world, 54 percent male and 46 percent female. Eighty percent of the student population boards and the remaining 20 percent are day students from surrounding towns. Students come from a variety of geographical, cultural, and economic backgrounds; have diverse personal strengths; and contribute a variety of interests and talents to the School community. Students who attend The White Mountain School value the small school community, the academic challenge and engagement, the unique extracurricular opportunities available to them, and the ready access they have to their teachers.

The White Mountain School believes that each member of the community is important and shares the responsibility for the well-being of the School. The *Community Handbook* outlines expectations to help provide structure for academic and personal success, as well as boundaries for safety. Through the Student-Faculty Citizenship Committee, students participate in the disciplinary process of the School.

The Student Council and the Student Social Committee serve as forums for student ideas. They also make recommendations to the administration regarding school policies, curricula, activities, and other aspects of community life. Student proctors assist faculty members with residential life activities, help out in the dorms on a daily basis, and serve as role models and mentors to other students. Other opportunities are provided for responsible leadership, individual initiative, and group decision-making.

In addition, all students, teachers and administrators share in community responsibilities. All participate in on-campus service through the Work Jobs Program. Duties include kitchen crew, recycling, or helping in the library. In addition to their campus jobs, all boarding students have rotating job assignments in their dormitories.

ACADEMIC FACILITIES

The McLane Academic Center houses the classroom wing; multimedia center; learning labs; music room with a recording studio; and extensive art studios that include a photo lab and ceramics, drawing, and printmaking rooms. The school library offers more than 7,000 volumes, an online catalog, several online databases, and an interlibrary loan system with Dartmouth College and the University of New Hampshire. The Fred Steele Science Center is equipped with SmartBoard interactive technology and state-of-the-art labs, which allow for a wide range of authentic projects.

BOARDING AND GENERAL FACILITIES

The School's clapboard and fieldstone dormitories are equipped with common rooms and wireless internet access. All dorm rooms contain beautiful light oak furniture (extra-long twin bed with four drawers, wardrobe with drawers, and a desk with a hutch) for each student. Most rooms are doubles. There are several faculty apartments in each dormitory. A school farm, including a student-built post and beam shed, a chicken coop with hens, an organic vegetable and fruit garden, and composting bins are integral parts of the School's commitment to sustainability practices and activities. A student center is located in McLane and provides a central location for students to gather and relax.

A state-of-the-art 3,000-square-foot indoor climbing wall is part of an indoor sports center outfitted with Nautilus equipment, free weights, and aerobic equipment. In addition, two athletic fields and an extensive trail system are part of the 250-acre property. The Health Services office is staffed by a registered nurse, who is also an emergency medical technician (EMT). The nurse is assisted by another EMT. Around-the-clock emergency services are available at Littleton Hospital, seven miles from campus.

ATHLETICS

The White Mountain School believes that athletics and healthy outdoor activities are essential. Teams and activities are open to all. Students participate in afternoon activities each season of the year and can choose from a variety of recreational and interscholastic sports. The School offers teams for boys and girls in lacrosse, soccer, basketball, cross-country running, sport climbing, Alpine skiing, Nordic skiing, freestyle skiing, snowboarding, road cycling, and mountain biking. Students can engage in instructional and recreational opportunities in rock climbing, white-water paddling, hiking, skiing, and snowboarding. In addition, students can pursue dance, yoga, theater, jewelry making, and community service in the afternoons.

The White Mountain School's rock climbing program was the first high school program, public or private, to earn accreditation from the American Mountain Guides Association (AMGA). The sport climbing program partners with USA Climbing to provide multiple opportunities for competition. Students who choose to pursue outdoor sports learn the technical aspects of their activity and explore such important topics as minimum-impact travel, first aid, navigation, orienteering, trip planning, and natural history. Team building and leadership are important components of the program.

EXTRACURRICULAR OPPORTUNITIES

Extracurricular opportunities vary from year to year, depending upon the interests of the student body. Current clubs include diversity club, astronomy club, electronics and robotics club, sustainability club, astronomy club, and film photography club. The yearbook, *The Pendulum,* is designed and produced by students. Students interested in the performing arts perform in A Capella, dance and theater productions, and informal coffee houses. With a focus on international song and dance, a diverse cultural events series brings professional performers and artists to the School.

Community service is an important part of The White Mountain School experience and gives students the opportunity to experience firsthand involvement with the larger world community. Each semester students can participate in community service trips that are often life-changing experiences. Opportunities are offered both within the United States and in international locations (the Dominican Republic and Nicaragua). Community service is offered as a winter sports option and is often part of weekend activities.

DAILY LIFE

Breakfast begins at 7 a.m. A student-led all-school Morning Meeting at 7:35 brings the community together for announcements followed by Morning Reading, an activity presented by one or more members of the faculty or student body. Morning Reading may include reading personal or reflective writing, sharing a video of a recent trip, engaging in Morning Sing, learning a new dance, or a skit.

Classes begin at 8. The academic day is based on a rotating block schedule. Each class meets four times per week, with one long block weekly to allow student project work, films, outdoor activities, or labs to take place without interruption. Students participate in Saturday project block classes every other week. Each course has one designated Saturday morning class each semester. This substantial block of time (3.5 hours) is set aside for collaborative projects, interdisciplinary explorations, hands-on learning, and field trips.

After classes, all students participate in afternoon sports or activities. Dinner is served at 5:45 p.m. Time is set aside after dinner for club meetings. Supervised study time for all students is from 7:30 to 9:30, Sundays through Thursdays. The library and computer labs are open for student use during study hall. For freshmen and sophomores, lights out is at 10:30; for juniors and seniors, lights out is at 11 during the academic week.

WEEKEND LIFE

On-campus activities are planned by students and teachers and include dances, movie marathons, intramural games, board game nights, bonfires, cider making, theater rehearsals, and art workshops. Studios in the art wing are open. Off-campus trips are made to Hanover (home of Dartmouth College), Boston, Portland, Burlington, or Montreal for a variety of cultural and sporting events. Students can also go to nearby Littleton to shop, enjoy a meal, or go to the movies. On weekends, transportation is provided to take students to optional religious services. There is a network of trails on campus available for hiking, running, biking, and cross-country skiing. Students are permitted to take weekends or overnights away from campus, if they have parental permission and all academic and community responsibilities have been met.

COSTS AND FINANCIAL AID

Tuition and room and board for 2012–13 are $46,900. Day student tuition is $22,600. A student expense account is required in the amount of $1500 ($1000 for day students). Learning Center tutorials and the ESL program have additional fees. Approximately 50 percent of the students receive financial aid. Eligibility is based on need as established by School and Student Services (SSS). Academic achievement, citizenship, and future promise are also taken into consideration when awards are made.

The White Mountain School is proud to announce two different scholarships opportunities. The E. E. Ford Sustainability Scholarship ($15,000 for boarding students and $7500 for day students) is for students with an active interest in sustainability and the environment. The North Country Scholarship ($10,000) is awarded to day students who have achieved high honors and who have been actively involved in their current school and/or community. Please contact the School or refer to the financial aid section of the School's Web site for more information regarding scholarship applications and deadlines.

ADMISSIONS INFORMATION

The White Mountain School encourages applications from students who wish to challenge themselves and enrich and broaden their educational experience through the various and unique programs it offers. Admissions candidates should be intellectually curious and motivated to perform at the college-preparatory level. The School encourages students from a variety of geographical and cultural backgrounds with a variety of interests and talents.

To complete the application process, the student must submit the application form and fee, references, and an official transcript of school records. The SSAT is encouraged, but not required. Admission staff members look forward to meeting and getting to know prospective students and their families through the campus visit and interview. Admission candidates are encouraged to visit the campus, but telephone or Skype interviews may be arranged. Families are welcome to request meetings with specific faculty members or administrators when they visit campus.

APPLICATION TIMETABLE

For March 10 notification, completed applications should be submitted by February 1. Applications submitted after February 1 are reviewed and considered on a rolling admission basis and are subject to the availability of spaces. Students generally enroll in September, and a small number of students may enroll in January, if there are spaces available.

ADMISSIONS CORRESPONDENCE

Allison Kimmerle
Director of Admission
The White Mountain School
371 West Farm Road
Bethlehem, New Hampshire 03574
United States
Phone: 603-444-2928 ext. 26
800-545-7813 (toll-free within the U.S. only)
Fax: 603-444-5568
E-mail: admissions@whitemountain.org
Web site: http://www.whitemountain.org

THE WILLISTON NORTHAMPTON SCHOOL

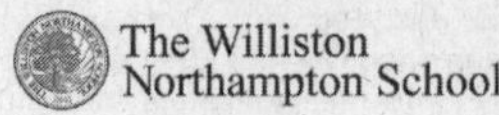

Easthampton, Massachusetts

Type: Coeducational boarding and day college-preparatory school
Grades: 7–PG: Middle School, 7–8; Upper School, 9–12, postgraduate year
Enrollment: School total: 534; Upper School: 454
Head of School: Robert W. Hill III, Head of School

THE SCHOOL

The Williston Northampton School was founded through the vision of 3 exceptional leaders: Samuel Williston, Sarah Whitaker, and Dorothy Bement.

Samuel Williston (1795–1874), one of New England's most successful industrialists, was passionate about education. After contributing to both Amherst and Mount Holyoke Colleges, he founded Williston Seminary in the thriving mill town of Easthampton. The school was renamed Williston Academy in 1924. That same year, Sarah Whitaker and Dorothy Bement cofounded the Northampton School for Girls. The school, built on Pomeroy Terrace in Northampton, emphasized a program of academic excellence and social simplicity for young women. By the 1930s, Williston Academy and Northampton School for Girls were holding joint dances, theater, and music events. In 1967 girls appeared in Williston classrooms for the first time in 103 years, as the schools began to share a few academic programs.

The merger agreement between Williston Academy and Northampton School for Girls was signed April 17, 1971. By September 1971, The Williston Northampton School opened as a fully coeducational institution. In the ensuing decades, Williston Northampton has continued to seek excellence in its academic, athletic, and extracurricular programs. Its mission is to inspire students to live with purpose, passion, and integrity.

The School is located on 125 acres in the heart of the Pioneer Valley near the base of Mount Tom, 85 miles west of Boston, and 150 miles north of New York. Within a 15-mile radius are the Five Colleges: Smith, Mount Holyoke, Hampshire, and Amherst Colleges, and the University of Massachusetts.

The current endowment is estimated at $40 million. The School's 10,000 alumni contributed more than $1.4 million in Annual Giving last year.

Williston is accredited by the New England Association of Schools and Colleges and is affiliated with the National Association of Independent Schools, the Association of Independent Schools of New England, the College Board, the School and College Conference on English, the Art Association of New England Preparatory Schools, and the Council for Advancement and Support of Education.

ACADEMIC PROGRAM

Williston's outstanding facilities and the exceptional recreational and cultural offerings nearby provide the setting for an outstanding education. Through its unique Williston+ Program, the School provides superior college preparation by bringing the rich resources of the nearby five colleges (Amherst, Hampshire, Mount Holyoke, and Smith Colleges and the University of Massachusetts, Amherst) into the classroom to enrich the School's curriculum.

At the heart of the School is a strong and varied academic program that seeks to strengthen, expand, and encourage students' skills and interests in the essential disciplines. Care is taken to place each student in the courses and sections most appropriate to his or her abilities. An average class size of 13 students enables faculty members to learn each student's abilities, and the flexibility of the program makes it possible for the School to structure programs that can best meet every individual student's needs. In addition, Williston offers numerous opportunities in competitive athletics, the arts, and leadership.

The School believes that each student should experience as many academic and creative disciplines as possible while they are at Williston. Therefore, Williston expects each of its students not only to satisfy the minimum basic requirements of 4 years of English, 3 years of math, 2 of science, 2 of a foreign language, and 2 in the social sciences, but also to select two trimester courses from the area of fine arts. Students may also choose a 1-credit directed studies course on a special topic not included in the regular curriculum. Students generally take five courses per trimester.

Williston also offers 37 Advanced Placement (AP) and honors classes. Qualified students may elect to complete extra work in consultation with the teacher to prepare to take the AP exam in two additional subject areas. Of the 169 Williston students who took the AP exams in 2012, which is required of all AP students at the School, 78 percent received scores of 3 or higher, earning college credit at participating institutions. Students attaining honor grades are recognized at the end of each term. The highest honor is election to the Cum Laude Society. Williston's chapter of Cum Laude is one of the oldest in the nation, founded in 1906.

The Writing Center plays a central part in Williston's academic program. Located in the library, the Writing Center is staffed by members of the English department, as well as by highly qualified student writers. The Writing Center provides support for students at all levels, on any writing assignment, so they can build critical thinking skills and clarity of expression, crucial tools that will be used again, in college and beyond. The Writing Center has over 1,000 visits annually.

Williston also offers the Writers' Workshop Series every fall. Founded by Williston parents and accomplished authors Madeleine Blais and Elinor Lipman in 1998, Williston's Writers' Workshop Series has hosted a variety of distinguished writers who give a public reading and then work with students enrolled in the Writers' Workshop course on the craft of writing. Authors who have participated include Augusten Burroughs, Gregory Maguire, Sue Miller, Richard Russo, and Curtis Sittenfeld.

During the winter and spring trimesters, Williston hosts the Photographers' Lecture series. Begun in 2000, this lecture series features internationally acclaimed photojournalists, filmmakers, and commercial photographers who share their work and ideas with the community and Williston's advanced photography students. Past distinguished visiting photographers have included John Willis, Sean Kerman, Lori Grinker, Nina Berman, and David Burnett.

FACULTY AND ADVISERS

The Williston Northampton School teaching faculty numbers 70 full-time members, and 64 percent hold advanced degrees (masters and doctorates). Almost half of the faculty members live in the School's dormitories. The School has established programs to support students with academic work, personal growth, and future educational goals and opportunities. Each boarding student has a faculty adviser who is also a dorm parent and may be easily consulted on academic or personal matters. Students can also consult with the Dean of Students, Chaplain, and Academic Dean. The School also employs the services of professional counselors in its Health Services.

In 2008, Williston instituted its Ninth Grade Program, which is designed to ease the transition for students from middle school to secondary school and to build camaraderie among ninth graders. The program includes an overnight orientation, special advisers, assemblies, and academic mentoring. The cornerstone of the program is C.O.R.E. (curiosity, organizations, reflection, and empathy). Each of these concepts is the focus of a special ninth grade–only assembly, where Williston adults and upperclass students address the ninth graders and discuss how these principles have helped them succeed. In addition, at the end of each trimester, the program holds final exam preparation clinics, where advisers outline for students the expectations for exam week and help the ninth graders fill out an hour-by-hour study schedule.

On July 1, 2010, Robert W. Hill III became Williston's nineteenth head of school. Mr. Hill came to Williston from the Carolina Day School in Asheville, North Carolina, where he had served as Associate Head of School and Principal of the Upper School since 2007. Prior to 2007, he served for nine years at St. Paul's School (Concord, New Hampshire) in a variety of roles, including Academic Dean, Director of College Advising, and Associate Dean of Faculty. His tenure there also included responsibilities as an English teacher, varsity girls' squash coach, and dorm resident. Hill started his teaching career at Westminster School (Simsbury, Connecticut), where he taught for fifteen years. He received his B.A. cum laude from Middlebury College and earned his M.A. in English literature from Middlebury's Bread Loaf School of English.

COLLEGE ADMISSION COUNSELING

Williston provides a thorough and personalized college counseling program for every student, beginning in their junior year. Three full-time counselors work with the junior and senior classes. From the beginning, the counselors collaborate with both parents and students to establish a dialogue between the School and the family. During the junior year, counselors and faculty members meet with students to acquaint them with standardized test-taking, financial aid, roles and functions of college officials, and campus lifestyles. In addition, all juniors visit the Five Colleges and participate in mock interviews at the different campuses.

The 125 members of the class of 2012 were accepted at over 450 colleges and universities, including Carnegie Mellon, Colby, Connecticut College, Duke, Hobart and William Smith, NYU, Skidmore, Williams College, and Yale.

STUDENT BODY AND CONDUCT

Most students enter Williston during the freshman or sophomore year. In 2012–13, grade 9 has 76 members (35 boys, 41 girls), of whom 35 were day students. Grade 10 has 123 members (62 boys, 61 girls), of whom 51 were day students. Grade 11 has 138 members (79 boys, 59 girls), of whom 50 were day students. Grade 12 has 116 members (67 boys, 49 girls), of whom 43 were day students. There are 9 postgraduate students. Sixteen percent of the students are members of minority groups. Students came from twenty-two states and twenty-four countries.

The rules and regulations of the School provide clear guidelines for everyone living in the Williston community. It is expected that students will follow both the spirit and the letter of these regulations as described in the *Student Handbook*, which is provided to all enrolling students.

Students who are reported to have violated School rules and regulations meet with the Discipline Committee, made up of faculty and student representatives. The committee's decisions and recommendations are reviewed by the head of school, who makes the final decision in disciplinary matters.

ACADEMIC FACILITIES

The campus is located on approximately 125 acres. Its facilities include the Reed Campus Center, the Scott Hall Science Building, the Boardman Theater, the Robert A. Ward Schoolhouse, the Robert Clapp Library, the Phillips Stevens Chapel, and the Whitaker-Bement Middle School Building. Renovations to the old gymnasium to create a new Campus Center that includes music and fine arts classrooms were completed in 1996. The Technology Center, the Science Tech Lab, the library, and the math floor house four student computer labs.

BOARDING AND GENERAL FACILITIES

The buildings on campus include the Head's House, the Zachs Admission Center at the Homestead, the Chapel, the Birch Dining Commons, five dormitories with facilities for 25 to 50 students, five residence houses with boarding facilities for 8 to 12 students, and faculty homes. Ford Hall and Memorial Dorm each house 50 students. Ford Hall received a million-dollar renovation in 1999, adding sun-splashed common rooms and other enhancements. All dorm rooms are wired into the campus computer network and have voice mail. A new ninth grade boys' dorm with housing for 32 students and three faculty families opened in 2008. The dorm, which is heated and cooled via seventeen geothermal wells, is the centerpiece of a planned residential quad.

Each dormitory or house is supervised by resident faculty houseparents to create an environment conducive to academic achievement and a warm and pleasant home atmosphere.

ATHLETICS

Sports are an integral part of student life at Williston, whether interscholastic or recreational. The School requires that each student be involved in the athletics program in each of the three sports seasons or enrolled in an arts alternative. The athletics department instills the principles of fair play, good sportsmanship, teamwork, and respect for rules and authority. Most of the academic faculty members also coach competitive teams, and the Director of Athletics oversees the program.

Interscholastic teams for girls include crew, cross-country, field hockey, soccer, and volleyball in the fall; basketball, ice hockey, skiing, squash, swimming and diving, and wrestling in the winter; and crew, golf, lacrosse, softball, tennis, track, and water polo in the spring. Boys may elect crew, cross-country, football, soccer, or water polo; basketball, ice hockey, skiing, squash, swimming and diving, or wrestling; and baseball, crew, golf, lacrosse, tennis, or track. Horseback riding at a nearby stable and modern dance are available every season. Fitness training, aerobics, yoga, and self-defense are choices open to upperclass students.

The Athletic Center houses two basketball courts, a six-lane pool with a diving well, five international squash courts, a weight room and fitness center, and a wrestling room. Other facilities include a lighted, synthetic-surface football/lacrosse field with stadium seating; a dance studio; facility renovated hockey rink; twelve tennis courts; an all-weather running track that surrounds a synthetic surface field for field hockey, soccer, and lacrosse; more than 30 acres of playing fields; and a 3.4-mile cross-country course. In addition, the School's golf teams play on several golf courses in the Easthampton area, and the ski team competes on the slopes in the eastern Berkshires.

EXTRACURRICULAR OPPORTUNITIES

The countryside offers excellent climbing, biking, and skiing opportunities, and the proximity of the Five Colleges provides a culturally rich environment of fine museums, libraries, and theater programs as well. The cities of Northampton and Springfield, Massachusetts, and Hartford, Connecticut, are near enough so that concerts and activities there are as readily available, as are those at the local colleges.

DAILY LIFE

The academic day runs from 8:30 a.m. until 2:40 p.m. on Monday, Tuesday, Thursday, and Friday and until 12:25 p.m. on Wednesday. Classes are held every other Saturday morning as well. Students take five courses in a six-period schedule, with classes lasting 60 minutes. All-school assemblies for announcements and special presentations are held once each week. Athletics are scheduled from the end of the class day until dinnertime. Except for theme-based formal dinners, most meals are served buffet-style. A free period immediately after classes end is frequently used for meetings of extracurricular organizations, library work, theater or music rehearsals, visiting between dormitories, or simply relaxing. Supervised evening study hours run from 8 to 10 p.m. All students are checked into the dorms at 8 p.m. by the dorm faculty.

WEEKEND LIFE

While the vast majority of students remain on campus, weekends at home or at the home of a friend are permitted with parental approval after all school obligations have been met. The Student Activities Director and students on the Activity Committee organize a variety of weekly activities, and students may take advantage of the events listed in the Five College calendar. Students travel off campus for college and professional athletic events, films, plays, dance performances, and concerts and to go skiing in Vermont. The many on-campus activities include dances and coffeehouse entertainment, talent shows, lectures by invited speakers, and a film series.

SUMMER PROGRAMS

Throughout the year, students have the opportunity to take part in several international excursions that enrich their studies. Trips to Canada and France during school vacations offer real-life practice for French language skills. A trip to Costa Rica allows students to perform community service while honing their Spanish. Ed Hing '77, Williston's photography instructor, helps students capture the beauty of locations in Italy, France, China, and other international destinations during summer photo trips. In the summer, the School also hosts many outside camps, offering theater, music, and athletics.

COSTS AND FINANCIAL AID

Tuition for boarders for 2012–13 is $49,400; for day students, it is $33,800. Additional expenses include books, insurance, laundry, and other incidental expenses. Tuition payment and insurance plans are recommended upon request.

Financial aid is awarded on the basis of need. The grants totaled $5.7 million for 2012–13.

ADMISSIONS INFORMATION

Williston seeks students who are interested in a challenging academic program, who can demonstrate solid academic achievement and outstanding personal character. Students should also be involved and caring contributors to life beyond the classroom. Admission is based upon an evaluation of these traits, a personal interview, and satisfactory scores on the SSAT or TOEFL. In 2012–13, 119 new students were enrolled in the Upper School.

APPLICATION TIMETABLE

The fall or winter prior to a candidate's prospective admission is usually the best time for a visit, which includes a faculty and student-guided tour of the School and an interview. The Admission Office is open Monday through Friday, from 8:30 a.m. to 4:30 p.m. during the academic year and 8 a.m. to 4 p.m. in the summer months, and on alternate Saturday mornings during the academic year.

An application for admission should be submitted by January 15 along with a nonrefundable fee of $50. The School abides by the March 10 notification date. After that date, a rolling admission plan is in effect.

ADMISSIONS CORRESPONDENCE

Christopher J. Dietrich, Director of Admission and Financial Aid
The Williston Northampton School
19 Payson Avenue
Easthampton, Massachusetts 01027
United States
Phone: 413-529-3241
Fax: 413-527-9494
E-mail: admissions@williston.com
Web site: http://www.williston.com

WINDWARD SCHOOL

Los Angeles, California

Type: Coeducational day college-preparatory school
Grades: 7–12; Middle School 7–8; Upper School 9–12
Enrollment: 550
Head of School: Thomas W. Gilder

THE SCHOOL

A dynamic education, a nurturing community—that's the mission of Windward School. Founded in 1971 in order to provide a unique educational opportunity for Westside young people, the School takes its name from Shirley Windward, one of Windward's founders, whose dedication to the School has become legendary.

Under the leadership of Tom Gilder, who became Head of School in 1987, the School has continued to broaden its academic programs and to incorporate areas of social concern and global awareness into the classroom and extracurricular activities.

From its founding, two concepts have been fundamental to Windward School. The first, that educators and young people should work together in an environment that encourages them to be responsible, caring, well informed, ethical, and prepared. Secondly, education should provide a basis for lifelong growth, and the School should therefore concern itself with every facet of the student's life.

Today, Windward School stands as a living tribute to its many graduates and the hard work of innumerable individuals. Windward students attend the colleges of their choice around the country, and as working adults they have shown that they can succeed and prosper. Never content to rest on its laurels, Windward continues to pursue innovation, even as it remains faithful to the vision of its founders.

A not-for-profit corporation, Windward is governed by a 25-member Board of Trustees and an administrative team centered by the Head of School. The Western Association of Schools and Colleges accredits Windward. The School holds membership in the National Association of Independent Schools, the Independent School Alliance for Minority Affairs, A Better Chance, Independent School Management, the Educational Records Bureau, and the California Association of Independent Schools.

ACADEMIC PROGRAM

Fundamental to the Windward School philosophy is the belief that secondary education must engage more than the mind alone. Allowing young people to participate in a range of academic and extracurricular experiences fosters social growth and responsibility, as well as personal development. Woven through the traditional college-preparatory courses—English language and literature, a complex social studies curriculum, mathematics, science, and foreign languages—are opportunities that enable students to be actively involved in their own education.

Windward's comprehensive and rigorous course of study teaches students to think independently, to reason with care and logic, to write and speak with clarity, and to identify and develop their aesthetic talents. This strong academic preparation is complemented by the development of ethics, character, and people skills. The School hopes its graduates will go forth from Windward with a strong sense of personal integrity, self-confidence, and pride in their particular talents, inspired by learning, and prepared for college and for life in the twenty-first century.

At Windward, the average class size is 15 students. In academic areas, courses are sectioned on the basis of interest and ability, and Advanced Placement courses are offered in every discipline. The minimum course load for students in grades 7–10 is six. Students in grades 11–12 may opt for an alteration of this pattern, though approval of the grade-level deans is required, and students are actively encouraged to take six or seven classes.

In the Upper School, minimum course requirements are one English course each year through grade 12, one history course each year through grade 12 (seniors who wish to take two courses in another discipline may petition to waive the grade 12 history requirement), one mathematics course each year through grade 11, one science course each year through grade 10, one science course in either grade 11 or grade 12 (this must include one year of laboratory science), completion of Level III in one foreign language or completion of Level II in each of two foreign languages (continuation of foreign language through grade 11 is required), one arts course each year through grade 10, and one physical education course each year through grade 10 (students in grades 9 and 10 who compete in an interscholastic team sport are excused from physical education during that sport's season).

Community service has long been at the heart of the Windward tradition. Beginning in Middle School, service learning is a core component of the program, and in the Upper School, all students are required to complete two separate and extensive community service projects prior to graduation.

Windward School provides numerous opportunities for students to learn far from the gates of the campus. These experiences provide our students with dynamic learning opportunities that prepare them to be twenty-first century learners, scholars, and global citizens. The School's World Language, Global Scholars, and Experiential Learning departments offer trips around the globe that focus on language study and immersion, global leadership, and service learning. Recent groups have travelled to Spain, France, Nicaragua, and Tahiti. The science department's active learning model enables students to do research in both the Florida Everglades and Guatemala. An extensive retreats program allows Windward students to travel as classes to retreat centers in scenic areas of California and to the East Coast as part of the School's highly regarded Junior college trip. Finally, students travel and represent Windward at conferences and competitions across the globe as members of clubs and teams such as debate, thespians, athletics, and peer writing tutors to name a few.

FACULTY AND ADVISERS

The Windward faculty consists of 75 full- and part-time members (37 women and 38 men). Seventy-three percent have advanced degrees, with 11 possessing doctorates. Thomas W. Gilder, Head of School, was appointed in 1987.

In selecting its faculty members, Windward looks for individuals who enjoy the art of teaching, who are enthusiastic about working with adolescents, who will involve themselves in the nonacademic life of the School, and who have lively personal interests of their own. Every faculty member at Windward is an integral component in the life of the School. Faculty benefits at Windward are generous on all accounts and include financial support for continuing education and the funding of faculty-generated betterment opportunities.

COLLEGE ADMISSION COUNSELING

The college counseling program is directly linked to Windward's mission of providing a dynamic education in a nurturing environment. As such, the School works closely to support its students and their families through every stage of the college search process, beginning in the tenth grade. Windward's college counselors not only serve students as academic-schedule advisers, but also help them explore extracurricular and summer options. The counseling program reflects both the depth and the breadth of students' interests, and the School strives to find the best colleges for Windward students. Representatives of more than 100 different colleges and universities come to Windward each year to meet its students. Additional support in exploring college options is provided through an East Coast college trip for eleventh grade students and workshops with topics ranging from interview tips to the college essay.

Last year's graduating class of 89 students matriculated to more than fifty different colleges and universities. Students in the last several graduating classes chose between such diverse opportunities as Barnard, Berkeley, Boston College, Colby, Columbia, Emory, George Washington, Harvard, Kenyon, Michigan, Princeton, Rhode Island School of Design, Rice, Stanford, Tufts, Vassar, Washington (St. Louis), Wesleyan, Yale, and the Universities of Pennsylvania, Texas, and Wisconsin. Windward places the utmost importance upon each senior having options from which to choose, and its college counselors seek to guide students to discover the college or university best suited to their individual needs and aspirations.

STUDENT BODY AND CONDUCT

Windward has 550 students in grades 7–12. The average class size is 15 students, allowing teachers to offer individualized attention.

The student government is directed by a group of 20 prefects, selected on the basis of community respect, personal integrity, and the ability to positively affect the life in the community. By working closely with the adults at Windward, acting as intermediaries, organizing School activities, and leading by example, the prefects help to set the tone of the School. Of primary importance is the cultivation of respect and consideration for others and their property, the enhancement of relationships between faculty members and students, and the general well-being of the student body. The prefects are expected to respect Windward's standards in their personal conduct and in the way in which they lead others.

At Windward, the breaking of major School rules (lying, cheating, stealing, or using or possessing drugs or alcohol) is a pressing matter and typically leads to dismissal. A committee headed by the appropriate division-level Dean of Students handles disciplinary matters and refers matters to the appropriate division head for final consideration. Beyond rules and regulations, however, the School's deeply ingrained code of honor expects all students to offer both civility and compassion to other students and to teachers, staff members, and their own families. In fact, this expectation is one of the defining characteristics of Windward School.

Under the oversight of the Head of School, the Middle and Upper School Directors oversee the successful operation of the School and ensure that appropriate procedures are in place for students to enjoy their Windward experience and to be safe in the knowledge that discipline is expected of all community members.

ACADEMIC FACILITIES

Windward moved to its present 9-acre site in 1982, envisioning then the pastoral campus familiar to today's Windward students. As the School's programs have expanded, new facilities have been added to the campus. In 2002, the School constructed a ten-room classroom building, the Lewis Jackson Memorial Sports Center, the Student Pavilion, the Arts Center, and renovated the playing fields. A state-of-the-art library/learning center with performing arts studios and broadcast production center and a science/math center opened in 2009.

ATHLETICS

There is a suitable level of athletics for every student. Some students seek out competitive accomplishment in one sport through years of participation, while others take advantage of Windward's breadth of offerings to begin new sports at the introductory level. The physical education and athletic programs emphasize acquiring lifetime skills, shaping confident attitudes about oneself as an individual and a contributing member of a group, and developing along the way a true sense of integrity and fairness.

There are junior varsity and varsity offerings in most sports, including football, soccer, baseball, cross-country, tennis, volleyball, basketball, and golf.

The Lewis Jackson Memorial Sports Center houses a weight training facility, meeting space, and trophy room display, while the gymnasium offers basketball and volleyball courts. The beauty of the playing fields, which are built to university and professional specifications, offers all participating students a chance to play at their best.

EXTRACURRICULAR OPPORTUNITIES

An array of extracurricular opportunities is available to students through period eight activity programs. Period eight is a block of scheduled time that is set aside twice a week for clubs, study hall, and other activities that provide extracurricular opportunities for Upper School students. Students choose from a wide variety of activities that include robotics, debate, yoga, ceramics, chorus, the yearbook, the newspaper, junior senate, and comedy sports. Students are encouraged to participate and to explore interests that support the development of talents and strengths that are not just limited to academic success.

DAILY LIFE

Beginning at 8 each morning and ending at 3 p.m., both Middle and Upper Schools utilize a five-day schedule cycle. Monday mornings offer an all-School meeting for both Middle and Upper School students and faculty members, and there is a morning nutrition period five days a week. Seniors may take lunch off campus.

COSTS AND FINANCIAL AID

Tuition for 2012–13 was $32,455. The School's philosophy is to avoid extra charges for sports, field trips, or other activities offered through the School. Approximately 19 percent of the students at the School receive need-based scholarship opportunities.

ADMISSIONS INFORMATION

In every year, more students wish to become members of the Windward community than can be admitted. The admissions office works diligently to ensure that students who are accepted offer positive contributions to the community and succeed in Windward's challenging academic environment. The School seeks qualified students of diverse economic, social, ethnic, and racial backgrounds. The ISEE, grades, recommendations from the previous school, and an interview with Windward admissions personnel are required for all applicants. Openings exist traditionally for grades 7 and 9, although students may apply for grades 8 and 10 with permission of the admissions office. Applicants to Windward should all possess admirable strengths of character, be positive contributors to school and community, and attain high grades at their present schools.

APPLICATION TIMETABLE

Inquiries are welcome throughout the year, though the deadline for application for the following year is in December. Interviews and tours of the campus begin as soon as all faculty and staff members have returned in September.

ADMISSIONS CORRESPONDENCE

Sharon Pearline
Director of Admission
Windward School
11350 Palms Boulevard
Los Angeles, California 90066
United States
Phone: 310-391-7127
Fax: 310-397-5655
Web site: http://www.windwardschool.org

YORK PREPARATORY SCHOOL

New York, New York

Type: Coeducational day college-preparatory school
Grades: 6–12: Middle School, 6–8; Upper School, 9–12
Enrollment: 357
Head of School: Ronald P. Stewart, Headmaster

THE SCHOOL

York Prep is a college-preparatory school where contemporary methods enliven a strong, academically challenging, traditional curriculum. In a city known for its diversity of private schools, York Prep has developed a unique program that leads students to their highest potential. The School's approach emphasizes independent thought, builds confidence, and sends graduates on to the finest colleges and universities. At York, every student finds opportunities to flourish. York Prep believes that success breeds success, and excellence in academics, arts, or sports creates self-confidence that enhances all aspects of life, both in and out of the classroom.

York Prep was established in 1969 by its current Headmaster, Ronald P. Stewart, and his wife, Jayme Stewart, Director of College Guidance. Situated on West 68th Street between Columbus Avenue and Central Park West, the School is well served by public transportation. Consequently, it attracts students from all over the metropolitan area. York Prep takes full advantage of the prime location, with regular visits to museums, parks, and theaters, all of which are easily accessible.

York Prep is approved by the New York State Board of Regents and accredited by the Middle States Association of Colleges and Schools.

ACADEMIC PROGRAM

The curriculum is designed to develop the superior academic skills necessary for future success. Close attention to each student's needs ensures that progress toward personal excellence is carefully guided.

Students must complete 21 credits for graduation: 4 in English, 4 in math, 4 in science, 4 in history, a minimum of 3 in foreign language, 1 in art or music, and ½ in health.

Eleventh and twelfth graders choose from a number of course offerings in every subject area. In addition to selecting one course from each required category, a student must choose an elective from a variety of options that range from the creative and performing arts to the analytical sciences. Students are required to carry at least five major subjects a year plus physical education.

York Prep is proud of its commitment to community service. Student volunteer work benefits others, helps students realize their full potential, builds a well-rounded individual, and establishes a closer relationship between the school and community. Colleges expect students to have volunteer experience and York Prep College Guidance strongly urges students to perform 25 hours of community service per year during high school as a mark of integrity, responsibility, and citizenship.

Classes at York are small—the average class has 15 students. There are close student-teacher relations and all students begin their day with a morning "house" period. Each student's academic and social progress is carefully monitored by the teachers, advisers, and deans of the Upper and Middle Schools. The deans, in turn, keep the Headmaster and the Principal informed at weekly meetings. In addition, the Headmaster and Principal maintain close relationships with the students. All of York's administrators, including the Headmaster and Principal, teach courses and are readily available to students and parents alike. At the close of each day, there is a period when students may go to faculty members or advisers for help.

Parents are kept informed of a student's progress through individual reports posted on "Edline," a component of the York Prep Web site, every Friday. Each family signs in with a unique password to see their child's progress in all academic subjects. The annual Curriculum Night, in which parents become students for an evening by attending their child's truncated classes, provides a good overview of the course work and the faculty members. Parent involvement is encouraged, and there is an active Parents' Association.

FACULTY AND ADVISERS

York Prep is proud of having maintained a stable faculty of outstanding and dedicated individuals. New teachers join the staff periodically, creating a nice balance between youth and experience.

There are 64 full-time faculty members, including 2 college guidance counselors, 15 reading and learning specialists, 2 computer specialists, and a librarian.

Mr. Ronald P. Stewart, the founding Headmaster, is a graduate of Oxford University (B.A., 1965; M.A., 1966; B.C.L., 1968), where he also taught.

COLLEGE ADMISSION COUNSELING

York Prep has a notable college guidance program. Mrs. Jayme Stewart, the Director of College Guidance, is well known for her expertise, experience, and authorship of *How to Get into the College of Your Choice.* She meets with all tenth graders to outline the program and then meets individually with eleventh graders and their parents. Extensive meetings continue through the twelfth grade on an individual basis. In addition, the eleventh and twelfth graders take college guidance as a course where they write their essays, research colleges, and complete their applications during school hours.

One hundred percent of York Prep's graduating students attend college. The ultimate aim of the college guidance program is the placement of each student in the college best suited to him or her. More than 85 percent of York Prep graduates are accepted to, attend, and finish at their first- or second-choice college. Graduates are currently attending schools that include Barnard, Berkeley, Bowdoin, Colgate, Columbia, Cornell, Franklin and Marshall, Hamilton, Harvard, Hobart, Johns Hopkins, MIT, Oberlin, Pennsylvania, Skidmore, Vassar, Wesley, and the University of Michigan. Numerous college representatives visit the School regularly to meet with interested students.

STUDENT BODY AND CONDUCT

There are 357 students enrolled at York Prep. York Prep students reside in all five boroughs of New York City as well as Long Island, northern New Jersey, and Westchester County. The School has a student code of conduct and a dress code. The elected student council is also an integral part of life at York Prep.

ACADEMIC FACILITIES

Located steps from Central Park at 40 West 68th Street, York Prep is a seven-story granite building housing two modern science laboratories, state-of-the-art computer equipment, performance and art studios, and a sprung hardwood gymnasium with weight and locker room facilities. The classrooms are spacious and airy, carpeted, and climate controlled. All classrooms have computers and audiovisual (AV) projectors. High-speed Internet access is available for the entire School and enables students to e-mail their teachers and review homework assignments. The building is wheelchair accessible and is located near Lincoln Center on a safe and lovely tree-lined street.

ATHLETICS

All students are required to take courses in physical education and health each year. A varied and extensive program and after-school selection offer students the opportunity to participate in competitive, noncompetitive, team, and individual sports. York Prep is a playing member of several athletics leagues.

EXTRACURRICULAR OPPORTUNITIES

The Student Council organizes regular social events and trips. The School provides a wide range of extracurricular activities, including Model UN, golf, electric blues band, beekeeping, and a drama club.

DAILY LIFE

The School day begins at 8:40 with a 10-minute house period. Academic classes of 42-minute duration begin at 8:56. There is a midmorning break at 10:24. Lunch period is from 12:08 to 12:50, Mondays through Thursdays, and classes end at 3:12. Following dismissal, teachers are available for extra help. During this time, clubs and sports teams also meet. On Fridays the school day ends at 1:35.

SUMMER PROGRAMS

The School provides workshops during the summer, both in study skills and in academic courses, most of which are set up on an individual tutorial basis. In addition, the athletic department provides summer sports camps.

COSTS AND FINANCIAL AID

Tuition for the 2012–13 academic year ranged from $40,700 to $41,300. More than 30 percent of the student body receives some financial assistance. During the previous year, $1 million was offered in scholarship assistance.

ADMISSIONS INFORMATION

York Prep seeks to enroll students of above-average intelligence with the will and ability to complete college-preparatory work. Students are accepted on the basis of their applications, ISEE or SSAT* test scores, writing samples, and interviews.

APPLICATION TIMETABLE

York conforms to the notification guidelines established by the Independent Schools Admissions Association of Greater New York. Subsequent applications are processed on a rolling admissions basis. Requests for financial aid should be made at the time of application for entrance.

ADMISSIONS CORRESPONDENCE

Elizabeth Norton, Director of Enrollment
Cathy Minaudo, Director of Admissions
York Preparatory School
40 West 68th Street
New York, New York 10023
United States
Phone: 212-362-0400
Fax: 212-362-7424
E-mail: enorton@yorkprep.org
cminaudo@yorkprep.org
Web site: http://www.yorkprep.org

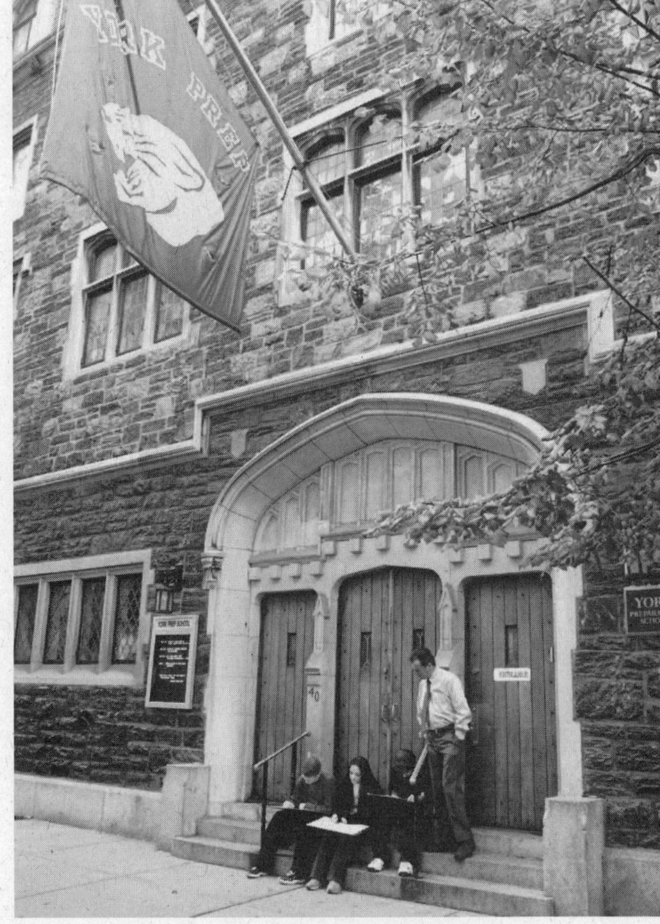

Special Needs Schools

AMERICAN ACADEMY

12200 West Broward Boulevard
Plantation, Florida 33325

Head of School: William R. Laurie

General Information Coeducational day college-preparatory, arts, and technology school; primarily serves underachievers, students with learning disabilities, individuals with Attention Deficit Disorder, dyslexic students, and slow learners, and those with lowered self-esteem and confidence. Grades 1–12. Founded: 1965. Setting: suburban. Nearest major city is Fort Lauderdale. 40-acre campus. 11 buildings on campus. Approved or accredited by Association of Independent Schools of Florida, Southern Association of Colleges and Schools, and Florida Department of Education. Total enrollment: 297. Upper school average class size: 14. Upper school faculty-student ratio: 1:12. There are 175 required school days per year for Upper School students. Upper School students typically attend 5 days per week. The average school day consists of 7 hours and 15 minutes.

Upper School Student Profile Grade 9: 34 students (22 boys, 12 girls); Grade 10: 39 students (29 boys, 10 girls); Grade 11: 44 students (32 boys, 12 girls); Grade 12: 33 students (18 boys, 15 girls).

Faculty School total: 32. In upper school: 3 men, 18 women; 19 have advanced degrees.

Subjects Offered Algebra, American history, American literature, anatomy, art, band, biology, business mathematics, ceramics, chemistry, chorus, computer graphics, computer science, creative writing, drafting, drama, drawing, earth science, English, English literature, environmental science, fine arts, French, geometry, health, jazz, mathematics, music appreciation, oceanography, orchestra, photography, physical education, physical science, science, sculpture, Spanish, theater, vocal music, weight training, word processing, world geography, world history, world literature, writing, yearbook.

Graduation Requirements 20th century history, arts and fine arts (art, music, dance, drama), computer science, English, mathematics, physical education (includes health), science, social studies (includes history), must be accepted to a college, 120 community service hours over 4 years of high school. Community service is required.

Special Academic Programs Honors section; independent study; academic accommodation for the gifted, the musically talented, and the artistically talented; remedial reading and/or remedial writing; remedial math; programs in English, mathematics, general development for dyslexic students; ESL (2 students enrolled).

College Admission Counseling 35 students graduated in 2012; all went to college, including Broward College; Florida Atlantic University; Lynn University; Nova Southeastern University; Palm Beach State College.

Student Life Upper grades have uniform requirement, student council. Discipline rests primarily with faculty.

Summer Programs Remediation, enrichment, advancement, ESL, art/fine arts, computer instruction programs offered; session focuses on remediation and make-up courses; held on campus; accepts boys and girls; open to students from other schools. 400 students usually enrolled. 2013 schedule: June 10 to August 8. Application deadline: none.

Tuition and Aid Day student tuition: $25,418–$29,399. Tuition installment plan (monthly payment plans, semester payment plan, annual payment plan). Tuition reduction for siblings, need-based scholarship grants available.

Admissions Traditional secondary-level entrance grade is 9. Psychoeducational evaluation, SAT and Slosson Intelligence required. Deadline for receipt of application materials: none. Application fee required: $100. On-campus interview required.

Athletics Interscholastic: baseball (boys), basketball (b,g), cheering (g), cross-country running (b,g), dance (g), dance squad (g), diving (b,g), football (b), golf (b,g), lacrosse (b,g), roller hockey (b), soccer (b,g), softball (g), swimming and diving (b,g), tennis (b,g), track and field (b,g), volleyball (b,g), weight lifting (b), weight training (b,g), winter soccer (b,g), wrestling (b). 7 PE instructors, 4 coaches, 1 athletic trainer.

Computers Computers are regularly used in graphic arts, literary magazine, newspaper, Web site design, word processing, writing, yearbook classes. Computer network features include on-campus library services, online commercial services, Internet access, Internet filtering or blocking technology, Questia. Student e-mail accounts and computer access in designated common areas are available to students. Students grades are available online. The school has a published electronic and media policy.

Contact William R. Laurie, President. 954-472-0022. Fax: 954-472-3088. Web site: www.ahschool.com

ARROWSMITH SCHOOL

245 St. Clair Avenue West
Toronto, Ontario M4V 1R3, Canada

Head of School: Ms. Barbara Arrowsmith Young

General Information Coeducational day school; primarily serves underachievers, students with learning disabilities, and dyslexic students. Ungraded, ages 6–20. Founded: 1980. Setting: urban. 1 building on campus. Approved or accredited by Ontario Ministry of Education and Ontario Department of Education. Language of instruction: English. Total enrollment: 75. Upper school average class size: 20. Upper school faculty-student ratio: 1:10. Upper School students typically attend 5 days per week. The average school day consists of 7 hours and 30 minutes.

Faculty School total: 9. In upper school: 2 men, 2 women.

Special Academic Programs Remedial reading and/or remedial writing; remedial math; programs in English, mathematics for dyslexic students.

College Admission Counseling 10 students graduated in 2012; 8 went to college, including University of Toronto; York University. Other: 2 went to work.

Student Life Upper grades have specified standards of dress. Discipline rests primarily with faculty.

Tuition and Aid Day student tuition: CAN$22,000. Tuition installment plan (monthly payment plans).

Admissions Traditional secondary-level entrance age is 14. For fall 2012, 20 students applied for upper-level admission, 20 were accepted, 20 enrolled. Achievement tests, Cognitive Abilities Test, Differential Aptitude Test, Oral and Written Language Scales, Otis-Lennon Mental Ability Test, Raven (Aptitude Test); school's own exam, Reading for Understanding, school's own test, Wide Range Achievement Test, WISC/Woodcock-Johnson or writing sample required. Deadline for receipt of application materials: none. No application fee required. Interview required.

Computers Computer resources include Internet access.

Contact Ms. Daina Luszczek, Receptionist. 416-963-4962. Fax: 416-963-5017. E-mail: dluzchek@arrowsmithprogram.ca. Web site: www.arrowsmithschool.org

ASSETS SCHOOL

One Ohana Nui Way
Honolulu, Hawaii 96818

Head of School: Mr. Paul Singer

General Information Coeducational day college-preparatory, arts, and technology school; primarily serves students with learning disabilities, individuals with Attention Deficit Disorder, dyslexic students, and gifted/talented students. Grades K–12. Founded: 1955. Setting: urban. 3-acre campus. 5 buildings on campus. Approved or accredited by Headmasters' Conference, The Hawaii Council of Private Schools, Western Association of Schools and Colleges, and Hawaii Department of Education. Member of National Association of Independent Schools. Endowment: $607,632. Total enrollment: 339. Upper school average class size: 7. Upper school faculty-student ratio: 1:8. There are 169 required school days per year for Upper School students. Upper School students typically attend 5 days per week. The average school day consists of 5 hours and 58 minutes.

Upper School Student Profile Grade 9: 24 students (19 boys, 5 girls); Grade 10: 30 students (20 boys, 10 girls); Grade 11: 34 students (21 boys, 13 girls); Grade 12: 29 students (20 boys, 9 girls).

Faculty School total: 68. In upper school: 9 men, 17 women; 18 have advanced degrees.

Subjects Offered 1 1/2 elective credits, algebra, American history, art, biology, business skills, calculus, chemistry, computer science, consumer education, creative writing, current events, earth science, economics, English, fine arts, fitness, general science, geometry, government/civics, health, humanities, independent study, integrated science, keyboarding, literature, marine biology, marine science, mathematics, music, music appreciation, philosophy, physical education, physics, pre-calculus, psychology, sign language, social studies, Spanish, statistics, theater, trigonometry, women's health, woodworking, word processing, world history, world literature.

Graduation Requirements Arts and fine arts (art, music, dance, drama), biology, business skills (includes word processing), computer science, English, foreign language, mathematics, physical education (includes health), science, social studies (includes history), study skills, participation in mentorship program in 10th-12th grades.

Special Academic Programs Academic accommodation for the gifted; remedial reading and/or remedial writing; remedial math; programs in English, mathematics, general development for dyslexic students.

College Admission Counseling 24 students graduated in 2012; 23 went to college, including Chaminade University of Honolulu; Hawai'i Pacific University; McMaster University; Oregon State University; University of Hawaii at Manoa. Other: 1 went to work.

Student Life Upper grades have specified standards of dress, student council, honor system. Discipline rests primarily with faculty.

Summer Programs Advancement programs offered; session focuses on learning strategies for students in the 9th and 10th grades; held on campus; accepts boys and girls; open to students from other schools. 40 students usually enrolled. 2013 schedule: June 10 to July 19. Application deadline: none.

Tuition and Aid Day student tuition: $21,730. Tuition installment plan (monthly payment plans, individually arranged payment plans, semester payment plan). Need-based scholarship grants, partial tuition remission for children of staff available. In 2012–13, 37% of upper-school students received aid. Total amount of financial aid awarded in 2012–13: $170,000.

Admissions Traditional secondary-level entrance grade is 9. For fall 2012, 23 students applied for upper-level admission, 11 were accepted, 8 enrolled. WISC III or other aptitude measures; standardized achievement test required. Deadline for receipt of application materials: none. Application fee required: $75. On-campus interview required.

Athletics Interscholastic: baseball (boys), basketball (b,g), bowling (b,g), canoeing/kayaking (b,g), cheering (g), cross-country running (b,g), diving (b,g), football (b), golf (b,g), gymnastics (g), judo (b,g), kayaking (b,g), sailing (b,g), soccer (b,g), softball (g), swimming and diving (b,g), tennis (b,g), track and field (b,g), volleyball (b,g), water polo (b,g), wrestling (b,g); intramural: basketball (b,g), volleyball (b,g); coed intramural: basketball, dance, flag football, kickball, Newcombe ball, soccer, softball, tai chi, touch football, ultimate Frisbee, volleyball, whiffle ball, yoga. 2 PE instructors, 4 coaches.

Computers Computers are regularly used in English, mathematics, photography, science classes. Computer network features include on-campus library services, Internet access, wireless campus network, Internet filtering or blocking technology, assistive technology for learning differences. Computer access in designated common areas is available to students. The school has a published electronic and media policy.

Contact Ms. Sandi Tadaki, Director of Admissions. 808-423-1356. Fax: 808-422-1920. E-mail: stadaki@assets-school.net. Web site: www.assets-school.net

ATLANTIS ACADEMY

9600 Southwest 107th Avenue
Miami, Florida 33176

Head of School: Mr. Carlos Aballi

General Information Coeducational day general academic school; primarily serves underachievers, students with learning disabilities, individuals with Attention Deficit Disorder, individuals with emotional and behavioral problems, dyslexic students, and Autism Spectrum Disorder. Ungraded, ages 5–18. Founded: 1976. Setting: suburban. 3-acre campus. 1 building on campus. Approved or accredited by Florida Council of Independent Schools, Southern Association of Colleges and Schools, and Florida Department of Education. Total enrollment: 156. Upper school average class size: 9. Upper school faculty-student ratio: 1:8. The average school day consists of 6 hours and 15 minutes.

Faculty School total: 26. In upper school: 5 men, 9 women; 3 have advanced degrees.

Subjects Offered Art, computer skills, French, language arts, mathematics, physical education, reading, science, social studies, Spanish.

Special Academic Programs Remedial reading and/or remedial writing; remedial math; programs in English, mathematics, general development for dyslexic students; ESL (3 students enrolled).

College Admission Counseling 12 students graduated in 2011; 8 went to college, including Florida International University; Lynn University; Miami Dade College; New York Institute of Technology. Other: 4 went to work.

Student Life Upper grades have uniform requirement. Discipline rests primarily with faculty.

Tuition and Aid Day student tuition: $14,000–$16,000. Tuition installment plan (monthly payment plans, semi-annual and annual payment plans). Need-based scholarship grants available. In 2011–12, 90% of upper-school students received aid. Total amount of financial aid awarded in 2011–12: $12,000.

Admissions Traditional secondary-level entrance age is 14. For fall 2011, 15 students applied for upper-level admission, 15 were accepted, 15 enrolled. Psychoeducational evaluation or school's own exam required. Deadline for receipt of application materials: none. No application fee required. On-campus interview required.

Athletics Interscholastic: basketball (boys, girls), flag football (b), tennis (b,g), volleyball (b,g); intramural: flag football (b); coed interscholastic: softball; coed intramural: golf, tennis. 1 PE instructor, 2 coaches.

Computers Computers are regularly used in art, English, foreign language, history, mathematics, science, social sciences classes. Computer network features include Internet access.

Contact Mr. Eric Smith, Assistant Director/Director of Admissions. 305-271-9771. Fax: 305-271-7078. E-mail: esmith@esa-education.com. Web site: miami.atlantisacademy.com

BACHMAN ACADEMY

414 Brymer Creek Road
McDonald, Tennessee 37353

Head of School: Mr. Mark A. Frizzell, M.Ed.

General Information Coeducational boarding and day college-preparatory, general academic, and vocational school; primarily serves underachievers, students with learning disabilities, individuals with Attention Deficit Disorder, dyslexic students, Non-verbal Learning Disorder, and Pervasive Developmental Disorder-Not Otherwise Specified. Grades 6–PG. Founded: 1999. Setting: rural. Nearest major city is Chattanooga. Students are housed in single-sex dormitories. 200-acre campus. 6 buildings on campus. Approved or accredited by Southern Association of Colleges and Schools, Southern Association of Independent Schools, and Tennessee Department of Education. Member of National Association of Independent Schools. Total enrollment: 35. Upper school average class size: 5. Upper school faculty-student ratio: 1:3. There are 169 required school days per year for Upper School students. Upper School students typically attend 5 days per week. The average school day consists of 7 hours and 30 minutes.

Upper School Student Profile Grade 9: 3 students (1 boy, 2 girls); Grade 10: 5 students (3 boys, 2 girls); Grade 11: 9 students (6 boys, 3 girls); Grade 12: 8 students (5 boys, 3 girls); Postgraduate: 2 students (1 boy, 1 girl). 69% of students are boarding students. 50% are state residents. 10 states are represented in upper school student body. 11% are international students. International students from Bermuda, China, India, and Nigeria.

Faculty School total: 12. In upper school: 6 men, 6 women; 3 have advanced degrees; 1 resides on campus.

Subjects Offered ACT preparation, agriculture, art, biology, calculus, carpentry, chemistry, English, equine management, equitation, leadership and service, mathematics, mechanics, personal finance, physics, pre-algebra, SAT preparation, social studies, Spanish, wellness, woodworking.

Graduation Requirements All courses as required by the State of TN Department of Education.

Special Academic Programs Honors section; accelerated programs; independent study; academic accommodation for the gifted; remedial reading and/or remedial writing; remedial math; programs in English, mathematics, general development for dyslexic students.

College Admission Counseling 5 students graduated in 2012; 4 went to college, including Chattanooga State Community College; Southern Adventist University. Other: 1 entered a postgraduate year.

Student Life Upper grades have uniform requirement, student council, honor system. Discipline rests primarily with faculty.

Summer Programs Remediation, enrichment, sports, art/fine arts programs offered; session focuses on learning disabilities; held on campus; accepts boys and girls; open to students from other schools. 150 students usually enrolled. 2013 schedule: July 1 to July 31. Application deadline: April 1.

Tuition and Aid Day student tuition: $18,779; 5-day tuition and room/board: $38,846; 7-day tuition and room/board: $48,275. Tuition installment plan (monthly payment plans, bi-annual payment plan, Your Tuition Solution). Need-based scholarship grants available. In 2012–13, 37% of upper-school students received aid. Total amount of financial aid awarded in 2012–13: $110,242.

Admissions Traditional secondary-level entrance grade is 9. For fall 2012, 52 students applied for upper-level admission, 19 were accepted, 10 enrolled. Any standardized test, Individual IQ, Achievement and behavior rating scale or WISC III or other aptitude measures; standardized achievement test required. Deadline for receipt of application materials: none. Application fee required: $100. Interview required.

Athletics Coed Intramural: archery, backpacking, basketball, billiards, bocce, bowling, canoeing/kayaking, dressage, drill team, equestrian sports, fishing, fitness, fitness walking, golf, hiking/backpacking, horseback riding, JROTC drill, kickball, outdoor activities, outdoor education, outdoor recreation, outdoor skills, outdoors, physical fitness, physical training, rafting, rappelling, rock climbing, ropes courses, strength & conditioning, swimming and diving, table tennis, tennis, volleyball, walking, wall climbing, weight training, wilderness, winter walking, yoga.

Computers Computers are regularly used in all academic classes. Computer network features include Internet access, wireless campus network, Internet filtering or blocking technology. Student e-mail accounts and computer access in designated common areas are available to students. The school has a published electronic and media policy.

Contact Mrs. Bridgette Owen, Director of Admissions. 423-479-4523 Ext. 41. Fax: 423-472-2718. E-mail: admissions@bachmanacademy.org. Web site: www.bachmanacademy.org/

BRIDGES ACADEMY

3921 Laurel Canyon Boulevard
Studio City, California 91604

Head of School: Carl Sabatino

General Information Coeducational day college-preparatory, arts, technology, and music, drama, talent development school; primarily serves gifted students with non-verbal learning differences. Grades 5–12. Founded: 1994. Setting: suburban. Nearest major city is Los Angeles. 4-acre campus. 3 buildings on campus. Approved or accredited by California Association of Independent Schools, Western Association of Schools and Colleges, and California Department of Education. Total enrollment: 134. Upper school average class size: 9. Upper school faculty-student ratio: 1:8. There are 174 required school days per year for Upper School students. Upper School students typically attend 5 days per week. The average school day consists of 5 hours and 15 minutes.

Upper School Student Profile Grade 9: 14 students (14 boys); Grade 10: 22 students (18 boys, 4 girls); Grade 11: 22 students (20 boys, 2 girls); Grade 12: 16 students (14 boys, 2 girls).

Faculty School total: 22. In upper school: 14 men, 8 women; 11 have advanced degrees.

Subjects Offered 20th century history, algebra, American government, American literature, anatomy and physiology, art, biology, calculus, chemistry, drama, economics, European history, European literature, film, genetics, geometry, Japanese, modern European history, music, non-Western literature, photography, physics, pre-calculus, senior project, Spanish, statistics, study skills, technology, U.S. history, world history.

Graduation Requirements Economics, English, foreign language, government, history, mathematics, performing arts, science, senior seminar, visual arts.

Special Academic Programs Honors section; academic accommodation for the gifted.

College Admission Counseling 15 students graduated in 2012; 13 went to college, including California State University, Northridge. Other: 2 had other specific plans. 56% scored over 600 on SAT critical reading, 24% scored over 600 on SAT math.
Student Life Discipline rests primarily with faculty.
Summer Programs Enrichment, sports, art/fine arts, computer instruction programs offered; session focuses on enrichment; held on campus; accepts boys and girls; open to students from other schools. 2013 schedule: June 1 to July 31. Application deadline: none.
Tuition and Aid Day student tuition: $31,411. Tuition installment plan (Insured Tuition Payment Plan, monthly payment plans). Need-based scholarship grants available. In 2012–13, 10% of upper-school students received aid.
Admissions Traditional secondary-level entrance grade is 9. For fall 2012, 11 students applied for upper-level admission, 7 were accepted, 5 enrolled. Deadline for receipt of application materials: March 1. Application fee required: $150. On-campus interview required.
Athletics Coed Interscholastic: basketball, cross-country running, track and field. 2 PE instructors, 1 coach.
Computers Computers are regularly used in all classes. Computer network features include Internet access, wireless campus network, Internet filtering or blocking technology. Campus intranet and student e-mail accounts are available to students. Students grades are available online.
Contact Doug Lenzini, Director of Admissions. 818-506-1091. Fax: 818-506-8094. E-mail: doug@bridges.edu. Web site: www.bridges.edu

CAMPHILL SPECIAL SCHOOL

1784 Fairview Road
Glenmoore, Pennsylvania 19343

Head of School: Mr. Bernard Wolf

General Information Coeducational boarding and day general academic, arts, and vocational school; primarily serves underachievers, intellectual and developmental disabilities, and mental retardation. Grades K–13. Founded: 1963. Setting: rural. Nearest major city is Philadelphia. Students are housed in on-campus single family homes. 82-acre campus. 1 building on campus. Approved or accredited by Association of Waldorf Schools of North America, Middle States Association of Colleges and Schools, National Council for Private School Accreditation, and Pennsylvania Department of Education. Total enrollment: 115. Upper school average class size: 9. Upper school faculty-student ratio: 1:5. There are 180 required school days per year for Upper School students. Upper School students typically attend 5 days per week. The average school day consists of 9 hours.
Upper School Student Profile Grade 9: 5 students (5 boys); Grade 10: 9 students (4 boys, 5 girls); Grade 11: 10 students (5 boys, 5 girls); Grade 12: 10 students (7 boys, 3 girls); Grade 13: 23 students (22 boys, 1 girl). 85% of students are boarding students. 72% are state residents. 12 states are represented in upper school student body. 3% are international students. International students from Jamaica; 1 other country represented in student body.
Faculty In upper school: 2 men, 2 women; 70 reside on campus.
Subjects Offered 20th century American writers, 20th century history, 20th century physics, 20th century world history, acting, agriculture, American Civil War, American culture, American democracy, American history, Ancient Greek, ancient history, ancient world history, animal husbandry, art, art and culture, art appreciation, astronomy, bell choir, biology, body human, botany, chemistry, choir, drama, drama performance, ecology, environmental education, eurythmy, gardening, geography, geometry, government, handbells, health and wellness, history, instruments, life skills, mathematics, medieval history, medieval literature, medieval/Renaissance history, meteorology, music, mythology, natural history, painting, physics, poetry, pottery, reading, science, Shakespeare, woodworking, zoology.
Special Academic Programs Remedial reading and/or remedial writing; remedial math.
Student Life Upper grades have student council. Discipline rests primarily with faculty.
Summer Programs Enrichment programs offered; session focuses on Extended School Year (ESY); held on campus; accepts boys and girls; not open to students from other schools. 45 students usually enrolled. 2013 schedule: June 29 to July 27.
Tuition and Aid Need-based scholarship grants available.
Admissions Traditional secondary-level entrance grade is 9. Deadline for receipt of application materials: none. No application fee required. On-campus interview required.
Contact 610-469-9236. Web site: www.camphillspecialschool.org

CHATHAM ACADEMY

4 Oglethorpe Professional Boulevard
Savannah, Georgia 31406

Head of School: Mrs. Carolyn M. Hannaford

General Information Coeducational day college-preparatory, general academic, and technology school; primarily serves underachievers, students with learning disabilities, individuals with Attention Deficit Disorder, dyslexic students, and different learning styles. Grades 1–12. Founded: 1978. Setting: suburban. 5-acre campus. 1 building on campus. Approved or accredited by Georgia Independent School Association, Southern Association of Colleges and Schools, and Georgia Department of Education. Endowment: $100,000. Total enrollment: 78. Upper school average class size: 10. Upper school faculty-student ratio: 1:10. There are 180 required school days per year for Upper School students. Upper School students typically attend 5 days per week. The average school day consists of 6 hours.
Upper School Student Profile Grade 9: 4 students (3 boys, 1 girl); Grade 10: 4 students (4 boys); Grade 11: 9 students (5 boys, 4 girls); Grade 12: 11 students (9 boys, 2 girls).
Faculty School total: 18. In upper school: 2 men, 8 women; 6 have advanced degrees.
Subjects Offered Algebra, American history, American literature, art, biology, earth science, economics, English, English literature, expository writing, geology, geometry, government/civics, grammar, history, keyboarding, mathematics, physical education, physical science, reading, SAT/ACT preparation, science, social studies, world history, world literature, writing.
Graduation Requirements Algebra, American government, American history, biology, British literature, chemistry, civics, composition, consumer economics, earth science, economics, electives, English, English composition, English literature, foreign language, French, grammar, marine biology, mathematics, physical education (includes health), physical science, reading/study skills, science, social studies (includes history), U.S. history.
Special Academic Programs Independent study; study at local college for college credit; remedial reading and/or remedial writing; remedial math; programs in English, mathematics, general development for dyslexic students.
College Admission Counseling 9 students graduated in 2011; 5 went to college, including Armstrong Atlantic State University; Savannah College of Art and Design. Other: 2 went to work, 2 had other specific plans.
Student Life Upper grades have uniform requirement, student council, honor system. Discipline rests primarily with faculty.
Tuition and Aid Day student tuition: $15,050. Tuition installment plan (monthly payment plans, individually arranged payment plans). Tuition reduction for siblings, need-based scholarship grants, Georgia Special Needs Scholarship available. In 2011–12, 33% of upper-school students received aid. Total amount of financial aid awarded in 2011–12: $90,200.
Admissions Traditional secondary-level entrance grade is 10. For fall 2011, 10 students applied for upper-level admission, 7 were accepted, 5 enrolled. Achievement tests, Individual IQ, Achievement and behavior rating scale, school's own test, Stanford Binet, Wechsler Individual Achievement Test, Wechsler Intelligence Scale for Children III, WISC or WAIS, WISC-R, Woodcock-Johnson Revised Achievement Test or writing sample required. Deadline for receipt of application materials: none. Application fee required: $50. Interview required.
Athletics Interscholastic: flag football (boys, girls), football (b), yoga (g); intramural: football (b), soccer (b,g); coed interscholastic: baseball, basketball, cheering, fitness, fitness walking, flag football; coed intramural: canoeing/kayaking, cheering, cooperative games, fitness, fitness walking, flag football, football, jump rope, kickball, Newcombe ball, outdoor activities, outdoor recreation, paddle tennis, physical fitness, physical training, soccer, whiffle ball. 1 PE instructor, 2 coaches.
Computers Computers are regularly used in all academic classes. Computer network features include Internet access, Internet filtering or blocking technology. The school has a published electronic and media policy.
Contact Mrs. Carolyn M. Hannaford, Principal. 912-354-4047. Fax: 912-354-4633. E-mail: channaford@chathamacademy.com. Web site: www.chathamacademy.com

CHELSEA SCHOOL

711 Pershing Avenue
Silver Spring, Maryland 20910

Head of School: Katherine Fedalen

General Information Coeducational day college-preparatory, general academic, arts, bilingual studies, and technology school; primarily serves students with learning disabilities, individuals with Attention Deficit Disorder, and dyslexic students. Grades 5–12. Founded: 1976. Setting: suburban. 10-acre campus. 3 buildings on campus. Approved or accredited by Maryland Department of Education. Total enrollment: 71. Upper school average class size: 8. Upper school faculty-student ratio: 1:8. There are 180 required school days per year for Upper School students. Upper School students typically attend 5 days per week. The average school day consists of 6 hours and 30 minutes.
Upper School Student Profile Grade 9: 13 students (10 boys, 3 girls); Grade 10: 12 students (11 boys, 1 girl); Grade 11: 17 students (11 boys, 6 girls); Grade 12: 17 students (12 boys, 5 girls).
Faculty School total: 19. In upper school: 10 men, 9 women.
Subjects Offered Algebra, American history, American literature, art, biology, calculus, career/college preparation, chemistry, community service, composition, computer graphics, computer technologies, computers, conceptual physics, earth and space science, earth science, English, English literature, environmental science, foreign language, geometry, health, health and wellness, independent study, information technology, math review, music, personal fitness, physical education, physics, pre-algebra, pre-calculus, reading, reading/study skills, remedial study skills, science, social skills, Spanish, state government, U.S. government, U.S. history, U.S. literature, wellness.

Graduation Requirements 20th century world history, algebra, American government, American history, art, biology, career/college preparation, chemistry, earth science, electives, English, English composition, English literature, general math, geometry, health and wellness, physical education (includes health), pre-algebra, Spanish, U.S. history.

Special Academic Programs Remedial reading and/or remedial writing; remedial math; programs in English, mathematics, general development for dyslexic students.

College Admission Counseling 25 students graduated in 2011; they went to Macalester College.

Student Life Upper grades have student council. Discipline rests primarily with faculty.

Tuition and Aid Day student tuition: $35,610. Tuition installment plan (individually arranged payment plans). Need-based scholarship grants available. In 2011–12, 14% of upper-school students received aid.

Admissions Traditional secondary-level entrance grade is 9. For fall 2011, 28 students applied for upper-level admission, 22 were accepted, 13 enrolled. Academic Profile Tests, Wechsler Individual Achievement Test, Wide Range Achievement Test, WISC III or other aptitude measures; standardized achievement test, WISC or WAIS, WISC-R or Woodcock-Johnson required. Deadline for receipt of application materials: none. Application fee required: $50. On-campus interview required.

Athletics Interscholastic: basketball (boys, girls), flagball (b); coed interscholastic: soccer, softball, track and field. 1 PE instructor.

Computers Computer network features include on-campus library services, Internet access, wireless campus network, Internet filtering or blocking technology. Campus intranet, student e-mail accounts, and computer access in designated common areas are available to students. The school has a published electronic and media policy.

Contact Debbie Lourie, Director of Admissions. 301-585-1430 Ext. 303. Fax: 301-585-0245. E-mail: dlourie@chelseaschool.edu. Web site: www.chelseaschool.edu

COPPER CANYON ACADEMY

PO Box 230
Rimrock, Arizona 86335

Head of School: Paul Taylor

General Information Girls' boarding college-preparatory and general academic school; primarily serves students with learning disabilities, individuals with Attention Deficit Disorder, and individuals with emotional and behavioral problems. Grades 9–12. Founded: 1998. Setting: rural. Nearest major city is Sedona. Students are housed in single-sex dormitories. 29-acre campus. 8 buildings on campus. Approved or accredited by CITA (Commission on International and Trans-Regional Accreditation), North Central Association of Colleges and Schools, and Arizona Department of Education. Total enrollment: 90. Upper school average class size: 10. Upper school faculty-student ratio: 1:10. Upper School students typically attend 5 days per week. The average school day consists of 6 hours.

Upper School Student Profile Grade 9: 20 students (20 girls); Grade 10: 20 students (20 girls); Grade 11: 25 students (25 girls); Grade 12: 25 students (25 girls). 100% of students are boarding students. 20% are state residents. 22 states are represented in upper school student body. 5% are international students.

Faculty School total: 12. In upper school: 5 men, 7 women; 3 have advanced degrees; 2 reside on campus.

Subjects Offered ACT preparation, acting, adolescent issues, advanced math, algebra, American Civil War, American government, American history, American literature, ancient history, ancient world history, applied arts, applied music, art, art and culture, art appreciation, art education, art history, arts, athletic training, athletics, ballet, ballet technique, basketball, biology, botany, British literature, business, business communications, business mathematics, calculus, career planning, character education, chemistry, child development, choir, chorus, civics, Civil War, civil war history, college admission preparation, college awareness, college counseling, college placement, college planning, college writing, communication skills, communications, community garden, community service, comparative civilizations, composition, computer applications, computer education, computer graphics, computer literacy, computer math, computer science, computer skills, computers, consumer mathematics, contemporary art, contemporary history, contemporary issues, creative arts, creative dance, creative writing, current events, dance, dance performance, decision making skills, drama, drama performance, drama workshop, dramatic arts, drawing, drawing and design, earth science, economics, economics and history, electives, English, English composition, English literature, equality and freedom, equestrian sports, equine management, equine science, ethical decision making, European history, European literature, experiential education, female experience in America, film appreciation, fine arts, fitness, food and nutrition, foreign language, foreign policy, French, gender issues, general science, geography, geology, geometry, global studies, government, government/civics, grammar, graphic arts, health, health and safety, health and wellness, health education, health science, heritage of American Women, history, history of dance, history of drama, home economics, human biology, human development, human sexuality, independent living, international studies, intro to computers, jazz dance, journalism, lab/keyboard, language, language and composition, language arts, leadership, leadership education training, learning strategies, library, life issues, life management skills, life skills, linear algebra, literature, literature by women, math applications, mathematics, modern dance, modern languages, moral and social development, music, music appreciation, music composition, music history, music performance, musical productions, musical theater, nature study, news writing, newspaper, non-Western literature, nutrition, oil painting, parenting, participation in sports, peer counseling, performing arts, personal development, personal growth, physical education, physics, play production, poetry, political science, political systems, portfolio art, pre-calculus, psychology, SAT preparation, SAT/ACT preparation, science, sex education, sexuality, Shakespeare, Shakespearean histories, social issues, sociology, softball, Spanish, Spanish literature, speech, speech and debate, sports, sports conditioning, stage and body movement, state history, statistics, student government, student publications, studio art, study skills, tap dance, theater, theater arts, theater history, theater production, trigonometry, U.S. government, U.S. government and politics, U.S. history, U.S. literature, visual and performing arts, visual arts, vocal music, volleyball, water color painting, weight fitness, weightlifting, wellness, Western literature, women in literature, women's health, women's literature, world civilizations, world cultures, world geography, world history, world studies, writing, writing, yoga.

Graduation Requirements Option of traditional academic graduation as well as graduation from the therapeutic side of school.

Special Academic Programs Accelerated programs; independent study; study at local college for college credit; academic accommodation for the gifted, the musically talented, and the artistically talented; programs in English, mathematics for dyslexic students.

Student Life Upper grades have uniform requirement, student council, honor system. Discipline rests primarily with faculty.

Tuition and Aid 7-day tuition and room/board: $6800. Middle-income loans, Keybank, prepGATE and Sallie Mae loans available. In 2012–13, 80% of upper-school students received aid. Total amount of financial aid awarded in 2012–13: $81,600.

Admissions Traditional secondary-level entrance grade is 10. For fall 2012, 400 students applied for upper-level admission, 150 were accepted, 90 enrolled. SAT required. Deadline for receipt of application materials: none. No application fee required.

Athletics Interscholastic: basketball, soccer, softball, volleyball; intramural: aerobics, aerobics/dance, badminton, ballet, basketball, cross-country running, dance, fitness, fitness walking, horseback riding, jogging, modern dance, physical fitness, physical training, soccer, softball, track and field, walking, yoga. 2 PE instructors, 1 coach, 1 athletic trainer.

Computers Computers are regularly used in all academic classes. Computer network features include Internet access, Internet filtering or blocking technology. Student e-mail accounts are available to students. Students grades are available online. The school has a published electronic and media policy.

Contact Stephanie Coleman, Admissions Counselor. 877-617-1222 Ext. 116. Fax: 928-567-1323. E-mail: stephaniecoleman@coppercanyonacademy.com. Web site: www.coppercanyonacademy.com

DENVER ACADEMY

4400 East Iliff Avenue
Denver, Colorado 80222

Head of School: Kevin Smith

General Information Coeducational day college-preparatory, general academic, arts, vocational, and technology school; primarily serves underachievers, students with learning disabilities, individuals with Attention Deficit Disorder, dyslexic students, and unique learning styles. Grades 1–12. Founded: 1972. Setting: urban. 22-acre campus. 19 buildings on campus. Approved or accredited by Association of Colorado Independent Schools and Colorado Department of Education. Member of National Association of Independent Schools. Endowment: $3 million. Total enrollment: 354. Upper school average class size: 14. Upper school faculty-student ratio: 1:8. There are 169 required school days per year for Upper School students. Upper School students typically attend 5 days per week. The average school day consists of 6 hours and 15 minutes.

Upper School Student Profile Grade 9: 38 students (27 boys, 11 girls); Grade 10: 51 students (43 boys, 8 girls); Grade 11: 48 students (35 boys, 13 girls); Grade 12: 63 students (44 boys, 19 girls).

Faculty School total: 63. In upper school: 26 men, 23 women; 18 have advanced degrees.

Subjects Offered ACT preparation, adolescent issues, algebra, American history, American literature, anatomy, art, art history, arts, baseball, basic skills, basketball, biology, botany, business, calculus, ceramics, chemistry, comparative cultures, computer applications, computer graphics, computer math, computer processing, computer programming, computer science, computer skills, creative writing, drama, dramatic arts, earth science, English, English literature, environmental science, ethics, European history, film, filmmaking, fine arts, geography, geometry, government/civics, grammar, health, history, life skills, mathematics, music, philosophy, photography, physical education, physics, physiology, psychology, science, social sciences, social studies, Spanish, speech, theater, trigonometry, values and decisions, world history, world literature, writing, yearbook.

Graduation Requirements Arts and fine arts (art, music, dance, drama), English, mathematics, physical education (includes health), science, social sciences, social studies (includes history).

Special Academic Programs Independent study; academic accommodation for the gifted; remedial reading and/or remedial writing; remedial math; programs in English, mathematics, general development for dyslexic students.

College Admission Counseling 54 students graduated in 2012; 48 went to college, including Colorado School of Mines; Metropolitan State University of Denver; University of Colorado Boulder; University of Colorado Denver; University of Northern Colorado. Other: 5 entered a postgraduate year, 1 had other specific plans.

Student Life Upper grades have specified standards of dress, student council, honor system. Discipline rests primarily with faculty.

Summer Programs Remediation, enrichment, advancement, art/fine arts, rigorous outdoor training, computer instruction programs offered; session focuses on academics, remediation, and summer fun camp; held both on and off campus; held at various locations around the city and the Rocky Mountains; accepts boys and girls; open to students from other schools. 150 students usually enrolled. 2013 schedule: June to July. Application deadline: June.

Tuition and Aid Day student tuition: $24,900. Tuition installment plan (monthly payment plans). Tuition reduction for siblings, need-based scholarship grants available. In 2012–13, 30% of upper-school students received aid.

Admissions For fall 2012, 35 students applied for upper-level admission, 32 were accepted, 28 enrolled. WISC/Woodcock-Johnson required. Deadline for receipt of application materials: none. Application fee required: $75. On-campus interview required.

Athletics Interscholastic: baseball (boys), basketball (b,g), cross-country running (b,g), golf (b), soccer (b,g), volleyball (g); intramural: volleyball (g); coed interscholastic: cheering, physical fitness, physical training; coed intramural: backpacking, basketball, boxing, canoeing/kayaking, climbing, cooperative games, fishing, flag football, golf, indoor hockey, indoor soccer, indoor track, jump rope, mountaineering, outdoor activities, rafting, rock climbing, skiing (downhill), soccer, swimming and diving, track and field, wall climbing. 4 PE instructors, 4 coaches.

Computers Computers are regularly used in basic skills, career exploration, career technology, college planning, drawing and design, English, foreign language, independent study, introduction to technology, mathematics, media arts, media production, media services, multimedia, music, occupational education, SAT preparation, science, writing, yearbook classes. Computer network features include on-campus library services, online commercial services, Internet access, wireless campus network, Internet filtering or blocking technology. Student e-mail accounts and computer access in designated common areas are available to students. Students grades are available online. The school has a published electronic and media policy.

Contact Janet Woolley, Director of Admissions. 303-777-5161. Fax: 303-777-5893. E-mail: jwoolley@denveracademy.org. Web site: www.denveracademy.org

EAGLE HILL SCHOOL

45 Glenville Road
Greenwich, Connecticut 06831

Head of School: Dr. Marjorie E. Castro

General Information Coeducational boarding college-preparatory, arts, and technology school; primarily serves students with learning disabilities, dyslexic students, and language-based learning disabilities. Grades 1–9. Founded: 1975. Setting: suburban. Nearest major city is New York, NY. Students are housed in single-sex by floor dormitories. 20-acre campus. 21 buildings on campus. Approved or accredited by Connecticut Association of Independent Schools and Connecticut Department of Education. Member of Secondary School Admission Test Board. Endowment: $18 million. Total enrollment: 230. Upper school average class size: 6. Upper school faculty-student ratio: 1:4.

Upper School Student Profile Grade 6: 45 students (45 boys); Grade 7: 45 students (45 boys); Grade 8: 45 students (45 boys); Grade 9: 25 students (25 boys). 30% of students are boarding students. 50% are state residents. 4 states are represented in upper school student body.

Faculty School total: 76. In upper school: 15 men, 20 women; 33 have advanced degrees; 35 reside on campus.

Subjects Offered Art, English, health, history, mathematics, music, physical education, science, technology.

Graduation Requirements Arts and fine arts (art, music, dance, drama), computer science, English, mathematics, physical education (includes health), science, social sciences, social studies (includes history), study skills.

Special Academic Programs Remedial reading and/or remedial writing; remedial math; programs in English, mathematics, general development for dyslexic students.

College Admission Counseling 70 students graduated in 2012; they went to Purnell School; Rumsey Hall School; The Forman School; The Harvey School.

Student Life Upper grades have specified standards of dress, student council, honor system. Discipline rests primarily with faculty.

Tuition and Aid Day student tuition: $59,125; 5-day tuition and room/board: $78,075. Tuition installment plan (monthly payment plans). Need-based scholarship grants available.

Admissions For fall 2012, 75 students applied for upper-level admission, 43 were accepted, 40 enrolled. Psychoeducational evaluation and Wechsler Intelligence Scale for Children III required. Deadline for receipt of application materials: none. Application fee required: $100. On-campus interview required.

Athletics Interscholastic: baseball, basketball (g), cheering (g), field hockey (g), lacrosse; intramural: aerobics (g), aerobics/dance (g), aerobics/Nautilus, flag football, football, lacrosse (g); coed interscholastic: basketball, cross-country running, ice hockey; coed intramural: basketball, bicycling, billiards, canoeing/kayaking, dance, fitness, fitness walking, floor hockey, Frisbee, golf, gymnastics, ice skating, jogging, judo, martial arts, outdoor activities, outdoor education, outdoor recreation, physical fitness, physical training, volleyball, yoga. 1 PE instructor, 1 athletic trainer.

Computers Computers are regularly used in English, history, mathematics, science classes. Computer network features include on-campus library services, online commercial services, Internet access, wireless campus network, Internet filtering or blocking technology, digital lab, iMovie, Active Boards, Intranet. The school has a published electronic and media policy.

Contact Mr. Thomas Cone, Director of Admissions and Placement. 203-622-9240 Ext. 648. Fax: 203-622-0914. E-mail: t.cone@eaglehill.org. Web site: www.eaglehillschool.org

EAGLE HILL SCHOOL

PO Box 116
242 Old Petersham Road
Hardwick, Massachusetts 01037

Head of School: Peter J. McDonald

General Information Coeducational boarding and day college-preparatory and arts school; primarily serves students with learning disabilities, individuals with Attention Deficit Disorder, dyslexic students, and non-verbal learning disabilities. Grades 8–12. Founded: 1967. Setting: small town. Nearest major city is Worcester. Students are housed in single-sex dormitories. 225-acre campus. 16 buildings on campus. Approved or accredited by Association of Independent Schools in New England, Massachusetts Office of Child Care Services, New England Association of Schools and Colleges, and The Association of Boarding Schools. Member of National Association of Independent Schools and Secondary School Admission Test Board. Endowment: $5 million. Total enrollment: 205. Upper school average class size: 5. Upper school faculty-student ratio: 1:4. There are 165 required school days per year for Upper School students. Upper School students typically attend 5 days per week. The average school day consists of 6 hours and 20 minutes.

Upper School Student Profile Grade 9: 49 students (31 boys, 18 girls); Grade 10: 48 students (32 boys, 16 girls); Grade 11: 48 students (21 boys, 27 girls); Grade 12: 51 students (31 boys, 20 girls). 90% of students are boarding students. 33% are state residents. 29 states are represented in upper school student body. 5% are international students. International students from Bermuda, Canada, Mexico, New Zealand, Norway, and United Kingdom; 2 other countries represented in student body.

Faculty School total: 54. In upper school: 23 men, 27 women; 35 have advanced degrees; 21 reside on campus.

Subjects Offered 1968, 20th century history, acting, advanced math, algebra, American foreign policy, American government, American history, American literature, anatomy and physiology, art, arts and crafts, athletics, biology, botany, British literature, calculus, career/college preparation, cell biology, ceramics, chemistry, chorus, civil war history, college admission preparation, college counseling, college planning, college writing, communication skills, composition, computer graphics, conceptual physics, contemporary issues, creative writing, critical writing, culinary arts, current events, desktop publishing, drama, dramatic arts, drawing, earth science, English, English composition, English literature, environmental science, expository writing, film appreciation, film studies, filmmaking, food and nutrition, foreign policy, forensics, French, French as a second language, gender issues, general science, geography, geometry, government, government/civics, graphic arts, graphics, guidance, health, history, history of music, history of rock and roll, Holocaust studies, illustration, Internet research, interpersonal skills, keyboarding, lab science, language arts, language development, Latin, leadership, life management skills, literacy, literary magazine, marine biology, mathematics, mentorship program, multicultural literature, music appreciation, music composition, music history, music performance, music theory, newspaper, outdoor education, Pacific Island studies, participation in sports, peer counseling, personal finance, personal fitness, philosophy, photo shop, photography, physical education, physical science, physics, poetry, pragmatics, pre-algebra, pre-calculus, printmaking, psychology, publishing, reading, reading/study skills, relationships, SAT/ACT preparation, science, sculpture, set design, Shakespeare, short story, silk screening, social sciences, social skills, social studies, Spanish, speech therapy, studio art, technical theater, technology, theater arts, trigonometry, U.S. government, U.S. history, video and animation, video film production, visual and performing arts, visual arts, Web site design, women in literature, women's literature, woodworking, work-study, world history, world literature, world wide web design, writing, writing, writing workshop, yearbook, zoology.

Graduation Requirements Art, college counseling, computer science, electives, history, literature, mathematics, physical education (includes health), science, writing. Community service is required.

Special Academic Programs Honors section; academic accommodation for the gifted, the musically talented, and the artistically talented; remedial reading and/or remedial writing; remedial math; programs in English, mathematics, general development for dyslexic students.

College Admission Counseling 42 students graduated in 2012; 41 went to college, including American University; Brandeis University; Curry College; Suffolk University; Syracuse University; University of Denver. Other: 1 entered a postgraduate year. Mean composite ACT: 30.
Student Life Upper grades have specified standards of dress, student council, honor system. Discipline rests primarily with faculty.
Summer Programs Remediation, enrichment, advancement, sports, art/fine arts, computer instruction programs offered; session focuses on academics and recreation; held on campus; accepts boys and girls; open to students from other schools. 74 students usually enrolled. 2013 schedule: July 1 to August 2. Application deadline: none.
Tuition and Aid Day student tuition: $46,249; 7-day tuition and room/board: $65,346. Tuition installment plan (Key Tuition Payment Plan). Need-based scholarship grants available. In 2012–13, 4% of upper-school students received aid. Total amount of financial aid awarded in 2012–13: $125,000.
Admissions Traditional secondary-level entrance grade is 9. For fall 2012, 252 students applied for upper-level admission, 64 were accepted, 57 enrolled. Achievement tests, WISC/Woodcock-Johnson and writing sample required. Deadline for receipt of application materials: none. Application fee required: $100. On-campus interview required.
Athletics Interscholastic: basketball (boys, girls), softball (b,g); intramural: dance (g), yoga (g); coed interscholastic: cross-country running, Frisbee, golf, lacrosse, running, soccer, tennis, ultimate Frisbee, wrestling; coed intramural: aerobics, aerobics/dance, aerobics/Nautilus, alpine skiing, badminton, basketball, bicycling, fencing, fitness, fitness walking, floor hockey, ice skating, jogging, mountain biking, Nautilus, outdoor adventure, paint ball, physical training, roller blading, roller skating, skiing (cross-country), skiing (downhill), snowboarding, snowshoeing, swimming and diving, touch football, weight lifting. 1 PE instructor.
Computers Computers are regularly used in college planning, creative writing, desktop publishing, English, foreign language, graphic arts, keyboarding, mathematics, music, music technology, newspaper, photojournalism, programming, research skills, theater arts, video film production, Web site design, writing, yearbook classes. Computer network features include on-campus library services, Internet access, wireless campus network, Internet filtering or blocking technology. Student e-mail accounts are available to students. Students grades are available online.
Contact Dana M. Harbert, Director of Admission. 413-477-6000. Fax: 413-477-6837. E-mail: admission@ehs1.org. Web site: www.ehs1.org

FAIRHILL SCHOOL

16150 Preston Road
Dallas, Texas 75248

Head of School: Ms. Jane Sego

General Information Coeducational day college-preparatory, arts, and technology school; primarily serves students with learning disabilities, individuals with Attention Deficit Disorder, and dyslexic students. Grades 1–12. Founded: 1971. Setting: suburban. 16-acre campus. 2 buildings on campus. Approved or accredited by Southern Association of Colleges and Schools and Texas Department of Education. Endowment: $4 million. Total enrollment: 220. Upper school average class size: 12. Upper school faculty-student ratio: 1:12. There are 175 required school days per year for Upper School students. Upper School students typically attend 5 days per week. The average school day consists of 7 hours and 30 minutes.
Upper School Student Profile Grade 9: 22 students (12 boys, 10 girls); Grade 10: 23 students (17 boys, 6 girls); Grade 11: 25 students (17 boys, 8 girls); Grade 12: 20 students (12 boys, 8 girls).
Faculty School total: 32. In upper school: 6 men, 10 women; 4 have advanced degrees.
Subjects Offered American history, American literature, art, biology, British literature, chemistry, computer science, economics, English, government, health, journalism, mathematics, music, performing arts, physical education, physical science, physics, psychology, reading, Spanish, speech, study skills, world geography.
Graduation Requirements Arts and fine arts (art, music, dance, drama), computer science, English, mathematics, physical education (includes health), science, social studies (includes history), 60 hours of volunteer service for seniors.
Special Academic Programs Remedial reading and/or remedial writing; remedial math; programs in English, mathematics, general development for dyslexic students.
College Admission Counseling 22 students graduated in 2012; 20 went to college, including Collin County Community College District; Southern Methodist University; St. Edward's University; Texas Tech University; University of Oklahoma. Other: 1 went to work, 1 entered military service.
Student Life Upper grades have uniform requirement, student council. Discipline rests primarily with faculty.
Summer Programs Remediation, advancement, computer instruction programs offered; session focuses on academics; held on campus; accepts boys and girls; open to students from other schools. 50 students usually enrolled. 2013 schedule: June 1 to June 26. Application deadline: none.
Tuition and Aid Day student tuition: $15,500. Need-based scholarship grants available. In 2012–13, 6% of upper-school students received aid. Total amount of financial aid awarded in 2012–13: $50,000.
Admissions Traditional secondary-level entrance grade is 9. For fall 2012, 7 students applied for upper-level admission, 5 were accepted, 5 enrolled. Psychoeducational evaluation required. Deadline for receipt of application materials: none. Application fee required: $1500. Interview required.
Athletics Interscholastic: baseball (boys), basketball (b,g), cheering (b,g), golf (b,g), soccer (b,g), tennis (b,g), volleyball (g); intramural: cheering (b,g); coed interscholastic: cheering, golf, soccer, tennis. 3 coaches.
Computers Computers are regularly used in college planning, English, technology, yearbook classes. Computer network features include on-campus library services, Internet access, wireless campus network, Internet filtering or blocking technology. Student e-mail accounts are available to students. Students grades are available online. The school has a published electronic and media policy.
Contact Mrs. Melinda Cameron, Head of Upper School. 972-233-1026. Fax: 972-233-8205. E-mail: mcameron@fairhill.org. Web site: www.fairhill.org

THE FAMILY FOUNDATION SCHOOL

431 Chapel Hill Road
Hancock, New York 13783

Head of School: Mr. Emmanuel A. Argiros

General Information Coeducational boarding college-preparatory, arts, religious studies, and character education school, affiliated with Christian faith, Jewish faith; primarily serves underachievers, individuals with Attention Deficit Disorder, individuals with emotional and behavioral problems, and alcohol and drug abuse. Grades 9–12. Founded: 1987. Setting: rural. Nearest major city is Binghamton. Students are housed in single-sex dormitories. 158-acre campus. 14 buildings on campus. Approved or accredited by Joint Commission on Accreditation of Healthcare Organizations, Middle States Association of Colleges and Schools, New York State Board of Regents, and New York Department of Education. Total enrollment: 120. Upper school average class size: 12. There are 210 required school days per year for Upper School students. Upper School students typically attend 5 days per week. The average school day consists of 6 hours and 20 minutes.
Upper School Student Profile Grade 9: 10 students (8 boys, 2 girls); Grade 10: 23 students (18 boys, 5 girls); Grade 11: 38 students (25 boys, 13 girls); Grade 12: 49 students (34 boys, 15 girls). 100% of students are boarding students. 40% are state residents. 22 states are represented in upper school student body. 1% are international students. International students from Canada. 97% of students are Christian, Jewish.
Faculty School total: 36. In upper school: 19 men, 17 women; 13 have advanced degrees; 5 reside on campus.
Subjects Offered Advanced chemistry, algebra, American government, American history, analysis and differential calculus, ancient world history, applied music, art, biology, British literature, character education, chemistry, choir, chorus, college writing, community service, dance, debate, drama, earth science, economics, English, family living, geometry, global studies, government, health and safety, health education, Jewish studies, journalism, modern dance, photography, physical education, physics, pre-calculus, religious education, Russian, sociology, Spanish, tap dance, trigonometry, woodworking, work-study, world history, World-Wide-Web publishing, yearbook.
Graduation Requirements Character education, English, foreign language, life skills, mathematics, physical education (includes health), science, social studies (includes history), New York State Board of Regents requirements, completion of character education program.
Special Academic Programs Study at local college for college credit; remedial reading and/or remedial writing.
College Admission Counseling 35 students graduated in 2011; 32 went to college, including Binghamton University, State University of New York; Marywood University; Montclair State University; Nassau Community College; St. John's University; The University of Scranton. Other: 3 had other specific plans. Mean SAT critical reading: 517, mean SAT math: 518, mean SAT writing: 502, mean combined SAT: 1537, mean composite ACT: 22.
Student Life Upper grades have specified standards of dress, student council, honor system. Discipline rests equally with students and faculty. Attendance at religious services is required.
Tuition and Aid 7-day tuition and room/board: $75,600. Tuition installment plan (monthly payment plans). Need-based scholarship grants, paying campus jobs available. In 2011–12, 15% of upper-school students received aid. Total amount of financial aid awarded in 2011–12: $500,000.
Admissions Iowa Tests of Basic Skills required. Deadline for receipt of application materials: none. Application fee required. On-campus interview required.
Athletics Interscholastic: basketball (boys, girls), soccer (b,g), softball (g); intramural: basketball (b,g), lacrosse (b), strength & conditioning (b,g); coed interscholastic: dance, golf; coed intramural: aerobics/dance, ballet, basketball, fishing, fitness, fitness walking, flag football, fly fishing, Frisbee, hiking/backpacking, horseback riding, horseshoes, ice skating, outdoor activities, outdoors, running, skateboarding, soccer, softball, tennis, ultimate Frisbee, volleyball, weight training, yoga. 3 PE instructors, 4 coaches.
Computers Computers are regularly used in English, history, journalism, science, Spanish, yearbook classes. Computer network features include on-campus library services, online commercial services, Internet access, wireless campus network, Internet

filtering or blocking technology. Computer access in designated common areas is available to students.

Contact Mr. Jeff Brain, MA, CTS, CEP, Dean of Admissions. 845-887-5213 Ext. 499. Fax: 845-887-4939. E-mail: jbrain@thefamilyschool.com. Web site: www.thefamilyschool.com

FOOTHILLS ACADEMY

745 37th Street NW
Calgary, Alberta T2N 4T1, Canada

Head of School: Mr. G.M. Bullivant

General Information Coeducational day college-preparatory, general academic, and technology school; primarily serves underachievers, students with learning disabilities, individuals with Attention Deficit Disorder, dyslexic students, and Asperger's Syndrome. Grades 3–12. Founded: 1979. Setting: urban. 7-acre campus. 1 building on campus. Approved or accredited by Association of Independent Schools and Colleges of Alberta and Alberta Department of Education. Affiliate member of National Association of Independent Schools. Language of instruction: English. Endowment: CAN$3 million. Total enrollment: 200. Upper school average class size: 12. Upper school faculty-student ratio: 1:12. There are 177 required school days per year for Upper School students. Upper School students typically attend 5 days per week. The average school day consists of 6 hours and 10 minutes.

Upper School Student Profile Grade 9: 36 students (20 boys, 16 girls); Grade 10: 26 students (10 boys, 16 girls); Grade 11: 24 students (18 boys, 6 girls); Grade 12: 29 students (19 boys, 10 girls).

Faculty School total: 40. In upper school: 10 men, 15 women; 7 have advanced degrees.

Subjects Offered Algebra, art, athletics, basic skills, biology, career and personal planning, career education, chemistry, college admission preparation, college awareness, college planning, community service, computer animation, computer applications, computer education, computer literacy, computer multimedia, computer skills, conflict resolution, consumer mathematics, decision making skills, digital photography, drama, drama performance, dramatic arts, electives, English composition, English literature, environmental studies, expository writing, food and nutrition, grammar, health education, information processing, Internet research, interpersonal skills, keyboarding, language arts, leadership, leadership and service, learning strategies, library research, library skills, mathematics, mechanics of writing, oral communications, painting, personal and social education, photography, physical fitness, poetry, reading, reading/study skills, remedial study skills, research and reference, research skills, science, Shakespeare, short story, social skills, social studies, speech therapy, study skills, technological applications, track and field, writing.

Graduation Requirements Athletics, career and personal planning, English, English composition, English literature, expository writing, grammar, keyboarding, language arts, learning strategies, mathematics, mechanics of writing, physical fitness, reading/study skills, research skills, science, social studies (includes history), study skills, Alberta education standards.

Special Academic Programs Remedial reading and/or remedial writing; remedial math; programs in English, mathematics, general development for dyslexic students.

College Admission Counseling 26 students graduated in 2012; 24 went to college, including Mount Allison University; Mount Royal University; University of Calgary; University of Victoria. Other: 2 went to work.

Student Life Upper grades have specified standards of dress, student council, honor system. Discipline rests primarily with faculty.

Summer Programs Remediation, enrichment programs offered; session focuses on remedial reading, language, organization skills; held on campus; accepts boys and girls; open to students from other schools. 50 students usually enrolled. 2013 schedule: July 4 to August 21. Application deadline: June 1.

Tuition and Aid Day student tuition: CAN$13,500–CAN$26,500. Tuition installment plan (The Tuition Plan, monthly payment plans, individually arranged payment plans). Bursaries, need-based scholarship grants available. In 2012–13, 60% of upper-school students received aid. Total amount of financial aid awarded in 2012–13: CAN$500,000.

Admissions Traditional secondary-level entrance grade is 9. For fall 2012, 30 students applied for upper-level admission, 10 were accepted, 10 enrolled. Achievement tests, CTBS, Stanford Achievement Test, any other standardized test, math, reading, and mental ability tests, Wechsler Intelligence Scale for Children or writing sample required. Deadline for receipt of application materials: none. Application fee required: CAN$50. On-campus interview required.

Athletics Interscholastic: badminton (boys, girls), basketball (b,g); intramural: badminton (b,g), basketball (b,g), football (b); coed interscholastic: cross-country running, golf, indoor track & field, tennis, track and field, volleyball; coed intramural: badminton, ball hockey, baseball, climbing, cooperative games, cross-country running, curling, fitness, flag football, floor hockey, golf, gymnastics, handball, hiking/backpacking, in-line skating, indoor soccer, indoor track & field, jogging, kickball, life saving, outdoor activities, outdoor adventure, outdoor education, outdoor recreation, outdoor skills, physical fitness, physical training, roller blading, running, skiing (downhill), snowboarding, snowshoeing, soccer, softball, strength & conditioning, tennis, touch football, track and field, volleyball, walking, weight training, wilderness, wilderness survival, wrestling. 1 PE instructor, 10 coaches, 2 athletic trainers.

Computers Computers are regularly used in all academic, animation, basic skills, career education, career exploration, computer applications, creative writing, desktop publishing, keyboarding, library skills, mentorship program, research skills, social studies, Web site design, word processing, writing, yearbook classes. Computer network features include on-campus library services, online commercial services, Internet access, wireless campus network, Internet filtering or blocking technology. Computer access in designated common areas is available to students. The school has a published electronic and media policy.

Contact Ms. A. Rose, Student Applications. 403-270-9400. Fax: 403-270-9438. E-mail: arose@foothillsacademy.org. Web site: www.foothillsacademy.org

THE FROSTIG SCHOOL

971 North Altadena Drive
Pasadena, California 91107

Head of School: Dr. Chris Schnieders

General Information Coeducational day arts, vocational, and technology school; primarily serves underachievers, students with learning disabilities, individuals with Attention Deficit Disorder, and dyslexic students. Grades 1–12. Founded: 1951. Setting: suburban. Nearest major city is Los Angeles. 2-acre campus. 1 building on campus. Approved or accredited by Western Association of Schools and Colleges and California Department of Education. Endowment: $3 million. Total enrollment: 95. Upper school average class size: 12. Upper school faculty-student ratio: 1:6. There are 180 required school days per year for Upper School students. Upper School students typically attend 5 days per week. The average school day consists of 6 hours and 10 minutes.

Upper School Student Profile Grade 9: 14 students (11 boys, 3 girls); Grade 10: 11 students (6 boys, 5 girls); Grade 11: 11 students (7 boys, 4 girls); Grade 12: 12 students (7 boys, 5 girls).

Faculty School total: 25. In upper school: 6 men, 7 women; 2 have advanced degrees.

Subjects Offered Algebra, American government, American history, art, athletics, basic skills, biology, career and personal planning, career education, computer animation, computer applications, consumer economics, creative drama, economics, English, filmmaking, geometry, government, health education, life science, music, physical education, U.S. history.

Special Academic Programs Remedial reading and/or remedial writing; remedial math; programs in English, mathematics, general development for dyslexic students.

College Admission Counseling 7 students graduated in 2012; 6 went to college, including Glendale Community College; Pasadena City College. Other: 1 went to work.

Student Life Upper grades have specified standards of dress, student council. Discipline rests equally with students and faculty.

Summer Programs Remediation, sports, art/fine arts programs offered; session focuses on maintaining skills obtained during the regular term, work experience for high school students; held on campus; accepts boys and girls; not open to students from other schools. 48 students usually enrolled. 2013 schedule: July 1 to July 29.

Tuition and Aid Day student tuition: $27,950. Tuition installment plan (monthly payment plans, individually arranged payment plans). Need-based scholarship grants available. In 2012–13, 5% of upper-school students received aid. Total amount of financial aid awarded in 2012–13: $50,000.

Admissions Traditional secondary-level entrance grade is 9. For fall 2012, 15 students applied for upper-level admission, 8 were accepted, 8 enrolled. Admissions testing required. Deadline for receipt of application materials: none. Application fee required: $100. On-campus interview required.

Athletics Coed Interscholastic: basketball, flag football, softball, touch football. 1 PE instructor, 2 coaches.

Computers Computers are regularly used in art, basic skills, career education, career exploration, college planning, computer applications, creative writing, current events, English, geography, health, history, keyboarding, lab/keyboard, library, library skills, life skills, mathematics, media, music, occupational education, photography, psychology, reading, remedial study skills, research skills, science, social sciences, social studies, study skills, technology, video film production, Web site design, word processing, writing, writing, yearbook classes. Computer network features include on-campus library services, Internet access, wireless campus network, Internet filtering or blocking technology, assistive technology services, laptops.

Contact Ms. Jacquie Knight, IEP and Admissions Administrator. 626-791-1255. Fax: 626-798-1801. E-mail: admissions@frostig.org. Web site: www.frostig.org

GATEWAY SCHOOL

2570 NW Green Oaks Boulevard
Arlington, Texas 76012

Head of School: Mrs. Harriet R. Walber

General Information Coeducational day college-preparatory, general academic, arts, and technology school; primarily serves underachievers, students with learning disabilities, individuals with Attention Deficit Disorder, and dyslexic students. Grades

5–12. Founded: 1980. Setting: urban. 7-acre campus. 1 building on campus. Approved or accredited by Southern Association of Colleges and Schools, Southern Association of Independent Schools, Texas Education Agency, and Texas Department of Education. Upper school average class size: 10. Upper school faculty-student ratio: 1:8. The average school day consists of 7 hours.

Faculty School total: 6. In upper school: 1 man, 5 women; 5 have advanced degrees.

Subjects Offered Algebra, American literature, art, biology, British literature, career planning, chemistry, college awareness, college counseling, community service, composition, computer education, computer literacy, computer science, computer skills, developmental math, drama, earth science, economics, English, English composition, English literature, environmental science, geometry, government, government/civics, grammar, health, health education, history, intro to computers, introduction to theater, journalism, keyboarding, language arts, literature, mathematics, music, music performance, music theater, newspaper, physical education, pre-algebra, reading, reading/study skills, science, social studies, Spanish, speech, state history, theater, U.S. government, U.S. history, word processing, world history, world literature, writing, writing workshop, yearbook.

Graduation Requirements Computer science, English, foreign language, mathematics, physical education (includes health), science, social studies (includes history). Community service is required.

Special Academic Programs Independent study; study at local college for college credit; remedial reading and/or remedial writing; remedial math; programs in English, mathematics, general development for dyslexic students.

College Admission Counseling 6 students graduated in 2012; 4 went to college, including Lon Morris College; Tarrant County College District; Texas Wesleyan University; The University of Texas at Arlington. Other: 1 went to work, 1 entered military service.

Student Life Upper grades have uniform requirement, student council. Discipline rests primarily with faculty.

Tuition and Aid Day student tuition: $13,500. Guaranteed tuition plan. Merit scholarship grants, need-based scholarship grants available.

Admissions Traditional secondary-level entrance grade is 9. School's own test, Wechsler Intelligence Scale for Children and Woodcock-Johnson required. Deadline for receipt of application materials: none. Application fee required: $150. On-campus interview required.

Athletics Interscholastic: basketball (boys, girls), golf (g); intramural: basketball (b,g), bowling (b,g), golf (b,g), jogging (b,g); coed interscholastic: fitness walking, golf, jogging, scuba diving; coed intramural: bowling. 1 PE instructor.

Computers Computers are regularly used in basic skills, English, mathematics, science classes. Computer network features include Internet access. The school has a published electronic and media policy.

Contact Harriet R. Walber, Executive Director. 817-226-6222. Fax: 817-226-6225. E-mail: walberhr@aol.com. Web site: www.gatewayschool.com

GLEN EDEN SCHOOL

8665 Barnard Street
Vancouver, British Columbia V6P 5G6, Canada

Head of School: Dr. Rick Brennan

General Information Coeducational day school; primarily serves underachievers, students with learning disabilities, individuals with Attention Deficit Disorder, individuals with emotional and behavioral problems, and Autism Spectrum Disorders. Grades K–12. Founded: 1976. Setting: urban. 1 building on campus. Approved or accredited by British Columbia Department of Education. Language of instruction: English. Upper school average class size: 4. Upper school faculty-student ratio: 1:5.

Faculty School total: 5. In upper school: 2 men, 1 woman; 2 have advanced degrees.

Special Academic Programs Remedial reading and/or remedial writing; remedial math.

Admissions Deadline for receipt of application materials: none. Application fee required: CAN$1000. Interview required.

Computers Computers are regularly used in journalism classes. Computer resources include Internet access.

Contact Dr. Rick Brennan, Director. 604-267-0394. Fax: 604-267-0544. E-mail: glenedenschool@gleneden.org. Web site: www.gleneden.org

THE GLENHOLME SCHOOL, DEVEREUX CONNECTICUT

81 Sabbaday Lane
Washington, Connecticut 06793

Head of School: Maryann Campbell

General Information Coeducational boarding and day college-preparatory, arts, vocational, technology, social coaching and motivational management, and self-discipline strategies and character development school; primarily serves underachievers, students with learning disabilities, individuals with Attention Deficit Disorder, individuals with emotional and behavioral problems, Aspergers Syndrome, ADHD, PDD, OCD, and anxiety disorders. Founded: 1968. Setting: small town. Nearest major city is Hartford. Students are housed in single-sex dormitories. 105-acre campus. 30 buildings on campus. Approved or accredited by Association of Independent Schools in New England, Connecticut Association of Independent Schools, Connecticut Department of Children and Families, Council of Accreditation and School Improvement, Massachusetts Department of Education, National Association of Private Schools for Exceptional Children, New England Association of Schools and Colleges, New Jersey Department of Education, New York Department of Education, US Department of State, and Connecticut Department of Education. Member of National Association of Independent Schools. Total enrollment: 89. Upper school average class size: 10. Upper school faculty-student ratio: 1:10. There are 215 required school days per year for Upper School students. Upper School students typically attend 5 days per week. The average school day consists of 5 hours and 45 minutes.

Upper School Student Profile Grade 9: 13 students (9 boys, 4 girls); Grade 10: 15 students (12 boys, 3 girls); Grade 11: 19 students (15 boys, 4 girls); Grade 12: 16 students (11 boys, 5 girls); Grade 13: 4 students (3 boys, 1 girl); Postgraduate: 8 students (4 boys, 4 girls). 92% of students are boarding students. 20% are state residents. 11 states are represented in upper school student body. 9% are international students. International students from China, Egypt, Hong Kong, India, Russian Federation, and Saudi Arabia; 1 other country represented in student body.

Faculty School total: 21. In upper school: 5 men, 16 women; 12 have advanced degrees; 3 reside on campus.

Subjects Offered ADL skills, adolescent issues, aerobics, algebra, art, basketball, biology, career and personal planning, career education, career exploration, career/college preparation, character education, chemistry, choral music, chorus, college admission preparation, college planning, communication skills, community service, computer animation, computer applications, computer art, computer education, computer graphics, computer literacy, computer skills, creative arts, creative dance, creative drama, creative thinking, creative writing, culinary arts, dance, decision making skills, digital photography, drama, drama performance, earth science, English, equine management, fine arts, geometry, graphic arts, guidance, health, health and wellness, health education, Internet research, interpersonal skills, keyboarding, library, life skills, mathematics, media arts, moral and social development, music, participation in sports, performing arts, personal fitness, photography, physical education, piano, play production, radio broadcasting, SAT preparation, science, social sciences, Spanish, theater, U.S. history, video and animation, world history, writing, yearbook.

Graduation Requirements Art, electives, English, language, mathematics, physical education (includes health), science, social studies (includes history), students must meet either Glenholme graduation requirements or the requirements of their home state, depending on the funding source.

Special Academic Programs Academic accommodation for the gifted; remedial reading and/or remedial writing; remedial math; programs in English, mathematics, general development for dyslexic students.

College Admission Counseling 14 students graduated in 2012; 5 went to college, including California College of the Arts; Meredith College; Western Connecticut State University. Other: 6 went to work, 3 entered a postgraduate year.

Student Life Upper grades have uniform requirement, student council, honor system. Discipline rests primarily with faculty.

Summer Programs Remediation, enrichment, sports, art/fine arts, computer instruction programs offered; session focuses on strengthening social skills and boosting academic proficiency; held on campus; accepts boys and girls; open to students from other schools. 90 students usually enrolled. 2013 schedule: July 8 to August 23.

Admissions Individual IQ, Achievement and behavior rating scale or psychoeducational evaluation required. Deadline for receipt of application materials: none. Application fee required: $150. On-campus interview required.

Athletics Intramural: aerobics (boys, girls), aerobics/dance (b,g), aquatics (b,g), archery (b,g), artistic gym (b,g), basketball (b,g), cheering (b,g), combined training (b,g), cooperative games (b,g), cross-country running (b,g), dance (b,g), dance squad (b,g), dance team (b,g), equestrian sports (b,g), figure skating (b,g), fishing (b,g), fitness (b,g), fitness walking (b,g), flag football (b,g), Frisbee (b,g), golf (b,g), hiking/backpacking (b,g), horseback riding (b,g), ice skating (b,g), jogging (b,g), jump rope (b,g), kickball (b,g), modern dance (b,g), outdoor activities (b,g), outdoor recreation (b,g), paddle tennis (b,g), physical fitness (b,g), physical training (b,g), roller blading (b,g), ropes courses (b,g), soccer (b,g), softball (b,g), strength & conditioning (b,g), tennis (b,g), ultimate Frisbee (b,g), volleyball (b,g), walking (b,g), weight training (b,g), yoga (b,g); coed interscholastic: basketball, cross-country running, soccer, softball, tennis; coed intramural: aerobics, aerobics/dance, aquatics, archery, artistic gym, basketball, cheering, combined training, cooperative games, cross-country running, dance, dance squad, dance team, equestrian sports, figure skating, fishing, fitness, fitness walking, flag football, Frisbee, golf, hiking/backpacking, horseback riding, ice skating, jogging, jump rope, kickball, modern dance, outdoor activities, outdoor recreation, paddle tennis, physical fitness, physical training, roller blading, ropes courses, soccer, softball, strength & conditioning, tennis, ultimate Frisbee, volleyball, walking, weight training, yoga. 1 PE instructor, 2 coaches, 1 athletic trainer.

Computers Computers are regularly used in all academic, technology classes. Computer network features include on-campus library services, Internet access, wireless campus network, Internet filtering or blocking technology, online learning, Web cam parent communications. Campus intranet, student e-mail accounts, and computer access in designated common areas are available to students. Students grades are available online. The school has a published electronic and media policy.

Contact David Dunleavy, Admissions. 860-868-7377 Ext. 285. Fax: 860-868-7413. E-mail: ddunleav@devereux.org. Web site: www.theglenholmeschool.org

THE HILL CENTER, DURHAM ACADEMY

3200 Pickett Road
Durham, North Carolina 27705

Head of School: Dr. Sharon Maskel

General Information Coeducational day college-preparatory school; primarily serves underachievers, students with learning disabilities, individuals with Attention Deficit Disorder, and dyslexic students. Grades K–12. Founded: 1977. Setting: small town. 5-acre campus. 1 building on campus. Approved or accredited by National Association of Private Schools for Exceptional Children, Southern Association of Colleges and Schools, Southern Association of Independent Schools, and North Carolina Department of Education. Member of National Association of Independent Schools. Endowment: $3.5 million. Total enrollment: 135. Upper school average class size: 4. Upper school faculty-student ratio: 1:4. There are 175 required school days per year for Upper School students. Upper School students typically attend 5 days per week. The average school day consists of 3 hours.

Upper School Student Profile Grade 9: 11 students (9 boys, 2 girls); Grade 10: 14 students (8 boys, 6 girls); Grade 11: 13 students (8 boys, 5 girls); Grade 12: 10 students (5 boys, 5 girls).

Faculty School total: 22. In upper school: 9 women; 7 have advanced degrees.

Subjects Offered Algebra, American literature, calculus, English, English literature, expository writing, geometry, grammar, mathematics, mechanics of writing, pre-algebra, pre-calculus, Spanish, writing.

Graduation Requirements Graduation requirements are determined by the student's home-based school.

Special Academic Programs Remedial reading and/or remedial writing; remedial math; programs in English, mathematics, general development for dyslexic students.

College Admission Counseling 14 students graduated in 2011; 12 went to college, including East Carolina University; The University of North Carolina at Asheville; The University of North Carolina at Charlotte; The University of North Carolina at Greensboro; The University of North Carolina Wilmington; University of Mississippi. Other: 2 went to work.

Student Life Upper grades have student council. Discipline rests primarily with faculty.

Tuition and Aid Day student tuition: $15,950. Guaranteed tuition plan. Tuition installment plan (The Tuition Plan, Key Tuition Payment Plan, monthly payment plans, The Tuition Refund Plan). Need-based scholarship grants available. In 2011–12, 18% of upper-school students received aid. Total amount of financial aid awarded in 2011–12: $59,700.

Admissions Traditional secondary-level entrance grade is 9. For fall 2011, 21 students applied for upper-level admission, 18 were accepted, 15 enrolled. WISC-III and Woodcock-Johnson required. Deadline for receipt of application materials: March 15. Application fee required: $50. On-campus interview required.

Computers Computers are regularly used in English, foreign language, mathematics, writing classes. Computer network features include Internet access, wireless campus network. Campus intranet is available to students.

Contact Ms. Wendy Speir, Director of Admissions. 919-489-7464 Ext. 7545. Fax: 919-489-7466. E-mail: wspeir@hillcenter.org. Web site: www.hillcenter.org

THE HILL TOP PREPARATORY SCHOOL

737 South Ithan Avenue
Rosemont, Pennsylvania 19010

Head of School: Mr. Thomas W. Needham

General Information Coeducational day college-preparatory, arts, and technology school; primarily serves students with learning disabilities, individuals with Attention Deficit Disorder, and Asperger's Syndrome, PDDNOS, LDNOS. Grades 5–12. Founded: 1971. Setting: suburban. Nearest major city is Philadelphia. 25-acre campus. 4 buildings on campus. Approved or accredited by Middle States Association of Colleges and Schools, Pennsylvania Association of Independent Schools, and Pennsylvania Department of Education. Member of National Association of Independent Schools. Total enrollment: 78. Upper school average class size: 8. Upper school faculty-student ratio: 1:6. There are 180 required school days per year for Upper School students. Upper School students typically attend 5 days per week.

Upper School Student Profile Grade 10: 16 students (13 boys, 3 girls); Grade 11: 10 students (8 boys, 2 girls); Grade 12: 16 students (14 boys, 2 girls).

Faculty School total: 26. In upper school: 10 men, 6 women.

Subjects Offered Algebra, American history, American literature, art, biology, ceramics, chemistry, civics, college counseling, computer math, computer science, computers, creative writing, drama, earth science, economics, electives, English, English literature, environmental science, European history, geography, geometry, government/civics, grammar, health, history, journalism, keyboarding, mathematics, media studies, music appreciation, Native American studies, photography, physical education, physics, psychology, public speaking, science, senior project, social studies, study skills, theater, U.S. history, world cultures, world history, writing.

Graduation Requirements English, mathematics, physical education (includes health), science, senior project, social sciences, social studies (includes history), study skills.

Special Academic Programs Independent study; study at local college for college credit; academic accommodation for the gifted and the artistically talented; programs in English, mathematics, general development for dyslexic students.

College Admission Counseling 12 students graduated in 2012; 11 went to college, including Eastern University; Muhlenberg College. Other: 1 entered a post-graduate year. Median SAT critical reading: 490, median SAT math: 540, median SAT writing: 540, median combined SAT: 1570. 25% scored over 600 on SAT critical reading, 33% scored over 600 on SAT math, 14% scored over 600 on SAT writing, 25% scored over 1800 on combined SAT.

Student Life Upper grades have specified standards of dress, student council, honor system. Discipline rests primarily with faculty.

Summer Programs Remediation, enrichment programs offered; session focuses on remediation, enrichment, recreation, teaching independence; held both on and off campus; held at Pathways to Independence 2012: One week at Eastern University, Pathways to Independence 2012: Overnight in Baltimore, MD, and Hill Top Summer trip to Alaska; accepts boys and girls; open to students from other schools. 9 students usually enrolled. 2013 schedule: July 1 to July 30. Application deadline: none.

Tuition and Aid Day student tuition: $38,050. Tuition installment plan (monthly payment plans, payment in full, 60% due June 1 and 40% due December 1, monthly payments over 10 months). Tuition reduction for siblings, need-based scholarship grants available. In 2012–13, 15% of upper-school students received aid.

Admissions Traditional secondary-level entrance grade is 10. For fall 2012, 9 students applied for upper-level admission, 9 were accepted, 6 enrolled. Achievement tests, psychoeducational evaluation, WISC or WAIS and WISC/Woodcock-Johnson required. Deadline for receipt of application materials: none. Application fee required: $100. On-campus interview required.

Athletics Interscholastic: wrestling (boys); coed interscholastic: basketball, golf, soccer, tennis; coed intramural: aerobics/Nautilus, basketball, bicycling, climbing, combined training, cooperative games, cross-country running, fitness, indoor soccer, martial arts, Newcombe ball, outdoor activities, outdoor adventure, outdoor recreation, outdoor skills, physical fitness, physical training, running, snowboarding, soccer, strength & conditioning, tennis, wall climbing, yoga. 2 PE instructors, 5 coaches.

Computers Computers are regularly used in English, mathematics, science, study skills classes. Computer network features include on-campus library services, Internet access, wireless campus network, Internet filtering or blocking technology, one to one student and faculty laptop initiative, online student information system, ACTIVBoards, projectors, and audio in all classrooms. Campus intranet, student e-mail accounts, and computer access in designated common areas are available to students. Students grades are available online. The school has a published electronic and media policy.

Contact Ms. Cindy Falcone, Assistant Headmaster. 610-527-3230 Ext. 697. Fax: 610-527-7683. E-mail: cfalcone@hilltopprep.org. Web site: www.hilltopprep.org

THE HOWARD SCHOOL

1192 Foster Street
Atlanta, Georgia 30318

Head of School: Ms. Marifred Cilella

General Information Coeducational day college-preparatory, general academic, arts, and technology school; primarily serves students with learning disabilities, individuals with Attention Deficit Disorder, dyslexic students, and students with language learning disabilities and differences. Grades PK–12. Founded: 1950. Setting: urban. 15-acre campus. 2 buildings on campus. Approved or accredited by Georgia Independent School Association, Southern Association of Colleges and Schools, Southern Association of Independent Schools, and Georgia Department of Education. Member of National Association of Independent Schools. Total enrollment: 244. Upper school average class size: 9. Upper school faculty-student ratio: 1:8.

Upper School Student Profile Grade 9: 24 students (17 boys, 7 girls); Grade 10: 10 students (6 boys, 4 girls); Grade 11: 24 students (13 boys, 11 girls); Grade 12: 15 students (10 boys, 5 girls).

Faculty School total: 62. In upper school: 8 men, 11 women; 11 have advanced degrees.

Subjects Offered Algebra, American history, American literature, art, biology, communications, computer science, creative writing, drama, ecology, economics, English, English literature, European history, film studies, geography, geometry, government/civics, grammar, history, journalism, mathematics, music, physical education, physical science, psychology, reading, science, service learning/internship, social studies, Spanish, study skills, trigonometry, world history, world literature, writing.

Graduation Requirements English, foreign language, health, mathematics, physical education (includes health), science, social studies (includes history).

Special Academic Programs Independent study; academic accommodation for the artistically talented; remedial reading and/or remedial writing; remedial math; programs in English, mathematics, general development for dyslexic students.

College Admission Counseling 18 students graduated in 2012; 16 went to college, including Andrew College; Georgia College & State University; Reinhardt

University; The University of Tampa; Washington and Lee University; Young Harris College. Other: 2 went to work.

Student Life Upper grades have specified standards of dress, student council, honor system. Discipline rests equally with students and faculty.

Summer Programs Remediation, advancement programs offered; session focuses on make-up of academic courses; held on campus; accepts boys and girls; open to students from other schools. 19 students usually enrolled. 2013 schedule: June 10 to July 26. Application deadline: May 1.

Tuition and Aid Day student tuition: $26,750. Tuition installment plan (SMART Tuition Payment Plan, 1-, 2-, 3- and 8-payment plans). Need-based scholarship grants available. In 2012–13, 30% of upper-school students received aid.

Admissions Psychoeducational evaluation required. Deadline for receipt of application materials: none. Application fee required: $150. On-campus interview required.

Athletics Interscholastic: basketball (boys, girls), soccer (b), track and field (b,g), volleyball (g), weight training (b,g); coed interscholastic: golf, soccer, track and field. 3 PE instructors, 6 coaches.

Computers Computers are regularly used in all classes. Computer network features include online commercial services, Internet access. The school has a published electronic and media policy.

Contact Ms. Dawn Splinter, Assistant to the Director of Admissions and Registrar. 404-377-7436 Ext. 259. Fax: 404-377-0884. E-mail: dsplinter@howardschool.org. Web site: www.howardschool.org

HUMANEX ACADEMY

2700 South Zuni Street
Englewood, Colorado 80110

Head of School: Mr. Daniel R. Toomey

General Information Coeducational day college-preparatory, general academic, and arts school; primarily serves underachievers, students with learning disabilities, individuals with Attention Deficit Disorder, individuals with emotional and behavioral problems, dyslexic students, and Asperger's Disorder, High Functioning Autism. Grades 6–12. Founded: 1983. Setting: suburban. Nearest major city is Denver. 1-acre campus. 1 building on campus. Approved or accredited by North Central Association of Colleges and Schools and Colorado Department of Education. Upper school average class size: 8. Upper school faculty-student ratio: 1:8. There are 170 required school days per year for Upper School students. Upper School students typically attend 5 days per week. The average school day consists of 6 hours and 30 minutes.

Upper School Student Profile Grade 6: 1 student (1 boy); Grade 7: 2 students (2 boys).

Faculty School total: 8. In upper school: 4 men, 4 women; all have advanced degrees.

Subjects Offered 1 1/2 elective credits, 1968, 20th century American writers, 20th century history, 20th century physics, 20th century world history, 3-dimensional art, 3-dimensional design, ACT preparation, addiction, ADL skills, adolescent issues, advanced biology, advanced math, advanced studio art-AP, advanced TOEFL/grammar, aerobics, American Civil War, American culture, American democracy, American foreign policy, American government, American history, American legal systems, American literature, American politics in film, anatomy, anatomy and physiology, ancient world history, animal behavior, animation, anthropology, art, art appreciation, art history, arts and crafts, athletic training, athletics, biology, British literature, calculus, career and personal planning, career exploration, cartooning/animation, chemistry, civics, civics/free enterprise, Civil War, civil war history, college counseling, college placement, comedy, composition, computer art, computer graphics, conflict resolution, consumer mathematics, creative writing, critical thinking, current events, drawing, English, English literature, epic literature, evolution, existentialism, expository writing, film, film and literature, fitness, foreign language, general, general math, general science, geography, geology, geometry, government, government/civics, grammar, graphic arts, graphic design, great books, Greek drama, guitar, Harlem Renaissance, health, health education, history, Holocaust, honors algebra, honors English, honors geometry, honors U.S. history, honors world history, human anatomy, human biology, human sexuality, illustration, independent living, keyboarding, language, language arts, language structure, languages, literacy, literary genres, literary magazine, literature, mathematics, media literacy, military history, newspaper, non-Western literature, North American literature, novels, nutrition, peer counseling, philosophy, physical fitness, physics, physiology, play/screen writing, poetry, politics, pottery, pre-algebra, pre-calculus, psychology, public speaking, reading, reading/study skills, remedial study skills, remedial/makeup course work, research, research skills, SAT preparation, SAT/ACT preparation, science, science fiction, sculpture, sexuality, Shakespeare, short story, speech, speech and debate, sports, statistics, U.S. government, U.S. government and politics, U.S. history, U.S. literature, Vietnam history, Vietnam War, weight fitness, weight training, weightlifting, Western civilization, Western literature, world geography, world governments, world history.

Graduation Requirements Research, speech.

Special Academic Programs Honors section; academic accommodation for the gifted; remedial reading and/or remedial writing; remedial math; programs in English, mathematics, general development for dyslexic students; special instructional classes for deaf students, blind students.

College Admission Counseling 14 students graduated in 2012; 8 went to college, including Colorado School of Mines; Colorado State University; Fort Lewis College; University of Colorado Boulder; University of Denver; University of Northern Colorado. Other: 4 went to work, 2 entered a postgraduate year. Median composite ACT: 24. 33% scored over 26 on composite ACT.

Student Life Upper grades have specified standards of dress, student council. Discipline rests equally with students and faculty.

Summer Programs Remediation, advancement, sports, art/fine arts programs offered; session focuses on academics, credit recovery, outdoor educ; held both on and off campus; held at Colorado Natl Parks; accepts boys and girls; open to students from other schools. 30 students usually enrolled. 2013 schedule: June 4 to June 30. Application deadline: June 5.

Tuition and Aid Day student tuition: $18,900. Guaranteed tuition plan. Tuition installment plan (FACTS Tuition Payment Plan). Tuition reduction for siblings, need-based scholarship grants, Sallie Mae available. In 2012–13, 20% of upper-school students received aid. Total amount of financial aid awarded in 2012–13: $5000.

Admissions Traditional secondary-level entrance grade is 9. For fall 2012, 5 students applied for upper-level admission, 5 were accepted, 4 enrolled. Wechsler Individual Achievement Test, Wechsler Intelligence Scale for Children III, WISC III or other aptitude measures; standardized achievement test, WISC or WAIS, WISC-III and Woodcock-Johnson, WISC-R, WISC-R or WISC-III and WISC/Woodcock-Johnson required. Deadline for receipt of application materials: none. No application fee required. On-campus interview required.

Athletics Coed Intramural: aerobics, ball hockey, basketball, bocce, bowling, cooperative games, fitness, flag football, Frisbee, handball, kickball, physical training, power lifting, ultimate Frisbee, weight lifting, weight training. 1 PE instructor.

Computers Computers are regularly used in art, English, health, history, literacy, mathematics, philosophy, psychology, reading, research skills, social studies, Spanish, speech, study skills, writing, writing classes. Computer resources include on-campus library services, online commercial services, Internet access, Internet filtering or blocking technology. Campus intranet is available to students. Students grades are available online. The school has a published electronic and media policy.

Contact 303-783-0137. Fax: 303-783-5901. Web site: www.humanexacademy.com

THE JOHN DEWEY ACADEMY

389 Main Street
Great Barrington, Massachusetts 01230

Head of School: Dr. Kenneth M. Steiner

General Information Coeducational boarding college-preparatory and arts school; primarily serves underachievers, students with learning disabilities, individuals with Attention Deficit Disorder, individuals with emotional and behavioral problems, and gifted, underachieving, self-destructive adolescents. Grades 10–PG. Founded: 1985. Setting: small town. Nearest major city is Hartford, CT. Students are housed in single-sex by floor dormitories. 90-acre campus. 3 buildings on campus. Approved or accredited by New England Association of Schools and Colleges and Massachusetts Department of Education. Member of Secondary School Admission Test Board. Total enrollment: 20. Upper school average class size: 6. Upper school faculty-student ratio: 1:3. There are 330 required school days per year for Upper School students. Upper School students typically attend 7 days per week. The average school day consists of 6 hours.

Upper School Student Profile Grade 10: 3 students (3 boys); Grade 11: 10 students (7 boys, 3 girls); Grade 12: 7 students (5 boys, 2 girls). 100% of students are boarding students. 10% are state residents. 11 states are represented in upper school student body. 10% are international students. International students from Jordan and Russian Federation.

Faculty School total: 10. In upper school: 5 men, 5 women; 9 have advanced degrees; 2 reside on campus.

Subjects Offered Adolescent issues, algebra, American literature, art, art history, biology, calculus, chemistry, creative writing, drama, English, English literature, environmental science, ethics, European history, fine arts, French, geometry, government/civics, grammar, health, history, Italian, moral reasoning, philosophy, physical education, physics, psychology, sociology, Spanish, statistics, theater, trigonometry, world history, world literature, writing.

Graduation Requirements American history, arts and fine arts (art, music, dance, drama), biology, English, English literature, European history, foreign language, leadership, literature, mathematics, moral reasoning, physical education (includes health), science, social studies (includes history), moral leadership qualities, minimum 18 months residency.

Special Academic Programs Honors section; accelerated programs; independent study; study at local college for college credit; academic accommodation for the gifted and the artistically talented; remedial reading and/or remedial writing; remedial math; programs in general development for dyslexic students.

College Admission Counseling 7 students graduated in 2011; all went to college, including Carleton College; Clark University; Columbia University; Peabody Conservatory of The Johns Hopkins University; Vassar College; Wheaton College. 95% scored over 600 on SAT critical reading, 95% scored over 600 on SAT math, 95% scored over 600 on SAT writing, 95% scored over 1800 on combined SAT.

Student Life Upper grades have specified standards of dress, student council, honor system. Discipline rests equally with students and faculty.

Tuition and Aid 7-day tuition and room/board: $92,000. Tuition installment plan (monthly payment plans, individually arranged payment plans). Need-based scholarship grants available. In 2011–12, 25% of upper-school students received aid.
Admissions Traditional secondary-level entrance grade is 10. Deadline for receipt of application materials: none. No application fee required. On-campus interview required.
Computers Computer resources include Internet access. Computer access in designated common areas is available to students.
Contact Dr. Lisa Sinsheimer, Parent Liaison/Admissions Counselor. 917-597-7814. E-mail: lisa@sinsheimer.net. Web site: www.jda.org

THE JUDGE ROTENBERG EDUCATIONAL CENTER

250 Turnpike Street
Canton, Massachusetts 02021-2341

Head of School: Glenda Crookes

General Information Coeducational boarding general academic and vocational school; primarily serves underachievers, students with learning disabilities, individuals with Attention Deficit Disorder, individuals with emotional and behavioral problems, dyslexic students, and autism and developmental disabilities. Founded: 1971. Setting: suburban. Nearest major city is Boston. 2 buildings on campus. Approved or accredited by Massachusetts Department of Education and Massachusetts Office of Child Care Services. Upper school average class size: 10. Upper School students typically attend 5 days per week. The average school day consists of 6 hours.
Special Academic Programs Remedial reading and/or remedial writing; remedial math; special instructional classes for deaf students, blind students.
Student Life Upper grades have specified standards of dress, honor system. Discipline rests primarily with faculty.
Admissions Deadline for receipt of application materials: none. No application fee required. Interview recommended.
Athletics Intramural: basketball (boys, girls); coed intramural: aerobics/dance, physical fitness. 2 PE instructors.
Computers Computers are regularly used in all academic classes. Computer network features include Internet access, Internet filtering or blocking technology. Student e-mail accounts are available to students.
Contact Julie Gomes, Director of Admissions. 781-828-2202 Ext. 4275. Fax: 781-828-2804. E-mail: j.gomes@judgerc.org. Web site: www.judgerc.org

THE KARAFIN SCHOOL

40-1 Radio Circle
PO Box 277
Mount Kisco, New York 10549

Head of School: Bart A. Donow, PhD

General Information Coeducational day college-preparatory and general academic school; primarily serves underachievers, students with learning disabilities, individuals with Attention Deficit Disorder, individuals with emotional and behavioral problems, emotionally disabled students, and Tourette's Syndrome. Grades 9–12. Founded: 1958. Setting: suburban. Nearest major city is New York. 1 building on campus. Approved or accredited by New York Department of Education and New York Department of Education. Total enrollment: 78. Upper school average class size: 6. Upper school faculty-student ratio: 1:6. There are 180 required school days per year for Upper School students. Upper School students typically attend 5 days per week. The average school day consists of 5 hours and 30 minutes.
Upper School Student Profile Grade 9: 15 students (7 boys, 8 girls); Grade 10: 21 students (11 boys, 10 girls); Grade 11: 21 students (10 boys, 11 girls); Grade 12: 21 students (11 boys, 10 girls).
Faculty School total: 25. In upper school: 9 men, 16 women; all have advanced degrees.
Subjects Offered Algebra, American history, American literature, art, art history, arts, biology, business, business skills, calculus, chemistry, computer math, computer programming, computer science, creative writing, earth science, ecology, economics, English, English literature, environmental science, European history, expository writing, fine arts, French, geography, geology, geometry, government/civics, grammar, history of science, Italian, Latin, mathematics, music, photography, physical education, physics, psychology, science, social sciences, social studies, sociology, Spanish, speech, trigonometry, typing, world history, world literature, writing, zoology.
Graduation Requirements Arts and fine arts (art, music, dance, drama), business skills (includes word processing), computer science, English, foreign language, mathematics, physical education (includes health), science, social sciences, social studies (includes history).
Special Academic Programs 1 Advanced Placement exam for which test preparation is offered; academic accommodation for the gifted, the musically talented, and the artistically talented; remedial reading and/or remedial writing; remedial math; programs in English, mathematics, general development for dyslexic students; special instructional classes for deaf students.
College Admission Counseling 20 students graduated in 2011; 15 went to college, including City College of the City University of New York; Hampshire College; John Jay College of Criminal Justice of the City University of New York; Manhattanville College; Purchase College, State University of New York; Westchester Community College. Other: 2 went to work, 1 entered a postgraduate year, 2 had other specific plans. Mean SAT critical reading: 500, mean SAT math: 550, mean SAT writing: 500.
Student Life Upper grades have student council. Discipline rests primarily with faculty.
Tuition and Aid Day student tuition: $27,945. Tuition installment plan (monthly payment plans).
Admissions Traditional secondary-level entrance grade is 9. For fall 2011, 350 students applied for upper-level admission, 50 were accepted, 25 enrolled. Deadline for receipt of application materials: none. No application fee required. On-campus interview required.
Athletics Coed Intramural: aerobics, aerobics/dance, archery, badminton, ball hockey, baseball, basketball, billiards, bowling, cooperative games, fitness, fitness walking, floor hockey, football, Frisbee, golf, gymnastics, jump rope, kickball, paddle tennis, physical fitness, physical training, pillo polo, power lifting, project adventure, racquetball, soccer, strength & conditioning, table tennis, team handball, tennis, touch football, volleyball, weight lifting, whiffle ball, wrestling. 1 PE instructor.
Computers Computers are regularly used in all academic classes. Computer resources include Internet access, Internet filtering or blocking technology. The school has a published electronic and media policy.
Contact Bart A. Donow, PhD, Director. 914-666-9211. Fax: 914-666-9868. E-mail: karafin@optonline.net. Web site: www.karafinschool.com

KEY SCHOOL

3947 East Loop 820 South
Fort Worth, Texas 76119

Head of School: Mary Ann Key

General Information Coeducational day college-preparatory, general academic, and technology school; primarily serves underachievers, students with learning disabilities, individuals with Attention Deficit Disorder, and dyslexic students. Grades K–12. Founded: 1966. Setting: suburban. Nearest major city is Dallas. 2-acre campus. 1 building on campus. Approved or accredited by Council of Accreditation and School Improvement, Southern Association of Colleges and Schools, and Texas Department of Education. Total enrollment: 87. Upper school average class size: 9. Upper school faculty-student ratio: 1:4. There are 140 required school days per year for Upper School students. Upper School students typically attend 4 days per week. The average school day consists of 6 hours and 45 minutes.
Upper School Student Profile Grade 9: 7 students (7 boys); Grade 10: 8 students (6 boys, 2 girls); Grade 11: 4 students (1 boy, 3 girls); Grade 12: 7 students (6 boys, 1 girl).
Faculty School total: 35. In upper school: 6 men, 29 women; 7 have advanced degrees.
Subjects Offered Algebra, art history, aviation, biology, chemistry, composition, current events, desktop publishing, economics, electives, English, geometry, government, grammar, journalism, keyboarding, language arts, life science, life skills, literature, mathematics, mathematics-AP, mechanics of writing, microbiology, novels, physical science, physics, pre-algebra, pre-calculus, reading, reading/study skills, SAT/ACT preparation, science, science fiction, social studies, Spanish, speech, speech communications, study skills, Texas history, U.S. history, world geography, world history, yearbook.
Graduation Requirements Graduation speech.
Special Academic Programs Study at local college for college credit; remedial reading and/or remedial writing; remedial math; programs in English, mathematics, general development for dyslexic students; special instructional classes for students with academic deficits, speech and auditory deficits, and ADD/ADHD; ESL (1 student enrolled).
College Admission Counseling 7 students graduated in 2011; all went to college, including Tarrant County College District; Texas Wesleyan University; Weatherford College; WyoTech Laramie. Median SAT critical reading: 420, median SAT math: 490, median SAT writing: 410.
Student Life Upper grades have specified standards of dress, honor system. Discipline rests primarily with faculty.
Tuition and Aid Tuition installment plan (individually arranged payment plans, quarterly and semester payment plans). Need-based tuition assistance available. In 2011–12, 18% of upper-school students received aid. Total amount of financial aid awarded in 2011–12: $30,000.
Admissions For fall 2011, 23 students applied for upper-level admission, 23 were accepted, 23 enrolled. Deadline for receipt of application materials: none. No application fee required. On-campus interview required.
Computers Computers are regularly used in desktop publishing, journalism, keyboarding, newspaper, writing, yearbook classes. Computer network features include Internet access, wireless campus network, Internet filtering or blocking technology. The school has a published electronic and media policy.
Contact Patricia Banks, Registrar. 817-446-3738. Fax: 817-446-8471. E-mail: registrar@ksfw.org. Web site: www.keyschoolfortworth.org

THE LAB SCHOOL OF WASHINGTON

4759 Reservoir Road NW
Washington, District of Columbia 20007

Head of School: Katherine Schantz

General Information Coeducational day college-preparatory and arts school; primarily serves students with learning disabilities, individuals with Attention Deficit Disorder, and dyslexic students. Grades 1–12. Founded: 1967. Setting: urban. 4-acre campus. 6 buildings on campus. Approved or accredited by Middle States Association of Colleges and Schools and District of Columbia Department of Education. Member of National Association of Independent Schools. Endowment: $4 million. Total enrollment: 344. Upper school average class size: 8. Upper school faculty-student ratio: 1:8. There are 180 required school days per year for Upper School students. Upper School students typically attend 5 days per week. The average school day consists of 6 hours and 30 minutes.

Upper School Student Profile Grade 9: 29 students (17 boys, 12 girls); Grade 10: 28 students (15 boys, 13 girls); Grade 11: 25 students (17 boys, 8 girls); Grade 12: 27 students (14 boys, 13 girls).

Faculty School total: 91. In upper school: 10 men, 17 women; 22 have advanced degrees.

Subjects Offered Algebra, American history, American literature, architecture, art, art history, biology, business, business skills, calculus, career education internship, chemistry, community service, computer science, creative writing, dance, digital art, drama, earth science, English, English literature, environmental science, expository writing, film, fine arts, geography, geometry, government, government/civics, grammar, health, internship, Latin, mathematics, music, music appreciation, physical education, physical science, physics, public policy, rhetoric, science, social sciences, social studies, Spanish, technology, theater, trigonometry, video and animation, word processing, world history, writing.

Graduation Requirements Arts and fine arts (art, music, dance, drama), career education internship, computer science, English, foreign language, mathematics, physical education (includes health), science, social sciences, social studies (includes history). Community service is required.

Special Academic Programs Study abroad; academic accommodation for the gifted, the musically talented, and the artistically talented; remedial reading and/or remedial writing; remedial math; programs in English, mathematics, general development for dyslexic students.

College Admission Counseling 36 students graduated in 2012; 28 went to college, including East Carolina University; Roanoke College; The University of Arizona. Other: 5 entered a postgraduate year, 3 had other specific plans.

Student Life Upper grades have specified standards of dress, student council. Discipline rests primarily with faculty.

Summer Programs Advancement programs offered; session focuses on environmental studies; held both on and off campus; held at Maine; accepts boys and girls; not open to students from other schools. 12 students usually enrolled.

Tuition and Aid Day student tuition: $38,025. Tuition installment plan (FACTS Tuition Payment Plan). Need-based scholarship grants, some funding by local public school systems available. Total amount of financial aid awarded in 2012–13: $150,000.

Admissions Traditional secondary-level entrance grade is 9. For fall 2012, 30 students applied for upper-level admission, 12 were accepted, 9 enrolled. Latest standardized score from previous school, psychoeducational evaluation, WISC or WAIS or WISC-III and Woodcock-Johnson required. Deadline for receipt of application materials: February 1. Application fee required: $100. On-campus interview required.

Athletics Interscholastic: basketball (boys, girls), cross-country running (b,g), lacrosse (b,g), soccer (b,g), swimming and diving (b,g), track and field (b,g), volleyball (g); coed interscholastic: cheering, golf, tennis. 6 PE instructors, 1 coach.

Computers Computers are regularly used in all classes. Computer network features include on-campus library services, Internet access, wireless campus network, iPads provided to all high school students. Computer access in designated common areas is available to students. Students grades are available online. The school has a published electronic and media policy.

Contact Susan Feeley, Director of Admissions. 202-944-2214. Fax: 202-965-5106. E-mail: susan.feeley@labschool.org. Web site: www.labschool.org

LA CHEIM SCHOOL

1413 F Street
Portable 1
Antioch, California 94509

Head of School: Ms. Sue Herrera

General Information Coeducational day general academic and vocational school; primarily serves underachievers, students with learning disabilities, individuals with Attention Deficit Disorder, individuals with emotional and behavioral problems, and bipolar. Grades 1–12. Founded: 1974. Setting: suburban. 5 buildings on campus. Approved or accredited by Western Association of Schools and Colleges and California Department of Education. Total enrollment: 15. Upper school average class size: 10. There are 180 required school days per year for Upper School students. Upper School students typically attend 5 days per week. The average school day consists of 6 hours.

Upper School Student Profile Grade 6: 1 student (1 boy); Grade 7: 2 students (1 boy, 1 girl); Grade 8: 1 student (1 boy); Grade 9: 1 student (1 girl); Grade 10: 2 students (2 boys); Grade 12: 2 students (1 boy, 1 girl).

Faculty School total: 3. In upper school: 2 men.

Subjects Offered Adolescent issues, American government, American history, art, basic skills, biology, economics, grammar, health, language arts, life science, life skills, mathematics, physical education, physical science, science, social studies, vocational skills, world history, writing.

Special Academic Programs Remedial reading and/or remedial writing; remedial math.

College Admission Counseling 1 student graduated in 2012. Other: 1 had other specific plans.

Student Life Upper grades have specified standards of dress. Discipline rests primarily with faculty.

Summer Programs Remediation, enrichment, art/fine arts programs offered; session focuses on continuing education and mental health services; held on campus; accepts boys and girls; not open to students from other schools. 20 students usually enrolled. 2013 schedule: June 18 to July 31.

Tuition and Aid Tuition installment plan (expenses covered by referring district and county agencies with no cost to parents).

Admissions Traditional secondary-level entrance grade is 9. Deadline for receipt of application materials: none. No application fee required. On-campus interview required.

Athletics Intramural: basketball (boys, girls), flag football (b,g).

Computers Computers are regularly used in all academic classes. Computer resources include Internet access.

Contact Ms. Sue Herrera, Director. 925-777-1133. Fax: 925-777-9933. E-mail: sue@lacheim.org. Web site: www.lacheim.org/schools/index.htm

LANDMARK SCHOOL

PO Box 227
429 Hale Street
Prides Crossing, Massachusetts 01965-0227

Head of School: Robert J. Broudo

General Information Coeducational boarding and day college-preparatory, general academic, and language arts tutorial, skill-based curriculum school; primarily serves students with learning disabilities, dyslexic students, and language-based learning disabilities. Boarding grades 9–12, day grades 2–12. Founded: 1971. Setting: suburban. Nearest major city is Boston. Students are housed in single-sex dormitories. 50-acre campus. 22 buildings on campus. Approved or accredited by Association of Independent Schools in New England, Massachusetts Department of Education, National Association of Private Schools for Exceptional Children, New England Association of Schools and Colleges, and Massachusetts Department of Education. Member of National Association of Independent Schools. Endowment: $10 million. Total enrollment: 459. Upper school average class size: 8. Upper school faculty-student ratio: 1:3. There are 180 required school days per year for Upper School students. Upper School students typically attend 5 days per week. The average school day consists of 7 hours.

Upper School Student Profile Grade 9: 72 students (27 boys, 45 girls); Grade 10: 69 students (20 boys, 49 girls); Grade 11: 82 students (39 boys, 43 girls); Grade 12: 76 students (24 boys, 52 girls). 54% of students are boarding students. 49% are state residents. 21 states are represented in upper school student body. 3% are international students. International students from Colombia, Mexico, Saudi Arabia, and United Kingdom.

Faculty School total: 232. In upper school: 72 men, 88 women; 125 have advanced degrees; 22 reside on campus.

Subjects Offered Advanced math, algebra, American government, American history, American literature, anatomy and physiology, art, auto mechanics, basketball, biology, boat building, calculus, calculus-AP, chemistry, chorus, communications, composition, computer programming, computer science, consumer mathematics, creative writing, cultural geography, dance, drama, early childhood, environmental science, expressive arts, filmmaking, geometry, grammar, integrated mathematics, language and composition, language arts, literature, marine science, modern world history, multimedia design, newspaper, oral communications, oral expression, photography, physical education, physical science, portfolio art, pragmatics, pre-algebra, pre-calculus, reading, reading/study skills, senior thesis, sociology, study skills, technical theater, technology, U.S. history, woodworking, world history, yearbook.

Graduation Requirements English, mathematics, physical education (includes health), science, social studies (includes history), Landmark School competency tests, minimum grade equivalents on standardized tests in reading and reading comprehension.

Special Academic Programs Study at local college for college credit; remedial reading and/or remedial writing; remedial math; programs in English, mathematics, general development for dyslexic students; special instructional classes for deaf students.

College Admission Counseling 72 students graduated in 2011; 69 went to college, including Curry College; Lynn University; The University of Arizona; University of Denver; Westfield State University. Other: 2 went to work, 1 entered a post-

graduate year. Mean SAT critical reading: 448, mean SAT math: 430, mean SAT writing: 441.
Student Life Upper grades have specified standards of dress, student council. Discipline rests primarily with faculty.
Tuition and Aid Day student tuition: $39,975–$46,575; 7-day tuition and room/board: $55,400–$62,000. Tuition installment plan (Key Tuition Payment Plan). Need-based scholarship grants, community and staff grants available. In 2011–12, 5% of upper-school students received aid. Total amount of financial aid awarded in 2011–12: $362,041.
Admissions Traditional secondary-level entrance grade is 9. For fall 2011, 317 students applied for upper-level admission, 196 were accepted, 121 enrolled. Achievement tests, psychoeducational evaluation and WISC or WAIS required. Deadline for receipt of application materials: none. Application fee required: $150. On-campus interview required.
Athletics Interscholastic: baseball (boys), basketball (b,g), dance (g), lacrosse (b,g), soccer (b,g), tennis (b,g), wrestling (b); intramural: basketball (b,g), floor hockey (b), volleyball (b,g); coed interscholastic: cross-country running, golf, swimming and diving, track and field; coed intramural: ropes courses, skateboarding, skiing (downhill). 5 PE instructors, 1 athletic trainer.
Computers Computers are regularly used in all academic, programming, publishing, technology, yearbook classes. Computer network features include on-campus library services, Internet access, wireless campus network, Internet filtering or blocking technology. Student e-mail accounts are available to students. The school has a published electronic and media policy.
Contact Carol Bedrosian, Admission Liaison. 978-236-3420. Fax: 978-927-7268. E-mail: cbedrosian@landmarkschool.org. Web site: www.landmarkschool.org

THE LAUREATE ACADEMY

100 Villa Maria Place
Winnipeg, Manitoba R3V 1A9, Canada

Head of School: Mr. Stino Siragusa

General Information Coeducational day college-preparatory school. Grades 1–12. Founded: 1987. Setting: suburban. 10-acre campus. 1 building on campus. Approved or accredited by Manitoba Department of Education. Language of instruction: English. Total enrollment: 80. Upper school average class size: 10. Upper school faculty-student ratio: 1:6. There are 186 required school days per year for Upper School students. Upper School students typically attend 5 days per week. The average school day consists of 6 hours and 30 minutes.
Faculty School total: 16. In upper school: 5 men, 4 women; 3 have advanced degrees.
Subjects Offered All academic.
Graduation Requirements Algebra, biology, Canadian geography, Canadian history, chemistry, communication skills, composition, computer skills, English, English literature, geometry, life issues, mathematics, physical education (includes health), physics, public speaking, science, social studies (includes history), writing, Department of Manitoba Education requirements, classical studies. Community service is required.
Special Academic Programs Academic accommodation for the gifted; remedial reading and/or remedial writing; remedial math; programs in English, mathematics for dyslexic students.
College Admission Counseling 6 students graduated in 2012; 5 went to college, including The University of Winnipeg; University of Manitoba. Other: 1 had other specific plans.
Student Life Upper grades have specified standards of dress, student council, honor system. Discipline rests primarily with faculty.
Summer Programs Remediation programs offered; session focuses on remedial reading; held on campus; accepts boys and girls; open to students from other schools. 8 students usually enrolled. 2013 schedule: July 4 to August 19. Application deadline: June 1.
Tuition and Aid Day student tuition: CAN$18,000. Tuition installment plan (monthly payment plans, quarterly payment plan). Tuition reduction for siblings, bursaries available. In 2012–13, 11% of upper-school students received aid. Total amount of financial aid awarded in 2012–13: CAN$66,000.
Admissions Traditional secondary-level entrance grade is 9. For fall 2012, 12 students applied for upper-level admission, 7 were accepted, 5 enrolled. WISC or WAIS and WISC-III and Woodcock-Johnson required. Deadline for receipt of application materials: none. Application fee required: CAN$75. Interview required.
Athletics Interscholastic: basketball (boys), volleyball (b); intramural: badminton (b), ball hockey (b), basketball (b); coed interscholastic: badminton, cross-country running, soccer, track and field, volleyball; coed intramural: aerobics, alpine skiing, badminton, ball hockey, basketball, broomball, combined training, cooperative games, fitness, flag football, floor hockey, Frisbee, jogging, martial arts, outdoor activities, outdoor adventure, outdoor education, outdoor recreation, paddle tennis, physical fitness, physical training, running, self defense, skiing (downhill), snowboarding, soccer, softball, strength & conditioning, table tennis, touch football, track and field, ultimate Frisbee, volleyball, weight lifting, weight training. 3 PE instructors, 3 coaches.
Computers Computers are regularly used in career education, career exploration, computer applications, creative writing, English, mathematics, research skills, science, social studies, writing, yearbook classes. Computer network features include Internet access, wireless campus network, Internet filtering or blocking technology. Campus intranet, student e-mail accounts, and computer access in designated common areas are available to students. The school has a published electronic and media policy.
Contact Mrs. Dora Lawrie, Admissions Coordinator. 204-831-7107. Fax: 204-885-3217. E-mail: dlawrie@laureateslanding.ca. Web site: www.laureateacademy.com

LAWRENCE SCHOOL

Upper School
10036 Olde Eight Road
Sagamore Hills, Ohio 44067

Head of School: Mr. Lou Salza

General Information Coeducational day college-preparatory school; primarily serves students with learning disabilities, individuals with Attention Deficit Disorder, and dyslexic students. Grades K–12. Founded: 1969. Setting: suburban. Nearest major city is Cleveland. 47-acre campus. 1 building on campus. Approved or accredited by Independent Schools Association of the Central States, North Central Association of Colleges and Schools, and Ohio Department of Education. Endowment: $2 million. Total enrollment: 280. Upper school average class size: 11. Upper school faculty-student ratio: 1:11. There are 185 required school days per year for Upper School students. Upper School students typically attend 5 days per week. The average school day consists of 6 hours.
Faculty School total: 34. In upper school: 12 men, 18 women; 10 have advanced degrees.
Subjects Offered 20th century history, accounting, Advanced Placement courses, algebra, American history, American sign language, anatomy, art, astronomy, biology, calculus, choir, chorus, college counseling, computer applications, consumer economics, creative writing, debate, drama, earth science, economics, English, English composition, forensics, geography, geometry, global studies, government, graphic arts, graphic design, health, integrated mathematics, journalism, keyboarding, language arts, Latin, law, life science, life skills, mathematics, meteorology, military history, music, mythology, painting, physical education, physical science, physics, physics-AP, poetry, pre-algebra, psychology, research skills, sign language, society, politics and law, sociology, Spanish, speech, speech communications, The 20th Century, U.S. history, U.S. history-AP, video, video communication, Web site design, weight training, world geography, world history, yearbook.
Graduation Requirements Independent study project for seniors, community service project.
Special Academic Programs Honors section; independent study; remedial reading and/or remedial writing; remedial math; programs in English, mathematics, general development for dyslexic students.
College Admission Counseling 30 students graduated in 2012; 27 went to college, including Kent State University; Ohio University; Rochester Institute of Technology; The University of Akron; University of Utah; Xavier University. Other: 1 entered military service, 2 entered a postgraduate year.
Student Life Upper grades have specified standards of dress, student council, honor system. Discipline rests equally with students and faculty.
Tuition and Aid Day student tuition: $16,900–$20,750. Tuition installment plan (FACTS Tuition Payment Plan, monthly payment plans, individually arranged payment plans). Need-based scholarship grants available. In 2012–13, 31% of upper-school students received aid. Total amount of financial aid awarded in 2012–13: $800,000.
Admissions Traditional secondary-level entrance grade is 9. Admissions testing required. Deadline for receipt of application materials: none. Application fee required: $100. Interview required.
Athletics Interscholastic: baseball (boys), basketball (b,g), cross-country running (b,g); coed interscholastic: golf; coed intramural: badminton, bowling, cooperative games, fishing, flag football, floor hockey, outdoor activities. 1 PE instructor.
Computers Computers are regularly used in all academic classes. Computer network features include on-campus library services, Internet access, wireless campus network, Internet filtering or blocking technology, one to one notebook laptop program for grades 9 to 12, laptop program for grades 7-8, school-wide social networking through Saywire. Student e-mail accounts are available to students. Students grades are available online. The school has a published electronic and media policy.
Contact Mrs. Janet Robinson, Admissions Assistant. 440-526-0717. Fax: 440-526-0595. E-mail: jrobinson@lawrenceschool.org. Web site: www.lawrenceschool.org

LITTLE KESWICK SCHOOL

PO Box 24
Keswick, Virginia 22947

Head of School: Marc J. Columbus

General Information Boys' boarding arts school; primarily serves underachievers, students with learning disabilities, individuals with Attention Deficit Disorder, individuals with emotional and behavioral problems, and dyslexic students. Founded: 1963. Setting: small town. Nearest major city is Washington, DC. Students are housed in single-sex dormitories. 25-acre campus. 10 buildings on campus. Approved or accredited by Virginia Association of Independent Specialized Education Facilities and Virginia Department of Education. Total enrollment: 34. Upper school average class size: 7. Upper school faculty-student ratio: 1:3. There are 205 required school days per year for Upper School students. The average school day consists of 5 hours and 30 minutes.

Upper School Student Profile 100% of students are boarding students. 17 states are represented in upper school student body. 10% are international students. International students from China and Mexico.

Faculty School total: 6. In upper school: 3 men, 3 women; 5 have advanced degrees.

Subjects Offered Algebra, American history, biology, computer applications, earth science, English, geography, government/civics, health, industrial arts, mathematics, physical education, practical arts, social studies, world history.

Special Academic Programs Academic accommodation for the gifted; remedial math; programs in English, mathematics, general development for dyslexic students.

Student Life Upper grades have specified standards of dress. Discipline rests primarily with faculty.

Tuition and Aid 7-day tuition and room/board: $101,546. Need-based scholarship grants available. In 2012–13, 2% of upper-school students received aid. Total amount of financial aid awarded in 2012–13: $20,000.

Admissions WISC-III and Woodcock-Johnson required. Deadline for receipt of application materials: none. Application fee required: $350. On-campus interview required.

Athletics Interscholastic: basketball (boys), combined training (b); intramural: basketball (b), bicycling (b), climbing (b), cross-country running (b), equestrian sports (b), fishing (b), fitness (b), gymnastics (b), hiking/backpacking (b), horseback riding (b), lacrosse (b), outdoor activities (b). 1 PE instructor, 2 coaches.

Computers Computer resources include Internet access. Computer access in designated common areas is available to students.

Contact Ms. Terry Columbus, Director. 434-295-0457 Ext. 14. Fax: 434-977-1892. E-mail: tcolumbus@littlekeswickschool.net. Web site: www.littlekeswickschool.net

MAPLEBROOK SCHOOL

5142 Route 22
Amenia, New York 12501

Head of School: Donna M. Konkolics

General Information Coeducational boarding and day general academic, vocational, and technology school; primarily serves underachievers, students with learning disabilities, individuals with Attention Deficit Disorder, and low average cognitive ability (minimum I.Q. of 70). Ungraded, ages 11–18. Founded: 1945. Setting: small town. Nearest major city is Poughkeepsie. Students are housed in single-sex dormitories. 100-acre campus. 25 buildings on campus. Approved or accredited by Middle States Association of Colleges and Schools, National Association of Private Schools for Exceptional Children, New York Department of Education, New York State Association of Independent Schools, New York State Board of Regents, US Department of State, United Private Schools Association of Pennsylvania, and New York Department of Education. Member of National Association of Independent Schools. Endowment: $500,000. Total enrollment: 70. Upper school average class size: 6. Upper school faculty-student ratio: 1:8. There are 180 required school days per year for Upper School students. Upper School students typically attend 7 days per week. The average school day consists of 6 hours and 5 minutes.

Upper School Student Profile 98% of students are boarding students. 15% are state residents. 24 states are represented in upper school student body. 20% are international students. International students from Bermuda, Canada, Hong Kong, Mexico, Morocco, and South Africa; 9 other countries represented in student body.

Faculty School total: 55. In upper school: 12 men, 14 women; 26 have advanced degrees; 50 reside on campus.

Subjects Offered Algebra, American history, art, biology, business skills, computer science, consumer mathematics, creative writing, drama, driver education, earth science, English, geography, global studies, government/civics, health, home economics, industrial arts, integrated mathematics, keyboarding, mathematics, music, occupational education, performing arts, photography, physical education, physical science, science, social skills, speech, theater, world history, writing.

Graduation Requirements Career and personal planning, computer science, English, mathematics, physical education (includes health), science, social sciences, social skills, social studies (includes history), attendance at Maplebrook School for a minimum of 2 years.

Special Academic Programs Study at local college for college credit; remedial reading and/or remedial writing; remedial math; programs in English, mathematics, general development for dyslexic students.

College Admission Counseling 8 students graduated in 2012; 3 went to college, including Dutchess Community College; Mitchell College. Other: 5 entered a postgraduate year.

Student Life Upper grades have specified standards of dress, student council, honor system. Discipline rests primarily with faculty.

Summer Programs Remediation, enrichment, sports, art/fine arts, computer instruction programs offered; session focuses on preventing regression of skills; held both on and off campus; held at various locations for New York City day and overnight trips; accepts boys and girls; open to students from other schools. 45 students usually enrolled. 2013 schedule: June 30 to August 10. Application deadline: none.

Tuition and Aid Day student tuition: $34,350; 5-day tuition and room/board: $50,200; 7-day tuition and room/board: $54,700. Tuition installment plan (Key Tuition Payment Plan, individually arranged payment plans, Tuition Management Systems Plan, Sallie Mae loans). Merit scholarship grants, need-based scholarship grants, need-based loans, middle-income loans, paying campus jobs, minority and cultural diversity scholarships, day student scholarships available. In 2012–13, 15% of upper-school students received aid; total upper-school merit-scholarship money awarded: $10,000. Total amount of financial aid awarded in 2012–13: $125,000.

Admissions Traditional secondary-level entrance age is 15. For fall 2012, 190 students applied for upper-level admission, 60 were accepted, 35 enrolled. Achievement tests, Bender Gestalt, TerraNova, Test of Achievement and Proficiency or WISC or WAIS required. Deadline for receipt of application materials: none. No application fee required. Interview required.

Athletics Interscholastic: basketball (boys, girls), cheering (g), field hockey (g); coed interscholastic: cooperative games, cross-country running, equestrian sports, fitness, freestyle skiing, horseback riding, running, skiing (cross-country), skiing (downhill), soccer, softball, swimming and diving, tennis, track and field, weight lifting, weight training; coed intramural: aerobics/dance, alpine skiing, basketball, bicycling, bowling, cooperative games, cricket, dance, figure skating, fitness, fitness walking, flag football, floor hockey, freestyle skiing, golf, hiking/backpacking, horseback riding, ice skating, indoor hockey, martial arts, outdoor education, outdoor recreation, roller blading, skiing (cross-country), skiing (downhill), soccer, softball, Special Olympics, swimming and diving, table tennis, tennis, volleyball, weight lifting, weight training, wrestling. 1 PE instructor, 12 coaches.

Computers Computers are regularly used in all academic classes. Computer network features include on-campus library services, Internet access, wireless campus network, Internet filtering or blocking technology. Campus intranet, student e-mail accounts, and computer access in designated common areas are available to students. Students grades are available online. The school has a published electronic and media policy.

Contact Jennifer L. Scully, Dean of Admissions. 845-373-8191. Fax: 845-373-7029. E-mail: admissions@maplebrookschool.org. Web site: www.maplebrookschool.org

MILL SPRINGS ACADEMY

13660 New Providence Road
Alpharetta, Georgia 30004

Head of School: Mr. Robert W. Moore

General Information Coeducational day college-preparatory and arts school; primarily serves students with learning disabilities, individuals with Attention Deficit Disorder, and dyslexic students. Grades 1–12. Founded: 1981. Setting: suburban. Nearest major city is Atlanta. 85-acre campus. 5 buildings on campus. Approved or accredited by Georgia Association of Private Schools for Exceptional Children, Georgia Independent School Association, Southern Association of Colleges and Schools, and Southern Association of Independent Schools. Member of National Association of Independent Schools. Endowment: $140,000. Total enrollment: 321. Upper school average class size: 10. Upper school faculty-student ratio: 1:4. There are 180 required school days per year for Upper School students. Upper School students typically attend 5 days per week. The average school day consists of 7 hours.

Upper School Student Profile Grade 9: 49 students (38 boys, 11 girls); Grade 10: 33 students (28 boys, 5 girls); Grade 11: 38 students (23 boys, 15 girls); Grade 12: 25 students (18 boys, 7 girls).

Faculty School total: 49. In upper school: 11 men, 10 women; 15 have advanced degrees.

Subjects Offered Algebra, American history, American literature, anatomy and physiology, art, band, biology, British literature, British literature (honors), calculus, career/college preparation, chemistry, chorus, composition, creative writing, diversity studies, drama, ecology, economics, film, geometry, government, health, history, honors algebra, honors English, honors geometry, honors U.S. history, honors world history, journalism, literature, media, music theater, performing arts, physical education, physics, play production, play/screen writing, playwriting and directing, political science, pre-algebra, pre-calculus, psychology, sculpture, senior project, set design, Spanish, state government, studio art, symphonic band, technology, theater, theater design and production, trigonometry, U.S. history, values and decisions, visual and performing arts, voice, world literature, yearbook.

Graduation Requirements Algebra, American history, American literature, anatomy and physiology, biology, British literature, British literature (honors), calculus, chemistry, civics, ecology, economics, geometry, physical education (includes health), physics, Spanish, trigonometry, world history, world literature, senior English, 6 units of electives.

Special Academic Programs Honors section; study at local college for college credit; academic accommodation for the gifted, the musically talented, and the artistically talented; programs in English, mathematics, general development for dyslexic students.

College Admission Counseling 12 students graduated in 2012; 9 went to college, including Andrew College; Georgia College & State University; Georgia Perimeter College; Reinhardt University; Valdosta State University; Young Harris College. Other: 1 went to work, 1 entered military service, 1 had other specific plans. Mean SAT critical reading: 459, mean SAT math: 436, mean SAT writing: 426, mean composite ACT: 18. 4% scored over 600 on SAT critical reading, 3% scored over 600 on SAT math, 1% scored over 600 on SAT writing, 1% scored over 26 on composite ACT.

Student Life Upper grades have uniform requirement, student council, honor system. Discipline rests equally with students and faculty.

Summer Programs Sports programs offered; session focuses on skills development or course credit; held on campus; accepts boys and girls; open to students from other schools. 160 students usually enrolled. 2013 schedule: June 10 to August 9. Application deadline: June 9.

Tuition and Aid Day student tuition: $20,570. Tuition installment plan (FACTS Tuition Payment Plan). Tuition reduction for siblings, need-based scholarship grants available. In 2012–13, 14% of upper-school students received aid. Total amount of financial aid awarded in 2012–13: $77,000.

Admissions Traditional secondary-level entrance grade is 9. For fall 2012, 34 students applied for upper-level admission, 26 were accepted, 24 enrolled. Psychoeducational evaluation required. Deadline for receipt of application materials: none. Application fee required: $100. On-campus interview required.

Athletics Interscholastic: baseball (boys), basketball (b,g), golf (b), lacrosse (b), tennis (b,g), volleyball (g), wrestling (b); intramural: cheering (g), strength & conditioning (b), weight lifting (b); coed interscholastic: cross-country running, soccer, swimming and diving, track and field; coed intramural: archery, dance, fencing, fishing, golf, mountain biking, outdoor activities, physical fitness, scuba diving, yoga. 2 coaches.

Computers Computers are regularly used in all academic classes. Computer network features include on-campus library services, Internet access, wireless campus network, Internet filtering or blocking technology, all students 4-12th grades have laptops, electronic textbooks/literature books, assignments online. Student e-mail accounts are available to students. Students grades are available online. The school has a published electronic and media policy.

Contact Mrs. Sheila FitzGerald, Admissions Director. 770-360-1336 Ext. 1707. Fax; 770-360-1341. E-mail: sfitzgerald@millsprings.org. Web site: www.millsprings.org

NOBLE ACADEMY

3310 Horse Pen Creek Road
Greensboro, North Carolina 27410

Head of School: Linda Hale

General Information Coeducational day college-preparatory, arts, and technology school; primarily serves students with learning disabilities, individuals with Attention Deficit Disorder, and dyslexic students. Grades K–12. Founded: 1987. Setting: suburban. Nearest major city is Greensboro/Winston-Salem. 40-acre campus. 3 buildings on campus. Approved or accredited by North Carolina Department of Exceptional Children, Southern Association of Colleges and Schools, Southern Association of Independent Schools, and North Carolina Department of Education. Endowment: $2.1 million. Total enrollment: 163. Upper school average class size: 9. Upper school faculty-student ratio: 1:9. There are 180 required school days per year for Upper School students. Upper School students typically attend 5 days per week. The average school day consists of 6 hours and 45 minutes.

Upper School Student Profile Grade 10: 19 students (15 boys, 4 girls); Grade 11: 14 students (11 boys, 3 girls); Grade 12: 6 students (6 boys).

Faculty School total: 34. In upper school: 3 men, 11 women; 5 have advanced degrees.

Subjects Offered Algebra, American history, art, basic skills, biology, career and personal planning, career exploration, chemistry, civics, college counseling, drama, earth science, economics, English, environmental science, geometry, health, journalism, life management skills, political systems, pre-algebra, pre-calculus, reading, reading/study skills, Spanish, world history, world history-AP, yearbook.

Graduation Requirements Algebra, American history, biology, earth science, economics, English, environmental science, geometry, physical education (includes health), Spanish, world history, 8th grade end-of-grade test, 20th percentile score on standardized reading test, North Carolina Computer Competency Test.

Special Academic Programs Study at local college for college credit; remedial reading and/or remedial writing; remedial math; programs in English, mathematics, general development for dyslexic students.

College Admission Counseling 14 students graduated in 2012; 10 went to college, including Brevard College; Elon University; Guilford College; St. Andrews University; The University of North Carolina at Greensboro; William Peace University. Other: 3 went to work, 1 had other specific plans. Median SAT critical reading: 510, median SAT math: 420, median SAT writing: 480. Mean combined SAT: 1458. 12% scored over 600 on SAT critical reading, 12% scored over 600 on SAT math, 12% scored over 600 on SAT writing.

Student Life Upper grades have student council, honor system. Discipline rests primarily with faculty.

Summer Programs Remediation, advancement, computer instruction programs offered; session focuses on courses for credit; held on campus; accepts boys and girls; open to students from other schools. 25 students usually enrolled. 2013 schedule: June 18 to August 2. Application deadline: June 4.

Tuition and Aid Day student tuition: $15,850. Tuition installment plan (monthly payment plans, individually arranged payment plans). Need-based scholarship grants available. In 2012–13, 8% of upper-school students received aid. Total amount of financial aid awarded in 2012–13: $52,700.

Admissions Traditional secondary-level entrance grade is 10. For fall 2012, 12 students applied for upper-level admission, 7 were accepted, 7 enrolled. WISC/Woodcock-Johnson required. Deadline for receipt of application materials: none. Application fee required: $75. On-campus interview required.

Athletics Interscholastic: cheering (girls); coed interscholastic: basketball, cross-country running, flag football, golf, soccer, tennis, volleyball; coed intramural: tennis. 1 PE instructor, 7 coaches.

Computers Computers are regularly used in art, career education, career exploration, career technology, college planning, computer applications, current events, graphic arts, graphic design, history, information technology, introduction to technology, journalism, keyboarding, lab/keyboard, photography, social studies, Spanish, study skills, word processing, writing, writing, yearbook classes. Computer network features include Internet access, wireless campus network, Internet filtering or blocking technology. Student e-mail accounts are available to students. Students grades are available online. The school has a published electronic and media policy.

Contact Tim Montgomery, Assistant Head and Director of Admissions. 336-282-7044. Fax: 336-282-2048. E-mail: tmontgomery@nobleknights.org. Web site: www.nobleknights.org

OAKLAND SCHOOL

Boyd Tavern
Keswick, Virginia 22947

Head of School: Ms. Carol Williams

General Information Coeducational boarding and day general academic school; primarily serves underachievers, students with learning disabilities, dyslexic students, processing difficulties, and organizational challenges. Boarding grades 2–9, day grades 1–9. Founded: 1950. Setting: rural. Nearest major city is Richmond. Students are housed in single-sex dormitories. 450-acre campus. 25 buildings on campus. Approved or accredited by Association of Independent Maryland Schools, Virginia Association of Independent Schools, Virginia Association of Independent Specialized Education Facilities, and Virginia Department of Education. Upper school average class size: 5. Upper school faculty-student ratio: 1:5. There are 180 required school days per year for Upper School students. Upper School students typically attend 5 days per week. The average school day consists of 6 hours and 45 minutes.

Upper School Student Profile 45% of students are boarding students. 38% are state residents. 9 states are represented in upper school student body. 15% are international students.

Faculty School total: 12. In upper school: 4 men, 8 women; 9 have advanced degrees; 2 reside on campus.

Subjects Offered Algebra, American history, earth science, English, expository writing, geometry, grammar, health, history of the Americas, keyboarding, life science, mathematics, physical education, physical science, remedial study skills, study skills, world history.

Graduation Requirements Skills must be at or above grade/ability level.

Special Academic Programs Remedial reading and/or remedial writing; remedial math; programs in English, mathematics for dyslexic students.

College Admission Counseling 19 students graduated in 2012.

Student Life Upper grades have specified standards of dress, student council, honor system. Discipline rests primarily with faculty.

Summer Programs Remediation, sports, art/fine arts, computer instruction programs offered; session focuses on academics; held on campus; accepts boys and girls; open to students from other schools. 135 students usually enrolled. 2013 schedule: July 1 to August 7.

Tuition and Aid Day student tuition: $27,500; 7-day tuition and room/board: $46,500. Tuition installment plan (SMART Tuition Payment Plan, individually arranged payment plans). Need-based scholarship grants available. In 2012–13, 20% of upper-school students received aid.

Admissions Wechsler Intelligence Scale for Children III required. Deadline for receipt of application materials: none. No application fee required. Interview required.

Athletics Interscholastic: basketball (boys, girls), cheering (g), cross-country running (b,g), equestrian sports (b,g), fishing (b,g), fitness (b,g), golf (b,g), handball (b,g), horseback riding (b,g), outdoor activities (b,g), outdoor adventure (b,g), outdoor education (b,g), outdoor recreation (b,g), outdoor skills (b,g), outdoors (b,g), physical fitness (b,g), physical training (b,g), roller skating (b,g), running (b,g), soccer (b,g), softball (b,g), table tennis (b,g), tennis (b,g), volleyball (b,g), weight training (b,g), wilderness (b,g), wildernessways (b,g); intramural: soccer (b,g), yoga (g); coed interscholastic: aerobics/dance, archery, basketball, bicycling, cross-country running, equestrian sports, fishing, fitness, golf, handball, horseback riding, kickball, outdoor activities, outdoor adventure, outdoor education, outdoor skills, outdoors, physical training, roller skating, running, soccer, softball, table tennis, tennis, volleyball, weight training, wilderness, wildernessways; coed intramural: archery, basketball, bicycling, billiards, cooperative games, cross-country running, equestrian sports, fishing, fitness, Frisbee, golf, hiking/backpacking, horseback riding, in-line skating, indoor soccer, kickball, lacrosse, mountain biking, outdoor activities, outdoor recreation, outdoors, paddle tennis, physical fitness, roller blading, roller skating, running, skateboarding, soccer, softball, swimming and diving, table tennis, tennis. 1 PE instructor.

Computers Computers are regularly used in English, word processing classes.
Contact Mrs. Jamie Cato, Admissions Director. 434-293-9059. Fax: 434-296-8930. E-mail: admissions@oaklandschool.net. Web site: www.oaklandschool.net

THE OLIVERIAN SCHOOL

PO Box 98
Mount Moosilauke Highway
Haverhill, New Hampshire 03765

Head of School: Mr. Randy Richardson

General Information Coeducational boarding and day and distance learning college-preparatory, arts, technology, and experiential education school; primarily serves students with learning disabilities, individuals with Attention Deficit Disorder, individuals with emotional and behavioral problems, and minor emotional and behavioral problems. Grades 9–PG. Distance learning grade X. Founded: 2002. Setting: rural. Nearest major city is Boston, MA. Students are housed in single-sex dormitories. 1,800-acre campus. 10 buildings on campus. Approved or accredited by Independent Schools of Northern New England and New Hampshire Department of Education. Candidate for accreditation by New England Association of Schools and Colleges. Member of National Association of Independent Schools and Secondary School Admission Test Board. Endowment: $50,000. Total enrollment: 50. Upper school average class size: 6. Upper school faculty-student ratio: 1:2. There are 180 required school days per year for Upper School students. Upper School students typically attend 5 days per week. The average school day consists of 7 hours and 30 minutes.
Upper School Student Profile Grade 9: 4 students (2 boys, 2 girls); Grade 10: 9 students (5 boys, 4 girls); Grade 11: 16 students (8 boys, 8 girls); Grade 12: 18 students (10 boys, 8 girls); Postgraduate: 3 students (2 boys, 1 girl). 100% of students are boarding students. 5% are state residents. 10 states are represented in upper school student body. 10% are international students. International students from Bermuda, Canada, Germany, Israel, and Kuwait.
Faculty School total: 19. In upper school: 9 men, 9 women; 10 have advanced degrees; 18 reside on campus.
Special Academic Programs 10 Advanced Placement exams for which test preparation is offered; honors section; accelerated programs; independent study; term-away projects; study at local college for college credit; study abroad; academic accommodation for the gifted and the artistically talented; remedial reading and/or remedial writing; remedial math; ESL (5 students enrolled).
College Admission Counseling 22 students graduated in 2011; 19 went to college, including St. Olaf College. Other: 1 went to work, 2 entered a postgraduate year.
Student Life Upper grades have specified standards of dress, student council, honor system. Discipline rests primarily with faculty.
Tuition and Aid 7-day tuition and room/board: $60,000. Tuition installment plan (FACTS Tuition Payment Plan). Merit scholarship grants, need-based scholarship grants available. In 2011–12, 20% of upper-school students received aid; total upper-school merit-scholarship money awarded: $50,000. Total amount of financial aid awarded in 2011–12: $200,000.
Admissions Traditional secondary-level entrance grade is 11. Deadline for receipt of application materials: none. Application fee required: $75. Interview required.
Athletics Intramural: flag football (boys, girls); coed interscholastic: soccer; coed intramural: alpine skiing, backpacking, basketball, bicycling, billiards, bowling, canoeing/kayaking, climbing, cooperative games, cross-country running, equestrian sports, fishing, fitness, Frisbee, golf, hiking/backpacking, horseback riding, indoor soccer, juggling, martial arts, mountain biking, mountaineering, nordic skiing, outdoor activities, outdoor adventure, outdoor education, outdoor recreation, outdoor skills, outdoors, physical fitness, physical training, rappelling, rock climbing, ropes courses, running, skateboarding, skiing (cross-country), skiing (downhill), snowboarding, snowshoeing, strength & conditioning, table tennis, touch football, triathlon, ultimate Frisbee, volleyball, walking, wall climbing, weight training, wilderness, wildernessways, yoga.
Computers Computer network features include online commercial services, Internet access, wireless campus network, Internet filtering or blocking technology. Campus intranet, student e-mail accounts, and computer access in designated common areas are available to students. Students grades are available online. The school has a published electronic and media policy.
Contact Mr. Barclay Mackinnon Jr., Director of Admissions/Headmaster Emeritus. 603-989-5100 Ext. 7103. Fax: 603-989-3055. E-mail: bmackinnon@oliverianschool.org. Web site: www.oliverianschool.org

THE PATHWAY SCHOOL

162 Egypt Road
Norristown, Pennsylvania 19403

Head of School: David Maola

General Information Coeducational day general academic, life skills/functional academics, and pre-vocational/career education school; primarily serves underachievers, students with learning disabilities, individuals with Attention Deficit Disorder, individuals with emotional and behavioral problems, neurologically impaired students, students with neuropsychiatric disorders, Asperger's Syndrome, Emotional Disturbance, and students needing speech/language therapy and occupational therapy. Ungraded, ages 7–21. Founded: 1961. Setting: suburban. Nearest major city is Philadelphia. 12-acre campus. 12 buildings on campus. Approved or accredited by Pennsylvania Department of Education. Endowment: $1 million. Upper school average class size: 9. Upper school faculty-student ratio: 1:6. There are 181 required school days per year for Upper School students. Upper School students typically attend 5 days per week. The average school day consists of 5 hours and 30 minutes.
Faculty School total: 23. In upper school: 4 men, 5 women; 4 have advanced degrees.
Subjects Offered Algebra, art, biology, career education, career experience, career/college preparation, computer skills, consumer mathematics, creative arts, drama, earth science, electives, English, environmental science, general math, geometry, health education, history, horticulture, interpersonal skills, language arts, mathematics, money management, physical education, pre-vocational education, senior seminar, social skills, social studies, work experience, world history.
Graduation Requirements Graduation requirements are as specified by the sending school district.
Special Academic Programs Study at local college for college credit; remedial reading and/or remedial writing; remedial math; programs in general development for dyslexic students; special instructional classes for emotional support program.
College Admission Counseling 10 students graduated in 2012; 3 went to college. Other: 6 went to work, 1 had other specific plans.
Student Life Upper grades have specified standards of dress, student council, honor system. Discipline rests equally with students and faculty.
Summer Programs Remediation programs offered; session focuses on providing consistency for the entire calendar year; held on campus; accepts boys and girls; open to students from other schools. 85 students usually enrolled. 2013 schedule: July 8 to August 16.
Tuition and Aid Day student tuition: $45,425. Tuition installment plan (individually arranged payment plans).
Admissions Traditional secondary-level entrance age is 16. For fall 2012, 4 students applied for upper-level admission, 2 were accepted, 1 enrolled. Deadline for receipt of application materials: none. No application fee required. On-campus interview required.
Athletics Interscholastic: basketball (boys, girls), softball (b,g), Special Olympics (b,g); coed interscholastic: soccer, Special Olympics; coed intramural: basketball, flag football, soccer. 2 PE instructors, 2 coaches.
Computers Computers are regularly used in basic skills, business education, business skills, career education, data processing, design, newspaper, typing classes. Computer network features include on-campus library services, Internet access, Internet filtering or blocking technology, computer access in classroom. Computer access in designated common areas is available to students. The school has a published electronic and media policy.
Contact Diana Phifer, Director of Admissions. 610-277-0660 Ext. 289. Fax: 610-539-1493. E-mail: dphifer@pathwayschool.org. Web site: www.pathwayschool.org

PINEHURST SCHOOL

10 Seymour Avenue
St. Catharines, Ontario L2P 1A4, Canada

Head of School: Mr. Dave Bird

General Information Coeducational boarding college-preparatory, arts, business, and technology school; primarily serves students with learning disabilities, individuals with Attention Deficit Disorder, and individuals with emotional and behavioral problems. Grades 7–12. Founded: 2000. Setting: urban. Students are housed in single-sex by floor dormitories. 5-acre campus. 1 building on campus. Approved or accredited by Ontario Ministry of Education and Ontario Department of Education. Language of instruction: English. Total enrollment: 22. Upper school average class size: 10. Upper school faculty-student ratio: 1:10. There are 165 required school days per year for Upper School students. Upper School students typically attend 5 days per week. The average school day consists of 5 hours and 50 minutes.
Upper School Student Profile Grade 11: 5 students (2 boys, 3 girls); Grade 12: 8 students (6 boys, 2 girls). 100% of students are boarding students. 90% are province residents. 2 provinces are represented in upper school student body. 10% are international students. International students from United States and Venezuela.
Faculty School total: 5. In upper school: 3 men, 2 women; 2 have advanced degrees.
Subjects Offered Science.
Graduation Requirements 20th century world history, art, business applications, Canadian geography, English, French, geography, health education, history, math applications, mathematics, science, outdoor education.
Special Academic Programs Honors section; accelerated programs; independent study; remedial reading and/or remedial writing; remedial math.
College Admission Counseling 8 students graduated in 2012; 1 went to college. Other: 7 entered a postgraduate year.
Student Life Upper grades have uniform requirement, student council, honor system. Discipline rests primarily with faculty.
Tuition and Aid 7-day tuition and room/board: CAN$35,000. Tuition installment plan (monthly payment plans).

Admissions Traditional secondary-level entrance grade is 11. For fall 2012, 5 students applied for upper-level admission, 5 were accepted, 5 enrolled. Deadline for receipt of application materials: none. No application fee required. On-campus interview required.

Athletics Coed Intramural: alpine skiing, aquatics, archery, backpacking, badminton, ball hockey, baseball, basketball, bicycling, billiards, blading, bocce, bowling, canoeing/kayaking, climbing, cooperative games, cricket, croquet, curling, field hockey, fishing, fitness, fitness walking, flag football, floor hockey, football, golf, hiking/backpacking, hockey, ice hockey, ice skating, in-line skating, indoor hockey, indoor soccer, kayaking, mountain biking, outdoor activities, outdoor adventure, outdoor education, outdoor skills, paddling, physical fitness, physical training, rock climbing, roller blading, ropes courses, running, scuba diving, skateboarding, skiing (cross-country), skiing (downhill), snowboarding, snowshoeing, soccer, softball, street hockey, strength & conditioning, swimming and diving, table tennis, touch football, volleyball, walking, wall climbing, weight lifting, weight training, wilderness, wilderness survival, wildernessways, winter soccer, winter walking, yoga. 1 PE instructor, 1 coach, 1 athletic trainer.

Computers Computers are regularly used in all classes. Computer network features include on-campus library services, Internet access, wireless campus network, Internet filtering or blocking technology. Student e-mail accounts are available to students.

Contact Mrs. Donna MacDonald, Admissions/Office Coordinator. 905-641-0993. Fax: 905-641-0399. E-mail: pinedonna@sympatico.ca. Web site: www.pinehurst.on.ca

ROBERT LAND ACADEMY

6727 South Chippawa Road
Wellandport, Ontario L0R 2J0, Canada

Head of School: Lt. Col. G. Scott Bowman

General Information Boys' boarding college-preparatory, arts, business, English and Math foundational building, and military school; primarily serves underachievers, students with learning disabilities, individuals with Attention Deficit Disorder, individuals with emotional and behavioral problems, dyslexic students, Oppositional Defiant Disorder, and Attention Deficit Hyperactive Disorder. Grades 6–12. Founded: 1978. Setting: rural. Nearest major city is Hamilton, Canada. Students are housed in single-sex dormitories and barracks. 168-acre campus. 14 buildings on campus. Approved or accredited by Ontario Ministry of Education and Ontario Department of Education. Language of instruction: English. Total enrollment: 125. Upper school average class size: 14. Upper school faculty-student ratio: 1:14. Upper School students typically attend 7 days per week. The average school day consists of 6 hours and 30 minutes.

Upper School Student Profile Grade 11: 15 students (15 boys); Grade 12: 6 students (6 boys). 100% of students are boarding students. 65% are province residents. 9 provinces are represented in upper school student body. 20% are international students. International students from Bahamas, China, Hong Kong, Japan, United Kingdom, and United States; 5 other countries represented in student body.

Faculty School total: 14. In upper school: 13 men, 1 woman; 7 have advanced degrees.

Subjects Offered Advanced biology, advanced chemistry, advanced math, algebra, all academic, American history, ancient history, art, art history, athletic training, athletics, band, basic language skills, biology, bookkeeping, British history, business, calculus, Canadian geography, Canadian history, Canadian literature, career planning, career/college preparation, chemistry, civics, computer applications, computer art, computer education, computer graphics, computer information systems, computer processing, computer programming, computer science, computer skills, computer studies, computers, consumer education, creative writing, culinary arts, economics, English, English literature, environmental geography, environmental science, environmental studies, ethical decision making, ethics, ethics and responsibility, European history, French, functions, geography, health education, history, keyboarding, language, language arts, leadership, life management skills, martial arts, military history, navigation, nutrition, personal fitness, physical education, physical fitness, physics, reading, science, scuba diving, sports, statistics, survival training, values and decisions, volleyball, weight fitness, weight training, weightlifting, wilderness education, wilderness experience, world literature, wrestling.

Graduation Requirements Ontario Literacy Equivalence Test, minimum 40 hours of community service.

Special Academic Programs Honors section; independent study; remedial reading and/or remedial writing; remedial math; programs in general development for dyslexic students.

College Admission Counseling 16 students graduated in 2011; 14 went to college, including Brock University; McMaster University; University of Guelph; University of Toronto; Wilfrid Laurier University. Other: 2 went to work.

Student Life Upper grades have uniform requirement, student council, honor system. Discipline rests primarily with faculty.

Tuition and Aid 7-day tuition and room/board: CAN$39,950. Tuition installment plan (monthly payment plans, individually arranged payment plans). Bursaries, merit scholarship grants, need-based scholarship grants, middle-income loans available. In 2011–12, 10% of upper-school students received aid.

Admissions Traditional secondary-level entrance grade is 11. Deadline for receipt of application materials: none. Application fee required: CAN$250. Interview required.

Athletics Interscholastic: badminton, basketball, cross-country running, ice hockey, rugby, running, soccer, track and field, volleyball, wall climbing, wrestling; intramural: aerobics/Nautilus, archery, backpacking, badminton, ball hockey, baseball, basketball, bicycling, boxing, canoeing/kayaking, climbing, cross-country running, drill team, fishing, fitness, fitness walking, flag football, floor hockey, Frisbee, hiking/backpacking, hockey, ice hockey, ice skating, indoor hockey, indoor soccer, jogging, JROTC drill, life saving, marksmanship, martial arts, mountain biking, mountaineering, Nautilus, outdoor activities, outdoor adventure, outdoor education, outdoor recreation, outdoor skills, outdoors, paddling, paint ball, physical fitness, physical training, rafting, rappelling, riflery, rock climbing, ropes courses, rugby, running, scuba diving, self defense, skydiving, soccer, softball, street hockey, strength & conditioning, touch football, track and field, ultimate Frisbee, volleyball, walking, wall climbing, weight lifting, weight training, wilderness, wilderness survival, winter walking, wrestling. 3 PE instructors, 10 coaches.

Computers Computer network features include on-campus library services, Internet access, Internet filtering or blocking technology.

Contact Admissions Officer. 905-386-6203. Fax: 905-386-6607. E-mail: admissions@rla.ca. Web site: www.robertlandacademy.com

ROBERT LOUIS STEVENSON SCHOOL

24 West 74th Street
New York, New York 10023

Head of School: Douglas Herron

General Information Coeducational day college-preparatory school; primarily serves underachievers, students with learning disabilities, individuals with Attention Deficit Disorder, individuals with emotional and behavioral problems, and dyslexic students. Grades 7–PG. Founded: 1908. Setting: urban. 1 building on campus. Approved or accredited by New York Department of Education. Member of National Association of Independent Schools. Total enrollment: 60. Upper school average class size: 8. Upper school faculty-student ratio: 1:5. There are 165 required school days per year for Upper School students. Upper School students typically attend 5 days per week. The average school day consists of 6 hours and 30 minutes.

Upper School Student Profile Grade 7: 1 student (1 boy); Grade 8: 4 students (3 boys, 1 girl); Grade 9: 6 students (3 boys, 3 girls); Grade 10: 12 students (8 boys, 4 girls); Grade 11: 18 students (10 boys, 8 girls); Grade 12: 19 students (11 boys, 8 girls).

Faculty School total: 16. In upper school: 6 men, 8 women; 8 have advanced degrees.

Subjects Offered Algebra, American history, American literature, anatomy, ancient history, ancient world history, ancient/medieval philosophy, art, biology, calculus, ceramics, chemistry, creative writing, current history, drama, earth and space science, earth science, English, English literature, environmental science, European civilization, European history, expository writing, film appreciation, geometry, government/civics, grammar, health, history, history of ideas, mathematics, philosophy, physical education, physics, physiology, poetry, political science, political thought, pre-algebra, pre-calculus, psychology, robotics, science, senior project, sex education, Shakespeare, social sciences, social studies, theater, trigonometry, world literature, writing.

Graduation Requirements American history, computer literacy, English, health education, mathematics, physical education (includes health), science, social sciences, social studies (includes history), portfolio of work demonstrating readiness to graduate.

Special Academic Programs Accelerated programs; independent study; academic accommodation for the gifted; remedial reading and/or remedial writing; remedial math; programs in English, mathematics, general development for dyslexic students.

College Admission Counseling 18 students graduated in 2011; 16 went to college, including City University of New York System; Pace University; State University of New York System. Other: 1 went to work, 1 had other specific plans.

Student Life Upper grades have student council. Discipline rests primarily with faculty.

Tuition and Aid Day student tuition: $49,000. Tuition installment plan (individually arranged payment plans). Need-based scholarship grants, need-based loans available. In 2011–12, 4% of upper-school students received aid. Total amount of financial aid awarded in 2011–12: $50,000.

Admissions Traditional secondary-level entrance grade is 10. For fall 2011, 65 students applied for upper-level admission, 43 were accepted, 38 enrolled. Psychoeducational evaluation required. Deadline for receipt of application materials: none. No application fee required. On-campus interview required.

Athletics Coed Interscholastic: basketball, bowling, cross-country running, fitness, floor hockey, jogging, soccer, softball, yoga; coed intramural: aerobics, ball hockey, basketball, bicycling, blading, bowling, cooperative games, fitness, flag football, floor hockey, jogging, judo, juggling, martial arts, physical fitness, physical training, soccer, softball, strength & conditioning, table tennis, tennis, touch football, volleyball, weight lifting, weight training, yoga. 1 PE instructor.

Computers Computers are regularly used in art, English, history, mathematics, science, technology classes. Computer network features include Internet access, wireless campus network, Internet filtering or blocking technology. Student e-mail accounts and computer access in designated common areas are available to students. The school has a published electronic and media policy.

Contact Dr. Dayana Jimenez, Clinical Director. 212-787-6400. Fax: 212-873-1872. E-mail: djimenez@stevenson-school.org. Web site: www.stevenson-school.org

SHELTON SCHOOL AND EVALUATION CENTER

15720 Hillcrest Road
Dallas, Texas 75248

Head of School: Linda Kneese

General Information Coeducational day college-preparatory and general academic school; primarily serves students with learning disabilities, individuals with Attention Deficit Disorder, and dyslexic students. Grades PS–12. Founded: 1976. Setting: suburban. 1-acre campus. 1 building on campus. Approved or accredited by Independent Schools Association of the Southwest and Southern Association of Independent Schools. Endowment: $3.5 million. Total enrollment: 868. Upper school average class size: 8. Upper school faculty-student ratio: 1:8. There are 170 required school days per year for Upper School students. Upper School students typically attend 5 days per week. The average school day consists of 6 hours.

Upper School Student Profile Grade 9: 65 students (38 boys, 27 girls); Grade 10: 63 students (39 boys, 24 girls); Grade 11: 69 students (45 boys, 24 girls); Grade 12: 65 students (40 boys, 25 girls).

Faculty School total: 147. In upper school: 14 men, 27 women; 27 have advanced degrees.

Subjects Offered All academic, American sign language, ethics, Spanish, theater arts.

Graduation Requirements Arts and fine arts (art, music, dance, drama), computers, English, ethics, foreign language, mathematics, physical education (includes health), reading, science, social studies (includes history), speech.

Special Academic Programs Programs in English, mathematics, general development for dyslexic students.

College Admission Counseling 46 students graduated in 2012; 43 went to college, including Collin County Community College District; Texas A&M University; The University of Arizona; University of Arkansas; University of Colorado Boulder; University of Oklahoma. Other: 3 had other specific plans.

Student Life Upper grades have uniform requirement, student council, honor system. Discipline rests primarily with faculty.

Summer Programs Enrichment programs offered; session focuses on enrichment; held on campus; accepts boys and girls; open to students from other schools. 39 students usually enrolled. 2013 schedule: July 1 to July 26. Application deadline: May 10.

Tuition and Aid Day student tuition: $19,990. Tuition installment plan (SMART Tuition Payment Plan, Sallie Mae). Need-based scholarship grants available. In 2012–13, 16% of upper-school students received aid. Total amount of financial aid awarded in 2012–13: $225,950.

Admissions Traditional secondary-level entrance grade is 9. For fall 2012, 25 students applied for upper-level admission, 14 were accepted, 14 enrolled. WISC/Woodcock-Johnson required. Deadline for receipt of application materials: none. No application fee required. Interview required.

Athletics Interscholastic: baseball (boys), basketball (b,g), cheering (g), cross-country running (b,g), dance squad (g), football (b), golf (b), soccer (b), tennis (b,g), track and field (b,g), volleyball (g). 4 PE instructors, 2 coaches.

Computers Computers are regularly used in all academic, English, foreign language, information technology, lab/keyboard, library, research skills, SAT preparation, video film production classes. Computer network features include on-campus library services, Internet access, wireless campus network, Internet filtering or blocking technology. Campus intranet and student e-mail accounts are available to students. Students grades are available online. The school has a published electronic and media policy.

Contact Diann Slaton, Director of Admissions. 972-774-1772. Fax: 972-991-3977. E-mail: dslaton@shelton.org. Web site: www.shelton.org

SHOORE CENTRE FOR LEARNING

801 Eglinton Avenue West
Suite 201
Toronto, Ontario M5N 1E3, Canada

Head of School: Mr. Michael I. Shoore

General Information Coeducational day general academic and literacy, study skills, high school credit courses school; primarily serves underachievers, students with learning disabilities, individuals with Attention Deficit Disorder, individuals with emotional and behavioral problems, dyslexic students, and Autism Spectrum Disorder and Acquired Brain Injury. Grades 8–12. Founded: 1975. Setting: urban. 1 building on campus. Approved or accredited by Ontario Department of Education. Language of instruction: English. Total enrollment: 30. Upper school average class size: 6. Upper school faculty-student ratio: 1:6. There are 200 required school days per year for Upper School students. Upper School students typically attend 5 days per week. The average school day consists of 5 hours.

Faculty School total: 8. In upper school: 5 men, 2 women; 3 have advanced degrees.

Subjects Offered Advanced math, anthropology, art, business studies, calculus, Canadian geography, Canadian history, Canadian law, career education, chemistry, civics, drama, dramatic arts, earth science, English, general science, health and safety, history, independent study, law, mathematics, media arts, parenting, physical education, physics, science, science and technology, technology, visual arts, writing.

Special Academic Programs Remedial reading and/or remedial writing; remedial math; programs in English, mathematics, general development for dyslexic students; special instructional classes for high school credits, skill building.

College Admission Counseling 6 students graduated in 2012. Other: 4 entered a postgraduate year.

Student Life Upper grades have specified standards of dress. Discipline rests primarily with faculty.

Summer Programs Remediation, enrichment, advancement programs offered; session focuses on English and math credits; held on campus; accepts boys and girls; open to students from other schools. 50 students usually enrolled. 2013 schedule: June 30 to August 31. Application deadline: May 15.

Tuition and Aid Day student tuition: CAN$27,500. Tuition installment plan (monthly payment plans, individually arranged payment plans). Financial aid available to upper-school students. In 2012–13, 10% of upper-school students received aid.

Admissions Deadline for receipt of application materials: none. No application fee required. Interview required.

Computers Computers are regularly used in aerospace science classes. Computer resources include Internet access.

Contact Mr. Michael I. Shoore, Director. 416-781-4754. Fax: 416-781 0163. E-mail: info@shoorecentre.com. Web site: www.shoorecentre.com

SMITH SCHOOL

131 West 86 Street
New York, New York 10024

Head of School: Karen Smith

General Information Coeducational day college-preparatory and music and art programs school; primarily serves students with learning disabilities, individuals with Attention Deficit Disorder, and depression or anxiety disorders; emotional and/or motivational issues. Grades 7–12. Founded: 1990. Setting: urban. 1 building on campus. Approved or accredited by Middle States Association of Colleges and Schools, New York State Board of Regents, Rhode Island State Certified Resource Progam, and New York Department of Education. Total enrollment: 57. Upper school average class size: 4. Upper school faculty-student ratio: 1:4. There are 160 required school days per year for Upper School students. Upper School students typically attend 5 days per week. The average school day consists of 6 hours and 30 minutes.

Upper School Student Profile Grade 9: 10 students (4 boys, 6 girls); Grade 10: 11 students (4 boys, 7 girls); Grade 11: 9 students (4 boys, 5 girls); Grade 12: 12 students (5 boys, 7 girls).

Faculty School total: 14. In upper school: 6 men, 8 women; all have advanced degrees.

Subjects Offered Algebra, American history, art, biology, chemistry, computer skills, earth science, English, environmental science, European history, film, French, geometry, lab science, life science, physical science, physics, pre-calculus, Spanish, trigonometry, U.S. government, U.S. history, world history.

Graduation Requirements Algebra, American history, art, biology, chemistry, conceptual physics, earth science, English, environmental science, European history, geometry, government, health education, languages, physical education (includes health), physical science, pre-algebra, pre-calculus, trigonometry, world history, community service/20 hours per year.

Special Academic Programs Accelerated programs; independent study; study at local college for college credit; remedial reading and/or remedial writing; remedial math; special instructional classes for peer mediation, socialization, and motivational issues.

College Admission Counseling 12 students graduated in 2012; all went to college, including American University; Fordham University; Purchase College, State University of New York; State University of New York at New Paltz; Syracuse University; Tulane University. Median SAT critical reading: 600, median SAT math: 620, median SAT writing: 620, median combined SAT: 600. 50% scored over 600 on SAT critical reading, 40% scored over 600 on SAT math, 50% scored over 600 on SAT writing, 45% scored over 1800 on combined SAT, 60% scored over 26 on composite ACT.

Student Life Upper grades have student council, honor system. Discipline rests primarily with faculty.

Summer Programs Remediation, enrichment, advancement, computer instruction programs offered; session focuses on academic courses for enrichment, remediation, or credit; held both on and off campus; held at local colleges; accepts boys and girls; open to students from other schools. 25 students usually enrolled. 2013 schedule: June 12 to August 16. Application deadline: June 1.

Tuition and Aid Day student tuition: $34,000–$48,000. Tuition installment plan (monthly payment plans, individually arranged payment plans, quarterly payment plan). Tuition reduction for siblings available. In 2012–13, 10% of upper-school students received aid. Total amount of financial aid awarded in 2012–13: $30,000.

Admissions Traditional secondary-level entrance grade is 9. For fall 2012, 47 students applied for upper-level admission, 26 were accepted, 21 enrolled. Comprehensive educational evaluation, psychoeducational evaluation, school placement exam, Wide Range Achievement Test or writing sample required. Deadline for receipt of application materials: none. Application fee required: $50. On-campus interview required.

Athletics Coed Interscholastic: basketball, dance, martial arts, physical fitness, running, volleyball, yoga. 2 PE instructors, 2 coaches.

Computers Computers are regularly used in English, history, research skills, writing, yearbook classes. Computer network features include Internet access, wireless campus network, Internet filtering or blocking technology, yearbook and monthly newsletter. Computer access in designated common areas is available to students. The school has a published electronic and media policy.

Contact Jennifer Sudary-Narine, Executive Assistant. 212-879-6317. Fax: 212-879-0962. E-mail: jsudary@smithschool.org. Web site: www.smithschool.org

TEMPLE GRANDIN SCHOOL

6446 Jay Road
Boulder, Colorado 80301

Head of School: Ms. Jennifer Wilger

General Information Coeducational day college-preparatory school; primarily serves underachievers, individuals with Attention Deficit Disorder, and Autism (Asperger's Syndrome). Grades 6–12. Founded: 1994. Setting: rural. Nearest major city is Denver. 1-acre campus. 1 building on campus. Approved or accredited by Colorado Department of Education. Member of National Association of Independent Schools. Total enrollment: 20. Upper school average class size: 7. Upper school faculty-student ratio: 1:4. There are 180 required school days per year for Upper School students. Upper School students typically attend 5 days per week. The average school day consists of 6 hours and 15 minutes.

Upper School Student Profile Grade 8: 2 students (2 boys); Grade 9: 2 students (2 boys); Grade 10: 3 students (1 boy, 2 girls); Grade 11: 2 students (1 boy, 1 girl); Grade 12: 2 students (2 boys).

Faculty School total: 6. In upper school: 1 man, 3 women; 3 have advanced degrees.

Subjects Offered 1 1/2 elective credits, acting, advanced math, algebra, alternative physical education, American history, American literature, analysis and differential calculus, analytic geometry, applied skills, biology, calculus, career and personal planning, career education, career education internship, career exploration, career planning, career/college preparation, cell biology, chemistry, civics, civil rights, college planning, communication skills, composition, computer literacy, conceptual physics, consumer economics, consumer mathematics, contemporary history, contemporary issues, contemporary math, decision making skills, drama, earth science, economics, English, English composition, English literature, general math, general science, genetics, geometry, government, human biology, humanities, independent study, inquiry into relationship, integrated physics, interpersonal skills, Japanese, lab science, lab/keyboard, language arts, learning cognition, literature, mathematics, media literacy, participation in sports, personal and social education, personal development, personal fitness, physical science, physics, practical living, pre-algebra, pre-calculus, public speaking, reading, research, science, senior internship, senior project, sexuality, social education, social psychology, social skills, vocational skills.

Graduation Requirements Participation in college course, Internship, individualized criteria for success in next steps.

Special Academic Programs Honors section; accelerated programs; independent study; study at local college for college credit; academic accommodation for the gifted, the musically talented, and the artistically talented.

College Admission Counseling 1 student graduated in 2012 and went to Colorado School of Mines.

Student Life Discipline rests equally with students and faculty.

Summer Programs Session focuses on perspective taking; held both on and off campus; held at local radio station; accepts boys and girls; open to students from other schools. 7 students usually enrolled. 2013 schedule: June 10 to June 30. Application deadline: June 1.

Tuition and Aid Day student tuition: $21,000. Tuition installment plan (individually arranged payment plans). Need-based scholarship grants available. In 2012–13, 40% of upper-school students received aid. Total amount of financial aid awarded in 2012–13: $60,000.

Admissions Traditional secondary-level entrance grade is 8. For fall 2012, 12 students applied for upper-level admission, 9 were accepted, 7 enrolled. Admissions testing, Cognitive Abilities Test, psychoeducational evaluation, WISC/Woodcock-Johnson or Woodcock-Johnson required. Deadline for receipt of application materials: none. Application fee required: $100. Interview required.

Computers Computers are regularly used in all classes. Computer network features include Internet access, wireless campus network, Internet filtering or blocking technology. Campus intranet, student e-mail accounts, and computer access in designated common areas are available to students. Students grades are available online. The school has a published electronic and media policy.

Contact Mr. Mark Inglis, Director of Admissions and Marketing. 303-554-7363. Fax: 303-554-7558. E-mail: info@templegrandinschool.org. Web site: www.templegrandinschool.org/

TURNING WINDS ACADEMIC INSTITUTE

6885 Bauman Street
Bonners Ferry, Idaho 83805

Head of School: David Warren

General Information Coeducational boarding college-preparatory, religious studies, bilingual studies, and technology school, affiliated with Christian faith; primarily serves individuals with Attention Deficit Disorder and individuals with emotional and behavioral problems. Grades 7–12. Founded: 2002. Setting: rural. Nearest major city is Troy, MT. Students are housed in single-sex dormitories. 149-acre campus. 4 buildings on campus. Approved or accredited by Christian Schools International, National Independent Private Schools Association, and Northwest Accreditation Commission. Upper school average class size: 12. Upper school faculty-student ratio: 1:7. There are 260 required school days per year for Upper School students. Upper School students typically attend 5 days per week. The average school day consists of 6 hours.

Upper School Student Profile Grade 7: 2 students (1 boy, 1 girl); Grade 8: 4 students (2 boys, 2 girls); Grade 9: 4 students (3 boys, 1 girl); Grade 10: 14 students (8 boys, 6 girls); Grade 11: 10 students (5 boys, 5 girls); Grade 12: 8 students (4 boys, 4 girls). 70% of students are Christian.

Faculty School total: 5. In upper school: 3 men, 2 women; 2 have advanced degrees.

Subjects Offered ACT preparation, advanced biology, advanced chemistry, advanced math, Advanced Placement courses, algebra, art and culture, biology, calculus, chemistry, Christian scripture, classical studies, college planning, computer science, fitness, gardening, geography, geology, geometry, health, history, honors English, mathematics, music appreciation, nutrition, physics, poetry, political science, pre-algebra, pre-calculus, pre-college orientation, psychology, radio broadcasting, Russian, SAT/ACT preparation, stock market, theater.

College Admission Counseling Median composite ACT: 19.

Student Life Upper grades have specified standards of dress, honor system. Discipline rests primarily with faculty.

Tuition and Aid Guaranteed tuition plan. Tuition installment plan (individually arranged payment plans, quarterly payments are required). Need-based scholarship grants available. In 2012–13, 10% of upper-school students received aid. Total amount of financial aid awarded in 2012–13: $100,000.

Admissions Deadline for receipt of application materials: none. Application fee required: $598. Interview required.

Athletics Intramural: backpacking (boys, girls), baseball (b,g), basketball (b,g), bicycling (b,g), bowling (b,g), canoeing/kayaking (b,g), cross-country running (b,g), flag football (b,g), fly fishing (b,g), football (b,g), Frisbee (b,g), hiking/backpacking (b,g), jogging (b,g), kayaking (b,g), kickball (b,g), mountain biking (b,g), outdoor activities (b,g), outdoor adventure (b,g), outdoor education (b,g), outdoor recreation (b,g), outdoor skills (b,g), outdoors (b,g), physical fitness (b,g), physical training (b,g), snowshoeing (b,g), volleyball (b,g), wilderness (b,g); coed intramural: backpacking, physical fitness, physical training, snowshoeing, volleyball, wilderness. 4 PE instructors.

Computers Computer network features include on-campus library services, Internet access. Campus intranet is available to students. Students grades are available online.

Contact Melanie Shreiner, Office Manager. 208-267-1500. Fax: 208-267-1600. E-mail: melanie@turningwinds.com. Web site: www.turningwinds.com

VALLEY VIEW SCHOOL

91 Oakham Road
PO Box 338
North Brookfield, Massachusetts 01535

Head of School: Dr. Philip G. Spiva

General Information Boys' boarding college-preparatory, general academic, arts, and vocational school; primarily serves underachievers, students with learning disabilities, individuals with Attention Deficit Disorder, individuals with emotional and behavioral problems, and difficulty socially adjusting to family and surroundings. Grades 5–12. Founded: 1970. Setting: rural. Nearest major city is Worcester. Students are housed in single-sex dormitories. 215-acre campus. 9 buildings on campus. Approved or accredited by Massachusetts Office of Child Care Services. Endowment: $530,000. Total enrollment: 56. Upper school average class size: 6. Upper school faculty-student ratio: 1:6. Upper School students typically attend 5 days per week.

Upper School Student Profile 100% of students are boarding students. 15% are state residents. 25 states are represented in upper school student body. 15% are international students. International students from Canada, France, Kenya, and Mexico; 2 other countries represented in student body.

Faculty School total: 11. In upper school: 5 men, 4 women; 4 have advanced degrees; 3 reside on campus.

Subjects Offered Algebra, American literature, anatomy, art, biology, chemistry, civics, composition, computer math, computer science, creative writing, drama, drama performance, drama workshop, dramatic arts, drawing, drawing and design, driver education, earth and space science, earth science, Eastern world civilizations, ecology, environmental systems, economics, economics and history, economics-AP, electronics, English, English composition, English language and composition-AP, English language-AP, English literature, English literature and composition-AP, English literature-AP, English-AP, English/composition-AP, environmental education, environmental geography, environmental science, environmental science-AP, epic literature, ethics and responsibility, ethnic studies, European history, European history-AP, general science, geography, geometry, government, grammar, health, history, life science, literature, mathematics, music, physical education, physical science, science, social studies, Spanish, study skills, theater, U.S. history, Western civilization, world history, world literature, writing, zoology.

Graduation Requirements English, mathematics, physical education (includes health), science, social studies (includes history).

Special Academic Programs Remedial reading and/or remedial writing; remedial math.

College Admission Counseling 1 student graduated in 2012.

Student Life Upper grades have specified standards of dress, student council, honor system. Discipline rests primarily with faculty.

Summer Programs Held on campus; accepts boys; not open to students from other schools. 45 students usually enrolled. 2013 schedule: July 8 to August 18. Application deadline: none.

Tuition and Aid 7-day tuition and room/board: $68,000. Tuition installment plan (quarterly payment plan).

Admissions Academic Profile Tests required. Deadline for receipt of application materials: none. No application fee required. On-campus interview required.

Athletics Interscholastic: basketball, cross-country running, golf, lacrosse, running, soccer, softball, tennis, ultimate Frisbee; intramural: alpine skiing, archery, backpacking, baseball, basketball, bicycling, billiards, blading, bocce, bowling, canoeing/kayaking, climbing, fishing, fitness, flag football, floor hockey, Frisbee, golf, hiking/backpacking, ice hockey, ice skating, in-line skating, indoor hockey, martial arts, mountain biking, outdoor recreation, riflery, rock climbing, roller blading, running, skateboarding, skiing (cross-country), skiing (downhill), snowboarding, softball, street hockey, swimming and diving, table tennis, touch football, ultimate Frisbee, volleyball, wall climbing, weight lifting, whiffle ball. 2 PE instructors.

Computers Computers are regularly used in English, mathematics, science classes. Computer network features include Internet access. Student e-mail accounts are available to students.

Contact Dr. Philip G. Spiva, Director. 508-867-6505. Fax: 508-867-3300. E-mail: valview@aol.com. Web site: www.valleyviewschool.org

WELLSPRING FOUNDATION

21 Arch Bridge Road
PO Box 370
Bethlehem, Connecticut 06751

Head of School: Dan Murray

General Information Coeducational boarding and day college-preparatory and general academic school; primarily serves students with learning disabilities, individuals with Attention Deficit Disorder, individuals with emotional and behavioral problems, and depression, mood disorders, eating disorders, and bipolar disorder. Boarding boys grades 1–6, boarding girls grades 1–12, day boys grades 1–12, day girls grades 1–12. Founded: 1977. Setting: rural. Nearest major city is Litchfield. Students are housed in single-sex dormitories. 13-acre campus. 6 buildings on campus. Approved or accredited by Connecticut Department of Children and Families and Connecticut Department of Education. Candidate for accreditation by New England Association of Schools and Colleges. Total enrollment: 51. Upper school average class size: 6. There are 189 required school days per year for Upper School students.

Faculty School total: 20.

Special Academic Programs Independent study.

Student Life Upper grades have specified standards of dress.

Summer Programs Enrichment programs offered; held on campus; accepts boys and girls; open to students from other schools. 36 students usually enrolled.

Admissions Deadline for receipt of application materials: none. No application fee required. On-campus interview required.

Computers Computer network features include Internet access, Internet filtering or blocking technology. Campus intranet is available to students. The school has a published electronic and media policy.

Contact Nancy Thurston. 203-266-8002. Fax: 203-266-8030. E-mail: nancy.thurston@wellspring.org. Web site: www.wellspring.org

WESTMARK SCHOOL

5461 Louise Avenue
Encino, California 91316

Head of School: Muir Meredith

General Information Coeducational day college-preparatory, general academic, arts, and technology school; primarily serves students with learning disabilities, individuals with Attention Deficit Disorder, dyslexic students, and students with language-based learning disabilities. Grades 4–12. Founded: 1982. Setting: suburban. Nearest major city is Los Angeles. 4.6-acre campus. 6 buildings on campus. Approved or accredited by California Association of Independent Schools, Western Association of Schools and Colleges, and California Department of Education. Member of National Association of Independent Schools. Upper school average class size: 12. Upper school faculty-student ratio: 1:12.

Faculty School total: 50.

Subjects Offered Algebra, American history, American literature, anatomy, art, biology, career exploration, chemistry, community service, computer science, creative writing, drama, earth science, economics, English, environmental science, European history, fine arts, general science, geography, geometry, health, history, home economics, literature, mathematics, music, physical education, physical science, physics, physiology, science, sign language, social sciences, social studies, Spanish, theater, trigonometry, video, world history, writing.

Graduation Requirements Arts and fine arts (art, music, dance, drama), English, foreign language, mathematics, physical education (includes health), science, social sciences, social studies (includes history), educational career plan. Community service is required.

Special Academic Programs Independent study; study at local college for college credit; remedial reading and/or remedial writing; remedial math; programs in English, mathematics, general development for dyslexic students.

College Admission Counseling 19 students graduated in 2011; all went to college, including The University of Arizona; University of Colorado Boulder; Whittier College.

Student Life Upper grades have uniform requirement, student council, honor system. Discipline rests equally with students and faculty.

Tuition and Aid Day student tuition: $31,000. Tuition installment plan (The Tuition Plan, individually arranged payment plans, Tuition Management Systems Plan). Need-based scholarship grants, sending district special education funding available.

Admissions Traditional secondary-level entrance grade is 9. Wechsler Intelligence Scale for Children III required. Deadline for receipt of application materials: none. Application fee required: $125. On-campus interview required.

Athletics Interscholastic: baseball (boys), basketball (b,g), cheering (b,g), equestrian sports (g), football (b,g), softball (g), volleyball (g); intramural: outdoor education (g); coed interscholastic: equestrian sports, flag football, golf, soccer, swimming and diving; coed intramural: basketball, outdoor education. 3 PE instructors, 6 coaches.

Computers Computers are regularly used in English, history, science classes. Computer network features include on-campus library services, Internet access.

Contact Polly Brophy, Director of Admissions. 818-986-5045 Ext. 306. Fax: 818-380-1377. Web site: www.westmarkschool.org

WINSTON PREPARATORY SCHOOL

126 West 17th Street
New York, New York 10011

Head of School: Mr. William DeHaven

General Information Coeducational day college-preparatory, general academic, and arts school; primarily serves underachievers, students with learning disabilities, individuals with Attention Deficit Disorder, dyslexic students, and non-verbal learning difficulties. Grades 6–12. Founded: 1981. Setting: urban. 2 buildings on campus. Approved or accredited by New York State Association of Independent Schools. Member of National Association of Independent Schools. Total enrollment: 191. Upper school average class size: 11. Upper school faculty-student ratio: 1:3. There are 170 required school days per year for Upper School students. Upper School students typically attend 5 days per week. The average school day consists of 6 hours and 45 minutes.

Faculty School total: 64. In upper school: 22 men, 42 women; 56 have advanced degrees.

Subjects Offered 3-dimensional art, acting, algebra, American Civil War, American history, American literature, art, biology, community service, creative writing, drama, English, English literature, expository writing, geography, geometry, grammar, health, history, mathematics, music, physical education, science, social skills, speech, theater, trigonometry, U.S. history, writing.

Graduation Requirements Art, English, history, mathematics, physical education (includes health), science.

Special Academic Programs Remedial reading and/or remedial writing; remedial math; programs in English, mathematics, general development for dyslexic students.

College Admission Counseling 49 students graduated in 2012; 41 went to college, including Adelphi University; Curry College; Keene State College; Manhattanville College; Mitchell College; University of Vermont. Other: 1 went to work, 3 entered a postgraduate year, 4 had other specific plans.

Student Life Upper grades have specified standards of dress, student council. Discipline rests primarily with faculty.

Summer Programs Remediation, enrichment, art/fine arts programs offered; session focuses on reading, writing, and math skill development as well as study skills; held on campus; accepts boys and girls; open to students from other schools. 35 students usually enrolled. 2013 schedule: June 30 to August 20. Application deadline: June.

Tuition and Aid Day student tuition: $51,250. Tuition installment plan (SMART Tuition Payment Plan, individually arranged payment plans). Need-based scholarship grants available. In 2012–13, 20% of upper-school students received aid. Total amount of financial aid awarded in 2012–13: $500,000.

Admissions Achievement tests, admissions testing, battery of testing done through outside agency, WISC or WAIS and writing sample required. Deadline for receipt of application materials: none. Application fee required: $70. On-campus interview required.
Athletics Interscholastic: basketball (boys, girls); coed interscholastic: cross-country running, golf, soccer, softball, track and field; coed intramural: fencing, outdoor education, physical fitness, physical training, sailing, weight training, yoga. 2 PE instructors, 3 coaches.
Computers Computers are regularly used in art, English, history, science, writing classes. Computer network features include Internet access, wireless campus network, Internet filtering or blocking technology. The school has a published electronic and media policy.
Contact Ms. Medry Rodriguez, Assistant to Director of Admissions. 646-638-2705 Ext. 619. Fax: 646-839-5457. E-mail: mrodriguez@winstonprep.edu. Web site: www.winstonprep.edu

See Display below and Close-Up on page 678.

THE WINSTON SCHOOL SAN ANTONIO

8565 Ewing Halsell Drive
San Antonio, Texas 78229

Head of School: Dr. Charles J. Karulak

General Information Coeducational day college-preparatory, general academic, arts, and technology school; primarily serves students with learning disabilities, individuals with Attention Deficit Disorder, and dyslexic students. Grades K–12. Founded: 1985. Setting: urban. 16-acre campus. 2 buildings on campus. Approved or accredited by Independent Schools Association of the Southwest and Texas Education Agency. Total enrollment: 197. Upper school average class size: 10. Upper school faculty-student ratio: 1:8. There are 170 required school days per year for Upper School students. Upper School students typically attend 5 days per week. The average school day consists of 7 hours and 5 minutes.
Upper School Student Profile Grade 9: 18 students (14 boys, 4 girls); Grade 10: 22 students (14 boys, 8 girls); Grade 11: 34 students (17 boys, 17 girls); Grade 12: 18 students (14 boys, 4 girls).
Faculty School total: 30. In upper school: 7 men, 9 women; 12 have advanced degrees.
Subjects Offered Algebra, American history, American literature, anatomy and physiology, art, athletics, basketball, biology, calculus, cheerleading, chemistry, college counseling, college planning, community service, computer graphics, computer literacy, computer multimedia, drama, economics, English, English composition, English literature, environmental science, geography, geometry, government, graphic design, health, health education, journalism, mathematical modeling, multimedia, music, photography, physical education, physical science, physics, pre-calculus, reading, Spanish, speech, student publications, world geography, world history, yearbook.
Graduation Requirements Arts and fine arts (art, music, dance, drama), computer science, English, foreign language, history, mathematics, physical education (includes health), science, social sciences, 20 hours of community service per year.
Special Academic Programs Independent study; study at local college for college credit; remedial reading and/or remedial writing; programs in English, mathematics, general development for dyslexic students.
College Admission Counseling 14 students graduated in 2012; 13 went to college, including San Antonio College; St. Mary's University; The University of Texas at Austin; The University of Texas at San Antonio; University of the Incarnate Word. Other: 1 went to work.
Student Life Upper grades have uniform requirement, student council, honor system. Discipline rests primarily with faculty.
Summer Programs Remediation, advancement, sports, art/fine arts, computer instruction programs offered; session focuses on high school classes for credit; held on campus; accepts boys and girls; open to students from other schools. 100 students usually enrolled. 2013 schedule: June 17 to July 12. Application deadline: May 31.
Tuition and Aid Day student tuition: $16,500. Tuition installment plan (monthly payment plans, individually arranged payment plans). Need-based scholarship grants available. In 2012–13, 25% of upper-school students received aid.
Admissions Traditional secondary-level entrance grade is 9. For fall 2012, 11 students applied for upper-level admission, 9 were accepted, 9 enrolled. Achievement tests, battery of testing done through outside agency, comprehensive educational evaluation, Individual IQ, Individual IQ, Achievement and behavior rating scale, psychoeducational evaluation, Wechsler Individual Achievement Test, Wechsler Intelligence Scale for Children, Wide Range Achievement Test or WISC or WAIS required. Deadline for receipt of application materials: none. Application fee required: $100. On-campus interview required.
Athletics Interscholastic: baseball (boys), basketball (b,g), football (b), volleyball (g); intramural: strength & conditioning (b); coed interscholastic: cheering, cross-country running, golf, outdoor education, physical fitness, strength & conditioning, track and field; coed intramural: cheering, golf, martial arts, outdoor education, physical fitness, physical training, tennis, track and field. 2 PE instructors.
Computers Computers are regularly used in all academic classes. Computer network features include on-campus library services, online commercial services, Internet access, wireless campus network, Internet filtering or blocking technology. Campus intranet is available to students. Students grades are available online. The school has a published electronic and media policy.
Contact Ms. Julie A. Saboe, Director of Admissions. 210-615-6544. Fax: 210-615-6627. E-mail: saboe@winston-sa.org. Web site: www.winston-sa.org

Special Needs Schools Close-Ups

WINSTON PREPARATORY SCHOOL

New York, New York

Type: coeducational day school for students with learning disabilities
Grades: 6–12
Enrollment: 193
Head of School: William DeHaven

THE SCHOOL

The Winston Preparatory School (WPS) was founded in 1981 by a group of concerned parents whose children had learning disabilities. These parents knew their children would soon be past elementary school age, but would be unlikely to flourish in a traditional mainstream junior high school program. Realizing that no suitable alternatives existed, they founded WPS as an academically oriented junior and senior high school for students with learning disabilities. The New York State charter was granted in May, and in September 1981 the school opened its doors to 18 students between the ages of 12 and 19.

Since 1998, the school has been under the direction of a new administration whose primary objective was to implement a more comprehensive, responsive, and outcome-driven model, which fully and precisely addresses the needs of each student and family. The essential elements of the new model developed at this time were the one-on-one remediation based Focus Program and an integrated skill-based approach to all curricular areas.

In order to accommodate increasing enrollment, WPS moved from its long time location on the Upper West Side of Manhattan to a larger facility in the Chelsea area in 2004. The success of WPS's education model, "Education for the individual," coupled with the paucity of available middle and secondary academic settings for students with learning disabilities in Connecticut, lead the Board of Trustees to approve the launching of WPS-CT in March 2007.

WPS's mission is to facilitate the independence of individuals with learning problems through assessment-driven individualized education, research, and outreach.

ACADEMIC PROGRAM

Educational programs at WPS center on facilitating the independence of students with learning difficulties through assessment-driven individualized education. To achieve this mission, Winston's curriculum focuses on skill-based learning with an underlying emphasis on social-emotional growth.

Key to the success of WPS's educational programs is the implementation of the Continuous Feedback System by all community members, which ensures that educational programs are developed around the needs of the students and are flexible and fluid. The Winston Prep program is designed to challenge each student's strengths while developing the essentials of reading, writing, mathematics, organization, and study skills. Each individualized educational program is based upon a continuously modified understanding of each student's dynamic learning profile that evolves as the student progresses and matures. Within the curriculum, skills are taught explicitly, including daily instruction in reading, writing, science, history, and mathematics through grade 12. Small classes of 8–12 students help to create a comfortable learning environment and facilitate the individualization of course work. Students participate in a daily one-to-one instructional period called Focus, designed to serve as the diagnostic, instructional, and mentoring centerpiece of their experience. Art, drama, music, and gym are offered within the school day as well as during the after-school program. Interscholastic athletic programs are also available after school. At the high-school level, students with appropriate levels of skill mastery may participate in college courses. Ninety percent of graduates in the last five years have been accepted to college.

FACULTY AND ADVISERS

Winston Prep teachers come from a variety of educational backgrounds. While many WPS teachers are professionals in the field of learning disabilities with degrees in speech and language, reading, or special education, WPS teachers are not required to be state certified due to the independent school status.

COLLEGE ADMISSION COUNSELING

Winston Prep provides support for students wishing to transition to a post-secondary setting. Prior to high school graduation, the school works with the family to identify the types of options that may be appropriate as the next step for the student and to facilitate any other parts of the investigation and application process. Consistent with the WPS mission and philosophy, the transition process is an individualized one that centers on the student and takes into consideration the same set of cognitive, academic, and social-emotional characteristics that drive the entire diagnostic educational process at WPS.

Over 90 percent of WPS students continue on to college or university after graduating. There are numerous opportunities for academic support that the School's graduates are utilizing at the college level, including extended time on exams, one-on-one tutoring, assistance with writing papers, and help planning long-term projects. In some instances, the School has been able to connect a current WPS student with members of the alumni community to share information about a school or program they might be considering.

The College Placement and Transition Office also provides instructional seminars to senior students that address topics aimed to educate them about changes that are commonly faced by students as they make the transition to college or other post-graduate programs. The goal of this seminar program is to directly teach seniors some things that most college students are expected to figure out independently once they arrive on a campus.

ATHLETICS

As a member of the Metro League, Winston Prep competes with other independent schools in New York City. Middle school students may participate in soccer (coed), track and field, and basketball. Sports for high school students include soccer (coed), cross-country, track and field, basketball, softball (coed) and golf.

EXTRACURRICULAR OPPORTUNITIES

Experiential education opportunities further the mission to create independent learners not only in the academic realm, but in the real-world realm as well. Students have participated in a variety of day trips in and around New York City, as well as overnight trips to Washington, D.C. and Philadelphia. These trips give students much-needed exposure to the immediate world around them as well as to the larger scheme of their city and country. They also provide new experiences such as visiting local museums and sites that reinforce or expand upon the classroom curriculum.

Students have participated in film screenings and lectures on the Holocaust at both the Museum of Jewish Heritage and the Jewish Museum. On "Explore NYC Day" students toured the New York Aquarium, the Intrepid Museum, the Financial District, and Ellis Island. Many students participated in a scavenger hunt around the city, which provided practice in reading maps and navigating the subways, as well as learning about some of New York's major attractions.

In the past several years, students have also traveled to Philadelphia to visit the National Constitution Center and Independence Hall and to Washington, D.C. to tour sites including the Supreme Court, Arlington National Cemetery, and the National Gallery of Art. Over 100 WPS students attended the inauguration of President Obama. Seniors are encouraged to participate in an annual a trip, which for the past two years has included hiking and camping in West Virginia. These programs are a major strength of WPS, as they simultaneously reinforce curricular goals and provide students with unique and important experiences.

DAILY LIFE

The typical WPS student has 42 minutes of instruction in writing, literature, history, and Focus, and 60 minutes of instruction in math, science, art, physical education, and music. In addition to the core classes, students may choose to participate in an array of after-school enrichment activities including athletics, drama, tutoring, and clubs; become a member of the student leadership team; attend experiential education activities; and participate in community service opportunities.

SUMMER PROGRAMS

The Summer Enrichment Program at WPS is an extension of the WPS philosophy, principles, and model that takes place during the summer months. It provides students with the unique opportunity to participate in an individually designed program aimed to enhance academic skills and foster independence.

The strength of the Summer Enrichment Program has always been and remains the individualized education for each student. Classes do not exceed 8 students per class, with most classes averaging 4 students per class.

Students from fourth through twelfth grades from private, public, and parochial schools from New York City and abroad participate in the program. Many of those enrolled are students with a variety of learning disabilities from WPS and other schools; however, the Summer Enrichment Program also benefits mainstream students from other schools who have difficulty in their full-time school environment and who come to WPS seeking to improve their academic skills.

Average enrollment in the Summer Program is approximately 40 students. Students from St. Bernard's School, Lycée Français de New York, United Nations International School, Birch Wathen Lenox School, and the Dwight School, as well as students from Turkey, Japan, China, Guam, and Trinidad, have all been enrolled in the summer program.

COSTS AND FINANCIAL AID

All questions regarding tuition, funding, and financial aid, should be directed to the admissions office, 646-638-2705, Ext. 619. The admissions team is able to guide families through the financial aid process and can help to answer families' questions about funding.

ADMISSIONS INFORMATION

The admissions process at WPS seeks to identify students with specific learning disabilities who the school can help achieve independence and actualization of their potential. WPS students have a wide variety of cognitive and academic profiles, including students who are dyslexic, have difficulties with expressive and receptive language, have nonverbal learning disabilities, and those who have difficulty with executive functions.

While WPS is committed to serving students with learning disabilities, the School is also committed to serving a diverse population of students. WPS accepts students of all races, nationalities, and ethnic groups, and the school works hard to maintain diversity in terms of gender, educational background, and socioeconomic status.

Admissions policies at WPS conform to the National Association of Independent Schools' (NAIS) *Principles of Good Practice for Admission to Independent Schools.* WPS also has professional associations with the International Dyslexia Association, Learning Disabilities Association, Independent School Association of Greater New York, New York State Association for College Admission Counseling, National Association of Independent Schools Parents League of New York, and, of course, the New York State Association of Independent Schools with whom the school is fully accredited.

APPLICATION TIMETABLE

Winston admissions operates on a rolling basis. Prospective families should contact the admissions office for an information packet and an application, or to sign up for an Open House.

More information can be found on the School's Web site, www.winstonprep.edu and by viewing the film *Able to Learn*, found on the home page.

ADMISSIONS CORRESPONDENCE

Winston Preparatory School
126 West 17th Street
New York, New York 10011
Web site: http://www.winstonprep.edu

Kristin Wisemiller
Director of Admissions
Phone: 646-638-2705 Ext. 634
E-mail: kwisemiller@winstonprep.edu

Medry Rodriguez
Assistant to the Admissions and Transitions Office
Phone: 646-638-2705 Ext. 619
Fax: 646-839-5457
E-mail: mrodriguez@winstonprep.edu

Junior Boarding Schools

THE AMERICAN BOYCHOIR SCHOOL

19 Lambert Drive
Princeton, New Jersey 08540

Head of School: Ms. Lisa Eckstrom

General Information Boys' boarding and day college-preparatory, arts, choral music, and music theory and literacy school. Grades 4–8. Founded: 1937. Setting: small town. Students are housed in single-sex dormitories. 17-acre campus. 5 buildings on campus. Approved or accredited by Middle States Association of Colleges and Schools. Member of Secondary School Admission Test Board. Endowment: $4 million. Total enrollment: 51. Upper school average class size: 11. Upper school faculty-student ratio: 1:5. Upper School students typically attend 5 days per week. The average school day consists of 8 hours.

Student Profile Grade 6: 12 students (12 boys); Grade 7: 18 students (18 boys); Grade 8: 12 students (12 boys). 70% of students are boarding students. 60% are state residents. 13 states are represented in upper school student body. 8% are international students. International students from Republic of Korea, Switzerland, and Taiwan.

Faculty School total: 13. In upper school: 5 men, 7 women; 6 have advanced degrees; 4 reside on campus.

Subjects Offered Computer music, computer skills, English, general science, health, mathematics, music, music performance, music theory, music theory-AP, physical education, physical fitness, social studies, Spanish.

Graduation Requirements Algebra, applied music, character education, choir, choral music, concert choir, English, eurythmics (guard), eurythmy, general science, geography, mathematics, music, music appreciation, music composition, music performance, music technology, music theory, musicianship, physical education (includes health), piano, pre-algebra, social studies (includes history), Spanish, values and decisions, vocal music, voice, participation in the concert choir.

Special Academic Programs Academic accommodation for the musically talented.

Secondary School Placement 13 students graduated in 2011; they went to St. Paul's School; The Hotchkiss School; The Lawrenceville School; The Pennington School.

Student Life Uniform requirement, student council, honor system. Discipline rests equally with students and faculty.

Tuition and Aid Day student tuition: $23,300; 7-day tuition and room/board: $29,550. Tuition installment plan (individually arranged payment plans). Tuition reduction for siblings, need-based scholarship grants available. In 2011–12, 70% of students received aid. Total amount of financial aid awarded in 2011–12: $38,000.

Admissions For fall 2011, 26 students applied for admission, 22 were accepted, 13 enrolled. Audition or standardized test scores required. Deadline for receipt of application materials: none. No application fee required. On-campus interview required.

Athletics Intramural: baseball, basketball. 1 PE instructor.

Computers Computers are regularly used in English, history, mathematics, music, science classes. Computer resources include Internet access, wireless campus network, Internet filtering or blocking technology. Computer access in designated common areas is available to students. The school has a published electronic and media policy.

Contact Ms. Lori Hoffman, Admissions Associate. 609-924-5858 Ext. 34. Fax: 801-934-5858. E-mail: lhoffman@americanboychoir.org. Web site: www.americanboychoir.org

ARTHUR MORGAN SCHOOL

60 AMS Circle
Burnsville, North Carolina 28714

Head of School: Michelle Rehfield

General Information Coeducational boarding and day college-preparatory, general academic, arts, service learning, and outdoor experiential learning school. Grades 7–9. Founded: 1962. Setting: rural. Nearest major city is Asheville. Students are housed in coed boarding homes. 100-acre campus. 7 buildings on campus. Approved or accredited by North Carolina Department of Non-Public Schools and North Carolina Department of Education. Member of Small Boarding School Association. Endowment: $1 million. Total enrollment: 27. Upper school average class size: 9. Upper school faculty-student ratio: 1:2. There are 180 required school days per year for Upper School students. Upper School students typically attend 5 days per week. The average school day consists of 8 hours.

Student Profile Grade 7: 4 students (1 boy, 3 girls); Grade 8: 16 students (11 boys, 5 girls); Grade 9: 4 students (1 boy, 3 girls). 75% of students are boarding students. 75% are state residents. 6 states are represented in upper school student body.

Faculty School total: 15. In upper school: 7 men, 8 women; 1 has an advanced degree; 14 reside on campus.

Subjects Offered 3-dimensional art, 3-dimensional design, acting, ADL skills, adolescent issues, African American history, African American studies, African history, agriculture, agroecology, algebra, alternative physical education, American culture, American government, American history, American literature, American minority experience, American studies, anatomy, ancient/medieval philosophy, animal behavior, animal husbandry, anthropology, art, arts and crafts, astronomy, athletics, audio visual/media, audition methods, auto mechanics, backpacking, baseball, biology, bookbinding, botany, career education, career education internship, carpentry, ceramics, character education, chemistry, civics, civil rights, clayworking, communication skills, community garden, community service, comparative cultures, comparative politics, composition, computer skills, computers, conflict resolution, conservation, constitutional history of U.S., consumer education, crafts, creative arts, creative dance, creative drama, creative thinking, creative writing, critical thinking, culinary arts, current events, dance, debate, decision making skills, democracy in America, design, drama, drama performance, dramatic arts, drawing, earth science, ecology, English, English composition, English literature, entrepreneurship, ethical decision making, ethics, ethics and responsibility, evolution, experiential education, expressive arts, fabric arts, family and consumer science, family living, family studies, fiber arts, first aid, fitness, food and nutrition, foreign language, forestry, gardening, gender issues, general science, geography, geology, geometry, global issues, global studies, grammar, guitar, health and wellness, health education, high adventure outdoor program, history, horticulture, human rights, human sexuality, humanities, independent living, integrated mathematics, interpersonal skills, jewelry making, journalism, language arts, leadership, leadership and service, life issues, mathematics, media studies, medieval/Renaissance history, meditation, mentorship program, metalworking, music, mythology, Native American studies, natural history, natural resources management, nature study, North Carolina history, oil painting, organic gardening, outdoor education, painting, peace and justice, peace education, peace studies, peer counseling, permaculture, personal growth, photo shop, photography, physical education, physics, piano, playwriting, poetry, politics, pottery, practical living, printmaking, probability and statistics, reading/study skills, relationships, sex education, shop, social justice, social sciences, social skills, social studies, socioeconomic problems, Spanish, sports, stained glass, study skills, swimming, travel, values and decisions, Vietnam War, visual and performing arts, visual arts, weaving, wilderness education, woodworking, work experience, writing, yearbook, yoga.

Graduation Requirements Annual 18-day field service learning trip, annual 3-, 6- and 8-day outdoor education trips.

Secondary School Placement 6 students graduated in 2012; they went to Carolina Friends School; George School; The Meeting School; Westtown School.

Student Life Honor system. Discipline rests primarily with faculty.

Tuition and Aid Day student tuition: $11,495; 5-day tuition and room/board: $21,945; 7-day tuition and room/board: $21,945. Tuition installment plan (40% by 8/15, 60% by Dec. 15; monthly payment 10% interest; full payment by 8/15- 2% discount). Need-based scholarship grants, individually negotiated barter arrangements may be made available. In 2012–13, 90% of students received aid. Total amount of financial aid awarded in 2012–13: $93,000.

Admissions Traditional entrance grade is 7. For fall 2012, 18 students applied for admission, 16 were accepted, 13 enrolled. Deadline for receipt of application materials: none. Application fee required: $35. On-campus interview required.

Athletics Coed Interscholastic: soccer; coed intramural: aquatics, backpacking, bicycling, billiards, blading, canoeing/kayaking, climbing, cooperative games, cross-country running, dance, fishing, Frisbee, hiking/backpacking, jogging, mountain biking, outdoor activities, rafting, running, skateboarding, soccer, swimming and diving, ultimate Frisbee, wilderness, winter walking, wrestling, yoga.

Computers Computers are regularly used in writing classes. Computer resources include supervised student access to computers for Web research, word processing, spreadsheet. Computer access in designated common areas is available to students.

Contact Bridget O'Hara, Admissions Coordinator. 828-675-4262. Fax: 828-675-0003. E-mail: admissions@arthurmorganschool.org. Web site: www.arthurmorganschool.org

CARDIGAN MOUNTAIN SCHOOL

62 Alumni Drive
Canaan, New Hampshire 03741-9307

Head of School: Mr. David J. McCusker Jr.

General Information Boys' boarding and day college-preparatory, arts, and technology school. Grades 6–9. Founded: 1945. Setting: rural. Nearest major city is Manchester. Students are housed in single-sex dormitories. 525-acre campus. 18 buildings on campus. Approved or accredited by Association of Independent Schools in New England, Independent Schools of Northern New England, Junior Boarding Schools Association, New England Association of Schools and Colleges, The Association of Boarding Schools, and New Hampshire Department of Education. Member of National Association of Independent Schools and Secondary School Admission Test Board. Total enrollment: 215. Upper school average class size: 12. Upper school faculty-student ratio: 1:4. There are 165 required school days per year for Upper School students. Upper School students typically attend 6 days per week. The average school day consists of 4 hours.

Student Profile Grade 6: 23 students (23 boys); Grade 7: 33 students (33 boys); Grade 8: 91 students (91 boys); Grade 9: 68 students (68 boys). 89% of students are boarding students. 16% are state residents. 21 states are represented in upper school student body. 41% are international students. International students from Canada, China, Hong Kong, Japan, Mexico, and Republic of Korea; 9 other countries represented in student body.

Faculty School total: 46. In upper school: 35 men, 10 women; 20 have advanced degrees; 39 reside on campus.

Subjects Offered Algebra, American history, American literature, art, biology, ceramics, computer math, computer science, creative writing, drama, earth science, ecology, English, English literature, environmental science, ethics, European history, expository writing, fine arts, French, geography, geology, geometry, grammar, health, history, industrial arts, Latin, life skills, mathematics, music, physical science, reading, science, social studies, Spanish, speech, study skills, theater, trigonometry, typing, world history, world literature, writing.

Graduation Requirements Arts and fine arts (art, music, dance, drama), computer science, English, foreign language, mathematics, reading, science, social studies (includes history), study skills.

Special Academic Programs Honors section; independent study; academic accommodation for the gifted; remedial reading and/or remedial writing; remedial math; ESL (12 students enrolled).

Secondary School Placement 70 students graduated in 2012; they went to Avon Old Farms School; Berkshire School; Kent School; Salisbury School; St. Paul's School.

Student Life Specified standards of dress, student council, honor system. Discipline rests primarily with faculty.

Summer Programs Remediation, enrichment, advancement, ESL, sports, art/fine arts, computer instruction programs offered; held on campus; accepts boys and girls; open to students from other schools. 135 students usually enrolled. 2013 schedule: June 25 to August 3. Application deadline: none.

Tuition and Aid Day student tuition: $27,690; 7-day tuition and room/board: $47,700. Tuition installment plan (The Tuition Plan, Insured Tuition Payment Plan, Academic Management Services Plan, Key Tuition Payment Plan, monthly payment plans). Need-based scholarship grants, need-based loans, prepGATE loans available. In 2012–13, 25% of students received aid. Total amount of financial aid awarded in 2012–13: $1,000,000.

Admissions For fall 2012, 220 students applied for admission, 155 were accepted, 80 enrolled. ISEE, SSAT, TOEFL or Wechsler Intelligence Scale for Children III required. Deadline for receipt of application materials: none. Application fee required: $50. Interview required.

Athletics Interscholastic: alpine skiing, baseball, basketball, climbing, cross-country running, football, freestyle skiing, ice hockey, independent competitive sports, lacrosse, mountain biking, nordic skiing, outdoor activities, physical training, rock climbing, running, sailing, skiing (cross-country), skiing (downhill), snowboarding, soccer, strength & conditioning, tennis, track and field, wall climbing, weight training, wrestling; intramural: archery, bicycling, bowling, boxing, climbing, equestrian sports, fitness, golf, ice hockey, martial arts, mountain biking, outdoor activities, physical training, riflery, rock climbing, ropes courses, sailing, skiing (downhill), snowboarding, swimming and diving, tennis, trap and skeet, weight lifting, whiffle ball. 1 coach, 1 athletic trainer.

Computers Computers are regularly used in English, history, mathematics, science, writing classes. Computer network features include on-campus library services, online commercial services, Internet access, wireless campus network, Internet filtering or blocking technology. Campus intranet, student e-mail accounts, and computer access in designated common areas are available to students. Students grades are available online. The school has a published electronic and media policy.

Contact Mrs. Karen Colburn, Administrative Assistant. 603-523-3748. Fax: 603-523-3565. E-mail: kcolburn@cardigan.orh. Web site: www.cardigan.org

See Display on this page and Close-Up on page 692.

EAGLEBROOK SCHOOL

271 Pine Nook Road
P.O. Box #7
Deerfield, Massachusetts 01342

Head of School: Mr. Andrew C. Chase

General Information Boys' boarding and day college-preparatory, arts, and technology school. Grades 6–9. Founded: 1922. Setting: rural. Nearest major city is Springfield. Students are housed in single-sex dormitories. 750-acre campus. 26 buildings on campus. Approved or accredited by Association of Independent Schools in New England, Junior Boarding Schools Association, and The Association of Boarding Schools. Member of National Association of Independent Schools and Secondary School Admission Test Board. Endowment: $75 million. Total enrollment: 253. Upper school average class size: 10. Upper school faculty-student ratio: 1:4.

Student Profile Grade 6: 30 students (30 boys); Grade 7: 57 students (57 boys); Grade 8: 83 students (83 boys); Grade 9: 83 students (83 boys). 80% of students are boarding students. 35% are state residents. 28 states are represented in upper school student body. 35% are international students. International students from China, Hong Kong, Mexico, Republic of Korea, Taiwan, and Venezuela; 22 other countries represented in student body.

Faculty School total: 84. In upper school: 48 men, 36 women; 34 have advanced degrees; 55 reside on campus.

Subjects Offered Acting, African-American history, algebra, American studies, anthropology, architectural drawing, architecture, art, astronomy, band, batik, biology, ceramics, Chinese, Chinese history, chorus, Civil War, civil war history, community service, computer art, computer science, computer-aided design, concert band, CPR, creative writing, current events, desktop publishing, digital music, digital photography, drafting, drama, drawing, drawing and design, earth science, ecology, English, English literature, environmental science, ESL, European history, expository writing, fine arts, first aid, French, general science, geography, geometry, grammar, health, history, industrial arts, instrumental music, journalism, keyboarding, Latin, mathematics, medieval history, music, newspaper, photography, physical education, pottery, pre-algebra, public speaking, publications, Russian history, science, sex education, social sciences, social studies, Spanish, study skills, swimming, theater, typing, U.S. history, Web site design, woodworking, world history, writing.

Graduation Requirements Arts and fine arts (art, music, dance, drama), English, foreign language, mathematics, physical education (includes health), science, social sciences, social studies (includes history). Community service is required.

Special Academic Programs Honors section; academic accommodation for the gifted, the musically talented, and the artistically talented; ESL (30 students enrolled).

Secondary School Placement 86 students graduated in 2012; they went to Choate Rosemary Hall; Deerfield Academy; Northfield Mount Hermon School; Phillips Exeter Academy; The Hotchkiss School; The Taft School.

Student Life Specified standards of dress, student council. Discipline rests primarily with faculty.

Summer Programs Enrichment, advancement, ESL, sports, art/fine arts, rigorous outdoor training, computer instruction programs offered; session focuses on enrichment; held on campus; accepts boys and girls; open to students from other schools. 60 students usually enrolled. 2013 schedule: July 7 to August 3. Application deadline: none.

Tuition and Aid Day student tuition: $31,800; 7-day tuition and room/board: $49,700. Tuition installment plan (individually arranged payment plans). Need-based scholarship grants available. In 2012–13, 30% of students received aid. Total amount of financial aid awarded in 2012–13: $1,650,000.

Admissions SSAT and Wechsler Intelligence Scale for Children required. Deadline for receipt of application materials: none. Application fee required: $50. On-campus interview required.

Athletics Interscholastic: alpine skiing, aquatics, baseball, basketball, cross-country running, diving, football, Frisbee, golf, hiking/backpacking, hockey, ice hockey, ice skating, in-line hockey, indoor hockey, indoor soccer, lacrosse, mountain biking, outdoor activities, outdoor recreation, ski jumping, skiing (downhill), snowboarding, soccer, squash, strength & conditioning, swimming and diving, tennis, track and field, triathlon, ultimate Frisbee, water polo, wrestling; intramural: backpacking, bicycling, broomball, canoeing/kayaking, climbing, fishing, fitness, floor hockey, fly fishing, hiking/backpacking, hockey, ice hockey, ice skating, in-line hockey, in-line skating, indoor hockey, indoor soccer, juggling, kayaking, life saving, mountain biking, nordic skiing, outdoor activities, physical training, rafting, riflery, rock climbing, roller blading, roller hockey, roller skating, ropes courses, scuba diving, ski jumping, skiing (cross-country), street hockey, table tennis, volleyball, wallyball, weight lifting, weight training, wilderness survival. 1 athletic trainer.

Computers Computer network features include on-campus library services, Internet access, wireless campus network, Internet filtering or blocking technology. Student e-mail accounts are available to students. The school has a published electronic and media policy.

Contact Mr. Theodore J. Low, Director of Admission. 413-774-9111. Fax: 413-774-9119. E-mail: tlow@eaglebrook.org. Web site: www.eaglebrook.org

See Display on this page and Close-Up on page 694.

FAY SCHOOL

48 Main Street
Southborough, Massachusetts 01772-9106

Head of School: Robert J. Gustavson

General Information Coeducational boarding and day college-preparatory, arts, bilingual studies, and technology school. Boarding grades 7–9, day grades PK–9. Founded: 1866. Setting: small town. Nearest major city is Boston. Students are housed in single-sex dormitories. 66-acre campus. 26 buildings on campus. Approved or accredited by Association of Independent Schools in New England and Massachusetts Department of Education. Member of National Association of Independent Schools and Secondary School Admission Test Board. Endowment: $35 million. Total enrollment: 450. Upper school average class size: 12. Upper school faculty-student ratio: 1:8. There are 166 required school days per year for Upper School students. Upper School students typically attend 5 days per week. The average school day consists of 7 hours.

Student Profile 12 states are represented in upper school student body.

Faculty School total: 71. In upper school: 21 men, 32 women; 35 have advanced degrees; 40 reside on campus.

Subjects Offered Algebra, American history, American literature, art, astronomy, biology, ceramics, computer science, creative writing, drama, English, English literature, environmental science, ethics, European history, expository writing, fine arts, French, geography, geometry, government/civics, grammar, Latin, Mandarin, mathematics, music, photography, physical education, science, social studies, Spanish, world history, writing.

Graduation Requirements Art, English, history, mathematics, music, science, technology.

Special Academic Programs Honors section; independent study; term-away projects; academic accommodation for the gifted, the musically talented, and the artistically talented; ESL (35 students enrolled).

Secondary School Placement 49 students graduated in 2012; they went to Choate Rosemary Hall; Middlesex School; Phillips Exeter Academy; Saint Mark's School; St. George's School.

Student Life Specified standards of dress, student council. Discipline rests primarily with faculty.

Summer Programs Enrichment, ESL, sports, art/fine arts, computer instruction programs offered; session focuses on ESL and enrichment; held on campus; accepts boys and girls; open to students from other schools. 70 students usually enrolled. 2013 schedule: June 29 to August 9. Application deadline: April 1.

Tuition and Aid Day student tuition: $19,525–$32,450; 7-day tuition and room/board: $54,025–$56,950. Tuition installment plan (monthly payment plans, individually arranged payment plans). Need-based scholarship grants available. In 2012–13, 19% of students received aid. Total amount of financial aid awarded in 2012–13: $1,110,900.

Admissions Traditional entrance grade is 7. ISEE or SSAT or WISC III required. Deadline for receipt of application materials: none. Application fee required: $50. Interview required.

Athletics Interscholastic: baseball (boys), basketball (b,g), cross-country running (b,g), field hockey (g), football (b), golf (b,g), hockey (b,g), ice hockey (b,g), independent competitive sports (b,g), lacrosse (b,g), soccer (b,g), softball (g), tennis (b,g), track and field (b,g), volleyball (g), wrestling (b); intramural: basketball (b,g), climbing (b,g), cooperative games (b,g), dance (b,g), fitness (b,g), golf (b,g), horseback riding (b,g), physical fitness (b,g), rock climbing (b,g), ropes courses (b,g), skiing (downhill) (b,g), snowboarding (b,g), soccer (b,g), strength & conditioning (b,g), tennis (b,g), trap and skeet (b,g), wall climbing (b,g), weight training (b,g), yoga (b,g); coed interscholastic: basketball, cross-country running, golf, hockey, ice hockey, independent competitive sports, lacrosse, soccer, tennis, track and field, volleyball; coed intramural: aerobics/Nautilus, alpine skiing, backpacking, basketball, bicycling, climbing, cooperative games, dance, fitness, golf, horseback riding, outdoor activities, outdoor adventure, outdoors, physical fitness, rock climbing, ropes courses, skiing (downhill), snowboarding, soccer, squash, strength & conditioning, tennis, trap and skeet, wall climbing, weight training, yoga. 2 PE instructors, 1 athletic trainer.

Computers Computers are regularly used in art, English, foreign language, history, information technology, mathematics, music, science classes. Computer network features include on-campus library services, Internet access, wireless campus network, Internet filtering or blocking technology. Campus intranet, student e-mail accounts, and computer access in designated common areas are available to students. Students grades are available online. The school has a published electronic and media policy.

Contact Elizabeth Lyons, Assistant to the Director of Admission. 508-490-8201. Fax: 508-481-7872. E-mail: elyons@fayschool.org. Web site: www.fayschool.org

See Display below, Close-Up on page 696, and Summer Program Close-Up on page 708.

THE FESSENDEN SCHOOL

250 Waltham Street
West Newton, Massachusetts 02465-1750

Head of School: Mr. David Stettler

General Information Boys' boarding and day college-preparatory, general academic, and arts school. Boarding grades 5–9, day grades K–9. Founded: 1903. Setting: suburban. Nearest major city is Boston. Students are housed in single-sex dormitories. 41-acre campus. 25 buildings on campus. Approved or accredited by Association of Independent Schools in New England, National Independent Private Schools Association, The Association of Boarding Schools, and Massachusetts Department of Education. Member of National Association of Independent Schools and Secondary School Admission Test Board. Endowment: $33 million. Total enrollment: 475. Upper school average class size: 12. Upper school faculty-student ratio: 1:7. There are 162 required school days per year for Upper School students. Upper School students typically attend 5 days per week. The average school day consists of 8 hours.

Student Profile Grade 7: 68 students (68 boys); Grade 8: 87 students (87 boys); Grade 9: 42 students (42 boys). 50% of students are boarding students. 70% are state residents. 17 states are represented in upper school student body. 19% are international students. International students from Bermuda, China, Mexico, Republic of Korea, Taiwan, and Thailand; 7 other countries represented in student body.

Faculty School total: 91. In upper school: 40 men, 51 women; 54 have advanced degrees; 43 reside on campus.

Subjects Offered Algebra, American history, American literature, anatomy, art, astronomy, biology, ceramics, chemistry, computer math, computer programming, computer science, creative writing, drama, earth science, English, English literature, European history, expository writing, fine arts, French, geography, geometry, government/civics, grammar, health, history, human sexuality, Latin, library studies, mathematics, music, photography, physical education, physics, science, social sciences, social studies, Spanish, theater, typing, world history, writing.

Graduation Requirements Arts and fine arts (art, music, dance, drama), computer science, English, foreign language, mathematics, science, social sciences, social studies (includes history).

Special Academic Programs Honors section; academic accommodation for the gifted, the musically talented, and the artistically talented; remedial reading and/or remedial writing; remedial math; ESL (14 students enrolled).

Secondary School Placement 49 students graduated in 2011; they went to Middlesex School; Milton Academy; Noble and Greenough School; Tabor Academy.

Student Life Specified standards of dress, student council, honor system. Discipline rests primarily with faculty.

Tuition and Aid Day student tuition: $23,775–$33,750; 5-day tuition and room/board: $42,750–$43,600; 7-day tuition and room/board: $48,750–$49,600. Tuition installment plan (Academic Management Services Plan, monthly payment plans). Need-based scholarship grants available. In 2011–12, 74% of students received aid. Total amount of financial aid awarded in 2011–12: $1,043,947.

Admissions Traditional entrance grade is 7. For fall 2011, 84 students applied for admission, 43 were accepted, 34 enrolled. ISEE, SLEP for foreign students, SSAT, Wechsler Intelligence Scale for Children or writing sample required. Deadline for receipt of application materials: February 1. Application fee required: $50. On-campus interview required.

Athletics Interscholastic: baseball, basketball, cross-country running, football, ice hockey, lacrosse, soccer, squash, tennis, track and field, wrestling; intramural: alpine skiing, baseball, basketball, canoeing/kayaking, fencing, football, golf, ice hockey, mountain biking, racquetball, sailing, skiing (cross-country), skiing (downhill), snowboarding, soccer, strength & conditioning, swimming and diving, tennis, weight training. 3 PE instructors, 1 athletic trainer.

Computers Computers are regularly used in English, mathematics, science classes. Computer network features include on-campus library services, Internet access, Internet filtering or blocking technology. Campus intranet and student e-mail accounts are available to students. The school has a published electronic and media policy.

Contact Mr. Caleb Thomson, Director of Admissions. 617-630-2300. Fax: 617-630-2303. E-mail: admissions@fessenden.org. Web site: www.fessenden.org

See Display below and Close-Up on page 698.

THE GREENWOOD SCHOOL

14 Greenwood Lane
Putney, Vermont 05346

Head of School: Mr. Stewart Miller

General Information Boys' boarding and day arts, woodshop, and music school; primarily serves underachievers, students with learning disabilities, individuals with Attention Deficit Disorder, dyslexic students, and Executive Functioning Difficulties. Grades 6–12. Founded: 1978. Setting: rural. Nearest major city is Boston, MA. Students are housed in single-sex dormitories. 100-acre campus. 13 buildings on campus. Approved or accredited by Association of Independent Schools in New England, Independent Schools of Northern New England, Junior Boarding Schools Association, National Association of Private Schools for Exceptional Children, New England Association of Schools and Colleges, The Association of Boarding Schools, and Vermont Department of Education. Member of National Association of Independent Schools. Endowment: $840,000. Total enrollment: 45. Upper school average class size: 4. Upper school faculty-student ratio: 1:2. There are 199 required school days per year for Upper School students. Upper School students typically attend 7 days per week. The average school day consists of 7 hours and 30 minutes.

Student Profile Grade 6: 3 students (3 boys); Grade 7: 6 students (6 boys); Grade 8: 10 students (10 boys); Grade 9: 18 students (18 boys); Grade 10: 8 students (8 boys). 93% of students are boarding students. 16% are state residents. 16 states are represented in upper school student body. 9% are international students. International students from Canada, Hong Kong, and Panama; 2 other countries represented in student body.

Faculty School total: 33. In upper school: 15 men, 14 women; 20 have advanced degrees; 15 reside on campus.

Subjects Offered American history, American literature, art, athletics, biology, crafts, creative writing, drama, earth science, ecology, English, geography, grammar, history, mathematics, music, physical education, pragmatics, speech, theater, woodworking, writing.

Special Academic Programs Academic accommodation for the gifted, the musically talented, and the artistically talented; remedial reading and/or remedial writing; remedial math; programs in English, mathematics, general development for dyslexic students; ESL.

Secondary School Placement 12 students graduated in 2012; they went to Dublin School; The Gow School.

Student Life Specified standards of dress, student council, honor system. Discipline rests primarily with faculty.

Summer Programs Session focuses on community service travel; held both on and off campus; held at Maine, Washington, DC, and Southwest and Alaska; accepts boys; open to students from other schools. 6 students usually enrolled. 2013 schedule: June 29 to July 18.

Tuition and Aid Day student tuition: $52,000; 7-day tuition and room/board: $65,870. Tuition installment plan (individually arranged payment plans). Need-based scholarship grants available. In 2012–13, 12% of students received aid. Total amount of financial aid awarded in 2012–13: $249,290.

Admissions Traditional entrance grade is 9. For fall 2012, 30 students applied for admission, 15 were accepted, 12 enrolled. Wechsler Intelligence Scale for Children III or Woodcock-Johnson Revised Achievement Test required. Deadline for receipt of application materials: none. Application fee required: $75. On-campus interview required.

Athletics Interscholastic: baseball, basketball, cross-country running, soccer, wrestling; intramural: alpine skiing, archery, backpacking, badminton, ball hockey, basketball, bicycling, billiards, canoeing/kayaking, climbing, cooperative games, cricket, equestrian sports, fishing, fitness, flag football, floor hockey, fly fishing, football, freestyle skiing, Frisbee, golf, hiking/backpacking, hockey, horseback riding, horseshoes, ice hockey, ice skating, in-line skating, indoor hockey, indoor soccer, jogging, judo, juggling, jump rope, kayaking, kickball, lacrosse, mountain biking, mountaineering, nordic skiing, outdoor activities, outdoor adventure, outdoor education, outdoor recreation, outdoor skills, outdoors, physical fitness, rock climbing, roller blading, ropes courses, running, skateboarding, skiing (cross-country), skiing (downhill), snowboarding, snowshoeing, telemark skiing, tennis, ultimate Frisbee, volleyball, walking, wilderness, winter soccer. 1 PE instructor, 6 coaches.

Computers Computers are regularly used in English, mathematics, science, social studies, writing classes. Computer network features include Internet access, wireless campus network, Internet filtering or blocking technology, individual laptop for each student. Campus intranet and student e-mail accounts are available to students. Students grades are available online. The school has a published electronic and media policy.

Contact Mrs. Melanie Miller, Director of Admissions. 802-387-4545 Ext. 199. Fax: 802-387-5396. E-mail: mmiller@greenwood.org. Web site: www.greenwood.org

HAMPSHIRE COUNTRY SCHOOL

28 Patey Circle
Rindge, New Hampshire 03461

Head of School: Bernd Foecking

General Information Boys' boarding college-preparatory and general academic school; primarily serves underachievers, individuals with Attention Deficit Disorder, and non-verbal learning disabilities and Asperger's Syndrome. Grades 3–12. Founded: 1948. Setting: rural. Nearest major city is Boston, MA. Students are housed in single-sex dormitories. 1,700-acre campus. 8 buildings on campus. Approved or accredited by New England Association of Schools and Colleges and New Hampshire Department of Education. Member of National Association of Independent Schools. Endowment: $1 million. Total enrollment: 21. Upper school average class size: 4. Upper school faculty-student ratio: 1:2. There are 180 required school days per year for Upper School students. Upper School students typically attend 5 days per week. The average school day consists of 5 hours and 30 minutes.

Student Profile Grade 7: 8 students (8 boys); Grade 8: 4 students (4 boys); Grade 9: 3 students (3 boys); Grade 10: 1 student (1 boy); Grade 12: 1 student (1 boy). 100% of students are boarding students. 10% are state residents. 13 states are represented in upper school student body. 15% are international students. International students from Bolivia and Saudi Arabia.

Faculty School total: 14. In upper school: 7 men, 7 women; 3 have advanced degrees; 13 reside on campus.

Subjects Offered Algebra, ancient history, chemistry, civics, earth science, English, geometry, German, history, mathematics, pre-algebra, science, Spanish, world history.

Graduation Requirements English, language arts, mathematics, science, social studies (includes history).

Special Academic Programs Academic accommodation for the gifted; remedial reading and/or remedial writing; remedial math.

Secondary School Placement 2 students graduated in 2012; 1 went to college, including American River College. Other: 1 had other specific plans.

Student Life Specified standards of dress. Discipline rests primarily with faculty.

Tuition and Aid 7-day tuition and room/board: $49,000.

Admissions Traditional entrance grade is 7. Academic Profile Tests, any standardized test or Individual IQ required. Deadline for receipt of application materials: none. No application fee required. On-campus interview required.

Athletics Intramural: alpine skiing, backpacking, basketball, bicycling, canoeing/kayaking, deck hockey, fishing, flag football, floor hockey, hiking/backpacking, ice skating, kickball, outdoor activities, outdoor recreation, skiing (downhill), snowshoeing, soccer, softball, tennis, touch football, walking, wall climbing, whiffle ball, winter walking.

Computers Computers are regularly used in foreign language, writing classes.

Contact William Dickerman, Admissions Director. 603-899-3325. Fax: 603-899-6521. E-mail: admissions@hampshirecountryschool.net. Web site: www.hampshirecountryschool.org

NORTH COUNTRY SCHOOL

4382 Cascade Road
Lake Placid, New York 12946

Head of School: David Hochschartner

General Information Coeducational boarding and day college-preparatory, general academic, and arts school. Grades 4–9. Founded: 1938. Setting: rural. Nearest major city is Albany. Students are housed in residential houses. 200-acre campus. 11 buildings on campus. Approved or accredited by New York Department of Education. Member of National Association of Independent Schools and Secondary School Admission Test Board. Endowment: $7 million. Total enrollment: 88. Upper school average class size: 12. Upper school faculty-student ratio: 1:3.

Student Profile Grade 6: 8 students (2 boys, 6 girls); Grade 7: 16 students (6 boys, 10 girls); Grade 8: 22 students (12 boys, 10 girls); Grade 9: 22 students (14 boys, 8 girls). 90% of students are boarding students. 30% are state residents. 19 states are represented in upper school student body. 18% are international students. International students from Bahamas, Bermuda, China, Colombia, Mexico, and Republic of Korea; 2 other countries represented in student body.

Faculty School total: 33. In upper school: 13 men, 20 women; 9 have advanced degrees; 20 reside on campus.

Subjects Offered Algebra, American history, biology, ceramics, computer science, creative writing, earth science, English, mathematics, music, performing arts, photography, physical education, social studies, Spanish, studio art.

Special Academic Programs Remedial reading and/or remedial writing; remedial math; ESL (10 students enrolled).

Secondary School Placement 23 students graduated in 2011; they went to Dublin School; Gould Academy; Northwood School; Vermont Academy.

Student Life Specified standards of dress, student council. Discipline rests primarily with faculty.

Tuition and Aid Day student tuition: $21,700; 7-day tuition and room/board: $52,500. Tuition installment plan (monthly payment plans, individually arranged payment plans, 2-payment plan). Need-based scholarship grants available. In 2011–12, 30% of students received aid. Total amount of financial aid awarded in 2011–12: $450,000.

Admissions Deadline for receipt of application materials: none. No application fee required. On-campus interview required.

Athletics Coed Interscholastic: aerobics/dance, alpine skiing, artistic gym, backpacking, basketball, bicycling, climbing, curling, drill team, equestrian sports, field hockey, fishing, fitness walking, Frisbee, hiking/backpacking, horseback riding, lacrosse, modern dance, mountain biking, mountaineering, nordic skiing, outdoor activities, outdoor adventure, outdoor education, outdoor recreation, outdoor skills, outdoors, physical fitness, rappelling, rock climbing, running, skateboarding, ski jumping, skiing (cross-country), skiing (downhill), snowboarding, snowshoeing, swimming and diving, telemark skiing, volleyball, walking, wall climbing, wilderness survival, yoga; coed intramural: basketball, biathlon, cross-country running, skiing (cross-country), skiing (downhill), soccer.

Computers Computer resources include on-campus library services, Internet access. Student e-mail accounts are available to students.

Contact Christine LeFevre, Director of Admissions. 518-523-9329 Ext. 6000. Fax: 518-523-4858. E-mail: admissions@northcountryschool.org. Web site: www.northcountryschool.org

THE RECTORY SCHOOL

528 Pomfret Street
Pomfret, Connecticut 06258

Head of School: Fred Williams

General Information Coeducational boarding and day college-preparatory, general academic, arts, technology, and music school, affiliated with Episcopal Church; primarily serves underachievers. Boarding grades 5–9, day grades K–9. Founded: 1920. Setting: rural. Nearest major city is Hartford. Students are housed in single-sex dormitories. 138-acre campus. 24 buildings on campus. Approved or accredited by Connecticut Association of Independent Schools, Junior Boarding Schools Association, National Independent Private Schools Association, The Association of Boarding Schools, and Connecticut Department of Education. Member of National Association of Independent Schools and Secondary School Admission Test Board. Endowment: $8.3 million. Total enrollment: 251. Upper school average class size: 10. Upper school faculty-student ratio: 1:4. There are 175 required school days per year for Upper School students. Upper School students typically attend 5 days per week. The average school day consists of 7 hours and 45 minutes.

Student Profile Grade 6: 19 students (12 boys, 7 girls); Grade 7: 41 students (26 boys, 15 girls); Grade 8: 76 students (52 boys, 24 girls); Grade 9: 61 students (42 boys, 19 girls). 69% of students are boarding students. 32% are state residents. 15 states are represented in upper school student body. 43% are international students. International students from Bermuda, China, Japan, Mexico, Nigeria, and Republic of Korea; 5 other countries represented in student body. 11% of students are members of Episcopal Church.

Faculty School total: 65. In upper school: 27 men, 38 women; 25 have advanced degrees; 26 reside on campus.

Subjects Offered Algebra, American Civil War, American history, American literature, ancient world history, art, biology, chorus, creative arts, creative writing, drama, earth science, ecology, English, English as a foreign language, English literature, environmental science, European history, expository writing, fine arts, foreign language, general science, geography, geometry, grammar, history, journalism, Latin, life science, mathematics, medieval history, medieval/Renaissance history, music, photography, physical education, physical science, reading, science, social studies, Spanish, study skills, theater, vocal music, world history, world literature, writing.

Graduation Requirements Arts and fine arts (art, music, dance, drama), literature, mathematics, physical education (includes health), science, social studies (includes history).
Special Academic Programs Honors section; academic accommodation for the gifted; remedial reading and/or remedial writing; remedial math; programs in English, mathematics, general development for dyslexic students; special instructional classes for students with learning disabilities, Attention Deficit Disorder, and dyslexia; ESL.
Secondary School Placement 62 students graduated in 2012; they went to Northfield Mount Hermon School; Pomfret School; St. George's School; Suffield Academy; The Ethel Walker School; The Hotchkiss School.
Student Life Specified standards of dress, student council, honor system. Discipline rests primarily with faculty. Attendance at religious services is required.
Summer Programs Remediation, enrichment, ESL, sports, art/fine arts, computer instruction programs offered; session focuses on study skills, academic enrichment, sports , music, off campus trips; held on campus; accepts boys and girls; open to students from other schools. 62 students usually enrolled. 2013 schedule: June 25 to July 20. Application deadline: none.
Tuition and Aid Day student tuition: $22,525; 5-day tuition and room/board: $45,000; 7-day tuition and room/board: $45,000. Tuition installment plan (Key Tuition Payment Plan, SMART Tuition Payment Plan). Need-based scholarship grants available. In 2012–13, 32% of students received aid. Total amount of financial aid awarded in 2012–13: $1,398,938.
Admissions Traditional entrance grade is 8. For fall 2012, 192 students applied for admission, 138 were accepted, 78 enrolled. Deadline for receipt of application materials: none. Application fee required: $50. Interview required.
Athletics Interscholastic: baseball (boys), basketball (b,g), cross-country running (b,g), football (b), golf (b,g), soccer (b,g), softball (g), wrestling (b); intramural: basketball (b,g), dance (g), soccer (b); coed interscholastic: cross-country running, equestrian sports, fencing, golf, horseback riding, ice hockey, lacrosse, running, soccer, tennis, track and field; coed intramural: basketball, bowling, climbing, cooperative games, cross-country running, equestrian sports, fencing, fitness, flag football, golf, ice hockey, lacrosse, life saving, outdoor adventure, ropes courses, skiing (downhill), snowboarding, snowshoeing, soccer, softball, squash, street hockey, strength & conditioning, table tennis, tennis, touch football, ultimate Frisbee, volleyball, weight training, whiffle ball, yoga. 4 coaches, 2 athletic trainers.
Computers Computers are regularly used in English, French, history, mathematics, multimedia, music, science, writing, yearbook classes. Computer network features include on-campus library services, online commercial services, Internet access, wireless campus network, Internet filtering or blocking technology. Campus intranet and student e-mail accounts are available to students. Students grades are available online. The school has a published electronic and media policy.
Contact Vincent Ricci, Director of Admissions and Marketing. 860-928-1328. Fax: 860-928-4961. E-mail: admissions@rectoryschool.org. Web site: www.rectoryschool.org

RUMSEY HALL SCHOOL

201 Romford Road
Washington Depot, Connecticut 06794

Head of School: Thomas W. Farmen

General Information Coeducational boarding and day college-preparatory, general academic, and arts school. Boarding grades 5–9, day grades K–9. Founded: 1900. Setting: rural. Nearest major city is Hartford. Students are housed in single-sex dormitories. 147-acre campus. 29 buildings on campus. Approved or accredited by Connecticut Association of Independent Schools, National Independent Private Schools Association, The Association of Boarding Schools, and Connecticut Department of Education. Member of National Association of Independent Schools and Secondary School Admission Test Board. Endowment: $8.5 million. Total enrollment: 333. Upper school average class size: 14. Upper school faculty-student ratio: 1:8. There are 180 required school days per year for Upper School students. Upper School students typically attend 6 days per week. The average school day consists of 6 hours and 40 minutes.
Student Profile Grade 6: 32 students (19 boys, 13 girls); Grade 7: 55 students (27 boys, 28 girls); Grade 8: 89 students (46 boys, 43 girls); Grade 9: 77 students (49 boys, 28 girls). 54% of students are boarding students. 21% are state residents. 16 states are represented in upper school student body. 20% are international students. International students from Bermuda, China, Japan, Mexico, Republic of Korea, and Russian Federation; 4 other countries represented in student body.
Faculty School total: 60. In upper school: 29 men, 31 women; 25 have advanced degrees; 42 reside on campus.
Subjects Offered Algebra, American history, American literature, art, art history, biology, computer science, creative writing, drama, earth science, English, English literature, environmental science, ESL, European history, fine arts, French, geography, geometry, government/civics, grammar, health, history, Japanese history, Latin, mathematics, music, physical education, science, social studies, Spanish, theater, world history, writing.
Graduation Requirements Arts and fine arts (art, music, dance, drama), computer science, English, foreign language, mathematics, physical education (includes health), science, social studies (includes history).
Special Academic Programs Academic accommodation for the gifted; remedial reading and/or remedial writing; programs in English for dyslexic students; special instructional classes for students with learning disabilities and Attention Deficit Disorder; ESL (23 students enrolled).
Secondary School Placement 72 students graduated in 2012; they went to Avon Old Farms School; Berkshire School; Kent School; St. George's School; The Gunnery; The Taft School.
Student Life Specified standards of dress, student council, honor system. Discipline rests primarily with faculty.
Summer Programs Enrichment, ESL programs offered; session focuses on academic enrichment; held on campus; accepts boys and girls; open to students from other schools. 60 students usually enrolled. 2013 schedule: June 30 to August 2. Application deadline: May 1.
Tuition and Aid Day student tuition: $22,470; 7-day tuition and room/board: $47,355. Tuition installment plan (monthly payment plans, individually arranged payment plans). Need-based scholarship grants available. In 2012–13, 24% of students received aid. Total amount of financial aid awarded in 2012–13: $819,000.
Admissions Traditional entrance grade is 8. For fall 2012, 152 students applied for admission, 85 were accepted, 60 enrolled. Psychoeducational evaluation, SLEP, SSAT, Wechsler Intelligence Scale for Children III or writing sample required. Deadline for receipt of application materials: none. Application fee required: $100. On-campus interview required.
Athletics Interscholastic: baseball (boys), basketball (b,g), crew (b,g), field hockey (g), football (b), ice hockey (b,g), lacrosse (b), soccer (b), softball (g), volleyball (g), wrestling (b); coed interscholastic: alpine skiing, cross-country running, horseback riding, skiing (downhill), soccer, tennis; coed intramural: alpine skiing, archery, backpacking, bicycling, broomball, canoeing/kayaking, climbing, cooperative games, equestrian sports, fishing, fly fishing, Frisbee, hiking/backpacking, ice skating, mountain biking, outdoor activities, outdoors, physical fitness, physical training, project adventure, roller blading, ropes courses, running, skateboarding, skiing (downhill), snowboarding, strength & conditioning, table tennis, tennis, track and field, ultimate Frisbee, wall climbing, weight lifting, weight training, whiffle ball. 1 PE instructor, 28 coaches, 1 athletic trainer.
Computers Computers are regularly used in all academic, English, history, mathematics, science classes. Computer network features include on-campus library services, Internet access, wireless campus network, Internet filtering or blocking technology. Student e-mail accounts and computer access in designated common areas are available to students.
Contact Matthew S. Hoeniger, Assistant Headmaster. 860-868-0535. Fax: 860-868-7907. E-mail: admiss@rumseyhall.org. Web site: www.rumseyhall.org

See Display on next page and Close-Up on page 700.

ST. CATHERINE'S ACADEMY

215 North Harbor Boulevard
Anaheim, California 92805

Head of School: Sr. Johnellen Turner, OP

General Information Boys' boarding and day college-preparatory, general academic, religious studies, leadership/military tradition, ESL, and military school, affiliated with Roman Catholic Church. Boarding grades 4–8, day grades K–8. Founded: 1889. Setting: suburban. Nearest major city is Los Angeles. Students are housed in single-sex dormitories. 8-acre campus. 8 buildings on campus. Approved or accredited by Military High School and College Association, National Catholic Education Association, The Association of Boarding Schools, Western Association of Schools and Colleges, Western Catholic Education Association, and California Department of Education. Total enrollment: 157. Upper school average class size: 16. Upper school faculty-student ratio: 1:14. There are 180 required school days per year for Upper School students. Upper School students typically attend 5 days per week. The average school day consists of 7 hours and 45 minutes.
Student Profile Grade 6: 18 students (18 boys); Grade 7: 35 students (35 boys); Grade 8: 46 students (46 boys). 74% of students are boarding students. 48% are state residents. 3 states are represented in upper school student body. 46% are international students. International students from China and Mexico. 58% of students are Roman Catholic.
Faculty School total: 21. In upper school: 2 men, 12 women; 9 have advanced degrees; 7 reside on campus.
Subjects Offered Art, band, Catholic belief and practice, character education, choir, Civil War, computer applications, computer literacy, computer skills, conflict resolution, decision making skills, English, environmental systems, ESL, ethical decision making, ethics and responsibility, fine arts, fitness, grammar, guidance, guitar, health and wellness, health education, healthful living, history, instrumental music, instruments, interpersonal skills, keyboarding, lab/keyboard, leadership, leadership education training, life skills, marching band, mathematics, military history, military science, moral and social development, music, music appreciation, music history, music performance, participation in sports, personal development, personal fitness, personal growth, physical education, physical fitness, piano, pre-algebra, reading/study skills, religion, religious education, science, service learning/internship, single survival, social studies, Spanish, sports, survival training, swimming, volleyball, wind instruments, word processing, yearbook.

Special Academic Programs Special instructional classes for students with Attention Deficit Disorder and learning disabilities; ESL (14 students enrolled).

Secondary School Placement 44 students graduated in 2012; they went to Army and Navy Academy; Mater Dei High School; New Mexico Military Institute; Servite High School.

Student Life Uniform requirement, honor system. Discipline rests equally with students and faculty. Attendance at religious services is required.

Summer Programs Remediation, enrichment, ESL, sports, art/fine arts, computer instruction programs offered; session focuses on academics and athletic activities; held both on and off campus; held at local attractions, (e.g., beach, aquarium, water park); accepts boys; open to students from other schools. 120 students usually enrolled. 2013 schedule: July 1 to July 31. Application deadline: none.

Tuition and Aid Day student tuition: $11,560; 5-day tuition and room/board: $30,675; 7-day tuition and room/board: $41,010. Tuition installment plan (FACTS Tuition Payment Plan, monthly payment plans, individually arranged payment plans, 4 payments). Tuition reduction for siblings, need-based scholarship grants available. In 2012–13, 48% of students received aid. Total amount of financial aid awarded in 2012–13: $355,000.

Admissions Any standardized test required. Deadline for receipt of application materials: none. Application fee required: $100. Interview required.

Athletics Interscholastic: basketball, flag football, volleyball; intramural: ball hockey, baseball, basketball, bowling, cooperative games, cross-country running, drill team, equestrian sports, field hockey, fitness, flag football, golf, handball, life saving, physical fitness, physical training, soccer, softball, swimming and diving, touch football, track and field, volleyball, water volleyball, weight lifting. 1 PE instructor, 7 coaches.

Computers Computers are regularly used in English, history, science, social studies classes. Computer network features include Internet access, Internet filtering or blocking technology. Students grades are available online.

Contact Graciela Salvador, Director of Admissions. 714-772-1363 Ext. 103. Fax: 714-772-3004. E-mail: admissions@stcatherinesacademy.org. Web site: www.StCatherinesAcademy.org

ST. THOMAS CHOIR SCHOOL

202 West 58th Street
New York, New York 10019-1406

Head of School: Rev. Charles Wallace

General Information Boys' boarding college-preparatory, general academic, arts, religious studies, technology, music, and pre-preparatory school, affiliated with Episcopal Church. Grades 3–8. Founded: 1919. Setting: urban. Students are housed in single-sex dormitories. 1 building on campus. Approved or accredited by National Association of Episcopal Schools, The Association of Boarding Schools, and New York Department of Education. Member of National Association of Independent Schools and Secondary School Admission Test Board. Endowment: $18 million. Total enrollment: 35. Upper school average class size: 8. Upper school faculty-student ratio: 1:5.

Student Profile Grade 6: 9 students (9 boys); Grade 7: 8 students (8 boys); Grade 8: 7 students (7 boys). 100% of students are boarding students. 10% are state residents. 12 states are represented in upper school student body. 67% of students are members of Episcopal Church.

Faculty School total: 7. In upper school: 5 men, 2 women; 6 have advanced degrees; all reside on campus.

Subjects Offered Algebra, applied music, art, choir, computers, English, French, Greek, history, Latin, mathematics, music theory, physical education, science, study skills, theology, visual arts.

Graduation Requirements Arts and fine arts (art, music, dance, drama), English, foreign language, mathematics, physical education (includes health), religion (includes Bible studies and theology), science, social studies (includes history).

Special Academic Programs Academic accommodation for the gifted and the musically talented; remedial reading and/or remedial writing; remedial math; programs in general development for dyslexic students.

Secondary School Placement 5 students graduated in 2011.

Student Life Uniform requirement. Discipline rests primarily with faculty. Attendance at religious services is required.

Tuition and Aid 7-day tuition and room/board: $13,500. Tuition installment plan (monthly payment plans, individually arranged payment plans). Need-based scholarship grants available. In 2011–12, 70% of students received aid. Total amount of financial aid awarded in 2011–12: $187,950.

Admissions Admissions testing and audition required. Deadline for receipt of application materials: none. No application fee required. On-campus interview required.

Athletics Interscholastic: basketball, soccer, softball; intramural: baseball, basketball, fitness, flag football, floor hockey, independent competitive sports, indoor hockey, indoor soccer, kickball, lacrosse, Newcombe ball, outdoor recreation, physical fitness, running, soccer, softball, strength & conditioning, table tennis, track and field, ultimate Frisbee, volleyball. 1 PE instructor.

Computers Computers are regularly used in art, English, foreign language, history, library, mathematics, music, science classes.

Contact Ms. Ruth S. Cobb, Director of Admissions, Alumni Relations, and Development. 212-247-3311 Ext. 304. Fax: 212-247-3393. E-mail: rcobb@choirschool.org. Web site: www.choirschool.org

Junior Boarding Schools Close-Ups

CARDIGAN MOUNTAIN SCHOOL

Canaan, New Hampshire

Type: Boys' junior boarding and day school
Grades: 6–9
Enrollment: 215
Head of School: David J. McCusker Jr. '80, Headmaster

THE SCHOOL

Cardigan Mountain School was founded in 1945 to serve the specific educational and developmental needs of boys during their formative middle school years. Two men whose vision and belief in their goal were unshakable—Harold P. Hinman, a Dartmouth College graduate, and William R. Brewster, then Headmaster of Kimball Union Academy—joined forces with legendary Dartmouth President Ernest M. Hopkins to obtain the land that is now the site of Cardigan Mountain's campus. Cardigan Mountain School opened with 24 boys, and, in 1954, upon merging with the Clark School of Hanover, New Hampshire, the School as it is known today began to emerge. Since that time, the School has grown to its current enrollment of more than 200 boys in grades six through nine, while the philosophy and objectives set forth by the founders have remained unchanged.

Cardigan was built upon an educational experience that emphasized rigorous academics and study habits, as well as spiritual guidance, physical training, and social orientation. In order to accomplish this purpose, Cardigan's program was tailored to each boy so that he made the best possible use of his potential in these areas. Thus, every boy had a balanced and well-rounded life: physically, mentally, and spiritually. This philosophy is the same today as it was in 1945.

The 425-acre campus, located on Canaan Street Lake, is 18 miles from Dartmouth College. Driving time from Boston is approximately 2½ hours. Some of the finest skiing in New England is only one hour away.

The self-perpetuating Board of Trustees is instrumental in guiding the School. The School's endowment is valued at more than $15.3 million. In 2011–12, Annual Giving was approximately $1 million.

Cardigan Mountain School is accredited by the New England Association of Schools and Colleges. Its memberships include the National Association of Independent Schools (NAIS), the Junior Boarding Schools Association, the Independent Schools Association of Northern New England (ISANNE), the Association of Independent Schools of New England (AISNE), the Secondary School Admission Test Board (SSATB), Boys' Schools, A Better Chance (ABC), the Federation of American Independent Schools, and the Educational Records Bureau (ERB).

ACADEMIC PROGRAM

Cardigan's curriculum is designed both to support and to challenge each student as the School prepares him for the demanding academic programs characteristic of the independent schools most graduates attend. In all disciplines, special emphasis is placed upon mastery of fundamental skills, content, and the study skills needed to become academically self-sufficient.

The curriculum provides each student with thorough instruction in all the major courses and substantial exposure to a number of other subject areas that round out a boy's education at this age. Cardigan requires all students to take yearlong courses in English, mathematics, social studies, and science. In addition, a world language (French, Latin, or Spanish) is required of boys not enrolled in English as a Second Language (ESL).

Beyond these major courses, the School also requires each boy to broaden his horizons and strengthen his scholastic preparation through additional course work in music, life skills, leadership, and art or woodworking. All students are required to attend evening study halls, with teachers from all subjects available for support. The advisory and conference period gives students another opportunity to work with faculty members on an individual basis.

Cardigan students also take a course called Personalized Education for the Acquisition of Knowledge and Skills (PEAKS®), which helps them become stronger learners and self-advocates. The PEAKS program provides students with guided self-development and helps each student, no matter his skill level, become a better learner and self-advocate. PEAKS facilitates collaboration among the members of the Cardigan Mountain School community to respond to the evolving needs of each student by focusing on the process of learning through the acquisition of developmentally appropriate knowledge and skills. Cardigan believes that every student learns differently. Through the PEAKS program, each boy comes to understand how he learns best, and becomes equipped with tools to use as he goes forward, enabling him to find success as a lifelong learner. The PEAKS program also offers additional resources for students in and out of the classroom.

PEAKS coaches are available for one-on-one assistance in the afternoons and evenings. Recognizing that some students require regular attention, while others may need less frequent support, the program is designed to maximize the accessibility of the coaches to their students.

The Charles C. Gates Invention & Innovation Competition is an academic and afternoon program offering at Cardigan made possible by a generous contribution from a past parent and Cardigan trustee through the Gates Frontiers Fund. Gates at Cardigan is designed to encourage creative thinking, risk-taking, and entrepreneurial spirit, and to develop an appreciation for hard work and accomplishment for students in grades six through nine. The competition offers students the opportunity to participate in the creative process, identify needs or new business opportunities, and develop practical solutions. Beginning each fall and concluding with competition presentations in the spring, each student or student team designs and builds an invention that must perform a practical function, make life easier or safer, entertain, or solve an everyday problem.

Cardigan Mountain School believes that students who learn to validate and appreciate different perspectives from across the United States, and around the world, are best prepared to meet the ever-changing needs of today's diverse society. Launched in the 2012–13 academic year, the *Global Community Initiative* (GCI) creates intentional opportunities for the entire school to come together to listen and learn from a wide range of life experiences and social identities. Each Cardigan student attends a weekly global leadership class in order to gain new insights and develop fundamental value-driven leadership skills such as critical thinking, open communication, innovative problem-solving, and ethical decision-making. This is further enhanced by the School's community service learning program, international spring break trips, Chapel services, and dining hall discussions. In addition, the entire community celebrates different cultural and religious holidays as well as attends GCI-related presentations and performances on campus and at Dartmouth College's Hopkins Center for the Arts.

FACULTY AND ADVISERS

The faculty consists of 46 full-time and 6 part-time members, the majority of whom reside on campus. Almost one quarter of the faculty members are women and 20 faculty members have earned advanced academic degrees. All faculty members teach, coach, supervise dormitories, and serve as advisers for the students. Cardigan has a 4:1 student-faculty ratio. Of the greatest importance to Cardigan are the faculty members who, by setting and attaining personal goals, serve as positive role models for the boys. Cardigan faculty members bring with them a love for learning and a variety of skills, experiences, and talents that broaden and enrich the educational experience and inject warmth and enthusiasm into campus life.

SECONDARY SCHOOL PLACEMENT

Cardigan offers extensive assistance to the students and their parents in selecting and then applying to independent secondary schools. The Secondary School Placement Office begins the counseling process in the spring of the eighth grade and continues to guide the student and his family throughout the application experience. The Placement Office offers workshops on interviewing techniques, SSAT preparation, and essay writing.

Cardigan graduates have matriculated to schools such as Avon Old Farms, Brooks, Deerfield, Holderness, Hotchkiss, Lawrence, Phillips Andover, Phillips Exeter, Pomfret, Salisbury, St. Mark's, St. Paul's, Tabor, Taft, and Westminster.

STUDENT BODY AND CONDUCT

For 2012–13, 215 boys are enrolled at Cardigan. There were 68 boys in the ninth grade, 91 in the eighth, 33 in the seventh, and 23 in the sixth. Almost 90 percent of the Cardigan students were boarders. In 2012–13, students came to Cardigan from 21 states and 13 countries.

Cardigan has a two-tiered disciplinary status system in order to inform students, their advisers, and parents when School expectations are not being met. This disciplinary system is used to correct patterns of misbehavior and to discipline those students who commit serious offenses. The Discipline Committee meets to hear cases deemed appropriate by the headmaster and the assistant headmaster. Two student leaders and 3 faculty members are selected by the assistant headmaster to join him on the committee. The committee hears cases and makes a recommendation for consequences to the headmaster.

Cardigan has a clearly stated honor code, and all students are expected to abide by the spirit of that code.

ACADEMIC FACILITIES

The numerous buildings that house academic facilities are highlighted by the Bronfman Center. Completed in 1996, Bronfman Center features, among other things, three Freda R. Caspersen state-of-the-art science laboratories, an art studio, the School Store, and classrooms for the sixth-grade class. Stoddard Center is the home of both the Kirk Library and the Humann Theatre. The Kirk Library is a three-tiered, well-equipped multimedia resource center that offers students and faculty members computer software, audio and video resources, as well as more than 10,000 volumes and numerous journals and periodicals. Thousands of newspaper and magazine articles are available through EbscoHost, a service provided by the New Hampshire State Library. Computers with Internet access are available in both the Kirk Library and the adjacent writing lab. Affiliation with the New Hampshire State Library's Automated Information Access System enables users at the School to obtain materials through the interlibrary loan process. The library is staffed by one full-time librarian and a part-time aid. A flexible access plan allows students and faculty members to work in groups, as well as individually, throughout the day and five evenings each week. Humann Theatre, the School's 250-seat auditorium, is the site of School meetings, lectures, films, concerts, and drama performances.

Cardigan encourages participation in the visual arts. The Williams Wood Shop and the Art Center are focal points for this important aspect of a boy's education. Hayward Hall houses the School's music facilities, where opportunities for vocal and instrumental instruction are available. The School's newest facility, the Cardigan Commons, is scheduled to open in spring 2013. The facility will feature bright spaces, a commanding view of Mount Cardigan, a new student center, a new dining hall, a large state-of-the-art multimedia classroom, and academic spaces. This facility is designed to enhance the campus and nurture Cardigan's already close-knit community.

BOARDING AND GENERAL FACILITIES

Eleven dormitories house from 8 to 16 students each. Each dormitory houses faculty members and their families. Students reside in double rooms, with some singles provided. Two dormitories, referred to as Dewar House and Funnell House, were completed in the fall of 2000 with each housing 3 faculty members, their families, and 12 students. In addition, all dormitory rooms and classrooms provide wireless access to the Internet. The School operates the on-campus Hamilton Family Student Health Center, where most of the students' medical needs can be met. For extended services, Cardigan students benefit from the Alice Peck Day Hospital and Dartmouth-Hitchcock Medical Center, both of which are located in Lebanon, New Hampshire. The Hamilton Family Student Health Center has a resident nurse and a visiting physician.

ATHLETICS

The objectives of the activities program at Cardigan are to provide the boys with opportunities to experience success, to offer healthy and enjoyable activities for the boys' free-time periods and weekends, to promote the physical and athletic development of each boy, to teach cooperation with and reliance on teammates, to allow the boys to experience sports and activities that may be new or unfamiliar to them, and to encourage good sportsmanship.

Over the years, Cardigan has been fortunate enough to acquire extensive athletics facilities, fields, and equipment. These include five fields for soccer, football, and lacrosse; 15 outdoor tennis courts; two baseball diamonds; a state-of-the-art hockey rink that can be converted to a multipurpose arena in the fall and spring; an on-campus, lighted ski slope; cross-country ski trails; ski team rooms; a wrestling room; an outing club room; a fully equipped weight-training room; an indoor climbing cave; and indoor and outdoor basketball courts.

As the School is situated on the shores of Canaan Street Lake, students and faculty members take full advantage of water-related activities. Sailing is offered as a competitive sporting activity, and motorboats kayaks, and canoes provide additional opportunities for students to enjoy the water. The waterfront area is well supervised, and instruction is available in all activities.

Cardigan has one of the top student-focused rock-climbing programs on the East Coast. When students complete the rock-climbing program at Cardigan they leave with a strong foundation of specific outdoor skills. Several former Cardigan rock climbers have continued to climb at secondary schools with great competence, strength, and problem-solving skills. The School's training facilities are some of the best in New England. The Cougar Cave is an 800-square-foot indoor bouldering room designed and built to train for sheer difficulty of movement, and it builds the athlete's endurance as well. In addition to the state-of-the art facilities, climbers travel two days a week to nearby Rumney, New Hampshire to rope up and challenge themselves on the high cliffs of Rattlesnake Mountain. This world-class climbing area has hundreds of moderate routes, which are perfect for middle school boys to learn new climbing skills, develop their technique, and have a great deal of fun.

The Sunapee Mountain ski area is close to the School and is used on weekdays by the Alpine ski team, recreational skiers, and snowboarders. On Sundays, there are day-long ski trips to major ski areas in New Hampshire and Vermont. Cardigan Mountain School skiers take advantage of the fully equipped, on-campus athletic training facilities for dry-land training beginning in the fall. The School's athletes train at three mountains—Mount Sunapee, Proctor, and Ragged Mountain—to offer the athletes varied terrain to develop and challenge their skills. The program focuses on the development of the fundamental skills needed to become a successful skier. During dry-land training the athletes work hard to develop strength, power, flexibility, speed, and coordination. The program also works hard on snow to develop tactical, mental, motivational, and the basic fundamental techniques that will allow young athletes to take their skiing to the next level. The racing program offers three levels of competition: USSA/Eastern, varsity, and junior varsity racing. Coaches use video analysis of on-snow performance to give the students yet another tool to improve their skills. Cardigan is committed to helping its athletes grow and develop both in sport and as good citizens.

Cardigan also offers a mountain biking program. Mountain bikers receive technical skills instruction and fitness, speed, and endurance training; learn about technical trail riding; and engage in competition against twelve New Hampshire, Vermont, and Maine high schools in the Lakes Region Interscholastic Mountain Bike Race League. Cardigan utilizes technical skills trails that feature typical New England single track (rocks and roots) and a newly built two-mile field conditioning loop with man-made technical trail features such as berms, drops, step-ups, log hops, rollers, log rolls, bridges, and log rides, most of which have been constructed by the team members. Team members also do conditioning rides on local dirt roads, woods roads, and snowmobile trails. For the 2012 season, Cardigan opened a new four-mile loop of woods single-track with technical flow adjacent to the field loop.

As in the classroom, the focus of interscholastic sports and individual activities is on learning the fundamentals. Teams are fielded on several levels in most sports, and they compete against local independent and public schools. Recreational sports are offered for the student who does not wish to compete interscholastically.

EXTRACURRICULAR OPPORTUNITIES

Many students and faculty members bring to Cardigan skills and interests that, though not included in the usual program of studies, may be pursued and developed in the informal setting of the Club Program. Clubs meet every Thursday afternoon in lieu of athletics, with the opportunity for additional meetings if the members and adviser so desire. Recent clubs have featured the following activities: community service, playing in a rock band, trap shooting, Lego building, ice fishing, chess, photography, SSAT prep, and culinary skills. Students have also played Whiffleball, broomball, Ultimate (Frisbee), and team handball.

A boy may participate in the optional drama program in each of the three seasons. The department mounts four productions a year: a series of one-act plays, the annual Christmas pageant, a full-length play/musical, and scenes from plays during the spring term talent show. Boys are given opportunities to act, serve backstage, learn to work lights and sound, build and decorate sets, produce, and, in some cases, direct. During the nights of performance, the student stage managers and student technical staff run the entire show. The audition process gives boys an excellent opportunity to learn the skills required to get a part.

DAILY LIFE

The typical academic day begins six days per week with a required family-style breakfast. After room inspection in the dormitories, classes begin at 7:45 a.m. and six class periods precede a family-style lunch. On Monday, Tuesday, Thursday, and Friday, lunch is followed by an advisory and conference period. On Wednesday and Saturday, the academic day ends with lunch and is followed by a full slate of athletics and recreational activities. Dinner is a family-style meal every evening except on Wednesday and Saturday, when a buffet is scheduled. A study period occurs each school night. Lights-out ranges from 9:20 to 10 p.m., depending on the evening and the age of the student.

Cardigan is nondenominational, yet the School seeks to strengthen each boy's spiritual development within his own religious heritage. All boys are required to attend the weekly Thursday afternoon chapel service. Arrangements are made for students of all faiths to attend appropriate weekly services in the immediate area.

WEEKEND LIFE

In addition to the regularly scheduled vacations, all boys may take weekends away from campus, and parents are invited to the campus to share in their son's experience at any time. The majority of Cardigan students are on campus on weekends, and the School provides an exciting array of options for them. A typical Saturday night's schedule might include a movie, a trip off campus, various other on-campus activities and programs, or an excursion to Dartmouth College to watch a hockey game.

SUMMER PROGRAMS

The Cardigan Mountain Summer Session, a coeducational experience for 170 girls and boys, was instituted in 1951 to meet the needs of four groups of students: those who may be seeking admission to Cardigan in the fall, those who desire advanced academic work and enrichment, those who require intensive work in basic academic skills, and those who require review. The Summer Session also serves a limited number of international students for whom English is not a first language. Cardigan's outstanding range of sports and activities, along with its academic offerings, makes the Summer Session a special blend of camp and school.

Academic enrichment offerings in the sciences are a focal point for the more able students. Courses in environmental sciences are designed to better prepare youngsters for the changing world. The visual and performing arts, long a part of the Summer Session's afternoon program, achieve curricular status, allowing students to pursue drama, dance, woodwork, ceramics, and photography as part of their morning academic program of study.

The six-week program is still known for its individualized instruction, close supervision of daily study time, and general emphasis on improving study skills. Academic offerings include English, advanced English composition, pre-algebra, algebra I and II, geometry, study skills, French, Spanish, and Latin.

The Summer Session is open to students who have completed third through ninth grade. The tuition for a student boarding for six weeks in 2013 is $8400 ($4300 for day students) and for students participating in the three-week program, the tuition is $5045 ($2570 for day students). Need-based aid is available.

COSTS AND FINANCIAL AID

In 2012–13, charges for boarding students are $47,700 and for day students, $27,690. There are additional charges for items such as textbooks, a one-to-one laptop program, laundry service, and athletic equipment.

Financial aid is available to families of qualified students who complete the School and Student Service for Financial Aid forms and demonstrate need. Information about loans and payment plans is available from the Cardigan Admissions Office. For 2012–13, approximately 25 percent of the student body received more than $1.27 million in financial assistance.

ADMISSIONS INFORMATION

Cardigan seeks to enroll students of good character and academic promise who will contribute to and benefit from the broad range of academic and extracurricular opportunities available. The Admissions Committee reviews applications on a rolling admissions basis for students wishing to enter the sixth through the ninth grades. Students in grades 3–9 are considered for the Summer Session. Decisions are based upon previous school records, teacher recommendations, aptitude testing, and a campus interview. Cardigan admits students of any race, color, nationality, or ethnic origin to all the rights, privileges, programs, and activities generally accorded or made available to students at the School.

APPLICATION TIMETABLE

Initial inquiries are welcome at any time. Office hours are 8:00 a.m. to 4:00 p.m., Monday through Friday, and 8:00 a.m. to 12:00 noon on Saturday. School catalogs and applications can be obtained through the Admissions Office. The application fee is $50 for domestic applicants and $125 for international applicants.

ADMISSIONS CORRESPONDENCE

Chip Audett, Director of Admissions and Director of Financial Aid
Cardigan Mountain School
62 Alumni Drive
Canaan, New Hampshire 03741
United States
Phone: 603-523-3510
Fax: 603-523-3565
E-mail: caudett@cardigan.org
Web site: http://www.cardigan.org

John Bayreuther, Associate Director of Admissions
Jessica Bayreuther, Associate Director of Admissions
Cardigan Mountain School
62 Alumni Drive
Canaan, New Hampshire 03741
United States
Phone: 603-523-3544
603-523-3528
E-mail: jbayreuther@cardigan.org
jebay@cardigan.org
Fax: 603-523-3565
Web site: http://www.cardigan.org

Matt Rinkin, Summer Session Programs Coordinator
Cardigan Mountain School
62 Alumni Drive
Canaan, New Hampshire 03741
United States
Phone: 603-523-3526
Fax: 603-523-3565
E-mail: mrinkin@cardigan.org

EAGLEBROOK SCHOOL

Deerfield, Massachusetts

Type: Boys' day and boarding school
Grades: 6–9
Enrollment: 253
Head of School: Andrew C. Chase, Headmaster

THE SCHOOL

Eaglebrook School was opened in 1922 by its Headmaster and founder, Howard B. Gibbs, a former faculty member of Deerfield Academy. One of the earliest members of his faculty was C. Thurston Chase. When Mr. Gibbs died in 1928, Mr. Chase became Headmaster, a position he held for thirty-eight years. From 1966 to 2002, Stuart and Monie Chase assumed leadership of the School. While continuing to foster the School's traditional commitment to excellence, the Chases have encouraged and developed many components of a vital school: expansion of both academic and recreational facilities, emphasis on the arts, increased endowment and financial aid, student and faculty diversity, and a balanced, healthful diet. Stuart and Monie's son, Andrew C. Chase, now assumes leadership duties as Headmaster. Eaglebrook's goals are simple—to help each boy come into full and confident possession of his innate talents, to improve the skills needed for the challenges of secondary school, and to establish values that will allow him to be a person who acts with thoughtfulness and humanity.

The School owns more than 750 acres on Mt. Pocumtuck, overlooking the Deerfield Valley and the historic town of Deerfield. It is located 100 miles west of Boston and 175 miles north of New York City.

The Allen-Chase Foundation was chartered in 1937 as a charitable, educational trust. It is directed by a 40-member self-perpetuating Board of Trustees, representing alumni, parents, and outside professionals in many fields.

Eaglebrook is a member of the National Association of Independent Schools, the Association of Independent Schools of New England, the Valley Independent School Association, the Junior Boarding School Association, and the Secondary School Admissions Test Board.

ACADEMIC PROGRAM

Sixth graders are taught primarily in a self-contained setting. Subjects include English, mathematics, reading, Latin, history, science, and trimester-length courses in studio art, computers, music, and woodworking. Required classes for grades 7 through 9 each year include foreign language study in Latin, French, Mandarin Chinese, or Spanish; a full year of mathematics; a full year of Colonial history in seventh grade, followed by a self-selected history the next two years; a full year of English; two trimesters of geography; two trimesters of science in seventh grade, followed by a full-year laboratory course; one trimester of human sexuality in eighth grade; and one trimester of ethics in the ninth grade. The School offers extensive trimester electives, including band and instrumental instruction, computer skills, word processing, current events, conditioning, chess, film classics, drama, public speaking, industrial field trips, music appreciation, first aid, publications, and an extensive variety of studio arts. Drug and alcohol education is required of all students in every grade.

Class enrollment averages 8 to 12 students. Teachers report directly to a student's adviser any time the student's work is noteworthy, either for excellence or deficiency. This allows the adviser to communicate praise or concern effectively and initiate appropriate follow-up. Midway through each trimester, teachers submit brief written evaluations to the advisers of each of their students. Advisers stay in close touch with the parents of their advisees. Grades, along with full academic reports from each of the student's teachers, are given to advisers each trimester and then sent home. The reports are accompanied by a letter from the adviser discussing the student's social adjustment progress, athletic and activity accomplishments, and academic progress and study habits.

FACULTY AND ADVISERS

Andrew C. Chase, the current Headmaster, is a graduate of Deerfield Academy and Williams College. Along with his wife, Rachel Blain, a graduate of Phillips Andover Academy and Amherst College, Andrew succeeded his father as Headmaster in 2002.

Eaglebrook's full- and part-time faculty consists of 72 men and women, 46 of whom live on campus, many with families of their own. Seventy hold undergraduate degrees, and 30 also hold graduate degrees. Leaves of absence, sabbaticals, and financial assistance for graduate study are available. The ratio of students to faculty members is 4.9:1.

Teachers endeavor to make learning an adventure and watch over each boy's personal growth. They set the academic tone, coach the teams, serve as dorm parents, and are available for a boy when he needs a friend. They help each individual establish lifelong study habits and set standards for quality. Eaglebrook's teachers have the skill not only to challenge the very able but also to make learning happen for those who need close supervision. Faculty members are chosen primarily for their appreciation of boys this age, their character and integrity as role models, and competence in their subject areas. The fact that many are married and have children of their own helps to create a warm, experienced family atmosphere.

SECONDARY SCHOOL PLACEMENT

The Director of Placement assists families in selecting, visiting, and applying to secondary schools. He meets with parents and students in the spring of a boy's eighth-grade year to discuss which schools might be appropriate based on each boy's aptitude, interests, achievements, and talent. He arranges visits from secondary schools and helps with applications. Parents and the Director of Placement work together until the boy has decided upon his secondary school in April of his ninth-grade year.

Schools frequently attended by Eaglebrook School graduates include Deerfield Academy, Choate Rosemary Hall, the Hotchkiss School, Loomis Chaffee, Northfield Mount Hermon School, Phillips Andover Academy, Phillips Exeter Academy, Pomfret School, St. George's School, St. Paul's School, Taft School, and Westminster School.

STUDENT BODY AND CONDUCT

In the 2012–13 school year, of the 195 boarding students and 58 day students, 30 are in grade 6, 57 in grade 7, 83 in grade 8, and 83 in grade 9. Twenty-four states and seventeen countries are represented.

There are specified standards of dress, which are neat and informal most of the time. Discipline is handled on an individual basis by those faculty members who are closely involved with the student.

ACADEMIC FACILITIES

The C. Thurston Chase Learning Center contains classrooms, an audiovisual center, and an assembly area. It also houses the Copley Library, which contains 18,000 volumes and subscriptions to eighty-five publications, books on tape, newspapers, DVDs, and Internet access. The computer room is equipped with state-of-the-art computers, color printers, scanners, digital cameras, and a projection board. The Bartlett Assembly Room is an all-purpose area with seats for the entire School. The Jean Flagler Matthews Science Building houses three laboratories, classrooms, a project room, a library, an online computerized weather station, and teachers' offices. The Bryant Arts Building houses studios for drawing, painting, stained glass, architectural design, computer-aided design, stone carving, ceramics, silk-screening, printmaking, and computer art; a darkroom for photography; a woodworking shop; a band rehearsal room; a publications office; a piano studio; piano practice rooms; and a drama rehearsal room. The campus has a high-speed fiber-optic network with e-mail and access to the Internet for research.

BOARDING AND GENERAL FACILITIES

Dormitories are relatively small; the five dormitories house between 18 and 36 students each, with at least one faculty family to every 8 to 10 boys.

Most students live in double rooms. A limited number of single rooms are available. After the first year, a boy may request a certain dormitory and adviser.

ATHLETICS

The athletics program is suitable for boys of all sizes and abilities. Teams are small enough to allow each boy a chance to play in the games, master skills, and develop a good sense of sportsmanship. The School's Athletic Director arranges a competitive schedule to ensure games with teams of equal ability. Fall sports include cross-country, tennis, hiking, football, water polo, and soccer. Winter sports include ice hockey, basketball, recreational and competitive skiing, swimming and diving, snowboarding, squash, and wrestling. The School maintains the Easton Ski Area, consisting of several ski trails, the Macomber Chair Lift, and snowmaking equipment. Spring sports are baseball, track and field, golf, Ultimate Disc, lacrosse, triathlon, mountain and road biking, and tennis. The School plays host to numerous students throughout the year in seasonal tournaments in ice hockey, soccer, skiing, basketball, Ultimate Disc, swimming, and wrestling. The Schwab Family Pool is a six-lane facility for both competitive and recreational swimming. The McFadden Rink at Alfond Arena features a state-of-the-art NHL-dimensioned 200-foot by 85-foot indoor ice surface. A multisport indoor surface is installed in the arena in the off-season to enable use of the facility for in-line skating, in-line hockey, soccer, lacrosse, and tennis. The Lewis Track and Field was dedicated in 2002.

EXTRACURRICULAR OPPORTUNITIES

Service and leadership opportunities build a sense of pride in the School and camaraderie in the student body. Elected Student Council representatives meet with the Headmaster as an advisory group and discuss School issues. Boys act as admissions guides, help with recycling, organize dances, serve as proctors in the dormitories and the dining room, act as headwaiters, and give the morning assemblies. Boys also assume responsibility, with faculty guidance, for the School newspaper, yearbook, and literary magazine.

Many of the students participate in numerous outdoor activities that are sponsored by the Mountain Club. They maintain an active weekend schedule that includes camping, hiking, backpacking, canoeing, kayaking, white-water rafting, fishing, rock climbing, and snowshoeing.

DAILY LIFE

On weekdays, students rise at 7:20 a.m.; breakfast is at 8. Academic class periods, including assembly, begin at 8:30. Lunch is at noon, and classes resume at 12:33. Study hall and special appointments begin at 2:15, athletics begin at 3:15, and tutorial periods and other activities begin at 5. Dinner is at 6, and evening activities are scheduled between 6:45 and 7:30; study hall is then held until 9:15 p.m. or later, according to the grade.

WEEKEND LIFE

A wide variety of weekend activities are available at Eaglebrook, both on campus and off, including community service, riflery, museum visits, dances, field trips, tournaments, movies, plays, concerts, town trips, Deerfield Academy games, bicycle trips, ski trips, hiking, camping, and mountain climbing. On Sunday, the Coordinator of Religion supervises a nondenominational and nonsectarian meeting for the student body. Attendance is required for boarding students. The aim is to share different beliefs and ways of worship. Transportation is provided for boys who wish to maintain their own religious commitment by attending local places of worship. Students with permission may leave the School for the weekend; 5–10 percent of the student body normally do so on a given weekend.

COSTS AND FINANCIAL AID

Eaglebrook School's tuition for the 2012–13 school year is $52,700 for boarding students and $32,400 for day students. Eaglebrook seeks to enroll boys from different backgrounds from this country and abroad, regardless of their ability to pay. Approximately 30 percent of the students receive financial aid. To apply for tuition assistance, a candidate must complete the School Scholarship Service's Parents' Financial Statement, which is obtainable from the Financial Aid Office.

ADMISSIONS INFORMATION

Most students enter in either the seventh or eighth grade, although students can be admitted to any grade. Information regarding required testing and transcripts can be obtained from the Admissions Office. A School visit and interview are required.

Eaglebrook welcomes boys of any race, color, religion, nation, or creed, and all share the same privileges and duties.

APPLICATION TIMETABLE

The School accepts applications throughout the year, but it is to the candidate's advantage to make application as early as possible. Decisions and notifications are made whenever a boy's file is complete. There is a $50 application fee ($100 for international students).

ADMISSIONS CORRESPONDENCE

Theodore J. Low
Director of Admissions
Eaglebrook School
Pine Nook Road
Deerfield, Massachusetts 01342
United States
Phone: 413-774-9111 (admissions)
413-774-7411 (main)
Fax: 413-774-9119 (admissions)
413-772-2394 (main)
E-mail: admissions@eaglebrook.org
Web site: http://www.eaglebrook.org

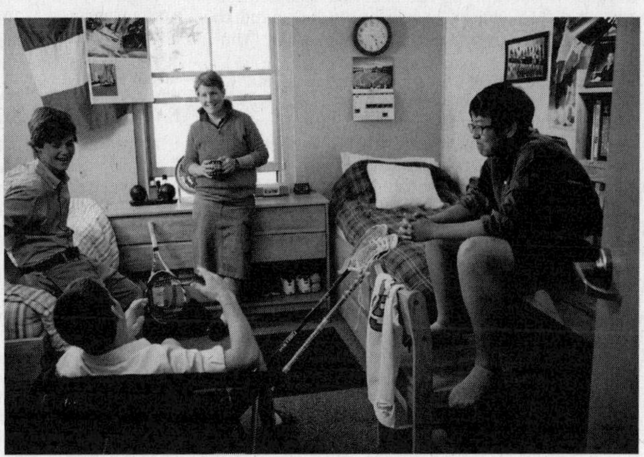

FAY SCHOOL

Southborough, Massachusetts

Type: Coeducational school for grades pre-K–9; boarding available for grades 7–9
Grades: Primary School (pre-K–2), Lower School (3–6), Upper School (7–9)
Enrollment: School total: 450; Boarding 110
Head of School: Robert J. Gustavson Jr., Head of School; David Liebmann, Assistant Head of School; Marie Beam, Director of Advancement; Matt Evans, Head of Upper School; Lainie Schuster, Head of Lower School; Anne Bishop, Head of Primary School

THE SCHOOL

A dynamic learning environment since 1866, Fay School exemplifies a coeducational tradition of academic excellence coupled with a dedication to maximize the potential of each individual child. With a structured environment that recognizes both effort and achievement, Fay School offers both breadth and depth in academic, artistic, and athletic programs. Multilevel course offerings and the availability of tutorial support ensure each student an appropriate level of academic challenge. In small advisory groups, students receive extensive individualized attention. Relationships between students and teachers mirror those of parent and child. At Fay, faculty members and parents work as partners during the critically important childhood and adolescent years. Fay's comprehensive secondary school placement program not only provides guidance in identifying and applying to model secondary schools but also assists students and their parents in selecting the best environment for continuing their education at the next level. Exceptional facilities and a faculty committed to ongoing professional development create an environment where living and learning thrive.

Established in 1866 by two sisters, Eliza Burnett Fay and Harriet Burnett, the School is situated on 66 acres in semirural surroundings 25 miles west of Boston. Fay School's day students come from thirty surrounding communities, and boarding students are drawn from across the United States and fifteen countries. Fay's graduates go on to thrive at independent secondary schools and area public high schools.

At Fay, each child's voice matters. Through its leadership opportunities, cultural program, comprehensive academic program, community service, arts, and sports offerings, the School caters to a wide range of interests and abilities. Students' endeavors are encouraged and supported by a dedicated and highly qualified faculty and monitored by an effort system that measures the level of engagement each student demonstrates in all aspects of campus life. Particular attention is given to the needs of boarding students and to making life in dormitories a "home away from home."

Fay School is a nonprofit institution and is governed by a self-perpetuating board of 29 trustees. Its endowment stands at $35 million and is supplemented by an annual fund of more than $1 million in total gifts, bridging the gap between tuition and the operating budget. Through its development efforts, the School annually receives support from more than 1,000 alumni, parents, and friends.

ACADEMIC PROGRAM

Fay's program seeks to achieve far more than a sound foundation in course work; the emphasis is on fostering positive attitudes toward learning and living in the world beyond the campus. By limiting class size to an average of 12 Upper School students, Fay provides an environment in which children are active participants in their own education. Each student's specific needs and academic background are carefully considered when scheduling classes. A rotating block schedule and more than 200 class offerings ensure maximum flexibility in designing programs of study.

The School offers different levels in most subject areas. In the Primary and Lower Schools, the program emphasizes individual growth and the development of sound fundamental skills. From the seventh grade onward, students experience increasingly demanding academic requirements. The School challenges students to do their best, and actively supports their efforts. Every student works closely with an adult adviser who serves as a counselor and role model. Students are prepared for the next step in their education, so they are ready to succeed academically, socially, and emotionally in secondary school. Fay also provides leadership training in grades 1–9 through a full-year program that stresses the leadership skills of conflict management, social responsibility, team building, communication, and positive role modeling.

Fay School offers a comprehensive technology education program. Technology is integrated across the curriculum and throughout the grades. The School also offers technology classes to Upper and Lower School students that are designed to help students use technology to enhance their studies and to become safe, ethical, and effective computer users. Technology offerings range from Lower School introductory courses to information literacy, digital video production, and Web site design in the upper grades.

To facilitate success in a student's academic endeavors, deliberate attention is paid to the development of study skills through a study skills curriculum administered by Learning Center staff members and reinforced in the classroom. In particular, research skills, note-taking, time management, and test-taking strategies are taught at the appropriate grade levels. In the academic and athletics programs, the School also monitors each student's progress by means of biweekly effort evaluations and by trimester reports at the middle and end of terms. Specialized help is available through the Learning Services Department for children who need support in following their regular course of study.

The International Student Program (ISP) offers English courses for students whose native language is not English. Three levels and small classes afford opportunities to tailor ISP courses to individual needs in the areas of speaking, listening, writing, reading, and skill building. As students' proficiency in English increases, they are integrated into mainstream courses. Full participation in art, music, technology classes, and sports activities helps students adapt quickly to life in their new community.

FACULTY AND ADVISERS

Children entering Fay School are welcomed into a family whose heart is the faculty. Faculty members are selected for their empathy and enthusiasm for working with students at the elementary and junior level, as well as for their expertise in a particular discipline. Students and teachers work, learn, play, and have meals together. In the boarding community they also spend weekends together, sharing many vibrant experiences both on and off campus.

Advisers are teachers and administrators who form the nuclei of small groups of 4 to 6 students, both day and boarding. Advisory groups meet at least three times a week. This peer support, combined with the guidance of a concerned and involved adult, makes advisory groups an important source of nurturing for youngsters at Fay. A major responsibility for advisers is communicating with parents.

SECONDARY SCHOOL PLACEMENT

Ensuring a good match between each graduating student and a secondary school is the primary objective in placement. The Director of Secondary School Placement and a second placement counselor work closely with American students, their families, their advisers, coaches, and teachers in identifying the students' needs, strengths, and talents. The Director of the International Student Program provides the same service for Fay's international students. Throughout the application process, the Placement Office provides counsel in selecting and applying to appropriate schools. Schools currently attended by Fay graduates include Berkshire School, Brooks School, Cate School, Choate Rosemary Hall, Concord Academy, Cushing Academy, Deerfield Academy, Emma Willard, Episcopal High School, Governor Dummer Academy, Groton School, Kent School, Lawrence Academy, Lawrenceville School, Loomis Chaffee School, Middlesex School, Milton Academy, Noble and Greenough School, Phillips Andover Academy, Phillips Exeter Academy, Pomfret School, Proctor Academy, Rivers School, St. George's School, St. Mark's School, St. Paul's School, Salisbury School, Suffield Academy, Tabor Academy, Thacher School, Westminster School, and Worcester Academy.

STUDENT BODY AND CONDUCT

At Fay, every effort is made to establish a balance between freedom and responsibility for the young people in its care. Through small advisory groups and the Leadership Program, unstated School rules such as ethical behavior and respect for others are reinforced. Minor misconduct is dealt with by advisers or by the Head of the Primary, Lower, or Upper Schools, depending on the child's grade. Where infractions of major School rules are involved, the Discipline Committee, composed of the appropriate Head and 5 faculty members, may convene.

ACADEMIC FACILITIES

The Root Academic Center (1984) houses most of the Upper and Lower School classrooms. The Primary School (2010) is LEED certified and contains classrooms, a multipurpose room, a music room, and a dining area for pre-K to grade 2. The Mars Wing (2001) includes the Learning Center, the media lab, four state-of-the-art science labs, a writing lab, and a multimedia lab. The Reinke Building (1971) contains a large auditorium and houses the Fay Extended Day Program, band room, School Counselor's office, and Summer and Special Programs office. The Picardi Art Center (1987) provides outstanding facilities for art classes, including a darkroom and ceramics studio. The Harris Events Center (1995) is home to Fay's Performing Arts Program and includes five music practice rooms, two music classrooms, a dance studio, and a 400-seat theater.

The School is completely networked and runs on PC and Mac technology in each classroom, in the library, the Learning Center, and in three computer labs. In addition, five multimedia carts are outfitted with the equipment necessary to create multimedia presentations, and three mobile laptop labs provide wireless Web connection for full class lessons. The library offers 18,000 volumes and nine computers for student use. The library Web page provides access to a fully automated catalog of Fay holdings, a connection to holdings outside of Fay via the Internet or the CD-ROM Catalogue of Independent Schools in Eastern Massachusetts, a subscription to 10 different databases to support teachers designing lessons and students accomplishing research, and links to many useful Web sites organized by subject and index. The library functions as a key point in the learning experience at Fay, providing students and faculty members with resources for study, research, and pleasure reading. The library program encourages a love of reading and an appreciation of quality literature, equips students with the knowledge and skills to become lifelong learners, and helps ensure that students are effective and responsible users of information and ideas.

BOARDING AND GENERAL FACILITIES

Boarding boys are housed in the Boys Village Dorm (2008) or Steward Dorm (1978), while girls live on the upper floors of the Girls Village Dorms (2008) and the Dining Room Building (1924), in Webster House (1880), and in East House (circa 1895). Family-style meals are served in the dining room. The Wellness Center, which opened in 2009, is situated in the lower level of the Steward Dorm and serves as the campus medical facility. Additional campus buildings include Brackett House (1860), home of advancement offices; Fay House (1860), the location for the Admission Office; and the Upjohn Building (1895), currently serving as a multiuse space.

ATHLETICS

Characterized by diversity, spirit, and sportsmanship, Fay's competitive athletics program involves all students and offers a wide range of sports and ability levels each term. Fay's interscholastic teams are noted for the high degree of pride and team spirit they bring with them. Fay's ten athletics fields and eight new tennis courts are in constant use for practices and games during the fall and spring terms, while in warmer weather the pool becomes a popular place to cool off. In snowy weather, the Harlow Gymnasium and the Mars Wrestling Room become the centers of activity, with the ice rinks at the nearby New England Sports Center providing facilities for Fay's hockey teams. Participants in the skiing program enjoy the slopes of SkiWard, a local ski area. Fay hosts annual basketball, wrestling, and tennis tournaments, and many individual athletes and teams participate in tournaments hosted by other schools. The following sports and activities are offered: fall—cross-country, field hockey, football, golf, photography, soccer, and tennis; winter—basketball, dance, drama, fitness, ice hockey, skiing, volleyball, woodworking, and wrestling; and spring—baseball, fitness, golf, lacrosse, softball, squash, tennis, and track.

The School's athletics facilities were greatly enhanced with the completion of the Fay School Athletic Campus in 2009. The campus comprises 30 acres of dedicated regulation-sized outdoor fields for soccer, field hockey, baseball, softball, and lacrosse. The campus also features a cross-country course and four batting cages—two for baseball and two for softball. Additional facilities include the Harlow Gymnasium (1993), a facility that incorporates four basketball courts, expanded locker room space, team rooms, a wrestling room, a weight room, and a training room.

EXTRACURRICULAR OPPORTUNITIES

Fay's academic program is augmented by a wide choice of extracurricular activities. Dramatic productions and musical groups such as band, bell ringers, and chorus offer performance opportunities; aspiring journalists, photographers, and artists work on the yearbook and student newspaper; and activities such as videotaping, woodworking, community service, chess, and computers offer something for everyone. In addition, an 800-square-foot textured rock-climbing wall has been added to the state-of-the-art gymnasium. The rock wall, 26 feet in height, provides an ideal setting for climbing, bouldering, and rappelling. Full advantage is taken of the School's proximity to Boston, and visits to museums, sports events, and historic sites take place throughout the year.

DAILY LIFE

Classes are held Monday through Friday in flexible blocks, starting at 8 and ending at 2:30 for all students. Grades pre-K–4 are dismissed at 3. All other students go on to sports, which continue until 4:30 for grades 5–9. Boarders have free time after sports until a family-style dinner at 6, followed by free time until 7:30 and a study period until 9. Lights-out is between 9:30 and 10, depending on the student's age.

WEEKEND LIFE

Due to the geographic diversity of Fay's boarding community, few boarding students return home on weekends. Boarders look forward to weekends, when the Weekend Coordinator schedules a wide range of activities, including daylong and weekend-long skiing, white-water rafting, and hiking trips; athletics contests; nature trips; attendance at a wide range of cultural events and performances; and visits to amusement and recreational parks, movies, Boston shops, and community service projects.

Families of day students are warmly supportive of the boarders, opening their homes to youngsters for weekends and some holidays. The number of off-campus weekends is not limited, with the exception of a few closed weekends, but permission must be granted by advisers and teachers.

SUMMER PROGRAMS

Fay School offers a safe, fun-filled co-ed camp for children ages 3 through 15, called Fay Discovery. Campers use the Fay campus and extensive facilities to participate in a variety of summertime activities, including swimming instruction. Eight 1-week sessions run Monday through Friday from 9 a.m. to 4 p.m., with extended care available. The School's highly qualified staff members and low camper-to-counselor ratio ensure individualized attention in all activities.

The Summer Session of Fay's International Student Program is designed to enrich international students' use of English and to provide an academic and cultural introduction to Fay School and the United States.

This is a six-week boarding program for students ages 10–15, running from late June to early August each year. The program provides a structured schedule throughout the day, beginning with academic classes in the morning and ending with sports and activities in the afternoon and evening. The weekends include exciting excursions to Boston and surrounding areas.

COSTS AND FINANCIAL AID

Tuition for 2012–13 ranged from $19,525 for day students in pre-K to $30,150 for fifth graders and $32,450 for ninth graders. Tuition for domestic boarding students in grades 7–9 ranged from $54,025 to $54,450; for mainstream international boarding students in grades 7–9 ranged from $56,525 to $56,950; and for international boarding students with ESL ranged from $59,525 to $59,950. The School offers several creative payment plans.

Financial aid is awarded on the basis of need to 14 percent of the student body. Amounts, based upon demonstrated need and procedures established by the School and Student Service for Financial Aid, range from $1000 to nearly full tuition.

ADMISSIONS INFORMATION

Fay School accepts day students for pre-K to grade 9 and boarding students for grades 7–9. The personal requirements for admission include satisfactory evidence of good character, an acceptable record of previous academic work, and the ability and motivation to successfully complete the work at Fay. All applicants must complete the application form and return it to the Director of Admission with the application fee, a transcript, and teacher recommendations. Applicants must visit the School for a personal interview and tour; interested students should call the Admission Office to arrange a time. If a student cannot visit the school a remote interview may be arranged via Skype. Candidates for grades 7–9 must take the SSAT or ISEE.

APPLICATION TIMETABLE

Applications for day students are due on February 1. Decisions on day student candidates whose folders are complete are announced on March 8. Fay continues to accept qualified candidates after this date until the grades are filled. Wait lists are often established. Decisions on boarding students are made once a candidate's folder is complete, beginning in January. Parents are asked to respond to the acceptance within thirty days. To hold a place for a child, a deposit and enrollment contract must be submitted. Information regarding clothing, course selection, and other pertinent items is sent upon enrollment.

ADMISSIONS CORRESPONDENCE

Beth Whitney, Director of Admission
Fay School
48 Main Street
Southborough, Massachusetts 01772-9106
United States
Phone: 508-490-8201
Fax: 508-481-7872
E-mail: admission@fayschool.org
Web site: http://www.fayschool.org

THE FESSENDEN SCHOOL

West Newton, Massachusetts

Type: Boys' boarding and day school
Grades: Pre-Kindergarten–9: Lower School, Pre-K–4; Middle School, 5–6; Upper School, 7–9
Enrollment: 492
Head of School: David B. Stettler, Headmaster

THE SCHOOL

The Fessenden School of West Newton, Massachusetts, has enjoyed a long history of providing high-quality education for boys in a supportive, yet challenging environment. The School was founded in 1903 by Mr. and Mrs. Frederick J. Fessenden. The founders' original educational philosophy was "to train a boy along the right lines, to teach him how to study and form correct habits of work, and to inculcate principles, which are to regulate his daily conduct and guide his future life." The Fessenden School brings out the best in boys by adhering to these principles today. The Fessenden School also recognizes the special requirements of a boy's elementary education and focuses on providing it in a nurturing environment where a boy can live up to his potential. Intellectual, physical, and emotional development share equal emphasis at Fessenden.

The mission of The Fessenden School is to teach, nurture, and celebrate growing boys, cultivating each student's individual potential and developing in balance his mind, character, heart, and body in an inclusive and joyful community that, through rigor, friendship, and service, reflects Fessenden's traditional values of honesty, compassion, and respect.

The Fessenden School campus is situated on 41 acres in a residential community just west of Boston. The School's proximity to the city presents a world of exciting possibilities for year-round activity, including well-known historic sites, first-class music and theater, world-renowned museums, and a multitude of professional and collegiate sporting events. The Fessenden campus is convenient to all major highway routes, and Logan International Airport is only a 20-minute drive from campus.

The Fessenden School is a nonprofit organization. The School's endowment currently stands at just over $35.8 million and is supported by alumni, current and former parents, and friends through an Annual Fund.

Fessenden's well-established character education program, based on the principles of honesty, compassion, respect, and commitment to academic and athletic excellence, seeks to ensure that every member of the school community is given the support and nurturing he needs to feel secure in his academic, physical, and social ability.

Fessenden holds membership in many academic associations, including the Association of Independent Schools in New England, the National Association of Independent Schools, the Junior Boarding School Association, the Secondary School Admission Test Board, and the Massachusetts Association of Nonprofit Schools and Colleges.

ACADEMIC PROGRAM

The Fessenden School's traditional curriculum is designed to be challenging yet developmentally appropriate and supportive of each student's learning style, providing him with a foundation of skills that are imperative for the secondary school experience. With an average class size of 12, each student's needs are carefully considered by his teachers, advisers, and division heads prior to placement in grade-level or honors classes.

Fessenden's Lower School (Pre-K–4) places emphasis on skills in reading, oral and written communication, and mathematics. These areas are complemented with work in social studies, FLES (Foreign Language in Elementary School), science, computers, library skills, art, drama, music, and physical education. A link to Upper School students is maintained through the Big Brother program, assemblies, and other all-school activities.

In the Middle School grades (5–6), students begin the transition from the self-contained classrooms of the Lower School toward the departmentalized structure of the Upper School. Courses in English, math, social studies, geography, science, art, music, woodworking, photography, and Spanish are required for all Middle School students. The Middle School focuses on organization, study skills, critical thinking, and writing, and benefits from a 1:1 laptop program.

The Upper School academic program ensures that each student is properly prepared for the educational programs he will encounter in secondary school. In the Upper School, an age-appropriate curriculum is augmented with a 1:1 laptop program that is designed to strengthen independent study habits and life skills that are imperative for high school and beyond. Grades 7–9 focus on the five major academic disciplines of English, history, mathematics, science, and foreign language (Spanish, Latin, Mandarin). Fessenden's commitment to the arts requires each student to choose a class each semester in the fine arts or performing arts. A "help and work" period each day provides additional opportunities for students to consult their teachers on an individual or small-group basis. Students must complete a half-year of computer studies and a course in personal growth and development prior to graduation. In addition, each boy is presented with a varied selection of electives, including computer programming and robotics, multimedia, student government, theater, art courses at various levels, woodworking, digital photography, video production, band, orchestra, and individual music instruction.

The Fessenden School recognizes that some students may need more specialized help with skill building and therefore offers a Skills Center staffed by professional reading and language specialists. The Skills Center provides individual skills instruction, administers tests, and makes evaluations and recommendations.

Fessenden's English Language Learning program (ELL) is offered in both intermediate and advanced levels to increase English proficiency. ELL students are educated using a variety of appropriate teaching resources. Class trips include visits to historic Plymouth, Massachusetts; Mystic Seaport, Connecticut; Boston's Freedom Trail; Old Sturbridge Village; and whale watches.

Fessenden's academic year is divided into four marking periods. The School acknowledges that a student's effort to learn is as important as letter or numerical grades. Teachers give both qualitative and quantitative marks four times during the year.

FACULTY AND ADVISERS

The 120 members of Fessenden's dedicated faculty and staff are committed to creating a family-oriented community by serving as teachers, coaches, advisers, dorm parents, and mentors. Seventy percent of the faculty and staff members for students in grades 5–9 live on campus, many with families of their own. The student-faculty ratio is approximately 6:1.

Each student has an academic faculty or staff adviser. Advisers foster close relationships with each student, becoming actively involved in all facets of the student's life at school. Each adviser is responsible for communicating to parents all aspects of their sons' experiences at Fessenden.

SECONDARY SCHOOL PLACEMENT

Fessenden seeks to provide each student with the placement guidance needed to ensure a positive secondary school experience. This is achieved by collaboration between the student and the Placement Officers, advisers, teachers, dorm parents, and coaches. Beginning in the spring of eighth grade, families start selecting an appropriate school based on academic ability, extracurricular activities, and athletic interests. Eighth and ninth grade students are encouraged to take the SSAT preparatory class in English and math. The Placement Office also works with students to teach specific interviewing techniques, including mock interviews.

Fessenden graduates have attended a variety of secondary schools, including Avon Old Farms, Belmont Hill, Brooks, Cate School, Choate Rosemary Hall, Deerfield, Exeter, Governor's Academy, Holderness, Loomis Chaffee, Middlesex, Noble and Greenough, Phillips Academy, Rivers, Roxbury Latin, St. Paul's, Tabor, and Westminster. However, it is ultimately the successful match between student and school that remains essential in the placement process.

STUDENT BODY AND CONDUCT

The Fessenden School seeks boys of solid character who can grow in a supportive environment where a balanced program of academics, athletics, the arts, and social life is vigorously pursued.

Of a total enrollment of 492 students for the academic year 2012–13, 392 are day students and 100 are boarders. Fessenden students come from fifty-eight cities and towns in Massachusetts, seventeen other states, and twelve other countries. International students represent 12 percent of the total student body.

Fessenden's character education program is modeled by its faculty, who have an extraordinary investment in caring for the boys and setting guidelines for them. Acknowledging boys for being active and positive contributors within the community places an emphasis on the reinforcement of positive role modeling. Teachers, coaches, and advisers handle disciplinary matters on an individual basis as warranted.

ACADEMIC FACILITIES

Fessenden's state-of-the-art academic building houses twenty-five classrooms that provide multiple data points, allowing the expanding world of information into each classroom via technology. The campus features a science center, a library, a study hall, a multimedia lab, a digital photography lab, a student health center, and a performing arts center that features a theater-size wide-screen projection monitor. The Fessenden School library contains more than 20,000 volumes, sixteen desktop computers, sixty laptop computers, twenty Chromebooks, Kindles, Nooks, iPods and iPads, twenty-five digital cameras, a color scanner, and a printer. There are two art studios with five electric pottery wheels and two kilns, a printmaking machine, and a music center that features two band rehearsal rooms and five individual practice rooms equipped with pianos. The Skills Center contains eight classrooms for one-to-one tutoring.

BOARDING AND GENERAL FACILITIES

Fessenden's boarding students live in home-like dormitories closely supervised by residential faculty members and their families. Dormitories are made up of students in grades 5–8, with proctors who are in grade 9. There are 11 to 19 students per hallway. Students in grade 9 live in two different dormitories. Weekday meals are served family style, with a buffet on weekends.

Students' everyday health-care needs are served at the campus Health Center and a registered nurse is always available. Newton-Wellesley Hospital is located only minutes away.

ATHLETICS

The School offers a variety of seasonal athletics for students of every age and ability level. Fessenden's long-standing tradition in sports embodies the philosophy of fair play, sportsmanship, and equal opportunity for all participants. Students may choose from competitive, intramural, or recreational activities each season. Competitive and intramural sports include baseball, basketball, crew, cross-country, football, hockey, lacrosse, soccer, squash, tennis, track and field, and wrestling. Boys may also choose from an exciting range of recreational sports, such as cross-country skiing, golf, mountain biking, sailing, and weight lifting and conditioning. The Fessenden School participates in several athletic tournaments each year, and also hosts annual soccer, wrestling, and tennis tournaments.

The Fessenden School has a state-of-the-art athletic facility, which houses two indoor basketball courts, a wrestling center with two regulation-size mats, a weight-training suite, and locker rooms for coaches and visiting teams. The facility overlooks six of Fessenden's outdoor tennis courts, which are lighted. Rounding out the sports facilities are an indoor hockey rink, two outdoor swimming pools, nine playing fields, and an additional four outdoor tennis courts.

EXTRACURRICULAR OPPORTUNITIES

The Fessenden School provides a variety of opportunities for students to develop leadership skills and exhibit their talents, thus enriching and balancing their academic program. Each year, the theater arts program presents several dramatic and musical productions. Faculty members offer club programs to share specific skills and interests with students, including art, board games, cooking, floor hockey, fly fishing, billiards, indoor soccer, model building, volleyball, science and aeronautics, and weight lifting.

Fessenden's Student Council is formed of elected officers in grade 9. The Council meets every two weeks for regular business and calls special meetings to discuss important issues. The Student Council has a voice in implementing School rules and planning special events.

DAILY LIFE

Boarding students begin their day with a family-style breakfast. The academic day encompasses eight periods. Athletic activities take place each weekday afternoon. Day students return home after sports; for boarding students, a structured study hall follows. There are also after-dinner study halls and free-time activities.

WEEKEND LIFE

Fessenden's weekend program is exceptionally full, providing the balance between academic and social life by satisfying the boys' many outside interests. The residential life staff works closely with the residential faculty to offer more than twenty exciting and interesting supervised activities every weekend and over 800 each year. A sampling of weekend trips includes college and professional sports events, museum trips, ski outings, movie nights, camping and mountain-biking trips, dances, plays, and concerts. The Fessenden School holds no religious affiliation but can provide transportation to services for boys of all faiths.

An indispensable aspect of Fessenden's boarding life is the Welcome Family Program. This program connects all new families with a current Fessenden family that has a boy in the same school division. Boarders may also spend some evenings, weekends, or holidays with their "Welcome Family," creating friendships that can last long after their Fessenden experience is over.

CO-ED SUMMER ELL PROGRAM

The Fessenden School's residential summer ELL program provides five weeks of immersion in the English language and American culture. This program is open to international boys and girls, ages 10 to 16.

The classes are offered at beginning, intermediate, and advanced levels and are designed to develop competent conversational skills and expand English vocabulary. Classes are small to enable every student to participate fully.

Fessenden's summer ELL program also offers films, videos, fun projects, and games, reinforcing classroom work and actively engaging students in the learning process. After-school and weekend trips bring students to such sites as Plymouth Plantation, Martha's Vineyard, Mystic Seaport, Harvard University, and New York City.

COSTS AND FINANCIAL AID

Day student tuition ranges from $22,000 to $35,000. Boarding tuition ranges from $44,750 to $57,100. Additional charges may be applicable to all students for supplies and laundry services.

The Fessenden School awards approximately $1.4 million in financial assistance to more than 9.75 percent of the student body each academic year. Scholarships are awarded on the basis of need.

ADMISSIONS INFORMATION

A viewbook, application, and financial aid material may be obtained by inquiring online at http://www.fessenden.org/inquiry or by contacting Fessenden's Admissions Office (admissions@fessenden.org, 617-630-2300).

APPLICATION TIMETABLE

Admissions inquiries are welcome at any time. The application deadline for day students is February 1. Boarding student applications are processed on a rolling admissions basis.

ADMISSIONS CORRESPONDENCE

Caleb W. Thomson '79
Director of Admission
Enrollment Manager
The Fessenden School
250 Waltham Street
West Newton, Massachusetts 02465
United States
Phone: 617-630-2300
Fax: 617-630-2303
E-mail: admissions@fessenden.org
Web site: http://www.fessenden.org

PHOTOS BY LEN RUBENSTEIN PHOTOGRAPHY

RUMSEY HALL SCHOOL

Washington Depot, Connecticut

RUMSEY HALL SCHOOL

Type: Coeducational Junior Boarding (grades 5–9) and Day Preparatory School
Grades: K–9: Lower School, K–5; Upper School, 6–9
Enrollment: School total: 333
Head of School: Thomas W. Farmen, Headmaster

THE SCHOOL

Rumsey Hall School was founded in 1900 by Mrs. Lillias Rumsey Sanford. Since its inception, Rumsey Hall School has retained its original philosophy: to help each child develop to his or her maximum stature as an individual, as a member of a family, and as a contributing member of society. The curriculum emphasizes basic academic skills, a complete athletic program, fine arts, computer literacy, and numerous extracurricular offerings, which are all designed to encourage individual responsibility for academic achievement, accomplishment in team sports, and service to the School community. The School believes that "effort is the key to success."

The 147-acre campus on the Bantam River provides landscaped and wooded areas in a rural environment located outside of Washington, Connecticut. Rumsey Hall School is 90 miles from New York City and within an hour of the major Connecticut cities of Hartford and New Haven. The School's location enables students to take advantage of major cultural and athletic events in New York City and Boston throughout the school year.

A nonprofit institution, Rumsey Hall School is governed by a 21-member Board of Trustees that meets quarterly. The 2012–13 operating budget totaled $8.3 million. Revenues include tuition and fees and contributions from alumni, parents, corporations, foundations, and friends of the School. The School's endowment is approximately $8.5 million. Annual fund giving was $1.88 million in 2012.

Rumsey Hall School is a member of the National Association of Independent Schools, the Connecticut Association of Independent Schools, the Junior Boarding Schools Association, the Educational Records Bureau, Western Connecticut Boarding Schools, and the Educational Testing Service, and is a voting member of the Secondary School Admission Test Board.

ACADEMIC PROGRAM

At Rumsey Hall, effort is as important as academic achievement. Effort as a criterion for success opens a new world to the students. Effort does not start and end with the student. It is a shared responsibility between the student and each faculty member. Just as the faculty members expect maximum effort from each student, they promise in return to give each student their very best effort.

Students in the Upper School (sixth through ninth grades) carry at least five major subjects. There are eight 40-minute periods in each day, including lunch. Extra help is available each day for students who need additional instruction or extra challenges. All classes are departmentalized.

Final examinations are given in all subjects twice a year. Report cards, with numerical grades, are sent home every other week throughout the school year. Anecdotal comments and individualized teacher, adviser, and Headmaster comments are sent home three times each academic year.

A supplementary feature of the academic program is the Language Skills Department, which is directed toward intellectually able students with dyslexia or learning differences. Students in this program carry a regular academic course load, with the exception of a foreign language. In 2012–13, 15 percent of the student body was involved in this program.

English as a Second Language (ESL) is offered to international students and is comprised of two levels with three courses in each level. The courses are designed to help students develop their conversational and academic English, reading comprehension, awareness of social and cultural differences, and to introduce them to American history.

The school year, divided into trimesters, begins in September and runs until the first weekend in June. Vacations are scheduled at Thanksgiving and Christmas and in the spring.

Class size averages 12 students. Honors courses are offered to exceptional ninth grade students who demonstrate talent and whose scholarship indicates a strong sense of responsibility and motivation.

Students have a study hall built into their daily schedules, and there is an evening study hall for all boarding students. Study halls are supervised by faculty members, and there is ample opportunity for assistance. The library and computer facilities adjoin the formal study hall and are available at all study times.

In the Lower School (K through fifth grade), the nine daily academic periods begin at 8 a.m. after class meetings. English, reading, mathematics, science, and social studies are taught by the classroom teachers. Classes in foreign languages, language skills, health, music, art, and physical education vary the students' schedules by requiring them to move to different classrooms with specialized teachers. Normal class size is between 12 and 14 students, which makes for a dynamic learning environment where everyone's voice is heard and encouraged.

FACULTY AND ADVISERS

All 60 full- and part-time faculty members (29 men and 31 women) hold baccalaureate degrees, and half have master's degrees. Forty-two faculty members live on campus, many with their families. This enables Rumsey to provide the close supervision and warm family atmosphere that is an essential part of the School's culture.

Thomas W. Farmen was appointed Headmaster of Rumsey Hall School in 1985. He holds a Bachelor of Arts degree from New England College and a master's in school administration from Western Connecticut State University. He has served as President of the Association of Boarding Schools for the National Association of Independent Schools, President of the Junior Boarding Schools Association, and as a director of the Connecticut Association of Independent Schools.

The Dean of Students supervises and coordinates the advisory program. Each faculty member has 7 or 8 student advisees. Advisors meet with their advisees individually and in a weekly group setting. The advisor is the first link in the line of communication between school and home.

Faculty members at Rumsey Hall are encouraged to continue their professional development by taking postgraduate courses and attending seminars and conferences throughout the year. The School generously funds these programs.

SECONDARY SCHOOL PLACEMENT

The Director of Secondary School Placement supervises all facets of the secondary school search. Beginning in the eighth grade, a process of testing and interviewing with students and parents takes place that enables the placement director to highlight certain schools that seem appropriate. After visits and interviews with the schools, the list is pared down to those to which the student wishes to apply. Members of the 2011–12 class matriculated to 43 secondary schools: Albuquerque Academy, NM; Avon Old Farms, CT (2); Berkshire School, MA (4); Brewster Academy, NH (3); Canterbury School, CT (5); Choate Rosemary Hall School, CT; Cheshire Academy, CT; Darlington School, GA; Deerfield Academy, MA; Episcopal High School, VA; Ethel Walker School, CT; Forman School, CT; Friends Select School, PA; The Greenwood School, VT; The Gunnery, CT (5); Hebron Academy, ME; Holy Cross High School, CT; Hotchkiss School, CT; Kents Hill School, ME; Kimball Union Academy, NH; Lawrenceville School, NJ; Loomis Chaffee School, CT (2); The Madeira School, VA; Mercersburg Academy, PA; Miss Hall's School, MA; Northfield Mt. Hermon School, MA; Peddie School, NJ (2); Phillips Academy Andover, MA; Proctor Academy, NH; St. Andrew's School, RI; St. George's School, RI; St. Joseph's High School, CT; Salisbury School, CT; Springside Chestnut Hill Academy, PA; South Kent School, CT (2); Suffield Academy, CT; The Taft School, CT (2); Thomas Jefferson School, MO; Tilton School, NH; Trinity-Pawling School, NY; Vermont Academy, VT; Webb Schools, CA; and Williston Northampton School, MA.

STUDENT BODY AND CONDUCT

In 2012–13, Rumsey Hall enrolled 333 students. The Lower School (grades K–5) enrolled 80 day students. The Upper School (grades 6–9) enrolled 253 students: 115 day students and 138 boarders. The School population was 54 percent boys and 46 percent girls.

In 2012–13, Rumsey students came from sixteen states, eleven countries, and thirty local communities. International students enrolled in the ESL program composed 8 percent of the community.

The dress code requires jackets, collared shirts, and ties for boys and dresses or skirts and collared shirts or blouses for girls. In the winter term, boys may wear turtlenecks and sweaters and girls may wear slacks.

The School values of honesty, kindness, and respect comprise the yardstick by which Rumsey measures a student's thoughts and actions. Students living outside the spirit of the community are asked to meet with the Disciplinary and Senior Committees. These committees represent a cross section of administrators, faculty members, and students.

ACADEMIC FACILITIES

Situated alongside the Bantam River on a 147-acre campus, the School is housed in thirty buildings, most of which have been constructed since 1950. Nine structures house a total of thirty classrooms, including the Dane W. Dicke Family Math and Science Buildings. Other buildings include the Dicke Family Library; the Sanford House, which houses the study and meeting hall; the J. Seward Johnson Sr. Fine Arts Center, with spacious art and music rooms; and the Satyvati Science Center. Students and faculty members meet as a community for meals in the D. G. Barr Dining Hall.

The Garassino Building is home to three lower school classrooms including an all-day kindergarten. The Maxwell A. Sarofim '05 Performing Arts Center (the MAX) is the setting for student performances, visiting artists, and school assemblies; students' art and exhibits of Rumsey community interest are displayed in the adjacent Allen Finkelson Gallery.

Rumsey has three fully interactive computer labs on campus and more than 120 wireless networked computers throughout the School. The schoolwide intranet system enhances communication within the community.

BOARDING AND GENERAL FACILITIES

The close relationship between teachers and students is a special part of Rumsey Hall School. Students live in dormitories with supportive dorm parents, and students become a part of their dorm parents' families.

Rumsey's boarding students live in one of eight dormitories. Dormitories are assigned by age, and most students have roommates, although single rooms are available in most dorms. Each dormitory has its own common room that is the shared living space for the dorm. A snack bar and store are open every afternoon. Laundry and dry cleaning are sent out on a weekly basis. Four registered nurses staff the School's infirmary, and the School doctor, a local pediatrician, is available on a daily basis. Emergency facilities are available at New Milford Hospital, which is 10 miles away. There are telephones in all dormitories, and every student has an e-mail account.

ATHLETICS

Athletics are a healthy and essential part of the Rumsey experience. On the playing field, lifelong attitudes, values, and habits are born. All students participate at their own level in athletics. Effort is rewarded through athletic letters and certificates at the end of the season.

Rumsey Hall fields thirty-nine interscholastic teams throughout the year. Most sports are offered on different levels so that students are able to compete with children of their own size and skill level. Over three seasons, 403 interscholastic teams are fielded in baseball, basketball, crew, cross-country, field hockey, football, boys' ice hockey, girls' ice hockey, lacrosse, skiing, soccer, softball, tennis, volleyball, and wrestling. Other activities available include horseback riding, Outdoor Club, Lower School games and activities, recreational skiing and snowboarding, biking, and ice-skating.

The John F. Schereschewsky, Sr. Memorial Center houses the Magnoli and Blue Dog Gymnasiums where basketball, volleyball, and wrestling activities are held. Recent renovations to the indoor athletic facilities include an indoor climbing wall, boys' and girls' locker rooms, and three new and improved tennis courts. The Cornell Common Room serves as the weight-training room and offers other training machines, as well as housing the athletic director and athletic training staff. Lufkin Rink is the newest of Rumsey Hall's athletic facilities. Opened in late 2008, the rink provides home ice for the boys' and girls' hockey teams. Intramural and recreational activities make the space available to skaters of all abilities.

There are several athletic fields on campus including the Pavek Athletic Field, in honor of Veronica D. and Charles H. Pavek; Scott Evans Seibert '92 Memorial Field; Paul Lincoln Cornell Athletic Field, and Roy Field. There are also three outdoor tennis courts and two ponds for outdoor recreation and winter skating.

Holt Beach at Lake Waramaug is the site for spring crew training. Off-season training is available for rowers in the state-of-the-art indoor rowing facility. Students who ski and snowboard in the winter term travel to Mohawk Mountain in nearby Cornwall, Connecticut on weekday afternoons.

EXTRACURRICULAR OPPORTUNITIES

Throughout the year, Upper School students may participate in many activities and clubs. The choices include fishing, computers, chorus, art club, bicycling, fly fishing, School newspaper, yearbook, art, swimming, hiking, rocketry, baking, community service, intramural sports, and participation in School dramatic and musical productions. The Rumsey Chamber Orchestra, Clef Club, and the a cappella singing group, Passing Notes, practice weekly and perform at various events throughout the year.

The Lower School features an exciting afternoon enrichment program for all students in kindergarten through fifth grade after their daily academic curriculum is complete. In keeping with Rumsey Hall's mission to educate the whole child, the varied activities offered each afternoon are organized to cultivate interests that can be nurtured as the children grow. Most activities are led by Rumsey teachers while others enlist the skills of specialists from surrounding communities. Activities include but are not limited to the arts (ceramics, printmaking, theater, crafts), athletics (field/gymnasium sports, martial arts), and recreational and outdoor games.

Traditional annual events for the School community include a Winter Concert, Parents' Day, Grandparents' Day, and Headmaster's Weekend and ski trip to Bromley Mountain, Vermont. Service to the School and to the greater community is encouraged throughout the year by the community service/service learning program. During the 2011–12 academic year the students amassed 903 total hours of volunteer service.

The student body is divided into red and blue color teams. These teams enjoy friendly competition throughout the school year in areas of community service, academic achievement, and athletics.

DAILY LIFE

The school day begins at 8 a.m. with an all-School meeting. All administrators, faculty members, and students are in attendance. It is a time to share the news of the School and the world as well as important information and announcements with the whole community. The rest of the academic day consists of eight 40-minute periods and supervised study halls, with a 20-minute recess in the middle of the morning. Extra help is available every day after lunch. Athletic practices or contests take place from 3 to 4:30 p.m. Dinner is served family style at 6 and is followed by study hall from 7 to 8:30. Free time follows, with bedtimes varying depending on the grade of the child.

WEEKEND LIFE

Weekends for boarding students include a variety of activities on and off campus. There are School dances, special theme weekends, off-campus trips, and intramural activities on campus. Rumsey's proximity to four major cities—New York, Boston, Hartford, and New Haven—allows for a wide variety of cultural events, sports events (collegiate and professional), and shopping excursions. All trips are fully supervised, and an appropriate student-teacher ratio is maintained. Day students are encouraged to participate in weekend activities and are also allowed to invite boarding students home with them for the weekend.

SUMMER PROGRAMS

The five-week Rumsey Hall summer session is open to students in the third through ninth grades. The program is designed for students who desire enrichment or need additional work in a subject area in order to move on to the next grade with confidence.

Special emphasis is placed on English, mathematics, study skills, and computer skills. Normal class size ranges from 6 to 10 students with individual attention and help available. Students who need support in language skills or developmental reading work daily with trained specialists. ESL is offered to international students. In the afternoon, students enjoy recreational activities such as swimming, hiking, tennis, fishing, horseback riding, baseball, soccer, lacrosse, and basketball. Off-campus trips to museums, movies, concerts, amusement parks, and sporting events occur each week. Considerable effort is made to cultivate students' interests and to expose them to new experiences. For the 2012 summer session, tuition, room, and board was $7100 for boarding students, $2540 for day students, and $1650 for half-day students. There are additional fees for individual tutoring in language skills and enrollment in ESL.

COSTS AND FINANCIAL AID

In 2012–13, full-year tuition is $18,270 for kindergarten and day students in grades 1 and 2, $22,470 for day students in grades 3–9, and $47,355 for boarding students. Additional fees included books, athletic fees, school supplies, and laundry and dry cleaning. A nonrefundable deposit of $2000 serves as the boarding student's drawing account for the year. The annual fee for language skills was $5245. The annual fee for ESL was $7350. Two thirds of the total tuition is due July 15 and the balance by December 15. A ten-installment payment agreement is available.

Rumsey Hall is a member of the School and Student Service for Financial Aid. In the 2011–12 academic year just over $1 million in tuition assistance was awarded to one third of the students.

ADMISSIONS INFORMATION

Rumsey Hall welcomes students of average to above-average intelligence and achievement. Students must show evidence of good citizenship and the willingness to live in a boarding community. Acceptance is based on past school performance, scores on standardized achievement tests, and a personal interview. Rumsey is able to accept a limited number of students with learning differences if their learning profile is compatible with the School's Orton-Gillingham–based language skills program. Rumsey Hall School admits students of any race, color, religion, or national or ethnic origin.

APPLICATION TIMETABLE

Inquiries are welcome at any time of the year, with most families beginning the admission process in the fall or winter in anticipation of September enrollment. Admission interviews and tours are scheduled throughout the year. Boarding student applications are accepted on a rolling basis. Day student applicants should complete the application process by February 15. Applicants are notified of acceptance by March 1.

ADMISSION CORRESPONDENCE

Matthew S. Hoeniger '81, Director of Admission
Rumsey Hall School
201 Romford Road
Washington Depot, Connecticut 06794
United States
Phone: 860-868-0535
Fax: 860-868-7907
E-mail: admiss@rumseyhall.org
Web site: http://www.rumseyhall.org

Summer Programs Close-Ups

CUSHING ACADEMY
LEARNING AT THE LEADING EDGE

CUSHING ACADEMY SUMMER SESSION

ASHBURNHAM, MASSACHUSETTS

Type of Program: Academic Enrichment
Participants: Coeducational; ages 12 through 18
Enrollment: 325
Program Dates: June 30 through August 2, 2013
Head of Program: Margaret H. Lee, Director of Summer Programs

LOCATION

Cushing's 162-acre campus lies in the small, rural town of Ashburnham in north-central Massachusetts, 55 miles west of Boston and 10 miles south of the New Hampshire border. Proximity to Boston permits extensive use of the city's cultural, entertainment, and commercial resources.

BACKGROUND AND PHILOSOPHY

Cushing Academy, founded in 1865, opened as a coeducational boarding school with funds provided by Thomas Parkman Cushing. Since its founding, Cushing Academy has prepared boys and girls in grades 9 through 12 and postgraduate to be contributing members of colleges and universities and of the modern world. Students live and learn with students from over thirty countries and thirty states in a quiet, safe, and supportive community 1 hour northwest of Boston. At Cushing Academy, students are prepared for the technological, political, artistic, environmental, scientific, cultural, and ethical issues already present in their lives—the big questions of this new century that frame their academics, athletics, activities, and life on campus. Cushing builds students' global awareness, helps them to fulfill their aspirations, and enables them to learn the skills they will need to succeed throughout their lives.

PROGRAM OFFERINGS

The Prep for Success program is for students aged 12–13, rising seventh and eighth graders. This program gives students the confidence and skills necessary to meet their academic success for the future. Core courses include literature and writing, mathematics or English as a second language. All students participate in a study, research, and technology skills course.

The College Prep program is for students aged 14–18, rising ninth through twelfth graders. College prep is a rigorous five-week program, which prepares students to meet the challenges of college-level curriculum confidently and successfully. Cushing offers a wide range of courses in English, mathematics, science, history, and college advising. Each class meets 5 hours per day, five days a week. One year of academic credit is given for successful completion of one course.

The Critical Skills Across the Curriculum program is for students aged 14–18, rising ninth through twelfth graders. This program focuses on the development of reading, writing, and mathematic skills. Study, organizational, and learning strategies, as well as appropriate use of technology, are woven into the curriculum.

The English as a Second Language (ESL) program is for students aged 14–18, rising ninth through twelfth graders. This course focuses on English immersion, intensive TOEFL preparation, and experiences in American culture.

The Studio Art and Portfolio Preparation program is for students aged 13–18, rising eighth through twelfth graders. This course focuses on the fundamentals of color, composition, line, and space used in media from pencil, canvas, metals, photographs, watercolor, and oil as students learn through hands-on practice of the techniques covered in class.

A wide variety of academic, athletic, and visual and performing arts courses, including advanced computer applications, music production, video and filmmaking, drama, jewelry-making, soccer, basketball, and tennis are offered in the afternoon.

ENROLLMENT

The 2012 Summer Session student body consisted of 328 students; 297 boarders and 31 day students. Students came from thirty countries and five continents.

DAILY SCHEDULE

See website at: http://www.cushing.org/summercalendar.

EXTRA OPPORTUNITIES AND ACTIVITIES

Cushing offers weekly all-school excursions, exciting weekend activities both on and off campus, a trip to High Meadow resort in Connecticut, educational class trips, International Dinner and Performances, an unforgettable talent show, Summer Fling, a dinner/dance cruise on the *Odyssey,* an art show, and graduation dinner.

FACILITIES

At the center of Cushing's campus is the Main Building, which houses classrooms, offices, and Cowell Chapel where members of the community gather for all-school meetings and performing arts productions. Also in the Main Building is the Fisher-Watkins Library, which was transformed in 2009 to a digital learning center. In addition to its collection of e-readers and online data sources, the library features collaborative instruction space, large-screen monitors for viewing interactive data and news feeds from around

the world, quiet study carrels, and a cyber café. The Joseph R. Curry Academic Center houses mathematics, the sciences, and the performing arts. This state-of-the-art facility of more than 56,000 square feet includes instructional laboratories, studios, student project rooms, and seminar space. The English Building houses seven newly renovated classrooms. The Emily Fisher Landau Center for Visual Arts has both studio and gallery space for students to create and display professional-quality work in a variety of media, including fused and stained glass, silver, ceramics, photography, painting, and sculpture.

In summer, Cushing houses students in seven dormitories that vary in capacity from 20 to 81 students each.

The Heslin Gymnasium contains four locker rooms, the John Biggs Jr. Memorial Fitness Center, a training room, and a basketball/volleyball court. There are also six playing fields and six tennis courts. In addition to year-round ice skating, the Theodore Iorio Ice Arena offers boys' and girls' locker rooms, workout facilities, a multipurpose function room, and a snack bar.

STAFF

Cushing Summer Session employs 95 full and part-time faculty and staff. The teacher-student ratio in the dormitories is 1:8, and 1:10 in the classroom.

MEDICAL CARE

Cushing has an on-campus health and wellness center that is staffed by a registered nurse at all times during Summer Session. A physician is on campus daily. Heywood Hospital is located just 4 miles from campus should a student require additional medical evaluation and/or treatment.

COSTS

Tuition and fees for the 2012 Summer Session were $6675 for boarding students and $3195 for day students. There are optional fees for sickness insurance, laundry service, Saturday in Boston trip, studio art materials, and transportation to and from the Academy during arrival and departure.

FINANCIAL AID

Limited need-based financial aid, as well as local and national scholarships, is available.

TRANSPORTATION

For a fee, Cushing provides chaperoned transportation to and from Logan International Airport in Boston on scheduled arrival and departure dates. Boston is 55 miles east of campus.

APPLICATION TIMETABLE

Applications are reviewed beginning in October, and students are accepted until all spaces in Summer Session are filled.

FOR MORE INFORMATION, CONTACT

Margaret H. Lee, Director of Summer Programs
Cushing Academy Summer Session
39 School Street
P.O. Box 8000
Ashburnham, MA 01430
United States
Phone: (978) 827-7700
Fax: (978) 827-6927
E-mail: summersession@cushing.org
Web site: http://www.cushing.org/summer

EMMA WILLARD SCHOOL

SUMMER ENGLISH IMMERSION PROGRAM

TROY, NEW YORK

Type of Program: Academic enrichment boarding program in English language and culture
Participants: Girls ages 12–17
Enrollment: 30
Program Dates: July 20–August 17, 2013
Heads of Program: Wendy Pattison, Director of Business Services

LOCATION

Emma Willard is situated in Troy, NY near the beautiful Adirondack Mountains and three hours from New York City and Boston. The region is rich with historically significant sites and cultural activities. The Emma Willard campus is on 137 beautifully maintained acres and includes our historic gothic, castle-like campus buildings and residences.

BACKGROUND AND PHILOSOPHY

The Immersion Program combines Emma Willard School's reputation for focused individualized study with fun and exciting weekend and evening activities designed to provide the girls with a sense of American culture. Evenings are filled with hall activities that quickly create a feeling of community. Students will improve their English speaking, listening, writing, and reading skills as well as gain a greater sense of American history and culture. This program is best for girls who have intermediate to advanced English language skills. The all-girls environment at Emma Willard creates a safe and comfortable place to explore American culture.

PROGRAM OFFERINGS

The program includes 18 hours of class time per week, plus field trips, physical education, and recreation. The girls taking part in the program also take day-long trips to New York City and Boston as well as visits to top regional colleges and universities to get acquainted with college life in the U.S. Students also enjoy practice interviewing for admissions to American preparatory schools or universities.

ENROLLMENT

The program is currently limited to 30 participants. The enrollment is kept intentionally small to provide individual instruction. In 2012, students from Thailand, Japan, Mexico, and China participated. Applicants to the program must submit an essay, teacher recommendation, school transcript, and scores from any standardized tests they have completed. Health forms and immunization documentation must be completed in order to attend.

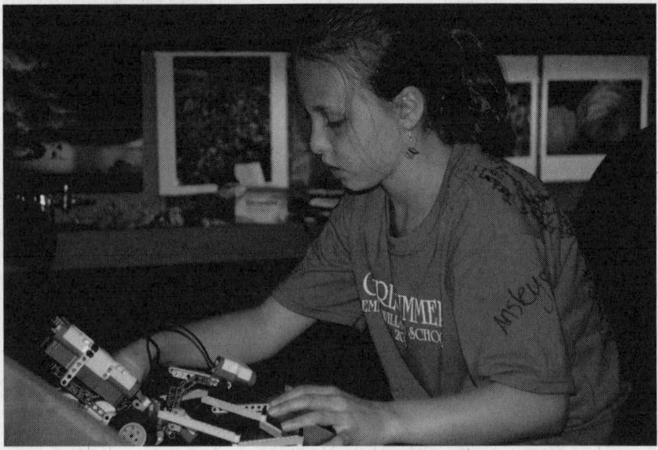

DAILY WEEKDAY SCHEDULE

A typical daily schedule includes breakfast starting at 7:45 followed by individualized and classroom English language instruction from 8:30 to 11:30. Students enjoy lunch and conversation from 11:30 to noon followed by instruction and activities in American history and culture from noon to 3:15. After the classroom time, the girls have access to a wide variety of health and wellness activities followed by dinner, evening activities, and quiet study. Girls must be in bed for the evening by 10:30. On field trip days, the girls experience a wide variety of cultural and historic activities in their destination city. During their time at the school, students are expected to follow the codes of conduct outlined in the student handbook.

EXTRA OPPORTUNITIES AND ACTIVITIES

Health and wellness activities include Zumba, yoga, pilates, tennis, Ultimate (Frisbee), basketball, and more. Campus facilities include a fitness gym, walking trails, an indoor pool, and 24-hour security. Local field trips include shopping, restaurants, museums, and parks. To assist in the learning process, American Emma Willard students participate in activities to enhance the American experience. Girls will make friends for a lifetime.

FACILITIES

Students live on the 137-acre, 23-building historic campus with resident faculty and current Emma Willard students. Spacious common rooms with wireless Internet and free laundry services are available.

STAFF

The school hires experienced teachers with university degrees in education and experience in language instruction. In addition, resident faculty members are adults who work regularly with students and live with them in the resident halls to meet their emotional and physical needs. They are the main point of contact for parents while the girls are away from home. Proctors assist the resident faculty and are often alumni of Emma Willard who are familiar with the routines and traditions of the school.

MEDICAL CARE

The school's Wellness Center is staffed with a nurse either on-site or on call 15 hours a day. Administrative on-call staff cover the remaining hours. In addition, a local pediatrician's office is contracted to provide health services. Students who do not have U.S. health insurance must purchase it on a per diem basis through the school. Medical forms documenting good health and specific health information are required. Documentation of immunizations is required by the New York State Department of Education and is required before starting the program.

RELIGIOUS LIFE

Participants may request a ride to a full range of religious serves available in the area. There is also a chapel on campus.

COSTS

The program cost for 2013 is $6500 U.S. dollars. The cost includes tuition, textbooks, and room and board. Additional costs include an application fee, health care, airfare, pick up from JFK Airport in New York City (no fee for Albany International Airport), eating out, and souvenirs. Participants should bring approximately $400 spending money. The signed contract and entire program fee must be paid in order to retain a place in the program. An enrolled student may only be withdrawn upon written notice received by the school. If such notice is received on or before July 20, 2013, tuition payments received minus a 50 percent fee will be refunded. Fees can be paid by U.S. check or money order or wire service. The application fee may be paid by credit card.

FINANCIAL AID

There is no financial aid available for this program.

TRANSPORTATION

Airport pick-up and drop-off are available for an additional fee.

APPLICATION TIMETABLE

Most of the application can be submitted online. Students can submit their application and application fee any time after September 1, 2012. Admissions decisions will be made on a rolling basis until June 1, 2013. Applications will only be taken after June 1, 2012 if any of the limited number of enrollments are still available. Upon receiving an enrollment contract, the family must then sign and submit their signed contract and the full payment of tuition to reserve a place in the program.

FOR MORE INFORMATION, CONTACT

Wendy A. Pattison, Director of Business Projects
Emma Willard School Summer English Immersion Program
285 Pawling Avenue
Troy, New York 12180
United States
Phone: 518-833-178
Fax: 518-833-1810
E-mail: wpattison@emmawillard.org
Web site: http://www.emmawillard.org/programs/summer-programs/summer-english-immersion

FAY SCHOOL

INTERNATIONAL STUDENT PROGRAM

SOUTHBOROUGH, MASSACHUSETTS

Type of Program: International families who want their children to be educated in the United States have a unique opportunity at Fay School each summer. The International Student Program offers academic programs in the morning and day camp activities in the afternoon, providing English language immersion and contact with domestic students of a comparable age.
Participants: Coeducational, international boarding students, ages 10–15
Enrollment: 60
Program Dates: Early July through mid-August
Head of Program: Courtney Sargent, Director of the Summer International Student Program

LOCATION

Fay School is situated on 66 beautiful acres in semirural surroundings in Southborough, Massachusetts, 25 miles west of Boston.

BACKGROUND AND PHILOSOPHY

The International Student Program (ISP) is integrated into the entire summer Fay experience. In addition to their daily academic program, international students spend part of each day with domestic students of similar age, choosing from a variety of fun and enriching activities that include day camp, athletics, visual and performing arts, trips, cultural experiences, test preparation, and public speaking. Each afternoon, students are immersed in English, putting their language skills to work, all while participating in engaging activities with other campers.

This summer boarding program makes it possible for international students ages 10 to 15 to participate in the Fay experience regardless of their level of English proficiency. It provides a meaningful introduction to Fay for students enrolling full-time in the upcoming academic year as well as an outstanding stand-alone program for international students who wish to focus on developing their English skills during the summer months.

The International Student Program supports students in all aspects of their summer experience. The School provides ground travel arrangements, academic scheduling, and continuous communication with parents. International students learn English by taking academic courses at their appropriate level.

PROGRAM OFFERINGS

Each morning, ISP students take academic classes designed to improve their English writing and speaking skills. There are three levels of classes: beginner (Level I), intermediate (Level II), and advanced (Level III). Students are placed in classes upon their arrival at Fay based on placement tests. At every level, classes emphasize grammar, composition, reading comprehension, and speaking and listening skills. Advanced electives include world geography, U.S. history, general science, and creative writing. As students become more proficient, they may progress to higher levels of the program. In addition to daily course work, students are expected to complete approximately 1 hour of homework each night.

Students are assessed in class on both effort and achievement. Just as in Fay's regular school year ISP program, students receive effort grades every two weeks in order to provide feedback on their level of engagement. In addition, students receive a midsummer grade and a final grade for each course, along with a written summary from the student's advisers.

Each afternoon, ISP students join children from the local area by participating in day camp or a specialty workshop, which includes academics, art, theater, music, outdoor adventures, and sports. This provides ISP students the opportunity to have an afternoon full of activities of their choice and to meet American friends of the same age.

The day camp activities offered in the afternoons include: archery, art, baseball, basketball, boating, ceramics, climbing wall, computers, cooking, crafts, dodge ball, drawing, fishing, flag football, free swim, gardening, GPS mapping and orienteering, high ropes course, improv, jewelry making, kickball, music, music with computers, nature, outdoor living, painting, photography, puppeteering, robotics and rockets, science, sculpture, sewing and fashion design, soccer, street hockey, swim lessons, tennis, theater, Ultimate (Frisbee), video production, woodshop, and writers' corner.

ENROLLMENT

During the summer of 2012, 60 students enrolled in Fay's Summer ISP program.

DAILY SCHEDULE

Mornings:	Academic classes
Noon:	Lunch
Afternoons:	Day Camp activities
4 p.m.:	Evening activities, dinner, and study hall

EXTRA OPPORTUNITIES AND ACTIVITIES

Summer weekends at Fay are a valuable time for students to put their language skills to use. They participate in academic and social activities on campus, explore Boston and the surrounding areas on field trips, and bond with faculty and other students. Weekend activities include Summer Olympics, which highlights students'

athletic, artistic, and other talents; a canoe trip down the Charles River; a trip to the New England seashore; an historical scavenger hunt throughout Boston; dance parties; and movie trips.

Students are also required to attend study hall each weekend in order to complete assignments for classes. The combination of trips and on-campus activities ensure that students remain engaged in the American experience while allowing them time to foster lasting relationships with students from all over the world.

FACILITIES

Fay's residential facilities are comfortable and well supervised. An adult is available at all times to answer questions and help resolve any issues that may arise. The School strives to create a family atmosphere based on respect for one's self and for others. Students live, work, and play together with guidance and supervision from dedicated teachers and staff.

The Root Academic Center (1984) houses most of the Upper and Lower School classrooms. The Mars Wing (2001) includes the Learning Center, the media lab, four state-of-the-art science labs, a writing lab, and a multimedia lab. The Picardi Art Center (1987) provides outstanding facilities for art classes, including a darkroom and ceramics studio. The Harris Events Center (1995) is home to Fay's performing arts program and includes five music practice rooms, two music classrooms, a dance studio, and a 400-seat theater.

Family-style meals are served in the dining room. The Wellness Center (2009) is situated in the lower level of the Steward Dorm and serves as the campus medical facility.

The School's athletic facilities were greatly enhanced with the completion of the Fay School athletic campus in 2009. The campus comprises 30 acres of dedicated regulation-sized outdoor fields for soccer, field hockey, baseball, softball, and lacrosse. The campus also features a cross-country course and four batting cages, two for baseball and two for softball. Additional facilities include the Harlow Gymnasium (1993), a facility that incorporates four basketball courts, expanded locker room space, team rooms, a wrestling room, a weight room, and a training room.

STAFF

ISP teachers and residential staff enjoy working with international students and are experienced and skillful instructors and mentors.

MEDICAL CARE

A school nurse is available on campus at all times.

COSTS

Tuition for ISP is $9000, which includes room and board. There is a $1200 incidentals fee (any unused portion is returned to the family).

FINANCIAL AID

Prospective families should contact Courtney Sargent, Director of the Summer International Student Program, to discuss the possible availability of financial aid.

TRANSPORTATION

Fay School will make ground transportation arrangements from and to the airport.

APPLICATION TIMETABLE

Student registration is conducted on a rolling basis throughout the 2012–13 school year.

FOR MORE INFORMATION, CONTACT:

Courtney Sargent, Director of the Summer International Student Program
Fay School
48 Main Street
Southborough, Massachusetts 01772
United States
Phone: 508-485-8371
E-mail: csargent@fayschool.org
Web site: http://www.fayschool.org

GRIER SCHOOL

GRIER SUMMER CAMP

TYRONE, PENNSYLVANIA

Type of Program: Allegheny Riding Camp, Allegheny Camp for the Arts
Participants: Girls, 7–17
Enrollment: 85 per session
Program Dates: June 23–August 2
Head of Program: Helen Zientek, Director

LOCATION

Grier Summer Camp is located in the Allegheny Mountains of central Pennsylvania and uses the facilities of the Grier School, an historic girls boarding school.

BACKGROUND AND PHILOSOPHY

Founded in 1975, Grier Summer is a very specialized all-girls camp with strong traditions in hunter/jumper horseback riding and intensive programs in the visual and performing arts.

PROGRAM OFFERINGS

Allegheny Riding Camp loves girls who love horses! The camp offers hunter/jumper riding lessons for the novice as well as the experienced rider, with two judged horse shows per session. There are 90-minute morning riding lessons and optional equine studies in the afternoon. There is also a travel show team for experienced riders who want to show at A and AA horse shows.

In order to provide a personalized experience for every camper, a horse is assigned to a rider for the entire session. The program welcomes beginners to experienced riders, maintains an excellent staff ratio for lessons, and groups riders by the same ability level for lessons. Instructors provide a progress report for each camper at the end of the session. The program teaches girls to realize their potential though horsemanship, friendship, and respect for animals.

There are two Friday morning, judged horse shows during each session of camp. Riders with show experience can practice their techniques and riders who have never shown can learn how to show. Sessions end with a Friday exhibition horse show for parents.

Campers are able to participate in a number of activities that do not involve riding, such as dance, theater, drama, art, digital photography, film studies, and pool games.

Grier Summer also offers Allegheny Camp for the Arts, a three-week program, perfect for girls, ages 7–17 looking for a fun camp experience in a beautiful, serene location with top-notch arts facilities.

Campers choose four different elective activities from a variety of creative and recreational options. There is intensive study in dance and musical theater, as well as a strong visual arts program with ceramics and pottery, mixed media, and drawing and painting. Activities may include; ceramics, mixed media, drawing, creative writing, sidewalk art, dance (modern, hip-hop, salsa, etc.), Grier Summer Players (on stage, back stage, musical heater, tech, make-up, and costume design), arts and crafts, tennis, outdoor sports, pool games, English for Fun (for international campers), and Spanish for Fun.

Summer campers can choose to participate with the Grier Summer Players for one or even two of their activity periods.

Students play theater games, act, sing, and dance. Each camper in Grier Summer Players learns and performs two large, ensemble Broadway tunes with singing, dancing, and acting. At the end of the camp session, GSP perform a final performance for friends and families.

ENROLLMENT

Grier Summer averages 85 participants per session. Sixty-five percent of those are from the greater tri-state area of New York, New Jersey, and Pennsylvania; 25 percent are international students; and 10 percent of participants come from other areas throughout the United States.

DAILY SCHEDULE

Campers are assigned to a unit of 6 to 10 girls the same age. At least two staff members are assigned to each unit. Each unit sits together for meals.

Breakfast is at 7:45 followed by two 90-minute activity sessions. Lunch is at noon followed by a 90-minute rest hour, two more activity sessions, and a snack. Dinner is served at 6:15 and there are unit activities before and after dinner. Evening programs feature both campwide events, such as camp fires, talent shows, color wars, and scavenger hunts, and small-group adventure activities, including pool parties, spa nights, and geocaching.

EXTRA OPPORTUNITIES AND ACTIVITIES

Saturdays are themed days, with daylong activities centered around a theme. The evening program is also themed and often includes professional performers. Sundays are adventure days. During a regular session there is one field trip that is campwide and off campus. The other Sunday is planned by the units and can include rails-to-trails hikes, small trips to local caverns and caves, geocaching, or the opportunity to stay on campus and relax. On weekends, breakfast is at 9, lunch is at 12:30 p.m., and dinner is at 6:15. Sunday night is call-home night for campers.

FACILITIES

For riders there are two indoor arenas, as well as stables for 55+ horses. Art facilities include a performing arts building as well as a visual arts building. A swimming pool is available; pool games are among the afternoon activities. Campers sleep in the dorm rooms of the Grier School and use the dining room for meals.

STAFF

Supervisory staff members include the director, assistant director, office manager, head counselor, and director of special programs. There is a pool director and visual arts manager. The dance and musical theater intensives are taught by Grier School teachers. The counselor to camper ratio is 1:4 for older campers and 1:3 for younger campers, with two counselors for every unit. The majority of the riding counselors are recruited from the United Kingdom.

Helen Zientek—affectionately named Mama Z by her campers—is the camp director. Helen's expertise includes creating and managing day camps for American families in El Khobar, Saudi Arabia. Helen is a retired library media specialist whose daughter is Emily Zientek, riding director of Grier Summer Camp and the Grier School. Helen and her husband, Chet, also known as Papa Z, divide their time between Florida and Pennsylvania.

MEDICAL CARE

The health center is staffed continually while children are at camp, from 7 a.m. until 11 p.m. Seasonal camp staff is certified in first aid and CPR, and the nearest emergency facility is about 10 minutes away. Health forms are in compliance with the standards of the American Camp Association.

RELIGIOUS LIFE

There are opportunities for participants to attend religious services.

COSTS

Program costs are $3400 per session for Allegheny Camp of the Arts and $3850 for Allegheny Riding Camp. Incidental fees are $75 for girls 7–14 and $175 for girls 15–17, which includes teen outing fees. Health insurance fee for international campers is $130.

Show Camper program costs are $7000–$10,000 for four- or six-week options. This fee is all-inclusive.

FINANCIAL AID

Financial assistance is determined on an individual basis.

TRANSPORTATION

Grier Summer staff will meet campers for arrival or accompany campers for departure at four designated airports: State College and Altoona Blair County Regional (45–60 minutes away), Pittsburgh International Airport (3 hours away), Dulles International Airport (4 hours away), and Philadelphia International Airport (5 hours away). There is a fee for airport transfers; $200 round-trip for the international airports

APPLICATION TIMETABLE

There are two camp open houses in the early spring, but parents and prospective campers may visit at any time with prior arrangements. There is a Grier Summer meet and greet in northern New Jersey in March. More information is available on the camp website at www.bestcamp.org.

FOR MORE INFORMATION, CONTACT

Helen Zientek, Director
Grier Summer Camp
2522 Grier School Road
Tyrone, PA 16686
United States
Phone: 814/684-3000, ext 113 May-September, 561/818-9753 September-April
Fax: 814/684-2177
E-mail: bestcamp@grier.org
Web site: www.bestcamp.org

PARTICIPANT/FAMILY COMMENTS

The Web address says it all—bestcamp.org—it is simply the best!

Best camp ever. My daughter loves it!

We could not be happier with the camp, the counselors, and the friends that she made. We will happily sign her up next year for even longer.

PHILLIPS EXETER ACADEMY

SUMMER SCHOOL

EXETER, NEW HAMPSHIRE

Type of Program: Academic enrichment
Participants: Coeducational, grades 8–12 and postgraduate year
Enrollment: 780
Program Dates: Five-week program; July 7–August 10, 2013
Head of Program: Ethan W. Shapiro, Director

LOCATION

The 400-acre Phillips Exeter Academy campus is located in the town of Exeter, the Colonial capital of New Hampshire, which is in the heart of the state's seacoast area. Boston, Newburyport, Portsmouth, and the White Mountains are all within easy access for excursions.

BACKGROUND AND PHILOSOPHY

Every summer, Phillips Exeter Academy welcomes to the campus more than 780 students for five weeks of academic study, athletics, and exploration that carry participants far beyond the classrooms and the playing fields. Typically, students come from more than forty states; Puerto Rico; Washington, D.C.; and several dozen foreign nations. Summer School students come from a variety of schools. Most reside in campus dormitories; others travel daily from their homes in the New Hampshire seacoast area. Together they embody a rich diversity of language, culture, religion, and race. They come to Exeter with that particular mix of intellectual curiosity and adventurous spirit that holds the promise of glimpsing new horizons and making new discoveries.

PROGRAM OFFERINGS

The UPPER SCHOOL offers a challenging academic experience for students who have completed grades 9, 10, 11, or 12. UPPER SCHOOL students are part of a richly international community in which students design their own programs of study by selecting courses from the more than 100 offered by the Academy. In shaping their own academic programs, students have the opportunity to expand their intellectual horizons. For instance, they might choose courses in math, art, and English, such as *Advanced Problem-Solving, Drawing,* and *Great Books/Great Reading.* Or they might sample offerings from science, history, and languages, like *Introduction to Biology, Great Issues in American History,* and *Introduction to Arabic.* Whatever their academic choices, students find themselves working in small classes with highly experienced, dedicated teachers. As students select their three classes, they are encouraged to venture into worlds rich in their personal appeal, worlds that may allow them to glimpse new horizons.

ACCESS EXETER offers students who have completed grades 7 or 8 access to a wide range of resources available at Phillips Exeter Academy. Participants will share in a partnership of cooperative learning and sharpen their skills of observation and expression. Students and their teachers will work together within the classroom and beyond. The ACCESS EXETER curriculum consists of six academic clusters. Each cluster has three courses organized around a central theme. Each cluster will include a two-night/three-day, off-campus excursion related to their topic of study midway through the session. Students choose to participate in one of six clusters: *Project*

Exeter: A Greener Earth; The Land and the Sea; Problem-Solving: An Odyssey of the Mind; A Global Community; The Creative Arts: Let Your Spirit Soar; and *Exeter C.S.I.: Crime Scene Investigation.*

Physical education, an important component of the Summer School, promotes fitness, cooperation, sportsmanship, and learning new skills. The offerings are designed to introduce fundamental rules and skills, provide some competition and recreation, and stimulate long-term participation in athletics. Each class meets four times per week for an hour each day. In the past, physical education offerings have included tennis, soccer, basketball, yoga, weight training, water polo, and many other options.

The Summer School also offers an opportunity for students to enjoy more intensive athletic experiences. UPPER SCHOOL students can sign up to participate in the crew program for the entire five weeks of Summer School. In addition, the Summer School and Seacoast United Soccer Club offer a special intensive instruction program for UPPER SCHOOL and ACCESS EXETER students. This program is for players who have a passion for soccer, have played at a competitive level, and want to continue a high level of training while at Summer School.

ENROLLMENT

Students come to the Summer School from forty-five countries and more than forty states. The UPPER SCHOOL is made up of 500 students while ACCESS EXETER can accommodate about 280 participants. Students of all racial, religious, and socioeconomic backgrounds are welcome.

DAILY SCHEDULE

Students attend classes six days a week, Monday through Saturday. On Wednesday and Saturday afternoons students may participate in off-campus excursions, on-campus activities, do homework, or simply relax. Twice a week the entire student body gathers for special assemblies where speakers and performers share their talents. Students have their meals in the dining hall, located in the center of campus. Here they have time to catch up with new friends or chat with faculty members and their families. Dormitory check-in is at 9 p.m. for UPPER SCHOOL students and 8 p.m. for ACCESS EXETER students (11 p.m. on Saturday). The dorm is expected to be conducive to study after this time.

EXTRA OPPORTUNITIES AND ACTIVITIES

Educational and recreational excursions are a regular feature of Wednesday afternoons and weekends, when there are no required appointments. Such excursions are optional and may consist of hikes in the White Mountains, tours of New England colleges, Boston museum visits, or whale watches. Extracurricular activities include theater, music, and various sports. Students are encouraged to enjoy the cultural and ethnic diversity that is at the heart of the Exeter Summer School experience.

FACILITIES

Exeter is proud of its outstanding academic and athletic facilities. The centerpiece of the campus is Louis Kahn's architectural landmark, The Class of 1945 Library, which has a capacity of 250,000 volumes and can seat approximately 400 students. The collection currently consists of 160,000 volumes in addition to an extensive collection of periodicals, DVDs, and CDs. Equally impressive is the Love Gymnasium, with its five basketball floors, Olympic pool, ten squash courts, and exercise and weight rooms. Outside there are acres of baseball diamonds, soccer fields, tennis courts, an all-weather 400-meter track, and a cross-country course through the nature preserve.

The Forrestal-Bowld Music Center has more than 24,000 square feet of space dedicated to the study of music. In addition to three large rehearsal rooms, there are eleven teacher studios, eight of them equipped with grand pianos, and sixteen practice rooms. The state-of-the-art Phelps Science Center offers students and teachers outstanding facilities for scientific investigation and study. Other highlights of the campus are the two-stage Fisher Theater, the Frederick R. Mayer Art Center and Lamont Gallery, and the Grainger Observatory.

STAFF

Many of the Summer School's instructors are Phillips Exeter Academy faculty members. Additional qualified instructors are recruited from other schools and universities from around the world, and many have made long-term commitments to teaching at Phillips Exeter Academy Summer School.

MEDICAL CARE

The Lamont Health and Wellness Center is staffed 24 hours a day. Exeter Hospital, which is just minutes away, offers emergency medical services. Enrollment in the Summer School Group Insurance Plan is included in the tuition.

RELIGIOUS LIFE

The Summer School is nondenominational; students may attend religious services at nearby churches and synagogues if they wish.

COSTS

The 2013 tuition for UPPER SCHOOL boarding students is $7600. UPPER SCHOOL day students pay $1150 per course. UPPER SCHOOL students can also register for SAT Prep for an additional $800. The ACCESS EXETER boarding student tuition is $7995 and day students pay $4900. A nonrefundable fee of $1500 is due at the time of enrollment.

FINANCIAL AID

Limited financial aid is available and awards are determined by demonstrated need. The deadline for financial aid applications is March 1.

APPLICATION TIMETABLE

Admission to the Phillips Exeter Academy Summer School is competitive and is based on academic achievement. The Summer School seeks students who are motivated to learn and prepared to contribute fully to classroom work and the community. There is a rolling admissions procedure, and only completed applications will be considered. Since many courses fill quickly, it is in the candidate's best interest to complete the application as early as possible. Application information and the course catalog can be found on the Summer School Web site at www.exeter.edu/summer.

FOR MORE INFORMATION, CONTACT:

Ethan W. Shapiro, Director
Phillips Exeter Academy
Summer School
20 Main Street
Exeter, New Hampshire 03833-2460
United States
Phone: 603-777-3488
800-828-4325 Ext. 3488 (toll-free)
Fax: 603-777-4385
E-mail: summer@exeter.edu
Web site: http://www.exeter.edu/summer
Facebook: www.facebook.com/ExeterSummerSchool

SOUTHWESTERN ACADEMY

SUMMER ADVENTURES

RIMROCK, ARIZONA

Type of Program: Academic enrichment, ESL courses, outdoor recreation, environmental education, field trips, and academic credit courses
Participants: Coeducational, ages 12–18
Enrollment: 40
Program Dates: Full- and half-summer, four-, six-, and eight-week sessions, from June 22 to August 14
Head of Program: Mr. Jack Leyden, Head of Campus

LOCATION

Southwestern Academy's Beaver Creek Ranch Campus is in a secluded red sandstone canyon that was carved by the creek around it. The Coconino National Forest surrounds the 180-acre campus. The campus rests at an elevation of 4,000 feet and is located 15 miles from Sedona, 45 miles south of Flagstaff, and 100 miles north of Phoenix, Arizona. Surrounded by large sycamores and cottonwoods, two ponds and a trout stream are located on campus, making this a perfect location for high school students to board, study, and enjoy the summer.

BACKGROUND AND PHILOSOPHY

Southwestern Academy offers a warm, friendly, safe, and supportive environment for boys and girls to grow toward success. Founded in 1924, Southwestern is an accredited, not-for-profit, independent school for students from across the United States and around the world. Southwestern offers classes for grade 6 through high school. Small classes promote individual interaction with teachers and encourage the pursuit of interests beyond course requirements. Southwestern Academy's vision is to offer American and international students personalized, stimulating classes and supportive, nurturing care that allow individual student success and an understanding of diverse cultures. Summer Adventures at Southwestern Academy offers students entering high school full/half-summer and four-, six-, and eight-week programs that uniquely combine college-preparatory, academic enrichment, and language skills with the fun and exciting activities that the season presents.

PROGRAM OFFERINGS

Students enroll in classes that provide opportunities to link academics with some of the most popular hot spots of the area. Students also discover that the Summer Adventures program enables them to develop self-reliance and confidence while making new friendships with other students from around the world. The low teacher-student ratio provides a nurturing and supportive environment, establishing a sense of community and trust that embraces the school's core values. Field trips and scholastics are designed to be achievement based, with individual attention made available to each student as needed—all surrounded by an energetic and spirited atmosphere.

The Summer Adventures program includes a core curriculum with comprehensive courses in English, history, science, math, Spanish, and art. Courses are selected individually to meet each student's academic needs. English as a second language is offered to international students who need to improve their skills in reading, writing, and speaking. Afternoons are left open for study time, enrichment through arts and crafts, elective course work, and travel. Electives also include outdoor and wilderness skills.

High school course credit and letters of achievement can be earned to make up credits for deficiencies, or students can gain a head start on the coming school year. Southwestern Academy, a college-preparatory school with a noncompetitive program, is accredited by the Western Association of Schools and Colleges.

ENROLLMENT

Campers and counselors generally come from the Southwest and are joined by other students from the U.S. and around the world. Southwestern Academy's programs are open to all qualified students without regard to race, creed, or national origin.

EXTRA OPPORTUNITIES AND ACTIVITIES

The canyon setting of the Beaver Creek Ranch Campus provides creek and pool swimming, archaeological and geological field trips, backpacking, rock climbing, and the exploration of nearby caves containing prehistoric remains. There is trout fishing in the creek as well as bass fishing in the campus ponds. The nights are clear for stargazing.

Recreational activities include basketball, softball, swimming, volleyball, horseback riding, hiking, billiards, table tennis, horseshoes, mountain biking, weight training, camping, and indoor games. A golf course is also nearby.

Weekend activities include overnight travel to Sunset Crater, the Grand Canyon, Lake Powell, Navajo and Hopi reservations, the Petrified Forest, and Canyon de Chelly. Camping skills are learned and applied during these trips. In addition, there are organized studies at each site that provide hands-on learning in history, geology, ecology, economics, and geography.

FACILITIES

Campus buildings include classic dorms with double and triple rooms; river-stone cottages for faculty members; classrooms and study assembly; a science lab; recreation halls; natural and man-made swimming pools; indoor tennis, basketball, and volleyball courts; weight and fitness rooms; an art building; and sports fields. There is a full gymnasium on campus. Computers and computer instruction are available to all students.

STAFF

The Beaver Creek Ranch Campus staff consists of the Head of School, teachers, and support staff members. Teachers from the school's regular term instruct the summer program classes. Resident teachers supervise all afternoon and evening travel and activities.

MEDICAL CARE

The application includes authorization for the school to coordinate any medical procedures that may be necessary during the program.

COSTS

Tuition, room, and board total $7950 for the four-week session, $11,925 for the six-week session, and $15,900 for the eight-week session. A deposit of $500 is required for the student's personal expenses. Updated costs and program dates are available online at http://www.southwesternacademy.edu.

FINANCIAL AID

Limited financial aid is available. Special grants are based on financial need.

TRANSPORTATION

Beaver Creek Ranch Campus is 7 hours from Los Angeles by car and 1½ hours from Phoenix. A private airstrip is nearby. Unless other arrangements are made, students fly into Phoenix Sky Harbor Airport and take a shuttle to Camp Verde, where they are greeted by a Southwestern Academy staff or faculty member and escorted to the campus.

APPLICATION TIMETABLE

The completed application includes an application form, an emergency medical form, a health statement, and the $100 application fee. The school accepts applications throughout the year and accepts students as long as space is available. On acceptance, the contract reserves space in the school. Southwestern's year-round campuses are always open for tours, interviews, and/or admission information. Summer applications are due by May 15.

FOR MORE INFORMATION, CONTACT

Director of Admissions
San Marino Campus
Southwestern Academy
2800 Monterey Road
San Marino, California 91108
United States
Phone: 626-799-5010 Ext. 5
Fax: 626-799-0407
E-mail: admissions@southwesternacademy.edu
Web site: http://www.southwesternacademy.edu

Beaver Creek Ranch Campus
Southwestern Academy
Rimrock, Arizona 86335
United States
Phone: 928-567-4581

PARTICIPANT/FAMILY COMMENTS

"Summer Adventures at Southwestern Academy is a place where everyone can find success."

"It was a good summer—the best of my life. The studying was difficult, but I'm so glad my parents sent me, or I never would have had this experience. You work for the teachers and counselors, and they work for you. There's not anything in the world they wouldn't do for us. They're just fantastic."

"Everybody works together as a unit. You know the teachers personally and respect their knowledge. But they're more than teachers, they're people who care. They teach you more than lessons—they teach you about life."

SOUTHWESTERN ACADEMY

SUMMER ADVENTURES

SAN MARINO, CALIFORNIA

Type of Program: Academic enrichment, credit, and English as a second language
Participants: Boys and girls in grades 6–12
Enrollment: 75
Program Dates: Full- and half-summer, four-, six-, and eight-week sessions, from June 10 to September 13
Head of Program: Kenneth Veronda, Headmaster

LOCATION

The San Marino campus is located in one of the most beautiful neighborhoods in Southern California, minutes from Pasadena and Los Angeles. The campus sprawls over more than 8 acres in a quiet and serene community, making this a perfect location for middle school and high school students to board, study, and enjoy the summer.

BACKGROUND AND PHILOSOPHY

Southwestern Academy offers a warm, friendly, safe, and supportive environment for boys and girls to grow toward success. Founded in 1924, Southwestern is an accredited, not-for-profit independent school for students from across the United States and around the world. Southwestern offers classes for grade 6 through high school. Small classes promote individual interaction with teachers and encourage the pursuit of interests beyond course requirements. Southwestern Academy's vision is to offer American and international students personalized, stimulating classes and supportive, nurturing care that allow individual student success and an understanding of diverse cultures. Summer Adventures at Southwestern Academy offers students entering high school full/half-summer and four-, six-, and eight-week programs that uniquely combine college-preparatory, academic enrichment, and language skills with the fun and exciting activities that the season presents.

PROGRAM OFFERINGS

The Southwestern Summer Adventures program consists of two components: an Intensive English as a Second Language (ESL)/American Culture Program and traditional college-prep classes. Courses range from four weeks to a full semester and are offered on the campuses in San Marino, California, and Beaver Creek, Arizona. Depending on the length of the program, students can earn academic credit.

The San Marino campus offers two English language programs. The **Intensive ESL Program** is designed to help students improve their English skills. There are three ability levels: beginning, intermediate, and advanced. Students improve their skills through listening and conversation, writing and grammar, and reading and vocabulary. There is also an SAT/TOEFL-preparation component. Students who enroll in the seven-week or fourteen-week program can earn half- or full-semester credit. The **American Culture Program** teaches English-speaking skills, but it also incorporates field trips in the region. Course work includes 20 hours of English per week, developing reading, vocabulary, and conversation skills. Students receive a certificate at the end of the program.

Students who do not need ESL can select from a wide range of core courses, such as math, science, history, and English.

Southwestern Academy is an accredited college-preparatory school with a noncompetitive program.

ENROLLMENT

Each program enrolls an average of 10 to 12 students, ages 12 through 18, who wish to improve their English skills and/or participate in a number of recreational and cultural activities in the region. Students are exposed to a multicultural learning atmosphere and gain a fresh perspective on academics. Students may commute to the program, or they can live in a dormitory at the school. Southwestern Academy's programs are open to all qualified students without regard to race, creed, or national origin.

EXTRA OPPORTUNITIES AND ACTIVITIES

Weekly educational and entertaining field trips are offered to a variety of popular attractions throughout Southern California. Such trips include Disneyland, Griffith Park, Huntington Library, the Los Angeles County Museum of Art, and the Getty Museum. For boarding students, there are three additional trips offered each weekend.

FACILITIES

All dorms are of modern masonry construction and have TVs, DVDs, and computers with Internet and e-mail access. Each dormitory is supervised by a resident counselor, who has an apartment adjacent to the dormitory. Boarding students are provided with a buffet-style cooked breakfast and a family-style lunch and dinner. Commuting students have a hot lunch with the whole school group at no additional charge. Teachers and staff members eat with the students.

STAFF

The San Marino campus staff consists of the school's Headmaster, Dean of ESL, Director of Admissions, and approximately 22 teachers and dorm counselors. Counseling, testing, and crisis-intervention services are provided by the school psychologist.

MEDICAL CARE

The application includes authorization for the school to coordinate any medical procedures that may be necessary during the program.

COSTS

Tuition, room, and board total $5500 for the four-week program, $8250 for the six-week program, $11,000 for the eight-week program, $9625 for the half-summer program, and $18,550 for the full-summer program. A deposit of $500 is required for the student's personal expenses. Updated costs and program dates are available online at http://www.southwesternacademy.edu.

FINANCIAL AID

Limited financial aid is available. Special grants are based on financial need.

TRANSPORTATION

Southwestern Academy is approximately 25 miles from Los Angeles International Airport (LAX).

APPLICATION TIMETABLE

The completed application for the regular school year includes an application form, an emergency medical form, a health statement, and the $100 application fee. The school accepts applications throughout the year and accepts students as long as space is available. On acceptance, the contract reserves space in the school. Southwestern's year-round campuses are always open for tours, interviews, and/or admission information. Applications are welcome all summer, though early submission is requested due to demand and to assure availability.

FOR MORE INFORMATION, CONTACT

Director of Admissions
Southwest Academy
2800 Monterey Road
San Marino, California 91108
United States
Phone: 626-799-5010 Ext. 5
Fax: 626-799-0407
E-mail: admissions@southwesternacademy.edu
Web site: http://www.southwesternacademy.edu

TASIS THE AMERICAN SCHOOL IN ENGLAND

TASIS ENGLAND SUMMER PROGRAMS

THORPE, SURREY, ENGLAND

Type of Program: Academic, enrichment, travel, sports

Participants: Coeducational, ages 11–18

Enrollment: 250

Program Dates: Three-week sessions, June 29–July 19 and July 21–August 10; or the full 6 weeks, June 29–August 10

Head of Program: Mr. Jeffrey Barton

LOCATION

The program takes place on TASIS The American School in England's beautiful 46-acre campus located in the heart of a small English village, 18 miles from London, 8 miles from Heathrow International Airport, and 6 miles from the royal residence of Windsor. The area is a popular tourist destination, rich in natural, leisure and cultural resources. King John sealed the Magna Carta in the nearby Runnymede, and the Royal Shakespeare Theatre and Stratford-upon-Avon attract classical drama lovers. The program takes full advantage of its proximity to London, the cultural capital of the English-speaking world.

BACKGROUND AND PHILOSOPHY

TASIS England was founded in 1976 by Mrs. M. Crist Fleming, and the summer school was inaugurated that same year. The Summer Programs offer an intensive enrichment learning experience for students seeking to strengthen skills or knowledge in one particular area, to explore the cultural riches of England, and to meet and form friendships with young people from around the world.

PROGRAM OFFERINGS

Algebra II and Geometry are six-week courses and can be taken for academic credit. Three-week enrichment courses include: ShakespeareXperience, Television Broadcasting, London Through a Lens, Theater in London, Art in London, International Business, Writing Enhancement, Public Speaking in English, Middle School Skills, Pre-IB/Advanced Math, SAT Review and College Admissions, English as a Second Language, and TOEFL Review. These major courses meet for 12.5 hours per week. Every student also spends 8 hours per week on additional course work or quiet study.

In addition to one major course, students select an elective course of their choice, such as art, dance, drama, music, computer skills, digital photography, or movie making.

The average class size of 14 allows for individualized instruction and attention. Grade reports and a summary of the work covered are sent at the end of each 3-week session.

ENROLLMENT

Approximately 250 students enroll for each 3-week session. The TASIS England Summer Programs attract young people from forty nations around the world, creating an international community, and exposing students to a variety of cultures, languages, and backgrounds.

DAILY SCHEDULE

Participants have a full day of activity, Mondays through Fridays. Breakfast begins at 7:45, followed by several periods of instruction, an all-school meeting, and lunch. There is more instruction as well as time designated for sports until 4:00 in the afternoon. Leisure time before dinner at 5:30 may include trips to the local town. Evenings include time for a study hall and on-campus activities; bedtime is at 10:30 (11:00 on Fridays and Saturdays).

Weekend schedules vary depending upon the activities scheduled.

EXTRA OPPORTUNITIES AND ACTIVITIES

Sports are integral to the program and include aerobic dance, fitness training, table tennis, softball, swimming, soccer, basketball, tennis, Ultimate (Frisbee), and volleyball. Horseback riding, waterskiing, and golf are offered at an additional cost. Other on-campus extracurricular activities include photography, drama, music, art, and social activities such as barbecues, laser tag, dances, and talent night.

All students participate in the off-campus travel program each weekend, choosing from trips to Bath, Brighton, Oxford, Stonehenge, Salisbury, and Windsor as well as frequent trips to London for shopping, theater, museums, and other attractions. Optional weekend trips are offered to Alton Towers Theme Park, Edinburgh, Oxford and Cambridge, and Paris at extra cost.

The final banquet is a highlight, followed by a memorable disco boat cruise along the Thames, with the historic buildings of London illuminating the background.

FACILITIES

The Summer Programs use the full facilities of TASIS The American School in England, a coeducational boarding and day school for 750 students during the academic year. Two Georgian mansions house dining rooms and serve as the main student residences. There are additional dormitories throughout the historic campus, staffed by teachers and counselors. Boys and girls are strictly segregated, but it is TASIS policy to mix nationalities and mother tongues within individual rooms.

Other facilities include computer centers, an art/music complex, a 350-seat theater, two gymnasiums, a fitness center, a 24-hour health center, and a café-style student center. Wi-Fi is available throughout the campus. Outdoors, there are tennis and basketball courts and extensive athletics fields. Off-campus facilities are used for swimming, horseback riding, golf, and waterskiing.

STAFF

The faculty consists of approximately forty qualified and experienced educators, and the faculty/student ratio is approximately 1:7. Staff are carefully chosen for the quality of their degrees, their relevant experience in American and international schools, and their energy and enthusiasm for interacting with young people in all aspects of the programs, as teachers, coaches, dormitory residents, and chaperones.

MEDICAL CARE

Two qualified nurses live on campus and are available 24 hours a day to attend to students' health needs. Should a student require the attention of a physician, this will be arranged by the nursing staff and parents will be notified immediately.

COSTS

Three-week sessions (enrichment and English language courses) cost £3,370. Six-week sessions (academic, enrichment, and English language courses) cost £6,540. Fees include room, board, tuition, excursions, sports, books, medical insurance, laundry, and airport transfers. Fees do not cover airfare. A recommended personal allowance is £150 per week.

A deposit of £500 is required with the application. Payment for the total tuition is due 30 days after receipt of the invoice.

TRANSPORTATION

TASIS The American School in England is located 18 miles from central London, and is convenient to London Heathrow International Airport, which is 8 miles away. The 35-mile journey from Gatwick International Airport takes approximately 1 hour.

After enrollment, students will be sent a Travel Information Request Form by the Admissions Office, requesting full arrival and departure information. Students will be met and transported from/to Heathrow or Gatwick International Airports free of charge if the student travels on the published arrival and departure dates. For students not arriving or departing on the published arrival and departure dates, TASIS will arrange private transportation at extra cost.

Students may not arrive before the published arrival date nor remain after the published departure date. Where possible, departing flights should be booked between 9 a.m. and 8 p.m. on the published departure date. A taxi will be booked for students departing outside of those times.

APPLICATION TIMETABLE

Applications are processed throughout the year. Visitors are welcome on campus at any time of the year other than the period between Christmas and New Year, when the School is closed. Visits should be scheduled by prior arrangement.

While early applications are encouraged, a rolling admissions policy exists. Upon receipt of all application documentation, confirmation of a student's acceptance to the program will be dispatched from the Summer Admissions Office.

FOR MORE INFORMATION, CONTACT

Faie Gilbert, Director of Summer Admissions
TASIS The American School in England
Coldharbour Lane
Thorpe, Nr Egham
Surrey TW20 8TE
England
Phone: +44-1932-582346
Fax: +44-1932-564644
E-mail: uksummer@tasisengland.org
Web site: http://www.tasisengland.org

TASIS Schools and Summer Programs in Europe
112 South Royal Street
Alexandria, Virginia 22314
United States
Phone: 703-299-8150
800-442-6005 (toll-free)
Fax: 703-299-8157
E-mail: usadmissions@tasis.com
Web site: http://www.tasis.org

TASIS–THE AMERICAN SCHOOL IN SWITZERLAND

LANGUAGES, PERFORMING AND VISUAL ARTS, SPORTS, AND CULTURAL EXCURSIONS IN EUROPE

LUGANO AND CHÂTEAU D'OEX, SWITZERLAND

Type of Program: *Lugano:* Intensive foreign language study, performing and visual arts; *Château d'Oex:* Intensive French language instruction, English as an Additional Language (EAL)

Participants: Coeducational, *Lugano:* ages 4+–18; *Château d'Oex:* ages 11–17

Enrollment: *Lugano:* 300; *Château d'Oex:* 65

Program Dates: *Lugano:* Four weeks, June–July; three weeks, July–August; *Château d'Oex:* Four weeks, June–July, plus one optional week in Paris

Heads of Programs: Betsy Newell, Marc Pierre Jansen, Jim Haley, and Marie-Josée Breton

LOCATION

Lugano, Switzerland: Nestled in the foothills of the southern Swiss Alps, with spectacular views, the TASIS campus is a compact cluster of historic buildings and new facilities. It overlooks the attractive resort town of Lugano and is 2 miles from Agno International Airport and less than an hour's drive from Milan (Malpensa) International Airport in Italy. The idyllic setting allows for a wide range of enjoyable activities, including windsurfing, pleasure cruises to lakeside hamlets, picnics, and hiking to picturesque villages.

Château d'Oex, Switzerland: Located in the French-speaking canton of Vaud, the area offers outstanding opportunities for French language learning and an appreciation of the area's natural beauty.

BACKGROUND AND PHILOSOPHY

Founded in 1956 by Mrs. M. Crist Fleming, TASIS is a coed college-preparatory American boarding school for students in grades 6–12 and postgraduates.

The Summer Programs began thirty-five years ago and were designed to offer American and international students an opportunity to study abroad and a chance to live in a truly international environment. The programs in Château d'Oex, were founded sixteen years ago.

PROGRAM OFFERINGS

TASIS Summer Program (TSP): This program combines languages, arts, and outdoor pursuits, and is based on the campus of The American School in Switzerland in Lugano. Offerings include intensive language courses in English as an additional language, French, and Italian for 14- to 18-year-olds. The program includes artistic activities, a wide choice of sports, alpine activities, and weekend excursions in Switzerland and Italy. Both four- and three-week sessions are available. Besides language courses, the program offers courses in digital photography, architecture and design, fashion and textile design, and musical theater.

Middle School Program (MSP): This program, on the Lugano campus, is designed for students aged 11 to 13 to study English as an additional language, French, Italian, or musical theater. The program provides appropriate academic challenges and recreational activities for this transitional age group within a warm and caring community. Students choose special workshops to attend two afternoons a week, including music and drama, art, special sports, or tennis. During the remaining afternoons, students participate in afternoon and weekend activities, sports, and excursions.

Optional intensive afternoon sports activities are offered in both MSP and TSP. TSP students can attend the AC Milan Junior Camp or Armani Junior Basketball Club four afternoons per week, while MSP offers four different special sports tracks that meet three afternoons per week. Students with proven previous experience can also choose the Golf Club or Tennis Academy.

Le Château des Enfants (CDE): This summer program offers learning and fun for 4+ to 10 year olds. Sharing the Lugano campus with TSP and MSP, but with its own separate living and dining facilities, the program teaches English, Italian, or French through lessons, games, activities, sports, and art in a close-knit, caring, family-style community specifically tailored to younger children. Picnics, excursions, and camping trips are also offered. Both

four- and three-week sessions are available. Children from 4+ to 6 years of age can attend the Minnows program as day students only.

The Summer Language Program (TSLP, ages 14–17) in Château-d'Oex: This program offers English- or French-language learning in an intimate alpine setting. Intensive outdoor sports options, arts and crafts workshops, excursions such as climbing and rafting, and special weekend activities make this program ideal for more adventurous students.

The Middle School Program (MSPCD, ages 11–13) in Châteu-d'Oex: This program is for students willing to improve or learn either English or French in this alpine setting of the Pays d'Enhaut. The study of the language is combined with mountain sports, cultural excursions, and a variety of activities which take advantage of the beautiful location.

ENROLLMENT

In Lugano, more than 300 students represent as many as forty different countries. In Château d'Oex, approximately 65 students enroll from all over the world, including the Americas, Europe, and Asia.

EXTRA OPPORTUNITIES AND ACTIVITIES

Lugano: All students participate in afternoon sports and activities. Students choose from a variety of sports, including swimming, aerobic dance, basketball, cross-country running, soccer, softball, tennis, and volleyball. The afternoon activities include art, photography, and computer club. Weekend excursions provide ample opportunity for students to explore local areas of interest. Full-day excursions to Como and Milan, Lucerne, and Valley Verzasca and half-day excursions to nearby places of interest, such as Swiss Miniature in Melide and the antique street markets in Como, are organized. Optional weekend travel destinations (at an extra cost) include such cities as Florence, Nice, Paris, Venice, and Verona. Students ages 11–18 may also choose to attend special sports afternoon tracks such as the AC Milan Junior Camp or the Armani Basketball Club, under the supervision of trained coaches. Middle school students can also participate in the Golf Club or Tennis Academy if they have previous experience in these sports.

Château d'Oex: Hiking, rock climbing, tennis, swimming, basketball, and soccer are offered. Weekend destinations include Geneva, Interlaken, Zermatt, and Gstaad.

FACILITIES

Lugano: The program uses all of the boarding school facilities of the American School in Switzerland. The historic Villa de Nobili houses the administrative offices, dining rooms/terraces, classrooms, and dormitory areas. Villa Monticello contains classrooms, a computer center, and dormitories. Hadsall House houses an audiovisual lab, a recreation center, and a snack bar, as well as dormitory accommodations. The M. Crist Fleming Library holds 20,000 volumes. In the brand-new Şahenk Arts Center, students of all ages will attend classes and workshops in the visual and creative arts. On-campus sports facilities include a gymnasium, an outdoor pool, a fitness center, and two multipurpose hard courts.

Château d'Oex: The historic wood-carved chalets, set in the heart of the village, are home to TASIS students. They house dormitories, classrooms, a dining room, and recreation areas. There are a tennis/basketball court and Ping-Pong tables in the garden of the main chalet. Nearby facilities include a swimming pool, soccer field, and beach volley. Tennis players of intermediate and advanced ability can enroll in the intensive tennis offering to improve their skills under the guidance of certified tennis instructors.

STAFF

There are 60 full-time summer staff members (the staff-student ratio is 1:5). Qualified classroom teachers also undertake supervisory responsibilities, including coaching sports, chaperoning trips, dormitory coverage, and the in loco parentis role. Counselors work alongside teachers in the dorms, on excursions, on the sports fields, and in recreational activities to help provide a caring environment for students.

Many of the staff members are current or former TASIS faculty members, and counselors are alumni from all TASIS programs.

COSTS

For Lugano and Château d'Oex, Switzerland, the all-inclusive cost for a four-week session in 2013 is CHF 7300. The cost for the three-week session is CHF 5900. The TASIS Summer Programs in Château-d'Oex, are four-week sessions only, and the boarding fee is CHF 7300. Students in the TSLP program can attend the optional fifth week to Paris, France, for an additional CHF 1550. There are no additional fees, with the exception of long-haul airfare, the optional European weekend travel costs, personal spending money, and medical expenses not covered by TASIS health insurance.

FOR MORE INFORMATION, CONTACT

TASIS U.S. Representative
The TASIS Schools
112 South Royal Street
Alexandria, Virginia 22314
United States
Phone: 703-299-8150
Fax: 703-299-8157
E-mail: usadmissions@tasis.com
Web site: http://www.tasis.com

Specialized Directories

COEDUCATIONAL DAY SCHOOLS

The Academy for Gifted Children (PACE), ON, Canada
Académie Ste Cécile International School, ON, Canada
Alexander Dawson School, CO
Allendale Columbia School, NY
Alpha Omega Academy, IA
American Academy, FL
American Heritage School, FL
American Heritage School, FL
American International School, Lusaka, Zambia
The American School Foundation, Mexico
The American School in El Salvador, FL
Anacapa School, CA
Annie Wright School, WA
Archbishop Mitty High School, CA
Arrowsmith School, ON, Canada
Arroyo Pacific Academy, CA
Arthur Morgan School, NC
ASSETS School, HI
The Athenian School, CA
Augusta Christian School (I), GA
Augusta Preparatory Day School, GA
The Awty International School, TX
Bachman Academy, TN
Bakersfield Christian High School, CA
Baldwin School of Puerto Rico, PR
The Baltimore Actors' Theatre Conservatory, MD
Baltimore Lutheran School, MD
Barrie School, MD
Battle Ground Academy, TN
Bay Ridge Preparatory School, NY
The Bay School of San Francisco, CA
Bayside Academy, AL
Bayview Glen School, ON, Canada
Bearspaw Christian School, AB, Canada
Beaver Country Day School, MA
The Beekman School, NY
Benet Academy, IL
Berkeley Preparatory School, FL
Berkshire School, MA
Beth Haven Christian School, KY
The Birch Wathen Lenox School, NY
Bishop Brady High School, NH
Bishop Denis J. O'Connell High School, VA
Bishop Eustace Preparatory School, NJ
Bishop Fenwick High School, OH
Bishop Guertin High School, NH
Bishop Ireton High School, VA
Bishop John J. Snyder High School, FL
Bishop Kelly High School, ID
Bishop Kenny High School, FL
Bishop Luers High School, IN
Bishop McGuinness Catholic High School, NC
Bishop McGuinness Catholic High School, OK
Bishop Montgomery High School, CA
Bishop O'Dowd High School, CA
Bishop's College School, QC, Canada
The Bishop's School, CA
Bishop Stang High School, MA
Blair Academy, NJ
The Blake School, MN
Blanchet School, OR
Blessed Trinity High School, GA
The Bolles School, FL
Boston Trinity Academy, MA
Boston University Academy, MA
Bradenton Christian School, FL
Breck School, MN
Brentwood College School, BC, Canada
Briarcrest Christian High School, TN
Briarwood Christian High School, AL
Bridges Academy, CA
Brimmer and May School, MA
The British School of Boston, MA
The Brook Hill School, TX
Brooks School, MA
Brookstone School, GA
Bulloch Academy, GA
Burr and Burton Academy, VT
Butte Central Catholic High School, MT
Buxton School, MA
Calvary Christian School, KY
Calvin Christian High School, CA
Campbell Hall (Episcopal), CA
Camphill Special School, PA
Cannon School, NC
The Canterbury Episcopal School, TX
Canterbury School, FL
The Canterbury School of Florida, FL
Canton Academy, MS
Canyonville Christian Academy, OR
Cape Cod Academy, MA
Cape Fear Academy, NC
Cape Henry Collegiate School, VA
Capistrano Valley Christian Schools, CA
Cardinal Gibbons High School, NC
Cardinal Mooney Catholic High School, FL
Cardinal Newman High School, FL
Cardinal O'Hara High School, PA
Carlisle School, VA
Carolina Day School, NC
Cascadilla School, NY
Cathedral High School, IN
Catholic Central High School, NY
Catholic Central High School, WI
The Catlin Gabel School, OR
Central Alberta Christian High School, AB, Canada
Central Catholic High School, CA
Central Catholic High School, MA
Chadwick School, CA
Chamberlain-Hunt Academy, MS
Chaminade College Preparatory, CA
Charlotte Country Day School, NC
Charlotte Latin School, NC
Chase Collegiate School, CT
Chattanooga Christian School, TN
Cheverus High School, ME
The Chicago Academy for the Arts, IL
Chicago Waldorf School, IL
Children's Creative and Performing Arts Academy of San Diego, CA
Chinese Christian Schools, CA
Choate Rosemary Hall, CT
Christa McAuliffe Academy School of Arts and Sciences, OR
Christ Church Episcopal School, SC
Christchurch School, VA
Christian Academy of Knoxville, TN
Christian Brothers Academy, NY
Christian Central Academy, NY
Christopher Dock Mennonite High School, PA
Chrysalis School, WA
Cincinnati Country Day School, OH
Clarksville Academy, TN
Colegio Bolivar, Colombia
Cole Valley Christian High School, ID
The Collegiate School, VA

The Colorado Springs School, CO
Columbia Academy, TN
Commonwealth Parkville School, PR
Community Christian Academy, KY
The Community School of Naples, FL
The Concept School, PA
Concord Academy, MA
Concordia Lutheran High School, IN
Concordia Preparatory School, UT
Contra Costa Christian High School, CA
Cotter Schools, MN
The Country Day School, ON, Canada
Crawford Adventist Academy, ON, Canada
Crosspoint Academy, WA
Crossroads School for Arts & Sciences, CA
Crystal Springs Uplands School, CA
Currey Ingram Academy, TN
Cushing Academy, MA
Dakar Academy, Senegal
Dallas Christian School, TX
Darlington School, GA
Darrow School, NY
Davidson Academy, TN
Deerfield Academy, MA
De La Salle North Catholic High School, OR
Denver Academy, CO
Denver Christian High School, CO
The Derryfield School, NH
Doane Stuart School, NY
Donelson Christian Academy, TN
Donna Klein Jewish Academy, FL
Dowling Catholic High School, IA
Dublin Christian Academy, NH
Dublin School, NH
DuBois Central Catholic High School/Middle School, PA
Durham Academy, NC
Eagle Hill School, MA
Eastern Mennonite High School, VA
Eaton Academy, GA
Edgewood Academy, AL
Edmund Burke School, DC
Eldorado Emerson Private School, CA
Elgin Academy, IL
Elyria Catholic High School, OH
The English College in Prague, Czech Republic
Episcopal Collegiate School, AR
Episcopal High School, TX
Episcopal High School of Jacksonville, FL
Escola Americana de Campinas, Brazil
Explorations Academy, WA
Ezell-Harding Christian School, TN
Fairhill School, TX
Faith Christian High School, CA
Faith Lutheran High School, NV
Falmouth Academy, MA
Father Lopez High School, FL
Father Ryan High School, TN
Fayetteville Academy, NC
Fay School, MA
The First Academy, FL
First Baptist Academy, TX
First Presbyterian Day School, GA
Flint Hill School, VA
Flintridge Preparatory School, CA
Flint River Academy, GA
Foothills Academy, AB, Canada
Forsyth Country Day School, NC
Fort Worth Christian School, TX
Fort Worth Country Day School, TX
Foundation Academy, FL
Fountain Valley School of Colorado, CO
Fox Valley Lutheran High School, WI
Frederica Academy, GA
Freeman Academy, SD
French-American School of New York, NY
Fresno Christian Schools, CA
Friends Academy, NY
Friends' Central School, PA
Front Range Christian High School, CO
The Frostig School, CA
Fryeburg Academy, ME
Gabriel Richard Catholic High School, MI
The Galloway School, GA
Gann Academy (The New Jewish High School of Greater Boston), MA
Gaston Day School, NC
Gateway School, TX
George Stevens Academy, ME
Georgetown Day School, DC
George Walton Academy, GA
Germantown Friends School, PA
Glades Day School, FL
Glenelg Country School, MD
The Glenholme School, Devereux Connecticut, CT
Gould Academy, ME
The Governor French Academy, IL
Grace Baptist Academy, TN
Grace Brethren School, CA
Grace Christian School, AK
The Grauer School, CA
Great Lakes Christian High School, ON, Canada
Greenhill School, TX
Greenhills School, MI
Guamani Private School, PR
The Gunston School, MD
The Harker School, CA
The Harley School, NY
Harrells Christian Academy, NC
The Harrisburg Academy, PA
Harvard-Westlake School, CA
Hawaii Baptist Academy, HI
Hawken School, OH
Hawthorne Christian Academy, NJ
Head-Royce School, CA
Hebrew Academy, CA
Hebrew Academy of the Five Towns & Rockaway, NY
Heritage Christian Academy, AB, Canada
Heritage Christian School, CA
Heritage Christian School, ON, Canada
The Heritage School, GA
Highland Hall Waldorf School, CA
The Hill School, PA
The Hill Top Preparatory School, PA
Holland Hall, OK
Holy Cross High School, CT
Holyoke Catholic High School, MA
Holy Savior Menard Catholic High School, LA
Holy Trinity Diocesan High School, NY
Holy Trinity School, ON, Canada
Hopkins School, CT
Houghton Academy, NY
The Howard School, GA
The Hudson School, NJ
Humanex Academy, CO

Huntington-Surrey School, TX
Hyde Park Baptist School, TX
Hyman Brand Hebrew Academy of Greater Kansas City, KS
Idyllwild Arts Academy, CA
Immaculata High School, KS
Immaculata High School, NJ
Immaculate Conception School, IL
Independent School, KS
Interlochen Arts Academy, MI
Intermountain Christian School, UT
International High School, CA
International School Bangkok, Thailand
International School of Amsterdam, Netherlands
The International School of London, United Kingdom
Istanbul International Community School, Turkey
Jack M. Barrack Hebrew Academy, PA
Jackson Preparatory School, MS
John Burroughs School, MO
John Hancock Academy, GA
The Journeys School of Teton Science School, WY
Kalamazoo Christian High School, MI
Kent Denver School, CO
Kent School, CT
Kents Hill School, ME
Kentucky Country Day School, KY
Keswick Christian School, FL
The Kew-Forest School, NY
Kimball Union Academy, NH
King Low Heywood Thomas, CT
Kings Christian School, CA
Kingsway College, ON, Canada
Kingswood-Oxford School, CT
The Lab School of Washington, DC
La Cheim School, CA
La Jolla Country Day School, CA
Lakehill Preparatory School, TX
Lancaster Country Day School, PA
Lancaster Mennonite High School, PA
Landmark Christian Academy, KY
Landmark Christian School, GA
Lansdale Catholic High School, PA
La Salle High School, CA
The Latin School of Chicago, IL
The Laureate Academy, MB, Canada
Lawrence School, OH
The Lawrenceville School, NJ
Lee Academy, ME
Lehigh Valley Christian High School, PA
Lehman High School, OH
Lexington Catholic High School, KY
Lincoln Academy, ME
Linden Christian School, MB, Canada
Linfield Christian School, CA
The Linsly School, WV
Lodi Academy, CA
Long Island Lutheran Middle and High School, NY
Los Angeles Lutheran High School, CA
Louisville Collegiate School, KY
The Lovett School, GA
Loyola School, NY
Lutheran High School North, MO
Lutheran High School Northwest, MI
Lutheran High School of Hawaii, HI
Lutheran High School of Indianapolis, IN
Lutheran High School of San Diego, CA
Luther College High School, SK, Canada
Luther North College Prep, IL
Lycee International de Los Angeles, CA
Lyndon Institute, VT
Madison Academy, AL
Maharishi School of the Age of Enlightenment, IA
Maine Central Institute, ME
Manhattan Christian High School, MT
Maplebrook School, NY
Maranatha High School, CA
Marian Central Catholic High School, IL
Marian High School, IN
Marion Academy, AL
Marist School, GA
Mars Hill Bible School, AL
Martin Luther High School, NY
The Marvelwood School, CT
Marymount International School, Italy
Matignon High School, MA
Maur Hill-Mount Academy, KS
McDonogh School, MD
McGill-Toolen Catholic High School, AL
Meadowridge School, BC, Canada
The Meadows School, NV
Memorial Hall School, TX
Memphis Catholic High School and Middle School, TN
Menaul School, NM
Mennonite Collegiate Institute, MB, Canada
Mesa Grande Seventh-Day Academy, CA
Middlesex School, MA
Middle Tennessee Christian School, TN
Mid-Pacific Institute, HI
Miller School of Albemarle, VA
Mill Springs Academy, GA
Milton Academy, MA
MMI Preparatory School, PA
Modesto Christian School, CA
Monsignor Donovan High School, NJ
Montclair Kimberley Academy, NJ
Moorestown Friends School, NJ
Moravian Academy, PA
Moreau Catholic High School, CA
Morristown-Beard School, NJ
Mount Carmel School, MP
Mt. De Sales Academy, GA
Mount Saint Charles Academy, RI
MPS Etobicoke, ON, Canada
MU High School, MO
Munich International School, Germany
Nazareth Academy, IL
Nebraska Christian Schools, NE
Newark Academy, NJ
New Covenant Academy, MO
Niagara Christian Community of Schools, ON, Canada
Noble Academy, NC
Noble and Greenough School, MA
The Nora School, MD
Norfolk Academy, VA
North Shore Country Day School, IL
North Toronto Christian School, ON, Canada
Northwest Academy, OR
Northwest Catholic High School, CT
The Northwest School, WA
Northwood School, NY
North Yarmouth Academy, ME
The Norwich Free Academy, CT
Notre Dame High School, NJ
Notre Dame High School, TN
Notre Dame Junior/Senior High School, PA

Oak Grove School, CA
The Oakland School, PA
Oakland School, VA
The Oakridge School, TX
Oakwood Friends School, NY
Ojai Valley School, CA
Oldenburg Academy, IN
The O'Neal School, NC
Oneida Baptist Institute, KY
Oregon Episcopal School, OR
Orinda Academy, CA
The Overlake School, WA
Pacific Academy, CA
Pacific Crest Community School, OR
Padua Franciscan High School, OH
Palmer Trinity School, FL
Palo Alto Preparatory School, CA
Paradise Adventist Academy, CA
Parish Episcopal School, TX
The Park School of Baltimore, MD
The Park School of Buffalo, NY
Parkview Adventist Academy, AB, Canada
The Pathway School, PA
Patten Academy of Christian Education, CA
Peddie School, NJ
The Pennington School, NJ
Pensacola Catholic High School, FL
Peoples Christian Academy, ON, Canada
Philadelphia-Montgomery Christian Academy, PA
Phillips Academy (Andover), MA
Phoenix Christian Unified Schools, AZ
Phoenix Country Day School, AZ
Pickens Academy, AL
Pickering College, ON, Canada
Piedmont Academy, GA
Pinecrest Academy, GA
Pine Crest School, FL
Pinewood - The International School of Thessaloniki, Greece, Greece
The Pingree School, MA
The Pingry School, NJ
Pioneer Valley Christian School, MA
Pope John XXIII Regional High School, NJ
Porter-Gaud School, SC
Portsmouth Abbey School, RI
Portsmouth Christian Academy, NH
Powers Catholic High School, MI
Prestonwood Christian Academy, TX
Proctor Academy, NH
Professional Children's School, NY
The Prout School, RI
Providence Country Day School, RI
Providence High School, CA
Punahou School, HI
Queen Margaret's School, BC, Canada
Quinte Christian High School, ON, Canada
Randolph-Macon Academy, VA
Randolph School, AL
Ranney School, NJ
Ransom Everglades School, FL
Ravenscroft School, NC
Realms of Inquiry, UT
The Rectory School, CT
Redwood Christian Schools, CA
Regis Jesuit High School, Girls Division, CO
Rejoice Christian Schools, OK
Ridley College, ON, Canada
Riverdale Country School, NY
River Oaks Baptist School, TX
The Rivers School, MA
Rockway Mennonite Collegiate, ON, Canada
Rolling Hills Preparatory School, CA
Ross School, NY
Rothesay Netherwood School, NB, Canada
Rowland Hall, UT
Royal Canadian College, BC, Canada
Roycemore School, IL
Rumsey Hall School, CT
Rundle College, AB, Canada
Rye Country Day School, NY
Sacramento Adventist Academy, CA
Sacramento Country Day School, CA
Sacred Heart/Griffin High School, IL
Sacred Heart School of Halifax, NS, Canada
Saddleback Valley Christian School, CA
Saddlebrook Preparatory School, FL
Sage Hill School, CA
Sage Ridge School, NV
St. Andrew's Episcopal School, MD
St. Andrew's School, RI
St. Andrew's–Sewanee School, TN
St. Anne's–Belfield School, VA
Saint Anthony High School, CA
Saint Anthony High School, IL
St. Anthony's Junior-Senior High School, HI
St. Benedict at Auburndale, TN
St. Bernard High School, CT
St. Bernard's Catholic School, CA
St. Brendan High School, FL
St. Croix Country Day School, VI
St. Croix Schools, MN
Saint Dominic Academy, ME
Saint Elizabeth High School, CA
St. Francis High School, KY
St. George's Independent School, TN
St. George's School, RI
St. George's School of Montreal, QC, Canada
St. Gregory College Preparatory School, AZ
Saint John's Preparatory School, MN
St. John's-Ravenscourt School, MB, Canada
St. Joseph High School, CT
Saint Joseph High School, IL
St. Joseph's Catholic School, SC
St. Jude's School, ON, Canada
Saint Lawrence Academy, CA
St. Martin's Episcopal School, LA
Saint Mary's Hall, TX
Saint Mary's High School, AZ
Saint Mary's High School, MD
St. Mary's School, OR
Saint Maur International School, Japan
Saint Patrick - Saint Vincent High School, CA
St. Patrick's Regional Secondary, BC, Canada
St. Paul Academy and Summit School, MN
St. Paul's Episcopal School, AL
St. Pius X Catholic High School, GA
St. Pius X High School, TX
St. Stephen's & St. Agnes School, VA
Saint Stephen's Episcopal School, FL
St. Stephen's Episcopal School, TX
St. Stephen's School, Rome, Italy
St. Thomas Aquinas High School, FL
Saint Thomas Aquinas High School, KS
St. Thomas Aquinas High School, NH

Saint Viator High School, IL
Salem Academy, OR
Salesian High School, CA
Salpointe Catholic High School, AZ
Sandia Preparatory School, NM
San Domenico School, CA
Sandy Spring Friends School, MD
San Marcos Baptist Academy, TX
Santa Fe Preparatory School, NM
SBEC (Southern Baptist Educational Center), MS
Scholar's Hall Preparatory School, ON, Canada
Scottsdale Christian Academy, AZ
Scotus Central Catholic High School, NE
Seabury Hall, HI
Seattle Academy of Arts and Sciences, WA
The Seven Hills School, OH
Severn School, MD
Shady Side Academy, PA
Shattuck-St. Mary's School, MN
Shawnigan Lake School, BC, Canada
Shelton School and Evaluation Center, TX
The Shipley School, PA
Shoore Centre for Learning, ON, Canada
Shoreline Christian, WA
Signet Christian School, ON, Canada
Smith School, NY
Solomon College, AB, Canada
Sonoma Academy, CA
Soundview Preparatory School, NY
Southfield Christian High School, MI
Southwest Christian School, Inc., TX
Southwestern Academy, AZ
Southwestern Academy, CA
Spartanburg Day School, SC
Stephen T. Badin High School, OH
Stevenson School, CA
The Storm King School, NY
Stratford Academy, GA
Strathcona-Tweedsmuir School, AB, Canada
Stratton Mountain School, VT
Stuart Hall, VA
The Sudbury Valley School, MA
Summerfield Waldorf School, CA
The Summit Country Day School, OH
Sunshine Bible Academy, SD
The Taft School, CT
Taipei American School, Taiwan
Tandem Friends School, VA
Tapply Binet College, ON, Canada
TASIS The American School in England, United Kingdom
TASIS, The American School in Switzerland, Switzerland
Telluride Mountain School, CO
Temple Grandin School, CO
The Tenney School, TX
The Thacher School, CA
Thomas Jefferson School, MO
Tidewater Academy, VA
Tilton School, NH
Timothy Christian High School, IL
TMI - The Episcopal School of Texas, TX
Tower Hill School, DE
Tri-City Christian Academy, AZ
Tri-City Christian Schools, CA
Trinity Christian Academy, TN
Trinity College School, ON, Canada
Trinity High School, NH
Trinity High School, OH
Trinity Preparatory School, FL
Tyler Street Christian Academy, TX
University Liggett School, MI
University of Chicago Laboratory Schools, IL
University Prep, WA
University School of Jackson, TN
University School of Milwaukee, WI
University School of Nova Southeastern University, FL
Valle Catholic High School, MO
Valley Christian High School, CA
Valley Lutheran High School, AZ
The Valley School, MI
Venta Preparatory School, ON, Canada
Vicksburg Catholic School, MS
Villa Angela-St. Joseph High School, OH
Villa Duchesne and Oak Hill School, MO
Wakefield School, VA
Waldorf High School of Massachusetts Bay, MA
The Waldorf School of Garden City, NY
The Waldorf School of Saratoga Springs, NY
Walnut Hill School for the Arts, MA
Walsingham Academy, VA
Wasatch Academy, UT
Washington International School, DC
The Waterford School, UT
Watkinson School, CT
Waynflete School, ME
Webb School of Knoxville, TN
The Webb Schools, CA
Wellspring Foundation, CT
Wellsprings Friends School, OR
Wesleyan Academy, PR
Westbury Christian School, TX
West Catholic High School, MI
Westchester Country Day School, NC
West Island College, AB, Canada
Westminster Christian Academy, LA
Westminster School, CT
West Sound Academy, WA
Westtown School, PA
Wheaton Academy, IL
The Wheeler School, RI
Whitefield Academy, GA
Whitefield Academy, KY
The Williams School, CT
The Williston Northampton School, MA
Wilmington Christian School, DE
Wilson Hall, SC
The Windsor School, NY
Windward School, CA
Winston Preparatory School, NY
The Winston School San Antonio, TX
Woodlynde School, PA
Worcester Preparatory School, MD
Wyoming Seminary, PA
York Catholic High School, PA
York Preparatory School, NY
York School, CA
Zurich International School, Switzerland

BOYS' DAY SCHOOLS

Academy of the New Church Boys' School, PA
All Hallows High School, NY
Archbishop Curley High School, MD
Army and Navy Academy, CA

** Coeducational in lower grades*

Belen Jesuit Preparatory School, FL
Bellarmine College Preparatory, CA
Brophy College Preparatory, AZ
Brother Rice High School, MI
Calvert Hall College High School, MD
Cardigan Mountain School, NH
Cathedral Preparatory School, PA
Central Catholic High School, TX
Chaminade College Preparatory School, MO
Christian Brothers Academy, NJ
Christopher Columbus High School, FL
The Church Farm School, PA
Cistercian Preparatory School, TX
Colegio San Jose, PR
Crespi Carmelite High School, CA
Damien High School, CA
De La Salle High School, CA
Delbarton School, NJ
DeMatha Catholic High School, MD
Devon Preparatory School, PA
Dexter School, MA
Eaglebrook School, MA
Fairfield College Preparatory School, CT
The Fessenden School, MA
Fishburne Military School, VA
Fordham Preparatory School, NY
Georgetown Preparatory School, MD
Gilman School, MD
Gonzaga College High School, DC
The Greenwood School, VT
Hargrave Military Academy, VA
Holy Cross School, LA
Holy Ghost Preparatory School, PA
Iona Preparatory School, NY
Jean and Samuel Frankel Jewish Academy of Metropolitan Detroit, MI
Jesuit High School of Tampa, FL
Junipero Serra High School, CA
Landon School, MD
Loyola-Blakefield, MD
Malvern Preparatory School, PA
Marmion Academy, IL
Merchiston Castle School, United Kingdom
Missouri Military Academy, MO
Montgomery Bell Academy, TN
Mount Michael Benedictine School, NE
Notre Dame College Prep, IL
Palma School, CA
Regis High School, NY
Riverside Military Academy, GA
The Roxbury Latin School, MA
St. Albans School, DC
St. Andrew's College, ON, Canada
St. Augustine High School, CA
Saint Augustine Preparatory School, NJ
St. Catherine's Academy, CA
St. Francis de Sales High School, OH
Saint Francis High School, CA
St. George's School, BC, Canada
St. John's Preparatory School, MA
Saint Joseph High School, NJ
St. Joseph's Preparatory School, PA
St. Mark's School of Texas, TX
St. Mary's Preparatory School, MI
St. Michael's College School, ON, Canada
Saint Patrick High School, IL
St. Paul's High School, MB, Canada
St. Stanislaus College, MS
Saint Thomas Academy, MN
St. Thomas High School, TX
Salesianum School, DE
Trinity High School, KY
Trinity-Pawling School, NY
University of Detroit Jesuit High School and Academy, MI
Upper Canada College, ON, Canada
Valley Forge Military Academy & College, PA
Vianney High School, MO
The Woodhall School, CT
Xaverian High School, NY

GIRLS' DAY SCHOOLS

Academy of Notre Dame de Namur, PA
Academy of Our Lady of Peace, CA
Academy of the Holy Cross, MD
Academy of the New Church Girls' School, PA
Academy of the Sacred Heart, LA
The Agnes Irwin School, PA
Alverno High School, CA
Balmoral Hall School, MB, Canada
Bishop Conaty-Our Lady of Loretto High School, CA
The Brearley School, NY
Buffalo Academy of the Sacred Heart, NY
Carondelet High School, CA
Castilleja School, CA
The Catholic High School of Baltimore, MD
Columbus School for Girls, OH
Convent of the Sacred Heart, CT
Convent of the Sacred Heart, NY
Country Day School of the Sacred Heart, PA
Dana Hall School, MA
Dominican Academy, NY
Duchesne Academy of the Sacred Heart, TX
Elizabeth Seton High School, MD
Emma Willard School, NY
The Ethel Walker School, CT
Fontbonne Hall Academy, NY
Foxcroft School, VA
Garrison Forest School, MD*
Georgetown Visitation Preparatory School, DC
Girls Preparatory School, TN
Grier School, PA
The Hewitt School, NY
Holy Angels Academy, NY
Immaculate Heart High School and Middle School, CA
Institute of Notre Dame, MD
Josephinum Academy, IL
Lauralton Hall, CT
Louisville High School, CA
Marylawn of the Oranges, NJ
The Mary Louis Academy, NY
Marymount High School, CA
Mercy High School College Preparatory, CA
Miss Edgar's and Miss Cramp's School, QC, Canada
Miss Porter's School, CT
Mother McAuley High School, IL
Mount Mercy Academy, NY
Mt. Saint Dominic Academy, NJ
Mount Saint Joseph Academy, PA
Nerinx Hall, MO
Notre Dame Academy, CA
Notre Dame High School, CA
Our Lady of Mercy Academy, NJ

** Coeducational in lower grades*

Ramona Convent Secondary School, CA
Roland Park Country School, MD
St. Agnes Academy, TX
Saint Joan Antida High School, WI
Saint Joseph Academy High School, OH
St. Joseph's Academy, LA
Saint Lucy's Priory High School, CA
St. Mary's Episcopal School, TN
Saint Mary's School, NC
Saint Teresa's Academy, MO
St. Timothy's School, MD
Saint Ursula Academy, OH
Salem Academy, NC
Santa Catalina School, CA
Southfield School, MA
The Spence School, NY
The Ursuline Academy of Dallas, TX
Villa Joseph Marie High School, PA
Villa Maria Academy, PA
Villa Victoria Academy, NJ
Villa Walsh Academy, NJ
Westover School, CT
Westridge School, CA
The Willows Academy, IL
The Woodward School, MA

SCHOOLS ACCEPTING BOARDING BOYS AND GIRLS

Académie Ste Cécile International School, ON, Canada†
Alliance Academy, Ecuador
Arthur Morgan School, NC†
The Athenian School, CA†
Bachman Academy, TN†
Berkshire School, MA†
Bishop's College School, QC, Canada†
Blair Academy, NJ†
The Bolles School, FL†
Brentwood College School, BC, Canada†
Brockwood Park School, United Kingdom
The Brook Hill School, TX†
Brooks School, MA†
Burr and Burton Academy, VT†
Buxton School, MA†
Camphill Special School, PA†
Canyonville Christian Academy, OR†
Carlisle School, VA†
Cascadilla School, NY†
Children's Creative and Performing Arts Academy of San Diego, CA†
Choate Rosemary Hall, CT†
Christchurch School, VA†
Christopher Dock Mennonite High School, PA†
Columbia International School, Japan
Concord Academy, MA†
Cotter Schools, MN†
Cushing Academy, MA†
Dakar Academy, Senegal†
Darlington School, GA†
Darrow School, NY†
Deerfield Academy, MA†
Dublin Christian Academy, NH†
Dublin School, NH†
Eagle Hill School, CT
Eagle Hill School, MA†
Episcopal High School, VA
Fay School, MA†
Forest Lake Academy, FL
Fountain Valley School of Colorado, CO†
Freeman Academy, SD†
Fryeburg Academy, ME†
George Stevens Academy, ME†
Gilmour Academy, OH
The Glenholme School, Devereux Connecticut, CT
Gould Academy, ME†
The Governor French Academy, IL†
Great Lakes Christian High School, ON, Canada†
The Harvey School, NY
The Hill School, PA†
Houghton Academy, NY†
Idyllwild Arts Academy, CA†
Interlochen Arts Academy, MI†
The Judge Rotenberg Educational Center, MA
Kent School, CT†
Kents Hill School, ME†
Kimball Union Academy, NH†
The King's Academy, TN
Kingsway College, ON, Canada†
Lakefield College School, ON, Canada
Lancaster Mennonite High School, PA†
The Lawrenceville School, NJ†
Lee Academy, ME†
The Linsly School, WV†
Luther College High School, SK, Canada†
Lyndon Institute, VT†
Maharishi School of the Age of Enlightenment, IA†
Maine Central Institute, ME†
Maplebrook School, NY
The Marvelwood School, CT†
Maur Hill-Mount Academy, KS†
McDonogh School, MD†
Menaul School, NM†
Mennonite Collegiate Institute, MB, Canada†
Middlesex School, MA†
Midland School, CA
Miller School of Albemarle, VA†
Milton Academy, MA†
Nebraska Christian Schools, NE†
Niagara Christian Community of Schools, ON, Canada†
Noble and Greenough School, MA†
North Central Texas Academy, TX
The Northwest School, WA†
Northwood School, NY†
Oak Grove School, CA†
Oakland School, VA†
Oakwood Friends School, NY†
Ojai Valley School, CA†
Oneida Baptist Institute, KY†
Oregon Episcopal School, OR†
Parkview Adventist Academy, AB, Canada†
Peddie School, NJ†
The Pennington School, NJ†
Phillips Academy (Andover), MA†
Pickering College, ON, Canada†
Pinehurst School, ON, Canada
Pinewood - The International School of Thessaloniki, Greece, Greece†
Portsmouth Abbey School, RI†
Presbyterian Pan American School, TX
Proctor Academy, NH†
Randolph-Macon Academy, VA†
The Rectory School, CT†
Ridley College, ON, Canada†

† Accepts day students

Rockway Mennonite Collegiate, ON, Canada†
Ross School, NY†
Rothesay Netherwood School, NB, Canada†
Rumsey Hall School, CT†
Saddlebrook Preparatory School, FL†
St. Andrew's School, RI†
St. Andrew's–Sewanee School, TN†
St. Anne's–Belfield School, VA†
St. Anthony Catholic High School, TX
St. Bernard's Catholic School, CA†
St. Croix Schools, MN†
St. George's School, RI†
Saint John's Preparatory School, MN†
St. John's-Ravenscourt School, MB, Canada†
St. Mary's School, OR†
St. Stephen's Episcopal School, TX†
St. Stephen's School, Rome, Italy†
Sandy Spring Friends School, MD†
San Marcos Baptist Academy, TX†
Shady Side Academy, PA†
Shattuck-St. Mary's School, MN†
Shawnigan Lake School, BC, Canada†
Southwestern Academy, AZ†
Southwestern Academy, CA†
Stevenson School, CA†
The Storm King School, NY†
Stratton Mountain School, VT†
Sunshine Bible Academy, SD†
The Taft School, CT†
TASIS The American School in England, United Kingdom†
TASIS, The American School in Switzerland, Switzerland†
The Thacher School, CA†
THINK Global School, CA
Thomas Jefferson School, MO†
Tilton School, NH†
TMI - The Episcopal School of Texas, TX†
Trinity College School, ON, Canada†
Turning Winds Academic Institute, ID
Venta Preparatory School, ON, Canada†
Walnut Hill School for the Arts, MA†
Wasatch Academy, UT†
The Webb Schools, CA†
Wellspring Foundation, CT†
Westminster School, CT†
West Sound Academy, WA†
Westtown School, PA†
The Williston Northampton School, MA†
Windells Academy, OR
Wyoming Seminary, PA†

SCHOOLS ACCEPTING BOARDING BOYS

Academy of the New Church Boys' School, PA†
Army and Navy Academy, CA†
Butte Central Catholic High School, MT†
Cardigan Mountain School, NH†
Chamberlain-Hunt Academy, MS†
Chaminade College Preparatory School, MO†
The Church Farm School, PA†
Eaglebrook School, MA†
The Fessenden School, MA†
Fishburne Military School, VA†
Georgetown Preparatory School, MD†
The Greenwood School, VT†
Hampshire Country School, NH
Hargrave Military Academy, VA†
Little Keswick School, VA
Marine Military Academy, TX
Merchiston Castle School, United Kingdom
Missouri Military Academy, MO†
Mount Michael Benedictine School, NE†
The Oxford Academy, CT
Riverside Military Academy, GA†
St. Albans School, DC†
St. Andrew's College, ON, Canada†
St. Catherine's Academy, CA†
St. George's School, BC, Canada†
St. Lawrence Seminary High School, WI
St. Mary's Preparatory School, MI†
St. Michael's Preparatory School of the Norbertine Fathers, CA
St. Stanislaus College, MS†
Trinity-Pawling School, NY†
Upper Canada College, ON, Canada†
Valley Forge Military Academy & College, PA†
Valley View School, MA
The Woodhall School, CT†

SCHOOLS ACCEPTING BOARDING GIRLS

Academy of the New Church Girls' School, PA†
Annie Wright School, WA†
Balmoral Hall School, MB, Canada†
Copper Canyon Academy, AZ
Dana Hall School, MA†
Emma Willard School, NY†
The Ethel Walker School, CT†
Foxcroft School, VA†
Garrison Forest School, MD†
Grier School, PA†
The Hockaday School, TX
Miss Porter's School, CT†
Queen Margaret's School, BC, Canada†
Saint Mary's School, NC†
St. Timothy's School, MD†
Salem Academy, NC†
San Domenico School, CA†
Santa Catalina School, CA†
Stuart Hall, VA†
Westover School, CT†

MILITARY SCHOOLS

Army and Navy Academy, CA
Chamberlain-Hunt Academy, MS
Fishburne Military School, VA
Hargrave Military Academy, VA
Marine Military Academy, TX
Missouri Military Academy, MO
Randolph-Macon Academy, VA
Riverside Military Academy, GA
St. Catherine's Academy, CA
Saint Thomas Academy, MN
Valley Forge Military Academy & College, PA

SCHOOLS WITH A RELIGIOUS AFFILIATION

Anglican Church of Canada
Queen Margaret's School, BC, Canada
Rothesay Netherwood School, NB, Canada

† Accepts day students

Assembly of God Church
Modesto Christian School, CA

Baptist Church
Beth Haven Christian School, KY
Bulloch Academy, GA
Calvary Christian School, KY
First Baptist Academy, TX
Foundation Academy, FL
Grace Baptist Academy, TN
Hyde Park Baptist School, TX
John Hancock Academy, GA
Landmark Christian Academy, KY
Linden Christian School, MB, Canada
SBEC (Southern Baptist Educational Center), MS
Tri-City Christian Academy, AZ
Whitefield Academy, KY

Baptist General Association of Virginia
Hargrave Military Academy, VA

Baptist General Conference
San Marcos Baptist Academy, TX

Bible Fellowship Church
Chinese Christian Schools, CA
Keswick Christian School, FL

Brethren Church
Grace Brethren School, CA

Brethren in Christ Church
Niagara Christian Community of Schools, ON, Canada

Christian
Academy of the New Church Girls' School, PA
Briarcrest Christian High School, TN
Christopher Dock Mennonite High School, PA
Cole Valley Christian High School, ID
Dublin Christian Academy, NH
Faith Christian High School, CA
The First Academy, FL
First Presbyterian Day School, GA
Fort Worth Christian School, TX
Grace Brethren School, CA
Harrells Christian Academy, NC
Hawthorne Christian Academy, NJ
Heritage Christian Academy, AB, Canada
Intermountain Christian School, UT
Marion Academy, AL
Mennonite Collegiate Institute, MB, Canada
Mesa Grande Seventh-Day Academy, CA
New Covenant Academy, MO
North Central Texas Academy, TX
Peoples Christian Academy, ON, Canada
Philadelphia-Montgomery Christian Academy, PA
Porter-Gaud School, SC
Quinte Christian High School, ON, Canada
Redwood Christian Schools, CA
River Oaks Baptist School, TX
St. Croix Schools, MN
SBEC (Southern Baptist Educational Center), MS
Scottsdale Christian Academy, AZ
Signet Christian School, ON, Canada
Timothy Christian High School, IL
TMI - The Episcopal School of Texas, TX
Turning Winds Academic Institute, ID
Valley Christian High School, CA

Christian Nondenominational
Alliance Academy, Ecuador
Alpha Omega Academy, IA
Bakersfield Christian High School, CA
Bearspaw Christian School, AB, Canada
Boston Trinity Academy, MA
Bradenton Christian School, FL
The Brook Hill School, TX
Canyonville Christian Academy, OR
Capistrano Valley Christian Schools, CA
Chattanooga Christian School, TN
Christian Academy of Knoxville, TN
Christian Central Academy, NY
Crosspoint Academy, WA
Dakar Academy, Senegal
Davidson Academy, TN
Donelson Christian Academy, TN
Dublin Christian Academy, NH
Fort Worth Christian School, TX
Front Range Christian High School, CO
Grace Christian School, AK
Hawthorne Christian Academy, NJ
Heritage Christian School, CA
The Hill School, PA
Landmark Christian School, GA
Linfield Christian School, CA
Manhattan Christian High School, MT
Maranatha High School, CA
Merchiston Castle School, United Kingdom
Missouri Military Academy, MO
Patten Academy of Christian Education, CA
Phoenix Christian Unified Schools, AZ
Portsmouth Christian Academy, NH
Riverside Military Academy, GA
Saddleback Valley Christian School, CA
St. Anne's–Belfield School, VA
St. George's Independent School, TN
Shoreline Christian, WA
Southfield Christian High School, MI
Southwest Christian School, Inc., TX
Sunshine Bible Academy, SD
Tri-City Christian Schools, CA
Tyler Street Christian Academy, TX
Westminster Christian Academy, LA
Wheaton Academy, IL
Whitefield Academy, GA

Christian Reformed Church
Central Alberta Christian High School, AB, Canada
Denver Christian High School, CO
Kalamazoo Christian High School, MI
Manhattan Christian High School, MT

Church of Christ
Columbia Academy, TN
Dallas Christian School, TX
Ezell-Harding Christian School, TN
Great Lakes Christian High School, ON, Canada
Madison Academy, AL
Mars Hill Bible School, AL
Middle Tennessee Christian School, TN
Westbury Christian School, TX

Church of England (Anglican)
Lakefield College School, ON, Canada
Ridley College, ON, Canada
Trinity College School, ON, Canada

Church of the New Jerusalem
Academy of the New Church Boys' School, PA
Academy of the New Church Girls' School, PA

Episcopal Church
Annie Wright School, WA
Berkeley Preparatory School, FL
The Bishop's School, CA
Breck School, MN
Brooks School, MA
Campbell Hall (Episcopal), CA
The Canterbury Episcopal School, TX
The Canterbury School of Florida, FL
Christ Church Episcopal School, SC
Christchurch School, VA
The Church Farm School, PA
Doane Stuart School, NY
Episcopal Collegiate School, AR
Episcopal High School, TX
Episcopal High School, VA
Episcopal High School of Jacksonville, FL
Harvard-Westlake School, CA
Holland Hall, OK
Kent School, CT
Oregon Episcopal School, OR
Palmer Trinity School, FL
Parish Episcopal School, TX
Porter-Gaud School, SC
The Rectory School, CT
St. Albans School, DC
St. Andrew's Episcopal School, MD
St. Andrew's–Sewanee School, TN
St. George's School, RI
St. Martin's Episcopal School, LA
St. Mary's Episcopal School, TN
Saint Mary's School, NC
St. Paul's Episcopal School, AL
St. Stephen's & St. Agnes School, VA
Saint Stephen's Episcopal School, FL
St. Stephen's Episcopal School, TX
St. Timothy's School, MD
Seabury Hall, HI
Shattuck-St. Mary's School, MN
Stuart Hall, VA
TMI - The Episcopal School of Texas, TX
Trinity-Pawling School, NY
Trinity Preparatory School, FL
York School, CA

Evangelical
Heritage Christian Academy, AB, Canada
Pioneer Valley Christian School, MA
Southfield Christian High School, MI

Evangelical Free Church of America
Intermountain Christian School, UT

Evangelical/Fundamental
Chinese Christian Schools, CA

Evangelical Lutheran Church in America
Faith Lutheran High School, NV
Luther North College Prep, IL

Free Will Baptist Church
Rejoice Christian Schools, OK

Jewish
Donna Klein Jewish Academy, FL
Gann Academy (The New Jewish High School of Greater Boston), MA
Hebrew Academy, CA
Hebrew Academy of the Five Towns & Rockaway, NY
Hyman Brand Hebrew Academy of Greater Kansas City, KS
Jack M. Barrack Hebrew Academy, PA
Jean and Samuel Frankel Jewish Academy of Metropolitan Detroit, MI

Lutheran Church
Concordia Preparatory School, UT
Long Island Lutheran Middle and High School, NY
Los Angeles Lutheran High School, CA
Lutheran High School North, MO
Lutheran High School of San Diego, CA
Luther College High School, SK, Canada
Martin Luther High School, NY

Lutheran Church&-Missouri Synod
Baltimore Lutheran School, MD
Concordia Lutheran High School, IN
Faith Lutheran High School, NV
Los Angeles Lutheran High School, CA
Lutheran High School Northwest, MI
Lutheran High School of Hawaii, HI
Lutheran High School of Indianapolis, IN
Luther North College Prep, IL
Valley Lutheran High School, AZ

Mennonite Church
Christopher Dock Mennonite High School, PA
Eastern Mennonite High School, VA
Freeman Academy, SD
Lancaster Mennonite High School, PA
Mennonite Collegiate Institute, MB, Canada

Mennonite Church USA
Rockway Mennonite Collegiate, ON, Canada

Methodist Church
Kents Hill School, ME
The Pennington School, NJ
Randolph-Macon Academy, VA

Moravian Church
Moravian Academy, PA
Salem Academy, NC

Pentecostal Church
Community Christian Academy, KY

Presbyterian Church
Blair Academy, NJ
Calvin Christian High School, CA
Chamberlain-Hunt Academy, MS
Menaul School, NM
Mount Vernon Presbyterian School, GA

Presbyterian Church (U.S.A.)
Presbyterian Pan American School, TX

Presbyterian Church in America
Briarwood Christian High School, AL
First Presbyterian Day School, GA

Protestant
Bulloch Academy, GA
Landmark Christian School, GA
Piedmont Academy, GA
Pioneer Valley Christian School, MA
Quinte Christian High School, ON, Canada
Wilmington Christian School, DE

Protestant Church
Salem Academy, OR

Protestant-Evangelical
Fresno Christian Schools, CA
Kings Christian School, CA
Lehigh Valley Christian High School, PA
Nebraska Christian Schools, NE
North Toronto Christian School, ON, Canada
Westminster Christian Academy, LA

Reformed Church
Calvin Christian High School, CA
Chamberlain-Hunt Academy, MS
Heritage Christian School, ON, Canada

Reformed Church in America
Kalamazoo Christian High School, MI

Roman Catholic Church
Academy of Notre Dame de Namur, PA
Academy of Our Lady of Peace, CA
Academy of the Holy Cross, MD
Academy of the Sacred Heart, LA
Académie Ste Cécile International School, ON, Canada
Alleman High School, IL
All Hallows High School, NY
Alverno High School, CA
Archbishop Curley High School, MD
Archbishop Mitty High School, CA
Belen Jesuit Preparatory School, FL
Bellarmine College Preparatory, CA
Benet Academy, IL
Bishop Brady High School, NH
Bishop Conaty-Our Lady of Loretto High School, CA
Bishop Denis J. O'Connell High School, VA
Bishop Eustace Preparatory School, NJ
Bishop Fenwick High School, OH
Bishop Guertin High School, NH
Bishop Ireton High School, VA
Bishop John J. Snyder High School, FL
Bishop Kelly High School, ID
Bishop Kenny High School, FL
Bishop Luers High School, IN
Bishop McGuinness Catholic High School, NC
Bishop McGuinness Catholic High School, OK
Bishop Montgomery High School, CA
Bishop O'Dowd High School, CA
Bishop Stang High School, MA
Blanchet School, OR
Blessed Trinity High School, GA
Brother Rice High School, MI
Buffalo Academy of the Sacred Heart, NY
Butte Central Catholic High School, MT
Calvert Hall College High School, MD
Cardinal Gibbons High School, NC
Cardinal Mooney Catholic High School, FL
Cardinal Newman High School, FL
Cardinal O'Hara High School, PA
Carondelet High School, CA
Cathedral High School, IN
Cathedral Preparatory School, PA
Catholic Central High School, NY
Catholic Central High School, WI
The Catholic High School of Baltimore, MD
Central Catholic High School, CA
Central Catholic High School, MA
Central Catholic High School, TX
Chaminade College Preparatory, CA
Chaminade College Preparatory School, MO
Christian Brothers Academy, NJ
Christian Brothers Academy, NY
Christopher Columbus High School, FL
Cistercian Preparatory School, TX
Colegio San Jose, PR
Convent of the Sacred Heart, CT
Convent of the Sacred Heart, NY
Cotter Schools, MN
Country Day School of the Sacred Heart, PA
Crespi Carmelite High School, CA
Damien High School, CA
De La Salle High School, CA
De La Salle North Catholic High School, OR
Delbarton School, NJ
DeMatha Catholic High School, MD
Devon Preparatory School, PA
Dominican Academy, NY
Dowling Catholic High School, IA
DuBois Central Catholic High School/Middle School, PA
Duchesne Academy of the Sacred Heart, TX
Elizabeth Seton High School, MD
Elyria Catholic High School, OH
Fairfield College Preparatory School, CT
Father Lopez High School, FL
Father Ryan High School, TN
Fontbonne Hall Academy, NY
Fordham Preparatory School, NY
Gabriel Richard Catholic High School, MI
Georgetown Preparatory School, MD
Georgetown Visitation Preparatory School, DC
Gilmour Academy, OH
Gonzaga College High School, DC
Holy Angels Academy, NY
Holy Cross High School, CT
Holy Cross School, LA
Holy Ghost Preparatory School, PA
Holyoke Catholic High School, MA
Holy Savior Menard Catholic High School, LA
Holy Trinity Diocesan High School, NY
Immaculata High School, KS
Immaculata High School, NJ
Immaculate Conception School, IL
Immaculate Heart High School and Middle School, CA
Institute of Notre Dame, MD
Iona Preparatory School, NY
Jesuit High School of Tampa, FL
Josephinum Academy, IL
Junipero Serra High School, CA
Lansdale Catholic High School, PA

La Salle High School, CA
Lauralton Hall, CT
Lehman High School, OH
Lexington Catholic High School, KY
Loretto Academy, TX
Louisville High School, CA
Loyola-Blakefield, MD
Malvern Preparatory School, PA
Marian Central Catholic High School, IL
Marian High School, IN
Marist School, GA
Marmion Academy, IL
Marylawn of the Oranges, NJ
The Mary Louis Academy, NY
Marymount High School, CA
Marymount International School, Italy
Matignon High School, MA
Maur Hill-Mount Academy, KS
McGill-Toolen Catholic High School, AL
Memphis Catholic High School and Middle School, TN
Mercy High School College Preparatory, CA
Monsignor Donovan High School, NJ
Moreau Catholic High School, CA
Mother McAuley High School, IL
Mount Carmel School, MP
Mt. De Sales Academy, GA
Mount Mercy Academy, NY
Mount Michael Benedictine School, NE
Mount Saint Charles Academy, RI
Mt. Saint Dominic Academy, NJ
Mount Saint Joseph Academy, PA
Nazareth Academy, IL
Nerinx Hall, MO
Northwest Catholic High School, CT
Notre Dame Academy, CA
Notre Dame College Prep, IL
Notre Dame High School, CA
Notre Dame High School, NJ
Notre Dame High School, TN
Notre Dame Junior/Senior High School, PA
Oldenburg Academy, IN
Our Lady of Mercy Academy, NJ
Padua Franciscan High School, OH
Palma School, CA
Pensacola Catholic High School, FL
Pinecrest Academy, GA
Pope John XXIII Regional High School, NJ
Portsmouth Abbey School, RI
Powers Catholic High School, MI
The Prout School, RI
Providence High School, CA
Ramona Convent Secondary School, CA
Regis High School, NY
Sacred Heart/Griffin High School, IL
Sacred Heart School of Halifax, NS, Canada
St. Agnes Academy, TX
Saint Albert Junior-Senior High School, IA
St. Anthony Catholic High School, TX
Saint Anthony High School, CA
Saint Anthony High School, IL
St. Anthony's Junior-Senior High School, HI
St. Augustine High School, CA
Saint Augustine Preparatory School, NJ
St. Benedict at Auburndale, TN
St. Bernard High School, CT
St. Bernard's Catholic School, CA
St. Brendan High School, FL
St. Catherine's Academy, CA
Saint Dominic Academy, ME
Saint Elizabeth High School, CA
St. Francis de Sales High School, OH
Saint Francis High School, CA
Saint Joan Antida High School, WI
St. John's Preparatory School, MA
Saint John's Preparatory School, MN
Saint Joseph Academy High School, OH
St. Joseph High School, CT
Saint Joseph High School, IL
Saint Joseph High School, NJ
St. Joseph's Academy, LA
St. Joseph's Catholic School, SC
St. Joseph's Preparatory School, PA
Saint Lawrence Academy, CA
St. Lawrence Seminary High School, WI
Saint Lucy's Priory High School, CA
Saint Mary's High School, AZ
Saint Mary's High School, MD
St. Mary's Preparatory School, MI
St. Mary's School, OR
Saint Maur International School, Japan
St. Michael's College School, ON, Canada
St. Michael's Preparatory School of the Norbertine Fathers, CA
Saint Patrick High School, IL
Saint Patrick - Saint Vincent High School, CA
St. Patrick's Regional Secondary, BC, Canada
St. Paul's High School, MB, Canada
St. Pius X Catholic High School, GA
St. Pius X High School, TX
St. Stanislaus College, MS
Saint Teresa's Academy, MO
Saint Thomas Academy, MN
St. Thomas Aquinas High School, FL
Saint Thomas Aquinas High School, KS
St. Thomas Aquinas High School, NH
St. Thomas High School, TX
Saint Ursula Academy, OH
Saint Viator High School, IL
Salesian High School, CA
Salesianum School, DE
Salpointe Catholic High School, AZ
San Domenico School, CA
Santa Catalina School, CA
Scotus Central Catholic High School, NE
Seisen International School, Japan
Stephen T. Badin High School, OH
The Summit Country Day School, OH
Trinity High School, KY
Trinity High School, NH
Trinity High School, OH
The Ursuline Academy of Dallas, TX
Valle Catholic High School, MO
Vianney High School, MO
Vicksburg Catholic School, MS
Villa Angela-St. Joseph High School, OH
Villa Duchesne and Oak Hill School, MO
Villa Joseph Marie High School, PA
Villa Maria Academy, PA
Villa Victoria Academy, NJ
Villa Walsh Academy, NJ
Walsingham Academy, VA
West Catholic High School, MI
The Willows Academy, IL
Xaverian High School, NY
York Catholic High School, PA

Roman Catholic Church (Jesuit Order)
Brophy College Preparatory, AZ
Cheverus High School, ME
Loyola School, NY
Regis Jesuit High School, Girls Division, CO
University of Detroit Jesuit High School and Academy, MI

Seventh-day Adventist Church
Crawford Adventist Academy, ON, Canada
Lodi Academy, CA
Parkview Adventist Academy, AB, Canada
Sacramento Adventist Academy, CA

Seventh-day Adventists
Forest Lake Academy, FL
Kingsway College, ON, Canada
Mesa Grande Seventh-Day Academy, CA
Paradise Adventist Academy, CA

Society of Friends
Friends Academy, NY
Friends' Central School, PA
Germantown Friends School, PA
Lincoln School, RI
Moorestown Friends School, NJ
Oakwood Friends School, NY
Sandy Spring Friends School, MD
Tandem Friends School, VA
Wellsprings Friends School, OR
Westtown School, PA

Southern Baptist Convention
First Baptist Academy, TX
Hawaii Baptist Academy, HI
The King's Academy, TN
Oneida Baptist Institute, KY
Prestonwood Christian Academy, TX

United Church of Christ
Mid-Pacific Institute, HI

United Methodist Church
John Hancock Academy, GA
Wyoming Seminary, PA

Wesleyan Church
Houghton Academy, NY
Wesleyan Academy, PR

Wisconsin Evangelical Lutheran Synod
Fox Valley Lutheran High School, WI
St. Croix Schools, MN

SCHOOLS WITH ELEMENTARY DIVISIONS
Academy of Notre Dame de Namur, PA
Academy of the Sacred Heart, LA
The Agnes Irwin School, PA
Alexander Dawson School, CO
Allendale Columbia School, NY
American Heritage School, FL
The American School Foundation, Mexico
The American School in El Salvador, FL
Annie Wright School, WA
Army and Navy Academy, CA
ASSETS School, HI
The Athenian School, CA
Augusta Preparatory Day School, GA
The Awty International School, TX
Bachman Academy, TN
Baldwin School of Puerto Rico, PR
Balmoral Hall School, MB, Canada
Barrie School, MD
Battle Ground Academy, TN
Bay Ridge Preparatory School, NY
Beaver Country Day School, MA
Berkeley Preparatory School, FL
The Birch Wathen Lenox School, NY
Bishop's College School, QC, Canada
The Bishop's School, CA
The Blake School, MN
The Bolles School, FL
Boston Trinity Academy, MA
Bradenton Christian School, FL
The Brearley School, NY
Breck School, MN
Brimmer and May School, MA
Brookstone School, GA
The Bryn Mawr School for Girls, MD
Bulloch Academy, GA
Campbell Hall (Episcopal), CA
Cannon School, NC
The Canterbury Episcopal School, TX
Canterbury School, FL
The Canterbury School of Florida, FL
Cape Cod Academy, MA
Cape Fear Academy, NC
Cape Henry Collegiate School, VA
Cardigan Mountain School, NH
Carlisle School, VA
Carolina Day School, NC
Castilleja School, CA
The Catlin Gabel School, OR
Chadwick School, CA
Chaminade College Preparatory School, MO
Charlotte Country Day School, NC
Charlotte Latin School, NC
Chase Collegiate School, CT
Chicago Waldorf School, IL
Christ Church Episcopal School, SC
The Church Farm School, PA
Cincinnati Country Day School, OH
Cistercian Preparatory School, TX
Clarksville Academy, TN
The Collegiate School, VA
The Colorado Springs School, CO
Columbus School for Girls, OH
Commonwealth Parkville School, PR
The Community School of Naples, FL
Convent of the Sacred Heart, CT
Convent of the Sacred Heart, NY
The Country Day School, ON, Canada
Country Day School of the Sacred Heart, PA
Crosspoint Academy, WA
Crossroads School for Arts & Sciences, CA
Crystal Springs Uplands School, CA
Currey Ingram Academy, TN
Dana Hall School, MA
Darlington School, GA
Delbarton School, NJ
Denver Academy, CO
The Derryfield School, NH
Devon Preparatory School, PA

Doane Stuart School, NY
Donna Klein Jewish Academy, FL
Durham Academy, NC
Eaglebrook School, MA
Eagle Hill School, MA
Edmund Burke School, DC
Elgin Academy, IL
Episcopal Collegiate School, AR
Episcopal High School of Jacksonville, FL
Escola Americana de Campinas, Brazil
The Ethel Walker School, CT
Falmouth Academy, MA
Fayetteville Academy, NC
Fay School, MA
The Fessenden School, MA
Flint Hill School, VA
Flintridge Preparatory School, CA
Foothills Academy, AB, Canada
Forsyth Country Day School, NC
Fort Worth Country Day School, TX
Frederica Academy, GA
French-American School of New York, NY
Friends Academy, NY
Friends' Central School, PA
The Galloway School, GA
Garrison Forest School, MD
Gaston Day School, NC
Georgetown Day School, DC
Germantown Friends School, PA
Gilman School, MD
Gilmour Academy, OH
Girls Preparatory School, TN
Glenelg Country School, MD
Greenhill School, TX
Greenhills School, MI
The Greenwood School, VT
Grier School, PA
Hampshire Country School, NH
Hargrave Military Academy, VA
The Harker School, CA
The Harley School, NY
The Harrisburg Academy, PA
Harvard-Westlake School, CA
The Harvey School, NY
Hawaii Baptist Academy, HI
Hawken School, OH
Head-Royce School, CA
The Heritage School, GA
The Hewitt School, NY
The Hill Top Preparatory School, PA
The Hockaday School, TX
Holland Hall, OK
Hopkins School, CT
Houghton Academy, NY
The Howard School, GA
The Hudson School, NJ
International High School, CA
International School Bangkok, Thailand
Istanbul International Community School, Turkey
Jack M. Barrack Hebrew Academy, PA
Jackson Preparatory School, MS
John Burroughs School, MO
The Journeys School of Teton Science School, WY
Kent Denver School, CO
Kentucky Country Day School, KY
The Kew-Forest School, NY
King Low Heywood Thomas, CT
Kingswood-Oxford School, CT
The Lab School of Washington, DC
La Jolla Country Day School, CA
Lakefield College School, ON, Canada
Lakehill Preparatory School, TX
Lancaster Country Day School, PA
Landon School, MD
The Latin School of Chicago, IL
Lincoln School, RI
The Linsly School, WV
Long Island Lutheran Middle and High School, NY
Louisville Collegiate School, KY
The Lovett School, GA
Maharishi School of the Age of Enlightenment, IA
Malvern Preparatory School, PA
Marist School, GA
McDonogh School, MD
The Meadows School, NV
Middle Tennessee Christian School, TN
Mid-Pacific Institute, HI
Miller School of Albemarle, VA
Mill Springs Academy, GA
Milton Academy, MA
Miss Edgar's and Miss Cramp's School, QC, Canada
Missouri Military Academy, MO
MMI Preparatory School, PA
Montclair Kimberley Academy, NJ
Montgomery Bell Academy, TN
Moorestown Friends School, NJ
Moravian Academy, PA
Morristown-Beard School, NJ
Mt. De Sales Academy, GA
Munich International School, Germany
Newark Academy, NJ
Noble and Greenough School, MA
Norfolk Academy, VA
North Central Texas Academy, TX
North Shore Country Day School, IL
Northwest Academy, OR
The Northwest School, WA
North Yarmouth Academy, ME
Oak Grove School, CA
The Oakridge School, TX
Oakwood Friends School, NY
Ojai Valley School, CA
The O'Neal School, NC
Oregon Episcopal School, OR
The Overlake School, WA
Palmer Trinity School, FL
Parish Episcopal School, TX
The Park School of Baltimore, MD
The Park School of Buffalo, NY
The Pennington School, NJ
Phoenix Country Day School, AZ
Pickering College, ON, Canada
Pine Crest School, FL
The Pingry School, NJ
Porter-Gaud School, SC
Professional Children's School, NY
Providence Country Day School, RI
Punahou School, HI
Queen Margaret's School, BC, Canada
Randolph-Macon Academy, VA
Randolph School, AL
Ranney School, NJ
Ransom Everglades School, FL
Ravenscroft School, NC

The Rectory School, CT
Ridley College, ON, Canada
Riverdale Country School, NY
River Oaks Baptist School, TX
Riverside Military Academy, GA
The Rivers School, MA
Roland Park Country School, MD
Rolling Hills Preparatory School, CA
Ross School, NY
Rothesay Netherwood School, NB, Canada
Rowland Hall, UT
The Roxbury Latin School, MA
Roycemore School, IL
Rumsey Hall School, CT
Rye Country Day School, NY
Sacramento Country Day School, CA
Sage Ridge School, NV
St. Albans School, DC
St. Andrew's College, ON, Canada
St. Andrew's Episcopal School, MD
St. Andrew's School, RI
St. Andrew's–Sewanee School, TN
St. Anne's–Belfield School, VA
St. Anthony's Junior-Senior High School, HI
St. Bernard High School, CT
St. Croix Country Day School, VI
St. George's Independent School, TN
St. George's School, BC, Canada
St. George's School of Montreal, QC, Canada
St. Gregory College Preparatory School, AZ
Saint John's Preparatory School, MN
St. Mark's School of Texas, TX
St. Martin's Episcopal School, LA
St. Mary's Episcopal School, TN
Saint Mary's Hall, TX
St. Mary's School, OR
St. Paul Academy and Summit School, MN
St. Paul's Episcopal School, AL
St. Stanislaus College, MS
St. Stephen's & St. Agnes School, VA
Saint Stephen's Episcopal School, FL
St. Stephen's Episcopal School, TX
Saint Thomas Academy, MN
Sandia Preparatory School, NM
San Domenico School, CA
Sandy Spring Friends School, MD
San Marcos Baptist Academy, TX
Santa Fe Preparatory School, NM
Seabury Hall, HI
Seattle Academy of Arts and Sciences, WA
The Seven Hills School, OH
Severn School, MD
Shady Side Academy, PA
Shattuck-St. Mary's School, MN
Shawnigan Lake School, BC, Canada
The Shipley School, PA
Soundview Preparatory School, NY
Southwest Christian School, Inc., TX
Spartanburg Day School, SC
The Spence School, NY
Stevenson School, CA
The Storm King School, NY
Stratford Academy, GA
Strathcona-Tweedsmuir School, AB, Canada
Stratton Mountain School, VT
Stuart Hall, VA
The Summit Country Day School, OH
Taipei American School, Taiwan
Tandem Friends School, VA
TASIS The American School in England, United Kingdom
TASIS, The American School in Switzerland, Switzerland
Telluride Mountain School, CO
Temple Grandin School, CO
Thomas Jefferson School, MO
Tower Hill School, DE
Trinity College School, ON, Canada
Trinity-Pawling School, NY
Trinity Preparatory School, FL
University Liggett School, MI
University of Chicago Laboratory Schools, IL
University Prep, WA
University School of Jackson, TN
University School of Milwaukee, WI
University School of Nova Southeastern University, FL
Upper Canada College, ON, Canada
Valley Forge Military Academy & College, PA
Villa Duchesne and Oak Hill School, MO
Villa Victoria Academy, NJ
Wakefield School, VA
The Waldorf School of Garden City, NY
Wasatch Academy, UT
Washington International School, DC
The Waterford School, UT
Watkinson School, CT
Waynflete School, ME
Webb School of Knoxville, TN
Westchester Country Day School, NC
Westridge School, CA
Westtown School, PA
The Wheeler School, RI
The Williams School, CT
The Williston Northampton School, MA
Windward School, CA
Winston Preparatory School, NY
Woodlynde School, PA
Worcester Preparatory School, MD
York Preparatory School, NY
York School, CA

SCHOOLS REPORTING ACADEMIC ACCOMMODATIONS FOR THE GIFTED AND TALENTED

The Academy for Gifted Children (PACE), ON, Canada G
Academy of Notre Dame de Namur, PA G,M,A
Academy of the Holy Cross, MD G,A
Academy of the New Church Boys' School, PA G,M,A
Academy of the New Church Girls' School, PA G,M,A
Académie Ste Cécile International School, ON, Canada G,M,A
The Agnes Irwin School, PA G
Alexander Dawson School, CO G,M,A
Alliance Academy, Ecuador G
Alverno High School, CA G
American Academy, FL G,M,A
American Heritage School, FL G,M,A
American Heritage School, FL G,M,A
Archbishop Mitty High School, CA G,M,A
ASSETS School, HI G
Augusta Preparatory Day School, GA G
Bachman Academy, TN G
Balmoral Hall School, MB, Canada G
The Baltimore Actors' Theatre Conservatory, MD G,M,A
Baltimore Lutheran School, MD G

G — gifted; M — musically talented; A — artistically talented

School	
Bay Ridge Preparatory School, NY	G,M,A
The Beekman School, NY	G,M,A
Benet Academy, IL	G
The Birch Wathen Lenox School, NY	G,M,A
Bishop Brady High School, NH	G
Bishop Denis J. O'Connell High School, VA	G
Bishop Eustace Preparatory School, NJ	G,M
Bishop Fenwick High School, OH	G
Bishop Guertin High School, NH	G
Bishop Ireton High School, VA	M
Bishop Luers High School, IN	G,M
Bishop McGuinness Catholic High School, OK	G,A
Bishop O'Dowd High School, CA	G,M,A
Bishop's College School, QC, Canada	G,M,A
Blueprint Education, AZ	M,A
Boston University Academy, MA	G
Breck School, MN	G,M,A
Briarcrest Christian High School, TN	G,M,A
Briarwood Christian High School, AL	G
Bridges Academy, CA	G
The British School of Boston, MA	G
Brockwood Park School, United Kingdom	G,M,A
The Bryn Mawr School for Girls, MD	G,M,A
Buffalo Academy of the Sacred Heart, NY	G,M,A
Bulloch Academy, GA	G,M,A
Buxton School, MA	G,M,A
Calvert Hall College High School, MD	G,M,A
Canton Academy, MS	G
Cape Henry Collegiate School, VA	G,M,A
Cardigan Mountain School, NH	G
Cardinal Mooney Catholic High School, FL	M,A
Cardinal Newman High School, FL	G
Cardinal O'Hara High School, PA	M
Carondelet High School, CA	G
Cascadilla School, NY	G,M,A
Castilleja School, CA	G
Cathedral High School, IN	G,M,A
Catholic Central High School, WI	G,A
The Catlin Gabel School, OR	G,M,A
Chadwick School, CA	G,M,A
Chamberlain-Hunt Academy, MS	G,M,A
Chaminade College Preparatory School, MO	G
Charlotte Country Day School, NC	G
Charlotte Latin School, NC	G
Chase Collegiate School, CT	G
Chattanooga Christian School, TN	G,A
The Chicago Academy for the Arts, IL	M,A
Children's Creative and Performing Arts Academy of San Diego, CA	G,M,A
Chinese Christian Schools, CA	G
Choate Rosemary Hall, CT	G,M,A
Christa McAuliffe Academy School of Arts and Sciences, OR	G,M,A
Christ Church Episcopal School, SC	G
Christchurch School, VA	G
Christopher Columbus High School, FL	G
Chrysalis School, WA	G
The Church Farm School, PA	G,M,A
The Colorado Springs School, CO	G
The Concept School, PA	G,A
Concord Academy, MA	G,M,A
Concordia Preparatory School, UT	G
Convent of the Sacred Heart, CT	G,A
Copper Canyon Academy, AZ	G,M,A
Cotter Schools, MN	G,M,A
Country Day School of the Sacred Heart, PA	M
Crossroads School for Arts & Sciences, CA	G,M,A
Currey Ingram Academy, TN	G,M,A
Cushing Academy, MA	G,M,A
Darlington School, GA	M
Darrow School, NY	M,A
Deerfield Academy, MA	G,M,A
DeMatha Catholic High School, MD	G,M,A
Denver Academy, CO	G
Doane Stuart School, NY	G,M,A
Donelson Christian Academy, TN	G
Dowling Catholic High School, IA	G,M,A
Dublin Christian Academy, NH	M,A
Dublin School, NH	G
Duchesne Academy of the Sacred Heart, TX	M,A
Eaglebrook School, MA	G,M,A
Eagle Hill School, MA	G,M,A
Eastern Mennonite High School, VA	G
Eaton Academy, GA	G,M,A
Eldorado Emerson Private School, CA	G,M,A
Elizabeth Seton High School, MD	G,M,A
Emma Willard School, NY	G,M,A
The English College in Prague, Czech Republic	G,M,A
Episcopal High School, VA	G,M,A
Episcopal High School of Jacksonville, FL	G
The Ethel Walker School, CT	G,M,A
Explorations Academy, WA	G
Faith Lutheran High School, NV	M
Father Ryan High School, TN	G,M,A
Fay School, MA	G,M,A
The Fessenden School, MA	G,M,A
Flint Hill School, VA	M,A
Flintridge Preparatory School, CA	G,M,A
Flint River Academy, GA	M,A
Forsyth Country Day School, NC	G
Fort Worth Country Day School, TX	G,M,A
Fountain Valley School of Colorado, CO	G,M,A
Foxcroft School, VA	G,M,A
Fox Valley Lutheran High School, WI	G
Freeman Academy, SD	M,A
Front Range Christian High School, CO	G
Fryeburg Academy, ME	M
The Galloway School, GA	G,M,A
Garrison Forest School, MD	G,M,A
Gaston Day School, NC	G
George Stevens Academy, ME	G,M,A
Georgetown Preparatory School, MD	G
George Walton Academy, GA	M,A
Germantown Friends School, PA	G,M,A
Gilman School, MD	G,M,A
Gilmour Academy, OH	G,M,A
Glenelg Country School, MD	G
The Glenholme School, Devereux Connecticut, CT	G
Gould Academy, ME	G,M,A
The Governor French Academy, IL	G,A
The Grauer School, CA	G,M,A
The Greenwood School, VT	G,M,A
Grier School, PA	G,M,A
The Gunston School, MD	G,M,A
Hampshire Country School, NH	G
The Harker School, CA	G
Harvard-Westlake School, CA	G,M,A
Head-Royce School, CA	G,M,A
Hebrew Academy of the Five Towns & Rockaway, NY	A
The Hill Top Preparatory School, PA	G,A
Ho'Ala School, HI	G,A
Holy Cross School, LA	G,M,A
The Howard School, GA	A
The Hudson School, NJ	G,M,A

G — gifted; M — musically talented; A — artistically talented

School	
Humanex Academy, CO	G
Huntington-Surrey School, TX	G
Hyman Brand Hebrew Academy of Greater Kansas City, KS	G
Immaculata High School, NJ	M
Independent School, KS	G,M,A
Institute of Notre Dame, MD	G
Interlochen Arts Academy, MI	G,M,A
International High School, CA	G,M,A
International School of Amsterdam, Netherlands	G,M,A
Iona Preparatory School, NY	G
Jack M. Barrack Hebrew Academy, PA	G
Jackson Preparatory School, MS	G,M,A
Jean and Samuel Frankel Jewish Academy of Metropolitan Detroit, MI	G
The Journeys School of Teton Science School, WY	G
Kent School, CT	G,M,A
Kents Hill School, ME	G,A
Kentucky Country Day School, KY	G,M,A
The Kew-Forest School, NY	G
King Low Heywood Thomas, CT	G,M,A
The Lab School of Washington, DC	G,M,A
Lancaster Country Day School, PA	G,M,A
Lancaster Mennonite High School, PA	M
Landmark Christian School, GA	G
The Latin School of Chicago, IL	G
The Laureate Academy, MB, Canada	G
Laurel Springs School, CA	G,M,A
Lehigh Valley Christian High School, PA	G
The Linsly School, WV	G
Little Keswick School, VA	G
Los Angeles Lutheran High School, CA	G,M,A
The Lovett School, GA	G,M,A
Loyola-Blakefield, MD	G,M,A
Lutheran High School of Hawaii, HI	M,A
Luther College High School, SK, Canada	G
Luther North College Prep, IL	G,M,A
Maharishi School of the Age of Enlightenment, IA	G,M,A
Maine Central Institute, ME	M
Maranatha High School, CA	A
Marine Military Academy, TX	G
Marmion Academy, IL	G
Marylawn of the Oranges, NJ	G,M,A
The Mary Louis Academy, NY	M,A
Maur Hill-Mount Academy, KS	G
Meadowridge School, BC, Canada	G
The Meadows School, NV	G,M,A
Menaul School, NM	G,A
Mennonite Collegiate Institute, MB, Canada	M
Merchiston Castle School, United Kingdom	G,M,A
Middlesex School, MA	G
Mid-Pacific Institute, HI	G,A
Miller School of Albemarle, VA	G,M,A
Mill Springs Academy, GA	G,M,A
Milton Academy, MA	G,M,A
Missouri Military Academy, MO	G,M,A
MMI Preparatory School, PA	G
Monsignor Donovan High School, NJ	G,M,A
Montclair Kimberley Academy, NJ	G
Mt. Saint Dominic Academy, NJ	G,M,A
Mount Saint Joseph Academy, PA	G,M,A
MU High School, MO	G
Munich International School, Germany	G
Newark Academy, NJ	G,M,A
Noble and Greenough School, MA	G,M,A
The Nora School, MD	G,A
Norfolk Academy, VA	G,M,A
North Central Texas Academy, TX	G,M,A

School	
Northwest Academy, OR	G,M,A
Notre Dame College Prep, IL	G
The Oakland School, PA	G,A
The Oakridge School, TX	G,M,A
Ojai Valley School, CA	G,A
Oregon Episcopal School, OR	G
Orinda Academy, CA	G
The Overlake School, WA	G,M,A
The Oxford Academy, CT	G
Pacific Academy, CA	G
Pacific Crest Community School, OR	G
Palmer Trinity School, FL	G,M,A
The Park School of Baltimore, MD	G,M,A
The Park School of Buffalo, NY	G
The Pennington School, NJ	G
Pensacola Catholic High School, FL	G
Philadelphia-Montgomery Christian Academy, PA	G,M,A
Phillips Academy (Andover), MA	G,M,A
The Pingry School, NJ	G
Portsmouth Abbey School, RI	G
Portsmouth Christian Academy, NH	G,M
Prestonwood Christian Academy, TX	G
Proctor Academy, NH	G
Providence Country Day School, RI	G,M,A
Providence High School, CA	M,A
Queen Margaret's School, BC, Canada	G,M,A
Ramona Convent Secondary School, CA	G,M,A
Randolph-Macon Academy, VA	G
Ravenscroft School, NC	G,M,A
Realms of Inquiry, UT	G,M,A
The Rectory School, CT	G
Regis Jesuit High School, Girls Division, CO	G,M,A
Ridley College, ON, Canada	M,A
Riverdale Country School, NY	G,M,A
Rockway Mennonite Collegiate, ON, Canada	G
Rolling Hills Preparatory School, CA	G
Rothesay Netherwood School, NB, Canada	G,M,A
The Roxbury Latin School, MA	G,M,A
Rumsey Hall School, CT	G
Rye Country Day School, NY	G
Sacred Heart/Griffin High School, IL	G,M,A
Sage Hill School, CA	G,M,A
Saint Albert Junior-Senior High School, IA	G
St. Andrew's–Sewanee School, TN	G,M,A
St. Anthony Catholic High School, TX	G
Saint Anthony High School, CA	G,A
St. Augustine High School, CA	G
St. Benedict at Auburndale, TN	G,M,A
St. Brendan High School, FL	G
St. Croix Schools, MN	G,M,A
St. Francis High School, KY	G,A
St. George's School, RI	G,M,A
St. George's School of Montreal, QC, Canada	G,M,A
St. Gregory College Preparatory School, AZ	G,M,A
St. John's Preparatory School, MA	G,M,A
St. Joseph High School, CT	G
Saint Joseph High School, NJ	G
St. Joseph's Preparatory School, PA	G,M,A
St. Mark's School of Texas, TX	G
St. Mary's Episcopal School, TN	G,M,A
Saint Mary's High School, MD	G
St. Mary's Preparatory School, MI	M,A
Saint Mary's School, NC	G,M,A
St. Mary's School, OR	G,M,A
Saint Maur International School, Japan	G,M,A
Saint Patrick - Saint Vincent High School, CA	G
St. Stephen's & St. Agnes School, VA	G,M,A

G — gifted; M — musically talented; A — artistically talented

Saint Thomas Aquinas High School, KS	G
Salem Academy, OR	M,A
Salesianum School, DE	G
Sandia Preparatory School, NM	G
San Domenico School, CA	M
Sandy Spring Friends School, MD	G,M,A
San Marcos Baptist Academy, TX	G,M,A
Santa Catalina School, CA	G,M,A
SBEC (Southern Baptist Educational Center), MS	G
Seabury Hall, HI	G
Seattle Academy of Arts and Sciences, WA	G,M,A
The Seven Hills School, OH	G
Severn School, MD	G,M,A
Shady Side Academy, PA	G,M,A
Shattuck-St. Mary's School, MN	G,M
Shawnigan Lake School, BC, Canada	G
The Shipley School, PA	G
Soundview Preparatory School, NY	G,A
Southwest Christian School, Inc., TX	G
Southwestern Academy, CA	M,A
Spartanburg Day School, SC	G,A
The Storm King School, NY	G,M,A
Stuart Hall, VA	G,M,A
The Summit Country Day School, OH	G
Sunshine Bible Academy, SD	M
The Taft School, CT	G,M,A
Tandem Friends School, VA	G
TASIS The American School in England, United Kingdom	G
Temple Grandin School, CO	G,M,A
The Tenney School, TX	G,M,A
The Thacher School, CA	G,M,A
Thomas Jefferson School, MO	G
Tower Hill School, DE	G,M,A
Trinity High School, KY	G,M,A
Trinity High School, OH	G,A
Trinity Preparatory School, FL	G,M,A
University Liggett School, MI	G,M,A
University School of Jackson, TN	G,M,A
University School of Nova Southeastern University, FL	G,M,A
Valle Catholic High School, MO	G,A
Valley Forge Military Academy & College, PA	M,A
Valley Lutheran High School, AZ	G
The Valley School, MI	G,A
Venta Preparatory School, ON, Canada	G
Villa Joseph Marie High School, PA	G,M,A
Villa Victoria Academy, NJ	G,M,A
Villa Walsh Academy, NJ	G,M,A
The Waldorf School of Garden City, NY	M,A
Walnut Hill School for the Arts, MA	G,M,A
The Waterford School, UT	G,M,A
Watkinson School, CT	G,M,A
The Webb Schools, CA	G
West Island College, AB, Canada	G
Westover School, CT	G,M,A
West Sound Academy, WA	G,M,A
Westtown School, PA	G,M,A
Wheaton Academy, IL	G,M,A
The Wheeler School, RI	G
Whitefield Academy, KY	G
The Williams School, CT	G,M,A
The Williston Northampton School, MA	G,M,A
The Windsor School, NY	G,M,A
Worcester Preparatory School, MD	G
Xaverian High School, NY	G,M
York Preparatory School, NY	G,M,A

SCHOOLS WITH ADVANCED PLACEMENT PREPARATION

The Academy for Gifted Children (PACE), ON, Canada
Academy of Our Lady of Peace, CA
Academy of the Holy Cross, MD
Academy of the New Church Boys' School, PA
Academy of the New Church Girls' School, PA
Academy of the Sacred Heart, LA
Académie Ste Cécile International School, ON, Canada
The Agnes Irwin School, PA
Alexander Dawson School, CO
Allendale Columbia School, NY
Alliance Academy, Ecuador
Alverno High School, CA
American Heritage School, FL
American Heritage School, FL
The American School Foundation, Mexico
The American School in El Salvador, FL
Anacapa School, CA
Archbishop Curley High School, MD
Archbishop Mitty High School, CA
Army and Navy Academy, CA
Arroyo Pacific Academy, CA
The Athenian School, CA
Augusta Christian School (I), GA
Bakersfield Christian High School, CA
Baldwin School of Puerto Rico, PR
Balmoral Hall School, MB, Canada
The Baltimore Actors' Theatre Conservatory, MD
Baltimore Lutheran School, MD
Barrie School, MD
Battle Ground Academy, TN
Bay Ridge Preparatory School, NY
Bayside Academy, AL
Bayview Glen School, ON, Canada
The Beekman School, NY
Belen Jesuit Preparatory School, FL
Bellarmine College Preparatory, CA
Benet Academy, IL
Berkeley Preparatory School, FL
Berkshire School, MA
The Birch Wathen Lenox School, NY
Bishop Brady High School, NH
Bishop Conaty-Our Lady of Loretto High School, CA
Bishop Denis J. O'Connell High School, VA
Bishop Eustace Preparatory School, NJ
Bishop Fenwick High School, OH
Bishop Guertin High School, NH
Bishop Ireton High School, VA
Bishop John J. Snyder High School, FL
Bishop Kelly High School, ID
Bishop Kenny High School, FL
Bishop Luers High School, IN
Bishop McGuinness Catholic High School, NC
Bishop McGuinness Catholic High School, OK
Bishop Montgomery High School, CA
Bishop O'Dowd High School, CA
Bishop's College School, QC, Canada
The Bishop's School, CA
Bishop Stang High School, MA
Blair Academy, NJ
The Blake School, MN
Blanchet School, OR
Blessed Trinity High School, GA
Blueprint Education, AZ
The Bolles School, FL
Boston Trinity Academy, MA

Bradenton Christian School, FL
The Brearley School, NY
Breck School, MN
Brentwood College School, BC, Canada
Briarcrest Christian High School, TN
Briarwood Christian High School, AL
Brimmer and May School, MA
The Brook Hill School, TX
Brooks School, MA
Brookstone School, GA
Brophy College Preparatory, AZ
Brother Rice High School, MI
The Bryn Mawr School for Girls, MD
Buffalo Academy of the Sacred Heart, NY
Bulloch Academy, GA
Burr and Burton Academy, VT
Butte Central Catholic High School, MT
Calvary Christian School, KY
Calvert Hall College High School, MD
Calvin Christian High School, CA
Campbell Hall (Episcopal), CA
Cannon School, NC
The Canterbury Episcopal School, TX
Canterbury School, FL
The Canterbury School of Florida, FL
Canyonville Christian Academy, OR
Cape Cod Academy, MA
Cape Fear Academy, NC
Cape Henry Collegiate School, VA
Capistrano Valley Christian Schools, CA
Cardinal Gibbons High School, NC
Cardinal Mooney Catholic High School, FL
Cardinal Newman High School, FL
Cardinal O'Hara High School, PA
Carlisle School, VA
Carolina Day School, NC
Carondelet High School, CA
Cascadilla School, NY
Castilleja School, CA
Cathedral High School, IN
Cathedral Preparatory School, PA
Catholic Central High School, NY
Catholic Central High School, WI
The Catholic High School of Baltimore, MD
Central Catholic High School, CA
Central Catholic High School, MA
Central Catholic High School, TX
Chadwick School, CA
Chaminade College Preparatory, CA
Chaminade College Preparatory School, MO
Charlotte Latin School, NC
Chase Collegiate School, CT
Chattanooga Christian School, TN
Cheverus High School, ME
The Chicago Academy for the Arts, IL
Children's Creative and Performing Arts Academy of San Diego, CA
Chinese Christian Schools, CA
Choate Rosemary Hall, CT
Christa McAuliffe Academy School of Arts and Sciences, OR
Christchurch School, VA
Christian Brothers Academy, NJ
Christian Brothers Academy, NY
Christian Central Academy, NY
Christopher Columbus High School, FL
Christopher Dock Mennonite High School, PA
The Church Farm School, PA
Cincinnati Country Day School, OH
Cistercian Preparatory School, TX
Clarksville Academy, TN
Colegio Bolivar, Colombia
Colegio San Jose, PR
Cole Valley Christian High School, ID
The Collegiate School, VA
The Colorado Springs School, CO
Columbia Academy, TN
Columbia International School, Japan
Columbus School for Girls, OH
Commonwealth Parkville School, PR
The Community School of Naples, FL
Concordia Lutheran High School, IN
Concordia Preparatory School, UT
Contra Costa Christian High School, CA
Convent of the Sacred Heart, CT
Convent of the Sacred Heart, NY
The Country Day School, ON, Canada
Country Day School of the Sacred Heart, PA
Crawford Adventist Academy, ON, Canada
Crespi Carmelite High School, CA
Cushing Academy, MA
Dakar Academy, Senegal
Damien High School, CA
Dana Hall School, MA
Darlington School, GA
Darrow School, NY
Davidson Academy, TN
Deerfield Academy, MA
De La Salle High School, CA
De La Salle North Catholic High School, OR
Delbarton School, NJ
DeMatha Catholic High School, MD
The Derryfield School, NH
Devon Preparatory School, PA
Dexter School, MA
Doane Stuart School, NY
Dominican Academy, NY
Donelson Christian Academy, TN
Donna Klein Jewish Academy, FL
Dowling Catholic High School, IA
Dublin Christian Academy, NH
Dublin School, NH
Duchesne Academy of the Sacred Heart, TX
Durham Academy, NC
Eastern Mennonite High School, VA
Edgewood Academy, AL
Edmund Burke School, DC
Eldorado Emerson Private School, CA
Elgin Academy, IL
Elizabeth Seton High School, MD
Elyria Catholic High School, OH
Emma Willard School, NY
Episcopal Collegiate School, AR
Episcopal High School, TX
Episcopal High School, VA
Episcopal High School of Jacksonville, FL
Escola Americana de Campinas, Brazil
The Ethel Walker School, CT
Explorations Academy, WA
Ezell-Harding Christian School, TN
Fairfield College Preparatory School, CT
Faith Christian High School, CA
Faith Lutheran High School, NV
Falmouth Academy, MA
Father Lopez High School, FL

Father Ryan High School, TN
Fayetteville Academy, NC
The First Academy, FL
First Baptist Academy, TX
First Presbyterian Day School, GA
Fishburne Military School, VA
Flint Hill School, VA
Flintridge Preparatory School, CA
Flint River Academy, GA
Fontbonne Hall Academy, NY
Fordham Preparatory School, NY
Forsyth Country Day School, NC
Fort Worth Christian School, TX
Fort Worth Country Day School, TX
Foundation Academy, FL
Fountain Valley School of Colorado, CO
Foxcroft School, VA
Fox Valley Lutheran High School, WI
Frederica Academy, GA
French-American School of New York, NY
Fresno Christian Schools, CA
Friends Academy, NY
Front Range Christian High School, CO
Fryeburg Academy, ME
Gabriel Richard Catholic High School, MI
The Galloway School, GA
Gann Academy (The New Jewish High School of Greater Boston), MA
Garrison Forest School, MD
Gaston Day School, NC
George Stevens Academy, ME
Georgetown Day School, DC
Georgetown Preparatory School, MD
Georgetown Visitation Preparatory School, DC
George Walton Academy, GA
Gilman School, MD
Gilmour Academy, OH
Girls Preparatory School, TN
Glades Day School, FL
Glenelg Country School, MD
Gonzaga College High School, DC
Gould Academy, ME
The Governor French Academy, IL
Grace Baptist Academy, TN
Grace Brethren School, CA
Grace Christian School, AK
The Grauer School, CA
Greenhill School, TX
Greenhills School, MI
Grier School, PA
Guamani Private School, PR
The Gunston School, MD
Hargrave Military Academy, VA
The Harker School, CA
The Harley School, NY
Harrells Christian Academy, NC
The Harrisburg Academy, PA
Harvard-Westlake School, CA
The Harvey School, NY
Hawaii Baptist Academy, HI
Hawken School, OH
Hawthorne Christian Academy, NJ
Head-Royce School, CA
Hebrew Academy, CA
Hebrew Academy of the Five Towns & Rockaway, NY
Heritage Christian School, CA
The Heritage School, GA
The Hewitt School, NY
The Hill School, PA
Ho'Ala School, HI
The Hockaday School, TX
Holland Hall, OK
Holy Angels Academy, NY
Holy Cross High School, CT
Holy Cross School, LA
Holy Ghost Preparatory School, PA
Holyoke Catholic High School, MA
Holy Savior Menard Catholic High School, LA
Holy Trinity Diocesan High School, NY
Holy Trinity School, ON, Canada
Hopkins School, CT
Houghton Academy, NY
The Hudson School, NJ
Hyde Park Baptist School, TX
Hyman Brand Hebrew Academy of Greater Kansas City, KS
Idyllwild Arts Academy, CA
Immaculata High School, NJ
Immaculate Conception School, IL
Independent School, KS
Institute of Notre Dame, MD
Interlochen Arts Academy, MI
Intermountain Christian School, UT
International School Bangkok, Thailand
Iona Preparatory School, NY
Jack M. Barrack Hebrew Academy, PA
Jackson Preparatory School, MS
Jean and Samuel Frankel Jewish Academy of Metropolitan Detroit, MI
Jesuit High School of Tampa, FL
John Burroughs School, MO
Josephinum Academy, IL
Junipero Serra High School, CA
Kalamazoo Christian High School, MI
Kent Denver School, CO
Kent School, CT
Kents Hill School, ME
Kentucky Country Day School, KY
Keswick Christian School, FL
The Kew-Forest School, NY
Kimball Union Academy, NH
King Low Heywood Thomas, CT
The King's Academy, TN
Kings Christian School, CA
Kingswood-Oxford School, CT
La Jolla Country Day School, CA
Lakefield College School, ON, Canada
Lakehill Preparatory School, TX
Lancaster Country Day School, PA
Lancaster Mennonite High School, PA
Landmark Christian School, GA
Landon School, MD
Lansdale Catholic High School, PA
La Salle High School, CA
La Scuola D'Italia Guglielmo Marconi, NY
The Latin School of Chicago, IL
Laurel Springs School, CA
Lee Academy, ME
Lehigh Valley Christian High School, PA
Lehman High School, OH
Lexington Catholic High School, KY
Lincoln Academy, ME
Lincoln School, RI
Linfield Christian School, CA
The Linsly School, WV

Lodi Academy, CA
Long Island Lutheran Middle and High School, NY
Loretto Academy, TX
Los Angeles Lutheran High School, CA
Louisville Collegiate School, KY
Louisville High School, CA
The Lovett School, GA
Loyola-Blakefield, MD
Loyola School, NY
Lutheran High School North, MO
Lutheran High School Northwest, MI
Lutheran High School of Hawaii, HI
Lutheran High School of Indianapolis, IN
Lutheran High School of San Diego, CA
Luther North College Prep, IL
Lyndon Institute, VT
Maine Central Institute, ME
Malvern Preparatory School, PA
Manhattan Christian High School, MT
Maranatha High School, CA
Marian Central Catholic High School, IL
Marian High School, IN
Marine Military Academy, TX
Marist School, GA
Marmion Academy, IL
Mars Hill Bible School, AL
Martin Luther High School, NY
The Marvelwood School, CT
Marylawn of the Oranges, NJ
The Mary Louis Academy, NY
Marymount High School, CA
Matignon High School, MA
Maui Preparatory Academy, HI
Maur Hill-Mount Academy, KS
McDonogh School, MD
McGill-Toolen Catholic High School, AL
The Meadows School, NV
Menaul School, NM
Mennonite Collegiate Institute, MB, Canada
Mercy High School College Preparatory, CA
Middlesex School, MA
Middle Tennessee Christian School, TN
Midland School, CA
Mid-Pacific Institute, HI
Miller School of Albemarle, VA
Milton Academy, MA
Miss Edgar's and Miss Cramp's School, QC, Canada
Missouri Military Academy, MO
Miss Porter's School, CT
MMI Preparatory School, PA
Modesto Christian School, CA
Monsignor Donovan High School, NJ
Montclair Kimberley Academy, NJ
Montgomery Bell Academy, TN
Moorestown Friends School, NJ
Moravian Academy, PA
Moreau Catholic High School, CA
Morristown-Beard School, NJ
Mother McAuley High School, IL
Mount Carmel School, MP
Mount Mercy Academy, NY
Mount Michael Benedictine School, NE
Mount Saint Charles Academy, RI
Mt. Saint Dominic Academy, NJ
Mount Saint Joseph Academy, PA
MU High School, MO
Nazareth Academy, IL
Nerinx Hall, MO
Newark Academy, NJ
Noble and Greenough School, MA
Norfolk Academy, VA
North Shore Country Day School, IL
Northwest Catholic High School, CT
Northwood School, NY
North Yarmouth Academy, ME
The Norwich Free Academy, CT
Notre Dame Academy, CA
Notre Dame College Prep, IL
Notre Dame High School, CA
Notre Dame High School, NJ
Notre Dame High School, TN
Notre Dame Junior/Senior High School, PA
Oak Grove School, CA
The Oakridge School, TX
Oakwood Friends School, NY
Ojai Valley School, CA
Oldenburg Academy, IN
The O'Neal School, NC
Oneida Baptist Institute, KY
Oregon Episcopal School, OR
Orinda Academy, CA
The Overlake School, WA
The Oxford Academy, CT
Pacific Academy, CA
Padua Franciscan High School, OH
Palma School, CA
Palmer Trinity School, FL
Palo Alto Preparatory School, CA
The Park School of Baltimore, MD
The Park School of Buffalo, NY
Peddie School, NJ
The Pennington School, NJ
Pensacola Catholic High School, FL
Philadelphia-Montgomery Christian Academy, PA
Phillips Academy (Andover), MA
Phoenix Christian Unified Schools, AZ
Phoenix Country Day School, AZ
Pinecrest Academy, GA
Pine Crest School, FL
The Pingree School, MA
The Pingry School, NJ
Pioneer Valley Christian School, MA
Pope John XXIII Regional High School, NJ
Porter-Gaud School, SC
Portsmouth Abbey School, RI
Portsmouth Christian Academy, NH
Powers Catholic High School, MI
Prestonwood Christian Academy, TX
Proctor Academy, NH
The Prout School, RI
Providence Country Day School, RI
Providence High School, CA
Punahou School, HI
Queen Margaret's School, BC, Canada
Ramona Convent Secondary School, CA
Randolph-Macon Academy, VA
Randolph School, AL
Ranney School, NJ
Ransom Everglades School, FL
Ravenscroft School, NC
Redwood Christian Schools, CA
Regis High School, NY
Regis Jesuit High School, Girls Division, CO
Ridley College, ON, Canada

Riverside Military Academy, GA
The Rivers School, MA
Roland Park Country School, MD
Rolling Hills Preparatory School, CA
Ross School, NY
Rowland Hall, UT
The Roxbury Latin School, MA
Roycemore School, IL
Rye Country Day School, NY
Sacramento Adventist Academy, CA
Sacramento Country Day School, CA
Sacred Heart/Griffin High School, IL
Sacred Heart School of Halifax, NS, Canada
Saddleback Valley Christian School, CA
Sage Hill School, CA
Sage Ridge School, NV
St. Agnes Academy, TX
St. Albans School, DC
Saint Albert Junior-Senior High School, IA
St. Andrew's College, ON, Canada
St. Andrew's Episcopal School, MD
St. Andrew's School, RI
St. Andrew's–Sewanee School, TN
St. Anne's–Belfield School, VA
St. Anthony Catholic High School, TX
Saint Anthony High School, CA
Saint Anthony High School, IL
St. Anthony's Junior-Senior High School, HI
St. Augustine High School, CA
Saint Augustine Preparatory School, NJ
St. Benedict at Auburndale, TN
St. Bernard's Catholic School, CA
St. Brendan High School, FL
St. Croix Country Day School, VI
St. Croix Schools, MN
Saint Dominic Academy, ME
Saint Elizabeth High School, CA
St. Francis de Sales High School, OH
Saint Francis High School, CA
St. Francis High School, KY
St. George's Independent School, TN
St. George's School, RI
St. George's School, BC, Canada
St. George's School of Montreal, QC, Canada
St. Gregory College Preparatory School, AZ
Saint Joan Antida High School, WI
St. John's Preparatory School, MA
Saint John's Preparatory School, MN
St. John's-Ravenscourt School, MB, Canada
Saint Joseph Academy High School, OH
St. Joseph High School, CT
Saint Joseph High School, IL
Saint Joseph High School, NJ
St. Joseph's Academy, LA
St. Joseph's Catholic School, SC
St. Joseph's Preparatory School, PA
Saint Lucy's Priory High School, CA
St. Mark's School of Texas, TX
St. Martin's Episcopal School, LA
St. Mary's Episcopal School, TN
Saint Mary's Hall, TX
Saint Mary's High School, AZ
Saint Mary's High School, MD
St. Mary's Preparatory School, MI
Saint Mary's School, NC
St. Mary's School, OR
Saint Maur International School, Japan
St. Michael's College School, ON, Canada
St. Michael's Preparatory School of the Norbertine Fathers, CA
Saint Patrick High School, IL
Saint Patrick - Saint Vincent High School, CA
St. Patrick's Regional Secondary, BC, Canada
St. Paul's Episcopal School, AL
St. Paul's High School, MB, Canada
St. Pius X Catholic High School, GA
St. Pius X High School, TX
St. Stanislaus College, MS
St. Stephen's & St. Agnes School, VA
Saint Stephen's Episcopal School, FL
St. Stephen's Episcopal School, TX
St. Stephen's School, Rome, Italy
Saint Teresa's Academy, MO
Saint Thomas Academy, MN
St. Thomas Aquinas High School, FL
Saint Thomas Aquinas High School, KS
St. Thomas Aquinas High School, NH
St. Thomas High School, TX
Saint Ursula Academy, OH
Salem Academy, NC
Salem Academy, OR
Salesian High School, CA
Salesianum School, DE
Salpointe Catholic High School, AZ
San Domenico School, CA
Sandy Spring Friends School, MD
San Marcos Baptist Academy, TX
Santa Catalina School, CA
Santa Fe Preparatory School, NM
SBEC (Southern Baptist Educational Center), MS
Scottsdale Christian Academy, AZ
Scotus Central Catholic High School, NE
Seabury Hall, HI
The Seven Hills School, OH
Severn School, MD
Shady Side Academy, PA
Shattuck-St. Mary's School, MN
Shawnigan Lake School, BC, Canada
The Shipley School, PA
Sonoma Academy, CA
Soundview Preparatory School, NY
Southfield Christian High School, MI
Southfield School, MA
Southwest Christian School, Inc., TX
Southwestern Academy, AZ
Southwestern Academy, CA
Spartanburg Day School, SC
The Spence School, NY
Spring Creek Academy, TX
Stephen T. Badin High School, OH
Stevenson School, CA
The Storm King School, NY
Stratford Academy, GA
Stuart Hall, VA
The Summit Country Day School, OH
The Taft School, CT
Taipei American School, Taiwan
Tandem Friends School, VA
TASIS The American School in England, United Kingdom
TASIS, The American School in Switzerland, Switzerland
The Tenney School, TX
The Thacher School, CA
Thomas Jefferson School, MO
Tidewater Academy, VA
Tilton School, NH

Timothy Christian High School, IL
TMI - The Episcopal School of Texas, TX
Tower Hill School, DE
Tri-City Christian Schools, CA
Trinity College School, ON, Canada
Trinity High School, KY
Trinity High School, NH
Trinity High School, OH
Trinity-Pawling School, NY
Trinity Preparatory School, FL
Tyler Street Christian Academy, TX
University of Chicago Laboratory Schools, IL
University of Detroit Jesuit High School and Academy, MI
University School of Jackson, TN
University School of Milwaukee, WI
University School of Nova Southeastern University, FL
The Ursuline Academy of Dallas, TX
Valle Catholic High School, MO
Valley Christian High School, CA
Valley Forge Military Academy & College, PA
Valley Lutheran High School, AZ
Vianney High School, MO
Vicksburg Catholic School, MS
Villa Angela-St. Joseph High School, OH
Villa Duchesne and Oak Hill School, MO
Villa Joseph Marie High School, PA
Villa Maria Academy, PA
Villa Victoria Academy, NJ
Villa Walsh Academy, NJ
Wakefield School, VA
The Waldorf School of Garden City, NY
Walnut Hill School for the Arts, MA
Walsingham Academy, VA
Wasatch Academy, UT
The Waterford School, UT
Webb School of Knoxville, TN
The Webb Schools, CA
Wesleyan Academy, PR
Westbury Christian School, TX
West Catholic High School, MI
Westchester Country Day School, NC
West Island College, AB, Canada
Westminster Christian Academy, LA
Westminster School, CT
Westover School, CT
Westridge School, CA
Westtown School, PA
Wheaton Academy, IL
The Wheeler School, RI
Whitefield Academy, GA
Whitefield Academy, KY
The Williams School, CT
The Williston Northampton School, MA
The Willows Academy, IL
Wilmington Christian School, DE
Wilson Hall, SC
The Windsor School, NY
Windward School, CA
The Woodhall School, CT
The Woodward School, MA
Worcester Preparatory School, MD
Wyoming Seminary, PA
Xaverian High School, NY
York Catholic High School, PA
York Preparatory School, NY
York School, CA
Zurich International School, Switzerland

SCHOOLS REPORTING A POSTGRADUATE YEAR

Bachman Academy, TN
The Beekman School, NY
Berkshire School, MA
Blair Academy, NJ
The Bolles School, FL
Cascadilla School, NY
Choate Rosemary Hall, CT
Cushing Academy, MA
Darlington School, GA
Deerfield Academy, MA
Emma Willard School, NY
Fishburne Military School, VA
Fryeburg Academy, ME
Gould Academy, ME
Grier School, PA
Hargrave Military Academy, VA
The Hill School, PA
Houghton Academy, NY
Idyllwild Arts Academy, CA
Interlochen Arts Academy, MI
Kent School, CT
Kents Hill School, ME
Kimball Union Academy, NH
The Lawrenceville School, NJ
Lee Academy, ME
Maine Central Institute, ME
Marine Military Academy, TX
Missouri Military Academy, MO
Northwood School, NY
The Oxford Academy, CT
Peddie School, NJ
Phillips Academy (Andover), MA
Randolph-Macon Academy, VA
Ridley College, ON, Canada
Saint John's Preparatory School, MN
St. Stanislaus College, MS
St. Stephen's School, Rome, Italy
Shattuck-St. Mary's School, MN
Soundview Preparatory School, NY
Southwestern Academy, AZ
Southwestern Academy, CA
Stratton Mountain School, VT
The Taft School, CT
TASIS, The American School in Switzerland, Switzerland
Thomas Jefferson School, MO
Tilton School, NH
Trinity-Pawling School, NY
Valley Forge Military Academy & College, PA
Walnut Hill School for the Arts, MA
Wasatch Academy, UT
Watkinson School, CT
Westminster School, CT
The Williston Northampton School, MA
The Windsor School, NY
The Woodhall School, CT
Wyoming Seminary, PA

SCHOOLS OFFERING THE INTERNATIONAL BACCALAUREATE PROGRAM

Academy of the Holy Cross, MD
Académie Ste Cécile International School, ON, Canada
American International School, Lusaka, Zambia
The American School Foundation, Mexico
Annie Wright School, WA

The Awty International School, TX
The British School of Boston, MA
Cardinal Newman High School, FL
Carlisle School, VA
Cathedral High School, IN
Central Catholic High School, MA
Chamberlain-Hunt Academy, MS
Charlotte Country Day School, NC
Christ Church Episcopal School, SC
Colegio San Jose, PR
DuBois Central Catholic High School/Middle School, PA
The English College in Prague, Czech Republic
The Harrisburg Academy, PA
Hebrew Academy, CA
International High School, CA
International School Bangkok, Thailand
International School of Amsterdam, Netherlands
The International School of London, United Kingdom
Istanbul International Community School, Turkey
John Hancock Academy, GA
The Journeys School of Teton Science School, WY
Keswick Christian School, FL
La Scuola D'Italia Guglielmo Marconi, NY
Luther College High School, SK, Canada
Lycee International de Los Angeles, CA
Marymount International School, Italy
Meadowridge School, BC, Canada
Mid-Pacific Institute, HI
Munich International School, Germany
Newark Academy, NJ
Niagara Christian Community of Schools, ON, Canada
Pinewood - The International School of Thessaloniki, Greece, Greece
The Prout School, RI
Regis Jesuit High School, Girls Division, CO
Ridley College, ON, Canada
Rothesay Netherwood School, NB, Canada
Saint Anthony High School, IL
Saint Dominic Academy, ME
Saint John's Preparatory School, MN
St. Joseph's Preparatory School, PA
Saint Maur International School, Japan
St. Stephen's School, Rome, Italy
St. Timothy's School, MD
Seisen International School, Japan
Strathcona-Tweedsmuir School, AB, Canada
Taipei American School, Taiwan
TASIS The American School in England, United Kingdom
TASIS, The American School in Switzerland, Switzerland
THINK Global School, CA
Tri-City Christian Schools, CA
Tyler Street Christian Academy, TX
Upper Canada College, ON, Canada
Villa Duchesne and Oak Hill School, MO
Washington International School, DC
West Sound Academy, WA
Zurich International School, Switzerland

SCHOOLS REPORTING THAT THEY AWARD MERIT SCHOLARSHIPS

Academy of Notre Dame de Namur, PA
Academy of the Holy Cross, MD
Academy of the Sacred Heart, LA
Académie Ste Cécile International School, ON, Canada
All Hallows High School, NY
Alverno High School, CA
American Heritage School, FL
American Heritage School, FL
Anacapa School, CA
Annie Wright School, WA
Archbishop Curley High School, MD
Balmoral Hall School, MB, Canada
Baltimore Lutheran School, MD
Battle Ground Academy, TN
Bay Ridge Preparatory School, NY
Berkeley Preparatory School, FL
The Birch Wathen Lenox School, NY
Bishop Brady High School, NH
Bishop Denis J. O'Connell High School, VA
Bishop Eustace Preparatory School, NJ
Bishop Fenwick High School, OH
Bishop Guertin High School, NH
Bishop Ireton High School, VA
Bishop Luers High School, IN
Bishop O'Dowd High School, CA
Bishop's College School, QC, Canada
Bishop Stang High School, MA
Blanchet School, OR
The British School of Boston, MA
Brookstone School, GA
Brother Rice High School, MI
Buffalo Academy of the Sacred Heart, NY
Calvert Hall College High School, MD
Canterbury School, FL
Canyonville Christian Academy, OR
Cape Fear Academy, NC
Cape Henry Collegiate School, VA
Cardinal Mooney Catholic High School, FL
Carolina Day School, NC
Cascades Academy of Central Oregon, OR
Cascadilla School, NY
Cathedral High School, IN
Cathedral Preparatory School, PA
The Catholic High School of Baltimore, MD
The Catlin Gabel School, OR
Central Catholic High School, CA
Central Catholic High School, MA
Central Catholic High School, TX
Chamberlain-Hunt Academy, MS
Chaminade College Preparatory, CA
Chaminade College Preparatory School, MO
Charlotte Latin School, NC
Chase Collegiate School, CT
Cheverus High School, ME
The Chicago Academy for the Arts, IL
Children's Creative and Performing Arts Academy of San Diego, CA
Chinese Christian Schools, CA
Christ Church Episcopal School, SC
Christian Brothers Academy, NJ
Christian Brothers Academy, NY
Christian Central Academy, NY
Cincinnati Country Day School, OH
The Colorado Springs School, CO
Columbia International School, Japan
Commonwealth Parkville School, PR
The Community School of Naples, FL
Concordia Lutheran High School, IN
Concordia Preparatory School, UT
Cotter Schools, MN
Country Day School of the Sacred Heart, PA
Crespi Carmelite High School, CA

Crossroads School for Arts & Sciences, CA
Cushing Academy, MA
Damien High School, CA
Darlington School, GA
DeMatha Catholic High School, MD
Denver Christian High School, CO
The Derryfield School, NH
Devon Preparatory School, PA
Dominican Academy, NY
DuBois Central Catholic High School/Middle School, PA
Duchesne Academy of the Sacred Heart, TX
Elgin Academy, IL
Elizabeth Seton High School, MD
Elyria Catholic High School, OH
Emma Willard School, NY
The English College in Prague, Czech Republic
Episcopal High School, VA
Explorations Academy, WA
Falmouth Academy, MA
Father Lopez High School, FL
First Presbyterian Day School, GA
Fontbonne Hall Academy, NY
Fordham Preparatory School, NY
Forest Lake Academy, FL
Fort Worth Country Day School, TX
Fountain Valley School of Colorado, CO
Foxcroft School, VA
Freeman Academy, SD
Fresno Christian Schools, CA
Gabriel Richard Catholic High School, MI
Gaston Day School, NC
Gateway School, TX
Georgetown Visitation Preparatory School, DC
Gilmour Academy, OH
Girls Preparatory School, TN
Glenelg Country School, MD
Gonzaga College High School, DC
Great Lakes Christian High School, ON, Canada
Grier School, PA
The Gunston School, MD
Hargrave Military Academy, VA
The Harrisburg Academy, PA
Hawken School, OH
Hawthorne Christian Academy, NJ
Holland Hall, OK
Holy Angels Academy, NY
Holy Cross High School, CT
Holy Cross School, LA
Holy Ghost Preparatory School, PA
Holyoke Catholic High School, MA
Holy Savior Menard Catholic High School, LA
Hyde Park Baptist School, TX
Immaculate Conception School, IL
Institute of Notre Dame, MD
Interlochen Arts Academy, MI
Iona Preparatory School, NY
Jack M. Barrack Hebrew Academy, PA
Josephinum Academy, IL
Junipero Serra High School, CA
Kent School, CT
Kentucky Country Day School, KY
Kingsway College, ON, Canada
Kingswood-Oxford School, CT
Lakefield College School, ON, Canada
Lancaster Country Day School, PA
Lancaster Mennonite High School, PA
Lansdale Catholic High School, PA
La Salle High School, CA
Lauralton Hall, CT
Lexington Catholic High School, KY
Lincoln School, RI
Linfield Christian School, CA
Lodi Academy, CA
Long Island Lutheran Middle and High School, NY
Los Angeles Lutheran High School, CA
Louisville Collegiate School, KY
Louisville High School, CA
Loyola-Blakefield, MD
Loyola School, NY
Lutheran High School North, MO
Lutheran High School Northwest, MI
Lutheran High School of Hawaii, HI
Lutheran High School of San Diego, CA
Luther College High School, SK, Canada
Luther North College Prep, IL
Maine Central Institute, ME
Malvern Preparatory School, PA
Maplebrook School, NY
Maranatha High School, CA
Marine Military Academy, TX
Marmion Academy, IL
Martin Luther High School, NY
The Marvelwood School, CT
Marylawn of the Oranges, NJ
The Mary Louis Academy, NY
Marymount High School, CA
Matignon High School, MA
Maui Preparatory Academy, HI
Maur Hill-Mount Academy, KS
Meadowridge School, BC, Canada
Mennonite Collegiate Institute, MB, Canada
Mercy High School College Preparatory, CA
Mid-Pacific Institute, HI
Miss Edgar's and Miss Cramp's School, QC, Canada
Missouri Military Academy, MO
Miss Porter's School, CT
MMI Preparatory School, PA
Monsignor Donovan High School, NJ
Moreau Catholic High School, CA
Morristown-Beard School, NJ
Mother McAuley High School, IL
Mount Carmel School, MP
Mt. De Sales Academy, GA
Mount Mercy Academy, NY
Mount Michael Benedictine School, NE
Mt. Saint Dominic Academy, NJ
Mount Saint Joseph Academy, PA
Nazareth Academy, IL
Nebraska Christian Schools, NE
Niagara Christian Community of Schools, ON, Canada
North Shore Country Day School, IL
Northwest Catholic High School, CT
Notre Dame Academy, CA
Notre Dame College Prep, IL
Notre Dame High School, CA
The Oakland School, PA
Oldenburg Academy, IN
The O'Neal School, NC
Our Lady of Mercy Academy, NJ
Padua Franciscan High School, OH
Palma School, CA
Paradise Adventist Academy, CA
The Park School of Buffalo, NY
Parkview Adventist Academy, AB, Canada

Peddie School, NJ
The Pennington School, NJ
Pickering College, ON, Canada
Pinewood - The International School of Thessaloniki, Greece, Greece
The Pingree School, MA
Portsmouth Abbey School, RI
Portsmouth Christian Academy, NH
Presbyterian Pan American School, TX
Providence High School, CA
Punahou School, HI
Queen Margaret's School, BC, Canada
Ramona Convent Secondary School, CA
Randolph-Macon Academy, VA
Ravenscroft School, NC
Redwood Christian Schools, CA
Ridley College, ON, Canada
Rolling Hills Preparatory School, CA
Rothesay Netherwood School, NB, Canada
Rowland Hall, UT
Royal Canadian College, BC, Canada
Roycemore School, IL
Rundle College, AB, Canada
Sacred Heart/Griffin High School, IL
Sacred Heart School of Halifax, NS, Canada
St. Agnes Academy, TX
Saint Albert Junior-Senior High School, IA
St. Andrew's College, ON, Canada
St. Andrew's–Sewanee School, TN
St. Anthony Catholic High School, TX
Saint Anthony High School, CA
St. Anthony's Junior-Senior High School, HI
St. Augustine High School, CA
Saint Augustine Preparatory School, NJ
St. Benedict at Auburndale, TN
St. Bernard High School, CT
St. Bernard's Catholic School, CA
St. Croix Country Day School, VI
St. Croix Schools, MN
Saint Dominic Academy, ME
Saint Elizabeth High School, CA
St. Francis de Sales High School, OH
Saint Francis High School, CA
St. Francis High School, KY
St. George's School, BC, Canada
Saint Joan Antida High School, WI
St. John's Preparatory School, MA
Saint John's Preparatory School, MN
St. John's-Ravenscourt School, MB, Canada
Saint Joseph Academy High School, OH
St. Joseph High School, CT
Saint Joseph High School, IL
Saint Joseph High School, NJ
St. Joseph's Catholic School, SC
St. Joseph's Preparatory School, PA
Saint Lawrence Academy, CA
Saint Lucy's Priory High School, CA
St. Martin's Episcopal School, LA
Saint Mary's Hall, TX
Saint Mary's High School, MD
St. Mary's Preparatory School, MI
Saint Mary's School, NC
St. Michael's College School, ON, Canada
Saint Patrick High School, IL
St. Pius X High School, TX
St. Stephen's Episcopal School, TX
St. Stephen's School, Rome, Italy
Saint Teresa's Academy, MO
Saint Thomas Academy, MN
St. Thomas High School, TX
St. Timothy's School, MD
Saint Ursula Academy, OH
Salem Academy, NC
Salesian High School, CA
Salesianum School, DE
Salpointe Catholic High School, AZ
Santa Catalina School, CA
The Seven Hills School, OH
Shady Side Academy, PA
Shattuck-St. Mary's School, MN
Shawnigan Lake School, BC, Canada
Spartanburg Day School, SC
Stephen T. Badin High School, OH
The Storm King School, NY
Stratford Academy, GA
Strathcona-Tweedsmuir School, AB, Canada
The Summit Country Day School, OH
Telluride Mountain School, CO
Thomas Jefferson School, MO
Tilton School, NH
TMI - The Episcopal School of Texas, TX
Tower Hill School, DE
Trinity High School, KY
Tyler Street Christian Academy, TX
University Liggett School, MI
University of Detroit Jesuit High School and Academy, MI
University School of Milwaukee, WI
Upper Canada College, ON, Canada
The Ursuline Academy of Dallas, TX
Valle Catholic High School, MO
Valley Forge Military Academy & College, PA
Valley Lutheran High School, AZ
The Valley School, MI
Venta Preparatory School, ON, Canada
Vianney High School, MO
Villa Angela-St. Joseph High School, OH
Villa Joseph Marie High School, PA
Villa Maria Academy, PA
Villa Victoria Academy, NJ
Villa Walsh Academy, NJ
Waldorf High School of Massachusetts Bay, MA
The Waldorf School of Garden City, NY
Wasatch Academy, UT
The Webb Schools, CA
Westbury Christian School, TX
West Sound Academy, WA
Westtown School, PA
Wheaton Academy, IL
The Williston Northampton School, MA
Windells Academy, OR
The Woodward School, MA
Wyoming Seminary, PA
Xaverian High School, NY
York Preparatory School, NY

SCHOOLS REPORTING A GUARANTEED TUITION PLAN

The Academy for Gifted Children (PACE), ON, Canada
Baldwin School of Puerto Rico, PR
Bayview Glen School, ON, Canada
Butte Central Catholic High School, MT
Capistrano Valley Christian Schools, CA

The Catholic High School of Baltimore, MD
Chamberlain-Hunt Academy, MS
Christa McAuliffe Academy School of Arts and Sciences, OR
Christian Academy of Knoxville, TN
Community Christian Academy, KY
Crawford Adventist Academy, ON, Canada
Damien High School, CA
Foundation Academy, FL
Gateway School, TX
Grace Brethren School, CA
Hargrave Military Academy, VA
Hawaii Baptist Academy, HI
Hebrew Academy, CA
The Hewitt School, NY
Humanex Academy, CO
Kingsway College, ON, Canada
Manhattan Christian High School, MT
Marion Academy, AL
Middlesex School, MA
Missouri Military Academy, MO
Nebraska Christian Schools, NE
New Covenant Academy, MO
Parish Episcopal School, TX
Pickens Academy, AL
Piedmont Academy, GA
Pope John XXIII Regional High School, NJ
Presbyterian Pan American School, TX
St. George's School of Montreal, QC, Canada
San Marcos Baptist Academy, TX
Scholar's Hall Preparatory School, ON, Canada
Trinity High School, KY
Trinity High School, OH
Turning Winds Academic Institute, ID
The Waterford School, UT
Wesleyan Academy, PR
Westchester Country Day School, NC
Windells Academy, OR

SCHOOLS REPORTING A TUITION INSTALLMENT PLAN

The Academy for Gifted Children (PACE), ON, Canada
Academy of Notre Dame de Namur, PA
Academy of Our Lady of Peace, CA
Academy of the Holy Cross, MD
Academy of the New Church Boys' School, PA
Academy of the New Church Girls' School, PA
Academy of the Sacred Heart, LA
Académie Ste Cécile International School, ON, Canada
The Agnes Irwin School, PA
Alexander Dawson School, CO
Allendale Columbia School, NY
Alliance Academy, Ecuador
Alpha Omega Academy, IA
Alverno High School, CA
American Academy, FL
American Heritage School, FL
American Heritage School, FL
The American School Foundation, Mexico
The American School in El Salvador, FL
Anacapa School, CA
Annie Wright School, WA
Archbishop Curley High School, MD
Archbishop Mitty High School, CA
Army and Navy Academy, CA
Arrowsmith School, ON, Canada
Arroyo Pacific Academy, CA
Arthur Morgan School, NC
ASSETS School, HI
The Athenian School, CA
Augusta Christian School (I), GA
The Awty International School, TX
Bachman Academy, TN
Bakersfield Christian High School, CA
Baldwin School of Puerto Rico, PR
Balmoral Hall School, MB, Canada
The Baltimore Actors' Theatre Conservatory, MD
Baltimore Lutheran School, MD
Barrie School, MD
Battle Ground Academy, TN
Bay Ridge Preparatory School, NY
Bayside Academy, AL
Bayview Glen School, ON, Canada
Bearspaw Christian School, AB, Canada
Beaver Country Day School, MA
The Beekman School, NY
Belen Jesuit Preparatory School, FL
Bellarmine College Preparatory, CA
Benet Academy, IL
Berkeley Preparatory School, FL
Berkshire School, MA
Beth Haven Christian School, KY
The Birch Wathen Lenox School, NY
Bishop Brady High School, NH
Bishop Conaty-Our Lady of Loretto High School, CA
Bishop Denis J. O'Connell High School, VA
Bishop Eustace Preparatory School, NJ
Bishop Fenwick High School, OH
Bishop Guertin High School, NH
Bishop Ireton High School, VA
Bishop John J. Snyder High School, FL
Bishop Kelly High School, ID
Bishop Kenny High School, FL
Bishop Luers High School, IN
Bishop McGuinness Catholic High School, NC
Bishop McGuinness Catholic High School, OK
Bishop Montgomery High School, CA
Bishop O'Dowd High School, CA
Bishop's College School, QC, Canada
The Bishop's School, CA
Bishop Stang High School, MA
Blair Academy, NJ
The Blake School, MN
Blanchet School, OR
Blessed Trinity High School, GA
The Bolles School, FL
Boston Trinity Academy, MA
Boston University Academy, MA
Bradenton Christian School, FL
The Brearley School, NY
Breck School, MN
Brentwood College School, BC, Canada
Briarcrest Christian High School, TN
Briarwood Christian High School, AL
Bridges Academy, CA
Brimmer and May School, MA
Brockwood Park School, United Kingdom
The Brook Hill School, TX
Brooks School, MA
Brookstone School, GA
Brophy College Preparatory, AZ
Brother Rice High School, MI
The Bryn Mawr School for Girls, MD

Buffalo Academy of the Sacred Heart, NY
Bulloch Academy, GA
Burr and Burton Academy, VT
Butte Central Catholic High School, MT
Buxton School, MA
Calvary Christian School, KY
Calvert Hall College High School, MD
Calvin Christian High School, CA
Campbell Hall (Episcopal), CA
Cannon School, NC
The Canterbury Episcopal School, TX
Canterbury School, FL
The Canterbury School of Florida, FL
Canton Academy, MS
Canyonville Christian Academy, OR
Cape Cod Academy, MA
Cape Fear Academy, NC
Cape Henry Collegiate School, VA
Capistrano Valley Christian Schools, CA
Cardigan Mountain School, NH
Cardinal Gibbons High School, NC
Cardinal Mooney Catholic High School, FL
Cardinal Newman High School, FL
Cardinal O'Hara High School, PA
Carlisle School, VA
Carolina Day School, NC
Carondelet High School, CA
Cascades Academy of Central Oregon, OR
Cascadilla School, NY
Castilleja School, CA
Cathedral High School, IN
Cathedral Preparatory School, PA
Catholic Central High School, NY
Catholic Central High School, WI
The Catholic High School of Baltimore, MD
The Catlin Gabel School, OR
Central Alberta Christian High School, AB, Canada
Central Catholic High School, CA
Central Catholic High School, MA
Central Catholic High School, TX
Chadwick School, CA
Chamberlain-Hunt Academy, MS
Chaminade College Preparatory, CA
Chaminade College Preparatory School, MO
C,harlotte Country Day School, NC
Charlotte Latin School, NC
Chase Collegiate School, CT
Chattanooga Christian School, TN
Cheverus High School, ME
The Chicago Academy for the Arts, IL
Chicago Waldorf School, IL
Children's Creative and Performing Arts Academy of San Diego, CA
Chinese Christian Schools, CA
Choate Rosemary Hall, CT
Christa McAuliffe Academy School of Arts and Sciences, OR
Christ Church Episcopal School, SC
Christchurch School, VA
Christian Academy of Knoxville, TN
Christian Brothers Academy, NJ
Christian Brothers Academy, NY
Christian Central Academy, NY
Christopher Columbus High School, FL
Christopher Dock Mennonite High School, PA
Chrysalis School, WA
The Church Farm School, PA
Cincinnati Country Day School, OH
Cistercian Preparatory School, TX
Clarksville Academy, TN
Colegio Bolivar, Colombia
Colegio San Jose, PR
Cole Valley Christian High School, ID
The Collegiate School, VA
The Colorado Springs School, CO
Columbia Academy, TN
Columbia International School, Japan
Columbus School for Girls, OH
Commonwealth Parkville School, PR
Community Christian Academy, KY
The Community School of Naples, FL
The Concept School, PA
Concord Academy, MA
Concordia Lutheran High School, IN
Concordia Preparatory School, UT
Contra Costa Christian High School, CA
Convent of the Sacred Heart, CT
Convent of the Sacred Heart, NY
Cotter Schools, MN
Country Day School of the Sacred Heart, PA
Crawford Adventist Academy, ON, Canada
Crespi Carmelite High School, CA
Crosspoint Academy, WA
Crossroads School for Arts & Sciences, CA
Crystal Springs Uplands School, CA
Currey Ingram Academy, TN
Cushing Academy, MA
Dallas Christian School, TX
Damien High School, CA
Dana Hall School, MA
Darlington School, GA
Darrow School, NY
Davidson Academy, TN
Deerfield Academy, MA
De La Salle High School, CA
De La Salle North Catholic High School, OR
Delbarton School, NJ
DeMatha Catholic High School, MD
Denver Academy, CO
Denver Christian High School, CO
The Derryfield School, NH
Devon Preparatory School, PA
Dexter School, MA
Doane Stuart School, NY
Dominican Academy, NY
Donelson Christian Academy, TN
Donna Klein Jewish Academy, FL
Dowling Catholic High School, IA
Dublin Christian Academy, NH
Dublin School, NH
DuBois Central Catholic High School/Middle School, PA
Duchesne Academy of the Sacred Heart, TX
Durham Academy, NC
Eaglebrook School, MA
Eagle Hill School, CT
Eagle Hill School, MA
Eastern Mennonite High School, VA
Edgewood Academy, AL
Edmund Burke School, DC
Eldorado Emerson Private School, CA
Elgin Academy, IL
Elizabeth Seton High School, MD
Elyria Catholic High School, OH
Emma Willard School, NY
Episcopal Collegiate School, AR

Episcopal High School, TX
Episcopal High School, VA
Episcopal High School of Jacksonville, FL
Escola Americana de Campinas, Brazil
The Ethel Walker School, CT
Explorations Academy, WA
Ezell-Harding Christian School, TN
Fairfield College Preparatory School, CT
Faith Christian High School, CA
Faith Lutheran High School, NV
Father Lopez High School, FL
Father Ryan High School, TN
Fayetteville Academy, NC
Fay School, MA
The Fessenden School, MA
The First Academy, FL
First Baptist Academy, TX
First Presbyterian Day School, GA
Flint Hill School, VA
Flintridge Preparatory School, CA
Flint River Academy, GA
Fontbonne Hall Academy, NY
Foothills Academy, AB, Canada
Fordham Preparatory School, NY
Forest Lake Academy, FL
Forsyth Country Day School, NC
Fort Worth Christian School, TX
Fort Worth Country Day School, TX
Foundation Academy, FL
Fountain Valley School of Colorado, CO
Foxcroft School, VA
Fox Valley Lutheran High School, WI
Frederica Academy, GA
Freeman Academy, SD
French-American School of New York, NY
Fresno Christian Schools, CA
Friends Academy, NY
Friends' Central School, PA
Front Range Christian High School, CO
The Frostig School, CA
Fryeburg Academy, ME
Gabriel Richard Catholic High School, MI
The Galloway School, GA
Gann Academy (The New Jewish High School of Greater Boston), MA
Garrison Forest School, MD
Gaston Day School, NC
George Stevens Academy, ME
Georgetown Day School, DC
Georgetown Preparatory School, MD
Georgetown Visitation Preparatory School, DC
George Walton Academy, GA
Germantown Friends School, PA
Gilman School, MD
Gilmour Academy, OH
Girls Preparatory School, TN
Glades Day School, FL
Glenelg Country School, MD
Gonzaga College High School, DC
Gould Academy, ME
The Governor French Academy, IL
Grace Baptist Academy, TN
Grace Brethren School, CA
Grace Christian School, AK
The Grauer School, CA
Great Lakes Christian High School, ON, Canada
Greenhills School, MI
The Greenwood School, VT
Grier School, PA
The Gunston School, MD
Hargrave Military Academy, VA
The Harley School, NY
Harrells Christian Academy, NC
The Harrisburg Academy, PA
Harvard-Westlake School, CA
The Harvey School, NY
Hawaii Baptist Academy, HI
Hawken School, OH
Hawthorne Christian Academy, NJ
Head-Royce School, CA
Hebrew Academy, CA
Hebrew Academy of the Five Towns & Rockaway, NY
Heritage Christian Academy, AB, Canada
Heritage Christian School, CA
Heritage Christian School, ON, Canada
The Heritage School, GA
The Hewitt School, NY
Highland Hall Waldorf School, CA
The Hill School, PA
The Hill Top Preparatory School, PA
Ho'Ala School, HI
Holland Hall, OK
Holy Angels Academy, NY
Holy Cross High School, CT
Holy Cross School, LA
Holy Ghost Preparatory School, PA
Holyoke Catholic High School, MA
Holy Savior Menard Catholic High School, LA
Holy Trinity Diocesan High School, NY
Hopkins School, CT
Houghton Academy, NY
Houston Learning Academy-North Houston, TX
The Howard School, GA
The Hudson School, NJ
Humanex Academy, CO
Huntington-Surrey School, TX
Hyde Park Baptist School, TX
Hyman Brand Hebrew Academy of Greater Kansas City, KS
Idyllwild Arts Academy, CA
Immaculata High School, NJ
Immaculate Conception School, IL
Immaculate Heart High School and Middle School, CA
Independent School, KS
Institute of Notre Dame, MD
Interlochen Arts Academy, MI
Intermountain Christian School, UT
International High School, CA
International School Bangkok, Thailand
International School of Amsterdam, Netherlands
Iona Preparatory School, NY
Jack M. Barrack Hebrew Academy, PA
Jackson Preparatory School, MS
Jesuit High School of Tampa, FL
John Burroughs School, MO
John Hancock Academy, GA
Josephinum Academy, IL
The Journeys School of Teton Science School, WY
Junipero Serra High School, CA
Kalamazoo Christian High School, MI
Kent Denver School, CO
Kent School, CT
Kents Hill School, ME
Kentucky Country Day School, KY
Keswick Christian School, FL

The Kew-Forest School, NY
Kimball Union Academy, NH
King Low Heywood Thomas, CT
The King's Academy, TN
Kings Christian School, CA
Kingsway College, ON, Canada
Kingswood-Oxford School, CT
The Lab School of Washington, DC
La Cheim School, CA
La Jolla Country Day School, CA
Lakefield College School, ON, Canada
Lakehill Preparatory School, TX
Lancaster Country Day School, PA
Lancaster Mennonite High School, PA
Landmark Christian Academy, KY
Landmark Christian School, GA
Landon School, MD
Lansdale Catholic High School, PA
La Salle High School, CA
The Latin School of Chicago, IL
The Laureate Academy, MB, Canada
Laurel Springs School, CA
Lauralton Hall, CT
Lawrence School, OH
The Lawrenceville School, NJ
Lee Academy, ME
Lehigh Valley Christian High School, PA
Lehman High School, OH
Lexington Catholic High School, KY
Lincoln School, RI
Linden Christian School, MB, Canada
Linfield Christian School, CA
The Linsly School, WV
Lodi Academy, CA
Long Island Lutheran Middle and High School, NY
Loretto Academy, TX
Los Angeles Lutheran High School, CA
Louisville Collegiate School, KY
Louisville High School, CA
The Lovett School, GA
Loyola-Blakefield, MD
Loyola School, NY
Lutheran High School North, MO
Lutheran High School Northwest, MI
Lutheran High School of Hawaii, HI
Lutheran High School of Indianapolis, IN
Lutheran High School of San Diego, CA
Luther College High School, SK, Canada
Luther North College Prep, IL
Lycee International de Los Angeles, CA
Lyndon Institute, VT
Madison Academy, AL
Maharishi School of the Age of Enlightenment, IA
Maine Central Institute, ME
Malvern Preparatory School, PA
Manhattan Christian High School, MT
Maplebrook School, NY
Maranatha High School, CA
Marian Central Catholic High School, IL
Marian High School, IN
Marine Military Academy, TX
Marist School, GA
Marmion Academy, IL
Mars Hill Bible School, AL
Martin Luther High School, NY
The Marvelwood School, CT
Marylawn of the Oranges, NJ
The Mary Louis Academy, NY
Marymount High School, CA
Matignon High School, MA
Maui Preparatory Academy, HI
Maur Hill-Mount Academy, KS
McDonogh School, MD
McGill-Toolen Catholic High School, AL
Meadowridge School, BC, Canada
The Meadows School, NV
Memorial Hall School, TX
Menaul School, NM
Mennonite Collegiate Institute, MB, Canada
Mercy High School College Preparatory, CA
Mesa Grande Seventh-Day Academy, CA
Middlesex School, MA
Middle Tennessee Christian School, TN
Midland School, CA
Mid-Pacific Institute, HI
Miller School of Albemarle, VA
Mill Springs Academy, GA
Milton Academy, MA
Miss Edgar's and Miss Cramp's School, QC, Canada
Missouri Military Academy, MO
Miss Porter's School, CT
MMI Preparatory School, PA
Modesto Christian School, CA
Monsignor Donovan High School, NJ
Montclair Kimberley Academy, NJ
Montgomery Bell Academy, TN
Moorestown Friends School, NJ
Moravian Academy, PA
Moreau Catholic High School, CA
Morristown-Beard School, NJ
Mother McAuley High School, IL
Mount Carmel School, MP
Mt. De Sales Academy, GA
Mount Mercy Academy, NY
Mount Michael Benedictine School, NE
Mount Saint Charles Academy, RI
Mt. Saint Dominic Academy, NJ
Mount Saint Joseph Academy, PA
MPS Etobicoke, ON, Canada
Munich International School, Germany
Nazareth Academy, IL
Nebraska Christian Schools, NE
Nerinx Hall, MO
Newark Academy, NJ
New Covenant Academy, MO
Niagara Christian Community of Schools, ON, Canada
Noble Academy, NC
Noble and Greenough School, MA
The Nora School, MD
Norfolk Academy, VA
North Central Texas Academy, TX
North Shore Country Day School, IL
North Toronto Christian School, ON, Canada
Northwest Academy, OR
Northwest Catholic High School, CT
The Northwest School, WA
Northwood School, NY
North Yarmouth Academy, ME
Notre Dame Academy, CA
Notre Dame College Prep, IL
Notre Dame High School, CA
Notre Dame High School, NJ
Notre Dame High School, TN
Notre Dame Junior/Senior High School, PA

Oak Grove School, CA
The Oakland School, PA
Oakland School, VA
The Oakridge School, TX
Oakwood Friends School, NY
Ojai Valley School, CA
Oldenburg Academy, IN
The O'Neal School, NC
Oneida Baptist Institute, KY
Oregon Episcopal School, OR
Orinda Academy, CA
Our Lady of Mercy Academy, NJ
The Overlake School, WA
The Oxford Academy, CT
Pacific Academy, CA
Pacific Crest Community School, OR
Padua Franciscan High School, OH
Palma School, CA
Palmer Trinity School, FL
Palo Alto Preparatory School, CA
Paradise Adventist Academy, CA
Parish Episcopal School, TX
The Park School of Baltimore, MD
The Park School of Buffalo, NY
Parkview Adventist Academy, AB, Canada
The Pathway School, PA
Patten Academy of Christian Education, CA
Peddie School, NJ
The Pennington School, NJ
Pensacola Catholic High School, FL
Peoples Christian Academy, ON, Canada
Philadelphia-Montgomery Christian Academy, PA
Phillips Academy (Andover), MA
Phoenix Christian Unified Schools, AZ
Phoenix Country Day School, AZ
Pickens Academy, AL
Pickering College, ON, Canada
Piedmont Academy, GA
Pinecrest Academy, GA
Pine Crest School, FL
Pinehurst School, ON, Canada
Pinewood - The International School of Thessaloniki, Greece, Greece
The Pingree School, MA
The Pingry School, NJ
Pioneer Valley Christian School, MA
Pope John XXIII Regional High School, NJ
Porter-Gaud School, SC
Portsmouth Abbey School, RI
Portsmouth Christian Academy, NH
Powers Catholic High School, MI
Presbyterian Pan American School, TX
Prestonwood Christian Academy, TX
Proctor Academy, NH
Professional Children's School, NY
The Prout School, RI
Providence Country Day School, RI
Providence High School, CA
Punahou School, HI
Queen Margaret's School, BC, Canada
Quinte Christian High School, ON, Canada
Ramona Convent Secondary School, CA
Randolph-Macon Academy, VA
Randolph School, AL
Ranney School, NJ
Ransom Everglades School, FL
Ravenscroft School, NC
Realms of Inquiry, UT
The Rectory School, CT
Redwood Christian Schools, CA
Rejoice Christian Schools, OK
Ridley College, ON, Canada
Riverdale Country School, NY
River Oaks Baptist School, TX
Riverside Military Academy, GA
The Rivers School, MA
Rockway Mennonite Collegiate, ON, Canada
Roland Park Country School, MD
Rolling Hills Preparatory School, CA
Ross School, NY
Rothesay Netherwood School, NB, Canada
Rowland Hall, UT
The Roxbury Latin School, MA
Roycemore School, IL
Rumsey Hall School, CT
Rundle College, AB, Canada
Rye Country Day School, NY
Sacramento Adventist Academy, CA
Sacramento Country Day School, CA
Sacred Heart/Griffin High School, IL
Sacred Heart School of Halifax, NS, Canada
Saddleback Valley Christian School, CA
Saddlebrook Preparatory School, FL
Sage Hill School, CA
Sage Ridge School, NV
St. Agnes Academy, TX
St. Albans School, DC
Saint Albert Junior-Senior High School, IA
St. Andrew's College, ON, Canada
St. Andrew's Episcopal School, MD
St. Andrew's School, RI
St. Andrew's–Sewanee School, TN
St. Anne's–Belfield School, VA
St. Anthony Catholic High School, TX
Saint Anthony High School, CA
Saint Anthony High School, IL
St. Anthony's Junior-Senior High School, HI
St. Augustine High School, CA
Saint Augustine Preparatory School, NJ
St. Benedict at Auburndale, TN
St. Bernard High School, CT
St. Bernard's Catholic School, CA
St. Brendan High School, FL
St. Catherine's Academy, CA
St. Croix Country Day School, VI
St. Croix Schools, MN
Saint Dominic Academy, ME
St. Francis de Sales High School, OH
Saint Francis High School, CA
St. Francis High School, KY
St. George's Independent School, TN
St. George's School, RI
St. George's School, BC, Canada
St. George's School of Montreal, QC, Canada
St. Gregory College Preparatory School, AZ
Saint Joan Antida High School, WI
St. John's Preparatory School, MA
Saint John's Preparatory School, MN
St. John's-Ravenscourt School, MB, Canada
Saint Joseph Academy High School, OH
St. Joseph High School, CT
Saint Joseph High School, IL
Saint Joseph High School, NJ
St. Joseph's Academy, LA

St. Joseph's Catholic School, SC
St. Joseph's Preparatory School, PA
St. Jude's School, ON, Canada
Saint Lawrence Academy, CA
St. Lawrence Seminary High School, WI
Saint Lucy's Priory High School, CA
St. Mark's School of Texas, TX
St. Martin's Episcopal School, LA
St. Mary's Episcopal School, TN
Saint Mary's Hall, TX
Saint Mary's High School, AZ
Saint Mary's High School, MD
St. Mary's Preparatory School, MI
Saint Mary's School, NC
St. Mary's School, OR
St. Michael's College School, ON, Canada
St. Michael's Preparatory School of the Norbertine Fathers, CA
Saint Patrick High School, IL
Saint Patrick - Saint Vincent High School, CA
St. Patrick's Regional Secondary, BC, Canada
St. Paul Academy and Summit School, MN
St. Paul's Episcopal School, AL
St. Paul's High School, MB, Canada
St. Pius X Catholic High School, GA
St. Pius X High School, TX
St. Stanislaus College, MS
St. Stephen's & St. Agnes School, VA
Saint Stephen's Episcopal School, FL
St. Stephen's Episcopal School, TX
St. Stephen's School, Rome, Italy
Saint Teresa's Academy, MO
Saint Thomas Academy, MN
St. Thomas Aquinas High School, FL
Saint Thomas Aquinas High School, KS
St. Thomas Aquinas High School, NH
St. Thomas High School, TX
St. Timothy's School, MD
Saint Ursula Academy, OH
Saint Viator High School, IL
Salem Academy, NC
Salem Academy, OR
Salesian High School, CA
Salesianum School, DE
Salpointe Catholic High School, AZ
Sandia Preparatory School, NM
San Domenico School, CA
Sandy Spring Friends School, MD
San Marcos Baptist Academy, TX
Santa Catalina School, CA
Santa Fe Preparatory School, NM
SBEC (Southern Baptist Educational Center), MS
Scholar's Hall Preparatory School, ON, Canada
Scottsdale Christian Academy, AZ
Scotus Central Catholic High School, NE
Seabury Hall, HI
Seattle Academy of Arts and Sciences, WA
Seisen International School, Japan
The Seven Hills School, OH
Severn School, MD
Shady Side Academy, PA
Shattuck-St. Mary's School, MN
Shawnigan Lake School, BC, Canada
Shelton School and Evaluation Center, TX
The Shipley School, PA
Shoore Centre for Learning, ON, Canada
Shoreline Christian, WA
Signet Christian School, ON, Canada
Smith School, NY
Sonoma Academy, CA
Southfield Christian High School, MI
Southfield School, MA
Southwest Christian School, Inc., TX
Southwestern Academy, AZ
Southwestern Academy, CA
Spartanburg Day School, SC
The Spence School, NY
Stephen T. Badin High School, OH
Stevenson School, CA
The Storm King School, NY
Stratford Academy, GA
Strathcona-Tweedsmuir School, AB, Canada
Stratton Mountain School, VT
Stuart Hall, VA
Summerfield Waldorf School, CA
The Summit Country Day School, OH
Sunshine Bible Academy, SD
The Taft School, CT
Taipei American School, Taiwan
Tandem Friends School, VA
TASIS The American School in England, United Kingdom
TASIS, The American School in Switzerland, Switzerland
Telluride Mountain School, CO
Temple Grandin School, CO
The Thacher School, CA
THINK Global School, CA
Thomas Jefferson School, MO
Tidewater Academy, VA
Tilton School, NH
Timothy Christian High School, IL
TMI - The Episcopal School of Texas, TX
Tower Hill School, DE
Tri-City Christian Academy, AZ
Tri-City Christian Schools, CA
Trinity Christian Academy, TN
Trinity College School, ON, Canada
Trinity High School, KY
Trinity High School, NH
Trinity High School, OH
Trinity-Pawling School, NY
Trinity Preparatory School, FL
Turning Winds Academic Institute, ID
Tyler Street Christian Academy, TX
University Liggett School, MI
University of Chicago Laboratory Schools, IL
University of Detroit Jesuit High School and Academy, MI
University Prep, WA
University School of Jackson, TN
University School of Milwaukee, WI
University School of Nova Southeastern University, FL
Upper Canada College, ON, Canada
The Ursuline Academy of Dallas, TX
Valle Catholic High School, MO
Valley Christian High School, CA
Valley Forge Military Academy & College, PA
Valley Lutheran High School, AZ
The Valley School, MI
Valley View School, MA
Venta Preparatory School, ON, Canada
Vianney High School, MO
Vicksburg Catholic School, MS
Villa Angela-St. Joseph High School, OH
Villa Duchesne and Oak Hill School, MO
Villa Joseph Marie High School, PA
Villa Maria Academy, PA

Villa Victoria Academy, NJ
Villa Walsh Academy, NJ
Wakefield School, VA
Waldorf High School of Massachusetts Bay, MA
The Waldorf School of Garden City, NY
The Waldorf School of Saratoga Springs, NY
Walnut Hill School for the Arts, MA
Walsingham Academy, VA
Wasatch Academy, UT
Washington International School, DC
The Waterford School, UT
Watkinson School, CT
Waynflete School, ME
Webb School of Knoxville, TN
The Webb Schools, CA
Wellsprings Friends School, OR
Wesleyan Academy, PR
Westbury Christian School, TX
West Catholic High School, MI
Westchester Country Day School, NC
West Island College, AB, Canada
Westminster Christian Academy, LA
Westminster School, CT
Westover School, CT
Westridge School, CA
West Sound Academy, WA
Westtown School, PA
Wheaton Academy, IL
The Wheeler School, RI
Whitefield Academy, GA
Whitefield Academy, KY
The Williams School, CT
The Williston Northampton School, MA
The Willows Academy, IL
Wilmington Christian School, DE
Wilson Hall, SC
Windells Academy, OR
The Windsor School, NY
Windward School, CA
Winston Preparatory School, NY
The Winston School San Antonio, TX
The Woodhall School, CT
Woodlynde School, PA
The Woodward School, MA
Worcester Preparatory School, MD
Wyoming Seminary, PA
Xaverian High School, NY
York Catholic High School, PA
York Preparatory School, NY
York School, CA
Zurich International School, Switzerland

SCHOOLS REPORTING THAT THEY OFFER LOANS

School	Loans
Academy of the New Church Girls' School, PA	M,N
Alexander Dawson School, CO	N
Bishop's College School, QC, Canada	N
Blair Academy, NJ	N
The Blake School, MN	N
The Brearley School, NY	N
Brookstone School, GA	M,N
The Bryn Mawr School for Girls, MD	M,N
Calvin Christian High School, CA	N
Cardigan Mountain School, NH	N
Choate Rosemary Hall, CT	N
Concord Academy, MA	N
Copper Canyon Academy, AZ	M
Dana Hall School, MA	N
Episcopal High School, TX	M
Explorations Academy, WA	N
Falmouth Academy, MA	N
Georgetown Preparatory School, MD	M
Gilman School, MD	N
Gilmour Academy, OH	N
Gould Academy, ME	N
Great Lakes Christian High School, ON, Canada	M,N
Grier School, PA	N
Hargrave Military Academy, VA	N
The Harker School, CA	N
Hawken School, OH	N
John Burroughs School, MO	N
Kent School, CT	N
The Latin School of Chicago, IL	M,N
Maplebrook School, NY	M,N
Marian High School, IN	N
Maur Hill-Mount Academy, KS	N
McDonogh School, MD	M,N
The Meadows School, NV	N
Mennonite Collegiate Institute, MB, Canada	M
Mesa Grande Seventh-Day Academy, CA	M,N
Middlesex School, MA	N
Missouri Military Academy, MO	N
Moorestown Friends School, NJ	N
Mount Michael Benedictine School, NE	N
Noble and Greenough School, MA	N
North Shore Country Day School, IL	M,N
Ojai Valley School, CA	N
Peddie School, NJ	N
Phillips Academy (Andover), MA	M
The Pingree School, MA	N
Randolph School, AL	M
Ravenscroft School, NC	N
Ridley College, ON, Canada	N
St. Albans School, DC	N
St. Andrew's School, RI	N
St. George's School, RI	M,N
Saint Joseph Academy High School, OH	N
St. Joseph's Preparatory School, PA	M,N
St. Paul's High School, MB, Canada	N
St. Stanislaus College, MS	N
St. Thomas High School, TX	M
St. Timothy's School, MD	N
Stratton Mountain School, VT	N
The Taft School, CT	N
Tilton School, NH	N
Trinity High School, OH	M
Trinity-Pawling School, NY	N
Wasatch Academy, UT	N
Westover School, CT	M,N
Windward School, CA	N
Wyoming Seminary, PA	N
Xaverian High School, NY	N

TOTAL AMOUNT OF UPPER SCHOOL FINANCIAL AID AWARDED FOR 2012–13

Academy of Notre Dame de Namur, PA	$449,500
Academy of Our Lady of Peace, CA	$2,400,000
Academy of the New Church Boys' School, PA	$750,000
Academy of the New Church Girls' School, PA	$750,000
Academy of the Sacred Heart, LA	$264,600

M — middle-income loans; N — need-based loans

Académie Ste Cécile International School, ON, Canada CAN$15,000
The Agnes Irwin School, PA $1,389,400
Alexander Dawson School, CO $1,300,000
Allendale Columbia School, NY $840,990
Alliance Academy, Ecuador $800,000
Alverno High School, CA $253,313
American Heritage School, FL $1,602,000
American Heritage School, FL $3,800,000
The American School Foundation, Mexico 7,534,193 Mexican pesos
Annie Wright School, WA $915,093
Archbishop Mitty High School, CA $3,000,000
Army and Navy Academy, CA $575,000
Arthur Morgan School, NC $93,000
ASSETS School, HI $170,000
The Athenian School, CA $2,002,000
The Awty International School, TX $407,857
Bachman Academy, TN $110,242
Bakersfield Christian High School, CA $170,000
Baldwin School of Puerto Rico, PR $54,420
Balmoral Hall School, MB, Canada CAN$253,096
The Baltimore Actors' Theatre Conservatory, MD $12,000
Baltimore Lutheran School, MD $70,000
Barrie School, MD $539,950
Battle Ground Academy, TN $1,180,000
Bearspaw Christian School, AB, Canada CAN$125,245
Beaver Country Day School, MA $3,335,098
Belen Jesuit Preparatory School, FL $400,000
Bellarmine College Preparatory, CA $3,700,000
Berkshire School, MA $4,955,292
Beth Haven Christian School, KY $8000
The Birch Wathen Lenox School, NY $1,200,000
Bishop Conaty-Our Lady of Loretto High School, CA $593,619
Bishop Denis J. O'Connell High School, VA $1,500,000
Bishop Eustace Preparatory School, NJ $800,000
Bishop Ireton High School, VA $580,000
Bishop John J. Snyder High School, FL $250,000
Bishop Kelly High School, ID $997,049
Bishop McGuinness Catholic High School, NC $288,550
Bishop McGuinness Catholic High School, OK $206,050
Bishop Montgomery High School, CA $30,000
Bishop O'Dowd High School, CA $2,300,000
The Bishop's School, CA $2,900,000
Bishop Stang High School, MA $500,000
Blair Academy, NJ $5,100,000
The Blake School, MN $1,912,893
Blanchet School, OR $240,000
The Bolles School, FL $3,000,000
Boston Trinity Academy, MA $1,223,000
Boston University Academy, MA $1,175,095
The Brearley School, NY $4,245,080
Briarwood Christian High School, AL $5000
Brimmer and May School, MA $1,474,565
The Brook Hill School, TX $400,000
Brooks School, MA $2,600,000
Brookstone School, GA $812,545
Brophy College Preparatory, AZ $2,098,895
Brother Rice High School, MI $900,000
The Bryn Mawr School for Girls, MD $1,300,000
Buffalo Academy of the Sacred Heart, NY $275,000
Bulloch Academy, GA $50,000
Butte Central Catholic High School, MT $68,000
Buxton School, MA $1,300,000
Calvary Christian School, KY $23,000
Calvert Hall College High School, MD $2,582,782
Calvin Christian High School, CA $228,000
Cannon School, NC $310,000
Canterbury School, FL $782,050
The Canterbury School of Florida, FL $588,000
Canton Academy, MS $64,000
Canyonville Christian Academy, OR $390,000
Cape Cod Academy, MA $1,600,000
Cape Fear Academy, NC $320,000
Capistrano Valley Christian Schools, CA $250,000
Cardigan Mountain School, NH $1,000,000
Cardinal Mooney Catholic High School, FL $200,000
Carlisle School, VA $250,000
Carolina Day School, NC $553,447
Carondelet High School, CA $1,300,000
Cascadilla School, NY $60,000
Castilleja School, CA $2,200,000
Cathedral High School, IN $2,300,000
Cathedral Preparatory School, PA $550,000
Catholic Central High School, NY $15,000
Catholic Central High School, WI $130,000
The Catholic High School of Baltimore, MD $523,116
The Catlin Gabel School, OR $2,900,000
Central Catholic High School, CA $392,671
Central Catholic High School, TX $717,000
Chadwick School, CA $1,750,500
Chamberlain-Hunt Academy, MS $250,000
Chaminade College Preparatory, CA $2,383,381
Chaminade College Preparatory School, MO $1,600,000
Charlotte Country Day School, NC $1,353,765
Charlotte Latin School, NC $827,525
Chase Collegiate School, CT $2,500,000
Chattanooga Christian School, TN $400,941
Cheverus High School, ME $1,919,108
Chicago Waldorf School, IL $361,783
Children's Creative and Performing Arts Academy of San Diego, CA $25,000
Chinese Christian Schools, CA $120,000
Choate Rosemary Hall, CT $10,000,000
Christ Church Episcopal School, SC $482,208
Christchurch School, VA $1,957,070
Christian Brothers Academy, NJ $994,100
Christian Central Academy, NY $51,527
Christopher Dock Mennonite High School, PA $533,185
The Church Farm School, PA $3,881,717
Cincinnati Country Day School, OH $1,400,000
Cistercian Preparatory School, TX $599,400
Colegio San Jose, PR $230,000
The Colorado Springs School, CO $224,825
Columbia Academy, TN $36,750
Columbia International School, Japan ¥3,360,000
Columbus School for Girls, OH $757,230
Commonwealth Parkville School, PR $82,318
Community Christian Academy, KY $9000
The Community School of Naples, FL $1,042,686
Concord Academy, MA $3,468,400
Concordia Preparatory School, UT $33,700
Convent of the Sacred Heart, CT $1,679,200
Convent of the Sacred Heart, NY $1,800,000
Copper Canyon Academy, AZ $81,600
Country Day School of the Sacred Heart, PA $424,500
Crawford Adventist Academy, ON, Canada CAN$35,000
Crosspoint Academy, WA $171,000
Crossroads School for Arts & Sciences, CA $3,114,960
Crystal Springs Uplands School, CA $2,200,000
Currey Ingram Academy, TN $1,500,000
Dallas Christian School, TX $180,000
Damien High School, CA $600,000
Dana Hall School, MA $3,395,219

Darlington School, GA	$3,405,880
Darrow School, NY	$950,000
Deerfield Academy, MA	$7,300,000
Delbarton School, NJ	$1,600,000
DeMatha Catholic High School, MD	$1,279,120
Denver Christian High School, CO	$40,000
The Derryfield School, NH	$1,527,520
Devon Preparatory School, PA	$1,030,000
Dexter School, MA	$3,000,000
Doane Stuart School, NY	$844,207
Donelson Christian Academy, TN	$125,757
Dowling Catholic High School, IA	$1,000,000
Dublin Christian Academy, NH	$45,000
Dublin School, NH	$1,200,000
DuBois Central Catholic High School/ Middle School, PA	$448,000
Duchesne Academy of the Sacred Heart, TX	$641,530
Durham Academy, NC	$916,540
Eaglebrook School, MA	$1,650,000
Eagle Hill School, MA	$125,000
Eastern Mennonite High School, VA	$129,736
Edmund Burke School, DC	$978,185
Eldorado Emerson Private School, CA	$50,000
Elizabeth Seton High School, MD	$500,000
Elyria Catholic High School, OH	$200,000
Emma Willard School, NY	$4,408,666
Episcopal Collegiate School, AR	$440,000
Episcopal High School, TX	$1,700,000
Episcopal High School, VA	$4,400,000
Episcopal High School of Jacksonville, FL	$2,000,000
Escola Americana de Campinas, Brazil	$51,000
The Ethel Walker School, CT	$3,058,789
Explorations Academy, WA	$140,000
Fairfield College Preparatory School, CT	$2,100,000
Fairhill School, TX	$50,000
Faith Christian High School, CA	$50,000
Faith Lutheran High School, NV	$461,000
Falmouth Academy, MA	$750,000
Father Lopez High School, FL	$1,275,284
Father Ryan High School, TN	$550,000
Fayetteville Academy, NC	$514,750
Fay School, MA	$1,110,900
First Presbyterian Day School, GA	$874,000
Flint Hill School, VA	$2,027,705
Fontbonne Hall Academy, NY	$121,500
Foothills Academy, AB, Canada	CAN$500,000
Fordham Preparatory School, NY	$2,200,000
Forest Lake Academy, FL	$347,000
Forsyth Country Day School, NC	$846,329
Fort Worth Christian School, TX	$111,000
Fort Worth Country Day School, TX	$980,225
Foundation Academy, FL	$300,000
Fountain Valley School of Colorado, CO	$2,180,000
Foxcroft School, VA	$1,200,000
Fox Valley Lutheran High School, WI	$325,000
Frederica Academy, GA	$500,000
Freeman Academy, SD	$38,000
French-American School of New York, NY	$138,499
Fresno Christian Schools, CA	$148,074
Friends Academy, NY	$1,664,000
Friends' Central School, PA	$3,515,676
Front Range Christian High School, CO	$118,822
The Frostig School, CA	$50,000
Fryeburg Academy, ME	$1,800,000
The Galloway School, GA	$1,134,000
Garrison Forest School, MD	$3,000,000
Gaston Day School, NC	$256,070
Georgetown Day School, DC	$1,000,000
Georgetown Preparatory School, MD	$2,000,000
Georgetown Visitation Preparatory School, DC	$1,700,000
Germantown Friends School, PA	$1,992,162
Gilman School, MD	$1,839,100
Gilmour Academy, OH	$3,500,000
Girls Preparatory School, TN	$1,388,888
Glenelg Country School, MD	$1,850,000
Gonzaga College High School, DC	$2,210,000
Gould Academy, ME	$1,355,000
Grace Christian School, AK	$200,000
The Grauer School, CA	$70,000
Great Lakes Christian High School, ON, Canada	CAN$150,000
Greenhill School, TX	$1,513,400
Greenhills School, MI	$1,000,000
The Greenwood School, VT	$249,290
Grier School, PA	$1,940,000
The Gunston School, MD	$860,000
Hargrave Military Academy, VA	$525,000
Harrells Christian Academy, NC	$62,500
The Harrisburg Academy, PA	$400,000
Harvard-Westlake School, CA	$8,069,000
The Harvey School, NY	$2,088,000
Hawaii Baptist Academy, HI	$283,240
Hawken School, OH	$5,102,962
Hawthorne Christian Academy, NJ	$74,440
Head-Royce School, CA	$2,062,725
Hebrew Academy, CA	$30,000
Heritage Christian School, CA	$820,000
The Heritage School, GA	$367,651
The Hewitt School, NY	$1,394,709
Highland Hall Waldorf School, CA	$204,600
Ho'Ala School, HI	$10,000
The Hockaday School, TX	$1,851,800
Holland Hall, OK	$928,525
Holy Angels Academy, NY	$400,000
Holy Cross High School, CT	$550,000
Holy Ghost Preparatory School, PA	$1,000,000
Holyoke Catholic High School, MA	$135,350
Holy Savior Menard Catholic High School, LA	$150,000
Hopkins School, CT	$2,900,000
Houghton Academy, NY	$95,000
The Hudson School, NJ	$363,025
Humanex Academy, CO	$5000
Hyde Park Baptist School, TX	$95,700
Hyman Brand Hebrew Academy of Greater Kansas City, KS	$66,850
Idyllwild Arts Academy, CA	$5,054,332
Immaculate Conception School, IL	$150,000
Institute of Notre Dame, MD	$843,000
Interlochen Arts Academy, MI	$8,844,645
Intermountain Christian School, UT	$14,662
International High School, CA	$748,000
Iona Preparatory School, NY	$325,000
Jack M. Barrack Hebrew Academy, PA	$1,483,690
Jackson Preparatory School, MS	$195,000
Jesuit High School of Tampa, FL	$1,213,590
John Burroughs School, MO	$2,034,000
The Journeys School of Teton Science School, WY	$240,150
Junipero Serra High School, CA	$2,100,000
Kent Denver School, CO	$2,000,000
Kent School, CT	$8,200,000
Kents Hill School, ME	$2,200,000
Kentucky Country Day School, KY	$857,180
Keswick Christian School, FL	$25,000
The Kew-Forest School, NY	$983,000
Kimball Union Academy, NH	$3,369,027

King Low Heywood Thomas, CT	$1,152,645
The King's Academy, TN	$89,610
Kings Christian School, CA	$275,000
Kingsway College, ON, Canada	CAN$200,000
Kingswood-Oxford School, CT	$2,300,000
The Lab School of Washington, DC	$150,000
La Jolla Country Day School, CA	$2,475,780
Lakefield College School, ON, Canada	CAN$1,648,600
Lancaster Country Day School, PA	$723,572
Lancaster Mennonite High School, PA	$2,000,000
Landmark Christian School, GA	$235,650
Landon School, MD	$1,436,765
La Salle High School, CA	$1,450,000
The Latin School of Chicago, IL	$1,999,129
The Laureate Academy, MB, Canada	CAN$66,000
Lauralton Hall, CT	$450,000
Lawrence School, OH	$800,000
The Lawrenceville School, NJ	$1,010,000
Lehigh Valley Christian High School, PA	$125,790
Lehman High School, OH	$353,850
Lexington Catholic High School, KY	$447,000
Lincoln School, RI	$2,000,000
Little Keswick School, VA	$20,000
Lodi Academy, CA	$33,000
Long Island Lutheran Middle and High School, NY	$325,000
Loretto Academy, TX	$240,000
Los Angeles Lutheran High School, CA	$100,000
Louisville High School, CA	$640,000
The Lovett School, GA	$1,237,420
Loyola-Blakefield, MD	$2,464,636
Loyola School, NY	$1,194,000
Lutheran High School North, MO	$750,000
Lutheran High School Northwest, MI	$20,000
Lutheran High School of Hawaii, HI	$500,000
Lutheran High School of Indianapolis, IN	$160,000
Lutheran High School of San Diego, CA	$60,000
Luther College High School, SK, Canada	CAN$165,000
Lycee International de Los Angeles, CA	$159,844
Madison Academy, AL	$100,000
Maine Central Institute, ME	$350,000
Malvern Preparatory School, PA	$855,650
Manhattan Christian High School, MT	$35,000
Maplebrook School, NY	$125,000
Marian Central Catholic High School, IL	$296,300
Marian High School, IN	$350,000
Marine Military Academy, TX	$300,000
Marist School, GA	$1,800,000
Marmion Academy, IL	$342,800
Mars Hill Bible School, AL	$150,000
Martin Luther High School, NY	$1,955,670
The Marvelwood School, CT	$950,000
Marylawn of the Oranges, NJ	$111,850
The Mary Louis Academy, NY	$421,200
Marymount High School, CA	$1,205,000
Matignon High School, MA	$300,000
Maui Preparatory Academy, HI	$465,785
Maur Hill-Mount Academy, KS	$291,000
McDonogh School, MD	$2,415,935
McGill-Toolen Catholic High School, AL	$958,000
Menaul School, NM	$307,000
Mennonite Collegiate Institute, MB, Canada	CAN$40,000
Mercy High School College Preparatory, CA	$1,200,000
Mesa Grande Seventh-Day Academy, CA	$35,000
Middlesex School, MA	$4,100,000
Midland School, CA	$1,000,000
Mid-Pacific Institute, HI	$2,900,000
Miller School of Albemarle, VA	$1,200,000
Mill Springs Academy, GA	$77,000
Miss Edgar's and Miss Cramp's School, QC, Canada	CAN$105,000
Missouri Military Academy, MO	$875,000
Miss Porter's School, CT	$3,100,000
MMI Preparatory School, PA	$881,500
Monsignor Donovan High School, NJ	$400,000
Montclair Kimberley Academy, NJ	$1,281,308
Montgomery Bell Academy, TN	$1,750,000
Moorestown Friends School, NJ	$1,717,400
Moravian Academy, PA	$1,124,920
Moreau Catholic High School, CA	$1,500,000
Morristown-Beard School, NJ	$2,000,000
Mother McAuley High School, IL	$1,000,000
Mount Carmel School, MP	$30,000
Mt. De Sales Academy, GA	$813,771
Mount Michael Benedictine School, NE	$556,449
Mount Saint Charles Academy, RI	$700,000
Mt. Saint Dominic Academy, NJ	$192,000
Mount Saint Joseph Academy, PA	$699,113
Munich International School, Germany	€27,250
Nazareth Academy, IL	$300,000
Nebraska Christian Schools, NE	$133,000
Nerinx Hall, MO	$670,640
Newark Academy, NJ	$2,109,625
Niagara Christian Community of Schools, ON, Canada	CAN$400,000
Noble Academy, NC	$52,700
Noble and Greenough School, MA	$3,433,400
The Nora School, MD	$167,000
North Shore Country Day School, IL	$1,000,000
Northwest Catholic High School, CT	$1,300,000
The Northwest School, WA	$1,142,451
North Yarmouth Academy, ME	$904,000
Notre Dame College Prep, IL	$3,600,000
Notre Dame High School, CA	$767,000
Notre Dame High School, NJ	$375,000
Notre Dame High School, TN	$378,271
Oak Grove School, CA	$60,000
The Oakland School, PA	$30,000
The Oakridge School, TX	$523,375
Oakwood Friends School, NY	$808,000
Ojai Valley School, CA	$347,360
Oldenburg Academy, IN	$65,000
The O'Neal School, NC	$471,500
Oregon Episcopal School, OR	$663,000
Orinda Academy, CA	$400,000
Our Lady of Mercy Academy, NJ	$35,000
The Overlake School, WA	$675,904
Pacific Crest Community School, OR	$50,000
Padua Franciscan High School, OH	$373,825
Palma School, CA	$229,000
Palmer Trinity School, FL	$940,300
Paradise Adventist Academy, CA	$50,000
The Park School of Baltimore, MD	$1,279,390
The Park School of Buffalo, NY	$567,832
Patten Academy of Christian Education, CA	$23,797
Peddie School, NJ	$5,000,000
The Pennington School, NJ	$2,500,000
Peoples Christian Academy, ON, Canada	CAN$30,000
Philadelphia-Montgomery Christian Academy, PA	$500,000
Phillips Academy (Andover), MA	$18,157,000
Phoenix Country Day School, AZ	$1,016,600
Pickering College, ON, Canada	CAN$100,000
Piedmont Academy, GA	$25,000
Pine Crest School, FL	$1,888,380
The Pingree School, MA	$2,500,000

The Pingry School, NJ	$199,259
Pioneer Valley Christian School, MA	$80,300
Porter-Gaud School, SC	$467,620
Portsmouth Abbey School, RI	$3,600,000
Portsmouth Christian Academy, NH	$180,000
Powers Catholic High School, MI	$450,300
Presbyterian Pan American School, TX	$1,196,250
Prestonwood Christian Academy, TX	$734,381
Proctor Academy, NH	$3,200,000
Professional Children's School, NY	$805,000
The Prout School, RI	$225,000
Providence Country Day School, RI	$1,500,000
Providence High School, CA	$382,000
Punahou School, HI	$2,386,690
Queen Margaret's School, BC, Canada	CAN$150,000
Ramona Convent Secondary School, CA	$350,000
Randolph-Macon Academy, VA	$436,000
Randolph School, AL	$258,240
Ranney School, NJ	$267,000
Ransom Everglades School, FL	$2,224,990
Realms of Inquiry, UT	$40,000
The Rectory School, CT	$1,398,938
Redwood Christian Schools, CA	$356,524
Ridley College, ON, Canada	CAN$3,000,000
The Rivers School, MA	$3,065,050
Rockway Mennonite Collegiate, ON, Canada	CAN$170,000
Roland Park Country School, MD	$1,208,315
Rolling Hills Preparatory School, CA	$560,000
Rowland Hall, UT	$591,190
The Roxbury Latin School, MA	$1,805,675
Royal Canadian College, BC, Canada	CAN$18,000
Roycemore School, IL	$699,821
Rumsey Hall School, CT	$819,000
Rundle College, AB, Canada	CAN$90,000
Sacramento Adventist Academy, CA	$10,000
Sacramento Country Day School, CA	$501,860
Sacred Heart/Griffin High School, IL	$443,093
Sacred Heart School of Halifax, NS, Canada	CAN$138,000
Saddleback Valley Christian School, CA	$175,000
Sage Hill School, CA	$1,857,570
Sage Ridge School, NV	$179,225
St. Agnes Academy, TX	$800,000
St. Albans School, DC	$2,482,572
Saint Albert Junior-Senior High School, IA	$380,000
St. Andrew's College, ON, Canada	CAN$1,897,830
St. Andrew's Episcopal School, MD	$2,193,800
St. Andrew's School, RI	$2,125,550
St. Andrew's–Sewanee School, TN	$1,365,590
St. Anne's–Belfield School, VA	$4,500,000
St. Anthony Catholic High School, TX	$175,000
St. Anthony's Junior-Senior High School, HI	$207,000
Saint Augustine Preparatory School, NJ	$1,010,000
St. Benedict at Auburndale, TN	$35,000
St. Bernard High School, CT	$354,257
St. Bernard's Catholic School, CA	$55,000
St. Brendan High School, FL	$266,000
St. Catherine's Academy, CA	$355,000
St. Croix Country Day School, VI	$265,550
St. Croix Schools, MN	$600,000
Saint Elizabeth High School, CA	$980,000
St. Francis de Sales High School, OH	$1,600,000
Saint Francis High School, CA	$500,000
St. Francis High School, KY	$615,000
St. George's Independent School, TN	$389,652
St. George's School, BC, Canada	CAN$800,000
St. Gregory College Preparatory School, AZ	$1,200,000
St. John's Preparatory School, MA	$2,900,000
Saint John's Preparatory School, MN	$700,000
St. John's-Ravenscourt School, MB, Canada	CAN$262,250
Saint Joseph Academy High School, OH	$900,000
St. Joseph High School, CT	$235,000
Saint Joseph High School, IL	$800,000
Saint Joseph High School, NJ	$250,000
St. Joseph's Academy, LA	$375,000
St. Joseph's Catholic School, SC	$446,439
St. Joseph's Preparatory School, PA	$2,000,000
St. Lawrence Seminary High School, WI	$778,110
Saint Lucy's Priory High School, CA	$90,000
St. Mark's School of Texas, TX	$1,064,791
St. Martin's Episcopal School, LA	$761,225
St. Mary's Episcopal School, TN	$318,200
Saint Mary's Hall, TX	$621,990
Saint Mary's High School, AZ	$2,200,000
Saint Mary's High School, MD	$250,000
St. Mary's School, OR	$650,000
St. Michael's College School, ON, Canada	CAN$1,800,000
St. Michael's Preparatory School of the Norbertine Fathers, CA	$350,000
Saint Patrick High School, IL	$1,025,000
Saint Patrick - Saint Vincent High School, CA	$680,000
St. Paul Academy and Summit School, MN	$1,797,260
St. Paul's High School, MB, Canada	CAN$320,000
St. Pius X Catholic High School, GA	$400,000
St. Pius X High School, TX	$711,000
St. Stephen's & St. Agnes School, VA	$2,198,325
Saint Stephen's Episcopal School, FL	$9250
St. Stephen's Episcopal School, TX	$2,800,000
St. Stephen's School, Rome, Italy	405,150
Saint Teresa's Academy, MO	$130,000
Saint Thomas Academy, MN	$2,500,000
St. Thomas High School, TX	$1,300,000
St. Timothy's School, MD	$2,500,000
Saint Ursula Academy, OH	$1,299,000
Saint Viator High School, IL	$1,200,000
Salem Academy, NC	$1,033,794
Salesian High School, CA	$1,400,000
Salesianum School, DE	$650,000
Salpointe Catholic High School, AZ	$1,350,000
Sandia Preparatory School, NM	$950,000
San Domenico School, CA	$1,000,000
San Marcos Baptist Academy, TX	$483,546
Santa Catalina School, CA	$2,094,575
SBEC (Southern Baptist Educational Center), MS	$67,675
Scholar's Hall Preparatory School, ON, Canada	CAN$20,000
Scotus Central Catholic High School, NE	$109,250
Seabury Hall, HI	$956,860
Seisen International School, Japan	¥1,990,000
The Seven Hills School, OH	$530,000
Severn School, MD	$1,115,305
Shady Side Academy, PA	$2,030,930
Shattuck-St. Mary's School, MN	$3,900,000
Shawnigan Lake School, BC, Canada	CAN$800,000
Shelton School and Evaluation Center, TX	$225,950
The Shipley School, PA	$2,453,825
Shoreline Christian, WA	$340,000
Smith School, NY	$30,000
Sonoma Academy, CA	$2,600,000
Soundview Preparatory School, NY	$420,000
Southfield School, MA	$3,000,000
Southwest Christian School, Inc., TX	$455,000
Southwestern Academy, AZ	$445,000
Southwestern Academy, CA	$450,000
The Spence School, NY	$2,014,982
Stephen T. Badin High School, OH	$300,000

Stevenson School, CA	$3,100,000
The Storm King School, NY	$405,575
Strathcona-Tweedsmuir School, AB, Canada	CAN$137,913
Stratton Mountain School, VT	$800,000
Stuart Hall, VA	$850,000
Sunshine Bible Academy, SD	$38,520
The Taft School, CT	$7,045,000
Tandem Friends School, VA	$379,110
Telluride Mountain School, CO	$117,000
Temple Grandin School, CO	$60,000
The Thacher School, CA	$2,181,350
Thomas Jefferson School, MO	$640,000
Tidewater Academy, VA	$125,000
Tilton School, NH	$2,237,570
TMI - The Episcopal School of Texas, TX	$555,500
Tower Hill School, DE	$1,022,687
Tri-City Christian Academy, AZ	$25,000
Tri-City Christian Schools, CA	$50,000
Trinity College School, ON, Canada	CAN$1,000,000
Trinity High School, KY	$2,200,000
Trinity High School, OH	$138,000
Trinity-Pawling School, NY	$3,200,000
Trinity Preparatory School, FL	$1,828,500
Turning Winds Academic Institute, ID	$100,000
Tyler Street Christian Academy, TX	$157,000
University Liggett School, MI	$2,600,000
University of Chicago Laboratory Schools, IL	$1,139,925
University of Detroit Jesuit High School and Academy, MI	$1,610,000
University Prep, WA	$1,392,423
University School of Jackson, TN	$130,000
University School of Milwaukee, WI	$1,000,450
University School of Nova Southeastern University, FL	$1,500,000
The Ursuline Academy of Dallas, TX	$851,300
Valle Catholic High School, MO	$165,000
Valley Christian High School, CA	$1,300,000
Valley Forge Military Academy & College, PA	$2,230,907
Valley Lutheran High School, AZ	$166,770
The Valley School, MI	$51,376
Vianney High School, MO	$316,127
Vicksburg Catholic School, MS	$75,000
Villa Duchesne and Oak Hill School, MO	$1,148,249
Villa Maria Academy, PA	$428,004
Villa Walsh Academy, NJ	$140,000
Wakefield School, VA	$1,000,000
Waldorf High School of Massachusetts Bay, MA	$357,455
The Waldorf School of Garden City, NY	$180,000
Walnut Hill School for the Arts, MA	$2,900,000
Walsingham Academy, VA	$190,000
Wasatch Academy, UT	$2,650,000
The Waterford School, UT	$140,162
Watkinson School, CT	$1,510,932
Waynflete School, ME	$1,553,768
Webb School of Knoxville, TN	$720,250
The Webb Schools, CA	$3,400,000
Wesleyan Academy, PR	$1000
Westbury Christian School, TX	$325,000
Westchester Country Day School, NC	$524,945
Westminster Christian Academy, LA	$70,000
Westminster School, CT	$4,020,700
Westridge School, CA	$1,523,099
West Sound Academy, WA	$254,180
Westtown School, PA	$4,848,091
Wheaton Academy, IL	$500,000
The Wheeler School, RI	$1,360,353
Whitefield Academy, GA	$800,000
Whitefield Academy, KY	$42,175
The Williams School, CT	$1,270,680
The Williston Northampton School, MA	$5,767,000
Wilmington Christian School, DE	$292,720
Wilson Hall, SC	$135,000
The Windsor School, NY	$30,000
Winston Preparatory School, NY	$500,000
Woodlynde School, PA	$525,475
The Woodward School, MA	$185,240
Wyoming Seminary, PA	$6,000,000
York Catholic High School, PA	$250,000
York Preparatory School, NY	$1,000,000
York School, CA	$1,463,100
Zurich International School, Switzerland	67,700 Swiss francs

SCHOOLS REPORTING THAT THEY OFFER ENGLISH AS A SECOND LANGUAGE

Academy of the New Church Boys' School, PA
Academy of the New Church Girls' School, PA
Académie Ste Cécile International School, ON, Canada
Alliance Academy, Ecuador
American Academy, FL
American Heritage School, FL
American Heritage School, FL
American International School, Lusaka, Zambia
Annie Wright School, WA
Army and Navy Academy, CA
The Athenian School, CA
Augusta Christian School (I), GA
The Awty International School, TX
Balmoral Hall School, MB, Canada
The Beekman School, NY
Berkshire School, MA
Bishop Brady High School, NH
Bishop's College School, QC, Canada
Blanchet School, OR
The Bolles School, FL
Boston Trinity Academy, MA
Brimmer and May School, MA
The British School of Boston, MA
Brockwood Park School, United Kingdom
The Brook Hill School, TX
Burr and Burton Academy, VT
Buxton School, MA
Canyonville Christian Academy, OR
Cape Henry Collegiate School, VA
Capistrano Valley Christian Schools, CA
Cardigan Mountain School, NH
Carlisle School, VA
Cascadilla School, NY
Catholic Central High School, NY
Chamberlain-Hunt Academy, MS
Chaminade College Preparatory School, MO
Charlotte Country Day School, NC
Children's Creative and Performing Arts Academy of San Diego, CA
Chinese Christian Schools, CA
Christ Church Episcopal School, SC
Christchurch School, VA
Colegió Bolivar, Colombia
Columbia International School, Japan
Contra Costa Christian High School, CA
Cotter Schools, MN
Crawford Adventist Academy, ON, Canada
Cushing Academy, MA

Darlington School, GA
Darrow School, NY
Deerfield Academy, MA
Donelson Christian Academy, TN
Dublin School, NH
Eaglebrook School, MA
Eastern Mennonite High School, VA
Eldorado Emerson Private School, CA
The English College in Prague, Czech Republic
Escola Americana de Campinas, Brazil
The Ethel Walker School, CT
Falmouth Academy, MA
Father Lopez High School, FL
Fay School, MA
The Fessenden School, MA
First Presbyterian Day School, GA
Forsyth Country Day School, NC
Fountain Valley School of Colorado, CO
French-American School of New York, NY
Fryeburg Academy, ME
Garrison Forest School, MD
George Stevens Academy, ME
Georgetown Preparatory School, MD
Germantown Friends School, PA
Gould Academy, ME
The Governor French Academy, IL
The Grauer School, CA
Great Lakes Christian High School, ON, Canada
The Greenwood School, VT
Grier School, PA
The Gunston School, MD
Hargrave Military Academy, VA
Heritage Christian School, CA
The Hockaday School, TX
Holy Angels Academy, NY
Holyoke Catholic High School, MA
Houghton Academy, NY
The Hudson School, NJ
Hyde Park Baptist School, TX
Idyllwild Arts Academy, CA
Interlochen Arts Academy, MI
International High School, CA
International School Bangkok, Thailand
International School of Amsterdam, Netherlands
The International School of London, United Kingdom
Istanbul International Community School, Turkey
Josephinum Academy, IL
Kent School, CT
Kents Hill School, ME
The Kew-Forest School, NY
The King's Academy, TN
Kingsway College, ON, Canada
Lancaster Country Day School, PA
Lancaster Mennonite High School, PA
La Scuola D'Italia Guglielmo Marconi, NY
Lee Academy, ME
Lehigh Valley Christian High School, PA
Long Island Lutheran Middle and High School, NY
Los Angeles Lutheran High School, CA
Luther College High School, SK, Canada
Lycee International de Los Angeles, CA
Lyndon Institute, VT
Maharishi School of the Age of Enlightenment, IA
Maine Central Institute, ME
Marine Military Academy, TX
The Marvelwood School, CT
Marymount International School, Italy
Matignon High School, MA
Maur Hill-Mount Academy, KS
Memorial Hall School, TX
Menaul School, NM
Mennonite Collegiate Institute, MB, Canada
Merchiston Castle School, United Kingdom
Mid-Pacific Institute, HI
Miller School of Albemarle, VA
Missouri Military Academy, MO
Miss Porter's School, CT
MPS Etobicoke, ON, Canada
Munich International School, Germany
Nebraska Christian Schools, NE
Niagara Christian Community of Schools, ON, Canada
North Central Texas Academy, TX
North Toronto Christian School, ON, Canada
The Northwest School, WA
Northwood School, NY
North Yarmouth Academy, ME
The Norwich Free Academy, CT
Notre Dame College Prep, IL
Oak Grove School, CA
The Oakland School, PA
Oakwood Friends School, NY
Ojai Valley School, CA
Oneida Baptist Institute, KY
Oregon Episcopal School, OR
Orinda Academy, CA
The Oxford Academy, CT
Palmer Trinity School, FL
The Park School of Buffalo, NY
Parkview Adventist Academy, AB, Canada
The Pennington School, NJ
Phoenix Christian Unified Schools, AZ
Pickering College, ON, Canada
Pine Crest School, FL
Pinewood - The International School of Thessaloniki, Greece, Greece
Pope John XXIII Regional High School, NJ
Portsmouth Christian Academy, NH
Presbyterian Pan American School, TX
Proctor Academy, NH
Professional Children's School, NY
Queen Margaret's School, BC, Canada
Randolph-Macon Academy, VA
The Rectory School, CT
Redwood Christian Schools, CA
Ridley College, ON, Canada
Riverside Military Academy, GA
Rockway Mennonite Collegiate, ON, Canada
Rolling Hills Preparatory School, CA
Ross School, NY
Rothesay Netherwood School, NB, Canada
Royal Canadian College, BC, Canada
Rumsey Hall School, CT
Sacramento Country Day School, CA
Sacred Heart School of Halifax, NS, Canada
Saddleback Valley Christian School, CA
Saddlebrook Preparatory School, FL
St. Andrew's College, ON, Canada
St. Andrew's Episcopal School, MD
St. Andrew's School, RI
St. Andrew's–Sewanee School, TN
St. Anne's–Belfield School, VA
St. Anthony Catholic High School, TX
St. Catherine's Academy, CA
St. Croix Schools, MN

St. Francis de Sales High School, OH
St. George's School of Montreal, QC, Canada
Saint John's Preparatory School, MN
St. John's-Ravenscourt School, MB, Canada
St. Jude's School, ON, Canada
St. Mary's Preparatory School, MI
St. Mary's School, OR
Saint Maur International School, Japan
St. Michael's Preparatory School of the Norbertine Fathers, CA
St. Patrick's Regional Secondary, BC, Canada
St. Stanislaus College, MS
St. Stephen's Episcopal School, TX
St. Stephen's School, Rome, Italy
St. Timothy's School, MD
Salem Academy, NC
Salem Academy, OR
San Domenico School, CA
Sandy Spring Friends School, MD
San Marcos Baptist Academy, TX
Scholar's Hall Preparatory School, ON, Canada
Seisen International School, Japan
Shattuck-St. Mary's School, MN
Shawnigan Lake School, BC, Canada
Signet Christian School, ON, Canada
Solomon College, AB, Canada
Southwestern Academy, AZ
Southwestern Academy, CA
Spartanburg Day School, SC
The Storm King School, NY
Stratton Mountain School, VT
Stuart Hall, VA
Taipei American School, Taiwan
TASIS The American School in England, United Kingdom
TASIS, The American School in Switzerland, Switzerland
The Tenney School, TX
Thomas Jefferson School, MO
Tilton School, NH
Tri-City Christian Academy, AZ
Trinity College School, ON, Canada
Trinity-Pawling School, NY
University School of Jackson, TN
University School of Nova Southeastern University, FL
Valley Forge Military Academy & College, PA
Villa Maria Academy, PA
Walnut Hill School for the Arts, MA
Wasatch Academy, UT
Washington International School, DC
Westover School, CT
West Sound Academy, WA
Westtown School, PA
Wheaton Academy, IL
The Williston Northampton School, MA
Wilmington Christian School, DE
The Windsor School, NY
The Woodhall School, CT
The Woodward School, MA
Wyoming Seminary, PA
Zurich International School, Switzerland

SCHOOLS REPORTING A COMMUNITY SERVICE REQUIREMENT

The Academy for Gifted Children (PACE), ON, Canada
Academy of Our Lady of Peace, CA
Academy of the Sacred Heart, LA
The Agnes Irwin School, PA
All Hallows High School, NY
American Academy, FL
American Heritage School, FL
American Heritage School, FL
Archbishop Curley High School, MD
The Athenian School, CA
The Awty International School, TX
Bakersfield Christian High School, CA
Barrie School, MD
Battle Ground Academy, TN
Beaver Country Day School, MA
Belen Jesuit Preparatory School, FL
Berkeley Preparatory School, FL
Berkshire School, MA
The Birch Wathen Lenox School, NY
Bishop Brady High School, NH
Bishop Conaty-Our Lady of Loretto High School, CA
Bishop Denis J. O'Connell High School, VA
Bishop Eustace Preparatory School, NJ
Bishop Fenwick High School, OH
Bishop Ireton High School, VA
Bishop Kelly High School, ID
Bishop McGuinness Catholic High School, NC
The Bishop's School, CA
Bishop Stang High School, MA
Blanchet School, OR
Boston University Academy, MA
Breck School, MN
Briarwood Christian High School, AL
Brimmer and May School, MA
The Brook Hill School, TX
Brooks School, MA
Brophy College Preparatory, AZ
The Bryn Mawr School for Girls, MD
Buffalo Academy of the Sacred Heart, NY
Burr and Burton Academy, VT
Butte Central Catholic High School, MT
Campbell Hall (Episcopal), CA
Cannon School, NC
Canterbury School, FL
The Canterbury School of Florida, FL
Canton Academy, MS
Cape Cod Academy, MA
Cape Fear Academy, NC
Cape Henry Collegiate School, VA
Cardinal Mooney Catholic High School, FL
Cardinal Newman High School, FL
Cascadilla School, NY
Cathedral High School, IN
Cathedral Preparatory School, PA
The Catholic High School of Baltimore, MD
The Catlin Gabel School, OR
Central Catholic High School, TX
Chaminade College Preparatory, CA
Chaminade College Preparatory School, MO
Charlotte Country Day School, NC
Chattanooga Christian School, TN
Cheverus High School, ME
Children's Creative and Performing Arts Academy of San Diego, CA
Choate Rosemary Hall, CT
Christian Brothers Academy, NY
Christian Central Academy, NY
Christopher Columbus High School, FL
The Church Farm School, PA
Cincinnati Country Day School, OH
Colegio San Jose, PR

The Collegiate School, VA
The Colorado Springs School, CO
Commonwealth Parkville School, PR
The Community School of Naples, FL
Concordia Lutheran High School, IN
Contra Costa Christian High School, CA
Convent of the Sacred Heart, CT
Cotter Schools, MN
Country Day School of the Sacred Heart, PA
Crespi Carmelite High School, CA
Crossroads School for Arts & Sciences, CA
Currey Ingram Academy, TN
Dana Hall School, MA
Darlington School, GA
Devon Preparatory School, PA
Donelson Christian Academy, TN
Donna Klein Jewish Academy, FL
Dowling Catholic High School, IA
Duchesne Academy of the Sacred Heart, TX
Durham Academy, NC
Eaglebrook School, MA
Eagle Hill School, MA
Edgewood Academy, AL
Edmund Burke School, DC
Eldorado Emerson Private School, CA
Elizabeth Seton High School, MD
Elyria Catholic High School, OH
Emma Willard School, NY
Episcopal High School of Jacksonville, FL
Escola Americana de Campinas, Brazil
The Ethel Walker School, CT
Explorations Academy, WA
Fairfield College Preparatory School, CT
Father Lopez High School, FL
First Baptist Academy, TX
Flint Hill School, VA
Flintridge Preparatory School, CA
Forest Lake Academy, FL
Forsyth Country Day School, NC
Fort Worth Christian School, TX
Fort Worth Country Day School, TX
Fountain Valley School of Colorado, CO
French-American School of New York, NY
Friends Academy, NY
Fryeburg Academy, ME
Gaston Day School, NC
Gateway School, TX
Georgetown Day School, DC
Georgetown Preparatory School, MD
Georgetown Visitation Preparatory School, DC
Gilmour Academy, OH
Glenelg Country School, MD
Gonzaga College High School, DC
The Grauer School, CA
Greenhill School, TX
Greenhills School, MI
Guamani Private School, PR
The Gunston School, MD
The Harker School, CA
The Harley School, NY
The Harrisburg Academy, PA
Harvard-Westlake School, CA
Hawken School, OH
Head-Royce School, CA
Highland Hall Waldorf School, CA
The Hockaday School, TX
Holy Angels Academy, NY
Holy Cross School, LA
Holy Ghost Preparatory School, PA
Holyoke Catholic High School, MA
Hopkins School, CT
The Hudson School, NJ
Hyde Park Baptist School, TX
Hyman Brand Hebrew Academy of Greater Kansas City, KS
Independent School, KS
Institute of Notre Dame, MD
Intermountain Christian School, UT
International School Bangkok, Thailand
International School of Amsterdam, Netherlands
The International School of London, United Kingdom
Iona Preparatory School, NY
Jack M. Barrack Hebrew Academy, PA
Jesuit High School of Tampa, FL
Josephinum Academy, IL
Junipero Serra High School, CA
Kalamazoo Christian High School, MI
Kent Denver School, CO
The Kew-Forest School, NY
Kingswood-Oxford School, CT
The Lab School of Washington, DC
La Jolla Country Day School, CA
Landon School, MD
The Latin School of Chicago, IL
The Laureate Academy, MB, Canada
Lauralton Hall, CT
Lawrence School, OH
The Lawrenceville School, NJ
Lincoln Academy, ME
Lincoln School, RI
Linfield Christian School, CA
Lodi Academy, CA
Louisville High School, CA
Lutheran High School North, MO
Lutheran High School Northwest, MI
Malvern Preparatory School, PA
Manhattan Christian High School, MT
Maranatha High School, CA
Marist School, GA
Marmion Academy, IL
Mars Hill Bible School, AL
The Marvelwood School, CT
Marylawn of the Oranges, NJ
Marymount High School, CA
Matignon High School, MA
Maui Preparatory Academy, HI
McDonogh School, MD
The Meadows School, NV
Memorial Hall School, TX
Menaul School, NM
Mesa Grande Seventh-Day Academy, CA
Miller School of Albemarle, VA
Missouri Military Academy, MO
Miss Porter's School, CT
Montclair Kimberley Academy, NJ
Moorestown Friends School, NJ
Moreau Catholic High School, CA
Morristown-Beard School, NJ
Mount Michael Benedictine School, NE
Mt. Saint Dominic Academy, NJ
Munich International School, Germany
Nerinx Hall, MO
Newark Academy, NJ
Noble and Greenough School, MA
The Nora School, MD

Norfolk Academy, VA
North Shore Country Day School, IL
North Toronto Christian School, ON, Canada
Northwest Academy, OR
Northwest Catholic High School, CT
Notre Dame Academy, CA
Notre Dame College Prep, IL
Notre Dame High School, CA
Notre Dame High School, NJ
Oak Grove School, CA
The Oakland School, PA
The Oakridge School, TX
Oakwood Friends School, NY
Oldenburg Academy, IN
The O'Neal School, NC
Orinda Academy, CA
The Overlake School, WA
The Oxford Academy, CT
Pacific Academy, CA
Palma School, CA
Palmer Trinity School, FL
Paradise Adventist Academy, CA
The Park School of Buffalo, NY
Patten Academy of Christian Education, CA
Peddie School, NJ
Phoenix Country Day School, AZ
Pickering College, ON, Canada
The Pingree School, MA
The Pingry School, NJ
Pioneer Valley Christian School, MA
Pope John XXIII Regional High School, NJ
Powers Catholic High School, MI
Providence Country Day School, RI
Punahou School, HI
Queen Margaret's School, BC, Canada
Ravenscroft School, NC
Riverdale Country School, NY
The Rivers School, MA
Roland Park Country School, MD
Ross School, NY
Sacramento Adventist Academy, CA
Sacramento Country Day School, CA
Sacred Heart School of Halifax, NS, Canada
Sage Ridge School, NV
St. Agnes Academy, TX
St. Albans School, DC
St. Andrew's College, ON, Canada
St. Andrew's Episcopal School, MD
St. Andrew's School, RI
St. Andrew's–Sewanee School, TN
St. Anne's–Belfield School, VA
Saint Anthony High School, CA
St. Bernard High School, CT
St. Bernard's Catholic School, CA
St. Brendan High School, FL
St. Croix Country Day School, VI
Saint Elizabeth High School, CA
St. Francis de Sales High School, OH
Saint Francis High School, CA
St. Francis High School, KY
St. George's School of Montreal, QC, Canada
St. Gregory College Preparatory School, AZ
St. Joseph High School, CT
Saint Joseph High School, IL
Saint Joseph High School, NJ
St. Joseph's Catholic School, SC
Saint Lawrence Academy, CA
St. Mark's School of Texas, TX
St. Martin's Episcopal School, LA
Saint Mary's Hall, TX
Saint Mary's High School, AZ
St. Mary's School, OR
St. Michael's College School, ON, Canada
Saint Patrick High School, IL
St. Paul's Episcopal School, AL
St. Pius X High School, TX
St. Stephen's & St. Agnes School, VA
Saint Stephen's Episcopal School, FL
St. Stephen's Episcopal School, TX
Saint Teresa's Academy, MO
Saint Thomas Academy, MN
St. Thomas Aquinas High School, NH
St. Timothy's School, MD
Saint Ursula Academy, OH
Salem Academy, OR
Salesianum School, DE
San Domenico School, CA
Sandy Spring Friends School, MD
Santa Fe Preparatory School, NM
Seabury Hall, HI
Seattle Academy of Arts and Sciences, WA
The Seven Hills School, OH
Severn School, MD
Shattuck-St. Mary's School, MN
The Shipley School, PA
Smith School, NY
Southwestern Academy, AZ
Southwestern Academy, CA
Stephen T. Badin High School, OH
The Storm King School, NY
Stratford Academy, GA
Stratton Mountain School, VT
Tandem Friends School, VA
TASIS The American School in England, United Kingdom
TASIS, The American School in Switzerland, Switzerland
Thomas Jefferson School, MO
Tilton School, NH
TMI - The Episcopal School of Texas, TX
Tower Hill School, DE
Tri-City Christian Schools, CA
Trinity Christian Academy, TN
Trinity College School, ON, Canada
Trinity High School, KY
University Liggett School, MI
University of Chicago Laboratory Schools, IL
University of Detroit Jesuit High School and Academy, MI
University Prep, WA
University School of Jackson, TN
University School of Milwaukee, WI
University School of Nova Southeastern University, FL
Upper Canada College, ON, Canada
The Ursuline Academy of Dallas, TX
Valle Catholic High School, MO
Vianney High School, MO
Villa Duchesne and Oak Hill School, MO
Villa Maria Academy, PA
Villa Victoria Academy, NJ
Waldorf High School of Massachusetts Bay, MA
Walsingham Academy, VA
Wasatch Academy, UT
Washington International School, DC
Waynflete School, ME
Webb School of Knoxville, TN
Wellsprings Friends School, OR

Wesleyan Academy, PR
Westbury Christian School, TX
Westchester Country Day School, NC
Westover School, CT
Westridge School, CA
The Wheeler School, RI
Whitefield Academy, GA
Wilmington Christian School, DE
Wilson Hall, SC
The Winston School San Antonio, TX
Woodlynde School, PA
The Woodward School, MA
Wyoming Seminary, PA
York Preparatory School, NY
York School, CA
Zurich International School, Switzerland

SCHOOLS REPORTING EXCHANGE PROGRAMS WITH OTHER U.S. SCHOOLS

Academy of the Sacred Heart, LA
The Athenian School, CA
Commonwealth Parkville School, PR
Convent of the Sacred Heart, CT
Convent of the Sacred Heart, NY
Country Day School of the Sacred Heart, PA
Crystal Springs Uplands School, CA
Doane Stuart School, NY
Dublin School, NH
Duchesne Academy of the Sacred Heart, TX
Emma Willard School, NY
Germantown Friends School, PA
Josephinum Academy, IL
La Scuola D'Italia Guglielmo Marconi, NY
Sacred Heart School of Halifax, NS, Canada
St. Stephen's School, Rome, Italy
Salesianum School, DE
University Prep, WA
Villa Duchesne and Oak Hill School, MO

SCHOOLS REPORTING PROGRAMS FOR STUDY ABROAD

Academy of Notre Dame de Namur, PA
The Agnes Irwin School, PA
Alexander Dawson School, CO
Annie Wright School, WA
The Athenian School, CA
Bayside Academy, AL
Berkeley Preparatory School, FL
Berkshire School, MA
The Birch Wathen Lenox School, NY
Bishop's College School, QC, Canada
The Bishop's School, CA
Blair Academy, NJ
The Blake School, MN
The Brearley School, NY
Brockwood Park School, United Kingdom
Brooks School, MA
Brophy College Preparatory, AZ
The Bryn Mawr School for Girls, MD
Burr and Burton Academy, VT
The Canterbury School of Florida, FL
Cape Cod Academy, MA
Cape Fear Academy, NC
Catholic Central High School, WI
The Catlin Gabel School, OR
Central Catholic High School, TX
Chadwick School, CA
Charlotte Country Day School, NC
Charlotte Latin School, NC
Chase Collegiate School, CT
Chicago Waldorf School, IL
Chinese Christian Schools, CA
Choate Rosemary Hall, CT
The Church Farm School, PA
Cincinnati Country Day School, OH
Columbia International School, Japan
Commonwealth Parkville School, PR
The Community School of Naples, FL
Concord Academy, MA
Convent of the Sacred Heart, CT
Convent of the Sacred Heart, NY
Cotter Schools, MN
The Country Day School, ON, Canada
Country Day School of the Sacred Heart, PA
Crystal Springs Uplands School, CA
Damien High School, CA
Dana Hall School, MA
Deerfield Academy, MA
Doane Stuart School, NY
Donna Klein Jewish Academy, FL
Eastern Mennonite High School, VA
Emma Willard School, NY
Episcopal High School, VA
Episcopal High School of Jacksonville, FL
Escola Americana de Campinas, Brazil
The Ethel Walker School, CT
Falmouth Academy, MA
Flintridge Preparatory School, CA
Foxcroft School, VA
Gann Academy (The New Jewish High School of Greater Boston), MA
George Stevens Academy, ME
Georgetown Preparatory School, MD
Germantown Friends School, PA
The Grauer School, CA
Grier School, PA
The Gunston School, MD
Harvard-Westlake School, CA
Hawken School, OH
Head-Royce School, CA
Hebrew Academy of the Five Towns & Rockaway, NY
The Hewitt School, NY
Highland Hall Waldorf School, CA
The Hill School, PA
The Hockaday School, TX
Holland Hall, OK
Holy Ghost Preparatory School, PA
Hopkins School, CT
The Hudson School, NJ
International High School, CA
Iona Preparatory School, NY
Jack M. Barrack Hebrew Academy, PA
Jean and Samuel Frankel Jewish Academy of Metropolitan Detroit, MI
Josephinum Academy, IL
Kents Hill School, ME
Kentucky Country Day School, KY
Kimball Union Academy, NH
Kingswood-Oxford School, CT
The Lab School of Washington, DC

La Jolla Country Day School, CA
Lakefield College School, ON, Canada
Lakehill Preparatory School, TX
Landon School, MD
La Scuola D'Italia Guglielmo Marconi, NY
The Latin School of Chicago, IL
The Lawrenceville School, NJ
Lee Academy, ME
Lincoln School, RI
Louisville Collegiate School, KY
The Lovett School, GA
Luther College High School, SK, Canada
Lycee International de Los Angeles, CA
Maine Central Institute, ME
Matignon High School, MA
Meadowridge School, BC, Canada
Merchiston Castle School, United Kingdom
Milton Academy, MA
Miss Porter's School, CT
Montclair Kimberley Academy, NJ
Montgomery Bell Academy, TN
Moorestown Friends School, NJ
Morristown-Beard School, NJ
Newark Academy, NJ
Noble and Greenough School, MA
Norfolk Academy, VA
North Shore Country Day School, IL
North Yarmouth Academy, ME
The Oakridge School, TX
Ojai Valley School, CA
Oregon Episcopal School, OR
The Overlake School, WA
Padua Franciscan High School, OH
Palmer Trinity School, FL
The Park School of Baltimore, MD
The Park School of Buffalo, NY
Peddie School, NJ
The Pennington School, NJ
Phillips Academy (Andover), MA
Phoenix Country Day School, AZ
The Pingry School, NJ
Proctor Academy, NH
Punahou School, HI
Ramona Convent Secondary School, CA
Randolph-Macon Academy, VA
Ravenscroft School, NC
Realms of Inquiry, UT
Regis High School, NY
Ridley College, ON, Canada
Riverdale Country School, NY
Roland Park Country School, MD
Rundle College, AB, Canada
Sacred Heart School of Halifax, NS, Canada
Saddleback Valley Christian School, CA
St. Albans School, DC
St. Andrew's College, ON, Canada
St. Andrew's–Sewanee School, TN
St. Anthony Catholic High School, TX
St. Augustine High School, CA
Saint Augustine Preparatory School, NJ
St. Francis High School, KY
St. George's School, RI
St. John's Preparatory School, MA
Saint John's Preparatory School, MN
Saint Joseph Academy High School, OH
St. Joseph's Preparatory School, PA
St. Mark's School of Texas, TX
Saint Mary's Hall, TX
Saint Mary's High School, MD
Saint Mary's School, NC
St. Paul Academy and Summit School, MN
St. Stephen's & St. Agnes School, VA
St. Stephen's Episcopal School, TX
Salem Academy, NC
Sandia Preparatory School, NM
Santa Fe Preparatory School, NM
Seattle Academy of Arts and Sciences, WA
The Seven Hills School, OH
Severn School, MD
Shady Side Academy, PA
The Shipley School, PA
Sonoma Academy, CA
Southwest Christian School, Inc., TX
The Spence School, NY
Stephen T. Badin High School, OH
Stevenson School, CA
Summerfield Waldorf School, CA
The Summit Country Day School, OH
The Taft School, CT
Telluride Mountain School, CO
The Thacher School, CA
THINK Global School, CA
Trinity College School, ON, Canada
Trinity High School, KY
University Liggett School, MI
University Prep, WA
Valley Forge Military Academy & College, PA
Villa Duchesne and Oak Hill School, MO
Waldorf High School of Massachusetts Bay, MA
The Waldorf School of Garden City, NY
The Waldorf School of Saratoga Springs, NY
Waynflete School, ME
Webb School of Knoxville, TN
West Island College, AB, Canada
Westminster School, CT
Westover School, CT
Westtown School, PA
The Wheeler School, RI
The Williams School, CT
The Williston Northampton School, MA
Wyoming Seminary, PA

SCHOOLS REPORTING SUMMER SESSIONS OPEN TO STUDENTS FROM OTHER SCHOOLS

Academy of Notre Dame de Namur, PA	A,C,S
Academy of Our Lady of Peace, CA	A
Academy of the Holy Cross, MD	A,C,F,S
Academy of the New Church Boys' School, PA	S
Academy of the New Church Girls' School, PA	S
Académie Ste Cécile International School, ON, Canada	A,F
The Agnes Irwin School, PA	A,C,F,S
Allendale Columbia School, NY	A,F,S
Alpha Omega Academy, IA	A
Alverno High School, CA	A,C,F,R,S
American Academy, FL	A,C,F
American Heritage School, FL	A
American Heritage School, FL	A,C,F
The American School in El Salvador, FL	A
Archbishop Curley High School, MD	A,C,F,S
Archbishop Mitty High School, CA	A,C,F,S
Army and Navy Academy, CA	A,C,F,R,S
Arroyo Pacific Academy, CA	A,F

A — academic; C — computer instruction; F — art/fine arts; R — rigorous outdoor training; S — sports; O — other

ASSETS School, HI A
The Athenian School, CA A,C,F,S
Augusta Christian School (I), GA A
Augusta Preparatory Day School, GA A,F,S
Bachman Academy, TN A,F,S
Baldwin School of Puerto Rico, PR A
The Baltimore Actors' Theatre Conservatory, MD A,F
Baltimore Lutheran School, MD A,S
Barrie School, MD S
Battle Ground Academy, TN A,C,F,S
Bearspaw Christian School, AB, Canada S
The Beekman School, NY A
Bellarmine College Preparatory, CA A,C,F,S
Berkeley Preparatory School, FL A,C,F,S
Bishop Brady High School, NH A,S
Bishop Conaty-Our Lady of Loretto High School, CA A,C,F
Bishop Denis J. O'Connell High School, VA A,C,F,S
Bishop Eustace Preparatory School, NJ A,S
Bishop Ireton High School, VA A,C,F
Bishop Luers High School, IN A,S
Bishop O'Dowd High School, CA A,C
Bishop's College School, QC, Canada A
The Bishop's School, CA A,C,F,S
Bishop Stang High School, MA A,C,F,S
The Blake School, MN A,S
Blanchet School, OR A,S
Blueprint Education, AZ A
The Bolles School, FL A,C,F
Boston Trinity Academy, MA A,F
The Brearley School, NY A,C,F,S
Bridges Academy, CA A,C,F,S
The Brook Hill School, TX A,F,S
Brooks School, MA A,C,S
Brophy College Preparatory, AZ A,C,F,S
Brother Rice High School, MI A,F
The Bryn Mawr School for Girls, MD A,F,S
Buffalo Academy of the Sacred Heart, NY C,F,S
Calvert Hall College High School, MD A,C,F,S
Calvin Christian High School, CA A,S
Cannon School, NC A,C,F,S
The Canterbury Episcopal School, TX A,S
Canterbury School, FL A,F,S
The Canterbury School of Florida, FL A,C,F,S
Canton Academy, MS A
Cape Fear Academy, NC A,F,S
Cape Henry Collegiate School, VA A,C,F,S
Capistrano Valley Christian Schools, CA A,F,S
Cardigan Mountain School, NH A,C,F,S
Cardinal Gibbons High School, NC F,S
Cardinal Mooney Catholic High School, FL A,S
Carlisle School, VA A,C,F,S
Carolina Day School, NC A,C,F,S
Cascadilla School, NY A,F
Cathedral Preparatory School, PA A,S
Catholic Central High School, WI S
The Catlin Gabel School, OR A,C,F
Central Catholic High School, CA A
Central Catholic High School, TX A,C,S
Chadwick School, CA C,F,S
Chamberlain-Hunt Academy, MS A,R,S
Chaminade College Preparatory, CA A,C,F,S
Chaminade College Preparatory School, MO A,F,S
Charlotte Country Day School, NC A,C,F,S
Charlotte Latin School, NC A,C,F,S
Chase Collegiate School, CT A,C,F,S
Chattanooga Christian School, TN A,F,S
Cheverus High School, ME A,S
Children's Creative and Performing Arts Academy of San Diego, CA A,C,F
Chinese Christian Schools, CA A,S
Choate Rosemary Hall, CT A,F,S
Christa McAuliffe Academy School of Arts and Sciences, OR A,C
Christ Church Episcopal School, SC A,S
Christchurch School, VA A,S
Christian Central Academy, NY S
Chrysalis School, WA A,C
Cincinnati Country Day School, OH A,C,F,S
Cistercian Preparatory School, TX A,C,F,S
Clarksville Academy, TN A,C,F,S
Colegio San Jose, PR A
The Collegiate School, VA A,C,F,S
The Colorado Springs School, CO A,C,F,S
Columbia International School, Japan A,C,F,S
Columbus School for Girls, OH A,C,F,R,S
Commonwealth Parkville School, PR A,C,F,S
The Community School of Naples, FL A,F,S
Concordia Lutheran High School, IN A,F,S
Convent of the Sacred Heart, NY C,F,S
Cotter Schools, MN A,F,S
The Country Day School, ON, Canada A,F,S
Crespi Carmelite High School, CA A,F,S
Crossroads School for Arts & Sciences, CA A,C,F,S
Currey Ingram Academy, TN A,F
Damien High School, CA A,C,F,S
Dana Hall School, MA A
Darlington School, GA A,C,F,S
Davidson Academy, TN A,F,S
Delbarton School, NJ A,C,S
DeMatha Catholic High School, MD A,C,F,S
Denver Academy, CO A,C,F,R
The Derryfield School, NH F
Dominican Academy, NY A
Duchesne Academy of the Sacred Heart, TX A,C,F
Durham Academy, NC A,C,F,S
Eaglebrook School, MA A,C,F,R,S
Eagle Hill School, MA A,C,F,S
Eaton Academy, GA A,C,F,S
Edgewood Academy, AL O
Edmund Burke School, DC A,C,F
Elgin Academy, IL A,F,S
Elizabeth Seton High School, MD A,C,F,S
Elyria Catholic High School, OH S
Emma Willard School, NY A
Episcopal Collegiate School, AR A,C,F,S
Episcopal High School, TX A,F
Episcopal High School, VA A,F,S
Episcopal High School of Jacksonville, FL A,C,F,R,S
The Ethel Walker School, CT F,S
Explorations Academy, WA A,F,R
Fairfield College Preparatory School, CT A,C,S
Fairhill School, TX A,C
Falmouth Academy, MA A,F
Father Ryan High School, TN A,C,F,S
Fayetteville Academy, NC A,C,F,S
Fay School, MA A,C,F,S
The First Academy, FL A,F,S
First Presbyterian Day School, GA A,F,S
Flint Hill School, VA A,C,F,R,S
Flintridge Preparatory School, CA A,C,F,R,S
Fontbonne Hall Academy, NY S
Foothills Academy, AB, Canada A
Forsyth Country Day School, NC A
Fort Worth Country Day School, TX A,F,S

A — academic; C — computer instruction; F — art/fine arts; R — rigorous outdoor training; S — sports; O — other

Foundation Academy, FL A,F,S
Fountain Valley School of Colorado, CO A,C,S
Frederica Academy, GA A,C,F,S
Friends Academy, NY F
Friends' Central School, PA A
The Galloway School, GA A,F,S
Garrison Forest School, MD F,S
Gaston Day School, NC A,F,S
George Stevens Academy, ME A,F,S
Georgetown Day School, DC A
Georgetown Preparatory School, MD A,S
George Walton Academy, GA A,F,S
Germantown Friends School, PA A
Gilman School, MD A,F,R,S
Gilmour Academy, OH A,S
Girls Preparatory School, TN A,C,F,S
Glenelg Country School, MD S
The Glenholme School, Devereux Connecticut, CT A,C,F,S
Gonzaga College High School, DC A
The Governor French Academy, IL A
Grace Baptist Academy, TN A
Grace Brethren School, CA A
Grace Christian School, AK A
The Grauer School, CA A,C,F,R,S
Greenhill School, TX A,C,F,S
Greenhills School, MI A,F,R,S
The Greenwood School, VT O
Grier School, PA A,F,S
Guamani Private School, PR A
The Gunston School, MD A,C,S
Hargrave Military Academy, VA A,C,R,S
The Harker School, CA A,S
The Harley School, NY A,C,F,S
The Harrisburg Academy, PA A,F
Harvard-Westlake School, CA A,C,F,R,S
The Harvey School, NY A
Hawaii Baptist Academy, HI A,C,F,S
Hawken School, OH A,C
Head-Royce School, CA A
Heritage Christian School, CA A,C,S
The Hill Top Preparatory School, PA A
The Hockaday School, TX A,C,F,S
Holland Hall, OK A,F,S
Holy Ghost Preparatory School, PA A,C,S
Hopkins School, CT A,S
Houston Learning Academy-North Houston, TX A
The Howard School, GA A
The Hudson School, NJ F
Humanex Academy, CO A,F,S
Huntington-Surrey School, TX A
Idyllwild Arts Academy, CA A,F
Independent School, KS A,C,F,S
Institute of Notre Dame, MD A,C,F,R,S
Interlochen Arts Academy, MI F
International High School, CA A
International School Bangkok, Thailand A,F
Jackson Preparatory School, MS A,C,F
John Hancock Academy, GA A
Josephinum Academy, IL A,C,F,S
Junipero Serra High School, CA A,C,F,S
Kent Denver School, CO A,C,F,S
Kentucky Country Day School, KY A,C,F,R,S
The Kew-Forest School, NY A
Kimball Union Academy, NH A,F,S
King Low Heywood Thomas, CT A,F,S
La Jolla Country Day School, CA A,C,F,S
Lakefield College School, ON, Canada A
Lakehill Preparatory School, TX A,C,F,S
Lancaster Mennonite High School, PA A,F,S
Landon School, MD A,F,S
Lansdale Catholic High School, PA A,F,S
La Salle High School, CA A,C,F,S
The Latin School of Chicago, IL A,C,F,R,S
The Laureate Academy, MB, Canada A
Laurel Springs School, CA A,C,F
Lee Academy, ME A
Linfield Christian School, CA F,S
Long Island Lutheran Middle and High School, NY C,F,S
Los Angeles Lutheran High School, CA A,S
Louisville Collegiate School, KY A,C,F,S
Louisville High School, CA S
The Lovett School, GA A
Loyola-Blakefield, MD A,C,F,S
Lutheran High School of Hawaii, HI A,C,F,S
Luther College High School, SK, Canada A
Luther North College Prep, IL A,C,S
Maine Central Institute, ME A,F
Malvern Preparatory School, PA A,C,F,S
Maplebrook School, NY A,C,F,S
Maranatha High School, CA A,F,S
Marian Central Catholic High School, IL A,S
Marian High School, IN C,F,S
Marine Military Academy, TX A,R,S
Marist School, GA A,F,S
Mars Hill Bible School, AL A,F,S
Martin Luther High School, NY A,C
The Marvelwood School, CT A,C,F
Marylawn of the Oranges, NJ A,C
The Mary Louis Academy, NY A,F,S
Marymount High School, CA A,C,F,S
Matignon High School, MA A
Maur Hill-Mount Academy, KS A
McDonogh School, MD A,C,F,S
The Meadows School, NV A,F,S
Memorial Hall School, TX A,C
Menaul School, NM A
Merchiston Castle School, United Kingdom A,S
Mercy High School College Preparatory, CA A
Mesa Grande Seventh-Day Academy, CA S
Mid-Pacific Institute, HI A,C,F
Mill Springs Academy, GA S
Missouri Military Academy, MO A,R,S
Miss Porter's School, CT A,F
MMI Preparatory School, PA A,C
Montclair Kimberley Academy, NJ A,C,F,S
Montgomery Bell Academy, TN A,C,F,R,S
Moravian Academy, PA A,F,S
Moreau Catholic High School, CA A,S
Morristown-Beard School, NJ A,C,F,S
Mother McAuley High School, IL A,C,F,S
Mount Carmel School, MP A,F
Mount Mercy Academy, NY A
Mount Saint Charles Academy, RI F,S
Mt. Saint Dominic Academy, NJ A,S
MPS Etobicoke, ON, Canada A,C,F,S
MU High School, MO A
Munich International School, Germany R,S
Nazareth Academy, IL A,F,S
Newark Academy, NJ A,C,F,S
Noble Academy, NC A,C
Norfolk Academy, VA A,F,S
North Shore Country Day School, IL A,C,F,R,S
Northwest Catholic High School, CT S
The Northwest School, WA A,C,F,S

A — academic; C — computer instruction; F — art/fine arts; R — rigorous outdoor training; S — sports; O — other

School	Sessions
Northwood School, NY	S
North Yarmouth Academy, ME	A,F,S
Notre Dame Academy, CA	A,C,F,S
Notre Dame College Prep, IL	A,C,F,S
Notre Dame High School, CA	A
Notre Dame High School, NJ	A,F,S
Notre Dame High School, TN	A,F,S
Oak Grove School, CA	A
Oakland School, VA	A,C,F,S
The Oakridge School, TX	A,C,F,R,S
Ojai Valley School, CA	A,C,F
Oneida Baptist Institute, KY	A
Oregon Episcopal School, OR	A,C,F,S
Orinda Academy, CA	A
The Oxford Academy, CT	A
Pacific Academy, CA	A
Padua Franciscan High School, OH	A,C,F,S
Palma School, CA	A
Palmer Trinity School, FL	A,C,F,R,S
Palo Alto Preparatory School, CA	A,R
Paradise Adventist Academy, CA	S
Parish Episcopal School, TX	A,C,F,S
The Park School of Buffalo, NY	A,F,S
The Pathway School, PA	A
Peddie School, NJ	A,F,S
Phillips Academy (Andover), MA	A,C,F
Phoenix Country Day School, AZ	A,C,F,S
Pickering College, ON, Canada	A
Pine Crest School, FL	A,S
The Pingry School, NJ	A,S
Pope John XXIII Regional High School, NJ	A,S
Porter-Gaud School, SC	A
Portsmouth Abbey School, RI	A,F,S
Portsmouth Christian Academy, NH	A,S
Prestonwood Christian Academy, TX	A,C,F,R,S
Providence High School, CA	A,C,F,S
Queen Margaret's School, BC, Canada	A,S
Ramona Convent Secondary School, CA	A,C,F,S
Randolph-Macon Academy, VA	A,C,F
Randolph School, AL	A,S
Ranney School, NJ	A,C,F,S
Ransom Everglades School, FL	A,C
Ravenscroft School, NC	A,C,F,S
Realms of Inquiry, UT	R
The Rectory School, CT	A,C,F,S
Riverside Military Academy, GA	A,C,F,R,S
Roland Park Country School, MD	A,F,S
Rolling Hills Preparatory School, CA	A,F
Ross School, NY	A,F,S
Rowland Hall, UT	A,C,F,S
The Roxbury Latin School, MA	A,C,S
Royal Canadian College, BC, Canada	A
Rumsey Hall School, CT	A
Sacred Heart/Griffin High School, IL	A,S
Sacred Heart School of Halifax, NS, Canada	A
Saddlebrook Preparatory School, FL	A,F,S
Sage Hill School, CA	A,F,S
Sage Ridge School, NV	A,F
St. Albans School, DC	A,C,F,R,S
St. Andrew's College, ON, Canada	A,F,S
St. Andrew's Episcopal School, MD	A,F,S
St. Andrew's School, RI	A,C,F,R,S
St. Andrew's–Sewanee School, TN	F,S
St. Anne's–Belfield School, VA	A,S
St. Anthony Catholic High School, TX	A,C,F,S
Saint Anthony High School, CA	A,S
St. Anthony's Junior-Senior High School, HI	A
St. Augustine High School, CA	A,R,S
Saint Augustine Preparatory School, NJ	A,F,R,S
St. Bernard's Catholic School, CA	A
St. Brendan High School, FL	A,C
St. Catherine's Academy, CA	A,C,F,S
St. Croix Schools, MN	A,S
Saint Dominic Academy, ME	A,F,S
Saint Francis High School, CA	A,S
St. Francis High School, KY	A,S
St. George's Independent School, TN	A,C,F,S
St. George's School, BC, Canada	A,C,F,S
St. John's Preparatory School, MA	A,C,F,S
Saint John's Preparatory School, MN	A,F
Saint Joseph High School, IL	A,S
Saint Joseph High School, NJ	A,C,S
St. Joseph's Catholic School, SC	F,S
St. Joseph's Preparatory School, PA	A,C,F,S
St. Jude's School, ON, Canada	O
St. Mark's School of Texas, TX	O
St. Martin's Episcopal School, LA	A,C,F,S
St. Mary's Episcopal School, TN	A,F,S
Saint Mary's Hall, TX	A,C,F,S
Saint Mary's High School, AZ	A,F,S
St. Mary's Preparatory School, MI	S
Saint Mary's School, NC	A,C,F,S
St. Mary's School, OR	A,S
Saint Maur International School, Japan	A,C,F,S
Saint Patrick High School, IL	A,C,F,S
Saint Patrick - Saint Vincent High School, CA	A,F,S
St. Paul Academy and Summit School, MN	A
St. Paul's Episcopal School, AL	A,C,F,S
St. Paul's High School, MB, Canada	S
St. Pius X Catholic High School, GA	A,F,S
St. Stanislaus College, MS	A
St. Stephen's & St. Agnes School, VA	A,C,F,S
Saint Stephen's Episcopal School, FL	A,C,F,S
St. Stephen's Episcopal School, TX	F,S
St. Stephen's School, Rome, Italy	A,F
Saint Teresa's Academy, MO	C,F,S
St. Thomas Aquinas High School, FL	A,C,F
Saint Thomas Aquinas High School, KS	A,C,S
St. Timothy's School, MD	A
Saint Ursula Academy, OH	A,C,F,S
Salesian High School, CA	A,C,F,S
Salpointe Catholic High School, AZ	A,C,S
Sandia Preparatory School, NM	A,C,F,S
Santa Catalina School, CA	A,F,S
SBEC (Southern Baptist Educational Center), MS	S
Scholar's Hall Preparatory School, ON, Canada	A
Scottsdale Christian Academy, AZ	F,S
Seabury Hall, HI	A,F,S
Seattle Academy of Arts and Sciences, WA	A,F,S
The Seven Hills School, OH	A
Severn School, MD	A,C,F,S
Shady Side Academy, PA	A,C,F,S
Shattuck-St. Mary's School, MN	A,F,S
Shawnigan Lake School, BC, Canada	S
Shelton School and Evaluation Center, TX	A
The Shipley School, PA	S
Shoore Centre for Learning, ON, Canada	A
Smith School, NY	A,C
Southwest Christian School, Inc., TX	A,C,F,S
Southwestern Academy, AZ	A,F,R
Southwestern Academy, CA	A,C,F
Spartanburg Day School, SC	A,C,F,S
Spring Creek Academy, TX	A,F
Stevenson School, CA	A

A — academic; C — computer instruction; F — art/fine arts; R — rigorous outdoor training; S — sports; O — other

Stratford Academy, GA A,F,S
The Summit Country Day School, OH A,C,F,S
The Taft School, CT A,F,S
Taipei American School, Taiwan A,C
Tandem Friends School, VA F
Tapply Binet College, ON, Canada A
Temple Grandin School, CO O
The Tenney School, TX A
Timothy Christian High School, IL F,S
TMI - The Episcopal School of Texas, TX A,S
Tower Hill School, DE A,S
Tri-City Christian Schools, CA A,S
Trinity College School, ON, Canada A,C,F
Trinity High School, OH A,F,S
Trinity Preparatory School, FL A,C,F,S
Tyler Street Christian Academy, TX O
University Liggett School, MI A,S
University of Chicago Laboratory Schools, IL A,S
University School of Jackson, TN A,C,F,S
University School of Milwaukee, WI A,C,F,S
University School of Nova Southeastern University, FL A,F,S
Upper Canada College, ON, Canada A,C,F
Valley Christian High School, CA A,C,F,S
Vianney High School, MO S
Villa Angela-St. Joseph High School, OH A,F,S
Villa Duchesne and Oak Hill School, MO A,C,F,S
Villa Joseph Marie High School, PA A,S
Villa Victoria Academy, NJ A,F
Wakefield School, VA A,C,F,S
The Waldorf School of Garden City, NY A
Walnut Hill School for the Arts, MA F
Wasatch Academy, UT A
Washington International School, DC A
Watkinson School, CT A
Waynflete School, ME A,F,S
Webb School of Knoxville, TN A,F,S
The Webb Schools, CA A,C,F,S
Wellspring Foundation, CT A
Wesleyan Academy, PR A
Westbury Christian School, TX S
Westchester Country Day School, NC A,C,F,S
Westminster School, CT A,S
West Sound Academy, WA A
Wheaton Academy, IL A,C,F,S
The Wheeler School, RI A,F,S
Whitefield Academy, GA A,F,S
Whitefield Academy, KY A,S
The Williams School, CT A,S
The Williston Northampton School, MA F,S
The Willows Academy, IL A,S
Wilmington Christian School, DE A
Windells Academy, OR R,S
The Windsor School, NY A,C,F
Winston Preparatory School, NY A,F
The Winston School San Antonio, TX A,C,F,S
Woodlynde School, PA A,F,S
Wyoming Seminary, PA A,F,S
Xaverian High School, NY A,S
Zurich International School, Switzerland O

SCHOOLS REPORTING THAT THEY ACCOMMODATE UNDERACHIEVERS

American Academy, FL
Arrowsmith School, ON, Canada
Bachman Academy, TN
Camphill Special School, PA
Denver Academy, CO
Foothills Academy, AB, Canada
The Frostig School, CA
Gateway School, TX
The Glenholme School, Devereux Connecticut, CT
The Greenwood School, VT
Hampshire Country School, NH
Humanex Academy, CO
The Judge Rotenberg Educational Center, MA
La Cheim School, CA
Little Keswick School, VA
Maplebrook School, NY
Marine Military Academy, TX
Oakland School, VA
The Pathway School, PA
Realms of Inquiry, UT
The Rectory School, CT
St. Jude's School, ON, Canada
Shoore Centre for Learning, ON, Canada
Temple Grandin School, CO
Valley View School, MA
Wellsprings Friends School, OR
Winston Preparatory School, NY

SCHOOLS REPORTING PROGRAMS FOR STUDENTS WITH SPECIAL NEEDS

Remedial Reading and/or Writing

Academy of the New Church Boys' School, PA
Academy of the New Church Girls' School, PA
Académie Ste Cécile International School, ON, Canada
Alexander Dawson School, CO
All Hallows High School, NY
Alliance Academy, Ecuador
Alverno High School, CA
American Academy, FL
American Heritage School, FL
The American School Foundation, Mexico
Archbishop Curley High School, MD
Arrowsmith School, ON, Canada
ASSETS School, HI
Bachman Academy, TN
Bay Ridge Preparatory School, NY
The Beekman School, NY
Bishop Conaty-Our Lady of Loretto High School, CA
Bishop Luers High School, IN
Bishop O'Dowd High School, CA
Bishop's College School, QC, Canada
Bishop Stang High School, MA
Blueprint Education, AZ
Brockwood Park School, United Kingdom
Brother Rice High School, MI
Burr and Burton Academy, VT
Butte Central Catholic High School, MT
Calvin Christian High School, CA
Camphill Special School, PA
Canton Academy, MS
Cardigan Mountain School, NH
Cardinal Newman High School, FL
Cascadilla School, NY
Cathedral High School, IN
Catholic Central High School, NY
The Catholic High School of Baltimore, MD
Central Catholic High School, CA

Chamberlain-Hunt Academy, MS
Chattanooga Christian School, TN
Children's Creative and Performing Arts Academy of San Diego, CA
Chinese Christian Schools, CA
Christa McAuliffe Academy School of Arts and Sciences, OR
Christ Church Episcopal School, SC
Christopher Columbus High School, FL
Christopher Dock Mennonite High School, PA
Colegio Bolivar, Colombia
Columbia International School, Japan
The Concept School, PA
Concordia Preparatory School, UT
Cotter Schools, MN
Crawford Adventist Academy, ON, Canada
Currey Ingram Academy, TN
Cushing Academy, MA
Damien High School, CA
De La Salle North Catholic High School, OR
DeMatha Catholic High School, MD
Denver Academy, CO
Dowling Catholic High School, IA
Dublin Christian Academy, NH
Eagle Hill School, CT
Eagle Hill School, MA
Eastern Mennonite High School, VA
Eaton Academy, GA
Elyria Catholic High School, OH
Fairhill School, TX
The Fessenden School, MA
Fishburne Military School, VA
Foothills Academy, AB, Canada
Foundation Academy, FL
Fox Valley Lutheran High School, WI
Fresno Christian Schools, CA
Friends Academy, NY
Front Range Christian High School, CO
The Frostig School, CA
Fryeburg Academy, ME
Gateway School, TX
George Stevens Academy, ME
The Glenholme School, Devereux Connecticut, CT
The Greenwood School, VT
Grier School, PA
Hampshire Country School, NH
Hargrave Military Academy, VA
Hebrew Academy, CA
Heritage Christian Academy, AB, Canada
Heritage Christian School, ON, Canada
Ho'Ala School, HI
Holy Angels Academy, NY
The Howard School, GA
The Hudson School, NJ
Humanex Academy, CO
Institute of Notre Dame, MD
International School of Amsterdam, Netherlands
Jack M. Barrack Hebrew Academy, PA
Jean and Samuel Frankel Jewish Academy of Metropolitan Detroit, MI
Josephinum Academy, IL
The Judge Rotenberg Educational Center, MA
Kings Christian School, CA
The Lab School of Washington, DC
La Cheim School, CA
Lancaster Mennonite High School, PA
Landmark Christian School, GA
La Scuola D'Italia Guglielmo Marconi, NY
The Latin School of Chicago, IL
The Laureate Academy, MB, Canada
Laurel Springs School, CA
Lawrence School, OH
Lutheran High School of Indianapolis, IN
Luther North College Prep, IL
Lyndon Institute, VT
Maharishi School of the Age of Enlightenment, IA
Maine Central Institute, ME
Manhattan Christian High School, MT
Maplebrook School, NY
Maranatha High School, CA
Marian Central Catholic High School, IL
Marian High School, IN
Marine Military Academy, TX
The Marvelwood School, CT
Marylawn of the Oranges, NJ
McGill-Toolen Catholic High School, AL
Memorial Hall School, TX
Mennonite Collegiate Institute, MB, Canada
Merchiston Castle School, United Kingdom
Missouri Military Academy, MO
Modesto Christian School, CA
Monsignor Donovan High School, NJ
MU High School, MO
Noble Academy, NC
The Nora School, MD
Northwood School, NY
The Norwich Free Academy, CT
Notre Dame College Prep, IL
Notre Dame High School, NJ
The Oakland School, PA
Oakland School, VA
Ojai Valley School, CA
Oneida Baptist Institute, KY
The Oxford Academy, CT
Padua Franciscan High School, OH
The Pathway School, PA
Pensacola Catholic High School, FL
Pinehurst School, ON, Canada
Pioneer Valley Christian School, MA
Powers Catholic High School, MI
The Rectory School, CT
Redwood Christian Schools, CA
Regis Jesuit High School, Girls Division, CO
Rumsey Hall School, CT
Saddleback Valley Christian School, CA
Saint Albert Junior-Senior High School, IA
St. Andrew's School, RI
St. Andrew's–Sewanee School, TN
Saint Anthony High School, CA
St. Augustine High School, CA
St. Benedict at Auburndale, TN
St. Bernard's Catholic School, CA
St. Brendan High School, FL
St. Croix Schools, MN
Saint Elizabeth High School, CA
St. George's School, BC, Canada
St. George's School of Montreal, QC, Canada
Saint Joan Antida High School, WI
Saint Joseph High School, IL
St. Jude's School, ON, Canada
Saint Lawrence Academy, CA
Saint Mary's High School, AZ
Saint Patrick High School, IL
St. Paul's Episcopal School, AL
St. Pius X High School, TX

St. Stanislaus College, MS
St. Thomas Aquinas High School, FL
Saint Thomas Aquinas High School, KS
Salesian High School, CA
Salesianum School, DE
Salpointe Catholic High School, AZ
San Marcos Baptist Academy, TX
SBEC (Southern Baptist Educational Center), MS
Seattle Academy of Arts and Sciences, WA
Seisen International School, Japan
Shattuck-St. Mary's School, MN
Shawnigan Lake School, BC, Canada
Shoore Centre for Learning, ON, Canada
Shoreline Christian, WA
Smith School, NY
Stephen T. Badin High School, OH
The Storm King School, NY
Tandem Friends School, VA
TASIS The American School in England, United Kingdom
The Tenney School, TX
Timothy Christian High School, IL
Trinity High School, KY
Trinity-Pawling School, NY
University School of Nova Southeastern University, FL
Valle Catholic High School, MO
Valley Forge Military Academy & College, PA
Valley View School, MA
Venta Preparatory School, ON, Canada
Villa Angela-St. Joseph High School, OH
Villa Duchesne and Oak Hill School, MO
Webb School of Knoxville, TN
Wellsprings Friends School, OR
West Catholic High School, MI
Wheaton Academy, IL
Wilmington Christian School, DE
The Windsor School, NY
Winston Preparatory School, NY
The Winston School San Antonio, TX
Woodlynde School, PA
Xaverian High School, NY
Zurich International School, Switzerland

Remedial Math

Academy of the New Church Boys' School, PA
Academy of the New Church Girls' School, PA
Académie Ste Cécile International School, ON, Canada
Alexander Dawson School, CO
All Hallows High School, NY
Alliance Academy, Ecuador
Alpha Omega Academy, IA
Alverno High School, CA
American Academy, FL
American Heritage School, FL
Archbishop Curley High School, MD
Arrowsmith School, ON, Canada
ASSETS School, HI
Bachman Academy, TN
Bay Ridge Preparatory School, NY
Bearspaw Christian School, AB, Canada
The Beekman School, NY
Bishop Conaty-Our Lady of Loretto High School, CA
Bishop Denis J. O'Connell High School, VA
Bishop Luers High School, IN
Bishop O'Dowd High School, CA
Bishop's College School, QC, Canada
Bishop Stang High School, MA
Blueprint Education, AZ
Brockwood Park School, United Kingdom
Brother Rice High School, MI
Buffalo Academy of the Sacred Heart, NY
Burr and Burton Academy, VT
Butte Central Catholic High School, MT
Camphill Special School, PA
Canton Academy, MS
Cardigan Mountain School, NH
Cardinal Newman High School, FL
Cascadilla School, NY
Cathedral High School, IN
Catholic Central High School, NY
The Catholic High School of Baltimore, MD
Central Catholic High School, CA
Chamberlain-Hunt Academy, MS
Chattanooga Christian School, TN
Children's Creative and Performing Arts Academy of San Diego, CA
Christa McAuliffe Academy School of Arts and Sciences, OR
Christ Church Episcopal School, SC
Columbia International School, Japan
The Concept School, PA
Cotter Schools, MN
Cushing Academy, MA
Damien High School, CA
De La Salle High School, CA
De La Salle North Catholic High School, OR
Denver Academy, CO
Dowling Catholic High School, IA
Dublin Christian Academy, NH
Eagle Hill School, CT
Eagle Hill School, MA
Eastern Mennonite High School, VA
Eaton Academy, GA
Elyria Catholic High School, OH
Ezell-Harding Christian School, TN
Fairhill School, TX
The Fessenden School, MA
Fishburne Military School, VA
Flint River Academy, GA
Foothills Academy, AB, Canada
Foundation Academy, FL
Fox Valley Lutheran High School, WI
Fresno Christian Schools, CA
Friends Academy, NY
Front Range Christian High School, CO
The Frostig School, CA
Fryeburg Academy, ME
Gateway School, TX
George Stevens Academy, ME
The Glenholme School, Devereux Connecticut, CT
Grace Brethren School, CA
The Grauer School, CA
The Greenwood School, VT
Grier School, PA
Hampshire Country School, NH
Hargrave Military Academy, VA
Hebrew Academy, CA
Heritage Christian Academy, AB, Canada
Heritage Christian School, ON, Canada
Ho'Ala School, HI
Holy Angels Academy, NY
The Howard School, GA
The Hudson School, NJ
Humanex Academy, CO
Institute of Notre Dame, MD
International School of Amsterdam, Netherlands

Jack M. Barrack Hebrew Academy, PA
Jean and Samuel Frankel Jewish Academy of Metropolitan Detroit, MI
Josephinum Academy, IL
The Judge Rotenberg Educational Center, MA
Kings Christian School, CA
The Lab School of Washington, DC
La Cheim School, CA
Lancaster Mennonite High School, PA
Landmark Christian School, GA
La Scuola D'Italia Guglielmo Marconi, NY
The Latin School of Chicago, IL
The Laureate Academy, MB, Canada
Laurel Springs School, CA
Lawrence School, OH
Little Keswick School, VA
Lutheran High School of Indianapolis, IN
Luther North College Prep, IL
Lyndon Institute, VT
Maharishi School of the Age of Enlightenment, IA
Maine Central Institute, ME
Manhattan Christian High School, MT
Maplebrook School, NY
Maranatha High School, CA
Marian Central Catholic High School, IL
Marian High School, IN
Marine Military Academy, TX
The Marvelwood School, CT
Marylawn of the Oranges, NJ
McGill-Toolen Catholic High School, AL
Memorial Hall School, TX
Mennonite Collegiate Institute, MB, Canada
Merchiston Castle School, United Kingdom
Missouri Military Academy, MO
Modesto Christian School, CA
Monsignor Donovan High School, NJ
Munich International School, Germany
Noble Academy, NC
The Nora School, MD
The Norwich Free Academy, CT
Notre Dame College Prep, IL
Notre Dame High School, NJ
The Oakland School, PA
Oakland School, VA
Ojai Valley School, CA
Oneida Baptist Institute, KY
The Oxford Academy, CT
Padua Franciscan High School, OH
The Pathway School, PA
Pensacola Catholic High School, FL
Pinehurst School, ON, Canada
Pioneer Valley Christian School, MA
Powers Catholic High School, MI
The Rectory School, CT
Redwood Christian Schools, CA
Regis Jesuit High School, Girls Division, CO
Sacramento Adventist Academy, CA
Saddleback Valley Christian School, CA
Saint Albert Junior-Senior High School, IA
St. Andrew's–Sewanee School, TN
Saint Anthony High School, CA
Saint Anthony High School, IL
St. Augustine High School, CA
St. Benedict at Auburndale, TN
St. Bernard's Catholic School, CA
St. Brendan High School, FL
St. Croix Schools, MN
Saint Elizabeth High School, CA
St. George's School of Montreal, QC, Canada
Saint Joan Antida High School, WI
Saint Joseph High School, IL
St. Jude's School, ON, Canada
Saint Lawrence Academy, CA
Saint Mary's High School, AZ
Saint Patrick High School, IL
Saint Patrick - Saint Vincent High School, CA
St. Paul's Episcopal School, AL
St. Paul's High School, MB, Canada
St. Pius X High School, TX
St. Stanislaus College, MS
St. Thomas Aquinas High School, FL
Saint Thomas Aquinas High School, KS
Salesian High School, CA
Salesianum School, DE
Salpointe Catholic High School, AZ
San Marcos Baptist Academy, TX
SBEC (Southern Baptist Educational Center), MS
Seattle Academy of Arts and Sciences, WA
Seisen International School, Japan
Shattuck-St. Mary's School, MN
Shawnigan Lake School, BC, Canada
Shoore Centre for Learning, ON, Canada
Smith School, NY
Stephen T. Badin High School, OH
Sunshine Bible Academy, SD
Tandem Friends School, VA
The Tenney School, TX
Trinity High School, KY
Trinity High School, OH
Valle Catholic High School, MO
Valley Forge Military Academy & College, PA
Valley Lutheran High School, AZ
Valley View School, MA
Venta Preparatory School, ON, Canada
Villa Angela-St. Joseph High School, OH
Villa Duchesne and Oak Hill School, MO
Webb School of Knoxville, TN
Wellsprings Friends School, OR
Westtown School, PA
Wheaton Academy, IL
Wilmington Christian School, DE
The Windsor School, NY
Winston Preparatory School, NY
Xaverian High School, NY
Zurich International School, Switzerland

Deaf Students

Alexander Dawson School, CO
American Heritage School, FL
Bishop Fenwick High School, OH
Blanchet School, OR
Brockwood Park School, United Kingdom
Burr and Burton Academy, VT
Cathedral High School, IN
The Catlin Gabel School, OR
The Colorado Springs School, CO
The Concept School, PA
Denver Christian High School, CO
Eaton Academy, GA
Foundation Academy, FL
Front Range Christian High School, CO
George Stevens Academy, ME
The Grauer School, CA
Heritage Christian Academy, AB, Canada

Holy Angels Academy, NY
Humanex Academy, CO
Jack M. Barrack Hebrew Academy, PA
Jean and Samuel Frankel Jewish Academy of Metropolitan Detroit, MI
The Judge Rotenberg Educational Center, MA
Lancaster Mennonite High School, PA
Merchiston Castle School, United Kingdom
Pensacola Catholic High School, FL
Phillips Academy (Andover), MA
Regis Jesuit High School, Girls Division, CO
Rye Country Day School, NY
Saint Albert Junior-Senior High School, IA
St. Andrew's Episcopal School, MD
Saint Anthony High School, IL
Saint Joseph High School, IL
San Marcos Baptist Academy, TX
The Tenney School, TX
Trinity High School, KY
University Liggett School, MI
Valley Lutheran High School, AZ
Watkinson School, CT
Westover School, CT
Whitefield Academy, GA
The Williston Northampton School, MA

Blind Students

American Heritage School, FL
Brockwood Park School, United Kingdom
Burr and Burton Academy, VT
Cathedral High School, IN
Dowling Catholic High School, IA
Front Range Christian High School, CO
George Stevens Academy, ME
Greenhills School, MI
Humanex Academy, CO
Jean and Samuel Frankel Jewish Academy of Metropolitan Detroit, MI
The Judge Rotenberg Educational Center, MA
Lancaster Mennonite High School, PA
Mennonite Collegiate Institute, MB, Canada
Merchiston Castle School, United Kingdom
MMI Preparatory School, PA
Pensacola Catholic High School, FL
Phillips Academy (Andover), MA
Regis Jesuit High School, Girls Division, CO
St. Augustine High School, CA
Saint Joseph High School, IL
Trinity High School, KY
Whitefield Academy, GA

Index

Alphabetical Listing of Schools

In the index that follows, page numbers for school profiles are shown in regular type, page numbers for Close-Ups are shown in **boldface** type, and page numbers for Displays are shown in *italics*.